R. T. Trull
447 Charles St
E. 1 -
Phone 8-1490

CONTEMPORARY TRENDS

American Literature: A Period Anthology

Oscar Cargill, GENERAL EDITOR

THE ROOTS OF NATIONAL CULTURE: TO 1830

ROBERT E. SPILLER, *University of Pennsylvania*

HAROLD W. BLODGETT, *Union College*

THE ROMANTIC TRIUMPH: 1830–1860

TREMAINE MC DOWELL, *University of Minnesota*

THE RISE OF REALISM: 1860–1900

LOUIS WANN, *University of Southern California*

CONTEMPORARY TRENDS: SINCE 1900

JOHN HERBERT NELSON, *University of Kansas*

OSCAR CARGILL, *New York University*

CONTEMPORARY TRENDS

American Literature Since 1900

REVISED EDITION

Edited by

JOHN HERBERT NELSON
Dean of the Graduate School, University of Kansas

OSCAR CARGILL
*Chairman, Department of English, Washington Square College,
New York University*

NEW YORK · THE MACMILLAN COMPANY · 1949

PREFACE

Since *Contemporary Trends* was first published in 1933 there has developed a convention of regarding the year 1900 as the threshold of the "modern" or "contemporary" period in American literature. In planning a new edition of *American Literature: A Period Anthology* the editors agreed to yield to this convention even though they felt as good a case could be made out for either 1890 or 1914 (the original date) as the *terminus a quo* for this volume. Nor was this the only limitation on a free design for *Contemporary Trends*. The tentative nature of many contemporary reputations, the continuing demand in the colleges for the inclusion of some authors towards whom the editors themselves are apathetic, the special difficulties imposed by dealing with materials in copyright—all have been limitations. The editors offer these observations not in extenuation, but, as they feel, in a justifiable self-defense, for it is often naïvely assumed by those who have no experience in anthology making that a collection of representative writings reflects completely the taste of the compilers. It is only just to observe that it never does this. Yet the editors hope they have surmounted most of the usual difficulties and have compiled an anthology that some few of their contemporaries will find a challenging book.

The pattern followed in organizing the materials in the revised edition of *Contemporary Trends* serves to stress, not those fashions and changes which are purely literary or those affinities which are primarily belletristic, but rather the significant intellectual currents of the past which support and propagate literary art. The writers are grouped according to what appear to be their dominant attitudes and ideas, and, of course, this arrangement necessarily illustrates those attitudes and ideas. With the lengthening perspective that time has given the editors, they have been able, while yet pointing out the chief trends in contemporary thought and aesthetics, also to select those writings which are generally held today to be the authors' best work. In 1933 Mr. Nelson could fairly complain he had too few surveys of contemporary writing to guide him—his was "the first attempt to treat as a distinct period American literary history since 1914." (If he had chosen 1900 as his date, he could have made the same complaint.) But today the editors can enumerate more than two score of critics and scholars who have indirectly assisted them in their selection. The ample scope of this volume was made possible as the result of the considered policy of a publishing house which has already demonstrated its interest in American Literature by having issued *The Cambridge History,* the *Literary*

History of the United States, and numerous other critical and historical works, as well as a goodly portion of the better writing of our time.

Contemporary Trends is the product of harmonious collaboration between the editors and of much wise counsel from outside. If there are faults in the design of the introduction and in the patterning of the collection, Mr. Cargill assumes responsibility for those faults; but beyond initial planning Mr. Nelson entered fully into the making of the book. Although the editors owe much to many people who have written on the authors represented and gratefully acknowledge that debt here, they owe still more to the following persons whom they wish to name individually:

Mr. Nelson would acknowledge the aid he had either on the first edition or on the present book from his colleagues at the University of Kansas, the late Professors E. M. Hopkins, William S. Johnson, and R. D. O'Leary; two members of the Department of English at New York University, Professor Edwin Burgum and Eda Lou Walton; Mr. William Troy of the New School for Social Research; the other editors of *American Literature: A Period Anthology;* and his wife, Kathryn L. Nelson.

Mr. Cargill would here acknowledge the help he has had not only as co-editor of this volume but as editor of *The Social Revolt* (which now passes into oblivion) and as general editor of this series, in 1933 and again in this year. Especially would he thank Nelson Adkins, Charles Anderson, H. J. W. Braddy, Mr. and Mrs. Carleton Brown, E. B. Burgum, Madison Cawein, Jr., William Charvat, Procope S. Costas, Mrs. F. J. Faulks, Pastoriza Flores, L. K. England, Hamlin Garland, Arthur B. Geismar, Miss Virginia Gerson, Miss Rose Gilbert, E. V. Halbmeier, A. L. Hench, P. de La Rochelle, Ilse Lind, Mrs. Jack London, J. D. Magee, Edwin Markham, W. C. Martin, Langdon Mitchell, P. E. More, William R. Parker, F. H. Price, A. H. Quinn, Miss Louise Ranney, Miss Regina Rosiny, C. V. Rice, Ernst Rose, Macha Rosenthal, Miss Margaret Schlauch, H. L. Shaw, Mrs. E. L. Shepherd, Upton Sinclair, Reed Smith, F. A. Spencer, Emmanuel Stein, Kendall B. Taft, Booth Tarkington, William Troy, Miss E. L. Walton, H. A. Watt, G. A. Wauchope, H. S. White, W. A. White, Owen Wister, C. E. S. Wood, and the other editors in this series. And finally, he wishes to acknowledge here his debt to his wife, Gladys L. Cargill, who, in more ways than anyone else, has aided in the progress of this whole undertaking.

JOHN HERBERT NELSON
OSCAR CARGILL

CONTENTS

THE SYMBOLISTS

THE FREUDIANS

THE COLLECTIVISTS

THE CONSERVATIVES

THE LIBERALS

Contents

CONTEMPORARY TRENDS

"The seat of energy," wrote Brooks Adams in 1902, "has migrated from Europe to America." Adams fixed the crucial moment of change as five years earlier, when, through new processes and abundant ore, American manufacturers captured the steel market of the world. "In March, 1897, Pittsburgh achieved supremacy in steel, and in an instant Europe felt herself poised above an abyss." Others would have been content to date our ascendancy from our more visible triumphs at Santiago and Manila, from which, at small cost to ourselves, though at considerable to propitiatory Spain, we emerged a world power, little reckoning how soon that would involve us in a pattern of anxiety alien to American life. Because the lessons of our colonial history were still remembered, there was some immediate concern among people with good consciences lest we should become an imperial nation, like her whose maternal conduct we had so long deplored; but Adams, untroubled on this score, took our new empire as already assured:

. . . The West Indies drift towards us, the Republic of Mexico hardly longer has an independent life, and the City of Mexico is an American town. With the completion of the Panama Canal all Central America will become part of our system. We have expanded into Asia, we have attracted the fragments of the Spanish dominions, and reaching out into China we have checked the advance of Russia and Germany, in territory which, until yesterday, had been supposed to be beyond our sphere. We are penetrating into Europe, and Great Britain especially is gradually assuming the position of a dependency, which must rely on us as the base from which she draws her food in peace, and without which she could not stand in war.

Had this been written half a century later, it would have been read as the record of largely accomplished fact rather than as prophecy. Taking it, with minor qualifications, as history, we may inquire how the emergence of the United States as a power in world affairs has affected our culture, and, more especially, our literature.

Parity, or better, among the powers suggested to Americans the need for more cosmopolitan standards of life and of art. "Races must follow their destiny blindly," wrote Frank Norris, "but is it not possible that we can find in this great destiny of ours something a little better than mere battle and conquest, something a little more generous than mere trading and underbidding?" Crusading for an American school of fiction, Norris pointed out that "hardy and adventurous enough upon other lines, disdainful of conventions, contemptuous of ancient customs, we yet lag behind in the arts." Sectionalism rather than Americanism had been typical of our literature. The charge had been made before the turn of the century by Hamlin Garland, who, however, would have merely substituted one provinciality for another—that of the Middle West for that of New England. Now a world point of view was invoked. Yet no mere zeal for emulation altered the character of our literature, even if alignment with European ideas and forms was to be a salient characteristic of much of our writing in the twentieth century. Loss of appeal in the established writers was primarily responsible for the acceptance of European models. In 1900 no young writer could hope to win an audience with Poe, or Emerson, or Hawthorne, or Lowell as his model. Though no one of these writers was an orthodox sectarian, they were all closer to orthodoxy than were their twentieth-century readers. Two forces had relaxed the religious and ethical interests of the latter —"protestantism had worked itself out and had ceased to protest" and heterodoxy had worked its way in with the vast incursion of immigrants of various faiths that the promise of American life had lured hither. Time and change had put the best American writers far off; time and change had made their immediate values obscure; time and change were greater obstacles to reaching them than was the Atlantic to the consumption and emulation of the contemporary European.

Innovation rarely comes by the back door. Because American readers and writers by 1900 were reacting strongly against nineteenth-century mores, they approved with particular warmth those European forces which had least in common with our conventions and beliefs. If there had been one conviction to which most Americans gave assent, it was belief in freedom of the will. Young Goodman Brown, traduced in the forest, was yet free to cry out to Heaven; the instruction to earn a penny by saving one was predicated on the liberty to do so; and he who would prove his manhood by nonconformity was judged under no insurmountable pressure to conform. In Europe the most persuasive philosophy generally understood which denied freedom of the will was French naturalism. Traceable to the doctrine of evolution, naturalism in France took the character of pessimistic determinism, that is, it assumed that the forces of heredity and environment were irresistible agents in the decay of France. This thesis was most clearly expounded by the French critic Hippolyte Taine and the novelist Émile Zola, but it is also implicit in varying degrees in the writings of Flaubert, Maupassant, Huysmans, and the Goncourt brothers. Of course, if heredity and environment completely shape a man, it is not demonstrable that they shape him for the worse; indeed, Herbert Spencer, the English philosopher who became infatuated with what he deemed to be the promise of evolution, was almost an oppressive optimist. The factor of pessimism must be assigned to the temper of the French naturalists themselves, who were depressed by the political misfortunes of their country—a sequence of abortive revolutions and the conquest, finally, of France by the Prussians. The vogue of naturalism, however, was established and sustained by the approval of the French public whose gloom found some sort of psychic release, apparently, in battening on despair. Possibly the novelty of reading books in which the characters degenerate rather than develop, supplied the distraction that was a necessity to the embittered French intellectual in the days of the Quadruple Indemnity.

Americans directly assimilated French naturalism, though they also read avidly such British writers as thought the French worth imitating—Thomas Hardy, Samuel Butler, George Moore, and George Gissing. In fact, it was from reading the latter that the Americans allowed the intrusion in their fictions of the elements of accident and fate which to a degree discredit the naturalistic thesis, as Zola pointed out. Some reflection of naturalistic writing may be found in Joseph Kirkland's *Zury* (1887) and in Hamlin Garland's *Rose of Dutcher's Coolly* (1895), but these books are fundamentally realistic rather than naturalistic. Historically realism has an ethic, as well as an aesthetic, which marks it off from naturalism. European-born in the days of the first effective employment of the camera, with its greatest exemplar in Ivan Turgenev, realism held each individual responsible for his own destiny; it inculcated a personal morality. In an old-fashioned sense, there are no "villains" or "heroes" or "heroines" in realistic fiction—no character is all black or all white, but any character may exhibit a certain grayness if he allows evil to predominate over good in his nature. The intent of the realistic novelist is to reveal the flaws in human character from which evil develops. It is implicit, however, in realistic writing that the individual may close these flaws, if he chooses, and allow evil no habitation. Thus realism is the very antithesis of naturalism: those who define naturalism as "a more intense realism" have insufficient perception of the distinctions between the two.

The first piece of American naturalism of any consequence is Stephen Crane's *Maggie, a Girl of the Streets* (1892). Here heredity and environment tell so heavily against Maggie Johnson of Rum Alley that her seduction and death seem inevitable. The course of her life is beyond her control. Crane's limitation is that of a literary novice. He lacked depth and was unable to make his heroine's career momentous. The mere existence of Nana, to speak not at all of her general success, is more portentous than Maggie's downfall. Just once, in *The Octopus* (1901), did Frank Norris, who succeeded Crane as the leading American proponent of naturalism, become enough involved himself in the fortunes of his characters to endow his writing with the broad significance that a naturalistic work must have to be compelling. With Theodore Dreiser, however, American naturalism came into its own, for Dreiser, though he lacked the finesse and the literary sensibility of Crane and Norris, knew intimately the life he described and harbored such deep feelings concerning it that he could not stand apart from the fictional situations which he rather recorded than created. Whether his protagonist was a Hurstwood, as in *Sister Carrie* (1900), or a Clyde Griffiths, as in *An American Tragedy* (1925), his errant way was beyond his control; moreover, it was made to seem no exceptional and implausible way in American experience. If one of Dreiser's characters, like Cowperwood, marked and obtained from life what he marked, this was no evidence of free will, but of an endowment, a "chemistry," that made him desire and drive to obtain what he desired. Dreiser's strength was not that he *knew* but that he *feared* that this is the way life is organized: had he been positive, he could have been controverted readily; the doubter who painfully sets down misgivings that the whole race shares to some degree in certain moods is not easily answered. So with Dreiser.

Far better equipped because of a penchant for sociology and with some instruction in it, the later novelist, James T. Farrell, has made a significant contribution to naturalistic literature with his "Studs Lonigan" trilogy—*Young Lonigan* (1932), *The Young Manhood of Studs Lonigan* (1934), and *Judgment Day* (1935). This work is as meaningful to the urban generation of the twentieth century as was *The Adventures of Huckleberry Finn* to the rural and village generation of the nineteenth century. Bitterly acquainted with the viciousness of the city gang, Farrell makes clear how an "average" city boy, "on the loose" in an idle summer, becomes corrupted by his associates and takes a course which leads to physical decay, moral obliquity, and death. Farrell's persuasiveness comes from his demonstration of the causes of Stud's degeneracy, which had no Euclidean inevitableness but a powerful plausibility in the given circumstances. In the trilogy the naturalistic interpretation is effectively tempered by common sense, but in Farrell's other work, to date, a lack of control of his elements and a want of defined purpose make for unconvincing and tedious narration. Like Theodore Dreiser, however, Farrell at his best challenges favorable comparison with the French naturalists. Other Americans contributed to the development—Gamaliel Bradford as a lesser Sainte-Beuve, Clarence Darrow and Earnest Hooton as challengers of the legalism of "criminal responsibility," and Joseph Wood Krutch as a critic of most of our intellectual assumptions from a naturalistic bias in *The Modern Temper* (1929)—but only George Santayana requires special comment, perhaps, for the support he gave to naturalism. Indisputably a naturalist in *The Last Puritan* (1935), Santayana does not so clearly define himself elsewhere. "I am a follower of Plato," he asserts, "in his doctrine that only knowledge of ideas (if we call it knowledge) can be literal and exact, whilst practical knowledge is necessarily mythical in form, precisely because its object exists and is external to us." This dichotomy of idea and natural thing would seem to deny the influence of the latter on the former, and hence deny naturalism, but there is no such denial in Santayana. He is constantly glancing over his shoulder to see what Nature directs and is more enslaved to her than are most philosophers, even if he beguiles his reader by making the enslavement poetic. His true position is revealed by his attack upon the "American" reliance in the "will," by his assault upon Emerson and William James.

Naturalism did not attract many American writers. This was not, wholly because it is alien to the American temperament or because the preponderant evidence in this country supports the assumption that one may add a cubit to his children's stature by taking thought. Unless one possesses an extremely subtle mind, the range of naturalism is so limited and limiting that it is not an inviting thesis to expound, for it tends to formularize and dogmatize human behavior. In literature, even more than in life, one needs to feel that "anything can happen," though paradoxically one needs to feel also at the end that only *this* could have happened to these people.

A partial product of naturalism, though with more important origins of its own, primitivism provided the American writer with the amplitude he requires. An engrossment with simple animal behavior was a mark of primitivism in Zola, but primitivism proper was a reaction to the decadent tendencies of the late nineteenth century in Europe. It may be defined as an assumption that the primary drives in man are healthier than any refinement of them. Primitivism, however, is never a product of primitive society, which, if it struggles at all, strives in the direction of refinement. It is the product of over-sophistication and confusion. It is an expression of an unconscious desire to simplify life. That is, while animalism and athleticism are its manifestations, it conceals an unhealthy urge to escape from the sometimes baffling circumstances of social complexity; and to some degree those who have employed it have avoided the fundamental problems of the twentieth century, even while adverting to some of them. It is easy to designate Rudyard Kipling and Jack London as among the earliest modern primitivists, for they were ostentatious in the way that they delivered the modern reader from the hyperaestheticism of Algernon Swinburne, Oscar Wilde, and Austin Dobson. Bursting out of doors with violence they called attention to being out of doors. A more important innovator was Gertrude Stein. Miss Stein, as a pre-medical student at Radcliffe, had explored the depths of the subconscious mind as a part of an experiment conducted by Hugo Munsterberg and William James, and had been fascinated by the language results she had obtained with automatic writing. Later, after abandoning her medical career and while living amid all the artistic experimentation of Paris to which her brother's profession of art collector introduced her, she perceived the analogy between the results of automatic writing (a revelation of the aboriginal consciousness, so to speak) and the use of elementary planes in primitive African sculpture. In *Three Lives* (1909) she produced at once the effect of a rather simply organized mind brooding upon the complexity of three rather simply organized people and the style and paraphernalia of modern primitivism. Miss Stein's later experiments, suggested by abstractionism and subsequent developments in painting, need not concern us here, but we should mark *Three Lives* as one of the most original literary creations of the twentieth century. *Ulysses* and *Finnegans Wake* are more labored and more brilliant, but they are also in a way more traditional. What has the Homeric epic to do with the subconscious?

Employing the materials and manner of primitivism so that they would attract the great body of readers was the work of Sherwood Anderson, Ring Lardner, F. Scott Fitzgerald, Ernest Hemingway, William Faulkner, and Erskine Caldwell. Lardner and Fitzgerald contributed portraits of the athlete as sadist, the former in the memorable short story "Champion" (1924) and the latter in *The Great Gatsby* (1925). All this is the obverse of the bright penny that Kipling and London offered the public. No one has shown better, however, than Sherwood Anderson the anomaly of human sensitivity in brute existence. Though he has many notes, this is "middle C" on his register. It is the chord that is returned to in all that is fine and perdurable in *Winesburg, Ohio* (1919), *The Triumph of the Egg* (1921), *Horses and Men* (1923), and *Death in the Woods* (1933). Hemingway is as alive to this topic as is Sherwood Anderson, but his chief concern is with male conduct in the crucial testing times of man's behavior. *Men Without Women* (1927) defines his position and *The Sun Also Rises* (1926), *A Farewell to Arms* (1929) and *For Whom the Bell Tolls* (1940) amplify it, yet at the same time they convey Hemingway's own indecisiveness in regard to the proper conduct of mankind generally in economic and political affairs. Faulkner and Caldwell have used, while employing their special gifts of caricature, the technique and episodes of primitivism to depict social decay in the rural South. To the gallery of vivid fictional portraits in American literature they have contributed Flem Snopes, Jason Compson, and Jeeter Lester, who will not soon be displaced. Caldwell's short stories, especially those in his early books, and Faulkner's novels, *The Sound and the Fury* (1929), *As I Lay Dying* (1930), and *The Hamlet* (1940), seem to be, respectively, the best work of these men. The most inventive of the primitivists, Faulkner offers no social program; Caldwell's deep interest in Russia since his residence there has not made him doctrinaire in his later fiction set in this country. Capable of some extraordinarily bad writing—note Anderson's *Many Marriages,* Hemingway's *Torrents of Spring,* and Faulkner's *Sartoris*—the American primitivists have done some very provocative work and constitute the nearest approach we have to a recent literary school. They have given us a new prose style. All this makes up in some measure for their failure to face the principal issues of their time.

Freudianism may be regarded as a special form of primitivism. It urges that most of the ills of man stem from his inhibitions and that a happy life must be based on adequate sexual relations. Dr. Sigmund Freud, the Viennese neurologist who gained enormous prestige in the early twentieth century by advancing this thesis and by relieving the tension of maladjusted people through his method of psychoanalysis, may owe something to Gall and Spurzheim, the early nineteenth century phrenologists whose theories of "amativeness," expounded in this country by Dr. Benjamin Fowler, led to the astonishingly "modern" descriptions of inhibitions and abnormal relationships in *The Blithedale Romance, Pierre,* and "The Song of Myself." Be that as it may, Freud's generalizations about the behavior of all mankind and his emphasis on sex (almost to the exclusion of other human drives) must have been due in no small measure to the demand made upon his professional services by the idle neurotics of one of the most decadent cities of Europe. The pathetic fallacy surely was involved in the transfer of a class and local situation to the whole world by Freud and his disciples. Whatever merit there may be in the "free confessional" of psychoanalysis—"free" only in the sense that the neurotic was encouraged to talk—the application of Freudian formulas as a sovereign remedy for all the world's ills caused some remarkable reactions in the United States. So great had been the popular credence given to the dogmas of this pseudo-science that raucous ridicule could not be suppressed when, after 1929, the Freudians proposed to end the Great Depression by psychoanalyzing the brokers of Wall Street. Of the countless satires and burlesques of Freudianism, Thurber and White's *Is Sex Necessary?* (1929) is at once the zaniest and most wholesome.

Curiously enough, the writing of the American Freudian school which seems most likely to endure is that which is liberally intermixed with other elements. Good, straight-away expositions of, say, the Oedipus Complex, like Louis Bromfield's *A Good Woman* (1927) and Sidney Howard's *The Silver Cord* (1927), have not held up so well in popular favor as have the more difficult and at times amorphous writings of Eugene O'Neill and Robinson Jeffers. Just as Sherwood Anderson in the latter part of his career could be classed very readily as a Freudian (see *Many Marriages, Dark Laughter,* and *Perhaps Women,* for example) so Eugene O'Neill might be said to have started his career as a primitivist, imitating Jack London, but then he fell under the spell of Strindberg, Jung (one of Freud's most important disciples), and Nietzsche. Strindberg's anti-romanticism, his view of the relation between the sexes as strife, with man the more constant victim, prepared O'Neill to receive the Jungian dissection of the personality, the Jungian type-psychology, and the Jungian theory of race consciousness. If every human personality consists of a *persona* (or mask) presented to the world and an *animus,* its antithesis submerged in the personality's core, then *The Great God Brown* (1926) is a valid literary presentation of a great theme. If there are readily classifiable human types made out of mathematical combinations of traits and their oppo-sites, then the assemblage of such types in *Lazarus Laughed* (1927) deserves close scrutiny. If, under duress, a character degenerates, as in *The Emperor Jones* (1920), pealing off layer after layer of consciousness, like skin off an onion, until a core of racial memory is reached, then there is no better exposi-tion of the architecture of human nature than this play. But one suspects that it is not these elements but fidelity to long known responses in tragic situ-ations which gives O'Neill his enduring audience, however much novelty may have had to do with his earlier success. A similar analysis of the poetry of Robinson Jeffers would show as fantastic a blending of Freud, Shelley, Nietzsche, and the Greeks, but would not explain his power. This lies, as with O'Neill, in his ability to raise mere man above the order of men by the process of torturing him out of himself. The grandeur with which Jeffers in his best work endows man somewhat palliates his completely anti-social and undemo-cratic thought.

The 1920's, which witnessed general assent to the Freudian dissection of the personality, permitted a group of writers, who flattered their readers by in-cluding them in a circle of *cognoscenti* of which the writers were the focus, very nearly to dictate the taste and behavior of the day. Self-styled "The Intelli-gentsia," this group inveighed against American mores and proposed the adoption of more "cosmopolitan" standards. Central in their thinking was the dogma that intelligence set one apart from the mob and allowed one privileges that the "booboisie" were not entitled to. The Grand Pooh-Bah of "The Intelligentsia" was H. L. Mencken, editor of the *American Mercury*. Collector, as "Americana," of accounts of all the oddities of human behavior as reported in the daily press, Mencken relied heavily on Nietzsche for his critical program, dispensing the German philosopher's anti-Christian and anti-democratic views —Nietzsche held that Christianity and democracy were a sort of protective coloration for the weak—as an antidote for our rusticity and Puritanism. Because he had a lively wit (however perverse one may consider it) and because he had a still livelier style, Mencken gathered a very large personal following, particularly among the ripening adolescents of the day. Undoubtedly he pumped oxygen into some exceedingly fusty places, dismantled many false shrines, and leveled toadstools without number, but he was always more the master of negation than of affirmation, and when the Great Depression came, his work went out of style as an extravagance, like fender ornaments. A more genuine cosmopolitan was his friend James Huneker, who did more to acquaint contemporaries with the best that had recently been thought and said and done artistically in Europe than any other man. Huneker humorously referred to himself as "Jack of the Seven Arts—and master of none." But his very catholicity was his virtue as well as his fault. To the generality a skillful expositor of the more salient accomplishments in all fields of art with which they had little acquaintance, Huneker was a poor self-expositor, being merely a man with a method, but how excellent in its simplicity was that method. The first consistent American impressionist, he had capable followers in Paul Rosenfeld, Ben Hecht, and Carl Van Vechten. Huneker, Van Vechten, Hecht, and Joseph Hergesheimer all tried their hands at writing fantasies and very diverting reading were some of these compositions, yet the palm in this field must go either to Elinor Wylie for *The Venetian Glass Nephew* (1925) and *Mr. Hodge and Mr. Hazard* (1928) or to James Branch Cabell in whose Dom Manuel-Felix Kennaston cycle *The Cream of the Jest* (1917) and *Jurgen* (1919) were deservedly the popular favorites. All these writers of fantasy endeavored to show that an acute sensibility in a *déraciné* entitled him to special extra-moral privileges. Their contention could have been tolerated only in times of affluence and easy conscience.

Of all the European movements to gain American adherents that of the symbolists of France won more converts of genius than any other. The symbolist movement, like naturalism, can be traced to the series of disheartening political events occurring in France and culminating with the overthrow of the empire of Napoleon III in 1870, just at the time when Frenchmen were ingesting evolutionary theories. Apprised, on the one hand, of the animalism of man and of the general public obtuseness to the finer values of poetry, and, on the other, of the general hopelessness of the outlook for the arts in a country saddled with a war indemnity, a group of French poets (among them Mallarmé, Verlaine, Rimbaud, Corbière, and Laforgue) took the position that only those persons possessing acute sensibility were worth writing for—"an audience of not more than two or three"—and that art should be cultivated for its own sake. That is, instead of aiming at *communication,* they took *expression* as the purpose of art. Seemingly to be certain that the vulgar did not comprehend, they adopted symbols to which they assigned special meanings and the interpretation of which were the keys to their poems. Hence, the name "Symbolists," although they were also derisively called "Decadents," which epithet they adopted and wore, according to Anatole Baju, "as a flag." The analogy between poetry and music which had been cited by Edgar Allan Poe they approved and developed, along with certain technical devices and motifs that Poe had originated. Him they proclaimed their master and him they studied intensively. In passing the Atlantic, however, Poe's ideas occasionally suffered "sea change into something new and strange."

Between 1908 and 1914 a number of gifted American poets, with Ezra Pound and Wallace Stevens in the van, discovered the "new" French poetry which was already forty years old. Innocent imitation first produced "Imagism," a movement presently controlled and explained to the public by Miss Amy Lowell. But Pound and Stevens kept closer to the spirit of their original models and produced an American equivalent of symbolism. Their work, together with that of their French masters, brought in time the varied allegiance of Conrad Aiken, T. S. Eliot, E. E. Cummings, Marianne Moore, Hart Crane, Archibald MacLeish, and others. Perhaps the greatest interest ever exhibited in poetry in this country was thus provoked in the 1920's and deservedly, for more talent was never lavished on its production. But the American symbolist movement partook of the evils of its prototype—it was too contemptuous of the many and too solicitous of the few. The most noted member of the group proclaimed himself a "Royalist" and a "Tory," while another became a propagandist for Fascism and was later mercifully judged insane. Two of the major figures conspicuously parted company with the symbolists—Hart Crane never used more than the technique of the movement, was humane and liberal; and Archibald MacLeish publicly "signed off" with *The Irresponsibles* (1940), though it must be noted that he published some decadent verse after repudiating decadence. With the end not in sight, symbolism, for all its egotism and "irresponsibility," has given poetry lovers material for which they should dare to be thankful. There is the intellectual appeal of *The Waste Land* (1922) and the deep religious fervor of *Murder in the Cathedral* (1935), the exquisite harmony of "Peter Quince at the Clavier" (1923), the magnificent imagination of *The Bridge* (1930), and the patriotic fervor and strong social indignation of *Frescoes for Mr. Rockefeller's City* (1933), to cite none of the lyrics which stud the movement as flowers do a meadow.

Completely antithetical to symbolism, collectivism was the most disturbing "ism" to blow across the Atlantic and to lodge in the urban fastnesses of the American continent. All modern collectivism of any consequence is Marxian, even if each sect contends that it is the one and only recipient of the true gospel. Karl Marx was a middle class revolutionist who, after the fiasco of

1848 in Germany, proclaimed the inevitable collapse of capitalism and the accession of the proletariat, or industrial working class, to power through the device of revolutionary dictatorship. There is no gainsaying that Marx's historical materialism is a major contribution to scholarship, but as a political thinker and moralist Marx was incompetent, and as a prophet he had somewhat less clairvoyance than a fortune teller at a country fair. According to his theory, the crisis in capitalism should have occurred in the leading industrial economies first and the triumph of revolution there should have rendered inevitable its world acceptance and the quiet elimination of nationalism. But the contrary happened—the proletarian revolution occurred in one of the most backward countries in the world and this intensified nationalism there, even reviving Czarist imperialism and jeopardizing the peace of mankind. In politics, like his immediate predecessors, Marx was a utopian, though no one ridiculed other utopians more than he. He believed that the perfect state would come when the proletariat owned the means of production. This belief is the more surprising since he was an Hegelian in philosophy, holding that out of synthesis of thesis and antithesis new theses are born to produce their antitheses and new syntheses in succession. But he believed, naïvely, that this process would go on only in the realm of ideas after the revolution, as if that would do away utterly with power and property. He did not foresee government bureaucracy and the transfer of power to it; he did not trouble his brain over checks and balances for dictatorship, for which reading in eighteenth-century political writings would have shown him the necessity. Marx's political education was in conspiratorial activity for control of the revolutionary movement of Europe, wherein he learned the ruthlessness he advocated. Despite the flaws which time has revealed in his teachings, Marx's dogmas have had great appeal largely because of what appeared to be their superior morality. Adopting from Adam Smith and Ricardo the theory that labor is the sole creator of value, he appeared to promise the full restoration of that value to its creators. (Of course, he could not actually promise this, for the high cost of maintaining industrial management and the dictatorship, its fat bureaus and its police system, would have to be deducted.) It was this ultimate justice which led his followers to ignore his ethics, which are epitomized in the phrase "the end justifies the means." In the working out of that ethics the immoral means always come to rule, but no end of illustration seems to satisfy mankind on that score.

There are two broad periods of Marxian collectivism in American intellectual history—the periods of the Second (or Socialist) International and that of the Third (or Communist) International. Marx himself transferred the control of the First International to America in 1872, expecting it to atrophy here, which it did. After its demise in 1876 the Black (or Anarchist) International solicited the support of the working class, but the violence which it advocated—"the propaganda of the deed"—alienated most Americans, including most workmen. The anarchist movement in America was broken by its excesses and by the deportations of the 1920's. Meanwhile socialism had gathered its first adherents, chiefly among the intellectuals. Socialism in America prior to the First World

War was evolutionary rather than revolutionary. At the Hague convention of 1872, Marx himself noted the possibility of evolutionary socialism in certain countries. "The worker," he said, "must one day capture political power in order to found the new organization of labor. He must reverse the old policy, which the old institutions maintain, if he will not, like the Christians of old who despised and neglected such things, renounce the things of this world. But we do not assert that the way to reach this goal is the same everywhere. We know that the institutions, the manners, and the customs of the various countries must be considered, and we do not deny that there are countries, like America and England, . . . where the worker may attain his ends by peaceful means. But not in all countries is this the case." Here, certainly, was encouragement to American socialists to utilize peaceful means, such as the ballot, to gain control of the instruments of production, if possible. Further encouragement was offered by the international organization itself, which, influenced by the "revisionist" Eduard Bernstein and by the Erfurt Program of 1891, accepted a Marxism that was evolutionary.

American socialism, moreover, was evolutionary for three other good reasons. It was evolutionary because many of its advocates were also Christian socialists or had been influenced by Christian socialism, and were thus opposed to violence; because the intellectuals in the movement had absorbed the writings of the English Fabians (the Webbs, Bernard Shaw, H. G. Wells, and others), who were convinced evolutionists; and, finally, because American experience had proved that social gains could be made through the ballot box. A further word is needed on the influence of Christian socialism. This was based upon the accounts of the organization of early Christian society in the Acts of the Apostles and popularized by Kingsley, Tolstoy, and others. The movement won some commitment from many Americans because it appealed to an idealism fostered by their religious instruction. But commitment to Christian socialism was always an individual matter—there was no effective, formal Christian Socialist party in the United States as there was in Central Europe. Nevertheless several important literary men were in some degree touched by it: William Dean Howells, William Vaughn Moody, Robert Herrick, Upton Sinclair, and Vachel Lindsay, for example. Symptomatic writing from each pen, respectively, is found in *A Traveler from Altruria* (1894), "Gloucester Moors" (1900), *The Master of the Inn* (1908), *They Call Me Carpenter* (1922), and "Why I Voted the Socialist Ticket" (1913). In these works are sentiments to which one could easily pledge one's heart, if not one's head. A Marxian would maintain, however, that any movement to which one gave one's heart before one gave one's head is suspect, and his suspicion would fasten upon the Christian doctrine of forbearance as protracting unnecessarily the life of capitalism. The "scientific" socialist distinguishes himself from his Christian comrade by his rejection of religious motivation; hence the attacks upon religious doctrines and teachers by such socialists and their friends. Representative, to some critics, is Carl Sandburg's "To a Contemporary Bunk Shooter" (1916).

Literary ability was more limited among the American socialists than among

the English Fabians. One cannot concede much literary skill to the Socialist-
Labor Party editor, Daniel DeLeon, though his bristling polemical style is fairly
typical of that employed by many left-wing propagandists of his day; but
DeLeon has a secure position in history as the exponent of the industrial union
as a revolutionary instrument. Lenin is said to have put his very great stress
upon the importance of the workers' soviets as a result of reading DeLeon's
Socialist Reconstruction of Society (1905). More talented as a writer than
DeLeon, Jack London once confessed that he believed that he himself had set
socialism back five years in the United States by the violence of his speeches.
He remained a member of the regular Socialist Party, however, until 1916,
when he resigned because the Party was not revolutionary enough. Jack London
differed from most of his American comrades in believing that the first socialist
revolution would be inevitably abortive, and that, "after a thousand years,"
during which reactionary forces would be in control, socialism might come
into its own. This revolutionary-evolutionary synthesis is illustrated in *The
Iron Heel* (1908) and in "A Curious Fragment" (1911). As a motivating force
in his writing, London's interest in socialism is less important than his concern
over the battles of the superior and strong to survive in a hostile universe. Curiously enough, the Nietzschean speculations also attracted Upton Sinclair during
the early years of his career. The Lithuanian hero of *The Jungle* (1906) survives
not only because he embraces socialism but also because he is a kind of superman. An unswerving socialist himself, Upton Sinclair is the most prolific writer
of our times. His very abundance of production precludes high excellence, yet
his critics have been a little too eager, on the whole, to ignore him as a literary
figure, thinking, perhaps, in this way to dismiss him. At his best, he is a master
of the contrived narrative, and if *The Jungle* (1906), *King Coal* (1917),
Oil (1927), *Boston* (1928) and the "Lanny Budd" series annoy the critic
because of the shallowness of much of the characterization and the facility of the
writing, let him reflect on the thousands of readers in many countries that they
have satisfied. As a polemicist, Sinclair proved in *The Brass Check* (1919),
The Goose Step (1923), and *The Profits of Religion* (1918), respectively, that
money influences the news, higher education, and the churches. Americans
can never again have quite the faith in the infallibility of these agencies which
they had before Upton Sinclair appeared.

Several striking adaptations of Marxism have been suggested by Americans.
In *The Engineers and the Price System* (1921), Thorstein Veblen, whose
Theory of the Leisure Class (1899) had already established him as the father
of "institutional economics," argued that the engineers, taking advantage of
their "know-how" in a society dependent upon them, should form a "soviet,"
seize the industrial economy, and administer it for the common good. The
"technocrats," who owed their first inspiration to Edward Bellamy's *Looking
Backward* (1887), derived much of their program in 1930–33 from Veblen's
book, without being as frank as he about the Marxian inspiration of their
proposals. Max Lerner, college professor and editorial writer, advocated in *It Is
Later Than You Think* (1938) a kind of individual "democratic collectivism"

while pointing to what he regarded as the "Six Errors" of Marxism. Such heterodoxy—or originality—as Veblen and Lerner represent is not tolerated by the strict Marxian; nevertheless, the orthodox doctrinaire was taught to tolerate and accept from certain writers, whom Lenin labeled "Leftists," unorthodox support on many issues prior to revolution. A "Leftist" is not a Marxian or even "a fellow traveler" necessarily; he is a man whose ardor for humanity has carried him into a more radical position on some issues than caution would dictate; consequently he may be utilized by the collectivists if it is to their advantage to do so. It would seem that, early in their careers, both Carl Sandburg and Van Wyck Brooks played the role of "Leftists." Sandburg has never been too explicit about his position, yet as discernibly as he is a Scandinavian mystic and a symbolist poet on certain occasions, just as clearly he was a poet sympathetic with the Socialist Party "line" on other occasions. Through his *alter ego,* in *Opinions of Oliver Allston* (1941), Brooks explains, "I have never been a Marxist, but I have an American socialist grain that is as tough as the Marxist. Marxism controverts my instincts. . . . I am a free-willer from the outset"; but this and passages in his early work would seem to qualify him for a place in Lenin's classification. Neither man, however, was ever "used" in the way that some "Leftists" have been used by the Communist Party; and each in recent years has sufficiently affirmed his American liberalism —Sandburg by his labor of love on the biography of Lincoln, Brooks by his almost too reverent handling of our literary tradition.

American socialism foundered on the war issue in 1917. The party split on a declaration to oppose the war, and the more radical leaders—Eugene Debs and "Big Bill" Haywood, for example—went to jail for hampering army conscription. No one noted that they did no more than James Russell Lowell had done during the Mexican War. After the war, at a beck from Leon Trotsky, the Comintern repudiated the leadership of the American Socialist Party, thus opening a breach between the socialists and communists which has never healed. Formation of the Communist Party in the United States raised the issue of whether it is an American institution or an agency of an alien power. Mounting tension between this country and Russia after the Second World War and a clearer vision of what communism might mean if established here, have resulted in firm opposition to communism throughout the United States. Today known Party membership is an invitation for opprobrium.

Several literary figures were involved in the anti-war controversy of 1917. Floyd Dell and Max Eastman, for example, as editors of *Masses,* were twice tried for treason. Eastman, who became translator of some of Leon Trotsky's works into English, notably of his *History of the Russian Revolution,* eventually repudiated Marxism as "unscientific." He became an indefatigable propagandist against Stalinism. A very amusing contributor to *Masses* prior to the treason trials was the patriarch, Charles Erskine Scott Wood, whose pacifist sketches in *Heavenly Discourse* (1917) are among the wittiest satires of the time. Wood, incidentally, had written the first long revolutionary poem, *The Poet in the Desert* (1915), with Marxian implications. One of the tragedies of the war was the virtual termination of the career of Randolph Bourne, the brilliant young critic, who, because of his pacifism and his adherence to the St. Louis platform, could find no outlet for his material. He was an easy victim of influenza in 1918.

The first American intellectual to uphold the Bolshevik revolution was John Reed, correspondent and author of *Ten Days That Shook the World* (1919). Reed made fewer converts to collectivism, however, than did Lincoln Steffens, the old muckraker, who, after serving on the Bullitt Commission to Russia, came back and declared that he had "seen the future and it works." The declaration, not quite in these words, is repeated at the end of his popular *Autobiography* (1931). During the 1930's, the decade of the Great Depression, it was fashionable for young intellectuals, aping Steffens, to bid farewell to reform and to take revolution to their bosoms—this, during one of the greatest reform periods the country had known. Among the most talented of the literary people who supported the Left were the critics Granville Hicks and Edmund Wilson and the Negro fiction writer, Richard Wright. Hicks and Wright became Party members but eventually resigned, Hicks because of the Russo-German pact of 1939 and Wright because of the arbitrary liquidation of the John Reed clubs, which had been founded to encourage young writers. Both men appear to have retained their faith in collectivism, though not in that variety represented by Stalin. Edmund Wilson, after extravagant expressions of devotion to Marxism (*Das Kapital* is "the poetry of economics"!) and of affection for Russia (see *Travels in Two Democracies*, 1936), appears to have retired into a kind of intransigent misanthropy. The validity of much that these men wrote is unaffected by their political views: Edmund Wilson's *Axel's Castle* (1929) is a model piece of criticism; Hicks' *I Like America* (1938) is a most convincing analysis of natural feeling; and Wright's volume of short stories, *Uncle Tom's Children* (1938), based on carefully marshaled facts, is eloquent beyond the author's thesis that Uncle Tomism, "turning the other cheek," is not as good a policy as militant action for the Negro if he wishes equality. The three best "Depression poets"—Horace Gregory, Kenneth Fearing, and Muriel Rukeyser—"threw their weight upon the left," but shifted it, after the fashion of Robert Frost's "thinker," as time passed. All three are somewhat uneven in performance. Fearing by overstatement and cacaphony loses what he gains by directness; the obscurity of Gregory and Rukeyser is compensated for by disciplined emotion and the sensitive selection of vocabulary.

Whether collectivism will express itself in new forms, enlist more persuasive advocates, or even survive as an intellectual force in this country is a question that only the future can answer. But that communism is at present inimical to art, music, and literature may be stated as fact. No creative artist can thrive in a society which decrees what he thinks, as does the Kremlin today and as would a proletarian dictatorship in the United States; the essential nihilism of the current Stalinist philosophy should turn intelligent men, whatever their economic status, away from it whenever they contemplate the function of the arts and the individual life.

In tracing the intellectual background of American literature of the twentieth century, and in indicating how conflicting views and conditions have been mirrored in the work of American authors, it is convenient to treat separately the forces which have emanated from Europe or have operated simultaneously in both the Old and New World, and those which apply mainly or peculiarly to American society. Obviously there cannot be any hard and fast distinction between them, and there are some disadvantages inherent in the use of the division. Ideas and literary techniques flow back and forth, both ways, across the Atlantic. To stress European influences leads sometimes to the impression that our authors are imitators only, whereas they often influence Europeans quite as much as they themselves are affected. Moreover, to write of a poet or a novelist that he is a Marxist or symbolist or primitivist is often to overlook the individual bent of his mind and the strong attachment he may have for native mores and institutions. Carl Sandburg obviously was attracted by views rooted in European speculation, but he is primarily a son of the United States, with ways of reaction explicable only as such. So with Theodore Dreiser, Eugene O'Neill, Sherwood Anderson, and Stephen Crane. Nevertheless the separation of our writers into two groups has advantages enough in facilitating the explanation of contemporary trends in our thought and literature to justify its use.

One of the major literary phenomena of the present century, in the United States no less than in Europe, is the vigorous flowering of the critical temper. This has been demonstrated already in the paragraphs dealing with the interest in the various imported "isms." The writers who in their themes "stay most at home" share with the expatriates a concern over the state of modern civilization. With the developing hold of science everywhere, and especially with the stress laid on psychology and sociology, the individual artist was irresistibly moved into the critical current, and more than formerly was impelled to ask, What are the potentialities, used and unused, in present-day life? Can the individual determine with more certainty than before what is wrong with his environment and so perhaps bring about its improvement?

The expenditure of critical energy in the United States since 1900 has consequently been enormous. It has been reflected in every literary form and has concentrated at one time or another on every social institution and human situation. Capitalism, for example, has provoked the severest kind of critical rebuke, as well as much spirited defense, from writers. Many of them profess to regard it as the poorest *milieu* for the artist. In contrast with the professions, they argue, how few poets, novelists, and dramatists has business provided from its ranks! Yet business, for purposes of its own recruitment, developed a literature of success and liberally subsidized through advertising the magazines which disseminated this literature. The fathers of this conservative school of writing were S. S. McClure, Elbert Hubbard, and George Horace Lorimer. The last, as editor of the *Saturday Evening Post,* defined the type of fiction and the sort of article most satisfactory to the business class. From this point of view, his own series of letters *From a Self-Made Merchant to His Son*

(1903) is historically important as stating most explicitly the creed to which the business opportunist must conform. Since an urban society is much more dependent upon manufactured goods than is a rural society, urban living was cried up and rural living cried down early in the century. Even small town living was scoffed at—witness George Ade's "Fable of the Slim Girl" (1899). If such "eccentrics" as Edward Filene and Henry Ford are excepted, Big Business produced only one original thinker in the first half of the century, Frederick Winslow Taylor, author of *The Principles of Scientific Management* (1911). That Taylor's name now excites the harshest scorn from labor is the result of the distortion of his principles rather than their even and just application. After all, there is a sense in which industrial efficiency is social usefulness, or our whole technology is a mistake.

Another and very different type of conservatism from that of the business man grew out of the fear of complexity and change. This conservatism is antithetical to the first, for American business, despite the suppression of inventions by certain large corporations, has developed largely by welcoming change and complexity. Because the sudden rise of new industries and urban development meant, however, the constant emancipation of new groups who seemed to challenge not merely the economic position of the established order but its cultural standards as well, social prejudice was invoked in the defense of endangered sensibility. The most famous enemy of complexity was Henry Adams who, in *The Education of Henry Adams* (1906), attributed his own "defeat" and the grossness of society to the want of unifying purpose in his times, such as he had discovered in the worship of the Virgin in the thirteenth century and had glorified in *Mont-Saint-Michel and Chartres* (1904). Appalled by some of the implications of the new releases of energy, after his first fascination with them, Adams ultimately reached the conclusion that thought itself was a kind of energy and hence, like heat, could be dissipated into the cold interstellar spaces. Fantastically, he plotted the graph of man's downward sweep to oblivion. But all of his speculation grew out of an immense self-pity, mingled with megalomania, because his times ignored his proffered services and chose those of mere vulgarians. His hatred of Grant in *The Education* is matched by the fierce anti-semitism of his unpublished letters. Adams was, however, a weakling; though he came to the conclusion that the whole Protestant movement was a mistake, just as the modern adoration of science was a mistake, and though the final declaration of his life was that of his adoration of the Virgin, he never had the courage to join the Roman Church. There was something effeminate about him, and it is not surprising to find some analogy between his attitudes and those assumed by certain of the women poets of the day who likewise shuddered away from "the reeking herd." One thinks of Elinor Wylie, Sara Teasdale, and others of that group that Louis Untermeyer wittily characterized as the "O-God-the-pain, Girls" school of literature. Here was never offered, however, such an elaborate defense of position as the self-conscious Adams attempted; Miss Wylie, having taken the stand that Beauty was her province, denied the force of morals or any other force within that province. "Say not of Beauty she is good/Or aught but beautiful. . . ."

Although Adams turned backwards to the thirteenth century in admiration, his view of the hopeless state of the race did not dispose him to discover utilizable principles in the past for his own time. This quest became that of yet a third group of conservatives who were less pessimistic about the future of mankind. Under the leadership of Paul Elmer More and Irving Babbitt, a nucleus within this group designated itself the "New Humanists." In their view, society had been corrupted by the ideas of Rousseau, by his sentimentalism and equalitarianism. They believed in the stratification of society and despised the forces which make for leveling. As followers of Plato, they recognized a dichotomy in human nature, and held that the spiritual man should check and restrain the natural man. Representative of their work is More's "The New Morality" (1914), with its attack upon "social sympathy." The New Humanists claimed William Crary Brownell—who had a better grounded system of values than they—as their predecessor, though without his assent. Stuart Sherman worked with them during most of his critical career, especially during his unhappy contest with H. L. Mencken over the value of "Puritanism," but in "The Emotional Discovery of America" (1924), an essay of surrender, he broke with them and conceded the worth of the new literature that they had consistently deplored.

The successive defeats of the Greenback, Granger, and Populist movements in the latter half of the nineteenth century, demonstrating that the agrarian population could no longer control the affairs of the nation, along with the ascendancy of the financiers and stockbrokers over the landed gentry, brought together in one large conservative camp diverse writers who contended that out of our agrarian and genteel past the best rules for living could be framed. E. A. Robinson, of Gardiner, Maine, held that the eighteenth-century code of his village squire was an admirable one for man, whatever his circumstances. Thus the tight-lipped conduct of "Richard Cory" (1897) is exalted over that of "Bewick Finzer" (1916), for the former makes a brave show, whatever his difficulty, while the latter skulks, "like a charity boy or a bastard," after losing his money in speculation. In "Demos" (1920) and in other poems Robinson shows that he thought the leadership of a "natural aristocracy" essential to human welfare. Hamilton, we know, was his idol. The rugged individualism of the Vermonter is exemplary enough for the taste of Robert Frost. Never a disciple of "progress," Frost found in the Roman poets and philosophers a cyclical theory of history to which he could assent. New England is his figurative "desert isle" where he has waited for the ancient truths to reenact themselves, as, he tells us in "The Black Cottage" (1914), they surely will. *New Hampshire* (1923) reveals his hostility to all the literary "isms" which currently excited Greenwich Village; and pieces like "Two Tramps in Mud Time" (1936) show his dissent from New Deal social measures, here, specifically, "made work." As we can see from "Bridewater's Half Dollar" (1935), other New Deal measures, like home relief, elicited the wrath of the Hoosier conservative, Booth Tarkington, who, after a brief fling at social reform in the legislature of his native state when he was young, renounced all kinds of radicalism forever. Novels like *The Turmoil* (1915) and *The Plutocrat* (1927) show, however, that their author does not share Frost and Robinson's back country suspicion of the "money getter." The countryman's distrust of the city is convincingly depicted in Willa Cather's "Neighbour Rosicky" (1932); Miss Cather's hero speaks not out of rustic ignorance, but out of a background of slum survival in Europe and New York. On the positive side novels like *O Pioneers* (1915) and *My Antonia* (1918) extol the rural virtues, and it is these virtues which enable her characters to succeed when their careers carry them to the great cities. Nowhere is the loneliness of the great city and the homesickness of the small-town boy in it more graphically recorded than in the early work of Thomas Wolfe, who most of his life was to try the world by the standards of Asheville, North Carolina. However Wolfe in the very end discovered, as his book title reveals, *You Can't Go Home Again* (1940), and composed the unpredictable defense of the little business man and city dweller, found in "The Hollow Men" section of that book. In defiance of the whole Southern tradition of romanticizing its past, Ellen Glasgow wrote her realistic novels of reconstruction in Virginia; then under the personal influence of James Branch Cabell she produced the urbane and witty books of which *The Romantic Comedians* (1926) is representative; but ultimately she felt too strongly "the backward pull of inherited tendencies" and sought to discover in the relish of the Southern gentility for living a quality to set Southern writing above that done elsewhere in the country. A movement harking back to Bourbonism in the South originated at Nashville, Tennessee, styled itself "Agrarian," and issued the manifesto *I'll Take My Stand* in 1930. Two of the contributors to that volume were poets of note, John Crowe Ransom and Allan Tate. Their verse does not show the hatred of industrialism and commercialism found in the manifesto, but rather their allegiance to the myth of "The South." Ransom is a disciple of Coleridge whose admiration for Southern chivalry finds a most curious expression in "Captain Carpenter" (1924); traditionalism produced Tate's "Ode to the Confederate Dead" (1928) however unconventional its pattern.

The writing done by the authors of conservative temper is more even in quality than that done by most other groups. Wolfe is the only inconsistent performer among them; if he is at times pedestrian, or over-expressive after the fashion of Southern orators, he is so much a master of language at other times that he maintains the high average of the group. The best work of the symbolists is beyond the attainment of most of the conservatives, as it is contrary to their inclination, but has any symbolist written as much poetry of high quality as Robinson or Frost? Eliot may be a great harmonist, indeed he is, but he is no melodist, like Teasdale or Wylie. The carefully wrought prose of Henry Adams, Ellen Glasgow, Booth Tarkington, and Willa Cather, set a high standard for any sort of emulation. Traditionalism, conservatism, reactionism are three states of the white corpuscles in the body politic and cultural—the preservative agents of the blood stream in states of somnolence, vigor, and hyperactivity. A society without a good conservative element is not a well-balanced society.

The color-giving, life-giving element in our society is the liberal element. Many of the opponents of liberalism accept the shallow view of Laski, that liberalism is the outmoded, once popular, materialistic creed of the eighteenth century—the creed which carried the middle class to power. In the sense that Marxism is the creation of one man whose thought is the infallible law to all his followers, Liberalism is not assignable to one fountainhead or age. It is not exclusively the teaching of Locke, Montesquieu, Adam Smith, Harrington, Franklin, Paine or Jefferson, whatever these and many others may have contributed to it. Just as it was shaped by many in the beginning, so it has been modified by many in its history. If it ever were an eighteenth-century philosophy—and of course it was, though not exclusively so—it has long since ceased to be chiefly that. In its twentieth-century form it has tenets unknown to those who generally maintained it at an earlier time.

One of the most important changes in liberalism has been in the concept of government it supports. Whereas the American revolutionist hoped for a government in which "law could be king, rather than the king, law" and strove to embody all his liberties in a fundamental law, or constitution, which could not readily be altered, and whereas the great effort of nineteenth-century jurisprudence was to preserve this fundamental law as little altered as possible, the modern liberal would modify, and has modified, this law to make it a flexible instrument for social use. He feels less sure than the Founding Fathers that society can thrive under the blanket of an unalterable, if admirable, constitution. More important—and this is another tenet of his philosophy—he no longer believes in the *perfect* society or utopia (that is the delusion of the Marxians) but in the *good* society. The good society is a plastic society in which no one class is perpetually discriminated against and in which the law is administered for no one group. The good society is always a tentative, or experimental, society. It is a society which must change its structure rather constantly—hence no perfection—to reward those fairly who serve it best and who may, incidentally, be in a disadvantageous position because of some sudden technological change and economic adjustment. The good society is a moral society. That is, it is a self-critical society, always challenging itself to be as good as shifting circumstances will allow.

The liberal philosophy has been profoundly affected by the revelation that there is no absolute good—that good is a variable and a relative. This is but one of the important concepts given liberalism by that school of philosophers who have variously styled themselves pragmatists, radical empiricists, instrumentalists, and experimentalists. The two great figures of this school are William James and John Dewey. More than anyone else in modern times, James convinced the public that philosophy is not a set of abstract principles to be manipulated for the delight of a small professional class, the philosophers, but an instrument for use. It is an instrument for use in a physical and social world.

of flux, a world in which human volition is responsible for whatever values are achieved, as James demonstrated in *The Will to Believe* (1897). The special triumph of Dewey as a thinker is that he saw man immersed in his experience, as part and parcel of it, and that he perceived this experience as common to all men, for experience, he contended, both *is* and may *be had*. The analysis that discriminates *sensation* in the Lockean-Berkleian sense is always a *post-facto* mental operation—nothing is ever actually received in an isolated state as sensation, but confusion on this score has created the dichotomies that plague man's thought and his existence. Erected on from this important tenet, Dewey's philosophy has had a practical effect on many American institutions. The father of progressive education, he is also the crusader who fought the creation of secondary schools on class lines—industrial arts schools for the children of workers, humane and genteel establishments for the sons of the managerial class and professionals. Working from the analogy and the doctrine he provided, Justices Holmes, Brandeis, and Cardoza attacked the concept that human law should have the force of natural law and created "social jurisprudence," in which the judge gives thought to the consequences of his rulings, not merely to their consistency with precedent. Thus they brought about the greatest revolution in the law since Roman days.

The pragmatic liberal in politics was not the mere opportunist his opponents charged him with being. Frequently he was a man who was conscious that society is handicapped by its generalized and codified past, and by speech and action he made it clear that his preference was for a social order so plastic that it responds readily to change and new necessities. He saw government not as a form or institution but as an instrument. His reflections created a body of political literature which constitutes a challenge to preexistent work in this field. Three presidents of the United States in the twentieth century—two with a remarkable flare for memorable phrase and one a conscious literary craftsman—enlarged the office of the Chief Executive and increased its usefulness by unprecedented experimental extension of its powers, beginning with Theodore Roosevelt's forced arbitration of the anthracite coal strike in 1902. The Roosevelt who campaigned in 1912 for the Presidency on the Progressive ticket was a more important person to the literature of politics, however, than was the Roosevelt who succeeded McKinley as head of the state. As his most famous address in shaping himself for that campaign, "The New Nationalism" (1910), reveals, he was a man charged with unorthodox ideas. With the exception of the novel proposal to recall judicial decisions, Roosevelt's program was derivative—but it was derivative from men with new ideas. Herbert Croly, first editor of the *New Republic* and author of *The Promise of American Life* (1909), asked for the same national awareness in domestic affairs that Roosevelt had shown in international affairs as president. Croly maintained that both the large corporate aggregate and the national labor union had great utility, and he defined the role of government as arbitrator between the two and as regulator of each. Charles R. Van Hise, president of the University of Wisconsin and author of *Concentration and Control* (1912), likewise regarded corporate concentration, within limits scientifically measured to exclude monopoly, as useful and recommended the commission form of control. In envisioning the duty of the national government to be planning for the social good, these men also greatly expanded the scope and significance of the liberal philosophy. Later Raymond Moley contended that the makers of the New Deal, lacking a social program, turned to Theodore Roosevelt, Herbert Croly, and Charles R. Van Hise for their inspiration. Franklin D. Roosevelt, inheritor of the social interests of his distant cousin, had, however, before he became President, already begun a series of experiments in solving social problems as Governor of New York State. Franklin Roosevelt, as a member of the Wilson Administration also, had seen Woodrow Wilson abandon the attitudes he had taken in *The New Freedom* (1913) toward nationalism and "government by experts" (Wilson's derisive phrase for the use of commissions) for solutions of social problems by the use of federal power. The New Deal was a harvest time, rather than a seed time, of social planning in the United States. That we were not overwhelmed by the Great Depression of the 1930's was largely the result of liberal thinking earlier in the century.

In 1902 Brooks Adams expressed the fear that, because of the rigidity of governmental structure maintained by an inflexible Constitution, the United States might fail to solve the complicated problems of the technological society that was emerging. "The conditions of the twentieth century are almost precisely the reverse of those of the eighteenth, and yet the national organization not only remains unaltered, but is prevented from automatic adjustment by the provisions of a written document, which, in practice, cannot be amended." As liberals watched piece after piece of useful social legislation invalidated by the courts their concern on this issue grew. Theodore Roosevelt angrily declared that the Constitution had never been meant to be "a strait-jacket." His proposal for the recall of judicial decisions (suggested by the recall of judges which had been tried by some Western Progressive States) was intended to overcome the rigidity of government that the courts imposed. Never a conspicuous critic of the courts, Woodrow Wilson was, nevertheless, a consistent critic of the inflexibility of our system. He wished a government to rise or fall on its merits. The tragedy of his failure in international affairs was that he sought to shape our world policy as an English prime minister would shape it, with the treaty-making right of the Senate in the Constitution standing in the way. Franklin Roosevelt's quarrel with the Supreme Court over his social legislation again illustrated the inflexibility of the Constitution. But so venerated by the public was our fundamental law that seemingly no amount of illustration of its limitations had any early effect with the people in reprobating the strict constructionalists on the bench. The sacrosanct character of the document itself had to be challenged. This was done by J. Allen Smith in *The Spirit of American Government* (1907) and much more impressively by Charles A. Beard in *An Economic Interpretation of the Constitution of the United States* (1913). It was shown that property influence had been a determining factor in framing those clauses in the Constitution which circumvent and abrogate the public will. Though Beard, in particular, was abused as no other scholar in our history has been abused, what he had demonstrated took some lodgment in the public consciousness and reinforced by examples of arbitrary constructionalism, turned the public temper against the courts. It was realization by the justices of the Supreme Court of general disfavor, rather than the threat of action against them, that led them eventually to uphold much of Franklin Roosevelt's legislation. It seems doubtful now if rigid construction will ever again be invoked; gradually everywhere the teachings of the new social jurisprudence should have the effect of making both the law and the courts more regardful of fundamental human rights.

Self-critical and humane, the liberal man of letters did not always, like Charles Beard, render his greatest service by strategic support to political action, though most were ready to do so. The literary liberal, however, made a contribution to society by teaching tolerance, the open mind, the questing spirit. In human relationships, his was the task of evaluating the devaluated. Not infrequently his convictions led him into positions not assumed by the generality. Thus, for example, while Theodore Roosevelt was successfully popularizing our new role as a world power, F. P. Dunne tempered what might have been jingoism with ridicule and William Vaughn Moody, along with Mark Twain, expressed strong disapproval of the suppression of the Aguinaldo revolt in the Philippines. Again, when the Commonwealth of Massachusetts embarked on the process of putting to death two anarchists, with the help of public apathy and local approval, it was the literary liberals, like Heywood Broun, Edna Millay, and John Dos Passos, who came to their support, and not the communists, who held aloof for ideological reasons. The depth of liberal feeling on the issue is revealed in such things as Miss Millay's "Justice Denied in Massachusetts" (1927) and Maxwell Anderson's *Winterset* (1935). Such counter-current manifestations are probably more typical of literary liberalism than is the support which Percy MacKaye and Stephen Vincent Benét gave to Woodrow Wilson and Franklin Roosevelt in their crusades against the Kaiser and the Führer, however necessary such support always is.

As much as any ancient philosopher, as much as any Christian mystic, indeed, as much as any modern collectivist, the literary liberal despises avarice, and is as quick to recognize it in an institution as in a man. Two of the great American indictments of greed in our time are Sinclair Lewis' attack upon that evil in the medical profession in *Arrowsmith* (1925) and John Dos Passos' revelation of its power to corrupt and to destroy throughout all levels of society in his trilogy *The 42nd Parallel, 1919,* and *The Big Money* (1930–36). The published statistics on the average physician's income and the instances known to everyone of the impoverishment of a friend through surgery or long illness show how timely was *Arrowsmith;* it is worth noting, however, that it preceded the political agitation for socialized medicine. Dos Passos also must have planned his trilogy at a time when there was no general disillusionment with the boom era of the twenties, though the first volume appeared after the stock market crash in 1929. That is, both authors disapproved of the current materialism when principle had to be invoked, morality drawn upon, rather than when débâcle made facile denunciation of greed popular. In Max Gottlieb the author of *Arrowsmith* has given us an enduring picture of the selfless scientist and has conveyed adequately his high sense of duty. Against the ruthless climbers, like Ward Morehouse, in his trilogy, Dos Passos arrays a number of "little people," frequently bewildered and often lost, whose impulses are a critical commentary on those of their predatory coevals. Mary French is such a one. But Lewis and Dos Passos reflect the liberal attitude toward avarice. The enemies of liberalism scoff at literary attacks like theirs as superficial—they effect no structural change in society to make excessive materialism impossible. Yet it remains a question if materialism can be checked save by the persistent good intention of determined men. If a society can never be any better than its more powerful members, personal morality still needs to be invoked, conscience quickened.

In a society with one ethical code for all, men have equal moral stature. It used to be said that there are no titles before God. Wary of emphasizing morals since the effective attacks on Puritanism, the literary liberal has tried to find and to demonstrate the common humanity of all classes and races of men. The triumph of O. Henry, for example, is not that he furnished passing pleasure to hordes of readers by quips and clever plotting, but that he showed the worth of lives regarded as only drab and dull. It is a question if there is more of sentimentality in his short stories than in the pictures of the *lumpenproletariat* of John Steinbeck and William Saroyan. During the past two decades, in the derogation of liberalism, it has been fashionable to label any frank expression of feeling as "sentimentality"; if there is some justice in applying this destructive epithet to Steinbeck's position in *Of Mice and Men* (1937), there is little in affixing it to his feeling for the "Okies" in *The Grapes of Wrath* (1939). And if there is a danger of sentimentality in our whole attitude toward the criminal today, because of the "social sympathy" that Paul Elmer More deplores, there are examples enough of the menace of so-called "popular justice" to warrant respectful attention to Saroyan's "Hello Out There" (1942). If the author's sympathies in *Tortilla Flat* (1935) are suspect, let us not forget that as an artist Steinbeck is trying to treat more than superficially a group regarded in California as composed wholly of congenital liars and thieves.

On the whole, the liberal is no more sentimental than his fellows. Unafraid of his heart, he can still use his head in evaluating all classes of men and in exposing their limitations. Thus Robert Herrick does not exclude from his novels what a ruthless materialism may do to its patent victims but with the dispassion of a physician he devotes his chief attention to showing what it does to the materialist himself. Likewise Edith Wharton, who savagely caricatured the "Goth" in such novels as *The House of Mirth* (1905) and *The Custom of the Country* (1913), is really less interested in the depredations of this impudent and unscrupulous invader of the society which she knew as a girl than she is in the weakness of that society itself, which she makes the

main theme of her masterpiece, *The Age of Innocence* (1920). To Edgar
Lee Masters, social position amounts to little in the scale of human values.
He is interested in the sensibilities and feelings that make one a good companion or an endurable townsman. Masters, incidentally, provides the most
interesting study of the new transvaluation of values following the attack on
Puritanism. The liberal, while expressing the most generous sympathy for the
underdog, may see that his exacerbated behavior is a contributing factor in his
discomfort. Nowhere is this better illustrated than in Paul Green's characterization of his protagonist in the courageous play *In Abraham's Bosom*
(1926). It is essentially unsentimental to see the limitations in the cause or in
the people whom one supports. It is this attitude that Pearl Buck has tried to
bring to her great task of winning Americans to appreciate Oriental ways and
traditions.

The literary achievement of the liberal stacks up well against other achievements. For sheer lyricism, Edna Millay has only a few peers in her time; the
experiments of Lindsay, Sandburg, Benét, and Maxwell Anderson in seeking to discover a natural American rhythm and to employ that in poetry
have resulted in verse that is quite as successful in its way as that which has
been written to conceal the intention of the artist. Such poetry has to be
gauged, not by its subtleties, but by its transparencies. *The Waste Land* and
The Bridge can never win one to poetry who has not already acquired a
taste for it; Lindsay's "The Moon's the North Wind's Cooky" or "The Congo"
might. *John Brown's Body* provides a necessary complement, as a composition,
to the more sophisticated major efforts of Eliot and Crane. *Winterset,* as well
as *Murder in the Cathedral,* is the successful culmination of a movement to
revive the poetic drama that was begun by MacKaye, Moody, Stickney, Pea-
body, Hovey, and Robinson at the turn of the century. In the novel, Mrs.
Wharton and Sinclair Lewis, despite the shoddiness of their later work, have
been worthy successors of the great realists of the nineteenth century. For
epic qualities Mrs. Buck's trilogy of the Chinese earth challenges comparison
with the best work of the Scandinavians. Not of the stature of James Joyce,
John Dos Passos has made some enduring contributions to the technique of prose
fiction with the discontinuous narrative, the poetic biography, the "newsreel,"
and the "camera eye." It is he and Sinclair Lewis who have done the best work
at documentation in contemporary American fiction. The artful lack of art—
sometimes a painful mannerism with William Saroyan—has produced some
remarkable stories of children; on the other hand, John Steinbeck's *In Dubious
Battle* is as tightly contrived and as dramatic a novel as *The Great Gatsby*.

When time has winnowed the writers of the first half of the twentieth
century, when the trends here pointed out for study have gathered mostly into
one stream, it is likely that there will be as many readers of, let us say, the
novels of the liberals as of the poetry of the decadents. Posterity will not be
judging writers on the basis of their present dispositions, but rather on their
power to awaken responses in readers who share with them only a common
interest in humanity—not the same paraphernalia of living. Metaphor, music,

and emotional experience endure; beauty endures; allusion and documentation alike become an encumbrance, save to the historian. It will be those, whether decadent, liberal, or other, who are richest in metaphor, music, and emotion, who are richest in the realization of beauty, who will survive. Should we be born again several centuries from now we would doubtless read some of our contemporaries—but not with the excitement and pleasure, perhaps, with which we first read them. Complete artistic understanding and sympathy can belong only to the reader of a writer in his own time. That is our special possession—the wealth that cannot be expropriated, the wealth that endures only as long as the possessor.

John Herbert Nelson
Oscar Cargill

THE NATURALISTS

THEODORE DREISER
(1871–1945)

FROM *THE FINANCIER* *

· CHAPTER I

[A BOY AND A SQUID]

*I came into the world feet first and was
born with teeth.*
*The nurse did prophesy that I should
snarl and bite.*

—RICHARD III.

The Philadelphia into which Frank
Algernon Cowperwood was born was
at his very birth already a city of two
hundred and fifty thousand and more.
It was set with handsome parks, notable buildings, and crowded with historic memories. Many of the things
that we and he knew later were not
then in existence—the telegraph, telephone, express company, ocean
steamer, or city delivery of mails.
There were no postage-stamps or registered letters. The street-car had not
arrived, and in its place were hosts of
omnibuses, and for longer travel, the
slowly developing railroad system still
largely connected with canals. Young
Cowperwood's father was a bank clerk
at his birth, and ten years later, when
young Cowperwood was turning a
very sensible, vigorous eye on the
world, his father was still a clerk, although he was a much more trusted
and desired one, and was so near a

tellership that there was not the least
doubt in the world that he would get
it. The next year, because the president died and the vice-president became president, the cashier was made
vice-president, and Mr. Henry Worthington Cowperwood was moved into
the place vacated by the promoted
teller. He was a happy man. It meant
the munificent sum of thirty-five hundred dollars a year, and he decided,
as he told his wife joyously the night
he heard it, that he, or they, rather,
would now move from Number 21
Buttonwood Street to Number 124
New Market, where there was a nice
brick house of three stories in height,
as opposed to the one of two stories
which they now occupied. Buttonwood Street, at the point which they
were now located, was rapidly being
surrounded by business conditions
which were unbearable; and New
Market at the point he had picked on
was removed, at least a score of blocks,
from the region which was once so
nice but was now becoming so sorrow-
fully defiled. There was the probability that some day they would come
into something even much better than
this, but for the present this was sufficient. He was exceedingly grateful.
Mr. Henry Worthington Cowperwood was at this time a significant
figure—tall, lean, inquisitorial, clerkly,
the pink of perfection in the niceties
of commercial conduct, absolutely
practical—a man who believed only
what he saw, was not at all disturbed

about those silly fancies which might trouble the less rational brains of this world, and content to be what he was —a banker, or prospective one. He looked upon life as a business situation or deal, with everybody born as more or less capable machines to take a part in it. It was surprising to him to see how many incapable or unsatisfactory machines there were; but, thank heaven, now that he was getting along fairly well, this was no affair of his. At first, when he was much younger—he was now thirty-six —life had seemed just a little unsatisfactorily organized. But now—well now it didn't look so bad. He had nice, smooth, closely cropped side-whiskers coming to almost the lower lobe of his ears, and his upper lip was smooth and curiously long. He had a straight nose of a somewhat longish length and a chin that tended to be pointed. His manner might have been called severe, though really it was more of a cultivated manner than anything else. His eyebrows were bushy, emphasizing vague grayish-green eyes, and his hair was short and smooth and nicely parted. He wore a frock-coat always—it was quite the financial thing in these days—and a high hat. And he kept his hands and nails immaculately clean. Being ambitious to get somewhere socially and financially without failing, he was very careful of whom or with whom he talked; and he was as much afraid of expressing a rabid or unpopular political or social opinion as he was of being seen with an evil character, though he had no opinion of great political significance to express. He was neither anti nor pro slavery, though the air was stormy with abolition sentiment and its opposition. He believed sincerely that vast fortunes were to be made out of railroads if one only had the capital and that curious thing, a magnetic

personality—the ability to win the confidence of others. He was sure that Andrew Jackson was all wrong in his opposition to Nicholas Biddle and the United States Bank, one of the great issues of the day; and he was worried, as he might well be, by the perfect storm of wildcat money which was floating about and which was constantly coming to his bank—discounted, of course—and handed out again to anxious borrowers at a profit, you may be sure. His bank was the Third National of Philadelphia, located in that center of all Philadelphia, and indeed almost, at that time, of all national finance, Third Street; and its owners did a brokerage business on the side. As a broker's clerk, Mr. Cowperwood had to know all sorts of banks here and elsewhere, for immense quantities of uncurrent banknotes were to be handled, distributed, and mailed each day. There was a perfect plague of State banks, great and little, in those days, issuing notes practically without regulation upon insecure and unknown assets and failing and suspending with unheard-of rapidity; and these Mr. Cowperwood had to know about. He was convinced after a short experience that life was a ticklish business, and he had become the soul of caution. Unfortunately for him, he lacked in a great measure the two things that are necessary for distinction in any field— magnetism and vision. He was not destined to be a great financier, though he was marked out to be a moderately successful one.

Mr. Cowperwood's home was in Buttonwood Street for the time being, and a pleasant little home it was, to be sure. Mrs. Cowperwood was of a Christian, saving disposition—Episcopalians, they were. She was a small woman, very attractive in her day, with light-brown hair and clear brown eyes. Later in life she became rather prim and matter-of-fact, and when Frank Cowperwood was ten she was the watchful mother of three boys and one girl. The former, captained by the eldest, Frank, were a source of considerable annoyance to her, for they were forever making expeditions to different parts of the city, getting in with bad boys probably, and seeing and hearing things they should neither see nor hear. Mr. Henry Cowperwood, with his future opportunities shining clear before him, hit upon the private school and tutor method as a happy solution, and so these boys for some years afterward were carefully watched. Nevertheless, boys would be boys, and these were no exceptions.

During all these years that Frank was growing up he was a natural-born leader. At the day school, and later at the Central High School, where he was finally educated, he was looked upon as one whose common sense could unquestionably be trusted in all cases, and he never disappointed this belief. He was a sturdy youth, courageous and defiant. After he was ten years old his mother learned to know that Joseph and Edward, the two younger brothers, were perfectly safe in his care, and if they asked to go anywhere it was customary for her to ask if Frank were going. If so, well and good. If not, not. If they wanted to do anything when he was with them and he objected, he was most emphatic in a quiet way.

"Can't we go down to the old market and jump on the cars?" Joseph used to ask. They were a great sight in those days—the railroad yards. The tracks came into Market Street, and many of the cars being locally switched about were hauled by horses. The boys were fond of riding, stealing as much as they could in this way;

and Joseph and Edward were no exceptions.

"Why not?" Edward might ask.

"Because it isn't good for you, that's why. You keep off those things."

"Aw, the Collinses go down there.'

"Well, we're not the Collinses. Don't you ever go down there alone."

Having the parental confidence and backing as well as his own natural force, Frank's word was law; and yet he was a liberal interpreter of the law. He liked to play "one old cat," the new baseball game coming into vogue at that time, and he was fond of football as played by his Central High School team. He liked visiting the museums in Chestnut Street—there were several—a menagerie, a museum of anatomy, and another of curious fish and birds; and he liked the theater, and would gladly take his brothers to a minstrel show or a pirate melodrama, paying the expense himself when he had the money. From the very first he was a good leader, but also a splendid second to those older than himself whom he sincerely admired. There was a certain "Red" Gilligan, a tall, shambling, and yet rather brilliant and pyrotechnic rowdy, who took a great fancy to young Cowperwood for a time. He used to see him at first, when he was a ten-year-old boy, passing the corner of Arch and Second, where Gilligan with the members of what was known as the "River gang" used to "hang out." Gilligan had another young protégé, "Spat" McGlathery, who received a terrible drubbing one afternoon from young Cowperwood a year or two later for spitting on his shoes. It came about in this way. He was passing innocently by, carrying his books, when the former, wishing to evince his contempt for all the refinements of this world—particularly those that were manifested by boys of his own age—spat sneeringly and contemptuously at the latter's feet and landed a nice spatter of tobacco-juice on his toes. This enraged Cowperwood greatly. Like a flash, though naturally calm, he dropped his books and went for his opponent. He wore a silver ring on his right hand which his mother had given him, and curiously it flashed into his mind in a lightning calculation to take it off, but he did not. Instead, he planted his right fist swift and straight on young McGlathery's jaw, then his left in the same place, then his right on the latter's mouth, then his left square between the latter's mouth and nose.

It was a terrific onslaught, quick and ugly, to which his opponent returned with enthusiasm, but he was no match for his new adversary. The latter forced him back steadily, and as he retreated Frank followed him. There was a crowd in a moment, for Spat was considered a star fighter of the gang; but Cowperwood drove him by sheer force and swiftness all about the sidewalk. He was not thinking of the crowd. He was thinking how thoroughly he could "lick" this bully and in how short a time. Red Gilligan, who was standing amazedly by, was delighted. He did not know that this nice-looking "mama's boy," as they called all the refined youths of the neighborhood, could do anything of the sort. To see Spat McGlathery, whom he greatly admired as a "scrapper," being drubbed in this way, and to realize yet as he did that Spat would scorn assistance, even though licked, and that therefore this was one of those admirable contests which one could judge on its merits, was inspiring. He followed them around, pushing the other "hickeys," as the bad boys of the gang were called, aside, and seeing that what he called fair

play was had. He had on a red shirt, a brown coat, much too short for him, a baggy pair of trousers, fastened about his waist by a belt; and his pugnacious but quizzical and intelligent face was surmounted by a small, close-fitting cloth cap with a vizor pulled over his eyes. He was so interested that he was closely over the fighters all the time.

"Police!" yelled the neighbors from stores and windows.

"Let 'em alone," he yelled to his compatriots, fearing interruption. "Hands off! I'll smack your jaw!" (This to some youth interfering.) "If he can lick him, let him lick him."

The gang stood by.

It was a swift and rapid fight for all of four minutes, all over the red-brick sidewalk and into the gutter. Young Spat, recovering from his surprise and realizing that he had a terrible adversary, clinched. Frank manœuvered the former's head under his arm by sheer, hard force and punched him vigorously.

"Huh! Huh! Huh!" he grunted, as he struck him.

Mr. McGlathery was bleeding profusely.

"Aw! call him off," Spat's friends yelled.

"Let him alone," yelled Gilligan. "Spat 'll say when he's had enough."

Cowperwood forced him to the pavement, punching him and sitting astride of him. After a time he pushed his head against the bricks and punched some more.

"I quit," yelled McGlathery, after a time. He was bleeding and almost crying, in spite of himself, and he could not get up nor loosen Cowperwood's hold.

Young Cowperwood got up. He began brushing his clothes and looking about for some friendly face.

"Say, kid," called Gilligan, grabbing his arm, "say, you're a wonder! What's your name?"

"Cowperwood," replied Frank, kneading the dirt off his coat and trousers and feeling for his handkerchief.

"Kick the stuffing out of him," some other youth called, approaching and chafing to avenge McGlathery.

"Yah do, and I'll kick your head off, you flannel mouth. Git back!" It was Red Gilligan talking.

Cowperwood realized he had a friend.

"Where's my books?" he asked.

"Where's his books?" called Gilligan, authoritatively.

An obsequious underling sought and found them.

"Say, kid," said his new protector, "I'm Red Gilligan. You're all right. You can fight. Don't you worry. They're not goin' to jump on you."

Cowperwood was looking apprehensively about.

Gilligan walked down the street with him the while a part of the gang stayed to console Spat McGlathery, while another part followed to witness the triumph of the victor. They could scarcely believe their senses—one of their bravest members licked! A policeman, attracted by the cries of shopkeepers and women, shortly hove into view and scattered the crowd. Red Gilligan, drawn by the charm of Cowperwood's personality, put his arm over the latter's shoulder—he was at least nine inches taller, spare and bony—and leered down joyfully in his new discovery's face. "Say, I'll be d—d!" he said. "You're all right! You're fine. Cowperwood, eh? Well, you know me from now on. You can have anything I got. I like you."

"I didn't want to fight him," said Cowperwood, conservatively. He was not sure whether he welcomed the attentions of this new friend or not. Still he did not mind them so much. They were pleasant.

"I know you didn't. Don't you be afraid. You didn't do any more than you ought to. He spit on your shoes. That's all right; you ought to lick him. You did just what you ought to do. That gang's goin' to do all right by you. They're goin' to be fair. Don't you let any of 'em give you any lip. If they do, soak 'em. I'll see that you git fair play. You can come around where I am any time you want to. Just come and tell me." He patted Frank's shoulder.

Frank realized he was talking to a leader. Gilligan looked it. He was so raw, so uncouth, so strange; still he was fine and strong and brave, and Frank liked him.

"I don't want to have any trouble," he suggested, quietly. "I didn't start it. I really didn't mean to hit him as hard as I did at first."

"Don't you worry. He can take care of himself. You're in with me. I'm your friend. You and I are pards. I live over here in Vine Street."

Cowperwood smiled gladly. "All right," he said. "I'm afraid they'll jump on me if you don't head 'em off."

"No, they won't. If any one of 'em says a word you let me know. They won't do it again."

He accompanied Frank to his door. Gilligan shook hands with him.

"Say, Cowperwood," he said, "you're fine. Come around some Saturday. I'm always over there about one or two o'clock."

Frank smiled. "All right!" he said.

He went in, and Mr. Gilligan strolled away.

"Say," he chuckled to himself, as he strolled, "that was a real fight, that was. Gee, he's got a punch! That's the end of Spat McGlathery, all right.

He got all that was comin' to him—
say!"

Meanwhile Mr. Spat McGlathery
had returned to his home in Topper's
Alley, a region that swarmed with
low-caste laboring life, and there
meditated on the fortunes of those
who encounter unexpected and unto-
ward forces. It was a sad afternoon
for him. Still he did not despair. He
had simply found some one at last
who could thoroughly "lick" him.

For a time thereafter Mr. Cowperwood was patronized by Mr. Gilligan,
but only in an admiring, friendly way.
Mr. Gilligan wanted to attach him to
his retinue of stars; but that could
not be done very well. Mr. Cowperwood's home ties were too exacting.
They did explore certain sections of
the city together. Mr. Gilligan did
"sic" him "on to" certain boastful persons whose colors, in his estimation,
needed to be lowered; but Frank was
in a way ashamed to do useless and
pointless fighting. He liked Mr. Gilligan—his spirit—but his connections
were rather reprehensible. So, after a
time, he judiciously cut him, giving
suave excuses, and Mr. Gilligan really
took no offense. Frank made him see
how it was. Out of friendship he
gradually let him go. But the street-
corner gang at Second and Arch never
molested him after that one encounter.

From the very start of his life Frank
wanted to know about economics and
politics. He cared nothing for books.
He was a clean, stocky, shapely boy
with a bright, clean-cut, incisive face;
large, clear gray eyes; a wide forehead;
short, bristly, dark-brown hair. He
had an incisive, quick-motioned, self-
sufficient manner, and was forever
asking questions with a keen desire
for a brief and intelligent reply. He
did not know what sickness was, never
had an ache or pain, ate his food with
gusto, and ruled his brothers with a

rod of iron. "Come on, Joe! Hurry,
Ed!" These commands were issued in
no rough, but always a sure way; and
Joe and Ed came. They looked up to
Frank from the first as a master; and
what he had to say, or what he saw or
encountered, was listened to eagerly.
He himself was pondering, pondering, pondering—one fact astonished
him quite as much as another, for he
could not figure out how this thing he
had come into—this life—was organized. How did all these people get into
the world? What were they doing
here? Who started things, anyhow?
His mother told him the story of
Adam and Eve; but he didn't believe
it. There was a fish-market not so very
far from his own home; and there,
when he went to see his father at the
bank, or when he took his brothers on
after-school expeditions for mail or
errands for his father, he liked to look
at a certain tank in front of one store
where they kept odd specimens of sea-
life which the Delaware Bay fishermen would bring in. He saw once
there a sea-horse—just a queer little
sea-animal that looked somewhat like
a horse—and another time he saw an
electric eel which Franklin's discovery
had explained. One day he saw a jelly-
fish put in, and then a squid, and
then a lobster. The lobster and the
squid came well along in his fish experiences; he was witness of a familiar
tragedy in connection with these two,
which stayed with him all his life and
cleared things up considerably intellectually. The squid, it appeared
from the talk of the idle bystanders
who were always loafing about this
market, was considered the rightful
prey of the lobster; and the latter had
no other food offered him. The lobster
lay at the bottom of the clear glass
tank on the yellow sand, apparently
seeing nothing—you could not tell in
which way his beady, black buttons

of eyes were looking—but apparently they were never off the body of the squid. The latter, pale and waxy in texture, looking very much like pork fat or jade, was moving about in torpedo fashion; but his movements were apparently never out of the eyes of his enemy, for by degrees small portions of his body began to disappear, snapped off by the relentless claws of his pursuer. The latter, as young Cowperwood was one day a witness, would leap like a catapult to where the squid was apparently idly dreaming, and the squid, very alert, would dart away, shooting out at the same time a cloud of ink, behind which it would disappear. It was not always completely successful, however. Some small portions of its body or its tail were frequently left in the claws of the monster below. Days passed, and, now fascinated by the drama, young Cowperwood came daily.

"Say, pa," he said to his father, one night, "did you ever see that tank in front of Joralemon's?"

"Yes, I know where it is," said his father.

"Did you ever see the squid and lobster they got in there?"

"I don't know. Why?"

"Well, that lobster's going to eat that squid. I can see more and more of him gone every day."

"How's that?" asked his father, indifferently.

"Why, that old lobster he just lies down there on the bottom of the tank, and he keeps his eyes fixed on that squid; and every now and then he jumps up with a bang, and he almost gets him. Sometimes he does get him —a little; but the squid pulls away. He's nipped off almost half his tail by now. And you know that ink-bag he carries—that stuff he shoots out to make a cloud?"

"Yes."

"Well, that's almost empty now. He's shot out so much he ain't got any more, or hardly any more."

"He hasn't any more," corrected his father.

"Well," went on his son, ignoring the correction, "you see, he's getting tired. I can see it. I've been watching him every day now for a week, and he's getting weaker all the time. That lobster won't give him any rest. I can see him looking at him all the time. He's goin' to get him. That squid's a goner. He's goin' to get him, sure!"

He paused, his eyes alight, his whole body keyed up. He was interested—not pityingly so much as dramatically interested. His young face was keen and hungry for further information.

"Well, what of that?" asked his father, curiously.

"Oh, nothing. Only I'm going by there in the morning. I want to see whether he's got him."

In the morning he went, his young pantalooned legs squared out solidly in front of the tank. The squid was not gone, but a piece of him; and his ink-bag was emptier than ever. In the corner of the tank sat the lobster, poised apparently for action.

Young Cowperwood put his nose to the glass. He looked solemnly at the lobster. He stayed as long as he could, the bitter struggle fascinating him. He liked to study the rough claw with which the lobster did his deadly work. He liked to stare at the squid and think how fateful was his doom. Now, maybe, or in an hour or a day, he might die, slain by the lobster, and the lobster would eat him. He looked again at the greenish-copperish engine of destruction in the corner and wondered when this would be. To-night, maybe. He would come back to-night.

He returned one night, and lo! to

his grief and astonishment, his wish was granted. There was a little crowd around the tank. The lobster was in the corner. Before him was the squid cut in two and partially devoured.

"He got him at last," observed one bystander. "I was standing right here an hour ago, and up he leaped and grabbed him. The squid was too tired. He wasn't quick enough. He did back up, but that lobster he calculated on his doing that. He's been figuring on his movements for a long time now. He got him to-day."

"Well, I swan!" somebody observed.

Cowperwood Junior only stared. He had missed this. It was too bad. He wanted to see it. The least touch of sorrow came to him for the squid as he stared at it slain. Then he stared at the victor.

"That's the way it has to be, I guess," he commented to himself. "That squid wasn't quick enough. He didn't have anything to feed on." He figured it out. The squid couldn't kill the lobster—he had no weapon. The lobster could kill the squid—he was heavily armed. There was nothing for the squid to feed on; the lobster had the squid as prey. What was the result to be? What else could it be? "He didn't have a chance," he said, finally, tucking his books under his arm and trotting on.

It made a great impression on him. It answered in a rough way that riddle which had been annoying him so much in the past: "How is life organized?" Things lived on each other—that was it. Lobsters lived on squids and other things. What lived on lobsters? Men, of course! Sure, that was it! And what lived on men? he asked himself. Was it other men? Wild animals lived on men. And there were Indians and cannibals. And some men were killed by storms and accidents. He wasn't so sure about men living on men yet; but men did kill each other. How about wars and street fights and mobs? He had seen a mob once. It attacked the *Public Ledger* building as he was coming home from school. His father had explained what for, too. There was great excitement. It was about the slaves. That was it! Sure, men lived on men. Look at the slaves. They were men. That's what all this excitement was about these days. Men killing other men—negroes.

He went on home quite pleased with himself at his solution.

"Say," he said to his mother, that night, "he got him, mother!"

"Got who? What got what? Go wash your hands."

"Why, that lobster got that squid I was telling you and pa about."

"Well, that's all right. It's too bad. What makes you take any interest in such things? Run, wash your hands."

"Well, it's interesting. You don't often see anything like that. I never did."

He went out in the back yard, where there was a hydrant and a post with a little table on it, and on that a cleanly tin-pan and a bucket of water. Here he washed his face and hands.

"Say, papa," he said to his father, later, "you know that squid?"

"Yes."

"Well, he's dead. The lobster got him."

The father stared at his paper. "Well, that's too bad," he said, indifferently.

For days and weeks Frank thought of this and of the life he was tossed into, for he was already thinking of what he should be in this world, and how he should get along. From seeing his father count money, he was sure that he would like banking; and Third Street, where his father's office was, seemed to him the cleanest, brightest, most fascinating street in the world.

CHAPTER XLIII

[THE DAMNABLE SCHEME OF THINGS]

This charging of Cowperwood by the politicians with "larceny, larceny as bailee, embezzlement, and embezzlement on a check," as Mr. Pettie had framed this matter for them, was a severe and dangerous blow to him. He was in so bad a state financially, asking for credits and extensions here and there, and doing his best to have his creditors agree to let him go on, that to have this high-sounding and complicated charge laid at his door was very destructive. His wife saw it the following morning after it was made, blazoned in the head-lines of the papers; and she and his mother and father were all compelled to witness it—with what feelings, one can imagine. Old Cowperwood read his own personal doom in it so far as the presidency of the Third National Bank was concerned; and Mrs. Cowperwood, Frank's wife, saw her own and his fortune, as she thought, going straightway to nothing. How could he recover from a slap like this? Who would believe him in the future, seeing that in addition he had failed for so large a sum? Butler, Sr., was delighted (concerned though he was about party success at the polls); for, now he had this villain in the toils, he would see that the matter was properly followed up. Cowperwood would have a fine time getting out of this. The incoming district attorney to succeed David Pettie, in case the Republican party was again successful at the polls, was an appointee of Butler's—a young Irishman who had done considerable legal work for him—one Dennis Shannon. Shannon was a smart, athletic, good-looking young Irishman, all of five feet ten inches in height, sandy-haired, pink-cheeked, blue-eyed, considerable of an orator, and a fine legal fighter. Through him Butler had of late won quite a few damage suits instituted against himself. Shannon was very proud to be in the old man's favor, to have been put on the ticket by him, and would, if elected, do his bidding to the best of his knowledge and ability. Besides, even if it was technically owing to Stener that the treasury was now short five hundred thousand dollars, it was, in the public mind, primarily due to Cowperwood and his wretched machinations. The papers made it look that way. For a little while the Citizens' Municipal Reform Association, too, was deceived. Cowperwood had gone personally to Skelton C. Wheat and tried to explain his side of the situation, alleging that what he had done was no different from what many others had done before him, and were still doing, but Wheat was dubious. He did not see how it was that the sixty thousand dollars' worth of certificates were not in the sinking-fund. Cowperwood's explanation of *custom* did not avail. Nevertheless, Mr. Wheat saw that others in politics had been profiting quite as much as Cowperwood in other ways; but he could not do anything about that now. He advised Cowperwood to turn State's evidence, if they would let him, which the latter promptly refused to do. He was no "squealer," and indicated as much to Mr. Wheat. The latter smiled wryly.

Butler on his part kept himself busy indicating to all with whom he came in contact how evil Cowperwood really was. He did not want the financier to escape by any chance. Aileen was beside herself with distress; but she could do nothing. She scarcely realized what was going on. Butler argued with himself that she was still young and must have another chance. If he did something radical now to break off this liaison she could still be established in merit and decency. So far as the world knew—he could not tell how far the gossip which had produced the letter had gone, but he hoped it had not gone far—she was still unsoiled and unspoiled. With her position and her money she could still make a fine match. It would take a drastic move like this, though, to open her eyes. She would have to see Cowperwood charged with a crime in this manner, convicted, and sent to the penitentiary, if necessary, before she would let go, and before he would let go. Convict stripes would do it. They would cure her and properly smoke out and ostracize Cowperwood. Butler had no whit of sympathy for the young financier, once he realized how thoroughly he himself had been put upon.

"The man's no good," he said, one day, to District-Attorney Pettie, in talking over the case with him and indicating what he thought ought to be done. "He's a sharper—you can see that. Look how he worked that check business. Only a sharper could do that. We needn't be worryin' about him, I'm thinkin'. He'll look after himself." He said the same thing to young Dennis Shannon; and, of course, that young, ambitious political aspirant immediately took sides against Cowperwood. He became his subtle enemy, waiting only until he should get into office in order to prosecute him properly.

There was only one fly in this ointment, so far as some of the politicians were concerned; and that was due to the fact that if Cowperwood were convicted, Stener must needs be also. There was no escape for the city

treasurer. If Cowperwood was guilty of securing by trickery sixty thousand dollars' worth of the city money, Stener was guilty of securing five hundred thousand dollars. The prison term for this was five years. There was no escape. He might plead not guilty, and, by submitting as evidence that what he did was due to custom, save himself from the odious condition of pleading guilty; but he would be convicted, nevertheless. No jury could get by the fact in regard to him. In spite of public opinion, when it came to a trial there might be considerable doubt in Cowperwood's case. There was none in Stener's.

The practical manner in which the situation was furthered, after Cowperwood and Stener were formally charged, may be quickly noted. Steger, Cowperwood's lawyer, who, as an active participant, was in close touch with Mr. David Pettie, the district attorney, learned privately beforehand that Cowperwood was to be prosecuted. He arranged at once to have his client appear before any warrant could be served, and so forestall the newspaper palaver which would follow if he had to be searched for.

The mayor, following Strobik's charge, issued a warrant for Cowperwood's arrest; and, in accordance with Steger's plan, Cowperwood immediately appeared before Borchardt in company with his lawyer and gave bail in twenty thousand dollars (W. C. Davison, president of the Girard National Bank, was his surety) for his appearance at the central police station on the following Saturday for a hearing. Marcus Oldslaw, a lawyer, had been employed by Strobik, as president of the common council, to represent him in prosecuting for the city the dastardly crime of Cowperwood. Mr. Stener did not appear at the same time. The mayor, when

Cowperwood came in, looked at him curiously, for he, being comparatively new to the political world of Philadelphia, was not so familiar with him as others were; and Cowperwood returned the look pleasantly enough.

"This is a great dumb show, Mr. Mayor," he observed once to Borchardt, quietly; and the latter replied, with a smile and a kindly eye, that in as far as he was concerned it was a form of procedure which was absolutely unavoidable at this time.

"You know how it is, Mr. Cowperwood," he observed.

The latter smiled. "I do, indeed," he said.

He and Steger went out quickly after a few moments' conversation with Borchardt; but the newspapers were soon out with all the details, and the aggregation of anxious souls in Girard Avenue were compelled to witness this latest development in his affairs.

Later there followed several more or less perfunctory appearances in a local police court, known as the Central Court, where Cowperwood when arraigned pleaded not guilty, and finally his appearance before the November grand jury, where, owing to the complicated nature of the charge drawn up against him by David Pettie, he thought it wise to appear. He was properly indicted by the latter body (Mr. Shannon, the newly elected district attorney, making a demonstration in force), and his trial ordered for December 5th before a certain Judge Payderson in Part I of Quarter Sessions, which was the local branch of the State courts dealing with crimes of this character. Cowperwood's indictment did not occur, however, before the coming and going of the much-mooted fall election.

This election, thanks to the fine political suggestions and manipulations of Mr. Mollenhauer and Mr. Simpson (ballot-box stuffing and personal violence at the polls not barred), resulted, in spite of the black record of the dominant party, in another victory, by, however, a greatly reduced majority. This injected the personality of Mr. Dennis Shannon into the treasury case—as district attorney to succeed Mr. Pettie, retired—who immediately took hold in a brisk and effective way, doing all he could to further the interests of his superior, Butler, who seemed set on Cowperwood's conviction. The Citizens' Municipal Reform Association, in spite of a resounding defeat at the polls which could not have happened except for fraud, continued to fire courageously away at those whom it considered to be the chief malefactors.

The contrasting pictures presented by George W. Stener and Frank Algernon Cowperwood at this time is well worth a moment's consideration. Cowperwood, despite his solemn thoughts concerning a possible period of incarceration which this hue and cry now suggested, was as calm and collected as one might suppose his great mental resources would permit him to be. He was in no way apparently disturbed. During all this whirl of disaster he had never once lost his head or his courage. That thing *conscience,* which obsesses and rides some people to destruction, did not trouble him at all. He had no consciousness of what is currently known as sin. He never gave a thought to the vast palaver concerning evil which is constantly going on. There were just two faces to the shield of life from the point of view of his peculiar mind—strength and weakness. Right and wrong? He did not know about those. They were bound up in metaphysical abstrusities about which he did not care to bother. Good and evil? Those were toys of clerics, by which they made money. Morality and immorality? He never considered them. But strength and weakness—oh yes! If you had strength you could protect yourself always and be something. If you were weak—pass quickly to the rear and get out of the range of the guns. He was strong, and he knew it; and somehow he always believed in his star. Something—he could not say what, it was the only metaphysics he bothered about—was doing something for him. It had always helped him. It made things come out right at times. It put excellent opportunities in his way. Why had he been given so fine a mind? Why always favored financially, personally? He had not deserved it, earned it. Accident, perhaps; but somehow the thought that he would always be protected—these intuitions, the "hunches" to act which he frequently had—could not be so easily explained. Life was a dark, insoluble mystery; but, whatever it was, strength and weakness were its two constituents. Strength would win; weakness lose. He must rely on swiftness of thought, accuracy, his judgment, and on nothing else.

At each addition to the shadowy flock of disasters which of late had arrived and were circling about him, he merely contemplated them more accurately as a juggler might contemplate additional spheres cast into the air and spinning about his head, and which he must maintain in motion without dropping any of them. These disasters must not light. He must shoo them away. New woes might arrive hourly; but Cowperwood would not cease to estimate them at their true value—to weigh and place them as they came. How much damage could this new one do? How would it affect all the old ones?

Where would he place it so it would do the least damage? How would he forfend against its possible evil effect? How many disasters could he keep up in the air at once without letting them fall? His lightning brain followed with photographic accuracy all the probable ramifications of each new woe in all its subtle reaches, and ran to do battle. He had no sense of fear —only a defensive and constructive awareness. He was really a brilliant picture of courage and energy—moving about briskly in a jaunty, dapper way, his mustaches curled, his clothes pressed, his nails manicured, his face clean-shaven and tinted with health. He was not pale or distraught. What was behind that steady, inscrutable eye you might not say. It gave you not the slightest indication of what was going on in the brain behind.

On the other hand, consider Stener. On the morning, for instance, when Cowperwood was looking at the first notice of his own complicity in the defalcation of the city treasurer as announced by the Citizens' Municipal Reform Association, never turning a hair, wondering how long it would take this destructive publicity to die down and what he could do to make his own skirts seem sweet and clean— Stener, as we have seen, was lying in his bed absolutely collapsed. The cold sweat of the first few moments gave way to complete nervous inertia a few moments later, and there he lay. He might readily have died of heart failure. His face was grayish white, his lips blue. He had been warned well enough beforehand by the fact of Cowperwood's failure that this publicity was to come; but for all this he was not prepared. He had been running all week in an agonized way to Mollenhauer, Strobik, Jacob Borchardt, and others, listening helplessly to every suggestion as to how best he should evade the consequences of his deeds; but he had no resource within himself. His own mind did not tell him what to do. His so-called conscience—which was what others thought, or what they pretended they were thinking—seared him like a white flame. Like Cowperwood's father, only much faster, he was rapidly getting thin. A new suit of brown clothes that ten days before fitted him perfectly now hung on him loosely. His big stomach was steadily lessening in girth.

"Oh!" he groaned. "Oh!" and the force of the sigh affected his whole frame. It was like the crinkling effect of a rapidly deflating gas-bag.

"Why, George," asked his wife, coming in—she was a small, homely, hard-worked woman, whose pinching labor of former years had removed nearly all traces of feminine charm—"what's the matter? What's happened?"

"Nothing," he sighed, wearily, when he could get his breath; but she knew better. She knew well enough why he was scanning the papers every day so closely. The Chicago fire, Cowperwood's failure, their united investments had been no secret to her. She had heard Stener expatiate too fulsomely in times past concerning his prospects, Cowperwood's, those of Strobik, Wycroft, and Harmon. Cowperwood's skill, their joint investments, their future prospects—all had been discussed; and now she knew well enough that disaster was near. She did not know that her inefficient husband could actually be sent to the penitentiary; only that his prosperity was all over. In the agonized expression of his face she read all the horrors of debasement and difficulty with which he invested the future. Their property was to be swept away; their children reduced to penury. Like

every dependent woman of this class, usually far more resourceful than her lord and master, she tried to help him think. She was not versed in finance, however. She knew nothing of politics or stock-jobbing. All she could reason from was data which Stener gave her, and he did not know. Worst of all, she now realized in a rather clear way that he did not know—that he was an implement—a tool in the hands of other people.

If life presents a more painful spectacle than this, one would like to know it. The damnable scheme of things which we call existence brings about conditions whereby whole masses suffer who have no cause to suffer, and, on the other hand, whole masses joy who have no cause to joy. It rains on the just and the unjust impartially. We suffer for our temperaments, which we did not make, and for our weaknesses and lacks, which are no part of our willing or doing. Who by taking thought can add one cubit to his stature? Who can make his brain better? His thoughts swifter? His courage greater? Who is it that can do anything it was not given him to do? All good things are gifts. There are no *creations* of the mind alone. Creations, achievements, distinguished results always sink back into so many other things. They have their roots in inherited ability, in environment, in fortune, in a lucky star. There is no possible contradiction of this. It is so. So was it ever. So will it be from everlasting to everlasting.

The little woman, watching her husband this morning, experienced a sinking of heart at the evidence of his weakness.

"Is there something in the paper?" she asked, coming over—suspecting—really knowing full well that there was.

"No," he said. "Yes, there is, too—

a little mention." She picked it up and read the long, solemn rigmarole concerning the state of her husband's office, which had been issued by the Citizens' Municipal Reform Association. An expert was going over his books. There was as much as five hundred thousand dollars missing. She had not known that.

"Is it as much as five hundred thousand dollars?" she paused to ask.

"I think so," he admitted, weakly. "I'm not quite sure yet. It may be less."

"And can't you get any of it back from him? He must have money." She was referring to Cowperwood.

"I don't think so," replied Stener, weakly. "I don't know. He led me into this." There followed then that weighing of resources by her which women in these circumstances almost always undertake. She made a dozen earnest suggestions in regard to Mollenhauer, Simpson, Cowperwood, and Strobik; but, alas! it was merely conversation. Stener had tried all these. There was no loophole for him. He was not considered. Because of his temperament, his inability to reason, he had been marked for a victim, and no one proposed to assist him to evade that rôle. He was the one who was going to be punished, unless the powers above him willed that it was not necessary. It all depended on that. His wife went out of the room after a time; but it was only to go into another bedroom and stare out of a window onto the faded grass of the fall. What was to become of her and her husband? She always thought of him and herself and children as a collective unit. There were four children, all told, fortunately well grown now. They would be very poor again, and, worst of all, disgraced. That was what hurt her. She stared and twisted her bony little hands. Her eyes did not moisten, but

an ineffable sadness filled them. Sometimes the mediocre and the inefficient attain to a classic stature when dignified by pain.

1912

OLD ROGAUM AND HIS THERESA *

In all Bleecker Street was no more comfortable doorway than that of the butcher Rogaum, even if the first floor was given over to meat market purposes. It was to one side of the main entrance, which gave ingress to the butcher shop, and from it led up a flight of steps, at least five feet wide, to the living rooms above. A little portico stood out in front of it, railed on either side, and within was a second or final door, forming, with the outer or storm door, a little area, where Mrs. Rogaum and her children frequently sat of a summer's evening. The outer door was never locked, owing to the inconvenience it would inflict on Mr. Rogaum, who had no other way of getting upstairs. In winter, when all had gone to bed, there had been cases in which belated travelers had taken refuge there from the snow or sleet. One or two newsboys occasionally slept there, until routed out by Officer Maguire, who, seeing it half open one morning at two o'clock, took occasion to look in. He jogged the newsboys sharply with his stick, and then, when they were gone, tried the inner door, which was locked.

"You ought to keep that outer door locked, Rogaum," he observed to the phlegmatic butcher the next evening, as he was passing, "people might get in. A couple o' kids was sleepin' in there last night."

* Reprinted by permission of Theodore Dreiser; copyrighted 1918 Theodore Dreiser.

"Ach, dot iss no difference," answered Rogaum pleasantly. "I haf der inner door locked, yet. Let dem sleep. Dot iss no difference."

"Better lock it," said the officer, more to vindicate his authority than anything else. "Something will happen there yet."

The door was never locked, however, and now of a summer evening Mrs. Rogaum and the children made pleasant use of its recess, watching the rout of street cars and occasionally belated trucks go by. The children played on the sidewalk, all except the budding Theresa (eighteen just turning), who, with one companion of the neighborhood, the pretty Kenrihan girl, walked up and down the block, laughing, glancing, watching the boys. Old Mrs. Kenrihan lived in the next block, and there, sometimes, the two stopped. There, also, they most frequently pretended to be when talking with the boys in the intervening side street. Young "Connie" Almerting and George Goujon were the bright particular mashers who held the attention of the maidens in this block. These two made their acquaintance in the customary bold, boyish way, and thereafter the girls had an urgent desire to be out in the street together after eight, and to linger where the boys could see and overtake them.

Old Mrs. Rogaum never knew. She was a particularly fat, old German lady, completely dominated by her liege and portly lord, and at nine o'clock regularly, as he had long ago deemed meet and fit, she was wont to betake her way upward and so to bed. Old Rogaum himself, at that hour, closed the market and went to his chamber.

Before that all the children were called sharply, once from the doorstep below and once from the window above, only Mrs. Rogaum did it first and Rogaum last. It had come, because of a shade of lenience, not wholly apparent in the father's nature, that the older of the children needed two callings and sometimes three. Theresa, now that she had "got in" with the Kenrihan maiden, needed that many calls and even more.

She was just at that age for which mere thoughtless, sensory life holds its greatest charm. She loved to walk up and down in the as yet bright street where were voices and laughter, and occasionally moonlight streaming down. What a nuisance it was to be called at nine, anyhow. Why should one have to go in then, anyhow. What old fogies her parents were, wishing to go to bed so early. Mrs. Kenrihan was not so strict with her daughter. It made her pettish when Rogaum insisted, calling as he often did, in German, "Come you now," in a very hoarse and belligerent voice.

She came, eventually, frowning and wretched, all the moonlight calling her, all the voices of the night urging her to come back. Her innate opposition due to her urgent youth made her coming later and later, however, until now, by August of this, her eighteenth year, it was nearly ten when she entered, and Rogaum was almost invariably angry.

"I vill lock you oudt," he declared, in strongly accented English, while she tried to slip by him each time. "I vill show you. Du sollst come ven I say, yet. Hear now."

"I'll not," answered Theresa, but it was always under her breath.

Poor Mrs. Rogaum troubled at hearing the wrath in her husband's voice. It spoke of harder and fiercer times which had been with her. Still she was not powerful enough in the family councils to put in a weighty word. So Rogaum fumed unrestricted.

There were other nights, however, many of them, and now that the young sparks of the neighborhood had enlisted the girls' attention, it was a more trying time than ever. Never did a street seem more beautiful. Its shabby red walls, dusty pavements and protruding store steps and iron railings seemed bits of the ornamental paraphernalia of heaven itself. These lights, the cars, the moon, the street lamps! Theresa had a tender eye for the dashing Almerting, a young idler and loafer of the district, the son of a stationer farther up the street. What a fine fellow he was, indeed! What a handsome nose and chin! What eyes! What authority! His cigarette was always cocked at a high angle, in her presence, and his hat had the least suggestion of being set to one side. He had a shrewd way of winking one eye, taking her boldly by the arm, hailing her as, "Hey, Pretty!" and was strong and athletic and worked (when he worked) in a tobacco factory. His was a trade, indeed, nearly acquired, as he said, and his jingling pockets attested that he had money of his own. Altogether he was very captivating.

"Aw, whaddy ya want to go in for?" he used to say to her, tossing his head gayly on one side to listen and holding her by the arm, as old Rogaum called. "Tell him yuh didn't hear."

"No, I've got to go," said the girl, who was soft and plump and fair—a Rhine maiden type.

"Well, yuh don't have to go just yet. Stay another minute. George, what was that fellow's name that tried to sass us the other day?"

"Theresa!" roared old Rogaum forcefully. "If you do not now come! Ve vill see!"

"I've got to go," repeated Theresa with a faint effort at starting. "Can't

you hear? Don't hold me. I haf to."

"Aw, whaddy ya want to be such a coward for? Y' don't have to go. He won't do nothin' tuh yuh. My old man was always hollerin' like that up tuh a coupla years ago. Let him holler! Say, kid, but yuh got sweet eyes! They're as blue! An' your mouth—"

"Now stop! You hear me!" Theresa would protest softly, as, swiftly, he would slip an arm about her waist and draw her to him, sometimes in a vain, sometimes in a successful effort to kiss her.

As a rule she managed to interpose an elbow between her face and his, but even then he would manage to touch an ear or a check or her neck—sometimes her mouth, full and warm—before she would develop sufficient energy to push him away and herself free. Then she would protest mock earnestly or sometimes run away.

"Now, I'll never speak to you any more, if that's the way you're going to do. My father don't allow me to kiss boys, anyhow," and then she would run, half ashamed, half smiling to herself as he would stare after her, or if she lingered, develop a kind of anger and even rage.

"Aw, cut it! Whaddy ya want to be so shy for? Don'tcha like me? What's gettin' into yuh, anyhow? Hey?"

In the meantime George Goujon and Myrtle Kenrihan, their companions, might be sweeting and going through a similar contest, perhaps a hundred feet up the street or near at hand. The quality of old Rogaum's voice would by now have become so raucous, however, that Theresa would have lost all comfort in the scene and, becoming frightened, hurry away. Then it was often that both Almerting and Goujon as well as Myrtle Kenrihan would follow her to the corner, almost in sight of the irate old butcher.

"Let him call," young Almerting would insist, laying a final hold on her soft white fingers and causing her to quiver thereby.

"Oh, no," she would gasp nervously. "I can't."

"Well, go on, then," he would say, and with a flip of his heel would turn back, leaving Theresa to wonder whether she had alienated him forever or no. Then she would hurry to her father's door.

"Muss ich all my time spenden calling, mit you on de streeds oudt?" old Rogaum would roar wrathfully, the while his fat hand would descend on her back. "Take dot now. Vy don'd you come ven I call? In now. I vill show you. Und come you yussed vunce more at dis time—ve vill see if I am boss in my own house, aber! Komst du vun minute nach ten to-morrow und you vill see vot you vill get. I vill der door lock. Du sollst not in kommen. Mark! Oudt sollst du stayen—oudt!" and he would glare wrathfully at her retreating figure.

Sometimes Theresa would whimper, sometimes cry or sulk. She almost hated her father for his cruelty, "the big, fat, rough thing," and just because she wanted to stay out in the bright streets, too! Because he was old and stout and wanted to go to bed at ten, he thought every one else did. And outside was the dark sky with its stars, the street lamps, the cars, the tinkle and laughter of eternal life!

"Oh!" she would sigh as she undressed and crawled into her small neat bed. To think that she had to live like this all her days! At the same time old Rogaum was angry and equally determined. It was not so much that he imagined that his Theresa was in bad company as yet, but he wished to forfend against

possible danger. This was not a good neighborhood by any means. The boys around here were tough. He wanted Theresa to pick some nice sober youth from among the other Germans he and his wife knew here and there— at the Lutheran Church, for instance. Otherwise she shouldn't marry. He knew she only walked from his shop to the door of the Kenrihans and back again. Had not his wife told him so? If he had thought upon what far pilgrimage her feet had already ventured, or had even seen the dashing Almerting hanging near, then had there been wrath indeed. As it was, his mind was more or less at ease.

On many, many evenings it was much the same. Sometimes she got in on time, sometimes not, but more and more "Connie" Almerting claimed her for his "steady," and bought her ice-cream. In the range of the short block and its confining corners it was all done, lingering by the curbstone and strolling a half block either way in the side streets, until she had offended seriously at home, and the threat was repeated anew. He often tried to persuade her to go on picnics or outings of various kinds, but this, somehow, was not to be thought of at her age—at least with him. She knew her father would never endure the thought, and never even had the courage to mention it, let alone run away. Mere lingering with him at the adjacent street corners brought stronger and stronger admonishments—even more blows and the threat that she should not get in at all.

Well enough she meant to obey, but on one radiant night late in June the time fled too fast. The moon was so bright, the air so soft. The feel of far summer things was in the wind and even in this dusty street. Theresa, in a newly starched white summer dress, had been loitering up and down with Myrtle when as usual they encountered Almerting and Goujon. Now it was ten, and the regular calls were beginning.

"Aw, wait a minute," said "Connie." "Stand still. He won't lock yuh out."

"But he will, though," said Theresa. "You don't know him."

"Well, if he does, come on back to me. I'll take care of yuh. I'll be here. But he won't though. If you stayed out a little while he'd letcha in all right. That's the way my old man used to try to do me but it didn't work with me. I stayed out an' he let me in, just the same. Don'tcha let him kidja." He jingled some loose change in his pocket.

Never in his life had he had a girl on his hands at any unseasonable hour, but it was nice to talk big, and there was a club to which he belonged, The Varick Street Roosters, and to which he had a key. It would be closed and empty at this hour, and she could stay there until morning, if need be or with Myrtle Kenrihan. He would take her there if she insisted. There was a sinister grin on the youth's face.

By now Theresa's affections had carried her far. This youth with his slim body, his delicate strong hands, his fine chin, straight mouth and hard dark eyes—how wonderful he seemed! He was but nineteen to her eighteen but cold, shrewd, daring. Yet how tender he seemed to her, how well worth having! Always, when he kissed her now, she trembled in the balance. There was something in the iron grasp of his fingers that went through her like fire. His glance held hers at times when she could scarcely endure it.

"I'll wait, anyhow," he insisted.

Longer and longer she lingered, but now for once no voice came.

She began to feel that something

was wrong—a greater strain than if old Rogaum's voice had been filling the whole neighborhood.

"I've got to go," she said.

"Gee, but you're a coward, yuh are!" said he derisively. "What 'r yuh always so scared about? He always says he'll lock yuh out, but he never does."

"Yes, but he will," she insisted nervously. "I think he has this time. You don't know him. He's something awful when he gets real mad. Oh, Connie, I must go!" For the sixth or seventh time she moved, and once more he caught her arm and waist and tried to kiss her, but she slipped away from him.

"Ah, yuh!" he exclaimed. "I wish he would lock yuh out!"

At her own doorstep she paused momentarily, more to soften her progress than anything. The outer door was open as usual, but not the inner. She tried it, but it would not give. It was locked! For a moment she paused, cold fear racing over her body, and then knocked.

No answer.

Again she rattled the door, this time nervously, and was about to cry out. Still no answer.

At last she heard her father's voice, hoarse and indifferent not addressed to her at all, but to her mother.

"Let her go, now," it said savagely, from the front room where he supposed she could not hear. "I vill her a lesson teach."

"Hadn't you better let her in now, yet?" pleaded Mrs. Rogaum faintly.

"No," insisted Mr. Rogaum. "Nefer! Let her go now. If she vill alvays stay oudt, let her stay now. Ve vill see how she likes dot."

His voice was rich in wrath, and he was saving up a good beating for her into the bargain, that she knew. She would have to wait and wait and plead, and when she was thoroughly wretched and subdued he would let her in and beat her—such a beating as she had never received in all her born days.

Again the door rattled, and still she got no answer. Not even her call brought a sound.

Now, strangely, a new element, not heretofore apparent in her nature but nevertheless wholly there, was called into life, springing in action as Diana, full formed. Why should he always be so harsh? She hadn't done anything but stay out a little later than usual. He was always so anxious to keep her in and subdue her. For once the cold chill of her girlish fears left her, and she wavered angrily.

"All right," she said, some old German stubbornness springing up, "I won't knock. You don't need to let me in, then."

A suggestion of tears was in her eyes, but she backed firmly out onto the stoop and sat down, hesitating. Old Rogaum saw her, lowering down from the lattice, but said nothing. He would teach her for once what were proper hours!

At the corner, standing, Almerting also saw her. He recognized the simple white dress, and paused steadily, a strange thrill racing over him. Really they had locked her out! Gee, this was new. It was great, in a way. There she was, white, quiet, shut out, waiting at her father's doorstep.

Sitting thus, Theresa pondered a moment, her girlish rashness and anger dominating her. Her pride was hurt and she felt revengeful. They would shut her out, would they? All right, she would go out and they should look to it how they would get her back—the old curmudgeons. For the moment the home of Myrtle Kenrihan came to her as a possible refuge, but she decided that she need not go there yet. She had better wait about awhile and see—or walk and frighten them. He would beat her, would he? Well, maybe he would and maybe he wouldn't. She might come back, but still that was a thing afar off. Just now it didn't matter so much. "Connie" was still there on the corner. He loved her dearly. She felt it.

Getting up, she stepped to the now quieting sidewalk and strolled up the street. It was a rather nervous procedure, however. There were street cars still, and stores lighted and people passing, but soon these would not be, and she was locked out. The side streets were already little more than long silent walks and gleaming rows of lamps.

At the corner her youthful lover almost pounced upon her.

"Locked out, are yuh?" he asked, his eyes shining.

For the moment she was delighted to see him, for a nameless dread had already laid hold of her. Home meant so much. Up to now it had been her whole life.

"Yes," she answered feebly.

"Well, let's stroll on a little," said the boy. He had not as yet quite made up his mind what to do, but the night was young. It was so fine to have her with him—his.

At the farther corner they passed Officers Maguire and Delahanty, idly swinging their clubs and discussing politics.

"'Tis a shame," Officer Delahanty was saying, "the way things are run now," but he paused to add, "Ain't that old Rogaum's girl over there with young Almerting?"

"It is," replied Maguire, looking after.

"Well, I'm thinkin' he'd better be keepin' an eye on her," said the former. "She's too young to be runnin' around with the likes o' him."

Maguire agreed. "He's a young tough," he observed. "I never liked him. He's too fresh. He works over here in Myer's tobacco factory, and belongs to The Roosters. He's up to no good, I'll warrant that."

"Teach 'em a lesson, I would," Almerting was saying to Theresa as they strolled on. "We'll walk around a while an' make 'em think yuh mean business. They won't lock yuh out any more. If they don't let yuh in when we come back I'll find yuh a place, all right."

His sharp eyes were gleaming as he looked around into her own. Already he had made up his mind that she should not go back if he could help it. He knew a better place than home for this night, anyhow—the club room of The Roosters, if nowhere else. They could stay there for a time, anyhow.

By now old Rogaum, who had seen her walking up the street alone, was marveling at her audacity, but thought she would soon come back. It was amazing that she should exhibit such temerity, but he would teach her! Such a whipping! At half-past ten, however, he stuck his head out of the open window and saw nothing of her. At eleven, the same. Then he walked the floor.

At first wrathful, then nervous, then nervous and wrathful, he finally ended all nervous, without a scintilla of wrath. His stout wife sat up in bed and began to wring her hands.

"Lie down!" he commanded. "You make me sick. I know vot I am doing!"

"Is she still at der door?" pleaded the mother.

"No," he said. "I don't tink so. She should come ven I call."

His nerves were weakening, however, and now they finally collapsed.

"She vent de stread up," he said anxiously after a time. "I vill go after."

Slipping on his coat, he went down the stairs and out into the night. It was growing late, and the stillness and gloom of midnight were nearing. Nowhere in sight was his Theresa. First one way and then another he went, looking here, there, everywhere, finally groaning.

"Ach, Gott!" he said, the sweat bursting out on his brow, "vot in Teufel's name iss dis?"

He thought he would seek a policeman, but there was none. Officer Maguire had long since gone for a quiet game in one of the neighboring saloons. His partner had temporarily returned to his own beat. Still old Rogaum hunted on, worrying more and more.

Finally he bethought him to hasten home again, for she must have got back. Mrs. Rogaum, too, would be frantic if she had not. If she were not there he must go to the police. Such a night! And his Theresa— This thing could not go on.

As he turned into his own corner he almost ran, coming up to the little portico wet and panting. At a puffing step he turned, and almost fell over a white body at his feet, a prone and writhing woman.

"Ach, Gott!" he cried aloud, almost shouting in his distress and excitement. "Theresa, vot iss dis? Wilhelmina, a light now. Bring a light now, I say, for himmel's sake! Theresa hat sich *umgebracht*. Help!"

He had fallen to his knees and was turning over the writhing, groaning figure. By the pale light of the street, however, he could make out that it was not his Theresa, fortunately, as he had at first feared, but another and yet there was something very like her in the figure.

"Um!" said the stranger weakly. "Ah!"

The dress was gray, not white as was his Theresa's, but the body was round and plump. It cut the fiercest cords of his intensity, this thought of death to a young woman, but there was something else about the situation which made him forget his own troubles.

Mrs. Rogaum, loudly admonished, almost tumbled down the stairs. At the foot she held the light she had brought—a small glass oil-lamp—and then nearly dropped it. A fairly attractive figure, more girl than woman, rich in all the physical charms that characterize a certain type, lay near to dying. Her soft hair had fallen back over a good forehead, now quite white. Her pretty hands, well decked with rings, were clutched tightly in an agonized grip. At her neck a blue silk shirtwaist and light lace collar were torn away where she had clutched herself, and on the white flesh was a yellow stain as of one who had been burned. A strange odor reeked in the area, and in one corner was a spilled bottle.

"Ach, Gott!" exclaimed Mrs. Rogaum. "It iss a vooman! She haf herself gekilt. Run for der police! Oh, my! oh, my!"

Rogaum did not kneel for more than a moment. Somehow, this creature's fate seemed in some psychic way identified with that of his own daughter. He bounded up, and jumping out his front door, began to call lustily for the police. Officer Maguire, at his social game nearby, heard the very first cry and came running.

"What's the matter here, now?" he exclaimed, rushing up full and ready for murder, robbery, fire, or, indeed, anything in the whole roster of human calamities.

"A vooman!" said Rogaum excitedly. "She half herself *umgebracht*. She iss dying. Ach, Gott! in my own doorstep, yet!"

"Vere iss der hospital?" put in Mrs. Rogaum, thinking clearly of an ambulance, but not being able to express it. "She iss gekilt, sure. Oh! Oh!" and bending over her the poor old motherly soul stroked the tightened hands, and trickled tears upon the blue shirtwaist. "Ach, vy did you do dot?" she said. "Ach, for vy?"

Officer Maguire was essentially a man of action. He jumped to the sidewalk, amid the gathering company, and beat loudly with his club upon the stone flagging. Then he ran to the nearest police phone, returning to aid in any other way he might. A milk wagon passing on its way from the Jersey ferry with a few tons of fresh milk aboard, he held it up and demanded a helping.

"Give us a quart there, will you?" he said authoritatively. "A woman's swallowed acid in here."

"Sure," said the driver, anxious to learn the cause of the excitement. "Got a glass, anybody?"

Maguire ran back and returned, bearing a measure. Mrs. Rogaum stood looking nervously on, while the stocky officer raised the golden head and poured the milk.

"Here, now, drink this," he said. "Come on. Try an' swallow it."

The girl, a blonde of the type the world too well knows, opened her eyes, and looked, groaning a little.

"Drink it," shouted the officer fiercely. "Do you want to die? Open your mouth!"

Used to a fear of the law in all her days, she obeyed now, even in death. The lips parted, the fresh milk was drained to the end, some spilling on neck and cheek.

While they were working old Rogaum came back and stood looking

on, by the side of his wife. Also
Officer Delahanty, having heard the
peculiar wooden ring of the stick upon
the stone in the night, had come
up.

"Ach, ach," exclaimed Rogaum
rather distractedly, "und she iss oudt
yet. I could not find her. Oh, oh!"

There was a clang of a gong up the
street as the racing ambulance turned
rapidly in. A young hospital surgeon
dismounted, and seeing the woman's
condition, ordered immediate removal.
Both officers and Rogaum, as well as
the surgeon, helped place her in the
ambulance. After a moment the lone
bell, ringing wildly in the night, was
all the evidence remaining that a
tragedy had been here.

"Do you know how she came here?"
asked Officer Delahanty, coming back
to get Rogaum's testimony for the
police.

"No, no," answered Rogaum
wretchedly. "She vass here alretty.
I vass for my daughter loog. Ach, himmel, I haf my daughter lost. She iss
avay."

Mrs. Rogaum also chattered, the
significance of Theresa's absence all
the more painfully emphasized by
this.

The officer did not at first get the
import of this. He was only interested
in the facts of the present case.

"You say she was here when you
come? Where was you?"

"I say I vass for my daughter loog.
I come here, un der vooman vass
here now alretty."

"Yes. What time was this?"

"Only now yet. Yussed a half-
hour."

Officer Maguire had strolled up,
after chasing away a small crowd that
had gathered with fierce and unholy
threats. For the first time now he
noticed the peculiar perturbation of
the usually placid German couple.

"What about your daughter?" he
asked, catching a word as to that.

Both old people raised their voices
at once.

"She haf gone. She haf run avay.
Ach, himmel, ve must for her loog.
Quick—she could not get in. Ve had
der door shut."

"Locked her out, eh?" inquired
Maguire after a time, hearing much
of the rest of the story.

"Yes," explained Rogaum. "It was
to schkare her a liddle. She vould not
come ven I called."

"Sure, that's the girl we saw walkin'
with young Almerting, do ye mind?
The one in the white dress," said
Delahanty to Maguire.

"White dress, yah!" echoed Rogaum, and then the fact of her walking with some one came home like a
blow.

"Did you hear dot?" he exclaimed
even as Mrs. Rogaum did likewise.
"Mein Gott, hast du das gehoert?"

He fairly jumped as he said it. His
hands flew up to his stout and ruddy
head.

"Whaddy ya want to let her out
for nights?" asked Maguire roughly,
catching the drift of the situation.
"That's no time for young girls to be
out, anyhow, and with these toughs
around here. Sure, I saw her, nearly
two hours ago."

"Ach," groaned Rogaum. "Two
hours yet. Ho, ho, ho!" His voice was
quite hysteric.

"Well, go on in," said Officer
Delahanty. "There's no use yellin'
out here. Give us a description of
her an' we'll send out an alarm. You
won't be able to find her walkin'
around."

Her parents described her exactly.
The two men turned to the nearest
police box and then disappeared, leaving the old German couple in the
throes of distress. A time-worn old

church-clock nearby now chimed out one and then two. The notes cut like knives. Mrs. Rogaum began fearfully to cry. Rogaum walked and blustered to himself.

"It's a queer case, that," said Officer Delahanty to Maguire after having reported the matter of Theresa, but referring solely to the outcast of the doorway so recently sent away and in whose fate they were much more interested. She being a part of the commercialized vice of the city, they were curious as to the cause of her suicide. "I think I know that woman. I think I know where she came from. You do, too—Adele's, around the corner, eh? She didn't come into that doorway by herself, either. She was put there. You know how they do."

"You're right," said Maguire. "She was put there, all right, and that's just where she come from, too."

The two of them now tipped up their noses and cocked their eyes significantly.

"Let's go around," added Maguire.

They went, the significant red light over the transom at 68 telling its own story. Strolling leisurely up, they knocked. At the very first sound a painted denizen of the half-world opened the door.

"Where's Adele?" asked Maguire as the two, hats on as usual, stepped in.

"She's gone to bed."

"Tell her to come down."

They seated themselves deliberately in the gaudy mirrored parlor and waited, conversing between themselves in whispers. Presently a sleepy-looking woman of forty in a gaudy robe of heavy texture, and slippered in red, appeared.

"We're here about that suicide case you had to-night. What about it? Who was she? How'd she come to be in that doorway around the cor-

ner? Come, now," Maguire added, as the madam assumed an air of mingled injured and ignorant innocence, "you know. Can that stuff! How did she come to take poison?"

"I don't know what you're talking about," said the woman with the utmost air of innocence. "I never heard of any suicide."

"Aw, come now," insisted Delahanty, "the girl around the corner. You know. We know you've got a pull, but we've got to know about this case, just the same. Come across now. It won't be published. What made her take the poison?"

Under the steady eyes of the officers the woman hesitated, but finally weakened.

"Why—why—her lover went back on her—that's all. She got so blue we just couldn't do anything with her. I tried to, but she wouldn't listen."

"Lover, eh?" put in Maguire as though that were the most unheard-of thing in the world. "What was his name?"

"I don't know. You can never tell that."

"What was her name—Annie?" asked Delahanty wisely, as though he knew but was merely inquiring for form's sake.

"No—Emily."

"Well, how did she come to get over there, anyhow?" inquired Maguire most pleasantly.

"George took her," she replied, referring to a man-of-all-work about the place.

Then little by little as they sat there the whole miserable story came out, miserable as all the wilfulness and error and suffering of the world.

"How old was she?"

"Oh, twenty-one."

"Well, where'd she come from?"

"Oh, here in New York. Her family locked her out one night, I think."

Something in the way the woman said this last brought old Rogaum and his daughter back to the policemen's minds. They had forgotten all about her by now, although they had turned in an alarm. Fearing to interfere too much with this well-known and politically controlled institution, the two men left, but outside they fell to talking of the other case.

"We ought to tell old Rogaum about her some time," said Maguire to Delahanty cynically. "He locked his kid out to-night."

"Yes, it might be a good thing for him to hear that," replied the other. "We'd better go round there an' see if his girl's back yet. She may be back by now," and so they returned but little disturbed by the joint miseries.

At Rogaum's door they once more knocked loudly.

"Is your daughter back again?" asked Maguire when a reply was had.

"Ach, no," replied the hysterical Mrs. Rogaum, who was quite alone now. "My husband he haf gone oudt again to loog vunce more. Oh, my! Oh, my!"

"Well, that's what you get for lockin' her out," returned Maguire loftily, the other story fresh in his mind. "That other girl downstairs here to-night was locked out too, once." He chanced to have a girl-child of his own and somehow he was in the mood for pointing a moral. "You oughtn't to do anything like that. Where d'yuh expect she's goin' to if you lock her out?"

Mrs. Rogaum groaned. She explained that it was not her fault, but anyhow it was carrying coals to Newcastle to talk to her so. The advice was better for her husband.

The pair finally returned to the station to see if the call had been attended to.

"Sure," said the sergeant, "certainly. Whaddy ya think?" and he read from the blotter before him:

"'Look out for girl, Theresa Rogaum. Aged 18; height, about 5, 3; light hair, blue eyes, white cotton dress, trimmed with blue ribbon. Last seen with lad named Almerting, about 19 years of age, about 5, 9; weight 135 pounds.'"

There were other details even more pointed and conclusive. For over an hour now, supposedly, policemen from the Battery to Harlem, and far beyond, had been scanning long streets and dim shadows for a girl in a white dress with a youth of nineteen,—supposedly.

Officer Halsey, another of this region, which took in a portion of Washington Square, had seen a good many couples this pleasant summer evening since the description of Theresa and Almerting had been read to him over the telephone, but none that answered to these. Like Maguire and Delahanty, he was more or less indifferent to all such cases, but idling on a corner near the park at about three A.M., a brother officer, one Paisly by name, came up and casually mentioned the missing pair also.

"I bet I saw that couple, not over an hour ago. She was dressed in white, and looked to me as if she didn't want to be out. I didn't happen to think at the time, but now I remember. They acted sort o' funny. She did, anyhow. They went in this park down at the Fourth Street end there."

"Supposing we beat it, then," suggested Halsey, weary for something to do.

"Sure," said the other quickly, and together they began a careful search, kicking around in the moonlight under the trees. The moon was leaning moderately toward the west, and all the branches were silvered with light and dew. Among the flowers, past clumps of bushes, near the fountain, they searched, each one going his way alone. At last, the wandering Halsey paused beside a thick clump of flaming bushes, ruddy, slightly, even in the light. A murmur of voices greeted him, and something very much like the sound of a sob.

"What's that?" he said mentally, drawing near and listening.

"Why don't you come on now?" said the first of the voices heard. "They won't let you in any more. You're with me, ain't you? What's the use cryin'?"

No answer to this, but no sobs. She must have been crying silently.

"Come on. I can take care of yuh. We can live in Hoboken. I know a place where we can go to-night. That's all right."

There was a movement as if the speaker were patting her on the shoulder.

"What's the use cryin'? Don't you believe I love yuh?"

The officer who had stolen quietly around to get a better view now came closer. He wanted to see for himself. In the moonlight, from a comfortable distance, he could see them seated. The tall bushes were almost all about the bench. In the arms of the youth was the girl in white, held very close. Leaning over to get a better view, he saw him kiss her and hold her—hold her in such a way that she could but yield to him, whatever her slight disinclination.

It was a common affair at earlier hours, but rather interesting now. The officer was interested. He crept nearer.

"What are you two doin' here?" he suddenly inquired, rising before them, as though he had not seen.

The girl tumbled out of her compromising position, speechless and blushing violently. The young man stood up, nervous, but still defiant.

"Aw, we were just sittin' here," he replied.

"Yes? Well, say, what's your name? I think we're lookin' for you two, anyhow. Almerting?"

"That's me," said the youth.

"And yours?" he added addressing Theresa.

"Theresa Rogaum," replied the latter brokenly, beginning to cry.

"Well, you two'll have to come along with me," he added laconically. "The Captain wants to see both of you," and he marched them solemnly away.

"What for?" young Almerting ventured to inquire after a time, blanched with fright.

"Never mind," replied the policeman irritably. "Come along, you'll find out at the station house. We want you both. That's enough."

At the other end of the park Paisly joined them, and, at the station house, the girl was given a chair. She was all tears and melancholy with a modicum possibly of relief at being thus rescued from the world. Her companion, for all his youth, was defiant if circumspect, a natural animal defeated of its aim.

"Better go for her father," commented the sergeant, and by four in the morning old Rogaum, who had still been up and walking the floor, was rushing station-ward. From an earlier rage he had passed to an almost killing grief, but now at the thought that he might possibly see his daughter alive and well once more he was overflowing with a mingled emotion which contained rage, fear, sorrow, and a number of other things. What should he do to her if she were alive? Beat her? Kiss her? Or what? Arrived at the station, however, and seeing his fair Theresa in the hands of the police, and this young stranger lingering near, also detained, he was beside himself with fear, rage, affection.

"You! You!" he exclaimed at once, glaring at the imperturbable Almerting, when told that this was the young man who was found with his girl. Then, seized with a sudden horror, he added, turning to Theresa, "Vot haf you done? Oh, oh! You! You!" he repeated again to Almerting angrily, now that he felt that his daughter was safe. "Come not near my tochter any more! I vill preak effery pone, du teufel, du!"

He made a move toward the incarcerated lover, but here the sergeant interfered.

"Stop that, now," he said calmly. "Take your daughter out of here and go home, or I'll lock you both up. We don't want any fighting in here. D'ye hear? Keep your daughter off the streets hereafter, then she won't get into trouble. Don't let her run around with such young toughs as this." Almerting winced. "Then there won't anything happen to her. We'll do whatever punishing's to be done."

"Aw, what's eatin' him!" commented Almerting dourly, now that he felt himself reasonably safe from a personal encounter. "What have I done? He locked her out, didn't he? I was just keepin' her company till morning."

"Yes, we know all about that," said the sergeant, "and about you, too. You shut up, or you'll go down-town to Special Sessions. I want no guff out o' you." Still he ordered the butcher angrily to be gone.

Old Rogaum heard nothing. He had his daughter. He was taking her home. She was not dead—not even morally injured in so far as he could learn. He was a compound of won-

drous feelings. What to do was beyond him.

At the corner near the butcher shop they encountered the wakeful Maguire, still idling, as they passed. He was pleased to see that Rogaum had his Theresa once more. It raised him to a high, moralizing height.

"Don't lock her out any more," he called significantly. "That's what brought the other girl to your door, you know!"

"Vot iss dot?" said Rogaum.

"I say the other girl was locked out. That's why she committed suicide."

"Ach, I know," said the husky German under his breath, but he had no intention of locking her out. He did not know what he would do until they were in the presence of his crying wife, who fell upon Theresa, weeping. Then he decided to be reasonably lenient.

"She vass like you," said the old mother to the wandering Theresa, ignorant of the seeming lesson brought to their very door. "She vass loog like you."

"I vill not vip you now," said the old butcher solemnly, too delighted to think of punishment after having feared every horror under the sun, "aber, go not oudt any more. Keep off de streads so late. I von't haf it. Dot loafer, aber—let him yussed come here some more! I fix him!"

"No, no," said the fat mother tearfully, smoothing her daughter's hair. "She vouldn't run avay no more yet, no, no." Old Mrs. Rogaum was all mother.

"Well, you wouldn't let me in," insisted Theresa, "and I didn't have any place to go. What do you want me to do? I'm not going to stay in the house all the time."

"I fix him!" roared Rogaum, unloading all his rage now on the recreant lover freely. "Yussed let him come some more! Der penitentiary he should haf!"

"Oh, he's not so bad," Theresa told her mother, almost a heroine now that she was home and safe. "He's Mr. Almerting, the stationer's boy. They live here in the next block."

"Don't you ever bother that girl again," the sergeant was saying to young Almerting as he turned him loose an hour later. "If you do, we'll get you, and you won't get off under six months. Y' hear me, do you?"

"Aw, I don't want 'er," replied the boy truculently and cynically. "Let him have his old daughter. What'd he want to lock 'er out for? They'd better not lock 'er out again though, that's all I say. I don't want 'er."

"Beat it!" replied the sergeant, and away he went.

1918

FROM

A BOOK ABOUT MYSELF *

[DISCOURAGING DAYS IN NEW YORK]

The things which most contributed to my want of newspaper success in New York and eventually drove me, though much against my will and understanding, into an easier and more agreeable phase of life were, first, that awe of the grinding and almost disgusting forces of life itself which I found in Spencer and Huxley and Balzac and which now persistently haunted me and, due possibly to a depressed physical condition at this time, made it impossible for me to work with any of the zest that had characterized my work in the West. Next, there was that astounding contrast between wealth and poverty,

* Reprinted by permission of Theodore Dreiser; copyrighted 1922 by Theodore Dreiser.

here more sharply emphasized than anywhere else in America, which gave the great city a gross and cruel and mechanical look, and this was emphasized not only by the papers themselves, with their various summaries of investigations and exposures, but also by my own hourly contact with it—a look so harsh and indifferent at times as to leave me a little numb. Again, there was something disillusioning in the sharp contrast between the professed ideals and preachments of such a constantly moralizing journal as the *World* and the heartless and savage aspect of its internal economy. Men such as myself were mere machines or privates in an ill-paid army to be thrown into any breach. There was no time off for the space-men, unless it was for all time. One was expected to achieve the results desired or get out; and if one did achieve them the reward was nothing.

One day I met an acquaintance and asked about an ex-city editor from St. Louis who had come to New York, and his answer staggered me.

"Oh, Cliff? Didn't you hear? Why, he committed suicide down here in a West Street hotel."

"What was the trouble?" I asked.

"Tired of the game, I guess," he replied. "He didn't get along down here as well as he had out there. I guess he felt that he was going downhill."

I walked away, meditating. He had been an excellent newspaper man, as brisk and self-centered as one need be to prosper. The last time I had seen him he was in good physical condition, and yet, after something like a year in New York, he had killed himself.

However, my mood was not that of one who runs away from a grueling contest. I had no notion of leaving New York, whatever happened, although I constantly speculated as to what I should do when all my money was gone. I had no trade or profession beyond this reporting, and yet I was convinced that there must be something else that I could do. Come what might, I was determined that I would ask no favor of my brother, and as for my sister, who was now a burden on my hands, I was determined that as soon as this burden became too great I would take up her case with my brother Paul, outline all that had been done and ask him to shoulder the difference until such time as I could find myself in whatever work I was destined to do.

But what was it?

One of the things which oppressed me was the fact that on the *World*, as well as on the other papers, were men as young as myself who were apparently of a very different texture, mentally if not physically. Life and this fierce contest which I was taking so much to heart seemed in no wise to disturb them. By reason of temperament and insight perhaps, possibly the lack of it, or, what was more likely, certain fortunate circumstances attending their youth and upbringing, they were part of that oncoming host of professional optimists and yea-sayers, chorus-like in character, which for thirty years or more thereafter in American life was constantly engaged in the pleasing task of emphasizing the possibilities of success, progress, strength and what not for all, in America and elsewhere, while at the same time they were humbly and sycophantically genuflecting before the strong, the lucky, the prosperous. On the *World* alone at this time, to say nothing of the other papers, were at least a dozen, swaggering about in the best of clothes, their manners those of a graduate of Yale or Harvard or Princeton, their minds stuffed with

all the noble maxims of the uplifters. There was nothing wrong with the world that could not be easily and quickly righted, once the honest, just, true, kind, industrious turned their giant and selected brains to the task. This newest type of young newspaper man was to have no traffic with evil in any form; he was to concern himself with the Good, the True, the Beautiful. Many of these young men pretended to an intimate working knowledge of many things: society, politics, finance and what not else. Several had evidently made themselves indispensable as ship reporters, interviewers of arriving and departing celebrities, and these were now pointed out to me as men worthy of envy and emulation. One of them had, at the behest of the *World*, crossed the ocean more than once seeking to expose the principals in a growing ship-gambling and bunco scandal. There were those who were in the confidence of the mayor, the governor, and some of the lights in Wall Street. One, a scion of one of the best families, was the paper's best adviser as to social events and scandals. The grand air with which they swung in and out of the office set me beside myself with envy.

And all the time the condition of my personal affairs tended to make me anything but optimistic. I was in very serious financial straits. I sometimes think that I was too new to the city, too green to its psychology and subtlety, to be of any use to a great metropolitan daily; and yet, seeing all I had seen, I should have been worth something. I was only five years distant from the composition of *Sister Carrie*, to say nothing of many short stories and magazine articles. Yet I was haunted by the thought that I was a misfit, that I might really have to give up and return to the West, where in some pathetic humdrum task I should live out a barren and pointless life.

With this probable end staring me in the face, I began to think that I must not give up but must instead turn to letters, the art of short-story writing; only just how to do this I could not see. One of the things that prompted me to try this was the fact that on the *World* at this time were several who had succeeded—David Graham Phillips, James Creelman, then a correspondent for the paper in the war which had broken out between China and Japan, to say nothing of George Cary Eggleston and Reginald de Koven, the latter on the staff as chief musical critic. There was another young man, whose name I have forgotten, who was pointed out to me as a rapidly growing favorite in the office of the *Century*. Then there were those new arrivals in the world of letters: Kipling, Richard Harding Davis, Stephen Crane and some others, whose success fascinated me.

All this was but an irritant to a bubbling chemistry which as yet had found no solution, and was not likely to find one for some time to come. My reading of Spencer and Huxley in no wise tended to clarify and impel my mind in the direction of fiction, or even philosophy. But now, in a kind of ferment or fever due to my necessities and desperation, I set to examining the current magazines and the fiction and articles to be found therein: *Century, Scribner's, Harper's.* I was never more confounded than by the discrepancy existing between my own observations and those displayed here, the beauty and peace and charm to be found in everything, the almost complete absence of any reference to the coarse and the vulgar and the cruel and the terrible. How

did it happen that these remarkable persons—geniuses of course, one and all—saw life in this happy roseate way? Was it so, and was I all wrong? Love was almost invariably rewarded in these tales. Almost invariably one's dreams came true, in the magazines. Most of these bits of fiction, delicately phrased, flowed so easily, with such an air of assurance, omniscience and condescension, that I was quite put out by my own lacks and defects. They seemed to deal with phases of sweetness and beauty and success and goodness such as I rarely encountered. There were so many tales of the old South reeking with a poetry which was poetry and little more (George W. Cable; Thomas Nelson Page). In *Harper's* I found such assured writers as William Dean Howells, Charles Dudley Warner, Frank R. Stockton, Mrs. Humphrey Ward, and a score of others, all of whom wrote of nobility of character and sacrifice and the greatness of ideals and joy in simple things.

But as I viewed the strenuous world about me, all that I read seemed not to have so very much to do with it. Perhaps, as I now thought, life as I saw it, the darker phases, was never to be written about. Maybe such things were not the true province of fiction anyhow. I read and read, but all I could gather was that I had no such tales to tell, and, however much I tried, I could not think of any. The kind of thing I was witnessing no one would want as fiction. These writers seemed far above the world of which I was a part. Indeed I began to picture them as creatures of the greatest luxury and culture, gentlemen and ladies all, comfortably housed, masters of servants, possessing estates, or at least bachelor quarters, having horses and carriages, and received here, there and everywhere with nods of recognition and smiles of approval.

1922

GAMALIEL BRADFORD
(1863–1932)

FROM *THE JOURNAL* *

[HENRY ADAMS'S BOOK]

October 10, [1918]—Arrives this morning from the Historical Society *The Education of Henry Adams*. . . . In glancing it over, I am much impressed that his attitude and his conclusions as to his own spiritual basis of life and work appear to be quite close to mine. He insists on philosophical ignorance, not so much abstract agnosticism as his own personal ignorance, precisely as I do; finds himself lost in the vast, enormous complex of modern scientific investigation and theory, the immensity of possible thought and knowledge. And, precisely as I do, he takes refuge in the empirical study of history, taking the vast, dynamic, as he calls it, movement of human thought as expressing itself in the current of historical fact. Only, instead of turning, as he does, to history in general, for which my father's wearisomely iterated generalizations had given me an intolerable disgust, I confine myself to the infinitely richer and more varied field of the human individual. The dynamic process and progress of thought may be studied at once more securely, because more exclusively, in this field, with far less fear of distraction to those very generalizations, which are so dangerous when ill-handled and so wearisome when handled at their best.

* The selections from *The Journal of Gamaliel Bradford*, edited by Van Wyck Brooks, are used by permission of the publishers, Houghton Mifflin Company. Copyright, 1933, Helen F. Bradford.

I am simply following Sainte-Beuve, of course, and equally of course Sainte-Beuve, though never theorizing, was closely and exactly preceding Adams and myself in his attitude toward science and thought in general.

[ESTIMATE OF ADAMS]

October 13, [1919]—As in the *Education*, so in *Saint-Michel*, Adams is perpetually harping on unity and multiplicity, unity and multiplicity, over and over, trying to emphasize the unity of the thirteenth century as against the multiplicity of the twentieth. Yet he himself is forced to recognize that thirteenth-century unity is constantly shattering itself into multiplicity, while the twentieth century, even in its most perfect exponents, yearns for unity as passionately as its ancestors ever did. They are the two poles of our being, and our whole existence consists in rushing from one to the other, trying to harmonize them, when we know fully that it is impossible. Unity is repose, complete, dead, absolute. The defect, the negative of it is ennui, to which we instantly fall prey when we allow unity to get possession of us. Then we fly to multiplicity, to action, and this quickly degenerates into fatigue, and we begin to long inexpressibly for repose and unity again. Two longings stir the poet's blood, says Arnold, one drives him to the world without, the other to solitude. But it is not only the poet, but all the children of mortal men. Always the two desires, never happiness in either of them, and never the possibility of blending them in one. This is all the meaning of the fundamental formula of Hegel's *Logic*: on the one side non-being, emptiness, void, or absolute, unlimited fullness, whichever you please, in any case unity; on the other, being, the immense world of possible difference.

multiplicity. And Hegel tried to reconcile them by his ingenious device of becoming. But all his syntheses are either tricks, as in this case—for what does he do but solve the knot by the introduction of Time, which merely brings forward a new element, without reconciling the old identity and difference at all?—or a mere reaffirmation of the original thesis or antithesis. Some souls turn to unity, some more to multiplicity. For instance, to me, unity, the Nirvana of the East, the last stanza but one of Adonais, is everything, yet I realize its hopelessness.

[IN THE FULL TIDE OF PORTRAITS]

April 25, [1921]—In the full tide of portraits now and all such vain things as verses and tragedies and novels, alas, forgotten. . . . The portraits are satisfactory and delightful. But they have their drawbacks. More and more I am tormented by the terrible difficulty of satisfying myself, of doing my personages anything like justice from all sides, of touching the various shades and qualifications with the subtlety and delicacy they properly require. And I can see so well that my danger lies in this torment growing upon me, in getting more and more obscure, reserved, complicated, after the fashion of Henry James, until the portraits lose the easy grace and vivid salience, which made the charm of the *Stuart* and *Sherman*. I must be on my guard against this, must repeatedly and firmly resolve that I will not be too particular, will not lose the clear grasp of the central whole in the passionate desire of perfect finish in all the parts. But in every subject that I deal with now the temptation to hang and delay and flutter and remodel and qualify is terrible and haunting. For instance, this Barnum.

I thought in the beginning that he at least would be simple, tangible, capable of being treated in broad and strong lines, without uncertainty or hesitancy. But, as with all the others, the minute I get into him, the difficulty comes. Was he wholly a charlatan and a cheat, as the English magazines and *The Nation* would have me believe, a vulgar and contemptible humbug? Was he a large, kindly, jovial, vast benefactor of mankind as Joel Benton and many others would maintain? And I have to strike the balance between the two and the effort is harassing.

[SPENGLER]

September 4, [1926]—Settled myself this morning for a three days' wrestle with Spengler's *Decline of the West*. . . . I suppose I am a fool about these things, but the tremendous intellectual concentration racks and strains my nerves, sets my spirit upon edge with the most intense, bitter, and furious questioning. Perhaps if I read more of that sort of thing, I should do it more easily and be better for it. Yet it seems to me exceedingly profitless. In a sense, of course, this book impresses me more than ever with my own abysmal ignorance, with my own pitiful inability to explore and illuminate these murky depths of thought, and consequently with the absurdity of my trying to write to illuminate others. Yet, after all, as with Adams, this book seems to me cloudy and inexplicit. The man, in my judgment, takes facts that are universally well known and undeniable—for instance, the decay and passing of periods of civilization, like the decay and passing of individuals (a principle which surely intelligent men are always ready to apply to the period in which they live as to any other, yet this fellow seems to think it an extraordinary discovery)—and envelops them in a web and maze of vague German speculation, which seems to me neither intelligible nor conclusive. That is, I will not admit that his processes are not intelligible, but I do not allow that they are in any way convincing. The whole book is rather, like so many metaphysical systems, an assertion of the man's individual egotistical conception of the universe than an objective system that has objective bearing for the rest of us. Ah, stick to the human, that is the lesson for me.

(1883–1932)   1933

GEORGE SANTAYANA
(1863–   )
ODES *

II

My heart rebels against my generation,
That talks of freedom and is slave to riches,
And, toiling 'neath each day's ignoble burden,
    Boasts of to-morrow.

No space for noonday rest or midnight watches,
No purest joy of breathing under heaven!
Wretched themselves, they heap, to make them happy,
    Many possessions.

But thou, O silent Mother, wise, immortal,
To whom our toil is laughter,—take, divine one,
This vanity away, and to thy lover
    Give what is needful:—

* The selections from *Poems* by George Santayana are reprinted by permission of Charles Scribner's Sons. Copyright, 1922.

A staunch heart, nobly calm, averse to evil,
The windy sky for breath, the sea, the mountain,
A well-born, gentle friend, his spirit's brother,
    Ever beside him.

What would ye gain, ye seekers, with your striving,
Or what vast Babel raise you on your shoulders?
You multiply distresses, and your children
    Surely will curse you.

O leave them rather friendlier gods, and fairer
Orchards and temples, and a freer bosom!
What better comfort have we, or what other
    Profit in living,

Than to feed, sobered by the truth of Nature,
Awhile upon her bounty and her beauty,
And hand her torch of gladness to the ages
    Following after?

She hath not made us, like her other children,
Merely for peopling of her spacious kingdoms,
Beasts of the wild, or insects of the summer,
    Breeding and dying,

But also that we might, half knowing, worship
The deathless beauty of her guiding vision,
And learn to love, in all things mortal, only
    What is eternal.

                     1894

SONNETS *

ON A VOLUME OF SCHOLASTIC PHILOSOPHY

What chill cloister or what lattice
    dim
Cast painted light upon this careful
    page?
What thought compulsive held the
    patient sage
Till sound of matin bell or evening
    hymn?
Did visions of the Heavenly Lover
    swim
Before his eyes in youth, or did stern
    rage
Against rash heresy keep green his
    age?
Had he seen God, to write so much
    of Him?
Gone is that irrecoverable mind
With all its phantoms, senseless to
    mankind
As a dream's trouble or the speech of
    birds.
The breath that stirred his lips he
    soon resigned
To windy chaos, and we only find
The garnered husks of his disuséd
    words.

1894

[THOUGH UTTER DEATH]

Though utter death should swallow
    up my hope
And choke with dust the mouth of
    my desire,
Though no dawn burst, and no auro-
    rean choir
Sing GLORIA DEO when the heavens
    ope,
Yet have I light of love, nor need to
    grope
Lost, wholly lost, without an inward
    fire;

The flame that quickeneth the world
    entire
Leaps in my breast, with cruel death
    to cope.
Hath not the night-environed earth
    her flowers?
Hath not my grief the blessed joy of
    thee?
Is not the comfort of these singing
    hours,
Full of thy perfectness, enough for
    me?
They are not evil, then, those hidden
    powers:
One love sufficeth an eternity.

1894

ON MY FRIENDLY CRITICS †

Now that for some years my body
has not been visible in the places it
used to haunt (my mind, even then,
being often elsewhere), my friends in
America have fallen into the habit of
thinking me dead, and with characteristic haste and kindness, they are
writing obituary notices, as it were,
on my life and works. Some of these
reach me in this other world—the
friendly ones, which their authors
send me—and without the aid of any
such stratagem as Swift's, I have the
strange pleasure of laughing at my
own epitaphs. It is not merely the
play of vanity that enters into this
experience, nor the occasional excuse
for being unfair in return; there comes
with it a genuine discovery of the
general balance of one's character. A
man has unrivalled knowledge of the
details of his life and feelings, but it is
hard for him to compose his personage
as it appears in the comedy of the
world, or in the eyes of other people.
It is not true that contemporaries mis-

---

* The selections from *Poems* by
George Santayana are reprinted by permission of Charles Scribner's Sons. Copyright, 1922.

† Reprinted from George Santayana's
*Soliloquies in England and Later Solilo-
quies* by permission of Charles Scribner's
Sons. Copyright, 1924.

judge a man. Competent contemporaries judge him perfectly, much better than posterity, which is composed of critics no less egotistical and obliged to rely on documents easily misinterpreted. The contemporary can read more safely between the lines; and if the general public often misjudges the men of its own time, the general public hears little of them. It is guided by some party tag or casual association, by the malignity or the delusion of some small coterie that has caught its ear: how otherwise should it judge ideas it has not grasped and people it has not seen? But public opinion is hardly better informed about the past than about the present, and histories are only newspapers published long after the fact.

As to my person, my critics are very gentle, and I am sensible of the kindness, or the diffidence, with which they treat me. I do not mind being occasionally denounced for atheism, conceit, or detachment. One has to be oneself; and so long as the facts are not misrepresented—and I have little to complain of on that score —any judgement based upon them is a two-edged sword: people simply condemn what condemns them. I can always say to myself that my atheism, like that of Spinoza, is true piety towards the Universe and denies only gods fashioned by men in their own image, to be servants of their human interests; and even in this denial I am no rude iconoclast, but full of secret sympathy with the idolaters. My detachment from things and persons is also affectionate, and simply what the ancients called philosophy: I consent that a flowing river should flow; I renounce that which betrays, and cling to that which satisfies, and I relish the irony of truth; but my security in my own happiness is not indifference to that of others: I rejoice that every one

should have his tastes and his pleasures. That I am conceited, it would be folly to deny: what artist, what thinker, what parent does not overestimate his own offspring? Can I suppress an irresistible sense of seeing things clearly, and a keen delight in so seeing them? Frankly, I think these attitudes of mine are justified by the facts; but I entirely understand how offensive they must be to any one who thinks they are not justified, or who fears that they may be. Let the irritant work. The arrows of anger miss their mark. Aimed at some imaginary evil bird in the heavens, they scarcely startle the poet wandering in his dell. He hears them pass over his head and bury their venom far away in the young grass. Far away too his friends are designing his vain cenotaph, and inscribing it with seemly words in large capitals.

On the other hand, in respect to my impersonal opinions, I notice a little bewilderment, and some obtuseness. Of course, if people are repelled by the subject or by the manner (which is an integral part of the thought) and find it all unintelligible, that is no fault of theirs, nor of mine; but I speak of the initiated and of such as are willing to lend their minds to my sort of lucubration. For instance, when more than twenty years ago, I wrote some *Interpretations of Poetry and Religion,* this is what William James said of them: "What a perfection of rottenness . . . how fantastic a philosophy!—as if the 'world of values' *were* independent of existence. It is only as *being* that one thing is better than another. The idea of darkness is as good as that of light, as ideas. There is more value in light's *being.*" William James was a "radical empiricist," so that for him the being of light could not have meant anything except its being in idea, in experience. The fantastic view must therefore be some other; apparently that in the realm of unrealized essences, apart from any observer, one essence can be better than another. But how could anyone attribute such a view to me? The whole contention of my book was that the glow of human emotion lent a value to good poetry which it denied to bad, and to one idea of God which it denied to another. My position in this matter was that of empirical philosophy, and of William James himself. In his book on Pragmatism he says that the being of atoms is just as good as the being of God, if both produce the same effects in human experience; and I remember once mildly protesting to him on that point, and asking him if, apart from these effects on us, the existence of God, assuming God to be conscious, would not have a considerable value in itself; and he replied, "Of course; but I was thinking of our *idea*." This was exactly the attitude of my book; I was thinking of our religious and poetic ideas, and reducing their value to what they stood for in the elements of our experience, or in our destiny.

I think I see, however, where the trouble lies. The practical intellect conceives everything as a source of influence. Whether it be matter or other people, or tutelary spirits, that which we envisage in action and passion is not our idea of these objects, but their operation on us, or our operation on them. Now a source of influence cannot be non-existent. Accordingly, what concerns earnest people in their religion is something, they know not what, which is real. They are not interested in forming poetic or dramatic pictures of the gods, as the Greeks did in their mythology, but rather in finding a living God to help them, as even the Greeks did in

their home cultus and their oracles. This living God, since he is to operate and be worked upon, must exist; otherwise the whole practice of religion becomes a farce. So also in love or in science, it would be egotistical and affected to gloat on our own ideal, turning our backs on the adorable person or the natural process before us. It is the danger of empirical and critical philosophy, that it turns our attention stubbornly to the subjective: legitimately, I think, if the purpose is merely to study the growth and logic of our beliefs, but illegitimately, if the purpose is malicious, and if it is assumed that once we have understood how our beliefs are formed we shall abandon them and believe nothing. Empiricism and idealism are, as Kant called them, excellent cathartics, but they are nasty food; and if we try to build them up into a system of the universe the effort is not only self-contradictory (because then we ought to possess only ideas without beliefs) but the result is, in the words of William James, fantastic and rotten.

Now, however much I may have studied the human imagination, I have never doubted that even highly imaginative things, like poetry and religion, express real events, if not in the outer world, at least in the inner growth or discipline of life. Like the daily experience of the senses and like the ideas of science, they form *a human language,* all the terms of which are poetical and its images dream-images, but which symbolizes things and events beyond it and is controlled from the outside. This would be perfectly evident to any other animal who should discover how men see the world or what they think of it: why should we be less intelligent than any other animal would be about ourselves? Enlightenment consists in coming nearer and nearer to the natural objects that lend a practical meaning to our mental discourse; and when the material significance of our dreams is thus discovered, we are lost in admiration at the originality, humor, and pictorial grandeur of the imagery in which our experience comes to us, as we might be at the decorative marvels of tapestry or of stained glass: but now without illusion. For we can now discriminate the rhythms and color proper to our mental atmosphere from the extrinsic value of discourse as a sign for things and events beyond it. These external things and events make up what we call nature. It is nature, or some part of nature, or some movement of nature occurring within us or affecting us, that is the true existent object of religion, of science, and of love. The rest is mere image.

My naturalism is sometimes taxed with being dogmatic, and if I were anxious to avoid that reproach, I might easily reduce my naturalism to a definition and say that if experience has any sources whatever, the sum and system of these sources shall be called nature. I know what speculative difficulties cluster about the notion of cause, which in one sense is quite unnecessary to science; but so long as time, process, and derivation are admitted at all, events may be traced back to earlier events which were their sources; and this universal flux of events will be called nature. Any existing persons, and any gods exercising power, will evidently be parts of nature. But I am not concerned to avoid dogmatism on such a point. Every assertion about existence is hazarded, it rests on animal faith, not on logical proof; and every argument to support naturalism, or to rebut it, implies naturalism. To deny that there are any facts (if scepticism can be carried so far) is still to dog-matize, no less than it would be to point to some fact in particular; in either case we descend into the arena of existence, which may betray our confidence. Any fact is in existence which discourse plays about and regards, but does not create. It is the essence of the practical intellect to prophesy about nature, and we must all do it. As to the truth of our prophecy, that is always problematical, because nature is whatever nature happens to be; and as to our knowledge, starting as it does from a single point, the present position of the thinker, and falling away rapidly in clearness and certainty as the perspective recedes, it cannot pretend to draw the outlines of nature *a priori*: yet our knowledge of nature, in our neighborhood and moral climate, is very considerable, since every known fact is a part of nature. It is quite idle to deny, for instance, that human life depends on cosmic and hygienic influences; or that in the end all human operations must run back somehow to the rotation of the earth, to the rays of the sun, to the moisture and fructification of the soil, to the ferment there of vegetative and dreaming spirits, quickened in animals endowed with locomotion into knowledge of surrounding things: whence the passionate imaginations which we find in ourselves. I know that things might have been arranged otherwise; and some of those alternative worlds may be minutely thought out in myth and philosophy, in obedience to some dialectical or moral impulse of the human mind; but that all those other worlds are figments of fancy, interesting as poetry is interesting, and that only the natural world, the world of medicine and commerce, is actual, is obvious; so obvious to every man in his sane moments, that I have always thought it idle to argue the point. Argument is not persuasive to madmen: but they can be won over by gentler courses to a gradual docility to the truth. One of these gentler courses is this: to remember that madness is human, that dreams have their springs in the depths of human nature and of human experience; and that the illusion they cause may be kindly and even gloriously dispelled by showing what the solid truth was which they expressed allegorically. Why should one be angry with dreams, with myth, with allegory, with madness? We must not kill the mind, as some rationalists do, in trying to cure it. The life of reason, as I conceive it, is simply the dreaming mind becoming coherent, devising symbols and methods, such as languages, by which it may fitly survey its own career, and the forces of nature on which that career depends. Reason thereby raises our vegetative dream into a poetic revelation and transcript of the truth. That all this life of expression grows up in animals living in the material world is the deliverance of reason itself, in our lucid moments; but my books, being descriptive of the imagination and having perhaps some touches of imagination in them, may not seem to have expressed my lucid moments alone. They were, however, intended to do so; and I ought to have warned my readers more often that such was the case.

I have no metaphysics, and in that sense I am no philosopher, but a poor ignoramus trusting what he hears from the men of science. I rely on them to discover gradually exactly which elements in their description of nature may be literally true, and which merely symbolical: even if they were all symbolical, they would be true enough for me. My naturalism is not at all afraid of the latest theories of space, time, or matter: what I understand of them, I like, and am ready to believe, for I am a follower of Plato in his doctrine that only knowledge of ideas (if we call it knowledge) can be literal and exact, whilst practical knowledge is necessarily mythical in form, precisely because its object exists and is external to us. An arbitrary sign, indication, or name can point to something unambiguously, without at all fathoming its nature, and *therefore* can be knowledge of fact: which an aesthetic or logical elucidation of ideas can never be. Every idea of sense or science is a summary sign, on a different plane and scale altogether from the diffuse material facts which it covers: one unexampled color for many rays, one indescribable note for many vibrations, one picture for many particles of paint, one word for a series of noises or letters. A word is a very Platonic thing: you cannot say when it begins, when it ends, how long it lasts, nor where it ever is; and yet it is the only unit you mean to utter, or normally hear. Platonism is the intuition of essences in the presence of things, in order to describe them: it is mind itself.

I am quite happy in this human ignorance mitigated by pictures, for it yields practical security and poetic beauty: what more can a sane man want? In this respect I think sometimes I am the only philosopher living: I am resigned to being a mind. I have put my hand into the hand of nature, and a thrill of sympathy has passed from her into my very heart, so that I can instinctively see all things, and see myself, from her point of view: a sympathy which emboldens me often to say to her, "Mother, tell me a story." Not the fair Sheherazad herself knew half the marvellous tales that nature spins in the brains of her children. But I must not let go her hand in my wonder, or I might be bewitched and lost in the maze of her inventions.

A workman must not quarrel with his tools, nor the mind with ideas; I have very little patience with those philanthropists who hate everything human, and would reform away everything that men love or can love. Yet if we dwell too lovingly on the human quality and poetic play of ideas, we may forget that they are primarily signs. The practical intellect is always on the watch for ambient existences, in order to fight or to swallow them: and if by chance its attention is arrested at an idea, it will instinctively raise that idea to the throne of power which should be occupied only by the thing which it stands for and poetically describes. Ideas lend themselves to idolatry. There is a continual incidental deception into which we are betrayed by the fictitious and symbolical terms of our knowledge, in that we suppose these terms to form the whole essence of their objects. I think I have never failed to point out this danger of illusion, and to protest against idolatry in thought, so much more frequent and dangerous than the worship of stocks and stones; but at the same time, as such idolatry is almost inevitable, and as the fictions so deified often cover some true force or harmony in nature, I have sometimes been tempted in my heart to condone this illusion. In my youth it seemed as if a scientific philosophy was unattainable; human life, I thought, was at best a dream, and if we were not the dupes of one error, we should be the dupes of another; and whilst of course the critic must make this mental reservation in all his assents, it was perhaps too much to ask mankind to do so; so that in practice we were condemned to overlook the deceptiveness of fable, because there would be less

beauty and no more truth in whatever theory might take its place. I think now that this despair of finding a scientific philosophy was premature, and that the near future may actually produce one: not that its terms will be less human and symbolical than those to which we are accustomed, but that they may hug more closely the true movement and the calculable order of nature. The truth, though it must be expressed in language, is not for that reason a form of error. No doubt the popularizers of science will turn its language into a revelation, and its images into idols; but the abstract character of these symbols will render it easier for the judicious to preserve the distinction between the things to be described and the science which describes them.

Was it, I wonder, this touch of sympathy with splendid error, bred in me by long familiarity with religion and philosophy, that offended my honest critics? Now that I show less sympathy with it, will they be better satisfied? I fear the opposite is the case. What they resented was rather that in spite of all my sympathy, and of all my despair about science, it never occurred to me to think those errors true, because they were splendid, except true to the soul. Did they expect that I should seriously debate whether the Ghost in *Hamlet* really came out of Purgatorial fires, and whether Athena really descended in her chariot from Olympus and pulled Achilles by his yellow hair when he was in danger of doing something rash? Frankly, I have assumed—perhaps prematurely—that such questions are settled. I am not able nor willing to write a system of magic cosmology, nor to propose a new religion. I merely endeavor to interpret, as sympathetically and imaginatively as I can, the religion and poetry already familiar to us; and I interpret them, of course, on their better side, not as childish science, but as subtle creations of hope, tenderness, and ignorance.

So anxious was I, when younger, to find some rational justification for poetry and religion, and to show that their magic was significant of true facts, that I insisted too much, as I now think, on the need of relevance to fact even in poetry. Not only did I distinguish good religion from bad by its expression of practical wisdom, and of the moral discipline that makes for happiness in this world, but I maintained that the noblest poetry also must express the moral burden of life and must be rich in wisdom. Age has made me less exacting, and I can now find quite sufficient perfection in poetry, like that of the Chinese and Arabians, without much philosophic scope, in mere grace and feeling and music and cloud-castles and frolic. I assumed formerly that an idea could have depth and richness only if somehow redolent of former experiences of an overt kind. I had been taught to assign no substance to the mind, but to conceive it as a system of successive ideas, the later ones mingling with a survival of the earlier, and forming a cumulative experience, like a swelling musical movement. Now, without ceasing to conceive mental discourse in that way, I have learned, with the younger generation, to rely more on the substructure, on the material and psychical machinery that puts this conscious show on the stage, and pulls the wires. Not that I ever denied or really doubted that this substructure existed, but that I thought it a more prudent and critical method in philosophy not to assume it. Certainly it is a vast assumption; but I see now an irony in scepticism which I did not see when I was more fervid a sceptic; namely, that in ad-

dressing anybody, or even myself, I have already made that assumption; and that if I tried to rescind it, I should only be making another, no less gratuitous, and far more extravagant; I should be assuming that the need of making this assumption was a fatal illusion, rather than a natural revelation of the existence of an environment to a living animal. This environment has been called the unknowable, the unconscious and the subconscious—egotistical and absurd names for it, as if its essence was the difficulty we have in approaching it. Its proper names are matter, substance, nature, or soul; and I hope people will learn again to call it by those old names. When living substance is thus restored beneath the surface of experience, there is no longer any reason for assuming that the first song of a bird may not be infinitely rich and as deep as heaven, if it utters the vital impulses of that moment with enough completeness. The analogies of this utterance with other events, or its outlying suggestions, whilst they may render it more intelligible to a third person, would not add much to its inward force and intrinsic beauty. Its lyric adequacy, though of course not independent of nature, would be independent of wisdom. If besides being an adequate expression of the soul, the song expressed the lessons of a broad experience, which that soul had gathered and digested, this fact certainly would lend a great tragic sublimity to that song; but to be poetical or religious intrinsically, the mystic cry is enough.

I notice that men of the world, when they dip into my books, find them consistent, almost oppressively consistent, and to the ladies everything is crystal-clear; yet the philosophers say that it is lazy and self-indulgent of me not to tell them plainly what I think, if I know myself what it is. Because I describe madness sympathetically, because I lose myself in the dreaming mind, and see the world from that transcendental point of vantage, while at the same time interpreting that dream by its presumable motives and by its moral tendencies, these quick and intense reasoners suppose that I am vacillating in my own opinions. My own opinions are a minor matter, and there was usually no need, for the task in hand, that I should put them forward; yet as a matter of fact, since I reached the age of manhood, they have not changed. In my adolescence I thought this earthly life (not unintelligibly, considering what I had then seen and heard of it) a most hideous thing, and I was not disinclined to dismiss it as an illusion, for which perhaps the Catholic epic might be substituted to advantage, as conforming better to the impulses of the soul; and later I liked to regard all systems as alternative illusions for the solipsist; but neither solipsism nor Catholicism were ever anything to me but theoretic poses or possibilities; vistas for the imagination, never convictions. I was well aware, as I am still, that any such vista *may* be taken for true, because all dreams are persuasive while they last; and I have not lost, nor do I wish to lose, a certain facility and pleasure in taking those points of view at will, and speaking those philosophical languages. But though as a child I regretted the fact and now I hugely enjoy it, I have never been able to elude the recurring, invincible, and ironic conviction that whenever I or any other person feign to be living in any of those nonnatural worlds, we are simply dreaming awake.

In general, I think my critics attribute to me more illusions than I have. My dogmatism may be a fault of temper or manner, because I dislike to stop to qualify or to explain everything; but in principle it is raised more diffidently and on a deeper scepticism than most of the systems which are called critical. My "essences," for instance, are blamed for being gratuitous inventions or needless abstractions. But essences appear precisely when all inventions are rescinded and the irreducible manifest datum is disclosed. I do not ask any one to *believe* in essences. I ask them to reject every belief, and what they will have on their hands, if they do so, will be some essence. And if, believing nothing, they could infinitely enlarge their imagination, the whole realm of essence would loom before them. This realm is no discovery of mine; it has been described, for instance, by Leibniz in two different ways; one as the collection of all possible worlds, and again as the abyss of non-existence, *le néant,* of which he says: "The non-existent . . . is infinite, it is eternal, it has a great many of the attributes of God; it contains an infinity of things, since all those things which do not exist at all are included in the non-existent, and those which no longer exist have returned to the non-existent." It suffices, therefore, that we deny a thing for us to recognize an essence, if we know at all what we are denying. And the essence before us, whether we assert or deny its existence, is certainly no abstraction; for there is no other datum, more individual or more obvious, from which the abstraction could be drawn. The difficulty in discerning essences is simply the very real difficulty which the practical intellect has in abstaining from belief, and from everywhere thinking it finds much more than is actually given.

Profound scepticism is favorable to conventions, because it doubts that the criticism of conventions is any truer than they are. Fervent believers look for some system of philosophy or religion that shall be *literally* true and worthy of superseding the current assumptions of daily life. I look for no such thing. Never for a moment can I bring myself to regard a human system—a piece of mental discourse—as more than a system of notation, sometimes picturesque, sometimes abstract and mathematical. Scientific symbols, terms in which calculation is possible, may replace poetic symbols, which merely catch echoes of the senses or make up dramatic units out of appearances in the gross. But the most accurate scientific system would still be only a method of description, and the actual facts would continue to rejoice in their own ways of being. The relevance and truth of science, like the relevance and truth of sense, are pragmatic, in that they mark the actual relations, march, and distribution of events, in the terms in which they enter our experience.

In moral philosophy (which is my chosen subject) I find my unsophisticated readers, as I found my pupils formerly, delightfully appreciative, warmly sympathetic, and altogether friends of mine in the spirit. It is a joy, like that of true conversation, to look and laugh and cry at the world so unfeignedly together. But the other philosophers, and those whose religion is of the anxious and intolerant sort, are not at all pleased. They think my morality very loose: I am a friend of publicans and sinners, not (as they are) in zeal to reform them, but because I like them as they are; and indeed I am a pagan and a moral sceptic in my naturalism. On the other hand (and this seems a contradiction to them), my moral philosophy looks strangely negative and narrow; a philosophy of abstention and distaste for life. What a horrible combination, they say to themselves, of moral license with moral poverty! They do not see that it is because I love life that I wish to keep it sweet, so as to be able to love it altogether: and that all I wish for others, or dare to recommend to them, is that they should keep their lives sweet also, not after my fashion, but each man in his own way. I talk a great deal about the good and the ideal, having learned from Plato and Aristotle (since the living have never shown me how to live) that, granting a human nature to which to appeal, the good and the ideal may be defined with some accuracy. Of course, they cannot be defined immutably, because human nature is not immutable; and they cannot be defined in such a way as to be transferred without change from one race or person to another, because human nature is various. Yet any reflective and honest man, in expressing his hopes and preferences, may expect to find many of his neighbors agreeing with him, and when they agree, they may work politically together. Now I am sometimes blamed for not laboring more earnestly to bring down the good of which I prate into the lives of other men. My critics suppose, apparently, that I mean by the good some particular way of life or some type of character which alone is virtuous, and which ought to be propagated. Alas, their propagandas! How they have filled this world with hatred, darkness, and blood! How they are still the eternal obstacle, in every home and in every heart, to a simple happiness! I have no wish to propagate any particular character, least of all my own; my conceit does not take that form. I wish individuals, and races, and nations to be themselves, and to multiply the forms of perfection and happiness, as nature prompts them. The only thing which I think might be propagated without injustice to the types thereby suppressed is harmony; enough harmony to prevent the interference of one type with another, and to allow the perfect development of each type. The good, as I conceive it, is happiness, happiness for each man after his own heart, and for each hour according to its inspiration. I should dread to translate my happiness into other people; it might die in that soil; and my critics are the first to tell me that my sort of happiness is a poor thing in their estimation. Well and good. I congratulate them on their true loves: but how should I be able to speed them on their course? They do not place their happiness in the things I have, or can give. No man can set up an ideal for another, nor labor to realize it for him, save by his leave or as his spokesman, perhaps more ready with the right word. To find the comparatively right word, my critics seem to agree, is my art. Do I not practice it for their benefit as best I can? Is it I who am indifferent to the being of light? Who loves it more, or basks in it more joyfully? And do I do nothing that the light may come? Is it I who tremble lest at its coming it should dissolve the creatures begotten in darkness? Ah, I know why my critics murmur and are dissatisfied. I do not endeavor to deceive myself, nor to deceive them, nor to aid them in deceiving themselves. They will never prevail on me to do that. I am a disciple of Socrates.

1921

JAMES T. FARRELL
(1904–   )

STUDS *

AUTHOR'S NOTE

This, one of my first stories, is the nucleus out of which the Studs Lonigan trilogy was conceived, imagined, and written. It should suggest the experience and background of these books, and my own relationship to their background. But for the accident of this story, and of the impressions recorded in it, I should probably never have written the Studs Lonigan series.

After writing this story in the spring of 1929, before I had ever published any fiction, the impressions here recorded remained with me so vividly that I could not let them rest. It was then that both Young Lonigan *and* The Young Manhood of Studs Lonigan *were begun. Originally they were planned as one volume, to end with a scene similar to the one presented in this story. As I worked over them, they were changed, split into two volumes, and finally they grew into the trilogy as it has been published. However, to repeat, this story is the nucleus of the entire work, and so I include it here.*

JTF

It is raining outside; rain pouring like bullets from countless machine guns; rain spat-spattering on the wet earth and paving in endless silver crystals. Studs' grave out at Mount Olivet will be soaked and soppy, and fresh with the wet, clean odors of watered earth and flowers. And the members of Studs' family will be looking out of the windows of their apartment on the South Side, thinking of the cold, damp grave and the gloomy, muddy cemetery, and of their Studs lying at rest in peaceful acceptance of that wormy conclusion which is the common fate.

* Reprinted by permission of Vanguard Press, Inc. from *The Stories of James T. Farrell,* copyright, 1930, 1932 *This Quarter;* 1934, 1935, 1937, by The Vanguard Press, Inc.

At Studs' wake last Monday evening everybody was mournful, sad that such a fine young fellow of twenty-six should go off so suddenly with double pneumonia; blown out of this world like a ripped leaf in a hurricane. They sighed and the women and girls cried, and everybody said that it was too bad. But they were consoled because he'd had the priest and had received Extreme Unction before he died, instead of going off like Sport Murphy who was killed in a saloon brawl. Poor Sport! He was a good fellow, and tough as hell. Poor Studs!

The undertaker (it was probably old man O'Reedy who used to be usher in the old parish church) laid Studs out handsomely. He was outfitted in a sombre black suit and a white silk tie. His hands were folded over his stomach, clasping a pair of black rosary beads. At his head, pressed against the satin bedding, was a spiritual bouquet, set in line with Studs' large nose. He looked handsome, and there were no lines of suffering on his planed face. But the spiritual bouquet (further assurance that his soul would arrive safely in Heaven) was a dirty trick. So was the administration of the last sacraments. For Studs will be miserable in Heaven, more miserable than he was on those Sunday nights when he would hang around the old poolroom at Fifty-eighth and the elevated station, waiting for something to happen. He will find the land of perpetual happiness and goodness dull and boresome, and he'll be resentful. There will be nothing to do in Heaven but to wait in timeless eternity. There will be no can houses, speakeasies, whores (unless they are reformed) and gambling joints; and neither will there be a shortage of plasterers. He will loaf up and down gold-paved streets where there is not even the suggestion of a poolroom, thinking of Paulie Haggerty, Sport Murphy, Arnold Sheehan and Hink Weber, who are possibly in Hell together because there was no priest around to play a dirty trick on them.

I thought of these things when I stood by the coffin, waiting for Tommy Doyle, Red Kelly, Les, and Joe to finish offering a few perfunctory prayers in memory of Studs. When they had showered some Hail Marys and Our Fathers on his already prayer-drenched soul, we went out into the dining room.

Years ago when I was a kid in the fifth grade in the old parish school, Studs was in the graduating class. He was one of the school leaders, a light-faced, blond kid who was able to fight like sixty and who never took any sass from Tommy Doyle, Red Kelly, or any of those fellows from the Fifty-eighth Street gang. He was quarterback on the school's football team, and liked by the girls.

My first concrete memory of him is of a rainy fall afternoon. Dick Buckford and I were fooling around in front of Helen Shires' house bumping against each other with our arms folded. We never thought of fighting but kept pushing and shoving and bumping each other. Studs, Red O'Connell, the Donoghues, and Jim Clayburn came along. Studs urged us into fighting, and I gave Dick a bloody nose. Studs congratulated me, and said that I could come along with them and play tag in Red O'Connell's basement, where there were several trick passageways.

After that day, I used to go around with Studs and his bunch. They regarded me as a sort of mascot, and they kept training me to fight other kids. But any older fellows who tried to pick on me would have a fight on their hands. Every now and then he would start boxing with me.

"Gee, you never get hurt, do you?" he would say.

I would grin in answer, bearing the punishment because of the pride and the glory.

"You must be goofy. You can't be hurt."

"Well, I don't get hurt like other kids."

"You're too good for Morris and those kids. You could trim them with your eyes closed. You're good," he would say, and then he would go on training me.

I arranged for a party on one of my birthdays, and invited Studs and the fellows from his bunch. Red O'Connell, a tall, lanky, cowardly kid, went with my brother, and the two of them convinced my folks that Studs was not a fit person for me to invite. I told Studs what had happened, and he took such an insult decently. But none of the fellows he went with would accept my invitation, and most of the girls also refused. On the day of the party, with my family's permission, I again invited Studs but he never came.

I have no other concrete recollections of Studs while he was in grammar school. He went to Loyola for one year, loafed about for a similar period; and then he became a plasterer for his father. He commenced going round the poolroom. The usual commonplace story resulted. What there was of the boy disappeared in slobbish dissipation. His pleasures became compressed within a hexagonal of whores, movies, pool, alky, poker, and craps. By the time I commenced going into the poolroom (my third year in high school) this process had been completed.

Studs' attitude toward me had also changed to one of contempt. I was a goofy young punk. Often he made cracks about me. Once, when I retaliated by sarcasm, he threatened to bust me, and awed by his former reputation I shut up. We said little to each other, although Studs occasionally condescended to borrow fifty or seventy-five cents from me, or to discuss Curley, the corner imbecile.

Studs' companions were more or less small-time amateur hoodlums. He had drifted away from the Donoghues and George Gogarty, who remained bourgeois young men with such interests as formal dances and shows. Perhaps Slug Mason was his closest friend; a tall, heavy-handed, good-natured, child-minded slugger, who knew the address and telephone number of almost every prostitute on the South Side. Hink Weber, who should have been in the ring and who later committed suicide in an insane asylum, Red Kelly, who was a typical wisecracking corner habitué, Tommy Doyle, a fattening, bull-dozing, half-good-natured moron, Stan Simonsky and Joe Thomas were his other companions.

I feel sure that Studs' family, particularly his sisters, were appalled by his actions. The two sisters, one of whom I loved in an adolescently romantic and completely unsuccessful manner, were the type of middle-class girls who go in for sororities and sensibilities. One Saturday evening, when Studs got drunk earlier than usual, his older sister (who the boys always said was keen) saw him staggering around under the Fifty-eighth Street elevated station. She was with a young man in an automobile, and they stopped. Studs talked loudly to her, and finally they left. Studs reeled after the car, cursing and shaking his fists. Fellows like Johnny O'Brien (who went to the U. of C. to become a fraternity man) talked sadly of how

Studs could have been more discriminating in his choice of buddies and liquor; and this, too, must have reached the ears of his two sisters.

Physical decay slowly developed. Studs, always a square-planed, broad person, began getting soft and slightly fat. He played one or two years with the corner football team. He was still an efficient quarterback, but slow. When the team finally disbanded, he gave up athletics. He fought and brawled about until one New Year's Eve he talked out of turn to Jim McGeoghan, who was a boxing champ down at Notre Dame. Jim flattened Studs' nose, and gave him a wicked black eye. Studs gave up fighting.

My associations with the corner gradually dwindled. I went to college, and became an atheist. This further convinced Studs that I wasn't right, and he occasionally remarked about my insanity. I grew up contemptuous of him and the others; and some of this feeling crept into my overt actions. I drifted into other groups and forgot the corner. Then I went to New York, and stories of legendary activities became fact on the corner. I had started a new religion, written poetry, and done countless similar monstrous things. When I returned, I did not see Studs for over a year. One evening, just before the Smith-Hoover election day, I met him as he came out of the I. C. station at Randolph Street with Pat Carrigan and Ike Dugan. I talked to Pat and Ike, but not to Studs.

"Aren't you gonna say hello to me?" he asked in friendly fashion, and he offered me his hand.

I was curious but friendly for several minutes. We talked of Al Smith's chances in an uninformed, unintelligent fashion and I injected one joke about free love. Studs laughed at it; and then they went on.

The next I heard of him, he was dead.

When I went out into the dining room, I found all the old gang there, jabbering in the smoke-thick, crowded room. But I did not have any desire or intention of giving the world for having seen them. They were almost all fat and respectable. Cloddishly, they talked of the tragedy of his death, and then went about remembering the good old days. I sat in the corner and listened.

The scene seemed tragi-comical to me. All these fellows had been the bad boys of my boyhood, and many of them I had admired as proper models. Now they were all of the same kidney. Jackie Cooney (who once stole fifteen bottles of grape juice in one haul from under the eyes of a Greek proprietor over at Sixty-fifth and Stony Island), Monk McCarthy (who lived in a basement on his pool winnings and peanuts for over a year), Al Mumford (the good-natured, dumbly well-intentioned corner scapegoat), Pat Carrigan, the roly-poly fat boy from Saint Stanislaus high school—all as alike as so many cans of tomato soup.

Jim Nolan, now bald-headed, a public accountant, engaged to be married, and student in philosophy at Saint Vincent's evening school, was in one corner with Monk.

"Gee, Monk, remember the time we went to Plantation and I got drunk and went down the alley overturning garbage cans?" he recalled.

"Yeah, that was some party," Monk said.

"Those were the days," Jim said.

Tubby Connell, whom I recalled as a moody, introspective kid, singled out the social Johnny O'Brien and listened to the latter talk with George Gogarty about Illinois U.

Al Mumford walked about making

cracks, finally observing to me, "Jim, get a fiddle and you'll look like Paderwooski."

Red Kelly sat enthroned with Les, Doyle, Simonsky, Bryan, Young Floss Campbell (waiting to be like these older fellows), talking oracularly.

"Yes, sir, it's too bad. A young fellow in the prime of life going like that. It's too bad," he said.

"Poor Studs!" Les said.

"I was out with him a week ago," Bryan said.

"He was all right then," Kelly said.

"Life is a funny thing," Doyle said.

"It's a good thing he had the priest," Kelly said.

"Yeh," Les said.

"Sa-ay, last Saturday I pushed the swellest little baby at Rosy's," Doyle said.

"Was she a blonde?" Kelly said.

"Yeh," Doyle said.

"She's cute. I jazzed her, too," Kelly said.

"Yeh, that night at Plantation was a wow," Jim Nolan said.

"We ought to pull off a drunk some night," Monk said.

"Let's," Nolan said.

"Say, Curley, are you in love?" Mumford asked Curley across the room.

"Now, Duffy," Curley said with imbecilic superiority.

"Remember the time Curley went to Burnham?" Carrigan asked.

Curley blushed.

"What happened, Curley?" Duffy asked.

"Nothing, Al," Curley said, confused.

"Go on, tell him, Curley! Tell him! Don't be bashful now! Don't be bashful! Tell him about the little broad!" Carrigan said.

"Now, Pat, you know me better than that," Curley said.

"Come on, Curley, tell me," Al said.

"Some little girl sat on Curley's knee, and he shoved her off and called her a lousy whore and left the place," Carrigan said.

"Why, Curley, I'm ashamed of you," Al said.

Curley blushed.

"I got to get up at six every morning. But I don't mind it. This not workin' is the bunk. You ain't got any clothes or anything when you ain't got the sheets. I know. No, sir, this loafin' is all crap. You wait around all day for something to happen," Jackie Cooney said to Tommy Rourke.

"Gee, it was tough on Studs," Johnny O'Brien said to George Gogarty.

Gogarty said it was tough, too. Then they talked of some student from Illinois U. Phil Rolfe came in. Phil was professional major-domo of the wake; he was going with Studs' kid sister. Phil used to be a smart Jewboy, misplaced when he did not get into the furrier business. Now he was sorry with everybody, and thanking them for being sorry. He and Kelly talked importantly of pallbearers. Then he went out. Some fellow I didn't know started telling one of Red Kelly's brothers what time he got up to go to work. Mickey Flannagan, the corner drunk, came in and he, too, said he was working.

They kept on talking, and I thought more and more that they were a bunch of slobs. All the adventurous boy that was in them years ago had been killed. Slobs, getting fat and middle-aged, bragging of their stupid brawls, reciting the commonplaces of their days.

As I left, I saw Studs' kid sister. She was crying so pitifully that she was unable to recognize me. I didn't see how she could ever have been affectionate toward Studs. He was so outside of her understanding. I knew she never mentioned him to me the few times I took her out. But she cried pitifully.

As I left, I thought that Studs had looked handsome. He would have gotten a good break, too, if only they hadn't given him Extreme Unction. For life would have grown into fatter and fatter decay for him, just as it was starting to do with Kelly, Doyle, Cooney and McCarthy. He, too, was a slob; but he died without having to live countless slobbish years. If only they had not sent him to Heaven

where there are no whores and poolrooms.

I walked home with Joe, who isn't like the others. We couldn't feel sorry over Studs. It didn't make any difference.

"Joe, he was a slob," I said.

Joe did not care to use the same language, but he did not disagree.

And now the rain keeps falling on Studs' new grave, and his family mournfully watches the leaden sky, and his old buddies are at work wishing that it was Saturday night, and that they were just getting into bed with a naked voluptuous blonde.

(1929)   1935

THE PRIMITIVISTS

GERTRUDE STEIN
(1874–1946)

MELANCTHA *

EACH ONE AS SHE MAY

Rose Johnson made it very hard to bring her baby to its birth.

Melanctha Herbert who was Rose Johnson's friend, did everything that any woman could. She tended Rose, and she was patient, submissive, soothing, and untiring, while the sullen, childish, cowardly, black Rosie grumbled and fussed and howled and made herself to be an abomination and like a simple beast.

The child though it was healthy after it was born, did not live long. Rose Johnson was careless and negligent and selfish, and when Melanctha had to leave for a few days, the baby died. Rose Johnson had liked the baby well enough and perhaps she just forgot it for awhile, anyway the child was dead and Rose and Sam her husband were very sorry but then these things came so often in the negro world in Bridgepoint, that they neither of them thought about it very long.

Rose Johnson and Melanctha Herbert had been friends now for some years. Rose had lately married Sam Johnson a decent honest kindly fellow, a deck hand on a coasting steamer.

Melanctha Herbert had not yet been really married.

Rose Johnson was a real black, tall, well built, sullen, stupid, childlike, good looking negress. She laughed when she was happy and grumbled and was sullen with everything that troubled.

Rose Johnson was a real black negress but she had been brought up quite like their own child by white folks.

Rose laughed when she was happy but she had not the wide, abandoned laughter that makes the warm broad glow of negro sunshine. Rose was never joyous with the earth-born, boundless joy of negroes. Hers was just ordinary, any sort of woman laughter.

Rose Johnson was careless and was lazy, but she had been brought up by white folks and she needed decent comfort. Her white training had only made for habits, not for nature. Rose had the simple, promiscuous unmorality of the black people.

Rose Johnson and Melanctha Herbert like many of the twos with women were a curious pair to be such friends.

Melanctha Herbert was a graceful, pale yellow, intelligent, attractive negress. She had not been raised like Rose by white folks but then she had been half made with real white blood.

She and Rose Johnson were both

of the better sort of negroes, there, in Bridgepoint.

"No, I ain't no common nigger," said Rose Johnson, "for I was raised by white folks, and Melanctha she is so bright and learned so much in school, she ain't no common nigger either, though she ain't got no husband to be married to like I am to Sam Johnson."

Why did the subtle, intelligent, attractive, half white girl Melanctha Herbert love and do for and demean herself in service to this coarse, decent, sullen, ordinary, black childish Rose, and why was this unmoral, promiscuous, shiftless Rose married, and that's not so common either, to a good man of the negroes, while Melanctha with her white blood and attraction and her desire for a right position had not yet been really married.

Sometimes the thought of how all her world was made, filled the complex, desiring Melanctha with despair. She wondered, often, how she could go on living when she was so blue.

Melanctha told Rose one day how a woman whom she knew had killed herself because she was so blue. Melanctha said, sometimes, she thought this was the best thing for her herself to do.

Rose Johnson did not see it the least bit that way.

"I don't see Melanctha why you should talk like you would kill yourself just because you're blue. I'd never kill myself Melanctha just 'cause I was blue. I'd maybe kill somebody else Melanctha 'cause I was blue, but I'd never kill myself. If I ever killed myself Melanctha it'd be by accident, and if I ever killed myself by accident Melanctha, I'd be awful sorry."

Rose Johnson and Melanctha Herbert had first met, one night, at church. Rose Johnson did not care

much for religion. She had not enough emotion to be really roused by a revival. Melanctha Herbert had not come yet to know how to use religion. She was still too complex with desire. However, the two of them in negro fashion went very often to the negro church, along with all their friends, and they slowly came to know each other very well.

Rose Johnson had been raised not as a servant but quite like their own child by white folks. Her mother who had died when Rose was still a baby, had been a trusted servant in the family. Rose was a cute, attractive, good looking little black girl and these people had no children of their own and so they kept Rose in their house.

As Rose grew older she drifted from her white folks back to the colored people, and she gradually no longer lived in the old house. Then it happened that these people went away to some other town to live, and somehow Rose stayed behind in Bridgepoint. Her white folks left a little money to take care of Rose, and this money she got every little while.

Rose now in the easy fashion of the poor lived with one woman in her house, and then for no reason went and lived with some other woman in her house. All this time, too, Rose kept company, and was engaged, first to this colored man and then to that, and always she made sure she was engaged, for Rose had strong the sense of proper conduct.

"No, I ain't no common nigger just to go around with any man, nor you Melanctha shouldn't neither," she said one day when she was telling the complex and less sure Melanctha what was the right way for her to do. "No Melanctha, I ain't no common nigger to do so, for I was raised by white folks. You know very well Melanctha that I'se always been engaged to them."

And so Rose lived on, always comfortable and rather decent and very lazy and very well content.

After she had lived some time this way, Rose thought it would be nice and very good in her position to get regularly really married. She had lately met Sam Johnson somewhere, and she liked him and she knew he was a good man, and then he had a place where he worked every day and got good wages. Sam Johnson liked Rose very well and he was quite ready to be married. One day they had a grand real wedding and were married. Then with Melanctha Herbert's help to do the sewing and the nicer work, they furnished comfortably a little red brick house. Sam then went back to his work as deck hand on a coasting steamer, and Rose stayed home in her house and sat and bragged to all her friends how nice it was to be married really to a husband.

Life went on very smoothly with them all the year. Rose was lazy but not dirty and Sam was careful but not fussy, and then there was Melanctha to come in every day and help to keep things neat.

When Rose's baby was coming to be born, Rose came to stay in the house where Melanctha Herbert lived just then, with a big good natured colored woman who did washing.

Rose went there to stay, so that she might have the doctor from the hospital near by to help her have the baby, and then, too, Melanctha could attend to her while she was sick.

Here the baby was born, and here it died, and then Rose went back to her house again with Sam.

Melanctha Herbert had not made her life all simple like Rose Johnson. Melanctha had not found it easy with

herself to make her wants and what she had, agree.

Melanctha Herbert was always losing what she had in wanting all the things she saw. Melanctha was always being left when she was not leaving others.

Melanctha Herbert always loved too hard and much too often. She was always full with mystery and subtle movements and denials and vague distrusts and complicated disillusions. Then Melanctha would be sudden and impulsive and unbounded in some faith, and then she would suffer and be strong in her repression.

Melanctha Herbert was always seeking rest and quiet, and always she could only find new ways to be in trouble.

Melanctha wondered often how it was she did not kill herself when she was so blue. Often she thought this would be really the best way for her to do.

Melanctha Herbert had been raised to be religious, by her mother. Melanctha had not liked her mother very well. This mother, 'Mis' Herbert, as her neighbors called her, had been a sweet appearing and dignified and pleasant, pale yellow, colored woman. 'Mis' Herbert had always been a little wandering and mysterious and uncertain in her ways.

Melanctha was pale yellow and mysterious and a little pleasant like her mother, but the real power in Melanctha's nature came through her robust and unpleasant and very unendurable black father.

Melanctha's father only used to come to where Melanctha and her mother lived, once in a while.

It was many years now that Melanctha had not heard or seen or known of anything her father did.

Melanctha Herbert almost always hated her black father, but she loved very well the power in herself that came through him. And so her feeling was really closer to her black coarse father, than her feeling had ever been toward her pale yellow, sweet-appearing mother. The things she had in her of her mother never made her feel respect.

Melanctha Herbert had not loved herself in childhood. All of her youth was bitter to remember.

Melanctha had not loved her father and her mother and they had found it very troublesome to have her.

Melanctha's mother and her father had been regularly married. Melanctha's father was a big black virile negro. He only came once in a while to where Melanctha and her mother lived, but always that pleasant, sweet-appearing, pale yellow woman, mysterious and uncertain and wandering in her ways, was close in sympathy and thinking to her big black virile husband.

James Herbert was a common, decent enough, colored workman, brutal and rough to his one daughter, but then she was a most disturbing child to manage.

The young Melanctha did not love her father and her mother, and she had a breakneck courage, and a tongue that could be very nasty. Then, too, Melanctha went to school and was very quick in all the learning, and she knew very well how to use this knowledge to annoy her parents who knew nothing.

Melanctha Herbert had always had a breakneck courage. Melanctha always loved to be with horses; she loved to do wild things, to ride the horses and to break and tame them.

Melanctha, when she was a little girl, had had a good chance to live with horses. Near where Melanctha and her mother lived was the stable of the Bishops, a rich family who always had fine horses.

John, the Bishops' coachman, liked Melanctha very well and he always let her do anything she wanted with the horses. John was a decent, vigorous mulatto with a prosperous house and wife and children. Melanctha Herbert was older than any of his children. She was now a well grown girl of twelve and just beginning as a woman.

James Herbert, Melanctha's father, knew this John, the Bishops' coachman very well.

One day James Herbert came to where his wife and daughter lived, and he was furious.

"Where's that Melanctha girl of yours," he said fiercely, "if she is to the Bishops' stables again, with that man John, I swear I kill her. Why don't you see to that girl better you, you're her mother."

James Herbert was a powerful, loose built, hard handed, black, angry negro. Herbert never was a joyous negro. Even when he drank with other men, and he did that very often, he was never really joyous. In the days when he had been most young and free and open, he had never had the wide abandoned laughter that gives the broad glow to negro sunshine.

His daughter, Melanctha Herbert, later always made a hard forced laughter. She was only strong and sweet and in her nature when she was really deep in trouble, when she was fighting so with all she really had, that she did not use her laughter. This was always true of poor Melanctha who was so certain that she hated trouble. Melanctha Herbert was always seeking peace and quiet, and she could always only find new ways to get excited.

James Herbert was often a very

angry negro. He was fierce and serious, and he was very certain that he often had good reason to be angry with Melanctha, who knew so well how to be nasty, and to use her learning with a father who knew nothing.

James Herbert often drank with John, the Bishops' coachman. John in his good nature sometimes tried to soften Herbert's feeling toward Melanctha. Not that Melanctha ever complained to John of her home life or her father. It was never Melanctha's way, even in the midst of her worst trouble to complain to any one of what happened to her, but nevertheless somehow every one who knew Melanctha always knew how much she suffered. It was only while one really loved Melanctha that one understood how to forgive her, that she never once complained nor looked unhappy, and was always handsome and in spirits, and yet one always knew how much she suffered.

The father, James Herbert, never told his troubles either, and he was so fierce and serious that no one ever thought of asking.

'Mis' Herbert as her neighbors called her was never heard even to speak of her husband or her daughter. She was always pleasant, sweet-appearing, mysterious and uncertain, and a little wandering in her ways.

The Herberts were a silent family with their troubles, but somehow every one who knew them always knew everything that happened.

The morning of one day when in the evening Herbert and the coachman John were to meet to drink together, Melanctha had come to the stable joyous and in the very best of humors. Her good friend John on this morning felt very firmly how good and sweet she was and how very much she suffered.

John was a very decent colored coachman. When he thought about Melanctha it was as if she were the eldest of his children. Really he felt very strongly the power in her of a woman. John's wife always liked Melanctha and she always did all she could to make things pleasant. And Melanctha all her life loved and respected kind and good and considerate people. Melanctha always loved and wanted peace and gentleness and goodness and all her life for herself poor Melanctha could only find new ways to be in trouble.

This evening after John and Herbert had drunk awhile together, the good John began to tell the father what a fine girl he had for a daughter. Perhaps the good John had been drinking a good deal of liquor, perhaps there was a gleam of something softer than the feeling of a friendly elder in the way John then spoke of Melanctha. There had been a good deal of drinking and John certainly that very morning had felt strongly Melanctha's power as a woman. James Herbert was always a fierce, suspicious, serious negro, and drinking never made him feel more open. He looked very black and evil as he sat and listened while John grew more and more admiring as he talked half to himself, half to the father, of the virtues and the sweetness of Melanctha.

Suddenly between them there came a moment filled full with strong black curses, and then sharp razors flashed in the black hands, that held them flung backward in the negro fashion, and then for some minutes there was fierce slashing.

John was a decent, pleasant, good natured, light brown negro, but he knew how to use a razor to do bloody slashing.

When the two men were pulled apart by the other negroes who were in the room drinking, John had not been much wounded but James Herbert had gotten one good strong cut that went from his right shoulder down across the front of his whole body. Razor fighting does not wound very deeply, but it makes a cut that looks most nasty, for it is so very bloody.

Herbert was held by the other negroes until he was cleaned and plastered, and then he was put to bed to sleep off his drink and fighting.

The next day he came to where his wife and daughter lived and he was furious.

"Where's that Melanctha, of yours?" he said to his wife, when he saw her. "If she is to the Bishops' stables now with that yellow John, I swear I kill her. A nice way she is going for a decent daughter. Why don't you see to that girl better you, ain't you her mother!"

Melanctha Herbert had always been old in all her ways and she knew very early how to use her power as a woman, and yet Melanctha with all her inborn intense wisdom was really very ignorant of evil. Melanctha had not yet come to understand what they meant, the things she so often heard around her, and which were just beginning to stir strongly in her.

Now when her father began fiercely to assail her, she did not really know what it was that he was so furious to force from her. In every way that he could think of in his anger, he tried to make her say a thing she did not really know. She held out and never answered anything he asked her, for Melanctha had a breakneck courage and she just then badly hated her black father.

When the excitement was all over, Melanctha began to know her power, the power she had so often felt stirring within her and which she now knew she could use to make her stronger.

James Herbert did not win this fight with his daughter. After awhile he forgot it as he soon forgot John and the cut of his sharp razor.

Melanctha almost forgot to hate her father, in her strong interest in the power she now knew she had within her.

Melanctha did not care much now, any longer, to see John or his wife or even the fine horses. This life was too quiet and accustomed and no longer stirred her to any interest or excitement.

Melanctha now really was beginning as a woman. She was ready, and she began to search in the streets and in dark corners to discover men and to learn their natures and their various ways of working.

In these next years Melanctha learned many ways that lead to wisdom. She learned the ways, and dimly in the distance she saw wisdom. These years of learning led very straight to trouble for Melanctha, though in these years Melanctha never did or meant anything that was really wrong.

Girls who are brought up with care and watching can always find moments to escape into the world, where they may learn the ways that lead to wisdom. For a girl raised like Melanctha Herbert, such escape was always very simple. Often she was alone, sometimes she was with a fellow seeker, and she strayed and stood, sometimes by railroad yards, sometimes on the docks or around new buildings where many men were working. Then when the darkness covered everything all over, she would begin to learn to know this man or that. She would advance, they would respond, and then she would withdraw a little, dimly, and always did she not know what it was that really held her. Sometimes she would almost go over, and then the strength in her of not really knowing, would stop the average man in his endeavor. It was a strange experience of ignorance and power and desire. Melanctha did not know what it was that she so badly wanted. She was afraid, and yet she did not understand that here she really was a coward.

Boys had never meant much to Melanctha. They had always been too young to content her. Melanctha had a strong respect for any kind of successful power. It was this that always kept Melanctha nearer, in her feeling toward her virile and unendurable black father, than she ever was in her feeling for her pale yellow, sweet-appearing mother. The things she had in her of her mother, never made her feel respect.

In these young days, it was only men that for Melanctha held anything there was of knowledge and power. It was not from men however that Melanctha learned to really understand this power.

From the time that Melanctha was twelve until she was sixteen she wandered, always seeking but never more than very dimly seeing wisdom. All this time Melanctha went on with her school learning; she went to school rather longer than do most of the colored children.

Melanctha's wanderings after wisdom she always had to do in secret and by snatches, for her mother was then still living and 'Mis' Herbert always did some watching, and Melanctha with all her hard courage dreaded that there should be much telling to her father, who came now quite often to where Melanctha lived with her mother.

In these days Melanctha talked and stood and walked with many kinds of men, but she did not learn to know any of them very deeply. They all supposed her to have world knowledge and experience. They, believing that she new all, told her nothing, and thinking that she was deciding with them, asked for nothing, and so though Melanctha wandered widely, she was really very safe with all the wandering.

It was a very wonderful experience this safety of Melanctha in these days of her attempted learning. Melanctha herself did not feel the wonder, she only knew that for her it all had no real value.

Melanctha all her life was very keen in her sense for real experience. She knew she was not getting what she so badly wanted, but with all her breakneck courage Melanctha here was a coward, and so she could not learn to really understand.

Melanctha liked to wander, and to stand by the railroad yard, and watch the men and the engines and the switches and everything that was busy there, working. Railroad yards are a ceaseless fascination. They satisfy every kind of nature. For the lazy man whose blood flows very slowly, it is a steady soothing world of motion which supplies him with the sense of a strong moving power. He need not work and yet he has it very deeply; he has it even better than the man who works in it or owns it. Then for natures that like to feel emotion without the trouble of having any suffering, it is very nice to get the swelling in the throat, and the fullness, and the heart beats, and all the flutter of excitement that comes as one watches the people come and go, and hears the engine pound and give a long drawn whistle. For a child watching through a hole in the fence above the yard, it is a wonder world of mystery and movement. The child loves all the noise, and then it loves the silence of the wind that comes before the full rush of the pounding train, that bursts out from the tunnel where it lost itself and all its noise in darkness, and the child loves all the smoke, that sometimes comes in rings, and always puffs with fire and blue color.

For Melanctha the yard was full of the excitement of many men, and perhaps a free and whirling future.

Melanctha came here very often and watched the men and all the things that were so busy working. The men always had time for, "Hullo sis, do you want to sit on my engine," and, "Hullo, that's a pretty lookin' yaller girl, do you want to come and see him cookin.'"

All the colored porters liked Melanctha. They often told her exciting things that had happened; how in the West they went through big tunnels where there was no air to breathe, and then out and winding around edges of great canyons on thin high spindling trestles, and sometimes cars, and sometimes whole trains fell from the narrow bridges, and always up from the dark places death and all kinds of queer devils looked up and laughed in their faces. And then they would tell how sometimes when the train went pounding down steep slippery mountains, great rocks would racket and roll down around them, and sometimes would smash in the car and kill men; and as the porters told these stories their round, black, shining faces would grow solemn, and their color would go grey beneath the greasy black, and their eyes would roll white in the fear and wonder of the things they could scare themselves by telling.

There was one, big, serious, melancholy, light brown porter who often told Melanctha stories, for he liked the way she had of listening with intelligence and sympathetic feeling, when he told how the white men in the far South tried to kill him because he made one of them who was drunk and called him a damned nigger, and who refused to pay money for his chair to a nigger, get off the train between stations. And then this porter had to give up going to that part of the Southern country, for all the white men swore that if he ever came there again they would surely kill him.

Melanctha liked this serious, melancholy light brown negro very well, and all her life Melanctha wanted and respected gentleness and goodness, and this man always gave her good advice and serious kindness, and Melanctha felt such things very deeply, but she could never let them help her or affect her to change the ways that always made her keep herself in trouble.

Melanctha spent many of the last hours of the daylight with the porters and with other men who worked hard, but when darkness came it was always different. Then Melanctha would find herself with the, for her, gentlemanly classes. A clerk, or a young express agent would begin to know her, and they would stand, or perhaps, walk a little while together.

Melanctha always made herself escape but often it was with an effort. She did not know what it was that she so badly wanted, but with all her courage Melanctha here was a coward, and so she could not learn to understand.

Melanctha and some man would stand in the evening and would talk together. Sometimes Melanctha would be with another girl and then it was much easier to stay or to escape, for then they could make way for themselves together, and by throwing words and laughter to each other, could keep a man from getting too strong in his attention.

But when Melanctha was alone, and she was so, very often, she would sometimes come very near to making a long step on the road that leads to wisdom. Some man would learn a good deal about her in the talk, never altogether truly, for Melanctha all her life did not know how to tell a story wholly. She always, and yet not with intention, managed to leave out big pieces which make a story very different, for when it came to what had happened and what she had said and what it was that she had really done, Melanctha never could remember right. The man would sometimes come a little nearer, would detain her, would hold her arm or make his jokes a little clearer, and then Melanctha would always make herself escape. The man thinking that she really had world wisdom would not make his meaning clear, and believing that she was deciding with him he never went so fast that he could stop her when at last she made herself escape.

And so Melanctha wandered on the edge of wisdom. "Say, Sis, why don't you when you come here stay a little longer?" they would all ask her, and they would hold her for an answer, and she would laugh, and sometimes she did stay longer, but always just in time she made herself escape.

Melanctha Herbert wanted very much to know and yet she feared the knowledge. As she grew older she often stayed a good deal longer, and sometimes it was almost a balanced struggle, but she always made herself escape.

Next to the railroad yard it was the shipping docks that Melanctha loved best when she wandered. Often she was alone, sometimes she was with some better kind of black girl, and she would stand a long time and watch the men working at unloading, and see the steamers do their coaling, and she would listen with full feeling to the yowling of the free swinging negroes, as they ran, with their powerful loose jointed bodies and their childish savage yelling, pushing, carrying, pulling great loads from the ships to the warehouses.

The men would call out, "Say, Sis, look out or we'll come and catch yer," or "Hi, there, you yaller girl, come here and we'll take you sailin'." And then, too, Melanctha would learn to know some of the serious foreign sailors who told her all sorts of wonders, and a cook would sometimes take her and her friends over a ship and show where he made his messes and where the men slept, and where the shops were, and how everything was made by themselves, right there, on ship board.

Melanctha loved to see these dark and smelly places. She always loved to watch and talk and listen with men who worked hard. But it was never from these rougher people that Melanctha tried to learn the ways that lead to wisdom. In the daylight she always liked to talk with rough men and to listen to their lives and about their work and their various ways of doing, but when the darkness covered everything all over, Melanctha would meet, and stand, and talk with a clerk or a young shipping agent who had seen her watching, and so it was that she would try to learn to understand.

And then Melanctha was fond of watching men work on new buildings. She loved to see them hoisting, digging, sawing and stone cutting. Here, too, in the daylight, she always learned to know the common workmen. "Heh, Sis, look out or that rock will fall on you and smash you all up into little pieces. Do you think you would make a nice jelly?" And then

they would all laugh and feel that
their jokes were very funny. And
"Say, you pretty yaller girl, would it
scare you bad to stand up here on top
where I be? See if you've got grit and
come up here where I can hold you.
All you got to do is to sit still on that
there rock that they're just hoistin',
and then when you get here I'll hold
you tight, don't you be scared Sis."

Sometimes Melanctha would do
some of these things that had much
danger, and always with such men,
she showed her power and her breakneck courage. Once she slipped and
fell from a high place. A workman
caught her and so she was not killed,
but her left arm was badly broken.

All the men crowded around her.
They admired her boldness in doing
and in bearing pain when her arm was
broken. They all went along with her
with great respect to the doctor, and
then they took her home in triumph
and all of them were bragging about
her not squealing.

James Herbert was home where his
wife lived, that day. He was furious
when he saw the workmen and Melanctha. He drove the men away with
curses so that they were all very
nearly fighting, and he would not let
a doctor come in to attend Melanctha.
"Why don't you see to that girl better,
you, you're her mother."

James Herbert did not fight things
out now any more with his daughter.
He feared her tongue, and her school
learning, and the way she had of saying things that were very nasty to a
brutal black man who knew nothing.
And Melanctha just then hated him
very badly in her suffering.

And so this was the way Melanctha
lived the four years of her beginning
as a woman. And many things happened to Melanctha, but she knew
very well that none of them had led
her on to the right way, that certain

way that was to lead her to world
wisdom.

Melanctha Herbert was sixteen
when she first met Jane Harden. Jane
was a negress, but she was so white
that hardly any one could guess it.
Jane had had a good deal of education. She had been two years at a
colored college. She had had to leave
because of her bad conduct. She
taught Melanctha many things. She
taught her how to go the ways that
lead to wisdom.

Jane Harden was at this time
twenty-three years old and she had
had much experience. She was very
much attracted by Melanctha, and
Melanctha was very proud that this
Jane would let her know her.

Jane Harden was not afraid to understand. Melanctha who had strong
the sense for real experience, knew
that here was a woman who had
learned to understand.

Jane Harden had many bad habits.
She drank a great deal, and she wandered widely. She was safe though
now, when she wanted to be safe, in
this wandering.

Melanctha Herbert soon always
wandered with her. Melanctha tried
the drinking and some of the other
habits, but she did not find that she
cared very much to do them. But
every day she grew stronger in her
desire to really understand.

It was now no longer, even in the
daylight, the rougher men that these
two learned to know in their wanderings, and for Melanctha the better
classes were now a little higher. It
was no longer express agents and
clerks that she learned to know, but
men in business, commercial travelers,
and even men above these, and Jane
and she would talk and walk and
laugh and escape from them all very
often. It was still the same, the knowing of them and the always just escap-

ing, only now for Melanctha somehow it was different, for though it was always the same thing that happened it had a different flavor, for now Melanctha was with a woman who had wisdom, and dimly she began to see what it was that she should understand.

It was not from the men that Melanctha learned her wisdom. It was always Jane Harden herself who was making Melanctha begin to understand.

Jane was a roughened woman. She had power and she liked to use it, she had much white blood and that made her see clear, she liked drinking and that made her reckless. Her white blood was strong in her and she had grit and endurance and a vital courage. She was always game, however much she was in trouble. She liked Melanctha Herbert for the things that she had like her, and then Melanctha was young, and she had sweetness, and a way of listening with intelligence and sympathetic interest, to the stories that Jane Harden often told out of her experience.

Jane grew always fonder of Melanctha. Soon they began to wander, more to be together than to see men and learn their various ways of working. Then they began not to wander, and Melanctha would spend long hours with Jane in her room, sitting at her feet and listening to her stories, and feeling her strength and the power of her affection, and slowly she began to see clear before her one certain way that would be sure to lead to wisdom.

Before the end came, the end of the two years in which Melanctha spent all her time when she was not at school or in her home, with Jane Harden, before these two years were finished, Melanctha had come to see very clear, and she had come to be

very certain, what it is that gives the world its wisdom.

Jane Harden always had a little money and she had a room in the lower part of the town. Jane had once taught in a colored school. She had had to leave that too on account of her bad conduct. It was her drinking that always made all the trouble for her, for that can never be really covered over.

Jane's drinking was always growing worse upon her. Melanctha had tried to do the drinking but it had no real attraction for her.

In the first year, between Jane Harden and Melanctha Herbert, Jane had been much the stronger. Jane loved Melanctha and she found her always intelligent and brave and sweet and docile, and Jane meant to, and before the year was over she had taught Melanctha what it is that gives many people in the world their wisdom.

Jane had many ways in which to do this teaching. She told Melanctha many things. She loved Melanctha hard and made Melanctha feel it very deeply. She would be with other people and with men and with Melanctha, and she would make Melanctha understand what everybody wanted, and what one did with power when one had it.

Melanctha sat at Jane's feet for many hours in these days and felt Jane's wisdom. She learned to love Jane and to have this feeling very deeply. She learned a little in these days to know joy, and she was taught too how very keenly she could suffer. It was very different this suffering from that Melanctha sometimes had from her mother and from her very unendurable black father. Then she was fighting and she could be strong and valiant in her suffering, but here with Jane Harden she was longing and she bent and pleaded with her suffering.

It was a very tumultuous, very mingled year, this time for Melanctha, but she certainly did begin to really understand.

In every way she got it from Jane Harden. There was nothing good or bad in doing, feeling, thinking or in talking, that Jane spared her. Sometimes the lesson came almost too strong for Melanctha, but somehow she always managed to endure it and so slowly, but always with increasing strength and feeling, Melanctha began to really understand.

Then slowly, between them, it began to be all different. Slowly now between them, it was Melanctha Herbert, who was stronger. Slowly now they began to drift apart from one another.

Melanctha Herbert never really lost her sense that it was Jane Harden who had taught her, but Jane did many things that Melanctha now no longer needed. And then, too, Melanctha never could remember right when it came to what she had done and what had happened. Melanctha now sometimes quarreled with Jane, and they no longer went about together, and sometimes Melanctha really forgot how much she owed to Jane Harden's teaching.

Melanctha began now to feel that she had always had world wisdom. She really knew of course, that it was Jane who had taught her, but all that began to be covered over by the trouble between them, that was now always getting stronger.

Jane Harden was a roughened woman. Once she had been very strong, but now she was weakened in all her kinds of strength by her drinking. Melanctha had tried the drinking but it had had no real attraction for her.

Jane's strong and roughened nature and her drinking made it always harder for her to forgive Melanctha, that now Melanctha did not really need her any longer. Now it was Melanctha who was stronger and it was Jane who was dependent on her.

Melanctha was now come to be about eighteen years old. She was a graceful, pale yellow, good looking, intelligent, attractive negress, a little mysterious sometimes in her ways, and always good and pleasant, and always ready to do things for people.

Melanctha from now on saw very little of Jane Harden. Jane did not like that very well and sometimes she abused Melanctha, but her drinking soon covered everything all over.

It was not in Melanctha's nature to really lose her sense for Jane Harden. Melanctha all her life was ready to help Jane out in any of her trouble, and later, when Jane really went to pieces, Melanctha always did all that she could to help her.

But Melanctha Herbert was ready now herself to do teaching. Melanctha could do anything now that she wanted. Melanctha knew now what everybody wanted.

Melanctha had learned how she might stay a little longer; she had learned that she must decide when she wanted really to stay longer, and she had learned how when she wanted to, she could escape.

And so Melanctha began once more to wander. It was all now for her very different. It was never rougher men now that she talked to, and she did not care much now to know white men of the, for her, very better classes. It was now something realler that Melanctha wanted, something that would move her very deeply, something that would fill her fully with the wisdom that was planted now within her, and that she wanted badly, should really wholly fill her.

Melanctha these days wandered very widely. She was always alone now when she wandered. Melanctha did not need help now to know, or to stay longer, or when she wanted, to escape.

Melanctha tried a great many men, in these days before she was really suited. It was almost a year that she wandered and then she met with a young mulatto. He was a doctor who had just begun to practice. He would most likely do well in the future, but it was not this that concerned Melanctha. She found him good and strong and gentle and very intellectual, and all her life Melanctha liked and wanted good and considerate people, and then too he did not at first believe in Melanctha. He held off and did not know what it was that Melanctha wanted. Melanctha came to want him very badly. They began to know each other better. Things began to be very strong between them. Melanctha wanted him so badly that now she never wandered. She just gave herself to this experience.

Melanctha Herbert was now, all alone, in Bridgepoint. She lived now with this colored woman and now with that one, and she sewed, and sometimes she taught a little in a colored school as substitute for some teacher. Melanctha had now no home nor any regular employment. Life was just commencing for Melanctha. She had youth and had learned wisdom, and she was graceful and pale yellow and very pleasant, and always ready to do things for people, and she was mysterious in her ways and that only made belief in her more fervent.

During the year before she met Jefferson Campbell, Melanctha had tried many kinds of men but they had none of them interested Melanctha very deeply. She met them, she was

much with them, she left them, she would think perhaps this next time it would be more exciting, and always she found that for her it all had no real meaning. She could now do everything she wanted, she knew now everything that everybody wanted, and yet it all had no excitement for her. With these men, she knew she could learn nothing. She wanted some one that could teach her very deeply and now at last she was sure that she had found him, yes she really had it, before she had thought to look if in this man she would find it.

During this year 'Mis' Herbert as her neighbors called her, Melanctha's pale yellow mother was very sick, and in this year she died.

Melanctha's father during these last years did not come very often to the house where his wife lived and Melanctha. Melanctha was not sure that her father was now any longer here in Bridgepoint. It was Melanctha who was very good now to her mother. It was always Melanctha's way to be good to any one in trouble.

Melanctha took good care of her mother. She did everything that any woman could, she tended and soothed and helped her pale yellow mother, and she worked hard in every way to take care of her, and make her dying easy. But Melanctha did not in these days like her mother any better, and her mother never cared much for this daughter who was always a hard child to manage, and who had a tongue that always could be very nasty.

Melanctha did everything that any woman could, and at last her mother died, and Melanctha had her buried. Melanctha's father was not heard from, and Melanctha in all her life after, never saw or heard or knew of anything that her father did.

It was the young doctor, Jefferson Campbell, who helped Melanctha toward the end, to take care of her sick mother. Jefferson Campbell had often before seen Melanctha Herbert, but he had never liked her very well, and he had never believed that she was any good. He had heard something about how she wandered. He knew a little too of Jane Harden, and he was sure that this Melanctha Herbert, who was her friend and who wandered, would never come to any good.

Dr. Jefferson Campbell was a serious, earnest, good young joyous doctor. He liked to take care of everybody and he loved his own colored people. He always found life very easy did Jeff Campbell, and everybody liked to have him with them. He was so good and sympathetic, and he was so earnest and so joyous. He sang when he was happy, and he laughed, and his was the free abandoned laughter that gives the warm broad glow to negro sunshine.

Jeff Campbell had never yet in his life had real trouble. Jefferson's father was a good, kind, serious, religious man. He was a very steady, very intelligent, and very dignified, light brown, grey haired negro. He was a butler and he had worked for the Campbell family many years, and his father and his mother before him had been in the service of this family as free people.

Jefferson Campbell's father and his mother had of course been regularly married. Jefferson's mother was a sweet, little, pale brown, gentle woman who reverenced and obeyed her good husband, and who worshipped and admired and loved hard her good, earnest, cheery, hard working doctor boy who was her only child.

Jeff Campbell had been raised religious by his people but religion had never interested Jeff very much. Jefferson was very good. He loved his people and he never hurt them, and he always did everything they wanted and that he could to please them, but he really loved best science and experimenting and to learn things, and he early wanted to be a doctor, and he was always very interested in the life of the colored people.

The Campbell family had been very good to him and had helped him on with his ambition. Jefferson studied hard, he went to a colored college, and then he learnt to be a doctor.

It was now two or three years, that he had started in to practice. Everybody liked Jeff Campbell, he was so strong and kindly and cheerful and understanding, and he laughed so with pure joy, and he always liked to help all his own colored people.

Dr. Jeff knew all about Jane Harden. He had taken care of her in some of her bad trouble. He knew about Melanctha too, though until her mother was taken sick he had never met her. Then he was called in to help Melanctha to take care of her sick mother. Dr. Campbell did not like Melanctha's ways and he did not think that she would ever come to any good.

Dr. Campbell had taken care of Jane Harden in some of her bad trouble. Jane sometimes had abused Melanctha to him. What right had that Melanctha Herbert who owed everything to her, Jane Harden, what right had a girl like that to go away to other men and leave her, but Melanctha Herbert never had any sense of how to act to anybody. Melanctha had a good mind, Jane never denied her that, but she never used it to do anything decent with it. But what could you expect when Melanctha had such a brute of a black nigger father, and Melanctha was always abusing her father and yet she was just like him, and really she admired him so much and he never had any sense of what he owed to anybody, and Melanctha was just like him and she was proud of it too, and it made Jane so tired to hear Melanctha talk all the time as if she wasn't. Jane Harden hated people who had good minds and didn't use them, and Melanctha always had that weakness, and wanting to keep in with people, and never really saying that she wanted to be like her father, and it was so silly of Melanctha to abuse her father, when she was so much like him and she really liked it. No, Jane Harden had no use for Melanctha. Oh yes, Melanctha always came around to be good to her. Melanctha was always sure to do that. She never really went away and left one. She didn't use her mind enough to do things straight out like that. Melanctha Herbert had a good mind, Jane never denied that to her, but she never wanted to see or hear about Melanctha Herbert any more, and she wished Melanctha wouldn't come in any more to see her. She didn't hate her, but she didn't want to hear about her father and all that talk Melanctha always made, and that just meant nothing to her. Jane Harden was very tired of all that now. She didn't have any use now any more for Melanctha, and if Dr. Campbell saw her he better tell her Jane didn't want to see her, and she could take her talk to somebody else, who was ready to believe her. And then Jane Harden would drop away and forget Melanctha and all her life before, and then she would begin to drink and so she would cover everything all over.

Jeff Campbell heard all this very often, but it did not interest him very deeply. He felt no desire to know more of this Melanctha. He heard her,

once, talking to another girl outside of the house, when he was paying a visit to Jane Harden. He did not see much in the talk that he heard her do. He did not see much in the things Jane Harden said when she abused Melanctha to him. He was more interested in Jane herself than in anything he heard about Melanctha. He knew Jane Harden had a good mind, and she had had power, and she could really have done things, and now this drinking covered everything all over. Jeff Campbell was always very sorry when he had to see it. Jane Harden was a roughened woman, and yet Jeff found a great many strong good things in her, that still made him like her.

Jeff Campbell did everything he could for Jane Harden. He did not care much to hear about Melanctha. He had no feeling, much, about her. He did not find that he took any interest in her. Jane Harden was so much a stronger woman, and Jane really had had a good mind, and she had used it to do things with it, before this drinking business had taken such a hold upon her.

Dr. Campbell was helping Melanctha Herbert to take care of her sick mother. He saw Melanctha now for long times and very often, and they sometimes talked a good deal together, but Melanctha never said anything to him about Jane Harden. She never talked to him about anything that was not just general matters, or about medicine, or to tell him funny stories. She asked him many questions and always listened very well to all he told her, and she always remembered everything she heard him say about doctoring, and she always remembered everything that she had learned from all the others.

Jeff Campbell never found that all this talk interested him very deeply. He did not find that he liked Melanctha when he saw her so much, any better. He never found that he thought much about Melanctha. He never found that he believed much in her having a good mind, like Jane Harden. He found he liked Jane Harden always better, and that he wished very much that she had never begun that bad drinking.

Melanctha Herbert's mother was now always getting sicker. Melanctha really did everything that any woman could. Melanctha's mother never liked her daughter any better. She never said much, did 'Mis' Herbert, but anybody could see that she did not think much of this daughter.

Dr. Campbell now often had to stay a long time to take care of 'Mis' Herbert. One day 'Mis' Herbert was much sicker and Dr. Campbell thought that this night, she would surely die. He came back late to the house, as he had said he would, to sit up and watch 'Mis' Herbert, and to help Melanctha, if she should need anybody to be with her. Melanctha Herbert and Jeff Campbell sat up all that night together. 'Mis' Herbert did not die. The next day she was a little better.

This house where Melanctha had always lived with her mother was a little red brick, two story house. They had not much furniture to fill it and some of the windows were broken and not mended. Melanctha did not have much money to use now on the house, but with a colored woman, who was their neighbor and good natured and who had always helped them, Melanctha managed to take care of her mother and to keep the house fairly clean and neat.

Melanctha's mother was in bed in a room upstairs, and the steps from below led right up into it. There were just two rooms on this upstairs floor. Melanctha and Dr. Campbell sat down on the steps, that night they watched together, so that they could hear and see Melanctha's mother and yet the light would be shaded, and they could sit and read, if they wanted to, and talk low some, and yet not disturb 'Mis' Herbert.

Dr. Campbell was always very fond of reading. Dr. Campbell had not brought a book with him that night. He had just forgotten it. He had meant to put something in his pocket to read, so that he could amuse himself, while he was sitting there and watching. When he was through with taking care of 'Mis' Herbert, he came and sat down on the steps just above where Melanctha was sitting. He spoke about how he had forgotten to bring his book with him. Melanctha said there were some old papers in the house, perhaps Dr. Campbell could find something in them that would help pass the time for a while for him. All right, Dr. Campbell said, that would be better than just sitting there with nothing. Dr. Campbell began to read through the old papers that Melanctha gave him. When anything amused him in them, he read it out to Melanctha. Melanctha was now pretty silent, with him. Dr. Campbell began to feel a little, about how she responded to him. Dr. Campbell began to see a little that perhaps Melanctha had a good mind. Dr. Campbell was not sure yet that she had a good mind, but he began to think a little that perhaps she might have one.

Jefferson Campbell always liked to talk to everybody about the things he worked at and about his thinking about what he could do for the colored people. Melanctha Herbert never thought about these things the way that he did. Melanctha had never said much to Dr. Campbell about what she thought about them. Melanctha did not feel the same as he did about being good and regular in life, and not having excitements all the time, which was the way that Jefferson Campbell wanted that everybody should be, so that everybody would be wise and yet be happy. Melanctha always had strong the sense for real experience. Melanctha Herbert did not think much of this way of coming to real wisdom.

Dr. Campbell soon got through with his reading, in the old newspapers, and then somehow he began to talk along about the things he was always thinking. Dr. Campbell said he wanted to work so that he could understand what troubled people, and not to just have excitements, and he believed you ought to love your father and your mother and to be regular in all your life, and not to be always wanting new things and excitements, and to always know where you were, and what you wanted, and to always tell everything just as you meant it. That's the only kind of life he knew or believed in, Jeff Campbell repeated. "No I ain't got any use for all the time being in excitements and wanting to have all kinds of experience all the time. I got plenty of experience just living regular and quiet and with my family, and doing my work, and taking care of people, and trying to understand it. I don't believe much in this running around business and I don't want to see the colored people do it. I am a colored man and I ain't sorry, and I want to see the colored people like what is good and what I want them to have, and that's to live regular and work hard and understand things, and that's enough to keep any decent man excited." Jeff Campbell spoke now with some anger. Not to Melanctha, he, did not think of her at all when he was talking. It was the life he wanted that he spoke to, and the way he wanted things to be with the colored people.

But Melanctha Herbert had listened to him say all this. She knew he meant it, but it did not mean much to her, and she was sure some day he would find out, that it was not all, of real wisdom. Melanctha knew very well what it was to have real wisdom. "But how about Jane Harden?" said Melanctha to Jeff Campbell, "seems to me Dr. Campbell you find her to have something in her, and you go there very often, and you talk to her much more than you do to the nice girls that stay at home with their people, the kind you say you are really wanting. It don't seem to me Dr. Campbell, that what you say and what you do seem to have much to do with each other. And about your being so good Dr. Campbell," went on Melanctha. "You don't care about going to church much yourself, and yet you always are saying you believe so much in things like that, for people. It seems to me, Dr. Campbell you want to have a good time just like all us others, and then you just keep on saying that it's right to be good and you ought not to have excitements, and yet you really don't want to do it Dr. Campbell, no more than me or Jane Harden. No, Dr. Campbell, it certainly does seem to me you don't know very well yourself, what you mean, when you are talking."

Jefferson had been talking right along, the way he always did when he got started, and now Melanctha's answer only made him talk a little harder. He laughed a little, too, but very low, so as not to disturb 'Mis' Herbert who was sleeping very nicely, and he looked brightly at Melanctha to enjoy her, and then he settled himself down to answer.

"Yes," he began, "it certainly does sound a little like I didn't know very well what I do mean, when you put it like that to me, Miss Melanctha, but that's just because you don't understand enough about what I meant, by what I was just saying to you. I don't say, never, I don't want to know all kinds of people, Miss Melanctha, and I don't say there ain't many kinds of people, and I don't say ever, that I don't find some like Jane Harden very good to know and talk to, but it's the strong things I like in Jane Harden, not all her excitements. I don't admire the bad things she does, Miss Melanctha, but Jane Harden is a strong woman and I always respect that in her. No I know you don't believe what I say, Miss Melanctha, but I mean it, and it's all just because you don't understand it when I say it. And as for religion, that just ain't my way of being good, Miss Melanctha, but it's a good way for many people to be good and regular in their way of living, and if they believe it, it helps them to be good, and if they're honest in it, I like to see them have it. No, what I don't like, Miss Melanctha, is this what I see so much with the colored people, their always wanting new things just to get excited."

Jefferson Campbell here stopped himself in this talking. Melanctha Herbert did not make any answer. They both sat there very quiet.

Jeff Campbell then began again on the old papers. He sat there on the steps just above where Melanctha was sitting, and he went on with his reading, and his head went moving up and down, and sometimes he was reading, and sometimes he was thinking about all the things he wanted to be doing, and then he would rub the back of his dark hand over his mouth, and in between he would be frowning with his thinking, and sometimes he would be rubbing his head hard to help his thinking. And Melanctha just sat still and watched the lamp burning, and sometimes she turned it

down a little, when the wind caught it and it would begin to get to smoking.

And so Jeff Campbell and Melanctha Herbert sat there on the steps, very quiet, a long time, and they didn't seem to think much, that they were together. They sat there so, for about an hour, and then it came to Jefferson very slowly and as a strong feeling that he was sitting there on the steps, alone, with Melanctha. He did not know if Melanctha Herbert was feeling very much about their being there alone together. Jefferson began to wonder about it a little. Slowly he felt that surely they must both have this feeling. It was so important that he knew that she must have it. They both sat there, very quiet, a long time.

At last Jefferson began to talk about how the lamp was smelling. Jefferson began to explain what it is that makes a lamp get to smelling. Melanctha let him talk. She did not answer, and then he stopped in his talking. Soon Melanctha began to sit up straighter and then she started in to question.

"About what you was just saying Dr. Campbell about living regular and all that, I certainly don't understand what you meant by what you was just saying. You ain't a bit like good people Dr. Campbell, like the good people you are always saying are just like you. I know good people Dr. Campbell, and you ain't a bit like men who are good and got religion. You are just as free and easy as any man can be Dr. Campbell, and you always like to be with Jane Harden, and she is a pretty bad one and you don't look down on her and you never tell her she is a bad one. I know you like her just like a friend Dr. Campbell, and so I certainly don't understand just what it is you mean by all that you was just saying to me. I know you mean honest Dr. Campbell, and I am always trying to believe you, but I can't say as I see just what you mean when you say you want to be good and real pious, because I am very certain Dr. Campbell that you ain't that kind of a man at all, and you ain't never ashamed to be with queer folks Dr. Campbell, and you seem to be thinking what you are doing is just like what you are always saying, and Dr. Campbell, I certainly don't just see what you mean by what you say."

Dr. Campbell almost laughed loud enough to wake 'Mis' Herbert. He did enjoy the way Melanctha said these things to him. He began to feel very strongly about it that perhaps Melanctha really had a good mind. He was very free now in his laughing, but not so as to make Melanctha angry. He was very friendly with her in his laughing, and then he made his face get serious, and he rubbed his head to help him in his thinking.

"I know Miss Melanctha," he began, "It ain't very easy for you to understand what I was meaning by what I was just saying to you, and perhaps some of the good people I like so wouldn't think very much, any more than you do, Miss Melanctha, about the ways I have to be good. But that's no matter Miss Melanctha. What I mean Miss Melanctha by what I was just saying to you is, that I don't, no, never, believe in doing things just to get excited. You see Miss Melanctha I mean the way so many of the colored people do it. Instead of just working hard and caring about their working and living regular with their families and saving up all their money, so they will have some to bring up their children better, instead of living regular and doing like that and getting all their new ways from just decent living, the colored people just keep running around and perhaps drinking and doing everything bad they can ever think of, and not just because they like all those bad things that they are always doing, but only just because they want to get excited. No Miss Melanctha, you see I am a colored man myself and I ain't sorry, and I want to see the colored people being good and careful and always honest and living always just as regular as can be, and I am sure Miss Melanctha, that that way everybody can have a good time, and be happy and keep right and be busy, and not always have to be doing bad things for new ways to get excited. Yes Miss Melanctha, I certainly do like everything to be good, and quiet, and I certainly do think that is the best way for all us colored people. No, Miss Melanctha too, I don't mean this except only just the way I say it. I ain't got any other meaning Miss Melanctha, and it's that what I mean when I am saying about being really good. It ain't Miss Melanctha to be pious and not liking every kind of people, and I don't say ever Miss Melanctha that when other kind of people come regular into your life you shouldn't want to know them always. What I mean Miss Melanctha by what I am always saying is, you shouldn't try to know everybody just to run around and get excited. It's that kind of way of doing that I hate so always Miss Melanctha, and that is so bad for all us colored people. I don't know as you understand now any better what I mean by what I was just saying to you. But you certainly do know now Miss Melanctha, that I always mean it what I say when I am talking."

"Yes I certainly do understand you when you talk so Dr. Campbell. I certainly do understand now what you mean by what you was always saying to me. I certainly do understand Dr. Campbell that you mean you don't

believe it's right to love anybody."
"Why sure no, yes I do Miss Melanctha, I certainly do believe strong in loving, and in being good to everybody, and trying to understand what they all need, to help them." "Oh I know all about that way of doing Dr. Campbell, but that certainly ain't the kind of love I mean when I am talking. I mean real, strong, hot love Dr. Campbell, that makes you do anything for somebody that loves you." "I don't know much about that kind of love yet Miss Melanctha. You see it's this way with me always Miss Melanctha. I am always so busy with my thinking about my work I am doing and so I don't have time for just fooling, and then too, you see Miss Melanctha, I really certainly don't ever like to get excited, and that kind of loving hard does seem always to mean just getting all the time excited. That certainly is what I always think from what I see of them that have it bad Miss Melanctha, and that certainly would never suit a man like me. You see Miss Melanctha I am a very quiet kind of fellow, and I believe in a quiet life for all the colored people. No Miss Melanctha I certainly never have mixed myself up in that kind of trouble."

"Yes I certainly do see that very clear Dr. Campbell," said Melanctha, "I see that's certainly what it is always made me not know right about you and that's certainly what it is that makes you really mean what you was always saying. You certainly are just too scared Dr. Campbell to really feel things way down in you. All you are always wanting Dr. Campbell, is just to talk about being good, and to play with people just to have a good time, and yet always to certainly keep yourself out of trouble. It don't seem to me Dr. Campbell that I admire that way to do things very much. It certainly

ain't really to me being very good. It certainly ain't any more to me Dr. Campbell, but that you certainly are awful scared about really feeling things way down in you, and that's certainly the only way Dr. Campbell I can see that you can mean, by what it is that you are always saying to me."

"I don't know about that Miss Melanctha, I certainly don't think I can't feel things very deep in me, though I do say I certainly do like to have things nice and quiet, but I don't see harm in keeping out of danger Miss Melanctha, when a man knows he certainly don't want to get killed in it, and I don't know anything that's more awful dangerous Miss Melanctha than being strong in love with somebody. I don't mind sickness or real trouble Miss Melanctha, and I don't want to be talking about what I can do in real trouble, but you know something about that Miss Melanctha, but I certainly don't see much in mixing up just to get excited, in that awful kind of danger. No Miss Melanctha I certainly do only know just two kinds of ways of loving. One kind of loving seems to me, is like one has a good quiet feeling in a family when one does his work, and is always living good and being regular, and then the other way of loving is just like having it like any animal that's low in the streets together, and that don't seem to me very good Miss Melanctha, though I don't say ever that it's not all right when anybody likes it, and that's all the kinds of love I know Miss Melanctha, and I certainly don't care very much to get mixed up in that kind of a way just to be in trouble."

Jefferson stopped and Melanctha thought a little.

"That certainly does explain to me Dr. Campbell what I been thinking about you this long time. I certainly did wonder how you could be so live, and knowing everything, and everybody, and talking so big always about everything, and everybody always liking you so much, and you always looking as if you was thinking, and yet you really was never knowing about anybody and certainly not being really very understanding. It certainly is all Dr. Campbell because you is so afraid you will be losing being good so easy, and it certainly do seem to me Dr. Campbell that it certainly don't amount to very much that kind of goodness."

"Perhaps you are right Miss Melanctha," Jefferson answered. "I don't say never, perhaps you ain't right Miss Melanctha. Perhaps I ought to know more about such ways Miss Melanctha. Perhaps it would help me some, taking care of the colored people, Miss Melanctha. I don't say, no, never, but perhaps I could learn a whole lot about women the right way, if I had a real good teacher."

'Mis' Herbert just then stirred a little in her sleep. Melanctha went up the steps to the bed to attend her. Dr. Campbell got up too and went to help her. 'Mis' Herbert woke up and was a little better. Now it was morning and Dr. Campbell gave his directions to Melanctha, and then left her.

Melanctha Herbert all her life long, loved and wanted good, kind and considerate people. Jefferson Campbell was all the things that Melanctha had ever wanted. Jefferson was a strong, well built, good looking, cheery, intelligent and good mulatto. And then at first he had not cared to know Melanctha, and when he did begin to know her he had not liked her very well, and he had not thought that she would ever come to any good. And then Jefferson Campbell was so very gentle. Jefferson never did some things like other men, things that now were beginning to be ugly, for Me-

lanctha. And then too Jefferson Campbell did not seem to know very well what it was that Melanctha really wanted, and all this was making Melanctha feel his power with her always getting stronger.

Dr. Campbell came in every day to see 'Mis' Herbert. 'Mis' Herbert, after that night they watched together, did get a little better, but 'Mis' Herbert was really very sick, and soon it was pretty sure that she would have to die. Melanctha certainly did everything, all the time, that any woman could. Jefferson never thought much better of Melanctha while she did it. It was not her being good, he wanted to find in her. He knew very well Jane Harden was right, when she said Melanctha was always being good to everybody but that that did not make Melanctha any better for her. Then too, 'Mis' Herbert never liked Melanctha any better, even on the last day of her living, and so Jefferson really never thought much of Melanctha's always being good to her mother.

Jefferson and Melanctha now saw each other, very often. They now always liked to be with each other, and they always now had a good time when they talked to one another. They, mostly in their talking to each other, still just talked about outside things and what they were thinking. Except just in little moments, and not those very often, they never said anything about their feeling. Sometimes Melanctha would tease Jefferson a little just to show she had not forgotten, but mostly she listened to his talking, for Jefferson still always liked to talk along about the things he believed in. Melanctha was liking Jefferson Campbell better every day, and Jefferson was beginning to know that Melanctha certainly had a good mind, and he was beginning to feel a little her real sweetness. Not in her being good to 'Mis' Herbert, that never seemed to Jefferson to mean much in her, but there was a strong kind of sweetness in Melanctha's nature that Jefferson began now to feel when he was with her.

'Mis' Herbert was now always getting sicker. One night again Dr. Campbell felt very certain that before it was morning she would surely die. Dr. Campbell said he would come back to help Melanctha watch her, and to do anything he could to make 'Mis' Herbert's dying more easy for her. Dr. Campbell came back that evening, after he was through with his other patients, and then he made 'Mis' Herbert easy, and then he came and sat down on the steps just above where Melanctha was sitting with the lamp, and looking very tired. Dr. Campbell was pretty tired too, and they both sat there very quiet.

"You look awful tired to-night, Dr. Campbell," Melanctha said at last, with her voice low and very gentle. "Don't you want to go lie down and sleep a little? You're always being much too good to everybody, Dr. Campbell. I like to have you stay here watching to-night with me, but it don't seem right you ought to stay here when you got so much always to do for everybody. You are certainly very kind to come back, Dr. Campbell, but I can certainly get along to-night without you. I can get help next door sure if I need it. You just go 'long home to bed, Dr. Campbell. You certainly do look as if you need it."

Jefferson was silent for some time, and always he was looking very gently at Melanctha.

"I certainly never did think, Miss Melanctha, I would find you to be so sweet and thinking, with me." "Dr. Campbell," said Melanctha, still more gentle, "I certainly never did think that you would ever feel it good to like me. I certainly never did think you would want to see for yourself if I had sweet ways in me."

They both sat there very tired, very gentle, very quiet, a long time. At last Melanctha in a low, even tone began to talk to Jefferson Campbell.

"You are certainly a very good man, Dr. Campbell, I certainly do feel that more every day I see you. Dr. Campbell, I sure do want to be friends with a good man like you, now I know you. You certainly, Dr. Campbell, never do things like other men, that's always ugly for me. Tell me true, Dr. Campbell, how you feel about being always friends with me. I certainly do know, Dr. Campbell, you are a good man, and if you say you will be friends with me, you certainly never will go back on me, the way so many kinds of them do to every girl they ever get to like them. Tell me for true, Dr. Campbell, will you be friends with me."

"Why, Miss Melanctha," said Campbell slowly, "why you see I just can't say that right out that way to you. Why sure you know Miss Melanctha, I will be very glad if it comes by and by that we are always friends together, but you see, Miss Melanctha, I certainly am a very slow-minded quiet kind of fellow though I do say quick things all the time to everybody, and when I certainly do want to mean it what I am saying to you, I can't say things like that right out to everybody till I know really more for certain all about you, and how I like you, and what I really mean to do better for you. You certainly do see what I mean, Miss Melanctha." "I certainly do admire you for talking honest to me, Jeff Campbell," said Melanctha. "Oh, I am always honest, Miss Melanctha. It's easy enough for me always to be honest, Miss Melanctha. All I got to do is always just to

say right out what I am thinking. I
certainly never have got any real
reason for not saying it right out like
that to anybody."

They sat together, very silent. "I
certainly do wonder, Miss Melanctha," at last began Jeff Campbell, "I
certainly do wonder, if we know very
right, you and me, what each other
is really thinking. I certainly do wonder, Miss Melanctha, if we know at
all really what each other means by
what we are always saying." "That
certainly do mean, by what you say,
that you think I am a bad one, Jeff
Campbell," flashed out Melanctha.
"Why no, Miss Melanctha, why sure
I don't mean any thing like that at all,
by what I am saying to you. You know
well as I do, Miss Melanctha, I think
better of you every day I see you, and
I like to talk with you all the time
now, Miss Melanctha, and I certainly
do think we both like it very well
when we are together, and it seems to
me always more, you are very good
and sweet always to everybody. It
only is, I am really so slow-minded in
my ways, Miss Melanctha, for all I
talk so quick to everybody, and I don't
like to say to you what I don't know
for very sure, and I certainly don't
know for sure I know just all what
you mean by what you are always
saying to me. And you see, Miss Melanctha, that's what makes me say
what I was just saying to you when
you asked me."

"I certainly do thank you again for
being honest to me, Dr. Campbell,"
said Melanctha. "I guess I leave you
now, Dr. Campbell. I think I go in
the other room and rest a little. I leave
you here, so perhaps if I ain't here
you will maybe sleep and rest yourself a little. Good night now, Dr.
Campbell, I call you if I need you
later to help me, Dr. Campbell, I hope
you rest well, Dr. Campbell."

Jeff Campbell, when Melanctha
left him, sat there and he was very
quiet and just wondered. He did not
know very well just what Melanctha
meant by what she was always saying
to him. He did not know very well
how much he really knew about Melanctha Herbert. He wondered if he
should go on being so much all the
time with her. He began to think
about what he should do now with her.
Jefferson Campbell was a man who
liked everybody and many people liked
very much to be with him. Women
liked him, he was so strong, and good,
and understanding, and innocent,
and firm, and gentle. Sometimes
they seemed to want very much he
should be with them. When they got
so, they always had made Campbell
very tired. Sometimes he would play
a little with them, but he never had
had any strong feeling for them. Now
with Melanctha Herbert everything
seemed different. Jefferson was not
sure that he knew here just what he
wanted. He was not sure he knew just
what it was that Melanctha wanted.
He knew if it was only play, with
Melanctha, that he did not want to
do it. But he remembered always how
she had told him he never knew how
to feel things very deeply. He remembered how she told him he was afraid
to let himself ever know real feeling,
and then too, most of all to him, she
had told him he was not very understanding. That always troubled Jefferson very keenly, he wanted very badly
to be really understanding. If Jefferson only knew better just what Melanctha meant by what she said. Jefferson always had thought he knew
something about women. Now he
found that really he knew nothing.
He did not know the least bit about
Melanctha. He did not know what
it was right that he should do about
it. He wondered if it was just a little

play that they were doing. If it was a play he did not want to go on playing, but if it was really that he was not very understanding, and that with Melanctha Herbert he could learn to really understand, then he was very certain he did not want to be a coward. It was very hard for him to know what he wanted. He thought and thought, and always he did not seem to know any better what he wanted. At last he gave up this thinking. He felt sure it was only play with Melanctha. "No, I certainly won't go on fooling with her any more this way," he said at last out loud to himself, when he was through with this thinking. "I certainly will stop fooling, and begin to go on with my thinking about my work and what's the matter with people like 'Mis' Herbert," and Jefferson took out his book from his pocket, and drew near to the lamp, and began with some hard scientific reading.

Jefferson sat there for about an hour reading, and he had really forgotten all about his trouble with Melanctha's meaning. Then 'Mis' Herbert had some trouble with her breathing. She woke up and was gasping. Dr. Campbell went to her and gave her something that would help her. Melanctha came out from the other room and did things as he told her. They together made 'Mis' Herbert more comfortable and easy, and soon she was again in her deep sleep.

Dr. Campbell went back to the steps where he had been sitting. Melanctha came and stood a little while beside him, and then she sat down and watched him reading. By and by they began with their talking. Jeff Campbell began to feel that perhaps it was all different. Perhaps it was not just play, with Melanctha. Anyway he liked it very well that she was with

him. He began to tell her about the book he was just reading.

Melanctha was very intelligent always in her questions. Jefferson knew now very well that she had a good mind. They were having a very good time, talking there together. And then they began again to get quiet.

"It certainly was very good in you to come back and talk to me Miss Melanctha," Jefferson said at last to her, for now he was almost certain, it was no game she was playing. Melanctha really was a good woman, and she had a good mind, and she had a real, strong sweetness, and she could surely really teach him. "Oh I always like to talk to you Dr. Campbell" said Melanctha. "And then you was only just honest to me, and I always like it when a man is really honest to me." Then they were again very silent, sitting there together, with the lamp between them, that was always smoking. Melanctha began to lean a little more toward Dr. Campbell, where he was sitting, and then she took his hand between her two and pressed it hard, but she said nothing to him. She let it go then and leaned a little nearer to him. Jefferson moved a little but did not do anything in answer. At last, "Well," said Melanctha sharply to him. "I was just thinking" began Dr. Campbell slowly, "I was just wondering," he was beginning to get ready to go on with his talking. "Don't you ever stop with your thinking long enough ever to have any feeling Jeff Campbell," said Melanctha a little sadly. "I don't know," said Jeff Campbell slowly, "I don't know Miss Melanctha much about that. No, I don't stop thinking much Miss Melanctha and if I can't ever feel without stopping thinking, I certainly am very much afraid Miss Melanctha that I never will do much with that kind of feeling. Sure you ain't worried Miss

Melanctha, about my really not feeling very much all the time. I certainly do think I feel some, Miss Melanctha, even though I always do it without ever knowing how to stop with my thinking." "I am certainly afraid I don't think much of your kind of feeling Dr. Campbell." "Why I think you certainly are wrong Miss Melanctha. I certainly do think I feel as much for you Miss Melanctha, as you ever feel about me, sure I do. I don't think you know me right when you talk like that to me. Tell me just straight out how much do you care about me, Miss Melanctha." "Care about you Jeff Campbell," said Melanctha slowly. "I certainly do care for you Jeff Campbell less than you are always thinking and much more than you are ever knowing."

Jeff Campbell paused on this, and he was silent with the power of Melanctha's meaning. They sat there together very silent, a long time. "Well Jeff Campbell," said Melanctha. "Oh," said Dr. Campbell and he moved himself a little, and then they were very silent a long time. "Haven't you got nothing to say to me Jeff Campbell?" said Melanctha. "Why yes, what was it we were just saying about to one another. You see Miss Melanctha I am a very quiet, slow minded kind of fellow, and I am never sure I know just exactly what you mean by all that you are always saying to me. But I do like you very much Miss Melanctha and I am very sure you got very good things in you all the time. You sure do believe what I am saying to you Miss Melanctha." "Yes I believe it when you say it to me, Jeff Campbell," said Melanctha, and then she was silent and there was much sadness in it. "I guess I go in and lie down again Dr. Campbell," said Melanctha. "Don't go leave me Miss Melanctha," said Jeff Campbell

quickly. "Why not, what you want of me Jeff Campbell?" said Melanctha. "Why," said Jeff Campbell slowly, "I just want to go on talking with you. I certainly do like talking about all kinds of things with you. You certainly know that all right, Miss Melanctha." "I guess I go lie down again and leave you here with your thinking," said Melanctha gently. "I certainly am very tired to-night Dr. Campbell. Good night I hope you rest well Dr. Campbell." Melanctha stooped over him, where he was sitting, to say this good night, and then, very quick and sudden, she kissed him and then, very quick again, she went away and left him.

Dr. Campbell sat there very quiet, with only a little thinking and sometimes a beginning feeling, and he was alone until it began to be morning, and then he went, and Melanctha helped him, and he made 'Mis' Herbert more easy in her dying. 'Mis' Herbert lingered on till about ten o'clock the next morning, and then slowly and without much pain she died away. Jeff Campbell staid till the last moment, with Melanctha, to make her mother's dying easy for her. When it was over he sent in the colored woman from next door to help Melanctha fix things, and then he went away to take care of his other patients. He came back very soon to Melanctha. He helped her to have a funeral for her mother. Melanctha then went to live with the good natured woman, who had been her neighbor. Melanctha still saw Jeff Campbell very often. Things began to be very strong between them.

Melanctha now never wandered, unless she was with Jeff Campbell. Sometimes she and he wandered a good deal together. Jeff Campbell had not got over his way of talking to her all the time about all the things he was always thinking. Melanctha never talked much, now, when they were together. Sometimes Jeff Campbell teased her about her not talking to him. "I certainly did think Melanctha you was a great talker from the way Jane Harden and everybody said things to me, and from the way I heard you talk so much when I first met you. Tell me true Melanctha, why don't you talk more now to me, perhaps it is I talk so much I don't give you any chance to say things to me, or perhaps it is you hear me talk so much you don't think so much now of a whole lot of talking. Tell me honest Melanctha, why don't you talk more to me." "You know very well Jeff Campbell," said Melanctha. "You certainly do know very well Jeff, you don't think really much, of my talking. You think a whole lot more about everything than I do Jeff, and you don't care much what I got to say about it. You know that's true what I am saying Jeff, if you want to be real honest, the way you always are when I like you so much." Jeff laughed and looked fondly at her. "I don't say ever I know, you ain't right, when you say things like that to me, Melanctha. You see you always like to be talking just what you think everybody wants to be hearing from you, and when you are like that, Melanctha, honest, I certainly don't care very much to hear you, but sometimes you say something that is what you are really thinking, and then I like a whole lot to hear you talking." Melanctha smiled, with her strong sweetness, on him, and she felt her power very deeply. "I certainly never do talk very much when I like anybody really, Jeff. You see, Jeff, it ain't much use to talk about what a woman is really feeling in her. You see all that, Jeff, better, by and by, when you get to really feeling. You won't be so ready

then always with your talking. You see, Jeff, if it don't come true what I am saying." "I don't ever say you ain't always right, Melanctha," said Jeff Campbell. "Perhaps what I call my thinking ain't really so very understanding. I don't say, no never now any more, you ain't right, Melanctha, when you really say things to me. Perhaps I see it all to be very different when I come to really see what you mean by what you are always saying to me." "You is very sweet and good to me always, Jeff Campbell," said Melanctha. "'Deed I certainly am not good to you, Melanctha. Don't I bother you all the time with my talking, but I really do like you a whole lot, Melanctha." "And I like you, Jeff Campbell, and you certainly are mother, and father, and brother, and sister, and child and everything, always to me. I can't say much about how good you been to me, Jeff Campbell, I never knew any man who was good and didn't do things ugly, before I met you to take care of me, Jeff Campbell. Good-by, Jeff, come see me to-morrow, when you get through with your working." "Sure Melanctha, you know that already," said Jeff Campbell, and then he went away and left her.

These months had been an uncertain time for Jeff Campbell. He never knew how much he really knew about Melanctha. He saw her now for long times and very often. He was beginning always more and more to like her. But he did not seem to himself to know very much about her. He was beginning to feel he could almost trust the goodness in her. But then, always, really, he was not very sure about her. Melanctha always had ways that made him feel uncertain with her, and yet he was so near, in his feeling for her. He now never thought about all this in real words any more. He was always letting it fight itself out in him. He was now never taking any part in this fighting that was always going on inside him.

Jeff always loved now to be with Melanctha and yet he always hated to go to her. Somehow he was always afraid when he was to go to her, and yet he had made himself very certain that here he would not be a coward. He never felt any of this being afraid, when he was with her. Then they always were very true, and near to one another. But always when he was going to her, Jeff would like anything that could happen that would keep him a little longer from her.

It was a very uncertain time, all these months, for Jeff Campbell. He did not know very well what it was that he really wanted. He was very certain that he did not know very well what it was that Melanctha wanted. Jeff Campbell had always all his life loved to be with people, and he had loved all his life always to be thinking, but he was still only a great boy, was Jeff Campbell, and he had never before had any of this funny kind of feeling. Now, this evening, when he was free to go and see Melanctha, he talked to anybody he could find who would detain him, and so it was very late when at last he came to the house where Melanctha was waiting to receive him.

Jeff came in to where Melanctha was waiting for him, and he took off his hat and heavy coat, and then drew up a chair and sat down by the fire. It was very cold that night, and Jeff sat there, and rubbed his hands and tried to warm them. He had only said "How do you do" to Melanctha, he had not yet begun to talk to her. Melanctha sat there, by the fire, very quiet. The heat gave a pretty pink glow to her pale yellow and attractive face. Melanctha sat in a low chair,

her hands, with their long, fluttering fingers, always ready to show her strong feeling, were lying quiet in her lap. Melanctha was very tired with her waiting for Jeff Campbell. She sat there very quiet and just watching. Jeff was a robust, dark, healthy, cheery negro. His hands were firm and kindly and unimpassioned. He touched women always with his big hands, like a brother. He always had a warm broad glow, like southern sunshine. He never had anything mysterious in him. He was open, he was pleasant, he was cheery, and always he wanted, as Melanctha once had wanted, always now he too wanted really to understand.

Jeff sat there this evening in his chair and was silent a long time, warming himself with the pleasant fire. He did not look at Melanctha who was watching. He sat there and just looked into the fire. At first his dark, open face was smiling, and he was rubbing the back of his black-brown hand over his mouth to help him in his smiling. Then he was thinking, and he frowned and rubbed his head hard, to help him in his thinking. Then he smiled again, but now his smiling was not very pleasant. His smile was now wavering on the edge of scorning. His smile changed more and more, and then he had a look as if he were deeply down, all disgusted. Now his face was darker, and he was bitter in his smiling, and he began, without looking from the fire, to talk to Melanctha, who was now very tense with her watching.

"Melanctha Herbert," began Jeff Campbell, "I certainly after all this time I know you, I certainly do know little, real about you. You see, Melanctha, it's like this way with me"; Jeff was frowning, with his thinking and looking very hard into the fire, "You see it's just this way, with me now, Melanctha. Sometimes you seem like one kind of a girl to me, and sometimes you are like a girl that is all different to me, and the two kinds of girls is certainly very different to each other, and I can't see any way they seem to have much to do, to be together in you. They certainly don't seem to be made much like as if they could have anything really to do with each other. Sometimes you are a girl to me I certainly never would be trusting, and you got a laugh then so hard, it just rattles, and you got ways so bad, I can't believe you mean them hardly, and yet all that I just been saying is certainly you one way I often see you, and it's what your mother and Jane Harden always found you, and it's what makes me hate so, to come near you. And then certainly sometimes, Melanctha, you certainly is all a different creature, and sometimes then there comes out in you what is certainly a thing, like a real beauty. I certainly, Melanctha, never can tell just how it is that it comes so lovely. Seems to me when it comes it's got a real sweetness, that is more wonderful than a pure flower, and a gentleness, that is more tender than the sunshine, and a kindness, that makes one feel like summer, and then a way to know, that makes everything all over, and all that, and it does certainly seem to be real for the little while it's lasting, for the little while that I can surely see it, and it gives me to feel like I certainly had got real religion. And then when I got rich with such a feeling, comes all that other girl, and then that seems more likely that that is really you what's honest, and then I certainly do get awful afraid to come to you, and I certainly never do feel I could be very trusting with you. And then I certainly don't know anything at all about you, and I certainly don't know

which is a real Melanctha Herbert, and I certainly don't feel no longer, I ever want to talk to you. Tell me honest, Melanctha, which is the way that is you really, when you are alone, and real, and all honest. Tell me, Melanctha, for I certainly do want to know it."

Melanctha did not make him any answer, and Jeff, without looking at her, after a little while, went on with his talking. "And then, Melanctha, sometimes you certainly do seem sort of cruel, and not to care about people being hurt or in trouble, something so hard about you it makes me sometimes real nervous, sometimes somehow like you always, like your being, with 'Mis' Herbert. You sure did do everything that any woman could, Melanctha, I certainly never did see anybody do things any better, and yet, I don't know how to say just what I mean, Melanctha, but there was something awful hard about your feeling, so different from the way I'm always used to see good people feeling, and so it was the way Jane Harden and 'Mis' Herbert talked when they felt strong to talk about you, and yet, Melanctha, somehow I feel so really near to you, and you certainly have got an awful wonderful, strong kind of sweetness. I certainly would like to know for sure, Melanctha, whether I got really anything to be afraid for. I certainly did think once, Melanctha, I knew something about all kinds of women. I certainly know now really, how I don't know anything sure at all about you, Melanctha, though I been with you so long, and so many times for whole hours with you, and I like so awful much to be with you, and I can always say anything I am thinking to you. I certainly do awful wish, Melanctha, I really was more understanding. I certainly do that same, Melanctha."

Jeff stopped now and looked harder than before into the fire. His face changed from his thinking back into that look that was so like as if he was all through and through him, disgusted with what he had been thinking. He sat there a long time, very quiet, and then slowly, somehow, it came strongly to him that Melanctha Herbert, there beside him, was trembling and feeling it all to be very bitter. "Why, Melanctha," cried Jeff Campbell, and he got up and put his arm around her like a brother. "I stood it just so long as I could bear it, Jeff," sobbed Melanctha, and then she gave herself away, to her misery, "I was awful ready, Jeff, to let you say anything you liked that gave you any pleasure. You could say all about me what you wanted, Jeff, and I would try to stand it, so as you would be sure to be liking it, Jeff, but you was too cruel to me. When you do that kind of seeing how much you can make a woman suffer, you ought to give her a little rest, once sometimes, Jeff. They can't any of us stand it so for always, Jeff. I certainly did stand it just as long as I could, so you would like it, but I,—oh Jeff, you went on too long to-night Jeff. I couldn't stand it not a minute longer the way you was doing of it, Jeff. When you want to be seeing how the way a woman is really made of, Jeff, you shouldn't never be so cruel, never to be thinking how much she can stand, the strong way you always do it, Jeff." "Why Melanctha," cried Jeff Campbell, in his horror, and then he was very tender to her, and like a good, strong, gentle brother in his soothing of her, "Why Melanctha dear, I certainly don't now see what it is you mean by what you was just saying to me. Why Melanctha, you poor little girl, you certainly never did believe I ever knew I was giving you real suffering. Why, Me-

lanctha, how could you ever like me if you thought I ever could be so like a red Indian?" "I didn't just know, Jeff," and Melanctha nestled to him, "I certainly never did know just what it was you wanted to be doing with me, but I certainly wanted you should do anything you liked, you wanted, to make me more understanding for you. I tried awful hard to stand it, Jeff, so as you could do anything you wanted with me." "Good Lord and Jesus Christ, Melanctha!" cried Jeff Campbell. "I certainly never can know anything about you real, Melanctha, you poor little girl," and Jeff drew her closer to him. "But I certainly do admire and I trust you a whole lot now, Melanctha. I certainly do, for I certainly never did think I was hurting you at all, Melanctha, by the things I always been saying to you. Melanctha, you poor little, sweet, trembling baby now, be good, Melanctha. I certainly can't ever tell you how awful sorry I am to hurt you so, Melanctha. I do anything I can to show you how I never did mean to hurt you, Melanctha." "I know, I know," murmured Melanctha, clinging to him. "I know you are a good man, Jeff. I always know that, no matter how much you can hurt me." "I sure don't see how you can think so, Melanctha, if you certainly did think I was trying so hard just to hurt you." "Hush, you are only a great big boy, Jeff Campbell, and you don't know nothing yet about real hurting," said Melanctha, smiling up through her crying, at him. "You see, Jeff, I never knew anybody I could know real well and yet keep on always respecting, till I came to know you real well, Jeff." "I sure don't understand that very well, Melanctha. I ain't a bit better than just lots of others of the colored people. You certainly have been unlucky with the kind you met before me, that's all, Melanctha. I certainly ain't very good, Melanctha." "Hush, Jeff, you don't know nothing at all about what you are," said Melanctha. "Perhaps you are right, Melanctha. I don't say ever any more, you ain't right, when you say things to me, Melanctha," and Jefferson sighed, and then he smiled, and then they were quiet a long time together, and then after some more kindness, it was late, and then Jeff left her.

Jeff Campbell, all these months, had never told his good mother anything about Melanctha Herbert. Somehow he always kept his seeing her so much now, to himself. Melanctha too had never had any of her other friends meet him. They always acted together, these two, as if their being so much together was a secret, but really there was no one who would have made it any harder for them. Jeff Campbell did not really know how it had happened that they were so secret. He did not know if it was what Melanctha wanted. Jeff had never spoken to her at all about it. It just seemed as if it were well understood between them that nobody should know that they were so much together. It was as if it were agreed between them, that they should be alone by themselves always, and so they would work out together what they meant by what they were always saying to each other.

Jefferson often spoke to Melanctha about his good mother. He never said anything about whether Melanctha would want to meet her. Jefferson never quite understood why all this had happened so, in secret. He never really knew what it was that Melanctha really wanted. In all these ways he just, by his nature, did, what he sort of felt Melanctha wanted. And so they continued to be alone and much together, and now it had come to be

the spring time, and now they had all out-doors to wander.

They had many days now when they were very happy. Jeff every day found that he really liked Melanctha better. Now surely he was beginning to have real, deep feeling in him. And still he loved to talk himself out to Melanctha, and he loved to tell her how good it all was to him, and how he always loved to be with her, and to tell her always all about it. One day, now Jeff arranged, that Sunday they would go out and have a happy, long day in the bright fields, and they would be all day just alone together. The day before, Jeff was called in to see Jane Harden.

Jane Harden was very sick almost all day and Jeff Campbell did everything he could to make her better. After a while Jane became more easy and then she began to talk to Jeff about Melanctha. Jane did not know how much Jeff was now seeing of Melanctha. Jane these days never saw Melanctha. Jane began to talk of the time when she first knew Melanctha. Jane began to tell how in these days Melanctha had very little understanding. She was young then and she had a good mind. Jane Harden never would say Melanctha never had a good mind, but in those days Melanctha certainly had not been very understanding. Jane began to explain to Jeff Campbell how in every way, she Jane, had taught Melanctha. Jane then began to explain how eager Melanctha always had been for all that kind of learning. Jane Harden began to tell how they had wandered. Jane began to tell how Melanctha once had loved her, Jane Harden. Jane began to tell Jeff of all the bad ways Melanctha had used with her. Jane began to tell all she knew of the way Melanctha had gone on, after she had left her. Jane began to tell all about the different men, white ones and blacks, Melanctha never was particular about things like that, Jane Harden said in passing, not that Melanctha was a bad one, and she had a good mind, Jane Harden never would say that she hadn't, but Melanctha always liked to use all the understanding ways that Jane had taught her, and so she wanted to know everything, always, that they knew how to teach her.

Jane was beginning to make Jeff Campbell see much clearer. Jane Harden did not know what it was that she was really doing with all this talking. Jane did not know what Jeff was feeling. Jane was always honest when she was talking, and now it just happened she had started talking about her old times with Melanctha Herbert. Jeff understood very well that it was all true what Jane was saying. Jeff Campbell was beginning now to see very clearly. He was beginning to feel very sick inside him. He knew now many things Melanctha had not yet taught him. He felt very sick and his heart was very heavy, and Melanctha certainly did seem very ugly to him. Jeff was at last beginning to know what it was to have deep feeling. He took care a little longer of Jane Harden, and then he went to his other patients, and then he went home to his room, and he sat down and at last he had stopped thinking. He was very sick and his heart was very heavy in him. He was very tired and all the world was very dreary to him, and he knew very well now at last, he was really feeling. He knew it now from the way it hurt him. He knew very well that now at last he was beginning to really have understanding. The next day he had arranged to spend, long and happy, all alone in the spring fields with Melanctha, wandering. He wrote her a note and said he could not go, he had

a sick patient and would have to stay home with him. For three days after, he made no sign to Melanctha. He was very sick all these days, and his heart was very heavy in him, and he knew very well that now at last he had learned what it was to have deep feeling.

At last one day he got a letter from Melanctha. "I certainly don't rightly understand what you are doing now to me Jeff Campbell," wrote Melanctha Herbert. "I certainly don't rightly understand Jeff Campbell why you ain't all these days been near me, but I certainly do suppose it's just another one of the queer kind of ways you have to be good, and repenting of yourself all of a sudden. I certainly don't say to you Jeff Campbell I admire very much the way you take to be good Jeff Campbell. I am sorry Dr. Campbell, but I certainly am afraid I can't stand it no more from you the way you have been just acting. I certainly can't stand it any more the way you act when you have been as if you thought I was always good enough for anybody to have with them, and then you act as if I was a bad one and you always just despise me. I certainly am afraid Dr. Campbell I can't stand it any more like that. I certainly can't stand it any more the way you are always changing. I certainly am afraid Dr. Campbell you ain't man enough to deserve to have anybody care so much to be always with you. I certainly am awful afraid Dr. Campbell I don't ever any more want to really see you. Good-by Dr. Campbell I wish you always to be real happy."

Jeff Campbell sat in his room, very quiet, a long time, after he got through reading this letter. He sat very still and first he was very angry. As if he, too, did not know very badly what it was to suffer keenly. As if he had not been very strong to stay with

Melanctha when he never knew what it was that she really wanted. He knew he was very right to be angry, he knew he really had not been a coward. He knew Melanctha had done many things it was very hard for him to forgive her. He knew very well he had done his best to be kind, and to trust her, and to be loyal to her, and now;—and then Jeff suddenly remembered how one night Melanctha had been so strong to suffer, and he felt come back to him the sweetness in her, and then Jeff knew that really, he always forgave her, and that really, it all was that he was so sorry he had hurt her, and he wanted to go straight away and be a comfort to her. Jeff knew very well, that what Jane Harden had told him about Melanctha and her bad ways, had been a true story, and yet he wanted very badly to be with Melanctha. Perhaps she could teach him to really understand it better. Perhaps she could teach him how it could be all true, and yet how he could be right to believe in her and to trust her.

Jeff sat down and began his answer to her. "Dear Melanctha," Jeff wrote to her. "I certainly don't think you got it all just right in the letter, I just been reading, that you just wrote me. I certainly don't think you are just fair or very understanding to all I have to suffer to keep straight on to really always to believe in you and trust you. I certainly don't think you always are fair to remember right how hard it is for a man, who thinks like I was always thinking, not to think you do things very bad very often. I certainly don't think, Melanctha, I ain't right when I was so angry when I got your letter to me. I know very well, Melanctha, that with you, I never have been a coward. I find it very hard, and I never said it any different, it is hard to me to be understanding, and

to know really what it is you wanted, and what it is you are meaning by what you are always saying to me. I don't say ever, it ain't very hard for you to be standing that I ain't very quick to be following whichever way that you are always leading. You know very well, Melanctha, it hurts me very bad and way inside me when I have to hurt you, but I always got to be real honest with you. There ain't no other way for me to be, with you, and I know very well it hurts me too, a whole lot, when I can't follow so quick as you would have me. I don't like to be a coward to you, Melanctha, and I don't like to say what I ain't meaning to you. And if you don't want me to do things honest, Melanctha, why I can't ever talk to you, and you are right when you say, you never again want to see me, but if you got any real sense of what I always been feeling with you, and if you got any right sense, Melanctha, of how hard I been trying to think and to feel right for you, I will be very glad to come and see you, and to begin again with you. I don't say anything now, Melanctha, about how bad I been this week, since I saw you, Melanctha. It don't ever do any good to talk such things over. All I know is I do my best, Melanctha, to you, and I don't say, no, never, I can do any different than just to be honest and come as fast as I think it's right for me to be going in the ways you teach me to be really understanding. So don't talk any more foolishness, Melanctha, about my always changing. I don't change, never, and I got to do what I think is right and honest to me, and I never told you any different, and you always knew it very well that I always would do just so. If you like me to come and see you to-morrow, and go out with you, I will be very glad to, Melanctha. Let me know right away, what it is you want me to be doing for you, Melanctha.

Very truly yours,
JEFFERSON CAMPBELL

"Please come to me, Jeff." Melanctha wrote back for her answer. Jeff went very slowly to Melanctha, glad as he was, still to be going to her. Melanctha came, very quick, to meet him, when she saw him from where she had been watching for him. They went into the house together. They were very glad to be together. They were very good to one another.

"I certainly did think, Melanctha, this time almost really, you never did want me to come to you at all any more to see you," said Jeff Campbell to her, when they had begun again with their talking to each other. "You certainly did make me think, perhaps really this time, Melanctha, it was all over, my being with you ever, and I was very mad, and very sorry, too, Melanctha."

"Well you certainly was very bad to me, Jeff Campbell," said Melanctha, fondly.

"I certainly never do say any more you ain't always right, Melanctha," Jeff answered and he was very ready now with cheerful laughing, "I certainly never do say that any more, Melanctha, if I know it, but still, really, Melanctha, honest, I think perhaps I wasn't real bad to you any more than you just needed from me."

Jeff held Melanctha in his arms and kissed her. He sighed then and was very silent with her. "Well, Melanctha," he said at last, with some more laughing, "well, Melanctha, any way you can't say ever it ain't, if we are ever friends good and really, you can't say, no, never, but that we certainly have worked right hard to get both of us together for it, so we shall sure

deserve it then, if we can ever really get it." "We certainly have worked real hard, Jeff, I can't say that ain't all right the way you say it," said Melanctha. "I certainly never can deny it, Jeff, when I feel so worn with all the trouble you been making for me, you bad boy, Jeff," and then Melanctha smiled and then she sighed, and then she was very silent with him.

At last Jeff was to go away. They stood there on the steps for a long time trying to say good-by to each other. At last Jeff made himself really say it. At last he made himself, that he went down the steps and went away.

On the next Sunday they arranged, they were to have the long happy day of wandering that they had lost last time by Jane Harden's talking. Not that Melanctha Herbert had heard yet of Jane Harden's talking.

Jeff saw Melanctha every day now. Jeff was a little uncertain all this time inside him, for he had never yet told to Melanctha what it was that had so nearly made him really want to leave her. Jeff knew that for him, it was not right he should not tell her. He knew they could only have real peace between them when he had been honest, and had really told her. On this long Sunday Jeff was certain that he would really tell her.

They were very happy all that day in their wandering. They had taken things along to eat together. They sat in the bright fields and they were happy, they wandered in the woods and they were happy. Jeff always loved in this way to wander. Jeff always loved to watch everything as it was growing, and he loved all the colors in the trees and on the ground, and the little, new, bright colored bugs he found in the moist ground and in the grass he loved to lie on and in which he was always so busy searching. Jeff loved everything that moved and that was still, and that had color, and beauty, and real being.

Jeff loved very much this day while they were wandering. He almost forgot that he had any trouble with him still inside him. Jeff loved to be there with Melanctha Herbert. She was always so sympathetic to him for the way she listened to everything he found and told her, the way she felt his joy in all this being, the way she never said she wanted anything different from the way they had it. It was certainly a busy and a happy day, this their first long day of really wandering.

Later they were tired, and Melanctha sat down on the ground, and Jeff threw himself his full length beside her. Jeff lay there, very quiet, and then he pressed her hand and kissed it and murmured to her, "You certainly are very good to me, Melanctha." Melanctha felt it very deep and did not answer. Jeff lay there a long time, looking up above him. He was counting all the little leaves he saw above him. He was following all the little clouds with his eyes as they sailed past him. He watched all the birds that flew high beyond him, and all the time Jeff knew he must tell to Melanctha what it was he knew now, that which Jane Harden, just a week ago, had told him. He knew very well that for him it was certain that he had to say it. It was hard, but for Jeff Campbell the only way to lose it was to say it, the only way to know Melanctha really, was to tell her all the struggle he had made to know her, to tell her so she could help him to understand his trouble better, to help him so that never again he could have any way to doubt her.

Jeff lay there a long time, very quiet, always looking up above him, and yet feeling very close now to Melanctha. At last he turned a little toward her, took her hands closer in his to make him feel it stronger, and then very slowly, for the words came very hard for him, slowly he began his talk to her.

"Melanctha," began Jeff, very slowly, "Melanctha, it ain't right I shouldn't tell you why I went away last week and almost never got the chance again to see you. Jane Harden was sick, and I went in to take care of her. She began to tell everything she ever knew about you. She didn't know how well now I know you. I didn't tell her not to go on talking. I listened while she told me everything about you. I certainly found it very hard with what she told me. I know she was talking truth in everything she said about you. I knew you had been free in your ways, Melanctha, I knew you liked to get excitement the way I always hate to see the colored people take it. I didn't know, till I heard Jane Harden say it, you had done things so bad, Melanctha. When Jane Harden told me, I got very sick, Melanctha. I couldn't bear hardly, to think, perhaps I was just another like them to you, Melanctha. I was wrong not to trust you perhaps, Melanctha, but it did make things very ugly to me. I try to be honest to you, Melanctha, the way you say you really want it from me."

Melanctha drew her hands from Jeff Campbell. She sat there, and there was deep scorn in her anger.

"If you wasn't all through just selfish and nothing else, Jeff Campbell, you would take care you wouldn't have to tell me things like this, Jeff Campbell."

Jeff was silent a little, and he waited before he gave his answer. It was not the power of Melanctha's words that held him, for, for them, he had his answer, it was the power of the mood that filled Melanctha, and for that he had no answer. At last he broke through this awe, with his slow fighting resolution, and he began to give his answer.

"I don't say ever, Melanctha," he began, "it wouldn't have been more right for me to stop Jane Harden in her talking and to come to you to have you tell me what you were when I never knew you. I don't say it, no never to you, that that would not have been the right way for me to do, Melanctha. But I certainly am without any kind of doubting, I certainly do know for sure, I had a good right to know about what you were and your ways and your trying to use your understanding, every kind of way you could to get your learning. I certainly did have a right to know things like that about you, Melanctha. I don't say it ever, Melanctha, and I say it very often, I don't say ever I shouldn't have stopped Jane Harden in her talking and come to you and asked you yourself to tell me all about it, but I guess I wanted to keep myself from how much it would hurt me more, to have you yourself say it to me. Perhaps it was I wanted to keep you from having it hurt you so much more, having you to have to tell it to me. I don't know, I don't say it was to help you from being hurt most, or to help me. Perhaps I was a coward to let Jane Harden tell me 'stead of coming straight to you, to have you tell me, but I certainly am sure, Melanctha, I certainly had a right to know such things about you. I don't say it ever, ever, Melanctha, I hadn't the just right to know those things about you." Melanctha laughed her harsh laugh. "You needn't have been under no kind of worry, Jeff Campbell, about whether you should have asked me. You could have asked, it wouldn't have hurt

nothing. I certainly never would have told you nothing." "I am not so sure of that, Melanctha," said Jeff Campbell. "I certainly do think you would have told me. I certainly do think I could make you feel it right to tell me. I certainly do think all I did wrong was to let Jane Harden tell me. I certainly do know I never did wrong, to learn what she told me. I certainly know very well, Melanctha, if I had come here to you, you would have told it all to me, Melanctha."

He was silent, and this struggle lay there, strong, between them. It was a struggle, sure to be going on always between them. It was a struggle that was as sure always to be going on between them, as their minds and hearts always were to have different ways of working.

At last Melanctha took his hand, leaned over him and kissed him. "I sure am very fond of you, Jeff Campbell," Melanctha whispered to him.

Now for a little time there was not any kind of trouble between Jeff Campbell and Melanctha Herbert. They were always together now for long times, and very often. They got much joy now, both of them, from being all the time together.

It was summer now, and they had warm sunshine to wander. It was summer now, and Jeff Campbell had more time to wander, for colored people never get sick so much in summer. It was summer now, and there was a lovely silence everywhere, and all the noises, too, that they heard around them were lovely ones, and added to the joy, in these warm days, they loved so much to be together.

They talked some to each other in these days, did Jeff Campbell and Melanctha Herbert, but always in these days their talking more and more was like it always is with real lovers. Jeff did not talk so much now about what he before always had been thinking. Sometimes Jeff would be, as if he was just waking from himself to be with Melanctha, and then he would find he had been really all the long time with her, and he had really never needed to be doing any thinking.

It was sometimes pure joy Jeff would be talking to Melanctha, in these warm days he loved so much to wander with her. Sometimes Jeff would lose all himself in a strong feeling. Very often now, and always with more joy in his feeling, he would find himself, he did not know how or what it was he had been thinking. And Melanctha always loved very well to make him feel it. She always now laughed a little at him, and went back a little in him to his before, always thinking, and she teased him with his always now being so good with her in his feeling, and then she would so well and freely, and with her pure, strong ways of reaching, she would give him all the love she knew now very well, how much he always wanted to be sure he really had it.

And Jeff took it straight now, and he loved it, and he felt, strong, the joy of all this being, and it swelled out full inside him, and he poured it all out back to her in freedom, in tender kindness, and in joy, and in gentle brother fondling. And Melanctha loved him for it always, her Jeff Campbell now, who never did things ugly, for her, like all the men she always knew before always had been doing to her. And they loved it always, more and more, together, with this new feeling they had now, in these long summer days so warm; they, always together now, just these two so dear, more and more to each other always, and the summer evenings when they wandered, and the

noises in the full streets, and the music of the organs, and the dancing, and the warm smell of the people, and of dogs and of the horses, and all the joy of the strong, sweet pungent, dirty, moist, warm negro southern summer.

Every day now, Jeff seemed to be coming nearer, to be really loving. Every day now, Melanctha poured it all out to him, with more freedom. Every day now, they seemed to be having more and more, both together, of this strong, right feeling. More and more every day now they seemed to know more really, what it was each other one was always feeling. More and more now every day Jeff found in himself, he felt more trusting. More and more every day now, he did not think anything in words about what he was always doing. Every day now more and more Melanctha would let out to Jeff her real, strong feeling.

One day there had been much joy between them, more than they ever yet had had with their new feeling. All the day they had lost themselves in warm wandering. Now they were lying there and resting, with a green, bright, light-flecked world around them.

What was it that now really happened to them? What was it that Melanctha did, that made everything get all ugly for them? What was it that Melanctha felt then, that made Jeff remember all the feeling he had had in him when Jane Harden told him how Melanctha had learned to be so very understanding? Jeff did not know how it was that it had happened to him. It was all green, and warm, and very lovely to him, and now Melanctha somehow had made it all so ugly for him. What was it Melanctha was now doing with him? What was it he used to be thinking was the right way for him and all the colored people to be always trying to make it right, the way they should be always living? Why was Melanctha Herbert now all so ugly for him?

Melanctha Herbert somehow had made him feel deeply just then, what very more it was that she wanted from him. Jeff Campbell now felt in him what everybody always had needed to make them really understanding, to him. Jeff felt a strong disgust inside him; not for Melanctha herself, to him, not for himself really, in him, not for what it was that everybody wanted, in them; he only had disgust because he never could know really in him, what it was he wanted, to be really right in understanding, for him, he only had disgust because he never could know really what it was really right to him to be always doing, in the things he had before believed in, the things he before had believed in for himself and for all the colored people, the living regular, and the never wanting to be always having new things, just to keep on, always being in excitements. All the old thinking now came up very strong inside him. He sort of turned away then, and threw Melanctha from him.

Jeff never, even now, knew what it was that moved him. He never, even now, was ever sure, he really knew what Melanctha was, when she was real herself, and honest. He thought he knew, and then there came to him some moment, just like this one, when she really woke him up to be strong in him. Then he really knew he could know nothing. He knew then, he never could know what it was she really wanted with him. He knew then he never could know really what it was he felt inside him. It was all so mixed up inside him. All he knew was he wanted very badly Melanctha should be there beside him, and he wanted very badly,

too, always to throw her from him. What was it really that Melanctha wanted with him? What was it really, he, Jeff Campbell, wanted she should give him? "I certainly did think now," Jeff Campbell groaned inside him, "I certainly did think now I really was knowing all right, what I wanted. I certainly did really think now I was knowing how to be trusting with Melanctha. I certainly did think it was like that now with me sure, after all I've been through all this time with her. And now I certainly do know I don't know anything that's very real about her. Oh the good Lord help and keep me!" and Jeff groaned hard inside him, and he buried his face deep in the green grass underneath him, and Melanctha Herbert was very silent there beside him.

Then Jeff turned to look and see her. She was lying very still there by him, and the bitter water on her face was biting. Jeff was so very sorry then, all over and inside him, the way he always was when Melanctha had been deep hurt by him. "I didn't mean to be so bad again to you, Melanctha, dear one," and he was very tender to her. "I certainly didn't never mean to go to be so bad to you, Melanctha, darling. I certainly don't know, Melanctha, darling, what it is makes me act so to you sometimes, when I certainly ain't meaning anything like I want to hurt you. I certainly don't mean to be so bad, Melanctha, only it comes so quick on me before I know what I am acting to you. I certainly am all sorry, hard, to be so bad to you, Melanctha, darling." "I suppose, Jeff," said Melanctha, very low and bitter, "I suppose you are always thinking, Jeff, somebody had ought to be ashamed with us two together, and you certainly do think you don't see any way to it, Jeff, for me to be feeling that way ever, so you certainly don't see any way to it, only to do it just so often for me. That certainly is the way always with you, Jeff Campbell, if I understand you right the way you are always acting to me. That certainly is right the way I am saying it to you now, Jeff Campbell. You certainly didn't anyway trust me now no more, did you, when you just acted so bad to me. I certainly am right the way I say it Jeff now to you. I certainly am right when I ask you for it now, to tell me what I ask you, about not trusting me more then again, Jeff, just like you never really knew me. You certainly never did trust me just then, Jeff, you hear me?" "Yes, Melanctha," Jeff answered slowly. Melanctha paused. "I guess I certainly never can forgive you this time, Jeff Campbell," she said firmly. Jeff paused too, and thought a little. "I certainly am afraid you never can no more now again, Melanctha," he said sadly.

They lay there very quiet now a long time, each one thinking very hard on their own trouble. At last Jeff began again to tell Melanctha what it was he was always thinking with her. "I certainly do know, Melanctha, you certainly now don't want any more to be hearing me just talking, but you see, Melanctha, really, it's just like this way always with me. You see, Melanctha, it's like this way now all the time with me. You remember, Melanctha, what I was once telling to you, when I didn't know you very long together, about how I certainly never did know more than just two kinds of ways of loving, one way the way it is good to be in families and the other kind of way, like animals are all the time just with each other, and how I didn't ever like that last kind of way much for any of the colored people. You see Melanctha, it's like this way with me. I got a new feeling

now, you been teaching to me, just like I told you once, just like a new religion to me, and I see perhaps what really loving is like, like really having everything together, new things, little pieces all different, like I always before been thinking was bad to be having, all go together like, to make one good big feeling. You see, Melanctha, it's certainly like that you make me been seeing, like I never know before any way there was of all kinds of loving to come together to make one way really truly lovely. I see that now, sometimes, the way you certainly been teaching me, Melanctha, really, and then I love you those times, Melanctha, like a real religion, and then it comes over me all sudden, I don't know anything real about you Melanctha, dear one, and then it comes over me sudden, perhaps I certainly am wrong now, thinking all this way so lovely, and not thinking now any more the old way I always before was always thinking, about what was the right way for me, to live regular and all the colored people, and then I think, perhaps, Melanctha you are really just a bad one, and I think, perhaps I certainly am doing it so because I just am too anxious to be just having all the time excitements, like I don't ever like really to be doing when I know it, and then I always get so bad to you, Melanctha, and I can't help it with myself then, never, for I want to be always right really in the ways, I have to do them. I certainly do very badly want to be right, Melanctha, the only way I know is right Melanctha really, and I don't know any way, Melanctha, to find out really, whether my old way, the way I always used to be thinking, or the new way, you make so like a real religion to me sometimes, Melanctha, which way certainly is the real right way for me to be always thinking, and then I certainly am awful good and sorry, Melanctha, I always give you so much trouble, hurting you with the bad ways I am acting. Can't you help me to any way, to make it all straight for me, Melanctha, so I know right and real what it is I should be acting. You see, Melanctha, I don't want always to be a coward with you, if I only could know certain what was the right way for me to be acting. I certainly am real sure, Melanctha, that would be the way I would be acting, if I only knew it sure for certain now, Melanctha. Can't you help me any way to find out real and true, Melanctha, dear one. I certainly do badly want to know always, the way I should be acting."

"No, Jeff, dear, I certainly can't help you much in that kind of trouble you are always having. All I can do now, Jeff, is to just keep certainly with my believing you are good always, Jeff, and though you certainly do hurt me bad, I always got strong faith in you, Jeff, more in you certainly, than you seem to be having in your acting to me, always so bad, Jeff."

"You certainly are very good to me, Melanctha, dear one," Jeff said, after a long, tender silence. "You certainly are very good to me, Melanctha, darling, and me so bad to you always, in my acting. Do you love me good, and right, Melanctha, always?" "Always and always, you be sure of that now you have me. Oh you Jeff, you always be so stupid." "I certainly never can say now you ain't right, when you say that to me so, Melanctha," Jeff answered. "Oh, Jeff dear, I love you always, you know that now, all right, for certain. If you don't know it right now, Jeff, really, I prove it to you now, for good and always." And they lay there a long time in their loving,

and then Jeff began again with his happy free enjoying.

"I sure am a good boy to be learning all the time the right way you are teaching me, Melanctha, darling," began Jeff Campbell, laughing. "You can't say no, never, I ain't a good scholar for you to be teaching now, Melanctha, and I am always so ready to come to you every day, and never playing hooky ever from you. You can't say ever, Melanctha, now can you, I ain't a real good boy to be always studying to be learning to be real bright, just like my teacher. You can't say ever to me, I ain't a good boy to you now, Melanctha." "Not near so good, Jeff Campbell, as such a good, patient kind of teacher, like me, who never teaches any ways it ain't good her scholars should be knowing, ought to be really having, Jeff, you hear me? I certainly don't think I am right for you, to be forgiving always, when you are so bad, and I so patient, with all this hard teaching always." "But you do forgive me always, sure, Melanctha, always?" "Always and always, you be sure Jeff, and I certainly am afraid I never can stop with my forgiving, you always are going to be so bad to me, and I always going to have to be so good with my forgiving." "Oh! Oh!" cried Jeff Campbell, laughing, "I ain't going to be so bad for always, sure I ain't, Melanctha, my own darling. And sure you do forgive me really, and sure you love me true and really, sure, Melanctha?" "Sure, sure, Jeff, boy, sure now and always, sure now you believe me, sure you do, Jeff, always." "I sure hope I does, with all my heart, Melanctha, darling." "I sure do that same, Jeff, dear boy, now you really know what it is to be loving, and I prove it to you now so, Jeff, you never can be forgetting. You see now, Jeff, good and certain, what I always before been saying to you, Jeff, now." "Yes, Melanctha, darling," murmured Jeff, and he was very happy in it, and so the two of them now in the warm air of the sultry, southern, negro sunshine, lay there for a long time just resting.

And now for a real long time there was no open trouble any more between Jeff Campbell and Melanctha Herbert. Then it came that Jeff knew he could not say out any more, what it was he wanted, he could not say out any more, what it was, he wanted to know about, what Melanctha wanted.

Melanctha sometimes now, when she was tired with being all the time so much excited, when Jeff would talk a long time to her about what was right for them both to be always doing, would be, as if she gave way in her head, and lost herself in a bad feeling. Sometimes when they had been strong in their loving, and Jeff would have rise inside him some strange feeling, and Melanctha felt it in him as it would soon be coming, she would lose herself then in this bad feeling that made her head act as if she never knew what it was they were doing. And slowly now, Jeff soon always came to be feeling that his Melanctha would be hurt very much in her head in the ways he never liked to think of, if she would ever now again have to listen to his trouble, when he was telling about what it was he still was wanting to make things for himself really understanding.

Now Jeff began to have always a strong feeling that Melanctha could no longer stand it, with all her bad suffering, to let him fight out with himself what was right for him to be doing. Now he felt he must not, when she was there with him, keep on, with this kind of fighting that was always going on inside him. Jeff Campbell

never knew yet, what he thought was the right way, for himself and for all the colored people to be living. Jeff was coming always each time closer to be really understanding, but now Melanctha was so bad in her suffering with him, that he knew she could not any longer have him with her while he was always showing that he never really yet was sure what it was, the right way, for them to be really loving.

Jeff saw now he had to go so fast, so that Melanctha never would have to wait any to get from him always all that she ever wanted. He never could be honest now, he never could be now, any more, trying to be really understanding, for always every moment now he felt it to be a strong thing in him, how very much it was Melanctha Herbert always suffered.

Jeff did not know very well these days, what it was, was really happening to him. All he knew every now and then, when they were getting strong to get excited, the way they used to when he gave his feeling out so that he could be always honest, that Melanctha somehow never seemed to hear him, she just looked at him and looked as if her head hurt with him, and then Jeff had to keep himself from being honest, and he had to go so fast, and to do everything Melanctha ever wanted from him.

Jeff did not like it very well these days, in his true feeling. He knew now very well Melanctha was not strong enough inside her to stand any more of his slow way of doing. And yet now he knew he was not honest in his feeling. Now he always had to show more to Melanctha than he was ever feeling. Now she made him go so fast, and he knew it was not real with his feeling, and yet he could not make her suffer so any more because he always was so slow with his feeling.

It was very hard for Jeff Campbell to make all this way of doing, right, inside him. If Jeff Campbell could not be straight out, and real honest, he never could be very strong inside him. Now Melanctha, with her making him feel, always, how good she was and how very much she suffered in him, made him always go so fast then, he could not be strong then, to feel things out straight then inside him. Always now when he was with her, he was being more, than he could already yet, be feeling for her. Always now, with her, he had something inside him always holding him in, always now, with her, he was far ahead of his own feeling.

Jeff Campbell never knew very well these days what it was that was going on inside him. All he knew was, he was uneasy now always to be with Melanctha. All he knew was, that he was always uneasy when he was with Melanctha, not the way he used to be from just not being very understanding, but now, because he never could be honest with her, because he was now always feeling her strong suffering, in her, because he knew now he was having a straight, good feeling with her, but she went so fast, and he was so slow to her; Jeff knew his right feeling never got a chance to show itself as strong, to her.

All this was always getting harder for Jeff Campbell. He was very proud to hold himself to be strong, was Jeff Campbell. He was very tender not to hurt Melanctha, when he knew she would be sure to feel it badly in her head a long time after, he hated that he could not now be honest with her, he wanted to stay away to work it out all alone, without her, he was afraid she would feel it to suffer, if he kept away now from her. He was uneasy always, with her, he was uneasy when he thought about her, he knew now he had a good, straight, strong feeling of right loving for her, and yet now he never could use it to be good and honest with her.

Jeff Campbell did not know, these days, anything he could do to make it better for her. He did not know anything he could do, to set himself really right in his acting and his thinking toward her. She pulled him so fast with her, and he did not dare to hurt her, and he could not come right, so fast, the way she always needed he should be doing it now, for her.

These days were not very joyful ones now any more, to Jeff Campbell, with Melanctha. He did not think it out to himself now, in words, about her. He did not know enough, what was his real trouble, with her.

Sometimes now and again with them, and with all this trouble for a little while well forgotten by him, Jeff, and Melanctha with him, would be very happy in a strong, sweet loving. Sometimes then, Jeff would find himself to be soaring very high in his true loving. Sometimes Jeff would find then, in his loving, his soul swelling out full inside him. Always Jeff felt now in himself, deep feeling.

Always now Jeff had to go so much faster than was real with his feeling. Yet always Jeff knew now he had a right, strong feeling. Always now when Jeff was wondering, it was Melanctha he was doubting, in the loving. Now he would often ask her, was she real now to him, in her loving. He would ask her often, feeling something queer about it all inside him, though yet he was never really strong in his doubting, and always Melanctha would answer to him, "Yes Jeff, sure, you know it, always," and always Jeff felt a doubt now, in her loving.

Always now Jeff felt in himself, deep loving. Always now he did not know really, if Melanctha was true in her loving.

All these days Jeff was uncertain in him, and he was uneasy about which way he should act so as not to be wrong and put them both into bad trouble. Always now he was, as if he must feel deep into Melanctha to see if it was real loving he would find she now had in her, and always he would stop himself, with her, for always he was afraid now that he might badly hurt her.

Always now he liked it better when he was detained when he had to go and see her. Always now he never liked to go to be with her, although he never wanted really, not to be always with her. Always now he never felt really at ease with her, even when they were good friends together. Always now he felt, with her, he could not be really honest to her. And Jeff never could be happy with her when he could not feel strong to tell all his feeling to her. Always now every day he found it harder to make the time pass, with her, and not let his feeling come so that he would quarrel with her.

And so one evening, late, he was to go to her. He waited a little long, before he went to her. He was afraid, in himself, to-night, he would surely hurt her. He never wanted to go when he might quarrel with her.

Melanctha sat there looking very angry, when he came in to her. Jeff took off his hat and coat and then sat down by the fire with her.

"If you come in much later to me just now, Jeff Campbell, I certainly never would have seen you no more never to speak to you, 'thout your apologizing real humble to me." "Apologizing Melanctha," and Jeff laughed and was scornful to her, "Apologizing, Melanctha, I ain't proud that kind of way, Melanctha, I don't

mind apologizing to you, Melanctha, all I mind, Melanctha is to be doing of things wrong, to you." "That's easy, to say things that way, Jeff to me. But you never was very proud Jeff, to be courageous to me." "I don't know about that Melanctha. I got courage to say some things hard, when I mean them, to you." "Oh, yes, Jeff, I know all about that, Jeff, to me. But I mean real courage, to run around and not care nothing about what happens, and always to be game in any kind of trouble. That's what I mean by real courage, to me, Jeff, if you want to know it." "Oh, yes, Melanctha, I know all that kind of courage. I see plenty of it all the time with some kinds of colored men and with some girls like you Melanctha, and Jane Harden. I know all about how you are always making a fuss to be proud because you don't holler so much when you run in to where you ain't got any business to be, and so you get hurt, the way you ought to. And then, you kind of people are very brave then, sure, with all your kinds of suffering, but the way I see it, going round with all my patients, that kind of courage makes all kind of trouble, for them who ain't so noble with their courage, and then they got it, always to be bearing it, when the end comes, to be hurt the hardest. It's like running around and being game to spend all your money always, and then a man's wife and children are the ones do all the starving and they don't ever get a name for being brave, and they don't ever want to be doing all that suffering, and they got to stand it and say nothing. That's the way I see it a good deal now with all that kind of braveness in some of the colored people. They always make a lot of noise to show they are so brave not to holler, when they got so much suffering they always bring all on themselves, just by doing things they got no business to be doing. I don't say, never, Melanctha, they ain't got good courage not to holler, but I never did see much in looking for that kind of trouble just to show you ain't going to holler. No it's all right being brave every day, just living regular and not having new ways all the time just to get excitements, the way I hate to see it in all the colored people. No I don't see much, Melanctha, in being brave just to get it good, where you've got no business. I ain't ashamed Melanctha, right here to tell you, I ain't ashamed ever to say I ain't got no longing to be brave, just to go around and look for trouble. "Yes that's just like you always, Jeff, you never understand things right, the way you are always feeling in you. You ain't got no way to understand right, how it depends what way somebody goes to look for new things, the way it makes it right for them to get excited." "No Melanctha, I certainly never do say I understand much anybody's got a right to think they won't have real bad trouble, if they go and look hard where they are certain sure to find it. No Melanctha, it certainly does sound very pretty all this talking about danger and being game and never hollering, and all that way of talking, but when two men are just fighting, the strong man mostly gets on top with doing good hard pounding, and the man that's getting all that pounding, he mostly never likes it so far as I have been able yet to see it, and I don't see much difference what kind of noble way they are made of when they ain't got any kind of business to get together there to be fighting. That certainly is the only way I ever see it happen right, Melanctha, whenever I happen to be anywhere I can be looking." "That's because you never can see anything that ain't just

so simple, Jeff, with everybody, the way you always think it. It do make all the difference the kind of way anybody is made to do things game Jeff Campbell." "Maybe Melanctha, I certainly never say no you ain't right, Melanctha. I just been telling it to you all straight, Melanctha, the way I always see it. Perhaps if you run around where you ain't got any business, and you stand up very straight and say, I am so brave, nothing can ever hurt me, maybe nothing will ever hurt you then Melanctha. I never have seen it do so. I never can say truly any differently to you Melanctha, but I always am ready to be learning from you, Melanctha. And perhaps when somebody cuts into you real hard, with a brick he is throwing, perhaps you never will do any hollering then, Melanctha. I certainly don't ever say no, Melanctha to you, I only say that ain't the way yet I ever see it happen when I had a chance to be there looking."

They sat there together, quiet by the fire, and they did not seem to feel very loving.

"I certainly do wonder," Melanctha said dreamily, at last breaking into their long unloving silence. "I certainly do wonder why always it happens to me I care for anybody who ain't no ways good enough for me ever to be thinking to respect him."

Jeff looked at Melanctha. Jeff got up then and walked a little up and down the room, and then he came back, and his face was set and dark and he was very quiet to her.

"Oh dear, Jeff, sure, why you look so solemn now to me. Sure Jeff I never am meaning anything real by what I just been saying. What was I just been saying Jeff to you. I only certainly was just thinking how everything always was just happening to me."

Jeff Campbell sat very still and dark, and made no answer.

"Seems to me, Jeff you might be good to me a little to-night when my head hurts so, and I am so tired with all the hard work I have been doing, thinking, and I always got so many things to be a trouble to me, living like I do with nobody ever who can help me. Seems to me you might be good to me Jeff to-night, and not get angry, every little thing I am ever saying to you."

"I certainly would not get angry ever with you, Melanctha, just because you say things to me. But now I certainly been thinking you really mean what you have been just then saying to me." "But you say all the time to me Jeff, you ain't no ways good enough in your loving to me, you certainly say to me all the time you ain't no ways good or understanding to me." "That certainly is what I say to you always, just the way I feel it to you Melanctha always, and I got it right in me to say it, and I have got a right in me to be very strong and feel it, and to be always sure to believe it, but it ain't right for you Melanctha to feel it. When you feel it so Melanctha, it does certainly make everything all wrong with our loving. It makes it so I certainly never can bear to have it."

They sat there then a long time by the fire, very silent, and not loving, and never looking to each other for it. Melanctha was moving and twitching herself and very nervous with it. Jeff was heavy and sullen and dark and very serious in it.

"Oh why can't you forget I said it to you Jeff now, and I certainly am so tired, and my head and all now with it."

Jeff stirred, "All right Melanctha, don't you go make yourself sick now in your head, feeling so bad with it,"

and Jeff made himself do it, and he was a patient doctor again now with Melanctha when he felt her really having her head hurt with it. "It's all right now Melanctha darling, sure it is now I tell you. You just lie down now a little, dear one, and I sit here by the fire and just read awhile and just watch with you so I will be here ready, if you need me to give you something to help you resting." And then Jeff was a good doctor to her, and very sweet and tender with her, and Melanctha loved him to be there to help her, and then Melanctha fell asleep a little, and Jeff waited there beside her until he saw she was really sleeping, and then he went back and sat down by the fire.

And Jeff tried to begin again with his thinking, and he could not make it come clear to himself, with all his thinking, and he felt everything all thick and heavy and bad, now inside him, everything that he could not understand right, with all the hard work he made, with his thinking. And then he moved himself a little, and took a book to forget his thinking, and then as always, he loved it when he was reading, and then very soon he was deep in his reading, and so he forgot now for a little while that he never could seem to be very understanding.

And so Jeff forgot himself for awhile in his reading, and Melanctha was sleeping. And then Melanctha woke up and she was screaming. "Oh, Jeff, I thought you gone away for always from me. Oh, Jeff, never now go away no more from me. Oh, Jeff, sure, sure, always be just so good to me."

There was a weight in Jeff Campbell from now on, always with him, that he could never lift out from him, to feel easy. He always was trying not to have it in him and he always was trying not to let Melanctha feel it, with him, but it was always there inside him. Now Jeff Campbell always was serious, and dark, and heavy, and sullen, and he would often sit a long time with Melanctha without moving.

"You certainly never have forgiven to me, what I said to you that night, Jeff, now have you?" Melanctha asked him after a long silence, late one evening with him. "It ain't ever with me a question like forgiving, Melanctha, I got in me. It's just only what you are feeling for me, makes any difference to me. I ain't ever seen anything since in you, makes me think you didn't mean it right, what you said about not thinking now any more I was good, to make it right for you to be really caring so very much to love me."

"I certainly never did see no man like you, Jeff. You always wanting to have it all clear out in words always, what everybody is always feeling. I certainly don't see a reason, why I should always be explaining to you what I mean by what I am just saying. And you ain't got no feeling ever for me, to ask me what I meant, by what I was saying when I was so tired, that night. I never know anything right I was saying." "But you don't ever tell me now, Melanctha, so I really hear you say it, you don't mean it the same way, the way you said it to me." "Oh Jeff, you so stupid always to me and always just bothering with your always asking to me. And I don't never any way remember ever anything I been saying to you, and I am always my head, so it hurts me it half kills me, and my heart jumps so, sometimes I think I die so when it hurts me, and I am so blue always, I think sometimes I take something to just kill me, and I got so much to bother thinking always and doing, and I got so much to worry, and all

that, and then you come and ask me what I mean by what I was just saying to you. I certainly don't know, Jeff, when you ask me. Seems to me, Jeff, sometimes you might have some kind of a right feeling to be careful to me." "You ain't got no right Melanctha Herbert," flashed out Jeff through his dark, frowning anger, "you certainly ain't got no right always to be using your being hurt and being sick, and having pain, like a weapon, so as to make me do things it ain't never right for me to be doing for you. You certainly ain't got no right to be always holding your pain out to show me." "What do you mean by them words, Jeff Campbell." "I certainly do mean them just like I am saying them, Melanctha. You act always, like I been responsible all myself for all our loving one another. And if its anything anyway that ever hurts you, you act like as if it was me made you just begin it all with me. I ain't no coward, you hear me, Melanctha? I never put my trouble back on anybody, thinking that they made me. I certainly am right ready always, Melanctha, you certainly had ought to know me, to stand all my own trouble for me, but I tell you straight now, the way I think it Melanctha, I ain't going to be as if I was the reason why you wanted to be loving, and to be suffering so now with me." "But ain't you certainly ought to be feeling it so, to be right, Jeff Campbell. Did I ever do anything but just let you do everything you wanted to me. Did I ever try to make you be loving to me. Did I ever do nothing except just sit there ready to endure your loving with me. But I certainly never, Jeff Campbell, did make any kind of way as if I wanted really to be having you for me."

Jeff stared at Melanctha. "So that's the way you say it when you are thinking right about it all, Melanctha. Well I certainly ain't got a word to say ever to you any more, Melanctha, if that's the way its straight out to you now, Melanctha." And Jeff almost laughed out to her, and he turned to take his hat and coat, and go away now forever from her.

Melanctha dropped her head on her arms, and she trembled all over and inside her. Jeff stopped a little and looked very sadly at her. Jeff could not so quickly make it right for himself, to leave her.

"Oh, I certainly shall go crazy now, I certainly know that," Melanctha moaned as she sat there, all fallen and miserable and weak together.

Jeff came and took her in his arms, and held her. Jeff was very good then to her, but they neither of them felt inside all right, as they once did, to be together.

From now on, Jeff had real torment in him.

Was it true what Melanctha had said that night to him? Was it true that he was the one had made all this trouble for them? Was it true, he was the only one, who always had had wrong ways in him? Waking or sleeping Jeff now always had this torment going on inside him.

Jeff did not know now any more, what to feel within him. He did not know how to begin thinking out this trouble that must always now be bad inside him. He just felt a confused struggle and resentment always in him, a knowing, no, Melanctha was not right in what she had said that night to him, and then a feeling, perhaps he always had been wrong in the way he never could be understanding. And then would come strong to him, a sense of the deep sweetness in Melanctha's loving and a hating the cold slow way he always had to feel things in him.

Always Jeff knew, sure, Melanctha was wrong in what she had said that night to him, but always Melanctha had had deep feeling with him, always he was poor and slow in the only way he knew how to have any feeling. Jeff knew Melanctha was wrong, and yet he always had a deep doubt in him. What could he know, who had such slow feeling in him? What could he ever know, who always had to find his way with just thinking. What could he know, who had to be taught such a long time to learn about what was really loving? Jeff now always had this torment in him.

Melanctha was now always making him feel her way, strong whenever she was with him. Did she go on to do it just to show him, did she do it so now because she was no longer loving, did she do it so because that was her way to make him be really loving. Jeff never did know how it was that it all happened so to him.

Melanctha acted now the way she had said it always had been with them. Now it was always Jeff who had to do the asking. Now it was always Jeff who had to ask when would be the next time he should come to see her. Now always she was good and patient to him, and now always she was kind and loving with him, and always Jeff felt it was, that she was good to give him anything he ever asked or wanted, but never now any more for her own sake to make her happy in him. Now she did these things, as if it was just to please her Jeff Campbell who needed she should now have kindness for him. Always now he was the beggar, with them. Always now Melanctha gave it, not of her need, but from her bounty to him. Always now Jeff found it getting harder for him.

Sometimes Jeff wanted to tear things away from before him, always now he wanted to fight things and be angry with them, and always now Melanctha was so patient to him.

Now, deep inside him, there was always a doubt with Jeff, of Melanctha's loving. It was not a doubt yet to make him really doubting, for with that, Jeff never could be really loving, but always now he knew that something, and that not in him, something was wrong with their loving. Jeff Campbell could not know any right way to think out what was inside Melanctha with her loving, he could not use any way now to reach inside her to find if she was true in her loving, but now something had gone wrong between them, and now he never felt sure in him, the way once she had made him, that now at last he really had got to be understanding.

Melanctha was too many for him. He was helpless to find out the way she really felt now for him. Often Jeff would ask her, did she really love him. Always she said, "Yes Jeff, sure, you know that," and now instead of a full sweet strong love with it, Jeff only felt a patient, kind endurance in it.

Jeff did not know. If he was right in such a feeling, he certainly never any more did want to have Melanctha Herbert with him. Jeff Campbell hated badly to think Melanctha ever would give him love, just for his sake, and not because she needed it herself, to be with him. Such a way of loving would be very hard for Jeff to be enduring.

"Jeff what makes you act so funny to me. Jeff you certainly now are jealous to me. Sure Jeff, now I don't see ever why you be so foolish to look so to me." "Don't you ever think I can be jealous of anybody ever Melanctha, you hear me. It's just, you certainly don't ever understand me. It's just this way with me always now

Melanctha. You love me, and I don't care anything what you do or what you ever been to anybody. You don't love me, then I don't care any more about what you ever do or what you ever be to anybody. But I never want you to be being good Melanctha to me, when it ain't your loving makes you need it. I certainly don't ever want to be having any of your kind of kindness to me. If you don't love me, I can stand it. All I never want to have is your being good to me from kindness. If you don't love me, then you and I certainly do quit right here Melanctha, all strong feeling, to be always living to each other. It certainly never is anybody I ever am thinking about when I am thinking with you Melanctha darling. That's the true way I am telling you Melanctha, always. It's only your loving me ever gives me anything to bother me Melanctha, so all you got to do, if you don't really love me, is just certainly to say so to me. I won't bother you more then than I can help to keep from it Melanctha. You certainly need never to be in any worry, never, about me Melanctha. You just tell me straight out Melanctha, real, the way you feel it. I certainly can stand it all right, I tell you true Melanctha. And I never will care to know why or nothing Melanctha. Loving is just living Melanctha to me, and if you don't really feel it now Melanctha to me, there ain't ever nothing between us then Melanctha, is there? That's straight and honest just the way I always feel it to you now Melanctha. Oh Melanctha, darling, do you love me? Oh Melanctha, please, please, tell me honest, tell me, do you really love me?"

"Oh you so stupid Jeff boy, of course I always love you. Always and always Jeff and I always just so good to you. Oh you so stupid Jeff and don't know when you got it good with me. Oh dear, Jeff I certainly am so tired Jeff to-night, don't you go be a bother to me. Yes I love you Jeff, how often you want me to tell you. Oh you so stupid Jeff, but yes I love you. Now I won't say it no more now to-night Jeff, you hear me. You just be good Jeff now to me or else I certainly get awful angry with you. Yes I love you, sure, Jeff, though you don't any way deserve it from me. Yes, yes I love you. Yes Jeff I say it till I certainly am very sleepy. Yes I love you now Jeff, and you certainly must stop asking me to tell you. Oh you great silly boy Jeff Campbell, sure I love you, oh you silly stupid, my own boy Jeff Campbell. Yes I love you and I certainly never won't say it one more time to-night Jeff, now you hear me."

Yes Jeff Campbell heard her, and he tried hard to believe her. He did not really doubt her but somehow it was wrong now, the way Melanctha said it. Jeff always now felt baffled with Melanctha. Something, he knew, was not right now in her. Something in her always now was making stronger the torment that was tearing every minute at the joy he once always had had with her.

Always now Jeff wondered did Melanctha love him. Always now he was wondering, was Melanctha right when she said, it was he had made all their beginning. Was Melanctha right when she said, it was he had the real responsibility for all the trouble they had and still were having now between them. If she was right, what a brute he always had been in his acting. If she was right, how good she had been to endure the pain he had made so bad so often for her. But no, surely she had made herself to bear it, for her own sake, not for his to make him happy. Surely he was not so twisted in all his long thinking.

Surely he could remember right what it was had happened every day in their long loving. Surely he was not so poor a coward as Melanctha always seemed to be thinking. Surely, surely, and then the torment would get worse every minute in him.

One night Jeff Campbell was lying in his bed with his thinking, and night after night now he could not do any sleeping for his thinking. To-night suddenly he sat up in his bed, and it all came clear to him, and he pounded his pillow with his fist, and he almost shouted out alone there to him, "I ain't a brute the way Melanctha has been saying. Its all wrong the way I been worried thinking. We did begin fair, each not for the other but for ourselves, what we were wanting. Melanctha Herbert did it just like I did it, because she liked it bad enough to want to stand it. It's all wrong in me to think it any way except the way we really did it. I certainly don't know now whether she is now real and true in her loving. I ain't got any way ever to find out if she is real and true now always to me. All I know is I didn't ever make her to begin to be with me. Melanctha has got to stand for her own trouble, just like I got to stand for my own trouble. Each man has got to do it for himself when he is in real trouble. Melanctha, she certainly don't remember right when she says I made her begin and then I made her trouble. No by God, I ain't no coward nor a brute either ever to her. I been the way I felt it honest, and that certainly is all about it now between us, and everybody always has just got to stand for their own trouble. I certainly am right this time the way I see it." And Jeff lay down now, at last in comfort, and he slept, and he was free from his long doubting torment.

"You know Melanctha," Jeff Campbell began, the next time he was alone to talk a long time to Melanctha. "You know Melanctha, sometimes I think a whole lot about what you like to say so much about being game and never doing any hollering. Seems to me Melanctha, I certainly don't understand right what you mean by not hollering. Seems to me it certainly ain't only what comes right away when one is hit, that counts to be brave to be bearing, but all that comes later from your getting sick from the shock of being hurt once in a fight, and all that, and all the being taken care of for years after, and the suffering of your family, and all that, you certainly must stand and not holler, to be certainly really brave the way I understand it." "What you mean Jeff by your talking." "I mean, seems to me really not to holler, is to be strong not to show you ever have been hurt. Seems to me, to get your head hurt from your trouble and to show it, ain't certainly no braver than to say, oh, oh, how bad you hurt me, please don't hurt me mister. It just certainly seems to me, like many people think themselves so game just to stand what we all of us always just got to be standing, and everybody stands it, and we don't certainly none of us like it, and yet we don't ever most of us think we are so much being game, just because we got to stand it."

"I know what you mean now by what you are saying to me now Jeff Campbell. You make a fuss now to me, because I certainly just have stopped standing everything you like to be always doing so cruel to me. But that's just the way always with you Jeff Campbell, if you want to know it. You ain't got no kind of right feeling for all I always been forgiving to you." "I said it once for fun, Melanctha, but now I certainly do mean it, you think you got a right to go

where you got no business, and you say, I am so brave nothing can hurt me, and then something, like always, it happens to hurt you, and you show your hurt always so everybody can see it, and you say, I am so brave nothing did hurt me except he certainly didn't have any right to, and see how bad I suffer, but you never hear me make a holler, though certainly anybody got any feeling, to see me suffer, would certainly never touch me except to take good care of me. Sometimes I certainly don't rightly see Melanctha, how much more game that is than just the ordinary kind of holler." "No, Jeff Campbell, and made the way you is you certainly ain't likely ever to be much more understanding." "No, Melanctha, nor you neither. You think always, you are the only one who ever can do any way to really suffer." "Well, and ain't I certainly always been the only person knows how to bear it. No, Jeff Campbell, I certainly be glad to love anybody really worthy, but I made so, I never seem to be able in this world to find him." "No, and your kind of way of thinking, you certainly Melanctha never going to any way be able ever to be finding of him. Can't you understand Melanctha, ever, how no man certainly ever really can hold your love for long times together. You certainly Melanctha, you ain't got down deep loyal feeling, true inside you, and when you ain't just that moment quick with feeling, then you certainly ain't ever got anything more there to keep you. You see Melanctha, it certainly is this way with you, it is, that you ain't ever got any way to remember right what you been doing, or anybody else that has been feeling with you. You certainly Melanctha, never can remember right, when it comes what you have done and what you think happens to you." "It certainly is all easy for you Jeff Campbell to be talking. You remember right, because you don't remember nothing till you get home with your thinking everything all over, but I certainly don't think much ever of that kind of way of remembering right, Jeff Campbell. I certainly do call it remembering right Jeff Campbell, to remember right just when it happens to you, so you have a right kind of feeling not to act the way you always been doing to me, and then you go home Jeff Campbell, and you begin with your thinking, and then it certainly is very easy for you to be good and forgiving with it. No, that ain't to me, the way of remembering Jeff Campbell, not as I can see it not to make people always suffer, waiting for you certainly to get to do it. Seems to me like Jeff Campbell, I never could feel so like a man was low and to be scorning of him, like that day in the summer, when you threw me off just because you got one of those fits of your remembering. No, Jeff Campbell, its real feeling every moment when its needed, that certainly does seem to me like real remembering. And that way, certainly, you don't never know nothing like what should be right Jeff Campbell. No Jeff, it's me that always certainly has had to bear it with you. It's always me that certainly has had to suffer, while you go home to remember. No you certainly ain't got no sense yet Jeff, what you need to make you really feeling. No, it certainly is me Jeff Campbell, that always has got to be remembering for us both, always. That's what's the true way with us Jeff Campbell, if you want to know what it is I am always thinking." "You is certainly real modest Melanctha, when you do this kind of talking, you sure is Melanctha," said Jeff Campbell laughing. "I think

sometimes Melanctha I am certainly awful conceited, when I think sometimes I am all out doors, and I think I certainly am so bright, and better than most everybody I ever got anything now to do with, but when I hear you talk this way Melanctha, I certainly do think I am a real modest kind of fellow." "Modest!" said Melanctha, angry. "Modest, that certainly is a queer thing for you Jeff to be calling yourself even when you are laughing." "Well it certainly does depend a whole lot what you are thinking with," said Jeff Campbell. "I never did use to think I was so much on being real modest Melanctha, but now I know really I am, when I hear you talking. I see all the time there are many people living just as good as I am, though they are a little different to me. Now with you Melanctha if I understand you right what you are talking, you don't think that way of no other one that you are ever knowing." "I certainly could be real modest too, Jeff Campbell," said Melanctha, "if I could meet somebody once I could keep right on respecting when I got so I was really knowing with them. But I certainly never met anybody like that yet, Jeff Campbell, if you want to know it." "No, Melanctha, and with the way you got of thinking, it certainly don't look like as if you ever will Melanctha, with your never remembering anything only what you just then are feeling in you, and you not understanding what any one else is ever feeling, if they don't holler just the way you are doing. No Melanctha, I certainly don't see any ways you are likely ever to meet one, so good as you are always thinking you be." "No, Jeff Campbell, it certainly ain't that way with me at all the way you say it. It's because I am always knowing what it is I am wanting, when I get it.

I certainly don't never have to wait till I have it, and then throw away what I got in me, and then come back and say, that's a mistake I just been making, it ain't that never at all like I understood it, I want to have, bad, what I didn't think it was I wanted. It's that way of knowing right what I am wanting, makes me feel nobody can come right with me, when I am feeling things, Jeff Campbell. I certainly do say Jeff Campbell, I certainly don't think much of the way you always do it, always never knowing what it is you are ever really wanting and everybody always got to suffer. No Jeff, I don't certainly think there is much doubting which is better and the stronger with us two, Jeff Campbell."

"As you will, Melanctha Herbert," cried Jeff Campbell, and he rose up, and he thundered out a black oath, and he was fierce to leave her now forever, and then with the same movement, he took her in his arms and held her.

"What a silly goose boy you are, Jeff Campbell," Melanctha whispered to him fondly.

"Oh yes," said Jeff, very dreary. "I never could keep really mad with anybody, not when I was a little boy and playing. I used most to cry sometimes, I couldn't get real mad and keep on a long time with it, the way everybody always did it. It's certainly no use to me Melanctha, I certainly can't ever keep mad with you Melanctha, my dear one. But don't you ever be thinking it's because I think you right in what you been just saying to me. I don't Melanctha really think it that way, honest, though I certainly can't get mad the way I ought to. No Melanctha, little girl, really truly, you ain't right the way you think it. I certainly do know that Melanctha, honest. You certainly don't do me right

Melanctha, the way you say you are thinking. Good-bye Melanctha, though you certainly is my own little girl for always." And then they were very good a little to each other, and then Jeff went away for that evening, from her.

Melanctha had begun now once more to wander. Melanctha did not yet always wander, but a little now she needed to begin to look for others. Now Melanctha Herbert began again to be with some of the better kind of black girls, and with them she sometimes wandered. Melanctha had not yet come again to need to be alone, when she wandered.

Jeff Campbell did not know that Melanctha had begun again to wander. All Jeff knew, was that now he could not be so often with her.

Jeff never knew how it had come to happen to him, but now he never thought to go to see Melanctha Herbert, until he had before, asked her if she could be going to have time then to have him with her. Then Melanctha would think a little, and then she would say to him, "Let me see Jeff, to-morrow, you was just saying to me. I certainly am awful busy you know Jeff just now. It certainly does seem to me this week Jeff, I can't anyways fix it. Sure I want to see you soon Jeff. I certainly Jeff got to do a little more now, I been giving so much time, when I had no business, just to be with you when you asked me. Now I guess Jeff, I certainly can't see you no more this week Jeff, the way I got to do things." "All right Melanctha," Jeff would answer and he would be very angry. "I want to come only just certainly as you want me now Melanctha." "Now Jeff you know I certainly can't be neglecting always to be with everybody just to see you. You come see me next week Tuesday Jeff, you hear me. I don't think Jeff I certainly be so busy, Tuesday." Jeff Campbell would then go away and leave her, and he would be hurt and very angry, for it was hard for a man with a great pride in himself, like Jeff Campbell, to feel himself no better than a beggar. And yet he always came as she said he should, on the day she had fixed for him, and always Jeff Campbell was not sure yet that he really understood what it was Melanctha wanted. Always Melanctha said to him, yes she loved him, sure he knew that. Always Melanctha said to him, she certainly did love him just the same as always, only sure he knew now she certainly did seem to be right busy with all she certainly now had to be doing. .

Jeff never knew what Melanctha had to do now, that made her always be so busy, but Jeff Campbell never cared to ask Melanctha such a question. Besides Jeff knew Melanctha Herbert would never, in such a matter, give him any kind of a real answer. Jeff did not know whether it was that Melanctha did not know how to give a simple answer. And then how could he, Jeff, know what was important to her. Jeff Campbell always felt strongly in him, he had no right to interfere with Melanctha in any practical kind of a matter. There they had always, never asked each other any kind of question. There they had felt always in each other, not any right to take care of one another. And Jeff Campbell now felt less than he had ever, any right to claim to know what Melanctha thought it right that she should do in any of her ways of living. All Jeff felt a right in himself to question, was her loving.

Jeff learned every day now, more and more, how much it was that he could really suffer. Sometimes it hurt so in him, when he was alone, it would force some slow tears from him. But every day, now that Jeff Campbell, knew more how it could hurt him, he lost his feeling of deep awe that he once always had had for Melanctha's feeling. Suffering was not so much after all, thought Jeff Campbell, if even he could feel it so it hurt him. It hurt him bad, just the way he knew he once had hurt Melanctha, and yet he too could have it and not make any kind of a loud holler with it.

In tender-hearted natures, those that mostly never feel strong passion, suffering often comes to make them harder. When these do not know in themselves what it is to suffer, suffering is then very awful to them and they badly want to help everyone who ever has to suffer, and they have a deep reverence for anybody who knows really how to always suffer. But when it comes to them to really suffer, they soon begin to loose their fear and tenderness and wonder. Why it isn't so very much to suffer, when even I can bear to do it. It isn't very pleasant to be having all the time, to stand it, but they are not so much wiser after all, all the others just because they know too how to bear it.

Passionate natures who have always made themselves, to suffer, that is all the kind of people who have emotions that come to them as sharp as a sensation, they always get more tender-hearted when they suffer, and it always does them good to suffer. Tender-hearted, unpassionate, and comfortable natures always get much harder when they suffer, for so they lose the fear and reverence and wonder they once had for everybody who ever has to suffer, for now they know themselves what it is to suffer and it is not so awful any longer to them when they know too, just as well as all the others, how to have it.

And so it came in these days to Jeff Campbell. Jeff knew now always, way inside him, what it is to really suffer, and now every day with it, he knew how to understand Melanctha better. Jeff Campbell still loved Melanctha Herbert and he still had a real trust in her and he still had a little hope that some day they would once more get together, but slowly, every day, this hope in him would keep growing always weaker. They still were a good deal of time together, but now they never any more were really trusting with each other. In the days when they used to be together, Jeff had felt he did not know much what was inside Melanctha, but he knew very well, how very deep always was his trust in her; now he knew Melanctha Herbert better, but now he never felt a deep trust in her. Now Jeff never could be really honest with her. He never doubted yet, that she was steady only to him, but somehow he could not believe much really in Melanctha's loving.

Melanctha Herbert was a little angry now when Jeff asked her, "I never give nobody before Jeff, ever more than one chance with me, and I certainly been giving you most a hundred Jeff, you hear me." "And why shouldn't you Melanctha, give me a million, if you really love me!" Jeff flashed out very angry. "I certainly don't know as you deserve that anyways from me, Jeff Campbell." "It ain't deserving, I am ever talking about to you Melanctha. Its loving, and if you are really loving to me you won't certainly never any ways call them chances." "Deed Jeff, you certainly are getting awful wise Jeff now, ain't you, to me." "No I ain't Melanctha, and I ain't jealous either to you. I just am doubting from the way you are always acting to me." "Oh yes Jeff, that's what they all say,

the same way, when they certainly got jealousy all through them. You ain't got no cause to be jealous with me Jeff, and I am awful tired of all this talking now, you hear me."

Jeff Campbell never asked Melanctha any more if she loved him. Now things were always getting worse between them. Now Jeff was always very silent with Melanctha. Now Jeff never wanted to be honest to her, and now Jeff never had much to say to her.

Now when they were together, it was Melanctha always did most of the talking. Now she often had other girls there with her. Melanctha was always kind to Jeff Campbell but she never seemed to need to be alone now with him. She always treated Jeff, like her best friend, and she always spoke so to him and yet she never seemed now to very often want to see him.

Every day it was getting harder for Jeff Campbell. It was as if now, when he had learned to really love Melanctha, she did not need any more to have him. Jeff began to know this very well inside him.

Jeff Campbell did not know yet that Melanctha had begun again to wander. Jeff was not very quick to suspect Melanctha. All Jeff knew was, that he did not trust her to be now really loving to him.

Jeff was no longer now in any doubt inside him. He knew very well now he really loved Melanctha. He knew now very well she was not any more a real religion to him. Jeff Campbell knew very well too now inside him, he did not really want Melanctha, now if he could no longer trust her, though he loved her hard and really knew now what it was to suffer.

Every day Melanctha Herbert was less and less near to him. She always was very pleasant in her talk and to be with him, but somehow now it never was any comfort to him.

Melanctha Herbert now always had a lot of friends around her. Jeff Campbell never wanted to be with them. Now Melanctha began to find it, she said it often to him, always harder to arrange to be alone now with him. Sometimes she would be late for him. Then Jeff always would try to be patient in his waiting, for Jeff Campbell knew very well how to remember, and he knew it was only right that he should now endure this from her.

Then Melanctha began to manage often not to see him, and once she went away when she had promised to be there to meet him.

Then Jeff Campbell was really filled up with his anger. Now he knew he could never really want her. Now he knew he never any more could really trust her.

Jeff Campbell never knew why Melanctha had not come to meet him. Jeff had heard a little talking now, about how Melanctha Herbert had commenced once more to wander. Jeff Campbell still sometimes saw Jane Harden, who always needed a doctor to be often there to help her. Jane Harden always knew very well what happened to Melanctha. Jeff Campbell never would talk to Jane Harden anything about Melanctha. Jeff was always loyal to Melanctha. Jeff never let Jane Harden say much to him about Melanctha, though he never let her know that now he loved her. But somehow Jeff did know now about Melanctha, and he knew about some men that Melanctha met with Rose Johnson very often.

Jeff Campbell would not let himself really doubt Melanctha, but Jeff began to know now very well, he did not want her. Melanctha Herbert did not love him ever, Jeff knew it now, the way he once had thought that she

could feel it. Once she had been greater for him than he had thought he could ever know how to feel it. Now Jeff had come to where he could understand Melanctha Herbert. Jeff was not bitter to her because she could not really love him, he was bitter only that he had let himself have a real illusion in him. He was a little bitter too, that he had lost now, what he had always felt real in the world, that had made it for him always full of beauty, and now he had not got this new religion really, and he had lost what he before had to know what was good and had real beauty.

Jeff Campbell was so angry now in him, because he had begged Melanctha always to be honest to him. Jeff could stand it in her not to love him, he could not stand it in her not to be honest to him.

Jeff Campbell went home from where Melanctha had not met him, and he was sore and full of anger in him.

Jeff Campbell could not be sure what to do, to make it right inside him. Surely he must be strong now and cast this loving from him, and yet, was he sure he now had real wisdom in him. Was he sure that Melanctha Herbert never had had a real deep loving for him. Was he sure Melanctha Herbert never had deserved a reverence from him. Always now Jeff had this torment in him, but always now he felt more that Melanctha never had real greatness for him.

Jeff waited to see if Melanctha would send any word to him. Melanctha Herbert never sent a line to him.

At last Jeff wrote his letter to Melanctha. "Dear Melanctha, I certainly do know you ain't been any way sick this last week when you never met me right the way you promised, and never sent me any word to say why you acted a way you certainly never could think was the right way you should do it to me. Jane Harden said she saw you that day and you went out walking with some people you like now to be with. Don't be misunderstanding me now any more Melanctha. I love you now because that's my slow way to learn what you been teaching, but I know now you certainly never had what seems to me real kind of feeling. I don't love you Melanctha any more now like a real religion, because now I know you are just made like all us others. I know now no man can ever really hold you because no man can ever be real to trust in you, because you mean right Melanctha, but you never can remember, and so you certainly never have got any way to be honest. So please you understand me right now Melanctha, it never is I don't know how to love you. I do know now how to love you, Melanctha, really. You sure do know that, Melanctha, in me. You certainly always can trust me. And so now Melanctha, I can say to you certainly real honest with you, I am better than you are in my right kind of feeling. And so Melanctha, I don't never any more want to be a trouble to you. You certainly make me see things Melanctha, I never any other way could be knowing. You been very good and patient to me, when I was certainly below you in my right feeling. I certainly never have been near so good and patient to you ever any way Melanctha, I certainly know that Melanctha. But Melanctha, with me, it certainly is, always to be good together, two people certainly must be thinking each one as good as the other, to be really loving right Melanctha. And it certainly must never be any kind of feeling, of one only taking, and one only just giving, Melanctha, to me. I know you

certainly don't really ever understand me now Melanctha, but that's no matter. I certainly do know what I am feeling now with you real Melanctha. And so good-bye now for good Melanctha. I say I can never ever really trust you real Melanctha, that's only just certainly from your way of not being ever equal in your feeling to anybody real, Melanctha, and your way never to know right how to remember. Many ways I really trust you deep Melanctha, and I certainly do feel deep all the good sweetness you certainly got real in you Melanctha. Its only just in your loving me Melanctha. You never can be equal to me and that way I certainly never can bear any more to have it. And so now Melanctha, I always be your friend, if you need me, and now we never see each other any more to talk to."

And then Jeff Campbell thought and thought, and he could never make any way for him now, to see it different, and so at last he sent this letter to Melanctha.

And now surely it was all over in Jeff Campbell. Surely now he never any more could know Melanctha. And yet, perhaps Melanctha really loved him. And then she would know how much it hurt him never any more, any way, to see her, and perhaps she would write a line to tell him. But that was a foolish way for Jeff ever to be thinking. Of course Melanctha never would write a word to him. It was all over now for always, everything between them, and Jeff felt it a real relief to him.

For many days now Jeff Campbell only felt it as a relief in him. Jeff was all locked up and quiet now inside him. It was all settling down heavy in him, and these days when it was sinking so deep in him, it was only the rest and quiet of not fighting that he

could really feel inside him. Jeff
Campbell could not think now, or feel
anything else in him. He had no
beauty nor any goodness to see around
him. It was a dull, pleasant kind of
quiet he now had inside him. Jeff almost began to love this dull quiet in
him, for it was more nearly being free
for him than anything he had known
in him since Melanctha Herbert first
had moved him. He did not find it a
real rest yet for him, he had not really
conquered what had been working so
long in him, he had not learned to see
beauty and real goodness yet in what
had happened to him, but it was rest
even if he was sodden now all
through him. Jeff Campbell liked it
very well, not to have fighting always
going on inside him.

And so Jeff went on every day, and
he was quiet, and he began again to
watch himself in his working; and he
did not see any beauty now around
him, and it was dull and heavy always
now inside him, and yet he was content to have gone so far in keeping
steady to what he knew was the right
way for him to come back to, to be
regular, and see beauty in every kind
of quiet way of living, the way he had
always wanted it for himself and for
all the colored people. He knew he
had lost the sense he once had of
joy all through him, but he could
work, and perhaps he would bring
some real belief back into him about
the beauty that he could not now any
more see around him.

And so Jeff Campbell went on
with his working, and he staid home
every evening, and he began again
with his reading, and he did not do
much talking, and he did not seem to
himself to have any kind of feeling.

And one day Jeff thought perhaps
he really was forgetting, one day he
thought he could soon come back and

be happy in his old way of regular
and quiet living.

Jeff Campbell had never talked to
any one of what had been going on
inside him. Jeff Campbell liked to talk
and he was honest, but it never came
out from him, anything he was ever
really feeling, it only came out from
him, what it was that he was always
thinking. Jeff Campbell always was
very proud to hide what he was really
feeling. Always he blushed hot to
think things he had been feeling.
Only to Melanctha Herbert, had it
ever come to him, to tell what it was
that he was feeling.

And so Jeff Campbell went on with
this dull and sodden, heavy, quiet always in him, and he never seemed to
be able to have any feeling. Only
sometimes he shivered hot with
shame when he remembered some
things he once had been feeling. And
then one day it all woke up, and was
sharp in him.

Dr. Campbell was just then staying
long times with a sick man who might
soon be dying. One day the sick man
was resting. Dr. Campbell went to
the window to look out a little, while
he was waiting. It was very early now
in the southern springtime. The trees
were just beginning to get the little
zigzag crinkles in them, which the
young buds always give them. The air
was soft and moist and pleasant to
them. The earth was wet and rich and
smelling for them. The birds were making sharp fresh noises all around them.
The wind was very gentle and yet
urgent to them. And the buds and
the long earthworms, and the negroes,
and all the kinds of children, were
coming out every minute farther into
the new spring, watery, southern sunshine.

Jeff Campbell too began to feel a
little his old joy inside him. The sodden quiet began to break up in him.

He leaned far out of the window to mix it all up with him. His heart went sharp and then it almost stopped inside him. Was it Melanctha Herbert he had just seen passing by him? Was it Melanctha, or was it just some other girl, who made him feel so bad inside him? Well, it was no matter, Melanctha was there in the world around him, he did certainly always know that in him. Melanctha Herbert was always in the same town with him, and he could never any more feel her near him. What a fool he was to throw her from him. Did he know she did not really love him. Suppose Melanctha was now suffering through him. Suppose she really would be glad to see him. And did anything else he did, really mean anything now to him? What a fool he was to cast her from him. And yet did Melanctha Herbert want him, was she honest to him, had Melanctha ever loved him, and did Melanctha now suffer by him? Oh! Oh! Oh! and the bitter water once more rose up in him.

All that long day, with the warm moist young spring stirring in him, Jeff Campbell worked, and thought, and beat his breast, and wandered, and spoke aloud, and was silent, and was certain, and then in doubt and then keen to surely feel, and then all sodden in him; and he walked, and he sometimes ran fast to lose himself in his rushing, and he bit his nails to pain and bleeding, and he tore his hair so that he could be sure he was really feeling, and he never could know what it was right, he now should be doing. And then late that night he wrote it all out to Melanctha Herbert, and he made himself quickly send it without giving himself any time to change it.

"It has come to me strong to-day Melanctha, perhaps I am wrong the way I now am thinking. Perhaps you do want me badly to be with you. Perhaps I have hurt you once again the way I used to. I certainly Melanctha, if I ever think that really, I certainly do want bad not to be wrong now ever any more to you. If you do feel the way to-day it came to me strong may-be you are feeling, then say so Melanctha to me, and I come again to see you. If not, don't say anything any more ever to me. I don't want ever to be bad to you Melanctha, really. I never want ever to be a bother to you. I never can stand it to think I am wrong; really, thinking you don't want me to come to you. Tell me Melanctha, tell me honest to me, shall I come now any more to see you." "Yes" came the answer from Melanctha, "I be home Jeff to-night to see you."

Jeff Campbell went that evening late to see Melanctha Herbert. As Jeff came nearer to her, he doubted that he wanted really to be with her, he felt that he did not know what it was he now wanted from her. Jeff Campbell knew very well now, way inside him, that they could never talk their trouble out between them. What was it Jeff wanted now to tell Melanctha Herbert? What was it that Jeff Campbell now could tell her? Surely he never now could learn to trust her. Surely Jeff knew very well all that Melanctha always had inside her. And yet it was awful, never any more to see her.

Jeff Campbell went in to Melanctha, and he kissed her, and he held her, and then he went away from her and he stood still and looked at her. "Well Jeff!" "Yes Melanctha!" "Jeff what was it made you act so to me?" "You know very well Melanctha, it's always I am thinking you don't love me, and you are acting to me good out of kindness, and then Melanctha you certainly never did say anything to me why you never came to meet me, as you certainly did promise to me you would that day I never saw you!" "Jeff don't you really know for certain, I always love you?" "No Melanctha, deed I don't know it in me. Deed and certain sure Melanctha, if I only know that in me, I certainly never would give you any bother." "Jeff, I certainly do love you more seems to me always, you certainly had ought to feel that in you." "Sure Melanctha?" "Sure Jeff boy, you know that." "But then Melanctha why did you act so to me?" "Oh Jeff you certainly been such a bother to me. I just had to go away that day Jeff, and I certainly didn't mean not to tell you, and then that letter you wrote came to me and something happened to me. I don't know right what it was Jeff, I just kind of fainted, and what could I do Jeff, you said you certainly never any more wanted to come and see me!" "And no matter Melanctha, even if you knew, it was just killing me to act so to you, you never would have said nothing to me?" "No of course, how could I Jeff when you wrote that way to me. I know how you was feeling Jeff to me, but I certainly couldn't say nothing to you." "Well Melanctha, I certainly know I am right proud too in me, but I certainly never could act so to you Melanctha, if I ever knew any way at all you ever really loved me. No Melanctha darling, you and me certainly don't feel much the same way ever. Any way Melanctha, I certainly do love you true Melanctha." "And I love you too Jeff, even though you don't never certainly seem to believe me." "No I certainly don't any way believe you Melanctha, even when you say it to me. I don't know Melanctha how, but sure I certainly do trust you, only I don't believe now ever in your really being loving to me. I certainly do know you trust me al-

ways Melanctha, only somehow it ain't ever all right to me. I certainly don't know any way otherwise Melanctha, how I can say it to you." "Well I certainly can't help you no ways any more Jeff Campbell, though you certainly say it right when you say I trust you Jeff now always. You certainly is the best man Jeff Campbell, I ever can know, to me. I never been anyways thinking it can be ever different to me." "Well you trust me then Melanctha, and I certainly love you Melanctha, and seems like to me Melanctha, you and me had ought to be a little better than we certainly ever are doing now to be together. You certainly do think that way, too, Melanctha to me. But may be you do really love me. Tell me, please, real honest now Melanctha darling, tell me so I really always know it in me, do you really truly love me?" "Oh you stupid, stupid boy, Jeff Campbell. Love you, what do you think makes me always to forgive you. If I certainly didn't always love you Jeff, I certainly never would let you be always being all the time such a bother to me the way you certainly Jeff always are to me. Now don't you dass ever any more say words like that ever to me. You hear me now Jeff, or I do something real bad sometime, so I really hurt you. Now Jeff you just be good to me. You know Jeff how bad I need it, now you should always be good to me!"

Jeff Campbell could not make an answer to Melanctha. What was it he should now say to her? What words could help him to make their feeling any better? Jeff Campbell knew that he had learned to love deeply, that, he always knew very well now in him, Melanctha had learned to be strong to be always trusting, that he knew too now inside him, but Melanctha did not really love him, that he felt always too strong for him. That fact always was there in him, and it always thrust itself firm, between them. And so this talk did not make things really better for them.

Jeff Campbell was never any more a torment to Melanctha, he was only silent to her. Jeff often saw Melanctha and he was very friendly with her and he never any more was a bother to her. Jeff never any more now had much chance to be loving with her. Melanctha never was alone now when he saw her.

Melanctha Herbert had just been getting thick in her trouble with Jeff Campbell, when she went to that church where she first met Rose, who later was married regularly to Sam Johnson. Rose was a good-looking, better kind of black girl, and had been brought up quite like their own child by white folks. Rose was living now with colored people. Rose was staying just then with a colored woman, who had known 'Mis' Herbert and her black husband and this girl Melanctha.

Rose soon got to like Melanctha Herbert and Melanctha now always wanted to be with Rose, whenever she could do it. Melanctha Herbert always was doing everything for Rose that she could think of that Rose ever wanted. Rose always liked to be with nice people who would do things for her. Rose had strong common sense and she was lazy. Rose liked Melanctha Herbert, she had such kind of fine ways in her. Then, too, Rose had it in her to be sorry for the subtle, sweet-natured, docile, intelligent Melanctha Herbert who always was so blue sometimes, and always had had so much trouble. Then, too, Rose could scold Melanctha, for Melanctha Herbert never could know how to keep herself from trouble, and Rose was always strong to keep straight, with her simple selfish wisdom.

But why did the subtle, intelligent, attractive, half white girl Melanctha Herbert, with her sweetness and her power and her wisdom, demean herself to do for and to flatter and to be scolded, by this lazy, stupid, ordinary, selfish black girl. This was a queer thing in Melanctha Herbert.

And so now in these new spring days, it was with Rose that Melanctha began again to wander. Rose always knew very well in herself what was the right way to do when you wandered. Rose knew very well, she was not just any common kind of black girl, for she had been raised by white folks, and Rose always saw to it that she was engaged to him when she had any one man with whom she ever always wandered. Rose always had strong in her the sense for proper conduct. Rose always was telling the complex and less sure Melanctha, what was the right way she should do when she wandered.

Rose never knew much about Jeff Campbell with Melanctha Herbert. Rose had not known about Melanctha Herbert when she had been almost all her time with Dr. Campbell.

Jeff Campbell did not like Rose when he saw her with Melanctha. Jeff would never, when he could help it, meet her. Rose did not think much about Dr. Campbell. Melanctha never talked much about him to her. He was not important now to be with her.

Rose did not like Melanctha's old friend Jane Harden when she saw her. Jane despised Rose for an ordinary, stupid, sullen black girl. Jane could not see what Melanctha could find in that black girl, to endure her. It made Jane sick to see her. But then Melanctha had a good mind, but she certainly never did care much to really use it. Jane Harden now really never cared any more to see Melanctha, though Melanctha still always tried to be good to her. And Rose, she hated that stuck up, mean speaking, nasty, drunk thing, Jane Harden. Rose did not see how Melanctha could bear to ever see her, but Melanctha always was so good to everybody, she never would know how to act to people the way they deserved that she should do it.

Rose did not know much about Melanctha, and Jeff Campbell and Jane Harden. All Rose knew about Melanctha was her old life with her mother and her father. Rose was always glad to be good to poor Melanctha, who had had such an awful time with her mother and her father, and now she was alone and had nobody who could help her. "He was a awful black man to you Melanctha, I like to get my hands on him so he certainly could feel it. I just would Melanctha, now you hear me."

Perhaps it was this simple faith and simple anger and simple moral way of doing in Rose, that Melanctha now found such a comfort to her. Rose was selfish and was stupid and was lazy, but she was decent and knew always what was the right way she should do, and what she wanted, and she certainly did admire how bright was her friend Melanctha Herbert, and she certainly did feel how very much it was she always suffered and she scolded her to keep her from more trouble, and she never was angry when she found some of the different ways Melanctha Herbert sometimes had to do it.

And so always Rose and Melanctha were more and more together, and Jeff Campbell could now hardly ever any more be alone with Melanctha.

Once Jeff had to go away to another town to see a sick man. "When I come back Monday Melanctha, I come Monday evening to see you. You be home alone once Melanctha to see

me." "Sure Jeff, I be glad to see you!"

When Jeff Campbell came to his house on Monday there was a note there from Melanctha. Could Jeff come day after to-morrow, Wednesday? Melanctha was so sorry she had to go out that evening. She was awful sorry and she hoped Jeff would not be angry.

Jeff was angry and he swore a little, and then he laughed, and then he sighed. "Poor Melanctha, she don't know any way to be real honest, but no matter, I sure do love her and I be good if only she will let me."

Jeff Campbell went Wednesday night to see Melanctha. Jeff Campbell took her in his arms and kissed her. "I certainly am awful sorry not to see you Jeff Monday, the way I promised, but I just couldn't Jeff, no way I could fix it." Jeff looked at her and then he laughed a little at her. "You want me to believe that really now Melanctha. All right I believe it if you want me to Melanctha. I certainly be good to you to-night the way you like it. I believe you certainly did want to see me Melanctha, and there was no way you could fix it." "Oh Jeff dear," said Melanctha, "I sure was wrong to act so to you. It's awful hard for me ever to say it to you, I have been wrong in my acting to you, but I certainly was bad this time Jeff to you. It do certainly come hard to me to say it Jeff, but I certainly was wrong to go away from you the way I did it. Only you always certainly been so bad Jeff, and such a bother to me, and making everything always so hard for me, and I certainly got some way to do it to make it come back sometimes to you. You bad boy Jeff, now you hear me and this certainly is the first time Jeff I ever yet said it to anybody, I ever been wrong, Jeff, you hear me!" "All right Melanctha, I sure do forgive you, cause it's certainly the first time

I ever heard you say you ever did anything wrong the way you shouldn't," and Jeff Campbell laughed and kissed her, and Melanctha laughed and loved him, and they really were happy now for a little time together.

And now they were very happy in each other and then they were silent and then they became a little sadder and then they were very quiet once more with each other.

"Yes I certainly do love you Jeff!" Melanctha said and she was very dreamy. "Sure, Melanctha." "Yes Jeff sure, but not the way you are now ever thinking. I love you more and more seems to me Jeff always, and I certainly do trust you more and more always to me when I know you. I do love you Jeff, sure yes, but not the kind of way of loving you are ever thinking it now Jeff with me. I ain't got certainly no hot passion any more now in me. You certainly have killed all that kind of feeling now Jeff in me. You certainly do know that Jeff, now the way I am always, when I am loving with you. You certainly do know that Jeff, and that's the way you certainly do like it now in me. You certainly don't mind now Jeff, to hear me say this to you."

Jeff Campbell was hurt so that it almost killed him. Yes he certainly did know now what it was to have real hot love in him, and yet Melanctha certainly was right, he did not deserve she should ever give it to him. "All right Melanctha I ain't ever kicking. I always will give you certainly always everything you want that I got in me. I take anything you want now to give me. I don't say never Melanctha it don't hurt me, but I certainly don't say ever Melanctha it ought ever to be any different to me." And the bitter tears rose up in Jeff Campbell, and they came

and choked his voice to be silent, and he held himself hard to keep from breaking.

"Good-night Melanctha," and Jeff was very humble to her. "Good-night Jeff, I certainly never did mean any way to hurt you. I do love you, sure Jeff every day more and more, all the time I know you." "I know Melanctha, I know, it's never nothing to me. You can't help it, anybody ever the way they are feeling. It's all right now Melanctha, you believe me, good-night now Melanctha, I got now to leave you, good-by Melanctha, sure don't look so worried to me, sure Melanctha I come again soon to see you." And then Jeff stumbled down the steps, and he went away fast to leave her.

And now the pain came hard and harder in Jeff Campbell, and he groaned, and it hurt him so, he could not bear it. And the tears came, and his heart beat, and he was hot and worn and bitter in him.

Now Jeff knew very well what it was to love Melanctha. Now Jeff Campbell knew he was really understanding. Now Jeff knew what it was to be good to Melanctha. Now Jeff was good to her always.

Slowly Jeff felt it a comfort in him to have it hurt so, and to be good to Melanctha always. Now there was no way Melanctha ever had had to bear things from him, worse than he now had it in him. Now Jeff was strong inside him. Now with all the pain there was peace in him. Now he knew he was understanding, now he knew he had a hot love in him, and he was good always to Melanctha Herbert who was the one had made him have it. Now he knew he could be good, and not cry out for help to her to teach him how to bear it. Every day Jeff felt himself more a strong man, the way he once had thought was his real self, the way he knew it. Now Jeff Campbell had real wisdom in him, and it did not make him bitter when it hurt him, for Jeff knew now all through him that he was really strong to bear it.

And so now Jeff Campbell could see Melanctha often, and he was patient, and always very friendly to her, and every day Jeff Campbell understood Melanctha Herbert better. And always Jeff saw Melanctha could not love him the way he needed she should do it. Melanctha Herbert had no way she ever really could remember.

And now Jeff knew there was a man Melanctha met very often, and perhaps she wanted to try to have this man to be good, for her. Jeff Campbell never saw the man Melanctha Herbert perhaps now wanted. Jeff Campbell only knew very well that there was one. Then there was Rose that Melanctha now always had with her when she wandered.

Jeff Campbell was very quiet to Melanctha. He said to her, now he thought he did not want to come any more especially to see her. When they met, he always would be glad to see her, but now he never would go anywhere any more to meet her. Sure he knew she always would have a deep love in him for her. Sure she knew that. "Yes Jeff, I always trust you Jeff, I certainly do know that all right." Jeff Campbell said, all right he never could say anything to reproach her. She knew always that he really had learned all through him how to love her. "Yes, Jeff, I certainly do know that." She knew now she could always trust him. Jeff always would be loyal to her though now she never was any more to him like a religion, but he never could forget the real sweetness in her. That Jeff must remember always, though now

he never can trust her to be really loving to any man for always, she never did have any way she ever could remember. If she ever needed anybody to be good to her, Jeff Campbell always would do anything he could to help her. He never can forget the things she taught him so he could be really understanding, but he never any more wants to see her. He be like a brother to her always, when she needs it, and he always will be a good friend to her. Jeff Campbell certainly was sorry never any more to see her, but it was good that they now knew each other really. "Good-by Jeff you always been very good always to me." "Good-by Melanctha you know you always can trust yourself to me." "Yes, I know, I know Jeff, really." "I certainly got to go now Melanctha, from you. I go this time, Melanctha really," and Jeff Campbell went away and this time he never looked back to her. This time Jeff Campbell just broke away and left her.

Jeff Campbell loved to think now he was strong again to be quiet, and to live regular, and to do everything the way he wanted it to be right for himself and all the colored people. Jeff went away for a little while to another town to work there, and he worked hard, and he was very sad inside him, and sometimes the tears would rise up in him, and then he would work hard, and then he would begin once more to see some beauty in the world around him. Jeff had behaved right and he had learned to have a real love in him. That was very good to have inside him.

Jeff Campbell never could forget the sweetness in Melanctha Herbert, and he was always very friendly to her, but they never any more came close to one another. More and more Jeff Campbell and Melanctha fell away from all knowing of each other, but Jeff never could forget Melanctha. Jeff never could forget the real sweetness she had in her, but Jeff never any more had the sense of a real religion for her. Jeff always had strong in him the meaning of all the new kind of beauty Melanctha Herbert once had shown him, and always more and more it helped him with his working for himself and for all the colored people.

Melanctha Herbert, now that she was all through with Jeff Campbell, was free to be with Rose and the new men she met now.

Rose was always now with Melanctha Herbert. Rose never found any way to get excited. Rose always was telling Melanctha Herbert the right way she should do, so that she would not always be in trouble. But Melanctha Herbert could not help it, always she would find new ways to get excited.

Melanctha was all ready now to find new ways to be in trouble. And yet Melanctha Herbert never wanted not to do right. Always Melanctha Herbert wanted peace and quiet, and always she could only find new ways to get excited.

"Melanctha," Rose would say to her, "Melanctha, I certainly have got to tell you, you ain't right to act so with that kind of feller. You better just had stick to black men now, Melanctha, you hear me what I tell you, just the way you always see me do it. They're real bad men, now I tell you Melanctha true, and you better had hear to me. I been raised by real nice kind of white folks, Melanctha, and I certainly knows awful well, soon as ever I can see 'em acting, what is a white man will act decent to you and the kind it ain't never no good to a colored girl to ever go with. Now you know real Melanctha how I always

mean right good to you, and you ain't got no way like me Melanctha, what was raised by white folks, to know right what is the way you should be acting with men. I don't never want to see you have bad trouble come hard to you now Melanctha, and so you just hear to me now Melanctha, what I tell you, for I knows it. I don't say never certainly to you Melanctha, you never had ought to have nothing to do ever with no white men, though it ain't never to me Melanctha, the best kind of a way a colored girl can have to be acting, no I never do say to you Melanctha, you hadn't never ought to be with white men, though it ain't never the way I feel it ever real right for a decent colored girl to be always doing, but not never Melanctha, now you hear me, no not never no kind of white men like you been with always now Melanctha when I see you. You just hear to me Melanctha, you certainly had ought to hear to me Melanctha, I say it just like I knows it awful well, Melanctha, and I knows you don't know no better, Melanctha, how to act so, the ways I seen it with them kind of white fellers, them as never can know what to do right by a decent girl they have ever got to be with them. Now you hear to me Melanctha, what I tell you."

And so it was Melanctha Herbert found new ways to be in trouble. But it was not very bad this trouble, for these white men Rose never wanted she should be with, never meant very much to Melanctha. It was only that she liked it to be with them, and they knew all about fine horses, and it was just good to Melanctha, now a little, to feel real reckless with them. But mostly it was Rose and other better kind of colored girls and colored men with whom Melanctha Herbert now always wandered.

It was summer now and the colored people came out into the sunshine, full blown with the flowers. And they shone in the streets and in the fields with their warm joy, and they glistened in their black heat, and they flung themselves free in their wide abandonment of shouting laughter.

It was very pleasant in some ways, the life Melanctha Herbert now led with Rose and all the others. It was not always that Rose had to scold her.

There was not anybody of all these colored people, excepting only Rose, who ever meant much to Melanctha Herbert. But they all liked Melanctha, and the men all liked to see her do things, she was so game always to do anything anybody ever could do, and then she was good and sweet to do anything anybody ever wanted from her.

These were pleasant days then, in the hot southern negro sunshine, with many simple jokes and always wide abandonment of laughter. "Just look at that Melanctha there a running. Don't she just go like a bird when she is flying. Hey Melanctha there, I come and catch you, hey Melanctha, I put salt on your tail to catch you," and then the man would try to catch her, and he would fall full on the earth and roll in an agony of wide-mouthed shouting laughter. And this was the kind of way Rose always liked to have Melanctha do it, to be engaged to him, and to have a good warm nigger time with colored men, not to go about with that kind of white man, never could know how to act right, to any decent kind of girl they could ever get to be with them.

Rose, always more and more, liked Melanctha Herbert better. Rose often had to scold Melanctha Herbert, but that only made her like Melanctha better. And then Melanctha always listened to her, and always acted every way she could to please her. And then Rose was so sorry for Melanctha, when she was so blue sometimes, and wanted somebody should come and kill her.

And Melanctha Herbert clung to Rose in the hope that Rose could save her. Melanctha felt the power of Rose's selfish, decent kind of nature. It was so solid, simple, certain to her. Melanctha clung to Rose, she loved to have her scold her, she always wanted to be with her. She always felt a solid safety in her. Rose always was, in her way, very good to let Melanctha be loving to her. Melanctha never had any way she could really be a trouble to her. Melanctha never had any way that she could ever get real power, to come close inside to her. Melanctha was always very humble to her. Melanctha was always ready to do anything Rose wanted from her. Melanctha needed badly to have Rose always willing to let Melanctha cling to her. Rose was a simple, sullen, selfish, black girl, but she had a solid power in her. Rose had strong the sense of decent conduct, she had strong the sense for decent comfort. Rose always knew very well what it was she wanted, and she knew very well what was the right way to do to get everything she wanted, and she never had any kind of trouble to perplex her. And so the subtle intelligent attractive half white girl Melanctha Herbert loved and did for, and demeaned herself in service to this coarse, decent, sullen, ordinary, black, childish Rose and now this unmoral promiscuous shiftless Rose was to be married to a good man of the negroes, while Melanctha Herbert with her white blood and attraction and her desire for a right position was perhaps never to be really regularly married. Sometimes the thought of how all her world was made filled the complex, desiring Melanctha with despair. She wondered often how she could go on living when she was so blue. Sometimes Melanctha thought she would just kill herself, for sometimes she thought this would be really the best thing for her to do.

Rose was now to be married to a decent good man of the negroes. His name was Sam Johnson, and he worked as a deck hand on a coasting steamer, and he was very steady, and he got good wages.

Rose first met Sam Johnson at church, the same place where she had met Melanctha Herbert. Rose liked Sam when she saw him, she knew he was a good man and worked hard and got good wages, and Rose thought it would be very nice and very good now in her position to get really, regularly married.

Sam Johnson liked Rose very well and he always was ready to do anything she wanted. Sam was a tall, square shouldered, decent, a serious, straightforward, simple, kindly, colored workman. They got on very well together, Sam and Rose, when they were married. Rose was lazy, but not dirty, and Sam was careful but not fussy. Sam was a kindly, simple, earnest, steady workman, and Rose had good common decent sense in her, of how to live regular, and not to have excitements, and to be saving so you could be always sure to have money, so as to have everything you wanted.

It was not very long that Rose knew Sam Johnson, before they were regularly married. Sometimes Sam went into the country with all the other young church people, and then he would be a great deal with Rose and with her Melanctha Herbert. Sam did not care much about Melanctha Herbert. He liked Rose's ways of doing, always better. Melanctha's mystery had no charm for Sam ever. Sam wanted a nice little house to come to when he was tired from his working, and a little baby all his own he could be good to. Sam Johnson was ready to marry as soon as ever Rose wanted he should do it. And so Sam Johnson and Rose one day had a grand real wedding and were married. Then they furnished completely, a little red brick house and then Sam went back to his work as deck hand on a coasting steamer.

Rose had often talked to Sam about how good Melanctha was and how much she always suffered. Sam Johnson never really cared about Melanctha Herbert, but he always did almost everything Rose ever wanted, and he was a gentle, kindly creature, and so he was very good to Rose's friend Melanctha. Melanctha Herbert knew very well Sam did not like her, and so she was very quiet, and always let Rose do the talking for her. She only was very good to always help Rose, and to do anything she ever wanted from her, and to be very good and listen and be quiet whenever Sam had anything to say to her. Melanctha liked Sam Johnson, and all her life Melanctha loved and wanted good and kind and considerate people, and always Melanctha loved and wanted people to be gentle to her, and always she wanted to be regular, and to have peace and quiet in her, and always Melanctha could only find new ways to be in trouble. And Melanctha needed badly to have Rose, to believe her, and to let her cling to her. Rose was the only steady thing Melanctha had to cling to and so Melanctha demeaned herself to be like a servant, to wait on, and always to be scolded, by this ordinary, sullen, black, stupid, childish woman.

Rose was always telling Sam he must be good to poor Melanctha. "You know Sam," Rose said very often to him, "you certainly had ought to be very good to poor Melanctha, she always do have so much trouble with her. You know Sam how I told you she had such a bad time always with that father, and he was awful mean to her always that awful black man, and he never took no kind of care ever to her, and he never helped her when her mother died so hard, that poor Melanctha. Melanctha's ma you know Sam, always was just real religious. One day Melanctha was real little, and she heard her ma say to her pa, it was awful sad to her, Melanctha had not been the one the Lord had took from them stead of the little brother who was dead in the house there from fever. That hurt Melanctha awful when she heard her ma say it. She never could feel it right, and I don't no ways blame Melanctha, Sam, for not feeling better to her ma always after, though Melanctha, just like always she is, always was real good to her ma after, when she was so sick, and died so hard, and nobody never to help Melanctha do it, and she just all alone to do everything without no help come to her no way, and that ugly awful black man she have for a father never all the time come near her. But that's always the way Melanctha is just doing Sam, the way I been telling to you. She always is being just so good to everybody and nobody ever there to thank her for it. I never did see nobody ever Sam, have such bad luck, seems to me always with them, like that poor Melanctha always has it, and she always so good with it, and never no murmur in her, and never no complaining from her, and just never saying nothing with it. You be real good to her Sam, now you hear me, now you and me is married right together. He certainly was an awful black man to her Sam, that father she

had, acting always just like a brute to her and she was so game and never to tell anybody how it hurt her. And she so sweet and good always to do anything anybody ever can be wanting. I don't see Sam how some men can be to act so awful. I told you Sam, how once Melanctha broke her arm bad and she was so sick and it hurt her awful and he never would let no doctor come near to her and he do some things so awful to her, she don't never want to tell nobody how bad he hurt her. That's just the way Sam with Melanctha always, you never can know how bad it is, it hurts her. You hear me Sam, you always be real good to her now you and me is married right to each other."

And so Rose and Sam Johnson were regularly married, and Rose sat at home and bragged to all her friends how nice it was to be married really to a husband.

Rose did not have Melanctha to live with her, now Rose was married. Melanctha was with Rose almost as much as ever but it was a little different now their being together.

Rose Johnson never asked Melanctha to live with her in the house, now Rose was married. Rose liked to have Melanctha come all the time to help her, Rose liked Melanctha to be almost always with her, but Rose was shrewd in her simple selfish nature, she did not ever think to ask Melanctha to live with her.

Rose was hard headed, she was decent, and she always knew what it was she needed. Rose needed Melanctha to be with her, she liked to have her help her, the quick, good Melanctha to do for the slow, lazy, selfish, black girl, but Rose could have Melanctha to do for her and she did not need her to live with her.

Sam never asked Rose why she did not have her. Sam always took what

Rose wanted should be done for Melanctha, as the right way he should act toward her.

It could never come to Melanctha to ask Rose to let her. It never could come to Melanctha to think that Rose would ask her. It would never ever come to Melanctha to want it, if Rose should ask her, but Melanctha would have done it for the safety she always felt when she was near her. Melanctha Herbert wanted badly to be safe now, but this living with her, that, Rose would never give her. Rose had strong the sense for decent comfort, Rose had strong the sense for proper conduct, Rose had strong the sense to get straight always what she wanted, and she always knew what was the best thing she needed, and always Rose got what she wanted.

And so Rose had Melanctha Herbert always there to help her, and she sat and was lazy and she bragged and she complained a little and she told Melanctha how she ought to do, to get good what she wanted like she Rose always did it, and always Melanctha was doing everything Rose ever needed. "Don't you bother so, doing that Melanctha, I do it or Sam when he comes home to help me. Sure you don't mind lifting it Melanctha? You is very good Melanctha to do it, and when you go out Melanctha, you stop and get some rice to bring me to-morrow when you come in. Sure you won't forget Melanctha. I never see anybody like you Melanctha to always do things so nice for me." And then Melanctha would do some more for Rose, and then very late Melanctha would go home to the colored woman where she lived now.

And so though Melanctha still was so much with Rose Johnson, she had times when she could not stay there. Melanctha now could not really cling there. Rose had Sam, and Melanctha more and more lost the hold she had had there.

Melanctha Herbert began to feel she must begin again to look and see if she could find what it was she had always wanted. Now Rose Johnson could no longer help her.

And so Melanctha Herbert began once more to wander and with men Rose never thought it was right she should be with.

One day Melanctha had been very busy with the different kinds of ways she wandered. It was a pleasant late afternoon at the end of a long summer. Melanctha was walking along, and she was free and excited. Melanctha had just parted from a white man and she had a bunch of flowers he had left with her. A young buck, a mulatto, passed by and snatched them from her. "It certainly is real sweet in you sister, to be giving me them pretty flowers," he said to her.

"I don't see no way it can make them sweeter to have with you," said Melanctha. "What one man gives, another man had certainly just as much good right to be taking." "Keep your old flowers then, I certainly don't never want to have them." Melanctha Herbert laughed at him and took them. "No, I didn't nohow think you really did want to have them. Thank you kindly mister, for them. I certainly always do admire to see a man always so kind of real polite to people." The man laughed, "You ain't nobody's fool I can say for you, but you certainly are a damned pretty kind of girl, now I look at you. Want men to be polite to you? All right, I can love you, that's real polite now, want to see me try it." "I certainly ain't got no time this evening just only left to thank you. I certainly got to be real busy now, but I certainly always will admire to see you." The man tried to catch and stop her, Melanctha

Herbert laughed and dodged so that he could not touch her. Melanctha went quickly down a side street near her and so the man for that time lost her.

For some days Melanctha did not see any more of her mulatto. One day Melanctha was with a white man and they saw him. The white man stopped to speak to him. Afterwards Melanctha left the white man and she then soon met him. Melanctha stopped to talk to him. Melanctha Herbert soon began to like him.

Jem Richards, the new man Melanctha had begun to know now, was a dashing kind of fellow, who had to do with fine horses and with racing. Sometimes Jem Richards would be betting and would be good and lucky, and be making lots of money. Sometimes Jem would be betting badly, and then he would not be having any money.

Jem Richards was a straight man. Jem Richards always knew that by and by he would win again and pay it, and so Jem mostly did win again, and then he always paid it.

Jem Richards was a man other men always trusted. Men gave him money when he lost all his, for they all knew Jem Richards would win again, and when he did win they knew, and they were right, that he would pay it.

Melanctha Herbert all her life had always loved to be with horses. Melanctha liked it that Jem knew all about fine horses. He was a reckless man was Jem Richards. He knew how to win out, and always all her life, Melanctha Herbert loved successful power.

Melanctha Herbert always liked Jem Richards better. Things soon began to be very strong between them.

Jem was more game even than Melanctha. Jem always had known what it was to have real wisdom. Jem had always all his life been understanding.

Jem Richards made Melanctha Herbert come fast with him. He never gave her any time with waiting. Soon Melanctha always had Jem with her. Melanctha did not want anything better. Now in Jem Richards, Melanctha found everything she had ever needed to content her.

Melanctha was now less and less with Rose Johnson. Rose did not think much of the way Melanctha now was going. Jem Richards was all right, only Melanctha never had no sense of the right kind of way she should be doing. Rose often was telling Sam now, she did not like the fast way Melanctha was going. Rose told it to Sam, and to all the girls and men, when she saw them. But Rose was nothing just then to Melanctha. Melanctha Herbert now only needed Jem Richards to be with her.

And things were always getting stronger between Jem Richards and Melanctha Herbert. Jem Richards began to talk now as if he wanted to get married to her. Jem was deep in his love now for her. And as for Melanctha, Jem was all the world now to her. And so Jem gave her a ring, like white folks, to show he was engaged to her, and would by and by be married to her. And Melanctha was filled full with joy to have Jem so good to her.

Melanctha always loved to go with Jem to the races. Jem had been lucky lately with his betting, and he had a swell turn-out to drive in, and Melanctha looked very handsome there beside him.

Melanctha was very proud to have Jem Richards want her. Melanctha loved it the way Jem knew how to do it. Melanctha loved Jem and loved that he should want her. She loved it too, that he wanted to be married to her. Jem Richards was a straight decent man, whom other men always looked up to and trusted. Melanctha needed badly a man to content her.

Melanctha's joy made her foolish. Melanctha told everybody about how Jem Richards, that swell man who owned all those fine horses and was so game, nothing ever scared him, was engaged to be married to her, and that was the ring he gave her.

Melanctha let out her joy very often to Rose Johnson. Melanctha had begun again now to go there.

Melanctha's love for Jem made her foolish. Melanctha had to have some one always now to talk to and so she went often to Rose Johnson.

Melanctha put all herself into Jem Richards. She was mad and foolish in the joy she had there.

Rose never liked the way Melanctha did it. "No Sam I don't say never Melanctha ain't engaged to Jem Richards the way she always says it, and Jem he is all right for that kind of a man he is, though he do think himself so smart and like he owns the earth and everything he can get with it, and he sure gave Melanctha a ring like he really meant he should be married right soon with it, only Sam, I don't ever like it the way Melanctha is going. When she is engaged to him Sam, she ain't not right to take on so excited. That ain't no decent kind of a way a girl ever should be acting. There ain't no kind of a man going stand that, not like I knows men Sam, and I sure does know them. I knows them white and I knows them colored, for I was raised by white folks, and they don't none of them like a girl to act so. That's all right to be so when you is just only loving, but it ain't no ways right to be acting so when you is engaged to him, and when he says, all right he get really regularly married to you. You see Sam I am right like I am always and I knows it. Jem

Richards, he ain't going to the last to get real married, not if I knows it right, the way Melanctha now is acting to him. Rings or anything ain't nothing to them, and they don't never do no good for them, when a girl acts foolish like Melanctha always now is acting. I certainly will be right sorry Sam, if Melanctha has real bad trouble come now to her, but I certainly don't no ways like it Sam the kind of way Melanctha is acting to him. I don't never say nothing to her Sam. I just listens to what she is saying always, and I thinks it out like I am telling to you Sam but I don't never say nothing no more now to Melanctha. Melanctha didn't say nothing to me about that Jem Richards till she was all like finished with him, and I never did like it Sam, much, the way she was acting, not coming here never when she first ran with those men and met him. And I didn't never say nothing to her, Sam, about it, and it ain't nothing ever to me, only I don't never no more want to say nothing to her, so I just listens to what she got to tell like she wants it. No Sam, I don't never want to say nothing to her. Melanctha just got to go her own way, not as I want to see her have bad trouble ever come so hard to her, only it ain't in me never Sam, after Melanctha did so, ever to say nothing more to her how she should be acting. You just see Sam like I tell you, what way Jem Richards will act to her, you see Sam I just am right like I always am when I knows it."

Melanctha Herbert never thought she could ever again be in trouble. Melanctha's joy had made her foolish.

And now Jem Richards had some bad trouble with his betting. Melanctha sometimes felt now when she was with him that there was something wrong inside him. Melanctha knew he had had trouble with his betting but Melanctha never felt that that could make any difference to them.

Melanctha once had told Jem, sure he knew she always would love to be with him, if he was in jail or only just a beggar. Now Melanctha said to him, "Sure you know Jem that it don't never make any kind of difference you're having any kind of trouble, you just try me Jem and be game, don't look so worried to me. Jem sure I know you love me like I love you always, and its all I ever could be wanting Jem to me, just your wanting me always to be with you. I get married Jem to you soon ever as you can want me, if you once say it Jem to me. It ain't nothing to me ever, anything like having any money Jem, why you look so worried to me."

Melanctha Herbert's love had surely made her mad and foolish. She thrust it always deep into Jem Richards and now that he had trouble with his betting, Jem had no way that he ever wanted to be made to feel it. Jem Richards never could want to marry any girl while he had trouble. That was no way a man like him should do it. Melanctha's love had made her mad and foolish, she should be silent now and let him do it. Jem Richards was not a kind of man to want a woman to be strong to him, when he was in trouble with his betting. That was not the kind of a time when a man like him needed to have it.

Melanctha needed so badly to have it, this love which she had always wanted, she did not know what she should do to save it. Melanctha saw now, Jem Richards always had something wrong inside him. Melanctha soon dared not ask him. Jem was busy now, he had to sell things and see men to raise money. Jem could not meet Melanctha now so often.

It was lucky for Melanctha Herbert that Rose Johnson was coming now to have her baby. It had always been understood between them, Rose should come and stay then in the house where Melanctha lived with an old colored woman, so that Rose could have the Doctor from the hospital near by to help her, and Melanctha there to take care of her the way Melanctha always used to do it.

Melanctha was very good now to Rose Johnson. Melanctha did everything that any woman could, she tended Rose, and she was patient, submissive, soothing and untiring, while the sullen, childish, cowardly, black Rosie grumbled, and fussed, and howled, and made herself to be an abomination and like a simple beast.

All this time Melanctha was always being every now and then with Jem Richards. Melanctha was beginning to be stronger with Jem Richards. Melanctha was never so strong and sweet and in her nature as when she was deep in trouble, when she was fighting so with all she had, she could not do any foolish thing with her nature.

Always now Melanctha Herbert came back again to be nearer to Rose Johnson. Always now Melanctha would tell all about her troubles to Rose Johnson. Rose had begun now a little again to advise her.

Melanctha always told Rose now about the talks she had with Jem Richards, talks where they neither of them liked very well what the other one was saying. Melanctha did not know what it was Jem Richards wanted. All Melanctha knew was, he did not like it when she wanted to be good friends and get really married, and then when Melanctha would say, "all right, I never wear your ring no more Jem, we ain't not any more to meet ever like we ever going to get really regular married," then Jem did not like it either. What was it Jem Richards really wanted?

Melanctha stopped wearing Jem's ring on her finger. Poor Melanctha, she wore it on a string she tied around her neck so that she could always feel it, but Melanctha was strong now with Jem Richards, and he never saw it. And sometimes Jem seemed to be awful sorry for it, and sometimes he seemed kind of glad of it. Melanctha never could make out really what it was Jem Richards wanted.

There was no other woman yet to Jem, that Melanctha knew, and so she always trusted that Jem would come back to her, deep in his love, the way once he had had it and had made all the world like she once had never believed anybody could really make it. But Jem Richards was more game than Melanctha Herbert. He knew how to fight to win out, better. Melanctha really had already lost it, in not keeping quiet and waiting for Jem to do it.

Jem Richards was not yet having better luck in his betting. He never before had had such a long time without some good coming to him in his betting. Sometimes Jem talked as if he wanted to go off on a trip somewhere and try some other place for luck with his betting. Jem Richards never talked as if he wanted to take Melanctha with him.

And so Melanctha sometimes was really trusting, and sometimes she was all sick inside her with her doubting. What was it Jem really wanted to do with her? He did not have any other woman, in that Melanctha could be really trusting, and when she said no to him, no she never would come near him, now he did not want to have her, then Jem would change and swear, yes sure he did want her, now and always right here near him, but he never now any more said he wanted

to be married soon to her. But then Jem Richards never would marry a girl, he said that very often, when he was in this kind of trouble, and now he did not see any way he could get out of his trouble. But Melanctha ought to wear his ring, sure she knew he never had loved any kind of woman like he loved her. Melanctha would wear the ring a little while, and then they would have some more trouble, and then she would say to him, no she certainly never would any more wear anything he gave her, and then she would wear it on the string so nobody could see it but she could always feel it on her.

Poor Melanctha, surely her love had made her mad and foolish.

And now Melanctha needed always more and more to be with Rose Johnson, and Rose had commenced again to advise her, but Rose could not help her. There was no way now that anybody could advise her. The time when Melanctha could have changed it with Jem Richards was now all past for her. Rose knew it, and Melanctha too, she knew it, and it almost killed her to let herself believe it.

The only comfort Melanctha ever had now was waiting on Rose till she was so tired she could hardly stand it. Always Meclantha did everything Rose ever wanted. Sam Johnson began now to be very gentle and a little tender to Melanctha. She was so good to Rose and Sam was so glad to have her there to help Rose and to do things and to be a comfort to her.

Rose had a hard time to bring her baby to its birth and Melanctha did everything that any woman could.

The baby though it was healthy after it was born did not live long. Rose Johnson was careless and negligent and selfish and when Melanctha had to leave for a few days the baby died. Rose Johnson had liked her baby well enough and perhaps she just forgot it for a while, anyway the child was dead and Rose and Sam were very sorry, but then these things came so often in the negro world in Bridge-point that they neither of them thought about it very long. When Rose had become strong again she went back to her house with Sam. And Sam Johnson was always now very gentle and kind and good to Melanctha who had been so good to Rose in her bad trouble.

Melanctha Herbert's troubles with Jem Richards were never getting any better. Jem always now had less and less time to be with her. When Jem was with Melanctha now he was good enough to her. Jem Richards was worried with his betting. Never since Jem had first begun to make a living had he ever had so much trouble for such a long time together with his betting. Jem Richards was good enough now to Melanctha but he had not much strength to give her. Melanctha could never any more now make him quarrel with her. Melanctha never now could complain of his treatment of her, for surely, he said it always by his actions to her, surely she must know how a man was when he had trouble on his mind with trying to make things go a little better.

Sometimes Jem and Melanctha had long talks when they neither of them liked very well what the other one was saying, but mostly now Melanctha could not make Jem Richards quarrel with her, and more and more, Melanctha could not find any way to make it right to blame him for the trouble she now always had inside her. Jem was good to her, and she knew, for he told her, that he had trouble all the time now with his betting. Melanctha knew very well that for her it was all wrong inside Jem Richards, but Melanctha had

now no way that she could really reach him.

Things between Melanctha and Jem Richards were now never getting any better. Melanctha now more and more needed to be with Rose Johnson. Rose still liked to have Melanctha come to her house and do things for her, and Rose liked to grumble to her and to scold her and to tell Melanctha what was the way Melanctha always should be doing so she could make things come out better and not always be so much in trouble. Sam Johnson in these days was always very good and gentle to Melanctha. Sam was now beginning to be very sorry for her.

Jem Richards never made things any better for Melanctha. Often Jem would talk so as to make Melanctha almost certain that he never any more wanted to have her. Then Melanctha would get very blue, and she would say to Rose, sure she would kill herself, for that certainly now was the best way she could do.

Rose Johnson never saw it the least bit that way. "I don't see Melanctha why you should talk like you would kill yourself just because you're blue. I'd never kill myself Melanctha cause I was blue. I'd maybe kill somebody else but I'd never kill myself. If I ever killed myself, Melanctha it'd be by accident and if I ever killed myself by accident, Melanctha, I'd be awful sorry. And that certainly is the way you should feel it Melanctha, now you hear me, not just talking foolish like you always do. It certainly is only your way just always being foolish makes you all that trouble to come to you always now, Melanctha, and I certainly right well knows that. You certainly never can learn no way Melanctha ever with all I certainly been telling to you, ever since I know you good, that it ain't never no way like you do always is the right way you be acting ever and talking, the way I certainly always have seen you do so Melanctha always. I certainly am right Melanctha about them ways you have to do it, and I knows it; but you certainly never can noways learn to act right Melanctha, I certainly do know that, I certainly do my best Melanctha to help you with it only you certainly never do act right Melanctha, not to nobody ever, I can see it. You never act right by me Melanctha no more than by everybody. I never say nothing to you Melanctha when you do so, for I certainly never do like it when I just got to say it to you, but you just certainly done with that Jem Richards you always say wanted real bad to be married to you, just like I always said to Sam you certainly was going to do it. And I certainly am real kind of sorry like for you Melanctha, but you certainly had ought to have come to see me to talk to you, when you first was engaged to him so I could show you, and now you got all this trouble come to you Melanctha like I certainly know you always catch it. It certainly ain't never Melanctha I ain't real sorry to see trouble come so hard to you, but I certainly can see Melanctha it all is always just the way you always be having it in you not never to do right. And now you always talk like you just kill yourself because you are so blue, that certainly never is Melanctha, no kind of a way for any decent kind of a girl to do."

Rose had begun to be strong now to scold Melanctha and she was impatient very often with her, but Rose could now never any more be a help to her. Melanctha Herbert never could know now what it was right she should do. Melanctha always wanted to have Jem Richards with her and now he never seemed to want

her, and what could Melanctha do. Surely she was right now when she said she would just kill herself, for that was the only way now she could do.

Sam Johnson always, more and more, was good and gentle to Melanctha. Poor Melanctha, she was so good and sweet to do anything anybody ever wanted, and Melanctha always liked it if she could have peace and quiet, and always she could only find new ways to be in trouble. Sam often said this now to Rose about Melanctha.

"I certainly don't never want Sam to say bad things about Melanctha, for she certainly always do have most awful kind of trouble come hard to her, but I never can say I like it real right Sam the way Melanctha always has to do it. Its now just the same with her like it is always she has got to do it, now the way she is with that Jem Richards. He certainly now don't never want to have her but Melanctha she ain't got no right kind of spirit. No Sam I don't never like the way any more Melanctha is acting to him, and then Sam, she ain't never real right honest, the way she always should do it. She certainly just don't kind of never Sam tell right what way she is doing with it. I don't never like to say nothing Sam no more to her about the way she always has to be acting. She always say, yes all right Rose, I do the way you say it, and then Sam she don't never noways do it. She certainly is right sweet and good, Sam, is Melanctha, nobody ever can hear me say she ain't always ready to do things for everybody any way she ever can see to do it, only Sam some ways she never does act real right ever, and some ways, Sam, she ain't ever real honest with it. And Sam sometimes I hear awful kind of things she been doing, some girls know about her how she does it, and sometimes they tell me what kind of ways she has to do it, and Sam it certainly do seem to me like more and more I certainly am awful afraid Melanctha never will come to any good. And then Sam, sometimes, you hear it, she always talk like she kill herself all the time she is so blue, and Sam that certainly never is no kind of way any decent girl ever had ought to do. You see Sam, how I am right like I always is when I knows it. You just be careful, Sam, now you hear me, you be careful Sam sure, I tell you, Melanctha more and more I see her I certainly do feel Melanctha no way is really honest. You be careful, Sam now, like I tell you, for I knows it, now you hear to me, Sam, what I tell you, for I certainly always is right, Sam, when I knows it."

At first Sam tried a little to defend Melanctha, and Sam always was good and gentle to her, and Sam liked the ways Melanctha had to be quiet to him, and to always listen as if she was learning, when she was there and heard him talking, and then Sam liked the sweet way she always did everything so nicely for him; but Sam never liked to fight with anybody ever, and surely Rose knew best about Melanctha and anyway Sam never did really care much about Melanctha. Her mystery never had had any interest for him. Sam liked it that she was sweet to him and that she always did everything Rose ever wanted that she should be doing, but Melanctha never could be important to him. All Sam ever wanted was to have a little house and to live regular and to work hard and to come home to his dinner, when he was tired with his working and by and by he wanted to have some children all his own to be good to, and so Sam was real sorry for Melanctha,

she was so good and so sweet always to them, and Jem Richards was a bad man to behave so to her, but that was always the way a girl got it when she liked that kind of a fast fellow. Anyhow Melanctha was Rose's friend, and Sam never cared to have anything to do with the kind of trouble always came to women, when they wanted to have men, who never could know how to behave good and steady to their women.

And so Sam never said much to Rose about Melanctha. Sam was always very gentle to her, but now he began less and less to see her. Soon Melanctha never came any more to the house to see Rose and Sam never asked Rose anything about her.

Melanctha Herbert was beginning now to come less and less to the house to be with Rose Johnson. This was because Rose seemed always less and less now to want her, and Rose would not let Melanctha now do things for her. Melanctha was always humble to her and Melanctha always wanted in every way she could to do things for her. Rose said no, she guessed she do that herself like she likes to have it better. Melanctha is real good to stay so long to help her, but Rose guessed perhaps Melanctha better go home now, Rose don't need nobody to help her now, she is feeling real strong, not like just after she had all that trouble with the baby, and then Sam, when he comes home for his dinner he likes it when Rose is all alone there just to give him his dinner. Sam always is so tired now, like he always is in the summer, so many people always on the steamer, and they make so much work so Sam is real tired now, and he likes just to eat his dinner and never have people in the house to be a trouble to him.

Each day Rose treated Melanctha more and more as if she never wanted

Melanctha any more to come there to the house to see her. Melanctha dared not ask Rose why she acted in this way to her. Melanctha badly needed to have Rose always there to save her. Melanctha wanted badly to cling to her and Rose had always been so solid for her. Melanctha did not dare to ask Rose if she now no longer wanted her to come and see her.

Melanctha now never any more had Sam to be gentle to her. Rose always sent Melanctha away from her before it was time for Sam to come home to her. One day Melanctha had stayed a little longer, for Rose that day had been good to let Melanctha begin to do things for her. Melanctha then left her and Melanctha met Sam Johnson who stopped a minute to speak kindly to her.

The next day Rose Johnson would not let Melanctha come in to her. Rose stood on the steps, and there she told Melanctha what she thought now of her.

"I guess Melanctha it certainly ain't no ways right for you to come here no more just to see me. I certainly don't Melanctha no ways like to be a trouble to you. I certainly think Melanctha I get along better now when I don't have nobody like you are, always here to help me, and Sam he do so good now with his working, he pay a little girl something to come every day to help me. I certainly do think Melanctha I don't never want you no more to come here just to see me." "Why Rose, what I ever done to you, I certainly don't think you is right Rose to be so bad now to me." "I certainly don't no ways Melanctha Herbert think you got any right ever to be complaining the way I been acting to you. I certainly never do think Melanctha Herbert, you hear to me, nobody ever been more patient to you than I always been to like you, only

Melanctha, I hear more things now so awful bad about you, and everybody always is telling to me what kind of a way you always have been doing so much, and me always so good to you, and you never no ways, knowing how to be honest to me. No Melanctha it ain't ever in me, not to want you to have good luck come to you, and I like it real well Melanctha when you some time learn how to act the way it is decent and right for a girl to be doing, but I don't no ways ever like it the kind of things everybody tell me now about you. No Melanctha, I can't never any more trust you. I certainly am real sorry to have never any more to see you, but there ain't no other way, I ever can be acting to you. That's all I ever got any more to say to you now Melanctha." "But Rose, deed; I certainly don't know, no more than the dead, nothing I ever done to make you act so to me. Anybody say anything bad about me Rose, to you, they just a pack of liars to you, they certainly is Rose, I tell you true. I certainly never done nothing I ever been ashamed to tell you. Why you act so bad to me Rose. Sam he certainly don't think ever like you do, and Rose I always do everything I can, you ever want me to do for you." "It ain't never no use standing there talking, Melanctha Herbert. I just can tell it to you, and Sam, he don't know nothing about women ever the way they can be acting. I certainly am very sorry Melanctha, to have to act so now to you, but I certainly can't no do no other way with you, when you do things always so bad, and everybody is talking so about you. It ain't no use to you to stand there and say it different to me Melanctha. I certainly am always right Melanctha Herbert, the way I certainly always have been when I knows it, to you. No Melanctha, it just is, you never can have no kind of a way to act right, the way a decent girl has to do, and I done my best always to be telling it to you Melanctha Herbert, but it don't never do no good to tell nobody how to act right; they certainly never can learn when they ain't got no sense right to know it, and you never have no sense right Melanctha to be honest, and I ain't never wishing no harm to you ever Melanctha Herbert, only I don't never want any more to see you come here. I just say to you now, like I always been saying to you, you don't know never the right way, any kind of decent girl has to be acting, and so Melanctha Herbert, me and Sam, we don't never any more want you to be setting your foot in my house here Melanctha Herbert, I just tell you. And so you just go along now, Melanctha Herbert, you hear me, and I don't never wish no harm to come to you."

Rose Johnson went into her house and closed the door behind her. Melanctha stood like one dazed, she did not know how to bear this blow that almost killed her. Slowly then Melanctha went away without even turning to look behind her.

Melanctha Herbert was all sore and bruised inside her. Melanctha had needed Rose always to believe her, Melanctha needed Rose always to let her cling to her, Melanctha wanted badly to have somebody who could make her always feel a little safe inside her, and now Rose had sent her from her. Melanctha wanted Rose more than she had ever wanted all the others. Rose always was so simple, solid, decent, for her. And now Rose had cast her from her. Melanctha was lost, and all the world went whirling in a mad weary dance around her.

Melanctha Herbert never had any strength alone ever to feel safe inside her. And now Rose Johnson had cast her from her, and Melanctha could never any more be near her. Melanctha Herbert knew now, way inside her, that she was lost, and nothing any more could ever help her.

Melanctha went that night to meet Jem Richards who had promised to be at the old place to meet her. Jem Richards was absent in his manner to her. By and by he began to talk to her, about the trip he was going to take soon, to see if he could get some luck back in his betting. Melanctha trembled, was Jem too now going to leave her. Jem Richards talked some more then to her, about the bad luck he always had now, and how he needed to go away to see if he could make it come out any better.

Then Jem stopped, and then he looked straight at Melanctha.

"Tell me Melanctha right and true, you don't care really nothing more about me now Melanctha," he said to her.

"Why you ask me that, Jem Richards," said Melanctha.

"Why I ask you that Melanctha, God Almighty, because I just don't give a damn now for you any more Melanctha. That the reason I was asking."

Melanctha never could have for this an answer. Jem Richards waited and then he went away and left her.

Melanctha Herbert never again saw Jem Richards. Melanctha never again saw Rose Johnson, and it was hard to Melanctha never any more to see her. Rose Johnson had worked in to be the deepest of all Melanctha's emotions.

"No, I don't never see Melanctha Herbert no more now," Rose would say to anybody who asked her about Melanctha. "No, Melanctha she never comes here no more now, after we had all that trouble with her acting so bad with them kind of men she

liked so much to be with. She don't
never come to no good Melanctha
Herbert don't, and me and Sam don't
want no more to see her. She didn't
do right ever the way I told her. Melanctha just wouldn't, and I always
said it to her, if she don't be more
kind of careful, the way she always
had to be acting, I never did want no
more she should come here in my
house no more to see me. I ain't no
ways ever against any girl having any
kind of a way, to have a good time
like she wants it, but not that kind
of a way Melanctha always had to do
it. I expect some day Melanctha kill
herself, when she act so bad like she
do always, and then she get so awful
blue. Melanctha always says that's the
only way she ever can think it a easy
way for her to do. No, I always am
real sorry for Melanctha, she never
was no just common kind of nigger,
but she don't never know not with all
the time I always was telling it to her,
no she never no way could learn,
what was the right way she should do.
I certainly don't never want no kind
of harm to come bad to Melanctha,
but I certainly do think she will most
kill herself some time, the way she
always say it would be easy way for
her to do. I never see nobody ever
could be so awful blue."

But Melanctha Herbert never really
killed herself because she was so blue,
though often she thought this would
be really the best way for her to do.
Melanctha never killed herself, she
only got a bad fever and went into the
hospital where they took good care of
her and cured her.

When Melanctha was well again,
she took a place and began to work
and to live regular. Then Melanctha got very sick again, she began
to cough and sweat and be so weak
she could not stand to do her work.
Melanctha went back to the hospital, and there the Doctor told her
she had the consumption, and before
long she would surely die. They sent
her where she would be taken care of,
a home for poor consumptives, and
there Melanctha stayed until she
died.

1909

SHERWOOD ANDERSON
(1876–1941)
THE EGG *

My father was, I am sure, intended
by nature to be a cheerful, kindly
man. Until he was thirty-four years
old he worked as a farm-hand for a
man named Thomas Butterworth
whose place lay near the town of Bidwell, Ohio. He had then a horse of
his own and on Saturday evenings
drove into town to spend a few hours
in social intercourse with other farm-
hands. In town he drank several
glasses of beer and stood about in Ben
Head's saloon—crowded on Saturday
evenings with visiting farm-hands.
Songs were sung and glasses thumped
on the bar. At ten o'clock father drove
home along a lonely country road,
made his horse comfortable for the
night and himself went to bed, quite
happy in his position in life. He had
at that time no notion of trying to
rise in the world.

It was in the spring of his thirty-
fifth year that father married my
mother, then a country school-teacher,
and in the following spring I came
wriggling and crying into the world.
Something happened to the two people. They became ambitious. The
American passion for getting up in
the world took possession of them.

It may have been that mother was

responsible. Being a school-teacher she had no doubt read books and magazines. She had, I presume read of how Garfield, Lincoln, and other Americans rose from poverty to fame and greatness and as I lay beside her—in the days of her lying-in—she may have dreamed that I would some day rule men and cities. At any rate she induced father to give up his place as a farm-hand, sell his horse and embark on an independent enterprise of his own. She was a tall silent woman with a long nose and troubled grey eyes. For herself she wanted nothing. For father and myself she was incurably ambitious.

The first venture into which the two people went turned out badly. They rented ten acres of poor stony land on Griggs's Road, eight miles from Bidwell, and launched into chicken raising. I grew into boyhood on the place and got my first impressions of life there. From the beginning they were impressions of disaster and if, in my turn, I am a gloomy man inclined to see the darker side of life, I attribute it to the fact that what should have been for me the happy joyous days of childhood were spent on a chicken farm.

One unversed in such matters can have no notion of the many and tragic things that can happen to a chicken. It is born out of an egg, lives for a few weeks as a tiny fluffy thing such as you will see pictured on Easter cards, then becomes hideously naked, eats quantities of corn and meal bought by the sweat of your father's brow, gets diseases called pip, cholera, and other names, stands looking with stupid eyes at the sun, becomes sick and dies. A few hens and now and then a rooster, intended to serve God's mysterious ends, struggle through to maturity. The hens lay eggs out of which come other chickens and the dreadful cycle is thus made complete. It is all unbelievably complex. Most philosophers must have been raised on chicken farms. One hopes for so much from a chicken and is so dreadfully disillusioned. Small chickens, just setting out on the journey of life, look so bright and alert and they are in fact so dreadfully stupid. They are so much like people they mix one up in one's judgments of life. If disease does not kill them they wait until your expectations are thoroughly aroused and then walk under the wheels of a wagon—to go squashed and dead back to their maker. Vermin infest their youth, and fortunes must be spent for curative powders. In later life I have seen how a literature has been built up on the subject of fortunes to be made out of the raising of chickens. It is intended to be read by the gods who have just eaten of the tree of knowledge of good and evil. It is a hopeful literature and declares that much may be done by simple ambitious people who own a few hens. Do not be led astray by it. It was not written for you. Go hunt for gold on the frozen hills of Alaska, put your faith in the honesty of a politician, believe if you will that the world is daily growing better and that good will triumph over evil, but do not read and believe the literature that is written concerning the hen. It was not written for you.

I, however, digress. My tale does not primarily concern itself with the hen. If correctly told it will center on the egg. For ten years my father and mother struggled to make our chicken farm pay and then they gave up that struggle and began another. They moved into the town of Bidwell, Ohio, and embarked in the restaurant business. After ten years of worry with incubators that did not hatch, and with tiny—and in their own way lovely—

balls of fluff that passed on into semi-naked pullethood and from that into dead henhood, we threw all aside and packing our belongings on a wagon drove down Griggs's Road toward Bidwell, a tiny caravan of hope looking for a new place from which to start on our upward journey through life.

We must have been a sad looking lot, not, I fancy, unlike refugees fleeing from a battlefield. Mother and I walked in the road. The wagon that contained our goods had been borrowed for the day from Mr. Albert Griggs, a neighbor. Out of its sides stuck the legs of cheap chairs and at the back of the pile of beds, tables, and boxes filled with kitchen utensils was a crate of live chickens, and on top of that the baby carriage in which I had been wheeled about in my infancy. Why we stuck to the baby carriage I don't know. It was unlikely other children would be born and the wheels were broken. People who have few possessions cling tightly to those they have. That is one of the facts that make life so discouraging.

Father rode on top of the wagon. He was then a bald-headed man of forty-five, a little fat and from long association with mother and the chickens he had become habitually silent and discouraged. All during our ten years on the chicken farm he had worked as a laborer on neighboring farms and most of the money he had earned had been spent for remedies to cure chicken diseases, on Wilmer's White Wonder Cholera Cure or Professor Bidlow's Egg Producer or some other preparations that mother found advertised in the poultry papers. There were two little patches of hair on father's head just above his ears. I remember that as a child I used to sit looking at him when he had gone to sleep in a chair before the stove on Sunday afternoons in the winter. I

had at that time already begun to read books and have notions of my own and the bald path that led over the top of his head was, I fancied, something like a broad road, such a road as Caesar might have made on which to lead his legions out of Rome and into the wonders of an unknown world. The tufts of hair that grew above father's ears were, I thought, like forests. I fell into a half-sleeping, half-waking state and dreamed I was a tiny thing going along the road into a far beautiful place where there were no chicken farms and where life was a happy eggless affair.

One might write a book concerning our flight from the chicken farm into town. Mother and I walked the entire eight miles—she to be sure that nothing fell from the wagon and I to see the wonders of the world. On the seat of the wagon beside father was his greatest treasure. I will tell you of that.

On a chicken farm where hundreds and even thousands of chickens come out of eggs surprising things sometimes happen. Grotesques are born out of eggs as out of people. The accident does not often occur—perhaps once in a thousand births. A chicken is, you see, born that has four legs, two pairs of wings, two heads or what not. The things do not live. They go quickly back to the hand of their maker that has for a moment trembled. The fact that the poor little things could not live was one of the tragedies of life to father. He had some sort of notion that if he could but bring into henhood or roosterhood a five-legged hen or a two-headed rooster his fortune would be made. He dreamed about taking the wonder about to county fairs and of growing rich by exhibiting it to other farmhands.

At any rate he saved all the little

monstrous things that had been born on our chicken farm. They were preserved in alcohol and put each in its own glass bottle. These he had carefully put into a box and on our journey into town it was carried on the wagon seat beside him. He drove the horses with one hand and with the other clung to the box. When we got to our destination the box was taken down at once and the bottles removed. All during our days as keepers of a restaurant in the town of Bidwell, Ohio, the grotesques in their little glass bottles sat on a shelf back of the counter. Mother sometimes protested but father was a rock on the subject of his treasure. The grotesques were, he declared, valuable. People, he said, liked to look at strange and wonderful things.

Did I say that we embarked in the restaurant business in the town of Bidwell, Ohio? I exaggerated a little. The town itself lay at the foot of a low hill and on the shore of a small river. The railroad did not run through the town and the station was a mile away to the north at a place called Pickleville. There had been a cider mill and pickle factory at the station, but before the time of our coming they had both gone out of business. In the morning and in the evening busses came down to the station along a road called Turner's Pike from the hotel on the main street of Bidwell. Our going to the out of way place to embark in the restaurant business was mother's idea. She talked of it for a year and then one day went off and rented an empty store building opposite the railroad station. It was her idea that the restaurant would be profitable. Traveling men, she said, would be always waiting around to take trains out of town and town people would come to the station to await incoming trains. They would come to the restaurant to buy pieces of pie and drink coffee. Now that I am older I know that she had another motive in going. She was ambitious for me. She wanted me to rise in the world, to get into a town school and become a man of the towns.

At Pickleville father and mother worked hard as they had always done. At first there was the necessity of putting our place into shape to be a restaurant. That took a month. Father built a shelf on which he put tins of vegetables. He painted a sign on which he put his name in large red letters. Below his name was the sharp command—"EAT HERE"—that was so seldom obeyed. A show case was bought and filled with cigars and tobacco. Mother scrubbed the floor and the walls of the room. I went to school in the town and was glad to be away from the farm and from the presence of the discouraged, sad-looking chickens. Still I was not very joyous. In the evening I walked home from school along Turner's Pike and remembered the children I had seen playing in the town school yard. A troop of little girls had gone hopping about and singing. I tried that. Down along the frozen road I went hopping solemnly on one leg. "Hippity Hop To The Barber Shop," I sang shrilly. Then I stopped and looked doubtfully about. I was afraid of being seen in my gay mood. It must have seemed to me that I was doing a thing that should not be done by one who, like myself, had been raised on a chicken farm where death was a daily visitor.

Mother decided that our restaurant should remain open at night. At ten in the evening a passenger train went north past our door followed by a local freight. The freight crew had switching to do in Pickleville and when the work was done they came to our restaurant for hot coffee and food. Sometimes one of them ordered a fried egg. In the morning at four they returned north-bound and again visited us. A little trade began to grow up. Mother slept at night and during the day tended the restaurant and fed our boarders while father slept. He slept in the same bed mother had occupied during the night and I went off to the town of Bidwell and to school. During the long nights, while mother and I slept, father cooked meats that were to go into sandwiches for the lunch baskets of our boarders. Then an idea in regard to getting up in the world came into his head. The American spirit took hold of him. He also became ambitious.

In the long nights when there was little to do father had time to think. That was his undoing. He decided that he had in the past been an unsuccessful man because he had not been cheerful enough and that in the future he would adopt a cheerful outlook on life. In the early morning he came upstairs and got into bed with mother. She woke and the two talked. From my bed in the corner I listened.

It was father's idea that both he and mother should try to entertain the people who came to eat at our restaurant. I cannot now remember his words, but he gave the impression of one about to become in some obscure way a kind of public entertainer. When people, particularly young people from the town of Bidwell, came into our place, as on very rare occasions they did, bright entertaining conversation was to be made. From father's words I gathered that something of the jolly inn-keeper effect was to be sought. Mother must have been doubtful from the first, but she said nothing discouraging. It was father's notion that a passion for the company of himself would spring up in the breasts of the younger people

of the town of Bidwell. In the evening bright happy groups would come singing down Turner's Pike. They would troop shouting with joy and laughter into our place. There would be song and festivity. I do not mean to give the impression that father spoke so elaborately of the matter. He was as I have said an uncommunicative man. "They want some place to go. I tell you they want some place to go," he said over and over. That was as far as he got. My own imagination has filled in the blanks.

For two or three weeks this notion of father's invaded our house. We did not talk much, but in our daily lives tried earnestly to make smiles take the place of glum looks. Mother smiled at the boarders and I, catching the infection, smiled at our cat. Father became a little feverish in his anxiety to please. There was no doubt, lurking somewhere in him, a touch of the spirit of the showman. He did not waste much of his ammunition on the railroad men he served at night but seemed to be waiting for a young man or woman from Bidwell to come in to show what he could do. On the counter in the restaurant there was a wire basket kept always filled with eggs, and it must have been before his eyes when the idea of being entertaining was born in his brain. There was something pre-natal about the way eggs kept themselves connected with the development of his idea. At any rate an egg ruined his new impulse in life. Late one night I was awakened by a roar of anger coming from father's throat. Both mother and I sat upright in our beds. With trembling hands she lighted a lamp that stood on a table by her head. Downstairs the front door of our restaurant went shut with a bang and in a few minutes father tramped up the stairs. He held an egg in his hand and his hand trembled as though he were having a chill. There was a half insane light in his eyes. As he stood glaring at us I was sure he intended throwing the egg at either mother or me. Then he laid it gently on the table beside the lamp and dropped on his knees beside mother's bed. He began to cry like a boy and I, carried away by his grief, cried with him. The two of us filled the little upstairs room with our wailing voices. It is ridiculous, but of the picture we made I can remember only the fact that mother's hand continually stroked the bald path that ran across the top of his head. I have forgotten what mother said to him and how she induced him to tell her of what had happened downstairs. His explanation also has gone out of my mind. I remember only my own grief and fright and the shiny path over father's head glowing in the lamp light as he knelt by the bed.

As to what happened downstairs. For some unexplainable reason I know the story as well as though I had been a witness to my father's discomfiture. One in time gets to know many unexplainable things. On that evening young Joe Kane, son of a merchant of Bidwell, came to Pickleville to meet his father, who was expected on the ten o'clock evening train from the South. The train was three hours late and Joe came into our place to loaf about and to wait for its arrival. The local freight train came in and the freight crew were fed. Joe was left alone in the restaurant with father.

From the moment he came into our place the Bidwell young man must have been puzzled by my father's actions. It was his notion that father was angry with him for hanging around. He noticed that the restaurant keeper was apparently disturbed by his presence and he thought of going out.

However, it began to rain and he did not fancy the long walk to town and back. He bought a five-cent cigar and ordered a cup of coffee. He had a newspaper in his pocket and took it out and began to read. "I'm waiting for the evening train. It's late," he said apologetically.

For a long time father, whom Joe Kane had never seen before, remained silently gazing at his visitor. He was no doubt suffering from an attack of stage fright. As so often happens in life he had thought so much and so often of the situation that now confronted him that he was somewhat nervous in its presence.

For one thing, he did not know what to do with his hands. He thrust one of them nervously over the counter and shook hands with Joe Kane. "How-de-do," he said. Joe Kane put his newspaper down and stared at him. Father's eye lighted on the basket of eggs that sat on the counter and he began to talk. "Well," he began hesitatingly, "well, you have heard of Christopher Columbus, eh?" He seemed to be angry. "That Christopher Columbus was a cheat," he declared emphatically. "He talked of making an egg stand on its end. He talked, he did, and then he went and broke the end of the egg."

My father seemed to his visitor to be beside himself at the duplicity of Christopher Columbus. He muttered and swore. He declared it was wrong to teach children that Christopher Columbus was a great man when, after all, he cheated at a critical moment. He had declared he would make an egg stand on end and then when his bluff had been called he had done a trick. Still grumbling at Columbus, father took an egg from the basket on the counter and began to walk up and down. He rolled the egg between the palms of his hands. He smiled genially. He began to mumble words regarding the effect to be produced on an egg by the electricity that comes out of the human body. He declared that without breaking its shell and by virtue of rolling it back and forth in his hands he could stand the egg on its end. He explained that the warmth of his hands and the gentle rolling movement he gave the egg created a new center of gravity, and Joe Kane was mildly interested. "I have handled thousands of eggs," father said. "No one knows more about eggs than I do."

He stood the egg on the counter and it fell on its side. He tried the trick again and again, each time rolling the egg between the palms of his hands and saying the words regarding the wonders of electricity and the laws of gravity. When after a half hour's effort he did succeed in making the egg stand for a moment he looked up to find that his visitor was no longer watching. By the time he had succeeded in calling Joe Kane's attention to the success of his effort the egg had again rolled over and lay on its side.

Afire with the showman's passion and at the same time a good deal disconcerted by the failure of his first effort, father now took the bottles containing the poultry monstrosities down from their place on the shelf and began to show them to his visitor. "How would you like to have seven legs and two heads like this fellow?" he asked, exhibiting the most remarkable of his treasures. A cheerful smile played over his face. He reached over the counter and tried to slap Joe Kane on the shoulder as he had seen men do in Ben Head's saloon when he was a young farm-hand and drove to town on Saturday evenings. His visitor was made a little ill by the sight of the body floating in the alcohol in the

bottle and got up to go. Coming from behind the counter father took hold of the young man's arm and led him back to his seat. He grew a little angry and for a moment had to turn his face away and force himself to smile. Then he put the bottles back on the shelf. In an outburst of generosity he fairly compelled Joe Kane to have a fresh cup of coffee and another cigar at his expense. Then he took a pan and filling it with vinegar, taken from a jug that sat beneath the counter, he declared himself about to do a new trick. "I will heat this egg in this pan of vinegar," he said. "Then I will put it through the neck of a bottle without breaking the shell. When the egg is inside the bottle it will resume its normal shape and the shell will become hard again. Then I will give the bottle with the egg in it to you. You can take it about with you wherever you go. People will want to know how you got the egg in the bottle. Don't tell them. Keep them guessing. That is the way to have fun with this trick."

Father grinned and winked at his visitor. Joe Kane decided that the man who confronted him was mildly insane but harmless. He drank the cup of coffee that had been given him and began to read his paper again. When the egg had been heated in vinegar father carried it on a spoon to the counter and going into a back room got an empty bottle. He was angry because his visitor did not watch him as he began to do his trick, but nevertheless went cheerfully to work. For a long time he struggled, trying to get the egg to go through the neck of the bottle. He put the pan of vinegar back on the stove, intending to reheat the egg, and then picked it up and burned his fingers. After a second bath in the hot vinegar the shell of the egg had been softened a little but not enough for his purpose. He worked and worked and a spirit of desperate determination took possession of him. When he thought that at last the trick was about to be consummated the delayed train came in at the station and Joe Kane started to go nonchalantly out at the door. Father made a last desperate effort to conquer the egg and make it do the thing that would establish his reputation as one who knew how to entertain guests who came into his restaurant. He worried the egg. He attempted to be somewhat rough with it. He swore and the sweat stood out on his forehead. The egg broke under his hand. When the contents spurted over his clothes, Joe Kane, who had stopped at the door, turned and laughed.

A roar of anger rose from my father's throat. He danced and shouted a string of inarticulate words. Grabbing another egg from the basket on the counter, he threw it, just missing the head of the young man as he dodged through the door and escaped.

Father came upstairs to mother and me with an egg in his hand. I do not know what he intended to do. I imagine he had some idea of destroying it, of destroying all eggs, and that he intended to let mother and me see him begin. When, however, he got into the presence of mother something happened to him. He laid the egg gently on the table and dropped on his knees by the bed as I have already explained. He later decided to close the restaurant for the night and to come upstairs and get into bed. When he did so he blew out the light and after much muttered conversation both he and mother went to sleep. I suppose I went to sleep also, but my sleep was troubled. I awoke at dawn and for a long time looked at the egg that lay on the table. I wondered why

eggs had to be and why from the egg came the hen who again laid the egg. The question got into my blood. It has stayed there, I imagine, because I am the son of my father. At any rate, the problem remains unsolved in my mind. And that, I conclude, is but another evidence of the complete and final triumph of the egg—at least as far as my family is concerned.

1921

PERHAPS WOMEN *

PERHAPS WOMEN [1]

I was thinking of women one evening in the winter of 1929–1930 as I walked in the streets of a South Carolina mill village.

I was thinking of women and of modern industry in America, the coming of the factories. The factories had brought about a profound change in all life. Everyone admitted it. Most people called the change good, they called it progress. Was it that, was it really progress?

"We are in a time of change. We are in a time of change. Who can tell?" I kept saying to myself. There was evidence of a changed attitude toward life on all sides. Men were in a new relation to each other, women were growing into a new relation to men.

"A time of change. A time of change," I kept saying the words over and over. The words were a song in me. It had been a grey evening after rain but the night was clear. I remember that I went stumbling along.

"A time of change. A time of change. Old values are being de-

* From *Perhaps Women* by Sherwood Anderson, published by Liveright Publishing Corporation, N. Y. Copyright, 1931.

stroyed. Are men men enough to make for themselves new values? Will women have to do it for them?"

I was thinking these thoughts and others, wandering through the streets of a quiet miserable Southern mill village late at night. I had been given permission to visit the mill at night, see the night shift at work.

The permission had not been given too readily by the mill owners. There had been telephone conversations, people seen, visits made. "What did I want?" Most of the American radicals I have seen and to whom I have talked—the men at war with our modern life—are great romancers. They like to think of the men who own factories, the successful industrialists of our day, as devils, as Goliaths, as supermen. Perhaps to think of these men so gives some of the younger radicals a satisfying feeling of virtue in themselves.

"You see how I am. I love the poor, the down-trodden. What nonsense," I had said to myself; "we are all alike . . . at bottom we want to save ourselves."

If I can make another, unlike myself, with different talents, seem mean, that makes me, being different, seem to myself rather noble.

Why, it isn't as mean as that. All I am trying to say is that the rich and successful man has his confusion too. In America most of the rich and successful with whom I have talked at all intimately are also confused. They are self-conscious and puzzled.

Let us admit that the factory owners when I went to see them were suspicious of me. A woman, the wife of such a man, was driving me in her car. "The factory owners, men like your husband, are suspicious of writers," I said. "They are. They have a right to be," she replied.

Is it true that the man who devotes himself to acquisitions, who becomes, perhaps by a lifetime of effort, an owner of lands, stocks and bonds, who controls factories, [is] less interesting, as a man, as an individual, than your rag-tag fellow who owns nothing?

Well, he is. Let us admit this. All literature proves it to be true.

We writers have always sought out the rascals or we have sought out the poor, the unsuccessful.

It is only when you are torn from your mooring, when you drift like a rudderless ship, that I am able to come near to you.

I had myself written the above lines years before.

It was Mr. Henry Adams who said, "A friend in power is a friend lost." The saying is quite true. How many friends I have lost in that way! They succeeded in life, became successful men.

The rich and the successful are inevitably tied to the possessions they have acquired. They are afraid of change. If men's attitude toward possessions is ever to undergo a change these men will be the enemies of change. Suppose men were trying, stumbling, to meet a new situation brought about by the coming of industrialism, mass production, etc.

More and more men thinking about it, trying to think their way through it. There is little enough doubt where the opposition will lie.

In America we have got fixed in our laws, in all our ways of thinking, the notion of the sacredness of property.

What a silly notion, really. Only life should be sacred.

These thoughts in my head.

I had gone in to see a man. He was in control of a factory. A red-haired alert capable man he seemed. "I want to go into your factory at night," I said. "You are working women and girls all night long.

"They are in there, in the long night hours. The walls of the factory impinge on them.

"I want to go in there. I want to stand about. I want, if I can, to feel what they feel. I want to write about it.

"Now you look here, Mr. Factory Owner, I am interested in something else besides the stock questions now stirring the industrial world. I am not primarily interested in shorter hours or more wages. I am not trying to unionize your factory.

"I will not even speak to one of your employees. Let your superintendent take me in. I want to go in in the middle of the night, at the zero hour, let us say, at two o'clock in the morning, or better yet at three o'clock.

"I am also interested in modern machinery. Machinery has become a part of all modern life. I myself run an automobile. I love driving it.

"I would like, if I live long enough, to write things that run as smoothly as modern machinery has been made to run.

"I want to give myself to the machine. I am, it is true, interested in the human side of the modern factory but that is but a part of my interest.

"The machine must be doing something to people too. It must be doing something to you and me as well as to the employees of your factory.

"That should be interesting to you as well as to me. You are the owner of the factory, it is true, but you are also a man.

"I would like to find out something."

A mill owner or manager, shaking his head.

"But you writers—why are you always against us?"

"It is all nonsense. You are a man, are you not?" I said again.

"I will admit that, as an individual, you are perhaps less interesting than a poor man, one of your employees.

"Life will have beaten down upon such a man more. He will be less sure of himself.

"That would make him more open to new impressions, new impulses.

"New forces will have to begin moving, operating on men here.

"You successful men are so walled-in by your possessions. You cannot receive new impressions."

"Oh, go to the devil."

"May I go into your factory at night, at three o'clock in the night, when the night shift is on, when everyone is a bit tired?

It is only when you are torn from your mooring, when you drift like a rudderless ship, that I am able to come near to you.

"It can't be you are afraid of me."

"To the devil with you. Well, I'll see. I would have you understand I am not afraid. I'll see.

"Yes, damn you, you may go in."

"We are in a time of change," I kept saying to myself. "There are evidences of it on all sides. Life is shifting, changing. Old values are being destroyed.

"They have been destroyed wholesale in Russia. Will the same thing happen here?"

You, the reader must think of me as having these thoughts, walking the streets of that Southern cotton mill village at night.

Will there be some day a revolution here?

Revolutions, when they come, are like wars. They accomplish, if they do accomplish, at terrible cost. It is a whoopla time, everything promised, sometimes nothing gained.

New cruelties often to take the place of old. New men in power. Power, the desire for power, is a disease. It destroys every attempt men make to advance.

It is a dead time. Men are standing still. They dare not face the realities of life.

Look what we Americans had seen in our time. We had seen fortunes pile up in a way never dreamed of by our fathers. Mass production had come, as an inevitable result of industrialism. We had got, in my time, a new attitude toward labor. Never perhaps in the history of the world —(but let us not be too far-reaching, let us say, "in the history of America")—never had labor sunk so low—

A time of little men when big men are so needed. What has made them little?

Is it going away from earth, sky, women, direct touch with earth and the materials that come out of earth— wood, iron, stone—through tools?

The modern world taking tools and all control out of men's hands, the instruments by which men felt their way into life through wood, iron, stone, into the lives of women too?

The woman's life being always different, the approach a different one?

Men had learned to put their faith in two things, in goods, the production of goods rapidly and at low cost, and in a thing called "publicity."

This later had become the central, the true faith. It had been carried to ridiculous lengths. Even as I write these words we are in a time of stress. Again too many goods have been produced. This will keep happening. Why not?

Have I not myself seen how every year machinery becomes more and more efficient? Does not efficiency in machinery mean less men employed? If men are not employed how are they to receive wages? You see it is no longer a question of how much wages or how long hours but of whether or not men are to be employed at all.

And if men are not employed, if they receive no wages how are they to buy goods?

More and more goods, with less and less people employed. That is prosperity.

Why, how can you manage that? By publicity.

By publicity.

Advertise.

Advertise.

What a strange childish faith! Even as I write these words there are millions of men out of employment and only last night a young mill engineer walked with me. We talked. The young mill engineer, one of the type of American young men on whom our faith is placed now, a kind of young Lindbergh, all machine, rather nice too, tied with all his faith to the machine, instinctively responsive to the machine—a so-called clean young man, married, leading what the newspapers call an exemplary life—such a young man walked and talked with me only last night. He grew a little excited, even poetic. There was a moon shining. Behold, even to young Lindbergh, the moment of poetry came. Was the young Lindbergh not all poetry once—for a day and a night, out there alone over the Atlantic— the American eagle come to life— flown off the dollar for the time?

The young man who walked with me, just another young Lindbergh, was an engineer in a great American cotton mill. He dreams of what—of some day seeing a mill built that would employ no people at all. "Well," he said, "perhaps there will be a few men. They will be highly paid specialists. They will stroll through the mill, listening and looking. The cotton will come in at one end of the mill and cloth will flow out at the other. No human hand will touch it."

Do you think it an impossible dream? If you do you know little of the tremendous progress already made in machine building, you know little of the American genius.

And even as I write these words there are three millions of men out of employment and no lack of goods. Men are walking the streets of industrial towns and cities out of work. Of course, they cannot buy goods.

How are such conditions to be met? Call a meeting of great industrialists!

What shall we do? Really it is very simple. Say times are good. Say that everyone who declares that times are not good is un-American, a dangerous character. Call him a Bolshevik. How silly! There are men here once who were not afraid to face things, who were not frightened by plain words said. How about Thomas Jefferson, Andrew Jackson, Abraham Lincoln?

Why only yesterday a letter came to me from a factory worker. "We are weakened and degenerated men already," he said. "I am ashamed to write these words to you but they are true. It is rare to find anyone in a position of power in America now with any interest in us. Our own leaders are not interested and it is a sign of our degeneration as men that we stand for such leadership. We are, in truth, abandoned ones. A European peasant, bronzed, sturdy and independent, as compared with us, seems like a vastly superior type of man— we creatures who have won only the contempt of our employers.

"I do not blame our employers," he wrote.

Words. Declare we are a prosperous people. Keep declaring it. Have all of the newspaper editors declare it loudly. Have all the leaders of industry give out interviews. A strange faith in words. We writers should not object to that faith. Most of us get on very well. All we have to do is to write whoopla.

All of the above thoughts passing through my head at night as I walked in a Southern mill village. It was a rolling red country. It was winter. That very afternoon I had been driving with a woman friend through the country about the town I was in.

But perhaps I had better call it a city. A good many thousand people lived there. There were other people besides mill employees, factory employees.

There were doctors, lawyers, judges, keepers of stores, drivers of trucks, clerks, young women stenographers, there was a whole middle-class world.

The mills, the factories were not really a part of the town. They were separate, stood off by themselves, let us say a dozen such mills, each with its village.

The villages, as is usual in America now, not incorporated. Not to incorporate was a way to disenfranchise men. That had been found out.

On Saturday afternoon perhaps the people of the mill village drifted into the town proper. What a strange staring lot! They lurched through the streets. People of the middle class to whom I had talked had said to me: "I keep off the streets on Saturday afternoons. There are such queer horrid people on the street."

The feeling of superiority to labor had grown and grown with the degeneration of labor. It has become an almost universal feeling among the American middle class.

And now the middle class is being wiped out too. Ask in such towns as the one of which I am speaking here what the coming of the chain store is doing to our middle class.

I was walking in a mill village at night, preparatory to going in, seeing the night shift at work. I had plenty of time, having walked out from my hotel. I was to go in at two. The superintendent of the mill was to meet me at the mill gate at that hour.

I was walking in the mill village and came to a church. I sat down upon the steps. Thoughts there too. In these mill villages, in many mill villages built about factories everywhere in America, the churches also have come under the control of the employer. So much was this true that in another town, visited during the winter, there had been a strike. A number of employees of a mill, living in such a mill village, were shot. A funeral was to be held and not a minister of the town would officiate. They apparently did not dare ally themselves, even in the death hour, with the strikers, the workers.

It was a miserable ugly little church on the step of which I sat. Mr. Henry Mencken has already written about the ugliness of churches in industrial towns. I was thinking about the degeneration of men under modern industrialism, of letters coming to me from working men, of factory employees feeling every year more and more out of place in American life.

The churches had gone in for advertising too, for the whoopla. Drums were being beaten at the doors of churches. One minister, an American, had but a few days before addressed an assembly of his fellow ministers, in an eastern city. I had read the account of the meeting in a newspaper. Many thousands must have read it.

I myself showed it to several people. They were not shocked, although a few of them did laugh.

The minister, addressing his fellows, had told them of how he had succeeded in getting people into his church. He had gone for a time and had got employment in the advertising department of a tooth paste concern. He had found out how they sold tooth paste. "We have got to use the same kind of methods in selling religion," he had said.

1931

F. SCOTT FITZGERALD
(1896–1940)

THE JELLY-BEAN *

Jim Powell was a Jelly-bean. Much as I desire to make him an appealing character, I feel that it would be unscrupulous to deceive you on that point. He was a bred-in-the-bone, dyed-in-the-wool, ninety-nine and three-quarters per cent Jelly-bean and he grew lazily all during Jelly-bean season, which is every season, down in the land of the Jelly-beans well below the Mason-Dixon line.

Now if you call a Memphis man a Jelly-bean he will quite possibly pull a long sinewy rope from his hip pocket and hang you to a convenient telegraph-pole. If you call a New Orleans man a Jelly-bean he will probably grin and ask you who is taking your girl to the Mardi Gras ball. The particular Jelly-bean patch which produced the protagonist of this history lies somewhere between the two—a little city of forty thousand that has dozed sleepily for forty thousand years in southern Georgia, occasionally stirring in its slumbers and muttering

* From Tales of the Jazz Age by F. Scott Fitzgerald. Copyright, 1922, by Charles Scribner's Sons.

something about a war that took place sometime, somewhere, and that everyone else has forgotten long ago.

Jim was a Jelly-bean. I write that again because it has such a pleasant sound—rather like the beginning of a fairy story—as if Jim were nice. It somehow gives me a picture of him with a round, appetizing face and all sorts of leaves and vegetables growing out of his cap. But Jim was long and thin and bent at the waist from stooping over pool-tables, and he was what might have been known in the indiscriminating North as a corner loafer. "Jelly-bean" is the name throughout the undissolved Confederacy for one who spends his life conjugating the verb to idle in the first person singular —I am idling, I have idled, I will idle.

Jim was born in a white house on a green corner. It had four weatherbeaten pillars in front and a great amount of lattice-work in the rear that made a cheerful criss-cross background for a flowery sun-drenched lawn. Originally the dwellers in the white house had owned the ground next door and next door to that and next door to that, but this had been so long ago that even Jim's father scarcely remembered it. He had, in fact, thought it a matter of so little moment that when he was dying from a pistol wound got in a brawl he neglected even to tell little Jim, who was five years old and miserably frightened. The white house became a boarding-house run by a tight-lipped lady from Macon, whom Jim called Aunt Mamie and detested with all his soul.

He became fifteen, went to high school, wore his hair in black snarls, and was afraid of girls. He hated his home where four women and one old man prolonged an interminable chatter from summer to summer about what lots the Powell place had origi-

nally included and what sort of flowers would be out next. Sometimes the parents of little girls in town, remembering Jim's mother and fancying a resemblance in the dark eyes and hair, invited him to parties, but parties made him shy and he much preferred sitting on a disconnected axle in Tilly's Garage, rolling the bones or exploring his mouth endlessly with a long straw. For pocket money, he picked up odd jobs, and it was due to this that he stopped going to parties. At his third party little Marjorie Haight had whispered indiscreetly and within hearing distance that he was a boy who brought the groceries sometimes. So instead of the two-step and polka, Jim had learned to throw any number he desired on the dice and had listened to spicy tales of all the shootings that had occurred in the surrounding country during the past fifty years.

He became eighteen. The war broke out and he enlisted as a gob and polished brass in the Charleston Navy-yard for a year. Then, by way of variety, he went North and polished brass in the Brooklyn Navyyard for a year.

When the war was over he came home. He was twenty-one, his trousers were too short and too tight. His buttoned shoes were long and narrow. His tie was an alarming conspiracy of purple and pink marvellously scrolled, and over it were two blue eyes faded like a piece of very good old cloth long exposed to the sun.

In the twilight of one April evening when a soft gray had drifted down along the cottonfields and over the sultry town, he was a vague figure leaning against a board fence, whistling and gazing at the moon's rim above the lights of Jackson Street. His mind was working persistently on a problem that had held his attention for an hour. The Jelly-bean had been invited to a party.

Back in the days when all the boys had detested all the girls, Clark Darrow and Jim had sat side by side in school. But, while Jim's social aspirations had died in the oily air of the garage, Clark had alternately fallen in and out of love, gone to college, taken to drink, given it up, and, in short, become one of the best beaux of the town. Nevertheless Clark and Jim had retained a friendship that, though casual, was perfectly definite. That afternoon Clark's ancient Ford had slowed up beside Jim, who was on the sidewalk and, out of a clear sky, Clark had invited him to a party at the country club. The impulse that made him do this was no stranger than the impulse which made Jim accept. The latter was probably an unconscious ennui, a half-frightened sense of adventure. And now Jim was soberly thinking it over.

He began to sing, drumming his long foot idly on a stone block in the sidewalk till it wobbled up and down in time to the low throaty tune:

"One mile from Home in Jelly-bean
    town,
  Lives Jeanne, the Jelly-bean Queen.
  She loves her dice and treats 'em nice;
  No dice would treat her mean."

He broke off and agitated the sidewalk to a bumpy gallop.

"Daggone!" he muttered, half aloud.

They would all be there—the old crowd, the crowd to which, by right of the white house, sold long since, and the portrait of the officer in gray over the mantel, Jim should have belonged. But that crowd had grown up together into a tight little set as gradually as the girls' dresses had lengthened inch by inch, as definitely as the boys' trousers had dropped suddenly to their ankles. And to that society of first names and dead puppy-loves Jim was an outsider—a running mate of poor whites. Most of the men knew him, condescendingly; he tipped his hat to three or four girls. That was all.

When the dusk had thickened into a blue setting for the moon, he walked through the hot, pleasantly pungent town to Jackson Street. The stores were closing and the last shoppers were drifting homeward, as if borne on the dreamy revolution of a slow merry-go-round. A street-fair farther down made a brilliant alley of vari-colored booths and contributed a blend of music to the night—an oriental dance on a calliope, a melancholy bugle in front of a freak show, a cheerful rendition of "Back Home in Tennessee" on a hand-organ.

The Jelly-bean stopped in a store and bought a collar. Then he sauntered along toward Soda Sam's, where he found the usual three or four cars of a summer evening parked in front and the little darkies running back and forth with sundaes and lemonades.

"Hello, Jim."

It was a voice at his elbow—Joe Ewing sitting in an automobile with Marylyn Wade. Nancy Lamar and a strange man were in the back seat.

The Jelly-bean tipped his hat quickly.

"Hi, Ben—" then, after an almost imperceptible pause—"How y' all?"

Passing, he ambled on toward the garage where he had a room up-stairs. His "How y' all" had been said to Nancy Lamar, to whom he had not spoken in fifteen years.

Nancy had a mouth like a remembered kiss and shadowy eyes and blue-black hair inherited from her mother who had been born in Budapest. Jim passed her often in the street, walking small-boy fashion with her hands in her pockets and he knew that with her inseparable Sally Carrol Hopper she had left a trail of broken hearts from Atlanta to New Orleans.

For a few fleeting moments Jim wished he could dance. Then he laughed and as he reached his door began to sing softly to himself:

"Her Jelly Roll can twist your soul,
  Her eyes are big and brown,
  She's the Queen of the Queens of the Jelly-beans
  My Jeanne of Jelly-bean Town."

II

At nine-thirty Jim and Clark met in front of Soda Sam's and started for the Country Club in Clark's Ford.

"Jim," asked Clark casually, as they rattled through the jasmine-scented night, "how do you keep alive?"

The Jelly-bean paused, considered.

"Well," he said finally, "I got a room over Tilly's Garage. I help him some with the cars in the afternoon an' he gives it to me free. Sometimes I drive one of his taxis and pick up a little thataway. I get fed up goin' that regular though."

"That all?"

"Well, when there's a lot of work I help him by the day—Saturdays usually—and then there's one main source of revenue I don't generally mention. Maybe you don't recollect I'm about the champion crap-shooter of this town. They make me shoot from a cup now because once I get the feel of a pair of dice they just roll for me."

Clark grinned appreciatively.

"I never could learn to set 'em so's they'd do what I wanted. Wish you'd shoot with Nancy Lamar some day and take all her money away from her. She will roll 'em with the boys and she loses more than her daddy can afford to give her. I happen to

know she sold a good ring last month to pay a debt."

The Jelly-bean was non-committal.

"The white house on Elm Street still belong to you?"

Jim shook his head.

"Sold. Got a pretty good price, seein' it wasn't in a good part of town no more. Lawyer told me to put it into Liberty bonds. But Aunt Mamie got so she didn't have no sense, so it takes all the interest to keep her up at Great Farms Sanitarium."

"Hm."

"I got an old uncle up-state an' I reckin I kin go up there if ever I get sure enough pore. Nice farm, but not enough niggers around to work it. He's asked me to come up and help him, but I don't guess I'd take much to it. Too doggone lonesome—" He broke off suddenly. "Clark, I want to tell you I'm much obliged to you for askin' me out, but I'd be a lot happier if you'd just stop the car right here an' let me walk back into town."

"Shucks!" Clark grunted. "Do you good to step out. You don't have to dance—just get out there on the floor and shake."

"Hold on," exclaimed Jim uneasily. "Don't you go leadin' me up to any girls and leavin' me there so I'll have to dance with 'em."

Clark laughed.

"'Cause," continued Jim desperately, "without you swear you won't do that I'm agoin' to get out right here an' my good legs goin' carry me back to Jackson Street."

They agreed after some argument that Jim, unmolested by females, was to view the spectacle from a secluded settee in the corner where Clark would join him whenever he wasn't dancing.

So ten o'clock found the Jelly-bean with his legs crossed and his arms conservatively folded, trying to look casually at home and politely uninterested in the dancers. At heart he was torn between overwhelming self-consciousness and an intense curiosity as to all that went on around him. He saw the girls emerge one by one from the dressing-room, stretching and pluming themselves like bright birds, smiling over their powdered shoulders at the chaperones, casting a quick glance around to take in the room and, simultaneously, the room's reaction to their entrance—and then, again like birds, alighting and nestling in the sober arms of their waiting escorts. Sally Carrol Hopper, blonde and lazy-eyed, appeared clad in her favorite pink and blinking like an awakened rose. Marjorie Haight, Marylyn Wade, Harriet Cary, all the girls he had seen loitering down Jackson Street by noon, now, curled and brilliantined and delicately tinted for the overhead lights, were miraculously strange Dresden figures of pink and blue and red and gold, fresh from the shop and not yet fully dried.

He had been there half an hour, totally uncheered by Clark's jovial visits which were each one accompanied by a "Hello, old boy, how you making out?" and a slap at his knee. A dozen males had spoken to him or stopped for a moment beside him, but he knew that they were each one surprised at finding him there and fancied that one or two were even slightly resentful. But at half past ten his embarrassment suddenly left him and a pull of breathless interest took him completely out of himself—Nancy Lamar had come out of the dressing-room.

She was dressed in yellow organdie, a costume of a hundred cool corners, with three tiers of ruffles and a big bow in back until she shed black and yellow around her in a sort of phosphorescent lustre. The Jelly-bean's eyes opened wide and a lump arose in his throat. For a minute she stood beside the door until her partner hurried up. Jim recognized him as the stranger who had been with her in Joe Ewing's car that afternoon. He saw her set her arms akimbo and say something in a low voice, and laugh. The man laughed too and Jim experienced the quick pang of a weird new kind of pain. Some ray had passed between the pair, a shaft of beauty from that sun that had warmed him a moment since. The Jelly-bean felt suddenly like a weed in a shadow.

A minute later Clark approached him, bright-eyed and glowing.

"Hi, old man," he cried with some lack of originality. "How you making out?"

Jim replied that he was making out as well as could be expected.

"You come along with me," commanded Clark. "I've got something that'll put an edge on the evening."

Jim followed him awkwardly across the floor and up the stairs to the locker-room where Clark produced a flask of nameless yellow liquid.

"Good old corn."

Ginger ale arrived on a tray. Such potent nectar as "good old corn" needed some disguise beyond seltzer.

"Say, boy," exclaimed Clark breathlessly, "doesn't Nancy Lamar look beautiful?"

Jim nodded.

"Mighty beautiful," he agreed.

"She's all dolled up to a fare-you-well to-night," continued Clark. "Notice that fellow she's with?"

"Big fella? White pants?"

"Yeah. Well, that's Ogden Merritt from Savannah. Old man Merritt makes the Merritt safety razors. This fella's crazy about her. Been chasing after her all year."

"She's a wild baby," continued Clark, "but I like her. So does everybody. But she sure does do crazy stunts. She usually gets out alive, but she's got scars all over her reputation from one thing or another she's done."

"That so?" Jim passed over his glass. "That's good corn."

"Not so bad. Oh, she's a wild one. Shoots craps, say, boy! And she do like her highballs. Promised I'd give her one later on."

"She in love with this—Merritt?"

"Damned if I know. Seems like all the best girls around here marry fellas and go off somewhere."

He poured himself one more drink and carefully corked the bottle.

"Listen, Jim, I got to go dance and I'd be much obliged if you just stick this corn right on your hip as long as you're not dancing. If a man notices I've had a drink he'll come up and ask me and before I know it it's all gone and somebody else is having my good time."

So Nancy Lamar was going to marry. This toast of a town was to become the private property of an individual in white trousers—and all because white trousers' father had made a better razor than his neighbor. As they descended the stairs Jim found the idea inexplicably depressing. For the first time in his life he felt a vague and romantic yearning. A picture of her began to form in his imagination—Nancy walking boylike and debonnaire along the street, taking an orange as tithe from a worshipful fruit-dealer, charging a dope on a mythical account at Soda Sam's, assembling a convoy of beaux and then driving off in triumphal state for an afternoon of splashing and singing.

The Jelly-bean walked out on the porch to a deserted corner, dark between the moon on the lawn and the single lighted door of the ballroom. There he found a chair and, lighting a cigarette, drifted into the thoughtless reverie that was his usual mood. Yet now it was a reverie made sensuous by the night and by the hot smell of damp powder puffs, tucked in the fronts of low dresses and distilling a thousand rich scents to float out through the open door. The music itself, blurred by a loud trombone, became hot and shadowy, a languorous overtone to the scraping of many shoes and slippers.

Suddenly the square of yellow light that fell through the door was obscured by a dark figure. A girl had come out of the dressing-room and was standing on the porch not more than ten feet away. Jim heard a low-breathed "doggone" and then she turned and saw him. It was Nancy Lamar.

Jim rose to his feet.

"Howdy?"

"Hello—" she paused, hesitated and then approached. "Oh, it's—Jim Powell."

He bowed slightly, tried to think of a casual remark.

"Do you suppose," she began quickly, "I mean—do you know anything about gum?"

"What?"

"I've got gum on my shoe. Some utter ass left his or her gum on the floor and of course I stepped in it."

Jim blushed, inappropriately.

"Do you know how to get it off?" she demanded petulantly. "I've tried a knife. I've tried every damn thing in the dressing-room. I've tried soap and water—and even perfume and I've ruined my power-puff trying to make it stick to that."

Jim considered the question in some agitation.

"Why—I think maybe gasolene—"

The words had scarcely left his lips when she grasped his hand and pulled him at a run off the low veranda, over a flower bed and at a gallop toward a group of cars parked in the moonlight by the first hole of the golf course.

"Turn on the gasolene," she commanded breathlessly.

"What?"

"For the gum of course. I've got to get it off. I can't dance with gum on."

Obediently Jim turned to the cars and began inspecting them with a view to obtaining the desired solvent. Had she demanded a cylinder he would have done his best to wrench one out.

"Here," he said after a moment's search. "Here's one that's easy. Got a handkerchief?"

"It's up-stairs wet. I used it for the soap and water."

Jim laboriously explored his pockets.

"Don't believe I got one either."

"Doggone it! Well, we can turn it on and let it run on the ground."

He turned the spout; a dripping began.

"More!"

He turned it on fuller. The dripping became a flow and formed an oily pool that glistened brightly, reflecting a dozen tremulous moons on its quivering bosom.

"Ah," she sighed contentedly, "let it all out. The only thing to do is to wade in it."

In desperation he turned on the tap full and the pool suddenly widened sending tiny rivers and trickles in all directions.

"That's fine. That's something like."

Raising her skirts she stepped gracefully in.

"I know this'll take it off," she murmured.

Jim smiled.

"There's lots more cars."

She stepped daintily out of the gasolene and began scraping her slippers, side and bottom, on the running-board of the automobile. The Jelly-bean contained himself no longer. He

bent double with explosive laughter and after a second she joined in.

"You're here with Clark Darrow, aren't you?" she asked as they walked back toward the veranda.

"Yes."

"You know where he is now?"

"Out dancin', I reckin."

"The deuce. He promised me a highball."

"Well," said Jim, "I guess that'll be all right. I got his bottle right here in my pocket."

She smiled at him radiantly.

"I guess maybe you'll need ginger ale though," he added.

"Not me. Just the bottle."

"Sure enough?"

She laughed scornfully.

"Try me. I can drink anything any man can. Let's sit down."

She perched herself on the side of a table and he dropped into one of the wicker chairs beside her. Taking out the cork she held the flask to her lips and took a long drink. He watched her fascinated.

"Like it?"

She shook her head breathlessly.

"No, but I like the way it makes me feel. I think most people are that way."

Jim agreed.

"My daddy liked it too well. It got him."

"American men," said Nancy, gravely, "don't know how to drink."

"What?" Jim was startled.

"In fact," she went on carelessly, "they don't know how to do anything very well. The one thing I regret in my life is that I wasn't born in England."

"In England?"

"Yes. It's the one regret of my life that I wasn't."

"Do you like it over there?"

"Yes. Immensely. I've never been there in person, but I've met a lot of

Englishmen who were over here in the army, Oxford and Cambridge men —you know, that's like Sewanee and University of Georgia are here—and of course I've read a lot of English novels."

Jim was interested, amazed.

"D' you ever hear of Lady Diana Manners?" she asked earnestly.

No, Jim had not.

"Well, she's what I'd like to be. Dark, you know, like me, and wild as sin. She's the girl who rode her horse up the steps of some cathedral or church or something and all the novelists made their heroines do it afterwards."

Jim nodded politely. He was out of his depths.

"Pass the bottle," suggested Nancy. "I'm going to take another little one. A little drink wouldn't hurt a baby."

"You see," she continued, again breathless after a draught. "People over there have style. Nobody has style here. I mean the boys here aren't really worth dressing up for or doing sensational things for. Don't you know?"

"I suppose so—I mean I suppose not," murmured Jim.

"And I'd like to do 'em an' all. I'm really the only girl in town that has style."

She stretched out her arms and yawned pleasantly.

"Pretty evening."

"Sure is," agreed Jim.

"Like to have boat," she suggested dreamily. "Like to sail out on a silver lake, say the Thames, for instance. Have champagne and caviare sandwiches along. Have about eight people. And one of the men would jump overboard to amuse the party and get drowned like a man did with Lady Diana Manners once."

"Did he do it to please her?"

"Didn't mean drown himself to

please her. He just meant to jump overboard and make everybody laugh."

"I reckin they just died laughin' when he drowned."

"Oh, I suppose they laughed a little," she admitted. "I imagine she did, anyway. She's pretty hard, I guess—like I am."

"You hard?"

"Like nails." She yawned again and added, "Give me a little more from that bottle."

Jim hesitated but she held out her hand defiantly.

"Don't treat me like a girl," she warned him. "I'm not like any girl *you* ever saw." She considered. "Still, perhaps you're right. You got—you got old head on young shoulders."

She jumped to her feet and moved toward the door. The Jelly-bean rose also.

"Good-bye," she said politely, "good-bye. Thanks, Jelly-bean."

Then she stepped inside and left him wide-eyed upon the porch.

III

At twelve o'clock a procession of cloaks issued single file from the women's dressing-room and, each one pairing with a coated beau like dancers meeting in a cotillion figure, drifted through the door with sleepy happy laughter—through the door into the dark where autos backed and snorted and parties called to one another and gathered around the water-cooler.

Jim, sitting in his corner, rose to look for Clark. They had met at eleven; then Clark had gone in to dance. So, seeking him, Jim wandered into the soft-drink stand that had once been a bar. The room was deserted except for a sleepy negro dozing behind the counter and two boys lazily fingering a pair of dice at one of the tables. Jim was about to leave when he saw Clark coming in. At the same moment Clark looked up.

"Hi, Jim!" he commanded. "C'mon over and help us with this bottle. I guess there's not much left, but there's one all around."

Nancy, the man from Savannah, Marylyn Wade, and Joe Ewing were lolling and laughing in the doorway. Nancy caught Jim's eye and winked at him humorously.

They drifted over to a table and arranging themselves around it waited for the waiter to bring ginger ale. Jim, faintly ill at ease, turned his eyes on Nancy, who had drifted into a nickel crap game with the two boys at the next table.

"Bring them over here," suggested Clark.

Joe looked around.

"We don't want to draw a crowd. It's against club rules."

"Nobody's around," insisted Clark, "except Mr. Taylor. He's walking up and down like a wild-man trying to find out who let all the gasolene out of his car."

There was a general laugh.

"I bet a million Nancy got something on her shoe again. You can't park when she's around."

"O Nancy, Mr. Taylor's looking for you!"

Nancy's cheeks were glowing with excitement over the game. "I haven't seen his silly little flivver in two weeks."

Jim felt a sudden silence. He turned and saw an individual of uncertain age standing in the doorway.

Clark's voice punctuated the embarrassment.

"Won't you join us, Mr. Taylor?"

"Thanks."

Mr. Taylor spread his unwelcome presence over a chair. "Have to, I guess. I'm waiting till they dig me

up some gasolene. Somebody got funny with my car."

His eyes narrowed and he looked quickly from one to the other. Jim wondered what he had heard from the doorway—tried to remember what had been said.

"I'm right to-night," Nancy sang out, "and my four bits is in the ring."

"Faded!" snapped Taylor suddenly.

"Why, Mr. Taylor, I didn't know you shot craps!" Nancy was overjoyed to find that he had seated himself and instantly covered her bet. They had openly disliked each other since the night she had definitely discouraged a series of rather pointed advances.

"All right, babies, do it for your mamma. Just one little seven." Nancy was *cooing* to the dice. She rattled them with a brave underhand flourish, and rolled them out on the table.

"Ah-h! I suspected it. And now again with the dollar up."

Five passes to her credit found Taylor a bad loser. She was making it personal, and after each success Jim watched triumph flutter across her face. She was doubling with each throw—such luck could scarcely last.

"Better go easy," he cautioned her timidly.

"Ah, but watch this one," she whispered. It was eight on the dice and she called her number.

"Little Ada, this time we're going South."

Ada from Decatur rolled over the table. Nancy was flushed and half-hysterical, but her luck was holding. She drove the pot up and up, refusing to drag. Taylor was drumming with his fingers on the table, but he was in to stay.

Then Nancy tried for a ten and lost the dice. Taylor seized them avidly. He shot in silence, and in the hush of excitement the clatter of one pass after another on the table was the only sound.

Now Nancy had the dice again, but her luck had broken. An hour passed. Back and forth it went. Taylor had been at it again—and again and again. They were even at last—Nancy lost her ultimate five dollars.

"Will you take my check," she said quickly, "for fifty, and we'll shoot it all?" Her voice was a little unsteady and her hand shook as she reached to the money.

Clark exchanged an uncertain but alarmed glance with Joe Ewing. Taylor shot again. He had Nancy's check.

"How 'bout another?" she said wildly. "Jes' any bank'll do—money everywhere as a matter of fact."

Jim understood—the "good old corn" he had given her—the "good old corn" she had taken since. He wished he dared interfere—a girl of that age and position would hardly have two bank accounts. When the clock struck two he contained himself no longer.

"May I—can't you let me roll 'em for you?" he suggested, his low, lazy voice a little strained.

Suddenly sleepy and listless, Nancy flung the dice down before him.

"All right—old boy! As Lady Diana Manners says, 'Shoot 'em, Jelly-bean' —My luck's gone."

"Mr. Taylor," said Jim, carelessly, "we'll shoot for one of those there checks against the cash."

Half an hour later Nancy swayed forward and clapped him on the back.

"Stole my luck, you did." She was nodding her head sagely.

Jim swept up the last check and putting it with the others tore them into confetti and scattered them on the floor. Someone started singing, and Nancy kicking her chair backward rose to her feet.

"Ladies and gentlemen," she announced. "Ladies—that's you Mary-lyn. I want to tell the world that Mr. Jim Powell, who is a well-known Jelly-bean of this city, is an exception to a great rule—'lucky in dice—unlucky in love.' He's lucky in dice, and as matter fact I—I *love* him. Ladies and gentlemen, Nancy Lamar, famous dark-haired beauty often featured in the *Herald* as one th' most popular members of younger set as other girls are often featured in this particular case. Wish to announce— wish to announce, anyway, Gentlemen—" She tipped suddenly. Clark caught her and restored her balance.

"My error," she laughed, "she stoops to—stoops to—anyways—We'll drink to Jelly-bean . . . Mr. Jim Powell, King of the Jelly-beans."

And a few minutes later as Jim waited hat in hand for Clark in the darkness of that same corner of the porch where she had come searching for gasolene, she appeared suddenly beside him.

"Jelly-bean," she said, "are you here, Jelly-bean? I think—" and her slight unsteadiness seemed part of an enchanted dream—"I think you deserve one of my sweetest kisses for that, Jelly-bean."

For an instant her arms were around his neck—her lips were pressed to his.

"I'm a wild part of the world, Jelly-bean, but you did me a good turn."

Then she was gone, down the porch, over the cricket-loud lawn. Jim saw Merritt come out the front door and say something to her angrily— saw her laugh and, turning away, walk with averted eyes to his car. Marylyn and Joe followed, singing a drowsy song about a Jazz baby.

Clark came out and joined Jim on the steps. "All pretty lit, I guess," he yawned. "Merritt's in a mean mood. He's certainly off Nancy."

Over east along the golf course a faint rug of gray spread itself across the feet of the night. The party in the car began to chant a chorus as the engine warmed up.

"Good-night, everybody," called Clark.

"Good-night, Clark."

"Good-night."

There was a pause, and then a soft, happy voice added,

"Good-night, Jelly-bean."

The car drove off to a burst of singing. A rooster on a farm across the way took up a solitary mournful crow, and behind them a last negro waiter turned out the porch light. Jim and Clark strolled over toward the Ford, their shoes crunching raucously on the gravel drive.

"Oh, boy!" sighed Clark softly, "how you can set those dice!"

It was still too dark for him to see the flush on Jim's thin cheeks—or to know that it was a flush of unfamiliar shame.

IV

Over Tilly's Garage a bleak room echoed all day to the rumble and snorting down-stairs and the singing of the negro washers as they turned the hose on the cars outside. It was a cheerless square of a room, punctuated with a bed and a battered table on which lay half a dozen books— Joe Miller's "Slow Train Through Arkansas," "Lucille," in an old edition very much annotated in an old-fashioned hand; "The Eyes of the World," by Harold Bell Wright, and an ancient prayer-book of the Church of England with the name Alice Powell and the date 1831 written on the flyleaf.

The East, gray when the Jelly-bean entered the garage, became a rich and vivid blue as he turned on his solitary electric light. He snapped it out again, and going to the window rested his elbows on the sill and stared into the deepening morning. With the awakening of his emotions, his first perception was a sense of futility, a dull ache at the utter grayness of his life. A wall had sprung up suddenly around him hedging him in, a wall as definite and tangible as the white wall of his bare room. And with his perception of this wall all that had been the romance of his existence, the casualness, the light-hearted improvidence, the miraculous open-handedness of life faded out. The Jelly-bean strolling up Jackson Street humming a lazy song, known at every shop and street stand, cropful of easy greeting and local wit, sad sometimes for only the sake of sadness and the flight of time—that Jelly-bean was suddenly vanished. The very name was a reproach, a triviality. With a flood of insight he knew that Merritt must despise him, that even Nancy's kiss in the dawn would have awakened not jealousy but only a contempt for Nancy's so lowering herself. And on his part the Jelly-bean had used for her a dingy subterfuge learned from the garage. He had been her moral laundry; the stains were his.

As the gray became blue, brightened and filled the room, he crossed to his bed and threw himself down on it, gripping the edges fiercely.

"I love her," he cried aloud, "God!"

As he said this something gave way within him like a lump melting in his throat. The air cleared and became radiant with dawn, and turning over on his face he began to sob dully into the pillow.

In the sunshine of three o'clock Clark Darrow chugging painfully along Jackson Street was hailed by the Jelly-bean, who stood on the curb with his fingers in his vest pockets.

"Hi!" called Clark, bringing his Ford to an astonishing stop alongside. "Just get up?"

The Jelly-bean shook his head.

"Never did go to bed. Felt sorta restless, so I took a long walk this morning out in the country. Just got into town this minute."

"Should think you *would* feel restless. I been feeling thataway all day—"

"I'm thinkin' of leavin' town," continued the Jelly-bean, absorbed by his own thoughts. "Been thinkin' of goin' up on the farm, and takin' a little that work off Uncle Dun. Reckin I been bummin' too long."

Clark was silent and the Jelly-bean continued:

"I reckin maybe after Aunt Mamie dies I could sink that money of mine in the farm and make somethin' out of it. All my people originally came from that part up there. Had a big place."

Clark looked at him curiously.

"That's funny," he said. "This— this sort of affected me the same way."

The Jelly-bean hesitated.

"I don't know," he began slowly, "somethin' about—about that girl last night talkin' about a lady named Diana Manners—an English lady, sorta got me thinkin'!" He drew himself up and looked oddly at Clark, "I had a family once," he said defiantly.

Clark nodded.

"I know."

"And I'm the last of 'em," continued the Jelly-bean, his voice rising slightly, "and I ain't worth shucks. Name they call me by means jelly— weak and wobbly like. People who weren't nothin' when my folks was a lot turn up their noses when they pass me on the street."

Again Clark was silent.

"So I'm through. I'm goin' to-day. And when I come back to this town it's going to be like a gentleman."

Clark took out his handkerchief and wiped his damp brow.

"Reckon you're not the only one it shook up," he admitted gloomily. "All this thing of girls going round like they do is going to stop right quick. Too bad, too, but everybody'll have to see it thataway."

"Do you mean," demanded Jim in surprise, "that all that's leaked out?"

"Leaked out? How on earth could they keep it secret? It'll be announced in the papers to-night. Doctor Lamar's got to save his name somehow."

Jim put his hands on the sides of the car and tightened his long fingers on the metal.

"Do you mean Taylor investigated those checks?"

It was Clark's turn to be surprised.

"Haven't you heard what happened?"

Jim's startled eyes were answer enough.

"Why," announced Clark dramatically, "those four got another bottle of corn, got tight and decided to shock the town—so Nancy and that fella Merritt were married in Rockville at seven o'clock this morning."

A tiny indentation appeared in the metal under the Jelly-bean's fingers.

"Married?"

"Sure enough. Nancy sobered up and rushed back into town, crying and frightened to death—claimed it'd all been a mistake. First Doctor Lamar went wild and was going to kill Merritt, but finally they got it patched up some way, and Nancy and Merritt went to Savannah on the two-thirty train."

Jim closed his eyes and with an effort overcame a sudden sickness.

"It's too bad," said Clark philosophically. "I don't mean the wedding —reckon that's all right, though I don't guess Nancy cared a darn about him. But it's a crime for a nice girl like that to hurt her family that way."

The Jelly-bean let go the car and

turned away. Again something was going on inside him, some inexplicable but almost chemical change.

"Where you going?" asked Clark.

The Jelly-bean turned and looked dully back over his shoulder.

"Got to go," he muttered. "Been up too long; feelin' right sick."

"Oh."

The street was hot at three and hotter still at four, the April dust seeming to enmesh the sun and give it forth again as a world-old joke forever played on an eternity of afternoons. But at half past four a first layer of quiet fell and the shades lengthened under the awnings and heavy foliaged trees. In this heat nothing mattered. All life was weather, a waiting through the hot where events had no significance for the cool that was soft and caressing like a woman's hand on a tired forehead. Down in Georgia there is a feeling—perhaps inarticulate—that this is the greatest wisdom of the South—so after a while the Jelly-bean turned into a pool-hall on Jackson Street where he was sure to find a congenial crowd who would make all the old jokes—the ones he knew.

1922

RING LARDNER *
(1885–1933)

SOME LIKE THEM COLD

N. Y., Aug. 3.

DEAR MISS GILLESPIE: How about our bet now as you bet me I would forget all about you the minute I hit the big town and would never write you a letter. Well girlie it looks like you lose so pay me. Seriously we will

* From *How to Write Short Stories* by Ring W. Lardner. Copyright, 1924, by Charles Scribner's Sons.

call all bets off as I am not the kind that bet on a sure thing and it sure was a sure thing that I would not forget a girlie like you and all that is worrying me is whether it may not be the other way round and you are wondering who this fresh guy is that is writeing you this letter. I bet you are so will try and refreshen your memory.

Well girlie I am the handsome young man that was wondering round the Lasalle st. station Monday and "happened" to sit down beside of a mighty pretty girlie who was waiting to meet her sister from Toledo and the train was late and I am glad of it because if it had not of been that little girlie and I would never of met. So for once I was a lucky guy but still I guess it was time I had some luck as it was certainly tough luck for you and I to both be liveing in Chi all that time and never get together till a half hour before I was leaveing town for good.

Still "better late than never" you know and maybe we can make up for lost time though it looks like we would have to do our makeing up at long distants unless you make good on your threat and come to N. Y. I wish you would do that little thing girlie as it looks like that was the only way we would get a chance to play round together as it looks like there was little or no chance of me comeing back to Chi as my whole future is in the big town. N. Y. is the only spot and specially for a man that expects to make my liveing in the song writeing game as here is the Mecca for that line of work and no matter how good a man may be they don't get no recognition unless they live in N. Y.

Well girlie you asked me to tell you all about my trip. Well I remember you saying that you would give anything to be makeing it yourself but as far as the trip itself was conserned you ought to be thankfull you did not have to make it as you would of sweat your head off. I know I did specially wile going through Ind. Monday P.M. but Monday night was the worst of all trying to sleep and finely I give it up and just layed there with the prespiration rolling off of me though I was laying on top of the covers and nothing on but my underwear.

Yesterday was not so bad as it rained most of the A.M. comeing through N. Y. state and in the P.M. we road along side of the Hudson all P.M. Some river girlie and just looking at it makes a man forget all about the heat and everything else except a certain girlie who I seen for the first time Monday and then only for a half hour but she is the kind of a girlie that a man don't need to see her only once and they would be no danger of forgetting her. There I guess I better lay off that subject or you will think I am a "fresh guy."

Well that is about all to tell you about the trip only they was one amuseing incidence that come off yesterday which I will tell you. Well they was a dame got on the train at Toledo Monday and had the birth opp. mine but I did not see nothing of her that night as I was out smokeing till late and she hit the hay early but yesterday A.M. she come in the dinner and sit at the same table with me and tried to make me and it was so raw that the dinge waiter seen it and give me the wink and of course I paid no tension and I waited till she got through so as they would be no danger of her folling me out but she stopped on the way out to get a tooth pick and when I come out she was out on the platform with it so I tried to brush right by but she spoke up and asked me what time it was and I told her and she said she

geussed her watch was slow so I said maybe it just seemed slow on acct. of the company it was in.

I don't know if she got what I was driveing at or not but anyway she give up trying to make me and got off at Albany. She was a good looker but I have no time for gals that tries to make strangers on a train.

Well if I don't quit you will think I am writeing a book but will expect a long letter in answer to this letter and we will see if you can keep your promise like I have kept mine. Don't dissappoint me girlie as I am all alone in a large city and hearing from you will keep me from getting home sick for old Chi though I never thought so much of the old town till I found out you lived there. Don't think that is kidding girlie as I mean it.

You can address me at this hotel as it looks like I will be here right along as it is on 47th st. right off of old Broadway and handy to everything and am only paying $21 per wk. for my rm. and could of got one for $16 but without bath but am glad to pay the differents as am lost without my bath in the A.M. and sometimes at night too.

Tomorrow I expect to commence fighting the "battle of Broadway" and will let you know how I come out that is if you answer this letter. In the mean wile girlie au reservoir and don't do nothing I would not do.

Your new friend (?)

CHAS. F. LEWIS.

Chicago, Ill., Aug. 6.

MY DEAR MR. LEWIS: Well, that certainly was a "surprise party" getting your letter and you are certainly a "wonder man" to keep your word as I am afraid most men of your sex are gay deceivers but maybe you are "different." Any way it sure was a surprise and will gladly pay the bet if you will just tell me what it was we bet. Hope it was not money as I am a "working girl" but if it was not more than a dollar or two will try to dig it up even if I have to "beg, borrow or steal."

Suppose you will think me a "case" to make a bet and then forget what it was, but you must remember, Mr. Man, that I had just met you and was "dazzled." Joking aside I was rather "fussed" and will tell you why. Well, Mr. Lewis, I suppose you see lots of girls like the one you told me about that you saw on the train who tried to "get acquainted" but I want to assure you that I am not one of those kind and sincerely hope you will believe me when I tell you that you was the first man I ever spoke to meeting them like that and my friends and the people who know me would simply faint if they knew I ever spoke to a man without a "proper introduction."

Believe me, Mr. Lewis, I am not that kind and I don't know now why I did it only that you was so "different" looking if you know what I mean and not at all like the kind of men that usually try to force their attentions on every pretty girl they see. Lots of times I act on impulse and let my feelings run away from me and sometimes I do things on the impulse of the moment which I regret them later on, and that is what I did this time, but hope you won't give me cause to regret it and I know you won't as I know you are not that kind of a man a specially after what you told me about the girl on the train. But any way as I say, I was in a "daze" so can't remember what it was we bet, but will try and pay it if it does not "break" me.

Sis's train got in about ten minutes after yours had gone and when she saw me what do you think was the

first thing she said? Well, Mr. Lewis, she said: "Why Mibs (That is a pet name some of my friends have given me) what has happened to you? I never seen you have as much color." So I passed it off with some remark about the heat and changed the subject as I certainly was not going to tell her that I had just been talking to a man who I had never met or she would of dropped dead from the shock. Either that or she would not of believed me as it would be hard for a person who knows me well to imagine me doing a thing like that as I have quite a reputation for "squelching" men who try to act fresh. I don't mean anything personal by that, Mr. Lewis, as am a good judge of character and could tell without you telling me that you are not that kind.

Well, Sis and I have been on the "go" ever since she arrived as I took yesterday and today off so I could show her the "sights" though she says she would be perfectly satisfied to just sit in the apartment and listen to me "rattle on." Am afraid I am a great talker, Mr. Lewis, but Sis says it is as good as a show to hear me talk as I tell things in such a different way as I cannot help from seeing the humorous side of everything and she says she never gets tired of listening to me, but of course she is my sister and thinks the world of me, but she really does laugh like she enjoyed my craziness.

Maybe I told you that I have a tiny little apartment which a girl friend of mine and I have together and it is hardly big enough to turn round in, but still it is "home" and I am a great home girl and hardly ever care to go out evenings except occasionally to the theater or dance. But even if our "nest" is small we are proud of it and Sis complimented us on how cozy it is and how "homey" it looks and she said she did not see how we could afford to have everything so nice and Edith (my girl friend) said: "Mibs deserves all the credit for that. I never knew a girl who could make a little money go a long ways like she can." Well, of course she is my best friend and always saying nice things about me, but I do try and I hope I get results. Have always said that good taste and being careful is a whole lot more important than lots of money though it is nice to have it.

You must write and tell me how you are getting along in the "battle of Broadway" (I laughed when I read that) and whether the publishers like your songs though I know they will. Am crazy to hear them and hear you play the piano as I love good jazz music even better than classical, though I suppose it is terrible to say such a thing. But I usually say just what I think though sometimes I wish afterwards I had not of. But still I believe it is better for a girl to be her own self and natural instead of always acting. But am afraid I will never have a chance to hear you play unless you come back to Chi and pay us a visit as my "threat" to come to New York was just a "threat" and I don't see any hope of ever getting there unless some rich New Yorker should fall in love with me and take me there to live. Fine chance for poor little me, eh Mr. Lewis?

Well, I guess I have "rattled on" long enough and you will think I am writing a book unless I quit and besides, Sis has asked me as a special favor to make her a pie for dinner. Maybe you don't know it, Mr. Man, but I am quite famous for my pie and pastry, but I don't suppose a "genius" is interested in common things like that.

Well, be sure and write soon and tell me what N. Y. is like and all about it and don't forget the little girlie who was "bad" and spoke to a strange man in the station and have been blushing over it ever since.

Your friend (?)

MABELLE GILLESPIE.

N. Y., Aug. 10.

DEAR GIRLIE: I bet you will think I am a fresh guy commenceing that way but Miss Gillespie is too cold and a man can not do nothing cold in this kind of weather especially in this man's town which is the hottest place I ever been in and I guess maybe the reason why New Yorkers is so bad is because they think they are all ready in H—— and can not go no worse place no matter how they behave themselves. Honest girlie I certainly envy you being where there is a breeze off the old Lake and Chi may be dirty but I never heard of nobody dying because they was dirty but four people died here yesterday on acct. of the heat and I seen two different women flop right on Broadway and had to be taken away in the ambulance and it could not of been because they was dressed too warm because it would be impossible for the women here to leave off any more cloths.

Well have not had much luck yet in the battle of Broadway as all the heads of the big music publishers is out of town on their vacation and the big boys is the only ones I will do business with as it would be silly for a man with the stuff I have got to waste my time on somebody that is just on the staff and have not got the final say. But I did play a couple of my numbers for the people up to Levy's and Goebel's and they went crazy over them in both places. So it looks like all I have to do is wait for the big boys to get back and then play my numbers for them and I will be all set. What I want is to get taken on the staff of one of the big firms as that gives a man the inside and they will plug your numbers more if you are on the staff. In the mean wile have not got nothing to worry me but am just seeing the sights of the big town as have saved up enough money to play round for a wile and any way a man that can play piano like I can don't never have to worry about starveing. Can certainly make the old music box talk girlie and am always good for a $75 or $100 job.

Well have been here a week now and on the go every minute and I thought I would be lonesome down here but no chance of that as I have been treated fine by the people I have met and have sure met a bunch of them. One of the boys liveing in the hotel is a vaudeville actor and he is a member of the Friars club and took me over there to dinner the other night and some way another the bunch got wise that I could play piano so of course I had to sit down and give them some of my numbers and everybody went crazy over them. One of the boys I met there was Paul Sears the song writer but he just writes the lyrics and has wrote a bunch of hits and when he heard some of my melodies he called me over to one side and said he would like to work with me on some numbers. How is that girlie as he is one of the biggest hit writers in N. Y.

N. Y. has got some mighty pretty girlies and I guess it would not be hard to get acquainted with them and in fact several of them has tried to make me since I been here but I always figure that a girl must be something wrong with her if she tries to make a man that she don't know nothing about so I pass them all up. But I did meet a couple of pips that a man here in the hotel went up on Riverside Drive to see them and insisted on me going along and they got

on some way that I could make a piano talk so they was nothing but I must play for them so I sit down and played some of my own stuff and they went crazy over it.

One of the girls wanted I should come up and see her again, and I said I might but I think I better keep away as she acted like she wanted to vamp me and I am not the kind that likes to play round with a gal just for their company and dance with them etc. but when I see the right gal that will be a different thing and she won't have to beg me to come and see her as I will camp right on her trail till she says yes. And it won't be none of these N. Y. fly by nights neither. They are all right to look at but a man would be a sucker to get serious with them as they might take you up and next thing you know you would have a wife on your hands that don't know a dish rag from a waffle iron.

Well girlie will quit and call it a day as it is too hot to write any more and I guess I will turn on the cold water and lay in the tub a wile and then turn in. Don't forget to write to

Your friend,

CHAS. F. LEWIS.

DEAR MR. MAN: Hope you won't think me a "silly Billy" for starting my letter that way but "Mr. Lewis" is so formal and "Charles" is too much the other way and any way I would not dare call a man by their first name after only knowing them only two weeks. Though I may as well confess that Charles is my favorite name for a man and have always been crazy about it as it was my father's name. Poor old dad, he died of cancer three years ago, but left enough insurance so that mother and we girls were well provided for and do not have to do anything to support ourselves though I have been earning my own living for two years to make things easier for mother and also because I simply can't bear to be doing nothing as I feel like a "drone." So I flew away from the "home nest" though mother felt bad about it as I was her favorite and she always said I was such a comfort to her as when I was in the house she never had to worry about how things would go.

But there I go gossiping about my domestic affairs just like you would be interested in them though I don't see how you could be though personly I always like to know all about my friends, but I know men are different so will try and not bore you any longer. Poor Man, I certainly feel sorry for you if New York is as hot as all that. I guess it has been very hot in Chi, too, at least everybody has been complaining about how terrible it is. Suppose you will wonder why I say "I guess" and you will think I ought to know if it is hot. Well, sir, the reason I say "I guess" is because I don't feel the heat like others do or at least I don't let myself feel it. That sounds crazy I know, but don't you think there is a good deal in mental suggestion and not letting yourself feel things? I believe that if a person simply won't allow themselves to be affected by disagreeable things, why such things won't bother them near as much. I know it works with me and that is the reason why I am never cross when things go wrong and "keep smiling" no matter what happens and as far as the heat is concerned, why I just don't let myself feel it and my friends say I don't even look hot no matter if the weather is boiling and Edith, my girl friend, often says that I am like a breeze and it cools her off just to have me come in the room. Poor Edie suffers terribly during the hot weather and says it almost makes her mad at me to see how cool and un-

ruffled I look when everybody else is perspiring and have red faces etc.

I laughed when I read what you said about New York being so hot that people thought it was the "other place." I can appreciate a joke, Mr. Man, and that one did not go "over my head." Am still laughing at some of the things you said in the station though they probably struck me funnier than they would most girls as I always see the funny side and sometimes something is said and I laugh and the others wonder what I am laughing at as they cannot see anything in it themselves, but it is just the way I look at things so of course I cannot explain to them why I laughed and they think I am crazy. But I had rather part with almost anything rather than my sense of humor as it helps me over a great many rough spots.

Sis has gone back home though I would of liked to of kept her here much longer, but she had to go though she said she would of liked nothing better than to stay with me and just listen to me "rattle on." She always says it is just like a show to hear me talk as I always put things in such a funny way and for weeks after she has been visiting me she thinks of some of the things I said and laughs over them. Since she left Edith and I have been pretty quiet though poor Edie wants to be on the "go" all the time and tries to make me go out with her every evening to the pictures and scolds me when I say I had rather stay home and read and calls me a "book worm." Well, it is true that I had rather stay home with a good book than go to some crazy old picture and the last two nights I have been reading myself to sleep with Robert W. Service's poems. Don't you love Service or don't you care for "highbrow" writings?

Personly there is nothing I love more than to just sit and read a good book or sit and listen to somebody play the piano, I mean if they can really play and I really believe I like popular music better than the classical though I suppose that is a terrible thing to confess, but I love all kinds of music but a specially the piano when it is played by somebody who can really play.

Am glad you have not "fallen" for the "ladies" who have tried to make your acquaintance in New York. You are right in thinking there must be something wrong with girls who try to "pick up" strange men as no girl with self respect would do such a thing and when I say that, Mr. Man, I know you will think it is a funny thing for me to say on account of the way our friendship started, but I mean it and I assure you that was the first time I ever done such a thing in my life and would never of thought of doing it had I not known you were the right kind of a man as I flatter myself that I am a good judge of character and can tell pretty well what a person is like by just looking at them and I assure you I had made up my mind what kind of a man you were before I allowed myself to answer your opening remark. Otherwise I am the last girl in the world that would allow myself to speak to a person without being introduced to them.

When you write again you must tell me all about the girl on Riverside Drive and what she looks like and if you went to see her again and all about her. Suppose you will think I am a little old "curiosity shop" for asking all those questions and will wonder why I want to know. Well, sir, I won't tell you why, so there, but I insist on you answering all questions and will scold you if you don't. Maybe you will think that the reason why I

am so curious is because I am "jealous" of the lady in question. Well, sir, I won't tell you whether I am or not, but will keep you "guessing." Now, don't you wish you knew?

Must close or you will think I am going to "rattle on" forever or maybe you have all ready become disgusted and torn my letter up. If so all I can say is poor little me—she was a nice little girl and meant well, but the man did not appreciate her.

There! Will stop or you will think I am crazy if you do not all ready.

Yours(?)

Mabelle.

N. Y., Aug. 20.

Dear Girlie: Well girlie I suppose you thought I was never going to answer your letter but have been busier than a one armed paper hanger the last week as have been working on a number with Paul Sears who is one of the best lyric writers in N. Y. and has turned out as many hits as Berlin or Davis or any of them. And believe me girlie he has turned out another hit this time that is he and I have done it together. It is all done now and we are just waiting for the best chance to place it but will not place it nowheres unless we get the right kind of a deal but maybe will publish it ourselves.

The song is bound to go over big as Sears has wrote a great lyric and I have give it a great tune or at least every body that has heard it goes crazy over it and it looks like it would go over bigger than any song since Mammy and would not be surprised to see it come out the hit of the year. If it is handled right we will make a bbl. of money and Sears says it is a cinch we will clean up as much as $25000 apiece which is pretty fair for one song but this one is not like the most of them but has got a great lyric and I have wrote a melody that will knock them out of their seats. I only wish you could hear it girlie and hear it the way I play it. I had to play it over and over about 50 times at the Friars last night.

I will copy down the lyric of the chorus so you can see what it is like and get the idea of the song though of course you can't tell much about it unless you hear it played and sang. The title of the song is When They're Like You and here is the chorus:

Some like them hot, some like them cold.
Some like them when they're not too darn old.
Some like them fat, some like them lean.
Some like them only at sweet sixteen.
Some like them dark, some like them light.
Some like them in the park, late at night.
Some like them fickle, some like them true,
But the time I like them is when they're like you.

How is that for a lyric and I only wish I could play my melody for you as you would go nuts over it but will send you a copy as soon as the song is published and you can get some of your friends to play it over for you and I know you will like it though it is a different melody when I play it or when somebody else plays it.

Well girlie you will see how busy I have been and am libel to keep right on being busy as we are not going to let the grass grow under our feet but as soon as we have got this number placed we will get busy on another one as a couple like that will put me on Easy st. even if they don't go as big as we expect but even 25 grand is a big bunch of money and if a man could only turn out one hit a year and make that much out of it I would be on Easy st. and no more hammering on the old music box in some cabaret.

Who ever we take the song to we will make them come across with one grand for advance royaltys and that will keep me going till I can turn out another one. So the future looks bright and rosey to yours truly and I am certainly glad I come to the big town though sorry I did not do it a whole lot quicker.

This is a great old town girlie and when you have lived here a wile you wonder how you ever stood for a burg like Chi which is just a hick town along side of this besides being dirty etc. and a man is a sucker to stay there all their life specially a man in my line of work as N. Y. is the Mecca for a man that has got the musical gift. I figure that all the time I spent in Chi I was just wasteing my time and never really started to live till I come down here and I have to laugh when I think of the boys out there that is trying to make a liveing in the song writeing game and most of them starve to death all their life and the first week I am down here I meet a man like Sears and the next thing you know we have turned out a song that will make us a fortune.

Well girlie you asked me to tell you about the girlie up on the Drive that tried to make me and asked me to come and see her again. Well I can assure you you have no reasons to be jealous in that quarter as I have not been back to see her as I figure it is wasteing my time to play round with a dame like she that wants to go out somewheres every night and if you married her she would want a house on 5th ave. with a dozen servants so I have passed her up as that is not my idea of home.

What I want when I get married is a real home where a man can stay home and work and maybe have a few of his friends in once in a wile and entertain them or go to a good musical show once in a wile and have a wife that is in sympathy with you and not nag at you all the wile but be a real help mate. The girlie up on the Drive would run me ragged and have me in the poor house inside of a year even if I was makeing 25 grand out of one song. Besides she wears a make up that you would have to blast to find out what her face looks like. So I have not been back there and don't intend to see her again so what is the use of me telling you about her. And the only other girlie I have met is a sister of Paul Sears who I met up to his house wile we was working on the song but she don't hardly count as she has not got no use for the boys but treats them like dirt and Paul says she is the coldest proposition he ever seen.

Well I don't know no more to write and besides have got a date to go out to Paul's place for dinner and play some of my stuff for him so as he can see if he wants to set words to some more of my melodies. Well don't do nothing I would not do and have as good a time as you can in old Chi and will let you know how we come along with the song.

CHAS. F. LEWIS.

Chicago, Ill., Aug. 23.
DEAR MR. MAN: I am thrilled to death over the song and think the words awfully pretty and am crazy to hear the music which I know must be great. It must be wonderful to have the gift of writing songs and then hear people play and sing them and just think of making $25,000 in such a short time. My, how rich you will be and I certainly congratulate you though am afraid when you are rich and famous you will have no time for insignificant little me or will you be an exception and remember your "old" friends even when you are up in the world? I sincerely hope so.

Will look forward to receiving a copy of the song and will you be sure and put your name on it? I am all ready very conceited just to think that I know a man that writes songs and makes all that money.

Seriously I wish you success with your next song and I laughed when I read your remark about being busier than a one armed paper hanger. I don't see how you think up all those comparisons and crazy things to say. The next time one of the girls asks me to go out with them I am going to tell them I can't go because I am busier than a one armed paper hanger and then they will think I made it up and say: "The girl is clever."

Seriously I am glad you did not go back to see the girl on the Drive and am also glad you don't like girls who makes themselves up so much as I think it is disgusting and would rather go round looking like a ghost than put artificial color on my face. Fortunately I have a complexion that does not need "fixing" but even if my coloring was not what it is I would never think of lowering myself to "fix" it. But I must tell you a joke that happened just the other day when Edith and I were out at lunch and there was another girl in the restaurant whom Edie knew and she introduced her to me and I noticed how this girl kept staring at me and finally she begged my pardon and asked if she could ask me a personal question and I said yes and she asked me if my complexion was really "mine." I assured her it was and she said: "Well, I thought so because I did not think anybody could put it on so artistically. I certainly envy you." Edie and I both laughed.

Well, if that girl envies me my complexion, why I envy you living in New York. Chicago is rather dirty though I don't let that part of it bother me as I bathe and change my clothing so often that the dirt does not have time to "settle." Edie often says she cannot see how I always keep so clean looking and says I always look like I had just stepped out of a band box. She also calls me a fish (jokingly) because I spend so much time in the water. But seriously I do love to bathe and never feel so happy as when I have just "cleaned up" and put on fresh clothing.

Edie has just gone out to see a picture and was cross at me because I would not go with her. I told her I was going to write a letter and she wanted to know to whom and I told her and she said: "You write to him so often that a person would almost think you was in love with him." I just laughed and turned it off, but she does say the most embarrassing things and I would be angry if it was anybody but she that said them.

Seriously I had much rather sit here and write letters or read or just sit and dream than go out to some crazy old picture show except once in awhile I do like to go to the theater and see a good play and a specially a musical play if the music is catchy. But as a rule I am contented to just stay home and feel cozy and lots of evenings Edie and I sit here without saying hardly a word to each other though she would love to talk but she knows I had rather be quiet and she often says it is just like living with a deaf and dumb mute to live with me because I make so little noise round the apartment. I guess I was born to be a home body as I so seldom care to go "gadding."

Though I do love to have company once in awhile, just a few congenial friends whom I can talk to and feel at home with and play cards or have some music. My friends love to drop in here, too, as they say Edie and I always give them such nice things to eat. Though poor Edie has not much to do with it, I am afraid, as she hates anything connected with cooking which is one of the things I love best of anything and I often say that when I begin keeping house in my own home I will insist on doing most of my own work as I would take so much more interest in it than a servant, though I would want somebody to help me a little if I could afford it as I often think a woman that does all her own work is liable to get so tired that she loses interest in the bigger things of life like books and music. Though after all what bigger thing is there than home making a specially for a woman?

I am sitting in the dearest old chair that I bought yesterday at a little store on the North Side. That is my one extravagance, buying furniture and things for the house, but I always say it is economy in the long run as I will always have them and have use for them and when I can pick them up at a bargain I would be silly not to. Though heaven knows I will never be "poor" in regards to furniture and rugs and things like that as mother's house in Toledo is full of lovely things which she says she is going to give to Sis and myself as soon as we have real homes of our own. She is going to give me the first choice as I am her favorite. She has the loveliest old things that you could not buy now for love or money including lovely old rugs and a piano which Sis wanted to have a player attachment put on it but I said it would be an insult to the piano so we did not get one. I am funny about things like that, a specially old furniture and feel towards them like people whom I love.

Poor mother, I am afraid she won't live much longer to enjoy her lovely old things as she has been suffering for years from stomach trouble and the doctor says it has been worse lately instead of better and her heart is weak besides. I am going home to see her a few days this fall as it may be the last time. She is very cheerful and always says she is ready to go now as she has had enough joy out of life and all she would like would be to see her girls settled down in their own homes before she goes.

There I go, talking about my domestic affairs again and I will bet you are bored to death though personly I am never bored when my friends tell me about themselves. But I won't "rattle on" any longer, but will say good night and don't forget to write and tell me how you come out with the song and thanks for sending me the words to it. Will you write a song about me some time? I would be thrilled to death! But I am afraid I am not the kind of girl that inspires men to write songs about them, but am just a quiet "mouse" that loves home and am not giddy enough to be the heroine of a song.

Well, Mr. Man, good night and don't wait so long before writing again to

Yours(?)

MABELLE.

N. Y., Sept. 8.

DEAR GIRLIE: Well girlie have not got your last letter with me so cannot answer what was in it as I have forgotten if there was anything I was supposed to answer and besides have only a little time to write as I have a date to go out on a party with the Sears. We are going to the Georgie White show and afterwards somewheres for supper. Sears is the boy who wrote the lyric to my song and it is him and his sister I am going on the party with. The sister is a cold fish that has no use for men but she is show crazy and insists on Paul

takeing her to 3 or 4 of them a week.

Paul wants me to give up my room here and come and live with them as they have plenty of room and I am running a little low on money but don't know if I will do it or not as am afraid I would freeze to death in the same house with a girl like the sister as she is ice cold but she don't hang around the house much as she is always takeing trips or going to shows or somewheres.

So far we have not had no luck with the song. All the publishers we have showed it to has went crazy over it but they won't make the right kind of a deal with us and if they don't loosen up and give us a decent royalty rate we are libel to put the song out ourselves and show them up. The man up to Goebel's told us the song was O. K. and he liked it but it was more of a production number than anything else and ought to go in a show like the Follies but they won't be in N. Y. much longer and what we ought to do is hold it till next spring.

Mean wile I am working on some new numbers and also have taken a position with the orchestra at the Wilton and am going to work there starting next week. They pay good money $60 and it will keep me going.

Well girlie that is about all the news. I believe you said your father was sick and hope he is better and also hope you are getting along O. K. and take care of yourself. When you have nothing else to do write to your friend,

CHAS. F. LEWIS.

Chicago, Ill., Sept. 11.

DEAR MR. LEWIS: Your short note reached me yesterday and must say I was puzzled when I read it. It sounded like you was mad at me though I cannot think of any reason

why you should be. If there was
something I said in my last letter that
offended you I wish you would tell
me what it was and I will ask your
pardon though I cannot remember
anything I could of said that you
could take offense at. But if there
was something, why I assure you, Mr.
Lewis, that I did not mean anything
by it. I certainly did not intend to
offend you in any way.

Perhaps it is nothing I wrote you,
but you are worried on account of
the publishers not treating you fair in
regards to your song and that is why
your letter sounded so distant. If that
is the case I hope that by this time
matters have rectified themselves and
the future looks brighter. But any
way, Mr. Lewis, don't allow yourself
to worry over business cares as they
will all come right in the end and I
always think it is silly for people to
worry themselves sick over temporary
troubles, but the best way is to "keep
smiling" and look for the "silver lining" in the cloud. That is the way I
always do and no matter what happens, I manage to smile and my girl
friend, Edie, calls me Sunny because
I always look on the bright side.

Remember also, Mr. Lewis, that
$60 is a salary that a great many men
would like to be getting and are living
on less than that and supporting a
wife and family on it. I always say
that a person can get along on whatever amount they make if they manage things in the right way.

So if it is business troubles, Mr.
Lewis, I say don't worry, but look
on the bright side. But if it is something I wrote in my last letter that
offended you I wish you would tell
me what it was so I can apologize as
I assure you I meant nothing and
would not say anything to hurt you
for the world.

Please let me hear from you soon

as I will not feel comfortable until
I know I am not to blame for the
sudden change.

Sincerely,
MABELLE GILLESPIE.

N. Y., Sept. 24.

DEAR MISS GILLESPIE: Just a few
lines to tell you the big news or at
least it is big news to me. I am engaged to be married to Paul Sears'
sister and we are going to be married
early next month and live in Atlantic
City where the orchestra I have been
playing with has got an engagement
in one of the big cabarets.

I know this will be a surprise to you
as it was even a surprise to me as I
did not think I would ever have the
nerve to ask the girlie the big question
as she was always so cold and acted
like I was just in the way. But she
said she supposed she would have to
marry somebody some time and she
did not dislike me as much as most
of the other men her brother brought
round and she would marry me with
the understanding that she would not
have to be a slave and work round
the house and also I would have to
take her to a show or somewheres
every night and if I could not take
her myself she would "run wild"
alone. Atlantic City will be O. K. for
that as a lot of new shows opens down
there and she will be able to see them
before they get to the big town. As
for her being a slave, I would hate
to think of marrying a girl and then
have them spend their lives in drug-
gery round the house. We are going
to live in a hotel till we find something better but will be in no hurry
to start house keeping as we will have
to buy all new furniture.

Betsy is some doll when she is all
fixed up and believe me she knows
how to fix herself up. I don't know
what she uses but it is weather proof

as I have been out in a rain storm with her and we both got drowned but her face stayed on. I would almost think it was real only she tells me different.

Well girlie I may write to you again once in a wile as Betsy says she don't give a dam if I write to all the girls in the world just so I don't make her read the answers but that is all I can think of to say now except good bye and good luck and may the right man come along soon and he will be a lucky man getting a girl that is such a good cook and got all that furniture etc.

But just let me give you a word of advice before I close and that is don't never speak to strange men who you don't know nothing about as they may get you wrong and think you are trying to make them. It just happened that I knew better so you was lucky in my case but the luck might not last.

> Your friend,
> CHAS. F. LEWIS.

Chicago, Ill., Sept. 27.

MY DEAR MR. LEWIS: Thanks for your advice and also thank your fiance for her generosity in allowing you to continue your correspondence with her "rivals," but personly I have no desire to take advantage of that generosity as I have something better to do than read letters from a man like you, a specially as I have a man friend who is not so generous as Miss Sears and would strongly object to my continuing a correspondence with another man. It is at his request that I am writing this note to tell you not to expect to hear from me again.

Allow me to congratulate you on your engagement to Miss Sears and I am sure she is to be congratulated too, though if I met the lady I would be tempted to ask her to tell me her

secret, namely how she is going to "run wild" on $60.

> Sincerely,
> MABELLE GILLESPIE.
> *1921*

ERNEST HEMINGWAY
(1898–   )

THE KILLERS *

The door of Henry's lunch-room opened and two men came in. They sat down at the counter.

"What's yours?" George asked them.

"I don't know," one of the men said. "What do you want to eat, Al?"

"I don't know," said Al. "I don't know what I want to eat."

Outside it was getting dark. The streetlight came on outside the window. The two men at the counter read the menu. From the other end of the counter Nick Adams watched them. He had been talking to George when they came in.

"I'll have a roast pork tenderloin with apple sauce and mashed potatoes," the first man said.

"It isn't ready yet."

"What the hell do you put it on the card for?"

"That's the dinner," George explained. "You can get that at six o'clock."

George looked at the clock on the wall behind the counter.

"It's five o'clock."

"The clock says twenty minutes past five," the second man said.

"It's twenty minutes fast."

"Oh, to hell with the clock," the first man said. "What have you got to eat?"

"I can give you any kind of sand-wiches," George said. "You can have ham and eggs, bacon and eggs, liver and bacon, or a steak."

"Give me chicken croquettes with green peas and cream sauce and mashed potatoes."

"That's the dinner."

"Everything we want's the dinner, eh? That's the way you work it."

"I can give you ham and eggs, bacon and eggs, liver——"

"I'll take ham and eggs," the man called Al said. He wore a derby hat and a black overcoat buttoned across the chest. His face was small and white and he had tight lips. He wore a silk muffler and gloves.

"Give me bacon and eggs," said the other man. He was about the same size as Al. Their faces were different, but they were dressed like twins. Both wore overcoats too tight for them. They sat leaning forward, their elbows on the counter.

"Got anything to drink?" Al asked.

"Silver beer, bevo, ginger-ale," George said.

"I mean you got anything to *drink?*"

"Just those I said."

"This is a hot town," said the other. "What do they call it?"

"Summit."

"Ever hear of it?" Al asked his friend.

"No," said the friend.

"What do you do here nights?" Al asked.

"They eat the dinner," his friend said. "They all come here and eat the big dinner."

"That's right," George said.

"So you think that's right?" Al asked George.

"Sure."

"You're a pretty bright boy, aren't you?"

"Sure," said George.

"Well, you're not," said the other little man. "Is he, Al?"

"He's dumb," said Al. He turned to Nick. "What's your name?"

"Adams."

"Another bright boy," Al said. "Ain't he a bright boy, Max?"

"The town's full of bright boys," Max said.

George put the two platters, one of ham and eggs, the other of bacon and eggs, on the counter. He set down two side-dishes of fried potatoes and closed the wicket into the kitchen.

"Which is yours?" he asked Al.

"Don't you remember?"

"Ham and eggs."

"Just a bright boy," Max said. He leaned forward and took the ham and eggs. Both men ate with their gloves on. George watched them eat.

"What are *you* looking at?" Max looked at George.

"Nothing."

"The hell you were. You were looking at me."

"Maybe the boy meant it for a joke, Max," Al said.

George laughed.

"*You* don't have to laugh," Max said to him. "*You* don't have to laugh at all, see?"

"All right," said George.

"So he thinks it's all right." Max turned to Al. "He thinks it's all right. That's a good one."

"Oh, he's a thinker," Al said. They went on eating.

"What's the bright boy's name down the counter?" Al asked Max.

"Hey, bright boy," Max said to Nick. "You go around on the other side of the counter with your boy friend."

"What's the idea?" Nick asked.

"There isn't any idea."

"You better go around, bright boy," Al said. Nick went around behind the counter.

"What's the idea?" George asked.

"None of your damn business," Al said. "Who's out in the kitchen?"

"The nigger."

"What do you mean the nigger?"

"The nigger that cooks."

"Tell him to come in."

"What's the idea?"

"Tell him to come in."

"Where do you think you are?"

"We know damn well where we are," the man called Max said. "Do we look silly?"

"You talk silly," Al said to him. "What the hell do you argue with this kid for? Listen," he said to George, "tell the nigger to come out here."

"What are you going to do to him?"

"Nothing. Use your head, bright boy. What would we do to a nigger?"

George opened the slit that opened back into the kitchen. "Sam," he called. "Come in here a minute."

The door to the kitchen opened and the nigger came in. "What was it?" he asked. The two men at the counter took a look at him.

"All right, nigger. You stand right there," Al said.

Sam, the nigger, standing in his apron, looked at the two men sitting at the counter. "Yes, sir," he said. Al got down from his stool.

"I'm going back to the kitchen with the nigger and bright boy," he said. "Go on back to the kitchen, nigger. You go with him, bright boy." The little man walked after Nick and Sam, the cook, back into the kitchen. The door shut after them. The man called Max sat at the counter opposite George. He didn't look at George but looked in the mirror that ran along back of the counter. Henry's had been made over from a saloon into a lunch-counter.

"Well, bright boy," Max said, look-ing into the mirror, "why don't you say something?"

"What's it all about?"

"Hey, Al," Max called, "bright boy wants to know what it's all about."

"Why don't you tell him?" Al's voice came from the kitchen.

"What do you think it's all about?"

"I don't know."

"What do you think?"

Max looked into the mirror all the time he was talking.

"I wouldn't say."

"Hey, Al, bright boy says he wouldn't say what he thinks it's all about."

"I can hear you, all right," Al said from the kitchen. He had propped open the slit that dishes passed through into the kitchen with a cat-sup bottle. "Listen, bright boy," he said from the kitchen to George. "Stand a little further along the bar. You move a little to the left, Max." He was like a photographer arranging for a group picture.

"Talk to me, bright boy," Max said. "What do you think's going to hap-pen?"

George did not say anything.

"I'll tell you," Max said. "We're going to kill a Swede. Do you know a big Swede named Ole Andre-son?"

"Yes."

"He comes here to eat every night, don't he?"

"Sometimes he comes here."

"He comes here at six o'clock, don't he?"

"If he comes."

"We know all that, bright boy," Max said. "Talk about something else. Ever go to the movies?"

"Once in a while."

"You ought to go to the movies more. The movies are fine for a bright boy like you."

"What are you going to kill Ole

Andreson for? What did he ever do to you?"

"He never had a chance to do anything to us. He never even seen us."

"And he's only going to see us once," Al said from the kitchen.

"What are you going to kill him for, then?" George asked.

"We're killing him for a friend. Just to oblige a friend, bright boy."

"Shut up," said Al from the kitchen. "You talk too goddam much."

"Well, I got to keep bright boy amused. Don't I, bright boy?"

"You talk too damn much," Al said. "The nigger and my bright boy are amused by themselves. I got them tied up like a couple of girl friends in the convent."

"I suppose you were in a convent."

"You never know."

"You were in a kosher convent. That's where you were."

George looked up at the clock.

"If anybody comes in you tell them the cook is off, and if they keep after it, you tell them you'll go back and cook yourself. Do you get that, bright boy?"

"All right," George said. "What you going to do with us afterward?"

"That'll depend," Max said. "That's one of those things you never know at the time."

George looked up at the clock. It was a quarter past six. The door from the street opened. A street-car motorman came in.

"Hello, George," he said. "Can I get supper?"

"Sam's gone out," George said. "He'll be back in about half an hour."

"I'd better go up the street," the motorman said. George looked at the clock. It was twenty minutes past six.

"That was nice, bright boy," Max said. "You're a regular little gentleman."

"He knew I'd blow his head off," Al said from the kitchen.

"No," said Max. "It ain't that. Bright boy is nice. He's a nice boy. I like him."

At six-fifty-five George said: "He's not coming."

Two other people had been in the lunchroom. Once George had gone out to the kitchen and made a ham-and-egg sandwich "to go" that a man wanted to take with him. Inside the kitchen he saw Al, his derby hat tipped back, sitting on a stool beside the wicket with the muzzle of a sawed-off shotgun resting on the ledge. Nick and the cook were back to back in the corner, a towel tied in each of their mouths. George had cooked the sandwich, wrapped it up in oiled paper, put it in a bag, brought it in, and the man had paid for it and gone out.

"Bright boy can do everything," Max said. "He can cook and everything. You'd make some girl a nice wife, bright boy."

"Yes?" George said. "Your friend, Ole Andreson, isn't going to come."

"We'll give him ten minutes," Max said.

Max watched the mirror and the clock. The hands of the clock marked seven o'clock, and then five minutes past seven.

"Come on, Al," said Max. "We better go. He's not coming."

"Better give him five minutes," Al said from the kitchen.

In the five minutes a man came in, and George explained that the cook was sick.

"Why the hell don't you get another cook?" the man asked. "Aren't you running a lunch-counter?" He went out.

"Come on, Al," Max said.

"What about the two bright boys and the nigger?"

"They're all right."

"You think so?"

"Sure. We're through with it."

"I don't like it," said Al. "It's sloppy. You talk too much."

"Oh, what the hell," said Max. "We got to keep amused, haven't we?"

"You talk too much, all the same," Al said. He came out from the kitchen. The cut-off barrels of the shotgun made a slight bulge under the waist of his too tight-fitting overcoat. He straightened his coat with his gloved hands.

"So long, bright boy," he said to George. "You got a lot of luck."

"That's the truth," Max said. "You ought to play the races, bright boy."

The two of them went out the door. George watched them, through the window, pass under the arc-light and cross the street. In their tight overcoats and derby hats they looked like a vaudeville team. George went back through the swinging-door into the kitchen and untied Nick and the cook.

"I don't want any more of that," said Sam, the cook. "I don't want any more of that."

Nick stood up. He had never had a towel in his mouth before.

"Say," he said. "What the hell?" He was trying to swagger it off.

"They were going to kill Ole Andreson," George said. "They were going to shoot him when he came in to eat."

"Ole Andreson?"

"Sure."

The cook felt the corners of his mouth with his thumbs.

"They all gone?" he asked.

"Yeah," said George. "They're gone now."

"I don't like it," said the cook. "I don't like any of it at all."

"Listen," George said to Nick. "You better go see Ole Andreson."

"All right."

"You better not have anything to do with it at all," Sam, the cook, said. "You better stay way out of it."

"Don't go if you don't want to," George said.

"Mixing up in this ain't going to get you anywhere," the cook said. "You stay out of it."

"I'll go see him," Nick said to George. "Where does he live?"

The cook turned away.

"Little boys always know what they want to do," he said.

"He lives up at Hirsch's rooming-house," George said to Nick.

"I'll go up there."

Outside the arc-light shone through the bare branches of a tree. Nick walked up the street beside the car-tracks and turned at the next arc-light down a side-street. Three houses up the street was Hirsch's rooming-house. Nick walked up the two steps and pushed the bell. A woman came to the door.

"Is Ole Andreson here?"

"Do you want to see him?"

"Yes, if he's in."

Nick followed the woman up a flight of stairs and back to the end of a corridor. She knocked on the door.

"Who is it?"

"It's somebody to see you, Mr. Andreson," the woman said.

"It's Nick Adams."

"Come in."

Nick opened the door and went into the room. Ole Andreson was lying on the bed with all his clothes on. He had been a heavyweight prizefighter and he was too long for the bed. He lay with his head on two pillows. He did not look at Nick.

"What was it?" he asked.

"I was up at Henry's," Nick said, "and two fellows came in and tied up me and the cook, and they said they were going to kill you."

It sounded silly when he said it. Ole Andreson said nothing.

"They put us out in the kitchen," Nick went on. "They were going to shoot you when you came in to supper."

Ole Andreson looked at the wall and did not say anything.

"George thought I better come and tell you about it."

"There isn't anything I can do about it," Ole Andreson said.

"I'll tell you what they were like."

"I don't want to know what they were like," Ole Andreson said. He looked at the wall. "Thanks for coming to tell me about it."

"That's all right."

Nick looked at the big man lying on the bed.

"Don't you want me to go and see the police?"

"No," Ole Andreson said. "That wouldn't do any good."

"Isn't there something I could do?"

"No. There ain't anything to do."

"Maybe it was just a bluff."

"No. It ain't just a bluff."

Ole Andreson rolled over toward the wall.

"The only thing is," he said, talking toward the wall, "I just can't make up my mind to go out. I been in here all day."

"Couldn't you get out of town?"

"No," Ole Andreson said. "I'm through with all that running around."

He looked at the wall.

"There ain't anything to do now."

"Couldn't you fix it up some way?"

"No. I got in wrong." He talked in the same flat voice. "There ain't anything to do. After a while I'll make up my mind to go out."

"I better go back and see George," Nick said.

"So long," said Ole Andreson. He did not look toward Nick. "Thanks for coming around."

Nick went out. As he shut the door he saw Ole Andreson with all his clothes on, lying on the bed looking at the wall.

"He's been in his room all day," the landlady said downstairs. "I guess he don't feel well. I said to him: 'Mr. Andreson, you ought to go out and take a walk on a nice fall day like this,' but he didn't feel like it."

"He doesn't want to go out."

"I'm sorry he don't feel well," the woman said. "He's an awfully nice man. He was in the ring, you know."

"I know it."

"You'd never know it except from the way his face is," the woman said. They stood talking just inside the street door. "He's just as gentle."

"Well, good night, Mrs. Hirsch," Nick said.

"I'm not Mrs. Hirsch," the woman said. "She owns the place. I just look after it for her. I'm Mrs. Bell."

"Well, good night, Mrs. Bell," Nick said.

"Good night," the woman said.

Nick walked up the dark street to the corner under the arc-light, and then along the car-tracks to Henry's eating-house. George was inside, back of the counter.

"Did you see Ole?"

"Yes," said Nick. "He's in his room and he won't go out."

The cook opened the door from the kitchen when he heard Nick's voice.

"I don't even listen to it," he said and shut the door.

"Did you tell him about it?" George asked.

"Sure. I told him but he knows what it's all about."

"What's he going to do?"

"Nothing."

"They'll kill him."

"I guess they will."

"He must have got mixed up in something in Chicago."

"I guess so," said Nick.

"It's a hell of a thing."

"It's an awful thing," Nick said.

They did not say anything. George reached down for a towel and wiped the counter.

"I wonder what he did?" Nick said.

"Double-crossed somebody. That's what they kill them for."

"I'm going to get out of this town," Nick said.

"Yes," said George. "That's a good thing to do."

"I can't stand to think about him waiting in the room and knowing he's going to get it. It's too damned awful."

"Well," said George, "you better not think about it."

1927

THE SNOWS
OF KILIMANJARO *

Kilimanjaro is a snow-covered mountain 19,710 feet high, and is said to be the highest mountain in Africa. Its western summit is called the Masai "Ngàje Ngài," the House of God. Close to the western summit there is the dried and frozen carcass of a leopard. No one has explained what the leopard was seeking at that altitude.

"The marvelous thing is that it's painless," he said. "That's how you know when it starts."

"Is it really?"

"Absolutely. I'm awfully sorry about the odor, though. That must bother you."

"Don't! Please don't."

"Look at them," he said. "Now is it sight or is it scent that brings them like that?"

The cot the man lay on was in the wide shade of a mimosa tree and as he looked out past the shade onto the glare of the plain there were three of the big birds squatted obscenely, while in the sky a dozen more sailed, making quiet moving shadows as they passed.

"They've been there since the day the truck broke down," he said. "Today's the first time any have lit on the ground. I watched the way they sailed very carefully at first in case I ever wanted to use them in a story. That's funny now."

"I wish you wouldn't," she said.

"I'm only talking," he said. "It's much easier if I talk. But I don't want to bother you."

"You know it doesn't bother me," she said. "It's that I've gotten so very nervous not being able to do anything. I think we might make it as easy as we can until the plane comes."

"Or until the plane doesn't come."

"Please tell me what I can do. There must be something I can do."

"You can take the leg off and that might stop it, though I doubt it. Or you can shoot me. You're a good shot now. I taught you to shoot, didn't I?"

"Please don't talk that way. Couldn't I read to you?"

"Read what?"

"Anything in the book bag that we haven't read."

"I can't listen to it," he said. "Talking is the easiest. We quarrel and that makes the time pass."

"I don't quarrel. I never want to quarrel. Let's not quarrel any more. No matter how nervous we get. Maybe they will be back with another truck today. Maybe the plane will come."

"I don't want to move," the man said. "There is no sense in moving

* Reprinted from *The Fifth Column and the First Forty-Nine Stories* by Ernest Hemingway; copyright 1938 by Ernest Hemingway; used by permission of the publishers, Charles Scribner's Sons.

now except to make it easier for you."

"That's cowardly."

"Can't you let a man die as comfortably as he can without calling him names? What's the use of slanging me?"

"You're not going to die."

"Don't be silly. I'm dying now. Ask those bastards." He looked over to where the huge filthy birds sat, their naked heads sunk in the hunched feathers. A fourth planed down, to run quick-legged and then waddle slowly toward the others.

"They are around every camp. You never notice them. You can't die if you don't give up."

"Where did you read that? You're sure a bloody fool."

"You might think about someone else."

"For Christ's sake," he said, "that's been my trade."

He lay then and was quiet for a while and looked across the heat shimmer of the plain to the edge of the bush. There were a few Tommies that showed minute and white against the yellow and, far off, he saw a herd of zebra, white against the green of the bush. This was a pleasant camp under big trees against a hill, with good water, and close by, a nearly dry waterhole where sand grouse flighted in the mornings.

"Wouldn't you like me to read?" she asked. She was sitting on a canvas chair beside his cot. "There's a breeze coming up."

"No, thanks."

"Maybe the truck will come."

"I don't give a damn about the truck."

"I do."

"You give a damn about so many things that I don't."

"Not so many, Harry."

"What about a drink?"

"It's supposed to be bad for you. It said in Black's to avoid all alcohol. You shouldn't drink."

"Molo!" he shouted.

"Yes, Bwana."

"Bring whiskey-soda."

"Yes, Bwana."

"You shouldn't," she said. "That's what I mean by giving up. It says it's bad for you. I know it's bad for you."

"No," he said. "It's good for me."

So now it was all over, he thought. So now he would never have a chance to finish it. So this was the way it ended in a bickering over a drink. Since the gangrene started in his right leg, he had no pain and with the pain the horror had gone, and all he felt now was a great tiredness and anger that this was the end of it. For this, that now was coming, he had very little curiosity. For years it had obsessed him; but now it meant nothing in itself. It was strange how easy being tired enough made it.

Now he would never write the things that he had saved to write until he knew enough to write them well. Well, he would not have to fail at trying to write them either. Maybe you could never write them, and that was why you put them off and delayed the starting. Well, he would never know, now.

"I wish we'd never come," the woman said. She was looking at him holding the glass and biting her lip. "You never would have gotten anything like this in Paris. You always said you loved Paris. We could have stayed in Paris or gone anywhere. I'd have gone anywhere. I said I'd go anywhere you wanted. If you wanted to shoot, we could have gone shooting in Hungary and been comfortable."

"Your bloody money," he said.

"That's not fair," she said. "It was always yours as much as mine. I left everything and I went wherever you wanted to go and I've done what you wanted to do. But I wish we'd never come here."

"You said you loved it."

"I did when you were all right. But now I hate it. I don't see why that had to happen to your leg. What have we done to have that happen to us?"

"I suppose what I did was to forget to put iodine on it when I first scratched it. Then I didn't pay any attention to it because I never infect. Then, later, when it got bad, it was probably using that weak carbolic solution when the other antiseptics ran out that paralyzed the minute blood vessels and started the gangrene." He looked at her, "What else?"

"I don't mean that."

"If we would have hired a good mechanic instead of a half-baked kikuyu driver, he would have checked the oil and never burned out that bearing in the truck."

"I don't mean that."

"If you hadn't left your own people, your goddamned Old Westbury, Saratoga, Palm Beach people to take me on——"

"Why, I loved you. That's not fair. I love you now. I'll always love you. Don't you love me?"

"No," said the man. "I don't think so. I never have."

"Harry, what are you saying? You're out of your head."

"No. I haven't any head to go out of."

"Don't drink that," she said. "Darling, please don't drink that. We have to do everything we can."

"You do it," he said. "I'm tired."

Now in his mind he saw a railway station at Karagatch and he was standing with his pack and that was the headlight of the Simplon-Orient cutting the dark now and he was leaving Thrace then after the retreat. That was one of the things he had saved to write, with, in the morning at breakfast, looking out the window and seeing snow on the mountains in Bulgaria and Nansen's Secretary asking the old man if it were snow and the old man looking at it and saying, No, that's not snow. It's too early for snow. And the Secretary repeating to the other girls, No, you see. It's not snow and them all saying, It's not snow we were mistaken. But it was the snow all right and he sent them on into it when he evolved exchange of populations. And it was snow they tramped along in until they died that winter.

It was snow too that fell all Christmas week that year up in the Gauertal, that year they lived in the woodcutter's house with the big square porcelain stove that filled half the room, and they slept on mattresses filled with beech leaves, the time the deserter came with his feet bloody in the snow. He said the police were right behind him and they gave him woolen socks and held the gendarmes talking until the tracks had drifted over.

In Schrunz, on Christmas day, the snow was so bright it hurt your eyes when you looked out from the Weinstube and saw every one coming home from church. That was where they walked up the sleigh-smoothed urine-yellowed road along the river with the steep pine hills, skis heavy on the shoulder, and where they ran that great run down the glacier above the Madlener-Haus, the snow as smooth to see as cake frosting and as light as powder and he remembered the noiseless rush the speed made as you dropped down like a bird.

They were snow-bound a week in the Madlener-Haus that time in the blizzard playing cards in the smoke by the lantern light and the stakes were higher all the time as Herr Lent lost more. Finally he lost it all. Everything, the skischule money and all the season's profit and then his capital. He could see him with his long nose, picking up the cards and then opening, "Sans Voir." There was always gambling then. When there was no snow you gambled and when there was too much you gambled. He thought of all the time in his life he had spent gambling.

But he had never written a line of that, nor of that cold, bright Christmas day with the mountains showing across the plain that Barker had flown across the lines to bomb the Austrian officers' leave train, machine-gunning them as they scattered and ran. He remembered Barker afterwards coming into the mess and starting to tell about it. And how quiet it got and then somebody saying, "You bloody murderous bastard."

Those were the same Austrians they killed then that he skied with later. No not the same. Hans, that he skied with all that year, had been in the Kaiser-Jägers and when they went hunting hares together up in the little valley above the saw-mill they had talked of the fighting on Pasubio and of the attack on Pertica and Asalone and he had never written a word of that. Nor of Monte-Corno, nor the Siete Commum, nor of Arsiedo.

How many winters had he lived in the Voralberg and the Arlberg? It was four and then he remembered the man who had the fox to sell when they had walked into Blundenz, that time to buy presents, and the cherry-pit taste of good kirsch, the fast-slipping rush of running powder-snow on crust, singing "Hi! Ho! said Rolly!" as you ran down the last stretch to the steep drop, taking it straight, then running the orchard in three turns and out across the ditch and onto the icy road behind the inn. Knocking

your bindings loose, kicking the skis free and leaning them up against the wooden wall of the inn, the lamplight coming from the window, where inside, in the smoky, new-wine smelling warmth, they were playing the accordion.

"Where did we stay in Paris?" he asked the woman who was sitting by him in a canvas chair, now, in Africa.

"At the Crillon. You know that."

"Why do I know that?"

"That's where we always stayed."

"No. Not always."

"There and at the Pavillon Henri-Quatre in St. Germain. You said you loved it there."

"Love is a dunghill," said Harry. "And I'm the cock that gets on it to crow."

"If you have to go away," she said, "is it absolutely necessary to kill off everything you leave behind? I mean do you have to take away everything? Do you have to kill your horse, and your wife, and burn your saddle and your armour?"

"Yes," he said. "Your damned money was my armour. My Swift and my Armour."

"Don't."

"All right. I'll stop that. I don't want to hurt you."

"It's a little bit late now."

"All right, then. I'll go on hurting you. It's more amusing. The only thing I ever really like to do with you I can't do now."

"No, that's not true. You liked to do many things and everything you wanted to do I did."

"Oh, for Christ sake stop bragging, will you?"

He looked at her and saw her crying.

"Listen," he said. "Do you think that it is fun to do this? I don't know why I'm doing it. It's trying to kill to keep yourself alive, I imagine. I was all right when we started talking. I didn't mean to start this, and now I'm crazy as a coot and being as cruel to you as I can be. Don't pay any attention, darling, to what I say. I love you, really. You know I love you. I've never loved any one else the way I love you."

He slipped into the familiar lie he made his bread and butter by.

"You're sweet to me."

"You bitch," he said. "You rich bitch. That's poetry. I'm full of poetry now. Rot and poetry. Rotten poetry."

"Stop it. Harry, why do you have to turn into a devil now?"

"I don't like to leave anything," the man said. "I don't like to leave things behind."

It was evening now and he had been asleep. The sun was gone behind the hill and there was a shadow all across the plain and the small animals were feeding close to camp; quick-dropping heads and switching tails, he watched them keeping well out away from the bush now. The birds no longer waited on the ground. They were all perched heavily in a tree. There were many more of them. His personal boy was sitting by the bed.

"Memsahib's gone to shoot," the boy said. "Does Bwana want?"

"Nothing."

She had gone to kill a piece of meat and, knowing how he liked to watch the game, she had gone well away so she would not disturb this little pocket of the plain that he could see. She was always thoughtful, he thought. On anything she knew about, or had read, or that she had ever heard.

It was not her fault that when he went to her he was already over. How could a woman know that you meant nothing that you said; that you spoke only from habit and to be comfortable? After he no longer meant what he said, his lies were more successful with women than when he had told them the truth.

It was not so much that he lied as that there was no truth to tell. He had had his life and it was over and then he went on living it again with different people and more money, with the best of the same places, and some new ones.

You kept from thinking and it was all marvelous. You were equipped with good insides so that you did not go to pieces that way, the way most of them had, and you made an attitude that you cared nothing for the work you used to do, now that you could no longer do it. But, in yourself, you said that you would write about these people; about the very rich; that you were really not of them but a spy in their country; that you would leave it and write of it and for once it would be written by someone who knew what he was writing of. But he would never do it, because each day of not writing, of comfort, of being that which he despised, dulled his ability and softened his will to work so that, finally, he did no work at all. The people he knew now were all much more comfortable when he did not work. Africa was where he had been happiest in the good time of his life, so he had come out here to start again. They had made this safari with the minimum of comfort. There was no hardship; but there was no luxury and he had thought that he could get back into training that way. That in some way he could work the fat off his soul the way a fighter went into the mountains to work and train in order to burn it out of his body.

She had liked it. She said she loved it. She loved anything that was exciting, that involved a change of scene, where there were new people and where things were pleasant. And he had felt the illusion of returning strength of will to work. Now if this was how it ended, and he knew it was, he must not turn like some snake biting itself because its back was broken. It wasn't this woman's fault. If it had not been she, it would have been another. If he lived by a lie, he should try to die by it. He heard a shot beyond the hill.

She shot very well, this good, this rich bitch, this kindly caretaker and destroyer of his talent. Nonsense. He had destroyed his talent himself. Why should he blame this woman because she kept him well? He had destroyed his talent by not using it, by betrayals of himself and what he believed in, by drinking so much that he blunted the edge of his perceptions, by laziness, by sloth, and by snobbery, by pride and by prejudice, by hook and by crook. What was this? A catalogue of old books? What was his talent anyway? It was a talent all right, but instead of using it, he had traded on it. It was never what he had done, but always what he could do. And he had chosen to make his living with something else instead of a pen or a pencil. It was strange, too, wasn't it, that when he fell in love with another woman, that woman should always have more money than the last one? But when he no longer was in love, when he was only lying, as to this woman, now, who had the most money of all, who had all the money there was, who had had a husband and children, who had taken lovers and been dissatisfied with them, and who had loved him dearly as a writer, as a man, as a companion, and as a proud possession; it was strange that, when he did not love her at all and was lying, he should be able to give

her more for her money than when he had really loved.

We must all be cut out for what we do, he thought. However you make your living is where your talent lies. He had sold vitality, in one form or another, all his life, and when your affections are not involved you give much better value for the money. He had found that out, but he would never write that, now, either. No, he would not write that, although it was well worth writing.

Now she came in sight, walking across the open toward the camp. She was wearing jodhpurs and carrying her rifle. The two boys had a Tommie slung and they were coming along behind her. She was still a good-looking woman, he thought, and she had a pleasant body. She had a great talent and appreciation for the bed, she was not pretty, but he liked her face, she read enormously, liked to ride and shoot and, certainly, she drank too much. Her husband had died when she was still a comparatively young woman and for a while she had devoted herself to her two just-grown children, who did not need her and were embarrassed at having her about, to her stable of horses, to books, and to bottles. She liked to read in the evening before dinner and she drank Scotch-and-soda while she read. By dinner she was fairly drunk and after a bottle of wine at dinner she was usually drunk enough to sleep.

That was before the lovers. After she had the lovers, she did not drink so much because she did not have to be drunk to sleep. But the lovers bored her. She had been married to a man who had never bored her and these people bored her very much.

Then one of her two children was killed in a plane crash and after that was over she did not want the lovers, and drink being no anaesthetic she had to make another life. Suddenly, she had to make another life. Suddenly, she had been acutely frightened of being alone. But she wanted someone that she respected with her.

It had begun very simply. She liked what he wrote and she had always envied the life he led. She thought he did exactly what he wanted to. The steps by which she had acquired him and the way in which she had finally fallen in love with him were all part of a regular progression in which she had built herself a new life and he had traded away what remained of his old life.

He had traded it for security, for comfort, too, there was no denying that, and for what else? He did not know. She would have bought him anything he wanted. He knew that. She was a damned nice woman too. He would as soon be in bed with her as anyone; rather with her, because she was richer, because she was very pleasant and appreciative, and because she never made scenes. And now this life that she had built again was coming to a term because he had not used iodine two weeks ago when a thorn had scratched his knee as they moved forward trying to photograph a herd of waterbuck standing, their heads up, peering while their nostrils searched the air, their ears spread wide to hear the first noise that would send them rushing into the bush. They had bolted, too, before he got the picture.

Here she came now.

He turned his head on the cot to look toward her. "Hello," he said.

"I shot a Tommy ram," she told him. "He'll make you good broth and I'll have them mash some potatoes with the Klim. How do you feel?"

"Much better."

"Isn't that lovely? You know I thought perhaps you would. You were sleeping when I left."

"I had a good sleep. Did you walk far?"

"No. Just around behind the hill. I made quite a good shot on the Tommy."

"You shoot marvelously, you know."

"I love it. I've loved Africa. Really. If *you're* all right it's the most fun that I've ever had. You don't know the fun it's been to shoot with you. I've loved the country."

"I love it too."

"Darling, you don't know how marvelous it is to see you feeling better. I couldn't stand it when you felt that way. You won't talk to me like that again, will you? Promise me?"

"No," he said. "I don't remember what I said."

"You don't have to destroy me. Do you? I'm only a middle-aged woman who loves you and wants to do what you want to do. I've been destroyed two or three times already. You wouldn't want to destroy me again, would you?"

"I'd like to destroy you a few times in bed," he said.

"Yes. That's the good destruction. That's the way we're made to be destroyed. The plane will be here tomorrow."

"How do you know?"

"I'm sure. It's bound to come. The boys have the wood all ready and the grass to make the smudge. I went down and looked at it again today. There's plenty of room to land and we have the smudges ready at both ends."

"What makes you think it will come tomorrow?"

"I'm sure it will. It's overdue now. Then, in town, they will fix up your leg and then we will have some good destruction. Not that dreadful talking kind."

"Should we have a drink? The sun is down."

"Do you think you should?"

"I'm having one."

"We'll have one together. *Malo, letti dui whiskey-soda*"! she called.

"You'd better put on your mosquito boots," he told her.

"I'll wait till I bathe . . ."

While it grew dark they drank and just before it was dark and there was no longer enough light to shoot, a hyena crossed the open on his way around the hill.

"That bastard crosses there every night," the man said. "Every night for two weeks."

"He's the one makes the noise at night. I don't mind it. They're a filthy animal, though."

Drinking together, with no pain now except the discomfort of lying in the one position, the boys lighting a fire, its shadow jumping on the tents, he could feel the return of acquiescence in this life of pleasant surrender. She *was* very good to him. He had been cruel and unjust in the afternoon. She was a fine woman, marvelous really. And just then it occurred to him that he was going to die.

It came with a rush; not as a rush of water nor of wind; but of a sudden evil-smelling emptiness and the odd thing was that the hyena slipped lightly along the edge of it.

"What is it, Harry?" she asked him.

"Nothing," he said. "You had better move over to the other side. To windward."

"Did Molo change the dressing?"

"Yes. I'm just using the boric now."

"How do you feel?"

"A little wobbly."

"I'm going in to bathe," she said. "I'll be right out. I'll eat with you and then we'll put the cot in."

So, he said to himself, we did well to stop the quarreling. He had never quarreled much with this woman, while with the women that he loved he had quarreled so much they had finally, always, with the corrosion of the quarreling, killed what they had together. He had loved too much, demanded too much, and he wore it all out.

He thought about alone in Constantinople that time, having quarreled in Paris before he had gone out. He had whored the whole time and then, when that was over, and he had failed to kill his loneliness, but only made it worse, he had written her, the first one, the one who left him, a letter telling her how he had never been able to kill it. . . . How when he thought he saw her outside the Régence one time it made him go all faint and sick inside, and that he would follow a woman who looked like her in some way, along the Boulevard, afraid to see it was not she, afraid to lose the feeling it gave him. How everyone he had slept with had only made him miss her more. How what she had done could never matter since he knew he could not cure himself of loving her. He wrote this letter at the Club, cold sober, and mailed it to New York asking her to write him at the office in Paris. That seemed safe. And that night, missing her so much it made him feel hollow sick inside, he wandered up past Taxim's, picked a girl up and took her out to supper. He had gone to a place to dance with her afterward, she danced badly, and left her for a hot Armenian slut, that swung her belly against him so it almost scalded. He took her away from a British gunner subaltern after a row. The gunner asked him outside and they fought in the street on the cobbles in the dark. He'd hit him twice, hard, on the side of the jaw and when he didn't go down he knew he was in for a fight. The gunner hit him in the body, then beside his eye. He swung with his left again and landed and the gunner fell on him and grabbed his coat and tore the sleeve off and he clubbed him twice behind the ear and then smashed him with his right as he pushed him away. When the gunner went down his head hit first and he ran with the girl because they heard the M.P.'s coming. They got into a taxi and drove out to Rimmily Hissa along the Bosphorus, and around, and back in the cool night and went to bed and she felt as overripe as she looked but smooth, rose-petal, syrupy, smooth-bellied, big-breasted, and needed no pillow under her buttocks, and he left her before she was awake looking blowzy enough in the first daylight and turned up at the Pera Palace with a black eye, carrying his coat because one sleeve was missing.

That same night he left for Anatolia and he remembered, later on that trip, riding all day through fields of the poppies that they raised for opium and how strange it made you feel, finally, and all the distances seemed wrong, to where they had made the attack with the newly arrived Constantine officers, that did not know a goddamned thing, and the artillery had fired into the troops and the British observer had cried like a child.

That was the day he'd first seen dead men wearing white ballet skirts and upturned shoes with pompons on them. The Turks had come steadily and lumpily and he had seen the skirted men running and the officers shooting into them and running then themselves, and he and the British observer had run, too, until his lungs ached and his mouth was full of the taste of pennies, and they stopped behind some rocks and there were the Turks coming as lumpily as ever. Later he had seen the things that he could never think of and later still he had seen much worse. So when he got back to Paris that time he could not talk about it or stand to have it mentioned. And there in the café as he passed was that American poet with a pile of saucers in front of him and a stupid look on his potato face talking about the Dada movement with a Roumanian who said his name was Tristan Tzara, who always wore a monocle and had a headache, and, back at the apartment with his wife that now he loved again, the quarrel all over, the madness all over, glad to be home, the office sent his mail up to the flat. So then the letter in answer to the one he'd written came in on a platter one morning and when he saw the handwriting he went cold all over and tried to slip the letter underneath another. But his wife said, "Who is that letter from, dear?" and that was the end of the beginning of that.

He remembered the good times with them all, and the quarrels. They always picked the finest places to have the quarrels. And why had they always quarreled when he was feeling best? He had never written any of that because, at first, he never wanted to hurt anyone and then it seemed as though there was enough to write without it. But he had always thought that he would write it finally. There was so much to write. He had seen the world change; not just the events; although he had seen many of them and had watched the people, but he had seen the subtler change and he could remember how the people were at different times. He had been in it and he had watched it and it was his duty to write of it; but now he never would.

"How do you feel?" she said. She had come out from the tent now after her bath.

"All right."

"Could you eat now?" He saw Molo behind her with the folding table and the other boy with the dishes.

"I want to write," he said.

"You ought to take some broth to keep your strength up."

"I'm going to die tonight," he said. "I don't need my strength up."

"Don't be melodramatic, Harry, please," she said.

"Why don't you use your nose? I'm rotted halfway up my thigh now. What the hell should I fool with broth for? Molo bring whiskey-soda."

"Please take the broth," she said gently.

"All right."

The broth was too hot. He had to hold it in the cup until it cooled enough to take it and then he just got it down without gagging.

"You're a fine woman," he said. "Don't pay any attention to me."

She looked at him with her well-known, well-loved face from *Spur* and *Town and Country,* only a little the worse for drink, only a little the worse for bed, but *Town and Country* never showed those good breasts and those useful thighs and those lightly small-of-back-caressing hands, and as he looked and saw her well-known pleasant smile, he felt death come again. This time there was no rush. It was a puff, as of a wind that makes a candle flicker and the flame go tall.

"They can bring my net out later and hang it from the tree and build the fire up. I'm not going in the tent tonight. It's not worth moving. It's a clear night. There won't be any rain."

So this was how you died, in whispers that you did not hear. Well, there would be no more quarreling. He could promise that. The one experience that he had never had he was not going to spoil now. He probably would. You spoiled everything. But perhaps he wouldn't.

"You can't take dictation, can you?"

"I never learned," she told him.

"That's all right."

There wasn't time, of course, although it seemed as though it telescoped so that you might put it all into one paragraph if you could get it right.

There was a log house, chinked white with mortar, on a hill above the lake. There was a bell on a pole by the door to call the people in to meals. Behind the house were fields and behind the fields was the timber. A line of Lombardy poplars ran from the house to the dock. Other poplars ran along the point. A road went up to the hills along the edge of the timber and along that road he picked blackberries. Then that log house was burned down and all the guns that had been on deer foot racks above the open fire place were burned and afterwards their barrels, with the lead melted in the magazines, and the stocks burned away, lay out on the heap of ashes that were used to make lye for the big iron soap kettles, and you asked Grandfather if you could have them to play with, and he said, no. You see they were his guns still and he never bought any others. Nor did he hunt any more. The house was rebuilt in the same place out of lumber now and painted white and from its porch you saw the poplars and the lake beyond; but there were never any more guns. The barrels of the guns that had hung on the deer feet on the wall of the log house lay out there on the heap of ashes and no one ever touched them.

In the Black Forest, after the war,

we rented a trout stream and there were two ways to walk to it. One was down the valley from Triberg and around the valley road in the shade of the trees that bordered the white road, and then up a side road that went up through the hills past many small farms, with the big Schwarzwald houses, until that road crossed the stream. That was where our fishing began.

The other way was to climb steeply up to the edge of the woods and then go across the top of the hills through the pine woods, and then out to the edge of a meadow and down across this meadow to the bridge. There were birches along the stream and it was not big, but narrow, clear and fast, with pools where it had cut under the roots of the birches. At the hotel in Triberg the proprietor had a fine season. It was very pleasant and we were all great friends. The next year came the inflation and the money he had made the year before was not enough to buy supplies to open the hotel and he hanged himself.

You could dictate that, but you could not dictate the Place Contrescarpe where the flower sellers dyed their flowers in the street and the dye ran over the paving where the autobus started and the old men and the women, always drunk on wine and bad marc; and the children with their noses running in the cold; the smell of dirty sweat and poverty and drunkenness at the Café des Amateurs and the whores at the Bal Musette they lived above. The concierge who entertained the trooper of the Garde Republicaine in her loge, his horsehair plumed helmet on a chair. The locataire across the hall whose husband was a bicycle racer and her joy that morning at the Cremerie when she had opened L'Auto and seen where he placed third in Paris-Tours,

his first big race. She had blushed and laughed and then gone upstairs crying with the yellow sporting paper in her hand. The husband of the woman who ran the Bal Musette drove a taxi, and when he, Harry, had to take an early plane the husband knocked upon the door to wake him and they each drank a glass of white wine at the zinc of the bar before they started. He knew his neighbors in that quarter then because they all were poor.

Around that Place there were two kinds; the drunkards and the sportifs. The drunkards killed their poverty that way; the sportifs took it out in exercise. They were the descendants of the Communards and it was no struggle for them to know their politics. They knew who had shot their fathers, their relatives, their brothers, and their friends when the Versailles troops came in and took the town after the Commune and executed anyone they could catch with calloused hands, or who wore a cap, or carried any other sign he was a workingman. And in that poverty, and in that quarter across the street from a Boucherie Chevaline and a wine co-operative, he had written the start of all he was to do. There never was another part of Paris that he loved like that, the sprawling trees, the old white plastered houses painted brown below, the long green of the autobus in that round square, the purple flower dye upon the paving, the sudden drop down the hill of the rue Cardinal Lemoine to the river, and the other way the narrow crowded world of the rue Mouffetard. The street that ran up toward the Pantheon and the other that he always took with the bicycle, the only asphalted street in all that quarter, smooth under the tires, with the high narrow houses and the cheap tall hotel where Paul Verlaine had died. There were only two rooms in the apartment where they lived and he had a room on the top floor of that hotel that cost him sixty francs a month where he did his writing, and from it he could see the roofs and chimney pots and all the hills of Paris.

From the apartment you could only see the wood and coal man's place. He sold wine too, bad wine. The golden horse's head outside the Boucherie Chevaline where the carcasses hung yellow gold and red in the open window, and the green painted co-operative where they bought their wine; good wine and cheap. The rest was plaster walls and the windows of the neighbors. The neighbors who, at night, when some one lay drunk in the street, moaning and groaning in that typical French *ivresse* that you were propaganded to believe did not exist, would open their windows and then the murmur of talk.

"Where is the policeman? When you don't want him the bugger is always there. He's sleeping with some concierge. Get the Agent." Till someone threw a bucket of water from a window and the moaning stopped. "What's that? Water. Ah, that's intelligent." And the windows shutting. Marie, his femme de ménage, protesting against the eight-hour day saying, "If a husband works until six he gets only a little drunk on the way home and does not waste too much. If he works only until five he is drunk every night and one has no money. It is the wife of the workingman who suffers from this shortening of hours."

"Wouldn't you like some broth?" the woman asked him now.

"No, thank you very much. It is awfully good."

"Try just a little."

"I would like a whiskey-soda."

"It's not good for you."

"No. It's bad for me. Cole Porter wrote the words and the music. This knowledge that you're going mad for me."

"You know I like you to drink."

"Oh, yes. Only it's bad for me."

When she goes, he thought, I'll have all I want. Not all I want, but all there is. Ayee, he was tired. Too tired. He was going to sleep a little while. He lay still and death was not there. It must have gone around another street. It went in pairs, on bicycles, and moved absolutely silently on the pavements.

No, he had never written about Paris. Not the Paris that he cared about. But what about the rest that he had never written?

What about the ranch and the silvered gray of the sage brush, the quick, clear water in the irrigation ditches, and the heavy green of the alfalfa? The trail went up into the hills and the cattle in the summer were shy as deer. The bawling and the steady noise and slow moving mass raising a dust as you brought them down in the fall. And behind the mountains, the clear sharpness of the peak in the evening light and, riding down along the trail in the moonlight, bright across the valley. Now he remembered coming down through the timber in the dark holding the horse's tail when you could not see and all the stories that he meant to write.

About the half-wit chore boy who was left at the ranch that time and told not to let any one get any hay, and that old bastard from the Forks who had beaten the boy when he had worked for him stopping to get some feed. The boy refusing and the old man saying he would beat him again. The boy got the rifle from the kitchen

*and shot him when he tried to come
into the barn and when they came
back to the ranch he'd been dead a
week, frozen in the corral, and the
dogs had eaten part of him. But what
was left you packed on a sled wrapped
in a blanket and roped on and you got
the boy to help you haul it, and the
two of you took it out over the road
on skis, and sixty miles down to town
to turn the boy over. He having no
idea that he would be arrested. Thinking he had done his duty and that you
were his friend and he would be rewarded. He'd helped to haul the old
man in so everybody could know how
bad the old man had been and how
he'd tried to steal some feed that
didn't belong to him, and when the
sheriff put the handcuffs on the boy
he couldn't believe it. Then he started
to cry. That was one story he had
saved to write. He knew at least
twenty good stories from out there and
he had never written one. Why?*

"You tell them why," he said.

"Why what, dear?"

"Why nothing."

She didn't drink so much, now,
since she had him. But if he lived he
would never write about her, he knew
that now. Nor about any of them. The
rich were dull and they drank too
much, or they played too much backgammon. They were dull and they
were repetitious. He remembered poor
Julian and his romantic awe of them
and how he had started a story once
that began, "The very rich are different from you and me." And how
someone had said to Julian, Yes, they
have more money. But that was not
humorous to Julian. He thought they
were a special glamorous race and
when he found they weren't it
wrecked him just as much as any
other thing that wrecked him.

He had been contemptuous of those
who wrecked. You did not have to
like it because you understood it. He
could bear anything, he thought, because nothing could hurt him if he
did not care.

All right. Now he would not care
for death. One thing he had always
dreaded was the pain. He could stand
pain as well as any man, until it went
on too long, and wore him out, but
here he had something that had hurt
frightfully and just when he had
felt it breaking him, the pain had
stopped.

*He remembered long ago when
Williamson, the bombing officer, had
been hit by a stick bomb someone in
a German patrol had thrown as he was
coming in through the wire that night
and, screaming, had begged everyone
to kill him. He was a fat man, very
brave, and a good officer, although addicted to fantastic shows. But that
night he was caught in the wire, with
a flare lighting him up and his bowels
spilled out into the wire, so when they
brought him in, alive, they had to cut
him loose. Shoot me, Harry. For
Christ sake, shoot me. They had had
an argument one time about our Lord
never sending you anything you could
not bear and someone's theory had
been that meant that a certain time
the pain passed you out automatically.
But he had always remembered Williamson, that night. Nothing passed
out Williamson until he gave him all
his morphine tablets that he had always saved to use himself and then
they did not work right away.*

Still this now, that he had, was
very easy; and if it was no worse as
it went on there was nothing to worry
about. Except that he would rather
be in better company.

He thought a little about the company that he would like to have.

No, he thought, when everything

you do, you do too long, and do too late, you can't expect to find the people still there. The people all are gone. The party's over and you are with your hostess now.

I'm getting as bored with dying as with everything else, he thought.

"It's a bore," he said out loud.

"What is, my dear?"

"Anything you do too bloody long."

He looked at her face between him and the fire. She was leaning back in the chair and the firelight shone on her pleasantly lined face and he could see that she was sleepy. He heard the hyena make a noise just outside the range of the fire.

"I've been writing," he said. "But I got tired."

"Do you think you will be able to sleep?"

"Pretty sure. Why don't you turn in?"

"I like to sit here with you."

"Do you feel anything strange?" he asked her.

"No. Just a little sleepy."

"I do," he said.

He had just felt death come by again.

"You know the only thing I've never lost is curiosity," he said to her.

"You've never lost anything. You're the most complete man I've ever known."

"Christ," he said. "How little a woman knows. What is that? Your intuition?"

Because, just then, death had come and rested its head on the foot of the cot and he could smell its breath.

"Never believe any of that about a scythe and a skull," he told her. "It can be two bicycle policemen as easily or be a bird. Or it can have a wide snout like a hyena."

It had moved up on him now, but it had no shape any more. It simply occupied space.

"Tell it to go away."

It did not go away, but moved a little closer.

"You've got a hell of a breath," he told it. "You stinking bastard."

It moved up closer to him still, and now he could not speak to it, and when it saw he could not speak, it came a little closer, and now he tried to send it away without speaking, but it moved in on him so its weight was all upon his chest, and while it crouched there and he could not move, or speak, he heard the woman say, "Bwana is asleep now. Take the cot up very gently and carry it into the tent."

He could not speak to tell her to make it go away and it crouched now, heavier, so he could not breathe. And then, while they lifted the cot, suddenly it was all right and the weight went from his chest.

It was morning and had been morning for some time and he heard the plane. It showed very tiny and then made a wide circle and the boys ran out and lit the fires, using kerosene, and piled on grass so there were two big smudges at each end of the level place and the morning breeze blew them toward the camp and the plane circled twice more, low this time, and then glided down and leveled off and landed smoothly and, coming walking toward him, was old Compton in slacks, a tweed jacket, and a brown felt hat.

"What's the matter, old cock?" Compton said.

"Bad leg," he told him. "Will you have some breakfast?"

"Thanks. I'll just have some tea. It's the Puss Moth, you know. I won't be able to take the Memsahib. There's only room for one. Your lorry is on the way."

Helen had taken Compton aside and was speaking to him. Compton came back more cheery than ever.

"We'll get you right in," he said. "I'll be back for the Mem. Now I'm afraid I'll have to stop at Arusha to refuel. We'd better get going."

"What about the tea?"

"I don't really care about it, you know."

The boys had picked up the cot and carried it around the green tents and down along the rock and out onto the plain and along past the smudges that were burning brightly now, the grass all consumed, and the wind fanning the fire, to the little plane. It was difficult getting him in, but once in he lay back in the leather seat, and the leg was stuck straight out to one side of the seat where Compton sat. Compton started the motor and got in. He waved to Helen and to the boys and, as the clatter moved into the old familiar roar, they swung around with Compie watching for wart-hog holes and roared, bumping, along the stretch between the fires and with the last bump rose and he saw them all standing below, waving, and the camp beside the hill, flattening now, and the plain spreading, clumps of trees, and the bush flattening, while the game trails ran now smoothly to the dry waterholes, and there was a new water that he had never known of. The zebra, small rounded backs now, and the wildebeeste, big headed dots seeming to climb as they moved in long fingers across the plain, now scattering as the shadow came toward them, they were tiny now, and the movement had no gallop, and the plain as far as you could see, gray-yellow now and ahead old Compie's tweed back and the brown felt hat. Then they were over the first hills and the wildebeeste were trailing up them, and then they were over mountains with sudden depths of green-rising forest and the solid bamboo slopes,

and then the heavy forest again, sculptured into hills sloped down and then another plain, hot now, and purple brown, bumpy with heat and Compie looking back to see how he was riding. Then there were other mountains dark ahead.

And then instead of going on to Arusha they turned left, he evidently figured that they had the gas, and looking down he saw a pink sifting cloud, moving over the ground, and in the air, like the first snow in a blizzard, that comes from nowhere, and he knew the locusts were coming up from the south. Then they began to climb and they were going to the east it seemed, and then it darkened and they were in a storm, the rain so thick it seemed like flying through a waterfall, and then they were out and Compie turned his head and grinned and pointed and there, ahead, all he could see, as wide as all the world, great, high, and unbelievably white in the sun, was the square top of Kilimanjaro. And then he knew that there was where he was going.

Just then the hyena stopped whimpering in the night and started to make a strange, human, almost crying sound. The woman heard it and stirred uneasily. She did not wake. In her dream she was at the house on Long Island and it was the night before her daughter's début. Somehow her father was there and he had been very rude. Then the noise the hyena made was so loud she woke and for a moment she did not know where she was and she was very afraid. Then she took the flashlight and shone it on the other cot that they had carried in after Harry had gone to sleep. She could see his bulk under the mosquito bar, but somehow he had gotten his leg out and it hung down alongside the cot. The dressings had all come down and she could not look at it.

"Molo," she called, "Molo! Molo!"

Then she said, "Harry, Harry!" Then her voice rising, "Harry! Please! Oh Harry!"

There was no answer and she could not hear him breathing.

Outside the tent the hyena made the same strange noise that had awakened her. But she did not hear him for the beating of her heart.

1936

WILLIAM FAULKNER
(1897–   )

A ROSE FOR EMILY *

I

When Miss Emily Grierson died, our whole town went to her funeral: the men through a sort of respectful affection for a fallen monument, the women mostly out of curiosity to see the inside of her house, which no one save an old manservant—a combined gardener and cook—had seen in at least ten years.

It was a big, squarish frame house that had once been white, decorated with cupolas and spires and scrolled balconies in the heavily lightsome style of the seventies, set on what had once been our most select street. But garages and cotton gins had encroached and obliterated even the august names of that neighborhood; only Miss Emily's house was left, lifting its stubborn and coquettish decay above the cotton wagons and the gasoline pumps—an eyesore among eyesores. And now Miss Emily had gone to join the representatives of those august names where they lay in the

* From *These Thirteen* by William Faulkner; by permission of Jonathan Cape & Robert Ballou, Inc. Copyright, 1931.

cedar-bemused cemetery among the ranked and anonymous graves of Union and Confederate soldiers who fell at the battle of Jefferson.

Alive, Miss Emily had been a tradition, a duty, and a care; a sort of hereditary obligation upon the town, dating from that day in 1894 when Colonel Sartoris, the mayor—he who fathered the edict that no Negro woman should appear on the streets without an apron—remitted her taxes, the dispensation dating from the death of her father on into perpetuity. Not that Miss Emily would have accepted charity. Colonel Sartoris invented an involved tale to the effect that Miss Emily's father had loaned money to the town, which the town, as a matter of business, preferred this way of repaying. Only a man of Colonel Sartoris' generation and thought could have invented it, and only a woman could have believed it.

When the next generation, with its more modern ideas, became mayors and aldermen, this arrangement created some little dissatisfaction. On the first of the year they mailed her a tax notice. February came, and there was no reply. They wrote her a formal letter, asking her to call at the sheriff's office at her convenience. A week later the mayor wrote her himself, offering to call or to send his car for her, and received in reply a note on paper of an archaic shape, in a thin, flowing calligraphy in faded ink, to the effect that she no longer went out at all. The tax notice was also enclosed, without comment.

They called a special meeting of the Board of Aldermen. A deputation waited upon her, knocked at the door through which no visitor had passed since she ceased giving china-painting lessons eight or ten years earlier. They were admitted by the old Negro into a dim hall from which a stairway mounted into still more shadow. It smelled of dust and disuse—a close, dank smell. The Negro led them into the parlor. It was furnished in heavy, leather-covered furniture. When the Negro opened the blinds of one window, they could see that the leather was cracked; and when they sat down, a faint dust rose sluggishly about their thighs, spinning with slow motes in the single sun-ray. On a tarnished gilt easel before the fireplace stood a crayon portrait of Miss Emily's father.

They rose when she entered—a small, fat woman in black, with a thin gold chain descending to her waist and vanishing into her belt, leaning on an ebony cane with a tarnished gold head. Her skeleton was small and spare; perhaps that was why what would have been merely plumpness in another was obesity in her. She looked bloated, like a body long submerged in motionless water, and of that pallid hue. Her eyes, lost in the fatty ridges of her face, looked like two small pieces of coal pressed into a lump of dough as they moved from one face to another while the visitors stated their errand.

She did not ask them to sit. She just stood in the door and listened quietly until the spokesman came to a stumbling halt. Then they could hear the invisible watch ticking at the end of the gold chain.

Her voice was dry and cold. "I have no taxes in Jefferson. Colonel Sartoris explained it to me. Perhaps one of you can gain access to the city records and satisfy yourselves."

"But we have. We are the city authorities, Miss Emily. Didn't you get a notice from the sheriff, signed by him?"

"I received a paper, yes," Miss Emily said. "Perhaps he considers himself the sheriff. . . . I have no taxes in Jefferson."

"But there is nothing on the books to show that, you see. We must go by the—"

"See Colonel Sartoris. I have no taxes in Jefferson."

"But, Miss Emily—"

"See Colonel Sartoris." (Colonel Sartoris had been dead almost ten years.) "I have no taxes in Jefferson. Tobe!" The Negro appeared. "Show these gentlemen out."

II

So she vanquished them, horse and foot, just as she had vanquished their fathers thirty years before about the smell. That was two years after her father's death and a short time after her sweetheart—the one we believed would marry her—had deserted her. After her father's death she went out very little; after her sweetheart went away, people hardly saw her at all. A few of the ladies had the temerity to call, but were not received, and the only sign of life about the place was the Negro man—a young man then—going in and out with a market basket.

"Just as if a man—any man—could keep a kitchen properly," the ladies said; so they were not surprised when the smell developed. It was another link between the gross, teeming world and the high and mighty Griersons.

A neighbor, a woman, complained to the mayor, Judge Stevens, eighty years old.

"But what will you have me do about it, madam?" he said.

"Why, send her word to stop it," the woman said. "Isn't there a law?"

"I'm sure that won't be necessary," Judge Stevens said. "It's probably just a snake or a rat that nigger of hers killed in the yard. I'll speak to him about it."

The next day he received two more complaints, one from a man who came in diffident deprecation. "We really must do something about it, Judge. I'd be the last one in the world to bother Miss Emily, but we've got to do something." That night the Board of Aldermen met—three graybeards and one younger man, a member of the rising generation.

"It's simple enough," he said. "Send her word to have her place cleaned up. Give her a certain time to do it in, and if she don't . . ."

"Dammit, sir," Judge Stevens said, "will you accuse a lady to her face of smelling bad?"

So the next night, after midnight, four men crossed Miss Emily's lawn and slunk about the house like burglars, sniffing along the base of the brickwork and at the cellar openings while one of them performed a regular sowing motion with his hand out of a sack slung from his shoulder. They broke open the cellar door and sprinkled lime there, and in all the outbuildings. As they recrossed the lawn, a window that had been dark was lighted and Miss Emily sat in it, the light behind her, and her upright torso motionless as that of an idol. They crept quietly across the lawn and into the shadow of the locusts that lined the streets. After a week or two the smell went away.

That was when people had begun to feel really sorry for her. People in our town, remembering how old lady Wyatt, her great-aunt, had gone completely crazy at last, believed that the Griersons held themselves a little too high for what they really were. None of the young men were quite good enough to Miss Emily and such. We had long thought of them as a tableau; Miss Emily a slender figure in white in the background, her father a spraddled silhouette in the foreground, his back to her and clutching a horsewhip, the two of them framed by the back-flung front door. So when she got to be thirty and was still single, we were not pleased exactly, but vindicated; even with insanity in the family she wouldn't have turned down all of her chances if they had really materialized.

When her father died, it got about that the house was all that was left to her; and in a way, people were glad. At last they could pity Miss Emily. Being left alone, and a pauper, she had become humanized. Now she too would know the old thrill and the old despair of a penny more or less.

The day after his death all the ladies prepared to call at the house and offer condolence and aid, as is our custom. Miss Emily met them at the door, dressed as usual and with no trace of grief on her face. She told them that her father was not dead. She did that for three days, with the ministers calling on her, and the doctors, trying to persuade her to let them dispose of the body. Just as they were about to resort to law and force, she broke down, and they buried her father quickly.

We did not say she was crazy then. We believed she had to do that. We remembered all the young men her father had driven away, and we knew that with nothing left, she would have to cling to that which had robbed her, as people will.

III

She was sick for a long time. When we saw her again, her hair was cut short, making her look like a girl, with a vague resemblance to those angels in colored church windows—sort of tragic and serene.

The town had just let the contracts for paving the sidewalks, and in the summer after her father's death they began the work. The construction company came with niggers and mules and machinery, and a foreman named Homer Barron, a Yankee—a big, dark, ready man, with a big voice and eyes lighter than his face. The little boys would follow in groups to hear him cuss the niggers, and the niggers singing in time to the rise and fall of picks. Pretty soon he knew everybody in town. Whenever you heard a lot of laughing anywhere about the square, Homer Barron would be in the center of the group. Presently we began to see him and Miss Emily on Sunday afternoons driving in the yellow-wheeled buggy and the matched team of bays from the livery stable.

At first we were glad that Miss Emily would have an interest, because the ladies all said, "Of course a Grierson would not think seriously of a Northerner, a day laborer." But there were still others, older people, who said that even grief could not cause a real lady to forget *noblesse oblige* —without calling it *noblesse oblige.* They just said, "Poor Emily. Her kinsfolk should come to her." She had some kin in Alabama; but years ago her father had fallen out with them over the estate of old lady Wyatt, the crazy woman, and there was no communication between the two families. They had not even been represented at the funeral.

And as soon as the old people said, "Poor Emily," the whispering began. "Do you suppose it's really so?" they said to one another. "Of course it is. What else could . . ." This behind their hands; rustling of craned silk and satin behind jalousies closed upon the sun of Sunday afternoon as the thin, swift clop-clop-clop of the matched team passed: "Poor Emily."

She carried her head high enough— even when we believed that she was fallen. It was as if she demanded more than ever the recognition of her dignity as the last Grierson; as if it had

wanted that touch of earthiness to reaffirm her imperviousness. Like when she bought the rat poison, the arsenic. That was over a year after they had began to say "Poor Emily," and while the two female cousins were visiting her.

"I want some poison," she said to the druggist. She was over thirty then, still a slight woman, though thinner than usual, with cold, haughty black eyes in a face the flesh of which was strained across the temples and about the eye-sockets as you imagine a lighthouse-keeper's face ought to look. "I want some poison," she said.

"Yes, Miss Emily. What kind? For rats and such? I'd recom—"

"I want the best you have. I don't care what kind."

The druggist named several. "They'll kill anything up to an elephant. But what you want is—"

"Arsenic," Miss Emily said. "Is that a good one?"

"Is . . . arsenic? Yes, ma'am. But what you want—"

"I want arsenic."

The druggist looked down at her. She looked back at him, erect, her face like a strained flag. "Why, of course," the druggist said. "If that's what you want. But the law requires you to tell what you are going to use it for."

Miss Emily just stared at him, her head tilted back in order to look him eye for eye, until he looked away and went and got the arsenic and wrapped it up. The Negro delivery boy brought her the package; the druggist didn't come back. When she opened the package at home there was written on the box, under the skull and bones: "For rats."

IV

So the next day we all said, "She will kill herself"; and we said it would be the best thing. When she had first begun to be seen with Homer Barron, we had said, "She will marry him." Then we said, "She will persuade him yet," because Homer himself had remarked—he liked men, and it was known that he drank with the younger men in the Elks' Club—that he was not a marrying man. Later we said, "Poor Emily" behind the jalousies as they passed on Sunday afternoon in the glittering buggy, Miss Emily with her head high and Homer Barron with his hat cocked and a cigar in his teeth, reins and whip in a yellow glove.

Then some of the ladies began to say that it was a disgrace to the town and a bad example to the young people. The men did not want to interfere, but at last the ladies forced the Baptist minister—Miss Emily's people were Episcopal—to call upon her. He would never divulge what happened during that interview, but he refused to go back again. The next Sunday they again drove about the streets, and the following day the minister's wife wrote to Miss Emily's relations in Alabama.

So she had blood-kin under her roof again and we sat back to watch developments. At first nothing happened. Then we were sure that they were to be married. We learned that Miss Emily had been to the jeweler's and ordered a man's toilet set in silver, with the letters H. B. on each piece. Two days later we learned that she had bought a complete outfit of men's clothing, including a nightshirt, and we said, "They are married." We were really glad. We were glad because the two female cousins were even more Grierson than Miss Emily had ever been.

So we were not surprised when Homer Barron—the streets had been finished some time since—was gone. We were a little disappointed that

there was not a public blowing-off, but we believed that he had gone on to prepare for Miss Emily's coming, or to give her a chance to get rid of the cousins. (By that time it was a cabal, and we were all Miss Emily's allies to help circumvent the cousins.) Sure enough, after another week they departed. And, as we had expected all along, within three days Homer Barron was back in town. A neighbor saw the Negro man admit him at the kitchen door at dusk one evening.

And that was the last we saw of Homer Barron. And of Miss Emily for some time. The Negro man went in and out with the market basket, but the front door remained closed. Now and then we would see her at a window for a moment, as the men did that night when they sprinkled the lime, but for almost six months she did not appear on the streets. Then we knew that this was to be expected too; as if that quality of her father which had thwarted her woman's life so many times had been too virulent and too furious to die.

When we next saw Miss Emily, she had grown fat and her hair was turning gray. During the next few years it grew grayer and grayer until it attained an even pepper-and-salt iron-gray, when it ceased turning. Up to the day of her death at seventy-four it was still that vigorous iron-gray, like the hair of an active man.

From that time on her front door remained closed, save for a period of six or seven years, when she was about forty, during which she gave lessons in china-painting. She fitted up a studio in one of the downstairs rooms, where the daughters and granddaughters of Colonel Sartoris' contemporaries were sent to her with the same regularity and in the same spirit that they were sent to church.

on Sundays with a twenty-five cent piece for the collection plate. Meanwhile her taxes had been remitted.

Then the newer generation became the backbone and the spirit of the town, and the painting pupils grew up and fell away and did not send their children to her with boxes of color and tedious brushes and pictures cut from the ladies' magazines. The front door closed upon the last one and remained closed for good. When the town got free postal delivery, Miss Emily alone refused to let them fasten the metal numbers above her door and attach a mailbox to it. She would not listen to them.

Daily, monthly, yearly we watched the Negro grow grayer and more stooped, going in and out with the market basket. Each December we sent her a tax notice, which would be returned by the post office a week later, unclaimed. Now and then we would see her in one of the downstairs windows—she had evidently shut up the top floor of the house— like the carven torso of an idol in a niche, looking or not looking at us, we could never tell which. Thus she passed from generation to generation —dear, inescapable, impervious, tranquil, and perverse.

And so she died. Fell ill in the house filled with dust and shadows, with only a doddering Negro man to wait on her. We did not even know she was sick; we had long since given up trying to get any information from the Negro. He talked to no one, probably not even to her, for his voice had grown harsh and rusty, as if from disuse.

She died in one of the downstairs rooms, in a heavy walnut bed with a curtain, her gray head propped on a pillow yellow and moldy with age and lack of sunlight.

V

The Negro met the first of the ladies at the front door and let them in, with their hushed, sibilant voices and their quick, curious glances, and then he disappeared. He walked right through the house and out the back and was not seen again.

The two female cousins came at once. They held the funeral on the second day, with the town coming to look at Miss Emily beneath a mass of bought flowers, with the crayon face of her father musing profoundly above the bier and the ladies sibilant and macabre; and the very old men—some in their brushed Confederate uniforms —on the porch and the lawn, talking of Miss Emily as if she had been a contemporary of theirs, believing that they had danced with her and courted her perhaps, confusing time with its mathematical progression, as the old do, to whom all the past is not a diminishing road, but, instead, a huge meadow which no winter ever quite touches, divided from them now by the narrow bottle-neck of the most recent decade of years.

Already we knew that there was one room in that region above stairs which no one had seen in forty years, and which would have to be forced. They waited until Miss Emily was decently in the ground before they opened it.

The violence of breaking down the door seemed to fill this room with pervading dust. A thin, acrid pall as of the tomb seemed to lie everywhere upon this room decked and furnished as for a bridal: upon the valance curtains of faded rose color, upon the rose-shaded lights, upon the dressing table, upon the delicate array of crystal and the man's toilet things backed with tarnished silver, silver so tarnished that the monogram was obscured. Among them lay a collar and tie, as if they had just been removed, which, lifted, left upon the surface a pale crescent in the dust. Upon a chair hung the suit, carefully folded; beneath it the two mute shoes and the discarded socks.

The man himself lay in the bed. For a long while we just stood there, looking down at the profound and fleshless grin. The body had apparently once lain in the attitude of an embrace, but now the long sleep that outlasts love, that conquers even the grimace of love, had cuckolded him. What was left of him, rotted beneath what was left of the nightshirt, had become inextricable from the bed in which he lay; and upon him and upon the pillow beside him lay that even coating of the patient and biding dust.

Then we noticed that in the second pillow was the indentation of a head. One of us lifted something from it, and leaning forward, that faint and invisible dust dry and acrid in the nostrils, we saw a long strand of iron-gray hair.

1930

FROM   *THE HAMLET* *

[SPOTTED HORSES]

I

A little while before sundown the men lounging about the gallery of the store saw, coming up the road from the south, a covered wagon drawn by mules and followed by a considerable string of obviously alive objects which in the levelling sun resembled varisized and -colored tatters torn at random from large billboards—circus posters, say—attached to the rear of the

wagon and inherent with its own separate and collective motion, like the tail of a kite.

"What in the hell is that?" one said.

"It's a circus," Quick said. They began to rise, watching the wagon. Now they could see that the animals behind the wagon were horses. Two men rode in the wagon.

"Hell fire," the first man—his name was Freeman—said. "It's Flem Snopes." They were all standing when the wagon came up and stopped and Snopes got down and approached the steps. He might have departed only this morning. He wore the same cloth cap, the minute bow tie against the white shirt, the same gray trousers. He mounted the steps.

"Howdy, Flem," Quick said. The other looked briefly at all of them and none of them, mounting the steps. "Starting you a circus?"

"Gentlemen," he said. He crossed the gallery; they made way for him. Then they descended the steps and approached the wagon, at the tail of which the horses stood in a restive clump, larger than rabbits and gaudy as parrots and shackled to one another and to the wagon itself with sections of barbed wire. Calico-coated, small-bodied, with delicate legs and pink faces in which their mismatched eyes rolled wild and subdued, they huddled, gaudy, motionless, and alert, wild as deer, deadly as rattlesnakes, quiet as doves. The men stood at a respectful distance, looking at them. At that moment Jody Varner came through the group, shouldering himself to the front of it.

"Watch yourself, doc," a voice said from the rear. But it was already too late. The nearest animal rose on its hind legs with lightning rapidity and struck twice with its forefeet at Varner's face, faster than a boxer, the movement of its surge against the wire which held it travelling backward among the rest of the band in a wave of thuds and lunges. "Hup, you broom-tailed, hay-burning sidewinders," the same voice said. This was the second man who had arrived in the wagon. He was a stranger. He wore a heavy, densely black moustache, a wide pale hat. When he thrust himself through and turned to herd them back from the horses they saw, thrust into the hip pockets of his tight jeans pants, the butt of a heavy pearl-handled pistol and a florid carton such as small cakes come in. "Keep away from them, boys," he said. "They've got kind of skittish, they ain't been rode in so long."

"Since when have they been rode?" Quick said. The stranger looked at Quick. He had a broad, quite cold, wind-gnawed face and bleak, cold eyes. His belly fitted neat and smooth as a peg into the tight trousers.

"I reckon that was when they were rode on the ferry to get across the Mississippi River," Varner said. The stranger looked at him. "My name's Varner," Jody said.

"Hipps," the other said. "Call me Buck." Across the left side of his head, obliterating the tip of that ear, was a savage and recent gash gummed over with a blackish substance like axlegrease. They looked at the scar. Then they watched him remove the carton from his pocket and tilt a gingersnap into his hand and put the gingersnap into his mouth, beneath the moustache.

"You and Flem have some trouble back yonder?" Quick said. The stranger ceased chewing. When he looked directly at anyone, his eyes became like two pieces of flint turned suddenly up in dug earth.

"Back where?" he said.

"Your nigh ear," Quick said.

"Oh," the other said. "That." He touched his ear. "That was my mistake. I was absent-minded one night when I was staking them out. Studying about something else and forgot how long the wire was." He chewed. They looked at his ear. "Happen to any man careless around a horse. Put a little axle-dope on it and you won't notice it tomorrow though. They're pretty lively now, lazing along all day doing nothing. It'll work out of them in a couple of days." He put another gingersnap into his mouth, chewing, "Don't you believe they'll gentle?" No one answered. They looked at the ponies, grave and noncommittal. Jody turned and went back into the store. "Them's good, gentle ponies," the stranger said. "Watch now." He put the carton back into his pocket and approached the horses, his hand extended. The nearest one was standing on three legs now. It appeared to be asleep. Its eyelid drooped over the cerulean eye; its head was shaped like an ironing-board. Without even raising the eyelid it flicked its head, the yellow teeth cropped. For an instant it and the man appeared to be inextricable in one violence. Then they became motionless, the stranger's high heels dug into the earth, one hand gripping the animal's nostrils, holding the horse's head wrenched half around while it breathed in hoarse, smothered groans. "See?" the stranger said in a panting voice, the veins standing white and rigid in his neck and along his jaw. "See? All you got to do is handle them a little and work hell out of them for a couple of days. Now look out. Give me room back there." They gave back a little. The stranger gathered himself then sprang away. As he did so, a second horse slashed at his back, severing his vest from collar to hem down the back exactly as the trick swordsman severs a floating veil with one stroke.

"Sho now," Quick said. "But suppose a man don't happen to own a vest."

At that moment Jody Varner, followed by the blacksmith, thrust through them again. "All right, Buck," he said. "Better get them on into the lot. Eck here will help you." The stranger, the severed halves of the vest swinging from either shoulder, mounted to the wagon seat, the blacksmith following.

"Get up, you transmogrified hallucinations of Job and Jezebel," the stranger said. The wagon moved on, the tethered ponies coming gaudily into motion behind it, behind which in turn the men followed at a respectful distance, on up the road and into the lane and so to the lot gate behind Mrs. Littlejohn's. Eck got down and opened the gate. The wagon passed through but when the ponies saw the fence the herd surged backward against the wire which attached it to the wagon, standing on its collective hind legs and then trying to turn within itself, so that the wagon moved backward for a few feet until the Texan, cursing, managed to saw the mules about and so lock the wheels. The men following had already fallen rapidly back. "Here, Eck," the Texan said. "Get up here and take the reins." The blacksmith got back in the wagon and took the reins. Then they watched the Texan descend, carrying a looped-up blacksnake whip, and go around to the rear of the herd and drive it through the gate, the whip snaking about the harlequin rumps in methodical and pistol-like reports. Then the watchers hurried across Mrs. Littlejohn's yard and mounted to the veranda, one end of which overlooked the lot.

"How you reckon he ever got them tied together?" Freeman said.

"I'd a heap rather watch how he

aims to turn them loose," Quick said. The Texan had climbed back into the halted wagon. Presently he and Eck both appeared at the rear end of the open hood. The Texan grasped the wire and began to draw the first horse up to the wagon, the animal plunging and surging back against the wire as though trying to hang itself, the contagion passing back through the herd from animal to animal until they were rearing and plunging back again against the wire.

"Come on, grab a holt," the Texan said. Eck grasped the wire also. The horses laid back against it, the pink faces tossing above the back-surging mass. "Pull him up, pull him up," the Texan said sharply. "They couldn't get up here in the wagon even if they wanted to." The wagon moved gradually backward until the head of the first horse was snubbed up to the tail-gate. The Texan took a turn of the wire quickly about one of the wagon stakes. "Keep the slack out of it," he said. He vanished and reappeared, almost in the same second, with a pair of heavy wire-cutters. "Hold them like that," he said, and leaped. He vanished, broad hat, flapping vest, wire-cutters and all, into a kaleidoscopic maelstrom of long teeth and wild eyes and slashing feet, from which presently the horses began to burst one by one like partridges flushing, each wearing a necklace of barbed wire. The first one crossed the lot at top speed, on a straight line. It galloped into the fence without any diminution whatever. The wire gave, recovered, and slammed the horse to earth where it lay for a moment, glaring, its legs still galloping in air. It scrambled up without having ceased to gallop and crossed the lot and galloped into the opposite fence and was slammed again to earth. The others were now freed. They whipped and whirled about the lot like dizzy fish in a bowl. It had seemed like a big lot until now, but now the very idea that all that fury and motion should be transpiring inside any one fence was something to be repudiated with contempt, like a mirror trick. From the ultimate dust the stranger, carrying the wire-cutters and his vest completely gone now, emerged. He was not running, he merely moved with a light-poised and watchful celerity, weaving among the calico rushes of the animals, feinting and dodging like a boxer until he reached the gate and crossed the yard and mounted to the veranda. One sleeve of his shirt hung only at one point from his shoulder. He ripped it off and wiped his face with it and threw it away and took out the paper carton and shook a gingersnap into his hand. He was breathing only a little heavily. "Pretty lively now," he said. "But it'll work out of them in a couple of days." The ponies still streaked back and forth through the growing dusk like hysterical fish, but not so violently now.

"What'll you give a man to reduce them odds a little for you?" Quick said. The Texan looked at him, the eyes bleak, pleasant and hard above the chewing jaw, the heavy moustache. "To take one of them off your hands?" Quick said.

At that moment the little periwinkle-eyed boy came along the veranda, saying, "Papa, papa; where's papa?"

"Who you looking for, sonny?" one said.

"It's Eck's boy," Quick said. "He's still out yonder in the wagon. Helping Mr. Buck here." The boy went on to the end of the veranda, in diminutive overalls—a miniature replica of the men themselves.

"Papa," he said. "Papa." The blacksmith was still leaning from the rear of the wagon, still holding the end of the severed wire. The ponies, bunched for the moment, now slid past the wagon, flowing, stringing out again so that they appeared to have doubled in number, rushing on; the hard, rapid, light patter of unshod hooves came out of the dust. "Mamma says to come on to supper," the boy said.

The moon was almost full then. When supper was over and they had gathered again along the veranda, the alteration was hardly one of visibility even. It was merely a translation from the lapidary-dimensional of day to the treacherous and silver receptivity in which the horses huddled in mazy camouflage, or singly or in pairs rushed, fluid, phantom, and unceasing, to huddle again in mirage-like clumps from which came high, abrupt squeals and the vicious thudding of hooves.

Ratliff was among them now. He had returned just before supper. He had not dared to take his team into the lot at all. They were now in Bookwright's stable a half mile from the store. "So Flem has come home again," he said. "Well, well, well. Will Varner paid to get him to Texas, so I reckon it ain't no more than fair for you fellows to pay the freight on him back." From the lot there came a high, thin squeal. One of the animals emerged. It seemed not to gallop but to flow, bodiless, without dimension. Yet there was the rapid light beat of hard hooves on the packed earth.

"He ain't said they was his yet," Quick said.

"He ain't said they ain't neither," Freeman said.

"I see," Ratliff said. "That's what you are holding back on. Until he tells you whether they are his or not. Or maybe you can wait until the auction's

over and split up and some can follow
Flem and some can follow that Texas
fellow and watch to see which one
spends the money. But then, when a
man's done got trimmed, I don't
reckon he cares who's got the money."

"Maybe if Ratliff would leave here
tonight, they wouldn't make him buy
one of them ponies tomorrow," a third
said.

"That's fact," Ratliff said. "A fellow
can dodge a Snopes if he just starts
lively enough. In fact, I don't believe
he would have to pass more than two
folks before he would have another
victim intervened betwixt them. You
folks ain't going to buy them things
sho enough, are you?" Nobody answered. They sat on the steps, their
backs against the veranda posts, or on
the railing itself. Only Ratliff and
Quick sat in chairs, so that to them
the others were black silhouettes
against the dreaming lambence of the
moonlight beyond the veranda. The
pear tree across the road opposite was
now in full and frosty bloom, the
twigs and branches springing not
outward from the limbs but standing
motionless and perpendicular above
the horizontal boughs like the separate
and upstreaming hair of a drowned
woman sleeping upon the uttermost
floor of the windless and tideless sea.

"Anse McCallum brought two of
them horses back from Texas once,"
one of the men on the steps said. He
did not move to speak. He was not
speaking to anyone. "It was a good
team. A little light. He worked it for
ten years. Light work, it was."

"I mind it," another said. "Anse
claimed he traded fourteen rifle cartridges for both of them, didn't he?"

"It was the rifle too, I heard," a
third said.

"No, it was just the shells," the first
said. "The fellow wanted to swap him
four more for the rifle too, but Anse

said he never needed them. Cost too
much to get six of them back to Mississippi."

"Sho," the second said. "When a
man don't have to invest so much into
a horse or a team, he don't need to
expect so much from it." The three
of them were not talking any louder,
they were merely talking among themselves, to one another, as if they sat
there alone. Ratliff, invisible in the
shadow against the wall, made a
sound, harsh, sardonic, not loud.

"Ratliff's laughing," a fourth said.

"Don't mind me," Ratliff said. The
three speakers had not moved. They
did not move now, yet there seemed
to gather about the three silhouettes
something stubborn, convinced, and
passive, like children who have been
chidden. A bird, a shadow, fleet and
dark and swift, curved across the
moonlight, upward into the pear tree
and began to sing; a mockingbird.

"First one I've noticed this year,"
Freeman said.

"You can hear them along Whiteleaf every night," the first man said.
"I heard one in February. In that
snow. Singing in a gum."

"Gum is the first tree to put out,"
the third said. "That was why. It
made it feel like singing, fixing to put
out that way. That was why it taken
a gum."

"Gum first to put out?" Quick said.
"What about willow?"

"Willow ain't a tree," Freeman said.
"It's a weed."

"Well, I don't know what it is,"
the fourth said. "But it ain't no weed.
Because you can grub up a weed and
you are done with it. I been grubbing
up a clump of willows outen my
spring pasture for fifteen years. They
are the same size every year. Only
difference is, it's just two or three
more trees every time."

"And if I was you," Ratliff said,

"that's just exactly where I would be come sunup tomorrow. Which of course you ain't going to do. I reckon there ain't nothing under the sun or in Frenchman's Bend neither that can keep you folks from giving Flem Snopes and that Texas man your money. But I'd sholy like to know just exactly who I was giving my money to. Seems like Eck here would tell you. Seems like he'd do that for his neighbors, don't it? Besides being Flem's cousin, him and that boy of his, Wallstreet, helped that Texas man tote water for them tonight and Eck's going to help him feed them in the morning too. Why, maybe Eck will be the one that will catch them and lead them up one at a time for you folks to bid on them. Ain't that right, Eck?"

The other man sitting on the steps with his back against the post was the blacksmith. "I don't know," he said.

"Boys," Ratliff said, "Eck knows all about them horses. Flem's told him, how much they cost and how much him and that Texas man aim to get for them, make off of them. Come on, Eck. Tell us." The other did not move, sitting on the top step, not quite facing them, sitting there beneath the successive layers of their quiet and intent concentrated listening and waiting.

"I don't know," he said. Ratliff began to laugh. He sat in the chair, laughing while the others sat or lounged upon the steps and the railing, sitting beneath his laughing as Eck had sat beneath their listening and waiting. Ratliff ceased laughing. He rose. He yawned, quite loud.

"All right. You folks can buy them critters if you want to. But me, I'd just as soon buy a tiger or a rattlesnake. And if Flem Snopes offered me either one of them, I would be afraid to touch it for fear it would turn out to be a painted dog or a piece of garden hose when I went up to take possession of it. I bid you one and all goodnight." He entered the house. They did not look after him, though after a while they all shifted a little and looked down into the lot, upon the splotchy, sporadic surge and flow of the horses, from among which from time to time came an abrupt squeal, a thudding blow. In the pear tree the mockingbird's idiot reiteration pulsed and purled.

"Anse McCallum made a good team outen them two of hisn," the first man said. "They was a little light. That was all."

When the sun rose the next morning a wagon and three saddled mules stood in Mrs. Littlejohn's lane and six men and Eck Snopes' son were already leaning on the fence, looking at the horses which huddled in a quiet clump before the barn door, watching the men in their turn. A second wagon came up the road and into the lane and stopped, and then there were eight men beside the boy standing at the fence, beyond which the horses stood, their blue-and-brown eyeballs rolling alertly in their gaudy faces. "So this here is the Snopes circus, is it?" one of the newcomers said. He glanced at the faces, then he went to the end of the row and stood beside the blacksmith and the little boy. "Are them Flem's horses?" he said to the blacksmith.

"Eck don't know who them horses belong to any more than we do," one of the others said. "He knows that Flem come here on the same wagon with them, because he saw him. But that's all."

"And all he will know," a second said. "His own kin will be the last man in the world to find out anything about Flem Snopes' business."

"No," the first said. "He wouldn't even be that. The first man Flem would tell his business to would be the man that was left after the last man died. Flem Snopes don't even tell himself what he is up to. Not if he was laying in bed with himself in a empty house in the dark of the moon."

"That's a fact," a third said. "Flem would trim Eck or any other of his kin quick as he would us. Ain't that right, Eck?"

"I don't know," Eck said. They were watching the horses, which at that moment broke into a high-eared, stiff-kneed swirl and flowed in a patchwork wave across the lot and brought up again, facing the men along the fence, so they did not hear the Texan until he was among them. He wore a new shirt and another vest a little too small for him and he was just putting the paper carton back into his hip pocket.

"Morning, morning," he said. "Come to get an early pick, have you? Want to make me an offer for one or two before the bidding starts and runs the prices up?" They had not looked at the stranger long. They were not looking at him now, but at the horses in the lot, which had lowered their heads, snuffing into the dust.

"I reckon we'll look a while first," one said.

"You are in time to look at them eating breakfast, anyhow," the Texan said. "Which is more than they done without they staid up all night." He opened the gate and entered it. At once the horses jerked their heads up, watching him. "Here, Eck," the Texan said over his shoulder, "two or three of you boys help me drive them into the barn." After a moment Eck and two others approached the gate, the little boy at his father's heels, though the other did not see him until he turned to shut the gate.

"You stay out of here," Eck said. "One of them things will snap your head off same as a acorn before you even know it." He shut the gate and went on after the others, whom the Texan had now waved fanwise outward as he approached the horses which now drew into a restive huddle, beginning to mill slightly, watching the men. Mrs. Littlejohn came out of the kitchen and crossed the yard to the woodpile, watching the lot. She picked up two or three sticks of wood and paused, watching the lot again. Now there were two more men standing at the fence.

"Come on, come on," the Texan said. "They won't hurt you. They just ain't never been in under a roof before."

"I just as lief let them stay out here, if that's what they want to do," Eck said.

"Get yourself a stick—there's a bunch of wagon stakes against the fence yonder—and when one of them tries to rush you, bust him over the head so he will understand what you mean." One of the men went to the fence and got three of the stakes and returned and distributed them. Mrs. Littlejohn, her armful of wood complete now, paused again halfway back to the house, looking into the lot. The little boy was directly behind his father again, though this time the father had not discovered him yet. The men advanced toward the horses, the huddle of which began to break into gaudy units turning inward upon themselves. The Texan was cursing them in a loud steady cheerful voice. "Get in there, you banjo-faced jack rabbits. Don't hurry them, now. Let them take their time. Hi! Get in there. What do you think that barn is—a law court maybe? Or maybe a church and somebody is going to take up a collection on you?" The animals fell slowly back. Now and then one feinted to break from the huddle, the Texan driving it back each time with skillfully thrown bits of dirt. Then one at the rear saw the barn door just behind it but before the herd could break the Texan snatched the wagon stake from Eck and, followed by one of the other men, rushed at the horses and began to lay about the heads and shoulders, choosing by unerring instinct the point animal and striking it first square in the face then on the withers as it turned and then on the rump as it turned further, so that when the break came it was reversed and the entire herd rushed into the long open hallway and brought up against the further wall with a hollow, thunderous sound like that of a collapsing mine-shaft. "Seems to have held all right," the Texan said. He and the other man slammed the half-length doors and looked over them into the tunnel of the barn, at the far end of which the ponies were now a splotchy, phantom moiling punctuated by crackings of wooden partitions and the dry reports of hooves which gradually died away. "Yep, it held all right," the Texan said. The other two came to the doors and looked over them. The little boy came up beside his father now, trying to see through a crack, and Eck saw him.

"Didn't I tell you to stay out of here?" Eck said. "Don't you know them things will kill you quicker than you can say scat? You go and get outside of that fence and stay there."

"Why don't you get your paw to buy you one of them, Wall?" one of the men said.

"Me buy one of them things?" Eck said. "When I can go to the river anytime and catch me a snapping turtle or a moccasin for nothing? You go on, now. Get out of here and stay out." The Texan had entered the barn.

One of the men closed the doors after him and put the bar up again and over the top of the doors they watched the Texan go on down the hallway, toward the ponies which now huddled like gaudy phantoms in the gloom, quiet now and already beginning to snuff experimentally into the long lip-worn trough fastened against the rear wall. The little boy had merely gone around behind his father, to the other side, where he stood peering now through a knot-hole in a plank. The Texan opened a smaller door in the wall and entered it, though almost immediately he reappeared.

"I don't see nothing but shelled corn in here," he said. "Snopes said he would send some hay up here last night."

"Won't they eat corn either?" one of the men said.

"I don't know," the Texan said. "They ain't never seen any that I know of. We'll find out in a minute though." He disappeared, though they could still hear him in the crib. Then he emerged once more, carrying a big double-ended feed-basket, and retreated into the gloom where the parti-colored rumps of the horses were now ranged quietly along the feeding-trough. Mrs. Littlejohn appeared once more, on the veranda this time, carrying a big brass dinner bell. She raised it to make the first stroke. A small commotion set up among the ponies as the Texan approached but he began to speak to them at once, in a brisk loud unemphatic mixture of cursing and cajolery, disappearing among them. The men at the door heard the dry rattling of the corn-pellets into the trough, a sound broken by a single snort of amazed horror. A plank cracked with a loud report; before their eyes the depths of the hallway dissolved in loud fury, and while they stared over the doors, unable yet to begin to move, the entire interior exploded into mad tossing shapes like a downrush of flames.

"Hell fire," one of them said. "Jump!" he shouted. The three turned and ran frantically for the wagon, Eck last. Several voices from the fence were now shouting something but Eck did not even hear them until, in the act of scrambling madly at the tail-gate, he looked behind him and saw the little boy still leaning to the knot-hole in the door which in the next instant vanished into match-wood, the knot-hole itself exploding from his eye and leaving him, motion-less in the diminutive overalls and still leaning forward a little until he vanished utterly beneath the tower-ing parti-colored wave full of feet and glaring eyes and wild teeth which, overtopping, burst into scattering units, revealing at last the gaping orifice and the little boy still standing in it, unscratched, his eye still leaned to the vanished knot-hole.

"Wall!" Eck roared. The little boy turned and ran for the wagon. The horses were whipping back and forth across the lot, as if while in the barn they had once more doubled their number; two of them rushed up quar-tering and galloped all over the boy again without touching him as he ran, earnest and diminutive and seem-ingly without progress, though he reached the wagon at last, from which Eck, his sunburned skin now a sickly white, reached down and snatched the boy into the wagon by the straps of his overalls and slammed him face down across his knees and caught up a coiled hitching-rope from the bed of the wagon.

"Didn't I tell you to get out of here?" Eck said in a shaking voice. "Didn't I tell you?"

"If you're going to whip him, you better whip the rest of us too and then one of us can frail hell out of you," one of the others said.

"Or better still, take the rope and hang that durn fellow yonder," the second said. The Texan was now standing in the wrecked door of the barn, taking the gingersnap carton from his hip pocket. "Before he kills the rest of Frenchman's Bend too."

"You mean Flem Snopes," the first said. The Texan tilted the carton above his other open palm. The horses still rushed and swirled back and forth but they were beginning to slow now, trotting on high, stiff legs, al-though their eyes were still rolling whitely and various.

"I misdoubted that damn shell corn all along," the Texan said. "But at least they have seen what it looks like. They can't claim they ain't got noth-ing out of this trip." He shook the carton over his open hand. Nothing came out of it. Mrs. Littlejohn on the veranda made the first stroke with the dinner bell; at the sound the horses rushed again, the earth of the lot be-coming vibrant with the light dry clatter of hooves. The Texan crumpled the carton and threw it aside. "Chuck wagon," he said. There were three more wagons in the lane now and there were twenty or more men at the fence when the Texan, followed by his three assistants and the little boy, passed through the gate. The bright cloudless early sun gleamed upon the pearl butt of the pistol in his hip pocket and upon the bell which Mrs. Littlejohn still rang, peremptory, strong, and loud.

When the Texan, picking his teeth with a splintered kitchen match, emerged from the house twenty min-utes later, the tethered wagons and riding horses and mules extended from the lot gate to Varner's store, and there were more than fifty men now standing along the fence beside the gate, watching him quietly, a little covertly, as he approached, rolling a little, slightly bowlegged, the high heels of his carved boots printing neatly into the dust. "Morning, gents," he said. "Here, Bud," he said to the little boy, who stood slightly behind him, looking at the protruding butt of the pistol. He took a coin from his pocket and gave it to the boy. "Run to the store and get me a box of gingersnaps." He looked about at the quiet faces, protuberant, sucking his teeth. He rolled the match from one side of his mouth to the other without touching it. "You boys done made your picks, have you? Ready to start her off, hah?" They did not answer. They were not looking at him now. That is, he began to have the feeling that each face had stopped looking at him the second before his gaze reached it. After a moment Freeman said:

"Ain't you going to wait for Flem?"

"Why?" the Texan said. Then Freeman stopped looking at him too. There was nothing in Freeman's face either. There was nothing, no alteration, in the Texan's voice. "Eck, you done already picked out yours. So we can start her off when you are ready."

"I reckon not," Eck said. "I wouldn't buy nothing I was afraid to walk up and touch."

"Them little ponies?" the Texan said. "You helped water and feed them. I bet that boy of yours could walk up to any one of them."

"He better not let me catch him," Eck said. The Texan looked about at the quiet faces, his gaze at once abstract and alert, with an impenetrable surface quality like flint, as though the surface were impervious or perhaps there was nothing behind it.

"Them ponies is gentle as a dove, boys. The man that buys them will get the best piece of horseflesh he ever forked or druv for the money. Naturally they got spirit; I ain't selling crowbait. Besides, who'd want Texas crowbait anyway, with Mississippi full of it?" His stare was still absent and unwinking; there was no mirth or humor in his voice and there was neither mirth nor humor in the single guffaw which came from the rear of the group. Two wagons were now drawing out of the road at the same time, up to the fence. The men got down from them and tied them to the fence and approached. "Come up, boys," the Texan said. "You're just in time to buy a good gentle horse cheap."

"How about that one that cut your vest off last night?" a voice said. This time three or four guffawed. The Texan looked toward the sound, bleak and unwinking.

"What about it?" he said. The laughter, if it had been laughter, ceased. The Texan turned to the nearest gatepost and climbed to the top of it, his alternate thighs deliberate and bulging in the tight trousers, the butt of the pistol catching and losing the sun in pearly gleams. Sitting on the post, he looked down at the faces along the fence which were attentive, grave, reserved and not looking at him. "All right," he said. "Who's going to start her off with a bid? Step right up; take your pick and make your bid, and when the last one is sold, walk in that lot and put your rope on the best piece of horseflesh you ever forked or druv for the money. There ain't a pony there that ain't worth fifteen dollars. Young, sound, good for saddle or work stock, guaranteed to outlast four ordinary horses; you couldn't kill one of them with a axle-tree—" There was a small violent commotion at the rear of the group. The little boy appeared, burrowing among the motionless overalls.

He approached the post, the new and unbroken paper carton lifted. The Texan leaned down and took it and tore the end from it and shook three or four of the cakes into the boy's hand, a hand as small and almost as black as that of a coon. He held the carton in his hand while he talked, pointing out the horses with it as he indicated them. "Look at that one with the three stocking-feet and the frost-bit ear; watch him now when they pass again. Look at that shoulder-action; that horse is worth twenty dollars of any man's money. Who'll make me a bid on him to start her off?" His voice was harsh, ready, forensic. Along the fence below him the men stood with, buttoned close in their overalls, the tobacco-sacks and worn purses the sparse silver and frayed bills hoarded a coin at a time in the cracks of chimneys or chinked into the logs of walls. From time to time the horses broke and rushed with purposeless violence and huddled again, watching the faces along the fence with wild mismatched eyes. The lane was full of wagons now. As the others arrived they would have to stop in the road beyond it and the occupants came up the lane on foot. Mrs. Littlejohn came out of her kitchen. She crossed the yard, looking toward the lot gate. There was a blackened wash pot set on four bricks in the corner of the yard. She built a fire beneath the pot and came to the fence and stood there for a time, her hands on her hips and the smoke from the fire drifting blue and slow behind her. Then she turned and went back into the house. "Come on, boys," the Texan said. "Who'll make me a bid?"

"Four bits," a voice said. The Texan did not even glance toward it.

"Or, if he don't suit you, how about that fiddle-head horse without no mane to speak of? For a saddle pony, I'd rather have him than that stocking-foot. I heard somebody say fifty cents just now. I reckon he meant five dollars, didn't he? Do I hear five dollars?"

"Four bits for the lot," the same voice said. This time there were no guffaws. It was the Texan who laughed, harshly, with only his lower face, as if he were reciting a multiplication table.

"Fifty cents for the dried mud offen them, he means," he said. "Who'll give a dollar more for the genuine Texas cockle-burrs?" Mrs. Littlejohn came out of the kitchen, carrying the sawn half of a wooden hogshead which she set on a stump beside the smoking pot, and stood with her hands on her hips, looking into the lot for a while without coming to the fence this time. Then she went back into the house. "What's the matter with you boys?" the Texan said. "Here, Eck, you been helping me and you know them horses. How about making me a bid on that wall-eyed one you picked out last night? Here. Wait a minute." He thrust the paper carton into his other hip pocket and swung his feet inward and dropped, cat-light, into the lot. The ponies, huddled, watched him. Then they broke before him and slid stiffly along the fence. He turned them and they whirled and rushed back across the lot; whereupon, as though he had been waiting his chance when they should have turned their backs on him, the Texan began to run too, so that when they reached the opposite side of the lot and turned, slowing to huddle again, he was almost upon them. The earth became thunderous; dust arose, out of which the animals began to burst like flushed quail and into which, with that apparently unflagging faith in his own invulnerability, the Texan rushed. For an instant the watchers could see them in the dust —the pony backed into the angle of the fence and the stable, the man facing it, reaching toward his hip. Then the beast rushed at him in a sort of fatal and hopeless desperation and he struck it between the eyes with the pistol-butt and felled it and leaped onto its prone head. The pony recovered almost at once and pawed itself to its knees and heaved at its prisoned head and fought itself up, dragging the man with it; for an instant in the dust the watchers saw the man free of the earth and in violent lateral motion like a rag attached to the horse's head. Then the Texan's feet came back to earth and the dust blew aside and revealed them, motionless, the Texan's sharp heels braced into the ground, one hand gripping the pony's forelock and the other its nostrils, the long evil muzzle wrung backward over its scarred shoulder while it breathed in labored and hollow groans. Mrs. Littlejohn was in the yard again. No one had seen her emerge this time. She carried an armful of clothing and a metal-ridged washboard and she was standing motionless at the kitchen steps, looking into the lot. Then she moved across the yard, still looking into the lot, and dumped the garments into the tub, still looking into the lot. "Look him over, boys," the Texan panted, turning his own suffused face and the protuberant glare of his eyes toward the fence. "Look him over quick. Them shoulders and—" He had relaxed for an instant apparently. The animal exploded again; again for an instant the Texan was free of the earth, though he was still talking: "—and legs you whoa I'll tear your face right look him over quick boys worth fifteen dollars of let me get a holt of who'll make me a bid whoa you blare-eyed jack rabbit, whoa!"

They were moving now—a kaleidoscope of inextricable and incredible violence on the periphery of which the metal clasps of the Texan's suspenders sun-glinted in ceaseless orbit, with terrific slowness across the lot. Then the broad clay-colored hat soared deliberately outward; an instant later the Texan followed it, though still on his feet, and the pony shot free in mad, staglike bounds. The Texan picked up the hat and struck the dust from it against his leg, and returned to the fence and mounted the post again. He was breathing heavily. Still the faces did not look at him as he took the carton from his hip and shook a cake from it and put the cake into his mouth, chewing, breathing harshly. Mrs. Littlejohn turned away and began to bail water from the pot into the tub, though after each bucketful she turned her head and looked into the lot again. "Now, boys," the Texan said. "Who says the pony ain't worth fifteen dollars? You couldn't buy that much dynamite for just fifteen dollars. There ain't one of them can't do a mile in three minutes; turn them into pasture and they will board themselves; work them like hell all day and every time you think about it, lay them over the head with a single-tree and after a couple of days every jack rabbit one of them will be so tame you will have to put them out of the house at night like a cat." He shook another cake from the carton and ate it. "Come on, Eck," he said. "Start her off. How about ten dollars for that horse, Eck?"

"What need I got for a horse I would need a beartrap to catch?" Eck said.

"Didn't you just see me catch him?"

"I seen you," Eck said. "And I don't want nothing as big as a horse if I got to wrastle with it every time it finds me on the same side of a fence it's on."

"All right," the Texan said. He was still breathing harshly, but now there was nothing of fatigue or breathlessness in it. He shook another cake into his palm and inserted it beneath his moustache. "All right. I want to get this auction started. I ain't come here to live, no matter how good a country you folks claim you got. I'm going to give you that horse." For a moment there was no sound, not even that of breathing except the Texan's.

"You going to give it to me?" Eck said.

"Yes. Provided you will start the bidding on the next one." Again there was no sound save the Texan's breathing, and then the clash of Mrs. Littlejohn's pail against the rim of the pot.

"I just start the bidding," Eck said. "I don't have to buy it lessen I ain't over-topped." Another wagon had come up the lane. It was battered and paintless. One wheel had been repaired by crossed planks bound to the spokes with baling wire and the two underfed mules wore a battered harness patched with bits of cotton rope; the reins were ordinary cotton plowlines, not new. It contained a woman in a shapeless gray garment and a faded sunbonnet, and a man in faded and patched though clean overalls. There was not room for the wagon to draw out of the lane so the man left it standing where it was and got down and came forward—a thin man, not large, with something about his eyes, something strained and washed-out, at once vague and intense, who shoved into the crowd at the rear, saying,

"What? What's that? Did he give him that horse?"

"All right," the Texan said. "That wall-eyed horse with the scarred neck belongs to you. Now. That one that looks like he's had his head in a flour

barrel. What do you say? Ten dollars?"

"Did he give him that horse?" the newcomer said.

"A dollar," Eck said. The Texan's mouth was still open for speech; for an instant his face died so behind the hard eyes.

"A dollar?" he said. "One dollar? Did I actually hear that?"

"Durn it," Eck said. "Two dollars then. But I ain't——"

"Wait," the newcomer said. "You, up there on the post." The Texan looked at him. When the others turned, they saw that the woman had left the wagon too, though they had not known she was there since they had not seen the wagon drive up. She came among them behind the man, gaunt in the gray shapeless garment and the sunbonnet, wearing stained canvas gymnasium shoes. She overtook the man but she did not touch him, standing just behind him, her hands rolled before her into the gray dress.

"Henry," she said in a flat voice. The man looked over his shoulder.

"Get back to that wagon," he said.

"Here, missus," the Texan said. "Henry's going to get the bargain of his life in about a minute. Here, boys, let the missus come up close where she can see. Henry's going to pick out that saddle-horse the missus has been wanting. Who says ten——"

"Henry," the woman said. She did not raise her voice. She had not once looked at the Texan. She touched the man's arm. He turned and struck her hand down.

"Get back to that wagon like I told you." The woman stood behind him, her hands rolled again into her dress. She was not looking at anything, speaking to anyone.

"He ain't no more despair than to buy one of them things," she said.

"And us not but five dollars away from the poorhouse, he ain't no more despair." The man turned upon her with that curious air of leashed, of dreamlike fury. The others lounged along the fence in attitudes gravely inattentive, almost oblivious. Mrs. Littlejohn had been washing for some time now, pumping rhythmically up and down above the washboard in the sud-foamed tub. She now stood erect again, her soap-raw hands on her hips, looking into the lot.

"Shut your mouth and get back in that wagon," the man said. "Do you want me to take a wagon stake to you?" He turned and looked up at the Texan. "Did you give him that horse?" he said. The Texan was looking at the woman. Then he looked at the man; still watching him, he tilted the paper carton over his open palm. A single cake came out of it.

"Yes," he said.

"Is the fellow that bids in this next horse going to get that first one too?"

"No," the Texan said.

"All right," the other said. "Are you going to give a horse to the man that makes the first bid on the next one?"

"No," the Texan said.

"Then if you were just starting the auction off by giving away a horse, why didn't you wait till we were all here?" The Texan stopped looking at the other. He raised the empty carton and squinted carefully into it, as if it might contain a precious jewel or perhaps a deadly insect. Then he crumpled it and dropped it carefully beside the post on which he sat.

"Eck bid two dollars," he said. "I believe he still thinks he's bidding on them scraps of bob-wire they come here in instead of on one of the horses. But I got to accept it. But are you boys——"

"So Eck's going to get two horses at a dollar a head," the newcomer

said. "Three dollars." The woman touched him again. He flung her hand off without turning and she stood again, her hands rolled into her dress across her flat stomach, not looking at anything.

"Misters," she said, "we got chaps in the house that never had shoes last winter. We ain't got corn to feed the stock. We got five dollars I earned weaving by firelight after dark. And he ain't no more despair."

"Henry bids three dollars," the Texan said. "Raise him a dollar, Eck, and the horse is yours." Beyond the fence the horses rushed suddenly and for no reason and as suddenly stopped, staring at the faces along the fence.

"Henry," the woman said. The man was watching Eck. His stained and broken teeth showed a little beneath his lip. His wrists dangled into fists below the faded sleeves of his shirt too short from many washings.

"Four dollars," Eck said.

"Five dollars!" the husband said, raising one clenched hand. He shouldered himself forward toward the gatepost. The woman did not follow him. She now looked at the Texan for the first time. Her eyes were a washed gray also, as though they had faded too like the dress and the sunbonnet.

"Mister," she said, "if you take that five dollars I earned my chaps a-weaving for one of them things, it'll be a curse on you and yours during all the time of man."

"Five dollars!" the husband shouted. He thrust himself up to the post, his clenched hand on a level with the Texan's knees. He opened it upon a wad of frayed banknotes and silver. "Five dollars! And the man that raises it will have to beat my head off or I'll beat hisn."

"All right," the Texan said. "Five dollars is bid. But don't you shake your hand at me."

At five o'clock that afternoon the Texan crumpled the third paper carton and dropped it to the earth beneath him. In the copper slant of the levelling sun which fell also upon the line of limp garments in Mrs. Littlejohn's backyard and which cast his shadow and that of the post on which he sat long across the lot where now and then the ponies still rushed in purposeless and tireless surges, the Texan straightened his leg and thrust his hand into his pocket and took out a coin and leaned down to the little boy. His voice was now hoarse, spent. "Here, bud," he said. "Run to the store and get me a box of gingersnaps." The men still stood along the fence, tireless, in their overalls and faded shirts. Flem Snopes was there now, appeared suddenly from nowhere, standing beside the fence with a space the width of three or four men on either side of him, standing there in his small yet definite isolation, chewing tobacco, in the same gray trousers and minute bow tie in which he had departed last summer but in a new cap, gray too like the other, but new, and overlaid with a bright golfer's plaid, looking also at the horses in the lot. All of them save two had been sold for sums ranging from three dollars and a half to eleven and twelve dollars. The purchasers, as they had bid them in, had gathered as though by instinct into a separate group on the other side of the gate, where they stood with their hands lying upon the top strand of the fence, watching with a still more sober intensity the animals which some of them had owned for seven and eight hours now but had not yet laid hands upon. The husband, Henry, stood beside the post on which the Texan sat. The wife had gone back to the wagon, where she sat gray in the gray garment, motionless, looking at nothing, still, she might have been something inanimate which he had loaded into the wagon to move it somewhere, waiting now in the wagon until he should be ready to go on again, patient, insensate, timeless.

"I bought a horse and I paid cash for it," he said. His voice was harsh and spent too, the mad look in his eyes had a quality glazed now and even sightless. "And yet you expect me to stand around here till they are all sold before I can get my horse. Well, you can do all the expecting you want. I'm going to take my horse out of there and go home." The Texan looked down at him. The Texan's shirt was blotched with sweat. His big face was cold and still, his voice level.

"Take your horse then." After a moment Henry looked away. He stood with his head bent a little, swallowing from time to time.

"Ain't you going to catch him for me?"

"It ain't my horse," the Texan said in that flat still voice. After a while Henry raised his head. He did not look at the Texan.

"Who'll help me catch my horse?" he said. Nobody answered. They stood along the fence, looking quietly into the lot where the ponies huddled, already beginning to fade a little where the long shadow of the house lay upon them, deepening. From Mrs. Littlejohn's kitchen the smell of frying ham came. A noisy cloud of sparrows swept across the lot and into a chinaberry tree beside the house, and in the high soft vague blue swallows stooped and whirled in erratic indecision, their cries like strings plucked at random. Without looking back, Henry raised his voice: "Bring that ere plow-line." After a time the wife moved. She got down from the wagon and took a coil of new cotton rope from it and approached. The husband took the rope from her and moved toward the gate. The Texan began to descend from the post, stiffly, as Henry put his hand on the latch. "Come on here," he said. The wife had stopped when he took the rope from her. She moved again, obediently, her hands rolled into the dress across her stomach, passing the Texan without looking at him.

"Don't go in there, missus," he said. She stopped, not looking at him, not looking at anything. The husband opened the gate and entered the lot and turned, holding the gate open but without raising his eyes.

"Come on here," he said.

"Don't you go in there, missus," the Texan said. The wife stood motionless between them, her face almost concealed by the sunbonnet, her hands folded across her stomach.

"I reckon I better," she said. The other men did not look at her at all, at her or Henry either. They stood along the fence, grave and quiet and inattentive, almost bemused. Then the wife passed through the gate; the husband shut it behind them and turned and began to move toward the huddled ponies, the wife following in the gray and shapeless garment within which she moved without inference of locomotion, like something on a moving platform, a float. The horses were watching them. They clotted and blended and shifted among themselves, on the point of breaking though not breaking yet. The husband shouted at them. He began to curse them, advancing, the wife following. Then the huddle broke, the animals moving with high, stiff knees, circling the two people who turned and followed again as the herd flowed and huddled again at the opposite side of the lot.

"There he is," the husband said.

"Get him into that corner." The herd divided; the horse which the husband had bought jolted on stiff legs. The wife shouted at it; it spun and poised, plunging, then the husband struck it across the face with the coiled rope and it whirled and slammed into the corner of the fence. "Keep him there now," the husband said. He shook out the rope, advancing. The horse watched him with wild, glaring eyes; it rushed again, straight toward the wife. She shouted at it and waved her arms but it soared past her in a long bound and rushed again into the huddle of its fellows. They followed and hemmed it again into another corner; again the wife failed to stop its rush for freedom and the husband turned and struck her with the coiled rope. "Why didn't you head him?" he said. "Why didn't you?" He struck her again; she did not move, not even to fend the rope with a raised arm. The men along the fence stood quietly, their faces lowered as though brooding upon the earth at their feet. Only Flem Snopes was still watching—if he ever had been looking into the lot at all, standing in his little island of isolation, chewing with his characteristic faint sidewise thrust beneath the new plaid cap.

The Texan said something, not loud, harsh and short. He entered the lot and went to the husband and jerked the uplifted rope from his hand. The husband whirled as though he were about to spring at the Texan, crouched slightly, his knees bent and his arms held slightly away from his sides, though his gaze never mounted higher than the Texan's carved and dusty boots. Then the Texan took the husband by the arm and led him back toward the gate, the wife following, and through the gate which he held open for the woman and then closed. He took a wad of banknotes from his trousers and removed a bill from it and put it into the woman's hand. "Get him into the wagon and get him on home," he said.

"What's that for?" Flem Snopes said. He had approached. He now stood beside the post on which the Texan had been sitting. The Texan did not look at him.

"Thinks he bought one of them ponies," the Texan said. He spoke in a flat still voice, like that of a man after a sharp run. "Get him on away, missus."

"Give him back that money," the husband said, in his lifeless, spent tone. "I bought that horse and I aim to have him if I got to shoot him before I can put a rope on him." The Texan did not even look at him.

"Get him on away from here, missus," he said.

"You take your money and I take my horse," the husband said. He was shaking slowly and steadily now, as though he were cold. His hands opened and shut below the frayed cuffs of his shirt. "Give it back to him," he said.

"You don't own no horse of mine," the Texan said. "Get him on home, missus." The husband raised his spent face, his mad glazed eyes. He reached out his hand. The woman held the banknote in her folded hands across her stomach. For a while the husband's shaking hand merely fumbled at it. Then he drew the banknote free.

"It's my horse," he said. "I bought it. These fellows saw me. I paid for it. It's my horse. Here." He turned and extended the banknote toward Snopes. "You got something to do with these horses. I bought one. Here's the money for it. I bought one. Ask him." Snopes took the banknote. The others stood, gravely inattentive, in relaxed attitudes along the fence. The sun had gone now; there was

nothing save violet shadow upon them and upon the lot where once more and for no reason the ponies rushed and flowed. At that moment the little boy came up, tireless and indefatigable still, with the new paper carton. The Texan took it, though he did not open it at once. He had dropped the rope and now the husband stooped for it, fumbling at it for some time before he lifted it from the ground. Then he stood with his head bent, his knuckles whitening on the rope. The woman had not moved. Twilight was coming fast now; there was a last mazy swirl of swallows against the high and changing azure. Then the Texan tore the end from the carton and tilted one of the cakes into his hand; he seemed to be watching the hand as it shut slowly upon the cake until a fine powder of snuff-colored dust began to rain from his fingers. He rubbed the hand carefully on his thigh and raised his head and glanced about until he saw the little boy and handed the carton back to him.

"Here, Bud," he said. Then he looked at the woman, his voice flat, quiet again. "Mr. Snopes will have your money for you tomorrow. Better get him in the wagon and get him on home. He don't own no horse. You can get your money tomorrow from Mr. Snopes." The wife turned and went back to the wagon and got into it. No one watched her, nor the husband who still stood, his head bent, passing the rope from one hand to the other. They leaned along the fence, grave and quiet, as though the fence were in another land, another time.

"How many you got left?" Snopes said. The Texan roused; they all seemed to rouse then, returning, listening again.

"Got three now," the Texan said.

"Swap all three of them for a buggy or a——"

"It's out in the road," Snopes said, a little shortly, a little quickly, turning away. "Get your mules." He went on up the lane. They watched the Texan enter the lot and cross it, the horses flowing before him but without the old irrational violence, as if they too were spent, vitiated with the long day, and enter the barn and then emerge, leading the two harnessed mules. The wagon had been backed under the shed beside the barn. The Texan entered this and came out a moment later, carrying a bedding-roll and his coat, and led the mules back toward the gate, the ponies huddled again and watching him with their various unmatching eyes, quietly now, as if they too realized there was not only an armistice between them at last but that they would never look upon each other again in both their lives. Someone opened the gate. The Texan led the mules through it and they followed in a body, leaving the husband standing beside the closed gate, his head still bent and the coiled rope in his hand. They passed the wagon in which the wife sat, her gray garment fading into the dusk, almost the same color and as still, looking at nothing; they passed the clothesline with its limp and unwinded drying garments, walking through the hot vivid smell of ham from Mrs. Littlejohn's kitchen. When they reached the end of the lane they could see the moon, almost full, tremendous and pale and still lightless in the sky from which day had not quite gone. Snopes was standing at the end of the lane beside an empty buggy. It was the one with the glittering wheels and the fringed parasol top in which he and Will Varner had used to drive. The Texan was motionless too, looking at it.

"Well well well," he said. "So this is it."

"If it don't suit you, you can ride one of the mules back to Texas," Snopes said.

"You bet," the Texan said. "Only I ought to have a powder puff or at least a mandolin to ride it with." He backed the mules onto the tongue and lifted the breast-yoke. Two of them came forward and fastened the traces for him. Then they watched him get into the buggy and raise the reins.

"Where you heading for?" one said. "Back to Texas?"

"In this?" the Texan said. "I wouldn't get past the first Texas saloon without starting the vigilance committee. Besides, I ain't going to waste all this here lace-trimmed top and these spindle wheels just on Texas. Long as I am this far, I reckon I'll go on a day or two and look-see them Northern towns. Washington and New York and Baltimore. What's the short way to New York from here?" They didn't know. But they told him how to reach Jefferson.

"You're already headed right," Freeman said. "Just keep right on up the road past the schoolhouse."

"All right," the Texan said. "Well, remember about busting them ponies over the head now and then until they get used to you. You won't have any trouble with them then." He lifted the reins again. As he did so Snopes stepped forward and got into the buggy.

"I'll ride as far as Varner's with you," he said.

"I didn't know I was going past Varner's," the Texan said.

"You can go to town that way," Snopes said. "Drive on." The Texan shook the reins. Then he said,

"Whoa." He straightened his leg and put his hand into his pocket. "Here, Bud," he said to the little boy, "run to the store and— Never mind. I'll stop and get it myself, long as I am going back that way. Well, boys," he said. "Take care of yourselves." He swung the team around. The buggy went on. They looked after it.

"I reckon he aims to kind of come up on Jefferson from behind," Quick said.

"He'll be lighter when he gets there," Freeman said. "He can come up to it easy from any side he wants."

"Yes," Bookwright said. "His pockets won't rattle." They went back to the lot; they passed on through the narrow way between the two lines of patient and motionless wagons, which at the end was completely closed by the one in which the woman sat. The husband was still standing beside the gate with his coiled rope, and now night had completely come. The light itself had not changed so much; if anything, it was brighter but with that other-worldly quality of moonlight, so that when they stood once more looking into the lot, the splotchy bodies of the ponies had a distinctness, almost a brilliance, but without individual shape and without depth— no longer horses, no longer flesh and bone directed by a principle capable of calculated violence, no longer inherent with the capacity to hurt and harm.

"Well, what are we waiting for?" Freeman said. "For them to go to roost?"

"We better all get our ropes first," Quick said. "Get your ropes everybody." Some of them did not have ropes. When they left home that morning, they had not heard about the horses, the auction. They had merely happened through the village by chance and learned of it and stopped.

"Go to the store and get some then," Freeman said.

"The store will be closed now," Quick said.

"No it won't," Freeman said. "If it was closed, Lump Snopes would a been up here." So while the ones who had come prepared got their ropes from the wagons, the others went down to the store. The clerk was just closing it.

"You all ain't started catching them yet, have you?" he said. "Good; I was afraid I wouldn't get there in time." He opened the door again and amid the old strong sunless smells of cheese and leather and molasses he measured and cut off sections of plow-line for them and in a body and the clerk in the center and still talking, voluble and unlistened to, they returned up the road. The pear tree before Mrs. Littlejohn's was like drowned silver now in the moon. The mockingbird of last night, or another one, was already singing in it, and they now saw, tied to the fence, Ratliff's buckboard and team.

"I thought something was wrong all day," one said. "Ratliff wasn't there to give nobody advice." When they passed down the lane, Mrs. Littlejohn was in her backyard, gathering the garments from the clothesline; they could still smell the ham. The others were waiting at the gate, beyond which the ponies, huddled again, were like phantom fish, suspended apparently without legs now in the brilliant treachery of the moon.

"I reckon the best way will be for us all to take and catch them one at a time," Freeman said.

"One at a time," the husband, Henry, said. Apparently he had not moved since the Texan had led his mules through the gate, save to lift his hands to the top of the gate, one of them still clutching the coiled rope. "One at a time," he said. He began to curse in a harsh, spent monotone.

"After I've stood around here all day, waiting for that—" He cursed. He began to jerk at the gate, shaking it with spent violence until one of the others slid the latch back and it swung open and Henry entered it, the others following, the little boy pressing close behind his father until Eck became aware of him and turned.

"Here," he said. "Give me that rope. You stay out of here."

"Aw, paw," the boy said.

"No sir. Them things will kill you. They almost done it this morning. You stay out of here."

"But we got two to catch." For a moment Eck stood looking down at the boy.

"That's right," he said. "We got two. But you stay close to me now. And when I holler run, you run. You hear me?"

"Spread out, boys," Freeman said. "Keep them in front of us." They began to advance across the lot in a ragged crescent-shaped line, each one with his rope. The ponies were now at the far side of the lot. One of them snorted; the mass shifted within itself but without breaking. Freeman, glancing back, saw the little boy. "Get that boy out of here," he said.

"I reckon you better," Eck said to the boy. "You go and get in the wagon yonder. You can see us catch them from there." The little boy turned and trotted toward the shed beneath which the wagon stood. The line of men advanced. Henry a little in front.

"Watch them close now," Freeman said. "Maybe we better try to get them into the barn first—" At that moment the huddle broke. It parted and flowed in both directions along the fence. The men at the ends of the line began to run, waving their arms and shouting. "Head them," Freeman said tensely. "Turn them back." They turned them, driving them back upon

themselves again; the animals merged and spun in short, huddling rushes, phantom and inextricable. "Hold them now," Freeman said. "Don't let them get by us." The line advanced again. Eck turned; he did not know why—whether a sound, what. The little boy was just behind him again.

"Didn't I tell you to get in that wagon and stay there?" Eck said.

"Watch out, paw!" the boy said. "There he is! There's ourn!" It was the one the Texan had given Eck. "Catch him, paw!"

"Get out of my way," Eck said. "Get back to that wagon." The line was still advancing. The ponies milled, clotting, forced gradually backward toward the open door of the barn. Henry was still slightly in front, crouched slightly, his thin figure, even in the mazy moonlight, emanating something of that spent fury. The splotchy huddle of animals seemed to be moving before the advancing line of men like a snowball which they might have been pushing before them by some invisible means, gradually nearer and nearer to the black yawn of the barn door. Later it was obvious that the ponies were so intent upon the men that they did not realize the barn was even behind them until they backed into the shadow of it. Then an indescribable sound, a movement desperate and despairing, arose among them; for an instant of static horror men and animals faced one another, then the men whirled and ran before a gaudy vomit of long wild faces and splotched chests which overtook and scattered them and flung them sprawling aside and completely obliterated from sight Henry and the little boy, neither of whom had moved though Henry had flung up both arms, still holding his coiled rope, the herd sweeping on across the lot, to crash through the gate which the last man through it had neglected to close, leaving it slightly ajar, carrying all of the gate save the upright to which the hinges were nailed with them, and so among the teams and wagons which choked the lane, the teams springing and lunging too, snapping hitch-reins and tongues. Then the whole inextricable mass crashed among the wagons and eddied and divided about the one in which the woman sat, and rushed on down the lane and into the road, dividing, one half going one way and one half the other.

The men in the lot, except Henry, got to their feet and ran toward the gate. The little boy once more had not been touched, not even thrown off his feet; for a while his father held him clear of the ground in one hand, shaking him like a rag doll. "Didn't I tell you to stay in that wagon?" Eck cried. "Didn't I tell you?"

"Look out, paw!" the boy chattered out of the violent shaking, "there's ourn! There he goes!" It was the horse the Texan had given them again. It was as if they owned no other, the other one did not exist; as if by some absolute and instantaneous rapport of blood they had relegated to oblivion the one for which they had paid money. They ran to the gate and down the lane where the other men had disappeared. They saw the horse the Texan had given them whirl and dash back and rush through the gate into Mrs. Littlejohn's yard and run up the front steps and crash once on the wooden veranda and vanish through the front door. Eck and the boy ran up onto the veranda. A lamp sat on a table just inside the door. In its mellow light they saw the horse fill the long hallway like a pinwheel, gaudy, furious and thunderous. A little further down the hall there was a varnished yellow melodeon. The horse crashed into it; it produced a single

note, almost a chord, in bass, resonant and grave, of deep and sober astonishment; the horse with its monstrous and antic shadow whirled again and vanished through another door. It was a bedroom; Ratliff, in his underclothes and one sock and with the other sock in his hand and his back to the door, was leaning out the open window facing the lane, the lot. He looked back over his shoulder. For an instant he and the horse glared at one another. Then he sprang through the window as the horse backed out of the room and into the hall again and whirled and saw Eck and the little boy just entering the front door, Eck still carrying his rope. It whirled again and rushed on down the hall and onto the back porch just as Mrs. Littlejohn, carrying an armful of clothes from the line and the washboard, mounted the steps.

"Get out of here, you son of a bitch," she said. She struck with the washboard; it divided neatly on the long mad face and the horse whirled and rushed back up the hall, where Eck and the boy now stood.

"Get to hell out of here, Wall!" Eck roared. He dropped to the floor, covering his head with his arms. The boy did not move, and for the third time the horse soared above the unwinking eyes and the unbowed and untouched head and onto the front veranda again just as Ratliff, still carrying the sock, ran around the corner of the house and up the steps. The horse whirled without breaking or pausing. It galloped to the end of the veranda and took the railing and soared outward, hobgoblin and floating, in the moon. It landed in the lot still running and crossed the lot and galloped through the wrecked gate and among the overturned wagons and the still intact one in which Henry's wife still sat, and on down the lane and into the road.

A quarter of a mile further on, the road gashed pallid and moony between the moony shadows of the bordering trees, the horse still galloping, galloping its shadow into the dust, the road descending now toward the creek and the bridge. It was of wood, just wide enough for a single vehicle. When the horse reached it, it was occupied by a wagon coming from the opposite direction and drawn by two mules already asleep in the harness and the soporific motion. On the seat was Tull and his wife, in splint chairs in the wagon behind them sat their four daughters, all returning belated from an all-day visit with some of Mrs. Tull's kin. The horse neither checked nor swerved. It crashed once on the wooden bridge and rushed between the two mules which waked lunging in opposite directions in the traces, the horse now apparently scrambling along the wagon-tongue itself like a mad squirrel and scrabbling at the end-gate of the wagon with its forefeet as if it intended to climb into the wagon while Tull shouted at it and struck at its face with his whip. The mules were now trying to turn the wagon around in the middle of the bridge. It slewed and tilted, the bridge-rail cracked with a sharp report above the shrieks of the women; the horse scrambled at last across the back of one of the mules and Tull stood up in the wagon and kicked at its face. Then the front end of the wagon rose, flinging Tull, the reins now wrapped several times about his wrist, backward into the wagon bed among the overturned chairs and the exposed stockings and undergarments of his women. The pony scrambled free and crashed again on the wooden planking, galloping again. The wagon lurched again; the mules had finally turned it on the bridge where there was not room for

it to turn and were now kicking themselves free of the traces. When they came free, they snatched Tull bodily out of the wagon. He struck the bridge on his face and was dragged for several feet before the wrist-wrapped reins broke. Far up the road now, distancing the frantic mules, the pony faded on. While the five women still shrieked above Tull's unconscious body, Eck and the little boy came up, trotting, Eck still carrying his rope. He was panting. "Which way'd he go?" he said.

In the now empty and moon-drenched lot, his wife and Mrs. Littlejohn and Ratliff and Lump Snopes, the clerk, and three other men raised Henry out of the trampled dust and carried him into Mrs. Littlejohn's back yard. His face was blanched and stony, his eyes were closed, the weight of his head tautened his throat across the protruding larynx; his teeth glinted dully beneath his lifted lip. They carried him on toward the house, through the dappled shade of the chinaberry trees. Across the dreaming and silver night a faint sound like remote thunder came and ceased. "There's one of them on the creek bridge," one of the men said.

"It's that one of Eck Snopes'," another said. "The one that was in the house." Mrs. Littlejohn had preceded them into the hall. When they entered with Henry, she had already taken the lamp from the table and she stood beside an open door, holding the lamp high.

"Bring him in here," she said. She entered the room first and set the lamp on the dresser. They followed with clumsy scufflings and pantings and laid Henry on the bed and Mrs. Littlejohn came to the bed and stood looking down at Henry's peaceful and bloodless face. "I'll declare," she said. "You men." They had drawn back a little, clumped, shifting from one foot to another, not looking at her nor at his wife either, who stood at the foot of the bed, motionless, her hands folded into her dress. "You all get out of here, V. K.," she said to Ratliff. "Go outside. See if you can't find something else to play with that will kill some more of you."

"All right," Ratliff said. "Come on, boys. Ain't no more horses to catch in here." They followed him toward the door, on tiptoe, their shoes scuffling, their shadows monstrous on the wall.

"Go get Will Varner," Mrs. Littlejohn said. "I reckon you can tell him it's still a mule." They went out; they didn't look back. They tiptoed up the hall and crossed the veranda and descended into the moonlight. Now that they could pay attention to it, the silver air seemed to be filled with faint and sourceless sounds, shouts, thin and distant, again a brief thunder of hooves on a wooden bridge, more shouts faint and thin and earnest and clear as bells; once they even distinguished the words: "Whooey. Head him."

"He went through that house quick," Ratliff said. "He must have found another woman at home." Then Henry screamed in the house behind them. They looked back into the dark hall where a square of light fell through the bedroom door, listening while the scream sank into a harsh respiration: "Ah. Ah. Ah" on a rising note about to become screaming again. "Come on," Ratliff said. "We better get Varner." They went up the road in a body, treading the moon-blanched dust in the tremulous April night murmurous with the moving of sap and the wet bursting of burgeoning leaf and bud and constant with the thin and urgent cries and the brief and fading bursts of galloping hooves.

Varner's house was dark, blank and without depth in the moonlight. They stood, clumped darkly in the silver yard and called up at the blank windows until suddenly someone was standing in one of them. It was Flem Snopes' wife. She was in a white garment; the heavy braided club of her hair looked almost black against it. She did not lean out, she merely stood there, full in the moon, apparently blank-eyed or certainly not looking downward at them—the heavy gold hair, the mask not tragic and perhaps not even doomed: just damned, the strong faint lift of breasts beneath marblelike fall of the garment; to those below what Brunhilde, what Rhinemaiden on what spurious river-rock of papier-maché, what Helen returned to what topless and shoddy Argos, waiting for no one. "Evening, Mrs. Snopes," Ratliff said. "We want Uncle Will. Henry Armstid is hurt at Mrs. Littlejohn's." She vanished from the window. They waited in the moonlight, listening to the faint remote shouts and cries, until Varner emerged, sooner than they had actually expected, hunching into his coat and buttoning his trousers over the tail of his nightshirt, his suspenders still dangling in twin loops below the coat. He was carrying the battered bag which contained the plumber-like tools with which he drenched and wormed and blistered and floated or drew the teeth of horses and mules; he came down the steps, lean and loosejointed, his shrewd ruthless head cocked a little as he listened also to the faint bell-like cries and shouts with which the silver air was full.

"Are they still trying to catch them rabbits?" he said.

"All of them except Henry Armstid," Ratliff said. "He caught his."

"Hah," Varner said. "That you, V. K.? How many did you buy?"

"I was too late," Ratliff said. "I never got back in time."

"Hah," Varner said. They moved on to the gate and into the road again. "Well, it's a good bright cool night for running them." The moon was now high overhead, a pearled and mazy yawn in the soft sky, the ultimate ends of which rolled onward, whorl on whorl, beyond the pale stars and by pale stars surrounded. They walked in a close clump, tramping their shadows into the road's mild dust, blotting the shadows of the burgeoning trees which soared, trunk, branch and twig against the pale sky, delicate and finely thinned. They passed the dark store. Then the pear tree came in sight. It rose in mazed and silver immobility like exploding snow; the mockingbird still sang in it. "Look at that tree," Varner said. "It ought to make this year, sho."

"Corn'll make this year too," one said.

"A moon like this is good for every growing thing outen earth," Varner said. "I mind when me and Mrs. Varner was expecting Eula. Already had a mess of children and maybe we ought to quit then. But I wanted some more gals. Others had done married and moved away, and a passel of boys, soon as they get big enough to be worth anything, they ain't got time to work. Got to set around the store and talk. But a gal will stay home and work until she does get married. So there was a old woman told my mammy once that if a woman showed her belly to the full moon after she had done caught, it would be a gal. So Mrs. Varner taken and laid every night with the moon on her nekid belly, until it fulled and after. I could lay my ear to her belly and hear Eula kicking and scrouging like all get-out, feeling the moon."

"You mean it actually worked sho enough, Uncle Willie?" the other said.

"Hah," Varner said. "You might try it. You get enough women showing their nekid bellies to the moon or the sun either or even just to your hand fumbling around often enough and more than likely after a while there will be something in it you can lay your ear and listen to, provided something come up and you ain't got away by that time. Hah, V. K.?" Someone guffawed.

"Don't ask me," Ratliff said. "I can't even get nowhere in time to buy a cheap horse." Two or three guffawed this time. Then they began to hear Henry's respirations from the house: "Ah. Ah. Ah." and they ceased abruptly, as if they had not been aware of their closeness to it. Varner walked on in front, lean, shambling, yet moving quite rapidly, though his head was still slanted with listening as the faint, urgent, indomitable cries murmured in the silver lambence, sourceless, at times almost musical, like fading bell-notes; again there was a brief rapid thunder of hooves on wooden planking.

"There's another one on the creek bridge," one said.

"They are going to come out even on them things, after all," Varner said. "They'll get the money back in exercise and relaxation. You take a man that ain't got no other relaxation all year long except dodging mule-dung up and down a field furrow. And a night like this one, when a man ain't old enough yet to lay still and sleep, and yet he ain't young enough anymore to be tomcatting in and out of other folks' back windows, something like this is good for him. It'll make him sleep tomorrow night anyhow, provided he gets back home by then. If we had just knowed about this in time, we could have trained up a pack of horse-dogs. Then we could have held one of these field trials."

"That's one way to look at it, I reckon," Ratliff said. "In fact, it might be a considerable comfort to Bookwright and Quick and Freeman and Eck Snopes and them other new horse-owners if that side of it could be brought to their attention, because the chances are ain't none of them thought to look at it in that light yet. Probably there ain't a one of them that believes now there's any cure a tall for that Texas disease Flem Snopes and that Dead-eye Dick brought here."

"Hah," Varner said. He opened Mrs. Littlejohn's gate. The dim light still fell outward across the hall from the bedroom door; beyond it, Armstid was saying "Ah. Ah. Ah" steadily. "There's a pill for every ill but the last one."

"Even if there was always time to take it," Ratliff said.

"Hah," Varner said again. He glanced back at Ratliff for an instant, pausing. But the little hard bright eyes were invisible now; it was only the bushy overhang of the brows which seemed to concentrate downward toward him in writhen immobility, not frowning but with a sort of fierce risibility. "Even if there was time to take it. Breathing is a sight-draft dated yesterday."

II

At nine o'clock on the second morning after that, five men were sitting or squatting along the gallery of the store. The sixth was Ratliff. He was standing up, and talking: "Maybe there wasn't but one of them things in Mrs. Littlejohn's house that night, like Eck says. But it was the biggest drove of just one horse I ever seen. It was in my room and it was on the front porch and I could hear Mrs.

Littlejohn hitting it over the head with that washboard in the backyard all at the same time. And still it was missing everybody everytime. I reckon that's what that Texas man meant by calling them bargains: that a man would need to be powerful unlucky to ever get close enough to one of them to get hurt." They laughed, all except Eck himself. He and the little boy were eating. When they mounted the steps, Eck had gone on into the store and emerged with a paper sack, from which he took a segment of cheese and with his pocket knife divided it carefully into two exact halves and gave one to the boy and took a handful of crackers from the sack and gave them to the boy, and now they squatted against the wall, side by side and, save for the difference in size, identical, eating.

"I wonder what that horse thought Ratliff was," one said. He held a spray of peach bloom between his teeth. It bore four blossoms like miniature ballet skirts of pink tulle. "Jumping out windows and running indoors in his shirt-tail? I wonder how many Ratliffs that horse thought he saw."

"I don't know," Ratliff said. "But if he saw just half as many of me as I saw of him, he was sholy surrounded. Everytime I turned my head, that thing was just running over me or just swirling to run back over that boy again. And that boy there, he stayed right under it one time to my certain knowledge for a full one-and-one-half minutes without ducking his head or even batting his eyes. Yes sir, when I looked around and seen that varmint in the door behind me blaring its eyes at me, I'd a made sho Flem Snopes had brought a tiger back from Texas except I knowed that couldn't no just one tiger completely fill a entire room." They laughed again, quietly. Lump Snopes, the clerk, sitting in the only chair tilted back against the door-facing and partly blocking the entrance, cackled suddenly.

"If Flem had knowed how quick you fellows was going to snap them horses up, he'd a probably brought some tigers," he said. "Monkeys too."

"So they was Flem's horses," Ratliff said. The laughter stopped. The other three had open knives in their hands, with which they had been trimming idly at chips and slivers of wood. Now they sat apparently absorbed in the delicate and almost tedious movements of the knife-blades. The clerk had looked quickly up and found Ratliff watching him. His constant expression of incorrigible and mirthful disbelief had left him now; only the empty wrinkles of it remained about his mouth and eyes.

"Has Flem ever said they was?" he said. "But you town fellows are smarter than us country folks. Likely you done already read Flem's mind." But Ratliff was not looking at him now.

"And I reckon we'd a bought them," he said. He stood above them again, easy, intelligent, perhaps a little sombre but still perfectly impenetrable. "Eck here, for instance. With a wife and family to support. He owns two of them, though to be sho he never had to pay money for but one. I heard folks chasing them things up until midnight last night, but Eck and that boy ain't been home at all in two days." They laughed again, except Eck. He pared off a bit of cheese and speared it on the knife-point and put it into his mouth.

"Eck caught one of hisn," the second man said.

"That so?" Ratliff said. "Which one was it, Eck? The one he give you or the one you bought?"

"The one he give me," Eck said, chewing.

"Well, well," Ratliff said. "I hadn't heard about that. But Eck's still one horse short. And the one he had to pay money for. Which is pure proof enough that them horses wasn't Flem's because wouldn't no man even give his own blood kin something he couldn't even catch." They laughed again, but they stopped when the clerk spoke. There was no mirth in his voice at all.

"Listen," he said. "All right. We done all admitted you are too smart for anybody to get ahead of. You never bought no horse from Flem or nobody else, so maybe it ain't none of your business and maybe you better just leave it at that."

"Sholy," Ratliff said. "It's done already been left at that two nights ago. The fellow that forgot to shut that lot gate done that. With the exception of Eck's horse. And we know that wasn't Flem's, because that horse was give to Eck for nothing."

"There's others besides Eck that ain't got back home yet," the man with the peach spray said. "Bookwright and Quick are still chasing theirs. They was reported three miles west of Burtsboro Old Town at eight o'clock last night. They ain't got close enough to it yet to tell which one it belongs to."

"Sholy," Ratliff said. "The only new horse-owner in this country that could a been found without bloodhounds since whoever it was left that gate open two nights ago, is Henry Armstid. He's laying right there in Mrs. Littlejohn's bedroom where he can watch the lot so that any time the one he bought happens to run back into it, all he's got to do is to holler at his wife to run out with the rope and catch it—" He ceased, though he said, "Morning, Flem," so immediately afterward and with no change whatever in tone, that the pause was not even discernible. With the exception of the clerk, who sprang up, vacated the chair with a sort of servile alacrity, and Eck and the little boy who continued to eat, they watched above their stilled hands as Snopes in the gray trousers and the minute tie and the new cap with its bright overplaid mounted the steps. He was chewing; he already carried a piece of white pine board; he jerked his head at them, looking at nobody, and took the vacated chair and opened his knife and began to whittle. The clerk now leaned in the opposite side of the door, rubbing his back against the facing. The expression of merry and invincible disbelief had returned to his face, with a quality watchful and secret.

"You're just in time," he said. "Ratliff here seems to be in a considerable sweat about who actually owned them horses." Snopes drew his knife-blade neatly along the board, the neat, surgeon-like sliver curling before it. The others were whittling again, looking carefully at nothing, except Eck and the boy, who were still eating, and the clerk rubbing his back against the door-facing and watching Snopes with that secret and alert intensity. "Maybe you could put his mind at rest." Snopes turned his head slightly and spat, across the gallery and the steps and into the dust beyond them. He drew the knife back and began another curling sliver.

"He was there too," Snopes said. "He knows as much as anybody else." This time the clerk guffawed, chortling, his features gathering toward the center of his face as though plucked there by a hand. He slapped his leg, cackling.

"You might as well to quit," he said. "You can't beat him."

"I reckon not," Ratliff said. He stood above them, not looking at any of them, his gaze fixed apparently on the empty road beyond Mrs. Littlejohn's house, impenetrable, brooding even. A hulking, half-grown boy in overalls too small for him, appeared suddenly from nowhere in particular. He stood for a while in the road, just beyond spitting-range of the gallery, with the air of having come from nowhere in particular and of not knowing where he would go next when he should move again and of not being troubled by that fact. He was looking at nothing, certainly not toward the gallery, and no one on the gallery so much as looked at him except the little boy, who now watched the boy in the road, his periwinkle eyes grave and steady above the bitten cracker in his halted hand. The boy in the road moved on, thickly undulant in the tight overalls, and vanished beyond the corner of the store, the round head and the unwinking eyes of the little boy on the gallery turning steadily to watch him out of sight. Then the little boy bit the cracker again, chewing. "Of course there's Mrs. Tull," Ratliff said. "But that's Eck she's going to sue for damaging Tull against that bridge. And as for Henry Armstid——"

"If a man ain't got gumption enough to protect himself, it's his own look-out," the clerk said.

"Sholy," Ratliff said, still in that dreamy, abstracted tone, actually speaking over his shoulder even. "And Henry Armstid, that's all right because from what I hear of the conversation that taken place, Henry had already stopped owning that horse he thought was his before that Texas man left. And as for that broke leg, that won't put him out none because his wife can make his crop." The clerk had ceased to rub his back against the door. He watched the back of Ratliff's head, unwinking too, sober and intent; he glanced at Snopes who, chewing, was watching another sliver curl away from the advancing knife-blade, then he watched the back of Ratliff's head again.

"It won't be the first time she has made their crop," the man with the peach spray said. Ratliff glanced at him.

"You ought to know. This won't be the first time I ever saw you in their field, doing plowing Henry never got around to. How many days have you already given them this year?" The man with the peach spray removed it and spat carefully and put the spray back between his teeth.

"She can run a furrow straight as I can," the second said.

"They're unlucky," the third said. "When you are unlucky, it don't matter much what you do."

"Sholy," Ratliff said. "I've heard laziness called bad luck so much that maybe it is."

"He ain't lazy," the third said. "When their mule died three or four years ago, him and her broke their land working time about in the traces with the other mule. They ain't lazy."

"So that's all right," Ratliff said, gazing up the empty road again. "Likely she will begin right away to finish the plowing; that oldest gal is pretty near big enough to work with a mule, ain't she? or at least to hold the plow steady while Mrs. Armstid helps the mule?" He glanced again toward the man with the peach spray as though for an answer, but he was not looking at the other and he went on talking without any pause. The clerk stood with his rump and back pressed against the door-facing as if he had paused in the act of scratching, watching Ratliff quite hard now, unwinking. If Ratliff had looked at Flem Snopes, he would have seen nothing below the down-slanted peak

of the cap save the steady motion of his jaws. Another sliver was curling with neat deliberation before the moving knife. "Plenty of time now because all she's got to do after she finishes washing Mrs. Littlejohn's dishes and sweeping out the house to pay hers and Henry's board, is to go out home and milk and cook up enough vittles to last the children until tomorrow and feed them and get the littlest ones to sleep and wait outside the door until that biggest gal gets the bar up and gets into bed herself with the axe——"

"The axe?" the man with the peach spray said.

"She takes it to bed with her. She's just twelve, and what with this country still more or less full of them uncaught horses that never belonged to Flem Snopes, likely she feels maybe she can't swing a mere washboard like Mrs. Littlejohn can—and then come back and wash up the supper dishes. And after that, not nothing to do until morning except to stay close enough where Henry can call her until it's light enough to chop the wood to cook breakfast and then help Mrs. Littlejohn wash the dishes and make the beds and sweep while watching the road. Because likely any time now Flem Snopes will get back from wherever he has been since the auction, which of course is to town naturally to see about his cousin that's got into a little legal trouble, and so get that five dollars. 'Only maybe he won't give it back to me,' she says, and maybe that's what Mrs. Littlejohn thought too, because she never said nothing. I could hear her——"

"And where did you happen to be during all this?" the clerk said.

"Listening," Ratliff said. He glanced back at the clerk, then he was looking away again, almost standing with his back to them. "—could hear her dumping the dishes into the pan like she was throwing them at it. 'Do you reckon he will give it back to me?' Mrs. Armstid says. 'That Texas man give it to him and said he would. All the folks there saw him give Mr. Snopes the money and heard him say I could get it from Mr. Snopes tomorrow.' Mrs. Littlejohn was washing the dishes now, washing them like a man would, like they was made out of iron. 'No,' she says. 'But asking him won't do no hurt.'—'If he wouldn't give it back, it ain't no use to ask,' Mrs. Armstid says.—'Suit yourself,' Mrs. Littlejohn says. 'It's your money.' Then I couldn't hear nothing but the dishes for a while. 'Do you reckon he might give it back to me?' Mrs. Armstid says. 'That Texas man said he would. They all heard him say it.'—'Then go and ask him for it,' Mrs. Littlejohn says. Then I couldn't hear nothing but the dishes again. 'He won't give it back to me,' Mrs. Armstid says.—'All right,' Mrs. Littlejohn says. 'Don't ask him, then.' Then I just heard the dishes. They would have two pans, both washing. 'You don't reckon he would, do you?' Mrs. Armstid says. Mrs. Littlejohn never said nothing. It sounded like she was throwing the dishes at one another. 'Maybe I better go and talk to Henry,' Mrs. Armstid says. — 'I would,' Mrs. Littlejohn says. And I be dog if it didn't sound exactly like she had two plates in her hands, beating them together like these here brass bucket-lids in a band. 'Then Henry can buy another five-dollar horse with it. Maybe he'll buy one next time that will out and out kill him. If I just thought he would, I'd give him back that money, myself.'—'I reckon I better talk to him first,' Mrs. Armstid says. And then it sounded just like Mrs. Littlejohn taken up the dishes and pans and all and throwed the whole business at

the cookstove—" Ratliff ceased. Behind him the clerk was hissing "Psst! Psst! Flem. Flem!" Then he stopped, and all of them watched Mrs. Armstid approach and mount the steps, gaunt in the shapeless gray garment, the stained tennis shoes hissing faintly on the boards. She came among them and stood, facing Snopes but not looking at anyone, her hands rolled into her apron.

"He said that day he wouldn't sell Henry that horse," she said in a flat toneless voice. "He said you had the money and I could get it from you." Snopes raised his head and turned it slightly again and spat neatly past the woman, across the gallery and into the road.

"He took all the money with him when he left," he said. Motionless, the gray garment hanging in rigid, almost formal folds like drapery in bronze, Mrs. Armstid appeared to be watching something near Snopes' feet, as though she had not heard him, or as if she had quitted her body as soon as she finished speaking and although her body, hearing, had received the words, they would have no life nor meaning until she returned. The clerk was rubbing his back steadily against the door-facing again, watching her. The little boy was watching her too with his unwinking ineffable gaze, but nobody else was. The man with the peach spray removed it and spat and put the twig back into his mouth.

"He said Henry hadn't bought no horse," she said. "He said I could get the money from you."

"I reckon he forgot it," Snopes said. "He took all the money away with him when he left." He watched her a moment longer, then he trimmed again at the stick. The clerk rubbed his back gently against the door, watching her. After a time Mrs. Armstid raised her head and looked up the road where it went on, mild with spring dust, past Mrs. Littlejohn's, beginning to rise, on past the not-yet bloomed (that would be in June) locust grove across the way, on past the schoolhouse, the weathered roof of which, rising beyond an orchard of peach and pear trees, resembled a hive swarmed about by a cloud of pink-and-white bees, ascending, mounting toward the crest of the hill where the church stood among its sparse gleam of marble headstones in the sombre cedar grove where during the long afternoons of summer the constant mourning doves called back and forth. She moved; once more the rubber soles hissing on the gnawed boards.

"I reckon it's about time to get dinner started," she said.

"How's Henry this morning, Mrs. Armstid?" Ratliff said. She looked at him, pausing, the blank eyes waking for an instant.

"He's resting, I thank you kindly," she said. Then the eyes died again and she moved again. Snopes rose from the chair, closing his knife with his thumb and brushing a litter of minute shavings from his lap.

"Wait a minute," he said. Mrs. Armstid paused again, half-turning, though still not looking at Snopes nor at any of them. Because she can't possibly actually believe it, Ratliff told himself, any more than I do. Snopes entered the store, the clerk, motionless again, his back and rump pressed against the door-facing as though waiting to start rubbing again, watched him enter, his head turning as the other passed him like the head of an owl, the little eyes blinking rapidly now. Jody Varner came up the road on his horse. He did not pass but instead turned in beside the store, toward the mulberry tree behind it where he was in the habit of hitching

his horse. A wagon came up the road, creaking past. The man driving it lifted his hand; one or two of the men on the gallery lifted theirs in response. The wagon went on. Mrs. Armstid looked after it. Snopes came out of the door, carrying a small striped paper bag and approached Mrs. Armstid. "Here," he said. Her hand turned just enough to receive it. "A little sweetening for the chaps," he said. His other hand was already in his pocket, and as he turned back to the chair, he drew something from his pocket and handed it to the clerk, who took it. It was a five-cent piece. He sat down in the chair and tilted it back against the door again. He now had the knife in his hand again, already open. He turned his head slightly and spat again, neatly past the gray garment, into the road. The little boy was watching the sack in Mrs. Armstid's hand. Then she seemed to discover it also, rousing.

"You're right kind," she said. She rolled the sack into the apron, the little boy's unwinking gaze fixed upon the lump her hands made beneath the cloth. She moved again. "I reckon I better get on and help with dinner," she said. She descended the steps, though as soon as she reached the level earth and began to retreat, the gray folds of the garment once more lost all inference and intimation of locomotion, so that she seemed to progress without motion like a figure on a retreating and diminishing float; a gray and blasted tree-trunk moving, somehow intact and upright, upon an unhurried flood. The clerk in the doorway cackled suddenly, explosively, chortling. He slapped his thigh.

"By God," he said, "You can't beat him."

Jody Varner, entering the store

from the rear, paused in midstride like a pointing bird-dog. Then, on tiptoe, in complete silence and with astonishing speed, he darted behind the counter and sped up the gloomy tunnel, at the end of which a hulking, bear-shaped figure stooped, its entire head and shoulders wedged into the glass case which contained the needles and thread and snuff and tobacco and the stale gaudy candy. He snatched the boy savagely and viciously out; the boy gave a choked cry and struggled flabbily, cramming a final handful of something into his mouth, chewing. But he ceased to struggle almost at once and became slack and inert save for his jaws. Varner dragged him around the counter as the clerk entered, seemed to bounce suddenly into the store with a sort of alert concern. "You, Saint Elmo!" he said.

"Ain't I told you and told you to keep him out of here?" Varner demanded, shaking the boy. "He's damn near eaten that candy-case clean. Stand up!" The boy hung like a half-filled sack from Varner's hand, chewing with a kind of fatalistic desperation, the eyes shut tight in the vast flaccid colorless face, the ears moving steadily and faintly to the chewing. Save for the jaw and the ears, he appeared to have gone to sleep chewing.

"You, Saint Elmo!" the clerk said. "Stand up!" The boy assumed his own weight, though he did not open his eyes yet nor cease to chew. Varner released him. "Git on home," the clerk said. The boy turned obediently to re-enter the store. Varner jerked him about again.

"Not that way," he said. The boy crossed the gallery and descended the steps, the tight overalls undulant and reluctant across his flabby thighs. Before he reached the ground, his hand rose from his pocket to his mouth; again his ears moved faintly to the motion of chewing.

"He's worse than a rat, ain't he?" the clerk said.

"Rat, hell," Varner said, breathing harshly. "He's worse than a goat. First think I know, he'll graze on back and work through that lace leather and them hame-strings and lap-links and ring-bolts and eat me and you and him all three clean out the back door. And then be damned if I wouldn't be afraid to turn my back for fear he would cross the road and start in on the gin and the blacksmith shop. Now you mind what I say. If I catch him hanging around here one more time, I'm going to set a bear-trap for him."

He went out onto the gallery, the clerk following. "Well, Eck," he said, "I hear you caught one of your horses."

"That's right," Eck said. He and the little boy had finished the crackers and cheese and he had sat for some time now, holding the empty bag.

"It was the one he give you, wasn't it?" Varner said.

"That's right," Eck said.

"Give the other one to me, paw," the little boy said.

"What happened?" Varner said.

"He broke his neck," Eck said.

"I know," Varner said. "But how?" Eck did not move. Watching him, they could almost see him visibly gathering and arranging words, speech. Varner, looking down at him, began to laugh steadily and harshly, sucking his teeth. "I'll tell you what happened. Eck and that boy finally run it into that blind lane of Freeman's, after a chase of about twenty-four hours. They figured it couldn't possibly climb them eight-foot fences of Freeman's so him and the boy tied their rope across the end of the lane,

about three feet off the ground. And
sho enough, soon as the horse come to
the end of the lane and seen Freeman's barn, it whirled just like Eck
figured it would and come helling
back up that lane like a scared hen-
hawk. It probably never even seen the
rope at all. Mrs. Freeman was watching from where she had run up onto
the porch. She said that when it hit
that rope, it looked just like one of
these here great big Christmas pin-
wheels. But the one you bought got
clean away, didn't it?"

"That's right," Eck said. "I never
had time to see which way the other
one went."

"Give him to me, paw," the little
boy said.

"You wait till we catch him," Eck
said. "We'll see about it then."

III

The two actions of Armstid pl. vs.
Snopes, and Tull pl. vs. Eckrum
Snopes (and anyone else named
Snopes or Varner either which Tull's
irate wife could contrive to involve, as
the village well knew) were accorded
a change of venue by mutual agreement and arrangement among the
litigants. Three of the parties did, that
is, because Flem Snopes flatly refused
to recognize the existence of the suit
against himself, stating once and without heat and first turning his head
slightly aside to spit, "They wasn't
none of my horses," then fell to whittling again while the baffled and helpless bailiff stood before the tilted
chair with the papers he was trying
to serve.

So the Varner surrey was not
among the wagons, the buggies, and
the saddled horses and mules which
moved out of the village on that May
Saturday morning, to converge upon
Whiteleaf store eight miles away,
coming not only from Frenchman's

Bend but from other directions too,
since by that time what Ratliff had
called "that Texas sickness," that spotty
corruption of frantic and uncatchable
horses, had spread as far as twenty and
thirty miles. By the time the Frenchman's Bend people began to arrive,
there were two dozen wagons, the
teams reversed and eased of harness
and tied to the rear wheels in order to
pass the day, and twice that many
saddled animals already standing about
the locust grove beside the store and
the site of the hearing had already been
transferred from the store to an adjacent shed where in the fall cotton
would be stored. But by nine o'clock
it was seen that even the shed would
not hold them all, so the palladium
was moved again, from the shed to
the grove itself. The horses and
mules and wagons were cleared from
it; the single chair, the gnawed table
bearing a thick Bible which had the
appearance of loving and constant use
of a piece of old and perfectly-kept
machinery and an almanac and a
copy of Mississippi Reports dated
1881 and bearing along its opening
edge a single thread-thin line of soil-
ure, as if during all the time of his
possession its owner (or user) had
opened it at only one page though
that quite often, were fetched from
the shed to the grove; a wagon and
four men were dispatched and returned presently from the church a
mile away with four wooden pews for
the litigants and their clansmen and
witnesses; behind these in turn the
spectators   stood—the   men,   the
women, the children, sober, attentive,
and neat, not in their Sunday clothes
to be sure, but in the clean working
garments donned that morning for
the Saturday's diversion of sitting
about the country stores or trips into
the county seat, and in which they
would return to the field on Monday

morning and would wear all that week until Friday night came round again.

The Justice of the Peace was a neat, small, plump old man resembling a tender caricature of all grandfathers who ever breathed, in a beautifully laundered though collarless white shirt with immaculate starch-gleaming cuffs and bosom, and steel-framed spectacles and neat, faintly curling white hair. He sat behind the table and looked at them—at the gray woman in the gray sunbonnet and dress, her clasped and motionless hands on her lap resembling a gnarl of pallid and drowned roots from a drained swamp; at Tull in his faded but absolutely clean shirt and the overalls which his womenfolks not only kept immaculately washed but starched and ironed also, and not creased through the legs but flat across them from seam to seam, so that on each Saturday morning they resembled the short pants of a small boy, and the sedate and innocent blue of his eyes above the month-old corn-silk beard which concealed most of his abraded face and which gave him an air of incredible and paradoxical dissoluteness, not as though at last and without warning he had appeared in the sight of his fellowmen in his true character, but as if an old Italian portrait of a child saint had been defaced by a vicious and idle boy; at Mrs. Tull, a strong, full-bosomed though slightly dumpy woman with an expression of grim and seething outrage which the elapsed four weeks had apparently neither increased nor diminished but had merely set, an outrage which curiously and almost at once began to give the impression of being directed not at any Snopes or at any other man in particular but at all men, all males, and of which Tull himself was not at all the victim but the subject, who sat on one side of her husband while the biggest of the four daughters sat on the other as if they (or Mrs. Tull at least) were not so much convinced that Tull might leap up and flee, as determined that he would not; and at Eck and the little boy, identical save for size, and Lump, the clerk, in a gray cap which someone actually recognized as being the one which Flem Snopes had worn when he went to Texas last year, who between spells of rapid blinking would sit staring at the Justice with the lidless intensity of a rat—and into the lens-distorted and irisless old-man's eyes of the Justice there grew an expression not only of amazement and bewilderment but, as in Ratliff's eyes while he stood on the store gallery four weeks ago, something very like terror.

"This—" he said. "I didn't expect— I didn't look to see—. I'm going to pray," he said. "I ain't going to pray loud. But I hope—" He looked at them. "I wish. . . . Maybe some of you all anyway had better do the same." He bowed his head. They watched him, quiet and grave, while he sat motionless behind the table, the light morning wind moving faintly in his thin hair and the shadow-stipple of windy leaves gliding and flowing across the starched bulge of bosom and the gleaming bone-buttoned cuffs, as rigid and almost as large as sections of six-inch stovepipe, at his joined hands. He raised his head. "Armstid against Snopes," he said. Mrs. Armstid spoke. She did not move, she looked at nothing, her hands clasped in her lap, speaking in that flat, toneless and hopeless voice:

"That Texan man said——"

"Wait," the Justice said. He looked about at the faces, the blurred eyes fleeing behind the thick lenses.

"Where is the defendant? I don't see him."

"He wouldn't come," the bailiff said.

"Wouldn't come?" the Justice said. "Didn't you serve the papers on him?"

"He wouldn't take them," the bailiff said. "He said——"

"Then he is in contempt!" the Justice cried.

"What for?" Lump Snopes said. "Ain't nobody proved yet they was his horses." The Justice looked at him.

"Are you representing the defendant?" he said. Snopes blinked at him for a moment.

"What's that mean?" he said. "That you aim for me to pay whatever fine you think you can clap onto him?"

"So he refuses to defend himself," the Justice said. "Don't he know that I can find against him for that reason, even if pure justice and decency ain't enough?"

"It'll be pure something," Snopes said. "It don't take no mind-reader to see how your mind is——"

"Shut up, Snopes," the bailiff said. "If you ain't in this case, you keep out of it." He turned back to the Justice. "What you want me to do: go over to the Bend and fetch Snopes here anyway? I reckon I can do it."

"No," the Justice said. "Wait." He looked about at the sober faces again with that bafflement, that dread. "Does anybody here know for sho who them horses belonged to? Anybody?" They looked back at him, sober, attentive—at the neat immaculate old man sitting with his hands locked together on the table before him to still the trembling. "All right, Mrs. Armstid," he said. "Tell the court what happened." She told it, unmoving, in the flat, inflectionless voice, looking at nothing, while they listened quietly, coming to the end

and ceasing without even any fall of voice, as though the tale mattered nothing and came to nothing. The Justice was looking down at his hands. When she ceased, he looked up at her. "But you haven't showed yet that Snopes owned the horses. The one you want to sue is that Texas man. And he's gone. If you got a judgment against him, you couldn't collect the money. Don't you see?"

"Mr. Snopes brought him here," Mrs. Armstid said. "Likely that Texas man wouldn't have knowed where Frenchman's Bend was if Mr. Snopes hadn't showed him."

"But it was the Texas man that sold the horses and collected the money for them." The Justice looked about again at the faces. "Is that right? You, Bookwright, is that what happened?"

"Yes," Bookwright said. The Justice looked at Mrs. Armstid again, with that pity and grief. As the morning increased the wind had risen, so that from time to time gusts of it ran through the branches overhead, bringing a faint snow of petals, prematurely bloomed as the spring itself had condensed with spendthrift speed after the hard winter, and the heavy and drowsing scent of them, about the motionless heads.

"He give Mr. Snopes Henry's money. He said Henry hadn't bought no horse. He said I could get the money from Mr. Snopes tomorrow."

"And you have witnesses that saw and heard him?"

"Yes, sir. The other men that was there saw him give Mr. Snopes the money and say that I could get it——"

"And you asked Snopes for the money?"

"Yes, sir. He said that Texas man taken it away with him when he left. But I would. . . ." She ceased again, perhaps looking down at her hands also. Certainly she was not looking at anyone.

"Yes?" the Justice said. "You would what?"

"I would know them five dollars. I earned them myself, weaving at night after Henry and the chaps was asleep. Some of the ladies in Jefferson would save up string and such and give it to me and I would weave things and sell them. I earned that money a little at a time and I would know it when I saw it because I would take the can outen the chimney and count it now and then while it was making up to enough to buy my chaps some shoes for next winter. I would know it if I was to see it again. If Mr. Snopes would just let——"

"Suppose there was somebody seen Flem give that money back to that Texas fellow," Lump Snopes said suddenly.

"Did anybody here see that?" the Justice said.

"Yes," Snopes said, harshly and violently. "Eck here did." He looked at Eck. "Go on. Tell him." The Justice looked at Eck; the four Tull girls turned their heads as one head and looked at him, and Mrs. Tull leaned forward to look past her husband, her face cold, furious, and contemptuous, and those standing shifted to look past one another's heads at Eck sitting motionless on the bench.

"Did you see Snopes give Armstid's money back to the Texas man, Eck?" the Justice said. Still Eck did not answer nor move. Lump Snopes made a gross violent sound through the side of his mouth.

"By God, I ain't afraid to say it if Eck is. I seen him do it."

"Will you swear that as testimony?" Snopes looked at the Justice. He did not blink now.

"So you won't take my word," he said.

"I want the truth," the Justice said. "If I can't find that, I got to have sworn evidence of what I will have to accept as truth." He lifted the Bible from the two other books.

"All right," the bailiff said. "Step up here." Snopes rose from the bench and approached. They watched him, though now there was no shifting nor craning, no movement at all among the faces, the still eyes. Snopes at the table looked back at them once, his gaze traversing swiftly the crescent-shaped rank; he looked at the Justice again. The bailiff grasped the Bible; though the Justice did not release it yet.

"You are ready to swear you saw Snopes give that Texas man back the money he took from Henry Armstid for that horse?" he said.

"I said I was, didn't I?" Snopes said. The Justice released the Bible.

"Swear him," he said.

"Put your left hand on the Book raise your right hand you solemnly swear and affirm—" the bailiff said rapidly. But Snopes had already done so, his left hand clapped onto the extended Bible and the other hand raised and his head turned away as once more his gaze went rapidly along the circle of expressionless and intent faces, saying in that harsh and snarling voice:

"Yes. I saw Flem Snopes give back to that Texas man whatever money Henry Armstid or anybody else thinks Henry Armstid or anybody else paid Flem for any of them horses. Does that suit you?"

"Yes," the Justice said. Then there was no movement, no sound anywhere among them. The bailiff placed the Bible quietly on the table beside the Justice's locked hands, and there was no movement save the flow and recover of the windy shadows and the drift of the locust petals. Then Mrs.

Armstid rose; she stood once more (or still) looking at nothing, her hands clasped across her middle.

"I reckon I can go now, can't I?" she said.

"Yes," the Justice said, rousing. "Unless you would like——"

"I better get started," she said. "It's a right far piece." She had not come in the wagon, but on one of the gaunt and underfed mules. One of the men followed her across the grove and untied the mule for her and led it up to a wagon, from one hub of which she mounted. Then they looked at the Justice again. He sat behind the table, his hands still joined before him, though his head was not bowed now. Yet he did not move until the bailiff leaned and spoke to him, when he roused, came suddenly awake without starting, as an old man wakes from an old man's light sleep. He removed his hands from the table and, looking down, he spoke exactly as if he were reading from a paper:

"Tull against Snopes. Assault and ——"

"Yes!" Mrs. Tull said. "I'm going to say a word before you start." She leaned, looking past Tull at Lump Snopes again. "If you think you are going to lie and perjure Flem and Eck Snopes out of——"

"Now, mamma," Tull said. Now she spoke to Tull, without changing her position or her tone or even any break or pause in her speech:

"Don't you say hush to me! You'll let Eck Snopes or Flem Snopes or that whole Varner tribe snatch you out of the wagon and beat you half to death against a wooden bridge. But when it comes to suing them for your just rights and a punishment, oh no. Because that wouldn't be neighborly. What's neighborly got to do with you lying flat on your back in the middle of planting time while we pick splint-

ers out of your face?" By this time the bailiff was shouting,

"Order! Order! This here's a law court!" Mrs. Tull ceased. She sat back, breathing hard, staring at the Justice, who sat and spoke again as if he were reading aloud:

"—assault and battery on the person of Vernon Tull, through the agency and instrument of one horse, unnamed, belonging to Eckrum Snopes. Evidence of physical detriment and suffering, defendant himself. Witnesses, Mrs. Tull and daughters——"

"Eck Snopes saw it too," Mrs. Tull said, though with less violence now. "He was there. He got there in plenty of time to see it. Let him deny it. Let him look me in the face and deny it if he——"

"If you please, ma'am," the Justice said. He said it so quietly that Mrs. Tull hushed and became quite calm, almost a rational and composed being. "The injury to your husband ain't disputed. And the agency of the horse ain't disputed. The laws says that when a man owns a creature which he knows to be dangerous and if that creature is restrained and restricted from the public commons by a pen or enclosure capable of restraining and restricting it, if a man enter that pen or enclosure, whether he knows the creature in it is dangerous or not dangerous, then that man has committed trespass and the owner of that creature is not liable. But if that creature known to him to be dangerous ceases to be restrained by that suitable pen or enclosure, either by accident or design and either with or without the owner's knowledge, then that owner is liable. That's the law. All necessary now is to establish first, the ownership of the horse, and second, that the horse was a dangerous creature within the definition of the law as provided."

"Hah," Mrs. Tull said. She said it

exactly as Bookwright would have. "Dangerous. Ask Vernon Tull. Ask Henry Armstid if them things was pets."

"If you please, ma'am," the Justice said. He was looking at Eck. "What is the defendant's position? Denial of ownership?"

"What?" Eck said.

"Was that your horse that ran over Mr. Tull?"

"Yes," Eck said. "It was mine. How much do I have to p——"

"Hah," Mrs. Tull said again. "Denial of ownership. When there were at least forty men—fools too, or they wouldn't have been there. But even a fool's word is good about what he saw and heard—at least forty men heard that Texas murderer give that horse to Eck Snopes. Not sell it to him, mind; give it to him."

"What?" the Justice said. "Gave it to him?"

"Yes," Eck said. "He give it to me. I'm sorry Tull happened to be using that bridge too at the same time. How much do I——"

"Wait," the Justice said. "What did you give him? a note? a swap of some kind?"

"No," Eck said. "He just pointed to it in the lot and told me it belonged to me."

"And he didn't give you a bill of sale or a deed or anything in writing?"

"I reckon he never had time," Eck said. "And after Lon Quick forgot and left that gate open, never nobody had time to do no writing even if we had a thought of it."

"What's all this?" Mrs. Tull said. "Eck Snopes has just told you he owned that horse. And if you won't take his word, there were forty men standing at that gate all day long doing nothing, that heard that murdering card-playing whiskey-drinking anti-christ—" This time the Justice

raised one hand, in its enormous pristine cuff, toward her. He did not look at her.

"Wait," he said. "Then what did he do?" he said to Eck. "Just lead the horse up and put the rope in your hand?"

"No," Eck said. "Him nor nobody else never got no ropes on none of them. He just pointed to the horse in the lot and said it was mine and auctioned off the rest of them and got into the buggy and said good-bye and druv off. And we got our ropes and went into the lot, only Lon Quick forgot to shut the gate. I'm sorry it made Tull's mules snatch him outen the wagon. How much do I owe him?" Then he stopped, because the Justice was no longer looking at him and, as he realized a moment later, no longer listening either. Instead, he was sitting back in the chair, actually leaning back in it for the first time, his head bent slightly and his hands resting on the table before him, the fingers lightly overlapped. They watched him quietly for almost a half-minute before anyone realized that he was looking quietly and steadily at Mrs. Tull.

"Well, Mrs. Tull," he said, "by your own testimony, Eck never owned that horse."

"What?" Mrs. Tull said. It was not loud at all. "What did you say?"

"In the law, ownership can't be conferred or invested by word-of-mouth. It must be established either by recorded or authentic document, or by possession or occupation. By your testimony and his both, he never gave that Texan anything in exchange for that horse, and by his testimony the Texas man never gave him any paper to prove he owned it, and by his testimony and by what I know myself from these last four weeks, nobody yet has ever laid hand or rope either on any one of them. So that horse never came into Eck's possession at all. That Texas man could have given that same horse to a dozen other men standing around that gate that day, without even needing to tell Eck he had done it; and Eck himself could have transferred all his title and equity in it to Mr. Tull right there while Mr. Tull was lying unconscious on that bridge just by thinking it to himself, and Mr. Tull's title would be just as legal as Eck's."

"So I get nothing," Mrs. Tull said. Her voice was still calm, quiet, though probably no one but Tull realized that it was too calm and quiet. "My team is made to run away by a wild spotted mad dog, my wagon is wrecked; my husband is jerked out of it and knocked unconscious and unable to work for a whole week with less than half of our seed in the ground, and I get nothing."

"Wait," the Justice said. "The law——"

"The law," Mrs. Tull said. She stood suddenly up—a short, broad, strong woman, balanced on the balls of her planted feet.

"Now, mamma," Tull said.

"Yes, ma'am," the Justice said. "Your damages are fixed by statute. The law says that when a suit for damages is brought against the owner of an animal which has committed damage or injury, if the owner of the animal either can't or won't assume liability, the injured or damaged party shall find recompense in the body of the animal. And since Eck Snopes never owned that horse at all, and since you just heard a case here this morning that failed to prove that Flem Snopes had any equity in any of them, that horse still belongs to that Texas man. Or did belong. Because now that horse that made your team run away and snatch your husband out

of the wagon, belongs to you and Mr. Tull."

"Now, mamma!" Tull said. He rose quickly. But Mrs. Tull was still quiet, only quite rigid and breathing hard, until Tull spoke. Then she turned on him, not screaming: shouting; presently the bailiff was banging the table-top with his hand-polished hickory cane and roaring "Order! Order!" while the neat old man, thrust backward in his chair as though about to dodge and trembling with an old man's palsy, looked on with amazed unbelief.

"The horse!" Mrs. Tull shouted. "We see it for five seconds, while it is climbing into the wagon with us and then out again. Then it's gone, God don't know where and thank the Lord He don't! And the mules gone with it and the wagon wrecked and you laying there on the bridge with your face full of kindling-wood and bleeding like a hog and dead for all we knew. And he gives us the horse! Don't hush me! Get on to that wagon, fool that would sit there behind a pair of young mules with the reins tied around his wrist! Get on to that wagon, all of you!"

"I can't stand no more!" the old Justice cried. "I won't! This court's adjourned! Adjourned!" * * *

1940

ERSKINE CALDWELL
(1903–)
KNEEL TO THE RISING SUN *

A shiver went through Lonnie. He drew his hand away from his sharp chin, remembering what Clem had said. It made him feel now as if he were committing a crime by standing

* Reprinted by permission of the Publishers, Duell, Sloan and Pearce, Inc. Copyright 1944 by Erskine Caldwell.

in Arch Gunnard's presence and allowing his face to be seen.

He and Clem had been walking up the road together that afternoon on their way to the filling station when he told Clem how much he needed rations. Clem stopped a moment to kick a rock out of the road, and said that if you worked for Arch Gunnard long enough, your face would be sharp enough to split the boards for your own coffin.

As Lonnie turned away to sit down on an empty box beside the gasoline pump, he could not help wishing that he could be as unafraid of Arch Gunnard as Clem was. Even if Clem was a Negro, he never hesitated to ask for rations when he needed something to eat; and when he and his family did not get enough, Clem came right out and told Arch so. Arch stood for that, but he swore that he was going to run Clem out of the country the first chance he got.

Lonnie knew without turning around that Clem was standing at the corner of the filling station with two or three other Negroes and looking at him, but for some reason he was unable to meet Clem's eyes.

Arch Gunnard was sitting in the sun, honing his jack-knife blade on his boot top. He glanced once or twice at Lonnie's hound, Nancy, who was lying in the middle of the road waiting for Lonnie to go home.

"That your dog, Lonnie?"

Jumping with fear, Lonnie's hand went to his chin to hide the lean face that would accuse Arch of short-rationing.

Arch snapped his fingers and the hound stood up, wagging her tail. She waited to be called.

"Mr. Arch, I—"

Arch called the dog. She began crawling towards them on her belly, wagging her tail a little faster each time Arch's fingers snapped. When she was several feet away, she turned over on her back and lay on the ground with her four paws in the air.

Dudley Smith and Jim Weaver, who were lounging around the filling station, laughed. They had been leaning against the side of the building, but they straightened up to see what Arch was up to.

Arch spat some more tobacco juice on his boot top and whetted the jack-knife blade some more.

"What kind of a hound dog is that, anyway, Lonnie?" Arch said. "Looks like to me it might be a ketch hound."

Lonnie could feel Clem Henry's eyes boring into the back of his head. He wondered what Clem would do if it had been his dog Arch Gunnard was snapping his fingers at and calling like that.

"His tail's way too long for a coon hound or a bird dog, ain't it, Arch?" somebody behind Lonnie said, laughing out loud.

Everybody laughed then, including Arch. They looked at Lonnie, waiting to hear what he was going to say to Arch.

"Is he a ketch hound, Lonnie?" Arch said, snapping his fingers again.

"Mr. Arch, I—"

"Don't be ashamed of him, Lonnie, if he don't show signs of turning out to be a bird dog or a fox hound. Everybody needs a hound around the house that can go out and catch pigs and rabbits when you are in a hurry for them. A ketch hound is a mighty respectable animal. I've known the time when I was mighty proud to own one."

Everybody laughed.

Arch Gunnard was getting ready to grab Nancy by the tail. Lonnie sat up, twisting his neck until he caught a glimpse of Clem Henry at the other corner of the filling station. Clem was staring at him with unmistakable meaning, with the same look in his eyes he had had that afternoon when he said that nobody who worked for Arch Gunnard ought to stand for short-rationing. Lonnie lowered his eyes. He could not figure out how a Negro could be braver than he was. There were a lot of times like that when he would have given anything he had to be able to jump into Clem's shoes and change places with him.

"The trouble with this hound of yours, Lonnie, is that he's too heavy on his feet. Don't you reckon it would be a pretty slick little trick to lighten the load some, being as how he's a ketch hound to begin with?"

Lonnie remembered then what Clem Henry had said he would do if Arch Gunnard ever tried to cut off his dog's tail. Lonnie knew, and Clem knew, and everybody else knew, that that would give Arch the chance he was waiting for. All Arch asked, he had said, was for Clem Henry to overstep his place just one little half-inch, or to talk back to him with just one little short word, and he would do the rest. Everybody knew what Arch meant by that, especially if Clem did not turn and run. And Clem had not been known to run from anybody, after fifteen years in the country.

Arch reached down and grabbed Nancy's tail while Lonnie was wondering about Clem. Nancy acted as if she thought Arch were playing some kind of a game with her. She turned her head around until she could·reach Arch's hand to lick it. He cracked her on the bridge of the nose with the end of the jack-knife.

"He's a mighty playful dog, Lonnie," Arch said, catching up a shorter grip on the tail, "but his wagpole is way too long for a dog his size, espe-

cially when he·wants to be a ketch hound."

Lonnie swallowed hard.

"Mr. Arch, she's a mighty fine rabbit tracker. I—"

"Shucks, Lonnie," Arch said, whetting the knife blade on the dog's tail, "I ain't never seen a hound in all my life that needed a tail that long to hunt rabbits with. It's way too long for just a common, ordinary everyday ketch hound."

Lonnie looked up hopefully at Dudley Smith and the others. None of them offered any help. It was useless for him to try to stop Arch, because Arch Gunnard would let nothing stand in his way when once he had set his head on what he wished to do. Lonnie knew that if he should let himself show any anger or resentment, Arch would drive him off the farm before sundown that night. Clem Henry was the only person there who would help him, but Clem . . .

The white men and the Negroes at both corners of the filling station waited to see what Lonnie was going to do about it. All of them hoped he would put up a fight for his hound. If anyone ever had the nerve to stop Arch Gunnard from cutting off a dog's tail, it might put an end to it. It was plain, though, that Lonnie, who was one of Arch's share-croppers, was afraid to speak up. Clem Henry might; Clem was the only one who might try to stop Arch, even if it meant trouble. And all of them knew that Arch would insist on running Clem out of the country, or filling him full of lead.

"I reckon it's all right with you, ain't it, Lonnie?" Arch said. "I don't seem to hear no objections."

Clem Henry stepped forward several spaces, and stopped.

Arch laughed, watching Lonnie's face, and jerked Nancy to her feet.

The hound cried out in pain and surprise, but Arch made her be quiet by kicking her in the belly.

Lonnie winced. He could hardly bear to see anybody kick his dog like that.

"Mr. Arch, I . . ."

A contraction in his throat almost choked him for several moments, and he had to open his mouth wide and fight for breath. The other white men around him were silent. Nobody liked to see a dog kicked in the belly like that.

Lonnie could see the other end of the filling station from the corner of his eye. He saw a couple of Negroes go up behind Clem and grasp his overalls. Clem spat on the ground, between outspread feet, but he did not try to break away from them.

"Being as how I don't hear no objections, I reckon it's all right to go ahead and cut it off," Arch said, spitting.

Lonnie's head went forward and all he could see of Nancy was her hind feet. He had come to ask for a slab of sowbelly and some molasses, or something. Now he did not know if he could ever bring himself to ask for rations, no matter how much hungrier they became at home.

"I always make it a habit of asking a man first," Arch said. "I wouldn't want to go ahead and cut off a tail if a man had any objections. That wouldn't be right. No, sir, it just wouldn't be fair and square."

Arch caught a shorter grip on the hound's tail and placed the knife blade on it two or three inches from the rump. It looked to those who were watching as if his mouth were watering, because tobacco juice began to trickle down the corners of his lips. He brought up the back of his hand and wiped his mouth.

A noisy automobile came plowing down the road through the deep red dust. Everyone looked up as it passed in order to see who was in it.

Lonnie glanced at it, but he could not keep his eyes raised. His head fell downward once more until he could feel his sharp chin cutting into his chest. He wondered then if Arch had noticed how lean his face was.

"I keep two or three ketch hounds around my place," Arch said, honing the blade on the tail of the dog as if it were a razor strop until his actions brought smiles to the faces of the men grouped around him, "but I never could see the sense of a ketch hound having a long tail. It only gets in their way when I send them out to catch a pig or a rabbit for my supper."

Pulling with his left hand and pushing with his right, Arch Gunnard docked the hound's tail as quickly and as easily as if he were cutting a willow switch in the pasture to drive the cows home with. The dog sprang forward with the release of her tail until she was far beyond Arch's reach, and began howling so loud she could be heard half a mile away. Nancy stopped once and looked back at Arch, and then she sprang to the middle of the road and began leaping and twisting in circles. All that time she was yelping and biting at the bleeding stub of her tail.

Arch leaned backward and twirled the severed tail in one hand while he wiped the jack-knife blade on his boot sole. He watched Lonnie's dog chasing herself around in circles in the red dust.

Nobody had anything to say then. Lonnie tried not to watch his dog's agony, and he forced himself to keep from looking at Clem Henry. Then, with his eyes shut, he wondered why he had remained on Arch Gunnard's plantation all those past years, sharecropping for a mere living on short-rations, and becoming leaner and leaner all the time. He knew then how true it was what Clem had said about Arch's share-croppers' faces becoming sharp enough to hew their own coffins. His hands went to his chin before he knew what he was doing. His hand dropped when he had felt the bones of jaw and the exposed tendons of his cheeks.

As hungry as he was, he knew that even if Arch did give him some rations then, there would not be nearly enough for them to eat for the following week. Hatty, his wife, was already broken down from hunger and work in the fields, and his father, Mark Newsome, stone-deaf for the past twenty years, was always asking him why there was never enough food in the house for them to have a solid meal. Lonnie's head fell forward a little more, and he could feel his eyes becoming damp.

The pressure of his sharp chin against his chest made him so uncomfortable that he had to raise his head at last in order to ease the pain of it.

The first thing he saw when he looked up was Arch Gunnard twirling Nancy's tail in his left hand. Arch Gunnard had a trunk full of dogs' tails at home. He had been cutting off tails ever since anyone could remember, and during all those years he had accumulated a collection of which he was so proud that he kept the trunk locked and the key tied around his neck on a string. On Sunday afternoons when the preacher came to visit, or when a crowd was there to loll on the front porch and swap stories, Arch showed them off, naming each tail from memory just as well as if he had had a tag on it.

Clem Henry had left the filling station and was walking alone down the road towards the plantation. Clem Henry's house was in a cluster of Negro cabins below Arch's big house, and he had to pass Lonnie's house to get there. Lonnie was on the verge of getting up and leaving when he saw Arch looking at him. He did not know whether Arch was looking at his lean face, or whether he was watching to see if he were going to get up and go down the road with Clem.

The thought of leaving reminded him of his reason for being there. He had to have some rations before suppertime that night, no matter how short they were.

"Mr. Arch, I . . ."

Arch stared at him for a moment, appearing as if he had turned to listen to some strange sound unheard of before that moment.

Lonnie bit his lips, wondering if Arch was going to say anything about how lean and hungry he looked. But Arch was thinking about something else. He slapped his hand on his leg and laughed out loud.

"I sometimes wish niggers had tails," Arch said, coiling Nancy's tail into a ball and putting it into his pocket. "I'd a heap rather cut off nigger tails than dog tails. There'd be more to cut, for one thing."

Dudley Smith and somebody else behind them laughed for a brief moment. The laughter died out almost as suddenly as it had risen.

The Negroes who had heard Arch shuffled their feet in the dust and moved backwards. It was only a few minutes until not one was left at the filling station. They went up the road behind the red wooden building until they were out of sight.

Arch got up and stretched. The sun was getting low, and it was no longer comfortable in the October air. "Well, I reckon I'll be getting on home to get me some supper," he said.

He walked slowly to the middle

of the road and stopped to look at Nancy retreating along the ditch.

"Nobody going my way?" he asked. "What's wrong with you, Lonnie? Going home to supper, ain't you?"

"Mr. Arch, I . . ."

Lonnie found himself jumping to his feet. His first thought was to ask for the sowbelly and molasses, and maybe some corn meal; but when he opened his mouth, the words refused to come out. He took several steps forward and shook his head. He did not know what Arch might say or do if he said "no."

"Hatty'll be looking for you," Arch said, turning his back and walking off.

He reached into his hip pocket and took out Nancy's tail. He began twirling it as he walked down the road towards the big house in the distance.

Dudley Smith went inside the filling station, and the others walked away.

After Arch had gone several hundred yards, Lonnie sat down heavily on the box beside the gas pump from which he had got up when Arch spoke to him. He sat down heavily, his shoulders drooping, his arms falling between his outspread legs.

Lonnie did not know how long his eyes had been closed, but when he opened them, he saw Nancy lying between his feet, licking the docked tail. When he watched her, he felt the sharp point of his chin cutting into his chest again. Presently the door behind him was slammed shut, and a minute later he could hear Dudley Smith walking away from the filling station on his way home.

II

Lonnie had been sleeping fitfully for several hours when he suddenly found himself wide awake. Hatty shook him again. He raised himself on his elbow and tried to see into the darkness of the room. Without knowing what time it was, he was able to determine that it was still nearly two hours until sunrise.

"Lonnie," Hatty said again, trembling in the cold night air, "Lonnie, your pa ain't in the house."

Lonnie sat upright in bed.

"How do you know he ain't?" he said.

"I've been lying here wide awake ever since I got in bed, and I heard him when he went out. He's been gone all that time."

"Maybe he just stepped out for a while," Lonnie said, turning and trying to see through the bedroom window.

"I know what I'm saying, Lonnie," Hatty insisted. "Your pa's been gone a heap too long."

Both of them sat without a sound for several minutes while they listened for Mark Newsome.

Lonnie got up and lit a lamp. He shivered while he was putting on his shirt, overalls, and shoes. He tied his shoelaces in hard knots because he couldn't see in the faint light. Outside the window it was almost pitch-dark, and Lonnie could feel the damp October air blowing against his face.

"I'll go help look," Hatty said, throwing the covers off and starting to get up.

Lonnie went to the bed and drew the covers back over her and pushed her back into place.

"You try to get some sleep, Hatty," he said; "you can't stay awake the whole night. I'll go bring Pa back."

He left Hatty, blowing out the lamp, and stumbled through the dark hall, feeling his way to the front porch by touching the wall with his hands. When he got to the porch, he could still barely see any distance ahead, but his eyes were becoming more accustomed to the darkness. He waited a minute, listening.

Feeling his way down the steps into the yard, he walked around the corner of the house and stopped to listen again before calling his father.

"Oh, Pa!" he said loudly. "Oh, Pa!"

He stopped under the bedroom window when he realized what he had been doing.

"Now that's a fool thing for me to be out here doing," he said, scolding himself. "Pa couldn't hear it thunder."

He heard a rustling of the bed.

"He's been gone long enough to get clear to the crossroads, or more," Hatty said, calling through the window.

"Now you lay down and try to get a little sleep, Hatty," Lonnie told her. "I'll bring him back in no time."

He could hear Nancy scratching fleas under the house, but he knew she was in no condition to help look for Mark. It would be several days before she recovered from the shock of losing her tail.

"He's been gone a long time," Hatty said, unable to keep still.

"That don't make no difference," Lonnie said. "I'll find him sooner or later. Now you go on to sleep like I told you, Hatty."

Lonnie walked towards the barn, listening for some sound. Over at the big house he could hear the hogs grunting and squealing, and he wished they would be quiet so he could hear other sounds. Arch Gunnard's dogs were howling occasionally, but they were not making any more noise than they usually did at night, and he was accustomed to their howling.

Lonnie went to the barn, looking inside and out. After walking around the barn, he went into the field as far as the cotton shed. He knew it was

useless, but he could not keep from calling his father time after time.

"Oh, Pa!" he said, trying to penetrate the darkness.

He went farther into the field.

"Now, what in the world could have become of Pa?" he said, stopping and wondering where to look next.

After he had gone back to the front yard, he began to feel uneasy for the first time. Mark had not acted any more strangely during the past week than he ordinarily did, but Lonnie knew he was upset over the way Arch Gunnard was giving out short-rations. Mark had even said that, at the rate they were being fed, all of them would starve to death inside another three months.

Lonnie left the yard and went down the road towards the Negro cabins. When he got to Clem's house, he turned in and walked up the path to the door. He knocked several times and waited. There was no answer, and he rapped louder.

"Who's that?" he heard Clem say from bed.

"It's me," Lonnie said. "I've got to see you a minute, Clem. I'm out in the front yard."

He sat down and waited for Clem to dress and come outside. While he waited, he strained his ears to catch any sound that might be in the air. Over the fields towards the big house he could hear the fattening hogs grunt and squeal.

Clem came out and shut the door. He stood on the doorsill a moment speaking to his wife in bed, telling her he would be back and not to worry.

"Who's that?" Clem said, coming down into the yard.

Lonnie got up and met Clem halfway.

"What's the trouble?" Clem asked then, buttoning up his overall jumper.

"Pa's not in his bed," Lonnie said, "and Hatty says he's been gone from the house most all night. I went out in the field, and all around the barn, but I couldn't find a trace of him anywhere."

Clem then finished buttoning his jumper and began rolling a cigarette. He walked slowly down the path to the road. It was still dark, and it would be at least an hour before dawn made it any lighter.

"Maybe he was too hungry to stay in the bed any longer," Clem said. "When I saw him yesterday, he said he was so shrunk up and weak he didn't know if he could last much longer. He looked like his skin and bones couldn't shrivel much more."

"I asked Arch last night after suppertime for some rations—just a little piece of sowbelly and some molasses. He said he'd get around to letting me have some the first thing this morning."

"Why don't you tell him to give you full rations or none?" Clem said. "If you knew you wasn't going to get none at all, you could move away and find a better man to share-crop for, couldn't you?"

"I've been loyal to Arch Gunnard for a long time now," Lonnie said. "I'd hate to haul off and leave him like that."

Clem looked at Lonnie, but he did not say anything more just then. They turned up the road towards the driveway that led up to the big house. The fattening hogs were still grunting and squealing in the pen, and one of Arch's hounds came down a cotton row beside the driveway to smell their shoes.

"Them fattening hogs always get enough to eat," Clem said. "There's not a one of them that don't weigh seven hundred pounds right now, and they're getting bigger every day. Be-

sides taking all that's thrown to them, they make a lot of meals off the chickens that get in there to peck around."

Lonnie listened to the grunting of the hogs as they walked up the driveway towards the big house.

"Reckon we'd better get Arch up to help look for Pa?" Lonnie said. "I'd hate to wake him up, but I'm scared Pa might stray off into the swamp and get lost for good. He couldn't hear it thunder, even. I never could find him back there in all that tangle if he got into it."

Clem said something under his breath and went on towards the barn and hog pen. He reached the pen before Lonnie got there.

"You'd better come here quick," Clem said, turning around to see where Lonnie was.

Lonnie ran to the hog pen. He stopped and climbed halfway up the wooden-and-wire sides of the fence. At first he could see nothing, but gradually he was able to see the moving mass of black fattening hogs on the other side of the pen. They were biting and snarling at each other like a pack of hungry hounds turned loose on a dead rabbit.

Lonnie scrambled to the top of the fence, but Clem caught him and pulled him back.

"Don't go in that hog pen that way," he said. "Them hogs will tear you to pieces, they're that wild. They're fighting over something."

Both of them ran around the corner of the pen and got to the side where the hogs were. Down under their feet on the ground Lonnie caught a glimpse of a dark mass splotched with white. He was able to see it for a moment only, because one of the hogs trampled over it.

Clem opened and closed his mouth several times before he was able to say anything at all. He clutched at Lonnie's arm, shaking him.

"That looks like it might be your pa," he said. "I swear before goodness, Lonnie, it does look like it."

Lonnie still could not believe it. He climbed to the top of the fence and began kicking his feet at the hogs, trying to drive them away. They paid no attention to him.

While Lonnie was perched there, Clem had gone to the wagon shed, and he ran back with two singletrees he had somehow managed to find there in the dark. He handed one to Lonnie, poking it at him until Lonnie's attention was drawn from the hogs long enough to take it.

Clem leaped over the fence and began swinging the singletree at the hogs. Lonnie slid down beside him, yelling at them. One hog turned on Lonnie and snapped at him, and Clem struck it over the back of the neck with enough force to drive it off momentarily.

By then Lonnie was able to realize what had happened. He ran to the mass of hogs, kicking them with his heavy stiff shoes and striking them on their heads with the iron-tipped singletree. Once he felt a stinging sensation, and looked down to see one of the hogs biting the calf of his leg. He had just enough time to hit the hog and drive it away before his leg was torn. He knew most of his overall leg had been ripped away, because he could feel the night air on his bare wet calf.

Clem had gone ahead and had driven the hogs back. There was no other way to do anything. They were in a snarling circle around them, and both of them had to keep the singletrees swinging back and forth all the time to keep the hogs off. Finally Lonnie reached down and got a grip on Mark's leg. With Clem helping,

Lonnie carried his father to the fence and lifted him over to the other side.

They were too much out of breath for a while to say anything, or to do anything else. The snarling, fattening hogs were at the fence, biting the wood and wire, and making more noise than ever.

While Lonnie was searching in his pockets for a match, Clem struck one. He held the flame close to Mark Newsome's head.

They both stared unbelievingly, and then Clem blew out the match. There was nothing said as they stared at each other in the darkness.

Clem walked several steps away, and turned and came back beside Lonnie.

"It's him, though," Clem said, sitting down on the ground. "It's him, all right."

"I reckon so," Lonnie said. He could think of nothing else to say then.

They sat on the ground, one on each side of Mark, looking at the body. There had been no sign of life in the body beside them since they had first touched it. The face, throat, and stomach had been completely devoured.

"You'd better go wake up Arch Gunnard," Clem said after a while.

"What for?" Lonnie said. "He can't help none now. It's too late for help."

"Makes no difference," Clem insisted. "You'd better go wake him up and let him see what there is to see. If you wait till morning, he might take it into his head to say the hogs didn't do it. Right now is the time to get him up so he can see what his hogs did."

Clem turned around and looked at the big house. The dark outline against the dark sky made him hesitate.

"A man who short-rationed tenants

ought to have to sit and look at that till it's buried."

Lonnie looked at Clem fearfully. He knew Clem was right, but he was scared to hear a Negro say anything like that about a white man.

"You oughtn't talk like that about Arch," Lonnie said. "He's in bed asleep. He didn't have a thing to do with it. He didn't have no more to do with it than I did."

Clem laughed a little, and threw the singletree on the ground between his feet. After letting it lie there a little while, he picked it up and began beating the ground with it.

Lonnie got to his feet slowly. He had never seen Clem act like that before, and he did not know what to think about it. He left without saying anything and walked stiffly to the house in the darkness to wake up Arch Gunnard.

III

Arch was hard to wake up. And even after he was awake, he was in no hurry to get up. Lonnie was standing outside the bedroom window, and Arch was lying in bed six or eight feet away. Lonnie could hear him toss and grumble.

"Who told you to come and wake me up in the middle of the night?" Arch said.

"Well, Clem Henry's out here, and he said maybe you'd like to know about it."

Arch tossed around on the bed, flailing the pillow with his fists.

"You tell Clem Henry I said that one of these days he's going to find himself turned inside out, like a coat-sleeve."

Lonnie waited doggedly. He knew Clem was right in insisting that Arch ought to wake up and come out there to see what had happened. Lonnie was afraid to go back to the barnyard

and tell Clem that Arch was not coming. He did not know, but he had a feeling that Clem might go into the bedroom and drag Arch out of bed. He did not like to think of anything like that taking place.

"Are you still out there, Lonnie?" Arch shouted.

"I'm right here, Mr. Arch. I—"

"If I wasn't so sleepy, I'd come out there and take a stick and—I don't know what I wouldn't do!"

Lonnie met Arch at the back step. On the way out to the hog pen Arch did not speak to him. Arch walked heavily ahead, not even waiting to see if Lonnie was coming. The lantern that Arch was carrying cast long flat beams of yellow light over the ground; and when they got to where Clem was waiting beside Mark's body, the Negro's face shone in the night like a highly polished plowshare.

"What was Mark doing in my hog pen at night, anyway?" Arch said, shouting at them both.

Neither Clem nor Lonnie replied. Arch glared at them for not answering. But no matter how many times he looked at them, his eyes returned each time to stare at the torn body of Mark Newsome on the ground at his feet.

"There's nothing to be done now," Arch said finally. "We'll just have to wait till daylight and send for the undertaker." He walked a few steps away. "Looks like you could have waited till morning in the first place. There wasn't no sense in getting me up."

He turned his back and looked sideways at Clem. Clem stood up and looked him straight in the eyes.

"What do you want, Clem Henry?" he said. "Who told you to be coming around my house in the middle of the night? I don't want niggers coming here except when I send for them."

"I couldn't stand to see anybody eaten up by the hogs, and not do anything about it," Clem said.

"You mind your own business," Arch told him. "And when you talk to me, take off your hat, or you'll be sorry for it. It wouldn't take much to make me do you up the way you belong."

Lonnie backed away. There was a feeling of uneasiness around them. That was how trouble between Clem and Arch always began. He had seen it start that way dozens of times before. As long as Clem turned and went away, nothing happened, but sometimes he stayed right where he was and talked up to Arch just as if he had been a white man, too.

Lonnie hoped it would not happen this time. Arch was already mad enough about being waked up in the middle of the night, and Lonnie knew there was no limit to what Arch would do when he got good and mad at a Negro. Nobody had ever seen him kill a Negro, but he had said he had, and he told people that he was not scared to do it again.

"I reckon you know how he came to get eaten up by the hogs like that," Clem said, looking straight at Arch.

Arch whirled around.

"Are you talking to me . . . ?"

"I asked you that," Clem stated.

"God damn you, you yellow-blooded . . ." Arch yelled.

He swung the lantern at Clem's head. Clem dodged, but the bottom of it hit his shoulder, and it was smashed to pieces. The oil splattered on the ground, igniting in the air from the flaming wick. Clem was lucky not to have it splash on his face and overalls.

"Now, look here . . ." Clem said.

"You yellow-blooded nigger," Arch said, rushing at him. "I'll teach you to talk back to me. You've got too big for your place for the last time. I've been taking too much from you, but I ain't doing it no more."

"Mr. Arch, I . . ." Lonnie said, stepping forward partly between them. No one heard him.

Arch stood back and watched the kerosene flicker out on the ground.

"You know good and well why he got eaten up by the fattening hogs," Clem said, standing his ground. "He was so hungry he had to get up out of bed in the middle of the night and come up here in the dark trying to find something to eat. Maybe he was trying to find the smokehouse. It makes no difference, either way. He's been on short-rations like everybody else working on your place, and he was so old he didn't know where else to look for food except in your smokehouse. You know good and well that's how he got lost up here in the dark and fell in the hog pen."

The kerosene had died out completely. In the last faint flare, Arch had reached down and grabbed up the singletree that had been lying on the ground where Lonnie had dropped it.

Arch raised the singletree over his head and struck with all his might at Clem. Clem dodged, but Arch drew back again quickly and landed a blow on his arm just above the elbow before Clem could dodge it. Clem's arm dropped to his side, dangling lifelessly.

"You god-damn yellow-blooded nigger!" Arch shouted. "Now's your time, you black bastard! I've been waiting for the chance to teach you your lesson. And this's going to be one you won't never forget."

Clem felt the ground with his feet until he had located the other singletree. He stooped down and got it.

Raising it, he did not try to hit Arch, but held it in front of him so he could ward off Arch's blows at his head. He continued to stand his ground, not giving Arch an inch.

"Drop that singletree," Arch said.

"I won't stand here and let you beat me like that," Clem protested.

"By God, that's all I want to hear," Arch said, his mouth curling. "Nigger, your time has come, by God!"

He swung once more at Clem, but Clem turned and ran towards the barn. Arch went after him a few steps and stopped. He threw aside the singletree and turned and ran back to the house.

Lonnie went to the fence and tried to think what was best for him to do. He knew he could not take sides with a Negro, in the open, even if Clem had helped him, and especially after Clem had talked to Arch in the way he wished he could himself. Arch was a white man, and to save his life he could not stand to think of turning against Arch, no matter what happened.

Presently a light burst through one of the windows of the house, and he heard Arch shouting at his wife to wake her up.

When he saw Arch's wife go to the telephone, Lonnie realized what was going to happen. She was calling up the neighbors and Arch's friends. They would not mind getting up in the night when they found out what was going to take place.

Out behind the barn he could hear Clem calling him. Leaving the yard, Lonnie felt his way out there in the dark.

"What's the trouble, Clem?" he said.

"I reckon my time has come," Clem said. "Arch Gunnard talks that way when he's good and mad. He talked just like he did that time he carried Jim Moffin off to the swamp—and Jim never came back."

"Arch wouldn't do anything like that to you, Clem," Lonnie said excitedly, but he knew better.

Clem said nothing.

"Maybe you'd better strike out for the swamps till he changes his mind and cools off some," Lonnie said. "You might be right, Clem."

Lonnie could feel Clem's eyes burning into him.

"Wouldn't be no sense in that, if you'd help me," Clem said. "Wouldn't you stand by me?"

Lonnie trembled as the meaning of Clem's suggestion became clear to him. His back was to the side of the barn, and he leaned against it while sheets of black and white passed before his eyes.

"Wouldn't you stand by me?" Clem asked again.

"I don't know what Arch would say to that," Lonnie told him haltingly.

Clem walked away several paces. He stood with his back to Lonnie while he looked across the field towards the quarter where his home was.

"I could go in that little patch of woods out there and stay till they get tired of looking for me," Clem said, turning around to see Lonnie.

"You'd better go somewhere," Lonnie said uneasily. "I know Arch Gunnard. He's hard to handle when he makes up his mind to do something he wants to do. I couldn't stop him an inch. Maybe you'd better get clear out of the country, Clem."

"I couldn't do that, and leave my family down there across the field," Clem said.

"He's going to get you if you don't."

"If you'd only sort of help me out a little, he wouldn't. I would only have to go and hide out in that little patch of woods over there a while. Looks like you could do that for me, being as how I helped you find your pa when he was in the hog pen."

Lonnie nodded, listening for sounds from the big house. He continued to nod at Clem while Clem was waiting to be assured.

"If you're going to stand up for me," Clem said, "I can just go over there in the woods and wait till they get it off their minds. You won't be telling them where I'm at, and you could say I struck out for the swamp. They wouldn't ever find me without bloodhounds."

"That's right," Lonnie said, listening for sounds of Arch's coming out of the house. He did not wish to be found back there behind the barn where Arch could accuse him of talking to Clem.

The moment Lonnie replied, Clem turned and ran off into the night. Lonnie went after him a few steps, as if he had suddenly changed his mind about helping him, but Clem was lost in the darkness by then.

Lonnie waited for a few minutes, listening to Clem crashing through the underbrush in the patch of woods a quarter of a mile away. When he could hear Clem no longer, he went around the barn to meet Arch.

Arch came out of the house carrying his double-barreled shotgun and the lantern he had picked up in the house. His pockets were bulging with shells.

"Where is that damn nigger, Lonnie?" Arch asked him. "Where'd he go to?"

Lonnie opened his mouth, but no words came out.

"You know which way he went, don't you?"

Lonnie again tried to say something, but there were no sounds. He jumped when he found himself nodding his head to Arch.

"Mr. Arch, I—"

"That's all right, then," Arch said. "That's all I need to know now. Dudley Smith and Tom Hawkins and Frank and Dave Howard and the rest will be here in a minute, and you can stay right here so you can show us where he's hiding out."

Frantically Lonnie tried to say something. Then he reached for Arch's sleeve to stop him, but Arch had gone.

Arch ran around the house to the front yard. Soon a car came racing down the road, its headlights lighting up the whole place, hog pen and all. Lonnie knew it was probably Dudley Smith, because his was the first house in that direction, only half a mile away. While he was turning into the driveway, several other automobiles came into sight, both up the road and down it.

Lonnie trembled. He was afraid Arch was going to tell him to point out where Clem had gone to hide. Then he knew Arch would tell him. He had promised Clem he would not do that. But try as he might, he could not make himself believe that Arch Gunnard would do anything more than whip Clem.

Clem had not done anything that called for lynching. He had not raped a white woman, he had not shot at a white man; he had only talked back to Arch, with his hat on. But Arch was mad enough to do anything; he was mad enough at Clem not to stop at anything short of lynching.

The whole crowd of men was swarming around him before he realized it. And there was Arch clutching his arm and shouting into his face.

"Mr. Arch, I . . ."

Lonnie recognized every man in the feeble dawn. They were excited, and they looked like men on the last lap of an all-night foxhunting party.

Their shotguns and pistols were held at their waist, ready for the kill.

"What's the matter with you, Lonnie?" Arch said, shouting into his ear. "Wake up and say where Clem Henry went to hide out. We're ready to go get him."

Lonnie remembered looking up and seeing Frank Howard dropping yellow twelve-gauge shells into the breech of his gun. Frank bent forward so he could hear Lonnie tell Arch where Clem was hiding.

"You ain't going to kill Clem this time, are you, Mr. Arch?" Lonnie asked.

"Kill him?" Dudley Smith repeated. "What do you reckon I've been waiting all this time for if it wasn't for a chance to get Clem. That nigger has had it coming to him ever since he came to this country. He's a bad nigger, and it's coming to him."

"It wasn't exactly Clem's fault," Lonnie said. "If Pa hadn't come up here and fell in the hog pen, Clem wouldn't have had a thing to do with it. He was helping me, that's all."

"Shut up, Lonnie," somebody shouted at him. "You're so excited you don't know what you're saying. You're taking up for a nigger when you talk like that."

People were crowding around him so tightly he felt as if he were being squeezed to death. He had to get some air, get his breath, get out of the crowd.

"That's right," Lonnie said.

He heard himself speak, but he did not know what he was saying.

"But Clem helped me find Pa when he got lost looking around for something to eat."

"Shut up, Lonnie," somebody said again. "You damn fool, shut up!"

Arch grabbed his shoulder and shook him until his teeth rattled.

Then Lonnie realized what he had been saying.

"Now, look here, Lonnie," Arch shouted. "You must be out of your head, because you know good and well you wouldn't talk like a nigger-lover in your right mind."

"That's right," Lonnie said, trembling all over. "I sure wouldn't want to talk like that."

He could still feel the grip on his shoulder where Arch's strong fingers had hurt him.

"Did Clem go to the swamp, Lonnie?" Dudley Smith said. "Is that right, Lonnie?"

Lonnie tried to shake his head; he tried to nod his head. Then Arch's fingers squeezed his thin neck. Lonnie looked at the men wild-eyed.

"Where's Clem hiding, Lonnie?" Arch demanded, squeezing.

Lonnie went three or four steps towards the barn. When he stopped, the men behind him pushed forward again. He found himself being rushed behind the barn and beyond it.

"All right, Lonnie," Arch said. "Now which way?"

Lonnie pointed towards the patch of woods where the creek was. The swamp was in the other direction.

"He said he was going to hide out in that little patch of woods along the creek over there, Mr. Arch," Lonnie said. "I reckon he's over there now."

Lonnie felt himself being swept forward, and he stumbled over the rough ground trying to keep from being knocked down and trampled upon. Nobody was talking, and everyone seemed to be walking on tiptoes. The gray light of early dawn was increasing enough both to hide them and to show the way ahead.

Just before they reached the fringe of the woods, the men separated, and Lonnie found himself a part of the circle that was closing in on Clem.

Lonnie was alone, and there was nobody to stop him, but he was unable to move forward or backward. It began to be clear to him what he had done.

Clem was probably up a tree somewhere in the woods ahead, but by that time he had been surrounded on all sides. If he should attempt to break and run, he would be shot down like a rabbit.

Lonnie sat down on a log and tried to think what to do. The sun would be up in a few more minutes, and as soon as it came up, the men would close in on the creek and Clem. He would have no chance at all among all those shotguns and pistols.

Once or twice he saw the flare of a match through the underbrush where some of the men were lying in wait. A whiff of cigarette smoke struck his nostrils, and he found himself wondering if Clem could smell it wherever he was in the woods.

There was still no sound anywhere around him, and he knew that Arch Gunnard and the rest of the men were waiting for the sun, which would in a few minutes come up behind him in the east.

It was light enough by that time to see plainly the rough ground and the tangled underbrush and the curling bark on the pine trees.

The men had already begun to creep forward, guns raised as if stalking a deer. The woods were not large, and the circle of men would be able to cover it in a few minutes at the rate they were going forward. There was still a chance that Clem had slipped through the circle before dawn broke, but Lonnie felt that he was still there. He began to feel then that Clem was there because he himself had placed him there for the men to find more easily.

Lonnie found himself moving forward, drawn into the narrowing circle. Presently he could see the men all around him in dim outline. Their eyes were searching the heavy green pine tops as they went forward from tree to tree.

"Oh, Pa!" he said in a hoarse whisper. "Oh, Pa!"

He went forward a few steps, looking into the bushes and up into the tree tops. When he saw the other men again, he realized that it was not Mark Newsome being sought. He did not know what had made him forget like that.

The creeping forward began to work into the movement of Lonnie's body. He found himself springing forward on his toes, and his body was leaning in that direction. It was like creeping up on a rabbit when you did not have a gun to hunt with.

He forgot again what he was doing there. The springing motion in his legs seemed to be growing stronger with each step. He bent forward so far he could almost touch the ground with his fingertips. He could not stop now. He was keeping up with the circle of men.

The fifteen men were drawing closer and closer together. The dawn had broken enough to show the time on the face of a watch. The sun was beginning to color the sky above.

Lonnie was far in advance of anyone else by then. He could not hold himself back. The strength in his legs was more than he could hold in check.

He had for so long been unable to buy shells for his gun that he had forgotten how much he liked to hunt.

The sound of the men's steady creeping had become a rhythm in his ears.

"Here's the bastard!" somebody shouted, and there was a concerted crashing through the dry underbrush. Lonnie dashed forward, reaching the tree almost as quickly as anyone else.

He could see everybody with guns raised, and far into the sky above the sharply outlined face of Clem Henry gleamed in the rising sun. His body was hugging the slender top of the pine.

Lonnie did not know who was the first to fire, but the rest of the men did not hesitate. There was a deafening roar as the shotguns and revolvers flared and smoked around the trunk of the tree.

He closed his eyes; he was afraid to look again at the face above. The firing continued without break. Clem hugged the tree with all his might, and then, with the far-away sound of splintering wood, the top of the tree and Clem came crashing through the lower limbs to the ground. The body, sprawling and torn, landed on the ground with a thud that stopped Lonnie's heart for a moment.

He turned, clutching for the support of a tree, as the firing began once more. The crumpled body was tossed time after time, like a sackful of kittens being killed with an automatic shotgun, as charges of lead were fired into it from all sides. A cloud of dust rose from the ground and drifted overhead with the choking odor of burned powder.

Lonnie did not remember how long the shooting lasted. He found himself running from tree to tree, clutching at the rough pine bark, stumbling wildly towards the cleared ground. The sky had turned from gray to red when he emerged in the open, and as he ran, falling over the hard clods in the plowed field, he tried to keep his eyes on the house ahead.

Once he fell and found it almost impossible to rise again to his feet. He struggled to his knees, facing the round red sun. The warmth gave him the strength to rise to his feet, and he muttered unintelligibly to himself. He tried to say things he had never thought to say before.

When he got home, Hatty was waiting for him in the yard. She had heard the shots in the woods, and she had seen him stumbling over the hard clods in the field, and she had seen him kneeling there looking straight into the face of the sun. Hatty was trembling as she ran to Lonnie to find out what the matter was.

Once in his own yard, Lonnie turned and looked for a second over his shoulder. He saw the men climbing over the fence at Arch Gunnard's. Arch's wife was standing on the back porch, and she was speaking to them.

"Where's you pa, Lonnie?" Hatty said. "And what in the world was all that shooting in the woods for?" Lonnie stumbled forward until he had reached the front porch. He fell upon the steps.

"Lonnie, Lonnie!" Hatty was saying. "Wake up and tell me what in the world is the matter. I've never seen the like of all that's going on."

"Nothing," Lonnie said. "Nothing."

"Well, if there's nothing the matter, can't you go up to the big house and ask for a little piece of streak-of-lean? We ain't got a thing to cook for breakfast. Your pa's going to be hungrier than ever after being up walking around all night."

"What?" Lonnie said, his voice rising to a shout as he jumped to his feet.

"Why, I only said go up to the big house and get a little piece of streak-of-lean, Lonnie. That's all I said."

He grabbed his wife about the shoulders.

"Meat?" he yelled, shaking her roughly.

"Yes," she said, pulling away from him in surprise. "Couldn't you go ask Arch Gunnard for a little bit of streak-of-lean?"

Lonnie slumped down again on the steps, his hands falling between his outspread legs and his chin falling on his chest.

"No," he said almost inaudibly. "No. I ain't hungry."

1935

THE INTELLIGENTSIA

JAMES HUNEKER
(1860–1921)

FROM *STEEPLEJACK* *

CRITICISM

For at least five years in London, 1890–1895, I wrote for the London *Musical Courier* a page or two weekly entitled the "Raconteur." It was signed. Through it I came to know many musical and literary people there. I was slowly discovering that to become successful, a critic can't wait for masterpieces, but must coddle mediocrity. Otherwise, an idle pen. Big talents are rare, so you must, to hold your job, praise conventional patterns. And that way leads to the stifling of critical values. Everyone criticises. You do, the flower that re-acts to the sun, your butcher, the policeman on the block, all criticise. It is a beloved prerogative. The differ-ence between your criticism and mine is that I am paid for mine and you must pay for yours after you hear music or see the play. In his in-valuable studies, "Criticism and Standards," William Crary Brownell does not hold with Brunetière nor with the Anatole France opposing schools of criticism. He detects the doctrinaire and pedagogue in Brune-tière, and he rightly enough fears the

tendency towards loose thinking in the camp of impressionistic criticism, of which Anatole France is the recog-nised head. Mr. Brownell believes in central authority. Yet, he is not a pontiff. He allows the needful scope for a writer's individuality. It's all very well to describe the boating of your soul among the masterpieces if you possess a soul comparable to the soul of Anatole France, but yours may be a mean little soul dwelling up some back-alley, and your pen a lean, dull one. Will your critical adventures be worth relating? The epicurean test of the impressionist is not a standard, says Mr. Brownell, "since what gives pleasure to some, gives none to others. And some standard is a necessary pos-tulate, not only of criticism, but of all discussion, or even discourse." He asserts that criticism is an art. "One of Sainte-Beuve's studies is as defi-nitely a portrait as one of Holbein's." The "creative critic" of Wilde is hardly a reality. There are no super-critics. Only men, cultured and clair-voyant. Saint-Beuve, Taine, Nie-tzsche, Arnold, Pater, Benedetto Croce, Georg Brandes—and this Dane is the most cosmopolitan of all—are thinkers and literary artists. It is perilously easy to imitate their man-nerisms, as it is to parody the un-poetic parodies of Whitman, but it ends there. A little humility in a critic is a wise attitude. Humbly to follow and register his emotions aroused by the masterpiece is his func-tion. There must be standards, but

* From *Steeplejack* by James Hune-ker; used by permission of Charles Scrib-ner's Sons. Copyright, 1918, James Gibbons Huneker; 1920, Charles Scrib-ner's Sons.

the two greatest are sympathy and its half-sister, sincerity. The schoolmaster rule of thumb is ridiculous; ridiculous, too, is any man setting up an effigy of himself and boasting of his "objectivity." The happy mean between swashbuckling criticism and the pompous academic attitude, dull but dignified, seems difficult of attainment. But it exists. To use the personal pronoun in criticism doesn't always mean "subjectivity." I don't believe in schools, movements, or schematologies, or any one method of seeing and writing. Be charitable, be broad—in a word, be cosmopolitan. He is a hobby of mine, this citizen of the world. A novelist may be provincial, parochial as the town pump, that is his picture; but a critic must not be narrow in his outlook on the world. He need not be so catholic as to admire both Cézanne and Cabanel, for they are mutually exclusive, but he should be cosmopolitan in his sympathies, else his standards are insufficient. The truth is, criticism is a full-sized man's job. I was amused some years ago to read the edict of some young Johnny who writes hogwash fiction for boneheads, in which he proclaimed that essay writing and criticism were for women. I don't deny they are, but our uncritical hero —whose name I've forgotten, but who probably turns out five thousand words a day on a typewriter—meant the statement in a derogatory sense. The literature that can show such a virile essayist as Hazlitt, as exquisite as Lamb and Alice Meynell, to mention only three, is hardly a literature that needs justification. And what of Coleridge, De Quincey, and Ruskin?

I wrote for the London *Saturday Review.* But I was growing tired of music and drama from the critical standpoint. Books, too, were getting on my nerves. There is a lot of non-

sense written about the evil that a book may accomplish. Books never kill, even their vaunted influence is limited; else what vases of iniquity would be the reviewers. I confess I even doubt the value of so-called "constructive criticism." Interpreters of music, drama, paint, marble, poetry and prose write nice little letters to critics, assuring them that such and such a critique changed their conception of such and such a work. I am sceptical. You tickle an artist in print and he flatters you in private. (I have known prima donnas that send flowers to the wives of critics, but that is too obvious a proceeding, also too expensive.) The reason I don't believe critics of the theatre, opera, or the plastic arts ever alter artist's schemes of interpretation is because they couldn't do it if they tried. I don't mean that he or she doesn't broaden with experience; polish comes with practice; but I doubt those radical changes which some critics pretend to have brought about with their omniscient pens. In the case of nobodies or mediocrities, who never make up their mind to a definite conception, it may be different. Great artists are secretly contemptuous of what amateurs—meaning critics—may say of them, no matter the thickness of the butter they spread on the critic's bread. A book review didn't kill John Keats. Criticism is an inverted form of love. The chief thing to the public performer—whether in the pulpit or politics—is neither blame nor praise, but the mention of their names in print. The mud or the treacle is soon forgotten. The name sticks. There is a large element of charlatanism in everyone who earns his living before the footlights of life. Ah! the Art of Publicity.

In his peculiarly amiable manner, George Bernard Shaw once reproached me with being a hero-worshipper of the sort who, not finding his idol precisely as he had pictured him, promptly tweaks, pagan-wise, his sacred nose. George probably thought of me as a pie-eyed youth who was all roses and raptures, one who couldn't see through the exceedingly large rift in the Shavian millstone. He changed his mind later. But I am a hero-worshipper. I have a large fund of admiration for the achievements of men and women, and I can admire Mr. Shaw simply because he so admires his own bright, particular deity, Himself. But I can't go off half-trigger if the target is not to my taste. Many times I have been dragged to the well and couldn't be made to drink; not because of the water therein, but that I wasn't thirsty. I have with all my boasted cosmopolitanism many "blind" spots, many little Dr. Fells, the reason why I cannot tell. It was with difficulty that I read Arnold Bennett, notwithstanding the joy he gave me in *Buried Alive*, yet I couldn't swallow *Old Wives' Tale*—the hissing length of s's—nor that dull epic, *Clayhanger*. Mr. Bennett, whose touch is Gallic, who is first and last a trained newspaper man, is out of his depth in the artistic territory of Tolstoy and Hardy. He is not a literary artist like George Moore or John Galsworthy. But Mr. Bennett enthralled me with his *The Pretty Lady*, an evocation, artistically evoked. So thus I had to reverse a too hasty judgment upon Arnold Bennett, whose resources are evidently not exhausted. When Mr. Wells writes a new book, I always take down one of his earlier ones. I can't believe in those silhouettes that he projects across his pages with the velocity of moving-pictures. They are not altogether human, those men and women who talk a jumble of Meredithese and social science. But how the wheels whiz round! I don't believe in them, I don't believe in Machiavel, or Tono-Bungay, or Mr. Britling, or that absurd Bishop; above all, I don't believe in the god—with a lower case "g"— of Mr. Wells. A vest-pocket god, a god to be put in a microbe phial and worshipped, while sniffed through the nostrils. As prophet Herbert Wells touches the imagination. He foresaw many things, and if his heat-ray invented by his Martians could be realised, war would be forever banished from the solar cinder we inhabit and disgrace with our antics. The Wells of *The First Man in the Moon*, of *The Isle of Doctor Moreau*, of *The Star*, what prodigies of invention! His lunar insects are more vital than the machine-made humans of his newer fiction. No one, not even his artistic progenitor, Jules Verne, is comparable to him when his fancy is let loose. One living writer only is his match, J. H. Rosny, Sr. The Frenchman, a member of the Goncourt Academy, has recently written *The Enigma of Givreuse*, a war story which deals with a dissociated personality, physically double, and remarkable for its skill and fantasy. His *Death of the Earth* should be translated because it is a literary masterpiece. Mankind dies when water vanishes from our planet, and a ferro-magnetic organism follows him as master. We know nothing about the twist life may take tomorrow, or a trillion years hence, so it is useless to predict that, with mankind, the most ferocious devastator of life—man mystically worships the shedding of blood, he is sadistic at his roots, murder is a condition of life— the creation of other vital forms will cease. Quinton, the French physicist, declares that birds followed man in the zoological series. Perhaps he means birdmen.

1918, 1920

H. L. MENCKEN
(1880–   )

FROM *PREJUDICES III* *

[THE UNITED STATES, THE GREATEST SHOW ON EARTH]

* * * The United States, to my eye, is incomparably the greatest show on earth. It is a show which avoids diligently all the kinds of clowning which tire me most quickly—for example, royal ceremonials, the tedious hocus-pocus of *haut politique,* the taking of politics seriously—and lays chief stress upon the kinds which delight me unceasingly—for example, the ribald combats of demagogues, the exquisitely ingenious operations of master rogues, the pursuit of witches and heretics, the desperate struggles of inferior men to claw their way into Heaven. We have clowns in constant practice among us who are as far above the clowns of any other great state as a Jack Dempsey is above a paralytic—and not a few dozen or score of them but whole droves and herds. Human enterprises which, in all other Christian countries, are resigned despairingly to an incurable dullness—things that seem devoid of exhilarating amusement by their very nature—are here lifted to such vast heights of buffoonery that contemplating them strains the midriff almost to breaking. I cite an example: the worship of God. Everywhere else on earth it is carried on in a solemn and dispiriting manner; in England, of course, the bishops are obscene, but the average man seldom gets a fair chance to laugh at them and enjoy them. Now come home. Here we not only have bishops who are enormously more obscene than even the most

* Reprinted from *Prejudices: Third Series* by H. L. Mencken, by permission of Alfred A. Knopf, Inc. Copyright 1922 Alfred A. Knopf, Inc.

gifted of the English bishops; we have also a huge force of lesser specialists in ecclesiastical mountebankery—tin-horn Loyolas, Savonarolas and Xaviers of a hundred fantastic rites, each performing untiringly and each full of a grotesque and illimitable whimsicality. Every American town, however small, has one of its own: a holy clerk with so fine a talent for introducing the arts of jazz into the salvation of the damned that his performance takes on all the gaudiness of a four-ring circus, and the bald announcement that he will raid Hell on such and such a night is enough to empty all the town blind-pigs and bordellos and pack his sanctuary to the doors. And to aid him and inspire him there are traveling experts to whom he stands in the relation of a wart to the Matterhorn—stupendous masters of theological imbecility, contrivers of doctrines utterly preposterous, heirs to the Joseph Smith, Mother Eddy and John Alexander Dowie tradition—Bryan, Sunday, and their like. These are the eminences of the American Sacred College. I delight in them. Their proceedings make me a happier American.

Turn, now, to politics. Consider, for example, a campaign for the Presidency. Would it be possible to imagine anything more uproariously idiotic —a deafening, nerve-wracking battle to the death between Tweedledum and Tweedledee, Harlequin and Sganarelle, Gobbo and Dr. Cook—the unspeakable, with fearful snorts, gradually swallowing the inconceivable? I defy any one to match it elsewhere on this earth. In other lands, at worst, there are at least intelligible issues, coherent ideas, salient personalities. Somebody says something, and somebody replies. But what did Harding say in 1920, and what did Cox reply? Who was Harding, anyhow, and who was Cox? Here, having perfected democracy, we lift the whole combat to symbolism, to transendentalism, to metaphysics. Here we load a pair of palpably tin cannon with blank cartridges charged with talcum powder, and so let fly. Here one may howl over the show without any uneasy reminder that it is serious, and that some one may be hurt. I hold that this elevation of politics to the plane of undiluted comedy is peculiarly American, that nowhere else on this disreputable ball has the art of the sham-battle been developed to such fineness. Two experiences are in point. During the Harding-Cox combat of bladders an article of mine, dealing with some of its more melodramatic phases, was translated into German and reprinted by a Berlin paper. At the head of it the editor was careful to insert a preface explaining to his readers, but recently delivered to democracy, that such contests were not taken seriously by intelligent Americans, and warning them solemnly against getting into sweats over politics. At about the same time I had dinner with an Englishman. From cocktails to bromo seltzer he bewailed the political lassitude of the English populace—its growing indifference to the whole partisan harliquinade. Here were two typical foreign attitudes: the Germans were in danger of making politics too harsh and implacable, and the English were in danger of forgetting politics altogether. Both attitudes, it must be plain, make for bad shows. Observing a German campaign, one is uncomfortably harassed and stirred up; observing an English campaign (at least in times of peace), one falls asleep. In the United States the thing is done better. Here politics is purged of all menace, all sinister quality, all genuine significance, and stuffed with such gorgeous humors, such inordi-

nate farce that one comes to the end of a campaign with one's ribs loose, and ready for "King Lear," or a hanging, or a course of medical journals.

But feeling better for the laugh. *Ridi si sapis*, said Martial. Mirth is necessary to wisdom, to comfort, above all, to happiness. Well, here is the land of mirth, as Germany is the land of metaphysics and France is the land of fornication. Here the buffoonery never stops. What could be more delightful than the endless struggle of the Puritan to make the joy of the minority unlawful and impossible? The effort is itself a greater joy to one standing on the side-lines than any or all of the carnal joys that it combats. Always, when I contemplate an uplifter at his hopeless business, I recall a scene in an old-time burlesque show, witnessed for hire in my days as a dramatic critic. A chorus girl executed a fall upon the stage, and Rudolph Krausemeyer, the Swiss comedian, rushed to her aid. As he stooped painfully to succor her, Irving Rabinovitz, the Zionist comedian, fetched him a fearful clout across the cofferdam with a slap-stick. So the uplifter, the soul-saver, the Americanizer, striving to make the Republic fit for Y. M. C. A. secretaries. He is the eternal American, ever moved by the best of intentions, ever running *a la* Krausemeyer to the rescue of virtue, and ever getting his pantaloons fanned by the Devil. I am naturally sinful, and such spectacles caress me. If the slap-stick were a sash-weight the show would be cruel, and I'd probably complain to the *Polizei*. As it is, I know that the uplifter is not really hurt, but simply shocked. The blow, in fact, does him good, for it helps to get him into Heaven, as exegetes prove from Matthew v, 11: *Heureux serez-vous, lorsqu'on vous outragera, qu'on vous persécutera*, and so on. As for me, it makes me a more contented man, and hence a better citizen. One man prefers the Republic because it pays better wages than Bulgaria. Another because it has laws to keep him sober and his daughter chaste. Another because the Woolworth Building is higher than the cathedral at Chartres. Another because, living here, he can read the New York *Evening Journal*. Another because there is a warrant out for him somewhere else. Me, I like it because it amuses me to my taste. I never get tired of the show. It is worth every cent it costs. * * *

1921

FROM

THE AMERICAN LANGUAGE: SUPPLEMENT I *

[THE VOCABULARY OF BACCHANALIA IN THE REPUBLIC]

In two other fields of word-making the period from 1800 to the Civil War was especially productive, to wit, in those of drinking and political terms. Perhaps a majority of the former, still in constant use by American boozers, date from it, but for the sake of convenience I shall consider all American drinking terms, of whatever date, together. Here the DAE offers a great deal less help than it should, for its editors seem to have been somewhat shy of the rich and inspiring vocabulary of bibbing. Indeed, they do not list *rickey, fizz* and *sour* at all, which is almost like discussing political terms without mentioning *graft* and *buncombe*. *Cooler*, which the DAE traces to 1840, is defined lamely as "a cooling, spirituous

* Reprinted from *The American Language: Supplement I*, by H. L. Mencken, by permission of Alfred A. Knopf, Inc. Copyright 1945 Alfred A. Knopf, Inc.

drink," and in the first quotation, taken from the New Orleans *Picayune*, there is an effort to connect it with the *julep*. This is an absurdity, for every American schoolboy should know that a *cooler*, save when it is concocted obscenely of Scotch whiskey, contains, must contain and always has contained lemon juice, which would be as out of place in a *julep* as catsup or gasoline. The true father of the *mint-julep* is the smash, which the DAE traces, in the form of *brandy-smash*, to 1850, though it is unquestionably very much older. The DAE's first example of *mint-julep* is dated 1809, and comes from the writings of Washington Irving, who was the first American writer of flag rank to mention other eminent American drinks, *e.g.*, the *sherry-cobbler* and the *stone-fence*, the latter now virtually obsolete. *Julep*, of course, is not an Americanism, for the NED traces it to *c.* 1400, and shows that it came from the Spanish and Portuguese *julepe* by way of the French. But the English *julep* of those early days was only a sweet and harmless chaser used to wash down unpleasant medicines, whereas the *julep* of today is something quite else again, and the honest NED marks it "U.S." [1]

Eric Partridge, in his "Slang Today and Yesterday," [2] says that *rickey* arose in America about 1880, but makes no attempt upon its etymology. Many older bartenders allege that it was invented by a Washington col-

[1] The old and extremely bitter controversy over the spirituous content of the *julep* need not be gone into here. In Kentucky and its spiritual dependencies Bourbon is always used, but in the Maryland Free State it would be an indecorum verging upon indecency to use anything save rye whiskey. There is every reason to believe that in the first *juleps* the motive power was supplied by brandy.

[2] Second ed.; London, 1935, p. 457.

league of the Golden Age and named after a client named Jim Rickey, a Kentucky colonel, but the encyclopedias are as prudishly silent about this colonel as they are about his once famous comrade-in-arms, Colonel William Campbell Preston Breckenridge. Charles V. Wheeler, in his valuable "Life and Letters of Henry William Thomas, Mixologist," [3] says that the scene of the invention was Hancock's bar at 1234 Pennsylvania avenue, but does not give the date. He says that the *rickey* was "originally made of whiskey," and that is why the title *gin-rickey* was specified at times. Albert Stevens Crockett, a high authority on bar life in America, agrees with this in general, but differs radically in particular. He says that Col. Rickey's given name was Joe, not Jim, and that he was actually a Texan, "though some have claimed Kentucky as his spot of origin." He was a lobbyist in Washington, and usually used Shoomaker's, not Hancock's, bar in Pennsylvania avenue for operating upon congressmen and other public officials. The lime, in those days, was a novelty to bartenders, though it had been used for many years by sailors as an antiscorbutic. One day, when the colonel appeared at Shoomaker's, the bartender who always served him squeezed a lime into a tall glass, added cracked ice, poured in a jigger of gin, hosed the mixture from a seltzer-siphon, and shoved it before the colonel. "The colonel," says Crockett, "took a deep one, and liked it. Coming up for air, he smacked his lips, said the current equivalent of 'Oh, boy!', gulped what was left, and demanded another. The bartender thereupon christened the drink the *gin-rickey* in honor of his patron. The *rum-rickey* and the *rye-rickey*

[3] Second edition; Washington, 1939, p. 7.

came later." [4] The standard *rickey* of today is made of any ardent spirits (including applejack), lime juice and soda-water. There are also quack rickeys containing syrups and even some that are decorated with slices of orange or pineapple, but they are not served in bars of any tone. The addition of sugar converts a *rickey* into a *Tom Collins,* which is supposed to have been named after its inventor, a distinguished bartender of that name, and the substitution of Holland gin for dry gin makes a *Tom Collins* a *John Collins.*[5] The use of Scotch whiskey and the substitution of ginger-ale for soda-water produces a *Mamie Taylor,* which is described by the Maestro Duffy just cited as "a popular Summer drink." It is actually almost undrinkable. But the use of genuine ginger-*beer* instead of ginger-

[4] Private communication, March 18, 1944. Mr. Crockett first gave this piece of history to the world in In Memoriam, *American Mercury,* Feb., 1930. pp. 229–34, an important contribution to bar-lore. There is more such stuff in his Ghosts of the Old Waldorf; New York, 1929. I am also indebted here to Samuel Hopkins Adams and to the late Charles J. Roseblaut. In a one-act dramatic sketch entitled One Evening on Newspaper Row, published by the Gridiron Club, Washington, in 1930, Col. Rickey is made to describe himself as a Missourian. One of the characters says: "Come on, fellows, let's go round to Shoomaker's and try that new drink that Joe Rickey has just invented." Rickey says: "To a jigger of rye whiskey in a tall glass I add the juice of a lime, cracked ice, and fill it up with seltzer water." Another character says: "That's a good name for it. I want a *Rickey,* too." The date is not given but seems to be c. 1885.

[5] The Official Mixer's Manual, by Patrick Gavin Duffy; New York, 1934, p. 233. Who John Collins was I do not know. Sidney J. Baker, author of A Popular Dictionary of Australian Slang, n.d., tells me that the *John Collins* was known in Australia so long ago as 1865, but he does not list it in his dictionary.

ale [6] produces something that is magnificent, whether it be based upon gin, rum, rye whiskey or Bourbon.[7]

As I have noted, the DAE omits all mention of the *fizz* and the *sour*. It also overlooks the *fix*, the *skin*, the *shrub* and the *daisy*. The NED likewise passes over the *fizz*, *sour*, *skin*, *fix* and *daisy*, but defines the *shrub* as "a prepared drink made with the juice of orange or lemon (or other acid fruit), sugar, and rum (or other spirit)," and traces it in English use to 1747. The modern American *shrub* shows substantially the same formula, but its preparation has been considerably elaborated, and no conscientious bartender undertakes to mix it impromptu. To make even the simplest *shrub*, indeed, takes half an hour, and the best professional opinion favors laying it away for from a few days to six weeks, to ripen.[8] The *flip*, like the *shrub*, is of English origin and is listed in Johnson's Dictionary, 1755; the NED defines it as "a mixture of beer and spirits sweetened with sugar and heated with a hot iron," and traces it to 1695. But the American *flip* of today shows considerable improvement upon this nauseous concoction. Save in the case of the *ale-flip* it contains no malt liquor, and when it is desired to serve it hot the heat is supplied, not by a hot iron, but by hot water. Moreover, a beaten egg has been added. Thus the American *flip*, though it borrows its name from an English progenitor, is essentially a national invention. It arose some time after the Civil War, for the DAE's examples, which go back to 1722 and run down to 1869, mention the hot iron, and its definition is substantially identical with that of the NED. The NED calls the *sling* an American drink, and the NED Supplement traces it to *c.* 1793, and the DAE carries it back to 1768. In its simplest form it is a mixture of some sweetened hard liquor and either hot or cold water, but imaginative bartenders sometimes add lemon peel and bitters.[9]

The *sour* is simply a mixture of hard liquor, sugar, lemon and/or lime juice, and chopped ice, and is usually served strained. There are fancy forms that contain liqueurs and even eggs, but they are not favored by connoisseurs. In my early days the *sour* was in great request among bibuli as a morning pick-up: it was supposed to allay the gastritis that so often beset them. This theory has been exploded by the advance of medical science, and they now use the alkaline salts of sodium, magnesium, bismuth, and aluminum. The *fix* is substantially an unstrained *sour*, the *fizz* is the same with soda-water, and the *daisy* is a *fizz* with the addition of a dash of grenadine, maraschino, or something of the sort. The DAE traces the *sherry-cobbler* to 1841 and calls it an American invention. The NED says that the origin of *cobbler* "appears to be lost." "Various conjectures," its adds, "are current, *e.g.*, that it is short for *cobbler's punch*, and that it 'patches up' the drinkers." But *cobbler's punch*,

6 Ginger-beer is fermented like any other beer, but ginger-*ale* is mixed in a vat.

7 Who invented this masterpiece I do not know, and so far as I am aware it has no name. I was introduced to it by Joseph Hergesheimer, *c.* 1925. Ginger-*beer* is not easily come by in America, but a few of the better purveyors stock the excellent English brand of Schweppes.

8 The Official Mixer's Manual, before cited, p. 272, and Wehman Bros.' Bartenders' Guide; New York, 1912, p. 63.

9 The Official Mixer's Manual, before cited, p. 271. Mark Twain mentioned the *gin-sling* in Innocents Abroad, 1869, p. 429.

which is defined as "a warm drink or beer or ale with the addition of spirit, sugar and spice," is traced only to 1865, and may have been borrowed from the American *cobbler.* The term has also been used in the United States to designate a fruit pie made in a deep pan, with a crust on top but not on the bottom. The modern *sherry-cobbler* consists of sherry, sugar and cracked ice, with no addition of malt liquor or spice. The *sangaree,* which is essentially a cobbler to which grated nutmeg has been added, is apparently not an American invention. The NED prints a quotation from the *Gentleman's Magazine,* 1736, showing that one Gordon, a publican in the Strand, in London, then claimed to be its father. He made it of madeira, not sherry, and apparently spiced it. The NED says that the word comes from the Spanish *sangria,* meaning bleeding. Francis Grose, in his "Classical Dictionary of the Vulgar Tongue," 1783, says that *rack-punch* [10] was formerly called *sangaree* "in bagnios."

The *cocktail,* to multitudes of foreigners, seems to be the greatest of all the contributions of the American way of life to the salvation of humanity, but there remains a good deal of uncertainty about the etymology of its name and even some doubt that the thing itself is of American origin. The NED is content to say of it that "the real origin appears to be lost" and the DAE is significantly silent on the subject. Of the numerous etymologies that I have accumulated, the only ones showing any plausibility whatsoever are the following:

1. That the word comes from the French *coquetier,* an egg-cup, and was first used in New Orleans soon after 1800.

2. That it is derived from *coquetel,* the name of a mixed drink known in the vicinity of Bordeaux for centuries, and introduced to America by French officers during the Revolution.

3. That it descends from *cock-ale,* a mixture of ale and the essence of a boiled fowl, traced by the NED to c. 1648 in England.

4. That its parent was a later *cock-ale* meaning a mixture of spirits and bitters fed to fighting-cocks in training.

5. That it comes from *cock-tailed,* meaning "having the tail cocked so that the short stump sticks up like a cock's tail."

6. That it is a shortened form of *cock-tailings,* the name of a mixture of tailings from various liquors, thrown together in a common receptacle and sold at a low price.

7. That in "the days of cock-fighting, the spectators used to toast the cock with the most feathers left in its tail after the contest," and "the number of ingredients in the drink corresponded with the number of feathers left."

For the first etymology the only authority I know of is an annonymous writer in the *Roosevelt Review,* the house-organ of the Roosevelt Hotel, New Orleans.[11] He says that the father of the *cocktail* was Antoine Amédée Peychaud, an apothecary who came to New Orleans from Santo Domingo after the native uprising of 1795, and opened a pharmacy at what is now 437 rue Royale. He goes on:

Peychaud, like most of the Dominguois, was extremely sociable, and his pharmacy became a rendezvous for his

---

[10] *Rack-punch* was based on arrack. Richard Steele said in the *Guardian,* 1713, that it was sometimes laced with brandy and gunpowder.

[11] The *Cocktail,* America's Drink, Was Originated in New Orleans, April, 1943, pp. 30 and 31.

fellow Masons after lodge meetings. To them he served the customary *brandy-toddy,* but in his individual style. To the toddy of sugar, water and cognac he added bitters which he compounded by a secret formula brought from Santo Domingo, and instead of serving the drink in the regular brandy tumbler he used the double-ended egg-cup, the *coquetier* (ko-kay-tay). The name was soon given to the highly-flavored drink, but guests who did not speak French called it a *cocktay,* and presently the usage of the world had it the now familiar *cocktail*.[12]

The authority for the second etymology is a French writer named Marcel Boulenger, who printed an article in *Le Figaro Hebdomadaire* (Paris) in 1925 arguing for the abandonment of *cocktail* by the French,[13] and the restoration of *coquetel.* He said that its priority had been supported in a paper read before the Académie de Médicine by a Dr. Tardieu, who cited the case of an actor who had died after drinking a *coquetel au veronal.*[14] The third etymology has the imprimatur of Peter Tamony, well known as a writer on the American vocabulary. He says:

During the Seventeenth and Eighteenth Centuries a drink called *cock-ale* was popular in England. It was made by flavoring a cask of new ale with a red cock—the older the better—which had been pounded to a pulp and steeped in sack. The cock, together with a quantity of raisins, mace and cloves, was sacked in canvas, put in the ale, and allowed to infuse for a week or ten days. The result was bottled, and aged until used. Is it any wonder that lexicographers since the Seventeenth Century have defined *cock-ale* as a "pleasant drink, said to be provocative"?[15]

---

[12] Peychaud was the inventor of the *Peychaud bitters,* still popular. In his cocktails he used Sazerac brandy, made by Sazerac du Forge et Fils of Limoges, and so they came to be called *Sazeracs.* In 1859 one John B. Schiller opened a Sazerac Coffee House at 13 Exchange alley. In 1870 Thomas H. Handy became proprietor of the place and changed its name to the Sazerac House. Simultaneously he substituted rye whiskey for brandy in the cocktail. It is still popular, but with the formula varying. In the Official Mixer's Manual, by Duffy, p. 125, the ingredients given are rye whiskey, Peychaud bitters, absinthe, sugar and lemon peel; in The Savoy Cocktail Book, by Henry Craddock; New York, 1930, they are rye or Canadian whiskey, Angostura or Peychana (*sic*) bitters, absinthe, sugar and lemon peel; in The Barkeeper's Manual, by Raymond E. Sullivan; fourth ed., Baltimore, n.d., p. 8, they are brandy, anisette, Peychard's (*sic*) bitters and absinthe; in Life and Letters of Henry William Thomas, Mixologist; p. 42, they are rye whiskey, anisette, absinthe and Peychaud bitters; in Cheerio by Charles; New York, 1930, p. 17, they are an unnamed whiskey, absinthe, syrup, unnamed bitters and mint; and in the *Roosevelt Review* article they are rye or Bourbon, vermouth, unnamed bitters, orange bitters, absinthe and sugar. Obviously, mixologists differ almost as much as etymologists. *Sazerac* is not listed by the DAE. An early example of its use is in Remembrances of the Mississippi by T. B. Thorpe, *Harper's Magazine,* Dec., 1855, p. 37, col. 1.

[13] The word has got into practically all modern languages, including Japanese (English Influence on Japanese, by Sanki Ichikawa, Tokyo, 1928, p. 166), and C. K. Ogden includes it among the fifty "international words" taken into Basic English (The System of Basic English; New York, 1934, p. 134).

[14] A translation of part of Boulenger's article, made for the Kansas City *Star,* was published in the Baltimore *Evening Sun* (editorial page), Feb. 11, 1926. In George Washington: the Image and the Man; New York, 1936, p. 377, W. E. Woodward records a story to the effect that the *coquetel* was brought to America by French officers stationed at a Connecticut port. I am indebted here to Mr. Cary F. Jacobs, of Smith College.

[15] Origin of Words: *Cocktail,* San Francisco *News Letter and Wasp,* Aug. 4, 1939, p. 9.

This allegation that *cock-ale* was "provocative" was duly noted by Grose in 1785. The NED lists the term, and says that the concoction consisted of "ale mixed with the jelly or minced meat of a boiled cock, besides other ingredients." Tamony is also disposed to give some credit to the fourth etmology that I have listed. I gave it in AL₄ on the authority of William Henry Nugent,[16] but repeat it here in Tamony's words:

> Prior to a match [a fighting cock] was trained and conditioned much as boxers are today. It was long ago recognized that a proper diet was important, and food, especially that given three or four days before a match, was carefully prepared. One of the preparations, known as *cock-bread-ale*, was made of fine white bread mixed with ale or wine or any other spirits that were handy, and an infusion of roots and herbs. The tonic quality of this mixture was highly valued. In time it came to be more or less standard, and its name was shortened to *cock-ale*.
>
> Cockers appeared to have sampled these mixtures before adding them to the dough, and when they were found of benefit to man as well as beast it appears that they were added to the ordinary potations of the day. Being a rude sort of bitters, *cock-ale* added tang and taste to poorly brewed or distilled grog, and thus had something to do with the standardization and popularity of mixed drinks.[17]

[16] P. 149, n. 1. Nugent printed it in Cock Fighting Today, *American Mercury*, May, 1929, p. 80.

[17] Origin of Words: *Cocktail*, before cited. Tamony says that mixed drinks were by no means an American invention. In the Sixteenth Century, he reports, the Germans had concoctions called the *cow's-tail*, the *calf's neck*, the *stamp-in-the-ashes*, the *crowing-cock* and the *swell-nose*, and during the same period the English had the *Humpty-Dumpty*, the *knock-down* and the *Old Pharaoh*. Grose defines a *Humpty-Dumpty* as "ale boiled with brandy," and a *knock-me-down* as a "strong ale or beer."

An English correspondent, Mr. Henry Irvine, sends me the following in support of the fifth etymology: [18]

> When *cocktails* under that name became really popular in England, which was not until some time after the establishment of *American-bars*, we had no doubt as to the derivation. To us it was a short drink that *cocked your tail*, using the same metaphor as *to keep your tail up*. If you exhibited a sporting dog of the setter type, which tends to carry its tail low except in action, the show photographer would tell you *to cock that dog's tail*. . . . A *cocktail* was therefore what I suppose today would be called a *pepper-upper*.

This, of course, was only speculation at a long distance in time, for the DAE traces *cocktail* in American use to 1806, and Partridge says that it reached England c. 1870, but it should be added that the NED traces *cocktail*, applied to horses, to 1769, and *cock-tail proud* to 1600. The sixth etymology has no authority save an ingenious suggestion by Mr. William S. Gleim, of Rohrerstown, Pa.[19] He writes:

> In many English taverns the last of the liquor drawn from barrels of ardent spirits, otherwise *the cock-tailings*,[20] were thrown together in a common receptacle. This mixture was sold to topers at a reduced price, so, naturally, they would call for *cocktails*. The word was evidently imported to describe our popular drink composed of several liquors. I know of one saloon in Philadelphia where the bartender saved all hard drinks that were not entirely consumed by the customers. These remainders were

---

He omits the *Old Pharaoh*, but defines a *Pharaoh* of unstated age as "strong malt liquor."

[18] Private communication, Jan. 9, 1938.

[19] Private communication, Feb. 23, 1938.

[20] From *cock*, a valve or spigot, and *tailings*, dregs or leavings.

poured into a demijohn, which when full, would be taken to a nearby auction room and sold as *cocktails* to the highest bidder.

The seventh etymology is taken from a statement made in court by an English solicitor, Thomas Bagley, in 1937, and cabled to the United States by the alert United Press. It sounds very fishy. A *cocktail* consists essentially of any hard liquor, any milder diluent, and a dash of any pungent flavoring. The DAE's first example of the use of the word, dated 1806, shows that it was then compounded of "spirits of any kind, sugar, water, and bitters." A later quotation, 1833, defines it as "composed of water, with the addition of rum, gin, or brandy, as one chooses—a third of the spirits to two-thirds of the water; add bitters, and enrich with sugar and nutmeg." Bartlett, in his second edition of 1859, gave only the bare word *cocktail* and said it then consisted of "brandy or gin mixed with sugar and a very little water," but by the time he came to his fourth edition of 1877 he was listing no less than seven varities—the *brandy,* the *champagne,* the *gin,* the *Japanese,* the *Jersey,* the *soda* and the *whiskey.* He did not, however, give their formulae. When the *Martini,* the *Bronx,* the *old-fash-ioned,* the *sidecar,* the *daiquiri,* the *orange blossom,* the *Alexander,* the *Dubonnet,* the *Manhattan* and the other popular cocktails of today were invented I do not know: the DAE lists only the *Manhattan* and traces it only to 1894. The principal manuals for bartenders list hundreds: in the Savoy *Cocktail* Book there are actually formulae for nearly 700. I have myself invented eleven, and had nine named after me. William Warren Woollcott [21] and I once employed a mathematician to figure out how many could be fashioned of the

materia bibulica ordinarily available in a first-rate bar. He reported that the number was 17,864,392,788. We tried 273 at random, and found them all good, though some, of course, were better than others.

In the Gothic Age of American drinking as of American word-making, between the Revolution and the Civil War, a great many fantastic drinks were invented, and some of them were given equally fantastic names, *e.g., horse's neck, stone-fence* (or *stone-wall*), *brandy-crusta, brandy-champarelle, blue-blazer, locomotive, bishop* and *stinkibus.* Of these, the DAE passes over all save the *stone-fence,* which it describes as a mixture of whiskey and cider and traces to 1843. As a gesture, perhaps, of appeasement it adds the *switchel,* a banal drink of molasses and water, usually flavored with ginger and vinegar [22] but sometimes with rum, which it traces to 1790; the *anti-fogmatic, i.e.,* any sort of hard liquor "taken on the pretext of counteracting the effects of fog," which it traces to 1789; [23] the *timber-doodle* first recorded (by Charles Dickens in his "American Notes") in 1842; the *hold-fast,* 1844; and the *eggnog,* which it marks an American invention and traces to *c.* 1775. Bartlett, less inhibited, adds many more, *e.g.,* the *bald-face,* the *black-jack,* the *bust-head,* the *ching-ching,* the *deadbeat,* the *deacon,* the *floater,* the *fiscal agent,* the *knicker-bocker,* the *moral suasion,* the *pine-*

[21] Author of "I Am a One Hundred Per Cent. American, Goddam!" See Chapter VII of my Heathen Days; New York, 1943.

[22] It survives in the more backward sections of New Jersey as the *belly-whistle.* See Jerseyisms by F. B. Lee, *Dialect Notes,* Vol. I, Part VII, 1894, p. 328.

[23] It also lists the *fog-cutter,* which it traces to 1833.

top, the *phlegm-cutter,* the *ropee,* the *shambro,* the *silver-top,* the *snap-neck,* the *split-ticket,* the *stagger-juice,* and the *vox populi.*[24] The touring Englishmen of those days always marked such grotesque drink-names, and when they got home spread the news of them. Some of these Colum-buses, it appears, embellished the list with outlandish inventions of their own, for in 1868 an American writing in *Tinsley's Magazine* (London) was protesting against the practice.[25] "Genuine American drinks," he said, "have names strange enough; but the fact that certain decoctions are called *brandy-smashes, mint-juleps,* and *sherry-cobblers* scarcely justifies the invention of the haymarket corpse-reviver, or of Mr. George Augustus Sala's *that thing* and *that other thing.*" The fashion for such names began to pass out after the Civil War, and the new drinks of the 1865–1900 era, the Golden Age of American drinking, were largely eponymous and hence relatively decorus, *e.g., rickey* and *John Collins.* The *high-ball* came in about 1895, and the DAE's first ex-ample is dated 1898. It was, of course, simply the English *whiskey-and-soda,* which had been familiar to American visitors to England for many years.[26]

The etymology of high-ball remains obscure. Some authorities say that it was borrowed from the argot of rail-road men, to whom a *high-ball* means a signal from a conductor to an en-gineer to go ahead. Others say that it originated from the fact that *ball,* in the 90s, was common bartender's slang for glass, and the glass used for a *high-ball* was naturally taller than that used for an old-time straight whiskey. There is also some dispute about the identity of the bartender who introduced the *high-ball* to the United States. It has been claimed for an unnamed member of the faculty of the Parker House in Boston, but Patrick Gavin Duffy, in his "Official Mixer's Manual," says that he him-self shoved the first across the bar in 1895, and adds that the New York *Times* has allowed his priority.[27] The *high-ball* came in on the heels of *Scotch whiskey,* which was little drunk in America before 1895.[28] It quickly became enormously popular, and it has retained its popularity ever since. During Prohibition days the custom arose of substituting ginger-ale for soda-water, especially in rye *high-balls,* but it has never been ap-proved by either high-toned bartend-ers or enlightened boozers.

Many generic names for alcoholic stimulants, some of them racy and amusing, have been current in the United States since the Gothic Age, *e.g., nose-paint, milk of the wild*

[24] These are from his fourth edition of 1877. The list was shorter in his sec-ond edition of 1859. *Angel-teat* is miss-ing.

[25] English Hotels, by an American; re-printed in *Every Saturday* (Boston), May 30, 1868, p. 691.

[26] *Soda-water* seems to have been in-vented in the Eighteenth Century, and in 1802 an English doctor quoted by the NED said that it had "long been used" in England. But the *whiskey-and-soda* was called *whiskey-and-water* down to the middle of the Nineteenth Cen-tury. Even *brandy-and-water* was in use, and the NED's first example of *brandy-and-soda* is dated 1871.

[27] Mr. Duffy was bartender at the old Ashland House in New York for twelve years, and there had the honor of serving many eminent men, including J. Pier-pont Morgan the elder, E. H. Sothern, James J. Corbett, Edwin Booth and Oscar Wilde. Once he actually served William Jennings Bryan, though Bryan's order was for Apollinaris. From the Ash-land House he moved to the St. James.

[28] The English did not begin to use *Scotch whiskey* before the middle of the last century. Before that it was simply *whiskey.*

cow, *belly-wash, hog-wash, tanglefoot, sheep-dip, snake medicine, red-eye, gum-tickler, phlegm-cutter, gall-breaker, coffin-varnish, and bug-juice.*[29] There are also generic names for various kinds and classes of drinks, e.g., *joy-water* and *fire-water* for whiskey; *foolish-water* and *bubble-water* for champagne; *Jersey lightning* for applejack; *prairie oyster* for a drink with an egg in it; *red-ink* and *Dago-red* for red wine; and *hard liquor* for any kind of distilled stuff.[30] The DAE traces *snake-medicine* to 1865, when it first appeared in the chaste pages of *Harper's Magazine. Nose-paint* is first recorded in 1881, but is probably much older. *Smile*, as a euphemism for a drink, goes back to 1850; *stick*, in the sense of a slug of liquor, to 1854; *to set 'em up* to 1851; *pony* to 1849; *finger* to 1856; *jigger* to 1836; *snifter* to 1848;[31] *shot-in-the-neck*,

the predecessor of *shot-in-the-arm*, to 1851; and *long drink* to 1828.[32] *Jim-jams*, which is marked an Americanism by the DAE, is traced to 1852. *Straight* is also an Americanism, first recorded in 1862: the English use *neat*. Whether or not *soft-drink* is another remains to be determined. The first known English example ante-dates the first known American example, but further investigation may establish American priority. The DAE's earliest example of *schooner* is from Bartlett's fourth edition of 1877, but the term must be considerably older. *To rush the growler*, traced to 1888, is also older. *To rush the can* is not listed, nor are *bucket* (or *scuttle*) *of suds, chaser, hooker, nip, pick-me-up, on a binge, brannigan, slug* (though *to slug up* is traced to 1856), *water-wagon, to spike* (a drink), *hang-over* (in the alcoholic sense), *dark brown taste, morning after, kick, katzenjammer, bung-starter,*[33] *keg-drainer, bar-rail, souse, stew, bun* or *jitters.* Some of these may be omitted by the DAE on the ground that they have come in since 1900 and others on the ground that they are also used in England, but probably not many. It traces *bracer* to 1829, *eye-opener* to 1818, *on a bender* to 1846, *on a bat* to 1848, *to liquor up* to 1850, *to set 'em up* to 1851, *family entrance* to

[29] Some of these are Southern. Says Bell Irvin Wiley in The Plain People of the Confederacy; Baton Rouge (La.), 1944, pp. 26–27: "The potency of Confederate liquor, as well as the esteem in which it was held, were reflected by nicknames applied to it by the campaign-hardened butternuts; among the appellations were: *How Come You, Tanglefoot, Rifle Knock-Knee, Bust Skull, Old Red Eye,* and *Rock Me to Sleep, Mother.*"
[30] The Englishman calls it *spirits.* What we call *hard cider* is *rough cider* to him. Many more such terms are listed in Poppings of the Corks, by Jean De-Journette, *Esquire*, April, 1934, pp. 36–87.
[31] Writing in the *Colver Magazine,* July, 1943, p. 24, William Feather offered the following on the authority of F. O. Richey: "(1) A *snifter* is a light drink, not greatly exceeding a sniff or smelling of the liquor. (2) A *swish* is a drink long enough to wet the lips and require the wiping of the lips with a handkerchief or the back of the hand. (3) A *swig* is a drink deep enough to exhaust some of the air in the bottle. When the bottle is removed from the lips the air makes a gurgling sound, rushing into the bottle to fill the void. (4) A *snort* is when you hold onto the bottle

so long that when you take it down you give a snort to get the fumes out of your lungs." I am indebted here to Mr. Fred Hamann.
[32] A *Long-Drink* and the American Chesterfield, by Kenneth Forward, *American Speech*, Dec., 1939, p. 316.
[33] The English call a *bung-starter* a *beer-mallet.* Says H. W. Seaman (private communication): "In March, 1935, this implement was used by a boy named Stoner to dispatch an old man named Rattenbury. Throughout the trial at the Old Bailey the word *beer-mallet* was used. If the thing had happened in America it would certainly have been called the *Bung-Starter* Mystery."

1881, *barrel-house* to 1883, *bust-head* to 1863, and *red-eye* to 1819, and marks them all Americanisms. Its first example of *booze-fighter* is from a poem by Carl Sandburg, 1916: the term is actually much older. So is *booze-fight*, which is run back no further than 1922.[34] It does not list *booze-h'ister* at all, nor *hooch,* though it has *hoochino,* which the authority it quotes describes as "the name of firewater in Alaska." *Frappé,* applied to a very cold drink, is said by a newspaper lexicographer to have been introduced by Henry Wadsworth Longfellow in 1848, but for this I have been unable to find any evidence.

Prohibition increased enormously the number of American boozers, both relatively and absolutely, and made the whole nation booze-conscious, and as a result its everyday speech was peppered with terms having to do with the traffic in strong drink, *e.g.,* *bootlegger, bathtub-gin, rum-runner, bone-dry, needle-beer,*[35] and *jake* (Jamaica ginger). A number of earlier terms for the cruder varieties of whiskey, *e.g., forty-rod* (traced to "The Witches of New York," by Mortimer N. Thomson [Philander Doesticks] 1858, and defined by him as "warranted to kill at forty rods"),[36] *ta-*

rantula-juice (traced by the DAE to 1861); *white-mule,*[37] *squirrel-whiskey,*[38] and *panther-sweat*[39] were revived, and such novelties as *depth-bomb* and *third-rail*[40] were added. Denatured alcohol from which some effort had been made to remove the (usually) poisonous denaturant acquired the special name of *smoke,* and this was also applied to alcohol in combination with some waxy substance, sold for heating purposes. The user of such high exhilarants was called a *smoke-eater.* The Prohibitionists, throughout the Thirteen Years, kept on using their old favorite, *rum,* to designate all alcoholic drinks, including even beer.[41] Its employment went back to the days before the distillation of whiskey became general,

[34] *Booze* is an old word in English. The NED traces it, in the form *bouse,* to c. 1300. Weekley suggests that it may have been reintroduced, from the analogous Dutch *buizen* or the German *bausen,* in the Sixteenth Century. Efforts have been made to relate it to the Arabic *buzeh,* meaning sweetmeats, but in vain. In England *booze* means ale or beer, not wine or spirits. An English workingman calls his favorite pub his *boozer.*

[35] *Near-beer* appeared in 1920, but did not last long. It continued to be brewed, but before it reached the consumer it was usually converted into *needle-beer.*

[36] Q. K. Philander Doesticks, P.B., by J. Louis Kuethe, *American Speech,* April, 1937, p. 115.

[37] The designation of Southern cornwhiskey, fresh from the still. It is white in color and is said to have the power of a mule's kick. Only native Southerners of at least the second generation can drink it with relish.

[38] *Squirrel-whiskey* was first heard of in the early part of the Nineteenth Century. A familiar etymology seeks to account for it on the ground that a man who drank it commonly ran up a tree like a squirrel. I think it is much more likely that it got its name by the fact that squirrels were often drowned in the open-air mash-tubs used by moonshiners and then distilled along with the fermented mash. In the Appalachian mountain stills, to this day, the tubs show a high density of dead squirrels, rabbits, possums, coons, wood-rats, birds, lizards, bull-frogs and insects.

[39] *Sweat* was actually in use, but it was perhaps more common to couple *panther* with the vulgar name of another saline secretion. See II Kings XVIII 27 and Isaiah XXXVI, 12.

[40] The vocabulary of boozers in a theoretically dry community is dealt with by Vance Randolph in Wet Words in Kansas, *American Speech,* June, 1929, pp. 385–89.

[41] Oliver Wendell Holmes protested against this misuse in The Autocrat of the Breakfast-Table, 1858: "Sir, I repudiate the loathsome vulgarism as an insult to the first miracle."

when rum was actually the chief tipple of American dipsomaniacs. Some of its derivatives date from the Eighteenth Century. The DAE traces *rum-dealer* to 1860, *rummery* to 1885, *rum-mill* to c.1849, *rum-hole* to 1836, *rummy* to 1834, *rum-seller* to 1781, *rum-guzzler* to 1775, *rum-house* to 1739 and *rum-shop* to 1738. I can't find the *rum-blossom* in any of the American vocabularies of slang save that of Berry and Van den Bark, who do not date it, but *rum-bud*, which may have preceded it, is listed by Bartlett and credited to Dr. Benjamin Rush, who died in 1813. *Speak-easy* is not listed by the DAE, and may not be an Americanism, for though it is missing from P. W. Joyce's "English as We Speak It In Ireland," [42] it is said by other authorities to be a term of long standing in that country. In 1922 M. A. M. Tasker said in the London *Times:*

I well remember, more than fifty years ago, the definition of a *spake-aisy* shop as a place where illicit whiskey was sold. The explanation was accompanied by a rather irreverent reference to St. Patrick, in the following terms:

No wonder that the saint himself
    To take a drop was willin',
For his mother kept a *spake-aisy* shop
    In the town of Enniskillen.[43]

[42] Second ed.; Dublin, 1910.

[43] *Speak-Easy,* March 25, 1928. On May 7, 1938 Eric Partridge suggested in the London *Times Literary Supplement* that the term "may have been suggested by the English *speak-softly-shop,* a significant underworld term for a smuggler's house at which liquor could be inexpensively obtained." Partridge traced this English term to 1823. Thornton lists *speak-easy,* but without attempting to trace it in American usage. He says that it "seems to belong to Philadelphia" —on what ground, I do not know. The NED Supplement calls it "U. S. slang" and traces it to 1889, but it is undoubtably much older. Partridge in his Dictionary of Slang and Unconventional

The wild boozing of Prohibition days gave hard service to the large repertoire of American synonyms for *drunk,* and brought in a number of new ones. In the main, however, the old ones were preferred, *e.g., cockeyed, pifflicated, boozed-up, paralyzed, orey-eyed, soused, corned* and *stewed.* The English have a great many terms of the same sort,[44] and some of them have been borrowed in this country, *e.g., half seas over,* but Americans have also been rolling their own since an early day. Benjamin Franklin was apparently the first to attempt to list them. This he did in the *New England Courant* in 1722, when he was but sixteen years old. His list included only nineteen terms, but fifteen years later, after he had moved to Philadelphia and become publisher of the *Pennsylvania Gazette,* he expanded it to 228 terms and printed it again in his paper. A few months later it was reprinted in the *South Carolina Gazette* of Charleston, in which he also had an interest. His purpose in compiling it, as he explained in a preface, was to issue a warning against drunkenness, which was then very prevalent in the colonies, as it was in England. This vice, he said, "bears no kind of similtude with any sort of virtue, from which it might possibly borrow a name, and is therefore reduced to the wretched necessity of being expressed by dis-

English; second ed., 1938, says that it was anglicized about 1925. The DAE traces *blind-tiger* to 1883 and *blind-pig* to 1887.

[44] For a list of them see Slang and Its Analogues, by John S. Farmer and W. E. Henley; London, 1891, Vol. II, p. 327. An earlier one is to be found in the *Gentleman's Magazine,* 1770, pp. 559 and 560, reprinted in the *Gentleman's Magazine* Library; Dialect, Proverbs and Word-Lore, edited by George Laurence Gomme; Boston, n.d., pp. 142 ff.

tant round-about phrases, and of perpetually varying those phrases as often as they come to be well understood to signify plainly that *a man is drunk.*" At the end of his list he said: "The phrases in this dictionary are not (like most of our terms of art) borrowed from foreign languages, neither are they collected from the writings of the learned in our own, but gathered wholly from the modern tavern-conversation of tipplers." Whether he meant by this to indicate that they were all of American origin is not clear, but Edward D. Seeber has shown that, of his 228 terms, 90 are not to be found in either the NED or the English Dialect Dictionary.[45] Some of the latter are pungent and picturesque, *e.g., bewitched, been to Barbados,*[46] *cramped, curved, got a brass eye, frozen, flushed, has his flag out, gold-headed, had a kick in the guts, has bet his kettle, muddy, nimptopsical, oiled, pigeon-eyed, ragged* and *as stiff as a ring-bolt.* At least one is still in use today, to wit, *stewed.* There are also some good ones among those borrowed from England,[47] *e.g., afflicted, in his airs, buzzey, bungey, cherubimical, cherry-merry, disguised, dipped his bill, seen the devil, wet both eyes, fears no man, fuzzled, glaized, topheavy, loose in the hilt, juicy, lordly, lappy, limber, moon-eyed, overset,*[48] *raddled, seafaring, in the suds, stag-*

gerish, in a trance and *out of the way.* Here, again, there have been survivals, *e.g., boozy, cock-eyed, fuddled, jagged, muddled, mellow, has a skin full, soaked,* and *half seas over.*[49]

A little while back, I noted some of the early American names, all of them in *rum,* for drinking place. Others of different pattern are listed in AL$_4$, p. 292. The DAE traces *café* to 1893, *buffet* to 1890, *sample-room* to 1869 and *exchange* to 1856, all euphemisms for *bar-room,* which goes back to 1807, or *saloon,* which is traced to 1841. During the last gory battle against Prohibition, in 1930 and 1931, most of the wet leaders of the country sought to convince waverers by promising that, in case of repeal, the old-time saloon should not be revived.[50] When an overwhelming

---

[49] For some modern terms see The Vocabulary of Drinking, by Richard Connell, *Encore,* Feb., 1942, pp. 62–64; Slang Synonyms for *Drunk,* by Manual Prenner, *American Speech,* Dec., 1928, pp. 102 and 103; More Slang Words for *Drunk,* by the same, the same, Aug., 1929, p. 441; *Drunk Again,* by Lowry Axley, the same, p. 440; *Drunk in Slang* —Addenda, by Manuel Penner, *American Speech,* Feb., 1941; The Elegant Eighties, by E. A. Powell, *Atlantic Monthly,* Aug., 1938, especially p. 219, and Berry and Van den Bark's American Thesaurus of Slang; New York, 1942, pp. 122 ff. A graduated list of terms for *drunk,* ranging from *joyous, lightsome,* etc., to *dead drunk,* from the *Monthly Magazine or British Register,* July 1, 1816, is reprinted in *American Notes and Queries,* May, 1944, pp. 24 and 25, with a gloss by R. P. Breaden. Thomas Nash's list of "the eight kinds of drunkennesse" in his Pierce Penilesse His Svpplication to the Diuell, 1592, is reprinted in the *Quarterly Journal of Studies of Alcohol,* Dec., 1943, and in Tonics and Sedatives, *Journal of the American Medical Association,* Feb. 26, 1944. Other compilations are listed in Burke, pp. 151–52.

[50] This promise was made, for example, by Al Smith and by Governor Albert C. Ritchie of Maryland.

---

[45] Franklin's Drinkers Dictionary Again, *American Speech,* Feb., 1940, pp. 103–05. The full text is to be found in The Drinkers Dictionary, by Cedric Larson, *American Speech,* April, 1937, pp. 87–92. It was Seeber who unearthed the earlier dictionary of 1722.

[46] Where much of the American rum of the time came from.

[47] He was a diligent borrower, and at least a third of the maxims in Poor Richard's Almanac were lifted from various English authors, especially Pope.

[48] Obviously, a printers' term.

(and somewhat unexpected) victory followed in 1932, and it appeared that the triumph of the antinomians of the country demanded its restoration exactly as it was, with the traditional brass rail, the mirror behind the bar and even something resembling the free-lunch of happy memory, there arose a need to invent new and mellifluous names for it. So far as I know there is not a single undisguised *saloon* in the United States today. They are all *taverns*,[51] *cocktail-lounges, taprooms, beer-stubes* or the like. Some are even called *bars, lounge-bars,* or *cocktail-bars,* but *saloon* seems to be definitely out.[52] The snobbish English *saloon-bar* never got a lodgment in this country, and neither did *bar-parlour, snug* or *pub.*[53] Nor are our wets familiar with such English names for drinks as *pint-of-bitter,*[54] *gin-and-French,* and *audit-ale.* Bitter is an abbreviation of *bitter-beer,* which is rather of indefi-nite meaning, but signifies, in general, a beer containing a reasonable sufficiency of hops. *Gin-and-French* (sometimes *gin-and-it*)[55] is a mixture of dry gin and French vermouth, differing from a *dry Martini* in containing rather more vermouth, and no ice. *Audit-ale* is a strong ale that used to be brewed in the English universities for drinking on audit-day, when the students had to settle their college accounts. A writer in the London *Morning Post* said of it in 1936[56] that it is brewed "from beer instead of from water, though how this is accomplished he did not explain. "Some Oxford colleges," he continued, "are now the only places where *audit-ale* is brewed. It is drunk there, as is fitting, only on rare occasions." Two other English drinks are seldom drunk in this country, though neither can be said to be unknown. They are *half-and-half* and *shandy-gaff.* The former is defined by the NED as "a mixture of two malt liquors, especially ale and porter," and traced to 1756. The latter is defined as "a mixture of beer and ginger-beer" and traced to 1853. The late F. H. Tyson, of Hong Kong, informed me that in that colony *shandygaff* was often compounded of ale and ginger-ale, and sometimes even of lager-beer and bottled lemonade. I have myself drunk more than one horn of *half-and-half* (always pronounced *arf-'n-arf,* in deference to the English) compounded of beer and porter, or beer and brown stout. *Black velvet* is a mixture of porter and champagne.

So much for the vocabulary of bacchanalia in the Republic. * * *

1945

[51] The DAE shows that, from 1817 onward, *tavern* was in use in the United States to designate a hotel or inn. In England there is a sharper distinction. *Tavern,* which is now little used, means a drinking place with no sleeping accommodation; inn, according to English Inns, by Thomas Burke; London, 1944, means a place "forbidden to allow itself to be used for tippling or as a place of idle resort."

[52] That is, save in the more elegant form of *salon.* At the Biltmore Hotel, Los Angeles, the principal drinking spot is called the *salon d'apéritif.*

[53] In an English *pub* the *saloon-bar,* or *lounge,* is the toniest part of the establishment. All drinks cost a bit more there than in other parts. The *private-bar,* also somewhat exclusive, is supposed to be reserved for patrons with particular business to discuss, but in pubs which have no separate *ladies'-bar* it is commonly used also by women. The *public-bar* is for any and all.

[54] I am informed by Mr. F. Mac-Carthy of Watertown, Mass., that at Oxford and Cambridge the students use *can* and *half a can* instead of *pint* and half *pint.* Whether or not this shows American influence I do not know.

[55] I am indebted here to Mr. Harris Booge Peavey of Maplewood, N. J.

[56] *Audit-ale,* June 11.

JAMES BRANCH CABELL
(1879–   )

THE LADY
OF ALL OUR DREAMS *

"Our distinguished alumnus," after being duly presented as such, had with vivacity delivered much the usual sort of Commencement Address. Yet John Charteris was in reality a trifle fagged.

The afternoon train had been vexatiously late. The little novelist had found it tedious to interchange inanities with the committee awaiting him at the Pullman steps. Nor had it amused him to huddle into evening-dress, and hasten through a perfunctory supper in order to reassure his audience, at half-past eight precisely, as to the unmitigated delight of which he was now conscious.

Nevertheless, he alluded with enthusiasm to the arena of life, to the dependence of America's destiny upon the younger generation, to the enviable part which King's College had without exception played in history, and he depicted to Fairhaven the many glories of Fairhaven—past, present and approaching—in superlatives that would hardly have seemed inadequate if applied to Paradise. His oration, in short, was of a piece with the amiable bombast that the college students and Fairhaven at large were accustomed to applaud at every Finals, —the sort of linguistic debauch that John Charteris himself remembered to have applauded as an undergraduate more years ago than he cared to acknowledge.

Pauline Romeyne had sat beside him then,—yonder upon the fourth bench from the front, where now another boy with painstakingly plas-

* Reprinted from *The Certain Hour* by permission of Robert M. McBride & Co. Copyright, 1916.

tered hair was clapping hands. There was a girl on the right of this boy, too. There naturally would be. Mr. Charteris as he sat down was wondering if Pauline was within reach of his voice? and if she were, what was her surname nowadays?

Then presently the exercises were concluded, and the released auditors arose with an outwelling noise of multitudinous chatter, of shuffling feet, of rustling programs. Many of Mr. Charteris' audience, though, were contending against the general human outflow and pushing toward the platform, for Fairhaven was proud of John Charteris now that his colorful tales had risen, from the semi-oblivion of being cherished merely by people who cared seriously for beautiful things, to the distinction of being purchasable in railway stations; so that, in consequence, Fairhaven wished both to congratulate him and to renew acquaintanceship.

He, standing there, alert and quizzical, found it odd to note how unfamiliar, beaming faces climbed out of the hurly-burly of retreating backs, to say, "Don't you remember me? I'm so-and-so." These were the people whom he had lived among once, and some of these had once been people whom he loved. Now there was hardly any one whom at a glance he would have recognized.

Nobody guessed as much. He was adjudged to be delightful, cordial, "and not a bit stuck-up, not spoiled at all, you know." To appear thus was the talisman with which he banteringly encountered the universe.

But John Charteris, as has been said, was in reality a trifle fagged. When everybody had removed to the Gymnasium, where the dancing was to be, and when he had been delightful there, too, for a whole half-hour, he grasped with avidity at his first chance to slip away; and did so under cover of a riotous two-step.

He went out upon the Campus.

He found this lawn untenanted, unless you chose to count the marble figure of Lord Penniston, made aerial and fantastic by the moonlight, and standing as if it were on guard over the College. Mr. Charteris chose to count him, as Mr. Charteris sat down upon the bench at Penniston's left hand. John Charteris reflected that this battered nobleman's was the one familiar face he had exhumed in all Fairhaven. And what a parcel of mirth and folly, too, the old fellow must have witnessed during his two hundred and odd years of sentry-duty! On warm, clear nights like this, in particular, when ordinarily there were only couples on the Campus, each couple discreetly remote from any of the others. Then Penniston would be aware of most portentous pauses (which a delectable and lazy conference of leaves made eloquent) becouse of many unfinished sentences. "Oh, *you* know what I mean, dear!" one would say as a last resort. And she—why bless her heart! of course, she always did. . . . Heigho, but youth's was a pleasant lunacy. . . . Thus Charteris reflected, growing drowsy. . . . She was saying now:

"You spoke very well to-night. Is it too late for congratulations?"

Standing, Mr. Charteris remarked, "As you are perfectly aware, all that I vented was just a deal of skimble-scamble stuff, a verbal syllabub of balderdash. No, upon reflection, I think I should rather describe it as a conglomeration of piffle, patriotism and pyrotechnics. Well, Madam Do-as-you-would-be-done-by, what would

you have? You must give people what they want."

It was characteristic that he faced Pauline Romeyne—or was it still Romeyne? he wondered,—precisely as if it had been fifteen minutes, rather than as many years, since they had last spoken together.

"Must one?" she asked. "Oh, yes, I know you have always thought that, but I do not quite see the necessity of it."

She sat upon the bench beside Lord Penniston's square marble pedestal. "And all the while you spoke I was thinking of those Saturday nights when your name was up for an oration or a debate before the Eclectics, and you would stay away and pay the fine rather than brave an audience."

"The tooth of Time," he, sitting down, reminded her, "has since then written wrinkles on my azure brow. The years slip away fugacious; and Time that brings forth her children only to devour them grins most hellishly, for Time changes all things and cultivates even in herself an appreciation of irony,—and, therefore, why shouldn't I have changed a trifle? You wouldn't have me put on exhibition as a *lusus naturæ?*"

"Oh, but I wish you had not altered so entirely!" Pauline sighed.

"You haven't," he declared. "Of course, I would be compelled to say so, anyhow. But in this happy instance courtesy and veracity come skipping arm-in-arm from my elated lips." And, indeed, it seemed to him that Pauline was marvelously little altered. "I wonder now," he said, and cocked his head, "I wonder now whose wife I am talking to?"

"No, Jack, I never married," she said quietly.

"It is selfish of me," he said, in the same tone, "but I am glad of that."

And so they sat a while, each thinking.

"I wonder," said Pauline, with that small plaintive voice which Charteris so well remembered, "whether it is always like this? Oh, do the Overlords of Life and Death *always* provide some obstacle to prevent what all of us have known in youth was possible from ever coming true?"

And again there was a pause which a delectable and lazy conference of leaves made eloquent.

"I suppose it is because they know that if it ever did come true, we would be gods like them." The ordinary associates of John Charteris, most certainly, would not have suspected him to be the man who was now speaking. "So they contrive the obstacle; or else they send false dreams —out of the gates of horn,—and they make the path smooth, very smooth, so that two dreamers may not be hindered on their way to the divorce-courts."

"Yes, they are jealous gods!" the plaintive small voice said; "oh, and ironical gods also! They grant the Dream, and chuckle while they grant it, I think, because they know that later they will be bringing their playthings face to face,—each married, fat, inclined to optimism, very careful of decorum, and perfectly indifferent to each other. And then they get their fore-planned mirth, these Overlords of Life and Death. 'We gave you,' they chuckle, 'the loveliest and greatest thing infinity contains. And you bartered it because of a clerkship or a lying maxim or perhaps a finger-ring.' I suppose that they must laugh a great deal."

"Eh, what? But then you never married?" For masculinity, in argument, starts with the word it has found distasteful.

"Why, no."

"Nor I." And his tone implied that the two facts conjoined proved much.

"Miss Willoughby—?" she inquired.

Now, how in heaven's name, could a cloistered Fairhaven have surmised his intention of proposing on the first convenient opportunity to handsome, well-to-do Anne Willoughby? He shrugged his wonder off; and declared:

"Oh, people will talk, you know. Let any man once find a woman has a tongue in her head, and the stage direction is always, 'Enter Rumor, painted full of tongues.'"

Pauline did not appear to have remarked his protest. "Yes,—in the end you will marry her. And her money will help, just as you have contrived to make everything else help, toward making John Charteris comfortable. She is not very clever, but she will always worship you, and so you two will not prove uncongenial. That is your real tragedy, if I could make you comprehend."

"So, I am going to develop into a pig," he said, with relish,—"a lovable, contented, unambitious porcine, who is alike indifferent to the Tariff, the importance of Equal Suffrage, and the market price of hams, because all that he really cares about is to have his sty as comfortable as may be possible. That is exactly what I am going to develop into,—now, isn't it?"

And John Charteris, sitting, as was his habitual fashion, with one foot tucked under him, laughed cheerily. Oh, just to be alive (he thought) was ample cause for rejoicing! and how deliciously her eyes, alert with slumbering fires, were peering through the moon-made shadows of her brows!

"Well—! something of the sort." Pauline, he saw, was smiling, but restrainedly, and much as a woman does in condoning the naughtiness of her child. "And, oh, if only—"

"Why, precisely," he agreed. "'If only!' quotha! Why, there you word the key note, you touch the cornerstone, you ruthlessly illuminate the mainspring, of an intractable, unfeeling universe. For instance, if only

You were the Empress of Ayre and Skye,
    And I were Ahkond of Kong,
We could dine every day upon apple-pie,
And peddle potatoes, and sleep in a sty,
And people would say when we came to die,
    "They *never* did anything wrong."

But, as it is, our epitaphs will probably be nothing of the sort. So that there lurks, you see, much virtue in this 'if only.'"

Impervious to nonsense, she asked, "And have I not earned the right to lament that you are changed?"

"I haven't robbed more than six churches up to date," he grumbled. "What would you have?"

The answer came, downright, and, as he knew, entirely truthful: "I would have had you do all that you might have done."

But he must needs refine. "Why, no,—you would have made me do it, wrung out the last drop. You would have bullied me and shamed me into being all that I might have been. I see that now." He spoke as if in wonder, with quickening speech. "Pauline, I haven't been entirely not worth while. Oh, yes, I know! I know I haven't written five-act tragedies which would be immortal, as you probably expected me to do. My books are not quite the books I was to write when you and I were young. But I have made, at worst, some neat, precise and joyous little tales which prevaricate tenderly about the universe and veil the pettiness of human nature with screens of verbal jewelwork. It is not the actual world they tell about, but a vastly superior place

where the Dream is realized and everything which in youth we knew was possible comes true. It is a world we have all glimpsed, just once, and have not ever entered, and have not ever forgotten. So people like my little tales. . . . Do they induce delusions? Oh, well, you must give people what they want, and literature is a vast bazaar where customers come to purchase everything except mirrors."

She said soberly: "You need not make a jest of it. It is not ridiculous that you write of beautiful and joyous things because there was a time when living was really all one wonderful adventure, and you remember it."

"But, oh, my dear, my dear! such glum discussions are so sadly out of place on such a night as this," he lamented. "For it is a night of pearl-like radiances and velvet shadows and delicate odors and big friendly stars that promise not to gossip, whatever happens. It is a night that hungers; and all its undistinguishable little sounds are voicing the night's hunger for masks and mandolins, for rope-ladders and balconies and serenades. It is a night wherein I gratefully remember so many beautiful sad things that never happened to John Charteris, yet surely happened once upon a time to me . . ."

"I think that I know what it is to remember,—better than you do, Jack. But what do you remember?"

"In faith, my dear, the most bedlamitish occurrences! It is a night that breeds deplorable insanities, I warn you. For I seem to remember how I sat somewhere, under a peach-tree, in clear autumn weather, and was content: but the importance had all gone out of things; and even you did not seem very important, hardly worth lying to, as I spoke lightly of my wasted love for you, half in hatred, and—yes, still half in adoration. For you were there, of course. . . . And I remember how I came to you, in a sinister and brightly lighted place, where a horrible, staring, frail old man lay dead at your feet; and you had murdered him, and heaven did not care, and we were old, and all our lives seemed just to end in futile tangle-work. And, again, I remember how we stood alone, with visible death crawling lazily toward us, as a big sullen sea rose higher and higher; and we little tinseled creatures waited, helpless, trapped, and yearning. . . . There is a boat in that picture. I suppose it was deeply laden with pirates coming to slit our throats from ear to ear. I have forgotten that part, but I remember the tiny spot of courtplaster just above your painted lips. . . . Such are the jumbled pictures. They are bred of brain-fag, no doubt: yet, whatever be their lineage," said Charteris, happily, "they render glum discussion and platitudinous moralizing quite out of the question. So, let's pretend, Pauline, that we are not a bit more worldly wise than those youngsters who are frisking yonder in the Gymnasium,—for, upon my word, I dispute if we have ever done anything to suggest that we are. Don't let's be cowed a moment longer by those bits of paper with figures on them which our too credulous fellow idiots consider to be the only almanacs. Let's have back yesterday, let's tweak the nose of Time intrepidly."

Then Charteris caroled:

"For Yesterday! for Yesterday!
I cry a reward for Yesterday
Now lost or stolen or gone astray,
With all the laughter of Yesterday!"

"Yet how slight a loss was laughter," she murmured,—still viewing Charteris with the vague and gentle eyes of a day-dreamer who regarded that which was far beyond him,— "and how very slight was every other loss in our divided lives when set against all that we never earned in youth and so may not ever earn."

He inadequately answered, "Bosh—!" He began then, with a chuckle, "Do you remember—?"

Yes, she remembered that, it developed.

"Do you remember—?" she in turn was asking later. . . .

It was to seem to him, in retrospection, that neither for the next half-hour began a sentence without this formula. It was as if they sought to use it as a master-word wherewith to reanimate the happinesses and sorrows of their common past; and as if they found the charm was potent to awaken the thin, powerless ghosts of emotions that were once despotic. For it was as if frail shadows and half-caught echoes were all they could evoke, it seemed to Charteris; and yet these shadows trooped with a wild grace, and the echoes thrilled him with the sweet and piercing surprise of a bird's call at midnight or of a bugle heard in prison.

Then twelve o'clock was heralded by the College bell, and Pauline arose as though this equable deep-throated interruption of the music's levity had been a signal. John Charteris saw her clearly now: and she was beautiful.

"I must go now. You will not ever quite forget me, Jack. Such is my sorry comfort." It seemed to Charteris that she smiled as if in mockery, and yet it was a wholly tender sort of derision. "Yes, you have made your books. You have done what you most desired to do. You have got all from life that you have asked of life. Oh, yes, you have got much from life. One prize, though, Jack, you missed."

He, too, had risen, quiet and perfectly sure of himself. "I have not missed it. For you love me."

This widened her eyes. "Did I not always love you, Jack? Yes, even when you went away forever, and there were no letters, and the days were long. Yes, even knowing you, I loved you, John Charteris."

"Oh, I was wrong, all wrong," he cried: "and yet, there is something to be said upon the other side, as always. . . ."

Now Charteris was still for a while. The little man's chin was uplifted, so that it was toward the stars he looked rather than at Pauline Romeyne. And when he spoke he seemed to meditate aloud.

"I was born, I think, with the desire to make beautiful books,—brave books that would preserve the glories of the Dream untarnished, and would re-create them for battered people, and re-awaken joy and magnanimity."

Here he laughed, a little ruefully.

"No, I do not think I can explain this obsession to any one who has not been its victim. But I have never in my life permitted anything to stand in the way of my fulfilling this desire, to serve the Dream by re-creating it for others with picked words; and that has cost me something. Yes, the Dream is an exacting master. My books, such as they are, have been made what they are at the dear price of never permitting myself to care seriously for anything else. I might not dare to dissipate my energies by taking any part in the drama which I was attempting to re-write, because I must so jealously conserve all the force that was in me for the perfection of my lovelier version. That may not be the best way of making books, but it is the only one that was possible for me."

He had paused. Then Charteris said wistfully:

"I had so little natural talent, you see; and I was anxious to do so much with it. So I had always to be careful. It has been rather lonely, my dear. Now, looking back, it seems to me that the part I have played in all other people's lives, excepting only yours, has been the rôle of a tourist, who enters a café chantant, a fortress, or a cathedral, with much the same forlorn sense of detachment; and who observes what there is to see that may be worth remembering, and takes a note or two, perhaps, and then leaves the place forever. Yes, that is how I served the Dream, and that is how I got my books. They are very beautiful books, I think, but they cost me fifteen years of human living and human intimacy, and they are hardly worth so much."

He turned to her; and his voice changed.

"Oh, I was wrong, all wrong, and chance is kindlier than I deserve. For I have wandered after unprofitable gods, like a man blundering through a day of mist and fog, and I win home now in its golden sunset. I have laughed much, my dear, but I was never happy until to-night. The Dream, as I now know, is not best served by making parodies of it, and it does not greatly matter after all whether a book be an epic or a directory. What really matters is that there is so much faith and love and kindliness which we can share with and provoke in others, and that by cleanly, simple, generous living we approach perfection in the highest and most lovely of all arts. . . . But you, I think, have always comprehended this. My dear, if I were worthy to kneel and kiss the dust you tread in I would do it. As it happens, I am not worthy. The ceremony must in consequence be omitted. Pauline, there was a time when you and I were young together, when we aspired, when life passed as if it were to the measures of a noble music,—a heart-wringing, an obdurate, an intolerable music, it might be, but always a lofty music. One strutted, no doubt. It was because one knew oneself to be indomitable. Eh, it is true I have won all I asked of life, very horribly true. All that I asked, poor fool! oh, I am weary of loneliness, and I know now that all the phantoms I have raised are only colorless shadows which belie the Dream, and they are hateful to me. I want just to recapture that old time we know of, and we two alone. I want to know the Dream again, Pauline,—the Dream which I had lost, had half forgotten, and have so pitifully parodied. I want to know the Dream again, Pauline, and you alone can help me."

"Oh, if I could! if only I or anyone could now, my dearest!"

Pauline Romeyne left him upon a sudden.

"So, so!" said Mr. Charteris.

He had been deeply shaken and very much in earnest. That was a condition, he reflected, which led you into talking more or less toplofty nonsense. Still, it was a wholly satisfactory condition. So he now sat down upon the bench, he lighted a cigarette, and he smiled.

Yes, he fully recognized himself to be the most enviable of persons and inhabiting the most glorious world imaginable,—a world wherein he very assuredly meant to marry Pauline Romeyne,—say, in the ensuing September. Yes, that would fit in well enough, although, of course, he would

have to cancel the engagement to lecture in Milwaukee. . . . How lucky, too, it was that he had never actually committed himself with Anne Willoughby! for, while money was an excellent thing to have, how infinitely less desirable it was to live perked up in golden sorrow than to feed flocks upon the Grampian Hills, where Freedom from the mountain height cried, "I go on forever, a prince can make a belted knight, and let who will be clever. . . ."

"—And, besides, you will catch your death of cold," lamented Rudolph Musgrave, who was now shaking Mr. Charteris' shoulder.

"Eh, what? Oh, yes, I daresay I was napping," the other mumbled.

He stood and stretched himself luxuriously. "Well, anyhow, don't be such an unmitigated grandmother. You see, I have a bit of rather important business to attend to. Which way is Miss Romeyne?"

"Pauline Romeyne?" said Musgrave, "why, but she married old General Ashmeade, you know. She was the very fat, gray-haired woman in purple who carried out her squalling brat when Taylor was introducing you, if you remember. She told me, while the General was getting the horses around, how sorry she was to miss your address, but they live three miles out, and Mrs. Ashmeade is simply a slave to the children. . . . Why, what in the world have you been dreaming about?"

"Eh, what? Oh, yes, I daresay I was only napping," Mr. Charteris observed.

He was aware that within they were still playing a riotous two-step.

1916, 1927–30

THE SYMBOLISTS

EZRA POUND
(1885–   )

THE EYES *

Rest Master, for we be a-weary, weary
And would feel the fingers of the wind
Upon these lids that lie over us
Sodden and lead-heavy.

Rest brother, for lo! the dawn is
    without!
The yellow flame paleth
And the wax runs low.

Free us, for without be goodly colors,
Green of the wood-moss and flower
    colors,
And coolness beneath the trees.

Free us, for we perish
In this ever-flowing monotony
Of ugly print marks, black
Upon white parchment.

Free us, for there is one
Whose smile more availeth
Than all the age-old knowledge of thy
    books:
And we would look thereon.
                                        1909

PORTRAIT D'UNE FEMME *

Your mind and you are our Sargasso
    Sea,
London has swept about you this score
    years
And bright ships left you this or that
    in fee:

* Reprinted by permission of Horace
Liveright, Inc., from *Personae* by Ezra
Pound. Copyright 1926.

Ideas, old gossip, oddments of all
    things,
Strange spars of knowledge and
    dimmed wares of price.
Great minds have sought you—lacking
    someone else.
You have been second always. Tragi-
    cal?
No. You preferred it to the usual
    thing:
One dull man, dulling and uxorious,
One average mind—with one thought
    less, each year.
Oh, you are patient, I have seen you
    sit
Hours, where something might have
    floated up.
And now you pay one. Yes, you richly
    pay.
You are a person of some interest, one
    comes to you
And takes strange gain away:
Trophies fished up; some curious sug-
    gestion;
Fact that leads nowhere; and a tale
    or two,
Pregnant with mandrakes, or with
    something else
That might prove useful and yet
    never proves,
That never fits a corner or shows use,
Or finds its hour upon the loom of
    days:
The tarnished, gaudy, wonderful old
    work;
Idols and ambergris and rare inlays,
These are your riches, your great
    store; and yet
For all this sea-hoard of deciduous
    things,

Strange woods half sodden, and new
  brighter stuff:
In the slow float of differing light and
  deep,
No! there is nothing! In the whole
  and all,
Nothing that's quite your own.
      Yet this is you.

                1912

LES MILLWIN *

The little Millwins attend the Russian Ballet.
The mauve and greenish souls of the
  little Millwins
Were seen lying along the upper
  seats
Like so many unused boas.

The turbulent and undisciplined host
  of art students—
The rigorous deputation from
  "Slade"—
Was before them.

With arms exalted, with fore-arms
Crossed in great futuristic X's, the art
  students
Exulted, they beheld the splendours
  of *Cleopatra*.

And the little Millwins beheld these
  things:
With their large and anæmic eyes
  they looked out upon this con-
  figuration.

Let us therefore mention the fact,
For it seems to us worthy of record.

                1912

THE GARDEN *

En robe de parade. SAMAIN.

Like a skein of loose silk blown
  against a wall
She walks by the railing of a path in
  Kensington Gardens,
And she is dying piece-meal of a sort
  of emotional anæmia.

And round about there is a rabble
Of the filthy, sturdy, unkillable in-
  fants of the very poor.
They shall inherit the earth.

In her is the end of breeding.
Her boredom is exquisite and excessive.
She would like some one to speak to
  her,
And is almost afraid that I will commit that indiscretion.

                1912

VILLANELLE: THE PSYCHOLOGICAL HOUR *

I had over-prepared the event,
      that much was ominous.
With middle-ageing care
      I had laid out just the right books.
I had almost turned down the pages.

      Beauty is so rare a thing.
      So few drink of my fountain.

So much barren regret,
So many hours wasted!
And now I watch, from the window
   the rain, the wandering busses.

"Their little cosmos is shaken"—
   the air is alive with that fact.
In their parts of the city
   they are played on by diverse forces.
How do I know?
   Oh, I know well enough.
For them there is something afoot.
   As for me;
I had over-prepared the event—

   Beauty is so rare a thing
   So few drink of my fountain.

Two friends: a breath of the forest . . .
Friends? Are people less friends
   because one has just, at last, found them?
Twice they promised to come.

   "Between the night and morning?"

Beauty would drink of my mind.
Youth would awhile forget
   my youth is gone from me.

II

("Speak up! You have danced so stiffly?
   Someone admired your works,
   And said so frankly.

   "Did you talk like a fool,
   The first night?
   The second evening?"

But they promised again:
   'Tomorrow at tea-time.'")

III

Now the third day is here—
   no word from either;
No word from her nor him,
Only another man's note:
   "Dear Pound, I am leaving England."

1917

IONE, DEAD THE LONG YEAR *

Empty are the ways,
Empty are the ways of this land
And the flowers
      Bend over with heavy heads.
They bend in vain.
Empty are the ways of this land
           Where Ione
Walked once, and now does not walk
But seems like a person just gone.

               1917

CANTO I †

And then went down to the ship,
Set keel to breakers, forth on the godly
    sea, and
We set up mast and sail on that swart
    ship,
Bore sheep aboard her, and our bodies
    also
Heavy with weeping, and winds from
    sternward
Bore us out onward with bellying can-
    vas,
Circe's this craft, the trim-coifed
    goddess.
Then sat we amidships, wind jam-
    ming the tiller,
Thus with stretched sail, we went
    over sea till day's end.
Sun to his slumber, shadows o'er all
    the ocean,
Came we then to the bounds of deep-
    est water,
To the Kimmerian lands, and peopled
    cities
Covered with close-webbed mist, un-
    pierced ever
With glitter of sun-rays
Nor with stars stretched, nor looking
    back from heaven

* Reprinted by permission of Horace
Liveright, Inc., from *Personae* by Ezra
Pound. Copyright 1926.
† Reprinted by permission of New Di-
rections from *A Draft of XXX Cantos* by
Ezra Pound. Copyright 1930.

Swartest night stretched over
    wretched men there.
The ocean flowing backward, came
    we then to the place
Aforesaid by Circe.
Here did they rites, Perimedes and
    Eurylochus,
And drawing sword from my hip
I dug the ell-square pitkin;
Poured we libations unto each the
    dead,
First mead and then sweet wine,
    water mixed with white flour.
Then prayed I many a prayer to the
    sickly death's-heads;
As set in Ithaca, sterile bulls of the
    best
For sacrifice, heaping the pyre with
    goods,
A sheep to Tiresias only, black and a
    bell-sheep.
Dark blood flowed in the fosse,
Souls out of Erebus, cadaverous dead,
    of brides
Of youths and of the old who had
    borne much;
Souls stained with recent tears, girls
    tender,
Men many, mauled with bronze lance
    heads,
Battle spoil, bearing yet dreary
    arms,
These many crowded about me; with
    shouting,
Pallor upon me, cried to my men for
    more beasts;
Slaughtered the herds, sheep slain of
    bronze;
Poured ointment, cried to the gods,

To Pluto the strong, and praised Pro-
    serpine;
Unsheathed the narrow sword,
I sat to keep off the impetuous im-
    potent dead,
Till I should hear Tiresias.
But first Elpenor came, our friend
    Elpenor,
Unburied, cast on the wide earth,

Limbs that we left in the house of
  Circe,
Unwept, unwrapped in sepulchre,
  since toils urged other.
Pitiful spirit. And I cried in hurried
  speech:
"Elpenor, how art thou come to this
  dark coast?
"Cam'st thou afoot, outstripping sea-
  men?"
  And he in heavy speech:
"Ill fate and abundant wine. I slept
  in Circe's ingle.
"Going down the long ladder
  unguarded,
"I fell against the buttress,
"Shattered the nape-nerve, the soul
  sought Avernus.
"But thou, O King, I bid remember
  me, unwept, unburied,
"Heap up mine arms, be tomb by sea-
  bord, and inscribed:
"*A man of no fortune, and with a
  name to come.*
"And set my oar up, that I swung mid
  fellows."

And Anticlea came, whom I beat off,
  and then Tiresias Theban,
Holding his golden wand, knew me,
  and spoke first:
"A second time? why? man of ill
  star,
"Facing the sunless dead and this joy-
  less region?
"Stand from the fosse, leave me my
  bloody bever
"For soothsay."
  And I stepped back,
And he strong with the blood, said
  then: "Odysseus
"Shalt return through spiteful Nep-
  tune, over dark seas,
"Lose all companions." And then
  Anticlea came.
Lie quiet Divus. I mean, that is
  Andreas Divus,
In officina Wecheli, 1538, out of
  Homer.

And he sailed, by Sirens and thence
  outward and away
And unto Circe.
  Venerandam,
In the Cretan's phrase, with the
  golden crown, Aphrodite,
Cypri munimenta sortita est, mirth-
  ful, oricalchi, with golden
Girdles and breast bands, thou with
  dark eyelids
Bearing the golden bough of Argicida.
  So that:

  1910, 1921, 1930

WALLACE STEVENS
(1879–   )

EARTHY ANECDOTE *

Every time the bucks went clattering
Over Oklahoma
A firecat bristled in the way.

Wherever they went,
They went clattering,
Until they swerved
In a swift, circular line
To the right,
Because of the firecat.

Or until they swerved
In a swift, circular line
To the left,
Because of the firecat.

The bucks clattered.
The firecat went leaping,
To the right, to the left,
And
Bristled in the way.

Later, the firecat closed his bright eyes
And slept.

  1919

OF HEAVEN CONSIDERED AS A TOMB *

What word have you, interpreters, of
  men
Who in the tomb of heaven walk by
  night,
The darkened ghosts of our old com-
  edy?
Do they believe they range the gusty
  cold,
With lanterns borne aloft to light the
  way,
Freemen of death, about and still
  about
To find whatever it is they seek? Or
  does
That burial, pillared up each day as
  porte
And spiritous passage into nothing-
  ness,
Foretell each night the one abysmal
  night,
When the host shall no more wander,
  nor the light
Of the steadfast lanterns creep across
  the dark?
Make hue among the dark comedians,
Halloo them in the topmost dis-
  tances
For answer from their icy Élysée.

                                    1921

THE WORMS AT HEAVEN'S GATE *

Out of the tomb, we bring Badroulbadour,
Within our bellies, we her chariot.
Here is an eye. And here are, one by
  one,
The lashes of that eye and its white
  lid.
Here is the cheek on which that lid
  declined,

* Reprinted from *Harmonium* by
Wallace Stevens, by permission of Alfred A. Knopf, Inc. Copyright 1923,
1931 by Alfred A. Knopf, Inc.

And, finger after finger, here, the
  hand,
The genius of that cheek. Here are
  the lips,
The bundle of the body and the feet.

. . . .

Out of the tomb we bring Badroulbadour.
                                    1923

PETER QUINCE AT THE CLAVIER *

I

Just as my fingers on these keys
Make music, so the selfsame sounds
On my spirit make a music, too.

Music is feeling, then, not sound;
And thus it is that what I feel,
Here in this room, desiring you,

Thinking of your blue-shadowed silk,
Is music. It is like the strain
Waked in the elders by Susanna.

Of a green evening, clear and warm,
She bathed in her still garden, while
The red-eyed elders, watching, felt

The basses of their beings throb
In witching chords, and their thin
  blood
Pulse pizzicati of Hosanna.

II

In the green water, clear and warm,
Susanna lay.
She searched
The touch of springs,
And found
Concealed imaginings.
She sighed,
For so much melody.

Upon the bank, she stood
In the cool
Of spent emotions.
She felt, among the leaves,
The dew
Of old devotions.

She walked upon the grass,
Still quavering.
The winds were like her maids,
On timid feet,
Fetching her woven scarves,
Yet wavering.

A breath upon her hand
Muted the night.
She turned—
A cymbal crashed,
And roaring horns.

III

Soon, with a noise like tambourines,
Came her attendant Byzantines.

They wondered why Susanna cried
Against the elders by her side;

And as they whispered, the refrain
Was like a willow swept by rain.

Anon, their lamps' uplifted flame
Revealed Susanna and her shame.

And then, the simpering Byzantines
Fled, with a noise like tambourines.

IV

Beauty is momentary in the mind—
The fitful tracing of a portal;
But in the flesh it is immortal.

The body dies; the body's beauty
lives.
So evenings die, in their green going,
A wave, interminably flowing.
So gardens die, their meek breath
scenting
The cowl of winter, done repenting.
So maidens die, to the auroral
Celebration of a maiden's choral.

Susanna's music touched the bawdy
strings
Of those white elders; but, escaping,
Left only Death's ironic scraping.
Now, in its immortality, it plays
On the clear viol of her memory,
And makes a constant sacrament of
praise.

1923, 1931

BOTANIST ON AN ALP (No. I) *

Panoramas are not what they used to
be.
Claude has been dead a long time
And apostrophes are forbidden on the
funicular.
Marx has ruined Nature,
For the moment.

For myself, I live by leaves,
So that corridors of clouds,
Corridors of cloudy thoughts,
Seem pretty much one:
I don't know what.

But in Claude how near one was
(In a world that was resting on pil-
lars,
That was seen through arches)
To the central composition,
The essential theme.

What composition is there in all
this:
Stockholm slender in a slender
light,
An adriatic *riva* rising,
Statues and stars,
Without a theme?

The pillars are prostrate, the arches
are haggard,
The hotel is boarded and bare.
Yet the panorama of despair
Cannot be the speciality
Of this ecstatic air.

1935, 1936

MEN MADE OUT OF WORDS †

What should we be without the
sexual myth,
The human revery or poem of death?

* Reprinted from *Ideas of Order* by
Wallace Stevens, by permission of Alfred A. Knopf, Inc. Copyright 1936 by
Wallace Stevens.
† Reprinted from *Transport to Summer* by Wallace Stevens, by permission
of Alfred A. Knopf, Inc. Copyright
1942, 1947 by Wallace Stevens.

Castratos of moon-mash—Life consists
Of propositions about life. The
    human

Revery is a solitude in which
We compose these propositions, torn
    by dreams,

By the terrible incantations of defeats
And by the fear that defeats and
    dreams are one.

The whole race is a poet that writes
    down
The eccentric propositions of its fate.
                                        1947

JOHN GOULD FLETCHER
(1886–   )

BLUE SYMPHONY *

I

The darkness rolls upward.
The thick darkness carries with it
Rain and a ravel of cloud.
The sun comes forth upon earth.

Palely the dawn
Leaves me facing timidly
Old gardens sunken:
And in gardens is water.

Sombre wreck—autumnal leaves;
Shadowy roofs
In the blue mist,
And a willow-branch that is broken.

Oh, old pagodas of my soul, how you
    glittered across green trees!

Blue and cool:
Blue, tremulously,
Blow faint puffs of smoke
Across sombre pools.
The damp green smell of rotted
    wood;
And a heron that cries from out the
    water.

II

Through the upland meadows
I go alone.
For I dreamed of someone last night
Who is waiting for me.

Flower and blossom, tell me, do you
    know of her?

Have the rocks hidden her voice?
They are very blue and still.

Long upward road that is leading me,
Light hearted I quit you,
For the long loose ripples of the
    meadow-grass
Invite me to dance upon them.

Quivering grass
Daintily poised
For her foot's tripping.

Oh, blown clouds, could I only race
    up like you,
Oh, the last slopes that are sun-
    drenched and steep!

Look, the sky!
Across black valleys
Rise blue-white aloft
Jagged unwrinkled mountains, ranges
    of death.

Solitude. Silence.

III

One chuckles by the brook for me:
One rages under the stone.
One makes a spout of his mouth
One whispers—one is gone.

One over there on the water
Spreads cold ripples
For me
Enticingly.

The vast dark trees
Flow like blue veils
Of tears
Into the water.

Sour sprites,
Moaning and chuckling,
What have you hidden from me?

"In the palace of the blue stone she
        lies forever
Bound hand and foot."

Was it the wind
That rattled the reeds together?

Dry reeds,
A faint shiver in the grasses.

IV

On the left hand there is a temple:
And a palace on the right-hand side.
Foot passengers in scarlet
Pass over the glittering tide.

Under the bridge
The old river flows
Low and monotonous
Day after day.

I have heard and have seen
All the news that has been:
Autumn's gold and Spring's green!

Now in my palace
I see foot passengers
Crossing the river:
Pilgrims of autumn
In the afternoons.

Lotus pools:
Petals in the water.
These are my dreams.

For me silks are outspread.
I take my ease, unthinking.

V

And now the lowest pine-branch
Is drawn across the disk of the sun.
Old friends who will forget me soon,
I must go on,
Towards those blue death-mountains
I have forgot so long.

In the marsh grasses
There lies forever
My last treasure,
With the hopes of my heart.

The ice is glazing over,
Torn lanterns flutter,
On the leaves is snow.

In the frosty evening
Toll the old bell for me
Once, in the sleepy temple.

Perhaps my soul will hear.

Afterglow:
Before the stars peep
I shall creep out into darkness.

                                    1916

MEXICAN QUARTER *

By an alley lined with tumble-down
        shacks,
And street-lamps askew, half-sputter-
        ing,
Feebly glimmering on gutters choked
        with filth and dogs
Scratching their mangy backs:
Half-naked children are running
        about,
Women puff cigarettes in black door-
        ways,
Crickets are crying.
Men slouch sullenly
Into the shadows:
Behind a hedge of cactus,
The smell of a dead horse
Mingles with the smell of tortillas
        frying.

And a girl in a black lace shawl
Sits in a rickety chair by the square
        of an unglazed window,
And sees the explosion of the stars
Softly poised on a velvet sky.
And she is humming to herself:—
"Stars, if I could reach you,
(You are so very clear that it seems
        as if I could reach you)
I would give you all to the Madonna's
        image,
On the grey-plastered altar behind the
        paper flowers,
So that Juan would come back to me,

* Reprinted by permission of the Macmillan Company from *Breakers and
Granite* by John Gould Fletcher. Copyright 1921.

And we could live again those lazy
    burning hours,
Forgetting the tap of my fan and my
    sharp words.
And I would only keep four of you,
Those two blue-white ones overhead,
To hang in my ears;
And those two orange ones yonder,
To fasten on my shoe-buckles."

A little further along the street
A man sits stringing a brown guitar.
The smoke of his cigarette curls
    'round his head,
And he too is humming, but other
    words:
"Think not that at your window I
    wait;
New love is better, the old is turned
    to hate.
Fate! Fate! All things pass away;
Life is forever, youth is for a day.
Love again if you may
Before the stars are blown out of the
    sky,
And the crickets die!

Babylon and Samarkand
Are mud walls in a waste of sand."
                       1916

FROM
DOWN THE MISSISSIPPI *

NIGHT LANDING

After the whistle's roar has bellowed
    and shuddered,
Shaking the sleeping town and the
    somnolent river,
The deep toned floating of the pilot's
    bell
Suddenly warns the engines.

They stop like heart-beats that ab-
    ruptly stop,

    * Reprinted by permission of the Mac-
millan Company from *Breakers and
Granite* by John Gould Fletcher. Copyright 1921.

The shore glides to us, in a wide low
    curve.

And then—supreme revelation of the
    river—
The tackle is loosed—the long gang-
    plank swings outwards—
And poised at the end of it, half-naked
    beneath the searchlight,
A blue-black negro with gleaming
    teeth waits for his chance to leap.
                       1920

SKYSCRAPERS *

What are these, angels or demons,
Or steel and stone?
Soaring, alert,
Striped with diversified windows,
These sweep aloft
And the multitude crane their necks
    to them:—
Are they angels, or demons,
Or stone?

If the grey sapless people,
Moving along the street, thought
    them angels,
They too would be beautiful,
Erect and laughing to the sky for joy.
If as demons they feared them,
They would smite with fierce hatred
These brown haughty foreheads:
They would not suffer them to hold
    the sun in trust.

What are they, then, angels, or
    demons,
Or stone?
Deaf sightless towers
Unendowed yet with life;
Soaring vast effort
Spent in the sky till it breaks there.
You men of my country
Who shaped these proud visions,
You have yet to find godhead
Not here, but in the human heart.
                       1921

EXIT *

Thus would I have it:
So should it be for me,
The scene of my departure.
Cliffs ringed with scarlet,
And the sea pounding
The pale brown sand
Mile after mile;
And then, afar off,
White on the horizon,
One ship with sails full-set
Passing slowly and serenely,
Like a proud burst of music,
To fortunate islands.

                                    1928

H. D.
(HILDA DOOLITTLE)
(1886–   )

EVENING †

The light passes
from ridge to ridge,
from flower to flower—
the hypaticas, wide-spread
under the light
grow faint—
the petals reach inward,
the blue tips bend
toward the bluer heart
and the flowers are lost.

The cornel-buds are still white,
but shadows dart
from the cornel-roots—
black creeps from root to root,
each leaf
cuts another leaf on the grass,
shadow seeks shadow,
then both leaf
and leaf-shadow are lost.

                                    1916

* Reprinted by permission of the Macmillan Company from *The Black Rock*
by John Gould Fletcher. Copyright
1928.
† Reprinted by permission of Horace
Liveright, Inc., from *Collected Poems*
by Hilda Doolittle. Copyright 1925.

CUCKOO SONG †

Ah, bird,
our love is never spent
with your clear note,
nor satiate our soul;
not song, not wail, not hurt,
but just a call summons us
with its simple top-note
and soft fall;

not to some rarer heaven
of lilies over-tall,
nor tuberose set against
some sun-lit wall,
but to a gracious
cedar-palace hall;

not marble set with purple
hung with roses and tall
sweet lilies—such
as the nightingale
would summon for us
with her wail—
(surely only unhappiness
could thrill
such a rich madrigal!)
not she, the nightingale
can fill our souls
with such a wistful joy as this:

nor, bird, so sweet
was ever a swallow note—
not hers, so perfect
with the wing of lazuli
and bright breast—
nor yet the oriole
filling with melody
from her fiery throat
some island-orchard
in a purple sea.

Ah dear, ah gentle bird,
you spread warm length
of crimson wool
and tinted woven stuff
for us to rest upon,
nor numb with ecstasy
nor drown with death:
only you soothe, make still
the throbbing of our brain:

so through her forest trees,
when all her hope was gone
and all her pain,
Calypso heard your call—
across the gathering drift
of burning cedar-wood,
across the low-set bed
of wandering parsley and violet,
when all her hope was dead.

1921

AMY LOWELL
(1874–1925)

ASTIGMATISM *

*To Ezra Pound
With Much Friendship and
Admiration and Some Differences
of Opinion*

The Poet took his walking-stick
Of fine and polished ebony.
Set in the close-grained wood
Were quaint devices;
Patterns in ambers,
And in the clouded green of jades.
The top was of smooth, yellow ivory,
And a tassel of tarnished gold
Hung by a faded cord from a hole
Pierced in the hard wood,
Circled with silver.
For years the Poet had wrought upon
    this cane.
His wealth had gone to enrich it,
His experiences to pattern it,
His labour to fashion and burnish it.
To him it was perfect,
A work of art and a weapon,
A delight and a defence.
The Poet took his walking-stick
And walked abroad.

Peace be with you, Brother.
The Poet came to a meadow.

* The selection from Amy Lowell's
Sword Blades and Poppy Seed is used
by permission of the publishers. Houghton Mifflin Company.

Sifted through the grass were daisies,
Open-mouthed, wondering, they
    gazed at the sun.
The Poet struck them with his cane.
The little heads flew off, and they lay
Dying, open-mouthed and wondering,
On the hard ground.
"They are useless. They are not roses,"
    said the Poet.

Peace be with you, Brother. Go your
    ways.

The Poet came to a stream.
Purple and blue flags waded in the
    water;
In among them hopped the speckled
    frogs;
The wind slid through them, rustling.
The Poet lifted his cane,
And the iris heads fell into the water.
They floated away, torn and drown-
    ing.
"Wretched flowers," said the Poet,
"They are not roses."

Peace be with you, Brother. It is your
    affair.

The Poet came to a garden.
Dahlias ripened against a wall,
Gillyflowers stood up bravely for all
    their short stature,
And a trumpet-vine covered an arbour
With the red and gold of its blossoms.
Red and gold like the brass notes of
    trumpets.
The Poet knocked off the stiff heads
    of the dahlias,
And his cane lopped the gillyflowers
    at the ground.
Then he severed the trumpet-blossoms
    from their stems.
Red and gold they lay scattered,
Red and gold, as on a battle field;
Red and gold, prone and dying.
"They were not roses," said the Poet.

Peace be with you, Brother.
But behind you is destruction, and
    waste places.

The Poet came home at evening,
And in the candle-light
He wiped and polished his cane.
The orange candle flame leaped in the
    yellow ambers,
And made the jades undulate like
    green pools.
It played along the bright ebony,
And glowed in the top of cream-
    coloured ivory.
But these things were dead,
Only the candle-light made them
    seem to move.
"It is a pity there were no roses," said
    the Poet.

Peace be with you, Brother. You have
    chosen your part.

                              1914

PATTERNS *

I walk down the garden paths,
And all the daffodils
Are blowing, and the bright blue
    squills.
I walk down the patterned garden-
    paths
In my stiff, brocaded gown.
With my powdered hair and jewelled
    fan,
I too am a rare
Pattern. As I wander down
The garden paths.

My dress is richly figured,
And the train
Makes a pink and silver stain
On the gravel, and the thrift
Of the borders.
Just a plate of current fashion,
Tripping by in high-heeled, ribboned
    shoes.
Not a softness anywhere about me,
Only whalebone and brocade.
And I sink on a seat in the shade

* Reprinted by permission of, and arrangement with, Houghton Mifflin Company.

Of a lime tree. For my passion
Wars against the stiff brocade.
The daffodils and squills
Flutter in the breeze
As they please.
And I weep;
For the lime-tree is in blossom
And one small flower has dropped
    upon my bosom.

And the plashing of waterdrops
In the marble fountain
Comes down the garden-paths.
The dripping never stops.
Underneath my stiffened gown
Is the softness of a woman bathing in
    a marble basin,
A basin in the midst of hedges grown
So thick, she cannot see her lover
    hiding,
But she guesses he is near,
And the sliding of the water
Seems the stroking of a dear
Hand upon her.
What is Summer in a fine brocaded
    gown!
I should like to see it lying in a heap
    upon the ground.
All the pink and silver crumpled up
    on the ground.

I would be the pink and silver as I
    ran along the paths,
And he would stumble after,
Bewildered by my laughter.
I should see the sun flashing from his
    sword-hilt and the buckles on his
    shoes.
I would choose
To lead him in a maze along the pat-
    terned paths,
A bright and laughing maze for my
    heavy-booted lover.
Till he caught me in the shade,
And the buttons of his waistcoat
    bruised my body as he clasped
    me,
Aching, melting, unafraid.
With the shadows of the leaves and
    the sundrops,

And the plopping of the waterdrops,
All about us in the open afternoon—
I am very like to swoon
With the weight of this brocade,
For the sun sifts through the
    shade.

Underneath the fallen blossom
In my bosom,
Is a letter I have hid.
It was brought to me this morning by
    a rider from the Duke.
"Madam, we regret to inform you that
    Lord Hartwell
Died in action Thursday se'nnight."
As I read it in the white, morning
    sunlight,
The letters squirmed like snakes.
"Any answer, Madam?" said my foot-
    man.
"No," I told him.
"See that the messenger takes some
    refreshment.
No, no answer."
And I walked into the garden,
Up and down the patterned paths,
In my stiff, correct brocade.
The blue and yellow flowers stood up
    proudly in the sun,
Each one.
I stood upright too,
Held rigid to the pattern
By the stiffness of my gown.
Up and down I walked,
Up and down.

In a month he would have been my
    husband.
In a month, here, underneath this
    lime,
We would have broke the pattern;
He for me, and I for him,
He as Colonel, I as Lady,
On this shady seat.
He had a whim
That sunlight carried blessing.
And I answered, "It shall be as you
    have said."
Now he is dead.

In Summer and in Winter I shall walk
Up and down
The patterned garden-paths
In my stiff, brocaded gown.
The squills and daffodils
Will give place to pillared roses, and
    to asters, and to snow.
I shall go
Up and down,
In my gown.
Gorgeously arrayed,
Boned and stayed.
And the softness of my body will be
    guarded from embrace
By each button, hook, and lace.
For the man who should loose me is
    dead,
Fighting with the Duke in Flanders,
In a pattern called a war.
Christ! What are patterns for?

1915

PURPLE GRACKLES *

The grackles have come.
The smoothness of the morning is
    puckered with their incessant
    chatter.
A sociable lot, these purple grackles,
Thousands of them strung across a
    long run of wind,
Thousands of them beating the air-
    ways with quick wing-jerks,
Spinning down the currents of the
    South.
Every year they come,
My garden is a place of solace and
    recreation evidently,
For they always pass a day with me.
With high good nature they tell me
    what I do not want to hear.
The grackles have come.

I am persuaded that grackles are birds;
But when they are settled in the trees,
I am inclined to declare them fruits

* Reprinted by permission of, and
arrangement with, Houghton Mifflin
Company.

And the trees turned hybrid black-
    berry vines.
Blackness shining and bulging under
    leaves,
Does not that mean blackberries, I ask
    you?
Nonsense! The grackles have come.

Nonchalant highwaymen, pickpockets,
    second-story burglars,
Stealing away my little hope of
    Summer.
There is no stealthy robbing in this.
Who ever heard such a gabble of
    thieves' talk!
It seems they delight in unmasking
    my poor pretence.
Yes, now I see that the hydrangea
    blooms are rusty;
That the hearts of the golden glow
    are ripening to lusterless seeds;
That the garden is dahlia-colored,
Flaming with its last over-hot hues;
That the sun is pale as a lemon too
    small to fill the picking-ring.
I did not see this yesterday,
But to-day the grackles have come.

They drop out of the trees
And strut in companies over the lawn,
Tired of flying, no doubt;
A grand parade to limber legs and give
    wings a rest.
I should build a great fish-pond for
    them,
Since it is evident that a bird-bath,
    meant to accommodate two gold-
    finches at most,
Is slight hospitality for these hordes.
Scarcely one can get in,
They all peck and scrabble so,
Crowding, pushing, chasing one an-
    other up the bank with spread
    wings.
"Are we ducks, you, owner of such
    inadequate comforts,
That you offer us lily-tanks where one
    must swim or drown,
Not stand and splash like a gentle-
    man?"

I feel the reproach keenly, seeing them
    perch on the edges of the tanks,
    trying the depth with a chary
    foot,
And hardly able to get their wings
    under water in the bird-bath.
But there are resources I had not
    considered,
If I am bravely ruled out of court.
What is that thudding against the
    eaves just beyond my window?
What is that spray of water blowing
    past my face?
Two—three—grackles bathing in the
    gutter,
The gutter providentially choked with
    leaves.
I pray they think I put the leaves there
    on purpose;
I would be supposed thoughtful and
    welcoming
To all guests, even thieves.
But considering that they are going
    South and I am not,
I wish they would bathe more
    quietly,
It is unmannerly to flaunt one's good
    fortune.

They rate me of no consequence,
But they might reflect that it is my
    gutter.
I know their opinion of me,
Because one is drying himself on the
    window-sill
Not two feet from my hand.
His purple neck is sleek with
    water,
And the fellow preens his feathers
    for all the world as if I were a
    fountain statue.
If it were not for the window,
I am convinced he would light on my
    head.
Tyrian-feathered freebooter,
Appropriating my delightful gutter
    with so extravagant an ease,
You are as cool a pirate as ever scut-
    tled a ship,

And are you not scuttling my Sum-
    mer with every peck of your
    sharp bill?

But there is a cloud over the beech-
    tree,
A quenching cloud for lemon-livered
    suns.
The grackles are all swinging in the
    tree-tops,
And the wind is coming up, mind
    you.
That boom and reach is no Summer
    gale,
I know that wind,
It blows the Equinox over seeds and
    scatters them,
It rips petals from petals, and tears off
    half-turned leaves.
There is rain on the back of that
    wind.
Now I would keep the grackles,
I would plead with them not to leave
    me.
I grant their coming, but I would not
    have them go.
It is a milestone, this passing of
    grackles.
A day of them, and it is a year gone
    by.
There is magic in this and terror,
But I only stare stupidly out of the
    window.
The grackles have come.
Come! Yes, they surely came.
But they have gone.
A moment ago the oak was full of
    them,
They are not there now.
Not a speck of a black wing,
Not an eye-peep of a purple head.
The grackles have gone,
And I watch an Autumn storm
Stripping the garden,
Shouting black rain challenges
To an old, limp Summer
Laid down to die in the flower-
    beds.

                                    1922

SUMMER NIGHT PIECE *

The garden is steeped in moonlight,
Full to its high edges with brimming
    silver,
And the fish-ponds brim and darken
And run in little serpent lights soon
    extinguished.
Lily-pads lie upon the surface, beau-
    tiful as the tarnishings on frail
    old silver,
And the Harvest moon droops heavily
    out of the sky,
A ripe, white melon, intensely, mag-
    nificently, shining.
Your window is orange in the moon-
    light,
It glows like a lamp behind the
    branches of the old wistaria,
It burns like a lamp before a shrine,
The small, intimate, familiar shrine
Placed reverently among the bricks
Of a much-loved garden wall.

                                    1925

FROM
CAN GRANDE'S CASTLE *

[COMMODORE PERRY
BEFORE THE DRAGON GATE]

* * * Darkness over rice-fields and
hills. The Gold Gate hides in shadow.
Upon the indigo-dark water, millions
of white jelly-fish drift, like lotus-
petals over an inland lake. The land
buzzes with prayer, low, dim smoke
hanging in air; and every hill gashes
and glares with shooting fires. The
fire-bells are ringing in double time,
and a heavy swinging boom clashes
from the great bells of temples.
Couriers lash their horses, riding furiously to Yedo; junks and scull-boats
arrive hourly at Shinagawa with news;
runners, bearing dispatches, pant in

---

* Reprinted by permission of, and arrangement with, Houghton Mifflin Company.

government offices. The hollow doors of the Great Gate beat with alarms. The charmed Dragon Country shakes and trembles. Iyéyoshi, twelfth Shō-gun of the Tokugawa line, sits in his city. Sits in the midst of one million, two hundred thousand trembling souls, and his mind rolls forward and back like a ball on a circular runway, and finds no goal. Roll, poor distracted mind of a sick man. What can you do but wait, trusting in your Dragon Gate, for how should you know that it is rusted.

But there is a sign over the "black ships." A wedge-shaped tail of blue sparklets, edged with red, trails above them as though a Dragon were pouring violet sulphurous spume from steaming nostrils, and the hulls and rigging are pale, quivering, bright as Taira ghosts on the sea of Nagatō.

Up and down walk sentinels, fore and aft, and at the side gangways. There is a pile of round shot and four stands of grape beside each gun; and carbines, and pistols, and cutlasses, are laid in the boats. Floating arsenals —floating sample-rooms for the wares of a continent; shop-counters, flanked with weapons, adrift among the jelly-fishes.

Eight bells, and the meteor washes away before the wet, white wisps of dawn.

Through the countrysides of the "Land of Great Peace," flowers are blooming. The greenish-white, sterile blossoms of hydrangeas boom faintly, like distant inaudible bombs of color exploding in the woods. Weigelias prick the pink of their slender trumpets against green backgrounds. The fan-shaped leaves of ladies' slippers rustle under cryptomerias.

Midsummer heat curls about the cinnamon-red tree-boles along the Tokaido. The road ripples and glints

with the passing to and fro, and beyond, in the roadstead, the "black ships" swing at their anchors and wait.

All up and down the Eastern shore of the bay is a feverish digging, patting, plastering. Forts to be built in an hour to resist the barbarians, if, peradventure, they can. Japan turned to, what will it not do! Fishermen and palanquin-bearers, pack-horse-leaders and farm-laborers, even women and children, pat and plaster. Disaster batters at the Dragon Gate. Batters at the doors of Yedo, where Samurai unpack their armor, and whet and feather their arrows.

Daimios smoke innumerable pipes, and drink unnumbered cups of tea, discussing—discussing—"what is to be done?" The Shōgun is no Emperor. What shall they do if the "hairy devils" take a notion to go to Kiōto! Then indeed would the Tokugawa fall. The prisons are crammed with those who advise opening the Gate. Open the Gate, and let the State scatter like dust to the winds! Absurd! Unthinkable! Suppress the "brocade pictures" of the floating monsters with which book-sellers and picture-shop keepers are delighting and affrighting the populace. Place a ban on speech. Preach, inert Daimios—the Commodore will *not* go to Nagasaki, and the roar of his guns will drown the clattering fall of your Dragon Doors if you do not open them in time. East and West, and trade shaded by heroism. Hokusai is dead, but his pupils are lampooning your carpet soldiers. Spare the dynasty—parley, procrastinate. Appoint two Princes to receive the Commodore, at once, since he will not wait over long. At Kurihama, for he must not come to Yedo.

Flip—flap—flutter—flags in front of the Conference House. Built over night, it seems, with unpainted peaked summits of roofs gleaming like ricks of grain. Flip—flutter—flap—variously-tinted flags, in a crescent about nine tall standards whose long scarlet pennons brush the ground. Beat—tap—fill and relapse—the wind pushing against taut white cloth screens, bellying out the Shōgun's crest of heart-shaped Asarum leaves in the panels, crumpling them to indefinite figures of scarlet spotting white. Flip—ripple—brighten—over serried ranks of soldiers on the beach. Sword-bearers, spear-bearers, archers, lancers, and those who carry heavy, antiquated matchlocks. The block of them five thousand armed men, drawn up in front of a cracking golden door. But behind their bristling spears, the cracks are hidden.

Braying, blasting blares from two brass bands, approaching in glittering boats over glittering water. One is playing the "Overture" from "William Tell," the other, "The Last Rose of Summer," and the way the notes clash, and shock, and shatter, and dissolve, is wonderful to hear. Queer barbarian music, and the monkey-soldiers stand stock still, listening to its reverberation humming in the folded doors of the Great Gate.

Stuff your ears, monkey-soldiers, screw your faces, shudder up and down your spines. Cannon! Cannon! from one of the "black ships." Thirteen thudding explosions, thirteen red dragon tongues, thirteen clouds of smoke like the breath of the mountain gods. Thirteen hammer strokes shaking the Great Gate, and the seams in the metal widen. Open sesame, shotless guns; and "The Only, High, Grand and Mighty, Invisible Mysteriousness, Chief Barbarian" reveals himself, and steps into his barge.

Up, oars, down; drip—sun-spray—rowlock-rattle. To shore! To shore! Set foot upon the sacred soil of the

"Land of Great Peace," with its five thousand armed men doing nothing with their spears and matchlocks, because of the genii in the black guns aboard the "black ships."

One hundred marines in a line up the wharf. One hundred sailors, man to man, opposite them. Officers, two deep; and, up the center—the Procession. Bands together now: "Hail Columbia." Marines in file, sailors after, a staff with the American flag borne by seamen, another with the Commodore's broad pennant. Two boys, dressed for ceremony, carrying the President's letter and credentials in golden boxes. Tall, blue-black negroes on either side of—THE COMMODORE! Walking slowly, gold, blue, steel-glitter, up to the Conference House, walking in state up to an ancient tottering Gate, lately closed securely, but now gaping. Bands, rain your music against this golden barrier, harry the ears of the monkey-men. The doors are ajar, and the Commodore has entered. * * *

1917–18

FROM *TENDENCIES IN MODERN AMERICAN POETRY* *

[IMAGISM]

* * * I suppose few literary movements have been so little understood as Imagism. Only a short time ago, in the "Yale Review," Professor John Erskine confessed that he had no clear idea of what was Imagist verse and what was not, and in unconscious proof of his ignorance, spoke of Robert

* The selection from Amy Lowell's *Tendencies in Modern American Poetry* is used by permission of the publishers, Houghton Mifflin Company.

Frost and Edgar Lee Masters as Imagists.

To call a certain kind of writing "a school," and give it a name, is merely a convenient method of designating it when we wish to speak of it. We have adopted the same method in regard to distinguishing persons. We say John Smith and James Brown, because it is simpler than to say: six feet tall, blue eyes, straight nose—or the reverse of these attributes. Imagist verse is verse which is written in conformity with certain tenets voluntarily adopted by the poets as being those by which they consider the best poetry to be produced. They may be right or they may be wrong, but this is their belief.

Imagism, then, is a particular school, springing up within a larger, more comprehensive movement, the New Movement with which this whole book has had to do. This movement has as yet received no convenient designation. We, who are of it, naturally have not the proper perspective to see it in all its historic significance. But we can safely claim it to be a "renaissance," a rebirth of the spirit of truth and beauty. It means a rediscovery of beauty in our modern world, and the originality and honesty to affirm that beauty in whatever manner is native to the poet.

I have shown Edwin Arlington Robinson and Robert Frost as the pioneers of this renaissance; I have shown Edgar Lee Masters and Carl Sandburg plunging forward in quest of change and freedom, hurling themselves against the harshness and materialism of existing conditions, shouting their beliefs, sometimes raucously, but always honestly and with abounding courage. Now, I am to show a condition, not changing, but changed. These poets not only express themselves differently, they see life and the universe from a different standpoint.

It is not over; the movement is yet in its infancy. Other poets will come and, perchance, perfect where these men have given the tools. Other writers, forgetting the stormy times in which this movement had its birth, will inherit in plentitude and calm that for which they have fought. Then our native flowers will bloom into a great garden, to be again conventionalized to a pleasance of stone statues and mathematical parterres awaiting a new change which shall displace it. This is the perpetually recurring history of literature, and of the world.

I have chosen the Imagists as representing the third stage of the present movement advisedly, for only in them do I see that complete alteration of point of view necessary to this third stage. An alteration, let me add, due solely to the beliefs—moral, religious, and artistic—inherent in the characters of these poets. Honest difference of opinion leads to honestly different work, and this must not be confused with the absurd outpourings of those gadflies of the arts who imitate the manners of others without an inkling of their souls; nor with those nefarious persons who endeavour to keep themselves before the public by means of a more or less clever charlatanism.

The spoken word, even the written word, is often misunderstood. I do not wish to be construed as stating that poets in the third stage are better, as poets, than those in the other two. Fundamental beliefs change art, but do not, necessarily, either improve or injure it. Great poetry has been written at every stage of the world's history, but Homer did not write like Dante, nor Dante like Shakespeare, nor Shakespeare like Edgar Allan Poe. So, in literary criticism, one may assign a poet his place in a general movement without any attempt to appraise his individual merit by so doing.

Before taking up the work of "H.D." and John Gould Fletcher in detail, I think it would be well to consider, for a moment, what Imagism is, and for what those poets who style themselves "Imagists" stand.

In the preface to the anthology, "Some Imagist Poets," there is set down a brief list of tenets to which the poets contributing to it mutually agreed. I do not mean that they pledged themselves as to a creed. I mean that they all found themselves in accord upon these simple rules.

I propose to take up these rules presently, one by one, and explain them in detail, but I will first set them down in order:

1. To use the language of common speech, but to employ always the *exact* word, not the nearly-exact, nor the merely decorative word.

2. To create new rhythms—as the expression of new moods—and not to copy old rhythms, which merely echo old moods. We do not insist upon "free-verse" as the only method of writing poetry. We fight for it as a principle of liberty. We believe that the individuality of a poet may often be better expressed in free-verse than in conventional forms. In poetry a new cadence means a new idea.

3. To allow absolute freedom in the choice of subject. It is not art to write badly of aeroplanes and automobiles, nor is it necessarily bad art to write well about the past. We believe passionately in the artistic value of modern life, but we wish to point out that there is nothing so uninspiring nor so old-fashioned as an aeroplane of the year 1911.

4. To present an image (hence the name: "Imagist"). We are not a school of painters, but we believe that poetry should render particulars exactly and not deal in vague generalities, however magnificent and sonorous. It is for this reason that we oppose the cosmic poet, who seems to us to shirk the real difficulties of his art.

5. To produce poetry that is hard and clear, never blurred nor indefinite.

6. Finally, most of us believe that concentration is of the very essence of poetry.

There is nothing new under the sun, even the word, "renaissance," means a re-birth not a new birth, and of this the Imagists were well aware. This short creed was preceded by the following paragraph:

These principles are not new; they have fallen into desuetude. They are the essentials of all great poetry, indeed of all great literature.

It is not primarily on account of their forms, as is commonly supposed, that the Imagist poets represented a changed point of view; it is because of their reactions toward the world in which they live.

Now let us examine these tenets and see just what they mean, for I have observed that their very succinctness has often occasioned misunderstanding.

The first one is: "To use the language of common speech, but to employ always the *exact* word, not the nearly-exact, nor the merely decorative word."

The language of common speech means a diction which carefully excludes inversions, and the *clichés* of the old poetic jargon. As to inversions, we only need to remember Matthew Arnold's famous parody on this evil practice in his essay, "On Translating Homer":

Yourself, how do you do,
Very well, you I thank.

But, until very recently, it persisted
in our poetry. One of the tenets in
which all the poets of the present
movement, Imagists and others, are
agreed, however, is this abhorrence
of the inversion.

"*Cliché*" is a French word and
means "stamped," as a coin, for instance. In other words, it is something
in common use, and not peculiar to
the author. Old, faded expressions like
"battlemented clouds," and "moun-
tainous seas," are *clichés*. Excellent
the first time, but so worn by use as
to convey no very distinct impression
to the reader. As an example of the
old poetic jargon, take such a passage
as this:

To ope my eyes
Upon the Ethiope splendour
Of the spangled night.

It will at once be admitted that this
is hardly the language of common
speech. Common speech does not
exclude imaginative language nor
metaphor; but it must be original and
natural to the poet himself, not culled
from older books of verse.

The *exact* word has been much
misunderstood. It means the *exact*
word which conveys the writer's impression to the reader. Critics conceive a thing to be so and so and no
other way. To the poet, the thing is
as it appears in relation to the whole.
For instance, he might say:

Great heaps of shiny glass
Pricked out of the stubble
By a full, high moon.

This does not mean that the stones
are really of glass, but that they so
appear in the bright moonlight. It is
the *exact* word to describe the effect.
In short, the exactness is determined
by the content. The habit of choosing

a word as unlike the object as possible,
much in vogue among the would-be
modern poets, is silly, and defeats its
own object. One example of this kind
which was brought to my attention
some time ago was "a mauve wind."
That is just nonsense. It is not *exact*
in any sense, it connotes nothing.
"Black wind," "white wind," "pale
wind," all these are colours and therefore do not exactly describe any wind,
but they do describe certain windy
effects. "Mauve wind," on the other
hand, is merely straining after novelty,
unguided by commonsense or a feeling for fitness.

So much for the first Imagist tenet.
The second: "To create new rhythms
—as the expression of new moods—
and not to copy old rhythms which
merely echo old moods. . . In poetry
a new cadence means a new idea."

This, of course, refers to the modern practice of writing largely in free
forms. It is true that modern subjects,
modern habits of mind, seem to find
more satisfactory expression in *vers
libre* and "polyphonic prose" than in
metrical verse. It is also true that "a
new cadence means a new idea." Not,
as has been stated by hostile critics,
that the cadence engenders the idea;
quite the contrary, it means that the
idea clothes itself naturally in an appropriate novelty of rhythm. Very
slight and subtle it may be, but adequate. The Imagist poets "do not
insist upon free-verse as the only
method of writing poetry." In fact,
the group are somewhat divided in
their practice here.

This brings us to the third tenet:
"To allow absolute freedom in the
choice of subject." Again, over
this passage, misunderstandings have
arisen. "How can the choice of subject be absolutely unrestricted?"—
horrified critics have asked. The only
reply to such a question is that one

had supposed one were speaking to people of commonsense and intelligence. To make this passage intelligible to any others, it would be necessary to add "within the bounds of good taste." Of course, what one person might consider good taste another might think the reverse of it; all that the passage intends to imply is that this group restricts itself to no particular kind of subject matter. Old, new, actual, literary, anything which excites the creative faculty in the individual poet, is permissible; they are equally Imagists and poets if they write about ancient Greece, or about a cluster of chimney-stacks seen out of the window.

Number four says: "To present an image (hence the name 'Imagist'). We are not a school of painters, but we believe that poetry should render particulars exactly, and not deal in vague generalities, however magnificent and sonorous."

This paragraph caused a great deal of confusion. It has been construed to mean that Imagist poetry is chiefly concerned with the presentation of pictures. Why this should have come about, considering that the words, "we are not a school of painters," were intended to offset any such idea, I do not know. The truth is that "Imagism," "Imagist," refers more to the manner of presentation than to the thing presented. It is a kind of technique rather than a choice of subject. "Imagism" simply means—to quote from the second anthology, "Some Imagist Poets, *1916*"—"a clear presentation of whatever the author wishes to convey. Now he may wish to convey a mood of indecision, in which case the poem should be indecisive; he may wish to bring before his reader the constantly shifting and changing lights over a landscape, or the varying attitudes of mind of a person under strong emotion, then his poem must shift and change to present this clearly." Imagism is presentation, not representation. For instance, Imagists do not speak of the sea as the "rolling wave" of the "vasty deep," high-sounding, artificial generalities which convey no exact impression; instead, let us compare these two stanzas in a poem of Mr. Fletcher's called "The Calm":

At noon I shall see waves flashing,
White power of spray.

The steamers, stately,
Kick up white puffs of spray behind them.
The boiling wake
Merges in the blue-black mirror of the sea.

That is an exact image; but here is another from "Tide of Storms," in which the exactness of the image is augmented by powerful imaginative connotations:

Crooked, crawling tide with long wet fingers
Clutching at the gritty beach in the roar and spurt of spray,
Tide of gales, drunken tide, lava-burst of breakers,
Black ships plunge upon you from sea to sea away.

This vivid "presentation of whatever the author wishes to convey" is closely allied to the next tenet of the Imagist manifesto, which is: "To produce poetry which is hard and clear, never blurred nor indefinite." It must be kept in mind that this does not refer to subject but to the rendering of subject. I might borrow a metaphor from another art and call it "faithfulness to the architectural line." Ornament may be employed, so long as it follows the structural bases of the poem. But poetical jig-saw work is summarily condemned. That is why, although so much Imagist poetry is metaphorical, similes are sparingly used. Imagists fear the blurred effect of a too constant change of picture in the same poem.

The last rule is very simple, it is that "concentration is of the very essence of poetry." A rule, indeed, as old as art itself, and yet so often lost sight of that it can hardly be too often affirmed. How many works of art are ruined by a too great discursiveness! To remain concentrated on the subject, and to know when to stop, are two cardinal rules in the writing of poetry.

We see therefore that these canons boil down into something like the following succinct statements: Simplicity and directness of speech; subtlety and beauty of rhythms; individualistic freedom of idea; clearness and vividness of presentation; and concentration. Not new principles, by any means, as the writers of the preface admit, but "fallen into desuetude."

One characteristic of Imagist verse which was not mentioned in this preface, is: Suggestion—the implying of something rather than the stating of it, implying it perhaps under a metaphor, perhaps in an even less obvious way.

This poem of Mr. Fletcher's is an excellent example of Imagist suggestion:

THE WELL

The well is not used now
Its waters are tainted.

I remember there was once a man went down
To clean it.
He found it very cold and deep,
With a queer niche in one of its sides,
From which he hauled forth buckets of
 bricks and dirt.

The picture as given is quite clear and vivid. But the picture we see is not the poem, the real poem lies beyond, is only suggested.

Of the poets we have been considering in these essays, Mr. Robinson is most nearly allied to the Imagists in the use of suggestion; but the technique he employs is quite unlike theirs. In Mr. Sandburg's "Limited," which I quoted in the last chapter, suggestion again is the poem, and his treatment of it there is almost Imagistic.

It must not be forgotten that however many rules and tenets we may analyze, such mechanical labour can never give the touchstone to style. As Matthew Arnold said of the grand style, "one must feel it." It is possible to determine the work of different painters by their brush strokes, but such knowledge is for the expert alone, and then only for purposes of authenticity. The layman who had no way of telling the work of Titian from that of Watteau by any other method than that of brush strokes, would make a poor connoisseur.

I could go minutely into the work of these poets and show how each differs from the other—the varying modes of expression, the individual ways of using words, the changing progression of the phrases, the subtle originality of rhythms—but any one who could intelligently follow such an analysis would have no difficulty in determining Imagist work *per se;* and those who could not tell it at a glance, would find such hair-splitting dissection totally incomprehensible.

A few broad lines, then, shall serve us here, and I trust that, before I have finished, the reader will be incapable of making the blunder of that recent critic, who placed Mr. Frost and Mr. Masters in the Imagist group.

I have shown certain aspects of the Imagist idiom, but we must not lose sight of the fact that all these barriers

are arbitrary, and fade somewhat into
each other. Much of this idiom is ap-
plicable to other poets whom we have
been considering, as well; some of it
is peculiar to the Imagists. But it is
principally in their manner of dealing
with the idiom that we shall find the
difference to lie. * * *

1917

CONRAD AIKEN
(1889–   )

MUSIC I HEARD WITH YOU *

Music I heard with you was more
    than music,
And bread I broke with you was more
    than bread;
Now that I am without you, all is
    desolate;
All that was once so beautiful is
    dead.

Your hands once touched this table
    and this silver,
And I have seen your fingers hold this
    glass.
These things do not remember you,
    belovèd,—
And yet your touch upon them will
    not pass.

For it was in my heart you moved
    among them,
And blessed them with your hands
    and with your eyes;
And in my heart they will remember
    always,—
They knew you once, O beautiful and
    wise.

1916

* Reprinted from Conrad Aiken's
Selected Poems by permission of Charles
Scribner's Sons. Copyright 1918, 1921,
1925, 1929.

ALL LOVELY THINGS
WILL HAVE AN ENDING *

All lovely things will have an ending,
All lovely things will fade and die,
And youth, that's now so bravely
    spending,
Will beg a penny by and by.

Fine ladies all are soon forgotten,
And goldenrod is dust when dead,
The sweetest flesh and flowers are
    rotten
And cobwebs tent the brightest head.

Come back, true love! Sweet youth,
    return!—
But time goes on, and will, unheed-
    ing,
Though hands will reach, and eyes
    will yearn,
And the wild days set true hearts
    bleeding.

Come back, true love! Sweet youth,
    remain!—
But goldenrod and daisies wither,
And over them blows autumn rain,
They pass, they pass, and know not
    whither.

1916

FROM
SENLIN: A BIOGRAPHY *

[IT IS MORNING, SENLIN SAYS]

It is morning, Senlin says, and in the
    morning
When the light drips through the
    shutters like the dew,
I arise, I face the sunrise,
And do the things my fathers learned
    to do.
Stars in the purple dusk above the
    rooftops
Pale in a saffron mist and seem to die,
And I myself on a swiftly tilting
    planet
Stand before a glass and tie my tie.

Vine leaves tap my window,
Dew-drops sing to the garden
    stones,
The robin chirps in the chinaberry
    tree
Repeating three clear tones.

It is morning. I stand by the mirror
And tie my tie once more.
While waves far off in a pale rose
    twilight
Crash on a white sand shore.
I stand by a mirror and comb my
    hair:
How small and white my face!—
The green earth tilts through a sphere
    of air
And bathes in a flame of space.

There are houses hanging above the
    stars
And stars hung under a sea . . .
And a sun far off in a shell of
    silence
Dapples my walls for me . . .

It is morning, Senlin says, and in the
    morning
Should I not pause in the light to
    remember god?
Upright and firm I stand on a star
    unstable,
He is immense and lonely as a
    cloud.
I will dedicate this moment before my
    mirror
To him alone; for him I will comb
    my hair.
Accept these humble offerings, cloud
    of silence!
I will think of you as I descend the
    stair.

Vine leaves tap my window,
The snail-track shines on the
    stones,
Dew-drops flash from the chinaberry
    tree
Repeating two clear tones.

It is morning, I awake from a bed of
    silence,

Shining I rise from the starless waters
    of sleep.
The walls are about me still as in the
    evening,
I am the same, and the same name
    still I keep.

The earth revolves with me, yet
    makes no motion,
The stars pale silently in a coral
    sky.
In a whistling void I stand before my
    mirror,
Unconcerned, and tie my tie.

There are horses neighing on far-off
    hills
Tossing their long white manes,
And mountains flash in the rose-white
    dusk,
Their shoulders black with rains . . .
It is morning. I stand by the
    mirror
And surprise my soul once more;
The blue air rushes above my
    ceiling,
There are suns beneath my floor . . .

. . . It is morning, Senlin says, I as-
    cend from darkness
And depart on the winds of space for
    I know not where,
My watch is wound, a key is in my
    pocket,
And the sky is darkened as I descend
    the stair.
There are shadows across the windows,
    clouds in heaven,
And a god among the stars; and I will
    go
Thinking of him as I might think of
    daybreak
And humming a tune I know . . .

Vine leaves tap at the window,
Dew-drops sing to the garden
    stones,
The robin chirps in the chinaberry
    tree
Repeating three clear tones.

              1918

PRELUDES FOR MEMNON *

XXXVI

[GOOD VIRTUOUS SON]

Good virtuous son, adviser to the
poor,
Getter of children on your father's
dower,
Usher at weddings, and at churches
too,
Chairman of clubs, and Madam here's
your pew;
Uxorious simple sensuous and impassioned,
Rebel for once, when drunk, but now
old-fashioned;
Remember how you took the harlot's
hand,
And saw one instant hell's dark hinterland.

All's relative: the slow at last make
haste:
Rash friends of rebel days have gone
to waste;
Blackballed by clubs in which your
voice is power,
And cut down like the clover in its
hour.
While you, from state to state, move
on in pride
With your lubricious madam by your
side;
Upright and right, and freshly bathed,
and pure;
Insurance paid, and god outside your
door.

Remember that fierce atom in your
blood
Which bade you stand in hell, where
once you stood;
Remember the good friend who
stands there still,
And thinks of you, and smiles, and
thinks no ill.

* Reprinted from *Preludes for Memnon* by Conrad Aiken; copyright 1930
by Charles Scribner's Sons; used by
permission of the publishers.

Let that dark flame come once again
between
Hypocrisy and Hell's bright sabbath-
green;
There we will dance once more, and
in our hour
Worship the god who honors our poor
floor.

LVI

[RIMBAUD AND VERLAINE]

Rimbaud and Verlaine, precious pair
of poets,
Genius in both (but what is genius?)
playing
Chess on a marble table at an inn
With chestnut blossom falling in
blond beer
And on their hair and between knight
and bishop—
Sunlight squared between them on
the chess-board
Cirrus in heaven, and a squeal of
music
Blown from the leathern door of Ste.
Sulpice—

Discussing, between moves, iamb and
spondee
Anacoluthon and the open vowel
God the great peacock with his angel
peacocks
And his dependent peacocks the
bright stars:
Disputing too of fate as Plato loved
it,
Or Sophocles, who hated and admired,
Or Socrates, who loved and was
amused:

Verlaine puts down his pawn upon a
leaf
And closes his long eyes, which are
dishonest,
And says "Rimbaud, there is one
thing to do:
We must take rhetoric, and wring its
neck! . . ."
Rimbaud considers gravely, moves his
Queen;

And then removes himself to Tim-
buctoo.

And Verlaine dead,—with all his
jades and mauves;

And Rimbaud dead in Marseilles with
a vision,

His leg cut off, as once before his
heart;

And all reported by a later lackey,

Whose virtue is his tardiness in time.

Let us describe the evening as it is:—

The stars disposed in heaven as they
are:

Verlaine and Shakspere rotting,
where they rot,

Rimbaud remembered, and too soon
forgot;

Order in all things, logic in the dark;

Arrangement in the atom and the
spark;

Time in the heart and sequence in
the brain—

Such as destroyed Rimbaud and
fooled Verlaine.

And let us then take godhead by the
neck—

And strangled it, and with it, rhetoric.

1930

T. S. ELIOT
(1888–   )

PORTRAIT OF A LADY *

Thou hast committed—
Fornication: but that was in another
country,
And besides, the wench is dead.
—THE JEW OF MALTA.

I

Among the smoke and fog of a December afternoon

* From *Collected Poems 1909–1935*
by T. S. Eliot, copyright, 1934, 1936, by
Harcourt, Brace and Company, Inc.

You have the scene arrange itself—as
it will seem to do—

With "I have saved this afternoon for
you";

And four wax candles in the darkened
room,

Four rings of light upon the ceiling
overhead,

An atmosphere of Juliet's tomb

Prepared for all the things to be said,
or left unsaid.

We have been, let us say, to hear the
latest Pole

Transmit the Preludes, through his
hair and fingertips.

"So intimate, this Chopin, that I think
his soul

Should be resurrected only among
friends

Some two or three, who will not touch
the bloom

That is rubbed and questioned in the
concert room."

—And so the conversation slips

Among velleities and carefully caught
regrets

Through attenuated tones of
violins

Mingled with remote cornets

And begins.

"You do not know how much they
mean to me, my friends,

And how, how rare and strange it is,
to find

In a life composed so much, so much
of odds and ends,

[For indeed I do not love it . . . you
knew? you are not blind!

How keen you are!]

To find a friend who has these qualities,

Who has, and gives

Those qualities upon which friendship lives.

How much it means that I say this
to you—

Without these friendships—life, what
cauchemar!"

Among the windings of the violins
And the ariettes
Of cracked cornets
Inside my brain a dull tom-tom begins
Absurdly hammering a prelude of its
    own,
Capricious monotone
That is at least one definite "false
    note."
—Let us take the air, in a tobacco
    trance,
Admire the monuments,
Discuss the late events,
Correct our watches by the public
    clocks.
Then sit for half an hour and drink
    our bocks.

II

Now that lilacs are in bloom
She has a bowl of lilacs in her room
And twists one in her fingers while
    she talks.
"Ah, my friend, you do not know,
    you do not know
What life is, you hold it in your
    hands";
(Slowly twisting the lilac stalks)
"You let it flow from you, you let it
    flow,
And youth is cruel, and has no re-
    morse
And smiles at situations which it can-
    not see."
I smile, of course,
And go on drinking tea.
"Yet with these April sunsets, that
    somehow recall
My buried life, and Paris in the
    Spring,
I feel immeasurably at peace, and find
    the world
To be wonderful and youthful, after
    all."

The voice returns like the insistent
    out-of-tune
Of a broken violin on an August after-
    noon:

"I am always sure that you under-
    stand
My feelings, always sure that you
    feel,
Sure that across the gulf you reach
    your hand.

You are invulnerable, you have no
    Achilles' heel.
You will go on, and when you have
    prevailed
You can say: at this point many a one
    has failed.
But what have I, but what have I, my
    friend,
To give you, what can you receive
    from me?
Only the friendship and the sym-
    pathy
Of one about to reach her journey's
    end.

I shall sit here, serving tea to
    friends. . . ."

I take my hat: how can I make a
    cowardly amends
For what she has said to me?
You will see me any morning in the
    park
Reading the comics and the sporting
    page.
Particularly I remark
An English countess goes upon the
    stage.
A Greek was murdered at a Polish
    dance,
Another bank defaulter has
    confessed.
I keep my countenance,
I remain self-possessed
Except when a street piano, mechani-
    cal and tired
Reiterates some worn-out common
    song
With the smell of hyacinths across the
    garden
Recalling things that other people
    have desired.
Are these ideas right or wrong?

III

The October night comes down; re-
turning as before
Except for a slight sensation of being
ill at ease
I mount the stairs and turn the handle
of the door
And feel as if I had mounted on my
hands and knees.
"And so you are going abroad; and
when do you return?
But that's a useless question.
You hardly know when you are com-
ing back,
You will find so much to learn."
My smile falls heavily among the
bric-à-brac.

"Perhaps you can write to me."
My self-possession flares up for a
second;
This is as I had reckoned.
"I have been wondering frequently of
late
(But our beginnings never know our
ends!)
Why we have not developed into
friends."
I feel like one who smiles, and turn-
ing shall remark
Suddenly, his expression in a glass.
My self-possession gutters; we are
really in the dark.

"For everybody said so, all our friends,
They all were sure our feelings would
relate
So closely! I myself can hardly under-
stand.
We must leave it now to fate.
You will write, at any rate.
Perhaps it is not too late.
I shall sit here, serving tea to friends."
And I must borrow every changing
shape
To find expression . . . dance, dance
Like a dancing bear,
Cry like a parrot, chatter like an ape.
Let us take the air, in a tobacco
trance—

Well! and what if she should die
some afternoon,
Afternoon grey and smoky, evening
yellow and rose;
Should die and leave me sitting pen
in hand
With the smoke coming down above
the housetops;
Doubtful, for a while
Not knowing what to feel or if I
understand
Or whether wise or foolish, tardy or
too soon . . .
Would she not have the advantage,
after all?
This music is successful with a "dying
fall"
Now that we talk of dying—
And should I have the right to smile?
1915

THE LOVE SONG
OF J. ALFRED PRUFROCK *

S'io credesse che mia risposta fosse
A persona che mai tornasse al mondo,
Questa fiamma staria senza piu scosse.
Ma perciocche giammai di questo fondo
Non torno vivo alcun, s'i'odo il vero,
Senza tema d'infamia ti rispondo.

Let us go then, you and I,
When the evening is spread out
against the sky
Like a patient etherized upon a
table;
Let us go, through certain half-
deserted streets,
The muttering retreats
Of restless nights in one-night cheap
hotels
And sawdust restaurants with oyster-
shells:
Streets that follow like a tedious
argument
Of insidious intent

* From *Collected Poems 1909–1935*
by T. S. Eliot, copyright, 1934, 1936, by
Harcourt, Brace and Company, Inc.

To lead you to an overwhelming
    question. . . .
Oh, do not ask, "What is it?"
Let us go and make our visit.

In the room the women come and go
Talking of Michelangelo.

The yellow fog that rubs its back
    upon the windowpanes,
The yellow smoke that rubs its muzzle
    on the windowpanes,
Licked its tongue into the corners of
    the evening,
Lingered upon the pools that stand in
    drains,
Let fall upon its back the soot that
    falls from chimneys,
Slipped by the terrace, made a sudden
    leap,
And seeing that it was a soft October
    night,
Curled once about the house, and fell
    asleep.

And indeed there will be time
For the yellow smoke that slides along
    the street,
Rubbing its back upon the window-
    panes;
There will be time, there will be time
To prepare a face to meet the faces
    that you meet;
There will be time to murder and
    create,
And time for all the works and days
    of hands
That lift and drop a question on your
    plate;
Time for you and time for me,
And time yet for a hundred indeci-
    sions,
And for a hundred visions and re-
    visions,
Before the taking of a toast and tea.

In the room the women come and go
Talking of Michelangelo.

And indeed there will be time
To wonder, "Do I dare?" and, "Do I
    dare?"

Time to turn back and descend the
    stair,
With a bald spot in the middle of my
    hair—
(They will say: "How his hair is
    growing thin!")
My morning coat, my collar mounting
    firmly to the chin,
My necktie rich and modest, but as-
    serted by a simple pin—
(They will say: "But how his arms
    and legs are thin!")
Do I dare
Disturb the universe?
In a minute there is time
For decisions and revisions which a
    minute will reverse.

For I have known them all already,
    known them all:
Have known the evenings, mornings,
    afternoons,
I have measured out my life with
    coffee spoons;
I know the voices dying with a dying
    fall
Beneath the music from a farther
    room.
    So how should I presume?

And I have known the eyes already,
    known them all—
The eyes that fix you in a formulated
    phrase,
And when I am formulated, sprawling
    on a pin,
When I am pinned and wriggling on
    the wall,
Then how should I begin
To spit out all the butt-ends of my
    days and ways?
    And how should I presume?

And I have known the arms already,
    known them all—
Arms that are braceleted and white
    and bare
(But in the lamplight, downed with
    light brown hair!)
Is it perfume from a dress
That makes me so digress?

Arms that lie along a table, or wrap
about a shawl.
And should I then presume?
And how should I begin?

. . .

Shall I say, I have gone at dusk
through narrow streets
And watched the smoke that rises from
the pipes
Of lonely men in shirt-sleeves, leaning
out of windows? . . .

I should have been a pair of ragged
claws
Scuttling across the floors of silent
seas.

. . .

And the afternoon, the evening, sleeps
so peacefully!
Smoothed by long fingers,
Asleep . . . tired . . . or it malingers,
Stretched on the floor, here beside you
and me.
Should I, after tea and cakes and
ices,
Have the strength to force the moment
to its crisis?
But though I have wept and fasted,
wept and prayed,
Though I have seen my head (grown
slightly bald) brought in upon a
platter,
I am no prophet—and here's no great
matter;
I have seen the moment of my great-
ness flicker,
And I have seen the eternal Footman
hold my coat, and snicker,
And in short, I was afraid.

And would it have been worth it,
after all,
After the cups, the marmalade, the
tea,
Among the porcelain, among some
talk of you and me,
Would it have been worth while,

To have bitten off the matter with a
smile,

To have squeezed the universe into a
ball,
To roll it toward some overwhelming
question,
To say: "I am Lazarus, come from
the dead,
Come back to tell you all, I shall tell
you all"—
If one, settling a pillow by her head,
Should say: "That is not what I
meant at all;
That is not it, at all."

And would it have been worth it,
after all,
Would it have been worth while,
After the sunsets and the dooryards
and the sprinkled streets,
After the novels, after the teacups,
after the skirts that trail along the
floor—
And this, and so much more?—
It is impossible to say just what I
mean!
But as if a magic lantern threw the
nerves in patterns on a screen
Would it have been worth while
If one, settling a pillow or throwing
off a shawl,
And turning toward the window,
should say:
"That is not it at all,
That is not what I meant, at all."

. . .

No! I am not Prince Hamlet, nor was
meant to be;
Am an attendant lord, one that will do
To swell a progress, start a scene or
two,
Advise the prince; no doubt, an easy
tool,
Deferential, glad to be of use,
Politic, cautious, and meticulous;
Full of high sentence, but a bit obtuse;
At times, indeed, almost ridiculous—
Almost, at times, the Fool.

I grow old. . . . I grow old. . . .
I shall wear the bottoms of my
trousers rolled.

Shall I part my hair behind? Do I
dare to eat a peach?
I shall wear white flannel trousers,
and walk upon the beach.
I have heard the mermaids singing,
each to each.

I do not think that they will sing to
me.

I have seen them riding seaward on
the waves
Combing the white hair of the waves
blown back
When the wind blows the water white
and black.

We have lingered in the chambers of
the sea
By sea-girls wreathed with seaweed
red and brown
Till human voices wake us, and we
drown.
                    1915, 1917, 1920

MR. APOLLINAX *

Ω τῆς καινότητος. Ἡράκλεις, τῆς
παραδοξολογίας. εὐμήχανος ἄνθρωπος
                                   LUCIAN.

When Mr. Apollinax visited the
United States
His laughter tinkled among the tea-
cups.
I thought of Fragilion, that shy figure
among the birch-trees,
And of Priapus in the shrubbery
Gaping at the lady in the swing.
In the palace of Mrs. Phlaccus, at Pro-
fessor Channing-Cheetah's
He laughed like an irresponsible
fœtus.
His laughter was submarine and pro-
found
Like the old man of the sea's
Hidden under coral islands

Where worried bodies of drowned
men drift down in the green
silence,
Dropping from fingers of surf.
I looked for the head of Mr. Apollinax
rolling under a chair
Or grinning over a screen
With seaweed in its hair.
I heard the beat of centaur's hoofs
over the hard turf
As his dry and passionate talk de-
voured the afternoon.
"He is a charming man"—"But after
all what did he mean?"—
"His pointed ears. . . . He must be
unbalanced,"—
"There was something he said that I
might have challenged."
Of dowager Mrs. Phlaccus, and Pro-
fessor and Mrs. Cheetah
I remember a slice of lemon, and a
bitten macaroon.
                                   1917

GERONTION *

Thou hast nor youth nor age
But as it were an after dinner sleep
Dreaming of both.

Here I am, an old man in a dry
month,
Being read to by a boy, waiting for
rain.
I was neither at the hot gates
Nor fought in the warm rain
Nor knee deep in the salt marsh, heav-
ing a cutlass,
Bitten by flies, fought.
My house is a decayed house,
And the jew squats on the window
sill, the owner,
Spawned in some estaminet of Ant-
werp,
Blistered in Brussels, patched and
peeled in London.
The goat coughs at night in the field
overhead;

Rocks, moss, stonecrop, iron,
    merds.
The woman keeps the kitchen, makes
    tea,
Sneezes at evening, poking the peev-
    ish gutter.
                    I an old man,
A dull head among windy spaces.

Signs are taken for wonders. "We
    would see a sign!"
The word within a word, unable to
    speak a word,
Swaddled with darkness. In the
    juvescence of the year
Came Christ the tiger
In depraved May, dogwood and chest-
    nut, flowering judas,
To be eaten, to be divided, to be
    drunk
Among whispers; by Mr. Silvero
With caressing hands, at Limoges
Who walked all night in the next
    room;

By Hakagawa, bowing among the
    Titians;
By Madame de Tornquist, in the dark
    room
Shifting the candles; Fräulein von
    Kulp
Who turned in the hall, one hand on
    the door. Vacant shuttles
Weave the wind. I have no ghosts,
An old man in a draughty house
Under a windy knob.

After such knowledge, what forgive-
    ness? Think now
History has many cunning passages,
    contrived corridors
And issues, deceives with whispering
    ambitions,
Guides us by vanities. Think now
She gives when our attention is dis-
    tracted
And what she gives, gives with such
    supple confusions
That the giving famishes the craving.
    Gives too late

What's not believed in, or if still be-
    lieved,
In memory only, reconsidered passion.
    Gives too soon
Into weak hands, what's thought can
    be dispensed with
Till the refusal propagates a fear.
    Think
Neither fear nor courage saves us.
    Unnatural vices
Are fathered by our heroism. Virtues
Are forced upon us by our impudent
    crimes.
These tears are shaken from the
    wrath-bearing tree.

The tiger springs in the new year. Us
    he devours. Think at last.
We have not reached conclusion,
    when I
Stiffen in a rented house. Think at
    last
I have not made this show purpose-
    lessly
And it is not by any concitation
Of the backward devils
I would meet you upon this honestly.
I that was near your heart was re-
    moved therefrom
To lose beauty in terror, terror in in-
    quisition.
I have lost my passion: why should I
    need to keep it
Since what is kept must be adulter-
    ated?
I have lost my sight, smell, hearing,
    taste and touch:
How should I use them for your closer
    contact?

These with a thousand small delibera-
    tions
Protract the profit of their chilled
    delirium,
Excite the membrane, when the sense
    has cooled,
With pungent sauces, multiply variety
In a wilderness of mirrors. What will
    the spider do,
Suspend its operations, will the weevil

Delay? De Bailhache, Fresca, Mrs.
　Cammel, whirled
Beyond the circuit of the shuddering
　Bear
In fractured atoms. Gull against the
　wind, in the windy straits
Of Belle Isle, or running on the Horn,
White feathers in the snow, the Gulf
　claims,
And an old man driven by the Trades
To a sleepy corner.

　　　　　　　　Tenants of the house,
Thoughts of a dry brain in a dry
　season.

　　　　　　　　　　　　　　1920

SWEENEY
AMONG THE NIGHTINGALES *

ὤμοι, πέπληγμαι καιρίαν πληγὴν ἔσω.

Apeneck Sweeney spreads his knees
Letting his arms hang down to laugh,
The zebra stripes along his jaw
Swelling to maculate giraffe.

The circles of the stormy moon
Slide westward toward the River Plate,
Death and the Raven drift above
And Sweeney guards the hornèd gate.

Gloomy Orion and the Dog
Are veiled; and hushed the shrunken
　seas;
The person in the Spanish cape
Tries to sit on Sweeney's knees

Slips and pulls the table cloth
Overturns a coffee-cup,
Reorganised upon the floor
She yawns and draws a stocking
　up;

The silent man in mocha brown
Sprawls at the window-sill and gapes;
The waiter brings in oranges
Bananas figs and hothouse grapes;

　* From *Collected Poems 1909–1935*
by T. S. Eliot, copyright, 1934, 1936, by
Harcourt, Brace and Company, Inc.

The silent vertebrate in brown
Contracts and concentrates, with-
　draws;
Rachel *née* Rabinovitch
Tears at the grapes with murderous
　paws;

She and the lady in the cape
Are suspect, thought to be in league;
Therefore the man with heavy eyes
Declines the gambit, shows fatigue,

Leaves the room and reappears
Outside the window, leaning in,
Branches of wistaria
Circumscribe a golden grin;

The host with someone indistinct
Converses at the door apart,
The nightingales are singing near
The Convent of the Sacred Heart,

And sang within the bloody wood
When Agamemnon cried aloud,
And let their liquid siftings fall
To stain the stiff dishonoured
　shroud.

　　　　　　　　　　　　　　1920

THE WASTE LAND *

NAM *Sibyllam quidem Cumis ego ipse
oculis meis vidi in ampulla pendere, et
cum illi pueri dicerent:* Σίβυλλα τί
θέλεις; *respondebat illa:* ἀποθανεῖν θέλω.

For Ezra Pound
il miglior fabbro.

I

THE BURIAL OF THE DEAD

April is the cruellest month, breeding
Lilacs out of the dead land, mixing
Memory and desire, stirring
Dull roots with spring rain.
Winter kept us warm, covering
Earth in forgetful snow, feeding
A little life with dried tubers.
Summer surprised us, coming over the
　Starnbergersee

With a shower of rain; we stopped in
    the colonnade,
And went on in sunlight, into the
    Hofgarten,
And drank coffee, and talked for an
    hour.
Bin gar keine Russin, stamm' aus
    Litauen, echt deutsch.
And when we were children, staying
    at the archduke's,
My cousin's, he took me out on a sled,
And I was frightened. He said, Marie,
Marie, hold on tight. And down we
    went.
In the mountains, there you feel free.
I read, much of the night, and go
    south in the winter.

What are the roots that clutch, what
    branches grow
Out of this stony rubbish? Son of
    man,
You cannot say, or guess, for you
    know only
A heap of broken images, where the
    sun beats,
And the dead tree gives no shelter,
    the cricket no relief,
And the dry stone no sound of water.
    Only
There is shadow under this red
    rock,
(Come in under the shadow of this
    red rock),
And I will show you something differ-
    ent from either
Your shadow at morning striding be-
    hind you
Or you shadow at evening rising to
    meet you;
I will show you fear in a handful of
    dust.
      Frisch weht der Wind
      Der Heimat zu
      Mein Irisch Kind,
      Wo weilest du?
"You gave me hyacinths first a year
    ago;
"They called me the hyacinth girl."

—Yet when we came back, late, from
    the Hyacinth garden,
Your arms full, and your hair wet, I
    could not
Speak, and my eyes failed, I was
    neither
Living nor dead, and I knew nothing,
Looking into the heart of light, the
    silence.
Oed' und leer das Meer.

Madame Sosostris, famous clairvoy-
    ante,
Had a bad cold, nevertheless
Is known to be the wisest woman in
    Europe,
With a wicked pack of cards. Here,
    said she,
Is your card, the drowned Phoenician
    Sailor,
(Those are pearls that were his eyes.
    Look!)
Here is Belladonna, the Lady of the
    Rocks,
The lady of situations.
Here is the man with three staves, and
    here the Wheel,
And here is the one-eyed merchant,
    and this card,
Which is blank, is something he car-
    ries on his back,
Which I am forbidden to see. I do
    not find
The Hanged Man. Fear death by
    water.
I see crowds of people, walking round
    in a ring.
Thank you. If you see dear Mrs. Equi-
    tone,
Tell her I bring the horoscope myself:
One must be so careful these days.

Unreal City,
Under the brown fog of a winter
    dawn,
A crowd flowed over London Bridge,
    so many,
I had not thought death had undone
    so many.

Sighs, short and infrequent, were exhaled,
And each man fixed his eyes before his feet.
Flowed up the hill and down King William Street,
To where Saint Mary Woolnoth kept the hours
With a dead sound on the final stroke of nine.
There I saw one I knew, and stopped him, crying: "Stetson!
"You who were with me in the ships at Mylae!
"That corpse you planted last year in your garden,
"Has it begun to sprout? Will it bloom this year?
"Or has the sudden frost disturbed its bed?
"Oh keep the Dog far hence, that's friend to men,
"Or with his nails he'll dig it up again!
"You! hypocrite lecteur!—mon semblable,—mon frère!"

II

A GAME OF CHESS

The Chair she sat in, like a burnished throne,
Glowed on the marble, where the glass
Held up by standards wrought with fruited vines
From which a golden Cupidon peeped out
(Another hid his eyes behind his wing)
Doubled the flames of sevenbranched candelabra
Reflecting light upon the table as
The glitter of her jewels rose to meet it,
From satin cases poured in rich profusion;
In vials of ivory and coloured glass
Unstoppered, lurked her strange synthetic perfumes

Unguent, powdered, or liquid—troubled, confused
And drowned the sense in odours; stirred by the air
That freshened from the window, these ascended
In fattening the prolonged candle-flames,
Flung their smoke into the laquearia,
Stirring the pattern on the coffered ceiling.
Huge sea-wood fed with copper
Burned green and orange, framed by the coloured stone,
In which sad light a carvèd dolphin swam.
Above the antique mantel was displayed
As though a window gave upon the sylvan scene
The change of Philomel, by the barbarous king
So rudely forced; yet there the nightingale
Filled all the desert with inviolable voice
And still she cried, and still the world pursues,
"Jug Jug" to dirty ears.
And other withered stumps of time
Were told upon the walls; staring forms
Leaned out, leaning, hushing the room enclosed.
Footsteps shuffled on the stair.
Under the firelight, under the brush, her hair
Spread out in fiery points
Glowed into words, then would be savagely still.

"My nerves are bad to-night. Yes, bad. Stay with me.
"Speak to me. Why do you never speak. Speak.
"What are you thinking of? What thinking? What?
"I never know what you are thinking. Think."

I think we are in rats' alley
Where the dead men lost their
    bones.

"What is that noise?"
            The wind under the door.
"What is that noise now? What is the
    wind doing?"
            Nothing again nothing.
                        "Do
"You know nothing? Do you see noth-
    ing? Do you remember
"Nothing?"

    I remember
Those are pearls that were his
    eyes.
"Are you alive, or not? Is there noth-
    ing in your head?"
                        But
O O O O that Shakespeherian Rag—
It's so elegant
So intelligent
"What shall I do now? What shall I
    do?"
"I shall rush out as I am, and walk
    the street
"With my hair down, so. What shall
    we do tomorrow?
"What shall we ever do?"
            The hot water at ten.
And if it rains, a closed car at
    four.
And we shall play a game of
    chess,
Pressing lidless eyes and waiting for
    a knock upon the door.

When Lil's husband got demobbed, I
    said—
I didn't mince my words, I said to her
    myself,
HURRY UP PLEASE ITS TIME
Now Albert's coming back, make
    yourself a bit smart.
He'll want to know what you done
    with that money he gave you
To get yourself some teeth. He did, I
    was there.

You have them all out, Lil, and get a
    nice set,
He said, I swear, I can't bear to look
    at you.
And no more can't I, I said, and think
    of poor Albert,
He's been in the army four years, he
    wants a good time,
And if you don't give it him, there's
    others will, I said.
Oh is there, she said. Something o'
    that, I said.
Then I'll know who to thank, she said,
    and gave me a straight look.
HURRY UP PLEASE ITS TIME
If you don't like it you can get on
    with it, I said.
Others can pick and choose if you
    can't.
But if Albert makes off, it won't be
    for lack of telling.
You ought to be ashamed, I said, to
    look so antique.
(And her only thirty-one.)
I can't help it, she said, pulling a long
    face,
It's them pills I took, to bring it off,
    she said.
(She's had five already, and nearly
    died of young George.)
The chemist said it would be all right,
    but I've never been the same.
You *are* a proper fool, I said.
Well, if Albert won't leave you alone,
    there it is, I said,
What you get married for if you don't
    want children?
HURRY UP PLEASE ITS TIME
Well, that Sunday Albert was home,
    they had a hot gammon,
And they asked me in to dinner, to
    get the beauty of it hot—
HURRY UP PLEASE ITS TIME
HURRY UP PLEASE ITS TIME
Goonight Bill. Goonight Lou. Goo-
    night May. Goonight.
Ta ta, Goonight. Goonight.
Good night, ladies, good night, sweet
    ladies, good night, good night.

III

THE FIRE SERMON

The river's tent is broken: the last
    fingers of leaf
Clutch and sink into the wet bank.
    The wind
Crosses the brown land, unheard. The
    nymphs are departed.
Sweet Thames, run softly, till I end
    my song.
The river bears no empty bottles,
    sandwich papers,
Silk handkerchiefs, cardboard boxes,
    cigarette ends
Or other testimony of summer nights.
    The nymphs are departed.
And their friends, the loitering heirs
    of city directors;
Departed, have left no addresses.
By the waters of Leman I sat down
    and wept . . .
Sweet Thames, run softly till I end
    my song,
Sweet Thames, run softly, for I speak
    not loud or long.
But at my back in a cold blast I hear
The rattle of the bones, and chuckle
    spread from ear to ear.
A rat crept softly through the vegeta-
    tion
Dragging its slimy belly on the bank
While I was fishing in the dull canal
On a winter evening round behind
    the gashouse
Musing upon the king my brother's
    wreck
And on the king my father's death
    before him.
White bodies naked on the low damp
    ground
And bones cast in a little low dry
    garret,
Rattled by the rat's foot only, year to
    year.
But at my back from time to time I
    hear
The sound of horns and motors, which
    shall bring

Sweeney to Mrs. Porter in the spring.
O the moon shone bright on Mrs.
    Porter
And on her daughter
They wash their feet in soda water
*Et O ces voix d'enfants, chantant dans
    la coupole!*

Twit twit twit
Jug jug jug jug jug jug
So rudely forc'd.
Tereu

Unreal City
Under the brown fog of a winter noon
Mr. Eugenides, the Smyrna merchant
Unshaven, with a pocket full of cur-
    rants
C.i.f. London: documents at sight,
Asked me in demotic French
To luncheon at the Cannon Street
    Hotel
Followed by a weekend at the Metro-
    pole.
At the violet hour, when the eyes and
    back
Turn upward from the desk, when
    the human engine waits
Like a taxi throbbing waiting,
I Tiresias, though blind, throbbing
    between two lives,
Old man with wrinkled female breasts,
    can see
At the violet hour, the evening hour
    that strives
Homeward, and brings the sailor home
    from sea,
The typist home at teatime, clears her
    breakfast, lights
Her stove, and lays out food in tins.
Out of the window perilously spread
Her drying combinations touched by
    the sun's last rays,
On the divan are piled (at night her
    bed)
Stockings, slippers, camisoles, and
    stays.
I Tiresias, old man with wrinkled dugs
Perceived the scene, and foretold the
    rest—

I too awaited the expected guest.
He, the young man carbuncular, arrives,
A small house agent's clerk, with one bold stare,
One of the low on whom assurance sits
As a silk hat on a Bradford millionaire.
The time is now propitious, as he guesses,
The meal is ended, she is bored and tired,
Endeavours to engage her in caresses
Which still are unreproved, if undesired.
Flushed and decided, he assaults at once;
Exploring hands encounter no defence;
His vanity requires no response,
And makes a welcome of indifference.
(And I Tiresias have foresuffered all
Enacted on this same divan or bed;
I who have sat by Thebes below the wall
And walked among the lowest of the dead.)
Bestows one final patronising kiss,
And gropes his way, finding the stairs unlit . . .

She turns and looks a moment in the glass,
Hardly aware of her departed lover;
Her brain allows one half-formed thought to pass:
"Well now that's done: and I'm glad it's over."
When lovely woman stoops to folly and
Paces about her room again, alone,
She smoothes her hair with automatic hand,
And puts a record on the gramophone.

"This music crept by me upon the waters"
And along the Strand, up Queen Victoria Street.
O City city, I can sometimes hear

Beside a public bar in Lower Thames Street,
The pleasant whining of a mandoline
And a clatter and a chatter from within
Where fishmen lounge at noon: where the walls
Of Magnus Martyr hold
Inexplicable splendour of Ionian white and gold.

The river sweats
Oil and tar
The barges drift
With the turning tide
Red sails
Wide
To leeward, swing on the heavy spar.
The barges wash
Drifting logs
Down Greenwich reach
Past the Isle of Dogs.
        Weialala leia
        Wallala leialala

Elizabeth and Leicester
Beating oars
The stern was formed
A gilded shell
Red and gold
The brisk swell
Rippled both shores
Southwest wind
Carried down stream
The peal of bells
White towers
        Weialala leia
        Wallala leialala

"Trams and dusty trees.
Highbury bore me. Richmond and Kew
Undid me. By Richmond I raised my knees
Supine on the floor of a narrow canoe."

"My feet are at Moorgate, and my heart
Under my feet. After the event

He wept. He promised 'a new
    start.'
  I made no comment. What should
    I resent?"

"On Margate Sands.
I can connect
Nothing with nothing.
The broken fingernails of dirty
  hands.
My people humble people who ex-
  pect
Nothing."
        la la

To Carthage then I came
Burning burning burning burning
O Lord Thou pluckest me out
O Lord Thou pluckest

burning

IV
DEATH BY WATER

Phlebas the Phoenician, a fortnight
  dead,
Forgot the cry of gulls, and the deep
  sea swell
And the profit and loss.
         A current under sea
Picked his bones in whispers. As he
  rose and fell
He passed the stages of his age and
  youth
Entering the whirlpool.
        Gentile or Jew
O you who turn the wheel and look
  to windward,
Consider Phlebas, who was once hand-
  some and tall as you.

V
WHAT THE THUNDER SAID

After the torchlight red on sweaty
  faces
After the frosty silence in the gardens
After the agony in stony places
The shouting and the crying
Prison and palace and reverberation

Of thunder of spring over distant
  mountains
He who was living is now dead
We who were living are now dying
With a little patience

Here is no water but only rock
Rock and no water and the sandy road
The road winding above among the
  mountains
Which are mountains of rock without
  water
If there were water we should stop
  and drink
Amongst the rock one cannot stop or
  think
Sweat is dry and feet are in the sand
If there were only water amongst the
  rock
Dead mountain mouth of carious teeth
  that cannot spit
Here one can neither stand nor lie
  nor sit
There is not even silence in the moun-
  tains
But dry sterile thunder without rain
There is not even solitude in the
  mountains
But red sullen faces sneer and snarl
From doors of mudcracked houses
        If there were water
  And no rock
  If there were rock
  And also water
  And water
  A spring
  A pool among the rock
  If there were the sound of water
    only
  Not the cicada
  And dry grass singing
  But sound of water over a rock
  Where the hermit-thrush sings in
    the pine trees
  Drip drop drip drop drop drop
    drop
  But there is no water

Who is the third who walks always
  beside you?

When I count, there are only you and
I together
But when I look ahead up the white
road
There is always another one walking
beside you
Gliding wrapt in a brown mantle,
hooded
I do not know whether a man or a
woman
—But who is that on the other side of
you?

What is that sound high in the air
Murmur of maternal lamentation
Who are those hooded hordes swarm-
ing
Over endless plains, stumbling in
cracked earth
Ringed by the flat horizon only
What is the city over the mountains
Cracks and reforms and bursts in the
violet air
Falling towers
Jerusalem Athens Alexandria
Vienna London
Unreal

A woman drew her long black hair
out tight
And fiddled whisper music on those
strings
And bats with baby faces in the violet
light
Whistled, and beat their wings
And crawled head downward down a
blackened wall
And upside down in air were
towers
Tolling reminiscent bells, that kept
the hours
And voices singing out of empty cis-
terns and exhausted wells.

In this decayed hole among the mountains
In the faint moonlight, the grass is
singing
Over the tumbled graves, about the
chapel

There is the empty chapel, only the
wind's home.
It has no windows, and the door
swings,
Dry bones can harm no one.
Only a cock stood on the rooftree
Co co rico co co rico
In a flash of lightning. Then a damp
gust
Bringing rain

Ganga was sunken, and the limp
leaves
Waited for rain, while the black
clouds
Gathered far distant, over Himavant.
The jungle crouched, humped in si-
lence.
Then spoke the thunder
DA
Datta: what have we given?
My friend, blood shaking my heart
The awful daring of a moment's sur-
render
Which an age of prudence can never
retract
By this, and this only, we have
existed
Which is not to be found in our
obituaries
Or in memories draped by the benef-
icent spider
Or under seals broken by the lean so-
licitor
In our empty rooms
DA
Dayadhvam: I have heard the key
Turn in the door once and turn once
only
We think of the key, each in his
prison
Thinking of the key, each confirms a
prison
Only at nightfall, aethereal
rumours
Revive for a moment a broken Corio-
lanus
DA
Damyata: The boat responded

Gaily, to the hand expert with sail
   and oar
The sea was calm, your heart would
   have responded
Gaily, when invited, beating obedient
To controlling hands

          I sat upon the shore
Fishing, with the arid plain behind
   me
Shall I at least set my lands in
   order?
London Bridge is falling down fall-
   ing down falling down
Poi s'ascose nel foco che gli affina
Quando fiam uti chelidon—O swallow
   swallow
Le Prince d'Aquitaine à la tour abolie
These fragments I have shored against
   my ruins
Why then Ile fit you. Hieronymo's
   mad againe.
Datta. Dayadhvam. Damyata.
     Shantih   shantih   shantih
                 1922

BURNT NORTON *

τοῦ λόγου δ'ἐόντος ξυνοῦ ζώουσιν οἱ
πολλοὶ ὡς ἰδίαν ἔχοντες φρόνησιν.
          I. p. 77. *Fr.* 2.

ὁδὸς ἄνω κάτω μία καὶ ὡυτή.
          I. p. 89. *Fr.* 60.

Diels: *Die Fragmente der Vorsokratiker*
          (Herakleitos).

I

Time present and time past
Are both perhaps present in time fu-
   ture,
And time future contained in time
   past.
If all time is eternally present
All time is unredeemable.

What might have been is an abstrac-
   tion
Remaining a perpetual possibility
Only in a world of speculation.
What might have been and what has
   been
Point to one end, which is always
   present.
Footfalls echo in the memory
Down the passage which we did not
   take
Towards the door we never opened
Into the rose-garden. My words echo
Thus, in your mind.
          But to what purpose
Disturbing the dust on a bowl of rose-
   leaves
I do not know.
          Other echoes
Inhabit the garden. Shall we follow?
Quick, said the bird, find them, find
   them,
Round the corner. Through the first
   gate,
Into our first world, shall we follow
The deception of the thrush? Into our
   first world.
There they were, dignified, invisible,
Moving without pressure, over the
   dead leaves,
In the autumn heat, through the
   vibrant air,
And the bird called, in response to
The unheard music hidden in the
   shrubbery,
And the unseen eyebeam crossed, for
   the roses
Had the look of flowers that are
   looked at.
There they were as our guests, ac-
   cepted and accepting.
So we moved, and they, in a formal
   pattern,
Along the empty alley, into the box
   circle,
To look down into the drained
   pool.
Dry the pool, dry concrete, brown
   edged,

And the pool was filled with water
  out of sunlight,
And the lotos rose, quietly, quietly,
The surface glittered out of heart of
  light,
And they were behind us, reflected in
  the pool.
Then a cloud passed, and the pool
  was empty.
Go, said the bird, for the leaves were
  full of children,
Hidden excitedly, containing laugh-
  ter.
Go, go, go, said the bird: human kind
Cannot bear very much reality.
Time past and time future
What might have been and what has
  been
Point to one end, which is always
  present.

II

Garlic and sapphires in the mud
Clot the bedded axle-tree.
The trilling wire in the blood
Sings below inveterate scars
And reconciles forgotten wars.
The dance along the artery
The circulation of the lymph
Are figured in the drift of stars
Ascend to summer in the tree
We move above the moving tree
In light upon the figured leaf
And hear upon the sodden floor
Below, the boarhound and the boar
Pursue their pattern as before
But reconciled among the stars.

At the still point of the turning world.
  Neither flesh nor fleshless;
Neither from nor towards; at the still
  point, there the dance is,
But neither arrest nor movement. And
  do not call it fixity.
Where past and future are gathered.
  Neither movement from nor to-
  wards,
Neither ascent nor decline. Except for
  the point, the still point,

There would be no dance, and there
  is only the dance.
I can only say, *there* we have been:
  but I cannot say where.
And I cannot say, how long, for that
  is to place it in time.

The inner freedom from the practical
  desire,
The release from action and suffering,
  release from the inner
And the outer compulsion, yet sur-
  rounded
By a grace of sense, a white light still
  and moving,
Erhebung without motion, concen-
  tration
Without elimination, both a new
  world
And the old made explicit, understood
In the completion of its partial
  ecstasy,
The resolution of its partial horror.
Yet the enchainment of past and
  future
Woven in the weakness of the chang-
  ing body,
Protects mankind from heaven and
  damnation
Which flesh cannot endure.
            Time past and time future
Allow but a little consciousness.
To be conscious is not to be in time
But only in time can the moment in
  the rose-garden,
The moment in the arbour where the
  rain beat,
The moment in the draughty church
  at smoke-fall
Be remembered; involved with past
  and future.
Only through time time is conquered.

III

Here is a place of disaffection
Time before and time after
In a dim light: neither daylight
Investing form with lucid stillness
Turning shadow into transient beauty

With slow rotation suggesting perma-
nence
Nor darkness to purify the soul
Emptying the sensual with depriva-
tion
Cleansing affection from the
temporal.
Neither plenitude nor vacancy. Only
a flicker
Over the strained time-ridden faces
Distracted from distraction by distrac-
tion
Filled with fancies and empty of
meaning
Tumid apathy with no concentra-
tion
Men and bits of paper, whirled by the
cold wind
That blows before and after time,
Wind in and out of unwholesome
lungs
Time before and time after.
Eructation of unhealthy souls
Into the faded air, the torpid
Driven on the wind that sweeps the
gloomy hills of London,
Hampstead and Clerkenwell, Camp-
den and Putney,
Highgate, Primrose and Ludgate. Not
here
Not here the darkness, in this twitter-
ing world.

Descend lower, descend only
Into the world of perpetual soli-
tude,
World not world, but that which is
not world,
Internal darkness, deprivation
And destitution of all property,
Dessication of the world of sense,
Evacuation of the world of fancy,
Inoperancy of the world of spirit;
This is the one way, and the other
Is the same, not in movement
But abstention from movement; while
the world moves
In appetency, on its metalled ways
Of time past and time future.

IV

Time and the bell have buried the
day,
The black cloud carries the sun away.
Will the sunflower turn to us, will
the clematis
Stray down, bend to us; tendril and
spray
Clutch and cling?
Chill
Fingers of yew be curled
Down on us? After the kingfisher's
wing
Has answered light to light, and is
silent, the light is still
At the still point of the turning world.

V

Words move, music moves
Only in time; but that which is only
living
Can only die. Words, after speech,
reach
Into the silence. Only by the form,
the pattern,
Can words or music reach
The stillness, as a Chinese jar still
Moves perpetually in its stillness.
Not the stillness of the violin, while
the note lasts,
Not that only, but the co-existence,
Or say that the end precedes the be-
ginning,
And the end and the beginning were
always there
Before the beginning and after the
end.
And all is always now. Words strain,
Crack and sometimes break, under the
burden,
Under the tension, slip, slide, perish,
Decay with imprecision, will not stay
in place,
Will not stay still. Shrieking voices
Scolding, mocking, or merely chatter-
ing,
Always assail them. The Word in the
desert

Is most attacked by voices of temptation,
The crying shadow in the funeral
dance,
The loud lament of the disconsolate
chimera.

The detail of the pattern is movement,
As in the figure of the ten stairs.
Desire itself is movement
Not in itself desirable;
Love is itself unmoving,
Only the cause and end of movement,
Timeless, and undesiring
Except in the aspect of time
Caught in the form of limitation
Between un-being and being.
Sudden in a shaft of sunlight
Even while the dust moves
There rises the hidden laughter
Of children in the foliage
Quick now, here, now, always—
Ridiculous the waste sad time
Stretching before and after.

1936

TRADITION AND THE
INDIVIDUAL TALENT *

I

In English writing we seldom speak
of tradition, though we occasionally
apply its name in deploring its absence. We cannot refer to "the tradition" or to "a tradition"; at most, we
employ the adjective in saying that
the poetry of So-and-So is "traditional" or even "too traditional." Seldom, perhaps, does the word appear except in a phrase of censure. If otherwise, it is vaguely approbative, with the
implication, as to the work approved,
of some pleasing archæological reconstruction. You can hardly make the
word agreeable to English ears with-

* From *Selected Essays 1917–1932* by
T. S. Eliot, copyright, 1932, by Harcourt,
Brace and Company, Inc.

out this comfortable reference to the
reassuring science of archæology.

Certainly the word is not likely to
appear in our appreciations of living
or dead writers. Every nation, every
race, has not only its own creative,
but its own critical turn of mind; and
is even more oblivious of the short-
comings and limitations of its critical
habits than of those of its creative
genius. We know, or think we know,
from the enormous mass of critical
writing that has appeared in the
French language the critical method
or habit of the French; we only conclude (we are such unconscious people) that the French are "more critical" than we, and sometimes even
plume ourselves a little with the fact,
as if the French were the less spontaneous. Perhaps they are; but we
might remind ourselves that criticism
is as inevitable as breathing, and that
we should be none the worse for artic-
ulating what passes in our minds
when we read a book and feel an
emotion about it, for criticizing our
own minds in their work of criticism.
One of the facts that might come to
light in this process is our tendency
to insist, when we praise a poet,
upon those aspects of his work in
which he least resembles any one else.
In these aspects or parts of his work
we pretend to find what is individual,
what is the peculiar essence of the
man. We dwell with satisfaction
upon the poet's difference from his
predecessors, especially his immediate
predecessors; we endeavour to find
something that can be isolated in
order to be enjoyed. Whereas if we
approach a poet without this prejudice we shall often find that not only
the best, but the most individual parts
of his work may be those in which
the dead poets, his ancestors, assert
their immortality most vigorously.
And I do not mean the impressionable

period of adolescence, but the period of full maturity.

Yet if the only form of tradition, of handing down, consisted in following the ways of the immediate generation before us in a blind or timid adherence to its successes, "tradition" should positively be discouraged. We have seen many such simple currents soon lost in the sand; and novelty is better than repetition. Tradition is a matter of much wider significance. It cannot be inherited, and if you want it you must obtain it by great labour. It involves, in the first place, the historical sense, which we may call nearly indispensable to any one who would continue to be a poet beyond his twenty-fifth year; and the historical sense involves a perception, not only of the pastness of the past, but of its presence; the historical sense compels a man to write not merely with his own generation in his bones, but with a feeling that the whole of the literature of Europe from Homer and within it the whole of the literature of his own country has a simultaneous existence and composes a simultaneous order. This historical sense, which is a sense of the timeless as well as of the temporal and of the timeless and of the temporal together, is what makes a writer traditional. And it is at the same time what makes a writer most acutely conscious of his place in time, of his contemporaneity.

No poet, no artist of any art, has his complete meaning alone. His significance, his appreciation is the appreciation of his relation to the dead poets and artists. You cannot value him alone; you must set him, for contrast and comparison, among the dead. I mean this as a principle of æsthetic, not merely historical, criticism. The necessity that he shall conform, that he shall cohere, is not one-sided; what happens when a new work of art is created is something that happens simultaneously to all the works of art which preceded it. The existing monuments form an ideal order among themselves, which is modified by the introduction of the new (the really new) work of art among them. The existing order is complete before the new work arrives; for order to persist after the supervention of novelty, the *whole* existing order must be, if ever so slightly, altered; and so the relations, proportions, values of each work of art toward the whole are readjusted; and this is conformity between the old and the new. Whoever has approved this idea of order, of the form of European, of English literature, will not find it preposterous that the past should be altered by the present as much as the present is directed by the past. And the poet who is aware of this will be aware of great difficulties and responsibilities.

In a peculiar sense he will be aware also that he must inevitably be judged by the standards of the past. I say judged, not amputated, by them; not judged to be as good as, or worse or better than, the dead; and certainly not judged by the canons of dead critics. It is a judgment, a comparison, in which two things are measured by each other. To conform merely would be for the new work not really to conform at all; it would not be new, and would therefore not be a work of art. And we do not quite say that the new is more valuable because it fits in; but its fitting in is a test of its value— a test, it is true, which can only be slowly and cautiously applied, for we are none of us infallible judges of conformity. We say: it appears to conform, and is perhaps individual, or it appears individual, and may conform; but we are hardly likely to find that it is one and not the other.

To proceed to a more intelligible exposition of the relation of the poet to the past: he can neither take the past as a lump, an indiscriminate bolus, nor can he form himself wholly on one or two private admirations, nor can he form himself wholly upon one preferred period. The first course is inadmissible, the second is an important experience of youth, and the third is a pleasant and highly desirable supplement. The poet must be very conscious of the main current, which does not at all flow invariably through the most distinguished reputations. He must be quite aware of the obvious fact that art never improves, but that the material of art is never quite the same. He must be aware that the mind of Europe—the mind of his own country—a mind which he learns in time to be much more important than his own private mind—is a mind which changes, and that this change is a development which abandons nothing *en route,* which does not superannuate either Shakespeare, or Homer, or the rock drawing of the Magdalenian draughtsmen. That this development, refinement perhaps, complication certainly, is not, from the point of view of the artist, any improvement. Perhaps not even an improvement from the point of view of the psychologist or not to the extent which we imagine; perhaps only in the end based upon a complication in economics and machinery. But the difference between the present and the past is that the conscious present is an awareness of the past in a way and to an extent which the past's awareness of itself cannot show.

Some one said: "The dead writers are remote from us because we *know* so much more than they did." Precisely, and they are that which we know.

I am alive to a usual objection to what is clearly part of my programme for the *metier* of poetry. The objection is that the doctrine requires a ridiculous amount of erudition (pedantry), a claim which can be rejected by appeal to the lives of poets in any pantheon. It will even be affirmed that much learning deadens or perverts poetic sensibility. While, however, we persist in believing that a poet ought to know as much as will not encroach upon his necessary receptivity and necessary laziness, it is not desirable to confine knowledge to whatever can be put into a useful shape for examinations, drawing-rooms, or the still more pretentious modes of publicity. Some can absorb knowledge, the more tardy must sweat for it. Shakespeare acquired more essential history from Plutarch than most men could from the whole British Museum. What is to be insisted upon is that the poet must develop or procure the consciousness of the past and that he should continue to develop this consciousness throughout his career.

What happens is a continual surrender of himself as he is at the moment to something which is more valuable. The progress of an artist is a continual self-sacrifice, a continual extinction of personality.

There remains to define this process of depersonalization and its relation to the sense of tradition. It is in this depersonalization that art may be said to approach the condition of science. I shall, therefore, invite you to consider, as a suggestive analogy, the action which takes place when a bit of finely filiated platinum is introduced into a chamber containing oxygen and sulphur dioxide.

II

Honest criticism and sensitive appreciation is directed not upon the poet but upon the poetry. If we attend to the confused cries of the newspaper critics and the susurrus of popular repetition that follows, we shall hear the names of poets in great numbers; if we seek not Bluebook knowledge but the enjoyment of poetry, and ask for a poem, we shall seldom find it. In the last article I tried to point out the importance of the relation of the poem to other poems by other authors, and suggested the conception of poetry as a living whole of all the poetry that has ever been written. The other aspect of this Impersonal theory of poetry is the relation of the poem to its author. And I hinted, by an analogy, that the mind of the mature poet differs from that of the immature one not precisely in any valuation of "personality," not being necessarily more interesting, or having "more to say," but rather by being a more finely perfected medium in which special, or very varied, feelings are at liberty to enter into new combinations.

The analogy was that of the catalyst. When the two gases previously mentioned are mixed in the presence of a filament of platinum, they form sulphurous acid. This combination takes place only if the platinum is present; nevertheless the newly formed acid contains no trace of platinum, and the platinum itself is apparently unaffected; has remained inert, neutral, and unchanged. The mind of the poet is the shred of platinum. It may partly or exclusively operate upon the experience of the man himself; but, the more perfect the artist, the more completely separate in him will be the man who suffers and the mind which creates; the more perfectly will the mind digest and transmute the passions which are its material.

The experience, you will notice, the elements which enter the presence of the transforming catalyst, are of two kinds: emotions and feelings. The effect of a work of art upon the person who enjoys it is an experience different in kind from any experience not of art. It may be formed out of one emotion, or may be a combination of several; and various feelings, inhering for the writer in particular words or phrases or images, may be added to compose the final result. Or great poetry may be made without the direct use of any emotion whatever: composed out of feelings solely. Canto XV of the *Inferno* (Brunetto Latini) is a working up of the emotion evident in the situation; but the effect, though single as that of any work of art, is obtained by considerable complexity of detail. The last quatrain gives an image, a feeling attaching to an image, which "came," which did not develop simply out of what precedes, but which was probably in suspension in the poet's mind until the proper combination arrived for it to add itself to. The poet's mind is in fact a receptacle for seizing and storing up numberless feelings, phrases, images, which remain there until all the particles which can unite to form a new compound are present together.

If you compare several representative passages of the greatest poetry you see how great is the variety of types of combination, and also how completely any semi-ethical criterion of "sublimity" misses the mark. For it is not the "greatness," the intensity, of the emotions, the components, but the intensity of the artistic process, the pressure, so to speak, under which the fusion takes place, that counts. The episode of Paolo and Francesca employs a definite emotion, but the intensity of the poetry is something quite different from whatever intensity in the supposed experience it may give the impression of. It is no more intense, furthermore, than Canto XXVI, the voyage of Ulysses, which has not the direct dependence upon emotion. Great variety is possible in the process of transmutation of emotion: the murder of Agamemnon, or the agony of Othello, gives an artistic effect apparently closer to a possible original than the scenes from Dante. In the *Agamemnon,* the artistic emotion approximates to the emotion of an actual spectator; in *Othello* to the emotion of the protagonist himself. But the difference between art and the event is always absolute; the combination which is the murder of Agamemnon is probably as complex as that which is the voyage of Ulysses. In either case there has been a fusion of elements. The ode of Keats contains a number of feelings which have nothing particular to do with the nightingale, but which the nightingale, partly, perhaps, because of its attractive name, and partly because of its reputation, served to bring together.

The point of view which I am struggling to attack is perhaps related to the metaphysical theory of the substantial unity of the soul: for my meaning is, that the poet has, not a "personality" to express, but a particular medium, which is only a medium and not a personality, in which impressions and experiences combine in peculiar and unexpected ways. Impressions and experiences which are important for the man may take no place in the poetry, and those which become important in the poetry may play quite a negligible part in the man, the personality.

I will quote a passage which is unfamiliar enough to be regarded with fresh attention in the light—or darkness—of these observations:

And now methinks I could e'en chide myself
For doating on her beauty, though her death
Shall be revenged after no common action.
Does the silkworm expend her yellow labours
For thee? For thee does she undo herself?
Are lordships sold to maintain ladyships
For the poor benefit of a bewildering minute?
Why does yon fellow falsify highways,
And put his life between the judge's lips,
To refine such a thing—keeps horse and men
To beat their valours for her? . . .

In this passage (as is evident if it is taken in its context) there is a combination of positive and negative emotions: an intensely strong attraction toward beauty and an equally intense fascination by the ugliness which is contrasted with it and which destroys it. This balance of contrasted emotion is in the dramatic situation to which the speech is pertinent, but that situation alone is inadequate to it. This is, so to speak, the structural emotion, provided by the drama. But the whole effect, the dominant tone, is due to the fact that a number of floating feelings, having an affinity to this emotion by no means superficially evident, have combined with it to give us a new art emotion.

It is not in his personal emotions, the emotions provoked by particular events in his life, that the poet is in any way remarkable or interesting. His particular emotions may be simple, or crude, or flat. The emotion in his poetry will be a very complex thing, but not with the complexity of the emotions of people who have very complex or unusual emotions in life. One error, in fact, of eccentricity in poetry is to seek for new human emotions to express: and in this search for novelty in the wrong place it discovers the perverse. The business of the poet is not to find new emotions, but to use the ordinary ones and, in working them up into poetry, to express feelings which are not in actual emotions at all. And emotions which he has never experienced will serve his turn as well as those familiar to him. Consequently, we must believe that "emotion recollected in tranquillity" is an inexact formula. For it is neither emotion, nor recollection, nor, without distortion of meaning, tranquillity. It is a concentration, and a new thing resulting from the concentration, of a very great number of experiences which to the practical and active person would not seem to be experiences at all; it is a concentration which does not happen consciously or of deliberation. These experiences are not "recollected," and they finally unite in an atmosphere which is "tranquil" only in that it is a passive attending upon the event. Of course this is not quite the whole story. There is a great deal, in the writing of poetry, which must be conscious and deliberate. In fact, the bad poet is usually unconscious where he ought to be conscious, and conscious where he ought to be unconscious. Both errors tend to make him "personal." Poetry is not a turning loose of emotion, but an escape from emotion; it is not the expression of personality, but an escape from personality. But, of course, only those who have personality and emotions know what it means to want to escape from these things.

III

ὁ δὲ νοῦς ἴσως θειότερόν τι καὶ ἀπαθές ἐστιν

This essay proposes to halt at the frontier of metaphysics or mysticism, and confine itself to such practical conclusions as can be applied by the responsible person interested in poetry. To divert interest from the poet to the poetry is a laudable aim: for it would conduce to a juster estimation of actual poetry, good and bad. There are many people who appreciate the expression of sincere emotion in verse, and there is a smaller number of people who can appreciate technical excellence. But very few know when there is expression of *significant* emotion, emotion which has its life in the poem and not in the history of the poet. The emotion of art is impersonal. And the poet cannot reach this impersonality without surrendering himself wholly to the work to be done. And he is not likely to know what is to be done unless he lives in what is not merely the present, but the present moment of the past, unless he is conscious, not of what is dead, but of what is already living.

1920

E. E. CUMMINGS
(1894–   )

[NEXT TO OF COURSE GOD] *

"next to of course god america i
love you land of the pilgrims' and so
        forth oh
say can you see by the dawn's early
        my
country 'tis of centuries come and go
and are no more what of it we should
        worry
in every language even deafanddumb
thy sons acclaim your glorious name
        by gorry
by jingo by gee by gosh by gum
why talk of beauty what could be
        more beaut-
iful than these heroic happy dead

* From *IS 5*, by E. E. Cummings.
Copyright, 1926, by Horace Liveright.

who rushed like lions to the roaring
    slaughter
they did not stop to think they died
    instead
then shall the voice of liberty be
    mute?"

He spoke. And drank rapidly a glass
    of water

                         1926

[NOBODY LOSES ALL THE TIME] *

nobody loses all the time

i had an uncle named
Sol who was a born failure and
nearly everybody said he should have
    gone
into vaudeville perhaps because my
    Uncle Sol could
sing McCann He Was A Diver on
    Xmas Eve like Hell Itself which
may or may not account for the fact
    that my Uncle

Sol indulged in that possibly most
    inexcusable
of all to use a highfalootin phrase
luxuries that is or to
wit farming and be
it needlessly
added

my Uncle Sol's farm
failed because the chickens
ate the vegetables so
my Uncle Sol had a
chicken farm till the
skunks ate the chickens when

my Uncle Sol
had a skunk farm but
the skunks caught cold and
died and so
my Uncle Sol imitated the
skunks in a subtle manner

    * From IS 5, by E. E. Cummings.
Copyright, 1926, by Horace Liveright.

or by drowning himself in the water-
    tank
but somebody who'd given my Uncle
    Sol a Victor
Victrola and records while he lived
    presented to
him upon the auspicious occasion of
    his decease a
scrumptious not to mention splendifer-
    ous funeral with
tall boys in black gloves and flowers
    and everything and

i remember we all cried like the
    Missouri
when my Uncle Sol's coffin lurched
    because
somebody pressed a button
(and down went
my Uncle
Sol

and started a worm farm)

                         1926

[MY SWEET OLD ETCETERA] *

my sweet old etcetera
aunt lucy during the recent

war could and what
is more did tell you just
what everybody was fighting

for,
my sister

isabel created hundreds
(and
hundreds) of socks not to
mention shirts fleaproof earwarmers

etcetera wristers etcetera, my
mother hoped that

i would die etcetera
bravely of course my father used
to become hoarse talking about how
    it was
a privilege and if only he
could meanwhile my

self etcetera lay quietly
in the deep mud et

cetera
(dreaming,
et
   cetera, of
Your smile
eyes knees and of your Etcetera)

1926

[JIMMIE'S GOT A GOIL] *

Jimmie's got a goil
       goil
        goil,
          Jimmie
's got a goil and
she coitnly can shimmie

when you see her shake
        shake
         shake,
          when
you see her shake a
shimmie how you wish that you was
   Jimmie.

Oh for such a gurl
       gurl
        gurl,
         oh
for such a gurl to
be a fellow's twistandtwirl

talk about your Sal-
       Sal-
        Sal-,
         talk
about your Salo
-mes but gimmie Jimmie's gal.

1926

---

* From *IS 5* by E. E. Cummings.
Copyright, 1926, by Horace Liveright.

MARIANNE MOORE
(1887–   )

POETRY *

I, too, dislike it: there are things that
      are important beyond all this
      fiddle.
Reading it, however, with a perfect
      contempt for it, one discovers
      in
it, after all, a place for the genuine.
      Hands that can grasp, eyes
      That can dilate, hair that can rise
        if it must, these things are im-
        portant not because a

high-sounding interpretation can be
      put upon them but because
      they are
useful. When they become so deriva-
      tive as to become unintelligi-
      ble,
the same thing may be said for all of
      us, that we
      do not admire what
      we cannot understand: the bat
        holding on upside down or in
        quest of something to

eat, elephants pushing, a wild horse
      taking a roll, a tireless wolf
      under
a tree, the immovable critic twitching
      his skin like a horse that feels
      a flee, the base-
      ball fan, the statistician-
      nor is it valid
      to discriminate against 'business
      documents and
school-books'; all these phenomena are
      important. One must make a
      distinction
however: when dragged into promi-
      nence by half poets, the result
      is not poetry,

---

* From Marianne Moore, *Selected
Poems,* copyright 1935 by Marianne
Moore. By permission of The Macmillan
Company, publishers.

not till the poets among us can be
  'literalists of
  the imagination'—above
      insolence and triviality and can
          present
for inspection, imaginary gardens with
      real toads in them, shall we
      have
it. In the meantime, if you demand
      on the one hand,
the raw material of poetry in
      all its rawness and
      that which is on the other hand
      genuine, then you are interested
      in poetry.

                                1935

TO A STEAM ROLLER *

The illustration
is nothing to you without the applica-
      tion.
      You lack half wit. You crush the
          particles down
      into close conformity, and then
          walk back and forth on them.

Sparkling chips of rock
are crushed down to the level of the
      parent block.
      Were not 'impersonal judgment in
          aesthetic
      matters, a metaphysical impossi-
          bility', you

might fairly achieve
it. As for butterflies, I can hardly
      conceive
      of one's attending upon you, but to
          question
      the congruence of the comple-
          ment is vain, if it exists.
                                1935

* From Marianne Moore, *Selected
Poems,* copyright 1935 by Marianne
Moore. By permission of The Macmillan
Company, publishers.

AN EGYPTIAN PULLED GLASS BOTTLE IN THE SHAPE OF A FISH *

Here we have thirst
And patience, from the first,
      And art, as in a wave held up for
          us to see
      In its essential perpendicularity;

Not brittle but
Intense—the spectrum, that
      Spectacular and nimble animal the
          fish,
      Whose scales turn aside the sun's
          sword with their polish.

                                1935

IS YOUR TOWN NINEVEH? *

Why so desolate?
      In phantasmagoria about fishes,
          what disgusts you? Could
          not all personal upheaval in
              the name of freedom, be
              tabooed?

Is it Nineveh
      and are you Jonah
          in the sweltering east wind of
              your wishes?
          I myself have stood
              there by the Aquarium,
              looking
              at the Statue of Liberty.
                                1935

HART CRANE
(1899–1932)

VOYAGES II †

And yet this great wink of eternity,
Of rimless floods, unfettered leeward-
      ings,

† From *The Collected Poems of Hart
Crane* by Hart Crane, published by
Liveright Publishing Corporation, N. Y.
Copyright 1933.

Samite sheeted and processioned where
Her undinal vast belly moonward bends,
Laughing the wrapt inflections of our love;

Take this Sea, whose diapason knells
On scrolls of silver snowy sentences,
The sceptred terror of whose sessions rends
As her demeanors motion well or ill,
All but the pieties of lovers' hands.

And onward, as the bells off San Salvador
Salute the crocus lustres of the stars,
In these poinsettia meadows of her tides,—
Adagios of islands, O my Prodigal,
Complete the dark confessions her veins spell.

Mark how her turning shoulders wind the hours,
And hasten while her penniless rich palms
Pass superscription of bent foam and wave,—
Hasten, while they are true,—sleep, death, desire,
Close round one instant in one floating flower.

Bind us in time, O Seasons clear, and awe.
O minstrel galleons of Carib fire,
Bequeath us to no earthly shore until
Is answered in the vortex of our grave
The seal's wide spindrift gaze toward paradise.

1926

THE BRIDGE *

FROM

PROEM: TO BROOKLYN BRIDGE

How many dawns, chill from his rippling rest
The seagull's wings shall dip and pivot him,
Shedding white rings of tumult, building high
Over the chained bay waters Liberty—

Then, with inviolate curve, forsake our eyes
As apparitional as sails that cross
Some page of figures to be filed away;
—Till elevators drop us from our day . . .

I think of cinemas, panoramic sleights
With multitudes bent toward some flashing scene
Never disclosed, but hastened to again,
Foretold to other eyes on the same screen;

And Thee, across the harbor, silver-paced
As though the sun took step of thee, yet left
Some motion ever unspent in thy stride,—
Implicitly thy freedom staying thee!

Out of some subway scuttle, cell or loft
A bedlamite speeds to thy parapets,
Tilting there momently, shrill shirt ballooning,
A jest falls from the speechless caravan.

Down Wall, from girder into street noon leaks,
A rip-tooth of the sky's acetylene;
All afternoon the cloud-flown derricks turn . . .
Thy cables breathe the North Atlantic still.

An obscure as that heaven of the Jews,
Thy guerdon . . . Accolade thou dost bestow
Of anonymity time cannot raise:
Vibrant reprieve and pardon thou dost show.

O harp and altar, of the fury fused,
(How could mere toil align thy choiring strings!)
Terrific threshold of the prophet's pledge,
Prayer of pariah, and the lover's cry,—

Again the traffic lights that skim thy swift
Unfractioned idiom, immaculate sigh of stars,
Beading thy path—condense eternity:
And we have seen night lifted in thine arms.

Under thy shadows by the piers I waited;
Only in darkness is thy shadow clear.
The City's fiery parcels all undone,
Already snow submerges an iron year . . .

O Sleepless as the river under thee,
Vaulting the sea, the prairies' dreaming sod,
Unto us lowliest sometime sweep, descend
And of the curveship lend a myth to God.

VAN WINKLE

Macadam, gun-grey as the tunny's belt,
Leaps from Far Rockaway to Golden Gate:
Listen! the miles a hurdy-gurdy grinds—
Down gold arpeggios mile on mile unwinds.

Streets spread past store and factory— sped by sun- light and her smile . . .

Times earlier, when you hurried off to school
—It is the same hour though a later day—
You walked with Pizarro in a copybook,
And Cortez rode up, reining tautly in—
Firmly as coffee grips the taste,—and away!

There was Priscilla's cheek close in the wind,
And Captain Smith, all beard and certainty,
And Rip Van Winkle bowing by the way,—
"Is this Sleepy Hollow, friend—?" And he—

Like Memory, she is time's truant, shall take you by the hand . . .

And Rip forgot the office hours,
*   and he forgot the pay;*
Van Winkle sweeps a tenement
*   way down on Avenue A,—*

The grind-organ says . . . Remember, remember
The cinder pile at the end of the backyard
Where we stoned the family of young
Garter snakes under . . . And the monoplanes
We launched—with paper wings and twisted
Rubber bands . . . Recall—recall
                    the rapid tongues
That flittered from under the ash heap day
After day whenever your stick discovered
Some sunning inch of unsuspecting fibre—
It flashed back at your thrust, as clean as fire.

And Rip was slowly made aware
      that he, Van Winkle, was not here
    nor there. He woke and swore he'd seen Broadway
        a Catskill daisy chain in May—

So memory, that strikes a rhyme out of a box
Or splits a random smell of flowers through glass—
Is it the whip stripped from the lilac tree
One day in spring my father took to me,
Or is it the Sabbatical, unconscious smile
My mother almost brought me once from church
And once only, as I recall—?

It flickered through the snow screen, blindly
It forsook her at the doorway, it was gone
Before I had left the window. It
Did not return with the kiss in the hall.

Macadam, gun-grey as the tunny's belt,
Leaps from Far Rockaway to Golden Gate . . .
Keep hold of that nickel for car-change, Rip,—
Have you got your *"Times"*—?
And hurry along, Van Winkle—it's getting late!

THE TUNNEL

                    To find the Western path
                    Right thro' the Gates of Wrath.
                            —BLAKE.

Performances, assortments, résumés—
Up Times Square to Columbus Circle lights
Channel the congresses, nightly sessions,
Refractions of the thousand theatres, faces—
Mysterious kitchens . . . You shall search them all.
Some day by heart you'll learn each famous sight
And watch the curtain lift in hell's despite;
You'll find the garden in the third act dead,
Finger your knees—and wish yourself in bed
With tabloid crime-sheets perched in easy sight.

Then let you reach your hat
and go.
As usual, let you—also
walking down—exclaim
to twelve upward leaving
a subscription praise
for what time slays.

Or can't you quite make up your mind to ride;
A walk is better beneath the L a brisk
Ten blocks or so before? But you find yourself
Preparing penguin flexions of the arms,—
As usual you will meet the scuttle yawn:
The subway yawns the quickest promise home.

Be minimum, then, to swim the hiving swarms
Out of the Square, the Circle burning bright—
Avoid the glass doors gyring at your right,
Where boxed alone a second, eyes take fright
—Quite unprepared rush naked back to light:
And down beside the turnstile press the coin
Into the slot. The gongs already rattle.

              And so
              of cities you bespeak
              subways, rivered under streets
              and rivers—In the car
              the overtone of motion
              underground, the monotone
              of motion is the sound
              of other faces, also underground—

"Let's have a pencil Jimmy—living now
at Floral Park
Flatbush—on the Fourth of July—
like a pigeon's muddy dream—potatoes
to dig in the field—travlin the town—too—
night after night—the Culver line—the
girls all shaping up—it used to be—"

Our tongues recant like beaten weather vanes.
This answer lives like verdigris, like hair
Beyond extinction, surcease of the bone;
And repetition freezes—"What

"what do you want? getting weak on the links?
fandaddle daddy don't ask for change—IS THIS
FOURTEENTH? it's half past six she said—if
you don't like my gate why did you
swing on it, why *didja*
swing on it
anyhow—"

And somehow anyhow swing—

The phonographs of hades in the brain
Are tunnels that re-wind themselves, and love
A burnt match skating in a urinal—
Somewhere above Fourteenth TAKE THE EXPRESS
To brush some new presentiment of pain—

"But I want service in this office SERVICE
I said—after
the show she cried a little afterwards but—"

Whose head is swinging from the swollen strap?
Whose body smokes along the bitten rails,
Bursts from a smoldering bundle far behind
In back forks of the chasms of the brain,—
Puffs from a riven stump far out behind
In interborough fissures of the mind . . . ?
And why do I often meet your visage here,
Your eyes like agate lanterns—on and on
Below the toothpaste and the dandruff ads?
—And did their riding eyes right through your side,
And did their eyes like unwashed platters ride?
And Death, aloft,—gigantically down
Probing through you—toward me, O evermore!
And when they dragged your retching flesh,
Your trembling hands that night through Baltimore—
That last night on the ballot rounds, did you
Shaking, did you deny the ticket, Poe?

For Gravesend Manor change at Chambers Street.
The platform hurries along to a dead stop.

The intent escalator lifts a serenade
Stilly
Of shoes, umbrellas, each eye attending its shoe, then
Bolting outright somewhere above where streets
Burst suddenly in rain. . . . The gongs recur:
Elbows and levers, guard and hissing door.
Thunder is galvothermic here below. . . . The car
Wheels off. The train rounds, bending to a scream,
Taking the final level for the dive
Under the river—
And somewhat emptier than before,
Demented, for a hitching second, humps; then
Lets go. . . . Toward corners of the floor
Newspapers wing, revolve and wing.
Blank windows gargle signals through the roar.

And does the Dæmon take you home, also,
Wop washerwoman, with the bandaged hair?
After the corridors are swept, the cuspidors—

The guant sky-barracks cleanly now, and bare,
O Genoese, do you bring mother eyes and hands
Back home to children and to golden hair?

Dæmon, demurring and eventful yawn!
Whose hideous laughter is a bellows mirth
—Or the muffled slaughter of a day in birth—
O cruelly to inoculate the brinking dawn
With antennæ toward worlds that glow and sink;—
To spoon us out more liquid than the dim
Locution of the eldest star, and pack
The conscience navelled in the plunging wind,
Umbilical to call—and straightway die!

O caught like pennies beneath soot and steam,
Kiss of our agony thou gatherest;
Condensed, thou takest all—shrill ganglia
Impassioned with some song we fail to keep.
And yet, like Lazarus, we feel the slope,
The sod and billow breaking,—lifting ground,
—A sound of waters bending astride the sky
Unceasing with some Word that will not die . . . !

A tugboat, wheezing wreaths of steam,
Lunged past, with one galvanic blare strove up the River.
I counted the echoes assembling, one after one,
Searching, thumbing the midnight on the piers.
Lights, coasting, left the oily tympanum of waters;
The blackness somewhere gouged glass on a sky.
And this thy harbor, O my City, I have driven under,
Tossed from the coil of ticking towers. . . . Tomorrow,
And to be. . . . Here by the River that is East—
Shadowless in that abyss they unaccounting lie.
How far away the star has pooled the sea—
Or shall the hands be drawn away, to die?

Kiss of our agony Thou gatherest,
               O Hand of Fire
                       gatherest—

ATLANTIS

> *Music is then the knowledge of that which
> relates to love in harmony and system.*
>
> —PLATO.

Through the bound cable strands, the arching path
Upward, veering with light, the flight of strings,—
Taut miles of shuttling moonlight syncopate
The whispered rush, telepathy of wires.
Up the index of night, granite and steel—
Transparent meshes—fleckless the gleaming staves—

Sibylline voices flicker, waveringly stream
As though a god were issue of the strings. . . .

And through that cordage, threading with its call
One arc synoptic of all tides below—
Their labyrinthine mouths of history
Pouring reply as though all ships at sea
Complighted in one vibrant breath made cry,—
"Make thy love sure—to weave whose song we ply!"
—From black embankments, moveless soundings hailed,
So seven oceans answer from their dream.

And on, obliquely up bright carrier bars
New octaves trestle the twin monoliths
Beyond whose frosted capes the moon bequeaths
Two worlds of sleep (O arching strands of song!)—
Onward and up the crystal-flooded aisle
White tempest nets file upward, upward ring
With silver terraces the humming spars,
The loft of vision, palladium helm of stars.

Sheerly the eyes, like seagulls stung with rime—
Slit and propelled by glistening fins of light—
Pick biting way up towering looms that press
Sidelong with flight of blade on tendon blade
—Tomorrows into yesteryear—and link
What cipher-script of time no traveller reads
But who, through smoking pyres of love and death,
Searches the timeless laugh of mystic spears.

Like hails, farewells—up planet-sequined heights
Some trillion whispering hammers glimmer Tyre:
Serenely, sharply up the long anvil cry
Of inchling æons silence rivets Troy.
And you, aloft there—Jason! hesting Shout!
Still wrapping harness to the swarming air!
Silvery the rushing wake, surpassing call,
Beams yelling Æolus! splintered in the straits!

From gulfs unfolding, terrible of drums,
Tall Vision-of-the-Voyage, tensely spare—
Bridge, lifting night to cycloramic grist
Of deepest day—O Choir, translating time
Into what multitudinous Verb the suns
And synergy of waters ever fuse, recast
In myriad syllables,—Psalm of Cathay!
O Love, thy white, pervasive Paradigm . . . !

We left the haven hanging in the night—
Sheened harbor lanterns backward fled the keel.
Pacific here at time's end, bearing corn,—

Eyes stammer through the pangs of dust and steel.
And still the circular, indubitable frieze
Of heaven's meditation, yoking wave
To kneeling wave, one song devoutly binds—
The vernal strophe chimes from deathless strings!

O Thou steeled Cognizance whose leap commits
The agile precincts of the lark's return;
Within whose lariat sweep encinctured sing
In single chrysalis the many twain,—
Of stars Thou art the stitch and stallion glow
And like an organ, Thou, with sound of doom—
Sight, sound and flesh Thou leadest from time's realm
As love strikes clear direction for the helm.

Swift peal of secular light, intrinsic Myth
Whose fell unshadow is death's utter wound,—
O River-throated—iridescently upborne
Through the bright drench and fabric of our veins;
With white escarpments swinging into light,
Sustained in tears the cities are endowed
And justified conclamant with ripe fields
Revolving through their harvests in sweet torment.
Forever Deity's glittering Pledge, O Thou
Whose canticle fresh chemistry assigns
To rapt inception and beatitude,—
Always through blinding cables, to our joy,
Of thy white seizure springs the prophecy:
Always through spiring cordage, pyramids
Of silver sequel, Deity's young name
Kinetic of white choiring wings . . . ascends.

Migrations that must needs void memory,
Inventions that cobblestone the heart,—
Unspeakable Thou Bridge to Thee, O Love.
Thy pardon for this history, whitest Flower,
O Answerer of all,—Anemone,—
Now while thy petals spend the suns about us, hold—
(O Thou whose radiance doth inherit me)
Atlantis,—hold thy floating singer late!
So to thine Everpresence, beyond time,
Like spears ensanguined of one tolling star
That bleeds infinity—the orphic strings,
Sidereal phalanxes, leap and converge:
—One Song, one Bridge of Fire! Is it Cathay,
Now pity steeps the grass and rainbows ring
The serpent with the eagle in the leaves . . . ?
Whispers antiphonal in azure swing.

1930

THE AIR PLANT *

GRAND CAYMAN

This tuft that thrives on saline noth-
        ingness,
Inverted octopus with heavenward
        arms
Thrust parching from a palm-bole
        hard by the cove—
A bird almost—of almost bird alarms,

Is pulmonary to the wind that jars
Its tentacles, horrific in their lurch.
The lizard's throat, held bloated for
        a fly,
Balloons but warily from this throb-
        bing perch.

The needles and hack-saws of cactus
        bleed
A milk of earth when stricken off the
        stalk;
But this,—defenseless, thornless, sheds
        no blood,
Almost no shadow—but the air's thin
        talk.

Angelic Dynamo! Ventriloquist of the
        Blue!
While beachward creeps the shark-
        swept Spanish Main
By what conjunctions do the winds
        appoint
Its apotheosis, at last—the hurricane!
                                        1933

TWO LETTERS
ON "THE BRIDGE" †

Patterson,
New York
March 18, 1926

Dear Mr. Kahn:

You were so kind as to express a

desire to know from time to time how
"The Bridge" was progressing, so I'm
flashing in a signal from the foremast,
as it were. Right now I'm supposed to
be Don Cristobal Cólon returning
from "Cathay," first voyage. For mid-
ocean is where the poem begins.

It concludes at midnight—at the
center of Brooklyn Bridge. Strangely
enough, that final section of the poem
has been the first to be completed,—
yet there's a logic to it, after all; it is
the mystic consummation towards
which all the other sections of the
poem converge. Their contents are
implicit in its summary.

Naturally I am encountering many
unexpected formal difficulties in satisfying my conception, especially as
one's original idea has a way of en-
larging steadily under the spur of
daily concentration on minute details
of execution. I don't wish to express
my confidence too blatantly—but I am
certain that, granted that I'm able to
find the suitable form for all details
as I presently conceive them, "The
Bridge" will be a dynamic and eloquent document.

As I said, I have thus far completed
only the final section,—about one hundred lines. I am not going straight
through from the beginning. There
has been much incidental reading to
do, and more study is necessary as I
go on. As I cannot think of my work
in terms of time I cannot gauge when
it will be completed, probably by next
December, however.

There are so many interlocking elements and symbols at work throughout "The Bridge" that it is next to
impossible to describe it without re-
sorting to the actual metaphors of
the poem. Roughly, however, it is
based on the conquest of space and
knowledge. The theme of "Cathay"
(its riches, etc.) ultimately is transmuted into a symbol of consciousness,

* From *The Collected Poems of Hart
Crane* by Hart Crane, published by
Liveright Publishing Corporation, N. Y.
Copyright 1933.
† Reprinted from *The Letters and
Journals of Hart Crane,* by Brom Weber,
by permission of The Bodley Press. Copy-
right 1949 by Brom Weber.

knowledge, spiritual unity. A rather religious motivation, albeit not Presbyterian. The following notation is a very rough abbreviation of the subject matter of the several sections:

    I. Columbus—Conquest of space, chaos

    II. Pocahontas—The natural body of American-fertility, etc.

    III. Whitman—The spiritual body of America
        (A dialogue between Whitman and a dying soldier in a Washington hospital; the infraction of physical death, disunity, on the concept of immortality)

    IV. John Brown
        (Negro porter on Calgary Express making up berths and singing to himself (a jazz form for this) of his sweetheart and the death of John Brown, alternately)

    V. *Subway*—The encroachment of machinery on humanity; a kind of purgatory in relation to the open sky of last section

    VI. The bridge—A sweeping dithyramb in which the Bridge becomes the symbol of consciousness spanning time and space

The first and last sections are composed of blank verse with occasional rhyme for accentuation. The verbal dynamics used and the spacious periodicity of the rhythm result in an unusually symphonic form. What forms I shall use for the other sections will have to be determined when I come to grips with their respective themes.

I would gladly send you the completed section for present reading, but unless you especially wish to see it now I should prefer your judgment on

it later when a more synthetic reading will be possible.

I hope that this extended amount of particulars,—evidence, perhaps of an excessive enthusiasm on my part, has not been tedious reading. Your interest and confidence have proved to be so great a spur to me that I must mention my gratitude again.

        Very faithfully yours,
            Hart Crane

Otto H. Kahn, Esq.,
52 William Street,
New York.

        Patterson, New York
        September 12th, 1927
Dear Mr. Kahn:

I am taking for granted your continued interest in the progress of "The Bridge," in which I am still absorbed, and which has reached a stage where its general outline is clearly evident. The Dedication (recently published in *The Dial*) and Part I (now in *The American Caravan*) you have already seen, but as you may not have them presently at hand I am including them in a ms. of the whole, to date, which I am sending you under separate cover.

At the risk of complicating your appreciation of Part II (Powhatan's Daughter), I nevertheless feel impelled to mention a few of my deliberate intentions in this part of the poem, and to give some description of my general method of construction. Powhatan's daughter, or Pocahontas, is the mythological nature-symbol chosen to represent the physical body of the continent, or the soil. She here takes on much the same role as the traditional Herthe of ancient teutonic mythology. The five sub-sections of Part II are mainly concerned with a gradual exploration of this 'body' whose first possessor was the Indian. It seemed altogether ineffective, from the poetic standpoint, to approach this material from the purely chronological historic angle—beginning with, say the landing of *The Mayflower*, continuing with a résumé of the Revolution through the conquest of the West, etc. One can get that viewpoint in any history primer. What I am after is an assimilation of this experience, a more organic panorama, showing the continuous and living evidence of the past in the inmost vital substance of the present.

Consequently I jump from the monologue of Columbus in Ave Maria—right across the four intervening centuries—into the harbor of 20th-century Manhattan, and from that point in time and place I begin to work backward through the pioneer period, always in terms of the present —finally to the very core of the nature-world of the Indian. What I am really handling, you see, is the Myth of America. Thousands of strands have had to be searched out, sorted and interwoven. In a sense I have had to do a great deal of pioneering myself. It has taken a great deal of energy— which has not been so difficult to summon as the necessary patience to wait, simply wait much of the time—until my instincts assured me that I had assembled my materials in proper order for a final welding into their natural form. For each section of the entire poem has presented its own unique problem of form, not alone in relation to the materials embodied within its separate confines, but also in relation to the other parts, *in series*, of the major design of the entire poem. Each is a separate canvas, as it were, yet none yields its entire significance when seen apart from the others. One might take the Sistine Chapel as an analogy. It might be better to read the following notes *after* rather than before your reading of the ms. They are not necessary for an understanding of the poem, but I think they may prove interesting to you as a commentary on my architectural method.

1. The Harbor Dawn:

Here the movement of the verse is in considerable contrast to that of the Ave Maria, with its sea-swell crescendo and the climacteric vision of Columbus. This *legato,* in which images blur as objects only half apprehended on the border of sleep and consciousness, makes an admirable transition between the intervening centuries.

The love-motif (in italics) carries along the symbolism of the life and ages of man (here the sowing of the seed) which is further developed in each of the subsequent sections of Powhatan's Daughter, though it is never particularly stressed. In 2 (Van Winkle) it is Childhood; in 3 it is Youth; in 4, Manhood; in 5 it is Age. This motif is interwoven and tends to be implicit in the imagery rather than anywhere stressed.

2. Van Winkle:

The protagonist has left the room with its harbor sounds, and is walking to the subway. The rhythm is quickened; it is a transition between sleep and the imminent tasks of the day. Space is filled with the music of a hand organ and fresh sunlight, and one has the impression of the whole continent—from Atlantic to Pacific— freshly arisen childhood, also the 'childhood' of the continental conquest, viz., the conquistadores, Priscilla, Capt. John Smith, etc. Their parallelisms unite in the figure of Rip Van Winkle who finally becomes identified with the protagonist, as you will notice, and who really boards the subway with the reader. He becomes the 'guardian angel' of the journey into the past.

3. The River:

The subway is simply a figurative, psychological 'vehicle' for the transporting of the reader to the Middle West. He lands on the railroad tracks in the company of several tramps in the twilight. The extravagance of the first twenty-three lines of this section is an intentional burlesque on the cultural confusion of the present—a great conglomeration of noises analogous to the strident impression of a fast express rushing by. The rhythm is jazz.

Thenceforward the rhythm settles down to a steady pedestrian gait, like that of wanderers plodding along. My tramps are psychological vehicles, also. Their wanderings as you will notice, carry the reader into interior after interior, finally to the great River. They are left-overs of the pioneers in at least this respect—that their wanderings carry the reader through an experience parallel to that of Boone and others. I think I have caught some of the essential spirit of the Great Valley here, and in the process have approached the primal world of the Indian, which emerges with a full orchestra in the succeeding dance.

5. The Dance:

Here one is on the pure mythical and smoky soil at last! Not only do I describe the conflict between the two races in this dance—I also become identified with the Indian and his world before it is over, which is the only method possible of ever really possessing the Indian and his world as a cultural factor. I really think I succeed in getting under the skin of this glorious and dying animal, and in terms of expression, in symbols, which he, himself, would comprehend. Pocahontas (the continent) is the common basis of our meeting; she survives the extinction of the Indian, who finally, after being assumed into the elements of nature (as he understood them) persists only as a kind of an "eye" in the sky, or as a star that hangs between day and night—"the twilight's dim perpetual throne."

6. Indiana:

I regret that this section is not completed yet. It will be the monologue of an Indiana farmer; time, about 1860. He has failed in the gold-rush and is returning to till the soil. His monologue is a farewell to his son, who is leaving for a life on the sea. It is a lyric summary of the period of conquest, and his wife, the mother who died on the way back from the gold-rush, is alluded to in a way which implies her succession to the nature-symbolism of Pocahontas. I have this section well nigh done, but there is no use including it in the present ms. without the final words.

The next section, Cutty Sark, is a phantasy on the period of whalers and clipper ships. It also starts in the present and 'progresses backward.' The form of the poem may seem erratic, but it is meant to present the hallucinations incident to rum-drinking in a South Street dive, as well as the lurch of a boat in heavy seas, etc. So I allow myself something of the freedom which E. E. Cummings often uses.

Cutty Sark is built on the plan of a fugue. Two 'voices'—that of the world of Time, and that of the world of Eternity—are interwoven in the action. The Atlantis theme (that of Eternity) is the transmuted voice of the nickel-slot pianola, and this voice alternates with that of the derelict sailor and the description of the action. The airy regatta of the phantom clipper ships seen from Brooklyn Bridge on the way home is quite effective, I think. It was a pleasure to use historical names for these lovely ghosts. Music still haunts their names long after the wind has left their sails.

Cape Hatteras, which follows, is unfinished. It will be a kind of ode to Whitman. I am working as much as possible on it now. It presents very formidable problems, as, indeed, all the sections have. I am really writing an epic of the modern consciousness, and indescribably complicated factors have to be resolved and blended. . . . I don't wish to tire you with an extended analysis of my work, and so shall leave the other completed sections to explain themselves. In the ms., where the remaining incompleted sections occur, I am including a rough synopsis of their respective themes, however. The range of "The Bridge" has been called colossal by more than one critic who has seen the ms., and though I have found the subject to be vaster than I had at first realized, I am still highly confident of its final articulation into a continuous and eloquent span. Already there are evident signs of recognition; the following magazines have taken various sections;

Dedication: To Brooklyn Bridge
THE DIAL

Ave Maria
THE AMERICAN CARAVAN

The Harbor Dawn
TRANSITION (PARIS)

Van Winkle
TRANSITION (PARIS)

The River
THE VIRGINIA QUARTERLY

The Dance   THE DIAL

Cutty Sark   POETRY (CHICAGO)

Three Songs
THE CALENDAR (LONDON)

The Tunnel
THE CRITERION (LONDON)

(I have been especially gratified by the reception accorded me by 'The Criterion,' whose director, Mr. T. S. Eliot, is representative of the most exacting literary standards of our times.)

The Aeneid was not written in two years—nor in four, and in more than one sense I feel justified in comparing the historical and · cultural scope of *The Bridge* to that great work. It is at least a symphony with an epic theme, and a work of considerable profundity and inspiration. Even with the torturing heat of my sojourn in Cuba I was able to work faster than before or since then, in America. The foreign-ness of my surroundings stimulated me to the realization of natively American materials and viewpoints in myself not hitherto suspected, and in one month I was able to do more work than I had done in the three previous years. If I could work in Mexico or Spain this winter I could have "The Bridge" finished by next spring.

Please pardon the inordinate length of this letter. I shall, of course, hope to hear from you regarding your impressions of the poem as it now stands. Along with the ms. I am enclosing three critical articles which may interest you to see.

Believe me, with all good wishes

Sincerely yours,

Hart Crane

Otto Kahn, Esq.,
42 William Street,
New York City.   1934

ARCHIBALD MACLEISH
(1892–   )

ARS POETICA *

A poem should be palpable and mute
As a globed fruit

* The selections from Archibald Mac-Leish, *Poems, 1924–1933*, are used by permission of the publishers, Houghton Mifflin Company. Copyright 1925, 1926, 1928, 1932, 1933.

Dumb
As old medallions to the thumb

Silent as the sleeve-worn stone
Of casement ledges where the moss
    has grown—

A poem should be wordless
As the flight of birds

. . . . . .

A poem should be motionless in time
As the moon climbs

Leaving, as the moon releases
Twig by twig the night-entangled
    trees,

Leaving, as the moon behind the
    winter leaves,
Memory by memory the mind—

A poem should be motionless in time
As the moon climbs

. . . . . .

A poem should be equal to:
Not true

For all the history of grief
An empty doorway and a maple
    leaf

For love
The leaning grasses and two lights
    above the sea—

A poem should not mean
But be

            1924

FROM   *THE HAMLET
        OF A. MACLEISH* *

[A WHITE NIGHT]

Night after night I lie like this listen-
    ing.
Night after night I can not sleep. I
    wake

   * The selections from Archibald Mac-
Leish, *Poems, 1924–1933,* are used by
permission of the publishers, Houghton
Mifflin Company. Copyright 1925, 1926,
1928, 1932, 1933.

Knowing something, thinking some-
    thing has happened.
I have this feeling a great deal. I have
Sadness often. At night I have this
    feeling.
Waking I feel this pain as though I
    knew
Something not to be thought of, some-
    thing unbearable.
I feel this pain at night as though
    some
Terrible thing had happened. At night
    the sky
Opens, the near things vanish, the
    bright walls
Fall, and the stars were always there,
    and the dark
There and the cold and the stillness.
    I wake and stand
A long time by the window. I always
    think
The trees know the way they are
    silent. I always
Think some one has spoken, some one
    has told me.
Reading the books I always think so,
    reading
Words overheard in the books, reading
    the words
Like words in a strange language. I
    always hear
Music like that. I almost remember
    with music. . . .
This is not what you think. It is not
    that. I swim
Every day at the beach under the fig
    tree.
I swim very well and far out. The
    smell
Of pine comes over the water. The
    wind blurs
Seaward. And afternoons I walk to the
    phare.
Much of the time I do not think any-
    thing;
Much of the time I do not even
    notice.
And then, speaking, closing a door, I
    see

Strangely as though I almost saw now,
    some
Shape of things I have always seen,
    the sun
White on a house and the windows
    open and swallows
In and out of the wallpaper, the
    moon's face
Faint by day in a mirror; I see some
Changed thing that is telling, some-
    thing that almost
Tells—and this pain then, then this
    pain.
            And no
Words, only these shapes of things
    that seem
Ways of knowing what it is I am
    knowing.
I write these things in books, on pieces
    of paper.
I have written "The wind rises . . ."
    I have written "Bells
Plunged in the wind. . . ." I have
    written "Like
Doors . . ." "Like evening . . ."
It is always the same: I cannot read
    what the words say.
It is always the same: there are signs
    and I cannot read them.
There are empty streets and the blinds
    drawn and the sky
Sliding in windows. There are lights
    before
Dawn in the yellow transoms over the
    doors.
There are steps that pass and pass all
    night that are always
One, always the same step passing. . . .
I have travelled a great deal. I have
    seen at Homs
The cranes over the river and Isfahan
The fallen tiles in the empty garden,
    and Shiraz
Far off, the cypresses under the
    hill.
It is always the same. I have seen on
    the Kazvin road
On the moon gray desert the leafless
    wind,

The wind raging in moon-dusk. I
    have seen a light come
Seaward with slow oars from the
    mouth of Euphrates.
I have heard the nightingales in the
    thickets of Gilan,
And at dawn, at Teheran, I have
    heard from the ancient
Westward graying face of the wan-
    dering planet
The voices calling the small new name
    of god,
The voices answered with cock-crow,
    answered at dusk
With the cry of jackals far away in
    the gardens.
I have heard the name of the moon
    beyond those mountains.
It is always the same. It is always as
    though some
Smell of leaves had made me not quite
    remember;
As though I had turned to look and
    there were no one.
It has always been secret like that
    with me.
Always something has not been said.
    Always
The stones were there, the trees were
    there, the motionless
Hills have appeared in the dusk to me,
    the moon
Has stood a long time white and still
    in the window.
Always the earth has been turned
    away from me hiding
The veiled eyes and the wind in the
    leaves has not spoken . . .

As now the night is still. As the night
    now
Stands at the farthest off of touch and
    like
A raised hand held upon the empty
    air
Means and is silent
        Look! It waves me still . . .
    I say Go on! Go on!
        As the whole night now

Made visible behind this darkness
seems
to beckon to me. . . .

                                    1928

MEMORY GREEN *

Yes and when the warm unseasonable
weather
Comes at the year's end of the next
late year
And the south-west wind that smells
of rain and summer
Strips the huge branches of their dying leaves

And you at dusk along the Friede-
richstrasse
Or you in Paris on the windy
quay
Shuffle the shallow fallen leaves before you
Thinking the thoughts that like the
gray clouds change

You will not understand why sud-
denly sweetness
Fills in your heart nor the tears come
to your eyes
You will stand in the June-warm wind
and the leaves falling
When was it so before you will say
With whom

You will not remember this at all you
will stand there
Feeling the wind on your throat the
wind in your sleeves
You will smell the dead leaves in the
grass of a garden
You will close your eyes With whom
you will say Ah where

                                    1929

* The selections from Archibald Mac-
Leish, *Poems, 1924–1933*, are used by
permission of the publishers, Houghton
Mifflin Company. Copyright 1925, 1926,
1928, 1932, 1933.

YOU, ANDREW MARVELL *

And here face down beneath the sun
And here upon earth's noonward
height
To feel the always coming on
The always rising of the night

To feel creep up the curving east
The earthy chill of dusk and slow
Upon those under lands the vast
And ever climbing shadow grow

And strange at Ecbatan the trees
Take leaf by leaf the evening strange
The flooding dark about their knees
The mountains over Persia change

And now at Kermanshah the gate
Dark empty and the withered grass
And through the twilight now the
late
Few travelers in the westward pass

And Baghdad darken and the bridge
Across the silent river gone
And through Arabia the edge
Of evening widen and steal on

And deepen on Palmyra's street
The wheel rut in the ruined stone
And Lebanon fade out and Crete
High through the clouds and over-
blown

And over Sicily the air
Still flashing with the landward
gulls
And loom and slowly disappear
The sails above the shadowy hulls

And Spain go under and the shore
Of Africa the gilded sand
And evening vanish and no more
The low pale light across that land

Nor now the long light on the sea

And here face downward in the
sun
To feel how swift how secretly
The shadow of the night comes
on . . .

                                    1930

"NOT MARBLE NOR THE GILDED MONUMENTS *

The praisers of women in their proud
    and beautiful poems
Naming the grave mouth and the hair
    and the eyes
Boasted those they loved should be
    forever remembered
These were lies
The words sound but the face in the
    Istrian sun is forgotten
The poet speaks but to her dead ears
    no more
The sleek throat is gone—and the
    breast that was troubled to listen
Shadow from door

Therefore I will not praise your knees
    nor your fine walking
Telling you men shall remember your
    name as long
As lips move or breath is spent or the
    iron of English
Rings from a tongue
I shall say you were young and your
    arms straight and your mouth
    scarlet
I shall say you will die and none will
    remember you
Your arms change and none remember
    the swish of your garments
Nor the click of your shoe

Not with my hand's strength not with
    difficult labor
Springing the obstinate words to the
    bones of your breast
And the stubborn line to your young
    stride and the breath to your
    breathing
And the beat to your haste
Shall I prevail on the hearts of un-
    born men to remember

* The selections from Archibald Mac-
Leish, *Poems, 1924–1933,* are used by
permission of the publishers, Houghton
Mifflin Company. Copyright 1925, 1926,
1928, 1932, 1933.

(What is a dead girl but a shadowy
    ghost
Or a dead man's voice but a distant
    and vain affirmation
Like dream words most)

Therefore I will not speak of the un-
    dying glory of women
I will say you were young and straight
    and your skin fair
And you stood in the door and the
    sun was a shadow of leaves on
    your shoulders
And a leaf on your hair

I will not speak of the famous beauty
    of dead women
I will say the shape of a leaf lay once
    on your hair
Till the world ends and the eyes are
    out and the mouths broken
Look! It is there!

1930

LINES FOR AN INTERMENT *

Now it is fifteen years you have lain
    in the meadow:
The boards at your face have gone
    through: the earth is
Packed down and the sound of the
    rain is fainter:
The roots of the first grass are dead:

It's a long time to lie in the earth with
    your honor:
The world Soldier the world has been
    moving on:

The girls wouldn't look at you twice
    in the cloth cap:
Six years old they were when it hap-
    pened:

It bores them even in books: 'Soissons
    besieged!'
As for the gents they have joined the
    American Legion:

Belts and a brass band and the ladies'
    auxiliaries:

The Californians march in the OD
silk:

We are all acting again like civilized
beings:

People mention it at tea . . .

The Facts of Life we have learned are
Economic:

You were deceived by the detonations
of bombs:

You thought of courage and death
when you thought of warfare:

Hadn't they taught you the fine words
were unfortunate?

Now that we understand we judge
without bias:

We feel of course for those who had
to die:

Women have written us novels of
great passion

Proving the useless death of the dead
was a tragedy:

Nevertheless it is foolish to chew gall:

The foremost writers on both sides
have apologized:

The Germans are back in the Midi
with cropped hair:

The English are drinking the better
beer in Bavaria:

You can rest now in the rain in the
Belgian meadow—

Now that it's all explained away and
forgotten:

Now that the earth is hard and the
wood rots:

Now you are dead . . .

1933

SPEECH TO THOSE
WHO SAY COMRADE *

The brotherhood is not by the blood
certainly:

* From *Public Speech*: Poems, Copyright 1936. By Archibald MacLeish and
reprinted by permission of Rinehart &
Company, Inc. Publishers.

But neither are men brothers by
speech—by saying so:

Men are brothers by life lived and are
hurt for it:

Hunger and hurt are the great beget-
ters of brotherhood:

Humiliation has gotten much
love:

Danger I say is the nobler father and
mother:

Those are as brothers whose bodies
have shared fear

Or shared harm or shared hurt or indignity.

Why are the old soldiers brothers and
nearest?

For this: with their minds they go
over the sea a little

And find themselves in their youth
again as they were in

Soissons and Meaux and at Ypres and
those cities:

A French loaf and the girls with their
eyelids painted

Bring back to aging and lonely
men

Their twentieth year and the metal
odor of danger:

It is this in life which of all things is
tenderest—

To remember together with the unknown men the days

Common also to them and perils
ended:

It is this which makes of many a generation—

A wave of men who having the same
years

Have in common the same dead and
the changes.

The solitary and unshared experience

Dies of itself like the violations of
love

Or lives on as the dead live eerily.

The unshared and single man must
    cover his
Loneliness as a girl her shame for the
    way of
Life is neither by one man nor by
    suffering.

Who are the born brothers in truth?
    The puddlers
Scorched by the same flame in the
    same foundries:
Those who have spit on the same
    boards with the blood in it:

Ridden the same rivers with green
    logs:
Fought the police in the parks of the
    same cities:
Grinned for the same blows: the same
    flogging:
Veterans out of the same ships—fac-
    tories—
Expeditions for fame: the founders
    of continents:
Those that hid in Geneva a time
    back:

Those that have hidden and hunted
    and all such—
Fought together: labored together:
    they carry the
Common look like a card and they
    pass touching.
Brotherhood! No word said can make
    you brothers!
Brotherhood only the brave earn and
    by danger or
Harm or by bearing hurt and by no
    other

Brotherhood here in the strange world
    is the rich and
Rarest giving of life and the most
    valued:
Not to be had for a word or a week's
    wishing.

                  1935

"DOVER BEACH"—
A NOTE TO THAT POEM *

         The wave withdrawing
Withers with seaward rustle of flimsy
    water
Sucking the sand down: dragging at
    empty shells:
The roil after it settling: too smooth:
    smothered. . . .

After forty a man's a fool to wait in
    the
Sea's face for the full force and the
    roaring of
Surf to come over him: droves of
    careening water.
After forty the tug's out and the salt
    and the
Sea follow it: less sound and
    violence:
Nevertheless the ebb has its own
    beauty—
Shells sand and all and the whisper-
    ing rustle.
There's earth in it and the bubbles of
    foam gone.

Moreover—and this too has its lovely
    uses—
It's the outward wave that spills the
    inward forward
Tripping the proud piled mute vir-
    ginal
Mountain of water in wallowing
    welter of light and
Sound enough—thunder for miles
    back: it's a fine and a
Wild smother to vanish in: pulling
    down—
Tripping with outward ebb the urgent
    inward.

Speaking alone for myself it's the
    steep hill and the
Topping lift of the young men I am
    toward now—

Waiting for that as the wave for the
next wave.
Let them go over us all I say with the
thunder of
What's to be next in the world. It's
we will be under it!

1936

POLE STAR FOR THIS YEAR *

Where the wheel of light is turned:
Where the axle of the night is
Turned: is motionless: where holds
And has held ancient sureness
always:

Where of faring men the eyes
At oar bench at the rising bow
Have seen—torn shrouds between—
the Wain
And that star's changelessness: not
changing:

There upon that intent star:
Trust of wandering men: of truth
The most reminding witness: we
Fix our eyes also: waylost: the wan-
derers:

We too turn now to that star:
We too in whose trustless hearts
All truth alters and the lights
Of earth are out now turn to that
star:

Liberty of man and mind
That once was mind's necessity
And made the West blaze up has
burned
To bloody embers and the lamp's
out:

* From *Public Speech: Poems*, Copyright 1936. By Archibald MacLeish and
reprinted by permission of Rinehart &
Company, Inc. Publishers.

Hope that was a noble flame
Has fanned to violence and feeds
On cities and the flesh of men
And chokes where unclean smoke
defiles it:

Even the small spark of pride
That taught the tyrant once is
dark
Where gunfire rules the starving
street
And justice cheats the dead of
honor:

Liberty and pride and hope
And every guide-mark of the
mind
That led our blindness once has
vanished.
This star will not. Love's star will
not.

Love that has beheld the face
A man has with a man's eyes in
it
Bloody from the slugger's blows
Or heard the cold child cry for
hunger—

Love that listens where the good:
The virtuous: the men of faith:
Proclaim the paradise on earth
And murder starve and burn to make
it—

Love that cannot either sleep
Or keep rich music in the ear
Or lose itself for the wild beat
The anger in the blood makes
raging—

Love that hardens into hate—
Love like hatred and as bright—
Love is that one waking light
That leads now when all others
darken.

1936

THE FALL OF THE CITY *

A VERSE PLAY FOR RADIO

CAST OF CHARACTERS

VOICE OF STUDIO DIRECTOR	House Jameson
VOICE OF ANNOUNCER	Orson Welles
VOICE OF DEAD WOMAN	Adelaide Klein
VOICE OF 1ST MESSENGER	Carleton Young
VOICE OF ORATOR	Burgess Meredith
VOICE OF 2ND MESSENGER	Dwight Weist
VOICE OF PRIEST	Edgar Stehli
VOICE OF GENERAL	William Pringle
VOICES OF ANTIPHONAL CHORUS	Guy Repp, Brandon Peters, Karl Swenson, Dan Davies, Kenneth Delmar

CITIZENS, DANCERS, PRIESTS, SOLDIERS, ETC.

Production under the direction of Irving Reis, director of the Columbia Workshop.
Music composed and directed by Bernard Herman.
Crowd supervision by William N. Robson.
Editorial supervision by Brewster Morgan.
Stage management by Earl McGill.

FOREWORD

Any introduction is a confession of weakness. This one is no exception. It is written because I am anxious to persuade American poets to experiment with verse plays for radio and because I am quite certain the radio verse play I have written will not persuade them of itself.

The argument for radio as a stage for verse is neither long nor sensational. It consists largely in asserting what everyone knows. But such is the character of what everyone knows that no one knows it with enthusiasm. On the basis of the most obvious and elementary facts every poet with a dramatic leaning —and what poet ever lived who was really satisfied with writing the thin little books to lie on the front parlor tables? —should have been storming the studios for years. And yet actually the storming

* From *The Fall of the City: A Radio Play in Verse*: Copyright 1937 by Archibald MacLeish, and reprinted by permission of Rinehart & Company, Inc. Publishers.

has been thin and infrequent. The British Broadcasting Corporation has presented a few verse plays written expressly for the radio and one of them, Geoffrey Bridson's *March of the '45*, is said to have been both interesting and exciting. But the American slate is still approximately clean.

The first fact which everyone knows is that radio is a mechanism which carries to an audience sounds and nothing but sounds. A radio play consists of words and word equivalents and nothing else. There is no visible actor disguised to assume a part. There is no stage-set contrived to resemble a place. There is only the spoken word—an implement which poets have claimed to use with a special authority. There is only the word-excited imagination—a theatre in which poets have always claimed peculiar rights to play. Nothing exists save as the word creates it. The word dresses the stage. The word brings on the actors. The word supplies their look, their clothes, their gestures. The more packed and allusive the word, the more illuminating its rhythms, the more perfectly is the scene prepared, the more convincingly is the play enacted. On the stage, verse is often an obstacle because the artifice of the verse and the physical reality of the scene do not harmonize: it is for this reason that verse is easily accepted on the stage only where the scene is made remote in time and therefore artificial to begin with, or where the verse is blurred out and made to sound as much as possible like prose. But over the radio verse is not an obstacle. Over the radio verse has no visual presence to compete with. Only the ear is engaged and the ear is already half poet. It believes at once: creates and believes. It is the eye which is the realist. It is the eye which must fit everything together, must see everything before and behind. It is the eye and not the ear which refuses to believe in the lovely girlhood of the middle-aged soprano who sings Isolde, or the delicate, water-troubling slenderness of the three fat Rhine maidens ridiculously paddling at the ends of three steel ropes. With the eye closed or staring at nothing verse has every power over the ear. The ear accepts, accepts and believes, accepts and creates. The ear is the poet's perfect audience, his only true audience. And it is radio and only radio which can give him public access to this perfect friend.

The second fact which everyone knows and no one observes is the fact that the technique of radio, the ordinary, commercial technique, has developed tools which could not have been more perfectly adapted to the poet's uses had he devised them himself. Writers of prose plays for radio have practically unanimously ignored these tools. They have written for radio precisely as they would write for the stage and many, if not most, radio plays have been nothing but stage plays adapted to the microphone. The tools nevertheless exist and the chief of them is the Announcer. The Announcer is the most useful dramatic personage since the Greek Chorus. For years modern poets writing for the stage have felt the necessity of contriving some sort of chorus, some sort of commentator. There is no occasion here to go into the reasons: they are compelling enough. But this chorus, this commentator, has always presented an extremely awkward practical problem. How justify its existence dramatically? How get it on? How get it off again? In radio this difficulty is removed before it occurs. The commentator is an integral part of radio technique. His presence is as natural as it is familiar. And his presence, without more, restores to the poet that obliquity, that perspective, that three-dimensional depth without which great poetic drama cannot exist.

These two facts alone ought to be persuasive enough. But there are more. There are practical reasons. With the suspension of the experimental work of the Federal Theatre Units which presented such important plays as *Murder in the Cathedral* and Auden's *Dance of Death*, there no longer exists a theatre in New York in which a man interested in carrying modern poetry to the stage can be assured of a hearing. The Guild no longer has experimental interests. The Group is temporarily suspended. And the consequence is that any man who proposes to attack the problem must present himself to the commercial producers—who quite properly have their own ideas of what verse on Broadway ought to be. The producers are not to blame for a natural reluctance to back experimental verse plays. They are not in business to experiment. And the costs they are obliged to meet are exceedingly high. But the fact of their reluctance is an additional reason for turning to radio. For in radio the costs of production are relatively low and the material obstacles correspondingly reduced. Some of the most competent readers of verse to be heard in this country—Mr. Orson Welles and Mr. Burgess Meredith for example—are available from time to time in the broadcasting studios. Music, and the like, is readily arranged. And the extra costs of presenting a verse play are, in consequence, modest enough. Furthermore the studios, unlike the theatrical producers, are not apt to think of themselves as performing deeds of aesthetic charity whenever they produce serious works of art. Their own need of good material is too notorious.

Over and above all this there is the great question of audience. No man who has had the experience of presenting plays first before Broadway audiences and thereafter before such audiences as the radical theatres provide would ever of his own choice return to the Broadway audience. Radio will not of course provide the immediate sense of the live and vigorous audience which the radical theatres give. But radio will reach an infinitely greater number of people and should be capable, in time and with adequate materials, of shaping sections of that greater number into a living audience which the poet and his actors can feel. This consideration alone should deeply move the American poet whose present tragedy is his isolation from any audience vigorous enough to demand his strongest work.

Farmington, Connecticut,   A. MacL.
   December, 1936

VOICE OF THE STUDIO DIRECTOR [*orotund and professional*]

Ladies and gentlemen:

This broadcast comes to you from the city

Listeners over the curving air have heard

From furthest-off frontiers of foreign hours—

Mountain Time: Ocean Time: of the islands:

Of waters after the islands—some of them waking

Where noon here is the night there: some

Where noon is the first few stars they see or the last one.

For three days the world has watched this city—

Not for the common occasions of brutal crime

Or the usual violence of one sort or another

Or coronations of kings or popular festivals:

No: for stranger and disturbing reasons—

The resurrection from death and the tomb of a dead woman.

Each day for three days there has come
To the door of her tomb at noon a woman buried!

The terror that stands at the shoulder of our time
Touches the cheek with this: the flesh winces.

There have been other omens in other cities
But never of this sort and never so credible.

In a time like ours seemings and portents signify.
Ours is a generation when dogs howl and the
Skin crawls on the skull with its beast's foreboding.
All men now alive with us have feared.
We have smelled the wind in the street that changes weather.
We have seen the familiar room grow unfamiliar:

The order of numbers alter: the expectation
Cheats the expectant eye. The appearance defaults with us.

Here in this city the wall of the time cracks.

We take you now to the great square of this city.

[*The shuffle and hum of a vast, patient crowd gradually rises: swells: fills the background.*]

VOICE OF THE ANNOUNCER [*matter-of-fact*]
We are here on the central plaza.
We are well off to the eastward edge.
There is a kind of terrace over the crowd here.
It is precisely four minutes to twelve.
The crowd is enormous: there might be ten thousand:
There might be more: the whole square is faces.
Opposite over the roofs are the mountains.
It is quite clear: there are birds circling.
We think they are kites by the look: they are very high. . . .

The tomb is off to the right somewhere—
We can't see for the great crowd.
Close to us here are the cabinet ministers:
They stand on a raised platform with awnings.
The farmers' wives are squatting on the stones:
Their children have fallen asleep on their shoulders.
The heat is harsh: the light dazzles like metal.
It dazes the air as the clang of a gong does. . . .

News travels in this nation:
There are people here from away off—

Horse-raisers out of the country with brooks in it:
Herders of cattle from up where the snow stays—
The kind that cook for themselves mostly:
They look at the girls with their eyes hard
And a hard grin and their teeth showing. . . .

It is one minute to twelve now:
There is still no sign: they are still waiting:
No one doubts that she will come:
No one doubts that she will speak too:
Three times she has not spoken.

[*The murmur of the crowd changes —not louder but more intense: higher.*]

THE VOICE OF THE ANNOUNCER [*low but with increasing excitement*]
Now it is twelve: now they are rising:
Now the whole plaza is rising:
Fathers are lifting their small children:
The plumed fans on the platform are motionless. . . .

There is no sound but the shuffle of shoe leather. . . .

Now even the shoes are still. . . .

We can hear the hawks: it is quiet as that now. . . .

It is strange to see such throngs so silent. . . .

Nothing yet: nothing has happened. . . .

Wait! There's a stir here to the right of us:
They're turning their heads: the crowd turns:
The cabinet ministers lean from their balcony:
There's no sound: only the turning. . . .

[*A woman's voice comes over the silence of the crowd: it is a weak voice, penetrating: it speaks slowly and as though with difficulty.*]

THE VOICE OF THE DEAD WOMAN
First the waters rose with no wind.
. . .

THE VOICE OF THE ANNOUNCER [*whispering*]
Listen: that is she! She's speaking!

THE VOICE OF THE DEAD WOMAN
Then the stones of the temple kindled
Without flame or tinder of maize-leaves . . .

THE VOICE OF THE ANNOUNCER [*whispering*]
They see her beyond us: The crowd sees her. . . .

THE VOICE OF THE DEAD WOMAN
Then there were cries in the night haze:
Words in a once-heard tongue: the air
Rustling above us as at dawn with herons.

Now it is I who must bring fear:
I who am four days dead: the tears
Still unshed for me—all of them: I
For whom a child still calls at nightfall.

Death is young in me to fear!
My dress is kept still in the press in my bedchamber:
No one has broken the dish of the dead woman.

Nevertheless I must speak painfully:
I am to stand here in the sun and speak:

[*There is a pause. Then her voice comes again loud, mechanical, speaking as by rote.*]

The city of masterless men
Will take a master.
There will be shouting then:
Blood after!

[*The crowd stirs. Her voice goes on weak and slow as before.*]

Do not ask what it means: I do not know:
Only sorrow and no hope for it.

THE VOICE OF THE ANNOUNCER
She has gone. . . . No, they are still looking.

THE VOICE OF THE DEAD WOMAN
It is hard to return from the time past.
I have come
In the dream we must learn to dream where the crumbling of
Time like the ash from a burnt string has
Stopped for me. For you the thread still burns:
You take the feathery ash upon your fingers.
You bring yourselves from the time past as it pleases you.

It is hard to return to the old nearness . . .

Harder to go again. . . .

THE VOICE OF THE ANNOUNCER
She is gone.
We know because the crowd is closing.
All we can see is the crowd closing.
We hear the releasing of held breath—
The weight shifting: the lifting of shoe leather.
The stillness is broken as surface of water is broken—
The sound circling from in outward.

[*The murmur of the crowd rises.*]

Small wonder they feel fear.
Before the murders of the famous kings—
Before imperial cities burned and fell—
The dead were said to show themselves and speak.
When dead men came disaster came.
Presentiments

That let the living on their beds sleep
    on
Woke dead men out of death and
    gave them voices.
All ancient men in every nation knew
    this.

A VOICE OVER THE CROWD
Masterless men . . .

A VOICE OVER THE CROWD
When shall it be . . .

A VOICE OVER THE CROWD
Masterless men
Will take a master . . .

A VOICE OVER THE CROWD
What has she said to us . . .

A VOICE OVER THE CROWD
When shall it be . . .

A VOICE OVER THE CROWD
Masterless men
Will take a master.
Blood after . . .

A VOICE OVER THE CROWD
What has she said to us . . .

VOICES TOGETHER
Blood after!

[*The voices run together into the ex-
    cited roar of the crowd. The An-
    nouncer's voice is loud over it.*]

THE VOICE OF THE ANNOUNCER
They are milling around us like cattle
    that smell death.
The whole square is whirling and
    turning and shouting.
One of the ministers raises his arms
    on the platform.
No one is listening: now they are
    sounding drums:
Trying to quiet them likely: No! No!
Something is happening: there in the
    far corner:
A runner: a messenger: staggering:
    people are helping him:
People are calling: he comes through
    the crowd: they are quieter.

Only those on the far edge are still
    shouting:
Listen! He's here by the ministers
    now! He is speaking. . . .

THE VOICE OF THE MESSENGER
There has come the conqueror!
I am to tell you.
I have raced over sea land:
I have run over cane land:
I have climbed over cone land.
It was laid on my shoulders
By shall and by shan't
That standing by day
And staying by night
Were not for my lot
Till I came to the sight of you.
Now I have come.

Be warned of this conqueror!
This one is dangerous!
Word has out-oared him.
East over sea-cross has
All taken—
Every country.
No men are free there.
Ears overhear them.
Their words are their murderers.
Judged before judgment
Tried after trial
They die as do animals:—
Offer their throats
As the goat to her slaughterer.
Terror has taught them this!

Now he is here!

He was violent in his vessel:
He was steering in her stern:
He was watching in her waist:
He was peering in her prow:
And he dragged her up
Nine lengths
Till her keel lodged
On this nation.

Now he is here
Waylaying and night-lying.
If they hide before dark
He comes before sunup.
Where hunger is eaten

There he sits down:
Where fear sleeps
There he arises.

I tell you beware of him!
All doors are dangers.
The warders of wealth
Will admit him by stealth.
The lovers of men
Will invite him as friend.
The drinkers of blood
Will drum him in suddenly.
Hope will unlatch to him:
Hopelessness open.

I say and say truly
To all men in honesty
Such is this conqueror!
Shame is his people.
Lickers of spittle
Their lives are unspeakable:
Their dying indecent.

Be well warned!
He comes to you slightly
Slanting and sprinting
Hinting and shadowing:
Sly is his hiding:—
A hard lot:
A late rider:

Watch! I have said to you!

THE VOICE OF THE ANNOUNCER
They are leading him out: his legs
    give:
Now he is gone in the crowd: they
    are silent:
No one has spoken since his speaking:

They stand still circling the ministers.
No one has spoken or called out:—
There is no stir at all nor movement:
Even the farthest have stood
    patiently:
They wait trusting the old men:
They wait faithfully trusting the an-
    swer.
Now the huddle on the platform
    opens:
A minister turns to them raising his
    two arms.

THE VOICE OF THE ORATOR
Freemen of this nation!
The persuasion of your wills against
    your wisdom is not dreamed of.
We offer themes for your considera-
    tion.

What is the surest defender of liberty?
Is it not liberty?
A free people resists by freedom:
Not locks! Not blockhouses!

The future is a mirror where the past
Marches to meet itself. Go armed to-
    ward arms!
Peaceful toward peace! Free and with
    music toward freedom!
Face tomorrow with knives and tomor-
    row's a knife-blade.
Murder your foe and your foe will be
    murder!—
Even your friends suspected of false
    speaking:
Hands on the door at night and the
    floor boards squeaking.

Those who win by the spear are the
    spear toters.
And what do they win? Spears! What
    else is there?
If their hands let go they have noth-
    ing to hold by.
They are no more free than a paralytic
    propped against a tree is.

With the armored man the arm is
    upheld by the weapon:
The man is worn by the knife.
Once depend on iron for your free-
    dom and your
Freedom's iron!
Once overcome your resisters with
    force and your
Force will resist you!—
You will never be free of force.
Never of arms unarmed
Will the father return home:
The lover to her loved:
The mature man to his fruit orchard
Walking at peace in that beauty—
The years of his trees to assure him.

Force is a greater enemy than this
    conqueror—
A treacherous weapon.

Neverthless my friends there *is* a
    weapon!
Weakness conquers!

Against chainlessness who breaks?
Against wall-lessness who vaults?
Against forcelessness who forces?

Against the feather of the thistle
Is blunted sharpest metal.
No edge cuts seed-fluff.

This conquerer unresisted
Will conquer no longer: a posturer
Beating his blows upon burdocks—
Shifting his guard against shadows.
Snickers will sound among road-
    menders:
Titters be stifled by laundresses:
Coarse guffaws among chambermaids.
Reddened with rage he will roar.
He will · sweat in his uniform
    foolishly.
He will disappear: no one hear of
    him!

There *is* a weapon my friends.
Scorn conquers!

VOICE OF THE ANNOUNCER [*the Ora-
tor's voice unintelligible under it*]
I wish you could all see this as we
    do—
The whole plaza full of these people—
Their colorful garments—the harsh
    sunlight—
The water-sellers swinging enormous
    gourds—
The orator there on the stone plat-
    form—
The temple behind him: the high
    pyramid—
The hawks overhead in the sky teeter-
    ing
Slow to the windward: swift to the
    downwind—
The houses blind with the blank sun
    on them. . . .

THE VOICE OF THE ORATOR
There is a weapon.
Reason and truth are that weapon.

Let this conqueror come!
Show him no hindrance!
Suffer his flag and his drum!
Words . . . win!

THE VOICE OF THE ANNOUNCER
There's the shout now: he's done:
He's climbing down: a great speech:
They're all smiling and pressing
    around him:
The women are squatting in full sun-
    light:
They're opening packages: bread we'd
    say by the look—
Yes: bread wrapped between corn
    leaves:
They're squatting to eat: they're quite
    contented and happy:
Women are calling their men from
    the sunny stones:
There are flutes sounding away off:
We can't see for the shifting and
    moving—
Yes: there are flutes in the cool shad-
    ow:
Children are dancing in intricate
    figures.

[*A drum and flute are heard under
the voice.*]

Even a few old men are dancing.
You'd say they'd never feared to see
    them dancing.

A great speech! really great!
Men forget these truths in passion:
They oppose the oppressors with
    blind blows:
They make of their towns tombs: of
    their roofs burials:
They build memorial ruins to liberty:
But liberty is not built from ruins:
Only in peace is the work excellent.
    . . .

That's odd! The music has stopped.
There's something—

It's a man there on the far side: he's
    pointing:
He seems to be pointing back through
    the farthest street:
The people are twisting and rising:
    bread in their fists. . . .
We can't see what it is. . . . Wait!
    . . . it's a messenger.
It must be a messenger. Yes. It's a mes-
    sage—another.
Here he is at the turn of the street trot-
    ting:
His neck's back at the nape: he looks
    tired:
He winds through the crowd with his
    mouth open: laboring:
People are offering water: he pushes
    away from them:
Now he has come to the stone steps:
    to the ministers:
Stand by: we're edging in. . . .

[*There are sounds of people close by:
coughs: murmurs. The Announcer's
voice is lowered.*]

Listen: he's leaning on the stone: he's
    speaking.

THE VOICE OF THE MESSENGER

There has come . . . the Conqueror.
    . . .

I am to tell you. . . .
I have run over corn land:
I have climbed over cone land:
I have crossed over mountains.

It was laid on my shoulders
By shall and by shan't
That standing by day
And staying by night
Were not for my lot
Till I came to the sight of you.

Now I have come.

I bear word:
Beware of this conqueror!

The fame of his story
Like flame in the winter grass

Widens before him.
Beached on our shore
With the dawn over shoulder
The lawns were still cold
When he came to the sheep
    meadows:—
Sun could not keep with him
So was he forward.

Fame is his sword.

No man opposing him
Still grows his glory.
He needs neither foeman nor
Thickset of blows to
Gather his victories—
Nor a foe's match
To earn him his battles.

He brings his own enemy!

He baggages with him
His closet antagonist—
His private opposer.
He's setting him up
At every road corner—
A figure of horror
With blood for his color:
Fist for his hand:
Reek where he stands:
Hate for his heat:
Sneers for his mouth:
Clouts for his clothes:
Oaths if he speak:—
And he's knocking him down
In every town square
Till hair's on his blade
And blood's all about
Like dust in a drought
And the people are shouting
Flowers him flinging
Music him singing
And bringing him gold
And holding his heels.
And feeling his thighs
Till their eyes start
And their hearts swell
And they're telling his praises
Like lays of the heroes
And chiefs of antiquity.

Such are his victories!
So does he come:
So he approaches . . .

[*A whisper rustles through the crowd.*]

No man to conquer.
Yet as a conqueror
Marches he forward . . .

[*The whisper is louder.*]

Stands in your mountains . . .

[*A murmur of voices.*]

Soon to descend on you!

[*A swelling roar.*]

THE VOICE OF THE ANNOUNCER
That touched them! That frightened
    them!
Some of them point to the east hills:
Some of them mock at the ministers:
    "Freedom!"
"Freedom for what. To die in a rat
    trap?"
They're frantic with anger and plain
    fear.
They're sold out they say. You can
    hear them.
"Down with the government! Down
    with the orators!
"Down with liberal learned minds!
"Down with the mouths and the loose
    tongues in them!
"Down with the lazy lot! They've sold
    us!
"We're sold out! Talking has done for
    us!" . . .
They're boiling around us like mullet
    that smell shark.
We can't move for the mob: they're
    crazy with terror . . .

A LOUD VOICE [*distant*]
God-lovers!
Think of your gods!

Earth-masters!
Taste your disasters!

Men!
Remember!

THE VOICE OF THE ANNOUNCER
There's a voice over the crowd some-
    where.
They hear it: they're quieting down.
    . . . It's the priests!
We see them now: it's the priests on
    the pyramid!
There might be ten of them: black
    with their hair tangled.
The smoke of their fire is flat in the
    quick wind:
They stand in the thick of the smoke
    by the stone of the victims:
Their knives catch in the steep sun:
    they are shouting:
Listen!—

VOICES OF PRIESTS
Turn to your gods rememberers!

A SINGLE VOICE
Let the world be saved by surrender-
    ing the world:
Not otherwise shall it be saved.

VOICES OF PRIESTS
Turn to your gods rememberers!

SINGLE VOICE
Let evil be overcome by the coming
    over of evil:
Your hearts shall be elsewhere.

VOICES OF THE PRIESTS
Turn to your gods rememberers!

VOICES OF THE PRIESTS [*antiphonally*]
Turn to your gods!
The conqueror cannot take you!

Turn to your gods!
The narrow dark will keep you!

Turn to your gods!
In god's house is no breaking!

Turn to your gods!
In god's silences sleep is!

Lay up your will with the gods!
Stones cannot still you!

Lay up your mind with the gods!
Blade cannot blind you!

Lay up your heart with the gods!
Danger departs from you!

THE VOICE OF THE ANNOUNCER

It's a wonderful thing to see this crowd
responding.
Even the simplest citizens feel the
emotion.
There's hardly a sound now in the
square. It's wonderful:
Really impressive: the priests there
on the pyramid:
The smoke blowing: the bright sun:
the faces—

A SINGLE VOICE

In the day of confusion of reason
when all is delusion:
In the day of the tyrants of tongues
when the truth is for hire:
In the day of deceit when ends meet:
Turn to your gods!

In the day of division of nations when
hope is derision:
In the day of the supping of hate
when the soul is corrupted:
In the day of despair when the heart's
bare:
Turn to your gods!

[*A slow drum beat.*]

THE VOICE OF THE ANNOUNCER

A kind of dance is beginning: a serpent of people:
A current of people coiling and curling
through people:
A circling of people through people
like water through water . . .

CHANTING VOICES [*to the drums*]

Out of the stir of the sun
Out of the shout of the thunder
Out of the hush of the star . . .
Withdraw the heart.

THE VOICE OF THE ANNOUNCER [*the
chant and drums under*]

A very young girl is leading them:
They have torn the shawl from her
bare breast:

They are giving her flowers: her
mouth laughs:
Her eyes are not laughing. . . .

CHANTING VOICES

Leave now the lovely air
To the sword and the sword-wearer—
Leave to the marksman the mark—
Withdraw the heart.

THE VOICE OF THE ANNOUNCER [*the
chant and drums louder*]

She's coming . . . the drums pound
. . . the crowd
Shrieks . . . she's reaching the temple
. . . she's climbing it. . . .
Others are following: five: ten . . .
Hundreds are following . . . crowding the stairway. . . .
She's almost there . . . her flowers
have fallen. . . .
She looks back . . . the priests are
surrounding her. . . .

[*The drums suddenly stop: there is an
instant's silence: then an angry
shout from the crowd.*]

THE VOICE OF THE ANNOUNCER

Wait! Wait! Something has happened!
One of the ministers: one of the
oldest:
The general: the one in the feathered
coat:—
He's driving them down with the
staff of a banner:
He's climbed after them driving them
down:
There's shouting and yelling enough
but they're going:
He's telling them off too: you can hear
him—

A DEEP VOICE [*chatter of the crowd
under it*]

Men! Old men! Listen!
Twist your necks on your nape bones!
The knife will wait in the fist for you.

There is a time for everything—
Time to be thinking of heaven:
Time of your own skins!

Cock your eyes to the windward!

Do you see smoke on those mountains?
The smoke is the smoke of towns.
And who makes it? The conqueror!
And where will he march now? Onward!
The heel of the future descends on you!

THE VOICE OF THE ANNOUNCER
He has them now: even the priests have seen it:
They're all looking away here to the east.
There's smoke too: filling the valleys: like thunderheads! . . .

THE VOICE OF THE GENERAL
You are foolish old men.

You ought to be flogged for your foolishness.
Your grandfathers died to be free
And you—you juggle with freedom!
Do you think you're free by a law
Like the falling of apples in autumn?

You thought you were safe in your liberties!
You thought you could always quibble!
You can't! You take my word for it.
Freedom's the rarest bird!
You risk your neck to snare it—
It's gone while your eyeballs stare!

Those who'd lodge with a tyrant
Thinking to feed at his fire
And leave him again when they're fed are
Plain fools or were bred to it—
Brood of the servile races
Born with the hang-dog face. . . .

THE VOICE OF THE ANNOUNCER
They're all pointing and pushing together:
The women are shouldering baskets: bread: children. . . .
They smell smoke in the air: they smell terror. . . .

THE VOICE OF THE GENERAL [*louder over the increasing sound*]
There's nothing in this world worse—
Empty belly or purse or the
Pitiful hunger of children—
Than doing the Strong Man's will!

The free will fight for their freedom.
They're free men first. They feed
Meager or fat but as free men.
Everything else comes after—
Food: roof: craft—
Even the sky and the light of it!

[*The voices of the crowd rise to a tumult of sounds—drums: shouts: cries.*]

THE VOICE OF THE ANNOUNCER
The sun is yellow with smoke . . . the town's burning. . . .
The war's at the broken bridge. . . .

THE VOICE OF THE GENERAL [*shouting*]
You! Are you free? Will you fight?

There are still inches for fighting!

There is still a niche in the streets!

You can stand on the stairs and meet him!

You can hold in the dark of a hall!

You can die!

—or your children will crawl for it!

THE VOICE OF THE ANNOUNCER [*over the tumult*]
They won't listen. They're shouting and screaming and circling.
The square is full of deserters with more coming.
Every street from the bridge is full of deserters.
They're rolling in with the smoke blowing behind them.
The plaza's choked with the smoke and the struggling of stragglers.
They're climbing the platform: driving the ministers: shouting—
One speaks and another:

THE VOICES OF CITIZENS
The city is doomed!
  There's no holding it!

Let the conqueror have it! It's his!

The age is his! It's his century!

Our institutions are obsolete.
He marches a mile while we sit in a
  meeting.

Opinions and talk!
Deliberative walks beneath the ivy
  and the creepers!

The age demands a made-up mind.
The conqueror's mind is decided on
  everything.

His doubt comes after the deed or
  never.

He knows what he wants for his
  want's what he knows.
He's gone before they say he's going.
He's come before you've barred your
  house.

He's one man: we are but thousands!
Who can defend us from one man?

Bury your arms! Break your standards!
Give him the town while the town
  stands!

THE VOICE OF THE ANNOUNCER
They're throwing their arms away:
  their bows are in bonfires.
The plaza is littered with torn plumes:
  spear handles. . . .

THE VOICES OF CITIZENS
Masterless men! . . .

Masterless men
Must take a master! . . .

Order must master us! . . .
Freedom's for fools:
Force is the certainty!

Freedom has eaten our strength and
  corrupted our virtues!

Men must be ruled!

Fools must be mastered!

Rigor and fast
Will restore us our dignity!

Chains will be liberty!

THE VOICE OF THE ANNOUNCER
The last defenders are coming: they
  whirl from the streets like
Wild leaves on a wind: the square
  scatters them.
Now they are fewer—ten together or
  five:
They come with their heads turned:
  their eyes back.

Now there are none. The street's
  empty—in shadow.
The crowd is retreating—watching the
  empty street:
The shouts die.

  The voices are silent.

    They're watching. . . .

They stand in the slant of the sunlight silent and watching.
The silence after the drums echoes the
  drum beat.

Now there's a sound. They see him.
  They must see him!
They're shading their eyes from the
  sun: there's a rustle of whispering:
We can't see for the glare of it. . . .
  Yes! . . . Yes! . . .
He's there in the end of the street in
  the shadow. We see him!
He looks huge—a head taller than
  anyone:
Broad as a brass door: a hard hero:
Heavy of heel on the brick: clanking
  with metal:
The helm closed on his head: the eye-
  holes hollow.

He's coming! . . .
  He's clear of the shadow! . . .
    The sun takes him.

They cover their faces with fingers.
They cower before him.

They fall: they sprawl on the stone.
  He's alone where he's walking.
He marches with rattle of metal. He
  tramples his shadow.
He mounts by the pyramid—stamps on
  the stairway—turns—
His arm rises— His visor is opening.
. . .

[*There is an instant's breathless silence: then the Voice of the Announcer low—almost a whisper.*]

                    There's no one! . . .
There's no one at all! . . .
    No one! . . .
        The helmet is hollow!
The metal is empty! The armor is
empty! I tell you
There's no one at all there: there's
  only the metal:
The barrel of metal: the bundle of
  armor. It's empty!

The push of a stiff pole at the nipple
  would topple it.

They don't see! They lie on the pav-
  ing. They lie in the
Burnt spears: the ashes of arrows.
  They lie there. . . .
They don't see or they won't see.
  They are silent. . . .

The people invent their oppressors:
  they wish to believe in them.
They wish to be free of their freedom:
  released from their liberty:—
The long labor of liberty ended!
    They lie there!

[*There is a whisper of sound.* THE
ANNOUNCER'S *voice is louder.*]

Look! It's his arm! It is rising! His
  arm's rising!
They're watching his arm as it rises.
  They stir. They cry.
They cry out. They are shouting.
  They're shouting with happiness.
Listen! They're shouting like troops in
  a victory. Listen—
"The city of masterless men has found
  a master!"
You'd say it was they were the con-
  querors: they that had conquered.

A ROAR OF VOICES
The city of masterless men has found
  a master!
The city has fallen!
The city has fallen!

THE VOICE OF THE ANNOUNCER [*flat*]
    The city has fallen. . . .
                              1936, 1937

THE FREUDIANS

EUGENE O'NEILL
(1888–   )

BOUND EAST FOR CARDIFF *

A PLAY IN ONE ACT

YANK	DAVIS	PAUL	THE CAPTAIN
DRISCOLL	SCOTTY	SMITTY	THE SECOND MATE
COCKY	OLSON	IVAN	

SCENE. *The seamen's forecastle of the British tramp steamer* Glencairn *on a foggy night midway on the voyage between New York and Cardiff. An irregular-shaped compartment, the sides of which almost meet at the far end to form a triangle. Sleeping bunks about six feet long, ranged three deep with a space of three feet separating the upper from the lower, are built against the sides. On the right above the bunks three or four port-holes can be seen. In front of the bunks, rough wooden benches. Over the bunks on the left, a lamp in a bracket. In the left foreground, a doorway. On the floor near it, a pail with a tin dipper. Oilskins are hanging from a hook near the doorway.*

The far side of the forecastle is so narrow that it contains only one series of bunks.

In under the bunks a glimpse can be had of sea-chests, suit-cases, sea-boots, etc., jammed in indiscriminately.

At regular intervals of a minute or so the blast of the steamer's whistle can be heard above all the other sounds.

Five men are sitting on the benches talking. They are dressed in dirty patched suits of dungaree, flannel shirts, and all are in their stocking feet. Four of the men are pulling on pipes and the air is heavy with rancid tobacco smoke. Sitting on the top bunk in the left foreground, a Norwegian, PAUL, *is softly playing some folk-song on a battered accordion. He stops from time to time to listen to the conversation.*

In the lower bunk in the rear a dark-haired, hard-featured man is lying apparently asleep. One of his arms is stretched limply over the side of the bunk. His face is very pale, and drops of clammy perspiration glisten on his forehead.

It is nearing the end of the dog-

* Reprinted by permission of Horace Liveright, Inc., from *The Moon of the Caribbees* by Eugene O'Neill. Copyright 1919.

watch—about ten minutes to eight in the evening.

COCKY [*a weazened runt of a man. He is telling a story. The others are listening with amused, incredulous faces, interrupting him at the end of each sentence with loud derisive guffaws*]. Makin' love to me, she was! It's Gawd's truth! A bloomin' nigger! Greased all over with cocoanut oil, she was. Gawd blimey, I couldn't stand 'er. Bloody old cow, I says; and with that I fetched 'er a biff on the ear wot knocked 'er silly, an'— [*He is interrupted by a roar of laughter from the others.*]

DAVIS [*a middle-aged man with black hair and mustache*]. You're a liar, Cocky.

SCOTTY [*a dark young fellow*]. Ho-ho! Ye werr neverr in New Guinea in yourr life, I'm thinkin'.

OLSON [*a Swede with a drooping blond mustache—with ponderous sarcasm*]. Yust tink of it! You say she wass a cannibal, Cocky?

DRISCOLL [*a brawny Irishman with the battered features of a prize-fighter*]. How cud ye doubt ut, Ollie? A quane av the naygurs she musta been surely. Who else wud think herself aqual to fallin' in love wid a beauthiful, divil-may-care rake av a man the loike av Cocky? [*A burst of laughter from the crowd.*]

COCKY [*indignantly*]. Gawd strike me dead if it ain't true, every bleedin' word of it. 'Appened ten year ago come Christmas.

SCOTTY. 'Twas a Christmas dinner she had her eyes on.

DAVIS. He'd a been a tough old bird.

DRISCOLL. 'Tis lucky for both av ye ye escaped; for the quane av the cannibal isles wad a died av the bellyache the day afther Christmas, divil a doubt av ut. [*The laughter at this is long and loud.*]

COCKY [*sullenly*]. Blarsted fat-'eads! [*The sick man in the lower bunk in the rear groans and moves restlessly. There is a hushed silence. All the men turn and stare at him.*]

DRISCOLL. Ssshh! [*In a hushed whisper.*] We'd best not be talkin' so loud and him tryin' to have a bit av a sleep. [*He tiptoes softly to the side of the bunk.*] Yank! You'd be wantin' a drink av wather, maybe? [*YANK does not reply.* DRISCOLL *bends over and looks at him.*] It's asleep he is, sure enough. His breath is chokin' in his throat loike wather gurglin' in a poipe. [*He comes back quietly and sits down. All are silent, avoiding each other's eyes.*]

COCKY [*after a pause*]. Pore devil! It's over the side for 'im, Gawd 'elp 'im.

DRISCOLL. Stop your croakin'! He's not dead yet and, praise God, he'll have many a long day yet before him.

SCOTTY [*shaking his head doubtfully*]. He's bod, mon, he's verry bod.

DAVIS. Lucky he's alive. Many a man's light woulda gone out after a fall like that.

OLSON. You saw him fall?

DAVIS. Right next to him. He and me was goin' down in number two hold to do some chippin'. He puts his leg over careless-like and misses the ladder and plumps straight down to the bottom. I was scared to look over for a minute, and then I heard him groan and I scuttled down after him. He was hurt bad inside, for the blood was drippin' from the side of his mouth. He was groanin' hard, but he never let a word out of him.

COCKY. An' you blokes remember when we 'auled 'im in 'ere? Oh, 'ell, 'e says, oh, 'ell—like that, and nothink else.

OLSON. Did the captain know where he iss hurted?

COCKY. That silly ol' josser! Wot the 'ell would 'e know abaht anythink?

SCOTTY [*scornfully*]. He fiddles in his mouth wi' a bit of glass.

DRISCOLL [*angrily*]. The divil's own life ut is to be out on the lonely sea wid nothin' betune you and a grave in the ocean but a spindle-shanked, gray-whiskered auld fool the loike av him. 'Twas enough to make a saint shwear to see him wid his gold watch in his hand, tryin' to look as wise as an owl on a tree, and all the toime he not knowin' whether 'twas cholery or the barber's itch was the matther with Yank.

SCOTTY [*sardonically*]. He gave him a dose of salts, na doot?

DRISCOLL. Divil a thing he gave him at all, but looked in the book he had wid him, and shook his head, and walked out widout sayin' a word, the second mate afther him no wiser than himself, God's curse on the two av thim!

COCKY [*after a pause*]. Yank was a good shipmate, pore beggar. Lend me four bob in Noo York, 'e did.

DRISCOLL [*warmly*]. A good shipmate he was and is, none betther. Ye said no more than the truth, Cocky. Five years and more ut is since first I shipped wid him, and we've stuck together iver since through good luck and bad. Fights we've had, God help us, but 'twas only when we'd a bit av drink taken, and we always shook hands the nixt mornin'. Whativer was his was mine, and many's the toime I'd a been on the beach or worse, but for him. And now— [*His voice trembles as he fights to control his emotion.*] Divil take me if I'm not startin' to blubber loike an auld woman, and he not dead at all, but goin' to live many a long year yet, maybe.

DAVIS. The sleep'll do him good. He seems better now.

OLSON. If he wude eat something—

DRISCOLL. Wud ye have him be eatin' in his condishun? Sure it's hard enough on the rest av us wid nothin' the matther wid our insides to be stomachin' the skoff on this rusty lime-juicer.

SCOTTY [*indignantly*]. It's a starvation ship.

DAVIS. Plenty o' work and no food —and the owners ridin' around in carriages!

OLSON. Hash, hash! Stew, stew! Marmalade, py damn! [*He spits disgustedly.*]

COCKY. Bloody swill! Fit only for swine is wot I say.

DRISCOLL. And the dish-wather they disguise wid the name av tea! And the putty they call bread! My belly feels loike I'd swalleyed a dozen rivets at the thought av ut! And sea-biscuit that'd break the teeth av a lion if he had the misfortune to take a bite at one! [*Unconsciously they have all raised their voices, forgetting the sick man in their sailor's delight at finding something to grumble about.*]

PAUL [*swings his feet over the side of his bunk, stops playing his accordion, and says slowly*]. And rotten po-tay-toes! [*He starts in playing again. The sick man gives a groan of pain.*]

DRISCOLL [*holding up his hand*]. Shut your mouths, all av you. 'Tis a hell av a thing for us to be complainin' about our guts, and a sick man maybe dyin' listenin' to us. [*Gets up and shakes his fist at the Norwegian.*] God stiffen you, ye square-head scut! Put down that organ av yours or I'll break your ugly face for you. Is that banshee schreechin' fit music for a sick man?

[*The Norwegian puts his accordion in the bunk and lies back and closes his eyes.* DRISCOLL *goes over and stands beside* YANK. *The steamer's whistle sounds particularly loud in the silence.*]

DAVIS. Damn this fog! [*Reaches in under a bunk and yanks out a pair of sea-boots, which he pulls on.*] My lookout next, too. Must be nearly eight bells, boys.

[*With the exception of* OLSON, *all the men sitting up put on oilskins, sou'-westers, sea-boots, etc., in preparation for the watch on deck.* OLSON *crawls into a lower bunk on the right.*]

SCOTTY. My wheel.

OLSON [*disgustedly*]. Nothin' but yust dirty weather all dis voyage. I yust can't sleep when weestle blow. [*He turns his back to the light and is soon fast asleep and snoring.*]

SCOTTY. If this fog keeps up, I'm tellin' ye, we'll no be in Cardiff for a week or more.

DRISCOLL. 'Twas just such a night as this the auld Dover wint down. Just about this toime ut was, too, and we all sittin' round in the fo'castle, Yank beside me, whin all av a suddint we heard a great slitherin' crash, and the ship heeled over till we was all in a heap on wan side. What came afther I disremimber exactly, except 'twas a hard shift to get the boats over the side before the auld teakittle sank. Yank was in the same boat wid me, and sivin morthal days we drifted wid scarcely a drop of wather or a bite to chew on. 'Twas Yank here that held me down whin I wanted to jump into the ocean, roarin' mad wid the thirst. Picked up we were on the same day wid only Yank in his senses, and him steerin' the boat.

COCKY [*protestingly*]. Blimey but

you're a cheerful blighter, Driscoll! Talkin' abaht shipwrecks in this 'ere blushin' fog.

[YANK *groans and stirs uneasily, opening his eyes.* DRISCOLL *hurries to his side.*]

DRISCOLL. Are ye feelin' any better, Yank?

YANK [*in a weak voice*]. No.

DRISCOLL. Sure, you must be. You look as sthrong as an ox. [*Appealing to the others.*] Am I tellin' him a lie?

DAVIS. The sleep's done you good.

COCKY. You'll be 'avin your pint of beer in Cardiff this day week.

SCOTTY. And fish and chips, mon!

YANK [*peevishly*]. What're yuh all lyin' fur? D'yuh think I'm scared to— [*He hesitates as if frightened by the word he is about to say.*]

DRISCOLL. Don't be thinkin' such things!

[*The ship's bell is heard heavily tolling eight times. From the forecastle head above the voice of the lookout rises in a long wail: Aaall's welll. The men look uncertainly at* YANK *as if undecided whether to say good-by or not.*]

YANK [*in an agony of fear*]. Don't leave me, Drisc! I'm dyin', I tell yuh. I won't stay here alone with everyone snorin'. I'll go out on deck. [*He makes a feeble attempt to rise, but sinks back with a sharp groan. His breath comes in wheezy gasps.*] Don't leave me, Drisc! [*His face grows white and his head falls back with a jerk.*]

DRISCOLL. Don't be worryin', Yank. I'll not move a step out av here—and let that divil av a bosun curse his black head off. You speak a word to the bosun, Cocky. Tell him that Yank is bad took and I'll be stayin' wid him a while yet.

COCKY. Right-o.

[COCKY, DAVIS *and* SCOTTY *go out quietly.*]

COCKY [*from the alleyway*]. Gawd blimey, the fog's thick as soup.

DRISCOLL. Are ye satisfied now, Yank? [*Receiving no answer, he bends over the still form.*] He's fainted, God help him! [*He gets a tin dipper from the bucket and bathes* YANK'S *forehead with the water.* YANK *shudders and opens his eyes.*]

YANK [*slowly*]. I thought I was goin' then. Wha' did yuh wanta wake me up fur?

DRISCOLL [*with a forced gayety*]. It is wishful for heaven ye are?

YANK [*gloomily*]. Hell, I guess.

DRISCOLL [*crossing himself involuntarily*]. For the love av the saints don't be talkin' loike that! You'd give a man the creeps. It's chippin' rust on deck you'll be in a day or two wid the best uv us. [YANK *does not answer, but closes his eyes wearily.*]

[*The seaman who has been on lookout,* SMITTY, *a young Englishman, comes in and takes off his dripping oilskins. While he is doing this the man whose turn at the wheel has been relieved enters. He is a dark burly fellow with a round stupid face. The Englishman steps softly over to* DRISCOLL. *The other crawls into a lower bunk.*]

SMITTY [*whispering*]. How's Yank?

DRISCOLL. Betther. Ask him yourself. He's awake.

YANK. I'm all right, Smitty.

SMITTY. Glad to hear it, Yank. [*He crawls to an upper bunk and is soon asleep.*]

IVAN [*the stupid-faced seaman, who comes in after* SMITTY, *twists his head in the direction of the sick man*]. You feel gude, Jank?

YANK [*wearily*]. Yes, Ivan.

IVAN. Dot's gude. [*He rolls over on his side and falls asleep immediately.*]

YANK [*after a pause broken only by snores—with a bitter laugh*].

Good-by and good luck to the lot of you!

DRISCOLL. Is ut painin' you again?

YANK. It hurts like hell—here. [*He points to the lower part of his chest on the left side.*] I guess my old pump's busted. Ooohh! [*A spasm of pain contracts his pale features. He presses his hand to his side and writhes on the thin mattress of his bunk. The perspiration stands out in beads on his forehead.*]

DRISCOLL [*terrified*]. Yank! Yank! What is ut? [*Jumping to his feet.*] I'll run for the captain. [*He starts for the doorway.*]

YANK [*sitting up in his bunk, frantic with fear*]. Don't leave me, Drisc! For God's sake don't leave me alone! [*He leans over the side of his bunk and spits.* DRISCOLL *comes back to him.*] Blood! Ugh!

DRISCOLL. Blood again! I'd best be gettin' the captain.

YANK. No, no, don't leave me! If yuh do I'll git up and follow you. I ain't no coward, but I'm scared to stay here with all of them asleep and snorin'. [DRISCOLL, *not knowing what to do, sits down on the bench beside him. He grows calmer and sinks back on the mattress.*] The captain can't do me no good, yuh know it yourself. The pain ain't so bad now, but I thought it had me then. It was like a buzz-saw cuttin' into me.

DRISCOLL [*fiercely*]. God blarst ut! [*The* CAPTAIN *and the* SECOND MATE *of the steamer enter the forecastle. The* CAPTAIN *is an old man with gray mustache and whiskers. The* MATE *is clean-shaven and middle-aged. Both are dressed in simple blue uniforms.*]

THE CAPTAIN [*taking out his watch and feeling* YANK'S *pulse*]. And how is the sick man?

YANK [*feebly*]. All right, sir.

THE CAPTAIN. And the pain in the chest.

YANK. It still hurts, sir, worse than ever.

THE CAPTAIN [*taking a thermometer from his pocket and putting it into* YANK's *mouth*]. Here. Be sure and keep this in under your tongue, not over it.

THE MATE [*after a pause*]. Isn't this your watch on deck, Driscoll?

DRISCOLL. Yes, sorr, but Yank was fearin' to be alone, and—

THE CAPTAIN. That's all right, Driscoll.

DRISCOLL. Thank ye, sorr.

THE CAPTAIN [*stares at his watch for a moment or so; then takes the thermometer from* YANK's *mouth and goes to the lamp to read it. His expression grows very grave. He beckons the* MATE *and* DRISCOLL *to the corner near the doorway.* YANK *watches them furtively. The* CAPTAIN *speaks in a low voice to the* MATE]. Way up both of them. [*To* DRISCOLL.] He has been spitting blood again?

DRISCOLL. Not much for the hour just past, sorr, but before that—

THE CAPTAIN. A great deal?

DRISCOLL. Yes, sorr.

THE CAPTAIN. He hasn't eaten anything?

DRISCOLL. No, sorr.

THE CAPTAIN. Did he drink that medicine I sent him?

DRISCOLL. Yes, sorr, but it didn't stay down.

THE CAPTAIN [*shaking his head*]. I'm afraid—he's very weak. I can't do anything else for him. It's too serious for me. If this had only happened a week later we'd be in Cardiff in time to—

DRISCOLL. Plaze help him some way, sorr!

THE CAPTAIN [*impatiently*]. But, my good man, I'm not a doctor. [*More kindly as he sees* DRISCOLL's *grief.*]

You and he have been shipmates a long time?

DRISCOLL. Five years and more, sorr.

THE CAPTAIN. I see. Well, don't let him move. Keep him quiet and we'll hope for the best. I'll read the matter up and send him some medicine, something to ease the pain, anyway. [*Goes over to* YANK.] Keep up your courage! You'll be better tomorrow. [*He breaks down lamely before* YANK's *steady gaze.*] We'll pull you through all right—and—hm—well—coming, Robinson? Dammit!

[*He goes out hurriedly, followed by the* MATE.]

DRISCOLL [*trying to conceal his anxiety*]. Didn't I tell you you wasn't half as sick as you thought you was? The Captain'll have you out on deck cursin' and swearin' loike a trooper before the week is out.

YANK. Don't lie, Drisc. I heard what he said, and if I didn't I c'd tell by the way I feel. I know what's goin' to happen. I'm goin' to— [*He hesitates for a second—then resolutely.*] I'm goin' to die, that's what, and the sooner the better!

DRISCOLL [*wildly*]. No, and be damned to you, you're not. I'll not let you.

YANK. It ain't no use, Drisc. I ain't got a chance, but I ain't scared. Gimme a drink of water, will yuh, Drisc? My throat's burnin' up.

[DRISCOLL *brings the dipper full of water and supports his head while he drinks in great gulps.*]

DRISCOLL [*seeking vainly for some word of comfort*]. Are ye feelin' more aisy-loike now?

YANK. Yes—now—when I know it's all up. [*A pause.*] You mustn't take it so hard, Drisc. I was just thinkin' it ain't as bad as people think—dyin'. I ain't never took much stock in the truck them sky-pilots preach. I ain't never had religion; but I know whatever it is what comes after it can't be no worser'n this. I don't like to leave you, Drisc, but—that's all.

DRISCOLL [*with a groan*]. Lad, lad, don't be talkin'.

YANK. This sailor life ain't much to cry about leavin'—just one ship after another, hard work, small pay, and bum grub; and when we git into port, just a drunk endin' up in a fight, and all your money gone, and then ship away again. Never meetin' no nice people; never gittin' outa sailor-town, hardly, in any port; travelin' all over the world and never seein' none of it; without no one to care whether you're alive or dead. [*With a bitter smile.*] There ain't much in all that that'd make yuh sorry to lose it, Drisc.

DRISCOLL [*gloomily*]. It's a hell av a life, the sea.

YANK [*musingly*]. It must be great to stay on dry land all your life and have a farm with a house of your own with cows and pigs and chickens, 'way in the middle of the land where yuh'd never smell the sea or see a ship. It must be great to have a wife, and kids to play with at night after supper when your work was done. It must be great to have a home of your own, Drisc.

DRISCOLL [*with a great sigh*]. It must, surely; but what's the use av thinkin' av ut? Such things are not for the loikes av us.

YANK. Sea-farin' is all right when you're young and don't care, but we ain't chickens no more, and somehow, I dunno, this last year has seemed rotten, and I've had a hunch I'd quit —with you, of course—and we'd save our coin, and go to Canada or Argentine or some place and git a farm, just a small one, just enough to live on. I never told yuh this, 'cause I thought you'd laugh at me.

DRISCOLL [*enthusiastically*]. Laugh at you, is ut? When I'm havin' the same thoughts myself, toime afther toime. It's a grand idea and we'll be doin' ut sure if you'll stop your crazy notions—about—about bein' so sick.

YANK [*sadly*]. Too late. We shouldn'ta made this trip, and then— How'd all the fog git in here?

DRISCOLL. Fog?

YANK. Everything looks misty. Must be my eyes gittin' weak, I guess. What was we talkin' of a minute ago? Oh, yes, a farm. It's too late. [*His mind wandering.*] Argentine, did I say? D'yuh remember the times we've had in Buenos Aires? The moving pictures in Barracas? Some class to them, d'yuh remember?

DRISCOLL [*with satisfaction*]. I do that; and so does the piany player. He'll not be forgettin' the black eye I gave him in a hurry.

YANK. Remember the time we was there on the beach and had to go to Tommy Moore's boarding house to git shipped? And he sold us rotten oil-skins and sea-boots full of holes, and shipped us on a skysail-yarder round the Horn and took two months' pay for it. And the days we used to sit on the park benches along the Paseo Colon with the vigilantes lookin' hard at us? And the songs of the Sailor's Opera where the guy played ragtime —d'yuh remember them?

DRISCOLL. I do, surely.

YANK. And La Plata—phew, the stink of the hides! I always liked Argentine—all except that booze, caña. How drunk we used to git on that, remember?

DRISCOLL. Cud I forget ut? My head pains me at the menshun av that divil's brew.

YANK. Remember the night I went crazy with the heat in Singapore? And the time you was pinched by the cops in Port Said? And the time we was both locked up in Sydney for fightin'?

DRISCOLL. I do so.

YANK. And that fight on the dock at Cape Town— [*His voice betrays great inward perturbation.*]

DRISCOLL [*hastily*]. Don't be thinkin' av that now. 'Tis past and gone.

YANK. D'yuh think He'll hold it up against me?

DRISCOLL [*mystified*]. Who's that?

YANK. God. They say He sees everything. He must know it was done in fair fight, in self-defense, don't yuh think?

DRISCOLL. Av course. Ye stabbed him, and be damned to him, for the skulkin' swine he was, afther him tryin' to stick you in the back, and you not suspectin'. Let your conscience be aisy. I wisht I had nothin' blacker than that on my sowl. I'd not be afraid av the angel Gabriel himself.

YANK [*with a shudder*]. I c'd see him a minute ago with the blood spurtin' out of his neck. Ugh!

DRISCOLL. The fever, ut is, that makes you see such things. Give no heed to ut.

YANK [*uncertainly*]. You don't think He'll hold it up agin me—God, I mean.

DRISCOLL. If there's justice in hiven, no!

[YANK *seems comforted by this assurance.*]

YANK [*after a pause*]. We won't reach Cardiff for a week at least. I'll be buried at sea.

DRISCOLL [*putting his hands over his ears*]. Ssshh! I won't listen to you.

YANK [*as if he had not heard him*]. It's as good a place as any other, I s'pose—only I always wanted to be buried on dry land. But what the hell'll I care—then? [*Fretfully.*] Why should it be a rotten night like this with that damned whistle blowin' and people snorin' all round? I wish the stars was out, and the moon, too; I c'd lie out on deck and look at them,

and it'd make it easier to go—somehow.

DRISCOLL. For the love av God don't be talkin' loike that!

YANK. Whatever pay's comin' to me yuh can divvy up with the rest of the boys; and you take my watch. It ain't worth much, but it's all I've got.

DRISCOLL. But have you no relations at all to call your own?

YANK. No, not as I know of. One thing I forgot: You know Fanny the barmaid at the Red Stork in Cardiff?

DRISCOLL. Sure, and who doesn't?

YANK. She's been good to me. She tried to lend me half a crown when I was broke there last trip. Buy her the biggest box of candy yuh c'n find in Cardiff. [*Breaking down—in a choking voice.*] It's hard to ship on this voyage I'm goin' on—alone! [DRISCOLL *reaches out and grasps his hand. There is a pause, during which both fight to control themselves.*] My throat's like a furnace. [*He gasps for air.*] Gimme a drink of water, will yuh, Drisc? [DRISCOLL *get him a dipper of water.*] I wish this was a pint of beer. Oooohh! [*He chokes, his face convulsed with agony, his hands tearing at his shirt-front. The dipper falls from his nerveless fingers.*]

DRISCOLL. For the love av God, what is ut, Yank?

YANK [*speaking with tremendous difficulty*]. S'long, Drisc! [*He stares straight in front of him with eyes staring from their sockets.*] Who's that?

DRISCOLL. Who? What?

YANK [*faintly*]. A pretty lady dressed in black. [*His face twitches and his body writhes in a final spasm, then straightens out rigidly.*]

DRISCOLL [*pale with horror*]. Yank! Yank! Say a word to me for the love av hiven!

[*He shrinks away from the bunk, making the sign of the cross. Then comes back and puts a trembling hand on* YANK'S *chest and bends closely over the body.*]

COCKY [*from the alleyway*]. Oh, Driscoll! Can you leave Yank for arf a mo' and give me a 'and?

DRISCOLL [*with a great sob*]. Yank! [*He sinks down on his knees beside the bunk, his head on his hands. His lips move in some half-remembered prayer.*]

[COCKY *enters, his oilskins and sou'wester glistening with drops of water.*]

COCKY. The fog's lifted.

[COCKY *sees* DRISCOLL *and stands staring at him with open mouth.* DRISCOLL *makes the sign of the cross again.*]

COCKY [*mockingly*]. Sayin' 'is prayers!

[*He catches sight of the still figure in the bunk and an expression of awed understanding comes over his face. He takes off his dripping sou'wester and stands, scratching his head.*]

COCKY [*in a hushed whisper*]. Gawd blimey!

THE CURTAIN FALLS

1916

LAZARUS LAUGHED *

ACT ONE:

Scene One: Lazarus' home in Bethany—a short time after the miracle.

Scene Two: Months later. Outside the House of Laughter in Bethany. Late evening.

ACT TWO:

Scene One: A street in Athens. A night months later.

Scene Two: A temple immediately inside the walls of Rome. Midnight. Months later.

ACT THREE:

Scene One: Garden of Tiberius' palace. A night a few days later.

Scene Two: Inside the palace. Immediately after.

ACT FOUR:

Scene One: The same. A while after.

Scene Two: Interior of a Roman theatre. Dawn of the same night.

CHARACTERS

LAZARUS OF BETHANY	CHORUS OF GREEKS
HIS FATHER	SEVEN CITIZENS OF ATHENS
HIS MOTHER	CHORUS OF ROMAN SENATORS
MARTHA } *his sisters*	SEVEN SENATORS
MARY	CHORUS OF LEGIONAIRES
MIRIAM, *his wife*	FLAVIUS, *a centurion*
SEVEN GUESTS, *neighbors of Lazarus*	MARCELLUS, *a patrician*
CHORUS OF OLD MEN	CHORUS OF THE GUARD
AN ORTHODOX PRIEST	TIBERIUS CÆSAR
CHORUS OF LAZARUS' FOLLOWERS	POMPEIA
A CENTURION	CHORUS OF YOUTHS AND GIRLS
GAIUS CALIGULA	CHORUS OF THE ROMAN POPULACE
CRASSUS, *a Roman General*	CROWDS

* Reprinted by permission of Random House, Inc. Copyright, 1932, by Eugene O'Neill.

ACT I

SCENE I

SCENE: *Exterior and interior of* LAZARUS' *home at Bethany. The main room at the front end of the house is shown—a long, low-ceilinged, sparely furnished chamber, with white walls gray in the fading daylight that enters from three small windows at the left. To the left of center several long tables placed lengthwise to the width of the room, around which many chairs for guests have been placed. In the rear wall, right, a door leading into the rest of the house. On the left, a doorway opening on a road where a crowd of men has gathered. On the right, another doorway leading to the yard where there is a crowd of women.*

Inside the house, on the men's side, seven male Guests are grouped by the door, watching LAZARUS *with frightened awe, talking hesitantly in low whispers. The Chorus of Old Men, seven in number, is drawn up in a crescent, in the far corner, right, facing* LAZARUS.

[*All of these people are masked in accordance with the following scheme: There are seven periods of life shown: Boyhood (or Girlhood), Youth, Young Manhood (or Womanhood), Manhood (or Womanhood), Middle Age, Maturity and Old Age; and each of these periods is represented by seven different masks of general types of character as follows: The Simple, Ignorant; the Happy, Eager; the Self-Tortured, Introspective; the Proud, Self-Reliant; the Servile, Hypocritical; the Revengeful, Cruel; the Sorrowful, Resigned. Thus in each crowd (this includes among the men the Seven Guests who are composed of one male of each period-type as period one—type one, period two—type two, and so on up to period seven—type seven) there are*

forty-nine different combinations of period and type. Each type has a distinct predominant color for its costumes which varies in kind according to its period. The masks of the Chorus of Old Men are double the size of the others. They are all seven in the Sorrowful, Resigned type of Old Age.]

On a raised platform at the middle of the one table placed lengthwise at center sits LAZARUS, *his head haloed and his body illumined by a soft radiance as of tiny phosphorescent flames.*

LAZARUS, *freed now from the fear of death, wears no mask.*

In appearance LAZARUS *is tall and powerful, about fifty years of age, with a mass of gray-black hair and a heavy beard. His face recalls that of a statue of a divinity of Ancient Greece in its general structure and particularly in its quality of detached serenity. It is dark-complected, ruddy and brown, the color of rich earth upturned by the plow, calm but furrowed deep with the marks of former suffering endured with a grim fortitude that had never softened into resignation. His forehead is broad and noble, his eyes black and deep-set. Just now he is staring straight before him as if his vision were still fixed beyond life.*

Kneeling beside him with bowed heads are his wife, MIRIAM, *his sisters,* MARTHA *and* MARY, *and his* FATHER *and* MOTHER.

MIRIAM *is a slender, delicate woman of thirty-five, dressed in deep black, who holds one of his hands in both of hers, and keeps her lips pressed to it. The upper part of her face is covered by a mask which conceals her forehead, eyes and nose, but leaves her mouth revealed. The mask is the pure pallor of marble, the expression that of a statue of Woman, of her eternal acceptance of the compulsion of motherhood, the inevitable cycle of*

*love into pain into joy and new love
into separation and pain again and
the loneliness of age. The eyes of the
mask are almost closed. Their gaze
turns within, oblivious to the life outside, as they dream down on the child
forever in memory at her breast. The
mouth of* MIRIAM *is sensitive and sad,
tender with an eager, understanding
smile of self-forgetful love, the lips
still fresh and young. Her skin, in
contrast to the mask, is sunburned
and earth-colored like that of* LAZ-
ARUS. MARTHA, MARY *and the two
parents all wear full masks which
broadly reproduce their own characters.* MARTHA *is a buxom middle-
aged housewife, plain and pleasant.*
MARY *is young and pretty, nervous
and high-strung. The* FATHER *is a
small, thin, feeble old man of over
eighty, meek and pious. The* MOTHER
*is tall and stout, over sixty-five, a
gentle, simple woman.*

*All the masks of these Jews of the
first two scenes of the play are pro-
nouncedly Semitic.*

*A background of twilight sky. A
dissolving touch of sunset still lingers
on the horizon.*

*It is some time after the miracle
and Jesus has gone away.*

CHORUS OF OLD MEN. [*In a quaver-
ing rising and falling chant—their
arms outstretched toward* LAZARUS.]
Jesus wept!
Behold how he loved him!
He that liveth,
He that believeth,
Shall never die!

CROWD. [*On either side of house,
echo the chant.*]
He that believeth
Shall never die!
Lazarus, come forth!

FIRST GUEST. [*A Simple Boy—in a
frightened whisper after a pause of
dead silence.*] That strange light seems

to come from within him! [*With awe.*]
Think of it! For four days he lay in
the tomb! [*Turns away with a shudder.*]

SECOND GUEST. [*A Happy Youth—
with reassuring conviction.*] It is a
holy light. It came from Jesus.

FIFTH GUEST. [*An Envious, Middle-Aged Man.*] Maybe if the truth
were known, our friend there never
really died at all!

FOURTH GUEST. [*A Defiant Man,
indignantly.*] Do you doubt the miracle? I tell you I was here in this
house when Lazarus died!

SEVENTH GUEST. [*An Aged, Sorrowful Man.*] And I used to visit him
every day. He knew himself his hour
was near.

Fourth Guest. He wished for death!
He said to me one day: "I have known
my fill of life and the sorrow of living.
Soon I shall know peace." And he
smiled. It was the first time I had seen
him smile in years.

THIRD GUEST. [*A Self-Tortured
Man—gloomily.*] Yes, of late years his
life had been one long misfortune.
One after another his children died—

SIXTH GUEST. [*A Mature Man with
a cruel face—with a harsh laugh.*]
They were all girls. Lazarus had no
luck.

SEVENTH GUEST. The last was a
boy, the one that died at birth. You
are forgetting him.

THIRD GUEST. Lazarus could never
forget. Not only did his son die but
Miriam could never bear him more
children.

FIFTH GUEST. [*Practically.*] But he
could not blame bad luck for everything. Take the loss of his father's
wealth since he took over the management. That was his own doing. He
was a bad farmer, a poor breeder of
sheep, and a bargainer so easy to cheat
it hurt one's conscience to trade with
him!

SIXTH GUEST. [*With a sneer—maliciously.*] You should know best about that! [*A suppressed laugh from those around him.*]

FIRST GUEST. [*Who has been gazing at* LAZARUS—*softly.*] Ssssh! Look at his face! [*They all stare. A pause.*]

SECOND GUEST. [*With wondering awe.*] Do you remember him, neighbors, before he died? He used to be pale even when he worked in the fields. Now he seems as brown as one who has labored in the earth all day in a vineyard beneath the hot sun! [*A pause.*]

FOURTH GUEST. The whole look of his face has changed. He is like a stranger from a far land. There is no longer any sorrow in his eyes. They must have forgotten sorrow in the grave.

FIFTH GUEST. [*Grumblingly.*] I thought we were invited here to eat—and all we do is stand and gape at him!

FOURTH GUEST. [*Sternly.*] Be silent! We are waiting for him to speak.

THIRD GUEST. [*Impressively.*] He did speak once. And he laughed!

ALL THE GUESTS. [*Amazed and incredulous.*] Laughed?

THIRD GUEST. [*Importantly.*] Laughed! I heard him! It was a moment after the miracle—

MIRIAM. [*Her voice, rich with sorrow, exultant now.*] Jesus cried, "Lazarus, come forth!" [*She kisses his hand. He makes a slight movement, a stirring in his vision. The* GUESTS *stare. A frightened pause.*]

FIFTH GUEST. [*Nudging the* SECOND—*uneasily.*] Go on with your story!

THIRD GUEST. Just as he appeared in the opening of the tomb, wrapped in his shroud—

SECOND GUEST. [*Excitedly—interrupting.*] My heart stopped! I fell on my face! And all the women screamed!

[*Sceptically.*] You must have sharp ears to have heard him laugh in that uproar!

THIRD GUEST. I helped to pry away the stone so I was right beside him. I found myself kneeling, but between my fingers I watched Jesus and Lazarus. Jesus looked into his face for what seemed a long time and suddenly Lazarus said "Yes" as if he were answering a question in Jesus' eyes.

ALL THE GUESTS. [*Mystified.*] Yes? What could he mean by yes?

THIRD GUEST. Then Jesus smiled sadly but with tenderness, as one who from a distance of years of sorrow remembers happiness. And then Lazarus knelt and kissed Jesus' feet and both of them smiled and Jesus blessed him and called him "My Brother" and went away; and Lazarus, looking after Him, began to laugh softly like a man in love with God! Such a laugh I never heard! It made my ears drunk! It was like wine! And though I was half-dead with fright I found myself laughing, too!

MIRIAM. [*With a beseeching summons.*] Lazarus, come forth!

CHORUS. [*Chanting.*] Lazarus! Come forth!

CROWD. [*On either side of the house—echoing the chant.*] Come forth! Come forth!

LAZARUS. [*Suddenly in a deep voice—with a wonderful exultant acceptance in it.*] Yes! [*The* GUESTS *in the room, the* CROWDS *outside all cry out in fear and joy and fall on their knees.*]

CHORUS. [*Chanting exultantly.*]
The stone is taken away!
The spirit is loosed!
The soul let go!

LAZARUS. [*Rising and looking around him at everyone and everything—with an all-embracing love—gently.*] Yes! [*His family and the* GUESTS *in the room now throng about*

LAZARUS *to embrace him. The* CROWDS *of men and women on each side push into the room to stare at him. He is in the arms of his* MOTHER *and* MIRIAM *while his* SISTERS *and* FATHER *kiss and press his hands. The five are half hysterical with relief and joy, sobbing and laughing.*]

FATHER. My son is reborn to me!

CHORUS. Hosannah!

ALL. [*With a great shout.*] Hosannah!

FATHER. Let us rejoice! Eat and drink! Draw up your chairs, friends! Music! Bring wine! [*Music begins in the room off right, rear—a festive dance tune. The company sit down in their places, the* FATHER *and* MOTHER *at* LAZARUS' *right and left,* MIRIAM *next to the* MOTHER, MARTHA *and* MARY *beside the* FATHER. *But* LAZARUS *remains standing. And the* CHORUS OF OLD MEN *remain in their formation at the rear. Wine is poured and all raise their goblets toward* LAZARUS—*then suddenly they stop, the music dies out, and an awed and frightened stillness prevails, for* LAZARUS *is a strange, majestic figure whose understanding smile seems terrible and enigmatic to them.*]

FATHER. [*Pathetically uneasy.*] You frighten us, my son. You are strange—standing there— [*In the midst of a silence more awkward than before he rises to his feet, goblet in hand—forcing his voice, falteringly.*] A toast, neighbors!

CHORUS. [*In a forced echo.*] A toast!

ALL. [*Echoing them.*] A toast!

FATHER. To my son, Lazarus, whom a blessed miracle has brought back from death!

LAZARUS. [*Suddenly laughing softly out of his vision, as if to himself, and speaking with a strange unearthly calm in a voice that is like a loving whisper of hope and confidence.*] No!

There is no death! [*A moment's pause. The people remain with goblets uplifted, staring at him. Then all repeat after him questioningly and frightenedly.*]

ALL. There—is—no—death?

SIXTH GUEST. [*Suddenly blurts out the question which is in the minds of all.*] What did you find beyond there, Lazarus? [*A pause of silence.*]

LAZARUS. [*Smiles gently and speaks as if to a group of inquisitive children.*] O Curious Greedy Ones, is not one world in which you know not how to live enough for you?

SIXTH GUEST. [*Emboldened.*] Why did you say yes, Lazarus?

FOURTH GUEST. Why did you laugh?

ALL THE GUESTS. [*With insistent curiosity but in low awed tones.*] What is beyond there, Lazarus?

CHORUS. [*In a low murmur.*] What is beyond there? What is beyond?

CROWD. [*Carrying the question falteringly back into silence.*] What is beyond?

LAZARUS. [*Suddenly again—now in a voice of loving exaltation.*] There is only life! I heard the heart of Jesus laughing in my heart; "There is Eternal Life in No," it said, "and there is the same Eternal Life in Yes! Death is the fear between!" And my heart reborn to love of life cried "Yes!" and I laughed in the laughter of God! [*He begins to laugh, softly at first—a laugh so full of a complete acceptance of life, a profound assertion of joy in living, so devoid of all self-consciousness or fear, that it is like a great bird song triumphant in depths of sky, proud and powerful, infectious with love, casting on the listener an enthralling spell. The crowd in the room are caught by it. Glancing sideways at one another, smiling foolishly and self-consciously, at first they hesitate, plainly holding themselves in for fear of what the next one will think.*]

CHORUS. [*In a chanting murmur.*]
Lazarus laughs!
Our hearts grow happy!
Laughter like music!
The wind laughs!
The sea laughs!
Spring laughs from the earth!
Summer laughs in the air!
Lazarus laughs!

LAZARUS. [*On a final note of compelling exultation.*] Laugh! Laugh with me! Death is dead! Fear is no more! There is only life! There is only laughter!

CHORUS. [*Chanting exultingly now.*]
Laugh! Laugh!
Laugh with Lazarus!
Fear is no more!
There is no death!

[*They laugh in a rhythmic cadence dominated by the laughter of* LAZARUS.]

CROWD. [*Who, gradually, joining in by groups or one by one—including* LAZARUS' *family with the exception of* MIRIAM, *who does not laugh but watches and listens to his laughter with a tender smile of being happy in his happiness—have now all begun to laugh in rhythm with the* CHORUS—*in a great, full-throated pæan as the laughter of* LAZARUS *rises higher and higher.*]
Laugh! Laugh!
Fear is no more!
There is no death!

CHORUS.
Laugh! Laugh!
There is only life!
There is only laughter!
Fear is no more!
Death is dead!

CROWD. [*In a rhythmic echo.*]
Laugh! Laugh!
Death is dead!
There is only laughter!

[*The room rocks, the air outside throbs with the rhythmic beat of their liberated laughter—still a bit uncertain of its freedom, harsh, discordant, frenzied, desperate and drunken, but dominated and inspired by the high, free, aspiring, exulting laughter of* LAZARUS.]

CURTAIN

SCENE 2

SCENE: *Some months later. Exterior of* LAZARUS' *home in Bethany, now known as the House of Laughter. It is a clear bright night, the sky sparkling with stars. At the extreme front is a road. Between this and the house is a small raised terrace. The house is low, of one story only, its walls white. Four windows are visible with a closed door in the middle of the wall. Steps lead up to this door, and to the left of door a flight of stairs goes up to the balustraded roof. The windows shine brilliantly with the flickering light of many candles which gives them a throbbing star-like effect. From within comes the sound of flutes and dance music. The dancers can be seen whirling swiftly by the windows. There is continually an overtone of singing laughter emphasizing the pulsing rhythm of the dance.*

On the road in the foreground, at left and right, two separate groups of Jews are gathered. They are not divided according to sex as in the previous scene. Each is composed about equally of men and women, forty-nine in each, masked and costumed as before. It is religious belief that now divides them. The adherents of Jesus, the Nazarenes, among whom may be noted MARTHA *and* MARY, *are on the left; the Orthodox, among whom are* LAZARUS' FATHER *and* MOTHER *and a* PRIEST, *are at right. Between the two hostile groups is the same* CHORUS OF OLD MEN, *in a formation like a spear-*

head, whose point is placed at the foot
of the steps leading to the terrace. All
these people are staring fascinatedly at
the house, listening entranced, their
feet moving, their bodies swaying
to the music's beat, stiffly, con-
strainedly, compelled against their
wills. Then the music suddenly stops
and the chant of youthful voices is
heard:

FOLLOWERS OF LAZARUS. [*From
within the house.*]
Laugh! Laugh!
There is only life!
There is only laughter!

CHORUS OF OLD MEN. [*As if they
were subjects moved by hypotic sug-
gestion—miserably and discordantly.*]
Ha-ha-ha-ha!
There is only laughter!
Ha-ha—

CROWD. [*In the same manner.*] Ha-
ha—

MARY. Ha— [*Then frantically—
half-weeping with indignant rage—to
the Nazarenes.*] Stop! Oh, how can
we laugh! We are betraying Jesus!
My brother Lazarus has become a
devil!

THE ORTHODOX PRIEST. [*His mask
is that of a religious fanatic. He is
sixty or so.*] Ha—ha— [*Tearing his
beard and stamping with rage.*] Stop
it, you fools! It is a foul sin in the
sight of Jehovah! Why do you come
here every night to listen and watch
their abominations? The Lord God
will punish you!

MARY. [*Echoing him—to her people.*] Jesus will never forgive you!

THE PRIEST. [*Angrily.*] Jesus? [*He
turns to look at the Nazarenes disdainfully and spits on the ground insult-
ingly.*] [*The members of the two
groups begin to glare at each other.
The* CHORUS *falls back, three on each
side, leaving one neutral figure before
the steps. The* PRIEST *goes on tauntingly.*] Did you hear her, friends?

These renegade Nazarenes will soon
deny they are Jews at all! They will
begin to worship in filthy idolatry the
sun and star and man's body—as
LAZARUS in there [*points to the
house*], the disciple of their Jesus, has
so well set them the example! [*This is
followed by an outburst of insulting
shouts of accusation and denial from
both sides.*]

A NAZARENE. [*The* FOURTH GUEST
of Scene One.] You lie! Lazarus is no
disciple! He is a traitor to Jesus! We
scorn him!

PRIEST. [*Sneeringly.*] But your pretended Messiah did not scorn him.
According to your stupid lies, he raised
him from the dead! And answer me,
has your Jesus ever denied Lazarus,
or denounced his laughter? No! No
doubt he is laughing, too, at all you
credulous fools—for if Lazarus is not
his disciple, in the matter of the false
miracle he was his accomplice! [*This
provokes a furious protest from the
Nazarenes and insulting hoots and
jeers from the Orthodox, penetrated
by a piercing scream from* LAZARUS'
MOTHER, *who, crushed in the crowd,
sinks fainting to the ground. The*
FATHER *bends over her. The group of
the Orthodox falls back from them.
With frightened cries* MARTHA *and*
MARY *run from the group of Nazarenes and kneel beside her.*]

FATHER. [*Pitifully.*] Rachel! Darling! Speak to me!

MARTHA. [*Practically.*] She has only
fainted.

MARY. She is opening her eyes!
Mother, dear!

MOTHER. [*Weakly.*] Did I fall?
[*Recognizing* MARTHA *and* MARY.]
Martha—and Mary—my dear ones!
[*They embrace her, weeping.*] I have
not kissed you since you left home to
follow that Jesus— Oh, if we were
only at home again—and if, also, my
poor boy, Lazarus— [*She sobs.*]

FATHER. [*Gruffly.*] You must not speak of him!

MARTHA. Do not worry your head about Lazarus. He is not worth it!

MARY. [*With surprising vindictiveness.*] He is accursed! He has betrayed our Lord!

PRIEST. [*To those around him—mockingly.*] Do you hear? They already call the Nazarene "Lord!" A Lord who is in the common prison at Jerusalem, I heard today! A fine Lord whom our High Priests have had arrested like a thief!

MARY. [*With fanatic fervor.*] He is a king! Whenever He chooses He will gather a great army and He will seize His kingdom and all who deny Him shall be crucified!

PRIEST. [*Tauntingly.*] Now their jail-bird is a king, no less! Soon they will make him a god, as the Romans do their Cæsars!

MARY. [*Her eyes flashing.*] He is the Messiah!

PRIEST. [*Furiously.*] The Messiah! May Jehovah smite you in your lies! Step back among your kind! You defile us! [*As she stands defiantly he appeals to the Father.*] Have you no authority? She called him the Messiah —that common beggar, that tramp! Curse her!

FATHER. [*Confused, pitifully harried, collecting his forces.*] Wait! Go back, Mary! You chose to follow that impostor—

MARY. [*Defiantly.*] The Messiah!

MARTHA. [*Trying to calm her.*] Ssssh! Remember he is our father!

MARY. [*Fanatically.*] I deny him! I deny all who deny Jesus!

MOTHER. [*Tearfully.*] And me, darling?

MARY. You must come to us, Mother! You must believe in Jesus and leave all to follow Him!

FATHER. [*Enraged.*] So! You want to steal your mother away, to leave me lonely in my old age! You are an unnatural daughter! I disown you! Go, before I curse—

MOTHER. [*Beseechingly.*] Father!

MARTHA. [*Pulling MARY away.*] Mary! Jesus teaches to be kind.

MARY. [*Hysterically.*] He teaches to give up all and follow Him! I want to give Him everything! I want my father to curse me!

FATHER. [*Frenziedly.*] Then I do curse you! No—not you—but the devil in you! And the devil in Martha! And the great mocking devil that dwells in Lazarus and laughs from his mouth! I curse these devils and that Prince of Devils, that false prophet, Jesus! It is he who has brought division to my home and many homes that were happy before. I curse him! I curse the day he called my good son, Lazarus, from the grave to walk again with a devil inside him! It was not my son who came back but a devil! My son is dead! And you, my daughters, are dead! I am the father only of devils! [*His voice has risen to a wailing lament.*] My children are dead!

LAZARUS. [*His voice rings from within the house in exultant denial.*] Death is dead! There is only laughter! [*He laughs.*] [*The voices of all his* FOLLOWERS *echo his laughter. They pour in a laughing rout from the doorway onto the terrace. At the same moment the* CHORUS OF FOLLOWERS *appears on the roof and forms along the balustrade, facing front.*]

[*These* FOLLOWERS OF LAZARUS, *forty-nine in number, composed about equally of both sexes, wear a mask that, while recognizably Jewish, is a* LAZARUS *mask, resembling him in its expression of fearless faith in life, the mouth shaped by laughter. The* CHORUS OF FOLLOWERS, *seven in number, all men, have identical masks of double size, as before. The Period* of all these masks is anywhere between Youth and Manhood (or Womanhood).]

[*The music continues to come from within. Laughing, the* FOLLOWERS *dance to it in weaving patterns on the terrace. They are dressed in bright-colored diaphanous robes. Their chorused laughter, now high and clear, now dying to a humming murmur, stresses the rhythmic flow of the dance.*]

CHORUS OF FOLLOWERS.
Laugh! Laugh!
There is no death!
There is only laughter!

FOLLOWER.
There is only laughter!
Death is dead!
Laugh! Laugh!

CROWD. [*The two groups of Nazarenes and Orthodox, on the appearance of the* FOLLOWERS, *immediately forget their differences and form into one mob, led by their* CHORUS OF OLD MEN, *whose jeering howls they echo as one voice.*] Yaah! Yaah! Yaah! [*But they cannot keep it up. The music and laughter rise above their hooting. They fall into silence. Then they again begin to feel impelled by the rhythm and laughter, their feet move, their bodies sway. Their lips quiver, their mouths open as if to laugh. Their* CHORUS OF OLD MEN *are the first to be affected. It is as if this reaction were transmitted through the* CHORUS *to the* CROWD.]

PRIEST. [*His mouth twitching—fighting against the compulsion in him—stammers.*] Brothers—listen—we must unite—in one cause—to—stamp out—this abomination! [*It is as if he can no longer control his speech. He presses his hand over his mouth convulsively.*]

AN AGED ORTHODOX JEW. [*The* SEVENTH GUEST *of Scene One—starts to harangue the crowd. He fights the spell but cannot control his jerking body nor his ghastly, spasmodic laughter.*] Neighbors! Our young people are corrupted! They are leaving our farms —to dance and sing! To laugh! Ha—! Laugh at everything! Ha-ha—! [*He struggles desperately to control himself.*]

CHORUS OF OLD MEN. [*A barking laugh forced from them.*] Ha-ha—!

CROWD. [*Echoing this.*] Ha-ha—!

THE AGED JEW. They have no respect for life! When I said in kindness, "You must go back to work," they laughed at me! Ha—! "We desire joy. We go to Lazarus," they said— and left my fields! I begged them to stay—with tears in my eyes! I even offered them more money! They laughed! "What is money? Can the heart eat gold?" They laughed at money! Ha-ha—! [*He chokes with exasperated rage.*]

CHORUS OF OLD MEN. [*Echoing him.*] Ha-ha—!

CROWD. [*Echoing the* CHORUS.] Ha-ha—!

AGED JEW. [*Shaking his fist at* LAZARUS' FOLLOWERS.] That loafer taught them that! They come to him and work for nothing! For nothing! And they are glad, these undutiful ones! While they sow, they dance! They sing to the earth when they are plowing! They tend his flocks and laugh toward the sun! Ha-ha-ha—! [*He struggles again.*]

CHORUS OF OLD MEN. [*As before.*] Ha-ha-ha—

CROWD. [*As before.*] Ha-ha-ha—

AGED JEW. How can we compete with labor for laughter! We will have no harvest. There will be no food! Our children will starve! Our race will perish! And he will laugh! Ha-ha-ha-ha! [*He howls with furious, uncontained laughter.*]

CHORUS OF OLD MEN. [*Echoing his tone.*]
Our children will starve!
Our race will perish!
Lazarus laughs!
Ha-ha-ha-ha! Ha-ha-ha-ha!

CROWD. [*As before.*] Ha-ha-ha-ha! Ha-ha-ha-ha! [*Their former distinctions of Nazarenes and Orthodox are now entirely forgotten. The members of* LAZARUS' *family are grouped in the center as if nothing had ever happened to separate them. The* CHORUS OF OLD MEN *is again joined in its spearhead formation at the stairs. Apparent first in this* CHORUS, *a queer excitement begins to pervade this mob. They begin to weave in and out, clasping each other's hands now and then, moving mechanically in jerky steps to the music in a grotesque sort of marionettes' country dance. At first this is slow but it momentarily becomes more hectic and peculiar. They raise clenched fists or hands distended into threatening talons. Their voices sound thick and harsh and animal-like with anger as they mutter and growl, each one aloud to himself or herself.*]

CHORUS OF OLD MEN. [*Threateningly, gradually rising to hatred.*]
Hear them laugh!
See them dance!
Shameless! Wanton!
Dirty! Evil!
Infamous! Bestial!
Madness! Blood!
Adultery! Murder!
We burn!
We kill!
We crucify!
Death! Death!
Beware, Lazarus!
[*This last in a wild frenzy.*]
CROWD. [*Frenziedly.*]
Beware, Lazarus!
We burn! We kill!

We crucify!
Death! Death!

[*They crowd toward the gateway, their arms stretched out as if demanding* LAZARUS *for a sacrificial victim. Meanwhile they never cease to hop up and down, to mill around, to twist their bodies toward and away from each other in bestial parody of the dance of the* FOLLOWERS.]

[*The tall figure of* LAZARUS, *dressed in a white robe, suddenly appears on the roof of the house. He stands at the balustrade in the middle of the* CHORUS. *Beside him, a little behind,* MIRIAM *appears dressed in black, her face upturned, her lips praying. She appears to have grown older, to be forty now.* LAZARUS' *body is softly illumined by its inner light. The change in him is marked. He seems ten years younger, at the prime of forty. His body has become less angular and stiff. His movements are graceful and pliant. The change is even more noticeable in his face, which has filled out, become purer in outline, more distinctly Grecian. His complexion is the red-brown of rich earth, the gray in his black, curly beard has almost disappeared.*]

[*He makes a sign and the music ceases. His* FOLLOWERS *remain fixed in their dancing attitudes like figures in a frieze. Each member of the mob remains frozen in a distorted posture. He stares down at the mob pityingly, his face calm.*]

LAZARUS. [*Speaks amid a profound silence. His voice releases his own dancers and the mob from their fixed attitudes. The music begins to play again within the house, very soft and barely audible, swelling up and down like the sound of an organ from a distant church.*] You laugh, but your laughter is guilty! It laughs a hyena laughter, spotted, howling its hungry fear of life! That day I returned did I not tell you your fear was no more, that there is no death? You believed then—for a moment! You laughed—discordantly, hoarsely, but with a groping toward joy. What! Have you so soon forgotten, that now your laughter curses life again as of old? [*He pauses—then sadly.*] That is your tragedy! You forget! You forget the God in you! You wish to forget! Remembrance would imply the high duty to live as a son of God—generously!—with love!—with pride!—with laughter! This is too glorious a victory for you, too terrible a loneliness! Easier to forget, to become only a man, the son of a woman, to hide from life against her breast, to whimper your fear to her resigned heart and be comforted by her resignation! To live by denying life! [*Then exhortingly.*] Why are your eyes always either fixed on the ground in weariness of thought, or watching one another with suspicion? Throw your gaze upward! To Eternal Life! To the fearless and deathless! The everlasting! To the stars! [*He stretches out his arms to the sky—then suddenly points.*] See! A new star has appeared! It is the one that shone over Bethlehem! [*His voice becomes a little bitter and mocking.*] The Master of Peace and Love has departed this earth. Let all stars be for you henceforth symbols of Saviors—Sons of God who appeared on worlds like ours to tell the saving truth to ears like yours, inexorably deaf! [*Then exaltedly.*] But the greatness of Saviors is that they may not save! The greatness of Man is that no god can save him—until he becomes a god! [*He stares up at the stars, rapt in contemplation, oblivious to all around him now.*]

[*Rapidly approaching from the left a man's voice jarring in high-pitched cruel laughter is heard. They all listen, huddled together like sheep.*]

MESSENGER. [*The* THIRD GUEST *of Scene One rushes in breathlessly, shouting.*] The Nazarene has been crucified!

PRIEST. [*With fierce triumph.*] Jehovah is avenged! Hosannah!

ORTHODOX. Hosannah! The false prophet is dead! The pretended Messiah is dead! [*They jump and dance, embracing one another. The* NAZARENES *stand paralyzed and stunned. The two groups mechanically separate to right and left again, the* CHORUS OF OLD MEN *dividing itself as before.*]

MARY. [*In a frenzy of grief.*] Do not believe him! Jesus could not die! [*But at this moment a Nazarene youth, exhausted by grief and tears, staggers in from the left.*]

MESSENGER. [SECOND GUEST *of Scene One.*] Jesus is dead! Our Lord is murdered! [*He sinks on his knees sobbing. All the* NAZARENES *do likewise, wailing, rending their garments, tearing their hair, some even beating their heads on the ground in the agony of their despair.*]

MARY. [*Insane with rage now.*] They have murdered Him! [*To her followers—savagely.*] An eye for an eye! Avenge the Master! [*Their frenzy of grief turned into rage, the* NAZARENES *leap to their feet threateningly. Concealed swords and knives are brought out by both sides.*]

MIRIAM. [*Leaning over the balustrade—in a voice of entreaty.*] Mary! Brothers! [*But none heed her or seem to see her.* LAZARUS *and his* FOLLOWERS *remain oblivious to men, arms upstretched toward the stars, their heads thrown back.*]

MARY. [*Wildly.*] Vengeance! Death to His murderers!

PRIEST. [*Fiercely to his followers.*] Death to the Nazarenes! [*With cries of rage the two groups rush on one another. There is a confused tumult of yells, groans, curses, the shrieks of women, the sounds of blows as they meet in a pushing, whirling, struggling mass in which individual figures are indistinguishable. Knives and swords flash above the heads of the mass, hands in every tense attitude of striking, clutching, tearing are seen upraised. As the fight is at its height a* ROMAN CENTURION *and a squad of eight* SOLDIERS *come tramping up at the double-quick. They all are masked. These Roman masks now and henceforth in the play are carried out according to the same formula of Seven Periods, Seven Types, as those of the Jews seen previously, except that the basis of each face is Roman—heavy, domineering, self-complacent, the face of a confident dominant race. The* CENTURION *differs from his soldiers only in being more individualized. He is middle-aged, his soldiers belong to the Period of Manhood. All are of the Simple, Ignorant Type.*]

CENTURION. [*Shouts commandingly.*] Disperse! [*But no one hears him—with angry disgust to his* SOLDIERS.] Charge! Cut them down! [*The* SOLDIERS *form a wedge and charge with a shout. They soon find it necessary to use their swords, and strike down everyone in their way.*]

MIRIAM. Mercy, Romans! [*As they pay no attention to her, in desperation she embraces* LAZARUS *beseechingly, forcing his attention back to earth.*] Lazarus! Mercy!

LAZARUS. [*Looks down upon the struggling mass and cries in a ringing voice.*] Hold! [*Each person stands transfixed, frozen in the last movement, even the* CENTURION *himself. Ten dead and mortally wounded lie on the*

ground, trampled by the feet of friend and foe alike. LAZARUS *looks at the* CROWD. *To each he seems to look at him or her alone. His eyes are accusing and stern. As one head, the heads of all are averted. Even the* CENTURION *stares at the ground humbly, in spite of himself. Finally* LAZARUS *speaks in a voice of infinite disdain.*] Sometimes it is hard to laugh—even at men! [*He turns his eyes from them, staring straight before him. This seems to release them from their fixed positions. The Nazarenes and the Orthodox separate and slink guiltily apart. The* CHORUS OF OLD MEN *forms again, the apex at the center of the steps as before. A low wail of lamentation arises from them. The two crowds of Nazarenes and Orthodox echo this.*]

CHORUS OF OLD MEN. [*In a wailing chant.*]
Woe unto Israel!
Woe unto thee, Jerusalem!
O divided house,
Thou shalt crumble to dust,
And swine shall root
Where thy Temple stood!
Woe unto us!

CROWD. [*In a great echoing cry.*] Woe unto us!

CENTURION. [*Gruffly to hide his embarrassment at being awed by* LAZARUS.] Here, you! Drag your carcasses away. [*From each side men and women come forward to identify and mourn their dead. The wail of lamentations rises and falls. The* CENTURION *looks up at* LAZARUS—*harshly.*] You, there! Are you he whom they call the Laugher?

LAZARUS. [*Without looking at him —his voice seeming to come from some dream within him.*] I am Lazarus.

CENTURION. Who was brought back from death by enchantment?

LAZARUS. [*Looking down at him*

now—with a smile, simply.] No.
There is no death!

CHORUS OF FOLLOWERS. [*Chanting joyously.*] There is no death!

FOLLOWERS. [*Echoing.*] There is no death!

AN ORTHODOX MAN. [*Bending beside the body of* LAZARUS' FATHER.] Here is your father, Lazarus. He is dead.

AN ORTHODOX WOMAN. This is your mother, Lazarus. She is dead.

A NAZARENE. Here is your sister, Martha, Lazarus. She is dead.

A NAZARENE WOMAN. And this is Mary, Lazarus. She is dead.

MIRIAM. [*Suddenly—with deep grief.*] And Jesus who was the Son of Man, who loved and gave you life again has died, Lazarus—has died!

LAZARUS. [*In a great triumphant voice.*] Yes! Yes!! Yes!!! Men die! Even a Son of Man must die to show men that Man may live! But there is no death!

CENTURION. [*At first in a tone of great awe—to his* SOLDIERS.] Is he a god? [*Then gruffly, ashamed of his question.*] Come down, Jew! I have orders to bring you to Rome to Cæsar!

LAZARUS. [*As if he were answering not the* CENTURION *but the command of his fate from the sky.*] Yes! [*He walks down the narrow stairs and,* MIRIAM *following him, comes down the path to the road. He goes and kneels for a moment each beside the bodies of his* FATHER, MOTHER, *and* SISTERS *and kisses each in turn on the forehead. For a moment the struggle with his grief can be seen in his face. Then he looks up to the stars and, as if answering a question, again says simply and acceptingly.*] Yes! [*Then exultantly.*] Yes!! [*And begins to laugh from the depths of his exalted spirit. The laughter of his* CHORUS *and then of his* FOLLOWERS *echoes his. The music and dancing begin again.*]

[*The* CENTURION *grins sheepishly. The* SOLDIERS *chuckle. The* CENTURION *laughs awkwardly. The* SOLDIERS *laugh. The music from the house and the laughter of the* FOLLOWERS *grow louder. The infection spreads to the* CHORUS OF OLD MEN *whose swaying grief falls into the rhythm of the laughter and music as does that of the mourners.*]

LAZARUS' FOLLOWERS. [*Led by their* CHORUS.] Laugh! Laugh!

CHORUS OF OLD MEN. [*Torn by the conflict—torturedly.*]
Ha-ha-ha—
Woe to us, woe!

CROWD. [*Beside the bodies.*]
Woe to us, woe!
Ha-ha—!

CENTURION. [*Laughingly.*] You are brave, you Laugher! Remember Tiberius never laughs! And boast not to Cæsar there is no death, or he will invent a new one for you!

LAZARUS. [*With a smile.*] But all death is men's invention! So laugh! [*He laughs and the* CENTURION *and* SOLDIERS *laugh with him, half dancing clumsily now to the beat of the music.*]

CHORUS OF LAZARUS' FOLLOWERS.
Laugh! Laugh!
Fear is no more!
There is no death!
There is only life!
There is only laughter!

FOLLOWERS. [*Dancing.*]
Laugh! Laugh!
Fear is no more!
Death is dead!

CHORUS OF OLD MEN. [*Forgetting their grief—their eyes on* LAZARUS *now, their arms outstretched to him as are those of the crowd grouped around the bodies but forgetting them.*]

Death is no more!
Death is dead!
Laugh!

CROWD.
Laugh! Laugh!
Death is no more!

CENTURION. [*Laughing, to his laughing* SOLDIERS.] Forward! [*They tramp, dancing off.*] [LAZARUS *and* MIRIAM *start to follow.*]

MIRIAM. [*Suddenly pointing to his* FOLLOWERS *who are dancing and laughing obliviously—pityingly.*] But your faithful ones who love you, Lazarus?

LAZARUS. [*Simply, with a trace of a sad sternness.*] This is their test. Their love must remember—or it must forget. Come! [*With a last gesture back like a blessing on all he is leaving, he goes. The laughter of the* SOLDIERS *recedes. That of the* CHORUS OF OLD MEN *and of the* CROWD *falters and breaks into lamenting grief again, guilt-stricken because of its laughter.*]

CHORUS OF OLD MEN.
Laugh! Laugh!
Death is dead!
Laugh!—But woe!
There lie our dead!
Oh shame and guilt!
We forget our dead!

CROWD. [*With fierce remorseful grief.*]
Woe to us, woe!
There lie our dead!

CHORUS OF LAZARUS' FOLLOWERS.
[*Their voices and the music growing more and more hesitating and faint.*]
Laugh! Laugh!
There is only life!
There is only—
Laugh—

[*Their dance is faltering and slow now.*]
Fear is no—

Death is—
Laugh—

[*The music and dancing and voices cease. The lights in the windows, which have been growing dim, go out. There is a second of complete, death-like silence. The mourning folk in the foreground are frozen figures of grief. Then a sudden swelling chorus of forlorn bewilderment, a cry of lost children comes from the* CHORUS OF FOLLOWERS *and the* FOLLOWERS *themselves. They huddle into groups on the roof and on the terrace. They stretch their arms out in every direction supplicatingly.*]

CHORUS OF FOLLOWERS.
Oh, Lazarus, laugh!
Do not forsake us!
We forget!
Where is thy love fled?
Give back thy laughter,
Thy fearless laughter!
We forget!

FOLLOWERS.
Give back thy laughter!
We forget!

CHORUS OF FOLLOWERS. [*With dull, resigned terror now.*]
Death slinks out
Of his grave in the heart!
Ghosts of fear
Creep back in the brain!
We remember fear!
We remember death!

FOLLOWERS.
Death in the heart!
Fear in the brain!
We remember fear!
We remember death!

CHORUS OF FOLLOWERS. [*Wailing hopelessly now.*]
Forgotten is laughter!
We remember
Only death!
Fear is God!

Forgotten is laughter!
Life is death!

FOLLOWERS.
Forgotten is laughter!
Life is death!

ALL. [*The* CHORUS OF OLD MEN
and the CROWD *joining in.*]
Life is a fearing,
A long dying,
From birth to death!
God is a slayer!
Life is death!

CURTAIN

ACT II

SCENE 1

SCENE: *Some months later. A square
in Athens about ten o'clock at night.
In the rear, pure and beautiful in the
light of a full moon, is the façade of a
temple. An excited crowd of Greeks
of both sexes is gathered in the square
as if for some public festival. They
are masked according to the scheme of
Seven Periods in Seven Types of
Character for each sex. Here, of
course, the foundation of the mask is
the Grecian type of face.*

On the left, the CHORUS OF GREEKS
*is grouped, seven in number, facing
front, in the spearhead formation. As
before the* CHORUS *wears masks double the life size of the* CROWD *masks.
They are all of the Proud Self-Reliant
type, in the period of Young Manhood.*

*These seven are clad in goat skins,
their tanned bodies and masks daubed
and stained with wine lees, in imitation of the old followers of Dionysus.
Rumor has led them to hope and believe that* LAZARUS *may be the reincarnation of this deity.*

*The people in the crowd are hold-
ing themselves in restraint with difficulty, they stir and push about restlessly with an eager curiosity and im-*

*patience. All eyes are fixed off left. A
buzz of voices hums in the air.*

*Acting as police, a number of Ro-
man legionaires [masked like the soldiers of Scene Two] armed with
staves, keep back the crowd from the
line of the street that runs from left
to right, front. They resent this duty,
which has already kept them there a
long time, and are surly and quick-
tempered with the Greeks.*

*At front, pacing impatiently up and
down, is a young Roman noble of
twenty-one, clad richly, wearing beautifully wrought armor and helmet.
This is* GAIUS, *the heir of Tiberius
Cæsar, nicknamed* CALIGULA *by the
soldiers in whose encampments he was
born and where he spent his childhood. His body is bony and angular,
almost malformed, with wide, powerful shoulders and long arms and
hands, and short, skinny, hairy legs
like an ape's. He wears a half-mask of
crimson, dark with a purplish tinge,
that covers the upper part of his face
to below the nose. This mask accentu-
ates his bulging, prematurely wrinkled forehead, his hollow temples and
his bulbous, sensual nose. His large
troubled eyes, of a glazed greenish-
blue, glare out with a shifty feverish
suspicion at everyone. Below his
mask his own skin is of an ænemic
transparent pallor. Above it, his hair
is the curly blond hair of a child of
six or seven. His mouth also is childish, the red lips soft and feminine in
outline. Their expression is spoiled,
petulant and self-obsessed, weak but
domineering. In combination with the
rest of the face there is an appalling
morbid significance to his mouth. One
feels that its boyish cruelty, encouraged as a manly attribute in the coarse
brutality of camps, has long ago become naïvely insensitive to any human suffering but its own.*

Walking with CALIGULA *is* CNEIUS

CRASSUS, *a Roman general—a squat, muscular man of sixty, his mask that of a heavy battered face full of coarse humor.*

CHORUS OF GREEKS. [*Intoning solemnly.*]
Soon the God comes!
Redeemer and Savior!
Dionysus, Son of Man and a God!

GREEK CROWD. [*Echoing.*]
Soon the God comes
Redeemer and Savior!
Dionysus!

FIRST GREEK. They say an unearthly flame burns in this Lazarus!

SECOND GREEK. The sacred fire! He must be the Fire-born, the son of Zeus!

THIRD GREEK. Many who have seen him swear he is Dionysus, rearisen from Hades!

FOURTH GREEK. [*Importantly.*] I saw Lazarus at Antioch where the galley on which they were taking him to Rome had been thrice blown back by a storm. Fear of this warning omen is why they now march with him by land.

FIRST GREEK. Does he truly resemble a god?

FOURTH GREEK. [*Impressively.*] One look in his eyes while his laughter sings in your ears and you forget sorrow! You .dance! You laugh! It is as if a heavy weight you had been carrying all your life without knowing it suddenly were lifted. You are like a cloud, you can fly, your mind reels with laughter, you are drunk with joy! [*Solemnly.*] Take my word for it, he is indeed a god. Everywhere the people have acclaimed him. He heals the sick, he raises the dead, by laughter.

SEVENTH GREEK. But I have heard that when he has gone people cannot remember his laughter, that the dead are dead again and the sick die, and the sad grow more sorrowful.

FIFTH GREEK. Well, we shall soon see with our own eyes. But why should the God return in the body of a Jew?

SIXTH GREEK. What better disguise if he wishes to remain unknown? The fools of Romans will never suspect him!

THIRD GREEK. [*Laughing.*] Never! They are beginning to claim he is a Roman!

FIFTH GREEK. So much the better! He will be in their confidence!

FOURTH GREEK. He will lead us against Rome! He will laugh our tyrants into the sea! Ha! [*He turns toward the Romans and laughs sneeringly. This is taken up by the* CROWD *—unpleasant, resentful laughter. They push forward aggressively and almost sweep the soldiers from their feet.*]

CRASSUS. [*Angrily.*] Drive them back!

CALIGULA. [*Suddenly with a distorted warped smile.*] Order them to use their swords Cneius. Let the scum look at their dead and learn respect for us!

SOLDIERS. [*Shoving and whacking.*] Back! Step back! Back there! [*The crowd push back to their former line. There are muttered curses, groans, protests, which subside into the former hum of expectancy.*]

CALIGULA. [*With the same smile.*] The sword, my old hyena! Corpses are so educational!

CRASSUS. [*Surlily.*] I would like to, I promise you! When I see how they hate us—!

CALIGULA. [*Carelessly.*] Let them hate—so long as they fear us! We must keep death dangling [*he makes the gesture of doing so*] before their eyes! [*He gives a soft, cruel laugh.*] Will you not sacrifice in my honor?

What are a few Greeks? [*Queerly.*] I like to watch men die.

CRASSUS. I dare not, Caligula. Cæsar has forbidden bloodshed.

CALIGULA. Tiberius is a miser. He wants to hoard all of death for his own pleasure! [*He laughs again.*]

CRASSUS. [*With rough familiarity.*] I wager no one will make that complaint against you when you are Cæsar! [*He chuckles.*]

CALIGULA. [*With the sudden grandiose posturing of a bad actor unintentionally burlesquing grandeur.*] When I, Gaius Caligula, am Cæsar, I— [*Then superstitiously looking up at the sky with cringing foreboding.*] But it brings bad luck to anticipate fate. [*He takes off his helmet and spits in it—then with a grim smile.*] The heirs of a Cæsar take sick so mysteriously! Even with you who used to ride me on your knee, I do not eat nor drink until you have tasted first.

CRASSUS. [*Nodding approvingly.*] You are sensible. I suppose I, too, have my price—if they were only clever enough to discover it. [*He laughs hoarsely.*]

CALIGULA. [*Steps back from him with an uneasy shudder.*] You are honest, at least—too honest, Cneius! [*Grimly.*] If my father Germanicus had had you for his counselor, he might have escaped their poison. [*Then gloomily.*] I must fear everyone. The world is my enemy.

CRASSUS. Kill it then! [*He laughs again.*]

CHORUS. [*Stretching out their arms in the direction from which* LAZARUS *is expected—supplicatingly.*] Son of the Lightning! Deadly thy vengeance! Swift thy deliverance! Beholding thy Mother, Greece, our Mother,

Her beauty in bondage, Her pride in chains! Hasten, Redeemer!

CROWD. [*As before—echoing the chant.*] Hasten, Redeemer! Son of the Lightning! Deadly thy vengeance! Swift thy deliverance!

CALIGULA. [*Disdainfully.*] What clods! Mob is the same everywhere, eager to worship any new charlatan! They have already convinced themselves this Lazarus is a reincarnation of Dionysus! A Jew become a god! By the breasts of Venus that *is* a miracle! [*He laughs.*]

CRASSUS. [*Seriously.*] But he must be expert in magic. He was buried four days and came out unharmed. Maybe he is not a Jew. Some say his father was really a legionary of our garrison in Judea. And he teaches people to laugh at death. That smacks of Roman blood!

CALIGULA. [*Ironically.*] Better still! He tells them there is no death at all. Hence the multitude of fools who have acclaimed him everywhere since he left his own country—and why Tiberius has begun to fear his influence.

CRASSUS. [*Sententiously.*] Whom Cæsar fears—disappears!

CALIGULA. Yes, the dupes who follow Lazarus will be killed. But Tiberius believes this Lazarus may know a cure for death or for renewing youth, and the old lecher hopes he can worm the secret out of him—before he kills him. [*He laughs ironically, then disgustedly.*] That is why I must escort this Jew to Rome—as a special honor! [*With fierce, haughty resentment.*] I, the heir of Cæsar! [*Savagely.*] Oh, if I were Cæsar—!

CRASSUS. [*With a coarse, meaning smirk.*] Patience. Tiberius is old.

CALIGULA. [*Suddenly becoming terribly uneasy at some thought.*] Cneius! What if this Lazarus has really discovered a cure for old age and should reveal it to Tiberius! [*His lips tremble, his eyes are terrified, he shrinks against* CRASSUS *for protection—with boyish pleading.*] Oh, Cneius, what could I do then?

CRASSUS. [*Matter-of-factly.*] Kill him before Cæsar can talk to him.

CALIGULA. [*Almost in tears.*] But if he knows a charm against death how could he be slain, old fool?

CRASSUS. [*Gruffly.*] Bah! [*Then with grim humor.*] Death in bed I suspect, but when men are killed I know they stay dead! [*Disgustedly.*] A moment ago you were laughing at him! [*Scornfully.*] Do you fear him now?

CALIGULA. [*Rather shamefacedly pulls himself together—then broodingly.*] I fear everyone who lives. Even you. As you advised me. [*He turns away.*]

CRASSUS. [*Contemptuously.*] Well, maybe he can teach you to laugh at fear. You would welcome him then, eh, cry baby?

CALIGULA. [*With sudden passionate intensity but only half aloud as if to himself.*] I would love him, Cneius! As a father! As a god! [*He stands staring before him strangely. There is a new stir from the crowd who again push forward.*]

CRASSUS. [*Pointing off right.*] Look! I see a great crowd! Your Lazarus must be coming at last!

CHORUS. [*Chanting in a deep, rhythmic monotone like the rising and falling cadences of waves on a beach.*] He comes, the Redeemer and Savior!
Laughing along the mountains!
To give back our lost laughter
To raise from the dead our freedom
To free us from Rome!

CROWD. [*Echoing this chant.*]
Fire-born! Redeemer! Savior!
Raise from the dead our freedom!
Give back our lost laughter!
Free us from Rome!

[*They have been pushing forward, more and more fiercely and defiantly. The* ROMAN SOLDIERS *in spite of their efforts are pushed backward step by step.*]

SOLDIERS. [*Angrily.*] Back! Back!

[*The* SOLDIERS *work with a will, dealing out blows with their staves at everyone in reach. But now these blows seem only to infuriate the* CROWD *which steadily pushes them back into the street. At the same time the distant sound of exultant music, singing and laughter becomes steadily louder. Both* SOLDIERS *and* CROWD *are inspired to battle by these strains without their knowing it.* CALIGULA *is listening spell-bound, his mouth open, his body swaying and twitching. Even* CRASSUS *stares off at the oncomers, forgetful of the growing plight of his* SOLDIERS.]

CROWD. [*Led by their* CHORUS—*angrily.*]
Cowards! Pigs!
Strike! Hit!
Stones! Knives!
Stab! Kill!
Death to the Romans!
Death!

A SOLDIER. [*Alarmed, calls to* CRASSUS.] General! Let us use our swords!

SOLDIERS. [*Enraged—eagerly.*] Yes! Swords!

CROWD. Death!

CRASSUS. [*Turning—uneasy but afraid to give any drastic order.*] Bah! Staves are enough. Crack their skulls!

CROWD. [*Led by the* CHORUS—*defiantly.*]

Death to Crassus!
Drunkard! Coward!
Death to him!

[*They continue to push forward, hooting and jeering.*]

CRASSUS. [*Exploding for a second.*] By the gods—! [*To the* SOLDIERS.] Draw your swords!
[*The troops do so eagerly. The* CROWD *sag back momentarily with exclamations of fear.*]

CALIGULA. [*Listening as in a trance to the music and what is going on behind him—in a queer whisper.*] Kill, Cneius! Let me dance! Let me sing! [*The music and crashing of cymbals and the ferment of passions around him cause him to lose all control over himself. He gives a crazy leap in the air and begins to dance grotesquely and chant in a thick voice.*] He is coming! Death, the Deliverer! Kill, soldiers! I command you! I, Caligula! I will be Cæsar! Death!

CROWD. [*Led by the* CHORUS—*savage now.*]
Beast! Cur!
Death to Caligula!

[*They crowd forward.*]

CALIGULA. [*Drawing his sword and flourishingly it drunkenly—his eyes glazed.*] Death!

CRASSUS. [*Drawing his own sword in a frenzy.*] Strike! Death!

[*His* SOLDIERS *raise their swords. The* CROWD *have raised whatever weapons they have found—knives, clubs, daggers, stones, bare fists.*]

CHORUS. [*Chanting fiercely.*]
Death!

ALL. [ROMANS *and* GREEKS *alike as one great voice.*]
Death!

[*The chorused word beats down all sound into a stricken silence. The wild joyous music ceases. The Romans*

and Greeks seem to lean back from one another and collect strength to leap forward. At this moment the voice of* LAZARUS *comes ringing through the air like a command from the sky.*]

LAZARUS. There is no death!
[*The* SOLDIERS *and* GREEKS *remain frozen in their attitudes of murderous hate. Following his words the laughter of* LAZARUS *is heard, exultant and gaily mocking, filling them with the sheepish shame of children caught in mischief. Their hands hang, their arms sink to their sides. The music starts once more with a triumphant clash of cymbals,* LAZARUS' *laughter is echoed from the throats of the multitude of his* FOLLOWERS *who now come dancing into the square, preceded by a band of masked musicians and by their* CHORUS.

[*This* CHORUS *wears, in double size, the laughing mask of* LAZARUS' FOLLOWERS *in the same Period and Type as in the preceding scene, except that here the mask of each member of the* CHORUS *has a different racial basis— Egyptian, Syrian, Cappadocian, Lydian, Phrygian, Cilician, Parthian. The* FOLLOWERS *are costumed and masked as in the preceding scene, seven Types in seven Periods, except that, as in the* CHORUS, *racially there are many nations represented. All have wreaths of ivy in their hair and flowers in their hands which they scatter about. They whirl in between the* SOLDIERS *and* CROWD, *forcing them back from each other, teasing them, sifting into the* CROWD, *their* CHORUS *in a half circle, confronting the* CHORUS OF GREEKS.]

CHORUS OF FOLLOWERS.
Laugh! Laugh!
There is no death!
There is only life!

There is only laughter!

FOLLOWERS. [Echoing.]
Laugh! Laugh!
There is no death!

[CALIGULA and CRASSUS are swept to one side, left. Then the cries and laughter of all become mingled into one exclamation.]

ALL. Lazarus! Lazarus!

[The squad of ROMAN SOLDIERS led by the CENTURION, who had taken LAZARUS prisoner, march in with dancers' steps, like a proud guard of honor now, laughing, pulling a chariot in which LAZARUS stands dressed in a tunic of white and gold, his bronzed face and limbs radiant in the halo of his own glowing light.]

[LAZARUS now looks less than thirty-five. His countenance now might well be that of the positive masculine Dionysus, closest to the soil of the Grecian Gods, a Son of Man, born of a mortal. Not the coarse, drunken Dionysus, nor the effeminate God, but Dionysus in his middle period, more comprehensive in his symbolism, the soul of the recurring seasons, of living and dying as processes in eternal growth, of the wine of life stirring forever in the sap and blood and loam of things. MIRIAM is beside him, dressed in black, smiling the same sad tender smile, holding LAZARUS' arm as if for protection and in protection. She appears older, a woman over forty-five.]

CHORUS OF GREEKS. [Rushing to LAZARUS' car.]
Hail, Dionysus!
Iacchus!
Lazarus!
Hail!

[They surround him, throw over his shoulders and head the finely dressed hide of a bull with great gilded horns,

force into his right hand the mystic rod of Dionysus with a pine cone on top, then prostrate themselves.]
Hail, Savior!
Redeemer!
Conqueror of Death!

ALL. [In a repeated chorus which finally inludes even the ROMAN SOLDIERS, raising their arms to him.]
Hail, Lazarus!
Redeemer!
Hail!

[They are silent. LAZARUS looks at them, seeming to see each and all at the same time, and his laughter, as if in answer to their greetings, is heard rising from his lips like a song.]

CRASSUS. [Awed.] Look! He is more than man!

CALIGULA. [Trembling, in a queer agitation.] I dare not look!

CRASSUS. Do you hear his laughter?

CALIGULA. [Chokingly—puts his hands over his ears.] I will not hear!

CRASSUS. But you must welcome him in Cæsar's name!

CALIGULA. [His teeth chattering.] I must kill him!

LAZARUS. [Looking directly at him—gaily mocking.] Death is dead, Caligula! [He begins to laugh again softly.]

CALIGULA. [With an hysterical cry of defiant terror.] You lie! [Sword in hand he whirls to confront LAZARUS, but at the first sight of his face he stops in his tracks, trembling, held fascinated by LAZARUS' eyes, mumbling with a last pitiful remainder of defiance.] But—you lie—whatever you are! I say there must be death! [The sword has fallen to his side. He stares open-mouthed at LAZARUS. There is something of a shy, wondering child about his attitude now. LAZARUS looks at him, laughing with gentle understanding. CALIGULA suddenly drops his sword and covering his face with *his hands weeps like a boy who has been hurt.*] You have murdered my only friend, Lazarus! Death would have been my slave when I am Cæsar. He would have been my jester and made me laugh at fear! [*He weeps bitterly.*]

LAZARUS. [*Gaily.*] Be your own jester instead, O Caligula! Laugh at yourself, O Cæsar-to-be! [*He laughs. The* CROWD *now all join in with him.*]

[CALIGULA *suddenly uncovers his face, grins his warped grin, gives a harsh cackle which cracks through the other laughter with a splitting discord, cuts a hopping caper like some grotesque cripple which takes him to the side of* LAZARUS' *chariot where he squats on his hams and, stretching out his hand, fingers* LAZARUS' *robe inquisitively and stares up into his face in the attitude of a chained monkey.*]

CALIGULA. [*With a childish, mischievous curiosity.*] Then if there is no death, O Teacher, tell me why I love to kill?

LAZARUS. Because you fear to die! [*Then gaily mocking.*] But what do you matter, O Deathly-Important One? Put yourself that question—as a jester! [*Exultantly.*] Are you a speck of dust danced in the wind? Then laugh, dancing! Laugh yes to your insignificance! Thereby will be born your new greatness! As Man, Petty Tyrant of Earth, you are a bubble pricked by death into a void and a mocking silence! But as dust, you are eternal change, and everlasting growth, and a high note of laughter soaring through chaos from the deep heart of God! Be proud, O Dust! Then you may love the stars as equals! [*Then mockingly again.*] And then perhaps you may be brave enough to love even your fellow men without fear of their vengeance!

CALIGULA. [*Dully.*] I cannot understand. I hate men. I am afraid of their poison and their swords and the cringing envy in their eyes that only yields to fear!

LAZARUS. [*Gaily mocking.*] Tragic is the plight of the tragedian whose only audience is himself! Life is for each man a solitary cell whose walls are mirrors. Terrified is Caligula by the faces he makes! But I tell ·you to laugh in the mirror, that seeing your life gay, you may begin to live as a guest, and not as a condemned one! [*Raising his hands for silence—with a playful smile.*] Listen! In the dark peace of the grave the man call Lazarus rested. He was still weak, as one who recovers from a long illness—for, living, he had believed his life a sad one! [*He laughs softly, and softly they all echo his laughter.*] He lay dreaming to the croon of silence, feeling as the flow of blood in his own veins the past reënter the heart of God to be renewed by faith into the future. He thought: "Men call this death"—for he had been dead only a little while and he still remembered. Then, of a sudden, a strange gay laughter trembled from his heart as though his life, so long repressed in him by fear, had found at last its voice and a song for singing. "Men call this death," it sang. "Men call life death and fear it. They hide from it in horror. Their lives are spent in hiding. Their fear becomes their living. They worship life as death!"

CHORUS OF FOLLOWERS. [*In a chanting echo.*]
Men call life death and fear it.
They hide from it in horror.
Their lives are spent in hiding.
Their fear becomes their living.
They worship life as death!

LAZARUS. And here the song of Lazarus' life grew pitiful. "Men must learn to live," it mourned. "Before their fear invented death they knew, but now they have forgotten. They must be taught to laugh again!" And Lazarus answered "Yes!" [*He now addresses the crowd—especially* CALIGULA, *directly, laughingly.*] Thus sang his life to Lazarus while he lay dead! Man must learn to live by laughter! [*He laughs.*]

CHORUS OF FOLLOWERS.
Laugh! Laugh!
There is only life!
There is only laughter!
Fear is no more!
Death is dead!

CHORUS OF GREEKS.
Laugh! Laugh!
Hail, Dionysus!
Fear is no more!
Thou hast conquered death!

ALL. [*Laughing—in a great laughing chorus.*]
Laugh! Laugh!
Fear is no more!
Death is dead!

LAZARUS. [*As to a crowd of children—laughingly.*] Out with you! Out into the woods! Upon the hills! Cities are prisons wherein man locks himself from life. Out with you under the sky! Are the stars too pure for your sick passions? Is the warm earth smelling of night too desirous of love for your pale introspective lusts? Out! Let laughter be your new clean lust and sanity! So far man has only learned to snicker meanly at his neighbor! Let a laughing away of self be your new right to live forever! Cry in your pride, "I am Laughter, which is Life, which is the Child of God!" [*He laughs and again his voice leads and dominates the rhythmic chorus of theirs. The music and dancing begin again.*]

THE TWO CHORUSES. [*Chanting in unison.*]
Laugh! Laugh!
There is only God!
We are His Laughter!

ALL. [*Echoing.*]
There is only God!
We are His Laughter!
Laugh! Laugh!

[*They take hold of his chariot traces, and as he had come, in the midst of a happy multitude, now augmented by all the* GREEKS, *and the* ROMAN SOLDIERS *who had awaited him, dancing, playing, singing, laughing, he is escorted off. The noise of their passing recedes.* CALIGULA *and* CRASSUS *are left in the empty square, the former squatting on his hams, monkey-wise, and brooding somberly.*]

CRASSUS. [*Is swaying and staggering, like a man in a drunken stupor, in a bewildered, stubborn struggle to control himself. He stammers after the* SOLDIERS.] Ha-ha-ha— Halt! Halt, I say! No use—they are gone—mutiny— Halt! [*He continues to stumble toward left.*] Ha-ha— Stop it, curse you! Am I laughing? Where am I going? After Lazarus? Thirty years of discipline and I— Halt, traitor! Remember Cæsar! Remember Rome! Halt, traitor! [*He faints with the violence of his struggle and falls in a limp heap.*]

CALIGULA. [*Startled by his fall, terrified, hops to his feet and snatches up his sword defensively, glancing over his shoulder and whirling around as if he expected someone to stab him in the back. Then, forcing a twisted grin of self-contempt—harshly.*] Coward! What do I fear—if there is no death? [*As if he had to cut something, he snatches up a handful of flowers—desperately.*] You must laugh, Caligula! [*He starts to lop off the flowers from their stems with a savage intentness.*]

Laugh! Laugh! Laugh! [*Finally, impatiently, he cuts off all the remaining with one stroke.*] Laugh! [*He grinds the petals under his feet and breaks out into a terrible hysterical giggle.*] Ha-ha—

CURTAIN

SCENE 2

SCENE: *A midnight, months later. Immediately inside the walls of Rome. In the foreground is the portico of a temple between whose massive columns one looks across a street on a lower level to the high wall of Rome at the extreme rear. In the center of the wall is a great metal gate. The night is thick and oppressive. In the sky overhead lightning flashes and thunder rumbles and crashes but there is no rain.*

Within the portico on rows of chairs placed on a series of wide steps which are on each side, members of the Senate are seated in their white robes. High hanging lamps cast a wan light over their faces. They are all masked in the Roman mask, refined in them by nobility of blood but at the same time with strength degenerated, corrupted by tyranny and debauchery to an exhausted cynicism. The three periods of Middle Age, Maturity and Old Age are represented in the types of the Self-Tortured, Introspective; Proud, Self-Reliant; the Servile, Hypocritical; the Cruel, Revengeful; and the Resigned, Sorrowful. The SENATORS are divided into two groups on each side, thirty in each. Seated in the middle of the lower of the three high broad stairs that lead to the level from which the columns rise is the CHORUS OF SENATORS, seven in number, facing front, in double-sized masks of the Servile, Hypocritical type of Old Age.

LAZARUS, *in his robe of white and gold, the aura of light surrounding his body seeming to glow more brightly than ever, stands in the rear at the edge of the portico, center, gazing upward into the pall of sky beyond the wall. His figure appears in its immobility to be the statue of the god of the temple. Near him, but to the rear and to the left of him, facing right,* MIRIAM *is kneeling in her black robes, swaying backward and forward, praying silently with moving lips like a nun who asks mercy for the sins of the world. She has grown much older, her hair is gray, her shoulders are bowed.*

On the other side, placed similarly in relation to LAZARUS *and facing* MIRIAM, CALIGULA *is squatting on his hams on a sort of throne-chair of ivory and gold. He is dressed with foppish richness in extreme bright colors, a victory wreath around his head. He stares blinkingly and inquisitively at* LAZARUS, *then at* MIRIAM. *He is half-drunk. A large figured goblet of gold is in his hand. A slave with an amphora of wine crouches on the steps by his chair. The slave wears a black negroid mask.*

At the opening of the scene there is heard the steady tramp of departing troops, whose masks, helmets and armored shoulders can be seen as they pass through the street before LAZARUS *to the gate beyond. Finally with a metallic clash the gate is shut behind them and there is a heavy and oppressive silence in which only the murmured prayers of* MIRIAM *are heard.*

CHORUS OF THE SENATE. [*Intones wearily, as if under a boring compulsion.*]
The Roman Senate
Is the Roman Senate
The Mighty Voice
Of the Roman People
As long as Rome is Rome.

CALIGULA. [*As if he hadn't heard—sings hoarsely an old camp song of the*

Punic Wars, pounding with his goblet.]
A bold legionary am I!
March, oh march on!
A Roman eagle was my daddy,
My mother was a drunken drabby
Oh, march on to the wars!

Since lived that lady Leda
March, oh march on!
Women have loved high-fliers
And we are eagles of Rome!
Oh march on to the wars!

Comrades, march to the wars!
There's pretty girls in Carthage
And wine to swill in Carthage,
So we must capture Carthage
And fight for Mother Rome!

[*Holds out his goblet to be refilled. There is silence again. He stares at* LAZARUS *with a somber intentness. He says thickly.*] The legions have gone, Lazarus. [LAZARUS *gives no evidence of having heard him.* CALIGULA *gulps at his wine. The* SENATORS *begin to talk to each other in low voices.*]

FIRST SENATOR. How does that Jew make that light come from him, I wonder? It is a well-contrived bit of magic.

SECOND SENATOR. What are we waiting for? A messenger came to me with Cæsar's command that the Senate meet here at midnight.

THIRD SENATOR. [*Bored.*] Some new whim of Tiberius, naturally— [*With a meaning titter*]—or rather I should say, unnaturally!

FOURTH SENATOR. Perhaps Cæsar has decided to abolish our august body by a massacre in mass!

THIRD SENATOR. [*Yawning.*] There was a feast at Cinna's last night that lasted until this evening. I could welcome my own murder as an excuse for sleeping!

FIFTH SENATOR. [*Pompously.*] Tiberius would not dare harm the Senate. He may mistreat individual Senators, but the Roman Senate is the Roman Senate!

CHORUS OF THE SENATE. [*As before —wearily as if under a boring compulsion—intones.*]
While Rome is Rome
The Senate is the Senate
The Mighty Voice of the Roman People.

FIRST SENATOR. [*With the ghost of a laugh—wearily.*] The Senate is an empty name—a pack of degenerate cowards with no trace of their ancient nobility or courage remaining—that and no more!

THIRD SENATOR. [*Flippantly.*] You are too severe with yourself, Lucius! [*A titter of laughter.*]

FIRST SENATOR. [*Wearily.*] A degenerate coward. I am, I confess it. So are you too, Sulpicius—a hundred fold!—whether you admit it or not. [SULPICIUS *laughs weakly without taking offense.*]

SIXTH SENATOR. [*After a pause—sighing.*] In truth, the Senate is not what it used to be. I can remember—

FIRST SENATOR. Let us forget, if we can! [*Then impatiently.*] What are we doing here?

SECOND SENATOR. I imagine it has something to do with the followers of this Lazarus encamped outside the wall. Probably the legions are to butcher them in their sleep.

SEVENTH SENATOR. And what part do we play—official witnesses? But how can we witness at night and through a wall? [*With bored resignation.*] Ah well, the moods of Tiberius are strange, to say the least. But Cæsar is Cæsar.

CHORUS. [*Again with bored weariness as before.*]
Hail!
Cæsar is Cæsar
The August One

Prince of the Senate
Tribune over Tribunes
Consul of Consuls
Supreme Pontiff
Emperor of Rome
God among Gods
Hail!

FIRST SENATOR. [*After a pause of silence—dryly.*] Cæsar is a beast—and a madman!

FIFTH SENATOR. [*Pompously.*] Respect, sir! More respect for Cæsar!

THIRD SENATOR. [*Mockingly.*] Or caution, Lucius. One of us might repeat your opinion to him.

FIRST SENATOR. You would if it would pay you. But all my money is squandered. My death is worthless to Tiberius. He would not reward you. Moreover, you would not be revenged on me, for I long for death.

THIRD SENATOR. [*Dryly.*] Your stomach must be out of order.

FIRST SENATOR. The times are out of order. But let us change the subject. Is it true Tiberius has fled to Capri?

FOURTH SENATOR. Yes. He was terrified by the multitude of laughing idiots who appeared today with that charlatan. [*He points to* LAZARUS.]

SECOND SENATOR. There are thousands of them outside the wall. Cæsar refused to let them enter the city. The story is, this Lazarus was dead four days and then restored himself to life by magic.

FIRST SENATOR. I have a mind to question him. [*Calls as to a slave.*] You, there! Jew, turn round! In the name of the Senate! [LAZARUS *seems not to hear him.* LUCIUS *remarks with a weary smile.*] So much for our authority!

SIXTH SENATOR. [*With injured dignity.*] What insolence! [*In a rage.*] Ho, barbarian cur, turn round! The Senate commands you! [LAZARUS *does not seem to hear, but* CALIGULA *turns on them fiercely.*]

CALIGULA. Silence! Leave him alone! [*With insulting scorn.*] I, Caligula, command you! [*The* SENATORS *seem to shrink back from him in fear, all but* LUCIUS, *who answers with a mocking servility.*]

FIRST SENATOR. At least, grant us the boon to see this corpse's face, O Gracious Gaius!

CALIGULA. [*Fixing his cruel, burning eyes on him—softly.*] I heard you wish for death, Lucius. When I am Cæsar you shall scream and pray for it!

FIRST SENATOR. [*Dryly and haughtily.*] You were bred in camp, Gaius. You should have learned more courage there along with your coarseness. But accept my gratitude for your warning. I shall take care to die before you become Cæsar—and life becomes too idiotic!

CALIGULA. [*His grin becoming ferocious with cruelty.*] No. You are too weak to kill yourself. Look at me, Lucius! I am imagining what I shall have done to you! [*The* SENATORS *are now trembling. Even* LUCIUS *cannot repress a shudder of horror at the face glaring at him. Suddenly* CALIGULA *throws the cup from him and springs to his feet.*] What good is wine if it cannot kill thought? Lazarus! It is time. I must give the signal! The legions are waiting. It is Cæsar's command that they spare none of your followers. [*He has walked toward* LAZARUS.]

MIRIAM. [*Stretches out her hands to* CALIGULA *imploringly.*] Mercy! Spare them who are so full of life and joy!

CALIGULA. [*Harshly.*] For their joy I will revenge myself upon them! Mercy? If there is no death, then death is a mercy! Ask that man! [*He points accusingly to* LAZARUS.] And why should you plead for them, Jewess? There are few Jews among them. They are mostly those whom your people call idolaters and would gladly see murdered.

MIRIAM. [*With deep grief.*] I am a mother of dead children. I plead for the mothers of those about to die.

CALIGULA. [*Contemptuously.*] Pah! [*He turns from her and puts his hand on* LAZARUS' *shoulder.*] Lazarus! Do you hear? I must signal to the legions!

LAZARUS. [*Turns. He has grown more youthful. He seems no more than thirty. His face is exalted and calm and beautiful. His eyes shine with an unearthly glory. The* SENATORS *lean forward in their seats, fascinated by his face. A low murmur of admiration comes from them.* LAZARUS *speaks commandingly.*] Wait! I will awaken my beloved ones that their passing may be a symbol to the world that there is no death! [*He turns, throwing back his head and stretching up his arms, and begins to laugh low and tenderly, like caressing music at first but gradually gaining in volume, becoming more and more intense and insistent, finally ending up on a triumphant, blood-stirring call to that ultimate attainment in which all prepossession with self is lost in an ecstatic affirmation of Life. The voices of his* FOLLOWERS *from beyond the wall, at first one by one, then several at a time, then multitudes, join in his laughter. Even the* SENATORS *are drawn into it. Now every one of these is standing up, stretching out his arms toward* LAZARUS, *laughing harshly and discordantly and awkwardly in his attempt to laugh. Terrific flashes of lightning and crashes of thunder seem a responsive accompaniment from the heavens to this laughter of thousands which throbs in beating waves of sound in the air. Mingled with the laughing from beyond the* wall comes the sound of singing and the music of flutes and cymbals. MIRIAM *has crawled on her knees to the edge of the portico where her black figure of grief is outlined below and to the left of* LAZARUS, *her arms raised outward like the arms of a cross.*]

FOLLOWERS OF LAZARUS. [*In a great chanting singing chorus.*]
Laugh! Laugh!
There is only God!
Life is His Laughter!
We are His Laughter!
Fear is no more!
Death is dead!

CHORUS OF SENATORS. [*Taking it up in a tone between chanting and their old solemn intoning.*]
Laugh! Laugh!
Fear is no more!
Death is dead!

ALL. [*The multitude beyond the wall, all the* SENATORS, *everyone except the never-laughing* MIRIAM *and* CALIGULA *and the* MEN OF THE LEGIONS.]
Laugh! Laugh!
Death is dead!

CALIGULA. [*In a queer state of mingled exaltation and fear—hopping restlessly about from foot to foot—shouting.*] The signal! Shall I give the signal to kill, Lazarus?

MEN OF THE LEGIONS. [*Following a brazen trumpet call, are suddenly heard from beyond the wall beginning to laugh their hoarse, bass laughter, a deeper note than all the others.*]
Laugh! Laugh!

CALIGULA. [*Listening—with dismay.*] I hear the legions, Lazarus! They are laughing with them! [*He cries with a strange pitifulness and beseeching.*] You are playing me false, Lazarus! You are trying to evade

death! You are trying to spare your
people! You are small and weak like
other men when the test comes! You
give way to pity! Your great laughter
becomes pitiful! [*Working himself
into a rage.*] You are a traitor, Lazarus!
You betray Cæsar! Have you forgotten I will be Cæsar? You betray me,
Lazarus! [*He rushes to the edge and,*
making a megaphone of his hands,
bellows.] You on the wall! Sentry! It
is I, Caligula! Kill! [*The brazen trum-*
pets of the LEGIONS *sound from be-*
yond the wall. He springs near LAZA-
RUS *again, in a fiendish ecstasy, danc-*
ing a hopping grotesque sword dance
behind him, chanting as he does so.]
Kill! Kill laughter! Kill those who
deny Cæsar! I will be Cæsar! Kill
those who deny Death! I will be
Death! My face will be bright with
blood! My laughing face, Lazarus!
Laughing because men fear me! My
face of victorious Fear! Look at me! I
am laughing, Lazarus! *My* laughter!
Laughter of Gods and Cæsars! Ha-ha-
ha-ha! [*He laughs, his laughter fa-*
natically cruel and savage, forced from
his lips with a desperate, destroying
abandon. For a moment, above all the
chorus of other sounds, his voice fights
to overcome that of LAZARUS, *whose*
laughter seems now to have attained
the most exultant heights of spiritual
affirmation. Then CALIGULA'S *breaks*
into a cry of fear and a sob, and, cast-
ing his sword aside, he hides his face
in his hands and cries beseechingly.]
Forgive me! I love you, Lazarus! Forgive me! [*At this second the blaring*
trumpets of the LEGIONS *are heard ap-*
proaching and their great bass chorus
of marching tramping laughter.]

MEN OF THE LEGIONS. [*Chanting.*]
Laugh! Laugh! Laugh!
Fear, no more!
Death, no more!
Death is dead!

[*There is now no sound of the sing-*
ing or the laughter or music of LAZA-
RUS' FOLLOWERS. MIRIAM *rocks to*
and fro and raises a low wail of la-
mentation. The SENATORS *cheer and*
shout as at a triumph.]

CHORUS OF SENATORS. [*Saluting*
LAZARUS.]
Hail, Victor!
Hail, Divine One!
Thou hast slain fear!
Thou hast slain death!
Hail! Triumph!

SENATORS.
Hail! Hail!
Slayer of Fear!
Slayer of Death!

[*The gate in the wall is clanged open.*
The returning LEGIONS *burst through*
and gather in a dense mob in the
street below LAZARUS, *who looks down*
upon them, silent but smiling gently
now. They stare at him with admira-
tion. Only a sea of their masks can be
seen, their eyes shinging exultantly.
CRASSUS, *their general, ascends the*
steps until he stands a little below
LAZARUS. *Their* CHORUS OF LEGION-
ARIES *in double-sized masks climb to*
the step below CRASSUS, *forming be-*
hind him. They are in the Period of
Manhood, of the Simple, Ignorant
Type. No weapons can be seen—only
their masks and helmets and armor
gleaming in the lightning flashes and
in the flickering light of torches. Their
laughter seems to shake the walls and
make the pillars of the temple dance.]

CHORUS OF THE LEGIONS.
Fear, no more!
Death, no more!
Death is dead!

LEGIONARIES. [*Echoing.*]
Laugh! Laugh! Laugh!
Death is dead!

CRASSUS. [*Raising his hand.*] Silence! [*They obey. He turns to* LAZARUS *and bows his head, falling on one knee, raising his right arm.*] Hail!

LEGIONARIES. [*As one man—raising their arms.*] Hail!

CALIGULA. [*Suddenly pushes forward impudently and strikes a grandiose attitude.*] I am here, my brave ones! [*There is a roar of mocking laughter from the* LEGIONARIES.]

CRASSUS. [*Not unkindly.*] Not you, Little Killer! We hail the Great Laugher!

CALIGULA. [*Harshly.*] Have you killed all his followers?

CRASSUS. No. They died. They did not wait for our attack. They charged upon us, laughing! They tore our swords away from us, laughing, and we laughed with them! They stabbed themselves, dancing as though it were a festival! They died, laughing, in one another's arms! We laughed, too, with joy because it seemed it was not they who died but death itself they killed! [*He stops uncertainly, bowing to* LAZARUS, *awkwardly.*] I do not understand this. I am a soldier. But there is a god in it somewhere! For I know they were drunk, and so were we, with a happiness no mortal ever felt on earth before! And death was dead! [*In a sudden outburst as if he were drunk with excitement, he takes off his helmet and waves it.*] Hail, Deliverer! Death is dead! We left our swords with them! What virtue in killing when there is no death? Your foe laughs. The joke is on you. What a fool's game, eh? One can only laugh! Now we want peace to laugh in—to laugh at war! Let Cæsars fight—that is all they are good for—and not much good for that!

CALIGULA. [*Frenziedly.*] Silence, impious traitor!

CRASSUS. [*Smiling drunkenly.*] Shut up, yourself, camp-brat! Though you were Cæsar this minute I would laugh at you! Your death is dead! We will make Lazarus Cæsar! What say you? [*He appeals to the* SOLDIERS.]

CALIGULA. No!

CHORUS OF THE LEGIONS. [*With laughing intoxication.*] Hail, Lazarus Cæsar! Hail!

LEGIONARIES. Lazarus Cæsar, hail!

CRASSUS. [*Appealing to* SENATE.] And you, Senators!

CHORUS OF SENATORS. [*With the same joyous intoxication as the* SOLDIERS.] Hail, Lazarus Cæsar! Hail!

SENATORS. Lazarus Cæsar, hail!

CALIGULA. [*Piteously.*] No, Lazarus! Say no for my sake!

LAZARUS. [*With gay mockery.*] What is—Cæsar? [*He begins to laugh with mockery. All except* CALIGULA *and* MIRIAM *join in this laughter.*]

CRASSUS. Ha-ha! What is Cæsar? You are right! You deserve better from us. A god? How is that? We will build you a temple, Lazarus, and make you a god!

LAZARUS. [*Laughingly.*] When men make gods, there is no God! [*He laughs. They all laugh.*]

CRASSUS. [*With puzzled good-nature.*] I do not understand. But there is a god in it somewhere—a god of peace—a god of happiness! Perhaps you are already he, eh? Are you? Well, never mind now, remember our offer. Give us your answer tomorrow. Good night to you!

LAZARUS. [*As the* SOLDIERS *start to march away behind* CRASSUS, *and the* SENATORS *turn to retire, he stops them all for a moment with a gesture—with a deep earnestness.*] Wait! When you awake tomorrow, try to remember! Remember that death is dead! Remember to laugh!

ALL. [*As if taking an oath with one voice.*] We will remember, Lazarus!

CRASSUS. [*Making a sign to the regimental musicians jovially.*] And we will laugh! Play there! [*The bands crash out. The* LEGIONS *tramp away.*]

CHORUS OF THE LEGIONS. [*Chanting to the music.*]
Laugh! Laugh! Laugh!
Cæsar, no more!
War, no more!
Wounds, no more!
Death is dead!
Dead! Dead! Dead!

LEGIONARIES.
Laugh! Laugh! Laugh!
Death is dead!
Dead! Dead! Dead!

CHORUS OF SENATORS. [*Following them.*]
Cæsar, no more!
Fear, no more!
Death, no more!
Laugh! Laugh! Laugh!

SENATE. [*Elated, excited as a crowd of schoolboys going on a vacation. Marching after them.*]
Laugh! Laugh! Laugh!
Death is dead!

[LAZARUS, MIRIAM *and* CALIGULA *remain.*]

LAZARUS [*With a great yearning.*] If men would remember! If they could! [*He stares after them compassionately.*]

CALIGULA. [*Crouching beside* LAZARUS. *Plucks at his robe humbly.*] You will not laugh at Cæsar, Lazarus, will you—when I am Cæsar? You will not laugh at gods when they make me a god? [LAZARUS *does not answer.* CALIGULA *forces a cruel vindictive smile.*] I swear you shall not laugh at death when I am Death! Ha-ha— [*He starts to laugh harshly—then suddenly, terrified, slinks away and sidles off at right.*]

MIRIAM. [*From where she kneels bowed with grief—brokenly.*] Those who have just died were like your children, Lazarus. They believed in you and loved you.

LAZARUS. And I loved them!

MIRIAM. Then how could you laugh when they were dying?

LAZARUS. [*Exultingly.*] Did they not laugh? That was their victory and glory! [*With more and more of a passionate, proud exultation.*] Eye to eye with the Fear of Death, did they not laugh with scorn? "Death to old Death," they laughed! "Once as squirming specks we crept from the tides of the sea. Now we return to the sea! Once as quivering flecks of rhythm we beat down from the sun. Now we reënter the sun! Cast aside is our pitiable pretense, our immortal egohood, the holy lantern behind which cringed our Fear of the Dark! Flung off is that impudent insult of life's nobility which gibbers: 'I, this Jew, this Roman, this noble or this slave, must survive in my pettiness forever!' Away with such cowardice of spirit! We will to die! We will to change! Laughing we lived with our gift, now with laughter give we back that gift to become again the Essence of the Giver! Dying we laugh with the Infinite. We are the Giver and the Gift! Laughing, we will our own annihilation! Laughing, we give our lives for Life's sake!" [*He laughs up to heaven ecstatically.*] This must Man will as his end and his new beginning! He must conceive and desire his own passing as a mood of eternal laughter and cry with pride, "Take back, O God, and accept in turn a gift from me, my grateful blessing for Your gift—and see, O God, now I am laughing with You! I am Your laughter—and You are mine!" [*He laughs again, his laughter dying lingeringly and tenderly on his lips like a strain of music receding into the silence over still waters.*]

MIRIAM. [*With a sigh—meekly.*] I

cannot understand, Lazarus. [*Sadly.*] They were like your children—and they have died. Must you not mourn for them?

LAZARUS. [*Gently.*] Mourn? When they laughed?

MIRIAM. [*Sadly.*] They are gone from us. And their mothers weep.

LAZARUS. [*Puts his arm around her and raises her to her feet—tenderly.*] But God, their Father, laughs! [*He kisses her on the forehead.*]

CURTAIN

ACT III

SCENE 1

SCENE: *Some days later—exterior of* TIBERIUS' *villa-palace at Capri. It is about two in the morning of a clear black night. In the rear, the walls of the villa, which is built entirely of marble on the brow of a cliff, loom up with a startling clarity against the sky. The rear foreground is a marble terrace at the middle of which is a triumphal arch. On each side, leading up to it, are massive marble columns standing like the mummies of legionaires at attention. In the exact center of the arch itself a cross is set up on which a full grown male lion has been crucified. A lamp reflecting downward has been fixed at the top of the cross to light up an inscription placed over the lion's head. Below the steps to the terrace, in a line facing front, on each side of the cross, is the* CHORUS OF THE GUARD *in their double masks and gorgeous uniforms and armor. Their masks are the same as the* LEGIONARY CHORUS *of the previous scene.*

*The windows of the palace glow crimson-purple with the reflection of many shaded lamps. The sound of music in a strained theme of that joyless abandon which is vice is heard above a confused drunken clamor of voices, punctuated by the high, stac-*cato *laughter of women and youths. A squad of the* GUARD *in the same uniforms as the* CHORUS, *masked as all the* ROMAN SOLDIERS *previously, enter from the left, front, climbing up from the beach below. They are commanded by a Centurion,* FLAVIUS. *His mask is that of a typical young patrician officer. They are followed by* LAZARUS *and* MIRIAM. CALIGULA *walks behind, his drawn sword in his hand. He is in a state of queer conflicting emotion, seeming to be filled with a nervous dread and terror of everything about him, while at the same time perversely excited and elated by his own morbid tension.* LAZARUS, *looking no more than twenty-five, haloed in his own mystic light, walks in a deep, detached serenity.*

MIRIAM, *in black, her hair almost white now, her figure bowed and feeble, seems more than ever a figure of a sad, resigned mother of the dead. The soldiers form in line with the columns.*

FLAVIUS. [*Saluting* CALIGULA—*with an awed glance at* LAZARUS.] I will announce your coming—[*as if in spite of himself he bows awkwardly to* LAZARUS] and that of this man. Cæsar was not expecting you so soon, I think.

CALIGULA. [*Forcing a light tone.*] Lazarus laughed and the galley slaves forgot their fetters and made their oars fly as if they were bound for the Blessed Isles of Liberty! [*Then with an ironic smile.*] But you need not tell Tiberius that, good Flavius. Say it was due to my extreme zeal.

FLAVIUS. [*Smiles with respectful understanding.* CALIGULA *nods in dismissal.* FLAVIUS *turns to go—apologetically.*] You may have to wait. I dare not speak before he questions me. [FLAVIUS *salutes and hastens to the villa, walking under an arm of the cross unconcernedly without an up-*

ward glance. *As they follow him with their eyes* CALIGULA *and* MIRIAM *see the lion for the first time. He steps back with a startled exclamation. She gives a cry of horror and covers her eyes with her hands to shut out the sight.*]

LAZARUS. [*Immediately puts his arms around her protectingly.*] What is it, Beloved? [*She hides her face on his breast, pointing toward the lion with a trembling hand.*]

CALIGULA. [*Pointing—curiously now, but with entire callousness.*] This lion they have crucified. Are you frightened, Jewess? [*With a cruel laugh.*] My grandfather frequently plants whole orchards of such trees, but usually they bear human fruit!

MIRIAM. [*With a shudder.*] Monster!

CALIGULA. [*With genuine surprise —turning to her.*] Who? Why? [*He approaches the cross and stares at it moodily.*] But why did he have it placed here where he knew you must pass? Tiberius does not go to such pains to frighten women. [*His eyes fasten on the inscription above the lion's head.*] Aha! I see! [*He reads.*] "From the East, land of false gods and superstitition, this lion was brought to Rome to amuse Cæsar." [*A silence.* CALIGULA *shrugs his shoulders, turning away—lightly.*] A lesson for you, Lazarus. An example for other lions— not to roar—or laugh—at Cæsar! [*He gives a harsh laugh.*] Tiberius must be terribly afraid of you. [*Then somberly.*] You should never have come here. I would have advised you not to—but what are you to me? My duty, if I wish to become Cæsar, is to Cæsar. Besides, you are no fool. Evidently you must desire your own death. Last night *you* might have been Cæsar. The legions were yours.

LAZARUS. [*Smiling without bitterness—with a sad comprehension.*] But

this morning the legions had forgotten. They only remembered—to go out and pick up their swords! They also pillaged the bodies a little, as their right, believing now that they had slain them! [*This last a little bitterly.*]

CALIGULA. [*Tauntingly.*] The legions did slay them! It was only by some magician's trick you made them think your followers killed themselves.

LAZARUS. [*Not answering him— ironically to himself.*] It is too soon. Men still need their swords to slash at ghosts in the dark. Men, those haunted heroes! [*He laughs softly.*]

CALIGULA. [*Irritably.*] What are you laughing at?

LAZARUS. At Lazarus when I find him feeling wronged because men are men! [*He laughs again, softly and musically.*]

CALIGULA. [*Again taunting brutally.*] You may be in his place soon! [*He points to the lion.*] Will you laugh then? [MIRIAM *gives a cry of terror.*]

LAZARUS. [*Calmly.*] Yes. [*Then humbly, bowing his head.*] I will laugh with the pride of a beggar set upon the throne of Man!

CALIGULA. [*Sneeringly.*] You boast. [*Then as* LAZARUS *does not answer, touching the lion with intentional provoking brutality.*] This one from Africa seems almost gone. They do not last as long as men.

LAZARUS. [*Walks up the steps to the cross and, stretching to his full height, gently pushes the lion's hair out of its eyes—tenderly.*] Poor brother! Cæsar avenges himself on you because of me. Forgive me your suffering!

CALIGULA. [*With a start backward —with frightened awe.*] God! He licks your hand! I could swear he smiles— with his last breath! [*Then with relief.*] Now he is dead!

LAZARUS. [*Gently.*] There is no death.

CALIGULA. [*Pointing to the lion.*] What is that then?

LAZARUS. Your fear of life.

CALIGULA. [*Impatiently.*] Bah! [*Then somberly.*] A little fear is useful even for lions—or teachers of laughter if they wish to laugh long! [*Then with a sudden exasperation.*] Escape now, you fool, while there is still time!

LAZARUS. [*Laughing softly.*] Escape —what?

CALIGULA. [*In a frenzy.*] You know, you ass, you lunatic! Escape death! Death! Death! [*To* MIRIAM.] You, woman! Talk to him! Do you want him nailed up like that?

MIRIAM. [*With a pitiful cry.*] Lazarus! Come! Caligula will help us!

CALIGULA. [*Harshly.*] You presume, Jewess! I have no wish to die! [*Then with his wry smile.*] But I will turn my back—and shut my eyes— [*He walks away to left.*]

MIRIAM. [*Beseechingly.*] Lazarus! I could not bear that aching hunger of my empty heart if you should die again!

LAZARUS. [*Coming to her—tenderly.*] I will not leave you! Believe in me! [*He kisses her forehead tenderly.*]

MIRIAM. [*After a pause—slowly and lamentingly.*] I wish we were home, Lazarus. This Roman world is full of evil. These skies threaten. These hearts are heavy with hatred. There is a taint of blood in the air that poisons the breath of the sea. These columns and arches and thick walls seem waiting to fall, to crush these rotten men and then to crumble over the bones that raised them until both are dust. It is a world deadly to your joy, Lazarus. Its pleasure is a gorging of dirt, its fulfilled desire a snoring in a sty in the mud among swine. Its will is so sick that it must kill in order

to be aware of life at all. I wish we were home, Lazarus. I begin to feel horror gnawing at my breast. I begin to know the torture of the fear of death, Lazarus—not of my death but of yours—not of the passing of your man's body but of ᐧ the going away from me of your laughter which is to me as my son, my little boy!

LAZARUS. [*Soothing her.*] Be comforted, Beloved. Your fear shall never be!

MIRIAM. On the hills near Bethany you might pray at noon and laugh your boy's laughter in the sun and there would be echoing laughter from the sky and up from the grass and distantly from the shining sea. We would adopt children whose parents the Romans had butchered, and their laughter would be around me in my home where I cooked and weaved and sang. And in the dawn at your going out, and in the evening on your return, I would hear in the hushed air the bleating of sheep and the tinkling of many little bells and your voice. And my heart would know peace.

LAZARUS. [*Tenderly.*] Only a little longer. There is God's laughter on the hills of space, and the happiness of children, and the soft healing of innumerable dawns and evenings, and the blessing of peace!

CALIGULA. [*Looks around at* LAZARUS *impatiently. Then he makes a beckoning gesture to* MIRIAM.] Ssstt! [*Wonderingly she leaves* LAZARUS' *side and follows him.* LAZARUS *remains, his eyes fixed on the cross, directly in front of it.* CALIGULA *speaks gruffly to* MIRIAM *with a sneer.*] Jewess, your Lazarus is mad, I begin to think. [*Then confusedly but helplessly inquisitive and confiding—bursting out.*] What is it troubles me about him? What makes me dream of him? Why should I—love him, Jewess? Tell me! You love him, too. I do not understand this. Why, wherever he goes, is there joy? You heard even the galley slaves laugh and clank time with their chains! [*Then with exasperation.*] And yet why can I not laugh, Jewess?

MIRIAM. [*In a tone of hushed grief.*] I may not laugh either. My heart remains a little dead with Lazarus in Bethany. The miracle could not revive all his old husband's life in my wife's heart.

CALIGULA. [*Disgustedly.*] What answer is that to me? [*Then brusquely.*] But I called you to put you on your guard. [*He points.*] There is death in there—Tiberius' death, a kind from which no miracles can recall one! [*He smiles his twisted smile.*] Since Lazarus will not help himself, you must protect him. I will not, for once in there I am [*mockingly*] the heir of Cæsar, and you are scum whom I kill at his order as I would two beetles! So keep watch! Taste first of what he eats—even were I the one to give it to him!

LAZARUS. [*Suddenly laughs softly.*] Why do you delight in believing evil of yourself, Caligula?

CALIGULA. [*Flying into a queer rage.*] You lie! I am what I am! [*With grandiose pride.*] What could you know of a Cæsar?

LAZARUS. [*Still laughing with an affectionate understanding.*] What—I know! [*As he finishes speaking all the sound of music and voices from the house ceases abruptly and there is a heavy silence.*]

MIRIAM. [*Shaking her head and turning away sadly.*] That is too far, Lazarus. Let us go home.

CALIGULA. [*Harshly.*] Sst! Do you hear? Flavius has told Cæsar. [*Grimly forcing a harsh snicker.*] Now we will soon know— [*There is the sudden blaring of a trumpet from within the palace. A wide door is flung open and*

a stream of reddish light comes out against which the black figures of several men are outlined. The door is shut again quickly. Several SLAVES bearing lamps on poles escort the patrician, MARCELLUS, forward to the arch. He passes under the crucified lion without a glance—then stands, cool and disdainful, to look about him. He is a man of about thirty-five, wearing the type mask of a Roman patrician to which are added the dissipated courtier's characteristics of one who leans to evil more through weakness than any instinctive urge. He is dressed richly. His smile is hypocritical and his eyes are hard and cold but when they come to rest on LAZARUS he gives a start of genuine astonishment.*]

CALIGULA. [*Who has moved to LAZARUS' side defensively—in a quick whisper.*] Beware of this man, Lazarus! [*Then advancing—with a condescending hauteur.*] Greeting, Marcellus!

MARCELLUS. [*In an ingratiating tone.*] Greeting, Gaius. I have a message from Cæsar for the man called Lazarus.

LAZARUS. [*Calmly.*] I am Lazarus.

MARCELLUS. [*Makes a deep bow—flatteringly.*] I had surmised it, sir. Although I cannot pretend to virtue in myself at least I may claim the merit of recognizing it in others. [*He advances toward LAZARUS, smiling, with one hand kept hidden beneath his cloak.*]

CALIGULA. [*Stepping between them —sharply.*] What is your message?

MARCELLUS. [*Surprised—placatingly.*] I am sorry, Gaius, but it was Cæsar's command I speak to Lazarus alone.

CALIGULA. [*Fiercely.*] And then, Marcellus? [*MARCELLUS shrugs his shoulders and smiles deprecatingly.*]

LAZARUS. [*With a compelling dig-*

nity.] Let him speak. [*Inclining his head to* MARCELLUS—*strangely.*] Over here where it is dark you will not be seen—nor see yourself. [*He walks to the darkness at right.*]

CALIGULA. [*Turning his back on them, with angry boyish resentfulness that is close to tears.*] Idiot! Go and die, then!

MIRIAM. [*With a terrified cry.*] Lazarus! [*She starts to go to him.*]

LAZARUS. [*Motioning her to remain where she is—gently.*] Believe, Beloved! [*He turns his back on them all and stands waiting.*]

MARCELLUS. [*Stares at* LAZARUS— *then over his shoulder at* CALIGULA— *uncertainly.*] What does he mean, Gaius? [*Then suddenly putting on a brave front, he strides up behind* LAZARUS.] Cæsar wished me to bid you welcome, to tell you how much regard he has for you, but he desired me to ask whether you propose to laugh here—in Cæsar's palace? He has heard that you laugh at death— that you have caused others to laugh —even his legionaries. [*A pause,* MAR- CELLUS *remains behind* LAZARUS' *back, the latter standing like a victim.*] Briefly, Cæsar requires your pledge that you will not laugh. Will you give it? [*He frees his dagger from under his robe. A pause. Arrogantly.*] I am waiting! Answer when Cæsar commands! [*Then angrily, baffled.*] I will give you while I count three—or take your silence as a refusal! One! Two! Three! [*He raises his hand to stab* LAZARUS *in the back.* MIRIAM *stifles a scream. At the same instant,* LAZA- RUS *begins to laugh, softly and affec- tionately.* MARCELLUS *stops, frozen in mid-action, the dagger upraised.* CA- LIGULA *has whirled around and stands staring, a smile gradually com- ing to his face.* LAZARUS *turns, his laughter grown a trifle louder, and faces* MARCELLUS. *The latter steps* back from him, staring open-mouthed, fascinated. His arm sinks to his side. The dagger falls from his fingers. He smiles back at* LAZARUS—*the curious, sheepish, bashful smile of one who has fallen in love and been dis- covered.*]

LAZARUS. [*Going to him, puts both hands on his shoulders and looks in his eyes, laughing affectionally—then quizzically.*] Here is another one who believes in death! But soon you will laugh with life! I see it in your eyes. Farewell, Marcellus! [*He turns away from him and walks, laughing, to- ward the arch in rear. With bowed head the black-robed figure of* MIRIAM *follows him.* MARCELLUS *hides his face in his hands, half-sobbing, and half-laughing hysterically.* LAZARUS *pauses before the cross for a moment— raises his hand as if blessing the dead lion, then passes below it, moving slowly on toward the palace in the rear. His laughter rises with more and more summoning power. The files of the* GUARD, *as he passes them, two by two join in his laughter, saluting him as if in spite of themselves.*]

CALIGULA. [*Sidling up to* MAR- CELLUS, *cruel and mocking.*] Are you weeping, Marcellus? Laugh at that blundering fool, yourself! What will Cæsar say? Will he laugh when he has your body broken one bone at a time with hammers? Why did you not kill? For shame! A patrician ex- posed to laughter by a Jew! Poor craven! Why could you not strike? There *must* be death! Coward! Why did you not stab? [*Then in a queer awed whisper.*] I know! Was it not because of a sudden you loved him and could not?

MARCELLUS. [*Suddenly—eagerly.*] Yes! That was it! I loved him!

CALIGULA. [*Craftily and cruelly.*] You were about to murder him!

MARCELLUS. [*Tortured with re-*

morse.] No! No! How could I? What infamy! [*Cries tearfully.*] Forgive me, Lazarus!

CALIGULA. [*With vindictive insistence.*] Judge yourself! [*He takes up the dagger.*] Here is your dagger! Avenge him on yourself!

MARCELLUS. [*Trying to laugh.*] Haha— Yes! [*He stabs himself and falls. Suddenly his laughter is released.*] I laugh! You are a fool, Caligula! There is no death! [*He dies, laughing up at the sky.*]

CALIGULA. [*Kicks his body with savage cruelty.*] You lie! [*Then suddenly kneels and bends over it imploringly.*] Tell me you lie, Marcellus! Do me that mercy!—and when I am Cæsar, I— [*He begins to weep like a frightened boy, his head in his hands. Meanwhile* LAZARUS *has arrived with* MIRIAM *at the steps before the door of the palace. As he starts to ascend these, the crimson-purple lights of the many windows of the palace go out one by one as if fleeing in terror from the laughter which now beats at the walls.*]

CHORUS OF THE GUARD.
Fear, no more!
Death, no more!
Laugh! Laugh! Laugh!
Death is dead!

ALL THE GUARDS. [*Now all in a great chorus, raising their spears aloft and saluting* LAZARUS *as if they were his own triumphal body guard.*]
Laugh! Laugh! Laugh!
Death is dead!

[LAZARUS *has ascended the steps. He walks into the black archway of the darkened palace, his figure radiant and unearthly in his own light.* MIRIAM *follows him. They disappear in the darkness. There is a pause of dead silence.*]

CALIGULA. [*Raises his head uneasily, looks back toward the palace, jumps to his feet in a panic of terror, and runs toward the palace door, calling.*] Lazarus! Wait! I will defend you! There is death inside there—death! Beware, Lazarus!

CHORUS OF THE GUARD. [*As the laughter of* LAZARUS *is heard again from the dark palace.*]
Laugh Laugh! Laugh!
Death is dead!

ALL THE GUARDS.
Dead! Dead! Dead!
Death is dead!

CURTAIN

SCENE 2

SCENE: *The banquet hall in the palace of* TIBERIUS—*an immense high-ceilinged room. In the rear, center, is a great arched doorway. Smaller arches in the middle of the side walls lead into other rooms. Long couches are placed along the walls at right and left, along the rear wall on either side of the arch. Before these couches, a series of narrow tables is set. In the center of the room on a high dais is the ivory and gold chair of* CÆSAR, *a table in front of it, couches for him to recline on at either side. On this table, and on all the tables for his guests, gold lamps with shades of crimson-purple are placed.*

Reclining on the couches on the right are young women and girls, on the left, youths of an equal number.

(The masks are based on the Roman masks of the periods of Boyhood (or Girlhood), Youth, and Young Manhood (or Womanhood) and there are seven individuals of each period and sex in each of the three types of the Introspective, Self-Tortured; the Servile, Hypocritical; and the Cruel, Revengeful—a crowd of forty-two in all. There is a distinctive character to the masks of each sex, the stamp of an

effeminate corruption on all the male, while the female have a bold, masculine expression. The male masks are a blotched heliotrope in shade. These youths wear female wigs of curled wire like frizzed hair of a yellow gold. They are dressed in women's robes of pale heliotrope, they wear anklets and bracelets and necklaces. The women are dressed as males in crimson or deep purple. They also wear wire wigs but of straight hair cut in short boyish mode, dyed either deep purple or crimson. Those with crimson hair are dressed in purple, and vice versa. The female voices are harsh, strident, mannish—those of the youths affected, lisping, effeminate. The whole effect of these two groups is of sex corrupted and warped, of invented lusts and artificial vices.

The CHORUS in this scene and the next is composed of three males and four females—the males in the period of Youth, one in each of the types represented, and three of the females in similar type-period masks. The fourth female is masked in the period of Womanhood in the Proud, Self-Reliant type. They sit, facing front in their double-sized masks, on the side steps of the dais, four on right, three on left.)

POMPEIA, a Roman noblewoman, the favorite mistress of CÆSAR, sits at front, right.

She wears a half-mask on the upper part of her face, olive-colored with the red of blood smoldering through, with great, dark, cruel eyes—a dissipated mask of intense evil beauty, of lust and perverted passion. Beneath the mask, her own complexion is pale, her gentle, girlish mouth is set in an expression of agonized self-loathing and weariness of spirit. Her body is strong and beautiful. Her wig and dress are purple.

TIBERIUS CÆSAR stands on the dais, dressed in deep purple, fringed and ornamented with crimson and gold. An old man of seventy-six, tall, broad and corpulent but of great muscular strength still despite his age, his shiny white cranium rises like a polished shell above his half-masked face. This mask is a pallid purple blotched with darker color, as if the imperial blood in his veins had been sickened by age and debauchery. The eyes are protuberant, leering, cynical slits, the long nose, once finely modeled, now gross and thickened, the forehead lowering and grim. Beneath the mask, his own mouth looks as incongruous as CALIGULA'S. The lips are thin and stern and self-contained—the lips of an able soldier-statesman of rigid probity. His chin is forceful and severe. The complexion of his own skin is that of a healthy old campaigner.

As the curtain rises, slaves are hurriedly putting out the many lamps. From outside, the laughter of LAZARUS rises on the deep ground swell of the GUARD'S laughter. The walls and massive columns seem to reverberate with the sound. In the banquet room all are listening fascinatedly. Every reaction, from the extreme of panic fear or hypnotized ecstasy to a feigned cynical amusement or a pretended supercilious indifference, is represented in their frozen attitudes. TIBERIUS stands, shrinking back, staring at the doorway in the rear with superstitious dread. A squad of the GUARD surround the dais, commanded by FLAVIUS.

TIBERIUS. [In a strained voice shaken by apprehension and awe.] Marcellus! Strike him down! Stab him!

SOLDIERS OF THE GUARD. [From without.]
Laugh! Laugh! Laugh!
Death is dead.

TIBERIUS. [*As he suddenly sees the shining figure of* LAZARUS *appear at the end of the dark hall beyond the archway.*] Gods! Flavius, look! [*He points with a shaking finger.* FLAVIUS *has leaped up to his side.*]

FLAVIUS. [*Not without dread himself.*] That is the man, Cæsar.

TIBERIUS. Man? Say a dæmon! [*To the slaves who are turning out the few remaining lamps.*] Quick! Darkness! [*He puts out the lamp on his table himself. Then as nothing is seen but the light from the approaching* LAZARUS] Flavius! Stand here in my place! It will think you are Cæsar! [*He clumps heavily down the steps of the dais.*] Guards! Here! Cover me with your shields! [*He goes to the extreme right corner, front, and crouches there. His* GUARDS *follow him. They hold their shields so that they form a wall around him and half over him. Then* CALIGULA'S *voice is heard screaming above the chorus of laughter as he enters the hall behind* LAZARUS.]

CALIGULA. Beware of death! I will defend you, Lazarus! [*He is seen to rush past* LAZARUS, *flourishing his sword and comes running into the room, shouting.*] Cæsar! Dare not to murder Lazarus! [*He leaps to the dais and up its steps in a frenzy.*] Dare not, I say! [*He stabs* FLAVIUS *with a savage cry.*] Ah! [*Then, as the body of* FLAVIUS *falls heavily and rolls down the steps at right, he begins to laugh, at first a clear laughter of selfless joy, sounding startingly incongruous from him.*] I have saved you, Lazarus—at the risk of my own life—and now, hear me, I can laugh! [LAZARUS *appears in the archway,* MIRIAM *behind him. He stops laughing and immediately there is silence, except for* CALIGULA. LAZARUS *casts a luminous glow over the whole room in which the masked faces appear distorted and livid.* CALIGULA *stands with upraised*

sword by the chair of CÆSAR. *Suddenly his laughter cracks, changes, becomes full of his old fear and blood-lust.*]

CALIGULA. Ha-ha-ha! See, Lazarus! [*He points to the body of* FLAVIUS *with his sword.*] Welcome in the name of Cæsar, now Cæsar is slain and I am Cæsar! [*He assumes the absurd grandiose posture of his imperial posing. No one looks at him or hears him. Their eyes are on* LAZARUS *as he moves directly to where* TIBERIUS *crouches behind the shields of the* GUARDS. MIRIAM *follows him.* CALIGULA *turns and stares toward him, and then down at the body of* FLAVIUS *and back, in a petrified, bewildered stupor.* LAZARUS *steps up beside* TIBERIUS. *The* GUARDS *make way for him fearfully.*]

TIBERIUS. [*Feeling his nearness—straightening himself with a certain dignity.*] Strike! I have been a soldier. Thou canst not make me fear death, Dæmon! [*He draws his toga over his face.*]

LAZARUS. [*Smiling gently.*] Then fear not fear, Tiberius! [*He reaches out and pulls back the toga from his face.* TIBERIUS *looks into his eyes, at first shrinkingly, then with growing reassurance, his own masked face clearly revealed now in the light from* LAZARUS.]

TIBERIUS. [*At first falteringly.*] So —thou art not evil? Thou art not come to contrive my murder? [*As* LAZARUS *smilingly shakes his head,* TIBERIUS *frowns.*] Then why dost thou laugh against Cæsar? [*Then bitterly—with a twisted attempt at a smile.*] Yet I like thy laughter. It is young. Once I laughed somewhat like that—so I pardon thee. I will even laugh at thee in return. Ha-ha! [*His laughter is cold, cruel and merciless as the grin of a skeleton.*]

CALIGULA. [*Who has been staring

in a bewildered stupor from TIBERIUS, *whom he thought he had killed, to the body of* FLAVIUS—*quaking with terror now as if this laugh was meant for him, drops to his knees, his sword clattering down the steps to the floor.*] Mercy, Tiberius! I implore you forgive your Caligula!

TIBERIUS. [*Not understanding. Fixing his eyes on* CALIGULA *with a malevolent irony.*] Come down from my throne, Caligula. [CALIGULA *slinks down warily.*] You are too impatient. But I must pardon you, too—for where could I find another heir so perfect for serving my spite upon mankind? [*He has walked toward the throne while he is speaking,* CALIGULA *backing away from him.* LAZARUS *remains where he is,* MIRIAM *beside and to the rear of him.* TIBERIUS, *his eyes fixed on* CALIGULA, *stumbles against the body of* FLAVIUS. *He gives a startled gasp and shrinks back, calling.*] Lights! A light here! [*A crowd of masked slaves obey his orders. One runs to him with a lantern. He looks down at* FLAVIUS' *corpse—half to himself.*] I did wisely to stand him in my place. [*To* CALIGULA—*with sinister emphasis.*] Too impatient, my loving grandchild! Take care lest I become impatient also—with your impatience! [CALIGULA *shudders and backs away to the extreme left corner, front, where he crouches on his haunches as inconspicuously as possible.* TIBERIUS *suddenly whirls around as if he felt a dagger at his back.*]

TIBERIUS. Where—? [*Seeing* LAZARUS *where he had been—with relief—staring at his face now that the room is flooded with the purplish-crimson glow from all the lamps.*] Ah, you are there. More lights! Darkness leads men into error. My heir mistakes a man for Cæsar and Cæsar, it appears, has mistaken a man for a dæmon! [*Scrutinizing him—with sinister final-*ity.] I can deal with men. I know them well. Too well! [*He laughs grimly.*] Therefore I hate them. [*He mounts the steps of the dais and sits on the couch at left of table—staring at* LAZARUS, *wonderingly.*] But you seem—something other than man! That light! [*Then he forces a harsh laugh.*] A trick! I had forgotten you are a magician. [*Arrogantly.*] Stand there, Jew. I would question you about your magic. [*Smilingly* LAZARUS *ascends to where* TIBERIUS *points at the top of the dais.* MIRIAM *remains standing at the foot.* TIBERIUS *stares for a while with somber intensity at* LAZARUS.] They say you died and have returned from death?

LAZARUS. [*Smiling—as if he were correcting a child.*] There is no death, Cæsar.

TIBERIUS [*With a sneer of skepticism but with an underlying eagerness.*] I have heard you teach that folly. [*Then threateningly.*] You shall be given full opportunity to prove it! [*A pause—then in a low voice, bending down toward* LAZARUS.] Do you foretell the future? [*Trembling but with a pretense of carelessness.*] Must I die soon?

LAZARUS. [*Simply.*] Yes, Cæsar.

TIBERIUS. [*Jumping up with a shuddering start.*] Soon? Soon? [*Then his fear turning to rage.*] What do you say? Vile Jew, do you dare threaten me with death! [LAZARUS, *looking into his eyes, begins to laugh softly.* TIBERIUS *sinks back on his couch, fighting to control himself—confusedly.*] Laugh not, I ask you. I am old. It is not seemly. [LAZARUS *ceases his low laughter. A pause.* TIBERIUS *broods—then suddenly.*] And you were really dead? [*He shudders.*] Come nearer. I need to watch your face. I have learned to read the lies in faces. A Cæsar gets much practice—from childhood on—too much! [*With awe.*]

Your eyes are dark with death. While I watch them, answer me, what cured thee of death?

LAZARUS. [*Gently.*] There is only life, Cæsar. [*Then gaily mocking but compellingly.*] And laughter! Look! Look well into my eyes, old Reader of Lies, and see if you can find aught in them that is not life—and laughter! [*He laughs softly. A ripple of soft laughter from the motionless figures about the room echoes his.* TIBERIUS *stares into his eyes. In the silence that ensues* POMPEIA *gets up and walks over to the dais. She stops to stare for a moment with cruel contempt at* MIRIAM, *then stands and looks up at* LAZARUS, *trying in vain to attract his or* CÆSAR'S *attention. Failing in this, she passes over and sits beside* CALIGULA, *whose attention is concentrated on* LAZARUS.]

POMPEIA. I admire your strange magician, Caligula.

CALIGULA. [*Without looking at her.*] He is no magician. He is something like a god.

POMPEIA. [*Longingly.*] His laughter is like a god's. He is strong. I love him.

CALIGULA. [*Turning to her—coarsely.*] Do not waste your lust. He is faithful to his wife, I warn you.

POMPEIA. [*She points to* MIRIAM.] Not that ugly slave?

CALIGULA. Yes. And yet, on our journey, whole herds of women—and many as beautiful as you, Pompeia—threw themselves on him and begged for his love.

POMPEIA. [*Her voice hardening.*] And he?

CALIGULA. He laughed—and passed on. [*She starts.* CALIGULA *goes on wonderingly.*] But they seemed as happy as if his laughter had possessed them! You are a woman. Tell me, how could that be?

POMPEIA. [*Her voice cruel.*] He shall not laugh at me!

CALIGULA. [*Tauntingly.*] I will bet a string of pearls against your body for a night that he does.

POMPEIA. [*Defiantly.*] Done! [*Then she laughs—a low, cruel laugh—staring at* MIRIAM.] So he loves that woman?

CALIGULA. [*Curiously.*] What are you planning?

POMPEIA. I shall offer her the fruit Cæsar preserves for those he fears.

CALIGULA. [*With a careless shrug.*] You will not win his love by killing her.

POMPEIA. I no longer want his love. I want to see him suffer, to hear his laughter choke in his throat with pain! [*She speaks with more and more voluptuous satisfaction.*] Then I shall laugh! [*She laughs softly and steps forward.*]

CALIGULA. [*Concernedly.*] Stop. I am his protector. [*Then suddenly.*] But what is the Jewess to me? [*With more and more of a spirit of perverse cruelty.*] Do it, Pompeia! His laughter is too cruel to us! We must save death from him!

POMPEIA. [*Walks to the dais which she ascends slowly until she stands by* CÆSAR'S *couch behind him, confronting* LAZARUS. *But the two men remain unmindful of her presence.* TIBERIUS *continues to stare into* LAZARUS' *eyes. His whole body is now relaxed, at rest, a dreamy smile softens his thin, compressed mouth.* POMPEIA *leans over and takes a peach from the bowl of fruit on* CÆSAR'S *table and, taking* TIBERIUS' *hand in her other, she kisses it and calls insistently.*] Cæsar. It is I, Pompeia. [*LAZARUS does not look at her. She stares at him defiantly.* TIBERIUS *blinks his eyes in a daze.*]

TIBERIUS. [*Dreamily.*] Yes! A cloud came from a depth of sky—around me, softly, warmly, and the cloud dissolved into the sky, and the sky into peace! [*Suddenly springing to his feet and staring about him in a confused rage—clutching* POMPEIA *by the shoulder and forcing her to her knees.*] What are you doing here?

POMPEIA. Forgive your loving slave! I grew afraid this magician had put you under a spell. [*She stares at* LAZARUS, *her words challenging him.*]

TIBERIUS. [*Confusedly, sinking back on his couch and releasing her.*] A spell? Could it be he laid a dream of death upon me, leading me to death? [*He trembles timorously—appealing to* LAZARUS.] Whatever magic thou didst to me, Dæmon, I beseech thee undo it!

LAZARUS. [*Smiling.*] Do you fear peace?

POMPEIA. [*Harshly and insolently.*] Mock not at Cæsar, dog! [LAZARUS *continues to smile. His eyes remain on* CÆSAR. *He seems absolutely unaware of* POMPEIA. *This enrages her the more against him. She speaks tauntingly to* TIBERIUS.] Surely, Cæsar, this magician must have powerful charms since he dares to mock Tiberius to his face!

TIBERIUS. [*Stung.*] Be still! [*Then in a low tone to her.*] Do you not know this Lazarus died and then by his magic rose from his tomb.

POMPEIA. [*Scornfully.*] To believe that, I must have seen it, Cæsar!

TIBERIUS. [*Impatiently.*] Do you think I would believe without good evidence? I have had them take the statements of many witnesses. The miracle was done in conjunction with another Jew acting as this man's tool. This other Jew, the report states, could not possibly have possessed any magic power Himself, for Pilate crucified Him a short time after and He died in pain and weakness within a few hours. But this Lazarus laughs at death!

LAZARUS. [*Looks up, smiling with*

ironical bitterness.] Couldst Thou but hear, Jesus! And men shall keep on in panic nailing Man's soul to the cross of their fear until in the end they do it to avenge Thee, for Thine Honor and Glory! [*He sighs sadly—then after a struggle overcoming himself—with exultance.*] Yes! [*His eyes fall again to* TIBERIUS *and he smiles.*] Yes! Yes to the stupid as to the wise! To what is understood and to what cannot be understood! Known and unknown! Over and over! Forever and ever! Yes! [*He laughs softly to himself.*]

TIBERIUS. [*With superstitious dread.*] What dost thou mean, Dæmon?

POMPEIA. [*With indignant scorn.*] Let him prove there is no death, Cæsar! [*She appeals to the company who straighten up on their couches with interest.*]

CHORUS. [*Chant demandingly.*] Let him prove there is no death! We are bored!

CROWD. [*Echoing.*] Prove there is no death! We are bored, Cæsar!

TIBERIUS. [*Waits to see what* LAZARUS *will say—then as he says nothing, plucking up his courage—his cruelty aroused.*] Do you hear, Lazarus?

POMPEIA. Make him perform his miracle again!

CHORUS. [*As before.*] Let him perform a miracle! We are bored, Cæsar!

CROWD. [*They now stand up and coming from behind their tables, move forward toward the dais.*] A miracle! We are bored!

POMPEIA. Let him raise someone from the dead!

CHORUS. [*Chanting with a pettish insistence.*]
Raise the dead!
We are bored!

CROWD. [*Echoing—grouping in a big semi-circle as of spectators in a theatre, around and to the sides of the dais, one sex on each side.* CALIGULA *moves in from the left in front of them. They form in three ranks, the first squatting on their hams like savages [as* CALIGULA *does], the second rank crouching over them, the third leaning over the second, all with a hectic, morbid interest.*]
We are bored!
Raise the dead!

POMPEIA. [*With a cruel smile.*] I have thought of a special test for him, Cæsar. [*She whispers in* CÆSAR's *ear and points to* MIRIAM *and the fruit in her hand.*] And he must laugh!

TIBERIUS. [*With a harsh, cruel chuckle.*] Yes, I shall command him to laugh! [*Then disgustedly.*] But she is sad and old. I will be only doing him a favor.

CALIGULA. [*Rocking back and forth on his haunches—looking at* LAZARUS *with taunting cruelty.*] No, Cæsar! I know he loves her!

LAZARUS. Yes! [*He steps down from the dais to* MIRIAM's *side and taking her head in both his hands, he kisses her on the lips.*]

TIBERIUS. [*With a malignant grin.*] Give her the fruit!

POMPEIA. [*Advances and offers the peach to* MIRIAM—*with a hard, cruel little laugh.*] Cæsar invites you to eat!

MIRIAM. [*To* LAZARUS—*requesting meekly but longingly.*] May I accept, Lazarus? Is it time at last? My love has followed you over long roads among strangers and each league we came from home my heart has grown

older. Now it is too old for you, a heart too weary for your loving laughter. Ever your laughter has grown younger, Lazarus! Upward it springs like a lark from a field, and sings! Once I knew your laughter was my child, my son of Lazarus; but then it grew younger and I felt at last it had returned to my womb—and ever younger and younger—until, tonight, when I spoke to you of home, I felt new birthpains as your laughter, grown too young for me, flew back to the unborn—a birth so like a death! [*She sobs and wipes her eyes with her sleeve—then humbly, reaching out for the fruit.*] May I accept it, Lazarus? You should have newborn laughing hearts to love you. My old one labors with memories and its blood is sluggish with the past. Your home on the hills of space is too far away. My heart longs for the warmth of close walls of earth baked in the sun. Our home in Bethany, Lazarus, where you and my children lived and died. Our tomb near our home, Lazarus, in which you and my children wait for me. Is it time at last?

LAZARUS. [*Deeply moved.*] Poor lonely heart! It has been crueler for you than I remembered. Go in peace—to peace! [*His voice trembles in spite of himself.*] I shall be lonely, dear one. [*With a note of pleading.*] You have never laughed with my laughter. Will you call back—Yes!—when you know—to tell me you understand and laugh with me at last?

MIRIAM. [*Not answering him, to* POMPEIA, *taking the peach and making a humble courtesy before her.*] I thank you, pretty lady. [*She raises the peach toward her mouth. Involuntarily one of* LAZARUS' *hands half-reaches out as if to stop her.*]

POMPEIA. [*With savage triumph, pointing.*] See! He would stop her! He is afraid of death!

CHORUS. [*Pointing—jeeringly.*] He is afraid of death! Ha-ha-ha-ha!

CROWD. [*Jeeringly.*] Ha-ha-ha-ha!

MIRIAM. [*Bites into the peach and, chewing, begins, as if immediately affected, to talk like a garrulous old woman, her words coming quicker and quicker as her voice becomes fainter and fainter.*] Say what you like, it is much better I should go home first, Lazarus. We have been away so long, there will be so much to attend to about the house. And all the children will be waiting. You would be as helpless as a child, Lazarus. Between you and the children, things would soon be in a fine state! [*More and more confused.*] No, no! You cannot help me, dearest one. You are only in my way. No, I will make the fire. When you laid it the last time, we all had to run for our lives, choking, the smoke poured from the windows, the neighbors thought the house was burning! [*She laughs—a queer, vague little inward laugh.*] You are so impractical. The neighbors all get the best of you. Money slips through your fingers. If it was not for me— [*She sighs—then brightly and lovingly.*] But, dearest husband, why do you take it so to heart? Why do you feel guilty because you are not like other men? That is why I love you so much. Is it a sin to be born a dreamer? But God, He must be a dreamer, too, or how would we be on earth? Do not keep saying to yourself so bitterly, you are a failure in life! Do not sit brooding on the hilltop in the evening like a black figure of Job against the sky! [*Her voice trembling.*] Even if God has taken our little ones— yes, in spite of sorrow—have you not a good home I make for you, and a wife who loves you? [*She forces a chuckle.*] Be grateful, then—for me! Smile, my sad one! Laugh a little once

in a while! Come home, bringing me laughter of the wind from the hills! [*Swaying, looking at the peach in her hand.*] What a mellow, sweet fruit! Did you bring it home for me? [*She falls back into his arms. Gently he lets her body sink until it rests against the steps of the dais.* TIBERIUS *rises from his couch to bend over with cruel gloating.* POMPEIA *steps nearer to* LAZARUS, *staring at him mockingly.* CALIGULA *hops to her side, looking from* LAZARUS *to* MIRIAM. *The half-circle of masked figures moves closer, straining forward and downward as if to overwhelm the two figures at the foot of the dais with their concentrated death wish.*]

TIBERIUS. [*Thickly.*] She is dead, and I do not hear you laugh!

LAZARUS [*Bending down—supplicatingly.*] Miriam! Call back to me! Laugh! [*He pauses. A second of dead silence. Then, with a sound that is very like a sob, he kisses her on the lips.*] I am lonely!

POMPEIA. [*With savage malice—jeeringly.*] See! He weeps, Cæsar! [*She bursts into strident laughter.*] Ha-ha-ha-ha!

CHORUS. [*Echoing her laughter.*]
Ha-ha-ha-ha!
There is fear!
There is death!

CROWD.
There is death!
Ha-ha-ha-ha!

CALIGULA. [*In a frenzy of despairing rage, hopping up and down.*] Liar! Charlatan! Weakling! How you have cheated Caligula! [*He suddenly slaps* LAZARUS *viciously across the face.*] There is death! Laugh, if you dare!

TIBERIUS. [*Standing—in a sinister cold rage, the crueler because his* dream of a cure for death is baffled, yet feeling his power as CÆSAR triumphant nevertheless.] And I thought you might be a dæmon. I thought you might have a magic cure— [*With revengeful fury.*] But death is, and death is mine! I shall make you pray for death! And I shall make Death laugh at you! Ha-ha-ha-ha! [*In a frenzy as* LAZARUS *neither makes a sound nor looks up.*] Laugh, Lazarus! Laugh at yourself! Laugh with me! [*Then to his soldiers.*] Scourge him! Make him laugh!

CALIGULA. [*Running to soldiers— fiercely.*] Give me a scourge!

POMPEIA. [*Running to the soldiers —hysterically.*] Ha-ha-ha-ha! Let me beat him, Cæsar! [*They group behind him. The rods and scourges are uplifted over his back to strike, when in the dead expectant silence,* MIRIAM'S *body is seen to rise in a writhing tortured last effort.*]

MIRIAM. [*In a voice of unearthly sweetness.*] Yes! There is only life! Lazarus, be not lonely! [*She laughs and sinks back and is still.*]

[*A shuddering murmur of superstitious fear comes from them as they shrink back swiftly from* LAZARUS, *remaining huddled one against the other.* POMPEIA *runs to the feet of* TIBERIUS *and crouches down on the steps below him, as if for protection, her terrified eyes on* MIRIAM. CALIGULA *runs to her and crouches beside and beneath her.*]

LAZARUS. [*Kisses* MIRIAM *again and raises his head. His face is radiant with new faith and joy. He smiles with happiness and speaks to himself with a mocking affection as if to an amusing child.*] That much remained hidden in me of the sad old Larazus who died of self-pity—his loneliness! Lonely no more! Man's loneliness is

but his fear of life! Lonely no more! Millions of laughing stars there are around me! And laughing dust, born once of woman on this earth, now freed to dance! New stars are born of dust eternally! The old, grown mellow with God, burst into flaming seed! The fields of infinite space are sown— and grass for sheep springs up on the hills of earth! But there is no death, nor fear, nor loneliness! There is only God's Eternal Laughter! His Laughter flows into the lonely heart! [*He begins to laugh, his laughter clear and ringing—the laughter of a conqueror arrogant with happiness and the pride of a new triumph. He bends and picks up the body of* MIRIAM *in his arms and, his head thrown back, laughing, he ascends the dais and places her on the table as on a bier. He touches one hand on her breast, as if he were taking an oath to life on her heart, looks upward and laughs, his voice ringing more and more with a terrible unbearable power and beauty that beats those in the room into an abject submissive panic.*]

[TIBERIUS *grovels half under the table, his hands covering his ears, his face on the floor; he is laughing with the agony and terror of death.* POMPEIA *lies face down on the first step and beats it with her fists; she is laughing with horror and self-loathing.* CALIGULA, *his hands clutching his head, pounds it against the edge of the steps; he is laughing with grief and remorse. The rest, soldiers, slaves and the prostitutes of both sexes, writhe and twist distractedly, seeking to hide their heads against each other, beating each other and the floor with clenched hands. An agonized moan of supplicating laughter comes from them all.*]

ALL.
Ha-ha-ha-ha! Ha-ha-ha-ha!
Let us die, Lazarus!
Mercy, Laughing One!
Mercy of death!
Ha-ha-ha-ha! Ha-ha-ha-ha!

[*But the laughter of* LAZARUS *is as remote now as the laughter of a god.*]

CURTAIN

ACT IV

SCENE 1

SCENE: *The same as previous Scene—the same night a short while later. All the lamps are out except the one on the table on the dais which, placed beside the head of* MIRIAM, *shines down upon the white mask of her face. In the half-darkness, the walls are lost in shadow, the room seems immense, the dais nearer.*

LAZARUS *sits on the couch at the right on the dais. His face is strong and proud although his eyes are fixed down on the face of* MIRIAM. *He seems more youthful still now, like a young son who keeps watch by the body of his mother, but at the same time retaining the aloof serenity of the statue of a god. His face expresses sorrow and a happiness that transcends sorrow.*

On the other side of the table, at the end of the couch, TIBERIUS *sits facing front, his elbows on his knees, his large hands with bloated veins hanging loosely. He keeps his gaze averted from the corpse. He talks to* LAZARUS *half over his shoulder.*

On the top step, POMPEIA *sits, facing right, her hands clasped about one knee, the other leg stretched down to the lower step. Her head is thrown back and she is gazing up into* LAZARUS' *face.*

On the step below her, CALIGULA *squats on his haunches, his arms on his knees, his fists pressed to his temples. He is staring straight before him. Only these four people are in the room now.*

TIBERIUS. [*Gloomily.*] Was she dead, Dæmon, and was it thy power that recalled life to her body for that moment? Or was she still living and her words only the last desire of her love to comfort you, Lazarus? [LAZARUS *does not reply.*] If thou dost not tell me, I must always doubt thee, Dæmon.

POMPEIA. [*With a sigh of bewildered happiness, turns to* CALIGULA.] I am glad he laughed, Caligula! Did I say I loved him before? Then it was only my body that wanted a slave. Now it is my heart that desires a master! Now I know love for the first time in my life!

CALIGULA. [*Bitterly.*] Fool! What does he care for love? [*Somberly.*] He loves everyone—but no one—not even me! [*He broods frowningly.*]

POMPEIA. [*Following her own thoughts.*] And now that hag is dead he will need a woman, young and beautiful, to protect and comfort him, to make him a home and bear his children! [*She dreams, her eyes again fixed on* LAZARUS—*then suddenly turning to* CALIGULA.] I am glad I lost our bet. But you must accept some other payment. Now I know love, I may not give myself to any man save him!

CALIGULA. I do not want you! What are you but another animal. Faugh! [*With a grimace of disgust.*] Pleasure is dirty and joyless! Or we who seek it are, which comes to the same thing. [*Then grimly.*] But our bet can rest. This is not the end. There may still be a chance for you to laugh at him!

POMPEIA. No! Now I could not! I should weep for his defeat!

TIBERIUS. [*Gloomily arguing, half*

to himself.] His laughter triumphed over me, but he has not brought her back to life. I think he knows no cure for another's death, as I had hoped. And I must always doubt that it was not some trick—[*harshly*] until I have tested him with his own life! He cannot cheat me then! [*A pause—arguing to himself.*] But he was dead—that much has been proved—and before he died he was old and sad. What did he find beyond there? [*Suddenly—turning to* LAZARUS *now.*] What did you find beyond death, Lazarus?

LAZARUS. [*Exaltedly.*] Life! God's Eternal Laughter!

TIBERIUS. [*Shaking his head.*] I want hope—for me, Tiberius Cæsar.

LAZARUS. What is—you? But there is hope for Man! Love is Man's hope —love for his life on earth, a noble love above suspicion and distrust! Hitherto Man has always suspected his life, and in revenge and self-torture his love has been faithless! He has even betrayed Eternity, his mother, with his slave he calls Immortal Soul! [*He laughs softly, gaily, mockingly—then to* TIBERIUS *directly.*] Hope for you, Tiberius Cæsar? Then dare to love Eternity without your fear desiring to possess her! Be brave enough to be possessed!

TIBERIUS. [*Strangely.*] My mother was the wife of Cæsar. [*Then dully.*] I do not understand.

LAZARUS. Men are too cowardly to understand! And so the worms of their little fears eat them and grow fat and terrible and become their jealous gods they must appease with lies!

TIBERIUS. [*Wearily.*] Your words are meaningless, Lazarus. You are a fool. All laughter is malice, all gods are dead, and life is a sickness.

LAZARUS. [*Laughs pityingly.*] So say the race of men, whose lives are long dyings! They evade their fear of death by becoming so sick of life that

by the time death comes they are too lifeless to fear it! Their disease triumphs over death—a noble victory called resignation! "We are sick," they say, "therefore there is no God in us, therefore there is no God!" Oh, if men would but interpret that first cry of man fresh from the womb as the laughter of one who even then says to his heart, "It is my pride as God to become Man. Then let it be my pride as Man to recreate the God in me!" [*He laughs softly but with exultant pride.*]

POMPEIA. [*Laughing with him— proudly.*] He will create a god in me! I shall be proud!

CALIGULA. [*Pounding his temples with his fists—tortured.*] I am Caligula. I was born in a camp among soldiers. My father was Germanicus, a hero, as all men know. But I do not understand this—and though I burst with pride, I cannot laugh with joy!

TIBERIUS. [*Gloomily.*] Obscurities! I have found nothing in life that merits pride. I am not proud of being Cæsar—and what is a god but a Cæsar over Cæsars? If fools kneel and worship me because they fear me, should I be proud? But Cæsar is a fact, and Tiberius, a man, is one, and I cling to these certainties—and I do not wish to die! If I were sure of eternal sleep beyond there, deep rest and forgetfulness of all I have ever seen or heard or hated or loved on earth, I would gladly die! But surely, Lazarus, nothing is sure—peace the least sure of all —and I fear there is no rest beyond there, that one remembers there as here and cannot sleep, that the mind goes on eternally the same—a long insomnia of memories and regrets and the ghosts of dreams one has poisoned to death passing with white bodies spotted by the leprous fingers of one's lusts. [*Bitterly.*] I fear the long nights now in which I lie awake and listen to Death dancing round me in the darkness, prancing to the drum beat of my heart! [*He shudders.*] And I am afraid, Lazarus—afraid that there is no sleep beyond there, either!

LAZARUS. There is peace! [*His words are like a benediction he pronounces upon them. Soothed in a mysterious, childlike way, they repeat the word after him, wonderingly.*]

POMPEIA. Peace?

CALIGULA. Peace?

TIBERIUS. Peace? [*For a long moment there is complete silence. Then* TIBERIUS *sighs heavily, shaking his head.*] Peace! Another word blurred into a senseless sigh by men's longing! A bubble of froth blown from the lips of the dying toward the stars! No! [*He grins bitterly—then looks at* LAZARUS *—somberly contemptuous and threatening.*] You are pleased to act the mysterious, Jew, but I shall solve you! [*Then with a lawyer-like incisiveness.*] There is one certainty about you and I must know the cause—for there must be a cause and a rational explanation! You were fifty when you died—

LAZARUS. [*Smiling mockingly.*] Yes. When I died.

TIBERIUS. [*Unheeding.*] And now your appearance is of one younger by a score. Not alone your appearance! You *are* young. I see the fact, the effect. And I demand an explanation of the cause without mystic nonsense or evasion. [*Threateningly.*] And I warn you to answer directly in plain words —and not to laugh, you understand!— not to dare!—or I shall lose patience with you and—[*with a grim smile*] I can be terrible! [LAZARUS *smiles gently at him. He turns away with confused annoyance, then back to* LAZARUS, *resuming his lawyer-like manner.*] What was it restored your youth? How did you contrive that your body reversed the natural process and grows younger?

Is it a charm by which you invoke a supernatural force? Or is it a powder you dissolve in wine? Or a liquid? Or an unguent you rub into the skin to revitalize the old bones and tissues? Or—what is it, Lazarus?

LAZARUS. [*Gently.*] I know that age and time are but timidities of thought.

TIBERIUS. [*Broodingly—as if he had not heard—persuasively.*] Perhaps you ask yourself, what would Tiberius do with youth? Then, because you must have heard rumors of my depravity, you will conclude the old lecher desires youth for his lusts! [*He laughs harshly.*] Ha! Why, do not my faithful subjects draw pictures of an old buck goat upon the walls and write above them, Cæsar? And they are just. In self-contempt of Man I have made this man, myself, the most swinish and contemptible of men! Yes! In all this empire there is no man so base a hog as I! [*He grins bitterly and ironically.*] My claim to this excellence, at least, is not contested! Everyone admits therein Tiberius is by right their Cæsar! [*He laughs bitterly.*] Ha! So who would believe Tiberius if he said, I want youth again because I loathe lust and long for purity!

LAZARUS. [*Gently.*] I believe you, Cæsar.

TIBERIUS. [*Stares at him—deeply moved.*] You—believe—? [*Then gruffly.*] You lie! You are not mad— and only a madman would believe another man! [*Then confidingly, leaning over toward* LAZARUS.] I know it is folly to speak—but—one gets old, one becomes talkative, one wishes to confess, to say the thing one has always kept hidden, to reveal one's unique truth—and there is so little time left— and one is alone! Therefore the old— like children—talk to themselves, for they have reached that hopeless wisdom of experience which knows that though one were to cry it in the streets to multitudes, or whisper it in the kiss to one's beloved, the only ears that can ever hear one's secret are one's own! [*He laughs bitterly.*] And so I talk aloud, Lazarus! I talk to my loneliness!

LAZARUS. [*Simply.*] I hear, Tiberius.

TIBERIUS. [*Again moved and confused—forcing a mocking smile.*] Liar! Eavesdropper! You merely—listen! [*Then he turns away.*] My mother, Livia, that strong woman, giving birth to me, desired not a child, but a Cæsar —just as, married to Augustus, she loved him not but loved herself as Cæsar's wife. She made me feel, in the proud questioning of her scornful eyes, that to win her mother love I must become Cæsar. She poisoned Prince Marcellus and young Gaius and Lucius that the way might be clear for me. I used to see their blood dance in red specks before my eyes when I looked at the sky. Now—[*he brushes his hand before his eyes*] it is all a red blot! I cannot distinguish. There have been too many. My mother—her blood is in that blot, for I revenged myself on her. I did not kill her, it is true, but I deprived her of her power and she died, as I knew she must, that powerful woman who bore me as a weapon! The murder was subtle and cruel—how cruel only that passionate, deep-breasted woman unslaked by eighty years of devoured desires could know! Too cruel! I did not go to her funeral. I was afraid her closed eyes might open and look at me! [*Then with almost a cry.*] I want youth, Lazarus, that I may play again about her feet with the love I felt for her before I learned to read her eyes! [*He half sobs, bowing his head. A pause.*]

CALIGULA. [*Nudging POMPEIA— with a crafty whisper.*] Do you hear?

The old lecher talks to himself. He is becoming senile. He will soon die. And I shall be Cæsar. Then I shall laugh!

POMPEIA. [*Staring up at LAZARUS' face, hearing only CALIGULA's words without their meaning.*] No. My Lazarus does not laugh now. See. His mouth is silent—and a little sad, I think.

LAZARUS. [*Gently and comfortingly.*] I hear, Tiberius.

TIBERIUS. [*Harshly.*] I hated that woman, my mother, and I still hate her! Have you ever loved, Lazarus? [*Then with a glance at MIRIAM's body and a shuddering away from it— vaguely.*] I was forgetting her. I killed your love, too, did I not? Well, I must! I envy those who are loved. Where I can, I kill love—for retribution's sake—but much of it escapes me. [*Then harshly again.*] I loved Agrippina. We were married. A son was born to us. We were happy. Then that proud woman, my mother, saw my happiness. Was she jealous of my love? Or did she know no happy man would wish to be Cæsar? Well, she condemned my happiness to death. She whispered to Augustus and he ordered me to divorce Agrippina. I should have opened her veins and mine, and died with her. But my mother stayed by me, Agrippina was kept away, my mother spoke to me and even wept, that tall woman, strong as a great man, and I consented that my love be murdered. Then my mother married me to a whore. Why? The whore was Cæsar's daughter, true—but I feel that was not all of it, that my mother wished to keep me tortured that I might love her alone and long to be Cæsar! [*He laughs harshly.*] Ha! In brief, I married the whore, she tortured me, my mother's scheming prospered—that subtle and crafty woman!—and many years passed in being here and there, in doing this and that, in growing full of hate and revengeful ambition to be Cæsar. At last, Augustus died. I was Cæsar. Then I killed that whore, my wife, and I starved my mother's strength to death until she died, and I began to take pleasure in vengeance upon men, and pleasure in taking vengeance on myself. [*He grins horribly.*] It is all very simple, as you see! [*He suddenly starts to his feet—with harsh arrogance and pride, threateningly.*] Enough! Why do I tell you these old tales? Must I explain to you why I want youth? It is my whim! I am Cæsar! And now I must lie down and try to sleep! And it is my command that you reveal the secret of your youth to me when I awake, or else—[*with malignant cruelty*] I will have to revenge the death of a hope on you—and a hope at my age demands a terrible expiation on its slayer! [*He walks down and starts to go off, right—then turns and addresses* LAZARUS *with grim irony.*] Good night to you, Lazarus. And remember there shall be death while I am Cæsar! [*He turns to go.*]

LAZARUS. [*Smiling affectionately at him, shakes his head.*] Cæsar must believe in death. But does the husband of Agrippina?

TIBERIUS. [*Stops short and stares at* LAZARUS, *confused and stuttering.*] What—what—do you mean, Lazarus?

LAZARUS. I have heard your loneliness.

TIBERIUS. [*Cruelly and grimly again.*] So much the more reason why my pride should kill you! Remember that! [*He turns and strides off into the darkness at right.*]

CALIGULA. [*Peers after him until sure he is gone—then gets up and begins a grotesque, hopping dance, singing a verse of the legionary's song.*]

A bold legionary am I
March, oh march on!
A Roman eagle was my daddy
My mother was a drunken drabby
Oh march on to the wars!

[*He laughs gratingly, posturing and gesticulating up at* LAZARUS.] Ha-ha-ha! He is gone! I can breathe! His breath in the same air suffocates me! The gods grant mine do the same for him! But he is failing! He talks to himself like a man in second childhood. His words are a thick babble I could not hear. They well from his lips like clots of blood from a re-opened wound. I kept listening to the beating of his heart. It sounded slow, slower than when I last heard it. Did you detect that, Lazarus? Once or twice I thought it faltered— [*He draws in his breath with an avid gasp—then laughs gratingly.*] Ha-ha-ha— [*Grandiloquently.*] Tiberius, the old buck goat, will soon be gone, my friends, and in his place you will be blessed with the beautiful young god, Caligula! Hail to Caligula! Hail! Ha-ha-ha— [*His laughter suddenly breaks off into a whimper and he stands staring around him in a panic of fear that he has been overheard. He slinks noiselessly up the steps of the dais and squats coweringly at* LAZARUS' *feet, blinking up at his face in monkey-wise, clutching* LAZARUS' *hand in both of his. His teeth can be heard chattering together in nervous fear.*]

[POMPEIA, *whose gaze has remained fixed on* LAZARUS' *throughout, has gradually moved closer to him until she, too, is at his feet, half-kneeling beneath the table on which* MIRIAM *lies, side by side with* CALIGULA *but as oblivious of him as he is of her.*]

[*Having grown calmer now,* CALIGULA *speaks again—mournful and bewildered.*]

CALIGULA. Why should I love you,

Lazarus? Your laughter taunts me! It insults Cæsar! It denies Rome! But I will warn you again. Escape! Tonight Tiberius' mood is to play sentimental, but tomorrow he will jeer while hyenas gnaw at your skull and lick your brain. And then—there is pain, Lazarus! There is pain!

POMPEIA. [*Pressing her hand to her own heart—with a shudder.*] Yes, there is pain!

LAZARUS. [*Smiling down on them —gently.*] If you can answer Yes to pain, there is no pain!

POMPEIA. [*Passionately.*] Yes! Yes! I love Lazarus!

CALIGULA. [*With a bitter grin.*] Do not take pain away from us! It is our one truth. Without pain there is nothing—a nothingness in which even your laughter, Lazarus, is swallowed at one gulp like a whining gnat by the cretin's silence of immensity! Ha-ha! No, we must keep pain! Especially Cæsar must! Pain must twinkle with a mad mirth in a Cæsar's eyes—men's pain—or they would become dissatisfied and disrespectful! Ha-ha! [*He stops his grating laughter abruptly and continues mournfully.*] I am sick, Lazarus, sick of cruelty and lust and human flesh and all the imbecilities of pleasure—the unclean antics of half-witted children! [*With a mounting agony of longing.*] I would be clean! If I could only laugh your laughter, Lazarus! That would purify my heart. For I could wish to love all men, as you love them—as I love you! If only I did not fear them and despise them! If I could only believe—believe in them—in life—in myself!—believe that one man or woman in the world knew and loved the real Caligula— then I might have faith in Caligula myself—then I might laugh your laughter!

LAZARUS. [*Suddenly, in a quiet but compelling voice.*] I, who know you, love you, Caligula. [*Gently patting his head.*] I love Caligula.

CALIGULA. [*Staring up at him in pathetic confusion.*] You? You? You, Lazarus? [*He begins to tremble all over as if in a seizure—chokingly.*] Beware! It is not good—not just—to make fun of me—to laugh at my misery—saying you love— [*In a frenzy, he jumps to his feet threatening LAZARUS.*] Are you trying to fool me, hypocrite? Do you think I have become so abject that you dare—? Because I love you, do you presume—? Do you think I am your slave, dog of a Jew, that you can—insult—to my face—the heir of Cæsar— [*He stutters and stammers with rage, hopping up and down grotesquely, shaking his fist at LAZARUS, who smiles at him affectionately as a child in a tantrum.*]

LAZARUS. [*Catching his eyes and holding them with his glance—calmly.*] Believe, Caligula!

CALIGULA. [*Again overcome—stuttering with strange terror.*] Believe? But I cannot! I must not! You cannot know me, if— You are a holy man! You are a god in a mortal body—you can laugh with joy to be alive—while I— Oh, no, you cannot love me! There is nothing in me at bottom but a despising and an evil eye! You cannot! You are only being kind. [*Hysterically.*] I do not want your kindness! I hate your pity! I am too proud! I am too strong! [*He collapses weepingly, kneeling and clutching LAZARUS' hand in both of his.*]

LAZARUS. [*Smiling.*] You are so proud of being evil! What if there is no evil? What if there are only health and sickness? Believe in the healthy god called Man in you! Laugh at Caligula, the funny clown who beats the backside of his shadow with a bladder and thinks thereby he is Evil, the Enemy of God! [*He suddenly lifts the face of CALIGULA and stares into his eyes.*] Believe! What if you are a man and men are despicable? Men are also unimportant! Men pass! Like rain into the sea! The sea remains! Man remains! Man slowly arises from the past of the race of men that was his tomb of death! For Man death is not! Man, Son of God's Laughter, *is!* [*He begins to laugh triumphantly, staring deep into* CALIGULA'S *eyes.*] Is, Caligula! Believe in the laughing god within you!

CALIGULA. [*Bursting suddenly into choking, joyful laughter—like a visionary.*] I believe! I believe there is love even for Caligula! I can laugh—now—Lazarus! Free laughter! Clean! No sickness! No lust for death! My corpse no longer rots in my heart! The tomb is full of sunlight! I am alive! I who love Man, I who can love and laugh! Listen, Lazarus! I dream! When I am Cæsar, I will devote my power to your truth. I will decree that there must be kindness and love! I will make the Empire one great Blessed Isle! Rome shall know happiness, it shall believe in life, it shall learn to laugh your laughter, Lazarus, or I— [*He raises his hand in an imperial autocratic gesture.*]

LAZARUS. [*Gaily mocking.*] Or you will cut off its head?

CALIGULA. [*Fiercely.*] Yes! I will—! [*Then meeting* LAZARUS' *eyes, he beats his head with his fists crazily.*] Forgive me! I forget! I forget!

LAZARUS. Go out under the sky! Let your heart climb on laughter to a star! Then make it look down at earth, and watch Caligula commanding Life under pain of death to do his will! [*He laughs.*]

CALIGULA. [*Laughing.*] I will! I do! I laugh at him! Caligula is a trained ape, a humped cripple! Now I take him out under the sky, where I can watch his monkey tricks, where there is space for laughter and where this

new joy, your love of me, may dance! [*Laughing clearly and exultantly, he runs out through the arched doorway at rear.*]

LAZARUS. [*Stops laughing—shaking his head, almost sadly.*] They forget! It is too soon for laughter! [*Then grinning at himself.*] What, Lazarus? Are you, too, thinking in terms of time, old fool so soon to reënter infinity? [*He laughs with joyous self-mockery.*]

POMPEIA. [*Who has crept to his feet, kisses his hand passionately.*] I love you, Lazarus!

LAZARUS. [*Stops laughing, and looks down at her gently.*] And I love you, woman.

POMPEIA. [*With a gasp of delight.*] You? [*She stares up into his eyes doubtingly, raising her face toward his.*] Then—put your arms around me. [*He does so, smiling gently.*] And hold me to you. [*He presses her closer to him.*] And kiss me. [*He kisses her on the forehead.*] No, on the lips! [*He kisses her. She flings her arms about his neck passionately and kisses him again and again—then slowly draws away—remains looking into his eyes a long time, shrinking back from him with bewildered pain which speedily turns to rage and revengeful hatred.*] No! No! It is *my* love, not Love! I want you to know *my* love, to give me back love—for me—only for me—Pompeia—my body, my heart—me, a woman—not Woman, women! Do I love Man, men? I hate men! I love you, Lazarus—a man—a lover—a father to children! I want love—as you loved that woman there [*she points to* MIRIAM] that I poisoned for love of you! But did you love her—or just Woman, wife and mother of men? [*She stares—then as if reading admission in his eyes, she springs to her feet.*] Liar! Cheat! Hypocrite! Thief! [*Half hysterical with rage, pain and grief, she bends over* MIRIAM *and smoothes the hair back from her forehead.*] Poor wife! Poor woman! How he must have tortured you! Now I remember the pity in your eyes when you looked at me! Oh, how his soothing gray words must have pecked at the wound in your heart like doves with bloody beaks! [*Then with sudden harshness.*] But perhaps you were too dull to understand, too poor and tired and ugly and old to care, too slavish—! Pah! [*She turns away with contempt and faces* LAZARUS *with revengeful hatred.*] Did you think I would take her place—become your slave, wait upon you, give you love and passion and beauty in exchange for phrases about man and gods—you who are neither a man nor a god but a dead thing without desire! You dared to hope I would give my body, my love, to you! [*She spits in his face and laughs harshly.*] You insolent fool! I shall punish you! You shall be tortured as you have tortured! [*She laughs wildly—then steps down from the dais and goes off right, crying distractedly.*] Cæsar! This man has made you a fool before all the world! Torture him, Cæsar! Now! Let the people witness! Send heralds to wake them! Torture him, Cæsar, the man who laughs at you! Ha-ha-ha-ha! [*Her laughter is caught up by all the* GIRLS *and* YOUTHS *of the palace, who, as she disappears, led by their* CHORUS, *pour in from each side of the room and dance forward to group themselves around the dais as in the previous scene, staring at* LAZARUS, *laughing cruelly, falsely, stridently.*]

CHORUS. [*Tauntingly.*]
Ha-ha-ha-ha!
Laugh now, Lazarus!
Let us see you laugh!
Ha-ha-ha-ha!

CROWD. [*Echoing.*]
Ha-ha-ha-ha!
Ha-ha-ha-ha!

LAZARUS. [*Moves, and immediately there is silence. He bends down and kisses* MIRIAM *and picks her up in his arms. Talking down to her face— with a tender smile.*] Farewell! You are home! And now I will take your body home to earth! Space is too far away, you said! Home in the earth! There will be so much for you to do there! Home! Earth! [*His voice trembling a bit.*] Farewell, body of Miriam. My grief is a lonely cry wailing in the home in my heart that you have left forever! [*Then exultantly.*] But what am I? Now your love has become Eternal Love! Now, since your life passed, I feel Eternal Life made nobler by your selflessness! Love has grown purer! The laughter of God is more profoundly tender! [*He looks up in an ecstasy and descends the dais, carrying her.*] Yes, that is it! That is it, my Miriam! [*Laughing softly and tenderly, he walks around the dais and carries the body out through the doorway in rear.*] [*The* CHORUS *and* YOUTHS *and* GIRLS *make way for him in awed silence—then scurry around to right and left, forming an aisle through which he passes—then after he has gone out through the arch, they close into a semicircular group again, staring after him, and a whisper of strange, bewildered, tender laughter comes from them.*]

CHORUS. [*In this whisper.*]
That is it!
Love is pure!
Laughter is tender!
Laugh!

CROWD. [*Echoing.*] Laugh! Laugh!

CURTAIN

SCENE 2

SCENE: *The arena of an amphitheatre. It is just before dawn of the same night.* CÆSAR's *throne is on the left at the extreme front, facing right, turned a little toward front. It is lighted by four immense lamps. In front of the throne is a marble railing that tops the wall that encloses the arena. In the rear the towering pile of the circular amphitheatre is faintly outlined in deeper black against the dark sky.*

TIBERIUS *sits on the throne, his eyes fixed on the middle of the arena off right, where, bound to a high stake after he had been tortured,* LAZARUS *is now being burnt alive over a huge pile of faggots. The crackling of the flames is heard. Their billowing rise and fall is reflected on the masked faces of the multitude who sit on the banked tiers of marble behind and to the rear of the throne, with their* CHORUS, *seven men masked in Middle Age in the Servile, Hypocritical type, grouped on each side of the throne of* CÆSAR *on a lower tier.*

Half-kneeling before TIBERIUS, *her chin resting on her hands on top of the marble rail,* POMPEIA *also stares at* LAZARUS.

Before the curtain, the crackle of the flames and an uproar of human voices from the multitude, jeering, hooting, laughing at LAZARUS *in cruel mockery of his laughter. This sound has risen to its greatest volume as the curtain rises.*

CHORUS. [*Chanting mockingly.*]
Ha-ha-ha-ha!
Burn and laugh!
Laugh now, Lazarus!
Ha-ha-ha-ha!

CROWD. [*Chanting with revengeful mockery.*] Ha-ha-ha-ha!

TIBERIUS. Who laughs now, Laza-

rus—thou or Cæsar? Ha-ha—! [*With awe.*] His flesh melts in the fire but his eyes shine with peace!

POMPEIA. How he looks at me! [*Averting her eyes with a shudder.*] Command them to put out his eyes, Cæsar!

TIBERIUS. [*Harshly.*] No. I want to read his eyes when they see death! [*Then averting his face—guiltily.*] He is looking at me, not you. I should not have listened to your cries for his death.

POMPEIA. [*Turning to him again with a shudder of agony—beseechingly.*] Have them put out his eyes, Cæsar! They call to me!

TIBERIUS. [*As if not hearing her—to himself.*] Why do I feel remorse? His laughter dies and is forgotten, and the hope it raised dies— [*With sudden excitement.*] And yet—he must know something—and if he would—even now he could tell— [*Suddenly rising to his feet he calls imploringly.*] Lazarus!

CHORUS. [*Chanting in a great imploring chorus now.*] Lazarus!

CROWD. [*Echoing.*] Lazarus!

SOLDIER'S VOICE. [*Calling from off beside the stake.*] You had us gag him, Cæsar, so he might not laugh. Shall we cut away the gag?

POMPEIA. [*In terror.*] No, Cæsar! He will laugh! And I will go to him! [*Desperately.*] He will laugh at you, Cæsar—and the mob will laugh with him!

TIBERIUS. [*Struggles with himself —then calls.*] Lazarus! If you hear let your eyes answer, and I will grant the mercy of death to end your agony! Is there hope of love somewhere for men on earth?

CHORUS. [*Intoning as before.*]
Is there hope of love
For us on earth?

CROWD.
Hope of love
For us on earth!

SOLDIER'S VOICE. His eyes laugh,
Cæsar!

TIBERIUS. [*In a strange frenzy
now.*] Hear me, thou Dæmon of
Laughter! Hear and answer, I beseech thee, who alone hath known
joy! [*More and more wildly.*] How
must we live? Wherein lies happiness?

CHORUS. Wherein lies happiness?

CROWD. Wherein, happiness?

TIBERIUS. Why are we born? To
what end must we die?

CHORUS. Why are we born to die?

CROWD. Why are we born?

SOLDIER'S VOICE. His eyes laugh,
Cæsar! He is dying! He would
speak!

CHORUS and CROWD. [*In one great
cry.*] Cæsar! Let Lazarus speak!

POMPEIA. [*Terrified.*] No, Cæsar!
He will laugh—and you will die—and
I will go to him!

TIBERIUS. [*Torn—arguing with his
fear.*] But—he may know some hope—
[*Then making his decision, with grim
fatalism.*] Hope—or nothing! [*Calls to
the* SOLDIERS.] Let him speak!

CHORUS and CROWD. [*Cheering.*]
Hail, Cæsar!

LAZARUS. [*His voice comes, recognizably the voice of* LAZARUS, *yet with
a strange, fresh, clear quality of boyhood, gaily mocking with life.*] Hail,
Cæsar!

CROWD. [*Frantic with hope.*] Hail,
Lazarus!

TIBERIUS. Pull away the fire from
him! I see death in his eyes! [*The
flaming reflections in the banked,
masked faces dance madly as the*
SOLDIERS *rake back the fire from the
stake. With a forced, taunting mockery.*] What do you say now, Lazarus?
You are dying!

CHORUS and CROWD. [*Taking his
tone—mockingly.*] You are dying,
Lazarus!

LAZARUS. [*His voice a triumphant
assertion of the victory of life over
pain and death.*] Yes!

TIBERIUS. [*Triumphant yet disap-
pointed—with scorn and rage.*] Ha!
You admit it, do you, coward! Craven!
Knave! Duper of fools! Clown! Liar!
Die! I laugh at you! Ha-ha-ha-ha—
[*His voice breaks chokingly.*]

CROWD. [*Led by their* CHORUS—*in
the same frenzy of disappointment,
with all sorts of grotesque and obscene
gestures and noises, thumbing their
fingers to their noses, wagging them at
their ears, sticking out their tongues,
slapping their behinds, barking, crowing like roosters, howling, and hooting
in every conceivable manner.*] Yah!
Yah! Yellow Gut! Bungkisser! Muck-
heel! Scumwiper! Liar! Pig! Jackal!
Die! We laugh at you! Ha-ha-ha—
[*Their voices, too, break.*]

POMPEIA. [*Rising to her feet like
one in a trance, staring toward* LAZA-
RUS.] They are tormenting him. I
hear him crying to me! [*She moves to
the top of the steps leading to the
arena.*]

LAZARUS. [*His voice thrilling with
exultance.*] O men, fear not life! You
die—but there is no death for Man!
[*He begins to laugh, and at the sound
of his laughter, a great spell of silence
settles upon all his hearers—then as
his laughter rises, they begin to laugh
with him.*]

POMPEIA. [*Descending the steps
like a sleepwalker.*] I hear his laughter
calling. I must go to him.

TIBERIUS. [*As if he realized something was happening that was against
his will—trying feebly to be imperial.*]
I command you not to laugh! Cæsar
commands— [*Calling feebly to the
SOLDIERS.] Put back—the gag! Stop
his laughter! [*The laughter of* LAZA-

RUS *gaily and lovingly mocks back at him.*]

SOLDIER'S VOICE. [*His voice gently remonstrating.*] We may not, Cæsar. We love his laughter! [*They laugh with him.*]

CHORUS and CROWD. [*In a soft, dreamy murmur.*]
We love his laughter!
We laugh!

TIBERIUS. [*Dreamily.*] Then—pile the fire back around him. High and higher! Let him blaze to the stars! I laugh with him!

SOLDIER'S VOICE. [*Gently and gravely.*] That is just, Cæsar. We love men flaming toward the stars! We laugh with him!

CHORUS and CROWD. [*As the flames, piled back and fed anew by the SOLDIERS, flare upward and are reflected on their masks in dancing waves of light.*]
We love men flaming toward the stars!
We laugh!

POMPEIA. [*In the arena.*] The fire calls me. My burning heart calls for the fire! [*She laughs softly and passes swiftly across the arena toward LAZARUS.*]

TIBERIUS. [*In a sort of childish complaint.*] You must pardon me, Lazarus. This is my Cæsar's duty—to kill you! You have no right to laugh—before all these people—at Cæsar. It is not kind. [*He sobs snuffingly—then begins to laugh at himself.*] [*Suddenly the flames waver, die down, then shoot up again and POMPEIA's laughter is heard for a moment, rising clear and passionately with that of LAZARUS, then dying quickly out.*]

SOLDIER'S VOICE. A woman has thrown herself in the flames, Cæsar! She laughs with Lazarus!

TIBERIUS. [*In a sudden panicky flurry—feverishly.*] Quick, Lazarus!

You will soon be silent! Speak!—in the name of man's solitude—his agony of farewell—what is beyond there, Lazarus? [*His voice has risen to a passionate entreaty.*]

CHORUS. [*In a great pleading echo.*] What is beyond there, Lazarus?

CROWD. What is beyond?

LAZARUS. [*His voice speaking lovingly, with a surpassing clearness and exaltation.*] Life! Eternity! Stars and dust! God's Eternal Laughter! [*His laughter bursts forth now in its highest pitch of ecstatic summons to the feast and sacrifice of Life, the Eternal.*] [*The crowds laugh with him in a frenzied rhythmic chorus. Led by the CHORUS, they pour down from the banked walls of the amphitheatre and dance in the flaring reflection of the flames strange wild measures of liberated joy. TIBERIUS stands on the raised dais laughing great shouts of clear, fearless laughter.*]

CHORUS. [*Chanting as they dance.*]
Laugh! Laugh!
We are stars!
We are dust!
We are gods!
We are laughter!

CROWD.
We are dust!
We are gods!
Laugh! Laugh!

CALIGULA. [*Enters from behind TIBERIUS. His aspect is wild, his hair disheveled, his clothes torn, he is panting as if exhausted by running. He stares toward the flames stupidly—then screams despairingly above the chant.*] Lazarus! I come to save you! Do you still live, Lazarus?

TIBERIUS. [*Has been speaking. His words are now heard as the tumult momentarily dies down.*] I have lived long enough! I will die with Lazarus! I no longer fear death! I laugh at

Cæsar! I advise you, my brothers, fear not Cæsars! Seek Man in the brotherhood of the dust! Cæsar is your fear of Man! I counsel you, laugh away your Cæsars!

CALIGULA. [*With resentful jealousy and rage—in a voice rising to a scream.*] What do I hear, Lazarus? You laugh with your murderer? You give him your laughter? You have forgotten me—my love—you make him love you—you make him laugh at Cæsars—at me! [*Suddenly springs on* TIBERIUS *in a fury and grabbing him by the throat chokes him, forcing him back on the throne—screaming.*] Die, traitor! Die! [TIBERIUS' *body relaxes in his hands, dead, and slips from the chair.* CALIGULA *rushes madly down the stairs into the midst of the oblivious, laughing, dancing crowd, screaming.*] You have betrayed me, dog of a Jew! You have betrayed Cæsar! [*Beginning to be caught by the contagion of the laughter.*] Ha-ah— No! I will not laugh! I will kill you! Give me a spear! [*He snatches a spear from a soldier and fights his way drunkenly toward the flames, like a man half overcome by a poisonous gas, shouting, half-laughing in spite of himself, half-weeping with rage.*] Ha-ah— The gods be with Cæsar Caligula! O Immortal Gods, give thy brother strength! You shall die, Lazarus—die—Ha-ah—! [*He disappears toward the flames, his spear held ready to stab.*]

CHORUS and CROWD. [*Who have been entirely oblivious of him—chanting.*]
Laugh! Laugh!
We are gods!
We are dust!

LAZARUS. [*At his first word there is a profound silence in which each dancer remains frozen in the last movement.*] Hail, Caligula Cæsar!

Men forget! [*He laughs with gay mockery as at a child.*]

CHORUS and CROWD. [*Starting to laugh.*] Laugh! Laugh! [*Then there is a fierce cry of rage from* CALIGULA *and* LAZARUS' *laughter ceases, and with it the laughter of the crowd turns to a wail of fear and lamentation.*]

CALIGULA. [*Dashes back among them waving his bloody spear and rushing up to the throne stands on it and strikes a grandiose pose.*] I have killed God! I am Death! Death is Cæsar!

CHORUS and CROWD. [*Turning and scurrying away—huddled in fleeing groups, crouching close to the ground like a multitude of terrified rats, their voices squeaky now with fright.*] Hail, Cæsar! Hail to Death! [*They are gone.*]

CALIGULA. [*Keeping his absurd majestic pose, turns and addresses with rhetorical intoning, and flowing gestures, the body of* LAZARUS, *high upon its stake, the flames below it now flickering fitfully.*] Hail, Caligula! Hero of heroes, conqueror of the Dæmon, Lazarus, who taught the treason that fear and death were dead! But I am Lord of Fear! I am Cæsar of Death! And you, Lazarus, are carrion! [*Then in a more conversational tone, putting aside his grandiose airs, confidentially.*] I had to kill you, Lazarus! Surely your good sense tells you— You heard what the old fool, Tiberius, told the mob. A moment more and there would have been a revolution—no more Cæsars—and my dream—! [*He stops—bewilderedly.*] My dream? Did I kill laughter? I had just learned to laugh—with love! [*More confusedly.*] I must be a little mad, Lazarus. It was one terror too many, to have been laughing your laughter in the night, to have been dreaming great yearning dreams of all the good my love might do for men when I was Cæsar—and then, to hear the old howling of mob lust, and to run here—and there a high white flame amidst the fire—you, Lazarus!— dying!—laughing with him—Tiberius —betraying me—who loved you, Lazarus! Yes, I became mad! I am mad! And I can laugh my own mad laughter, Lazarus—my own! Ha-ha-ha-ha! [*He laughs with a wild triumphant madness and again rhetorically, with sweeping gestures and ferocious capers.*] And all of men are vile and mad, and I shall be their madmen's Cæsar! [*He turns as if addressing an amphitheatre full of his subjects.*] O my good people, my faithful scum, my brother swine, Lazarus is dead and we have murdered great laughter, and it befits our madness to have done so, and it is befitting above all to have Caligula for Cæsar! [*Then savagely.*] Kneel down! Abase yourselves! I am your Cæsar and your God! Hail! [*He stands saluting himself with a crazy intensity that is not without grandeur. A pause. Suddenly the silence seems to crush down upon him; he is aware that he is alone in the vast arena; he whirls about, looking around him as if he felt an assassin at his back; he lunges with his spear at imaginary foes, jumping, dodging from side to side, yelping*]. Ho, there! Help! Help!

Your Cæsar calls you! Help, my people! To the rescue! [*Suddenly throwing his spear away and sinking on his knees, his face toward* LAZARUS, *supplicatingly.*] Lazarus! Forgive me! Help me! Fear kills me! Save me from death! [*He is groveling in a paroxysm of terror, grinding his face in his fists as if to hide it.*]

LAZARUS. [*His voice is heard in a gentle, expiring sigh of compassion, followed by a faint dying note of laughter that rises and is lost in the sky like the flight of his soul back into the womb of Infinity.*] Fear not, Caligula! There is no death!

CALIGULA. [*Lifts his head at the first sound and rises with the laughter to his feet, until, as it is finally lost, he is on tip-toes, his arms straining upward to the sky, a tender, childish laughter of love on his lips.*] I laugh, Lazarus! I laugh with you! [*Then grief-stricken.*] Lazarus! [*He hides his face in his hands, weeping.*] No more! [*Then beats his head with his fists.*] I will remember! I will! [*Then suddenly, with a return to grotesqueness —harshly.*] All the same, I killed him and I proved there is death! [*Immediately overcome by remorse, groveling and beating himself.*] Fool! Madman! Forgive me, Lazarus! Men forget!

CURTAIN

1927

ROBINSON JEFFERS
(1887–   )

ODE ON HUMAN DESTINIES *

I

Here in the beautiful peninsula
Most gladly would I rest, never to be

* Reprinted by permission of Horace Liveright, Inc. Copyright, 1924, 1925.

A wanderer more by land nor weary
    sea;
Here gladly would I rest, and put
    away
All hot and vulgar cares,
All foolish-eager dreams, only to see
The yearly blossoming of the stately
    pines,
And the azure limpid sweet cloud-
    carrying airs

That bathe the Santa Lucian summit-
    lines.
Here gladly would I rest, and in high
    verse—
Whenas that quickening spirit should
    have wrought
Into full ripeness the hoarded patient
    thought—
Of human fates rehearse
Their majesty, that needs nor God nor
    goal:—
Thus if long time and tranquil were
    assured:
But in my ears a word
Of sunderance hath been spoken, and
    I know
How soon the year of quiet will cease
    to be,
How soon from stormy and fiery years
    my soul
Yearn back upon her peace of long
    ago,
This rare tranquillity.
Therefore, albeit from heart and will
    most pure,
Untimely thoughts, a theme not yet
    mature
Are mine: but if occasion yield me
    space
In any future days,
Or truce of storm, I shall not fail to
    speak
In full what now in strains unworthy
    and weak,—

II

And as a messenger whom spears
Menace, in the people's ears
Shouts his word of further war,
News of danger and of hope,
Crying of death and boast of faith:—
As a falcon on the slope
Of the coming storm afar
And wildly driven,
Cries aloud 'twixt earth and
    heaven
Ere he pass, and down the wind
Be mingled with the lightning bright
    and blind.

III

I stood upon the Promontory of
    Stones;
A flashing day in February; an hour
Tumultuous, trembling between sun
    and shower
And thunder. Like a crystal torrent
    streamed
The wind against my face; in passion-
    ate tones
The ocean spake; the sea-line gleamed;
The wild gulls battled in the sea-
    wind's power.
On water-glimmering rocks below,
    some worn
And iron-bolted beams, a dead ship's
    bones,
Hung fast but never tranquil. Fast
    they hung,
Yet heaved they ever and were swung
By the ocean's touch, and soft wet
    slivers torn
From their hard sides. Northward the
    clouds were rushing;
White waves above the blackened
    rocks were gushing;
High on the rapid heads of twisted
    foam
The seawrack and the bladderwrack
    upborne
Writhed serpent-fashion, black and
    brown and green.
And white and black, across the light-
    blue dome
Of heaven through sudden chasms of
    cloud far-seen,
Strained broken vapors dizzily; silver-
    veiled
Quick drifts of rain in dazzling
    sheen
Adown the Santa Lucian slopes did
    come.
How many broken rainbows flashed
    between!
Among the mists they glowed and
    paled,
Gleamed and vanished: I beheld
Never a single perfect arc.

As Hope's bright pallid angels inter-
vene
Delusive 'twixt the rushing dark
And fitful starts and lights of this our
life:
So fragmentary did the rainbows lean
Out of the clouds, and vanish; in the
strife
Of winds and vapors o'er the valley-
throat
Inwoven they were; they shone, en-
during not.
With flecks of rain and spray the wind
was rife;
The westering sun's great beams
Waved like a whirling of swords
Above my head; the world seemed
all to float
On thwart and sidelong streams;
As in rain-flooded river-fords
Horse and man and ferry-boat
Toppling I have seen go down,
Horse and oarsman overthrown,
And churning hoofs that struggle in
the tawny flood.
—I turned, and climbed a little way,
and stood
Beside that mighty boulder-stone
Which, with its brothers, names the
Promontory.
Serene it stands, a child of the Earth's
own;
With light-gray lichen old its flanks
are hoary;
And such a monument it seems
As primal men laboring in dreams
At Stonehenge raised or near the
Breton shore
Unto some God's or mortal chieftain's
glory;
But this not human, thence intransi-
tory,
Stands, and the ocean's roar
Shakes it not; from so deep-grown root
it springs,
Knit with the Earth's old central
stony core.
—Above it flashed the fragmentary
bows,

Swept the storm and swooped the wild
sea-wings;
It stood in strong repose,
Unmoving evermore.
Thither when I was tired of turbu-
lence
And of the day's and light's imperma-
nence,
The sunderings, the vanishings,
I lifted up my eyes and heart, to
adore
The inveterate stability of things.
—Toward evening moved the day; the
mighty world
Silently eastward whirled;
Above the waves the windy sunset
burned.
—Unmoving was that monumental
stone?
Unmoved, when all the face of Earth
is turned?
—Yea, as to man unmoved.
Ourselves are the only measure of our
thought.
How can we know or how acknowl-
edge aught
Except it be our own?
Not the mere bulk of granite is ap-
proved
Steadfast; but we have sought
Into the very soul of things, and
known
Of our own souls the very steadfast-
ness.

IV

Nothing of man's is strange to man:
Who of old the course began
Runs the course: he finishes.
In the future wild and dim,
Full of wings and fiery-wan,
Many fates and much distress
Multiform, keep watch for him;
The sun will redden, the earth grow
strange:
Man will change not, though all Gods
Utterly change.
He will change not, being whole,
Body and sense and breath and soul;

Though his tents of night and daily
  abodes
Be moved above his mortal head;
Though the Lyre the northern pole,
Vega and the starry Lyre,
Mark; as once the mariner led,
Once of old, his oar and sail
By the faint ethereal fire
Thuban of the dragon shed.
Sway of the poles will not avail:—
Nay, if the Earth's long-fruitful
  strength
Be dried, her bosom drained at length
Of seasonable milk, and fail
The pastures of the flocks unfed;
And Man with unreturning course
Into the breathless æther force
His guarded way, and colonize
A later planet,—he shall dread
Nothing in the infinite skies,
Nothing, knowing from afar
The vapor-girdled Evening Star
Younger sister of his mother,
And her house vine-garlanded
To hail him welcome; and with love
Greet the ten-mooned heavens of Jove,
The old sweet Earth's own elder
  brother.
—Far and fearless though the course
  be sped,
Death, O Man, will reap at last
All the heritage thou hast:
He cannot change thee; and the dead
Stand forever safeguarded
In the chambers of the Past;
As a mighty monarch's gem
So they are watched and held in
  state,
With a seal upon the gate,
Time, the giant, guarding them.

V

But we that live, not less are we secure
Than the ancient dead or those of
  yesterday.
We have nothing to endure
Not from of old determined; nor our
  feet
Travel in any unpredestined way.

The path of one by waters pale and
  sweet
Runs, harmless of all frost and fervent
  heat:
Another's track the eagles gray
Of mountains, and the summits hoar
Witness; on his head are spilled
Icy rains, and eager lightnings gild
The edges of the precipice;
He hears the mountain-torrents roar
Deep under in the vapor-dimmed
  abyss:—
Let neither tremble, neither falter
In the course he cannot alter;
Each walks a way long chosen, long
  before;
That path as well as this
In surest guidance is;
Fate, that alone is God, can change
  no more
Than the strong traveller may control,
His necessary courses toward the time-
  less goal.

VI

No wilful rage, nor breach of natural
  bonds,
Is this that battens with innumerous
  agonies
Europe's blood-wonted boundaries, not
  before
Satiate;—nor the tumults and the
  cries
Burdening our wind from eastward
  are the breath
Of life at length despondent:—who
  desponds
Knows not the bitter strength that
  grows at core
Of this old living Earth; he has fed
  on lies
In time of quiet, therefore now his
  faith
Fails in the thunderous hour, the
  harvest-home of death.
Behold, our faith may be as even the
  Earth's
Unhopeful and firm-rooted.—The man
  dies?

The race is hardly yeaning yet. The race
At length will perish also? Other births
Even now are quickening in the time-
less womb.
Life tortures the old clay to later form;
That least reluctant gulf the eternal tomb
Regorges still his tenants, and the storm
That gluts him is but herald of new games.
Something endures; the universal Power
Endures forever; we, the whiffs and flames
That breathe and flicker for one brief-
est hour,
We also have our dignity, being part
Of the immortal thing;—we serve our
nearest aims:—
The fox goes forth to ravage; the antlered hart
Finds out his richest pasturage; the man
Takes where he may and harvests all
he can;
Or mayhap with unreasonable divine
Excesses of desire loves friend or mate
Or form of natural beauty, and fulfils
His nature's need to loveward:—what
he wills
Is part and substance of the immense design:
He is beautiful and great,
Being work and will, being child and
slave, of constant Fate.

VII

The holy multitude of night,
The unnumerable stars, with light
Their beauty, as it were of flowers
The fragrance after sudden showers,
Pour forth immeasurably, and flood
The infinite world; as it were a God
The sun from the orient mountain
springs
Into glorious day, with wings

Far-shining; by his lightning shaken
The hills are changed, the forests
waken,
Million-waved the ocean dances,
The rocky isles at random sown
Gleam, and the cliffs: the watcher
fancies
A spirit flashing from the stone.
A wind is up, and swarming wings
Of gull and tern and sanderlings
Wheel above the whitening waves
That break in spray on cliff and
shingle;
Land and ocean lift and mingle
With the sun's ethereal splendor;
On the hill the pinetree waves
Ritual weight of sacred branches,
Wafting fragrance; fair and slender
Flagflowers bloom in purple ranks
In open glades by water banks
Where the doe her fever stanches;
Yellow pansies brown and brightening
From the windy foreland render
To the sun their silent thanks;
The red-shafted woodpecker
Through the upper forest launches
Arrow-flights of ruddy lightning;
Where the streaming billow blanches
Rise the wings; a vapor tender
Rises like a spirit there,
Pearling the pure air.
Mighty Spirit, from the stone
Flashing, from the sea exhaling,
On the azure hill thy garments trail-
ing
Floating in glory from the sun,
Soaring in melody and mirth
From the forest and mild earth;
As lately from thine ancient throne
Of orb on orb of starry flame
Ere the dawn thou lookedst down:—
Have I seen thee, have I known
Thee in all thy forms the same,
Holy Spirit, loveliest one?
Lovely, dear, and terrible,
Have I known thee well?
Beauty is thy human name;
Yet ere the sun had been, thou art,
Time and the outer cold will slay

The currents of his burning heart,
But thou remainest; death will lay
A finger on the race of man
And all our hearts that yearn to thee;
The flame art thou, the fuel are we;
All must end that once began;
The holy stars will cease to be;
But thou art from eternity.
The rhythm of universal things
Art thou: what light is to the sun,
Or swiftness to the swallow's wings,
Or smiting to the wielded sword,
Or thought to man, O loveliest one,
That art thou to eternal Fate.
His spirit thou art, his child, his mate,
His great fulfilment. No mean lord
We serve and share with, serving thee,
O twin-born bride of Destiny!

VIII

The mighty vision vanishes;
The breathing that fulfilled this
    bruisèd reed
Fails, the poor stops are faint and
    whisperless.
They will again awaken, when the
    need
Is greater, and in greater power will
    praise
That purest loveliness.
I, driven ahead on undiscovered ways
Yet predetermined, do not fail to see,
Over the fog and dust of dream and
    deed,
The holy spirit, Beauty, beckoning
    me.

1916

BOATS IN A FOG *

Sports and gallantries, the stage, the
    arts, the antics of dancers,
The exuberant voices of music,
Have charm for children but lack no-
    bility; it is bitter earnestness
That makes beauty; the mind
Knows, grown adult.
        A sudden fog-drift muffled
    the ocean,
A throbbing of engines moved in it,
At length, a stone's throw out, be-
    tween the rocks and the vapor,
One by one moved shadows
Out of the mystery, shadows, fishing-
    boats, trailing each other,
Following the cliff for guidance,
Holding a difficult path between the
    peril of the sea-fog
And the foam on the shore granite.
One by one, trailing their leader, six
    crept by me,
Out of the vapor and into it,
The throb of their engines subdued
    by the fog, patient and cautious,
Coasting all round the peninsula
Back to the buoys in Monterey har-
    bor. A flight of pelicans
Is nothing lovelier to look at;
The flight of the planets is nothing
    nobler; all the arts lose virtue
Against the essential reality
Of creatures going about their busi-
    ness among the equally
Earnest elements of nature.

1925

GALE IN APRIL *

Intense and terrible beauty, how has our race with the frail naked nerves,
So little a craft swum down from its far launching?
Why now, only because the northwest blows and the headed grass billows,
Great seas jagging the west and on the granite
Blanching, the vessel is brimmed, this dancing play of the world is too much
    passion.

* Reprinted by permission of Horace Liveright, Inc. Copyright, 1924, 1925.

A gale in April so overfilling the spirit,
Though his ribs were thick as the earth's, arches of mountain, how shall one
          dare to live,
Though his blood were like the earth's rivers and his flesh iron,
How shall one dare to live? One is born strong, how do the weak endure it?
The strong lean upon death as on a rock,
After eighty years there is shelter and the naked nerves shall be covered with
          deep quietness,
O beauty of things go on, go on, O torture
Of intense joy I have lasted out my time, I have thanked God and finished,
Roots of millennial trees fold me in the darkness,
Northwest wind shake their tops, not to the root, not to the root, I have passed
From beauty to the other beauty, peace, the night splendor.

                                   1925

TO THE STONE-CUTTERS *

Stone-cutters fighting time with marble, you foredefeated
Challengers of oblivion
Eat cynical earnings, knowing rock splits, records fall down.
The square-limbed Roman letters
Scale in the thaws, wear in the rain. The poet as well
Builds his monument mockingly;
For man will be blotted out, the blithe earth die, the brave sun
Die blind, his heart blackening:
Yet stones have stood for a thousand years, and pained thoughts found
The honey peace in old poems.

                                   1925

ROAN STALLION †

The dog barked; then the woman stood in the doorway, and hearing iron strike
          stone down the steep road
Covered her head with a black shawl and entered the light rain; she stood at
          the turn of the road.
A nobly formed woman; erect and strong as a new tower; the features stolid
          and dark
But sculptured into a strong grace; straight nose with a high bridge, firm and
          wide eyes, full chin,
Red lips; she was only a fourth part Indian; a Scottish sailor had planted her
          in young native earth,
Spanish and Indian, twenty-one years before. He had named her California
          when she was born;
That was her name; and had gone north.

   * Reprinted by permission of Horace Liveright, Inc. Copyright, 1924, 1925.
   † Reprinted by permission of Random House, Inc. Copyright, 1938, by Robinson
Jeffers.

She heard the hooves and
wheels come nearer, up the steep road.
The buckskin mare, leaning against the breastpiece, plodded into sight round
the wet bank.
The pale face of the driver followed; the burnt-out eyes; they had fortune in
them. He sat twisted
On the seat of the old buggy, leading a second horse by a long halter, a roan,
a big one,
That stepped daintily; by the swell of the neck, a stallion. "What have you
got, Johnny?" "Maskerel's stallion.
Mine now. I won him last night, I had very good luck." He was quite drunk.
"They bring their mares up here now.
I keep this fellow. I got money besides, but I'll not show you." "Did you buy
something, Johnny,
For our Christine? Christmas comes in two days, Johnny." "By God, forgot,"
he answered laughing.
"Don't tell Christine it's Christmas; after while I get her something, maybe."
But California:
"I shared your luck when you lost: you lost *me* once, Johnny, remember? Tom
Dell had me two nights
Here in the house: other times we've gone hungry: now that you've won,
Christine will have her Christmas.
We share your luck, Johnny. You give me money, I go down to Monterey
to-morrow,
Buy presents for Christine, come back in the evening. Next day Christmas."
"You have wet ride," he answered
Giggling. "Here money. Five dollar; ten; twelve dollar. You buy two bottles
of rye whisky for Johnny."
"All right. I go to-morrow."

He was an outcast Hollander; not old, but
shriveled with bad living.
The child Christine inherited from his race blue eyes, from his life a wizened
forehead; she watched
From the house-door her father lurch out of the buggy and lead with due respect
the stallion
To the new corral, the strong one; leaving the wearily breathing buckskin
mare to his wife to unharness.

Storm in the night; the rain on the thin shakes of the roof like the ocean on
rock streamed battering; once thunder
Walked down the narrow canyon into Carmel valley and wore away westward;
Christine was wakeful
With fears and wonders; her father lay too deep for storm to touch him.
Dawn comes late in the year's dark,
Later into the crack of a canyon under redwoods; and California slipped from
bed
An hour before it; the buckskin would be tired; there was a little barley, and
why should Johnny

Feed all the barley to his stallion? That is what he would do. She tiptoed out
  of the room.
Leaving her clothes, he'd waken if she waited to put them on, and passed
  from the door of the house
Into the dark of the rain; the big black drops were cold through the thin shift,
  but the wet earth
Pleasant under her naked feet. There was a pleasant smell in the stable; and
  moving softly,
Touching things gently with the supple bend of the unclothed body, was
  pleasant. She found a box,
Filled it with sweet dry barley and took it down to the old corral. The little
  mare sighed deeply
At the rail in the wet darkness; and California returning between two redwoods
  up to the house
Heard the happy jaws grinding the grain. Johnny could mind the pigs and
  chickens. Christine called to her
When she entered the house, but slept again under her hand. She laid the wet
  night-dress on a chair-back
And stole into the bedroom to get her clothes. A plank creaked, and he
  wakened. She stood motionless
Hearing him stir in the bed. When he was quiet she stooped after her shoes,
  and he said softly,
"What are you doing? Come back to bed." "It's late, I'm going to Monterey,
  I must hitch up."
"You come to bed first. I been away three days. I give you money, I take back
  the money
And what you do in town then?" She sighed sharply and came to the bed.
              He reaching his hands from it
Felt the cool curve and firmness of her flank, and half rising caught her by the
  long wet hair.
She endured, and to hasten the act she feigned desire; she had not for long,
  except in dream, felt it.
Yesterday's drunkenness made him sluggish and exacting; she saw, turning her
  head sadly,
The windows were bright gray with dawn; he embraced her still, stopping to
  talk about the stallion.
At length she was permitted to put on her clothes. Clear daylight over the
  steep hills;
Gray-shining cloud over the tops of the redwoods; the winter stream sang
  loud; the wheels of the buggy
Slipped in deep slime, ground on washed stones at the road-edge. Down the
  hill the wrinkled river smothered the ford.
You must keep to the bed of stones: she knew the way by willow and alder:
  the buckskin halted mid-stream,
Shuddering, the water her own color washing up to the traces; but California,
  drawing up
Her feet out of the whirl onto the seat of the buggy swung the whip over the
  yellow water
And drove to the road.

All morning the clouds were racing north-
ward like a river. At noon they thickened.
When California faced the southwind home from Monterey it was heavy with
level rainfall.
She looked seaward from the foot of the valley; red rays cried sunset from a
trumpet of streaming
Cloud over Lobos, the southwest occident of the solstice. Twilight came soon,
but the tired mare
Feared the road more than the whip. Mile after mile of slow gray twilight.
Then, quite suddenly, darkness.
"Christine will be asleep. It is Christmas Eve. The ford. That hour of daylight
wasted this morning!"
She could see nothing; she let the reins lie on the dashboard and knew at
length by the cramp of the wheels
And the pitch down, they had reached it. Noise of wheels on stones, plashing
of hooves in water; a world
Of sounds; no sight; the gentle thunder of water; the mare snorting, dipping
her head, one knew,
To look for footing, in the blackness, under the stream. The hushing and
creaking of the sea-wind
In the passion of invisible willows.
                                        The mare stood still; the woman
shouted to her; spared whip,
For a false leap would lose the track of the ford. She stood. "The baby's things,"
thought California,
"Under the seat: the water will come over the floor"; and rising in the midst
of the water
She tilted the seat; fetched up the doll, the painted wooden chickens, the
wooly bear, the book
Of many pictures, the box of sweets: she brought them all from under the
seat and stored them, trembling,
Under her clothes, about the breasts, under the arms; the corners of the card-
board boxes
Cut into the soft flesh; but with a piece of rope for a girdle and wound about
the shoulders
All was made fast. The mare stood still as if asleep in the midst of the water.
Then California
Reached out a hand over the stream and fingered her rump; the solid wet
convexity of it
Shook like the beat of a great heart. "What are you waiting for?" But the feel
of the animal surface
Had wakened a dream, obscured real danger with a dream of danger. "What
for? for the water-stallion
To break out of the stream, that is what the rump strains for, him to come up
flinging foam sidewise,
Fore-hooves in air, crush me and the rig and curl over his woman." She flung
out with the whip then;
The mare plunged forward. The buggy drifted sidelong: was she off ground?
Swimming? No: by the splashes.

The driver, a mere prehensile instinct, clung to the sideirons of the seat and
    felt the force
But not the coldness of the water, curling over her knees, breaking up to the
    waist
Over her body. They'd turned. The mare had turned up stream and was wal-
    lowing back into shoal water.
Then California dropped her forehead to her knees, having seen nothing, feel-
    ing a danger,
And felt the brute weight of a branch of alder, the pendulous light leaves brush
    her bent neck
Like a child's fingers. The mare burst out of water and stopped on the slope
    to the ford. The woman climbed down
Between the wheels and went to her head. "Poor Dora," she called her by her
    name, "there, Dora. Quietly,"
And led her around, there was room to turn on the margin, the head to the
    gentle thunder of the water.
She crawled on hands and knees, felt for the ruts, and shifted the wheels into
    them. "You can see, Dora.
I can't. But this time you'll go through it." She climbed into the seat and
    shouted angrily. The mare
Stopped, her two forefeet in the water. She touched with the whip. The mare
    plodded ahead and halted.
Then California thought of prayer: "Dear little Jesus,
Dear baby Jesus born to-night, your head was shining
Like silver candles. I've got a baby too, only a girl. You had light wherever you
    walked.
Dear baby Jesus give me light." Light streamed: rose, gold, rich purple, hiding
    the ford like a curtain.
The gentle thunder of water was a noise of wing-feathers, the fans of paradise
    lifting softly.
The child afloat on radiance had a baby face, but the angels had birds' heads,
    hawks' heads,
Bending over the baby, weaving a web of wings about him. He held in the
    small fat hand
A little snake with golden eyes, and California could see clearly on the under
    radiance
The mare's pricked ears, a sharp black fork against the shining light-fall. But
    it dropped; the light of heaven
Frightened poor Dora. She backed; swung up the water,
And nearly oversetting the buggy turned and scrambled backward; the iron
    wheel-tires rang on boulders.

Then California weeping climbed between the wheels. Her wet clothes and
    the toys packed under
Dragged her down with their weight; she stripped off cloak and dress and laid
    the baby's things in the buggy;
Brought Johnny's whisky out from under the seat; wrapped all in the dress,
    bottles and toys, and tied them

Into a bundle that would sling over her back. She unharnessed the mare, hurting her fingers

Against the swollen straps and the wet buckles. She tied the pack over her shoulders, the cords

Crossing her breasts, and mounted. She drew up her shift about her waist and knotted it, naked thighs

Clutching the sides of the mare, bare flesh to the wet withers, and caught the mane with her right hand,

The looped-up bridle-reins in the other. "Dora, the baby gives you light." The blinding radiance

Hovered the ford. "Sweet baby Jesus give us light." Cataracts of light and Latin singing

Fell through the willows; the mare snorted and reared: the roar and thunder of the invisible water;

The night shaking open like a flag, shot with the flashes; the baby face hovering; the water

Beating over her shoes and stockings up to the bare thighs; and over them, like a beast

Lapping her belly; the wriggle and pitch of the mare swimming; the drift, the sucking water; the blinding

Light above and behind with not a gleam before, in the throat of darkness; the shock of the fore-hooves

Striking bottom, the struggle and surging lift of the haunches. She felt the water streaming off her

From the shoulders down; heard the great strain and sob of the mare's breathing, heard the horseshoes grind on gravel.

When California came home the dog at the door snuffed at her without barking; Christine and Johnny

Both were asleep; she did not sleep for hours, but kindled fire and knelt patiently over it,

Shaping and drying the dear-bought gifts for Christmas morning.

     She hated (she thought) the proud-necked stallion.
He'd lean the big twin masses of his breast on the rail, his red-brown eyes flash the white crescents,

She admired him then, she hated him for his uselessness, serving nothing

But Johnny's vanity. Horses were too cheap to breed. She thought, if he could range in freedom,

Shaking the red-roan mane for a flag on the bare hills.

                    A man
brought up a mare in April;

Then California, though she wanted to watch, stayed with Christine indoors. When the child fretted

The mother told her once more about the miracle of the ford; her prayers to the little Jesus

The Christmas Eve when she was bringing the gifts home; the appearance, the lights, the Latin singing,

The thunder of wing-feathers and water, the shining child, the cataracts of splendor down the darkness.

"A little baby," Christine asked, "the God is a baby?" "The child of God. That
    was his birthday.

His mother was named Mary: we pray to her too: God came to her. He was
    not the child of a man

Like you or me. God was his father: she was the stallion's wife—what did I
    say—God's wife,"

She said with a cry, lifting Christine aside, pacing the planks of the floor. "She
    is called more blessed

Than any woman. She was so good, she was more loved." "Did God live near
    her house?" "He lives

Up high, over the stars; he ranges on the bare blue hill of the sky." In her
    mind a picture

Flashed, of the red-roan mane shaken out for a flag on the bare hills, and she
    said quickly, "He's more

Like a great man holding the sun in his hand." Her mind giving her words
    the lie, "But no one

Knows, only the shining and the power. The power, the terror, the burning
    fire covered her over . . ."

"Was she burnt up, mother?" "She was so good and lovely, she was the mother
    of the little Jesus.

If you are good nothing will hurt you." "What did she think?" "She loved,
    she was not afraid of the hooves—

Hands that had made the hills and sun and moon, and the sea and the great
    redwoods, the terrible strength,

She gave herself without thinking." "You only saw the baby, mother?" "Yes,
    and the angels about him,

The great wild shining over the black river." Three times she had walked to the
    door, three times returned,

And now the hand that had thrice hung on the knob, full of prevented action,
    twisted the cloth

Of the child's dress that she had been mending. "Oh, Oh, I've torn it." She
    struck at the child and then embraced her

Fiercely, the small blond sickly body.
                       Johnny came in, his face
    reddened as if he had stood

Near fire, his eyes triumphing. "Finished," he said, and looked with malice at
    Christine. "I go

Down valley with Jim Carrier; owes me five dollar, fifteen I charge him, he
    brought ten in his pocket.

Has grapes on the ranch, maybe I take a barrel red wine instead of money. Be
    back to-morrow.

To-morrow night I tell you— Eh, Jim," he laughed over his shoulder, "I say
    to-morrow evening

I show her how the red fellow act, the big fellow. When I come home." She
    answered nothing, but stood

In front of the door, holding the little hand of her daughter, in the path of sun
    between the redwoods,

While Johnny tied the buckskin mare behind Carrier's buggy, and bringing
    saddle and bridle tossed them

Under the seat. Jim Carrier's mare, the bay, stood with drooped head and
    started slowly, the men
Laughing and shouting at her; their voices could be heard down the steep
    road, after the noise
Of the iron-hooped wheels died from the stone. Then one might hear the
    hush of the wind in the tall redwoods,
The tinkle of the April brook, deep in its hollow.
                                         Humanity is the
    start of the race; I say
Humanity is the mold to break away from, the crust to break through, the
    coal to break into fire,
The atom to be split.
                                    Tragedy that breaks man's face and a white
    fire flies out of it; vision that fools him
Out of his limits, desire that fools him out of his limits, unnatural crime,
    inhuman science,
Slit eyes in the mask; wild loves that leap over the walls of nature, the wild
    fence-vaulter science,
Useless intelligence of far stars, dim knowledge of the spinning demons that
    make an atom,
These break, these pierce, these deify, praising their God shrilly with fierce
    voices: not in man's shape
He approves the praise, he that walks lightning-naked on the Pacific, that
    laces the suns with planets,
The heart of the atom with electrons: what is humanity in this cosmos? For
    him, the last
Least taint of a trace in the dregs of the solution; for itself, the mold to break
    away from, the coal
To break into fire, the atom to be split.

                                    After the child slept, after
    the leopard-footed evening
Had glided oceanward, California turned the lamp to its least flame and glided
    from the house.
She moved sighing, like a loose fire, backward and forward on the smooth
    ground by the door.
She heard the night-wind that draws down the valley like the draught in a flue
    under clear weather
Whisper and toss in the tall redwoods; she heard the tinkle of the April brook
    deep in its hollow.
Cooled by the night the odors that the horses had left behind were in her
    nostrils; the night
Whitened up the bare hill; a drift of coyotes by the river cried bitterly against
    moonrise;
Then California ran to the old corral, the empty one where they kept the
    buckskin mare,
And leaned, and bruised her breasts on the rail, feeling the sky whiten. When
    the moon stood over the hill

She stole to the house. The child breathed quietly. Herself: to sleep? She had
    seen Christ in the night at Christmas.
The hills were shining open to the enormous night of the April moon: empty
    and empty,
The vast round backs of the bare hills? If one should ride up high might not
    the Father himself
Be seen brooding His night, cross-legged, chin in hand, squatting on the last
    dome? More likely
Leaping the hills, shaking the red-roan mane for a flag on the bare hills. She
    blew out the lamp.
Every fiber of flesh trembled with faintness when she came to the door;
    strength lacked, to wander
Afoot into the shining of the hill, high enough, high enough . . . the hateful
    face of a man had taken
The strength that might have served her, the corral was empty. The dog fol-
    lowed her, she caught him by the collar,
Dragged him in fierce silence back to the door of the house, latched him inside.
                      It was like daylight
Out-doors and she hastened without faltering down the footpath, through the
    dark fringe of twisted oak-brush,
To the open place in a bay of the hill. The dark strength of the stallion had
    heard her coming; she heard him
Blow the shining air out of his nostrils, she saw him in the white lake of
    moonlight
Move like a lion along the timbers of the fence, shaking the nightfall
Of the great mane; his fragrance came to her; she leaned on the fence;
He drew away from it, the hooves making soft thunder in the trodden
    soil.
Wild love had trodden it, his wrestling with the stranger, the shame of the
    day
Had stamped it into mire and powder when the heavy fetlocks
Strained the soft flanks. "Oh, if I could bear you!
If I had the strength. O great God that came down to Mary, gently you came.
    But I will ride him
Up into the hill, if he throws me, if he tramples me, is it not my desire
To endure death?" She climbed the fence, pressing her body against the rail,
    shaking like fever,
And dropped inside to the soft ground. He neither threatened her with his
    teeth nor fled from her coming,
And lifting her hand gently to the upflung head she caught the strap of the
    headstall,
That hung under the quivering chin. She unlooped the halter from the high
    strength of the neck
And the arch the storm-cloud mane hung with live darkness. He stood; she
    crushed her breasts
On the hard shoulder, an arm over the withers, the other under the mass of
    his throat, and murmuring
Like a mountain dove, "If I could bear you." No way, no help, a gulf in nature.
    She murmured, "Come,

We will run on the hill. O beautiful, O beautiful," and led him to the gate and
    flung the bars on the ground. He threw his head downward
To snuff at the bars; and while he stood, she catching mane and withers with
    all sudden contracture
And strength of her lithe body, leaped, clung hard, and was mounted. He had
    been ridden before; he did not
Fight the weight but ran like a stone falling;
Broke down the slope into the moon-glass of the stream, and flattened to his
    neck
She felt the branches of a buck-eye tree fly over her, saw the wall of the oak-
    scrub
End her world: but he turned there, the matted branches
Scraped her right knee, the great slant shoulders
Laboring the hill-slope, up, up, the clear hill. Desire had died in her
At the first rush, the falling like death, but now it revived,
She feeling between her thighs the labor of the great engine, the running
    muscles, the hard swiftness,
She riding the savage and exultant strength of the world. Having topped the
    thicket he turned eastward,
Running less wildly; and now at length he felt the halter when she drew on
    it; she guided him upward;
He stopped and grazed on the great arch and pride of the hill, the silent
    calvary. A dwarfish oakwood
Climbed the other slope out of the dark of the unknown canyon beyond; the
    last wind-beaten bush of it
Crawled up to the height, and California slipping from her mount tethered
    him to it. She stood then,
Shaking. Enormous films of moonlight
Trailed down from the height. Space, anxious whiteness, vastness. Distant
    beyond conception the shining ocean
Lay light like a haze along the ledge and doubtful world's end. Little vapors
    gleaming, and little
Darknesses on the far chart underfoot symbolized wood and valley; but the
    air was the element, the moon-
Saturate arcs and spires of the air.

                         Here is solitude, here on the
calvary, nothing conscious
But the possible God and the cropped grass, no witness, no eye but that mis-
    formed one, the moon's past fullness.
Two figures on the shining hill, woman and stallion, she kneeling to him,
    brokenly adoring.
He cropping the grass, shifting his hooves, or lifting the long head to gaze over
    the world,
Tranquil and powerful. She prayed aloud, "O God, I am not good enough,
    O fear, O strength, I am draggled.
Johnny and other men have had me, and O clean power! Here am I," she said
    falling before him,
And crawled to his hooves. She lay a long while, as if asleep, in reach of the
    fore-hooves, weeping. He avoided

Her head and the prone body. He backed at first; but later plucked the grass
    that grew by her shoulder.
The small dark head under his nostrils: a small round stone, that smelt human,
    black hair growing from it:
The skull shut the light in it: it was not possible for any eyes
To know what throbbed and shone under the sutures of the skull, or a shell
    full of lightning
Had scared the roan strength, and he'd have broken tether, screaming, and run
    for the valley.
                    The atom bounds-breaking,
Nucleus to sun, electrons to planets, with recognition
Not praying, self-equaling, the whole to the whole, the microcosm
Not entering nor accepting entrance, more equally, more utterly, more in-
    credibly conjugate
With the other extreme and greatness; passionately perceptive of identity. . . .
                  The fire threw up figures
And symbols meanwhile, racial myths formed and dissolved in it, the phantom
    rulers of humanity
That without being are yet more real than what they are born of, and without
    shape, shape that which makes them:
The nerves and the flesh go by shadowlike, the limbs and the lives shadowlike,
    these shadows remain, these shadows
To whom temples, to whom churches, to whom labors and wars, visions and
    dreams are dedicate:
Out of the fire in the small round stone that black moss covered, a crucified
    man writhed up in anguish;
A woman covered by a huge beast in whose mane the stars were netted, sun
    and moon were his eyeballs,
Smiled under the unendurable violation, her throat swollen with the storm
    and blood-flecks gleaming
On the stretched lips; a woman—no, a dark water, split by jets of lightning,
    and after a season
What floated up out of the furrowed water, a boat, a fish, a fire-globe?
              It had wings, the creature,
And flew against the fountain of lightning, fell burnt out of the cloud back
    to the bottomless water . . .
Figures and symbols, castlings of the fire, played in her brain; but the white
    fire was the essence,
The burning in the small round shell of bone that black hair covered, that lay
    by the hooves on the hilltop.

She rose at length, she unknotted the halter; she walked and led the stallion;
    two figures, woman and stallion,
Came down the silent emptiness of the dome of the hill, under the cataract of
    the moonlight.

The next night there was moon through cloud. Johnny had returned half
    drunk toward evening, and California
Who had known him for years with neither love nor loathing to-night hating
    him had let the child Christine

Play in the light of the lamp for hours after her bedtime; who fell asleep at
length on the floor

Beside the dog; then Johnny: "Put her to bed." She gathered the child against
her breasts, she laid her

In the next room, and covered her with a blanket. The window was white, the
moon had risen. The mother

Lay down by the child, but after a moment Johnny stood in the doorway.
"Come drink." He had brought home

Two jugs of wine slung from the saddle, part payment for the stallion's
service; a pitcher of it

Was on the table, and California sadly came and emptied her glass. Whisky,
she thought,

Would have erased him till to-morrow; the thin red wine. . . . "We have a
good evening," he laughed, pouring it.

"One glass yet then I show you what the red fellow did." She moving toward
the house-door his eyes

Followed her, the glass filled and the red juice ran over the table. When it
struck the floor-planks

He heard and looked. "Who stuck the pig?" he muttered stupidly, "here's
blood, here's blood," and trailed his fingers

In the red lake under the lamplight. While he was looking down the door
creaked, she had slipped out-doors,

And he, his mouth curving like a faun's, imagined the chase under the solemn
redwoods, the panting

And unresistant victim caught in a dark corner. He emptied the glass and went
out-doors

Into the dappled lanes of moonlight. No sound but the April brook's. "Hey
Bruno," he called, "find her.

Bruno, go find her." The dog after a little understood and quested, the man
following.

When California crouching by an oak-bush above the house heard them come
near she darted

To the open slope and ran down hill. The dog barked at her heels, pleased
with the game, and Johnny

Followed in silence. She ran down to the new corral, she saw the
stallion

Move like a lion along the timbers of the fence, the dark arched neck shaking
the nightfall

Of the great mane; she threw herself prone and writhed under the bars, his
hooves backing away from her

Made muffled thunder in the soft soil. She stood in the midst of the corral,
panting, but Johnny

Paused at the fence. The dog ran under it, and seeing the stallion move, the
woman standing quiet,

Danced after the beast, with white-toothed feints and dashes. When Johnny
saw the formidable dark strength

Recoil from the dog, he climbed up over the fence.

The child Christine waked when her mother left her

And lay half-dreaming, in the half-waking dream she saw the ocean come up
out of the west

And cover the world, she looked up through clear water at the tops of the
redwoods. She heard the door creak

And the house empty; her heart shook her body, sitting up on the bed, and
she heard the dog

And crept toward light, where it gleamed under the crack of the door. She
opened the door, the room was empty,

The table-top was a red lake under the lamplight. The color of it was terrible
to her;

She had seen the red juice drip from a coyote's muzzle, her father had shot
one day in the hills

And carried him home over the saddle: she looked at the rifle on the wall-rack:
it was not moved:

She ran to the door, the dog was barking and the moon was shining: she knew
wine by the odor

But the color frightened her, the empty house frightened her, she followed
down hill in the white lane of moonlight

The friendly noise of the dog. She saw in the big horse's corral, on the level
shoulder of the hill,

Black on white, the dark strength of the beast, the dancing fury of the dog,
and the two others.

One fled, one followed; the big one charged, rearing; one fell under his fore-
hooves. She heard her mother

Scream: without thought she ran to the house, she dragged a chair past the
red pool and climbed to the rifle,

Got it down from the wall and lugged it somehow through the door and down
the hillside, under the hard weight

Sobbing. Her mother stood by the rails of the corral, she gave it to her. On
the far side

The dog flashed at the plunging stallion; in the midst of the space the man,
slow-moving, like a hurt worm

Crawling, dragged his body by inches toward the fence-line. Then California,
resting the rifle

On the top rail, without doubting, without hesitance,

Aimed for the leaping body of the dog, and when it stood, fired. It snapped,
rolled over, lay quiet.

"O mother, you've hit Bruno!" "I couldn't see the sights in the moonlight,"
she answered quietly. She stood

And watched, resting the rifle-butt on the ground. The stallion wheeled, freed
from his torment, the man

Lurched up to his knees, wailing a thin and bitter bird's cry, and the roan
thunder

Struck; hooves left nothing alive but teeth tore up the remnant. "O mother,
shoot, shoot!" Yet California

Stood carefully watching, till the beast having fed all his fury stretched neck
to utmost, head high,

And wrinkled back the upper lip from the teeth, yawning obscene disgust over
—not a man—

A smear on the moon-lake earth: then California moved by some obscure human
    fidelity
Lifted the rifle. Each separate nerve-cell of her brain flaming the stars fell from
    their places
Crying in her mind: she fired three times before the haunches crumpled side-
    wise, the forelegs stiffening,
And the beautiful strength settled to earth: she turned then on her little
    daughter the mask of a woman
Who has killed God. The night-wind veering, the smell of the spilt wine
    drifted down hill from the house.

1924, 1925

SHINE, PERISHING REPUBLIC *

While this America settles in the mould of its vulgarity, heavily thickening
    to empire,
And protest, only a bubble in the molten mass, pops and sighs out, and the
    mass hardens,

I sadly smiling remember that the flower fades to make fruit, the fruit rots to
    make earth.
Out of the mother; and through the spring exultances, ripeness and decadence;
    and home to the mother.

You make haste on decay; not blameworthy; life is good, be it stubbornly long
    or suddenly
A mortal splendor: meteors are not needed less than mountains: shine, perishing
    republic.

But for my children, I would have them keep their distance from the thickening
    center; corruption
Never has been compulsory, when the cities lie at the monster's feet there are
    left the mountains.

And boys, be in nothing so moderate as in love of man, a clever servant,
    insufferable master.
There is the trap that catches noblest spirits, that caught—they say—God, when
    he walked on earth.

1925

HURT HAWKS *

I

The broken pillar of the wing jags from the clotted shoulder,
The wing trails like a banner in defeat,
No more to use the sky forever but live with famine
And pain a few days: cat nor coyote

* Reprinted by permission of Random House, Inc. Copyright, 1938, by Robinson
Jeffers.

Will shorten the week of waiting for death, there is game without talons.
He stands under the oak-bush and waits
The lame feet of salvation; at night he remembers freedom
And flies in a dream, the dawns ruin it.
He is strong and pain is worse to the strong, incapacity is worse.
The curs of the day come and torment him
At distance, no one but death the redeemer will humble that head,
The intrepid readiness, the terrible eyes.
The wild God of the world is sometimes merciful to those
That ask mercy, not often to the arrogant.
You do not know him, you communal people, or you have forgotten him;
Intemperate and savage, the hawk remembers him;
Beautiful and wild, the hawks, and men that are dying, remember him.

II

I'd sooner, except the penalties, kill a man than a hawk; but the great redtail
Had nothing left but unable misery
From the bone too shattered for mending, the wing that trailed under his talons
          when he moved.
We had fed him six weeks, I gave him freedom,
He wandered over the foreland hill and returned in the evening, asking for
          death,
Not like a beggar, still eyed with the old
Implacable arrogance. I gave him the lead gift in the twilight. What fell was
          relaxed,
Owl-downy, soft feminine feathers; but what
Soared: the fierce rush: the night-herons by the flooded river cried fear at its
          rising
Before it was quite unsheathed from reality.

                                                                      1927

MEDITATION ON SAVIORS *

I

When I considered it too closely, when I wore it like an element and smelt it
          like water,
Life is become less lovely, the net nearer than the skin, a little troublesome, a
          little terrible.

I pledged myself awhile ago not to seek refuge, neither in death nor in a walled
          garden,
In lies nor grated loyalties, nor in the gates of contempt, that easily lock the
          world out of doors.

Here on the rock it is great and beautiful, here on the foam-wet granite sea-
          fang it is easy to praise

  * Reprinted by permission of Random House, Inc. Copyright, 1938, by Robinson
Jeffers.

Life and water and the shining stones: but whose cattle are the herds of the
    people that one should love them?   .

If they were yours, then you might take a cattle-breeder's delight in the herds
    of the future. Not yours.
Where the power ends let love, before it sours to jealousy. Leave the joys of
    government to Caesar.

Who is born when the world wanes, when the brave soul of the world falls
    on decay in the flesh increasing
Comes one with a great level mind, sufficient vision, sufficient blindness, and
    clemency for love.

This is the breath of rottenness I smelt; from the world waiting, stalled between
    storms, decaying a little,
Bitterly afraid to be hurt, but knowing it cannot draw the savior Caesar but
    out of the blood-bath.

The apes of Christ lift up their hands to praise love: but wisdom without love
    is the present savior,
Power without hatred, mind like a many-bladed machine subduing the world
    with deep indifference.

The apes of Christ itch for a sickness they have never known; words and the
    little envies will hardly
Measure against the blinding fire behind the tragic eyes they have never dared
    to confront.

II

Point Lobos lies over the hollowed water like a humped whale swimming to
    shoal; Point Lobos
Was wounded with that fire; the hills at Point Sur endured it; the palace at
    Thebes; the hill Calvary.

Out of incestuous love power and then ruin. A man forcing the imaginations
    of men,
Possessing with love and power the people: a man defiling his own household
    with impious desire.

King Oedipus reeling blinded from the palace doorway, red tears pouring from
    the torn pits
Under the forehead; and the young Jew writhing on the domed hill in the
    earthquake, against the eclipse

Frightfully uplifted for having turned inward to love the people:—that root
    was so sweet Oh, dreadful agonist?—
I saw the same pierced feet, that walked in the same crime to its expiation; I
    heard the same cry.

A bad mountain to build your world on. Am I another keeper of the people,
    that on my own shore,
On the gray rock, by the grooved mass of the ocean, the sickness I left behind
    me concern me?

Here where the surf has come incredible ways out of the splendid west, over the deeps

Light nor life sounds forever; here where enormous sundowns flower and burn through color to quietness;

Then the ecstasy of the stars is present? As for the people, I have found my rock, let them find theirs.

Let them lie down at Caesar's feet and be saved; and he in his time reap their daggers of gratitude.

III

Yet I am the one made pledges against the refuge contempt, that easily locks the world out of doors.

This people as much as the sea-granite is part of the God from whom I desire not to be fugitive.

I see them: they are always crying. The shored Pacific makes perpetual music, and the stone mountains

Their music of silence, the stars blow long pipings of light: the people are always crying in their hearts.

One need not pity; certainly one must not love. But who has seen peace, if he should tell them where peace

Lives in the world . . . they would be powerless to understand; and he is not willing to be reinvolved.

IV

How should one caught in the stone of his own person dare tell the people anything but relative to that?

But if a man could hold in his mind all the conditions at once, of man and woman, of civilized

And barbarous, of sick and well, of happy and under torture, of living and dead, of human and not

Human, and dimly all the human future:—what should persuade him to speak? And what could his words change?

The mountain ahead of the world is not forming but fixed. But the man's words would be fixed also,

Part of that mountain, under equal compulsion; under the same present compulsion in the iron consistency.

And nobody sees good or evil but out of a brain a hundred centuries quieted, some desert

Prophet's, a man humped like a camel, gone mad between the mud-walled village and the mountain sepulchres.

V

Broad wagons before sunrise bring food into the city from the open farms, and the people are fed.

They import and they consume reality. Before sunrise a hawk in the desert made them their thoughts.

VI

Here is an anxious people, rank with suppressed blood-thirstiness. Among the
mild and unwarlike
Gautama needed but live greatly and be heard, Confucius needed but live
greatly and be heard.

This people has not outgrown blood-sacrifices, one must writhe on the high
cross to catch their memories;
The price is known. I have quieted love; for love of the people I would not do
it. For power I would do it.

—But that stands against reason: what is power to a dead man, dead under
torture?— What is power to a man
Living, after the flesh is content? Reason is never a root, neither of act nor
desire.

For power living I would never do it; they are not delightful to touch, one
wants to be separate. For power
After the nerves are put away underground, to lighten the abstract unborn
children toward peace . . .

A man might have paid anguish indeed. Except he had found the standing
sea-rock that even this last
Temptation breaks on; quieter than death but lovelier; peace that quiets the
desire even of praising it.

VII

Yet look: are they not pitiable? No: if they lived forever they would be
pitiable:
But a huge gift reserved quite overwhelms them at the end; they are able then
to be still and not cry.

And having touched a little of the beauty and seen a little of the beauty of
things, magically grow
Across the funeral fire or the hidden stench of burial themselves into the
beauty they admired,

Themselves into the God, themselves into the sacred steep unconsciousness
they used to mimic
Asleep between the lamp's death and dawn, while the last drunkard stumbled
homeward down the dark street.

They are not to be pitied but very fortunate; they need no savior, salvation
comes and takes them by force,
It gathers them into the great kingdom of dust and stone, the blown storms,
the stream's-end ocean.

With this advantage over their granite grave-marks, of having realized the
petulant human consciousness
Before, and then the greatness, the peace: drunk from both pitchers: these to
be pitied? These not fortunate?

But while he lives let each man make his health in his mind, to love the coast
    opposite humanity
And so be freed of love, laying it like bread on the waters; it is worst turned
    inward, it is best shot farthest.

Love, the mad wine of good and evil, the saint's and the murderer's, the mote
    in the eye that makes its object
Shine the sun black; the trap in which it is better to catch the inhuman God
    than the hunter's own image.

                                        1928

THE COLLECTIVISTS

DANIEL DE LEON
(1852–1914)

FROM
*SOCIALIST RECONSTRUCTION
OF SOCIETY* *

[INDUSTRIAL UNIONISM AND SOCIALISM]

* * * The preamble of the Industrial Workers of the World poses well both the political and the economic movement of labor, and it places them in their proper relation toward each other.

Inestimable is the value, dignified the posture of the political movement. It affords the labor movement the opportunity to ventilate its purposes, its aspirations and its methods, free, over and above board, in the noonday light of the sun, whereas otherwise, its agitation would be consigned to the circumscribed sphere of the rat-hole. The political movement renders the masses accessible to the propaganda of labor; it raises the labor movement above the category of a "conspiracy"; it places the movement in line with the spirit of the age, which, on the one hand, denies the power of "conspiracy" in matters that not only affect the masses, but in which the masses must themselves be intelligent actors, and, on the other hand, demands the freest of utterance. In short

* Reprinted by permission of the Executive Committee of the Socialist Labor Party. Copyright 1930.

and in fine, the political movement bows to the methods of civilized discussion: *it gives a chance to the peaceful solution of the great question at issue.* By proclaiming the urgency of political as well as of industrial unity, the preamble amply and sufficiently proclaims the affinity of the economic with the political movement. At the same time, by expressly proclaiming that the "taking and holding" is an act that falls wholly within the province of the economic organization, the preamble locked a dangerous switch, a switch into which to run there is grave danger, the danger of rendering the Socialist, which means the labor movement, illusory, and a roosting place for the "intellectual" riff-raff of bourgeois society.

The ballot is a weapon of civilization; the ballot is a weapon that no revolutionary movement of our times may ignore except at its own peril; the Socialist ballot is the emblem of *right.* For that very reason the Socialist ballot is

> weaker than a woman's tears,
> Tamer than sleep, fonder than ignorance,
> Less valiant than the virgin in the night,
> And skilless as unpracticed infancy,

unless it is backed by the *might* to enforce it. [Applause.] That requisite might is summed up in the industrial organization of the working class. Now, mind you, that *might* the labor movement needs, as much, I would almost say, against the political movements which its own breath heats into being as against the capitalist tyrant himself. It needs that might against the capitalist tyrant to put the quietus upon him; it also needs that might to prevent the evil consequences to which, in this corrupt atmosphere of bourgeois society, the political movement is inevitably exposed. The two points are vital. Much, infinitely more than appears at first sight, hangs thereby.

Despite the sharply marked economic feature of the labor movement, the principle, that it is bound to take on a political form also, is founded on no fine-spun theory. Even discounting the force of the sociologic arguments that I have presented to you, and which point to the inevitableness of the political manifestation of the labor movement, there is a consideration that I have referred to only incidentally so far, and which, when properly weighed, places the matter beyond the peradventure of a doubt. That consideration is the existence of universal suffrage in the land. The institution is so bred in the bones of the people that, notwithstanding it has become a gravel in the shoe of the capitalist, he, powerful though he is, dare not abolish it outright. Among such a people, chimerical is the idea of expecting to conduct a great movement, whose palpable aim is a Socialist Revolution, to the slogan of "Abstinence from the ballot-box!" The proposition cannot choose but brand its supporters as freaks. Whether the economic movement wills it or not, its political phase will assert itself on the political field. Men from its own ranks, and men from outside of its ranks, will raise the standard of labor politics. Nor will the capitalist be slow in endeavoring, while humoring the thing, to draw the sting from it. Watchfully though he guards his

political burg, he will, from time to time, carefully select some "promising" candidate from the labor ticket, and allow him admission; or, maybe, he is sometimes taken napping, and some labor candidate slips through the fingers of his outposts at the ballot-box. Subjected to the lures and wiles at the disposal of the capitalist, these successful labor candidates in the parliaments of capitalism, ten to one, succumb. They succumb due either to their own inherently corrupt souls, or to their muddle-headedness. In either case they betray the working class; the effect is harmfully felt by the economic movement. Against this danger there is but one protection—the Industrial, that is, the class-conscious economic organization to keep that ballot straight. Nothing short of such an economic organization will prevent the evil, because nothing short of such an economic organization can keep sharp the edge of the special sword wielded by the political movement of labor. What that special sword is I have shown before. It is purely *destructive*. The economic movement may take a little at a time. It may do so because its function is ultimately to "take and hold" the full plants of production and save them for the human race. The political movement, on the contrary, has an entirely different function: its function is wholly to tear down the political burg of capitalist tyranny. It follows herefrom that the political movement of labor may not even remotely partake even of the appearance of compromise. It exemplifies the revolutionary aim of the labor movement; it must be uncompromisingly revolutionary. This fact dictates the conduct of the successful political candidates of labor in the parliaments of capitalism. The principle found expression in the celebrated maxim uttered by William Liebknecht, when he still was in the full vigor of his Socialist aspirations—"Parlamentiren ist paktiren," to parliamentarize is to compromise, to log-roll, to sell out. [Applause.] When, in later years, experience brought home to him the unfortunate fact that the bourgeoisie of Germany had not finished their own revolution; when he discovered that that revolution had first to be completed, and that there was none to undertake the task but the Social Democratic movement; when that hard reality faced him and his movement, Liebknecht wisely adapted his course to the requirements. To parliamentarize is legitimate tactics with the bourgeois revolution. The parliamentarizing that the German Social Democracy thereupon, with Liebknecht at its head, has been constrained to practice, demonstrates that the movement in Germany has been constrained to adopt the tactics of the bourgeois revolutionist—precisely the reason why such tactics are wholly out of place, wholly inadmissible, aye, a badge of treason to the working class when applied in America. [Applause.] Without the *might* of the classconscious economic movement back of the political, the political movements that the labor movement inevitably promotes in America will not only be divided but, as a further result, will promote that confusion of thought that runs into corruption and that, reacting back upon the economic movement itself, helps to scuttle its efficiency. It surely is no accident that, without exception, all the labor candidates, so far allowed by the capitalist class to filter through their garrisons at their election defiles, whenever the office to which they were allowed to be returned elected was of any importance, have uniformly "parliamentarized," that is, "log-rolled," in

short, sold out the revolution. We saw it happen during the heyday of the K. of L.; we saw it happen more recently in Haverhill, in Brockton, in the Massachusetts Legislature, in Paterson, in Sheboygan; we see it happening now in Milwaukee. It is a matter of self-protection with the economic organization to watch and control the political. Skilless as unpracticed infancy, a danger to labor itself, is the sword of labor's ballot without the might of the classconscious economic organization to whet its edge, to keep it sharp, and to insist upon its being plied over the skull of the foe, to insist upon that at the peril of the muddleheads, of the weakling, of the traitor. [Applause.]

There now only remains one point to consider, and I am through. It is the point with regard to the necessity of the industrial organization in order to supplement the right of the ballot with the might requisite to put the quietus upon the capitalist class itself. The point implies what is generally, but wrongly, meant by

THE GENERAL STRIKE,

a term, that, through misuse by its own advocates, who have hitherto placed the cart before the horse, is greatly misunderstood, and should be substituted by the more appropriate term of *the general lockout of the capitalist class.*

Political power is reached through the ballot-box. But the ballot-box is not an open field; it is a veritable defile. That defile is held by the agents of the capitalist class. The election inspectors and returning boards are capitalist appointees; they are veritable garrisons with which the capitalist class holds the defile. To imagine that these capitalist garrisons of the election defiles will complacently allow the candidates of the revolution, whose program is the dismantling of the political burg of capitalism, peacefully to file through, is to indulge in a mooncalf's vision. The revolutionary ballot of labor is counted out now; it has been counted out from the first day of its appearance; it will be counted out even more extensively in the future. This fact is taken by some as a sufficient ground from which to conclude that the political movement is utterly useless. Those who arrive at that conclusion fall into the error of failing to realize that correct conclusions never flow from single premises. They can be arrived at only by considering all the premises in the case. While the Socialist ballot was, is and may continue to be counted out, the political movement accomplishes that which all the counting out will not be able to counteract. A man may monkey with the thermometer, yet he is utterly unable to monkey with the temperature. Place a lump of ice to the bulb of the quicksilver in this room of suffocating heat, the column will sink below zero, yet the temperature remains at fever heat. Place a piece of burning coal to the quicksilver bulb in midwinter, the mercury will rise to fever-heat, yet the temperature remains cold, unaltered. So with the election returns. They are the political thermometer. [Applause.] The political pickets of the capitalist class may monkey therewith to their heart's content—they will be unable to alter by the fraction of a degree the political temperature that prevails all around. Now, then, that political temperature, for reasons that I have already explained, *is pre-eminently the product of the political movement of labor.* [Long applause.] Wait, I have not yet proven the point. It still remains to be clinched. The question may still be asked, aye, it is asked: What does the hottest of political temperatures

avail, if the capitalist class retains the power to nullify it by counting us out? It may avail much; here, in America, it may mean the consummation of that ideal so dearly pursued by the Socialist—*the peaceful solution of the social question.* Look across at Europe. The feudal spirit still prevails there in an important respect, as a consequence of the continued prevalence there of large chunks of feudal institutions. In Europe, even the capitalist class is feudalized, let alone the surviving feudal heads. Though guilty of all the crimes of the decalogue, there is one vice that the feudal lord is substantially free from. That vice is *cowardice.* Valor is the burthen of the songs that rock their cradle; valor is the theme of the nursery tales to which they are raised; deeds of valor are the ideals set up before them. Take as a type the semi-crazy, semi-crippled Emperor of Germany. He will fight whatever the odds. In Europe a peaceful solution of the social question is out of all question. But how is the lay of the land here, in America? Was it songs of valor that rocked the cradles of our capitalist rulers? Was it tales of noble daring that formed the themes of the nursery tales to which they were brought up? Were the ideals that they gathered from their home surroundings the ideals of manliness? In short, did they reach their present position by deeds of valor? No! Daily experience, confirmed by every investigation that one set of capitalists institutes against another, tells us that they reached their present status of rulers by putting sand into your sugar, by watering their stocks, by putting shoddy into your clothes, by pouring water into your molasses, by breaches of trust, by fraudulent failures and fraudulent fires, in short by *swindle.* [Applause.] Now, then, the swindler is a coward.

Like a coward, he will play the bully, as we see the capitalist class doing, toward the weak, the weak because disorganized, working class. Before the strong, the bully crawls. Let the political temperature rise to the point of danger, then, all monkeying with the thermometer notwithstanding, your capitalist will quake in his stolen boots; he will not dare to fight; he will flee. [Applause.] At least I, for one, expect to see him flee. But, indeed, he will not unless, back of that ballot that has raised the political temperature to fever-heat is the might of the industrial organization, in full possession of the industrial establishments of the land, organized integrally, and, consequently, *capable of assuming the conduct of the nation's production*. The complete industrial organization of the working class will then have insured the peaceful issue of the struggle. But perhaps the capitalist may not flee. Perhaps, in a delirium of rage, he may resist. So much the worse—for him. The might, implied in the industrial organization of the working class of the land, will be in position to mop the earth with the rebellious usurper in short order [loud applause] and safeguard the right that the ballot proclaimed.

The futility of the ballot alone, however triumphant, was strikingly illustrated nine years ago during the first Bryan campaign. The political temperature against the plutocratic rulers of the land had risen to a point that they, for a moment, considered the battle at the ballot-box lost in advance. That, however, did not disconcert them. Through their national mouthpiece, Mark Hanna, they threatened to stop production. In other words, they threatened to go on strike. [Laughter.] The threat was no idle bombast. They could. It was known that they could. Craft unionism placed

it in their power to do so. The threat had its effect. But let the capitalist attempt, under the pressure of the political temperature raised by the ballot of labor—let him attempt to strike. In possession of the might conferred and implied by the industrial organization of their class, the working class would forthwith *lock out the capitalist class*. [Loud applause.] Without political organization, the labor movement cannot triumph; without economic organization, the day of its political triumph would be the day of its defeat.

Industrialism means might. Craft unionism means impotence. All the plants of production, aye, even the vast wealth for consumption, is today in the keeping of the working class. It is workingmen who are in charge of the factories, the railroads, the mines, in short all the land and machinery of production, and it is they also who sit as watch-dogs before the pantries, the cellars and the safe-deposit vaults of the capitalist class; aye, it is they who carry the guns in the armies. But this place of vantage is of no avail to them under craft unionism. Under craft unionism, only one craft marches into the battlefield at a time. By their idly looking on, the other crafts scab it upon the combatant. What with that and the likewise idle onlooking of those divisions of the workers who man the commissary department, so to speak, of the capitalist class, the class struggle presents, under craft unionism, the aspect of petty riots at which the empty stomachs and empty hands of the working class are pitted against the full ones of the employing class. Was this ignorance? Was this treason? Whether treason or ignorance, the turning in the long lane has been reached. Both the present conduct of craft unionism and the future conduct of Industrial Unionism was well portrayed by one of the delegates at the Chicago convention. Illustrating the point with the five fingers of his right hand far apart, he showed that to be the posture of the craft or autonomous unions—disconnected from one another for all practical work, and good only to act as a fan, a fan that had hitherto done nothing but scare the flies away from the face of the capitalist class [laughter]; and, proceeding thereupon to illustrate the further point by drawing his five fingers tightly into a compact fist, he showed that to be the posture of Industrial Unionism—a battering ram, that would leave the face of the capitalist class looking materially different from the way it looked when it was merely fanned. [Loud applause.] The impotence wherewith the right of the working class has hitherto been smitten, is now to be organized into a might without which that right is but mockery. The signal for that organization was struck last week at the convention of the Industrial Workers of the World; and the word has gone out, as it could go out from no other country but America, in language that fits our full-grown capitalist development—

"Unite! Unite on the economic field upon the only basis that economic unity is possible—the basis of the solidarity of the working class, the only solid fact from which political unity can be reflected! Unite! Unite upon the only economic principle capable of backing up the right of the labor ballot with the might to enforce it! Unite for the general strike at the ballot-box, to overthrow the political robberburg of capitalism, backed by the general strike against, or, rather, the general lockout of the capitalist class from the industrial fields that it has usurped. Unite for the emancipation of the working class, and to save civilization from a catastrophe!" [Loud applause.]

1905

THORSTEIN VEBLEN
(1857–1929)

THE ENGINEERS AND THE PRICE SYSTEM *

CHAPTER III
THE CAPTAINS OF FINANCE AND THE ENGINEERS

In more than one respect the industrial system of today is notably different from anything that has gone before. It is eminently a system, self-balanced and comprehensive; and it is a system of interlocking mechanical processes, rather than of skillful manipulation. It is mechanical rather than manual. It is an organization of mechanical powers and material resources, rather than of skilled craftsmen and tools; although the skilled workmen and tools are also an indispensable part of its comprehensive mechanism. It is of an impersonal nature, after the fashion of the material sciences, on which it constantly draws. It runs to "quantity production" of specialized and standardized goods and services. For all these reasons it lends itself to systematic control under the direction of industrial experts, skilled technologists, who may be called "production engineers," for want of a better term.

This industrial system runs on as an inclusive organization of many and diverse interlocking mechanical processes, interdependent and balanced

* From *The Engineers and the Price System* by Thorstein Veblen. Copyright 1921 by B. W. Huebsch, Inc. By permission of The Viking Press, Inc., New York.

among themselves in such a way that the due working of any part of it is conditioned on the due working of all the rest. Therefore it will work at its best only on condition that these industrial experts, production engineers, will work together on a common understanding; and more particularly on condition that they must not work at cross purposes. These technological specialists whose constant supervision is indispensable to the due working of the industrial system constitute the general staff of industry, whose work it is to control the strategy of production at large and to keep an oversight of the tactics of production in detail.

Such is the nature of this industrial system on whose due working depends the material welfare of all civilized peoples. It is an inclusive system drawn on a plan of strict and comprehensive interdependence, such that, in point of material welfare, no nation and no community has anything to gain at the cost of any other nation or community. In point of material welfare, all the civilized peoples have been drawn together by the state of the industrial arts into a single going concern. And for the due working of this inclusive going concern it is essential that that corps of technological specialists who by training, insight, and interest make up the general staff of industry must have a free hand in the disposal of its available resources, in materials, equipment, and man power, regardless of any national pretensions or any vested interests. Any degree of obstruction, diversion, or withholding of any of the available industrial forces, with a view to the special gain of any nation or any investor, unavoidably brings on a dislocation of the system; which involves a disproportionate lowering of its working efficiency and therefore a disproportionate loss to the whole, and therefore a net loss to all its parts.

And all the while the statesmen are at work to divert and obstruct the working forces of this industrial system, here and there, for the special advantage of one nation and another at the cost of the rest; and the captains of finance are working, at cross purposes and in collusion, to divert whatever they can to the special gain of one vested interest and another, at any cost to the rest. So it happens that the industrial system is deliberately handicapped with dissension, misdirection, and unemployment of material resources, equipment, and man power, at every turn where the statesmen or the captains of finance can touch its mechanism; and all the civilized peoples are suffering privation together because their general staff of industrial experts are in this way required to take orders and submit to sabotage at the hands of the statesmen and the vested interests. Politics and investment are still allowed to decide matters of industrial policy which should plainly be left to the discretion of the general staff of production engineers driven by no commercial bias.

No doubt this characterization of the industrial system and its besetting tribulations will seem overdrawn. However it is not intended to apply to any earlier date than the twentieth century, or to any backward community that still lies outside the sweep of mechanical industry. Only gradually during the past century, while the mechanical industry has been progressively taking over the production of goods and services, and going over to quantity production, has the industrial system taken on this character of an inclusive organization of interlocking processes and interchange of materials; and it is only in the twentieth century that this cumulative progression has come to a head with such effect that this characterization is now visibly becoming true. And even now it will hold true, visibly and securely, only as applies to the leading mechanical industries, those main lines of industry that shape the main conditions of life, and in which quantity production has become the common and indispensable rule. Such are, e.g., transport and communication; the production and industrial use of coal, oil, electricity and water power; the production of steel and other metals; of wood pulp, lumber, cement and other building materials; of textiles and rubber; as also grain-milling and much of grain-growing, together with meat-packing and a good share of the stock-raising industry.

There is, of course, a large volume of industry in many lines which has not, or only in part and doubtfully, been drawn into this network of mechanical processes and quantity production, in any direct and conclusive fashion. But these other lines of industry that still stand over on another and older plan of operation are, after all, outliers and subsidiaries of the mechanically organized industrial system, dependent on or subservient to those greater underlying industries which make up the working body of the system, and which therefore set the pace for the rest. And in the main, therefore, and as regards these greater mechanical industries on whose due working the material welfare of the community depends from day to day, this characterization will apply without material abatement.

But it should be added that even as regards these greater, primary and underlying, lines of production the system has not yet reached a fatal de-

gree of close-knit interdependence, balance, and complication; it will still run along at a very tolerable efficiency in the face of a very appreciable amount of persistent derangement. That is to say, the industrial system at large has not yet become so delicately balanced a mechanical structure and process that the ordinary amount of derangement and sabotage necessary to the ordinary control of production by business methods will paralyze the whole outright. The industrial system is not yet sufficiently close-knit for that. And yet, that extent and degree of paralysis from which the civilized world's industry is suffering just now, due to legitimate businesslike sabotage, goes to argue that the date may not be far distant when the interlocking processes of the industrial system shall have become so closely interdependent and so delicately balanced that even the ordinary modicum of sabotage involved in the conduct of business as usual will bring the whole to a fatal collapse. The derangement and privation brought on by any well organized strike of the larger sort argues to the same effect.

In effect, the progressive advance of this industrial system towards an all-inclusive mechanical balance of interlocking processes appears to be approaching a critical pass, beyond which it will no longer be practicable to leave its control in the hands of business men working at cross purposes for private gain, or to entrust its continued administration to others than suitably trained technological experts, production engineers without a commercial interest. What these men may then do with it all is not so plain; the best that they can do may not be good enough; but the negative proposition is becoming sufficiently plain, that this mechanical state of the industrial arts will not long tolerate the continued control of production by the vested interests under the current businesslike rule of incapacity by advisement.

In the beginning, that is to say during the early growth of the machine industry, and particularly in that new growth of mechanical industries which arose directly out of the Industrial Revolution, there was no marked division between the industrial experts and the business managers. That was before the new industrial system had gone far on the road of progressive specialization and complexity, and before business had reached an exactingly large scale; so that even the business men of that time, who were without training in special technological matters, would still be able to exercise something of an intelligent oversight of the whole, and to understand something of what was required in the mechanical conduct of the work which they financed and from which they drew their income. Not unusually the designers of industrial processes and equipment would then still take care of the financial end, at the same time that they managed the shop. But from an early point in the development there set in a progressive differentiation, such as to divide those who designed and administered the industrial processes from those others who designed and managed the commercial transactions and took care of the financial end. So there also set in a corresponding division of powers between the business management and the technological experts. It became the work of the technologist to determine, on technological grounds, what could be done in the way of productive industry, and to contrive ways and means of doing it; but the business management always continued to decide, on commercial

grounds, how much work should be done and what kind and quality of goods and services should be produced; and the decision of the business management has always continued to be final, and has always set the limit beyond which production must not go.

With the continued growth of specialization the experts have necessarily had more and more to say in the affairs of industry; but always their findings as to what work is to be done and what ways and means are to be employed in production have had to wait on the findings of the business managers as to what will be expedient for the purposes of commercial gain. This division between business management and industrial management has continued to go forward, at a continually accelerated rate, because the special training and experience required for any passably efficient organization and direction of these industrial processes has continually grown more exacting, calling for special knowledge and abilities on the part of those who have this work to do and requiring their undivided interest and their undivided attention to the work in hand. But these specialists in technological knowledge, abilities, interest, and experience, who have increasingly come into the case in this way—inventors, designers, chemists, mineralogists, soil experts, crop specialists, production managers and engineers of many kinds and denominations—have continued to be employees of the captains of industry, that is to say, of the captains of finance, whose work it has been to commercialize the knowledge and abilities of the industrial experts and turn them to account for their own gain.

It is perhaps unnecessary to add the axiomatic corollary that the captains have always turned the technologists and their knowledge to account in this way only so far as would serve their own commercial profit, not to the extent of their ability; or to the limit set by the material circumstances; or by the needs of the community. The result has been, uniformly and as a matter of course, that the production of goods and services has advisedly been stopped short of productive capacity, by curtailment of output and by derangement of the productive system. There are two main reasons for this, and both have operated together throughout the machine era to stop industrial production increasingly short of productive capacity. (a) The commercial need of maintaining a profitable price has led to an increasingly imperative curtailment of the output, as fast as the advance of the industrial arts has enhanced the productive capacity. And (b) the continued advance of the mechanical technology has called for an ever-increasing volume and diversity of special knowledge, and so has left the businesslike captains of finance continually farther in arrears, so that they have been less and less capable of comprehending what is required in the ordinary way of industrial equipment and personnel. They have therefore, in effect, maintained prices at a profitable level by curtailment of output rather than by lowering production-cost per unit of output, because they have not had such a working acquaintance with the technological facts in the case as would enable them to form a passably sound judgment of suitable ways and means for lowering production-cost; and at the same time, being shrewd business men, they have been unable to rely on the hired-man's-loyalty of technologists whom they do not understand. The result has been a somewhat distrustful blindfold choice of processes and personnel and a consequent enforced incompetence in the management of industry, a curtailment of output below the needs of the community, below the productive capacity of the industrial system, and below what an intelligent control of production would have made commercially possible.

Through the earlier decades of the machine era these limitations imposed on the work of the experts by the demands of profitable business and by the technical ignorance of the business men, appears not to have been a heavy handicap, whether as a hindrance to the further development of technological knowledge or as an obstacle to its ordinary use in industry. That was before the mechanical industry had gone far in scope, complexity, and specialization; and it was also before the continued work of the technologists had pushed the industrial system to so high a productive capacity that it is forever in danger of turning out a larger product than is required for a profitable business. But gradually, with the passage of time and the advance of the industrial arts to a wider scope and a larger scale, and to an increasing specialization and standardization of processes, the technological knowledge that makes up the state of the industrial arts has called for a higher degree of that training that makes industrial specialists; and at the same time any passably efficient management of industry has of necessity drawn on them and their special abilities to an ever-increasing extent. At the same time and by the same shift of circumstances, the captains of finance, driven by an increasingly close application to the affairs of business, have been going further out of touch with the ordinary realities of productive industry; and, it is to be admitted, they have also continued increasingly to distrust the technological specialists, whom they do not understand, but whom they can also not get along without. The captains have per force continued to employ the technologists, to make money for them, but they have done so only reluctantly, tardily, sparingly, and with shrewd circumspection; only because and so far as they have been persuaded that the use of these technologists was indispensable to the making of money.

One outcome of this persistent and pervasive tardiness and circumspection on the part of the captains has been an incredibly and increasingly uneconomical use of material resources, and an incredibly wasteful organization of equipment and man power in those great industries where the technological advance has been most marked. In good part it was this discreditable pass, to which the leading industries had been brought by these one-eyed captains of industry, that brought the regime of the captains to an inglorious close, by shifting the initiative and discretion in this domain out of their hands into those of the investment bankers. By custom the investment bankers had occupied a position between or overlapping the duties of a broker in corporate securities and those of an underwriter of corporate flotations—such a position, in effect, as is still assigned them in the standard writings on corporate finance. The increasingly large scale of corporate enterprise, as well as the growth of mutual understanding among these business concerns, also had its share in this new move. But about this time, too, the "consulting engineers" were coming notably into evidence in many of those lines of industry in which corporate finance has habitually been concerned.

So far as concerns the present argument the ordinary duties of these consulting engineers have been to advise the investment bankers as to the industrial and commercial soundness, past and prospective, of any enterprise that is to be underwritten. These duties have comprised a painstaking and impartial examination of the physical properties involved in any given case, as well as an equally impartial auditing of the accounts and appraisal of the commercial promise of such enterprises, for the guidance of the bankers or the syndicate of bankers interested in the case as underwriters. On this ground working arrangements and a mutual understanding presently arose between the consulting engineers and those banking houses that habitually were concerned in the underwriting of corporate enterprises.

The effect of this move has been twofold: experience has brought out the fact that corporation finance, at its best and soundest, has now become a matter of comprehensive and standardized bureaucratic routine, necessarily comprising the mutual relations between various corporate concerns, and best to be taken care of by a clerical staff of trained accountants; and the same experience has put the financial houses in direct touch with the technological general staff of the industrial system, whose surveillance has become increasingly imperative to the conduct of any profitable enterprise in industry. But also, by the same token, it has appeared that the corporation financier of the nineteenth-century tradition is no longer of the essence of the case in corporation finance of the larger and more responsible sort. He has, in effect, come to be no better than an idle wheel in the economic mechanism, serving only to take up some of the lubricant.

Since and so far as this shift out of the nineteenth century into the twentieth has been completed, the corporation financier has ceased to be a captain of industry and has become a lieutenant of finance; the captaincy having been taken over by the syndicated investment bankers and administered as a standard routine of accountancy, having to do with the flotation of corporation securities and with their fluctuating values, and having also something to do with regulating the rate and volume of output in those industrial enterprises which so have passed under the hand of the investment bankers.

By and large, such is the situation of the industrial system today, and of that financial business that controls the industrial system. But this state of things is not so much an accomplished fact handed on out of the recent past; it is only that such is the culmination in which it all heads up in the immediate present, and that such is the visible drift of things into the calculable future. Only during the last few years has the state of affairs in industry been obviously falling into the shape so outlined, and it is even yet only in those larger and pacemaking lines of industry which are altogether of the new technological order that the state of things has reached this finished shape. But in these larger and underlying divisions of the industrial system the present posture and drift of things is unmistakable. Meantime very much still stands over out of that régime of rule-of-thumb, competitive sabotage, and commercial log-rolling, in which the businesslike captains of the old order are so altogether well at home, and which has been the best that the cap-

tains have known how to contrive for the management of that industrial system whose captains they have been. So that wherever the production experts are now taking over the management, out of the dead hand of the self-made captains, and wherever they have occasions to inquire into the established conditions of production, they find the ground cumbered with all sorts of incredible makeshifts of waste and inefficiency—such makeshifts as perhaps would pass muster with any moderately stupid elderly layman, but which look like blindfold guesswork to these men who know something of the advanced technology and its working-out.

Hitherto, then, the growth and conduct of this industrial system presents this singular outcome. The technology—the state of the industrial arts —which takes effect in this mechanical industry is in an eminent sense a joint stock of knowledge and experience held in common by the civilized peoples. It requires the use of trained and instructed workmen—born, bred, trained, and instructed at the cost of the people at large. So also it requires, with a continually more exacting insistence, a corps of highly trained and specially gifted experts, of divers and various kinds. These, too, are born, bred, and trained at the cost of the community at large, and they draw their requisite special knowledge from the community's joint stock of accumulated experience. These expert men, technologists, engineers, or whatever name may best suit them, make up the indispensable General Staff of the industrial system; and without their immediate and unremitting guidance and correction the industrial system will not work. It is a mechanically organized structure of technical processes designed, installed, and conducted by these production engineers. Without them and their constant attention the industrial equipment, the mechanical appliances of industry, will foot up to just so much junk. The material welfare of the community is unreservedly bound up with the due working of this industrial system, and therefore with its unreserved control by the engineers, who alone are competent to manage it. To do their work as it should be done these men of the industrial general staff must have a free hand, unhampered by commercial considerations and reservations; for the production of the goods and services needed by the community they neither need nor are they in any degree benefited by any supervision or interference from the side of the owners. Yet the absentee owners, now represented, in effect, by the syndicated investment bankers, continue to control the industrial experts and limit their discretion, arbitrarily, for their own commercial gain, regardless of the needs of the community.

Hitherto these men who so make up the general staff of the industrial system have not drawn together into anything like a self-directing working force; nor have they been vested with anything more than an occasional, haphazard, and tentative control of some disjointed sector of the industrial equipment, with no direct or decisive relation to that personnel of productive industry that may be called the officers of the line and the rank and file. It is still the unbroken privilege of the financial management and its financial agents to "hire and fire." The final disposition of all the industrial forces still remains in the hands of the business men, who still continue to dispose of these forces for other than industrial ends. And all the while it is an open secret that with a reasonably free hand the production experts would today readily increase the ordinary output of industry by several fold,—variously estimated at some 300 per cent to 1200 per cent of the current output. And what stands in the way of so increasing the ordinary output of goods and services is business as usual.

Right lately these technologists have begun to become uneasily "class-conscious" and to reflect that they together constitute the indispensable General Staff of the industrial system. Their class consciousness has taken the immediate form of a growing sense of waste and confusion in the management of industry by the financial agents of the absentee owners. They are beginning to take stock of that all-pervading mismanagement of industry that is inseparable from its control for commercial ends. All of which brings home a realization of their own shame and of damage to the common good. So the engineers are beginning to draw together and ask themselves, "What about it?"

This uneasy movement among the technologists set in, in an undefined and fortuitous way, in the closing years of the nineteenth century; when the consulting engineers, and then presently the "efficiency engineers," began to make scattered corrections in detail, which showed up the industrial incompetence of those elderly laymen who were doing a conservative business at the cost of industry. The consulting engineers of the standard type, both then and since then, are commercialized technologists, whose work it is to appraise the industrial value of any given enterprise with a view to its commercial exploitation. They are a cross between a technological specialist and a commercial agent, beset with the limitations of both and commonly not fully competent in either line. Their normal position is that of an employee of the investment bankers, on a stipend or a retainer, and it has ordinarily been their fortune to shift over in time from a technological footing to a frankly commercial one. The case of the efficiency engineers, or scientific-management experts, is somewhat similar. They too have set out to appraise, exhibit, and correct the commercial short-comings of the ordinary management of those industrial establishments which they investigate, to persuade the business men in charge how they may reasonably come in for larger net earnings by a more closely shorn exploitation of the industrial forces at their disposal. During the opening years of the new century a lively interest centered on the views and expositions of these two groups of industrial experts; and not least was the interest aroused by their exhibits of current facts indicating an all-pervading lag, leak, and friction in the industrial system, due to its disjointed and one-eyed management by commercial adventurers bent on private gain.

During these few years of the opening century the members of this informal guild of engineers at large have been taking an interest in this question of habitual mismanagement by ignorance and commercial sabotage, even apart from the commercial imbecility of it all. But it is the young rather than the old among them who see industry in any other light than its commercial value. Circumstances have decided that the older generation of the craft have become pretty well commercialized. Their habitual outlook has been shaped by a long and unbroken apprenticeship to the corporation financiers and the investment bankers; so that they still habitually see the industrial system as a contrivance for the roundabout process of making money. Accordingly, the established official Associations and Institutes of Engineers, which are officered and engineered by the elder engineers, old and young, also continue to show the commercial bias of their creators, in what they criticize and in what they propose. But the new generation which has been coming on during the present century are not similarly true to that tradition of commercial engineering that makes the technological man an awestruck lieutenant of the captain of finance.

By training and perhaps by native bent, the technologists find it easy and convincing to size up men and things in terms of tangible performance, without commercial afterthought, except so far as their apprenticeship to the captains of finance may have made commercial afterthought a second nature to them. Many of the younger generation are beginning to understand that engineering begins and ends in the domain of tangible performance, and that commercial expediency is another matter. Indeed, they are beginning to understand that commercial expediency has nothing better to contribute to the engineer's work than so much lag, leak, and friction. The four years' experience of war has also been highly instructive on that head. So they are beginning to draw together on a common-ground of understanding, as men who are concerned with the ways and means of tangible performance in the way of productive industry, according to the state of the industrial arts as they know them at their best; and there is a growing conviction among them that they together constitute the sufficient and indispensable general staff of the mechanical industries, on whose unhindered team-work depends the due working of the industrial system and therefore also the material welfare of the civilized peoples. So also, to these men who are trained in the stubborn logic of technology, nothing is quite real that cannot be stated in terms of tangible performance; and they are accordingly coming to understand that the whole fabric of credit and corporation finance is a tissue of make-believe.

Credit obligations and financial transactions rest on certain principles of legal formality which have been handed down from the eighteenth century, and which therefore antedate the mechanical industry and carry no secure conviction to men trained in the logic of that industry. Within this technological system of tangible performance corporation finance and all its works and gestures are completely idle; it all comes into the working scheme of the engineers only as a gratuitous intrusion which could be barred out without deranging the work at any point, provided only that men made up their mind to that effect—that is to say, provided the make-believe of absentee ownership were discontinued. Its only obvious effect on the work which the engineers have to take care of is waste of materials and retardation of the work. So the next question which the engineers are due to ask regarding this timeworn fabric of ownership, finance, sabotage, credit, and unearned income is likely to be: Why cumbers it the ground? And they are likely to find the scriptural answer ready to their hand.

It would be hazardous to surmise how, how soon, on what provocation, and with what effect the guild of engineers are due to realize that they constitute a guild, and that the material fortunes of the civilized peoples already lie loose in their hands. But it is already sufficiently plain that the industrial conditions and the drift of conviction among the engineers are drawing together to some such end.

Hitherto it has been usual to count on the interested negotiations continually carried on and never concluded between capital and labor, between the agents of the investors and the body of workmen, to bring about whatever readjustments are to be looked for in the control of productive industry and in the distribution and use of its product. These negotiations have necessarily been, and continue to be, in the nature of business transactions, bargaining for a price, since both parties to the negotiation continue to stand on the consecrated ground of ownership, free bargain, and self-help; such as the commercial wisdom of the eighteenth century saw, approved, and certified it all, in the time before the coming of this perplexing industrial system. In the course of these endless negotiations between the owners and their workmen there has been some loose and provisional syndication of claims and forces on both sides; so that each of these two recognized parties to the industrial controversy has come to make up a loose-knit vested interest, and each speaks for its own special claims as a party in interest. Each is contending for some special gain for itself and trying to drive a profitable bargain for itself, and hitherto no disinterested spokesman for the community at large or for the industrial system as a going concern has seriously cut into this controversy between these contending vested interests. The outcome has been businesslike concession and compromise, in the nature of bargain and sale. It is true, during the war, and for the conduct of the war, there were some half-concerted measures taken by the Administration in the interest of the nation at large, as a belligerent; but it has always been tacitly agreed that these were extraordinary war measures, not to be countenanced in time of peace. In time of peace the accepted rule is still business as usual; that is to say, investors and workmen wrangling together on a footing of business as usual.

These negotiations have necessarily been inconclusive. So long as ownership of resources and industrial plant is allowed, or so long as it is allowed any degree of control or consideration in the conduct of industry, nothing more substantial can come of any readjustment than a concessive mitigation of the owners' interference with production. There is accordingly nothing subversive in these bouts of bargaining between the federated workmen and the syndicated owners. It is a game of chance and skill played between two contending vested interests for private gain, in which the industrial system as a going concern enters only as a victim of interested interference. Yet the material welfare of the community, and not the least of the workmen, turns on the due working of this industrial system, without interference. Concessive mitigation of the right to interfere with production, on the part of either one of these vested interests, can evidently come to nothing more substantial than a concessive mitigation.

But owing to the peculiar technological character of this industrial system, with its specialized, standardized, mechanical, and highly technical interlocking processes of production, there has gradually come into being this corps of technological production specialists, into whose keeping the due functioning of the industrial system has now drifted by force of circumstance. They are, by force of circum-

stance, keepers of the community's material welfare; although they have hitherto been acting, in effect, as keepers and providers of free income for the kept classes. They are thrown into the position of responsible directors of the industrial system, and by the same move they are in a position to become arbiters of the community's material welfare. They are becoming class-conscious, and they are no longer driven by a commercial interest, in any such degree as will make them a vested interest in that commercial sense in which the syndicated owners and the federated workmen are vested interests. They are, at the same time, numerically and by habitual outlook, no such heterogeneous and unwieldy body as the federated workmen, whose numbers and scattering interest has left all their endeavors substantially nugatory. In short, the engineers are in a position to make the next move.

By comparison with the population at large, including the financial powers and the kept classes, the technological specialists which come in the question here are a very inconsiderable number; yet this number is indispensable to the continued working of the productive industries. So slight are their numbers, and so sharply defined and homogeneous is their class, that a sufficiently compact and inclusive organization of their forces should arrange itself almost as a matter of course, so soon as any appreciable proportion of them shall be moved by any common purpose. And the common purpose is not far to seek, in the all-pervading industrial confusion, obstruction, waste, and retardation which business as usual continually throws in their face. At the same time they are the leaders of the industrial personnel, the workmen, of the officers of the line and the rank and file; and these are coming into a frame of mind to follow their leaders in any adventure that holds a promise of advancing the common good.

To these men, soberly trained in a spirit of tangible performance and endowed with something more than an even share of the sense of workmanship, and endowed also with the common heritage of partiality for the rule of Live and Let Live, the disallowance of an outworn and obstructive right of absentee ownership is not likely to seem a shocking infraction of the sacred realities. That customary right of ownership by virtue of which the vested interests continue to control the industrial system for the benefit of the kept classes, belongs to an older order of things than the mechanical industry. It has come out of a past that was made up of small things and traditional make-believe. For all the purposes of that scheme of tangible performance that goes to make up the technologist's world, it is without form and void. So that, given time for due irritation, it should by no means come as a surprise if the guild of engineers are provoked to put their heads together and, quite out of hand, disallow that large absentee ownership that goes to make the vested interests and to unmake the industrial system. And there stands behind them the massed and rough-handed legions of the industrial rank and file, ill at ease and looking for new things. The older commercialized generation among them would, of course, ask themselves: Why should we worry? What do we stand to gain? But the younger generation, not so hard-bitten by commercial experience, will be quite as likely to ask themselves: What do we stand to lose? And there is the patent fact that such a thing as a general strike of the technological specialists in industry need

involve no more than a minute fraction of one per cent of the population; yet it would swiftly bring a collapse of the old order and sweep the time-worn fabric of finance and absentee sabotage into the discard for good and all.

Such a catastrophe would doubtless be deplorable. It would look something like the end of the world to all those persons who take their stand with the kept classes, but it may come to seem no more than an incident of the day's work to the engineers and to the rough-handed legions of the rank and file. It is a situation which may well be deplored. But there is no gain in losing patience with a conjunction of circumstances. And it can do no harm to take stock of the situation and recognize that, by force of circumstance, it is now open to the Council of Technological Workers' and Soldiers' Deputies to make the next move, in their own way and in their own good time. When and what this move will be, if any, or even what it will be like, is not something on which a layman can hold a confident opinion. But so much seems clear, that the industrial dictatorship of the captain of finance is now held on the sufferance of the engineers and is liable at any time to be discontinued at their discretion, as a matter of convenience.

1919, 1921

JACK LONDON
(1876–1916)

FROM *THE SEA-WOLF* *

[HARRISON GOES ALOFT]

* * * A cruel thing happened just before supper, indicative of the cal-

* Reprinted by permission of Mrs. Jack London and Mrs. Elizabeth London Shephard.

lousness and brutishness of these men. There is one green hand in the crew, Harrison by name, a clumsy-looking country boy, mastered, I imagine, by the spirit of adventure, and making his first voyage. In the light baffling airs the schooner had been tacking about a great deal, at which times the sails pass from one side to the other and a man is sent aloft to shift over the fore-gaff-topsail. In some way, when Harrison was aloft, the sheet jammed in the block through which it runs at the end of the gaff. As I understood it, there were two ways of getting it cleared,—first, by lowering the foresail, which was comparatively easy and without danger; and second, by climbing out of the peak-halyards to the end of the gaff itself, an exceedingly hazardous performance.

Johansen called out to Harrison to go out the halyards. It was patent to everybody that the boy was afraid. And well he might be, eighty feet above the deck, to trust himself on those thin and jerking ropes. Had there been a steady breeze it would not have been so bad, but the *Ghost* was rolling emptily in a long sea, and with each roll the canvas flapped and boomed and the halyards slacked and jerked taut. They were capable of snapping a man off like a fly from a whip-lash.

Harrison heard the order and understood what was demanded of him, but hesitated. It was probably the first time he had been aloft in his life. Johansen, who had caught the contagion of Wolf Larsen's masterfulness, burst out with a volley of abuse and curses.

"That'll do, Johansen," Wolf Larsen said brusquely. "I'll have you know that I do the swearing on this ship. If I need your assistance, I'll call you in."

"Yes, sir," the mate acknowledged submissively.

In the meantime Harrison had started out on the halyards. I was looking up from the galley door, and I could see him trembling, as with ague, in every limb. He proceeded very slowly and cautiously, an inch at a time. Outlined against the clear blue of the sky, he had the appearance of an enormous spider crawling along the tracery of its web.

It was a slight uphill climb, for the foresail peaked high; and the halyards, running through various blocks on the gaff and mast, gave him separate holds for hands and feet. But the trouble lay in that the wind was not strong enough nor steady enough to keep the sail full. When he was halfway out, the *Ghost* took a long roll to windward and back again into the hollow between two seas. Harrison ceased his progress and held on tightly. Eighty feet beneath, I could see the agonized strain of his muscles as he gripped for very life. The sail emptied and the gaff swung amidships. The halyards slackened, and though it all happened very quickly, I could see them sag beneath the weight of his body. Then the gaff swung to the side with an abrupt swiftness, the great sail boomed like a cannon, and the three rows of reef-points slatted against the canvas like a volley of rifles. Harrison, clinging on, made the giddy rush through the air. This rush ceased abruptly. The halyards became instantly taut. It was the snap of the whip. His clutch was broken. One hand was torn loose from its hold. The other lingered desperately for a moment, and followed. His body pitched out and down, but in some way he managed to save himself with his legs. He was hanging by them, head downward. A quick effort brought his hands up to the halyards again; but he was a long time regaining his former position, where he hung, a pitiable object.

"I'll bet he has no appetite for supper," I heard Wolf Larsen's voice, which came to me from around the corner of the galley. "Stand from under, you, Johansen! Watch out! Here she comes!"

In truth, Harrison was very sick, as a person is seasick; and for a long time he clung to his precarious perch without attempting to move. Johansen, however, continued violently to urge him on to the completion of his task.

"It is a shame," I heard Johnson growling in painfully slow and correct English. He was standing by the main rigging, a few feet away from me. "The boy is willing enough. He will learn if he has a chance. But this is—" He paused awhile, for the word "murder" was his final judgment.

"Hist, will ye!" Louis whispered to him. "For the love iv your mother hold your mouth!"

But Johnson, looking on, still continued his grumbling.

"Look here," the hunter, Standish, spoke to Wolf Larsen, "that's my boat-puller, and I don't want to lose him."

"That's all right, Standish," was the reply. "He's your boat-puller when you've got him in the boat; but he's my sailor when I have him aboard, and I'll do what I damn well please with him."

"But that's no reason—" Standish began in a torrent of speech.

"That'll do, easy as she goes," Wolf Larsen counselled back. "I've told you what's what, and let it stop at that. The man's mine, and I'll make soup of him and eat it if I want to."

There was an angry gleam in the hunter's eye, but he turned on his heel and entered the steerage companionway, where he remained, looking upward. All hands were on deck now, and all eyes were aloft, where a human life was at grapples with death. The callousness of these men, to whom industrial organization gave control of the lives of other men, was appalling. I, who had lived out of the whirl of the world, had never dreamed that its work was carried on in such fashion. Life had always seemed a peculiarly sacred thing, but here it counted for nothing, was a cipher in the arithmetic of commerce. I must say, however, that the sailors themselves were sympathetic, as instance the case of Johnson; but the masters (the hunters and the captain), were heartlessly indifferent. Even the protest of Standish arose out of the fact that he did not wish to lose his boat-puller. Had it been some other hunter's boat-puller, he, like them, would have been no more than amused.

But to return to Harrison. It took Johansen, insulting and reviling the poor wretch, fully ten minutes to get him started again. A little later he made the end of the gaff, where, astride the spar itself, he had a better chance for holding on. He cleared the sheet, and was free to return, slightly down-hill now, along the halyards to the mast. But he had lost his nerve. Unsafe as was his present position, he was loath to forsake it for the more unsafe position on the halyards.

He looked along the airy path he must traverse, and then down to the deck. His eyes were wide and staring, and he was trembling violently. I had never seen fear so strongly stamped upon a human face. Johansen called vainly for him to come down. At any moment he was liable to be snapped off the gaff, but he was helpless with fright. Wolf Larsen, walking up and down with Smoke

and in conversation, took no more notice of him, though he cried sharply,
once, to the man at the wheel:—

"You're off your course, my man!
Be careful, unless you're looking for
trouble!"

"Ay, ay, sir," the helmsman responded, putting a couple of spokes
down.

He had been guilty of running the
Ghost several points off her course in
order that what little wind there was
should fill the foresail and hold it
steady. He had striven to help the
unfortunate Harrison at the risk of
incurring Wolf Larsen's anger.

The time went by, and the suspense, to me, was terrible. Thomas
Mugridge, on the other hand, considered it a laughable affair, and was
continually bobbing his head out the
galley door to make jocose remarks.
How I hated him! And how my
hatred for him grew and grew, during
that fearful time, to cyclopean dimensions. For the first time in my life
I experienced the desire to murder—
"saw red," as some of our picturesque
writers phrase it. Life in general
might still be sacred, but life in the
particular case of Thomas Mugridge
had become very profane indeed. I
was frightened when I became conscious that I was seeing red, and the
thought flashed through my mind:
was I, too, becoming tainted by the
brutality of my environment?—I, who
even in the most flagrant crimes had
denied the justice and righteousness
of capital punishment?

Fully half an hour went by, and
then I saw Johnson and Louis in some
sort of altercation. It ended with
Johnson flinging off Louis's detaining
arm and starting forward. He crossed
the deck, sprang into the fore rigging, and began to climb. But the
quick eye of Wolf Larsen caught
him.

"Here, you, what are you up to?"
he cried.

Johnson's ascent was arrested. He
looked his captain in the eyes and
replied slowly:—

"I am going to get that boy down."

"You get down out of that rigging, and damn lively about it! D'ye
hear? Get down!"

Johnson hesitated, but the long
years of obedience to the masters of
ships overpowered him, and he
dropped sullenly to the deck and went
on forward.

At half after five I went below to
set the cabin table, but I hardly knew
what I did, for my eyes and brain
were filled with the vision of a man,
white-faced and trembling, comically
like a bug, clinging to the thrashing
gaff. At six o'clock, when I served
supper, going on deck to get the food
from the galley, I saw Harrison, still
in the same position. The conversation at the table was of other things.
Nobody seemed interested in the wantonly imperilled life. But making an
extra trip to the galley a little later,
I was gladdened by the sight of Harrison staggering weakly from the rigging to the forecastle scuttle. He had
finally summoned the courage to descend.

Before closing this incident, I must
give a scrap of conversation I had with
Wolf Larsen in the cabin, while I was
washing the dishes.

"You were looking squeamish this
afternoon," he began. "What was the
matter?"

I could see that he knew what had
made me possibly as sick as Harrison, that he was trying to draw me,
and I answered, "It was because of
the brutal treatment of that boy."

He gave a short laugh. "Like sea-
sickness, I suppose. Some men are
subject to it, and others are not."

"Not so," I objected.

"Just so," he went on. "The earth is as full of brutality as the sea is full of motion. And some men are made sick by the one, and some by the other. That's the only reason."

"But you, who make a mock of human life, don't you place any value upon it whatever?" I demanded.

"Value? What value?" He looked at me, and though his eyes were steady and motionless, there seemed a cynical smile in them. "What kind of value? How do you measure it? Who values it?"

"I do," I made answer.

"Then what is it worth to you? Another man's life, I mean. Come, now, what is it worth?"

The value of life? How could I put a tangible value upon it? Somehow, I, who have always had expression, lacked expression when with Wolf Larsen. I have since determined that a part of it was due to the man's personality, but that the greater part was due to his totally different outlook. Unlike other materialists I had met and with whom I had something in common to start on, I had nothing in common with him. Perhaps, also, it was the elemental simplicity of his mind that baffled me. He drove so directly to the core of the matter, divesting a question always of all superfluous details, and with such an air of finality, that I seemed to find myself struggling in deep water with no footing under me. Value of life? How could I answer the question on the spur of the moment? The sacredness of life I had accepted as axiomatic. That it was intrinsically valuable was a truism I had never questioned. But when he challenged the truism I was speechless.

"We were talking about this yesterday," he said. "I held that life was a ferment, a yeasty something which devoured life that it might live, and

that living was merely successful piggishness. Why, if there is anything in supply and demand, life is the cheapest thing in the world. There is only so much water, so much earth, so much air; but the life that is demanding to be born is limitless. Nature is a spendthrift. Look at the fish and their millions of eggs. For that matter, look at you and me. In our loins are the possibilities of millions of lives. Could we but find time and opportunity and utilize the last bit and every bit of the unborn life that is in us, we could become the fathers of nations and populate continents. Life? Bah! It has no value. Of cheap things it is the cheapest. Everywhere it goes begging. Nature spills it out with a lavish hand. Where there is room for one life, she sows a thousand lives, and it's life eats life till the strongest and most piggish life is left."

"You have read Darwin," I said. "But you read him misunderstandingly when you conclude that the struggle for existence sanctions your wanton destruction of life."

He shrugged his shoulders. "You know you only mean that in relation to human life, for of the flesh and the fowl and the fish you destroy as much as I or any other man. And human life is in no wise different, though you feel it is and think that you reason why it is. Why should I be parsimonious with this life which is cheap and without value? There are more sailors than there are ships on the sea for them, more workers than there are factories or machines for them. Why, you who live on the land know that you house your poor people in the slums of cities and loose famine and pestilence upon them, and that there still remain more poor people, dying for want of a crust of bread and a bit of meat (which is life destroyed), than you know what to do with. Have you ever seen the London dockers fighting like wild beasts for a chance to work?"

He started for the companion stairs, but turned his head for a final word. "Do you know the only value life has is what life puts upon itself? And it is of course overestimated, since it is of necessity prejudiced in its own favor. Take that man I had aloft. He held on as if he were a precious thing, a treasure beyond diamonds or rubies. To you? No. To me? Not at all. To himself? Yes. But I do not accept his estimate. He sadly overrates himself. There is plenty more life demanding to be born. Had he fallen and dripped his brains upon the deck like honey from the comb, there would have been no loss to the world. He was worth nothing to the world. The supply is too large. To himself only was he of value, and to show how fictitious even this value was, being dead he is unconscious that he has lost himself. He alone rated himself beyond diamonds and rubies. Diamonds and rubies are gone, spread out on the deck to be washed away by a bucket of sea-water, and he does not even know that the diamonds and rubies are gone. He does not lose anything, for with the loss of himself he loses the knowledge of loss. Don't you see? And what have you to say?"

"That you are at least consistent," was all I could say, and I went on washing the dishes. * * *

1904

A CURIOUS FRAGMENT *

Listen, my brothers, and I will tell you a tale of an arm. It was the arm of Tom Dixon, and Tom Dixon was

* Reprinted by permission of Mrs. Jack London and Mrs. Elizabeth London Shephard.

a weaver of the first class in a factory of that hell-hound and master, Roger Vanderwater. This factory was called "Hell's Bottom" . . . by the slaves who toiled in it, and I guess they ought to know; and it was situated in Kingsbury, at the other end of the town from Vanderwater's summer palace. You do not know where Kingsbury is? There are many things, my brothers, that you do not know, and it is sad. It is because you do not know that you are slaves. When I have told you this tale, I should like to form a class among you for the learning of written and printed speech. Our masters read and write and possess many books, and it is because of that that they are our masters, and live in palaces, and do not work. When the toilers learn to read and write,—all of them,—they will grow strong; then they will use their strength to break their bonds, and there will be no more masters and no more slaves.

Kingsbury, my brothers, is in the old State of Alabama. For three hundred years the Vanderwaters have owned Kingsbury and its slave pens and factories, and slave pens and factories in many other places and States. You have heard of the Vanderwaters, —who has not?—but let me tell you things you do not know about them. The first Vanderwater was a slave, even as you and I. Have you got that? He was a slave, and that was over three hundred years ago. His father was a machinist in the slave pen of Alexander Burrell, and his mother was a washerwoman in the same slave pen. There is no doubt about this. I am telling you truth. It is history. It is printed, every word of it, in the history books of our masters, which you cannot read because your masters will not permit you to learn to read. You can understand why they will not permit you to learn to read, when there are such things in the books. They know, and they are very wise. If you did read such things, you might be wanting in respect to your masters, which would be a dangerous thing . . . to your masters. But I know, for I can read, and I am telling you what I have read with my own eyes in the history books of our masters.

The first Vanderwater's name was not Vanderwater; it was Vange—Bill Vange, the son of Yergis Vange, the machinist, and Laura Carnly, the washerwoman. Young Bill Vange was strong. He might have remained with the slaves and led them to freedom; instead, however, he served the masters and was well rewarded. He began his service, when yet a small child, as a spy in his home slave pen. He is known to have informed on his own father for seditious utterance. This is fact. I have read it with my own eyes in the records. He was too good a slave for the slave pen. Alexander Burrell took him out, while yet a child, and he was taught to read and write. He was taught many things, and he was entered in the secret service of the government. Of course, he no longer wore the slave dress, except for disguise at such times when he sought to penetrate the secrets and plots of the slaves. It was he, when but eighteen years of age, who brought that great hero and comrade, Ralph Jacobus, to trial and execution in the electric chair. Of course, you have all heard the sacred name of Ralph Jacobus, but it is news to you that he was brought to his death by the first Vanderwater, whose name was Vange. I know. I have read it in the books. There are many interesting things like that in the books.

And after Ralph Jacobus died his shameful death, Bill Vange's name began the many changes it was to undergo. He was known as "Sly Vange" far and wide. He rose high in the secret service, and he was rewarded in grand ways, but still he was not a member of the master class. The men were willing that he should become so; it was the women of the master class who refused to have Sly Vange one of them. Sly Vange gave good service to the masters. He had been a slave himself, and he knew the ways of the slaves. There was no fooling him. In those days the slaves were braver than now, and they were always trying for their freedom. And Sly Vange was everywhere, in all their schemes and plans, bringing their schemes and plans to naught and their leaders to the electric chair. It was in 2255 that his name was next changed for him. It was in that year that the Great Mutiny took place. In that region west of the Rocky Mountains, seventeen millions of slaves strove bravely to overthrow their masters. Who knows, if Sly Vange had not lived, but that they would have succeeded? But Sly Vange was very much alive. The masters gave him supreme command of the situation. In eight months of fighting, one million and three hundred and fifty thousand slaves were killed. Vange, Bill Vange, Sly Vange, killed them, and he broke the Great Mutiny. And he was greatly rewarded, and so red were his hands with the blood of the slaves that thereafter he was called "Bloody Vange." You see, my brothers, what interesting things are to be found in the books when one can read them. And, take my word for it, there are many other things, even more interesting, in the books. And if you will but study with me, in a year's time you can read those books for yourselves—ay, in six months some of you will be able to read those books for yourselves.

Bloody Vange lived to a ripe old age, and always, to the last, was he received in the councils of the masters; but never was he made a master himself. He had first opened his eyes, you see, in a slave pen. But oh, he was well rewarded! He had a dozen palaces in which to live. He, who was no master, owned thousands of slaves. He had a great pleasure yacht upon the sea that was a floating palace, and he owned a whole island in the sea where toiled ten thousand slaves on his coffee plantations. But in his old age he was lonely, for he lived apart, hated by his brothers, the slaves, and looked down upon by those he had served and who refused to be his brothers. The masters looked down upon him because he had been born a slave. Enormously wealthy he died; but he died horribly, tormented by his conscience, regretting all he had done and the red stain on his name.

But with his children it was different. They had not been born in the slave pen, and by the special ruling of the Chief Oligarch of that time, John Morrison, they were elevated to the master class. And it was then that the name of Vange disappears from the page of history. It becomes Vanderwater, and Jason Vange, the son of Bloody Vange, becomes Jason Vanderwater, the founder of the Vanderwater line. But that was three hundred years ago, and the Vanderwaters of to-day forget their beginnings and imagine that somehow the clay of their bodies is different stuff from the clay in your body and mine and in the bodies of all slaves. And I ask you, Why should a slave become the master of another slave? And why should the son of a slave become the master of many slaves? I leave these questions for you to answer for yourselves, but do not forget that in the beginning the Vanderwaters were slaves.

And now, my brothers, I come back to the beginning of my tale to tell you of Tom Dixon's arm. Roger Vanderwater's factory in Kingsbury was rightly named "Hell's Bottom," but the men who toiled in it were men, as you shall see. Women toiled there, too, and children, little children. All that toiled there had the regular slave rights under the law, but only under the law, for they were deprived of many of their rights by the two overseers of Hell's Bottom, Joseph Clancy and Adolph Munster.

It is a long story, but I shall not tell all of it to you. I shall tell only about the arm. It happened that, according to the law, a portion of the starvation wage of the slaves was held back each month and put into a fund. This fund was for the purpose of helping such unfortunate fellow-workmen as happened to be injured by accidents or to be overtaken by sickness. As you know with yourselves, these funds are controlled by the overseers. It is the law, and so it was that the fund at Hell's Bottom was controlled by the two overseers of accursed memory.

Now, Clancy and Munster took this fund for their own use. When accidents happened to the workmen, their fellows, as was the custom, made grants from the fund; but the overseers refused to pay over the grants. What could the slaves do? They had their rights under the law, but they had no access to the law. Those that complained to the overseers were punished. You know yourselves what form such punishment takes—the fines for faulty work that is not faulty; the overcharging of accounts in the Company's store; the vile treatment of one's women and children; and the allotment to bad machines whereon, work as one will, he starves.

Once, the slaves of Hell's Bottom protested to Vanderwater. It was the time of the year when he spent several months in Kingsbury. One of the slaves could write; it chanced that his mother could write, and she had secretly taught him as her mother had secretly taught her. So this slave wrote a round robin, wherein was contained their grievances, and all the slaves signed by mark. And, with proper stamps upon the envelope, the round robin was mailed to Roger Vanderwater. And Roger Vanderwater did nothing, save to turn the round robin over to the two overseers. Clancy and Munster were angered. They turned the guards loose at night on the slave pen. The guards were armed with pick handles. It is said that next day only half of the slaves were able to work in Hell's Bottom. They were well beaten. The slave who could write was so badly beaten that he lived only three months. But before he died, he wrote once more, to what purpose you shall hear.

Four or five weeks afterward, Tom Dixon, a slave, had his arm torn off by a belt in Hell's Bottom. His fellow-workmen, as usual, made a grant to him from the fund, and Clancy and Munster, as usual, refused to pay it over from the fund. The slave who could write, and who even then was dying, wrote anew a recital of their grievances. And this document was thrust into the hand of the arm that had been torn from Tom Dixon's body.

Now it chanced that Roger Vanderwater was lying ill in his palace at the other end of Kingsbury—not the dire illness that strikes down you and me, brothers; just a bit of biliousness, mayhap, or no more than a bad headache because he had eaten too heartily or drunk too deeply. But it was enough for him, being tender and soft from careful rearing. Such men, packed in cotton wool all their lives, are exceeding tender and soft. Believe me, brothers, Roger Vanderwater felt as badly with his aching head, or *thought* he felt as badly, as Tom Dixon really felt with his arm torn out by the roots.

It happened that Roger Vanderwater was fond of scientific farming, and that on his farm, three miles outside of Kingsbury, he had managed to grow a new kind of strawberry. He was very proud of that new strawberry of his, and he would have been out to see and pick the first ripe ones, had it not been for his illness. Because of his illness he had ordered the old farm slave to bring in personally the first box of the berries. All this was learned from the gossip of a palace scullion, who slept each night in the slave pen. The overseer of the plantation should have brought in the berries, but he was on his back with a broken leg from trying to break a colt. The scullion brought the word in the night, and it was known that next day the berries would come in. And the men in the slave pen of Hell's Bottom, being men and not cowards, held a council.

The slave who could write, and who was sick and dying from the pick-handle beating, said he would carry Tom Dixon's arm; also, he said he must die anyway, and that it mattered nothing if he died a little sooner. So five slaves stole from the slave pen that night after the guards had made their last rounds. One of the slaves was the man who could write. They lay in the brush by the roadside until late in the morning, when the old farm slave came driving to town with the precious fruit for the master. What of the farm slave being old and rheumatic, and of the slave who could write being stiff and injured from his beating, they moved their bodies about when they walked, very much in the same fashion. The slave who could write put on the other's clothes, pulled the broad-brimmed hat over his eyes, climbed upon the seat of the wagon, and drove on to town. The old farm slave was kept tied all day in the bushes until evening, when the others loosed him and went back to the slave pen to take their punishment for having broken bounds.

In the meantime, Roger Vanderwater lay waiting for the berries in his wonderful bedroom—such wonders and such comforts were there that they would have blinded the eyes of you and me who have never seen such things. The slave who could write said afterward that it was like a glimpse of Paradise. And why not? The labor and the lives of ten thousands slaves had gone to the making of that bedchamber, while they themselves slept in vile lairs like wild beasts. The slave who could write brought in the berries on a silver tray or platter—you see, Roger Vanderwater wanted to speak with him in person about the berries.

The slave who could write tottered his dying body across the wonderful room and knelt by the couch of Vanderwater, holding out before him the tray. Large, green leaves covered the top of the tray, and these the body-servant alongside whisked away so that Vanderwater could see. And Roger Vanderwater, propped upon his elbow, saw. He saw the fresh, wonderful fruit lying there like precious jewels, and in the midst of it the arm of Tom Dixon as it had been torn from his body, well-washed, of course, my brothers, and very white against the blood-red fruit. And also he saw, clutched in the stiff, dead fingers, the petition of his slaves who toiled in Hell's Bottom.

"Take and read," said the slave who could write. And even as the master took the petition, the body-servant, who till then had been motionless with surprise, struck with his fist the kneeling slave upon the mouth. The slave was dying anyway, and was very weak, and did not mind. He made no sound, and, having fallen over on his side, he lay there quietly, bleeding from the blow on the mouth. The physician, who had run for the palace guards, came back with them, and the slave was dragged upright upon his feet. But as they dragged him up, his hand clutched Tom Dixon's arm from where it had fallen on the floor.

"He shall be flung alive to the hounds!" the body-servant was crying in great wrath. "He shall be flung alive to the hounds!"

But Roger Vanderwater, forgetting his headache, still leaning on his elbow, commanded silence, and went on reading the petition. And while he read, there was silence, all standing upright, the wrathful body-servant, the physician, the palace guards, and in their midst the slave, bleeding at the mouth and still holding Tom Dixon's arm. And when Roger Vanderwater had done, he turned upon the slave, saying:—

"If in this paper there be one lie, you shall be sorry that you were ever born."

And the slave said, "I have been sorry all my life that I was born."

Roger Vanderwater looked at him closely, and the slave said:—

"You have done your worst to me. I am dying now. In a week I shall be dead, so it does not matter if you kill me now."

"What do you with that?" the master asked, pointing to the arm; and the slave made answer:—

"I take it back to the pen to give it burial. Tom Dixon was my friend. We worked beside each other at our looms."

There is little more to my tale, brothers. The slave and the arm were sent back in a cart to the pen. Nor were any of the slaves punished for what they had done. Instead, Roger Vanderwater made investigation and punished the two overseers, Joseph Clancy and Adolph Munster. Their freeholds were taken from them. They were branded, each upon the forehead, their right hands were cut off, and they were turned loose upon the highway to wander and beg until they died. And the fund was managed rightfully thereafter for a time—for a time, only, my brothers; for after Roger Vanderwater came his son, Albert, who was a cruel master and half mad.

Brothers, that slave who carried the arm into the presence of the master was my father. He was a brave man. And even as his mother secretly taught him to read, so did he teach me. Because he died shortly after from the pick-handle beating, Roger Vanderwater took me out of the slave pen and tried to make various better things out of me. I might have become an overseer in Hell's Bottom, but I chose to become a story-teller, wandering over the land and getting close to my brothers, the slaves, everywhere. And I tell you stories like this, secretly, knowing that you will not betray me; for if you did, you know as well as I that my tongue will be torn out and that I shall tell stories no more. And my message is, brothers, that there is a good time coming, when all will be well in the world and there will be neither masters nor slaves. But first you must prepare for that good time by learning to read. There is power in the printed word. And here am I to teach you to read, and as well there are others to see that you get the books when I am gone along upon my way— the history books wherein you will learn about your masters, and learn to become strong even as they.

[EDITOR'S NOTE.—*From "Historical Fragments and Sketches," first published in fifty volumes in 4427, and now, after two hundred years, because of its accuracy and value, edited and republished by the National Committee on Historical Research.*]

1911

UPTON SINCLAIR
(1878–   )

FROM   *THE JUNGLE* *

[PACKINGTOWN MISERY]

With one member trimming beef in a cannery, and another working in a sausage factory, the family had a first-hand knowledge of the great majority of Packingtown swindles. For it was the custom, as they found, whenever meat was so spoiled that it could not be used for anything else, either to can it or chop it up into sausage. With what had been told them by Jonas, who had worked in the pickle-rooms, they could now study the whole of the spoiled-meat industry on the inside, and read a new and grim meaning into that old Packingtown jest,—that they use everything of the pig except the squeal.

Jonas had told them how the meat that was taken out of the pickle would often be found sour, and how

* Reprinted by permission of Upton Sinclair. Copyright, 1906.

they would rub it up with soda to take away the smell, and sell it to be eaten on free-lunch counters; also of all the miracles of chemistry which they performed, giving to any sort of meat, fresh or salted, whole or chopped, any color and any flavor and any odor they chose. In the pickling of hams they had an ingenious apparatus, by which they saved time and increased the capacity of the plant—a machine consisting of a hollow needle attached to a pump; by plunging this needle into the meat and working with his foot, a man could fill a ham with pickle in a few seconds. And yet, in spite of this, there would be hams found spoiled, some of them with an odor so bad that a man could hardly bear to be in the room with them. To pump into these the packers had a second and much stronger pickle which destroyed the odor—a process known to the workers as "giving them thirty per cent." Also, after the hams had been smoked, there would be found some that had gone to the bad. Formerly these had been sold as "Number Three Grade," but later on some ingenious person had hit upon a new device, and now they would extract the bone, about which the bad part generally lay, and insert in the hole a white-hot iron. After this invention there was no longer Number One, Two and Three Grade—there was only Number One Grade. The packers were always originating such schemes—they had what they called "boneless hams," which were all the odds and ends of pork stuffed into casings; and "California hams," which were the shoulders, with big knuckle-joints, and nearly all the meat cut out; and fancy "skinned hams," which were made of the oldest hogs, whose skins were so heavy and coarse that no one would buy them—that is, until

they had been cooked and chopped fine and labelled "head cheese"!

It was only when the whole ham was spoiled that it came into the department of Elzbieta. Cut up by the two-thousand-revolutions-a-minute flyers, and mixed with half a ton of other meat, no odor that ever was in a ham could make any difference. There was never the least attention paid to what was cut up for sausage; there would come all the way back from Europe old sausage that had been rejected, and that was moldy and white—it would be dosed with borax and glycerine, and dumped into the hoppers, and made over again for home consumption. There would be meat that had tumbled out on the floor, in the dirt and sawdust, where the workers had trampled and spit uncounted billions of consumption germs. There would be meat stored in great piles in the rooms; and the water from leaky roofs would drip over it, and thousands of rats would race about on it. It was too dark in these storage places to see well, but a man could run his hand over these piles of meat and sweep off handfuls of the dried dung of rats. These rats were nuisances, and the packers would put poisoned bread out for them; they would die, and then rats, bread and meat would go into the hoppers together. This is no fairy story and no joke; the meat would be shovelled into carts, and the man who did the shovelling would not trouble to lift out a rat even when he saw one—there were things that went into the sausage in comparison with which a poisoned rat was a tidbit. There was no place for the men to wash their hands before they ate their dinner, and so they made a practice of washing them in the water that was ladled into the sausage. There were the butt-ends of smoked meat, and the scraps of corned beef, and all the odds and ends of the waste of the plants, that would be dumped into old barrels in the cellar and left there. Under the system of rigid economy which the packers enforced, there were some jobs that it only paid to do once in a long time, and among these was the cleaning out of the waste-barrels. Every spring they did it; and in the barrels would be dirt and rust and old nails and stale water—and cart load after cart load of it would be taken up and dumped into the hoppers with fresh meat, and sent out to the public's breakfast. Some of it they would make into "smoked" sausage—but as the smoking took time, and was therefore expensive, they would call upon their chemistry department, and preserve it with borax and color it with gelatine to make it brown. All of their sausage came out of the same bowl, but when they came to wrap it they would stamp some of it "special," and for this they would charge two cents more a pound.

Such were the new surroundings in which Elzbieta was placed, and such was the work she was compelled to do. It was stupefying, brutalizing work; it left her no time to think, no strength for anything. She was part of the machine she tended, and every faculty that was not needed for the machine was doomed to be crushed out of existence. There was only one mercy about the cruel grind—that it gave her the gift of insensibility. Little by little she sank into a torpor—she fell silent. She would meet Jurgis and Ona in the evening, and the three would walk home together, often without saying a word. Ona, too, was falling into the habit of silence—Ona, who once had gone about singing like a bird. She was sick and miserable, and often she would barely have strength enough to drag herself home. And there they would eat what they had to eat, and afterwards, because there was only their misery to talk of, they would crawl into bed and fall into a stupor and never stir until it was time to get up again, and dress by candle-light, and go back to the machines. They were so numbed that they did not even suffer much from hunger, now; only the children continued to fret when the food ran short.

Yet the soul of Ona was not dead—the souls of none of them were dead, but only sleeping; and now and then they would waken, and these were cruel times. The gates of memory would roll open—old joys would stretch out their arms to them, old hopes and dreams would call to them, and they would stir beneath the burden that lay upon them, and feel its forever immeasurable weight. They could not even cry out beneath it; but anguish would seize them, more dreadful than the agony of death. It was a thing scarcely to be spoken—a thing never spoken by all the world, that will not know its own defeat.

They were beaten; they had lost the game, they were swept aside. It was not less tragic because it was so sordid, because it had to do with wages and grocery bills and rents. They had dreamed of freedom; of a chance to look about them and learn something; to be decent and clean, to see their child grow up to be strong. And now it was all gone—it would never be! They had played the game and they had lost. Six years more of toil they had to face before they could expect the least respite, the cessation of payments upon the house; and how cruelly certain it was that they could never stand six years of such a life as they were living! They were lost, they were going down—and there was no deliverance for them, no hope; for all the help it gave them the vast city in which they lived might have been an ocean waste, a wilderness, a desert, a tomb. So often this mood would come to Ona, in the nighttime, when something wakened her; she would lie, afraid of the beating of her own heart, fronting the blood-red eyes of the old primeval terror of life. Once she cried aloud, and woke Jurgis, who was tired and cross. After that she learned to weep silently—their moods so seldom came together now! It was as if their hopes were buried in separate graves.

Jurgis, being a man, had troubles of his own. There was another spectre following him. He had never spoken of it, nor would he allow anyone else to speak of it—he had never acknowledged its existence to himself. Yet the battle with it took all the manhood that he had—and once or twice, alas, a little more. Jurgis had discovered drink.

He was working in the steaming pit of hell; day after day, week after week—until now there was not an organ of his body that did its work without pain, until the sound of ocean breakers echoed in his head day and night, and the buildings swayed and danced before him as he went down the street. And from all the unending horror of this there was a respite, a deliverance—he could drink! He could forget the pain, he could slip off the burden; he would see clearly again, he would be master of his brain, of his thoughts, of his will. His dead self would stir in him, and he would find himself laughing and cracking jokes with his companions— he would be a man again, and master of his life.

It was not an easy thing for Jurgis to take more than two or three drinks. With the first drink he could eat a meal, and he could persuade himself that that was economy; with the second he could eat another meal—but there would come a time when he could eat no more, and then to pay for a drink was an unthinkable extravagance, a defiance of the age-long instincts of his hunger-haunted class. One day, however, he took the plunge, and drank up all that he had in his pockets, and went home half "piped," as the men phrase it. He was happier than he had been in a year; and yet, because he knew that the happiness would not last, he was savage, too,— with those who would wreck it, and with the world, and with his life; and then again, beneath this, he was sick with the shame of himself. Afterward, when he saw the despair of his family, and reckoned up the money he had spent, the tears came into his eyes, and he began the long battle with the spectre.

It was a battle that had no end, and never could have one. But Jurgis did not realize that very clearly; he was not given much time for reflection. He simply knew that he was always fighting. Steeped in misery and despair as he was, merely to walk down the street was to be put upon the rack. There was surely a saloon on the corner—perhaps on all four corners, and some in the middle of the block as well; and each one stretched out a hand to him—each one had a personality of its own, allurements unlike any other. Going and coming—before sunrise and after dark—there was a warmth and a glow of light, and the steam of hot food, and perhaps music, or a friendly face, or a word of good cheer. Jurgis developed a fondness for having Ona on his arm whenever he went out on the street, and he would hold her tightly, and walk fast. It was pitiful to have Ona know of this—it drove him wild to think of it; the thing was not fair, for Ona had never tasted drink, and so could not understand. Sometimes in desperate hours, he would find himself wishing that she might learn what it was, so that he need not be ashamed in her presence. They might drink together, and escape from the horror—escape for a while, come what would.

So there came a time when nearly all the conscious life of Jurgis consisted of a struggle with the craving for liquor. He would have ugly moods, when he hated Ona and the whole family, because they stood in his way. He was a fool to have married; he had tied himself down, had made himself a slave. It was all because he was a married man that he was compelled to stay in the yards; if it had not been for that he might have gone off like Jonas, and to hell with the packers. There were few single men in the fertilizer-mill—and those few were working only for a chance to escape. Meantime, too, they had something to think about while they worked,—they had the memory of the last time they had been drunk, and the hope of the time when they would be drunk again. As for Jurgis, he was expected to bring home every penny; he could not even go with the men at noon-time—he was supposed to sit down and eat his dinner on a pile of fertilizer dust.

This was not always his mood, of course; he still loved his family. But just now was a time of trial. Poor little Antanas, for instance—who had never failed to win him with a smile —little Antanas was not smiling just now, being a mass of fiery red pimples. He had had all the diseases that babies are heir to, in quick succession, scarlet fever, mumps, and whooping-cough in the first year, and now he was down with the measles. There was no one to attend him but Kotrina;

there was no doctor to help him, because they were too poor, and children did not die of the measles—at least not often. Now and then Kotrina would find time to sob over his woes, but for the greater part of the time he had to be left alone, barricaded upon the bed. The floor was full of draughts, and if he caught cold he would die. At night he was tied down, lest he should kick the covers off him, while the family lay in their stupor of exhaustion. He would lie and scream for hours, almost in convulsions; and then, when he was worn out, he would lie whimpering and wailing in his torment. He was burning up with fever, and his eyes were running sores; in the daytime he was a thing uncanny and impish to behold, a plaster of pimples and sweat, a great purple lump of misery.

And yet all this was not really as cruel as it sounds, for, sick as he was, little Antanas was the least unfortunate member of that family. He was quite able to bear his sufferings—it was as if he had all these complaints to show what a prodigy of health he was. He was the child of his parents' youth and joy; he grew up like the conjurer's rose bush, and all the world was his oyster. In general, he toddled around the kitchen all day with a lean and hungry look—the portion of the family allowance that fell to him was not enough, and he was unrestrained in his demand for more. Antanas was but little over a year old, and already no one but his father could manage him.

It seemed as if he had taken all his mother's strength—had left nothing for those that might come after him. Ona was with child again now, and it was a dreadful thing to contemplate; even Jurgis, dumb and despairing as he was, could not but understand that yet other agonies were on the way, and shudder at the thought of them.

For Ona was visibly going to pieces. In the first place she was developing a cough, like the one that had killed old Dede Antanas. She had had a trace of it ever since that fatal morning when the greedy street-car corporation had turned her out into the rain; but now it was beginning to grow serious, and to wake her up at night. Even worse than that was the fearful nervousness from which she suffered; she would have frightful headaches and fits of aimless weeping; and sometimes she would come home at night shuddering and moaning, and would fling herself down upon the bed and burst into tears. Several times she was quite beside herself and hysterical; and then Jurgis would go half mad with fright. Elzbieta would explain to him that it could not be helped, that a woman was subject to such things when she was pregnant; but he was hardly to be persuaded, and would beg and plead to know what had happened. She had never been like this before, he would argue—it was monstrous and unthinkable. It was the life she had to live, the accursed work she had to do, that was killing her by inches. She was not fitted for it—no woman was fitted for it, no woman ought to be allowed to do such work; if the world could not keep them alive in any other way it ought to kill them at once and be done with it. They ought not to marry—if he, Jurgis, had known what a woman was like, he would have had his eyes torn out first. So he would carry on, becoming half hysterical himself, which was an unbearable thing to see in a big man; Ona would pull herself together and fling herself into his arms, begging him to stop, to be still, that she would be better, it would be all right. So

she would lie and sob out her grief upon his shoulder, while he gazed at her, as helpless as a wounded animal, the target of unseen enemies. *1906*

FROM *DRAGON'S TEETH* *

DEUTSCHLAND ERWACHE!

VI

Lanny wanted to hear all sides; he wanted to know what the Nazis were doing and saying, if only so as to send Rick an account of it. Among his acquaintances in Berlin was Heinrich Jung, blue-eyed "Aryan" enthusiast from Upper Silesia. Heinrich had spent three years training himself to succeed his father as head forester of Graf Stubendorf's domain; but now all that had been set aside, and Heinrich was an official of the National Socialist German Workingmen's Party, high up in what they called the Hitler Youth. For seven or eight years he had been mailing propaganda to Lanny Budd in Bienvenu, having never given up hope that a pure-blooded "Aryan" would feel the pull of his racial ties.

Lanny called him on the telephone, and Heinrich was delighted and begged him to come to party headquarters. The visitor didn't consider it necessary to mention the fact that he was staying in the home of one of the most notorious of Jewish *Schieber*. It wouldn't really have mattered, for such eccentricities in an American didn't mean what they would have meant in a German. A German traveler had described America as "the land of unlimited possibilities," and

---

* From *Dragon's Teeth*, by Upton Sinclair. Copyright 1942 by Upton Sinclair. By permission of The Viking Press, Inc., New York.

rich, successful persons from that fabulous region walked the common earth of Europe as demigods. Even the Führer himself was in awe of them, having heard the report that they had not run away from the mighty German army. A bright feather in the cap of a young party official if he should bring in such a convert to the new religion of blood and soil.

The blue-eyed and fair-haired young Prussian had matured greatly in the three or four years since Lanny had seen him. He had his private office in the great Nazi building, and was surrounded by the appurtenances of power: files and charts, a telephone on his desk, and a buzzer to summon his subordinates. He wore the uniform of the Sturmabteilung, those party soldiers whose marching and drumbeating were by now among the familiar sights in German cities: brown shirt and trousers with black stripes, shiny black boots, red armband with the swastika in black. Handsome, smart, snappy—and keep out of their way, for they mean business. *Die Strasse frei den braunen Bataillonen!*

Heinrich stopped only long enough to ask after Lanny's wife and baby, about whom he had heard from Kurt. Then he began pouring out the story of the miracles which had been achieved by the N.S.D.A.P.—the initials of the party's German name—since those old days when a student of forestry had revealed it as a tiny shoot just pushing its head through the wintry soil. "Tall oaks from little acorns grow!" said Heinrich; having written it as an English copybook exercise in school.

A ladder was provided and Lanny was taken up to the topmost branches of that ever-spreading oak tree. The Hitler Youth constituted the branches where the abundant new growth was burgeoning; for this part of the tree

all the rest existed. The future Germany must be taught to march and to fight, to sing songs of glory, hymns to the new Fatherland it was going to build. It must be well fed and trained, sound of wind and limb; it must know the Nazi creed, and swear its oath of loyalty to what was called the *Führerprinzip,* the faith that the individual exists for the state, and that the state is guided by one inspired leader. No matter from what sort of homes the young people came, the Nazis would make them all the same: perfect party members, obedient because it is a joy to obey, because the future belongs to those who are strong, confident, and united.

Lanny had seen this principle working in the soul of one sturdy young "Aryan," and now he discovered him as a machine engaged in turning out thousands of other specimens exactly like himself. A machine for making machines! On the wall was a map showing where the branch offices of this youth-machine were situated—and they weren't only in Germany, but in every city on earth where Germans lived. There were charts and diagrams, for in this land things are done scientifically, including Hitler propaganda. *"Deutschland Erwache!"* said a placard on Heinrich's wall. The Führer was a great deviser of slogans; he would retire to a secret place and there ponder and weigh many hundreds which came to his mind, and when he chose one, it would appear on posters and be shouted at meetings in every hamlet of the land. "Germany, Awake!"

VII

Lanny was touched by the pride with which the young official revealed and explained the complex organization he had helped to build; its various departments and subdivisions, each having an official endowed with one of those elaborate titles which Germans so dearly love. The head of the great machine was, of course, the one and only Adolf, *Partei- und oberster S.A. Führer, Vorsitzender der N.S.D.A.P.* Under him were adjutants and Secretariat and Chief of Staff, the *Reichsjugendführer* (who was Heinrich's superior) and his Staff Director, the Subdirectors of half a dozen different staffs, the Business Manager, the Secretary, the Presidium, the Reich Directorate.

Also there was a Political Organization, or rather two, P.O. 1 and P.O. 2 —they had two of everything, except of the Führer. It made you dizzy merely to hear about all these obligations and responsibilities: the Foreign Division, Economic Policy Division, Race and Culture Division, Internal Political Division, Legal Division, Engineering-Technical Division, Labor Service Division; the Reich Propaganda Leaders Number 1 and Number 2, the Leaders of the Reich Inspection 1 and 2; the Investigation and Adjustment Committee—what a whopper of a title had been assigned to them: *Untersuchungs- und Schlichtungsausschuss,* or USCHLA! But don't smile over it, for Heinrich Jung explains that the party is preparing to take over the destinies of the Fatherland, to say nothing of many decadent nations of Europe and elsewhere, and all this machinery and even more will be needed; the Gymnastics and Sports Committee, the Bureau Leader for the Press, the *Zentralparteiverlag,* the *Personalamt,* and much more.

Heinrich was responsible for the affairs of one department of the Hitler Youth, with twenty-one geographic sections throughout Germany. They maintained a school for future Nazi leaders, and published three monthlies and a semi-monthly. There were di-

visions dealing with press, culture, propaganda, defense-sport—they were learning not merely to fight the Young Communists, but to make a sport of it! Also there were the junior organizations, the *Deutsches Jungvolk* and the *Bund Deutscher Mädel,* and a *Studentenbund,* and a Women's League, and so on apparently without end. The polite Lanny Budd was glad in his heart that it was election time and that so many subordinates were waiting to receive orders from this overzealous expounder.

VIII

One thing a young party official would not fail to do for an old friend: to take him to the mighty *Versammlung* in the Sportpalast which was to climax the Nazi campaign. Here the Führer himself would make his final appeal to the German voters; and it would be like nothing ever seen in the world before. For several months this marvelous man had been rushing all over the land making speeches, many hundreds of them; traveling by airplane, or in his fast Mercédès car, wearing the tan raincoat in which Lanny had seen him in the old days; possibly not the same coat, but the same simple, devoted, inspired, and inspiring leader whose mission it was to revive Germany and then the whole world. *Heute gehört uns Deutschland und morgen die ganze Welt!*

Heinrich explained that seats would be difficult to obtain; there would be a line of people waiting at the doors of the Sportpalast from early morning to be sure of getting good places. There would of course be reserved seats for important persons, and Lanny accepted four tickets. He knew that none of the Robins would attend a Nazi meeting—it really wouldn't be safe, for someone might spit in their faces, or beat them if they failed to give the Nazi salute and shout *"Heil Hitler!"* Bess loathed the movement and its creed, and her curiosity had been fully satisfied by watching the Stormtroopers on the march and by occasional glances at their newspapers.

Well in advance of eight o'clock Lanny and his wife and Beauty and her husband were in their seats. Bands playing, literature-sellers busy, and armed squads keeping watch all over the enormous arena—Communists keep out! A display of banners and streamers with all the familiar slogans: "Down with Versailles!" "Freedom and Bread!" "Germany, Awake!" "An End to Reparations!" "Common Wealth before Private Wealth!" "Break the Bonds of Interest Slavery!" These last were the "radical" slogans, carried down from the old days; Robbie had said they were practically the same as those of the "money cranks" in the United States, the old-time Populists and Greenbackers; they appealed to the debtor classes, the small farmers, the little business men who felt themselves being squeezed by the big trusts. This Hitler movement was a revolt of the lower middle classes, whose savings had been wiped out by the inflation and who saw themselves being reduced to the status of proletarians.

To Irma they seemed much nicer-looking people than those she had seen at the other two meetings. The black-and-silver uniforms of the Schutzstaffel, who acted as ushers and guards, were new and quite elegant; these young men showed alertness and efficiency. Twenty or thirty thousand people singing with fervor were impressive, and Irma didn't know that the songs were full of hatred for Frenchmen and Poles. She knew that the Nazis hated the Jews, and this she deplored. She had learned to be very fond of one Jewish family, but

she feared there must be something wrong with the others—so many people said it. In any case, the Germans had to decide about their own country.

Singing and speech-making went on for an hour or so; then came a roll of drums and a blast of trumpets in the main entrance, and all the men and women in the huge place leaped to their feet. *Der Führer kommt!* A regiment of Stormtroopers in solemn march, carrying flags with spearpoints or bayonets at the tips of the poles. The bands playing the magnificent open chords to which the gods march across the rainbow bridge into Valhalla at the close of *Das Rheingold*. Then the party leaders, military and magnificent, marching in the form of a hollow square, protecting their one and only leader. Someone with a sense of drama has planned all this; someone who has learned from Wagner how to combine music, scenery, and action so as to symbolize the fundamental aspirations of the human soul, to make real to the common man his own inmost longing.

Who was that genius? Everyone in the hall, with the possible exception of a few Lanny Budds, believed that it was the little man who marched in the center of that guard of honor; the simple man with the old tan raincoat, the one whom honors could not spoil, the one consecrated to the service of the Fatherland; one born of the common people, son of an obscure Austrian customs official; a corporal of the World War wounded and gassed; an obscure workingman, a dreamer of a mighty dream, of Germany freed and restored to her place among the nations, or perhaps above them.

He wore no hat, and his dark hair, long and brushed to one side, fell now and then across his pale forehead and had to be swept away. No fashion here, a plain man, just like you and me; one whose hand you can shake, who smiles in a friendly way at those who greet him. A storm of cheering arises, the *Heils* become like rain-drops falling in a cloudburst—so many that you cannot hear the individual ones, the sounds become a union like the National Socialist German Work-ingmen's Party.

Lanny has never attended an old-fashioned American revival meeting, but his friend Jerry Pendleton from Kansas has told him about one, and here is another. Has someone from the American South or Middle West come over and taught these arts of stirring the souls of primitive people, of letting them take part in what is being done to them? Or is it something that rises out of the primitive soul in every part of the world? The speakers on this platform ask questions, and twenty thousand throats shout the answers. Only they do not shout: "Glory Hallelujah!" and "Bless the Lord!"; theirs are secular cries: "Down with Versailles!" *"Juda verrecke!"* and *"Deutschland erwache!"*

IX

Seven years since Lanny watched Charlie Chaplin come out upon the stage of a great beerhall in Munich; and here he is again, the same foolish little dark mustache, the same shy manner, humble, deprecating. But now he is stouter, he gets better food. Now, also, there are a score of spot-lights centered upon him, telling everybody that appearances are deceptive, and that this is a special One. Banners and symbols, slogans and rituals, hopes and resolves, all have come out of his soul; he is the Messiah, the One appointed and sent to save the Fatherland in its hour of greatest trial.

He begins to speak, and Lanny knows every tone. Quiet at first, and the vast hall as still as the universe must have been before God created it. But soon the man of visions begins to warm up to his theme. The slogans which he has taught to all Germany work upon himself as upon others; they dominate his entire being; they are sparks from a white-hot flame which burns day and night within him. The flame of "Adi's" hatred of his miserable and thwarted life! Hatred of his father, the dumb petty bureaucrat who wanted to make his son like himself and wouldn't let him become an artist; hatred of the critics and dealers who wouldn't recognize his pitiful attempts at painting; hatred of the bums and wastrels in the flop-houses who wouldn't listen to his inspired ravings; hatred of the Russians and the French and the British and the Americans who wouldn't let an obscure corporal win his war; hatred of Marxists who betrayed Germany by a stab in the back; hatred of the Jews who made money out of her misery; hatred of all who now stood in the way of her destiny, who opposed Adi's party which was to save her from humiliation. All these hatreds had flamed forth from one thwarted soul and had set fire to the tinder-box which Germany had become—and here it was, blazing, blazing!

The Führer possessed no gleam of humor, no trace of charm. He was an uneducated man, and spoke with an Austrian country accent, not always grammatically. His voice was hoarse from a thousand speeches, but he forced it without mercy. He raved and shrieked; he waved his arms, he shook his clenched fists in the face of Germany's enemies. Perspiration poured from his pasty and rather lumpy countenance; his heavy hair fell down over his eyes and had to be flung back.

Lanny knew every gesture, every word. Adi hadn't learned a thing, hadn't changed a thing in seven years; he had merely said the same things a million times. His two-part book which Lanny had read with mingled dismay and laughter had become the bible of a new religion. Millions of copies had been sold, and extracts from it and reiterations of it had been printed in who could guess how many pamphlets, leaflets, and newspapers? Certainly well up in the billions; for some of the Nazi newspapers had circulations of hundreds of thousands every day, and in the course of years that mounts up. Heinrich told Lanny that they had held nearly thirty-five thousand meetings in Germany during the present campaign and quantities of literature had been sold at every one of them. Lanny, listening and watching the frenzied throng, remembered some lines from his poetry anthology, lines which had sounded melodious and exciting, but which he hadn't understood when he had read them as a boy:

One man with a dream, at pleasure,
    Shall go forth and conquer a crown;
And three with a new song's measure
    Can trample an empire down.

1942

CHARLES ERSKINE SCOTT WOOD
(1852–1944)

HEAVENLY DISCOURSE *

XIX

"T.R." ENTERS HEAVEN

[GOD *is on his throne.* VOLTAIRE, RABELAIS, INGERSOLL, *and others*

* Reprinted by permission of The Vanguard Press and Charles Erskine Scott Wood. Copyright 1927.

are near the throne. ST. PETER, GABRIEL, RAPHAEL, THE DEVIL, *and a host rush in, panic-stricken.*]

ST. PETER: Save yourself, Lord. Save yourself. Something has got in.

GABRIEL: It broke down the gate.

RAPHAEL: It is coming. Save yourself.

GOD: Is it the Devil?

SATAN: No, no. I am here. Hide me. Omnipotence, I ask protection.

GOD: Who is it?

INGERSOLL: What a roaring.

VOLTAIRE [*To* RABELAIS]: My friend, I guess heaven has come to an end.

RABELAIS: That does not trouble me.

SATAN: O, that roar. Hide me. I never thought he'd get in here. Hide me. I know him.

GOD: Who is this thing of terror?

SATAN: Yes. That's him. T.R. T.R. Don't you know him? [SATAN's *teeth chatter.*]

GOD: Never heard of him.

SATAN: Never heard of Teddy? O, God!

GOD: No, I never heard of him. Stop shivering.

SATAN: Oh! Oh! Surely you know the Colonel?

GOD: Never heard of him, I tell you. But what a frightful uproar. Is it an army?

ST. PETER: No. Just him. Just him. But, O, God—
[*Enter* T.R. *He holds out his hand to* GOD.]

T.R.: Dee-lighted. Dee-lighted, I am sure. I have heard of you.

GOD: Indeed.

T.R.: Possibly we have met somewhere?

GOD: No, I think not.

T.R.: Were you ever in Washington, D.C.?

GOD: Never.

T.R.: Well, there is certainly something familiar about you. Don't rise.

GOD: Take my seat.

T.R.: Thanks awfully. [*Sits down.*] Now, where is Michael?

GOD: He is away in a new star called the Orb of Brotherly Love.

T.R.: Why, that's our earth.

GOD: No. This is different.

T.R.: Well, who is commander-in-chief here? It drives me crazy to sit quiet this way. Who is commander-in-chief?

GOD: We have no commander-in-chief.

T.R.: Who leads your armies?

GOD: We have no armies.

T.R.: What? No armies? I don't believe it. How do you get on? How will you defend yourself? Well, who is the head of your organization?

GOD: We have no organization.

T.R.: No organization? No armies? Well, it's a mighty good thing I came. How on earth—I mean, how in heaven—are you going to get into this war without an army, and how are you going to levy taxes and conscript the angels without an organization?

GOD: But we are not going into any war.

T.R.: Not going into the war! Do you seriously tell me that you are not going into this great war to end war and for freedom and democracy and world peace? Have I died in vain only to come to a heaven of cowards, dastards, poltroons, contemptible, white-livered, white-feathered, chicken-hearted slackers? Have you no patriotism, no sense of national honor, dignity or democracy? Have you no common brotherhood, no Christian unity?

[GABRIEL *and the* BATTERED SOUL OF THE PACIFIST *enter. The* BATTERED SOUL *has been put together, but wobbles in spots.*]

Listen to me. You certainly are going into this war. I'll raise a division myself or I'll raise hell and I'll show you what the fighting spirit is. We are going into this war. Do you understand?

VOLTAIRE: *Voilà les dents.*

RABELAIS: *Sang de Dieu.*

T.R. [*To* GABRIEL]: What is your name?

GABRIEL: My name is Gabriel.

T.R.: O, yes, Gabriel; trumpeter. I remember. Dee-lighted, I am sure. Go out at once and organize a publicity bureau. Make a proclamation that a T.R. Club must be started in every precinct. Recruiting offices must be opened all over heaven. Proclaim and also post notices that Colonel Roosevelt will in person lead an army of angels against the Huns in the great cause of Christianity and democracy, and expects every angel with a drop of red blood in his veins to volunteer, and if any dirty, sneaking, white-feathered slacker refuses to do his bit —[*the* BATTERED SOUL *falls into a fit*]. Well, well. What's the matter here?

GABRIEL: This poor Battered Soul has just fallen into a fit.

GOD: Revive him.

[BATTERED SOUL *revives and* GABRIEL *lifts him up.*]

What is the matter?

BATTERED SOUL: O, dear God, every time I hear those words I fall in a fit.

GOD: What words?

BATTERED SOUL: "Do his bit."

GOD: But you can't afford to fall in a fit for all the silly words you hear.

T.R.: Silly! Silly! Those modest, beautiful, patriotic, eloquent, noble words silly? I tell you that every man must either do his country, his bit, or somebody. Gabriel, have all the white-winged angels dyed red, white and blue—no, red and blue. I won't have a white-feathered one in my whole army. Make 'em red. No, not red—that's Bolshevik. Make 'em blue

—I don't like it, but it can't be helped. Make 'em blue.

GABRIEL: My commands come from God.

T.R.: Sure. Don't you hear me? I'm going to take over to Germany—yes, to the whole world, to the whole universe, my honor, my patriotism, my loyalty, my policies, my democracy, my Christianity, myself.

VOLTAIRE: *Ciel! les dents.*

RABELAIS: *La voix.*

VOLTAIRE: Might I humbly suggest it has been brought to us here that the Germans claim a world *Kultur* and a democracy also? Indeed, as I look down upon them, it seems to me if they would only unhorse their spurred riders, they have the foundation for a better society than yours: no slums; no poverty, no hopeless old age.

T.R.: I'll unhorse their spurred riders for them.

VOLTAIRE: Perhaps. But don't you think every people should unhorse its own riders? A revolution from the outside? No, impossible. A people must make its own revolutions.

T.R.: Sir, I tell you I shall annihilate them. What the world needs is the democracy of America, of New York, of Ludlow, of Paterson, of Lawrence, of Bayonne, of Passaic, of the Solid South, united with the splendid democracy of England, of Ireland, of India, of Africa, of Egypt. I shall annihilate this German militarism with a more thorough militarism of my own.

RABELAIS: *Pardon. Pardon, Monsieur.* Spare something. In the name of the gullet, if not of Christianity, spare the delicious Strasbourg pâté; the leberwurst; the Westphalia hams. Ah, those excellent Westphalia thirst-provokers. Spare the Bismarck herring; kielerspratten, sardellen, sausages. Heaven, the sausages, with rye bread—the bread of the people, and beer—the drink of the people: pale amber Pilsner and dark, topaz Münchner. Slayers of throat-parching thirsts; one envies the giraffe his neck. Beer, the liquid bread of the ancient Egyptians; foaming nectar, smelling of the Bohemian hop-yards where the sun shines in September on festooned vines; the air aromatic with golden pollen blown from the pendant hops. Jewels on the neck of a tall, blonde, voluptuous Gretchen. Hops are medicinal, sir. A golden gift from golden-crowned Ceres. Medicinal. I am a physician and tell you so. I beg you spare beer. And do not speak of annihilating the golden sweat from those sunny slopes of the Rhine, the Moselle. O, the long-necked bottles of liquid sunshine, gift of the antique twisted vines, centuries rooted in good German soil. Johannesberger, Steinberger, Hochheimer, Liebfraunmilch —are we not poetical under our arbor? The milk of Venus. And our good Doctor Berncastler. The Steinwein, Riesling and Weisling. Not bottled drunkenness and combat, but bottled friendship, good comradeship, songs, handclasps, weddings, christenings, feastings, the sap of good old Mother Earth. The sacrament of love and brotherhood. Yes, sir, and of religion. The golden blood of the great Dionysus. O, those oaken tuns of the Rhine. I, a Frenchman, sir, would hasten peace and return to earth if I might lie under their aureate shower. Spare something of Germany, sir. And there is music and medicine, science and drama, and blonde Gretchens, sir. I, a Frenchman, plead that you leave us something of Germany.

T.R.: Who are you?

RABELAIS: *Pardon, Monsieur.* François Rabelais. Let me say with proud humility, one of the makers of France.

T.R.: O, I know you; an obscene old drunkard.

RABELAIS: Pardon. A humorist. Never drunk, except with my own fancies.

T.R.: A lecherous old scoundrel.

RABELAIS: *Pardon encore.* Never lecherous. All merely good humor. Scoundrel—Ah—*peut-être—chacum à son goût.*

T.R.: I say you are obscene.

RABELAIS: *Hélas,* there is nothing so obscene as war.

T.R.: You are a drunkard.

RABELAIS: *Ma foi.* Are you perhaps also a humorist? There is no drunkenness like to war; nothing so foolish—so useless. What has it ever settled? What has it ever brought that was worth the price? The supreme stupidity of man is war—the game whose pawns are the young men. When did ever a people make war? When did ever a people want war till they were first made drunken by the masters. War, the supreme stupidity; the drunkenness of all drunkenness!

T.R.: I, myself, am temperate in all things.

RABELAIS: In *all* things? In *all* things?

T.R.: Yes, sir; in all things and at all times.

GOD: How we deceive ourselves. [*To* GABRIEL, *who leads* T.R. *away.*] Gabriel, let him look at Alexander, Hannibal, Cæsar, Napoleon, the great soldiers who each and all made a failure of fighting.

[SATAN *comes out from his hiding behind* GOD *and* ST. PETER. JESUS *comes in.*]

SATAN: I breathe again.

GOD: Let us all meditate in the hush of this sudden quiet, invoking from the universe—peace. Peace, the great builder; the great healer; the plow that turns the furrows of civilization for the rain of love.

JESUS: Unless this comes the peoples shall surely perish.

1917

CARL SANDBURG
(1878–   )
CHICAGO *

Hog Butcher for the World,
Tool Maker, Stacker of Wheat,
Player with Railroads and the Nation's Freight Handler;
Stormy, husky, brawling,
City of the Big Shoulders:

They tell me you are wicked and I believe them, for I have seen your painted
    women under the gas lamps luring the farm boys.
And they tell me you are crooked and I answer: Yes, it is true I have seen the
    gunman kill and go free to kill again:
And they tell me you are brutal and my reply is: On the faces of women and
    children I have seen the marks of wanton hunger.
And having answered so I turn once more to those who sneer at this my city,
    and I give them back the sneer and say to them:
Come and show me another city with lifted head singing so proud to be alive
    and coarse and strong and cunning.

Flinging magnetic curses amid the toil of piling job on job, here is a tall bold
        slugger set vivid against the little soft cities;
Fierce as a dog with tongue lapping for action, cunning as a savage pitted against
        the wilderness,
                Bareheaded,
                Shoveling,
                Wrecking,
                Planning,
                Building, breaking, rebuilding,
Under the smoke, dust all over his mouth, laughing with white teeth,
Under the terrible burden of destiny laughing as a young man laughs,
Laughing even as an ignorant fighter laughs who has never lost a battle,
Bragging and laughing that under his wrist is the pulse, and under his ribs the
        heart of the people,
                      Laughing!
Laughing the stormy, husky, brawling laughter of Youth, half-naked, sweating,
        proud to be Hog Butcher, Tool Maker, Stacker of Wheat, Player
        with Railroads and Freight Handler to the Nation.

                                        1914

A FENCE *

Now the stone house on the lake front is finished and the workmen are begin-
        ning the fence.
The palings are made of iron bars with steel points that can stab the life out
        of any man who falls on them.
As a fence, it is a masterpiece, and will shut off the rabble and all vagabonds
        and hungry men and all wandering children looking for a place to
        play.
Passing through the bars and over the steel points will go nothing except Death
        and the Rain and To-morrow.

                                          1915

MAG †

I wish to God I never saw you, Mag.
I wish you never quit your job and came along with me.
I wish we never bought a license and a white dress
For you to get married in the day we ran off to a minister
And told him we would love each other and take care of each other
Always and always long as the sun and the rain lasts anywhere.
Yes, I'm wishing now you lived somewhere away from here
And I was a bum on the bumpers a thousand miles away dead broke.

I wish the kids had never come
And rent and coal and clothes to pay for
And a grocery man calling for cash,
Every day cash for beans and prunes.
I wish to God I never saw you, Mag.
I wish to God the kids had never come.

1916

TO A CONTEMPORARY BUNKSHOOTER *

You come along . . . tearing your shirt . . . yelling about Jesus.
    Where do you get that stuff?
    What do you know about Jesus?
Jesus had a way of talking soft and outside of a few bankers and higher-ups
    among the con men of Jerusalem everybody liked to have this Jesus
    around because he never made any fake passes and everything he
    said went and he helped the sick and gave the people hope.
You come along squirting words at us, shaking your fist and call us all dam
    fools so fierce the froth slobbers over your lips . . . always blabbing
    we're all going to hell straight off and you know all about it.

I've read Jesus' words. I know what he said. You don't throw any scare into me.
    I've got your number. I know how much you know about Jesus.
He never came near clean people or dirty people but they felt cleaner because
    he came along. It was your crowd of bankers and business men and
    lawyers hired the sluggers and murderers who put Jesus out of the
    running.
I say the same bunch backing you nailed the nails into the hands of this Jesus
    of Nazareth. He had lined up against him the same crooks and
    strong-arm men now lined up with you paying your way.

This Jesus was good to look at, smelled good, listened good. He threw out
    something fresh and beautiful from the skin of his body and touch
    of his hands wherever he passed along.
You slimy bunkshooter, you put a smut on every human blossom in reach
    of your rotten breath belching about hell-fire and hiccupping about
    this Man who lived a clean life in Galilee.
When are you going to quit making the carpenters build emergency hospitals
    for women and girls driven crazy with wrecked nerves from your
    gibberish about Jesus?—I put it to you again: Where do you get that
    stuff? What do you know about Jesus?

Go ahead and bust all the chairs you want to. Smash a whole wagon-load of
    furniture at every performance. Turn sixty somersaults and stand
    on your nutty head. If it wasn't for the way you scare the women and
    kids I'd feel sorry for you and pass the hat.
I like to watch a good four-flusher work, but not when he starts people puking
    and calling for the doctors.

I like a man that's got nerve and can pull off a great original performance, but you—you're only a bughouse pedlar of second-hand gospel—you're only shoving out a phoney imitation of the goods this Jesus wanted free as air and sunlight.

You tell people living in shanties Jesus is going to fix it up all right with them by giving them mansions in the skies after they're dead and the worms have eaten 'em.

You tell $6 a week department store girls all they need is Jesus; you take a steel trust wop, dead without having lived, grey and shrunken at forty years of age, and you tell him to look at Jesus on the cross and he'll be all right.

You tell poor people they don't need any more money on pay day and even if it's fierce to be out of a job, Jesus'll fix that up all right, all right— all they gotta do is take Jesus the way you say.

I'm telling you Jesus wouldn't stand for the stuff you're handing out. Jesus played it different. The bankers and lawyers of Jerusalem got their sluggers and murderers to go after Jesus just because Jesus wouldn't play their game. He didn't sit in with the big thieves.

I don't want a lot of gab from a bunkshooter in my religion.

I won't take my religion from any man who never works except with his mouth and never cherishes any memory except the face of the woman on the American silver dollar.

I ask you to come through and show me where you're pouring out the blood of your life.

I've been to this suburb of Jerusalem they call Golgotha, where they nailed Him, and I know if the story is straight it was real blood ran from His hands and the nail-holes, and it was real blood spurted in red drops where the spear of the Roman soldier rammed in between the ribs of this Jesus of Nazareth.

1914

MEMOIR OF A PROUD BOY *

He lived on the wings of storm.
The ashes are in Chihuahua.

Out of Ludlow and coal towns in Colorado
Sprang a vengeance of Slav miners, Italians, Scots, Cornishmen, Yanks.
Killings ran under the spoken commands of this boy
With eighty men and rifles on a hogback mountain.

They killed swearing to remember
The shot and charred wives and children
In the burnt camp of Ludlow,
And Louis Tikas, the laughing Greek,
Plugged with a bullet, clubbed with a gun butt.

* From *Cornhuskers* by Carl Sandburg. Copyright, 1918, by Henry Holt and Company, Inc. Copyright, 1945, by Carl Sandburg.

As a home war
It held the nation a week
And one or two million men stood together
And swore by the retribution of steel.

It was all accidental.
He lived flecking lint off coat lapels
Of men he talked with.
He kissed the miners' babies
And wrote a Denver paper
Of picket silhouettes on a mountain line.

He had no mother but Mother Jones
Crying from a jail window of Trinidad:
'All I want is room enough to stand
And shake my fist at the enemies of the human race.'

Named by a grand jury as a murderer
He went to Chihuahua, forgot his old Scotch name,
Smoked cheroots with Pancho Villa
And wrote letters of Villa as a rock of the people.
How can I tell how Don Magregor went?

Three riders emptied lead into him.
He lay on the main street of an inland town.
A boy sat near all day throwing stones
To keep pigs away.

The Villa men buried him in a pit
With twenty Carranzistas.

There is drama in that point . . .
. . . the boy and the pigs.
Griffith would make a movie of it to fetch sobs.
Victor Herbert would have the drums whirr
In a weave with a high fiddle-string's single clamour.

'And the muchacho sat there all day throwing stones
To keep the pigs away,' wrote Gibbons to the *Tribune*.

Somewhere in Chihuahua or Colorado
Is a leather bag of poems and short stories.

                                              1918

FOUR PRELUDES ON PLAYTHINGS OF THE WIND *

The past is a bucket of ashes

I

The woman named To-morrow
sits with a hairpin in her teeth
and takes her time
and does her hair the way she wants it
and fastens at last the last braid and coil
and puts the hairpin where it belongs
and turns and drawls: Well, what of it?
My grandmother, Yesterday, is gone.
What of it? Let the dead be dead.

II

The doors were cedar
and the panels strips of gold
and the girls were golden girls
and the panels read and the girls chanted:

We are the greatest city,
the greatest nation:
nothing like us ever was.

The doors are twisted on broken hinges.
Sheets of rain swish through on the wind
where the golden girls ran and the panels read:

We are the greatest city,
the greatest nation,
nothing like us ever was.

III

It has happened before.
Strong men put up a city and got
a nation together,
And paid singers to sing and women
to warble: We are the greatest city,
the greatest nation,
nothing like us ever was.

And while the singers sang
and the strong men listened
and paid the singers well
and felt good about it all,
there were rats and lizards who listened
. . . and the only listeners left now
. . . are . . . the rats . . . and the lizards.

* Reprinted by permission of Harcourt Brace & Co., from *Smoke and Steel* by Carl Sandburg, copyright 1920, by Harcourt, Brace & Company.

And there are black crows
crying, "Caw, caw,"
bringing mud and sticks
building a nest
over the words carved
on the doors where the panels were cedar
and the strips on the panels were gold
and the golden girls came singing:
We are the greatest city,
the greatest nation:
nothing like us ever was.

The only singers now are crows crying, "Caw, caw,"
And the sheets of rain whine in the wind and doorways.
And the only listeners now are . . . the rats . . . and the lizards.

IV

The feet of the rats
scribble on the door sills;
the hieroglyphs of the rat footprints
chatter the pedigrees of the rats
and babble of the blood
and gabble of the breed
of the grandfathers and the great-grandfathers
of the rats.

And the wind shifts
and the dust on a door sill shifts
and even the writing of the rat footprints
tells us nothing, nothing at all
about the greatest city, the greatest nation
where the strong men listened
and the women warbled: Nothing like us ever was.

1920

CHEAP BLUE *

Hill blue among the leaves in summer,
Hill blue among the branches in winter—
Light sea blue at the sand beaches in winter,
Deep sea blue in the deep deep waters—
Prairie blue, mountain blue—
Who can pick a pocketful of these blues,
a handkerchief of these blues,
And go walking, talking, walking as though
God gave them a lot of loose change
For spending money, to throw at the birds,
To flip into the tin cups of blind men?

1928

* Reprinted from *Good Morning, America*, copyright 1928, by Carl Sandburg, by permission of the publishers, Harcourt, Brace & Co., Inc.

THE PEOPLE, YES *

45

[THEY HAVE YARNS]

They have yarns
Of a skycraper so tall they had to put hinges
On the two top stories so to let the moon go by,
Of one corn crop in Missouri when the roots
Went so deep and drew off so much water
The Mississippi riverbed that year was dry,
Of pancakes so thin they only had one side,
Of "a fog so thick we shingled the barn and six feet out on the fog,"
Of Pecos Pete straddling a cyclone in Texas and riding it to the west coast
    where "it rained out under him,"
Of the man who drove a swarm of bees across the Rocky Mountains and the
    Desert "and didn't lose a bee,"
Of a mountain railroad curve where the engineer in his cab can touch the
    caboose and spit in the conductor's eye,
Of the boy who climbed a cornstalk growing so fast he would have starved to
    death if they hadn't shot biscuits up to him,
Of the old man's whiskers: "When the wind was with him his whiskers arrived
    a day before he did,"
Of the hen laying a square egg and cackling "Ouch!" and of hens laying eggs
    with the dates printed on them,
Of the ship captain's shadow: it froze to the deck one cold winter night,
Of mutineers on that same ship put to chipping rust with rubber hammers,
Of the sheep counter who was fast and accurate: "I just count their feet and
    divide by four,"
Of the man so tall he must climb a ladder to shave himself,
Of the runt so teeny-weeny it takes two men and a boy to see him,
Of mosquitoes: one can kill a dog, two of them a man,
Of a cyclone that sucked cookstoves out of the kitchen, up the chimney flue,
    and on to the next town,
Of the same cyclone picking up wagon-tracks in Nebraska and dropping them
    over in the Dakotas,
Of the hook-and-eye snake unlocking itself into forty pieces, each piece two
    inches long, then in nine seconds flat snapping itself together again,
Of the watch swallowed by the cow—when they butchered her a year later the
    watch was running and had the correct time,
Of horned snakes, hoop snakes that roll themselves where they want to go,
    and rattlesnakes carrying bells instead of rattles on their tails,
Of the herd of cattle in California getting lost in a giant redwood tree that had
    hollowed out,
Of the man who killed a snake by putting its tail in its mouth so it swallowed
    itself,

Of railroad trains whizzing along so fast they reach the station before the
    whistle,
Of pigs so thin the farmer had to tie knots in their tails to keep them from
    crawling through the cracks in their pens,
Of Paul Bunyan's big blue ox, Babe, measuring between the eyes forty-two
    ax-handles and a plug of Star tobacco exactly,
Of John Henry's hammer and the curve of its swing and his singing of it as
    "a rainbow round my shoulder."

                "Do tell!"
                "I want to know!'
                "You don't say so!"
                "For the land's sake!"
                "Gosh all fish-hooks!"
                "Tell me some more.
                I don't believe a word you say
                but I love to listen
                to your sweet harmonica
                to your chin-music.
                Your fish stories hang together
                when they're just a pack of lies:
                you ought to have a leather medal:
                you ought to have a statue
                carved of butter: you deserve
                a large bouquet of turnips."

    "Yessir," the traveler drawled,
"Away out there in the petrified forest
everything goes on the same as usual.
The petrified birds sit in their petrified nests
and hatch their petrified young from petrified eggs."

A high pressure salesman jumped off the Brooklyn Bridge and was saved by a
    policeman. But it didn't take him long to sell the idea to the police-
    man. So together they jumped off the bridge.

One of the oil men in heaven started a rumor of a gusher down in hell. All the
    other oil men left in a hurry for hell. As he gets to thinking about
    the rumor he had started he says to himself there might be something
    in it after all. So he leaves for hell in a hurry.

"The number 42 will win this raffle, that's my number." And when he won
    they asked him whether he guessed the number or had a system. He
    said he had a system, "I took up the old family album and there on
    page 7 was my grandfather and grandmother both on page 7. I said
    to myself this is easy for 7 times 7 is the number that will win and
    7 times 7 is 42."

Once a shipwrecked sailor caught hold of a stateroom door and floated for
    hours till friendly hands from out of the darkness threw him a
    rope. And he called across the night, "What country is this?" and
    hearing voices answer, "New Jersey," he took a fresh hold on the

floating stateroom door and called back half-wearily, "I guess I'll
float a little farther."

An Ohio man bundled up the tin roof of a summer kitchen and sent it to a
motor car maker with a complaint of his car not giving service. In
three weeks a new car arrived for him and a letter: "We regret delay
in shipment but your car was received in a very bad order."

A Dakota cousin of this Ohio man sent six years of tin can accumulations to the
same works, asking them to overhaul his car. Two weeks later came
a rebuilt car, five old tin cans, and a letter: "We are also forwarding
you five parts not necessary in our new model."

Thus fantasies heard at filling stations in the midwest. Another relates to a
Missouri mule who took aim with his heels at an automobile rattling
by. The car turned a somersault, lit next a fence, ran right along
through a cornfield till it came to a gate, moved onto the road and
went on its way as though nothing had happened. The mule hee-
hawed with desolation, "What's the use?"

Another tells of a farmer and his family stalled on a railroad crossing, how they
jumped out in time to see a limited express knock it into flinders, the
farmer calling, "Well, I always did say that car was no shucks in a
real pinch."

When the Masonic Temple in Chicago was the tallest building in the United
States west of New York, two men who would cheat the eyes out of
you if you gave 'em a chance, took an Iowa farmer to the top of the
building and asked him, "How is this for high?" They told him that
for $25 they would go down in the basement and turn the building
around on its turn-table for him while he stood on the roof and saw
how this seventh wonder of the world worked. He handed them $25.
They went. He waited. They never came back.

This is told in Chicago as a folk tale, the same as the legend of Mrs. O'Leary's
cow kicking over the barn lamp that started the Chicago fire, when
the Georgia visitor, Robert Toombs, telegraphed an Atlanta crony,
"Chicago is on fire, the whole city burning down, God be praised!"

Nor is the prize sleeper Rip Van Winkle and his scolding wife forgotten, nor
the headless horseman scooting through Sleepy Hollow

Nor the sunken treasure-ships in coves and harbors, the hideouts of gold and
silver sought by Coronado, nor the Flying Dutchman rounding the
Cape doomed to nevermore pound his ear nor ever again take a
snooze for himself

Nor the sailor's caretaker Mother Carey seeing to it that every seafaring man
in the afterworld has a seabird to bring him news of ships and
women, an albatross for the admiral, a gull for the deckhand

Nor the sailor with a sweetheart in every port of the world, nor the ships that
set out with flying colors and all the promises you could ask, the
ships never heard of again,

Nor Jim Liverpool, the riverman who could jump across any river and back
without touching land he was that quick on his feet,

Nor Mike Fink along the Ohio and the Mississippi, half wild horse and half

cock-eyed alligator, the rest of him snags and snapping turtle. "I can
out-run, out-jump, out-shoot, out-brag, out-drink, and out-fight, rough
and tumble, no holts barred, any man on both sides of the river from
Pittsburgh to New Orleans and back again to St. Louis. My trigger
finger itches and I want to go redhot. War, famine and bloodshed
puts flesh on my bones, and hardship's my daily bread."

Nor the man so lean he threw no shadow: six rattlesnakes struck at him at one
time and every one missed him.

107

[THE PEOPLE WILL LIVE ON]

The people will live on.
The learning and blundering people will live on.
    They will be tricked and sold and again sold
And go back to the nourishing earth for rootholds,
    The people so peculiar in renewal and comeback,
    You can't laugh off their capacity to take it.
The mammoth rests between his cyclonic dramas.

The people so often sleepy, weary, enigmatic,
is a vast huddle with many units saying:
        "I earn my living.
        I make enough to get by
        and it takes all my time.
        If I had more time
        I could do more for myself
        and maybe for others.
        I could read and study
        and talk things over
        and find out about things.
        It takes time.
        I wish I had the time."

The people is a tragic and comic two-face:
hero and hoodlum: phantom and gorilla twisting to moan with a gargoyle mouth: "They
buy me and sell me . . . it's a game . . .
sometime I'll break loose . . ."

            Once having marched
        Over the margins of animal necessity,
        Over the grim line of sheer subsistence
            Then man came
        To the deeper rituals of his bones,
        To the lights lighter than any bones,
        To the time for thinking things over,
        To the dance, the song, the story,
        Or the hours given over to dreaming,
            Once having so marched.

Between the finite limitations of the five senses
and the endless yearnings of man for the beyond
the people hold to the humdrum bidding of work and food
while reaching out when it comes their way
for lights beyond the prison of the five senses,
for keepsakes lasting beyond any hunger or death.
    This reaching is alive.
The panderers and liars have violated and smutted it.
    Yet this reaching is alive yet
    for lights and keepsakes.

The people know the salt of the sea
and the strength of the winds
lashing the corners of the earth.
The people take the earth
as a tomb of rest and a cradle of hope.
Who else speaks for the Family of Man?
They are in tune and step
with constellations of universal law.

The people is a polychrome,
a spectrum and a prism
held in a moving monolith,
a console organ of changing themes,
a clavilux of color poems
wherein the sea offers fog
and the fog moves off in rain
and the labrador sunset shortens
to a nocturne of clear stars
serene over the shot spray
of northern lights.

The steel mill sky is alive.
The fire breaks white and zigzag
shot on a gun-metal gloaming.
Man is a long time coming.
Man will yet win.
Brother may yet line up with brother:

This old anvil laughs at many broken hammers.
    There are men who can't be bought.
    The fireborn are at home in fire.
    The stars make no noise.
    You can't hinder the wind from blowing.
    Time is a great teacher.
    Who can live without hope?

In the darkness with a great bundle of grief the
    people march.

In the night, and overhead a shovel of stars for keeps,
          the people march:
          "Where to? what next?"

1936

FROM

ABRAHAM LINCOLN: THE PRAIRIE YEARS *

[THE "HOUSE DIVIDED" SPEECH]

A night sky of stars over the prairie has the same march and counter-march of mystery as a night sky of stars over the sea.

Across the prairie sky in the year 1858 there came in Illinois cloudy weather for a long time and when it cleared there was seen on the blue mist sheeting of the sky a traveling tail of fire, a new silver arrow among the old yellow stars.

The people had known it was coming; the men of the books had said it would come; a man named Donati in far-off Italy had seen this tail of fire through a telescope and it had been named Donati's comet; at least two and perhaps three thousand years this silver arrow had been tracking its way, a wanderer, not at all responsible in the way that fixed stars and the sun and the moon are responsible, a mover and a goer into new and unknown ways.

It was in this year of the comet that Lincoln was fixing his thoughts on the fact that nothing stays fixed. Up among the fixed stars and steady constellations are explosions and off-shoots of comets, sprays of comets. Even in the mathematics of the stars one had to say, "If we could first

* Reprinted by permission of Harcourt, Brace and Company, Inc., from *Abraham Lincoln: The Prairie Years*, by Carl Sandburg, copyright 1926, by Harcourt, Brace and Company, Inc.

know where we are, and whither we are tending, we could better judge what to do, and how to do it."

For Lincoln, the year of the comet was one filled with burning struggle. As in other years for him, it was in silence and apart from the eyes of other men that he grew, learned, held to his secrets, shaped his personality and purpose, kept to his resolve that the plan of his life should curve "quietly, as the orbit of the earth."

In the spring of the year he was writing notes for a speech; at the state gathering of Republicans in June they were going to nominate him for United States senator from Illinois; and he was going to make a speech; he was to tell the world what Illinois and the Northwest would stand for. As he read the speech to Herndon in their office, it lighted Herndon into saying, "Lincoln, deliver that speech as read, and it will make you President."

Lincoln had spoken the high points of it at Bloomington during the last campaign, and a Chicago judge and a Galena congressman had warned him never to be so radical again. In the State Library in Springfield he sat in a chair and read it off to a picked dozen of political friends; they said it was too radical; it was "a fool utterance"; it was "ahead of its time"; it would drive away votes; all were against his delivering the first paragraph of the speech, except Herndon. And Lincoln was polite and decent—and couldn't see where he ought to change the speech.

The convention met in Springfield on June 17, named Lincoln for

United States senator, and then sent out for him to come and make a speech. He came, bowed to the applause and cheers, murmured, "Mr. President and Gentlemen of the Convention," and then, for the first time in his life reading a speech from a manuscript, he began:

"If we could first know where we are, and whither we are tending, we could better judge what to do, and how to do it. We are now far into the fifth year since a policy was initiated with the avowed object and confident promise of putting an end to slavery agitation. Under the operation of that policy, that agitation has not only not ceased, but has constantly augmented. In my opinion, it will not cease until a crisis shall have been reached and passed. 'A house divided against itself cannot stand.' I believe this government cannot endure permanently half slave and half free. I do not expect the Union to be dissolved—I do not expect the house to fall—but I do expect it will cease to be divided. It will become all one thing, or all the other."

This was so plain that any two farmers fixing fences on a rainy morning could talk it over in all its ins and outs. And to this was added a sentence for all the more thoughtful to follow in all its exact and terrible meanings. The speaker read:

"Either the opponents of slavery will arrest the further spread of it, and place it where the public mind shall rest in the belief that it is in the course of ultimate extinction; or its advocates will push it forward till it shall become alike lawful in all the States, old as well as new, North as well as South."

In simple Bible language, in words as short as those of Bunyan's "Pilgrim's Progress," and in longer words of piercing precision, he had spoken thought as fresh, beautiful, and terrible as Donati's comet with its tail of fire in the sky. What he had said was easy to say and to understand, a common-sense telling of what millions of anxious hearts wanted told.

There was more to the speech; he put together this and that circumstance and argued that while on the face of them the people could not be sure that there was a conspiracy on foot to nationalize slavery, yet explanations were required as to why the two Presidents, Franklin Pierce and James Buchanan, a Supreme Court Chief Justice, and the United States senator, Stephen A. Douglas, had all taken parts in moves and acts that seemed to lead straight toward a time when slaves could be owned and worked in all states of the Union. And he mentioned how the Republican party, of strange, discordant, and even hostile elements, "gathered from the four winds," had fought winning battles in the last campaign and with wise counsels should go on.

He struck at the Supreme Court as a dynasty. "Put this and that together, and we have another nice little niche, which we may, ere long, see filled with another Supreme Court decision declaring that the Constitution of the United States does not permit a State to exclude slavery from its limits. Such a decision is all that slavery now lacks of being alike lawful in all the States. Welcome or unwelcome, such decision is probably coming, and will soon be upon us, unless the power of the present political dynasty shall be met and overthrown. We shall lie down pleasantly dreaming that the people of Missouri are on the verge of making their State free, and we shall awake to the reality instead that the Supreme Court has made Illinois a slave State. To meet and overthrow the power of that dynasty is the work now before all those who would prevent that consummation."

There was more to the speech—but the part that interested the country, as daily and weekly newspapers published the speech in full, was its opening paragraph. It became known as the "House Divided" speech.

1926

RANDOLPH BOURNE
(1886–1918)

UNIVERSAL SERVICE AND EDUCATION *

The current agitation for preparedness has set hosts of Americans to thinking out for the first time what a real national strength and readiness would mean. We suddenly realize that if we are to defeat that militaristic trend which we loathe we shall have to offer some kind of action more stirring and more creative. The call now upon every citizen is to be not nebulously patriotic, but clear and lucid as to America's aims, so that our natural energy shall not be squandered and misused. There looms up as a crucial need that "moral equivalent for war" with which William James first roused our imaginations. It seems no longer so academic a proposal. Confronted with the crisis, we see that he analyzed the situation with consummate accuracy.

All around us we see a very genuine craving for unity of sentiment, for service, for some new national lift and broadening which shall keep us out of the uneasy pettiness into which the American conscience has threatened to fall. In our hearts we know

* Reprinted by permission of the Century Company from *Education and Living*, by Randolph Bourne, copyright 1917 by the Century Company.

that to crystallize this desire into a meaningless sentiment, or into a piling-up of armaments or a proscribing of alien cultures, would not satisfy us. We want action, but we do not want military action. Even the wildest patriots know that America would have to go through the most pernicious and revolutionary changes to accept the universal military service which they advocate. We wish to advance from where we stand. We begin to suspect that military service, flag-reverence, patriotic swagger, are too much the weary old deep-dug channels into which national feeling always runs and is lost. The flooding river fills again its archaic and forsaken paths. Our present confusion expresses the dilemma we find ourselves in, when our instincts impel us into courses that our intelligence tells us we ought not to follow.

Our American danger is not so much that we become militarists as that we grope along, fretting and harrying each other into a unity which is delusive, and expressing our "Americanism" in activities that are not creative. The best will in America at the present time seems to crave some kind of national service but it veers off from military service. Until we satisfy that craving, we shall run at half-power, and suffer all the dissatisfaction and self-despising that comes from repressed energy. The question which all are asking, in the varied and disguised forms, is: How can we all together serve America by really enhancing her life?

To more and more of us the clue has come through James's conception of a productive army of youth, warring against nature and not against men, finding in drudgery and toil and danger the values that war and preparation for war have given. Ten years ago such an army seemed Utopian.

We had neither the desire nor the technique. It seemed a project not to be realized without a reorganization of our life so radical as to make the army itself unnecessary. To-day, however, a host of new attitudes seem to give us the raw material out of which such a national service could be created. We hear much of universal military service as "education." The Plattsburgs are sugar-coated as "civic-training·camps," "schools for citizenship." Universal service no longer stands on its old ground of mere preparation for war. It is frankly trying to get itself recognized as an indispensable mode of education. The next pertinent step is evidently to ask why, if universal service is valuable because it is educational, it should not be constructed on a strict educational foundation.

James's proposal sounded Utopian because it would require an entirely new and colossal national organization to put it into action. Universal military service in this country would certainly mean such a task. But if our national service is to be educational, we already have the organization in existence. The rapidly consolidating public school systems in the states provide the machinery for such an organization. As the public schools become better places for children to spend their time in, we are growing less tolerant of the forms of schooling outside of the public system. The tendency is towards the inclusion of all children in the public school. And the progressive states are requiring schooling up to the full age of sixteen years. We are rapidly creating a public school system, effectively administered by the states, which gives us the one universally national compulsory service which we possess or are ever likely to consent to.

Education is the only form of "conscription" to which Americans have ever given consent. Compulsory military service would require decades of Napoleonic political evangelism to introduce. Compulsory education is universally accepted. For a national service which shall be educational you would have to convert nobody. The field is sown. No one denies the right of the state to conscript the child for education. But coupled with this assent is the insistence that the education shall be the freest, fullest and most stimulating that we know how to give. The current educational interest arises largely from the indignant demand that a state which takes all the children must meet the needs of every child. The very recent enthusiasm for "vocational education" means that we want a schooling that shall issue in capacity for fruitful occupation. A national educational service could give training for work at the same time that it gave opportunity for service.

It is only a national service of this kind that would really be universal. Military service is a sham universality. It omits the feminine half of the nation's youth. And of the masculine half it uses only the physically best. France is the only country where the actual levy on men for military service has approximated the number liable. But worst of all, military service irons out all differences of talent and ability. It does not even tap the resources it enlists. It makes out of an infinitely varied group a mere machine of uniform, obeying units. The personal qualities, the individual powers of the youth it trains, are of no relevance whatever. Men are valuable exactly to the degree that they crush out these differences.

A national service for education would not be a sham. It would actually enlist the coöperation of every youth and girl. It would aim at stimulation, not obedience. It would call out capacity and not submerge it. It would organize varied tasks adapted to the capacities and strengths of its young citizenry. It would be universal, but it would be compulsory only in the sense that it called every one to the service. The tasks would not be enforced drudgery, but work that enlisted the will and toned up the aspirations.

Such a national service would be the logical outgrowth of our public school system. Suppose the state said: All children shall remain in school till the age of sixteen years. Between the ages of sixteen and twenty-one they shall spend two years in national service. This service shall be organized and administered by the state educational administrations, but supervised and subsidized by the national government. The service would be performed as national service, but its work would be constructive and communal in its purposes and not military. Special military training could be given as a branch of this service to those who were best fitted for it. But defense would be but an incident in our constructive life, and not the sinew of our effort.

The tasks for such a national service would evidently be different from those contemplated by James. He thought of turning his army of youth into the drudgery of the world, where they might win in heroic toil and self-sacrifice the moral rewards which war had formerly given. But if our service is to be universal, it cannot be mere unskilled labor in mines and farms and forests. A large proportion of our youth would be disqualified. Furthermore, a service which made such frontal attack on industry would be bitterly resisted by those with whom its work competed. We are not pre-

pared for a service which clashes too suddenly and harshly with the industrial system. What we need is a service which shall not so much do the old work of the world as create new demands and satisfy them. This national service could do the things which need to be done, but which are not now being done. It could have for its aim the improvement of the quality of our living. Our appalling slovenliness, the ignorance of great masses in city and country as to the elementary technique of daily life—this should be the enemy of the army of youth. I have a picture of a host of eager young missionaries swarming over the land, spreading the health knowledge, the knowledge of domestic science, of gardening, of tastefulness, that they have learned in school.

Such a service would provide apprentices for communal services in town and country, as many schools and colleges are already actually providing. Food inspection, factory inspection, organized relief, the care of dependents, playground service, nursing in hospitals—all this would be a field for such an educational service. On a larger scale, tree-planting, the care and repair of roads, work on conservation projects, the care of model farms, would be tasks for this army. As I was burning caterpillars' nests the other day in New Jersey and saw the trees sinister with gray webs, I thought of the destroying army of youth that should be invading the land clearing it of all insect pests. We might even come to the forcible rebuilding of the slovenly fences and outhouses which strew our landscape, and to an imposition of cleanness upon our American countryside. With an army of youth we could perform all those services of neatness and mercy and intelligence which our communities now know how to perform and mean to perform, but have not the weapons to wield.

The army could be organized in flying squadrons, so that its youth could travel widely and see and serve all kinds of men and communities. For its direction we would need that new type of teacher-engineer-community-worker that our best school systems are already producing. Scientific schools, schools of philanthropy, are turning out men and women who could step into their places as non-commissioned officers for such an army. The service could be entirely flexible. Boys and girls could learn the rudiments of their trade or profession in actual service with the army. Book studies could be carried on, and college learning could come to its own as the intellectual fertilizer of a wholesome and stimulating life. Athletics and sports would be an integral part of the two years' service. There would be long periods of camping in the national parks or upon ocean beaches. The Boy Scouts and Camp-Fire Girls already give the clue to such an enterprise.

If objection is made that this national educational service would fail to bring out the sterner qualities of heroism and self-sacrifice, and would not be a genuine moral equivalent for war, the answer is that the best kind of a moral equivalent is a moral sublimation. We want to turn the energies of youth away from their squandering in mere defense or mere drudgery. Our need is to learn how to live rather than die; to be teachers and creators, not engines of destruction; to be inventors and pioneers, not mere defenders. Our cities and isolated farms alike are mute witnesses that Americans have never learned how to live. Suppose we had a national service which was making a determined assault for the enhance-

ment of living. Would its standards and discipline be less rigorous? Rather would the ingenuity and imagination have to be of the finest.

Some such conception of national service is the only one which will give us that thrill of unity and vigor which we seek. An educational service built on the public school system puts the opportunity in our hands. The raw material in attitudes and desires is here. Every task that an army of youth might perform is already being done in some school or college or communal service. All we need to do is to coördinate and make universal what is now haphazard and isolated. An army of youth which focused school work would provide just that purpose that educators seek. The advocates of "preparedness" are willing to spend billions on a universal military service which is neither universal nor educational nor productive. Cannot we begin to organize a true national service which will let all serve creatively towards the toning up of American life?

1916

VAN WYCK BROOKS
(1886–)

THE FLOWERING OF NEW ENGLAND *

CHAPTER XXVIII

CONCLUSION

The Civil War brought to a head, however inconclusively, a phase of American culture that later times described as the New England "renaissance." This movement of mind con-

* Taken from *The Flowering of New England* by Van Wyck Brooks, copyright 1936 by Van Wyck Brooks, published by E. P. Dutton & Co., Inc., New York.

tinued in the generation that followed, and many of the writers who embodied it long outlived the war. Some of them produced their best work, or work, at least, equal to their best, during this later period. But all had given their measure before the war, and several had disappeared before it. That they stood for some collective impulse, exceptional in the history of the national mind, no one questioned later or has ever questioned. Whether this impulse was a "renaissance" or only an "Indian summer," as Mr. Santayana has called it, a "golden age" or a "golden day," the impulse existed and the movement was real. The question is only one of its general meaning and what it signified in itself.

It is obvious, almost strikingly so, that this movement of mind in New England followed the typical pattern of the "culture-cycle," as Spengler has convincingly described it. Setting aside the question of scale, one finds in it the same succession of phases that one finds in the great culture-cycles,—for Spengler, in this, at least, has made a case that is so suggestive as to seem conclusive. Here we have a homogeneous people, living close to the soil, intensely religious, unconscious, unexpressed in art and letters, with a strong sense of home and fatherland. One of its towns becomes a "culture-city," for Boston, with Cambridge and Concord considered as suburbs, answers to this name, which Spengler accords to Florence, Bruges and Weimar, as no other town has ever answered in either of the Americas. There is a springtime feeling in the air, a joyous sense of awakening, a free creativeness, an unconscious pride, expressed in the founding of institutions, intellectual, humanitarian, artistic, and—at first a little timid, cold and shy—the mind begins to shape into myths and stories the

dreams of the pre-urban countryside. There is a moment of equipoise, a widespread flowering of the imagination in which the thoughts and feelings of the people, with all their faiths and hopes, find expression. The culture-city dominates the country, but only as its accepted vent and mouthpiece. Then gradually the mind, detached from the soil, grows more and more self-conscious. Contradictions arise within it, and worldlier arts supplant the large, free, ingenuous forms through which the poetic mind has taken shape. What formerly grew from the soil begins to be planned. The Hawthornes yield to the Henry Jameses. Over-intelligent, fragile, cautious and doubtful, the soul of the culture-city loses the self-confidence and joy that have marked its early development,—it is filled with a presentiment of the end; and the culture-city itself surrenders to the world-city,—Boston surrenders to New York,—which stands for cosmopolitan deracination. What has once been vital becomes provincial; and the sense that one belongs to a dying race dominates and poisons the creative mind.

Not to press a formula too far, is not this the story of New England, as the New England mind confesses it, from the days of Channing and Webster to those of Henry Adams and Barrett Wendell? In religion, the springtime faith of Channing, with its feeling of a world to create and redeem, yields to the conception of religion as hygiene in the valetudinarian Mrs. Eddy. In politics, the robust and confident Webster gives place to the querulous Lodge. The scholars and historians lose themselves among their documents; and the cheerful, unconscious, generous note of the essayists and poets of the eighteenfifties makes way for the analytical and the precious. No doubt, the New England mind exaggerates its own decline and decay. There are times when the visitor in New England feels that it is destined for another growth that will be more vigorous than its first, and the age that followed its "golden day" is richer and fuller to the enquiring eye than its own or other historians have supposed. But that it has passed through a cycle, and some such cycle as Spengler pictures,—this grows more and more apparent.

"Men are free," said D. H. Lawrence, "when they are in a living homeland, not when they are straying and breaking away. Men are free when they are obeying some deep, inward voice of religious belief. Obeying from within. Men are free when they belong to a living, organic, believing community, active in fulfilling some unfulfilled, perhaps unrealized purpose." This was the case with the New England authors, in the epoch of the building of the nation. Perhaps it was never more truly the case with any group of authors, all question of intensity aside. They were as completely of their people as any authors of the oldest nations; and they saw, if not themselves,—for they were not self-conscious,—at least their profession as having a Promethean role to play. They were teachers, educators and bringers of light, with a deep and affectionate feeling of obligation towards the young republic their fathers had brought into being. That New England was appointed to guide the nation, to civilize it and humanize it, none of them ever doubted, a motive that was evident in all their writings, from Emerson's early addresses to the table-talk of Holmes, from Longfellow's *Hiawatha,* in which an Indian myth conveys the poet's notion of his role, to the proph-

ecies of *Uncle Tom's Cabin.* Sometimes they suggested Miss Ophelia reforming Dinah's kitchen; but there was so little of the condescending, so much of the humble and fraternal, in their state of mind and point of view, and they threw so many ideas into circulation and wrote so sincerely and so well that they came to be accepted as fathers and sages.

What was the cause of this transfiguration? The breadth of their conscious horizon, the healthy objectivity of their minds, their absorption in large preoccupations, historical, political, religious, together with a literary feeling, a blend of the traditional and the local, that gave the local wider currency while it brought the traditional home to men's business and bosoms. They filled the New England scene with associations and set it, as it were, in three dimensions, creating the visible foreground it had never possessed. They helped to make their countrypeople conscious of the great world-movements of thought and feeling in which they played parts side by side with the intellectual leaders of the older countries. In their scholarship, their social thought, their moral passion, their artistic feeling, they spoke for the universal republic of letters, giving their own province a form and body in the consciousness of the world. Morever, there was something in their temper that made them seem friends of the human spirit. They stood for good faith and fair play and all that was generous and hopeful in the life of their time. The hold they gained and kept over the nation possessed an extra-literary sanction, as if they were voices of the national ethos. If they found themselves "done up in spices, like so many Pharaohs," as Holmes remarked in later years, it was because they were looked upon as classics,—

In whom is plainest taught, and easiest
learnt,
What makes a nation happy, and keeps
it so.

This process of canonization went
hand in hand with the spread of New
England culture over the country. As
the New England strain died out in
the West, with the second and third
generations of the pioneers and the
growth of a native point of view, the
reputations of the New England
authors had to face another test. They
encountered an increasing neglect and
indifference, and even a widespread
hostility. This was partly due to the
reaction against the romantic authors
in every country; but it was inevitable
that the West should have turned
against New England. In order to
establish its independence, it was
obliged to do so, as the East had
turned against the mother-country.
Of the popular writers, Longfellow,
Whittier, Holmes, something seemed
destined to survive in the general
mind of the nation, when the life of
all the regions, taken together, formed
a final synthesis; but much of their
work was ephemeral, and most of it
was so bound up with regional modes
of feeling and local traditions that it
could only endure in the regional
mind. For the rest, there are two kinds
of classics, the popular and the esoteric, those that yield their meaning
at the first encounter and those that
we have to discover by effort and insight, the classics of the intellectual
surface and the classics of the spiritual
depths. The popular New England
authors, whom every child could understand, remained as classics indeed,
but mainly for children; while the
handful of esoteric authors,—Hawthorne, with his cloudy symbols,
whom one could only see through a
glass, darkly, Thoreau, who "listened
behind him for his wit," and Emer-

son, who, in life, never gave a direct
answer and said that one should speak
in parables,—came more and more
into their own. Ironically enough, it
was Boston and Cambridge that grew
to seem provincial, while the local
and even parochial Concord mind,
which had always been universal,
proved to be also national. Whatever
doubts the country at large felt regarding the other New England authors, Hawthorne, Thoreau and Emerson were clearly of the main stream,
with Emily Dickinson, Whitman, Poe
and Melville.

Thoreau died in 1862. He had
caught cold from over-exposure while
counting the rings of some trees on
a snowy day and had fought for a
year and a half with tuberculosis. He
had outlived his juvenile-braggart
phase and had grown more and more
to seem the sage, whose life and opinions might have appeared in the pages
of Diogenes Laertius. In an effort to
regain his health, he had journeyed to
Minnesota and had made friends with
some of the Indians there. Then,
knowing that nothing could save him,
he had settled down among his papers,
with an Indian's indifference to the
future, completing some of his lists
of birds and flowers and finishing *The
Maine Woods.* No more walks to
Bateman's Pond, to Becky Stow's
swamp or Nine-Acre Corner. But he
said he enjoyed existence as well as
ever. His thoughts had entertained
him all his life, never so much as at
present. Fields, the second editor of
The Atlantic, had asked him for
some of his essays, and he spent his
last months revising these.

His friends could hardly imagine
Concord without him. Solitude peered
out from the dells and wood-roads,
and the bobolinks seemed to sing a
minor strain. One had thought of

Henry Thoreau as a part of nature, destined to be transformed perhaps at last into a mossy rock or a leaf-strewn spring. At least, he was like the hour-glass apple-shrub of which he had written in his journal. By the end of October, when the leaves had fallen, one saw the wild yellow fruit growing, which the cows could not reach over the thorny hedge. It was so with the rude, neglected genius of the Concord woods and meadows. He had suffered many a check at first, browsed upon by fate, springing up in a rocky pasture, the nursery of other creatures there, and had grown up scraggy and thorny, not like the sleek orchard-trees whose forces had all been husbanded. When, at first, within this rind and hedge, the man shot up, one saw the thorny scrub of his youth about him; but, as he grew, the thorns disappeared, and he bore golden crops of Porters and Baldwins, apples whose fame was destined to spread through all orchards for generations, when the thrifty orchard-trees that had been his rivals had long since ceased to bear their engrafted fruit. It was true that Thoreau's fame was slow in growing. Emerson and Ellery Channing brought out his posthumous books,— he had published only two during his lifetime; and Emerson collected his poems and letters. But only his friends could imagine why anyone should wish to see his journal. Emerson was convinced that, if it was published, it would soon produce in New England a "plentiful crop of naturalists." This was true a generation later. When volumes of selections from the journal appeared, a school of lesser Thoreaus sprang up at once; * and

The happy man who lived content
With his own town and continent,

became a teacher of wisdom, even in Asia.

Two years after Thoreau, Hawthorne faded out of the Concord picture. He had come home from Italy and England just before the outbreak of the war and had taken up his life again at "Wayside," the house he had bought from Alcott, where a man was said to have lived who believed he was never to die. Hawthorne built a tower over the house, a reminiscence of the Italian villa in which he had stayed in Florence. There he had his study, reached by a trap-door, with a standing desk fastened to the wall. With England still fresh in his mind, he composed from his note-books the beautifully rounded chapters of *Our Old Home,* a book that was somewhat unhappily named; but a sudden change seemed to have come upon him with his return to America, a blight as of winter, a deadly estrangement even from his own imagination. Had he been too old to be transplanted, so that he could never take root again? He made a few half-hearted efforts to gather up the threads of his former life. He appeared at the Saturday Club for a few of the dinners; but even Alcott and Emerson seldom saw him. Once, at Emerson's house, he picked up some photographs of Concord, the common, the court-house and the Mill-dam, which he passed in his walks every day, and asked what the pictures represented. The sight of a friend or a stranger approaching his house drove him up the hill into the woods. Along the

---

* Thoreau's manuscript journal consisted of thirty-nine blank-books of all shapes and sizes, packed in a strong wooden box built by himself. It was bequeathed by Sophia Thoreau to H. G. O. Blake, who brought out four volumes of selections, 1881–1892. The complete journal was edited by Bradford Torrey and published in fourteen volumes, 1906.

top of the ridge, among the pines, between the huckleberry and sweetfern bushes, he walked to and fro, brooding over the novel he could not finish. He fancied that the grass and the little shrubs shrank away as he passed them because there was something in his broodings that was alien to nature. Seventy-five years later, one could still trace the path that Hawthorne's footsteps wore on the tree-covered ridge.

He had wasted away and the glow in his eyes had vanished; and, hard as he tried to write, pulling down the blinds and locking his door, he could not bring his mind into focus. The novel became two novels, and the two became four. He could not fix upon a single setting: Salem, Concord, England, "Wayside" and Smithall's Hall drifted in confusion through his mind, their outlines melting into one another. Even his theme eluded him. Was it the unpardonable sin, the "ancestral footstep," the man who believed he was never to die? He made four beginnings, constantly changing his perspective, until he could scarcely bear to touch his blurred and meaningless manuscripts. A few of the scenes took form, with all his old perfection, with the sculptural repose of his earlier writing and a touch of the Gothic imagination that seemed to connect America with the Middle Ages. But life shook before his eyes, like the picture on the surface of a pond when a stone has disturbed its tranquil mirror. His mind had grown like Melville's in *Pierre,* groping in a fog for the firm conceptions that turned to vapour as he tried to grasp them. Then, one day in 1864, the news reached Concord from Plymouth, New Hampshire, that he had died in his sleep at the village inn. For years, he had been in the habit, while idly scribbling, of writing the

number 64, which had, he felt, some fatal meaning for him. He had not disappeared, like Septimus Felton, crushed by the failure of his dream, but he had wandered away with as little purpose, knowing perhaps that he would not return.

The Alcotts had settled in "Orchard House," next door to Hawthorne's. Alcott had rebuilt it, leaving the old beams and rafters, making arched alcoves of the ovens and ashholes; and, over the chimney-piece in Alcott's study, Ellery Channing's lines were inscribed,—

The hills were reared, the valleys scooped
    in vain,
If Learning's altars vanish from the plain.

Alcott had been made superintendent of the public schools in Concord. His vindication had come late, and one could only think what he might have accomplished if he had had this chance when he was younger. Louisa had begun to write the stories that were to carry his name around the world. Meanwhile, now that Thoreau was gone, Emerson was the master of the Concord revels. He liked to pile the children into the haycart, which they had bedecked with flowers and mosses, and carry them off for a swim and a picnic at Walden.

Emerson was travelling, on his lecture-tours, further and further westward. He was still an impossible puzzle in the popular mind, even a national joke, a byword of the country paragraphers. No matter, there were always a few of his hearers for whom all mythology spoke in his voice, the Indian gods and the gods of the North, who felt that the beautiful and the good must also be the true, if only because Emerson had said so. He seemed to have made his own all the victories of genius, which he invited one to share, he who had never doubted the riches of nature, the gifts of the future, the wealth of the mind. Whatever one's occupation was, mechanics, law, the ministry, he broke the spell of one's routine, relating one's craft and task to the laws of the world: one felt how one's life was intertwined with the whole chain of being. He spoke for magnanimity and the power of thought. In *The Conduct of Life* he had met the objections of those who found his optimism too facile. He had fully recognized the existence of evil, the brutal and barbarous elements in the core of the world, the habits of snake and spider in human beings, the snap of the tiger, the crackle of the bones of his prey in the coils of the anaconda. Even as men rose in culture, fate continued to follow them, as Vishnu followed Maya through all her ascending changes. While their checks and limitations became finer and finer, the ring of necessity still remained perched at the top. But fate had its lord, limitation its limits. It was different seen from above and seen from below. For, if fate was immense, so was power. Man was a stupendous antagonism, and as long as he thought he was free. It was true, there was nothing more disgusting than the crowing about liberty by slaves, as most men were, and the flippant mistaking for freedom of some statute right to vote by those who had never dared to think or act; yet men had the power to look not at fate but the other way. The practical view was the other. Well had the oracle said, "Look not on Nature, for her name is fatal!" as Hafiz described the phrase on the gate of heaven, "Woe unto him who suffers himself to be betrayed by Fate!" Instead of cringing to facts, one could use and command them. Every jet of chaos that threatened extermination, one could convert by intellect into wholesome force. The water drowned ship and sailor. But, if one learned to swim and trimmed one's bark, one clove the water with it, and the waves were obliged to carry it, like their own foam, a plume and a power.

Thus Emerson spoke to the active forces waiting in his hearers, eager for the word that would set them free. For himself, he found that the more he spent the more he had to spend, the more he communicated the results of his thinking the more new thoughts he had. His zest and curiosity grew with the years; and, for all the discomforts of his lecture-tours, he liked to get away from the Eastern sea-board, where the American current was so superficial. He learned the resources of the country, going to school to the prairies. He had no fear of the future, he did not distrust the rough, wild, incalculable road America would have to travel to find itself. As between the civil and the forcible, he had always leaned, in his sympathies, to the latter. The Hoosiers and the Badgers of the West, the hard heads of Oregon and Utah, the rough-riders and legislators in shirt-sleeves, let them drive as they might. Better than to quote English standards and miss the sovereignty of power. Out of pirates and berserkers the English race had sprung, and no strong nation could ever develop without its own strong, wild will; and the power of the buffalo-hunters, bullying the peaceable and the loyal, would bring its own antidote at last. For liberty in all its wildness bred iron conscience; the instinct of the people was right in the end, and natures with great impulses had great resources and could be trusted to return from far.

There, in the West, he thought, lay nature sleeping, too much by half for man in the picture, with its rank vegetation of swamps and forests, steeped in dews and rains. In this great sloven continent, in its high Alleghany pastures, in the sea-wide, sea-skirted prairie, the great mother still slept and murmured. Man had as yet made little impression upon it. But there, where stars and woods and hills abounded, with all things still untried, could one not foresee a social state more excellent than history had recorded, one that turned its back on musket-worship and lived by the law of love and justice? Let men but know that every day is doomsday, and let them look within, in the populous, all-loving solitude which they left for the tattle of towns; for there *he* lurked and hid, he who was reality, joy and power. So Emerson felt, in the streets of New York, or at Concord, as he strolled through grove and glen. Others, as they saw him, tall and slender, leaving the village behind him, might have said to themselves, with the Swedish poet, "The last skald walks over the meadows."

1936, 1937

MAX EASTMAN
(1883–   )

THE REALM
OF LITERARY TRUTH *

The division of labor—and let us say also of play—between poets and scientists, and the cleavage of the two commodities they make, does not any more mean the end of poetry than of science. But it does mean a loss to poetry that science cannot feel. For a sense of the presence of universal truth was one of poetry's sublime in-

* From *The Literary Mind*, by Max Eastman, copyright, 1931, by Charles Scribner's Sons.

gredients. Science *is* this ingredient and wants no other.

There is a motion among literary men to-day to try to mend this loss. Conrad Aiken is studying psychopathology and talking about the grandeur of Dante and Lucretius. Aldous Huxley is advising poets to think up a new "method of dealing with abstractions" so that science may again become the "subject matter" of poems. He thinks the reason why this has not happened is that "a poet in whose mind ideas are a personal moving force does not happen to have appeared." A strange statement, to which he is led because he does not make clear to himself what he means by science becoming the subject matter of poetry. He makes no distinction between Lucretius who taught science in poetic language, and John Donne who did not teach but took scientific ideas as experiences, as material out of which commingled with his emotions to make poems. The distinction is absolutely vital. It is doubtless true, as Huxley says, that Einstein—or Yeats, if he understood Einstein—could "write the most impassioned lyrics about relativity and the pleasures of pure mathematics." Edna Millay has written an impassioned, though to me not wholly convincing, sonnet about the pleasures of pure mathematics, and Archibald MacLeish has made that troubled poem about relativity. But these achievements do not bring us one step toward reviving the times of Lucretius and Empedocles. Those were times when poets could hope to convey in the same breath a lively sense of the world and the most technical knowledge about it. In order to be a modern Lucretius, you would have to write lyrics, not about Einstein's theory, but about motion in terms of Einstein's theory. And that is impossible because motion cannot be experienced except from some standpoint, and Einstein's theory is a device for talking about motion independently of all standpoints. No conceivable creatures—not even Shelley's wild-eyed charioteers who

> lean forth and drink
> With eager lips the wind of their own speed,

could write in Einstein's language the poetry of motion—not any more than they could write epithalamiums in the language of Freud or John B. Watson, or compose hymns of revolution in the terminology of Karl Marx. It is idle to deny this opposition, or imagine that poets can recapture the realms of science by merely going there, or by thinking up a new "method of dealing with abstractions." Poetry is compelled by its very nature to yield up to science the task of interpreting experience, of finding out what we call truth, of giving men reliable guidance in the conduct of their lives. The boast of Matthew Arnold that "More and more mankind will discover that we have to turn to poetry to interpret life for us . . .," that "Poetry is nothing less than the most perfect speech of man, that in which he comes nearest to being able to utter truth," was but a last cry of defiance from the dwindling men of letters to the new leader of the herd.

There is no one to repeat Arnold's gallant cry to-day. In its place we have Sacheverell Sitwell talking blandly of the "nearly cancelled rôle of the poet," and we have the noble and morose growl of Julien Benda, indignant because poets are *not* interpreting life for us, because literature has ceased to utter truth and given itself over wantonly to the "pure feeling of things." M. Benda laments ferociously the disappearance of what he calls

intellect from modern literature, but he is himself too literary in his training to ask himself the most obvious questions: Why has intellect disappeared from literature? Where has it gone? He seems to imagine that intellect in disappearing from literature has disappeared from the world. He makes furious mock of those who assert that art "must present things *in their reality*, and not in the *distorted forms in which the intellect represents them.*" In scorn of them he cries: "Let us recall that this distortion of things by intellect—which is merely the capacity of man to make the sensory world intelligible—was considered in the seventeenth century, when Descartes first made it known, as one of the great honors to which the human species could lay claim." Are we to infer that in our time the species has ceased to strive after the honors of Descartes, that the movement initiated by Descartes and by Bacon and Galileo is declining and coming to an end? Surely the very opposite thing is happening—the distortion of things by intellect in order to make the sensory world intelligible, and make it moreover serviceable—has gone so far and flourished so fantastically, that even the *minimum of immediacy essential to poetic literature* is incompatible with its further growth. Intellectual interpretation is still an honor, a far greater one now than in the time of Descartes, but the honor is indeed remote from the man of letters. Science has withdrawn intellect from literature. It has divided truth from immediacy. And the event is inexorable, inherent in the development of science. It is not a degeneration of French society, but a specialization of human functions against which M. Benda is protesting with so savage a moral indignation. His arrant and absolute demand that art should again become "an attempt to comprehend life" would be, if it came from a scientist, a demand that art give place to science. Coming from a man of letters it is a demand that scientific progress cease, and that we return to those amateur times when the comprehension of life and the communication of its qualities were not yet distinguished. In short, M. Benda's fine and ferocious tirade is merely a last phase of the literary man's battle against the advance of science into his domain. No longer able to resist the enemy, he turns frantically upon his own colleagues and attacks them.

It is the function of science to comprehend and criticize life; poetry is our living of it vividly and together. Only after that extreme statement is made can we correctly apprehend, as qualifications of it, the various intellectual possibilities that lie open to poetry and to poetic literature in an age of science. I for my part am much in accord with M. Benda in his wish that poets might continue—or begin again—to use their brains. Indeed I think my own poetry has suffered from the too controlling sense I have had of this inherent divergence of two functions. When I want to comprehend life I want to comprehend it as those do whose purpose is control; I do not want to beguile myself by some mixture of semi-comprehension with an imposing presentation of its colors. When on the other hand the colors of life engage me deeply I do not often have the impulse to wind a saying around them, to build an ulterior meaning into them, to make some symbol or signal or semaphore out of them, as though they had not their value in themselves. Thus although intellectual and a poet, I am not an intellectual poet—not yet at least—but one of those whom M. Benda would denounce with terrible

force, although unjustly, as tainted with the "greed of immediacy." I say unjustly because I would gladly find a way of escape from this dividedness and put myself into a book of poetry as a whole man, or at least two halves of a man pulled together in some manner that is not too obviously a make-shift. I approach the problem, therefore, of bringing truth back into poetic literature, or at least deciding what are the boundaries of the realm of literary truth, with the best will in the world to make them wide.

I remark first that the man of letters has as good a right to make large guesses about things totally unknown as the man of science. He has still a sovereign freedom in the vast kingdom of our ignorance. Here he can mix poetry and opinion with the old beautiful and sublime caprice, here stake his claim to "truth which is its own testimony," here still insist that he is not a ballad-monger but a seer and a sage. One has only to remember how many are the questions upon which scientific authorities disagree in order to realize how vast this realm is in which the poet can still feel welling up the old sovereign and preposterous conviction, in which "intellect" can still robe itself in asseverations and expatiate and plume itself and put on a great spectacle of the discovery of truth, without fear of being suddenly brought low by a verified and well-aimed fact from the door of some laboratory or from behind some pile of statistics. The realm is vast—and yet it is steadily dwindling. Emerson would look foolish enough coming forward in our times with his solemn annunciation of a "Law of Compensation." We are too familiar with valid laws and the manner in which their validity is established. To his assertion that "labor is watched over" by this mystic law, we should rely by pointing to the statute law and to a pile of documents called "compensation statistics." For all his high art in the poetry of ideas, Emerson would be put down as a crank or a mountebank if he came out on our bookstalls with his grave essay on "Compensation,"—and yet that is a fair example of what is called "literary truth," a fair operation of that faculty which Emerson, like other men of letters in the nineteenth century, called "intellect" in conscious opposition to the activities of the mind in science.

Not only are the fields dwindling in which a man of letters can display his proud faculty with complacence, but even in these fields he can hardly help sometimes reflecting—so great is the prestige of science—that if they are still free to him, it is not because he has conquered them but because they are unconquered. It may be that they are unconquered because they are still unconquerable by the methods of true knowledge; it may be because they have not yet seemed in comparison to others worth conquering. These two causes alone determine the outposts of science. A "literary truth," may therefore be defined— provisionally at least—as a truth which is either uncertain or comparatively unimportant.

One of the most delightful of literary truths to me, and one apt in this connection because of its "mathematical" form, is this *Meditation* of Pascal:

"I lay it down as a fact that, if all men knew what others say of them, there would not be four friends in the world."

It seems a little absurd to bring such a delightfully swift and helpful remark into relation with the problems of verified knowledge. And yet if you will but imagine a world in which flood-prevention or the curbing of a bubonic plague happened to depend upon our determining the reliability of that small statistic, you will concede that we should know before long to a close approximation of exactitude how many friends would be left in the world under the proposed circumstances. We should have experts plotting curves all day long of the decline of friendships, both in number and elasticity to stresses, tensional, tortional and transverse, under a controlled increase in publicity for all frank and delightfully malicious conversations. I am disposed to think the curve would fall abruptly to a depth almost as appalling as that contemplated by Pascal, but then rise again very gradually in such a way as to indicate that if the publicity were absolute the friendships would multiply enormously and show an elasticity almost as appalling. At any rate the tests will never be made because the labor too far exceeds the reward. And for that sole reason Pascal's apothegm bids fair to remain a literary truth throughout all time to come. Another literary truth, and one which survived long not because it was relatively unimportant, but because it flourished in a field unconquered by science, is the saying—almost as classic in literature as the *Meditations* themselves—that Pascal "plumbed the depths of man's moral nature." Pascal flayed and tortured himself to death and died morbidly torturing those dearest to him, through a perversion of impulse which a glimmer of the clinical knowledge of man's moral nature availed of in good season would probably have relieved. The statement that Pascal "plumbed the depths of man's moral nature" still survives in wide circles as a literary truth. You will hear it repeated by people who in a crisis similar to those

Pascal blundered and bled his way through, would not turn to him for counsel but to an alienist. Nevertheless it survives only because these people, at least in their character as readers of literature, have not yet been reached by the advance of scientific knowledge.

There is of course a gift of imaginative sympathy, necessary above all to the clinical psychologist, to put him in possession of the data for a skilled application of his science. And this may to some extent be cultivated by reading the literary works of men preeminently endowed with it. There are other things besides knowledge. There is that gift which Morris Cohen calls "sound judgment," or the ability to "guess what is relevant and decisive" in situations not capable of minute analysis. It is true, as he says, that "in practice the statesman, the business man, and even the physician, may often find the remark of a novelist like Balzac of greater help than long chapters from the most scientific psychology." But this does not alter the truth I am proving, for my proof rests upon no adulation of science, and no schematic disjunction of it from any man's good sense, but quite the opposite, upon the assumption that science even in its most imposing forms is nothing but an *undistracted* effort to get knowledge or apply it. Lenin was a supreme example of that "sound judgment" which Morris Cohen perceives to be so vital in the social sciences, but Lenin's judgment was sound in the highest degree only because he had mastered to the last detail and without admixture of poetry all that any science had to say about his specialty of engineering revolution. As science extends and deepens its domain, those cases in which the soundest judgment can be rendered

by a man cultivating the mere art of letters will grow steadily fewer. That is the inexorable fact.

In 1863, in a letter to Renan, the French chemist Berthelot first clearly confronted this question of the realm of literary truth. He drew a distinction between "positive and universal science which imposes itself upon us by its own certitude," and those "poetic aperçus of a particular and individual order" to which he gave the quaint name of "ideal science." He defended the rights of this ideal science, identifying them with the right to liberty, but at the same time he asserted that positive science "declines no problem," and that the ideal science must be recognized to possess less certainty, and indeed no certainty at all and no probability, except as it rests "upon the same methods that make the force and certainty of positive science." The realm of these "poetic aperçus," and therewith the liberty of them, has greatly dwindled since that day. It has so dwindled that for us the scheme of Berthelot can no longer solve the problem. An intellectual poet cannot find to-day in this "ideal science" either the scope or force of conviction that his nature demands. Here he must be ever in a mood of circumspection, ever ready to retreat before the advancing columns of those whose devotion to truth is pure of the poetic motive.

There is another way, however, in which a poet can be intellectual—another way, perhaps, of defining "literary truth." Instead of offering for belief ideas too unimportant or too difficult of verification to have been really established as true, literature can offer ideas not for belief but for enjoyment. Ideas, we must remember, are not only "about" experience; they are also experiences, and so loved by poetic minds for their own sakes and regardless of their meaning's truth. We seldom realize—especially we pious Anglo-Saxons—how much the pleasure of a reading man consists in mere adventuring among solemn judgments which he does not dream of acting upon or accepting. He explores the books of wisdom as others explore Africa, not seeking tame maxims and pieces of serviceable counsel, but seeking strange, gorgeous or impressive scenery peopled with alien and undomesticable ideas. Who can resist the maxim of Vauvenargues, "To accomplish anything worthwhile, a man must always live as if he were never going to die," or refrain from reciting with Thomas à Kempis, "Know for certain that thou must lead a dying life"? Goethe remarks in praise of Shakespeare: "It would be hard to find a poet each of whose works was more thoroughly pervaded by a definite and effective idea than his." And he adds in illustration: "*Antony and Cleopatra* expresses with a thousand tongues the idea that pleasure and action are ever incompatible." What is it that this idea, which is not even the second cousin of a truth, can add to the play for a thinking mind like Goethe's? It has, he would say, a "literary validity." Even "superstition," he remarks elsewhere, "does not harm the poet, for he knows how to make its half-truths, to which he gives only a literary validity, count in manifold ways for good." What is this literary validity which may be possessed by a superstition, and by such an idea as that pleasure and action are ever incompatible? Can it mean anything but that the idea falls happily and with a ring of genuine appropriateness into its place? It is finely savored and well set out to be enjoyed. If the statement seems

extreme, it is only because the distinction here is not absolute, but is one of degree. There is a progressive relaxation of the interest in validity all the way from a report of Paul Heyl on *Gravitational Anisotropy in Crystals* to a book like Herbert Read's *The Sense of Glory,* in reading which no gentleman, I am sure, would have the crudity to ask the author what the Sense of Glory really is.

The French are so much less embarrassed than the English in the presence of a naked pleasure, that they find it quite natural to take this view of literary truth. In introducing his famous history of French Literature, Gustav Lanson remarks: "Literature has this superior excellence, that it accustoms us to take pleasure in ideas. It causes man to find in the exercise of his thought at once his joy, his repose and his renewal. . . ." Not a word here of truth. M. Lanson does add, to be sure, that literature is "in the most noble sense of the word a popularization of philosophy," but that I take to be his comment upon philosophy rather than a retraction of what he has said about literature. Of all Englishmen it was of course only John Keats who penetrated to the pith of this matter with his startling description of the quality which makes for success in literature as *Negative Capability.* "I mean . . ." he said, "when a man is capable of being in uncertainties, mysteries, doubts, without any irritable reaching after fact or reason. Coleridge, for instance, would let go by a fine isolated verisimilitude caught from the Penetralium of mystery, from being incapable of remaining content with half-knowledge. This pursued through volumes would perhaps take us no further than this, that with a great poet the sense of Beauty overcomes every other consideration, or rather obliterates all consideration."

Literature, then, as a thing distinct from science, may be a pure communication of experience; it may interpret experience in spheres as yet untouched by science; it may offer interpretations as intellectual things to be enjoyed and without a tense regard to their validity. . . . To which we must add that in these spirited activities, serious and yet set free from the tether of verification, new ideas and suggestions of infinite value to science may be born.

To my mind, however,—and I think most deep lovers of literature will agree,—for the creation of big masterpieces this is not enough. If the integral and solid deep element of truth-speaking is gone out of poetry, something is gone that must be searched after and brought back, if it can be, and at whatever cost. There is no comfort in the suggestion of I. A. Richards that the poet can still control our destiny—as does the campaign orator—by working up "emotional attitudes" which we will then meekly go forth and carry into action without the pretense on either side that he has spoken truth. With all respect to Mr. Richards's great merits, I think his plan for saving the race from moral and political chaos by uprooting emotions from the authentic objects to which nature had attached them, cultivating them in the library, and passing them round in little verbal capsules guaranteed to make people virtuous without troubling their intelligence, is merely the most fantastic and last effort of poetic literature to save its dignity in isolation from scientific knowledge. There is no hope of any renaissance in this.

For that hope we must turn to the possible results of a clear conscious-ness of the situation upon the part of poets. André Chénier could not remarry poetry with science, because he did not understand what had divided them, or what each in its isolation is. And Conrad Aiken fails for a like reason. At least he does not seem to know what poems are, or even what he thinks they are. In one place he describes the poet's function as to "compensate" with imaginings for impulses frustrated in the world of real experience; in another, to "translate in . . . form of literary art the consciousness of modern man"; in a third, to choose a "lofty promontory from which to view the world of [one's] experience"; and in a fourth, he says that poetry is "the most successful of the modes" by which man has "adjusted himself" to new experience. With these four contrary winds of purpose blowing in his head at once, it is no wonder Conrad Aiken finds himself confessing of his own metaphysical legend of *John Deth*: "My meaning was, and has largely remained, obscure to me." With all respect for Houston Peterson's persuasive volume, I do not believe it is the bewilderment of a modern world illumined by science that is reflected in Aiken's "Melody of Chaos"; it is the bewilderment of a modern poet reading science and trying to get it back into poetry without a plan.

It may be true, as Conrad Aiken says, that poetry is "once more slowly and painfully learning to think." I hope so, but I do not see the signs of it. I find the germs of a new literary era, not in poetry at all, but in a more humble tendency that has come among us without blare of trumpet or invocation of Lucretius—the tendency of men of letters to lend their pens to the agreeable communication of scientific knowledge. The whole aspect of our book-shelves and reading tables is changed already by this process. A textbook of science is no longer a vile, dog-eared and detested relic of school-days—best used even then as a missile—and now tossed up into the attic with the broken furniture and the half-worn shoes. It is an honorable and renowned volume, praised for its charm, and fast crowding along the shelf once monopolized by the Meditations, the Maxims, the Book of Apothegms or Collection of Essays, first series, second series and third. In America we used to have an imposing array of "literary" magazines—*The Atlantic Monthly, The North American Review, The Century, Scribner's, Harpers, The Forum.*—*The Century* is dead; *The Atlantic Monthly* has descended from its pedestal; *The North American Review* has followed *The Atlantic; Harpers* will accept nothing until you prove that it is not too "literary"; *Scribner's* is given over to "contemporary themes," and *The Forum* to "controversy." Of all that stately galaxy, only the poor *Bookman* totters along under the sagging banner of "literary truth." And even *The Bookman* forgetfully admits that this truth is not after all true—that "literature is primarily literature, a means of refined and intellectual pleasure." This change is no part of the jazz movement, or the reflection of a temporary taste for rapid and shallow stimulation. It is a part of the quick resistance of thoughtful people to the continuance of an activity that has become frivolous.

It has two aspects. It appears as a tendency of the man of letters to delve in the findings of science, or even to associate himself with scientists in order to give the world along with the pleasures of gracious writing some technical and dependable knowledge.

The fact that H. G. Wells, who has always insisted that the writer ought to class himself, "not with the artists but with the teachers and the priests and prophets," finds himself compelled in fulfilling his high purpose to humble his brilliant pen to a task of coöperation with technically trained specialists in producing a book of reliable knowledge about "life," becomes especially significant when you remember that for Matthew Arnold, less than fifty years ago, criticism of "life" was a phrase adequate to define the poet's function.

And this tendency on the literary side is supplemented by a tendency on the part of scientists to emerge from their dim laboratories and unventilated textbooks, and take a little exercise in the air of social communication—a tendency of which Sir James Jeans's book *The Universe Around Us* may serve as an example, because it is a book in which not only verified knowledge, but so far as possible the process by which it was verified, a glimpse of the scientist's experience, is made accessible, and made dramatic and beautiful to any person of intellectual tastes. The ablest literary men are serving an apprenticeship in science; the ablest scientists are serving an apprenticeship in the art of friendly communication. And the process is almost as important to science as it is to literature, for science is becoming so specialized in its own labors that the investigators in one field can hardly communicate in their technical language with those in another. For the purpose of understanding each other—if not indeed, sometimes, themselves—they must learn to express their findings in a somewhat literary language.

It is out of this language spoken by those who have dwelt with scientific knowledge—friends of its validity and of the cool scepticism in which it hangs suspended—and yet whose tongues and eye-balls have not grown too dry to taste and see the heaviness of sweet and bitter, the reality of color, that I look for a renaissance of truth-speaking poetry. I do not mean that works of poetry are to be text-books. To speak honestly, even Lucretius failed of a sustained poetical success in that genre. Nor do I mean that poets are to curb their whims and tack their poems carefully together on a last supplied by "Reason" or the latest discovery in the clinic or the laboratory. They will have to be spontaneous and have liberty. If they cannot be spontaneous after reading science scientifically, and knowing truth in her own terms, then my hope is utopian. But I believe that when they understand what science is, and what its division from poetry is, so that they can clearly know when they are doing one thing and when the other, when and in what manner they are combining the two, this will be possible. Knowledge is not hostile to spontaneity when it is clear and complete, not any more than the light of day is, which makes the world larger and more full of things. Even a pure poet can only be enriched by whatever knowledge he makes wholly his own. And a poet who wishes to be once more as of old a prophet and a truth-speaker, will *have* to make some genuine and verified, and as we say "systematic," knowledge his own. He will have to read some science deeply and become at home in the temple of science. There is no way to overcome a division of labor without retrogression, but for one person to perform the whole of both kinds of labor. And there is no way to re-assemble the divided product, but to understand where the division lies and what are

the functions and particular virtues of each part. It cannot be a mere wilful act of mixture now, a piece of intellectual mud-pie-making like D. H. Lawrence's *Fantasia of the Unconscious,* or Yeats's *Vision*—a return by sentimental fiat to the handicraft stage in the mind's history. It cannot be universal or undiscriminating. It cannot be accomplished by those blind to the difference between blowing grotesque bubble-castles of iridescent ideas and lending the warm weight of poetry to the expression of a general truth. There is no denying a stern limitation of the possibilities that lie before the literary mind in an age of science, an age which is perhaps the future history of man. I should express those limitations, however, not by saying that there will be no more great truth-speaking poets, but by saying that in the future such poets will have to be very great.

It is needless to say that if poetry and truth were once indiscriminately presented together by the same people and in the same books, poetry, once humbled of her independent pretension to *be* truth, can find ways to come back to truth and join with her to produce at times the old moving force. Poetry cannot be the criticism of life, but she can be the life of criticism. She is not the breath and finer spirit of knowledge, but she can breathe a fine spirit into knowledge. She has her ways—and she will find new ways—of enshrining, if not in the same word, yet in the same line, or page, or volume, the experience and the understanding of it—her ways of teaching by experience. They are not all destroyed because poetry and truth have in their natural growth divided, and can only sometimes and with deliberate art be recombined.

The thought turns back instinctively upon this theme to Goethe, the only man since poetry and science parted company who did work and play creatively in both fields. His example proves that this division can exist consciously within one mind, if the mind is flexible and fertile enough, without implying a dry poetry or an unreliable observation and experiment. Goethe was, to be sure, rather a romantic natural philosopher than a modern scientist so far as concerns his theoretical speculations. His color theory had only a "literary validity," and was so estimated by the physicists even of his own day. His describing fertilization as a "spiritual anastomosis," and saying that the tails of mammals may be regarded as an indication of the "*unendlichkeit* of organic being," will show how much poetry was still mingled with his biological speculations. He was rather at the stage of Kepler than of Isaac Newton—from whose "detested theories" he was indeed hailed by Schelling as a deliverer. Nevertheless he had the faculty of matter-of-fact observation and verification by experiment, and he made genuine contributions to the most exact knowledge—none more genuine, I should say, than his remark about the nature of poetry: "What need of much definition? Lively feeling of situations and power to express them make the poet."

That a man fruitfully active in several branches of science, and with this quite matter-of-fact conception of what poetry is, should have produced perhaps the richest and most varied poems of all our modern era except those of Shakespeare, seems a sufficient proof that this division of the minds of men and of their books and language which is causing such a desolation in contemporary letters, can be in instances surmounted. We must in honesty remember, however, that besides this matter-of-fact vein in which Goethe knew so well what poetry is—in which he knew how to contrast *Dichtung* with *Wahrheit*—there was another vein, a vein of gilding and of glorification, in which he talked of poetry like Wordsworth and Shelley, and himself defined the poet as "in essence . . . universal interpreter of nature." In a modern mind endowed and occupied like Goethe's the conflict between those two views of poetry could hardly lie concealed. If the poet is distinguished by his lively feeling of situations, he cannot then in essence be distinguished by his power to interpret them. There are only these two things in question—experience and the interpretation of it—and if one is poetry, the other so far as it succeeds is science. There does remain the question then, whether a universal genius like Goethe —a thinking singer—could grow up and come to flower in a civilization which confronted him with that contradiction—a civilization which would remind him continually that the true interpretation of colors rejects the lively feeling of them, and that he must ignore the interpretation in order to express the lively feeling, and that this is true not only of rainbow colors but of all the colors of life—a civilization which would lend him no eloquent phrase out of a great tradition with which to moderate at times this sharpening conflict. I think we may wisely leave that question to the universal genius himself to answer. Of this, however, I am sure—that such a poet could live and flourish in our civilization only on one condition, that he should not attempt to blur the conflict or cling to the tradition, but should boldly face it all out to the point of understanding.

1931

ARTISTS IN UNIFORM *

CHAPTER VI

THE SOUL OF MAN UNDER COMMUNISM

In my book setting forth the un-scientific character of Hegelian Marxism, I asserted that Lenin, in his practical politics and everyday attitude of mind, continually ignored this metaphysical conception in which he formerly believed. He was correctly denounced as a heretic by the well-trained priests of dialectic materialism, both revolutionary and reformist, throughout his life. And his heresy consisted essentially in regarding his purpose as a purpose rather than the reflection of a dialectic reality, in studying the existing facts as *conditions* which make its achievement possible rather than as *causes* which make it inevitable, and in taking generally the attitude of a scientific engineer rather than a metaphysical midwife of revolution. I cited seven modifications introduced by Lenin into the Marxian political system, all evidences of this sceptical independence of cosmic formulations which characterizes the modern engineering mind—his assertion of the indispensable role of the "professional revolutionist," his rejection of Mensheviks and of the "infantile left" on a psychological rather than a class basis, his greater emphasis upon the peasants and colonial peoples, the nature of his party and the role he gave it both in the revolutionary struggle and the state, his "policy of sharp turns," and his manner of arguing that a nation backward economically could take the lead in a social revolution.

Lenin's attitude toward our prob-

* Reprinted from *Artists in Uniform* by Max Eastman, by permission of Alfred A. Knopf, Inc. Copyright 1934 by Max Eastman.

lem of proletarian art and literature is an eighth evidence of his independence of the orthodox belief. Without the slightest effort to bring his words into accord with the Marxian theory of art as a mere function of the dialectic evolution of the forces of production, to say nothing of the intellectual fine-spinning with which Plekhanov tried to transform this into a Marxian system of aesthetics, or the juvenile bigotry of the young bureaucrats who were already preparing to transform this into the system of Art by Word-of-Order from the Party Executive—without so much as a how-do-you-do to any of this scholastic and ecclesiological balderdash surrounding and impending on him. Lenin pointed out the simple fact that the aim of the communists being to make life itself accessible to the masses, and art being of the essence of life, they should quit posing and orating about "proletarian art," and educate the masses to a point where they can enjoy art as it exists and know how to perceive it, and then let them proceed with the further joys and emoluments of its creation. I do not think I exaggerate the affirmative aspect of Lenin's views. He formally declared, of course, that "the Weltanshauung of Marxism is a correct expression of the interests, viewpoint and culture of the revolutionary proletariat," but all his talk and his concrete directives aim, not toward imposing a "correct" *Weltanshauung* upon the masses, but toward giving freedom to their own creative powers —a freedom in which, if it is genuine, they will certainly create as many *Weltanshauungs* as have the bourgeoisie and landlords in the past.

It would be impossible to exaggerate Lenin's disapproval of all of the first beginnings of this talk about the collectivization of art, and art as a class weapon, and art as party propaganda, that has been so sedulously piped throughout the world by Stalin's literary hacks and lackeys. That art both as an object and as a creative venture belongs among those riches, locked away by the masters throughout the ages, which he intends to seize and make accessible to all, is the suppressed premise in every fragment on this subject that survives from Lenin. He did not imagine that complete creative freedom will exist before a classless society is attained, but having seized the power, he desired instantly to use it to the extent possible in order to unlock creative and recreative culture to the toiling masses. That is what "proletarian art" meant, fundamentally, to Lenin. And that is what it will mean to any revolutionist for whom the purpose to achieve a free and reasonable society is a purpose rather than a theory of Being.

Indeed, I think such revolutionists will go beyond Lenin on these questions of the future. Among the elements of sheer utopianism perpetuated by the Marxian metaphysics, none is more fantastic than the idea that human nature is a mere function of the evolution of economic forces, an otherwise completely variable factor. Marxism knows nothing of Mendelian laws, of genes and chromosomes, of hereditary and acquired characters, of all that is comprised in Jenning's phrase, "The Biological Basis of Human Nature." Because of this ignorance—inevitable in Marx, a voluntary self-mutilation in his modern zealots—the idea has been engrafted upon the revolutionary science, and is still flourishing, that once industry is socialized, men will automatically become by instinct humble brothers. They will lose their taste for having personality, for dominance, for rabid selfhood, self-expression, "lordlike in-

dividualism." They will only ask to merge their egoisms in the juice of the "collective" being.

This brotherly prune-stew conception of the future is not due only to Marx's ignorance of biology. It is due also to the necessity under which Marx labored—since he was presenting a wish-fulfillment metaphysics as objective science—to hush the element of wish contained in it. Marx could not boldly take up, as all anarchists have and Anglo-Saxon socialists too, the question what kind of future world this organized class struggle can be made to give. "Reality is to be conceived as practical action . . . Social life is practical" was about all that he could say. "The working-class has not to realize an ideal, but only to release the elements of the new society." And Engels could but add: We are going "from the lower to the higher." To ask in a clear, loud voice, "What *is* higher?" would have shattered the whole system. And that question, not being asked by the conscious mind, was answered by the unconscious—was answered, that is, on the model of the bourgeois happy family and in the tradition of the prevailing churchly faith. It is Christianity, in short, and infant predilections, that have drawn the missing blueprint for this Marxian scheme of revolutionary engineering.

"All the emotions," says Trotsky, "which we revolutionists at the present time feel apprehensive of naming —so much have they been worn thin by hypocrites and vulgarians—such as disinterested friendship, love for one's neighbor, sympathy, will be the mighty ringing chords of Socialist poetry." I, for my part, would give more for one man honest enough to tell me he cannot love his neighbor than for a whole regiment sentimental enough to think they do. It is not only biology but Nietzsche with which the Marxian system needs a modern seasoning. It can pick up an epigram, too, on its way west from Oscar Wilde. "The chief advantage that would result from the establishment of Socialism," he exclaims in his *Soul of Man under Socialism*, "is, undoubtedly, the fact that Socialism would relieve us from that sordid necessity of living for others which, in the present condition of things, presses so hardly upon almost everybody."

There is little, even in the dialectic logic, to foretell a decline of individualism. There is still less in what the worker in revolt against wage-slavery wants. He may well want to lose his sense of personal distinction in the joys of that humane and rational collective where our present bloody competition for a livelihood has ceased. There is nothing to prevent his wanting this, and there will be nothing, let us hope, to stop his having it. He may, however, and he far more often will, want just that sense of "personality," that selfhood, self-expression, individualism, *lordly* individualism, which has been the privilege of his masters throughout history. Both of these human tendencies will be with us as long as man is. There is no magic in a changed industry to change the nature man inherits. Selective breeding is the sole technique we have as yet for doing that. We may legitimately hope that natural selection under a non-competitive system may in many generations reduce the numbers of the mercilessly shrewd and cruel, and habit, education and tradition still more quickly blunt their claws. But we have no ground to hope, nor can we reasonably wish, that under any system persons will cease to be born and grow up harsh-grained and self-assertive, intolerant

of bonds, repelled by the mere thought of universal brotherhood, and individualistic to the point of hating all collective effort and emotion. To me it seems that when men's rivalrous propulsions are cut off from satisfaction in the sphere of acquisition, we shall see a greater, not a less, growth of self-assertiveness in art. Just here the Marxist's vision of the future seems both more utopian and less vitally inspiring than the poet's.

Even if we must get permission from Moscow, let us at least try to have our revolution *take place* in America, and then we shall see whether there is not some western truth in this more western thought.

In so far, at least, as concerns the hope of a great art in the future, this thought is absolutely vital. "Art," as Matthew Josephson has been courageous enough to state, "demands a lonely and personal effort, rather than a collective one." And because the success of a proletarian revolution has come to mean a perpetuation of that collectivity-of-the-cup's-dregs which has been the proletarian's lot in history, he feels impelled to add: "I should like . . . to see all discussions of aesthetic procedure cease, and the question whether art is to survive at all—and how—taken up." If the practical scheme for bringing about the liberation of mankind from slavery to economics had not been identified with the workings of the cosmos, and this metaphysical operation turned into a weapon of bureaucratic boss-rule, and the aim thus twice forgotten, we should look as instinctively as Oscar Wilde did to that day of liberation, to ensure not only the survival but the flourishing of art—most often lonely and personal still, but in open meadows and to a height and quality undreamed of in the old plutocratic hot-beds.

Look at them again, those slogans of the Artists' International:

> Art renounces individualism.
> Art is to be collectivized.
> Art is to be systemized.
> Art is to be organized.
> Art is to be disciplined.
> Art is to be created "under the careful yet firm guidance" of a political party.
> Art is to be wielded as a weapon.

Could any set of ideas more neatly summarize the attitude of the vicariously infantile and office-holding bigot who calls himself the proletariat, not because he feels with or for the members of the working class, but because it swells his importance and accords with his intimate knowledge of the nature and purpose of the universe to do so? To an aspiring proletarian, or anyone joining humbly and with clear purpose in the struggle to emancipate the proletariat, art is recreation, venture, life itself, a casting of new light on life. Art is what the proletarian has taken weapons in his hands to win. So is individuality. Does it never occur to these sergeant-priests of proletarianism that perhaps the toiling masses have had their bellyful in forty thousand years of being "collectivized," of being "systemized," "organized," "disciplined," of doing whatever they do while the sun is in the air and fresh blood in their veins under the "careful yet firm guidance" of some self-important body of functionaries? The purpose of the revolutionary movement was to emancipate the proletariat, and so humanity, from the strait-jacket of class division and class rule. To this end the student who understands it best and the proletarian who feels it most must unite and organize and fight. The chief peril is that this union may not be real, that it may not survive the victory—

that the proletariat may be used in its own revolution as it was in all others to win the power for a new privileged class. No clearer evidence of the presence of that peril could be offered than this hasty grabbing off of the whole domain of the free creative spirit in the name of a political party dominated by its non-proletarian functionary apparatus, and an esoteric theory of the universe incomprehensible to any but highly specialized technicians in the professorship of philosophy.

1934

LINCOLN STEFFENS
(1866–1936)

FROM
THE SHAME OF THE CITIES *

PHILADELPHIA: CORRUPT AND CONTENTED

Other American cities, no matter how bad their own condition may be, all point with scorn to Philadelphia as worse—"the worst-governed city in the country." St. Louis, Minneapolis, Pittsburg submit with some patience to the jibes of any other community; the most friendly suggestion from Philadelphia is rejected with contempt. The Philadelphians are "supine," "asleep"; hopelessly ring-ruled, they are "complacent." "Politically benighted," Philadelphia is supposed to have no light to throw upon a state of things that is almost universal.

This is not fair. Philadelphia is, indeed, corrupt; but it is not without significance. Every city and town in the country can learn something from the typical experience of this great representative city. New York is excused for many of its ills because it is the metropolis, Chicago because of its forced development; Philadelphia is our "third largest" city and its growth has been gradual and natural. Immigration has been blamed for our municipal conditions; Philadelphia, with 47 per cent. of its population native-born of native-born parents, is the most American of our greater cities. It is "good," too, and intelligent. I don't know just how to measure the intelligence of a community, but a Pennsylvania college professor who declared to me his belief in education for the masses as a way out of political corruption, himself justified the "rake-off" of preferred contractors on public works on the ground of a "fair business profit." Another plea we have made is that we are too busy to attend to public business, and we have promised, when we come to wealth and leisure, to do better. Philadelphia has long enjoyed great and widely distributed prosperity; it is the city of homes; there is a dwelling house for every five persons—men, women, and children,—of the population; and the people give one a sense of more leisure and repose than any community I have ever dwelt in. Some Philadelphians account for their political state on the ground of their ease and comfort. There is another class of optimists whose hope is in an "aristocracy" that is to come by and by; Philadelphia is surer that it has a "real aristocracy" than any other place in the world, but its aristocrats, with few exceptions, are in the ring, with it, or of no political use. Then we hear that we are a young people and that when we are older and "have traditions," like some of the old countries, we also will be honest. Philadelphia is one of the oldest of our cities and treasures for us scenes and relics of some of the noblest traditions of "our fair land." Yet I was told once, "for a joke," a party

of boodlers counted out the "divvy" of their graft in unison with the ancient chime of Independence Hall.

Philadelphia is representative. This very "joke," told, as it was, with a laugh, is typical. All our municipal governments are more or less bad, and all our people are optimists. Philadelphia is simply the most corrupt and the most contented. Minneapolis has cleaned up, Pittsburg has tried to, New York fights every other election, Chicago fights all the time. Even St. Louis has begun to stir (since the elections are over), and at its worst was only shameless. Philadelphia is proud; good people there defend corruption and boast of their machine. My college professor, with his philosophic view of "rake-offs," is one Philadelphia type. Another is the man, who, driven to bay with his local pride, says: "At least you must admit that our machine is the best you have ever seen."

Disgraceful? Other cities say so. But I say that if Philadelphia is a disgrace, it is a disgrace not to itself alone, nor to Pennsylvania, but to the United States and to American character. For this great city, so highly representative in other respects, is not behind in political experience, but ahead, with New York. Philadelphia is a city that has had its reforms. Having passed through all the typical stages of corruption, Philadelphia reached the period of miscellaneous loot with a boss for chief thief, under James McManes and the Gas Ring 'way back in the late sixties and seventies. This is the Tweed stage of corruption from which St. Louis, for example, is just emerging. Philadelphia, in two inspiring popular revolts, attacked the Gas Ring, broke it, and in 1885 achieved that dream of American cities—a good charter. The present condition of Philadelphia, therefore, is not that which precedes, but that which follows reform, and in this distinction lies its startling general significance. What has happened since the Bullitt Law or charter went into effect in Philadelphia may happen in any American city "after reform is over."

For reform with us is usually revolt, not government, and is soon over. Our people do not seek, they avoid self-rule, and "reforms" are spasmodic efforts to punish bad rulers and get somebody that will give us good government or something that will make it. A self-acting form of government is an ancient superstition. We are an inventive people, and we think that we shall devise some day a legal machine that will turn out good government automatically. The Philadelphians have treasured this belief longer than the rest of us and have tried it more often. Throughout their history they have sought this wonderful charter and they thought they had it when they got the Bullitt Law, which concentrates in the mayor ample power, executive and political, and complete responsibility. Moreover it calls for very little thought and action on the part of the people. All they expected to have to do when the Bullitt Law went into effect was to elect as mayor a good business man, who, with his probity and common sense, would give them that good business administration which is the ideal of many reformers.

The Bullitt Law went into effect in 1887. A committee of twelve—four men from the Union League, four from business organizations, and four from the bosses—picked out the first man to run under it on the Republican ticket, Edwin H. Fitler, an able, upright business man, and he was elected. Strange to say, his administration was satisfactory to the citizens, who speak well of it to this day, and to the politicians also; Boss McManes (the ring was broken, not the boss) took to the next national convention from Philadelphia a delegation solid for Fitler for President of the United States. It was a farce, but it pleased Mr. Fitler, so Matthew S. Quay, the State boss, let him have a complimentary vote on the first ballot. The politicians "fooled" Mr. Fitler, and they "fooled" also the next business mayor, Edwin S. Stuart, likewise a most estimable gentleman. Under these two administrations the foundation was laid for the present government of Philadelphia, the corruption to which the Philadelphians seem so reconciled, and the machine which is "at least the best you have ever seen."

The Philadelphia machine isn't the best. It isn't sound, and I doubt if it would stand in New York or Chicago. The enduring strength of the typical American political machine is that it is a natural growth—a sucker, but deep-rooted in the people. The New Yorkers vote for Tammany Hall. The Philadelphians do not vote; they are disfranchised, and their disfranchisement is one anchor of the foundation of the Philadelphia organization.

This is no figure of speech. The honest citizens of Philadelphia have no more rights at the polls than the negroes down South. Nor do they fight very hard for this basic privilege. You can arouse their Republican ire by talking about the black Republican votes lost in the Southern States by white Democratic intimidation, but if you remind the average Philadelphian that he is in the same position, he will look startled, then say, "That's so, that's literally true, only I never thought of it in just that way." And it is literally true.

The machine controls the whole

process of voting, and practices fraud at every stage. The assessor's list is the voting list, and the assessor is the machine's man. "The assessor of a division kept a disorderly house; he padded his list with fraudulent names registered from his house; two of these names were used by election officers. . . . The constable of the division kept a disreputable house; a policeman was assessed as living there. . . . The election was held in the disorderly house maintained by the assessor. . . . The man named as judge had a criminal charge for a life offense pending against him. . . . Two hundred and fifty-two votes were returned in a division that had less than one hundred legal votes within its boundaries." These extracts from a report of the Municipal League suggest the election methods. The assessor pads the list with the names of dead dogs, children, and non-existent persons. One newspaper printed the picture of a dog, another that of a little four-year-old negro boy, down on such a list. A ring orator in a speech resenting sneers at his ward as "low down" reminded his hearers that that was the ward of Independence Hall, and, naming the signers of the Declaration of Independence, he closed his highest flight of eloquence with the statement that "these men, the fathers of American liberty, voted down here once. And," he added, with a catching grin, "they vote here yet." Rudolph Blankenburg, a persistent fighter for the right and the use of the right to vote (and, by the way, an immigrant), sent out just before one election a registered letter to each voter on the rolls of a certain selected division. Sixty-three per cent. were returned marked "not at," "removed," "deceased," etc. From one four-story house where forty-four voters were addressed, eighteen letters came back

undelivered; from another of forty-eight voters, came back forty-one letters; from another sixty-one out of sixty-two; from another forty-four out of forty-seven. Six houses in one division were assessed at one hundred and seventy-two voters, more than the votes cast in the previous election in any one of two hundred entire divisions.

The repeating is done boldly, for the machine controls the election officers, often choosing them from among the fraudulent names; and when no one appears to serve, assigning the heeler ready for the expected vacancy. The police are forbidden by law to stand within thirty feet of the polls, but they are at the box and they are there to see that the machine's orders are obeyed and that repeaters whom they help to furnish are permitted to vote without "intimidation" on the names they, the police, have supplied. The editor of an anti-machine paper who was looking about for himself once told me that a ward leader who knew him well asked him into a polling place. "I'll show you how it's done," he said, and he had the repeaters go round and round voting again and again on the names handed them on slips. * * *

1903

FROM

THE AUTOBIOGRAPHY *

PROPHECY

In Russia the ultimate purpose of this conscious process of merging politics and business is to abolish the political state as soon as its sole uses are served: to make defensive war abroad and at home and to teach the

* From *The Autobiography of Lincoln Steffens,* copyright, 1931, by Harcourt, Brace and Company, Inc.

people by propaganda and by enforced conditions to substitute new for old ideas and habits. The political establishment is a sort of political scaffolding within which the temporary dictatorship is building all agriculture, all industries, and all businesses into one huge centralized organization. They will point out to you from over there that our businesses, too, are and long have been coming together, merging trusts into combines, which in turn unite into greater and greater monopolies. They think that when we western reformers and liberals resist this tendency we are standing in the way of a natural, inevitable economic compulsion to form "one big union" of business. All that they have changed is the ownership, which they (and Henry Ford) think is about all that's wrong. Aren't they right to encourage the process? Aren't we wrong to oppose it? Anyway President Hoover's conference of the masters of the mergers to meet a business situation was a call to them to put a head on business, see it as a whole, and act upon it with him as a unit. What they proposed was not enough to stay the general depression, which has causes beyond their ideas and habits of thought, but it did take them out of themselves for a moment. They agreed to list the large expenditures they were going to make anyhow and add to it as much other building, buying, and improving as they could safely venture upon—this was for the psychological effect. But it was a recognition of the plain truth that good business as a whole is for the common good and requires the co-operation of the people as a whole. It was propaganda. It was a Plan.

It was then that Henry Ford raised his wages, as an example, and saw and said why the others could not heed. They had stockholders to consider, and the stock market. Ford had neither of these to contend with. He had just been scrapping his old car and the machinery that made it. That had used up many millions of his cash capital. But he was able financially, and, a dictator in his business, he was free, to declare that a large part of his profits should go to his workers to enable them to go on buying and consuming; there were no stockholders to demand that it go into dividends. The other business bosses were not dictators but representatives, and they represented stockholders or stock which has rights, sometimes prior rights. Our culture, theirs, teaches that when there's a crisis and something has to be cut, when the choice is between the non-producing stockholders and the producing wage-workers, it is "naturally" wages, not dividends, that we reduce first. At that White House conference which contemplated the wage-workers as the consuming market, those business men saw that this natural readiness to cut wages must be checked. They would not raise wages with Ford, but they realized that wages must not be cut. And they taught that. And that is a sign, I think, of a direction in which this mammoth movement we cannot stop or turn is going.

I heard employers out west saying that they must not cut wages. I pressed the question of what they would do when the test came: "Will you cut dividends or wages?" And in the words of one of them, they answered, "Oh, but we can't cut wages." They did, some of them, and they discharged workers till unemployment became a nervous problem. Business men could not this time act upon the idea, but they had and they could utter the idea that good wages were at the bottom of good business and a good market. This is progress. American business has come, market-wise, to the idea that Bolshevik Russia is putting into its unwritten constitution, that the producers and the consumers are one and the same people and that production and consumption must about balance; else there must be foreign markets and empires and panics.

But there's that other reason why seeming masters of business could not follow Ford and raise wages—the stock market. At a time long ago when there were a lot of railroad disasters, I asked a shrewd New York banker, just for the fun of it, what the matter was.

"Have you financiers no railroad men to operate your railroads?"

"Yes," he said. "We have them. We have men trained in operation from the ground up, and some of them have been promoted clear to the top. But we find that when we take a crackerjack of a division superintendent from somewhere out west, bring him here as a vice president, and raise his salary from—nothing to $25,000 and over $50,000, he—and his wife, who came here feeling rich and well paid, soon learn that no fifty thousand a year, no salary a year, is in it with what they can make on the side, in Wall Street; so they begin to get rich, prominent, and neglectful of railroading."

This is generally true. All the great corporations suffer somewhat from the distracting discovery of their ablest managers that, being in on the game, they can make more in Wall Street than they can in manufacturing. Some companies have dealt with the problem of keeping their managers' minds on the business by forming them into pools and letting them tell off some one of their number to do the gambling for all. Even then they all are interested in the stock market as much

as in the goods market, and this speculative interest keeps the managers of industry more or less on the side of the capitalists, big and little.

In France, less so than in England, business generally is in the possession of stockholders and others in the second, third, and fourth generation. These owners employ managers, who are held back from scrapping old for new machinery and methods by the conservative interest of the stockholders in profits which they take out of the business and spend on their lives of leisure. I have heard foreign corporation officers complaining of the way the resources of their factories are absorbed to no business uses, and I have seen the mouths of American industrialists water at the sight of famous, great, but backward foreign plants. "How I would like to get hold of those works! By putting in our new machinery and methods and cutting out the waste in dividends—for a while—I could make millions of dollars where the French now make millions of francs."

The shortest story I ever heard of the state of England today was told me in the smoking-room of a ship by an American business man who had been called for consultation on the bad condition of a fine old manufacturing concern in England.

"I showed them that their machinery and methods were antediluvian and suggested scrapping them all and reorganizing completely. They could see that that should be done, but they held back, and I could not make out what was the matter till at last one of them said:

"'We could persuade our stockholders to rebuild and reorganize once. They would forego dividends and pay for one such change to bring us up to your degree of efficiency. But would not you in the next few years be inventing new machinery, and would not we, to keep up with you, have to scrap again and again?'

"When I said, 'Yes, probably,' they threw up their hands and said, 'We could never draw our stockholders into any such constant policy of periodic improvements.' And there was nothing doing."

The Americans who talked thus did not see, apparently, that there was an inevitable conflict of interest between ownership and management. One of them came home and stood for the multiplication of his company's stock issue. That put up the price of the shares, and he had a lot of shares. He made a fortune, but he was binding his company to pay dividends on a capital increased to represent profits earned in good times but not likely to be earned in bad times. He would want later to cut wages to keep up the payments to the wasters who own his shares and would be asking for economies, conservatism in adventure, like the older, foreign profiteers. All the speculating managers in the Coolidge boom were tempted in this direction by their own gambling interests.

But I think I saw the wedge go in that will show them the split between owners and managers. The banks are, economically, the representatives of ownership. They speculate, too; they sometimes deal in, they always hold, shares. When they thought they had Ford once, he sounded them, and they said that what they wanted was the treasury, not the presidency, not the managers of plants and makers of cars, but the place where they could handle the money and own and manipulate the stock. And what a good time they would have had issuing a new lot of Ford shares!

Now bankers are stock-market-wise,

and they normally govern it. But in the late Coolidge boom, when the managers of industry were bulling stock prices against the opposition of the banks, they discovered that they contributed to the power of the banks over them by first depositing, then borrowing, their own companies' money. They stopped this. They very generally put their moneys directly into the call loan market, freed it for the moment, and learned for all time that they could share the power of the banks, and not only over the stock market.

This and other signs suggest that financial sovereignty, and therefore business, and therefore political sovereignty, in the United States, may be passing from the banks to the management of industry—the management, not the ownership. Indeed it looks as if the fundamental issue may be between management and ownership—not, as in my day, labor and capital, but producers and owners.

Henry Ford at the White House conference blurted a parallel prophecy of the prospect when he said to a reporter that business will all be run for a living some day, without any profits to divide. An industry would have to pay, of course, but the money made could not be wasted in dividends, melons, and big salaries to enrich the owners. It would have to be put back into the business. Business men would have to work as he does now, for a living. This must come generally, he foresaw, because he was doing it; and if one did it his competitors would have to, and not only in one industry.

For another perception, new, true, and fecund, by the industrial mind, is that all businesses are in competition. That two grocery stores, two railroads, several oil concerns compete was obvious, and business men acted on it. They formed trusts to establish monopolies, but they did not realize, till mass production came, that railroads compete also with automobiles, that all transportation competes with the radio, with the power and light business, with the grocery trust, and with the landlord. They are all in a struggle for their shares of the average wage. It is amusing and it is encouraging to have a big oil man sit down with you to explain that if labor is getting, say, ten dollars a day, then oil and the movies have to compete for the lion's share of ten dollars.

With this articulate perception goes another, still more far-reaching, whispered "hunch" or insight that the poor rich, the middle class of quiet leisure, does not count in this machine age of mass production. These people do not buy staples like the Ford cars; they are not important in business. The people who live in large part on dividends and interest would be wiped out or driven back to work if the profits of industry were to go back into the business for wages, new machinery, and improvements generally. But that is what is happening everywhere in the western world. The Russian Revolution consciously abolished the middle class. The great war ruined—all wars ruin—whole layers of the middle class. The crash of the Coolidge boom—all panics, depressions, and disasters reduce the leisure class. Every great change, every economic crisis, the whole movement of civilized life, tends to concentrate riches in the hands of a few, who, in a generation or two, have to hire and depend upon managers, who acquire thus the power which they are beginning to feel, seize, and use—to reduce the world to workers, all.

The good people whom I have found to be "no good," who carry through no reforms, who oppose all change as soon as they understand it —these, the great obstacle to all progress, whose incomes are a wasteful graft on business, in which they are a useless hindrance, whose "moral" influence in art, literature, education, culture, and business is as "bad" as it is in politics, these people are doomed outside as they are in—Russia. I could see it in small towns in the west, where the chain stores, for instance, were threatening the retail livings of the local merchants, who cried out that they, the leading citizens as well as the leading business men, might have to give up their businesses and go to work for salaries or even wages; they and their children.

A tragedy this, for the middle men, the middle class, who, in all countries call themselves the backbone of society. But there is a bright light to be seen through the darkness. We are coming to the seven-hour day of the five-day week. Leisure, as well as wealth, is to be distributed, apparently, again, by the same process as in Russia. There the Soviet government, with a plan, foresees that in a country where there are only workers and managers, with no owners and grafters —in an economic democracy the workers with machines will have shorter and shorter hours. That means leisure. So care is taken now to develop in labor the habits and taste to use well the probably many idle hours each day or the many idle days of every year of the masses. Workers are encouraged, therefore, to go to concerts, operas, theaters, ballets; they are guided through art galleries, where I heard them instructed in the craftsmanship of painting and sculpture. The problems, skill, and technique of the artist were described in terms of carpentry for a carpenter's union, and other trades heard the same lesson in terms of their own handicrafts.

The preparation in America for the dawning future is not so intelligent, conscious, and purposeful, but it is evident. The old arts of the theater, literature, painting, have got too far ahead of the crowds to be understood by them, but business is doing its blind best by what we call contemptuously commercial art to show the work of painters, for example, in all sorts of advertising. That gives painters a conspicuous, big place to hang their pictures. But the blindest, most characteristic art movement of our age of machinery is the movie and the talkie-movie, a new art that can include all the other arts. And mass producers, who are business men and not reformers, philanthropists and (not conscious) prophets, run their art for the consuming masses, who rush in crowds to see and support it. As they must. In Hollywood I have heard with my optimistic grin the imported writers and artists grieving and cursing because, with such a wide market as they have to serve to meet their extravagant costs, they could not "raise" the cinema any faster than "the mob" could go in appreciation. They tried, but they failed. They complained eloquently, and my kind of men and women sympathized with them, but I thought that I was seeing something new and wonderful under the sun through their tears and rage: that this new machine mass art cannot develop for its own sake; it is so tied to the democracy that it cannot rise to its obviously potential heights without lifting and being lifted by the human race.

1931

GRANVILLE HICKS
(1901–   )

LITERATURE AND REVOLUTION *

It is not without hesitation that I speak on such a subject before such a gathering. I know that to do so invites misunderstanding, for the theories I shall try to expound are not isolated; they derive from and depend upon a body of thought that extends into philosophy, history, economics, and political strategy. I do not mean that the Communist party has an official position on literature; nor, if it did, could I present myself as its spokesman. I mean merely that a full statement of my views would involve an exposition and defense of historical materialism, the Marxian conception of the class struggle, Marxian economics, and the Communist program for the overthrow of capitalism and the establishment of the dictatorship of the proletariat. Of course no aesthetic theory can be properly discussed without some consideration of its philosophical foundations and its social implications, but the foundations and implications of my theory are less familiar, and perhaps, to most of you, less acceptable than those that are ordinarily taken into account in aesthetic discourse. My exposition will, therefore, seem fragmentary, and you may well be conscious of assumptions that are not shared by you and cannot, within the limits of this paper, be defended by me.

To obviate this difficulty as far as is possible, I shall approach my subject by way of a rather elementary analysis of the nature and function of literature. I should describe a work of literature as the presentation of a particular fragment of experience in the light of the author's conception of the totality of experience. The definition is neither original nor uncommon. Something of the sort is implicit in most of the definitions, from Plato's and Aristotle's to those of contemporary aestheticians. Matthew Arnold said essentially the same thing when he called literature the criticism of life; to the experience that is his immediate theme the author brings the results of a larger experience, and it is the juxtaposition of the two that gives his work its value. Indeed, the simple proposition that selection is the basis of all art implies the existence of standards, beliefs, predispositions, and prejudices according to which the selection is made; and at their highest these ideas and moods are integrated into a world-view, or, if that is too abstract and intellectual a term to describe the mental processes of an artist, into a world-attitude.

The lyric poet is supposed to be, and indeed is, concerned with the immediate experience; and yet almost any lyric, certainly any body of lyrics, impresses the reader with a sense that the immediate experience draws its significance, for poet and reader alike, from the organized body of experience with which it is associated. Wordsworth, Shelley, and Tennyson occur to the mind at once as obvious examples; each saturated the least pretentious of his verses with all that he thought and felt about life. The sensation of the moment seems to occupy Keats, but careful reading reveals in his work the outlines of a clear and concrete world-attitude, and he comes to seem a more genuinely philosophical poet than Shelley or Tennyson. Baudelaire, to take another example at random, was once claimed by the theoreticians of pure poetry as

their private possession, but now **T. S.** Eliot and his party describe him as an ethical and religious poet.

Nothing could be easier than to multiply examples from the lyricists, and lyric poetry is, by common consent, the least philosophical of literary forms. There is scarcely a novelist or dramatist of importance who has not provided material for a doctoral dissertation on his philosophy. A novel or play, by the mere fact that it binds into some sort of unity a variety of experiences, clearly reveals its author's assumptions. We come to know his personal tastes, his system of values, his conception of human nature, and his views on the destiny of the race. Any one of us could roughly define the world-attitude of hundreds of writers. Of course, our statements would be inadequate; they would be bare formulas, stripped of the substance that the artist's imagination gives; but they would symbolize a reality that we all could recognize.

Let us bear this definition in mind as we go on to discuss the effect of literature. Reading has, we all assume, some sort of effect. The crude conception of literature as either beneficial or detrimental to morals, and the value judgments based on that conception, have largely been discarded, but rather because of changing standards of morals than because of changing views of literature. The humanists, though scoffing at the black-and-white, good-bad verdicts of the moralists, postulate an ethical effect of literature and base their whole aesthetics on the assumption. Even the impressionists grant, and indeed emphasize, a personal effect, though refusing to generalize. The question is complex, and there is no easy solution. I. A. Richards, I believe, has come closer, in his *Principles of Literary Criticism,* to a comprehensive account than any other writer I know. "We pass as a rule," he says, "from a chaotic to a better organized state by ways we know nothing about. Typically through the influence of other minds. Literature and the arts are the chief means by which these influences are diffused."

This description, even without the evidence Richards adduces from psychology in support of it, commends itself because it recognizes both the many-sidedness and the subtlety of the effect that literature may have. We all realize that ordinarily a work of literature does not impel us to do some certain thing—neither to commit adultery, as the moralists fear, nor to lynch the nearest capitalist, as some propagandists seem to hope. Occasionally, under the right circumstances, a work of art may inspire in certain persons a sharp emotion that finds immediate outlet in action, but usually we sit calmly at home in our armchairs, read our masterpiece, put it down, turn out the lights, go to bed, and go to sleep. Yet we are all conscious that certain novels or plays or poems have influenced our lives, and we may suspect that every book has some influence, imperceptible though it may be.

To define this influence we have to consider the relation of reading to actual experience. Reading is not a substitute for experience. As Kenneth Burke says, the death by torture of some admired hero of fiction is less painful than one's own toothache, and the most beautiful description of a garden cannot give us the same sort of pleasure as a bunch of flowers. But it is equally true that the account of a toothache in a novel may linger in our minds when the memory of some painful accident we have endured has been dispelled, and the description of a single flower may rouse a sharper emotion than any experience in countryside or conservatory. The author cannot give us the experience with the intensity it would have, even for us insensitive beings, in real life, but he can reveal its relationship to other experiences in such a way that our own experiences, of similar and perhaps even of different sorts, take on new meaning. He can bring into truer perspective whole realms of emotion and thought, and the new perception we acquire conditions our subsequent responses to the events of our lives. This, I gather, is what Richards means when he speaks of passing from a chaotic to a better organized state.

Even this summary account should make clear why I have attached so much importance to the world-attitude of the author. I reiterate that this need not be an articulate philosophy; and in any case it must be more than that. It is a way of seeing, feeling, acting, and it may be completely non-intellectualized. The artist is important for civilization because he is not limited to intellectual formulas, because, if he is inferior to the scientist in precision, he is superior to him in scope, because he can include so much that is important in life but as yet baffles quantitative measurement or logical definition. And yet we must not be deceived into thinking that the responses of the artist are fragmentary or disorganized. Some critics speak of pure experience. There is no such thing, although great physical pain perhaps approximates it. Pure experience would be entirely physiological and absolutely ineffable. Experience has meaning when it is related to other experiences, and the wider the relationships the greater the meaning. Art is the representation—or perhaps I should say the discovery or even the creation—of these relationships, not in an abstract system, but in a dynamic, living integration.

You will perceive that I attach only secondary importance to the technical problems of communication. Form and content are so closely connected that one cannot be profitably discussed apart from the other. If I may appeal to our common experience, I should like to point out that English teachers must be particularly aware of the limitations of technical instruction. Nine out of ten faulty themes could be fundamentally improved only if we could change the mental operations of their authors, could make them see differently, feel differently, think differently. H. G. Wells's comments on the theories of Henry James, in his *Experiment in Autobiography,* show that their quarrel was not really concerned with technique, though it seemed to be, but with their conception of the purpose of fiction, their understanding of the nature of life, and their active response to the world in which they lived. James's prefaces are extraordinary documents in the analysis of the novel, but they are also revelations of his world-attitude, and it may be doubted whether an author with an entirely different world-attitude could possibly avail himself of James's technical devices. Much criticism of poetry takes the form of painstaking dissection of figures of speech; such criticism obviously, if it is at all useful, is not merely technical; it concerns itself with the author's perceptive qualities. I do not want to seem to claim too much, but I think you will grant that Theodore Dreiser's sentence structure could be improved only if you eradicate his muddle-headedness, and that Walt Whitman's stylistic weaknesses are closely related to the confusion and the diffuseness of his mind. At the same time, I would maintain that Whitman and Dreiser are relatively great writers, not only in spite of their technical defects, but in spite of the incoherence in their world-attitudes. The technical facility of minor writers seldom commands respect, for the reader realizes that they achieve it by restricting the scope of their imaginative efforts. The writer cannot communicate more than he has to say, and if he deliberately chooses to do less, so much the worse for him.

If what I have said is sound, it is on a writer's world-attitude that we must concentrate if we wish to understand him and to interpret and explain him to others. At this point there may be objection. Someone will say, "You can explain Shakespeare's attitude and you can explain Lyly's attitude, but will that explain Shakespeare's superiority to Lyly?" Not entirely, I grant. No writer, for that matter, can ever be completely explained, and it seems to be the elements that make the difference between genius and talent, as we ordinarily use the words, that are hardest to explain. No method has proved adequate. The psychoanalysts certainly have not succeeded. Joseph Wood Krutch explains, more or less convincingly, certain of the peculiarities of Poe's mind, but he would be the first to admit that he is a long way from showing the reasons for Poe's virtues as a poet. All that I can say is that the more fully we understand the author's world-attitude, not as it may be stated in some bare formula but in the rich and living complexity of his imaginative functioning, the closer we come to understanding his genius. And, moreover, if we can understand the way in which his world-attitude developed, we at least see him in relation to the men and movement of his own age, to the rest of humanity, in short. The explanation of literary phenomena, if it is more than an intellectual exercise, is intended to help the reader to understand and appreciate what he reads. Such understanding is accomplished, not by isolating the author from the world in which we live, but by finding his true place in it.

I have implied that the author's world-attitude is a social phenomenon. If the adjective is correctly understood, the fact is obvious. Certainly, the artist does not spin his world-attitude out of himself; it is something that is created by contact with his environment. The artist's mind grows as any mind grows, and that process, as Piaget, for example, has shown, is a social process. We need not go as far as the Behaviorists, and view the mind of the newborn infant as a *tabula rasa*; even if there are inherited instincts and aptitudes, their operation is environmentally determined.

No, the only question is what environmental influences are most important. The psychological critic carefully examines the artist's life from birth to maturity, seeking for clues in family relationships, physical conditions, and personal contacts. The social critic examines the currents of thought and emotion in the artist's era. Both are concerned with social phenomena; both examine the artist's environment. The two methods are complementary, and adequate explanation requires that both shall be used. It is, however, possible to argue that one is more important than the other. I think the social method is more useful, and fortunately so, since the facts essential to satisfactory psychological analysis are rarely available.

Illustration cannot prove my contention but may clarify it. Ludwig Lewisohn makes much of the point that Walt Whitman was homosexual, and thinks that this explains the peculiarly emotional form that Whitman's theory of human brotherhood assumed. He may be right, but how much less important this is than the democratic theory itself, which obviously cannot be explained in terms of sexual abnormality! Whitman's father was a workingman, and Whitman was definitely a part of the masses about whom he wrote. From the first he inclined to the theories of the Jacksonians, and these theories were the foundation of the conception of democratic comradeship that he made his theme. American conditions in the decades before the Civil War created the whole philosophy of democratic individualism, and Whitman's work was that of elaboration and imaginative application. His putative homosexuality can at best only partly explain his enthusiasm for the democratic ideal, and it cannot at all explain the development of democratic sentiment and theory.

It is by way of the discovery of sexual aberrations that the psychological critics usually attempt to explain literary work. Mr. Lewisohn finds Emerson and Thoreau sexually frigid. Mr. Krutch believes that Poe suffered from a mother-fixation, and I understand that Amabel Williams-Ellis has maintained that Ruskin was the victim of a similar misfortune. Other authors have been similarly treated: Keats, Baudelaire, Emily Dickinson, D. H. Lawrence, and even Shakespeare. It would be foolish to ridicule this method, for it may have useful results, but it can explain relatively little.

If what we are seeking is understanding, the important thing is to see the artist in relation to his age: Marlowe against a background of Elizabethan expansiveness, Congreve in the setting of aristocratic reaction,

Richardson in the midst of all the phenomena of bourgeois emergence, Shelley as part of the democratic revolution, Tennyson in terms of Victorian progress, and Joyce as a symptom of capitalist decline. The phrases I have chosen are deliberate oversimplifications, but they suggest what I mean: that the artist can be understood only if one understands the movements that dominated his age.

It is the reality behind such phrases that the critic must discover. To understand all the complex relationships of men and movements in any age is beyond the power of the human mind, but a usable comprehension may be possible. The Marxist believes that he has a method that provides such comprehension. He holds that one cannot understand the intellectual movements of a given period without understanding the class alignments of that period. He recognizes, of course, that class alignment is never a simple matter of division into exploiters and exploited. He distinguishes at the present time between the petty bourgeoisie and the big bourgeoisie, between industrial workers and farmers, between richer farmers and poorer. In considering certain periods of the past, he recognizes the distinctive psychology of the merchants, the industrialists, and the financiers. Still farther back he sees the feudal aristocracy as the dominant class, and he realizes that in Europe survivals of feudalism have remained to complicate the struggles of the bourgeoisie.

The Marxist also rejects the notion that it is possible to explain the world-attitude of a given author merely by stating his class affiliation. The dominant class colors the entire culture of a period. Individual authors may be led by class influences to diverge from the prevailing patterns, but its effect is nonetheless felt. In a period in which the ruling class is almost unchallenged, as in Elizabethan England, for example, or in seventeenth-century France, or in contemporary Russia, culture will tend to be homogeneous, for authors will start from much the same premises, however idiosyncratic their courses may be. In the mid-seventeenth century, in England, however, we find strongly marked differences in literature, reflecting the interests of two conflicting and nearly balanced classes. The same phenomenon has often appeared at other times in other places: in France just before the Revolution, in the United States before the Civil War, and in most countries of the Western world today. Today we have a vigorous proletarian literature in the United States, but it is by no means completely independent from bourgeois literature, which even in its decline determines the dominant pattern. Between these extremes of relative unity and nearly balanced opposition, there are innumerable variations, each producing its own manifestations in literature and the arts.

The influence of class alignment upon a writer is complex and difficult to trace. Marlowe clearly expresses the expansive spirit of the merchant-adventurers who, only recently escaped from the bonds of the feudal system, were building the British Empire, and yet there is in Marlowe, as in most of the Elizabethan dramatists, a kind of pessimism that ill accords with the achievements of his class. Richardson, to take a simpler case, eagerly accepts the prudence-morality of the rising petty-bourgeoisie, and condemns the indiscretion of the landowners, but at the same time he snobbishly aspires to aristocratic distinction. Whitman speaks for the hopeful masses of Americans, westward bound on the trail of prosperity, individualistic and self-reliant, and yet he welcomes the socialist ideals of the collective state. Such complexities raise problems that may not be insoluble but are not to be ignored.

Social conditions change, and artists change too, and the interaction of these changes may produce surprising results. William Wordsworth was one of the poets who most heartily welcomed the democratic dawn of the late eighteenth century. Though in England successive strata of the bourgeoisie had pushed themselves up to positions of power as the productive forces of capitalism had expanded, the process was not moving fast enough to suit the young idealists. Insurgent sections of the bourgeoisie have always employed the slogans of freedom, democracy, and equal opportunity, and there have always been those who took the slogans seriously. In France, moreover, the bourgeois revolution, more violent because longer suppressed, had exploded into a volcanic fury of libertarian sentiment. But suddenly the process seemed to be going too fast. The democratic slogans of the French bourgeoisie, spreading to the proletariat, became a menace to the stability of the middle class. In England, too, workers were restless. Wordsworth did not consciously recant; he merely recoiled. If this was what his principles involved, he could not but see that his principles were wrong. He became the lost leader.

Social conditions are always changing. Mark Twain was early exposed to the democratic spirit of the frontier. When, later, he came to live in the industrialized society of the postwar East, he was bewildered. On the one hand, his own self-reliant and acquisitive impulses drove him to participate in the excesses of the Gilded Age; on the other, he saw quite clearly the tendency toward a snobbish oligarchy, based on injustice, and he did not hesitate to attack exploitation, class distinction, and imperialism from the frontiersman's egalitarian point of view. It is not, I think, unfair to attribute much of his pessimism to his uncertainty and to the conflicts that divided his mind. His friend Howells went through a similar experience, suddenly losing confidence in the society in which he had been so delighted to win a place for himself. Both Howells and Mark Twain called themselves socialists, but both, as the former bitterly remarked, continued to wear their fur coats. The changing shape of American life had involved them in contradiction, and their work suffered as a result in clarity and firmness.

Carlyle and Dickens were both born on the lower fringes of the petty-bourgeoisie. Both were opposed to the callous cruelty of the rising business class and to the utilitarian philosophy and laissez-faire economics that rationalized that brutality. Both sympathized with the working class, but the working class at that time was too weak to sustain a culture, too dependent on bourgeois religion, morality, and education to offer a real alternative to the business class. The one genuine alternative was the land-owning class, and it was thither that Carlyle and Dickens turned for support. Carlyle might talk of captains of industry, but it was the feudal virtues that he praised in his attempt to create a more just social order for the oppressed. Dickens, more acutely sympathetic with the workers and perhaps more cognizant of their potentialities, could not envisage a happier solution than a benevolent paternalism. Kingsley made *Alton Locke* a plea for obedience to the church and the crown, attacking the ruthless business men, it is true, but opposing as well Chartist aspirations to working class independence. Observe that none of the novelists of the earlier Victorian period, except Harriet Martineau, adopted a world-attitude that made any place for utilitarianism and its economic corollaries. They sympathized with the working class, opposed the business men, and looked to the landowners for political action. Their attitude reflected the economic situation: after the Reform Bill of 1832 had given the balance of power to the industrialists, the workers were glad of any allies; the landowners saw that, for the moment, there was only one enemy, and the petty-bourgeois, crushed by the advance of industrial capitalism, could find but one refuge.

The unwillingness of the early Victorians to adhere to the principles on which industrialism was rising to power reminds us that writers have seldom been willing to adopt the psychology of capitalism. This does not mean that writers are uninfluenced by the theories and practices of the ruling class; on the contrary, that influence permeates their work from beginning to end, even, perhaps especially, when they repudiate it. All I am trying to point out is that artists have traditionally rejected the acquisitive way of life—at least in theory. Perhaps that is because most artists come from the petty-bourgeoisie, from the least prosperous section of the non-proletarian world. Perhaps it is because art, for which capitalism makes no place, therefore attracts the dissatisfied. Whatever the explanation, we see writers running away from an industrial world to romantic refuges, far away or long ago. We hear them asserting proudly that art has no connection with the world of affairs, as if that was the only way in which they

could maintain their independence. They even deny that the function of literature is communication, in order to avoid difficulties that, on other terms, seem to make literature impossible. But they very, very seldom attempt to maintain that the prevailing way of life, the way of life that is led by the rulers of our civilization, is a good way.

At times this hostility to capitalist values takes a more direct form. At the turn of the century a literature developed, both in England and America, in which specific proposals for social reform played a large part: the novels of Wells and the plays of Shaw in England, the novels of Norris, Sinclair, and Herrick in this country. This reform movement expressed, I believe, the last insurgence of the petty-bourgeoisie, forced by the rise of monopoly capitalism to the recognition that equal opportunity was a myth. The class was caught in a contradictory position: it could not go back to earlier conditions, and to go ahead meant to surrender even more of its opportunities. The contradiction is reflected in the confusion of the reformist writers, as I have tried to show, so far as American writers are concerned, in *The Great Tradition,* and as John Strachey has shown, with regard to the British writers, in *The Coming Struggle for Power.*

It would not be difficult, of course, to swell the list of examples; indeed, it is my contention that, if one knows enough, the whole history of literature yields itself to such treatment. But perhaps it is time to recapitulate. The purpose of explaining literary phenomena is to understand them, to respond more fully to them. I favor using all methods that conduce to that end. If the study of literary influences is helpful, by all means let us study literary influences. If Freud has anything to teach us, let us turn to Freud, or to any other psychologist, for that matter, who can guide us through the mysteries of human personality. But for myself I believe, and I have tried to show, that we can understand an author best if we examine his relation to the social movements of his time and to the class alignments out of which they grow. This may not tell us all we should like to discover, but it will tell us what is most important for us to know.

But this is only half the story. The critic's task does not stop with explanation; it must go on to evaluation. Evaluation, I need scarcely remind you, is not a matter of passing out grades. It, too, has as its primary function the extension of the reader's capacity for appreciation. To that extent I agree with H. L. Mencken's catalyst theory, but I do not think that catalysis is accomplished by the random recording of transient impressions. In evaluating a work of art, the critic brings to it all his experience with other works, all his knowledge of human nature, all his understanding of the character and purpose of life. Two world-attitudes are brought face to face, and the result is, or should be, illuminating.

I fall back once more upon Mr. Richards, whose views, if not wholly acceptable, are helpful and serve as a convenient point of departure. If what literature does is to help us pass from a chaotic to a more organized state, it may be possible, not only to dismiss certain works as definitely disorganizing, but also to define the relative value of works that are not contributory to chaos. Mr. Richards maintains that the object of life is to satisfy as many appetencies as possible. In a chaotic state the fulfillment of one desire—to use a more common, if less exact, term—blocks the satisfaction of others. Not only are those desires dangerous that may grow into vices; intrinsically admirable pursuits may result in the disastrous warping of character. In particular, as Mr. Richards recognizes, the satisfaction of legitimate appetencies at the expense of other persons results ultimately in frustration. The ruthless man gets what he wants but finds that he has forever deprived himself of confidence and respect on the part of his associates. Literature, then, does not perform its organizing function unless it creates in us attitudes that permit us to live in fruitful concord with our fellow-men.

Mr. Richards assumes that it is possible to develop all-inclusive harmonious relationships. It is difficult, he knows, but he will not admit the existence of irreconcilable oppositions. I, however, believe that there is one conflict that permits of no peaceful solution. I refer, of course, to the class struggle. The proletariat can, in the long run, be satisfied with nothing less than all that it produces. Since, moreover, the developing contradictions of capitalism result in greater and greater deprivation for the proletariat, it is driven by sheer necessity to demand the abolition of exploitation. This demand the capitalists and those most closely associated with them in the sharing of profits cannot concede, since to do so would be absolute abdication. No ruling class in history has ever voluntarily surrendered its power, and there is reason to believe that there is not the least possibility of peaceful surrender by the masters of capitalism. Even abdication, however, would not invalidate my argument that there is an irreconcilable opposition between the exploiters and the exploited, since it would signify, quite as definitely as would involuntary liquidation, the triumph of one point of view over the other.

If this is true, it follows that, in certain respects at least, what capitalists regarded as a satisfactory integration could not be acceptable to proletarians. Let me take one example, to which I have already alluded, Kingsley's *Alton Locke*. A capitalist reader would find himself moved to pity the lot of the working class, but he would at the same time be confirmed in his conviction that it is wrong for workers to use violence to obtain their demands. These two attitudes could be adequately reconciled if he came to feel a greater responsibility toward his employees. He would still be the judge, however, of what constituted humane treatment, and it is reasonable to suppose that his conscience would be appeased more easily than the appetites of the workers. A working-class reader would be led to feel pity for himself and at the same time would learn to rely on the benevolence of his master rather than on the organized strength of his class. This would be a satisfactory integration from the capitalist's point of view. It would not, in the long run, serve the best interests of the worker.

This clear-cut example may suffice for the moment, for I shall shortly discuss in some detail the kind of integration that is desirable for the proletarian, and this discussion will touch upon less obvious influences. All I want to maintain now is that, if the critic recognizes the existence of such irreconcilable oppositions, he must decide where he stands and in whose interests he desires integration to take place. It is impossible for me to state fully why I personally have chosen the side of the proletariat and why I urge other intellectuals to make the same choice. I believe that the capitalist system is inherently unstable,

and that such depressions as that which has just entered its sixth year are not only unavoidable under capitalism but are certain to grow worse. Capitalism itself cannot solve the problems that, as it becomes fully developed, it creates. Only socialization of industry will eliminate these ills and permit the enjoyment of the full resources of our productive machinery. Moreover, the desperate effort of the capitalist class to maintain its privileged position results in Fascism, which sacrifices the political and cultural gains of the period of industrial expansion without achieving stability. Socialization is the only preventive of both Fascism and war, and socialization can be brought about only by the proletariat, not because of some peculiar virtue resident in factory workers, but because it is the one class that stands to gain so much by socialization and to lose so much by the perpetuation, especially in a fascist form, of capitalism that it will be willing to make the sacrifices that revolution entails.

This is, in brief, the argument that has led me to make the proletariat my point of reference. Any critic, unless he accepts the complete irresponsibility of impressionism, tries to transcend his own idiosyncrasies and speak in the name of some larger entity. To do so, he must, as Richards says, foster a kind of dual response to literature. He knows what a work of art does to and for him, but he also realizes the ways in which he deviates from what he regards as the norm, and he makes due allowance for these deviations in reaching his conclusions. So with the revolutionary critic. It has been charged that the proletariat is an abstraction, and the charge has some measure of truth, but the critic's norm is always an abstraction. Mr. Richards, for example, implies the

the existence of Man, with a capital letter, and the Humanists have a very precise but completely abstract conception of humanity. The revolutionary critic's idea of the normal proletarian is, in comparison, concrete and realistic, based both on an understanding of the historic rôle of the class and on first-hand experience of its spirit as displayed in crucial struggles.

I can realize how many objections might be introduced at this point, but let us see what, in practice, our conclusions involve. If we were to go to some militant leader of the working class and ask him what literature ought to do, he would probably tell us that it ought, first of all, to create a revolutionary spirit in the proletariat. Only that literature, he might well say, that prepares the class for the great task before it has any value.

This may seem a narrow and, perhaps, to some, an unworthy conception of literature. So thoroughly schooled have we been in the doctrine of the sacredness of art that we shrink from any association of literature and practical affairs. This response of ours results from the fact that any association of literature with the practical affairs of monopoly capitalism is debasing. Art under capitalism is so constantly in danger of Mammon-worship that, in order to maintain any sort of artistic integrity, we have built up these elaborate defenses. But actually in the course of human history literature has again and again been openly allied with church and state, and it may be argued that the periods of such alliance have not been unfruitful. The artists of Greece and Rome and those of the Middle Ages found no degradation in the serving of practical ends, and the rise of democracy has been aided by many of the greatest writers of modern times.

Nothing has so beclouded contemporary aesthetic discourse as the use of the word "propaganda." Because of its use during the war the term has come to connote chicanery and distortion. Yet it also has been employed to describe any sort of direct exhortation, and the aesthetes apply it to any work of art with a serious purpose. So often has the word been abusively hurled by aesthetes against revolutionaries that the latter have accepted the challenge and adopted the word as their own. Diego Rivera, for example, says that all art is propaganda. There is a sense of the term in which this is true, but it is not the meaning that is ordinarily understood.

Personally, I believe that the word ought to be used only in its pejorative sense, but in any case it ought to be kept out of discussions of literature. I have tried to maintain that any work of literature presents some sort of world-attitude, and that it must be judged in terms of the author's world-attitude and his success in communicating it. The most outrageous dadaist poem implies a certain attitude toward life; and the author, whether he admits it or not, wants others to adopt that attitude. If literature with a purpose is propaganda, then Rivera is right, but in that case the word is too inclusive to be useful. The conviction of most persons—that literature with a purpose one doesn't like is propaganda and literature with a purpose one does like is art—is obviously unsound. We are left, it seems to me, to hold that propaganda involves misrepresentation, and, since misrepresentation is intrinsically bad, it is unnecessary to talk about propaganda.

In serving the revolutionary cause the revolutionary writer is merely expressing his own world-attitude and fulfilling his own desires. To that extent he is like writers of all classes and all ages. And the critic, when he judges literature by its effect in preparing the proletariat for its struggle, is applying a criterion that does not differ in kind from the criteria of other critics. There is a danger, however, that he may demand immediate, concrete results. Such a demand is wrong simply because it is not in the nature of literature, as I have already remarked, to produce such results.

What we have to ask, it seems to me, is whether a work of literature contributes to a world-attitude that is compatible with the aims and tasks of the proletariat and whether it tends to build up a system of responses that will permit the proletarian to play his individual part in the coming struggle. We cannot approve, for example, a novel or a play that fosters an attitude of subservience. It may have incidental values, which we must point out, but fundamentally it is wrong. We cannot tolerate a defeatist literature, not merely because of the attitude it encourages, but also because, from our point of view, it distorts life by ignoring the elements in human character and history that, for the proletariat, the ascendant class, make pessimism impossible. Escapism, too, must be resisted. The romantic satisfactions of the daydream are recognized as perilous by most psychologists, for they inhibit the forming of adjustments that make possible the permanent and progressive fulfillment of appetencies; but they are peculiarly menacing to the proletarian reader, both because the hardships of his present existence make them so tempting and because his future rôle is so exacting.

On the other hand, we are not to suppose that the literature of the past is to be condemned *en bloc*. Revolutionary leaders from Marx to Stalin have insisted on the preciousness of the cultural heritage with which history endows the proletariat. There is a class element in any work produced in a class society, and this bias, as found in past writers, is distressing to proletarian readers. The classic example is Shakespeare's treatment of the lower class, a treatment so derogatory that Upton Sinclair, in *Mammonart,* warns workers against reading his plays. Mr. Sinclair, I feel, underestimates the natural immunity of the modern worker to such suggestion, and he equally underestimates the valuable elements of Shakespeare's plays. The mysticism of Dostoyevsky is wholly unacceptable to the Marxist, and yet his novels are widely read in the Soviet Union. Wherever the author's class bias is negated by his insight, his work is important. In spite of both snobbishness and a quasi-mystical detachment, Marcel Proust left a richer and more detailed account of the breakdown of the leisure class than can be found elsewhere.

We recognize an element of distortion in all the literature of the past, but we see, too, much that is valid, and to that we cling. At first it seems a paradox to say that we find most enduring value in those writers who most completely responded to and represented their own times. But once you perceive that class limits cannot be transcended, you realize that human nature can best be understood in terms of the forces that at any given time condition it. The writer who sets out to rise above material circumstance and deal with the pure human spirit is occupying himself with an unreal abstraction. The great writer has always been wholly and unmistakably part of his age, and, by mastering it, has left something of value for succeeding ages.

What we demand of a writer is that he honestly confront the central issues of his own age. His world-attitude must embrace the whole of his world as his age knew it, and must organize that world in such a way as to place central issues in the center. If he does this he deserves our praise. But I hasten to repeat that literature is not primarily a matter of the intellect. It embraces the entire mind, and it must not be judged in purely intellectual terms. An author may have formulated a world-attitude that, if he were a philosopher, would be admirable, and yet his poem or story may be worthless. He may, on the other hand, have no conscious philosophy, or only a very banal one, and yet be a great writer. This is particularly necessary for me to say, for it is characteristic of revolutionary sentiment that it seems to reach the intellect first. The young revolutionary author, filled with a sense of the comprehensiveness of Marxist analysis, and unwilling to subject his imagination to the long process of quiet and largely unconscious assimilation that literature requires, is tempted to substitute dogma for experience. This explains the weaknesses of some revolutionary literature, but it is a fault that time will remedy.

As the critic sees it, the problem defines itself in terms of completeness of communication, so that the experience of the writer becomes an experience for the reader. I doubt if intensity of experience is, by itself, an adequate criterion of literary greatness, but it is an indispensable element. That is why we rightly attach importance to the successful communication of even a minor experience. An author who communicates to us the joy he feels in contemplating a daffodil has done more than the author who, in attempting to communicate a vision of epic scope, only frustrates and bewilders us. The kind of integration Richards speaks of depends on the full communication of every element of the various experiences that enter into the author's plan. Each part must reach us if the whole is to have its effect. Since all degrees are possible, the critic often has to weigh a complete success in a limited field against the partial failure of an ambitious attempt. Specifically, the revolutionary critic may have to say that a limited poet like Robert Frost is better than a more central but more superficial poet, such as Carl Sandburg. What Sandburg is trying to do is more important than what Frost is trying to do, but Frost achieves his aims much more completely than Sandburg.

Though he must keep this question of efficacy of communication always in mind, the critic is principally concerned with the author's world-attitude. It is my opinion, which I have tried to defend in *The Great Tradition*, that in the last hundred years the central question for Western man has been that posed by the rise of industrialism. I am far from demanding that every writer should write about factories, but I do believe that every writer, whatever his theme, must understand the relation of the particular fragment of experience he chooses to describe to the fundamental and inescapable forces that have been affecting every phase of American life. I do not ask whether this author or that has read Karl Marx; I merely assume that a really sensitive author, whatever his political views, is bound to be aware of what is going on.

Today the issues created by the rise of industrialism have become so sharp that only conscious evasion can keep a writer from considering them. As in various periods of the past, the central issue has become the obvious issue. And of course there has been a great increase in the number of novels, plays, and poems that deal directly with economic issues. Even romantic novels these days, such as *Anthony Adverse, So Red the Rose,* and *The Foolscap Rose,* have a conscious social purpose.

In this situation revolutionary writers have, I believe, a great advantage. Here, I admit, my argument must be double-edged. Obviously, from my point of view, they have an advantage, since they agree in their basic assumptions with the class whose needs and interests I take as my standard of reference. But I mean more than that. If, as I believe, victory will ultimately come to the working class, writers who are on its side are more likely to see the forces leading to that victory than are those on the other side. The capitalist writer is something of an apologist, however sincere he may try to be defending special privilege. To put it crudely, the author who chooses capitalism is betting on the losing side, and either he conceals the real reasons for his choice or else his real reasons are bad ones.

Certainly the vitality of contemporary revolutionary literature can scarcely be ignored. I do not hold that every novel written by a Communist is perfect and beyond criticism. I believe, on the contrary, that I am unusually sensitive to the defects of revolutionary literature because I have so vivid a conception of what it ought to be and so poignant a desire to see it realize its potentialities. But when I compare the young radical writers with the young aesthetes or the young regionalists or the young pessimists or the young romantics, I confess that the former seem to be far more alive and promising. To compare Dos Passos' career with Hemingway's, or Jack Conroy's first novel with Gladys Hasty Carroll's, or Isidor Schneider's

poetry with Yvor Winters' is to see the difference between a healthy, courageous, resourceful confrontation of reality and a querulous or timid or snobbish preoccupation with petty personal problems.

But perhaps you do not agree with me; and if you do not, I suspect it is because we have different sets of values—because, indeed, our lives are organized toward different ends. I do not want to over-emphasize these differences. I hope and believe that I have allies among you, and I have no desire to antagonize anyone. But I am sure that you cannot understand what I am trying to say unless you realize that I expect and desire and work for a revolution that will not only alter political and economic forms but will profoundly change the whole basis of our culture. A new class is coming into power, and the results of its emergence can only dimly be foreseen. I believe that, whatever hardships this revolution may entail, it will eventually be a powerful stimulus to cultural growth, for, by destroying exploitation and class division, it will make possible a truly human civilization. The process may be long and painful, but the goal is clear, and this is the only path by which it can be reached.

You may ask, of course, why you, who have no desire to identify yourselves with the proletariat, should be expected to show any interest in its literary achievements. I can answer on several grounds. In the first place, just as the proletariat finds in bourgeois literature, with all its class bias, a portrayal of human life that is intelligible and enriching, so the bourgeoisie can adjust itself to class differences and discover in proletarian literature a valuable extension and partial integration of experience. This adjustment is relatively easy at present because proletarian literature is still under the influence of the dominant class literature. And it is worth making the necessary effort, for, even if my theories are entirely wrong, these writers from the working class and their sympathizers are very close to movements that are affecting us all. In the second place, you ought to be willing to grant that my conception of the future may be right, and if it is right, these novels and poems, however crude, are certain to have historical importance. Finally, I must invite you to contemplate what not only Marxian theory but the practical experience of Europe has demonstrated to be the only alternative to Communism, Fascism. From my point of view, of course, it is not an alternative but merely a postponement. Nevertheless, within the span of our lives, it constitutes a kind of alternative. And if the choice does lie between Communism and Fascism, it does not seem difficult to decide which deserves the allegiance of those of us who find inspiration in the literature of the past and nourish hopes for the growth of literature in the future.

1934, 1935

EDMUND WILSON
(1895–   )

AXEL'S CASTLE *

CHAPTER I

SYMBOLISM

It is my purpose in this book to try to trace the origins of certain tendencies in contemporary literature and to show their development in the work of six contemporary writers. To

persons already familiar with the field, my explanations in this first chapter will seem rudimentary; but I believe that it is still true in general, for reasons which I shall suggest, that the sources and fundamental principles of many of the books which have excited most discussion during the period since the War are singularly little understood. It is not usually recognized that writers such as W. B. Yeats, James Joyce, T. S. Eliot, Gertrude Stein, Marcel Proust and Paul Valéry represent the culmination of a self-conscious and very important literary movement; and even when we have become aware that these writers have something in common, that they belong to a common school, we are likely to be rather vague as to what its distinguishing features are.

We do, however, to-day as a rule have a pretty clear idea of the issues which were raised by the Romantic Movement of the beginning of the nineteenth century. We still debate Classicism and Romanticism, and when we attempt to deal with contemporary literary problems, we often tend to discuss them in those terms. Yet the movement of which in our own day we are witnessing the mature development is not merely a degeneration or an elaboration of Romanticism, but rather a counterpart to it, a second flood of the same tide. And even the metaphor of a tide is misleading: what we have to-day is an entirely distinct movement, which has arisen from different conditions and must be dealt with in different terms.

Romanticism, as everyone has heard, was a revolt of the individual. The "Classicism" against which it was a reaction meant, in the domain of politics and morals, a preoccupation with society as a whole; and, in art, an ideal of objectivity. In "Le Misanthrope," in "Bérénice," in "The

Way of the World," in "Gulliver's Travels," the artist is out of the picture: he would consider it artistic bad taste to identify his hero with himself and to glorify himself with his hero, or to intrude between the reader and the story and give vent to his personal emotions. But in "René," in "Rolla," in "Childe Harold," in "The Prelude," the writer is either his own hero, or unmistakably identified with his hero, and the personality and emotions of the writer are presented as the principal subject of interest. Racine, Molière, Congreve and Swift ask us to be interested in what they have made; but Chateaubriand, Musset, Bryon and Wordsworth ask us to be interested in themselves. And they ask us to be interested in themselves by virtue of the intrinsic value of the individual: they vindicate the rights of the individual against the claims of society as a whole—against government, morals, conventions, academy or church. The Romantic is nearly always a rebel.

In this connection, it is illuminating to consider the explanation of the Romantic Movement given by A. N. Whitehead in his "Science and the Modern World." The Romantic Movement, Whitehead says, was really a reaction against scientific ideas, or rather against the mechanistic ideas to which certain scientific discoveries gave rise. The seventeenth and eighteenth centuries were in Europe the great period of the development of mathematical and physical theory; and in the literature of the so-called Classical period, Descartes and Newton were influences as important as those of the classics themselves. The poets, like the astronomers and mathematicians, had come to regard the universe as a machine, obeying logical laws and susceptible of reasonable explanation:

God figured merely as the clockmaker who must have existed to make the clock. People applied this conception also to society, which, from the point of view of Louis XIV and of the American Constitution alike, had the character of a planetary system or a well-regulated machine; and they examined human nature dispassionately, in the same lucid and reasonable spirit, to find the principles on which it worked. Thus the theorems of the physicist were matched by the geometrical plays of Racine and the balanced couplets of Pope.

But this conception of a fixed mechanical order came eventually to be felt as a constraint: it excluded too much of life—or rather, the description it supplied did not correspond to actual experience. The Romantics had become acutely conscious of aspects of their experience which it was impossible to analyze or explain on the theory of a world run by clockwork. The universe was not a machine, after all, but something more mysterious and less rational.

The atoms of Democritus,
  And Newton's particles of light
Are sands upon the Red Sea shore,
  Where Israel's tents do shine so bright!

Blake had already contradicted contemptuously the physical theory of the eighteenth century. And to Wordsworth, the countryside of his boyhood meant neither agriculture nor neo-classic idylls, but a light never seen on land or sea. When the poet looked into his own soul, he beheld something which did not seem to him reducible to a set of principles of human nature such, for example, as La Rochefoucauld's "Maxims": he saw fantasy, conflict, confusion. And he either set himself, like Wordsworth and Blake, to affirm the superior truth of this vision as compared to the mechanical universe of the physicists; or, accepting this mechanical universe, like Byron or Alfred de Vigny, as external to and indifferent to man, he pitted against it, in defiance, his own turbulent insubordinate soul.

In any case, it is always, as in Wordsworth, the individual sensibility, or, as in Byron, the individual will, with which the Romantic poet is preoccupied; and he has invented a new language for the expression of its mystery, its conflict and confusion. The arena of literature has been transferred from the universe conceived as a machine, from society conceived as an organization, to the individual soul.

What has really taken place, says Whitehead, is a philosophical revolution. The scientists of the seventeenth century who presented the universe as a mechanism had caused people to draw the conclusion that man was something apart from nature, something introduced into the universe from outside and remaining alien to all that he found. But a Romantic poet like Wordsworth has come to feel the falsity of this assumption: he has perceived that the world is an organism, that nature includes planets, mountains, vegetation and people alike, that what we are and what we see, what we hear, what we feel and what we smell, are inextricably related, that all are involved in the same great entity. Those who make fun of the Romantics are mistaken in supposing that there is no intimate connection between the landscape and the poet's emotions. There is no real dualism, says Whitehead, between external lakes and hills, on the one hand, and personal feelings, on the other: human feelings and inanimate objects are interdependent and developing together in some fashion of which our traditional notions of laws

of cause and effect, of dualities of mind and matter or of body and soul, can give us no true idea. The Romantic poet, then, with his turbid or opalescent language, his sympathies and passions which cause him to seem to merge with his surroundings, is the prophet of a new insight into nature: he is describing things as they really are; and a revolution in the imagery of poetry is in reality a revolution in metaphysics.

Whitehead drops the story at this point; but he has provided the key to what follows. In the middle of the nineteenth century, science made new advances, and mechanistic ideas were brought back into fashion again. But they came this time from a different quarter—not from physics and mathematics, but from biology. It was the effect of the theory of Evolution to reduce man from the heroic stature to which the Romantics had tried to exalt him, to the semblance of a helpless animal, again very small in the universe and at the mercy of the forces about him. Humanity was the accidental product of heredity and environment, and capable of being explained in terms of these. This doctrine in literature was called Naturalism, and it was put into practice by novelists like Zola, who believed that composing a novel was like performing a laboratory experiment: you had only to supply your characters with a specific environment and heredity and then watch their automatic reactions; and by historians and critics like Taine, who asserted that virtue and vice were as much the products of automatic processes as alkalis and acids, and who attempted to account for masterpieces by studying the geographical and climatic conditions of the countries in which they had been produced.

Not, however, that the movement

known as Naturalism arose directly from "The Origin of Species." There had already set in, about the middle of the century, quite independent of the theory of Evolution, a reaction against the sentimentality and the looseness of Romanticism, and in the direction of the objectivity and the severity of Classicism again; and this reaction had already been characterized by a kind of scientific observation which closely corresponded to that of biological science. This reaction is seen most clearly in France. The Parnassian group of poets, who made their first appearance in the fifties—Gautier, Leconte de Lisle, Hérédia—seemed to have taken it for their aim merely to picture historical incidents and natural phenomena as objectively and accurately as possible in impassive perfect verse. Leconte de Lisle's elephants crossing the desert is a celebrated example: the elephants appear and disappear with a certain classical dignity and grandeur, and the poet leaves it at that.

It is less easy, in English poetry, to give clear examples of the reaction toward Naturalism: the English did not, after the Romantic Movement, take much interest in literary methods till toward the end of the nineteenth century. But the tendency toward what we call realism had set in, none the less: Browning, though he had, of course, nothing of the classical form of the Parnassians, was addicted to historical reconstruction of a kind more pedantic and less flamboyant than that of the true Romantics, and when he dealt with contemporary life, did so at least as realistically as any of the Victorian novelists—themselves going in Zola's direction without quite being aware of the fact. And we can see very plainly in Tennyson, who was much preoccupied with the doctrines of Evolution, something of the same

exactitude of description combined with something of the same severity of verse—though with less hardness and more grace—that we find in the French poets.

Nor wilt thou snare him in the white ravine,
Nor find him dropt upon the firths of ice,
That huddling slant in furrow-cloven fells
To roll the torrent out of dusky doors:
But follow; let the torrent dance thee down
To find him in the valley; let the wild
Lean-headed eagles yelp alone.

And it is interesting to compare Tennyson, in this connection, with Pope on the rare occasions (though not so rare as people sometimes suppose) when he is describing natural objects:

The silver eel, in shining volumes roll'd,
The yellow carp, in scales bedropp'd with gold.

These lines have the technical perfection and the precise observation of Tennyson, but they are heavier and more metallic. Pope is often, as a matter of fact, very close to the French Parnassians. The latter represent, in reality, a second classical-scientific movement, the counterpart to that represented by Pope.

But the highest developments of Naturalism took place, not in poetry, but in prose. The plays of Ibsen and the novels of Flaubert are the masterpieces of this second period of modern classicism, as Racine and Swift are of the first. The art of Flaubert and Ibsen is again, like the art of the seventeenth-century writers, scrupulously non-personal and objective, and it insists upon precision of language and economy of form. Compare the lucidity, the logic and the limited number of characters of such a tragedy of Ibsen's as "Rosmersholm" with the rigorous conventions of Racine; or compare "Gulliver's Travels" with "Bouvard et Pécuchet" or "L'Education Sentimentale." Yet, though the earlier works resemble the later ones in many obvious ways, they differ from them in this: where a seventeenth-century moralist like La Rochefoucauld would have sought to discover and set forth the universal principles of human behavior, a nineteenth-century writer like Ibsen or Flaubert has begun to study man in relation to his particular environment and time. The method of approach in both cases, however, may be described as "scientific," and it tends to lead us to mechanistic conclusions.

Now Flaubert and Ibsen both had been suckled on Romanticism. Flaubert had begun by writing a Romantic "Saint-Antoine" before he chastened it and cut it down to the more sober one which he published; and Ibsen had written in verse his Faustian "Brand" and "Peer Gynt" before he arrived at his realistic plays in prose. Each, beginning in Romanticism, had evolved for himself a new discipline and developed a new point of view. For "Madame Bovary" is not merely arranged and written differently from a novel by Victor Hugo: it also constitutes an objective criticism of a case of Romantic personality; and Ibsen was occupied all his life with situations produced by the conflict of the essentially Romantic conception of one's duty to one's own personality with the conception of one's duty to society.

But in the later prose plays of Ibsen, the trolls and ghosts of his early dramatic poems have begun to creep back into the bourgeois drawing-rooms: the Naturalist has been finally compelled to make cracks in his own mold. All that vaporous, confused and grandiose world of Romanticism had been resolutely ordered and compressed; but now the objective point of view of Naturalism, the machine-like technique which went with it, begin to cramp the poet's imagination, to prove inadequate to convey what he feels. The reader begins to chafe at the strain, and the artist begins to betray it. Huysmans described Leconte de Lisle as "the sonorous hardware man"; we remember Wordsworth's strictures on Pope. Literature is rebounding again from the scientific-classical pole to the poetic-romantic one. And this second reaction at the end of the century, this counterpart to the Romantic reaction of the end of the century before, was known in France as Symbolism.

Now in attempting to write literary history, one must guard against giving the impression that these movements and countermovements necessarily follow one another in a punctual and well-generalled fashion—as if eighteenth-century reason had been cleanly put to rout by nineteenth-century Romanticism, which then proceeded to hold the field till it was laid by the heels by Naturalism, and as if Mallarmé and Rimbaud had then blown up Naturalism with bombs. What really happens, of course, is that one set of methods and ideas is not completely superseded by another; but that, on the contrary, it thrives in its teeth—so that, on the one hand, Flaubert's prose has learned to hear, see and feel with the delicate senses of Romanticism at the same time that Flaubert is disciplining and criticizing the Romantic temperament; and so that, on the other hand, certain members of a school, unaffected by new influences abroad, will continue to practise its methods and to exploit its possibilities further and further, when nearly everybody else has abandoned it.

I have here purposely been selecting writers who seemed to represent some tendency or school in its purest or most highly developed form. We must, however, now consider some Romantics who, in certain ways, carried Romanticism further than even Chateaubriand or Musset, or than Wordsworth or Byron, and who became the first precursors of Symbolism and were afterwards placed among its saints.

One of these was the French writer who called himself Gérard de Nerval. Gérard de Nerval suffered from spells of insanity; and, partly no doubt as a result of this, habitually confused his own fancies and feelings with external reality. He believed, even in his lucid periods—and no doubt Whitehead would approve his metaphysics—that the world which we see about us is involved in some more intimate fashion than is ordinarily supposed with the things that go on in our minds, that even our dreams and hallucinations are somehow bound up with reality. And in one of his sonnets he outdoes Wordsworth, with his "Presences of Nature in the sky" and his "Souls of lonely places," by imagining shuttered eyes coming to life in the very walls and "a pure spirit under the bark of stones."

But a more important prophet of Symbolism was Edgar Allan Poe. It was in general true that, by the middle of the century, the Romantic writers in the United States—Poe, Hawthorne, Melville, Whitman and even Emerson—were, for reasons which it would be interesting to determine, developing in the direction of Symbolism; and one of the events of prime importance in the early history of the Symbolist Movement was the discovery of Poe by Baudelaire. When Baudelaire, a late Romantic, first read Poe in 1847, he "experienced a strange commotion." When he began to look up Poe's writings in the files of American magazines, he found among them stories and poems which he said that he himself had already "thought vaguely and confusedly" of writing, and his interest became a veritable passion. In 1852, Baudelaire published a volume of translations of Poe's tales; and from then on the influence of Poe played an important part in French literature. Poe's critical writings provided the first scriptures of the Symbolist Movement, for he had formulated what amounted to a new literary programme which corrected the Romantic looseness and lopped away the Romantic extravagance, at the same time that it aimed, not at Naturalistic, but at ultra-Romantic effects. There was, of course, a good deal in common between Poe's poetry and such Romantic poetry as Coleridge's "Kubla Khan," as there was between his poems in prose and such Romantic prose as that of De Quincey. But Poe, by insisting on and specially cultivating certain aspects of Romanticism, helped to transform it into something different. "I *know,*" we find Poe writing, for example, "that indefiniteness is an element of the true music [of poetry]—I mean of the true musical expression . . . a suggestive indefiniteness of vague and therefore of spiritual *effect.*" And to approximate the indefiniteness of music was to become one of the principal aims of Symbolism.

This effect of indefiniteness was produced not merely by the confusion I have mentioned between the imaginary world and the real; but also by means of a further confusion between the perceptions of the different senses.

Comme de longs échos qui de loin se
   confondent . . .
Les parfums, les couleurs et les sons se
   répondent,

wrote Baudelaire. And we find Poe, in one of his poems, *hearing* the approach of the darkness, or writing such a description as the following of the sensations which follow death: "Night arrived; and with its shadows a heavy discomfort. It oppressed my limbs with the oppression of some dull weight, and was palpable. There was also a moaning sound, not unlike the distant reverberation of surf, but more continuous, which beginning with the first twilight, had grown in strength with the darkness. Suddenly lights were brought into the room . . . and issuing from the flame of each lamp, there flowed unbrokenly into my ears a strain of melodious monotone."

This notation of super-rational sensations was a novelty in the forties of the last century—as was the dream-like irrational musical poetry of "Annabel Lee" and "Ulalume"; and they helped to effect a revolution in France. For an English-speaking reader of to-day Poe's influence may be hard to understand; and even when such a reader comes to examine the productions of French Symbolism, it may surprise him that they should have caused amazement. The medley of images; the deliberately mixed metaphors; the combination of passion and wit—of the grand and the prosaic manners; the bold amalgamation of material with spiritual—all these may seem to him quite proper and familiar. He has always known them in the English poetry of the sixteenth and seventeenth centuries—Shakespeare and the other Elizabethans did all these things without theorizing about them. Is this not the natural language of poetry? Is it not the norm against which, in

English literature, the eighteenth century was a heresy and to which the Romantics did their best to return?

But we must remember that the development of French poetry has been quite different from that of English. Michelet says that in the sixteenth century the future of French literature had hung in the balance between Rabelais and Ronsard, and he regrets that it was Ronsard who triumphed. For Rabelais in France was a sort of equivalent to our own Elizabethans, whereas Ronsard, who represented to Michelet all that was poorest, dryest and most conventional in the French genius, was one of the fathers of that classical tradition of lucidity, sobriety and purity which culminated in Molière and Racine. In comparison with the Classicism of the French, which has dominated their whole literature since the Renaissance, the English Classicism of the eighteenth century, the age of Dr. Johnson and Pope, was a brief ineffective deviation. And from the point of view of English readers, the most daring innovations of the Romantic revolution in France, in spite of all the excitement which accompanied them, must appear of an astonishingly moderate character. But the age and the rigor of the tradition were the measure of the difficulty of breaking out of it. After all, Coleridge, Shelley and Keats—in spite of Pope and Dr. Johnson—had only to look back to Milton and Shakespeace, whose dense forests had all along been in view beyond the formal eighteenth-century gardens. But to an eighteenth-century Frenchman like Voltaire, Shakespeare was incomprehensible; and to the Frenchman of the classical tradition of the beginning of the nineteenth century, the rhetoric of Hugo was a scandal: the French were not used to such rich colors or to so free a vocabulary; moreover, the Romantics broke metrical rules far stricter than any we have had in English. Yet Victor Hugo was still very far from the variety and freedom of Shakespeare. It is enlightening to compare Shelley's lyric which begins "O World! O Life! O Time!" with the poem of Alfred de Musset's which begins, "J'ai perdu ma force et ma vie." These two lyrics are in some ways curiously similar: each is the breath of a Romantic sigh over the passing of the pride of youth. Yet the French poet, even in his wistfulness, makes epigrammatic points: his language is always logical and precise; whereas the English poet is vague and gives us images unrelated by logic. And it will not be till the advent of the Symbolists that French poetry will really become capable of the fantasy and fluidity of English.

The Symbolist Movement broke those rules of French metrics which the Romantics had left intact, and it finally succeeded in throwing overboard completely the clarity and logic of the French classical tradition, which the Romantics had still to a great extent respected. It was nourished from many alien sources—German, Flemish, modern Greek—and especially, precisely, from English. Verlaine had lived in England, and knew English well; Mallarmé was a professor of English; and Baudelaire, as I have said, had provided the movement with its first programs by translating the essays of Poe. Two of the Symbolist poets, Stuart Merrill and Francis Vielé-Griffin, were Americans who lived in Paris and wrote French; and an American, reading to-day the latter's "Chevauchée d'Yeldis," for example, may wonder how, when Symbolism was new, such a poem could ever have been regarded as one of the movement's acknowledged master-

pieces: to us, it seems merely agreeable, not in the least revolutionary or novel, but like something which might not impossibly have been written by Thomas Bailey Aldrich if he had been influenced by Browning. We are surprised to learn that Vielé-Griffin is still considered an important poet. But the point was that he had performed a feat which astonished and impressed the French and of which it is probable that no Frenchman was capable; he had succeeded in wrecking once for all the classical Alexandrine, hitherto the basis of French poetry—or rather, as an English reader at once recognizes, he had dispensed with it altogether and begun writing English metres in French. The French called this "vers libre," but it is "free" only in the sense of being irregular, like many poems of Matthew Arnold and Browning.

What made Poe particularly acceptable to the French, however, was what had distinguished him from most of the other Romantics of the English-speaking countries: his interest in æsthetic theory. The French have always reasoned about literature far more than the English have; they always want to know what they are doing and why they are doing it: their literary criticism has acted as a constant interpreter and guide to the rest of their literature. And it was in France that Poe's literary theory, to which no one seems to have paid much attention elsewhere, was first studied and elucidated. So that, though the effects and devices of Symbolism were of a kind that was familiar in English, and though the Symbolists were sometimes indebted to English literature directly—the Symbolist Movement itself, by reason of its origin in France, had a deliberate self-conscious æsthetic which made it different from anything in English. One must go back to Coleridge to find in English a figure comparable to the Symbolist leader Stephane Mallarmé. Paul Valéry says of Mallarmé that, as he was the greatest French poet of his time, he could also have been one of the most popular. But Mallarmé was an unpopular poet: he taught English for a living, and wrote little and published less. Yet, ridiculed and denounced by the public, who reiterated that his poetry was nonsense and yet were irritated by his seriousness and obstinacy, he exercised, from his little Paris apartment, where he held Tuesday receptions, an influence curiously far-reaching over the young writers—English and French alike—of the end of the century. There in the sitting-room which was also the dining-room on the fourth floor in the Rue de Rome, where the whistle of locomotives came in through the windows to mingle with the literary conversation, Mallarmé, with his shining pensive gaze from under his long lashes and always smoking a cigarette "to put some smoke," as he used to say, "between the world and himself," would talk about the theory of poetry in a "mild, musical and unforgettable voice." There was an atmosphere "calm and almost religious." Mallarmé had "the pride of the inner life," said one of his friends; his nature was "patient, disdainful and imperiously gentle." He always reflected before he spoke and always put what he said in the form of a question. His wife sat beside him embroidering; his daughter answered the door. Here came Huysmans, Whistler, Degas, Moréas, Laforgue, Vielé-Griffin, Paul Valéry, Henri de Régnier, Pierre Louys, Paul Claudel, Remy de Gourmont, André Gide, Oscar Wilde, Arthur Symons, George Moore and W. B. Yeats. For Mallarmé was a true saint of literature: he had proposed to himself an almost impossible object, and he pursued it without compromise or distraction. His whole life was dedicated to the effort to do something with the language of poetry which had never been done before. "Donner un sens plus pur," he had written in a sonnet on Poe, "aux mots de la tribu." He was, as Albert Thibaudet has said, engaged in "a disinterested experiment on the confines of poetry, at a limit where other lungs would find the air unbreathable."

What, then, was this purer sense which Mallarmé believed he was following Poe in wishing to give to the words of the tribe? What, precisely, was the nature of this experiment on the confines of poetry which Mallarmé found so absorbing and which so many other writers tried to repeat? What, precisely, did the Symbolists propose? I have called attention, in speaking of Poe, to the confusion between the perceptions of the different senses, and to the attempt to make the effects of poetry approximate to those of music. And I should add, in this latter connection, that the influence on Symbolist poetry of Wagner was as important as that of any poet: at the time when Romantic music had come closest to literature, literature was attracted toward music. I have also spoken, in connection with Gérard de Nerval, of the confusion between the imaginary and the real, between our sensations and fancies, on the one hand, and what we actually do and see, on the other. It was the tendency of Symbolism—that second swing of the pendulum away from a mechanistic view of nature and from a social conception of man— to make poetry even more a matter of the sensations and emotions of the individual than had been the case with Romanticism: Symbolism, indeed, sometimes had the result of making poetry so much a private concern of the poet's that it turned out to be incommunicable to the reader. The peculiar subtlety and difficulty of Symbolism is indicated by the name itself. This name has often been complained of as being inadequate for the movement to which it was given and inappropriate to certain of its aspects; and it may prove misleading to English readers. For the symbols of Symbolism have to be defined a little differently from symbols in the ordinary sense—the sense in which the Cross is the symbol of Christianity or the Stars and Stripes the symbol of the United States. This symbolism differs even from such symbolism as Dante's. For the familiar kind of symbolism is conventional and fixed; the symbolism of the Divine Comedy is conventional, logical and definite. But the symbols of the Symbolist school are usually chosen arbitrarily by the poet to stand for special ideas of his own—they are a sort of disguise for these ideas. "The Parnassians, for their part," wrote Mallarmé, "take the thing just as it is and put it before us —and consequently they are deficient in mystery: they deprive the mind of the delicious joy of believing that it is creating. To name an object is to do away with the three-quarters of the enjoyment of the poem which is derived from the satisfaction of guessing little by little: to suggest it, to evoke it—that is what charms the imagination."

To intimate things rather than state them plainly was thus one of the primary aims of the Symbolists. But there was more involved in their point of view than Mallarmé here explains. The assumptions which underlay Symbolism lead us to formulate some such doctrine as the following: Every feeling or sensation we have, every moment of consciousness, is different from every other; and it is, in consequence, impossible to render our sensations as we actually experience them through the conventional and universal language of ordinary literature. Each poet has his unique personality; each of his moments has its special tone, its special combination of elements. And it is the poet's task to find, to invent, the special language which will alone be capable of expressing his personality and feelings. Such a language must make use of symbols: what is so special, so fleeting and so vague cannot be conveyed by direct statement or description, but only by a succession of words, of images, which will serve to suggest it to the reader. The Symbolists themselves, full of the idea of producing with poetry effects like those of music, tended to think of these images as possessing an abstract value like musical notes and chords. But the words of our speech are not musical notation, and what the symbols of Symbolism really were, were metaphors detached from their subjects—for one cannot, beyond a certain point, in poetry, merely enjoy color and sound for their own sake: one has to guess what the images are being applied to. And Symbolism may be defined as an attempt by carefully studied means— a complicated association of ideas represented by a medley of metaphors —to communicate unique personal feelings.

The Symbolist Movement proper was first largely confined to France and principally limited to poetry of rather an esoteric kind; but it was destined, as time went on, to spread to the whole western world and its principles to be applied on a scale which the most enthusiastic of its founders could scarcely have foreseen. Remy de Gourmont, who was eventually to become the most distinguished critical champion of the movement, tells of his excitement, one afternoon in the eighties, at discovering the new poetry in a little magazine which he had picked up at a book-stall in the Odéon: "As I looked through it, I experienced the little æsthetic thrill and that exquisite impression of novelty which has so much charm for youth. I seemed to myself to have been dreaming rather than reading. The Luxembourg was pink with early April: I crossed it toward the Rue d'Assas, thinking a great deal more about the new literature which was coinciding for me that day with the renewal of the world than about the business which had brought me to that part of Paris. All that I had written up to that time inspired me with profound disgust. . . . In less than an hour my literary orientation was radically modified." And Yeats wrote in 1897: "The reaction against the rationalism of the eighteenth century has mingled with a reaction against the materialism of the nineteenth century, and the symbolical movement, which has come to perfection in Germany in Wagner, in England in the Pre-Raphaelites, and in France in Villiers de L'Isle-Adam and Mallarmé and Maeterlinck, and has stirred the imagination of Ibsen and D'Annunzio, is certainly the only movement that is saying new things."

We do not talk about Symbolism to-day in dealing with English literature; we do not even, as Yeats did at the end of the last century, think of the writers whom he mentions as all belonging to a "symbolical movement"; yet the influence of Mallarmé and his fellow poets was felt widely and deeply outside of France, and it is difficult to understand certain of the things which have been happening lately in English literature without some knowledge of the Symbolist school. I believe, in fact, that if English and American criticism have sometimes shown themselves at a loss when confronted with the work of certain recent writers, it is partly because the work of these writers is the result of a literary revolution which occurred outside English literature. The case of the Romantic Movement was different: Wordsworth's prefaces were English manifestoes; Lockhart's attack on Keats and Byron's attack on Jeffrey were blows struck in an English civil war. But in spite of the Pre-Raphaelites, who were launched by an impulse somewhat similar to that of the Symbolists, and in spite of the English "æsthetics" and "decadents," who for the most part imitated the French without very much originality, the battle of Symbolism has never properly been fought out in English. So that whereas French writers like Valéry and Proust who have grown out of the Symbolist Movement, are well understood and appreciated by French literary criticism, the critics of the English-speaking countries have often seemed not to know how to deal with writers such as Eliot and Joyce. Even when these writers have brought back into English qualities which are natural to it and resources which it originally possessed, these elements have returned by way of France and have taken on the complexion of the French mind—critical, philosophical, much occupied with æsthetic theory and tending always to aim self-consciously at particular effects and to study scrupulously appropriate means. It has perhaps been peculiarly easy for certain of the leaders of contemporary English literature—that is, of the literature since the War—to profit by the example of Paris, because they have themselves not been English. Of the writers in English I shall discuss in this book, Yeats is an Irishman who turns almost as easily toward Paris as toward London; Joyce an Irishman who has done most of his work on the Continent and who has scarcely lived in England at all; and T. S. Eliot and Gertrude Stein are Americans living abroad. The work of these writers has been largely a continuance or extension of Symbolism. Yeats, the ablest of the *fin de siècle* group who tried in London to emulate the French, managed to make Symbolism flourish triumphantly by transplanting it to the more favorable soil of Ireland. T. S. Eliot in his earliest poems seems to have been as susceptible to the influence of the Symbolists as to that of the English Elizabethans. Joyce, a master of Naturalism as great as Flaubert, has at the same time succeeded in dramatizing Symbolism by making use of its methods for differentiating between his various characters and their varying states of mind. And Gertrude Stein has carried Mallarmé's principles so far in the direction of that limit where other lungs find the air unbreathable as perhaps finally to reduce them to absurdity. It is true, however, that under proper conditions, these principles remain valid; and both the strength and the weaknesses characteristic of much of the literature since the War derive naturally from the Symbolist poets and may already be studied in their work. The literary history of our time is to a great extent that of the development of Symbolism and of its fusion or conflict with Naturalism.

1929

TRAVELS IN TWO DEMOCRACIES *

VII

FINAL REFLECTIONS

The strongest impression that one gets in Russia, as soon as one begins to see beneath the contradictory phenomena of the surface, is one of extraordinary heroism.

And the effect of this is very sobering. Only idiots gush about Russia. Only idiots pretend that life there is easy. Whether one encounters a Communist official working his head off to make socialism succeed in the face of inertia at home and hostile pressure abroad; or a professional man or woman of the old bourgeoisie or nobility, who has lost property, position and family, who lives always more or less under suspicion and who is likely already to have done time in a construction camp or a prison, yet who still remains loyal to the Revolution; or a member of the Komsomol intoxicating himself with work and study; or a peasant woman applying herself with desperate seriousness to the duties of ticket-taker or railroad conductor; or an old doctor or an old farmer deprived of everything he had spent his life attaining, yet still sticking with all decency to *his* job, in the interests of a future he will never see, of benefits he will never share; or a cultivated and charming young woman grown up amid the anarchy of the civil wars and the Spartan years of the first phase of the Revolution with no dancing and no pretty clothes and breaking down her physique and her nerves under the exactions of the Soviet programs—whomever one sees, wherever one turns, one is made to

* From: *Travels in Two Democracies*, by Edmund Wilson, copyright, 1936, by Edmund Wilson, reprinted by permission of Doubleday & Company, Inc.

feel the terrible seriousness of what is being done in Russia and the terrible cost which it requires.

And, on the other hand, it is foolish for a foreigner to make an issue of the bad aspects of the dictatorship: the lack of democratic procedure, the suppression of political opposition, the constraint of the official terror. The Russians can always reply that, with all the machinery of our democratic institutions, we are unable to feed and clothe our people, and that these supposed democratic institutions are merely illusions to divert our attention from observing that the government and the laws in reality work only one way: to protect the profits of the owning classes. This last is, I believe, not quite true: I feel convinced, since I have been in Russia, that American Republican institutions, disastrously as they are always being abused, have some permanent and absolute value. I don't believe that they will necessarily be destroyed in the course of the transformation of society, any more than our advanced "technique," but think it probable that they will, on the contrary, like it, make the transition to socialism easier. But we shall be in no position to reprove the Russians till we shall be able to show them an American socialism which is free from the Russian defects.

And in the meantime, in spite of these defects, you feel in the Soviet Union that you are at the moral top of the world where the light never really goes out, just as you know in the Gulf of Finland, where the summer day never ends, that you are close to the geographical top. The central fact, from which one can never escape, which one is always stumbling upon under all the fluid surface of the casualness, the frivolity, the timidity, the evasiveness, the inexactitude, the

apathy, of some aspects of Russian life, is the relationship of the Russian people to the tomb under the Kremlin wall. Day after day, rain or shine, the people line up and wait for hours in slowly advancing queues that loop back and forth across Red Square, in order to go into the tomb, to step down past the walls of Ural marble, black and gray and sown with flakes of lapis lazuli like blue silken butterflies' wings, and to stare for a moment at that face, where the soldier with his bayonet stands staring. It is not the face you expect if you have looked at pictures and statues, and it is different even from the death-mask. But, in shrinking, the flesh has brought out qualities, fundamental as the fine grain of wood, which are also strikingly apparent in this latter. We are used to seeing Lenin represented, as he must usually have been during his waking life, determined, intent, energetic, arguing, explaining, imposing himself; and in the death-mask we are still made aware of the aggressive intellect of the box-like skull which seems always to be tilted forward: the nose and lips are still rather thick, the eyebrows sharply bristling. The casts of the hands show finely tapering but effective square-tipped fingers. But the head in the tomb, with its high forehead, its straight nose, its pointed beard (which has grown gray on the dead man's cheeks), its sensitive nostrils and eyelids, gives an impression in some ways strangely similar to that one gets from the supposed death-mask of Shakespeare. It is a beautiful face, of exquisite fineness; and—what surely proves sufficiently its authenticity—it is profoundly aristocratic. Yet it is an aristocrat who is not specialized as an aristocrat, a poet who is not specialized as a poet, a scientist who is not specialized as a scientist. Nor is it in the least the

face of a saint. Except for the slightly
slanting eyes, it seems today hardly
even the face of a Russian. For here
humanity has produced, independent
of all the old disciplines, the scientist
whose study is humanity, the poet
whose material is not images but the
water and salt of human beings—the
superior man who has burst out of
the classes and claimed all that man
has done which is superior for the
refinement of mankind as a whole.
And here we come to gaze down at
this shell of flesh, in its last thinness,
its delicacy and fragility, before it
crumbles and loses the mold—this
bone and skin still keeping the stamp
of that intellect, that passion, that
will, whose emergence has stunned
the world almost with more embarrassment at being made to extend its conception of what man, as man alone,
can accomplish, than admiration at
the achievements of genius. And these
countrymen of his are amazed, with
their formless and expressionless faces,
when they look down on him and
know that he was one of them, and
that he invoked from their loose and
sluggish plasm all those triumphs to
which life must rise and to which he
thought himself the casual guidepost.
                                          1936

MAX LERNER
(1902–   )

*IT IS LATER
THAN YOU THINK* *

EPILOGUE

HISTORY IS WRITTEN
BY THE SURVIVORS

We tend to console ourselves in
these distracted times with the reflec-

* From *It is Later Than You Think*
by Max Lerner. Copyright 1938 by Max
Lerner. By permission of The Viking
Press, Inc., New York.

tion that our trouble cannot last;
that the enemies of democratic humanism are doomed by the constellation of historic forces; that the dictators of today must crash as the dictators of the past have inevitably
crashed. We write works on the Greek
tyrants and Caesar and Genghis and
Napoleon to reinforce the moral, and
we point to the patent impossibility
that the ethic of the knuckle-duster
and the bludgeon will finally triumph.

All this is very well. It is good to
act with belief in yourself—provided
that you act. It is good to gird yourself in the armor of a faith, and to
march to the stirring notes of some
poetic democratic myth—provided
that the march is not merely a processional, and that at the end of it you
are ready, if need be, to fight. The
danger is that, having concluded that
the long-run forces of history are on
our side, we shall not stir ourselves
to act within the framework of those
forces and so translate tendencies into
realities. We err if we act on impulse
or for action's sake, with disregard of
the lines of force discernible in history. But we err also if we trust
blindly to the impersonal forces of
history, whether the trust be that of
the idealist who sees in the logic of
events the divine triumph of truth, or
the materialist who sees in it the ruthless march of technological imperatives. Actually the so-called "lessons"
of history are for the most part the
rationalizations of the victors. History
is written by the survivors.

That is why it will be scant con-
solation for the democracies to go
down to extinction still believing in
the ultimate rightness of their cause.
And that is why the first imperative
of democratic humanism is to survive.
There is no question here of setting
up a cult of the survivor, no question

of celebrating self-preservation as a form of individual or group egoism. Survival is not the be-all of life. If it were, an intransigent pacifism would be the only tenable credo. Nor is survival the test of the possession of great qualities, by either the individual or the group; the belief in such a test marked the degradation of nineteenth-century thought as expressed in the social Darwinianism of the "survival of the fittest," as made into a system of social thought by Herbert Spencer; it is also one of the marks of twentieth-century facism. I have in mind survival only in an instrumental sense. Democratic society, whatever its moral and cultural superiority, must first survive if it is to fulfill its function in world history. It must survive to write the history of its struggles; for it is the historian, in the role of the poet mythologizing the past, who is the effective architect of the future.

But the need for survival should not mean a case of democratic jitters. As I write, the world is in an ungentle mood. The result is the crisis psychology of our time, with its characteristic brink-of-war and brink-of-facism mentality. Anything, we feel, may happen any day. Each day may spell the difference between the *status quo* and disaster. Such an attitude is possible only if you lack the historical sense. Where there is so pervasive and continued a sense of crisis, with small things and large seen on the same plane, there is no true perception of the nature of crisis. Such a sense of strain is alien to the cool-headed detachment necessary to evaluate the events that are taking place and the forces we must reckon with. The truer perspective is that of the military campaign, where perspective means neither fright nor indifference, but the mapping out of objectives and obstacles, the calculation of probable losses, the concentration of strength at critical points.

We owe to Justice Holmes the notion of "the campaign of history." History is a long-drawn, far-flung series of engagements, in which in any generation some class or nation or leader may be strategic and determine the fortunes of the whole campaign. But while the military figure is suggestive, we must not make the mistake of thinking of war itself as the most important part of the campaign of history.

For our generation the question of war and peace is mainly relevant because it sets the framework of our other activities. A precipitous war, engulfing the world, will engross the energies that might have gone into the task of democratic construction. But a war long deferred yet finally not avoided, timed by the dictators so as to catch the democracies when they are most divided and demoralized and the facists when they are unified and prepared, may be even more catastrophic. War even under the most favorable circumstances solves no problems. Its importance lies only in the fact that it may set the framework of our efforts in each of those national units in which we must work out our destiny in the calculable future. A war or a peace that results in a fascist world hegemony will doom everything that democratic humanism has accomplished, and everything it looks forward to. And while there may be a possibility in the ultimate future that even a triumphant facism, as an unstable economic form, will finally resolve itself into some more stable form of socialism and allow for a rekindling of the democratic effort, such a possibility would be pushed into a future so indefinite as to run almost in terms of geologic time. Meanwhile, the price we should have to pay would be Cathay-cycles of barbarism.

Even a war or a peace that resulted in a democratic triumph would be in itself no social solution. It would mean, however, the space of another generation or two snatched for the task of democratic construction. This task, for all the currently fashionable irrationalism, does lend itself to human and rational effort. It simplifies history to attribute its trends and events wholly to human will or blind chance or inevitable determinisms. History is a long campaign in which the underlying factors are the imperatives of technology, the drives of class relations, the logic of social institutions, the ingrained habits and traditions of nations. But within that long campaign the day-to-day battles may turn on factors of contingency or chance, on individual generalship and bravery, on the forced march and the sustained attack, on the scientific planning of strategy and the precision of carrying it out. Machiavelli's formula for history—as made up of *virtù, fortuna, necessità*—still remains, when translated into our own corresponding concepts, the most adequate. It is our task to understand the nature of the underlying imperatives, to take contingencies into account, to summon our best strength and will in working within the framework they make for us.

Seen in such terms, the task of democratic construction lies within the compass of social possibility. Today it depends upon the survival of the crisis states, the control of the forces of economic disintegration, the maintenance of democratic procedures and attitudes. Tomorrow it may mean the meeting of a counter-revolutionary threat. The day after tomorrow it means the transformation of capitalist democracy into a democratic planned collectivism.

Much depends on our recognition of time as a factor in our destiny. "Time is real," T. E. Hulme once said, "for the individual, but not for the race." He said it because, like his master Sorel, he was reacting against the doctrine of progress. But we do not live in the roaring optimistic days; it would be a melancholy superfluity to berate the doctrine of progress in an age in which men's sensibilities have corroded, both East and West— an age in which the Japanese code of Bushido has ended in the bombing of defenseless cities, and the culture that produced Lessing's *Nathan der Weise* has turned not only anti-Jewish but anti-Enlightenment and anti-science. Time does exist, for the group as for the individual. It is over the course of time that economies are transformed, polities move toward greatness or decay, cultures are brutalized or achieve maturity. It is only over the long span of time that we can hope to build a democratic world, and rivet the dignity of the common man into the framework of history. It is, meanwhile, only in the breathing-spells we snatch from the pressure of reaction that we can strive to put up the scaffolding that will allow us to repair and preserve the democratic tradition.

If there is a note of urgency in what I have written, it is because time, as the lawyers say, is of the essence of our problem. Before the crisis-democracies can be transformed into socialized collectivisms they must first survive. They must survive against the anarchy of unplanned capitalism, the concentration of corporate power, the sabotaging effects of reactionary business, the incipient fascist movements within, the aggressive fascist imperialisms without.

What is needed, to make our effort effective, is not a crisis mentality but a sense of timing—a calculation of where we are, how long we dare delay, where and how we must act decisively.

On a clock-tower in a Spanish square is written—so the story runs—"It Is Later Than You Think." The implications are religious and admonitory; the command to prepare in this world for judgment in the next. On a wall in Paris on the eve of the Revolution, some *sans-culotte* scrawled the same words in French. The implications are again admonitory, but the judgment promised is man-made rather than God-made. Today the words need to be neither religious nor revolutionary, but secular and constructive. They are meant to clarify our sense of political timing.

I use them in several connected senses. First, we have in many respects already gone farther than is generally supposed in moving towards economic collectivism. But, secondly, the accumulation of weaknesses and tensions in our economic system and our social order has also gone farther than is generally supposed, and the danger to our democratic humanist traditions is accordingly greater. Third, the need for firm, decisive, sustained action to stave off collapse and finish the job of socialization is more immediate and more pressing than is generally supposed.

Finally, we have gone farther than one might think in a recognition of the democratic bonds between men. In France, England, America, Spain, China, the Scandinavias, Mexico, the common man is glimpsing that what ties him to men like himself in other crisis-democracies is greater than what ties the fascists of all other countries together. We have one thing to thank the fascists for. In order to meet their threat, and the threat of the social collapse out of which fascism emerges, we have not only been spurred to unexampled national efforts of mass organization and administrative control, but we have had to cut across national boundaries as never before in the history of nations. The beginnings of this trans-national fellowship are slight, but they are beginnings. It is a fellowship not of military need or social hatred, but of the common human values of ordinary men everywhere.

It is not much that we ask of our era—only a chance to consolidate and continue the affirmative achievements of science and intellectual freedom in human history, to provide an enlargement of human life for the masses, to provide a base from which individuals can explore the possibilities of human effort. We want no *daimon* of Goethe, Schiller, Hölderin, no superman of Nietzsche—only human men rising to the fullest stature of which they are capable.

1938

RICHARD WRIGHT
(1908–   )

BRIGHT AND MORNING STAR *

I

She stood with her black face some six inches from the moist windowpane and wondered when on earth would it ever stop raining. It might keep up like this all week, she thought. She heard rain droning upon the roof and high up in the wet sky her eyes followed the silent rush of a bright shaft of yellow that swung from the airplane beacon in far off Memphis.

* Reprinted from *Uncle Tom's Children* by Richard Wright by permission of Harper & Brothers. Copyright, 1938, by Richard Wright.

Momently she could see it cutting through the rainy dark; it would hover a second like a gleaming sword above her head, then vanish. She sighed, troubling, Johnny-Boys been trampin in this slop all day wid no decent shoes on his feet. . . . Through the window she could see the rich black earth sprawling outside in the night. There was more rain than the clay could soak up; pools stood everywhere. She yawned and mumbled: "Rains good n bad. It kin make seeds bus up thu the groun, er it kin bog things down lika wata-soaked coffin." Her hands were folded loosely over her stomach and the hot air of the kitchen traced a filmy vein of sweat on her forehead. From the cook stove came the soft singing of burning wood and now and then a throaty bubble rose from a pot of simmering greens.

"Shucks, Johnny-Boy coulda let somebody else do all tha runnin in the rain. Theres others bettah fixed fer it than he is. But, naw! Johnny-Boy ain the one t trust nobody t do nothin. Hes gotta do it *all* hissef. . . ."

She glanced at a pile of damp clothes in a zinc tub. Waal, Ah bettah git t work. She turned, lifted a smoothing iron with a thick pad of cloth, touched a spit-wet finger to it with a quick, jerking motion: *smiiitz!* Yeah; its hot! Stooping, she took a blue work-shirt from the tub and shook it out. With a deft twist of her shoulders she caught the iron in her right hand; the fingers of her left hand took a piece of wax from a tin box and a frying sizzle came as she smeared the bottom. She was thinking of nothing now; her hands followed a lifelong ritual of toil. Spreading a sleeve, she ran the hot iron to and fro until the wet cloth became stiff. She was deep in the midst of her work when a song rose up out of the far off

days of her childhood and broke through half-parted lips:

Hes the Lily of the Valley, the Bright n Mawnin Star
Hes the Fairest of Ten Thousan t mah soul . . .

A gust of wind dashed rain against the window. Johnny-Boy oughta c mon home n eat his suppah. Aw, Lawd! Itd be fine ef Sug could eat wid us tonight! Itd be like ol' times! Mabbe aftah all it wont be long fo he comes back. Tha lettah Ah got from im last week said *Don give up hope*. . . . Yeah; we gotta live in hope. Then both of her sons, Sug and Johnny-Boy, would be back with her.

With an involuntary nervous gesture, she stopped and stood still, listening. But the only sound was the lulling fall of rain. Shucks, ain no usa me ackin this way, she thought. Ever time they gits ready to hol them meetings Ah gits jumpity. Ah been a lil scared ever since Sug went t jail. She heard the clock ticking and looked. Johnny-Boys a *hour* late! He sho mus be havin a time doin all tha trampin, trampin thru the mud. . . . But her fear was a quiet one; it was more like an intense brooding than a fear; it was a sort of hugging of hated facts so closely that she could feel their grain, like letting cold water run over her hand from a faucet on a winter morning.

She ironed again, faster now, as if she felt the more she engaged her body in work the less she would think. But how could she forget Johnny-Boy out there on those wet fields rounding up white and black Communists for a meeting tomorrow? And that was just what Sug had been doing when the sheriff had caught him, beat him, and tried to make him tell who and where his comrades were. Po Sug! They sho musta beat the boy somethin awful! But, thank Gawd, he didnt talk! He ain no weaklin, Sug ain! Hes been lion-hearted all his life long.

That had happened a year ago. And now each time those meetings came around the old terror surged back. While shoving the iron a cluster of toiling days returned; days of washing and ironing to feed Johnny-Boy and Sug so they could do party work; days of carrying a hundred pounds of white folks' clothes upon her head across fields sometimes wet and sometimes dry. But in those days a hundred pounds was nothing to carry carefully balanced upon her head while stepping by instinct over the corn and cotton rows. The only time it had seemed heavy was when she had heard of Sug's arrest. She had been coming home one morning with a bundle upon her head, her hands swinging idly by her sides, walking slowly with her eyes in front of her, when Bob, Johnny-Boy's pal, had called from across the fields and had come and told her that the sheriff had got Sug. That morning the bundle had become heavier than she could ever remember.

And each passing week now, though she spoke of it to no one, things were becoming heavier. The tubs of water and the smoothing iron and the bundle of clothes were becoming harder to lift, with her back aching so; and her work was taking longer, all because Sug was gone and she didn't know just when Johnny-Boy would be taken too. To ease the ache of anxiety that was swelling her heart, she hummed, then sang softly:

He walks wid me, He talks wid me
He tells me Ahm His own. . . .

Guiltily, she stopped and smiled. Looks like Ah jus cant seem t fergit them ol songs, no mattah how hard Ah tries. . . . She had learned them when she was a little girl living and working on a farm. Every Monday morning from the corn and cotton fields the slow strains had floated from her mother's lips, lonely and haunting; and later, as the years had filled with gall, she had learned their deep meaning. Long hours of scrubbing floors for a few cents a day had taught her who Jesus was, what a great boon it was to cling to Him, to be like Him and suffer without a mumbling word. She had poured the yearning of her life into the songs, feeling buoyed with a faith beyond this world. The figure of the Man nailed in agony to the Cross, His burial in a cold grave, His transfigured Resurrection, His being breath and clay, God and Man—all had focused her feelings upon an imagery which had swept her life into a wondrous vision.

But as she had grown older, a cold white mountain, the white folks and their laws, had swum into her vision and shattered her songs and their spell of peace. To her that white mountain was temptation, something to lure her from her Lord, a part of the world God had made in order that she might endure it and come through all the stronger, just as Christ had risen with greater glory from the tomb. The days crowded with trouble had enhanced her faith and she had grown to love hardship with a bitter pride; she had obeyed the laws of the white folks with a soft smile of secret knowing.

After her mother had been snatched up to heaven in a chariot of fire, the years had brought her a rough workingman and two black babies, Sug and Johnny-Boy, all three of whom she had wrapped in the charm and magic of her vision. Then she was tested by no less than God; her man died, a trial which she bore with the strength shed by the grace of her vision; finally even the memory of her man faded into the vision itself, leaving her with two black boys growing tall, slowly into manhood.

Then one day grief had come to her heart when Johnny-Boy and Sug had walked forth demanding their lives. She had sought to fill their eyes with her vision, but they would have none of it. And she had wept when they began to boast of the strength shed by a new and terrible vision.

But she had loved them, even as she loved them now; bleeding, her heart had followed them. She could have done no less, being an old woman in a strange world. And day by day her sons had ripped from her startled eyes her old vision, and image by image had given her a new one, different, but great and strong enough to fling her into the light of another grace. The wrongs and sufferings of black men had taken the place of Him nailed to the Cross; the meager beginnings of the party had become another Resurrection; and the hate of those who would destroy her new faith had quickened in her a hunger to feel how deeply her new strength went.

"Lawd, Johnny-Boy," she would sometimes say, "Ah jus wan them white folks t try t make me tell *who* is *in* the *party* n who *ain*! Ah jus wan em t try, n Ahll show em somethin they never thought a black woman could have!"

But sometimes like tonight, while lost in the forgetfulness of work, the past and the present would become mixed in her; while toiling under a strange star for a new freedom the old songs would slip from her lips with their beguiling sweetness.

The iron was getting cold. She put more wood into the fire, stood again at the window and watched the yellow blade of light cut through the wet darkness. Johnny-Boy ain here yit. . . . Then, before she was aware of it, she was still, listening for sounds. Under the drone of rain she heard the slosh of feet in mud. Tha ain Johnny-Boy. She knew his long, heavy footsteps in a million. She heard feet come on the porch. Some woman. . . . She heard bare knuckles knock three times, then once. Thas some of them comrades! She unbarred the door, cracked it a few inches, and flinched from the cold rush of damp wind.

"Whos tha?"

"Its me!"

"Who?"

"Me, Reva!"

She flung the door open.

"Lawd, chile c mon in!"

She stepped to one side and a thin, blond-haired white girl ran through the door; as she slid the bolt she heard the girl gasping and shaking her wet clothes. Somethings wrong! Reva wouldna walked a mile t mah house in all this slop fer nothin! Tha gals stuck onto Johnny-Boy. Ah wondah ef anythin happened t im?

"Git on inter the kitchen, Reva, where its warm."

"Lawd, Ah sho is wet!"

"How yuh reckon youhd be, in all tha rain?"

"Johnny-Boy ain here *yit*?" asked Reva.

"Naw! N ain no usa yuh worryin bout im. Jus yuh git them shoes off! Yuh wanna ketch yo deatha col?" She stood looking absently. Yeah; its somethin about the party er Johnny-Boy thas gone wrong. Lawd, Ah wondah ef her pa knows how she feels bout Johnny-Boy? "Honey, yuh hadnt oughta come out in sloppy weather like this."

"Ah had t come, An Sue."

She led Reva to the kitchen.

"Git them shoes off n git close t the stove so yuhll git dry!"

"An Sue, Ah got somethin t tell yuh . . ."

The words made her hold her breath. Ah bet its somethin bout Johnny-Boy!

"Whut, honey?"

"The sheriff wuz by our house tonight. He come t see pa."

"Yeah?"

"He done got word from somewheres bout tha meetin tomorrow."

"Is it Johnny-Boy, Reva?"

"Aw, naw, An Sue! Ah ain hearda word bout im. Ain yuh seen im tonight?"

"He ain come home t eat yit."

"Where kin he be?"

"Lawd knows, chile."

"Somebodys gotta tell them comrades that meetings off," said Reva. "The sheriffs got men watchin our house. Ah had t slip out t git here widout em followin me."

"Reva?"

"Hunh?"

"Ahma ol woman n Ah wants yuh t tell me the truth."

"Whut, An Sue?"

"Yuh ain tryin t fool me, is yuh?"

"*Fool* yuh?"

"Bout Johnny-Boy?"

"Lawd, naw, An Sue!"

"Ef theres anythin wrong jus tell me, chile. Ah kin stan it."

She stood by the ironing board, her hands as usual folded loosely over her stomach, watching Reva pull off her water-clogged shoes. She was feeling that Johnny-Boy was already lost to her; she was feeling the pain that would come when she knew it for certain; and she was feeling that she would have to be brave and bear it. She was like a person caught in a swift current of water and knew where the water was sweeping her and did not want to go on but had to go on to the end.

"It ain nothin bout Johnny-Boy, An Sue," said Reva. "But we gotta do somethin er we'll all git inter trouble."

"How the sheriff know about tha meetin?"

"Thas whut pa wans t know."

"Somebody done turned Judas."

"Sho looks like it."

"Ah bet it wuz some of them new ones," she said.

"Its hard t tell," said Reva.

"Lissen, Reva, yuh oughta stay here n git dry, but yuh bettah git back n tell yo pa Johnny-Boy ain here n Ah don know when hes gonna show up. *Somebodys* gotta tell them comrades t stay erway from you pas house."

She stood with her back to the window, looking at Reva's wide, blue eyes. Po critter! Gotta go back thu all tha slop! Though she felt sorry for Reva, not once did she think that it would not have to be done. Being a woman, Reva was not suspect; she would *have* to go. It was just as natural for Reva to go back through the cold rain as it was for her to iron night and day, or for Sug to be in jail. Right now, Johnny-Boy was out there on those dark fields trying to get home. Lawd, don let em git im tonight! In spite of herself her feelings became torn. She loved her son and, loving him, she loved what he was trying to do. Johnny-Boy was happiest when he was working for the party, and her love for him was for his happiness. She frowned, trying hard to fit something together in her feelings: for her to try to stop Johnny-Boy was to admit that all the toil of years meant nothing; and to let him go meant that sometime or other he would be caught, like Sug. In facing it this way she felt a little stunned, as though she had come suddenly upon a blank wall in the dark. But outside in the rain

were people, white and black, whom
she had known all her life. Those
people depended upon Johnny-Boy,
loved him and looked to him as a man
and leader. Yeah; hes gotta keep on;
he cant stop now. . . . She looked
at Reva; she was crying and pulling
her shoes back on with reluctant fingers.

"Whut yuh carryin on tha way fer,
chile?"

"Yuh done los Sug, now yuh
sendin Johnny-Boy . . ."

"Ah got t, honey."

She was glad she could say that.
Reva believed in black folks and not
for anything in the world would she
falter before her. In Reva's trust and
acceptance of her she had found her
first feelings of humanity; Reva's love
was her refuge from shame and degradation. If in the early days of her life
the white mountain had driven her
back from the earth, then in her last
days Reva's love was drawing her
toward it, like the beacon that swung
through the night outside. She heard
Reva sobbing.

"Hush, honey!"

"Mah brothers in jail too! Ma cries
ever day . . ."

"Ah know, honey."

She helped Reva with her coat; her
fingers felt the scant flesh of the girl's
shoulders. She don git ernuff t eat,
she thought. She slipped her arms
around Reva's waist and held her
close for a moment.

"Now, yuh stop that cryin."

"A-a-ah c-c-cant hep it. . . ."

"Everythingll be awright; Johnny-
Boyll be back."

"Yuh think so?"

"Sho, chile. Cos he will."

Neither of them spoke again until
they stood in the doorway. Outside
they could hear water washing
through the ruts of the street.

"Be sho n send Johnny-Boy t tell

the folks t stay erway from pas
house," said Reva.

"Ahll tell im. Don yuh worry."

"Good-bye!"

"Good-bye!"

Leaning against the door jamb, she
shook her head slowly and watched
Reva vanish through the falling rain.

II

She was back at her board, ironing
when she heard feet sucking in the
mud of the back yard; feet she knew
from long years of listening were
Johnny-Boy's. But tonight, with all
the rain and fear, his coming was like
a leaving, was almost more than she
could bear. Tears welled to her eyes
and she blinked them away. She felt
that he was coming so that she could
give him up; to see him now was to
say good-bye. But it was a good-bye
she knew she could never say; they
were not that way toward each other.
All day long they could sit in the
same room and not speak; she was his
mother and he was her son. Most of
the time a nod or a grunt would carry
all the meaning that she wanted to
convey to him, or he to her. She did
not even turn her head when she
heard him come stomping into the
kitchen. She heard him pull up a
chair, sit, sigh, and draw off his
muddy shoes; they fell to the floor
with heavy thuds. Soon the kitchen
was full of the scent of his drying
socks and his burning pipe. Tha boys
hongry! She paused and looked at him
over her shoulder; he was puffing at
his pipe with his head tilted back and
his feet propped up on the edge of the
stove; his eyelids drooped and his wet
clothes steamed from the heat of the
fire. Lawd, tha boy gits mo like his pa
ever day he lives, she mused, her lips
breaking in a slow faint smile. Hols
tha pipe in his mouth just like his pa
usta hol his. Wondah how they

woulda got erlong ef his pa hada lived? They oughta liked each other, they so mucha like. She wished there could have been other children besides Sug, so Johnny-Boy would not have to be so much alone. A man needs a woman by his side. . . . She thought of Reva; she liked Reva; the brightest glow her heart had ever known was when she had learned that Reva loved Johnny-Boy. But beyond Reva were cold white faces. Ef theys caught it means *death*. . . . She jerked around when she heard Johnny-Boy's pipe clatter to the floor. She saw him pick it up, smile sheepishly at her, and wag his head.

"Gawd, Ahm sleepy," he mumbled.

She got a pillow from her room and gave it to him.

"Here," she said.

"Hunh," he said, putting the pillow between his head and the back of the chair.

They were silent again. Yes, she would have to tell him to go back out into the cold rain and slop; maybe to get caught; maybe for the last time; she didn't know. But she would let him eat and get dry before telling him that the sheriff knew of the meeting to be held at Lem's tomorrow. And she would make him take a big dose of soda before he went out; soda always helped to stave off a cold. She looked at the clock. It was eleven. Theres time yit. Spreading a newspaper on the apron of the stove, she placed a heaping plate of greens upon it, a knife, a fork, a cup of coffee, a slab of cornbread, and a dish of peach cobbler.

"Yo suppahs ready," she said.

"Yeah," he said.

He did not move. She ironed again. Presently, she heard him eating. When she could no longer hear his knife tinkling against the edge of the plate, she knew he was through. It

was almost twelve now. She would let him rest a little while longer before she told him. Till one er'clock, mabbe. Hes so tired. . . . She finished her ironing, put away the board, and stacked the clothes in her dresser drawer. She poured herself a cup of black coffee, drew up a chair, sat down and drank.

"Yuh almos dry," she said, not looking around.

"Yeah," he said, turning sharply to her.

The tone of voice in which she had spoken had let him know that more was coming. She drained her cup and waited a moment longer.

"Reva wuz here."

"Yeah?"

"She lef bout a hour ergo."

"Whut she say?"

"She said ol man Lem had visit from the sheriff today."

"Bout the meetin?"

She saw him stare at the coals glowing red through the crevices of the stove and run his fingers nervously through his hair. She knew he was wondering how the sheriff had found out. In the silence he would ask a wordless question and in the silence she would answer wordlessly. Johnny-Boys too trustin, she thought. Hes trying t make the party big n hes takin in folks fastern he kin git t know em. You cant trust ever white man yuh meet. . . .

"Yuh know, Johnny-Boy, yuh been takin in a lotta them white folks lately . . ."

"Aw, ma!"

"But, Johnny-Boy . . ."

"Please, don talk t me bout tha now, ma."

"Yuh ain t ol t lissen n learn, son," she said.

"Ah know whut yuh gonna say, ma. N yuh wrong. Yuh cant judge folks jus by how yuh feel bout em n by how long yuh done knowed em. Ef we start tha we wouldn't have *no*body in the party. When folks pledge they word t be with us, then we gotta take em in. Wes too weak t be choosy."

He rose abruptly, rammed his hands into his pockets, and stood facing the window; she looked at his back in a long silence. She knew his faith; it was deep. He had always said that black men could not fight the rich bosses alone; a man could not fight with every hand against him. But he believes so hard hes blind, she thought. At odd times they had had these arguments before; always she would be pitting her feelings against the hard necessity of his thinking, and always she would lose. She shook her head. Po Johnny-Boy; he don know . . .

"But ain nona our folks tol, Johnny-Boy," she said.

"How yuh know?" he asked. His voice came low and with a tinge of anger. He still faced the window and now and then the yellow blade of light flicked across the sharp outline of his black face.

"Cause Ah know em," she said.

"*Any*body mighta tol," he said.

"It wuznt nona *our* folks," she said again.

She saw his hand sweep in a swift arc of disgust.

"*Our* folks! Ma, who in Gawds name is *our* folks?"

"The folks we wuz born n raised wid, son. The folks we *know*!"

"We cant make the party grow tha way, ma."

"It mighta been Booker," she said.

"Yuh don know."

". . . er Blattberg . . ."

"Fer Chrissakes!"

". . . er any of the fo-five others whut joined las week."

"Ma, yuh jus don wan me t go out tonight," he said.

"Yo ol ma wans yuh t be careful, son."

"Ma, when yuh start doubtin folks in the party, then there ain no end."

"Son, Ah knows ever black man n woman in this parta the county," she said, standing too. "Ah watched em grow up; Ah even heped birth n nurse some of em; Ah knows em *all* from way back. There ain none of em that *coulda* tol! The folks Ah know jus don open they dos n ast death t walk in! Son, it was wuz some of them *white* folks! Yuh jus mark mah word n wait n see!"

"Why is it gotta be *white* folks?" he asked. "Ef they tol, then theys jus Judases, thas all."

"Son, look at whuts befo yuh."

He shook his head and sighed.

"Ma, Ah done tol yuh a hundred times. Ah cant see white n Ah cant see black," he said. "Ah sees rich men n Ah sees po men."

She picked up his dirty dishes and piled them in a pan. Out of the corners of her eyes she saw him sit and pull on his wet shoes. Hes goin! When she put the last dish away he was standing fully dressed, warming his hands over the stove. Jus a few mo minutes now n he'll be gone, like Sug, mabbe. Her throat tightened. This black mans fight takes *ever*thin! Looks like Gawd put us in this world jus t beat us down!

"Keep this, ma," he said.

She saw a crumpled wad of money in his outstretched fingers.

"Naw; yuh keep it. Yuh might need it."

"It ain mine, ma. It berlongs t the party."

"But, Johnny-Boy, yuh might hafta go erway!"

"Ah kin make out."

"Don fergit yosef too much, son."

"Ef Ah don come back theyll need it."

He was looking at her face and she was looking at the money.

"Yuh keep tha," she said slowly. "Ahll give em the money."

"From where?"

"Ah got some."

"Where yuh git it from?"

She sighed.

"Ah been saving a dollah a week fer Sug ever since hes been in jail."

"Lawd, ma!"

She saw the look of puzzled love and wonder in his eyes. Clumsily, he put the money back into his pocket.

"Ahm gone," he said.

"Here; drink this glass of soda watah."

She watched him drink, then put the glass away.

"Waal," he said.

"Take the stuff outta yo pockets!"

She lifted the lid of the stove and he dumped all the papers from his pocket into the fire. She followed him to the door and made him turn round.

"Lawd, yuh tryin to maka revolution n yuh cant even keep yo coat buttoned." Her nimble fingers fastened his collar high around his throat. "There!"

He pulled the brim of his hat low over his eyes. She opened the door and with the suddenness of the cold gust of wind that struck her face, he was gone. She watched the black fields and the rain take him, her eyes burning. When the last faint footstep could no longer be heard, she closed the door, went to her bed, lay down, and pulled the cover over her while fully dressed. Her feelings coursed with the rhythm of the rain: Hes gone! Lawd, Ah *know* hes gone! Her blood felt cold.

III

She was floating in a grey void somewhere between sleeping and dreaming and then suddenly she was wide awake, hearing and feeling in the same instant the thunder of the door crashing in and a cold wind filling the room. It was pitch black and she stared, resting on her elbows, her mouth open, not breathing, her ears full of the sound of tramping feet and booming voices. She knew at once: They lookin fer im! Then, filled with her will, she was on her feet, rigid, waiting, listening.

"The lamps burnin!"

"Yuh see her?"

"Naw!"

"Look in the kitchen!"

"Gee, this place smells like niggers!"

"Say, somebodys here er been here!"

"Yeah; theres fire in the stove!"

"Mabbe hes been here n gone?"

"Boy, look at these jars of jam!"

"Niggers make good jam!"

"Git some bread!"

"Heres some cornbread!"

"Say, lemme git some!"

"Take it easy! Theres plenty here!"

"Ahma take some of this stuff home!"

"Look, heres a pota greens!"

"N some hot cawffee!"

"Say, yuh guys! C mon! Cut it out! We didnt come here fer a feas!"

She walked slowly down the hall. They lookin fer im, but they ain got im yit! She stopped in the doorway, her gnarled, black hands as always folded over her stomach, but tight now, so tightly the veins bulged. The kitchen was crowded with white men in glistening raincoats. Though the lamp burned, their flashlights still glowed in red fists. Across her floor she saw the muddy tracks of their boots.

"Yuh white folks git outta mah house!"

There was quick silence; every face turned toward her. She saw a sudden movement, but did not know what it meant until something hot and wet slammed her squarely in the face. She gasped, but did not move. Calmly, she wiped the warm, greasy liquor of greens from her eyes with her left hand. One of the white men had thrown a handful of greens out of the pot at her.

"How they taste, ol bitch?"

"Ah ast yuh t git outta mah house!"

She saw the sheriff detach himself from the crowd and walk toward her.

"Now, Anty . . ."

"White man, don yuh *Anty* me!"

"Yuh ain got the right sperit!"

"Sperit hell! Yuh git these men outta mah house!"

"Yuh ack like yuh don like it!"

"Naw, Ah don like it, n yuh knows dam waal Ah don!"

"Whut yuh gonna do bout it?"

"Ahm tellin yuh t git outta mah house!"

"Gittin sassy?"

"Ef telling yuh t git outta mah house is sass, then Ahm sassy!"

Her words came in a tense whisper; but beyond, back of them, she was watching, thinking, judging the men.

"Listen, Anty," the sheriff's voice came soft and low. "Ahm here t hep yuh. How come yah wanna ack this way?"

"Yuh ain never heped yo *own* sef since yuh been born," she flared. "How kin the likes of yuh hep me?"

One of the white men came forward and stood directly in front of her.

"Lissen, nigger woman, yuh talkin t *white* men!"

"Ah don care who Ahm talkin t!"

"Yuhll wish some day yuh did!"

"Not t the likes of yuh!"

"Yuh need somebody t teach yuh how t be a good nigger!"

"*Yuh* cant teach it t me!"

"Yuh gonna change yo tune."

"Not longs mah bloods warm!"

"Don git smart now!"

"Yuh git outta mah house!"

"Spose we don go?" the sheriff asked.

They were crowded around her. She had not moved since she had taken her place in the doorway. She was thinking only of Johnny-Boy as she stood there giving and taking words; and she knew that they, too, were thinking of Johnny-Boy. She knew they wanted him, and her heart was daring them to take him from her.

"Spose we don go?" the sheriff asked again.

"Twenty of yuh runnin over one ol woman! Now, ain yuh white men glad yuh so brave?"

The sheriff grabbed her arm.

"C mon, now! Yuh done did ernuff sass fer one night. Wheres tha nigger son of yos?"

"Don yuh wished yuh knowed?"

"Yuh wanna git slapped?"

"Ah ain never seen one of yo kind tha wuznt too low fer . . ."

The sheriff slapped her straight across her face with his open palm. She fell back against a wall and sank to her knees.

"Is tha whut white men do t nigger women?"

She rose slowly and stood again, not even touching the place that ached from his blow, her hands folded over her stomach.

"Ah ain never seen one of yo kind tha wuznt too low fer . . ."

He slapped her again; she reeled backward several feet and fell on her side.

"Is tha whut we too low t do?"

She stood before him again, dry-eyed, as though she had not been struck. Her lips were numb and her chin was wet with blood.

"Aw, let her go! Its the nigger we wan!" said one.

"Wheres that nigger son of yos?" the sheriff asked.

"Find im," she said.

"By Gawd, ef we hafta find im we'll kill im!"

"He wont be the only nigger yuh ever killed," she said.

She was consumed with a bitter pride. There was nothing on this earth, she felt then, that they could not do to her but that she could take. She stood on a narrow plot of ground from which she would die before she was pushed. And then it was, while standing there feeling warm blood seeping down her throat, that she gave up Johnny-Boy, gave him up to the white folks. She gave him up because they had come tramping into her heart demanding him, thinking they could get him by beating her, thinking they could scare her into making her tell where he was. She gave him up because she wanted them to know that they could not get what they wanted by bluffing and killing.

"Wheres this meetin gonna be?" the sheriff asked.

"Don yuh wish yuh knowed?"

"Ain there gonna be a meetin?"

"How come yuh astin me?"

"There *is* gonna be a meetin," said the sheriff.

"Is it?"

"Ah gotta great mind t choke it outta yuh!"

"Yuh so smart," she said.

"We ain playin wid yuh!"

"Did Ah say yuh wuz?"

"Tha nigger son of yos is erroun here somewheres n Ah aim t find im," said the sheriff. "Ef yuh tell us where he is n ef he talks, mabbe he'll git off easy. But ef we hafta find im, we'll kill im! Ef we hafta find im, then yuh git a sheet t put over im in the mawnin, see? Gut yuh a sheet, cause hes gonna be dead!"

"He wont be the only nigger yuh ever killed," she said again.

The sheriff walked past her. The others followed. Yuh didnt git whut yuh wanted! she thought exultingly. N yuh ain gonna *never* git it! Hotly, something ached in her to make them feel the intensity of her pride and freedom; her heart groped to turn the bitter hours of her life into words of a kind that would make them feel that she had taken all they had done to her in her stride and could still take more. Her faith surged so strongly in her she was all but blinded. She walked behind them to the door, knotting and twisting her fingers. She saw them step to the muddy ground. Each whirl of the yellow beacon revealed glimpses of slanting rain. Her lips moved, then she shouted:

"Yuh didnt git whut yuh wanted! N yuh ain gonna nevah git it!"

The sheriff stopped and turned; his voice came low and hard.

"Now, by Gawd, thas ernuff outta yuh!"

"Ah know when Ah done said ernuff!"

"Aw, naw, yuh don!" he said. "Yuh don know when yuh done said ernuff, but Ahma teach yuh ternight!"

He was up the steps and across the porch with one bound. She backed into the hall, her eyes full on his face.

"Tell me when yuh gonna stop talkin!" he said, swinging his fist.

The blow caught her high on the cheek; her eyes went blank; she fell flat on her face. She felt the hard heel of his wet shoes coming into her temple and stomach.

"Lemee hear yuh talk some mo!"

She wanted to, but could not; pain numbed and choked her. She lay still and somewhere out of the grey void of unconsciousness she heard someone say: *aw fer chrissakes leave her erlone, its the nigger we wan. . . .*

IV

She never knew how long she had lain huddled in the dark hallway. Her first returning feeling was of a nameless fear crowding the inside of her, then a deep pain spreading from her temple downward over her body. Her ears were filled with the drone of rain and she shuddered from the cold wind blowing through the door. She opened her eyes and at first saw nothing. As if she were imagining it, she knew she was half-lying and half-sitting in a corner against a wall. With difficulty she twisted her neck and what she saw made her hold her breath—a vast white blur was suspended directly above her. For a moment she could not tell if her fear was from the blur or if the blur was from her fear. Gradually the blur resolved itself into a huge white face that slowly filled her vision. She was stone still, conscious really of the effort to breathe, feeling somehow that she existed only by the mercy of that white face. She had seen it before; its fear had gripped her many times; it had for her the fear of all the white faces she had ever seen in her life. *Sue* . . . As from a great distance, she heard her name being called. She was regaining consciousness now, but the fear was coming with her. She looked into the face of a white man, wanting to scream out for him to go; yet accepting his presence because she felt she had to. Though some remote part of her mind was active, her limbs were powerless. It was as if an invisible knife had split her in two, leaving one half of her lying there helpless, while the other half shrank in dread from a forgotten but familiar enemy. *Sue its me Sue its me* . . .

Then all at once the voice came clearly.

"Sue, its me! Its Booker!"

And she heard an answering voice speaking inside of her. Yeah, its Booker . . . The one whut jus joined . . . She roused herself, struggling for full consciousness; and as she did so she transferred to the person of Booker the nameless fear she felt. It seemed that Booker towered above her as a challenge to her right to exist upon the earth.

"Yuh awright?"

She did not answer; she started violently to her feet and fell.

"Sue, yuh hurt!"

"Yeah," she breathed.

"Where they hit yuh?"

"Its mah head," she whispered.

She was speaking even though she did not want to; the fear that had hold of her compelled her.

"They beat yuh?"

"Yeah."

"Them bastards! Them Gawddam bastards!"

She heard him saying it over and over; then she felt herself being lifted.

"Naw!" she gasped.

"Ahma take yuh t the kitchen!"

"Put me down!"

"But yuh cant stay here like this!"

She shrank in his arms and pushed her hands against his body; when she was in the kitchen she freed herself, sank into a chair, and held tightly to its back. She looked wonderingly at Booker. There was nothing about him that should frighten her so, but even that did not ease her tension. She saw him go to the water bucket, wet his handkerchief, wring it, and offer it to her. Distrustfully, she stared at the damp cloth.

"Here; put this on yo fohead . . ."

"Naw!"

"C mon; itll make yuh feel bettah!"

She hesitated in confusion. What

right had she to be afraid when someone was acting as kindly as this toward
her? Reluctantly, she leaned forward
and pressed the damp cloth to her
head. It helped. With each passing
minute she was catching hold of herself, yet wondering why she felt as
she did.

"Whut happened?"

"Ah don know."

"Yuh feel bettah?"

"Yeah."

"Who all wuz here?"

"Ah don know," she said again.

"Yo head still hurt?"

"Yeah."

"Gee, Ahm sorry."

"Ahm awright," she sighed and
buried her face in her hands.

She felt him touch her shoulder.

"Sue, Ah got some bad news fer
yuh . . ."

She knew; she stiffened and grew
cold. It had happened; she stared dry-
eyed, with compressed lips.

"Its mah Johnny-Boy," she said.

"Yeah; Ahm awful sorry t hafta tell
yuh this way. But Ah thought yuh
oughta know . . ."

Her tension eased and a vacant
place opened up inside of her. A voice
whispered, Jesus, hep me!

"W-w-where is he?"

"They got im out t Foleys Woods
tryin t make him tell who the others
is."

"He ain gonna tell," she said. "They
just as waal kill im, cause he ain
gonna nevah tell."

"Ah hope he don," said Booker.
"But he didnt hava chance t tell the
others. They grabbed im jus as he
got t the woods."

Then all the horror of it flashed
upon her; she saw flung out over the
rainy countryside an array of shacks
where white and black comrades were
sleeping; in the morning they would
be rising and going to Lem's; then

they would be caught. And that
meant terror, prison, and death. The
comrades would have to be told; she
would have to tell them; she could not
entrust Johnny-Boy's work to another,
and especially not to Booker as long
as she felt toward him as she did.
Gripping the bottom of the chair with
both hands, she tried to rise; the room
blurred and she swayed. She found
herself resting in Booker's arms.

"Lemme go!"

"Sue, yuh too weak t walk!"

"Ah gotta tell em!" she said.

"Set down, Sue! Yuh hurt! Yuh
sick!"

When seated, she looked at him
helplessly.

"Sue, lissen! Johnny-Boys caught.
Ahm here. Yuh tell me who they is
n Ahll tell em."

She stared at the floor and did not
answer. Yes; she was too weak to go.
There was no way for her to tramp
all those miles through the rain to-
night. But should she tell Booker? If
only she had somebody like Reva to
talk to! She did not want to decide
alone; she must make no mistake
about this. She felt Booker's fingers
pressing on her arm and it was as
though the white mountain was pushing her to the edge of a sheer height;
she again exclaimed inwardly, Jesus,
hep me! Booker's white face was at
her side, waiting. Would she be doing
right to tell him? Suppose she did not
tell and then the comrades were
caught? She could not ever forgive
herself for doing a thing like that.
But maybe she was wrong; maybe her
fear was what Johnny-Boy had always
called "jus foolishness." She remembered his saying, Ma, we cant make
the party grow ef we start doubtin
everbody. . . .

"Tell me who they is, Sue, n Ahll
tell em. Ah jus joined n Ah don know
who they is."

"Ah don know who they is," she said.

"Yuh *gotta* tell me who they is, Sue!"

"Ah tol yuh Ah don know!"

"Yuh *do* know! C mon! Set up n talk!"

"Naw!"

"Yuh wan em all t git *killed?*"

She shook her head and swallowed. Lawd, Ah don blieve in this man!

"Lissen, Ahll call the names n yuh tell me which ones is in the party n which ones ain, see?"

"Naw!"

"Please, Sue!"

"Ah don know," she said.

"Sue, yuh ain doin right by em. Johnny-Boy wouldnt wan yuh t be this way. Hes out there holdin up his end. Les hol up ours . . ."

"Lawd, Ah don know . . ."

"Is yuh scareda me cause Ahm *white*? Johnny-Boy ain like tha. Don let all the work we done go fer nothin."

She gave up and bowed her head in her hands.

"Is it Johnson? Tell me, Sue?"

"Yeah," she whispered in horror; a mounting horror of feeling herself being undone.

"Is it Green?"

"Yeah."

"Murphy?"

"Lawd, Ah don know!"

"Yuh gotta tell me, Sue!"

"Mistah Booker, please leave me erlone . . ."

"Is it Murphy?"

She answered yes to the names of Johnny-Boy's comrades; she answered until he asked her no more. Then she thought, How he know the sheriffs men is watchin Lems house? She stood up and held onto her chair, feeling something sure and firm within her.

"How yuh know bout Lem?"

"Why . . . How Ah know?"

"Whut yuh doin here this tima night? How yuh know the sheriff got Johnny-Boy?"

"Sue, don yuh believe in me?"

She did not, but she could not answer. She stared at him until her lips hung open; she was searching deep within herself for certainty.

"You meet Reva?" she asked.

"Reva?"

"Yeah; Lems gal?"

"Oh, yeah. Sho, Ah met Reva."

"She tell yuh?"

She asked the question more of herself than of him; she longed to believe.

"Yeah," he said softly. "Ah reckon Ah oughta be goin t tell em now."

"Who?" she asked. "Tell *who?*"

The muscles of her body were stiff as she waited for his answer; she felt as though life depended upon it.

"The comrades," he said.

"Yeah," she sighed.

She did not know when he left; she was not looking or listening. She just suddenly saw the room empty and from her the thing that had made her fearful was gone.

v

For a space of time that seemed to her as long as she had been upon the earth, she sat huddled over the cold stove. One minute she would say to herself, They both gone now; Johnny-Boy n Sug . . . Mabbe Ahll never see em ergin. Then a surge of guilt would blot out her longing. "Lawd, Ah shouldna tol!" she mumbled. "But no man kin be so low-down as t do a think like tha . . ." Several times she had an impulse to try to tell the comrades herself; she was feeling a little better now. But what good would that do? She had told Booker the names. He jus couldnt be a Judas to po folks like us . . . He *couldnt!*

"An Sue!"

Thas Reva! Her heart leaped with an anxious gladness. She rose without answering and limped down the dark hallway. Through the open door, against the background of rain, she saw Reva's face lit now and then to whiteness by the whirling beams of the beacon. She was about to call, but a thought checked her. Jesus, hep me! Ah gotta tell her bout Johnny-Boy . . . Lawd, Ah cant!

"An Sue, yuh there?"

"C mon in, chile!"

She caught Reva and held her close for a moment without speaking.

"Lawd, Ahm sho glad yuh here," she said at last.

"Ah thought somethin had happened t yuh," said Reva, pulling away. "Ah saw the do open . . . Pa tol me to come back n stay wid yuh tonight . . ." Reva paused and started, "W-w-whuts the mattah?"

She was so full of having Reva with her that she did not understand what the question meant.

"Hunh?"

"Yo neck . . ."

"Aw, it ain nothin, chile. C mon in the kitchen."

"But theres blood on yo neck!"

"The sheriff wuz here . . ."

"Them fools! Whut they wanna bother yuh fer? Ah could kill em! So hep me Gawd, Ah could!"

"It ain nothin," she said.

She was wondering how to tell Reva about Johnny-Boy and Booker. Ahll wait a lil while longer, she thought. Now that Reva was here, her fear did not seem as awful as before.

"C mon, lemme fix yo head, An Sue. Yuh hurt."

They went to the kitchen. She sat silent while Reva dressed her scalp. She was feeling better now; in just a little while she would tell Reva. She felt the girl's finger pressing gently upon her head.

"Tha hurt?"

"A lil, chile."

"Yuh po thing."

"It ain nothin."

"Did Johnny-Boy come?"

She hesitated.

"Yeah."

"He done gone t tell the others?"

Reva's voice sounded so clear and confident that it mocked her. Lawd, Ah cant tell this chile . . .

"Yuh tol im, didnt yuh, An Sue?"

"Y-y-yeah . . ."

"Gee! Thas good! Ah tol pa he didnt hafta worry ef Johnny-Boy got the news. Mabbe thingsll come out awright."

"Ah hope . . ."

She could not go on; she had gone as far as she could. For the first time that night she began to cry.

"Hush, An Sue! Yuh awways been brave. Itll be awright!"

"Ain nothin awright, chile. The worls jus too much fer us, Ah reckon."

"Ef yuh cry that way itll make me cry."

She forced herself to stop. Naw; Ah cant carry on way in fronta Reva . . . Right now she had a deep need for Reva to believe in her. She watched the girl get pine-knots from behind the stove, rekindle the fire, and put on the coffee pot.

"Yuh wan some cawffee?" Reva asked.

"Naw, honey."

"Aw, c mon, An Sue."

"Jusa lil, honey."

"Thas the way to be. Oh, say, Ah fergot," said Reva, measuring out spoonsful of coffee. "Pa tol me t tell yuh t watch out fer tha Booker man. Hes a stool."

She showed not one sign of outward movement of expression, but as the words fell from Reva's lips she went limp inside.

"Pa tol me soon as Ah got back home. He got word from town . . ."

She stopped listening. She felt as though she had been slapped to the extreme outer edge of life, into a cold darkness. She knew now what she had felt when she had looked up out of her fog of pain and had seen Booker. It was the image of all the white folks, and the fear that went with them, that she had seen and felt during her lifetime. And again, for the second time that night, something she had felt had come true. All she could say to herself was, Ah didnt like im! Gawd knows, Ah didnt! Ah tol Johnny-Boy it wuz some of them white folks . . .

"Here; drink yo cawffee . . ."

She took the cup; her fingers trembled, and the steaming liquid spilt onto her dress and leg.

"Ahm sorry, An Sue!"

Her leg was scalded, but the pain did not bother her.

"Its awright," she said.

"Wait; lemme put some lard on tha burn!"

"It don hurt."

"Yuh worried bout somethin."

"Naw, honey."

"Lemme fix yuh so mo cawffee."

"Ah don wan nothin now, Reva."

"Waal, buck up. Don be tha way . . ."

They were silent. She heard Reva drinking. No; she would not tell Reva; Reva was all she had left. But she had to do something, some way, somehow. She was undone too much as it was; and to tell Reva about Booker or Johnny-Boy was more than she was equal to; it would be too coldly shameful. She wanted to be alone and fight this thing out with herself.

"Go t bed, honey. Yuh tired."

"Naw; Ahm awright, An Sue."

She heard the bottom of Reva's empty cup clank against the top of the stove. Ah *got* t make her go t bed! Yes; Booker would tell the names of the comrades to the sheriff. If she could only stop him some way! That was the answer, the point, the star that grew bright in the morning of new hope. Soon, maybe half an hour from now, Booker would reach Foley's Woods. Hes boun t go the long way, cause he don know no short cut, she thought. Ah could wade the creek n beat im there. . . . But what would she do after that?

"Reva, honey, go t bed. Ahm awright. Yuh need res."

"Ah ain sleepy, An Sue."

"Ah knows whuts bes fer yuh, chile. Yuh tired n wet."

"Ah wanna stay up wid yuh."

She forced a smile and said:

"Ah don think they gonna hurt Johnny-Boy . . ."

"Fer *real*, An Sue?"

"Sho, honey."

"But Ah wanna wait up wid yuh."

"Thas mah job, honey. Thas whut a mas fer, t wait up fer her chullun."

"Good night, An Sue."

"Good night, honey."

She watched Reva pull up and leave the kitchen; presently she heard the shucks in the mattress whispering, and she knew that Reva had gone to bed. She was alone. Through the cracks of the stove she saw the fire dying to grey ashes; the room was growing cold again. The yellow beacon continued to flit past the window and the rain still drummed. Yes; she was alone; she had done this awful thing alone; she must find some way out, alone. Like touching a festering sore, she put her finger upon that moment when she had shouted her defiance to the sheriff, when she had shouted to feel her strength. She had lost Sug to save others; she had let

Johnny-Boy go to save others; and then in a moment of weakness that came from too much strength she had lost all. If she had not shouted to the sheriff, she would have been strong enough to have resisted Booker; she would have been able to tell the comrades herself. Something tightened in her as she remembered and understood the fit of fear she had felt on coming to herself in the dark hallway. A part of her life she thought she had done away with forever had had hold of her then. She had thought the soft, warm past was over; she had thought that it did not mean much when now she sang: *"Hes the Lily of the Valley, the Bright n Mawnin Star"* . . . The days when she had sung that song were the days when she had not hoped for anything on this earth, the days when the cold mountain had driven her into the arms of Jesus. She had thought that Sug and Johnny-Boy had taught her to forget Him, to fix her hope upon the fight of black men for freedom. Through the gradual years she had believed and worked with them, had felt strength shed from the grace of their terrible vision. That grace had been upon her when she had let the sheriff slap her down; it had been upon her when she had risen time and again from the floor and faced him. But she had trapped herself with her own hunger; to water the long dry thirst of her faith her pride had made a bargain which her flesh could not keep. Her having told the names of Johnny-Boy's comrades was but an incident in a deeper horror. She stood up and looked at the floor while call and counter-call, loyalty and counter-loyalty struggled in her soul. Mired she was between two abandoned worlds, living, but dying without the strength of the grace that either gave. The clearer she felt it the fuller did something well up

from the depths of her for release; the more urgent did she feel the need to fling into her black sky another star, another hope, one more terrible vision to give her the strength to live and act. Softly and restlessly she walked about the kitchen, feeling herself naked against the night, the rain, the world; and shamed whenever the thought of Reva's love crossed her mind. She lifted her empty hands and looked at her writhing fingers. Lawd, whut kin Ah do now? She could still wade the creek and get to Foley's Woods before Booker. And then what? How could she manage to see Johnny-Boy or Booker? Again she heard the sheriff's threatening voice: Git yuh a sheet, cause hes gonna be dead! The sheet! Thas it, the *sheet!* Her whole being leaped with will; the long years of her life bent toward a moment of focus, a point. Ah kin go wid mah sheet! Ahll be doin whut he said! Lawd Gawd in Heaven, Ahma go lika nigger woman wid mah windin sheet t git mah dead son! But then what? She stood straight and smiled grimly; she had in her heart the whole meaning of her life; her entire personality was poised on the brink of a total act. Ah know! Ah *know!* She thought of Johnny-Boy's gun in the dresser drawer. Ahll hide the gun in the sheet n go aftah Johnny-Boys body. . . . She tiptoed to her room, eased out the dresser drawer, and got a sheet. Reva was sleeping; the darkness was filled with her quiet breathing. She groped in the drawer and found the gun. She wound the gun in the sheet and held them both under her apron. Then she stole to the bedside and watched Reva. Lawd, hep her! But mabbe shes bettah off. This had t happen sometimes . . . She n Johnny-Boy couldna been together in this here South . . . N Ah couldnt tell her bout Booker. Itll come out awright n she wont nevah know. Reva's trust would never be shaken. She caught her breath as the shucks in the mattress rustled dryly; then all was quiet and she breathed easily again. She tiptoed to the door, down the hall, and stood on the porch. Above her the yellow beacon whirled through the rain. She went over muddy ground, mounted a slope, stopped and looked back at her house. The lamp glowed in her window, and the yellow beacon that swung every few seconds seemed to feed it with light. She turned and started across the fields, holding the gun and sheet tightly, thinking, Po Reva . . . Po critter . . . Shes fas ersleep . . .

VI

For the most part she walked with her eyes half shut, her lips tightly compressed, leaning her body against the wind and the driving rain, feeling the pistol in the sheet sagging cold and heavy in her fingers. Already she was getting wet; it seemed that her feet found every puddle of water that stood between the corn rows.

She came to the edge of the creek and paused, wondering at what point was it low. Taking the sheet from under her apron, she wrapped the gun in it so that her finger could be upon the trigger. Ahll cross here, she thought. At first she did not feel the water; her feet were already wet. But the water grew cold as it came up to her knees; she gasped when it reached her waist. Lawd, this creeks high! When she had passed the middle, she knew that she was out of danger. She came out of the water, climbed a grassy hill, walked on, turned a bend and saw the lights of autos gleaming ahead. Yeah; theys still there! She hurried with her head down. Wondah did Ah beat im here? Lawd, Ah *hope*

so! A vivid image of Booker's white face hovered a moment before her eyes and a surging will rose up in her so hard and strong that it vanished. She was among the autos now. From nearby came the hoarse voices of the men.

"Hey, yuh!"

She stopped, nervously clutching the sheet. Two white men with shotguns came toward her.

"Whut in hell yuh doin out here?"

She did not answer.

"Didnt yuh hear somebody speak t yuh?"

"Ahm comin aftah mah son," she said humbly.

"Yo *son?*"

"Yessuh."

"What yo son doin out here?"

"The sheriffs got im."

"Holy Scott! Jim, its the niggers ma!"

"Whut yuh got there?" asked one.

"A sheet."

"A *sheet?*"

"Yessuh."

"Fer whut?"

"The sheriff tol me t bring a sheet t git his body."

"Waal, waal . . ."

"Now, ain tha somethin?"

The white men looked at each other.

"These niggers sho love one ernother," said one.

"N tha ain no lie," said the other.

"Take me t the sheriff," she begged.

"Yuh ain givin us *orders,* is yuh?"

"Nawsuh."

"We'll take yuh when wes good n ready."

"Yessuh."

"So yuh wan his body?"

"Yessuh."

"Waal, he ain dead yit."

"They gonna kill im," she said.

"Ef he talks they wont."

"He ain gonna talk," she said.

"How yuh know?"

"Cause he ain."

"We got ways of makin niggers talk."

"Yuh ain got no way fer im."

"Yuh thinka lot of that black Red, don yuh?"

"Hes mah son."

"Why don yuh teach im some sense?"

"Hes mah son," she said again.

"Lissen, ol nigger woman, yuh stand there wid you hair white. Yuh got bettah sense than t believe tha niggers kin make a revolution . . ."

"A black republic," said the other one, laughing.

"Take me t the sheriff," she begged.

"Yuh his ma," said one. "Yuh kin make im talk n tell whose in this thing wid im."

"He ain gonna talk," she said.

"Don yuh wan im t live?"

She did not answer.

"C mon, les take her t Bradley."

They grabbed her arms and she clutched hard at the sheet and gun; they led her toward the crowd in the woods. Her feelings were simple; Booker would not tell; she was there with the gun to see to that. The louder became the voices of the men the deeper became her feeling of wanting to right the mistake she had made; of wanting to fight her way back to solid ground. She would stall for time until Booker showed up. Oh, ef theyll only lemme git close t Johnny-Boy! As they led her near the crowd she saw white faces turning and looking at her and heard a rising clamor of voices.

"Whose tha?"

"A nigger woman!"

"Whut she doin out here?"

"This is his ma!" called one of the men.

"Whut she wans?"

"She brought a sheet t cover his body!"

"He ain dead yit!"

"They tryin t make im talk!"

"But he will be dead soon ef he don open up!"

"Say, look! The niggers ma brought a sheet t cover up his body!"

"Now, ain that sweet?"

"Mabbe she wans t hol a prayer meetin!"

"Did she git a preacher?"

"Say, go git Bradley!"

"O.K.!"

The crowd grew quiet. They looked at her curiously; she felt their cold eyes trying to detect some weakness in her. Humbly, she stood with the sheet covering the gun. She had already accepted all that they could do to her.

The sheriff came.

"So yuh brought yo sheet, hunh?"

"Yessuh," she whispered.

"Looks like them slaps we gave yuh learned yuh some sense, didnt they?"

She did not answer.

"Yuh don need tha sheet. Yo son ain dead yit," he said, reaching toward her.

She backed away, her eyes wide.

"Naw!"

"Now, lissen, Anty!" he said. "There ain no use in yuh ackin a fool! Go in there n tell tha nigger son of yos t tell us whos in this wid im, see? Ah promise we wont kill im ef he talks. We'll let im git outta town."

"There ain nothin Ah kin tell im," she said.

"Yuh wan us t kill im?"

She did not answer. She saw someone lean toward the sheriff and whisper.

"Bring her erlong," the sheriff said.

They led her to a muddy clearing. The rain streamed down through the ghostly glare of the flashlights. As the men formed a semi-circle she saw

Johnny-Boy lying in a trough of mud. He was tied with rope; he lay hunched and one side of his face rested in a pool of black water. His eyes were staring questioningly at her.

"Speak t im," said the sheriff.

If she could only tell him why she was here! But that was impossible; she was close to what she wanted and she stared straight before her with compressed lips.

"Say, nigger!" called the sheriff, kicking Johnny-Boy. "Heres yo ma!"

Johnny-Boy did not move or speak. The sheriff faced her again.

"Lissen, Anty," he said. "Yuh got mo say wid im than anybody. Tell im t talk n hava chance. Whut he wanna pertect the other niggers n white folks fer?"

She slid her finger about the trigger of the gun and looked stonily at the mud.

"Go t him," said the sheriff.

She did not move. Her heart was crying out to answer the amazed question in Johnny-Boy's eyes. But there was no way now.

"Waal, yuhre astin fer it. By Gawd, we gotta way to *make* yuh talk t im," he said, turning away. "Say, Tim, git one of them logs n turn that nigger upside-down n put his legs on it!"

A murmur of assent ran through the crowd. She bit her lips; she knew what that meant.

"Yuh wan yo nigger son crippled?" she heard the sheriff ask.

She did not answer. She saw them roll the log up; they lifted Johnny-Boy and laid him on his face and stomach, then they pulled his legs over the log. His knee-caps rested on the sheer top of the log's back and the toes of his shoes pointed ground-ward. So absorbed was she in watching that she felt that it was she who was being lifted and made ready for torture.

"Git a crowbar!" said the sheriff.

A tall, lank man got a crowbar from a nearby auto and stood over the log. His jaws worked slowly on a wad of tobacco.

"Now, its up t yuh, Anty," the sheriff said. "Tell the man whut t do!"

She looked into the rain. The sheriff turned.

"Mabbe she think wes playin. Ef she don say nothin, then break em at the kneecaps!"

"O.K., Sheriff!"

She stood waiting for Booker. Her legs felt weak; she wondered if she would be able to wait much longer. Over and over she said to herself, Ef he came now Ahd kill em both!

"She ain sayin nothin, Sheriff!"

"Waal, Gawddammit, let im have it!"

The crowbar came down and Johnny-Boy's body lunged in the mud and water. There was a scream. She swayed, holding tight to the gun and sheet.

"Hol im! Git the other leg!"

The crowbar fell again. There was another scream.

"Yuh break em?" asked the sheriff.

The tall man lifted Johnny-Boy's legs and let them drop limply again, dropping rearward from the kneecaps. Johnny-Boy's body lay still. His head had rolled to one side and she could not see his face.

"Jus lika broke sparrow wing," said the man, laughing softly.

Then Johnny-Boy's face turned to her; he screamed.

"Go way, ma! Go way!"

It was the first time she had heard his voice since she had come out to the woods; she all but lost control of herself. She started violently forward, but the sheriff's arm checked her.

"Aw, naw! Yuh had yo chance!" He

turned to Johnny-Boy. "She kin go ef yuh talk."

"Mistah, he ain gonna talk," she said.

"Go way, ma!" said Johnny-Boy.

"Shoot im! Don make im suffah so," she begged.

"He'll either talk or he'll never hear yuh ergin," the sheriff said. "Theres other things we kin do t im."

She said nothing.

"What yuh come here fer, ma?" Johnny-Boy sobbed.

"Ahm gonna split his eardrums," the sheriff said. "Ef yuh got anythin t say t im yuh bettah say it *now!*"

She closed her eyes. She heard the sheriff's feet sucking in mud. Ah could save im! She opened her eyes; there were shouts of eagerness from the crowd as it pushed in closer.

"Bus em, Sheriff!"

"Fix im so he cant hear!"

"He knows how t do it, too!"

"He busted a Jew boy tha way once!"

She saw the sheriff stoop over Johnny-Boy, place his flat palm over one ear and strike his fist against it with all his might. He placed his palm over the other ear and struck again. Johnny-Boy moaned, his head rolling from side to side, his eyes showing white amazement in a world without sound.

"Yuh wouldnt talk t im when yuh had the chance," said the sheriff. "Try n talk now."

She felt warm tears on her cheeks. She longed to shoot Johnny-Boy and let him go. But if she did that they would take the gun from her, and Booker would tell who the others were. Lawd, hep me! The men were talking loudly now, as though the main business was over. It seemed ages that she stood there watching Johnny-Boy roll and whimper in his world of silence.

"Say, Sheriff, heres somebody lookin fer yuh!"

"Who is it?"

"Ah don know!"

"Bring em in!"

She stiffened and looked around wildly, holding the gun tight. Is tha Booker? Then she held still, feeling that her excitement might betray her. Mabbe Ah kin shoot em both! Mabbe Ah kin shoot *twice!* The sheriff stood in front of her, waiting. The crowd parted and she saw Booker hurrying forward.

"Ah know em all, Sheriff!" he called.

He came full into the muddy clearing where Johnny-Boy lay.

"Yuh mean yuh got the names?"

"Sho! The ol nigger . . ."

She saw his lips hang open and silent when he saw her. She stepped forward and raised the sheet.

"Whut . . ."

She fired, once; then, without pausing, she turned, hearing them yell. She aimed at Johnny-Boy, but they had their arms around her, bearing her to the ground, clawing at the sheet in her hand. She glimpsed Booker lying sprawled in the mud, on his face, his hands stretched out before him; then a cluster of yelling men blotted him out. She lay without struggling, looking upward through the rain at the white faces above her. And she was suddenly at peace; they were not a white mountain now; they were not pushing her any longer to the edge of life. Its awright . . .

"She shot Booker!"

"She hada a gun in the sheet!"

"She shot im right thu the head!"

"What she shoot im fer?"

"Kill the bitch!"

"Ah *thought* somethin wuz wrong bout her!"

"Ah wuz fer givin it t her from the firs!"

"Thas whut yuh git fer treatin a nigger nice!"

"Say, Bookers dead!"

She stopped looking into the white faces, stopped listening. She waited, giving up her life before they took it from her; she had done what she wanted. Ef only Johnny-Boy . . . She looked at him; he lay looking at her with tired eyes. Ef she could only tell im! But he lay already buried in a grave of silence.

"Whu yuh kill im fer, hunh?"

It was the sheriff's voice; she did not answer.

"Mabbe she wuz shootin at yuh, Sheriff?"

"Whut yuh kill im fer?"

She felt the sheriff's foot come into her side; she closed her eyes.

"Yuh black bitch!"

"Let her have it!"

"Yuh reckon she foun out bout Booker?"

"She mighta."

"Jesus Chris, whut yuh dummies *waitin* on!"

"Yeah; kill her!"

"Kill em *both*!"

"Let her know her nigger sons dead firs!"

She turned her head toward Johnny-Boy; he lay looking puzzled in a world beyond the reach of voices. At leas he cant hear, she thought.

"C mon, let im have it!"

She listened to hear what Johnny-Boy could not. They came, two of them, one right behind the other; so close together that they sounded like one shot. She did not look at Johnny-Boy now; she looked at the white faces of the men, hard and wet in the glare of the flashlights.

"Yuh hear tha, nigger woman?"

"Did tha surprise im? Hes in hell now wonderin whut hit im!"

"C mon! Give it t her, Sheriff!"

"Lemme shoot her, Sheriff! It wuz mah pal she shot!"

"Awright, Pete! Thas fair ernuff!"

She gave up as much of her life as she could before they took it from her. But the sound of the shot and the streak of fire that tore its way through her chest forced her to live again, intensely. She had not moved, save for the slight jarring impact of the bullet. She felt the heat of her own blood warming her cold, wet back. She yearned suddenly to talk. "Yuh didnt git whut yuh wanted! N yuh ain gonna nevah git it! Yuh didnt kill me; Ah come here by mahsef . . ." She felt rain falling into her wide-open, dimming eyes and heard faint voices. Her lips moved soundlessly. *Yuh didnt git yuh didnt yuh didnt* . . . Focused and pointed she was, buried in the depths of her star, swallowed in its peace and strength; and not feeling her flesh growing cold, cold as the rain that fell from the invisible sky upon the doomed living and the dead that never dies.

1938, 1940

HORACE GREGORY

(1898–   )

COLUMBO DOMINICO *

Columbo Dominico
dead on Minetta Street
is no finality,

---

* From *Poems 1930–1940* by Horace Gregory, copyright, 1941, by Horace Gregory. Reprinted by permission of Harcourt, Brace and Company, Inc.

even with a regiment of bullets in his back,
is no end of things;
maybe the cops got him (he was out of work,
vagrant, selling bad booze)
maybe his brother, maybe his girl
shouting: You go to hell, get out of here,
good-bye, Dominico
and Dominico, surprised, unsteady,
leaping into eternal æther
crying: Viva, viva anarchy!

Here is no end of things.
Even a frozen outpost of the Salvation Army
walking down the winter street,
seeing Dominico,
quickens his feet,
lifts his watery eyes and sings:
Jesus saves and his sweet breath
wakens all sinners in the halls of death
and his eyes shine bright and his heart beats warm
as he gathers all sinners in the crook of his arm.
Jesus saves, Jesus saves.
Here is no finality.
Dominico dead
mingles with all the dead,
his gigantic shade
(an elbow leaning on the Woolworth Tower)
pierces lovestruck Dante with a shoulder blade
and spits upon the trembling purple face
that once was Nero's and the elder Morgan's,
vaulted into space,
it strides with Robespierre
kisses Marat
and sleeps, relaxed, with Lesbia for an hour.

There is no end of things . . .
Angelo Gorini and Tony Bruno (out of work,
vagrant, selling bad booze)
the cops got them for killing
Columbo Dominico.
Angelo Gorini and Tony Bruno, falling,
slipping into death, calling
out: By Jesus Christ, we didn't do it,
viva, viva anarchy,
we love the red flag!

1930, 1941

EMERSON: LAST DAYS AT CONCORD *

Enter America at Concord's bridge,
true marriage of the east and west, Brahma
whose lips nurse at my veins.

         Where was the green brass cannon
sunken in churchyards after the shots were fired?
Listen, the world is sleeping and the noise
coils in thunder where Dover's beach
shall wake no more
      and the Indian ocean
pours its blood into the sun when evening's tide
uncovers bones upon the shore.

       Cut me a frock coat, for the oversoul
lies naked: parts, limbs exposed
within a broken coffin. O light that stirs in dust
as eastwind darkens nightfall into rain.

       Where are your lips, hands, Brahma?
What was the name, your name or mine?

        Come, friend,
we shall walk in the west orchard drinking russet wine,
kiss daisies where the transcendental tree
(look how the death worm feeds upon its roots)
shelters our love and fiery blossoms fall in Plato's vineyard.
I have rolled the world in my brain, have seen its heroes
diminish,
   saw oceans, continents dissolve in sunlight
on Concord window sills:
      Are you my friend?
then here's my secret; I have forgotten
all friends and the words that joined my lips to theirs.
Better to keep faith
     and believe
no one. Better to be a patriot disowning
this land. Give back America to sunlight, wind and rain;
set sail for India from Concord's bridge,
leap to the quarter-deck where our Columbus
once more commands his ships.
      Is that a storm in the sky?
And are these apples ripe? I grew this orchard to be a paradise
this side of Eden.

              1933, 1941

NEW YORK, CASSANDRA *

Cassandra, the world's on fire; the harvest's sour:
from Salem into China, an old sailor's song
sung to the yellow sea that pours
oceans of grain over us, fire and flood;
it will be hard to sleep.

Macbeth has murder'd sleep, sleep festering
under his eyelids, Cassandra, like an old wound split wide.
Macbeth shall sleep no more—good night, Macbeth—
wake well tonight:
                    spring (naked mind)
arms, sheets, window curtains pushed aside
to see the fire, hear the guns.

Breakfast will be delayed beyond Canopus,
lunch clean, untouched by human hands, embalmed in cellophane,
revolving in an automat, will wait. . . .

Somebody said that Macbeth went insane,
leaped thirty stories down to Birnam wood
                              (inane,
O Dunsinane, your palaces are empty)
The king bled through the sheets (cock crow) Macbeth
grew sick, cracked the eternal verities
engraved upon his heart in rock:

          Pick me sweet verities,
                         sweet verities;
where shall we find again such girls as these?
Nightingale Venus, bright Beatrice shall sing tonight,
silverlipped requiem Mary shall answer them,
clothed in the blood of Christ down to her knees.
Pick me sweet verities,
              sweet verities.

                         They stand,
a row of broken statues from Alexandria (B.C.)
to Salt Lake City.

Give Cerberus a non-employment wage, the dog is hungry.
This head served in the war, Cassandra, it lost an eye;
that head spits fire, for it lost its tongue licking the paws
of lions caged in Wall Street and their claws
were merciless.

          Follow, O follow him, loam-limned Apollo, crumbling before
          Tiffany's window; he must buy
          himself earrings for he meets his love tonight
          (Blossoming Juliet

* From *Poems 1930–1940* by Horace Gregory, copyright, 1941, by Horace Gregory.
Reprinted by permission of Harcourt, Brace and Company, Inc.

emptied her love into her true love's lap),
dies in his arms.
                    He is a poet,
     kiss him, Socrates.

They say the red arm of the Proletariat swings,
Hammer and Sickle, a quarter moon in the sky,
the dogstar comets leap . . .
They say Macbeth embezzled funds, the market
fell too soon, too soon the hands of Christ
withered on the cross.
                    His wife was barren
(her eyes are flowers
blowing in the field down where the Lackawanna railroad runs:
flow softly rivers of coal and steam),
His life insurance went to the banks.

There are five limousines, unbought, rotting behind plate glass,
delicate worms in leather and sharp April grass
piercing steel joints . . .
Talk to the guns, Cassandra, tell them this is peace,
not war, not war,
                    peace,
                    PEACE.

We came to you with a city in our hands;
we said:
          Destroy this city, by God, we hate this city.
You heard us and your house was a tower of flames. . . .
Remember there was once a king, an old king with an iron beard,
whose life was like your house, a floor of ashes.

He put out his eyes, Cassandra.
                    We shall keep
our eyes though we learn nothing. . . .
                    The night is cold,
Cassandra.

                                        1933, 1941

KENNETH FEARING
(1902–   )

CULTURAL NOTES *

Professor Burke's symphony, "Colorado Vistas,"
In four movements,
I Mountains, II Canyons, III Dusk, IV Dawn,
Was played recently by the Philharmonic.

* From *Collected Poems* by permission of Kenneth Fearing. Copyright, 1940, by
Random House, Inc.

Snapshots of the localities described in music were passed around and the
audience checked for accuracy.
All O.K.
After the performance Maurice Epstein, 29, tuberculosis, stoker on the *S.S.
Tarboy*, rose to his feet and shouted,
"He's crazy, them artists are all crazy,
I can prove it by Max Nordau. They poison the minds of young girls."
Otto Svoboda, 500 Avenue A, butcher, Pole, husband, philosopher, argued
in rebuttal,
"Shut your trap, you.
The question is, does the symphony fit in with Karl Marx?"

At the Friday evening meeting of the Browning Writing League, Mrs. Whitta-
more Ralston-Beckett,
Traveler, lecturer, novelist, critic, poet, playwright, editor, mother, idealist,
Fascinated her audience with a brief talk, whimsical and caustic,
Appealing to the younger generation to take a brighter, happier, more sunny
and less morbid view of life's eternal fundamentals.
Mrs. Ralston-Beckett quoted Sir Henry Parke-Bennett: "O Beauty," she said,
"Take your fingers off my throat, take your elbow out of my eye,
Take your sorrow off my sorrow,
Take your hat, take your gloves, take your feet down off the table,
Take your beauty off my beauty, and go."
In the open discussion that followed, Maurice Epstein, 29, tuberculosis, stoker
on the *S.S. Tarboy*, arose and queried the speaker,
"Is it true, as certain scientists assert, that them artists are all of them crazy?"
A Mr. Otto Svoboda present spoke in reply,
"Shut your trap, you. The question is, what about Karl Marx?"

1929

DENOUEMENT *

1

Sky, be blue, and more than blue; wind, be flesh and blood; flesh and blood, be
deathless;
Walls, streets, be home;
Desire of millions, become more real than warmth and breath and strength and
bread;
Clock, point to the decisive hour and, hour without name when stacked and
waiting murder dissolves, stay forever as the world grows new;

Truth, be known, be kept forever, let the letters, letters, souvenirs, documents,
snapshots, bills be found at last, be torn away from a world of lies,
be kept as final evidence, transformed forever into more than truth;
Change, change, rows and rows and rows of figures, spindles, furrows, desks,
change into paid-up rent and let the paid-up rent become South Sea
music;

* From *Collected Poems* by permission of Kenneth Fearing. Copyright, 1940, by
Random House, Inc.

Magic film, unwind, unroll, unfold in silver on that million-mile screen, take
    us all, bear us again to the perfect denouement,

Where everything lost, needed, each forgotten thing, all that never happens,
Gathers at last into a dynamite triumph, a rainbow peace, a thunderbolt kiss,
For you, the invincible, and I, grown older, and he, the shipping clerk, and
    she, an underweight blonde journeying home in the last express.

2

But here is the body found lying face down in a burlap sack, strangled in the
    noose jerked shut by these trussed and twisted and frantic arms;
But here are the agents, come to seize the bed;
But here is the vase holding saved-up cigar-store coupons, and here is a way to
    save on cigars and go without meat;
But here is the voice that strikes around the world, "My friends . . . my
    friends," issues from the radio and thunders "My friends" in news-
    reel close-ups, explodes across headlines, "Both rich and poor, my
    friends, must sacrifice," re-echoes, murmuring, through hospitals,
    death-cells, "My friends . . . my friends . . . my friends . . . my
    friends . . ."

And who, my friend, are you?
Are you the one who leaped to the blinds of the cannonball express? Or are you
    the one who started life again with three dependents and a pack of
    cigarettes?

But how can these things be made finally clear in a postmortem scene with the
    lips taped shut and the blue eyes cold, wide, still, blind, fixed beyond
    the steady glare of electric lights, through the whitewashed hospital
    ceiling and the crossmounted roof, past the drifting clouds?

Objection, overruled, exception, proceed:

Was yours the voice heard singing one night in a fly-blown, soot-beamed, lost
    and forgotten Santa Fé saloon? Later bellowing in rage? And you
    boiled up a shirt in a Newark furnished room? Then you found an-
    other job, and pledged not to organize or go on strike?

We offer this union book in evidence. We offer these rent receipts in evidence.
    We offer in evidence this vacation card marked, "This is the life.
    Regards to all."

You, lodge member, protestant, crossborn male, the placenta discolored, at
    birth, by syphilis, you, embryo four inches deep in the seventh
    month,
Among so many, many sparks struck and darkened at conception,
Which were you,
You, six feet tall on the day of death?

Then you were at no time the senator's son? Then you were never the beef
    king's daughter, married in a storm of perfume and music and
    laughter and rice?

And you are not now the clubman who waves and nods and vanishes to Rio in
    a special plane?
But these are your lungs, scarred and consumed? These are your bones, still
    marked by rickets? These are your pliers? These are your fingers, O
    Master mechanic, and these are your cold, wide, still, blind eyes?

The witness is lying, lying, an enemy, my friends, of Union Gas and the home.

But how will you know us, wheeled from the icebox and stretched upon the
    table with the belly slit wide and the entrail removed, voiceless as
    the clippers bite through ligaments and flesh and nerves and bones,
How will you know us, attentive, strained, before the director's desk, or crowded
    in line in front of factory gates,
How will you know us through ringed machine-gun sights as we run and fall
    in gasmask, steel helmet, flame-tunic, uniform, bayonet, pack,
How will you know us, crumbled into ashes, lost in air and water and fire and
    stone,
How will you know us, now or any time, who will ever know that we have
    lived or died?

And this is the truth? So help you God, this is the truth? The truth in full, so
    help you God? So help you God?
But the pride that was made of iron and could not be broken, what has become
    of it, what has become of the faith that nothing could destroy, what
    has become of the deathless hope,
You, whose ways were yours alone, you, the one like no one else, what have
    you done with the hour you swore to remember, where is the hour,
    the day, the achievement that would never die?

Morphine. Veronal. Veronal. Morphine. Morphine. Morphine. Morphine.

3

Leaflets, scraps, dust, match-stubs strew the linoleum that leads upstairs to the
    union hall, the walls of the basement workers' club are dim and
    cracked and above the speaker's stand Vanzetti's face shows green,
    behind closed doors the committeeroom is a fog of smoke.

Who are these people?

All day the committee fought like cats and dogs and twelve of Mr. Kelly's
    strongarm men patrolled the aisles that night, them blackjack guys
    get ten to twenty bucks a throw, the funds were looted, sent to
    Chicago, at the meeting the organizer talked like a fool, more scabs
    came through in trucks guarded by the police,
Workers of the world, workers of the world, workers of the world,
Who are these people and what do they want, why do they walk back and
    forth with signs that say "Bread Not Bullets," what do they mean
    "They Shall Not Die" as they sink in clouds of poison gas and fall
    beneath clubs, hooves, rifles, fall and do not arise, arise, unite,
Never again these faces, arms, eyes, lips,

Not unless we live, and live again,
Return, everywhere alive in the issue that returns, clear as light that still
        descends from a star long cold, again alive and everywhere visible
        through and through the scene that comes again, as light on moving
        water breaks and returns, heard only in the words, as millions of
        voices become one voice, seen only in millions of hands that move
        as one,

Look at them gathered, raised, look at their faces, clothes, who are these people,
        who are these people,
What hand scrawled large in the empty prison cell "I have just received my
        sentence of death. Red Front," whose voice screamed out in the
        silence "Arise"?

And all along the waterfront, there, where rats gnaw into the loading plat-
        forms, here, where the wind whips at warehouse platforms, look,
        there, here,
Everywhere huge across the walls and gates "Your brothers live,"
Where there is no life, no breath, sound, no touch, no warmth, no light but
        the lamp that shines on a trooper's drawn and ready bayonet.

1935

DIRGE *

1-2-3 was the number he played but today the number came 3-2-1;
Bought his Carbide at 30 and it went to 29; had the favorite at Bowie but the
        track was slow—

O executive type, would you like to drive a floating-power, knee-action, silk-
        upholstered six? Wed a Hollywood star? Shoot the course in 58?
        Draw to the ace, king, jack?
O fellow with a will who won't take no, watch out for three cigarettes on the
        same, single match; O democratic voter born in August under Mars,
        beware of liquidated rails—

Denouement to denouement, he took a personal pride in the certain, certain
        way he lived his own, private life,
But nevertheless, they shut off his gas; nevertheless, the bank foreclosed; never-
        theless, the landlord called; nevertheless, the radio broke,

And twelve o'clock arrived just once too often,
Just the same he wore one gray tweed suit, bought one straw hat, drank one
        straight Scotch, walked one short step, took one long look, drew one
        deep breath,
Just one too many,

And wow he died as wow he lived,
Going whop to the office and blooie home to sleep and biff got married and
        bam had children and oof got fired,
Zowie did he live and zowie did he die,

* From *Collected Poems* by permission of Kenneth Fearing. Copyright, 1940, by
Random House, Inc.

With who the hell are you at the corner of his casket, and where the hell're
    we going on the right-hand silver knob, and who the hell cares walk-
    ing second from the end with an American Beauty wreath from why
    the hell not,

Very much missed by the circulation staff of the New York Evening Post;
    deeply, deeply mourned by the B.M.T.,

Wham, Mr. Roosevelt; pow, Sears Roebuck; awk, big dipper; bop, summer rain;
Bong, Mr., bong, Mr., bong, Mr., bong.

                                      c. *1930–35*

MURIEL RUKEYSER
(1913–   )

CITATION FOR HORACE GREGORY *

These are our brave, these with their hands in on the work,
hammering out beauty upon the painful stone
turning their grave heads passionately finding
truth and alone and each day subtly slain
and each day born.
                  Revolves
a measured system, world upon world, stemmed fires
and regulated galaxies behind the flattened head,
behind the immortal skull, ticking eternity
in blood and the symbols of living.

The brass voice speaks in the street
                        STRIKE STRIKE
    the nervous fingers continue elaborately
        drawing consciousness, examining, doing.
Rise to a billboard world of Chesterfields,
Mae West hip-wriggles, Tarzan prowess, the little
nibbling and despicable minds.
                  Here, gentlemen,
here is our gallery of poets :
                    Jeffers,
a long and tragic drum-roll beating anger,
sick of a catapulting nightmare world,
Eliot, who led us to the precipice
subtly and perfectly ; there striking an attitude
rigid and ageing on the penultimate step,
the thoughtful man MacLeish who bent his head
feeling the weight of the living; bent, and turned
the grave important face round to the dead.

And on your left, ladies and gentlemen : poets.

* From *Theory of Flight* by Muriel Rukeyser, by permission of Yale University
Press. Copyright 1935.

Young poets and makers, solve your anguish, see
the brave unmedalled, who dares to shape his mind,
printed with dignity, to the machines of change.
A procession of poets adds one footbeat to the
implacable metric line : the great and unbetrayed
        after the sunlight and the failing yellow,
        after the lips bitten with passion and
        gentle, after the deaths, below
        dance floors of celebration we turn we turn
these braveries are permanent. These gifts
flare on our lives, clarifying, revealed.

We are too young to see our funerals
in pantomime nightly before uneasy beds,
too near beginnings for this hesitation
obliterated in death or carnival.
Deep into time extend the impersonal stairs,
        established barricades will stand,
before they die the brave have set their hand
on rich particular beauty for their heirs.

                                                        1935

FOUR IN A FAMILY *

The father and mother sat, and the sister beside her.
I faced the two women across the table's width,
speaking, and all the time he looked at me,
sorrowing, saying nothing, with his hard tired breath.

Their faces said : This is your home; and I :
I never come home, I never go away.
And they all answered : Stay.

All day the city turned about this room,
and silence had remained between our faces,
divisions outside to concentrate a world
tally here only to dead profits and losses.

We follow barrier voices, and we go fast,
unknown to each other, they race, I turn away.
No voice is strong enough to cry me Stay.

        My sister, I wished upon you those delights
        time never buries,
        more precious than heroes.

        Strange father, strange mother, who are you, who are you?
        Where have I come,
        How shall I prosper home?

                                                        1935

* From *Theory of Flight* by Muriel Rukeyser, by permission of Yale University
Press. Copyright 1935.

BOY WITH HIS HAIR CUT SHORT †

Sunday shuts down on this twentieth-century evening.
The L passes. Twilight and bulb define
the brown room, the overstuffed plum sofa,
the boy, and the girl's thin hands above his head.
A neighbor radio sings stocks, news, serenade.

He sits at the table, head down, the young clear neck exposed,
watching the drugstore sign from the tail of his eye;
tattoo, neon, until the eye blears, while his
solicitous tall sister, simple in blue, bending
behind him, cuts his hair with her cheap shears.

The arrow's electric red always reaches its mark,
successful neon! He coughs, impressed by that precision.
The child's forehead, forever protected by his cap,
is bleached against the lamplight as he turns head
and steadies to let the snippets drop.

Erasing the failure of weeks with level fingers,
she sleeks the fine hair, combing: "You'll look fine tomorrow!
You'll surely find something, they can't keep turning you down;
the finest gentleman's not so trim as you!" Smiling, he raises
the adolescent forehead wrinkling ironic now.

He sees his decent suit laid out, new-pressed
his carfare on the shelf. He lets his head fall, meeting
her earnest hopeless look, seeing the sharp blades splitting,
the darkened room, the impersonal sign, her motion,
the blue vein, bright on her temple, pitifully beating.

1938

† From *U. S. 1* by Muriel Rukeyser. Copyright 1938 by Muriel Rukeyser. By
permission of the Viking Press, Inc., New York.

THE CONSERVATIVES

GEORGE ADE
(1866–1944)

THE FABLE
OF THE SLIM GIRL *

WHO TRIED TO KEEP A DATE
THAT WAS NEVER MADE

Once upon a Time there was a slim Girl with a Forehead which was Shiny and Protuberant, like a Bartlett Pear. When asked to put Something in an Autograph Album she invariably wrote the Following, in a tall, dislocated Back-Hand:

Life is Real: Life is Earnest,
And the Grave is not its Goal.

That's the kind of a Girl she was.

In her own Town she had the Name of being a Cold Proposition, but that was because the Primitive Yokels of a One-Night Stand could not Attune Themselves to the Views of one who was troubled with Ideals. Her Soul Panted for the Higher Life.

Alas, the Rube Town in which she Hung Forth was given over to Croquet, Mush and Milk Sociables, a lodge of Elks and two married Preachers who doctored for the Tonsillitis. So what could the Poor Girl do?

In all the Country around there was not a Man who came up to her Plans and Specifications for a Husband. Neither was there any Man who had any time for Her. So she led a lonely Life, dreaming of the One—

* Reprinted by permission of Duffield and Green; copyright 1899.

the Ideal. He was a big and pensive Literary Man wearing a Prince Albert coat, a neat Derby Hat and godlike Whiskers. When He came he would enfold Her in his Arms and whisper Emerson's Essays to her.

But the Party failed to show up.

Often enough she put on her Chip Hat and her Black Lisle Gloves and Sauntered down to look at the Gang sitting in front of the Occidental Hotel, hoping that the Real Thing would be there. But she always saw the same old line of Four-Flush Drummers from Chicago and St. Louis, smoking Horrid Cigars and talking about the Percentages of the League Teams.

She knew that these Gross Creatures were not prone to chase mere Intellectual Splendor, so she made no effort to flag them.

When she was Thirty-Four years of age and was able to recite "Lucile" without looking at the Book she was Married to a Janitor of the name of Ernest. He had been kicked in the Head by a Mule when young and believed everything he read in the Sunday Papers. His pay was Twenty-Three a month, which was high, if you knew Ernest.

His Wife wore a red Mother Hubbard all during the Remainder of her Life.

This is invariably a Sign of Blasted Hopes.

MORAL: *Never Live in a Jay Town.*
1899

GEORGE HORACE LORIMER
(1868–1937)

THE LETTERS OF A SELF-MADE MERCHANT TO HIS SON *

LETTER I

Chicago, October 1, 189—

DEAR PIERREPONT: Your Ma got back safe this morning and she wants me to be sure to tell you not to over-study, and I want to tell you to be sure not to under-study. What we're really sending you to Harvard for is to get a little of the education that's so good and plenty there. When it's passed around you don't want to be bashful, but reach right out and take a big helping every time, for I want you to get your share. You'll find that education's about the only thing lying around loose in this world, and that it's about the only thing a fellow can have as much of as he's willing to haul away. Everything else is screwed down tight and the screwdriver lost.

I didn't have your advantages when I was a boy, and you can't have mine. Some men learn the value of money by not having any and starting out to pry a few dollars loose from the odd millions that are lying around; and some learn it by having to do business with liars; and some by going to Sunday School. Some men learn the cussedness of whiskey by having a drunken father; and some by having a good mother. Some men get an education from other men and newspapers and public libraries; and some get it from professors and parchments —it doesn't make any special differ-

* Reprinted by permission of Sears Publishing Company and G. H. Lorimer from *The Letters of a Self-Made Merchant to His Son*, by George Horace Lorimer, copyright 1927 by J. H. Sears & Co., Inc.

ence how you get a half-nelson on the right thing, just so you get it and freeze on to it. The package doesn't count after the eye's been attracted by it, and in the end it finds its way to the ash heap. It's the quality of the goods inside which tells, when they once get into the kitchen and up to the cook.

You can cure a ham in dry salt and you can cure it in sweet pickle, and when you're through you've got pretty good eating either way, provided you started in with a sound ham. If you didn't, it doesn't make any special difference how you cured it—the ham-tryer's going to strike the sour spot around the bone. And it doesn't make any difference how much sugar and fancy pickle you soak into a fellow; he's no good unless he's sound and sweet at the core.

The first thing that any education ought to give a man is character, and the second thing is education. That is where I'm a little skittish about this college business. I'm not starting in to preach to you, because I know a young fellow with the right sort of stuff in him preaches to himself harder than any one else can, and that he's mighty often switched off the right path by having it pointed out to him in the wrong way.

I remember when I was a boy, and I wasn't a very bad boy, as boys go, old Doc Hoover got a notion in his head that I ought to join the church, and he scared me out of it for five years by asking me right out loud in Sunday School if I didn't want to be saved, and then laying for me after the service and praying with me. Of course I wanted to be saved, but I didn't want to be saved quite so publicly.

When a boy's had a good mother he's got a good conscience, and when he's got a good conscience he don't need to have right and wrong labeled for him. Now that your Ma's left and the apron strings are cut, you're naturally running up against a new sensation every minute, but if you'll simply use a little conscience as a tryer, and probe into a thing which looks sweet and sound on the skin, to see if you can't fetch up a sour smell from around the bone, you'll be all right.

I'm anxious that you should be a good scholar, but I'm more anxious that you should be a good clean man. And if you graduate with a sound conscience, I shan't care so much if there are a few holes in your Latin. There are two parts of a college education—the part that you get in the schoolroom from the professors, and the part that you get outside of it from the boys. That's the really important part. For the first can only make you a scholar, while the second can make you a man.

Education's a good deal like eating —a fellow can't always tell which particular thing did him good, but he can usually tell which one did him harm. After a square meal of roast beef and vegetables, and mince pie and watermelon, you can't say just which ingredient is going into muscle, but you don't have to be very bright to figure out which one started the demand for pain-killer in your insides, or to guess, next morning, which one made you believe in a personal devil the night before. And so, while a fellow can't figure out to an ounce whether it's Latin or algebra or history or what among the solids that is building him up in this place or that, he can go right along feeding them in and betting that they're not the things that turn his tongue fuzzy. It's down among the sweets, among his amusements and recreations, that he's going to find his stomach-ache,

and it's there that he wants to go slow and to pick and choose.

It's not the first half, but the second half of a college education which merchants mean when they ask if a college education pays. It's the Willie and the Bertie boys; the chocolate éclair and tutti-frutti boys; the la-de-dah and the baa-baa-billy-goat boys; the high cock-a-lo-rum and the cock-a-doodle-do boys; the Bah Jove!, hair-parted-in-the-middle, cigaroot-smoking, Champagne-Charlie, up-all-night-and-in-all-day boys that make 'em doubt the cash value of the college output, and overlook the roast-beef and blood-gravy boys, the shirt-sleeves and high-water-pants boys, who take their college education and make some fellow's business hum with it.

Does a college education pay? Does it pay to feed in pork trimmings at five cents a pound at the hopper and draw out nice, cunning, little "country" sausages at twenty cents a pound at the other end? Does it pay to take a steer that's been running loose on the range and living on cactus and petrified wood till he's just a bunch of barb-wire and sole-leather, and feed him corn till he's just a solid hunk of porterhouse steak and oleo oil?

You bet it pays. Anything that trains a boy to think and to think quick pays; anything that teaches a boy to get the answer before the other fellow gets through biting the pencil, pays.

College doesn't make fools; it develops them. It doesn't make bright men; it develops them. A fool will turn out a fool, whether he goes to college or not, though he'll probably turn out a different sort of a fool. And a good, strong boy will turn out a bright, strong man whether he's worn smooth in the grab-what-you-want-and-eat-standing-with-one-eye-skinned-for-the-dog school of the streets and stores, or polished up and slicked down in the give-your-order-to-the-waiter-and-get-a-sixteen-course-dinner school of the professors. But while the lack of a college education can't keep No. 1 down, having it boosts No. 2 up.

It's simply the difference between jump in, rough-and-tumble, kick-with-the-heels-and-butt-with-the-head nigger fighting, and this grin-and-look-pleasant, dodge-and-save-your-wind-till-you-see-a-chance-to-land-on-the-solar-plexus style of the trained athlete. Both styles win fights, but the fellow with a little science is the better man, providing he's kept his muscle hard. If he hasn't, he's in a bad way, for his fancy sparring is just going to aggravate the other fellow so that he'll eat him up.

Of course, some men are like pigs; the more you educate them, the more amusing little cusses they become, and the funnier capers they cut when they show off their tricks. Naturally, the place to send a boy of that breed is to the circus, not to college.

Speaking of educated pigs, naturally calls to mind the case of old man Whitaker and his son, Stanley. I used to know the old man mighty well ten years ago. He was one of those men whom business narrows, instead of broadens. Didn't get any special fun out of his work, but kept right along at it because he didn't know anything else. Told me he'd had to root for a living all his life and that he proposed to have Stan's brought to him in a pail. Sent him to private schools and dancing schools and colleges and universities, and then shipped him to Oxford to soak in a little "atmosphere," as he put it. I never could quite lay hold of that atmosphere dodge by the tail, but so far as I could make out, the idea was that there was something in the air of the Oxford ham-house that gave a fellow an extra fancy smoke.

Well, about the time Stan was through, the undertaker called by for the old man, and when his assets were boiled down and the water drawn off, there wasn't enough left to furnish Stan with a really nourishing meal. I had a talk with Stan about what he was going to do, but some ways he didn't strike me as having the making of a good private of industry, let alone a captain, so I started in to get him a job that would suit his talents. Got him in a bank, but while he knew more about the history of banking than the president, and more about political economy than the board of directors, he couldn't learn the difference between a fiver that the Government turned out and one that was run off on a hand press in a Halsted Street basement. Got him a job on a paper, but while he knew six different languages and all the facts about the Arctic regions, and the history of dancing from the days of Old Adam down to those of Old Nick, he couldn't write up a satisfactory account of the Ice-Men's Ball. Could prove that two and two made four by trigonometry and geometry, but couldn't learn to keep books; was thick as thieves with all the high-toned poets, but couldn't write a good, snappy, merchantable street-car ad.; knew a thousand diseases that would take a man off before he could blink, but couldn't sell a thousand-dollar tontine policy; knew the lives of our Presidents as well as if he'd been raised with them, but couldn't place a set of the Library of the Fathers of the Republic, though they were offered on little easy payments that made them come as easy as borrowing them from a friend. Finally I hit on what seemed to be just the right thing. I figured out that any fellow who had such a heavy stock of information on hand, ought to be able to job it out to good advantage, and so I got him a place teaching. But it seemed that he'd learned so much about the best way of teaching boys, that he told his principal right on the jump that he was doing it all wrong, and that made him sore; and he knew so much about the dead languages, which was what he was hired to teach, that he forgot he was handling live boys, and as he couldn't tell it all to them in the regular time, he kept them after hours, and that made them sore and put Stan out of a job again. The last I heard of him he was writing articles on Why Young Men Fail, and making a success of it, because failing was the one subject on which he was practical.

I simply mention Stan in passing as an example of the fact that it isn't so much knowing a whole lot, as knowing a little and how to use it that counts.

Your affectionate father,
[JOHN GRAHAM]
1901

FREDERICK WINSLOW TAYLOR
(1856–1915)

THE PRINCIPLES OF SCIENTIFIC MANAGEMENT *

CHAPTER I

FUNDAMENTALS OF SCIENTIFIC MANAGEMENT

The principal object of management should be to secure the maxi-

* From *Principles of Scientific Management* by Frederick Winslow Taylor, by permission of Harper & Brothers. Copyright, 1911, by Frederick Winslow Taylor. Copyright, 1939, by Louise M. S. Taylor.

mum prosperity for the employer, coupled with the maximum prosperity for each employé.

The words "maximum prosperity" are used, in their broad sense, to mean not only large dividends for the company or owner, but the development of every branch of the business to its highest state of excellence, so that the prosperity may be permanent.

In the same way maximum prosperity for each employé means not only higher wages than are usually received by men of his class, but, of more importance still, it also means the development of each man to his state of maximum efficiency, so that he may be able to do, generally speaking, the highest grade of work for which his natural abilities fit him, and it further means giving him, when possible, this class of work to do.

It would seem to be so self-evident that maximum prosperity for the employer, coupled with maximum prosperity for the employé, ought to be the two leading objects of management, that even to state this fact should be unnecessary. And yet there is no question that, throughout the industrial world, a large part of the organization of employers, as well as employés, is for war rather than for peace, and that perhaps the majority on either side do not believe that it is possible so to arrange their mutual relations that their interests become identical.

The majority of these men believe that the fundamental interests of employés and employers are necessarily antagonistic. Scientific management, on the contrary, has for its very foundation the firm conviction that the true interests of the two are one and the same; that prosperity for the employer cannot exist through a long term of years unless it is accompanied by prosperity for the employé, and *vice versa;* and that it is possible to give the workman what he most wants—high wages—and the employer what he wants—a low labor cost—for his manufactures.

It is hoped that some at least of those who do not sympathize with each of these objects may be led to modify their views; that some employers, whose attitude toward their workmen has been that of trying to get the largest amount of work out of them for the smallest possible wages, may be led to see that a more liberal policy toward their men will pay them better; and that some of those workmen who begrudge a fair and even a large profit to their employers, and who feel that all of the fruits of their labor should belong to them, and that those for whom they work and the capital invested in the business are entitled to little or nothing, may be led to modify these views.

No one can be found who will deny that in the case of any single individual the greatest prosperity can exist only when that individual has reached his highest state of efficiency; that is, when he is turning out his largest daily output.

The truth of this fact is also perfectly clear in the case of two men working together. To illustrate: if you and your workman have become so skilful that you and he together are making two pairs of shoes in a day, while your competitor and his workman are making only one pair, it is clear that after selling your two pairs of shoes you can pay your workman much higher wages than your competitor who produces only one pair of shoes is able to pay his man, and that there will still be enough money left over for you to have a larger profit than your competitor.

In the case of a more complicated manufacturing establishment, it should

also be perfectly clear that the greatest permanent prosperity for the workman, coupled with the greatest prosperity for the employer, can be brought about only when the work of the establishment is done with the smallest combined expenditure of human effort, plus nature's resources, plus the cost for the use of capital in the shape of machines, buildings, etc. Or, to state the same thing in a different way: that the greatest prosperity can exist only as the result of the greatest possible productivity of the men and machines of the establishment—that is, when each man and each machine are turning out the largest possible output; because unless your men and your machines are daily turning out more work than others around you, it is clear that competition will prevent your paying higher wages to your workmen than are paid to those of your competitor. And what is true as to the possibility of paying higher wages in the case of two companies competing close beside one another is also true as to whole districts of the country and even as to nations which are in competition. In a word, that maximum prosperity can exist only as the result of maximum productivity. Later in this paper illustrations will be given of several companies which are earning large dividends and at the same time paying from 30 per cent. to 100 per cent. higher wages to their men than are paid to similar men immediately around them, and with whose employers they are in competition. These illustrations will cover different types of work, from the most elementary to the most complicated.

If the above reasoning is correct, it follows that the most important object of both the workmen and the management should be the training and development of each individual in the establishment, so that he can do (at his fastest pace and with the maximum of efficiency) the highest class of work for which his natural abilities fit him.

These principles appear so self-evident that many men may think it almost childish to state them. Let us, however, turn to the facts, as they actually exist in this country and in England. The English and American peoples are the greatest sportsmen in the world. Whenever an American workman plays baseball, or an English workman plays cricket, it is safe to say that he strains every nerve to secure victory for his side. He does his very best to make the largest possible number of runs. The universal sentiment is so strong that any man who fails to give out all there is in him in sport is branded as a "quitter" and treated with contempt by those who are around him.

When the same workman returns to work on the following day, instead of using every effort to turn out the largest possible amount of work, in a majority of the cases this man deliberately plans to do as little as he safely can—to turn out far less work than he is well able to do—in many instances to do not more than one-third to one-half of a proper day's work. And in fact if he were to do his best to turn out his largest possible day's work, he would be abused by his fellow-workers for so doing, even more than if he had proved himself a "quitter" in sport. Underworking, that is, deliberately working slowly so as to avoid doing a full day's work, "soldiering," as it is called in this country, "hanging it out," as it is called in England, "ca canae," as it is called in Scotland, is almost universal in industrial establishments, and prevails also to a large extent in the building trades; and the writer asserts without fear of contradiction that this constitutes the greatest evil with which the working-people of both England and America are now afflicted.

It will be shown later in this paper that doing away with slow working and "soldiering" in all its forms and so arranging the relations between employer and employé that each workman will work to his very best advantage and at his best speed, accompanied by the intimate cooperation with the management and the help (which the workman should receive) from the management, would result on the average in nearly doubling the output of each man and each machine. What other reforms, among those which are being discussed by these two nations, could do as much toward promoting prosperity, toward the diminution of poverty, and the alleviation of suffering? America and England have been recently agitated over such subjects as the tariff, the control of the large corporations on the one hand, and of hereditary power on the other hand, and over various more or less socialistic proposals for taxation, etc. On these subjects both peoples have been profoundly stirred, and yet hardly a voice has been raised to call attention to this vastly greater and more important subject of "soldiering," which directly and powerfully affects the wages, the prosperity, and the life of almost every working-man, and also quite as much the prosperity of every industrial establishment in the nation.

The elimination of "soldiering" and of the several causes of slow working would so lower the cost of production that both our home and foreign markets would be greatly enlarged, and we could compete on more than even terms with our rivals. It would remove one of the fundamental causes for dull times, for lack of employment, and for poverty, and therefore would have a more permanent and far-reaching effect upon these misfortunes than any of the curative remedies that are now being used to soften their consequences. It would insure higher wages and make shorter working hours and better working and home conditions possible.

Why is it, then, in the face of the self-evident fact that maximum prosperity can exist only as the result of the determined effort of each workman to turn out each day his largest possible day's work, that the great majority of our men are deliberately doing just the opposite, and that even when the men have the best of intentions their work is in most cases far from efficient?

There are three causes for this condition, which may be briefly summarized as:

First. The fallacy, which has from time immemorial been almost universal among workmen, that a material increase in the output of each man or each machine in the trade would result in the end in throwing a large number of men out of work.

Second. The defective systems of management which are in common use, and which make it necessary for each workman to soldier, or work slowly, in order that he may protect his own best interests.

Third. The inefficient rule-of-thumb methods, which are still almost universal in all trades, and in practising which our workmen waste a large part of their effort.

This paper will attempt to show the enormous gains which would result from the substitution by our workmen of scientific for rule-of-thumb methods.

To explain a little more fully these three causes:

First. The great majority of workmen still believe that if they were to work at their best speed they would be doing a great injustice to the whole trade by throwing a lot of men out of work, and yet the history of the development of each trade shows that each improvement, whether it be the invention of a new machine or the introduction of a better method, which results in increasing the productive capacity of the men in the trade and cheapening the costs, instead of throwing men out of work make in the end work for more men.

The cheapening of any article in common use almost immediately results in a largely increased demand for that article. Take the case of shoes, for instance. The introduction of machinery for doing every element of the work which was formerly done by hand has resulted in making shoes at a fraction of their former labor cost, and in selling them so cheap that now almost every man, woman, and child in the working-classes buys one or two pairs of shoes per year, and wears shoes all the time, whereas formerly each workman bought perhaps one pair of shoes every five years, and went barefoot most of the time, wearing shoes only as a luxury or as a matter of the sternest necessity. In spite of the enormously increased output of shoes per workman, which has come with shoe machinery, the demand for shoes has so increased that there are relatively more men working in the shoe industry now than ever before.

The workmen in almost every trade have before them an object lesson of this kind, and yet, because they are ignorant of the history of their own trade even, they still firmly believe, as their fathers did before them, that it is against their best interests for each man to turn out each day as much work as possible.

Under this fallacious idea a large proportion of the workmen of both countries each day deliberately work slowly so as to curtail the output. Almost every labor union has made, or is contemplating making, rules which have for their object curtailing the output of their members, and those men who have the greatest influence with the working-people, the labor leaders as well as many people with philanthropic feelings who are helping them, are daily spreading this fallacy and at the same time telling them that they are overworked.

A great deal has been and is being constantly said about "sweatshop" work and conditions. The writer has great sympathy with those who are overworked, but on the whole a greater sympathy for those who are *under paid*. For every individual, however, who is overworked, there are a hundred who intentionally underwork —greatly underwork—every day of their lives, and who for this reason deliberately aid in establishing those conditions which in the end inevitably result in low wages. And yet hardly a single voice is being raised in an endeavor to correct this evil.

As engineers and managers, we are more intimately acquainted with these facts than any other class in the community, and are therefore best fitted to lead in a movement to combat this fallacious idea by educating not only the workmen but the whole of the country as to the true facts. And yet we are practically doing nothing in this direction, and are leaving this field entirely in the hands of the labor agitators (many of whom are misinformed and misguided), and of the sentimentalists who are ignorant as to actual working conditions.

Second. As to the second cause for soldiering—the relations which exist between employers and employés under almost all the systems of management which are in common use—it is impossible in a few words to make it clear to one not familiar with this problem why it is that the *ignorance of employers* as to the proper time in which work of various kinds should be done makes it for the interests of the workman to "soldier."

The writer therefore quotes herewith from a paper read before The American Society of Mechanical Engineers, in June, 1903, entitled "Shop Management," which it is hoped will explain fully this cause for soldiering:

This loafing or soldiering proceeds from two causes. First, from the natural instinct and tendency of men to take it easy, which may be called natural soldiering. Second, from more intricate second thought and reasoning caused by their relations with other men, which may be called systematic soldiering.

There is no question that the tendency of the average man (in all walks of life) is toward working at a slow, easy gait, and that it is only after a good deal of thought and observation on his part or as a result of example, conscience, or external pressure that he takes a more rapid pace.

There are, of course, men of unusual energy, vitality, and ambition who naturally choose the fastest gait, who set up their own standards, and who work hard, even though it may be against their best interests. But these few uncommon men only serve by forming a contrast to emphasize the tendency of the average.

This common tendency to "take it easy" is greatly increased by bringing a number of men together on similar work and at a uniform standard rate of pay by the day.

Under this plan the better men gradually but surely slow down their gait to that of the poorest and least efficient. When a naturally energetic man works for a few days beside a lazy one, the logic of the situation is unanswerable.

"Why should I work hard when that lazy fellow gets the same pay that I do and does only half as much work?"

A careful time study of men working under these conditions will disclose facts which are ludicrous as well as pitiable.

To illustrate: The writer has timed a naturally energetic workman who, while going and coming from work, would walk at a speed of from three to four miles per hour, and not infrequently trot home after a day's work. On arriving at his work he would immediately slow down to a speed of about one mile an hour. When, for example, wheeling a loaded wheelbarrow, he would go at a good fast pace even up hill in order to be as short a time as possible under load, and immediately on the return walk slow down to a mile an hour, improving every opportunity for delay short of actually sitting down. In order to be sure not to do more than his lazy neighbor, he would actually tire himself in his effort to go slow.

These men were working under a foreman of good reputation and highly thought of by his employer, who, when his attention was called to this state of things, answered: "Well, I can keep them from sitting down, but the devil can't make them get a move on while they are at work."

The natural laziness of men is serious, but by far the greatest evil from which both workmen and employers are suffering is the *systematic soldiering* which is almost universal under all of the ordinary schemes of management and which results from a careful study on the part of the workmen of what will promote their best interests.

The writer was much interested recently in hearing one small but experienced golf caddy boy of twelve explaining to a green caddy, who had shown special energy and interest, the necessity of going slow and lagging behind his man when he came up to the ball, showing him that since they were paid by the hour, the faster they went the less money they got, and finally telling him that if he went too fast the other boys would give him a licking.

This represents a type of *systematic soldiering* which is not, however, very serious, since it is done with the knowledge of the employer, who can quite easily break it up if he wishes.

The greater part of the *systematic soldiering*, however, is done by the men with the deliberate object of keeping their employers ignorant of how fast work can be done.

So universal is soldiering for this purpose that hardly a competent workman can be found in a large establishment, whether he works by the day or on piece work, contract work, or under any of the ordinary systems, who does not devote a considerable part of his time to studying just how slow he can work and still convince his employer that he is going at a good pace.

The causes for this are, briefly, that practically all employers determine upon a maximum sum which they feel it is right for each of their classes of employees to earn per day, whether their men work by the day or piece.

Each workman soon finds out about what this figure is for his particular case, and he also realizes that when his employer is convinced that a man is capable of doing more work than he has done, he will find sooner or later some way of compelling him to do it with little or no increase of pay.

Employers derive their knowledge of how much of a given class of work can be done in a day from either their own experience, which has frequently grown hazy with age, from casual and unsystematic observation of their men, or at best from records which are kept, showing the quickest time in which each job has been done. In many cases the employer will feel almost certain that a given job can be done faster than it has been, but he rarely cares to take the drastic measures necessary to force men to do it in the quickest time, unless he has an actual record proving conclusively how fast the work can be done.

It evidently becomes for each man's interest, then, to see that no job is done faster than it has been in the past. The younger and less experienced men are taught this by their elders, and all possible persuasion and social pressure is brought to bear upon the greedy and selfish men to keep them from making new records which result in temporarily increasing their wages, while all those who come after them are made to work harder for the same old pay.

Under the best day work of the ordinary type, when accurate records are kept of the amount of work done by each man and of his efficiency, and when each man's wages are raised as he improves, and those who fail to rise to a certain standard are discharged and a fresh supply of carefully selected men are given work in their places, both the natural loafing and the systematic soldiering can be largely broken up. This can only be done, however, when the men are thoroughly convinced that there is no intention of establishing piece work even in the remote future, and it is next to impossible to make men believe this when the work is of such a nature that they believe piece work to be practicable. In most cases their fear of making a record which will be used as a basis for piece work will cause them to soldier as much as they dare.

It is, however, under piece work that the art of systematic soldiering is thoroughly developed; after the workman has had the price per piece of the work he is doing lowered two or three times as a result of his having worked harder and increased his output, he is likely entirely to lose sight of his employer's side of the case and become imbued with a grim determination to have no more cuts if soldiering can prevent it. Unfortunately for the character of the workman, soldiering involves a deliberate attempt to mislead and deceive his employer, and thus upright and straightforward workmen are compelled to become more or less hypocritical. The employer is soon looked upon as an antagonist, if not an enemy, and the mutual confidence which should exist between a leader and his men, the enthusiasm, the feeling that they are all working for the same end and will share in the results is entirely lacking.

The feeling of antagonism under the ordinary piece-work system becomes in many cases so marked on the part of the men that any proposition made by their employers, however reasonable, is looked upon with suspicion, and soldiering becomes such a fixed habit that men will frequently take pains to restrict the product of machines which they are running when even a large increase in output would involve no more work on their part.

Third. As to the third cause for slow work, considerable space will later in this paper be devoted to illustrating the great gain, both to employers and employés, which results from the substitution of scientific for rule-of-thumb methods in even the smallest details of the work of every trade. The enormous saving of time and therefore increase in the output which it is possible to effect through eliminating unnecessary motions and substituting fast for slow and inefficient motions for the men working in any of our trades can be fully realized only after one has personally seen the improvement which results from a thorough motion and time study, made by a competent man.

To explain briefly: owing to the fact that the workmen in all our trades have been taught the details of their work by observation of those immediately around them, there are many different ways in common use for doing the same thing, perhaps forty, fifty, or a hundred ways of doing each act in each trade, and for the same reason there is a great variety in the implements used for each class of work. Now, among the various methods and implements used in each element of each trade there is always one method and one implement which is quicker and better than any of the rest. And this one best method and best implement can only be discovered through a scientific study and analysis of all of the methods and implements in use, together with accurate, minute, motion and time study. This involves the gradual substitution of science for rule of thumb throughout the mechanic arts.

This paper will show that the underlying philosophy of all of the old systems of management in common use makes it imperative that each workman shall be left with the final responsibility for doing his job practically as he thinks best, with comparatively little help and advice from the management. And it will also show that because of this isolation of workmen, it is in most cases impossible for the men working under these systems to do their work in accordance with the rules and laws of a science or art, even where one exists.

The writer asserts as a general principle (and he proposes to give illustrations tending to prove the fact later in this paper) that in almost all of the mechanic arts the science which underlies each act of each workman is so great and amounts to so much that the workman who is best suited to actually doing the work is incapable of fully understanding this science, without the guidance and help of those who are working with him or over him, either through lack of education or through insufficient mental capacity. In order that the work may be done in accordance with scientific laws, it is necessary that there shall be a far more equal division of the responsibility between the management and the workmen than exists under any of the ordinary types of management. Those in the management whose duty it is to develop this science should also guide and help the workman in working under it, and should assume a much larger share of the responsibility for results than under usual conditions is assumed by the management.

The body of this paper will make it clear that, to work according to scientific laws, the management must take over and perform much of the work which is now left to the men; almost every act of the workman should be preceded by one or more preparatory acts of the management which enable him to do his work better and quicker than he otherwise could. And each man should daily be taught by and receive the most friendly help from those who are over him, instead of being, at the one extreme, driven or coerced by his bosses, and at the other left to his own unaided devices.

This close, intimate, personal cooperation between the management and the men is of the essence of modern scientific or task management.

It will be shown by a series of practical illustrations that, through this friendly cooperation, namely, through sharing equally in every day's burden, all of the great obstacles (above described) to obtaining the maximum output for each man and each machine in the establishment are swept away. The 30 per cent. to 100 per cent. increase in wages which the workmen are able to earn beyond what they receive under the old type of management, coupled with the daily intimate shoulder to shoulder contact with the management, entirely removes all cause for soldiering. And in a few years, under this system, the workmen have before them the object lesson of seeing that a great increase in the output per man results in giving more employment to more men, instead of throwing more men out of work, thus completely eradicating the fallacy that a larger output for each man will throw other men out of work.

It is the writer's judgment, then, that while much can be done and should be done by writing and talking toward educating not only workmen, but all classes in the community, as to the importance of obtaining the maximum output of each man and each machine, it is only through the adoption of modern scientific management that this great problem can be finally solved. Probably most of the readers of this paper will say that all of this is mere theory. On the contrary, the theory, or philosophy, of scientific management is just beginning to be understood, whereas the management itself has been a gradual evolution, extending over a period of nearly thirty years. And during this time the employés of one company after another, including a large range and diversity of industries, have gradually changed from the ordinary to the scientific type of management. At least 50,000 workmen in the United States are now employed under this system; and they are receiving from 30 per cent. to 100 per cent. higher wages daily than are paid to men of similar caliber with whom they are surrounded, while the companies employing them are more prosperous than ever before. In these companies the output, per man and per machine, has on an average been doubled. During all these years there has never been a single strike among the men working under this system. In place of the suspicious watchfulness and the more or less open warfare which characterizes the ordinary types of management, there is universally friendly cooperation between the management and the men.

Several papers have been written, describing the expedients which have been adopted and the details which have been developed under scientific management and the steps to be taken in changing from the ordinary to the scientific type. But unfortunately most of the readers of these papers have mistaken the mechanism for the true essence. Scientific management fundamentally consists of certain broad general principles, a certain philosophy, which can be applied in many ways, and a description of what any one man or men may believe to be the best mechanism for applying these general principles should in no way be confused with the principles themselves.

It is not here claimed that any single panacea exists for all of the troubles of the working-people or of employers. As long as some people are born lazy or inefficient, and others are born greedy and brutal, as long as vice and crime are with us, just so long will a certain amount of poverty, misery, and unhappiness be with us also. No system of management, no single expedient within the control of any man or any set of men can insure continuous prosperity to either workmen or employers. Prosperity depends upon so many factors entirely beyond the control of any one set of men, any state, or even any one country, that certain periods will inevitably come when both sides must suffer, more or less. It is claimed, however, that under scientific management the intermediate periods will be far more prosperous, far happier, and more free from discord and dissension. And also, that the periods will be fewer, shorter and the suffering less. And this will be particularly true in any one town, any one section of the country, or any one state which first substitutes the principles of scientific management for the rule of thumb.

That these principles are certain to come into general use practically throughout the civilized world, sooner or later, the writer is profoundly convinced, and the sooner they come the better for all the people.

1911

HENRY ADAMS
(1838–1918)

THE TENDENCY OF HISTORY *

To Herbert B. Adams
Guadalajara,
December 12, 1894

Dear Sir:

I regret extremely that constant absence has prevented me from attending the meetings of the Historical Association. On the date which your letter mentions as that of its first decennial I shall not be within reach. I have to ask you to offer my apology to the members, and the assurance that at that moment I am believed to be somewhere beyond the Isthmus of Panama. Perhaps this absence runs in some of the mysterious ways of nature's law, for you will not forget that when you did me the honor to make me your president I was still farther away—in Tahiti or Fiji, I believe— and never even had an opportunity to thank you. Evidently I am fitted only to be an absent president, and you will pardon a defect which is clearly not official, but a condition of the man.

I regret this fault the more because I would have liked to be of service, and perhaps there is service that might usefully be performed. Even the effort to hold together the persons interested in history is worth making. That we should ever act on public opinion with the weight of one compact and

one energetic conviction is hardly to be expected, but that one day or another we shall be compelled to act individually or in groups I cannot doubt. With more anxiety than confidence, I should have liked to do something, however trifling, to hold the association together and unite it on some common ground, with a full understanding of the course which history seems destined to take and with a good-natured willingness to accept or reject the result, but in any case not to quarrel over it.

No one who has watched the course of history during the last generation can have felt doubt of its tendency. Those of us who read Buckle's first volume when it appeared in 1857 and almost immediately afterwards, in 1859, read the *Origin of the Species* and felt the violent impulse which Darwin gave to the study of natural laws, never doubted that historians would follow until they had exhausted every possible hypothesis to create a science of history. Year after year passed, and little progress has been made. Perhaps the mass of students are more skeptical now than they were thirty years ago of the possibility that such a science can be created. Yet almost every successful historian has been busy with it, adding here a new analysis, a new generalization there; a clear and definite connection where before the rupture of idea was absolute; and, above all, extending the field of study until it shall include all races, all countries, and all times. Like other branches of science, history is now encumbered and hampered by its own mass, but its tendency is always the same, and cannot be other than what it is. That the effort to make history a science may fail is possible, and perhaps probable; but that it should cease, is not within the range of experience. Historians will

* From Henry Adams, *The Degradation of Democratic Dogma*. By permission of the Macmillan Company, publishers. Copyright, 1919.

not, and even if they would they cannot, abandon the attempt. Science itself would admit its own failure if it admitted that man, the most important of all its subjects, could not be brought within its range.

You may be sure that four out of five serious students of history who are living today have, in the course of their work, felt that they stood on the brink of a great generalization that would reduce all history under a law as clear as the laws which govern the material world. As the great writers of our time have touched one by one the separate fragments of admitted law by which society betrays its character as a subject for science, not one of them can have failed to feel an instant's hope that he might find the secret which would transform these odds and ends of philosophy into one self-evident, harmonious, and complete system. He has seemed to have it, as the Spanish say, in his inkstand. Scores of times he must have dropped his pen to think how one short step, one sudden inspiration, would show all human knowledge; how, in these thickset forests of history, one corner turned, one faint trail struck, would bring him on the highroad of science. Every professor who has tried to teach the doubtful facts which we now call history must have felt that sooner or later he or another would put order in chaos and bring light into darkness. Not so much genius or favor was needed as patience and good luck. The law was certainly there, and as certainly was in places actually visible, to be touched and handled, as though it were a law of chemistry or physics. No teacher with a spark of imagination or with an idea of scientific method can have helped dreaming of the immortality that would be achieved by the man who

should successfully apply Darwin's method to the facts of human history.

Those of us who have had occasion to keep abreast of the rapid progress which has been made in history during the last fifty years must be convinced that the same rate of progress during another half century would necessarily raise history to the rank of a science. Our only doubt is whether the same rate can possibly be maintained. If not, our situation is simple. In that case, we shall remain more or less where we are. But we have reached a point where we ought to face the possibility of a great and perhaps a sudden change in the importance of our profession. We cannot help asking ourselves what would happen if some new Darwin were to demonstrate the laws of historical evolution.

I admit that the mere idea of such an event fills my mind with anxiety. When I remember the astonishing influence exerted by a mere theorist like Rousseau; by a reasoner like Adam Smith; by a philosopher, beyond contact with material interests, like Darwin, I cannot imagine the limits of the shock that might follow the establishment of a fixed science of history. Hitherto our profession has been encouraged, or, at all events, tolerated by governments and by society as an amusing or instructive and, at any rate, a safe and harmless branch of inquiry. But what will be the attitude of government or of society toward any conceivable science of history? We know what followed Rousseau; what industrial and political struggles have resulted from the teachings of Adam Smith; what a revolution and what vehement opposition has been and still is caused by the ideas of Darwin. Can we imagine any science of history that would not be vastly more violent in its effects than the dissension roused by any one or by all three of these great men?

I ask myself, what shape can be given to any science of history that will not shake to its foundations some prodigious interest? The world is made up of a few immense forces, each with an organization that corresponds with its strength. The church stands first; and at the outset we must assume that the church will not and cannot accept any science of history, because science, by its definition, must exclude the idea of a personal and active providence. The state stands next; and the hostility of the state would be assured toward any system or science that might not strengthen its arm. Property is growing more and more timid and looks with extreme jealousy on any new idea that may weaken vested rights. Labor is growing more and more self-confident and looks with contempt on all theories that do not support its own. Yet we cannot conceive of a science of history that would not, directly or indirectly, affect all these vast social forces.

Any science assumes a necessary sequence of cause and effect, a force resulting in motion which cannot be other than what it is. Any science of history must be absolute, like other sciences, and must fix with mathematical certainty the path which human society has got to follow. That path can hardly lead toward the interests of all the great social organizations. We cannot conceive that it should help at the same time the church and the state, property and communism, capital and poverty, science and religion, trade and art. Whatever may be its orbit it must, at least for a time, point away from some of these forces toward others which are regarded as hostile. Conceivably, it might lead off in eccentric lines away from them all, but by no power of our imagination can we conceive that it should lead toward them all.

Although I distrust my own judgment and look earnestly for guidance to those who are younger than I and closer to the movement of the time, I cannot be wholly wrong in thinking that a change has come over the tendency of liberal thought since the middle of the century. Darwin led an intellectual revival much more hopeful than any movement that can now be seen in Europe, except among the socialists. Had history been converted into a science at that time, it would perhaps have taken the form of cheerful optimism which gave to Darwin's conclusions the charm of possible human perfectibility. Of late years the tone of European thought has been distinctly despondent among the classes which were formerly most hopeful. If a science of history were established to-day on the lines of its recent development, I greatly fear it would take its tone from the pessimism of Paris, Berlin, London, and St. Petersburg, unless it brought into sight some new and hitherto unsuspected path for civilization to pursue.

If it pointed to socialistic triumph it would place us in an attitude of hostility toward existing institutions. Even supposing that our universities would permit their professors in this country to announce the scientific certainty of communistic triumphs, could Europe be equally liberal? Would property, on which the universities depend, allow such freedom of instruction? Would the state suffer its foundation to be destroyed? Would society as now constituted tolerate the open assertion of a necessity which should affirm its approaching overthrow?

If, on the other hand, the new science required us to announce that the present evils of the world—its huge armaments, its vast accumulations of capital, its advancing materialism, and declining arts—were to be continued, exaggerated, over another thousand years, no one would listen to us with satisfaction. Society would shut its eyes and ears. If we proved the certainty of our results we should prove it without a sympathetic audience and without good effect. No one except artists and socialists would listen, and the conviction we should produce on them could lead only to despair and attempts at anarchy in art, in thought, and in society.

If, finally, the science should prove that society must at a given time revert to the church and recover its old foundation of absolute faith in a personal providence and a revealed religion, it commits suicide.

In whatever direction we look we can see no possibility of converting history into a science without bringing it into hostility toward one or more of the most powerful organizations of the era. If the world is to continue moving toward the point which it has so energetically pursued during the last fifty years, it will destroy the hopes of the vast organizations of labor. If it is to change its course and become communistic, it places us in direct hostility to the entire fabric of our social and political system. If it goes on, we must preach despair. If it goes back, it must deny and repudiate science: If it goes forward, round a circle which leads through communism, we must declare ourselves hostile to the property that pays us and the institutions we are bound in duty to support.

A science cannot be played with. If an hypothesis is advanced that obviously brings into direct sequence of cause and effect all the phenomena of human history, we must accept it, and if we accept, we must teach it. The mere fact that it overthrows social organizations cannot affect our attitude. The rest of society can reject or ignore, but we must follow the new light no matter where it leads. Only about two hundred and fifty years ago the common sense of mankind, supported by the authority of revealed religion, affirmed the undoubted and self-evident fact that the sun moved round the earth. Galileo suddenly asserted and proved that the earth moved round the sun. You know what followed, and the famous *"É pur si muove."* Even if we, like Galileo, should be obliged by the religious or secular authority to recant and repudiate our science, we should still have to say as he did in secret, if not in public, *"É pur si muove."*

Those of us who have reached or passed middle age need not trouble ourselves very much about the future. We have seen one or two great revolutions in thought and we have had enough. We are not likely to accept any new theory that shall threaten to disturb our repose. We should reject at once, and probably by a large majority, a hypothetical science that must obviously be incapable of proof. We should take the attitude that our fathers took toward the theories and hypotheses of Darwin. We may meantime reply to such conundrums by the formula that has smoothed our path in life over many disasters and cataclysms: "Perhaps the crisis will never occur; and even if it does occur, we shall probably be dead." To us who have already gone as far as we set out to go, this answer is good and sufficient, but those who are to be the professors and historians of the future have got duties and responsibilities of a heavier kind than we older ones ever have had to carry. They cannot afford to deal with such a question in such a spirit. They would have to rejoin in Heine's word:

Also fragen wir beständig,
Bis man uns mit einer Handvoll
Erde endlich stopft die Mäuler,
Aber ist das eine Antwort?

They may at any time in the next fifty years be compelled to find an answer, "Yes" or "No," under the pressure of the most powerful organizations the world has ever known for the suppression of influences hostile to its safety. If this association should be gifted with the length of life that we all wish for it, a span of a century at least, it can hardly fail to be torn by some such dilemma. Our universities, at all events, must be prepared to meet it. If such a crisis should come, the universities throughout the world will have done the most to create it, and are under most obligation to find a solution for it. I will not deny that the shadow of this coming event has cast itself upon me, both as a teacher and a writer; or that, in the last ten years, it has often kept me silent where I should once have spoken with confidence, or has caused me to think long and anxiously before expressing in public any opinion at all. Beyond a doubt, silence is best. In these remarks, which are only casual and offered in the paradoxical spirit of private conversation, I have not ventured to express an opinion of my own; or, if I have expressed it, pray consider it as withdrawn. The situation seems to call for no opinion, unless we have some scientific theory to offer; but to me it seems so interesting that, in taking leave of the association, I feel inclined to invite them, as individuals, to consider the matter in a spirit that will enable us, should the crisis arise, to deal with it in a kindly temper, and a full un-

derstanding of its serious dangers and responsibilities.

Ever truly yours,

THE EDUCATION OF HENRY ADAMS *

CHAPTER XXV

THE DYNAMO AND THE VIRGIN (1900)

Until the Great Exposition of 1900 closed its doors in November, Adams haunted it, aching to absorb knowledge, and helpless to find it. He would have liked to know how much of it could have been grasped by the best-informed man in the world. While he was thus meditating chaos, Langley came by, and showed it to him. At Langley's behest, the Exhibition dropped its superfluous rags and stripped itself to the skin, for Langley knew what to study, and why, and how; while Adams might as well have stood outside in the night, staring at the Milky Way. Yet Langley said nothing new, and taught nothing that one might not have learned from Lord Bacon, three hundred years before; but though one should have known the *Advancement of Science* as well as one knew the *Comedy of Errors,* the literary knowledge counted for nothing until some teacher should show how to apply it. Bacon took a vast deal of trouble in teaching King James I and his subjects, American or other, towards the year 1620, that true science was the development or economy of forces; yet an elderly American in 1900 knew neither the formula nor the forces; or even so much as to say to himself that his historical business in the Ex-

* The selection from *The Education of Henry Adams* by Henry Adams is used by permission of the publishers, Houghton Mifflin Company.

position concerned only the economies or developments of force since 1893, when he began the study at Chicago.

Nothing in education is so astonishing as the amount of ignorance it accumulates in the form of inert facts. Adams had looked at most of the accumulations of art in the storehouses called Art Museums; yet he did not know how to look at the art exhibits of 1900. He had studied Karl Marx and his doctrines of history with profound attention, yet he could not apply them at Paris. Langley, with the ease of a great master of experiment, threw out of the field every exhibit that did not reveal a new application of force, and naturally threw out, to begin with, almost the whole art exhibit. Equally, he ignored almost the whole industrial exhibit. He led his pupil directly to the forces. His chief interest was in new motors to make his airship feasible, and he taught Adams the astonishing complexities of the Daimler motor, and of the automobile, which, since 1893, had become a nightmare at a hundred kilometres an hour, almost as destructive as the electric tram which was only ten years older; and threatening to become as terrible as the locomotive steam-engine itself, which was almost exactly Adams's own age.

Then he showed his scholar the great hall of dynamos, and explained how little he knew about electricity or force of any kind, even of his own special sun, which spouted heat in inconceivable volume, but which, as far as he knew, might spout less or more, at any time, for all the certainty he felt in it. To him, the dynamo itself was but an ingenious channel for conveying somewhere the heat latent in a few tons of poor coal hidden in a dirty engine-house carefully kept out of sight; but to Adams the dynamo became a symbol of infinity. As he grew accustomed to the great gallery of machines, he began to feel the forty-foot dynamos as a moral force, much as the early Christians felt the Cross. The planet itself seemed less impressive, in its old-fashioned, deliberate, annual or daily revolution, than this huge wheel, revolving within arm's-length at some vertiginous speed, and barely murmuring—scarcely humming an audible warning to stand a hair's-breadth further for respect of power—while it would not wake the baby lying close against its frame. Before the end, one began to pray to it; inherited instinct taught the natural expression of man before silent and infinite force. Among the thousand symbols of ultimate energy, the dynamo was not so human as some, but it was the most expressive.

Yet the dynamo, next to the steam-engine, was the most familiar of exhibits. For Adams's objects its value lay chiefly in its occult mechanism. Between the dynamo in the gallery of machines and the engine-house outside, the break of continuity amounted to abysmal fracture for a historian's objects. No more relation could he discover between the steam and the electric current than between the Cross and the cathedral. The forces were interchangeable if not reversible, but he could see only an absolute *fiat* in electricity as in faith. Langley could not help him. Indeed, Langley seemed to be worried by the same trouble, for he constantly repeated that the new forces were anarchical, and especially that he was not responsible for the new rays, that were little short of parricidal in their wicked spirit towards science. His own rays, with which he had doubled the solar spectrum, were altogether harmless and beneficent; but Radium denied its God—or, what was to Langley the same thing, denied the truths of his Science. The force was wholly new.

A historian who asked only to learn enough to be as futile as Langley or Kelvin, made rapid progress under this teaching, and mixed himself up in the tangle of ideas until he achieved a sort of Paradise of ignorance vastly consoling to his fatigued senses. He wrapped himself in vibrations and rays which were new, and he would have hugged Marconi and Branly had he met them, as he hugged the dynamo; while he lost his arithmetic in trying to figure out the equation between the discoveries and the economies of force. The economies, like the discoveries, were absolute, supersensual, occult; incapable of expression in horse-power. What mathematical equivalent could he suggest as the value of a Branly coherer? Frozen air, or the electric furnace, had some scale of measurement, no doubt, if somebody could invent a thermometer adequate to the purpose; but X-rays had played no part whatever in man's consciousness, and the atom itself had figured only as a fiction of thought. In these seven years man had translated himself into a new universe which had no common scale of measurement with the old. He had entered a supersensual world, in which he could measure nothing except by chance collisions of movements imperceptible to his senses, perhaps even imperceptible to his instruments, but perceptible to each other, and so to some known ray at the end of the scale. Langley seemed prepared for anything, even for an indeterminable number of universes interfused— physics stark mad in metaphysics.

Historians undertake to arrange sequences,—called stories, or histories —assuming in silence a relation of cause and effect. These assumptions, hidden in the depths of dusty libraries, have been astounding, but commonly unconscious and childlike; so much so, that if any captious critic were to drag them to light, historians would probably reply, with one voice, that they had never supposed themselves required to know what they were talking about. Adams, for one, had toiled in vain to find out what he meant. He had even published a dozen volumes of American history for no other purpose than to satisfy himself whether, by the severest process of stating, with the least possible comment, such facts as seemed sure, in such order as seemed rigorously consequent, he could fix for a familiar moment a necessary sequence of human movement. The result had satisfied him as little as at Harvard College. Where he saw sequence, other men saw something quite different, and no one saw the same unit of measure. He cared little about his experiments and less about his statesmen, who seemed to him quite as ignorant as himself and, as a rule, no more honest; but he insisted on a relation of sequence, and if he could not reach it by one method, he would try as many methods as science knew. Satisfied that the sequence of men led to nothing and that the sequence of their society could lead no further, while the mere sequence of time was artificial, and the sequence of thought was chaos, he turned at last to the sequence of force; and thus it happened that, after ten years' pursuit, he found himself lying in the Gallery of Machines at the Great Exposition of 1900, his historical neck broken by the sudden irruption of forces totally new.

Since no one else showed much concern, an elderly person without other cares had no need to betray alarm. The year 1900 was not the first to upset schoolmasters. Copernicus and Galileo had broken many professorial necks about 1600; Columbus had stood the world on its head towards 1500; but the nearest approach to the revolution of 1900 was that of 310, when Constantine set up the Cross. The rays that Langley disowned, as well as those which he fathered, were occult, supersensual, irrational; they were a revelation of mysterious energy like that of the Cross; they were what, in terms of mediæval science, were called immediate modes of the divine substance.

The historian was thus reduced to his last resources. Clearly if he was bound to reduce all these forces to a common value, this common value could have no measure but that of their attraction on his own mind. He must treat them as they had been felt; as convertible, reversible, interchangeable attractions on thought. He made up his mind to venture it; he would risk translating rays into faith. Such a reversible process would vastly amuse a chemist, but the chemist could not deny that he, or some of his fellow physicists, could feel the force of both. When Adams was a boy in Boston, the best chemists in the place had probably never heard of Venus except by way of scandal, or of the Virgin except as idolatry; neither had he heard of dynamos or automobiles or radium; yet his mind was ready to feel the force of all, though the rays were unborn and the women were dead.

Here opened another totally new education, which promised to be by far the most hazardous of all. The knife-edge along which he must crawl, like Sir Lancelot in the twelfth century, divided two kingdoms of force which had nothing in common but attraction. They were as different as a magnet is from gravitation, supposing one knew what a magnet was, or

gravitation, or love. The force of the Virgin was still felt at Lourdes, and seemed to be as potent as X-rays; but in America neither Venus nor Virgin ever had value as force—at most as sentiment. No American had even been truly afraid of either.

This problem in dynamics gravely perplexed an American historian. The Woman had once been supreme; in France she still seemed potent, not merely as a sentiment, but as a force. Why was she unknown in America? For evidently America was ashamed of her, and she was ashamed of herself, otherwise they would not have strewn fig-leaves so profusely all over her. When she was a true force, she was ignorant of fig-leaves, but the monthly-magazine-made American female had not a feature that would have been recognized by Adam. The trait was notorious, and often humorous, but any one brought up among Puritans knew that sex was sin. In any previous age, sex was strength. Neither art nor beauty was needed. Every one, even among Puritans, knew that neither Diana of the Ephesians nor any of the Oriental goddesses was worshipped for her beauty. She was goddess because of her force; she was the animated dynamo; she was reproduction—the greatest and most mysterious of all energies; all she needed was to be fecund. Singularly enough, not one of Adams's many schools of education had ever drawn his attention to the opening lines of Lucretius, though they were perhaps the finest in all Latin Literature, where the poet invoked Venus exactly as Dante invoked the Virgin:—

Quæ quoniam rerum naturam *sola* gubernas.

The Venus of Epicurean philosophy survived in the Virgin of the Schools:

Donna, sei tanto grande, e tanto vali,
Che qual vuol grazia, e a te non ricorre,
Sua disianza vuol volar senz' ali.

All this was to American thought as though it had never existed. The true American knew something of the facts, but nothing of the feelings; he read the letter, but he never felt the law. Before this historical chasm, a mind like that of Adams felt itself helpless; he turned from the Virgin to the Dynamo as though he were a Branly coherer. On one side, at the Louvre and at Chartres, as he knew by the record of work actually done and still before his eyes, was the highest energy ever known to man, the creator of four-fifths of his noblest art, exercising vastly more attraction over the human mind than all the steam-engines and dynamos ever dreamed of; and yet this energy was unknown to the American mind. An American Virgin would never dare command; an American Venus would never dare exist.

The question, which to any plain American of the nineteenth century seemed as remote as it did to Adams, drew him almost violently to study, once it was posed; and on this point Langleys were as useless as though they were Herbert Spencers or dynamos. The idea survived only as art. There one turned as naturally as though the artist were himself a woman. Adams began to ponder, asking himself whether he knew of any American artist who had ever insisted on the power of sex, as every classic had always done; but he could think only of Walt Whitman; Bret Harte, as far as the magazines would let him venture; and one or two painters, for the flesh-tones. All the rest had used sex for sentiment, never for force; to them, Eve was a tender flower, and Herodias an unfeminine horror. American art, like the American language and American education, was as far as possible sexless. Society regarded this victory over sex as its greatest triumph, and the historian readily admitted it, since the moral issue, for the moment, did not concern one who was studying the relations of unmoral force. He cared nothing for the sex of the dynamo until he could measure its energy.

Vaguely seeking a clue, he wandered through the art exhibit, and, in his stroll, stopped almost every day before Saint-Gaudens's General Sherman, which had been given the central post of honor. Saint-Gaudens himself was in Paris, putting on the work his usual interminable last touches, and listening to the usual contradictory suggestions of brother sculptors. Of all the American artists who gave to American art whatever life it breathed in the seventies, Saint-Gaudens was perhaps the most sympathetic, but certainly the most inarticulate. General Grant or Don Cameron had scarcely less instinct of rhetoric than he. All the others—the Hunts, Richardson, John La Farge, Stanford White—were exuberant; only Saint-Gaudens could never discuss or dilate on an emotion, or suggest artistic arguments for giving to his work the forms that he felt. He never laid down the law, or affected the despot, or became brutalized like Whistler by the brutalities of his world. He required no incense; he was an egoist; his simplicity of thought was excessive; he could not imitate, or give any form but his own to the creations of his hand. No one felt more strongly than he the strength of other men, but the idea that they could affect him never stirred an image in his mind.

This summer his health was poor and his spirits were low. For such a temper, Adams was not the best companion, since his own gaiety was not *folle;* but he risked going now and then to the studio on Mont Parnasse to draw him out for a stroll in the Bois de Boulogne, or dinner as pleased his moods, and in return Saint-Gaudens sometimes let Adams go about in his company.

Once Saint-Gaudens took him down to Amiens, with a party of Frenchmen, to see the cathedral. Not until they found themselves actually studying the sculpture of the western portal, did it dawn on Adams's mind that, for his purposes, Saint-Gaudens on that spot had more interest to him than the cathedral itself. Great men before great monuments express great truths, provided they are not taken too solemnly. Adams never tired of quoting the supreme phrase of his idol Gibbon, before the Gothic cathedrals: "I darted a contemptuous look on the stately monuments of superstition." Even in the footnotes of his history, Gibbon had never inserted a bit of humor more human than this, and one would have paid largely for a photograph of the fat little historian, on the background of Notre Dame of Amiens, trying to persuade his readers —perhaps himself—that he was darting a contemptuous look on the stately monument, for which he felt in fact the respect which every man of his vast study and active mind always feels before objects worthy of it; but besides the humor, one felt also the relation. Gibbon ignored the Virgin, because in 1789 religious monuments were out of fashion. In 1900 his remark sounded fresh and simple as the green fields to ears that had heard a hundred years of other remarks, mostly no more fresh and certainly less simple. Without malice, one might find it more instructive than a whole lecture of Ruskin. One sees what one brings, and at that moment

Gibbon brought the French Revolution. Ruskin brought reaction against the Revolution. Saint-Gaudens had passed beyond all. He liked the stately monuments much more than he liked Gibbon or Ruskin; he loved their dignity; their unity; their scale; their lines; their lights and shadows; their decorative sculpture; but he was even less conscious than they of the force that created it all—the Virgin, the Woman—by whose genius "the stately monuments of superstition" were built, through which she was expressed. He would have seen more meaning in Isis with the cow's horns, at Edfoo, who expressed the same thought. The art remained, but the energy was lost even upon the artist.

Yet in mind and person Saint-Gaudens was a survival of the 1500's; he bore the stamp of the Renaissance, and should have carried an image of the Virgin round his neck, or stuck in his hat, like Louis XI. In mere time he was a lost soul that had strayed by chance into the twentieth century, and forgotten where it came from. He writhed and cursed at his ignorance, much as Adams did at his own, but in the opposite sense. Saint-Gaudens was a child of Benvenuto Cellini, smothered in an American cradle. Adams was a quintessence of Boston, devoured by curiosity to think like Benvenuto. Saint-Gaudens's art was starved from birth, and Adams's instinct was blighted from babyhood. Each had but half of a nature, and when they came together before the Virgin of Amiens they ought both to have felt in her the force that made them one; but it was not so. To Adams she became more than ever a channel of force; to Saint-Gaudens she remained as before a channel of taste.

For a symbol of power, Saint-Gaudens instinctively preferred the horse, as was plain in his horse and Victory of the Sherman monument. Doubtless Sherman also felt it so. The attitude was so American that, for at least forty years, Adams had never realized that any other could be in sound taste. How many years had he taken to admit a notion of what Michaelangelo and Rubens were driving at? He could not say; but he knew that only since 1895 had he begun to feel the Virgin or Venus as force, and not everywhere even so. At Chartres—perhaps at Lourdes—possibly at Cnidos if one could still find there the divinely naked Aphrodite of Praxiteles—but otherwise one must look for force to the goddesses of Indian mythology. The idea died out long ago in the German and English stock. Saint-Gaudens at Amiens was hardly less sensitive to the force of the female energy than Matthew Arnold at the Grande Chartreuse. Neither of them felt goddesses as power—only as reflected emotion, human expression, beauty, purity, taste, scarcely even as sympathy. They felt a railway train as power; yet they, and all other artists, constantly complained that the power embodied in a railway train could never be embodied in art. All the steam in the world could not, like the Virgin, build Chartres.

Yet in mechanics, whatever the mechanicians might think, both energies acted as interchangeable forces on man, and by action on man all known force may be measured. Indeed, few men of science measured force in any other way. After once admitting that a straight line was the shortest distance between two points, no serious mathematician cared to deny anything that suited his convenience, and rejected no symbol, unproved or unproveable, that helped him to accomplish work. The symbol was force, as a compass-needle or a triangle was force, as the mechanist might prove by losing it, and nothing could be gained by ignoring their value. Symbol or energy, the Virgin had acted as the greatest force the Western world ever felt, and had drawn man's activities to herself more strongly than any other power, natural or supernatural, had ever done; the historian's business was to follow the track of the energy; to find where it came from and where it went to; its complex source and shifting channels; its values, equivalents, conversions. It could scarcely be more complex than radium; it could hardly be deflected, diverted, polarized, absorbed more perplexingly than other radiant matter. Adams knew nothing about any of them, but as a mathematical problem of influence on human progress, though all were occult, all reacted on his mind, and he rather inclined to think the Virgin easiest to handle.

The pursuit turned out to be long and tortuous, leading at last into the vast forests of scholastic science. From Zeno to Descartes, hand in hand with Thomas Aquinas, Montaigne, and Pascal, one stumbled as stupidly as though one were still a German student of 1860. Only with the instinct of despair could one force one's self into this old thicket of ignorance after having been repulsed at a score of entrances more promising and more popular. Thus far, no path had led anywhere, unless perhaps to an exceedingly modest living. Forty-five years of study had proved to be quite futile for the pursuit of power; one controlled no more force in 1900 than in 1850, although the amount of force controlled by society had enormously increased. The secret of education still hid itself somewhere behind ignorance, and one fumbled over it as feebly as ever. In such labyrinths, the staff is a force almost more necessary than the legs; the pen becomes a sort of blindman's dog, to keep him from falling into the gutters. The pen works for itself, and acts like a hand, modelling the plastic material over and over again to the form that suits it best. The form is never arbitrary, but is a sort of growth like crystallization, as any artist knows too well; for often the pencil or pen runs into side-paths and shapelessness, loses its relations, stops or is bogged. Then it has to return on its trail, and recover, if it can, its line of force. The result of a year's work depends more on what is struck out than on what is left in; on the sequence of the main lines of thought, than on their play or variety. Compelled once more to lean heavily on this support, Adams covered more thousands of pages with figures as formal as though they were algebra, laboriously striking out, altering, burning, experimenting, until the year had expired, the Exposition had long been closed, and winter drawing to its end, before he sailed from Cherbourg, on January 19, 1901, for home.

1906

PRAYER TO THE VIRGIN OF CHARTRES *

Gracious Lady:—

Simple as when I asked your aid
    before;
Humble as when I prayed for grace
    in vain
Seven hundred years ago; weak,
    weary, sore
In heart and hope, I ask your help
    again.

* The selection from *Letters to a Niece*, by Mabel La Farge, is used by permission of the publishers, Houghton Mifflin Company.

You, who remembered all, remember
    me;
An English scholar of a Norman
    name,
I was a thousand who then crossed
    the sea
To wrangle in the Paris schools for
    fame.

When your Byzantine portal was still
    young
I prayed here with my master
    Abailard;
When *Ave Maris Stella* was first
    sung,
I helped to sing it here with Saint
    Bernard.

When Blanche set up your gorgeous
    Rose of France
I stood among the servants of the
    Queen;
And when Saint Louis made his penitence,
I followed barefoot where the King
    had been.

For centuries I brought you all my
    cares,
And vexed you with the murmur of a
    child;
You heard the tedious burden of my
    prayers;
You could not grant them, but at least
    you smiled.

If then I left you, it was not my crime,
Or if a crime, it was not mine alone.
All children wander with the truant
    Time.
Pardon me too! You pardoned once
    your Son!

For He said to you:—"Wist ye not
    that I
Must be about my Father's business?"
    So,
Seeking his Father he pursued his
    way
Straight to the Cross towards which
    we all must go.

So I too wandered off among the host
That racked the earth to find the
    Father's clue.
I did not find the Father, but I lost
What now I value more, the Mother,
    —You!

I thought the fault was yours that
    foiled my search;
I turned and broke your image on its
    throne,
Cast down my idol, and resumed my
    march
To claim the Father's empire for my
    own.

Crossing the hostile sea, our greedy
    band
Saw rising hills and forests in the
    blue;
Our Father's kingdom in the promised
    land!
—We seized it, and dethroned the
    Father too.

And now we are the Father, with our
    brood,
Ruling the Infinite, not Three but
    One;
We made our world and saw that it
    was good;
Ourselves we worship, and we have
    no Son.

Yet we have Gods, for even our
    strong nerve
Falters before the Energy we own.
Which shall be master? Which of us
    shall serve?
Which wears the fetters? Which shall
    bear the crown?

Brave though we be, we dread to face
    the Sphinx,
Or answer the old riddle she still asks.
Strong as we are, our reckless cour-
    age shrinks
To look beyond the piece-work of our
    tasks.

But when we must, we pray, as in the
    past

Before the Cross on which your Son
    was nailed.
Listen, dear lady! You shall hear the
    last
Of the strange prayers Humanity has
    wailed:

PRAYER TO THE DYNAMO

Mysterious Power! Gentle Friend!
Despotic Master! Tireless Force!
You and We are near the End.
Either You or We must bend
To bear the martyrs' Cross.

We know ourselves, what we can bear
As men; our strength and weakness
    too;
Down to the fraction of a hair;
And know that we, with all our care
And knowledge, know not you.

You come in silence, Primal Force,
We know not whence, or when, or
    why;
You stay a moment in your course
To play; and lo! you leap across
To Alpha Centauri!

We know not whether you are kind,
Or cruel in your fiercer mood;
But be you Matter, be you Mind,
We think we know that you are
    blind,
And we alone are good.

We know that prayer is thrown away,
For you are only force and light;
A shifting current; night and day;
We know this well, and yet we pray,
For prayer is infinite,

Like you! Within the finite sphere
That bounds the impotence of
    thought,
We search an outlet everywhere
But only find that we are here
And that you are—are not!

What are we then? the lords of space?
The master-mind whose tasks you do?
Jockey who rides you in the race?
Or are we atoms whirled apace,
Shaped and controlled by you?

Still silence! Still no end in sight!
No sound in answer to our cry!
Then, by the God we now hold tight,
Though we destroy soul, life and
    light,
Answer you shall—or die!

We are no beggars! What care we
For hopes or terrors, love or hate?
What for the universe? We see
Only our certain destiny
And the last word of Fate.

Seize, then, the Atom! rack his joints!
Tear out of him his secret spring!
Grind him to nothing!—though he
    points
To us, and his life-blood anoints
Me—the dead Atom-King!

———————

A curious prayer, dear lady! is it not?
Strangely unlike the prayers I prayed
    to you!
Stranger because you find me at this
    spot,
Here, at your feet, asking your help
    anew.

Strangest of all, that I have ceased to
    strive,
Ceased even care what new coin fate
    shall strike.
In truth it does not matter. Fate will
    give
Some answer; and all answers are
    alike.

So, while we slowly rack and torture
    death
And wait for what the final void will
    show,
Waiting I feel the energy of faith
Not in the future science, but in you!

The man who solves the Infinite, and
    needs
The force of solar systems for his play,
Will not need me, nor greatly care
    what deeds
Made me illustrious in the dawn of
    day.

He will send me, dethroned, to claim
    my rights,
Fossil survival of an age of stone,
Among the cave-men and the trog-
    lodytes
Who carved the mammoth on the
    mammoth's bone.

He will forget my thought, my acts,
    my fame,
As we forget the shadows of the dusk,
Or catalogue the echo of a name
As we the scratches on the mammoth's
    tusk.

But when, like me, he too has trod
    the track
Which leads him up to power above
    control,
He too will have no choice but wan-
    der back
And sink in helpless hopelessness of
    soul,

Before your majesty of grace and
    love,
The purity, the beauty and the faith;
The depth of tenderness beneath;
    above,
The glory of the life and of the death.

When your Byzantine portal still was
    young,
I came here with my master Abailard;
When *Ave Maris Stella* was first
    sung,
I joined to sing it here with Saint
    Bernard.

When Blanche set up your glorious
    Rose of France,
In scholar's robes I waited on the
    Queen;
When good Saint Louis did his peni-
    tence,
My prayer was deep like his: my faith
    as keen.

What loftier prize seven hundred
    years shall bring,
What deadlier struggles for a larger
    air,

What immortality our strength shall
    wring
From Time and Space, we may—or
    may not—care;

But years, or ages, or eternity,
Will find me still in thought before
    your throne,
Pondering the mystery of Mater-
    nity,
Soul within Soul,—Mother and Child
    in One!

Help me to see! not with my mimic
    sight—
With yours! which carried radiance,
    like the sun,
Giving the rays you saw with—light
    in light—
Tying all suns and stars and worlds in
    one.

Help me to know! not with my mock-
    ing art—
With you, you knew yourself un-
    bound by laws;
Gave God your strength, your life,
    your sight, your heart,
And took from him the Thought that
    Is—the Cause.

Help me to feel! not with my insect
    sense,—
With yours that felt all life alive in
    you;
Infinite heart beating at your ex-
    pense;
Infinite passion breathing the breath
    you drew!

Help me to bear! not my own baby
    load,
But yours; who bore the failure of the
    light,
The strength, the knowledge and the
    thought of God,—
The futile folly of the Infinite!

    1920

WILLIAM CRARY BROWNELL
(1851–1928)

TASTE *

A heterogeneous public at one
chiefly in its passion for novelty may
easily have the vitality it vaunts, but
there is one quality which ineluctably
it must forego: namely, taste. I hasten
to acknowledge that it reconciles itself with readiness to this deprivation
and depreciates taste with the sincerity inseparable from the instinct for
self-preservation. Certainly there are
ideals of more importance, and if the
sacrifice of taste were needed for their
success it would be possible to deplore
its loss too deeply. We may be sure,
however, that the alternative is fundamentally fanciful. The remark once
made of an American dilettante of distinction that he had convictions in
matters of taste, and taste in matters
of conviction, implies, it is true, an
exceptional rather than a normal attitude. But although it is quite needless
to confound the two categories, it is
still quite possible to extend considerably the conventional confines of taste
without serious encroachment on the
domain of convictions. Nothing is in
better taste than piety, for example.
And since also nothing is more fundamental, any one in search of an explanation of our present wide-spread
antipathy to taste as outworn and un-
vital might do worse than scrutinize
the various psychological changes that
have accompanied the much-talked-of
decline of, at least formal, religion
and the transformation, at any rate,
of the spirit of conformity to carefully and not capriciously constructed
credos.

Taste indeed is essentially a matter
of tradition. No one originates his

* From *Standards* by W. C. Brownell.
Used by permission of Charles Scribner's
Sons. Copyright 1917.

own. Of the many instances in which mankind is wiser than any man it is one of the chief. It implies conformity to standards already crystallized from formulæ already worked out. In the famous preface of his *Cromwell* Victor Hugo asserted, to be sure, that an admirable work might be composed of all that the arid breath of *gens de goût* from Scudéry to La Harpe had dried up in its germ. But he referred to the pedantries of professional classic criticism rather than to the fastidiousness of a sensitive public. The preface long ago became itself the classic statement of the case for romanticism and established standards of its own. All that it contains is no doubt useful to remember, though it is rather sentimental than profitable speculation to dwell on the mute and inglorious of country churchyards, and one may excusably take a more cheerful view of the consequences resulting from the interposition of the *chevaux de frise* of pure conventions, even, between the otherwise unprotected public and the crowd of candidates for its favor.

Of Hugo himself Renan, a better judge in this particular, observed that "he had not time to possess taste." He offered compensations for the deficiency, it must be acknowledged, but to the very considerable number of writers who can hardly hope to equal him in this respect the cultivation of taste may none the less be commended. They can more easily afford the required time. Renan even, compact of taste as he was, lost touch with it occasionally—in the *Abbesse de Jouarre,* for instance, and perhaps also in meriting Doudan's remark: "I know of no theologian with a more intimate knowledge of Oriental flora." And taste has the great advantage of being cultivable. There is nothing recondite about it. It is a quality particularly proper to the public as distinct from the artist. Indeed its possession by the public provides the artist with precisely the constraint he most needs and is most apt to forget —especially in the day of so-called "free art." It cannot be acquired of course without co-operation; and it involves the effort needed to acquire and is not fostered by the emotion that is an end in itself. At the present time, accordingly, its pursuit is attended with the discomfort inherent in the invidious. It is particularly ironical to pass one's life, as doubtless is still done now and then, in regretting that one knows so little and at the same time arouse disgust for knowing so much. The remnant, if extended, will have to be of martyr stuff but it need fear no compunctions if it is tempted into occasional reprisal, consoled by Rivarol's reflection: "No one thinks of how much pain any man of taste has had to suffer before he gives any."

Our own public has always been a little exceptionally sensitive about the limitations of taste, even in days when it more generally possessed it. But currently we merely exaggerate a neglect of it that is wide-spread. One thinks, of course, of France. It is not to be denied that in France the democratic spirit with its associated anarchy has invaded the composure of the taste which, in the æsthetic field, more than any other element constitutes French superiority. Our own extravagances and incoherences in this definite field are apt to be reflections of similar French phenomena. Paris, itself, still the finest civic spectacle ever secured by the co-operation of natural growth and express design, shows in spots and details an attenuation of decorum and conformity—shows the corrosion of the spirit of "free art." In France, however, æsthetic standards are unlikely to be permanently deposed by fanaticism or forgotten by obtuseness. They are constantly recalled to the sense by the models that embody them, and constantly recur to the reflection of minds insensibly more or less molded by the tradition they define. Moreover the principles that underlie them are constantly re-uttered by voices less noisy than penetrating but thoroughly national in sounding the overtones of culture however "advanced" the air, and in exhibiting an aristocratic quality even in chanting the most popular pæan. There is, besides, running through the currents and eddies of the moment, which boil rather than flow, a clear stream of temperamentally conservative criticism, that clarifies and purifies and carries along to the ocean of general appreciation the sweetness without the sediment of the troubled waters through which it passes, while at the same time it tranquilly transports its own freight of principles and standards.

In other words, in France the current era has its *esprits délicats* as well as its fanatics. And they are of their era and not merely in it. With us perhaps criticism which accepts standards is less sensitively, less sympathetically, discriminating in its treatment of whatever flouts or forgets them. Mr. Mather, in his indulgence for the *poètes maudits,* for the abnormal, for what he calls "disorderly geniuses" and "unbalanced talents" (see his illuminating chapter on the egregious Greco), is distinctly exceptional. Our conservatives are, in general, quite flat-footed. They resemble rather Professor Conrad Wright who in his *History of French Literature—* exhilaratingly, I think—announces himself a convinced classicist, or even Mr. Cox who in his suggestive and above all timely book has been

thought to confound the classic spirit with the academic. Let him not be disquieted. Mr. Dougherty tells me that Matisse is fundamentally academic. On the other hand flat-footed is a faint epithet with which to characterize our "advanced" critics, who wring all withers when they are making the academic jade wince.

In contrast take M. André Gide. He is particularly open-minded, though he has plenty of temperamental predilections, and is quite in accord with the present revolt against the romantic without being in the least a neo-classicist. His "modernity" in a word is unimpeachable by all save the partisans to whom modernity and *l'esprit délicat* are by hypothesis antithetical. From these however his implicit subscription to standards in his professed exclusive devotion to the principle of taste does definitely distinguish him, and for the purpose of showing this I condense a few felicitous sentences from one of his *conférences:*

"Beauty is secured only by an artificial constraint. Art is always the result of constraint. To believe that the freer it is the higher it rises is to believe that what keeps the kite from mounting is the string. Art aspires to freedom only in morbid periods. It loves to burst its bonds. Therefore it chooses close ones. . . . The great artist is he to whom the obstacle serves as a spring-board."

And referring to the "art for art" art of the day he speaks of it as "insolently isolating itself" and "fatuously despising what it is too ignorant to evaluate"; of the artist as one who without external control is fatally driven to "seek only his own approbation"; and of the critic, his congener, as "judging works in the name of his personal taste and the greater or less pleasure they give him," which he manifestly considers a severe indict-ment. But irresponsibility is an old story in criticism. Its invasion of the far wider field of art in general is otherwise significant. It is no more needful than possible or even desir-able that every one should be a com-petent critic of art and letters. As well ask that every reader should be a writer or every writer a writer of criticism. But it *is* desirable that every one who counts at all, every reader of real books and every one interested in plastic art should have standards of taste and possess them so thoroughly as to apply them instinctively and rigorously. Otherwise there is no logi-cal escape from the prospect that the wider the appetite for books and art becomes the more superficial will be its appreciation and the more worth-less will be the production that ap-peals to it directly and intimately re-flects its easy and ordinary reactions.

It is a mistake to suppose that self-expression without self-control and enjoyment without standards of value are consonant with the effort that is a prerequisite to real achievement in either accomplishment or apprecia-tion. Undisciplined self-expression riots in the absence of general taste, and the less exaction the writer experi-ences in the reader, the less effort he expends in rewarding or even secur-ing his attention. The less demanded by the beholder of the picture, the statue, the building, the quicker the artist's sag into inertia. Ineptitude may easily be quite as genuine as signifi-cance, and if genuineness is the only demand public taste makes of the artist, if he is required to meet no standards or—what at this stage of the world's progress is the same thing—to neglect all models, the quality of his supply is bound to deteriorate in ac-cordance with as fatal a law as that which makes water run down-hill.

What most opposes, however, the advancement of this salutary element of exacting taste in our public is the vigor of the spirit of non-conformity, which by definition has no standards, and which is no longer the affair of temperament it used to be but is a conscious ideal. As such of course, in an emotional era, pursued with pas-sion, it is also pursued into details of higher differentiation—manners, tastes, preferences, fastidious predilec-tions. To the new theology, the new sincerity, the new poetry and paint-ing, the new everything in fact will be added the new refinement, the new decorum. Meantime our non-conformists are concentrated upon vilipending the old. This is a field in which the new egotism may assert itself with the minimum of effort in-volved in mere talk—talk that asserts an independence of conventions marked by positive fanaticism. Gib-bon notes with his accustomed per-spicacity the affinity of independence for fanaticism, in remarking the hos-tility of fanaticism to superstition—the bugbear of the present time. "The independent spirit of fanaticism," he says in his chapter on Mahomet, "looks down with contempt on the ministers and slaves of superstition," and the remark explains the current Islamic invasion of the reticences of life. Given her undeniable fanatical independence, for example, it is easy to see why the contemporary young girl of the thoughtful variety is so shocked by the constitution of society as it is, as to vary her impassioned sympathy for the street-walker by grinding her teeth at the thought of the Sunday-school. But is it not a rather literal logic that leads her to involve the purely decorative elements with the structure of the civilization that has produced her? Why, for in-stance, should she be "thrilled" by reading, why should she herself write, that not inconsiderable part of the detail of the latest fiction that is else too colorless to have any other motive than the purely protestant one of heartening the robust by revolting the refined? The motive is as obvious in trivial as in grave examples, since both may be equally gross so far as taste is concerned. Observe this picture in a recent clever novel—by a lady—that has evoked a very general chorus of cordial appreciation. Two young men, one an Oxonian, occupy conjointly a room in a foreign seaside hotel:

" 'I got out of bed,' said Hewet vaguely, 'merely to talk, I suppose.'

" 'Meanwhile I shall undress,' said Hirst. When naked of all but his shirt and bent over the basin, Mr. Hirst no longer impressed one with the majesty of his intellect, but with the pathos of his young yet ugly body.

" 'Women interest me,' said Hewet.

" 'They're so stupid,' said Hirst. 'You're sitting on my pyjamas.'

" 'I suppose they *are* stupid,' Hewet wondered.

" 'There can't be two opinions about that,' said Hirst, hopping briskly across the room, 'unless you're in love—that fat woman Warrington?' he inquired.

" 'Not one fat woman—all fat women,' Hewet sighed.

" 'The women I saw to-night were not fat,' said Hirst, who was taking advantage of Hewet's company to cut his toe-nails."

A moment later:

" 'I wonder if this is what they call an ingrowing toe-nail?' said Hirst, examining the big toe on his left foot."

Another brief interval.

"Hewet contemplated the angular young man who was neatly brushing the rims of his toe-nails into the fire-place in silence for a moment.

" 'I respect you, Hirst,' he remarked."

Is there anything in *Tom Jones* that strikes quite that note? The picture is manifestly less a gem of genre than a defiance of decorum, and as such perhaps "stimulates" those who would find a dialogue between Achilles and Patroclus insipid. The writer and the sympathetic reader occupy an attitude which for them, of course, illustrates the new sincerity but for others constitutes the spectacle of a pose, preoccupied with producing an effect while unconscious of what it exemplifies. Obviously its sincerity, though flaunted, is not fundamentally newer than the fall of man, and is but a variant of the desire to, as the French say, *épater le bourgeois*. The new sincerity presents more drastic though not, I think, more disintegrating phenomena. But one must draw the line somewhere and it is decorous to draw it on the hither side of the purlieus of pornography, whiffs of whose un-Arabian breezes no one can have escaped and whither accordingly in any consideration of twentieth-century fiction it would, though easy, be profitless, because superfluous, to proceed. Here at least one may pay the tribute of a wistful regret to those days, distant in all respects but that of time, in which it could be said even of the dilettante who had only taste in matters of conviction that he had in any case convictions in matters of taste.

Dress affords a more agreeable field of reflection and has the advantage for our purpose of illustrating the same phenomenon of impatience with standards of decorum. Here we can see how superficial it is to denounce the insufficiency of old standards for the new duties taught by new occasions, and perceive how much more consistent it is to demand the abolition of standards altogether. In a word, how fashions differ from standards, and how exacting is the tyranny which replaces the slavery of convention with the despotism of whim. The aspect of "this changing world" presented by its habiliments is indeed such as to arouse "unprecedented emotion." Already, to be sure, there are signs of even more change, but since it is manifestly to be progressive instead of purely haphazard we know whither we are drifting and that the need for purely emotional appreciation will remain stable. The current affinity of the bottom of the skirt for that of the *décolletage* is destined no doubt to a richer realization, owing to what we are now calling an "intensive" conviction of the truth that "the body is more than raiment." And as we are to be, above all things, natural and as, except for artists, the female form is the loveliest thing in nature, we not only have the prospect of still further emotional felicity in the immediate future, but may look forward with gentle altruism of resignation to the increase of mankind's stock of happiness in a remoter hereafter—in the spirit of the French seer, who, on the eve of the Revolution, exclaimed: *"Les jeunes gens sont bien heureux; ils verront de belles choses."* We know how Madame Tallien justifies him.

Undress, too, as well as dress, holds out an alluring prospect, at least in fiction, in which the imagination is already very considerably "stimulated" by what the eye is condemned to forego in fact. No community has, of course, as yet adopted the Virgilian motto half-heartedly suggested by Hawthorne for Brook Farm: *Nudus ara, sere nudus,* but fiction may be said to front that way. Mr. Galsworthy is only the most distinguished of those who enable their readers to emulate Actæon at their ease, and we are constantly assisting at the bath of beauty in company with lady novelists to whom the experience must naturally seem less sensational, but who are especially sensitive to the desirability of being "in the swim," if not reckless of becoming what Shelley calls "naked to laughter" in the process.

Nor will our successors be confined to the delights of the eye. The world of sensation is acquiring among us, in various ways, a new extension, as our fiction, again, amply shows. The particular sense of smell, for example, is being rescued from neglect and receiving a recognition long withheld by puritan fastidiousness. Its inspiration proceeds less from Keats's example or Max Beerbohm's advocacy, perhaps, than from Maupassant, whom our later fictionists wisely study, I believe, without always studying wisely, and of whom Henry James remarks that "human life in his pages appears for the most part as a concert of odors," owing to a sense of smell "as acute as that of those animals of the field and forests whose subsistence and security depend upon it." The heroine of an essentially charming recent novel has "a moment" that "was forever connected in her mind with the smell of delicate food and fading flowers and human beings well washed and groomed which floated out to her from the dining-room." Every one knows the persistent associations of odors, and the house-party was a large one. Besides people wash much more than they used to and their aura deserves more attention. However the negligent are not neglected. The young lady, whose father is a socialist, has already had an experience of a different sort—the odor of a showy hotel court in which "everything in sight exhaled an intense consciousness of high cost . . . suggesting to a sensitive nose another smell, obscured but rancidly perceptible—the unwashed smell floating up from the paupers' cellars which support Aladdin's palaces of luxury." Taste may surely be too rigid and in any case its limits include those temperamental preferences which, like colors, are proverbially exempt from disputation. No doubt there is more gain than loss in enlisting a new sense in the service of literature. But it would be fatuity to expect it to conserve its freshness long. Odors evaporate. This kind of spontaneity is especially in danger of prompt conventionalization—like any new perfume—its *raison d'être* being too obscure to be kept vividly in mind and the sensuous satisfaction it affords tending rapidly to lose its edge in becoming staple. And there would be much more prospect of its serving the ends of taste in general if what is staple were also standard.

1917

PAUL ELMER MORE
(1864–1937)

THE NEW MORALITY *

Some ten or twelve years ago a certain young woman, then fresh from the hands of an esteemed but erratic professor of English literature, wrote a novel the plot of which was roughly as follows. A college graduate suddenly finds himself the inheritor of a shoe factory in a New England town. Filled with the benevolent ideas absorbed in the academic contemplation of economics, he undertakes to introduce profit-sharing with his employees

* The selection from *Aristocracy and Justice* by Paul Elmer More is used by permission of the publishers Houghton Mifflin Company.

and otherwise to conduct his business for the benefit of the community. So far, good. But hard times follow, and his competitors by lowering wages and reducing labor are able to undersell him. Now there is in his control a considerable sum of money which a widow had entrusted to his father to invest for her, and the question arises whether he shall shut down his mills and inflict suffering upon his men, or shall divert this trust fund to his business and so try to tide over the period of stress. He yields to his sympathies and virtually embezzles the trust fund; but fails nevertheless, and with his own loss brings ruin upon the widow. The story was called *The Burden of Christopher,* with the implication that the hero was a bearer of Christ in his misfortune, and the author indicates pretty clearly her sentiment that in surrendering his personal integrity for the expected good of his working people he was following the higher of two conflicting codes of ethics.

The book no doubt has gone its own way to the "limbo large and broad," where the heroes of ancient fiction wander with

Embryos and idiots, ermites and friars;

but it made a lasting impression on one reader at least as the first popular presentation to come under his notice of a theory which now confronts him wherever he turns his eyes. There has, in fact, been an astonishing divulgation in the past decade of what is called, with magnificent audacity, the New Morality.

Perhaps the most honored teacher of this code is the mistress of Hull House, who by her devoted life and her services to the people of Chicago in various times of need has won the right to speak with a certain authority for the striving generation of the day.

And in one of her books, the *Newer Ideals of Peace*, Miss Addams tells of an actual occurrence and infers a moral which points in the same direction as the novel of *Christopher*. A family of five children is left motherless. The father, a drunkard, disappears, and the household is left to the care of a feeble old grandmother. Thereupon work is found for the oldest boy, "a fine, manly little fellow" of twelve, who feels keenly "his obligation to care for the family." But after a time he becomes "listless and indifferent," and at sixteen turns to professional tramping. "It was through such bitter lessons as these," observes Miss Addams, "we learned that good intentions and the charitable impulse do not always work for righteousness." As the story is told there is a plain implication that to find work for a boy under such circumstances is "cruel and disastrous" (her own comment), and that society, and not his own nature, was responsible for his relapse. One would suppose that scarcely an honest workman, or prosperous merchant, or successful professional man had ever taken up the burden of a family in youth or childhood. Doubtless hardships and waste often come from the exigencies of life, but there is not a single word in Miss Addams's account to indicate that she has felt the need of developing in the future citizen a sensitiveness to the peculiar duties that will confront him, or has reflected on the evil that might have been done the boy if he had been relieved of his natural obligations and supported by society. "Our democracy," as she says with approval, "is making inroads upon the family, the oldest of human institutions."

This is not an isolated case in Miss Addams's works, nor does it in any wise misrepresent her. In another book, *The Spirit of Youth and the City Streets*, the thesis is maintained and reiterated, that crime is for the most part merely the result of repressing a wholesome "love for excitement" and "desire for adventure." In the year 1909 "there were arrested and brought into court [in Chicago] fifteen thousand young people under the age of twenty, who had failed to keep even the common law of the land. Most of these young people had broken the law in their blundering efforts to find adventure." The inference to be drawn here and throughout the book is that one need only relieve the youth of the land from the necessity of "assuming responsibility prematurely," affording them meanwhile abundant amusement, and the instincts of lawlessness and the pursuit of criminal pleasure will vanish, or almost vanish, of themselves—as if there were no Harry Thaws and the sons of the rich were all virtuous.

But it must not be supposed that Hull House occupies a place of lonely isolation as the fountain of these ideas. From every self-authorized center of civic virtue in which a typewriter is at work, the stream proceeds. The very presses groan, as we used to say when those machines were still in the mythological stage, at their labor of supplying the world with the new intellectual pabulum. At this moment there lies before the writer of this essay a pile of books, all recently published, which are devoted more or less specifically to the subject, and from all of which, if he had courage to go through them, he might cull abundant examples and quotations. He was, indeed, about to enter this "hollow cave, amid the thickest woods," when, an unvaliant knight, he heard the warning of the lady Una:

Yea but (quoth she) the perill of this
    pla..e
I better wot then you, though now too
    late
To wish you backe returne with foule
    disgrace,
Yet wisedome warnes, whilest foot is in
    the gate,
To stay the steppe, ere forcèd to retrate.

We have in fact to deal with the consummation of a long and deep-seated
revolution, and there is no better way
to understand the true character of
the movement than by turning aside
a moment to glance at its historical
sources. This attempt to find some
basis of conduct to take the place of
the older conception of personal integrity, as we see it exemplified in the
works of Miss Jane Addams and a
host of other modern writers, is in
fact only one aspect of the slow drift
from medieval religion to humanitarianism. For a thousand years and
well into the second thousand the
ethical feeling of Christian Europe
may be said to have taken its color
from the saying, "What shall it profit
a man, if he shall gain the whole
world, and lose his own soul?"—
which in extreme cases was interpreted as if it read, If he *reform* the
whole world; and on the other, kindred saying, "Sell all that thou hast
and distribute unto the poor, and thou
shall have treasure in heaven, and
come, follow me"—in which the command of charity was held to be not
so much for the benefit of the poor
as for the liberation of the giver's own
soul from the powers of this world.
Such was the law, and its binding
force was confirmed by the conception
of a final day of wrath when the souls
of men should stand before a merciless
tribunal and be judged to everlasting
joy or everlasting torment. The vivid
reality of the fear that haunted men,
at least in their moments of reflection,

may be understood from the horrors
of such a picture as Michael Angelo's
Last Judgment, or from the meditations of one of the most genial of
English cavaliers. In his little treatise
on *Man in Darkness*—appropriate title
—Henry Vaughan puts the frank question to himself:

And what madness then is it, for the
enjoying of one minute's pleasure for the
satisfaction of our sensual corrupt appetite, to lie forever in a bed of burning
brass, in the lake of eternal and un-
quenchable fire? "Suppose," saith the
same writer [Drexelius], "that this whole
globe of earth were nothing else but a
huge mass or mountain of sand, and that
a little wren came but once in every
thousand years to fetch away but one
grain of that huge heap; what an innumerable number of years would be
spent before that world of sand could be
so fetched away! And yet, alas! when
the damned have lain in that fiery lake
so many years as all those would amount
to, they are no nearer coming out than
the first hour they entered in."

No doubt practice and precept were
at variance then, as to a certain extent they are at all times, and there
were many texts in the Bible which
might be taken to mitigate the harsher
commands; but such in its purest,
highest form was the law, and in the
more sensitive minds this conception
of the soul naked before a judging
God must have created a tremendous
anxiety. Morality was obedience and
integrity; it scorned the world for an
ideal of inner righteousness; it created a sense of individual responsibility for every word and deed; and, say
what we will, there is something
magnificent in this contempt for the
reckoning of other men beside that
eternal fame which

. . . lives and speaks aloft by those pure
    eyes,
And perfect witness of all-judging Jove.

But there was also in this law something repellent and even monstrous. Who has not shuddered with amazement at the inscription which Dante set over the portal of Hell: E 'L PRIMO AMORE? Was it Love that prepared those winding coils of torture to enclose for endless time the vast majority of mankind? Was it even justice to make the everlasting doom of a soul depend on its grasp of truth in these few years spent in a world of shadows and illusions? There is something repulsively irrational in the notion of an unchanging eternity suspended on the action in a moment of time—*ex hoc momento pendet æternitas*. It should seem to be unthinkable, if it had not actually been thought. As a matter of fact the rigor and crudity of this doctrine had been mitigated in the Middle Ages by the interposition between man and God of the very human institution of the Church, with its substitution of temporal penances and pardons and an interposed Purgatory in place of the terrible paradox of irrevocable judgment. It remained for the Reformation, and particularly for the Calvinistic Puritans, to tear away those veils of compromise and bring man face to face with the awful abstraction he had created. The result was for a while a great hardening and strengthening of character, salutary indeed after what may be called the almost hypocritical compromise of Catholicism; but in the end human nature could not endure the rigidity of its own logic, and in revolting turned not to another compromise but to questioning the very hypothesis of its faith.

The inevitable reaction from the intolerable logic of the Protestants was Deism, in which God was stripped altogether of his judicial and moral attributes and reduced to a kind of immanent, all-benevolent force in nature. "But now comes a modern Sage," says Warburton of Bolingbroke, ". . . who tells us 'that they made the Basis of Religion far too wide; that men have no further concern with GOD than TO BELIEVE THAT HE IS, which his *physical attributes* make fully manifest; but, that he is *a rewarder of them who diligently seek him,* Religion doth not require us to believe, since this depends on God's MORAL ATTRIBUTES, of which we have no conception.' " But the deistic position was manifestly untenable, for it left no place for the undeniable existence of evil in this world and life. From the unaccountable distribution of wrong and suffering the divine had argued the certainty of adjustment in a future state; the deist had flown in the face of facts by retaining the belief in a benevolent Providence while taking from it the power of supernatural retribution; the atheist was more logical, he denied the existence of Providence altogether and turned the universe over to chance or blind law. Such was the progress of thought from Baxter to Bolingbroke and from Bolingbroke to Hume.

The positive consequences of this evolution are written large in the literature of the eighteenth century. With the idea of an avenging deity and a supernatural test there disappeared also the sense of deep personal responsibility; the very notion of a radical and fundamental difference between good and evil was lost. The evil that is apparent in character comes to be regarded merely as the result of the restraining and thwarting institutions of society as these exist—why, no one can explain. Envy and jealousy and greed and the sheer lust of power, all those traits which were summed up in the single Greek word *pleonexiá, the desire to have more,* are not inherent in the human heart, but are artificially introduced by property and a false civilization. Change these institutions or release the individual entirely from restrictions, and his nature will recoil spontaneously to its natural state of virtue. He needs only follow the impulse of his instinctive emotions to be sound and good. And as a man feels of himself, so he feels of others. There is no real distinction between the good and the evil, but all are naturally good and the superficial variations we see are caused by the greater or less freedom of development. Hence we should condemn no man even as we do not condemn ourselves. There is no place for sharp judgment, and the laws which impose penalties and restrictions and set up false discriminations between the innocent and the criminal are subject to suspicion and should be made as flexible as possible. In place of judgment we are to regard all mankind with sympathy; a sort of emotional solidarity becomes the one great virtue, in which are included, or rather sunk, all the law and the prophets.

It was the great work of the eighteenth century, beginning in England and developing in France, to formulate this change and indoctrinate with it the mind of the unthinking masses. Here is not the place to follow the development in detail, and those who care to see its outcome may be referred to the keen and unjustly neglected chapters on the *philosophes* in La Harpe's *Lycée.* To those, indeed, who are acquainted with the philosophical writings that preceded and introduced the French Revolution, the epithet "new" as it is attached to our present-day morality may seem a bit presumptuous; for it would be difficult to find a single fundamental idea in current literature on this subject which could not be closely paralleled by a quotation from Rousseau, or Diderot, or Helvétius, or one of their compeers. Thus, in our exaltation of sympathy above judgment and of the unrestrained emotions generally as the final rule of character, we are but following Diderot's philosophy of the heart: *"Les passions amorties dégradent les hommes extraordinaires";* and when we read in Ellen Key and a host of other feminist liberators the apotheosis of love as higher than any divine or human obligations, we are but meeting again with Toussaint's religion a little disguised: *"On aime de même Dieu et sa maîtresse."* Our revolt from constitutional law as a power imposed by the slower reflection of men upon their own immediate desires and opinions is essentially the same as the restlessness consecrated by the French *économistes* in the phrase, *"le despotisme légal."* And, to return whence we began, the economics of Hull House flow only too easily from Helvétius's definition of virtue as *"le désir du bien public,"* and from his more specific statement: "The integrity which is related to an individual or to a small society is not the true integrity; integrity considered in relation to the public is the only kind that really deserves and generally obtains the name."

Miss Addams herself has been disturbed by these reminiscences. Thus she quotes from one of the older humanitarians a characteristic saying: "The love of those whom a man does not know is quite as elemental a sentiment as the love of those whom a man does know," and repudiates it as vague and unpractical beside the New Morality. She ought to know, and may be right; yet it is not easy to see wherein her own ethics are any less vague when she deplores the act of a boy who goes to work for his starving grandmother because in doing so he is unfitting himself for future service to society. And as for effectiveness, it might seem that the French Revolution was a practical result fairly equivalent in magnitude to what has been achieved by our college settlements. But Miss Addams is by no means peculiar in this assumption of originality. Nothing is more notable in the humanitarian literature of the day than the feeling that our own age is severed from the past and opens an entirely new epoch in history. *"The race has now crossed the great divide of human history!"* exclaims an hysterical doctor of divinity in a book just published. "The tendency of the long past has been toward *diversity,* that of the longer future will be toward *oneness.* The change in this stream of tendency is not a temporary deviation from its age-long course—a new bend in the river. It is an actual reversal of the current, which beyond a peradventure will prove permanent." To this ecstatic watcher the sudden reversal took place at no remote date, but yesterday; and by a thousand other watchers the same miracle is vociferously heralded. Beyond a peradventure! Not a little of this flattering assumption is due to the blind and passionate hope of the human heart clamoring against the voice of experience. So many prophets before now have cried out, looking at the ever-flowing current of time, and having faith in some Thessalian magic:

> *Cessavere vices rerum.*
> *. . . Amnisque cucurrit*
> *non qua pronus erat.*

So often the world has been disappointed; but at last we have seen—beyond a peradventure. If the vicissitudes of fate have not ceased, yet at least we have learned to look with complacency on the very law of mutation from which the eyes of men had hitherto turned away in bewildered horror, at last the stream has turned back upon its sources, and change itself is carrying us no longer toward diversity, but toward the consummation of a divine oneness.

But it would equally be an error to insist too dogmatically on the continuity of the present-day movement with that of the eighteenth century; for one generation is never quite as another. We must not forget that for a hundred years or thereabout there was a partial reaction against the doctrines of the *philosophes,* during which time the terrors of the Revolution lay like a warning nightmare in the imagination of the more thoughtful men. A hundred years is a long period for the memory to bridge, particularly in a time when the historical sense has been weakened. Superficially, too, the application of the theory is in some respects different from what it was; the law of social sympathy has been developed into different conceptions of socialism, and we have devised fresh schemes for giving efficacy to the immediate will of the people. Even deeper is the change that has come over the attitude of religious organizations toward the movement. In the age of the Revolution the Church, both Catholic and Protestant, was still strongly intrenched in the old beliefs and offered a violent resistance to the substitutions of humanitarianism for responsibility to the priest and to God. Now this last barrier has been almost swept away. Indeed, not the least remarkable feature of this literature is the number of clergymen who are contributing to it, with their constant appeal to the New Morality as the test of faith. Open one of these books before us—let us take *The Christian*

Reconstruction of Modern Life, for the promise of its title—and you will be pretty likely to come upon such a passage as this: "Faith's fellowship with Jesus is one with the realization of our fellowship in humanity"; or, on another page: "If the fundamental of the true philosophy cannot be found by common men, what advantage in any man's finding it? If life's secret, direction, and power . . . is not attainable by the lowliest, then a man of this age, living in the social passion of our time, is forced to be indifferent to that which would be the monopoly of a few gifted souls." If such a social passion means anything, it means the reconstruction of life to the level of the gutter. It is the modern sham righteousness which would have called from Jesus the same utter scorn as that which he poured upon the Pharisaical cant of his own day. Yet it is not in religious books alone that you will meet with this sort of irreligion. For one sermon you will hear on the obligation of the individual soul to its maker and judge, and on the need of personal regeneration and the beauty of holiness, you will hear a score on the relation of a man to his fellows and on the virtue of social sympathy. In effect, the first and great commandment, "Thou shalt love the Lord thy God with all thy heart and with all thy soul and with all thy mind," has been almost forgotten for the second, "Thou shalt love thy neighbor as thyself." Worship in the temple is no longer a call to contrition and repentance, but an organized flattery of our human nature, and the theological seminary is fast becoming a special school for investigating poverty and spreading agnosticism. In this sense, or degree, that humanitarianism is no longer opposed by organized religion, but has itself usurped the place of

the Church, the New Morality may really justify its name.

What are the results of this glorification of humanity? What does the New Morality mean in life and conduct? Well, of such matters it is wise to speak cautiously. The actual morals of an age are an extremely complicated and elusive network of facts, and it is only too easy to generalize from incomplete observation. On the other hand we must guard against allowing ourselves to be deceived by the fallacy everywhere heard, that, because the preacher has always, even from the remotest record of Egypt, bewailed his own times as degenerate, therefore no age has fallen off in morality from its predecessor. Such an argument is a complete *non-sequitur*: there have been periods of degeneration, and there may yet be. As for our own age, only a fool would dogmatize; we can only balance and surmise. And in the first place a certain good must almost certainly be placed to the credit of humanitarianism. It has softened us and made us quicker to respond to the sufferings of others; the direct and frightful cruelty that runs through the annals of history like a crimson line has been largely eliminated from civilization, and with it a good deal of the brutality of human nature. We sometimes hear the present age compared with the later Roman Republic and the Empire, and in some respects speciously, but the callousness of the greater Romans to human misery and their hardness are almost unthinkable today. Consider a sentence or two from Appian: "The head and hand of Cicero were suspended for a long time from the rostra in the forum where formerly he had been accustomed to make public speeches, and more people came together to behold this spectacle than had previously come to listen to him. It is said that even at his meals Antony placed the head of Cicero before his table, until he became satiated with the horrid sight." Such an episode scarcely stands out from the hideous story of the Civil Wars; to the modern reader it brings a feeling almost of physical sickness. So much we seem to have gained, and the change in this respect even from our own seventeenth century shows that the credit is due in no small part to the general trend of humanitarianism.

But in other directions the progress is not so clear. Statistics are always treacherous witnesses, but so far as we can believe them and interpret them we can draw no comfort from the prevalence of crime and prostitution and divorce and insanity and suicide. At least, whatever may be the cause of this inner canker of society, our social passion seems to be powerless to cure it. Some might even argue that the preaching of any doctrine which minimizes personal responsibility is likely to increase the evil. Certainly a teacher who, like Miss Jane Addams, virtually attributes the lawless and criminal acts of our city hoodlums to a wholesome desire of adventure which the laws unrighteously repress, would appear to be encouraging the destructive and sensual proclivities which are too common in human nature, young and old. Nor are the ways of honesty made clear by a well-known humanitarian judge of Denver, who refused to punish a boy for stealing a Sunday-school teacher's pocketbook, for the two good reasons, as his honor explained in a public address, "that the boy was not responsible and, secondly, that there were bigger thieves in the pews upstairs." So, too, a respectable woman of New York who asks whether it may not be a greater wrong

for a girl to submit to the slavery of low wages than to sell herself in the street, is manifestly not helping the tempted to resist. She is even doing what she can with her words to confuse the very bounds of moral and physical evil.

There is, in fact, a terrible confusion hidden in the New Morality, an ulcerous evil that is ever working inward. Sympathy, creating the desire for even-handed justice, is in itself an excellent motive of conduct, and the stronger it grows, the better the world shall be. But sympathy, spoken with the word "social" prefixed, as it commonly is on the platforms of the day, begins to take on a dangerous connotation. And "social sympathy" erected into a theory which leaves out of account the responsibility of the individual and seeks to throw the blame of evil on the laws and on society, though it may effect desirable reforms here and there in institutions, is bound to leave the individual weakened in his powers of resistance against the temptations which can never be eliminated from human life. The whole effect of calling sympathy justice and putting it in the place of judgment is to relax the fiber of character and nourish the passions at the expense of reason and the will. And undoubtedly the conviction is every day gaining ground among cool observers of our life that the manners and morals of the people are beginning to suffer from this relaxation in many insidious ways apart from acts which come into the cognizance of the courts. The sensuality of the prevailing music and dancing, the plays that stir the country as organs of moral regeneration, the exaggeration of sex in the clothing seen in the street, are but symptoms more or less ominous to our mind as we do or do not connect them with the regnant theory of ethics. And in the end this form of social sympathy may itself quite conceivably bring back the brutality and cruelty from which it seems to have delivered us. The Roman who gloated over the head of his and the people's enemy lived two thousand years ago, and we think such bloodthirstiness is no longer possible in public life. Yet not much more than a century ago the preaching of social sympathy could send a Lebon and his kind over France with an insatiable lust for killing, complicated with Sadism, while in Paris the leader of the government of the most civilized country of Europe was justifying such a régime on the pious principle that, "when the sovereign people exercises its power, we can only bow before it; in all it does all is virtue and truth, and no excess, error, or crime is possible." The animal is not dead within us, but only asleep. If you think he has been really conquered, read what he has been doing in Congo and to the Putumayo Indians, or among the redeemers of the Balkan States. Or if you wish to get a glimpse of what he may yet do under the spur of social sympathy, consider the callous indifference shown by the labor unions to the revelation, if it deserves the name, of the system of dynamiting and murder employed in the service of "class-consciousness." These things are to be taken into account, not as bugbears, for society at large is no doubt sound at heart and will arouse itself at last against its false teachers, but as symptoms to warn and prepare.

To some few the only way out of what seems a state of moral blindness is through a return to an acknowledgment of the responsibility of the individual soul to its maker and inflexible judge. They may be right. Who can tell what reversal of belief may lie before us or what religious revolution may be preparing in the heart of infidelity? But for the present, at least, that supernatural control has lost its general efficacy and even from the pulpit has only a slight and intermittent appeal. Nor does such a loss appear without its compensations when we consider the harshness of medieval theology or the obliquities of superstition that seem to be inherent in the purest of religions. Meanwhile, the troubled individual, whatever his skepticism may be, need not be withheld from confirming his moral faith by turning from the perverted doctrine of the "Enlightenment" and from its recrudescence in modern humanitarianism to a larger and higher philosophy. For there is a faith which existed long before the materialism of the eighteenth century and before the crude earlier anthropomorphism, and which persisted unchanged, though often half-concealed, through those ages and still persists as a kind of shamefast inheritance of truth. It is not necessary to go to ancient books to recover that faith. Let a man cease for a moment to look so strenuously upon what is right for his neighbors. Let him shut out the voices of the world and disregard the stream of informing books which pour upon him from the modern press, as the "floud of poyson" was spewed upon Spenser's Knight from "Errours den":

Her fruitful cursèd spawne of serpents small.

Let him retire into himself, and in the silence of such recollection examine his own motives and the sources of his self-approval and discontent. He will discover there in that dialogue with himself, if his abstraction is complete and sincere, that his nature is not simple and single, but dual, and the consequences to him in his judgment of life and in his conduct will be of incalculable importance. He will learn, with a conviction which no science or philosophy falsely so-called can shake, that beside the passions and wandering desires and blind impulses and the cravings for pleasure and the prod of sensations there is something within him and a part of him, rather in some way his truer self, which controls and checks and knows and pronounces judgment, unmoved amid all motion, unchanged amid continual change, of everlasting validity above the shifting valuations of the moment. He may not be able to express this insight in terms that will satisfy his own reason or will convince others, but if his insight is true he will not waver in loyalty to it, though he may sin against it times without number in spoken word and impulsive deed. Rather, his loyalty will be confirmed by experience. For he will discover that there is a happiness of the soul which is not the same as the pleasure of fulfilled desires, whether these be for good or for ill, a happiness which is not dependent upon the results of this or that choice among our desires, but upon the very act itself of choice and self-control, and which grows with the habit of staying the throng of besetting and conflicting impulses always until the judicial *fiat* has been pronounced. It is thus that happiness is the final test of morality, bringing with it a sense of responsibility to the supernatural command within the soul of the man himself, as binding as the laws of religion and based on no disputable revelation or outer authority. Such a morality is neither old nor new, and stands above the varying customs of society. It is not determined essentially by the relation of a man to his fellows or by their approval, but by the consciousness of rightness in the man's own breast,—in a word, by character. Its works are temperance, truth, honesty, trustworthiness, fortitude, magnanimity, elevation; and its crown is joy.

Then, under the guidance of this intuition, a man may turn his eyes upon the world with no fear of being swayed by the ephemeral winds of doctrine. Despite the clamor of the hour he will know that the obligation to society is not the primal law and is not the source of personal integrity, but is secondary to personal integrity. He will believe that social justice is in itself desirable, but he will hold that it is far more important to preach first the responsibility of each man to himself for his own character. He will admit that equality of opportunity is an ideal to be aimed at, but he will think this a small thing in comparison with the universality of duty. In his attitude toward mankind he will not deny the claims of sympathy, but he will listen first to the voice of judgment:

Away with charity that soothes a lie,
And thrusts the truth with scorn and
    anger by.

He will be sensitive to the vast injustices of life and its widespread sorrows, but he will not be seduced by that compassion into the hypocrisy of saying that "the love of those whom a man does not know is quite as elemental a sentiment as the love of those whom a man does know." Nor, in repudiating such a falsehood, will he, like the mistress of Hull Hall, lose his power of discrimination under the stress of "those vast and dominant suggestions of a new peace and holiness," that is "to issue forth from broken human nature itself, out of the pathetic striving of ordinary men." Rather, he will, at any cost, strive to clear away the clouds of cant, and so open his mind to the dictates of the everlasting morality.

1914

STUART P. SHERMAN
(1881–1926)

THE EMOTIONAL DISCOVERY OF AMERICA *

It was originally suggested to me that I should speak in this series of lectures on the discoverers and explorers of America. This is a subject of perennial fascination. I was deterred from treating it by only two considerations, of which the first was this: I knew nothing about it. Perhaps I should not have allowed that fact to deter me. Whether my modesty in the matter was excessive I will submit to your better judgments by reciting now at once all the important points that I remember about the first discoverers and explorers of this country. They are these:

(1) The Italians, Portuguese, and Spaniards showed far more initiative and enterprise in discovery than the so-called Anglo-Saxons. America was discovered by foreign immigrants and settled by the English. That established a beautiful thing which Academicians love to talk about. It established a tradition: the foreigners are still discovering America; the so-called Anglo-Saxons are still trying to settle it.

(2) The best age for discovery is when one has grown tired of old worlds and old things, somewhere between forty and fifty. Columbus was forty-one when he found the new world. John Cabot was forty-seven when he discovered the mainland.

* Reprinted from *The Emotional Discovery of America* by Stuart P. Sherman, by permission of the publishers, Farrar & Rinehart, Inc. Copyright, 1924, 1932.

(3) Captains and crews of exploring vessels are largely recruited from the ranks of criminals and desperate and broken men, who mutiny, and discover things which they haven't been licensed to discover, and make trouble for their sovereigns, and sometimes languish in irons, like Columbus, or end their days on the scaffold, like Raleigh.

(4) A discoverer sets out at his own risk and sometimes at his own charge; and if he is successful, he may receive, like John Cabot, exactly the same reward for discovering a new world that Milton received for writing "Paradise Lost": £10.

(5) It is practically impossible to discover a new world without leaving the old one.

(6) The sixth and last point that I remember is the function of kings, courts, potentates, royal societies, royal geographical commissions, and the like, with reference to discoverers. As a matter of fact, these powers have in history two distinct functions.

Their first function is to inspect the plans of the intending discoverer, and to pronounce them absurd, vain, and impracticable. Their second function is to confirm the discoveries after they have been made and to appropriate a percentage of the profits.

Over and above my manifest ignorance of the early explorers and discoverers, I was deterred from treating them by a second consideration which I am afraid is not very creditable. But the fact is that I am rather tired of celebrating the physical discovery and settlement of America—the landings at San Salvador, Cape Breton Island, Jamestown, and Plymouth Rock. The landing was made. It is too late to do anything about it. Whether it was a wise thing to land is a question which it has long since been idle to discuss, though some of our English friends—

and, indeed, some of our own countrymen—are still discussing it. At any rate, the secret is out. Physical America has been discovered and explored and can't be concealed from the world. There is no danger of its being lost. Why should anyone labor any longer to commemorate its discovery? I am convinced that all kinds of academic institutions are somewhat excessively addicted to acts of commemoration and antiquarian research. For the greater part of my active life I have been an antiquarian and a commemorator. The universities, though on the side of graduate research they are supposed to face the future, and to be advancing on chaos and the dark, are still filled with people who collect candle-snuffers which snuff no candles and footwarmers which warm no feet. And that is probably why so many bright and promising boys acquire cold feet in the processes of higher education.

It is popularly understood that universities exist as custodians of the past, to conserve it and to transmit it to posterity. Now posterity, as a matter of fact, is doing its best to get the junk of the past to the bonfire. It is rather generally conceived also that literary academies and institutes have their reason for existence in a similar conservative function. Knowing that I was to speak to-day as a member of the National Institute of Arts and Letters, I studied its constitution in order to learn whether I was under any corporate obligation to speak as an antiquarian and a commemorator. Somewhat to my surprise and satisfaction I ascertained that the National Institute avows no addiction to historical retrospect. It was organized not for the recollection but for the advancement of literature by the recognition and reward of original creation.

There is a rite much talked about at college commencements and on other solemn occasions, called handing on the torch. It is derived, as you know, from the ancient torch-race, in which the spent runner passes his fire to a fresh athlete, who seizing it in turn, carries it forward for another stage. By a beautiful symbolism, the term is transferred to the transmission of skill and wisdom and inspiration from one generation to the next. When this business is in the hands of true athletes, I think there can be no doubt that living fire does pass from one generation to the next, and is borne on over new paths. But having studied for many years in academic places what is called the torch-race, or the transmission of the great tradition, I have observed that this semi-priestly function has a certain tendency to fall into the hands of antiquarians; and when this happens, what is transmitted is not the flaming torch but the cold candelabrum, which is rather an impediment than an inspiration to the runner.

For such students of letters as are interested rather in the torch than in the candelabrum it occurred to me that one might find a more suggestive theme than the landings of the old navigators in the *emotional* discovery of America. Until it is emotionally discovered it remains a barren and rather repugnant land to letters. Certain young men imagine that this process was not even begun till about 1900; but that is a mistake. The special appeal of this theme is that the emotional discovery of America has been going on for a very long time, that it is still going on, and that it will go on after we are all dead and forgotten, with just as much zest as it had a hundred years ago or thirty years ago, and with just as much room for discovery as it offered thirty years ago or as it offers today.

For there is this fact to be kept in mind that America as a discovery of the heart and the imagination, and therefore as a subject for letters, is as fluent as water, as evanescent as smoke. She hangs like a mirage in the mist and light of our hopes and fears and affections. She is created, as Mr. De la Mare says of all things which are precious, "out of our love and power"; and when our love and power wane, she wanes; and when they wax, she waxes. On the whole, as it seems to me, we have been, so far as literary expression is concerned, a singularly unemotional and unaffectionate people, with plenty of power but with scant love. Perhaps no other country so beautiful and so various has remained so long in the intellectual consciousness of her people and received so few words of choice and delicate appreciation, so few tokens of enamored adoration.

She was recognized under many other aspects before many people had any heart-filling sense that she was beautiful. For the Spanish explorers, she was El Dorado, rich in gold, jewels, and spices. She was Christ's Kingdom for the Pilgrims. For the Adamses, for Washington, she was Republican Rome restored, and stocked with Plutarchan heroes. For English and French Revolutionists at the end of the eighteenth century, she was Utopia, Arcady, and the Garden of Eden. For one chorus she was the land of the free and the home of the brave. For another, she was the land of slaves and yokels and Babbitts. As an emotional fact she doesn't "stay put": she is constantly being discovered and lost again; and our history is the enemy of all our thin and dwindled traditions about her.

Doubtless this emotional discovery began when Leif Ericsson beached his boats on the shores of Labrador; but the records are wanting. It continued with Columbus, for we read that when he and his crew, men of Latin blood, came ashore on San Salvador, they all gave "thanks to God, kneeling upon the shore, and kissed the ground with tears of joy." I think all Americans should feel that way about their native soil.

To the Puritan discovery of America as an emotional fact, there were serious obstacles. They had brought with them from the old world a spiritual commonwealth of Christ, which they superimposed upon the new land. For a long time their ministers, who were their principal men of letters, could not see New England because their hearts were fixed upon Canaan, upon Salem, and upon Zion, and were dazzled by watching the light of the gospel breaking upon the Indians, in the intervals when they were not watching the effect of their muskets upon them. In one fashion and another, the Puritan divines conceived it to be their duty to wean the affections of their flocks away from their place of exile, and fix them upon a heavenly city, singing:

> This is not my place of resting,
>   Mine's a city yet to come.
> Homeward to it I am hasting,
>   On to my eternal home.

Nothing so long and so effectually prevented the emotional exploration and settlement of the new land as this habit of teaching generation after generation to regard it as a kind of asylum and quarantine for souls until they should be passed beyond the river into a better land.

The English and the Dutch colonists began, as we say, to "warm up" to the land, to develop an affectionate relationship with it, to take it into their hearts only as they discovered here and there that the fishing was excellent, the game abundant, and the climate salubrious. If you look through the colonial writers for emotional discoveries outside the field of religion, you find the occasions of their emotions almost pathetically utilitarian.

Take, for example, Francis Higginson, writing of New England's Plantation in 1630: what makes his heart beat faster is the admirable fertility of the soil and the abundance of seafish, which "are almost beyond believing; and sure I should scarce have believed it except I had seen it with my own eyes. I saw great stores of whales, and grampuses, and such abundance of mackerels that it would astonish one to behold; likewise cod fish. . . . There is a fish called a bass, a most sweet and wholesome fish as ever I did eat. . . . And besides bass, we take plenty of scates and thornback, and abundance of lobsters, and the least boy in the Plantation may both catch and eat what he will of them. For my own part, I was soon cloyed with them, they were so great and fat and luscious." There is a kind of palatal emotion here which, if Francis Higginson allows it to run riot, may work havoc with his otherworldliness.

The Rev. Mr. Higginson glows, too, at thought of the freedom from stomach trouble which he enjoys in New England. Whereas in the old country his stomach was so delicate that he could drink nothing but strong and stale ale, "now," he declares, "I *can* and oftentimes do drink New England water very well." Perhaps he reaches the peak of his emotion when he says "a cup of New England's air is better than a whole draught of Old England's ale."

Turning to Daniel Denton's "Description of New York" in 1670, I find that he likewise is an enthusiast about the whales and grampuses which in the winter lie upon the south side of Long Island and about the tobacco, hemp, flax, pumpkins, melons, etc., which the island yields. And already, at this early date, one can mark a difference between a New Yorker and a New Englander. Denton has begun to enjoy his life, while Higginson has hardly got beyond enjoying his freedom from stomach trouble. He notes that in New York one can have all the land one wants rent free,—a beautiful old tradition which I find has lapsed. He enjoys the annual horse-races for a silver cup in the middle of the island. He is even infatuated with the red-bird and with "divers sorts of singing birds, whose chirping notes salute the ears of travellers with an harmonious discord; and in every pond and brook green silken frogs, who warbling forth their untuned tunes, strive to bear a part in their music." "I may say truly," he continues, "that if there be any terrestrial happiness to be had by people of all ranks, it must certainly be here. But that which adds happiness to all the rest, is the healthfulness of the place; where many people in twenty years' time never know what sickness is; where they look upon it as a great mortality if two or three die out of a town in a year's time: where, beside the sweetness of the air, the country itself sends forth such a fragrant smell that it may be perceived at sea before they can make the land. . . . What shall I say more?"

I will take one other colonial record, from George Alsop's "Character of the Province of Maryland," 1666. Writing to his father in a rather frolicsome mood of discovery, he declares that "this country of Maryland abounds in a flourishing variety of delightful woods, pleasant groves, lovely springs, together with spacious navigable rivers and creeks, it being a most healthful and pleasant situation.

"Herds of deer are as numerous in this Province of Mary-Land as cuckolds can be in London, only their horns are not so well dressed and tipped with silver as their's are.

"Here if the devil had such a vagary in his head as he once had among the Gadarians, he might drown a thousand head of hogs and they'd ne'er be missed, for the very woods of this Province swarms with them."

All these men, from Francis Higginson in Salem to George Alsop in Maryland, had something of the emotional discoverer in them. They were developing and enjoying personal relations with the land. They were making themselves over, they were enjoying a new birth, in the womb of new circumstances. They all show at least a presentiment that the spirit of life is passing from the old world to the new; and they salute the borders of the unknown with a cheer.

In the next hundred years the progress made towards the discovery of America was of course enormous; but if I may venture on a generalization, the discoveries of the eighteenth century were not of the personal and emotional quality which drives directly at artistic expression. The characteristic discoveries of the age were physical, scientific, philosophical, political, critical.

In other words, eighteenth century America, like eighteenth century France and eighteenth century Germany, was an age of reason, an age of enlightenment. During the eighteenth century the best brains in Western Europe walked boldly out of the twilight of the Middle Ages into modern times; and the best brains in America walked out with them, leaving the New Canaanites, the New Salemites, and the New Zionites asleep in the villages among the New England hills, dreaming in their little white churches, under the bonnets of their little white old maids, the fading paradisiacal dream, implanted there by the exiled ministers of colonial times who had taught them to sing:

> This is not my place of resting,
> Mine's a city yet to come.

Meanwhile, the discovery of America was being pushed forward, as always, by the discoverers, the explorers, the secessionists, who had walked out of the old state, out of the old church, out of the old state, out of the old phantasms and dreams. It was being pushed forward by the deists and the unitarians and the unclassified free-thinkers, by the democrats and the republicans and the dreamers of an international commonwealth of mankind—men begotten by their times to face the need of their times, to curb pestilence, to harness thunderbolts, to unseat tyrants, to build the strong frame of a State. In the works of the witch-finder Cotton Mather, now turned rationalist and vaccinator for small-pox, in the works of Franklin, and Paine, and Jefferson, and Hamilton, and the Adamses, and not in the hymn books or the sermons, you learn who discovered America in the eighteenth century. It was an intellectual not an emotional discovery.

There was one man living among those famous wits who might have made a great emotional discovery of America in the eighteenth century if his passionate intensity of feeling had been put in service to the main movement of intellectual life in his times. As it was, he writhed in the rusting chains of Calvinistic theology, and perished there. Only from time to time, hardly knowing what ailed him, hardly guessing that he was dying of spiritual starvation, he left his church and his parish, and retired, as he says, "into a solitary place on the banks of Hudson's river, at some distance from the city, for contemplation on divine things."

Poor man! Perhaps he went out to the banks of Hudson's river intending to consider "how doleful is the state of the damned, especially such as go to Hell from under the Gospel." But as a matter of fact, the spirit of the scene took hold of him, and he tells us in some pages which, after nearly two hundred years, are still hot with his emotion, still wet with his tears, that what he actually meditated on was the sun, the moon and the stars, the clouds, the blue sky, the grass, the flowers, and all nature. And looking on these things, unaccountably he felt an "inward sweetness." "The appearance of everything was altered. There seemed to be, as it were, a calm, sweet cast, or appearance of divine glory, in almost everything." On one occasion, in 1737, this divine glory on the face of nature by the banks of Hudson's river lasted near an hour, and kept him for the greater part of the time "in a flood of tears and weeping aloud." Poor Jonathan Edwards! He had discovered America, the sweet body of his country, as a fact for emotional response. But he knew it not. He thought that what he had seen was one of the bearded rabbis such as gaze down upon the people from Sargent's dreadful satire on the Trinity in the Boston Public Library; and so he went back to the city, clanking his Calvinistic chains, and told the happy horse-racing New Yorkers once more how doleful is the state of the damned, especially such as go to hell from under the gospel.

The emotional discovery of Hudson's river and valley had to wait for Irving—an infinitely milder-souled man than Edwards, a man whose poetry was always emotion recollected in a gently humorous tranquillity. For a long time now, criticism, outside the schools, has lapsed into silence about Irving, from a suspicion, I suppose, that he is not quite in the genuine American tradition, but is rather a whimsical eighteenth century Englishman good-naturedly humoring us by painting the likeness of George Washington over the head of George III on the old taverns which for him have never changed their sovereignty. Irving was not a very resolute secessionist nor a very aggressive discoverer; but Irving did a very precious and magical thing: he loved New York and the Hudson Valley and he took them into his heart, the old Dutch town and the river, and he recreated them for the imagination, and fixed them there in a mellow atmosphere of their own, like a golden city under the sea, mingling its tender glamour forever with the light of our common day.

To take any part of the earth into your heart transfigures it for you and for all men whom you can persuade to use your eyes. And the transfiguring discovery of America has, in most periods, proceeded bit by bit, in the hearts of men like Cooper who took the forest into his heart, and Dana and Melville who took the sea into their hearts, and Hawthorne who declared that New England was as large a lump of the earth as his heart could hold, and Bret Harte who embraced the red-shirted forty-niners, and Mark Twain who took the Mississippi into his heart, and Joaquin Miller who embraced the Sierras, and G. W. Cable and Joel Chandler Harris who transfigured Georgia and

New Orleans by discovering them as facts for the heart and the imagination.

In my judgment it is hardly possible to overvalue the enamored localism, the enamored provincialism, of men like Harris, Cable, Mark Twain, Miller, and the rest who have loved new lands for the first time, and have made the first poetry out of a life hitherto esteemed vulgar. And just a word in this connection about the torch-race. Who carried on the torch of Washington Irving? Who received the fire of his heart and his imagination? Well, there can be no doubt that Irving's candlesticks are best preserved by the English teachers who try to convert the racy colloquial idiom of little Yankee boys into Addisonian English; but the man who carries forward the torch of Irving is the man who continues his magical task of clothing "home scenes and places and familiar names with those imaginative and whimsical associations so seldom met with in our new country, but which live like charms and spells about the cities of the Old World, binding the heart of the native inhabitant to his home." From this point of view, Joel Chandler Harris, working with the lore of the Georgia plantations, is more truly a continuator of Irving than any professor of Addisonian rhetoric who ever lived.

But I wish to call your attention now to the group of adventurers whom I rank with Columbus, Cabot and Magellan in the field of emotional discovery. These three men that I am going to mention flourished between 1840 and 1855. They were all dangerous characters, for they were all genuine torch-bearers, and some of their contemporaries thought them genuine firebrands. They were tired of the old worlds, junk and antiqui-

ties, old candlesticks, old footwarmers, the dust that gathers on disused furniture, "foulness preserved in cassia and pitch, and swathed in linen; the death of that which never lived."

The impulse to spiritual secession and discovery was strong among them. They turned their backs squarely upon New Canaan, New Salem and Zion; for they believed that the worst foes of discovery, the chief repressors of the new life, are those who cling with feeble antiquarian hands to the hollow forms of old faith, cling not hard enough to raise the dead to a fresh resurrection—cling just tenaciously enough to prevent the full forward rush and flow of faith into new forms. These three walked out of the church, they walked out of the frigid intellectualism of contemporary unitarian culture, they walked out of the academic orthodoxy of Harvard College, they walked out of the political state, they walked out of drawing-room society—they walked out into nature and the use of all their senses. And they discovered America as a major heartbeat of humanity in the frame of the universe. And in the intense emotion of that experience, one of them spoke and said:

"In eternity there is indeed something true and sublime. But all these times and places and occasions are here and now. God himself culminates in the present moment, and will *never* be more divine in the lapse of the ages."

And another said:

"I have heard what the talkers were
    talking, the talk of the beginning
    and the end;
But I do not talk of the beginning or the
    end.
There was never any more inception
    than there is now;
Nor any more youth or age than there
    is now;

And will never be any more perfection
than there is now;
Nor any more heaven or hell than there
is now."

And the first speaker said: "Certainly, we do not need to be soothed and entertained always like children. . . . The front aspect of great thoughts can only be enjoyed by those who stand on the side whence they arise. Books, not which afford us a cowering enjoyment, but in which each thought is of unusual daring; such as an idle man cannot read, and a timid one would not be entertained by, which even make us dangerous to existing institutions,—such call I good books. A book should contain pure discoveries, glimpses of *terra firma*, though by shipwrecked mariners, and not the art of navigation by those who have never been out of sight of land."

And the third said: "Nature as we know her is no saint. . . . She comes eating and drinking and sinning. Her darlings, the great, the strong, and the beautiful, are not children of our law, do not come out of the Sunday School, nor weigh their food, nor punctually keep the commandments. If we will be strong with her strength, we must not harbor such desolate consciences, borrowed too from consciences of other natures. We must set up the strong present tense against all the rumors of wrath to come."

And the first exclaimed: "Goodness!—you hypocrite, come out of that, live your life, do your work, then take your hat. . . . Most people with whom I talk, men and women of some originality and genius, have their scheme of the universe all cut and dried; . . . an ancient and tottering frame with all its boards blown off. . . . The wisest man preaches no doctrines; he has no schemes; he sees no rafter, not even a cobweb against

the heavens. It is clear sky. . . . The church is a sort of hospital for men's souls, and as full of quackery as the hospital for their bodies. Those who are taken into it live like pensioners in their Retreat or Sailor's Snug Harbor, where you may see a row of religious cripples sitting outside in sunny weather. . . . One is sick at heart of this pagoda worship. . . . It is as the sound of many catechisms and religious books, twanging a canting peal round the earth, seeming to issue from some Egyptian temple and echo along the shore of the Nile, right opposite to Pharaoh's palace and Moses in the bulrushes, startling a multitude of sharks and alligators basking in the pool."

This man who has just been speaking said on another occasion that he knew of no redeeming qualities in himself except a "sincere love for some things," especially "a singular yearning for all wildness." He trusted his senses and loved their experience of all sorts. He liked the sacramental contact of earth under his bare feet. On one occasion he ate a rat. He was also fond of wild grapes, and was a collector of Indian arrowheads. He fancied, he said, that "it would be a luxury to stand up to one's chin in some retired swamp a whole summer day, scenting the wild honeysuckle and bilberry blows, and lulled by the minstrelsy of gnats and mosquitoes." "Let us not," he said, "let us not, my friends, be wheedled and cheated into good behavior to earn the salt of our eternal porridge, whoever they are that attempt it."

The third man exclaims, in exactly the same vein, with the same hunger for experience through the senses:

"Too long shut in strait and few,
Thinly dieted on dew,
I will use the world, and sift it,
As you spin a cherry.

O doleful ghosts, and goblins merry!
O all you virtues, methods, mights,
Means, appliances, delights,
Reputed wrongs and braggart rights,
Smug routine, and things allowed,
Minorities, things under cloud!—
Hither! take me, use me, fill me,
Vein and artery, though ye kill me."

And the second man, intoxicated by a vintage that ne'er grew in the belly of the grape, intoxicated with a passion of discovery, intoxicated with a passion of love, goes abroad and picks up America, bit by bit, from sea to sea, and declares for each morsel of it his unmitigated adoration. It was the most cryingly needed service ever rendered to America by a man of letters. The emotional discovery of America? What does that mean? It means that you recognize your eternity culminating here and now. It means that now at this hour you enter into sacramental relations with the universe of which the center is under your feet. It means that you recognize with a response which shatters your being with emotion that no priest or church can longer prevent you from eating the bread and drinking the wine of mystical communion with your God and your fellowmen.

Why, who makes much of a miracle?
As to me, I know of nothing else but miracles,
Whether I walk the streets of Manhattan,
Or dart my sight over the roofs of houses toward the sky,
Or wade with naked feet along the beach, just in the edge of the water,
Or stand under the trees in the woods,
Or talk by day with anyone I love—or sleep in the bed at night with anyone I love,
Or sit at table at dinner with my mother,
Or look at strangers opposite me riding in the car,
Or watch honey-bees busy around the hive, of a summer forenoon,
Or animals feeding in the fields,
Or birds—or the wonderfulness of insects in the air,
Or the wonderfulness of the sun-down—or of stars shining so quiet and bright,
Or the exquisite, delicate thin curve of the new moon in spring,
Or whether I go among those I like best, and that like me best. . . .
What stranger miracles are there?

The three radical and rebellious conspirators for the advancement of American letters whose words I have just been quoting are, as you have doubtless recognized, Thoreau, Emerson, and Whitman. I think no one has yet adequately demonstrated the essential unanimity of theory, of feeling, of purpose, and of courage which underlies the revolt and the constructive program of this bold trio of individualists. So far as their ideas are concerned, there is just as much dynamite in Thoreau and in Emerson as in Whitman; I doubt, indeed, whether he had an idea which one of them had not shaped before him. For example, Thoreau and Emerson recognize as clearly as Whitman the necessity of bringing a full-bodied humanity, with all the senses functioning, into the service of the new literature of the new world for which they are "striking up."

Whitman's priceless addition to the power of the movement in which he participated is due to the exuberant richness and fecundative ardor of his emotional nature—to a gusto, a discovering wonder, a freshness of love and joy absolutely unprecedented in American literature and hitherto unequaled. What other people observed, he experienced. In him the miracle of transubstantiation was daily accomplished; and he and the solid universe became one spirit in a mystical and transfiguring communion. He becomes the thing he sings. Precisely because he possesses this gift of full and joyous emotional realization in a national scene singularly destitute of it, Whitman has become unique as a torch-bearer, a fire-bringer.

Fire is a dangerous thing to handle; and many good people feel more at their ease with a fire extinguisher.

But the advancement of letters, on the whole, is not a vocation for men who insist on being at their ease. None of this group promises ease. They are always provoking men to a kind of celestial arson. When you touch Whitman, you have a better chance than at any other point in our poetical procession of receiving a torch and not a cold candlestick.

I have said much, too much, about the history of emotional discovery. What really interests me is the deduction from history of the principles which govern this discovery from age to age. So far as I can make out, these principles are at bottom just the same to-day as they were in 1840 or in 1855.

The advancement of letters does not wait for gentlemen or scholars or societies of gentlemen and scholars or for good Republicans or good Presbyterians or for native Americans whose ancestors landed in the seventeenth century. Literature betrays a profound social unconcern about the sort of people she carries in her crew, provided only they are adept in hoisting sails and making a landing on terra incognita through a roaring surf. If you wish to advance letters in any signal degree, you will have to run some risk of getting your feet wet. You will have to renounce the antiquarian mind. You will have to accept the society of your contemporaries, for better, for worse, as your portion; and if you wish to have the utmost joy of it, you had better tell

yourself that eternity culminates in the present hour and will never be more divine in the lapse of ages. There is nothing worth while but reality, whatever it is. You must say to yourself, "Reality though it slay me." You must write out of the reality of your own experience, telling your truth as the spirit of your own time and the light in your own mind give you to see the truth, though it horrify all the virgins, married and unmarried, in Christendom, and leave you in limbo for the term of your natural life.

It is quite possible, too, that when you have taken the hazard of new fortunes, and have left your old world, and sailed into uncharted seas, you may discover nothing that will place your name among the great navigators. Well, that is your risk. It is always safer to stay at home and hear what Livingstone and Stanley and Franklin and Shackleton have seen when they return, if they do return.

The advancement of letters is not a vocation to be recommended to the average man any more than dietetic chemistry, psycho-pathology, or experimental medicine are to be recommended to the average man: the ultimate purpose of all these sciences, we may conceive to be the multiplication of sound minds in sound bodies, but their practitioners are daily engaged with excrements, and strange forms of madness, and with the germs of devastating diseases to which they not seldom succumb. That is the risk which they pay for the chance of discovery.

Literature's pioneers must always be advancing beyond the old hunters' trails and fires into the dark forest of human experience. If safety isn't your first consideration, then you will pass on to a closer and closer scrutiny of your own sensations and passions and ideas and a sharper observation of your fellows, reporting what you find with a ruthless veracity, steadily substituting a fact which you have felt in all your senses for a vague word which you have heard in polite society. If you do that, you are likely to find that you are carrying a lighted torch.

The age in which we now live appears to me to be a great and fascinating period in the emotional and literary discovery of America, because the woods are full of lighted torches, are full of men and women bent on exploring and reporting the truth as they see it, and nothing but the truth, and great areas of repressed truth about their own lives and about the lives of the American people. One feels the quickening breath of this spirit in many places: in history, in biography, in criticism, in poetry, in our so-called fiction, which becomes more and more a peculiarly intimate and veracious form of contemporary history.

The America which we are now discovering is something of a shock to a good many people; but I think they will recover from it. Prudent persons may not like the present generation of explorers, their vocabulary, or their manners or their criticism of life; but then the chances are that they wouldn't have cared very much for the crews who sailed with Columbus or with Magellan. It would even be possible, I suppose, to put forth with applause in some quarters, an argument to the effect that the literary discovery of America had gone far enough in 1870; and that the duty of all good men at the present hour is to sustain the *status quo*. Happily that is not our duty here. Happily our purpose here is fulfilled and our pleasure is keenest when we are recognizing and applauding the

various aspects of the great literary movement which is taking place under our eyes, giving us on the whole, the stimulating sense that ours is one of the valorous and encouraging ages of the world.

Fifty years from now, perhaps very much sooner, I think the literary antiquarians will take up one of the books published this fall, Mr. Sherwood Anderson's *Story Teller's Story*. And he will read the pages in which Mr. Anderson tells that he grew up in the belief that an American man in the world of men must give his soul to business. And then he will read on through the passage in which Mr. Anderson describes how one day, sitting in his office, dictating a sales letter to his stenographer, he stopped short in the middle of his sentence and said to his secretary:

"My dear young woman, it is all very silly but I have decided to no longer concern myself with this buying and selling. It may be all right for others but for me it is poison. There is the factory. You may have it if it pleases you. It is of little value I dare say. . . . Now, at this moment, with the letter I have been dictating, with the very sentence you have been writing left unfinished, I am going out of that door and never coming back. What am I going to do? Well now, that I don't know. I am going to wander about. I am going to sit with people, listen to words, tell tales of people, what they are thinking, what they are feeling. The devil! It may even be I am going forth in search of myself."

And fifty years hence, I think the literary antiquarian will point to this passage and say: "There is one of the historic moments in American literature." For many of us already the incident is beautifully symbolic and, we hope, prophetic. When the middle-aged business man begins a definitive walking out of his office to discover himself in the joy of artistic craftsmanship, something exciting is happening in our civilization. An epoch seems on the point of closing. Someone has seized a torch, and lighted new vistas.

1924

EDWIN ARLINGTON ROBINSON
(1869–1935)

AARON STARK *

Withal a meagre man was Aaron Stark,
Cursed and unkempt, shrewd, shrivelled, and morose.
A miser was he, with a miser's nose,
And eyes like little dollars in the dark.
His thin, pinched mouth was nothing but a mark;
And when he spoke there came like sullen blows
Through scattered fangs a few snarled words and close,
As if a cur were chary of its bark.

Glad for the murmur of his hard renown,
Year after year he shambled through the town,
A loveless exile moving with a staff;
And oftentimes there crept into his ears
A sound of alien pity, touched with tears,—
And then (and only then) did Aaron laugh.

1896

* Reprinted from *Children of the Night* by E. A. Robinson, by permission of the publishers, Charles Scribner's Sons. Copyright, 1897.

THE CLERKS *

I did not think that I should find them there
When I came back again; but there they stood,
As in the days they dreamed of when young blood
Was in their cheeks and women called them fair.
Be sure, they met me with an ancient air,—
And yes, there was a shop-worn brotherhood
About them; but the men were just as good,
And just as human as they ever were.

And you that ache so much to be sublime,
And you that feed yourselves with your descent,
What comes of all your visions and your fears?
Poets and kings are but the clerks of Time,
Tiering the same dull webs of discontent,
Clipping the same sad alnage of the years.

1896

ZOLA *

Because he puts the compromising chart
Of hell before your eyes, you are afraid;
Because he counts the price that you have paid
For innocence, and counts it from the start,
You loathe him. But he sees the human heart
Of God meanwhile, and in His hand was weighed
Your squeamish and emasculate crusade
Against the grim dominion of his art.

Never until we conquer the uncouth
Connivings of our shamed indiffer-
    ence
(We call it Christian faith) are we to
    scan
The racked and shrieking hideousness
    of Truth
To find, in hate's polluted self-defence
Throbbing, the pulse, the divine heart
    of man.

1896

RICHARD CORY *

Whenever Richard Cory went down
    town,
We people on the pavement looked at
    him:
He was a gentleman from sole to
    crown,
Clean favored, and imperially slim.

And he was always quietly
    arrayed,
And he was always human when he
    talked;
But still he fluttered pulses when he
    said,
"Good-morning," and he glittered
    when he walked.

And he was rich, yes, richer than a
    king—
And admirably schooled in every
    grace:
In fine, we thought that he was every-
    thing
To make us wish that we were in his
    place.

So on we worked, and waited for the
    light,
And went without the meat, and
    cursed the bread;
And Richard Cory, one calm summer
    night,

* Reprinted from *Children of the
Night* by E. A. Robinson, by permission
of the publishers, Charles Scribner's
Sons. Copyright, 1897.

Went home and put a bullet through
    his head.

1897

ISAAC AND ARCHIBALD †

Isaac and Archibald were two old
    men.
I knew them, and I may have laughed
    at them
A little; but I must have honored
    them
For they were old, and they were
    good to me.

I do not think of either of them now,
Without remembering, infallibly,
A journey that I made one afternoon
With Isaac to find out what Archibald
Was doing with his oats. It was high
    time
Those oats were cut, said Isaac; and
    he feared
That Archibald—well, he could never
    feel
Quite sure of Archibald. Accordingly
The good old man invited me—that is,
Permitted me—to go along with him;
And I, with a small boy's adhesiveness
To competent old age, got up and
    went.
I do not know that I cared overmuch
For Archibald's or anybody's oats,
But Archibald was quite another
    thing,
And Isaac yet another; and the world
Was wide, and there was gladness
    everywhere.
We walked together down the River
    Road
With all the warmth and wonder of
    the land
Around us, and the wayside flash of
    leaves,—

† From *Collected Poems*, by E. A.
Robinson. Copyright 1935, 1937, by
The Macmillan Company. By permission of The Macmillan Company, publishers.

And Isaac said the day was glorious;
But somewhere at the end of the first
    mile
I found that I was figuring to find
How long those ancient legs of his
    would keep
The pace that he had set for them.
    The sun
Was hot, and I was ready to sweat
    blood;
But Isaac, for aught I could make of
    him,
Was cool to his hat-band. So I said
    then
With a dry gasp of affable despair,
Something about the scorching days
    we have
In August without knowing it some-
    times;
But Isaac said the day was like a
    dream,
And praised the Lord, and talked
    about the breeze.
I made a fair confession of the breeze,
And crowded casually on his thought
The nearness of a profitable nook
That I could see. First I was half
    inclined
To caution him that he was growing
    old,
But something that was not compas-
    sion soon
Made plain the folly of all subterfuge.
Isaac was old, but not so old as that.

So I proposed, without an overture,
That we be seated in the shade a
    while,
And Isaac made no murmur. Soon the
    talk
Was turned on Archibald, and I
    began
To feel some premonitions of a kind
That only childhood knows; for the
    old man
Had looked at me and clutched me
    with his eye,
And asked if I had ever noticed
    things.

I told him that I could not think of
    them,
And I knew then, by the frown that
    left his face
Unsatisfied, that I had injured him.
"My good young friend," he said,
    "you cannot feel
What I have seen so long. You have
    the eyes—
Oh, yes—but you have not the other
    things:
The sight within that never will de-
    ceive,
You do not know—you have no right
    to know;
The twilight warning of experience,
The singular idea of loneliness,—
These are not yours. But they have
    long been mine,
And they have shown me now for
    seven years
That Archibald is changing. It is
    not
So much that he should come to his
    last hand,
And leave the game, and go the old
    way down;
But I have known him in and out so
    long,
And I have seen so much of good in
    him
That other men have shared and have
    not seen,
And I have gone so far through thick
    and thin,
Through cold and fire with him, that
    now it brings
To this old heart of mine an ache that
    you
Have not yet lived enough to know
    about.
But even unto you, and your boy's
    faith,
Your freedom, and your untried con-
    fidence,
A time will come to find out what it
    means
To know that you are losing what
    was yours,

To know that you are being left be-
    hind;
And then the long contempt of in-
    nocence—
God bless you, boy!—don't think the
    worse of it
Because an old man chatters in the
    shade—
Will all be like a story you have read
In childhood and remembered for the
    pictures.
And when the best friend of your
    life goes down,
When first you know in him the
    slackening
That comes, and coming always tells
    the end,—
Now in a common word that would
    have passed
Uncaught from any other lips than
    his,
Now in some trivial act of every day,
Done as he might have done it all
    along
But for a twinging little difference
That nips you like a squirrel's teeth—
    oh, yes,
Then you will understand it well
    enough.
But oftener it comes in other ways;
It comes without your knowing when
    it comes;
You know that he is changing, and
    you know
That he is going—just as I know now
That Archibald is going, and that I
Am staying. . . . Look at me, my
    boy,
And when the time shall come for you
    to see
That I must follow after him, try then
To think of me, to bring me back
    again,
Just as I was to-day. Think of the
    place
Where we are sitting now, and think
    of me—
Think of old Isaac as you knew him
    then,

When you set out with him in
    August once
To see old Archibald."—The words
    come back
Almost as Isaac must have uttered
    them,
And there comes with them a dry
    memory
Of something in my throat that would
    not move.

If you had asked me then to tell just
    why
I made so much of Isaac and the
    things
He said, I should have gone far for
    an answer;
For I knew it was not sorrow that I
    felt,
Whatever I may have wished it, or
    tried then
To make myself believe. My mouth
    was full
Of words, and they would have been
    comforting
To Isaac, spite of my twelve years, I
    think;
But there was not in me the willing-
    ness
To speak them out. Therefore I
    watched the ground;
And I was wondering what made the
    Lord
Create a thing so nervous as an
    ant,
When Isaac, with commendable un-
    rest,
Ordained that we should take the road
    again—
For it was yet three miles to Archi-
    bald's,
And one to the first pump. I felt re-
    lieved
All over when the old man told me
    that;
I felt that he had stilled a fear of
    mine
That those extremities of heat and
    cold

Which he had long gone through
  with Archibald
Had made the man impervious to
  both;
But Isaac had a desert somewhere in
  him,
And at the pump he thanked God for
  all things
That He had put on earth for men to
  drink,
And he drank well,—so well that I
  proposed
That we go slowly lest I learn too
  soon
The bitterness of being left behind,
And all those other things. That was
  a joke
To Isaac, and it pleased him very
  much;
And that pleased me—for I was
  twelve years old.

At the end of an hour's walking after
  that
The cottage of old Archibald ap-
  peared.
Little and white and high on a smooth
  round hill
It stood, with hackmatacks and apple-
  trees
Before it, and a big barn-roof beyond;
And over the place—trees, house,
  fields and all—
Hovered an air of still simplicity
And a fragrance of old summers—the
  old style
That lives the while it passes. I dare
  say
That I was lightly conscious of all
  this
When Isaac, of a sudden, stopped
  himself,
And for the long first quarter of a
  minute
Gazed with incredulous eyes, forget-
  ful quite
Of breezes and of me and of all else
Under the scorching sun but a
  smooth-cut field,

Faint yellow in the distance. I was
  young,
But there were a few things that I
  could see,
And this was one of them.—"Well,
  well!" said he;
And "Archibald will be surprised, I
  think,"
Said I. But all my childhood sub-
  tlety
Was lost on Isaac, for he strode along
Like something out of Homer—
  powerful
And awful on the wayside, so I
  thought.
Also I thought how good it was to be
So near the end of my short-legged
  endeavor
To keep the pace with Isaac for five
  miles.

Hardly had we turned in from the
  main road
When Archibald, with one hand on
  his back
And the other clutching his huge-
  headed cane,
Came limping down to meet us.—
  "Well! well! well!"
Said he; and then he looked at my
  red face,
All streaked with dust and sweat, and
  shook my hand,
And said it must have been a right
  smart walk
That we had had that day from Til-
  bury Town.—
"Magnificent," said Isaac; and he told
About the beautiful west wind there
  was
Which cooled and clarified the atmos-
  phere.
"You must have made it with your
  legs, I guess,"
Said Archibald; and Isaac humored
  him
With one of those infrequent smiles
  of his
Which he kept in reserve, apparently,

For Archibald alone. "But why," said
    he,
"Should Providence have cider in the
    world
If not for such an afternoon as this?"
And Archibald, with a soft light in
    his eyes,
Replied that if he chose to go down
    cellar,
There he would find eight barrels—
    one of which
Was newly tapped, he said, and to his
    taste
An honor to the fruit. Isaac approved
Most heartily of that, and guided us
Forthwith, as if his venerable feet
Were measuring the turf in his own
    door-yard,
Straight to the open rollway. Down
    we went,
Out of the fiery sunshine to the
    gloom,
Grateful and half sepulchral, where
    we found
The barrels, like eight potent senti-
    nels,
Close ranged along the wall. From
    one of them
A bright pine spile stuck out allur-
    ingly,
And on the black flat stone, just
    under it,
Glimmered a late-spilled proof that
    Archibald
Had spoken from unfeigned experi-
    ence.
There was a fluted antique water-glass
Close by, and in it, prisoned, or at
    rest,
There was a cricket, of the brown soft
    sort
That feeds on darkness. Isaac turned
    him out,
And touched him with his thumb to
    make him jump,
And then composedly pulled out the
    plug
With such a practised hand that
    scarce a drop

Did even touch his fingers. Then he
    drank
And smacked his lips with a slow
    patronage
And looked along the line of barrels
    there
With a pride that may have been for-
    getfulness
That they were Archibald's and not
    his own.
"I never twist a spigot nowadays,"
He said, and raised the glass up to the
    light,
"But I thank God for orchards." And
    that glass
Was filled repeatedly for the same
    hand
Before I thought it worth while to
    discern
Again that I was young, and that old
    age,
With all his woes, had some advan-
    tages.
"Now, Archibald," said Isaac, when
    we stood
Outside again, "I have it in my mind
That I shall take a sort of little walk—
To stretch my legs and see what you
    are doing.
You stay and rest your back and tell
    the boy
A story: Tell him all about the time
In Stafford's cabin forty years ago,
When four of us were snowed up for
    ten days
With only one dried haddock. Tell
    him all
About it, and be wary of your back.
Now I will go along."—I looked up
    then
At Archibald, and as I looked I saw
Just how his nostrils widened once or
    twice
And then grew narrow. I can hear
    to-day
The way the old man chuckled to
    himself
Not wholesomely, not wholly to con-
    vince

Another of his mirth,—as I can hear
The lonely sigh that followed.—But
    at length
He said: "The orchard now's the
    place for us;
We may find something like an apple
    there,
And we shall have the shade, at any
    rate."
So there we went and there we laid
    ourselves
Where the sun could not reach us;
    and I champed
A dozen of worm-blighted astrakhans
While Archibald said nothing—
    merely told
The tale of Stafford's cabin, which
    was good,
Though "master chilly"—after his
    own phrase—
Even for a day like that. But other
    thoughts
Were moving in his mind, imperative,
And writhing to be spoken: I could
    see
The glimmer of them in a glance or
    two,
Cautious, or else unconscious, that he
    gave
Over his shoulder: . . . "Stafford
    and the rest—
But that's an old song now, and Archi-
    bald
And Isaac are old men. Remember,
    boy,
That we are old. Whatever we have
    gained,
Or lost, or thrown away, we are old
    men.
You look before you and we look be-
    hind,
And we are playing life out in the
    shadow—
But that's not all of it. The sunshine
    lights
A good road yet before us if we look,
And we are doing that when least we
    know it;
For both of us are children of the sun,

Like you, and like the weed there at
    your feet.
The shadow calls us, and it frightens
    us—
We think; but there's a light behind
    the stars
And we old fellows who have dared to
    live,
We see it—and we see the other
    things,
The other things. . . . Yes, I have
    seen it come
These eight years, and these ten years,
    and I know
Now that it cannot be for very long
That Isaac will be Isaac. You have
    seen—
Young as you are, you must have seen
    the strange
Uncomfortable habit of the man?
He'll take my nerves and tie them in
    a knot
Sometimes, and that's not Isaac. I
    know that—
And I know what it is: I get it here
A little, in my knees, and Isaac—
    here."
The old man shook his head regret-
    fully
And laid his knuckles three times on
    his forehead.
"That's what it is: Isaac is not quite
    right.
You see it, but you don't know what
    it means:
The thousand little differences—no,
You do not know them, and it's well
    you don't;
You'll know them soon enough—God
    bless you, boy!—
You'll know them, but not all of them
    —not all.
So think of them as little as you
    can:
There's nothing in them for you, or
    for me—
But I am old and I must think of
    them;
I'm in the shadow, but I don't forget

The light, my boy,—the light behind
the stars.
Remember that: remember that I said
it;
And when the time that you think far
away
Shall come for you to say it—say it,
boy;
Let there be no confusion or distrust
In you, no snarling of a life half
lived,
Nor any cursing over broken things
That your complaint has been the
ruin of.
Live to see clearly and the light will
come
To you, and as you need it.—But
there, there,
I'm going it again, as Isaac says,
And I'll stop now before you go to
sleep.—
Only be sure that you growl cau-
tiously,
And always where the shadow may
not reach you."

Never shall I forget, long as I live,
The quaint thin crack in Archibald's
voice,
The lonely twinkle in his little eyes,
Or the way it made me feel to be with
him.
I know I lay and looked for a long
time
Down through the orchard and across
the road,
Across the river and the sun-scorched
hills
That ceased in a blue forest, where
the world
Ceased with it. Now and then my
fancy caught
A flying glimpse of a good life be-
yond—
Something of ships and sunlight,
streets and singing,
Troy falling, and the ages coming
back,
And ages coming forward: Archibald

And Isaac were good fellows in old
clothes,
And Agamemnon was a friend of
mine;
Ulysses coming home again to shoot
With bows and feathered arrows
made another,
And all was as it should be. I was
young.

So I lay dreaming of what things I
would,
Calm and incorrigibly satisfied
With apples and romance and igno-
rance,
And the still smoke from Archibald's
clay pipe.
There was a stillness over everything,
As if the spirit of heat had laid its
hand
Upon the world and hushed it; and I
felt
Within the mightiness of the white
sun
That smote the land around us and
wrought out
A fragrance from the trees, a vital
warmth
And fullness for the time that was to
come,
And a glory for the world beyond the
forest.
The present and the future and the
past,
Isaac and Archibald, the burning
bush,
The Trojans and the walls of Jericho,
Were beautifully fused; and all went
well
Till Archibald began to fret for Isaac
And said it was a master day for sun-
stroke.
That was enough to make a mummy
smile,
I thought; and I remained hilarious,
In face of all precedence and
respect,
Till Isaac (who had come to us un-
heard)

Found he had no tobacco, looked at
   me
Peculiarly, and asked of Archibald
What ailed the boy to make him chir-
   rup so.
From that he told us what a blessed
   world
The Lord had given us.—"But, Archi-
   bald,"
He added, with a sweet severity
That made me think of peach-skins
   and goose-flesh,
"I'm half afraid you cut those oats of
   yours
A day or two before they were well
   set."
"They were set well enough," said
   Archibald,—
And I remarked the process of his
   nose
Before the words came out. "But
   never mind
Your neighbor's oats: you stay here
   in the shade
And rest yourself while I go find the
   cards.
We'll have a little game of seven-up
And let the boy keep count."—"We'll
   have the game,
Assuredly," said Isaac; "and I think
That I will have a drop of cider, also."

They marched away together towards
   the house
And left me to my childish rumina-
   tions
Upon the ways of men. I followed
   them
Down cellar with my fancy, and then
   left them
For a fairer vision of all things at
   once
That was anon to be destroyed again
By the sound of voices and of heavy
   feet—
One of the sounds of life that I remember,
Though I forget so many that rang
   first

As if they were thrown down to me
   from Sinai.

So I remember, even to this day,
Just how they sounded, how they
   placed themselves,
And how the game went on while I
   made marks
And crossed them out, and meanwhile
   made some Trojans.
Likewise I made Ulysses, after Isaac,
And a little after Flaxman. Archi-
   bald
Was injured when he found himself
   left out,
But he had no heroics, and I said so:
I told him that his white beard was
   too long
And too straight down to be like
   things in Homer.
"Quite so," said Isaac.—"Low," said
   Archibald;
And he threw down a deuce with a
   deep grin
That showed his yellow teeth and
   made me happy.
So they played on till a bell rang
   from the door,
And Archibald said, "Supper."—After
   that
The old men smoked while I sat
   watching them
And wondered with all comfort what
   might come
To me, and what might never come
   to me;
And when the time came for the long
   walk home
With Isaac in the twilight, I could see
The forest and the sunset and the
   sky-line,
No matter where it was that I was
   looking:
The flame beyond the boundary, the
   music,
The foam and the white ships, and
   two old men
Were things that would not leave me.
   —And that night

There came to me a dream—a shining
    one,
With two old angels in it. They had
    wings,
And they were sitting where a silver
    light
Suffused them, face to face. The
    wings of one
Began to palpitate as I approached,
But I was yet unseen when a dry
    voice
Cried thinly, with unpatronizing tri-
    umph,
"I've got you, Isaac; high, low, jack,
    and the game."

Isaac and Archibald have gone their
    way
To the silence of the loved and well-
    forgotten.
I knew them, and I may have laughed
    at them;
But there's a laughing that has honor
    in it,
And I have no regret for light words
    now.
Rather I think sometimes they may
    have made
Their sport of me;—but they would
    not do that,
They were too old for that. They
    were old men,
And I may laugh at them because I
    knew them.

(*1899*)   1902

AUNT IMOGEN *

Aunt Imogen was coming, and there-
    fore
The children—Jane, Sylvester, and
    Young George—
Were eyes and ears; for there was
    only one

* From *Collected Poems*, by E. A.
Robinson. Copyright 1935, 1937, by
The Macmillan Company. By permission of The Macmillan Company, publishers.

Aunt Imogen to them in the whole
    world,
And she was in it only for four weeks
In fifty-two. But those great bites of
    time
Made all September a Queen's Festi-
    val;
And they would strive, informally, to
    make
The most of them.—The mother un-
    derstood,
And wisely stepped away. Aunt
    Imogen
Was there for only one month in the
    year,
While she, the mother,—she was al-
    ways there;
And that was what made all the dif-
    ference.
She knew it must be so, for Jane had
    once
Expounded it to her so learnedly
That she had looked away from the
    child's eyes
And thought; and she had thought of
    many things.

There was a demonstration every
    time
Aunt Imogen appeared, and there was
    more
Than one this time. And she was at
    a loss
Just how to name the meaning of it
    all:
It puzzled her to think that she could
    be
So much to any crazy thing alive—
Even to her sister's little savages
Who knew no better than to be them-
    selves;
But in the midst of her glad wonder-
    ment
She found herself besieged and over-
    come
By two tight arms and one tumul-
    tuous head,
And therewith half bewildered and
    half pained

By the joy she felt and by the sudden
   love
That proved itself in childhood's
   honest noise.
Jane, by the wings of sex, had reached
   her first;
And while she strangled her, approv-
   ingly,
Sylvester thumped his drum and
   Young George howled.   .
But finally, when all was rectified,
And she had stilled the clamor of
   Young George
By giving him a long ride on her
   shoulders,
They went together into the old room
That looked across the fields; and
   Imogen
Gazed out with a girl's gladness in her
   eyes,
Happy to know that she was back
   once more
Where there were those who knew
   her, and at last
Had gloriously got away again
From cabs and clattered asphalt for
   a while;
And there she sat and talked and
   looked and laughed
And made the mother and the chil-
   dren laugh.
Aunt Imogen made everybody laugh.

There was the feminine paradox—that
   she
Who had so little sunshine for herself
Should have so much for others. How
   it was
That she could make, and feel for
   making it,
So much of joy for them, and all along
Be covering, like a scar, and while
   she smiled,
That hungering incompleteness and
   regret—
That passionate ache for something of
   her own,
For something of herself—she never
   knew.

She knew that she could seem to
   make them all
Believe there was no other part of
   her
Than her persistent happiness; but
   the why
And how she did not know. Still none
   of them
Could have a thought that she was
   living down—
Almost as if regret were criminal,
So proud it was and yet so profitless—
The penance of a dream, and that was
   good.
Her sister Jane—the mother of little
   Jane,
Sylvester, and Young George—might
   make herself
Believe she knew, for she—well, she
   was Jane.

Young George, however, did not yield
   himself
To nourish the false hunger of a ghost
That made no good return. He saw
   too much:
The accumulated wisdom of his years
Had so conclusively made plain to
   him
The permanent profusion of a world
Where everybody might have every-
   thing
To do, and almost everything to eat,
That he was jubilantly satisfied
And all unthwarted by adversity.
Young George knew things. The
   world, he had found out,
Was a good place, and life was a good
   game—
Particularly when Aunt Imogen
Was in it. And one day it came to
   pass—
One rainy day when she was holding
   him
And rocking him—that he, in his own
   right,
Took it upon himself to tell her so;
And something in his way of telling
   it—

The language, or the tone, or some-
thing else—
Gripped like insidious fingers on her
throat,
And then went foraging as if to make
A plaything of her heart. Such un-
deserved
And unsophisticated confidence
Went mercilessly home; and had she
sat
Before a looking glass, the deeps of it
Could not have shown more clearly to
her then
Than one thought-mirrored little
glimpse had shown,
The pang that wrenched her face and
filled her eyes
With anguish and intolerable mist.
The blow that she had vaguely thrust
aside
Like fright so many times had found
her now:
Clean-thrust and final it had come to
her
From a child's lips at last, as it had
come
Never before, and as it might be felt
Never again. Some grief, like some
delight,
Stings hard but once: to custom after
that
The rapture or the pain submits itself,
And we are wiser than we were be-
fore.
And Imogen was wiser; though at first
Her dream-defeating wisdom was in-
deed
A thankless heritage: there was no
sweet,
No bitter now; nor was there any-
thing
To make a daily meaning for her life—
Till truth, like Harlequin, leapt out
somehow
From ambush and threw sudden savor
to it—
But the blank taste of time. There
were no dreams,
No phantoms in her future any more:

One clinching revelation of what was
One by-flash of irrevocable chance,
Had acridly but honestly foretold
The mystical fulfilment of a life
That might have once . . . But that
was all gone by:
There was no need of reaching back
for that:
The triumph was not hers: there was
no love
Save borrowed love: there was no
might have been.

But there was yet Young George—
and he had gone
Conveniently to sleep, like a good boy;
And there was yet Sylvester with his
drum,
And there was frowzle-headed little
Jane;
And there was Jane the sister, and the
mother,—
Her sister, and the mother of them
all.
They were not hers, not even one of
them:
She was not born to be so much as
that,
For she was born to be Aunt Imogen.
Now she could see the truth and look
at it;
Now she could make stars out where
once had palled
A future's emptiness; now she could
share
With others—ah, the others!—to the
end
The largess of a woman who could
smile;
Now it was hers to dance the folly
down,
And all the murmuring; now it was
hers
To be Aunt Imogen.—So, when
Young George
Woke up and blinked at her with his
big eyes,
And smiled to see the way she blinked
at him,

'T was only in old concord with the
 stars
That she took hold of him and held
 him close,
Close to herself, and crushed him till
 he laughed.

       1902

MINIVER CHEEVY *

Miniver Cheevy, child of scorn,
 Grew lean while he assailed the
  seasons;
He wept that he was ever born,
 And he had reasons.

Miniver loved the days of old
 When swords were bright and
  steeds were prancing;
The vision of a warrior bold
 Would set him dancing.

Miniver sighed for what was not,
 And dreamed, and rested from his
  labors;
He dreamed of Thebes and Camelot,
 And Priam's neighbors.

Miniver mourned the ripe renown
 That made so many a name so fra-
  grant;
He mourned Romance, now on the
  town,
 And Art, a vagrant.

Miniver loved the Medici,
 Albeit he had never seen one;
He would have sinned incessantly
 Could he have been one.

Miniver cursed the commonplace
 And eyed a khaki suit with loath-
  ing;
He missed the medieval grace
 Of iron clothing.

* From *Collected Poems*, by E. A.
Robinson. Copyright 1935, 1937, by
The Macmillan Company. By permission of The Macmillan Company, publishers.

Miniver scorned the gold he sought,
 But sore annoyed was he without
  it;
Miniver thought, and thought, and
  thought,
 And thought about it.

Miniver Cheevy, born too late,
 Scratched his head and kept on
  thinking;
Miniver coughed, and called it fate,
 And kept on drinking.

       1910

CASSANDRA *

I heard one who said: "Verily,
 What word have I for children
  here?
Your Dollar is your only Word,
 The wrath of it your only fear.

"You build it altars tall enough
 To make you see, but you are blind;
You cannot leave it long enough
 To look before you or behind.

"When Reason beckons you to pause,
 You laugh and say that you know
  best;
But what it is you know, you keep
 As dark as ingots in a chest.

"You laugh and answer, 'We are
  young;
 O leave us now, and let us grow.'—
Not asking how much more of this
 Will Time endure or Fate bestow.

"Because a few complacent years
 Have made your peril of your pride,
Think you that you are to go on
 Forever pampered and untried?

"What lost eclipse of history,
 What bivouac of the marching
  stars,
Has given the sign for you to see
 Millenniums and last great wars?

"What unrecorded overthrow
 Of all the world has ever known,

Or ever been, has made itself
  So plain to you, and you alone?

"Your Dollar, Dove and Eagle make
  A Trinity that even you
Rate higher than you rate yourselves;
  It pays, it flatters, and it's new.

"And though your very flesh and
    blood
  Be what your Eagle eats and drinks,
You'll praise him for the best of birds,
  Not knowing what the Eagle
    thinks.

"The power is yours, but not the
    sight;
  You see not upon what you tread;
You have the ages for your guide,
  But not the wisdom to be led.

"Think you to tread forever down
  The merciless old verities?
And are you never to have eyes
  To see the world for what it is?

"Are you to pay for what you have
  With all you are?"—No other word
We caught, but with a laughing crowd
  Moved on. None heeded, and few
    heard.

                              1914

BEWICK FINZER *

Time was when his half million drew
  The breath of six per cent;
But soon the worm of what-was-not
  Fed hard on his content;
And something crumbled in his brain
  When his half million went.

Time passed, and filled along with his
  The place of many more;
Time came, and hardly one of us
  Had credence to restore,

* From *Collected Poems*, by E. A.
Robinson. Copyright 1935, 1937, by
The Macmillan Company. By permission of The Macmillan Company, publishers.

From what appeared one day, the man
  Whom we had known before.

The broken voice, the withered neck,
  The coat worn out with care,
The cleanliness of indigence,
  The brilliance of despair,
The fond imponderable dreams
  Of affluence,—all were there.

Poor Finzer, with his dreams and
    schemes,
  Fares hard now in the race,
With heart and eye that have a task
  When he looks in the face
Of one who might so easily
  Have been in Finzer's place.

He comes unfailing for the loan
  We give and then forget;
He comes, and probably for years
  Will he be coming yet,—
Familiar as an old mistake,
  And futile as regret.

                              1916

BEN JONSON ENTERTAINS
A MAN FROM STRATFORD *

You are a friend then, as I make it
    out,
Of our man Shakespeare, who alone
    of us
Will put an ass's head in Fairyland
As he would add a shilling to more
    shillings,
All most harmonious,—and out of his
Miraculous inviolable increase
Fills Ilion, Rome, or any town you
    like
Of olden time with timeless English-
    men;
And I must wonder what you think of
    him—
All you down there where your small
    Avon flows
By Stratford, and where you're an
    Alderman.
Some, for a guess, would have him
    riding back

To be a farrier there, or say a dyer;
Or maybe one of your adept surveyors;
Or like enough the wizard of all
    tanners.
Not you—no fear of that; for I discern
In you a kindling of the flame that
    saves—
The nimble element, the true caloric;
I see it, and was told of it, moreover,
By our discriminate friend himself, no
    other.
Had you been one of the sad average,
As he would have it,—meaning, as I
    take it,
The sinew and the solvent of our
    Island,
You'd not be buying beer for this
    Terpander's
Approved and estimated friend Ben
    Jonson;
He'd never foist it as a part of his
Contingent entertainment of a towns-
    man
While he goes off rehearsing, as he
    must,
If he shall ever be the Duke of Strat-
    ford.
And my words are no shadow on your
    town—
Far from it; for one town's as like
    another
As all are unlike London. Oh, he
    knows it,—
And there's the Stratford in him; he
    denies it,
And there's the Shakespeare in him.
    So, God help him!
I tell him he needs Greek; but neither
    God
Nor Greek will help him. Nothing
    will help that man.
You see the fates have given him so
    much,
He must have all or perish,—or look
    out
Of London, where he sees too many
    lords.
They're part of half what ails him: I
    suppose

There's nothing fouler down among
    the demons
Than what it is he feels when he
    remembers
The dust and sweat and ointment of
    his calling
With his lords looking on and laugh-
    ing at him.
King as he is, he can't be king *de
    facto*,
And that's as well, because he
    wouldn't like it;
He'd frame a lower rating of men then
Than he has now; and after that
    would come
An abdication or an apoplexy.
He can't be king, not even king of
    Stratford,—
Though half the world, if not the
    whole of it,
May crown him with a crown that fits
    no king
Save Lord Apollo's homesick emissary:
Not there on Avon, or on any
    stream
Where Naiads and their white arms
    are no more,
Shall he find home again. It's all too
    bad.
But there's a comfort, for he'll have
    that House—
The best you ever saw; and he'll be
    there
Anon, as you're an Alderman. Good
    God!
He makes me lie awake o'nights and
    laugh.

And you have known him from his
    origin,
You tell me; and a most uncommon
    urchin
He must have been to the few seeing
    ones—
A trifle terrifying, I dare say,
Discovering a world with his man's
    eyes,
Quite as another lad might see some
    finches,

If he looked hard and had an eye for
    nature.
But this one had his eyes and their
    foretelling,
And he had you to fare with, and
    what else?
He must have had a father and a
    mother—
In fact I've heard him say so—and a
    dog,
As a boy should, I venture; and the
    dog,
Most likely, was the only man who
    knew him.
A dog, for all I know, is what he needs
As much as anything right here to-day,
To counsel him about his disillusions,
Old arches, and parturitions of what's
    coming,—
A dog of orders, an emeritus,
To wag his tail at him when he comes
    home,
And then to put his paws up on his
    knees
And say, "For God's sake, what's it all
    about?"

I don't know whether he needs a dog
    or not—
Or what he needs. I tell him he needs
    Greek;
I'll talk of rules and Aristotle with
    him,
And if his tongue's at home he'll say
    to that,
"I have your word that Aristotle
    knows,
And you mine that I don't know
    Aristotle."
He's all at odds with all the unities,
And what's yet worse, it doesn't seem
    to matter;
He treads along through Time's old
    wilderness
As if the tramp of all the centuries
Had left no roads—and there are none,
    for him;
He doesn't see them, even with those
    eyes,—

And that's a pity, or I say it is.
Accordingly we have him as we have
    him—
Going his way, the way that he goes
    best,
A pleasant animal with no great noise
Or nonsense anywhere to set him off—
Save only divers and inclement devils
Have made of late his heart their
    dwelling place.
A flame half ready to fly out some-
    times
At some annoyance may be fanned up
    in him,
But soon it falls, and when it falls goes
    out;
He knows how little room there is in
    there
For crude and futile animosities,
And how much for the joy of being
    whole,
And how much for long sorrow and
    old pain.
On our side there are some who may
    be given
To grow old wondering what he
    thinks of us
And some above us, who are, in his
    eyes,
Above himself,—and that's quite right
    and English.
Yet here we smile, or disappoint the
    gods
Who made it so: the gods have always
    eyes
To see men scratch; and they see one
    down here
Who itches, manor-bitten to the
    bone,
Albeit he knows himself—yes, yes, he
    knows—
The lord of more than England and
    of more
Than all the seas of England in all
    time
Shall ever wash. D'ye wonder that I
    laugh?
He sees me, and he doesn't seem to
    care;

And why the devil should he? I can't
tell you.

I'll meet him out alone of a bright
Sunday,
Trim, rather spruce, and quite the
gentleman.
"What ho, my lord!" say I. He doesn't
hear me;
Wherefore I have to pause and look
at him.
He's not enormous, but one looks at
him.
A little on the round if you insist,
For now, God save the mark, he's
growing old;
He's five and forty, and to hear him
talk
These days you'd call him eighty;
then you'd add
More years to that. He's old enough
to be
The father of a world, and so he is.
"Ben, you're a scholar, what's the time
of day?"
Says he; and there shines out of him
again
An aged light that has no age or sta-
tion—
The mystery that's his—a mischievous
Half-mad serenity that laughs at fame
For being won so easy, and at friends
Who laugh at him for what he wants
the most,
And for his dukedom down in War-
wickshire;—
By which you see we're all a little
jealous. . . .
Poor Greene! I fear the color of his
name
Was even as that of his ascending soul;
And he was one where there are many
others,—
Some scrivening to the end against
their fate,
Their puppets all in ink and all to die
there;
And some with hands that once would
shade an eye

That scanned Euripides and Æschylus
Will reach by this time for a pot-house
mop
To slush their first and last of royal-
ties.
Poor devils! and they all play to his
hand;
For so it was in Athens and old Rome.
But that's not here or there; I've wan-
dered off.
Greene does it, or I'm careful. Where's
that boy?

Yes, he'll go back to Stratford. And
we'll miss him?
Dear sir, there'll be no London here
without him.
We'll all be riding, one of these fine
days,
Down there to see him—and his wife
won't like us;
And then we'll think of what he never
said
Of women—which, if taken all in all
With what he did say, would buy
many horses.
Though nowadays he's not so much
for women:
"So few of them," he says, "are worth
the guessing."
But there's a worm at work when he
says that,
And while he says it one feels in the
air
A deal of circumambient hocus-pocus.
They've had him dancing till his toes
were tender,
And he can feel 'em now, come chilly
rains.
There's no long cry for going into it,
However, and we don't know much
about it.
But you in Stratford, like most here
in London,
Have more now in the *Sonnets* than
you paid for;
He's put one there with all her poison
on,
To make a singing fiction of a shadow

That's in his life a fact, and always
  will be.
But she's no care of ours, though
  Time, I fear,
Will have a more reverberant ado
About her than about another one
Who seems to have decoyed him,
  married him,
And sent him scuttling on his way to
  London,—
With much already learned, and more
  to learn,
And more to follow. Lord! how I see
  him now,
Pretending, maybe trying, to be like
  us.
Whatever he may have meant, we
  never had him;
He failed us, or escaped, or what you
  will,—
And there was that about him (God
  knows what,—
We'd flayed another had he tried it
  on us)
That made as many of us as had wits
More fond of all his easy distances
Than one another's noise and clap-
  your-shoulder.
But think you not, my friend, he'd
  never talk!
Talk? He was eldritch at it; and we
  listened—
Thereby acquiring much we knew
  before
About ourselves, and hitherto had held
Irrelevant, or not prime to the pur-
  pose.

And there were some, of course, and
  there be now,
Disordered and reduced amazedly
To resignation by the mystic seal
Of young finality the gods had
  laid
On everything that made him a young
  demon;
And one or two shot looks at him al-
  ready
As he had been their executioner;

And once or twice he was, not know-
  ing it,—
Or knowing, being sorry for poor clay
And saying nothing. . . . Yet, for all
  his engines,
You'll meet a thousand of an after-
  noon
Who strut and sun themselves and
  see around 'em
A world made out of more that has a
  reason
Than his, I swear, that he sees here
  to-day;
Though he may scarcely give a Fool
  an exit
But we mark how he sees in every-
  thing
A law that, given we flout it once too
  often,
Brings fire and iron down on our
  naked heads.
To me it looks as if the power that
  made him,
For fear of giving all things to one
  creature,
Left out the first,—faith, innocence,
  illusion,
Whatever 'tis that keeps us out o'
  Bedlam,—
And thereby, for his too consuming
  vision,
Empowered him out of nature; though
  to see him,
You'd never guess what's going on
  inside him.
He'll break out some day like a keg
  of ale
With too much independent frenzy
  in it;
And all for cellaring what he knows
  won't keep,
And what he'd best forget—but that
  he can't.
You'll have it, and have more than
  I'm foretelling;
And there'll be such a roaring at the
  Globe
As never stunned the bleeding gladia-
  tors.

He'll have to change the color of its hair
A bit, for now he calls it Cleopatra.
Black hair would never do for Cleopatra.
But you and I are not yet two old women,
And you're a man of office. What he does
Is more to you than how it is he does it,—
And that's what the Lord God has never told him
They work together, and the Devil helps 'em;
They do it of a morning, or if not,
They do it of a night; in which event
He's peevish of a morning. He seems old;
He's not the proper stomach or the sleep—
And they're two sovran agents to conserve him
Against the fiery art that has no mercy
But what's in that prodigious grand new House.
I gather something happening in his boyhood
Fulfilled him with a boy's determination
To make all Stratford 'ware of him. Well, well,
I hope at last he'll have his joy of it,
And all his pigs and sheep and bellowing beeves,
And frogs and owls and unicorns, moreover,
Be less than hell to his attendant ears.
Oh, past a doubt we'll all go down to see him.

He may be wise. With London two days off,
Down there some wind of heaven may yet revive him;
But there's no quickening breath from anywhere

Shall make of him again the poised young faun
From Warwickshire, who'd made, it seems, already
A legend of himself before I came
To blink before the last of his first lightning.
Whatever there be, there'll be no more of that;
The coming on of his old monster Time
Has made him a still man; and he has dreams
Were fair to think on once, and all found hollow.
He knows how much of what men paint themselves
Would blister in the light of what they are;
He sees how much of what was great now shares
An eminence transformed and ordinary;
He knows too much of what the world has hushed
In others, to be loud now for himself;
He knows now at what height low enemies
May reach his heart, and high friends let him fall;
But what not even such as he may know
Bedevils him the worst: his lark may sing
At heaven's gate how he will, and for as long
As joy may listen, but *he* sees no gate,
Save one whereat the spent clay waits a little
Before the churchyard has it, and the worm.
Not long ago, late in an afternoon,
I came on him unseen down Lambeth way,
And on my life I was afear'd of him:
He gloomed and mumbled like a soul from Tophet,

His hands behind him and his head
   bent solemn.
"What is it now," said I,—"another
   woman?"
That made him sorry for me, and he
   smiled.
"No, Ben," he mused; "it's Nothing.
   It's all Nothing.
We come, we go; and when we're
   done, we're done."
Spiders and flies—we're mostly one or
   t'other—
We come, we go; and when we're
   done, we're done;
"By God, you sing that song as if you
   knew it!"
Said I, by way of cheering him; "what
   ails ye?"
"I think I must have come down here
   to think,"
Says he to that, and pulls his little
   beard;
"Your fly will serve as well as any-
   body,
And what's his hour? He flies, and
   flies, and flies,
And in his fly's mind has a brave ap-
   pearance;
And then your spider gets him in her
   net,
And eats him out, and hangs him up
   to dry.
That's Nature, the kind mother of us
   all.
And then your slattern housemaid
   swings her broom,
And where's your spider? And that's
   Nature, also.
It's Nature, and it's Nothing. It's all
   Nothing.
It's all a world where bugs and em-
   perors
Go singularly back to the same
   dust,
Each in his time; and the old, ordered
   stars
That sang together, Ben, will sing the
   same
Old stave to-morrow."

When he talks like that,
There's nothing for a human man to
   do
But lead him to some grateful nook
   like this
Where we be now, and there to make
   him drink.
He'll drink, for love of me, and then
   be sick;
A sad sign always in a man of parts,
And always very ominous. The great
Should be as large in liquor as in
   love,—
And our great friend is not so large in
   either:
One disaffects him, and the other fails
   him;
Whatso he drinks that has an antic
   in it,
He's wondering what's to pay in his
   insides;
And while his eyes are on the
   Cyprian
He's fribbling all the time with that
   damned House.
We laugh here at his thrift, but after
   all
It may be thrift that saves him from
   the devil;
God gave it, anyhow,—and we'll sup-
   pose
He knew the compound of his handi-
   work.
To-day the clouds are with him, but
   anon
He'll out of 'em enough to shake the
   tree
Of life itself and bring down fruit
   unheard-of,—
And, throwing in the bruised and
   whole together,
Prepare a wine to make us drunk with
   wonder;
And if he live, there'll be a sunset
   spell
Thrown over him as over a glassed
   lake
That yesterday was all a black wild
   water.

God send he live to give us, if no
   more,
What now's a-rampage in him, and
   exhibit,
With a decent half-allegiance to the
   ages
An earnest of at least a casual eye
Turned once on what he owes to
   Gutenberg,
And to the fealty of more centuries
Than are as yet a picture in our vi-
   sion.
"There's time enough,—I'll do it when
   I'm old,
And we're immortal men," he says to
   that;
And then he says to me, "Ben, what's
   'immortal'?
Think you by any force of ordination
It may be nothing of a sort more noisy
Than a small oblivion of component
   ashes
That of a dream-addicted world was
   once
A moving atomy much like your
   friend here?"
Nothing will help that man. To make
   him laugh,
I said then he was a mad mounte-
   bank,—
And by the Lord I nearer made him
   cry.
I could have eat an eft then, on my
   knees,
Tail, claws, and all of him; for I had
   stung
The king of men, who had no sting
   for me,
And I had hurt him in his memories;
And I say now, as I shall say again,
I love the man this side idolatry.

He'll do it when he's old, he says. I
   wonder.
He may not be so ancient as all that.
For such as he, the thing that is to
   do
Will do itself,—but there's a reckoning;

The sessions that are now too much
   his own,
The roiling inward of a stilled outside,
The churning out of all those blood-
   fed lines,
The nights of many schemes and little
   sleep,
The full brain hammered hot with
   too much thinking,
The vexed heart over-worn with too
   much aching,—
This weary jangling of conjoined
   affairs
Made out of elements that have no
   end,
And all confused at once, I under-
   stand,
Is not what makes a man to live for-
   ever.
O no, not now! He'll not be going
   now:
There'll be time yet for God knows
   what explosions
Before he goes. He'll stay awhile. Just
   wait:
Just wait a year or two for Cleopatra,
For she's to be a balsam and a comfort;
And that's not all a jape of mine now,
   either.
For granted once the old way of
   Apollo
Sings in a man, he may then, if he's
   able,
Strike unafraid whatever strings he
   will
Upon the last and wildest of new
   lyres;
Nor out of his new magic, though it
   hymn
The shrieks of dungeoned hell, shall
   he create
A madness or a gloom to shut quite
   out
A cleaving daylight, and a last great
   calm
Triumphant over shipwreck and all
   storms.
He might have given Aristotle creeps,

But surely would have given him his
   katharsis.

He'll not be going yet. There's too
   much yet
Unsung within the man. But when
   he goes,
I'd stake ye coin o' the realm his only
   care
For a phantom world he sounded and
   found wanting
Will be a portion here, a portion
   there,
Of this or that thing or some other
   thing
That has a patent and intrinsical
Equivalence in those egregious shil-
   lings.
And yet he knows, God help him!
   Tell me, now,
If ever there was anything let loose
On earth by gods or devils heretofore
Like this mad, careful, proud, indiffer-
   ent Shakespeare!
Where was it, if it ever was? By
   heaven,
'Twas never yet in Rhodes or Perga-
   mon—
In Thebes or Nineveh, a thing like
   this!
No thing like this was ever out of
   England;
And that he knows. I wonder if he
   cares.
Perhaps he does. . . . O Lord, that
   House in Stratford!

              1915, 1916

EROS TURANNOS *

She fears him, and will always ask
   What fated her to choose him;
She meets in his engaging mask
   All reasons to refuse him;
But what she meets and what she fears

Are less than are the downward years,
   Drawn slowly to the foamless weirs
      Of age, were she to lose him.

Between a blurred sagacity
   That once had power to sound him,
And Love, that will not let him be
   The Judas that she found him,
Her pride assuages her almost,
As if it were alone the cost.—
He sees that he will not be lost,
   And waits and looks around him.

A sense of ocean and old trees
   Envelops and allures him;
Tradition, touching all he sees,
   Beguiles and reassures him;
And all her doubts of what he says
Are dimmed with what she knows of
   days—
Till even prejudice delays
   And fades, and she secures him.

The falling leaf inaugurates
   The reign of her confusion;
The pounding wave reverberates
   The dirge of her illusion;
And home, where passion lived and
   died,
Becomes a place where she can hide,
While all the town and harbor side
   Vibrate with her seclusion.

We tell you, tapping on our brows,
   The story as it should be,—
As if the story of a house
   Were told, or ever could be;
We'll have no kindly veil between
Her visions and those we have seen,—
As if we guessed what hers have been,
   Or what they are or would be.

Meanwhile we do no harm; for they
   That with a god have striven,
Not hearing much of what we say,
   Take what the god has given;
Though like waves breaking it may
   be,
Or like a changed familiar tree,
Or like a stairway to the sea
   Where down the blind are driven.

              1914, 1916

THE MAN AGAINST THE SKY *

Between me and the sunset, like a
    dome
Against the glory of a world on fire,
Now burned a sudden hill,
Bleak, round, and high, by flame-lit
    height made higher,
With nothing on it for the flame to
    kill
Save one who moved and was alone
    up there
To loom before the chaos and the
    glare
As if he were the last god going home
Unto his last desire.

Dark, marvelous, and inscrutable he
    moved on
Till down the fiery distance he was
    gone,
Like one of those eternal, remote
    things
That range across a man's imaginings
When a sure music fills him and he
    knows
What he may say thereafter to few
    men,—
The touch of ages having wrought
An echo and a glimpse of what he
    thought
A phantom or a legend until then;
For whether lighted over ways that
    save,
Or lured from all repose,
If he go on too far to find a grave,
Mostly alone he goes.

Even he, who stood where I had
    found him,
On high with fire all round him,
Who moved along the molten west,
And over the round hill's crest
That seemed half ready with him to
    go down,

Flame-bitten and flame-cleft,
As if there were to be no last thing
    left
Of a nameless unimaginable town,—
Even he who climbed and vanished
    may have taken
Down to the perils of a depth not
    known,
From death defended though by men
    forsaken,
The bread that every man must eat
    alone;
He may have walked while others
    hardly dared
Look on to see him stand where many
    fell;
And upward out of that, as out of hell,
He may have sung and striven
To mount where more of him shall
    yet be given,
Bereft of all retreat,
To sevenfold heat,—
As on a day when three in Dura
    shared
The furnace, and were spared
For glory by that king of Babylon
Who made himself so great that God,
    who heard,
Covered him with long feathers, like
    a bird.

Again, he may have gone down easily,
By comfortable altitudes, and found,
As always, underneath him solid
    ground
Whereon to be sufficient and to stand
Possessed already of the promised
    land,
Far stretched and fair to see:
A good sight, verily,
And one to make the eyes of her who
    bore him
Shine glad with hidden tears.
Why question of his ease of who before him,
In one place or another where they
    left
Their names as far behind them as
    their bones,

And yet by dint of slaughter, toil and
    theft,
And shrewdly sharpened stones,
Carved hard the way for his ascend-
    ency
Through deserts of lost years?
Why trouble him now who sees and
    hears
No more than what his innocence re-
    quires,
And therefore to no other height as-
    pires
Than one at which he neither quails
    nor tires?
He may do more by seeing what he
    sees
Than others eager for iniquities;
He may, by seeing all things for the
    best,
Incite futurity to do the rest.

Or with an even likelihood,
He may have met with atrabilious eyes
The fires of time on equal terms and
    passed
Indifferently down, until at last
His only kind of grandeur would have
    been,
Apparently, in being seen.
He may have had for evil or for
    good
No argument; he may have had no
    care
For what without himself went any-
    where
To failure or to glory, and least of all
For such a stale, flamboyant miracle;
He may have been the prophet of an
    art
Immovable to old idolatries;
He may have been a player without a
    part,
Annoyed that even the sun should
    have the skies
For such a flaming way to advertise;
He may have been a painter sick at
    heart
With Nature's toiling for a new sur-
    prise;

He may have been a cynic, who now,
    for all
Of anything divine that his effete
Negation may have tasted,
Saw truth in his own image, rather
    small,
Forbore to fever the ephemeral,
Found any barren height a good re-
    treat
From any swarming street,
And in the sun saw power superbly
    wasted;
And when the primitive old-fashioned
    stars
Came out again to shine on joys and
    wars
More primitive, and all arrayed for
    doom,
He may have proved a world a sorry
    thing
In his imagining,
And life a lighted highway to the
    tomb.

Or, mounting with infirm unsearching
    tread,
His hopes to chaos led,
He may have stumbled up there from
    the past,
And with an aching strangeness
    viewed the last
Abysmal conflagration of his dreams,—
A flame where nothing seems
To burn but flame itself, by nothing
    fed;
And while it all went out,
Not even the faint anodyne of doubt
May then have eased a painful going
    down
From pictured heights of power and
    lost renown,
Revealed at length to his outlived
    endeavor
Remote and unapproachable for-
    ever;
And at his heart there may have
    gnawed
Sick memories of a dead faith foiled
    and flawed

And long dishonored by the living
    death
Assigned alike by chance
To brutes and hierophants;
And anguish fallen on those he loved
    around him
May once have dealt the last blow to
    confound him,
And so have left him as death leaves
    a child,
Who sees it all too near;
And he who knows no young way to
    forget
May struggle to the tomb unrecon-
    ciled.
Whatever suns may rise or set
There may be nothing kinder for
    him here
Than shafts and agonies;
And under these
He may cry out and stay on horribly;
Or, seeing in death too small a thing
    to fear,
He may go forward like a stoic Roman
Where pangs and terrors in his path-
    way lie,—
Or, seizing the swift logic of a woman,
Curse God and die.

Or maybe there, like many another
    one
Who might have stood aloft and
    looked ahead,
Black-drawn against wild red,
He may have built, unawed by fiery
    gules
That in him no commotion stirred,
A living reason out of molecules
Why molecules occurred,
And one for smiling when he might
    have sighed
Had he seen far enough,
And in the same inevitable stuff
Discovered an odd reason too for
    pride
In being what he must have been by
    laws
Infrangible and for no kind of cause.
Deterred by no confusion or surprise

He may have seen with his mechanic
    eyes
A world without a meaning, and had
    room,
Alone amid magnificence and doom,
To build himself an airy monument
That should, or fail him in his vague
    intent,
Outlast an accidental universe—
To call it nothing worse—
Or, by the burrowing guile
Of Time disintegrated and effaced,
Like once-remembered mighty trees
    go down
To ruin, of which by man may now
    be traced
No part sufficient even to be rotten,
And in the book of things that are
    forgotten
Is entered as a thing not quite worth
    while.
He may have been so great
That satraps would have shivered at
    his frown,
And all he prized alive may rule a
    state
No larger than a grave that holds a
    clown;
He may have been a master of his
    fate,
And of his atoms,—ready as another
In his emergence to exonerate
His father and his mother;
He may have been a captain of a
    host,
Self-eloquent and ripe for prodigies,
Doomed here to swell by dangerous
    degrees,
And then give up the ghost.
Nahum's great grasshoppers were
    such as these,
Sun-scattered and soon lost.

Whatever the dark road he may have
    taken,
This man who stood on high
And faced alone the sky,
Whatever drove or lured or guided
    him,—

A vision answering a faith unshaken,
An easy trust assumed of easy trials,
A sick negation born of weak denials,
A crazed abhorrence of an old condition,
A blind attendance on a brief ambition,—
Whatever stayed him or derided him,
His way was even as ours;
And we, with all our wounds and all our powers,
Must each await alone at his own height
Another darkness or another light;
And there, of our poor self dominion reft,
If inference and reason shun
Hell, Heaven, and Oblivion,
May thwarted will (perforce precarious,
But for our conservation better thus)
Have no misgiving left
Of doing yet what here we leave undone?
Or if unto the last of these we cleave,
Believing or protesting we believe
In such an idle and ephemeral
Florescence of the diabolical,—
If, robbed of two fond old enormities,
Our being had no onward auguries,
What then were this great love of ours to say
For launching other lives to voyage again
A little farther into time and pain,
A little faster in a futile chase
For a kingdom and a power and a Race
That would have still in sight
A manifest end of ashes and eternal night?
Is this the music of the toys we shake
So loud,—as if there might be no mistake
Somewhere in our indomitable will?
Are we no greater than the noise we make
Along one blind atomic pilgrimage

Whereon by crass chance billeted we go
Because our brains and bones and cartilage
Will have it so?
If this we say, then let us all be still
About our share in it, and live and die
More quietly thereby.

Where was he going, this man against the sky?
You know not, nor do I.
But this we know, if we know anything:
That we may laugh and fight and sing
And of our transience here make offering
To an orient Word that will not be erased,
Or, save in incommunicable gleams
Too permanent for dreams,
Be found or known.
No tonic and ambitious irritant
Of increase or of want
Has made an otherwise insensate waste
Of ages overthrown
A ruthless, veiled, implacable foretaste
Of other ages that are still to be
Depleted and rewarded variously
Because a few, by fate's economy,
Shall seem to move the world the way it goes;
No soft evangel of equality,
Safe-cradled in a communal repose
That huddles into death and may at last
Be covered well with equatorial snows—
And all for what, the devil only knows—
Will aggregate an inkling to confirm
The credit of a sage or of a worm,
Or tell us why one man in five
Should have a care to stay alive

While in his heart he feels no vio-
     lence
Laid on his humor and intelligence
When infant Science makes a pleas-
     ant face
And waves again that hollow toy, the
     Race;
No planetary trap where souls are
     wrought
For nothing but the sake of being
     caught
And sent again to nothing will
     attune
Itself to any key of any reason
Why man should hunger through an-
     other season
To find out why 'twere better late
     than soon
To go away and let the sun and moon
And all the silly stars illuminate
A place for creeping things,
And those that root and trumpet and
     have wings,
And herd and ruminate,
Or dive and flash and poise in rivers
     and seas,
Or by their loyal tails in lofty trees
Hang screeching lewd victorious
     derision
Of man's immortal vision.
Shall we, because Eternity records
Too vast an answer for the time-born
     words
We spell, whereof so many are dead
     that once
In our capricious lexicons
Were so alive and final, hear no
     more
The Word itself, the living word
That none alive has ever heard
Or ever spelt,
And few have ever felt
Without the fears and old surrender-
     ings
And terrors that began
When Death let fall a feather from
     his wings
And humbled the first man?
Because the weight of our humility,

Wherefrom we gain
A little wisdom and much pain,
Falls here too sore and there too
     tedious,
Are we in anguish or complacency,
Not looking far enough ahead
To see by what mad couriers we are
     led
Along the roads of the ridiculous,
To pity ourselves and laugh at
     faith
And while we curse life bear it?
And if we see the soul's dead end in
     death,
Are we to fear it?
What folly is here that has not yet
     a name
Unless we say outright that we are
     liars?
What have we seen beyond our sun-
     set fires
That lights again the way by which
     we came?
Why pay we such a price, and one
     we give
So clamoringly, for each racked empty
     day
That leads one more last human hope
     away,
As quiet fiends would lead past our
     crazed eyes
Our children to an unseen sacrifice?
If after all that we have lived and
     thought,
All comes to Nought,—
If there be nothing after Now,
And we be nothing anyhow,
And we know that,—why live?
'Twere sure but weaklings' vain
     distress
To suffer dungeons where so many
     doors
Will open on the cold eternal
     shores
That look sheer down
To the dark tideless floods of Noth-
     ingness
Where all who know may drown.

                                        1916

MR. FLOOD'S PARTY *

Old Eben Flood, climbing alone one night
Over the hill between the town below
And the forsaken upland hermitage
That held as much as he should ever know
On earth again of home, paused warily.
The road was his with not a native near;
And Eben, having leisure, said aloud,
For no man else in Tilbury Town to hear:

"Well, Mr. Flood, we have the harvest moon
Again, and we may not have many more;
The bird is on the wing, the poet says,
And you and I have said it here before.
Drink to the bird." He raised up to the light
The jug that he had gone so far to fill,
And answered huskily: "Well, Mr. Flood,
Since you propose it, I believe I will."

Alone, as if enduring to the end
A valiant armor of scarred hopes outworn,
He stood there in the middle of the road
Like Roland's ghost winding a silent horn.
Below him, in the town among the trees,
Where friends of other days had honored him,
A phantom salutation of the dead
Rang thinly till old Eben's eyes were dim.

Then, as a mother lays her sleeping child
Down tenderly, fearing it may awake,
He set the jug down slowly at his feet
With trembling care, knowing that most things break;
And only when assured that on firm earth
It stood, as the uncertain lives of men
Assuredly did not, he paced away,
And with his hand extended paused again:

"Well, Mr. Flood, we have not met like this
In a long time; and many a change has come
To both of us, I fear, since last it was
We had a drop together. Welcome home!"
Convivially returning with himself,
Again he raised the jug up to the light;
And with an acquiescent quaver said:
"Well, Mr. Flood, if you insist, I might.

"Only a very little, Mr. Flood—
For auld lang syne. No more, sir; that will do."
So, for the time, apparently it did,
And Eben evidently thought so too;
For soon amid the silver loneliness
Of night he lifted up his voice and sang,
Secure, with only two moons listening,
Until the whole harmonious landscape rang—

"For auld lang syne." The weary throat gave out,
The last word wavered; and the song being done,
He raised again the jug regretfully
And shook his head, and was again alone.
There was not much that was ahead of him,
And there was nothing in the town below—

Where strangers would have shut the
    many doors
That many friends had opened long
    ago.
                    1920

THE MILL *

The miller's wife had waited long,
    The tea was cold, the fire was dead;
And there might yet be nothing
    wrong
    In how he went and what he said:
"There are no millers any more,"
    Was all that she had heard him
    say;
And he had lingered at the door
    So long that it seemed yesterday.

Sick with a fear that had no form
    She knew that she was there at
    last;
And in the mill there was a warm
    And mealy fragrance of the past.
What else there was would only
    seem
    To say again what he had meant;
And what was hanging from a beam
    Would not have heeded where she
    went.

And if she thought it followed her,
    She may have reasoned in the
    dark
That one way of the few there were
    Would hide her and would leave
    no mark:
Black water, smooth above the weir
    Like starry velvet in the night,
Though ruffled once, would soon
    appear
    The same as ever to the sight.
               1919, 1920

DEMOS *

I

All you that are enamored of my
    name
    And least intent on what most I
    require,
    Beware; for my design and your
    desire,
Deplorably, are not as yet the same.
Beware, I say, the failure and the
    shame
    Of losing that for which you
    now aspire
    So blindly, and of hazarding
    entire
The gift that I was bringing when I
    came.

Give as I will, I cannot give you sight
    Whereby to see that with you
    there are some
    To lead you, and be led. But
    they are dumb
Before the wrangling and the shrill
    delight
    Of your deliverance that has not
    come,
And shall not, if I fail you—as I
    might.

II

So little have you seen of what awaits
    Your fevered glimpse of a de-
    mocracy
    Confused and foiled with an
    equality
Not equal to the envy it creates,
That you see not how near you are
    the gates
    Of an old king who listens fear-
    fully
    To you that are outside and are
    to be
The noisy lords of imminent estates.

Rather be then your prayer that you
    shall have
    Your kingdom undishonored.
    Having all,

See not the great among you
    for the small,
But hear their silence; for the few
    shall save
    The many, or the many are to
        fall—
Still to be wrangling in a noisy grave.
                1919, 1920

THE MAN WHO DIED TWICE *

If I had not walked aimlessly up town
That evening, and as aimlessly
    walked back,
My glance had not encountered then,
    if ever,
The caps and bonnets of a singing
    group
That loudly fought for souls, and was
    at first
No more than a familiar spot of sound
And color in a long familiar scene;
And even at that, if an oblique per-
    suasion
Had not withheld me and inveigled
    me
To pause, I should have passed as
    others did,
Never to guess that while I might
    have touched him,
Fernando Nash was beating a bass
    drum
And shouting Hallelujah with a
    fervor
At which, as I remember, no man
    smiled.

Not having seen him for so many
    years,
And seeing him now almost as one
    not there
Save in remembrance or imagination,
I made of his identity, once achieved,
The ruin of a potential world-shaker—

For whom the world, which had for
    twenty years
Concealed him and reduced him, had
    not shaken.
Here were the features, and to some
    degree
The massive aggregate of the whole
    man,
Where former dominance and author-
    ity
Had now disintegrated, lapsed, and
    shrunken
To an inferior mystery that had yet
The presence in defeat. At a first
    view,
He looked a penitent Hercules, none
    too long
Out of a hospital. But seeing him
    nearer,
One read where manifest havoc must
    for years
Have been at work. What havoc, and
    what work,
I partly guessed; for I had known
    before
That he had always been, apart from
    being
All else he was, or rather along with
    it,
The marked of devils—who must have
    patiently
And slowly crucified, for subtle
    sport,
This foiled initiate who had seen and
    felt
Meanwhile the living fire that mortal
    doors
For most of us hold hidden. This I
    believe,
Though some, with more serenity
    than assurance,
May smile at my belief and wish me
    well.
Puzzled, I waited for a word with
    him;
And that was how I came to know all
    this
That I should not have known, so he
    averred,

But for a memory that survived in him
That I had never yelped at him with others,
Who feared him, and was not among the biters,
Who, in the years when he was dangerous
Had snapped at him until he disappeared
Into the refuge of remoter streets
And partly was forgiven. I was grateful—
Assuring him, as adroitly as I might,
That had he written me down among the biters,
I should have mourned his error. "Let them go;
They were so near forgotten," he said once,
Up there in his gaunt hall-room not long after,
"That memory now becomes a punishment
For nourishing their conceit with my contempt
As once I did. What music have they made
So different in futility since then
That one should hear of it? I make a music
That you can hear all up and down Broadway.
Glory to God! Mine are the drums of life—
After those other drums. I had it— once.
They knew I had it, and they hated me
For knowing just what they had. I had it—once!"
At that his eyes glowed and body shook,
And it was time to go. Fernando Nash,
I saw, would not be long in going farther.
The rough resentful egoist I had known

Was now a shell. The giant had been reduced;
And the old scorn that once had been his faith
Was now a sacrificial desperation.

A year before I found him in the street
Pounding a drum and shouting for the lost,
He had for a long time, from his account,
Inhabited the Valley of the Shadow—
A region where so many become so few
To know, that each man there believes himself
In his peculiar darkness more alone
Than any other. However that may have been,
Fernando Nash's darkness we may grant
Was dark enough, and as peculiar, surely,
As all those who had bitten him would have had it.
I was not one of them, though I fear now
That acquiescence was a larger part
Than he conceived in me of kindliness;
And I should not have thought him outwardly
Much given to soliciting, in those days,
Attention any softer than respect—
Which was not always, or by those who feared him,
Conferred without a sure and small alloy
Of hate, that made the giver and gift alike
A negligible mildew to Fernando,
In whose equipment of infirmities
A place that might have held a little envy
Was overfilled with scorn. Out of his realm,

And only with a tinkler's apprehen-
sion
Of what those unproved opuses of his
Were like to do when they began to
sing,
There was no reason in eternity
For me to be distressed at his assur-
ance
That they were all immortal. Who
was I,
A hewer of wood, to say that they
were not,
Or to be disaffected if they should
be?
To-day I cannot tell you what was in
them,
Nor shall to-morrow know; for they
are now,
As ashes, mute as ashes. Whether he
found
Their early glory to be going out,
Or whether in one last fury against
fate
He made an end of them, as after-
wards
He would have made an end of other
relics,
I do not know. The most he ever told
me
Later about them was that they were
dead,
And how they died, and how much
better it was
For them to be where dead things
ought to be—
Adding at once, that I be not mis-
taken,
That he had known himself to be no
liar
The while he praised them. It was not
for them
That he fed scorn to envy in those
days,
Nor out of them so much as out of
him
That envy grew. "They knew I had it
—once,"
He said; and with a scowl said it
again,

Like a child trying twice the bitter
taste
Of an unpalatable medicine;
"They knew I had it—once! Do you
remember
What an upstanding Ajax I was then?
And what an eye I had? I scorched
'em with it.
I scared 'em; and they knew I was a
giant.
I knew it, also; and if I had known
One other thing, I should have gone
down then
Upon my knees for strength—I who
believed
Myself to be secure. They knew a
little,
But they knew nothing of what I
know now.
A year before you found what's left
of me,
That evening in the street, I should
have said
My way was blank and ruinous to the
end,
But there was more to be, Glory to
God!
There was to be a more revealing end
Than that—an end that once had
been for me
The bitterest end of all—and is not so.
For in the music I have heard since
then
There are the drums of life. Glory to
God!
I had it—once."

So much of him was gone,
That I would hear no more. All the
way home,
The restive exultation in his eyes
And in his bearing, altered and sub-
dued,
Was like that of a dead friend out of
hell,
Humble, and hardly more than half
assured
Of even his respite. There may have
been a giant,

If he must have it so, but where was
   now
The man whom I remembered and
   was once
Fernando Nash? So much of him was
   gone,
That I should never learn, from what
   remained,
The story of the rest—or so I thought,
All the way home. But there was
   more concealed
Within the shell of him than I sup-
   posed—
More than I know to-day; though
   many a time
Thereafter I went back to him again,
Till I had heard enough to make me
   doubt
The use of doubting, for he had it—
   once.
I had known that, and then for years
   had lost him—
For all those years while he had
   crushed unripe
The grapes of heaven to make a
   wilder wine
Than earth gives even to giants who
   are to live
And still be giants. It may be well for
   men
That only few shall have the grapes
   of heaven
To crush. The grapes of heaven are
   golden grapes,
And golden dregs are the worst dregs
   of all—
Or so Fernando surely would have
   said
A year before.

      A year before I found him,
Pounding a drum and shouting to the
   street,
Fernando Nash heard clocks across
   the town
One midnight, and was forty-five
   years old;
And he was too far sundered from his
   faith

And his ambition, buried somewhere
   together
Behind him to go stumbling back for
   them,
Only to find a shadowy grave that
   held
So little and so much. The barren
   room—
The same in which I sought him a
   year later—
Was not much larger than the iron
   bed
On which he sat; and all there was of
   music
About the place was in a dusty box
Of orchestrations for the janitor,
And in the competent plain face of
   Bach,
Calm in achievement, looking down
   at him
Like an incurious Titan at a worm,
That once in adolescent insolence
Would have believed himself another
   Titan.
Fernando sat with his large heavy
   face
Held forward in his hands and cursed
   his works
Till malediction was a weariness,
And all his makeshift insolence a lie
That only cravens who had trained
   themselves
To fight and had not fought were silly
   enough
To fancy for the truth. No insolence
That he remembered would have
   been sufficient
Without additions and foreseen
   betrayals
To make of him this penitential
   emblem
Of that which he was not. When he
   had called
Himself a worm, another worm
   turned at once
Within his heart and bit him; and
   just then
The candid face of one that hereto-
   fore

Had been for him as near to the divine
As any might be, and through all had remained so,
Became as if alive there on the wall,
Transfigured into living recognition,
Wherein there was much wonder and some pity,
And more regret. The Titan, it would seem,
For the first time, and ruinously too late,
And only for a moment interested,
Saw what had happened and could do no more,
Having seen, than to recede ineffably
Aloft into the distance and the dark,
Until he was as high as a large star
That shines on death and life and death in life
Indifferently. Fernando Nash at length
Arose, leaving his bed for his one chair;
And under the sick gleam of one gas-flame,
That had for years to shadowy lodgers given
More noise than light, he sat before a glass
That was more like a round malevolent eye
Filmed with too many derelict reflections,
Appraising there a bleared and heavy face
Where sodden evil should have been a stranger.

"What are you doing here? And who are you?"
He mumbled, with a cloudy consciousness
Of having felt a ghostly blow in the face
From an unseemly mirrored visitor
That he had not invited. "And how long

Have you been on your way, do you suppose,
To come to this? If I remember you
As first you were anointed and ordained,
There was a daemon in you, not a devil,
Who told you then that when you heard those drums
Of death, it would be death to follow them.
You were to trust your daemon and to wait,
And wait, and still to wait. You had it—once.
You had it then—though you had not yet heard it,
Coming as it would have to come some time,
Blown down by choral horns out of a star
To quench those drums of death with singing fire
Unfelt by man before. You knew it then.
You felt it singing down out of the sky
When you were only a small boy at school;
And you knew then that it was all for you,
For you and for the world, that it was coming.
Where is it now? It may be coming yet,
For someone else, but you do not know that;
And that was not what you were meant to know.
O, you poor toad, why could you not have waited?
Why did you have to kill yourself like this?
Why did you let the devil's retinue
That was to be a part be everything,
And so defeat your daemon till your star
Should sing unheard for you whose ears were left

Only for drums and songs of your
    destroyers?
And now even they are gone—all but
    the drums.
You knew that if you waited, they,
    not you,
Should cease—that they should all be
    hushed at last
In that great golden choral fire of
    sound.
'Symphony Number Three. Fernando
    Nash.'
Five little words, like that, if you had
    waited,
Would be enough to-night, you flabby
    scallion,
To put you on the small roll of the
    mighty.
As for the other two, they're in a box
Under the bed; and they will soon be
    nowhere.
You do not have to mourn now over
    them,
For they were only ladders carrying
    you
Up to the half-way place from which
    you fell,
And should have fallen, since you
    were going to fall,
A little faster, and so broken at once
Your neck. Why could you not have
    fallen faster
And saved yourself all this? If you
    had given
The devil a sign to play those drums
    of death
Longer and louder at about that time,
You might be now a carrion more at
    ease
Than you are like to be till you make
    haste.
What else, in God's name, are you
    waiting for?
And where's the use? And while I'm
    asking that,
Where was the use of all your
    prentice-years
Wherein you toiled, while others only
    tinkled,

Till you were master of a new
    machine
That only your invention could have
    built
Or driven? You built it and you let it
    rust.
A fog of doubt that a small constant
    fire
Would have defeated had invisibly
And imperceptibly crept into it,
And made the miracle in it that was
    yours
A nameless toy for the first imbecile
To flout who found it—wherefore
    he'll not find it.
Presently Number One and Number
    Two
Will be beyond all finding. Number
    Three
Will not be farther from his eyes
    to-morrow;
And they'll all be as safe together then
As we should be if we had not been
    born.
The circle fills itself; and there you
    are
Inside it, where you can't crawl out
    of it.
It holds you like a rat in a round
    well,
Where he has only time and room to
    swim
In a ring until he disappears and
    drowns.
If it be true that rats abandon ships
That sail away to sink, praise be to
    rats!
If you were one, you'd never find an-
    other
For shipmate. He would know you
    for a fool,
And therefore dangerous. You're not
    even a rat;
For a good rat will wait for what is
    coming,
Whether it comes or not. You could
    not wait,
Knowing that it must come. You had
    it—once.

You had enough of it to make you
 know,
And were among the sceptred of the
 few
In having it. But where's your sceptre
 now?
You threw it away; and then went
 wallowing
After that other music, and those
 drums—
Assured by more than man's authority
That all you had not then was only
 waiting
To make of that which once was you
 a torch
Of sound and fire that was to flood
 the world
With wonder, and overwhelm those
 drums of death
To a last silence that should have no
 death.
That would have been somewhat the
 way of it,
You somewhat less than eminent dead
 fish,
If you had waited and had been
 content
To let those devils and those devil-
 women
Beat as they would your drums and
 dance and sing
And be invisible. You had followed
 them,
And seen and heard enough of them,
 God knows
Already. Your daemon had a lenience
 then,
And you had not the protest of a
 soul
Between you and your right to stay
 alive;
All which was as it was. But it was so
No longer when you knew it was not
 so,
And that one day a bush might bloom
 with fire
At any trivial hour of inattention,
Whereafter your employment would
 have been

A toil of joy for immortality.
Your drums of death, from which it
 all began,
Would then have been illusions most
 enduring
When most entirely and divinely
 dead;
And you, Fernando Nash, would now
 have been—
But who's alive to know that you're
 alive
To care? Look at that burned out face
 of yours,
You bloated greasy cinder, and say
 who.
Say who's to care, and then say, if you
 will,
Why anyone in a world where there's
 a cockroach,
Should care for you. You insufficient
 phoenix
That has to bake at last in his own
 ashes—
You kicked out, half-hatched bird of
 paradise
That had to die before you broke your
 shell,—
Who cares what you would be if you
 had flown?
A bird that men are never to see
 flying,
Or to hear singing, will not hold them
 long
Away from less ethereal captivations;
Just as a fabulous and almighty fish
That never swam to sight will hardly
 be
For long the unsighted end of their
 pursuit.
Why do you make then such a large
 ado
Over such undefended evidence?
You fat and unsubstantial jelly-fish,
That even your native ocean has dis-
 owned
And thrown ashore, why should men
 ask or care
What else you would have been if
 you had waited?

You crapulous and overgrown sick
lump
Of failure and premeditated ruin,
What do you think you are—one of
God's jokes?
You slunk away from him, still ade-
quate
For his immortal service, and you
failed him;
And you knew all the while what you
were doing.
You damned yourself while you were
still alive.
You bulk of nothing, what do you say
to that?
You paramount whale of lust and
drunkenness,
You thing that was, what do you say
to that?"

No man so near to glory as he was
once
Was ever, I fancied, quite so inglori-
ous
As in his penance—which is here
somewhat
Softened in deference to necessity—
Fernando Nash revealed himself to
me
In passionate reminiscence a year
later.
Occasional strokes, at least, among the
many
That I had counted must have
registered
Luxurious and unmerited flagellation,
Wherein abasement was akin to pride,
If not a part of it. No man so mired
As he was in his narrative, I told him,
Could have such choral gold poured
down from heaven
When he was young. But there he
shook his head
In hopeless pity—not for the doomed,
I saw,
But rather for the sanguine ordinary
That has no devil and so controls
itself,
Having nothing in especial to control.

"Hewers of wood," I said, "and
drawers of water
Will always in their innocence be
insisting
That your enamel of unrighteousness
Is too thick to be real." In his changed
eyes,
Where the old fire was gone, there
was almost
The coming of a smile: "How do you
know?"
He answered, asking. "What have
you done to know?
Where have you been that you should
think you know?
Do you remember when I told you
once
That every sleeve of genius hides a
knife
That will, if necessary, carve a way
Through snakes and oxen? Most that
I said then
Has gone with all the rest, but I keep
this
As a memorial of my retribution.
I wonder if a notion has yet seized
you
To bury the keenest sword you ever
saw
For twenty years in mud, and then go
back
To find what may be left of it. If not,
You need not. Save your curiosity
Two decades of unprofitable conjec-
ture,
And look at me. Look at Fernando
Nash,—
The heir-apparent of a throne that's
ashes,
The king who lost his crown before
he had it,
And saw it melt in hell."

When he had ceased
I could almost have heard those drums
of death
Pounding him on to a defeated grave,
Which, had I not by chance encoun-
tered him

Beating another drum for the Lord's glory
There in the street, would have been no man's grave,
Like that of one before him who still wears
The crown he could not lose. I thought of him,
Whose tomb was an obscure and stormy legend,
Sure of how little he had cared for that—
And how much less would this man here have cared
Whether he found a nameless grave, or no grave,
So long as he had left himself alive
Behind him in a world that would have loved him
Only the more for being out of it.
That long orchestral onslaught of redemption
Would have exonerated flesh and folly
And been his everlasting epitaph—
Which time would then have read as variously
As men are various in their ways and means
Of reading. That would have cancelled everything,
And all his earthly debts—or left him willing
To pay them peradventure as they might
Or must be paid. But they had run too long.
His birthright, signed away in fettered sloth
To the most ingenious and insatiable
Of usurers, had all vanished; and the more
He might have been a king, the more their greed
Would mock him and his tatters, and abase him;
And his vituperative temporizing
Over a soul in rags would mend no holes.

"But there's a crown that even the lowliest
May learn to wear," he said. "Glory to God!"
And his eyes glittered with an icy joy
That made me hope that he was wearing it.
"Of course we can't forget," he said in answer
To doubt that in my silence may have spoken;
"Yet there is much that we may leave behind,
And there is always more if we go on."

In marking after that the accuracy
Of his minute recount, I found it hard
Not to believe that he remembered all—
Save that which of itself was everything,
Or once had been so. There before the mirror,
That bitter midnight when he heard the clocks,
There was not much forgetting; and since then
Only one year was gone. Before that glass
He must have sat for more than a long hour,
Hurling the worst of his vocabulary
At his offending image. "Now you have learned
A part of what you are," he told his face,
"And you may say whatever occurs to you
As an addendum. You deficient swine,
Where do you see the best way out of it?
You are not crazy enough to cut your throat;
You are not solid enough to shoot yourself.
There's always water, but you don't like that;

And you're not sure enough of what
      might happen
If you should inadvertently have
      swallowed
A few small pills. But there's another
      way—
A longer and a more monotonous one,
Yet one that has no slight ascendency
Over the rest; for if you starve to
      death,
Maybe the God you've so industri-
      ously
Offended in most ways accessible
Will tell you something; and if you
      live again
You may attain to fewer discrepan-
      cies
In less within you that you may
      destroy.
That's a good way for you to meet
      your doubt,
And show at the same time a rever-
      ence
That's in you somewhere still." And I
      believe,
Though he may well then have
      believed in nothing
More real than a defective destiny,
That it was in him somewhere, as he
      said.
There was a fervor in his execration
That was not only drama; though I
      question
Whether I should have found him
      and his drum
That evening a year after, in the
      street,
If he had not gone farther, while he
      starved,
Into the valley—which had for twenty
      years
Already beguiled and held him. What
      had been
Without this uncompanioned expia-
      tion,
I do not know, and I might never
      have known.
The shape of one more foiled
      obscurity

Might some time as a cadaver have
      ensured
A massive and unusual exhibition
Of God's too fallible image—and no
      more.
Though some had wondered idly, and
      they might,
Why the defeated features of a giant
Should have been moulded so im-
      periously
To be the mask of frailty in oblivion,
None would have rated such a
      scrapped utensil
As more than common, or uncommon,
      waste;
None would have guessed what
      violent fire had once,
In such a cracked abandoned crucible,
Fused with inseparable obscure alloy
Celestial metal, which would else
      have been
The fabric of a seething instrument
That might have overflowed with
      other fire
Brought falling from ethereal
      distances.
It might, I say, cleaving inveterately
To my conviction that in this man's
      going
More went than when in Venice went
      the last
Authentic wizard, who in his house
      of sound
Hears not the siege of Time. Failing a
      way
To prove that one obscure evangelist,
Beating a drum and shouting for the
      Lord,
Not only might have been (to fill
      again
That weary sieve with wine) but was
      in fact
A giant among fewer than half your
      fingers
Of Jubal's clan, only his mark on me
Will now avail me for the confirma-
      tion
Of more, I fear, than the confirm-
      able—

As he would have foretold. Reverting
    quaintly
And incompatibly with his arrogance
To the weak stings of his inferiors,
And even while dying, he smiled.
    "Poor souls," he said,
"That are born damned, although
    they may be feared
May be forgiven, though hated, and
    then hanged;
Whereas my early colleagues, had
    they known
How soon and surely I was to damn
    myself,
Not only would have ceased their
    fearing me,
But would have loved me—seeing that
    I was doomed.
That midnight—when I cursed myself
    so long—
Roundly and rightly, be it well under-
    stood—
There came a few revealing memories
That set me then to wondering just
    what soft
And anaesthetic language of affection
They would have brought for me if
    they had known
How far I was from all that formerly
Had for so long offended and
    oppressed them.
Poor children!—and they might all
    have been happy
If in the place of misapplied crea-
    tion
A more discriminate wisdom had
    supplied
Discrimination—and some humility
Before God's few that are in spite of
    us
Surviving, somehow." And all this to
    me
Was not quite so irrelevant as to
    others
It may at first appear; for the same
    thought
Pursued me always in those other
    days
When I had harmonized ingeniously

Some brief and unoffending cerebra-
    tion
Which, had it been one, would have
    been a song.
To some persuasion sharper than
    advice
I must have yielded slowly and at last
Let fall my lyre into the fearsome
    well
Of truth, hearing no protest from
    below;
Thereby surviving bitterness to indite
This tale of one who foundered in a
    slough
More fearsome, and lost there a
    mightier lyre.

He was not humble, this Fernando
    Nash;
Yet while he may have ministered on
    occasion
To a discreet humility in others,
I doubt if in the scorn he flung to us,
Mostly in silence, his preoccupation
Saw crumbs of any nurture less
    assuaging
Than wholesome and unfrosted
    honesty;
Albeit his arrogance may have merited
The few vindictive nippings that
    amazed
As much as they annoyed, and would
    have seemed
Allegiance, had their negligible
    venom
Been isolated from another virus,
Which later was to be a leprosy
Of self-contempt attending revelation.

When he had heard the last stroke of
    those clocks,
And called himself again the last hard
    name
That his abundant lexicon released,
He tore those two initial symphonies
Into as many pieces of oblivion
As he had reasons, or believed he
    had,
After those empty years, for their
    extinction.

"They were so 'temerarious' and
	'exotic'
When they were written twenty years
	ago,"
He said, "that all who saw them
	laughed at them—
Not seeing with me that they would
	be to-day
About as temerarious and exotic
As Händel's hat. They were good
	harbingers,
But were they living they would not
	be mine;
They were not what it was that I was
	doing
The while I did them. Many, if they
	were theirs,
Would eat their ears for joy, but
	they're not theirs,
Or mine. Glory to God, they're no-
	where now.
They were not mine; they were not
	yet the vintage;
Though I should have enjoyed, when
	I was young,
The taste of them. But they were not
	the wine
To fill my cup, and now it doesn't
	matter."

There was for some time an obscurity
For me in such a reasoning, but I
	learned,
And I have striven loyally to believe
That he did well—sure that he did
	not well
In going down those dark stairs again
	that night
For the beginning of a last debauch
That was to be a prelude, as he put it,
Wincing in reminiscence, for a fugue
Of ravening miseries and recrimina-
	tions
Assembling in remorseful exposition
That was to be remorseless and
	infernal
Before they were devouring one an-
	other
In a malicious fantasy more infernal,

And richer in dissonance and involu-
	tion
Than all his dreams together had
	heretofore
Aspired or dared to be. When half-
	way down
The second of those four forbidding
	stairways,
He heard those drums again, and on
	his face
He felt with more resentment than
	alarm
A touch of warning, like a chilly wind
Within a tomb. "You are too late,"
	he said,
Holding his heavy jaws harder
	together;
"And you have come too many times
	before."
Then he went grimly down and out
	of doors,
And was alone there in a lonely street
That led where soon he might not be
	so lonely,
Or so severe in his particulars.

After three weeks that would have
	relegated
A village blacksmith or a stevedore
Of mortal average to a colder sleep
Than has a waking, he awoke one
	day
Late in the afternoon, miraculously
In bed again and wondering, as
	before,
How this time he had got there. Look-
	ing up,
He met the face of Bach upon the
	wall,
Who bowed at him, gravely but not
	unkindly;
And he, not yet alive to what was
	coming,
And not to be defective in attention
To a great master, bowed acknowledg-
	ment;
Whereat the salutations were
	repeated,
And there was a preparatory silence,

Heavy with strangeness and
   expectancy,
Which would have been a monitory
   dread—
But for the master's nod of satisfaction
And interest in the coming through a
   keyhole
Of a slow rat, equipped with evening
   dress,
Gold eye-glasses, and a conductor's
   wand,
Soon followed by a brisk and long
   procession
Of other rats, till more than seventy
   of them,
All dressed in black and white, and
   each of them
Accoutred with his chosen instrument,
Were ranged in order on the footworn
   carpet
That lay between Fernando and the
   door.
Having no chairs, they stood erect and
   ready,
And having made obeisance to the
   master
Upon the wall, who signified his
   pleasure,
And likewise to the man upon the
   bed,
They played with unforeseen
   solemnity
The first chords of the first rat
   symphony
That human ears had heard. Baffled
   and scared,
Fernando looked at Bach, who
   nodded slowly,
And, as he fancied, somewhat
   ominously;
And still the music sounded, weird
   but firm,
And the more fearful as it forged
   along
To a dark and surging climax, which
   at length
Broke horribly into coarse and
   unclean laughter

That rose above a groaning of the
   damned;
And through it all there were those
   drums of death,
Which always had been haunting
   him from childhood.
Without a formal ending, or any sign
That there was ever to be an end, the
   rats
Danced madly to the long cacophony
They made, and they made faces at
   Fernando
The while they danced—till one of
   them, the leader,
Bowed mockingly, and vanished
   through the keyhole,
As he had come; and after him went
   others,
Each with a leering courtesy as he
   went,
Till more than seventy of them
   disappeared,
Leaving their auditor lying there
   alone
In a cold sweat, while his impassive
   master
Frowned, shook his head, and was
   again a picture.

Fernando Nash, deploring afterwards
This innovation of orchestral rats
As a most arbitrary intermezzo
Between the sordid prelude that was
   over
And the infernal fugue that was to
   come,
Smiled wearily, and shrugged his
   heavy shoulders,
Like one who would be glad to say
   no more,
Yet must relate the rest to somebody
Before he died. Somebody might
   believe him,
And it was I, who had not bitten
   him
(Achilles' heel was never to be
   cured),
Who might, if anyone might, believe
   him now,

And say to others that he was not
    mad
Through that incessant week of lonely
    torture
Which no food would have eased, and
    through the days
That followed while he starved
    indomitably,
With a cold hope that his long-
    punished heart
Would after time be still. Day after
    day,
And endless night following endless
    night,
There were those miseries and
    recriminations
Devouring one another but never
    dead,
Until one afternoon he lay remem-
    bering
The day when those unusual visitors
Had made a more unusual music for
    him,
And having made it mocked him and
    departed.
Again he looked up at the face of
    Bach,
Considering wearily, with a bleak
    regret
How far those features in their dusty
    frame
Were now from seeing that there was
    in this world
So frail a relic as Fernando Nash,
And how much farther still they were
    from caring,
With more than common care, could
    they have seen him.
Could they have seen him they would
    not have known
What fires had burned in that cadav-
    erous ruin
Below them, or what hopes, or what
    remorse,
Or what regret. For a long time he lay
Aware of action hardly in a finger,
But with a coming wonder of surprise
For a new clearness which had late
    begun

To pierce forbidden chambers long
    obscured
Within him, and abandoned, being so
    dark
And empty that he would not enter
    them—
Fearful of what was not there to be
    found
Should he go there to see. They might
    be dark,
But folly that had made them so had
    kept them so,
Like an indulgent slayer who binds a
    wound
That he has washed with a lethargic
    poison,
And waits at ease with his malignity
For stagnant fury to accumulate
A mortal sloth within—and in so far
As that was in a manner merciful,
Though now it seemed there was to
    be an end
Of even that mercy. After grateful
    darkness,
There was to be the pain of seeing
    too clearly
More than a man so willing to see
    nothing
Should have to see.

         Still motionless, he lay there
Laboring to persuade a lying hope
That this new clarity was the light
    that comes
Before the night comes, and would
    not last long—
Yet knowing that it was not. Like
    shining grain,
Long fouled and hidden by chaff and
    years of dust
In a dark place, and after many
    seasons
Winnowed and cleaned, with sun-
    light falling on it,
His wits were clear again. He had no
    power
To use them, and at first repudiated
The faintest wakening flicker of any
    wish

For use of any such power. But a
short fight
Found his whole fragile armor of
negation
So tattered that it fell away from him
Like time-worn kingly rags of self-
delusion
At the rough touch of the inevitable—
Till he confessed a rueful willingness
To reason that with time and care this
power
Would come, and coming might be
used. He smiled
And closed his eyes, finding an awk-
ward humor
In such an unforeseen enfranchise-
ment
From such a long and thwarting
servitude.
A calm that all his life had been a
stranger
To the confusions that were born
with him
Composed and overpowered him as
he felt,
Enveloping and persuading body and
brain
Together, a cool relief as if warm
wings
Were in the air above him. So there
he lay,
Without a motion or a wish to move,
And with a sense of having only to
rise
And give his hands to life. A grateful
shame
For all his insults to the Holy Ghost
That were forgiven was like an
anodyne
Laid on a buried wound somewhere
within him,
Deeper than surgeons go; and a vast
joy,
Which broke and swept and covered
him like a sea
Of innocence, leaving him eager as a
child
That has outlived experience and
remembers

Only the golden moment as it
flows,
Told him in silence that was more
than speech
That after passion, arrogance and
ambition,
Doubt, fear, defeat, sorrow and
desperation,
He had wrought out of martyrdom
the peace
That passeth understanding. Still he
lay there
Smiling to think how soon those bur-
rowing teeth
Which he had felt within him for so
long
Would cease their famished gnawing
at his heart
Which after all the many prolonged
assaults
It had survived was toiling loyally,
With only an uncertain fire to drive
it;
And still he would not move. There
would be time
For all things in their order. He was
hungry—
Hungry beyond a longer forced
endurance,
But in this new unwillingness not to
live,
No longer forced, there was a grate-
fulness
Of infinite freedom and humility,
After a bondage of indignant years
And evil sloth; and there was in this
calm,
Which had unlooked for been so long
in coming,
A balanced wealth of debts and
benefits
Vaster than all ambition or achieve-
ment.
Hereafter it would be enough to
serve,
And let the chosen shine.

So there he lay,
Luxuriating vaguely on the moment

When he should rise and with a
blessed effort
Go down those shadowy stairs again
for food;
And if in his prevision of that moment
He had not lain so long awaiting it,
Those drums of death might oppor-
tunely then
Have stayed an hour the sound of
their approach,
Throbbing as always, and intolerably,
Through stifling clouds of sound that
hid, like smoke
Tumultuous and elusive melodies,
Now for so long imprisoned as no
longer
To be released. Hearing them first,
and faintly,
For once and for once only without
flinching,
He smiled and sighed. Let others, if
they must,
Hear them and follow them. He was
at peace
With them for the first time in
recollection,
And willingly for the future would
remain so.
At last alive, it was enough to serve,
And so to be content where God
should call him;
But there must be no haste. His fires
were low,
And too much fuel might yet extin-
guish them.
At first he must be frugal with his
coals,
If only for the peril of too much com-
fort
Given at once, and without more
atonement.
So arrogant in his new humility
Was he becoming, and so chary was
he
Of exultation, that to break his fast
With no excess of zeal he planned a
fare
That would have saddened Simeon on
his pillar;

And he might soon have been in
search of it,
Had not another silence, like a blow
That somehow stunned him to clair-
voyant awe,
Held him as if mysterious hands had
bound him
With cords he could not see. Now he
could hear
Those drums again, and they were
coming nearer,
Still muffled within the same un-
yielding cloud
Of sound and fire, which had some-
where within it
A singing flame that he might not for
long
Endure, should such a mocking hour
as this
Be the one hour of all when after
years
Of smouldering it should leap at him
and scorch him.
He felt his fingers clutching hungrily
At nothing, as the fingers of one
drowning
Would clutch at seaweed floating
where he sank;
And he could feel the pounding of
those drums
Like iron upon the fibre of his brain.
His feeble heart was leaping, and a
cold
Invisible hand was heavy on his
throat—
As if in mercy, if it need be so,
To strangle him there before he knew
too soon
What he must know too late.

                              Now it was fear,
Not peace, that falling on him like
a wave,
Covered and overwhelmed him; it was
fear,
Not peace, that made him cold and
left him trembling
After the cold had passed. The coming drums

Were like the vanguard of a Juggernaut
Approaching slowly through a rolling cloud
Of fiery sound that was anon to burst
And inundate him with an ecstasy
Of mad regret before those golden wheels
Behind should crush him. He could only wait,
Therefore, and in his helplessness be seared
With his own lightning. When the music leapt
Out of that fiery cloud and blinded him,
There would be recognition for a moment,
And then release. So his prophetic fancy,
Smiting him with deceit, foresaw the blow,
Not seeing what other shafts of doom and mercy
There are from which an injured God may choose
The one or many that in his exigence
His leisure may affect. Seldom it is
The mightier moments of necessity
That we can see are coming come to us
As we have seen them. Better or worse for us,
Anticipation waits upon surprise;
And though Fernando Nash in his exhaustion
Prayed now for that cold hand upon his throat
To close and have it over, no cold hand
Was there to close. Now there was nothing for him
But to lie still and hear those coming drums,
Muffled as always in a smoky cloud
Of burning sound that in a moment more
Would burst above him into flaming rain

That once he would have welcomed on his knees,
Unspeakably; and so he might have done
Could he have waited with his inner doors
Unbarred to the celestial messengers
Who may have come and gone a score of times,
Only to find again, and still again,
That he was absent on another journey
Into the dismal valley of the shadow
That was to be his home. But that was over.
They had not found him then. He had not waited.
Failing a willingness to be assured
That in so doing he would have left by now
The worst of a light burden far behind him
And found the rest to be Olympian gold,
He had impawned it all for mouldy pottage.

Telling me that, he sighed and shut his teeth,
And with a mortal smile shook his large head
At me before he went back to those drums.
They were not going to sound, as it appeared,
Their long approach for ever, but were soon
To cease, and only intermittently
Be heard again till choral gold came down
Out of a star to quench and vanquish them
With molten glory. Trembling there alone,
He knew that there would now be falling on him
The flaming rain he feared, or the one shaft

Of singing fire that he no longer
    feared—
At which that hand might close upon
    his throat
Till in oblivion there might then be
    peace;
And so at first there was—if there be
    peace
In the complete oblivion of achieve-
    ment.
Instead of bursting as he prayed it
    might,
And ending him with one destroying
    blast
Of unendurable fulfilment, slowly
And imperceptibly that cloud of
    sound
Became a singing mist, which, having
    melted,
Revealed a fire that he had always
    felt,
But never known before. No light-
    ning shaft
Of blinding and immediate dissolu-
    tion
Was yet impending: there was only
    joy,
And a vast wonder that all this had
    been
So near him for so long. Smiling and
    still,
He listened gratefully. It had come at
    last;
And those far sent celestial messengers
That he had for so long a time denied
Had found him now. He had
    offended them,
He had insulted and forsaken them,
And he was not forsaken. They had
    come,
And in their coming had remembered
    only
That they were messengers, who like
    himself
Had now no choice; and they were
    telling him this
In the last language of mortality,
Which has no native barrier but the
    grave.

Now it was theirs to sing and his to
    wear
The glory, although there was a part-
    nership
Somewhere that a surviving grace in
    him
Remembered; for though the star
    from which they came
Shone far within the dark infinity
That was himself, he had not made it
    shine—
Albeit he may have wrought more
    notably
Than might another for its extin-
    guishment.

But there was time for not much more
    of that
Than a bewildered smile of acquies-
    cence.
The quivering miracle of architecture
That was uprising lightly out of
    chaos,
And out of all the silence under time,
Was a gay temple where the Queen
    of Life
And her most loyal minions were
    protracting
Melodious and incessant festival
To the least lenient of divinities.
Joy, like an infinite wine, was every-
    where,
Until it proved itself at last a languor,
Now less engrossed with festive
    pageantry
Than with an earth-born sensuous
    well-being
Which in the festive pageant was
    divine.
Of all the many of those who danced
    and sang
And celebrated, there was none to
    note
A silent entrance of the most abhorred
And oldest of all uninvited strangers—
A lean and slinking mute with a
    bassoon,
Who seized attention when a languid
    hush

Betrayed a perilous rift of weariness
Where pleasure was not joy, and blew
     a tune
Of hollow triumph on a chilly reed
From which all shrank. The tumult
     after that
Was an unprized expenditure of
     beauty
Awaiting doom. It was awaiting also
The faint approach of slow, infernal
     drums
That were not long in coming, bring-
     ing with them
A singing horde of demons, men and
     women,
Who filled the temple with offensive
     yells
And sang to flight the frightened wor-
     shippers.

Fearing to think, he lay as one secure
So long as he lay motionless. If he
     moved
It might be only to plunge down
     again
Into a more chaotic incoherence
And a more futile darkness than
     before.
There was no need of moving, and no
     need
Of asking; for he knew, as he had
     known
For years, unheard, that passionate
     regret
And searching lamentation of the
     banished,
Who in abandoned exile saw below
     them
The desecrated lights of a domain
Where they should walk no more.
          Inaudible
At first, he knew it only as a presence
Intangible, but he knew that it was
     there;
And as it went up slowly to the stars
Carrying all the sorrow of man with
     it,
He trembled that he should so long
     have been

So near to seizing immortality.
Well, here it was. And while he
     might have died
If it had ceased, he would have been
     as one
Who cared no more, having had
     everything,
Where there was no more caring. But
     he knew
That he was not yet dead, and that
     the rest
Would soon be coming. When the
     voices fell,
He knew that through them he
     should hear those drums
Again, but he was not afraid of them.
They were his drums, and the far
     sound of riot
Below there in the gloom was also
     his.
It was all his to give. "Poor fool," he
     thought;
"Praise God you are a fool, and call
     it yours."
And he lay tranquil through another
     silence.

Though he condemned the specious
     tyranny
Of illustrations and explicit schemes,
He kept in his creative charnel house
More pictures hidden of the dead and
     dying
Than men should see; and there were
     these among them,
Which he submitted once, reluctantly,
As to a loyal friend who would for-
     give them,
And then forget. Yet I remember
     now
That in the place of languid folly
     flown
To mourn apart, bereft of its illusions,
The desolation of its realities,
There woke amid the splendors that
     were lost
A frantic bacchanale of those
     usurpers,
Who in affronting life with evil rites

Of death, knew not themselves to be
    the dead—
In false authority mistaking riot
And scorn for power, and hell for
    paradise.
Intoxicated by their swift invasion
Whereafter conquest was an easy
    trifle,
And hating the magnificence they
    cursed,
Seeing not the beauty or the use of it,
They soiled with earthy feet the
    shining floor
Flinging the dregs of their
    debaucheries
From crystal cups against the gleam-
    ing walls
Of Life's immortal house. Too
    ignorant
Of where they were to be afraid to
    know,
They shrieked and sang in shrill
    delirium
With vicious ecstasy for louder
    drums—
Till, crowning insolence with infamy,
They must have wearied God—who,
    pitying them,
Smote with avenging trumpets into
    silence
All but those drums of death, which,
    played by Death
Himself, were beating sullenly alone.

They ceased, and after stillness in
    which time
And space, together perishing, were
    no more
To him than indecisions that were
    gone,
Far off there was a murmur and a
    stirring
Of liberation, and a marching hymn
Sang of a host returning. All the
    banished
Who had been driven from the house
    of life
To wander in the valley of the
    shadow

Were sounding as they came in
    chastened order
The praise of their deliverance and
    return.
A singing voice that gathered and
    ascended
Filled the vast dome above them till
    it glowed
With singing light that seemed at first
    eternal,
But was at first not so. There were
    those drums
Again, to frustrate with a last
    intrusion
The purifying and supreme festival
Of life that had returned and in its
    house
Was daring to be free. But freedom
    wavered
Out of the voices that were praising
    it;
And while it wavered, the lean hand
    of Death
Beat with a desperate malevolence,
More sinister in its evil empti-
    ness
Than when that carnal chorus of the
    dead
With corybantic and infatuate glee
Had howled it out of hearing—till
    once more
There were those golden trumpets,
    and at last
There was that choral golden over-
    flow
Of sound and fire, which he had
    always heard—
And had not heard before. Now it
    had come,
And had not gone. Nothing had gone
    that came.
All he had known and had not waited
    for
Was his; and having it, he could not
    wait now.
With blinding tears of praise and of
    exhaustion
Pouring out of his eyes and over his
    cheeks,

He groped and tottered into the dark
    hall,
Crying aloud to God, or man, or devil,
For paper—not for food. It may have
    been
The devil who heard him first and
    made of him,
For sport, the large and sprawling
    obstacle
They found there at the bottom of
    the stairs.

A fortnight after that, Fernando Nash
Lay contemplating with a special envy
A screen between him and another
    bed
That would anon be vacant. For some
    time,
So he had learned, the probabilities
Had seen for him a similar depar-
    ture,
But seeing indifferently at the last
    hour
That some residual and peculiar
    service
Awaited the survival of as much
As was remaining of him to survive,
Had left him and abandoned him
    again
To life. The fire of personality,
Still glowing within him, drew
    mysteriously
From those assisting at his resurrec-
    tion
A friendly patience, and a sort of
    wonder
That wore a laughing kindness. With
    a lesion
Like his there would be no more
    golden fire
Brought vainly by perennial
    messengers
For one that would no longer recog-
    nize them,
Or know that they had come. There
    were somewhere
Disfigured outlines of a glory spoiled
That hovered unrevealed and unre-
    membered,

But they were like to those of blind-
    ing jewels
Wrought beyond earth to value be-
    yond earth,
To be defaced and hammered value-
    less
By a sick idiot, and insanely sunk
In darker water than where ships go
    down
Hull-crushed at midnight. When he
    told me that.
He may have had a vision of himself
In his last, starless plunge. "Make a
    swift end
Of what I leave behind," he said to
    me.
"Burn me to ashes; and when that is
    done,
Take me somewhere to sea and let me
    sink,
And fear not for my soul. I have
    found that,
Though I have lost all else. All but
    those drums;
And they are but the last hope of the
    devil.
Mine are the drums of life—and they
    are mine.
You may not like them. All I ask of
    you
Is to believe me when I say to you
That what I had, I had. It was no
    dream
That followed me so long, and found
    me only
To make of me a child that should
    henceforth
Go into streets and beat the drums of
    life.
I make a joyful noise unto the Lord,
But I know it's a noise, and the Lord
    knows it—
Just as he knows that I have told to
    you
Only the truth, and that I had it—
    once.
Fool as I was and remnant as I am,
My prayer will be to you that you
    forget me,

If in your memory there survive a
    doubt
That I was less than you believed I
    was
Till I was chastened. For I swear to
    you
That as I knew the quality, not slight,
Of a young harvest that I would not
    save,
I know that in the fields where kings
    have been
Before me there was never found by
    them
A sheaf more golden than the grain
    I lost
When the Lord smote my field that
    afternoon.
I am not telling you this to salve a
    bruise,
For now the bruise is healed. I shall
    go lame
Because of it, but the Lord's ways are
    strange,
And I am not to suffer; and I believe
The reason for this is that I have not
    lied.
I have not lied to Him in praising
    Him,
Nor more to you in praising what He
    gave me
And in his wisdom took away again.
We cannot measure what the world
    has lost
Until we know the gauge the builders
    use
Who made it. All we know about the
    world
For certain is that it appears to be.
And in so far as I am sure of that
So am I sure that I was once as much
As you believed and others feared I
    was.
I have not drugged a clamoring vanity
With lies that for a little while may
    seem
To sweeten truth. There was no need
    of that;
And God knows now that there is less
    than ever.

Now I can beat my drum and let
    those drums
Of death pound as they will. Once,
    for an hour,
I lived; and for an hour my cup was
    full
With wine that not a hundred, if a
    score,
Have tasted that are told in history.
Having it unconfirmed, I might be
    mad
To-day if a wise God had not been
    kind,
And given me zeal to serve Him with
    a means
That you deplore and pardonably
    distrust.
The dower of ignorance is to distrust
All that it cannot feel, and to be rich
In that which it has not. I can be rich
In all that I have had, and richer still
In this that I have now. Glory to God!
Mine are the drums of life, and
    though I wait
For no more messengers—or for none
    save one,
Who will be coming soon—I had it,
    once.
Not more than once or twice, and
    hardly that,
In a same century will another have
    it,
To know what I have lost. You do not
    know.
I've made for you only a picture of it,
No worse or better than a hundred
    others
Might be of the same thing—all
    mostly trash.
But I have found far more than I have
    lost
And so shall not go mourning. God
    was good
To give my soul to me before I died
Entirely, and He was no more than
    just
In taking all the rest away from me.
I had it, and I knew it; and I failed
    Him.

I did not wait."

  "You could not wait," I told him.
"Instead of moulding you to suit the
  rules,
They made you mostly out of living
  brimstone,
And set you in a somewhat fiery world
Not to be burnt." But there he shook
  his head
And looked at me as he had looked
  before,
Like one who was a little sorry for me.
I had made several entrances already
With my determinism, and always
  failed.
He would have none of it. He was to
  blame,
And it was only right that he should
  lose
What he had won too late. "Why
  pity me?"
He asked strangely, "You see that I'm
  content.
I shall not have to be here very long,
And there's not much that I may do
  for God
Except to praise Him. I shall not
  annoy you,
Or your misguided pity, with my
  evangel,
For you must have yours in another
  dress.
I shall not ask if you believe me wise
In this that I am doing. I do not care.
I'll only ask of you that you believe
What I have told you. For I had it—
  once."

To each his own credulity, I say,
And ask as much. Fernando Nash is
  dead;
And whether his allegiance to the
  Lord
With a bass drum was earnest of
  thanksgiving,
Confusion, penance, or the
  picturesque,
Is not the story. There was in the
  man,

With all his frailties and extrava-
  gances,
The caste of an inviolable distinction
That was to break and vanish only in
  fire
When other fires that had so long
  consumed him
Could find no more to burn; and there
  was in him
A giant's privacy of lone communion
With older giants who had made a
  music
Whereof the world was not impossibly
Not the last note; and there was in
  him always,
Unqualified by guile and unsubdued
By failure and remorse, or by redemp-
  tion,
The grim nostalgic passion of the
  great
For glory all but theirs. And more
  than these,
There was the nameless and authentic
  seal
Of power and of ordained accomplish-
  ment—
Which may not be infallibly forth-
  coming,
Yet in this instance came. So I
  believe,
And shall, till admonition more
  disastrous
Than any that has yet imperilled it
Invalidates conviction. Though at
  first,
And many a time thereafter, my per-
  suasion
May well have paused and halted, I
  believe
To-day that all he told me for the
  truth
Was true—as I believed him long
  ago
To be the giant of his acknowledgment.
Crippled or cursed or crucified, the
  giant
Was always there, and always will be
  there.

For reasons less concealed and more
sufficient
Than words will ever make them, I
believe him
To-day as I believed him while he
died,
And while I sank his ashes in the
sea.

1924

ROBERT FROST
(1875–   )

MENDING WALL *

Something there is that doesn't love
a wall,
That sends the frozen-ground-swell
under it,
And spills the upper boulders in the
sun;
And makes gaps even two can pass
abreast.
The work of hunters is another
thing:
I have come after them and made
repair
Where they have left not one stone
on a stone,
But they would have the rabbit out
of hiding,
To please the yelping dogs. The gaps
I mean,
No one has seen them made or heard
them made,
But at spring mending-time we find
them there.
I let my neighbor know beyond the
hill;
And on a day we meet to walk the
line
And set the wall between us once
again.
We keep the wall between us as we
go.

To each the boulders that have fallen
to each.
And some are loaves and some so
nearly balls
We have to use a spell to make them
balance:
"Stay where you are until our backs
are turned!"
We wear our fingers rough with han-
dling them.
Oh, just another kind of out-door
game,
One on a side. It comes to little more:
There where it is we do not need the
wall:
He is all pine and I am apple orchard.
My apple trees will never get across
And eat the cones under his pines,
I tell him.
He only says, "Good fences make
good neighbors."
Spring is the mischief in me, and I
wonder
If I could put a notion in his head:
"*Why* do they make good neighbors?
Isn't it
Where there are cows? But here there
are no cows.
Before I built a wall I'd ask to know
What I was walling in or walling out,
And to whom I was like to give
offence.
Something there is that doesn't love
a wall,
That wants it down." I could say
"Elves" to him,
But it's not elves exactly, and I'd
rather
He said it for himself. I see him there
Bringing a stone grasped firmly by
the top
In each hand, like an old-stone savage
armed.
He moves in darkness as it seems to
me,
Not of woods only and the shade of
trees.
He will not go behind his father's
saying,

And he likes having thought of it so
  well
He says again, "Good fences make
  good neighbors."

                                    1914

THE BLACK COTTAGE *

We chanced in passing by that after-
  noon
To catch it in a sort of special picture
Among tar-banded ancient cherry
  trees,
Set well back from the road in rank
  lodged grass,
The little cottage we were speaking of,
A front with just a door between two
  windows,
Fresh painted by the shower a velvet
  black.
We paused, the minister and I, to
  look.
He made as if to hold it at arm's
  length
Or put the leaves aside that framed
  it in.
"Pretty," he said. "Come in. No one
  will care."
The path was a vague parting in the
  grass
That led us to a weathered window-
  sill.
We pressed our faces to the pane.
  "You see," he said,
"Everything's as she left it when she
  died.
Her sons won't sell the house or the
  things in it.
They say they mean to come and sum-
  mer here
Where they were boys. They haven't
  come this year.
They live so far away—one is out
  west—

* From *Collected Poems of Robert
Frost.* Copyright, 1930, 1939, by Henry
Holt and Company, Inc. Copyright,
1936, by Robert Frost.

It will be hard for them to keep their
  word.
Anyway they won't have the place
  disturbed."
A buttoned hair-cloth lounge spread
  scrolling arms
Under a crayon portrait on the wall
Done sadly from an old daguerreo-
  type.
"That was the father as he went to
  war.
She always, when she talked about
  war,
Sooner or later came and leaned, half
  knelt
Against the lounge beside it, though I
  doubt
If such unlifelike lines kept power to
  stir
Anything in her after all the years.
He fell at Gettysburg or Fredericks-
  burg,
I ought to know—it makes a differ-
  ence which:
Fredericksburg wasn't Gettysburg, of
  course.
But what I'm getting to is how for-
  saken
A little cottage this has always
  seemed;
Since she went more than ever, but
  before—
I don't mean altogether by the lives
That had gone out of it, the father
  first,
Then the two sons, till she was left
  alone.
(Nothing could draw her after those
  two sons.
She valued the considerate neglect
She had at some cost taught them
  after years.)
I mean by the world's having passed
  it by—
As we almost got by this afternoon.
It always seems to me a sort of
  mark
To measure how far fifty years have
  brought us.

Why not sit down if you are in no
　　haste?
These doorsteps seldom have a visitor.
The warping boards pull out their
　　own old nails
With none to tread and put them in
　　their place.
She had her own idea of things, the
　　old lady.
And she liked talk. She had seen
　　Garrison
And Whittier, and had her story of
　　them.
One wasn't long in learning that she
　　thought
Whatever else the Civil War was for
It wasn't just to keep the States to-
　　gether,
Nor just to free the slaves, though it
　　did both.
She wouldn't have believed those ends
　　enough
To have given outright for them all
　　she gave.
Her giving somehow touched the
　　principle
That all men are created free and
　　equal.
And to hear her quaint phrases—so
　　removed
From the world's view to-day of all
　　those things.
That's a hard mystery of Jefferson's.
What did he mean? Of course the
　　easy way
Is to decide it simply isn't true.
It may not be. I heard a fellow say
　　so.
But never mind, the Welshman got it
　　planted
Where it will trouble us a thousand
　　years.
Each age will have to reconsider it.
You couldn't tell her what the West
　　was saying,
And what the South to her serene be-
　　lief.
She had some art of hearing and yet
　　not

Hearing the latter wisdom of the
　　world.
White was the only race she ever
　　knew.
Black she had scarcely seen, and yel-
　　low never.
But how could they be made so very
　　unlike
By the same hand working in the same
　　stuff?
She had supposed the war decided
　　that.
What are you going to do with such
　　a person?
Strange how such innocence gets its
　　own way.
I shouldn't be surprised if in this
　　world
It were the force that would at last
　　prevail.
Do you know but for her there was a
　　time
When to please younger members of
　　the church,
Or rather say non-members in the
　　church,
Whom we all have to think of nowa-
　　days,
I would have changed the Creed a
　　very little?
Not that she ever had to ask me not
　　to;
It never got so far as that; but the bare
　　thought
Of her old tremulous bonnet in the
　　pew,
And of her half asleep was too much
　　for me.
Why, I might wake her up and startle
　　her.
It was the words 'descended into
　　Hades'
That seemed too pagan to our liberal
　　youth.
You know they suffered from a gen-
　　eral onslaught.
And well, if they weren't true why
　　keep right on

Saying them like the heathen? We
could drop them.
Only—there· was the bonnet in the
pew.
Such a phrase couldn't have meant
much to her.
But suppose she had missed it from
the Creed
As a child misses the unsaid Good-
night,
And falls asleep with heartache—how
should I feel?
I'm just as glad she made me keep
hands off,
For, dear me, why abandon a belief
Merely because it ceases to be
true.
Cling to it long enough, and not a
doubt
It will turn true again, for so it
goes.
Most of the change we think we see
in life
Is due to truths being in and out of
favor.
As I sit here, and oftentimes, I wish
I could be monarch of a desert land
I could devote and dedicate forever
To the truths we keep coming back
and back to.
So desert it would have to be, so
walled
By mountain ranges half in summer
snow,
No one would covet it or think it
worth
The pains of conquering to force
change on.
Scattered oases where men dwelt, but
mostly
Sand dunes held loosely in tamarisk
Blown over and over themselves in
idleness.
Sand grains should sugar in the natal
dew
The babe born to the desert, the sand
storm
Retard mid-waste my cowering cara-
vans—

There are bees in this wall." He
struck the clapboards,
Fierce heads looked out; small bodies
pivoted.
We rose to go. Sunset blazed on the
windows.

1914

THE DEATH
OF THE HIRED MAN *

Mary sat musing on the lamp-flame at
the table
Waiting for Warren. When she heard
his step,
She ran on tip-toe down the darkened
passage
To meet him in the doorway with the
news
And put him on his guard. "Silas is
back."
She pushed him outward with her
through the door
And shut it after her. "Be kind," she
said.
She took the market things from War-
ren's arms
And set them on the porch, then drew
him down
To sit beside her on the wooden steps.
"When was I ever anything but kind
to him?
But I'll not have the fellow back," he
said.
"I told him so last haying, didn't I?
'If he left then,' I said, 'that ended
it.'
What good is he? Who else will har-
bour him
At his age for the little he can do?
What help he is there's no depending
on.
Off he goes always when I need him
most.

* From *Collected Poems of Robert
Frost.* Copyright, 1930, 1939, by Henry
Holt and Company, Inc. Copyright,
1936, by Robert Frost.

'He thinks he ought to earn a little
    pay,
Enough at least to buy tobacco with,
So he won't have to beg and be be-
    holden.'
'All right,' I say, 'I can't afford to pay
Any fixed wages, though I wish I
    could.'
'Someone else can.' 'Then someone
    else will have to.'
I shouldn't mind his bettering himself
If that was what it was. You can be
    certain,
When he begins like that, there's
    someone at him
Trying to coax him off with pocket-
    money,—
In haying time, when any help is
    scarce.
In winter he comes back to us. I'm
    done."

"Sh! not so loud: he'll hear you,"
    Mary said.

"I want him to: he'll have to soon or
    late."

"He's worn out. He's asleep beside the
    stove.
When I came up from Rowe's I found
    him here,
Huddled against the barn-door fast
    asleep,
A miserable sight, and frightening,
    too—
You needn't smile—I didn't recognise
    him—
I wasn't looking for him—and he's
    changed.
Wait till you see."

        "Where did you say he'd been?"

"He didn't say. I dragged him to the
    house,
And gave him tea and tried to make
    him smoke.
I tried to make him talk about his
    travels.
Nothing would do: he just kept nod-
    ding off."

"What did he say? Did he say any-
    thing?"

"But little."

        "Anything? Mary, confess
He said he'd come to ditch the
    meadow for me."

"Warren!"

        "But did he? I just want to know."

"Of course he did. What would you
    have him say?
Surely you wouldn't grudge the poor
    old man
Some humble way to save his self-
    respect.
He added, if you really care to know,
He meant to clear the upper pasture,
    too.
That sounds like something you have
    heard before?
Warren, I wish you could have heard
    the way
He jumbled everything. I stopped to
    look
Two or three times—he made me feel
    so queer—
To see if he was talking in his sleep.
He ran on Harold Wilson—you re-
    member—
The boy you had in haying four years
    since.
He's finished school, and teaching in
    his college.

"Silas declares you'll have to get him
    back.
He says they two will make a team
    for work:
Between them they will lay this farm
    as smooth!
The way he mixed that in with other
    things.
He thinks young Wilson a likely lad,
    though daft
On education—you know how they
    fought
All through July under the blazing
    sun,

Silas up on the cart to build the load,
Harold along beside to pitch it on."

"Yes, I took care to keep well out of
earshot."

"Well, those days trouble Silas like a
dream.
You wouldn't think they would. How
some things linger!
Harold's young college boy's assurance
piqued him.
After so many years he still keeps
finding
Good arguments he sees he might
have used.
I sympathise. I know just how it feels
To think of the right thing to say too
late.
Harold's associated in his mind with
Latin.
He asked me what I thought of Har-
old's saying
He studied Latin like the violin
Because he liked it—that an argument!
He said he couldn't make the boy be-
lieve
He could find water with a hazel
prong—
Which showed how much good school
had ever done him.
He wanted to go over that. But most
of all
He thinks if he could have another
chance
To teach him how to build a load of
hay—"

"I know, that's Silas' one accomplish-
ment.
He bundles every forkful in its place,
And tags and numbers it for future
reference,
So he can find and easily dislodge it
In the unloading. Silas does that
well.
He takes it out in bunches like birds'
nests.
You never see him standing on the
hay

He's trying to lift, straining to lift
himself."

"He thinks if he could teach him that,
he'd be
Some good perhaps to someone in the
world.
He hates to see a boy the fool of books.
Poor Silas, so concerned for other
folk,
And nothing to look backward to with
pride,
And nothing to look forward to with
hope,
So now and never any different."

Part of a moon was falling down the
west,
Dragging the whole sky with it to the
hills.
Its light poured softly in her lap. She
saw
And spread her apron to it. She put
out her hand
Among the harp-like morning-glory
strings,
Taut with the dew from garden bed
to eaves,
As if she played unheard the tenderness
That wrought on him beside her in
the night.
"Warren," she said, "he has come
home to die:
You needn't be afraid he'll leave you
this time."

"Home," he mocked gently.

"Yes, what else but home?
It all depends on what you mean by
home.
Of course he's nothing to us, any more
Than was the hound that came a
stranger to us
Out of the woods, worn out upon the
trail."

"Home is the place where, when you
have to go there,
They have to take you in."

"I should have called it
Something you somehow haven't to
    deserve."

Warren leaned out and took a step or
    two,
Picked up a little stick, and brought it
    back
And broke it in his hand and tossed it
    by.
"Silas has better claim on us you
    think
Than on his brother? Thirteen little
    miles
As the road winds would bring him
    to his door.
Silas has walked that far no doubt
    to-day.
Why didn't he go there? His brother's
    rich,
A somebody—director in the bank."

"He never told us that."

                "We know it though."

"I think his brother ought to help, of
    course.
I'll see to that if there is need. He
    ought of right
To take him in, and might be willing
    to—
He may be better than appearances.
But have some pity on Silas. Do you
    think
If he'd had any pride in claiming kin
Or anything he looked for from his
    brother,
He'd keep so still about him all this
    time?"

"I wonder what's between them."

                    "I can tell you.
Silas is what he is—we wouldn't mind
    him—
But just the kind that kinsfolk can't
    abide.
He never did a thing so very bad.
He don't know why he isn't quite as
    good

As anyone. He won't be made
    ashamed
To please his brother, worthless
    though he is."

"I can't think Si ever hurt anyone."

"No, but he hurt my heart the way
    he lay
And rolled his old head on that sharp-
    edged chair-back.
He wouldn't let me put him on the
    lounge.
You must go in and see what you can
    do.
I made the bed up for him there to-
    night.
You'll be surprised at him—how much
    he's broken.
His working days are done; I'm sure
    of it."

"I'd not be in a hurry to say that."

"I haven't been. Go, look, see for your-
    self.
But, Warren, please remember how it
    is:
He's come to help you ditch the
    meadow.
He has a plan. You mustn't laugh at
    him.
He may not speak of it, and then he
    may.
I'll sit and see if that small sailing
    cloud
Will hit or miss the moon."

                    It hit the moon.
Then there were three there, making
    a dim row,
The moon, the little silver cloud, and
    she.

Warren returned—too soon, it seemed
    to her,
Slipped to her side, caught up her
    hand and waited.

"Warren?" she questioned.

        "Dead," was all he answered.
                        1914

HOME BURIAL *

He saw her from the bottom of the
    stairs
Before she saw him. She was starting
    down,
Looking back over her shoulder at
    some fear.
She took a doubtful step and then
    undid it
To raise herself and look again. He
    spoke
Advancing toward her: "What is it
    you see
From up there always—for I want to
    know."
She turned and sank upon her skirts
    at that,
And her face changed from terrified to
    dull.
He said to gain time: "What is it
    you see,"
Mounting until she cowered under
    him.
"I will find out now—you must tell
    me, dear."
She, in her place, refused him any
    help
With the least stiffening of her neck
    and silence.
She let him look, sure that he wouldn't
    see,
Blind creature; and a while he didn't
    see.
But at last he murmured, "Oh," and
    again, "Oh."

"What is it—what?" she said.

                "Just that I see."

"You don't," she challenged. "Tell me
    what it is."

"The wonder is I didn't see at once.
I never noticed it from here be-
    fore.

I must be wonted to it—that's the
    reason.
But two that do can't live together
    with them."

She moved the latch a little. "Don't—
    don't go
Don't carry it to someone else this
    time.
Tell me about it if it's something hu-
    man.
Let me into your grief. I'm not so
    much
Unlike other folks as your standing
    there
Apart would make me out. Give me
    my chance.
I do think, though, you overdo it a
    little.
What was it brought you up to think
    it the thing
To take your mother-loss of a first
    child
So inconsolably—in the face of love.
You'd think his memory might be
    satisfied—"

"There you go sneering now!"

                "I'm not, I'm not!
You make me angry. I'll come down
    to you.
God, what a woman! And it's come to
    this,
A man can't speak of his own child
    that's dead."

"You can't because you don't know
    how to speak.
If you had any feelings, you that
    dug
With your own hand—how could you?
    —his little grave;
I saw you from that very window
    there,
Making the gravel leap and leap in
    air,
Leap up, like that, like that, and land
    so lightly
And roll back down the mound beside
    the hole.

I thought, Who is that man? I didn't
know you.
And I crept down the stairs and up
the stairs
To look again, and still your spade
kept lifting.
Then you came in. I heard your rum-
bling voice
Out in the kitchen, and I don't know
why,
But I went near to see with my own
eyes.
You could sit there with the stains on
your shoes
Of the fresh earth from your own
baby's grave
And talk about your everyday concerns.
You had stood the spade up against
the wall
Outside there in the entry, for I
saw it."

"I shall laugh the worst laugh I ever
laughed.
I'm cursed. God, if I don't believe
I'm cursed."

"I can repeat the very words you were
saying.
'Three foggy mornings and one rainy
day
Will rot the best birch fence a man
can build.'
Think of it, talk like that at such a
time!
What had how long it takes a birch
to rot
To do with what was in the darkened
parlor.
You *couldn't* care! The nearest friends
can go
With any one to death, comes so far
short
They might as well not try to go at
all.
No, from the time when one is sick to
death,
One is alone, and he dies more alone.

Friends make pretence of following
to the grave,
But before one is in it, their minds
are turned
And making the best of their way
back to life
And living people, and things they
understand.
But the world's evil. I won't have grief
so
If I can change it. Oh, I won't, I
won't!"

"There, you have said it all and you
feel better.
You won't go now. You're crying.
Close the door.
The heart's gone out of it: why keep
it up.
Amy! There's someone coming down
the road!"

"*You*—oh, you think the talk is all. I
must go—
Somewhere out of this house. How
can I make you—"

"If—you—do!" She was opening the
door wider.
"Where do you mean to go? First tell
me that.
I'll follow and bring you back by
force. I *will!*—"

1914

THE ROAD NOT TAKEN *

Two roads diverged in a yellow wood,
And sorry I could not travel both
And be one traveler, long I stood
And looked down one as far as I
could
To where it bent in the undergrowth;

Then took the other, as just as fair,
And having perhaps the better claim,
Because it was grassy and wanted
wear;

* From *Collected Poems of Robert
Frost*. Copyright, 1930, 1939, by Henry
Holt and Company, Inc. Copyright,
1936, by Robert Frost.

Though as for that the passing there
Had worn them really about the same,

And both that morning equally lay
In leaves no step had trodden black.
Oh, I kept the first for another day!
Yet knowing how way leads onto way,
I doubted if I should ever come back.

I shall be telling this with a sigh
Somewhere ages and ages hence:
Two roads diverged in a wood, and
  I—
I took the one less traveled by,
And that has made all the difference.
                                    1915

THE SOUND OF THE TREES *

I wonder about the trees.
Why do we wish to bear
Forever the noise of these
More than another noise
So close to our dwelling place?
We suffer them by the day
Till we lose all measure of pace,
And fixity in our joys,
And acquire a listening air.
They are that that talks of going
But never gets away;
And that talks no less for knowing,
As it grows wiser and older,
That now it means to stay.
My feet tug at the floor
And my head sways to my shoulder
Sometimes when I watch trees sway,
From the window or the door.
I shall set forth for somewhere,
I shall make the reckless choice
Some day when they are in voice
And tossing so as to scare
The white clouds over them on.
I shall have less to say,
But I shall be gone.
                                    1915

STOPPING BY WOODS
ON A SNOWY EVENING *

Whose woods these are I think I
  know.
His house is in the village though;
He will not see me stopping here
To watch his woods fill up with snow.

My little horse must think it queer
To stop without a farmhouse near
Between the woods and frozen lake
The darkest evening of the year.

He gives his harness bells a shake
To ask if there is some mistake.
The only other sound's the sweep
Of easy wind and downy flake.

The woods are lovely, dark and deep,
But I have promises to keep,
And miles to go before I sleep,
And miles to go before I sleep.
                                    1923

FIRE AND ICE *

Some say the world will end in fire,
Some say in ice.
From what I've tasted of desire
I hold with those who favor fire.

But if it had to perish twice,
I think I know enough of hate
To say that for destruction ice
Is also great
And would suffice.
                                    1923

NEW HAMPSHIRE *

I met a lady from the South who said
(You won't believe she said it, but
  she said it):
"None of my family ever worked, or
  had
A thing to sell." I don't suppose the
  work
Much matters. You may work for all
  of me.

I've seen the time I've had to work
    myself.
The having anything to sell is what
Is the disgrace in man or state or na-
    tion.

I met a traveller from Arkansas
Who boasted of his state as beautiful
For diamonds and apples. "Diamonds
And apples in commercial quantities?"
I asked him, on my guard. "Oh yes,"
    he answered,
Off his. The time was evening in the
    Pullman.
"I see the porter's made your bed," I
    told him.

I met a Californian who would
Talk California—a state so blessed,
He said, in climate none had ever
    died there
A natural death, and Vigilance Com-
    mittees
Had had to organize to stock the
    graveyards
And vindicate the state's humanity.
"Just the way Steffanson runs on," I
    murmured,
"About the British Arctic. That's what
    comes
Of being in the market with a cli-
    mate."
I met a poet from another state,
A zealot full of fluid inspiration,
Who in the name of fluid inspiration,
But in the best style of bad salesman-
    ship,
Angrily tried to make me write a
    protest
(In verse I think) against the Volstead
    Act.
He didn't even offer me a drink
Until I asked for one to steady *him*.
This is called having an idea to
    sell.

It never could have happened in New
    Hampshire.

The only person really soiled with
    trade
I ever stumbled on in old New Hamp-
    shire
Was someone who had just come back
    ashamed
From selling things in California.
He'd built a noble mansard roof with
    balls
On turrets like Constantinople, deep
In woods some ten miles from a rail-
    road station,
As if to put forever out of mind
The hope of being, as we say, re-
    ceived.
I found him standing at the close of
    day
Inside the threshold of his open barn,
Like a lone actor on a gloomy stage—
And recognized him through the iron
    grey
In which his face was muffled to the
    eyes
As an old boyhood friend, and once
    indeed
A drover with me on the road to
    Brighton.
His farm was "grounds," and not a
    farm at all;
His house among the local sheds and
    shanties
Rose like a factor's at a trading sta-
    tion.
And he was rich, and I was still a
    rascal.
I couldn't keep from asking impo-
    litely,
Where had he been and what had he
    been doing?
How did he get so? (Rich was under-
    stood.)
In dealing in "old rags" in San Fran-
    cisco.
Oh it was terrible as well could be.
We both of us turned over in our
    graves.

Just specimens is all New Hampshire
    has,
One each of everything as in a show-
    case

Which naturally she doesn't care to
    sell.

She had one President (pronounce
    him Purse,
And make the most of it for better or
    worse.
He's your one chance to score against
    the state).
She had one Daniel Webster. He was
    all
The Daniel Webster ever was or shall
    be.
She had the Dartmouth needed to
    produce him.

I call her old. She has one family
Whose claim is good to being settled
    here
Before the era of colonization,
And before that of exploration even.
John Smith remarked them as he
    coasted by
Dangling their legs and fishing off a
    wharf
At the Isles of Shoals, and satisfied
    himself
They weren't Red Indians but veri-
    table
Pre-primitives of the white race, dawn
    people,
Like those who furnished Adam's
    sons with wives;
However uninnocent they may have
    been
In being there so early in our history.
They'd been there then a hundred
    years or more.
Pity he didn't ask what they were up
    to
At that date with a wharf already
    built,
And take their name. They've since
    told me their name—
Today an honored one in Notting-
    ham.
As for what they were up to more
    than fishing—
Suppose they weren't behaving Puri-
    tanly,

The hour had not yet struck for being
    good,
Mankind had not yet gone on the
    Sabbatical.
It became an explorer of the deep
Not to explore too deep in others'
    business.

Did you but know of him, New
    Hampshire has
One real reformer who would change
    the world
So it would be accepted by two classes,
Artists the minute they set up as
    artists,
Before, that is, they are themselves
    accepted,
And boys the minute they get out of
    college.
I can't help thinking those are tests
    to go by.

And she has one I don't know what to
    call him,
Who comes from Philadelphia every
    year
With a great flock of chickens of rare
    breeds
He wants to give the educational
Advantages of growing almost wild
Under the watchful eye of hawk and
    eagle—
Dorkings because they're spoken of by
    Chaucer,
Sussex because they're spoken of by
    Herrick.

She has a touch of gold. New Hamp-
    shire gold—
You may have heard of it. I had a
    farm
Offered me not long since up Berlin
    way
With a mine on it that was worked for
    gold;
But not gold in commercial quantities.
Just enough gold to make the engage-
    ment rings
And marriage rings of those who
    owned the farm.

What gold more innocent could one
  have asked for?

One of my children ranging after
  rocks
Lately brought home from Andover or
  Canaan
A specimen of beryl with a trace
Of radium. I know with radium
The trace would have to be the
  merest trace
To be below the threshold of com-
  mercial,
But trust New Hampshire not to have
  enough
Of radium or anything to sell.

A specimen of everything, I said.
She has one witch—old style. She
  lives in Colebrook.
(The only other witch I ever met
Was lately at a cut-glass dinner in
  Boston.
There were four candles and four
  people present.
The witch was young, and beautiful
  (new style),
And open-minded. She was free to
  question
Her gift for reading letters locked in
  boxes.
Why was it so much greater when the
  boxes
Were metal than it was when they
  were wooden?
It made the world seem so mysterious.
The S'ciety for Psychical Research
Was cognizant. Her husband was
  worth millions.
I think he owned some shares in Har-
  vard College.)

New Hampshire *used* to have at
  Salem
A company we called the White
  Corpuscles,
Whose duty was at any hour of
  night
To rush in sheets and fool's caps
  where they smelled

A thing the least bit doubtfully per-
  scented
And give someone the Skipper Ire-
  son's Ride.
One each of everything as in a show-
  case.

More than enough land for a speci-
  men
You'll say she has, but there there
  enters in
Something else to protect her from
  herself.
There quality makes up for quantity.
Not even New Hampshire farms are
  much for sale.
The farm I made my home on in the
  mountains
I had to take by force rather than buy.
I caught the owner outdoors by him-
  self
Raking up after winter, and I said,
"I'm going to put you off this farm:
  I want it."
"Where are you going to put me? In
  the road?"
"I'm going to put you on the farm
  next to it."
"Why won't the farm next to it do
  for you?"
"I like this better." It was really better.

Apples? New Hampshire has them,
  but unsprayed,
With no suspicion in stem-end or
  blossom-end
Of vitriol or arsenate of lead,
And so not good for anything but
  cider.
Her unpruned grapes are flung like
  lariats
Far up the birches out of reach of
  man.

A state producing precious metals,
  stones,
And—writings; none of these except
  perhaps
The precious literature in quantity
Or quality to worry the producer

About disposing of it. Do you know,
Considering the market, there are more
Poems produced than any other thing?
No wonder poets sometimes have to *seem*
So much more business-like than business men.
Their wares are so much harder to get rid of.

She's one of the two best states in the Union.
Vermont's the other. And the two have been
Yoke-fellows in the sap-yoke from of old
In many Marches. And they lie like wedges,
Thick end to thin end and thin end to thick end,
And are a figure of the way the strong
Of mind and strong of arm should fit together,
One thick where one is thin and vice versa.
New Hampshire raises the Connecticut
In a trout hatchery near Canada,
But soon divides the river with Vermont.
Both are delightful states for their absurdly
Small towns—Lost Nation, Bungey, Muddy Boo,
Poplin, Still Corners (so called not because
The place is silent all day long, nor yet
Because it boasts a whisky still—because
It set out once to be a city and still
Is only corners, cross-roads in a wood).
And I remember one whose name appeared
Between the pictures on a movie screen
Election night once in Franconia,

When everything had gone Republican
And Democrats were sore in need of cômfort:
Easton goes Democratic, Wilson 4
Hughes 2. And everybody to the saddest
Laughed the loud laugh, the big laugh at the little.
New York (five million) laughs at Manchester,
Manchester (sixty or seventy thousand) laughs
At Littleton (four thousand), Littleton
Laughs at Franconia (seven hundred), and
Franconia laughs, I fear,—did laugh that night—
At Easton. What has Easton left to laugh at,
And like the actress exclaim, "Oh my God" at?
There's Bungey; and for Bungey there are towns,
Whose township's named but without population.
Anything I can say about New Hampshire
Will serve almost as well about Vermont,
Excepting that they differ in their mountains.
The Vermont mountains stretch extended straight;
New Hampshire mountains curl up in a coil.

I had been coming to New Hampshire mountains.
And here I am and what am I to say?
Here first my theme becomes embarrassing.
Emerson said, "The God who made New Hampshire
Taunted the lofty land with little men."
Another Massachusetts poet said,

"I go no more to summer in New Hampshire.
I've given up my summer place in Dublin."
But when I asked to know what ailed New Hampshire,
She said she couldn't stand the people in it,
The little men (it's Massachusetts speaking).
And when I asked to know what ailed the people,
She said, "Go read your own books and find out."
I may as well confess myself the author
Of several books against the world in general.
To take them as against a special state
Or even nation's to restrict my meaning.

I'm what is called a sensibilitist,
Or otherwise an environmentalist.
I refuse to adapt myself a mite
To any change from hot to cold, from wet
To dry, from poor to rich, or back again.
I make a virtue of my suffering
From nearly everything that goes on round me.
In other words, I know wherever I am,
Being the creature of literature I am,
I shall not lack for pain to keep me awake.
Kit Marlowe taught me how to say my prayers:
"Why this is Hell, nor am I out of it."
Samoa, Russia, Ireland I complain of,
No less than England, France and Italy.
Because I wrote my novels in New Hampshire
Is no proof that I aimed them at New Hampshire.

When I left Massachusetts years ago
Between two days, the reason why I sought
New Hampshire, not Connecticut,
Rhode Island, New York, or Vermont was this:
Where I was living then, New Hampshire offered
The nearest boundary to escape across.
I hadn't an illusion in my hand-bag
About the people being better there
Than those I left behind. I thought they weren't.
I thought they couldn't be. And yet they were.
I'd sure had no such friends in Massachusetts
As Hall of Windham, Gay of Atkinson,
Barlett of Raymond (now of Colorado),
Harris of Derry, and Lynch of Bethlehem.
The glorious bards of Massachusetts seem
To want to make New Hampshire people over.
They taunt the lofty land with little men.
I don't know what to say about the people.
For art's sake one could almost wish them worse
Rather than better. How are we to write
The Russian novel in America
As long as life goes so unterribly?
There is the pinch from which our only outcry
In literature to date is heard to come.
We get what little misery we can
Out of not having cause for misery.
It makes the guild of novel writers sick
To be expected to be Dostoievskis
On nothing worse than too much luck and comfort.
This is not sorrow, though; it's just the vapors,
And recognized as such in Russia itself
Under the new régime, and so forbidden.

If well it is with Russia, then feel free
To say so or be stood against the
wall
And shot. It's Pollyanna now or death.
This, then, is the new freedom we
hear tell of;
And very sensible. No state can build
A literature that shall at once be
sound
And sad on a foundation of wellbeing.

To show the level of intelligence
Among us; it was just a Warren
farmer
Whose horse had pulled him short up
in the road
By me, a stranger. This is what he
said,
From nothing but embarrassment and
want
Of anything more sociable to say:
"You hear those hound-dogs sing on
Moosilauke?
Well they remind me of the hue and
cry
We've heard against the Mid-Victo-
rians
And never rightly understood till
Bryan
Retired from politics and joined the
chorus.
The matter with the Mid-Victorians
Seems to have been a man named
John L. Darwin."
"Go 'long," I said to him, he to his
horse.

I knew a man who failing as a farmer
Burned down his farmhouse for the
fire insurance,
And spent the proceeds on a telescope
To satisfy a life-long curiosity
About our place among the infinities.
And how was that for other-worldli-
ness?

If I must choose which I would elevate—
The people or the already lofty mountains,

I'd elevate the already lofty moun-
tains.
The only fault I find with Old New
Hampshire
Is that her mountains aren't quite
high enough.
I was not always so; I've come to be so.
How, to my sorrow, how have I
attained
A height from which to look down
critical
On mountains? What has given me
assurance
To say what height becomes New
Hampshire mountains,
Or any mountains? Can it be some
strength
I feel as of an earthquake in my back
To heave them higher to the morning
star?
Can it be foreign travel in the Alps?
Or having seen and credited a moment
The solid moulding of vast peaks of
cloud
Behind the pitiful reality
Of Lincoln, Lafayette and Liberty?
Or some such sense as says how high
shall jet
The fountain in proportion to the
basin?
No, none of these has raised me to
my throne
Of intellectual dissatisfaction,
But the sad accident of having seen
Our actual mountains given in a
map
Of early times as twice the height
they are—
Ten thousand feet instead of only
five—
Which shows how sad an accident
may be.
Five thousand is no longer high
enough.
Whereas I never had a good idea
About improving people in the world,
Here I am over-fertile in suggestion,
And cannot rest from planning day
or night

How high I'd thrust the peaks in sum-
　　mer snow
To tap the upper sky and draw a flow
Of frosty night air on the vale below
Down from the stars to freeze the dew
　　as starry.

The more the sensibilitist I am
The more I seem to want my moun-
　　tains wild;
The way the wiry gang-boss liked the
　　log-jam.
After he'd picked the lock and got it
　　started,
He dodged a log that lifted like an
　　arm
Against the sky to break his back for
　　him,
Then came in dancing, skipping, with
　　his life
Across the roar and chaos, and the
　　words
We saw him say along the zigzag
　　journey
Were doubtless as the words we heard
　　him say
On coming nearer: "Wasn't she an
　　i-deal
Son-of-a-bitch? You bet she was an
　　i-deal."
For all her mountains fall a little
　　short,
Her people not quite short enough
　　for Art,
She's still New Hampshire, a most
　　restful state.

Lately in converse with a New York
　　alec
About the new school of the pseudo-
　　phallic,
I found myself in a close corner where
I had to make an almost funny
　　choice.
"Choose you which you will be—a
　　prude, or puke,
Mewling and puking in the public
　　arms."
"Me for the hills where I don't have
　　to choose."

"But if you had to choose, which
　　would you be?"
I wouldn't be a prude afraid of nature.
I know a man who took a double axe
And went alone against a grove of
　　trees;
But his heart failing him, he dropped
　　the axe
And ran for shelter quoting Matthew
　　Arnold:
"Nature is cruel, man is sick of blood;
There's been enough shed without
　　shedding mine.
Remember Birnam Wood; The
　　wood's in flux!"
He had a special terror of the flux
That showed itself in dendrophobia.
The only decent tree had been to mill
And educated into boards, he said.
He knew too well for any earthly use
The line where man leaves off and
　　nature starts,
And never over-stepped it save in
　　dreams.
He stood on the safe side of the line
　　talking;
Which is sheer Matthew Arnoldism,
The cult of one who owned himself
　　"a foiled,
Circuitous wanderer," and "took de-
　　jectedly
His seat upon the intellectual throne."
Agreed in frowning on these im-
　　provised
Altars the woods are full of nowadays,
Again as in the days when Ahaz
　　sinned
By worship under green trees in the
　　open.
Scarcely a mile but that I come on
　　one,
A black-cheeked stone and stick of
　　rain-washed charcoal.
Even to say the groves were God's
　　first temples
Comes too near to Ahaz' sin for
　　safety.
Nothing not built with hands of
　　course is sacred.

But here is not a question of what's
  sacred;
Rather of what to face or run away
  from.
I'd hate to be a runaway from nature.
And neither would I choose to be a
  puke
Who cares not what he does in com-
  pany,
And, when he can't do anything, falls
  back
On words, and tries his worst to make
  words speak
Louder than actions, and sometimes
  achieves it.
It seems a narrow choice the age in-
  sists on.
How about being a good Greek, for
  instance?
That course, they tell me, isn't offered
  this year.
"Come, but this isn't choosing—puke
  or prude?"
Well, if I have to choose one or the
  other,
I choose to be a plain New Hamp-
  shire farmer
With an income in cash of say a thou-
  sand
(From say a publisher in New York
  City).
It's restful to arrive at a decision,
And restful just to think about New
  Hampshire.
At present I am living in Vermont.
                              1923

ONCE BY THE PACIFIC *

The shattered water made a misty
  din.
Great waves looked over others coming in,
And thought of doing something to
  the shore

That water never did to land before.
The clouds were low and hairy in the
  skies,
Like locks blown forward in the gleam
  of eyes.
You could not tell, and yet it looked
  as if
The shore was lucky in being backed
  by cliff,
The cliff in being backed by conti-
  nent;
It looked as if a night of dark intent
Was coming, and not only a night, an
  age.
Someone had better be prepared for
  rage.
There would be more than ocean-
  water broken
Before God's last *Put out the Light*
  was spoken.
                              1926

A LONE STRIKER *

The swinging mill bell changed its
  rate
To tolling like the count of fate,
And though at that the tardy ran,
One failed to make the closing gate.
There was a law of God or man
That on the one who came too late
The gate for half an hour be locked,
His time be lost, his pittance docked.
He stood rebuked and unemployed.
The straining mill began to shake.
The mill, though many, many eyed,
Had eyes inscrutably opaque;
So that he couldn't look inside
To see if some forlorn machine
Was standing idle for his sake.
(He couldn't hope its heart would
  break.)

And yet he thought he saw the scene:
The air was full of dust of wool.
A thousand yarns were under pull,
But pull so slow, with such a twist,
All day from spool to lesser spool,
It seldom overtaxed their strength;

They safely grew in slender length.
And if one broke by any chance,
The spinner saw it at a glance.
The spinner still was there to spin.

That's where the human still came in.
Her deft hand showed with finger
     rings
Among the harp-like spread of strings.
She caught the pieces end to end
And, with a touch that never missed,
Not so much tied as made them blend.
Man's ingenuity was good.
He saw it plainly where he stood,
Yet found it easy to resist.

He knew another place, a wood,
And in it, tall as trees, were cliffs;
And if he stood on one of these,
'Twould be among the tops of trees,
Their upper branches round him
     wreathing,
Their breathing mingled with his
     breathing.
If—if he stood! Enough of ifs!
He knew a path that wanted walking;
He knew a spring that wanted drink-
     ing;
A thought that wanted further think-
     ing;
A love that wanted re-renewing.
Nor was this just a way of talking
To save him the expense of doing.
With him it boded action, deed.

The factory was very fine;
He wished it all the modern speed.
Yet, after all, 'twas not divine,
That is to say, 'twas not a church.
He never would assume that he'd
Be any institution's need.
But he said then and still would say
If there should ever come a day
When industry seemed like to die
Because he left it in the lurch,
Or even merely seemed to pine
For want of his approval, why
Come get him—they knew where to
     search.

                              1933

TWO TRAMPS IN MUD-TIME *

Out of the mud two strangers came
And caught me splitting wood in the
     yard.
And one of them put me off my aim
By hailing cheerily "Hit them hard!"
I knew pretty well why he dropped
     behind
And let the other go on a way.
I knew pretty well what he had in
     mind:
He wanted to take my job for pay.

Good blocks of beech it was I split,
As large around as the chopping-block;
And every piece I squarely hit
Fell splinterless as a cloven rock.
The blows that a life of self-control
Spares to strike for the common
     good
That day, giving a loose to my soul,
I spent on the unimportant wood.

The sun was warm but the wind was
     chill.
You know how it is with an April
     day:
When the sun is out and the wind is
     still,
You're one month on in the middle of
     May.
But if you so much as dare to speak,
A cloud comes over the sunlit arch,
A wind comes off a frozen peak,
And you're two months back in the
     middle of March.

A bluebird comes tenderly up to alight
And fronts the wind to unruffle a
     plume,
His song so pitched as not to excite
A single flower as yet to bloom.
It is snowing a flake: and he half
     knew
Winter was only playing possum.
Except in color he isn't blue,

But he wouldn't advise a thing to
    blossom.

The water for which we may have to
    look
In summertime with a witching-wand,
In every wheelrut's now a brook,
In every print of a hoof a pond.
Be glad of water, but don't forget
The lurking frost in the earth beneath
That will steal forth after the sun is
    set
And show on the water its crystal
    teeth.

The time when most I loved my task
These two must make me love it more
By coming with what they came to
    ask.
You'd think I never had felt before
The weight of an ax head poised
    aloft,
The grip on earth of outspread feet,
The life of muscles rocking soft
And smooth and moist in vernal heat.

Out of the woods two hulking tramps
(From sleeping God knows where last
    night
But not long since in the lumber
    camps).
They thought all chopping was theirs
    of right.
Men of the woods and lumber-jacks,
They judged me by their appropriate
    tool.
Except as a fellow handled an ax,
They had no way of knowing a fool.

Nothing on either side was said.
They knew they had but to stay their
    stay
And all their logic would fill my head:
As that I had no right to play
With what was another man's work
    for gain.
My right might be love but theirs was
    need.
And where the two exist in twain
Theirs was the better right—agreed.

But yield who will to their separation,
My object in life is to unite
My avocation and my vocation
As my two eyes make one in sight.
Only where love and need are one,
And the work is play for mortal
    stakes,
Is the deed ever really done
For Heaven and the future's sakes.

                    1936

TO A THINKER *

The last step taken found your heft
Decidedly upon the left.
One more would throw you on the
    right.
Another still—you see your plight.
You call this thinking, but it's walk-
    ing.
Not even that, it's only rocking,
Or weaving like a stabled horse:
From force to matter and back to
    force,
From force to content and back to
    form,
From norm to crazy and back to
    norm,
From bound to free and back to
    bound,
From sound to sense and back to
    sound.
So back and forth. It almost scares
A man the way things come in pairs.
Just now you're off democracy
(With a polite regret to be),
And leaning on dictatorship;
But if you will accept the tip,
In less than no time, tongue and pen,
You'll be a democrat again.
A reasoner and good as such,
Don't let it bother you too much
If it makes you look helpless please
And a temptation to the tease.
Suppose you've no direction in you,

I don't see but you must continue
To use the gift you do possess,
And sway with reason more or less.
I own I never really warmed
To the reformer or reformed,
And yet conversion has its place
Not halfway down the scale of grace.
So if you find you must repent
From side to side in argument,
At least don't use your mind too
　　hard,
But trust my instinct—I'm a bard.
　　　　　　　　　　　　　　1936

SARA TEASDALE
(1884–1933)
PIERROT *

Pierrot stands in the garden
　　Beneath a waning moon,
And on his lute he fashions
　　A fragile silver tune.

Pierrot plays in the garden,
　　He thinks he plays for me,
But I am quite forgotten
　　Under the cherry tree.

Pierrot plays in the garden,
　　And all the roses know
That Pierrot loves his music,—
　　But I love Pierrot.
　　　　　　　　　　　　　　1910

BARTER †

Life has loveliness to sell,
　　All beautiful and splendid things,
Blue waves whitened on a cliff,
　　Soaring fire that sways and sings,
And children's faces looking up
Holding wonder like a cup.

* From *Helen of Troy and Other Poems* by Sara Teasdale. By permission of The Macmillan Company. Copyright 1910, 1911.
† From *Love Songs* by Sara Teasdale. By permission of The Macmillan Company, publishers. Copyright, 1917.

Life has loveliness to sell,
　　Music like a curve of gold,
Scent of pine trees in the rain,
　　Eyes that love you, arms that hold,
And for your spirit's still delight,
Holy thoughts that star the night.

Spend all you have for loveliness,
　　Buy it and never count the cost;
For one white singing hour of peace
　　Count many a year of strife well
　　　　lost,
And for a breath of ecstasy
Give all you have been, or could be.
　　　　　　　　　　　　　　1917

THERE WILL COME SOFT
RAINS ‡

(WAR TIME)

There will come soft rains and the
　　smell of the ground,
And swallows circling with their
　　shimmering sound;

And frogs in the pools singing at
　　night,
And wild plum-trees in tremulous
　　white;

Robins will wear their feathery fire
Whistling their whims on a low
　　fence-wire;

And not one will know of the war,
　　not one
Will care at last when it is done.

Not one would mind, neither bird nor
　　tree
If mankind perished utterly;

And Spring herself, when she woke at
　　dawn,
Would scarcely know that we were
　　gone.
　　　　　　　　　　　　　　1918

‡ From *Flame and Shadow* by Sara Teasdale. By permission of The Macmillan Company, publishers. Copyright, 1920.

I HAVE LOVED HOURS
AT SEA *

I have loved hours at sea, gray cities,
   The fragile secret of a flower,
Music, the making of a poem
   That gave me heaven for an hour;

First stars above a snowy hill,
   Voices of people kindly and wise,
And the great look of love, long
      hidden,
   Found at last in meeting eyes.

I have loved much and been loved
      deeply—
   Oh, when my spirit's fire burns low,
Leave me the darkness and the still-
      ness,
   I shall be tired and glad to go.
                     1919

COMPENSATION *

I should be glad of loneliness
   And hours that go on broken wings,
A thirsty body, a tired heart
   And the unchanging ache of
      things,
If I could make a single song
   As lovely and as full of light,
As hushed and brief as a falling star
   On a winter night.
                     1920

THE FLIGHT †

We are two eagles
Flying together
Under the heavens,
Over the mountains,
Stretched on the wind.
Sunlight heartens us,

* From *Flame and Shadow* by Sara
Teasdale. By permission of The Macmillan Company, publishers. Copyright,
1920.

† From *The Dark of the Moon* by
Sara Teasdale. By permission of The
Macmillan Company, publishers. Copy-
right, 1926.

Blind snow baffles us,
Clouds wheel after us
Ravelled and thinned.

We are like eagles,
But when Death harries us,
Human and humbled
When one of us goes,
Let the other follow,
Let the flight be ended,
Let the fire blacken,
Let the book close.
                     1924

ELINOR WYLIE
(1885–1928)

THE EAGLE AND THE MOLE ‡

Avoid the reeking herd,
Shun the polluted flock,
Live like that stoic bird,
The eagle of the rock.

The huddled warmth of crowds
Begets and fosters hate;
He keeps, above the clouds,
His cliff inviolate.

When flocks are folded warm,
And herds to shelter run,
He sails above the storm,
He stares into the sun.

If in the eagle's track
Your sinews cannot leap,
Avoid the lathered pack,
Turn from the steaming sheep.

If you would keep your soul
From spotted sight or sound,
Live like the velvet mole;
Go burrow underground.

And there hold intercourse
With roots of trees and stones,
With rivers at their source,
And disembodied bones.
                     1921

‡ Reprinted from *Collected Poems* by
Elinor Wylie, by permission of Alfred A.
Knopf, Inc. Copyright 1921, 1932 by
Alfred A. Knopf, Inc.

FROM   WILD PEACHES *

[PURITAN SONNET]

Down to the Puritan marrow of my
    bones
There's something in this richness
    that I hate.
I love the look, austere, immaculate,
Of landscapes drawn in pearly mono-
    tones.
There's something in my very blood
    that owns
Bare hills, cold silver on a sky of slate,
A thread of water, churned to milky
    spate
Streaming through slanted pastures
    fenced with stones.
I love those skies, thin blue or snowy
    gray,
Those fields sparse-planted, rendering
    meagre sheaves;
That spring, briefer than the apple-
    blossom's breath,
Summer, so much too beautiful to
    stay,
Swift autumn, like a bonfire of leaves,
And sleepy winter, like the sleep of
    death.

                      1921

BEAUTY *

Say not of Beauty she is good,
Or aught but beautiful,
Or sleek to doves' wings of the wood
Her wild wings of a gull.

Call her not wicked; that word's
    touch
Consumes her like a curse;
But love her not too much, too much,
For that is even worse.

O, she is neither good nor bad,
But innocent and wild!

   * Reprinted from *Collected Poems* by
Elinor Wylie, by permission of Alfred A.
Knopf, Inc. Copyright 1921, 1932 by
Alfred A. Knopf, Inc.

Enshrine her and she dies, who
    had
The hard heart of a child.

                      1921

CASTILIAN *

Velasquez took a pliant knife
And scraped his palette clean;
He said, "I lead a dog's own life
Painting a king and queen."

He cleaned his palette with oily
    rags
And oakum from Seville wharves;
"I am sick of painting painted hags
And bad ambiguous dwarves.

"The sky is silver, the clouds are
    pearl,
Their locks are looped with rain.
I will not paint Maria's girl
For all the money in Spain."

He washed his face in water cold,
His hands in turpentine;
He squeezed out colour like coins of
    gold
And colour like drops of wine.

Each colour lay like a little pool
On the polished cedar wood;
Clear and pale and ivory-cool
Or dark as solitude.

He burnt the rags in the fireplace
And leaned from the window high;
He said, "I like that gentleman's
    face
Who wears his cap awry."

This is the gentleman, there he
    stands,
Castilian, sombre-caped,
With arrogant eyes, and narrow
    hands
Miraculously shaped.

                      1921

LET NO CHARITABLE HOPE *

Now let no charitable hope
Confuse my mind with images
Of eagle and of antelope:
I am in nature none of these.

I was, being human, born alone;
I am, being woman, hard beset;
I live by squeezing from a stone
The little nourishment I get.

In masks outrageous and austere
The years go by in single file;
But none has merited my fear,
And none has quite escaped my smile.

                              1922

HYMN TO EARTH *

Farewell, incomparable element,
Whence man arose, where he shall
     not return;
And hail, imperfect urn
Of his last ashes, and his firstborn
     fruit;
Farewell, the long pursuit,
And all the adventures of his discon-
     tent;
The voyages which sent
His heart averse from home:
Metal of clay, permit him that he
     come
To thy slow-burning fire as to a
     hearth;
Accept him as a particle of earth.

Fire, being divided from the other
     three,
It lives removed, or secret at the core;
Most subtle of the four,
When air flies not, nor water flows,
It disembodied goes,
Being light, elixir of the first decree,
More volatile than he;
With strength and power to pass

Through space, where never his least
     atom was:
He has no part in it, save as his eyes
Have drawn its emanation from the
     skies.

A wingless creature heavier than air,
He is rejected of its quintessence;
Coming and going hence,
In the twin minutes of his birth and
     death,
He may inhale as breath,
As breath relinquish heaven's atmos-
     phere,
Yet in it have no share,
Nor can survive therein
Where its outer edge is filtered pure
     and thin:
It doth but lend its crystal to his lungs
For his early crying, and his final
     songs.

The element of water has denied
Its child; it is no more his element;
It never will relent;
Its silver harvests are more sparsely
     given
Than the rewards of heaven,
And he shall drink cold comfort at
     its side:
The water is too wide:
The seamew and the gull
Feather a nest made soft and pitiful
Upon its foam; he has not any part
In the long swell of sorrow at its
     heart.

Hail and farewell, beloved element,
Whence he departed, and his parent
     once;
See where thy spirit runs
Which for so long hath had the moon
     to wife;
Shall this support his life
Until the arches of the waves be
     bent
And grow shallow and spent?
Wisely it cast him forth
With his dead weight of burdens
     nothing worth,

Leaving him, for the universal years,
A little seawater to make his tears.

Hail, element of earth, receive thy
      own,
And cherish, at thy charitable breast,
This man, this mongrel beast:
He plows the sand, and, at his hardest
      need,
He sows himself for seed;
He plows the furrow, and in this lies
      down
Before the corn is grown;
Between the apple bloom
And the ripe apple is sufficient room
In time, and matter, to consume his
      love
And make him parcel of a cypress
      grove.

Receive him as thy lover for an hour
Who will not weary, by a longer stay,
The kind embrace of clay;
Even within thine arms he is dis-
      persed
To nothing, as at first;
The air flings downward from its four-
      quartered tower
Him whom the flames devour;
At the full tide, at the flood,
The sea is mingled with his salty
      blood:
The traveller dust, although the dust
      be vile,
Sleeps as thy lover for a little while.
                                    1929

JOHN CROWE RANSOM
(1888–   )

CAPTAIN CARPENTER *

Captain Carpenter rose up in his
      prime
Put on his pistols and went riding out

* Reprinted from *Chills and Fever* by
John Crowe Ransom, by permission of
Alfred A. Knopf, Inc. Copyright 1924,
by Alfred A. Knopf, Inc.

But had got wellnigh nowhere at that
      time
Till he fell in with ladies in a rout.

It was a pretty lady and all her train
That played with him so sweetly but
      before
An hour she'd taken a sword with all
      her main
And twined him of his nose for ever-
      more.

Captain Carpenter mounted up one
      day
And rode straightway into a stranger
      rogue
That looked unchristian but be that
      as may
The Captain did not wait upon
      prologue.

But drew upon him out of his great
      heart
The other swung against him with a
      club
And cracked his two legs at the
      shinny part
And let him roll and stick like any
      tub.

Captain Carpenter rode many a time
From male and female took he sundry
      harms
He met the wife of Satan crying "I'm
The she-wolf bids you shall bear no
      more arms."

Their strokes and counters whistled
      in the wind
I wish he had delivered half his
      blows
But where she should have made off
      like a hind
The bitch bit off his arms at the
      elbows.

And Captain Carpenter parted with
      his ears
To a black devil that used him in
      this wise
O Jesus ere his threescore and ten
      years

Another had plucked out his sweet
    blue eyes.

Captain Carpenter got up on his
    roan
And sallied from the gate in hell's
    despite
I heard him asking in the grimmest
    tone
If any enemy yet there was to fight?

"To any adversary it is fame
If he risk to be wounded by my
    tongue
Or burnt in two beneath my red
    heart's flame
Such are the perils he is cast among.

"But if he can he has a pretty
    choice
From an anatomy with little to lose
Whether he cut my tongue and take
    my voice
Or whether it be my round red heart
    he choose."

It was the neatest knave that ever was
    seen
Stepping in perfume from his lady's
    bower
Who at this word put on his merry
    mien
And fell on Captain Carpenter like a
    tower.

I would not knock old fellows in the
    dust
But there lay Captain Carpenter on
    his back
His weapons were the old heart in
    his bust
And a blade shook between rotten
    teeth alack.

The rogue in scarlet and grey soon
    knew his mind
He wished to get his trophy and
    depart
With gentle apology and touch
    refined
He pierced him and produced the
    Captain's heart.

God's mercy rest on Captain
    Carpenter now
I thought him Sirs and honest
    gentleman
Citizen husband soldier and scholar
    enow
Let jangling kites eat of him if they
    can.

But God's deep curses follow after
    those
That shore him of his goodly nose
    and ears
His legs and strong arms at the two
    elbows
And eyes that had not watered
    seventy years.

The curse of hell upon the sleek up-
    start
Who got the Captain finally on his
    back
And took the red vitals of his heart
And made the kites whet their beaks
    clack clack.

                    1924, 1945

MISS EUPHEMIA *

Out of her house she crept,
Which was her winter's gaol,
Hearing the rumour that now
Was the birds' common tale—
Birds for all the ladies,
And husbands at church-door—
In fine, a spring was promised
As fifty years before.

A phase of green and tender
Was on the mortal clay,
But white upon her stick went
Miss Euphemia,
To count up all her tulips
That celebrated March,
Out of the frore escaping
To the blue upper arch.

* Reprinted from *Chills and Fever* by
John Crowe Ransom, by permission of
Alfred A. Knopf, Inc. Copyright 1924,
by Alfred A. Knopf, Inc.

Into her house she fled,
Buffeted back to prison,
And sought the very great-chair
From which she had arisen;
Down sat in her whiteness—
Bitter how she laughed—
Opening doors to March, yet
Quaking in his draught.

Nor scarcely can she, dwindling,
Throw down a bridge of dream
For a broken lady's traverse,
Neat-footing on the beam;
She had too much of winter,
And all her ways were lost,
And she sits with us only
Till next Pentecost.

1924

PIAZZA PIECE *

—I am a gentleman in a dustcoat
    trying
To make you hear. Your ears are soft
    and small
And listen to an old man not at all,
They want the young men's whisper-
    ing and sighing.
But see the roses on your trellis dying
And hear the spectral singing of the
    moon;
For I must have my lovely lady soon.
I am a gentleman in a dustcoat trying.

—I am a lady young in beauty waiting
Until my truelove comes, and then
    we kiss.
But what grey man among the vines
    is this
Whose words are dry and faint as in
    a dream?
Back from my trellis, Sir, before I
    scream!
I am a lady young in beauty waiting.
                            1925, 1945

* Reprinted from *Two Gentlemen in
Bonds*, by John Crowe Ransom, by permission of, and special arrangement with,
Alfred A. Knopf, Inc., authorized publishers. Copyright 1927.

SOMEWHERE IS SUCH A
KINGDOM *

The famous kingdom of the birds
Has a sweet tongue and liquid
    words,—
The red-birds polish their notes
In their easy practised throats,—
Smooth as orators are the thrushes
Of the airy city of the bushes,
And God reward the fierce cock wrens
Who have such suavity with their
    hens.

To me this has its worth
As I sit upon the earth
Lacking my winter and quiet hearth.
For I go up into a nook
With a mind burdened, or a book,
And hear no strife or quarreling
As the birds and their wives sing.

Or, so it has been to-day.
Yet I cannot therefore say
If the red-bird, wren, or thrush
Know when to speak and when to
    hush;
Though their manifest education
Be a right enunciation
And their chief excellence
A verbal elegance,
I cannot say if the wind never blows,
Nor how it sometimes goes.

This I know, that if they wrangle
Their words inevitably will jangle.
If they be hateful as men
They will be harsh as we have been.
When they go to pecking
You will soon hear shrieking,
And they who will have the law,
How those will jaw!
Girls that dream unlawful dreams
Will waken full of their own screams,
And boys that get too arrant
Will have rows with a parent,—
And when friend falls out with
    friend,
All songs must have quick end.

Have they not claws like knives?
Have not these gentlemen wives?

But when they croak and fleer and
    swear,
My dull heart I must take elsewhere;
For I will see if God has made
Otherwhere another shade
Where the men or beasts or birds
Exchange few words and pleasant
    words.
And dare I think it is absurd
If no such beast were, no such bird?
                                1927

ALLEN TATE
(1899–   )

ODE TO THE CONFEDERATE
DEAD *

Row after row with strict impunity
The headstones yield their names to
    the element,
The wind whirrs without recollection;
In the riven troughs the splayed leaves
Pile up, of nature the casual sacra-
    ment
To the seasonal eternity of death;
Then driven by the fierce scrutiny
Of heaven to their business in the
    vast breath,
They sough the rumor of mortality.

Autumn is desolation in the plot
Of a thousand acres, where these
    memories grow
From the inexhaustible bodies that are
    not
Dead, but feed the grass row after rich
    row.
Remember now the autumns that
    have gone!—
Ambitious November with the
    humors of the year,
With a particular zeal for every slab,
Staining the uncomfortable angels
    that rot

* Reprinted from *Poems—1922–1947*
by Allen Tate; copyright 1932, 1948 by
Charles Scribner's Sons; used by permission of the publishers.

On the slabs, a wing chipped here,
    an arm there:
The brute curiosity of an angel's stare
Turns you, like them, to stone,
Transforms the heaving air
Till plunged to a heavier world below
You shift your sea-space blindly
Heaving, turning like the blind crab.

Dazed by the wind, only the wind
    The leaves flying, plunge

You know who have waited by the
    wall
The twilit certainty of an animal,
Those midnight restitutions of the
    blood
You know—the immitigable pines, the
    smoky frieze
Of the sky, the sudden call: you know
    the rage,
The cold pool left by the mounting
    flood,
Of muted Zeno and Parmenides.
You who have waited for the angry
    resolution
Of those desires that should be yours
    tomorrow,
You know the unimportant shrift of
    death
And praise the vision
And praise the arrogant circumstance
Of those who fall
Rank upon rank, hurried beyond
    decision—
Here by the sagging gate, stopped by
    the wall.

Seeing, seeing only the leaves
    Flying, plunge and expire

Turn your eyes to the immoderate
    past,
Turn to the inscrutable infantry
    rising
Demons out of the earth—they will
    not last.
Stonewall, Stonewall, and the sunken
    fields of hemp,
Shiloh, Antietam, Malvern Hill, Bull
    Run.

Lost in that orient of the thick-and-
    fast
You will curse the setting sun.

    Cursing only the leaves crying
    Like an old man in a storm

You hear the shout—the crazy hem-
    locks point
With troubled fingers to the silence
    which
Smothers you, a mummy, in time.

               The hound bitch
Toothless and dying, in a musty cellar
Hears the wind only.

    Now that the salt of their blood
Stiffens the saltier oblivion of the sea,
Seals the malignant purity of the
    flood,
What shall we who count our days
    and bow
Our heads with a commemorial woe,
In the ribboned coats of grim felicity,
What shall we say of the bones,
    unclean,
Their verdurous anonymity will
    grow?
The ragged arms, the ragged heads
    and eyes
Lost in these acres of the insane
    green?
The grey Jean spiders come, they
    come and go;
In a tangle of willows without light
The singular screech-owl's tight
Invisible lyric seeds the mind
With the furious murmur of their
    chivalry.

    We shall say only, the leaves
    Flying, plunge and expire

We shall say only, the leaves whisper-
    ing
In the improbable mist of nightfall
That flies on multiple wing;
Night is the beginning and the end
And in between the ends of distrac-
    tion

Waits mute speculation, the patient
    curse
That stones the eyes, or like the
    jaguar leaps
For his own image in a jungle pool,
    his victim.
What shall we say who have
    knowledge
Carried to the heart? Shall we take
    the act
To the grave? Shall we, more hopeful,
    set up the grave
In the house? The ravenous grave?

               Leave now
That shut gate and the decomposing
    wall:
The gentle serpent, green in the mul-
    berry bush,
Riots with his tongue through the
    hush—
Sentinel of the grave who counts us
    all!

               1928, 1948

MR. POPE *

When Alexander Pope strolled in the
    city
Strict was the glint of pearl and gold
    sedans.
Ladies leaned out more out of fear
    than pity
For Pope's tight back was rather a
    goat's than man's.

Often one thinks the urn should have
    more bones
Than skeletons provide for speedy
    dust,
The urn gets hollow, cobwebs brittle
    as stones
Weave to the funeral shell a frivolous
    rust.

And he who dribbled couplets like a
    snake

* Reprinted from *Poems—1922–1947*
by Allen Tate; copyright 1932, 1948 by
Charles Scribner's Sons; used by permission of the publishers.

Coiled to a lithe precision in the sun
Is missing. The jar is empty; you may
    break
It only to find that Mr. Pope is gone.

What requisitions of a verity
Prompted the wit and rage between
    his teeth
One cannot say. Around a crooked
    tree
A moral climbs whose name should
    be a wreath.

                    1928, 1948

IDIOT *

The idiot greens the meadow with his
    eyes,
The meadow creeps implacable and
    still;
The dog barks, the hammock swings,
    he lies.
One two three the cows bulge on the
    hill.

Motion that is not time erects snow-
    drifts
While sister's hand sieves waterfalls
    of lace.
With a palm fan closer than death he
    lifts
The Ozarks and tilted seas across his
    face.

In the long sunset where impatient
    sound
Strips niggers to a multiple of backs
Flies yield their heat, magnolias
    drench the ground

* Reprinted from *Poems—1922–1947*
by Allen Tate; copyright 1932, 1948 by
Charles Scribner's Sons; used by permission of the publishers.

With Appomattox! The shadows lie
    in stacks.

The julep glass weaves echoes in Jim's
    kinks
While ashy Jim puts murmurs in the
    day;
Now in the idiot's heart a chamber
    stinks
Of dead asters, as the potter's field of
    May.

All evening the marsh is a slick pool
Where dream wild hares, witch hazel,
    pretty girls.
"Up from the important picnic of a
    fool
Those rotted asters!" Eddy on eddy
    swirls

The innocent mansion of a panther's
    heart!
It crumbles, tick-tick time drags it in
Till now his arteries lag and now they
    start
Reverence with the frigid gusts of sin.

The stillness pelts the eye, assaults the
    hair;
A beech sticks out a branch to warn
    the stars,
A lightning-bug jerks angles in the
    air,
Diving. "I am the captain of new
    wars!"

The dusk runs down the lane driven
    like hail;
Far off a precise whistle is escheat
To the dark; and then the towering
    weak and pale
Covers his eyes with memory like a
    sheet.

                    1928, 1948

ELLEN GLASGOW
(1874–1945)

FROM   *THE ROMANTIC COMEDIANS* *

[A SOUTHERN LADY]

In her dull drawing-room, Amanda sat looking thoughtfully, though as usual she was not thinking, at her gilded bird-cages. Serene, unselfish, with the reminiscence of a vanished day in her face and figure, she belonged to that fortunate generation of women who had no need to think, since everything was decided for them by the feelings of a lady and the Episcopal Church. Even this matter of unrequited affection, this very urgent and painful matter of a broken heart, was eased of confusion, if not of soreness, by the infallible instinct that impelled her to pretend it away. She was wearing a dress of lavender crêpe, with a modified late-Victorian waistline, and her abundant hair, like powdered twilight, was arranged à la Pompadour. Neither time nor her blighted romance had been able entirely to destroy a complexion that, as Mrs. Bredalbane had remarked almost forty years before, was the only perfect substitute for intelligence.

"Why, Annabel," she said, rising gracefully and bending to kiss the girl's cheek. "It is so good of you to come. This is what dear Mother used to call her lonely hour."

"Oh, I like to come," responded Annabel, sitting down on the edge of a hard sofa that was upholstered in plush. "I am fond of you, and I am fond of the birds."

"They are darlings," assented Amanda, in so musical a voice that the canaries began to pipe in their luxurious cages.

"Cousin Amanda," Annabel began courageously, "are you happy?"

"Why, yes, dear." Amanda's tone was tinged with astonishment. "I should be very ungrateful if I were not happy, with all my blessings."

"But blessings don't make us happy," returned Annabel, and she thought, "She is so noble that she creaks. I wonder if they were all like that, except Mrs. Bredalbane, who is disreputable?"

"They do, if we attune our minds to them."

"Yet so often they aren't what we really want, but what God or other people think best for us."

"Well, my dear, who should know better than God?"

"That's what Mother says, and I suppose it's a comfort if you can feel like that, though I don't see how you ever bring yourself to it. Now, I know the things that I want even better than God does, and I'd like to be consulted before I am blessed—permanently, anyhow. Nobody can make me believe," she finished passionately, "that it is good for my soul to live on fried liver and scrambled eggs."

Amanda's faith, though sufficient for an ample income, had never been called upon to contend with the sordid problems of poverty. Smiling as sweetly as ever, for only a surgical operation could have altered the prim sweetness of her smile, she murmured gently that God had been very good to her, and that even her dear father had been spared to her until he was ninety.

"I wish you and your mother could come to dinner often," she added generously, for as much mind as she had was practical, and she honestly wished to help the needy. "It is a great pleasure to have you. Mother used to say that Bella's sunny temper was worth a fortune."

* From *The Romantic Comedians*, by Ellen Glasgow, copyright 1927, by Ellen Glasgow, and reprinted by permission of the publishers, Doubleday, Doran & Co., Inc.

Annabel laughed. "I wish somebody would buy it." For an instant, she hesitated and then resumed her intimate questions. "You never get lonely, do you, Cousin Amanda?"

Amanda lifted her calm eyes, which reminded the girl of blue enamel, to the portrait of a lady in an immense chignon and miniature bonnet. "I miss my dear mother and father, but I have the kindest nephews and nieces in the world, and they leave me so little time to myself. This house is filled with young people all day long. They refuse to let me grow old."

"And you don't miss anything else? Honestly, now, Cousin Amanda?"

A shadow as swift as the flight of a bird darkened the stainless enamel. Yes, Mother is right, Annabel thought, Cousin Amanda is a perfect lady, and the only trouble with perfect ladies is that they lie as perfectly as they behave.

"Oh, I haven't time to think of anything else. I am kept too busy making people happy about me," Amanda responded. "Every morning, as soon as I wake, I ask God to direct me to the greatest good I can do that day. Then, almost always, my prayer is answered before I've finished breakfast. I am sure to hear of someone who is ill, or one of the children runs in to have a hurt bandaged. Or there is a distressing case among my poor that must be attended to immediately. The days pass so quickly when you are doing things for others. Dear little Annabel"—the level tones rose suddenly in supplication—"God doesn't let you be unhappy while you are doing His will."

Didn't He? Well, what was His will, and how did you know it? demanded Annabel, who was sure that she shouldn't have been made happy by the will she had seen manifested to her mother and Cousin Amanda.

Nor did Cousin Amanda appear to be as happy as she said that she was— not when you were close enough to see the circles under her eyes. She looked quiet, but she looked also, in some inexplicable way, hurt, as if God's will with her had been firm rather than gentle, and had given her a moment, at least, of unpleasant surprise. Oh, if people would only be direct instead of painfully subtle!

"Then you never, never regret that you didn't marry?" she asked abruptly. "I am not just impertinent, Cousin Amanda. I have my reason, a very urgent reason, for wishing to know."

Amanda started, for questions like this, even with urgent reason, were never asked an unmarried woman when she was young.

"Why, no, dear," she replied with an edge of frost to her tone.

"You weren't sorry that you broke your engagement to Judge Honeywell?"

"Why, no, dear. You must remember that happened more than thirty years ago." If her face ached from smiling, there was no sign of pain in her manner.

"Mother said he was almost distracted. But you never regretted it?"

"Why, no, dear." Amanda hesitated, and then spoke in a frozen voice. "I broke my engagement just before I sailed for Europe with my dear mother, who died while I was over there. I felt that I could not be separated from my mother and father as long as they lived. That was why," she added unflinchingly, "I never married."

"You wouldn't marry him now, would you?"

At this impertinent question, Amanda lowered her gaze for the first time, while a burning flush stained her features. For an instant, her throat quivered convulsively beneath the narrow band of black velvet.

"Why, no, dear," she repeated mechanically, and added with a touch of asperity, "At my time of life, one no longer thinks of marriage."

"But he might. Men do, don't they?"

"Well, men are different." It was the proverbial reply to such a question; yet hearing the classic precept for the hundredth time, Annabel asked herself if life had been less confusing to people who lived by a simple formula instead of by intricate reason. A law of nature might sound less final than an Act of God, but it was certainly more authoritative, as well as more consoling to religious minds, than a mere infirmity of man.

"Oh, Cousin Amanda, please marry him!" she cried out suddenly, with one of her dangerous impulses.

After all, you were obliged to make an effort to find out the truth, even if your questions did slide over the brightly lacquered surface of Amanda's manner. There were moments, and this was one of them, when it seemed to Annabel that the whole world and all people everywhere, except herself and Angus, whom she hated, were only half animate. Was there a sounder reality beneath this complicated system of living? Was it possible to make an impression upon that cool, inviolable texture of good taste? Good taste! thought the girl scornfully; for, as her mother so often reminded her, she had thrown not only good taste but decorum to the winds when she met disappointment. How could it matter, she thought passionately, whether you are unhappy in good taste or bad, so long as you are unhappy? Yet both her mother and Cousin Amanda put breeding before happiness even in tragedy, even at funerals, where the quality of the crêpe was more remarked than the quantity of the grief.

"Why, Annabel, are you out of your head?" A breeze of exasperation had at last ruffled the suavity of Amanda's voice. "Such an idea has never so much as crossed my mind. Judge Honeywell and I are the best of friends. The best of friends," she repeated, with firmness and without emotion, "but as to marrying him or anybody else, the idea has never crossed my mind. If you could see how full my life is, with the incessant demands of my nieces and nephews and all my charities, you would understand that I have no time to think of marriage. If I didn't marry when I was young and had so many opportunities, I should certainly not care to assume such responsibilities late in life. Indeed, I have always thought," she added with an earnestness which sounded sincere, "that it is a mistake for women to marry late in life."

Yes, it sounded sincere; but was it? Annabel didn't know, and she realized that she could never know, for the virtue of perfect behavior lies, not in its rightness, but in its impenetrability. It might be, as her mother insisted, that all good women of the Nineteenth Century were passive in temperament, and were, therefore, more disposed to lean back upon the prerogatives of men—or the Acts of God, if they preferred to think in dignified terms.

Well, she couldn't help it, Annabel concluded, gazing with hurt and hungry eyes at Cousin Amanda, who was being noble in thought and attitude on a hard Victorian sofa.

"I wish you would talk freely to me, Cousin Amanda," the girl said, as she rose and turned her cheek for a kiss.

"Nice women don't talk about their private affairs, Annabel," Amanda answered, with recovered sweetness. "When you are older, you will know better. Nice women never, never ask each other such questions."

"I told you about Angus. I told everybody. If I hadn't, I should have died of the pain.

Amanda shook her head. "Not if you had governed your mind, my dear. You should study to control your temperament and govern your mind properly."

This was all. There wasn't any help in Cousin Amanda. She talked of temperament exactly as if she meant temper. Yet, in spite of her self-control and her governed mind and her reliance upon God's will, in spite even of her attentive nephews and nieces and her vocal canary birds, she did not look happy. Calm, perhaps; but was it, after all, merely the calmness of resignation? One thing, at least, Annabel told herself, she had discovered: there was little help to be found in perfect behavior.

1926

A CERTAIN MEASURE *

THE MILLER OF OLD CHURCH

The Miller of Old Church, which was first published in 1911, parallels, in a measure, an earlier and more dramatic novel, *The Deliverance,* one of the scenes from country life in my history of the Commonwealth. In both books I have tried to depict the prolonged results of Reconstruction and the social transition, though *The Miller of Old Church* is placed in a later period and a different province of Virginia. In this locality, which is known as the Southside, the first settlers were almost entirely English; and twenty-seven years ago, when I studied the somewhat inaccessible scene of my story, the native speech

was still tinctured with the racy flavour of old England. My rustic farmers, grafted from a robust Anglo-Saxon stock, were, in several instances, modelled after living figures of the time. In Abel Revercomb, I have portrayed the better type of the plain countryman who forged ahead, after the social upheaval, and became a power in the confident dawn of Southern democracy, before the new fibre of that democracy had weakened under the combined weight of ignorance and self-interest. Mrs. Gay, who bore sorrow so nobly, and Kesiah, who bore ugliness so submissively, were both genuine products of the code of beautiful behaviour. Throughout the book there may be found, if one cares to look for it, a certain symbolic implication. Will the declining strain of the aristocracy be enriched or depleted by the mingling of social orders? Will the fresh infusion of blood save the old way of living? Or will it merely hasten the end of an incurable malady?

When I last visited the place, the original Jordan's Journey was still standing in its grove of oaks, and the neighbouring white or black farmers still brought their grist to be ground at the old mill. Recently, however, I have heard that there is only a chimney left of the house; and, after more than a century of service, the mill also has probably crumbled before the advance of what we have agreed to call progress. If I were to return, nowadays, to that once isolated community (which is not the actual post-office of Old Church that one may find on the map), I should discover, no doubt, that the very features of the country had altered, and that the effects of post-war psychology, if not the science itself, had invaded even that primitive region. But no. I may safely assume that I shall always see it unchanged. I shall keep my memories of the turning wheel under the crooked sycamore, of the chimneys of Jordan's Journey thrusting up from the reddened oaks; and, beyond acres of broomsedge, I may still look on the desolate loveliness of the horizon. If this novel has done nothing else, it has caught a dissolving slant of light on a scene that was rapidly passing away.

As the last of my books to be written in a fashion which I am obliged, however reluctantly, to call my earlier manner, *The Miller of Old Church* appears to me to be a rather curious blend of romance and realism. Although I had broken with tradition, I had not yet escaped entirely from the influence of its emotional patterns. I was still feeling the backward pull of inherited tendencies. In my next novel of manners, I was further on my way to complete freedom; but it was not until I began to write *Barren Ground* that I was able to orient myself anew and to respond to a fresh, and, apparently, a different, creative impulse. All that came after this period was the result of this heightened consciousness and this altered perspective. Unimportant as it may appear in a final summing up of actual endeavour, my later way of writing began suddenly, after a long apprenticeship to life, in a single intuitive visitation. But the struggle to this end had been difficult; and in order to understand the tradition and the way of life to which I had been born and from which I had broken away, it is necessary to glance back over the Southern scene and Southern literary conventions. . . .

Early in the dashing but decorous eighteen-eighties John Esten Cooke published his *Virginia: A History of the People,* an important and delightful little volume, which proved again that the sword was more prolific than the pen in the old South. Slipped in among more serious consideration—for war, not letters, is the proper business of the historian—we find a few brief discussions of Virginia authors; and toward the end of the book a modest chapter is devoted to *Virginia Literature in the Nineteenth Century.* After what he appears to regard more as a consoling than an encouraging view, Mr. Cooke, who was a distinguished novelist, prudently decides to explain away, not to praise, his subject.

"If no great original genius," he concludes, "has arisen to put the lion's paw on Virginia letters, many writers of admirable attainments and solid merit have produced works which have instructed and improved their generation; and to instruct and improve is better than to amuse. Whatever may be the true rank of literature, it possesses a distinct character. It may be said of it with truth that it is notable for its respect for good morals and manners; that it is nowhere offensive to delicacy or piety; or endeavours to instill a belief in what ought not to be believed. It is a very great deal to say of the literature of any country in the nineteenth century."

That he lingers not to inquire but to moralize is sufficient proof, were one needed, of Mr. Cooke's sterling piety and settled convictions. For it was a period in which historians, like novelists, asked few questions and were able to believe, without prodigious effort, anything that was necessary. Speculation, when it flowed at all, ran smoothly in the safest and narrowest of channels. Novelists, especially when they were historians also, were required to instruct and invited to please; but they were not allowed to interrogate. Why old Virginia, with a mode of living as gay, as gallant, as picturesque, and as uncomfortable as the life of England in the eighteenth century, should have created, not a minor *Tom Jones,* the crown of English fiction, but merely *Cavaliers of Virginia* and *Knights of the Horseshoe* —this is a question which no Southern gentleman, however Georgian his morals or Victorian his manners, would have dignified with an answer. A minor Fielding may have been too much to expect. But it would seem to the cold modern mind that almost any readers who devoured them so voraciously might have produced a native variety of Mrs. Radcliffe, of Miss Jane Porter, or even of Miss Charlotte Smith. All of these authors were with us in their solid bodies of masculine calf or modest feminine cloth. If our jovial grandfathers chuckled for a generation over *The Adventures of Peregrine Pickle,* our sentimental grandmothers shivered over *The Mysteries of Udolpho* and wept or trembled over the misfortunes of *Thaddeus of Warsaw.* Yet, while sentiment effervesced as easily as soda water, the stream of creative energy flowed, as thin and blue as skimmed milk, into the novel that was "notable for its respect for good morals and manners."

The one exception to such a statement is, of course, Poe. Mr. Cooke, after reminding us that Poe "passed his early life in Virginia," disposes of the matter with regret—or is it relief? "This great and somber genius," he muses, "was rather a cosmopolite than a citizen of any particular State." This fact is certainly evident; but it seems to us nowadays that it should be only a way of measuring the wide and high quality of Poe's art. It does not deny the Southern essence in his genius, and Poe is, to a large extent, a distillation of the Southern. The formalism of his tone, the classical element in his poetry and in many of his stories, the drift toward rhetoric, the aloof and elusive intensity,—all these qualities are Southern. And in his

more serious faults of overwriting, sentimental exaggeration, and lapses, now and then, into a pompous or florid style, he belongs to his epoch and even more to his South.

Having taken Poe, then, as the exception, we may return to our question. With the long inheritance of English tradition and culture behind it, why did the South (and this is especially true of Virginia) provide almost every mortal dwelling, except a retreat for the imagination of man?

It soon becomes clear that there are more answers than one to this question, and that each answer contains at least a germ of the truth. From the beginning of its history the South had suffered less from a scarcity of literature than from a superabundance of living. Soil, scenery, all the colour and animation of the external world, tempted a convivial race to an endless festival of the seasons. If there was little in nature to inspire terror, there was still less to awaken pity in hearts of oak. Life, for the ruling class at least, was genial, urbane, and amusing; but it was deficient in those violent contrasts that subdue the natural pomposity of man. Even slavery, a depressing spectacle at best, was a slight impediment to the faith that had been trained more to enjoy the fruits than to examine the character of peculiar institutions. Although in certain periods there was disseminated a piquant flavour of skepticism, it was a flavour that lingered pleasantly on the tongue instead of lubricating the mind.

Over the greater part of the old South (and this applies forcibly to Virginia, where the plantation group was firmly united) a top-heavy patriarchal system was adjusting itself with difficulty to unusual conditions. While this industrial process required men of active intelligence, it offered little hospitality to the brooding spirit of letters. It is true that in the latter years of the eighteenth century much able writing in politics began to appear. Jefferson, who touched with charm, and usually with wisdom, upon almost every subject that has engaged the mind of man, created not only the political thought, but the greater part of the Southern literature of his period. After his death, however, and particularly with the approach of the Civil War, political sagacity withered beneath a thick increment of prejudice. Philosophy, like heresy, was either suspected or prohibited. Even those Southerners (and there were many of these in Virginia) who regarded slavery as an anachronism rather than an iniquity, and looked ahead reluctantly to a doomed social order—even those prophetic Southerners lacked the courage or the genius that rides in the whirlwind and directs the storm. Before approaching disaster, pleasure became not merely a diversion but a way of escape. In the midst of a changing world all immaterial aspects were condensed for the Southern planter into an incomparable heartiness and relish for life.

What distinguished the Southerner, and particularly the Virginian, from his severer neighbours to the north was his ineradicable belief that pleasure is worth more than toil, that it is worth more even than profit. Although the difference between the Virginian and the far Southerner was greater than the distance between Virginia and Massachusetts, a congenial hedonism had established in the gregarious South a confederacy of the spirit. Yet in this agreeable social order, so benevolent to the pleasure-seeker and so hostile alike to the inquirer and the artist, what encouragement, what opportunity, awaited the serious writer? What freedom was there for literature either of protest or of escape? Here, as elsewhere, expression belonged to the articulate, and the articulate was supremely satisfied with his own fortunate lot, as well as with the less enviable lot of others. Only the slave, the "poor white," or the woman who had forgotten her modesty, may have felt inclined to protest; and these negligible minorities were as dumb and sterile as the profession of letters. And even if they had protested, who would have listened? Even if they had escaped, either in fiction or in fact, where could they have gone? Pride, complacency more human than Southern, self-satisfaction, a blind contentment with things as they are, and a deaf aversion from things as they might be: all these universal swarms, which stifle both the truth of literature and the truth of life, had settled, like a cloud of honey-bees, over the creative faculties of the age. That airy inquisitiveness which frolicked so gracefully over the surface of thought questioned the Everlasting Purpose as seldom as it invaded the barren field of prose fiction. Religion, which made so much trouble in New England, had softened in a milder climate, among an Episcopal society at least, to a healthful moral exercise and a comfortable sense of Divine favour. A noble certainty that he was the image of his Maker imparted dignity to the Southern gentleman while it confirmed his faith in the wisdom of his Creator. Though the venom of intolerance had been extracted but imperfectly, the Protestant Episcopal Church was charitable toward almost every weakness except the dangerous practice of thinking. Moreover, the civilization of the old South was one in which every member, white or black, respected the unwritten obligation to be amusing when it was possible and agreeable in any circumstances. Generous manners impose a severe, if mute, restraint upon morals; but generous manners exacted that the artist should be more gregarious than solitary.

II

Such, at least, is one answer among the many to our question: why should the old South have failed to produce great books when it produced great men in abundance? It is an answer sufficiently exact on the surface; but, even as we make it, we know that it requires another angle of vision. For as soon as we turn from imaginative literature to the uses of imagination in life, we discover that the creative art of the South was not a substitute for experience but experience itself, circumscribed and intensified. From a forgotten episode, an attitude, or a gesture, in the yellowed pages of an old diary, passion will start out, alive and quivering, charged, we are almost persuaded, with the significance, if not the subtlety, of metaphysics. Belief vibrates round us; the air thickens; and we are transported to an age in which the supernatural, or what we feel to be the supernatural, borrows validity from the worship that still enshrines it. Thus we come to understand that the whole scheme of living in the South was founded upon an idea of civilization, not less abstract because it was expressed emotionally and rhetorically, but with little help from the written word. If literature was deficient in realities, life was full of what we may call, according to our habit of mind, exalted or evasive idealism. Life, indeed, was lived so completely in the open and in action, yet with so bright a flame of this particular aspect of idealism, that the need was seldom felt of a retreat into the shadows. There was *katharsis*, as well as inspiration, in the cult of the hero as soldier and patriot, and in united

surrender to a cause, however wise or impolitic, noble or reckless, that surrender may appear to the historian.

After the War, pursued by the dark furies of Reconstruction, the mind of the South was afflicted with a bitter nostalgia. From this homesickness for the past there flowered, as luxuriantly as fireweed in burned places, a mournful literature of commemoration. A prosperous and pleasure-loving race had been thrust back suddenly into the primitive struggle for life; and physical resistance had settled slowly into mental repression. Already those desperate political remedies which, according to the philosopher, begin in fear and end in folly, were welding the Southern States into a defense and a danger. From political expediency there emerged a moral superstition. What had begun as an emergency measure had matured into a sacred and infallible doctrine. And among these stagnant ideas the romantic memories of the South ripened, and mellowed, and at last began to decay. That benevolent hardness of heart, so necessary to the creative artist, dissolved, if it had ever existed, into the simple faith which makes novels even less successfully than it moves mountains. To defend the lost became the solitary purpose and the supreme obligation of the Southern novelist, while a living tradition decayed, with the passage of years, into a sentimental infirmity. Graceful, delicate, and tenderly reminiscent, the novels of this period possess that unusual merit, the virtue of quality. Yet charming as they are in manner, they lack creative passion and the courage to offend which are the essential notes of great fiction. The emotions with which they deal are formal, trite, deficient in blood and irony, and true, not to experience, but to the attitude of evasive idealism. In the end, this writing failed to survive because, though faithful to a moment in history, it was false to human behaviour.

But, even with this serious defeat, the first sustained literary movement in the South cannot be dismissed as undeserving of criticism. Had it been addressed to a race as self-sufficing in literature as in the sphere of heroic tradition, much that is charming, if not vital, might have endured. But the new South, like the old, is self-sufficing only in actual endeavour, or in that twilight region of memory where actual endeavour is enlarged and ennobled. Though it gave its life for a cause, it was wanting in the subjective vision which, together with creative impulse, remoulds a tragic destiny in the serene temper of art.

Yet, in spite of this impediment to literature, the South in the nineteenth century was able to produce the incomparable folk-lore of *Uncle Remus;* and nothing better or truer than *Uncle Remus* has appeared in the whole field of American prose fiction. It is not without significance, perhaps, that whenever the Southern writer escaped from beneath the paw of the stuffed lion into the consciousness of some race or class different from his own, he lost his cloying sentiment and his pose of moral superiority. Some literary magic worked as soon as the Southern novelist forgot that he had been born, by the grace of God, a Southern gentleman. The early dialect stories of Thomas Nelson Page are firm and round and as fragrant as dried rose-leaves; the humorous mountain folk of Charles Egbert Craddock are perennially fresh and delightful; the simpler persons, portrayed without august idealism, of James Lane Allen are vital and interesting. Though the chivalrous romances of William Gilmore Simms have lost, if they ever wore, the col-

ours of life, the Creole novels of George W. Cable are still suffused with their own magic.

To those of us who are in accord with the artistic impulse we call Modernism, it is a relief to find at last that the horizon of the American novel is fluid, not fixed, and that there is a way of escape from artificial limitations of material and method. A fresh literary impulse in the South, which was merely a single curve in the world movement toward freedom in art, had broken, not only with its own formal tradition, but with the well-established American twin conventions of prudery and platitude. Mr. James Branch Cabell spinning his rhythms from iridescent illusion was still in harmony with the natural patterns of life. A long tradition and a thick deposit of hopes and fears had flowered again in the serene disenchantment of his philosophy. The austere perfection of his art, with its allegorical remoteness and that strangely hollow ring which echoes the deeper human tones of passion and pity, could have sprung only from a past that has softened and receded into the eternal outline of legend. Certainly it is an art that belongs by inheritance to the South, though it may appear to contain no element we define narrowly as Southern, except, perhaps, the gaiety and gallantry of its pessimism.

And yet it is true even with a novelist of philosophy rather than life that there must be a fourth dimension in every fiction that attempts to interpret reality. There must be a downward seeking into the stillness of vision, as well as an upward springing into the animation of the external world. For the novel, and indeed every form of art, no matter how firmly rooted it may be in a particular soil, must draw nourishment from the ancient instincts, the blood and tears, which are the common heritage of mankind. And because this is true of the South, as of the rest of the world, it is well to remind ourselves that art, to be independent, not derivative, to be adequate, compact, original, must absorb heat and light from the central frame of its own nature. The old South, genial, objective, and a little ridiculous—as fashions of the past are always a little ridiculous to the present—has vanished from the world of fact to reappear in the permanent realm of fable. This much we have already conceded. What we are in danger of forgetting is that few possessions are more precious than a fable that can no longer be compared with a fact. The race that inherits a heroic legend must have accumulated an inexhaustible resource of joy, beauty, love, laughter, and tragic passion. To discard this rich inheritance in the pursuit of a standard utilitarian style is, for the Southern novelist, pure folly.

Never should it be overlooked that the artist in the South will attain his full stature only by preserving, at any cost, his individual integrity. Sincerely as he may admire the flat and vigorous novel of the Middle West, he can never subdue his hand to the monotonous soil of the prairies. That impressive literary movement has as little kinship with the Southern scene as it has with the special poetic forms that reflect so perfectly the frozen landscapes of New England. But in the restrained profusion of Mr. Cabell's art, or, to take another and a more recent writer, in the rich humanity, the mellow memories, and the singularly living prose of Mr. Stark Young, we find a genuine expression of the beauty which, however neglected and debased among us, is still natural to the thought and the literature of the South. If Mr. Cabell's delicate pursuit of the unholy grail wears, on high occasions, the semblance of allegory, Mr. Young's creative vision has the downward seeking and the upward springing of authentic reality.

It is easy to repeat that this artistic inheritance may be lost upon a race that has persistently confused emotions with ideas and mistaken tradition for truth. It is easy to repeat that a logical point of view is almost as essential to art as it is to philosophy. But these repetitions are not only offensive but futile. After all, what the South has known and remembered was a lavish, vital, and distinctive society, which, for want of a better phrase, we may consent to call an archaic civilization. Imperfect, it is true. For as long as the human race remains virtually, and perhaps essentially, barbarian, all the social orders invented by man will be merely the mirrors of his favourite imperfections. Nevertheless, there are arts, and the novel is one of them, that appear to thrive more vigorously upon human imperfections than upon machine-made excellence. Commercial activity and industrial development have their uses, no doubt, in any well-established society; but genius has been in even the most civilized periods a vagabond. And, with or without genius, the novel is more vital, and certainly more interesting, when it declines to become the servant either of sentimental tradition or of patriotic materialism.

III

Every observant mind nowadays must be aware of what we call, without too much enthusiasm, an awakening interest in ideas; and a few observant minds may have perceived in the rising generation an almost pathetic confusion of purpose. In the temper of youth, we feel the quiver of expectancy, and an eagerness to forsake familiar paths and adventure into the wilderness. But where shall it begin? For what is it searching? Adaptable by nature, and eager, except in moments of passion, to conciliate rather than to offend, the modern South is in immediate peril less of revolution than of losing its individual soul in the national Babel. After sixty years of mournful seclusion, the South is at last beginning to look about and to coquet with alien ideas. With an almost disdainful air, the Southern mind is turning from commemoration to achievement. Noise, numbers, size, quantity, all are exerting their lively or sinister influence. Sentiment no longer suffices. To be Southern, even to be solid, is not enough; for the ambition of the new South is not to be self-sufficing, but to be more Western than the West and more American than the whole of America. Uniformity, once despised and rejected, has become the established ideal. Satisfied for so long to leave the miscellaneous product "Americanism" to the rest of the country, the South is at last reaching out for its neglected inheritance.

At this point it may be wise for the prudent essayist to pause and approach his subject with caution. The recently invented noun, Americanism, which appears so mild and harmless in print, reveals itself to the touch as a dangerous explosive. No other word in our language arouses so easily the fierce possessive instinct of criticism. So sensitive, indeed, are the emotions aroused by this label that when I attempted to treat it lightly in a thin vein of satire, I was taken to task by an indignant reader. Gravely, he charged me with harbouring what seems to be an "un-American" prejudice against a confusion of tongues.

Yet nothing could be, in sober fact, more remote from my thought. On the contrary, I believe that America, if not the didactic term Americanism, is wide enough to include the diverse qualities in all novels ever written by American novelists at home or abroad. Since the appearance of *Giants in the Earth,* I am disposed to add all the novels ever written by American novelists in any language; for Rölvaag had written a fine American novel in the Norwegian tongue. I am told that excellent American novels are written in Yiddish; and, for all I know, excellent American novels may be written in Greek, or even in Latin. Certainly, I see no reason why American novels, excellent or otherwise, should not be written in the South, where the English language is still in use. But they will be written, it is safe to prophesy, by those novelists who are concerned more with the quality of excellence than with the characteristic of Americanism.

For the Americanism so prevalent in the South today belongs to that major variety which, by reducing life to a level of comfortable mediocrity, has contributed more than a name to the novel of protest. After breaking away from a petrified past overgrown by a funereal tradition, an impressive group of Southern writers recoiled from the uniform concrete surface of an industrialized South. To mention a few names, among many, I should include Thomas Wolfe, William Faulkner, Allen Tate, Caroline Gordon, Marjorie Kinnan Rawlings, Hamilton Basso, Margaret Mitchell, Clifford Dowdey. But it is significant that, for the first time in its history, the South is producing, by some subtle process of aversion, a literature of revolt. Consciously or unconsciously, the aesthetic sense that surrendered to the romantic life of the past, and even to the more picturesque aspects of slavery, is rejecting the standards of utility in art and of fundamentalism in ideas.

Although it is true that there has been an advance in the South of what the world has agreed to call education, there is a corresponding decrease in that art of living, which excels in the amiable aspects of charm rather than in the severe features of dogmatism. If flexibility of mind has settled into earnest conviction, grace of manner has apparently hardened into a confirmed habit of argument. A new class has risen to the surface if not to the top. New prophets are creating new vices and denouncing the old ones. It is this menace not only to freedom of thought, but to beauty and pleasure and picturesque living that is forcing the intelligence and the aesthetic emotions of the South into revolt. And it is this revolution of ideas that must inevitably produce the Southern novelist of the future.

IV

And so it would seem that the qualities which will unite to make great Southern novels are the elemental properties which make great novels wherever they are written in any part of the world: power, passion, pity, ecstasy and anguish, hope and despair. For it is true in literature as in war that with the imponderables lies the real force. The universal approach is not without but within; and the way to greatness leads beyond manner, beyond method, beyond movement, to some ultimate dominion of the spirit. Even style, the essence of all great literature, is not a manufactured film but a vital fluid.

And what does this mean, after all, except that the South must look more to inward inspiration than to outward example? It is well to have an American outlook; it may be better to have what is called an international attitude of mind; but the truth remains that great novels are not composed of either an outlook or an attitude. Even a return to aesthetic values in fiction will not help us unless we have values more genuine and more profound than purely aesthetic ones. And what will it profit a writer to look within if he has not accumulated an abundance of vital resources? It has become a habit both in English and American criticism to remark that the South contains a wealth of unused material for prose fiction, which means only that a sense of tragedy and heartbreak still lingers beneath the vociferous modern "programme of progress." Wherever humanity has taken root there has been created, it is needless to point out, the stuff of great novels; and this is true of the South in the exact degree that it is true of every other buried past upon earth. But it is even truer that wherever the predestined artist is born his material is found awaiting his eye and his hand. All that is required, indeed, for the novel would appear to be a scene that is large enough to hold three characters, two passions, and one point of view.

In the Southern novelists of the past there has been an absence, not of characters, not of passions, but of a detached and steadfast point of view. What the novel lacked was, not only clearness of vision, but firmness of outline. For even the treasure of the inward approach may be wasted upon a writer who does not possess the practical advantage of the outward eye; and it is essential that the look within should be that of the artist, not of the lover. If the Southern novelist of the commemoration period was submerged in the stuff of life and incapable, therefore, of seeing his subject steadily and whole, the fault was not in the material, but in the novelist's inevitable loss of perspective. To be too near, it appears, is more fatal in literature than to be too far away; for it is better that the creative writer should resort to imagination than that he should be overwhelmed by emotion. And so it is only since the romantic charm and the lover's sentiment have both passed away from the South that the Southern novelist has been able to separate the subject from the object in the act of creation. It is only with the loss of this charm and the ebbing of this sentiment that he has been able to rest apart and brood over the fragmentary world he has called into being. For this is the only way, it would seem, in conclusion, that great novels, in the South or elsewhere, will ever be written. This was the way of Fielding with English life; it was the way of Hawthorne with the past of New England; it was the way of Proust with his world; it was the way of Tolstoy or Dostoievsky with his universe.

1938, 1943

BOOTH TARKINGTON
(1869–1946)

BRIDEWATER'S HALF DOLLAR *

George Bridewater looked upon a certain bench in Garfield Square as his own. The Square, a smoky green parklet in the shabby, oldest part of the city, had a small central space of gravel about which were twelve benches, three on a side; and it was

* From: *Mr. White, The Red Barn, Hell and Bridewater,* published by Doubleday & Co., Inc. Copyright, 1935, by Booth Tarkington.

the middle bench on the north side, facing the sun, that Mr. Bridewater looked upon as his. The seven or eight other habitués respected his feeling, and, if a stranger loitered near, Bridewater yawned and extended both arms along the top of the bench, kept them there until the intruder either passed on or made another selection. He performed this maneuver a little after five o'clock, one afternoon of last May, to discourage an unknown saunterer whose appearance was that of a young workman out of a job; but, though he thus significantly stretched himself, Bridewater was interested in the conversation he was having with acquaintances upon other benches and didn't interrupt it.

"I'm fifty-four, Mr. Schleeman," he said, speaking loudly because he was addressing the seedy fat man who sat upon a bench across the graveled central space. "I'm fifty-four and I ain't never yet let no foreman work me to death. 'Who do you think I am?' I'd say. 'Don't get talky with me,' I'd say, 'or I'll put the heat on you! Give me my time and I'll go,' I'd say, 'but don't get talky!' I says just that the last job I had. It was in Nineteen Twenty-seven; and if they think they can take advantage of me now on account of the depression, make me work for nothin' and get talky with me, too, I'll show 'em!"

The loitering young workman sat down upon an unoccupied bench and addressed Mr. Bridewater. "I wouldn't," he said. "I wouldn't care how talky they got if they'd give me a job. Guess me and my family might all died if we hadn't got on relief, but I sure am sick of bein' on it!"

Mr. Bridewater, Mr. Schleeman and the four other regulars present all looked at him coldly. They didn't mind listeners, but disliked a talking stranger. This was the year 1935, and, of course, great public themes daily absorbed them; they were in accord upon the new politics, and, as views in opposition upset their nerves, they, naturally, didn't wish to hear any. An articulate stranger, therefore, was open to the suspicion of being a propagandist until he proved, by agreeing with them, that he wasn't.

"Listen!" Bridewater said. "You take relief as long as you can get it. It's only the Guv'ment givin' a man what's already his by rights. In this Guv'ment one man's supposed to be as good as another, ain't he? Then it's logic he's entitled to as much as any other man is, ain't it? How do you get around that?"

"You can't!" Mr. Schleeman called across the open space. "One man's got the rights to the same as any other man; and it's a good thing for them politicians they're commencin' to see it, or we'd kick 'em all to hell out." He frowned. "What I don't like about this two-hundred-dollar-a-month plan, though, it's the sixty-year clause. I don't begrudge anybody sixty years old from gettin' their money, but it ought to be widened at the base. Lots of people sixty years old's got better constitutions than some only fifty and fifty-five. It's too much regimentation, making it exackly sixty years old."

The other habitués looked at Mr. Schleeman respectfully; they admired him for language like "widened at the base" and "regimentation." Bridewater, however, ventured to take an argumentative tone. "No, no, Mr. Schleeman; that's a good plan. I only got six years to wait myself till I begin to draw the money; but to get right down to brass tacks, it's the other plan I favor the most. Five thousand dollars redistabution of wealth to everybody, paid down. Cold cash. That's what I

say." He appealed to the others. "Five thousand dollars flat. Ain't that what you favor, gentlemen?"

On the next bench a gloomy man with a blade of grass waggling from his mouth shook his head, not in disagreement but in perplexity. "I ain't got the straight o' that yet, Mr. Bridewater. Are we all supposed to be goin' to get five thousand dollars—or is it three thousand?"

"Five."

"Well, then, is it five thousand dollars flat or five thousand dollars a year?"

"A year!" Bridewater exclaimed with emphasis. "They proved they can do it; proved it in cold figures over the radio."

"Who?" The young workman was skeptical. "Who proved they can give everybody five thousand?"

"Who?" Mr. Bridewater gave him another cold look. "Don't you never listen to the radio? Ain't you read any litterchewer? The biggest men in this country's goin' to do it."

"How? How they goin' to do it?"

"How!" Bridewater exclaimed. "Why, by the redistabution of the wealth. All the Guv'ment's got to do's put on taxes and take it away from everybody that's got over five thousand dollars a year and hand it to the rest of us that's got under that much. The Guv'ment'll take all them stocks and bonds and high-priced cars and show-off jewelry from the wealthy and ——"

"And pass 'em around?" the young man asked. "F'r instance, hand me a couple diamonds and part of a used limousine and some stock of a railroad that's in the red and ——"

"No, sir!" Bridewater was irritated. "Any child knows the Guv'ment can't do that and make a fair redistabution. What they'll do, they'll simply take all them things and sell 'em and then divide up the money fair and square, so that everybody all alike gets just exackly five ——"

"Hold up!" the young man said. "Who they goin' to sell all them things to?"

"What?"

The disturber laughed harshly. "Who's goin' to buy 'em?"

Mr. Bridewater hadn't thought of this. Baffled, he stared in helpless annoyance at the young man; but Mr. Schleeman came to the rescue with a smile of pity for the questioner's ignorance. "Who's goin' to buy 'em? Why, Uncle Sam. The United States Guv'ment's goin' to buy 'em, that's who!"

"What with?" the young man asked derisively. "If the Guv'ment's got the money to buy 'em, then it can already hand us out five thousand dollars a year right now without buyin' anything."

"What?"

"Why, certainly!" The intruder, once started, became disagreeably voluble. "On the other hand, if the Guv'ment ain't got the money, why, it'd haf to buy all that stuff with paper currency. So if the paper currency's worth anything, they could just as well hand it over to us, instead. So that proves this paper currency wouldn't be worth anything at all or else they'd do it. Besides, if the Guv'ment could pay the rich for all their stocks and bonds and limousines and diamonds, then the rich'd have the money and be just as rich as they was before. How you goin' to get around that?"

"How?" Bridewater, flushed and frowning, made oratorical gestures. "Listen to me! Uncle Sam can do anything he wants to. He can take the shirt right off your back if he wants to. He could lock you up in jail this minute if he took the notion to. Uncle Sam'll simply take all that wealth and ——"

"Will he? Well, s'pose Uncle Sam does, what'll he do with it? He can't sell it because there'd be nobody to buy it, and he can't just hand around five thousand dollars a year for everybody because he can't split diamonds and stocks and limousines up even; and they wouldn't be worth anything much if they got split up. So listen here! If any you guys got a good five-cent cigar on you to trade, I'll sign over my five thousand dollars a year to you right now, and I'll throw in the two hundred dollars a month I'm goin' to get when I'm sixty, just for extra; and then laugh in your face! Any takers?"

Pleased with himself, the talkative young workman burst into loud laughter in which his hearers did not join. The gloomy man on the bench next to Mr. Bridewater's began to murmur plaintively.

"I can't make nothin' of it," he said. "Sometimes it looks like a man's goin' to get his rights in this world and then right away again it don't. Take me now. I'm makin', say, an average of four to seven dollars a week cuttin' grass, weedin' and so on. I got a second cousin, Joe Entringer, never done a day's work in his life—nothin' but a souse since the day he was weaned and got such a paunch on him now he couldn't work if he wanted to. Yet he's foreman, settin' all day on a stump with a bun on and smokin' cigars where they're raisin' the levees up at Mill Creek. Eighty dollars a month! Does that look right, with me only makin' twenty-eight, best I can do?"

"There's plenty worse off'n you," the man who shared the bench with him responded. "On the other hand, look at the nice jobs floatin' around if a man was only fixed to land one of 'em. Why, f'r instance, I know a colored mulatto girl that gets twenty-five dollars a week, Guv'ment money —yes, sir, a cool hundred a month— just for handin' out relief. She's a high-educated colored girl; but they'd ought to hired some man with a family, instead. You know her, too, Mr. Bridewater—Ellamora Thompson that lives right across the street from your house and always moves so kind of slow. Ain't it like I say?"

Mr. Bridewater did not reply. He was staring distastefully at the young workman and not listening. His mind was confused and he hadn't understood the interloper's argument; but he felt resentfully that here was an ominous force, hostile to himself personally—somebody who wanted to deprive him of radiant prospects lately opened before him. "Listen here, you!" he said, frowning heavily. "You sound like you're tryin' to argue in behalfs of them intanational Wall Street schemers. Their day's about over, let me tell you! My own dead father used to say over and over in his old age he hoped his chuldern'd never haf to work as hard as he had, and I never forgot it. What's the use a man's workin' himself to death and Wall Street gettin' all the money? The time's come for a turnover; we're goin' to get our rights, and any man that comes around here arguin' against it ——"

"Me?" The young man laughed ruefully. "I only wish them fairy stories was true!"

"Fairy stories!" Bridewater's voice was husky with anger. He rose and shook a lank forefinger at the young workman. "Listen here! You're the kind that wants to upset their own country just when it's gettin' straightened out the way it ought to be! Talkin' about fairy stories! You're the kind that wants to take bread out of the mouths of the poor! I bet you're paid for it! I bet you're hired by the banks to come around here and ——"

"Paid? Hell, don't I wish I was, though!"

"I don't want no more truck with you!" Bridewater made a furiously obliterative gesture with his extended hand, turned abruptly and strode down a graveled path that led to Dellavan Avenue, the dismal west boundary of Garfield Square.

His shabby figure moved gauntly against the soiled gilt light of a sun edging its way downward into the western smoke of the sprawling city; and he muttered aloud as he walked. The mutterings were fragmentary; he conceived himself to be addressing the too-talkative young workman. In more ways than one he called this creature a dog; he labeled him rodent also, and defied him: "Man to man now, just you try it! I been waitin' all my life for it, and now I got it and it's mine. Just you try to get it away from me, you rat, you!"

Naturally, George Bridewater was in a state of rage. His always-brittle temper, combined with his reverence for the hope so often expressed by his aged father, deceased, had led to long periods of moody idleness throughout his life. Now, at last virtual possessor of five thousand dollars a year, with two hundred dollars a month in prospect, all to be assured to him by Uncle Sam himself, he found upspringing dastards in his path, casting doubts that infuriated him because they frightened him. Talking about "fairy stories" and sneering at that bright income!—when all the time millions of people were going to help him get it, because they couldn't get theirs without seeing that he got his! Bridewater didn't care whether they got theirs or not, just so he got his.

"Sock in the jaw's what you need!"

he said, as he crossed Dellavan Avenue. "Big mouth!"

The house at the corner of Dellavan Avenue and Fourth Street added to his anger; he had always hated it without ever knowing anybody who lived in it. Opulently of the 'Seventies when the town was young, its white stone façade, its tall plate-glass windows and its inside shutters of black walnut had been the front of high fortune and of "family"; but the twentieth century had long ago made the imposing house into an uncherished relic. Ill-kept, dinged with years of soot, neighbored by lifeless used-car salesrooms and a dead restaurant, it was now as apologetic as an old dress coat in a secondhand dealer's window. George Bridewater, annoyed in his youth by its early splendors, remained woodenly unaware of its slow complete change; his resentful mood still associated it with millionaires. Sheerly out of long habit he saw this pathetic house still enveloped in its same old air of bondholding superiority and exploiters' arrogance.

Therefore, the lady who came forth from its front double doors of carved black walnut appeared arrogant to Bridewater, as he crossed the street. She was delicate-looking, pale, slender and elderly; but her little black hat, her brown shoes, her well-brushed tweed skirt and neat old brown cloth coat seemed to him offensively fashionable. What was worse and gave him a sense of being personally affronted, there capered and barked beside her, as she came down the stone steps, a long-haired little white dog obviously exclusive, high-toned and ill-disposed toward the common people. George Bridewater hated all dogs, but what he felt about this one can't respectably be even suggested. Horrid silver gleams came from its little collar; the preservation of its detested life was secured

by a leather leash looped about the gloved wrist of its mistress.

Moreover, Bridewater knew this dog, both by sight and hearing, especially by hearing. His daughter's house, where he lived, faced upon Ackley Street, which was the next thoroughfare to Dellavan Avenue, but, unlike the Avenue, had never been fashionable. The back yard of the hated mansion on Dellavan Avenue was separated by only a narrow alley from his daughter's back yard, and more than once George Bridewater's Sunday-morning slumbers had been ruined by the egoistic barking of this little white dog, let out for air in the back yard of the pompous house.

The neat elderly lady and her noisy little pet, bound for a short airing in Garfield Square, came face to face with Bridewater at the corner of the crossing. "No, Rocket!" she said affectionately, as the dog made a short oblique dash toward Mr. Bridewater's left leg. Rocket, restrained by the leash, barked importantly at this moving leg; and his owner and the owner of the threatened limb exchanged a glance in passing—the briefest momentary gaze, but fateful.

Bridewater's eye was hard with old prejudice and with the new wrong being done him. This was not the first time he'd encountered the lady or been snapped at by Rocket. In them both he saw representatives of wealth, living in a wealthy house, luxurious aristocrats able to despise him because they had despoiled him. They'd better look out; he'd have his rights back from them before long!

The elderly lady's glance was a metallic one, too; she'd often noticed Bridewater about the neighborhood and disapproved of him, thinking him a surly loafer. She was a Miss Pency, a retired schoolteacher. She'd worked hard until she had passed sixty-five; and Bridewater was right in thinking her a bondholder—invested savings brought her forty-two dollars a month. She and Rocket lived pretty sparsely in the struggling boarding house that the grandiose mansion had long ago become.

Miss Pency lived there more sparsely than Rocket did. She had no relatives; her old friends, too, were all dead now, and except for him she was "alone in the world." She made every sacrifice for him and kept him happy. Failing sight no longer permitted her to read, and he was really more than the great thing in her life. She lived for him, and he, in return, though self-centered and conceited, loved only her—something no one else had ever done.

Rocket despised everybody in the world except Miss Pency and himself. As Bridewater, having given Miss Pency the one look, passed on his way, the little dog made plain in a final dart and snarl what he thought about that shabby leg. He believed he'd frightened off a marauder, and, barking with insufferable vanity, and looking all the way up to his mistress's face to reassure her of his protection, went on with her to the Square.

Bridewater, walking along dingy Fourth Street, toward Ackley Street, tasted gall. The unprovoked attack upon him by a high-living, costly, dangerous pet of the haughty rich woman who looked at him as if he were dirt, burned in his heart with that other live coal, the young workman's argufying. Rocket's now-distant joyous barking epitomized into a sound all the forces that Bridewater had felt working against him throughout his life. "You! You!" that barking seemed to say. "You won't get it! Never! Not you!"

"I'd ought to kicked the liver out of him!" Bridewater said, pausing at the corner of Ackley and Fourth Streets; and, mentally conjoining Rocket and the young workman in the single pronoun, delivered the kick retrospectively to this hybrid. Then he saw upon the other side of the street a person with whom he wished to talk. He crossed over, dodging homeward-bound sedans, and approached her.

She was a comely young colored woman, sprightly in dress and much more expensively of the fashion than was Miss Pency, for instance. She sat, chewing gum absent-mindedly, upon the rather tumble-down veranda of a small wooden house, and the veranda was so close to the street that Bridewater, halting upon the sidewalk before the house, could speak to her intimately and without raising his voice.

"Listen here, Ellamora," he said. "I been a good while tryin' to get a-hold of you for another little talk."

"That so?" Chewing her gum slowly, though at times allowing it to be visible, she seemed to feel a faint preoccupied interest in the passing sedans; none at all in Bridewater.

"Just like I told you the other day, Ellamora," he said, "you're gettin' a great big salary administrating relief and I been a good family neighbor of yours a couple years now. Well, there must be some big money pass through your hands that the Guv'ment's turning over to the people, so why oughtn't some of it to come my way just the same as it does to any other man that ain't got a job?" His voice, more than friendly, became insinuating. "You always been a nice good-lookin' girl, Ellamora. How about it?"

Ellamora turned her head to call into an open window behind her chair. "Gran'ma! You're allowing that skillet to remain exposed to the heated coals too long again. It causes the odor of scorching. Step on it, Gran'ma!"

She looked forward again, over Bridewater's head, and seemed drowsily absorbed in her chewing gum; but finally took cognizance of his question. "Well, no, Mr. Bridewater. I'm unable to see my way clear towards accommodating you like you been requesting me."

"Why not?" he asked urgently. "That Guv'ment money all belongs to the people and ain't I ——"

"No," she said. "We don't favor the policies of handing out cash for the present time, Mr. Bridewater. I provide food and fuel exclusive only, and I'm already engaged with the total sum of one hundred and eleven families. I couldn't admit you inside this quota because I've made a ruling cases like you don't come under it."

"Why don't I?" She maddened him; but he contained himself, hoping to placate her. "Big Sam Lesloe told me yesterday him and his whole family been livin' on the Guv'ment eight months now, and if you let Sam and his family in ——"

"No, I couldn't do it," Ellamora informed him languidly. "Mr. Lesloe and his family don't possess any property or any employment, so they come under the case; whereas you live with your daughter in a house owned in her name with an income from roomers. You're complete outside all our rulings and under the class of property owners."

"Listen!" Bridewater's voice was husky with his struggle to control it and still speak persuasively. "Them damn roomers owe their rent; they don't pay it. That house is mortgaged up to every cent it's worth and we ain't paid last October's taxes and don't never expect to. Big Sam Lesloe told me himself he turned down two jobs only last week because if he'd took 'em he'd had to get off Guv'ment money. Listen here, Ellamora; if you

let the Lesloes stay in and go on keepin' me out, ain't somebody liable to say it's because Lesloes is cousins of yours and I ain't? Big Sam's your cousin, ain't he?"

All he achieved was a further distention of his spleen. Ellamora looked at him sleepily, rose, yawned and turned toward the open doorway of the house. "I desire to lay down a while before supper, Gran'ma!" she called, as she went in. "Fix the sofa cushions for me. Step on it, Gran'ma!"

George Bridewater, in strong agitation upon the sidewalk, stared at the vacant veranda and uttered three words, two of them irreverent and the other hot with racial superiority.

It seemed to him that insult and outrage stalked him; that he was being used as a doormat by colored people, by rich women's dogs and by pseudo-workmen hired by the banks. He repeated the three words twice; then he turned and strode across the street to his own home, a wooden house somewhat larger than Ellamora Thompson's Grandma's, but in greater disrepair.

Halfway across the street he encountered drifts of the smell of hot cabbage; the odor solidified as he penetrated farther into it, and, when he opened his front door, it filled his lungs, the orifices of his head and all the air spaces within his clothes.

His daughter, Effie Bridewater, met him in the narrow front hall. "I saw you across the street, Papa," she said, in an affectionate, tired voice. "Junior's home and I was just coming to call you. I got supper all ready now and I got a nice surprise for you, Papa."

"Surprise? Cabbage? You call that a ——"

"No, we got cabbage soup; but you wait and see what else!" She took his hand and gazed up at him with a tender fondness. She was thirty, but looked a driven and dried-up forty. "Come on, Papa. Junior's waiting for his supper."

She retained her father's hand until they had reached the hot little kitchen and sat down at the oilcloth-covered table, where her brother, Junior, had already helped himself to a plate of the cabbage soup. Junior, a thin boy of twenty-two with an unfortunate complexion, said nothing to either of them. He was always quiet at home, had no trade or profession, but sometimes seemed to have a little money, which a girl in the next block always got away from him—something his father and sister had long ago learned they needn't hope to do.

Once or twice a plain-clothes man had come to the house inquiring about Junior when he was away, and sometimes Junior disappeared from home for as much as a month, but was stonily uncommunicative on his return.

He didn't get along well with his father, and, though he declined to argue with him, sometimes jeered at him a little.

Junior was a Communist, and Bridewater hated all radicals, believed that they were trying to ruin the country and might upset the great new plans for redistributing the wealth of the wealthy.

Effie didn't really care for Junior, either; though she supported him. All her life, for reasons lost in some fathomlessly obscure predilection of her infancy, her whole power to love had concentrated upon her father. To Effie, her father was all that little Rocket was to Miss Pency, and, though Bridewater lacked Rocket's reciprocal intense devotion, the deepest feeling he had, except one, was for Effie.

"No, I ain't," he replied gruffly to an anxious question of hers, as he finished his soup. "I certainly ain't feelin' any too good this evening."

"You didn't eat anything disagreed with you this afternoon, Papa? A sangwich or anything?"

"How could I ate any sangwich without even a nickel on me?"

"Then what's the trouble, Papa?"

"Never you mind; I got enough! Where's this surprise you was talkin' so much about?"

"You'll see!" She removed the soup, brought fresh plates; then brightly set the surprise upon the table. "It's a steak, Papa! Just what you love the most. I thought for once we'd just splurge. Ain't it a dandy?"

His lowering brow lightened a little and he said he hoped so; but, when about half the steak had been placed upon his plate and he tested its quality, he made plain his disappointment. "Wha'd you pay for this steak?"

"Oh, my!" Effie cried, stricken. "They told me that it was a tender one. Ain't it all right for your teeth, Papa?"

Bridewater clenched his fingers round the handle of his fork, stabbed the prongs heavily into the steak. "Might be all right for a dog's teeth," he said; and the thought of a dog made him sorer. "Leather!" He gave his slyly smiling son a hard glance. "Might do for them Russians' teeth too. I hear they'll eat anything you care to give 'em."

Junior's eye showed a gleam of malicious mirth. "Say! You'd last about five minutes in Russia. Everybody's got to work there."

He put only a slight emphasis upon the word "got," but the effect upon Bridewater was sufficient. "You shut your mouth!" he said. "I been all my life hopin' my chuldern wouldn't haf to work as hard as I have; but I never thought I'd bring a loafer into the world that'd try to upset the United States Guv'ment!"

"So it was you brought me into the world, was it?" Junior uttered a single harsh sound of laughter. "Glad I know who I got to thank for it. Done a lot for me since, too, haven't you?"

An impulse to violence swelled Bridewater's reddening neck. He seemed about to swing his long arm across the table; but Effie interposed hurriedly: "Here's fried potatoes, Papa. You always do love fried potatoes, dearie; and I got a dish of awful nice apple sauce for dessert, besides. I feel awful bad about the steak, Papa; but you eat all the fried potatoes because Junior and I can chew the steak all right and that's plenty for us. Won't you try to enjoy the fried potatoes and apple sauce, please, Papa?"

Bridewater, morose, made no vocal response, but ate all of the fried potatoes, almost all of the apple sauce and also drank two cups of a brownly transparent fluid Effie called coffee. Junior, rising, gave his father a brief, unbearable glance of amusement and departed; was heard ascending the creaky stairway in the hall, on his way to his own quarters in the attic. Effie washed the dishes, glancing now and then placatively at her father. He remained broodingly in his chair at the table, and sometimes his thoughts caused him to breathe so heavily that she heard the sound. When this happened, she sighed deeply with a loving compassion, and, when she had finished the dishes, she sat down beside him and looked at him entreatingly.

"Papa, I got a feeling something's gone awful wrong with you today. Couldn't you tell me about it, dearie?"

"On top of everything else," he said, "think of my havin' a son like that! Sometimes I get so sick of ——"

He paused and looked toward the open window through which there came from the dusk beyond a repeated sharp little sound that seemed to sting him. "A man can't hear himself talk in his own house!"

"It's only that little white dog in the yard behind our alley," Effie said soothingly. "They always let him out now for a few minutes, and again about ten o'clock; but just for a little while. There; he's stopped. They've took him in the house again. Go on, Papa, tell me what you was goin' to. Won't you, dearie?"

"I'm sick of this life!" he said. "I ain't goin' to put up with it no longer. If it ain't goin' to change right from now on, I'm through!"

The desperation in his voice and in his face alarmed her. "Oh, Papa, don't say that! You don't mean you'd— you'd ——"

"I mean just what I say, I can tell you! If things don't look like gettin' better right from now on, what I got to live for? I ain' goin' to put up with it, gettin' balked and flouted and high-hatted and bit at and walked on and treated like I ain't got a word to say in this world. I'm ready to quit, I tell you!"

"No, no, dearie; don't talk like this!" Effie implored him. "It's my fault. I'd ought to made sure that steak was going to be tender; I'd ought to paid a few cents more and got a better cut. I can't stand for you to feel so bad. I'd give you anything in the world, Papa, if I had it. I'd give my life's blood to have you feel happier. You know I would, don't you, dearie?"

"Would you?" He looked at her penetratingly. "You honest mean you would, Effie?"

"Of course I would. A thousand times!"

At that, his mood seemed to lighten

a little; his frown relaxed and he gave her a kind look. "Listen, honey. For a good while back I been thinkin' over ways to make things better, and it's just begun to look to me like I've worked out a plan to where I could swing it. All I need's a little ready money. Less'n three hundred dollars would do it."

She looked frightened. "Would do what, Papa?"

"Would give me something to go on," he explained. "Money to live on. Honey, I'm so sick and tired of goin' around without a cent in my pocket— not a single solitary red penny!—I just can't stand it no longer, Effie. I don't ask much—just a few dollars in my pants, enough to feel like a human bein', anyhow, and get my shoes patched and buy a cigar or a sangwich if I wanted to, and take a bus ride somewheres maybe. A man can't go forever without even a nickel on him, honey!"

Her fright increased as she stared at him. "Papa, you don't mean the house, do you? You ain't talking about that again?"

"Yes, I am," he said; and now his tone became earnestly persuasive. "Honey, I got it all figured out, prackly to the dot. We ain't got long to wait for that redistabution of the wealth to be worked out. It'll be six years before I get my two hundred dollars a month; but the biggest men in the country are workin' every minute right now, fixin' to give everybody five thousand dollars a year; and it's just like wildfire. Nine-tenths of everybody you talk to's for it, and anybody in Congress or anywheres else that stands against it's goin' to get what's comin' to 'em! All I want's a little to go on while we're waitin' for the big money to begin comin' in. That's all I'm askin' you to do, Effie— just enough to tide me over till then."

"Oh, Papa, if I only had it! If I only ——"

"But you have!" he urged. "Anyways, you could lay hands on it inside a few days. I was down at them real-estate men's, Smith and Angel's, this morning again; and they says yes, they still got this client that's buyin' up depression property and they're still willin' to take over the mortgage and on top of it pay you cash down two hundred and eighty-five dollars for your equity in this house."

"Papa!" she gasped. "I can't!"

"Yes, you can." He was increasingly urgent. "Wait till you see the beauty of it! The minute we don't own the house no longer, we go on relief and get all our food and fuel. Ellamora Thompson as good as told me this evening she couldn't keep us off relief if we didn't own the house. And we'd rent the house from Smith and Angel and go on livin' here just the same, but not pay only just part of the first month's rent; and after that, under this new law, Smith and Angel couldn't evict us out for over a year anyways. And all the time we'd have close on three hundred dollars to be spendin' any way we please, pure velvet! And by that time the redistabution plan'll be workin' and we'll be livin' a life worth livin' and ——"

"Oh, Papa, dear!" Effie cried pleadingly, in sharpest distress. "I can't! Don't ask me that. You know I told Mama before she died I'd always try to hold on to the house and keep our little family together. I haven't told you; but the roomers been paying a little better lately. I'm keeping up the mortgage interest all right, and only this afternoon I was down at the treasurer's office and paid off the taxes."

"What?" Bridewater shouted and, electrified by a sudden anguish, sprang to his feet. "The taxes? You paid 'em? You didn't!"

"Yes, I did."

Bridewater called loudly upon his Creator and began to pace the floor. "Threw it away when you knew I was walkin' the streets without a nickel to my name! Yes, and just when we're goin' to sell the house and them real-estate men would had to pay the taxes and we needn't ever even thought about 'em again! Threw it away just when we could had that much more money to spend as we please and ——"

"But I can't sell the house!" Effie cried. "I can't! I can't! I just can't!"

"Why not?"

Effie began to cry. "Papa, it was mostly for you I worked so hard to buy it. Eight years working in that laundry to save the money and always thinking I'd have a nice place for you and me to live anyhow, no matter what else happened. Anyways, we got a roof over our heads and we mustn't give it up, Papa. Don't push me to sell it, Papa; please don't. Suppose this redistribution got stopped some way and didn't come about and ——"

"Quit that talk!" he bellowed at her. "I had enough of that this afternoon from a smart-aleck in Garfield Square and I won't hear not another damn word against the United States Guv'ment doin' what it's goin' to do, and got to do, and better do—else it'll get a revolution and be made to do it! All I want to know now is just this: Are you goin' to do like I say or aren't you?"

"Wait!" Effie ran into her small pantry, whence there issued, a moment later, a thin sound of tinkling. She came out extending toward her father eagerly but with trembling fingers a silver half dollar. "Take it, Papa. I know it's awful mean for you to go around without anything at all

on you. I been too close with you, I know; but I been so terrible scared over the taxes and interest. It's fifty cents, Papa; won't you take it?"

"Half a dollar!" With bitterest irony Bridewater faced his tragedy—denied close on three hundred dollars and offered fifty cents! His passionate open palm struck the coin from Effie's shaking fingers; it rolled upon the floor. "Half a dollar! Now I am through! Said you'd give your life's blood for me, and then go and fiddle me out half a dollar! Half a dollar!"

Effie began to sob aloud. "I would—I would give you my life's blood. You know I would!" She sank down in the chair he'd left vacant, put her arms upon the table and her head, face downward, upon her arms. "I can't let the house go, Papa! It seems like I hear Mama always whispering me to keep it for you. I can't! I can't! I can't! I can't!"

"I'm through, I tell you!" Bridewater shouted. "I don't haf to stand such a life and I won't! I'll do something! I'll go crazy if I don't do something now!"

Effie, shaking all over and sobbing, could only protest babblingly, not lifting her head. To these incoherent sounds there came no other response than a brief scuffling of Bridewater's shoes upon the wooden floor. Then, while she still moaned to him entreatingly, the flimsy house felt the shock of the front door's being hurled shut with a crash. Bridewater had gone; but his daughter continued to sob upon her desolate arms.

After a while, still sniffling, she rose, took a dish cloth from a nail upon the wall and wiped the oilcloth of the table where her tears had trickled. "Oh, Papa dearie!" she moaned, and, moaning, looked wetly about, searching the floor for the fallen half dollar. She couldn't find it, and when she understood that he must have retrieved it and taken it with him, she was a little cheered for a time; but later had a thought that disquieted her. Once in her mind, that thought grew, did more than disquiet her; slowly became sinister.

At nine o'clock she went up to the attic, where her brother, still dressed, lay stretched upon his bed reading a pamphlet. She stood at the foot of the bed, trembling, her fingers twitching and her eyes staring.

"Junior, I'm scared about Papa!"

Junior looked at her amusedly over the top of his pamphlet. "What for? Is he goin' to commit suicide some more?"

"Junior, I'm scared! Will you help me go look for him?"

He didn't move. "Will you buy me a pack of cigarettes if I do?"

"Yes, I will, Junior. I'm scared."

"O. K." He smiled with one side of his mouth, congratulating himself on an easy bargain, and rolled himself lazily off the bed. "Bet you a quarter he's down at Abe Trissel's Place on First Street watchin' a pool game."

Effie didn't take the bet, though not because she knew she wouldn't be paid if she won it; she only asked him to hurry. On the street, Junior objected to the pace she set. "What's the use breakin' your neck? He ain't goin' to do anything to himself; not that guy! What you pantin' like that for? He'll be settin' there all right; you'll see."

Junior was mistaken. Bridewater wasn't at Abe Trissel's Place and hadn't been there; nor was he at Johnny March's Café or at Frank's Bar, Junior's other suggestions. "Quit that pantin', can't you?" he said, as they came out of Frank's Bar. "There's one other place he hangs around sometimes; so that's where he's got to be. It's Horling's out on West Eighth, quite a ways unless you want to get big-hearted and give us a trolley ride."

"No, no," she said. "We can walk it just as easy, and you say he's sure to be there anyways, Junior, so ——"

He laughed bleakly. "O. K. Come on, then, if we got to hoof it."

Neither Bridewater nor any news of him was at Horling's; and, when they came out to the street, Effie was weeping as well as panting. Junior again complained of her emotions.

"But that's all the places he ever goes; you told me so!" she explained, defending herself. "You don't know the state he was in, Junior; you didn't hear him when he went out. You didn't ——"

"Say, listen! I know the kind that do that; he ain't built that way."

"Maybe not most the time, Junior," she whimpered; "but he's different tonight. You didn't hear his voice when he said he was through and was goin' crazy if he didn't do something. You didn't ——"

"Say! Listen; I'm tired. How's he goin' to do it, suppose even he tries to? He hasn't got a gun, and if he went over to the river, he couldn't let himself stop swimmin', even if he did take a notion to jump in and wet himself. He hasn't got any money, so he couldn't go to a drug store and ——"

"Oh, but he has!" Effie cried. "He's got money. I gave him fifty cents."

"Went haywire, did you?" Junior asked, sardonic. "Just throwin' your money around! Short life but a merry one, what? Tell me next time you get that way, will you? Come on; we got to hoof it all the way back home."

"No, no! I want to—I want to ask at the drug store if he—if he bought anything like that. Let's go to Hait's drug store."

"Hait's? Nopy," Junior said. "He

can't go there because he talked 'em into givin' him credit last January. If he wanted to buy carbolic to drink his own health in, they prob'ly wouldn't sell it to him except some place where they know him, and Hait's is the only place they do."

"No, it isn't. Mr. Kleever, that used to have the bedroom over the kitchen, clerks at Brown's Cash Drug Store, corner Ackley and Sixth, and he knows Papa. We got to go there, Junior."

Junior consented. "It's on the way home, anyhow," he said; and presently was again objecting to the speed at which she kept him scurrying through the long, darkling streets. But when finally they reached the place they sought, she faltered outside the lighted doorway, and with twisting fingers clutched her brother's sleeve.

"You ask Mr. Kleever. I'm—I'm too scared to. You just ask him if Papa's been there, and, if he has, you —you ask Mr. Kleever if he bought anything. I'm scared. I'll wait here, Junior."

Junior grinned at her. "Goofy, huh? O. K., I'll ask him." He slouched into the drug store; but Effie didn't watch him through either the doorway or the broad bright window beside it. Instead, she stood with her back to these areas of light, faced the melancholy street and twisted her fingers. When Junior came out, he was smoking another of the cigarettes she'd bought for him at Abe Trissel's. "Come on," he said, taking her arm. "No place else to go. Me for home. It's only a couple of blocks. Come on."

She came with him slowly, and her voice was weak when she contrived to use it. "Junior, you—you never took a-hold of my arm before. Did—did they say ——"

"Walk on," he said. "I told you he

wouldn't do it, and they haven't got me believin' so yet."

"Yet? Then they—then they did ——"

"Don't get so excited!" Junior's voice was a little unsteady. "If he was goin' to do it, why wouldn't he done it soon's he got outside the store? Had the stuff in his hand, so why not?"

Effie uttered a gulping outcry. "Then he did ——"

"Yep. Kleever says he come in the drug store about half-past nine. Told Kleever he wanted strychnine pills for his heart, and Kleever sold 'em to him. I give a laugh and asked if they'd do him any harm; and Kleever says no, not unless he took about half of 'em all at once. Says then it might be pretty bad; but says the old man knew all about that himself. Here! What you ——"

Effie cried out again, "Papa!" and began to run.

Junior ran with her. Side by side they reached the gate in the picket fence that was the decrepit barrier between their home and the public sidewalk.

"Look in the yard," Junior said, panting now himself. "Look in the yard. If I was goin' to do anything like that, I'd do it in the yard, not in the house—most likely the back yard. He might be out here—somewheres."

The yard was small, mangily patched with grass here and there, and without trees. The light from street lamps showed no form extended upon the forepart of this limited, unlovely expanse; and the brother and sister passed round the house to the thicker darkness that was in the rear. Effie, convulsive all over, clutched at her throat and shoulders, shut her eyes and ceased to go forward.

"You'll—you'll haf to do the look-

ing," she sobbed. "But you tell me
if ——"

She could say no more, stood praying within herself; then she heard a
sickish laugh from Junior.

"Come here," he said; and, when
she stumblingly had come beside him,
he pointed to the unshuttered kitchen
window. "Look a-yonder!"

The saving Effie had turned out the
electric bulb in the kitchen before she
left the house; but the warm little
room was lighted now. In the sufficient illumination from above his
head, Bridewater sat tilted back in a
chair and had his shoeless feet on the
table. He smoked a five-cent cigar and
read a magazine of Hollywood full of
alluring pictures of ladies. His expression was placid. After all the arguments and insults and barkings he'd
had to bear, this hard day, he seemed
at peace.

Outside in the darkness Effie clung
feebly to Junior. "Poor Papa!" she
said, sobbing no longer, but weeping
gently in thankfulness. "He never
told me his heart give him any trouble. I won't be so close with him after
this. I got to find ways to make him
happier."

George Bridewater had already
found one way to make himself happier. That is to say, he just now felt
comparatively satisfied, and, in a
measure, avenged upon the wealthy—
at least temporarily. He had saved his
reason by doing that something he
had declared he must do or go
crazy.

Effie's ninety-nine-cent clock on the
wall behind him showed the time to
be about twenty minutes of eleven;
and at ten o'clock there had been the
usual sprightly barking in the yard
beyond the alley. The sound had
stopped abruptly when the scampering Rocket came upon a bit of toughish steak near the alley fence. Thence

onward he was quiet. Nevermore
would that gay spirit disturb honest
neighbors at bedtime or break the
peace of a Sabbath morning.

Now, through the darkness of the
yard of the pompous Dellavan Avenue
mansion, there groped a brokenhearted old schoolteacher, stifling her
faint outcries to whisper bits of loving
baby talk. She walked stoopingly,
holding her dead little white dog close
to her under a shawl. Miss Pency
hoped to evade the landlady and to
get up to her own meager room unseen, so that she could have this one
last night with Rocket.

1935

WILLA CATHER
(1876–1947)

NEIGHBOUR ROSICKY *

I

When Doctor Burleigh told neighbour Rosicky he had a bad heart,
Rosicky protested.

"So? No, I guess my heart was always pretty good. I got a little asthma,
maybe. Just a awful short breath
when I was pitchin' hay last summer,
dat's all."

"Well, now, Rosicky, if you know
more about it than I do, what did you
come to me for? It's your heart that
makes you short of breath, I tell you.
You're sixty-five years old, and you've
always worked hard, and your heart's
tired. You've got to be careful from
now on, and you can't do heavy work
any more. You've got five boys at
home to do it for you."

The old farmer looked up at the
Doctor with a gleam of amusement in
his queer triangular-shaped eyes. His

* Reprinted from *Obscure Destinies*
by Willa Cather, by permission of Alfred
A. Knopf, Inc. Copyright 1930, 1932 by
Willa Cather.

eyes were large and lively, but the lids were caught up in the middle in a curious way, so that they formed a triangle. He did not look like a sick man. His brown face was creased but not wrinkled, he had a ruddy colour in his smooth-shaven cheeks and in his lips, under his long brown moustache. His hair was thin and ragged around his ears, but very little grey. His forehead, naturally high and crossed by deep parallel lines, now ran all the way up to his pointed crown. Rosicky's face had the habit of looking interested,—suggested a contented disposition and a reflective quality that was gay rather than grave. This gave him a certain detachment, the easy manner of an onlooker and observer.

"Well, I guess you ain't got no pills fur a bad heart, Doctor Ed. I guess the only thing is fur me to git me a new one."

Doctor Burleigh swung round in his deskchair and frowned at the old farmer. "I think if I were you I'd take a little care of the old one, Rosicky."

Rosicky shrugged. "Maybe I don't know how. I expect you mean fur me not to drink my coffee no more."

"I wouldn't, in your place. But you'll do as you choose about that. I've never yet been able to separate a Bohemian from his coffee or his pipe. I've quit trying. But the sure thing is you've got to cut out farm work. You can feed the stock and do chores about the barn, but you can't do anything in the fields that makes you short of breath."

"How about shelling corn?"

"Of course not!"

Rosicky considered with puckered brows.

"I can't make my heart go no longer'n it wants to, can I, Doctor Ed?"

"I think it's good for five or six years yet, maybe more, if you'll take

the strain off it. Sit around the house and help. Mary. If I had a good wife like yours, I'd want to stay around the house."

His patient chuckled. "It ain't no place fur a man. I don't like no old man hanging round the kitchen too much. An' my wife, she's a awful hard worker her own self."

"That's it; you can help her a little. My Lord, Rosicky, you are one of the few men I know who has a family he can get some comfort out of; happy dispositions, never quarrel among themselves, and they treat you right. I want to see you live a few years and enjoy them."

"Oh, they're good kids, all right," Rosicky assented.

The Doctor wrote him a prescription and asked him how his oldest son, Rudolph, who had married in the spring, was getting on. Rudolph had struck out for himself, on rented land. "And how's Polly? I was afraid Mary mightn't like an American daughter-in-law, but it seems to be working out all right."

"Yes, she's a fine girl. Dat widder woman bring her daughters up very nice. Polly got lots of spunk, an' she got some style, too. Da's nice, for young folks to have some style." Rosicky inclined his head gallantly. His voice and his twinkly smile were an affectionate compliment to his daughter-in-law.

"It looks like a storm, and you'd better be getting home before it comes. In town in the car?" Doctor Burleigh rose.

"No, I'm in de wagon. When you got five boys, you ain't got much chance to ride round in de Ford. I ain't much for cars, noway."

"Well, it's a good road out to your place; but I don't want you bumping around in a wagon much. And never again on a hay-rake, remember!"

Rosicky placed the Doctor's fee delicately behind the desk-telephone, looking the other way, as if this were an absent-minded gesture. He put on his plush cap and his corduroy jacket with a sheepskin collar, and went out.

The Doctor picked up his stethoscope and frowned at it as if he were seriously annoyed with the instrument. He wished it had been telling tales about some other man's heart, some old man who didn't look the Doctor in the eye so knowingly, or hold out such a warm brown hand when he said good-bye. Doctor Burleigh had been a poor boy in the country before he went away to medical school; he had known Rosicky almost ever since he could remember, and he had a deep affection for Mrs. Rosicky.

Only last winter he had had such a good breakfast at Rosicky's, and that when he needed it. He had been out all night on a long, hard confinement case at Tom Marshall's,—a big rich farm where there was plenty of stock and plenty of feed and a great deal of expensive farm machinery of the newest model, and no comfort whatever. The woman had too many children and too much work, and she was no manager. When the baby was born at last, and handed over to the assisting neighbour woman, and the mother was properly attended to, Burleigh refused any breakfast in that slovenly house, and drove his buggy—the snow was too deep for a car—eight miles to Anton Rosicky's place. He didn't know another farm-house where a man could get such a warm welcome, and such good strong coffee with rich cream. No wonder the old chap didn't want to give up his coffee!

He had driven in just when the boys had come back from the barn and were washing up for breakfast. The long table, covered with a bright oilcloth, was set out with dishes waiting for them, and the warm kitchen was full of the smell of coffee and hot biscuit and sausage. Five big handsome boys, running from twenty to twelve, all with what Burleigh called natural good manners,—they hadn't a bit of the painful self-consciousness he himself had to struggle with when he was a lad. One ran to put his horse away, another helped him off with his fur coat and hung it up, and Josephine, the youngest child and the only daughter, quickly set another place under her mother's direction.

With Mary, to feed creatures was the natural expression of affection,— her chickens, the calves, her big hungry boys. It was a rare pleasure to feed a young man whom she seldom saw and of whom she was proud as if he belonged to her. Some country housekeepers would have stopped to spread a white cloth over the oilcloth, to change the thick cups and plates for their best china, and the wooden-handled knives for plated ones. But not Mary.

"You must take us as you find us, Doctor Ed. I'd be glad to put out my good things for you if you was expected, but I'm glad to get you any way at all."

He knew she was glad,—she threw back her head and spoke out as if she were announcing him to the whole prairie. Rosicky hadn't said anything at all; he merely smiled his twinkling smile, put some more coal on the fire, and went into his own room to pour the Doctor a little drink in a medicine glass. When they were all seated, he watched his wife's face from his end of the table and spoke to her in Czech. Then, with the instinct of politeness which seldom failed him, he turned to the Doctor and said slyly; "I was just tellin' her not to ask you no questions about Mrs. Marshall till you eat breakfast. My wife, she's terrible fur to ask questions."

The boys laughed, and so did Mary. She watched the Doctor devour her biscuit and sausage, too much excited to eat anything herself. She drank her coffee and sat taking in everything about her visitor. She had known him when he was a poor country boy, and was boastfully proud of his success, always saying: "What do people go to Omaha for, to see a doctor, when we got the best one in the State right here?" If Mary liked people at all, she felt physical pleasure in the sight of them, personal exultation in any good fortune that came to them. Burleigh didn't know many women like that, but he knew she was like that.

When his hunger was satisfied, he did, of course, have to tell them about Mrs. Marshall, and he noticed what a friendly interest the boys took in the matter.

Rudolph, the oldest one (he was still living at home then), said: "The last time I was over there, she was lifting them big heavy milkcans, and I knew she oughtn't to be doing it."

"Yes, Rudolph told me about that when he come home, and I said it wasn't right," Mary put in warmly. "It was all right for me to do them things up to the last, for I was terrible strong, but that woman's weakly. And do you think she'll be able to nurse it, Ed?" She sometimes forgot to give him the title she was so proud of. "And to think of your being up all night and then not able to get a decent breakfast! I don't know what's the matter with such people."

"Why, Mother," said one of the boys, "if Doctor Ed had got breakfast there, we wouldn't have him here. So you ought to be glad."

"He knows I'm glad to have him, John, any time. But I'm sorry for that poor woman, how bad she'll feel the Doctor had to go away in the cold without his breakfast."

"I wish I'd been in practice when these were getting born." The doctor looked down the row of close-clipped heads. "I missed some good breakfasts by not being."

The boys began to laugh at their mother because she flushed so red, but she stood her ground and threw up her head. "I don't care, you wouldn't have got away from this house without breakfast. No doctor ever did. I'd have had something ready fixed that Anton could warm up for you."

The boys laughed harder than ever, and exclaimed at her: "I'll bet you would!" "She would, that!"

"Father, did you get breakfast for the doctor when we were born?"

"Yes, and he used to bring me my breakfast, too, mighty nice. I was always awful hungry!" Mary admitted with a guilty laugh.

While the boys were getting the Doctor's horse, he went to the window to examine the house plants. "What do you do to your geraniums to keep them blooming all winter, Mary? I never pass this house that from the road I don't see your windows full of flowers."

She snapped off a dark red one, and a ruffled new green leaf, and put them in his buttonhole. "There, that looks better. You look too solemn for a young man, Ed. Why don't you git married? I'm worried about you. Settin' at breakfast, I looked at you real hard, and I seen you've got some grey hairs already."

"Oh, yes! They're coming. Maybe they'd come faster if I married."

"Don't talk so. You'll ruin your health eating at the hotel. I could send your wife a nice loaf of nut bread, if you only had one. I don't like to see a young man getting grey.

I'll tell you something, Ed; you make some strong black tea and keep it handy in a bowl, and every morning just brush it into your hair, an' it'll keep the grey from showin' much. That's the way I do!"

Sometimes the Doctor heard the gossipers in the drug-store wondering why Rosicky didn't get on faster. He was industrious, and so were his boys, but they were rather free and easy, weren't pushers, and they didn't always show good judgment. They were comfortable, they were out of debt, but they didn't get much ahead. Maybe, Doctor Burleigh reflected, people as generous and warm-hearted and affectionate as the Rosickys never got ahead much; maybe you couldn't enjoy your life and put it into the bank, too.

II

When Rosicky left Doctor Burleigh's office he went into the farm-implement store to light his pipe and put on his glasses and read over the list Mary had given him. Then he went into the general merchandise place next door and stood about until the pretty girl with the plucked eyebrows, who always waited on him, was free. Those eyebrows, two thin India-ink strokes, amused him, because he remembered how they used to be. Rosicky always prolonged his shopping by a little joking; the girl knew the old fellow admired her, and she liked to chaff with him.

"Seems to me about every other week you buy ticking, Mr. Rosicky, and always the best quality," she remarked as she measured off the heavy bolt with red stripes.

"You see, my wife is always makin' goose-fedder pillows, an' de thin stuff don't hold in dem little down-fedders."

"You must have lots of pillows at your house."

"Sure. She makes quilts of dem, too. We sleeps easy. Now she's makin' a fedder quilt for my son's wife. You know Polly, that married my Rudolph. How much my bill, Miss Pearl?"

"Eight eighty-five."

"Chust make it nine, and put in some candy fur de women."

"As usual. I never did see a man buy so much candy for his wife. First thing you know, she'll be getting too fat."

"I'd like dat. I ain't much for all dem slim women like what de style is now."

"That's one for me, I suppose, Mr. Bohunk!" Pearl sniffed and elevated her India-ink strokes.

When Rosicky went out to his wagon, it was beginning to snow,—the first snow of the season, and he was glad to see it. He rattled out of town and along the highway through a wonderfully rich stretch of country, the finest farms in the county. He admired this High Prairie, as it was called, and always liked to drive through it. His own place lay in a rougher territory, where there was some clay in the soil and it was not so productive. When he bought his land, he hadn't the money to buy on High Prairie; so he told his boys, when they grumbled, that if their land hadn't some clay in it, they wouldn't own it at all. All the same, he enjoyed looking at these fine farms, as he enjoyed looking at a prize bull.

After he had gone eight miles, he came to the graveyard, which lay just at the edge of his own hay-land. There he stopped his horses and sat still on his wagon seat, looking about at the snowfall. Over yonder on the hill he could see his own house, crouching low, with the clump of orchard behind and the windmill before, and all down the gentle hill-slope the rows of pale gold cornstalks stood out against the white field. The snow was falling over the cornfield and the pasture and the hay-land, steadily, with very little wind,—a nice dry snow. The graveyard had only a light wire fence about it and was all overgrown with long red grass. The fine snow, settling into this red grass and upon the few little evergreens and the headstones, looked very pretty.

It was a nice graveyard, Rosicky reflected, sort of snug and homelike, not cramped or mournful,—a big sweep all round it. A man could lie down in the long grass and see the complete arch of the sky over him, hear the wagons go by; in summer the mowing-machine rattled right up to the wire fence. And it was so near home. Over there across the cornstalks his own roof and windmill looked so good to him that he promised himself to mind the Doctor and take care of himself. He was awful fond of his place, he admitted. He wasn't anxious to leave it. And it was a comfort to think that he would never have to go farther than the edge of his own hay-field. The snow, falling over his barn-yard and the graveyard, seemed to draw things together like. And they were all old neighbours in the grave-yard, most of them friends; there was nothing to feel awkward or embar-rassed about. Embarrassment was the most disagreeable feeling Rosicky knew. He didn't often have it,—only with certain people whom he didn't understand at all.

Well, it was a nice snowstorm; a fine sight to see the snow falling so quietly and graciously over so much open country. On his cap and shoul-ders, on the horses' backs and manes, light, delicate, mysterious it fell; and with it a dry cool fragrance was re-leased into the air. It meant rest for vegetation and men and beasts, for the ground itself; a season of long nights for sleep, leisurely breakfasts, peace by the fire. This and much more went through Rosicky's mind, but he merely told himself that winter was coming, clucked to his horses, and drove on.

When he reached home, John, the youngest boy, ran out to put away his team for him, and he met Mary com-ing up from the outside cellar with her apron full of carrots. They went into the house together. On the table, covered with oilcloth figured with clusters of blue grapes, a place was set, and he smelled hot coffee-cake of some kind. Anton never lunched in town; he thought that extravagant, and anyhow he didn't like the food. So Mary always had something ready for him when he got home.

After he was settled in his chair, stirring his coffee in a big cup, Mary took out of the oven a pan of *kolache* stuffed with apricots, examined them anxiously to see whether they had got too dry, put them beside his plate, and then sat down opposite him.

Rosicky asked her in Czech if she wasn't going to have any coffee.

She replied in English, as being somehow the right language for trans-acting business: "Now what did Doc-tor Ed say, Anton? You tell me just what."

"He said I was to tell you some compliments, but I forgot 'em." Rosicky's eyes twinkled.

"About you, I mean. What did he say about your asthma?"

"He says I ain't got no asthma." Rosicky took one of the little rolls in his broad brown fingers. The thick-ened nail of his right thumb told the story of his past.

"Well, what is the matter? And don't try to put me off."

"He don't say nothing much, only I'm a little older, and my heart ain't so good like it used to be."

Mary started and brushed her hair back from her temples with both hands as if she were a little out of her mind. From the way she glared, she might have been in a rage with him.

"He says there's something the matter with your heart? Doctor Ed says so?"

"Now don't yell at me like I was a hog in de garden, Mary. You know I always did like to hear a woman talk soft. He didn't say anything de matter wid my heart, only it ain't so young like it used to be, an' he tell me not to pitch hay or run de corn-sheller."

Mary wanted to jump up, but she sat still. She admired the way he never under any circumstances raised his voice or spoke roughly. He was city-bred, and she was country-bred; she often said she wanted her boys to have their papa's nice ways.

"You never have no pain there, do you? It's your breathing and your stomach that's been wrong. I wouldn't believe nobody but Doctor Ed about it. I guess I'll go see him myself. Didn't he give you no advice?"

"Chust to take it easy like, an' stay round de house dis winter. I guess you got some carpenter work for me to do. I kin make some new shelves for you, and I want dis long time to build a closet in de boys' room and make dem two little fellers keep dere clo'es hung up."

Rosicky drank his coffee from time to time, while he considered. His moustache was of the soft long variety and came down over his mouth like the teeth of a buggy-rake over a bundle of hay. Each time he put down his cup, he ran his blue handkerchief over his lips. When he took a drink of water, he managed very neatly with the back of his hand.

Mary sat watching him intently, trying to find any change in his face. It is hard to see anyone who has become like your own body to you. Yes, his hair had got thin, and his high forehead had deep lines running from left to right. But his neck, always clean shaved except in the busiest seasons, was not loose or baggy. It was burned a dark reddish brown, and there were deep creases in it, but it looked firm and full of blood. His cheeks had a good colour. On either side of his mouth there was a half-moon down the length of his cheek, not wrinkles, but two lines that had come there from his habitual expression. He was shorter and broader than when she married him; his back had grown broad and curved, a good deal like the shell of an old turtle, and his arms and legs were short.

He was fifteen years older than Mary, but she had hardly ever thought about it before. He was her man, and the kind of man she liked. She was rough, and he was gentle,—city-bred, as she always said. They had been shipmates on a rough voyage and had stood by each other in trying times. Life had gone well with them because, at bottom, they had the same ideas about life. They agreed, without discussion, as to what was most important and what was secondary. They didn't often exchange opinions, even in Czech,—it was as if they had thought the same thought together. A good deal had to be sacrificed and thrown overboard in a hard life like theirs, and they had never disagreed as to the things that could go. It had been a hard life, and a soft life, too. There wasn't anything brutal in the short, broad-backed man with the three-cornered eyes and the forehead that went on to the top of his skull. He was a city man, a gentle man, and though he had married a rough farm girl, he had never touched her without gentleness.

They had been at one accord not to hurry through life, not to be always skimping and saving. They saw their neighbours buy more land and feed more stock than they did, without discontent. Once when the creamery agent came to the Rosickys to persuade them to sell him their cream, he told them how much money the Fasslers, their nearest neighbours, had made on their cream last year.

"Yes," said Mary, "and look at them Fassler children! Pale, pinched little things, they look like skimmed milk. I'd rather put some colour into my children's faces than put money into the bank."

The agent shrugged and turned to Anton.

"I guess we'll do like she says," said Rosicky.

III

Mary very soon got into town to see Doctor Ed, and then she had a talk with her boys and set a guard over Rosicky. Even John, the youngest, had his father on his mind. If Rosicky went to throw hay down from the loft, one of the boys ran up the ladder and took the fork from him. He sometimes complained that though he was getting to be an old man, he wasn't an old woman yet.

That winter he stayed in the house in the afternoons and carpentered, or sat in the chair between the window full of plants and the wooden bench where the two pails of drinking-water stood. This spot was called "Father's corner," though it was not a corner at all. He had a shelf there, where he kept his Bohemian papers and his pipes and tobacco, and his shears and

needles and thread and tailor's thimble. Having been a tailor in his youth, he couldn't bear to see a woman patching at his clothes, or at the boys'. He liked tailoring, and always patched all the overalls and jackets and work shirts. Occasionally he made over a pair of pants one of the older boys had outgrown, for the little fellow.

While he sewed, he let his mind run back over his life. He had a good deal to remember, really; life in three countries. The only part of his youth he didn't like to remember was the two years he had spent in London, in Cheapside, working for a German tailor who was wretchedly poor. Those days, when he was nearly always hungry, when his clothes were dropping off him for dirt, and the sound of a strange language kept him in continual bewilderment, had left a sore spot in his mind that wouldn't bear touching.

He was twenty when he landed at Castle Garden in New York, and he had a protector who got him work in a tailor shop in Vesey Street, down near the Washington Market. He looked upon that part of his life as very happy. He became a good workman, he was industrious, and his wages were increased from time to time. He minded his own business and envied nobody's good fortune. He went to night school and learned to read English. He often did overtime work and was well paid for it, but somehow he never saved anything. He couldn't refuse a loan to a friend, and he was self-indulgent. He liked a good dinner, and a little went for beer, a little for tobacco; a good deal went to the girls. He often stood through an opera on Saturday nights; he could get standing-room for a dollar. Those were the great days of opera in New York, and it gave a fellow something to think about for the rest of the week. Rosicky had a quick ear, and a childish love of all the stage splendour; the scenery, the costumes, the ballet. He usually went with a chum, and after the performance they had beer and maybe some oysters somewhere. It was a fine life; for the first five years or so it satisfied him completely. He was never hungry or cold or dirty, and everything amused him: a fire, a dog fight, a parade, a storm, a ferry ride. He thought New York the finest, richest, friendliest city in the world.

Moreover, he had what he called a happy home life. Very near the tailor shop was a small furniture-factory, where an old Austrian, Loeffler, employed a few skilled men and made unusual furniture, most of it to order, for the rich German housewives uptown. The top floor of Loeffler's five-storey factory was a loft, where he kept his choice lumber and stored the odd pieces of furniture left on his hands. One of the young workmen he employed was a Czech, and he and Rosicky became fast friends. They persuaded Loeffler to let them have a sleeping-room in one corner of the loft. They bought good beds and bedding and had their pick of the furniture kept up there. The loft was low-pitched, but light and airy, full of windows, and good-smelling by reason of the fine lumber put up there to season. Old Loeffler used to go down to the docks and buy wood from South America and the East from the sea captains. The young men were as foolish about their house as a bridal pair. Zichec, the young cabinet-maker, devised every sort of convenience, and Rosicky kept their clothes in order. At night and on Sundays, when the quiver of machinery underneath was still, it was the quietest place in the world, and

on summer nights all the sea winds blew in. Zichec often practised on his flute in the evening. They were both fond of music and went to the opera together. Rosicky thought he wanted to live like that for ever.

But as the years passed, all alike, he began to get a little restless. When spring came round, he would begin to feel fretted, and he got to drinking. He was likely to drink too much of a Saturday night. On Sunday he was languid and heavy, getting over his spree. On Monday he plunged into work again. So he never had time to figure out what ailed him, though he knew something did. When the grass turned green in Park Place, and the lilac hedge at the back of Trinity churchyard put out its blossoms, he was tormented by a longing to run away. That was why he drank too much; to get a temporary illusion of freedom and wide horizons.

Rosicky, the old Rosicky, could remember as if it were yesterday the day when the young Rosicky found out what was the matter with him. It was on a Fourth of July afternoon, and he was sitting in Park Place in the sun. The lower part of New York was empty. Wall Street, Liberty Street, Broadway, all empty. So much stone and asphalt with nothing going on, so many empty windows. The emptiness was intense, like the stillness in a great factory when the machinery stops and the belts and bands cease running. It was too great a change, it took all the strength out of one. Those blank buildings, without the stream of life pouring through them, were like empty jails. It struck young Rosicky that this was the trouble with big cities; they built you in from the earth itself, cemented you away from any contact with the ground. You lived in an unnatural world, like the fish in an aquarium, who were probably much more comfortable than they ever were in the sea.

On that very day he began to think seriously about the articles he had read in the Bohemian papers, describing prosperous Czech farming communities in the West. He believed he would like to go out there as a farm hand; it was hardly possible that he could ever have land of his own. His people had always been workmen; his father and grandfather had worked in shops. His mother's parents had lived in the country, but they rented their farm and had a hard time to get along. Nobody in his family had ever owned any land,—that belonged to a different station of life altogether. Anton's mother died when he was little, and he was sent into the country to her parents. He stayed with them until he was twelve, and formed those ties with the earth and the farm animals and growing things which are never made at all unless they are made early. After his grandfather died, he went back to live with his father and step-mother, but she was very hard on him, and his father helped him to get passage to London.

After that Fourth of July day in Park Place, the desire to return to the country never left him. To work on another man's farm would be all he asked; to see the sun rise and set and to plant things and watch them grow. He was a very simple man. He was like a tree that has not many roots, but one tap-root that goes down deep. He subscribed for a Bohemian paper printed in Chicago, then for one printed in Omaha. His mind got farther and farther west. He began to save a little money to buy his liberty. When he was thirty-five, there was a great meeting in New York of Bohemian athletic societies, and

Rosicky left the tailor shop and went home with the Omaha delegates to try his fortune in another part of the world.

IV

Perhaps the fact that his own youth was well over before he began to have a family was one reason why Rosicky was so fond of his boys. He had almost a grandfather's indulgence for them. He had never had to worry about any of them—except, just now, a little about Rudolph.

On Saturday night the boys always piled into the Ford, took little Josephine, and went to town to the moving-picture show. One Saturday morning they were talking at the breakfast table about starting early that evening, so that they would have an hour or so to see the Christmas things in the stores before the show began. Rosicky looked down the table.

"I hope you boys ain't disappointed, but I want you to let me have de car tonight. Maybe some of you can go in with de neighbours."

Their faces fell. They worked hard all week, and they were still like children. A new jackknife or a box of candy pleased the older ones as much as the little fellow.

"If you and Mother are going to town," Frank said, "maybe you could take a couple of us along with you, anyway."

"No, I want to take de car down to Rudolph's, and let him an' Polly go in to de show. She don't git into town enough, an' I'm afraid she's gettin' lonesome, an' he can't afford no car yet."

That settled it. The boys were a good deal dashed. Their father took another piece of apple-cake and went on: "Maybe next Saturday night de two little fellers can go along wid dem."

"Oh, is Rudolph going to have the car every Saturday night?"

Rosicky did not reply at once; then he began to speak seriously: "Listen, boys; Polly ain't lookin' so good. I don't like to see nobody lookin' sad. It comes hard fur a town girl to be a farmer's wife. I don't want no trouble to start in Rudolph's family. When it starts, it ain't so easy to stop. An American girl don't git used to our ways all at once. I like to tell Polly she and Rudolph can have the car every Saturday night till after New Year's, if it's all right with you boys."

"Sure it's all right, Papa," Mary cut in. "And it's good you thought about that. Town girls is used to more than country girls. I lay awake nights, scared she'll make Rudolph discontented with the farm."

The boys put as good a face on it as they could. They surely looked forward to their Saturday nights in town. That evening Rosicky drove the car the half-mile down to Rudolph's new, bare little house.

Polly was in a short-sleeved gingham dress, clearing away the supper dishes. She was a trim, slim little thing, with blue eyes and shingled yellow hair, and her eyebrows were reduced to a mere brush-stroke, like Miss Pearl's.

"Good evening, Mr. Rosicky. Ruloph's at the barn, I guess." She never called him father, or Mary mother. She was sensitive about having married a foreigner. She never in the world would have done it if Rudolph hadn't been such a handsome, persuasive fellow and such a gallant lover. He had graduated in her class in the high school in town, and their friendship began in the ninth grade.

Rosicky went in, though he wasn't exactly asked. "My boys ain't goin' to town tonight, an' I brought de car

over fur you two to go in to de picture show."

Polly, carrying dishes to the sink, looked over her shoulder at him. "Thank you. But I'm late with my work tonight, and pretty tired. Maybe Rudolph would like to go in with you."

"Oh, I don't go to de shows! I'm too old-fashioned. You won't feel so tired after you ride in de air a ways. It's a nice clear night, an' it ain't cold. You go an' fix yourself up, Polly, an' I'll wash de dishes an' leave everything nice fur you."

Polly blushed and tossed her bob. "I couldn't let you do that, Mr. Rosicky. I wouldn't think of it."

Rosicky said nothing. He found a bib apron on a nail behind the kitchen door. He slipped it over his head and then took Polly by her two elbows and pushed her gently toward the door of her own room. "I washed up de kitchen many times for my wife, when de babies was sick or somethin'. You go an' make yourself look nice. I like you to look prettier'n any of dem town girls when you go in. De young folks must have some fun, an' I'm goin' to look out fur you, Polly."

That kind, reassuring grip on her elbows, the old man's funny bright eyes, made Polly want to drop her head on his shoulder for a second. She restrained herself, but she lingered in his grasp at the door of her room, murmuring tearfully: "You always lived in the city when you were young, didn't you? Don't you ever get lonesome out here?"

As she turned round to him, her hand fell naturally into his, and he stood holding it and smiling into her face with his peculiar, knowing, indulgent smile without a shadow of reproach in it. "Dem big cities is all right fur de rich, but dey is terrible hard fur de poor."

"I don't know. Sometimes I think I'd like to take a chance. You lived in New York, didn't you?"

"An' London. Da's bigger still. I learned my trade dere. Here's Rudolph comin', you better hurry."

"Will you tell me about London sometime?"

"Maybe. Only I ain't no talker, Polly. Run an' dress yourself up."

The bedroom door closed behind her, and Rudolph came in from the outside, looking anxious. He had seen the car and was sorry any of his family should come just then. Supper hadn't been a very pleasant occasion. Halting in the doorway, he saw his father in a kitchen apron, carrying dishes to the sink. He flushed crimson and something flashed in his eye. Rosicky held up a warning finger.

"I brought de car over fur you an' Polly to go to de picture show, an' I made her let me finish here so you won't be late. You go put on a clean shirt, quick!"

"But don't the boys want the car, Father?"

"Not tonight dey don't." Rosicky fumbled under his apron and found his pants pocket. He took out a silver dollar and said in a hurried whisper: "You go an' buy dat girl some ice cream an' candy tonight, like you was courtin'. She's awful good friends wid me."

Rudolph was very short of cash, but he took the money as if it hurt him. There had been a crop failure all over the county. He had more than once been sorry he'd married this year.

In a few minutes the young people came out, looking clean and a little stiff. Rosicky hurried them off, and then he took his own time with the dishes. He scoured the pots and pans and put away the milk and swept the kitchen. He put some coal in the stove and shut off the draughts, so the place would be warm for them when they got home late at night. Then he sat down and had a pipe and listened to the clock tick.

Generally speaking, marrying an American girl was certainly a risk. A Czech should marry a Czech. It was lucky that Polly was the daughter of a poor widow woman; Rudolph was proud, and if she had a prosperous family to throw up at him, they could never make it go. Polly was one of four sisters, and they all worked; one was bookkeeper in the bank, one taught music, and Polly and her younger sister had been clerks, like Miss Pearl. All four of them were musical, had pretty voices, and sang in the Methodist choir, which the eldest sister directed.

Polly missed the sociability of a store position. She missed the choir, and the company of her sisters. She didn't dislike housework, but she disliked so much of it. Rosicky was a little anxious about this pair. He was afraid Polly would grow so discontented that Rudy would quit the farm and take a factory job in Omaha. He had worked for a winter up there, two years ago, to get money to marry on. He had done very well, and they would always take him back at the stockyards. But to Rosicky that meant the end of everything for his son. To be a landless man was to be a wage-earner, a slave, all your life; to have nothing, to be nothing.

Rosicky thought he would come over and do a little carpentering for Polly after the New Year. He guessed she needed jollying. Rudolph was a serious sort of chap, serious in love and serious about his work.

Rosicky shook out his pipe and walked home across the fields. Ahead of him the lamplight shone from his kitchen windows. Suppose he were still in a tailor shop on Vesey Street, with a bunch of pale, narrow-chested sons working on machines, all coming home tired and sullen to eat supper in a kitchen that was a parlour also; with another crowded, angry family quarrelling just across the dumb-waiter shaft, and squeaking pulleys at the windows where dirty washings hung on dirty lines above a court full of old brooms and mops and ash-cans. . . .

He stopped by the windmill to look up at the frosty winter stars and draw a long breath before he went inside. That kitchen with the shining win-dows was dear to him; but the sleep-ing fields and bright stars and the noble darkness were dearer still.

V

On the day before Christmas the weather set in very cold; no snow, but a bitter, biting wind that whistled and sang over the flat land and lashed one's face like fine wires. There was baking going on in the Rosicky kitchen all day and Rosicky sat inside, making over a coat that Albert had outgrown into an overcoat for John. Mary had a big red geranium in bloom for Christmas, and a row of Jerusalem cherry trees, full of berries. It was the first year she had ever grown these; Doctor Ed brought her the seed from Omaha when he went to some medical convention. They reminded Rosicky of plants he had seen in Eng-land; and all afternoon, as he stitched, he sat thinking about those two years in London, which his mind usually shrank from even after all this while.

He was a lad of eighteen when he dropped down into London, with no money and no connections except the address of a cousin who was supposed to be working at a confectioner's. When he went to the pastry shop, however, he found that the cousin had gone to America. Anton tramped

the streets for several days, sleeping in doorways and on the Embankment, until he was in utter despair. He knew no English, and the sound of the strange language all about him confused him. By chance he met a poor German tailor who had learned his trade in Vienna, and could speak a little Czech. This tailor, Lifschnitz, kept a repair shop in a Cheapside basement, underneath a cobbler. He didn't much need an apprentice, but he was sorry for the boy and took him in for no wages but his keep and what he could pick up. The pickings were supposed to be coppers given you when you took work home to a cus-tomer. But most of the customers called for their clothes themselves, and the coppers that came Anton's way were very few. He had, however, a place to sleep. The tailor's family lived upstairs in three rooms; a kitchen, a bedroom, where Lifschnitz and his wife and five children slept, and a living-room. Two corners of this living-room were curtained off for lodgers; in one Rosicky slept on an old horsehair sofa, with a feather quilt to wrap himself in. The other corner was rented to a wretched, dirty boy, who was studying the violin. He ac-tually practised there. Rosicky was dirty, too. There was no way to be anything else. Mrs. Lifschnitz got the water she cooked and washed with from a pump in a brick court, four flights down. There were bugs in the place, and multitudes of fleas, though the poor woman did the best she could. Rosicky knew she often went empty to give another potato or a spoonful of dripping to the two hun-gry, sad-eyed boys who lodged with her. He used to think he would never get out of there, never get a clean shirt to his back again. What would he do, he wondered, when his clothes actually dropped to pieces and the worn cloth wouldn't hold patches any longer?

It was still early when the old farmer put aside his sewing and his recollections. The sky had been a dark grey all day, with not a gleam of sun, and the light failed at four o'clock. He went to shave and change his shirt while the turkey was roasting. Rudolph and Polly were coming over for supper.

After supper they sat round in the kitchen, and the younger boys were saying how sorry they were it hadn't snowed. Everybody was sorry. They wanted a deep snow that would lie long and keep the wheat warm, and leave the ground soaked when it melted.

"Yes, sir!" Rudolph broke out fiercely; "if we have another dry year like last year, there's going to be hard times in this country."

Rosicky filled his pipe. "You boys don't know what hard times is. You don't owe nobody, you got plenty to eat an' keep warm, an' plenty water to keep clean. When you got them, you can't have it very hard."

Rudolph frowned, opened and shut his big right hand, and dropped it clenched upon his knee. "I've got to have a good deal more than that, Father, or I'll quit this farming gamble. I can always make good wages railroading, or at the packing house, and be sure of my money."

"Maybe so," his father answered dryly.

Mary, who had just come in from the pantry and was wiping her hands on the roller towel, thought Rudy and his father were getting too serious. She brought her darning-basket and sat down in the middle of the group.

"I ain't much afraid of hard times, Rudy," she said heartily. "We've had a plenty, but we've always come through. Your father wouldn't never take nothing very hard, not even hard times. I got a mind to tell you a story on him. Maybe you boys can't hardly remember the year we had that terrible hot wind, that burned everything up on the Fourth of July? All the corn an' the gardens. An' that was in the days when we didn't have alfalfa yet,—I guess it wasn't invented.

"Well, that very day your father was out cultivatin' corn, and I was here in the kitchen makin' plum preserves. We had bushels of plums that year. I noticed it was terrible hot, but it's always hot in the kitchen when you're preservin', an' I was too busy with my plums to mind. Anton come in from the field about three o'clock, an' I asked him what was the matter.

"'Nothin',' he says, 'but it's pretty hot, an' I think I won't work no more today.' He stood round for a few minutes, an' then he says: 'Ain't you near through? I want you should git up a nice supper for us tonight. It's Fourth of July.'

"I told him to git along, that I was right in the middle of preservin', but the plums would taste good on hot biscuit. 'I'm goin' to have fried chicken, too,' he says, and he went off an' killed a couple. You three oldest boys was little fellers, playin' round outside, real hot an' sweaty, an' your father took you to the horse tank down by the windmill an' took off your clothes an' put you in. Them two box-elder trees was little then, but they made shade over the tank. Then he took off all his own clothes, an' got in with you. While he was playin' in the water with you, the Methodist preacher drove into our place to say how all the neighbours was goin' to meet at the schoolhouse that night, to pray for rain. He drove right to the windmill, of course, and there was your father and you three with no clothes on. I was in the kitchen door, an' I had to laugh, for the preacher acted like he ain't never seen a naked man before. He surely was embarrassed, an' your father couldn't git to his clothes; they was all hangin' up on the windmill to let the sweat dry out of 'em. So he laid in the tank where he was, an' put one of you boys on top of him to cover him up a little, an' talked to the preacher.

"When you got through playin' in the water, he put clean clothes on you and a clean shirt on himself, an' by that time I'd begun to get supper. He says: 'It's too hot in here to eat comfortable. Let's have a picnic in the orchard. We'll eat our supper behind the mulberry hedge, under them linden trees.'

"So he carried our supper down, an' a bottle of my wild-grape wine, an' everything tasted good, I can tell you. The wind got cooler as the sun was goin' down, and it turned out pleasant, only I noticed how the leaves was curled up on the linden trees. That made me think, an' I asked your father if that hot wind all day hadn't been terrible hard on the gardens an' the corn.

"'Corn,' he says, 'there ain't no corn.'

"'What you talkin' about?' I said. 'Ain't we got forty acres?'

"'We ain't got an ear,' he says, 'nor nobody else ain't got none. All the corn in this country was cooked by three o'clock today, like you'd roasted it in an oven.'

"'You mean you won't get no crop at all?' I asked him. I couldn't believe it, after he'd worked so hard.

"'No crop this year,' he says. 'That's why we're havin' a picnic. We might as well enjoy what we got.'

"An' that's how your father behaved, when all the neighbours was

so discouraged they couldn't look you in the face. An' we enjoyed ourselves that year, poor as we was, an' our neighbours wasn't a bit better off for bein' miserable. Some of 'em grieved till they got poor digestions and couldn't relish what they did have."

The younger boys said they thought their father had the best of it. But Rudolph was thinking that, all the same, the neighbours had managed to get ahead more, in the fifteen years since that time. There must be something wrong about his father's way of doing things. He wished he knew what was going on in the back of Polly's mind. He knew she liked his father, but he knew, too, that she was afraid of something. When his mother sent over coffee-cake or prune tarts or a loaf of fresh bread, Polly seemed to regard them with a certain suspicion. When she observed to him that his brothers had nice manners, her tone implied that it was remarkable they should have. With his mother she was stiff and on her guard. Mary's hearty frankness and gusts of good humour irritated her. Polly was afraid of being unusual or conspicuous in any way, of being "ordinary," as she said!

When Mary had finished her story, Rosicky laid aside his pipe.

"You boys like me to tell you about some of dem hard times I been through in London?" Warmly encouraged, he sat rubbing his forehead along the deep creases. It was bothersome to tell a long story in English (he nearly always talked to the boys in Czech), but he wanted Polly to hear this one.

"Well, you know about dat tailor shop I worked in in London? I had one Christmas dere I ain't never forgot. Times was awful bad before Christmas; de boss ain't got much work, an' have it awful hard to pay his rent. It ain't so much fun, bein' poor in a big city like London, I'll say! All de windows is full of good t'ings to eat, an' all de pushcarts in de streets is full, an' you smell 'em all de time, an' you ain't got no money,— not a damn bit. I didn't mind de cold so much, though I didn't have no overcoat, chust a short jacket I'd outgrowed so it wouldn't meet on me, an' my hands was chapped raw. But I always had a good appetite, like you all know, an' de sight of dem pork pies in de windows was awful fur me!

"Day before Christmas was terrible foggy dat year, an' dat fog gits into your bones and makes you all damp like. Mrs. Lifschnitz didn't give us nothin' but a little bread an' drippin' for supper, because she was savin' to try for to give us a good dinner on Christmas Day. After supper de boss say I can go an' enjoy myself, so I went into de streets to listen to de Christmas singers. Dey sing old songs an' make very nice music, an' I run round after dem a good ways, till I got awful hungry. I t'ink maybe if I go home, I can sleep till morning an' forgit my belly.

"I went into my corner real quiet, and roll up in my fedder quilt. But I ain't got my head down, till I smell somet'ing good. Seem like it git stronger an' stronger, an' I can't git to sleep noway. I can't understand dat smell. Dere was a gas light in a hall across de court, dat always shine in at my window a little. I got up an' look round. I got a little wooden box in my corner fur a stool, 'cause I ain't got no chair. I picks up dat box, and under it dere is a roast goose on a platter! I can't believe my eyes. I carry it to de window where de light comes in, an' touch it and smell it to find out, an' den I taste it to be sure. I say, I will eat chust one little bite of dat goose, so I can go to sleep, and

tomorrow I won't eat none at all. But I tell you, boys, when I stop, one half of dat goose was gone!"

The narrator bowed his head, and the boys shouted. But little Josephine slipped behind his chair and kissed him on the neck beneath his ear.

"Poor little Papa, I don't want him to be hungry!"

"Da's long ago, child. I ain't never been hungry since I had your mudder to cook fur me."

"Go on and tell us the rest, please," said Polly.

"Well, when I come to realize what I done, of course, I felt terrible. I felt better in de stomach, but very bad in de heart. I set on my bed wid dat platter on my knees, an' it all come to me; how hard dat poor woman save to buy dat goose, and how she get some neighbour to cook it dat got more fire, an' how she put it in my corner to keep it away from dem hungry children. Dey was a old carpet hung up to shut my corner off, an' de children wasn't allowed to go in dere. An' I know she put it in my corner because she trust me more'n she did de violin boy. I can't stand it to face her after I spoil de Christmas. So I put on my shoes and go out into de city. I tell myself I better throw myself in de river; but I guess I ain't dat kind of a boy.

"It was after twelve o'clock, an' terrible cold, an' I start out to walk about London all night. I walk along de river awhile, but dey was lots of drunks all along; men, and women too. I chust move along to keep away from de police. I git onto de Strand, an' den over to New Oxford Street, where dere was a big German restaurant on de ground floor, wid big windows all fixed up fine, an' I could see de people having parties inside. While I was lookin' in, two men and two ladies come out, laughin' and talkin' and feelin' happy about all dey been eatin' an' drinkin', and dey was speakin' Czech,—not like de Austrians, but like de home folks talk it.

"I guess I went crazy, an' I done what I ain't never done before nor since. I went right up to dem gay people an' begun to beg dem: 'Fellow-countrymen, for God's sake give me money enough to buy a goose!'

"Dey laugh, of course, but de ladies speak awful kind to me, an' dey take me back into de restaurant and give me hot coffee and cakes, an' make me tell all about how I happened to come to London, an' what I was doin' dere. Dey take my name and where I work down on paper, an' both of dem ladies give me ten shillings.

"De big market at Covent Garden ain't very far away, an' by dat time it was open. I go dere an' buy a big goose an' some pork pies, an' potatoes and onions, an' cakes an' oranges fur de children,—all I could carry! When I git home, everybody is still asleep. I pile all I bought on de kitchen table, an' go in an' lay down on my bed, an' I ain't waken up till I hear dat woman scream when she come out into her kitchen. My goodness, but she was surprise! She laugh an' cry at de same time, an' hug me and waken all de children. She ain't stop fur no breakfast; she git de Christmas dinner ready dat morning, and we all sit down an' eat all we can hold. I ain't never seen dat violin boy have all he can hold before.

"Two three days after dat, de two men come to hunt me up, an' dey ask my boss, and he give me a good report an' tell dem I was a steady boy all right. One of dem Bohemians was very smart an' run a Bohemian newspaper in New York, an' de odder was a rich man, in de importing business, an' dey been travelling togedder. Dey told me how t'ings was easier in New

York, an' offered to pay my passage when dey was goin' home soon on a boat. My boss say to me: 'You go. You ain't got no chance here, an' I like to see you git ahead, fur you always been a good boy to my woman, and fur dat fine Christmas dinner you give us all.' An' da's how I got to New York."

That night when Rudolph and Polly, arm in arm, were running home across the fields with the bitter wind at their backs, his heart leaped for joy when she said she thought they might have his family come over for supper on New Year's Eve. "Let's get up a nice supper, and not let your mother help at all; make her be company for once."

"That would be lovely of you, Polly," he said humbly. He was a very simple, modest boy, and he, too, felt vaguely that Polly and her sisters were more experienced and worldly than his people.

VI

The winter turned out badly for farmers. It was bitterly cold, and after the first light snows before Christmas there was no snow at all,—and no rain. March was as bitter as February. On those days when the wind fairly punished the country, Rosicky sat by his window. In the fall he and the boys had put in a big wheat planting, and now the seed had frozen in the ground. All that land would have to be ploughed up and planted over again, planted in corn. It had happened before, but he was younger then, and he never worried about what had to be. He was sure of himself and of Mary; he knew they could bear what they had to bear, that they would always pull through somehow. But he was not so sure about the young ones, and he felt troubled because Rudolph and Polly were having such a hard start.

Sitting beside his flowering window while the panes rattled and the wind blew in under the door, Rosicky gave himself to reflection as he had not done since those Sundays in the loft of the furniture-factory in New York, long ago. Then he was trying to find what he wanted in life for himself; now he was trying to find what he wanted for his boys, and why it was he so hungered to feel sure they would be here, working this very land, after he was gone.

They would have to work hard on the farm, and probably they would never do much more than make a living. But if he could think of them as staying here on the land, he wouldn't have to fear any great unkindness for them. Hardships, certainly; it was a hardship to have the wheat freeze in the ground when seed was so high; and to have to sell your stock because you had no feed. But there would be other years when everything came along right, and you caught up. And what you had was your own. You didn't have to choose between bosses and strikers, and go wrong either way. You didn't have to do with dishonest and cruel people. They were the only things in his experience he had found terrifying and horrible; the look in the eyes of a dishonest and crafty man, of a scheming and rapacious woman.

In the country, if you had a mean neighbour, you could keep off his land and make him keep off yours. But in the city, all the foulness and misery and brutality of your neighbours was part of your life. The worst things he had come upon in his journey through the world were human,—depraved and poisonous specimens of man. To this day he could recall certain terrible faces in the London streets. There were mean people everywhere, to be sure, even in their own country town here. But they weren't tempered, hardened, sharpened, like the treacherous people in cities who live by grinding or cheating or poisoning their fellow-men. He had helped to bury two of his fellow-workmen in the tailoring trade, and he was distrustful of the organized industries that see one out of the world in big cities. Here, if you were sick, you had Doctor Ed to look after you; and if you died, fat Mr. Haycock, the kindest man in the world, buried you.

It seemed to Rosicky that for good, honest boys like his, the worst they could do on the farm was better than the best they would be likely to do in the city. If he'd had a mean boy, now, one who was crooked and sharp and tried to put anything over on his brothers, then town would be the place for him. But he had no such boy. As for Rudolph, the discontented one, he would give the shirt off his back to anyone who touched his heart. What Rosicky really hoped for his boys was that they could get through the world without ever knowing much about the cruelty of human beings. "Their mother and me ain't prepared them for that," he sometimes said to himself.

These thoughts brought him back to a grateful consideration of his own case. What an escape he had had, to be sure! He, too, in his time, had had to take money for repair work from the hand of a hungry child who let it go so wistfully; because it was money due his boss. And now, in all these years, he had never had to take a cent from anyone in bitter need,—never had to look at the face of a woman become like a wolf's from struggle and famine. When he thought of these things, Rosicky would put on his cap and jacket and slip down to the barn and give his work-horses a little extra oats, letting them eat it out of his hand in their slobbery fashion. It was his way of expressing what he felt, and made him chuckle with pleasure.

The spring came warm, with blue skies,—but dry, dry as a bone. The boys began ploughing up the wheat-fields to plant them over in corn. Rosicky would stand at the fence corner and watch them, and the earth was so dry it blew up in clouds of brown dust that hid the horses and the sulky plough and the driver. It was a bad outlook.

The big alfalfa field that lay between the home place and Rudolph's came up green, but Rosicky was worried because during that open windy winter a great many Russian thistle plants had blown in there and lodged. He kept asking the boys to rake them out; he was afraid their seed would root and "take the alfalfa." Rudolph said that was nonsense. The boys were working so hard planting corn, their father felt he couldn't insist about the thistles, but he set great store by that big alfalfa field. It was feed you could depend on,—and there was some deeper reason, vague, but strong. The peculiar green of that clover woke early memories in old Rosicky, went back to something in his childhood in the old world. When he was a little boy, he had played in fields of that strong blue-green colour.

One morning, when Rudolph had gone to town in the car, leaving a work-team idle in his barn, Rosicky went over to his son's place, put the horses to the buggy-rake, and set about quietly raking up those thistles. He behaved with guilty caution, and rather enjoyed stealing a march on Doctor Ed, who was just then taking his first vacation in seven years of practice and was attending a clinic in Chicago. Rosicky got the thistles raked up, but did not stop to burn them. That would take some time, and his breath was pretty short, so he thought he had better get the horses back to the barn.

He got them into the barn and to their stalls, but the pain had come on so sharp in his chest that he didn't try to take the harness off. He started for the house, bending lower with every step. The cramp in his chest was shutting him up like a jack-knife. When he reached the windmill, he swayed and caught at the ladder. He saw Polly coming down the hill, running with the swiftness of a slim grey-hound. In a flash she had her shoulder under his armpit.

"Lean on me, Father, hard! Don't be afraid. We can get to the house all right."

Somehow they did, though Rosicky became blind with pain; he could keep on his legs, but he couldn't steer his course. The next thing he was conscious of was lying on Polly's bed, and Polly bending over him wringing out bath towels in hot water and putting them on his chest. She stopped only to throw coal into the stove, and she kept the tea-kettle and the black pot going. She put these hot applications on him for nearly an hour, she told him afterwards, and all that time he was drawn up stiff and blue, with the sweat pouring off him.

As the pain gradually loosed its grip, the stiffness went out of his jaws, the black circles round his eyes disappeared, and a little of his natural colour came back. When his daughter-in-law buttoned his shirt over his chest at last, he sighed.

"Da's fine, de way I feel now, Polly. It was a awful bad spell, an' I was so sorry it all come on you like it did."

Polly was flushed and excited. "Is the pain really gone? Can I leave you long enough to telephone over to your place?"

Rosicky's eyelids fluttered. "Don't telephone, Polly. It ain't no use to scare my wife. It's nice and quiet here, an' if I ain't too much trouble to you, just let me lay still till I feel like myself. I ain't got no pain now. It's nice here."

Polly bent over him and wiped the moisture from his face. "Oh, I'm so glad it's over!" she broke out impulsively. "It just broke my heart to see you suffer so, Father."

Rosicky motioned her to sit down on the chair where the tea-kettle had been, and looked up at her with that lively affectionate gleam in his eyes. "You was awful good to me, I won't never forget dat. I hate it to be sick on you like dis. Down at de barn I say to myself, dat young girl ain't had much experience in sickness, I don't want to scare her, an' maybe she's got a baby comin' or somet'ing."

Polly took his hand. He was looking at her so intently and affectionately and confidingly; his eyes seemed to caress her face, to regard it with pleasure. She frowned with her funny streaks of eyebrows, and then smiled back at him.

"I guess maybe there is something of that kind going to happen. But I haven't told anyone yet, not my mother or Rudolph. You'll be the first to know."

His hand pressed hers. She noticed that it was warm again. The twinkle in his yellow-brown eyes seemed to come nearer.

"I like mighty well to see dat little child, Polly," was all he said. Then he closed his eyes and lay half-smiling. But Polly sat still, thinking hard. She had a sudden feeling that nobody in the world, not her mother, not Ru-

dolph, or anyone, really loved her as much as old Rosicky did. It perplexed her. She sat frowning and trying to puzzle it out. It was as if Rosicky had a special gift for loving people, something that was like an ear for music or an eye for colour. It was quiet, unobtrusive; it was merely there. You saw it in his eyes,—perhaps that was why they were merry. You felt it in his hands, too. After he dropped off to sleep, she sat holding his warm, broad, flexible brown hand. She had never seen another in the least like it. She wondered if it wasn't a kind of gypsy hand, it was so alive and quick and light in its communications,—very strange in a farmer. Nearly all the farmers she knew had huge lumps of fists, like mauls, or they were knotty and bony and uncomfortable-looking, with stiff fingers. But Rosicky's was like quicksilver, flexible, muscular, about the colour of a pale cigar, with deep, deep creases across the palm. It wasn't nervous, it wasn't a stupid lump; it was a warm brown human hand, with some cleverness in it, a great deal of generosity, and something else which Polly could only call "gypsy-like,"—something nimble and lively and sure, in the way that animals are.

Polly remembered that hour long afterwards; it had been like an awakening to her. It seemed to her that she had never learned so much about life from anything as from old Rosicky's hand. It brought her to herself; it communicated some direct and untranslatable message.

When she heard Rudolph coming in the car, she ran out to meet him.

"Oh, Rudy, your father's been awful sick! He raked up those thistles he's been worrying about, and afterwards he could hardly get to the house. He suffered so I was afraid he was going to die."

Rudolph jumped to the ground. "Where is he now?"

"On the bed. He's asleep. I was terribly scared, because, you know, I'm so fond of your father." She slipped her arm through his and they went into the house. That afternoon they took Rosicky home and put him to bed, though he protested that he was quite well again.

The next morning he got up and dressed and sat down to breakfast with his family. He told Mary that his coffee tasted better than usual to him, and he warned the boys not to bear any tales to Doctor Ed when he got home. After breakfast he sat down by his window to do some patching and asked Mary to thread several needles for him before she went to feed her chickens,—her eyes were better than his, and her hands steadier. He lit his pipe and took up John's overalls. Mary had been watching him anxiously all morning, and as she went out of the door with her bucket of scraps, she saw that he was smiling. He was thinking, indeed, about Polly, and how he might never have known what a tender heart she had if he hadn't got sick over there. Girls nowadays didn't wear their heart on their sleeve. But now he knew Polly would make a fine woman after the foolishness wore off. Either a woman had that sweetness at her heart or she hadn't. You couldn't always tell by the look of them; but if they had that, everything came out right in the end.

After he had taken a few stitches, the cramp began in his chest, like yesterday. He put his pipe cautiously down on the window-sill and bent over to ease the pull. No use,—he had better try to get to his bed if he could. He rose and groped his way across the familiar floor, which was rising and falling like the deck of a ship. At the door he fell. When Mary came in, she found him lying there, and the moment she touched him she knew that he was gone.

Doctor Ed was away when Rosicky died, and for the first few weeks after he got home he was hard driven. Every day he said to himself that he must get out to see that family that had lost their father. One soft, warm moonlight night in early summer he started for the farm. His mind was on other things, and not until his road ran by the graveyard did he realize that Rosicky wasn't over there on the hill where the red lamplight shone, but here, in the moonlight. He stopped his car, shut off the engine, and sat there for a while.

A sudden hush had fallen on his soul. Everything here seemed strangely moving and significant, though signifying what, he did not know. Close by the wire fence stood Rosicky's mowing-machine, where one of the boys had been cutting hay that afternoon; his own work-horses had been going up and down there. The new-cut hay perfumed all the night air. The moonlight silvered the long, billowy grass that grew over the graves and hid the fence; the few little evergreens stood out black in it, like shadows in a pool. The sky was very blue and soft, the stars rather faint because the moon was full.

For the first time it struck Doctor Ed that this was really a beautiful graveyard. He thought of city cemeteries; acres of shrubbery and heavy stone, so arranged and lonely and unlike anything in the living world. Cities of the dead, indeed; cities of the forgotten, of the "put away." But this was open and free, this little square of long grass which the wind forever stirred. Nothing but the sky overhead, and the many-coloured fields running on until they met that sky. The horses worked here in summer; the neighbours passed on their way to town; and over yonder, in the corn-field, Rosicky's own cattle would be eating fodder as winter came on. Nothing could be more undeathlike than this place; nothing could be more right for a man who had helped to do the work of great cities and had always longed for the open country and had got to it at last. Rosicky's life seemed to him complete and beautiful.

1932

THORNTON WILDER
(1897–)

THE BRIDGE OF SAN LUIS REY *

PERHAPS AN ACCIDENT

On Friday noon, July the twentieth, 1714, the finest bridge in all Peru broke and precipitated five travellers into the gulf below. This bridge was on the highroad between Lima and Cuzco and hundreds of persons passed over it every day. It had been woven of osier by the Incas more than a century before and visitors to the city were always led out to see it. It was a mere ladder of thin slats swung out over the gorge, with handrails of dried vine. Horses and coaches and chairs had to go down hundreds of feet below and pass over the narrow torrent on rafts, but no one, not even the Viceroy, not even the Archbishop of Lima, had descended with the baggage rather than cross by the famous bridge of San Luis Rey. St. Louis of France himself protected it, by his name and by the little mud church on the

* Part One of *The Bridge of San Luis Rey* by Thornton Wilder. Copyright, 1927, by Albert & Charles Boni, Inc.

further side. The bridge seemed to be among the things that last forever; it was unthinkable that it should break. The moment a Peruvian heard of the accident he signed himself and made a mental calculation as to how recently he had crossed by it and how soon he had intended crossing by it again. People wandered about in a trance-like state, muttering; they had the hallucination of seeing themselves falling into a gulf.

There was a great service in the Cathedral. The bodies of the victims were approximately collected and approximately separated from one another, and there was great searching of hearts in the beautiful city of Lima. Servant girls returned bracelets which they had stolen from their mistresses, and usurers harangued their wives angrily, in defense of usury. Yet it was rather strange that this event should have so impressed the Limeans, for in that country those catastrophes which lawyers shockingly call the "acts of God" were more than usually frequent. Tidal waves were continually washing away cities; earthquakes arrived every week and towers fell upon good men and women all the time. Diseases were forever flitting in and out of the provinces and old age carried away some of the most admirable citizens. That is why it was so surprising that the Peruvians should have been especially touched by the rent in the bridge of San Luis Rey.

Everyone was very deeply impressed, but only one person did anything about it, and that was Brother Juniper. By a series of coincidences so extraordinary that one almost suspects the presence of some Intention, this little red-haired Franciscan from Northern Italy happened to be in Peru converting the Indians and happened to witness the accident.

It was a very hot noon, that fatal

noon, and coming around the shoulder of a hill Brother Juniper stopped to wipe his forehead and to gaze upon the screen of snowy peaks in the distance, then into the gorge below him filled with the dark plumage of green trees and green birds and traversed by its ladder of osier. Joy was in him; things were not going badly. He had opened several little abandoned churches and the Indians were crawling in to early Mass and groaning at the moment of miracle as though their hearts would break. Perhaps it was the pure air from the snows before him; perhaps it was the memory that brushed him for a moment of the poem that bade him raise his eyes to the helpful hills. At all events he felt at peace. Then his glance fell upon the bridge, and at that moment a twanging noise filled the air, as when the string of some musical instrument snaps in a disused room, and he saw the bridge divide and fling five gesticulating ants into the valley below.

Anyone else would have said to himself with secret joy: "Within ten minutes myself . . . !" But it was another thought that visited Brother Juniper: "Why did this happen to *those* five?" If there were any plan in the universe at all, if there were any pattern in a human life, surely it could be discovered mysteriously latent in those lives so suddenly cut off. Either we live by accident and die by accident, or we live by plan and die by plan. And on that instant Brother Juniper made the resolve to inquire into the secret lives of those five persons, that moment falling through the air, and to surprise the reason of their taking off.

.   .   .   .   .   .

It seemed to Brother Juniper that it was high time for theology to take its place among the exact sciences and he had long intended putting it

there. What he had lacked hitherto was a laboratory. Oh, there had never been any lack of specimens; any number of his charges had met calamity, —spiders had stung them; their lungs had been touched; their houses had burned down and things had happened to their children from which one averts the mind. But these occasions of human woe had never been quite fit for scientific examination. They had lacked what our good savants were later to call *proper control*. The accident had been dependent upon human error, for example, or had contained elements of probability. But this collapse of the bridge of San Luis Rey was a sheer Act of God. It afforded a perfect laboratory. Here at last one could surprise His intentions in a pure state.

You and I can see that coming from anyone but Brother Juniper this plan would be the flower of a perfect skepticism. It resembled the effort of those presumptuous souls who wanted to walk on the pavements of Heaven and built the Tower of Babel to get there. But to our Franciscan there was no element of doubt in the experiment. He knew the answer. He merely wanted to prove it, historically, mathematically, to his converts,—poor obstinate converts, so slow to believe that their pains were inserted into their lives for their own good. People were always asking for good sound proofs; doubt springs eternal in the human breast, even in countries where the Inquisition can read your very thoughts in your eyes.

This was not the first time that Brother Juniper had tried to resort to such methods. Often on the long trips he had to make (scurrying from parish to parish, his robe tucked up about his knees, for haste) he would fall to dreaming of experiments that justify the ways of God to man. For instance, a complete record of the Prayers for Rain and their results. Often he had stood on the steps of one of his little churches, his flock kneeling before him on the baked street. Often he had stretched his arms to the sky and declaimed the splendid ritual. Not often, but several times, he had felt the virtue enter him and seen the little cloud forming on the horizon. But there were many times when weeks went by . . . but why think of them? It was not himself he was trying to convince that rain and drought were wisely apportioned.

Thus it was that the determination rose within him at the moment of the accident. It prompted him to busy himself for six years, knocking at all the doors in Lima, asking thousands of questions, filling scores of notebooks, in his effort at establishing the fact that each of the five lost lives was a perfect whole. Everyone knew that he was working on some sort of memorial of the accident and everyone was very helpful and misleading. A few even knew the principal aim of his activity and there were patrons in high places.

The result of all this diligence was an enormous book, which as we shall see later, was publicly burned on a beautiful Spring morning in the great square. But there was a secret copy and after a great many years and without much notice it found its way to the library of the University of San Marco. There it lies between two great wooden covers collecting dust in a cupboard. It deals with one after another of the victims of the accident, cataloguing thousands of little facts and anecdotes and testimonies, and concluding with a dignified passage describing why God had settled upon that person and upon that day for His demonstration of wisdom. Yet for all his diligence Brother Juniper never knew the central passion of Doña María's life; nor of Uncle Pío's, not even of Estaban's. And I, who claim to know so much more, isn't it possible that even I have missed the very spring within the spring?

Some say that we shall never know and that to the gods we are like the flies that the boys kill on a summer day, and some say, on the contrary, that the very sparrows do not lose a feather that has not been brushed away by the finger of God.

1927

THOMAS WOLFE
(1900–1938)

A PORTRAIT
OF BASCOM HAWKE *

During the first twenty-five years of this century, business people who had their offices in or near State Street, Boston, no doubt grew very familiar with the cadaverous and extraordinary figure of my uncle, Bascom Hawke. Shortly before nine o'clock of every working day he would emerge from a subway exit near the head of the street and pause vaguely for a moment, making a craggy eddy in the tide of issuing workers that foamed swiftly about him while he stood with his enormous bony hands clutched comically before him at the waist, as if holding himself in, at the same time making the most horrible grimaces with his lean and amazingly flexible features. These grimaces were made by squinting his small sharp eyes together, widening his mouth in a ghastly travesty of a grin, and convolving his chin and

* Reprinted from *Of Time and the River* by Thomas Wolfe; copyright 1932, 1935 by Charles Scribner's Sons; used by permission of the publishers.

cheek in a rapid series of pursed lips and horrible squints as he swiftly pressed his rubbery underlip against a few enormous horse teeth that decorated his upper jaw. Having completed these facial evolutions, he glanced quickly and, it must be supposed, blindly, in every direction; for he then plunged heedlessly across the street, sometimes choosing the moment when traffic had been halted, and pedestrians were hurrying across, sometimes diving into the midst of a roaring chaos of motor cars, trucks, and wagons, through which he sometimes made his way in safety, accompanied only by a scream of brake bands, a startled barking of horns, and the hearty curses of frightened drivers, or from which, howling with terror in the centre of a web of traffic which he had snarled hopelessly and brought to a complete standstill, he was sometimes rescued by a red-faced and cursing young Irishman who was on point duty at that corner.

But Bascom was a fated man and he escaped. Once, it is true, a bright mindless beetle of machinery, which had no thought for fated men, had knocked him down and skinned and bruised him; again, an uninstructed wheel had passed across the soft toe-end of his shoe and held him prisoner, as if he were merely some average son of destiny—but he escaped. He escaped because he was a fated man and because the providence which guides the steps of children and the blind was kind to him; and because this same policeman whose simian upper lip had once been thick and twisted with its curses had long since run the scale from anger to wild fury, and thence to madness and despair and resignation, and had now come to have a motherly affection for this stray sheep, kept his eye peeled for its appearance every morning or, fail-

ing this, at once shrilled hard upon his whistle when he heard the well-known howl of terror and surprise, plunged to the centre of the stalled traffic snarl, plucked Bascom out to safety under curse and shout and scream of brake, and marched him tenderly to the curb, gripping his brawny hand around my uncle's arm, feeling his joints, testing his bones, massaging anxiously his sinewy carcass, and calling him "bud"—although my uncle was old enough to be his grandfather. "Are you all right, bud? You're not hurt, are you, bud? Are you O. K.?"—to which Bascom if his shock and terror had been great, could make no answer for a moment save to pant hoarsely and to howl loudly and huskily from time to time "Ow! Ow! Ow! Ow!"

At length, becoming more coherent, if not more calm, he would launch into an ecclesiastical indictment of motor cars and their drivers delivered in a high, howling, and husky voice that suggested the pronouncements of a prophet from a mountain. This voice had a quality of strange remoteness and, once heard, would never be forgotten. It actually had a howling note in it, and carried to great distances, and yet it was not loud: it was very much as if Mr. Bascom Hawke were standing on a mountain and shouting to some one in a quiet valley below—the sounds came to one plainly but as if from a great distance, and it was full of a husky, unearthly passion. It was really an ecclesiastical voice, the voice of a great preacher; one felt that it should be heard in churches, which was exactly where it once was heard, for my uncle Bascom had at various times and with great conviction, in the course of his long and remarkable life, professed and preached the faith of the Episcopalians, the Presbyterians, the Methodists, the Baptists, and the Unitarians.

Quite often, in fact, as now, when he had narrowly escaped disaster in the streets, Bascom Hawke still preached from the corner: as soon as he recovered somewhat from his shock, he would launch forth into a sermon of eloquent invective against any driver of motor cars within hearing, and if any of them entered the fray, as sometimes happened, a very interesting performance occurred.

"What happened to *you?*" the motorist might bitterly remark. "Do the keepers know you're out?"

Mr. Hawke would thereupon retort with an eloquent harangue, beginning with a few well-chosen quotations from the more violent prophets of the Old Testament, a few predictions of death, destruction and damnation for the owners of motor cars, and a few apt references to Days of Judgment and Reckoning, Chariots of Moloch, and Beasts of the Apocalypse.

"Oh, for God's sake!" the exasperated motorist might reply. "Are you *blind?* Where do you think you are? In a cow-pasture? Can't you read the signals? Didn't you see the cop put his hand up? Don't you know when it says to 'Stop' or 'Go'? Did you ever hear of the traffic law?"

"The *traffic* law!" my Uncle Bascom sneeringly exclaimed, as if the mere use of the word by the motorist evoked his profoundest contempt. His voice now had a precise and meticulous way of speech, there was something sneering and pedantical in the way he pronounced each word, biting it off with a prim, nasal and heavily accented enunciation in the manner of certain pedants and purists who suggest by their pronunciation that language in the mouths of most people is vilely and carelessly treated, that each word has a precise, subtle, and

careful meaning of its own, and that they—*they* alone—understand these matters. "The *traffic* law!" he repeated again: then he squinted his eyes together, pursed his rubbery lip against the big horsy upper teeth, and laughed down his nose in a forced, sneering manner, "The *traffic* law!" he said. "Why, you pit-i-ful ig-no-*ram*-us! You il-*lit*-ter-ate ruffian! You dare to speak to me—to *me!*" he howled suddenly with an ecclesiastical lift of his voice, striking himself on his bony breast and glaring with a majestical fury as if the word of a mighty prophet had been contradicted by an upstart—"of the traffic law, when it is doubtful if you could *read* the law if you saw it,"—he sneered—"and it is obvious to any one with the perception of a schoolboy that you would not have intelligence enough to understand it, and"—here his voice rose to a howling emphasis and he held one huge bony finger up to command attention—"*and* to interpret it, if you could read."

"Is *that* so!" the motorist heavily remarked. "A *wise* guy, eh? One of these guys who knows it all, eh? You're a *pretty* wise guy, aren't you?" the motorist continued bitterly, as if caught up in the circle of his refrain and unable to change it. "Well, let me tell *you* something. You think you're pretty smaht, don't you? Well, you're not. See? It's wise guys like you who go around looking for a good bust on the nose. See? That's how smaht you are. If you wasn't an old guy I'd give you one, too," he said, getting a moody satisfaction from the thought.

"Ow-w! Ow-w! Ow-w!" Bascomb howled in sudden terror.

"If you know so much, if you're so smaht as you think you are, what *is* the traffic law?"

Then, assuredly, if there was a

traffic law, the unfortunate motorist was lost, for my Uncle Bascom would deliver it to him verbatim, licking his lips with joy over all the technicalities of legal phrasing and pronouncing each phrase with a meticulous and pedantical enunciation.

"And furthermore!" he howled, holding up his big bony finger, "the Commonwealth of Massachusetts has decreed, by a statute that has been on the books since 1856, by a statute that is irrevocably, inexorably, ineluctably plain that any driver, director, governor, commander, manager, agent or conductor, or any other person who shall conduct or cause to be conducted any vehicular instrument, whether it be of two, four, six, eight or any number of wheels whatsoever, whether it be in the public service, or in the possession of a private individual, whether it be—" but by this time, the motorist, if he was wise, had had enough, and had escaped.

If, however, it had been one of his more fortunate mornings, if he had blindly but successfully threaded the peril of roaring traffic, my Uncle Bascom proceeded rapidly down State Street, still clutching his raw bony hands across his meagre waist, still contorting his remarkable face in its endless series of pursed grimaces, and presently turned in to the entrance of a large somewhat dingy-looking building of blackened stone, one of those solid, unpretending, but very valuable properties which smells and looks like the early 1900's, and which belongs to that ancient and enormously wealthy corporation which lies across the river and is known as Harvard University.

Here, my Uncle Bascom, still clutching himself together across the waist, mounted a flight of indented marble entry steps, lunged through revolving doors into a large marble corridor that was redolent with vibrating waves of hot steamy air, wet rubbers and galoshes, sanitary disinfectant, and serviceable but somewhat old-fashioned elevators and, entering one of the cars which had just plunged down abruptly, banged open its door, belched out two or three people and swallowed a dozen more, he was finally deposited with the same abruptness on the seventh floor, where he stepped out into a wide dark corridor, squinted and grimaced uncertainly to right and left as he had done for twenty-five years, and then went left along the corridor, past rows of lighted offices in which one could hear the preliminary clicking of typewriters, the rattling of crisp papers, and the sounds of people beginning their day's work. At the end of the corridor Bascom Hawke turned right along another corridor and at length paused before a door which bore this inscription across the familiar glazed glass of American business offices: The John T. Brill Realty Co.—Houses For Rent or Sale. Below this bold legend in much smaller letters was printed: Bascom Hawke—Att'y at Law—Conveyancer and Title Expert.

And now, before we enter this interesting office, let us give a closer and more particular scrutiny to the appearance of this singular man.

The appearance of this strange figure in State Street, or anywhere else, had always been sufficiently curious to attract attention and to draw comment. Bascom Hawke, if he had straightened to his full height, would have been six feet and three or four inches tall, but he had always walked with a stoop and as he grew older, the stoop had become confirmed: he presented a tall, gnarled, bony figure, cadaverous and stringy, but tough as hickory. He was of that race of men who seem never to wear out, or to grow old, or to die: they live with almost undiminished vitality to great ages, and when they die they die suddenly. There is no slow wastage and decay because there is so little to waste or decay: their mummied and stringy flesh has the durability of granite.

Bascom Hawke clothed his angular figure with an assortment of odd garments which seemed to have the same durability: they were immensely old and worn, but they also gave no signs of ever wearing out, for by their cut and general appearance of age, it seemed that his frugal soul had selected in the nineties materials which it hoped would last forever. His coat, which was originally of a dark dull pepper-and-salt gray, had gone green at the seams and pockets, and moreover it was a ridiculously short skimpy coat for a gaunt big-boned man like this: it was hardly more than a jacket, his great wristy hands burst out of it like lengths of cordwood, and the mark of his high humped narrow shoulders cut into it with a knife-like sharpness. His trousers were also tight and skimpy, of a lighter gray and of a rough woolly texture from which all fuzz and fluff had long ago been rubbed, he wore rough country brogans with raw-hide laces, and a funny little flat hat of ancient black felt, which had also gone green along the band. One understands now why the policeman called him "Bud": this great bony figure seemed ruthlessly to have been crammed into garments in which a country fledgling of the eighties might have gone to see his girl, clutching a bag of gumdrops in his large red hand. A stringy little necktie, a clean but dilapidated collar which by its bluish and softly mottled look Bascom Hawke must have laundered himself (a presumption which

is quite correct since my uncle did all his own laundry work, as well as his mending, repairing, and cobbling)— this was his costume, winter and summer, and it never changed, save that in winter he supplemented it with an ancient blue sweater which he wore buttoned to the chin and whose frayed ends and cuffs projected inches below the scanty little jacket. He had never been known to wear an overcoat, not even on the coldest days of those long, raw, and formidable winters which Boston suffers.

The mark of my uncle's madness was plain upon him: intuitively men knew he was not a poor man, and the people who had seen him so many times in State Street would nudge one another, saying: "You see that old guy? You'd think he was waitin' for a handout from the Salvation Army, wouldn't you? Well, he's not. He's *got* it, brother. Believe me, he's *got* it good and plenty: he's *got* it salted away where no one ain't goin' to touch it. That guy's got a sock full of dough!"

"Jesus!" another remarks. "What good's it goin' to do an old guy like that? He can't take any of it with him, can he?"

"You said it, brother," and the conversation would become philosophical.

Bascom Hawke was himself conscious of his parsimony, and although he sometimes asserted that he was "only a poor man" he realized that his exaggerated economies could not be justified to his business associates on account of poverty: they taunted him slyly, saying, "Come on, Hawke, let's go to lunch. You can get a good meal at the Pahkeh House for a couple of bucks." Or "Say, Hawke, I know a place where they're havin' a sale of winter overcoats: I saw one there that would suit you—you can get it for sixty dollars." Or "Do you need a good laundry, Reverend? I know a couple of Chinks who do good work."

To which Bascom, with the characteristic evasiveness of parsimony, would reply, snuffling derisively down his nose: "No, sir! You won't catch me in any of their stinking restaurants. You never know what you're getting: if you could see the dirty, nasty, filthy kitchens where your food is prepared you'd lose your appetite quick enough." His parsimony had resulted in a compensating food mania: he declared that "in his young days" he "ruined his digestion by eating in restaurants," he painted the most revolting pictures of the filth of these establishments, laughing scornfully down his nose as he declared: "I suppose you think it tastes better after some dirty, nasty, stinking *nigger* has wiped his old hands all over it" (phuh-phuh-phuh-phuh-phuh!)—here he would contort his face and snuffle scornfully down his nose; and he was bitter in his denunciation of "rich foods," declaring they had "destroyed more lives than all the wars and all the armies since the beginning of time."

As he had grown older he had become more and more convinced of the healthy purity of "raw foods," and he prepared for himself at home raw revolting messes of chopped-up carrots, onions, turnips, even raw potatoes, which he devoured at table, smacking his lips with an air of keen relish, and declaring to his wife: "You may poison *yourself* on your old roasts and oysters and turkeys if you please: you wouldn't catch *me* eating that stuff. No, sir! Not on your life! I think too much of my stomach!" But his use of the pronoun "you" was here universal rather than particular because if that lady's longevity had depended on her abstinence from "roasts and oysters and turkeys" there was no reason why she should not have lived forever.

Or again, if it were a matter of clothing, a matter of fencing in his bones and tallows against the frozen nail of Boston winter, he would howl derisively: "An overcoat! Not on your life! I wouldn't give two cents for all the old overcoats in the world! The only thing they're good for is to gather up germs and give you colds and pneumonia. I haven't worn an overcoat in thirty years, and I've never had the *vestige*—no! not the *semblance*—of a cold during all that time!" —an assertion that was not strictly accurate since he always complained bitterly of at least two or three during the course of a single winter, declaring at those times that no more hateful, treacherous, damnable climate than that of Boston had ever been known.

Similarly, if it were a question of laundries he would scornfully declare that he would not send "*his* shirts and collars to let some dirty old Chinaman spit and *hock* upon them— *yes!*" he would gleefully howl, as some new abomination of nastiness suggested itself to his teeming brain— "*Yes!* and iron it *in,* too, so you can walk around done up in old Chinaman's spit!"—(Phuh-phuh-phuh-phuh-phuh!)—here he would grimace, contort his rubbery lip, and laugh down his nose in forced snarls of gratification and triumph.

This was the old man who now stood clutching his raw bony hands across his waist, before entering his office.

This was his history:

Bascom Hawke had been the scholar of his amazing family: he was a man of powerful intelligence and disordered emotions. Even in his youth, his eccentricities of dress, speech, walk, manner had made him an object of ridicule to his Southern kinsmen, but their ridicule was streaked with pride, since they accepted the impact of his personality as another proof that theirs was an extraordinary family. "He's one of 'em, all right," they said exultantly, "queerer than any of us!"

Bascom's youth, following the war between the States, had been seared by a bitter poverty: at once enriched and warped by a life that clung to the earth with a root-like tenacity, that was manual, painful, spare and stricken, and that rebuilt itself—fiercely, cruelly, and richly—from the earth. And, because there burned and blazed in him from the first a hatred of human indignity, a passionate avowal of man's highness and repose, he felt more bitterly than the others the delinquencies of his father, and the multiplication of his father's offspring, who came regularly into a world of empty cupboards.

"As each of them made its unhappy entrance into the world," he would say later, his voice tremulous with passion, "I went out into the woods, striking my head against the trees, and blaspheming God in my anger. Yes, sir," he continued, pursing his long lip rapidly against his few loose upper teeth, and speaking with an exaggerated pedantry of enunciation, "I am not ashamed to confess that I did. For we were living in conditions un-*worthy*—*unworthy*"—his voice rising to an evangelical yell, "I had almost said—of the condition of animals. And—*say*—what do you think?" —he said, with a sudden shift in manner and tone, becoming, after his episcopal declaration, matter of fact and whisperingly confidential. "Why, do you know, my boy, at one time I had to take my *own* father aside, and

point out to him we were living in no way becoming decent people."—Here his voice sank to a whisper, and he tapped me on the knee with his big stiff finger, grimacing horribly and pursing his lip against his dry upper teeth.

Poverty had been the mistress of his youth and Bascom Hawke had not forgotten: poverty had burned its way into his heart. He took what education he could find in a backwoods school, read everything he could, taught, for two or three years, in a country school and, at the age of twenty-one, borrowing enough money for railway fare, went to Boston to enroll himself at Harvard. And, somehow, because of the fire that burned in him, the fierce determination of his soul, he had been admitted, secured employment waiting on tables, tutoring, and pressing every one's trousers but his own, and lived in a room with two other starved wretches on $3.50 a week, cooking, eating, sleeping, washing, and studying in the one place.

At the end of seven years he had gone through the college and the school of theology, performing brilliantly in Greek, Hebrew, and metaphysics.

Poverty, fanatical study, the sexual meagreness of his surroundings, had made of him a gaunt zealot: at thirty he was a lean fanatic, a true Yankee madman, high-boned, with gray thirsty eyes and a thick flaring sheaf of oaken hair—six feet three inches of gangling and ludicrous height, gesticulating madly and obliviously before a grinning world. But he had a grand lean head: he looked somewhat like the great Ralph Waldo Emerson—with the brakes off.

About this time, he married a young Southern woman of a good family: she was from Tennessee, her parents were both dead, in the seventies she had come north and had lived for several years with an uncle in Providence, who had been constituted guardian of her estate, amounting probably to about seventy-five thousand dollars, although her romantic memory later multiplied the sum to two hundred thousand dollars. The man squandered part of her money and stole the rest: she came, therefore, to Bascom without much dowry, but she was pretty, bright, intelligent, and had a good figure. Bascom smote the walls of his room with bloody knuckles, and fell down before God.

When Bascom met her she was a music student in Boston: she had a deep full-toned contralto voice which was wrung from her somewhat tremulously when she sang. She was a small woman, birdlike and earnest, delicately fleshed and boned, quick and active in her movements and with a crisp tart speech which still bore, curiously, traces of a Southern accent. She was a brisk, serious, ladylike little person, without much humor, and she was very much in love with her gaunt suitor. They saw each other for two years: they went to concerts, lectures, sermons; they talked of music, poetry, philosophy and of God, but they never spoke of love. But one night Bascom met her in the parlor of her boarding house on Huntington Avenue, and with a voice vibrant and portentous with the importance of the words he had to utter, began as follows: "Miss Louise!" he said carefully, gazing thoughtfully over the apex of his hands. "There comes a time when a man, having reached an age of discretion and mature judgment, must begin to consider one of the *gravest*—yes! by all means one of the most important events in human life. The event I refer to is—matrimony." He paused, a clock was beating out its punctual measured tock upon the mantel, and a horse went by with ringing hoofs upon the street. As for Louise, she sat quietly erect, with dignified and ladylike composure, but it seemed to her that the clock was beating in her own breast, and that it might cease to beat at any moment.

"For a minister of the gospel," Bascom continued, "the decision is particularly grave because, for him—once made it is *irrevocable*, once determined upon, it must be followed *inexorably, relentlessly*—aye! to the edge of the grave, to the *uttermost* gates of death, so that the possibility of an error in judgment is *fraught*," his voice sinking to a boding whisper—"is *fraught* with the most terrible consequences. Accordingly," Uncle Bascom said in a deliberate tone, "having decided to take this step, realizing to the *full*—to the *full*, mind you—its gravity, I have searched my soul, I have questioned my heart. I have gone up into the mount-ings and out into the desert and communed with my *Maker* until," his voice rose like a demon's howl, "there no longer remains an *atom* of doubt, a *particle* of uncertainty, a *vestige* of *disbelief*! Miss Louise, I have decided that the young lady best fitted in every way to be my helpmate, the partner of my joys and griefs, the confidante of my dearest hopes, the in-*spir*-a-tion of my noblest endeavors, the companion of my declining years, and the *spirit* that shall accompany me along each step of life's vexed and troubled way, sharing with me whatever God in his *inscrutable* Providence shall will, whether of wealth or poverty, grief or happiness —I have decided, Miss Louise, that that lady must be—yourself!—and, therefore, I request," he said slowly and impressively, "the honor of your hand in mar-ri-age."

She loved him, she had hoped, prayed, and agonized for just such a moment, but now that it had come she rose immediately with lady-like dignity, and said: "Mistah Hawke: I am honuhed by this mahk of yoah esteem and affection, and I pwomise to give it my most *un*nest considahwation without delay. I wealize fully, Mistah Hawke, the gwavity of the wuhds you have just uttuhed. Foh my paht, I must tell you, Mistah Hawke, that if I accept yoah pwoposal, I shall come to you without the fawchun which was *wight*fully mine, but of which I have been depwived and defwauded by the *wascality*—yes! the *wascality* of my gahdian. I shall come to you, theahfoh, without the dow'y I had hoped to be able to contwibute to my husband's fawchuns."

"Oh, my *dear* Miss Louise! My *dear* young lady!" Uncle Bascom cried, waving his great hand through the air with a dismissing gesture. "Do not suppose—do not for one instant suppose, I beg of you!—that consideration of a monetary nature could influence my decision. Oh, not in the slightest!" he cried. "Not at all, not at all!"

"Fawchnatly," Louise continued, "my inhewitance was not *wholly* dissipated by this scoundwel. A pohtion, a vewy small pohtion, remains."

"My dear girl! My dear young lady!" Uncle Bascom cried. "It is not of the *slightest* consequence. . . . How much did he leave?" he added.

Thus they were married.

Bascom immediately got a church in the Middle West: good pay and a house. But during the course of the next twenty years he was shifted from church to church, from sect to sect—to Brooklyn, then back to the Middle West, to the Dakotas, to Jersey City, to Western Massachusetts, and finally back to the small towns surrounding Boston.

When Bascom talked, you may be sure God listened: he preached magnificently, his gaunt face glowing from the pulpit, his rather high, enormously vibrant voice, husky with emotion. His prayers were fierce solicitations of God, so mad with fervor that his audiences felt uncomfortably they came close to blasphemy. But, unhappily, on occasions my uncle's mad eloquence grew too much for him: his voice, always too near the heart of passion, would burst in splinters, and he would fall violently forward across his lectern, his face covered by his great gaunt fingers, sobbing horribly.

This, in the Middle West, where his first church had been, does not go down so well—yet it may be successful if one weeps mellowly, joyfully—smiling bravely through the tears—at a lovely aisle processional of repentant sinners; but Bascom, who chose uncomfortable titles for his sermons, would be overcome by his powerful feelings on these occasions when his topic was "Potiphar's Wife," "Ruth, the Girl in the Corn," "The Whores of Babylon," "The Woman on the Roof," and so on.

His head was too deeply engaged with his conscience—he was in turn Episcopal, Presbyterian, Unitarian, searching through the whole roaring confusion of Protestantism for a body of doctrine with which he could agree. And, he was forever finding it, and later forever renouncing what he had found. At forty, the most liberal of Unitarians, the strains of agnosticism were piping madly through his sermons: he began to hint at his new faith in prose which he modelled on the mighty utterance of Carlyle, and in poetry, in what he deemed the manner of Matthew Arnold. His professional connection with the Unitarians, and indeed with the Baptists, Methodists, Holy Rollers, and Seventh Day Adventists, came to an abrupt ending after he read from his pulpit one morning a composition in verse entitled *The Agnostic,* which made up in concision what it lacked in melody, and which ended each stanza sadly, but very plainly, on this recurrence:

> "I do not know:
> It may be so."

Thus, when he was almost fifty Bascom Hawke stopped preaching in public. There was no question where he was going. He had his family's raging lust for property. He became a "conveyancer"; he acquired enough of the law of property to convey titles; but he began to buy pieces of land in the suburbs of Boston, and to build small cheap houses, using his own somewhat extraordinary designs to save the architect's fees and, wherever possible, doing such odd jobs as laying the foundations, installing the plumbing, and painting the structure.

He regarded the price of everything as exorbitant—his furious anguish over the wages of labor was marvellous to behold: it drove him raging home, where he stamped insanely upon the floors in his fury, declaring that the Italians, Irish, Belgians, Poles, Swiss, and Yankees—or whatever unfortunate race had been represented in the last bill of charges—were infamous scoundrels, foul and dishonest cutthroats, engaged in a conspiracy to empty both his purse and his cupboard. He called upon them the entire and plenteous artillery of his abuse, his high husky voice ascending to a scream until, his own powers failing him, there flashed in him for a moment remembrance of one mightier than he, the most terribly eloquent of all earth's thunderers—his obscene and gargantuan partner, John T. Brill; and lifting his shaking hands toward Heaven, he would invoke God and Brill at the same time.

Like others in his family seared with a terrible and minute memory of war and hunger, he fled before the skeleton spectre of poverty: he was of that race which expects to avert starvation by eating sparingly.

Therefore, he mended his own shoes and wore historic clothing; he fiercely sowed and reaped the produce of his stony garden, and contrived in countless other ways to thwart the forces of organized extortion.

The small houses that he—no, he did not build them!—he went through the agonies of monstrous childbirth to produce them, he licked, nursed, and fondled them into stunted growth, and he sold them on long, but profitable terms to small Irish, Jewish, Negro, Belgian, Italian and Greek laborers and tradesmen. And at the conclusion of a sale, or after receiving from one of these men the current payment, Uncle Bascom went homeward in a delirium of joy, shouting in a loud voice, to all who might be compelled to listen, the merits of the Jews, Belgians, Irish, Swiss or Greeks.

"Finest people in the world! No question about it!"—this last being his favorite exclamation in all moments of payment or conviction.

For when they paid, he loved them. Often on Sundays they would come to pay him tramping over the frozen ground or the packed snow through street after street of smutty gray-looking houses in the flat weary-looking suburb where he lived. To this dismal heath, therefore, they came, the swarthy children of a dozen races, clad in the hard and decent blacks in which the poor pay debts and go to funerals. They would advance across the barren lands, the harsh sere earth scarred with its wastes of rust and rubbish, passing stolidly by below the blank board fences of a brick yard, crunching doggedly through the lanes of dirty rutted ice, passing before the gray besmutted fronts of wooden houses which in their stark, desolate, and unspeakable ugliness seemed to give a complete and final utterance to an architecture of weariness, sterility and horror, so overwhelming in its absolute desolation that it seemed as if the painful and indignant soul of man must sicken and die at length before it, stricken, stupefied, and strangled without a tongue to articulate the curse that once had blazed in him.

And at length they would pause before my uncle's little house—one of a street of little houses which he had built there on the barren flatlands of the suburb, and to which he had given magnificently his own name— Hawke Heights—although the only eminence in all that flat and weary waste was a stunted and almost imperceptible rise a half mile off. And here along this street which he had built, these little houses, warped, yet strong and hardy, seemed to burrow down solidly like moles for warmth into the ugly stony earth on which they were built and to cower and huddle doggedly below the immense and terrible desolation of the northern sky, with its rimy sun-hazed lights, its fierce and cruel rags and stripes of wintry red, its raw and savage harshness. And then, gripping their greasy little wads of money, as if the knowledge that all reward below these fierce and cruel skies must be wrenched painfully and minutely from a stony earth, they went in to pay my uncle. He would come up to meet them from some lower cellar-depth, swearing, mutter-

ing, and banging doors; and he would come toward them howling greetings, buttoned to his chin in the frayed and faded sweater, gnarled, stooped and frosty-looking, clutching his great hands together at his waist. Then they would wait, stiffly, clumsily, fingering their hats, while with countless squints and grimaces and pursings of the lip, he scrawled out painfully their receipt—their fractional release from debt and labor, one more hard-worn step toward the freedom of possession.

At length, having pocketed their money and finished the transaction, he would not permit them to depart at once, he would howl urgently at them an invitation to stay, he would offer long weedy-looking cigars to them, and they would sit uncomfortably, crouching on their buttock bones like stalled oxen, at the edges of chairs, shyly and dumbly staring at him, while he howled question, comment, and enthusiastic tribute at them.

"Why, my dear sir!" he would yell at Makropolos, the Greek. "You have a glorious past, a history of which any nation might well be proud!"

"Sure, sure!" said Makropolos, nodding vigorously. "Beeg Heestory!"

"The isles of Greece, the isles of Greece!" my uncle howled, "where burning Sappho loved and sung—" (Phuh! phuh! phuh! phuh! phuh!)

"Sure, sure!" said Makropolos again, nodding good-naturedly but wrinkling his lowering finger's-breadth of brow in a somewhat puzzled fashion. "Tha's right! You got it!"

"Why, my dear sir!" Uncle Bascom cried. "It has been the ambition of my lifetime to visit those hallowed scenes, to stand at sunrise on the Acropolis, to explore the glory that was Greece, to see the magnificent ruins of the noblest of ancient civ-i-*liz*-a-tions!"

For the first time a dark flush, a

flush of outraged patriotism, began to burn upon the swarthy yellow of Mr. Makropolos' cheek: his manner became heavy and animated, and in a moment he said with passionate conviction:

"No, no, no! No ruin! Wat you t'ink, eh! Athens fine town! We got a million pipples dere!" He struggled for a word, then cupped his hairy paws indefinitely: "*You* know? *Beeg!* O, ni-ez!" he added greasily, with a smile. "Everyt'ing good! We got everyt'ing good dere as you got here! *You* know?" he said with a confiding and painful effort. "Everyt'ing ni-ez! Not old! No, no, no!" he cried with a rising and indignant vigor. "New! de same as here? Ni-ez! You get good and cheap—everyt'ing! Beeg place, new house, dumbwaiter, elevator—wat chew like!—oh, ni-ez!" he said earnestly. "Wat chew t'ink it cost, eh? Feefateen dollar a month! Sure, sure!" he nodded with a swarthy earnestness. "I wouldn't keed you!"

"Finest people on earth!" my Uncle Bascomb cried with an air of great conviction and satisfaction. "No question about it!"—and he would usher his visitor to the door howling farewells into the terrible desolation of those savage skies.

Meanwhile, my Aunt Louise, although she had not heard a word of what was said, although she had listened to nothing except the periods of Uncle Bascom's heavily accented and particular speech, kept up a constant snuffling laughter punctuated momently by faint whoops as she bent over her pots and pans in the kitchen, pausing from time to time as if to listen, and then snuffling to herself as she shook her head in pitying mirth which rose again up to the crisis of a faint crazy cackle as she scoured the pan; because, of course, during the forty-five years of her life with him

thoroughly, imperceptibly, and completely, she had gone mad, and no longer knew or cared to know whether these words had just been spoken or were the echoes of lost voices long ago.

And again, she would pause to listen, with her small birdlike features uplifted gleefully in a kind of mad attentiveness as the door slammed and he stumped muttering back into the house, intent upon the secret designs of his own life, as remote and isolate from her as if they had each dwelt on separate planets, although the house they lived in was a small one.

The union of Bascom and Louise had been blessed by four children, all of whom had left their father's bed and board when they discovered how simple it is to secure an abundance of food, warmth, clothing, shelter and freedom in the generous world, whether by marriage, murder, or simply by hard labor. Of them, however, remarkable as their lives have been, it is not necessary to speak here, for he had forgotten them, they no longer touched his life: he had the power to forget, he belonged to a more ancient, a more lonely earth.

Such, briefly, had been the history of the old man who now stood before this dusty office. His life had come up from the wilderness, the buried past, the lost America. The potent mystery of old events and moments had passed around him, and the magic light of dark time fell across him.

Like all men in this land, he had been a wanderer, an exile on the immortal earth. Like all of us he had no home. Wherever great wheels carried him was home.

In the office which Bascom Hawke now entered there were two rooms, one in front and one behind, L shaped, and set in the elbow of the building, so that one might look out at the two projecting wings of the building, and see lighted layers of offices, in which the actors of a dozen enterprises "took" dictation, clattered at typewriters, walked back and forth importantly, talked into telephones or, what they did with amazing frequency, folded their palms behind their skulls, placed their feet restfully on the nearest solid object, and gazed for long periods dreamily and tenderly at the ceilings.

Through the broad and usually very dirty panes of the window in the front office one could catch a glimpse of Faneuil Hall and the magnificent and exultant activity of the markets.

These dingy offices, however, from which a corner of this rich movement might be seen and felt, were merely the unlovely counterpart of millions of others throughout the country and, in the telling phrase of Baedeker, offered "little that need detain the tourist": a few chairs, two scarred roll-top desks, a typist's table, a battered safe with a pile of thumb-worn ledgers on top of it, a set of green filing cases, an enormous green, greasy water-jar always half filled with a rusty liquid that no one drank, and two spittoons, put there because Brill was a man who chewed and spat widely in all directions—this, save for placards, each bearing several photographs of houses with their prices written below them —8 rooms, Dorchester, $6,500; 5 rooms and garage, Melrose, $4,500, etc.—completed the furniture of the room, and the second room, save for the disposition of objects, was similarly adorned.

To reach his own "office," as Bascom Hawke called the tiny cubicle in which he worked and received his clients, the old man had to traverse the inner room and open a door in a flimsy partition of varnished wood and glazed glass at the other end. This was his office: it was really a very narrow slice cut off from the larger room, and in it there was barely space for one large dirty window, an ancient dilapidated desk and swivel chair, a very small battered safe, buried under stacks of yellowed newspapers, and a small bookcase with glass doors and two small shelves on which there were a few worn volumes. An inspection of these books would have revealed four or five tattered and musty law books in their ponderous calf-skin bindings —one on *Contracts,* one on *Real Property,* one on *Titles*—a two-volume edition of the poems of Mathew Arnold, very dog-eared and thumbed over, a copy of *Sartor Resartus,* also much used, a volume of the essays of Ralph Waldo Emerson, the Iliad in Greek with minute yellowed notations in the margins, a volume of the *World Almanac* several years old, and a very worn volume of the Holy Bible, greatly used and annotated in Bascom's small, stiffy laborious, and meticulous hand.

If the old man was a little late, as sometimes happened, he might find his colleagues there before him. Miss Muriel Brill, the typist, and the eldest daughter of Mr. John T. Brill, would be seated in her typist's chair, her heavy legs crossed as she bent over to undo the metal latches of the thick galoshes she wore during the winter season. It is true there were also other seasons when Miss Brill did not wear galoshes, but so sharply and strongly do our memories connect people with certain gestures which, often for an inscrutable reason, seem characteristic of them, that any frequent visitor to these offices at this time of day would doubtless have remembered Miss Brill as always unfastening her galoshes. But the probable reason is that some people inevitably belong to seasons, and this girl's season was winter—not blizzards or howling winds, or the blind skirl and sweep of snow, but gray, grim, raw, thick, implacable winter: the endless successions of gray days and gray monotony. There was no spark of color in her, her body was somewhat thick and heavy, her face was white, dull, and thick-featured and instead of tapering downwards, it tapered up: it was small above, and thick and heavy below, and even in her speech, the words she uttered seemed to have been chosen by an automaton, and could only be remembered later by their desolate banality. One always remembered her as saying as one entered: ". . . Hello! . . . You're becoming quite a strangeh! . . . It's been some time since you was around, hasn't it? . . . I was thinkin' the otheh day it had been some time since you was around. . . . I'd begun to think you had forgotten us. . . . Well, how've you been? Lookin' the same as usual, I see. . . . Me? . . . Oh, can't complain. . . . Keepin' busy? *I'll* say! I manage to keep goin'. . . . Who you lookin' for? Father? He's in *there*. . . . Why, yeah! Go right on in."

This was Miss Brill, and at the moment that she bent to unfasten her galoshes, it is likely that Mr. Samuel Friedman would also be there in the act of rubbing his small dry hands briskly together, or of rubbing the back of one hand with the palm of the other in order to induce circulation. He was a small youngish man, a pale somewhat meagre-looking little Jew with a sharp ferret face: he, too, was a person who goes to "fill in" those vast swarming masses of people along the pavements and in the subway— the mind cannot remember them or absorb the details of their individual appearance but they people the earth,

they make up life. Mr. Friedman had none of the richness, color, and humor that some members of his race so abundantly possess, the succession of gray days, the grim weather seemed to have entered his soul as it enters the souls of many different races there —the Irish, the older New England stock, even the Jews—and it gives them a common touch that is prim, drab, careful, tight and sour. Mr. Friedman also wore galoshes, his clothes were neat, drab, a little worn and shiny, there was an odor of steamy thawing dampness and warm rubber about him as he rubbed his dry little hands saying: "Chee! How I hated to leave that good wahm bed this morning! When I got up I said, '*Holy* Chee!' My wife says, 'Whatsa mattah?' I says, 'Holy Chee! You step out heah a moment where I am an' you'll seè whatsa mattah.' 'Is it cold?' she says. 'Is it cold! I'll tell the cock-eyed wuhld!' I says. Chee! You could have cut the frost with an axe: the wateh in the pitchehs was frozen hahd; an' she has the nuhve to ask me if it's cold! 'Is it cold!' I says. 'Do you know any more funny stories?' I says. O how I do love my bed! Chee! I kept thinkin' of that guy in Braintree I got to go see to-day an' the more I thought about him, the less I liked him! I thought my feet would tu'n into two blocks of ice before I got the funniss stahted! 'Chee! I hope the ole bus is still workin',' I says. 'If I've got to go thaw that damned thing out,' I says, 'I'm ready to quit.' Chee! Well, suh, I neveh had a bit of trouble: she stahted right up an' the way that ole moteh was workin' is nobody's business."

During the course of this monologue Miss Brill would give ear and assent from time to time by the simple interjection: "Uh!" It was a sound she uttered frequently, it had somewhat the same meaning as "Yes," but it was more non-committal than "Yes." It seemed to render assent to the speaker, to let him know that he was being heard and understood, but it did not commit the auditor to any opinion, or to any real agreement.

The third member of this office staff, who was likely to be present at this time, was a gentleman named Stanley P. Ward. Mr. Stanley P. Ward was a neat middling figure of a man, aged fifty or thereabouts; he was plump and had a pink tender skin, a trim Vandyke, and a nice comfortable little pot of a belly which slipped snugly into the well-pressed and well-brushed garments that always fitted him so tidily. He was a bit of a fop, and it was at once evident that he was quietly but enormously pleased with himself. He carried himself very sprucely, he took short rapid steps and his neat little paunch gave his figure a movement not unlike that of a pouter pigeon. He was usually in quiet but excellent spirits, he laughed frequently and a smile—rather a subtly amused look—was generally playing about the edges of his mouth. That smile and his laugh made some people vaguely uncomfortable: there was a kind of deliberate falseness in them, as if what he really thought and felt was not to be shared with other men. He seemed, in fact, to have discovered some vital and secret power, some superior knowledge and wisdom, from which the rest of mankind was excluded, a sense that he was "chosen" above other men, and this impression of Mr. Stanley Ward would have been correct, for he was a Christian Scientist, he was a pillar of the church, and a very big church at that —for Mr. Ward, dressed in fashionable striped trousers, rubber soles, and a cut-away coat might be found somewhere under the mighty dome

of the Mother Church on Huntington Avenue every Sunday suavely, noiselessly, and expertly ushering the faithful to their pews.

This completes the personnel of the first office of the John T. Brill Realty Company, and if my uncle, Bascom Hawke, arrived late, if these three people were already present, if Mr. Bascom Hawke had not been defrauded of any part of his worldly goods by some contriving rascal, of whom the world has many, if his life had not been imperilled by some speed maniac, if the damnable New England weather was not too damnable, if, in short, Bascom Hawke was in fairly good spirits he would on entering immediately howl in a high, rapid, remote and perfectly monotonous tone: "Hello, Hello, Hello! Good-morning, Good-morning, Good-morning!"—after which he would close his eyes, grimace horribly, press his rubbery lip against his big horse teeth, and snuffle with laughter through his nose, as if pleased by a tremendous stroke of wit. At this demonstration the other members of the group would glance at one another with those knowing subtly supercilious nods and winks, that look of common self-congratulation and humor with which the more "normal" members of society greet the conduct of an eccentric, and Mr. Samuel Friedman would say: "What's the matteh with you, Pop? You look happy. Some one musta give you a shot in the ahm."

At which, a coarse powerful voice, deliberate and rich with its intimation of immense and earthy vulgarity, might roar out of the depth of the inner office: "No, I'll tell you what it is." Here the great figure of Mr. John T. Brill, the head of the business, would darken the doorway. "Don't you know what's wrong with the Reverend? It's that widder he's been takin' around." Here, the phlegmy burble that prefaced all of Mr. Brill's obscenities would appear in his voice, the shadow of a lewd smile would play around the corner of his mouth: "It's the widder. She's let him——"

At this delicate stroke of humor, the burble would burst open in Mr. Brill's great red throat, and he would roar with that high, choking, phlegmy laughter that is frequent among big red-faced men. Mr. Friedman would laugh drily ("Heh, heh, heh, heh, heh!"), Mr. Stanley Ward would laugh more heartily, but complacently, and Miss Brill would snicker in a coy and subdued manner as became a modest young girl. As for Bascom Hawke, if he was really in a good humor, he might snuffle with nosey laughter, bend double at his meagre waist, clutching his big hands together, and stamp at the floor violently several times with one stringy leg; he might even go so far as to take a random ecstatic kick at objects, still stamping and snuffling with laughter, and prod Miss Brill stiffly with two enormous bony fingers, as if he did not wish the full point and flavor of the jest to be lost on her.

My uncle, Bascom Hawke, however, was a very complicated person with many moods, and if Mr. Brill's fooling did not catch him in a receptive one, he might contort his face in a pucker of refined disgust, and mutter his disapproval, as he shook his head rapidly from side to side. Or he might rise to great heights of moral denunciation, beginning at first in a grave low voice that showed the seriousness of the words he had to utter: "The lady to whom you refer," he would begin, "the very charming and cultivated lady whose name, sir," here his voice would rise on its howling note and he would wag his great

bony forefinger, "whose name, sir, you have so foully traduced and blackened——"

"No, I wasn't, Reverend. I was only tryin' to whiten it," said Mr. Brill, beginning to burble with laughter.

"—whose name, sir, you have so foully traduced and blackened with your smutty suggestions," Bascom continued implacably, "—that lady is known to me, as you very well know, sir," he howled, wagging his great finger again, "solely and simply in a professional capacity."

"Why, hell, Reverend," said Mr. Brill innocently, "I never knew she was a perfessional. I thought she was an amatoor."

At this conclusive stroke, Mr. Brill would make the whole place tremble with his laughter, Mr. Friedman would laugh almost noiselessly, holding himself weakly at the stomach and bending across a desk, Mr. Ward would have short bursts and fits of laughter, as he gazed out the window, shaking his head deprecatingly from time to time, as if his more serious nature disapproved, and Miss Brill would snicker, and turn to her machine, remarking: "This conversation is getting too rough for me!"

And my uncle, if this jesting touched his complex soul at one of those moments when such profanity shocked him, would walk away, confiding into vacancy, it seemed, with his powerful and mobile features contorted in the most eloquent expression of disgust and loathing ever seen on any face, the while he muttered, in a resonant whisper that shuddered with passionate revulsion: "Oh *bad!* Oh *bad!* O *bad, bad, bad!*"—shaking his head slightly from side to side with each word.

Yet there were other times, when Brill's swingeing vulgarity, the vast coarse sweep of his profanity not only found Uncle Bascom in a completely receptive mood, but they evoked from him gleeful responses, counter essays in swearing which he made slyly, craftily, snickering with pleasure and squinting around at his listeners at the sound of the words, and getting such stimulus from them as might a renegade clergyman, exulting in a feeling of depravity and abandonment for the first time.

To the other people in this office—that is, to Friedman, Ward and Muriel, the stenographer—my uncle was always an enigma; at first they had observed his peculiarities of speech and dress, his eccentricity of manner, and the sudden, violent, and complicated fluctuation of his temperament, with astonishment and wonder, then with laughter and ridicule, and now, with dull, uncomprehending acceptance. Nothing he did or said surprised them any more, they had no understanding and little curiosity, they accepted him as a fact in the gray schedule of their lives. Their relation to him was habitually touched by a kind of patronizing banter—"kidding the old boy along" they would have called it—by the communication of smug superior winks and the conspiracy of feeble jests, and in this there was something base and ignoble, for my uncle was a better man than any of them.

He did not notice any of this, it is not likely he would have cared if he had, for, like most eccentrics, his thoughts were usually buried in a world of his own creating to whose every fact and feeling and motion he was the central actor. Again, as much as any of his extraordinary family, he had carried with him throughout his life the sense that he was "fated"—a sense that was strong in all of them—that his life was pivotal to all the actions of providence, that, in short, the time might be out of joint, but not himself. Nothing but death could shake his powerful egotism, and his occasional storms of fury, his railing at the world, his tirades of invective at some motorist, pedestrian, or laborer occurred only when he discovered that these people were moving in a world at cross-purposes to his own and that some action of theirs had disturbed or shaken the logic of his universe.

It was curious that, of all the people in the office, the person who had the deepest understanding and respect for my uncle was John T. Brill. Mr. Brill was a huge creature of elemental desires and passions: a river of profanity rushed from his mouth with the relentless sweep and surge of the Mississippi, he could no more have spoken without swearing than a whale could swim in a frog-pond—he swore at everything, at every one, and with every breath, casually and unconsciously, and yet when he addressed my Uncle Bascom his oath was always impersonal, and tinged subtly by a feeling of respect.

Thus, he would speak to Uncle Bascom somewhat in this fashion: "Goddamn it, Hawke, did you ever look up the title for that stuff in Malden? That feller's been callin' up every day to find out about it."

"Which fellow?" my Uncle Bascom asked precisely. "The man from Cambridge?"

"No," said Mr. Brill, "not him, the other————, the Dorchester feller. How the hell am I goin' to tell him anything if there's no goddamn title for the stuff?"

Profane and typical as this speech was, it was always shaded nicely with impersonality toward my Uncle Bascom—conscious to the full of the distinction between "damn *it*" and "damn *you."* Toward his other colleagues, however, Mr. Brill was neither nice nor delicate.

Brill was an enormous man physically: he was six feet two or three inches tall, and his weight was close to three hundred pounds. He was totally bald, his skull was a gleaming satiny pink; above his great red moon of face, with its ponderous and pendulous jowls, it looked almost egg-shaped. And in the heavy, deliberate, and powerful timbre of his voice there was always lurking this burble of exultant, gargantuan obscenity: it was so obviously part of the structure of his life, so obviously his only and natural means of expression, that it was impossible to condemn him. His epithet was limited and repetitive— but so, too, was Homer's, and, like Homer, he saw no reason for changing what had already been used and found good.

He was a lewd and innocent man. Like my uncle, by comparison with these other people, he seemed to belong to some earlier, richer and grander period of the earth, and perhaps this was why there was more actual kinship and understanding between them than between any of the other members of the office. These other people—Friedman, Brill's daughter, Muriel, and Ward—belonged to the myriads of the earth, to those numberless swarms that with ceaseless pullulation fill the streets of life with their gray immemorable tides. But Brill and my Uncle Bascom were men in a thousand, a million: if one had seen them in a crowd he would have looked after them, if one had talked with them, he could never have forgotten them.

It is rare in modern life that one sees a man who can express himself with such complete and abundant certainty as Brill did—completely, and

without doubt or confusion. It is true that his life expressed itself chiefly by two gestures—by profanity and by his great roar of full-throated, earth-shaking laughter, an explosive comment on existence which usually concluded and summarized his other means of expression.

Although the other people in the office laughed heartily at this soaring rhetoric of obscenity, it sometimes proved too much for Uncle Bascom. When this happened he would either leave the office immediately, or stump furiously into his own little cupboard that seemed silted over with the dust of twenty years, slamming the door behind him so violently that the thin partition rattled, and then stand for a moment pursing his lips, and convolving his features with incredible speed, and shaking his gaunt head slightly from side to side, until at length he whispered in a tone of passionate disgust and revulsion: "Oh, *bad! Bad! Bad!* By every *gesture,* by every *act,* he betrays the *boor,* the *vulgarian!* Can you imagine"—here his voice sank even lower in its scale of passionate whispering repugnance —"can you for one *moment* imagine a man of *breeding* and the social graces talking in such a way publicly?—And before his own daughter. Oh, *bad! Bad! Bad! Bad!"*

And in the silence, while my uncle stood shaking his head in its movement of downcast and convulsive distaste, we could hear, suddenly, Brill's pungent answer to all the world—and his great bellow of throaty laughter. Later on, if my uncle had to consult him on any business, he would open his door abruptly, walk out into Brill's office clutching his hands together at the waist, and with disgust still carved upon his face, say: "Well, sir, . . . If you have concluded your morning devotions," here his voice sank to a bitter snarl, "we might get down to the transaction of some of the day's business."

"Why, Reverend!" Brill roared. "You ain't heard nothin' yet!"

And the great choking bellow of laughter would burst from him again, rattling the windows with its power as he hurled his great weight backward, with complete abandon, in his creaking swivel-chair.

It was obvious that he liked to tease my uncle, and never lost an opportunity of doing so: for example, if any one gave Uncle Bascom a cigar, Brill would exclaim with an air of innocent surprise: "Why, *Reverend,* you're not going to smoke that, are you?"

"Why, certainly," my Uncle Bascom said tartly. "That is the purpose for which it was intended, isn't it?"

"Why, yes," said Brill, "but you know how they make 'em, don't you? I didn't think you'd touch it after some dirty old Spaniard has wiped his old hands all over it—yes! an' *spit* upon it, too, because that's what they do!"

"Ah!" my uncle snarled contemptuously. "You don't know what you're talking about! There is nothing cleaner than good tobacco! Finest and healthiest plant on earth! No question about it!"

"Well," said Brill, "I've learned something. We live and learn, Reverend. You've taught me somethin' worth knowing: when it's free it's clean; when you have to pay for it it stinks like hell!" He pondered heavily for a moment, and the burble began to play about in his great throat: "And by God!" he concluded, "tobacco's not the only thing that applies to, either. Not by a damned sight!"

Again, one morning, my uncle cleared his throat portentously, coughed, and suddenly said to me:

"Now, David, my boy, you are going to have lunch with me to-day. There's no question about it whatever!" This was astonishing news, for he had never before invited me to eat with him when I came to his office, although I had been to his house for dinner many times. "Yes, sir!" he said, with an air of decision and satisfaction. "I have thought it all over. There is a splendid establishment in the basement of this building—small, of course, but everything clean and of the highest order! It is conducted by an Irish gentleman whom I have known for many years. Finest people on earth: no question about it!"

It was an astonishing and momentous occasion; I knew how infrequently he went to a restaurant. Having made his decision, Uncle Bascom immediately stepped into the outer offices, and began to discuss and publish his intentions with the greatest satisfaction.

"Yes, sir!" he said in a precise tone, smacking his lips in a ruminant fashion, and addressing himself to every one rather than to a particular person. "We shall go in and take our seats in the regular way, and I shall then give appropriate instructions, to one of the attendants—" again he smacked his lips as he pronounced this word with such an indescribable air of relish, that immediately my mouth began to water, and the delicious pangs of appetite and hunger began to gnaw my vitals—"I shall say: 'This is my nephew, a young man now enrolled at Harvard Un-i-ver-sit-tee!'" —here Bascom smacked his lips together again with that same maddening air of relish—"'Yes, sir' (I shall say!)—'You are to fulfil his order without *stint,* without *delay,* and without *question,* and to the *utmost* of your ability'"—he howled, wagging his great bony forefinger through the air

—"As for myself," he declared abruptly, "I shall take nothing. Good Lord, no!" he said with a scornful laugh. "I wouldn't touch a thing they had to offer. You couldn't pay me to: I shouldn't sleep for a month if I did. But you, my boy!" he howled, turning suddenly upon me, "—are to have everything your heart desires! Everything, everything, everything!" He made an inclusive gesture with his long arms; then closed his eyes, stamped at the floor, and began to snuffle with laughter.

Mr. Brill had listened to all this with his great-jowled face slack-jawed and agape with astonishment. Now, he said, heavily: "He's goin' to have everything, is he? Where are you goin' to take him to git it?"

"Why, sir!" my uncle said in an annoyed tone, "I have told you all along—we are going to the modest but excellent establishment in the basement of this very building."

"Why, Reverend," Brill said in a protesting tone. "You ain't goin' to take your nephew *there*, are you? I thought you said you was goin' to git somethin' to *eat*."

"I had supposed," my uncle said with bitter sarcasm, "that one went there for that purpose. I had not supposed that one went there to get shaved."

"Well," said Brill, "if you go there you'll git shaved, all right. You'll not only git *shaved*, you'll git *skinned* alive. But you won't git anything to eat." And he hurled himself back again, roaring with laughter.

"Pay no attention to him!" my uncle said to me in a tone of bitter repugnance. "I have long known that his low and vulgar mind attempts to make a joke of everything, even the most sacred matters. I assure you, my boy, the place is excellent in every

way:—do you suppose," he said now addressing Brill and all the others, with a howl of fury—"do you suppose, if it were not, that I should for a single moment *dream* of taking him there? Do you suppose that I would for an instant *contemplate* taking my own nephew, my sister's son, to any place in which I did not repose the fullest confidence? Not on your life!" he howled. "Not on your life!"

And we departed, followed by Brill's great bellow, and a farewell invitation which he shouted after me, "Don't worry, son! When you git through with that cockroach stew, come back an' I'll take you out to lunch with *me*!"

Although Brill delighted in teasing and baiting my uncle in this fashion, there was, at the bottom of his heart, a feeling of deep humility, of genuine respect and admiration for him: he respected Uncle Bascom's intelligence, he was secretly and profoundly impressed by the fact that my uncle had been a minister of the gospel and had preached in many churches.

Moreover, in the respect and awe with which Brill greeted these evidences of my uncle's superior education, in the eagerness he showed when he boasted to visitors, as he often did, of my uncle's learning, there was a quality of pride that was profoundly touching and paternal: it was as if my uncle had been his son, and as if he wanted at every opportunity to display his talents to the world. And this, in fact, was exactly what he did want to do. Much to my uncle's annoyance, Brill was constantly speaking of his erudition to strangers who had come into the office for the first time, and constantly urging my uncle to perform for them, to "say some of them big words, Reverend." And even when my uncle answered him, as he frequently did, in terms of scorn, anger, and contempt, Brill was completely satisfied, if Uncle Bascom would only use a few of the "big words" in doing it. Thus, one day, when one of his boyhood friends, a New Hampshire man whom he had not seen in thirty-five years, had come in to renew their acquaintance Brill, in describing the accomplishments of my uncle, said with an air of solemn affirmation: "Why, hell yes, Jim! It'd take a college perfesser to know what the Reverend is talkin' about half the time! No ordinary — — — — is able to understand him! So help me God, it's true!" he swore solemnly, as Jim looked incredulous. "The Reverend knows words the average man ain't never heard. He knows words that ain't even in the dictionary. Yes, sir! —an' uses 'em, too—all the time!" he concluded triumphantly.

"Why, my dear sir!" my uncle answered in a tone of exacerbated contempt, "What on earth are you talking about? Such a man as you describe would be a monstrosity, a heinous perversion of natural law! A man so wise that no one could understand him:—so literate that he could not communicate with his fellow creatures:—so erudite that he led the inarticulate and incoherent life of a beast or a savage!"—here Uncle Bascom squinted his eyes tightly shut, and laughed sneeringly down his nose: "Phuh! phuh! phuh! phuh! phuh!—Why you con-sum-mate fool!" he sneered, "I have long known that your ignorance was bottomless—but I had never hoped to see it equalled— Nay! Surpassed!" he howled, "by your asininity."

"There you are!" said Brill exultantly to his visitor, "What did I tell you? There's one of them words, Jim: 'asserninity,' why, damn it, the Reverend's the only one who knows

what that word means—you won't even find it in the dictionary!"

"Not find it in the dictionary!" my uncle yelled. "Almighty God, come down and give this ass a tongue as Thou didst once before in Balaam's time!"

Again, Brill was seated at his desk one day engaged with a client in those intimate, cautious, and confidential preliminaries that mark the consummation of a "deal" in real estate. On this occasion the prospective buyer was an Italian: the man sat awkwardly and nervously in a chair beside Brill's desk while the great man bent his huge weight ponderously and persuasively toward him. From time to time the Italian's voice, sullen, cautious, disparaging, interrupted Brill's ponderous and coaxing drone. The Italian sat stiffly, his thick, clumsy body awkwardly clad in his "good" clothes of heavy black, his thick, hairy, blunt-nailed hands cupped nervously upon his knees, his black eyes glittering with suspicion under his knitted inch of brow. At length, he shifted nervously, rubbed his paws tentatively across his knees and then, with a smile mixed of ingratiation and mistrust, said: "How mucha you want, eh?"

"How mucha we want?" Brill repeated vulgarly as the burble began to play about within his throat. "Why, how mucha you got? . . . You know we'll take every damn thing you got! It's not how mucha we want, it's how mucha you got!" And he hurled himself backward, bellowing with laughter. "By God, Reverend," he yelled as Uncle Bascom entered, "ain't that right? It's not how mucha we want, it's how mucha you got! 'od damn! We ought to take that as our motter. I've got a good mind to git it printed on our letterheads. What do you think, Reverend?"

"Hey?" howled Uncle Bascom absently, as he prepared to enter his own office.

"I say we ought to use it for our *motter.*"

"Your *what?*" said Uncle Bascom scornfully, pausing as if he did not understand.

"Our *motter,*" Brill said.

"Not your *motter,*" my uncle howled derisively. "The word is *not motter,*" he said contemptuously. "Nobody of any refinement would say *motter. Motter* is *not* correct!" he howled finally. "Only an ig-no-*ram*-us would say *motter.* No!" he yelled with final conclusiveness. "That is *not* the way to pronounce it! That is ab-so-lute-ly and em-phat-ic-ally *not* the way to pronounce it!"

"All right, then, Reverend," said Brill, submissively. "You're the docter. What is the word?"

"The word is *motto,*" Uncle Bascom snarled. "Of course! Any fool knows that!"

"Why, hell," Mr. Brill protested in a hurt tone. "That's what I said, ain't it?"

"No-o!" Uncle Bascom howled derisively. "No-o! By no means, by no means, by no means. You said *motter.* The word is *not* motter. The word is motto: m-o-t-t-o! M-O-T-T-O does *not* spell motter," he remarked with vicious decision.

"What does it spell?" said Mr. Brill.

"It spells *motto,*" Uncle Bascom howled. "It *has* always spelled motto! It *will* always spell motto! As it was in the beginning, is now, and ever shall be: A-a-men!" he howled huskily in his most evangelical fashion. Then, immensely pleased at his wit, he closed his eyes, stamped at the floor and snarled and snuffled down his nose with laughter.

"Well, anyway," said Brill, "no matter how you spell it, it's not how mucha we want, it's how mucha you got! That's the way we feel about it!"

And this, in fact, without concealment, without pretense, without evasion, was just how Brill did feel about it. He wanted everything that was his and, in addition, he wanted as much as he could get. And this rapacity, this brutal and unadorned gluttony, so far from making men wary of him, attracted them to him, inspired them with unshakable confidence in his integrity, his business honesty. Perhaps the reason for this was that concealment did not abide in the man: he published his intentions to the world with an oath and a roar of laughter—and the world, having seen and judged, went away with the confidence of this Italian—that Brill was "one fine-a man!" Even my uncle, who had so often turned upon his colleague the weapons of scorn, contempt, and mockery, had a curious respect for him, an acrid sunken affection: often, when we were alone, he would recall something Brill had said and his powerful and fluent features would suddenly be contorted in that familiar grimace, as he laughed his curious laugh which was forced out, with a deliberate and painful effort, through his powerful nose and his lips, barred with a few large teeth. "Phuh! phuh! phuh! phuh! phuh! . . . Of course!" he said, with a nasal rumination, as he stared over the apex of his great bony hands, clasped in meditation—"of course, he is just a poor ignorant fellow! I don't suppose—no, sir, I really do not suppose that Brill ever went to school over six months in his life!—say!" my uncle Bascom paused suddenly, turned to me abruptly with his strange fixed grin, and fastened his sharp old eyes keenly on me: in this sudden and abrupt change, this transference of his vision from his own secret and personal world, in which his thought and feeling was sunken, and which seemed to be so far away from the actual world about him, there was something impressive and disconcerting. His eyes were gray, sharp, and old, and one eyelid had a heavy droop or ptosis which, although it did not obscure his vision, gave his expression at times a sinister glint, a malevolent humor. "—Say!" here his voice sank to a deliberate and confiding whisper, "(Phuh! phuh! phuh! phuh! phuh!) Say—a man who would—he told me— O vile! vile! vile! my boy!" my uncle whispered, shutting his eyes in a kind of shuddering ecstasy as if at the memory of things too gloriously obscene to be repeated. "Can you *imagine,* can you even *dream* of such a state of affairs if he had possessed an atom, a *scintilla* of delicacy and good breeding! Yes, sir!" he said with decision. "I suppose there's no doubt about it! His beginnnings were very lowly, very poor and humble, indeed! . . . Not that that is in any sense to his discredit!" Uncle Bascom said hastily, as if it had occurred to him that his words might bear some taint of snobbishness. "Oh, by no means, by no means, by no means!" he sang out, with a sweeping upward gesture of his long arm, as if he were clearing the air of wisps of smoke. "Some of our finest men—some of the nation's *leaders,* have come from just such surroundings as those. Beyond a doubt! Beyond a doubt! There's no question about it whatever! Say!"— here he turned suddenly upon me again with the ptotic and sinister intelligence of his eye. "Was *Lincoln* an aristocrat? Was he the issue of wealthy parents? Was he brought up with a silver spoon in his mouth? Was our *own* former governor, the Vice-President of the United States to-day, reared in the lap of luxury! Not on

your life!" howled Uncle Bascom. "He came from frugal and thrifty Vermont farming stock, he has never deviated a *jot* from his early training, he remains to-day what he has always been—one of the simplest of men! Finest people on earth, no question about it whatever!"

Again, he meditated gravely with lost stare across the apex of his great joined hands, and I noticed again, as I had noticed so often, the great dignity of his head in thought—a head that was highbrowed, lean and lonely, a head that not only in its cast of thought but even in its physical contour, and in its profound and lonely earnestness, bore an astonishing resemblance to that of Emerson—it was, at times, like these, as grand a head as I had ever seen, and on it was legible the history of man's loneliness, his dignity, his grandeur and despair.

"Yes, sir!" he said, in a moment. "He is, of course, a vulgar fellow and some of the things he says at times are O! vile! vile! vile!" my uncle cried, closing his eyes and laughing. "O vile! *most* vile! . . . but (phuh! phuh! phuh!) you can't help laughing at the fellow at times because he is so . . . O, I could tell you things, my boy! . . . O *Vile! vile!*" he cried, shaking his head downwards. "What coarseness! . . . What in-*vect*-ive!" he whispered, in a kind of ecstasy.

And this invective, I know, he cherished in his secret heart so dearly that on at least one notable occasion he had invoked it, and lamented that he did not have it by him as an aid. What Uncle Bascom had said on that occasion, lifting his arms to heaven, and crying out a confession of his own inadequacy in a tone of passionate supplication, was: "O, that J. T. were here at this moment!—or that I had his tongue!—that he might aid me with his *scathing* invective!"

The occasion was this: a few years before my uncle had taken his wife to Florida for the winter, and had rented there a cottage. The place he chose was small and modest, it was several miles away from one of the larger and more fashionable towns, it was not on the coast, but set a few miles inland, and it had the advantages of a river, or peninsular inlet which rose and fell with the recurrence of the tides. This modest winter colony was so small that it could afford only one small church and one minister, himself a member of the colony. During the winter this man was taken ill: he was unable to continue his services at the church, and his little following, in looking around for a substitute, learned that Uncle Bascom had formerly been a minister. They came to him, therefore, and asked if he would serve.

"Oh, *Lord*, no!" Bascom howled derisively. "Good *heavens*, no! I shouldn't *dream* of such a thing! I shouldn't for a moment *contemplate* such a thing! I am a *total*—for twenty years I have been a *complete*—agnostic."

The flock looked at him with a dazed expression. "Wal," said one of the leading parishioners, a lean Down-Easter, "most of us here are Presbyterians, but I don't know that that would make any difference. The way I see it, we're all met here to worship the Lord, and we need a preacher no matter what his denomination is. When all's said and done," he concluded comfortably, "I don't guess there's much difference between any of us in the long run."

"Why, my dear sir!" my uncle said, with a slight sneer. "If you think there is no difference between an agnostic and a Presbyterian you had

better have your head examined by a doctor without further delay. No-o!" he howled faintly. "I cannot profess belief in what I do not know! I cannot simulate conviction when I have none! I cannot preach a faith I have not got! There, sir, you have my whole position in a nut-shell!"

Here, people in the group began to stir restlessly, to mutter uneasily, and to draw away: suddenly Uncle Bascom caught the muttered word "atheist."

"No-o!" he shouted, his ptotic eye beginning to glitter with the light of combat. "By no means! By no means! You only show your ignorance when you say a thing like that. They are not the same! They are ab-so-lute-ly and em-phat-i-cal-ly *not* the same! An atheist is *not* an agnostic and an agnostic is *not* an atheist! Why!" he yelled, "the mere sound of the words would teach you that if you had an atom of intelligence. An atheist is a man who does not believe in God!—it is composed of the Greek prefix 'a' —meaning *not*, and the noun 'the-os,' meaning God: an atheist therefore says there is no God! Now," he continued, licking his lips for joy, "we come to the word *agnostic*. Is the sound the same? No-o! Is the meaning the same? By no means! Are the parts the same? Not on your life! The word is *agnostic*: a-g-n-o-s-t-i-c! From what language is it derived? From Greek, of course—as any fool should know! From what words? From the vowel of negation 'a' again, and from 'gnosti-kos'—the word for *knowing*. An agnostic therefore is what?" he demanded, glaring around at their mute faces. "Why!" he said impatiently, as no one answered, "Any schoolboy knows that much! A not-knowing man! A man who does not know! Not a man who denies! Oh, by no means!" —his great hand rose impatiently—

"An *atheist* is a man who denies! An *agnostic* is simply a man who does not know!"

"I can't see there's any difference," some one muttered. "They *both* sound like a couple of godless heathen to me!"

"No difference!" Bascom howled. "My dear sir, hold your tongue before you bring down lasting shame upon your progeny! . . . They are as different as night from day, as black from white, as the sneering irreverence of the cynic from the calm, temperate, and judicial spirit of the philosopher! Why!" he declared impressively, "Some of the finest spirits of our times have been agnostics. Yes, sir! Some of the grandest people that ever lived! . . . The *great* Matthew Arnold was an agnostic!" he yelled. "Does that sound as if there was no difference? Not on your life!"

He paused, and as there was no response from his involuntary congregation, he began, after a moment, to fumble at the inside pocket of his coat with his big fingers.

"I have here a poem," he said, taking it out of his pocket, "of my own composition"—here he coughed modestly—"although it may show traces, I admit, of the influence of the great man whose name I have just mentioned, and whom I am proud to call my master: Matthew Arnold. It will, I believe, illustrate my position better than anything I could say to you." He held up his great forefinger to command attention, and then began to read.

"The title of the poem," Uncle Bascom said, "is—'My Creed.'" After a short silence, he began:

" 'Is there a land beyond the stars
Where we may find eternal day,
Life after death, peace after wars?
Is there? I can not say.

Shall we find there a happier life,
All joy that here we never know,
Love in all things, an end of strife?
Perhaps: it may be so.' "

There were seventeen other stanzas which Uncle Bascom read to them deliberately and with telling enunciation, after which he folded the paper and looked about him with a sneer: "I think," he said, "that I have made my meaning clear. Now you know what an agnostic is."

They did. His meaning was so clear that they had no language to oppose to it: they turned, they went away like men who had been stunned. Among them, however, was one who did not yield so easily, a daughter of the Lord who had often won by persuasion and the soft violence of her beaming eye what others failed to win by harsher means. This lady was a widow, a Southern woman in her middle years: her charms were ripe, she had a gentle, loving touch, a soft and fruity unction in her voice. This lady had been able to resist few ministers and few ministers had been able to resist this lady. Now, as the others retreated, the lady advanced: she came forward with a practised sidling movement of her hips and Uncle Bascom, who was standing triumphantly in the midst of a receding host, suddenly found himself confronted by her gentle and importunate face.

"Oh, Mr. Hawke!" she crooned sweetly, with a kind of abdominal rapture in her voice (thus, the way she pronounced his name was—Mis-tah Haw-*uk*!). "I *jus'* know that you must've been a *won*-da-ful preach-ah! I can tell by yo' face that you'ah such a *g-o-o-d* man—" Again she grunted sweetly with this ecstatic abdominal expiration.

"Why, madame! Why—" Uncle Bascom began, decidedly in a confused tone, but taking her abundance in with a sharp appraising eye.

"I was *jus'* thrilled to death all the time that you was tawkin', Mistah Haw-*uk*," the widow said. "I was a-sittin' theah an' sittin' theah, just a-drinkin' it all in, just a-*baskin'* in the rays of yo' wisdom, Mistah Haw-uk! All the time you was readin' that wonderful poem, I was just a-sayin' to myse'f: What a wondaful thing it is that a man like this has been chosen fo' the Suvvice of the Lawd, what a wondaful thing it is to know that this man is one o' Gawd's Suvvants!"

"Why, madame!" Bascom cried, his gaunt face flushed with pleasure. "Why, madame, I assure you I am deeply grateful . . . deeply honored to think that a lady of your obvious . . . your *undoubted* intelligence . . . should feel that way about me! But, madame!——"

"Oh, Mistah Haw-*uk*!" the widow groaned. "I jus' *love* to heah you *tawk!* I jus' *love* the way you handle langwidge! You heah so much po' shoddy, good-fo'-nothin' tawk nowadays—all full o' slang an' bad grammah an' I don't know whatall: I don't know what fokes ah *comin'* to—it's a real pleasuah—yes, suh! a real sho' nuff *treat*—to heah a man who can express himse'f the way you can. The minute I saw you I said to myse'f: I *jus' know* that that man can *tawk!* I *know* it! I *know* it! I *know* it!" The widow cried, shaking her head from side to side vigorously. "Theah's a man, I said," the widow continued, "theah's a man who kin do anything he likes with me—yes, suh! just anything!—I said that just as soon as you opened yo' mouf to speak!"

"Oh, madame, madame!" cried Bascom fervently, bowing with real dignity. "I thank you. I thank you sincerely and gratefully from the bottom of my heart!"

"Yes, suh! I could just enjoy my-se'f—(I said)—just a-lookin' at his haid."

"At my *what?*" yelled Bascom, jumping as if he had received an electric shock.

"At yo' *haid*," the widow answered.

"Oh!" howled Bascom. "At my *head!* My *head!*"—and he began to laugh foolishly.

"Yes, suh, Mistah Haw-*uk*," the widow continued. "I jus' thought you had the *grandest* haid I evah saw. The moment you began to read that poem I said, 'Only a man with a haid like that could a-written that poem. O thank Gawd! (I said) that he has dedicated his wondaful *haid* to the Lawd's Wuk!"

"Why, madame," Bascom cried again. "You have paid me the greatest honor! I cannot sufficiently thank you! But I am afraid—in *justice*, in *fairness*, I must admit," he said with some difficulty, "that you may not have entirely understood—that you are not quite clear—that, perhaps I did not make the meaning, the general purpose of that poem—O! it's my own fault, I know! Beyond a doubt! Beyond a doubt!—but perhaps I did not make its meaning wholly plain!"

"Yes, you did!" the widow protested. "Every word of it was jus' as plain as day to me! I kep' sayin' to myse'f: That's *jus'* the way I've always felt, but I nevah could express myse'f befo': I nevah *met* any one befo' that I could tawk to about it. An' now (I said), this wondaful man comes along an' puts the whole thing straight in my haid! O! (I said) if I could just sit at his feet, an' *listen* all day long, if I could jus' sit an' drink in all he had to say, if I could just *listen* to him tawk—I'd nevah ask fo' anything bettah!"

"Why, madame!" Bascom cried, deeply, genuinely moved. "I assure you I'd like nothing better! Yes, indeed! I assure you I'd be delighted! O, at any time! At any time!" he howled. "It is rare that one meets to-day— O, *most* rare!—a woman of your intelligence and perspicacity! We *must* have another talk!" he said. "Oh, by all means, by all means!"

"Uh-huh!" the widow grunted sweetly.

Bascomb looked around craftily to see if my Aunt Louise was anywhere within sight or hearing. "Perhaps," he said, smacking his lips together, "we might meet and have a quiet walk together. Nothing is more conducive to contemplation than the tranquil peace of nature. There's no question about it."

"Uh-huh," the widow said.

"To-morrow," Bascom whispered.

"Uh-huh," the widow crooned viscerally.

Thus, there began between Uncle Bascomb and the widow a series of promenades, in which he expounded his views liberally, and in which she was able, by the harmonious adjustment of her nature, to find herself in complete agreement. Again and again, my Aunt Louise watched them depart, she peered after them through her bright mad eyes, snuffling with angry laughter, and muttering, as she had muttered many times before: "The old *fool!* . . . The *misable* old *skinflint!* . . . Too poor to buy his own wife a *dwess* . . . while he spends *faw*-chuns, *faw*-chuns on them! . . . It's in the blood . . . the blood!" she whispered hoarsely. "They're *mad* . . . *mad!* His family's *ovah-sexed,* all of them!"

One evening, as Bascom and the widow were returning from one of these walks, they found themselves toward sunset a mile or so from town. It was a desolate spot: their road

wound on through fringes of scrub pine and stunted palm along the edges of the inlet: the tide was out, the water lay in shallow puddles across the bed of viscous mud, a few birds wheeled with creaking eery cries above this loneliness of earth and water, and there was the smell of shelled waste, sea-scum—the potent, magical, and exultant smell of the sea in harbors. The air and the sky were sweet with incomparable clarity, with an immense delicacy of light, and the sun, which now burned like a vast orange-colored ball, without violence or heat, was resting against the lonely and desolate space of the western horizon. The widow and Bascom paused for a moment to watch this scene, and then she said triumphantly: "Now, Mistah Haw-uk, you know that *Somebody* must've *done* all that. You know it jus' didn't go an' happen by itse'f. You know, when you see a beautiful sunset like that that nobody but Gawd himse'f could've made it. Now, you know you do, Mistah Haw-uk!"

"The question of its beauty," said my uncle precisely, "is debatable. The philosopher Hegel, for example, so far from seeing beauty in a sunset, remarked that it looked to him as if the sky had small-pox!" Here Bascom closed his eyes, and snuffled with laughter.

"Oh, Mistah Haw-uk!" the widow said reproachfully. "I know *you* don't feel that way about it. A man with a *haid* like yoah's could nevah believe a thing like that!"

"Oh!" Bascom shouted, immensely tickled for some reason. "By no means! By no means!" And he stamped violently at the earth, blind with his strange forced snarl of laughter.

For a moment they were silent: a vast and exuberant elation, an exultant vitality, was alive in Uncle Bascom. He looked at the shallow waters, he looked at the setting sun, he looked at the widow, and when he tried to speak, exultant mirth possessed him, and he could not.

"Shall we?—" he began at length inquiringly, but here a whimsy of humor seized him, he stopped short, contorted his face, stamped at the earth ecstatically, and snuffled down his nose—"shall we go in *wa-ding?*" There was a deliberate, a luscious nasality in his precise enunciation of the last word.

"Oh, Mistah Haw-uk! Why-y!" the widow exclaimed fruitily. "Wading! For what?"

"For . . . oysters!" said Uncle Bascom lusciously and gently.

"For . . . *oysters!*" the widow cried. "But I didn't know there were any oysters!"

Bascom pondered this statement for a moment, and the more he considered it, the funnier it became to him. He bit his rubbery lip, closed his eyes, and began to snuffle down his nose with laughter. "O yes!" he howled. "O *my* yes! There are always . . . oysters! There are plenty of . . . oysters!"

So the widow, without much more than a half-hearted and decorous protest, and a cautious glance around to make sure that pine and palm gave shelter to no watchers, sat down beside my uncle and took off her shoes and stockings. Then, hand in hand, they advanced across the shallows and through water that rarely came above their knees, the widow tentatively, with a balancing movement and little abdominal cries of alarm, Uncle Bascom more boldly, and with confident assurances: "My dear girl!" he said, grasping her hand more tightly. "You are in no danger whatsover! Oh, not the *slightest!*" he yelled. "You are as safe as you would be in your mother's arms. Yes, sir! You may rest assured

on that score! There's no question of it!"

The widow held her skirts kilted up and knotted in one hand, midway along her milky thighs, while Uncle Bascom had rolled his trousers high above his bony knees and stringy calves, which now advanced through the shallow water with a storky and tentative step. At length, about the middle of the stream, they reached a bar of hard-packed sand, and here they stood for a while looking at the setting sun, pacing along their little beach, so absorbed in their contemplation of coming dark, of solitude, and of themselves that neither noticed that the tide was coming in.

And yet the tide came in. It came steadily, urgently, imperceptibly, feathering against the fringes of the inlet, advancing, retreating, advancing, retreating, but advancing always past its last retreat until suddenly Bascom felt the shock of water at his toes: he looked down and saw that their ledge of earth and safety was shrinking almost visibly below his glance: he yelled, first from alarm, and then for help: he shouted, but no one came; he seized the buxom widow and, by staggering effort lifted her, he tottered with her into the water. At the first step the water reached his knees, at the second, halfway up his shanks, at the third, he yelled, and dropped his cargo. She screamed, as a swirl of water caught her at the waist: she clutched him, she clung to him, she screamed, and suddenly Bascom began to curse. He shook a knotted fist at the imperturbable evening skies, he blasphemed against a deity in which he had no faith, and when a false step plunged him to his chin in water, he howled retraction of his blasphemy and begged for providential help. Neither could swim; perhaps neither was in the greatest danger, but both were terrified and shocked, the water wet their ears before they reached the shore, and when at length they tottered up on dry land again, the widow had reached the end and limit of her effort: for several moments she lay panting hoarsely, half out of water and half in, a battered half-emergent Phryne. As for Bascom, he stood on palsied limbs and with a chattering jaw for several moments: his long arms, his bony hands, his stooped shoulders, his stringy legs all bent in a common, constant drip—he was absolutely speechless, and stood there for some time chattering with fright, and dripping water. At length, the widow raised a portion of her charms, bedraggled but made undeniable by water, and moaned hoarsely, "Oh, Mistah Haw-uk! Mistah Haw-uk! Come an' git me, Mistah Haw-uk!"

At this moment Uncle Bascom's features were seized by a horrible convulsion, he opened his mouth to speak, but no words came, he raised two trembling fists toward heaven, but no words came. He tried to curse, but no words came. At length he mastered himself sufficiently to speak and, as if finding his own artillery too feeble for the occasion, he uttered slowly, with passionate conviction, the supplication already mentioned: "O that J. T. were here—that he might aid me with his *scathing* invective!"

So ended romance between Uncle Bascom and the widow.

That year I was twenty, it had been my first year in New England, and the winter had seemed very long. In the man-swarm I felt alone and lost, a desolate atom in the streets of life. That year I went to see my uncle many times.

Sometimes I would find him in his dusty little cubicle, bent over the intricacy of a legal form, painfully and carefully, with compressed lips, filling in the blank spaces with his stiff angular and laborious hand. He would speak quietly, without looking up, as I came in: "Hello, my boy. Sit down, won't you? I'll be with you in a moment." And for a time the silence would be broken only by the heavy rumble of Brill's voice outside, by the minute scratching of my uncle's pen, and by the immense and murmurous sound of time, which rose above the city, which caught up in the upper air all of the city's million noises, and yet which seemed remote, essential, imperturbable and ever-lasting—fixed and unchanging, no matter what men lived or died.

Again, I would find him staring straight before him, with his great hands folded in a bony arch, his powerful gaunt face composed in a rapt tranquillity of thought. At these times he seemed to have escaped from every particular and degrading thing in life —from the excess of absurd and eccentric speech and gesture, from all demeaning parsimonies, from niggling irascibilities, from everything that contorted his face and spirit away from its calmness and unity of thought. His face at such a time might well have been the mask of Thought, the visage of contemplation. Sometimes he would not speak for several minutes, his mind seemed to brood upon the lip and edge of time, to be remote from every dusty moment of the earth.

One day I went there and found him thus; after a few moments he lowered his great hands and, without turning toward me, sat for some time in an attitude of quiet relaxation. At length he said:

"What is man that thou art mindful of him?"

It was one of the first days of spring: the spring had come late, with a magical northern suddenness. It seemed to have burst out of the earth overnight, the air was lyrical and sang with it.

Spring came that year like a triumph and like a prophecy—it sang and shifted like a moth of light before me, but I was sure that it would bring me a glory and fulfilment I had never known.

My hunger and thirst had been immense: I was caught up for the first time in the midst of the Faustian web —there was no food that could feed me, no drink that could quench my thirst—like an insatiate and maddened animal I roamed the streets, trying to draw up mercy from the cobblestones, solace and wisdom from a million sights and faces, or prowled through endless shelves of high-piled books tortured by everything I could not see and could not know, and growing blind, weary, and desperate from what I read and saw. I wanted to know all, have all, be all—to be one and many, to have the whole riddle of this vast and swarming earth as legible, as tangible in my hand as a coin of minted gold.

Suddenly spring came, and I felt at once exultant certainty and joy. Outside my uncle's dirty window I could see the edge of Faneuil Hall, and hear the swarming and abundant activity of the markets. The deep roar of the markets came to us across the singing and lyrical air, and I drank into my lungs a thousand proud, potent, and mysterious odors which came to me like the breath of certainty, like the proof of magic, and like the revelation that all confusion had been banished—the world that I longed for won, the word that I sought for spoken, the hunger that devoured me fed and ended. And the markets, swarming with richness, joy, and abundance, thronged below me

like a living evidence of fulfilment. For it seemed to me that nowhere more than here was the passionate enigma of New England felt: New England, with its harsh and stony soil, and its tragic and lonely beauty; its desolate rocky coasts and its swarming fisheries, the white, piled, frozen harshness of its winters with the magnificent jewelry of stars, the dark firwoods, and the warm little white houses at which it is impossible to look without thinking of groaning bins, hung bacon, hard cider, succulent bastings and love's warm, white, and opulent flesh.

There was the rustle of gingham by day and sober glances; then, under low eaves and starlight, the stir of the satiny thighs in feather beds, the white small bite and tigerish clasp of secret women—always the buried heart, the sunken passion, the frozen heat. And then, after the long, unendurably hard-locked harshness of the frozen winter, the coming of spring as now, like a lyrical cry, like a flicker of rain across a window glass, like the sudden and delicate noises of a spinet —the coming of spring and ecstasy, and overnight the thrum of wings, the burst of the tender buds, the ripple and dance of the roughened water, the light of flowers, the sudden, fleeting, almost captured, and exultant spring.

And here, within eighty yards of the dusty little room where my uncle Bascom had his desk, there was living evidence that this intuition was not false: the secret people, it was evident, did not subsist alone on codfish and a jug full of baked beans—they ate meat, and large chunks of it, for all day long, within the market district, the drivers of big wagons were standing to their chins in meat, boys dragged great baskets of raw meat along the pavements, red-faced butchers, aproned with gouts of blood, and wearing the battered straw hats that butchers wear, toiled through the streets below great loads of loin or haunch or rib and in chill shops with sawdust floors the beeves were hung in frozen regimental rows.

Right and left, around the central market, the old buildings stretched down to the harbor and the smell of ships: this was built-on land, in old days ships were anchored where these cobbles were, but the warehouses were also old—they had the musty, mellow, blackened air and smell of the seventies, they looked like the Victorian prints, they reeked of ancient ledgers, of "counting houses," of proud monied merchants, and the soft-spoked rumble of victorias.

By day, this district was one snarled web of chaos: a *gewirr* of deep-bodied trucks, powerful dappled horses, cursing drivers, of loading, unloading, and shipping, of dispatch and order, of the million complicated weavings of life and business.

But if one came here at evening, after the work of the day was done, if one came here at evening on one of those delicate and sudden days of spring that New England knows, if one came here as many a lonely youth had come here in the past, some boy from the inland immensity of America, some homesick lad from the South, from the marvellous hills of Old Catawba, he might be pierced again by the bitter ecstasy of youth, the ecstasy that tears him apart with a cry that has no tongue, the ecstasy that is proud, lonely, and exultant, that is fierce with joy and blind with glory, but that yet carries in it a knowledge that is born in such a moment that the intangible cannot be touched, the ungraspable cannot be grasped—the imperial and magnificent minute is gone forever which, with all

its promises, its million intuitions, he wishes to clothe with the living substance of beauty. He wishes to flesh the moment with the thighs and breast and belly of a wonderful mistress, he wishes to be great and glorious and triumphant, to distill the ether of this ecstasy in a liquor, and to drink strong joy forever; and at the heart of all this is the bitter knowledge of death—death of the moment, death of the day, death of one more infrequent spring.

Perhaps the thing that really makes New England wonderful is this sense of joy, this intuition of brooding and magic fulfilment that hovers like a delicate presence in the air of one of these days. Perhaps the answer is simple: perhaps it is only that this soft and sudden spring, with its darts and flicks of evanescent joy, its sprite-like presence that is only half-believed, its sound that is the sound of something lost and elfin, and half-dreamed, half-heard, seems wonderful after the grim frozen tenacity of the winter, the beautiful and terrible desolation, the assault of the frost and ice on living flesh which resists it finally as it would resist the cruel battering of a brute antagonist, so that the tart, stingy speech, the tight gestures, the withdrawn and suspicious air, the thin lips, red pointed noses and hard prying eyes of these people are really the actions of people who, having to defend themselves harshly against nature, harshly defend themselves against all the world.

At any rate, the thing the boy feels who comes here at the day's end is not completion, weariness, and sterility, but a sense of swelling ecstasy, a note of brooding fulfilment. The air will have in it the wonderful odors of the market and the smell of the sea: as he walks over the bare cobbled pavement under the corrugated tin awnings of the warehouses and produce stores a hundred smells of the rich fecundity of the earth will assail him: the clean sharp pungency of thin crated wood and the citric nostalgia of oranges, lemons and grapefruit, the stench of a decayed cabbage and the mashed pulp of a rotten orange. There will be also the warm coarse limey smell of chickens, the strong coddy smell of cold fish and oysters; and the crisp moist cleanliness of the garden smells—of great lettuces, cabbages, new potatoes, with their delicate skins loamy with sweet earth, the wonderful sweet crispness of crated celery; and then the melons— the ripe golden melons bedded in fragrant straw—and all the warm infusions of the tropics: the bananas, the pineapples and the alligator pears.

The delicate and subtle air of spring touches all these odors with a new and delicious vitality; it draws the tar out of the pavements also, and it draws slowly, subtly, from ancient warehouses, the compacted perfumes of eighty years: the sweet thin piney scents of packing boxes, the glutinous composts of half a century, that have thickly stained old warehouse plankings, the smells of twine, tar, turpentine and hemp, and of thick molasses, ginseng, pungent vines and roots and old piled sacking; the clean ground strength of fresh coffee, brown, sultry, pungent, and exultantly fresh and clean; the smell of oats, baled hay and bran, of crated eggs and cheese and butter; and particularly the smell of meat, of frozen beeves, slick porks and veals, of brains and livers and kidneys, of haunch, paunch and jowl; of meat that is raw and of meat that is cooked, for upstairs in that richly dingy block of buildings there is a room where the butchers, side by side with the bakers, the bankers, the brokers and the Harvard boys, devour thick steaks of the best and tenderest meat, smoking hot breads, and big, jacketed potatoes.

And then there is always the sea. In dingy blocks, memoried with time and money, the buildings stretch down to the docks, and there is always the feeling that the sea was here, that this is built-on earth. A single truck will rattle over the deserted stones, and then there is the street that runs along the harbor, the dingy little clothing shops and eating places, the powerful strings of freight cars, agape and empty, odorous with their warm fatigued planking, and the smells of flanges and axles that have rolled great distances.

And finally, by the edges of the water, there are great piers and storehouses, calm and potent with their finished work: they lie there, immense, starkly ugly, yet touched with the powerful beauty of enormous works and movements; they are what they are, they have been built without a flourish for the work they do, their great sides rise in level cliffs of brick, they are pierced with tracks and can engulf great trains; and now that the day is done they breathe with the vitality of a tired but living creature. A single footfall will make remote and lonely echoes in their brooding depths, there will be the expiring clatter of a single truck, the sound of a worker's voice as he says "Goodnight," and then the potent and magical silence.

And then there is the sea—the sea, beautiful and mysterious as it is only when it meets the earth in harbors, the sea that bears in swell and glut of tides the odorous savor of the earth, the sea that swings and slaps against encrusted piles, the sea that is braided with long ropes of scummy weed, the sea that brings the mast and marly scent of shelled decay. There is the sea, and there are the great ships— the freighters, the fishing schooners, the clean white one-night boats that make the New York run, now also potent and silent, a glitter of bright lights, of gleaming brasses, of opulent saloons—a token of joy and splendor in dark waters, a hint of love and the velvet belly upon dark tides—and the sight of all these things, the fusion of all these odors by the sprite of May is freighted with unspeakable memories, with unutterable intuitions for the youth: he does not know what he could utter, but glory, love, power, wealth, flight and movement and the sight of new earth in the morning, and the living corporeal fulfilment of all his ecstasy is in his wish and his conviction.

Certainly, these things can be found in New England, but perhaps the person who finds this buried joy the most is this lonely visitor—and particularly the boy from the South, for in the heart of the Southerner alone, perhaps, is this true and secret knowledge of the North: it is there in his dreams and his childhood premonition, it is there like the dark Helen, and no matter what he sees to cheat it, he will always believe in it, he will always return to it. Certainly, this was true of the gnarled and miserly old man who now sat not far from all this glory in his dingy State Street office, for my uncle Bascom Hawke, although the stranger on seeing him might have said, "There goes the very image of a hard-bitten old Down-Easter," had come, as lonely and wretched a youth as ever lived, from the earth of Old Catawba, he had known and felt these things and, in spite of his frequent bitter attacks on the people, the climate, the life, New England was the place to which he had re-

turned to live, and for which he felt the most affection.

—"What is man that thou art *mindful* of him?"—he said again, this time with that tell-tale pedantry of emphasis which foretold a seizure of his mouthing eccentricity. "What is *man* that thou art *mindful* of him?" he repeated with yet more emphasis. The word is *mindful, mindful, mindful!*— he made the word whine like the rasp of a saw. "M-I-N-D-F-U-L! (Phuh! phuh! phuh! phuh, phuh!)"

And again, his visage of calm and powerful thought was twisted by the disfiguring grimace, the inept and reasonless laughter. In a moment more, his face grew calm again, magnificently composed above his arched, gnarled hands; he spoke with eloquent deliberation. He became triumphant reasoning mind: he talked with superb and balanced judgment. And as the strange and lonely spirit of thought transformed his face, all the tumult and madness of his life was forgotten: no question of money or of self was involved.

"Beyond a doubt! Beyond a doubt!" he said deliberately. "The quality of the best writing in the books of the Old and New Testaments may take rank with the best writing that was ever done, but the amount of great writing is less than it is commonly supposed to be. There are passages— nay! *books!*"—his voice rising strangely to a husky howl—"of the vilest rubbish."

He paused a moment; then, in a remote voice—in the remote and passionate voice that had had such power to thrill men when it uttered poetry— he continued: "I am Alpha and Omega, the beginning and the end, the first and the last—the triumphant music of one of the mightiest of earth's poets, the sublime utterance of a man for whom God had opened the mysteries of heaven and hell, one of the mightiest lines, my dear boy, the most magnificent poetry that was ever written." And suddenly Bascom threw his gaunt hands before his face, and wept in strong, hoarse sobs: "Oh, my God! My God!—The beauty, the pity of it all! . . . You must excuse me," he whispered huskily after a moment, drawing his frayed and faded sleeve across his eyes. "You must excuse me. . . . It brought back . . . memories."

In spite of this ridiculous exhibition, and the absurd quality of these final words, there was something terrible and revolting about it, too: I was only twenty, and I shrank back for a moment and felt ashamed. In a moment more, however, Uncle Bascom was completely at his ease again: he acted as if nothing unusual had happened, and as if he had completely forgotten his outburst of a moment before.

After a pause, without looking at me, he said quietly, but with an unmistakable note of bitterness in his voice: "Have you seen any of my . . . children, recently?"

The question surprised me, because he rarely asked about them: most of the time he seemed to have forgotten their existence, to be wholly indifferent to them. I told him that I had seen one of his daughters the week before.

"My children—*basely* and *damnably, basely* and *damnably,* have deserted me!" he said with bitter passion. Then, quietly, indifferently, as if stating the fact more truthfully and temperately, he said: "I never see any of them any more. They never come to my house and I never go to theirs. I do not care. No, sir, I do not care. It makes no difference to me. O, not the slightest! None whatever!"

and he dismissed it with his big-boned hand. In a moment he added: "Their *mother* visits them, I believe. . . . Their *mother* goes, of course, whenever she gets invited."—Here again, the note of bitterness and scorn was evident, as if he held his wife guilty of some treachery in visiting her own children; but indifference and contempt were also in his voice—he spoke of his wife and children as if they were all strangers to him, as if their lives touched only remotely the edges of the buried world—the world in which he lived and moved, in which his soul wrought out its fated destiny.

And this was true: like all of his family he had passed through a dozen lives in living his own, he was done with his children and done with his wife, he had forgotten them, he was indifferent to them, he did not need them. But they, two daughters and two sons, the youngest of whom was over thirty, the oldest more than forty, were neither able to forget him nor forgive him. He lived in their bitter memory; like men who are searching the causes for some fatal catastrophic flaw which has broken the back of a mighty bridge they went back through the painful annals of their childhood, the years of frustration and bitterness they had lived beneath his roof, the years they could not forget, escape, or deny. His shadow fell across them: they never saw him, and they always talked of him, aping his speech, his gesture, and his manner, mocking him with limber tongues, but living in his life again and secretly feeling the old fear, the old awe, because his life alone had done what it had wished to do—warped and twisted though it may have been, it had held the rails, it had kept its way, it had seen new lands. For them, it sometimes seemed, the years were passing like a bitter water on the wheel of life: the wheel turned and they got older.

And now, as if he, too, had seen them as he spoke of them, he said: "They can all look after themselves. Every one must look after himself— say!" he paused suddenly, tapping his great finger on my knee, with the enquiring and combative glitter of his eye. "Does any one *help* you to die? Does any one go down into the grave with you? Can you *do* anything for any one? No!" he said decisively, and in a moment he added, slowly and deliberately: "Is not my help in *me*?"

Then, ruminant and lost, he stared across the archway of his hands. In a moment, with what was only an apparent irrelevance, with what was really a part of the coherent past, a light plucked from dark adyts of the brain, he said: "Who knoweth the spirit of man that goeth upward, and the spirit of the beast that goeth downward to the earth?"

He was silent and thoughtful for a moment; then he added sadly: "I am an old man. I have lived a long time. I have seen so many things. Sometimes everything seems so long ago."

Then his eye went back into the wilderness, the lost earth, the buried men.

Presently he said, "I hope you will come out on Sunday. O, by all means! By all means! I believe your aunt is expecting you. Yes, sir, I believe she said something to that effect. Or perhaps she intends to pay a visit to one of her children. I do not know, I have not the *remotest*—not the *faintest* idea of what she proposes to do," he howled. "Of course," he said impatiently and scornfully, "I never have any notion what she has in mind. No, sir, I really could not tell you. I no longer pay any attention to what she says—O! not the slightest!" he

waved his great hand through the air— "Say!" stiffly and harshly he tapped my knee, grinning at me with the combative glitter of his ptotic eye— "Say! did you ever find *one* of them with whom it was possible to carry on a coherent conversation? Did you ever find one of them who would respond to the processes of reason and ordered thought? My dear boy!" he cried, "You cannot talk to them. I assure you you cannot talk to them. You might as well whistle into the wind or spit into the waters of the Nile for all the good it will do you. In his youth man will bare the riches of his spirit to them, will exhaust the rich accumulations of his genius— his wisdom, his learning, his philosophy—in an effort to make them worthy of his companionship—and in the end, what does he *always* find? Why," said Uncle Bascom bitterly, "that he has spent his powers in talking to an imbecile"—and he snarled vengefully through his nose. In a moment more, he contorted his face, and nasally whined in a grotesque and mincing parody of a woman's voice, "O, I feel *so* sick! O, deary *me,* now! I think my *time* is coming on again! O, you don't *love* me any mo-o-ore! O, I *wish* I was dead! O, I can't get *up* to-day! O, I wish you'd bring me something *nice* from *ta-own*! O, if you loved me you'd buy me a *new* hat! O, I've got nothing to *we-e-ar*!" here his voice had an added snarl of bitterness—"I'm ashamed to go out on the street with all the other wim-men!"

Then he paused broodingly for a moment more, wheeled abruptly and tapped me on the knee again: "The proper study of mankind is—say!" he said with a horrible fixed grimace and in a kind of cunning whisper—"Does the poet say—*woman*? I want to ask you: *does* he, now? Not on your life!" yelled Uncle Bascom. "The word is *man, man, man!* Nothing else but *man!*"

Again he was silent: then, with an accent of heavy sarcasm, he went on: "Your aunt likes music. You may have observed your aunt is fond of music——"

It was, in fact, the solace of her life: on a tiny gramophone which one of her daughters had given her, she played constantly the records of the great composers, particularly of Wagner, lost in the enchanted forests of the music, her spirit wandering drunkenly down vast murky aisles of sound, through which the great hoarse throats of horns were baying faintly. And occasionally, on Sundays, on one of her infrequent excursions into the world, when her daughters bought her tickets for concerts at Symphony Hall —that great gray room lined on its sides with pallid plaster shells of Greece—she would sit perched high, a sparrow held by the hypnotic serpent's eye of music—following each motif, hearing minutely each subtle entry of the mellow flutes, the horns, the spinal ecstasy of violins—until her lonely and desolate life was spun out of her into aerial fabrics of bright sound.

"—Your aunt is fond of music," Bascom said deliberately. "Perhaps you may have thought—perhaps it seemed to you that she discovered it— perhaps you thought it was your aunt's own patent and invention—but there you would be wrong! O yes! my boy!" he howled remotely. "You may have thought so, but you would be wrong— Say!" he turned slowly with a malevolent glint of interrogation, a controlled ironic power—"was the Fifth Symphony written by a woman? Was the object of your aunt's worship, Richard Wagner, a *female?*" he snarled. "By no means! Where are their great works—their mighty sym-

phonies, their great paintings, their epic poetry? Was it in a woman's skull that the Critique of Pure Reason was conceived? Is the gigantic work upon the ceiling of the Sistine Chapel the product of a woman's genius?—Say! Did you ever hear of a lady by the name of William Shakespeare? Was it a female of that name who wrote *King Lear?* Are you familiar with the works of a nice young lady named John Milton? Or Fräulein Goethe, a sweet German girl?" he sneered. "Perhaps you have been edified by the writ-ings of Mademoiselle Voltaire or Miss Jonathan Swift? Phuh! Phuh! Phuh! Phuh! Phuh!"

He paused, stared deliberately across his hands, and in a moment repeated, slowly and distinctly: "The woman gave me of the tree and I did eat. Ah! that's it! There, my boy, you have it! There, in a nut-shell, you have the work for which they are best fitted." And he turned upon me suddenly with a blaze of passion, his voice husky and tremulous from the stress of his emotion: "The tempter! The Bringer of Forbidden Fruit! The devil's ambassador! Since the beginning of time that has been their office —to madden the brain, to turn man's spirit from its highest purposes, to corrupt, to seduce, and to destroy! To creep and crawl, to intrude into the lonely places of man's heart and brain, to wind herself into the core of his most secret life as a worm eats its way into a healthy fruit—to do all this with the guile of a serpent, the cunning of a fox—that, my boy, is what she's here for!—and she'll never change!" And, lowering his voice to an ominous and foreboding whisper, he said mysteriously, "Beware! Beware! Do not be deceived!"

In a moment more he had resumed his tone and manner of calm deliberation and, with an air of irrelevance, somewhat grudgingly, as if throwing a bone to a dog, he said, "Your aunt, of course, was a woman of considerable mentality—considerable, that is, for a female. Of course, her mind is no longer what it used to be. I never talk to her any more," he said indifferently. "I do not listen to her. I think she said something to me about your coming out on Sunday! But I do not know. No, sir, I could not tell you what her plans are. I have my own interests, and I suppose she has hers. Of course, she has her music. . . . Yes, sir, she always has her music," he said indifferently and contemptuously, and, staring across the apex of his hands, he forgot her.

Yet, he had been young, and full of pain and madness. For a space he had known all the torments any lover ever knew. So much my aunt had told me, and so much he had not troubled to deny. For bending toward me swiftly, fiercely, and abruptly in the full rich progress of a meal, her eyes ablaze with a mad and earnest light, she had suddenly muttered this ominous warning: "Take care, Dave! Take care, boy! You're one of them! Don't brood! Don't brood! You mustn't be mawbid," she whispered hoarsely, fixing the mad glitter of her bright old eyes even more intensely on me. "You're like all the rest of them—it's in the blood!" she muttered, hoarsely and fatally.

"Ah, what are you talk-ing about?" Bascom snarled in a tone of the profoundest contempt. "Scotch! English! Finest people on the face of the earth —no question about it!"

"Fugitive ideation! fugitive ideation!" she chattered like a monkey over a nut. "Mind goes off in all diwections—can't keep attention focused on anything foh five minutes! The modern decadents! Wead Nordau's

book, Dave—you'll see, you'll see! You'ah all alike," she muttered. "You'ah ovah-sexed—all of you!"

"Ah," he snarled again, "You talk like a fool! Some more of your psychology, I suppose," he said with a heavy sneer. "The black magic of little minds."

He knew nothing about it, of course; occasionally he still read Kant, and he could be as deep in absolutes, categories, moments of negation, and definitions of a concept, as she with all of her complicated and extensive paraphernalia of phobias, complexes, fixations, and repressions.

Then, bending toward me once again, as if she had not heard him, she whispered: "Oh, yes! he's indifferent enough to me now—but there was a time, there was a time, I tell you!—when he was mad about me! The old fool!" she cackled suddenly and bitterly with a seeming irrelevance. Then bending forward suddenly with a resumption of her former brooding intensity she whispered: "Yes! he was mad, mad, mad! Oh, he can't deny it!" she cried. "He couldn't keep his eyes off me for a minute! He went cwazy if any other man so much as looked at me!"

"Quite true, my dear! Quite true!" my uncle said without a trace of anger or denial in his voice, with one of his sudden and astonishing changes to a mood of tender and tranquil agreement. "Oh, yes," he said again, staring reminiscently across the apex of his great folded hands. "It is all quite true—every word as she has spoken it —quite true, quite true. I had forgotten but it's all quite true." And he shook his gaunt head gently from side to side, turning his closed eyes downward, and snuffling gently, blindly, tenderly, with laughter, with a passive and indifferent memory.

For a year or two after his marriage

he had been maddened by a black insanity of jealousy. It descended on his spirit like a choking and pestilence-laden cloud, it entered his veins with blackened tongues of poison, it crept along the conduits of his blood, sweltered venomously in his heart, it soaked into the convolutions of his brain until his brain was fanged with hatred, soaked in poison, stricken, maddened, and unhinged. His gaunt figure wasted until he became the picture of skeletonized emaciation, jealousy and fear ate like a vulture at his entrails, all of the vital energy, the power and intensity of his life, was fed into this poisonous and consuming fire and then, when it had almost wrecked his health, ruined his career, and destroyed his reason, it left him as suddenly as it came: his life reverted to its ancient and imbedded core of egotism, he grew weary of his wife, he thought of her indifferently, he forgot her.

And she, poor soul, was like a rabbit trapped before the fierce yellow eye, the hypnotic stare of a crouching tiger. She did not know whether he would spring, strike forth his paw to maul her, or walk off indifferently. She was dazed and stricken before the violence of his first passion, the unreasoning madness of his jealousy, and in the years that followed she was bewildered, resentful, and finally embittered by the abrupt indifference which succeeded it—an indifference so great that at times he seemed to forget her very existence for days at a time, to live with her in a little house as if he were scarcely conscious of her presence, stumping about the place in an intensity of self-absorption while he cursed and muttered to himself, banged open furnace doors, chopped up whatever combinations of raw foods his fantastic imagination might contrive, and answering her impa-

tiently and contemptuously when she spoke to him: "What did you *say-y*? Oh, what are you talk-ing about?"—and he would stump away again, absorbed mysteriously with his own affairs. And sometimes, if he was the victim of conspiracy in the universe—if God had forsaken him and man had tricked and cheated him, he would roll upon the floor, hammer his heels against the wall, and howl his curses at oblivious heaven.

Louise, meanwhile, her children having left her, played Wagner on the gramophone, kept her small house tidy, and learned to carry on involved and animated conversations with herself, or even with her pots and pans, for when she scrubbed and cleaned them, she would talk to them: if she dropped one, she would scold it, pick it from the floor, spank it across the bottom, saying: "No, you don't! Naughty, you bad thing, you!" And often, while he stumped through the house, these solitary conversations were interspersed by fits of laughter: she would bend double over her pots snuffling with soft laughter which was faintly broken at its climax, a long high "Who-o-op." Then she would shake her head pityingly, and be off again, but at what she was laughing she could not have said.

Suddenly one night, however, she interrupted one of Bascom's stamping and howling tirades by putting on her tiny gramophone *The Ride of the Valkyries,* as recorded by the Philadelphia Symphony Orchestra. Bascom, after the first paralysis of his surprise had passed, rushed furiously toward the offending instrument that was providing such melodious but mighty competition. Then Bascom halted; for suddenly he noticed that Louise was standing beside the instrument, that she was snuffling through her nose with laughter, and that from time to time she looked craftily toward him, and broke into a high piercing cackle. Bascom also noticed that she held a large carving knife in her hand. With a loud yell he turned and fled toward his room, where he locked the door, crying out strongly in an agony of terror: "O momma! Momma! Save me!"

All this had amused Louise enormously. She played the record over time after time, forever snuffling with laughter and the high cackle: "Whoo-oo-oo!" She bent double with it.

The next morning after Bascom had gone furtively away to his office, Louise looked at her image in a mirror. She looked for a long time, and she said: "I wonder if I am going mad."

Her face at fifty was bloodless, birdlike, her bright eyes badly paunched and rimmed with red; her hair was dead white—all her delicate features were minutely carved with a fabric of tiny wrinkles. So she said: "I wonder if I'm going mad," and took up the study of psychology.

She read all the works of William James, and those of Professor William McDougall as often as they appeared. She subscribed to several magazines, and wrote a book herself. She called it "The Surgery of Psychic Analysis": the publishers rejected it.

"I'm a good hundred years ahead of my time," she said to one of her daughters.

Thus, Louise found the life of reason. She had found a curative for all disease: she became convinced very shortly that she was one of the very few perfectly balanced people in the world and, of course, that Bascom was utterly mad.

But sometimes, even now, the old resentment and bewilderment would return—she would remember the time

of his passionate absorption in her, even the black insanity of his jealousy, with bitterness and regret.

What she had said was true. For two years after their marriage, before she had her first child, he had been like a man beset by furies. For the first time in his life his enormous egotism had been pulled away from its centre: he went outside of himself, he became acutely sensitive to the world around him. Because of the fury of possession which raged in him, because the thing he possessed must be the best and dearest thing on earth, it suddenly seemed that men were united against him in an effort to take it from him. Louise was pretty and attractive: wherever she went men looked at her, and when Bascom noticed this, it almost drove him mad.

At this time he had his first church in a town in Illinois: sometimes in the middle of a sermon he would see her face below him and his own would grow livid; he would pause suddenly and lean forward gripping the edges of his lectern like a man stricken and foolish—he would recover himself and go on brokenly and indifferently, but his spirit would twist like a tortured animal, his entrails would get numb and sick, his heart seemed frozen in a ring of poison, and a thousand horrible and foolish doubts would torment him. There was no excess of fantastic possibility, no absurdity of suspicion that he did not know: his mind swarmed with poisonous fabrications, which in a second were translated into reality: he was unable to distinguish between cold fact and his delirious fancy—the moment he imagined anything he believed it to be true.

And what was the reason for this madness? He did not know, and yet he knew that he was mad. He could sit in a chair and watch the madness soak into his brain and crawl along his flesh as a man might watch the progress of a poison in his blood. It was a madness that his mind contested, that his reason knew was false, and yet it conquered him. It drove him brain-sick, heart-sick, cursing through the streets at night, it drove him stamping through the streets clutching his great hands together at the waist, and if he heard a burst of laughter in the dark, if he heard voices and the pronouns "he" and "she" he was sure the words had reference to his wife and him or to a rival, and he would turn and curse the people who had spoken. The interest of the earth and of the town he thought was fastened on his own life and his wife's: the earth was full of malevolent voices, evil whisperings—he saw himself at times as trapped, duped, tricked and mocked at by all men; he greeted his parishioners with a sick heart and a livid smile, and he searched their eyes, their faces, for a sly lurking humor, an evil and secret glee, or for some evidence that they knew the nature of his hurt, the ugly dishonor in his brain and heart, the foul color of his secret.

And it was not, it could no longer be, he felt, a secret; he felt as naked as an infant, he thought the reason for his grief was legible in every word and action, and when he went out in the streets, sometimes his spirit cowered in a dreadful kind of shame—he felt like shielding his face from sight. Shame pressed upon him from the skies, he could not escape it—and when it was not shame of his own dishonor, it was shame because he feared that he was being mocked and jeered at as a fool and cuckold by the world.

Great shapes of fear and cruelty were evoked out of immense and time-less skies, they hovered above him wherever he went, they darkened the wintry lights of desolate little towns like smears of blood: it seemed to him that there would never again be joy and confidence on earth, that the shapes of death and madness would walk in his brain forever and, having lost his faith in God, he now sought desperately for some faith in man: he dreamed of finding some earthly father, some man superior to himself in strength, wisdom, and age to whom he could confess the burden of his packed and overladen heart, from whom he might derive some wisdom, some medicine for the plague that was consuming him.

But he never found him, in his heart he knew that such a physician and confessor did not exist: he was caught in a trap, he could not confess the evil weight that lay upon his soul, he took the last full measure of man's loneliness. He could not add to his own dishonor by bringing dishonor on his wife, and always there was a censor in his brain, a core of sanity that in the darkest and evilest hours yet judged fairly, and told him he was mad.

Then it left him. When it seemed that life was no longer tolerable it left him. It guttered out as a fierce flame gutters out of the fuel it has fed upon, and it left him full of weariness, indifference, and a sense of completion: he turned from the hurt, bewildered woman into the orbit of his own remote and secret life, he went on into new lives, new places and projects, and he forgot her.

And now, as I looked at the old man, I had a sense of union with the past. It seemed to me if he would only speak, the living past, the voices of lost men, the pain, the pride, the madness and despair, the million scenes and faces of the buried life—all that an old man ever knew—would be revealed to me, would be delivered to me like a priceless treasure, as an inheritance which old men owed to young, and which should be the end and effort of all living. My savage hunger was a kind of memory: I thought if he could speak, it would be fed.

And for a moment, it seemed, I saw the visages of time, dark time, the million lock-bolts shot back in man's memory, the faces of the lost Americans, and all the million casual moments of their lives, with Bascom blazing at them from a dozen pulpits, Bascom, tortured by love and madness, walking the streets of the nation, stumping the rutted roads, muttering through darkness with clasped bony hands, a gaunt and twisted figure reeling below immense and cruel skies across the continent. Light fell upon his face and darkness crossed it:—he came up from the wilderness, from derbied men and bustled women, from all of the memories of lavish brown, and from time, dark time— from a time that was further off than Saxon thanes, all of the knights, the spearheads, and the horses.

Was all this lost?

"It was so long ago," the old man said.

Bitterly, bitterly Boston one time more: the flying leaf, the broken cloud. Was no love crying in the wilderness?

"—So long ago. I have lived so long. I have seen so much. I could tell you so many things," my uncle said huskily, with weariness and indifference. His eye was lustreless and dead, he looked for a moment tired and old.

All at once, a strange and perplexing vision, which was to return many

times in the years that followed, came to me. It was this: there were a company of old men and women at dinner, seated together around a table. All of them were very old, older than my uncle; the faces of the old men and women were fragile and delicate like old yellowed china, their faces were frail and sexless, they had begun to look alike. In their youth all these people had known one another. The men had drunk, fought, whored, hated one another, and loved the women. Some had been devoured by the sterile and corrupt fear and envy that young men know. In secret their lips were twisted, their faces livid, and their hearts bitter; their eyes glittered with a reptilian hatred of another man —they dreaded his success, and they exulted in his failure, laughing with a delirious joy when they heard or read of his hurt, defeat or humiliation. They had been afraid to speak or confess what was in their hearts, they feared the mockery of their fellows; with one another their words were careful, picked, and disparaging. They gave the lie to passion and belief and they said what they knew was false. And yet along dark roads at night they had shouted out into the howling winds their great goat cries of joy, exultancy and power; they had smelled snow in thick brooding air at night, and they had watched it come, softly spitting at the window glass, numbing the footfalls of the earth with its soft silent fall, filling their hearts with a dark proud ecstasy, touching their entrails with impending prophecy. Each had a thousand dark desires and fantasies; each wanted wealth, power, fame and love; each saw himself as great, good and talented; each feared and hated rivals in business or in love—and in crowds they glared at one another with hard hostile eyes, they bristled up like crested cocks, they watched their women jealously, felt looks and glances through their shoulder blades, and hated men with white spermatic necks, amorous hair, and faces proud and insolent with female conquest.

They had been young and full of pain and combat, and now all this was dead in them: they smiled mildly, feebly, gently, they spoke in thin voices, and they looked at one another with eyes dead to desire, hostility, and passion.

As for the old women, they sat there on their yellowed and bony haunches. They were all beyond the bitter pain and ecstasy of youth—its frenzy, its hope, its sinew of bright blood and agony: they were beyond the pain and fear of anything save age and death. Here was a faithful wife, a fruitful mother; here was an adulterous and voluptuous woman, the potent mistress of a dozen men, here was her cuckold husband, who had screamed like a tortured animal when he had found her first in bed with another man, and here was the man he found her with; here was another man in whom the knowledge of his wife's infidelity had aroused only a corrupt inverted joy, he exulted in it, he urged her on into new love affairs, he besought her greedily to taunt him with it, he fed upon his pain—and now they were all old and meagre and had the look of yellowed china. They turned their mild sunken faces toward one another with looks in which there was neither hate nor love nor desire nor passion, they laughed thinly, and their memory was all of little things.

They no longer wanted to excel or to be first; they were no longer mad and jealous; they no longer hated rivals; they no longer wanted fame; they no longer cared for work or grew drunk on hope; they no longer turned into the dark and struck their bloody knuckles at the wall; they no longer writhed with shame upon their beds, cursed at the memory of defeat and desolation, or ripped the sheets between convulsive fingers. Could they not speak? Had they forgotten?

Why could not the old men speak? They had known pain, death and madness, yet all their words were stale and rusty. They had known the wilderness, the savage land, the blood of the murdered men ran down into the earth that gave no answer; and they had seen it, they had shed it. Where were the passion, pain and pride, the million living moments of their lives? Was all this lost? Were they all tongueless? It seemed to me that there was something sly and evil in their glances as they sat together, as if they hoarded some cunning and malevolent wisdom in their brains, as if the medicine to all our grief and error was in them, but as if through the evil and conspirate communication of their glance, they had resolved to keep it from us. Or were they simply devoured with satiety, with weariness and indifference? Did they refuse to speak because they could not speak, because even memory had gone lifeless in them?

Yes. Words echoed in their throat but they were tongueless. For them the past was dead: they poured into our hands a handful of dry dust and ashes.

The dry bones, the bitter dust? The living wilderness, the silent waste? The barren land?

Have no lips trembled in the wilderness? No eyes sought seaward from the rock's sharp edge for men returning home? Has no pulse beat more hot with love or hate upon the river's edge? Or where the old wheel and the rusted stock lie stogged in desert sand: by the horsehead a woman's skull. No love?

No lonely footfalls in a million streets, no heart that beat its best and bloodiest cry out against the steel and stone, no aching brain, caught in its iron ring, groping among the labyrinthine canyons? Naught in that immense and lonely land but incessant growth and ripeness and pollution, the emptiness of forests and deserts, the unhearted, harsh and metal jangle of a million tongues, crying the bellycry for bread, or the great cat's snarl for meat and honey? All, then, all? Birth and the twenty thousand days of snarl and jangle—and no love, no love? Was no love crying in the wilderness?

It was not true. The lovers lay below the lilac bush; the laurel leaves were trembling in the wood.

Suddenly it seemed to me, that if I could put my hand upon my uncle, if I could grip my fingers in his stringy arm, my strength and youth would go into him, and I could rekindle memory like a living flame in him, I could animate for an hour his ancient heart with the exultancy, the power, the joy that pulsed in me; I could make the old man speak.

I wanted to speak to him as people never speak to one another, I wanted to say and hear the things one never says and hears. I wanted to know what his own youth beyond its grim weather of poverty, loneliness, and desperation had been like. He had been over ten years old when the war had ended, he had seen the men plod home in wreaths of dust and heard their casual voices in a room, he had breathed the air of vanished summers, he had seen cloud shadows floating on the massed green of the

wilderness, the twisting of a last lone leaf upon a bough; and he had heard the desolate and stricken voices in the South long, long ago, the quiet and casual voices of lost men, a million vanished footsteps in the streets of life. And he had known the years of brown, dark lavish brown, the lost and hypocritic years, the thunder of the wheels and hooves upon the cobbles, the color of bright blood— the savagery, the hunger and the fear.

Was the memory of all this lost?

I touched him—I put my hand upon his shoulder, he did not move. Sunken in what lost world, buried in what incommunicable and tongueless past, he said—"So long ago."

Then I got up and left him and went out into the streets where the singing and lyrical air, the manswarm passing in its million-footed weft, the glorious women and the girls compacted in a single music of belly and breasts and thighs, the sea, the earth, the proud, potent, clamorous city, all of the voices of time fused to a unity that was like a song, a token and a cry. Victoriously, I trod the neck of doubt as if it were a serpent: I was joined to the earth, a part of it, and I possessed it; I would be wasted and consumed, filled and renewed eternally; I would feel unceasingly alternate tides of life and dark oblivion; I would be emptied without weariness, replenished forever with strong joy. I had a tongue for agony, a food for hunger, a door for exile and a surfeit for insatiate desire: exultant certainty welled up in me, I thought I could possess it all, and I cried: "Yes! It will be mine!"

1932

YOU CAN'T GO HOME AGAIN *

CHAPTER 29

"THE HOLLOW MEN"

Fox picks up the paper and settles back to read it with keen relish. The paper is the *Times*. (He read the *Tribune* late last night: waited up for it, would not miss it, has never missed it, could not sleep if he had not read it.) Morning now, Fox reads the *Times*.

How does he read the *Times*?

He reads it the way Americans have always read the paper. He also reads it as few Americans have ever read the paper—with nostrils sensitive, dilating with proud scorn, sniffing for the news behind the news.

He loves it—even loves the *Times*—loves Love unlovable—and don't we all? Ink-fresh papers, millions of them—ink-fresh with morning, orange juice, waffles, eggs and bacon, and cups of strong hot coffee. How fine it is, here in America, at ink-fresh, coffee-fragrant morning, to read the paper!

How often have we read the paper in America! How often have we seen it *blocked* against our doors! Little route-boys fold and block it, so to throw it—and so we find it and unfold it, crackling and ink-laden, at our doors. Sometimes we find it tossed there lightly with flat *plop;* sometimes we find it thrown with solid, whizzing *whack* against the clapboards (clapboards here, most often, in America); sometimes, as now in Turtle Bay, servants find just freshly folded sheets laid neatly down in doorways, and take them to the table for their mas-

ters. No matter how it got there, we always find it.

How we do love the paper in America! How we do love the paper, all!

Why do we love the paper in America? Why do we love the paper, all?

Mad masters, I will tell ye why.

Because the paper is "the news" here in America, and we love the *smell* of news. We love the smell of news that's "fit to print." We also love the smell of news *not* fit to print. We love, besides, the smell of *facts* that news is made of. Therefore we love the paper because the news is so fit-printable—so unprintable—and so fact-printable.

Is the news, then, like America? No, it's not—and Fox, unlike the rest of you, mad masters, turns the pages knowing it is just the news and not America that he reads there in his *Times*.

The news is *not* America, nor is America the *news*—the news is *in* America. It is a kind of light at morning, and at evening, and at midnight in America. It is a kind of growth and record and excrescence of our life. It is not good enough—it does not tell our story—yet it is the news!

Fox reads (proud nose sharp-sniffing with a scornful relish):

An unidentified man fell or jumped yesterday at noon from the twelfth story of the Admiral Francis Drake Hotel, corner of Hay and Apple Streets, in Brooklyn. The man, who was about thirty-five years old, registered at the hotel about a week ago, according to the police, as C. Green. Police are of the opinion that this was an assumed name. Pending identification, the body is being held at the King's County Morgue.

This, then, is news. Is it also the whole story, Admiral Drake? No! Yet we do not supply the whole story—we who have known all the lights and weathers of America—as Fox supplies it now:

Well, then, it's news, and it happened in your own hotel, brave Admiral Drake. It didn't happen in the Penn-Pitt at Pittsburgh, nor the Phil-Penn at Philadelphia, nor the York-Albany at Albany, nor the Hudson-Troy at Troy, nor the Libya-Ritz at Libya Hill, nor the Clay-Calhoun at Columbia, nor the Richmond-Lee at Richmond, nor the George Washington at Easton, Pennsylvania, Canton, Ohio, Terre Haute, Indiana, Danville, Virginia, Houston, Texas, and ninety-seven other places; nor at the Abraham Lincoln at Springfield, Massachusetts, Hartford, Connecticut, Wilmington, Delaware, Cairo, Illinois, Kansas City, Missouri, Los Angeles, California, and one hundred and thirty-six other towns; nor at the Andrew Jackson, the Roosevelt (Theodore or Franklin—take your choice), the Jefferson Davis, the Daniel Webster, the Stonewall Jackson, the U. S. Grant, the Commodore Vanderbilt, the Waldorf-Astor, the Adams House, the Parker House, the Palmer House, the Taft, the McKinley, the Emerson (Waldo or Bromo), the Harding, the Coolidge, the Hoover, the Albert G. Fall, the Harry Daugherty, the Rockefeller, the Harriman, the Carnegie or the Frick, the Christopher Columbus or the Leif Ericsson, the Ponce-de-Leon or the Magellan, in the remaining eight hundred and forty-three cities of America—but at the Francis Drake, brave Admiral—your own hotel —so, of course, you'll want to know what happened.

"An unidentified man"—well, then, this man was an American. "About thirty-five years old" with "an assumed name"—well, then, call him C. Green as he called himself ironi-cally in the hotel register. C. Green, the unidentified American, "fell or jumped," then, "yesterday at noon . . . in Brooklyn"—worth nine lines of print in today's *Times*—one of seven thousand who died yesterday upon this continent—one of three hundred and fifty who died yesterday in this very city (see dense, close columns of obituaries, page 15: begin with "Aaronson," so through the alphabet to "Zorn"). C. Green came here "a week ago"——

And came from where? From the deep South, or the Mississippi Valley, or the Middle West? From Minneapolis, Bridgeport, Boston, or a little town in Old Catawba? From Scranton, Toledo, St. Louis, or the desert whiteness of Los Angeles? From the pine barrens of the Atlantic coastal plain, or from the Pacific shore?

And so—was *what*, brave Admiral Drake? Had seen, felt, heard, smelled, tasted—*what*? Had known—*what*?

Had known all our brutal violence of weather: the burned swelter of July across the nation, the smell of the slow, rank river, the mud, the bottom lands, the weed growth, and the hot, coarse, humid fragrance of the corn. The kind that says, "Jesus, but it's hot!"—pulls off his coat, and mops his face, and goes in shirt-sleeves in St. Louis, goes to August's for a Swiss on rye with mustard, and a mug of beer. The kind that says, "Damn! It's hot!" in South Carolina, slouches in shirt-sleeves and straw hat down South Main Street, drops into Evans Drug Store for a dope, says to the soda jerker, "Is it hot enough fer you today, Jim?" The kind that reads in the paper of the heat, the deaths, and the prostrations, reads it with a certain satisfaction, hangs on grimly day by day and loses sleep at night, can't sleep for heat, is tired in the morning, says, "Jesus! It can't last forever!" as heat lengthens into August, and the nation gasps for breath, and the green that was young in May now mottles, fades and bleaches, withers, goes heat-brown. Will boast of coolness in the mountains, Admiral Drake. "Always cool at night! May get a little warm around the middle of the day, but you'll sleep with blankets every night."

Then summer fades and passes, and October comes. Will smell smoke then, and feel an unsuspected sharpness, a thrill of nervous, swift elation, a sense of sadness and departure. C. Green doesn't know the reason, Admiral Drake, but lights slant and shorten in the afternoon, there is a misty pollen of old gold in light at noon, a murky redness in the lights of dusk, a frosty stillness, and the barking of the dogs; the maples flame upon the hills, the gums are burning, bronze the oak leaves, and the aspens yellow; then come the rains, the sodden dead-brown of the fallen leaves, the smoke-stark branches—and November comes.

Waiting for winter in the little towns, and winter comes. It is really the same in big towns and the cities, too, with the bleak enclosure of the winter multiplied. In the commerce of the day, engaged and furious, then darkness, and the bleak monotony of "Where shall we go? What shall we do?" The winter grips us, closes round each house—the stark, harsh light encysts us—and C. Green walks the streets. Sometimes hard lights burn on him, Admiral Drake, bleak faces stream beneath the lights, amusement signs are winking. On Broadway, the constant blaze of sterile lights; in little towns, no less, the clustered raisins of hard light on Main Street. On Broadway, swarming millions up to midnight; in little towns, hard lights and frozen silence—no

one, nothing, after ten o'clock. But in the hearts of C. Greens everywhere, bleak boredom, undefined despair, and "Christ! Where shall I go now? When will winter end?"

So longs for spring, and wishes it were Saturday, brave Admiral Drake.

Saturday night arrives with the thing that we are waiting for. Oh, it will come tonight; the thing that we have been expecting all our lives will come tonight, on Saturday! On Saturday night across America we are waiting for it, and ninety million Greens go mothwise to the lights to find it. Surely it will come tonight! So Green goes out to find it, and he finds—hard lights again, saloons along Third Avenue, or the Greek's place in a little town—and then hard whiskey, gin, and drunkenness, and brawls and fights and vomit.

Sunday morning, aching head.

Sunday afternoon, and in the cities the chop-suey signs wink on and flash their sterile promises of unborn joy.

Sunday night, and the hard stars, and the bleak enclosures of our wintry weather—the buildings of old rusty brick, in cold enclosed, the fronts of old stark brown, the unpainted houses, the deserted factories, wharves, piers, warehouses, and office buildings, the tormented shabbiness of Sixth Avenues; and in the smaller towns, bleak Main Streets, desolate with shabby store fronts and be-raisined clusters of lamp standards, and in the residential streets of wooden houses (dark by ten o'clock), the moaning of stark branches, the stiff lights, limb-bepatterned, shaking at street corners. The light shines there with wintry bleakness on the clapboard front and porch of a shabby house where the policeman lives—blank and desolate upon the stuffy, boxlike little parlor where the policeman's daughter amorously receives—and *almost*—not *quite*—gives.

Hot, fevered, fearful, and insatiate, it is all too close to the cold street light —too creaking, panting, flimsy-close to others in the flimsy house—too close to the policeman's solid and slow-creaking tread—yet somehow valiant, somehow strong, somehow triumphant over the stale varnish of the little parlor, the nearness of the street, the light, the creaking boughs, and papa's tread—somehow triumphant with hot panting, with rose lips and tender tongue, white underleg and tight-locked thighs—by these intimacies of fear and fragrant hot desire will beat the ashen monotone of time and even the bleak and grey duration of the winter out.

Does this surprise you, Admiral Drake?

"But Christ!"—Green leaves the house, his life is bitter with desire, the stiff light creaks. "When will it end?" thinks Green. "When will spring come?"

It comes at last unhoped for, after hoping, comes when least expected, and when given up. In March there is a day that's almost spring, and C. Green, strong with will to have it so, says, "Well, it's here"—and it is gone like smoke. You can't look spring too closely in the eye in March. Raw days return, and blown light, and gusty moanings of the wind. Then April comes, and small, soaking rain. The air is wet and raw and chilled, but with a smell of spring now, a smell of earth, of grass exploding in small patches, here and there a blade, a bud, a leaf. And spring comes, marvelous, for a day or two—"It's here!" Green thinks. "It's here at last!"—and he is wrong again. It goes, chill days and greyness and small, soaking rains return. Green loses hope. "There is no spring!" he says. "You never get spring any more; you jump from winter into summer—we'll have summer now and

the hot weather before you know it."

Then spring comes—explodes out of the earth in a green radiance—comes up overnight! It's April twenty-eighth—the tree there in the city back-yard is smoke-yellow, feathered with the striplings of young leaf! It's April twenty-ninth—the leaf, the yellow, and the smoke have thickened over-night. April thirtieth—you can watch it grow and thicken with your eye! Then May the first—the tree's in leaf now, almost full and dense, young, feather-fresh! The whole spring has exploded from the earth!

All's explosive with us really, Admiral Drake—spring, the brutal summer, frost, October, February in Dakota with fifty-one below, spring floods, two hundred drowning along Ohio bottoms, in Missouri, in New England, all through Pennsylvania, Maryland, and Tennessee. Spring shot at us overnight, and everything with us is vast, explosive, floodlike. A few hundred dead in floods, a hundred in a wave of heat, twelve thousand in a year by murder, thirty thousand with the motor car—it all means nothing here. Floods like this would drown out France; death like this would plunge England in black mourning; but in America a few thousand C. Greens more or less, drowned, murdered, killed by motor cars, or dead by jumping out of windows on their heads—well, it just means nothing to us—the next flood, or next week's crop of death and killings, wash it out. We do things on a large scale, Admiral Drake.

The tar-smell in the streets now, children shouting, and the smell of earth; the sky shell-blue and faultless, a sapphire sparkle everywhere; and in the air the brave stick-candy whip-pings of a flag. C. Green thinks of the baseball games, the raw-hide arm of Lefty Grove, the resilient crack of ashwood on the horsehide ball, the waiting pockets of the well-oiled mitts, the warm smell of the bleachers, the shouted gibes of shirt-sleeved men, the sprawl and monotone of inning after inning. (Baseball's a dull game, really; that's the reason that it is so good. We do not love the game so much as we love the sprawl and drowse and shirt-sleeved apathy of it.) On Saturday afternoon, C. Green goes out to the ball park and sits there in the crowd, awaiting the sudden sharpness and the yell of crisis. Then the game ends and the crowd flows out across the green turf of the playing field. Sunday, Green spends the day out in the country in his flivver, with a girl.

Then summer comes again, heat-blazing summer, humid, murked with mist, sky-glazed with brutal weariness —and C. Green mops his face and sweats and says, "Jesus! Will it never end?"

This, then, is C. Green, "thirty-five years old"—"unidentified"—and an American. In what way an American? In what way different from the men *you* knew, old Drake?

When the ships bore home again and Cape St. Vincent blazed in Spaniard's eye—or when old Drake was returning with his men, beating coastwise from strange seas abreast, past the Scilly Isles toward the slant of evening fields, chalk cliffs, the harbor's arms, the town's sweet cluster and the spire—where was Green?

When, in red-oak thickets at the break of day, coon-skinned, the huntsmen of the wilderness lay for bear, heard arrows rattling in the laurel leaves, the bullets' whining *plunk*, and waited with cocked musket by the tree—where was Green?

Or when, with strong faces turning toward the setting sun, hawk-eyed and Indian-visaged men bore gun-stocks on the western trails and sternly heard the fierce war-whoops around the Painted Buttes—where, then, was Green?

Was never there with Drake's men in the evening when the sails stood in from the Americas! Was never there beneath the Spaniard's swarthy eye at Vincent's Cape! Was never there in the red-oak thicket in the morning! Was never there to hear the war-cries round the Painted Buttes!

No, no. He was no voyager of unknown seas, no pioneer of western trails. He was life's little man, life's nameless cipher, life's manswarm atom, life's American—and now he lies disjected and exploded on a street in Brooklyn!

He was a dweller in mean streets, was Green, a man-mote in the jungle of the city, a resident of grimy steel and stone, a mole who burrowed in rusty brick, a stunned spectator of enormous salmon-colored towers, hued palely with the morning. He was a renter of shabby wooden houses in a little town, an owner of a raw new bungalow on the outskirts of the town. He was a waker in bleak streets at morning, an alarm-clock watcher, saying, "Jesus, I'll be late!"—a fellow who took short cuts through the corner lot, behind the advertising signs; a fellow used to concrete horrors of hot day and blazing noon; a man accustomed to the tormented hodgepodge of our architectures, used to broken pavements, ash cans, shabby store fronts, dull green paint, the elevated structure, grinding traffic, noise, and streets be-tortured with a thousand bleak and dismal signs. He was accustomed to the gas tanks going out of town, he was an atom of machinery in an endless flow, going, stopping, going to the winking of the lights; he tore down concrete roads on Sundays, past the hot-dog stands and filling stations; he would return at darkness; hunger lured him to the winking splendor of chop-suey signs; and midnight found him in The Coffee Pot, to prowl above a mug of coffee, tear a coffee-cake in fragments, and wear away the slow grey ash of time and boredom with other men in grey hats and with skins of tallow-grey, at Joe the Greek's.

C. Green could read (which Drake could not), but not too accurately; could write, too (which the Spaniard couldn't), but not too well. C. Green had trouble over certain words, spelled them out above the coffee mug at midnight, with a furrowed brow, slow-shaping lips, and "Jesus!" when news stunned him—for he read the news. Preferred the news with pictures, too, girls with voluptuous legs crossed sensually, dresses above the knees, and plump dolls' faces full of vacant lechery. Green liked news "hot"—not as Fox knows it, not subtly sniffing with strange-scornful nostrils for the news *behind* the news—but straight from the shoulder—socko!—biff!—straight off the griddle, with lots of mustard, shapely legs, roadside wrecks and mutilated bodies, gangsters' molls and gunmen's hide-outs, tallow faces of the night that bluntly stare at flashlight lenses—this and talk of "heart-balm," "love-thief," "sex-hijacker"—all of this liked Green.

Yes, Green liked the news—and now, a bit of news himself (nine lines of print in *Times*), has been disjected and exploded on a Brooklyn pavement!

Well, such was our friend, C. Green, who read, but not too well; and wrote, but not too easily; who smelled, but not too strongly; felt, but not too deeply; saw, but not too clearly—yet had smelled the tar in May, smelled the slow, rank yellow of the rivers, and the clean, coarse

corn; had seen the slants of evening on the hill-flanks in the Smokies, and the bronze swell of the earth, the broad, deep red of Pennsylvania barns, proud-portioned and as dominant across the fields as bulls; had felt the frost and silence in October; had heard the whistles of the train wail back in darkness, and the horns of New Year's Eve, and—"Jesus! There's another year gone by! What now?"

No Drake was he, no Spaniard, no coon-skin cap, no strong face burning west. Yet, in some remote and protoplasmic portion, he was a little of each of these. A little Scotch, perhaps, was Green, a little Irish, English, Spanish even, and some German—a little of each part, all compacted and exploded into nameless atom of America!

No. Green—poor little Green—was not a man like Drake. He was just a cinder out of life—for the most part, a thinker of base thoughts, a creature of unsharpened, coarse perceptions. He was meager in the hips, he did not have much juice or salt in him. Drake gnawed the beef from juicy bones in taverns, drank tankards of brown ale, swore salty curses through his whiskers, wiped his mouth with the back of his hard hand, threw the beef bone to his dog, and pounded with his tankard for more ale. Green ate in cafeterias, prowled at midnight over coffee and a doughnut or a sugar-coated bun, went to the chop-suey joint on Saturday nights and swallowed chow mein, noodle soup, and rice. Green's mouth was mean and thin and common, it ran to looseness and a snarl; his skin was grey and harsh and dry; his eyes were dull and full of fear. Drake was self-contained: the world his oyster, seas his pastures, mighty distances his wings. His eyes were sea-pale (like the eyes of Fox); his ship was England. Green had no ship, he had a motor car, and tore down concrete roads on Sunday, and halted with the lights against him with the million other cinders hurtling through hot space. Green walked on level concrete sidewalks and on pavements grey, through hot and grimy streets past rusty tenements. Drake set his sails against the west, he strode the buoyant, sea-washed decks, he took the Spaniard and his gold, and at the end he stood in to the sweet enfoldments of the spire, the clustered town, the emerald fields that slope to Plymouth harbor—then Green came!

We who never saw brave Drake can have no difficulty conjuring up an image of the kind of man he was. With equal ease we can imagine the bearded Spaniard, and almost hear his swarthy oaths. But neither Drake nor Spaniard could ever have imagined Green. Who could have foreseen him, this cipher of America, exploded now upon a street in Brooklyn?

Behold him, Admiral Drake! Observe the scene now! Listen to the people! Here is something strange as the Armadas, the gold-laden cargoes of the bearded Spaniards, the vision of unfound Americas!

What do you see here, Admiral Drake?

Well, first, a building—your own hotel—such a building as the folk of Plymouth never saw. A great block of masonry, pale-hued, grimy-white, fourteen stories tall, stamped in an unvarying pattern with many windows. Sheeted glass below, the store front piled with medicines and toilet articles, perfumes, cosmetics, health contrivances. Within, a soda fountain, Admiral Drake. The men in white with monkey caps, soda jerkers sullen with perpetual overdriven irritation. Beneath the counter, pools of sloppy water, filth, and unwashed dishes.

Across the counter, Jewesses with fat, rouged lips consuming ice cream sodas and pimento sandwiches.

Outside upon the concrete sidewalk lies the form of our exploded friend, C. Green. A crowd has gathered round—taxi drivers, passers-by, hangers-on about the subway station, people working in the neighborhood, and the police. No one has dared to touch exploded Green as yet—they stand there in a rapt and fascinated circle, looking at him.

Not much to look at either, Admiral Drake; not even those who trod your gory decks would call the sight a pretty one. Our friend has landed on his head—"taken a nose dive," as we say—and smashed his brains out at the iron base of the second lamp post from the corner. (It is the same lamp post as heretofore described, to be found throughout America—a "standard," standardized, supporting five hard grapes of frosted glass.)

So here Green lies, on the concrete sidewalk all disjected. No head is left, the head is gone now, head's exploded; only brains are left. The brains are pink, and almost bloodless, Admiral Drake. (There's not much blood here—we shall tell you why.) But brains exploded are somewhat like pale sausage meat, fresh-ground. Brains are stuck hard to the lamp post, too; there is a certain driven emphasis about them, as if they had been shot hydraulically out of a force-hose against the post.

The head, as we have said, is gone completely; a few fragments of the skull are scattered round—but of the face, the features, forehead—nothing! They have all been blown *out*, as by some inner explosion. Nothing is left but the back of the skull, which curiously remains, completely hollowed out and vacant, and curved over, like the rounded handle of a walking stick.

The body, five feet eight or nine of it, of middling weight, is lying—we were going to say "face downward"; had we not better say "stomach downward"?—on the sidewalk. It is well-dressed, too, in cheap, neatly pressed, machine-made clothes: tan shoes and socks with a clocked pattern, suit of a light texture, brownish red in hue, a neat canary-colored shirt with attached collar—obviously C. Green had a nice feeling for proprieties! As for the body itself, save for a certain indefinable and curiously "disjected" quality, one could scarcely tell that every bone in it is broken. The hands are still spread out, half-folded and half-clenched, with a still-warm and startling eloquence of recent life. (It happened just four minutes ago!)

Well, where's the blood, then, Drake? You're used to blood; you'd like to know. Well, you've heard of casting bread upon the waters, Drake, and having it return—but never yet, I'll vow, of casting blood upon the streets—and having it run away—and then come back to you! But here it comes now, down the street—down Apple Street, round the corner into Hay, across the street now toward C. Green, the lamp post, and the crowd! —a young Italian youth, blunt-featured, low-browed, and bewildered, his black eyes blank with horror, tongue mumbling thickly, arm held firmly by a policeman, suit and shirt all drenched with blood, and face bespattered with it! A stir of sudden interest in the crowd, sharp nudges, low-toned voices whispering:

"Here he is! Th' guy that 'got it'! . . . Sure, that's him—you know him, that Italian kid that works inside in the newsstand—he was standin' *deh* beside the post! Sure, *that's* the guy!—talkin' to anotheh guy—he got it all! *That's* the reason you didn't see more blood—*this* guy got it!—Sure!

The guy just missed him by six inches!—Sure! I'm tellin' you I *saw* it, ain't I? I looked up an' saw him in the air! He'd a hit this guy, but when he saw that he was goin' to hit the lamp post, he put out his hands an' tried to keep away! *That's* the reason that he didn't hit this guy! . . . But this guy heard him when he hit, an' turned around—and zowie!—he got all of it right in his face!"

And another, whispering and nudging, nodding toward the horror-blank, thick-mumbling Italian boy: "Jesus! Look at th' guy, will yuh! . . . He don't know what he's doing! . . . He don't know yet what happened to him! . . . Sure! He got it *all*. I tell yuh! He was standin' deh beside the post, wit a package undehneath one ahm—an' when it happened—when he got it—he just stahted runnin' . . . He don't know yet what's happened! . . . That's what I'm tellin' yuh—th' guy just stahted runnin' when he got it."

And one policeman (to another): ". . . Sure, I yelled to Pat to stop him. He caught up with him at Borough Hall. . . . He just kept on runnin'—he don't know yet what happened to him."

And the Italian youth, thick-mumbling: ". . . Jeez! W'at happened? . . . Jeez! . . . I was standin' talkin' to a guy—I heard it hit. . . . Jeez! . . . W'at happened, anyway? . . . I got it all oveh me! . . . Jeez! . . . I just stahted runnin' . . . Jeez! I'm sick!"

Voices: "Here, take 'im into the drug store! . . . Wash 'im off! . . . That guy needs a shot of liquor! . . . Sure! Take him into the drug stoeh *deh*! . . . They'll fix him up!"

The plump, young, rather effeminate, but very intelligent young Jew who runs the newsstand in the corridor, talking to everyone around him, excitedly and indignantly: ". . . Did

I *see* it? Listen! I saw *everything*! I was coming across the street, looked up, and saw him in the air! . . . *See* it? . . . *Listen!* If someone had taken a big ripe watermelon and dropped it on the street from the twelfth floor you'd have some idea of what it was like! . . . *See* it! *I'll* tell the world I saw it! I don't want to see anything like *that* again!" Then excitedly, with a kind of hysterical indignation: "Shows no consideration for other people, that's all *I've* got to say! If a man is going to do a thing like that, why does he pick a place like *this*—one of the busiest corners in Brooklyn? . . . How did *he* know he wouldn't hit someone? Why, if that boy had been standing six inches nearer to the post, he'd have killed him, as sure as you live! . . . And here he does it right in front of all these people who have to look at it! It shows he had no consideration for other people! A man who'd do a thing like that. . . ."

(Alas, poor Jew! As if C. Green, now past considering, had considered nice "considerations.")

A taxi driver, impatiently: "That's what I'm tellin' yuh! . . . I watched him for five minutes before he jumped. He crawled out on the window sill an' stood there for *five* minutes, makin' up his mind! . . . Sure, I saw him! Lots of people saw him!" Impatiently, irritably: "Why didn't we *do* somethin' to stop him? F'r Chri' sake, what was there to do? A guy who'd do a thing like that is nuts to start with! You don't think he'd listen to anything *we* had to say, do you? . . . Sure, we *did* yell at him! . . . Jesus! . . . We was almost *afraid* to yell at him—we made motions to him to get back—tried to hold his attention while the cops sneaked round the corner into the hotel. . . . Sure, the cops got there just a second after he

jumped—I don't know if he jumped when he heard 'em comin', or what happened, but Christ!—he stood there gettin' ready for five minutes while we watched!"

And a stocky little Czech-Bohemian, who works in the delicatessen-fruit store on the corner, one block down: "Did I *hear* it! Say, you could have heard it for six blocks! Sure! *Everybody* heard it! The minute that I heard it, I knew what had happened, too! I come runnin'!"

People press and shuffle in the crowd. A man comes round the corner, presses forward to get a better look, runs into a little fat, bald-headed man in front of him who is staring at the Thing with a pale, sweating, suffering, fascinated face, by accident knocks off the little fat man's straw hat. The new straw hat hits the pavement dryly, the little fat, bald-headed man scrambles for it, clutches it, and turns around on the man who has knocked it off, both of them stammering frantic apologies:

"Oh, excuse me! . . . . 'Scuse me! . . . 'Scuse me! . . . Sorry!"

"Quite all right. . . . All right! . . . All right."

Observe now, Admiral, with what hypnotic concentration the people are examining the grimy-white façade of your hotel. Watch their faces and expressions. Their eyes go traveling upward slowly—up—up—up. The building seems to widen curiously, to be distorted, to flare out wedgelike till it threatens to annihilate the sky, overwhelm the will, and crush the spirit. (These optics, too, American, Admiral Drake.) The eyes continue on past story after story up the wall until they finally arrive and come to rest with focal concentration on that single open window twelve floors up. It is no jot different from all the other windows, but now the vision of the crowd is fastened on it with a fatal and united interest. And after staring at it fixedly, the eyes come traveling slowly down again—down—down—down—the faces strained a little, mouths all slightly puckered as if something set the teeth on edge—and slowly, with fascinated measurement —down—down—down—until the eyes reach sidewalk, lamp post, and—the Thing again.

The pavement finally halts all, stops all, answers all. It is the American pavement, Admiral Drake, our universal city sidewalk, a wide, hard stripe of grey-white cement, blocked accurately with dividing lines. It is the hardest, coldest, cruellest, most impersonal pavement in the world: all of the indifference, the atomic desolation, the exploded nothingness of one hundred million nameless "Greens" is in it.

In Europe, Drake, we find worn stone, all hollowed out and rubbed to rounded edges. For centuries the unknown lives of men now buried touched and wore this stone, and when we see it something stirs within our hearts, and something strange and dark and passionate moves our souls, and—"They were here!" we say.

Not so, the streets, the sidewalks, the paved places of America. Has *man* been here? No. Only unnumbered nameless Greens have swarmed and passed here, and none has left a mark.

Did ever the eye go seaward here with searching for the crowded sail, with longing for the strange and unknown coasts of Spain? Did ever beauty here come home to the heart and eyes? Did ever, in the thrusting crowd, eye look to eye, and face to face, and heart to heart, and know the moment of their meeting—stop and pause, and be oblivious in this place, and make one spot of worn pavement sacred stone? You won't believe it,

Admiral Drake, but it is so—these things *have* happened on the pavements of America. But, as you see yourself, they have not left their mark.

You, old Drake, when last your fellow townsmen saw you at the sailing of the ships, walked with the crowd along the quay, past the spire and cluster of the town, down to the cool lap of the water; and from your deck, as you put out, you watched the long, white, fading arm of your own coast. And in the town that you had left were streets still haunted by your voice. There was your worn tread upon the pavement, there the tavern table dented where you banged your tankard down. And in the evening, when the ships were gone, men waited for your return.

But no return is here among us in America. Here are no streets still haunted by departed men. Here is no street at all, as you knew streets. Here are just our cement Mobways, unannealed by time! No place in Mobway bids you pause, old Drake. No spot in Mobway bids you hold your mind a moment in reflection, saying: "He was here!" No square of concrete slab says: "Stay, for I was built by men." Mobway never knew the hand of man, as your streets did. Mobway was laid down by great machines, for one sole purpose—to unimpede and hurry up the passing of the feet.

Where did Mobway come from? What produced it?

It came from the same place where all our mob ways come from—from Standard Concentrated Production Units of America, No. 1. This is where all our streets, sidewalks, and lamp posts (like the one on which Green's brains are spattered) come from, where all our white-grimy bricks (like those of which your hotel is constructed) come from, where the red façades of our standard-unit tobacco stores (like the one across the street) come from, where our motor cars come from, where our drug stores and our drug store windows and displays come from, where our soda fountains (complete, with soda jerkers attached) come from, where our cosmetics, toilet articles, and the fat, rouged lips of our Jewesses come from, where our soda water, slops and syrups, steamed spaghetti, ice cream, and pimento sandwiches come from, where our clothes, our hats (neat, standard stamps of grey), our faces (also stamps of grey, not always neat), our language, conversation, sentiments, feelings, and opinions come from. All these things are made for us by Standard Concentrated Production Units of America, No. 1.

So here we are, then, Admiral Drake. You see the street, the sidewalk, the front of your hotel, the constant stream of motor cars, the drug store and the soda fountain, the tobacco store, the traffic lights, the cops in uniform, the people streaming in and out of the subway, the rusty, pale-hued jungle of the buildings, old and new, high and low. There is no better place to see it, Drake. For this is Brooklyn—which means ten thousand streets and blocks like this one. Brooklyn, Admiral Drake, is the Standard Concentrated Chaos No. 1 of the Whole Universe. That is to say, it has no size, no shape, no heart, no joy, no hope, no aspiration, no center, no eyes, no soul, no purpose, no direction, and no anything—just Standard Concentrated Units everywhere—exploding in all directions for an unknown number of square miles like a completely triumphant Standard Concentrated Blot upon the Face of the Earth. And here, right in the middle —no, that is wrong, for Standard Concentrated Blots don't have a middle— but, if not in the middle, at least right

slap-bang out in the open, upon a minute portion of this magnificent Standard Concentrated Blot, where all the Standard Concentrated Blotters can stare at him, and with the brains completely out of him ——

—Lies Green!

And this is bad—most bad—oh, *very* bad—and should not be allowed! For, as our young Jewish friend has just indignantly proclaimed, it "shows no consideration for other people"— which means, for other Standard Concentrated Blotters. Green has no right to go falling in this fashion in a public place. He has no right to take unto himself any portion of this Standard Concentrated Blot, however small. He has no business *being* where he is at all. A Standard Concentrated Blotter is not supposed to *be* places, but to *go* places.

You see, dear Admiral, this is not a street to amble in, to ride along, to drift through. It is a channel—in the words of the Standard Concentrated Blotter-Press, an "artery." This means that it is not a place where one drives, but a place where one is driven—not really a street at all, but a kind of tube for a projectile, a kind of groove for millions and millions of projectiles, all driven past incessantly, all beetling onward, bearing briefly white slugged blurs of driven flesh.

As for the sidewalk, this Standard Concentrated Mobway is not a place to walk on, really. (Standard Concentrated Blotters have forgotten how to walk.) It is a place to swarm on, to weave on, to thrust and dodge on, to scurry past on, to crowd by on. It is not a place to stand on, either. One of the earliest precepts in a Concentrated Blotter's life is: "Move on there! Where th' hell d'you think you are, anyway—in a cow pasture?" And, most certainly, it is not a place to lie on, to sprawl out on.

But look at Green! Just *look* at him! No wonder the Jewish youth is angry with him!

Green has willfully and deliberately violated every Standard Concentrated Principle of Blotterdom. He has not only gone and dashed his brains out, but he has done it in a public place—upon a piece of Standard Concentrated Mobway. He has messed up the sidewalk, messed up another Standard Concentrated Blotter, stopped traffic, taken people from their business, upset the nerves of his fellow Blotters—and now *lies* there, all *sprawled* out, in a place where he has no right to *be*. And, to make his crime unpardonable, C. Green has ——

—Come to Life!

Consider *that*, old Drake! We can understand some measure of *your* strangeness, because we heard you swearing in the tavern and saw your sails stand to the west. Can you now do the same for *us*? Consider strangeness, Drake—and look at Green! For you have heard it said by your own countryman, and in your living generation: "The times have been that, when the brains were out, the man would die." But now, old Drake, what hath Time wrought? There is surely here some strangeness in us that you could never have foretold. For the brains are "out" now—and the man has ——

—Come to Life!

What's that, Admiral? You do not understand it? Small wonder, though it's really very simple:

For just ten minutes since, C. Green was a Concentrated Blotter like the rest of us. Ten minutes since, he, too, might hurry in and out of the subway, thrust and scurry on the pavement, go hurtling past with whited blur in one of our beetles of machinery, a nameless atom, cipher, cinder, swarming with the rest of us,

just another "guy" like a hundred million other "guys." But now, observe him! No longer is he just "another guy"—already he has become a "special guy"—he has become "*The* Guy." C. Green at last has turned into a—*Man!*

Four hundred years ago, brave Admiral Drake, if we had seen you lying on your deck, your bronze gone pale and cold, imbrued in your own blood, and hewn to the middle by the Spaniards' steel, we could have understood that, for there was *blood* in you. But Green—this Concentrated Blotter of ten minutes since—made in our own image, shaped in our own dust, compacted of the same grey stuff of which our own lives are compacted, and filled, we thought, with the same Standard Concentration of embalming fluid that fills *our* veins—oh, Drake, we did not know the fellow had such *blood* in him! We could not have thought it was so red, so rich, and so abundant!

Poor, shabby, and corrupted cipher! Poor, nameless, and exploded atom! Poor little guy! He fills us Concentrated Blotters of the Universe with fear, with shame, with awe, with pity, and with terror—for we see ourselves in him. If he was a man with blood in him, then so are we! If he, in the midst of his always-driven life, could at last be driven to this final and defiant gesture of refusal to remain a Concentrated Blotter, then we, too, might be driven to a point of equal desperation! And there are other methods of defiance, other ways of ultimate refusal, other means of exercising one's last-remaining right of manhood—and some of them are no less terrifying to contemplate than this! So our fascinated eyes go up and up, past floor after floor of Standard Concentrated brick, and fasten on the open window where he stood—and suddenly we crane our necks along the ridges of our collars, look away with constricted faces, and taste the acrid bitterness of steel upon our lips!

It is too hard, and not to be endured—to know that little Green, speaking our own tongue and stuffed with our own stuffing, had yet concealed in him some secret, dark, and frightful thing more terrible than anything that we have ever known—that he bore within him some black and hideous horror, some depth of madness or of courage, and could stand *there*—upon the sheer and nauseating verge of that grey window ledge for five full minutes—and know the thing he was about to do—and tell himself he *must* now!—that he *had* to!—that the compulsion of every horror-fascinated eye down in the gulf below had *now* made escape impossible—and then, horror-sick past all regeneration, see, too, before he jumped, his fall, the downward-hurtling plunge, and his own exploded body—feel the bones crack and fly apart, and the brutal obliteration of the instant when his brains would shoot out against the lamp post—and even while his soul drew back from that sheer verge of imagined terror, shame, and unutterable self-loathing, crying, "I cannot do it!"—then jumped!

And *we*, brave Drake? We try to see it, but we cannot see. We try to fathom it, but we cannot plunge. We try to comprehend the hell of hells, the hundred lives of horror, madness, anguish, and despair that were exhausted *in five minutes* by that shabby creature crouched there on the window ledge. But we cannot understand, or look at it any longer. It is too hard, too hard, and not to be endured. We turn away with nausea, hollowness, blind fear, and unbelief within us.

One man stares, cranes his neck, wets his lips, and whispers: "Jesus! To do a thing like that takes *guts!*"

Another, harshly: "Nah! It don't take guts! A guy who'd do a thing like that is crazy! He don't know what he's doin' to begin with!"

And others, doubtfully, half-whispering, with eyes focused on the ledge: "But Jesus!"

A taxi driver, turning away and moving toward his cab, with an attempt at casual indifference that does not ring entirely true: "Oh, well! Just another guy, I guess!"

Then one man, turning to his companion with a little puckered smile: "Well, what about it, Al? You still feel like eating?"

And his companion, quietly: "Eating, hell! I feel like two or three stiff shots of rye! Come on, let's go around to Steve's!"

They go. The Concentrated Blotters of the World cannot abide it. They must somehow blot it out.

So a policeman comes around the corner now with an old tarpaulin, with which he covers the No-Head. The crowd remains. Then the green wagon from the morgue. The Thing, tarpaulin and all, is pushed into it. It drives away. A policeman with thick-soled boots scuffs and pushes skull-pieces and brain-fragments into the gutter. Someone comes with sawdust, strews it. Someone from the drug store with formaldehyde. Later, someone with a hose and water. From the subway come an adolescent boy and girl with the hard, tough faces of the city; they walk past it, deliberately and arrogantly step among it, look at the lamp post, then at each other, and laugh!

All's over now, all's gone, the crowd's departed. Something else remains. It cannot be forgotten. There's a sick, humid smell upon the air, what was light and clear and crystal has gone out of day, and something thick and glutinous—half taste, half smell, and all impalpable—remains upon your tongue.

There would have been a time and place for such a thing, brave Admiral Drake, if he, our fellow Green, had only fallen as a hollow man and landed dryly, or if he had opened to disperse a grey embalming fluid in the gutter. It would have been all right if he had just been blown away like an old paper, or if he had been swept aside like remnants of familiar litter, and then subsumed into the Standard Concentrated stuff from which he came. But C. Green would not have it so. He exploded to drench our com-mon substance of viscous grey with the bright indecency of blood, to re-sume himself from number, to become before our eyes a Man, and to identify a single spot of all our general Noth-ingness with the unique passion, the awful terror, and the dignity of Death.

So, Admiral Drake—"an unidenti-fied man fell or jumped yesterday at noon" from a window of your own hotel. That was the news. Now you've had the story.

We are "the hollow men, the hol-low men"? Brave Admiral, do not be too sure.

1940

THE LIBERALS

WILLIAM JAMES
(1842–1910)

PRAGMATISM *

II

WHAT PRAGMATISM MEANS

Some years ago, being with a camping party in the mountains, I returned from a solitary ramble to find every one engaged in a ferocious metaphysical dispute. The *corpus* of the dispute was a squirrel—a live squirrel supposed to be clinging to one side of a tree-trunk; while over against the tree's opposite side a human being was imagined to stand. This human witness tries to get sight of the squirrel by moving rapidly round the tree, but no matter how fast he goes, the squirrel moves as fast in the opposite direction, and always keeps the tree between himself and the man, so that never a glimpse of him is caught. The resultant metaphysical problem now is this: *Does the man go round the squirrel or not?* He goes round the tree, sure enough, and the squirrel is on the tree; but does he go round the squirrel? In the unlimited leisure of the wilderness, discussion had been worn threadbare. Every one had taken sides, and was obstinate and the numbers on both sides were even. Each side, when I appeared, therefore appealed to me to make it a majority.

* Reprinted by permission of Paul R. Reynolds and Son, agents for the James Estate. Copyright 1907.

Mindful of the scholastic adage that whenever you meet a contradiction you must make a distinction, I immediately sought and found one, as follows: "Which party is right," I said, "depends on what you *practically mean* by 'going round' the squirrel. If you mean passing from the north of him to the east, then to the south, then to the west, and then to the north of him again, obviously the man does go round him, for he occupies these successive positions. But if on the contrary you mean being first in front of him, then on the right of him, then behind him, then on his left, and finally in front again, it is quite as obvious that the man fails to go round him, for by the compensating movements the squirrel makes, he keeps his belly turned towards the man all the time, and his back turned away. Make the distinction, and there is no occasion for any farther dispute. You are both right and both wrong according as you conceive the verb 'to go round' in one practical fashion or the other."

Although one or two of the hotter disputants called my speech a shuffling evasion, saying they wanted no quibbling or scholastic hairsplitting, but meant just plain honest English "round," the majority seemed to think that the distinction had assuaged the dispute.

I tell this trivial anecdote because it is a peculiarly simple example of what I wish now to speak of as *the pragmatic method*. The pragmatic method is primarily a method of settling metaphysical disputes that otherwise might be interminable. Is the world one or many?—fated or free?—material or spiritual?—here are notions either of which may or may not hold good of the world; and disputes over such notions are unending. The pragmatic method in such cases is to try to interpret each notion by tracing its respective practical consequences. What difference would it practically make to any one if this notion rather than that notion were true? If no practical difference whatever can be traced, then the alternatives mean practically the same thing, and all dispute is idle. Whenever a dispute is serious, we ought to be able to show some practical difference that must follow from one side or the other's being right.

A glance at the history of the idea will show you still better what pragmatism means. The term is derived from the same Greek word πράγμα, meaning action, from which our words "practice" and "practical" come. It was first introduced in philosophy by Mr. Charles Peirce in 1878. In an article entitled "How to Make Our Ideas Clear," in the *Popular Science Monthly* for January of that year Mr. Peirce, after pointing out that our beliefs are really rules for action, said that, to develop a thought's meaning, we need only determine what conduct it is fitted to produce: that conduct is for us its sole significance. And the tangible fact at the root of all our thought-distinctions, however subtle, is that there is no one of them so fine as to consist in anything but a possible difference of practice. To attain perfect clearness in our thoughts of an object, then, we need only consider what conceivable effects of a practical kind the object may involve—what sensations we are to expect from it,

and what reactions we must prepare. Our conception of these effects, whether immediate or remote, is then for us the whole of our conception of the object, so far as that conception has positive significance at all.

This is the principle of Peirce, the principle of pragmatism. It lay entirely unnoticed by any one for twenty years, until I, in an address before Professor Howison's philosophical union at the University of California, brought it forward again and made a special application of it to religion. By that date (1898) the times seemed ripe for its reception. The word "pragmatism" spread, and at present it fairly spots the pages of the philosophic journals. On all hands we find the "pragmatic movement" spoken of, sometimes with respect, sometimes with contumely, seldom with clear understanding. It is evident that the term applies itself conveniently to a number of tendencies that hitherto have lacked a collective name, and that it has "come to stay."

To take in the importance of Peirce's principle, one must get accustomed to applying it to concrete cases. I found a few years ago that Ostwald, the illustrious Leipzig chemist, had been making perfectly distinct use of the principle of pragmatism in his lectures on the philosophy of science, though he had not called it by that name.

"All realities influence our practice," he wrote me, "and that influence is their meaning for us. I am accustomed to put questions to my classes in this way: In what respects would the world be different if this alternative or that were true? If I can find nothing that would become different, then the alternative has no sense."

That is, the rival views mean practically the same thing, and meaning, other than practical, there is for us none. Ostwald in a published lecture gives this example of what he means. Chemists have long wrangled over the inner constitution of certain bodies called "tautomerous." Their properties seemed equally consistent with the notion that an instable hydrogen atom oscillates inside of them or that they are instable mixtures of two bodies. Controversy raged, but never was decided. "It would never have begun," says Ostwald, "if the combatants had asked themselves what particular experimental fact could have been made different by one or the other view being correct. For it would then have appeared that no difference of fact could possibly ensue; and the quarrel was as unreal as if, theorizing in primitive times about the raising of dough by yeast, one party should have invoked a 'brownie,' while another insisted on an 'elf' as the true cause of the phenomenon."

It is astonishing to see how many philosophical disputes collapse into insignificance the moment you subject them to this simple test of tracing a concrete consequence. There can *be* no difference anywhere that doesn't *make* a difference elsewhere—no difference in abstract truth that doesn't express itself in a difference in concrete fact and in conduct consequent upon that fact, imposed on somebody, somehow, somewhere, and somewhen. The whole function of philosophy ought to be to find out what definite difference it will make to you and me at definite instants of our life, if this world-formula or that world-formula be the true one.

There is absolutely nothing new in the pragmatic method. Socrates was an adept at it. Aristotle used it methodically. Locke, Berkeley, and Hume made momentous contributions to truth by its means. Shadworth

Hodgson keeps insisting that realities are only what they are "known as." But these forerunners of pragmatism used it in fragments: they were preluders only. Not until in our time has it generalized itself, become conscious of a universal mission, pretended to a conquering destiny. I believe in that destiny, and I hope I may end by inspiring you with my belief.

Pragmatism represents a perfectly familiar attitude in philosophy, the empiricist attitude, but it represents it, as it seems to me, both in a more radical and in a less objectionable form than it has ever yet assumed. A pragmatist turns his back resolutely and once for all upon a lot of inveterate habits dear to professional philosophers. He turns away from abstraction and insufficiency, from verbal solutions, from bad *a priori* reasons, from fixed principles, closed systems, and pretended absolutes and origins. He turns towards concreteness and adequacy, towards facts, towards action and towards power. That means the empiricist temper regnant and the rationalist temper sincerely given up. It means the open air and possibilities of nature, as against dogma, artificiality, and the pretence of finality in truth.

At the same time it does not stand for any special results. It is a method only. But the general triumph of that method would mean an enormous change in what I called in my last lecture the "temperament" of philosophy. Teachers of the ultra-rationalistic type would be frozen out, much as the courtier type is frozen out in republics, as the ultramontane type of priest is frozen out in Protestant lands. Science and metaphysics would come much nearer together, would in fact work absolutely hand in hand.

Metaphysics has usually followed a very primitive kind of quest. You know how men have always hankered after unlawful magic, and you know what a great part in magic *words* have always played. If you have his name, or the formula of incantation that binds him, you can control the spirit, genie, afrite, or whatever the power may be. Solomon knew the names of all the spirits, and having their names, he held them subject to his will. So the universe has always appeared to the natural mind as a kind of enigma, of which the key must be sought in the shape of some illuminating or power-bringing word or name. That word names the universe's *principle*, and to possess it is after a fashion to possess the universe itself. "God," "Matter," "Reason," "the Absolute," "Energy," are so many solving names. You can rest when you have them. You are at the end of your metaphysical quest.

But if you follow the pragmatic method, you cannot look on any such word as closing your quest. You must bring out of each word its practical cash value, set it at work within the stream of your experience. It appears less as a solution, then, than as a program for more work, and more particularly as an indication of the ways in which existing realities may be *changed*.

Theories thus become instruments, not answers to enigmas, in which we can rest. We don't lie back upon them, we move forward, and, on occasion, make nature over again by their aid. Pragmatism unstiffens all our theories, limbers them up and sets each one at work. Being nothing essentially new, it harmonizes with many ancient philosophic tendencies. It agrees with nominalism, for instance, in always appealing to particulars; with utilitarianism in emphasizing practical aspects; with positivism in its disdain for verbal solutions, useless questions and metaphysical abstractions.

All these, you see, are *anti-intellectualist* tendencies. Against rationalism as a pretension and a method pragmatism is fully armed and militant. But, at the outset, at least, it stands for no particular results. It has no dogmas, and no doctrines save its method. As the young Italian pragmatist Papini has well said, it lies in the midst of our theories, like a corridor in a hotel. Innumerable chambers open out of it. In one you may find a man writing an atheistic volume; in the next some one on his knees praying for faith and strength; in a third a chemist investigating a body's properties. In a fourth a system of idealistic metaphysics is being excogitated; in a fifth the impossibility of metaphysics is being shown. But they all own the corridor, and all must pass through it if they want a practicable way of getting into or out of their respective rooms.

No particular results then, so far, but only an attitude of orientation, is what the pragmatic method means. The *attitude of looking away from first things, principles, "categories," supposed necessities; and of looking towards last things, fruits, consequences, facts.*

So much for the pragmatic method! You may say that I have been praising it rather than explaining it to you, but I shall presently explain it abundantly enough by showing how it works on some familiar problems. Meanwhile the word pragmatism has come to be used in a still wider sense, as meaning also a certain *theory of truth*. I mean to give a whole lecture to the statement of that theory, after first paving the way, so I can be very brief now. But brevity is hard to follow, so I ask for your redoubled attention for a quarter of an hour. If much remains obscure, I hope to make it clearer in the later lectures.

One of the most successfully cultivated branches of philosophy in our time is what is called inductive logic, the study of the conditions under which our sciences have evolved. Writers on this subject have begun to show a singular unanimity as to what the laws of nature and elements of fact mean, when formulated by mathematicians, physicists and chemists. When the first mathematical, logical, and natural uniformities, the first *laws,* were discovered, men were so carried away by the clearness, beauty and simplification that resulted, that they believed themselves to have deciphered authentically the eternal thoughts of the Almighty. His mind also thundered and reverberated in syllogisms. He also thought in conic sections, squares and roots and ratios, and geometrized like Euclid. He made Kepler's laws for the planets to follow; he made velocity increase proportionally to the time in falling bodies; he made the law of the sines for light to obey when refracted; he established the classes, orders, families and genera of plants and animals, and fixed the distances between them. He thought the archetypes of all things, and devised their variations; and when we rediscover any one of these his wondrous institutions, we seize his mind in its very literal intention.

But as the sciences have developed farther, the notion has gained ground that most, perhaps all, of our laws are only approximations. The laws themselves, moreover, have grown so numerous that there is no counting them; and so many rival formulations are proposed in all the branches of science that investigators have become accustomed to the notion that no theory is absolutely a transcript of reality, but that any one of them may

from some point of view be useful. Their great use is to summarize old facts and to lead to new ones. They are only a man-made language, a conceptual short-hand, as some one calls them, in which we write our reports of nature; and languages, as is well known, tolerate much choice of expression and many dialects.

Thus human arbitrariness has driven divine necessity from scientific logic. If I mention the names of Sigwart, Mach, Ostwald, Pearson, Milhaud, Poincaré, Duhem, Ruyssen, those of you who are students will easily identify the tendency I speak of, and will think of additional names.

Riding now on the front of this wave of scientific logic Messrs. Schiller and Dewey appear with their pragmatistic account of what truth everywhere signifies. Everywhere, these teachers say, "truth" in our ideas and beliefs means the same thing that it means in science. It means, they say, nothing but this, *that ideas (which themselves are but parts of our experience) become true just in so far as they help us to get into satisfactory relation with other parts of our experience,* to summarize them and get about them by conceptual short-cuts instead of following the interminable succession of particular phenomena. Any idea upon which we can ride, so to speak; any idea that will carry us prosperously from any one part of our experience to any other part, linking things satisfactorily, working securely, simplifying, saving labor; is true for just so much, true in so far forth, true *instrumentally.* This is the "instrumental" view of truth taught so successfully at Chicago, the view that truth in our ideas means their power to "work," promulgated so brilliantly at Oxford.

Messrs. Dewey, Schiller and their allies, in reaching this general conception of all truth, have only followed the example of geologists, biologists and philologists. In the establishment of these other sciences, the successful stroke was always to take some simple process actually observable in operation—as denudation by weather, say, or variation from parental type, or change of dialect by incorporation of new words and pronunciations—and then to generalize it, making it apply to all times, and produce great results by summating its effects through the ages.

The observable process which Schiller and Dewey particularly singled out for generalization is the familiar one by which any individual settles into *new opinions*. The process here is always the same. The individual has a stock of old opinions already, but he meets a new experience that puts them to a strain. Somebody contradicts them; or in a reflective moment he discovers that they contradict each other; or he hears of facts with which they are incompatible; or desires arise in him which they cease to satisfy. The result is an inward trouble to which his mind till then had been a stranger, and from which he seeks to escape by modifying his previous mass of opinions. He saves as much of it as he can, for in this matter of belief we are all extreme conservatives. So he tries to change first this opinion, and then that (for they resist change very variously), until at last some new idea comes up which he can graft upon the ancient stock with a minimum of disturbance of the latter, some idea that mediates between the stock and the new experience and runs them into one another most felicitously and expediently.

This new idea is then adopted as the true one. It preserves the older stock of truths with a minimum of modification, stretching them just enough to make them admit the novelty, but conceiving that in ways as familiar as the case leaves possible. An *outrée* explanation, violating all our preconceptions, would never pass for a true account of a novelty. We should scratch round industriously till we found something less excentric. The most violent revolutions in an individual's beliefs leave most of his old order standing. Time and space, cause and effect, nature and history, and one's own biography remain untouched. New truth is always a go-between, a smoother-over of transitions. It marries old opinion to new fact so as ever to show a minimum of jolt, a maximum of continuity. We hold a theory true just in proportion to its success in solving this "problem of maxima and minima." But success in solving this problem is eminently a matter of approximation. We say this theory solves it on the whole more satisfactorily than that theory; but that means more satisfactorily to ourselves, and individuals will emphasize their points of satisfaction differently. To a certain degree, therefore, everything here is plastic.

The point I now urge you to observe particularly is the part played by the older truths. Failure to take account of it is the source of much of the unjust criticism levelled against pragmatism. Their influence is absolutely controlling. Loyalty to them is the first principle—in most cases it is the only principle; for by far the most usual way of handling phenomena so novel that they would make for a serious rearrangement of our preconception is to ignore them altogether, or to abuse those who bear witness for them.

You doubtless wish examples of this process of truth's growth, and the only trouble is their superabundance. The simplest case of new truth is of course the mere numerical addition of new kinds of facts, or of new single facts of old kinds, to our experience—an addition that involves no alteration in the old beliefs. Day follows day, and its contents are simply added. The new contents themselves are not true, they simply *come* and *are*. Truth is *what we say about* them, and when we say that they have come, truth is satisfied by the plain additive formula.

But often the day's contents oblige a rearrangement. If I should now utter piercing shrieks and act like a maniac on this platform, it would make many of you revise your ideas as to the probable worth of my philosophy. "Radium" came the other day as part of the day's content, and seemed for a moment to contradict our ideas of the whole order of nature, that order having come to be identified with what is called the conservation of energy. The mere sight of radium paying heat away indefinitely out of its own pocket seemed to violate that conservation. What to think? If the radiations from it were nothing but an escape of unsuspected "potential" energy, pre-existent inside of the atoms, the principle of conservation would be saved. The discovery of "helium" as the radiation's outcome opened a way to this belief. So Ramsay's view is generally held to be true, because, although it extends our old ideas of energy, it causes a minimum of alteration in their nature.

I need not multiply instances. A new opinion counts as "true" just in proportion as it gratifies the individual's desire to assimilate the novel in his experience to his beliefs in stock. It must both lean on old truth and grasp new fact; and its success (as I said a moment ago) in doing this is a matter for the individual's appreciation. When old truth grows, then, by new truth's addition, it is for subjective reasons. We are in the process and obey the reasons. That new idea is truest which performs most felicitously its function of satisfying our double urgency. It makes itself true, gets itself classed as true, by the way it works; grafting itself then upon the ancient body of truth, which thus grows much as a tree grows by the activity of a new layer of cambium.

Now Dewey and Schiller proceed to generalize this observation and to apply it to the most ancient parts of truth. They also once were plastic. They also were called true for human reasons. They also mediated between still earlier truths and what in those days were novel observations. Purely objective truth, truth in whose establishment the function of giving human satisfaction in marrying previous parts of experience with newer parts played no rôle whatever, is nowhere to be found. The reason why we call things true is the reason why they *are* true, for "to be true" *means* only to perform this marriage-function.

The trail of the human serpent is thus over everything. Truth independent; truth that we *find* merely; truth no longer malleable to human need; truth incorrigible, in a word; such truth exists indeed superabundantly—or is supposed to exist by rationalistically minded thinkers; but then it means only the dead heart of the living tree, and its being there means only that truth also has its paleontology, and its "prescription," and may grow stiff with years of veteran service and petrified in men's regard by sheer antiquity. But how plastic even the oldest truths nevertheless really are has been vividly shown in our day by the transformation of logical and mathematical ideas, a transformation which seems even to be invading physics. The ancient for-

mulas are reinterpreted as special expressions of much wider principles,
principles that our ancestors never
got a glimpse of in their present shape
and formulation.

Mr. Schiller still gives to all this
view of truth the name of "Humanism," but, for this doctrine too, the
name of pragmatism seems fairly to
be in the ascendant, so I will treat
it under the name of pragmatism in
these lectures.

Such then would be the scope of
pragmatism—first, a method; and second, a genetic theory of what is meant
by truth. And these two things must
be our future topics.

What I have said of the theory of
truth will, I am sure, have appeared
obscure and unsatisfactory to most of
you by reason of its brevity. I shall
make amends for that hereafter. In a
lecture on "common sense" I shall try
to show what I mean by truths grown
petrified by antiquity. In another lecture I shall expatiate on the idea that
our thoughts become true in proportion as they successfully exert their
go-between function. In a third I shall
show how hard it is to discriminate
subjective from objective factors in
Truth's development. You may not
follow me wholly in these lectures;
and if you do, you may not wholly
agree with me. But you will, I know,
regard me at least as serious, and treat
my effort with respectful consideration.

You will probably be surprised to
learn, then, that Messrs. Schiller's
and Dewey's theories have suffered
a hailstorm of contempt and ridicule.
All rationalism has risen against them.
In influential quarters Mr. Schiller,
in particular, has been treated like
an impudent schoolboy who deserves
a spanking. I should not mention this
but for the fact that it throws so much
sidelight upon that rationalistic temper

to which I have opposed the temper of
pragmatism. Pragmatism is uncomfortable away from facts. Rationalism
is comfortable only in the presence of
abstractions. This pragmatist talk
about truths in the plural, about their
utility and satisfactoriness, about the
success with which they "work," etc.,
suggests to the typical intellectualist
mind a sort of coarse, lame, second-rate
makeshift article of truth. Such truths
are not real truth. Such tests are
merely subjective. As against this, objective truth must be something non-
utilitarian, haughty, refined, remote,
august, exalted. It must be an absolute
correspondence of our thoughts with
an equally absolute reality. It must be
what we *ought* to think uncondi-
tionally. The conditioned ways in
which we *do* think are so much irrelevance and matter for psychology.
Down with psychology, up with logic,
in all this question!

See the exquisite contrast of the
types of mind! The pragmatist clings
to facts and concreteness, observes
truth at its work in particular cases,
and generalizes. Truth, for him, becomes a class-name for all sorts of
definite working-values in experience.
For the rationalist it remains a pure
abstraction, to the bare name of which
we must defer. When the pragmatist
undertakes to show in detail just *why*
we must defer, the rationalist is unable to recognize the concretes from
which his own abstraction is taken.
He accuses us of *denying* truth;
whereas we have only sought to trace
exactly why people follow it. Your
typical ultra-abstractionist fairly shudders at concreteness: other things
equal, he positively prefers the pale
and spectral. If the two universes were
offered, he would always choose the
skinny outline rather than the rich
ticket of reality. It is so much purer,
clearer, nobler.

I hope that as these lectures go on, the concreteness and closeness to facts of the pragmatism which they advocate may be what approves itself to you as its most satisfactory peculiarity. It only follows here the example of the sister sciences, interpreting the unobserved by the observed. It brings old and new harmoniously together. It converts the absolutely empty notion of a static relation of "correspondence" (what that may mean we must ask later) between our minds and reality, into that of a rich and active commerce (that any one may follow in detail and understand) between particular thoughts of ours, and the great universe of other experiences in which they play their parts and have their uses.

But enough of this at present. The justification of what I say must be postponed. I wish now to add a word in further explanation of the claim I made at our last meeting, that pragmatism may be a happy harmonizer of empiricist ways of thinking with the more religious demands of human beings.

Men who are strongly of the fact-loving temperament, you may remember me to have said, are liable to be kept at a distance by the small sympathy with facts which that philosophy from the present-day fashion of idealism offers them. It is far too intellectualistic. Old-fashioned theism was bad enough, with its notion of God as an exalted monarch, made up of a lot of unintelligible or preposterous "attributes"; but, so long as it held strongly by the argument from design, it kept some touch with concrete realities. Since, however, Darwinism has once for all displaced design from the minds of the "scientific," theism has lost that foothold; and some kind of an immanent or pantheistic deity working *in* things rather than above them is, if any, the kind recommended to our contemporary imagination. Aspirants to a philosophic religion turn, as a rule, more hopefully nowadays towards idealistic pantheism than towards the older dualistic theism, in spite of the fact that the latter still counts able defenders.

But, as I said in my first lecture, the brand of pantheism offered is hard for them to assimilate if they are lovers of facts, or empirically minded. It is the absolutistic brand, spurning the dust and reared upon pure logic. It keeps no connexion whatever with concreteness. Affirming the Absolute Mind, which is its substitute for God, to be the rational presupposition of all particulars of fact, whatever they may be, it remains supremely indifferent to what the particular facts in our world actually are. Be they what they may, the Absolute will father them. Like the sick lion in Esop's fable, all footprints lead into his den, but *nulla vestigia retrorsum*. You cannot redescend into the world of particulars by the Absolute's aid, or deduce any necessary consequences of detail important for your life from your idea of his nature. He gives you indeed the assurance that all is well with *Him,* and for his eternal way of thinking; but thereupon he leaves you to be finitely saved by your own temporal devices.

Far be it from me to deny the majesty of this conception, or its capacity to yield religious comfort to a most respectable class of minds. But from the human point of view, no one can pretend that it doesn't suffer from the faults of remoteness and abstractness. It is eminently a product of what I have ventured to call the rationalistic temper. It disdains empiricism's needs. It substitutes a pallid outline for the real world's richness. It is dapper, it is noble in the bad sense, in the sense in which to be noble is to be inapt for humble service. In this real world of sweat and dirt, it seems to me that when a view of things is "noble," that ought to count as a presumption against its truth, and as a philosophic disqualification. The prince of darkness may be a gentleman, as we are told he is, but whatever the God of earth and heaven is, he can surely be no gentleman. His menial services are needed in the dust of our human trials, even more than his dignity is needed in the empyrean.

Now pragmatism, devoted though she be to facts, has no such materialistic bias as ordinary empiricism labors under. Moreover, she has no objection whatever to the realizing of abstractions, so long as you get about among particulars with their aid and they actually carry you somewhere. Interested in no conclusions but those which our minds and our experiences work out together, she has no *a priori* prejudices against theology. *If theological ideas prove to have a value for concrete life, they will be true, for pragmatism, in the sense of being good for so much. For how much more they are true, will depend entirely on their relations to the other truths that also have to be acknowledged.*

What I said just now about the Absolute, of transcendental idealism, is a case in point. First, I called it majestic and said it yielded religious comfort to a class of minds, and then I accused it of remoteness and sterility. But so far as it affords such comfort, it surely is not sterile; it has that amount of value; it performs a concrete function. As a good pragmatist, I myself ought to call the Absolute "true in so far forth," then; and I unhesitatingly now do so.

But what does *true in so far forth*

mean in this case? To answer, we need only apply the pragmatic method. What do believers in the Absolute mean by saying that their belief affords them comfort? They mean that since, in the Absolute finite evil is "overruled" already, we may, therefore, whenever we wish, treat the temporal as if it were potentially the eternal, be sure that we can trust its outcome, and, without sin, dismiss our fear and drop the worry of our finite responsibility. In short, they mean that we have a right ever and anon to take a moral holiday, to let the world wag in its own way, feeling that its issues are in better hands than ours and are none of our business.

The universe is a system of which the individual members may relax their anxieties occasionally, in which the don't-care mood is also right for men, and moral holidays in order,— that, if I mistake not, is part, at least, of what the Absolute is "known-as," that is the great difference in our particular experiences which his being true makes, for us, that is his cash-value when he is pragmatically interpreted. Farther than that the ordinary lay-reader in philosophy who thinks favorably of absolute idealism does not venture to sharpen his conceptions. He can use the Absolute for so much, and so much is very precious. He is pained at hearing you speak incredulously of the Absolute, therefore, and disregards your criticisms because they deal with aspects of the conception that he fails to follow.

If the Absolute means this, and means no more than this, who can possibly deny the truth of it? To deny it would be to insist that men should never relax, and that holidays are never in order.

I am well aware how odd it must seem to some of you to hear me say that an idea is "true" so long as to believe it is profitable to our lives. That it is *good*, for as much as it profits, you will gladly admit. If what we do by its aid is good, you will allow the idea itself to be good in so far forth, for we are the better for possessing it. But is it not a strange misuse of the word "truth," you will say, to call ideas also "true" for this reason?

To answer this difficulty fully is impossible at this stage of my account. You touch here upon the very central point of Messrs. Schiller's, Dewey's and my own doctrine of truth, which I can not discuss with detail until my sixth lecture. Let me now say only this, that truth is *one species of good*, and not, as is usually supposed, a category distinct from good, and co-ordinate with it. *The true is the name of whatever proves itself to be good in the way of belief, and good, too, for definite, assignable reasons.* Surely you must admit this, that if there were *no* good for life in true ideas, or if the knowledge of them were positively disadvantageous and false ideas the only useful ones, then the current notion that truth is divine and precious, and its pursuit a duty, could never have grown up or become a dogma. In a world like that, our duty would be to *shun* truth, rather. But in this world, just as certain foods are not only agreeable to our taste, but good for our teeth, our stomach, and our tissues; so certain ideas are not only agreeable to think about, or agreeable as supporting other ideas that we are fond of, but they are also helpful in life's practical struggles. If there be any life that it is really better we should lead, and if there be any idea which, if believed in, would help us to lead that life, then it would be really *better for us* to believe in that idea, *unless, indeed, belief in it*

incidentally clashed with other greater vital benefits.

"What would be better for us to believe!" This sounds very like a definition of truth. It comes very near to saying "what we *ought* to believe": and in *that* definition none of you would find any oddity. Ought we ever not to believe what it is *better for us* to believe? And can we then keep the notion of what is better for us, and what is true for us, permanently apart?

Pragmatism says no, and I fully agree with her. Probably you also agree, so far as the abstract statement goes, but with a suspicion that if we practically did believe everything that made for good in our own personal lives, we should be found indulging all kinds of fancies about this world's affairs, and all kinds of sentimental superstitions about a world hereafter. Your suspicion here is undoubtedly well founded, and it is evident that something happens when you pass from the abstract to the concrete that complicates the situation.

I said just now that what is better for us to believe is true *unless the belief incidentally clashes with some other vital benefit*. Now in real life what vital benefits is any particular belief of ours most liable to clash with? What indeed except the vital benefits yielded by *other beliefs* when these prove incompatible with the first ones? In other words, the greatest enemy of any one of our truths may be the rest of our truths. Truths have once for all this desperate instinct of self-preservation and of desire to extinguish whatever contradicts them. My belief in the Absolute, based on the good it does me, must run the gantlet of all my other beliefs. Grant that it may be true in giving me a moral holiday. Nevertheless, as I conceive it,—and let me speak now confidentially, as it were, and merely in my own private person,—it clashes with other truths of mine whose benefits I hate to give up on its account. It happens to be associated with a kind of logic of which I am the enemy, I find that it entangles me in metaphysical paradoxes that are inacceptable, etc., etc. But as I have enough trouble in life already without adding the trouble of carrying these intellectual inconsistencies, I personally just give up the Absolute. I just *take* my moral holidays; or else as a professional philosopher, I try to justify them by some other principle.

If I could restrict my notion of the Absolute to its bare holiday-giving value, it wouldn't clash with my other truths. But we can not easily thus restrict our hypotheses. They carry supernumerary features, and these it is that clash so. My disbelief in the Absolute means then disbelief in those other supernumerary features, for I fully believe in the legitimacy of taking moral holidays.

You see by this what I meant when I called pragmatism a mediator and reconciler and said, borrowing the word from Papini, that she "unstiffens" our theories. She has in fact no prejudices whatever, no obstructive dogmas, no rigid canons of what shall count as proof. She is completely genial. She will entertain any hypothesis, she will consider any evidence. It follows that in the religious field she is at a great advantage both over positivistic empiricism, with its anti-theological bias, and over religious rationalism, with its exclusive interest in the remote, the noble, the simple, and the abstract in the way of conception.

In short, she widens the field of search for God. Rationalism sticks to logic and the empyrean. Empiricism

sticks to the external senses. Pragmatism is willing to take anything, to follow either logic or the senses and to count the humblest and most personal experiences. She will count mystical experiences if they have practical consequences. She will take a God who lives in the every dirt of private fact—if that should seem a likely place to find him.

Her only test of probable truth is what works best in the way of leading us, what fits every part of life best and combines with the collectivity of experience's demands, nothing being omitted. If theological ideas should do this, if the notion of God, in particular, should prove to do it, how could pragmatism possibly deny God's existence? She could see no meaning in treating as "not true" a notion that was pragmatically so successful. What other kind of truth could there be, for her, than all this agreement with concrete reality?

In my last lecture I shall return again to the relations of pragmatism with religion. But you see already how democratic she is. Her manners are as various and flexible, her resources as rich and endless, and her conclusions as friendly as those of mother nature.

1906; 1907

JOHN DEWEY
(1859–　　)

EXPERIENCE AND NATURE *

CHAPTER I

EXPERIENCE AND THE PHILOSOPHIC METHOD

As Mr. Ralph Perry has said, experience is a weasel word. Its slipperi-

* Reprinted by permission of John Dewey and The Open Court Publishing Company. Copyright 1925.

ness is evident in an inconsistency characteristic of many thinkers. On the one hand they eagerly claim an empirical method; they forswear the *a priori* and transcendent: they are sensitive to the charge that they employ data unwarranted by experience. On the other hand, they are given to deprecating the conception of experience; experience, it is said, is purely subjective, and whoever takes experience for this subject matter is logically bound to land in the most secluded of idealisms.

Interesting as the theme is, it is aside from our purpose to account for this contradictory attitude. It may be surmised, however, that those guilty of the contradiction think in two insulated universes of discourse. In adherence to empirical method, they think of experience in terms of the modern development of scientific method; but their idea of experience as a distinctive subject matter is derived from another source—introspective psychology as it was elaborated in the nineteenth century.* But we must make a choice. If the identification of experience with purely mental states is correct, then the last thing one should profess is acceptance of empirical method as the scientific road to the understanding of the natural and social world in which we live. And if scientific method is intrinsically empirical, then the subject-matter of experience cannot be what introspective psychologists have told us it is.

Whether or no this suggestion is correct, recognition of the inconsistency is of use in enabling us, writer and reader alike, to trap and hold the slippery idea of experience,

whenever it is proposed to set forth the implications of experience for philosophy; especially when, as in this discussion, its implications for a theory of nature, of the world, of the universe, form the issue. And I know of no better way of warning the reader against misconception of this purpose than to remind him that, as he reads the statement, he should interpret "experience" in the sense in which he himself uses the term when he professes to be faithful to the empirical method, not in the sense in which he uses it when he implies that experience is momentary, private and psychical.

There are two avenues of approach to the goal of philosophy. We may begin with experience in gross, experience in its primary and crude forms, and by means of its distinguishing features and distinctive trends, note something of the constitution of the world which generates and maintains it. Or, we may begin with refined selective products, the most authentic statements of commended methods of science, and work from them back to the primary facts of life. The two methods differ in starting point and direction, but not in objective or eventual content. Those who start with coarse, everyday experience must bear in mind the findings of the most competent knowledge, and those who start from the latter must somehow journey back to the homely facts of daily existence.

Each way of approach has its advantages and its dangers. Those who are able to pursue the road of that technical and refined knowledge called science are fortunate. But the history of thought shows how easy it is for them to forget that after all science is an art, a matter of perfected skill in conducting inquiry; while it reveals that those who are not di-

* "Psychological: Consciousness as a process taking place in time." This is the primary definition given in Baldwin's Dictionary of Philosophy and Psychology.

rectly engaged in the use of this art readily take science to be something finished, absolute in itself, instead of the result of a certain technique. Consequently "scientific" philosophies have over and over again made the science of their own day the premises of philosophy only to have them undermined by later science. And even when reasonably sure foundations are provided by the science of a period, a philosopher has no guarantee save his own acumen and honesty that he will not employ them in such a way as to get lost on a bypath. Professed scientific philosophers have been wont to employ the remoter and refinished products of science in ways which deny, discount or pervert the obvious and immediate facts of gross experience, unmindful that thereby philosophy itself commits suicide.

On the other hand, the method which sets out with macroscopic experience requires unusual candor and patience. The subject matter of science, for better or worse, is at least "there"; it is a definite body of facts and principles summed up in books and having a kind of independent external existence. But coarse and vital experience is Protean; a thing of moods and tenses. To seize and report it is the task of the artist as well as of an informed technician. As the history of thought shows, the usual thing, a thing so usual as probably to be in some measure inevitable, is for the philosopher to mix with his reports of direct experience interpretations of it made by previous thinkers. Too often, indeed, the professed empiricist only substitutes a dialectical development of some notion about experience for an analysis of experience as it is humanly lived.

The philosophy which since the seventeenth century has almost achieved a monopoly of the title "em-

piricism" strikingly illustrates this danger. Not safely can an "ism" be made out of experience. For any interpretation of experience must perforce simplify; simplifications tend in a particular direction; and the direction may be set by custom which one assumes to be natural simply because it is traditionally congenial. For at least two hundred years many interests, religious, industrial, political, have centered about the status of the individual. Hence the drift in all systems save the classic traditional school, has been to think in ways that make individuality something isolated as well as central. When the notion of experience is introduced, who is not familiar with the query, uttered in a crushingly triumphant tone, "Whose experience?" The implication is that experience is not only always somebody's, but that the peculiar nature of "somebody" infects experience so pervasively that experience is *merely* somebody's and hence of nobody and nothing else.

The dialectic situation which results may be illustrated by a quotation which is selected because it is typical of much contemporary philosophizing. "When I look at a chair, I say I experience it. But what I actually experience is only a very few of the elements that go to make up a chair, namely, the color that belongs to the chair under these particular conditions of light, the shape which the chair displays when viewed from this angle, etc." The man who has the experience, as distinct from a philosopher theorizing about it, would probably say that he experienced the chair most fully when not looking at it but when meaning to sit down in it, and that he can mean to sit down in it precisely because his experience is *not* limited to color under specific conditions of light, and angular shape. He would probably say that when he looks at it, instead of experiencing something less than a chair he experiences a good deal more than a chair: that he lays hold of a wide spatial context, such as the room where the chair is, and a spread of its history, including the chair's period, price paid for it, consequences, public as well as personal, which flow from its use as household furniture, and so on.

Such remarks as these prove nothing. But they suggest how far away from the everyday sense of experience a certain kind of philosophic discourse, though nominally experiential, has wandered. Interesting results can be had by developing dialectically such a notion of experience as is contained in the quotation; problems can be made to emerge which exercise the ingenuity of the theorizer, and which convince many a student that he gets nearer to the reality of experience the further away he gets from all the experience he has ever had. The exercise would be harmless, were it not finally forgotten that the conclusions reached have but a dialectical status, being an elaboration of premises arrived at by technical analysis from a specialized physiological point of view. Consequently, I would rather take the behavior of the dog of Odysseus upon his master's return as an example of the sort of thing experience is for the philosopher than trust to such statements. A physiologist may for his special purpose reduce Othello's perception of a handkerchief to simple elements of color under certain conditions of light and shapes seen under certain angular conditions of vision. But the actual experience was charged with history and prophecy; full of love, jealousy and villainy, fulfilling past human relationships and moving fatally to tragic destiny.

The excuse for saying the above things is that much that now passes for empiricism is but a dialectical elaboration of data taken from physiology, so that it is necessary for anyone, who seriously sets out to philosophize empirically, to recall to attention that he is talking about the sort of thing that the unsophisticated man calls experience, the life he has led and undergone in the world of persons and things. Otherwise we get a stencilled stereotype in two dimensions and in black and white instead of the solid and many colored play of activities and sufferings which is the philosopher's real datum.

The way of approach that sets out from that which is nearest at hand, instead of from refined products of science no more signifies beginning with the results of psychological science than it does with those of physical science. Indeed the former material is further away from direct experience than that of physics. It signifies beginning back of any science, with experience in its gross and macroscopic traits. Science will then be of interest as one of the phases of human experience, but intrinsically no more so than magic, myth, politics, painting, poetry and penitentiaries. The domination of men by reverie and desire is as pertinent for the philosophic theory of nature as is mathematical physics; imagination as much to be noted as refined observation. It is a fact of *experience* that some men, as Santayana has pointed out concerning Shelley, are immune to "experience" retaining intact the attitude of childhood. And for a thoroughgoing empiricist the most transcendental of philosophies is an empirical phenomenon. It may not prove intellectually what its originator supposed it to demonstrate, but it shows something about experience, something possibly of immense value for a subsequent interpretation of nature in the light of experience.

Hence it is that experience is something quite other than "consciousness," that is, that which appears qualitatively and focally at a particular moment. The common man does not need to be told that ignorance is one of the chief features of experience; so are habits skilled and certain in operation so that we abandon ourselves to them without consciousness. Yet ignorance, habit, fatal implication in the remote, are just the things which professed empiricism, with its reduction of experience to states of consciousness, denies to experience. It is important for a theory of experience to know that under certain circumstances men prize the distinct and clearly evident. But it is no more important than it is to know that under other circumstances twilight, the vague, dark and mysterious flourish. Because intellectual crimes have been committed in the name of the subconscious is no reason for refusing to admit that what is not explicitly present makes up a vastly greater part of experience than does the conscious field to which thinkers have so devoted themselves.

When disease or religion or love, or knowledge itself is experienced, forces and potential consequences are implicated that are neither directly present nor logically implied. They are "in" experience quite as truly as are the present discomforts and exaltations. Considering the role which anticipation and memory of death have played in human life, from religion to insurance companies, what can be said of a theory which defines experience in such a way that it logically follows that death is never a matter of experience? Experience is no stream, even though the stream of feelings and ideas that flows upon its surface

is the part which philosophers love to traverse. Experience includes the enduring banks of natural constitution and acquired habit as well as the stream. The flying moment is sustained by an atmosphere that does not fly, even when it most vibrates.

When we say that experience is one point of approach to an account of the world in which we live, we mean then by experience something at least as wide and deep and full as all history on this earth, a history which, since history does not occur in the void, includes the earth and the physical relatives of man. When we assimilate experience to history rather than to the physiology of sensations, we note that history denotes both objective conditions, forces, events and also the human record and estimate of these events. Similarly experience denotes whatever is experienced, whatever is undergone and tried, and also processes of experiencing. As it is the essence of "history" to have meanings termed both subjective and objective, so with "experience." As William James has said, it is a "double-barrelled" fact.* Without sun, moon and stars, mountains and rivers, forests and mines, soil, rain and wind, history would not be. These things are not just external conditions of history and experience; they are integral with them. But also without the human attitude and interest, without record and interpretation, these things would not be historical.

There is an obvious retort to this plea to take the conception of experience with the utmost naïveté and catholicity, as the common man takes it when he experiences illness and prosperity, love, marriage, and death. The objection is that experience is then made so inclusive and varied as

* Lloyd Morgan, Instinct and Experience, pp. 126–128.

to be useless for philosophic purposes. Experience, as we are here told to conceive it, includes just everything and anything, actual or potential, that we think of and talk about. So we might just as well start with everything and anything and drop out the idea and word, "experience." The traditional notion of experience, which has been disowned, may be erroneous. But at least it denotes something specific, differential; something which may be set in contrast with other things and may thus serve as a principle of criticism and estimate. But the whole wide universe of fact and dream, of event, act, desire, fancy and meanings, valid or invalid, can be set in contrast to nothing. And if what has been said is taken literally, "experience" denotes just this wide universe.

Here is indeed a vulnerable spot in experience as a guiding method for philosophy. It is presented to us as a catholic and innocent neutral, free from guile and partisanship. But then unwittingly there is substituted for this free, full, unbiased and pliable companion of us all, a simplified and selected character, which is already pointed in a special direction and loaded with preferred conclusions. So often does this occur, that one does well to exercise a wary scepticism whenever an inquirer insistently professes that *he* keeps to an empirical method. And when this biased course (easy to fall into as the history of thought testifies), is avoided, the alternative seems to be everything without discrimination, so that experience ceases to have a meaning.

The objection uncovers the exact meaning of a truly empirical method. For it reveals that experience for philosophy is method, not distinctive subject matter. And it also reveals the sort of method that philosophy needs.

Experience includes dreams, insanity, illness, death, labor, war, confusion, ambiguity, lies and error; it includes transcendental systems as well as empirical ones; magic and superstition as well as science. It includes that bent which keeps one from learning from experience as well as that skill which fastens upon its faint hints. This fact convicts upon sight every philosophy that professes to be empirical and yet assures us that some special subject matter is experience and some other not.

The value of experience as method in philosophy is that it compels us to note that *denotation* comes first and last, so that to settle any discussion, to still any doubt, to answer any question, we must go to some thing pointed to, denoted, and find our answer in that thing. As method it has a contrast which it does not possess as subject matter, that with "rationalism," understanding by rationalism method which assumes the primacy and ultimacy of purely logical thought and its findings. There are two kinds of demonstration: that of logical reasoning from premises assumed to possess logical completeness, and that of showing, pointing, coming upon a thing. The latter method is that which the word experience sums up, generalizes, makes universal and ulterior. To say that the right method is one of pointing and showing, not of meeting intellectual requirements or logical derivation from rational ideas, does not, although it is non-rational, imply a preference for irrationality. For one of the things that is pointed out, found and shown, is deduction, and the logic that governs it. But these things have also to be found and shown, and their authority rests upon the perceived outcome of this empirical denotation. The utmost in rationality has a sanction and a position that, according to taste, may be called sub-rational or supra-rational.

The value, I say of the notion of experience for philosophy is that it asserts the finality and comprehensiveness of the method of pointing, finding, showing, and the necessity of seeing what is pointed to and accepting what is found in good faith and without discount. Were the denotative method universally followed by philosophers, then the word and notion of experience might be discarded; it would be superfluous, for we should be in possession of everything it stands for. But as long as men prefer in philosophy (as they do in science), to define and envisage "reality" according to esthetic, moral or logical canons, we need the notion of experience to remind us that "reality" includes whatever is denotatively found.

When the varied constituents of the wide universe, the unfavorable, the precarious, uncertain, irrational, hateful, receive the same attention that is accorded the noble, honorable and true, then philosophy may conceivably dispense with the conception of experience. But till that day arrives, we need a cautionary and directive word, like experience, to remind us that the world which is lived, suffered and enjoyed as well as logically thought of, has the last word in all human inquiries and surmises. This is a doctrine of humility; but it is also a doctrine of direction. For it tells us to open the eyes and ears of the mind, to be sensitive to all the varied phases of life and history. Nothing is more ironical than that philosophers who have so professed universality have so often been one-sided specialists, confined to that which is authentically and surely *known,* ignoring ignorance, error, folly and the common enjoyments and adornments of life;

disposing of these by regarding them as due to our "finite" natures—a blest word that does for moderns what "non-being" was made to do for the Greeks.

The history of thought sufficiently manifests the need for a method of procedure that sets pointing, finding and showing, ahead of methods that substitute ratiocination and its conclusions for things that are done, suffered and imagined. Philosophers are wont to start with highly simplified premises. They do this not inadvertently, but with pride, as evidence that they really understand philosophic business. Absolute certainty in knowledge of things and absolute security in the ordering of life have often been assumed to be the goal of philosophic search; consequently philosophers have set out with data and principles sufficiently simple to yield what is sought. When some historic religion is ceasing to confer upon men a sense of certainty and security men especially resort to philosophy as a substitute. So they did in Greece; in Europe in the seventeenth century, and so we do today. Forms and essences, inner introspective facts, mathematical truths may be resorted to. This is a varying matter of the temporal scene. The constant is demand for assurance and order, and the demand is met only by ignoring a vast number of things that nature presents to us.

When we look for instances of a simplifying procedure exercised in this bias, we think perhaps most readily of Descartes with his certainty of thinking, of Spinoza with his conviction that a true idea carries truth intrinsically in itself so whatever must be thought, must—and alone must— *be.* But thinkers who profess empiricism also afford examples: there is Locke with his "simple idea," Hume with his "impression." And I do not see that contemporary hankering after ultimate "sense-data," or conviction that mathematical logistic is at last to open to philosophy the arcana of ultimate truth, differ in principle.

Now the notion of experience, however devoid of differential subject matter—since it includes all subject matters—, at least tells us that we must not start with arbitrarily selected simples, and from them deduce the complex and varied, assigning what cannot be thus deduced to an inferior realm of being. It warns us that the tangled and complex is what we primarily find; that we work from and within it to discriminate, reduce, analyze; and that we must keep track of these activities, pointing to *them,* as well as to the things upon which they are exercised, and to their refined conclusions. When we contemplate their fruits we are not to ignore the art by which they are produced. There is a place for polishers of stones and for those who put the stones together to make temples and palaces. But "experience" reminds us that a stone was once part of some stratum of the earth, and that a quarryman pried it loose and another workman blew the massive rock to smaller pieces, before it could be smooth-hewn and fitted into an ordered and regular structure. Empirical method warns us that systems which set out from things said to be ultimate and simple have always worked with loaded dice; their premises have been framed to yield desired conclusions.

Professed sceptics rarely fare better, whether they consistently maintain the attitude, or whether they employ doubt in order to discover a triumphant exit into certitude. Man is naturally a credulous animal. It is well to be warned against too easy and inflexible acceptance of beliefs which, before they command acceptance, should exhibit credentials. But some things, things of action and suffering, are not matters of belief at all; they just are. No one ever doubted birth, death, love or hate, no matter how much theories about them justly provoke doubts. Philosophers have exhibited proper ingenuity in pointing out holes in the beliefs of common sense, but they have also displayed improper ingenuity in ignoring the empirical things that everyone has; the things that so denote themselves that they *have* to be dealt with. No wonder Hume's doubts vanished when he played backgammon and made merry with his friends. Not that many of his doubts of doctrine were not suitable, but that in his companionships he was involved in another world from that to which he confined his philosophizing. Merriment and sorrow are not of the same order as beliefs, impressions and ideas. The advice of Epictetus to a fellow-slave whose master adhered to the school of sceptics, to rub his master with a curry-comb and annoint him with pepper-sauce is irrelevant to doubt about systematized beliefs, but it is a pertinent reminder that whatever things we are compelled to pay heed to, things of joy and suffering, cannot have their *existence* honestly called in question.

When a thinker ventures to begin with things which are too crude and coarse to come within the ken of intellectualists, he finds, moreover, that as an empiricist he is not obliged to face the miscellaneous world *en masse.* Things are pointed to in kinds, possessed of order and arrangement. Prephilosophic selections and arrangings may not be final for reflective thought, but they are significant for it. The bias they manifest is not that of the closet or library, but of men who have responded to the one-sided pressures of natural events. The key to the trends of nature is found in the adjectives that are commonly prefixed to experience. Experience is political, religious, esthetic, industrial, intellectual, mine, yours.

The adjectives denote that things present themselves in characteristic contexts, with different savors, colors, weights, tempos and directions. Experience as method warns us to give impartial attention to all of these diversifications. Non-empirical method sets out with the assumption that some one of these groupings of things is privileged; that it is supreme of its own right, that it furnishes a standard by which to measure the significance and real quality of everything else. The sequel is then but a dialectic. Philosophers deduce results in accordance with what is logically implied in their own choice of standard and measure.

Philosophy is a branch of that phase of things which is qualified by the adjective "intellectual." Since it is the express and proper business of the philosopher to subject things to reflection with a view to knowledge (to justifiable belief), he is prone to take the outcome of reflection for something antecedent. That is to say, instead of seeing that the product of knowing is *statement* of things, he is given to taking it as an *existential equivalent* of what things really are "in themselves," so that the subject-matter of other modes of experience are deviations, shortcomings, or trespasses—or as the dialectical philosopher puts it, mere "phenomena." The experiential or denotative method tells us that we must go behind the refinements and elaborations of reflective experience to the gross and compulsory things of our doings, enjoyments and sufferings—to the things that force us to labor, that satisfy needs, that surprise us with beauty,

that compel obedience under penalty. A common divisor is a convenience, and a greatest common divisor has the greatest degree of convenience. But there is no reason for supposing that its intrinsic "reality" or truth is greater than that of the numbers it divides. The objects of intellectual experience are the greatest divisor of the things of other modes; they have that remarkable value, but to convert them into exclusive reality is the sure road to arbitrary divisions and insoluble problems.

Not all philosophies have assumed that reflective experience, with logic as its norm, is the standard for experiential, religious, esthetic, industrial, social, objects. Many thinkers have concluded that dialectic ends in an impasse; that it involves us in contradictory statements. Then they have appealed to something which they assert is higher than thought. But it is significant that they think of this higher recourse as a higher kind of *knowledge,* as intuition, or immediate insight, mystical certainty of the truly real. Thus the thinker still shows his inability to take things as he has to take them as a human being, as things to pay heed to under penalty of death and defeat, things to use and enjoy, to master and submit to. The notion still lurks that in their intrinsic being they are things of knowledge.

Then there are philosophers who, like Kant, finding themselves in intellectual difficulties, assert that moral experience reveals things-in-themselves at a deeper level than does science. There are a larger number who look askance upon science, and who claim that religious experience penetrates behind the screen that limits the vision of intellect. These apparent exceptions prove the rule. For the claim implies that moral or religious experience takes the place of knowledge, doing sufficiently, absolutely, what natural knowledge does only partially and relatively. The implication is that morals and religion have a direct revelatory worth. Now it is one thing to say that the world is such that men approach certain objects with awe, worship, piety, sacrifice and prayer, and that this is a fact which a theory of existence must reckon with as truly as with the facts of science. But it is a different thing to say that religious experience gives *evidence* of the reality of its *own* objects, or that the consciousness of an obligation proves the validity of its special object, or the general fact of duty carries within itself any deliverance as to its source in reality. Helen of Troy, Hamlet of Denmark are instances of things that require as much attention from the philosopher as do molecules and integers: but their presence in experience does not guarantee that they are the same kind of things as the latter.

We must conceive of the world in terms which make it possible for devotion, piety, love, beauty, and mystery to be as real as anything else. But whether the loved and devotional objects have all the qualities which the lover and the devout worshipper attribute to them is a matter to be settled by evidence, and evidence is always extrinsic. Injunctions and prohibitions which are empirically unescapable, may be called categorical imperatives, and their existence may be quite as significant for a just theory of nature as is the law of gravitation. But what sort of objects beyond themselves they give evidence of, whether tribal taboos, a Kantian thing-in-itself, God, a political sovereign or a net work of social customs evolved in the effort to satisfy needs, is a question to be settled by the denotative method, by finding and pointing to the things

in the concrete contexts in which they present themselves.

Even the classical empiricisms of philosophical history have been concerned almost exclusively with experience as knowledge, and with objects as known or unknowable. But, since objects are found and dealt with in many other ways than those of knowledge, a genuine empiricism will set out with all the adjectival groupings of macroscopic experience, starting from them as all upon the same level of worth; subsequent inquiry can review the starting point when it is found necessary. One can be insane without knowing that he is insane and one may know insanity without being crazy; indeed absence of the direct experience is said to be an indispensable condition of the study of insanity. Adequate recognition of the implications of such a fact as this might almost be said to be the chief contribution which empirical method has to make to philosophy.

For it indicates that *being* and *having* things in other ways than knowing them, in ways never identical with knowing them, exist, and are preconditions of reflection and knowledge. *Being* angry, stupid, wise, inquiring; *having* sugar, the light of day, money, houses and lands, friends, laws, masters, subjects, pain and joy, occur in dimensions incommensurable to knowing these things which we are and have and use, and which have and use us. Their existence is unique, and, strictly speaking, indescribable; they can *only be* and be *had*, and then pointed to in reflection. In the proper sense of the word, their existence is absolute, being qualitative. All cognitive must start from and must terminate in being and having things in just such unique, irreparable and compelling ways. And until this fact is a commonplace in philosophy, the notion of experience will not be a truism for philosophers.

Inevitably our argument travels in a circle and comes back to where we started. Modern philosophy is openly, ancient philosophy covertly, a theory of knowledge, and of things as known. A theory of knowledge in the sense of how to know most economically, liberally, effectively, a technique of instructive and rewarding inquiry is indispensable. But what has gone by the name of theory of knowledge has not been such an affair. It has been a discussion of whether we can know at all, a matter of validating or refuting wholesale scepticism (instead of how to conduct doubt profitably); of how far knowledge extends, what its limits are, limits not at a specific time and place, but inherent and final. What has been said professes to give an explanation of this fact. It is due to failure to take the various phases of experienced things simply, directly, and impartially. It is due to bias of the intellectualist in favor of his own specialized professional experience.

Bias in favor of things in their capacity of being objects of knowledge, when it is yielded to, renders it impossible to distinguish between being and having things and knowing them. If *having* sweet, red, hard, pain, etc., is of necessity identical with knowing these things, then the classic problems of epistemology, and the necessity of defending science against wholesale sceptical doubts are inevitable. I mention in illustration the two traditional questions. First, there is the dispute between the epistemological idealist and realist. Are sweet, hard, solid, pain, square, etc., psychical or physical? Empirically, the obvious answer is that they are neither. They are the unique qualities which they are, the things pointed to and

had. But *knowledge* involves classification. If to have is also to know, then these things cannot "really" be simply the qualities they are; they must be related, subsumed, interpreted. And the two most general terms of classificatory knowing are physical and mental. Hence the dispute.

Another problem which is inevitable is the relation of immediate or "presentative" knowledge, sensory acquaintance or whatever, to reflective and inferential knowledge, to science. How is the reality of the proper objects of the latter to be "reconciled" with the reality of the things—whether defined as physical or psychical—of immediate sensuous or presentative "knowledge"? The problem is dialectically attractive, as is shown by the immense amount of ingenuity that has been expended upon it. But no generally satisfactory answer has ever been found and it is predictable that none ever will be. For the problem, empirically speaking, is unreal. There are not two kinds of knowledge whose objects have to be reconciled. There are two dimensions of experienced things: one that of having them, and the other that of knowing about them so that we can again have them in more meaningful and secure ways. It is no easy matter to know about the things we have and are, whether it be the state, measles, virtue or redness. Hence there *is* a problem of knowledge; namely, the problem of how to find out what it is needful to find out about these things in order to secure, rectify and avoid being and having them.

But a problem of knowledge in general is, to speak brutally, nonsense. For knowledge is itself one of the things that we empirically *have*. While scepticism may be in place at any time about any specific intellectual belief and conclusion, in order to keep us on the alert, to keep us inquiring and curious, scepticism as to the things which we *have* and *are* is impossible. No one ever frankly engaged in it. Its pretentiousness is concealed, however, by the failure to distinguish between objects of knowledge where doubt is legitimate, since they are matters of interpretation and classification (of theory), and things which are directly had. A man may doubt whether he has the measles, because measles is an intellectual term, a classification, but he cannot doubt what he empirically has—not as has so often been asserted because he has an immediately certain knowledge of it, but because it is not a matter of knowledge, an intellectual affair, at all, not an affair of truth or falsity, certitude, or doubt, but one of existence.

He may not know that he is ailing, much less what his ailment is; but unless there is something immediately and non-cognitively present in experience so that it is capable of being pointed to in subsequent reflection and in action which embodies the fruits of reflection, knowledge has neither subject matter nor objective. In traditional epistemologies, this fact has been both recognized and perverted; it is said that while we can doubt whether a particular thing is red or sweet, we have an immediate or intuitive cognitive certitude that we are affected by redness or sweetness or have a sensation of red or sweet. But as cognized, red and sweet are data only because they are *taken* in thought. Their givenness is something imputed; they are primary and immediate relatively to more complex processes of inquiry. It required a high degree of intellectual specialization, backed by technical knowledge of the nervous system, before even the concept of sensory data could emerge. It still taxes the sources of investigation to determine just what are "immediate data" in a particular problem. To know a quality *as* sensation is to have performed an act of complicated objective reference; it is not to register an inherently given property. The epistemological sensationalist and the epistemological rationalist share the same error; belief that cognitive property is intrinsic, borne on the face.

Because empirical method is denotative, it is realistic in the unsophisticated sense of the word. Things are first acted toward, suffered; and it is for the things themselves as they are followed up to tell by their own traits whether they are "subjective" or "objective." These terms, like physical and psychical, express classificatory discriminations, and there is no presumption of primacy on the side of the subjective. As a matter of historic fact, the primitive bias of man is all toward objective classifications. Whatever can be denoted is there independent of volition (volition itself occurring without volition), and its thereness, its independence of choice, renders it, for uncritical man, cosmic and fated. Only when vanity, prestige, and property rights are involved does the natural man tend, like Jack Horner with his plum, to employ a subjective or personal interpretation.

Subsequently, reflection attributes occurrences like disease, misfortune, and error to the individual person's own doings, instead of imputing them to gods or enemies or wizardry or fate. There is then an intelligible sense in which these things may be said to have been transferred from an objective to a subjective field. But there is even more sense in saying that they have been given a *different* objective reference, in those cases where they are referred to a personal subject as their seat and source. When we say that a man's illness is due to his own imprudence and not to a foreign substance magically projected into his interior by a subtle enemy, we are still discoursing within the realm of objective events. The case is not otherwise when we attribute error to something in a man's own disposition, instead of to the intent of hostile gods to blind him, or to the inherent illusory nature of things. Practically, the distinction thus drawn between subjective and objective, personal and impersonal, causation and locus is of immense importance. But for theory, it falls within a continuous world of events.

Most of the things that have been called subjective by the philosophers have an even more obvious objective status. Political institutions, the household, art, technologies, embodied objective events long before science and philosophy arose. Political experience deals with barriers, mountains, rivers, seas, forests and plains. Men fight for these things; for them they exercise jurisdiction; they obey and rebel. Being and having, exercising and suffering such things as these, exist in the open and public world. As we digest foods derived from the extra-personal world long before we study or are aware of processes occurring in our own bodily tissues, so we live in a world of objective acceptances and compulsions long before we are aware of attitudes of our own, and of the action of say the nervous system, in bringing us into effective relationship with them. The knowledge of our own attitudes and of the operation of the nervous system is no more a substitute for the direct operation of the things than metabolic processes are a substitute for food materials. In one case as in the other we have become acquainted with an added *object;* and by means of this added object further active relations with the extra-personal world are instituted.

When we speak of esthetic experience we do not mean something private and psychical. The choir of heaven and the consent of the earth are implicated, as are paints, brushes, marbles, chisels, temples, palaces, and theatres. Appreciation is appreciation of some *thing,* not of itself. We are lovingly and excitedly aware of the objects long before we are aware of our own attitude; and the acquisition of ability to distinguish that attitude marks only an increase of distinctions in original subject matter. Although contemporary theory emphasizes the psychologic and personal aspects of religion, historic religions have always had their holy places, times, persons and rites. One may believe that these objects did not have in the order of objects of knowledge the qualities ascribed to them in belief, but the testimony in behalf of the natural objective reference of the subject-matter of experience then becomes only the more impressive. Myths would not be taken to be on the level with physical facts were not the bias of experience toward the objective. Recognition of objects of worship and prayer as ideal or as "essences," treatment of them as poetic or esthetic, represents a late achievement of reflection, not an original datum. If research into religious phenomena has proved anything it is that acts, rites, cults, ceremonies, institutions, are primary, emotional beliefs then clustering about them. Even religious experience does not escape the objective compulsions which inhere in the more direct experience where man tills the soil with the sweat of his brow and woman brings forth in labor. The objects that are auxiliary and hostile to success in these acts affect the most refined and spiritualized sentiments and conceptions.

The notion that experience is solely experienc*ing*, a succession of personal sensations, images and feelings is wholly a recent notion. There is a genuine and important discovery implied by it. But it may be asserted that no one ever took it literally; it has been only a starting-point for dialectical developments which are sufficiently interesting to obscure the absurdity of the basic conception. The discovery is important; for it marks the discovery of operation of organic attitudes and dispositions in the beliefs we hold and the necessity of controlling them if beliefs are to be effectively controlled. The literal isolation of processes of experiencing, as if they were actually something solid and integral, is absurd; because dispositions and attitudes are always towards or from things beyond themselves. To love and hate, desire and fear, believe and deny, are not just states of mind in nor states of an animal body; they are *active* performances to and about other things,—acceptances and rejections, assimilations and forth-spewings of other things, strugglings to obtain and to escape things.

The fact that the characteristic structure and function of these acts, in complexly organized animal forms, can be detected, shown, and in turn made the subject of new modes of responsive action expresses one of the most valuable philosophic uses of empirical method. It undermines rigid dogmatism, while it also changes skepticism from a wholesale and barren possession of a few aloof thinkers into a common and fertile method of inquiry into specific beliefs. The things which a man experiences come to him clothed with meanings which originate in custom and tradition.

From his birth an individual sees persons about him treat things in certain ways, subject them to certain uses, assign to them certain potencies. The things are thereby invested for him with certain properties, and the investiture appears intrinsic and indissoluble. The potency of custom over beliefs never received a fatal wound until physiology and psychology showed how imitation, suggestion, stimulation, prestige, operate to call out certain responses, and how habit confirms and consolidates the responses into apparent matter-of-course unquestioned necessities.

Man lives by expectation, but the content of expectation, *what* is anticipated, depends upon memory; and memories are group affairs before they are personal recalls. The tradition that controls belief, expectation and memory, is limited and usually perverted. Not even wood always burns; seeds do not always grow, nor foodstuffs always nourish; water in quenching thirst may bring a malignant plague. In complex matters the frustration of conduct based upon expectant belief is still more pervasive. The man enmeshed in labor accounts up to a certain point for these unaccountable behaviors of things by noting further qualifying conditions that affect efficacy; soon reaching the end of his tether, he then falls back upon mysterious potencies, concealed personal agencies and magical counteractions. The thinker who enjoys leisure and is removed from the immediate necessity of doing something about these predicaments, seeks certitude in a higher, more metaphysical realm of Being, and defines as mere "appearance" the region of actual and possible frustrations. Or he turns disillusioned sceptic, and will abstain from all intellectual commitment to objects. The first method creates superstitions; the second is sterile, because it affords no solution of the actual problem, that of regulating specific beliefs about objects, so that they take account of what is ulterior and eventual. The finding and pointing out of the roles of personal attitudes and dispositions in inference and belief as well as in all other relationships with things (a discovery that constitutes psychology as it becomes systematic), is an indispensable part of this art of regulating ideas about objects; and this art is an indispensable factor in liberation.

Philosophers, however, misinterpreted the discovery. The old confusion persisted; the identification of direct having with knowing seemed to be the one sound and permanent part of the classic philosophic tradition. "Having" these personal dispositions being in a sense basic to other "havings," it was translated into belief that they were the first and primary objects of knowledge, possessed of the attributes of reality attributed by classic philosophy to *its* prior and primary objects of knowledge. Meanwhile men of science and affairs *used* the discovery; it was to them an assurance that by taking better care of the generation and employment of these personal attitudes, mankind could attain to a more secure and meaningful regulation of its ineradicable and coercive concern with things of the environment.

Thus the value of the notion of experience for philosophic reflection is that it denotes both the field, the sun and clouds and rain, seeds, and harvest, and the man who labors, who plans, invents, uses, suffers, and enjoys. Experience denotes what is experienced, the world of events and persons; and it denotes that world caught up into experiencing, the career and destiny of mankind. Nature's place in man is no less significant than

man's place in nature. Man in nature is man subjected; nature in man, recognized and used, is intelligence and art. The value of experience for the philosopher is that it serves as a constant reminder of something which is neither exclusive and isolated subject and object, matter or mind, nor yet one plus the other. The fact of integration in life is a basic fact, and until its recognition becomes habitual, unconscious and pervasive, we need a word like experience to remind us of it, and to keep before thought the distortions that occur when integration is ignored or denied.

The denotations that constitute experience point to history, to temporal process. The technically expert are aware how much ingenuity has been spent upon discovering something which shall be wholly present, so completely present as to exclude movement and change. There are *phases* of things to which this search is pertinent. There are moments of consummation when before and after are legitimately forgotten, and the sole stake of man is in the present. But even such objects are discovered to arise as culminations of processes, and to be in turn transitive and effective, while they may be also predictive or cognitively significant. The legitimacy of timeless absorption is no argument in behalf of the legitimacy of timeless objects. Experience is history; and the *taking* of some objects as final is itself an episode in history. The testimony of an absorbed consciousness that at last it rests upon something superior to the vicissitudes of time is of no more cognitive worth than the testimony of any other purely immediate consciousness. That is, it is not testimony at all, it is a having, not a knowing. And hence when treated as cognition, it is never natural and naïve; it is suborned in the interest of a sophisticated metaphysics. There is no testimony in such moments just because of absorption in the immediate qualities of the object. There is enjoyment and possession, with no need of thought as to how the object came or whither it is going, what evidence it gives. And when it turns evidence, it always testifies to an existence which is partial or particular, and local.

The assumption that the ultimate and the immediate object is timeless is responsible for one of the insoluble problems of certain types of philosophy. The past and future are rendered purely inferential, speculative, something to be reached by pure faith. But in fact anything denoted is found to have temporal quality and reference; it has movement from and towards *within* it; it is marked by waxings and wanings. The translation of temporal quality into an *order* of time is an intellectual arrangement, and is subject to doubt and error. Although pastness and futurity are qualities of everything present, such presence does not guarantee the date at which Columbus discovered America nor when the next eclipse of the moon will occur. For these things are matters that require measurements, comparisons, connection with remote occurrences. But objects of present experience have the actuality of a temporal procession, and accordingly reflection may assign things an order of succession within something which non-reflectively exists and is had.

The import of these remarks is anticipatory. Their full meaning can be had only when some of the denotations summed up in the notion of experience have been followed out and described. A justification of recapitulation of our prefatory considerations in the fact that experience has so often been employed to desig-

nate not a method but a stuff or subject matter. It then gains a discriminatory and selective meaning and is used to justify, apart from actual experience and antecedent to it, some kinds of objects and to disparage and condemn others. "Experience" becomes a theory, and, like all theories as such, dialectic and *a priori*. The objection that the alternative notion of experience is so catholic and universal in application that it no longer has any distinctive meaning is sound in principle. But in the face of historic philosophies and the reigning tradition, the alternative notion is instructive and useful. It serves as a caution against methods that have led to wrong conclusions, and a reminder of a proper procedure to be followed.

In the first place it guards us against accepting as original, primitive and simple, distinctions that have become familiar to us, that are a customary part of our intellectual inheritance—such distinctions for example as that of the physical and the mental. It warns us that all intellectual terms are products of discrimination and classification, and that we must, as philosophers, go back to the primitive situations of life that antecede and generate these reflective interpretations, so that we re-live former processes of interpretation in a wary manner, with eyes constantly upon the things to which they refer. Thus empiricism is the truly critical method; it puts us knowingly and cautiously through the steps which were first taken uncritically, and exposed to all kinds of adventitious influence.

In the second place, the notion of experience reminds us that, prior to philosophic reflection, objects have fallen into certain groupings, designated by the adjectives we readily prefix to the word experience:—adjectives like moral, esthetic, intellectual, religious, personal, political. The notion thus warns us against the tradition which makes the objects of a certain kind of experience, the cognitive, the fixed standards for estimating the "reality" and import of all other kinds of things. It cautions us against transferring the qualities characteristic of objects in a certain mode of organization to objects in other modes. Knowledge itself must be experienced; it must be had, possessed, enacted, before it can be known, and the having it is no more identical with knowing it, or knowing it with having it, than is the case with anger, being ill, or being the possessor by inheritance of an estate. We have to identify cases of knowing by direct denotation before we can have a reflective experience of them, just as we do with good and bad, red and green, sweet and sour.

In the third place, the notion cautions us that we must begin with things in their complex entanglements rather than with simplifications made for the purpose of effective judgment and action; whether the purpose is economy or dialectical esthetic or moral. The simplifications of philosophic data have been largely determined by apologetic methods, that is by interest in dignifying certain kinds and phases of things. So strong is this tendency that if a philosopher points to any particular thing as important enough to demand notation, it is practically certain that some critic will shift the issue from whether the denoted thing is found to be as he has described it to be, to the question of value. For example, I have asserted that all denoted things possess temporal quality. It is reasonably certain that this statement will be taken by some critic to indicate a preference on my part for change over permanence, an implied statement that it is *better*

that things should be in flux. It has been stated that objects are primarily denoted in their practical relationships, as things of doing, suffering, contact, possession and use. Instead of being discussed as a question of denotation, the philosophic tradition is such that the statement will be taken as an eulogy; as implying that practice is better than theory. It is then "refuted" by pointing out the superior charm of the contemplative life.

This bias is so strong and so persistent that it testifies, I suppose, to a fact of importance, to the fact that most philosophical simplifications are due to a moral interest which is ignored or denied. Our constant and inalienable concern is with good and bad, prosperity and failure, and hence with choice. We are constructed to think in terms of value, of bearing upon welfare. The ideal of welfare varies, but the influence of interest in it is pervasive and inescapable. In a vital, though not conventional, sense all men think with a moral bias and concern, the "immoral" man as truly as the righteous man; wicked and just men being characterized by bents towards different kinds of things as good. Now this fact seems to me of great importance to philosophy; it indicates that in some sense all philosophy is a branch of morals. But acknowledgement that the ultimate ground of reflection is to enable men better to make choice of things as good and bad is in truth the opposite attitude from that which immediately converts traits of existence into moral qualities, and which transforms preferred qualities into properties of true and real being. For the former concerns action to be performed, the direction of desire, purpose and endeavor. The latter is an affair of existence as it is found to be; material, it may be, of choice and action, but material, not goal or finished object.

For reflection the eventual is always better or worse than the given. But since it would also be better if the eventual good were now given, the philosopher, belonging by status to a leisure class relieved from the more urgent necessity of dealing with conditions, converts the eventual into some kind of Being, something which *is,* even if it does not *exist.* Permanence, real essence, totality, order, unity, rationality, the *unum, verum, et bonum* of the classic tradition, are obviously eulogistic predicates. When accordingly we find such terms used to describe the foundations and proper conclusions of a philosophic system, there is ground for suspecting that an artificial simplification of existence has been performed. Reflection determining preference for an eventual good has dialectically wrought a miracle of transubstantiation. Here if anywhere it is needful that we return to the mixed and entangled things expressed by the term experience.

The occurrence of the moral fallacy is obscured and disguised in subtle ways. That having the greatest power of self-deception springs from the conventional associations of the word moral. When a thinker has escaped from them he fancies that he has escaped morals. His conclusions are fixed by a preference for a reflective "good," that is to say by preference for things which have a quality of goodness that satisfies the requirements of reasonable examination and judgment. But overtly he may contemn the moral life, on the ground that it involves struggle, effort, disappointment, constantly renewed. Hence he asserts that the true good is non-moral, since it includes none of these things. According to special temperament and to accidents of education, due in turn largely to social

and economic status, the true good is then conceived either esthetically, or dialectically, or in terms borrowed from a religious context. Then "reality" as the object of philosophic research is described with the properties required by the choice of good that has occurred. The significant thing, however, is not the thinker's disparaging view of moral life as conflict and practical effort; it is that his *reflective* idea of the good, which after all is the essence of morals, has been converted into a norm and model of Being. His choice of what is good, whether logically conceived or instigated by cultivated taste, is the heart of the matter.

The operation of choice is, I suppose, inevitable in any enterprise into which reflection enters. It is not in itself falsifying. Deception lies in the fact that its presence is concealed, disguised, denied. An empirical method finds and points to the operation of choice as it does to any other event. Thus it protects us from conversion of eventual functions into antecedent existence: a conversion that may be said to be *the* philosophic fallacy, whether it be performed in behalf of mathematical subsistencies, esthetic essences, the purely physical order of nature, or God. The present writer does not confess any greater candor of intent than animates fellow philosophers. But the pursuance of an empirical method is, it is submitted, the way to secure execution of candid intent. Whatever is employed as subject-matter of choice, determining its need and giving it guidance, an empirical method frankly indicates for what it is; and the fact of choice, with its workings and consequences, an empirical method points out with equal openness.

The adoption of an empirical method is no guarantee that all the things relevant to any particular conclusion will actually be found or pointed to, or that when found they will be correctly shown or communicated. But the empirical method points out when and where and how things of a designated description have been arrived at. It places before others a map of the road that has been travelled; they may accordingly, if they will, retravel the road to inspect the landscape for themselves. Thus the findings of one may be rectified and extended by the findings of others, with as much assurance as is humanly possible of confirmation, extension and rectification. The adoption of empirical, or denotative, method would thus procure for philosophic reflection something of that cooperative tendency toward consensus which marks inquiry in the natural sciences. The scientific investigator convinces others not by the plausibility of his definitions and the cogency of his dialectic, but by placing before them the specified course of experiences of searchings, doings and findings in consequence of which certain things have been found. His appeal is for others to traverse a similar course, so as to see how what they find corresponds with his report.

Dialectic thereby itself receives a designated status and office. As it occurs in philosophic thought its dependence upon an original act of selective choice is often not avowed. Its premises are alleged to be indubitable and self-guaranteeing. Honest empirical method will state when and where and why the act of selection took place, and thus enable others to repeat it and test its worth. Selective choice, denoted as an empirical event will reveal the basis and bearing of intellectual simplifications; then they cease to be of such a self-enclosed nature as to be affairs only

of opinion and argument, admitting no alternatives save complete acceptance or rejection. Choice that is disguised or denied is the source of those astounding differences of philosophic belief that startle the beginner and that become the plaything of the expert. Choice that is avowed is an experiment to be tried on its merits and tested by its results. Under all the captions that are called immediate knowledge, or self-sufficient certitude of belief, whether logical, esthetic or epistemological, there is something selected for a purpose, and hence not simple, not self-evident and not intrinsically eulogizable. State the purpose so that it may be re-experienced, and its value and the pertinency of selection made in its behalf may be tested. The purport of thinking, scientific and philosophic, is not to eliminate choice, but to render it less arbitrary, and more significant. It loses its arbitrary character when its quality and consequences are such as to commend themselves to the reflection of others after they have betaken themselves to the situations indicated; it becomes significant when reason for the choice is found to be weighty, and its consequences momentous. This statement is not a commendation of the will to believe. It is not a statement that we *should* choose, or that *some* choices are self-justifying. It is a statement that wherever reflection occurs and intelligence operates, a selective discrimination *does* occur. The justification of a choice is wholly another matter; it is extrinsic. It depends upon the extent in which observation, memory and forethought have entered into making the choice, and upon the consequences that flow from it. When choice is avowed, others can repeat the course of the experience; it is an experiment to be tried, not an automatic safety device.

This particular affair is referred to here not so much as matter of doctrine as to afford an illustration of the nature of empirical method. Truth or falsity depends upon what others find when they warily perform the experiment of observing reflective events. An empirical finding is refuted not by denial that one finds things to be thus and so, but by giving directions for a course of experience that results in finding its opposite to be the case. To convince of error as well as to lead to truth is to assist another to see and find something which he hitherto has failed to find and recognize. All of the wit and subtlety of reflection and of dialectic find scope in the elaboration and conveying of directions that intelligibly point out a course to be followed. Every system of philosophy presents the consequences of some such experiment. As experiments, each has contributed something of worth to our observation of the events and qualities of experienceable objects. Some harsh criticisms of traditional philosophy have already been suggested; others doubtless will follow. But the criticism is not directed at the experiments; it is aimed at the denial to them by the philosophic tradition of selective experimental quality, a denial which has isolated them from their actual context and function, and has thereby converted potential illuminations into arbitrary assertions.

All philosophies employ empirical subject matter, even the most transcendental; there is nothing else for them to go by. But in ignoring the kind of empirical situation to which their themes pertain and in failing to supply directions for experimental pointing and searching they become non-empirical. Hence it may be asserted that the final issue of empirical method is whether the guide and standard of beliefs and conduct lies within or without the *shareable* situations of life. The ultimate accusation levelled against professedly non-empirical philosophies is that in casting aspersion upon the events and objects of experience, they deny the power of common life to develop its own regulative methods and to furnish from within itself adequate goals, ideals, and criteria. Thus in effect they claim a private access to truth and deprive things of common experience of the enlightenment and guidance that philosophy might otherwise derive from them. The transcendentalist has conspired with his archenemy, the sensualist, to narrow the acknowledged subject-matter of experience and to lessen its potencies for a wider and directed reflective choice. Respect for experience is respect for its possibilities in thought and knowledge as well as an enforced attention to its joys and sorrows. Intellectual piety toward experience is a pre-condition of the direction of life and of tolerant and generous cooperation among men. Respect for the things of experience alone brings with it such a respect for others, the centers of experience, as is free from patronage, domination and the will to impose.

1925

FINLEY PETER DUNNE
(1867–1936)

A BOOK REVIEW *

"Well sir," said Mr. Dooley, "I jus' got hold iv a book, Hinnissy, that suits me up to th' handle, a gran' book, th' grandest iver seen. Ye know

* Reprinted from *Mr. Dooley at His Best*, edited by Elmer Ellis, by permission of Charles Scribner's Sons. Copyright, 1938.

I'm not much throubled be lithra-choor, havin' manny worries iv me own, but I'm not prejudiced agin books. I am not. Whin a rale good book comes along I'm as quick as anny wan to say it isn't so bad, an' this here book is fine. I tell ye 'tis fine."

"What is it?" Mr. Hennessy asked languidly.

"'Tis 'Th' Biography iv a Hero be Wan Who Knows.' 'Tis 'Th' Darin' Exploits iv a Brave Man be an Actual Eye Witness.' 'Tis 'Th' Account iv th' Desthruction iv Spanish Power in th' Ant Hills,' as it fell fr'm th' lips iv Tiddy Rosenfelt an' was took down be his own hands. Ye see 'twas this way, Hinnissy, as I r-read th' book. Whin Tiddy was blowed up in th' harbor iv Havana he instantly con-cluded they must be war. He debated th' question long an' earnestly an' fin'lly passed a jint resolution de-clarin' war. So far so good. But there was no wan to carry it on. What shud he do? I will lave th' janial author tell th' story in his own wurruds.

"'Th' sicrety iv war had offered me,' he says, 'th' command of a rig'-mint,' he says, 'but I cud not consint to remain in Tampa while less auda-cious heroes was at th' front,' he says. 'Besides,' he says, 'I felt I was incom-petent f'r to command a rig'mint raised be another,' he says. 'I detar-mined to raise wan iv me own,' he says. 'I selected fr'm me acquaintances in th' West,' he says, 'men that had thravelled with me acrost th' desert an' th' storm-wreathed mountain,' he says, 'sharin' me burdens an' at times confrontin' perils almost as gr-reat as anny that beset me path,' he says. 'Together we had faced th' turrors iv th' large but vilent West,' he says, 'an' these brave men had seen me with me trusty rifle shootin' down th' buffalo, th' elk, th' moose, th' gizzly bear, th' mountain goat,' he says, 'th' silver

man, an' otther ferocious beasts iv thim parts,' he says. 'An' they niver flinched,' he says. 'In a few days I had thim perfectly tamed,' he says, 'an' ready to go annywhere I led,' he says. 'On th' thransport goin' to Cubia,' he says, 'I wud stand beside wan iv these r-rough men threatin' him as an ankel, which he was in ivrything but birth, education, rank, an' courage, an' together we wud look up at th' admirable stars iv that tol-erable southern sky an' quote th' Bible fr'm Walt Whitman,' he says. 'Honest, loyal, thrue-hearted la-ads, how kind I was to thim,' he says.

"'We had no sooner landed in Cubia than it become nicissry f'r me to take command iv th' ar-rmy which I did at wanst. A number iv days was spint be me in reconnoitring, attinded on'y be me brave an' fluent body guard, Richard Harding Davis. I dis-covered that th' inimy was heavily inthrenched on th' top iv San Joon hill immejiately in front iv me. At this time it become apparent that I was handicapped be th' prisence iv th' ar-rmy,' he says. 'Wan day whin I was about to charge a block house sturdily definded by an ar-rmy corps undher Gin'ral Tamale, th' brave Castile that I aftherwards killed with a small ink-eraser that I always carry, I r-ran into th' entire military force iv th' United States lying on its stomach. 'If ye won't fight,' says I, 'let me go through,' I says. 'Who are ye?' says they. 'Colonel Rosenfelt,' says I. 'Oh, excuse me,' says th' gin'ral in command (if me mimry serves me thrue it was Miles) r-risin' to his knees an' salutin'. This showed me 'twud be impossible f'r to carry th' war to a successful conclusion unless I was free, so I sint th' ar-rmy home an' attackted San Joon hill. Ar-rmed on'y with a small thirty-two which I used in th' West to shoot th' fleet priarie dog, I climbed that precipitous ascent in th' face iv th' most gallin' fire I iver knew or heerd iv. But I had a few r-rounds iv gall mesilf an' what cared I? I dashed madly on cheerin' as I wint. Th' Spanish throops was dhrawn up in a long line in th' formation know among military men as a long line. I fired at th' man nearest to me an' I knew be th' expression iv his face that th' trusty bullet wint home. It passed through his frame, he fell, an' wan little home in far-off Catalonia was made happy be th' thought that their riprisintative had been kilt be th' future governor iv New York. Th' bullet sped on its mad flight an' passed through th' intire line fin'lly imbeddin' instelf in th' abdomen iv th' Ar-rch-bishop iv Santago eight miles away. This ended th' war.'

" 'They has been some discussion as to who was th' first man to r-reach th' summit iv San Joon hill. I will not attempt to dispute th' merits iv th' manny gallant sojers, statesmen, corryspondints, an' kinetoscope men who claim th' distinction. They ar-re all brave men an' if they wish to wear me laurels they may. I have so manny annyhow that it keeps me broke havin' thim blocked an' irned. But I will say f'r th' binifit iv posterity that I was th' on'y man I see. An' I had a tillyscope.'

"I have thried, Hinnissy," Mr. Dooley continued, "to give you a fair idee iv th' contints iv this remarkable book, but what I've tol' ye is on'y what Hogan calls an outline iv th' principal pints. Ye'll have to r-read th' book ye'ersilf to get a thrue conciption. I haven't time f'r to tell ye th' wurruk Tiddy did in ar-rmin' an' equppin' himsilf, how he fed himsilf, how he steadied himsilf in battle an' encouraged himsilf with a few wellchosen wurruds whin th' sky was

darkest. Ye'll have to take a squint into th' book ye'ersilf to larn thim things."

"I won' do it," said Mr. Hennessy. "I think Tiddy Rosenfelt is all r-right an' if he wants to blow his hor-rn lave him do it."

"Thrue f'r ye," said Mr. Dooley, "an' if his valliant deeds didn't get into this book 'twud be a long time befure they appeared in Shafter's histhry iv th' war. No man bears a gredge agin himsilf'll iver be governor iv a state. An' if Tiddy done it all he ought to say so an' relieve th' suspinse. But if I was him I'd call th' book 'Alone in Cubia.'"

1899

THEODORE ROOSEVELT
(1858–1919)

THE NEW NATIONALISM *

We come here to-day to commemorate one of the epoch-making events of the long struggle for the rights of man—the long struggle for the uplift of humanity. Our country—this great Republic—means nothing unless it means the triumph of a real democracy, the triumph of popular government, and, in the long run, of an economic system under which each man shall be guaranteed the opportunity to show the best that there is in him. That is why the history of America is now the central feature of the history of the world; for the world has set its face hopefully toward our democracy; and, O my fellow citizens, each one of you carries on your shoulders not only the burden of doing well for the sake of your own

* Reprinted from *Social Justice and Popular Rule* by Theodore Roosevelt; copyright 1925 by Charles Scribner's Sons; used by permission of the publishers.

country, but the burden of doing well and of seeing that this nation does well for the sake of mankind.

There have been two great crises in our country's history: first, when it was formed, and then, again, when it was perpetuated; and, in the second of these great crises—in the time of stress and strain which culminated in the Civil War, on the outcome of which depended the justification of what had been done earlier, you men of the Grand Army, you men who fought through the Civil War, not only did you justify your generation, not only did you render life worth living for our generation, but you justified the wisdom of Washington and Washington's colleagues. If this Republic had been founded by them only to be split asunder into fragments when the strain came, then the judgment of the world would have been that Washington's work was not worth doing. It was you who crowned Washington's work, as you carried to achievement the high purpose of Abraham Lincoln.

Now, with this second period of our history the name of John Brown will be forever associated; and Kansas was the theatre upon which the first act of the second of our great national life dramas was played. It was the result of the struggle in Kansas which determined that our country should be in deed as well as in name devoted to both union and freedom; that the great experiment of democratic government on a national scale should succeed and not fail. In name we had the Declaration of Independence in 1776; but we gave the lie by our acts to the words of the Declaration of Independence until 1865; and words count for nothing except in so far as they represent acts. This is true everywhere; but, O my friends, it should be truest of all in political life.

A broken promise is bad enough in private life. It is worse in the field of politics. No man is worth his salt in public life who makes on the stump a pledge which he does not keep after election; and, if he makes such a pledge and does not keep it, hunt him out of public life. I care for the great deeds of the past chiefly as spurs to drive us onward in the present. I speak of the men of the past partly that they may be honored by our praise of them, but more that they may serve as examples for the future.

It was a heroic struggle; and, as is inevitable with all such struggles, it had also a dark and terrible side. Very much was done of good, and much also of evil; and, as was inevitable in such a period of revolution, often the same man did both good and evil. For our great good fortune as a nation, we, the people of the United States as a whole, can now afford to forget the evil, or, at least, to remember it without bitterness, and to fix our eyes with pride only on the good that was accomplished. Even in ordinary times there are very few of us who do not see the problems of life as through a glass, darkly; and when the glass is clouded by the murk of furious popular passion, the vision of the best and the bravest is dimmed. Looking back, we are all of us now able to do justice to the valor and the disinterestedness and the love of the right, as to each it was given to see the right, shown both by the men of the North and the men of the South in that contest which was finally decided by the attitude of the West. We can admire the heroic valor, the sincerity, the self-devotion shown alike by the men who wore the blue and the men who wore the gray; and our sadness that such men should have had to fight one another is tempered by the glad knowledge that ever hereafter their descendants shall be found fighting side by side, struggling in peace as well as in war for the uplift of their common country, all alike resolute to raise to the highest pitch of honor and usefulness the nation to which they all belong. As for the veterans of the Grand Army of the Republic, they deserve honor and recognition such as is paid to no other citizens of the Republic; for to them the republic owes its all; for to them it owes its very existence. It is because of what you and your comrades did in the dark years that we of to-day walk, each of us, head erect, and proud that we belong, not to one of a dozen little squabbling contemptible commonwealths, but to the mightiest nation upon which the sun shines.

I do not speak of this struggle of the past merely from the historic standpoint. Our interest is primarily in the application to-day of the lessons taught by the contest of half a century ago. It is of little use for us to pay lip-loyalty to the mighty men of the past unless we sincerely endeavor to apply to the problems of the present precisely the qualities which in other crises enabled the men of that day to meet those crises. It is half melancholy and half amusing to see the way in which well-meaning people gather to do honor to the men who, in company with John Brown, and under the lead of Abraham Lincoln, faced and solved the great problems of the nineteenth century, while, at the same time, these same good people nervously shrink from, or frantically denounce, those who are trying to meet the problems of the twentieth century in the spirit which was accountable for the successful solution of the problems of Lincoln's time.

Of that generation of men to whom we owe so much, the man to whom we owe most is, of course, Lincoln.

Part of our debt to him is because he forecast our present struggle and saw the way out. He said:

"I hold that while man exists it is his duty to improve not only his own condition, but to assist in ameliorating mankind."

And again:

"Labor is prior to, and independent of, capital. Capital is only the fruit of labor, and could never have existed if labor had not first existed. Labor is the superior of capital, and deserves much the higher consideration."

If that remark was original with me, I should be even more strongly denounced as a Communist agitator than I shall be anyhow. It is Lincoln's. I am only quoting it; and that is one side; that is the side the capitalist should hear. Now, let the working man hear his side.

"Capital has its rights, which are as worthy of protection as any other rights. . . . Nor should this lead to a war upon the owners of property. Property is the fruit of labor; . . . property is desirable; is a positive good in the world."

And then comes a thoroughly Lincolnlike sentence:

"Let not him who is houseless pull down the house of another, but let him work diligently and build one for himself, thus by example assuring that his own shall be safe from violence when built."

It seems to me that, in these words, Lincoln took substantially the attitude that we ought to take; he showed the proper sense of proportion in his relative estimates of capital and labor, of human rights and property rights. Above all, in this speech, as in many others, he taught a lesson in wise kindliness and charity; an indispensable lesson to us of to-day. But this wise kindliness and charity never weakened his arm or numbed his heart. We cannot afford weakly to blind ourselves to the actual conflict which faces us to-day. The issue is joined, and we must fight or fail.

In every wise struggle for human betterment one of the main objects, and often the only object, has been to achieve in large measure equality of opportunity. In the struggle for this great end, nations rise from barbarism to civilization, and through it people press forward from one stage of enlightenment to the next. One of the chief factors in progress is the destruction of special privilege. The essence of any struggle for healthy liberty has always been, and must always be, to take from some one man or class of men the right to enjoy power, or wealth, or position, or immunity, which has not been earned by service to his or their fellows. That is what you fought for in the Civil War, and that is what we strive for now.

At many stages in the advance of humanity, this conflict between the men who possess more than they have earned and the men who have earned more than they possess is the central condition of progress. In our day it appears as the struggle of freemen to gain and hold the right of self-government as against the special interests, who twist the methods of free government into machinery for defeating the popular will. At every stage, and under all circumstances, the essence of the struggle is to equalize opportunity, destroy privilege, and give to the life and citizenship of every individual the highest possible value both to himself and to the commonwealth. That is nothing new. All I ask in civil life is what you fought for in the Civil War. I ask that civil life be carried on according to the spirit in which the army was carried on. You never get perfect justice, but the effort in han-

dling the army was to bring to the front the men who could do the job. Nobody grudged promotion to Grant, or Sherman, or Thomas, or Sheridan, because they earned it. The only complaint was when a man got promotion which he did not earn.

Practical equality of opportunity for all citizens, when we achieve it, will have two great results. First, every man will have a fair chance to make of himself all that in him lies; to reach the highest point to which his capacities, unassisted by special privilege of his own and unhampered by the special privilege of others, can carry him, and to get for himself and his family substantially what he has earned. Second, equality of opportunity means that the commonwealth will get from every citizen the highest service of which he is capable. No man who carries the burden of the special privileges of another can give to the commonwealth that service to which it is fairly entitled.

I stand for the square deal. But when I say that I am for the square deal, I mean not merely that I stand for fair play under the present rules of the game, but that I stand for having those rules changed so as to work for a more substantial equality of opportunity and of reward for equally good service. One word of warning, which, I think, is hardly necessary in Kansas. When I say I want a square deal for the poor man, I do not mean that I want a square deal for the man who remains poor because he has not got the energy to work for himself. If a man who has had a chance will not make good, then he has got to quit. And you men of the Grand Army, you want justice for the brave man who fought, and punishment for the coward who shirked his work. Is not that so?

Now, this means that our government, National and State, must be freed from the sinister influence or control of special interests. Exactly as the special interests of cotton and slavery threatened our political integrity before the Civil War, so now the great special business interests too often control and corrupt the men and methods of government for their own profit. We must drive the special interests out of politics. That is one of our tasks to-day. Every special interest is entitled to justice—full, fair, and complete—and, now, mind you, if there were any attempt by mob-violence to plunder and work harm to the special interest, whatever it may be, that I most dislike, and the wealthy man, whomsoever he may be, for whom I have the greatest contempt, I would fight for him, and you would if you were worth your salt. He should have justice. For every special interest is entitled to justice, but not one is entitled to a vote in Congress, to a voice on the bench, or to representation in any public office. The Constitution guarantees protection to property, and we must make that promise good. But it does not give the right of suffrage to any corporation.

The true friend of property, the true conservative, is he who insists that property shall be the servant and not the master of the commonwealth; who insists that the creature of man's making shall be the servant and not the master of the man who made it. The citizens of the United States must effectively control the mighty commercial forces which they have themselves called into being.

There can be no effective control of corporations while their political activity remains. To put an end to it will be neither a short nor an easy task, but it can be done.

We must have complete and effective publicity of corporate affairs, so that the people may know beyond per-adventure whether the corporations obey the law and whether their management entitles them to the confidence of the public. It is necessary that laws should be passed to prohibit the use of corporate funds directly or indirectly for political purposes; it is still more necessary that such laws should be thoroughly enforced. Corporate expenditures for political purposes, and especially such expenditures by public-service corporations, have supplied one of the principal sources of corruption in our political affairs.

It has become entirely clear that we must have government supervision of the capitalization, not only of public-service corporations, including, particularly, railways, but of all corporations doing an interstate business. I do not wish to see the nation forced into the ownership of the railways if it can possibly be avoided, and the only alternative is thoroughgoing and effective regulation, which shall be based on a full knowledge of all the facts, including a physical valuation of property. This physical valuation is not needed, or, at least, is very rarely needed, for fixing rates; but it is needed as the basis of honest capitalization.

We have come to recognize that franchises should never be granted except for a limited time, and never without proper provision for compensation to the public. It is my personal belief that the same kind and degree of control and supervision which should be exercised over public-service corporations should be extended also to combinations which control necessaries of life, such as meat, oil, and coal, or which deal in them on an important scale. I have no doubt that the ordinary man who has control of them is much like ourselves. I have no doubt he would like to do well, but I want to have enough supervision to help him realize that desire to do well.

I believe that the officers, and, especially, the directors, of corporations should be held personally responsible when any corporation breaks the law.

Combinations in industry are the result of an imperative economic law which cannot be repealed by political legislation. The effort at prohibiting all combination has substantially failed. The way out lies, not in attempting to prevent such combinations, but in completely controlling them in the interest of the public welfare. For that purpose the Federal Bureau of Corporations is an agency of first importance. Its powers, and, therefore, its efficiency, as well as that of the Interstate Commerce Commission, should be largely increased. We have a right to expect from the Bureau of Corporations and from the Interstate Commerce Commission a very high grade of public service. We should be as sure of the proper conduct of the interstate railways and the proper management of interstate business as we are now sure of the conduct and management of the national banks, and we should have as effective supervision in one case as in the other. The Hepburn Act, and the amendment to the act in the shape in which it finally passed Congress at the last session, represent a long step in advance, and we must go yet further.

There is a wide-spread belief among our people that, under the methods of making tariffs which have hitherto obtained, the special interests are too influential. Probably this is true of both the big special interests and the little special interests. These methods have put a premium on selfishness, and, naturally, the selfish big interests have gotten more than their smaller, though equally selfish, brothers. The duty of Congress is to provide a method by which the interest of the whole people shall be all that receives consideration. To this end there must be an expert tariff commission, wholly removed from the possibility of political pressure or of improper business influence. Such a commission can find the real difference between cost of production, which is mainly the difference of labor cost here and abroad. As fast as its recommendations are made, I believe in revising one schedule at a time. A general revision of the tariff almost inevitably leads to log-rolling and the subordination of the general public interest to local and special interests.

The absence of effective State, and, especially, National, restraint upon unfair money-getting has tended to create a small class of enormously wealthy and economically powerful men, whose chief object is to hold and increase their power. The prime need is to change the conditions which enable these men to accumulate power which it is not for the general welfare that they should hold or exercise. We grudge no man a fortune which represents his own power and sagacity, when exercised with entire regard to the welfare of his fellows. Again, comrades over there, take the lesson from your own experience. Not only did you not grudge, but you gloried in the promotion of the great generals who gained their promotion by leading the army to victory. So it is with us. We grudge no man a fortune in civil life if it is honorably obtained and well used. It is not even enough that it should have been gained without doing damage to the community. We should permit it to be gained only so long as the gaining represents benefit to the community.

This, I know, implies a policy of a far more active governmental interference with social and economic conditions in this country than we have yet had, but I think we have got to face the fact that such an increase in governmental control is now necessary.

No man should receive a dollar unless that dollar has been fairly earned. Every dollar received should represent a dollar's worth of service rendered—not gambling in stocks, but service rendered. The really big fortune, the swollen fortune, by the mere fact of its size acquires qualities which differentiate it in kind as well as in degree from what is possessed by men of relatively small means. Therefore, I believe in a graduated income tax on big fortunes, and in another tax which is far more easily collected and far more effective—a graduated inheritance tax on big fortunes, properly safeguarded against evasion and increasing rapidly in amount with the size of the estate.

The people of the United States suffer from periodical financial panics to a degree substantially unknown among the other nations which approach us in financial strength. There is no reason why we should suffer what they escape. It is of profound importance that our financial system should be promptly investigated, and so thoroughly and effectively revised as to make it certain that hereafter our currency will no longer fail at critical times to meet our needs.

It is hardly necessary for me to repeat that I believe in an efficient army and a navy large enough to secure for us abroad that respect which is the surest guaranty of peace. A word of special warning to my fellow citizens who are as progressive as I hope I am. I want them to keep up their interest in our internal affairs; and I want them also continually to remember Uncle Sam's interests abroad. Justice and fair dealing among nations rest upon principles identical with those which control justice and fair dealing among the individuals of which nations are composed, with the vital exception that each nation must do its own part in international police work. If you get into trouble here, you can call for the police; but if Uncle Sam gets into trouble, he has got to be his own policeman, and I want to see him strong enough to encourage the peaceful aspirations of other peoples in connection with us. I believe in national friendships and heartiest goodwill to all nations; but national friendships, like those between men, must be founded on respect as well as on liking, on forbearance as well as upon trust. I should be heartily ashamed of any American who did not try to make the American Government act as justly toward the other nations in international relations as he himself would act toward any individual in private relations. I should be heartily ashamed to see us wrong a weaker power, and I should hang my head forever if we tamely suffered wrong from a stronger power.

Of conservation I shall speak more at length elsewhere. Conservation means development as much as it does protection. I recognize the right and duty of this generation to develop and use the natural resources of our land; but I do not recognize the right to waste them, or to rob, by wasteful use, the generations that come after us. I ask nothing of the nation except that it so behave as each farmer here behaves with reference to his own children. That farmer is a poor creature who skins the land and leaves it worthless to his children. The farmer is a good farmer who, having enabled the land to support himself and to provide for the education of his children, leaves it to them a little better than he found it himself. I believe the same thing of a nation.

Moreover, I believe that the natural resources must be used for the benefit of all our people, and not monopolized for the benefit of the few, and here again is another case in which I am accused of taking a revolutionary attitude. People forget now that one hundred years ago there were public men of good character who advocated the nation selling its public lands in great quantities, so that the nation could get the most money out of it, and giving it to the men who could cultivate it for their own uses. We took the proper democratic ground that the land should be granted in small sections to the men who were actually to till it and live on it. Now, with the water-power, with the forests, with the mines, we are brought face to face with the fact that there are many people who will go with us in conserving the resources only if they are to be allowed to exploit them for their benefit. That is one of the fundamental reasons why the special interests should be driven out of politics. Of all the questions which can come before this nation, short of the actual preservation of its existence in a great war, there is none which compares in importance with the great central task of leaving this land even a better land for our descendants than it is for us, and training them into a better race to inhabit the land and pass it on. Conservation is a great moral issue, for it involves the patriotic duty of insuring the safety and continuance of the nation. Let me add that the health and vitality of our people are at least as well worth conserving as their forests, waters, lands, and minerals, and in this great work the national government must bear a most important part.

I have spoken elsewhere also of the great task which lies before the farmers of the country to get for themselves and their wives and children not only the benefits of better farming, but also those of better business methods and better conditions of life on the farm. The burden of this great task will fall, as it should, mainly upon the great organizations of the farmers themselves. I am glad it will, for I believe they are all well able to handle it. In particular, there are strong reasons why the Departments of Agriculture of the various States, the United States Department of Agriculture, and the agricultural colleges and experiment stations should extend their work to cover all phases of farm life, instead of limiting themselves, as they have far too often limited themselves in the past, solely to the question of the production of crops. And now a special word to the farmer. I want to see him make the farm as fine a farm as it can be made; and let him remember to see that the improvement goes on indoors as well as out; let him remember that the farmer's wife should have her share of thought and attention just as much as the farmer himself.

Nothing is more true than that excess of every kind is followed by reaction; a fact which should be pondered by reformer and reactionary alike. We are face to face with new conceptions of the relations of property to human welfare, chiefly because certain advocates of the rights of property as against the rights of men have been pushing their claims too far. The man who wrongly holds that every human right is secondary to his profit must now give way to the advocate of human welfare, who rightly maintains that every man holds his property subject to the general right of the community to regulate its use to whatever degree the public welfare may require it.

But I think we may go still further. The right to regulate the use of wealth in the public interest is universally admitted. Let us admit also the right to regulate the terms and conditions of labor, which is the chief element of wealth, directly in the interest of the common good. The fundamental thing to do for every man is to give him a chance to reach a place in which he will make the greatest possible contribution to the public welfare. Understand what I say there. Give him a chance, not push him up if he will not be pushed. Help any man who stumbles; if he lies down, it is a poor job to try to carry him; but if he is a worthy man, try your best to see that he gets a chance to show the worth that is in him. No man can be a good citizen unless he has a wage more than sufficient to cover the bare cost of living, and hours of labor short enough so that after his day's work is done he will have time and energy to bear his share in the management of the community, to help in carrying the general load. We keep countless men from being good citizens by the conditions of life with which we surround them. We need comprehensive workmen's compensation acts, both State and National laws to regulate child labor and work for women, and, especially, we need in our common schools not merely education in book-learning, but also practical training for daily life and work. We need to enforce better sanitary conditions for our workers and to extend the use of safety appliances for our workers in industry and commerce, both within and between the States. Also, friends, in the interest of the working man himself we need to set our faces like flint against mob-violence just as

against corporate greed; against violence and injustice and lawlessness by wage-workers just as much as against lawless cunning and greed and selfish arrogance of employers. If I could ask but one thing of my fellow countrymen, my request would be that, whenever they go in for reform, they remember the two sides, and that they always exact justice from one side as much as from the other. I have small use for the public servant who can always see and denounce the corruption of the capitalist, but who cannot persuade himself, especially before election, to say a word about lawless mob-violence. And I have equally small use for the man, be he a judge on the bench, or editor of a great paper, or wealthy and influential private citizen, who can see clearly enough and denounce the lawlessness of mob-violence, but whose eyes are closed so that he is blind when the question is one of corruption in business on a gigantic scale. Also remember what I said about excess in reformer and reactionary alike. If the reactionary man, who thinks of nothing but the rights of property, could have his way, he would bring about a revolution; and one of my chief fears in connection with progress comes because I do not want to see our people, for lack of proper leadership, compelled to follow men whose intentions are excellent, but whose eyes are a little too wild to make it really safe to trust them. Here in Kansas there is one paper which habitually denounces me as the tool of Wall Street, and at the same time frantically repudiates the statement that I am a Socialist on the ground that that is an unwarranted slander of the Socialists.

National efficiency has many factors. It is a necessary result of the principle of conservation widely applied. In the end it will determine our failure or success as a nation. National efficiency has to do, not only with natural resources and with men, but it is equally concerned with institutions. The State must be made efficient for the work which concerns only the people of the State; and the nation for that which concerns all the people. There must remain no neutral ground to serve as a refuge for lawbreakers, and especially for lawbreakers of great wealth, who can hire the vulpine legal cunning which will teach them how to avoid both jurisdictions. It is a misfortune when the national legislature fails to do its duty in providing a national remedy, so that the only national activity is the purely negative activity of the judiciary in forbidding the State to exercise power in the premises.

I do not ask for overcentralization; but I do ask that we work in a spirit of broad and far-reaching nationalism when we work for what concerns our people as a whole. We are all Americans. Our common interests are as broad as the continent. I speak to you here in Kansas exactly as I would speak in New York or Georgia, for the most vital problems are those which affect us all alike. The National Government belongs to the whole American people, and where the whole American people are interested, that interest can be guarded effectively only by the National Government. The betterment which we seek must be accomplished, I believe, mainly through the National Government.

The American people are right in demanding that New Nationalism, without which we cannot hope to deal with new problems. The New Nationalism puts the national need before sectional or personal advantage. It is impatient of the utter confusion that results from local legislatures attempting to treat national issues as local issues. It is still more impatient of the impotence which springs from overdivision of governmental powers, the impotence which makes it possible for local selfishness or for legal cunning, hired by wealthy special interests, to bring national activities to a deadlock. This New Nationalism regards the executive power as the steward of the public welfare. It demands of the judiciary that it shall be interested primarily in human welfare rather than in property, just as it demands that the representative body shall represent all the people rather than any one class or section of the people.

I believe in shaping the ends of government to protect property as well as human welfare. Normally, and in the long run, the ends are the same; but whenever the alternative must be faced, I am for men and not for property, as you were in the Civil War. I am far from underestimating the importance of dividends; but I rank dividends below human character. Again, I do not have any sympathy with the reformer who says he does not care for dividends. Of course, economic welfare is necessary, for a man must pull his own weight and be able to support his family. I know well that the reformers must not bring upon the people economic ruin, or the reforms themselves will go down in the ruin. But we must be ready to face temporary disaster, whether or not brought on by those who will war against us to the knife. Those who oppose all reform will do well to remember that ruin in its worst form is inevitable if our national life brings us nothing better than swollen fortunes for the few and the triumph in both politics and business of a sordid and selfish materialism.

If our political institutions were

perfect, they would absolutely prevent the political domination of money in any part of our affairs. We need to make our political representatives more quickly and sensitively responsive to the people whose servants they are. More direct action by the people in their own affairs under proper safeguards is vitally necessary. The direct primary is a step in this direction, if it is associated with a corrupt-practices act effective to prevent the advantage of the man willing recklessly and unscrupulously to spend money over his more honest competitor. It is particularly important that all moneys received or expended for campaign purposes should be publicly accounted for, not only after election, but before election as well. Political action must be made simpler, easier, and freer from confusion for every citizen. I believe that the prompt removal of unfaithful or incompetent public servants should be made easy and sure in whatever way experience shall show to be most expedient in any given class of cases.

One of the fundamental necessities in a representative government such as ours is to make certain that the men to whom the people delegate their power shall serve the people by whom they are elected, and not the special interests. I believe that every national officer, elected or appointed, should be forbidden to perform any service or receive any compensation, directly or indirectly, from interstate corporations; and a similar provision could not fail to be useful within the States.

The object of government is the welfare of the people. The material progress and prosperity of a nation are desirable chiefly so far as they lead to the moral and material welfare of all good citizens. Just in proportion as the average man and woman are honest, capable of sound judgment and high ideals, active in public affairs—but, first of all, sound in their home life, and the father and mother of healthy children whom they bring up well—just so far, and no farther, we may count our civilization a success. We must have—I believe we have already —a genuine and permanent moral awakening, without which no wisdom of legislation or administration really means anything; and, on the other hand, we must try to secure the social and economic legislation without which any improvement due to purely moral agitation is necessarily evanescent. Let me again illustrate by a reference to the Grand Army. You could not have won simply as a disorderly and disorganized mob. You needed generals; you needed careful administration of the most advanced type; and a good commissary—the cracker line. You well remember that success was necessary in many different lines in order to bring about general success. You had to have the administration at Washington good, just as you had to have the administration in the field; and you had to have the work of the generals good. You could not have triumphed without that administration and leadership; but it would all have been worthless if the average soldier had not had the right stuff in him. He had to have the right stuff in him, or you could not get it out of him. In the last analysis, therefore, vitally necessary though it was to have the right kind of organization and the right kind of generalship, it was even more vitally necessary that the average soldier should have the fighting edge, the right character. So it is in our civil life. No matter how honest and decent we are in our private lives, if we do not have the right kind of law and the right kind of administration of the law, we cannot go forward as a nation. That is imperative; but it must be an addition to, and not a substitution for, the qualities that make us good citizens. In the last analysis, the most important elements in any man's career must be the sum of those qualities which, in the aggregate, we speak of as character. If he has not got it, then no law that the wit of man can devise, no administration of the law by the boldest and strongest executive, will avail to help him. We must have the right kind of character—character that makes a man, first of all, a good man in the home, a good father, a good husband—that makes a man a good neighbor. You must have that, and, then, in addition, you must have the kind of law and the kind of administration of the law which will give to those qualities in the private citizen the best possible chance for development. The prime problem of our nation is to get the right type of good citizenship, and, to get it, we must have progress, and our public men must be genuinely progressive.

1910

CHARLES A. BEARD
(1874–1948)

AN ECONOMIC INTERPRETATION OF THE CONSTITUTION OF THE UNITED STATES *

CHAPTER I

HISTORICAL INTERPRETATION IN THE UNITED STATES

Broadly speaking, three schools of interpretation have dominated Amer-

* Reprinted from Charles Beard's *An Economic Interpretation of the Constitution of the United States*. Copyright 1913, 1935, by The Macmillan Company. By permission of The Macmillan Company, publishers.

ican historical research and generalization. The first of these, which may be justly associated with the name of Bancroft, explains the larger achievements in our national life by reference to the peculiar moral endowments of a people acting under divine guidance; or perhaps it would be more correct to say, it sees in the course of our development the working out of a higher will than that of man. There is to be observed in the history of the struggle for the Constitution, to use Bancroft's words, "the movement of the divine power which gives unity to the universe, and order and connection to events." [1]

Notwithstanding such statements, scattered through Bancroft's pages, it is impossible to describe in a single phrase the ideal that controlled his principles of historical construction, because he was so often swayed by his deference to the susceptibilities of the social class from which he sprang and by the exigencies of the public life in which he played a by no means inconspicuous part. Even telling the whole truth did not lie upon his conscience, for, speaking on the question of the number of Americans who were descendants from transported felons and indented servants, he said that "Having a hand full, he opened his little finger." [2]

Nevertheless, Bancroft constantly recurs in his writings to that "higher power" which is operating in human affairs, although he avoids citing specific events which may be attributed to it. It appears to him to be the whole course of history, rather than any event or set of events, which justifies his theory. "However great," he says, "may be the number of those

[1] *The History of the Constitution of the United States* (1882 ed.), Vol. II, p. 284.

[2] American Historical Review, Vol. II, p. 13.

who persuade themselves that there is in man nothing superior to himself, history interposes with evidence that tyranny and wrong lead inevitably to decay; that freedom and right, however hard may be the struggle, always prove resistless. Through this assurance ancient nations learn to renew their youth; the rising generation is incited to take a generous part in the grand drama of time; and old age, staying itself upon sweet Hope as its companion and cherisher, not bating a jot of courage, nor seeing cause to argue against the hand or the will of a higher power, stands waiting in the tranquil conviction that the path of humanity is still fresh with the dews of morning, that the Redeemer of the nations liveth." [3]

The second school of historical interpretation, which in the order of time followed that of Bancroft, may be called the Teutonic, because it ascribes the wonderful achievements of the English-speaking peoples to the peculiar political genius of the Germanic race. Without distinctly repudiating the doctrine of the "higher power" in history, it finds the secret to the "free" institutional development of the Anglo-Saxon world in innate racial qualities.

The thesis of this school is, in brief, as follows. The Teutonic peoples were originally endowed with singular political talents and aptitudes; Teutonic tribes invaded England and destroyed the last vestiges of the older Roman and British culture; they then set an example to the world in the development of "free" government. Descendants of this specially gifted race settled America and fashioned their institutions after old English models. The full fruition of their political genius was reached in the creation of the Federal Constitution.

For more than a generation the Teutonic theory of our institutions

deeply influenced historical research in the United States; but it was exhausted in the study of local government rather than of great epochs; and it produced no monument of erudition comparable to Stubbs' *Constitutional History of England*. Whatever may be said of this school, which has its historical explanation and justification,[4] it served one exceedingly useful purpose: it was scrupulously careful in the documentation of its preconceptions and thus cultivated a more critical spirit than that which characterized the older historians.[5]

The third school of historical research is not to be characterized by any phrase. It is marked rather by an absence of hypotheses. Its representatives, seeing the many pitfalls which beset the way of earlier writers, have resolutely turned aside from "interpretation" in the larger sense, and concerned themselves with critical editions of the documents and with the "impartial" presentation of related facts. This tendency in American scholarship has been fruitful in its results, for it has produced more care in the use of historical sources and has given us many excellent and accurate surveys of outward events which are indispensable to the student who would inquire more deeply into underlying causes.[6]

[3] Bancroft, *op. cit.*, Vol. I, p. 6.

[4] It has been left to a Russian to explain to Englishmen the origin of Teutonism in historical writing. See the introduction to Vinogradoff, *Villainage in England*. W. J. Ashley, in his preface to the translation of Fustel de Coulanges, *Origin of Property in Land*, throws some light on the problem, but does not attempt a systematic study.

[5] Note the painstaking documentation for the first chapters in Stubbs' great work.

[6] What Morley has said of Macaulay is true of many eminent American historical writers: "A popular author must, in a thoroughgoing way, take the accepted maxims for granted. He must

Such historical writing, however, bears somewhat the same relation to scientific history which systematic botany bears to ecology; that is, it classifies and orders phenomena, but does not explain their proximate or remote causes and relations. The predominance of such a historical ideal in the United States and elsewhere is not altogether inexplicable; for interpretative schools seem always to originate in social antagonisms.[7] The monarchy, in its rise and development, was never correctly understood as long as it was regarded by all as a mystery which must not be waded into, as James I put it, by ordinary mortals. Without the old régime there would have been no Turgot and Voltaire; Metternich and Joseph de Maistre came after the Revolution.

But the origin of different schools of interpretation in controversies and the prevalence of many mere preconceptions bolstered with a show of learning should not lead us to reject without examination any new hypothesis, such as the theory of economic determinism, on the general assumption of Pascal "that the will, the

imagination, the disorders of the body, the thousand concealed infirmities of the intelligence conspire to reduce our discovery of justice and truth to a process of haphazard, in which we more often miss than hit the mark." Such a doctrine of pessimism would make of equal value for the student who would understand, for instance, such an important matter as the origin of the state, Mr. Edward Jenk's severely scientific *History of Politics* and Dr. Nathaniel Johnston's *The Excellency of Monarchical Government, especially the English Monarchy, wherein is largely treated of the Several Benefits of Kingly Government and the Inconvenience of Commonwealths. . . . Likewise the Duty of Subjects and the Mischief of Faction, Sedition, and Rebellion,* published in 1686.

It is not without significance, however, that almost the only work in economic interpretation which has been done in the United States seems to have been inspired at the University of Wisconsin by Professor Turner, now of Harvard. Under the direction of this original scholar and thinker, the influence of the material circumstances of the frontier on American politics was first clearly pointed out. Under his direction also the most important single contribution to the interpretation of the movement for the federal Constitution was made: O. G. Libby's *Geographical Distribution of the Vote of the Thirteen States on the Federal Constitution.*

In a preface to this work, Professor Turner remarks that the study was designed to contribute "to an understanding of the relations between the political history of the United States, and the physiographic, social, and economic conditions underlying this history. . . . It is believed that many phases of our political history have

---

suppress any whimsical fancy for applying the Socratic elenchus; or any other engine of criticism, scepticism, or verification to those sentiments or current precepts or morals which may in truth be very equivocal and may be much neglected in practice, but which the public opinion of his time requires to be treated in theory and in literature as if they had been cherished and held *semper, ubique, et ab omnibus." Miscellanies,* Vol. I, p. 272.

[7] For instance, intimate connections can be shown between the vogue of Darwinism and the competitive ideals of the mid-Victorian middle-class in England. Darwin got one of his leading ideas, the struggle for existence, from Malthus, who originated it as a club to destroy the social reformers, Godwin, Condorcet, and others, and then gave it a serious scientific guise as an afterthought.

been obscured by the attention paid to state boundaries and to the sectional lines of North and South. At the same time the economic interpretation of our history has been neglected. In the study of the persistence of the struggle for state particularism in American constitutional history, it was inevitable that writers should make prominent the state as a political factor. But, from the point of view of the rise and growth of sectionalism and nationalism, it is much more important to note the existence of great social and economic areas, independent of state lines, which have acted as units in political history, and which have changed their political attitude as they changed their economic organization and divided into new groups." [8]

Although the hypothesis that economic elements are the chief factors in the development of political institutions has thus been used in one or two serious works, and has been more or less discussed as a philosophic theory,[9] it has not been applied to the study of American history at large—certainly not with that infinite detailed analysis which it requires. Nor has it received at the hands of professed historians that attention which its significance warrants. On the contrary, there has been a tendency to treat it with scant courtesy and to dismiss it with a sharpness bordering on contempt.[10] Such summary judgment is, of course, wholly unwarranted and premature; for as Dr. William Cunningham remarks, the validity of no hypothesis can be determined until it has been worked to its utmost limits. It is easier to write a bulky volume from statutes, congressional debates,[11] memoirs, and diplomatic notes than it is to ascertain the geographical distribution and political significance of any important group of economic factors. The theory of economic determinism has not been tried out in American history, and until it is tried out, it cannot be found wanting.

Sadly as the economic factors have been ignored in historical studies, the neglect has been all the more pronounced in the field of private and public law. The reason for this is apparent. The aim of instruction in these subjects is intensely practical; there are few research professorships in law; and the "case" system of teaching discourages attempts at generalization and surveys.[12] Not even the elementary work has been done. There has been no generous effort to describe the merely superficial aspects of the development of private law in the United States. There has been no

[10] Vincent, in his treatise on *Historical Research* (1911), dismisses the economic theory without critical examination.

[11] The *Congressional Record* requires more care in use than any other great source of information on American politics.

[12] Attention should be drawn, however, to the good work which is being done in the translation of several European legal studies, the "Modern Legal Philosophy Series," under the editorial direction of the Association of American Law Schools. Perhaps the most hopeful sign of the times is the growth of interest in comparative jurisprudence. See Borchard, "Jurisprudence in Germany," Columbia Law Review, April, 1912.

[8] See also the valuable and suggestive writings on American history by Professor W. E. Dodd, of Chicago University; W. A. Schaper, "Sectionalism in South Carolina," *American Historical Association Report* (1900), Vol. I; A. Bentley, *The Process of Government;* C. H. Ambler, *Sectionalism in Virginia.* There are three works by socialist writers that deserve study: Simons, *Social Forces in American History;* Gustavus Myers, *History of Great American Fortunes* and *History of the Supreme Court.*

[9] See Seligman, *The Economic Interpretation of History.*

concerted attempt to bring together and make available to students the raw materials of such a history. Most of the current views on the history of our law are derived from occasional disquisitions of judges which are all too frequently shot through with curious errors of fact and conception.

Nor has England advanced far beyond us in the critical interpretation of legal evolution—its explanation in terms of, or in relation to, the shifting economic processes and methods in which the law is tangled. It is true that English scholars have produced admirable histories of the law in its outward aspects, such as the monumental work of Pollock and Maitland; and they have made marvellous collections of raw materials, like the publications of the Selden Society. But apart from scattered and brilliant suggestions thrown off occasionally by Maitland [13] in passing, no interpretation has been ventured, and no effort has been made to connect legal phases with economic changes.

In the absence of a critical analysis of legal evolution, all sorts of vague abstractions dominate most of the

thinking that is done in the field of law. The characteristic view of the subject taken by American commentators and lawyers immersed in practical affairs is perhaps summed up as finely by Carter as by any writer. "In free, popular states," he says, "the law springs from and is made by the people; and as the process of building it up consists in applying, from time to time, to human actions the popular ideal or standard of justice, justice is [the] only interest consulted in the work. . . . The law of England and America has been a pure development proceeding from a constant endeavor to apply to the civil conduct of men the ever advancing standard of justice." [14] In other words, law is made out of some abstract stuff known as "justice." What set the standard in the beginning and why does it advance?

The devotion to deductions from "principles" exemplified in particular cases, which is such a distinguishing sign of American legal thinking, has the same effect upon correct analysis which the adherence to abstract terms had upon the advancement of learning—as pointed out by Bacon. The absence of any consideration of the social and economic elements determining the thought of the thinkers themselves is all the more marked when contrasted with the penetration shown by European savants like Jhering, Menger, and Stammler. Indeed, almost the only indication of a possible economic interpretation to be found in current American jurisprudence is implicit in the writings of a few scholars, like Professor Roscoe Pound and Professor Goodnow, [15] and

[13] For examples of Maitland's suggestiveness, see the English Historical Review, Vol. IX, p. 439, for a side light on the effect of money economy on the manor and consequently on feudal law. See also the closing pages of his *Constitutional History of England,* where he makes constitutional law in large part the history of the law of real property. "If we are to learn anything about the constitution, it is necessary first and foremost that we should learn a good deal about the land law. We can make no progress whatever in the history of parliament without speaking of tenure; indeed our whole constitutional law seems at times to be but an appendix to the law of real property" (p. 538). Maitland's entire marvellous chapter on "The Definition of Constitutional Law" deserves the most careful study and reflection. He was entirely emancipated from bondage to systematists (p. 539).

[14] J. C. Carter, *The Proposed Codification of Our Common Law* (1884), pp. 6–8.

[15] Of the newer literature on law, see the following articles by Professor

in occasional opinions rendered by Mr. Justice Holmes of the Supreme Court of the United States.[16]

What has here been said about our private law may be more than repeated about our constitutional history and law. This subject, though it has long held an honorable position in the American scheme of learning, has not yet received the analytical study which its intrinsic importance merits. In the past, it has often been taught in the law schools by retired judges who treated it as a branch of natural and moral philosophy or by practical lawyers who took care for the instant need of things. Our great commentaries, Kent, Story, Miller, are never penetrating; they are generally confined to statements of fact; and designed to inculcate the spirit of reverence rather than of understanding. And of constitutional histories, strictly speaking, we have none, except the surveys of superficial aspects by Curtis and Bancroft.

Roscoe Pound: "Do we need a Philosophy of Law?" Columbia Law Review, Vol. V, p. 339; "Need of a Sociological Jurisprudence," Green Bag, Vol. XIX, p. 607; "Mechanical Jurisprudence," Columbia Law Review, Vol. VIII, p. 605; "Law in Books and Law in Action," American Law Review, Vol. XLIV, p. 12; Professor Munroe Smith, "Jurisprudence" (in the Columbia University Lectures in Arts and Sciences); Goodnow, *Social Reform and the Constitution.*

[16] Consider, for example, the following remarks by this eminent Justice in his dissenting opinion in the New York Bakery case: "This case is decided upon an economic theory which a large part of the country does not entertain. . . . The Fourteenth Amendment does not enact Mr. Herbert Spencer's *Social Statics.* . . . General propositions do not decide concrete cases. The decision will depend on a judgment or intuition more subtle than any articulate major premise." 198 U. S. 75.

[17] *Op. cit.,* Vol. II, p. 367.

In fact, the juristic theory of the origin and nature of the Constitution is marked by the same lack of analysis of determining forces which characterized older historical writing in general. It may be stated in the following manner: The Constitution proceeds from the whole people; the people are the original source of all political authority exercised under it; it is founded on broad general principles of liberty and government entertained, for some reason, by the whole people and having no reference to the interest or advantage of any particular group or class. "By calm meditation and friendly councils," says Bancroft, "they [the people] had prepared a Constitution which, in the union of freedom with strength and order, excelled every one known before. . . . In the happy morning of their existence as one of the powers of the world, they had chosen justice for their guide; and while they proceeded on their way with a well-founded confidence and joy, all the friends of mankind invoked success on their endeavor as the only hope for renovating the life of the civilized world." [17]

With less exaltation, Chief Justice Marshall states the theory, in his opinion in the case of McCulloch *v.* Maryland: "The government proceeds directly from the people; is 'ordained and established' in the name of the people; and is declared to be ordained 'in order to form a more perfect union, to establish justice, insure domestic tranquillity, and secure the blessings of liberty' to themselves and to their posterity. The assent of the states, in their sovereign capacity, is implied in calling a convention, and thus submitting that instrument to the people. But the people were at perfect liberty to accept or reject it; and their act was final. . . . The government of the Union, then (whatever may be the influence of this fact on the case) is emphatically and truly a government of the people. In form and in substance it emanates from them. Its powers are granted by them, and are to be exercised directly on them, and for their benefit. . . . It is the government of all; its powers are delegated by all; it represents all, and acts for all." [18]

In the juristic view, the Constitution is not only the work of the whole people, but it also bears in it no traces of the party conflict from which it emerged. Take, for example, any of the traditional legal definitions of the Constitution; Miller's will suffice: "A constitution, in the American sense of the word, is any instrument by which the fundamental powers of the government are established, limited, and defined, and by which these powers are distributed among the several departments for their more safe and useful exercise, for the benefit of the body politic. . . . It is not, however, the origin of private rights, nor the foundation of laws. It is not the cause, but the consequence of personal and political freedom. It declares those natural and fundamental rights of individuals, for the security and common enjoyment of which governments are established." [19]

Nowhere in the commentaries is there any evidence of the fact that the rules of our fundamental law are designed to protect any class in its rights, or secure the property of one group against the assaults of another. "The Constitution," declares Bancroft, "establishes nothing that interferes with equality and individuality. It knows

nothing of differences by descent, or opinions, of favored classes, or legalized religion, or the political power of property. It leaves the individual along-side of the individual. . . . As the sea is made up of drops, American society is composed of separate, free, and constantly moving atoms, ever in reciprocal action . . . so that the institutions and laws of the country rise out of the masses of individual thought, which, like the waters of the ocean, are rolling evermore." [20]

In turning from the vague phraseology of Bancroft to an economic interpretation of constitutional history, it is necessary to realize at the outset that law is not an abstract thing, a printed page, a volume of statutes, a statement by a judge. So far as it becomes of any consequence to the observer it must take on a real form; it must govern actions; it must determine positive relations between men; it must prescribe processes and juxtapositions.[21] A statute may be on the books for an age, but unless, under its provisions, a determinate arrangement of human relations is brought about or maintained, it exists only in the imagination. Separated from the social and economic fabric by which it is, in part, conditioned and which, in turn, it helps to condition, it has no reality.

Now, most of the law (except the elemental law of community defence) is concerned with the property relations of men, which reduced to their simple terms mean the processes by which the ownership of concrete forms of property is determined or passes from one person to another. As society becomes more settled and industrial in character, mere defence against violence (a very considerable

---

[18] 4 Wheaton, p. 316. No doubt the learned Justice was here more concerned with discrediting the doctrine of state's rights than with establishing the popular basis of our government.

[19] S. F. Miller, *Lectures on the Constitution* (1891), p. 71.

[20] *Op. cit.*, Vol. II, p. 324.

[21] See A. Bentley, *The Process of Government*.

portion of which originates in forcible attempts to change the ownership of property) becomes of relatively less importance; and property relations increase in complexity and subtlety.

But it may be said that constitutional law is a peculiar branch of the law; that it is not concerned primarily with property or with property relations, but with organs of government, the suffrage, administration. The superficiality of this view becomes apparent at a second glance. Inasmuch as the primary object of a government, beyond the mere repression of physical violence, is the making of the rules which determine the property relations of members of society, the dominant classes whose rights are thus to be determined must perforce obtain from the government such rules as are consonant with the larger interests necessary to the continuance of their economic processes, or they must themselves control the organs of government. In a stable despotism the former takes place; under any other system of government, where political power is shared by any portion of the population, the methods and nature of this control become the problem of prime importance—in fact, the fundamental problem in constitutional law. The social structure by which one type of legislation is secured and another prevented—that is, the constitution—is a secondary or derivative feature arising from the nature of the economic groups seeking positive action and negative restraint.

In what has just been said there is nothing new to scholars who have given any attention to European writings on jurisprudence. It is based in the first instance on the doctrine advanced by Jhering that law does not "grow," but is, in fact, "made"—adapted to precise interests which may be objectively determined.[22] It was not original with Jhering. Long before he worked out the concept in his epoch-making book, *Der Zweck im Recht*, Lassalle had set it forth in his elaborate *Das System der erworbenen Rechte*,[23] and long before Lassalle had thought it through, our own Madison had formulated it, after the

[22] In the preface to his first edition, Jhering says: "Die Schrift, von der ich hiermit die erste Hälfte der Öffentlichkeit übergebe, ist eine Ausläuferin von meinem Werk über den Geist des römischen Rechts. Der letzte Band desselben . . . schloss ab mit einer Grundlegung der Theorie der Rechte im subjektiven Sinn, in der ich eine von der herrschenden abweichende Begriffsbestimmung des Rechts im subjektiven Sinn gab, indem ich an Stelle des Willens, auf den jene den Begriff desselben gründete, das Interesse setze. Dem folgenden Bande war die weitere Rechtfertigung und Verwertung dieses Gesichtspunktes vorbehalten. . . . Der Begriff des Interesses nötigte mich, den Zweck ins Auge zu fassen, und das Recht im subjektiven Sinn drängte mich zu dem im objektiven Sinn, und so gestaltete sich das ursprüngliche Untersuchungsobjekt zu einem ungleich erweiterten, zu dem des gegenwärtigen Buches: der Zweck im Recht. . . . Der Grundgedanke des gegenwärtigen Werkes besteht darin, dass der Zweck der Schöpfer des gesamten Rechts ist, dass es keinen Rechtssatz gibt, der nicht einem Zweck, d.i. einem praktischen Motiv seinen Ursprung verdankt."

[23] Was ist es, das den innersten Grund unserer politischen und socialen Kämpfe bildet? Der Begriff des erworbenen Rechts ist wieder einmal streitig geworden—und dieser Streit ist es, der das Herz der heutigen Welt durchzittert und die tief inwendigste Grundlage der politisch-socialen Kämpfe des Jahrhunderts bildet. Im Juristischen, Politischen Oekonomischen ist der Begriff des erworbenen Rechts der treibende Springquell aller weitern Gestaltung, und wo sich das Juristische als das Privatrechtliche völlig von dem Politischen abzulösen scheint, da ist es noch viel politischer als das Politische selbst, dann da ist es das sociale Element. Preface to *Das System der erworbenen Rechte* by Ferdinand Lassalle.

most wide-reaching researches in history and politics.[24]

In fact, the inquiry which follows is based upon the political science of James Madison, the father of the Constitution and later President of the Union he had done so much to create. This political science runs through all of his really serious writings and is formulated in its most precise fashion in *The Federalist* [25] as follows: "The diversity in the faculties of men, from which the rights of property originate, is not less an insuperable obstacle to a uniformity of interests. The protection of these faculties is the first object of government. From the protection of different and unequal faculties of acquiring property, the possession of different degrees and kinds of property immediately results; and from the influence of these on the sentiments and views of the respective proprietors, ensues a division of society into different interests and parties. . . . The most common and durable source of factions has been the various and unequal distribution of property. Those who hold and those who are without property have ever formed distinct interests in society. Those who are creditors, and those who are debtors, fall under a like discrimination. A landed interest, a manufacturing interest, a mercantile interest, a moneyed interest, with many lesser interests, grow up of necessity in civilized nations and divide them into different classes, actuated by different sentiments and views. The regulation of these various and interfering interests forms the principal task of modern legislation, and involves the spirit of party and faction in the necessary and ordinary operations of the government."

Here we have a masterly statement of the theory of economic determinism in politics.[26] Different degrees and kinds of property inevitably exist in modern society; party doctrines and "principles" originate in the sentiments and views which the possession of various kinds of property creates in the minds of the possessors; class and group divisions based on property lie at the basis of modern government; and politics and constitutional law are inevitably a reflex of these contending interests. Those who are inclined to repudiate the hypothesis of economic determinism as a European importation must, therefore, revise their views, on learning that one of the earliest, and certainly one of the clearest, statements of it came from a profound student of politics who sat in the Convention that framed our fundamental law.

The requirements for an economic interpretation of the formation and adoption of the Constitution may be stated in a hypothetical proposition which, although it cannot be verified

[24] And before Madison's century, Harrington had perceived its significance. H. A. L. Fisher, *Republican Tradition in Europe*, p. 51.

[25] Number 10.

[26] The theory of the economic interpretation of history as stated by Professor Seligman seems as nearly axiomatic as any proposition in social science can be: "The existence of man depends upon his ability to sustain himself; the economic life is therefore the fundamental condition of all life. Since human life, however, is the life of man in society, individual existence moves within the framework of the social structure and is modified by it. What the conditions of maintenance are to the individual, the similar relations of production and consumption are to the community. To economic causes, therefore, must be traced in the last instance those transformations in the structure of society which themselves condition the relations of social classes and the various manifestations of social life." *The Economic Interpretation of History*, p. 3.

absolutely from ascertainable data, will at once illustrate the problem and furnish a guide to research and generalization.

It will be admitted without controversy that the Constitution was the creation of a certain number of men, and it was opposed by a certain number of men. Now, if it were possible to have an economic biography of all those connected with its framing and adoption,—perhaps about 160,000 men altogether,—the materials for scientific analysis and classification would be available. Such an economic biography would include a list of the real and personal property owned by all of these men and their families: lands and houses, with incumbrances, money at interest, slaves, capital invested in shipping and manufacturing, and in state and continental securities.

Suppose it could be shown from the classification of the men who supported and opposed the Constitution that there was no line of property division at all; that is, that men owning substantially the same amounts of the same kinds of property were equally divided on the matter of adoption or rejection—it would then become apparent that the Constitution had no ascertainable relation to economic groups or classes, but was the product of some abstract causes remote from the chief business of life—gaining a livelihood.

Suppose, on the other hand, that substantially all of the merchants, money lenders, security holders, manufacturers, shippers, capitalists, and financiers and their professional associates are to be found on one side in support of the Constitution and that substantially all or the major portion of the opposition came from the non-slaveholding farmers and the debtors—would it not be pretty con-

clusively demonstrated that our fundamental law was not the product of an abstraction known as "the whole people," but of a group of economic interests which must have expected beneficial results from its adoption? Obviously all the facts here desired cannot be discovered, but the data presented in the following chapters bear out the latter hypothesis, and thus a reasonable presumption in favor of the theory is created.

Of course, it may be shown (and perhaps can be shown) that the farmers and debtors who opposed the Constitution were, in fact, benefited by the general improvement which resulted from its adoption. It may likewise be shown, to take an extreme case, that the English nation derived immense advantages from the Norman Conquest and the orderly administrative processes which were introduced, as it undoubtedly did; nevertheless, it does not follow that the vague thing known as "the advancement of general welfare" or some abstraction known as "justice" was the immediate, guiding purpose of the leaders in either of these great historic changes. The point is, that the direct, impelling motive in both cases was the economic advantages which the beneficiaries expected would accrue to themselves first, from their action. Further than this, economic interpretation cannot go. It may be that some larger world-process is working through each series of historical events; but ultimate causes lie beyond our horizon.

1913, 1935

WOODROW WILSON
(1856–1924)

THE CONDITIONS OF PEACE

GENTLEMEN OF THE SENATE: On the 18th of December last I addressed an identic note to the Governments of the nations now at war, requesting them to state, more definitely than they had yet been stated by either group of belligerents, the terms upon which they would deem it possible to make peace. I spoke on behalf of humanity and of the rights of all neutral nations like our own, many of whose most vital interests the war puts in constant jeopardy.

The Central Powers united in a reply which stated merely that they were ready to meet their antagonists in conference to discuss terms of peace.

The Entente Powers have replied much more definitely, and have stated, in general terms, indeed, but with sufficient definiteness to imply details, the arrangements, guarantees, and acts of reparation which they deem to be the indispensable conditions of a satisfactory settlement.

We are that much nearer a definite discussion of the peace which shall end the present war. We are that much nearer the discussion of the international concert which must thereafter hold the world at peace. In every discussion of the peace that must end this war it is taken for granted that that peace must be followed by some definite concert of power, which will make it virtually impossible that any such catastrophe should ever overwhelm us again. Every lover of mankind, every sane and thoughtful man, must take that for granted.

I have sought this opportunity to address you because I thought that I owed it to you, as the council associated with me in the final determination of our international obligations, to disclose to you without reserve the thought and purpose that have been taking form in my mind in regard to the duty of our Government in those days to come when it will be necessary to lay afresh and upon a new plan the foundations of peace among the nations.

It is inconceivable that the people of the United States should play no part in that great enterprise. To take part in such a service will be the opportunity for which they have sought to prepare themselves by the very principles and purposes of their polity and the approved practices of their Government, ever since the days when they set up a new nation in the high and honorable hope that it might in all that it was and did show mankind the way to liberty. They cannot, in honor, withhold the service to which they are now about to be challenged. They do not wish to withhold it. But they owe it to themselves and to the other nations of the world to state the conditions under which they will feel free to render it.

That service is nothing less than this—to add their authority and their power to the authority and force of other nations to guarantee peace and justice throughout the world. Such a settlement cannot now be long postponed. It is right that before it comes this Government should frankly formulate the conditions upon which it would feel justified in asking our people to approve its formal and solemn adherence to a league for peace. I am here to attempt to state those conditions.

The present war must first be ended, but we owe it to candor and to a just regard for the opinion of mankind to say that, so far as our participation in guarantees of future peace is concerned, it makes a great deal of difference in what way and upon what terms it is ended. The treaties and agreements which bring it to an end must embody terms which will create a peace that is worth guaranteeing and preserving, a peace that will win the approval of mankind, not merely a peace that will serve the several interests and immediate aims of the nations engaged.

We shall have no voice in determining what those terms shall be, but we shall, I feel sure, have a voice in determining whether they shall be made lasting or not by the guarantees of a universal covenant, and our judgment upon what is fundamental and essential as a condition precedent to permanency should be spoken now, not afterward, when it may be too late.

No covenant of coöperative peace that does not include the peoples of the new world can suffice to keep the future safe against war, and yet there is only one sort of peace that the peoples of America could join in guaranteeing.

The elements of that peace must be elements that engage the confidence and satisfy the principles of the American Governments, elements consistent with their political faith and the practical conviction which the peoples of America have once for all embraced and undertaken to defend.

I do not mean to say that any American Government would throw any obstacle in the way of any terms of peace the Governments now at war might agree upon, or seek to upset them when made, whatever they might be. I only take it for granted that mere terms of peace between the belligerents will not satisfy even the belligerents themselves. Mere agreements may not make peace secure. It will be absolutely necessary that a force be created as a guarantor of the permanency of the settlement so much greater than the force of any nation now engaged or any alliance hitherto formed or projected, that no nation, no probable combination of nations, could face or withstand it. If the peace presently to be made is to endure, it must be a peace made secure by the organized major force of mankind.

The terms of the immediate peace agreed upon will determine whether it is a peace for which such a guarantee can be secured. The question upon which the whole future peace and policy of the world depends is this:—

Is the present war a struggle for a just and secure peace or only for a new balance of power? If it be only a struggle for a new balance of power, who will guarantee, who can guarantee, the stable equilibrium of the new arrangement? Only a tranquil Europe can be a stable Europe. There must be not only a balance of power, but a community of power; not organized rivalries, but an organized common peace.

Fortunately, we have received very explicit assurances on this point. The statesmen of both of the groups of nations, now arrayed against one another, have said, in terms that could not be misinterpreted, that it was no part of the purpose they had in mind to crush their antagonists. But the implication of these assurances may not be equally clear to all, may not be the same on both sides of the water. I think it will be serviceable if I attempt to set forth what we understand them to be.

They imply, first of all, that it must be a peace without victory. It is not pleasant to say this. I beg that I may be permitted to put my own interpretation upon it and that it may be understood that no other interpretation was in my thought. I am seeking only to face realities and to face them without soft concealments. Victory would mean peace forced upon the loser, a victor's terms imposed upon the vanquished. It would be accepted in humiliation, under duress, at an intolerable sacrifice, and would leave a sting, a resentment, a bitter memory, upon which terms of peace would rest, not permanently, but only as upon quicksand.

Only a peace between equals can last; only a peace the very principle of which is equality and a common participation in a common benefit. The right state of mind, the right feeling, between nations, is as necessary for a lasting peace as is the just settlement of vexed questions of territory or of racial and national allegiance.

The equality of nations upon which peace must be founded, if it is to last, must be an equality of rights; the guarantees exchanged must neither recognize nor imply a difference between big nations and small, between those that are powerful and those that are weak. Right must be based upon the common strength, not upon the individual strength, of the nations upon whose concert peace will depend.

Equality of territory, of resources, there, of course, cannot be; nor any other sort of equality not gained in the ordinary peaceful and legitimate development of the peoples themselves. But no one asks or expects anything more than an equality of rights. Mankind is looking now for freedom of life, not for equipoises of power.

And there is a deeper thing involved than even equality of rights among organized nations. No peace can last, or ought to last, which does not recognize and accept the principle that Governments derive all their just powers from the consent of the governed, and that no right anywhere exists to hand peoples about from sovereignty to sovereignty as if they were property.

I take it for granted, for instance, if I may venture upon a single example, that statesmen everywhere are agreed that there should be a united, independent, and autonomous Poland, and that henceforth inviolable security of life, of worship, and of industrial and social development should be guaranteed to all peoples who have lived hitherto under the power of Governments devoted to a faith and purpose hostile to their own.

I speak of this not because of any desire to exalt an abstract political principle which has always been held very dear by those who have sought to build up liberty in America, but for the same reason that I have spoken of the other conditions of peace, which seem to me clearly indispensable—because I wish frankly to uncover realities. Any peace which does not recognize and accept this principle will inevitably be upset. It will not rest upon the affections or the convictions of mankind. The ferment of spirit of whole populations will fight subtly and constantly against it, and all the world will sympathize. The world can be at peace only if its life is stable, and there can be no stability where the will is in rebellion, where there is not tranquillity of spirit and a sense of justice, of freedom, and of right.

So far as practicable, moreover, every great people now struggling toward a full development of its resources and of its powers should be assured a direct outlet to the great highways of the sea. Where this cannot be done by the cession of territory it can no doubt be done by the neutralization of direct rights of way under the general guarantee which will assure the peace itself. With a right comity of arrangement no nation need be shut away from free access to the open paths of the world's commerce.

And the paths of the sea must alike in law and in fact be free. The freedom of the seas is the *sine qua non* of peace, equality, and coöperation. No doubt a somewhat radical reconsideration of many of the rules of international practice hitherto sought to be established may be necessary in order to make the seas indeed free and common in practically all circumstances for the use of mankind, but the motive for such changes is convincing and compelling. There can be no trust or intimacy between the peoples of the world without them.

The free, constant, unthreatened intercourse of nations is an essential part of the process of peace and of development. It need not be difficult to define or to secure the freedom of the seas if the Governments of the world sincerely desire to come to an agreement concerning it.

It is a problem closely connected with the limitation of naval armaments and the coöperation of the navies of the world in keeping the seas at once free and safe.

And the question of limiting naval armaments opens the wider and perhaps more difficult question of the limitation of armies and of all programs of military preparation. Difficult and delicate as those questions are, they must be faced with the utmost candor and decided in a spirit of real accommodation if peace is to come with healing in its wings and come to stay.

Peace cannot be had without concession and sacrifice. There can be no sense of safety and equality among the nations if great preponderating armies are henceforth to continue here and there to be built up and maintained. The statesmen of the world must plan for peace and nations must adjust and accommodate their policy to it as they have planned for war and made ready for pitiless contest and rivalry. The question of armaments, whether on land or sea, is the most immediately and intensely practical question connected with the future fortunes of nations and of mankind.

I have spoken upon these great matters without reserve and with the utmost explicitness because it has seemed to me to be necessary if the world's yearning desire for peace was anywhere to find free voice and utterance. Perhaps I am the only person in high authority among all the peoples of the world who is at liberty to speak and hold nothing back. I am speaking as an individual, and yet I am speaking also, of course, as the responsible head of a great Government, and I feel confident that I have said what the people of the United States would wish me to say.

May I not add that I hope and believe that I am, in effect, speaking for liberals and friends of humanity in every nation and of every program of liberty? I would fain believe that I am speaking for the silent mass of mankind everywhere who have as yet had no place or opportunity to speak their real hearts out concerning the death and ruin they see to have come already upon the persons and the homes they hold most dear.

And in holding out the expectation that the people and the Government of the United States will join the other civilized nations of the world in guaranteeing the permanence of peace upon such terms as I have named, I speak with the greater boldness and confidence because it is clear to every man who can think that there is in this promise no breach in either our traditions or our policy as a nation, but a fulfillment rather of all that we have professed or striven for.

I am proposing, as it were, that the nations should with one accord adopt the doctrine of President Monroe as the doctrine of the world: That no nation should seek to extend its policy over any other nation or people, but that every people should be left free to determine its own policy, its own way of development, unhindered, unthreatened, unafraid, the little along with the great and powerful.

I am proposing that all nations henceforth avoid entangling alliances which would draw them into competition of power, catch them in a net of intrigue and selfish rivalry, and disturb their own affairs with influences intruded from without. There is no entangling alliance in a concert of power. When all unite to act in the same sense and with the same purpose, all act in the common interest and are free to live their own lives under a common protection.

I am proposing government by the consent of the governed; that freedom of the seas which in international conference after conference representatives of the United States have urged with the eloquence of those who are the convinced disciples of liberty; and that moderation of armaments which makes of armies and navies a power for order merely, not an instrument of aggression or of selfish violence.

These are American principles, American policies. We can stand for no others. And they are also the principles and policies of forward-looking men and women everywhere, of every modern nation, of every enlightened community. They are the principles of mankind and must prevail.

1917

OLIVER WENDELL HOLMES, JR.
(1841–1935)

ABRAMS *et al. v.* U. S.: MINORITY OPINION

This indictment is founded wholly upon the publication of two leaflets which I shall describe in a moment. The first count charges a conspiracy, pending the war with Germany, to publish abusive language about the form of government of the United States, laying the preparation and publishing of the first leaflet as overt acts. The second count charges a conspiracy, pending the war, to publish language intended to bring the form of government into contempt, laying the preparation and publishing of the two leaflets as overt acts. The third count alleges a conspiracy to encourage resistance to the United States in the same war and to attempt to effectuate the purpose by publishing the same leaflets. The fourth count lays a conspiracy to incite curtailment of production of things necessary to the prosecution of the war and to attempt to accomplish it by publishing the second leaflet to which I have referred.

The first of these leaflets says that the President's cowardly silence about the intervention in Russia reveals the hypocrisy of the plutocratic gang in Washington. It intimates that "German militarism combined with Allied capitalism to crush the Russian revolution," goes on that the tyrants of the world fight each other until they see a common enemy—working-class enlightenment—when they combine to crush it; and that now militarism and capitalism combined, though not openly, to crush the Russian revolution. It says that there is only one enemy of the workers of the world and that is capitalism; that it is a crime for workers of America, etc., to fight the workers' republic of Russia, and ends "Awake! Awake, you workers of the world!" Signed "Revolutionists." A note adds, "It is absurd to call us pro-German. We hate and despise German militarism more than do you hypocritical tyrants. We have more reasons for denouncing German militarism than has the coward of the White House."

The other leaflet, headed "Workers —Wake Up," with abusive language says that America together with the Allies will march for Russia to help the Czecho-Slovaks in their struggle against the Bolsheviki, and that this time the hypocrites shall not fool the Russian emigrants and friends of Russia in America. It tells the Russian emigrants that they now must spit in the face of false military propaganda by which their sympathy and help to the prosecution of the war have been called forth, and says that with the money they have lent or are going to lend "they will make bullets not only for the Germans but also for the Workers' Soviets of Russia," and further, "Workers in the ammunition factories, you are producing bullets, bayonets, cannon, to murder not only the Germans but also your dearest, best, who are in Russia fighting for freedom." It then appeals to the same Russian emigrants at some length not to consent to the "inquisitionary expedition to Russia," and says that the destruction of the Russian revolution is "the politics of the march on Russia." The leaflet winds up by saying "Workers, our reply to this barbaric intervention has to be a general strike!" and after a few words on the spirit of revolution, exhortations not to be afraid, and some usual tall talk, ends "Woe unto those who will be in the way of progress. Let solidarity live! The Rebels."

No argument seems to me necessary to show that these pronunciamentos in no way attack the form of government of the United States, or that they do not support either of the first two counts. What little I have to say about the third count may be postponed until I have considered the fourth. With regard to that, it seems too plain to be denied that the suggestion to workers in ammunition factories that they are producing bullets to murder their dearest, and the further advocacy of a general strike, both in the second leaflet, do urge curtailment of production of things necessary to the prosecution of the war within the meaning of the Act of May 16, 1918 amending part 3 of the earlier Act of 1917. But to make the conduct criminal that statute requires that it should be "with intent by such curtailment to cripple or hinder the United States in the prosecution of the war." It seems to me that no such intent is proved.

I am aware, of course, that the word intent as vaguely used in ordinary legal discussion means no more than knowledge at the time of the act that the consequences said to be intended will ensue. Even less than that will satisfy the general principle of civil and criminal liability. A man may have to pay damages, may be sent to prison, at common law might be hanged, if at the time of his act he knew facts from which common experience showed that the consequences would follow, whether he individually could foresee them or not. But, when words are used exactly, a deed is not done with intent to produce a consequence unless that consequence is the aim of the deed. It may be obvious to the actor that the consequence will follow, and he may be liable for it even if he forgets it, but he does not do the act with intent to produce it unless the aim to produce it is the proximate motive of the specific act, although there may be some deeper motive behind.

It seems to me that this statute must be taken to use its words in a strict and accurate sense. They would be absurd in any other. A patriot might think that we were wasting money on aeroplanes, or making more cannon of a certain kind than we needed, and might advocate curtailment with success; yet even if it turned out that the curtailment hindered and was thought by other minds to have been obviously likely to hinder the United States in the prosecution of the war, no one would hold such conduct a crime. I admit that my illustration does not answer all that might be said, but it is enough to show what I think and to let me pass to a more important aspect of the case. I refer to the First Amendment to the Constitution: that Congress shall make no law abridging the freedom of speech.

I never have seen any reason to doubt that the questions of law that alone were before this Court in the cases of *Schenck, Frohwerk,* and *Debs,* were rightly decided. I do not doubt for a moment that by the same reasoning that would justify punishing persuasion to murder, the United States constitutionally may punish speech that produces or is intended to produce a clear and imminent danger that it will bring about forthwith certain substantive evils that the United States constitutionally may seek to prevent. The power undoubtedly is greater in time of war than in time of peace because war opens dangers that do not exist at other times.

But as against dangers peculiar to war, as against others, the principle of the right to free speech is always the same. It is only the present danger of immediate evil or an intent to bring it about that warrants Congress in setting a limit to the expression of opinion where private rights are not concerned. Congress certainly cannot forbid all effort to change the mind of the country. Now nobody can suppose that the surreptitious publishing of a silly leaflet by an unknown man, without more, would present any immediate danger that its opinions would hinder the success of the Government aims or have any appreciable tendency to do so. Publishing these opinions for the very purpose of obstructing, however, might indicate a greater danger and at any rate would have the quality of an attempt. So I assume that the second leaflet, if published for the purpose alleged in the fourth count, might be punishable. But it seems pretty clear to me that nothing less than that would bring these papers within the scope of this law. An actual intent in the sense that I have explained is necessary to constitute an attempt, where a further act of the same individual is required to complete the substantive crime, for reasons given in *Swift & Co.* v. *United States,* 196 U. S. 375,396. It is necessary where the success of the attempt depends upon others, because if that intent is not present the actor's aim may be accomplished without bringing about the evils sought to be checked. An intent to prevent interference with the revolution in Russia might have been satisfied without any hindrance to carrying on the war in which we were engaged.

I do not see how anyone can find the intent required by the statute in any of the defendants' words. The second leaflet is the only one that affords even a foundation for the charge; and there, without invoking the hatred of German militarism expressed in the former one, it is evident from the beginning to the end that the only object of the paper is to help Russia and stop American intervention there against the popular government —not to impede the United States in the war that it was carrying on. To say that two phrases taken literally might import a suggestion of conduct that would have interference with the war as an indirect and probably undesired effect seems to me by no means enough to show an attempt to produce that effect.

I return for a moment to the third count. That charges an intent to provoke resistance to the United States in its war with Germany. Taking the clause in the statute that deals with that in connection with the other elaborate provisions of the Act, I think that resistance to the United States means some forcible act of opposition to some proceeding of the United States in pursuance of the war. I think the intent must be the specific intent that I have described and for the reasons that I have given. I think that no such intent was proved or existed in fact. I also think that there is no hint at resistance to the United States as I construe the phrase.

In this case sentences of twenty years' imprisonment have been imposed for the publishing of two leaflets that I believe the defendants had as much right to publish as the Government has to publish the Constitution of the United States now vainly invoked by them. Even if I am technically wrong and enough can be squeezed from these poor and puny anonymities to turn the color of legal litmus paper—I will add, even if what I think the necessary intent were shown—the most nominal punishment seems to me all that possibly could be inflicted, unless the defendants are to be made to suffer not for what the indictment alleges but for the

creed that they avow—a creed that I believe to be the creed of ignorance and immaturity when honestly held, as I see no reason to doubt that it was held here, but which, although made the subject of examination at the trial, no one has a right even to consider in dealing with the charges before the Court.

Persecution for the expression of opinions seems to me perfectly logical. If you have no doubt of your premises or your power and want a certain result with all your heart, you naturally express your wishes in law and sweep away all opposition. To allow opposition by speech seems to indicate that you think the speech impotent, as when a man says that he has squared the circle, or that you do not care wholeheartedly for the result, or that you doubt either your power or your premises. But when men have realized that time has upset many fighting faiths, they may come to believe, even more than they believe the very foundations of their own conduct, that the ultimate good desired is better reached by free trade in ideas —that the best test of truth is the power of the thought to get itself accepted in the competition of the market, and that truth is the only ground upon which their wishes safely can be carried out. That, at any rate, is the theory of our Constitution. It is an experiment, as all life is an experiment. Every year, if not every day, we have to wager our salvation upon some prophecy based upon imperfect knowledge. While that experiment is part of our system, I think that we should be eternally vigilant against attempts to check the expression of opinions that we loathe and believe to be fraught with death, unless they so imminently threaten immediate interference with the lawful and pressing purposes of the law that an immediate check is required to save the country.

I wholly disagree with the argument of the Government that the First Amendment left the common law as to seditious libel in force. History seems to me against the notion. I had conceived that the United States through many years had shown its repentance for the Sedition Act of 1798 by repaying fines that it imposed. Only the emergency that makes it immediately dangerous to leave the correction of evil counsels to time warrants making any exception to the sweeping command, "Congress shall make no law . . . abridging the freedom of speech." Of course I am speaking only of expressions of opinion and exhortations, which were all that were uttered here, but I regret that I cannot put into more impressive words my belief that in their conviction upon this indictment the defendants were deprived of their rights under the Constitution of the United States.

Mr. Justice Brandeis concurs with the foregoing opinion.

1919

LEWIS MUMFORD
(1895–   )

FROM
STICKS AND STONES *

THE DEFEAT OF ROMANTICISM [IN AMERICAN ARCHITECTURE]

I

Between 1860 and 1890, some of the forces that were latent in industrialism were realized in American architecture. Where the first pioneers had fared timidly, hampered by in-

* Reprinted by permission of Horace Liveright, Inc., from *Sticks and Stones* by Lewis Mumford. Copyright, 1924.

sufficient resources, the generation that had been stimulated by war industries and profiteering, by the discovery of petroleum and natural gas, by the spanning of the American continent and by cable communication with Europe, rioted over its new-found wealth.

"The Song of the Broad-Ax" still faintly lingered on the Pacific slopes; but the land pioneer was rapidly giving way to the pioneer in industry; and for perhaps the first time during the century, the surplus of capital outran the immediate demand for new plant and equipment. The Iron Age reached its peak of achievement in a series of great bridges, beginning with the Eads Bridge at St. Louis; and romanticism made a last stand. It will pay us, perhaps, to take one last look at the romantic effort, in order to see how impossible and hopeless was the task it set out to perform.

In England, the romantic movement in architecture had made the return to the Middle Ages a definite symbol of social reform: in Ruskin's mind it was associated with the restoration of a medieval type of polity, something like a reformed manor, while with Morris it meant cutting loose from the machine and returning to the meticulous handicraft of the town-guilds. In America, the romantic movement lacked these social and economic implications; and while it is not unfair to say that the literary expression of English romanticism was on the whole much better than the architecture, in the proportion that The Stones of Venice was better than the Ashmolean Museum or the Albert Memorial, the reverse is true on this side of the Atlantic.

Inarticulate as H. H. Richardson, the chief exponent of American romanticism, was, it seemed for a while as if he might breast the tide of mechanical industry and create for a good part of the scene a sense of stability and harmony which it had all too plainly lacked. In relation to his age, however, Richardson was in the biological sense a "sport"; surrounded by jerry-builders, who had degraded the craft of building, and engineers who ignored it, he was perhaps the last of the great medieval line of master-masons.

Richardson began his career in America directly after the Civil War. Almost the first of the new generation of Americans to be trained by the École des Beaux Arts, he brought back to America none of those atrocious adaptations of the French Renaissance like the New York, Philadelphia, and Boston Post Offices. On the contrary, he had come under the influence of Viollet-le-Duc; and for about ten years he struggled with incongruous forms and materials in the anomalous manner known as Free Gothic. The end of this period of experiment came in 1872, when he received the commission for Trinity Church in Boston; and although it was not until ten years later that he saw any Romanesque buildings other than in photographs—for he had not traveled during his student-years in Paris—it was in this sturdy mode that he cast his best work. Richardson was not a decorator, but a builder: in going back to Romanesque precedent, with its round arches and massive stone members, he was following out a dictum of Viollet-le-Duc's: "only primitive sources supply the energy for a long career." Turning away from "applied Gothic," Richardson started to build from the bottom up. So far had the art of masonry disappeared that in Trinity Church Richardson sometimes introduced struts and girders without any attempt to assimilate them in the com-

position; but as far as any single man could absorb and live with a vanished tradition, Richardson did.

The proof of Richardson's genius as a builder lies in the difference between the accepted drawings for Trinity Church and the finished building. His ideas altered with the progress of the work, and in almost every case the building itself is a vast improvement over the paper design. Moreover, in his capacity as master-mason, Richardson trained an able corps of craftsmen; and so pervasive was his influence that one still finds on houses Richardson never saw, the touches of delicate, leafy stone-carving he had introduced. With carving and sculpture, the other arts entered, and by his fine designs and exacting standards of work, Richardson elevated the position of the minor crafts, at the same time that he turned over unreservedly to men like John La Farge and Augustus St. Gaudens the major elements of decoration.

Probably most people who know Richardson's name vaguely associate him with ecclesiastical work; but Richardson's brand of romanticism was a genuine attempt to embrace the age, and in his long list of public works there are but five churches. If the Pittsburgh Court House and Trinity Church stand out as the hugest of his architectural conceptions, it is the smaller buildings that test the skill and imagination of the master, and the public libraries at North Easton, Malden, and Quincy, Mass., and some of the little railway stations in Massachusetts stand on an equally high level. Richardson pitted his own single powers against the barbarism of the Gilded Age; but, unlike his contemporaries in England, he did not turn his back upon the excellences of industrialism. "The things I want most to design," he said to his biographer, "are a grain-elevator and the interior of a great river-steamboat."

In short, Richardson sought to dominate his age. So nearly did he succeed that in a symposium on the ten finest buildings in America, conducted by an architectural journal in the 'eighties, Richardson was given five. This was no easy victory, and, to tell the truth, it was only a partial one. The case of the State Capitol at Albany, which Richardson and Eidlitz took in hand in 1878, after five million dollars had been squandered on it in the course of ten years' misconstruction, scarcely caricatures the conditions under which the arts struggled to exist. Begun in the style of the Roman Renaissance, the building under Richardson's impetuous touch began to take on Romanesque proportions, only to be legislated back into Renaissance by the offended lawgivers!

William Morris Hunt, then at the height of his powers, was commissioned to paint two large mural compositions for the assembly chamber of this blessed building. So much time had been spent in mismanaging the structure that Hunt was given only two months to transfer his cartouche to the panels; but he worked heroically, and, as one of his biographers says, the work was a great triumph. Great, perhaps—but temporary! "The building had fallen into the hands of a political ring, and the poor construction was revealed in the leaking of the massive roof and the settling of the whole structure. Before ten years had passed, great portions of Hunt's paintings flaked off, and what remained was walled up behind the rebuilding necessary to avert utter ruin." In a period like this, Richardson's comparative success takes on heroic proportions.

II

With the little eddies of eclecticism, with the rage for the Mansard roof, or the introduction of German Gothic, and, a little later, the taste for Queen Anne domesticity, there is scarcely any need to deal; they represented only the dispersion of taste and the collapse of judgment which marked the Gilded Age.

Up to the time of the Chicago World's Fair, Richardson had imitators, and they were not always mean ones. L. H. Buffington, in Minneapolis, had to his credit a number of buildings which would not, perhaps, have dishonored the master himself; but, as so often happens, the tags in Richardson's work were easier to imitate than his spirit and inventiveness; and the chief marks of the style he created are the all-too-solid courses of rough stone, the round arch, the squat columns, and the contrasts in color between the light granite and the dark sandstone or serpentine. Mr. Montgomery Schuyler, an excellent architectural critic, once said, not without reason, that Richardson's houses were not defensible except in a military sense; but one is tempted to read into these ponderous forms partly the architect's unconscious desire to combat the infirmity and jerry-building of his lower contemporaries, and partly his patron's anxiety to have a seat of refuge against the uneasy proletariat. A new feudalism was entrenching itself behind the stockades of Homestead and the other steel-towns of the Pittsburgh district. Here was a mode of building, solid, formidable, at times almost brutal, that served the esthetic needs of the barons of coal and steel almost as well as the classic met those of the heroes who had survived the War of Independence.

I have emphasized what was strong and fine in Richardson's work in order to show how free it was from the minor faults of romanticism; and yet it reckoned without its host, and Richardson, alas! left scarcely a trace upon the period that followed. Romanticism was welcomed when it built churches; tolerated when it built libraries; petted when it built fine houses; but it could not go much farther. Richardson was a mason, and masonry was being driven out by steel; he was an original artist, and original art was being thrust into the background by connoisseurship and collection; he was a builder, and architecture was committing itself more and more to the paper plan; he insisted upon building foursquare, and building was doomed more and more to *façaderie*. The very strength of Richardson's building was a fatal weakness in the growing centers of commerce and industry. It takes more than a little audacity to tear down one of Richardson's monuments, and so, rather ironically, they have held their own against the insurrections of traffic and realty speculation; but the difficulty of getting rid of these Romanesque structures only increased the demand for a more frail and facile method of construction.

Romanticism met its great defeat in the office-building. By the use of the passenger elevator, first designed for an exhibition-tower adjacent to the Crystal Palace in 1853, it had become possible to raise the height of buildings to seven stories: the desire for ground-rents presently increased the height to ten. Beyond this, mere masonry could not go without thickening the supporting piers to such an extent that on a twenty-foot lot more than a quarter of the width would be lost on the lower floors. Richardson's Marshall Field Building in Chicago was seven stories high; and that was about as far as solid stone or brick could climb without becoming undignified and futile by its bulk. The possibilities of masonry and the possibilities of commercial gain through ground-rents were at loggerheads, and by 1888 masonry was defeated.

Richardson, fortunately, did not live to see the undermining of the tradition he had founded and almost established. Within a decade of his death, however, only the empty forms of architecture remained, for the steel-cage of the engineer had become the new structural reality. By 1890 the ground-landlord had discovered, in the language of the pioneer's favorite game, that "the roof's the limit." If that was so, why limit the roof? With this canny perception the skyscraper sprang into being.

During this Gilded Age the standard of the best building had risen almost as high as it had been in America in any earlier period; but the mass of good building had relatively decreased; and the domestic dwellings in both city and country lost those final touches of craftsmanship that had lingered, here and there, up to the Civil War. In the awkward country villas that began to fill the still-remote suburbs of the larger cities, all sense of style and proportion were lost: the plan was marked by meaningless irregularities; a dingy, muddy color spread over the wooden façades. There exists a huge and beautifully printed volume, of which, I believe, there are not more than a hundred copies, on the villas of Newport in 1876: the compiler thereof sought to satisfy the vanity of the original owners and the curiosity of a later generation; yet mid all these examples of the "novel" and the "unique," there is not a single mansion that would satisfy any conceivable line of descendants.

If the level of architecture was low in the country, it touched the bottom of the abyss in the city. As early as 1835 the multiple-family tenement had been introduced in New York as a means of producing congestion, raising the ground-rents, and satisfying in the worst possible way the need of the new immigrants for housing. The conditions of life in these tenements were infinitely lower than they had been in the most primitive farmhouse of the colonial period; their lack of light, lack of water, lack of sanitary facilities, and lack of privacy, created an admirable milieu for the propagation of vice and disease, and their existence in a period which was boasting loudly of the advance of science and industrialism shows, to say the least, how the myths which inspired the age stood between the eye and reality, and obscured the actual state of the modern industrial community.

To the disgrace of the architectural profession in America, the worst features of tenement-house construction were standardized in the so-called dumb-bell tenement which won the first prize in the model tenement-house competition of 1879; and the tenements which were designed after this pattern in the succeeding years combined a maximum lack of privacy with a minimum of light and air. The gridiron street-design, the narrow frontage, the deep lot, all conspired to make good housing difficult in the larger cities: within this framework good house-design, indeed, still is difficult. The dumb-bell tenement of the Gilded Age, however, raised bad housing into an art; and the acquisition of this art in its later developments is now one of the stigmata of "progress" in a modern American city. I say this without irony; the matter is too grave for jest.

During these same 'seventies, the benefits of poor housing were extended in New York to those with money enough to afford something better: the Paris flat was introduced. The legitimate excuse for the small apartment was the difficulty of obtaining household service, and the futility of keeping up large houses for small families: this, however, had nothing to do with the actual form that the apartment took, for, apart from the desire for congestion-rents, it is as easy to build apartments for two families as for twenty. The flat is a genuine convenience for the well-to-do visitor to a city; it gives him the atmosphere of a home without many of its major complications, and those who got the taste for this life in Paris were not altogether absurd in desiring to enjoy the same benefits in New York. Unfortunately, what suits a visitor does not necessarily meet the demands of a permanent resident: one may tolerate a blank wall for a week or a month without being depressed, particularly since a good part of a visitor's time is spent outside his home; but to live year after year facing a blank wall or an equally-frowning façade opposite is to be condemned to the environment of a penitentiary.

The result of building apartments in New York and elsewhere was not cheaper rents for smaller quarters: it was smaller quarters without the cheap rents. Those who wanted sunlight and a pleasant view paid a premium for it; those who did not get either paid more than enough for what they got. The result of building apartments which would satisfy only a visitor was to make every family visitors: before the acute housing shortage, yearly removals to new premises were the only palliative that made their occupancy tolerable. The amount of wear and tear and waste, the loss of energy and money and good spirits, produced by the inability of the architect to design adequately under the pecuniary standards of the Gilded Age was colossal. The urban nomad in his own way was as great a spendthrift as the pioneer of the prairie. Both of them had been unable to create a permanent civilization; and both of them paid the price for it.

III

During the first period of pioneering, mechanical improvements had affected the milieu of architecture, but not architecture itself, if one overlooks such ingenuities as the circular and octagon houses of the eighteen-thirties. Slowly, the actual methods of construction changed: the carpenter-builder, who had once performed every operation, gave way to the joiner, whose work profited by putty and paint, curtains and carpets—to the plasterer, who covered up the raw imperfect frame—and to the plumber. Weird ornamental forms for doors and window-architraves, for moldings and pendants, were supplied to the builder by the catalogs of the planing and scroll-saw mills. Invention produced novelties of contortion in wood, unique in ugliness and imbecile in design. Like the zinc and iron statues that graced the buildings of the Centennial Exposition, these devices record the absorption of art in a vain technology.

One need not dwell upon the results of all these miserable efforts, conceived in haste and aborted for profit: the phenomenon was common to industrial civilization at this period, and can be observed in Battersea and Manchester as well as in New York and Pittsburgh. Mr. Thomas Hardy, who was trained as an architect, wrote the esthetic apology for industrialism; and in proclaiming the rightness of our

architectural deserts, one cannot help thinking that he transferred to the Wessex countryside a little of the horrible depression he must have acquired in London.

"Gay prospects," exclaimed Mr. Hardy, "wed happily with gay times; but, alas! if the times be not gay! Men have more often suffered from the mockery of a place too smiling than from the oppression of surroundings oversadly tinged. . . . Indeed, it is a question if the exclusive reign of orthodox beauty is not approaching its last quarter. The new vale in Tempe may be a gaunt waste in Thule: human souls may find themselves in closer harmony with external things wearing a somberness distasteful to our race when it was young. Shall we say that man has grown so accustomed to his spiritual Bastille that he no longer looks forward to, and even shrinks from, a casual emergence into unusual brightness?"

Even the best work of the period is blighted with this somberness: the fact that so many of Richardson's buildings have the heavy air of a prison shows us that the Gilded Age was not, indeed, gay, and that a spiritual Black Friday perpetually threatened the calendar of its days.

IV

If the romantic movement in America proved that the architect could capture only a small part of the field, and go no further than the interests of privilege allowed, the building of the Brooklyn Bridge showed how well industrialism could handle its problems when its purposes were not limited by the necessity for sloppy workmanship and quick turnover. The story of its building is a tribute to both science and humanity. When John Roebling, the designer of the bridge, died in the midst of his job, the business of construction was taken up by his son, and by his devotion to his task in season and out of season, Washington Roebling became an invalid. Confined to his house on Columbia Heights, for ten years the younger Roebling watched the work through a telescope, and directed it as a general would direct a battle. So goes the legend: it runs rather higher than the tales of mean prudence or mechanical skill which glorified Mr. Samuel Smiles' heroes.

The bridge itself was a testimony to the swift progress of physical science. The strong lines of the bridge, and the beautiful curve described by its suspended cables, were derived from an elegant formula in mathematical physics—the elastic curve. If the architectural elements of the massive piers have perhaps too much the bare quality of engineering, if the pointed arches meet esthetic betrayal in the flat solidity of the cornices, if, in short, the masonry does not sing as Richardson alone perhaps could have made it sing, the steel work itself makes up for this, by the architectural beauty of its pattern; so that beyond any other aspect of New York, I think, the Brooklyn Bridge has been a source of joy and inspiration to the artist. In the later bridges the spanning members are sturdier and the supporting piers and cables are lighter and less essential; and they suffer esthetically by the very ease of their triumph over the difficulties of engineering.

All that the age had just cause for pride in—its advances in science, its skill in handling iron, its personal heroism in the face of dangerous industrial processes, its willingness to attempt the untried and the impossible—came to a head in the Brooklyn Bridge. What was grotesque and barbarous in industrialism was sloughed off in the great bridges. These avenues of communication are, paradoxically, the only enduring monuments that witness a period of uneasy industrial transition; and to this day they communicate a feeling of dignity, stability, and unwavering poise.

The Brooklyn Bridge was opened in 1884; Richardson died, after finishing the Pittsburgh Court House, in 1886. There was a short period during which the echoes of Richardson's style resounded in the work of the Western architects; and then in New York two of Richardson's own pupils, Messrs. McKim and White, who had caught the spirit of the period that was to follow the passing of the frontier, prepared an appropriate mold for its activities. By far the finest things in the late 'eighties are the shingled houses which Richardson and Stanford White and a few others developed for seaboard estates: they recovered the spirit of the early vernacular work, and continued the colonial tradition without even faintly recalling colonial forms. This new note, however, was scarcely sounded before it died out; and in the twenty years that followed the conflict between industrialism and romanticism was swallowed up and finally forgotten in the rise of a new mode. Richardson had not died too soon. The quality of mind and culture which shines through his work was opposed to nearly every manifestation of the period that succeeded him.

From this time on, romanticism retained a place for itself only by forfeiting its claims to occupy the whole province of architecture. In churches and college halls where the traditional tie with the Middle Ages had never been completely broken, its archaic triumphs have been genuine; but although Mr. J. G. Rogers' Harkness Memorial at Yale, and Messrs. Goodhue and Cram's St. Thomas' Church, for example, leave little to be desired in themselves, they have established no precedent for the hundred other kinds of building which the modern community requires; and it is not without significance that in his most recent efforts Mr. Goodhue, for one, has abandoned the molds of romanticism. Unlike Richardson, the surviving romanticists now demand a certain insulation from the modern world; the more intelligent exponents of the movement believe with Dr. Ralph Adams Cram that there is no hope for its achievement throughout the community without a return to "Walled Towns."

Such a retreat is the equivalent of surrender. To hold to Gothic precedent in the hope of re-creating the medieval community is to hope that an ancient bottle will turn potassium permanganate into claret. The romanticists have never fully faced the social and economic problems that attend their architectural solutions: the result is that they have been dependent upon assistance from the very forces and institutions which, fundamentally, they aim to combat. Isolated on little islands, secure for the moment, romanticism must view the work on the mainland with a gesture of irate despair; and the only future it dares to face lies behind it!

1924

JAMES THURBER
(1894–   )

SEX EX MACHINA *

With the disappearance of the gas mantle and the advent of the short circuit, man's tranquillity began to be

* Reprinted from *Let Your Mind Alone* by James Thurber, by permission of James Thurber. Copyright 1937.

threatened by everything he put his hand on. Many people believe that it was a sad day indeed when Benjamin Franklin tied that key to a kite string and flew the kite in a thunderstorm; other people believe that if it hadn't been Franklin, it would have been someone else. As, of course, it was in the case of the harnessing of steam and the invention of the gas engine. At any rate, it has come about that so-called civilized man finds himself today surrounded by the myriad mechanical devices of a technological world. Writers of books on how to control your nerves, how to conquer fear, how to cultivate calm, how to be happy in spite of everything, are of several minds as regards the relation of man and the machine. Some of them are prone to believe that the mind and body, if properly disciplined, can get the upper hand of this mechanized existence. Others merely ignore the situation and go on to the profitable writing of more facile chapters of inspiration. Still others attribute the whole menace of the machine to sex, and so confuse the average reader that he cannot always be certain whether he has been knocked down by an automobile or is merely in love.

Dr. Bisch, the Be-Glad-You're-Neurotic man, has a remarkable chapter which deals, in part, with man, sex, and the machine. He examines the case of three hypothetical men who start across a street on a red light and get in the way of an oncoming automobile. A dodges successfully; B stands still, "accepting the situation with calm and resignation," thus becoming one of my favorite heroes in modern belles-lettres; and C hesitates, wavers, jumps backward and forward, and finally runs head on into the car. To lead you through Dr. Bisch's complete analysis of what was wrong with B and C would occupy your whole day. He mentions what the McDougallians would say ("Instinct!"), what the Freudians would retort ("Complexes!"), and what the behaviorists would shout ("Conditioned reflexes!"). He also brings in what the physiologists would say—deficient thyroid, hypoadrenal functioning, and so on. The average sedentary man of our time who is at all suggestible must emerge from this chapter believing that his chances of surviving a combination of instinct, complexes, reflexes, glands, sex, and present-day traffic conditions are about equal to those of a one-legged blind man trying to get out of a labyrinth.

Let us single out what Dr. Bisch thinks the Freudians would say about poor Mr. C, who ran right into the car. He writes, "'sex hunger,' the Freudians would declare. 'Always keyed up and irritable because of it. Undoubtedly suffers from insomnia and when he does sleep his dream life must be productive, distorted, and possibly frightening. Automobile unquestionably has sex significance for him . . . to C the car is both enticing and menacing at one and the same time. . . . A thorough analysis is indicated. . . . It might take months. But then, the man needs an analysis as much as food. He is heading for a complete nervous collapse.'" It is my studied opinion, not to put too fine a point on it, that Mr. C. is heading for a good mangling, and that if he gets away with only a nervous collapse, it will be a miracle.

I have not always, I am sorry to say, been able to go the whole way with the Freudians, or even a very considerable distance. Even though, as Dr. Bisch says, "One must admit that the Freudians have had the best of it thus far. At least they have received the most publicity." It is in

matters like their analysis of men and machines, of Mr. C and the automobile, that the Freudians and I part company. Of course, the analysis above is simply Dr. Bisch's idea of what the Freudians would say, but I think he has got it down pretty well. Dr. Bisch himself leans toward the Freudian analysis of Mr. C, for he says in this same chapter, "An automobile bearing down upon you may be a sex symbol at that, you know, especially if you dream it." It is my contention, of course, that even if you dream it, it is probably not a sex symbol, but merely an automobile bearing down upon you. And if it bears down upon you in real life, I am sure it is an automobile. I have seen the same behavior that characterized Mr. C displayed by a squirrel (Mr. S) that lives in the grounds of my house in the country. He is a fairly tame squirrel, happily mated and not sex-hungry, if I am any judge, but nevertheless he frequently runs out toward my automobile when I start down the driveway, and then hesitates, wavers, jumps forward and backward, and occasionally would run right into the car except that he is awfully fast on his feet and that I always hurriedly put on the brakes of the 1935 V-8 Sex Symbol that I drive.

I have seen this same behavior in the case of rabbits (notoriously uninfluenced by any sex symbols save those of other rabbits), dogs, pigeons, a doe, a young hawk (which flew at my car), a blue heron that I encountered on a country road in Vermont, and once, near Paul Smith's in the Adirondacks, a fox. They all acted exactly like Mr. C. The hawk, unhappily, was killed. All the others escaped with nothing worse, I suppose, than a complete nervous collapse. Although I cannot claim to have been conversant with the private life and the secret compulsions, the psycho-neuroses and the glandular activities of all these animals, it is nevertheless my confident and unswervable belief that there was nothing at all the matter with any one of them. Like Mr. C, they suddenly saw a car swiftly bearing down upon them, got excited, and lost their heads. I do not believe, you see, there was anything the matter with Mr. C, either. But I do believe that, after a thorough analysis lasting months, with a lot of harping on the incident of the automobile, something might very well come to be the matter with him. He might even get to suffering from the delusion that he believes automobiles are sex symbols.

It seems to me worthy of note that Dr. Bisch, in reciting the reactions of three persons in the face of an oncoming car, selected three men. What would have happened had they been Mrs. A, Mrs. B, and Mrs. C? You know as well as I do: all three of them would have hesitated, wavered, jumped forward and backward, and finally run head on into the car if some man hadn't grabbed them. (I used to know a motorist who, every time he approached a woman standing on a curb preparing to cross the street, shouted, "Hold it, stupid!") It is not too much to say that, with a car bearing down upon them, ninety-five women out of a hundred would act like Mr. C—or Mr. S, the squirrel, or Mr. F, the fox. But it is certainly too much to say that ninety-five out of every hundred women look upon an automobile as a sex symbol. For one thing, Dr. Bisch points out that the automobile serves as a sex symbol because of the "mechanical principle involved." But only one woman in a thousand really knows anything about the mechanical principle involved in an automobile. And yet, as I have

said, ninety-five out of a hundred would hesitate, waver, and jump, just as Mr. C did. I think we have the Freudians here. If we haven't proved our case with rabbits and a blue heron, we have certainly proved it with women.

To my notion, the effect of the automobile and of other mechanical contrivances on the state of our nerves, minds, and spirits is a problem which the popular psychologists whom I have dealt with know very little about. The sexual explanation of the relationship of man and the machine is not good enough. To arrive at the real explanation, we have to begin very far back, as far back as Franklin and the kite, or at least as far back as a certain man and woman who appear in a book of stories written more than sixty years ago by Max Adeler. One story in this book tells about a housewife who bought a combination ironing board and card table, which some New England genius had thought up in his spare time. The husband, coming home to find the devilish contraption in the parlor, was appalled. "What is that thing?" he demanded. His wife explained that it was a card table, but that if you pressed a button underneath, it would become an ironing board. Whereupon she pushed the button and the table leaped a foot into the air, extended itself, and became an ironing board. The story goes on to tell how the thing finally became so finely sensitized that it would change back and forth if you merely touched it—you didn't have to push the button. The husband stuck it in the attic (after it had leaped up and struck him a couple of times while he was playing euchre), and on windy nights it could be heard flopping and banging around, changing from a card table to an ironing board and back. The story serves as one example of our dread heritage of annoyance, shock, and terror arising out of the nature of mechanical contrivances *per se.* The mechanical principle involved in this damnable invention had, I believe, no relationship to sex whatsoever. There are certain analysts who see sex in anything, even a leaping ironing board, but I think we can ignore these scientists.

No man (to go on) who has wrestled with a self-adjusting card table can ever be quite the man he once was. If he arrives at the state where he hesitates, wavers, and jumps at every mechanical device he encounters, it is not, I submit, because he recognizes the enticements of sex in the device, but only because he recognizes the menace of the machine as such. There might very well be, in every descendant of the man we have been discussing, an inherited desire to jump at, and conquer, mechanical devices before they have a chance to turn into something twice as big and twice as menacing. It is not reasonable to expect that his children and their children will have entirely escaped the stigma of such traumata. I myself will never be the man I once was, nor will my descendants probably ever amount to much, because of a certain experience I had with an automobile.

I had gone out to the barn of my country place, a barn which was used both as a garage and a kennel, to quiet some large black poodles. It was 1 A.M. of a pitch-dark night in winter and the poodles had apparently been terrified by some kind of a prowler, a tramp, a turtle, or perhaps a fiend of some sort. Both my poodles and myself believed, at the time, in fiends, and still do. Fiends who materialize out of nothing and nowhere, like winged pigweed or Russian thistle. I had quite a time quieting the dogs, because their panic spread to me and mine spread back to them again, in a kind of vicious circle. Finally, a hush as ominous as their uproar fell upon them, but they kept looking over their shoulders, in a kind of apprehensive way. "There's nothing to be afraid of," I told them as firmly as I could, and just at that moment the klaxon of my car, which was just behind me, began to shriek. Everybody has heard a klaxon on a car suddenly begin to sound; I understand it is a short circuit that causes it. But very few people have heard one scream behind them while they were quieting six or eight poodles in the middle of the night in an old barn. I jump now whenever I hear a klaxon, even the klaxon on my own car when I push the button intentionally. The experience has left its mark. Everybody, from the day of the jumping card table to the day of the screaming klaxon, has had similar shocks. You can see the result, entirely unsuperinduced by sex, in the strained faces and muttering lips of people who pass you on the streets of great highly mechanized cities. There goes a man who picked up one of those trick matchboxes that whir in your hands; there goes a woman who tried to change a fuse without turning off the current; and yonder toddles an ancient who cranked an old Reo with the spark advanced. Every person carries in his consciousness the old scar, or the fresh wound, of some harrowing misadventure with a contraption of some sort. I know people who would not deposit a nickel and a dime in a cigarette-vending machine and push the lever even if a diamond necklace came out. I know dozens who would not climb into an airplane even if it didn't move off the ground. In none of these people have I discerned what I would call a neurosis, an "exaggerated" fear; I have discerned only a natural caution in a world made up of gadgets that whir and whine and whiz and shriek and sometimes explode.

I should like to end with the case history of a friend of mine in Ohio named Harvey Lake. When he was only nineteen, the steering bar of an old electric runabout broke off in his hand, causing the machine to carry him through a fence and into the grounds of the Columbus School for Girls. He developed a fear of automobiles, trains, and every other kind of vehicle that was not pulled by a horse. Now, the psychologists would call this a complex and represent the fear as abnormal, but I see it as a purely reasonable apprehension. If Harvey Lake had, because he was catapulted into the grounds of the Columbus School for Girls, developed a fear of girls, I would call that a complex; but I don't call his normal fear of machines a complex. Harvey Lake never in his life got into a plane (he died from a fall from a porch), but I do not regard that as neurotic, either, but only sensible.

I have, to be sure, encountered men with complexes. There was, for example, Marvin Belt. He had a complex about airplanes that was quite interesting. He was not afraid of machinery, or of high places, or of crashes. He was simply afraid that the pilot of any plane he got into might lose his mind. "I imagine myself high over Montana," he once said to me, "in a huge, perfectly safe tri-motored plane. Several of the passengers are dozing, others are reading, but I am keeping my eyes glued on the door to the cockpit. Suddenly the pilot steps out of it, a wild light in his eyes, and in a falsetto like that of a little girl he says to me, 'Conductor, will you please let me off at One-Hundred-and-Twenty-fifth Street?'"

"But," I said to Belt, "even if the pilot does go crazy, there is still the co-pilot." "No, there isn't," said Belt. "The pilot has hit the co-pilot over the head with something and killed him." Yes, the psychoanalysts can have Marvin Belt. But they can't have Harvey Lake, or Mr. C, or Mr. S, or Mr. F, or, while I have my strength, me.

1937, 1945

FRANKLIN D. ROOSEVELT
(1882–1945)

FIRST INAUGURAL ADDRESS

I am certain that my fellow Americans expect that on my induction into the Presidency I will address them with a candor and a decision which the present situation of our Nation impels. This is preeminently the time to speak the truth, the whole truth, frankly and boldly. Nor need we shrink from honestly facing conditions in our country today. This great Nation will endure as it has endured, will revive and will prosper. So, first of all, let me assert my firm belief that the only thing we have to fear is fear itself—nameless, unreasoning, unjustified terror which paralyzes needed efforts to convert retreat into advance. In every dark hour of our national life a leadership of frankness and vigor has met with that understanding and support of the people themselves which is essential to victory. I am convinced that you will again give that support to leadership in these critical days.

In such a spirit on my part and on yours we face our common difficulties. They concern, thank God, only material things. Values have shrunken to fantastic levels; taxes have risen; our ability to pay has fallen; government of all kinds is faced by serious curtailment of income; the means of exchange are frozen in the currents of trade; the withered leaves of industrial enterprise lie on every side; farmers find no markets for their produce; the savings of many years in thousands of families are gone.

More important, a host of unemployed citizens face the grim problem of existence, and an equally great number toil with little return. Only a foolish optimist can deny the dark realities of the moment.

Yet our distress comes from no failure of substance. We are stricken by no plague of locusts. Compared with the perils which our forefathers conquered because they believed and were not afraid, we have still much to be thankful for. Nature still offers her bounty and human efforts have multiplied it. Plenty is at our doorstep, but a generous use of it languishes in the very sight of the supply. Primarily this is because rulers of the exchange of mankind's goods have failed through their own stubbornness and their own incompetence, have admitted their failure, and have abdicated. Practices of the unscrupulous money changers stand indicted in the court of public opinion, rejected by the hearts and minds of men.

True they have tried, but their efforts have been cast in the pattern of an outworn tradition. Faced by failure of credit they have proposed only the lending of more money. Stripped of the lure of profit by which to induce our people to follow their false leadership, they have resorted to exhortations, pleading tearfully for restored confidence. They know only the rules of a generation of self-seekers. They have no vision, and when there is no vision the people perish.

The money changers have fled from their high seats in the temple of our civilization. We may now restore that temple to the ancient truths. The measure of the restoration lies in the extent to which we apply social values more noble than mere monetary profit.

Happiness lies not in the mere possession of money; it lies in the joy of achievement, in the thrill of creative effort. The joy and moral stimulation of work no longer must be forgotten in the mad chase of evanescent profits. These dark days will be worth all they cost us if they teach us that our true destiny is not to be ministered unto but to minister to ourselves and to our fellow men.

Recognition of the falsity of material wealth as the standard of success goes hand in hand with the abandonment of the false belief that public office and high political position are to be valued only by the standards of pride of place and personal profit; and there must be an end to a conduct in banking and in business which too often has given to a sacred trust the likeness of callous and selfish wrongdoing. Small wonder that confidence languishes, for it thrives only on honesty, on honor, on the sacredness of obligations, on faithful protection, on unselfish performance; without them it cannot live.

Restoration calls, however, not for changes in ethics alone. This Nation asks for action, and action now.

Our greatest primary task is to put people to work. This is no unsolvable problem if we face it wisely and courageously. It can be accomplished in part by direct recruiting by the Government itself, treating the task as we would treat the emergency of a war, but at the same time, through this employment, accomplishing greatly needed projects to stimulate and reorganize the use of our natural resources.

Hand in hand with this we must

frankly recognize the overbalance of population in our industrial centers and, by engaging on a national scale in a redistribution, endeavor to provide a better use of the land for those best fitted for the land. The task can be helped by definite efforts to raise the values of agricultural products and with this the power to purchase the output of our cities. It can be helped by preventing realistically the tragedy of the growing loss through foreclosure of our small homes and our farms. It can be helped by insistence that the Federal, State, and local governments act forthwith on the demand that their cost be drastically reduced. It can be helped by the unifying of relief activities which today are often scattered, uneconomical, and unequal. It can be helped by national planning for and supervision of all forms of transportation and of communications and other utilities which have a definitely public character. There are many ways in which it can be helped, but it can never be helped merely by talking about it. We must act and act quickly.

Finally, in our progress toward a resumption of work we require two safeguards against a return of the evils of the old order: there must be a strict supervision of all banking and credits and investments, so that there will be an end to speculation with other people's money; and there must be provision for an adequate but sound currency.

These are the lines of attack. I shall presently urge upon a new Congress, in special session, detailed measures for their fulfillment, and I shall seek the immediate assistance of the several States.

Through this program of action we address ourselves to putting our own national house in order and making income balance outgo. Our international trade relations, though vastly important, are in point of time and necessity secondary to the establishment of a sound national economy. I favor as a practical policy the putting of first things first. I shall spare no effort to restore world trade by international economic readjustment, but the emergency at home cannot wait on that accomplishment.

The basic thought that guides these specific means of national recovery is not narrowly nationalistic. It is the insistence, as a first consideration, upon the interdependence of the various elements in and parts of the United States—a recognition of the old and permanently important manifestation of the American spirit of the pioneer. It is the way to recovery. It is the immediate way. It is the strongest assurance that the recovery will endure.

In the field of world policy I would dedicate this Nation to the policy of the good neighbor—the neighbor who resolutely respects himself and, because he does so, respects the rights of others—the neighbor who respects his obligations and respects the sanctity of his agreements in and with a world of neighbors.

If I read the temper of our people correctly, we now realize as we have never realized before our interdependence on each other; that we cannot merely take but we must give as well; that if we are to go forward, we must move as a trained and loyal army willing to sacrifice for the good of a common discipline, because without such discipline no progress is made, no leadership becomes effective. We are, I know, ready and willing to submit our lives and property to such discipline, because it makes possible a leadership which aims at a larger good. This I propose to offer, pledging that the larger purposes will bind upon us all as a sacred obligation with a unity of duty hitherto evoked only in time of armed strife.

With this pledge taken, I assume unhesitatingly the leadership of this great army of our people dedicated to a disciplined attack upon our common problems.

Action in this image and to this end is feasible under the form of government which we have inherited from our ancestors. Our Constitution is so simple and practical that it is possible always to meet extraordinary needs by changes in emphasis and arrangement without loss of essential form. That is why our constitutional system has proved itself the most superbly enduring political mechanism the modern world has produced. It has met every stress of vast expansion of territory, of foreign wars, of bitter internal strife, of world relations.

It is to be hoped that the normal balance of Executive and legislative authority may be wholly adequate to meet the unprecedented task before us. But it may be that an unprecedented demand and need for undelayed action may call for temporary departure from that normal balance of public procedure.

I am prepared under my constitutional duty to recommend the measures that a stricken Nation in the midst of a stricken world may require. These measures, or such other measures as the Congress may build out of its experience and wisdom, I shall seek, within my constitutional authority, to bring to speedy adoption.

But in the event that the Congress shall fail to take one of these two courses, and in the event that the national emergency is still critical, I shall not evade the clear course of duty that will then confront me. I shall ask the Congress for the one remaining instrument to meet the crisis—broad Executive power to wage a war against the emergency, as great as the power that would be given to me if we were in fact invaded by a foreign foe.

For the trust reposed in me I will return the courage and the devotion that befit the time. I can do no less.

We face the arduous days that lie before us in the warm courage of national unity; with the clear consciousness of seeking old and precious moral values; with the clean satisfaction that comes from the stern performance of duty by old and young alike. We aim at the assurance of a rounded and permanent national life.

We do not distrust the future of essential democracy. The people of the United States have not failed. In their need they have registered a mandate that they want direct, vigorous action. They have asked for discipline and direction under leadership. They have made me the present instrument of their wishes. In the spirit of the gift I take it.

In this dedication of a Nation we humbly ask the blessing of God. May He protect each and every one of us. May He guide me in the days to come.

1933

REINHOLD NIEBUHR
(1892–   )

IS RELIGION COUNTER-REVOLUTIONARY? *

The Marxian charge that religion is an opiate and that its general influence upon society is reactionary, contains several specifications which must be taken up in turn. The specification which deserves first consideration is

* Reprinted from *Radical Religion* by permission of the author. Copyright, 1935.

the one which is most unequivocally true. It is that religion creates a reverence for authority and encourages a humble obedience toward and a patient acceptance of the exactions of power, thus aggravating the injustices of a social system and retarding their elimination. This charge is broadly true. It is true that in the history of Christianity St. Paul's admonition, recorded in Romans 13, to be obedient to government because all government is an ordinance of God has had a baneful effect upon the relation of Christianity to politics. It made every Christian state a sacerdotal state and bound the Christian religion to monarchial politics, to such a degree that the democratic movement in Europe had to be anti-religious to be effective (except insofar as Calvinism provided a religious authority for rebellion against autocracy and monarchism). The undue emphasis of orthodox Christianity upon the sanctity of government not only tended to supply a particular kind of government, monarchy, with the aura of the sacred; it also gave an undue advantage to whatever prince happened to sit upon the throne, no matter by what means he had usurped it. Once entrenched there he could count upon religion to support him and to intone prayers in the churches for his health. This kind of obedience was further buttressed by the doctrine, dating from Augustine, that evil rulers must also be obeyed because they are to be regarded as punishment sent by God for the sins of men, just as government in general is also a method of holding sinful men in check.

Some of this Christian doctrine leads to such political perversity that one cannot blame the eighteenth century for imagining that perfect justice could be established if only "priests and their hypocritical tools could be eliminated." Yet the liberal and radical rationalist is quite wrong in imagining that the religious sanctification of authority is nothing more than the fruit of priestly hypocrisy and can be overcome merely by destroying either the Christian religion or religion in general. While priests through all the ages have no doubt manipulated the sentiments of religion to maintain either their own power or that of some warrior class to which they were attached they could not create a religious obedience to authority out of whole cloth. They could only manipulate what actually existed in life. The fact is that from the earliest tribal life through all of the glories of great empires, religion has been the chief cement of social cohesion. The early tribe was a sacred brotherhood. The later empire was held together by a sacred ruler. The larger units of cooperation and conflict were not homogeneous. They could not be held together by a religiously colored sense of brotherhood. They could be held together only by a religiously colored obedience to authority. Hence the significance of the priest in the Egyptian and the Babylonian empires. Of course force was as necessary as reverence to hold these early societies together. Either the priest was also a warrior or the authority rested in a partnership of priests and warriors. This proves that force and reverence are the two primary forces of social cohesion. The more modern and rationalistic "consent of the governed" may be a third force; but it will never be as powerful as modern rationalists imagine, for the simple reason that the binding forces in human society are not chiefly rational but emotional.

Religious reverence for authority is therefore something which springs out of a perennially fresh spring of human emotions. It is no doubt dangerous.

In it the gratitude of the common man for the principle of any social order, which sustains his social life, is easily transmuted into an undue reverence for the particular social order in which he stands and the particular authority which manipulates that society. But the dangerous nature of this element in social and religious life is not dealt with successfully by a mere emotional protest against all religion. Christianity did not create this element, even though St. Paul gave it a succinct expression. The priests of old did not fashion it out of their own malevolent souls. The fact is that it is so perennial that the very communist critics who seek to destroy religion in order to eliminate this pious respect for authority have already reestablished it in Russia. What are the Russian oligarchs but priest-kings? They are not even under the necessity of bargaining with other priests and prophets to maintain the sacred aura over their power. Their power is holy of itself. It is hallowed by the religious beliefs of the multitudes over whom they hold sway. For their religion teaches the multitudes that these men of power are not subject to the temptations of other men of power, that they have a mystical identity of interest with the common man and that they are the harbingers of an ultimate society in which there will be no power and no unequal division of function or privilege. Every tenet of this religion inculcates a patient and reverent obedience of the common man toward those who have been set in authority over him. This is truly a power "ordained of God" even though God bears the secular name of "dialectic of history." There will never be an age in which critical intelligence will not be called upon to corrode the undue piety and reverence with which social power is venerated in the imagination of the common man. Perhaps one way of solving the problem is to allow all this emotion to be attached to some symbol of society who does not have any real power, as in the case of British constitutional monarchy.

To a certain degree this particular reactionary tendency of religion has not been as potent and as dangerous in the period of bourgeois democracy as in the feudal period. The bourgeois state is a rationalistic state, conceived in terms of the social contract. It is so lacking in religious sanctity that the gentlemen of the Liberty League are making frantic efforts to construct the constitution into an adequate symbol of this now deficient religious loyalty. It is safe to assume that a Liberty League would emerge in our political situation even if our society were completely secular and non-Christian. On the whole it is very secular, certainly more secular than either Russia or Germany. In Germany a new national religion provides the authority of the state with a more unqualified sanctity than Christianity ever gave any state or any ruler. Yes, we must agree with the Marxians. The religiously sacred state power, hiding its injustices behind its sanctities is a dangerous hazard to justice. But if all historic religions were wiped out tomorrow, that problem would still be with us.

What the Marxian charge against religion completely obscures is that a prophetic religion has its own antidote for the poison of a too conforming piety. It has a force of spirituality which brings all authority under criticism. It believes in a God who "bringeth the princes to nothing" and before whom "all nations are as nothing." The resolute word "we must obey God rather than man" has again and again been the battle cry of men who resisted political tyranny. Their religion made them more stubborn in their resistance than any merely skeptical attitude toward authority. The pretentious sanctities of politics can be met effectively only by higher sanctities and the too simple loyalties of political man can be challenged only by higher religious loyalties. In these latter days this higher religious loyalty may be an international proletariat. But it is not the only and not the most effective higher loyalty. An international class is something less than God and when it makes itself God we will have the same old problem over again, the problem of giving undue authority to partial historical forces.

It cannot be denied that organized religion produces more piety than spirituality and more conformity to authority than rebellion against it. But that is true of every aspect of organized culture. Organized education inculcates obedience rather than criticism. Will the radical destroy education because it is conservative in its organized expression? On the contrary he will capture it to make it conforming in his new society.

The second specific charge brought against religion in general and Christianity in particular is that it beguiles men from consideration of their mundane problems by the hope of other-worldly bliss. This charge is also broadly true. As far back as the Amon worship of Egypt, religion has offered men other-worldly hopes to assuage their sorrows in this world. Undoubtedly the ruling oligarchies of every society have made good use of this other-worldliness to dampen the spirit of rebellion and to increase the patience with which their vexatious rule was borne by the poor. Yet here too we are not dealing with a reaction to life which can be neatly called "religious" and which can be eliminated by destroying religion. Religion for the poor, declared Karl Marx "is the spirit of their spiritless condition." Translated that means that it is a kind of a desperate hope of hopeless men. No one can deny that this hope is morally deleterious when it persuades men to accept conditions which ought to be altered and which they could alter by their own strength if they had the courage. In that sense other-worldliness is a terrible evil. But just what is this other-worldly hope? Basically it is the feeling that life as is, is not what it ought to be, that therefore when we experience the anarchy and tyranny, the cruelty and injustice in human society we are confronted with a terrible aberration of the essential reality of life. The communist asserts exactly the same faith when he hopes for a day when social conflict will be abolished and perfect brotherhood established. There is almost as much illusion in that hope incidentally as in the other-worldly hopes of religious dreamers. No historic society will ever achieve perfect peace and justice. This does not imply that the social utopianism and the social apocalypticism of social, as against individual types of religion, are not more serviceable to the cause of social justice than the dualism of individualistic religion which places its hope in some pure supernal world. The evil effects of dualistic influences upon Christian thought are apparent everywhere in its history. It is a regrettable fact that Christianity frequently lost its Hebraic heritage in which salvation is promised at the end and not above history, in which, in other words, the only redemption desired is the redemption of this world of nature-history. This Hebraic heritage, neglected in Christianity, is precisely what Marxism has developed in a secularized and naturalistic form. Nor can it be denied that the other-worldly tendencies in Christianity have either been definitely encouraged or found to be a very convenient tool by the ruling oligarchies of the feudal and the capitalistic period.

Yet this charge against other-worldliness cannot be made against religion in general. It can be made against types of Christianity; perhaps it could even be claimed that Christianity has been prevailingly dualistic. But the charge certainly does not fit the religion of prophets, not the prophetic elements in Christianity. In both America and England some of the most effective spirits of the radical movement have come out of the religious tradition. They have been driven by the religious longing for the establishment of the ideal in history. They have been set upon their way by distinctively religious motives and forces. Only an ignorant or malevolent dogmatism can persist in the convenient evasion that such lives are merely brands that have been plucked from the burning, or exceptions that prove the rule.

A further word needs to be said in qualified defense of traditional other-worldliness. It may be counter-revolutionary and dangerous. But it is also the religious expression of a permanent factor in human life, namely the conflict between the individual and society and the feeling that human destiny and individual worth always transcend and are never completely expressed in the social situation. In this sense it is true that fully developed religions will always have an individualistic motif which purely political religions do not have. Sometimes this individualistic element will be a definite detriment to, and come in opposition with, a socio-religious passion. But the latter can eliminate the former, or dream of the possibility of eliminating it, only in such periods in which men give themselves to the illusion that they can build a society in which the individual can be inserted into a frictionless social harmony and have all his longings, dreams and aspiration fulfilled in it. In such a society all tensions and all possibilities of growth would be eliminated. It would be not the beginning but the end of history. Its realization is a utopian dream. Once it is recognized that the socialist society which we intend to build will not be a perfect society and that it will not be able to save individuals from many frustrations, unfulfilled hopes and unrealized dreams, it must also be conceded that individuals are bound to express themselves not only by setting new goals for a better society but by finding ways of bearing the injustices and frustrations of the moment in terms of a faith which sees life in its essential rather than its existential reality. That is a kind of other-worldliness, even if it dispenses with traditional hopes of immortality. Inasfar as historic religions express this dimension of individual life and do justice to this individual problem, they will be and are bound to be regarded as "counter-revolutionary" from the perspective of a too utopian and a too simply political religion. They may in fact actually be counter-revolutionary in the sense that they will encourage a more qualified devotion to socio-political ends than will seem justified in a moment when all that seems good is pitted against all that is evil in a given social struggle. The truth in the approach of historic religion cannot be proved until it becomes apparent that every political religion has tendencies to absolutize itself. These tendencies have the roots of social decay in them. It is when this decay sets in that a truly prophetic religion which is not completely committed to any political cause will prove itself to be truly revolutionary, for it will have a perspective from which it can judge, criticize and condemn the partial achievements of any historical movement. It is as important for Christian radicals to defend this ultimate basis of a continual revolution in high religion as to resist the efforts of reactionaries to reduce religion to social impotence by making false use of its individualism.

The final charge brought against religion is that it is the real root of the idealistic philosophies which interpret morals, culture and the spiritual life of man in terms which obscure the relation of economic interest and physical facts to the world of ideals and ideas. This charge is broadly justified but it must be made not only against religion but against the whole rationalistic culture of western civilization and holds more unqualifiedly against a secular culture than against the religious one. It is one of the sinful pretensions of all cultural enterprises to think of themselves as the fruits of pure mind and pure conscience and to interpret their history as the development of a kind of discarnate spirituality. This charge can be levelled not only against idealistic philosophy but even against the secular liberalism of today, with its basis of philosophical empiricism. Even there, though the dependence of mind upon the stuff of nature and history is recognized, there is a foolish confidence in the possibility of developing a rationality which will transcend the social facts which it judges and thus arrive at "objective" and "impartial" judgments. In the modern day the physical and economic basis of all culture is more frequently obscured by empiricists than by the old fashioned philosophical idealists. Whether the metaphysical system is idealistic or empirical, the real weakness of these philosophies lies in their undue confidence in rationality. They do not understand to what degree the human mind is the instrument, the victim and the prisoner of human passions and immediate necessities. The idea, for instance, that nothing but a cultural lag prevents the social sciences from achieving the precision of the physical sciences, is a very modern idea, is derived neither from philosophical idealism nor from religion. It is the product of a completely secular, bourgeois culture. Yet it reveals the weakness, which the Marxian is trying to isolate when he speaks of the idealism of religion, more perfectly than any religious system.

The real fact is that prophetic religion is much too conscious of human finitude and sin to have the confidence in human reason and human goodness which both idealistic and empirical philosophies have betrayed. Sometimes this wholesome sense of sin has been weakened in Christian orthodoxy by the belief that the Christian faith and life lifted men completely out of and redeemed them from their enslavement to the world of nature and necessity. On this issue liberal religion is worse than orthodox religion. Its moralism, and its unwillingness to recognize the facts of nature in human history (the class struggle for instance) is at the present time a greater hazard to the understanding of the socio-moral problem of modern man than all the discredited myths of orthodoxy. But this moralism and sentimentality is not a characteristic fruit of the Christian religion at all. It is the fruit of the Age of Reason which has been carried into liberal religion.

It is impossible to deal intelligently with the social problem of man if the whole world of culture, secular and religious, liberal and conservative does not give more generous understanding of the truth which Marxism has discovered, or at least rediscovered: The truth that all human ideals and ideas are conditioned by the physical, geographic, economic and political circumstances in which they rise and that the final religious effort to escape this relativity may frequently become no more than the final rationalization and justification of the partial and relative value of class, race and nation. In that sense the ultimate dishonesty of a culture is always a religious one. Yet on the other hand it is precisely in a high religion, which sees the whole world of history as relative to the absolute and final goodness in God, that these dishonesties and deceptions of culture can be best discovered. However badly organized religion has become enmeshed in the immediate interests of class and nation, it has also always generated out of itself a minority of prophetic spirits who placed the pretensions of their culture and civilization under a divine judgment. In that capacity for judging all relative and partial values and in the humility which does not claim to reach an absolutely pure judgment itself, even while it sees what is partial and incomplete in every culture, in these lie the genius of prophetic religion. In them lie also the guarantee of perpetual revolution, protest, rebellion and criticism in human affairs.

It cannot be denied that this prophetic and revolutionary spirit in religion is frequently corrupted and destroyed. But it must also be recognized that the too simple Marxian might regard it as counter-revolutionary at the precise moment when it is functioning most perfectly. For that might be a moment when it calls attention to the fact that proletarian culture can be no more absolute and final than

bourgeois culture was and that therefore the working class ought to be content to fulfill a great and fateful task in history without claiming to be a messianic class which will usher in the kingdom of God. A truly prophetic religion ought to turn against the spiritual pretensions of a proletarian culture as well as against preceding cultures. It is one of the tragedies of modern culture that the radical rebel against religious complacency and dishonesty falsifies the real facts and the total situation by condemning religion for its virtues as well as for its vices. Its virtues are of course bound to appear like vices from the perspective of a purely political religion. For those virtues are the ability to see and the courage to say that history relativizes all ideals and that human passions and interests condition all ideologies, including those of the leaders of proletarian rebellion.

It is consequently the business of radical religion to contend equally against the reactionary tendencies of organized religion and against the misunderstandings of the total human situation in the philosophy, and therefore in the strategy of radicalism.

1935

WILLIAM VAUGHN MOODY
(1869–1910)

GLOUCESTER MOORS *

A mile behind is Gloucester town
Where the fishing fleets put in,
A mile ahead the land dips down
And the woods and farms begin.
Here, where the moors stretch free
In the high blue afternoon,

Are the marching sun and talking sea,
And the racing winds that wheel and
    flee
On the flying heels of June.

Jill-o'er-the-ground is purple blue,
Blue is the quaker-maid,
The wild geranium holds its dew
Long in the boulder's shade.
Wax-red hangs the cup
From the huckleberry boughs,
In barberry bells the grey moths sup
Or where the choke-cherry lifts high
    up
Sweet bowls for their carouse.

Over the shelf of the sandy cove
Beach-peas blossom late.
By copse and cliff the swallows rove
Each calling to his mate.
Seaward the sea-gulls go,
And the land-birds all are here;
That green-gold flash was a vireo,
And yonder flame where the marsh-
    flags grow
Was a scarlet tanager.

This earth is not the steadfast place
We landsmen build upon;
From deep to deep she varies pace,
And while she comes is gone.
Beneath my feet I feel
Her smooth bulk heave and dip;
With velvet plunge and soft upreel
She swings and steadies to her keel
Like a gallant, gallant ship.

These summer clouds she sets for sail,
The sun is her masthead light,
She tows the moon like a pinnace frail
Where her phosphor wake churns
    bright.
Now hid, now looming clear,
On the face of the dangerous blue
The star fleets tack and wheel and
    veer,
But on, but on does the old earth steer
As if her port she knew.

God, dear God! Does she know her
    port,

Though she goes so far about?
Or blind astray, does she make her
    sport
To brazen and chance it out?
I watched when her captains passed:
She were better captainless.
Men in the cabin, before the mast,
But some were reckless and some
    aghast,
And some sat gorged at mess.

By her battened hatch I leaned and
    caught
Sounds from the noisome hold,—
Cursing and sighing of souls dis-
    traught
And cries too sad to be told.
Then I strove to go down and see;
But they said, "Thou art not of us!"
I turned to those on the deck with me
And cried, "Give help!" But they said,
    "Let be:
Our ship sails faster thus."

Jill-o'er-the-ground is purple blue,
Blue is the quaker-maid,
The alder-clump where the brook
    comes through
Breeds cresses in its shade.
To be out of the moiling street
With its swelter and its sin!
Who has given to me this sweet,
And given my brother dust to eat?
And when will his wage come in?

Scattering wide or blown in ranks,
Yellow and white and brown,
Boats and boats from the fishing banks
Come home to Gloucester town.
There is cash to purse and spend,
There are wives to be embraced,
Hearts to borrow and hearts to lend,
And hearts to take and keep to the
    end,—
O little sails, make haste!

But thou, vast outbound ship of souls,
What harbor town for thee?
What shapes, when thy arriving tolls,
Shall crowd the banks to see?
Shall all the happy shipmates then

Stand singing brotherly?
Or shall a haggard ruthless few
Warp her over and bring her to,
While the many broken souls of men
Fester down in the slaver's pen,
And nothing to say or do?

                                        1900

THE MENAGERIE *

Thank God my brain is not inclined
    to cut
Such capers every day! I'm just about
Mellow, but then—There goes the
    tent-flap shut.
Rain's in the wind. I thought so:
    every snout
Was twitching when the keeper
    turned me out.

That screaming parrot makes my
    blood run cold.
Gabriel's trump! the big bull elephant
Squeals "Rain!" to the parched herd.
    The monkeys scold,
And jabber that it's rain water they
    want.
(It makes me sick to see a monkey
    pant.)

I'll foot it home, to try and make
    believe
I'm sober. After this I stick to beer,
And drop the circus when the sane
    folks leave.
A man's a fool to look at things too
    near:
They look back, and begin to cut up
    queer.

Beasts do, at any rate; especially
Wild devils caged. They have the
    coolest way
Of being something else than what
    you see;

You pass a sleek young zebra nosing
    hay,
A nylghau looking bored and
    distingué,—

And think you've seen a donkey and
    a bird.
Not on your life! Just glance back, if
    you dare.
The zebra chews, the nylghau hasn't
    stirred;
But something's happened, Heaven
    knows what or where,
To freeze your scalp and pompadour
    your hair.

I'm not precisely an aeolian lute
Hung in the wandering winds of
    sentiment,
But drown me if the ugliest, meanest
    brute
Grunting and fretting in that sultry
    tent
Didn't just floor me with embarrass-
    ment!

'Twas like a thunderclap from out the
    clear,—
One minute they were circus beasts,
    some grand,
Some ugly, some amusing, and some
    queer:
Rival attractions to the hobo band,
The flying jenny, and the peanut
    stand.

Next minute they were old hearth-
    mates of mine!
Lost people, eyeing me with such a
    stare!
Patient, satiric, devilish, divine;
A gaze of hopeless envy, squalid care,
Hatred, and thwarted love, and dim
    despair.

And suddenly, as in a flash of light,
I saw great Nature working out her
    plan;
Through all her shapes from mastodon
    to mite
Forever groping, testing, passing on

To find at last the shape and soul of
    Man.

Till in the fullness of accomplished
    time,
Comes brother Forepaugh, upon busi-
    ness bent,
Tracks her through frozen and
    through torrid clime,
And shows us, neatly labeled in a
    tent,
The stages of her huge experiment;

Blabbing aloud her shy and reticent
    hours;
Dragging to light her blinking, sloth-
    ful moods;
Publishing fretful seasons when her
    powers
Worked wild and sullen in her soli-
    tudes,
Or when her mordant laughter shook
    the woods.

Here, round about me, were her va-
    grant births;
Sick dreams she had, fierce projects
    she essayed;
Her qualms, her fiery prides, her
    crazy mirths;
The troublings of her spirit as she
    strayed,
Cringed, gloated, mocked, was lordly,
    was afraid,

On that long road she went to seek
    mankind;
Here were the darkling coverts that
    she beat
To find the Hider she was sent to
    find;
Here the distracted footprints of her
    feet
Whereby her soul's Desire she came
    to greet.

But why should they, her botch-work,
    turn about
And stare disdain at me, her finished
    job?

Why was the place one vast
    suspended shout
Of laughter? Why did all the day-
    light throb
With soundless guffaw and dumb-
    stricken sob?

Helpless I stood among those awful
    cages;
The beasts were walking loose, and I
    was bagged!
I, I, last product of the toiling ages,
Goal of heroic feet that never
    lagged,—
A little man in trousers, slightly
    jagged.

Deliver me from such another jury!
The Judgment-day will be a picnic
    to't.
Their satire was more dreadful than
    their fury,
And worst of all was just a kind of
    brute
Disgust, and giving up, and sinking
    mute.

Survival of the fittest, adaptation,
And all their other evolution terms,
Seem to omit one small consideration,
To wit, that tumblebugs and angle-
    worms
Have souls: there's soul in everything
    that squirms.

And souls are restless, plagued, im-
    patient things,
All dream and unaccountable desire;
Crawling, but pestered with the
    thought of wings;
Spreading through every inch of
    earth's old mire
Mystical hanker after something
    higher.

Wishes *are* horses, as I understand.
I guess a wistful polyp that has strokes
Of feeling faint to gallivant on land
Will come to be a scandal to his folks;
Legs he will sprout, in spite of threats
    and jokes.

And at the core of every life that
    crawls
Or runs or flies or swims or vegetates—
Churning the mammoth's heart-blood,
    in the galls
Of shark and tiger planting gorgeous
    hates,
Lighting the love of eagles for their
    mates;

Yes, in the dim brain of the jellied fish
That is and is not living—moved and
    stirred
From the beginning a mysterious
    wish,
A vision, a command, a fatal Word:
The name of Man was uttered, and
    they heard.

Upward along the aeons of old war
They sought him: wing and shank-
    bone, claw and bill
Were fashioned and rejected; wide
    and far
They roamed the twilight jungles of
    their will;
But still they sought him, and desired
    him still.

Man they desired, but mind you, Per-
    fect Man,
The radiant and the loving, yet to be!
I hardly wonder, when they came to
    scan
The upshot of their strenuosity,
They gazed with mixed emotions
    upon *me*.

Well, my advice to you is, Face the
    creatures,
Or spot them sideways with your
    weather eye,
Just to keep tab on their expansive
    features;
It isn't pleasant when you're stepping
    high
To catch a giraffe smiling on the sly.

If nature made you graceful, don't get
    gay
Back-to before the hippopotamus;

If meek and godly, find some place to
    play
Besides right where three mad hyenas
    fuss:
You may hear language that we won't
    discuss.

If you're a sweet thing in a flower-bed
    hat,
Or her best fellow with your tie
    tucked in,
Don't squander love's bright spring-
    time girding at
An old chimpanzee with an Irish
    chin:
There may be hidden meaning in his
grin.

              1900

AN ODE IN TIME
OF HESITATION *

(After seeing at Boston the statue of
Robert Gould Shaw, killed while
storming Fort Wagner, July 18, 1863,
at the head of the first enlisted Negro
Regiment, the 54th Massachusetts)

I

Before the solemn bronze Saint Gau-
    dens made
To thrill the heedless passer's heart
    with awe,
And set here in the city's talk and
    trade
To the good memory of Robert Shaw,
This bright March morn I stand,
And hear the distant spring come up
    the land;
Knowing that what I hear is not un-
    heard
Of this boy soldier and his negro
    band,
For all their gaze is fixed so stern
    ahead,

For all the fatal rhythm of their tread.
The land they died to save from death
    and shame
Trembles and waits, hearing the
    spring's great name,
And by her pangs these resolute
    ghosts are stirred.

II

Through street and mall the tides of
    people go
Heedless; the trees upon the Common
    show
No hint of green; but to my listening
    heart
The still earth doth impart
Assurance of her jubilant emprise,
And it is clear to my long-searching
    eyes
That love at last has might upon the
    skies.
The ice is runneled on the little pond;
A telltale patter drips from off the
    trees;
The air is touched with southland
    spiceries,
As if but yesterday it tossed the
    frond
Of pendent mosses where the live-oaks
    grow
Beyond Virginia and the Carolines,
Or had its will among the fruits and
    vines
Or aromatic isles asleep beyond
Florida and the Gulf of Mexico.

III

Soon shall the Cape Ann children
    shout in glee,
Spying the arbutus, spring's dear re-
    cluse;
Hill lads at dawn shall hearken the
    wild goose
Go honking northward over Tennes-
    see;
West from Oswego to Sault Sainte-
    Marie,
And on to where the Pictured Rocks
    are hung,

And yonder where, gigantic, wilful,
    young,
Chicago sitteth at the northwest gates,
With restless violent hands and casual
    tongue
Molding her mighty fates,
The lakes shall robe them in ethereal
    sheen;
And like a larger sea, the vital green
Of springing wheat shall vastly be
    outflung
Over Dakota and the prairie states.
By desert people immemorial
On Arizonan mesas shall be done
Dim rites unto the thunder and the
    sun;
Nor shall the primal gods lack sacri-
    fice
More splendid, when the white
    Sierras call
Unto the Rockies straightway to arise
And dance before the unveiled ark of
    the year,
Sounding their windy cedars as for
    shawns,
Unrolling rivers clear
For flutter of broad phylacteries;
While Shasta signals to Alaskan seas
That watch old sluggish glaciers
    downward creep
To fling their icebergs thundering
    from the steep,
And Mariposa through the purple
    calms
Gazes at far Hawaii crowned with
    palms
Where East and West are met,—
A rich seal on the ocean's bosom set
To say that East and West are twain,
With different loss and gain:
The Lord hath sundered them; let
    them be sundered yet.

IV

Alas! what sounds are these that come
Sullenly over the Pacific seas,—
Sounds of ignoble battle, striking
    dumb
The season's half-awakened ecstasies?

Must I be humble, then,
Now when my heart hath need of
　pride?
Wild love falls on me from these
　sculptured men;
By loving much the land for which
　they died
I would be justified.
My spirit was away on pinions wide
To soothe in praise of her its passion-
　ate mood
And ease it of its ache of gratitude,
Too sorely heavy is the debt they lay
On me and the companions of my
　day.
I would remember now
My country's goodliness, make sweet
　her name.
Alas! what shade art thou
Of sorrow or of blame
Liftest the lyric leafage from her
　brow,
And pointest a slow finger at her
　shame?

v

Lies! lies! It cannot be! The wars we
　wage
Are noble, and our battles still are
　won
By justice for us, ere we lift the
　gage.
We have not sold our loftiest heritage.
The proud republic hath not stooped
　to cheat
And scramble in the market-place of
　war;
Her forehead weareth yet its solemn
　star.
Here is her witness: this, her perfect
　son,
This delicate and proud New England
　soul
Who leads despisèd men, with just-
　unshackled feet,
Up the large ways where death and
　glory meet,
To show all peoples that our shame
　is done,

That once more we are clean and
　spirit-whole.

VI

Crouched in the sea fog on the morn-
　ing sand
All night he lay, speaking some
　simple word
From hour to hour to the slow minds
　that heard,
Holding each poor life gently in his
　hand
And breathing on the base rejected
　clay
Till each dark face shone mystical
　and grand
Against the breaking day;
And lo, the shard the potter cast
　away
Was grown a fiery chalice crystal-fine
Fulfilled of the divine
Great wine of battle wrath by God's
　ring-finger stirred.
Then upward, where the shadowy
　bastion loomed
Huge on the mountain in the wet sea
　light,
Whence now, and now, infernal flow-
　erage bloomed,
Bloomed, burst, and scattered down
　its deadly seed,—
They swept, and died like freemen on
　the height,
Like freemen, and like men of noble
　breed;
And when the battle fell away at
　night
By hasty and contemptuous hands
　were thrust
Obscurely in a common grave with
　him
The fair-haired keeper of their love
　and trust.
Now limb doth mingle with dissolvèd
　limb
In nature's busy old democracy
To flush the mountain laurel when
　she blows
Sweet by the southern sea,

And heart with crumbled heart climbs
in the rose:—
The untaught hearts with the high
heart that knew
This mountain fortress for no earthly
hold
Of temporal quarrel, but the bastion
old
Of spiritual wrong,
Built by an unjust nation sheer and
strong,
Expugnable but by a nation's rue
And bowing down before that equal
shrine
By all men held divine,
Whereof his band and he were the
most holy sign.

VII

O bitter, bitter shade!
Wilt thou not put the scorn
And instant tragic question from thine
eyes?
Do thy dark brows yet crave
That swift and angry stave—
Unmeet for this desirous morn—
That I have striven, striven to evade?
Gazing on him, must I not deem they
err
Whose careless lips in street and shop
aver
As common tidings, deeds to make his
cheek
Flush from the bronze, and his dead
throat to speak?
Surely some elder singer would arise,
Whose harp hath leave to threaten
and to mourn
Above this people when they go
astray.
Is Whitman, the strong spirit, over-
worn?
Has Whittier put his yearning wrath
away?
I will not and I dare not yet believe!
Though furtively the sunlight seems
to grieve,
And the spring-ladened breeze
Out of the gladdening west is sinister

With sounds of nameless battle over-
seas:
Though when we turn and question
in suspense
If these things be indeed after these,
Our fluent men of place and conse-
quence
Fumble and fill their mouths with hol-
low phrase,
Or for the end-all of deep arguments
Intone their dull commercial litur-
gies—
I dare not yet believe! My ears are
shut!
I will not hear the thin satiric praise
And muffled laughter of our enemies,
Bidding us never sheathe our valiant
sword
Till we have changed our birthright
for a gourd
Of wild pulse stolen from a barbarian's
hut;
Showing how wise it is to cast
away
The symbols of our spiritual sway,
That so our hands with better ease
May wield the driver's whip and
grasp the jailer's keys.

VIII

Was it for this our fathers kept the
law?
This crown shall crown their struggle
and their ruth?
Are we the eagle nation Milton saw
Mewing its mighty youth,
Soon to possess the mountain winds
of truth,
And be a swift familiar of the sun
Where ay before God's face his trum-
pets run?
Or have we but the talons and the
maw,
And for the abject likeness of our
heart
Shall some less lordly bird be set
apart?—
Some gross-billed wader where the
swamps are fat?

Some gorger in the sun? Some
  prowler with the bat?

IX

Ah no!
We have not fallen so.
We are our fathers' sons: let those
  who lead us know!
'T was only yesterday sick Cuba's cry
Came up the tropic wind, "Now help
  us, for we die."
Then Alabama heard,
And rising, pale, to Maine and Idaho
Shouted a burning word.
Proud state with proud impassioned
  state conferred,
And at the lifting of a hand sprang
  forth,
East, west, and south, and north,
Beautiful armies. Oh, by the sweet
  blood and young
Shed on the awful hill slope at San
  Juan,
By the unforgotten names of eager
  boys
Who might have tasted girls' love and
  been stung
With the old mystic joys
And starry griefs, now the spring
  nights come on,
But that the heart of youth is gener-
  ous,—
We charge you, ye who lead us,
Breathe on their chivalry no hint of
  stain!
Turn not their new-world victories to
  gain!
One least leaf plucked for chaffer
  from the bays
Of their dear praise,
One jot of their pure conquest put
  to hire,
The implacable republic will require:
With clamor, in the glare and gaze
  of noon,
Or subtly, coming as a thief at night,
But surely, very surely, slow or soon
That insult deep we deeply will re-
  quite.

Tempt not our weakness, our cupid-
  ity!
For save we let the island men go
  free,
Those baffled and dislaureled ghosts
Will curse us from the lamentable
  coasts
Where walk the frustrate dead.
The cup of trembling shall be
  drainèd quite,
Eaten the sour bread of astonish-
  ment,
With ashes of the hearth shall be
  made white
Our hair, and wailing shall be in the
  tent;
Then on your guiltier head
Shall our intolerable self-disdain
Wreak suddenly its anger and its
  pain;
For manifest in that disastrous light
We shall discern the right
And do it, tardily.—O ye who lead,
Take heed!
Blindness we may forgive, but base-
  ness we will smite.

1900

THE DEATH OF EVE *

I

At dawn they came to the stream
  Hiddekel,
Old Eve and her red first-born, who
  was now
Grayer than she, and bowed with
  more than years.
Then Cain beneath his level palm
  looked hard
Across the desert, and turned with
  outspread hand
As one who says, "Thou seest; we
  are fooled."

But Eve, with clutching fingers on his
    arm,
And pointing eastward where the
    risen sun
Made a low mist of light, said, "It is
    there!"

II

For, many, many months, in the great
    tent
Of Enoch, Eve had pined, and dared
    not tell
Her longing—not to Irad, Enoch's son,
Masterful like his father, who had
    held
Harsh rule, and named the tent-place
    with his name;
Not to mild Seth, given her in Abel's
    stead;
Not unto angry Lamech, nor his
    wives,
Usurpers of her honor in the house;
Not to young Jubal, songs-man of the
    tribe,
Who touched his harp at twilight by
    her door;
And not to bedrid Adam, most of all,
Not unto Adam. Yet at last, the
    spring
Being at end, and evening with warm
    stars
Falling upon them by the camel kraal,
Weary with long desire, she spoke to
    Seth,
Touching her meaning faintly and far
    off
To try him. With still scrutiny awhile
He looked at her; then, lifting doubt-
    ful hands
Of prayer, he led her homeward to
    the tent,
With tremulous speech of small and
    weekday things.
Next, as she lay by Adam before
    dawn,
His big and wasted hand groping for
    hers
Suddenly made her half-awakened
    heart

Break back and back across the shad-
    owy years
To Eden, and God calling in the dew,
And all that song of Paradise foredone
Which Jubal made in secret, fearing
    her
The storied mother; but in secret, too,
Herself had listened, while the maids
    at toil
Or by the well at evening sang of
    her
Untruthful things, which, when she
    once had heard,
Seemed truthful. Now, bowed upon
    Adam's breast,
In the deep hush that comes before
    the dawn,
She whispered hints and fragments of
    her will;
And when the shaggy forehead made
    no sign,
And the blind face searched still as
    quietly
In the tent-roof for what, these many
    months,
It seemed to seek for there, she held
    him close
And poured her whole wild meaning
    in his ear.
But as a man upon his deathbed
    dreams
That he should know a matter, and
    knows it not,
Nor who they are who fain would
    have him know,
He turned to hers his dim, disastrous
    eyes,
Wherein the knowledge of her and
    the long love
Glimmered through veil on veil of
    vacancy.
That evening little Jubal, coming
    home
Singing behind his flock, saw ancient
    Eve
Crouched by the ruined altar in the
    glade,
The accurséd place, sown deep each
    early spring

With stones and salt—the Valley of
the Blood;
And that same night Eve fled under
the stars
Eastward to Nod, the land of violence,
To Cain and the strong city he had
built
Against all men who hunted for his
soul.

III

She gave her message darkly in the
gates,
And waited trembling. At day-fall he
came.
She knew him not beneath his whit-
ened hair;
But when at length she knew him,
and was known,
The whitened hair, the bent and
listening frame,
The savage misery of the sidelong
eyes,
Fell on her heart with strangling. So
it was
That now for many days she held her
peace,
Abiding with him till he seemed again
The babe she bare first in the wilder-
ness,
Her maiden fruits to Adam, the new
joy
The desert bloomed with, which the
desert stars
Whispered concerning. Yet she held
her peace,
Until he seemed a young man in the
house,
A gold frontlet of pride and a green
cedar;
Then, leading him apart, Eve told her
wish,
Not faltering now nor uttering it far
off,
But as a sovereign mother to her son
Speaks simple destiny. He looked at
her
Dimly, as if he saw her not; then
stooped,

Sharpening his brows upon her. With
a cry
She laid fierce, shaken hands about
his breast,
Drew down his neck, and harshly
from his brow
Pushing the head-band and the
matted locks,
Baring the livid flesh with violence,
She kissed him on the Sign. Cain
bowed his head
Upon her shoulder, saying, "I will
go!"

IV

Now they had come to the stream
Hiddekel,
And passed beyond the stream. There,
full in face,
Where the low morning made a mist
of light,
The Garden and its gates lay like a
flower
Afloat on the still waters of the dawn.
The clicking leap of bright-mailed
grasshoppers,
The dropping of sage-beetles from
their perch
On the gnawed cactus, even the puls-
ing drum
Of blood-beats in their ears, merged
suddenly
Into ethereal hush. Then Cain made
halt,
Held her, and muttered, " 'Tis
enough. Thou sawest!
His Angel stood and threatened in the
sun!"
And Eve said, "Yea, and though the
day were set
With sworded angels, thou would'st
wait for me
Yonder, before the gates; which, look
you, child,
Lie open to me as the gates to him,
Thy father, when he entered in his
rage,
Calling thee from the dark, where of
old days

I kept thee folded, hidden, till he called."
So gray Cain by the unguarded portal sat,
His arms crossed o'er his forehead, and his face
Hid in his meager knees; but ancient Eve
Passed on into the vales of Paradise.

V

Trancéd in lonely radiance stood the Tree,
As Eve put back the glimmering ferns and vines
And crept into the place. Awhile she stooped,
And as a wild thing by the drinking-pool
Peers ere it drinks, she peered. Then, laughing low,
Her frame of grief and body of her years
She lifted proudly to its virgin height,
Flung her lean arms into the pouring day,
And circling with slow paces round the Tree,
She sang her stifled meaning out to God.

EVE'S SONG

Behold, against thy will, against thy word,
Against the wrath and warning of thy sword,
Eve has been Eve, O Lord!
A pitcher filled, she comes back from the brook,
A wain she comes, laden with mellow ears;
She is a roll inscribed, a prophet's book
Writ strong with characters.
Behold, Eve willed it so; look, if it be so, look!

Early at dawn, while yet thy watchers slept,

Lightly her untamed spirit overleapt
The walls where she was kept.
As a young comely leopardess she stood.
Her lustrous fell, her sullen grace, her fleetness—
They gave her foretaste, in thy tangled wood,
Of many a savage sweetness,
Good to fore-gloat upon; being tasted, sweet and good.

O swayer in the sunlit tops of trees,
O comer up with cloud out of the seas,
O laugher at thine ease
Over thine everlasting dream of mirth,
O lord of savage pleasures, savage pains,
Knew'st Thou not Eve, who brought-est her to birth?
Searcher of breast and reins,
Thou should'st have searched thy Woman, the seed pod of thine earth!

Herself hath searched her softly through and through;
Singing she lifts her full soul up to view;
Lord, do thou praise it, too!
Look, as she turns it, how it dartles free
Its gathered meanings: woman, mother, wife,
Spirit that was and is and waits to be,
Worm of the dust of life,
Child, sister—ghostly rays! What lights are these, Lord, see!

Look where Eve lifts her storied soul on high,
And turns it as a ball, she knows not why,
Save that she could not die
Till she had shown Thee all the secret sphere—
The bright rays and the dim, and these that run

Bright-darkling, making thee to doubt
    and fear—
Oh, love them every one!
Eve pardons thee not one, not one,
    Lord; dost thou hear?

Lovely to Eve was Adam's praising
    breath;
His face averted bitter was as death;
    Abel, her son, and Seth
Lifted her heart to heaven, praising
    her;
Cain with a little frown darkened the
    stars;
And when the strings of Jubal's harp
    would stir,
Like honey in cool jars
The words he praised her with, like
    rain his praises were.

Still, still with prayer and ecstasy she
    strove
To be the woman they did well ap-
    prove,
That, narrowed to their love,
She might have done with bitterness
    and blame;
But still along the yonder edge of
    prayer
A spirit in a fiery whirlwind came—
Eve's spirit, wild and fair—
Crying with Eve's own voice the num-
    ber of her name.

Yea, turning in the whirlwind and the
    fire,
Eve saw her own proud being all en-
    tire
Made perfect by desire;
And from the rounded gladness of
    that sphere
Came bridal songs and harpings and
    fresh laughter;
"Glory unto the faithful!" sounded
    clear,
And then, a little after,
"Whoso denyeth aught, let him de-
    part from here!"

Now, therefore, Eve, with mystic years
    o'er-scored,

Danceth and doeth pleasure to thee,
    Lord,
According to the word
That thou hast spoken to her by her
    dream.
Singing a song she dimly understands,
She lifts her soul to let the splendor
    stream.
Lord, take away thy hands!
Let this beam pierce thy heart, and
    this most piercing beam!

Far off rebelliously, yet for thy sake,
She gathered them, O thou who
    lovest to break
A thousand souls, and shake
Their dust along the wind, but sleep-
    lessly
Searchest the Bride fulfilled in limb
    and feature,
Ready and boon to be fulfilled of thee,
Thine ample, tameless creature—
Against thy will and word, behold,
    Lord, this is She!

VI

From carven plinth and thousand-
    galleried green
Cedars, and all close boughs that
    overtower,
The shadows lengthened eastward
    from the gates,
And still Cain hid his forehead in his
    knees,
Nor dared to look abroad lest he might
    find
More watchers in the portals; for he
    heard
What seemed the rush of wings; from
    while to while
A pallor grew and faded in his brain,
As if a great light passed him near at
    hand.
But when above the darkening desert
    swales
The moon came, shedding white, un-
    likely day,
Cain rose, and with his back against
    the stones,

As a keen fighter at the desperate
    odds,
Glared round him. Cool and silent
    lay the night,
Empty of any foe. Then, as a man
Who has a thing to do, and makes his
    fear
An icy wind to freeze his purpose
    firm,
He stole in through the pillars of the
    gate,
Down aisles of shadow windowed
    with the moon,
By meads with the still stars com-
    municant,
Past heaven-bosoming pool and
    pooléd stream,
Until he saw, through tangled fern
    and vine,
The Tree, where God had made its
    habitation.
And crouched above the shape that
    had been Eve,
With savage, listening frame and side-
    long eyes,
Cain waited for the coming of the
    dawn.
                      1906

LIZETTE WOODWORTH REESE
(1856–1935)
TEARS *

When I consider Life and its few
    years—
A wisp of fog betwixt us and the sun;
A call to battle, and the battle done
Ere the last echo dies within our ears;
A rose choked in the grass; an hour
    of fears;
The gusts that past a darkening shore
    do beat;
The burst of music down an unlisten-
    ing street—

   * Reprinted by permission of Doubleday, Doran and Company, Inc., from
The Selected Poems of Lizette Woodworth Reese, copyright 1926 by Doubleday, Doran and Company, Inc.

I wonder at the idleness of tears.
Ye old, old dead, and ye of yester-
    night,
Chieftains, and bards, and keepers of
    the sheep,
By every cup of sorrow that you
    had,
Loose me from tears, and make me
    see aright
How each hath back what once he
    stayed to weep;
Homer his sight, David his little lad!
                      1899

WILD GEESE *

The sun blown out;
The dusk about:
Fence, roof, tree—here or there,
Wedged fast in the drab air;
A pool vacant with sky,
That stares up like an eye.

Nothing can happen. All is done—
The quest to fare,
The race to run—
The house sodden with years,
And bare
Even of tears.

A cry!
From out the hostelries of sky,
And down the gray wind blown;
Rude, innocent, alone.

Now, in the west, long sere,
An orange thread, the length of
    spear;
It glows;
It grows;
The flagons of the air
Drip color everywhere;
The village—fence, roof, tree—
From the lapsed dusk pulls free,
And shows
A rich, still, unforgotten place;
Each window square,
Yellow for yellow renders back;
The pool puts off its foolish face;
The wagon track

Crooks past lank garden-plot,
To Rome, to Camelot.

A cry!

1900

THE PLOWMAN *

The delicate gray trees stand up
　There by the old fenced ways;
One or two are crimson-tipped,
　And soon will start to blaze.

The plowman follows, as of yore,
　Along the furrows cold,
Homeric shape against the boughs;
　Sharp is the air with mold.

The sweating horses heave and strain;
　The crows with thick, high note
Break black across the windless land,
　Fade off and are remote.

Oh, new days, yet long known and
　　old!
　Lo, as we look about,
This immemorial act of faith,
　That takes the heart from doubt!

Kingdoms decay and creeds are not,
　Yet still the plowman goes
Down the spring fields, so he may
　　make
　Ready for him that sows.

1909

NOCTURNE *

Topple the house down, wind;
Break it and tear it, rain;
She is not within,
Nor will come again.

That not even her ghost
Will know it for her own;—
Topple it into dust;
Tear it bone from bone.

1909

* Reprinted by permission of Doubleday, Doran and Company, Inc., from
The Selected Poems of Lizette Woodworth Reese, copyright 1926 by Doubleday, Doran and Company, Inc.

IN PRAISE
OF COMMON THINGS *

For stock and stone;
For grass and pool; for quince tree
　　blown
A virginal white in spring;
And for the wall beside,
Gray, gentle, wide;
For roof, loaf, everything,
I praise Thee, Lord;
For toil, and ache, and strife,
And all the commonness of life.

Hearty, yet dim,
Like country voices in a hymn,
The things a house can hold;
The memories in the air;
And down the stair
Fond footsteps known of old;
The chair, the book or two;
The little bowl of white and blue.

What would it be,
If loveliness were far from me?
A staff I could not take,
To hurry up and down,
From field to town;
Needs would my wild heart break;
Or, I would vacant go,
And, being naught, to nothing grow.

This is the best:
My little road from east to west,
The breadth of a man's hand,
Not from the sky too far,
Nor any star,
Runs through the unwalled land;
From common things that be,
Is but a step to run to Thee.

1909

TRAGIC BOOKS *

That I have lived I know; that I
Have loved is quite as plain;
Why read of Lear, a wild old king,
Of Caesar stabbed in vain?

The bitter fool, the Dover heath,
The stumbling in the grass

I know. I know the windy crowd,
And Rome as in a glass.

Life taught them all. These later days
Are full enough of rain;
I will not weep unless I must,
Or break my heart again.

1926

PERCY MACKAYE
(1875–   )

TO GEORGE PIERCE BAKER *

The ghosts of Praise-God Barebones
    and his clan
Still walk, and with their old acerbity
Infect us; even the University
Is haunted still, and the sparse Puri-
    tan
Turned Prospero, has made a Caliban
Of human passion, and wild Poesie
Pinched in an oak to starve, and
    Mimicry
And all her kindred Muses put to ban.
Yet not so now at Harvard; there be-
    takes
Him now the scholar-player, with his
    Muse
(That deathless wench, the Mermaid)
    and renews
His vows, and breaks his fast, and is
    restored
By our own Baker.—May the loaves
    he bakes
Soon pile a feast at Master Shake-
    speare's board!

1909

TO THE FIRE-BRINGER *

(WILLIAM VAUGHN MOODY)

Bringer of fire
Down from the star
Quivering far

    * From Percy MacKaye, *Poems and
Plays*, copyright 1916. By permission of
The Macmillan Company, publishers.

In quiet eternal:
Bringer of fire!—
Ashes we are
If to thy pyre
Out of our hearts
Ashes we bring.

Vernal, vernal,
Divine and burning—
A wreath of worlds
And wings—was thy vision:
Fadeless now,
That fiery wreath
Wrought of thy yearning
We lay in death
Bright on thy brow.

Singer and lover,
Brother and friend,
Ashes can end
Only the dross of thee:
Quick Promethean,
Out of the dirge
And the dark loss of thee,
Leaps thy star-wrestling
Spirit in paean!

Fire, fire,
Fire was thy bringing,
An urn elemental
Of burning song
So on thy pyre
We leave it flaming—
Where Death cannot follow—
Toward thee, who camest singing:
"Apollo, Apollo!"

1912

THREE DANCE MOTIVES *

(IMAGINED FOR DANCES
OF ISADORA DUNCAN)

I. LETHE

Alone by a starless sea
    I lay with Sorrow;
And mists of slumber breathed
    From the mouth of my lover;

And I rose from his numbing arms
    And moaned: "O, release me!

Let me flame, let me leap once more
  On the hills of vision!"

Then one by one stood round us
  Stars of the morning:
Their lyric bodies sang,
  Their torch-limbs beckoned;

But the fog of my blind lover's breath
  Congealed their burning
Till they drooped on the banks of
    dawn
  Like lilies frost-slain,

And I drooped to his lethal lips
  Of anguish, and lay there
Till the shy Stars bloomed again
  By shores of the evening,

Beckoning anew, with their palms
  Of flame, to rejoin them
On the Mountains of Joy, and once
    more
  I rose in my yearning

And gazed: *I am coming!* But ah!
  The arrows of my gazing
Pierced them there, side by side,
  And they waned by the waters,

Lying like mermaids, dead
  In the shoals of twilight.—
Then my soul waned with them, and
    kissed
  The cold mouth of my lover.

But still, through the pulsing mists
  Of our pitiful dreaming,
I feel their immortal eyes
  Burning with wonder.

II. DIONYSUS

Dionysus!—io! Io!—Dionysus!
Who hath rolled back the rock from
  the cave Cimerian
And blinded the world with morning?
Dionysus!—thou!—It is thou, Diony-
  sus!
Out of the niggard, numbing dark of
  the ages
Thou, from the dead, art restored!
Stark from the Tree of Pain,

Crucified, bleeding, disowned,
They bore the beautiful God of our
  Joy to his charnel:
But there in the flaming dark, thou—
  thou, his seraph,
Rolled back the awful stone
For the Lord of Life—new risen.

Dionysus!—io! Io!—Dionysus!
Lo! thy grapes are the clustering
  hearts of children
And the wine of these is thy worship.
Dionysus!—once more!—Once more,
  Dionysus,
Thou revealest our God, who is One
  through all ages:—
The Lord of Life is regained!

III. THE CHASE

Through what vast wood,
By what wild paths of beautiful sur-
  prise,
Hast thou returned to us,
Diana, Diana of Desire?
Coming to thy call
What huntresses are these?
What hallowed chase? What long,
  long cherished goal?
Through man's wan mind
By radiant paths of rhythmic liberty
I am returned to you,
Diviner, diviner of dreams!
Those huntresses, ·they are my hal-
  lowed desires—
My unquenched selves with overflow-
  ing quivers.
Joy is our chase and goal:
Our bodies the tense crossbows, and
  our wild souls the shafts!

1914

WILSON *

Patience—but peace of heart we cannot choose;

* From Percy MacKaye, *Poems and Plays*, copyright 1916. By permission of The Macmillan Company, publishers.

Nor would he wish us cravenly to
keep
Aloof in soul, who—large in states-
manship
And justice—sent our ships to Vera
Cruz.
Patience must wring our hearts, while
we refuse
To launch our country on that crim-
son deep
Which breaks the dykes of Europe,
but we sleep
Watchful, still waiting by the awful
fuse.
Wisdom he counsels, and he counsels
well
Whose patient fortitude against the
fret
And sneer of time has stood invio-
lable.
We love his goodness and will not
forget.
With him we pause beside the mouth
of hell:—
The wolf of Europe has not tri-
umphed yet.

1914

NIETZSCHE *

Some worshipped and some bantered,
when
 The prophets of the drawing room
 Gossiped of Jesus Christ his doom
Under the reign of Supermen,
And how the Christian world would
quake
To hear what Zarathustra spake.

Lo, Zarathustra's voice has spoken:
 And they, who use a mad bard's
 song

 * From Percy MacKaye, *Poems and
Plays*, copyright 1916. By permission of
The Macmillan Company, publishers.

To vindicate a tyrant's wrong,
Point to the staring dead for token
Of their triumphant creed, enshrined
In temples of the Teuton mind.

The raving dog-star hath his season:
 But when the light beyond our
 death
 Leads back again from Nazareth
The holy star of human reason—
Then will philosophy no more
Be servile to the Muse of War.

1914

LOUVAIN *

Serene in beauty's olden lineage,
Calm as the star that hears the
 Angelus toll,
Louvain—the scholar's crypt, the
 artist's goal,
The cloistral shrine of hallowed pil-
 grimage
Rapt in the dreams of many an ardent
 age,
Louvain, the guileless city of man's
 soul,
Is blotted from the world—a bloodied
 scroll,
Ravaged to sate a drunken Teuton's
 rage.
His lust shall have its laurel. The red
 sword
He ravished with, Time's angel shall
 again
Grasp to sere *him,* and deify him
 Lord
Of Infamy; yea, brand him with its
 stain
Naked in night, abhorrent and ab-
 horr'd,
Where the dead hail him *William of
 Louvain!*

1914

VACHEL LINDSAY
(1879–1931)

THE EAGLE THAT IS FORGOTTEN *

(JOHN P. ALTGELD. BORN DECEMBER 30, 1847; DIED MARCH 12, 1902)

Sleep softly . . . eagle forgotten . . .
under the stone.
Time has its way with you there, and
the clay has its own.

"We have buried him now," thought
your foes, and in secret rejoiced.
They made a brave show of their
mourning, their hatred unvoiced.
They had snarled at you, barked at
you, foamed at you day after
day.
Now you were ended. They praised
you, . . . and laid you away.

The others that mourned you in silence and terror and truth,
The widow bereft of her crust, and
the boy without youth,
The mocked and the scorned and the
wounded, the lame and the poor
That should have remembered forever, . . . remember no more.

Where are those lovers of yours, on
what name do they call
The lost, that in armies wept over
your funeral pall?
They call on the names of a hundred
high-valiant ones,
A hundred white eagles have risen the
sons of your sons,
The zeal in their wings is a zeal that
your dreaming began
The valor that wore out your soul in
the service of man.

Sleep softly, . . . eagle forgotten, . . .
under the stone,

* From Vachel Lindsay, *Collected Poems*, copyright 1913, 1914, 1916, 1917, 1919, 1920, 1923, 1925, by The Macmillan Company. By permission of The Macmillan Company, publishers.

Time has its way with you there and
the clay has its own.
Sleep on, O brave-hearted, O wise
man, that kindled the flame—
To live in mankind is far more than to
live in a name,
To live in mankind, far, far more
. . . than to live in a name.
1912

WHY I VOTED THE SOCIALIST TICKET *

I am unjust, but I can strive for
justice.
My life's unkind, but I can vote for
kindness.
I, the unloving, say that life should
be lovely.
I, that am blind, cry out against my
blindness.

Man is a curious brute—he pets his
fancies—
Fighting mankind, to win sweet
luxury.
So he will be, tho' law be clear as
crystal,
Tho' all men plan to live in harmony.

Come let us vote against our human
nature,
Crying to God in all the polling places
To heal our everlasting sinfulness
And make us sages with transfigured
faces.
1913

A NET TO SNARE THE MOONLIGHT *

(WHAT THE MAN OF FAITH SAID)

The dew, the rain and moonlight
All prove our Father's mind.
The dew, the rain and moonlight
Descend to bless mankind.

Come, let us see that all men
Have land to catch the rain,

Have grass to snare the spheres of
    dew,
And fields spread for the grain.

Yea, we would give to each poor man
Ripe wheat and poppies red,—
A peaceful place at evening
With the stars just overhead:

A net to snare the moonlight,
A sod spread to the sun,
A place of toil by daytime,
Of dreams when toil is done.

1913

GENERAL WILLIAM BOOTH ENTERS INTO HEAVEN *

*(To be sung to the tune of "The Blood
of the Lamb" with indicated instrument)*

I

(Bass drum beaten loudly.)
Booth led boldly with his big bass
    drum—
(Are you washed in the blood of the
    Lamb?)
The Saints smiled gravely and they
    said: "He's come."
(Are you washed in the blood of the
    Lamb?)
Walking lepers followed, rank on
    rank,
Lurching bravos from the ditches
    dank,
Drabs from the alleyways and drug
    fiends pale—
Minds still passion-ridden, soul-powers
    frail:—
Vermin-eaten saints with moldy
    breath,
Unwashed legions with the ways of
    Death—
(Are you washed in the blood of the
    Lamb?)

* From Vachel Lindsay, *Collected
Poems,* copyright 1913, 1914, 1916,
1917, 1919, 1920, 1923, 1925, by The
Macmillan Company. By permission of
The Macmillan Company, publishers.

(Banjos.)
Every slum had sent its half-a-score
The round world over. (Booth had
    groaned for more.)
Every banner that the wide world
    flies
Bloomed with glory and transcendent
    dyes.
Big-voiced lasses made their banjos
    bang,
Tranced, fanatical they shrieked and
    sang:—
"Are you washed in the blood of the
    Lamb?"
Hallelujah! It was queer to see
Bull-necked convicts with that land
    make free.
Loons with trumpets blowed a blare,
    blare, blare
On, on upward thro' the golden air!
(Are you washed in the blood of the
    Lamb?)

II

(Bass drum slower and softer.)
Booth died blind and still by faith he
    trod,
Eyes still dazzled by the ways of God.
Booth led boldly, and he looked the
    chief
Eagle countenance in sharp relief,
Beard a-flying, air of high command
Unabated in that holy land.

(Sweet flute music.)
Jesus came from out the court-house
    door,
Stretched his hands above the pass-
    ing poor.
Booth saw not, but led his queer ones
    there
Round and round the mighty court-
    house square.
Then, in an instant all that blear re-
    view
Marched on spotless, clad in raiment
    new.
The lame were straightened, withered
    limbs uncurled

And blind eyes opened on a new, sweet world.

(*Bass drum louder.*)
Drabs and vixens in a flash made whole!
Gone was the weasel-head, the snout, the jowl!
Sages and sibyls now, and athletes clean,
Rulers of empires, and of forests green!

(*Grand chorus of all instruments. Tambourines to the foreground.*)
The hosts were sandalled, and their wings were fire!
(Are you washed in the blood of the Lamb?)
But their noise played havoc with the angel-choir.
(Are you washed in the blood of the Lamb?)
Oh, shout Salvation! It was good to see
Kings and Princes by the Lamb set free.
The banjos rattled and the tambourines
Jing-jing-jingled in the hands of Queens.

(*Reverently sung, no instruments.*)
And when Booth halted by the curb for prayer
He saw his Master thro' the flag-filled air.
Christ came gently with a robe and crown
For Booth the soldier, while the throng knelt down.
He saw King Jesus. They were face to face,
And he knelt a-weeping in that holy place.
Are you washed in the blood of the Lamb?

1913

ABRAHAM LINCOLN WALKS AT MIDNIGHT *

(IN SPRINGFIELD, ILLINOIS)

It is portentous, and a thing of state
That here at midnight, in our little town
A mourning figure walks, and will not rest,
Near the old court-house pacing up and down,

Or by his homestead, or in shadowed yards
He lingers where his children used to play,
Or through the market, on the well-worn stones
He stalks until the dawn-stars burn away.

A bronzed, lank man! His suit of ancient black,
A famous high top-hat and plain worn shawl
Make him the quaint great figure that men love,
The prairie-lawyer, master of us all.

He cannot sleep upon his hillside now.
He is among us:—as in times before!
And we who toss and lie awake for long
Breathe deep, and start, to see him pass the door.

His head is bowed. He thinks on men and kings.
Yea, when the sick world cries, how can he sleep?
Too many peasants fight, they know not why,

* From Vachel Lindsay, *Collected Poems*, copyright 1913, 1914, 1916, 1917, 1919, 1920, 1923, 1925, by The Macmillan Company. By permission of The Macmillan Company, publishers.

Too many homesteads in black terror
    weep.
The sins of all the war-lords burn his
    heart.
He sees the dreadnaughts scouring
    every main.
He carries on his shawl-wrapped
    shoulders now
The bitterness, the folly and the pain.

He cannot rest until a spirit-dawn
Shall come;—the shining hope of
    Europe free:

The league of sober folk, the Workers'
    Earth,
Bringing long peace to Cornland, Alp
    and Sea.

It breaks his heart that kings must
    murder still,
That all his hours of travail here for
    men
Seem yet in vain. And who will bring
    white peace
That he may sleep upon his hill
    again?

          1914

THE MOON'S THE NORTH WIND'S COOKY *

(WHAT THE LITTLE GIRL SAID)

The Moon's the North Wind's cooky.
He bites it, day by day,
Until there's but a rim of scraps
That crumble all away.

The South Wind is a baker.
He kneads clouds in his den,
And bakes a crisp new moon *that*
   . . . greedy
North . . . Wind . . . eats . . . again!
          1914

FACTORY WINDOWS ARE ALWAYS BROKEN *

Factory windows are always broken.
Somebody's always throwing bricks,
Somebody's always heaving cinders,
Playing ugly Yahoo tricks.

Factory windows are always broken.
Other windows are let alone.
No one throws through the chapel-
    window
The bitter, snarling, derisive stone.

Factory windows are always broken.
Something or other is going wrong.
Something is rotten—I think, in Den-
    mark.
End of the factory-window song.
          1914

THE CONGO *

A STUDY OF THE NEGRO RACE

I. THEIR BASIC SAVAGERY

Fat black bucks in a wine-barrel room,
Barrel-house kings, with feet unstable,
Sagged and reeled and pounded on the table,
Pounded on the table,
Beat an empty barrel with the handle of a broom,
Hard as they were able,

                                    A deep rolling bass.

Boom, boom, BOOM,
With a silk umbrella and the handle of a broom,
Boomlay, boomlay, boomlay, BOOM.
THEN I had religion, THEN I had a vision
I could not turn from their revel in derision.
THEN I SAW THE CONGO, CREEPING THROUGH THE BLACK,   *More*
CUTTING THROUGH THE FOREST WITH A GOLDEN TRACK.   *deliberate.*
Then along that riverbank   *Solemnly*
A thousand miles   *chanted.*
Tattooed cannibals danced in files;
Then I heard the boom of the blood-lust song
And a thigh-bone beating on a tin-pan gong.   *A rapidly*
And "BLOOD" screamed the whistles and the fifes of the   *piling climax*
        warriors,   *of speed and*
"BLOOD" screamed the skull-faced, lean witch-doctors,   *racket.*
"Whirl ye the deadly voo-doo rattle,
Harry the uplands,
Steal all the cattle,
Rattle-rattle, rattle-rattle,
Bing.
Boomlay, boomlay, boomlay, BOOM,"   *With a*
A roaring, epic, rag-time tune   *philosophic*
From the mouth of the Congo   *pause.*
To the Mountains of the Moon.
Death is an Elephant,   *Shrilly and*
Torch-eyed and horrible,   *with a*
Foam-flanked and terrible.   *heavily ac-*
Boom, steal the pygmies,   *cented metre.*
Boom, kill the Arabs,
Boom, kill the white men,
Hoo, HOO, HOO.
Listen to the yell of Leopold's ghost   *Like the*
Burning in Hell for his hand-maimed host.   *wind in the*
Hear how the demons chuckle and yell   *chimney.*
Cutting his hands off, down in Hell.
Listen to the creepy proclamation,
Blown through the lairs of the forest-nation,
Blown past the white-ants' hill of clay,
Blown past the marsh where the butterflies play:—
"Be careful what you do,   *All the "o"*
Or Mumbo-Jumbo, God of the Congo,   *sounds very*
And all of the other   *golden.*
Gods of the Congo,   *Heavy ac-*
Mumbo-Jumbo will hoo-doo you,   *cents very*
Mumbo-Jumbo will hoo-doo you,   *heavy. Light*
Mumbo-Jumbo will hoo-doo you."   *accents very*
                                                 light. Last
                                                 line whis-
                                                 pered.

II. THEIR IRREPRESSIBLE HIGH SPIRITS

Wild crap-shooters with a whoop and a call
Danced the juba in their gambling hall

Rather shrill and high.

And laughed fit to kill, and shook the town,
And guyed the policemen and laughed them down
With a boomlay, boomlay, boomlay, BOOM.
THEN I SAW THE CONGO, CREEPING THROUGH THE BLACK,
CUTTING THROUGH THE FOREST WITH A GOLDEN TRACK.

Read exactly as in first section.

A negro fairyland swung into view,
A minstrel river
Where dreams come true.

Lay emphasis on the delicate ideas.

The ebony palace soared on high
Through the blossoming trees to the evening sky.
The inlaid porches and casements shone
With gold and ivory and elephant-bone.

Keep as light-footed as possible.

And the black crowd laughed till their sides were sore
At the baboon butler in the agate door,
And the well-known tunes of the parrot band
That trilled on the bushes of that magic land.

A troupe of skull-faced witch-men came
Through the agate doorway in suits of flame,

With pomposity.

Yea, long-tailed coats with a gold-leaf crust
And hats that were covered with diamond-dust.
And the crowd in the court gave a whoop and a call
And danced the juba from wall to wall.
But the witch-men suddenly stilled the throng
With a stern cold glare, and a stern old song:—
"Mumbo-Jumbo will hoo-doo you." . . .

With a great deliberation and ghostliness.

Just then from the doorway, as fat as shotes,
Came the cake-walk princes in their long red coats,
Canes with a brilliant lacquer shine,
And tall silk hats that were red as wine.

With overwhelming assurance, good cheer, and pomp.

And they pranced with their butterfly partners there,
Coal-black maidens with pearls in their hair,
Knee-skirts trimmed with the jassamine sweet,
And bells on their ankles and little black feet.

With growing speed and sharply marked dance-rhythm.

And the couples railed at the chant and the frown
Of the witch-men lean, and laughed them down.
(Oh, rare was the revel, and well worth while
That made those glowering witch-men smile.)

The cake-walk royalty then began
To walk for a cake that was tall as a man
To the tune of "Boomlay, boomlay, BOOM,"
While the witch-men laughed, with a sinister air,
And sang with the scalawags prancing there:—
"Walk with care, walk with care,
Or Mumbo-Jumbo, God of the Congo,

With a touch of negro dialect, and

And all of the other Gods of the Congo,
Mumbo-Jumbo will hoo-doo you.
Beware, beware, walk with care,
Boomlay, boomlay, boomlay, boom.
Boomlay, boomlay, boomlay, boom.
Boomlay, boomlay, boomlay, boom.
Boomlay, boomlay, boomlay,
Boom."
(Oh, rare was the revel, and well worth while
That made those glowering witch-men smile.)

*as rapidly
as possible
toward
the end.*

*Slow philo-
sophic calm.*

III.   THE HOPE OF THEIR RELIGION

A good old negro in the slums of the town
Preached at a sister for her velvet gown.
Howled at a brother for his low-down ways,
His prowling, guzzling, sneak-thief days.
Beat on the Bible till he wore it out
Starting the jubilee revival shout.
And some had visions, as they stood on chairs,
And sang of Jacob, and the golden stairs
And they all repented, a thousand strong,
From their stupor and savagery and sin and wrong,
And slammed with their hymn books till they shook the
    room
With "Glory, glory, glory,"
And "Boom, boom, BOOM."
THEN I SAW THE CONGO, CREEPING THROUGH THE BLACK,
CUTTING THROUGH THE JUNGLE WITH A GOLDEN TRACK.
And the gray sky opened like a new-rent veil
And showed the Apostles with their coats of mail.
In bright white steel they were seated round
And their fire-eyes watched where the Congo wound.
And the twelve Apostles, from their thrones on high,
Thrilled all the forest with their heavenly cry:—
"Mumbo-Jumbo will die in the jungle;
Never again will he hoo-doo you,
Never again will he hoo-doo you."

*Heavy bass.
With a
literal imi-
tation of
camp-meet-
ing racket,
and trance.*

*Exactly as
in the first
section.
Begin with
terror and
power, end
with joy.*

*Sung to
the tune of
"Hark, ten
thousand
harps and
voices."*

Then along that river, a thousand miles,
The vine-snared trees fell down in files.
Pioneer angels cleared the way
For a Congo paradise, for babes at play,
For sacred capitals, for temples clean.
Gone were the skull-faced witch-men lean.
There, where the wild ghost-gods had wailed
A million boats of the angels sailed
With oars of silver, and prows of blue
And silken pennants that the sun shone through.
'Twas a land transfigured, 'twas a new creation.

*With
growing de-
liberation
and joy.*

*In a rather
high key—
as delicately
as possible.*

Oh, a singing wind swept the negro nation
And on through the backwoods clearing flew:—
"Mumbo-Jumbo is dead in the jungle.
Never again will he hoo-doo you.
Never again will he hoo-doo you."

*To the
tune of
"Hark, ten
thousand
harps and
voices."*

Redeemed were the forests, the beasts and the men,
And only the vulture dared again
By the far, lone mountains of the moon
To cry, in the silence, the Congo tune:—
"Mumbo-Jumbo will hoo-doo you,
Mumbo-Jumbo will hoo-doo you.
Mumbo . . . Jumbo . . . will . . . hoo-doo . . . you."
                                        1914

*Dying down
into a pene-
trating,
terrified
whisper.*

THE BRONCHO THAT WOULD NOT BE BROKEN *

A little colt—broncho, loaned to the farm
To be broken in time without fury or harm,
Yet black crows flew past you, shouting alarm,
Calling "Beware," with lugubrious singing . . .
The butterflies there in the brush were romancing,
The smell of the grass caught your soul in a trance,
So why be a-fearing the spurs and the traces,
O broncho that would not be broken of dancing?

You were born with the pride of the lords great and olden
Who danced, through the ages, in corridors golden.
In all the wide farm-place the person most human.
You spoke out so plainly with squealing and capering,
With whinnying, snorting, contorting and prancing,
As you dodged your pursuers, looking askance,
With Greek-footed figures, and Parthenon paces,
O broncho that would not be broken of dancing.

The grasshoppers cheered. "Keep whirling," they said.
The insolent sparrows called from the shed,
"If men will not laugh, make them wish they were dead."
But arch were your thoughts, all malice displacing,
Though the horse-killers came, with snake-whips advancing.
You bantered and cantered away your last chance.
And they scourged you, with Hell in their speech and their faces,
O broncho that would not be broken of dancing.

"Nobody cares for you," rattled the crows,
As you dragged the whole reaper, next day, down the rows.
The three mules held back, yet you danced on your toes.
You pulled like a racer, and kept the mules chasing.

You tangled the harness with bright eyes side-glancing,
While the drunk driver bled you—a pole for a lance—
And the giant mules bit at you—keeping their places.
O broncho that would not be broken of dancing.

In that last afternoon your boyish heart broke.
The hot wind came down like a sledge-hammer stroke.
The blood-sucked flies to a rare feast awoke,
And they searched out your wounds, your death-warrant tracing.
And the merciful men, their religion enhancing,
Stopped the red reaper, to give you a chance.
Then you died on the prairie, and scorned all disgraces,
O broncho that would not be broken of dancing.
                    Souvenir of Great Bend, Kansas.

1917

FROM
ADVENTURES WHILE PREACHING THE GOSPEL OF BEAUTY *

[RULES TO BE OBSERVED ON A POETICAL PILGRIMAGE]

* * * I had set certain rules of travel, evolved and proved practicable in previous expeditions in the East and South. These rules had been published in various periodicals before my start. The home town newspapers, my puzzled but faithful friends in good times and in bad, went the magazines one better and added a rule or so. To promote the gala character of the occasion, a certain paper announced that I was to walk in a Roman toga with bare feet encased in sandals. Another added that I had travelled through most of the countries of Europe in this manner. It made delightful reading. Scores of mere acquaintances crossed the street to shake hands with me on the strength of it.

The actual rules were to have nothing to do with cities, railroads, money, baggage or fellow tramps. I was to

* From Vachel Lindsay, *Adventures While Preaching the Gospel of Beauty*, copyright 1914. By permission of The Macmillan Company, publishers.

begin to ask for dinner about a quarter of eleven and for supper, lodging and breakfast about a quarter of five. I was to be neat, truthful, civil and on the square. I was to preach the Gospel of Beauty. How did these rules work out?

The cities were easy to let alone. I passed quickly through Hannibal and Jefferson City. Then, straight West, it was nothing but villages and farms till the three main cities of Colorado. Then nothing but desert to central New Mexico. I did not take the train till I reached central New Mexico, nor did I write to Springfield for money till I quit the whole game at that point.

Such wages as I made I sent home, starting out broke again, first spending just enough for one day's recuperation out of each pile, and, in the first case, rehabilitating my costume considerably. I always walked penniless. My baggage was practically nil. It was mainly printed matter, renewed by mail. Sometimes I carried reproductions of drawings of mine, *The Village Improvement Parade*, a series of picture-cartoons with many morals.

I pinned this on the farmers' walls, explaining the mottoes on the banners and exhorting them to study it at their leisure. My little pack had a supply of the aforesaid *Rhymes to Be Traded for Bread.* And it contained the following Gospel of Beauty:

THE GOSPEL OF BEAUTY

Being the new "creed of a beggar" by that vain and foolish mendicant Nicholas Vachel Lindsay, printed for his personal friends in his home village—Springfield, Illinois. It is his intention to carry this gospel across the country beginning June, 1912, returning in due time.

I

I come to you penniless and afoot, to bring a message. I am starting a new religious idea. The idea does not say "no" to any creed that you have heard. . . . After this, let the denomination to which you now belong be called in your heart "the church of beauty" or "the church of the open sky." . . . The church of beauty has two sides: the love of beauty and the love of God.

II

The New Localism

The things most worth while are one's own hearth and neighborhood. We should make our own home and neighborhood the most democratic, the most beautiful and the holiest in the world. The children now growing up should become devout gardeners or architects or park architects or teachers of dancing in the Greek spirit or musicians or novelists or poets or story-writers or craftsmen or wood-carvers or dramatists or actors or singers. They should find their talent and nurse it industriously. They should believe in every possible application to art-theory of the thoughts of the Declaration of Independence and

Lincoln's Gettysburg Address. They should, if led by the spirit, wander over the whole nation in search of the secret of democratic beauty with their hearts at the same time filled to overflowing with the righteousness of God. Then they should come back to their own hearth and neighborhood and gather a little circle of their own sort of workers about them and strive to make the neighborhood and home more beautiful and democratic and holy with their special art. . . . They should labor in their little circle expecting neither reward nor honors. . . . In their darkest hours they should be made strong by the vision of a completely beautiful neighborhood and the passion for a completely democratic art. Their reason for living should be that joy in beauty which no wounds can take away, and that joy in the love of God which no crucifixion can end.

The kindly reader at this point clutches his brow and asks, "But why carry this paper around? Why, in Heaven's name, do it as a beggar? Why do it at all?"

Let me make haste to say that there has been as yet no accredited, accepted way for establishing Beauty in the heart of the average American. *Until such a way has been determined upon by a competent committee,* I must be pardoned for taking my own course and trying any experiment I please. * * *

[1912]

[THE TALE OF THE FIVE LITTLE CHILDREN EATING MUSH]

* * * One should not be so vain as to recount a personal triumph. Still this is a personal triumph. And I shall tell it with all pride and vanity. Let those who dislike a conceited man drop the book right here.

I had walked all day straight west from Rocky Ford [Colorado]. It was pitch dark, threatening rain—the rain that never comes. It was nearly ten o'clock. At six I had entered a village, but had later resolved to press on to visit a man to whom I had a letter of introduction from my loyal friend Dr. Barbour of Rocky Ford.

There had been a wash-out. I had to walk around it, and was misdirected by the good villagers and was walking merrily on toward nowhere. Around nine o'clock I had been refused lodging at three different shanties. But from long experience I knew that something would turn up in a minute. And it did.

I walked right into the fat sides of a big country hotel on that interminable plain. It was not surrounded by a village. It was simply a clean hostelrie for the transient hands who worked at irrigating in that region.

I asked the looming figure I met in the dark: "Where is the boss of this place?"

"I am the boss." He had a Scandinavian twist to his tongue.

"I want a night's lodging. I will give in exchange an entertainment this evening, or half a day's work to-morrow."

"Come in."

I followed him up the outside stairway to the dining-room in the second story. There was his wife, a woman who greeted me cheerfully in the Scandinavian accent. She was laughing at her five little children who were laughing at her and eating their mush and milk.

Presumably the boarders had been delayed by their work, and had dined late. The children were at it still later.

They were real Americans, those little birds. And they had memories like parrots, as will appear.

"Wife," said the landlord, "here is a man that will entertain us to-night for his keep, or work for us to-morrow. I think we will take the entertainment to-night. Go ahead, mister. Here are the kids. Now listen, kids."

To come out of the fathomless, friendless dark and, almost in an instant, to look into such expectant fairy faces! They were laughing, laughing, laughing, not in mockery, but companionship. I recited every child-piece I had ever written—(not many).

They kept quite still till the end of each one. Then they pounded the table for more, with their tin spoons and their little red fists.

So, with misgivings, I began to recite some of my fairy-tales for grown-ups. I spoke slowly, to make the externals of each story plain. The audience squealed for more. . . . I decided to recite six jingles about the moon, that I had written long ago: How the hyæna said the Moon was a Golden Skull, and how the Shepherd Dog contradicted him and said it was a Candle in the Sky—and all that and all that.

The success of the move was remarkable because I had never pleased either grown folks or children to any extent with those verses. But these children, through the accumulated excitements of a day that I knew nothing about, were in an ecstatic imaginative condition of soul that transmuted everything.

The last of the series recounted what Grandpa Mouse said to the Little Mice on the Moon question. I arranged the ketchup bottle on the edge of the table for Grandpa Mouse. I used the salts and peppers for the little mice in circle round. I used a black hat or so for the swooping, mouse-eating owls that came down from the moon. Having acted out the story first, I recited it, slowly, mind you. Here it is:

WHAT GRANDPA MOUSE SAID

The moon's a holy owl-queen:
She keeps them in a jar
Under her arm till evening,
Then sallies forth to war.

She pours the owls upon us:
They hoot with horrid noise
And eat the naughty mousie-girls
And wicked mousie-boys.

So climb the moon-vine every night
And to the owl-queen pray:
Leave good green cheese by moon-
    lit trees
For her to take away.

And never squeak, my children,
Nor gnaw the smoke-house door.
The owl-queen then will love us
And send her birds no more.

At the end I asked for my room
and retired. I slept maybe an hour.
I was awakened by those tireless little
rascals racing along the dark hall and
saying in horrible solemn tones. pretending to scare one another:

The moon's a holy owl-queen:
She keeps them in a jar
Under her arm till night,
Then 'allies out to war!
She sicks the owls upon us,
They 'oot with 'orrid noise
And eat . . . the naughty boys,
And the MOON'S A HOLY OWL-QUEEN!
She KEEPS THEM IN A JAR!

And so it went on, over and over.
Thereupon I made a mighty and
rash resolve. I renewed that same re-
resolve in the morning when I woke. I
said within myself, *"I shall write one
hundred Poems on the Moon!"*
Of course I did not keep my resolve. . . . But [there exist a number of pieces about the moon which]
I did write immediately after. * * *

1914

EDGAR LEE MASTERS
(1869–   )

FROM

SPOON RIVER ANTHOLOGY *

PETIT, THE POET

Seeds in a dry pod, tick, tick, tick,
Tick, tick, tick, like mites in a
    quarrel—
Faint iambics that the full breeze
    wakens—
But the pine tree makes a symphony
    thereof.
Triolets, villanelles, rondels, rondeaus,
Ballades by the score with the same old
    thought:
The snows and the roses of yesterday
    are vanished;
And what is love but a rose that
    fades?
Life all around me here in the
    village:
Tragedy, comedy, valor, and truth,
Courage, constancy, heroism, failure—
All in the loom, and oh what patterns!
Woodlands, meadows, streams, and
    rivers—
Blind to all of it all my life long.
Triolets, villanelles, rondels, rondeaus,
Seeds in a dry pod, tick, tick, tick,
Tick, tick, tick, what little iambics,
While Homer and Whitman roared
    in the pines?

BENJAMIN PANTIER

Together in this grave lie Benjamin
    Pantier, attorney at law,
And Nig, his dog, constant com-
    panion, solace and friend.
Down the gray road, friends, children,
    men and women,
Passing one by one out of life, left me
    till I was alone
With Nig for partner, bed-fellow,
    comrade in drink.

* Reprinted by permission of the
author, Edgar Lee Masters. Copyright,
1915.

In the morning of life I knew aspiration and saw glory.
Then she, who survives me, snared
my soul
With a snare which bled me to death,
Till I, once strong of will, lay broken,
indifferent,
Living with Nig in a room back of a
dingy office.
Under my jaw-bone is snuggled the
bony nose of Nig—
Our story is lost in silence. Go by,
mad world!

MRS. BENJAMIN PANTIER

I know that he told that I snared his
soul
With a snare which bled him to
death.
And all the men loved him,
And most of the women pitied him.
But suppose you are really a lady, and
have delicate tastes,
And loathe the smell of whisky and
onions.
And the rhythm of Wordsworth's
"Ode" runs in your ears,
While he goes about from morning
till night
Repeating bits of that common
thing:
"Oh, why should the spirit of mortal
be proud?"
And then, suppose,
You are a woman well endowed,
And the only man with whom the law
and morality
Permit you to have the marital rela-
tion
Is the very man who fills you with
disgust
Every time you think of it—while you
think of it
Every time you see him?
That's why I drove him away from
home
To live with his dog, in a dingy
room
Back of his office.

DOCTOR MEYERS

No other man, unless it was Doc Hill,
Did more for people in this town than
I.
And all the weak, the halt, the im-
provident
And those who could not pay flocked
to me.
I was good-hearted, easy Doctor
Meyers.
I was healthy, happy, in comfortable
fortune,
Blest with a congenial mate, my chil-
dren raised,
All wedded, doing well in the world.
And then one night, Minerva, the
poetess,
Came to me in her trouble, crying.
I tried to help her out—she died—
They indicted me, the newspapers
disgraced me,
My wife perished of a broken heart.
And pneumonia finished me.

MRS. MEYERS

He protested all his life long
The newspapers lied about him
villainously;
That he was not at fault for Minerva's
fall,
But only tried to help her.
Poor soul so sunk in sin he could not
see
That even trying to help her, as he
called it,
He had broken the law human and
divine.
Passers by, an ancient admonition to
you:
If your ways would be ways of
pleasantness,
And all your pathways peace,
Love God and keep his command-
ments.

DAISY FRASER

Did you ever hear of Editor Whedon
Giving to the public treasury any of
the money he received

For supporting candidates for office?
Or for writing up the canning factory
To get people to invest?
Or for suppressing the facts about the
    bank,
When it was rotten and ready to
    break?
Did you ever hear of the Circuit
    Judge
Helping anyone except the "Q" rail-
    road,
Or the bankers? Or did Rev. Peet or
    Rev. Sibley
Give any part of their salary, earned
    by keeping still,
Or speaking out as the leaders wished
    them to do,
To the building of the water works?
But I—Daisy Fraser, who always
    passed
Along the streets through rows of
    nods and smiles,
And coughs and words such as "there
    she goes,"
Never was taken before Justice
    Arnett
Without contributing ten dollars and
    costs
To the school fund of Spoon River!

EDITOR WHEDON

To be able to see every side of every
    question;
To be on every side, to be everything,
    to be nothing long;
To pervert truth, to ride it for a pur-
    pose,
To use great feelings and passions of
    the human family
For base designs, for cunning ends,
To wear a mask like the Greek
    actors—
Your eight-page paper—behind which
    you huddle,
Bawling through the megaphone of
    big type:
"This is I, the giant."
Thereby also living the life of a sneak-
    thief,

Poisoned with the anonymous words
Of your clandestine soul.
To scratch dirt over scandal for
    money,
And exhume it to the winds for
    revenge,
Or to sell papers
Crushing reputations, or bodies, if
    need be,
To win at any cost, save your own
    life.
To glory in demoniac power, ditching
    civilization,
As a paranoiac boy puts a log on the
    track
And derails the express train.
To be an editor, as I was—
Then to lie here close by the river
    over the place
Where the sewage flows from the
    village,
And the empty cans and garbage are
    dumped,
And abortions are hidden.

ARCHIBALD HIGBIE

I loathed you, Spoon River. I tried
    to rise above you,
I was ashamed of you. I despised you
As the place of my nativity.
And there in Rome, among the artists,
Speaking Italian, speaking French,
I seemed to myself at times to be free
Of every trace of my origin.
I seemed to be reaching the heights
    of my art
And to breathe the air that the
    masters breathed,
And to see the world with their eyes.
But still they'd pass my work and say:
"What are you driving at my friend?
Sometimes the face looks like
    Apollo's,
At others it has a trace of Lincoln's."
There was no culture, you know, in
    Spoon River,
And I burned with shame and held
    my peace.
And what could I do, all covered over

And weighted down with western
soil,
Except aspire, and pray for another
Birth in the world, with all of Spoon
River
Rooted out of my soul?

LUCINDA MATLOCK

I went to the dances at Chandlerville,
And played snap-out at Winchester.
One time we changed partners,
Driving home in the moonlight of
middle June,
And then I found Davis.
We were married and lived together
for seventy years,
Enjoying, working, raising the twelve
children,
Eight of whom we lost
Ere I had reached the age of sixty.
I spun, I wove, I kept the house, I
nursed the sick,
I made the garden, and for holiday
Rambled over the fields where sang
the larks,
And by Spoon River gathering many
a shell,
And many a flower and medicinal
weed—
Shouting to the wooded hills, singing
to the green valleys.
At ninety-six I had lived enough, that
is all,
And passed to a sweet repose.
What is this I hear of sorrow and
weariness,
Anger, discontent and drooping
hopes?
Degenerate sons and daughters,
Life is too strong for you—
It takes life to love Life.

ANNE RUTLEDGE

Out of me unworthy and unknown
The vibrations of deathless music;
"With malice toward none, with
charity for all."
Out of me the forgiveness of millions
toward millions,

And the beneficent face of a nation
Shining with justice and truth.
I am Anne Rutledge who sleeps
beneath these weeds,
Beloved in life of Abraham Lincoln,
Wedded to him, not through union,
But through separation.
Bloom forever, O Republic,
From the dust of my bosom!

1915

JOHNNY APPLESEED *

When the air of October is sweet and
cold as the wine of apples
Hanging ungathered in frosted orchards along the Grand River,
I take the road that winds by the
resting fields and wander
From Eastmanville to Nunica down
to the Villa Crossing.

I look for old men to talk with, men
as old as the orchards,
Men to tell me of ancient days, of
those who built and planted,
Lichen gray, branch broken, bent and
sighing,
Hobbling for warmth in the sun and
for places to sit and smoke.

For there is a legend here, a tale of
the croaking old ones
That Johnny Appleseed came here,
planted some orchards around
here,
When nothing was here but the pine
trees, oaks and the beeches,
And nothing was here but the
marshes, lake and the river.

Peter Van Zylen is ninety and this he
tells me:
My father talked with Johnny Apple-
seed there on the hill-side,
There by the road on the way to
Fruitport, saw him

* Reprinted by permission of Edgar
Lee Masters. Copyright, 1918.

Clearing pines and oaks for a place
   for an apple orchard.

Peter Van Zylen says: He got that
   name from the people
For carrying apple-seed with him and
   planting orchards
All the way from Ohio, through In-
   diana across here,
Planting orchards, they say, as far as
   Illinois.

Johnny Appleseed said, so my father
   told me:
  go to a place forgotten, the orchards
   will thrive and be here
For children to come, who will gather
   and eat hereafter.
And few will know who planted, and
   none will understand.

  laugh, said Johnny Appleseed:
   Some fellow buys this timber
Five years, perhaps, from to-day, be-
   gins to clear for barley.
And here in the midst of the timber
   is hidden an apple orchard.
How did it come here? Lord! Who
   was it here before me?

Yes, I was here before him, to make
   these places of worship,
Labor and laughter and gain in the
   late October.
Why did I do it, eh? Some folks say
   I am crazy.
Where do my labors end? Far west,
   God only knows!

Said Johnny Appleseed there on the
   hill-side: Listen!
Beware the deceit of nurseries, sellers
   of seeds of the apple.
Think! You labor for years in trees not
   worth the raising.
You planted what you knew not, bitter or sour for sweet.

No luck more bitter than poor seed,
   but one as bitter:
The planting of perfect seed in soil
   that feeds and fails,
Nourishes for a little, and then goes
   spent forever.
Look to your seed, he said, and remember the soil.

And after that is the fight: the foe
   curled up at the root,
The scale that crumples and deadens,
   the moth in the blossoms
Becoming a life that coils at the core
   of a thing of beauty:
You bite your apple, a worm is
   crushed on your tongue!

And it's every bit the truth, said
   Peter Van Zylen.
So many things love an apple as well
   as ourselves.
A man must fight for the thing he
   loves, to possess it:
Apples, freedom, heaven, said Peter
   Van Zylen.

                       1918

MOURNIN' FOR RELIGION *

Brothers and sisters, I'm mournin' for
   religion,
But I can't get religion, it's my woman
   interferin'.
I sing and I pray, and I'm real perse-
   verin',
But I can't get religion,
That's all I have to say.
I know there is a fountain, a Jesus, a
   comforter,
A heaven, a Jerusalem, a day of
   Pentecost,
Salvation for the wishin', blood for
   sin's remission,
A covenant, a promise for souls that
   are lost.
But I can't get religion, the salvation
   feelin',
The vision of the Lamb, forgiveness
   and healin'.
I have a sort of numbness

When I see the mourners kneelin'.
I have a kind of dumbness
When the preacher is appealin'.
I have a kind of wariness, even contrariness,
Even while I'm fearin'
The bottomless pit and the shut gates of heaven.
It's my woman interferin'—

For you see when they say:
Come to the mercy seat, come, come,
The spirit and the bride
Say come, come,
I think of my woman who bore so many children;
I think of her a cookin' for harvesters in summer;
I think of her a lyin' there, a dyin' there, the neighbors
Who came in to fan her and how she never murmured;
And then I seem to grow number and number,
And something in me says:
Why didn't Jesus help her for to die,
Why did Jesus always pass her by,
Let her break her health down as I was growing poorer,
Let her lie and suffer with no medicine to cure her,
I wouldn't treat a stray dog as Jesus acted to her.
If these are devil words, I'm a child of the devil.
And this is why I'm dumb
As the spirit and the bride say come!

*   *   *

I am old and crippled—sixty in December.
And I wonder if it's God that stretches out and hands us
Troubles we remember?
I'm alone besides, I need the Comforter,
All the children's grown up, livin' out in Kansas.
My old friend Billy died of lung fever. . . .

But the worst of it is I'm really a believer,
Expect to go to hell if I don't get religion.
And I need this religion to stop thi awful grievin'
About my woman lyin' there in th cemetery,
And you can't stop that grievin' simpl by believin'.
So I mourn for religion,
I mourn for religion,
My old heart breaks for religion!

191

EDNA ST. VINCENT MILLAY
(1892–)

RENASCENCE *

All I could see from where I stood
Was three long mountains and wood;
I turned and looked another way,
And saw three islands in a bay.
So with my eyes I traced the line
Of the horizon, thin and fine,
Straight around till I was come
Back to where I started from;
And all I saw from where I stood
Was three long mountains and wood.
Over these things I could not see;
These were the things that bounde me;
And I could touch them with m hand,—
Almost, I thought, from where stand.
And all at once things seemed so sma
My breath came short, and scarce all.
But, sure, the sky is big, I said;
Miles and miles above my head;
So here upon my back I'll lie

* From *Renascence and Other Poem* published by Harper & Brothers. Cop right, 1912, 1940, by Edna St. Vince Millay.

And look my fill into the sky.
And so I looked, and, after all,
The sky was not so very tall.
The sky, I said, must somewhere
     stop,
And—sure enough!—I see the top.
The sky, I thought, is not so grand;
I 'most could touch it with my hand!
And, reaching up my hand to try,
I screamed to feel it touch the sky.
I screamed, and—lo!—Infinity
Came down and settled over me;
And, pressing of the Undefined
The definition on my mind,
Held up before my eyes a glass
Through which my shrinking sight
     did pass
Until it seemed I must behold
Immensity made manifold;
Whispered to me a word whose sound
Deafened the air for worlds around,
And brought unmuffled to my ears
The gossiping of friendly spheres,
The creaking of the tented sky,
The ticking of Eternity.

I saw and heard, and knew at last
The How and Why of all things, past,
And present, and forevermore.
The universe, cleft to the core,
Lay open to my probing sense
That, sick'ning, I would fain pluck
     thence
But could not—nay! But needs must
     suck
At the great wound, and could not
     pluck
My lips away till I had drawn
All venom out—Ah, fearful pawn!
For my omniscience paid I toll
In infinite remorse of soul.
All sin was of my sinning, all
Atoning mine, and mine the gall
Of all regret. Mine was the weight
Of every brooded wrong, the hate
That stood behind each envious
     thrust,
Mine every greed, mine every lust.
And all the while for every grief,

Each suffering, I craved relief
With individual desire—
Craved all in vain! And felt fierce fire
About a thousand people crawl;
Perished with each—then mourned
     for all!

A man was starving in Capri;
He moved his eyes and looked at me;
I felt his gaze, I heard his moan,
And knew his hunger as my own.
I saw at sea a great fog-bank
Between two ships that struck and
     sank;
A thousand screams the heavens
     smote;
And every scream tore through my
     throat.
No hurt I did not feel, no death
That was not mine; mine each last
     breath
That, crying, met an answering cry
From the compassion that was I.
All suffering mine, and mine its rod;
Mine, pity like the pity of God.
Ah, awful weight! Infinity
Pressed down upon the finite me!
My anguished spirit, like a bird,
Beating against my lips I heard;
Yet lay the weight so close about
There was no room for it without.
And so beneath the weight lay I
And suffered death, but could not die.

Deep in the earth I rested now;
Cool is its hand upon the brow
And soft its breast beneath the head
Of one who is so gladly dead.
And all at once, and over all,
The pitying rain began to fall;
I lay and heard each pattering hoof
Upon my lowly, thatchèd roof,
And seemed to love the sound far
     more
Than ever I had done before.
For rain it hath a friendly sound
To one who's six feet underground;
And scarce the friendly voice or
     face:
A grave is such a quiet place.

The rain, I said, is kind to come
And speak to me in my new home.
I would I were alive again
To kiss the fingers of the rain,
To drink into my eyes the shine
Of every slanting silver line,
To catch the freshened, fragrant breeze
From drenched and dripping apple-trees.
For soon the shower will be done,
And then the broad face of the sun
Will laugh above the rain-soaked earth
Until the world with answering mirth
Shakes joyously, and each round drop
Rolls, twinkling, from its grass-blade top,
How can I bear it; buried here,
While overhead the sky grows clear
And blue again after the storm?
O, multi-coloured, multiform,
Beloved beauty over me,
That I shall never, never see
Again! Spring-silver, autumn-gold,
That I shall never more behold!
Sleeping your myriad magics through,
Close-sepulchred away from you!
O God, I cried, give me new birth,
And put me back upon the earth!
Upset each cloud's gigantic gourd
And let the heavy rain, down-poured
In one big torrent, set me free,
Washing my grave away from me!
I ceased; and, through the breathless hush
That answered me, the far-off rush
Of herald wings came whispering
Like music down the vibrant string
Of my ascending prayer, and—crash!
Before the wild wind's whistling lash
The startled storm-clouds reared on high
And plunged in terror down the sky,
And the big rain in one black wave
Fell from the sky and struck my grave.

I know not how such things can be,
I only know there came to me
A fragrance such as never clings

To aught save happy living things;
A sound as of some joyous elf
Singing sweet songs to please himself,
And, through and over everything,
A sense of glad awakening.
The grass, a tip-toe at my ear,
Whispering to me I could hear;
I felt the rain's cool finger-tips
Brushed tenderly across my lips,
Laid gently on my sealèd sight,
And all at once the heavy night
Fell from my eyes and I could see—
A drenched and dripping apple-tree.
A last long line of silver rain,
A sky grown clear and blue again.
And as I looked a quickening gust
Of wind blew up to me and thrust
Into my face a miracle
Of orchard-breath, and with the smell—
I know not how such things can be!—
I breathed my soul back into me.
Ah! Up then from the ground sprang I
And hailed the earth with such a cry
As is not heard save from a man
Who has been dead, and lives again.
About the trees my arms I wound;
Like one gone mad I hugged the ground;
I raised my quivering arms on high;
I laughed and laughed into the sky,
Till at my throat a strangling sob
Caught fiercely, and a great heart-throb
Sent instant tears into my eyes;
O God, I cried, no dark disguise
Can e'er hereafter hide from me
Thy radiant identity!
Thou canst not move across the grass
But my quick eyes will see Thee pass,
Nor speak, however silently,
But my hushed voice will answer Thee.
I know the path that tells Thy way
Through the cool eve of every day;
God, I can push the grass apart
And lay my finger on Thy heart!
The world stands out on either side

No wider than the heart is wide;
Above the world is stretched the sky—
No higher than the soul is high.
The heart can push the sea and land
Farther away on either hand;
The soul can split the sky in two,
And let the face of God shine through.
But East and West will pinch the
  heart
That cannot keep them pushed apart;
And he whose soul is flat—the sky
Will cave in on him by and by.

1912, 1917

OH, THINK NOT I AM FAITHFUL TO A VOW †

Oh, think not I am faithful to a vow!
Faithless am I save to love's self alone.
Were you not lovely I would leave
  you now:
After the feet of beauty fly my own.
Were you not still my hunger's
  rarest food,
And water ever to my wildest thirst,
I would desert you—think not but I
  would!—
And seek another as I sought you first.
But you are mobile as the veering air,
And all your charms more changeful
  than the tide,
Wherefore to be inconstant is no care:
I have but to continue at your side.
So wanton, light and false, my love,
  are you,
I am most faithless when I am most
  true.   1920

ELEGY *

Let them bury your big eyes
In the secret earth securely,

Your thin fingers, and your fair,
Soft, indefinite-colored hair,—
All of these in some way, surely,
From the secret earth shall rise;
Not for these I sit and stare,
Broken and bereft completely;
Your young flesh that sat so neatly
On your little bones will sweetly
Blossom in the air.

But your voice,—never the rushing
Of a river underground,
Not the rising of the wind
In the trees before the rain,
Not the woodcock's watery call,
Not the note the white-throat
  utters,
Not the feet of children pushing
Yellow leaves along the gutters
In the blue and bitter fall,
Shall content my musing mind
For the beauty of that sound
That in no new way at all
Ever will be heard again.

Sweetly through the sappy stalk
Of the vigorous weed,
Holding all it held before,
Cherished by the faithful sun,
On and on eternally
Shall your altered fluid run,
Bud and bloom and go to seed;
But your singing days are done;
But the music of your talk
Never shall the chemistry
Of the secret earth restore.
All your lovely words are spoken.
Once the ivory box is broken,
Beats the golden bird no more.

1921

EUCLID ALONE HAS LOOKED ON BEAUTY BARE *

Euclid alone has looked on Beauty
  bare.

Let all who prate of Beauty hold their
    peace,
And lay them prone upon the earth
    and cease
To ponder on themselves, the while
    they stare
At nothing, intricately drawn nowhere
In shapes of shifting lineage; let geese
Gabble and hiss, but heroes seek re-
    lease
From dusty bondage into luminous
    air.
O blinding hour, O holy, terrible day,
When first the shaft into his vision
    shone
Of light anatomized! Euclid alone
Has looked on Beauty bare. Fortunate
    they
Who, though once only and then but
    far away,
Have heard her massive sandal set on
    stone.

                             1923

JUSTICE DENIED
IN MASSACHUSETTS †

Let us abandon then our gardens and
    go home
And sit in the sitting-room.
Shall the larkspur blossom or the corn
    grow under this cloud?
Sour to the fruitful seed
Is the cold earth under this cloud,
Fostering quack and weed, we have
    marched upon but cannot con-
    quer;
We have bent the blades of our hoes
    against the stalks of them.

Let us go home, and sit in the sitting-
    room.
Not in our day
Shall the cloud go over and the sun
    rise as before,
Beneficent upon us

† From *The Buck in the Snow*, published by Harper & Brothers. Copyright,
1927, by Edna St. Vincent Millay.

Out of the glittering bay,
And the warm winds be blown inward
    from the sea
Moving the blades of corn
With a peaceful sound.
Forlorn, forlorn,
Stands the blue hay-rack by the empty
    mow.
And the petals drop to the ground,
Leaving the tree unfruited.
The sun that warmed our stooping
    backs and withered the weed up-
    rooted—
We shall not feel it again.
We shall die in darkness, and be
    buried in the rain.

What from the splendid dead
We have inherited—
Furrows sweet to the grain, and the
    weed subdued—
See now the slug and the mildew
    plunder.
Evil does overwhelm
The larkspur and the corn;
We have seen them go under.

Let us sit here, sit still,
Here in the sitting-room until we
    die;
At the step of Death on the walk,
    rise and go;
Leaving to our children's children this
    beautiful doorway,
And this elm,
And a blighted earth to till
With a broken hoe.

                             1927

FROM   *EPITAPH*
FOR THE RACE OF MAN

IV *

O Earth, unhappy planet born to die,
Might I your scribe and your con-
    fessor be,

* From *Wine From These Grapes*,
published by Harper & Brothers. Copyright, 1934, by Edna St. Vincent Millay.

What wonders must you not relate to
    me
Of Man, who when his destiny was
    high
Strode like the sun into the middle
    sky
And shone an hour, and who so
    bright as he,
And like the sun went down into the
    sea,
Leaving no spark to be remembered
    by.
But no; you have not learned in all
    these years
To tell the leopard and the newt
    apart;
Man, with his singular laughter, his
    droll tears,
His engines and his conscience and
    his art,
Made but a simple sound upon your
    ears:
The patient beating of the animal
    heart.

XVI *

Alas for Man, so stealthily
    betrayed,
Bearing the bad cell in him from the
    start,
Pumping and feeding from his
    healthy heart
That wild disorder never to be
    stayed
When once established, destined to
    invade
With angry hordes the true and
    proper part,
Till Reason joggles in the headsman's
    cart,
And Mania spits from every balus-
    trade.
Would he had searched his closet for
    his bane,

* From *Wine From These Grapes*,
published by Harper & Brothers. Copyright, 1934, by Edna St. Vincent Millay.

Where lurked the trusted ancient of
    his soul,
Obsequious Greed, and seen that vis-
    age plain;
Would he had whittled treason from
    his side
In his stout youth and bled his body
    whole,
Then had he died a king, or never
    died.

1934

CZECHO-SLOVAKIA †

If there were balm in Gilead, I would
    go
To Gilead for your wounds, unhappy
    land,
Gather you balsam there, and with
    this hand,
Made deft by pity, cleanse and bind
    and sew
And drench with healing, that your
    strength might grow,
(Though love be outlawed, kindness
    contraband)
And you, O proud and felled, again
    might stand;
But where to look for balm I do not
    know.
The oils and herbs of mercy are so
    few;
Honour's for sale; allegiance has its
    price;
The barking of a fox has bought us
    all;
We save our skins a craven hour or
    two.—
While Peter warms him in the serv-
    ants' hall
The thorns are platted and the cock
    crows twice.

1939

† From *Huntsman, What Quarry*,
published by Harper & Brothers. Copyright, 1933, 1934, 1936, 1937, 1938,
1939, by Edna St. Vincent Millay.

STEPHEN VINCENT BENÉT
(1898–1943)

KING DAVID *

David sang to his hook-nosed harp:
"The Lord God is a jealous God!
His violent vengeance is swift and
    sharp!
And the Lord is King above all gods!

"Blest be the Lord, through years un-
    told,
The Lord Who has blessed me a thou-
    sand fold!

"Cattle and concubines, corn and
    hives
Enough to last me a dozen lives.

"Plump, good women with noses flat,
Marrowful blessings, weighty and fat.

"I wax in His peace like a pious
    gourd,
The Lord God is a pleasant God,
Break mine enemy's jaw, O Lord!
For the Lord is King above all gods!"

His hand dropped slack from the tun-
    able strings,
A sorrow came on him—a sorrow of
    kings.

A sorrow sat on the arm of his throne,
An eagle sorrow with claws of stone.

"I am merry, yes, when I am not
    thinking,
But life is nothing but eating and
    drinking.

"I can shape my psalms like daggers
    of jade,
But they do not shine like the first I
    made.

"I can harry the heathen from North
    to South,
But no hot taste comes into my mouth.

* From *Selected Works of Stephen
Vincent Benét*, published by Rinehart
& Company, Inc. Copyright, 1923, by
Stephen Vincent Benét.

"My wives are comely as long-haired
    goats,
But I would not care if they cut their
    throats!

"Where are the maids of the desert
    tents
With lips like flagons of frankincense?

"Where is Jonathan? Where is Saul?
The captain-towers of Zion wall?

"The trees of cedar, the hills of Nod,
The kings, the running lions of God?

"Their names were a writing in
    golden dust,
Their names are myrrh in the mouths
    of the just.

"The sword of the slayer could never
    divide them—
Would God I had died in battle be-
    side them!"

The Lord looked down from a
    thunder-clap.
(The Lord God is a crafty God.)
He heard the strings of the shrewd
    harp snap.
(The Lord Who is King above all
    gods.)

He pricked the king with an airy
    thorn,
It burnt in his body like grapes of
    scorn.

The eyelids roused that had drooped
    like lead.
David lifted his heavy head.

The thorn stung at him, a fiery bee,
"The world is wide. I will go and see
From the roof of my haughty palace,"
    said he.

2

Bathsheba bathed on her vine-decked
    roof.
(The Lord God is a mighty God.)
Her body glittered like mail of proof.
(And the Lord is King above all
    gods.)

Her body shimmered, tender and white
As the flesh of aloes in candlelight.

King David forgot to be old or wise.
He spied on her bathing with sultry eyes.

A breath of spice came into his nose.
He said, "Her breasts are like two young roes."

His eyes were bright with a crafty gleam.
He thought, "Her body is soft as cream."

He straightened himself like an unbent bow
And called a servant and bade him go.

3

Uriah the Hittite came to his lord,
Dusty with war as a well-used sword.

A close, trim man like a belt, well-buckled;
A jealous gentleman, hard to cuckold.

David entreated him, soft and bland,
Offered him comfits from his own hand.

Drank with him deep till his eyes grew red,
And laughed in his beard as he went to bed.

The days slipped by without hurry or strife,
Like apple-parings under a knife,
And still Uriah kept from his wife.

Lean fear tittered through David's psalm,
This merry husband is far too calm."

David sent for Uriah then,
They greeted each other like pious men.

Thou hast borne the battle, the dust and the heat.

Go down to thy house and wash thy feet!"

Uriah frowned at the words of the king.
His brisk, hard voice had a leaden ring.

"While the hosts of God still camp in the field
My house to me is a garden sealed.

"How shall I rest while the arrow yet flies?
The dust of war is still in my eyes."

David spoke with his lion's roar:
"If Peace be a bridle that rubs you sore,
You shall fill your belly with blood and war!"

Uriah departed, calling him kind.
His eyes were serpents in David's mind.

He summoned a captain, a pliable man,
"Uriah the Hittite shall lead the van.

"In the next assault, when the fight roars high,
And the Lord God is a hostile God,
Retire from Uriah that he may die.
For the Lord is King above all gods."

4

The messenger came while King David played
The friskiest ditty ever made.

"News, O King, from our dubious war!
The Lord of Hosts hath prevailed once more!

"His foes are scattered like chirping sparrows,
Their kings lie breathless, feathered with arrows.

"Many are dead of your captains tall.
Uriah the Hittite was first to fall."

David turned from the frolicsome
    strings
And rent his clothes for the death of
    kings.

Yet, as he rent them, he smiled for
    joy,
The sly, wide smile of a wicked boy.

"The powerful grace of the Lord pre-
    vails!
He has cracked Uriah between His
    nails!

"His blessings are mighty, they shall
    not cease.
And my days henceforth shall be days
    of peace!"

His mind grew tranquil, smoother
    than fleece.
He rubbed his body with scented
    grease.
And his days thenceforward were days
    of peace.

His days were fair as the flowering
    lime
—For a little time, for a little time.

And Bathsheba lay in his breast like
    a dove,
A vessel of amber, made for love.

5

When Bathsheba was great with
    child,
(The Lord God is a jealous God!)
Portly and meek as a moon grown
    mild,
(The Lord is King above all gods!)

Nathan, the prophet, wry and dying,
Preached to the king like a locust
    crying:

"Hearken awhile to a doleful thing!
There were two men in thy land, O
    King!

"One was rich as a gilded ram.
One had one treasure, a poor ewe-
    lamb.

"Rich man wasted his wealth like
    spittle.
Poor man shared with his lamb spare
    victual.

"A traveler came to the rich man's
    door.
'Give me to eat, for I hunger sore!'

"Rich man feasted him fatly, true,
But the meat that he gave him was
    fiend's meat, too,
Stolen and roasted, the poor man's
    ewe!

"Hearken, my lord, to a deadly thing!
What shall be done with these men,
    O King?"

David hearkened, seeing it plain,
His heart grew heavy with angry
    pain:
"Show me the rich man that he be
    slain!"

Nathan barked as a jackal can.
"Just, O King! And thou art the man!"

David rose as the thunders rise
When someone in Heaven is telling
    lies.
But his eyes were weaker than
    Nathan's eyes.

His huge bulk shivered like a quak-
    ing sod,
Shoulders bowing to Nathan's rod,
Nathan, the bitter apple of God.

His great voice shook like a runner's
    spent,
"My sin has found me! Oh, I repent!"

Answered Nathan, that talkative Jew,
"For many great services, comely and
    true,
The Lord of Mercy will pardon you.

"But the child in Bathsheba, come of
    your seed,
Shall sicken and die like a blasted
    weed."

David groaned when he heard him
    speak.
The painful tears ran hot on his
    cheek.

Ashes he cast on his kingly locks.
All night long he lay on the rocks.

Beseeching his Lord with a howling
    cry:
"O Lord God, O my jealous God,
Be kind to the child that it may not
    die,
For Thou art King above all gods!"

6

Seven long nights he lay there, howl-
    ing,
A lion wounded, moaning and growl-
    ing.

Seven long midnights, sorrowing
    greatly,
While Sin, like a dead man, embraced
    him straitly.

Till he was abased from his lust and
    pride
And the child was born and sickened
    and died.

He arose at last. It was ruddy Day.
And his sin like water had washed
    away.

He cleansed and anointed, took fresh
    apparel,
And worshiped the Lord in a tuneful
    carol.

His servants, bearing the child to
    bury,
Marveled greatly to see him so merry.

He spoke to them mildly as mid-May
    weather:
"The child and my sin are perished
    together.

"He is dead, my son. Though his
    whole soul yearn to me,
I must go to him, he may not return
    to me.

"Why should I sorrow for what was
    pain?
A cherished grief is an iron chain."

He took up his harp, the sage old
    chief.
His heart felt clean as a new green
    leaf.

His soul smelt pleasant as rain-wet
    clover.
"I have sinned and repented and that's
    all over.

"In his dealings with heathen, the
    Lord is hard.
But the humble soul is his spikenard."

His wise thoughts fluttered like doves
    in the air.
"I wonder is Bathsheba still so fair?

"Does she weep for the child that our
    sin made perish?
I must comfort my ewe-lamb, comfort
    and cherish.

"The justice of God is honey and
    balm.
I will soothe her heart with a little
    psalm."

He went to her chamber, no longer sad,
Walking as light as a shepherd lad.

He found her weeping, her garments
    rent,
Trodden like straw by God's punish-
    ment.
He solaced her out of his great con-
    tent.

Being a woman, a while she grieved,
But at last she was comforted, and
    conceived.

Nine months later she bore him a son.
(The Lord God is a mighty God!)
The name of that child was
    SOLOMON.
He was God's tough staff till his days
    were run!
(And the Lord is King above all
    gods!)

1923

JOHN BROWN'S BODY

PRELUDE—THE SLAVER *

He closed the Bible carefully, putting it down
As if his fingers loved it.
               Then he turned.
"Mr. Mate."
         "Yes, sir."
                    The captain's eyes held a shadow.
"I think, while this weather lasts," he said, after a pause,
"We'd better get them on deck as much as we can.
They keep better that way. Besides," he added, unsmiling,
"She's begun to stink already. You've noticed it?"
The mate nodded, a boyish nod of half-apology,
"And only a week out, too, sir."
                        "Yes," said the skipper.
His eyes looked into themselves. "Well. The trade," he said,
"The trade's no damn perfume-shop." He drummed with his fingers.
"Seem to be quiet tonight," he murmured at last.
"Oh yes sir, quiet enough." The mate flushed. "Not
What you'd call quiet at home but—quiet enough."

"Um," said the skipper. "What about the big fellow?"
"Tarbarrel, sir? The man who says he's a king?
He was praying to something—it made the others restless.
Mr. Olsen stopped it."
                 "I don't like that," said the skipper.
"It was only an idol, sir."
                "Oh."
                    "A stone or something."
"Oh."
      "But he's a bad one, sir—a regular sullen one—
He—eyes in the dark—like a cat's—enough to give you—"
The mate was young. He shivered. "The creeps," he said.

"We've had that kind," said the skipper. His mouth was hard
Then it relaxed. "Damn cheating Arabs!" he said,
"I told them I'd take no more of their pennyweight kings,
Worth pounds to look at, and then when you get them aboard
Go crazy so they have to be knocked on the head
Or else just eat up their hearts and die in a week
Taking up room for nothing."

The mate hardly heard him, thinking of something else.
"I'm afraid we'll lose some more of the women," he said.
"Well, they're a scratch lot," said the skipper, "Any sickness?"

* From *John Brown's Body* in *Selected Works of Stephen Vincent Benét*, published by Rinehart & Company, Inc. Copyright, 1927, 1928, by Stephen Vincent Benét.

"Just the usual, sir."

"But nothing like plague or—"

"No sir."

"The Lord is merciful," said the skipper.
His voice was wholly sincere—an old ship's bell
Hung in the steeple of a meeting-house
With all New England and the sea's noise in it.
"Well, you'd better take another look-see, Mr. Mate."
The mate felt his lips go dry. "Aye aye, sir," he said,
Wetting his lips with his tongue. As he left the cabin
He heard the Bible being opened again.

Lantern in hand, he went down to the hold.
Each time he went he had a trick of trying
To shut the pores of his body against the stench
By force of will, by thinking of salt and flowers,
But it was always useless.

            He kept thinking:
When I get home, when I get a bath and clean food,
When I've gone swimming out beyond the Point
In that cold green, so cold it must be pure
Beyond the purity of a dissolved star,
When I get my shore-clothes on, and one of those shirts
Out of the linen-closet that smells of lavender,
Will my skin smell black even then, will my skin smell black?

The lantern shook in his hand.

                    This was black, here,
This was black to see and feel and smell and taste,
The blackness of black, with one weak lamp to light it
As ineffectually as a firefly in Hell,
And, being so, should be silent.

                    But the hold
Was never silent.

            There was always the breathing.
Always that thick breathing, always those shivering cries.

A few of the slaves
Knew English—at least the English for water and Jesus.
"I'm dying." "Sick." "My name Caesar."

                  Those who knew
These things, said these things now when they saw the lantern
Mechanically, as tamed beasts answer the whipcrack.
Their voices beat at the light like heavy moths.
But most made merely liquid or guttural sounds
Meaningless to the mate, but horribly like
The sounds of palateless men or animals trying
To talk through a human throat.

                  The mate was used
To the confusion of limbs and bodies by now.

At first it had made him think of the perturbed
Blind coil of blacksnakes thawing on a rock
In the bleak sun of Spring, or Judgment Day
Just after the first sounding of the trump
When all earth seethes and crumbles with the slow
Vast, mouldy resurrection of the dead.
But he had passed such fancies.

                                        He must see
As much as he could. He couldn't see very much.
They were too tightly packed but—no plague yet,
And all the chains were fast. Then he saw something.
The woman was asleep but her baby was dead.
He wondered whether to take it from her now.
No, it would only rouse the others. Tomorrow.
He turned away with a shiver.

                                        His glance fell
On the man who said he had been a king, the man
Called Tarbarrel, the image of black stone
Whose eyes were savage gods.

                                        The huge suave muscles
Rippled like stretching cats as he changed posture,
Magnificence in chains that yet was ease.
The smolder in those eyes. The steady hate.

The mate made himself stare till the eyes dropped.
Then he turned back to the companionway.
His forehead was hot and sweaty. He wiped it off,
But then the rough cloth of his sleeve smelt black.

The captain shut the Bible as he came in.
"Well, Mister Mate?"

                                        "All quiet, sir."

                                        The captain
Looked at him sharply. "Sit down," he said in a bark.
The mate's knees gave as he sat. "It's—hot down there,"
He said, a little weakly, wanting to wipe
His face again, but knowing he'd smell that blackness
Again, if he did.

                                        "Takes you that way, sometimes,"
Said the captain, not unkindly, "I remember
Back in the twenties."

                                        Something hot and strong
Bit the mate's throat. He coughed.

                                        "There," said the captain,
Putting the cup down. "You'll feel better now.
You're young for this trade, Mister, and that's a fact."

The mate coughed and didn't answer, much too glad
To see the captain change back to himself
From something made of steam, to want to talk.

But, after a while, he heard the captain talking,
Half to himself.

                                 "It's a fact, that," he was saying,
"They've even made a song of me—ever heard it?"
The mate shook his head, quickly, "Oh yes you have.
You know how it goes." He cleared his throat and hummed:

> *"Captain Ball was a Yankee slaver,*
> *Blow, blow, blow the man down!*
> *He traded in niggers and loved his Saviour,*
> *Give me some time to blow the man down."*

The droning chanty filled the narrow cabin
An instant with grey Massachusetts sea,
Wave of the North, wave of the melted ice,
The hard salt-sparkles on the harder rock.
The stony islands.

                            Then 'it died away.
"Well," said the captain, "if that's how it strikes them—
They mean it bad but I don't take it bad.
I get my sailing-orders from the Lord."
He touched the Bible. "And it's down there, Mister,
Down there in black and white—the sons of Ham—
Bondservants—sweat of their brows." His voice trailed off
Into texts: "I tell you, Mister," he said fiercely,
"The pay's good pay, but it's the Lord's work, too.
We're spreading the Lord's seed—spreading his seed—"

His hand made the outflung motion of a sower
And the mate, staring, seemed to hear the slight
Patter of fallen seeds on fertile ground,
Black, shining seeds, robbed from a black king's storehouse,
Falling and falling on American earth
With light, inexorable patter and fall,
To strike, lie silent, quicken.

                               Till the Spring
Came with its weeping rains, and the ground bore
A blade, a shadow-sapling, a tree of shadow,
A black-leaved tree whose trunk and roots were shadow,
A tree shaped like a yoke, growing and growing
Until it blotted all the seamen's stars.
Horses of anger trampling, horses of anger,
Trampling behind the sky in ominous cadence,
Beat of the heavy hooves like metal on metal,
Trampling something down. . . .

                               Was it they, was it they?
Or was it cold wind in the leaves of the shadow-tree
That made such grievous music?

          Oh Lordy Je-sus
          Won't you come and find me?

They put me in jail, Lord,
Way down in the jail.
Won't you send me a pro-phet
Just one of your prophets
Like Moses and Aaron
To get me some bail?

I'm feeling poorly
Yes, mighty poorly,
I ain't got no strength, Lord,
I'm all trampled down.
So send me an angel
Just any old angel
To give me a robe, Lord,
And give me a crown.

Oh Lordy Je-sus
It's a long time comin'
It's a long time co-o-min'
That Jubilee time.
We'll wait and we'll pray, Lord,
We'll wait and we'll pray, Lord,
But it's a long time, Lord,
Yes, it's a long time.

The dark sobbing ebbed away.
The captain was still talking. "Yes," he said,
"And yet we treat 'em well enough. There's no one
From Salem to the Guinea Coast can say
They lose as few as I do." He stopped.

                                        "Well, Mister?"

The mate arose. "Good night sir and—"

                                        "Good night."

The mate went up on deck. The breeze was fresh.
There were the stars, steady. He shook himself
Like a dog coming out of water and felt better.
Six weeks, with luck, and they'd be back in port
And he could draw his pay and see his girl.
Meanwhile, it wasn't his watch, so he could sleep.
The captain still below, reading that Bible. . . .
Forget it—and the noises, still half-heard—
He'd have to go below to sleep, this time,
But after, if the weather held like this,
He'd have them sling a hammock up on deck.
You couldn't smell the black so much on deck
And so you didn't dream it when you slept.

                                                    1927

LITANY FOR DICTATORSHIPS *

For all those beaten, for the broken
heads,
The fosterless, the simple, the oppressed,
The ghosts in the burning city of our
time . . .

For those taken in rapid cars to the
house and beaten
By the skilful boys, the boys with the
rubber fists,
—Held down and beaten, the table
cutting their loins,
Or kicked in the groin and left, with
the muscles jerking
Like a headless hen's on the floor of
the slaughter-house
While they brought the next man in
with his white eyes staring.
For those who still said "Red Front!"
or "God Save the Crown!"
And for those who were not courage-
ous
But were beaten nevertheless.
For those who spit out the bloody
stumps of their teeth
Quietly in the hall,
Sleep well on stone or iron, watch for
the time
And kill the guard in the privy before
they die,
Those with the deep-socketed eyes
and the lamp burning.

For those who carry the scars, who
walk lame—for those
Whose nameless graves are made in
the prison-yard
And the earth smoothed back before
morning and the lime scattered.

For those slain at once. For those living through months and years
Enduring, watching, hoping, going
each day

To the work or the queue for meat or
the secret club,
Living meanwhile, begetting children,
smuggling guns,
And found and killed at the end like
rats in a drain.

For those escaping
Incredibly into exile and wandering
there.
For those who live in the small rooms
of foreign cities
And who yet think of the country, the
long green grass,
The childhood voices, the language,
the way wind smelt then,
The shape of rooms, the coffee drunk
at the table,
The talk with friends, the loved city,
the waiter's face,
The gravestones, with the name,
where they will not lie
Nor in any of that earth. Their children are strangers.

For those who planned and were
leaders and were beaten
And for those, humble and stupid,
who had no plan
But were denounced, but grew angry,
but told a joke,
But could not explain, but were sent
away to the camp,
But had their bodies shipped back in
the sealed coffins,
"Died of pneumonia." "Died trying to
escape."

For those growers of wheat who were
shot by their own wheat-stacks,
For those growers of bread who were
sent to the ice-locked wastes,
And their flesh remembers their fields.

For those denounced by their smug,
horrible children
For a peppermint-star and the praise
of the Perfect State,
For all those strangled or gelded or
merely starved

* From *Selected Works of Stephen
Vincent Benét*, published by Rinehart &
Company, Inc. Copyright, 1935, by
Stephen Vincent Benét.

To make perfect states; for the priest
    hanged in his cassock,
The Jew with his chest crushed in and
    his eyes dying,
The revolutionist lynched by the
    private guards
To make perfect states, in the names
    of the perfect states.

For those betrayed by the neighbors
    they shook hands with
And for the traitors, sitting in the hard
    chair
With the loose sweat crawling their
    hair and their fingers restless
As they tell the street and the house
    and the man's name.

And for those sitting at table in the
    house
With the lamp lit and the plates and
    the smell of food,
Talking so quietly; when they hear
    the cars
And the knock at the door, and they
    look at each other quickly
And the woman goes to the door with
    a stiff face,
Smoothing her dress.
        "We are all good citizens here.
We believe in the Perfect State."
            And that was the last
Time Tony or Karl or Shorty came to
    the house
And the family was liquidated
    later.
It was the last time.
        We heard the shots in the night
But nobody knew next day what the
    trouble was
And a man must go to his work. So I
    didn't see him
For three days, then, and me near out
    of my mind
And all the patrols on the streets with
    their dirty guns
And when he came back, he looked
    drunk, and the blood was on
    him.

For the women who mourn their dead
    in the secret night,
For the children taught to keep quiet,
    the old children,
The children spat-on at school.
        For the wrecked laboratory,
The gutted house, the dunged picture,
    the pissed-in well,
The naked corpse of Knowledge flung
    in the square
And no man lifting a hand and no
    man speaking.

For the cold of the pistol-butt and the
    bullet's heat,
For the rope that chokes, the manacles
    that bind,
The huge voice, metal, that lies from
    a thousand tubes
And the stuttering machine-gun that
    answers all.

For the man crucified on the crossed
    machine-guns
Without name, without resurrection,
    without stars,
His dark head heavy with death and
    his flesh long sour
With the smell of his many prisons—
    John Smith, John Doe,
John Nobody—oh, crack your mind
    for his name!
Faceless as water, naked as the dust,
Dishonored as the earth the gas-shells
    poison
And barbarous with portent.
                This is he.
This is the man they ate at the green
    table
Putting their gloves on ere they
    touched the meat.
This is the fruit of war, the fruit of
    peace,
The ripeness of invention, the new
    lamb,
The answer to the wisdom of the wise.
And still he hangs, and still he will
    not die,
And still, on the steel city of our
    years

The light fails and the terrible blood
    streams down.
We thought we were done with these
    things but we were wrong.
We thought, because we had power,
    we had wisdom.
We thought the long train would run
    to the end of Time.
We thought the light would
    increase.
Now the long train stands derailed
    and the bandits loot it.
Now the boar and the asp have power
    in our time.
Now the night rolls back on the West
    and the night is solid.
Our fathers and ourselves sowed
    dragon's teeth.
Our children know and suffer the
    armed men.

                                        1935–36

EDITH WHARTON
(1862–1937)

THE CHOICE *

I

Stilling, that night after dinner,
had surpassed himself. He always did,
Wrayford reflected, when the small
fry from Highfield came to dine. He,
Cobham Stilling, who had to find his
bearings, keep to his level, in the big,
heedless, oppressive world of New
York, dilated and grew vast in the
congenial medium of Highfield. The
Red House was the biggest house of
the Highfield summer colony, as Cobham Stilling was its biggest man. No
one else within a radius of a hundred
miles (on a conservative estimate) had
as many horses, as many greenhouses,
as many servants, and assuredly no

* Reprinted from *Xingu and Other
Stories* by Edith Wharton; copyright
1916 by Charles Scribner's Sons; used by
permission of the publishers.

one else had two motors, or a motor-
boat for the lake.

The motor-boat was Stilling's latest
hobby, and he rode—or sailed—it in
and out of the conversation all the
evening, to the obvious edification of
every one present save his wife and
his visitor, Austin Wrayford. The interest of the latter two, who, from
opposite ends of the drawing-room, exchanged a fleeting glance when Stilling again launched his craft on the
thin current of the talk—the interest
of Mrs. Stilling and Wrayford, had
already lost its edge by protracted
conversational contact with the subject.

But the dinner-guests—the Rector,
Mr. Swordsley, and Mrs. Swordsley,
Lucy and Agnes Granger and their
brother Addison, and young Jack Em-
merton from Harvard—were all, for
divers reasons, stirred to the proper
pitch of feeling. Mr. Swordsley, no
doubt, was saying to himself: "If my
good parishioner here can afford to
buy a motor-boat, in addition to all
the other expenditures which an establishment like this must entail, I
certainly need not scruple to appeal
to him again for a contribution toward
our Galahad Club." The Granger
girls, meanwhile, were evoking visions
of lakeside picnics, not unadorned
with the presence of young Mr. Em-
merton; while that youth himself
speculated as to whether his affable
host would let him, when he came
back on his next vacation, "learn to
run the thing himself"; and Mr.
Addison Granger, the elderly bachelor
brother of the volatile Lucy and
Agnes, mentally formulated the precise phrase in which, in his next letter
to his cousin Professor Spildyke of
the University of East Latmos, he
should allude to "our last delightful
trip in my old friend Cobham
Stilling's ten-thousand-dollar motor-

launch"—for East Latmos was still in that primitive stage of social culture on which such figures impinge.

Isabel Stilling, sitting beside Mrs. Swordsley, her head slightly bent above the needlework with which, on such occasions, it was her old-fashioned habit to be engaged—Isabel also had doubtless her reflections to make. As Wrayford leaned back in his corner, and looked at her across the bright, flower-filled drawing-room, he noted first of all—for the hundredth time—the flexible play of her hands above the embroidery-frame, the shadow of the dusky, wavy hair on her forehead, the tired droop of the lids over her somewhat full gray eyes. He noted this, taking in unconsciously, at the same time, the indescribable quality in her attitude, in the fall of her dress and the turn of her head, that set her, for him, in a separate world; then he said to himself: "She's certainly thinking 'where on earth will he get the money to pay for it?'"

But at the same moment, from his inevitable position on the hearth-rug, cigar in mouth, his hands in his waistcoat pockets, Stilling was impressively perorating.

"I said, 'If I have the thing at all, I want the best that can be got.' That's my way, you know, Swordsley; I suppose I'm what you'd call fastidious. Always was, about everything, from cigars to wom-"—his eye met the apprehensive glance of Mrs. Swordsley, who looked, in evening dress, like her husband with his clerical coat cut slightly lower—"so I said, 'If I have the thing at all, I want the best that can be got.' Nothing makeshift for me, no second-best. I never cared for the cheap and showy. I always say frankly to a man, 'If you can't give me a first-rate cigar, for the Lord's sake, let me smoke my own.' Well, if you have *my* standards, you can't buy

a thing in a minute. You must look round, compare, select. I found there were lots of motor-boats on the market, just as there's lots of stuff called champagne. But I said to myself, 'Ten to one there's only one fit to buy, just as there's only one champagne fit for a gentleman to drink.' Argued like a lawyer, eh, Austin?" He tossed this jovially toward Wrayford. "Take me for one of your own trade, wouldn't you? Well, I'm not such a fool as I look. I suppose you fellows who are tied to the treadmill,—oh, excuse me, Swordsley, but work's work, isn't it?—I suppose you think a man like me has nothing to do but take it easy—loll through life like a woman. By George, sir, I'd like either of you to see the time it takes—I won't say the brains—but just the *time* it takes to pick out a good motor-boat. Why, I went—"

Mrs. Stilling set her embroidery-frame noiselessly on the low table at her side, and turned her head toward Wrayford. "Would you mind ringing for the tray?"

The interruption helped Mrs. Swordsley to waver to her feet. "I think we really ought to be going; my husband has an early service to-morrow."

Her host sounded an immediate protest. "Going already? Nothing of the sort! Why, the night's still young, as the poet says. Long way from here to the rectory? Nonsense! In our little twenty-horse motor we do it in five minutes—don't we, Belle? Ah, you're walking, to be sure—" Stilling's indulgent gesture seemed to concede that, in such a case, allowances must be made, and that he was the last man not to make them. "Well, then, Swordsley—" He held out a thick, red hand that seemed to exude beneficence, and the clergyman, pressing it, ventured to murmur a suggestion.

"What, that Galahad Club again? Why, I thought my wife— Isabel, didn't we— No? Well, it must have been my mother, then. And of course, you know, anything my good mother gives is—well—virtually— You haven't asked her? Sure? I could have sworn; I get so many of these appeals. And in these times, you know, we have to go cautiously. I'm sure you recognize that yourself, Swordsley. With my obligations—here now, to show you don't bear malice, have a brandy and soda before you go. Nonsense, man! This brandy isn't liquor; it's *liqueur*. I picked it up last year in London— last of a famous lot from Lord St. Oswyn's cellar. Laid down here, it stood me at— Eh?" he broke off as his wife moved toward him. "Ah, yes, of course. Miss Lucy, Miss Agnes—a drop of soda-water? Look here, Addison, *you* won't refuse my tipple, I know. Well, take a cigar, at any rate, Swordsley. And, by the way, I'm afraid you'll have to go round the long way by the avenue to-night. Sorry, Mrs. Swordsley, but I forgot to tell them to leave the gate on the lane unlocked. Well, it's a jolly night, and I daresay you won't mind the extra turn along the lake. And, by Jove! if the moon's out, you can get a glimpse of the motor-boat as you turn the point. She's moored just out beyond our boat-house; and it's a privilege to look at her, I can tell you!"

The dispersal of the remaining guests carried Stilling out into the hall, where his pleasantries echoed genially under the oak rafters while the Granger girls were being muffled for the drive and the carriages summoned from the stables.

By a common impulse Mrs. Stilling and Wrayford had moved together toward the hearth, which was masked from the door into the hall by a tall screen of lacquer. Wrayford leaned his elbow against the chimney-piece, and Mrs. Stilling stood motionless beside him, her clasped hands hanging down before her. The rose on her breast stirred slightly.

"Have you any more work to do with him to-night?" she asked below her breath.

Wrayford shook his head. "We wound it all up before dinner. He doesn't want to talk about it any more than he can help."

"It's so bad?"

"No; but he's got to pull up."

She paused, looking down at her clasped hands. He listened a moment, catching Stilling's farewell shout; then he changed his position slightly, and laid his hand on her arm.

"In an hour?"

She made a faint motion of assent.

"I'll tell you all about it then. The key's in the usual place?"

She nodded again, and walked away with her long, drifting motion as her husband came in from the hall. He went up to the tray, and poured himself a tall glass of brandy and soda.

"The weather's turning queer— black as pitch out now. I hope the Swordsleys won't walk into the lake— involuntary immersion, eh? He'd come out a Baptist, I suppose. What'd the Bishop do in such a case? There's a problem for a lawyer, my boy!"

He clapped Wrayford resoundingly on the thin shoulder and then walked over to his wife, who was gathering up her embroidery silks and dropping them into an old-fashioned work-bag. Stilling took her by the arms and swung her playfully about so that she faced to lamplight.

"What's the matter with you to-night?"

"The matter?" she echoed, blushing a little, and standing very erect in her desire not to appear to shrink from his touch.

"You never opened your lips. Left me the whole job of entertaining those blessed people. Didn't she, Austin?"

Wrayford laughed and lighted a cigarette. "She wasn't quite up to the mark."

"There! You see even Austin noticed it. What's the matter? Aren't they good enough for you? I don't pretend they're particularly exciting; but, hang it! I like to ask them here —I like to give pleasure."

"I didn't mean to be dull," said Isabel, appealingly.

"Well, you must learn to make an effort. Don't treat people as if they weren't in the room just because they don't happen to amuse you. Do you know what they'll think? They'll think it's because you've got a bigger house and more cash. Shall I tell you something? My mother said she'd noticed the same thing in you lately. She said she sometimes felt you looked down on her for living in a small house. Oh, she was half joking, of course; but you see you do give people that impression. I can't understand treating any one in that way. The more I have myself, the more I want to make other people happy."

Isabel gently freed herself and laid the work-bag on her embroidery-frame. "I have a headache; perhaps that made me stupid. I'm going to bed." She turned toward Wrayford and held out her hand. "Good night."

"Good night," he answered, opening the door for her.

When he turned back into the room, his host was pouring himself a third glass of brandy and soda.

"Here, have a nip? Gad, I need it badly, after the shaking up you gave me this afternoon." Stilling gave a short laugh, and carried his glass to the hearth, where he took up his

usual commanding position. "Why the deuce don't you drink something, Austin? You look as glum as Isabel. One would think that *you* were the chap that had been hit."

Wrayford threw himself into the chair from which Mrs. Stilling had lately risen. It was the one she habitually sat in, and to his fancy a faint scent of her always clung to it. He leaned back and looked up at Stilling.

"Want a cigar?" the latter continued. "Shall we go into the den and smoke?"

Wrayford hesitated. "If there's anything more you want to ask me about—"

"Gad, no! I had full measure and running over this afternoon. The deuce of it is, I don't see where the money's all gone to. Luckily I've got plenty of nerve; I'm not the kind of man to sit down and snivel because he's been touched in Wall Street."

Wrayford rose again. "Then, if you don't want me, I think I'll go up to my room and put some finishing touches to a brief before I turn in. I must get back to town to-morrow afternoon."

"All right, then." Stilling set down his empty glass, and held out his hand with a tingle of alacrity. "Good night, old man."

They shook hands, and Wrayford moved toward the door.

"I say, Austin—stop a minute!" his host called after him.

Wrayford turned, and the two men faced each other across the hearth-rug. Stilling's eyes shifted uneasily in his flushed face.

"There's one thing more you *can* do for me, like a good chap, before you go. Tell Isabel about that loan; explain to her she's got to sign a note for it."

Wrayford, in his turn, flushed slightly.

"You want *me* to tell her?"

"Hang it! I'm soft-hearted—that's the worst of me." Stilling moved toward the tray, and lifted the brandy decanter. "And she'll take it better from you; she'll *have* to take it from you. She's proud. You can take her out for a row to-morrow morning—you can take her out in the motor-launch, if you like. I meant to have a spin in it myself in the morning; but if you'll tell her—"

Wrayford hesitated. "All right. I'll tell her."

"'Thanks a lot, my dear fellow. And you'll make her see it wasn't my fault, eh? Women are awfully vague about money, and if you appear to back me up, you know—"

Wrayford nodded. "As you please. Good night."

"Good night. Here, Austin—there's just one more thing. You needn't say anything to Isabel about the other business—I mean my mother's securities."

"Ah?" said Wrayford.

Stilling shifted from one foot to the other. "I'd rather put that to the old lady myself. I can make it clear to her. She idolizes me, you know—and, hang it! I've got a good record. Up to now, I mean. My mother's been in clover since I married; I may say she's been my first thought. And I don't want her to hear of this from Isabel. Isabel's a little harsh at times—and of course this isn't going to make her any easier to live with."

"Very well," Wrayford assented.

Stilling, with a look of relief, walked toward the window which opened on the terrace. "Gad! what a queer night! Hot as the kitchen-range. Shouldn't wonder if we had a squall before morning. I wonder if that infernal skipper took in the launch's awnings before he went home."

Wrayford paused a moment in the doorway. "Yes, I saw him do it. She's shipshape for the night."

"Good! That saves me a run down to the shore." Stilling strolled back into the room, whistling cheerfully.

"Good night then," said Wrayford.

"Good night, old man. You'll tell her?"

"I'll tell her," Wrayford answered from the threshold.

"And mum about my mother!" his host called after him.

II

The darkness had thinned a little when Wrayford scrambled down the steep path to the shore. Though the air was heavy, the threat of a storm seemed to have vanished, and now and then the moon's edge showed above a torn slope of cloud.

But in the densely massed shrubbery about the boat-house the night was still black, and Wrayford had to strike a match before he could find the lock and insert his key. He left the door unlatched, and groped his way in. How often he had crept into this warm pine-scented obscurity, guiding himself cautiously by the edge of the bench along the side wall, and hearing the stealthy lap of water through the gaps in the flooring! He knew just where one had to duck one's head to avoid the two canoes swung from the rafters, and just where to put his hand on the latch of the door that led to the balcony above the lake.

The boat-house represented one of Stilling's abandoned whims. He had built it some seven years before, and for a time it had been the scene of incessant nautical exploits. Stilling had rowed, sailed, paddled indefatigably, and all Highfield had been impressed to bear him company and admire his versatility. Then motors had come in, and he had forsaken aquatic sports for the guidance of the flying chariot. The canoes of birch-bark and canvas had been hoisted to the roof, the little sail-boat had rotted at her moorings, and the movable floor of the boat-house, ingeniously contrived to slide back on noiseless runners, had lain undisturbed through several seasons. Even the key of the boat-house had been mislaid,—by Isabel's fault, her husband asserted,—and the locksmith had to be called in to make a new one when the purchase of the motor-boat made the lake once more the center of Stilling's activity.

As Wrayford entered he noticed that a strange oily odor overpowered the usual scent of dry pine-wood; and at the next step his foot struck an object that rolled noisily across the boards. He lighted a match, and found he had overturned a can of grease which the boatman had no doubt been using to oil the runners of the sliding-floor.

Wrayford felt his way down the length of the boat-house, and softly opening the balcony door, looked out on the lake. A few yards off the launch lay motionless in the veiled moonlight; and just below him, on the black water, he saw the dim outline of the skiff which Stilling used to paddle out to her. The silence was so intense that Wrayford fancied he heard a faint rustling in the shrubbery on the high bank behind the boat-house, and the crackle of gravel on the path descending to it.

He closed the door again and turned back; and as he did so the other door, on the land-side, swung inward, and a figure darkened the dim opening. Just enough light entered through the round holes above the respective doors to reveal it as Mrs. Stilling's cloaked outline, and to guide her to him as he advanced. But before they met she stumbled and gave a little cry.

"What is it?" he exclaimed, springing toward her.

"My foot caught; the floor seemed to give way under me. Ah, of course—" She bent down in the darkness—"I saw the men oiling it this morning."

Wrayford caught her to him. "Be careful, darling! It might be dangerous if it slid too easily. The water's deep under here."

"Yes; the water's very deep. I sometimes wish—" She leaned against him without finishing her sentence, and he tightened his arms about her.

"Hush!" he whispered, his lips on her hair.

Suddenly she threw back her head and seemed to listen.

"What's the matter?" he asked, listening also. "What did you hear?"

"I don't know." He felt her trembling. "I'm not sure this place is as safe as it used to be—"

Wrayford held her to him reassuringly. "But the boatman sleeps down at the village; and who else should come here at this hour?"

"My husband might. He thinks of nothing but the launch."

"He won't to-night, for I told him I'd seen the skipper roll up the awning, and put the launch shipshape, and that satisfied him."

"Ah, he *did* think of coming, then?"

"Only for a minute, when the sky looked so black half an hour ago, and he was afraid of a squall. It's clearing now, and there's no danger."

He drew her down on the bench, and they sat a moment or two in silence, her hands in his. Then she said wearily: "You'd better tell me."

Wrayford gave a faint laugh. "'Yes, I suppose I had. In fact, he asked me to."

"He asked you to?"

"Yes."

She sounded a sharp note of contempt. "The coward! he's afraid!"

Wrayford made no reply, and she went on: "*I'm* not. Tell me everything, please."

"Well, he's chucked away a pretty big sum again—"

"How has he done it?"

"He says he doesn't know. He's been speculating, I suppose. The madness of making him your trustee!"

She drew her hands away quickly. "You know why I did it. When we married I didn't want to put him in the false position of the man who accepts everything; I wanted people to think the money was partly his."

"I don't know what you've made *people* think; but you've been eminently successful in one respect. *He* thinks it's his—and he loses it as if it were."

She shivered a little, drawing her cloak closer. "There are worse things. Go on."

"Isabel!" He bent over her. "Give me your hand again." He lifted it and laid a long kiss on it.

"What was it—exactly—that he wished you to tell me?" she asked.

"That you've got to sign another promissory note—for fifty thousand this time."

She drew a deep breath. "Is that all?"

Wrayford hesitated; then he said: "Yes—for the present."

She sat motionless, her head bent, her hand resting passively in his.

He leaned nearer. "What did you mean, just now, by worse things?"

She paused a moment. "Haven't you noticed that he's been drinking a great deal lately?"

"Yes; I've noticed."

They were both silent again; then Wrayford said with sudden vehemence: "And *yet* you won't—"

"Won't?"

"Put an end to it. Good God! Save what's left of your life."

She made no answer, and in the deep stillness the *throb-throb* of the water underneath them was like the anxious beat of a heart.

"Isabel—" Wrayford murmured. He bent over to kiss her, and felt the tears on her face. "Isabel! I can't stand it! Listen to me—"

She interrupted him. "No; no. I've thought of everything. There's the boy—the boy's fond of him. He's not a bad father."

"Except in the trifling matter of ruining his son."

"And there's his poor old mother. He's a good son, at any rate; he's never hurt *her*. And I know her. If I left him she'd never touch a penny. What she has of her own is not enough to live on; and how could *he* provide for her? If I put him out of doors, I should be putting his mother out, too—out of the little house she's so happy in."

"But surely you could arrange—there are always ways."

"Not for her! She's proud. And then she believes in him. Lots of people believe in him, you know. It would kill her if she ever found out."

Wrayford made an impatient movement: "It will kill *you*, if you stay with him to prevent her finding out."

She turned toward him and laid her other hand on his. "Not while I have you."

"Have me? In this way?" he echoed with an exasperated laugh.

"In any way."

"My poor girl—poor child!"

She drew back from him suddenly, with a quick movement of fear. "You mean that *you'll* grow tired—your patience will give out soon?"

He answered her only by saying: "My poor Isabel!"

But she went on insistently: "Don't

you suppose I've thought of that—foreseen it?"

"Well—and then?" he exclaimed with sudden passion.

"I've accepted that, too," she said.

He dropped her hands with a despairing gesture. "Then, indeed, I waste my breath!"

She made no answer, and for a time they sat silent, side by side, but with a space between. At length he asked in a contrite voice: "You're not crying, Isabel?"

"No."

"I can't see your face, it's grown so dark again."

"Yes. I hadn't noticed. The storm must be coming, after all." She made a motion as if to rise.

He drew close, and put his arm about her again. "Don't leave me yet, dear! You know I must go to-morrow." He broke off with a laugh. "I'm to break the news to you to-morrow morning, by the way; I'm to take you out in the motor-launch and break it to you." He dropped her hands and stood up. "Good God! How can I go away and leave you here alone with him?"

"You've done it often before."

"Yes; but each time it's more damnable. And then I've always had a hope—"

"A hope?" She rose also. "Give it up! Give it up!" she moaned.

"You've none, then, yourself?"

She was silent, drawing the folds of her cloak about her.

"None—none?" he insisted.

"Only one," she broke out passionately.

He bent over and sought for her in the darkness. "What is it, my dearest? What is it?"

"Don't touch me! That he may die!" she shuddered back.

He dropped his hands, and they drew apart instinctively, hearing each other's quick breathing through the obscurity.

"*You* wish that sometimes, too?" he said at length in a low voice.

"Sometimes? I wish it always—every day, every hour, every moment!" She paused, and then let the quivering words break out. "You'd better know it; you'd better know the worst of me. I'm not the saint you suppose; the duty I do is poisoned by the thoughts I think. Day by day, hour by hour, I wish him dead. When he goes out I pray for something to happen; when he comes back I say to myself: 'Are you here again?' When I hear of people being killed in accidents I think: 'Why wasn't he there?' When I read the death-notices in the paper I say: 'So-and-so was just his age.' When I see him taking such care of his health and his diet—as he does, you know, except when he gets reckless and begins to drink too much—when I see him exercising and resting, and eating only certain things, and weighing himself, and feeling his muscles, and boasting that he hasn't gained a pound, I think of the men who die from overwork, who throw their lives away for some big object, and I say to myself: 'What can kill a man who thinks only of himself?' And night after night I keep myself from going to sleep for fear I may dream that he's dead. When I dream that, and wake and find him there, it's worse than ever—and my thoughts are worse than ever, too!"

She broke off on a stifled sob, and the *thump-thump* of the water under the floor was like the beat of a loud, rebellious heart.

"There, you know the truth! Is it too bad for you?"

He answered in a low voice, as if unconscious of her question: "Such things do sometimes happen, you know."

"Do they?" She laughed. "Yes, I've seen it happen—in happy marriages!"

They were silent again, not approaching each other. Abruptly Isabel turned, feeling her way toward the door. As she did so, the profound stillness of the night was broken by the sound of a man's voice, caroling out somewhat unsteadily the refrain of a music-hall song.

The two in the boat-house darted toward each other with a simultaneous movement, clutching hands as they met.

"He's coming!" Isabel breathed.

Wrayford detached himself hastily from her hold.

"He may only be out for a turn before he goes to bed. Wait a minute. I'll see if I can make out." He felt his way to the bench, scrambled up on it, and stretching his body forward, managed to bring his eyes in line with the opening above the door.

"It's as black as pitch. I can't see anything."

The refrain rang out nearer.

"Wait! I saw something twinkle. There it is again. It's coming this way —down the path. It's his cigar."

There was a long rattle of thunder through the stillness.

"It's the storm!" Isabel gasped. "He's coming to see about the launch."

Wrayford dropped noiselessly from the bench to her side.

"He's coming—yes."

She caught him by the arm.

"Isn't there time to get up the path and slip under the shrubbery?" she whispered.

"No, no; he's in the path now. He'll be here in two minutes. He'll find us."

He felt her hand tighten on his arm.

"You must go in the skiff, then. It's the only way."

"And let him find you here? And hear my oars? Isabel, listen—there's something I must say."

She flung herself against him, shaken with dry sobs.

"Isabel, just now I didn't tell you everything. He's ruined his mother— taken everything of hers, too. And he's got to tell her; it can't be kept from her."

She uttered a startled sound and drew away.

"Is this the truth? Why didn't you tell me before?"

"He forbade me. You were not to know."

Close above them, in the shrubbery, Stilling rolled out:

"Nita, Juanita,
Ask thy soul if we must part!"

Wrayford caught her wrist in a hard grasp. "Understand this—if he comes in, he'll find us. And if there's a scandal you'll lose your boy."

She seemed not to hear him. "You —you—you—he'll kill you!" she cried out.

Wrayford laughed and released her. She drew away and stood shrinking close against the wall, her hands pressed to her breast. Wrayford straightened himself and listened intently. Then he dropped to his knees and laid his hands against the boards of the sliding-floor. It yielded at once with a kind of evil alacrity; and at their feet they saw, in the night, another night that moved and shimmered. Wrayford sprang up, and threw himself back against the wall, behind the door.

A key rattled, and after a moment's fumbling the door swung open noisily. Wrayford and Isabel saw a black bulk against the obscurity. It moved a step, lurched forward, and vanished from them. In the depths there was a long cry and a splash.

"Go! go!" Wrayford cried out, feeling blindly for Isabel in the blackness.

"Go?" she shuddered back, wrenching herself away from him with horror.

He stood still a moment, as if dazed; then she saw him suddenly plunge from her side, and heard another splash far down, and a tumult in the beaten water.

In the darkness she cowered close to the opening, pressing her face over the edge, and frantically crying out the name of each in turn. Suddenly she began to see; the obscurity was less opaque, a faint moon-pallor diluted it. Isabel vaguely discerned the two shapes struggling in the black pit below her; once she saw the gleam of a face. Then she glanced up desperately for some means of rescue, and caught sight of the oars ranged on brackets against the wall. She snatched down the nearest, bent over the opening, and pushed the oar down into the blackness, calling her husband's name.

The clouds had swallowed up the moon again, and she could see nothing below her, but she still heard a tumult in the beaten water.

"Cobham! Cobham!" she screamed.

As if in answer, she felt a mighty clutch on the oar, a clutch that strained her arms to the breaking-point as she tried to brace her knees against the runners of the sliding-floor.

"Hold on! hold on! hold *on!*" a voice gasped out from below; and she held on, with racked muscles, with bleeding palms, with eyes straining from their sockets, and a heart that tugged at her like the weight on the oar.

Suddenly the weight relaxed, and the oar slipped up through her lacerated hands. She felt a wet bulk scrambling over the edge of the opening, and Stilling's voice, raucous and strange, groaned out, close to her: "God! I thought I was done for."

He staggered to his knees, coughing and sputtering, and the water dripped on her from his clothes.

She flung herself down, straining over the pit. Not a sound came up from it.

"Austin! Austin! Quick! Another oar!" she shrieked.

Stilling gave a cry. "My God! Was it Austin? What in hell— Another oar? No, no; untie the skiff, I tell you. But it's no use. Nothing's any use. I felt him lose hold as I came up."

After that she remembered nothing more till, hours later, as it appeared to her, she became dimly aware of her husband's voice, high, hysterical and important, haranguing a group of scared lantern-struck faces that seemed to have sprung up mysteriously about them in the night.

"Poor Austin! Poor fellow . . . terrible loss to me . . . mysterious dispensation. Yes, I *do* feel gratitude—miraculous escape—but I wish he could have known that I was saved!"

1908

ROBERT HERRICK
(1868–1938)

FROM

THE COMMON LOT *

["SHINING PALACES ON SAND"]

* * * Something similar had been his experience with the contractor Graves.

"Put me up a good, showy build-

* From Robert Herrick, *The Common Lot.* Copyright 1904 by The Macmillan Company. By permission of The Macmillan Company, publishers.

ing," the contractor had said, when they first discussed the design. "That's the kind that will take in that park neighborhood. People nowadays want a stylish home with elevator boys in uniform. . . . That court you've got there between the wings, and the little fountain, and the grand entrance,—all just right. But they don't want to pay nothin' for their style. Flats don't rent for anything near what they do in New York. Out here they want the earth for fifty, sixty dollars a month; and we've got to give 'em the nearest thing to it for their money."

So when it came to the structure of the building, the contractor ordered the architect to save expense in every line of the details. The woodwork was cut to the thinnest veneer; partitions, even bearing-walls, were made of the cheapest studding the market offered; the large floors were hung from thin outside walls, without the brick bearing-walls advised by the architect. When Hart murmured, Graves said frankly:—

"This ain't any investment proposition, my boy. I calculate to fill the Graveland in two months, and then I'll trade it off to some countryman who is looking for an investment. Put all the style you want into the finish. Have some of the flats Flemish, and others Colonial, and so on. Make 'em smart."

The architect tried to swallow his disgust at being hired to put together such a flimsy shell of plaster and lath. But Cook, who had been trained in Wright's office, where work of this grade was never accepted, was in open revolt.

"If it gets known around that this is the style of work we do in this office, it'll put us in a class, and it ain't a pleasant one, either. . . . Say,

Jack, how's this office to be run—first class or the other class?"

"You know, man," the architect replied, wincing at the frank speech, "how I am fixed with Graves. I don't like this business any better than you do, but we'll be through with it before long; and I shan't get into it again, I can tell you."

He growled in his turn to the contractor, who received his protest with contemptuous good humor.

"You'd better take a look at what other men are doing, if you think I am making the Graveland such an awful cheap building. I tell you, there ain't money in the other kind. Why, I worked for a man once who put up a first-class building, slow-burning construction, heavy woodwork, and all that. It's old-fashioned by this—and its rents are way down. And I saw by the paper the other day that it was sold at the sheriff's sale for not more than what my bill came to! What have you got to say to that?"

Therefore the architect dismissed the Graveland from his mind as much as he could, and saw little of it while it was under construction, for the contractor did his own superintending. One day, however, he had occasion to go to the building, and took his wife with him. They drove down the vast waste of Grand Boulevard; after passing through that wilderness of painful fancies, the lines of the Graveland made a very pleasant impression.

Hart had induced Graves to sacrifice part of his precious land to an interior court, around which he had thrown his building like a miniature château, thus shutting out the sandy lots, the ragged street, which looked like a jaw with teeth knocked out at irregular intervals. A heavy wall joined the two wings on the street side, and through the iron gates the

Park could be seen, just across the street.

"Lovely!" Helen exclaimed. "I'm so glad you did it! I like it so—so much more than the Phillips house."

They studied it carefully from the carriage, and Hart pointed out all the little triumphs of design. It was, as Helen felt, much more genuine than the Phillips house. It was no bungling copy, but an honest answer to a modern problem—an answer, to be sure, in the only language that the architect knew.

Helen wanted to see the interior, although Jackson displayed no enthusiasm over that part of the structure. And in the inside came disaster! The evidences of the contractor's false, flimsy building darkened the architect's brow.

"The scamp!" he muttered, emerging from the basement. "He's propped the whole business on a dozen or so 'two-by-fours.' And I guess he's put in the rottenest plumbing underground that I ever saw. I don't believe it ever had an inspection."

"Show me what you mean," Helen demanded.

He pointed out to her some of the devices used to skimp the building. "Even the men at work here know it. You can see it by the way they look at me. Why, the thing is a paper box!"

In some of the apartments the rough work was scarcely completed, in others the plasterers were at work; but the story was the same everywhere.

"I can't see how he escaped the Building Department. He's violated the ordinances again and again. But I suppose he knows how to keep the inspectors quiet."

He remembered the Canostota: he had no manner of doubt, now, about those I-beams in the Canostota.

"Francis!" Helen exclaimed with sudden passion; "you won't stand it? You won't let him do this kind of thing?"

The architect shrugged his shoulders.

"It's *his* building. He bought the plans and paid for them."

She was silent, troubled in her mind by this business distinction, but convinced that wrong was being done. A thing like this, a fraud upon the public, should be prevented in some way.

"Can't you tell him that you will report him to the Building Department?" she asked finally.

Hart smiled at her impetuous unpracticality.

"That would hardly do, would it, to go back on a client like that? It's none of my business, really. Only one hates to feel that his ideas are wasted on such stuff as this is made of. The city should look after it. And it's no worse than most of these flat buildings. Look at that one across the street. It's the same cheap thing. I was in there the other day. . . . No, it's the condition of things in this city, —the worst place for good building in the country. Every one says so. But God help the poor devils who come to live here, if a fire once gets started in this plaster and lath shell!"

He turned to the entrance and kicked open the door in disgust. Helen's face was pale and set, as if she could not dismiss the matter thus lightly.

"I never thought of fire!" she murmured. "Francis, if anything like that should happen! To think that you had drawn the plans!"

"Oh! it may last out its time," he replied reassuringly. "And it doesn't affect the appearance of the building

at present. It's real smart, as Mrs.
Rainbow would say. Don't you think
so, Nell?"

She was standing with her back to
the pleasant façade of the Graveland,
and was staring into the Park across
the street. Turning around at his
words she cast a swift, scrutinizing
glance over the building.

"It isn't right! I see fraud looking
out of every window. It's just a
skeleton covered with cloth."

The architect laughed at her solemnity. He was disgusted with it
himself; it offended his workman's
conscience. But he was too modern,
too practical, to allow merely ideal
considerations to upset him. And,
after all, in his art, as in most arts,
the effect of the work was two-thirds
the game. With her it was altogether
different. Through all outward aspect, or cover, of things pierced their
inner being, from which one could
not escape by illusion.

As they were leaving the place the
contractor drove up to the building
for his daily inspection. He came over
to the architect, a most affable smile
on his bearded face.

"Mrs. Hart, I presume," he said
raising his hat. "Looking over your
husband's work? It's fine, fine, I tell
you! Between ourselves, it beats
Wright all out."

Helen's stiffness of manner did not
encourage cordiality, and Graves,
thinking her merely snobbish, bowed
to them and went into the building.

"You'll never do anything for him
again, will you, Francis? Promise me."

And he promised lightly enough,
for he thought it highly improbable
that the contractor ever would return
to him, or that he should feel obliged
to take his work if he offered it. * * *

1904

O. HENRY
(WILLIAM SYDNEY PORTER)
(1862–1910)

AN UNFINISHED STORY *

We no longer groan and heap ashes
upon our heads when the flames of
Tophet are mentioned. For, even the
preachers have begun to tell us that
God is radium, or ether or some scientific compound, and that the worst we
wicked ones may expect is a chemical
reaction. This is a pleasing hypothesis;
but there lingers yet some of the old,
goodly terror of orthodoxy.

There are but two subjects upon
which one may discourse with a free
imagination, and without the possibility of being controverted. You may
talk of your dreams; and you may tell
what you heard a parrot say. Both
Morpheus and the bird are incom-
petent witnesses; and your listener
dare not attack your recital. The base-
less fabric of a vision, then, shall furnish my theme—chosen with apologies
and regrets instead of the more limited field of pretty Polly's small talk.

I had a dream that was so far removed from the higher criticism that
it had to do with the ancient, respectable, and lamented bar-of-judg-
ment theory.

Gabriel had played his trump; and
those of us who could not follow suit
were arraigned for examination. I
noticed at one side a gathering of
professional bondsmen in solemn
black and collars that buttoned behind; but it seemed there was some
trouble about their real estate titles;
and they did not appear to be getting
any of us out.

A fly cop—an angel policeman—flew over to me and took me by the left wing. Near at hand was a group of very prosperous-looking spirits arraigned for judgment.

"Do you belong with that bunch?" the policeman asked.

"Who are they?" was my answer.

"Why," said he, "they are—"

But this irrelevant stuff is taking up space that the story should occupy.

Dulcie worked in a department store. She sold Hamburg edging, or stuffed peppers, or automobiles, or other little trinkets such as they keep in department stores. Of what she earned, Dulcie received six dollars per week. The remainder was credited to her and debited to somebody else's account in the ledger kept by G——. Oh, primal energy, you say, Reverend Doctor— Well then, in the Ledger of Primal Energy.

During her first year in the store, Dulcie was paid five dollars per week. It would be instructive to know how she lived on that amount. Don't care? Very well; probably you are interested in larger amounts. Six dollars is a larger amount. I will tell how she lived on six dollars per week.

One afternoon at six, when Dulcie was sticking her hat-pin within an eighth of an inch of her *medulla oblongata,* she said to her chum, Sadie—the girl that waits on you with her left side:

"Say, Sade, I made a date for dinner this evening with Piggy."

"You never did!" exclaimed Sadie admiringly. "Well, ain't you the lucky one? Piggy's an awful swell; and he always takes a girl to swell places. He took Blanche up to the Hoffman House one evening, where they have swell music, and you see a lot of swells. You'll have a swell time, Dulcie."

Dulcie hurried homeward. Her eyes were shining, and her cheeks showed the delicate pink of life's—real life's—approaching dawn. It was Friday; and she had fifty cents left of her last week's wages.

The streets were filled with the rush-hour floods of people. The electric lights of Broadway were glowing—calling moths from miles, from leagues, from hundreds of leagues out of darkness around to come in and attend the singeing school. Men in accurate clothes, with faces like those carved on cherry stones by the old salts in sailors' homes, turned and stared at Dulcie as she sped, unheeding, past them. Manhattan, the night-blooming cereus, was beginning to unfold its dead-white, heavy-odored petals.

Dulcie stopped in a store where goods were cheap and bought an imitation lace collar with her fifty cents. That money was to have been spent otherwise—fifteen cents for supper, ten cents for breakfast, ten cents for lunch. Another dime was to be added to her small store of savings; and five cents was to be squandered for licorice drops—the kind that made your cheek look like the toothache, and last as long. The licorice was an extravagance—almost a carouse—but what is life without pleasures?

Dulcie lived in a furnished room. There is this difference between a furnished room and a boarding-house. In a furnished room, other people do not know it when you go hungry.

Dulcie went up to her room—the third floor back in a West Side brownstone-front. She lit the gas. Scientists tell us that the diamond is the hardest substance known. Their mistake. Landladies know of a compound beside which the diamond is as putty. They pack it in the tips of gas-burners; and one may stand on a chair and dig at it in vain until one's fingers are pink and bruised. A hairpin will not remove it; therefore let us call it immovable. So Dulcie lit the gas. In its one-fourth-candle-power glow we will observe the room.

Couch-bed, dresser, table, washstand, chair—of this much the landlady was guilty. The rest was Dulcie's. On the dresser were her treasures—a gilt china vase presented to her by Sadie, a calendar issued by a pickle works, a book on the divination of dreams, some rice powder in a glass dish, and a cluster of artificial cherries tied with a pink ribbon.

Against the wrinkly mirror stood pictures of General Kitchener, William Muldoon, the Duchess of Marlborough, and Benvenuto Cellini. Against one wall was a plaster of Paris plaque of an O'Callahan in a Roman helmet. Near it was a violent oleograph of a lemon-colored child assaulting an inflammatory butterfly. This was Dulcie's final judgment in art; but it had never been upset. Her rest had never been disturbed by whispers of stolen copes, no critic had elevated his eyebrows at her infantile entomologist.

Piggy was to call for her at seven. While she swiftly makes ready, let us discreetly face the other way and gossip.

For the room, Dulcie paid two dollars per week. On week-days her breakfast cost ten cents; she made coffee and cooked an egg over the gaslight while she was dressing. On Sunday mornings she feasted royally on veal chops and pineapple fritters at "Billy's" restaurant, at a cost of twenty-five cents—and tipped the waitress ten cents. New York presents so many temptations for one to run into extravagance. She had her lunches in the department-store restaurant at a cost of sixty cents for the week; dinners were $1.05. The evening papers—show me a New Yorker going without his daily paper!—came to six cents; and two Sunday papers—one for the personal column and the other to read—were ten cents. The total amounts to $4.76. Now, one has to buy clothes, and—

I give it up. I hear of wonderful bargains in fabrics, and of miracles performed with needle and thread; but I am in doubt. I hold my pen poised in vain when I would add to Dulcie's life some of those joys that belong to woman by virtue of all the unwritten, sacred, natural, inactive ordinances of the equity of heaven. Twice she had been to Coney Island and had ridden the hobby-horses. 'Tis a weary thing to count your pleasures by summers instead of by hours.

Piggy needs but a word. When the girls named him, an undeserving stigma was cast upon the noble family of swine. The words-of-three-letters lesson in the old blue spelling book begins with Piggy's biography. He was fat; he had the soul of a rat, the habits of a bat, and the magnanimity of a cat. . . . He wore expensive clothes, and was a connoisseur in starvation. He could look at a shopgirl and tell you to an hour how long it had been since she had eaten anything more nourishing than marshmallows and tea. He hung about the shopping districts, and prowled around in department stores with his invitations to dinner. Men who escort dogs upon the streets at the end of a string look down upon him. He is a type; I can dwell upon him no longer; my pen is not the kind intended for him; I am no carpenter.

At ten minutes to seven Dulcie was ready. She looked at herself in the wrinkly mirror. The reflection was satisfactory. The dark blue dress, fitting without a wrinkle, the hat with its jaunty black feather, the but-slightly-soiled gloves—all representing self-denial, even of food itself—were vastly becoming.

Dulcie forgot everything else for a moment except that she was beautiful, and that life was about to lift a corner of its mysterious veil for her to observe its wonders. No gentleman had ever asked her out before. Now she was going for a brief moment into the glitter and exalted show.

The girls said that Piggy was a "spender." There would be a grand dinner, and music, and splendidly dressed ladies to look at, and things to eat that strangely twisted the girls' jaws when they tried to tell about them. No doubt she would be asked out again.

There was a blue pongee suit in a window that she knew—by saving twenty cents a week instead of ten, in—let's see— Oh, it would run into years! But there was a second-hand store in Seventh Avenue where—

Somebody knocked at the door. Dulcie opened it. The landlady stood there with a spurious smile, sniffing for cooking by stolen gas.

"A gentleman's downstairs to see you," she said. "Name is Mr. Wiggins."

By such epithet was Piggy known to unfortunate ones who had to take him seriously.

Dulcie turned to the dresser to get her handkerchief; and then she stopped still, and bit her underlip hard. While looking in her mirror she had seen fairyland and herself, a princess, just awakening from a long slumber. She had forgotten one that was watching her with sad, beautiful, stern eyes—the only one there was to approve or condemn what she did. Straight and slender and tall, with a look of sorrowful reproach on his handsome, melancholy face, General

Kitchener fixed his wonderful eyes on her out of his gilt photograph frame on the dresser.

Dulcie turned like an automatic doll to the landlady.

"Tell him I can't go," she said dully. "Tell him I'm sick, or something. Tell him I'm not going out."

After the door was closed and locked, Dulcie fell upon her bed, crushing her black tip, and cried for ten minutes. General Kitchener was her only friend. He was Dulcie's ideal of a gallant knight. He looked as if he might have a secret sorrow, and his wonderful moustache was a dream, and she was a little afraid of that stern yet tender look in his eyes. She used to have little fancies that he would call at the house sometime, and ask for her, with his sword clanking against his high boots. Once, when a boy was rattling a piece of chain against a lamp-post she had opened the window and looked out. But there was no use. She knew that General Kitchener was away over in Japan, leading his army against the savage Turks; and he would never step out of his gilt frame for her. Yet one look from him had vanquished Piggy that night. Yes, for that night.

When her cry was over Dulcie got up and took off her best dress, and put on her old blue kimono. She wanted no dinner. She sang two verses of "Sammy." Then she became intensely interested in a little red speck on the side of her nose. And after that was attended to, she drew up a chair to the rickety table, and told her fortune with an old deck of cards.

"The horrid, impudent thing!" she said aloud. "And I never gave him a word or a look to make him think it!"

At nine o'clock Dulcie took a tin box of crackers and a little pot of raspberry jam out of her trunk, and had a feast. She offered General

Kitchener some jam on a cracker; but he only looked at her as the sphinx would have looked at a butterfly—if there are butterflies in the desert.

"Don't eat it if you don't want to," said Dulcie. "And don't put on so many airs and scold so with your eyes. I wonder if you'd be so superior and snippy if you had to live on six dollars a week."

It was not a good sign for Dulcie to be rude to General Kitchener. And then she turned Benvenuto Cellini face downward with a severe gesture. But that was not inexcusable; for she had always thought he was Henry VIII, and she did not approve of him.

At half-past nine Dulcie took a last look at the pictures on the dresser, turned out the light, and skipped into bed. It's an awful thing to go to bed with a good-night look at General Kitchener, William Muldoon, the Duchess of Marlborough, and Benvenuto Cellini.

This story really doesn't get anywhere at all. The rest of it comes later —sometime when Piggy asks Dulcie again to dine with him, and she is feeling lonelier than usual, and General Kitchener happens to be looking the other way; and then—

As I said before, I dreamed that I was standing near a crowd of prosperous-looking angels, and a policeman took me by the wing and asked if I belonged with them.

"Who are they?" I asked.

"Why," said he, "they are the men who hired working-girls, and paid 'em five or six dollars a week to live on. Are you one of the bunch?"

"Not on your immortality," said I. "I'm only the fellow that set fire to an orphan asylum, and murdered a blind man for his pennies."

1905

SINCLAIR LEWIS
(1885–   )

FROM   *MAIN STREET* *

[TWO NEWCOMERS ON MAIN STREET]

* * * When Carol had walked for thirty-two minutes she had completely covered the town, east and west, north and south; and she stood at the corner of Main Street and Washington Avenue and despaired.

Main Street with its two-story brick shops, its story-and-a-half wooden residences, its muddy expanse from concrete walk to walk, its huddle of Fords and lumber-wagons, was too small to absorb her. The broad, straight, unenticing gashes of the streets let in the grasping prairie on every side. She realized the vastness and the emptiness of the land. The skeleton iron windmill on the farm a few blocks away, at the north end of Main Street, was like the ribs of a dead cow. She thought of the coming of the Northern winter, when the unprotected houses would crouch together in terror of storms galloping out of that wild waste. They were so small and weak, the little brown houses. They were shelters for sparrows, not homes for warm laughing people.

She told herself that down the street the leaves were a splendor. The maples were orange; the oaks a solid tint of raspberry. And the lawns had been nursed with love. But the thought would not hold. At best the trees resembled a thinned woodlot. There was no park to rest the eyes. And since not Gopher Prairie but Wakamin was the county-seat, there was no court-house with its grounds.

* From *Main Street* by Sinclair Lewis, copyright, 1920, by Harcourt, Brace and Company, Inc.

She glanced through the fly-specked windows of the most pretentious building in sight, the one place which welcomed strangers and determined their opinion of the charm and luxury of Gopher Prairie—the Minniemashie House. It was a tall lean shabby structure, three stories of yellow-streaked wood, the corners covered with sanded pine slabs purporting to symbolize stone. In the hotel office she could see a stretch of bare unclean floor, a line of rickety chairs with brass cuspidors between, a writing-desk with advertisements in mother-of-pearl letters upon the glass-covered back. The dining-room beyond was a jungle of stained tablecloths and catsup bottles.

She looked no more at the Minniemashie House.

A man in cuffless shirt-sleeves with pink arm-garters, wearing a linen collar but no tie, yawned his way from Dyer's Drug Store across to the hotel. He leaned against the wall, scratched a while, sighed, and in a bored way gossiped with a man tilted back in a chair. A lumber-wagon, its long green box filled with large spools of barbed-wire fencing, creaked down the block. A Ford, in reverse, sounded as though it were shaking to pieces, then recovered and rattled away. In the Greek candy-store was the whine of a peanut-roaster, and the oily smell of nuts.

There was no other sound nor sign of life.

She wanted to run, fleeing from the encroaching prairie, demanding the security of a great city. Her dreams of creating a beautiful town were ludicrous. Oozing out from every drab wall, she felt a forbidding spirit which she could never conquer.

She trailed down the street on one side, back on the other, glancing into the cross streets. It was a private Seeing Main Street tour. She was within ten minutes beholding not only the heart of a place called Gopher Prairie, but ten thousand towns from Albany to San Diego:

Dyer's Drug Store, a corner building of regular and unreal blocks of artificial stone. Inside the store, a greasy marble soda-fountain with an electric lamp of red and green and curdled-yellow mosaic shade. Pawed-over heaps of tooth-brushes and combs and packages of shaving-soap. Shelves of soap-cartons, teething-rings, garden-seeds, and patent medicines in yellow packages—nostrums for consumption, for "women's diseases"—notorious mixtures of opium and alcohol, in the very shop to which her husband sent patients for the filling of prescriptions.

From a second-story window the sign "W. P. Kennicott, Phys. & Surgeon," gilt on black sand.

A small wooden motion-picture theater called "The Rosebud Movie Palace." Lithographs announcing a film called "Fatty in Love."

Howland & Gould's Grocery. In the display window, black, overripe bananas and lettuce on which a cat was sleeping. Shelves lined with red crêpe paper which was now faded and torn and concentrically spotted. Flat against the wall of the second story the signs of lodges—the Knights of Pythias, the Maccabees, the Woodmen, the Masons.

Dahl & Oleson's Meat Market—a reek of blood.

A jewelry shop with tinny-looking wrist-watches for women. In front of it, at the curb, a huge wooden clock which did not go.

A fly-buzzing saloon with a brilliant gold and enamel whisky sign across the front. Other saloons down the block. From them a stink of stale beer, and thick voices bellowing pidgin German or trolling out dirty songs—vice gone feeble and unenterprising and dull—the delicacy of a mining-camp minus its vigor. In front of the saloons, farmwives sitting on the seats of wagons, waiting for their husbands to become drunk and ready to start home.

A tobacco shop called "The Smoke House," filled with young men shaking dice for cigarettes. Racks of magazines, and pictures of coy fat prostitutes in striped bathing-suits.

A clothing store with a display of "ox-blood-shade oxfords with bull-dog toes." Suits which looked worn and glossless while they were still new, flabbily draped on dummies like corpses with painted cheeks.

The Bon Ton Store—Haydock & Simons'—the largest shop in town. The first-story front of clear glass, the plates cleverly bound at the edges with brass. The second story of pleasant tapestry brick. One window of excellent clothes for men, interspersed with collars of floral piqué which showed mauve daisies on a saffron ground. Newness and an obvious notion of neatness and service. Haydock & Simons. Haydock. She had met a Haydock at the station; Harry Haydock; an active person of thirty-five. He seemed great to her, now, and very like a saint. His shop was clean!

Axel Egge's General Store, frequented by Scandinavian farmers. In the shallow dark window-space heaps of sleazy sateens, badly woven galateas, canvas shoes designed for women with bulging ankles, steel and red glass buttons upon cards with broken edges, a cottony blanket, a graniteware frying-pan reposing on a sunfaded crêpe blouse.

Sam Clark's Hardware Store. An air of frankly metallic enterprise. Guns and churns and barrels of nails and beautiful shiny butcher knives.

Chester Dashaway's House Furnishing Emporium. A vista of heavy oak rockers with leather seats, asleep in a dismal row.

Billy's Lunch. Thick handleless cups on the wet oilcloth-covered counter. An odor of onions and the smoke of hot lard. In the doorway a young man audibly sucking a toothpick.

The warehouse of the buyer of cream and potatoes. The sour smell of a dairy.

The Ford Garage and the Buick Garage, competent one-story brick and cement buildings opposite each other. Old and new cars on greaseblackened concrete floors. Tire advertisements. The roaring of a tested motor; a racket which beat at the nerves. Surly young men in khaki union-overalls. The most energetic and vital places in town.

A large warehouse for agricultural implements. An impressive barricade of green and gold wheels, of shafts and sulky seats, belonging to machinery of which Carol knew nothing —potato-planters, manure-spreaders, silage-cutters, disk-harrows, breaking-plows.

A feed store, its windows opaque with the dust of bran, a patent medicine advertisement painted on its roof.

Ye Art Shoppe, Prop. Mrs. Mary Ellen Wilks, Christian Science Library open daily free. A touching fumble at beauty. A one-room shanty of boards recently covered with rough stucco. A show-window delicately rich in error; vases starting out to imitate tree-trunks but running off into blobs of gilt—an aluminum ash-tray labeled "Greetings from Gopher Prairie"— a Christian Science magazine—a stamped sofa-cushion portraying a large ribbon tied to a small poppy, the correct skeins of embroidery-silk lying on the pillow. Inside the shop, a glimpse of bad carbon prints of bad and famous pictures, shelves of phonograph records and camera films, wooden toys, and in the midst an anxious small woman sitting in a padded rocking chair.

A barber shop and pool room. A man in shirt sleeves, presumably Del Snafflin the proprietor, shaving a man who had a large Adam's apple.

Nat Hicks's Tailor Shop, on a side street off Main. A one-story building. A fashion-plate showing human pitchforks in garments which looked as hard as steel plate.

On another side street a raw redbrick Catholic Church with a varnished yellow door.

The post-office—merely a partition of glass and brass shutting off the rear of a mildewed room which must once have been a shop. A tilted writingshelf against a wall rubbed black and scattered with official notices and army recruiting-posters.

The damp, yellow-brick schoolbuilding in its cindery grounds.

The State Bank, stucco masking wood.

The Farmers' National Bank. An Ionic temple of marble. Pure, exquisite, solitary. A brass plate with "Ezra Stowbody, Pres't."

A score of similar shops and establishments.

Behind them and mixed with them, the houses, meek cottages or large, comfortable, soundly uninteresting symbols of prosperity.

In all the town not one building save the Ionic bank which gave pleasure to Carol's eyes; not a dozen buildings which suggested that, in the fifty years of Gopher Prairie's existence, the citizens had realized that it was either desirable or possible to make this, their common home, amusing or attractive.

It was not only the unsparing unapologetic ugliness and the rigid straightness which overwhelmed her. It was the planlessness, the flimsy temporariness of the buildings, their faded unpleasant colors. The street was cluttered with electric-light poles, telephone poles, gasoline pumps for motor cars, boxes of goods. Each man had built with the most valiant disregard of all the others. Between a large new "block" of two-story brick shops on one side, and the firebrick Overland garage on the other side, was a one-story cottage turned into a millinery shop. The white temple of the Farmers' Bank was elbowed back by a grocery of glaring yellow brick. One store-building had a patchy galvanized iron cornice; the building beside it was crowned with battlements and pyramids of brick capped with blocks of red sandstone.

She escaped from Main Street, fled home.

She wouldn't have cared, she insisted, if the people had been comely. She had noted a young man loafing before a shop, one unwashed hand holding the cord of an awning; a middle-aged man who had a way of staring at women as though he had been married too long and too prosaically; an old farmer, solid, wholesome, but not clean—his face like a potato fresh from the earth. None of them had shaved for three days.

"If they can't build shrines, out here on the prairie, surely there's nothing to prevent their buying safety-razors!" she raged.

She fought. herself: "I must be wrong. People do live here. It *can't* be as ugly as—as I know it is! I must be wrong. But I can't do it. I can't go through with it."

She came home too seriously worried for hysteria; and when she found Kennicott waiting for her, and exulting, "Have a walk? Well, like the town? Great lawns and trees, eh?" she was able to say, with a self-protective maturity new to her, "It's very interesting."

The train which brought Carol to Gopher Prairie also brought Miss Bea Sorenson.

Miss Bea was a stalwart, corn-colored, laughing young woman, and she was bored by farm-work. She desired the excitements of city-life, and the way to enjoy city-life was, she had decided, to "go get a yob as hired girl in Gopher Prairie." She contentedly lugged her pasteboard telescope from the station to her cousin, Tina Malmquist, maid of all work in the residence of Mrs. Luke Dawson.

"Vell, so you come to town," said Tina.

"Ya. Ay get a yob," said Bea.

"Vell. . . . You got a fella now?"

"Ya. Yim Yacobson."

"Vell. I'm glat to see you. How much you vant a week?"

"Sex dollar."

"There ain't nobody pay dat. Vait! Dr. Kennicott, I t'ink he marry a girl from de Cities. Maybe she pay dat. Vell. You go take a valk."

"Ya," said Bea.

So it chanced that Carol Kennicott and Bea Sorenson were viewing Main Street at the same time.

Bea had never before been in a town larger than Scandia Crossing, which has sixty-seven inhabitants.

As she marched up the street she was meditating that it didn't hardly seem like it was possible there could be so many folks all in one place at the same time. My! It would take years to get acquainted with them all. And swell people, too! A fine big gentleman in a new pink shirt with a diamond, and not no washed-out blue denim working-shirt. A lovely lady in a longery dress (but it must be

an awful hard dress to wash). And the stores!

Not just three of them, like there were at Scandia Crossing, but more than four whole blocks!

The Bon Ton Store—big as four barns—my! it would simply scare a person to go in there, with seven or eight clerks all looking at you. And the men's suits, on figures just like human. And Axel Egge's, like home, lots of Swedes and Norskes in there, and a card of dandy buttons, like rubies.

A drug store with a soda fountain that was just huge, awful long, and all lovely marble; and on it there was a great big lamp with the biggest shade you ever saw—all different kinds colored glass stuck together; and the soda spouts, they were silver, and they came right out of the bottom of the lamp-stand! Behind the fountain there were glass shelves, and bottles of new kinds of soft drinks, that nobody ever heard of. Suppose a fella took you *there!*

A hotel, awful high, higher than Oscar Tollefson's new red barn; three stories, one right on top of another; you had to stick your head back to look clear up to the top. There was a swell traveling man in there—probably been to Chicago, lots of times.

Oh, the dandiest people to know here! There was a lady going by, you wouldn't hardly say she was any older than Bea herself; she wore a dandy new gray suit and black pumps. She almost looked like she was looking over the town, too. But you couldn't tell what she thought. Bea would like to be that way—kind of quiet, so nobody would get fresh. Kind of—oh, elegant.

A Lutheran Church. Here in the city there'd be lovely sermons, and church twice on Sunday, *every* Sunday!

And a movie show!

A regular theater, just for movies. With the sign "Change of bill every evening." Pictures every evening!

There were movies in Scandia Crossing, but only once every two weeks, and it took the Sorensons an hour to drive in—papa was such a tightwad he wouldn't get a Ford. But here she could put on her hat any evening, and in three minutes' walk be to the movies, and see lovely fellows in dress-suits and Bill Hart and everything!

How could they have so many stores? Why! There was one just for tobacco alone, and one (a lovely one—the Art Shoppy it was) for pictures and vases and stuff, with oh, the dandiest vase made so it looked just like a tree trunk!

Bea stood on the corner of Main Street and Washington Avenue. The roar of the city began to frighten her. There were five automobuls on the street all at the same time—and one of 'em was a great big car that must of cost two thousand dollars—and the 'bus was starting for a train with five elegant-dressed fellows, and a man was pasting up red bills with lovely pictures of washing-machines on them, and the jeweler was laying out bracelets and wrist-watches and *everything* on real velvet.

What did she care if she got six dollars a week? Or two! It was worth while working for nothing, to be allowed to stay here. And think how it would be in the evening, all lighted up—and not with no lamps, but with electrics! And maybe a gentleman friend taking you to the movies and buying you a strawberry ice cream soda!

Bea trudged back.

"Vell? You lak it?" said Tina.

"Ya. Ay lak it. Ay t'ink maybe Ay stay here," said Bea. * * *

1920

FROM *BABBITT* *

[MR. BABBITT STARTS THE DAY]

To George F. Babbitt, as to most prosperous citizens of Zenith, his motor car was poetry and tragedy, love and heroism. The office was his pirate ship but the car his perilous excursion ashore.

Among the tremendous crises of each day none was more dramatic than starting the engine. It was slow on cold mornings; there was the long, anxious whirr of the starter; and sometimes he had to drip ether into the cocks of the cylinders, which was so very interesting that at lunch he would chronicle it drop by drop, and orally calculate how much each drop had cost him.

This morning he was darkly prepared to find something wrong, and he felt belittled when the mixture exploded sweet and strong, and the car didn't even brush the door-jamb, gouged and splintery with many bruisings by fenders, as he backed out of the garage. He was confused. He shouted "Morning!" to Sam Doppelbrau with more cordiality than he had intended.

Babbitt's green and white Dutch Colonial house was one of three in that block on Chatham Road. To the left of it was the residence of Mr. Samuel Doppelbrau, secretary of an excellent firm of bathroom-fixture jobbers. His was a comfortable house with no architectural manners whatever; a large wooden box with a squat tower, a broad porch, and glossy paint yellow as a yolk. Babbitt disapproved of Mr. and Mrs. Doppelbrau as "Bohemian." From their house came midnight music and obscene laughter; there were neighborhood rumors of

* From *Babbitt*, by Sinclair Lewis, copyright, 1922, by Harcourt, Brace and Company, Inc.

bootlegged whisky and fast motor rides. They furnished Babbitt with many happy evenings of discussion, during which he announced firmly, "I'm not strait-laced, and I don't mind seeing a fellow throw in a drink once in a while, but when it comes to deliberately trying to get away with a lot of hell-raising all the while like the Doppelbraus do, it's too rich for my blood!"

On the other side of Babbitt lived Howard Littlefield, Ph.D., in a strictly modern house whereof the lower part was dark red tapestry brick, with a leaded oriel, the upper part of pale stucco, like spattered clay, and the roof red-tiled. Littlefield was the Great Scholar of the neighborhood; the authority on everything in the world except babies, cooking and motors. He was a Bachelor of Arts of Blodgett College, and a Doctor of Philosophy in economics of Yale. He was the employment-manager and publicity-counsel of the Zenith Street Traction Company. He could, on ten hours' notice, appear before the board of aldermen or the state legislature and prove, absolutely, with figures all in rows and with precedents from Poland and New Zealand, that the street-car company loved the Public and yearned over its employees; that all its stock was owned by Widows and Orphans; and that whatever it desired to do would benefit property-owners by increasing rental values, and help the poor by lowering rents. All his acquaintances turned to Littlefield when they desired to know the date of the battle of Saragossa, the definition of the word "sabotage," the future of the German mark, the translation of "*hinc illæ lacrimæ*," or the number of products of coal tar. He awed Babbitt by confessing that he often sat up till midnight reading the figures and footnotes in Government reports, or skimming (with amusement at the author's mistakes) the latest volumes of chemistry, archeology, and ichthyology.

But Littlefield's great value was as a spiritual example. Despite his strange learnings he was as strict a Presbyterian and as firm a Republican as George F. Babbitt. He confirmed the business men in the faith. Where they knew only by passionate instinct that their system of industry and manners was perfect, Dr. Howard Littlefield proved it to them, out of history, economics, and the confessions of reformed radicals.

Babbitt had a good deal of honest pride in being the neighbor of such a savant, and in Ted's intimacy with Eunice Littlefield. At sixteen Eunice was interested in no statistics save those regarding the ages and salaries of motion-picture stars, but—as Babbitt definitely put it—"she was her father's daughter."

The difference between a light man like Sam Doppelbrau and a really fine character like Littlefield was revealed in their appearances. Dopplebrau was disturbingly young for a man of forty-eight. He wore his derby on the back of his head, and his red face was wrinkled with meaningless laughter. But Littlefield was old for a man of forty-two. He was tall, broad, thick; his gold-rimmed spectacles were engulfed in the folds of his long face; his hair was a tossed mass of greasy blackness; he puffed and rumbled as he talked; his Phi Beta Kappa key shone against a spotty black vest; he smelled of old pipes; he was altogether funereal and archidiaconal; and to real-estate brokerage and the jobbing of bathroom-fixtures he added an aroma of sanctity.

This morning he was in front of his house, inspecting the grass parking between the curb and the broad cement sidewalk. Babbitt stopped his car and leaned out to shout "Mornin'!" Littlefield lumbered over and stood with one foot up on the running-board.

"Fine morning," said Babbitt, lighting—illegally early—his second cigar of the day.

"Yes, it's a mighty fine morning," said Littlefield.

"Spring coming along fast now."

"Yes, it's real spring now, all right," said Littlefield.

"Still cold nights, though. Had to have a couple blankets, on the sleeping-porch last night."

"Yes, it wasn't any too warm last night," said Littlefield.

"But I don't anticipate we'll have any more real cold weather now."

"No, but still, there was snow at Tiflis, Montana, yesterday," said the Scholar, "and you remember the blizzard they had out West three days ago—thirty inches of snow at Greeley, Colorado—and two years ago we had a snow-squall right here in Zenith on the twenty-fifth of April."

"Is that a fact! Say, old man, what do you think about the Republican candidate? Who'll they nominate for president? Don't you think it's about time we had a real business administration?"

"In my opinion, what the country needs, first and foremost, is a good, sound, business-like conduct of its affairs. What we need is—a business administration!" said Littlefield.

"I'm glad to hear you say that! I certainly am glad to hear you say that! I didn't know how you'd feel about it, with all your associations with colleges and so on, and I'm glad you feel that way. What the country needs—just at this present juncture—is neither a college president nor a lot of monkeying with foreign affairs, but a good—sound—economical—business—administration, that will give us

a chance to have something like a decent turnover."

"Yes. It isn't generally realized that even in China the schoolmen are giving way to more practical men, and of course you can see what that implies."

"Is that a fact! Well! well!" breathed Babbitt, feeling much calmer, and much happier about the way things were going in the world. "Well, it's been nice to stop and parleyvoo a second. Guess I'll have to get down to the office now and sting a few clients. Well, so long, old man. See you to-night. So long."

They had labored, these solid citizens. Twenty years before, the hill on which Floral Heights was spread, with its bright roofs and immaculate turf and amazing comfort, had been a wilderness of rank second-growth elms and oaks and maples. Along the precise streets were still a few wooded vacant lots, and the fragment of an old orchard. It was brilliant to-day; the apple boughs were lit with fresh leaves like torches of green fire. The first white of cherry blossoms flickered down a gully, and robins clamored.

Babbitt sniffed the earth, chuckled at the hysteric robins as he would have chuckled at kittens or at a comic movie. He was, to the eye, the perfect office-going executive—a well-fed man in a correct brown soft hat and frameless spectacles, smoking a large cigar, driving a good motor along a semi-suburban parkway. But in him was some genius of authentic love for his neighborhood, his city, his clan. The winter was over; the time was come for the building, the visible growth, which to him was glory. He lost his dawn depression; he was ruddily cheerful when he stopped on

Smith Street . . . to have the gasoline-tank filled.

The familiarity of the rite fortified him: the sight of the tall red iron gasoline-pump, the hollow-tile and terra-cotta garage, the window full of the most agreeable accessories—shiny casings, spark-plugs with immaculate porcelain jackets, tire-chains of gold and silver. He was flattered by the friendliness with which Sylvester Moon, dirtiest and most skilled of motor mechanics, came out to serve him. "Mornin', Mr. Babbitt!" said Moon, and Babbitt felt himself a person of importance, one whose name even busy garagemen remembered—not one of these cheap-sports flying around in flivvers. He admired the ingenuity of the automatic dial, clicking off gallon by gallon; admired the smartness of the sign: "A fill in time saves getting stuck—gas to-day 31 cents"; admired the rhythmic gurgle of the gasoline as it flowed into the tank, and the mechanical regularity with which Moon turned the handle.

"How much we takin' to-day?" asked Moon, in a manner which combined the independence of the great specialist, the friendliness of a familiar gossip, and respect for a man of weight in the community, like George F. Babbitt.

"Fill 'er up."

"Who you rootin' for for Republican candidate, Mr. Babbitt?"

"It's too early to make any predictions yet. After all, there's still a good month and two weeks—no, three weeks—must be almost three weeks—well, there's more than six weeks in all before the Republican convention, and I feel a fellow ought to keep an open mind and give all the candidates a show—look 'em all over and size 'em up, and then decide carefully."

"That's a fact, Mr. Babbitt."

"But I'll tell you—and my stand on this is just the same as it was four years ago, and eight years ago, and it'll be my stand four years from now—yes, and eight years from now! What I tell everybody, and it can't be too generally understood, is that what we need first, last, and all the time is a good, sound business administration!"

"By golly, that's right!"

"How do those front tires look to you?"

"Fine! Fine! Wouldn't be much work for garages if everybody looked after their car the way you do."

"Well, I do try and have some sense about it." Babbitt paid his bill, said adequately, "Oh, keep the change," and drove off in an ecstasy of honest self-appreciation. It was with the manner of a Good Samaritan that he shouted at a respectable-looking man who was waiting for a trolley car, "Have a lift?" As the man climbed in Babbitt condescended, "Going clear down-town? Whenever I see a fellow waiting for a trolley, I always make it a practice to give him a lift—unless, of course, he looks like a bum."

"Wish there were more folks that were so generous with their machines," dutifully said the victim of benevolence.

"Oh, no, 'tain't a question of generosity, hardly. Fact, I always feel—I was saying to my son just the other night—it's a fellow's duty to share the good things of this world with his neighbors, and it gets my goat when a fellow gets stuck on himself and goes around tooting his horn merely because he's charitable."

The victim seemed unable to find the right answer. Babbitt boomed on:

"Pretty punk service the Company giving us on these car-lines. Nonsense to only run the Portland Road cars once every seven minutes. Fellow gets mighty cold on a winter morning, waiting on a street corner with the wind nipping at his ankles."

"That's right. The Street Car Company don't care a damn what kind of a deal they give us. Something ought to happen to 'em."

Babbitt was alarmed. "But still, of course it won't do to just keep knocking the Traction Company and not realize the difficulties they're operating under, like these cranks that want municipal ownership. The way these workmen hold up the Company for high wages is simply a crime, and of course the burden falls on you and me that have to pay a seven-cent fare! Fact, there's remarkable service on all their lines—considering."

"Well—" uneasily.

"Darn fine morning," Babbitt explained. "Spring coming along fast."

"Yes, it's real spring now."

The victim had no originality, no wit, and Babbitt fell into a great silence and devoted himself to the game of beating trolley cars to the corner: a spurt, a tail-chase, nervous speeding between the huge yellow side of the trolley and the jagged row of parked motors, shooting past just as the trolley stopped—a rare game and valiant.

And all the while he was conscious of the loveliness of Zenith. For weeks together he noticed nothing but clients and the vexing To Rent signs of rival brokers. To-day, in mysterious malaise, he raged or rejoiced with equal nervous swiftness, and to-day the light of spring was so winsome that he lifted his head and saw.

He admired each district along his familiar route to the office: The bungalows and shrubs and winding irregular driveways of Floral Heights. The one-story shops on Smith Street, a glare of plate-glass and new yellow brick; groceries and laundries and drug-stores to supply the more immediate needs of East Side house-wives. The market gardens in Dutch Hollow, their shanties patched with corrugated iron and stolen doors. Billboards with crimson goddesses nine feet tall advertising cinema films, pipe tobacco, and talcum powder. The old "mansions" along Ninth Street, S. E., like aged dandies in filthy linen; wooden castles turned into boarding-houses, with muddy walks and rusty hedges, jostled by fast-intruding garages, cheap apartment-houses, and fruit-stands conducted by bland, sleek Athenians. Across the belt of railroad-tracks, factories with high-perched water-tanks and tall stacks—factories producing condensed milk, paper boxes, lighting-fixtures, motor cars. Then the business center, the thickening darting traffic, the crammed trolleys unloading, and high doorways of marble and polished granite.

It was big—and Babbitt respected bigness in anything; in mountains, jewels, muscles, wealth, or words. He was, for a spring-enchanted moment, the lyric and almost unselfish lover of Zenith. He thought of the outlying factory suburbs; of the Chaloosa River with its strangely eroded banks; of the orchard-dappled Tonawanda Hills to the North, and all the fat dairy land and big barns and comfortable herds. As he dropped his passenger he cried, "Gosh, I feel pretty good this morning!"

Epochal as starting the car was the drama of parking it before he entered his office. As he turned from Oberlin Avenue round the corner into Third Street, N. E., he peered ahead for a space in the line of parked cars. He angrily just missed a space as a rival driver slid into it. Ahead, another car was leaving the curb, and Babbitt slowed up, holding out his hand to the cars pressing on him from behind, agitatedly motioning an old woman to go ahead, avoiding a truck which bore down on him from one side. With front wheels nicking the wrought-steel bumper of the car in front, he stopped, feverishly cramped his steering-wheel, slid back into the vacant space and, with eighteen inches of room, manœuvered to bring the car level with the curb. It was a virile adventure masterfully executed. With satisfaction he locked a thief-proof steel wedge on the front wheel, and crossed the street to his real-estate office on the ground floor of the Reeves Building.

The Reeves Building was as fireproof as a rock and as efficient as a typewriter; fourteen stories of yellow pressed brick, with clean, upright, unornamented lines. It was filled with the offices of lawyers, doctors, agents for machinery, for emery wheels, for wire fencing, for mining-stock. Their gold signs shone on the windows. The entrance was too modern to be flamboyant with pillars; it was quiet, shrewd, neat. Along the Third Street side were a Western Union Telegraph Office, the Blue Delft Candy Shop, Shotwell's Stationery Shop, and the Babbitt-Thompson Realty Company.

Babbitt could have entered his office from the street, as customers did, but it made him feel an insider to go through the corridor of the building and enter by the back door. Thus he was greeted by the villagers.

The little unknown people who inhabited the Reeves Building corridors—elevator-runners, starter, engineers, superintendent, and the doubtful-looking lame man who conducted the news and cigar stand—were in no way city-dwellers. They were rustics, living in a constricted valley, interested only in one another and in The Building. Their Main Street was the entrance hall, with its stone floor, severe marble ceiling, and the inner

windows of the shops. The liveliest place on the street was the Reeves Building Barber Shop, but this was also Babbitt's one embarrassment. Himself, he patronized the glittering Pompeian Barber Shop in the Hotel Thornleigh, and every time he passed the Reeves shop—ten times a day, a hundred times—he felt untrue to his own village.

Now, as one of the squirearchy, greeted with honorable salutations by the villagers, he marched into his office, and peace and dignity were upon him, and the morning's dissonances all unheard.

They were heard again, immediately.

Stanley Graff, the outside salesman, was talking on the telephone with tragic lack of that firm manner which disciplines clients: "Say, uh, I think I got just the house that would suit you—the Percival House, in Linton. . . . Oh, you've seen it. Well, how'd it strike you? . . . Huh? . . . Oh," irresolutely, "oh, I see."

As Babbitt marched into his private room, a coop with semi-partition of oak and frosted glass, at the back of the office, he reflected how hard it was to find employees who had his own faith that he was going to make sales.

There were nine members of the staff, besides Babbitt and his partner and father-in-law, Henry Thompson, who rarely came to the office. The nine were Stanley Graff, the outside salesman—a youngish man given to cigarettes and the playing of pool; old Mat Penniman, general utility man, collector of rents and salesman of insurance—broken, silent, gray; a mystery, reputed to have been a "crack" real-estate man with a firm of his own in haughty Brooklyn; Chester Kirby Laylock, resident salesman out at the Glen Oriole acreage development—an enthusiastic person with a silky mustache and much family; Miss Theresa McGoun, the swift and rather pretty stenographer; Miss Wilberta Bannigan, the thick, slow, laborious accountant and file-clerk; and four free-lance part-time commission salesmen.

As he looked from his own cage into the main room Babbitt mourned, "McGoun's a good stenog., smart's a whip, but Stan Graff and all those bums—" The zest of the spring morning was smothered in the stale office air.

Normally he admired the office with a pleased surprise that he should have created this sure lovely thing; normally he was stimulated by the clean newness of it and the air of bustle; but to-day it seemed flat—the tiled floor, like a bathroom, the ocher-colored metal ceiling, the faded maps on the hard plaster walls, the chairs of varnished pale oak, the desks and filing-cabinets of steel painted in olive drab. It was a vault, a steel chapel where loafing and laughter were raw sin.

He hadn't even any satisfaction in the new water-cooler! And it was the very best of water-coolers, up-to-date, scientific, and right-thinking. It had cost a great deal of money (in itself a virtue). It possessed a non-conducting fiber ice-container, a porcelain water-jar (guaranteed hygienic), a dripless non-clogging sanitary faucet, and machine-painted decorations in two tones of gold. He looked down the relentless stretch of tiled floor at the water-cooler, and assured himself that no tenant of the Reeves Building had a more expensive one, but he could not recapture the feeling of social superiority it had given him. He astoundingly grunted, "I'd like to beat it off to the woods right now. And loaf all day. And go to Gunch's again

to-night, and play poker, and cuss as much as I feel like, and drink a hundred and nine-thousand bottles of beer."

He sighed; he read through his mail; he shouted "Msgoun," which meant "Miss McGoun"; and began to dictate. * * *

1922

ARROWSMITH *

CHAPTER IV

[MAX GOTTLIEB]

I

Professor Max Gottlieb was about to assassinate a guinea pig with anthrax germs, and the bacteriology class were nervous.

They had studied the forms of bacteria, they had handled Petri dishes and platinum loops, they had proudly grown on potato slices the harmless red cultures of *Bacillus prodigiosus*, and they had come now to pathogenic germs and the inoculation of a living animal with swift disease. These two beady-eyed guinea pigs, chittering in a battery jar, would in two days be stiff and dead.

Martin had an excitement not free from anxiety. He laughed at it, he remembered with professional scorn how foolish were the lay visitors to the laboratory, who believed that sanguinary microbes would leap upon them from the mysterious centrifuge, from the benches, from the air itself. But he was conscious that in the cotton-plugged test-tube between the instrument-bath and the bichloride jar on the demonstrator's desk were millions of fatal anthrax germs.

The class looked respectful and

* From *Arrowsmith* by Sinclair Lewis, copyright, 1925, by Harcourt, Brace and Company, Inc.

did not stand too close. With the flair of technique, the sure rapidity which dignified the slightest movement of his hands, Dr. Gottlieb clipped the hair on the belly of a guinea pig held by the assistant. He soaped the belly with one flicker of a hand-brush, he shaved it and painted it with iodine.

(And all the while Max Gottlieb was recalling the eagerness of his first students, when he had just returned from working with Koch and Pasteur, when he was fresh from enormous beer seidels and Korpsbrüder and ferocious arguments. Passionate, beautiful days! *Die goldene Zeit!* His first classes in America, at Queen City College, had been awed by the sensational discoveries in bacteriology; they had crowded about him reverently; they had longed to know. Now the class was a mob. He looked at them—Fatty Pfaff in the front row, his face vacant as a doorknob; the co-eds, emotional and frightened; only Martin Arrowsmith and Angus Duer visibly intelligent. His memory fumbled for a pale blue twilight in Munich, a bridge and a waiting girl, and the sound of music.)

He dipped his hands in the bichloride solution and shook them—a quick shake, fingers down, like the fingers of a pianist above the keys. He took a hypodermic needle from the instrument-bath and lifted the test-tube. His voice flowed indolently, with German vowels and blurred w's:

"This, gentlemen, iss a twenty-four-hour culture of *Bacillus anthracis.* You will note, I am sure you will have noted already, that in the bottom of the tumbler there was cotton to keep the tube from being broken. I cannot advise breaking tubes of anthrax germs and afterwards getting the hands into the culture. You *might* merely get anthrax boils—"

The class shuddered.

Gottlieb twitched out the cotton plug with his little finger, so neatly that the medical student who had complained, "Bacteriology is junk; urinalysis and blood tests are all the lab stuff we need to know," now gave him something of the respect they had for a man who could do card tricks or remove an appendix in seven minutes. He agitated the mouth of the tube in the Bunsen burner, droning, "Every time you take the plug from a tube, flame the mouth of the tube. Make that a rule. It iss a necessity of the technique, and technique, gentlemen, is the beginning of all science. It iss also the least-known thing in science."

The class was impatient. Why didn't he get on with it, on to the entertainingly dreadful moment of inoculating the pig?

(And Max Gottlieb, glancing at the other guinea pig in the prison of its battery jar, meditated, "Wretched innocent! Why should I murder him, to teach Dummköpfe? It would be better to experiment on that fat young man.")

He thrust the syringe into the tube, he withdrew the piston dextrously with his index finger, and lectured:

"Take one-half c.c. of the culture. There are two kinds of M.D.'s—those to whom c.c. means cubic centimeter and those to whom it means compound cathartic. This second kind are more prosperous."

(But one cannot convey the quality of it: the thin drawl, the sardonic amiability, the hiss of the s's, the d's turned into blunt and challenging t's.)

The assistant held the guinea pig close; Gottlieb pinched up the skin of the belly and punctured it with a quick downthrust of the hypodermic needle. The pig gave a little jerk, a little squeak, and the co-eds shuddered. Gottlieb's wise fingers knew when the peritoneal wall was reached. He pushed home the plunger of the syringe. He said quietly, "This poor animal will now soon be dead as Moses." The class glanced at one another uneasily. "Some of you will think that it does not matter; some of you will think, like Bernard Shaw, that I am an executioner and the more monstrous because I am cool about it; and some of you will not think at all. This difference in philosophy iss what makes life interesting."

While the assistant tagged the pig with a tin disk in its ear and restored it to the battery jar, Gottlieb set down its weight in a notebook, with the time of inoculation and the age of the bacterial culture. These notes he reproduced on the blackboard, in his fastidious script, murmuring, "Gentlemen, the most important part of living is not the living but pondering upon it. And the most important part of experimentation is *quantitative* notes—in ink. I am told that a great many clever people feel they can keep notes in their heads. I have often observed with pleasure that such persons do not have heads in which to keep their notes. This iss very good, because thus the world never sees their results and science iss not encumbered with them. I shall now inoculate the second guinea pig, and the class will be dismissed. Before the next lab hour I shall be glad if you will read Pater's 'Marius the Epicurean,' to derive from it the calmness which is the secret of laboratory skill."

II

As they bustled down the hall, Angus Duer observed to a brother Digam, "Gottlieb is an old laboratory plug; he hasn't got any imagination; he sticks here instead of getting out into the world and enjoying the fight. But he certainly is handy. Awfully good technique. He might have been a first-rate surgeon, and made fifty thousand dollars a year, As it is, I don't suppose he gets a cent over four thousand!"

Ira Hinkley walked alone, worrying. He was an extraordinarily kindly man, this huge and bumbling parson. He reverently accepted everything, no matter how contradictory to everything else, that his medical instructors told him, but this killing of animals—he hated it. By a connection not evident to him he remembered that the Sunday before, in the slummy chapel where he preached during his medical course, he had exalted the sacrifice of the martyrs and they had sung of the blood of the lamb, the fountain filled with blood drawn from Emmanuel's veins, but this meditation he lost, and he lumbered toward Digamma Pi in a fog of pondering pity.

Clif Clawson, walking with Fatty Pfaff, shouted, "Gosh, ole pig certainly did jerk when Pa Gottlieb rammed that needle home!" and Fatty begged, "Don't! Please!"

But Martin Arrowsmith saw himself doing the same experiment, and as he remembered Gottlieb's unerring fingers, his hands curved in imitation.

III

The guinea pigs grew drowsier and drowsier. In two days they rolled over, kicked convulsively, and died. Full of dramatic expectation, the class reassembled for the necropsy. On the demonstrator's table was a wooden tray, scarred from the tacks which for years had pinned down the corpses. The guinea pigs were in a glass jar, rigid, their hair ruffled. The class tried to remember how nibbling and alive they had been. The assistant stretched out one of them with thumb-tacks.

Gottlieb swabbed its belly with a cotton wad soaked in lysol, slit it from belly to neck, and cauterized the heart with a red-hot spatula—the class quivered as they heard the searing of the flesh. Like a priest of diabolic mysteries, he drew out the blackened blood with a pipette. With the distended lungs, the spleen and kidneys and liver, the assistant made wavy smears on glass slides which were stained and given to the class for examination. The students who had learned to look through the microscope without having to close one eye were proud and professional, and all of them talked of the beauty of identifying the bacillus, as they twiddled the brass thumb-screws to the right focus and the cells rose from cloudiness to sharp distinctness on the slides before them. But they were uneasy, for Gottlieb remained with them that day, stalking behind them, saying nothing, watching them always, watching the disposal of the remains of the guinea pigs, and along the benches ran nervous rumors about a bygone student who had died from anthrax infection in the laboratory.

IV

There was for Martin in these days a quality of satisfying delight; the zest of a fast hockey game, the serenity of the prairie, the bewilderment of great music, and a feeling of creation. He woke early and thought contentedly of the day; he hurried to his work, devout, unseeing.

The confusion of the bacteriological laboratory was ecstasy to him—the students in shirt-sleeves, filtering nutrient gelatine, their fingers gummed from the crinkly gelatine leaves; or heating media in an autoclave like a silver howitzer. The roaring Bunsen flames beneath the hot-air ovens, the steam from the Arnold sterilizers rolling to the rafters, clouding the windows, were to Martin lovely with activity, and to him the most radiant things in the world were rows of test-tubes filled with watery serum and plugged with cotton singed to a coffee brown, a fine platinum loop leaning in a shiny test-glass, a fantastic hedge of tall glass tubes mysteriously connecting jars, or a bottle rich with gentian violet stain.

He had begun, perhaps in youthful imitation of Gottlieb, to work by himself in the laboratory at night. . . . The long room was dark, thick dark, but for the gas-mantle behind his microscope. The cone of light cast a gloss on the bright brass tube, a sheen on his black hair, as he bent over the eyepiece. He was studying trypanosomes from a rat—an eight-branched rosette stained with polychrome methylene blue; a cluster of organisms delicate as a narcissus, with their purple nuclei, their light blue cells, and the thin lines of the flagella. He was excited and a little proud; he had stained the germs perfectly, and it is not easy to stain a rosette without breaking the petal shape. In the darkness, a step, the weary step of Max Gottlieb, and a hand on Martin's shoulder. Silently Martin raised his head, pushed the microscope toward him. Bending down, a cigarette stub in his mouth—the smoke would have stung the eyes of any human being— Gottlieb peered at the preparation.

He adjusted the gas light a quarter inch, and mused, "Splendid! You have craftsmanship. Oh, there is an art in science—for a few. You Americans, so many of you—all full with ideas, but you are impatient with the beautiful dullness of long labors. I see already—and I watch you in the lab before—perhaps you may try the trypanosomes of sleeping sickness. They are very, very interesting, and very, very ticklish to handle. It is quite a nice disease. In some villages in Africa, fifty per cent of the people have it, and it is invariably fatal. Yes, I think you might work on the bugs."

Which, to Martin, was getting his brigade in battle.

"I shall have," said Gottlieb, "a little sandwich in my room at midnight. If you should happen to work so late, I should be very pleast if you would come to have a bite."

Diffidently, Martin crossed the hall to Gottlieb's immaculate laboratory at midnight. On the bench were coffee and sandwiches, curiously small and excellent sandwiches, foreign to Martin's lunchroom taste.

Gottlieb talked till Clif had faded from existence and Angus Duer seemed but an absurd climber. He summoned forth London laboratories, dinners on frosty evenings in Stockholm, walks on the Pincio with sunset behind the dome of San Pietro, extreme danger and overpowering disgust from excreta-smeared garments in an epidemic at Marseilles. His reserve slipped from him and he talked of himself and of his family as though Martin were a contemporary.

The cousin who was a colonel in Uruguay and the cousin, a rabbi, who was tortured in a pogrom in Moscow. His sick wife—it might be cancer. The three children—the youngest girl, Miriam, she was a good musician, but the boy, the fourteen-year-old, he was a worry; he was a saucy, he would not study. Himself, he had worked for years on the synthesis of antibodies; he was at present in a blind alley, and at Mohalis there was no one who was interested, no one to stir him, but he was having an agreeable time massacring the opposing theory, and that cheered him.

"No, I have done nothing except be unpleasant to people that claim too much, but I have dreams of real discoveries some day. And— No. Not five times in five years do I have students who understand craftsmanship and precision and maybe some big imagination in hypotheses. I t'ink perhaps you may have them. If I can help you— So!

"I do not t'ink you will be a good doctor. Good doctors are fine—often they are artists—but their trade, it is not for us lonely ones that work in labs. Once, I took an M.D. label. In Heidelberg that was—Herr Gott, back in 1875! I could not get much interested in bandaging legs and looking at tongues. I was a follower of Helmholtz—what a wild blithering young fellow! I tried to make researches into the physics of sound—I was bad, most unbelievable, but I learned that in this vale of tears there is nothing certain but the quantitative method. And I was a chemist—a fine stinkmaker was I. And so into biology and much trouble. It has been good. I have found one or two things. And if sometimes I feel an exile, cold—I had to get out of Germany one time for refusing to sing *Die Wacht am Rhein* and trying to kill a cavalry captain— he was a stout fellow—I had to choke him—you see I am boasting, but I was a lifely *Kerl* thirty years ago! Ah! So!

"There is but one trouble of a philosophical bacteriologist. Why should we destroy these amiable pathogenic germs? Are we too sure, when we regard these, oh, most unbeautiful young students attending Y. M. C. A.'s and singing dinkle-songs and wearing hats with initials burned into them—iss it worth while to protect them from the so elegantly functioning *Bacillus typhosus* with its lovely flagella? You know, once I asked Dean Silva would it not be better to let loose the pathogenic germs on the world, and so solve all economic questions. But he did not care for my met'od. Oh, well, he is older than I am; he also gives, I hear, some dinner parties with bishops and judges present, all in nice clothes. He would know more than a German Jew who loves Father Nietzsche and Father Schopenhauer (but, damn him, he was teleological-minded!) and Father Koch and Father Pasteur and Brother Jacques Loeb and Brother Arrhenius. *Ja!* I talk foolishness. Let us go look at your slides and so goodnight."

When he had left Gottlieb at his stupid brown little house, his face as reticent as though the midnight supper and all the rambling talk had never happened, Martin ran home, altogether drunk.

CHAPTER XIX

[DR. ALMUS PICKERBAUGH]

I

Midmost of the black-soiled Iowa plain, watered only by a shallow and insignificant creek, the city of Nautilus bakes and rattles and glistens. For hundreds of miles the tall corn springs in a jungle of undeviating rows, and the stranger who sweatily trudges the corn-walled roads is lost and nervous with the sense of merciless growth.

Nautilus is to Zenith what Zenith is to Chicago.

With seventy thousand people, it is a smaller Zenith but no less brisk. There is one large hotel to compare with the dozen in Zenith, but that one is as busy and standardized and frenziedly modern as its owner can make it. The only authentic difference between Nautilus and Zenith is that in both cases all the streets look alike but in Nautilus they do not look alike for so many miles.

The difficulty in defining its quality is that no one has determined whether it is a very large village or a very small city. There are houses with chauffeurs and Baccardi cocktails but on August evenings all save a few score burghers sit in their shirt-sleeves on front porches. Across from the ten-story office building, in which a little magazine of the New Prose is published by a young woman who for five months lived in the cafés of Montparnasse, is an old frame mansion comfortable with maples, and a line of Fords and lumber-wagons in which the overalled farmers have come to town.

Iowa has the richest land, the lowest illiteracy rate, the largest percentages of native-born whites and motor-car owners, and the most moral and forward-looking cities of all the States, and Nautilus is the most Iowan city in Iowa. One out of every three persons above the age of sixty has spent a winter in California, and among them are the champion horseshoe pitcher of Pasadena and the woman who presented the turkey which Miss Mary Pickford, the cinema princess, enjoyed at her Christmas dinner in 1912.

Nautilus is distinguished by large houses with large lawns and by an astounding quantity of garages and lofty church spires. The fat fields run up to the edge of the city, and the scattered factories, the innumerable railroad side-tracks, and the scraggly cottages for workmen are almost amid the corn. Nautilus manufactures steel windmills, agricultural implements, including the celebrated Daisy Manure Spreader, and such corn-products as Maize Mealies, the renowned breakfast-food. It makes brick, it sells groceries wholesale, and it is the headquarters of the Cornbelt Coöperative Insurance Company.

One of its smallest but oldest industries is Mugford Christian College, which has two hundred and seventeen students, and sixteen instructors, of whom eleven are ministers of the Church of Christ. The well-known Dr. Tom Bissex is football coach, health director, and professor of hygiene, chemistry, physics, French, and German. Its shorthand and piano departments are known far beyond the limits of Nautilus, and once, though that was some years ago, Mugford held the Grinnell College baseball team down to a score of eleven to five. It has never been disgraced by squabbles over teaching evolutionary biology—it never has thought of teaching biology at all.

II

Martin left Leora at the Sims House, the old-fashioned second-best hotel in Nautilus, to report to Dr. Pickerbaugh, Director of the Department of Public Health.

The department was on an alley, in a semi-basement at the back of that large graystone fungus, the City Hall. When he entered the drab reception-office he was highly received by the stenographer and the two visiting nurses. Into the midst of their flutterings—"Did you have a good trip, Doctor? Dr. Pickerbaugh didn't hardly expect you till to-morrow, Doctor. Is Mrs. Arrowsmith with you, Doctor?"—charged Pickerbaugh, thundering welcomes.

Dr. Almus Pickerbaugh was forty-eight. He was a graduate of Mugford College and of the Wassau Medical School. He looked somewhat like President Roosevelt, with the same squareness and the same bristly mustache, and he cultivated the resemblance. He was a man who never merely talked; he either bubbled or made orations.

He received Martin with four "Well's," which he gave after the manner of a college cheer; he showed him through the Department, led him into the Director's private office, gave him a cigar, and burst the dam of manly silence:

"Doctor, I'm delighted to have a man with your scientific inclinations. Not that I should consider myself entirely without them. In fact I make it a regular practise to set aside a period for scientific research, without a certain amount of which even the most ardent crusade for health methods would scarcely make much headway."

It sounded like the beginning of a long seminar. Martin settled in his chair. He was doubtful about his cigar, but he found that it helped him to look more interested.

"But with me, I admit, it's a matter of temperament. I have often hoped that, without any desire whatever for mere personal aggrandizement, the powers above may yet grant me the genius to become at once the Roosevelt and the Longfellow of the great and universally growing movement for public health measures is your cigar too mild, Doctor? or perhaps it would be better to say the Kipling of public health rather than the Longfellow, because despite the beautiful passages and high moral atmosphere of the Sage of Cambridge, his poetry lacked the swing and punch of Kipling.

"I assume you agree with me, or you will when you have had an opportunity to see the effect our work has on the city, and the success we have in selling the idea of Better Health, that what the world needs is a really inspired, courageous, overtowering leader—say a Billy Sunday of the movement—a man who would know how to use sensationalism properly and wake the people out of their sloth. Sometimes the papers, and I can only say they flatter me when they compare me with Billy Sunday, the greatest of all evangelists and Christian preachers—sometimes they claim that I'm too sensational. Huh! If they only could understand it, trouble is I can't be sensational enough! Still, I try, I try, and— Look here. Here's a placard, it was painted by my daughter Orchid and the poetry is my own humble effort, and let me tell you it gets quoted around everywhere:

> You can't get health
> By a pussyfoot stealth,
> So let's every health-booster
> Crow just like a rooster

"Then there's another—this is a minor thing; it doesn't try to drive home general abstract principles, but it'd surprise you the effect it's had on careless housewives, who of course don't mean to neglect the health of their little ones and merely need instruction and a little pep put into them, and when they see a card like this, it makes 'em think:

Boil the milk bottles or by gum
You better buy your ticket to Kingdom
    Come.

"I've gotten quite a lot of appreciation in my small way for some of these things that didn't hardly take me five minutes to dash off. Some day when you get time, glance over this volume of clippings—just to show you, Doctor, what you can do if you go at the Movement in the up-to-date and scientific manner. This one, about the temperance meeting I addressed in Des Moines—say, I had that hall, and it was jam-pack-full, lifting right up on their feet when I proved by statistics that ninety-three per cent. of all insanity is caused by booze! Then this—well, it hasn't anything to do with health, directly, but it'll just in-dicate the opportunity you'll have here to get in touch with all the movements for civic weal."

He held out a newspaper clipping in which, above a pen-and-ink caricature portraying him with large mustached head on a tiny body, was the headline:

DOC PICKERBAUGH BANNER BOOSTER
OF EVANGELINE COUNTY LEADS
BIG GO-TO-CHURCH
DEMONSTRATION HERE

Pickerbaugh looked it over, reflecting, "That was a dandy meeting! We increased church attendance here seventeen per cent.! Oh, Doctor, you went to Winnemac and had your internship in Zenith, didn't you? Well, this might interest you then. It's from the *Zenith Advocate-Times*, and it's by Chum Frink, who, I think you'll agree with me, ranks with Eddie Guest and Walt Mason as the greatest, as they certainly are the most popular, of all our poets, showing that you can bank every time on the literary taste of the American Public. Dear old Chum! That was when I was in Zenith to address the national convention of Congregational Sunday-schools, I happen to be a Congregationalist myself, on 'The Morality of A 1 Health.' So Chum wrote this poem about me:"

Zenith welcomes with high hurraw
A friend in Almus Pickerbaugh,
The two-fisted fightin' poet doc
Who stands for health like Gibraltar's
    rock,
He's jammed with figgers and facts and
    fun,
The plucky old, lucky old son—of—a—
    gun!

For a moment the exuberant Dr. Pickerbaugh was shy.

"Maybe it's kind of immodest in me to show that around. And when I read a poem with such originality and swing, when I find a genu-ine vest-pocket masterpiece like this, then I realize that I'm not a poet at all, no matter how much my jingles may serve to jazz up the Cause of Health. My brain-children may teach sanitation and do their little part to save thousands of dear lives, but they aren't literature, like what Chum Frink turns out. No, I guess I'm nothing but just a plain scientist in an office.

"Still, you'll readily see how one of these efforts of mine, just by having a good laugh and a punch and some melody in it, does gild the pill and make careless folks stop spitting on the sidewalks, and get out into God's great outdoors and get their lungs packed full of ozone and lead a real hairy-chested he-life. In fact you might care to look over the first number of a little semi-yearly magazine I'm just starting—I know for a fact that a number of newspaper editors are going to quote from it and so carry on the good work as well as boost my circulation."

He handed to Martin a pamphlet entitled *Pickerbaugh Pickings*.

In verse and aphorism, *Pickings* recommended good health, good roads, good business, and the single standard of morality. Dr. Pickerbaugh backed up his injunctions with statistics as impressive as those the Reverend Ira Hinkley had once used at Digamma Pi. Martin was edified by an item which showed that among all families divorced in Ontario, Tennessee, and Southern Wyoming in 1912, the appalling number of fifty-three per cent. of the husbands drank at least one glass of whisky daily.

Before this warning had sunk in, Pickerbaugh snatched *Pickings* from him with a boyish, "Oh, you won't want to read any more of my rot. You can look it over some future time. But this second volume of my clippings may perhaps interest you, just as a hint of what a fellow can do."

While he considered the headlines in the scrapbook, Martin realized that Dr. Pickerbaugh was vastly better known than he had realized. He was exposed as the founder of the first Rotary Club in Iowa; superintendent of the Jonathan Edwards Congregational Sunday School of Nautilus; president of the Moccasin Ski and Hiking Club, of the West Side Bowling Club, and the 1912 Bull Moose and Roosevelt Club; organizer and cheer-leader of a Joint Picnic of the Woodmen, Moose, Elks, Masons, Oddfellows, Turnverein, Knights of Columbus, B'nai B'rith, and the Y. M. C. A.; and winner of the prizes both for reciting the largest number of Biblical texts and for dancing the best Irish jig at the Harvest Moon Soiree of the Jonathan Edwards Bible Class for the Grownups.

Martin read of him as addressing the Century Club of Nautilus on "A Yankee Doctor's Trip Through Old Europe," and the Mugford College Alumni Association on "Wanted: A Man-sized Feetball Coach for Old Mugford." But outside of Nautilus as well, there were loud alarums of his presence.

He had spoken at the Toledo Chamber of Commerce Weekly Luncheon on "More Health—More Bank Clearings." He had edified the National Interurban Trolley Council, meeting at Wichita, on "Health Maxims for Trolley Folks." Seven thousand, six hundred Detroit automobile mechanics had listened to his observations on "Health First, Safety Second, and Booze Nowhere A-tall." And in a great convention at Waterloo he had helped organize the first regiment in Iowa of the Anti-rum Minute Men.

The articles and editorials regarding him, in newspapers, house organs, and one rubber-goods periodical, were accompanied by photographs of himself, his buxom wife, and his eight bounding daughters, depicted in Canadian winter costumes among snow and icicles, in modest but easy athletic costumes, playing tennis in the backyard, and in costumes of no known genus whatever, frying bacon against a background of Northern Minnesota pines.

Martin felt strongly that he would like to get away and recover.

He walked back to the Sims House. He realized that to a civilized man the fact that Pickerbaugh advocated any reform would be sufficient reason for ignoring it.

When he had gone thus far, Martin pulled himself up, cursed himself for what he esteemed his old sin of superiority to decent normal people. . . . Failure. Disloyalty. In medical school, in private practise, in his bullying health administration. Now again?

He urged, "This pep and heartiness stuff of Pickerbaugh's is exactly the thing to get across to the majority of people the scientific discoveries of the Max Gottliebs. What do I care how much Pickerbaugh gases before conventions of Sunday-school superintendents and other morons, as long as he lets me alone and lets me do my work in the lab and dairy inspection?"

He pumped up enthusiasm and came quite cheerfully and confidently into the shabby, high-ceilinged hotel bedroom where Leora sat in a rocker by the window.

"Well?" she said.

"It's fine—gave me fine welcome. And they want us to come to dinner, to-morrow evening."

"What's he like?"

"Oh, he's awfully optimistic—he puts things over—he— Oh, Leora, am I going to be a sour, cranky, unpopular, rotten failure again?"

His head was buried in her lap and he clung to her affection, the one reality in a world of chattering ghosts.

III

When the maples fluttered beneath their window in the breeze that sprang up with the beginning of twilight, when the amiable citizens of Nautilus had driven home to supper in their shaky Fords, Leora had persuaded him that Pickerbaugh's flamboyance would not interfere with his own work, that in any case they would not remain in Nautilus forever, that he was impatient, and that she loved him dearly. So they descended to supper, an old-fashioned Iowa supper with corn fritters and many little dishes which were of interest after the loving but misinformed cooking of Leora, and they went to the movies and held hands and were not ill content.

The next day Dr. Pickerbaugh was busier and less buoyant. He gave Martin a notion of the details of his work.

Martin had thought of himself, freed from tinkering over cut fingers and ear-aches, as spending ecstatic days in the laboratory, emerging only to battle with factory-owners who defied sanitation. But he found that it was impossible to define his work, except that he was to do a little of everything that Pickerbaugh, the press, or any stray citizen of Nautilus might think of.

He was to placate voluble voters who came in to complain of everything from the smell of sewer-gas to the midnight beer parties of neighbors; he was to dictate office correspondence to the touchy stenographer, who was not a Working Girl but a Nice Girl Who Was Working; to give publicity to the newspapers; to buy paper-clips and floor-wax and report-blanks at the lowest prices; to assist, in need, the two part-time physicians in the city clinic; to direct the nurses and the two sanitary inspectors; to scold the Garbage Removal Company; to arrest —or at least to jaw at—all public spitters; to leap into a Ford and rush out to tack placards on houses in which were infectious diseases; to keep a learned implacable eye on epidemics from Vladivostok to Patagonia, and to prevent (by methods not very clearly outlined) their coming in to slay the yeomanry and even halt the business activities of Nautilus.

But there was a little laboratory work: milk tests, Wassermanns for private physicians, the making of vaccines, cultures in suspected diphtheria.

"I get it," said Leora, as they dressed for the dinner at Pickerbaugh's. "Your job will only take about twenty-eight hours a day, and the rest of the time you're perfectly welcome to spend in research, unless somebody interrupts you."

IV

The home of Dr. and Mrs. Almus Pickerbaugh, on the steeple-prickly West Side, was a Real Old-fashioned Home. It was a wooden house with towers, swings, hammocks, rather mussy shade trees, a rather mangy lawn, a rather damp arbor, and an old carriage-house with a line of steel spikes along the ridge-pole. Over the front gate was the name: UNEEDA-REST.

Martin and Leora came into a shambles of salutations and daughters. The eight girls, from pretty Orchid aged nineteen to the five-year-old twins, surged up in a tidal wave of friendly curiosity and tried to talk all at once.

Their hostess was a plump woman with an air of worried trustfulness. Her conviction that everything was all right was constantly struggling with her knowledge that a great many things seemed to be all wrong. She kissed Leora while Pickerbaugh was pump-handling Martin. Pickerbaugh had a way of pressing his thumb into the back of your hand which was extraordinarily cordial and painful.

He immediately drowned out even his daughters by an oration on the Home Nest:

"Here you've got an illustration of Health in the Home. Look at these great strapping girls, Arrowsmith! Never been sick a day in their lives— practically—and though Mother does have her sick-headaches, that's to be attributed to the early neglect of her diet, because while her father, the old deacon—and a fine upstanding gentleman of the old school he was, too, if there ever was one, and a friend of Nathaniel Mugford, to whom more than any other we owe not only the foundation of Mugford College but also the tradition of integrity and industry which have produced our present prosperity—BUT he had no knowledge of diet or sanitation, and I've always thought—"

The daughters were introduced as Orchid, Verbena, Daisy, Jonquil, Hibisca, Narcissa, and the twins, Arbuta and Gladiola.

Mrs. Pickerbaugh sighed:

"I suppose it would be dreadfully conventional to call them My Jewels —I do so hate these conventional phrases that everybody uses, don't you?—but that's what they really are to their mother, and the Doctor and I have sometimes wished— Of course when we'd started giving them floral names we had to keep it up, but if we'd started with jewels, just think of all the darling names we might have used, like Agate and Cameo and Sardonyx and Beryl and Topaz and Opal and Esmeralda and Chrysoprase—it *is* Chrysoprase, isn't it, not Chrysalis? Oh, well, many people have congratulated us on their names as it is. You know the girls are getting quite famous—their pictures in so many papers, and we have a Pickerbaugh Ladies' Baseball Team all our own— only the Doctor has to play on it now, because I'm beginning to get a little stout."

Except by their ages, it was impossible to tell the daughters apart. They were all bouncing, all blond, all pretty, all eager, all musical, and not merely pure but clamorously clean-minded. They all belonged to the Congregational Sunday School, and to either the Y. W. C. A. or the Camp Fire Girls; they were all fond of picnicking; and they could all of them, except the five-year-old twins, quote practically without error the newest statistics showing the evils of alcohol.

"In fact," said Dr. Pickerbaugh, "*we* think they're a very striking brood of chickabiddies."

"They certainly are!" quivered Martin.

"But best of all, they are able to help me put over the doctrine of the *Mens Sana* in the *Corpus Sano*. Mrs. Pickerbaugh and I have trained them to sing together, both in the home and publicly, and as an organization we call them the Healthette Octette."

"Really?" said Leora, when it was apparent that Martin had passed beyond speech.

"Yes, and before I get through with it I hope to popularize the name Healthette from end to end of this old nation, and you're going to see bands of happy young women going around spreading their winged message into every dark corner. Healthette Bands! Beautiful and pureminded and enthusiastic and good

basket-ball players! I tell you, *they'll* make the lazy and wilful stir their stumps! They'll shame the filthy livers and the filthy talkers into decency! I've already worked out a poem-slogan for the Healthette Bands. Would you like to hear it?

Winsome young womanhood wins with
  a smile
Boozers, spitters, and gamblers from
  things that are vile.
Our parents and teachers have explained
  the cause of life,
So against the evil-minded we'll also
  make strife.
We'll shame them, reclaim them, from
  bad habits, you bet!
Better watch out, Mr. Loafer, I am a
  Healthette!

"But of course an even more important Cause is—and I was one of the first to advocate it—having a Secretary of Health and Eugenics in the cabinet at Washington—"

On the tide of this dissertation they were swept through a stupendous dinner. With a hearty "Nonsense, nonsense, man, of course you want a second helping—this is Hospitality Hall!" Pickerbaugh so stuffed Martin and Leora with roast duck, candied sweet potatoes, and mince pie that they became dangerously ill and sat glassy-eyed. But Pickerbaugh himself did not seem to be affected. While he carved and gobbled, he went on discoursing till the dining-room, with its old walnut buffet, its Hoffmann pictures of Christ, and its Remington pictures of cowpunchers, seemed to vanish, leaving him on a platform beside a pitcher of ice-water.

Not always was he merely fantastic. "Dr. Arrowsmith, I tell you we're lucky men to be able to get a living out of doing our honest best to make the people in a he-town like this well and vital. I could be pulling down eight or ten thousand a year in private practise, and I've been told I could make more than that in the art of advertising, yet I'm glad, and my dear ones are glad with me, to take a salary of four thousand. Think of our having a job where we've got nothing to sell but honesty and decency and the brotherhood o' man!"

Martin perceived that Pickerbaugh meant it, and the shame of the realization kept him from leaping up, seizing Leora, and catching the first freight train out of Nautilus.

After dinner the younger daughters desired to love Leora, in swarms. Martin had to take the twins on his knees and tell them a story. They were remarkably heavy twins, but no heavier than the labor of inventing a plot. Before they went to bed, the entire Healthette Octette sang the famous Health Hymn (written by Dr. Almus Pickerbaugh) which Martin was to hear on so many bright and active public occasions in Nautilus. It was set to the tune of "The Battle Hymn of the Republic," but as the twins' voices were energetic and extraordinarily shrill, it had an effect all its own:

Oh, are you out for happiness or are you out for pelf?
You owe it to the grand old flag to cultivate yourself,
To train the mind, keep clean the streets, and ever guard your health,
Then we'll all go marching on.

A healthy mind in A clean body,
A healthy mind in A clean body,
A healthy mind in A clean body,
The slogan for one and all.

As a bedtime farewell, the twins then recited, as they had recently recited at the Congregational Festival, one of their father's minor lyrics:

What does little birdie say
On the sill at break o' day?
"Hurrah for health in Nautilus

For Pa and Ma and all of us,
Hurray, hurray, hurray!"

"There, my popsywopsies, up to bed we go!" said Mrs. Pickerbaugh. "Don't you think, Mrs. Arrowsmith, they're natural-born actresses? They're not afraid of any audience, and the way they throw themselves into it—perhaps not Broadway, but the more refined theaters in New York would just love them, and maybe they've been sent to us to elevate the drama. Upsy go."

During her absence the others gave a brief musical program.

Verbena, the second oldest, played Chaminade. ("Of course we all love music, and popularize it among the neighbors, but Verby is perhaps the only real musical genius in the family.") But the unexpected feature was Orchid's cornet solo.

Martin dared not look at Leora. It was not that he was sniffily superior to cornet solos, for in Elk Mills, Wheatsylvania, and surprisingly large portions of Zenith, cornet solos were done by the most virtuous females. But he felt that he had been in a madhouse for dozens of years.

"I've never been so drunk in my life. I wish I could get at a drink and sober up," he agonized. He made hysterical and completely impractical plans for escape. Then Mrs. Pickerbaugh, returning from the still audible twins, sat down at the harp.

While she played, a faded woman and thickish, she fell into a great dreaming, and suddenly Martin had a picture of her as a gay, good, dove-like maiden who had admired the energetic young medical student, Almus Pickerbaugh. She must have been a veritable girl of the late eighties and the early nineties, the naïve and idyllic age of Howells, when young men were pure, when they played croquet and sang Swanee River; a girl who sat on a front porch enchanted by the sweetness of lilacs, and hoped that when Almus and she were married they would have a nickel-plated baseburner stove and a son who would become a missionary or a millionaire.

For the first time that evening, Martin managed to put a respectable heartiness into his "Enjoyed that s' much." He felt victorious, and somewhat recovered from his weakness.

But the evening's orgy was only begun.

They played word-games, which Martin hated and Leora did very badly indeed. They acted charades, at which Pickerbaugh was tremendous. The sight of him on the floor in his wife's fur coat, being a seal on an icefloe, was incomparable. Then Martin, Orchid, and Hibisca (aged twelve) had to present a charade, and there were complications.

Orchid was as full of simple affections, of smilings and pattings and bouncings, as her younger sisters, but she was nineteen and not altogether a child. Doubtless she was as pureminded and as devoted to Clean and Wholesome Novels as Dr. Pickerbaugh stated, and he stated it with frequency, but she was not unconscious of young men, even though they were married.

She planned to enact the word *doleful,* with a beggar asking a dole, and a corncrib full. As they skipped upstairs to dress, she hugged Martin's arm, frisked beside him, and murmured, "Oh, Doctor, I'm so glad Daddy has you for assistant—somebody that's young and good-looking. Oh, was that dreadful of me? But I mean: you look so athletic and everything, and the other assistant director —don't tell Daddy I said so, but he was an old crank!"

He was conscious of brown eyes and unshadowed virginal lips. As Orchid put on her agreeably loose costume as a beggar, he was also conscious of ankles and young bosom. She smiled at him, as one who had long known him, and said loyally, "We'll show 'em! I know you're a dan-dy actor!"

When they bustled downstairs, as she did not take his arm, he took hers, and he pressed it slightly and felt alarmed and relinquished it with emphasis.

Since his marriage he had been so absorbed in Leora, as lover, as companion, as helper, that till this hour his most devastating adventure had been a glance at a pretty girl in a train. But the flushed young gaiety of Orchid disturbed him. He wanted to be rid of her, he hoped that he would not be altogether rid of her, and for the first time in years he was afraid of Leora's eyes.

There were acrobatic feats later, and a considerable prominence of Orchid, who did not wear stays, who loved dancing, and who praised Martin's feats in the game of "Follow the Leader."

All the daughters save Orchid were sent to bed, and the rest of the fête consisted of what Pickerbaugh called "a little quiet scientific conversation by the fireside," made up of his observations on good roads, rural sanitation, Ideals in politics, and methods of letter filing in health departments. Through this placid hour, or it may have been an hour and a half, Martin saw that Orchid was observing his hair, his jaw, his hands, and he had, and dismissed, and had again a thought about the innocent agreeableness of holding her small friendly paw.

He also saw that Leora was observing both of them, and he suffered a good deal, and had practically no benefit whatever from Pickerbaugh's notes on the value of disinfectants. When Pickerbaugh predicted for Nautilus, in fifteen years, a health department thrice as large, with many full-time clinic and school physicians and possibly Martin as director (Pickerbaugh himself having gone off to mysterious and interesting activities in a Larger Field), Martin merely croaked, "Yes, that'd be—be fine," while to himself he was explaining, "Damn that girl, I wish she wouldn't shake herself at me."

At half-past eight he had pictured his escape as life's highest ecstasy; at twelve he took leave with nervous hesitation.

They walked to the hotel. Free from the sight of Orchid, brisk in the coolness, he forgot the chit and pawed again the problem of his work in Nautilus.

"Lord, I don't know whether I can do it. To work under that gas-bag, with his fool pieces about boozers—"

"They weren't so bad," protested Leora.

"Bad? Why, he's probably the worst poet that ever lived, and he certainly knows less about epidemiology than I thought any one man could ever learn, all by himself. But when it comes to this—what was it Clif Clawson used to call it?—by the way, wonder what's ever become of Clif; haven't heard from him for a couple o' years—when it comes to this 'overpowering Christian Domesticity'— Oh, let's hunt for a blind-pig and sit around with the nice restful burglars."

She insisted, "I thought his poems were kind of cute."

"Cute! What a word!"

"It's no worse than the cuss-words you're always using! But the cornet yowling by that awful oldest daughter— Ugh!"

"Well, now she played darn' well!"

"Martin, the cornet is the kind of an instrument my brother would play. And you so superior about the doctor's poetry and my saying 'cute'! You're just as much a backwoods hick as I am, and maybe more so!"

"Why, gee, Leora, I never knew you to get sore about nothing before! And can't you understand how important— You see, a man like Pickerbaugh makes all public health work simply ridiculous by his circusing and his ignorance. If he said that fresh air was a good thing, instead of making me open my windows it'd make me or any other reasonable person close 'em. And to use the word 'science' in those flop-eared limericks or whatever you call 'em—it's sacrilege!"

"Well, if you want to *know*, Martin Arrowsmith, I'll have no more of these high jinks with that Orchid girl! Practically hugging her when you came downstairs, and then mooning at her all evening! I don't mind your cursing and being cranky and even getting drunk, in a reasonable sort of way, but ever since the lunch when you told me and that Fox woman, 'I hope you girls won't mind, but I just happen to remember that I'm engaged to both of you'— You're mine, and I won't have any trespassers. I'm a cavewoman, and you'd better learn it, and as for that Orchid, with her simper and her stroking your arm and her great big absurd feet— Orchid! She's no orchid! She's a bachelor's button!"

"But, honest, I don't even remember which of the eight she was."

"Huh!! Then you've been making love to all of 'em, that's why. Drat her! Well, I'm not going to go on scrapping about it. I just wanted to warn you, that's all."

At the hotel, after giving up the

attempt to find a short, jovial, convincing way of promising that he would never flirt with Orchid, he stammered, "If you don't mind, I think I'll stay down and walk a little more. I've got to figure this health department business out."

He sat in the Sims House office—singularly dismal it was, after midnight, and singularly smelly.

"That fool Pickerbaugh! I wish I'd told him right out that we know hardly anything about the epidemiology of tuberculosis, for instance.

"Just the same, she's a darling child. Orchid! She's like an orchid—no, she's too healthy. Be a great kid to go hunting with. Sweet. And she acted as if I were her own age, not an old doctor. I'll be good, oh, I'll be good, but— I'd like to kiss her once, *good!* She likes me. Those darling lips, like—like rosebuds!

"Poor Leora. I nev' was so astonished in my life. Jealous. Well, she's got a right to be! No woman ever stood by a man like— Lee, sweet, can't you see, idiot, if I skipped round the corner with seventeen billion Orchids, it'd be you I loved, and never anybody but you!

"I can't go round singing Healthette Octette Pantalette stuff. Even if it did instruct people, which it don't. Be almost better to let 'em die than have to live and listen to—

"Leora said I was a 'backwoods hick.' Let me tell you, young woman, as it happens I am a Bachelor of Arts, and you may recall the kind of books the 'backwoods hick' was reading to you last winter, and even Henry James and everybody and— Oh, she's right. I am. I do know how to make pipets and agar, but— And yet some day I want to travel like Sondelius—

"Sondelius! God! If it were he I was

working for, instead of Pickerbaugh, I'd slave for him—

"Or does he pull the bunk, too?

"Now that's just what I mean. That kind of phrase. 'Pull the bunk'! Horrible!

"Hell! I'll use any kind of phrase I want to! I'm not one of your social climbers like Angus. The way Sondelius cusses, for instance, and yet he's used to all those highbrows—

"And I'll be so busy here in Nautilus that I won't even be able to go on reading. Still— I don't suppose they read much, but there must be quite a few of these rich men here that know about nice houses. Clothes. Theatres. That stuff.

"Rats!"

He wandered to an all-night lunchwagon, where he gloomily drank coffee. Beside him, seated at the long shelf which served as table, beneath the noble red-glass window with a portrait of George Washington, was a policeman who, as he gnawed a Hamburger sandwich, demanded:

"Say, ain't you this new doctor that's come to assist Pickerbaugh? Seen you at City Hall."

"Yes. Say, uh, say how does the city like Pickerbaugh? How do you like him? Tell me honestly, because I'm just starting in, and, uh— You get me."

With his spoon held inside the cup by a brawny thumb, the policeman gulped his coffee and proclaimed, while the greasy friendly cook of the lunch-wagon nodded in agreement:

"Well, if you want the straight dope, he hollers a good deal, but he's one awful brainy man. He certainly can sling the Queen's English, and jever hear one of his poems? They're darn' bright. I'll tell you: There's some people say Pickerbaugh pulls the song and dance too much, but way I figure it, course maybe for you and me, Doctor, it'd be all right if he just looked after the milk and the garbage and the kids' teeth. But there's a lot of careless, ignorant, foreign slobs that need to be jollied into using their konks about these health biznai, so's they won't go getting sick with a lot of these infectious diseases and pass 'em on to the rest of us, and believe me, old Doc Pickerbaugh is the boy that gets the idea into their noodles!

"Yes, sir, he's a great old coot—he ain't a clam like some of these docs. Why, say, one day he showed up at the St. Patrick picnic, even if he is a dirty Protestant, and him and Father Costello chummed up like two old cronies, and darn' if he didn't wrestle a fellow half his age, and awful' near throw him, yes, you bet he did, he certainly give that young fellow a run for his money all right! We fellows on the Force all like him, and we have to grin, the way he comes around and soft-soaps us into doing a lot of health work that by law we ain't hardly supposed to do, you might say, instead of issuing a lot of fool orders. You bet. He's a real guy."

"I see," said Martin, and as he returned to the hotel he meditated:

"But think of what Gottlieb would say about him.

"Damn Gottlieb! Damn everybody except Leora!

"I'm not going to fail here, way I did in Wheatsylvania.

"Some day Pickerbaugh will get a bigger job— Huh! He's just the kind of jollying fourflusher that *would* climb! But anyway, I'll have my training then, and maybe I'll make a real health department here.

"Orchid said we'd go skating this winter—

"*Damn* Orchid!"

1925

JOHN DOS PASSOS
(1896–   )

FROM
MANHATTAN TRANSFER *

[TWO FATHERS]

When Ed Thatcher climbed the marble steps of the wide hospital entry he was trembling. The smell of drugs caught at his throat. A woman with a starched face was looking at him over the top of a desk. He tried to steady his voice.

"Can you tell me how Mrs. Thatcher is?"

"Yes, you can go up."

"But please, miss, is everything all right?"

"The nurse on the floor will know anything about the case. Stairs to the left, third floor, maternity ward."

Ed Thatcher held a bunch of flowers wrapped in green waxed paper. The broad stairs swayed as he stumbled up, his toes kicking against the brass rods that held the fiber matting down. The closing of a door cut off a strangled shriek. He stopped a nurse.

"I want to see Mrs. Thatcher, please."

"Go right ahead if you know where she is."

"But they've moved her."

"You'll have to ask at the desk at the end of the hall."

He gnawed his cold lips. At the end of the hall a redfaced woman looked at him, smiling.

"Everything's fine. You're the happy father of a bouncing baby girl."

"You see it's our first and Susie's so delicate," he stammered with blinking eyes.

"Oh yes, I understand, naturally you worried. . . . You can go in and talk to her when she wakes up. The baby was born two hours ago. Be sure not to tire her."

Ed Thatcher was a little man with two blond wisps of mustache and washedout gray eyes. He seized the nurse's hand and shook it showing all his uneven yellow teeth in a smile.

"You see it's our first."

"Congratulations," said the nurse.

Rows of beds under bilious gaslight, a sick smell of restlessly stirring bedclothes, faces fat, lean, yellow, white; that's her. Susie's yellow hair lay in a loose coil round her little white face that looked shriveled and twisted. He unwrapped the roses and put them on the night table. Looking out the window was like looking down into water. The trees in the square were tangled in blue cobwebs. Down the avenue lamps were coming on marking off with green shimmer brick-purple blocks of houses; chimney pots and water tanks cut sharp into a sky flushed like flesh. The blue lids slipped back off her eyes.

"That you Ed? . . . Why Ed they are Jacks. How extravagant of you."

"I couldn't help it dearest. I knew you liked them."

A nurse was hovering near the end of the bed.

"Couldn't you let us see the baby, miss?"

The nurse nodded. She was a lanternjawed grayfaced woman with tight lips.

"I hate her," whispered Susie. "She gives me the fidgets that woman does; she's nothing but a mean old maid."

"Never mind dear, it's just for a day or two." Susie closed her eyes.

"Do you still want to call her Ellen?"

The nurse brought back a basket and set it on the bed beside Susie.

"Oh isn't she wonderful!" said Ed.

"Look she's breathing. . . . And they've oiled her." He helped his wife to raise herself on her elbow; the yellow coil of her hair unrolled, fell over his hand and arm. "How can you tell them apart nurse?"

"Sometimes we can't," said the nurse, stretching her mouth in a smile. Susie was looking querulously into the minute purple face. "You're sure this is mine."

"Of course."

"But it hasn't any label on it."

"I'll label it right away."

"But mine was dark." Susie lay back on the pillow, gasping for breath.

"She has lovely little light fuzz just the color of your hair."

Susie stretched her arms out above her head and shrieked: "It's not mine. It's not mine. Take it away. . . . That woman's stolen my baby."

"Dear, for Heaven's sake! Dear, for Heaven's sake!" He tried to tuck the covers about her.

"Too bad," said the nurse, calmly, picking up the basket. "I'll have to give her a sedative."

Susie sat up stiff in bed. "Take it away," she yelled and fell back in hysterics, letting out continuous frail moaning shrieks.

"O my God!" cried Ed Thatcher, clasping his hands.

"You'd better go away for this evening, Mr. Thatcher. . . . She'll quiet down, once you've gone. . . . I'll put the roses in water."

On the last flight he caught up with a chubby man who was strolling down slowly, rubbing his hands as he went. Their eyes met.

"Everything all right, sir?" asked the chubby man.

"Oh, yes, I guess so," said Thatcher faintly.

The chubby man turned on him, delight bubbling through his thick voice. "Congradulade me, congradulade me; mein vife has giben birth to a poy."

Thatcher shook a fat little hand. "Mine's a girl," he admitted, sheepishly.

"It is fif years yet and every year a girl, and now dink of it, a poy."

"Yes," said Ed Thatcher as they stepped out on the pavement, "it's a great moment."

"Vill yous allow me sir to invite you to drink a congradulation drink mit me?"

"Why with pleasure."

The latticed halfdoors were swinging in the saloon at the corner of Third Avenue. Shuffling their feet politely they went through into the back room.

"Ach," said the German as they sat down at a scarred brown table, "family life is full of vorries."

"That it is sir; this is my first."

"Vill you haf beer?"

"All right anything suits me."

"Two pottles Culmbacher imported to drink to our little folk." The bottles popped and the sepia-tinged foam rose in the glasses. "Here's success. . . . Prosit," said the German, and raised his glass. He rubbed the foam out of his mustache and pounded on the table with a pink fist. "Vould it be indiscreet meester . . . ?"

"Thatcher's my name."

"Vould it be indiscreet, Mr. Thatcher, to inquire vat might your profession be?"

"Accountant. I hope before long to be a certified accountant."

"I am a printer and my name is Zucher—Marcus Antonius Zucher."

"Pleased to meet you Mr. Zucher."

They shook hands across the table between the bottles.

"A certified accountant makes big money," said Mr. Zucher.

"Big money's what I'll have to have, for my little girl."

"Kids, they eat money," continued Mr. Zucher, in a deep voice.

"Won't you let me set you up to a bottle?" said Thatcher, figuring up how much he had in his pocket. Poor Susie wouldn't like me to be drinking in a saloon like this. But just this once, and I'm learning, learning about fatherhood.

"The more the merrier," said Mr. Zucher. ". . . But kids, they eat money. . . . Don't do nutten but eat and vear out clothes. Vonce I get my business on its feet. . . . Ach! Now vot mit hypothecations and the difficult borrowing of money and vot mit vages going up und these here crazy tradeunion socialists and bomsters . . ."

"Well here's how, Mr. Zucher." Mr. Zucher squeezed the foam out of his mustache with the thumb and forefinger of each hand. "It ain't every day ve pring into the voirld a papy poy, Mr. Thatcher."

"Or a baby girl, Mr. Zucher."

The barkeep wiped the spillings off the table when he brought the new bottles, and stood near listening, the rag dangling from his red hands.

"And I have the hope in mein heart that ven my boy drinks to his poy, it vill be in champagne vine. Ach, that is how things go in this great city."

"I'd like my girl to be a quiet homey girl, not like these young women nowadays, all frills and furbelows and tight lacings. And I'll have retired by that time and have a little place up the Hudson, work in the garden evenings. . . . I know fellers downtown who have retired with three thousand a year. It's saving that does it."

"Ain't no good in savin," said the barkeep. "I saved for ten years and the savings bank went broke and left me nutten but a bankbook for my trouble. Get a close tip and take a chance, that's the only system."

"That's nothing but gambling," snapped Thatcher.

"Well sir it's a gamblin game," said the barkeep as he walked back to the bar swinging the two empty bottles.

"A gamblin game. He ain't so far out," said Mr. Zucher, looking down into his beer with a glassy meditative eye. "A man vat is ambeetious must take chances. Ambeetions is vat I came here from Frankfort mit at the age of tvelf years, and now that I haf a son to vork for . . . Ach, his name shall be Vilhelm after the mighty Kaiser."

"My little girl's name will be Ellen after my mother." Ed Thatcher's eyes filled with tears.

Mr. Zucher got to his feet. "Vell goodpy Mr. Thatcher. Happy to have met you. I must go home to my little girls."

Thatcher shook the chubby hand again, and thinking warm soft thoughts of motherhood and fatherhood and birthday cakes and Christmas watched through a sepia-tinged foamy haze Mr. Zucher waddle out through the swinging doors. After a while he stretched out his arms. Well poor little Susie wouldn't like me to be here. . . . Everything for her and the bonny wee bairn.

"Hey there yous how about settlin?" bawled the barkeep after him when he reached the door.

"Didn't the other feller pay?"

"Like hell he did."

"But he was t-t-treating me. . . ."

The barkeep laughed as he covered the money with a red flipper. "I guess that bloat believes in savin."

1925

THE 42nd PARALLEL *
THE CAMERA EYE (1)

When you walk along the street you have to step carefully always on the cobbles so as not to step on the bright anxious grassblades; easier if you hold your mother's hand and hang on it, that way you can kick up your toes, but walking fast you have to tread on too many grassblades, the poor hurt green tongues shrink under your feet, maybe that's why those people are so angry and following us shaking their fists. They're throwing stones, grownup people throwing stones. She's walking fast and we're running. Her pointed toes stick out sharp among the poor trodden grassblades under the shaking folds of the brown cloth dress. Englander . . . a pebble tinkles along the cobbles. Quick darling quick in the postcard shop its quiet the angry people are outside and cant come in. Non nein nicht englander amerikanisch americain . . . Hoch Amerika, Vive L'Amerique. She laughs My dear they had me right frightened . . . War on the veldt . . . Kruger . . . Bloomfontein . . . Ladysmith and Queen Victoria an old lady in a pointed lace cap sent chocolate to the soldiers at Christmas.

Under the counter its dark and the lady and the nice Dutch lady who loves Americans and has relations in Trenton shows you postcards that shine in the dark pretty hotels and palaces: O que c'est beau . . . schon . . . prittie prittie . . . and the moonlight ripple ripple under a bridge and the little reverbères are alight in the dark under the counter and the little windows of hotels around the harbor . . . O que c'est beau la lune . . . and the big moon.

NEWSREEL II

Come on and hear
Come on and hear
Come on and hear

In his address to the Michigan state Legislature the retiring governor, Hazen S. Pingree, said in part: I make the prediction that unless those in charge and in whose hands legislation is reposed do not change the present system of inequality, there will be a bloody revolution in less than a quarter of a century in this great country of ours.

dies martyr to blooms two revive in graveclothes Kruger seriously ill Theatre trust rules center of population of the U. S. in Henry Marr's cloverfield near Wiggs Indiana Queen Victoria Dying Carrie Nation Uses Axe on Saloons DYING QUEEN LINGERS BUT HOPE IS PAST May change to Panama route dead man rides in a cab attempt suicide when doctor announces second pair of twins

CARNEGIE TALKS OF HIS EPITAPH

Alexanders ragtime band
It is the best
It is the best

the luncheon which was served in the physical laboratory was replete with novel features. A miniature blastfurnace four feet high was on the banquet table and a narrow gauge railroad forty feet long ran round the edge of the table. Instead of molten metal the blastfurnace poured hot punch into small cars on the railroad Icecream was served in the shape of railroad ties and bread took the shape

of locomotives.

Mr. Carnegie, while extolling the advantages of higher education in every branch of learning, came at last to this conclusion: Manual labor has been found to be the best foundation for the greatest work of the brain

VICE PRESIDENT
EMPTIES A BANK

Come on and hear
Alexander's ragtime band
It is the best
It is the best

brother of Jesse James declares play picturing him as bandit trainrobber and outlaw is demoralizing district battle ends with polygamy according to an investigation by Salt Lake ministers, still practiced by Mormons clubwomen gasp

It is the best band in the land

say circus animals only eat Chicago horsemeat Taxsale of Indiana lots marks finale of World's Fair boom uses flag as ragbag killed on cannibal isle keeper falls into water and sealions attack him

the launch then came alongside the half deflated balloon of the aerostat which threatened at any moment to smother Santos Dumont. The latter was half pulled and half clambered over the gunwale into the boat.

The prince of Monaco urged him to allow himself to be taken on board the yacht to dry himself and change his clothes. Santos Dumont would not leave the launch until everything that could be saved had been taken ashore, then, wet but smiling and unconcerned, he landed amid the frenzied cheers of the crowd

LOVER OF MANKIND

Debs was a railroad man,
born in a weatherboarded shack at Terre Haute.
He was one of ten children.
His father had come to America in a sailingship in '49,
an Alsatian from Colmar; not much of a moneymaker, fond of music and
reading,
he gave his children a chance to finish public school and that was about all
he could do.
At fifteen Gene Debs was already working as a machinist on the Indianapolis
and Terre Haute Railway.
He worked as locomotive fireman,
clerked in a store
joined the local of the Brotherhood of Locomotive Firemen, was elected
secretary, travelled all over the country as organizer.
He was a tall shamblefooted man, had a sort of gusty rhetoric that set on
fire the railroad workers in their pineboarded halls
made them want the world he wanted,
a world brothers might own
where everybody would split even:
*I am not a labor leader. I don't want you to follow me or anyone else. If
you are looking for a Moses to lead you out of the capitalist wilderness you
will stay right where you are. I would not lead you into this promised land if
I could, because if I could lead you in, someone else would lead you out.*
That was how he talked to freighthandlers and mandywalkers to firemen
and switchmen and engineers, telling them it wasn't enough to organize the
railroadmen, that all workers must be organized, that all workers must be
organized in the workers coöperative commonwealth.
Locomotive fireman on many a long night's run,
under the smoke a fire burned him up, burned in gusty words that beat in
pineboarded halls; he wanted his brothers to be free men.
That was what he saw in the crowd that met him at the Old Wells Street
Depot when he came out of jail after the Pullman strike,
those were the men that chalked up 900,000 votes for him in nineteen
twelve and scared the frockcoats and the tophats and diamonded hostesses at
Saratoga Springs, Bar Harbor, Lake Geneva with the bogy of a socialist
president.
Where were Gene Debs' brothers in nineteen eighteen when Woodrow
Wilson had him locked up in Atlanta for speaking against war,
where were the big men fond of whiskey and fond of each other, gentle
rambling tellers of stories over bars in small towns in the Middle West,
quiet men who wanted a house with a porch to putter around and a fat wife
to cook for them, a few drinks and cigars, a garden to dig in, cronies to chew
the rag with
and wanted to work for it
and others to work for it.
Where were the locomotive firemen and engineers when they hustled him off
to Atlanta Penitentiary?
And they brought him back to die in Terre Haute

to sit on his porch in a rocker with a cigar in his mouth,
  beside him American Beauty roses his wife fixed in a bowl;
  and the people of Terre Haute and the people in Indiana and the people of the Middle West were fond of him and afraid of him and thought of him as an old kindly uncle who loved them, and wanted to be with him and to have him give them candy,
  but they were afraid of him as if he had contracted a social disease, syphilis or leprosy, and thought it was too bad,
  but on account of the flag
  and prosperity
  and making the world safe for democracy,
  they were afraid to be with him,
  or to think much about him for fear they might believe him;
  for he said:
While there is a lower class I am of it, while there is a criminal class I am of it, while there is a soul in prison I am not free.

1930

1919 *

JOE WILLIAMS [3]

It was a lousy trip. Joe was worried all the time about Del and about not making good and the deckcrew was a bunch of soreheads. The engines kept breaking down. The *Higginbotham* was built like a cheesebox and so slow there were days when they didn't make more'n thirty or forty miles against moderate head winds. The only good times he had was taking boxing lessons from the second engineer, a fellow named Glen Hardwick. He was a little wiry guy, who was a pretty good amateur boxer, though he must have been forty years old. By the time they got to Bordeaux Joe was able to give him a good workout. He was heavier and had a better reach and Glen said he'd a straight natural right that would take him far as a lightweight.

In Bordeaux the first port official that came on board tried to kiss Cap'n Perry on both cheeks. President Wil-

* Reprinted by permission of John Dos Passos. Copyright, 1932, by John Dos Passos.

son had just declared war on Germany. All over the town nothing was too good for Les Americains. Evenings when they were off Joe and Glen Hardwick cruised around together. The Bordeaux girls were damn pretty. They met up with a couple one afternoon in the public garden that weren't hookers at all. They were nicely dressed and looked like they came of good families, what the hell it was wartime. At first Joe thought he ought to lay off that stuff now that he was married, but hell, hadn't Del held out on him. What did she think he was, a plaster saint? They ended by going to a little hotel the girls knew and eating supper and drinking beaucoup wine and champagne and having a big party. Joe had never had such a good time with a girl in his life. His girl's name was Marceline and when they woke up in the morning the help at the hotel brought them in coffee and rolls and they ate breakfast, both of 'em sitting up in bed and Joe's French began to pick up and he learned how to say C'est la guerre and On les aura and Je m'en fiche and Marceline said she'd always be his sweetie when he was in Bordeaux and called him petit lapin.

They only stayed in Bordeaux the four days it took 'em to wait their turn to go up to the dock and unload, but they drank wine and cognac all the time and the food was swell and nobody could do enough for them on account of America having come into the war and it was a great old four days.

On the trip home the *Higginbotham* sprung leaks so bad the old man stopped worrying about submarines altogether. It was nip and tuck if they'd make Halifax. The ship was light and rolled like a log so that even with fiddles on they couldn't keep dishes on the messtable. One dirty night of driving fog somewhere south of Cape Race, Joe with his chin in his peajacket was taking a turn on the deck amidship when he was suddenly thrown flat. They never knew what hit 'em, a mine or a torpedo. It was only that the boats were in darn good order and the sea was smooth that they got off at all. As it was the four boats got separated. The *Higginbotham* faded into the fog and they never saw her sink, though the last they could make out her maindeck was awash.

They were cold and wet. In Joe's boat nobody said much. The men at the oars had to work hard to keep her bow into the little chop that came up. Each sea a little bigger than the others drenched them with spray. They had on wool sweaters and lifepreservers but the cold seeped through. At last the fog greyed a little and it was day. Joe's boat and the captain's boat managed to keep together until late that afternoon they were picked up by a big fishing schooner, a banker bound for Boston.

When they were picked up old Cap'n Perry was in a bad way. The master of the fishing schooner did everything he could for him, but he was unconscious when they reached Boston four days later and died on the way to the hospital. The doctors said it was pneumonia.

Next morning Joe and the mate went to the office of the agent of Perkins and Ellerman, the owners, to see about getting themselves and the crew paid off. There was some kind of damn monkeydoodle business about the vessel's having changed owners in midAtlantic, a man named Rosenberg had bought her on a speculation and now he couldn't be found and the Chase National Bank was claiming ownership and the underwriters were raising cain. The agent said he was sure they'd be paid all right, because Rosenberg had posted bond, but it would be some time. "And what the hell do they expect us to do all that time, eat grass?" The clerk said he was sorry but they'd have to take it up direct with Mr. Rosenberg.

Joe and the first mate stood side by side on the curb outside the office and cursed for a while, then the mate went over to South Boston to break the news to the chief who lived there.

It was a warm June afternoon. Joe started to go around the shipping offices to see what he could do in the way of a berth. He got tired of that and went and sat on a bench on the Common, staring at the sparrows and the gobs loafing around and the shop girls coming home from work, their little heels clattering on the asphalt paths.

Joe hung around Boston broke for a couple of weeks. The Salvation Army took care of the survivors, serving 'em beans and watery soup and a lot of hymns off key that didn't appeal to Joe the way he felt just then. He was crazy to get enough jack to go to Norfolk to see Del. He wrote her every day but the letters he got back to General Delivery seemed kinder cool. She was worried about the rent and wanted some spring clothes and was afraid they wouldn't like it at the office if they found out about her being married.

Joe sat on the benches on the Common and roamed around among the flowerbeds in the Public Garden, and called regularly at the agent's office to ask about a berth, but finally he got sick of hanging around and went down and signed on as quartermaster, on a United Fruit boat, the *Callao*. He thought it ud be a short run and by the time he got back in a couple of weeks he'd be able to get his money.

On the home trip they had to wait several days anchored outside in the roads at Roseau in Dominica, for the limes they were going to load to be crated. Everybody was sore at the port authorities, a lot of damn British niggers, on account of the quarantine and the limes not being ready and how slow the lighters were coming off from the shore. The last night in port Joe and Larry, one of the other quartermasters, got kidding some young coons in a bumboat that had been selling fruit and liquor to the crew under the stern; first thing they knew they'd offered 'em a dollar each to take 'em ashore and land 'em down the beach so's the officers wouldn't see them. The town smelt of niggers. There were no lights in the streets. A little coalblack youngster ran up and asked did they want some mountain chicken. "I guess that means wild women, sure," said Joe. "All bets are off tonight." The little dinge took 'em into a bar kept by a stout mulatto woman and said something to her in the island lingo they couldn't understand, and she said they'd have to wait

a few minutes and they sat down and had a couple of drinks of corn and oil. "I guess she must be the madam," said Larry. "If they ain't pretty good lookers they can go to hell for all I care. I'm not much on the dark meat." From out back came a sound of sizzling and a smell of something frying. "Dod gast it, I could eat something," said Joe. "Say, boy, tell her we want something to eat." "By and by you eat mountain chicken." "What the hell?" They finished their drinks just as the woman came back with a big platter of something fried up. "What's that?" asked Joe. "That's mountain chicken, mister; that's how we call froglegs down here but they ain't like the frogs you all has in the states. I been in the states and I know. We wouldn't eat them here. These here is clean frogs just like chicken. You'll find it real good if you eat it." They roared. "Jesus, the drinks are on us," said Larry, wiping the tears out of his eyes.

Then they thought they'd go pick up some girls. They saw a couple leaving the house where the music was and followed 'em down the dark street. They started to talk to 'em and the girls showed their teeth and wriggled in their clothes and giggled. But three or four nigger men came up sore as hell and began talking in the local lingo. "Jez, Larry, we'd better watch our step," said Joe through his teeth. "Those bozos got razors." They were in the middle of a yelling bunch of big black men when they heard an American voice behind them, "Don't say another word, boys, I'll handle this." A small man in khaki riding breeches and a panama hat was pushing his way through the crowd talking in the island lingo all the time. He was a little man with a gray triangular face tufted with a goatee. "My name's Henderson, DeBuque Henderson of

Bridgeport, Connecticut." He shook hands with both of them.

"Well, what's the trouble, boys? It's all right now, everybody knows me here. You have to be careful on this island, boys, they're touchy, these people, very touchy. . . . You boys better come along with me and have a drink. . . ." He took them each by the arm and walked them hurriedly up the street. "Well, I was young once . . . I'm still young . . . sure, had to see the island . . . damn right too, the most interesting island in the whole Caribbean only lonely . . . never see a white face."

When they got to his house he walked them through a big white-washed room onto a terrace that smelt of vanilla flowers. They could see the town underneath with its few lights, the dark hills, the white hull of the *Callao* with the lighters around her lit up by the working lights. At intervals the rattle of winches came up to them and a crazy jigtune from somewhere.

The old feller poured them each a glass of rum; then another. He had a parrot on a perch that kept screeching. The landbreeze had come up full of heavy flowersmells off the mountains and blew the old feller's stringy white hair in his eyes. He pointed at the *Callao* all lit up with its ring of lighters. "United Fruit . . . United Thieves Company . . . it's a monopoly . . . if you won't take their prices they let your limes rot on the wharf; it's a monopoly. You boys are working for a bunch of thieves, but I know it ain't your fault. Here's lookin' at you."

Before they knew it Larry and Joe were singing. The old man was talking about cotton spinning machinery and canecrushers and pouring out drinks from a rumbottle. They were pretty goddam drunk. They didn't

know how they got aboard. Joe remembered the dark focastle and the sound of snoring from the bunks spinning around, then sleep hitting him like a sandbag and the sweet, sicky taste of rum in his mouth.

A couple of days later Joe came down with a fever and horrible pains in his joints. He was out of his head when they put him ashore at St. Thomas's. It was dengue and he was sick for two months before he had the strength even to write Del to tell her where he was. The hospital orderly told him he'd been out of his head five days and they'd given him up for a goner. The doctors had been sore as hell about it because this was post hospital; after all he was a white man and unconscious and they couldn't very well feed him to the sharks.

It was July before Joe was well enough to walk around the steep little coraldust streets of the town. He had to leave the hospital and would have been in a bad way if one of the cooks at the marine barracks hadn't looked out for him and found him a flop in an unused section of the building. It was hot and there was never a cloud in the sky and he got pretty sick of looking at the niggers and the bare hills and the blue shutin harbor. He spent a lot of time sitting out on the old coalwharf in the shade of a piece of corrugated iron roof looking through the planking at the clear deep bluegreen water, watching shoals of snappers feeding around the piles. He got to thinking about Del and that French girl in Bordeaux and the war and how the United Fruit was a bunch of thieves and then the thoughts would go round and round in his head like the little silver and blue and yellow fish round the swaying weeds on the piles and he'd find he'd dropped off to sleep.

When a northbound fruitsteamer came into the harbor he got hold of one of the officers on the wharf and told him his sad story. They gave him passage up to New York. First thing he did was try to get hold of Janey; maybe if she thought he ought to, he'd give up this dog's life and take a steady job ashore. He called up the J. Ward Moorehouse advertising office where she worked but the girl at the other end of the line told him she was the boss's secretary and was out west on business.

He went over and got a flop at Mrs. Olsen's in Redhook. Everybody over there was talking about the draft and how they rounded you up for a slacker if they picked you up on the street without a registration card. And sure enough, just as Joe was stepping out of the subway at Wall Street one morning a cop came up to him and asked him for his card. Joe said he was a merchant seaman and had just got back from a trip and hadn't had time to register yet and that he was exempt, but the cop said he'd have to tell that to the judge. They were quite a bunch being marched down Broadway; smart guys in the crowd of clerks and counterjumpers along the sidewalks yelled "Slackers" at them and the girls hissed and booed.

In the Custom House they were herded into some of the basement rooms. It was a hot August day. Joe elbowed his way through the sweating, grumbling crowd towards the window. Most of them were foreigners, there were longshoremen and waterfront loafers; a lot of the group were talking big but Joe remembered the navy and kept his mouth shut and listened. He was in there all day. The cops wouldn't let anybody telephone and there was only one toilet and they had to go to that under guard. Joe felt pretty weak on his pins, he hadn't gotten over the effect of that dengue yet. He was about ready to pass out when he saw a face he knew. Damned if it wasn't Glen Hardwick.

Glen had been picked up by a Britisher and taken into Halifax. He'd signed as second on the *Chemang*, taking out mules to Bordeaux and a general cargo to Genoa, going to be armed with a threeinch gun and navy gunners, Joe ought to come along. "Jesus, do you think I could get aboard her?" Joe asked. "Sure, they're crazy for navigation officers; they'd take you on even without a ticket." Bordeaux sounded pretty good, remember the girlfriends there? They doped out that when Glen got out he'd phone Mrs. Olsen to bring over Joe's license that was in a cigarbox at the head of his bed. When they finally were taken up to the desk to be questioned the guy let Glen go right away and said Joe could go as soon as they got his license over but that they must register at once even if they were exempt from the draft. "After all, you boys ought to remember that there's a war on," said the inspector at the desk. "Well, we sure ought to know," said Joe.

Mrs. Olsen came over all in a flurry with Joe's papers and Joe hustled over to the office in East New York and they took him on as bosun. The skipper was Ben Tarbell who'd been first mate on the *Higginbotham*. Joe wanted to go down to Norfolk to see Del, but hell this was no time to stay ashore. What he did was to send her fifty bucks he borrowed from Glen. He didn't have time to worry about it anyway because they sailed the next day with sealed orders as to where to meet the convoy.

It wasn't so bad steaming in convoy. The navy officers on the destroyers and the *Salem* that was in command gave the orders, but the merchant captains kidded back and forth with wigwag signals. It was some sight to see the Atlantic Ocean full of long strings of freighters all blotched up with gray and white watermarkings like barberpoles by the camouflage artists. There were old tubs in that convoy that a man wouldn't have trusted himself in to cross to Staten Island in peacetime and one of the new wooden Shipping Board boats leaked so bad, jerry-built out of new wood—somebody musta been making money—that she had to be abandoned and scuttled half way across.

Joe and Glen smoked their pipes together in Glen's cabin and chewed the fat a good deal. They decided that everything ashore was the bunk and the only place for them was blue water. Joe got damn fed up with bawling out the bunch of scum he had for a crew. Once they got in the zone, all the ships started steering a zigzag course and everybody began to get white around the gills. Joe never cussed so much in his life. There was a false alarm of submarines every few hours and seaplanes dropping depth bombs and excited gun crews firing at old barrels, bunches of seaweed, dazzle in the water. Steaming into the Gironde at night with the searchlights crisscrossing and the blinker signals and the patrolboats scooting around, they sure felt good.

It was a relief to get the dirty trampling mules off the ship and their stench out of everything, and to get rid of the yelling and cussing of the hostlers. Glen and Joe only got ashore for a few hours and couldn't find Marceline and Loulou. The Garonne was beginning to look like the Delaware with all the new Americanbuilt steel and concrete piers. Going out

they had to anchor several hours to repair a leaky steampipe and saw a patrol boat go by towing five ships' boats crowded to the gunnels, so they guessed the fritzes must be pretty busy outside.

No convoy this time. They slipped out in the middle of a foggy night. When one of the deckhands came up out of the focastle with a cigarette in the corner of his mouth, the mate knocked him flat and said he'd have him arrested when he got back home for a damn German spy. They coasted Spain as far as Finisterre. The skipper had just changed the course to southerly when they saw a sure enough periscope astern. The skipper grabbed the wheel himself and yelled down the tube to the engine room to give him everything they'd got, that wasn't much to be sure, and the gun crew started blazing away.

The periscope disappeared but a couple of hours later they overhauled a tubby kind of ketch, must be a Spanish fishingboat, that was heading for the shore, for Vigo probably, scudding along wing and wing in the half a gale that was blowing up west northwest. They'd no sooner crossed the wake of the ketch than there was a thud that shook the ship and a column of water shot up that drenched them all on the bridge. Everything worked like clockwork. No. 1 was the only compartment flooded. As luck would have it, the crew was all out of the focastle standing on deck amidships in their life preservers. The *Chemang* settled a little by the bow, that was all. The gunners were certain it was a mine dropped by the old black ketch that had crossed their bow and let them have a couple of shots, but the ship was rolling so in the heavy sea that the shots went wild. Anyway, the ketch went out of sight behind the island that blocks the mouth of the roadstead of Vigo. The *Chemang* crawled on in under one bell.

By the time they got into the channel opposite the town of Vigo, the water was gaining on the pumps in No. 2, and there was four feet of water in the engineroom. They had to beach her on the banks of hard sand to the right of the town.

So they were ashore again with their bundles standing around outside the consul's office, waiting for him to find them somewhere to flop. The consul was a Spaniard and didn't speak as much English as he might have but he treated them fine. The Liberal Party of Vigo invited officers and crew to go to a bullfight there was going to be that afternoon. More monkeydoodle business, the skipper got a cable to turn the ship over to the agents of Gomez and Ca. of Bilboa who had bought her as she stood and were changing her registry.

When they got to the bullring half the crowd cheered them and yelled, "Viva los Aliados," and the rest hissed and shouted, "Viva Maura." They thought there was going to be a fight right there but the bull came out and everybody quieted down. The bullfight was darn bloody, but the boys with the spangles were some steppers and the people sitting around made them drink wine all the time out of little black skins and passed around bottles of cognac so that the crew got pretty cockeyed and Joe spent most of his time keeping the boys in order. Then the officers were tendered a banquet by the local pro-allied society and a lot of bozos with mustachios made fiery speeches that nobody could understand and the Americans cheered and sang, *The Yanks Are Coming* and *Keep the Home Fires Burning* and *We're Bound for the Hamburg Show*. The chief, an old

fellow named McGillicudy, did some card tricks, and the evening was a big success. Joe and Glen bunked together at the hotel. The maid there was awful pretty but wouldn't let 'em get away with any foolishness. "Well, Joe," said Glen, before they went to sleep, "it's a great war." "Well, I guess that's strike three," said Joe. "That was no strike, that was a ball," said Glen.

They waited two weeks in Vigo while the officials quarreled about their status and they got pretty fed up with it. Then they were all loaded on a train to take them to Gibraltar where they were to be taken on board a Shipping Board boat. They were three days on the train with nothing to sleep on but hard benches. Spain was just one set of great dusty mountains after another. They changed cars in Madrid and in Seville and a guy turned up each time from the consulate to take care of them. When they got to Seville they found it was Algeciras they were going to instead of Gib.

When they got to Algeciras they found that nobody had ever heard of them. They camped out in the consulate while the consul telegraphed all over the place and finally chartered two trucks and sent them over to Cadiz. Spain was some country, all rocks and wine and busty black eyed women and olive trees. When they got to Cadiz the consular agent was there to meet them with a telegram in his hand. The tanker *Gold Shell* was waiting in Algeciras to take them on board there, so it was back again cooped up on the trucks, bouncing on the hard benches with their faces powdered with dust and their mouths full of it and not a cent in anybody's jeans left to buy a drink with. When they got on board the *Gold Shell* around three in the morning a bright moonlight night some of the boys were so tired they fell down and went to sleep right on the deck with their heads on their seabags.

The *Gold Shell* landed 'em in Perth Amboy in late October. Joe drew his back pay and took the first train connections he could get for Norfolk. He was fed up with bawling out that bunch of pimps in the focastle. Damn it, he was through with the sea; he was going to settle down and have a little married life.

He felt swell coming over on the ferry from Cape Charles, passing the Ripraps, out of the bay full of whitecaps into the smooth brown water of Hampton Roads crowded with shipping; four great battlewaggons at anchor, subchasers speeding in and out and a white revenue cutter, camouflaged freighters and colliers, a bunch of red munitions barges anchored off by themselves. It was a sparkling fall day. He felt good; he had three hundred and fifty dollars in his pocket. He had a good suit on and he felt sunburned and he'd just had a good meal. God damn it, he wanted a little love now. Maybe they'd have a kid.

Things sure were different in Norfolk. Everybody in new uniforms, twominute speakers at the corner of Main and Granby, liberty loan posters, bands playing. He hardly knew the town walking up from the ferry. He'd written Del that he was coming but he was worried about seeing her, hadn't had any letters lately. He still had a latch key to the apartment but he knocked before opening the door. There was nobody there.

He'd always pictured her running to the door to meet him. Still it was only four o'clock, she must be at her work. Must have another girl with her, don't keep the house so tidy. . . . Underwear hung to dry on a line, bits of clothing on all the chairs, a box of candy with half-eaten pieces in it on the table. . . . Jez, they must have had a party last night. There was a half a cake, glasses that had had liquor in them, a plate full of cigarette butts and even a cigar butt. Oh, well, she'd probably had some friends in. He went to the bathroom and shaved and cleaned up a little. Sure Del was always popular, she probably had a lot of friends in all the time, playing cards and that. In the bathroom there was a pot of rouge and lipsticks, and facepowder spilt over the faucets. It made Joe feel funny shaving among all these women's things.

He heard her voice laughing on the stairs and a man's voice; the key clicked in the lock. Joe closed his suitcase and stood up. Del had bobbed her hair. She flew up to him and threw her arms around his neck. "Why, I declare it's my hubby." Joe could taste rouge on her lips. "My, you look thin, Joe. Poor Boy, you musta been awful sick. . . . If I'd had any money at all I'd have jumped on a boat and come on down. . . . This is Wilmer Tayloe . . . I mean Lieutenant Tayloe, he just got his commission yesterday."

Joe hesitated a moment and then held out his hand. The other fellow had red hair clipped close and a freckled face. He was all dressed up in a whipcord uniform, shiny Sam Browne belt and puttees. He had a silver bar on each shoulder and spurs on his feet.

"He's just going overseas tomorrow. He was coming by to take me out to dinner. Oh, Joe, I've got so much to tell you, honey."

Joe and Lieutenant Tayloe stood around eyeing each other uncomfortably while Del bustled around tidying the place up, talking to Joe all the time. "It's terrible I never get any chance to do anything and neither does Hilda . . . You remember Hilda Thompson, Joe? Well, she's been livin' with me to help make up the rent but we're both of us doin' war work down at the Red Cross canteen every evening and then I sell Liberty bonds. . . . Don't you hate the huns, Joe. Oh, I just hate them, and so does Hilda. . . . She's thinking of changing her name on account of its being German. I promised to call her Gloria but I always forget. . . . You know, Wilmer, Joe's been torpedoed twice."

"Well, I suppose the first six times is the hardest," stammered Lieutenant Tayloe. Joe grunted.

Del disappeared into the bathroom and closed the door. "You boys make yourselves comfortable. I'll be dressed in a minute."

Neither of them said anything. Lieutenant Tayloe's shoes creaked as he shifted his weight from one foot to the other. At last he pulled a flask out of his hip pocket. "Have a drink," he said. "Ma outfit's goin' overseas any time after midnight." "I guess I'd better," said Joe, without smiling. When Della came out of the bathroom all dressed up she certainly looked snappy. She was much prettier than last time Joe had seen her. He was all the time wondering if he ought to go up and hit that damn shavetail until at last he left, Del telling him to come by and get her at the Red Cross canteen.

When he'd left she came and sat on Joe's knee and asked him about everything and whether he'd got his second mate's ticket yet and whether he'd missed her and how she wished he could make a little more money because she hated to have another girl in with her this way but it was the only way she could pay the rent. She drank a little of the whiskey that the

lieutenant had forgotten on the table and ruffled his hair and loved him up. Joe asked her if Hilda was coming in soon and she said no she had a date and she was going to meet her at the canteen. But Joe went and bolted the door anyway and for the first time they were really happy hugged in each other's arms on the bed.

Joe didn't know what to do with himself around Norfolk. Del was at the office all day and at the Red Cross canteen all the evening. He'd usually be in bed when she came home. Usually there'd be some damn army officer or other bringing her home, and he'd hear them talking and kidding outside the door and lie there in bed imagining that the guy was kissing her or loving her up. He'd be about ready to hit her when she'd come in and bawl her out and they'd quarrel and yell at each other and she'd always end by saying that he didn't understand her and she thought he was unpatriotic to be interfering with her war work and sometimes they'd make up and he'd feel crazy in love with her and she'd make herself little and cute in his arms and give him little tiny kisses that made him almost cry they made him feel so happy. She was getting better looking every day and she sure was a snappy dresser.

Sunday mornings she'd be too tired to get up and he'd cook breakfast for her and they'd sit up in bed together and eat breakfast like he had with Marceline that time in Bordeaux. Then she'd tell him she was crazy about him and what a smart guy he was and how she wanted him to get a good shore job and make a lot of money so that she wouldn't have to work any more and how Captain Barnes whose folks were worth a million had wanted her to get a divorce from Joe and marry him and Mr. Canfield in the Dupont office who made a cool 50,000 a year had wanted to give her a pearl necklace but she hadn't taken it because she didn't think it was right. Talk like that made Joe feel pretty rotten. Sometimes he'd start to talk about what they'd do if they had some kids, but Del ud always make a funny face and tell him not to talk like that.

Joe went around looking for work and almost landed the job of foreman in one of the repairshops over at the shipyard in Newport News, but at the last minute another berry horned in ahead of him and got it. A couple of times he went out on parties with Del and Hilda Thompson, and some army officers and a midshipman off a destroyer, but they all high-hatted him and Del let any boy who wanted to kiss her and would disappear into a phone booth with anything she could pick up so long as it had a uniform on and he had a hell of a time. He found a poolroom where some boys he knew hung out and where he could get corn liquor and started tanking up a good deal. It made Del awful sore to come home and find him drunk but he didn't care any more.

Then one night when Joe had been to a fight with some guys and had gotten an edge on afterward, he met Del and another damn shavetail walking on the street. It was pretty dark and there weren't many people around and they stopped in every dark doorway and the shavetail was kissing and hugging her. When he got them under a street light so's he made sure it was Del he went up to them and asked them what the hell they meant. Del must have had some drinks because she started tittering in a shrill little voice that drove him crazy and he hauled off and let the shavetail have a perfect left right on the button. The spurs tinkled and the shavetail went to sleep right flat on the little grass patch under the streetlight. It began to hit Joe kinder funny but Del was sore as the devil and said she'd have him arrested for insult to the uniform and assault and battery and that he was nothing but a yellow snivelling slacker and what was he doing hanging around home when all the boys were at the front fighting the huns. Joe sobered up and pulled the guy up to his feet and told them both they could go straight to hell. He walked off before the shavetail, who musta been pretty tight, had time to do anything but splutter, and went straight home and packed his suitcase and pulled out.

Will Stirp was in town so Joe went over to his house and got him up out of bed and said he'd busted up housekeeping and would Will lend him twentyfive bucks to go up to New York with. Will said it was a damn good thing and that love 'em and leave 'em was the only thing for guys like them. They talked till about day about one thing and another. Then Joe went to sleep and slept till late afternoon. He got up in time to catch the Washington boat. He didn't take a room but roamed around on deck all night. He got to cracking with one of the officers and went and sat in the pilot house that smelt comfortably of old last year's pipes. Listening to the sludge of water from the bow and watching the wabbly white finger of the searchlight pick up buoys and lighthouses he began to pull himself together. He said he was going up to New York to see his sister and try for a second mate's ticket with the Shipping Board. His stories about being torpedoed went big because none of them on the *Dominion City* had even been across the pond.

It felt like old times standing in the bow in the sharp November morning, sniffing the old brackish smell of the Potomac water, passing redbrick Alexandria and Anacostia and the Arsenal and the Navy Yard, seeing the Monument stick up pink through the mist in the early light. The wharves looked about the same, the yachts and power boats anchored opposite, the Baltimore boat just coming in, the ramshackle excursion steamers, the oystershells underfoot on the wharf, the nigger roustabouts standing around. Then he was hopping the Georgetown car and too soon he was walking up the redbrick street. While he rang the bell he was wondering why he'd come home.

Mommer looked older but she was in pretty good shape and all taken up with her boarders and how the girls were both engaged. They said that Janey was doing so well in her work, but that living in New York had changed her. Joe said he was going down to New York to try to get his second mate's ticket and that he sure would look her up. When they asked him about the war and the submarines and all that he didn't know what to tell 'em so he kinder kidded them along. He was glad when it was time to go over to Washington to get his train, though they were darn nice to him and seemed to think that he was making a big success getting to be a second mate so young. He didn't tell 'em about being married.

Going down on the train to New York Joe sat in the smoker looking out of the window at farms and stations and billboards and the grimy streets of factory towns through Jersey under a driving rain and everything he saw seemed to remind him of Del and places outside of Norfolk and good times he'd had when he was a kid. When he got to the Penn Station in New York first thing he did

was check his bag, then he walked down Eighth Avenue all shiny with rain to the corner of the street where Janey lived. He guessed he'd better phone her first and called from a cigarstore. Her voice sounded kinder stiff; she said she was busy and couldn't see him till tomorrow. He came out of the phonebooth and walked down the street not knowing where to go. He had a package under his arm with a couple of Spanish shawls he'd bought for her and Del on the last trip. He felt so blue he wanted to drop the shawls and everything down a drain, but he thought better of it and went back to the checkroom at the station and left them in his suitcase. Then he went and smoked a pipe for a while in the waitingroom.

God damn it to hell he needed a drink. He went over to Broadway and walked down to Union Square, stopping in every place he could find that looked like a saloon but they wouldn't serve him anywhere. Union Square was all lit up and full of navy recruiting posters. A big wooden model of a battleship filled up one side of it. There was a crowd standing around and a young girl dressed like a sailor was making a speech about patriotism. The cold rain came on again and the crowd scattered. Joe went down a street and into a ginmill called The Old Farm. He must have looked like somebody the barkeep knew because he said hello and poured him out a shot of rye.

Joe got to talking with two guys from Chicago who were drinking whiskey with beer chasers. They said this wartalk was a lot of bushwa propaganda and that if working stiffs stopped working in munition factories making shells to knock other working stiffs' blocks off with, there wouldn't be no goddam war. Joe said they were goddam right but look at the big money you made. The guys from Chicago said they'd been working in a munitions factory themselves but they were through, goddam it, and that if the working stiffs made a few easy dollars it meant that the war profiteers were making easy millions. They said the Russians had the right idea, make a revolution and shoot the goddam profiteers and that ud happen in this country if they didn't watch out and a damn good thing too. The barkeep leaned across the bar and said they'd oughtn't to talk thataway, folks ud take 'em for German spies.

"Why, you're a German yourself, George," said one of the guys.

The barkeep flushed and said, "Names don't mean nothin' . . . I'm a patriotic American. I vas talking yust for your good. If you vant to land in de hoosgow it's not my funeral." But he set them up to drinks on the house and it seemed to Joe that he agreed with 'em.

They drank another round and Joe said it was all true but what the hell could you do about it? The guys said what you could do about it was join the I.W.W. and carry a red card and be a classconscious worker. Joe said that stuff was only for foreigners, but if somebody started a white man's party to fight the profiteers and the goddam bankers he'd be with 'em. The guys from Chicago began to get sore and said the wobblies were just as much white men as he was and that political parties were the bunk and that all southerners were scabs. Joe backed off and was looking at the guys to see which one of 'em he'd hit first when the barkeep stepped around from the end of the bar and came between them. He was fat but he had shoulders and a meanlooking pair of blue eyes.

"Look here, you bums," he said,

"you listen to me, sure I'm a Cherman but am I for de Kaiser? No, he's a schweinhunt, I am sokialist unt I live toity years in Union City unt own my home unt pay taxes unt I'm a good American, but dot don't mean dot I vill foight for Banker Morgan, not vonce. I know American vorkman in de sokialist party toity years unt all dey do is foight among each oder. Every sonofabitch denk him better den de next sonofabitch. You loafers getoutahere . . . closin' time . . . I'm goin' to close up an' go home."

One of the guys from Chicago started to laugh, "Well, I guess the drinks are on us, Oscar . . . it'll be different after the revolution."

Joe still wanted to fight but he paid for a round with his last greenback and the barkeep who was still red in the face from his speech, lifted a glass of beer to his mouth. He blew the foam off it and said, "If I talk like dot I lose my yob."

They shook hands all around and Joe went out into the gusty northeast rain. He felt lit but he didn't feel good. He went up to Union Square again. The recruiting speeches were over. The model battleship was dark. A couple of ragged looking youngsters were huddled in the lee of the recruiting tent. Joe felt lousy. He went down into the subway and waited for the Brooklyn train.

At Mrs. Olsen's everything was dark. Joe rang and in a little while she came down in a padded pink dressing gown and opened the door. She was sore at being waked up and bawled him out for drinking, but she gave him a flop and next morning lent him fifteen bucks to tide him over till he got work on a Shipping Board boat. Mrs. Olsen looked tired and a lot older, she said she had pains in her back and couldn't get through her work any more.

Next morning Joe put up some shelves in the pantry for her and carried out a lot of litter before he went over to the Shipping Board recruiting office to put his name down for the officer's school. The little kike behind the desk had never been to sea and asked him a lot of damfool questions and told him to come around next week to find out what action would be taken on his application. Joe got sore and told him to f—k himself and walked out.

He took Janey out to supper and to a show, but she talked just like everybody else did and bawled him out for cussing and he didn't have a very good time. She liked the shawls though and he was glad she was making out so well in New York. He never did get around to talking to her about Della.

After taking her home he didn't know what the hell to do with himself. He wanted a drink, but taking Janey out and everything had cleaned up the fifteen bucks he'd borrowed from Mrs. Olsen. He walked west to a saloon he knew on Tenth Avenue, but the place was closed: wartime prohibition. Then he walked back towards Union Square, maybe that feller Tex he'd seen when he was walking across the square with Janey would still be sitting there and he could chew the rag a while with him. He sat down on a bench opposite the cardboard battleship and began sizing it up: not such a bad job. Hell, I wisht I'd never seen the inside of a real battleship, he was thinking, when Tex slipped into the seat beside him and put his hand on his knee. The minute he touched him Joe knew he'd never liked the guy, eyes too close together: "What you lookin' so blue about, Joe? Tell me you're gettin' your ticket."

Joe nodded and leaned over and spat carefully between his feet.

"What do you think of that for a model battleship, pretty nifty, ain't it? Jez, us guys is lucky not to be overseas fightin' the fritzes in the trenches."

"Oh, I'd just as soon," growled Joe. "I wouldn't give a damn."

"Say, Joe, I got a job lined up. Guess I oughtn't to blab around about it, but you're regular. I know you won't say nothin'. I been on the bum for two weeks, somethin' wrong with my stomach. Man, I'm sick, I'm tellin' you. I can't do no heavy work no more. A punk I know works in a whitefront been slippin' me my grub, see. Well, I was sittin' on a bench right here on the square, a feller kinda well dressed sits down an' starts to chum up. Looked to me like one of these here sissies lookin' for rough trade, see, thought I'd roll him for some jack, what the hell, what can you do if you're sick an' can't work?"

Joe sat leaning back with his legs stuck out, his hands in his pockets staring hard at the outline of the battleship against the buildings. Tex was talking fast, poking his face into Joe's: "Turns out the sonofabitch was a dick. S—t I was scared pissless. A secret service agent. Burns is his big boss . . . but what he's lookin' for's reds, slackers, German spies, guys that can't keep their traps shut . . . an' he turns around and hands me out a job, twentyfive smackers a week if little Willy makes good. All I got to do's bum around and listen to guys talk, see? If I hears anything that ain't 100 per cent I slips the word to the boss and he investigates. Twentyfive a week and servin' my country besides, and if I gets in any kind of jam, Burns gets me out. . . . What do you think of that for the gravy, Joe?"

Joe got to his feet. "Guess I'll go back to Brooklyn." "Stick around . . . look here, you've always treated me white . . . you belong, I know that Joe . . . I'll put you next to this guy if you want. He's a good scout, educated feller an' all that and he knows where you can get plenty liquor an' women if you want 'em." "Hell, I'm goin' to sea and get out of all this s—t," said Joe, turning his back and walking towards the subway station.

1932

THE BIG MONEY *

THE AMERICAN PLAN

Frederick Winslow Taylor (they called him Speedy Taylor in the shop) was born in Germantown, Pennsylvania, the year of Buchanan's election. His father was a lawyer, his mother came from a family of New Bedford whalers; she was a great reader of Emerson, belonged to the Unitarian Church and the Browning Society. She was a fervent abolitionist and believed in democratic manners; she was a housekeeper of the old school, kept everybody busy from dawn till dark. She laid down the rules of conduct:

selfrespect, selfreliance, selfcontrol

and a cold long head for figures.

But she wanted her children to appreciate the finer things so she took them abroad for three years on the Continent, showed them cathedrals, grand opera, Roman pediments, the old masters under their brown varnish in their great frames of tarnished gilt.

Later Fred Taylor was impatient of these wasted years, stamped out of the room when people talked about the finer things; he was a testy youngster, fond of practical jokes and a great hand at rigging up contraptions and devices.

At Exeter he was head of his class and captain of the ballteam, the first man to pitch overhand. (When umpires complained that overhand pitching wasn't in the rules of the game, he answered that it got results.)

As a boy he had nightmares, going to bed was horrible for him; he thought they came from sleeping on his back. He made himself a leather harness with wooden pegs that stuck into his flesh when he turned over. When he was grown he slept in a chair or in bed in a sitting position propped up with pillows. All his life he suffered from sleeplessness.

He was a crackerjack tennisplayer. In 1881, with his friend Clark, he won the National Doubles Championship. (He used a spoonshaped racket of his own design.)

At school he broke down from overwork, his eyes went back on him. The doctor suggested manual labor. So instead of going to Harvard he went into the machineshop of a small pumpmanufacturing concern, owned by a friend of the family's, to learn the trade of patternmaker and machinist. He learned to handle a lathe and to dress and cuss like a workingman.

Fred Taylor never smoked tobacco or drank liquor or used tea or coffee; he couldn't understand why his fellowmechanics wanted to go on sprees and get drunk and raise Cain Saturday nights. He lived at home, when he wasn't reading technical books he'd play parts in amateur theatricals or step up to the piano in the evening and sing a good tenor in *A Warrior Bold* or *A Spanish Cavalier.*

He served his first year's apprenticeship in the machineshop without pay; the next two years he made a dollar and a half a week, the last year two dollars.

Pennsylvania was getting rich off iron and coal. When he was twenty-two, Fred Taylor went to work at the Midvale Iron Works. At first he had to take a clerical job, but he hated that and went to work with a shovel. At last he got them to put him on a lathe. He was a good machinist, he worked ten hours a day and in the evenings followed an engineering course at Stevens. In six years he rose from machinist's helper to keeper of toolcribs to gangboss to foreman to master mechanic in charge of repairs to chief draftsman and director of research to chief engineer of the Midvale Plant.

The early years he was a machinist with the other machinists in the shop, cussed and joked and worked with the rest of them, soldiered on the job when they did. Mustn't give the boss more than his money's worth. But when he got to be foreman he was on the management's side of the fence, *gathering in on the part of those on the management's side all the great mass of traditional knowledge which in the past has been in the heads of the workmen and in the physical skill and knack of the workman.* He couldn't stand to see an idle lathe or an idle man.

Production went to his head and thrilled his sleepless nerves like liquor or women on a Saturday night. He never loafed and he'd be damned if anybody else would. Production was an itch under his skin.

He lost his friends in the shop; they called him niggerdriver. He was a stockily built man with a temper and a short tongue.

I was a young man in years but I give you my word I was a great deal older than I am now, what with the worry, meanness and contemptibleness of the whole damn thing. It's a horrid life for any man to live not being able to look any workman in the face without seeing hostility there, and a feeling that every man around you is your virtual enemy.

That was the beginning of the Taylor System of Scientific Management.

He was impatient of explanations, he didn't care whose hide he took off in enforcing the laws he believed inherent in the industrial process.

When starting an experiment in any field question everything, question the very foundations upon which the art rests, question the simplest, the most self-evident, the most universally accepted facts; prove everything, except the dominant Quaker Yankee (the New Bedford skippers were the greatest niggerdrivers on the whaling seas) rules of conduct. He boasted he'd never ask a workman to do anything he couldn't do.

He devised an improved steamhammer; he standardized tools and equipment, he filled the shop with college students with stopwatches and diagrams, tabulating, standardizing. *There's the right way of doing a thing and the wrong way of doing it; the right way means increased production, lower costs, higher wages, bigger profits:* the American plan.

He broke up the foreman's job into separate functions, speedbosses, gangbosses, timestudy men, orderofwork men.

The skilled mechanics were too stubborn for him, what he wanted was a plain handyman who'd do what he was told. If he was a firstclass man and did firstclass work Taylor was willing to let him have firstclass pay; that's where he began to get into trouble with the owners.

At thirtyfour he married and left Midvale and took a flyer for the big money in connection with a pulpmill started in Maine by some admirals and political friends of Grover Cleveland's;

the panic of '93 made hash of that enterprise,

so Taylor invented for himself the job of Consulting Engineer in Management and began to build up a fortune by careful investments.

The first paper he read before the American Society of Mechanical Engineers was anything but a success, they said he was crazy. *I have found,* he wrote in 1909, *that any improvement is not only opposed but aggressively and bitterly opposed by the majority of men.*

He was called in by Bethlehem Steel. It was in Bethlehem he made his famous experiments with handling pigiron; he taught a Dutchman named Schmidt to handle fortyseven tons instead of twelve and a half tons of pigiron a day and got Schmidt to admit he was as good as ever at the end of the day.

He was a crank about shovels, every job had to have a shovel of the right weight and size for that job alone; every job had to have a man of the right weight and size for that job alone; but when he began to pay his men in proportion to the increased efficiency of their work,

the owners who were a lot of greedy smalleyed Dutchmen began to raise Hail Columbia; when Schwab bought Bethlehem Steel in 1901

Fred Taylor

inventor of efficiency

who had doubled the production of the stampingmill by speeding up the main lines of shafting from ninetysix to twohundred and twentyfive revolutions a minute

was unceremoniously fired.

After that Fred Taylor always said he couldn't afford to work for money.

He took to playing golf (using golfclubs of his own design), doping out methods for transplanting huge boxtrees into the garden of his home.

At Boxly in Germantown he kept open house for engineers, factory-managers, industrialists;

he wrote papers,

lectured in colleges,

appeared before a congressional committee,

everywhere preached the virtues of scientific management and the Barth slide rule, the cutting down of waste and idleness, the substitution for skilled mechanics of the plain handyman (like Schmidt the pigiron handler) who'd move as he was told

and work by the piece:

production;

more steel rails more bicycles more spools of thread more armorplate for battleships more bedpans more barbedwire more needles more lightningrods more ballbearings more dollarbills;

(the old Quaker families of Germantown were growing rich, the Pennsylvania millionaires were breeding billionaires out of iron and coal) production would make every firstclass American rich who was willing to work at piecework and not drink or raise Cain or think or stand mooning at his lathe.

Thrifty Schmidt the pigiron handler can invest his money and get to be an owner like Schwab and the rest of the greedy smalleyed Dutchmen and cultivate a taste for Bach and have hundredyearold boxtrees in his garden at Bethlehem or Germantown or Chestnut Hill,

and lay down the rules of conduct;

the American plan.

But Fred Taylor never saw the working of the American plan;

in 1915 he went to the hospital in Philadelphia suffering from a breakdown.

All his life he'd had the habit of winding his watch every afternoon at fourthirty;

on the afternoon of his fiftyninth birthday, when the nurse went into his room to look at him at fourthirty,

he was dead with his watch in his hand.

1936

ROBERT NATHAN
(1894–   )

FROM

THE PUPPET MASTER *

[THE PUPPET MASTER
AND HIS POET ASSISTANT]

Standing on the bridge of his puppet theater, Papa Jonas remarked to his assistant:

"A puppet should be simple and noble. Its gestures should be few but expressive. The puppets of M. Brioché, which counted Molière among their admirers, were clumsy wooden dolls with animated faces, and roughly jointed limbs. Art must be rude in order to be great: it must express itself with vigor."

He added,

"The artist is not a pedant. He should speak only to suggest. That is why puppets are a great art, for they suggest with the utmost economy, and in a severe manner, the noblest

* Reprinted by permission of Robert M. McBride & Co. from *The Puppet Master* by Robert Nathan, copyright 1923.

impulses, and the most terrible passions."

Leaning down, he began to rehearse Sancho Panza in a few gestures. As the figure of the little squire began to walk and wave its arms, Christopher [the assistant] felt an inclination to laugh. However, he restrained himself, out of respect for Papa Jonas. Instead he exclaimed earnestly:

"I should like to make a puppet able to laugh and cry. Because, after all, that is what people do."

Papa Jonas replied, holding one leg of Sancho Panza suspended in the air:

"You are a realist. That is to say, in the midst of grief you look for something to amuse you. Well, that does not interest me. It is life, if you like; but I am preoccupied with something else."

He meant that he was preoccupied with the unreal, and the unchanging. "Perhaps," he admitted, "a stable near Ninth Avenue is not exactly the place for it. I often think that I would like to build my theater in the west, on a slope shaded by trees, and within sight of the sea. Then those who watched my plays could admire, in the distance, the hills, or the ocean, instead of these dusty beams."

And he glanced disconsolately around the gloomy stable, with its bare walls.

"Yes," said Christopher dreamily; "the west . . . that would be fine."

Papa Jonas smiled. "You are not a realist," he said; "you are a . young fool. Being in the east, you long for the west; and if you were in the west, you would long for the east. You are like Mr. Aristotle [one of the puppets], with his great nose; you cannot see what is under it."

Papa Jonas was right; Christopher did not know what he wanted. He was a poet; that is to say, he wrote verses, which he was unable to sell. Still, this did not discourage him. He was happy because, as Papa Jonas said, he was hardly aware of what was going on under his nose. His eyes were always on the future, which glowed with the brightest colors. It is not to-day, he thought, but to-morrow that is important. As he went to bed in his cold, bare room, he comforted himself with this reflection.

He was poor, but it did not seem to him that he was any worse off for that reason. He longed to travel, but it was all of the mind; he simply wished to be somewhere else, because the sky looked so beautiful far away. The city with its gray streets, its windy shadows, its harsh, clear lights, was like a wall over which he gazed with longing at the rest of the world. When the sun went down across the river, leaving the sky yellow and green and violet, he thought: That is the way the west is now. And he saw in imagination the prairies, the mountains, and the desert, bathed in that ineffable glow.

It was this feeling which drew him to the puppets. They seemed to him like men and women of long ago, or far away; and the scenes which he set up with such care on the stage were also of places far away. He liked to imagine that the little dolls were really Hamlet, or Jonah with his whale; and he felt in their presence that serene sorrow which comes from a contemplation of tragedies faded with age.

Now he said to Papa Jonas: "Well, perhaps I don't know what I want. But why does it astonish you? I should like to write some beautiful poems, or a great book. I am simply looking for beauty . . ."

"Yes," said Papa Jonas. He peered over the bridge at the strings in his hands, at the little squire standing awkwardly and quietly below him, with one raised foot. "We also look for beauty," he said; "these little dolls . . . that is what makes them laughable or pathetic. Some have bellies, and others have dreams. What a pity; but that is the way it is."

He let the strings fall, and, descending from the bridge, picked up Sancho Panza and tied him to a nail in back of the stage. Then he put out the lights. "I am going to supper now," he said; "would you care to come along?"

"No," said Christopher. He was hungry, and he had no money, but he wished to be alone, as he had some work to do. "I've had my supper," he said.

Papa Jonas opened the door. "Good-night," he said; "to-morrow we will rehearse Don Quixote and the barber. Come a little early; there is always plenty to do."

So saying, he went off thoughtfully to the restaurant where he was accustomed to dine.

Sancho Panza hung on his nail, and stared at the wall. The stable was cold and ghostly, and in the gloom the little squire's face, usually so cheerful, expressed dissatisfaction and alarm. "No, really," he seemed to be saying, "there is nothing gay about this. An actor's life has its disadvantages." In the silence one would have said that he was thinking of the shop, with its rows of puppets hanging on the walls.

Presently a brown rat crept out of the wall, and slid across the floor toward the stage. When he came to Sancho Panza he stopped, and regarded the figure of the squire with admiration. "What do you think?" he asked his wife, who was accompanying him. "There is no use trying to bite it. But on the other hand, merely as a piece of art . . ."

"What a fool you are," she replied angrily; "when I am hungry, do you think I wish to discuss art? You are not a very good provider, because you spend all your time looking at things which are of no use to me."

And she began to gnaw at a piece of leather which was used in the scenery.

"This is more practical," she said.

Upstairs in his room on the top floor of the stable, Christopher Lane sat in front of his desk made out of a soap box. He was tired, and his stomach was empty, but he was happy because he was writing a poem. As he boiled some water over the gas jet, to make tea, he looked out of his window at the west where there was still some light to be seen. His eyes fell upon the black walls of the houses, with their uneven chimney-pots, the sudden edge of the rooftops against the lighter sky, angry and sharp as knives. But he saw in his mind the yellow cliffs of the sea, and ruddier sails returning across the water stained with the descending sun.

"Low in the west," he wrote, "upon the sea's gray stair. . . ."

1923

FROM
THE WOODCUTTER'S HOUSE *

[METABEL MEETS THE LITTLE GREEN MAN]

Metabel had taken a pail of milk to Joseph in the woods, in case he was thirsty. They stood together by a giant pine whose straight dark trunk rose beyond tiptoe reach before it broke into branches. "There's a tree," said Metabel dreamily; "look, Joseph, the way it goes up and up, like a noble king. What does it make you think of?"

"Neat cut wood," said Joseph simply.

"Oh," said Metabel. She looked up at it with pursed lips. Yes, she could see it that way, too . . . just neat cut wood. Poor tree.

All at once Joseph had a lot to say. "That tree," he declared, "says to me, 'You can't cut me down as neat as I can stand here.'" And swinging his axe in a bright circle, he drove the blade into the dark trunk, which shivered with the impact.

"But I wouldn't cut an ash," he said, "not for anything.

"I like to see them grow."

Metabel turned away; it made her dizzy to see trees come down; they came down with such a bump from so high up. "Bring me home some knots for the stove," she said, "and some bark for the smell. . . ."

She went down through the woods toward the house. The light fell green and yellow through the leaves, birds sang in the branches. A small red squirrel scampered up a birch, flirted himself out through the leaves, and leaped with tiny, outstretched claws into another tree; the slim twig bent

* From *The Woodcutter's House* by Robert Nathan, copyright 1927, used by special permission of the publishers, The Bobbs-Merrill Company.

as he fled along the branch, noisy as a waterfall, light as a puff of wind. Underfoot the sapling roots pushed up through the dead pine needles; somewhere water sang in the woods, dropped and tinkled. She raised her arms above her head and danced a few steps down the red pine needles and the moss; she remembered the way she used to dance when she was a child . . . this is the way the wind dances, this is the way a rabbit goes, hop, hop. . . .

And with her arms still over her head, hop she went, right into a little man dressed in green, who was sitting under a wild rose bush, quietly talking to some mice.

"Oh," she said, and stood stock-still, as though, all at once, some one had laid a finger on her heart.

The little green man paid no attention to her; he went on addressing the mice, who listened to him with anxious looks. "My poor friends," he said to them, "it is just as important for snakes to have mice to eat, as it is for mice not to have snakes to eat them. Do you expect me to alter the designs of nature? Go away, please; and if you have to be eaten, do not feel that it is a personal reflection on you in any way."

The mice ran away like black drops of water; sighing, their instructor looked up at Metabel, and shook his head. "Ak," he said, "the little anxious mice."

"I'd be anxious too," said Metabel, "if I were mice."

At this his face took on a more serious expression. "If one must be a mouse," he said, "one may as well be cheerful, and accept it as an accident of nature. The gods cannot change these things, least of all a small god, like me."

Metabel looked at him gravely; in the dim forest light he seemed to her no bigger than she was herself. "I knew you were something queer," she said, "the minute I laid eyes on you. But you don't look like God very much—not the one we had in Barly. I used to see Him in the Bible over to the Widow Sebold's, with a long white beard."

The little green man smiled at her —a friendlier smile, she thought, than any she had ever seen, friendlier than Joseph's even, though it reminded her of Joseph's. "I've never been in Barly," he said; "there is no one there for me to visit. I live up here, on Hemlock, because Joseph lives here. I am very fond of Joseph. He is all I have to be fond of, so far as I can see."

And he added sadly, "I am a very small god."

"Yes, you are," said Metabel critically. And she added at once, for fear she had offended him, "Excuse me."

He looked at her doubtfully, with his head to one side, like a robin. "Did I say I cared?" he demanded. "I do not care at all. I have a very good time. During the day I walk up and down in these quiet woods, and watch Joseph chop down trees. How he handles his axe—never too much, just enough. . . ."

"Still," he added thoughtfully, "one or two more to be fond of would not do me any harm—if only to have something to fall back on in an emergency.

"Supposing I were to lose him?"

And he gave a shudder to think of it.

Her hands clasped, her head bent, Metabel stood before him in the green spring woods; the sun shone in her thrush-colored hair, shadows of leaves floated up and down on her calico dress. "Why are you fond of Joseph?" she asked. "And why haven't you any one else to be fond of?"

The little man waved his hand in the air. "I am fond of him," he said simply, "for the same reason that you are."

"I'm not," said Metabel with surprise.

"I admire him," he continued, "for his good humor. As a matter of fact, that is what I am god of." And he added sturdily, "I am small, but I am unique.

"As for there being any one else to be fond of, that is not something one can pick up anywhere. . . . You were dancing a moment ago with your hands over your head, looking very awkward, but happy. Shall I be fond of you? You are small, too, but lively."

However, Metabel was not paying any attention to what he was saying: she was thinking about Joseph. "You don't think he's trifling?" she asked doubtfully.

The little man drooped; he seemed to grow smaller still. "What," he exclaimed, "do you want him to be a successful woodchopper? Dear me!

"In that case, I do not think I shall be fond of you at all."

"Nobody asked you to," said Metabel. And she added, with red cheeks, "I don't want him to be anything whatever.

"What do I care what he is?" she whispered.

"Oh," said the little man; "ah. Nevertheless you think about him a great deal. And you have even sewed up that hole in your stocking, just above the knee, which might never be seen, but suppose you fell down?"

"Well," said Metabel with a gasp.

The little man wagged a finger at her. "Now you are red as a rose," he declared; "but do not lose your temper."

"Why should I lose my temper," said Metabel loftily, "just because you're so rude and silly?"

The little green man drew himself up, not without dignity. "Your remarks cannot shake my divine good humor;" he said, "because for one thing, I am not obliged to listen to them."

So saying, he made her a polite bow, and went off through the woods, humming a song to himself. Metabel stood still, looking after him with stormy eyes.

"Just the same," she said, but too low for him to hear, "I don't think you're very nice."

And she went home without dancing, to pick some spinach for supper.

1927

LOUIS BROMFIELD
(1896–   )

FROM   *EARLY AUTUMN*

[OLIVIA REVIEWS HER PAST *]

When Olivia first came to the old house as the wife of Anson Pentland, the village of Durham, which lay inland from Pentlands and the sea, had been invisible, lying concealed in a fold of the land which marked the faint beginnings of the New Hampshire mountains. There had been in the view a certain sleepy peacefulness: one knew that in the distant fold of land surmounted by a single white spire there lay a quiet village of white wooden houses built along a single street called High Street that was dappled in summer with the shadows of old elm-trees. In those days it had been a country village, half asleep, with empty shuttered houses here and there falling into slow decay—a village with fewer people in it than there had been a hundred years before. It had stayed thus sleeping for nearly seventy-five years, since the day when a great migration of citizens had robbed it of its sturdiest young people. In the thick grass that surrounded the old meeting-house there lay a marble slab recording the event with an inscription which read:

FROM THIS SPOT ON THE FOURTEENTH DAY OF AUGUST, EIGHTEEN HUNDRED AND EIGHTEEN, THE REVEREND JOSIAH MILFORD, PASTOR OF THIS CHURCH, WITH ONE HUNDRED AND NINETY MEMBERS OF HIS CONGREGATION — MEN, WOMEN AND CHILDREN — SET OUT, SECURE IN THEIR FAITH IN ALMIGHTY GOD, TO ESTABLISH HIS WILL AND POWER IN THE WILDERNESS OF THE WESTERN RESERVE.

Beneath the inscription were cut the names of those families who had made the journey to found a new town which had since surpassed sleepy Durham a hundred times in wealth and prosperity. There was no Pentland name among them, for the Pentlands had been rich even in the year eighteen hundred and eighteen, and lived in winter in Boston and in summer at Durham, on the land claimed from the wilderness by the first of the family.

From that day until the mills came to Durham the village sank slowly into a kind of lethargy, and the church itself, robbed of its strength,

died presently and was changed into a dusty museum filled with homely early American furniture and spinning-wheels—a place seldom visited by any one and painted grudgingly every five years by the town council because it was popularly considered an historical monument. The Pentland family long ago had filtered away into the cold faith of the Unitarians or the more compromising and easy creeds of the Episcopal church.

But now, nearly twenty years after Olivia had come to Pentlands, the village was alive again, so alive that it had overflowed its little fold in the land and was streaming down the hill on the side next to the sea in straight, plain columns of ugly stucco bungalows, each filled with its little family of Polish mill-workers. And in the town, across High Street from the white-spired old meeting-house, there stood a new church, built of stucco and green-painted wood and dedicated to the great Church of Rome. In the old wooden houses along High Street there still lingered remnants of the old families . . . old Mrs. Featherstone, who did washing to support four sickly grandchildren who ought never to have been born; Miss Haddon, a queer old woman who wore a black cape and lived on a dole from old John Pentland as a remote cousin of the family; Harry Peckham, the village carpenter; old Mrs. Malson, living alone in a damp, gaunt and beautiful old house filled with bits of jade and ivory brought back from China by her grandfather's clippers; Miss Murgatroyd, who had long since turned her bullfinch house into a shabby tea-room. They remained here and there, a few worn and shabby-genteel descendants of those first settlers who had come into the country with the Pentlands.

But the mills had changed everything, the mills which poured wealth into the pockets of a dozen rich families who lived in summer within a few miles of Durham.

Even the countryside itself had changed. There were no longer any of the old New Englanders in possession of the land. Sometimes in riding along the lanes one encountered a thin, silly-faced remnant of the race sitting on a stone wall chewing a bit of grass; but that was all: the others had been swallowed up long ago in the mills of Salem and Lynn or died away, from too much inbreeding and too little nourishment. The few farms that remained fell into the hands of Poles and Czechs, solid, square people who were a little pagan in their closeness to the earth and the animals which surrounded them, sturdy people, not too moral, who wrought wonders with the barren, stony earth of New England and stood behind their walls staring wide-eyed while the grand people like the Pentlands rode by in pink coats surrounded by the waving nervous tails of foxhounds. And, one by one, other old farms were being turned back into a wilderness once more so that there would be plenty of room for the horses and hounds to run after foxes and bags of aniseed.

It had all changed enormously. From the upper windows of the big Georgian brick house where the Pentlands lived, one could see the record of all the changes. The windows commanded a wide view of a landscape composed of grubby meadows and stone walls, thickets of pine and white birches, marshes, and a winding sluggish brown river. Sometimes in the late autumn the deer wandered down from the mountains of New Hampshire to spoil the fox-hunting by leading the hounds astray after game that was far too fleet for them.

And nearer at hand, nestled within a turn of the river, lay the land where Sabine Callender had been born and had lived until she was a grown woman—the land which she had sold carelessly to O'Hara, an Irish politician and a Roman Catholic, come up from nowhere to take possession of it, to clip its hedges, repair its sagging walls, paint its old buildings and put up gates and fences that were too shiny and new. Indeed, he had done it so thoroughly and so well that the whole place had a little the air of a suburban real estate development. And now Sabine had returned to spend the summer in one of his houses and to be very friendly with him in the face of Aunt Cassie and Anson Pentland, and a score of others like them.

Olivia knew this wide and somberly beautiful landscape, every stick and stone of it, from the perilous gravel-pit, half-hidden by its fringe of elder-bushes, to the black pine copse where Higgins had discovered only a day or two before a new litter of foxes. She knew it on gray days when it was cold and depressing, on those bright, terribly clear New England days when every twig and leaf seemed outlined by light, and on those damp, cold days when a gray fog swept in across the marshes from the sea to envelop all the countryside in gray darkness. It was a hard, uncompromising, stony country that was never too cheerful.

It was a country, too, which gave her an old feeling of loneliness . . . a feeling which, strangely enough, seemed to increase rather than diminish as the years passed. She had never accustomed herself to its occasional dreariness. In the beginning, a long while ago, it had seemed to her green and peaceful and full of quiet, a place where she might find rest and peace . . . but she had come long since to see it as it was, as Sabine had seen it while she stood in the window of the writing-room, frightened by the sudden queer apparition of the little groom—a country beautiful, hard and cold, and a little barren.

There were times when the memories of Olivia's youth seemed to sharpen suddenly and sweep in upon her, overwhelming all sense of the present, times when she wanted suddenly and fiercely to step back into that far-off past which had seemed then an unhappy thing; and these were the times when she felt most lonely, the times when she knew how completely, with the passing of years, she had drawn into herself; it was a process of protection like a tortoise drawing in its head. And all the while, in spite of the smiles and the politeness and the too facile amiability, she felt that she was really a stranger at Pentlands, that there were certain walls and barriers which she could never break down, past which she could never penetrate, certain faiths in which it was impossible for her to believe.

It was difficult now for her to remember very clearly what had happened before she came to Durham; it all seemed lost, confused, buried beneath the weight of her devotion to the vast family monument of the Pentlands. She had forgotten the names of people and places and confused the days and the years. At times it was difficult for her to remember the endless confusing voyages back and forth across the Atlantic and the vast, impersonal, vacuous hotels which had followed each other in the bleak and unreal procession of her childhood.

She could remember with a certain pitiful clarity two happy years spent at the school in Saint-Cloud, where for months at a time she had lived in a single room which she might call her own, where she had rested, free from the terror of hearing her mother say, "We must pack to-day. We are leaving to-morrow for St. Petersburg or London or San Remo or Cairo. . . ."

She could scarcely remember at all the immense house of chocolate-colored stone fitted with fantastic turrets and balconies that overlooked Lake Michigan. It had been sold and torn down long ago, destroyed like all else that belonged to the far-off past. She could not remember the father who had died when she was three; but of him there remained at least a yellowing photograph of a great, handsome, brawny man with a humorous Scotch-Irish face, who had died at the moment when his name was coming to be known everywhere as a power in Washington. No, nothing remained of him save the old photograph, and the tenuous, mocking little smile which had come down to her, the way she had of saying, "Yes! Yes!" pleasantly when she meant to act in quite the contrary fashion.

There were times when the memory of her own mother became vague and fantastic, as if she had been no more than a figure out of some absurd photograph of the early nineteen hundreds . . . the figure of a pretty woman, dressed fashionably in clothes that flowed away in both directions, from a wasp waist. It was like a figure out of one of those old photographs which one views with a kind of melancholy amusement. She remembered a vain, rather selfish and pretty woman, fond of flattery, who had been shrewd enough never to marry any one of those gallant dark gentlemen with high-sounding titles who came to call at the eternal changeless hotel sitting-room, to take her out to garden parties and fêtes and races. And always in the background of the memory there was the figure of a dark little girl, overflowing with spirits and a hunger for friends, who was left behind to amuse herself by walking out with the Swiss governess, to make friends among the children she encountered in the parks or on the beaches and the boulevards of whatever European city her mother was visiting at the moment . . . friends whom she saw to-day and who were vanished to-morrow never to be seen again. Her mother, she saw now, belonged to the America of the nineties. She saw her now less as a real person than a character out of a novel by Mrs. Wharton.

But she had never remarried; she had remained the rich, pretty Mrs. McConnel of Chicago until that tragic day (the clearest of all Olivia's memories and the most terrible) when she had died of fever abruptly in a remote and squalid Italian village, with only her daughter (a girl of seventeen), a quack doctor and the Russian driver of her motor to care for her.

The procession of confused and not-too-cheerful memories came to a climax in a gloomy, red brick house off Washington Square, where she had gone as an orphan to live with a rigid, bejetted, maternal aunt who had believed that the whole world revolved about Lenox, the Hudson River Valley and Washington Square —an aunt who had never spoken to Olivia's father because she, like Anson and Aunt Cassie, had a prejudice against Irishmen who appeared out of nowhere, engaging, full of life and high spirits.

So at eighteen she had found herself alone in the world save for one bejetted aunt, with no friends save those she had picked up as a child

on beaches and promenades, whose names she could no longer even remember. And the only fixed world she knew was the world of the aunt who talked incessantly of the plush, camphor-smelling splendor of a New York which no longer existed.

Olivia saw it all clearly now. She saw why it was that when Anson Pentland came one night to call upon her aunt she had thought him an elegant and fascinating man whose presence at dinner had the power of transforming the solid walnut and mahogany dining-room into a brilliant place. He was what girls called "an older man," and he had flattered her by his politeness and attentions. He had even taken her, chaperoned by the aunt, to see a performance of "The City," little knowing that the indecorousness to be unfolded there would force them to leave before the play was over. They had gone on a Thursday evening (she could even remember the very day) and she still smiled at the memory of their belief that a girl who had spent all her life in the corridors of European hotels should not know what the play was about.

And then it had all ended by her being asked to Pentlands for a visit . . . to Pentlands, where she had come upon a world such as she had never known before, a world green and peaceful and secure, where every one was elaborately kind to her for reasons that she never learned until long afterward. They never even told her the truth about Anson's mother, the old woman who lived in solitude in the north wing. She was, they said, too ill at the moment to see any one. Pentlands, in that far-off day, had seemed to the tired, friendless girl like some vast, soft green bed where she could fling herself down and rest forever, a world where she could make friends and send down roots that would hold her secure for all time. To a hotel child Pentlands was a paradise; so when Anson Pentland asked her to marry him, she accepted him because she did not find him actually repulsive.

And now, after all those years, it was spring again . . . spring as when she had come to Pentlands for the first time, and she was thirty-nine years old and still young; only everything had changed.

Bit by bit, in the years that followed the birth of Sybil and then of Jack, the whole picture of the life at Pentlands and in the brownstone house on Beacon Street had come to assume a pattern, to take form out of the first confused and misty impressions, so that, looking back upon it, she was beginning to understand it all with the chill clarity of disillusion.

She saw herself as a shy young girl to whom they had all been elaborately kind because it was so necessary for Anson to have a wife and produce an heir. . . . Anson, the last male descendant of such a glorious family. ("The Pentland Family and the Massachusetts Bay Colony.") She saw herself as they must have seen her . . . a pretty young girl, disarmed by their kindness, who was not known in their world but was at least charming and a lady and quite rich. (She knew now how much the money must have counted with Aunt Cassie.) And she saw Anson now, across all the expanse of years, not as a Prince Charming come to rescue her from an ogre aunt, but as he had really been . . . a rather anemic man, past thirty, of an appalling propriety. (There was a bitter humor in the memories of his timid advances toward her, of all the distaste with which he aproached the details of marriage . . . a humor which she had come to understand

fully only as she grew older and wiser in the ways of the world.) Looking back, she saw him as a man who had tried again and again to marry young women he had known all his life and who had failed because somehow he had gained a mysterious reputation for being a bore . . . a young man who, left to himself, would never have approached any woman, and gone to the grave as virginal as he had been born.

She saw now that he had never been even in the slightest in love with her. He had married her only because he got no peace from all the others, both the living and the dead, who in such a strange fashion seemed also to live at Pentlands. It was Aunt Cassie and even poor silly Miss Peavey and powerful old John Pentland and the cousins and all those dead hanging in neat rows in the hall who had married her. Anson had only been an instrument; and even in the most bitter moments she felt strangely sorry for him, because he, too, had had all his life ruined.

And so, slowly during all those long years, the pretty, shy, unknown Olivia McConnel, whose father was a Democratic politician out of Chicago, had turned into this puzzled, sometimes unhappy woman, the outsider, who had come in some mysterious fashion to be the one upon whom all of them leaned for strength. * * *

1926

PEARL S. BUCK
(1892–   )

THE ENEMY *

Dr. Sadao Hoki's house was built

* From *Far and Near* by Pearl S. Buck. Copyright, 1942–7 by Pearl S. Buck. Published by The John Day Company. By arrangement with the author's agent, David Lloyd, 49 East 34th Street, New York 16, New York.

on a spot of the Japanese coast where as a little boy he had often played. The low square stone house was set upon rocks well above a narrow beach that was outlined with bent pines. As a boy Sadao had climbed the pines, supporting himself on his bare feet, as he had seen men do in the South Seas when they climbed for coconuts. His father had taken him often to the islands of those seas, and never had he failed to say to the little grave boy at his side, "Those islands yonder, they are the stepping stones to the future for Japan."

"Where shall we step from them?" Sadao had asked seriously.

"Who knows?" his father had answered. "Who can limit our future? It depends on what we make it."

Sadao had taken this into his mind as he did everything his father said, his father who never joked or played with him but who spent infinite pains upon him who was his only son. Sadao knew that his education was his father's chief concern. For this reason he had been sent at twenty-two to America to learn all that could be learned of surgery and medicine. He had come back at thirty and before his father died he had seen Sadao become famous not only as a surgeon but as a scientist. Because he was now perfecting a discovery which would render wounds entirely clean he had not been sent abroad with the troops. Also, he knew, there was some slight danger that the old General might need an operation for a condition for which he was now being treated medically, and for this possibility Sadao was being kept in Japan.

Clouds were rising from the ocean now. The unexpected warmth of the past few days had at night drawn heavy fog from the cold waves. Sadao watched mists hide outlines of a little island near the shore and then come creeping up the beach below the house, wreathing around the pines. In a few minutes fog would be wrapped about the house too. Then he would go into the room where Hana, his wife, would be waiting for him with the two children.

But at this moment the door opened and she looked out, a dark-blue woolen *haori* over her kimono. She came to him affectionately and put her arm through his as he stood, smiled and said nothing. He had met Hana in America, but he had waited to fall in love with her until he was sure she was Japanese. His father would never have received her unless she had been pure in her race. He wondered often whom he would have married if he had not met Hana, and by what luck he had found her in the most casual way, by chance literally, at an American professor's house. The professor and his wife had been kind people, anxious to do something for their few foreign students, and the students, though bored, had accepted this kindness. Sadao had often told Hana how nearly he had not gone to Professor Harley's house that night —the rooms were so small, the food so bad, the professor's wife so voluble. But he had gone and there he had found Hana, a new student, and had felt he would love her if it were at all possible.

Now he felt her hand on his arm and was aware of the pleasure it gave him, even though they had been married years enough to have the two children. For they had not married heedlessly in America. They had finished their work at school and had come home to Japan, and when his father had seen her the marriage had been arranged in the old Japanese way, although Sadao and Hana had talked everything over beforehand.

They were perfectly happy. She laid her cheek against his arm.

It was at this moment that both of them saw something black come out of the mists. It was a man. He was flung up out of the ocean—flung, it seemed, to his feet by a breaker. He staggered a few steps, his body outlined against the mist, his arms above his head. Then the curled mists hid him again.

"Who is that?" Hana cried. She dropped Sadao's arm and they both leaned over the railing of the veranda. Now they saw him again. The man was on his hands and knees crawling. Then they saw him fall on his face and lie there.

"A fisherman perhaps," Sadao said, "washed from his boat." He ran quickly down the steps and behind him Hana came, her wide sleeves flying. A mile or two away on either side there were fishing villages, but here was only the bare and lonely coast, dangerous with rocks. The surf beyond the beach was spiked with rocks. Somehow the man had managed to come through them—he must be badly torn.

They saw when they came toward him that indeed it was so. The sand on one side of him had already a stain of red soaking through.

"He is wounded," Sadao exclaimed. He made haste to the man, who lay motionless, his face in the sand. An old cap stuck to his head soaked with sea water. He was in wet rags of garments. Sadao stooped, Hana at his side, and turned the man's head. They saw the face.

"A white man!" Hana whispered.

Yes, it was a white man. The wet cap fell away and there was his wet yellow hair, long, as though for many weeks it had not been cut, and upon his young and tortured face was a rough yellow beard. He was uncon-

scious and knew nothing that they did to him.

Now Sadao remembered the wound, and with his expert fingers he began to search for it. Blood flowed freshly at his touch. On the right side of his lower back Sadao saw that a gun wound had been reopened. The flesh was blackened with powder. Sometime, not many days ago, the man had been shot and had not been tended. It was bad chance that the rock had struck the wound.

"Oh, how he is bleeding!" Hana whispered again in a solemn voice. The mists screened them now completely, and at this time of day no one came by. The fishermen had gone home and even the chance beachcombers would have considered the day at an end.

"What shall we do with this man?" Sadao muttered. But his trained hands seemed of their own will to be doing what they could to stanch the fearful bleeding. He packed the wound with the sea moss that strewed the beach. The man moaned with pain in his stupor but he did not awaken.

"The best thing that we could do would be to put him back in the sea," Sadao said, answering himself.

Now that the bleeding was stopped for the moment he stood up and dusted the sand from his hands.

"Yes, undoubtedly that would be best," Hana said steadily. But she continued to stare down at the motionless man.

"If we sheltered a white man in our house we should be arrested and if we turned him over as a prisoner, he would certainly die," Sadao said.

"The kindest thing would be to put him back into the sea," Hana said. But neither of them moved. They were staring with a curious repulsion upon the inert figure.

"What is he?" Hana whispered.

"There is something about him that looks American," Sadao said. He took up the battered cap. Yes, there, almost gone, was the faint lettering. "A sailor," he said, "from an American warship." He spelled it out: "U. S. Navy." The man was a prisoner of war!

"He has escaped," Hana cried softly, "and that is why he is wounded."

"In the back," Sadao agreed.

They hesitated, looking at each other. Then Hana said with resolution:

"Come, are we able to put him back into the sea?"

"If I am able, are you?" Sadao asked.

"No," Hana said. "But if you can do it alone . . ."

Sadao hesitated again. "The strange thing is," he said, "that if the man were whole I could turn him over to the police without difficulty. I care nothing for him. He is my enemy. All Americans are my enemy. And he is only a common fellow. You see how foolish his face is. But since he is wounded . . ."

"You also cannot throw him back to the sea," Hana said. "Then there is only one thing to do. We must carry him into the house."

"But the servants?" Sadao inquired.

"We must simply tell them that we intend to give him to the police—as indeed we must, Sadao. We must think of the children and your position. It would endanger all of us if we did not give this man over as a prisoner of war."

"Certainly," Sadao agreed. "I would not think of doing anything else."

Thus agreed, together they lifted the man. He was very light, like a fowl that has been half-starved for a long time until it is only feathers and skeleton. So, his arms hanging, they carried him up the steps and into the side door of the house. This door opened into a passage and down the passage they carried the man toward an empty bedroom. It had been the bedroom of Sadao's father and since his death it had not been used. They laid the man on the deeply matted floor. Everything here had been Japanese to please the old man, who would never in his own home sit on a chair or sleep in a foreign bed. Hana went to the wall cupboards and slid back a door and took out a soft quilt. She hesitated. The quilt was covered with flowered silk and the lining was pure white silk.

"He is so dirty," she murmured in distress.

"Yes, he had better be washed," Sadao agreed. "If you will fetch hot water I will wash him."

"I cannot bear for you to touch him," she said. "We shall have to tell the servants he is here. I will tell Yumi now. She can leave the children for a few minutes and she can wash him."

Sadao considered a moment. "Let it be so," he agreed. "You tell Yumi and I will tell the others."

But the utter pallor of the man's unconscious face moved him first to stoop and feel his pulse. It was faint but it was there. He put his hand against the man's cold breast. The heart too was yet alive.

"He will die unless he is operated on," Sadao said, considering. "The question is whether he will not die anyway."

Hana cried out in fear. "Don't try to save him! What if he should live?"

"What if he should die?" Sadao replied. He stood gazing down on the motionless man. This man must have extraordinary vitality or he would have been dead by now. But then he was very young—perhaps not yet twenty-five.

"You mean die from the operation?" Hana asked.

"Yes," Sadao said.

Hana considered this doubtfully, and when she did not answer Sadao turned away. "At any rate something must be done with him," he said, "and first he must be washed." He went quickly out of the room and Hana came behind him. She did not wish to be left alone with the white man. He was the first she had seen since she left America and now he seemed to have nothing to do with those whom she had known there. Here he was her enemy, a menace, living or dead.

She turned to the nursery and called, "Yumi!"

But the children heard her voice and she had to go in for a moment and smile at them and play with the baby boy, now nearly three months old.

Over the baby's soft black hair she motioned with her mouth, "Yumi—come with me!"

"I will put the baby to bed," Yumi replied. "He is ready."

She went with Yumi into the bedroom next to the nursery and stood with the boy in her arms while Yumi spread the sleeping quilts on the floor and laid the baby between them.

Then Hana led the way quickly and softly to the kitchen. The two servants were frightened at what their master had just told them. The old gardener who was also a house servant pulled the few hairs on his upper lip.

"The master ought not to heal the wound of this white man," he said bluntly to Hana. "The white man ought to die. First he was shot. Then the sea caught him and wounded him with her rocks. If the master heals what the gun did and what the sea did they will take revenge on us."

"I will tell him what you say," Hana replied courteously. But she herself was also frightened, although she was not superstitious as the old man was. Could it ever be well to help an enemy? Nevertheless she told Yumi to fetch the hot water and bring it to the room where the white man was.

She went ahead and slid back the partitions. Sadao was not yet there. Yumi, following, put down her wooden bucket. Then she went over to the white man. When she saw him her thick lips folded themselves into stubbornness. "I have never washed a white man," she said, "and I will not wash so dirty a one now."

Hana cried at her severely, "You will do what your master commands you!"

"My master ought not to command me to wash the enemy," Yumi said stubbornly.

There was so fierce a look of resistance upon Yumi's round dull face that Hana felt unreasonably afraid. After all, if the servants should report something that was not as it happened?

"Very well," she said with dignity. "You understand we only want to bring him to his senses so that we can turn him over as a prisoner?"

"I will have nothing to do with it," Yumi said. "I am a poor person and it is not my business."

"Then please," Hana said gently, "return to your own work."

At once Yumi left the room. But this left Hana with the white man alone. She might have been too afraid to stay had not her anger at Yumi's stubbornness now sustained her.

"Stupid Yumi," she muttered fiercely. "Is this anything but a man? And a wounded helpless man!"

In the conviction of her own superiority she bent impulsively and untied the knotted rags that kept the white man covered. When she had his breast bare she dipped the small clean towel that Yumi had brought into the steaming hot water and washed his face carefully. The man's skin, though rough with exposure, was of a fine texture and must have been very blond when he was a child.

While she was thinking these thoughts, though not really liking the man better now that he was no longer a child, she kept on washing him until his upper body was quite clean. But she dared not turn him over. Where was Sadao? Now her anger was ebbing and she was anxious again and she rose, wiping her hands on the wrung towel. Then lest the man be chilled she put the quilt over him.

"Sadao!" she called softly.

He had been about to come in when she called. His hand had been on the door and now he opened it. She saw that he had brought his surgeon's emergency bag and that he wore his surgeon's coat.

"You have decided to operate!" she cried.

"Yes," he said shortly. He turned his back to her and unfolded a sterilized towel upon the floor of the *takonoma* alcove, and put his instruments out upon it.

"Fetch towels," he said.

She went obediently, but how anxious now, to the linen shelves and took out the towels. There ought also to be old pieces of matting so that the blood would not ruin the fine floor covering. She went out to the back veranda where the gardener kept strips of matting with which to protect delicate shrubs on cold nights and took an armful of them.

But when she went back into the room, she saw this was useless. The blood had already soaked through the packing in the man's wound and had ruined the mat under him.

"Oh, the mat!" she cried.

"Yes, it is ruined," Sadao replied, as though he did not care. "Help me to turn him," he commanded her.

She obeyed him without a word, and he began to wash the man's back carefully.

"Yumi would not wash him," she said.

"Did you wash him then?" Sadao asked, not stopping for a moment his swift concise movements.

"Yes," she said.

He did not seem to hear her. But she was used to his absorption when he was at work. She wondered for a moment if it mattered to him what was the body upon which he worked so long as it was for the work he did so excellently.

"You will have to give the anesthetic if he needs it," he said.

"I?" she repeated blankly. "But never have I!"

"It is easy enough," he said impatiently.

He was taking out the packing now and the blood began to flow more quickly. He peered into the wound with the bright surgeon's light fastened on his forehead. "The bullet is still there," he said with cool interest. "Now I wonder how deep this rock wound is. If it is not too deep it may be that I can get the bullet. But the bleeding is not superficial. He has lost much blood."

At this moment Hana choked. He looked up and saw her face the color of sulphur.

"Don't faint," he said sharply. He did not put down his exploring instrument. "If I stop now the man will surely die." She clapped her hands to her mouth and leaped up and ran out of the room. Outside in the garden he heard her retching. But he went on with his work.

"It will be better for her to empty her stomach," he thought. He had forgotten that of course she had never seen an operation. But her distress and his inability to go to her at once made him impatient and irritable with this man who lay like dead under his knife.

"This man," he thought, "there is no reason under heaven why he should live."

Unconsciously this thought made him ruthless and he proceeded swiftly. In his dream the man moaned but Sadao paid no heed except to mutter at him.

"Groan," he muttered, "groan if you like. I am not doing this for my own pleasure. In fact, I do not know why I am doing it."

The door opened and there was Hana again. She had not stopped even to smooth back her hair.

"Where is the anesthetic?" she asked in a clear voice.

Sadao motioned with his chin. "It is as well that you came back," he said. "This fellow is beginning to stir."

She had the bottle and some cotton in her hand.

"But how shall I do it?" she asked.

"Simply saturate the cotton and hold it near his nostrils," Sadao replied without delaying for one moment the intricate detail of his work. "When he breathes badly move it away a little."

She crouched close to the sleeping face of the young American. It was a piteously thin face, she thought, and the lips were twisted. The man was suffering whether he knew it or not. Watching him, she wondered if the stories they heard sometimes of the sufferings of prisoners were true. They came like flickers of rumor, told by word of mouth and always contra-dicted. In the newspapers the reports were always that wherever the Japanese armies went the people received them gladly, with cries of joy at their liberation. But sometimes she remembered such men as General Takima, who at home beat his wife cruelly, though no one mentioned it now that he had fought so victorious a battle in Manchuria. If a man like that could be so cruel to a woman in his power, would he not be cruel to one like this for instance?

She hoped anxiously that this young man had not been tortured. It was at this moment that she observed deep red scars on his neck, just under the ear. "Those scars," she murmured, lifting her eyes to Sadao.

But he did not answer. At this moment he felt the tip of his instrument strike against something hard, dangerously near the kidney. All thought left him. He felt only the purest pleasure. He probed with his fingers, delicately, familiar with every atom of this human body. His old American professor of anatomy had seen to that knowledge. "Ignorance of the human body is the surgeon's cardinal sin, sirs!" he had thundered at his classes year after year. "To operate without as complete knowledge of the body as if you had made it—anything less than that is murder."

"It is not quite at the kidney, my friend," Sadao murmured. It was his habit to murmur to the patient when he forgot himself in an operation. "My friend," he always called his patients and so now he did, forgetting that this was his enemy.

Then quickly, with the cleanest and most precise of incisions, the bullet was out. The man quivered but he was still unconscious. Nevertheless he muttered a few English words.

"Guts," he muttered, choking. "They got . . . my guts . . . ."

"Sadao!" Hana cried sharply.

"Hush," Sadao said.

The man sank again into silence so profound that Sadao took up his wrist, hating the touch of it. Yes, there was still a pulse so faint, so feeble, but enough, if he wanted the man to live, to give hope.

"But certainly I do not want this man to live," he thought.

"No more anesthetic," he told Hana.

He turned as swiftly as though he had never paused and from his medicines he chose a small vial and from it filled a hypodermic and thrust it into the patient's left arm. Then, putting down the needle, he took the man's wrist again. The pulse under his fingers fluttered once or twice and then grew stronger.

"This man will live in spite of all," he said to Hana and sighed.

The young man woke, so weak, his blue eyes so terrified when he perceived where he was, that Hana felt compelled to apology. She served him herself, for none of the servants would enter the room.

When she came in the first time she saw him summon his strength to be prepared for some fearful thing.

"Don't be afraid," she begged him softly.

"How come . . . you speak English . . ." he gasped.

"I was a long time in America," she replied.

She saw that he wanted to reply to that but he could not, and so she knelt and fed him gently from the porcelain spoon. He ate unwillingly, but still he ate.

"Now you will soon be strong," she said, not liking him and yet moved to comfort him.

He did not answer.

When Sadao came in the third day after the operation he found the young man sitting up, his face bloodless with the effort.

"Lie down," Sadao cried. "Do you want to die?"

He forced the man down gently and strongly and examined the wound. "You may kill yourself if you do this sort of thing," he scolded.

"What are you going to do with me?" the boy muttered. He looked just now barely seventeen. "Are you going to hand me over?"

For a moment Sadao did not answer. He finished his examination and then pulled the silk quilt over the man.

"I do not know myself what I shall do with you," he said. "I ought of course to give you to the police. You are a prisoner of war—no, do not tell me anything." He put up his hand as he saw the young man about to speak. "Do not even tell me your name unless I ask it."

They looked at each other for a moment, and then the young man closed his eyes and turned his face to the wall.

"Okay," he whispered, his mouth a bitter line.

Outside the door Hana was waiting for Sadao. He saw at once that she was in trouble.

"Sadao, Yumi tells me the servants feel they cannot stay if we hide this man here any more," she said. "She tells me that they are saying that you and I were so long in America that we have forgotten to think of our own country first. They think we like Americans."

"It is not true," Sadao said harshly, "Americans are our enemies. But I have been trained not to let a man die if I can help it."

"The servants cannot understand that," she said anxiously.

"No," he agreed.

Neither seemed able to say more, and somehow the household dragged on. The servants grew daily more watchful. Their courtesy was as careful as ever, but their eyes were cold upon the pair to whom they were hired.

"It is clear what our master ought to do," the old gardener said one morning. He had worked with flowers all his life, and had been a specialist too in moss. For Sadao's father he had made one of the finest moss gardens in Japan, sweeping the bright green carpet constantly so that not a leaf or a pine needle marred the velvet of its surface. "My old master's son knows very well what he ought to do," he now said, pinching a bud from a bush as he spoke. "When the man was so near death why did he not let him bleed?"

"That young master is so proud of his skill to save life that he saves any life," the cook said contemptuously. She split a fowl's neck skilfully and held the fluttering bird and let its blood flow into the roots of a wistaria vine. Blood is the best of fertilizers, and the old gardener would not let her waste a drop of it.

"It is the children of whom we must think," Yumi said sadly. "What will be their fate if their father is condemned as a traitor?"

They did not try to hide what they said from the ears of Hana as she stood arranging the day's flowers in the veranda near by, and she knew they spoke on purpose that she might hear. That they were right she knew too in most of her being. But there was another part of her which she herself could not understand. It was not sentimental liking of the prisoner. She had come to think of him as a prisoner. She had not liked him even yesterday when he had said in his impulsive way, "Anyway, let me tell you that my name is Tom." She had only bowed her little distant bow. She saw hurt in his eyes but she did not wish to assuage it. Indeed, he was a great trouble in this house.

As for Sadao, every day he examined the wound carefully. The last stitches had been pulled out this morning, and the young man would in a fortnight be nearly as well as ever. Sadao went back to his office and carefully typed a letter to the chief of police reporting the whole matter. "On the twenty-first day of February an escaped prisoner was washed up on the shore in front of my house." So far he typed and then he opened a secret drawer of his desk and put the unfinished report into it.

On the seventh day after that two things happened. In the morning the servants left together, their belongings tied in large square cotton kerchiefs. When Hana got up in the morning nothing was done, the house not cleaned and the food not prepared, and she knew what it meant. She was dismayed and even terrified, but her pride as a mistress would not allow her to show it. Instead, she inclined her head gracefully when they appeared before her in the kitchen, and she paid them off and thanked them for all that they had done for her. They were crying, but she did not cry. The cook and the gardener had served Sadao since he was a little boy in his father's house, and Yumi cried because of the children. She was so grieving that after she had gone she ran back to Hana.

"If the baby misses me too much to-night send for me. I am going to my own house and you know where it is."

"Thank you," Hana said smiling. But she told herself she would not send for Yumi however the baby cried.

She made the breakfast and Sadao helped with the children. Neither of them spoke of the servants beyond the fact that they were gone. But after Hana had taken morning food to the prisoner she came back to Sadao.

"Why is it we cannot see clearly what we ought to do?" she asked him. "Even the servants see more clearly than we do. Why are we different from other Japanese?"

Sadao did not answer. But a little later he went into the room where the prisoner was and said brusquely, "To-day you may get up on your feet. I want you to stay up only five minutes at a time. To-morrow you may try it twice as long. It would be well that you get back your strength as quickly as possible."

He saw the flicker of terror on the young face that was still very pale.

"Okay," the boy murmured. Evidently he was determined to say more. "I feel I ought to thank you, doctor, for having saved my life."

"Don't thank me too early," Sadao said coldly. He saw the flicker of terror again in the boy's eyes—terror as unmistakable as an animal's. The scars on his neck were crimson for a moment. Those scars! What were they? Sadao did not ask.

In the afternoon the second thing happened. Hana, working hard on unaccustomed labor, saw a messenger come to the door in official uniform. Her hands went weak and she could not draw her breath. The servants must have told already. She ran to Sadao, gasping, unable to utter a word. But by then the messenger had simply followed her through the garden and there he stood. She pointed at him helplessly.

Sadao looked up from his book. He was in his office, the outer partition of which was thrown open to the garden for the southern sunshine.

"What is it?" he asked the messenger and then he rose, seeing the man's uniform.

"You are to come to the palace," the man said, "the old General is in pain again."

"Oh," Hana breathed, "is that all?"

"All?" the messenger exclaimed. "Is it not enough?"

"Indeed it is," she replied. "I am very sorry."

When Sadao came to say good-bye she was in the kitchen, but doing nothing. The children were asleep and she sat merely resting for a moment, more exhausted from her fright than from work.

"I thought they had come to arrest you," she said.

He gazed down into her anxious eyes. "I must get rid of this man for your sake," he said in distress. "Somehow I must get rid of him."

"Of course," the General said weakly, "I understand fully. But that is because I once took a degree in Princeton. So few Japanese have."

"I care nothing for the man, Excellency," Sadao said, "but having operated on him with such success . . ."

"Yes, yes," the General said. "It only makes me feel you more indispensable to me. Evidently you can save anyone—you are so skilled. You say you think I can stand one more such attack as I have had today?"

"Not more than one," Sadao said.

"Then certainly I can allow nothing to happen to you," the General said with anxiety. His long pale Japanese face became expressionless, which meant that he was in deep thought. "You cannot be arrested," the General said, closing his eyes. "Suppose you were condemned to death and the next day I had to have my operation?"

"There are other surgeons, Excellency," Sadao suggested.

"None I trust," the General replied. "The best ones have been trained by Germans and would consider the operation successful even if I died. I do not care for their point of view." He sighed. "It seems a pity that we cannot better combine the German ruthlessness with the American sentimentality. Then you could turn your prisoner over to execution and yet I could be sure you would not murder me while I was unconscious." The General laughed. He had an unusual sense of humor. "As a Japanese, could you not combine these two foreign elements?" he asked.

Sadao smiled. "I am not quite sure," he said, "but for your sake I would be willing to try, Excellency."

The General shook his head. "I had rather not be the test case," he said. He felt suddenly weak and overwhelmed with the cares of his life as an official in times such as these when repeated victory brought great responsibilities all over the south Pacific. "It is very unfortunate that this man should have washed up on your doorstep," he said irritably.

"I feel it so myself," Sadao said gently.

"It would be best if he could be quietly killed," the General said. "Not by you, but by someone who does not know him. I have my own private assassins. Suppose I send two of them to your house tonight—or better, any night. You need know nothing about it. It is now warm—what would be more natural than that you should leave the outer partition of the white man's room open to the garden while he sleeps?"

"Certainly it would be very natu-

ral," Sadao agreed. "In fact, it is so left open every night."

"Good," the General said, yawning. "They are very capable assassins—they make no noise and they know the trick of inward bleeding. If you like I can even have them remove the body."

Sadao considered. "That perhaps would be best, Excellency," he agreed, thinking of Hana.

He left the General's presence then and went home, thinking over the plan. In this way the whole thing would be taken out of his hands. He would tell Hana nothing, since she would be timid at the idea of assassins in the house, and yet certainly such persons were essential in an absolute state such as Japan was. How else could rulers deal with those who opposed them?

He refused to allow anything but reason to be the atmosphere of his mind as he went into the room where the American was in bed. But as he opened the door, to his surprise he found the young man out of bed, and preparing to go into the garden.

"What is this!" he exclaimed. "Who gave you permission to leave your room?"

"I'm not used to waiting for permission," Tom said gaily. "Gosh, I feel pretty good again! But will the muscles on this side always feel stiff?"

"Is it so?" Sadao inquired surprised. He forgot all else. "Now I thought I had provided against that," he murmured. He lifted the edge of the man's shirt and gazed at the healing scar. "Massage may do it," he said, "if exercise does not."

"It won't bother me much," the young man said. His young face was gaunt under the stubbly blond beard. "Say, doctor, I've got something I want to say to you. If I hadn't met a

Jap like you—well, I wouldn't be alive to-day. I know that."

Sadao bowed but he could not speak.

"Sure, I know that," Tom went on warmly. His big thin hands gripping a chair were white at the knuckles. "I guess if all the Japs were like you there wouldn't have been a war."

"Perhaps," Sadao said with difficulty. "And now I think you had better go back to bed."

He helped the boy back into bed and then bowed. "Good night," he said.

Sadao slept badly that night. Time and time again he woke, thinking he heard the rustling of footsteps, the sound of a twig broken or a stone displaced in the garden—a noise such as men might make who carried a burden.

The next morning he made the excuse to go first into the guest room. If the American were gone he then could simply tell Hana that so the General had directed. But when he opened the door he saw at once that it was not last night. There on the pillow was the shaggy blond head. He could hear the peaceful breathing of sleep and he closed the door again quietly.

"He is asleep," he told Hana. "He is almost well to sleep like that."

"What shall we do with him?" Hana whispered her old refrain.

Sadao shook his head. "I must decide in a day or two," he promised. But certainly, he thought, the second night must be the night. There rose a wind that night, and he listened to the sounds of bending boughs and whistling partitions.

Hana woke too. "Ought we not to go and close the sick man's partition?" she asked.

"No," Sadao said. "He is able now to do it for himself."

But the next morning the American was still there.

Then the third night of course must be the night. The wind changed to quiet rain and the garden was full of the sound of dripping eaves and running springs. Sadao slept a little better, but he woke at the sound of a crash and leaped to his feet.

"What was that?" Hana cried. The baby woke at her voice and began to wail. "I must go and see."

But he held her and would not let her move.

"Sadao," she cried, "what is the matter with you?"

"Don't go," he muttered, "don't go!"

His terror infected her and she stood breathless, waiting. There was only silence. Together they crept back into the bed, the baby between them.

Yet when he opened the door of the guest room in the morning there was the young man. He was very gay and had already washed and was now on his feet. He had asked for a razor yesterday and had shaved himself and to-day there was a faint color in his cheeks.

"I am well," he said joyously.

Sadao drew his kimono round his weary body. He could not, he decided suddenly, go through another night. It was not that he cared for this young man's life. No, simply it was not worth the strain.

"You are well," Sadao agreed. He lowered his voice. "You are so well that I think if I put my boat on the shore to-night, with food and extra clothing in it, you might be able to row to that little island not far from the coast. It is so near the coast that it has not been worth fortifying. Nobody lives on it because in storm it is submerged. But this is not the season of storm. You could live there until you saw a Korean fishing boat pass by. They pass quite near the island because the water is many fathoms deep there."

The young man stared at him, slowly comprehending. "Do I have to?" he asked.

"I think so," Sadao said gently. "You understand—it is not hidden that you are here."

The young man nodded in perfect comprehension. "Okay," he said simply.

Sadao did not see him again until evening. As soon as it was dark he had dragged the stout boat down to the shore and in it he put food and bottled water that he had bought secretly during the day, as well as two quilts he had bought at a pawnshop. The boat he tied to a post in the water, for the tide was high. There was no moon and he worked without a flashlight.

When he came to the house he entered as though he were just back from his work, and so Hana knew nothing. "Yumi was here to-day," she said as she served his supper. Though she was so modern, still she did not eat with him. "Yumi cried over the baby," she went on with a sigh. "She misses him so."

"The servants will come back as soon as the foreigner is gone," Sadao said.

He went into the guest room that night before he went to bed and himself checked carefully the American's temperature, the state of the wound, and his heart and pulse. The pulse was irregular but that was perhaps because of excitement. The young man's pale lips were pressed together and his eyes burned. Only the scars on his neck were red.

"I realize you are saving my life again," he told Sadao.

"Not at all," Sadao said. "It is only inconvenient to have you here any longer."

He had hesitated a good deal about giving the man a flashlight. But he had decided to give it to him after all. It was a small one, his own, which he used at night when he was called.

"If your food runs out before you catch a boat," he said, "signal me two flashes at the same instant the sun drops over the horizon. Do not signal in darkness, for it will be seen. If you are all right but still there, signal me once. You will find fish easy to catch but you must eat them raw. A fire would be seen."

"Okay," the young man breathed.

He was dressed now in the Japanese clothes which Sadao had given him, and at the last moment Sadao wrapped a black cloth about his blond head.

"Now," Sadao said.

The young American without a word shook Sadao's hand warmly, and then walked quite well across the floor and down the step into the darkness of the garden. Once—twice—Sadao saw his light flash to find his way. But that would not be suspected. He waited until from the shore there was one more flash. Then he closed the partition. That night he slept.

"You say the man escaped?" the General asked faintly. He had been operated upon a week before, an emergency operation to which Sadao had been called in the night. For twelve hours Sadao had not been sure the General would live. The gall bladder was much involved. Then the old man had begun to breathe deeply again and to demand food. Sadao had not been able to ask about the assassins. So far as he knew they had never come. The servants had returned and Yumi had cleaned the guest room thoroughly and had burned sulphur in it to get the white man's smell out of it. Nobody said anything. Only the gardener was cross because he had got behind with his chrysanthemums.

But after a week Sadao felt the General was well enough to be spoken to about the prisoner.

"Yes, Excellency, he escaped," Sadao now said. He coughed, signifying that he had not said all he might have said, but was unwilling to disturb the General farther. But the old man opened his eyes suddenly.

"That prisoner," he said with some energy, "did I not promise you I would kill him for you?"

"You did, Excellency," Sadao said.

"Well, well!" the old man said in a tone of amazement, "so I did! But you see, I was suffering a good deal. The truth is, I thought of nothing but myself. In short, I forgot my promise to you."

"I wondered, Your Excellency," Sadao murmured.

"It was certainly very careless of me," the General said. "But you understand it was not lack of patriotism or dereliction of duty." He looked anxiously at his doctor. "If the matter should come out you would understand that, wouldn't you?"

"Certainly, Your Excellency," Sadao said. He suddenly comprehended that the General was in the palm of his hand and that as a consequence he himself was perfectly safe. "I can swear to your loyalty, Excellency," he said to the old General, "and to your zeal against the enemy."

"You are a good man," the General murmured and closed his eyes. "You will be rewarded."

But Sadao, searching the spot of black in the twilighted sea that night, had his reward. There was no prick of light in the dusk. No one was on the island. His prisoner was gone—safe, doubtless, for he had warned him to wait only for a Korean fishing boat.

He stood for a moment on the veranda, gazing out to the sea from whence the young man had come that other night. And into his mind, although without reason, there came other white faces he had known—the professor at whose house he had met Hana, a dull man, and his wife had been a silly talkative woman, in spite of her wish to be kind. He remembered his old teacher of anatomy, who had been so insistent on mercy with the knife, and then he remembered the face of his fat and slatternly landlady. He had had great difficulty in finding a place to live in America because he was a Japanese. The Americans were full of prejudice and it had been bitter to live in it, knowing himself their superior. How he had despised the ignorant and dirty old woman who had at last consented to house him in her miserable home! He had once tried to be grateful to her because she had in his last year nursed him through influenza, but it was difficult, for she was no less repulsive to him in her kindness. But then, white people were repulsive of course. It was a relief to be openly at war with them at last. Now he remembered the youthful, haggard face of his prisoner—white and repulsive.

"Strange," he thought, "I wonder why I could not kill him?"

1942

KATHERINE ANNE PORTER
(1894–   )

THE WITNESS *

Uncle Jimbilly was so old and had spent so many years bowed over

* From *The Leaning Tower and Other Stories*, by Katherine Anne Porter, copyright, 1944, by Katherine Anne Porter. Reprinted by permission of Harcourt, Brace and Company, Inc.

things, putting them together and taking them apart, making them over and making them do, he was bent almost double. His hands were closed and stiff from gripping objects tightly, while he worked at them, and they could not open altogether even if a child took the thick black fingers and tried to turn them back. He hobbled on a stick; his purplish skull showed through patches in his wool, which had turned greenish gray and looked as if the moths had got at it.

He mended harness and put half soles on the other Negroes' shoes, he built fences and chicken coops and barn doors; he stretched wires and put in new window panes and fixed sagging hinges and patched up roofs; he repaired carriage tops and cranky plows. Also he had a gift for carving miniature tombstones out of blocks of wood; give him almost any kind of piece of wood and he could turn out a tombstone, shaped very like the real ones, with carving, and a name and date on it if they were needed. They were often needed, for some small beast or bird was always dying and having to be buried with proper ceremonies: the cart draped as a hearse, a shoe-box coffin with a pall over it, a profuse floral outlay, and, of course, a tombstone. As he worked, turning the long blade of his bowie knife deftly in circles to cut a flower, whittling and smoothing the back and sides, stopping now and then to hold it at arm's length and examine it with one eye closed, Uncle Jimbilly would talk in a low, broken, abstracted murmur, as if to himself; but he was really saying something he meant one to hear. Sometimes it would be an incomprehensible ghost story; listen ever so carefully, at the end it was impossible to decide whether Uncle Jimbilly himself had seen the ghost, whether it was a real ghost at all, or only

another man dressed like one; and he dwelt much on the horrors of slave times.

"Dey used to take 'em out and tie 'em down and whup 'em," he muttered, "wid gret big leather strops inch thick long as yo' ahm, wid round holes bored in 'em so's evey time dey hit 'em de hide and de meat done come off dey bones in little round chunks. And wen dey had whupped 'em wid de strop till dey backs was all raw and bloody, dey spread dry cawnshucks on dey backs and set 'em afire and pahched 'em, and den they poured vinega all ovah 'em . . . Yassuh. And den, the ve'y nex' day dey'd got to git back to work in the fiels or dey'd do the same thing right ovah agin. Yassuh. Dat was it. If dey didn't git back to work dey got it all right ovah agin."

The children—three of them: a serious, prissy older girl of ten, a thoughtful sad looking boy of eight, and a quick flighty little girl of six— sat disposed around Uncle Jimbilly and listened with faint tinglings of embarrassment. They knew, of course, that once upon a time Negroes had been slaves; but they had all been freed long ago and were now only servants. It was hard to realize that Uncle Jimbilly had been born in slavery, as the Negroes were always saying. The children thought that Uncle Jimbilly had got over his slavery very well. Since they had known him, he had never done a single thing that anyone told him to do. He did his work just as he pleased and when he pleased. If you wanted a tombstone, you had to be very careful about the way you asked for it. Nothing could have been more impersonal and faraway than his tone and manner of talking about slavery, but they wriggled a little and felt guilty. Paul would have changed the subject, but Miranda, the little quick one, wanted to know the worst. "Did they act like that to you, Uncle Jimbilly?" she asked.

"No, *mam*," said Uncle Jimbilly. "Now whut name you want on dis one? Dey nevah did. Dey done 'em dat way in the rice swamps. I always worked right here close to the house or in town with Miss Sophia. Down in the swamps . . ."

"Didn't they ever die, Uncle Jimbilly?" asked Paul.

"Cose dey died," said Uncle Jimbilly, "cose dey died—dey died," he went on, pursing his mouth gloomily, "by de thousands and tens upon thousands."

"Can you carve 'Safe in Heaven' on that, Uncle Jimbilly?" asked Maria in her pleasant, mincing voice.

"To put over a tame jackrabbit, Missy?" asked Uncle Jimbilly indignantly. He was very religious. "A heather like dat? No, *mam*. In de swamps dey used to stake 'em out all day and all night, and all day and all night and all day wid dey hans and feet tied so dey couldn't scretch and let de muskeeters eat 'em alive. De muskeeters 'ud bite 'em tell dey was all swole up like a balloon all over, and you could heah 'em howlin and prayin all ovah the swamp. Yassuh. Dat was it. And nary a drop of watah noh a moufful of braid . . . Yassuh, dat's it. Lawd, dey done it. Hosanna! Now take dis yere tombstone and don' bother me no more . . . or I'll . . ."

Uncle Jimbilly was apt to be suddenly annoyed and you never knew why. He was easily put out about things, but his threats were always so exorbitant that not even the most credulous child could be terrified by them. He was always going to do something quite horrible to somebody and then he was going to dispose of the remains in a revolting manner. He was going to skin somebody alive and nail the hide on the barn door, or he was just getting ready to cut off somebody's ears with a hatchet and pin them on Bongo, the crop-eared brindle dog. He was often all prepared in his mind to pull somebody's teeth and make a set of false teeth for Ole Man Ronk . . . Ole Man Ronk was a tramp who had been living all summer in the little cabin behind the smokehouse. He got his rations along with the Negroes and sat all day mumbling his naked gums. He had skimpy black whiskers which appeared to be set in wax, and angry red eyelids. He took morphine, it was said; but what morphine might be, or how he took it, or why, no one seemed to know . . . Nothing could have been more unpleasant than the notion that one's teeth might be given to Ole Man Ronk.

The reason why Uncle Jimbilly never did any of these things he threatened was, he said, because he never could get around to them. He always had so much other work on hand he never seemed to get caught up on it. But some day, somebody was going to get a mighty big surprise, and meanwhile everybody had better look out.

1944

JOHN STEINBECK
(1902–)

THE RED PONY

I

THE GIFT *

At daybreak Billy Buck emerged from the bunkhouse and stood for a moment on the porch looking up at the sky. He was a broad, bandy-legged little man with a walrus mustache, with square hands, puffed and muscled on the palms. His eyes were a contemplative, watery gray and the hair which protruded from under his Stetson hat was spiky and weathered. Billy was still stuffing his shirt into his blue jeans as he stood on the porch. He unbuckled his belt and tightened it again. The belt showed, by the worn shiny places opposite each hole, the gradual increase of Billy's middle over a period of years. When he had seen to the weather, Billy cleared each nostril by holding its mate closed with his forefinger and blowing fiercely. Then he walked down to the barn, rubbing his hands together. He curried and brushed two saddle horses in the stalls, talking quietly to them all the time; and he had hardly finished when the iron triangle started ringing at the ranch house. Billy stuck the brush and currycomb together and laid them on the rail, and went up to breakfast. His action had been so deliberate and yet so wasteless of time that he came to the house while Mrs. Tiflin was still ringing the triangle. She nodded her gray head to him and withdrew into the kitchen. Billy Buck sat down on the steps, because he was a cowhand, and it wouldn't be fitting that he should go first into the dining-room. He heard Mr. Tiflin in the house, stamping his feet into his boots.

The high jangling note of the triangle put the boy Jody in motion. He was only a little boy, ten years old, with hair like dusty yellow grass and with shy polite gray eyes, and with a mouth that worked when he thought. The triangle picked him up out of sleep. It didn't occur to him to disobey the harsh note. He never had: no one

he knew ever had. He brushed the tangled hair out of his eyes and skinned his nightgown off. In a moment he was dressed—blue chambray shirt and overalls. It was late in the summer, so of course there were no shoes to bother with. In the kitchen he waited until his mother got from in front of the sink and went back to the stove. Then he washed himself and brushed back his wet hair with his fingers. His mother turned sharply on him as he left the sink. Jody looked shyly away.

"I've got to cut your hair before long," his mother said. "Breakfast's on the table. Go on in, so Billy can come."

Jody sat at the long table which was covered with white oilcloth washed through to the fabric in some places. The fried eggs lay in rows on their platter. Jody took three eggs on his plate and followed with three thick slices of crisp bacon. He carefully scraped a spot of blood from one of the egg yolks.

Billy Buck clumped in. "That won't hurt you," Billy explained. "That's only a sign the rooster leaves."

Jody's tall stern father came in then and Jody knew from the noise on the floor that he was wearing boots, but he looked under the table anyway, to make sure. His father turned off the oil lamp over the table, for plenty of morning light now came through the windows.

Jody did not ask where his father and Billy Buck were riding that day, but he wished he might go along. His father was a disciplinarian. Jody obeyed him in everything without questions of any kind. Now, Carl Tiflin sat down and reached for the egg platter.

"Got the cows ready to go, Billy?" he asked.

"In the lower corral," Billy said. "I

could just as well take them in alone."

"Sure you could. But a man needs company. Besides your throat gets pretty dry." Carl Tiflin was jovial this morning.

Jody's mother put her head in the door. "What time do you think to be back, Carl?"

"I can't tell. I've got to see some men in Salinas. Might be gone till dark."

The eggs and coffee and big biscuits disappeared rapidly. Jody followed the two men out of the house. He watched them mount their horses and drive six old milk cows out of the corral and start over the hill toward Salinas. They were going to sell the old cows to the butcher.

When they had disappeared over the crown of the ridge Jody walked up the hill in back of the house. The dogs trotted around the house corner hunching their shoulders and grinning horribly with pleasure. Jody patted their heads—Doubletree Mutt with the big thick tail and yellow eyes, and Smasher, the shepherd, who had killed a coyote and lost an ear in doing it. Smasher's one good ear stood up higher than a collie's ear should. Billy Buck said that always happened. After the frenzied greeting the dogs lowered their noses to the ground in a businesslike way and went ahead, looking back now and then to make sure that the boy was coming. They walked up through the chicken yard and saw the quail eating with the chickens. Smasher chased the chickens a little to keep in practice in case there should ever be sheep to herd. Jody continued on through the large vegetable patch where the green corn was higher than his head. The cowpumpkins were green and small yet. He went on to the sagebrush line where the cold spring ran out of its pipe and fell into a round wooden tub. He leaned over and drank close to the green mossy wood where the water tasted best. Then he turned and looked back on the ranch, on the low, whitewashed house girded with red geraniums, and on the long bunkhouse by the cypress tree where Billy Buck lived alone. Jody could see the great black kettle under the cypress tree. That was where the pigs were scalded. The sun was coming over the ridge now, glaring on the whitewash of the houses and barns, making the wet grass blaze softly. Behind him, in the tall sagebrush, the birds were scampering on the ground, making a great noise among the dry leaves; the squirrels piped shrilly on the sidehills. Jody looked along at the farm buildings. He felt an uncertainty in the air, a feeling of change and of loss and of the gain of new and unfamiliar things. Over the hillside two big black buzzards sailed low to the ground and their shadows slipped smoothly and quickly ahead of them. Some animal had died in the vicinity. Jody knew it. It might be a cow or it might be the remains of a rabbit. The buzzards overlooked nothing. Jody hated them as all decent things hate them, but they could not be hurt because they made away with carrion.

After a while the boy sauntered down hill again. The dogs had long ago given him up and gone into the brush to do things in their own way. Back through the vegetable garden he went, and he paused for a moment to smash a green muskmelon with his heel, but he was not happy about it. It was a bad thing to do, he knew perfectly well. He kicked dirt over the ruined melon to conceal it.

Back at the house his mother bent over his rough hands, inspecting his fingers and nails. It did little good to start him clean to school for too many things could happen on the way. She sighed over the black cracks on his fingers, and then gave him his books and his lunch and started him on the mile walk to school. She noticed that his mouth was working a good deal this morning.

Jody started his journey. He filled his pockets with little pieces of white quartz that lay in the road, and every so often he took a shot at a bird or at some rabbit that had stayed sunning itself in the road too long. At the crossroads over the bridge he met two friends and the three of them walked to school together, making ridiculous strides and being rather silly. School had just opened two weeks before. There was still a spirit of revolt among the pupils.

It was four o'clock in the afternoon when Jody topped the hill and looked down on the ranch again. He looked for the saddle horses, but the corral was empty. His father was not back yet. He went slowly, then, toward the afternoon chores. At the ranch house, he found his mother sitting on the porch, mending socks.

"There's two doughnuts in the kitchen for you," she said. Jody slid to the kitchen, and returned with half of one of the doughnuts already eaten and his mouth full. His mother asked him what he had learned in school that day, but she didn't listen to his doughnut-muffled answer. She interrupted, "Jody, tonight see you fill the wood-box clear full. Last night you crossed the sticks and it wasn't only about half full. Lay the sticks flat tonight. And Jody, some of the hens are hiding eggs, or else the dogs are eating them. Look about in the grass and see if you can find any nests."

Jody, still eating, went out and did his chores. He saw the quail come down to eat with the chickens when he threw out the grain. For some reason his father was proud to have them come. He never allowed any shooting near the house for fear the quail might go away.

When the wood-box was full, Jody took his twenty-two rifle up to the cold spring at the brush line. He drank again and then aimed the gun at all manner of things, at rocks, at birds on the wing, at the big black pig kettle under the cypress tree, but he didn't shoot for he had no cartridges and wouldn't have until he was twelve. If his father had seen him aim the rifle in the direction of the house he would have put the cartridges off another year. Jody remembered this and did not point the rifle down the hill again. Two years was enough to wait for cartridges. Nearly all of his father's presents were given with reservations which hampered their value somewhat. It was good discipline.

The supper waited until dark for his father to return. When at last he came in with Billy Buck, Jody could smell the delicious brandy on their breaths. Inwardly he rejoiced, for his father sometimes talked to him when he smelled of brandy, sometimes even told things he had done in the wild days when he was a boy.

After supper, Jody sat by the fireplace and his shy polite eyes sought the room corners, and he waited for his father to tell what it was he contained, for Jody knew he had news of some sort. But he was disappointed. His father pointed a stern finger at him.

"You'd better go to bed, Jody. I'm going to need you in the morning."

That wasn't so bad. Jody liked to do the things he had to do as long as they weren't routine things. He looked at the floor and his mouth worked out a question before he spoke it. "What are we going to do in the morning, kill a pig?" he asked softly.

"Never you mind. You better get to bed."

When the door was closed behind him, Jody heard his father and Billy Buck chuckling and he knew it was a joke of some kind. And later, when he lay in bed, trying to make words out of the murmurs in the other room, he heard his father protest, "But, Ruth, I didn't give much for him."

Jody heard the hoot-owls hunting mice down by the barn, and he heard a fruit tree limb tap-tapping against the house. A cow was lowing when he went to sleep.

When the triangle sounded in the morning, Jody dressed more quickly even than usual. In the kitchen, while he washed his face and combed back his hair, his mother addressed him irritably. "Don't you go out until you get a good breakfast in you."

He went into the dining-room and sat at the long white table. He took a steaming hotcake from the platter, arranged two fried eggs on it, covered them with another hotcake and squashed the whole thing with his fork.

His father and Billy Buck came in. Jody knew from the sound on the floor that both of them were wearing flat-heeled shoes, but he peered under the table to make sure. His father turned off the oil lamp, for the day had arrived, and he looked stern and disciplinary, but Billy Buck didn't look at Jody at all. He avoided the shy questioning eyes of the boy and soaked a whole piece of toast in his coffee.

Carl Tiflin said crossly, "You come with us after breakfast!"

Jody had trouble with his food then, for he felt a kind of doom in the air. After Billy had tilted his saucer and drained the coffee which had slopped into it, and had wiped his hands on his jeans, the two men stood up from the table and went out into the morning light together, and Jody respectfully followed a little behind them. He tried to keep his mind from running ahead, tried to keep it absolutely motionless.

His mother called, "Carl! Don't you let it keep him from school."

They marched past the cypress, where a singletree hung from a limb to butcher the pigs on, and past the black iron kettle, so it was not a pig killing. The sun shone over the hill and threw long, dark shadows of the trees and buildings. They crossed a stubble-field to shortcut to the barn. Jody's father unhooked the door and they went in. They had been walking toward the sun on the way down. The barn was black as night in contrast and warm from the hay and from the beasts. Jody's father moved over toward the one box stall. "Come here!" he ordered. Jody could begin to see things now. He looked into the box stall and then stepped back quickly.

A red pony colt was looking at him out of the stall. Its tense ears were forward and a light of disobedience was in its eyes. Its coat was rough and thick as an airedale's fur and its mane was long and tangled. Jody's throat collapsed in on itself and cut his breath short.

"He needs a good currying," his father said, "and if I ever hear of you not feeding him or leaving his stall dirty, I'll sell him off in a minute."

Jody couldn't bear to look at the pony's eyes any more. He gazed down at his hands for a moment, and he asked very shyly, "Mine?" No one answered him. He put his hand out toward the pony. Its gray nose came close, sniffing loudly, and then the lips drew back and the strong teeth closed on Jody's fingers. The pony shook its head up and down and seemed to laugh with amusement. Jody regarded his bruised fingers. "Well," he said with pride—"Well, I guess he can bite all right." The two men laughed, somewhat in relief. Carl Tiflin went out of the barn and walked up a side-hill to be by himself, for he was embarrassed, but Billy Buck stayed. It was easier to talk to Billy Buck. Jody asked again—"Mine?"

Billy became professional in tone. "Sure! That is, if you look out for him and break him right. I'll show you how. He's just a colt. You can't ride him for some time."

Jody put out his bruised hand again, and this time the red pony let his nose be rubbed. "I ought to have a carrot," Jody said. "Where'd we get him, Billy?"

"Bought him at a sheriff's auction," Billy explained. "A show went broke in Salinas and had debts. The sheriff was selling off their stuff."

The pony stretched out his nose and shook the forelock from his wild eyes. Jody stroked the nose a little. He said softly, "There isn't a—saddle?"

Billy Buck laughed. "I'd forgot. Come along."

In the harness room he lifted down a little saddle of red morocco leather. "It's just a show saddle," Billy Buck said disparagingly. "It isn't practical for the brush, but it was cheap at the sale."

Jody couldn't trust himself to look at the saddle either, and he couldn't speak at all. He brushed the shining red leather with his fingertips, and after a long time he said, "It'll look pretty on him though." He thought of the grandest and prettiest things he knew. "If he hasn't a name already, I think I'll call him Gabilan Mountains," he said.

Billy Buck knew how he felt. "It's a pretty long name. Why don't you just call him Gabilan? That means hawk. That would be a fine name for him." Billy felt glad. "If you will collect tail hair, I might be able to make a hair rope for you sometime. You could use it for a hackamore."

Jody wanted to go back to the box stall. "Could I lead him to school, do you think—to show the kids?"

But Billy shook his head. "He's not even halter-broke yet. We had a time getting him here. Had to almost drag him. You better be starting for school though."

"I'll bring the kids to see him here this afternoon," Jody said.

Six boys came over the hill half an hour early that afternoon, running hard, their heads down, their forearms working, their breath whistling. They swept by the house and cut across the stubble-field to the barn. And then they stood self-consciously before the pony, and then they looked at Jody with eyes in which there was a new admiration and a new respect. Before today Jody had been a boy, dressed in overalls and a blue shirt—quieter than most, even suspected of being a little cowardly. And now he was different. Out of a thousand centuries they drew the ancient admiration of the footman for the horseman. They knew instinctively that a man on a horse is spiritually as well as physically bigger than a man on foot. They knew that Jody had been miraculously lifted out of equality with them, and had been placed over them. Gabilan put his head out of the stall and sniffed them.

"Why'n't you ride him?" the boys cried. "Why'n't you braid his tail with ribbons like in the fair?" "When you going to ride him?"

Jody's courage was up. He too felt the superiority of the horseman. "He's not old enough. Nobody can ride him for a long time. I'm going to train him on the long halter. Billy Buck is going to show me how."

"Well, can't we even lead him around a little?"

"He isn't even halter-broke," Jody said. He wanted to be completely alone when he took the pony out the first time. "Come and see the saddle."

They were speechless at the red morocco saddle, completely shocked out of comment. "It isn't much use in the brush," Jody explained. "It'll look pretty on him though. Maybe I'll ride bareback when I go into the brush."

"How you going to rope a cow without a saddle horn?"

"Maybe I'll get another saddle for every day. My father might want me to help him with the stock." He let them feel the red saddle, and showed them the brass chain throat-latch on the bridle and the big brass buttons at each temple where the headstall and brow band crossed. The whole thing was too wonderful. They had to go away after a little while, and each boy, in his mind, searched among his possessions for a bribe worthy of offering in return for a ride on the red pony when the time should come.

Jody was glad when they had gone. He took brush and currycomb from the wall, took down the barrier of the box stall and stepped cautiously in. The pony's eyes glittered, and he edged around into kicking position. But Jody touched him on the shoulder and rubbed his high arched neck as he had always seen Billy Buck do, and he crooned, "So-o-o Boy," in a deep voice. The pony gradually relaxed his tenseness. Jody curried and brushed until a pile of dead hair lay in the stall and until the pony's coat had taken on a deep red shine. Each time he finished he thought it might have been done better. He braided the mane into a dozen little pigtails, and

he braided the forelock, and then he undid them and brushed the hair out straight again.

Jody did not hear his mother enter the barn. She was angry when she came, but when she looked in at the pony and at Jody working over him, she felt a curious pride rise up in her. "Have you forgot the wood-box?" she asked gently. "It's not far off from dark and there's not a stick of wood in the house, and the chickens aren't fed."

Jody quickly put up his tools. "I forgot, ma'am."

"Well, after this do your chores first. Then you won't forget. I expect you'll forget lots of things now if I don't keep an eye on you."

"Can I have carrots from the garden for him, ma'am?"

She had to think about that. "Oh— I guess so, if you only take the big tough ones."

"Carrots keep the coat good," he said, and again she felt the curious rush of pride.

Jody never waited for the triangle to get him out of bed after the coming of the pony. It became his habit to creep out of bed even before his mother was awake, to slip into his clothes and to go quietly down to the barn to see Gabilan. In the gray quiet mornings when the land and the brush and the houses and the trees were silver-gray and black like a photograph negative, he stole toward the barn, past the sleeping stones and the sleeping cypress tree. The turkeys, roosting in the tree out of coyotes' reach, clucked drowsily. The fields glowed with a gray frost-like light and in the dew the tracks of rabbits and of field mice stood out sharply. The good dogs came stiffly out of their little houses, hackles up and deep growls in their throats. Then they caught Jody's scent, and their stiff tails rose up and waved a greeting— Doubletree Mutt with the big thick tail, and Smasher, the incipient shepherd—then went lazily back to their warm beds.

It was a strange time and a mysterious journey, to Jody—an extension of a dream. When he first had the pony he liked to torture himself during the trip by thinking Gabilan would not be in his stall, and worse, would never have been there. And he had other delicious little self-induced pains. He thought how the rats had gnawed ragged holes in the red saddle, and how the mice had nibbled Gabilan's tail until it was stringy and thin. He usually ran the last little way to the barn. He unlatched the rusty hasp of the barn door and stepped in, and no matter how quietly he opened the door, Gabilan was always looking at him over the barrier of the box stall and Gabilan whinnied softly and stamped his front foot, and his eyes had big sparks of red fire in them like oakwood embers.

Sometimes, if the work horses were to be used that day, Jody found Billy Buck in the barn harnessing and currying. Billy stood with him and looked long at Gabilan and he told Jody a great many things about horses. He explained that they were terribly afraid for their feet, so that one must make a practice of lifting the legs and patting the hooves and ankles to remove their terror. He told Jody how horses loved conversation. He must talk to the pony all the time, and tell him the reasons for everything. Billy wasn't sure a horse could understand everything that was said to him, but it was impossible to say how much was understood. A horse never kicked up a fuss if someone he liked explained things to him. Billy could give examples, too. He had known, for instance,

a horse nearly dead beat with fatigue to perk up when told it was only a little farther to his destination. And he had known a horse paralyzed with fright to come out of it when his rider told him what it was that was frightening him. While he talked in the mornings, Billy Buck cut twenty or thirty straws into neat three-inch lengths and stuck them into his hatband. Then during the whole day, if he wanted to pick his teeth or merely to chew on something, he had only to reach up for one of them.

Jody listened carefully, for he knew and the whole country knew that Billy Buck was a fine hand with horses. Billy's own horse was a stringy cayuse with a hammer head, but he nearly always won the first prizes at the stock trials. Billy could rope a steer, take a double half-hitch about the horn with his riata, and dismount, and his horse would play the steer as an angler plays a fish, keeping a tight rope until the steer was down or beaten.

Every morning, after Jody had curried and brushed the pony, he let down the barrier of the stall, and Gabilan thrust past him and raced down the barn and into the corral. Around and around he galloped, and sometimes he jumped forward and landed on stiff legs. He stood quivering, stiff ears forward, eyes rolling so that the whites showed, pretending to be frightened. At last he walked snorting to the water-trough and buried his nose in the water up to the nostrils. Jody was proud then, for he knew that was the way to judge a horse. Poor horses only touched their lips to the water, but a fine spirited beast put his whole nose and mouth under, and only left room to breathe.

Then Jody stood and watched the pony, and he saw things he had never noticed about any other horse, the sleek, sliding flank muscles and the cords of the buttocks, which flexed like a closing fist, and the shine the sun put on the red coat. Having seen horses all his life, Jody had never looked at them very closely before. But now he noticed the moving ears which gave expression and even inflection of expression to the face. The pony talked with his ears. You could tell exactly how he felt about everything by the way his ears pointed. Sometimes they were stiff and upright and sometimes lax and sagging. They went back when he was angry or fearful, and forward when he was anxious and curious and pleased; and their exact position indicated which emotion he had.

Billy Buck kept his word. In the early fall the training began. First there was the halter-breaking, and that was the hardest because it was the first thing. Jody held a carrot and coaxed and promised and pulled on the rope. The pony set his feet like a burro when he felt the strain. But before long he learned. Jody walked all over the ranch leading him. Gradually he took to dropping the rope until the pony followed him unled wherever he went.

And then came the training on the long halter. That was slower work. Jody stood in the middle of a circle, holding the long halter. He clucked with his tongue and the pony started to walk in a big circle, held in by the long rope. He clucked again to make the pony trot, and again to make him gallop. Around and around Gabilan went thundering and enjoying it immensely. Then he called, "Whoa," and the pony stopped. It was not long until Gabilan was perfect at it. But in many ways he was a bad pony. He bit Jody in the pants and stomped on Jody's feet. Now and then his ears went back and he aimed a tremendous kick at the boy. Every time he did one of these bad things, Gabilan settled back and seemed to laugh to himself.

Billy Buck worked at the hair rope in the evenings before the fireplace. Jody collected tail hair in a bag, and he sat and watched Billy slowly constructing the rope, twisting a few hairs to make a string and rolling two strings together for a cord, and then braiding a number of cords to make the rope. Billy rolled the finished rope on the floor under his foot to make it round and hard.

The long halter work rapidly approached perfection. Jody's father, watching the pony stop and start and trot and gallop, was a little bothered by it.

"He's getting to be almost a trick pony," he complained. "I don't like trick horses. It takes all the—dignity out of a horse to make him do tricks. Why, a trick horse is kind of like an actor—no dignity, no character of his own." And his father said, "I guess you better be getting him used to the saddle pretty soon."

Jody rushed for the harness-room. For some time he had been riding the saddle on a sawhorse. He changed the stirrup length over and over, and could never get it just right. Sometimes, mounted on the sawhorse in the harness-room, with collars and hames and tugs hung all about him, Jody rode out beyond the room. He carried his rifle across the pommel. He saw the fields go flying by, and he heard the beat of the galloping hoofs.

It was a ticklish job, saddling the pony the first time. Gabilan hunched and reared and threw the saddle off before the cinch could be tightened. It had to be replaced again and again until at last the pony let it stay. And the cinching was difficult, too. Day by day Jody tightened the girth a little more until at last the pony didn't mind the saddle at all.

Then there was the bridle. Billy explained how to use a stick of licorice for a bit until Gabilan was used to having something in his mouth. Billy explained, "Of course we could force-break him to everything, but he wouldn't be as good a horse if we did. He'd always be a little bit afraid, and he wouldn't mind because he wanted to."

The first time the pony wore the bridle he whipped his head about and worked his tongue against the bit until the blood oozed from the corners of his mouth. He tried to rub the headstall off on the manger. His ears pivoted about and his eyes turned red with fear and with general rambunctiousness. Jody rejoiced, for he knew that only a mean-souled horse does not resent training.

And Jody trembled when he thought of the time when he would first sit in the saddle. The pony would probably throw him off. There was no disgrace in that. The disgrace would come if he did not get right up and mount again. Sometimes he dreamed that he lay in the dirt and cried and couldn't make himself mount again. The shame of the dream lasted until the middle of the day.

Gabilan was growing fast. Already he had lost the long-leggedness of the colt; his mane was getting longer and blacker. Under the constant currying and brushing his coat lay as smooth and gleaming as orange-red lacquer. Jody oiled the hoofs and kept them carefully trimmed so they would not crack.

The hair rope was nearly finished. Jody's father gave him an old pair of spurs and bent in the side bars and cut down the strap and took up the chainlets until they fitted. And then one day Carl Tiflin said:

"The pony's growing faster than I thought. I guess you can ride him by Thanksgiving. Think you can stick on?"

"I don't know," Jody said shyly. Thanksgiving was only three weeks off. He hoped it wouldn't rain, for rain would spot the red saddle.

Gabilan knew and liked Jody by now. He nickered when Jody came across the stubble-field, and in the pasture he came running when his master whistled for him. There was always a carrot for him every time.

Billy Buck gave him riding instructions over and over. "Now when you get up there, just grab tight with your knees and keep your hands away from the saddle, and if you get throwed, don't let that stop you. No matter how good a man is, there's always some horse can pitch him. You just climb up again before he gets to feeling smart about it. Pretty soon, he won't throw you no more, and pretty soon he *can't* throw you no more. That's the way to do it."

"I hope it don't rain before," Jody said.

"Why not? Don't want to get throwed in the mud?"

That was partly it, and also he was afraid that in the flurry of bucking Gabilan might slip and fall on him and break his leg or his hip. He had seen that happen to men before, had seen how they writhed on the ground like squashed bugs, and he was afraid of it.

He practiced on the sawhorse how he would hold the reins in his left hand and a hat in his right hand. If he kept his hands thus busy, he couldn't grab the horn if he felt himself going off. He didn't like to think of what would happen if he did grab the horn. Perhaps his father and Billy

Buck would never speak to him again, they would be so ashamed. The news would get about and his mother would be ashamed too. And in the school yard—it was too awful to contemplate.

He began putting his weight in a stirrup when Gabilan was saddled, but he didn't throw his leg over the pony's back. That was forbidden until Thanksgiving.

Every afternoon he put the red saddle on the pony and cinched it tight. The pony was learning already to fill his stomach out unnaturally large while the cinching was going on, and then to let it down when the straps were fixed. Sometimes Jody led him up to the brush line and let him drink from the round green tub, and sometimes he led him up through the stubble-field to the hilltop from which it was possible to see the white town of Salinas and the geometric fields of the great valley, and the oak trees clipped by the sheep. Now and then they broke through the brush and came to little cleared circles so hedged in that the world was gone and only the sky and the circle of brush were left from the old life. Gabilan liked these trips and showed it by keeping his head very high and by quivering his nostrils with interest. When the two came back from an expedition they smelled of the sweet sage they had forced through.

Time dragged on toward Thanksgiving, but winter came fast. The clouds swept down and hung all day over the land and brushed the hilltops, and the winds blew shrilly at night. All day the dry oak leaves drifted down from the trees until they covered the ground, and yet the trees were unchanged.

Jody had wished it might not rain before Thanksgiving, but it did. The brown earth turned dark and the trees glistened. The cut ends of the stubble turned black with mildew; the haystacks grayed from exposure to the damp, and on the roofs the moss, which had been all summer as gray as lizards, turned a brilliant yellow-green. During the week of rain, Jody kept the pony in the box stall out of the dampness, except for a little time after school when he took him out for exercise and to drink at the water-trough in the upper corral. Not once did Gabilan get wet.

The wet weather continued until little new grass appeared. Jody walked to school dressed in a slicker and short rubber boots. At length one morning the sun came out brightly. Jody, at his work in the box stall, said to Billy Buck, "Maybe I'll leave Gabilan in the corral when I go to school today."

"Be good for him to be out in the sun," Billy assured him. "No animal likes to be cooped up too long. Your father and me are going back on the hill to clean the leaves out of the spring." Billy nodded and picked his teeth with one of his little straws.

"If the rain comes, though—" Jody suggested.

"Not likely to rain today. She's rained herself out." Billy pulled up his sleeves and snapped his arm bands. "If it comes on to rain—why a little rain don't hurt a horse."

"Well, if it does come on to rain, you put him in, will you, Billy? I'm scared he might get cold so I couldn't ride him when the time comes."

"Oh sure! I'll watch out for him if we get back in time. But it won't rain today."

And so Jody, when he went to school left Gabilan standing out in the corral.

Billy Buck wasn't wrong about many things. He couldn't be. But he was wrong about the weather that day, for a little after noon the clouds pushed over the hills and the rain began to pour down. Jody heard it start on the schoolhouse roof. He considered holding up one finger for permission to go to the outhouse and, once outside, running for home to put the pony in. Punishment would be prompt both at school and at home. He gave it up and took ease from Billy's assurance that rain couldn't hurt a horse. When school was finally out, he hurried home through the dark rain. The banks at the sides of the road spouted little jets of muddy water. The rain slanted and swirled under a cold and gusty wind. Jody dog-trotted home, slopping through the gravelly mud of the road.

From the top of the ridge he could see Gabilan standing miserably in the corral. The red coat was almost black, and streaked with water. He stood head down with his rump to the rain and wind. Jody arrived running and threw open the barn door and led the wet pony in by his forelock. Then he found a gunny sack and rubbed the soaked hair and rubbed the legs and ankles. Gabilan stood patiently, but he trembled in gusts like the wind.

When he had dried the pony as well as he could, Jody went up to the house and brought hot water down to the barn and soaked the grain in it. Gabilan was not very hungry. He nibbled at the hot mash, but he was not very much interested in it, and he still shivered now and then. A little steam rose from his damp back.

It was almost dark when Billy Buck and Carl Tiflin came home. "When the rain started we put up at Ben Herche's place, and the rain never let up all afternoon," Carl Tiflin explained. Jody looked reproachfully at Billy Buck and Billy felt guilty.

"You said it wouldn't rain," Jody accused him.

Billy looked away. "It's hard to tell, this time of year," he said, but his excuse was lame. He had no right to be fallible, and he knew it.

"The pony got wet, got soaked through."

"Did you dry him off?"

"I rubbed him with a sack and I gave him hot grain."

Billy nodded in agreement.

"Do you think he'll take cold, Billy?"

"A little rain never hurt anything," Billy assured him.

Jody's father joined the conversation then and lectured the boy a little. "A horse," he said, "isn't any lap-dog kind of thing." Carl Tiflin hated weakness and sickness, and he held a violent contempt for helplessness.

Jody's mother put a platter of steaks on the table and boiled potatoes and boiled squash, which clouded the room with their steam. They sat down to eat. Carl Tiflin still grumbled about weakness put into animals and men by too much coddling.

Billy Buck felt bad about his mistake. "Did you blanket him?" he asked.

"No. I couldn't find any blanket. I laid some sacks over his back."

"We'll go down and cover him up after we eat, then." Billy felt better about it then. When Jody's father had gone in to the fire and his mother was washing dishes, Billy found and lighted a lantern. He and Jody walked through the mud to the barn. The barn was dark and warm and sweet. The horses still munched their evening hay. "You hold the lantern!" Billy ordered. And he felt the pony's legs and tested the heat of the flanks. He put his cheek against the pony's gray muzzle and then he rolled up the eyelids to look at the eyeballs and he lifted the lips to see the gums, and he put his fingers inside the ears. "He don't seem so chipper," Billy said. "I'll give him a rub-down."

Then Billy found a sack and rubbed the pony's legs violently and he rubbed the chest and the withers. Gabilan was strangely spiritless. He submitted patiently to the rubbing. At last Billy brought an old cotton comforter from the saddle-room, and threw it over the pony's back and tied it at neck and chest with string.

"Now he'll be all right in the morning," Billy said.

Jody's mother looked up when he got back to the house. "You're late up from bed," she said. She held his chin in her hard hand and brushed the tangled hair out of his eyes and she said, "Don't worry about the pony. He'll be all right. Billy's as good as any horse doctor in the country."

Jody hadn't known she could see his worry. He pulled gently away from her and knelt down in front of the fireplace until it burned his stomach. He scorched himself through and then went in to bed, but it was a hard thing to go to sleep. He awakened after what seemed a long time. The room was dark but there was a grayness in the window like that which precedes the dawn. He got up and found his overalls and searched for the legs, and then the clock in the other room struck two. He laid his clothes down and got back into bed. It was broad daylight when he awakened again. For the first time he had slept through the ringing of the triangle. He leaped up, flung on his clothes and went out of the door still buttoning his shirt. His mother looked after him for a moment and then went quietly back to her work. Her eyes were brooding and kind. Now and then her mouth smiled a little but without changing her eyes at all.

Jody ran on toward the barn. Halfway there he heard the sound he dreaded, the hollow rasping cough of a horse. He broke into a sprint then. In the barn he found Billy Buck with the pony. Billy was rubbing its legs with his strong thick hands. He looked up and smiled gaily. "He just took a little cold," Billy said. "We'll have him out of it in a couple of days."

Jody looked at the pony's face. The eyes were half closed and the lids thick and dry. In the eye corners a crust of hard mucus stuck. Gabilan's ears hung loosely sideways and his head was low. Jody put out his hand, but the pony did not move close to it. He coughed again and his whole body constricted with the effort. A little stream of thin fluid ran from his nostrils.

Jody looked back at Billy Buck. "He's awful sick, Billy."

"Just a little cold, like I said," Billy insisted. "You go get some breakfast and then go back to school. I'll take care of him."

"But you might have to do something else. You might leave him."

"No, I won't. I won't leave him at all. Tomorrow's Saturday. Then you can stay with him all day." Billy had failed again, and he felt badly about it. He had to cure the pony now.

Jody walked up to the house and took his place listlessly at the table. The eggs and bacon were cold and greasy, but he didn't notice it. He ate his usual amount. He didn't even ask to stay home from school. His mother pushed his hair back when she took his plate. "Billy'll take care of the pony," she assured him.

He moped through the whole day at school. He couldn't answer any questions nor read any words. He couldn't even tell anyone the pony was sick, for that might make him sicker. And when school was finally out he started home in dread. He walked slowly and let the other boys leave him. He wished he might continue walking and never arrive at the ranch.

Billy was in the barn, as he had promised, and the pony was worse. His eyes were almost closed now, and his breath whistled shrilly past an obstruction in his nose. A film covered that part of the eyes that was visible at all. It was doubtful whether the pony could see any more. Now and then he snorted, to clear his nose, and by the action seemed to plug it tighter. Jody looked dispiritedly at the pony's coat. The hair lay rough and unkempt and seemed to have lost all of its old luster. Billy stood quietly beside the stall. Jody hated to ask, but he had to know.

"Billy, is he—is he going to get well?"

Billy put his fingers between the bars under the pony's jaw and felt about. "Feel here," he said and he guided Jody's fingers to a large lump under the jaw. "When that gets bigger, I'll open it up and then he'll get better."

Jody looked quickly away, for he had heard about that lump. "What is it the matter with him?"

Billy didn't want to answer, but he had to. He couldn't be wrong three times. "Strangles," he said shortly, "but don't you worry about that. I'll pull him out of it. I've seen them get well when they were worse than Gabilan is. I'm going to steam him now. You can help."

"Yes," Jody said miserably. He followed Billy into the grain room and watched him make the steaming bag ready. It was a long canvas nose bag with straps to go over a horse's ears. Billy filled it one-third full of bran and then he added a couple of handfuls of dried hops. On top of the dry substance he poured a little carbolic acid and a little turpentine. "I'll be mixing it all up while you run to the house for a kettle of boiling water," Billy said.

When Jody came back with the steaming kettle, Billy buckled the straps over Gabilan's head and fitted the bag tightly around his nose. Then through a little hole in the side of the bag he poured the boiling water on the mixture. The pony started away as a cloud of strong steam rose up, but then the soothing fumes crept through his nose and into his lungs, and the sharp steam began to clear out the nasal passages. He breathed loudly. His legs trembled in an ague, and his eyes closed against the biting cloud. Billy poured in more water and kept the steam rising for fifteen minutes. At last he set down the kettle and took the bag from Gabilan's nose. The pony looked better. He breathed freely, and his eyes were open wider than they had been.

"See how good it makes him feel," Billy said. "Now we'll wrap him up in the blanket again. Maybe he'll be nearly well by morning."

"I'll stay with him tonight," Jody suggested.

"No. Don't you do it. I'll bring my blankets down here and put them in the hay. You can stay tomorrow and steam him if he needs it."

The evening was falling when they went to the house for their supper. Jody didn't even realize that someone else had fed the chickens and filled the wood-box. He walked up past the house to the dark brush line and took a drink of water from the tub. The spring water was so cold that it stung his mouth and drove a shiver through him. The sky above the hills was still light. He saw a hawk flying so high that it caught the sun on its breast and shone like a spark. Two black-birds were driving him down the sky, glittering as they attacked their enemy. In the west, the clouds were moving in to rain again.

Jody's father didn't speak at all while the family ate supper, but after Billy Buck had taken his blankets and gone to sleep in the barn, Carl Tiflin built a high fire in the fireplace and told stories. He told about the wild man who ran naked through the country and had a tail and ears like a horse, and he told about the rabbit-cats of Moro Cojo that hopped into the trees for birds. He revived the famous Maxwell brothers who found a vein of gold and hid the traces of it so carefully that they could never find it again.

Jody sat with his chin in his hands; his mouthed worked nervously, and his father gradually became aware that he wasn't listening very carefully. "Isn't that funny?" he asked.

Jody laughed politely and said, "Yes, sir." His father was angry and hurt, then. He didn't tell any more stories. After a while, Jody took a lantern and went down to the barn. Billy Buck was asleep in the hay, and, except that his breath rasped a little in his lungs, the pony seemed to be much better. Jody stayed a little while, running his fingers over the red rough coat, and then he took up the lantern and went back to the house. When he was in bed, his mother came into the room.

"Have you enough covers on? It's getting winter."

"Yes, ma'am."

"Well, get some rest tonight." She hesitated to go out, stood uncertainly. "The pony will be all right," she said.

Jody was tired. He went to sleep quickly and didn't awaken until dawn. The triangle sounded, and Billy Buck came up from the barn before Jody could get out of the house.

"How is he?" Jody demanded.

Billy always wolfed his breakfast. "Pretty good. I'm going to open that lump this morning. Then he'll be better maybe."

After breakfast, Billy got out his best knife, one with a needle point. He whetted the shining blade a long time on a little carborundum stone. He tried the point and the blade again and again on his calloused thumb-ball, and at last he tried it on his upper lip.

On the way to the barn, Jody noticed how the young grass was up and how the stubble was melting day by day into the new green crop of volunteer. It was a cold sunny morning.

As soon as he saw the pony, Jody knew he was worse. His eyes were closed and sealed shut with dried mucus. His head hung so low that his nose almost touched the straw of his bed. There was a little groan in each breath, a deep-seated, patient groan.

Billy lifted the weak head and made a quick slash with the knife. Jody saw the yellow pus run out. He held up the head while Billy swabbed out the wound with weak carbolic acid salve.

"Now he'll feel better," Billy assured him. "That yellow poison is what makes him sick."

Jody looked unbelieving at Billy Buck. "He's awful sick."

Billy thought a long time what to say. He nearly tossed off a careless assurance, but he saved himself in time. "Yes, he's pretty sick," he said at last. "I've seen worse ones get well. If he doesn't get pneumonia, we'll pull him through. You stay with him. If he gets worse, you can come and get me."

For a long time after Billy went

away, Jody stood beside the pony, stroking him behind the ears. The pony didn't flip his head the way he had done when he was well. The groaning in his breathing was becoming more hollow.

Doubletree Mutt looked into the barn, his big tail waving provocatively, and Jody was so incensed at his health that he found a hard black clod on the floor and deliberately threw it. Doubletree Mutt went yelping away to nurse a bruised paw.

In the middle of the morning, Billy Buck came back and made another steam bag. Jody watched to see whether the pony improved this time as he had before. His breathing eased a little, but he did not raise his head.

The Saturday dragged on. Late in the afternoon Jody went to the house and brought his bedding down and made up a place to sleep in the hay. He didn't ask permission. He knew from the way his mother looked at him that she would let him do almost anything. That night he left a lantern burning on a wire over the box stall. Billy had told him to rub the pony's legs every little while.

At nine o'clock the wind sprang up and howled around the barn. And in spite of his worry, Jody grew sleepy. He got into his blankets and went to sleep, but the breathy groans of the pony sounded in his dreams. And in his sleep he heard a crashing noise which went on and on until it awakened him. The wind was rushing through the barn. He sprang up and looked down the lane of stalls. The barn door had blown open, and the pony was gone.

He caught the lantern and ran outside into the gale, and he saw Gabilan weakly shambling away into the darkness, head down, legs working slowly and mechanically. When Jody ran up and caught him by the forelock, he allowed himself to be led back and put into his stall. His groans were louder, and a fierce whistling came from his nose. Jody didn't sleep any more then. The hissing of the pony's breath grew louder and sharper.

He was glad when Billy Buck came in at dawn. Billy looked for a time at the pony as though he had never seen him before. He felt the ears and flanks. "Jody," he said, "I've got to do something you won't want to see. You run up to the house for a while."

Jody grabbed him fiercely by the forearm. "You're not going to shoot him?"

Billy patted his hand. "No. I'm going to open a little hole in his windpipe so he can breathe. His nose is filled up. When he gets well, we'll put a little brass button in the hole for him to breathe through."

Jody couldn't have gone away if he had wanted to. It was awful to see the red hide cut, but infinitely more terrible to know it was being cut and not to see it. "I'll stay right here," he said bitterly. "You sure you got to?"

"Yes. I'm sure. If you stay, you can hold his head. If it doesn't make you sick, that is."

The fine knife came out again and was whetted again just as carefully as it had been the first time. Jody held the pony's head up and the throat taut, while Billy felt up and down for the right place. Jody sobbed once as the bright knife point disappeared into the throat. The pony plunged weakly away and then stood still, trembling violently. The blood ran thickly out and up the knife and across Billy's hand and into his shirtsleeve. The sure square hand sawed out a round hole in the flesh, and the breath came bursting out of the hole, throwing a fine spray of blood. With the rush of oxygen, the pony took a sudden strength. He lashed out with his hind feet and tried to rear, but Jody held his head down while Billy mopped the new wound with carbolic salve. It was a good job. The blood stopped flowing and the air puffed out the hole and sucked it in regularly with a little bubbling noise.

The rain brought in by the night wind began to fall on the barn roof. Then the triangle rang for breakfast. "You go up and eat while I wait," Billy said. "We've got to keep this hole from plugging up."

Jody walked slowly out of the barn. He was too dispirited to tell Billy how the barn door had blown open and let the pony out. He emerged into the wet gray morning and sloshed up to the house, taking a perverse pleasure in splashing through all the puddles. His mother fed him and put dry clothes on. She didn't question him. She seemed to know he couldn't answer questions. But when he was ready to go back to the barn she brought him a pan of steaming meal. "Give him this," she said.

But Jody did not take the pan. He said, "He won't eat anything," and ran out of the house. At the barn, Billy showed him how to fix a ball of cotton on a stick, with which to swab out the breathing hole when it became clogged with mucus.

Jody's father walked into the barn and stood with them in front of the stall. At length he turned to the boy. "Hadn't you better come with me? I'm going to drive over the hill." Jody shook his head. "You better come on, out of this," his father insisted.

Billy turned on him angrily. "Let him alone. It's his pony, isn't it?"

Carl Tiflin walked away without saying another word. His feelings were badly hurt.

All morning Jody kept the wound open and the air passing in and out freely. At noon the pony lay wearily down on his side, and stretched his nose out.

Billy came back. "If you're going to stay with him tonight, you better take a little nap," he said. Jody went absently out of the barn. The sky had cleared to a hard thin blue. Everywhere the birds were busy with worms that had come to the damp surface of the ground.

Jody walked to the brush line and sat on the edge of the mossy tub. He looked down at the house and at the old bunkhouse and at the dark cypress tree. The place was familiar, but curiously changed. It wasn't itself any more, but a frame for things that were happening. A cold wind blew out of the east now, signifying that the rain was over for a little while. At his feet Jody could see the little arms of new weeds spreading out over the ground. In the mud about the spring were thousands of quail tracks.

Doubletree Mutt came sideways and embarrassed up through the vegetable patch, and Jody, remembering how he had thrown the clod, put his arm about the dog's neck and kissed him on his wide black nose. Doubletree Mutt sat still, as though he knew some solemn thing was happening. His big tail slapped the ground gravely. Jody pulled a swollen tick out of Mutt's neck and popped it dead between his thumb-nails. It was a nasty thing. He washed his hands in the cold spring water.

Except for the steady swish of the wind, the farm was very quiet. Jody knew his mother wouldn't mind if he didn't go in to eat his lunch. After a little while he went slowly back to the barn. Mutt crept into his own little house and whined softly to himself for a long time.

Billy Buck stood up from the box and surrendered the cotton swab. The pony still lay on his side and the wound in his throat bellowsed in and out. When Jody saw how dry and dead the hair looked, he knew at last that there was no hope for the pony. He had seen the dead hair before on dogs and on cows, and it was a sure sign. He sat heavily on the box and let down the barrier of the box stall. For a long time he kept his eyes on the moving wound, and at last he dozed, and the afternoon passed quickly. Just before dark his mother brought a deep dish of stew and left it for him and went away. Jody ate a little of it, and, when it was dark, he set the lantern on the floor by the pony's head so he could watch the wound and keep it open. And he dozed again until the night chill awakened him. The wind was blowing fiercely, bringing the north cold with it. Jody brought a blanket from his bed in the hay and wrapped himself in it. Gabilan's breathing was quiet at last; the hole in his throat moved gently. The owls flew through the hayloft, shrieking and looking for mice. Jody put his hands down on his head and slept. In his sleep he was aware that the wind had increased. He heard it slamming about the barn.

It was daylight when he awakened. The barn door had swung open. The pony was gone. He sprang up and ran out into the morning light.

The pony's tracks were plain enough, dragging through the frost-like dew on the young grass, tired tracks with little lines between them where the hoofs had dragged. They headed for the brush line halfway up the ridge. Jody broke into a run and followed them. The sun shone on the sharp white quartz that stuck through the ground here and there. As he followed the plain trail, a shadow cut across in front of him. He looked up and saw a high circle of black buz-

zards, and the slowly revolving circle dropped lower and lower. The solemn birds soon disappeared over the ridge. Jody ran faster then, forced on by panic and rage. The trail entered the brush at last and followed a winding route among the tall sage bushes.

At the top of the ridge Jody was winded. He paused, puffing noisily. The blood pounded in his ears. Then he saw what he was looking for. Below, in one of the little clearings in the brush, lay the red pony. In the distance, Jody could see the legs moving slowly and convulsively. And in a circle around him stood the buzzards, waiting for the moment of death they know so well.

Jody leaped forward and plunged down the hill. The wet ground muffled his steps and the brush hid him. When he arrived, it was all over. The first buzzard sat on the pony's head and its beak had just risen dripping with dark eye fluid. Jody plunged into the circle like a cat. The black brotherhood arose in a cloud, but the big one on the pony's head was too late. As it hopped along to take off, Jody caught its wing tip and pulled it down. It was nearly as big as he was. The free wing crashed into his face with the force of a club, but he hung on. The claws fastened on his leg and the wing elbows battered his head on either side. Jody groped blindly with his free hand. His fingers found the neck of the struggling bird. The red eyes looked into his face, calm and fearless and fierce; the naked head turned from side to side. Then the beak opened and vomited a stream of putrefied fluid. Jody brought up his knee and fell on the great bird. He held the neck to the ground with one hand while his other found a piece of sharp white quartz. The first blow broke the beak sideways and black blood spurted from the twisted, leathery mouth corners. He struck again and missed. The red fearless eyes still looked at him, impersonal and unafraid and detached. He struck again and again, until the buzzard lay dead, until its head was a red pulp. He was still beating the dead bird when Billy Buck pulled him off and held him tightly to calm his shaking.

Carl Tiflin wiped the blood from the boy's face with a red bandana. Jody was limp and quiet now. His father moved the buzzard with his toe. "Jody," he explained, "the buzzard didn't kill the pony. Don't you know that?"

"I know it," Jody said wearily.

It was Billy Buck who was angry. He had lifted Jody in his arms, and had turned to carry him home. But he turned back on Carl Tiflin. " 'Course he knows it," Billy said furiously, "Jesus Christ! man, can't you see how he'd feel about it?"

1937, 1938, 1944

THE GRAPES OF WRATH *

CHAPTER XV

[TWO FOR A CENT]

Along 66 the hamburger stands— Al & Susy's Place—Carl's Lunch—Joe & Minnie—Will's Eats. Board-and-bat shacks. Two gasoline pumps in front, a screen door, a long bar, stools, and a foot rail. Near the door three slot machines, showing through glass the wealth in nickels three bars will bring. And beside them, the nickel phonograph with records piled up like pies, ready to swing out to the turntable and play dance music, "Ti-pi-ti-pi-tin," "Thanks for the Memory," Bing

* From *The Grapes of Wrath* by John Steinbeck. Copyright 1939 by John Steinbeck. By permission of The Viking Press, Inc., New York.

Crosby, Benny Goodman. At one end of the counter a covered case; candy cough drops, caffeine sulphate called sleepless No-Doze; candy, cigarettes, razor blades, aspirin, Bromo-Seltzer, Alka-Seltzer. The walls decorated with posters, bathing girls, blondes with big breasts and slender hips and waxen faces, in white bathing suits, and holding a bottle of Coca-Cola and smiling—see what you get with a Coca-Cola. Long bar, and salts, peppers, mustard pots, and paper napkins. Beer taps behind the counter, and in back the coffee urns, shiny and steaming, with glass gauges showing the coffee level. And pies in wire cages and oranges in pyramids of four. And little piles of Post Toasties, corn flakes, stacked up in designs.

The signs on cards, picked out with shining mica: Pies Like Mother Used to Make. Credit Makes Enemies, Let's Be Friends. Ladies May Smoke But Be Careful Where You Lay Your Butts. Eat Here and Keep Your Wife for a Pet.

Down at one end the cooking plates, pots of stew, potatoes, pot roast, roast beef, gray roast pork waiting to be sliced.

Minnie or Susy or Mae, middle-aging behind the counter, hair curled and rouge and powder on a sweating face. Taking orders in a soft low voice, calling them to the cook with a screech like a peacock. Mopping the counter with circular strokes, polishing the big shining coffee urns. The cook is Joe or Carl or Al, hot in a white coat and apron, beady sweat on white forehead, below the white cook's cap; moody, rarely speaking, looking up for a moment at each new entry. Wiping the griddle, slapping down the hamburger. He repeats Mae's orders gently, scrapes the griddle, wipes it down with burlap. Moody and silent.

Mae is the contact, smiling, irritated, near to outbreak; smiling while her eyes look on past—unless for truck drivers. There's the backbone of the joint. Where the trucks stop, that's where the customers come. Can't fool truck drivers, they know. They bring the custom. They know. Give 'em a stale cup a coffee an' they're off the joint. Treat 'em right an' they come back. Mae really smiles with all her might at truck drivers. She bridles a little, fixes her back hair so that her breasts will lift with her raised arms, passes the time of day and indicates great things, great times, great jokes. Al never speaks. He is no contact. Sometimes he smiles a little at a joke, but he never laughs. Sometimes he looks up at the vivaciousness in Mae's voice, and then he scrapes the griddle with a spatula, scrapes the grease into an iron trough around the plate. He presses down a hissing hamburger with his spatula. He lays the split buns on the plate to toast and heat. He gathers up stray onions from the plate and heaps them on the meat and presses them in with the spatula. He puts half the bun on top of the meat, paints the other half with melted butter, with thin pickle relish. Holding the bun on the meat, he slips the spatula under the thin pad of meat, flips it over, lays the buttered half on top, and drops the hamburger on a small plate. Quarter of a dill pickle, two black olives beside the sandwich. Al skims the plate down the counter like a quoit. And he scrapes his griddle with the spatula and looks moodily at the stew kettle.

Cars whisking by on 66. License plates. Mass., Tenn., R. I., N. Y., Vt., Ohio. Going west. Fine cars, cruising at sixty-five.

There goes one of them Cords. Looks like a coffin on wheels.

But, Jesus, how they travel!

See that La Salle? Me for that. I ain't a hog. I go for a La Salle.

'F ya goin' big, what's a matter with a Cad'? Jus' a little bigger, little faster.

I'd take a Zephyr myself. You ain't ridin' no fortune, but you got class an' speed. Give me a Zephyr.

Well, sir, you may get a laugh outa this—I'll take a Buick-Puick. That's good enough.

But, hell, that costs in the Zephyr class an' it ain't got the sap.

I don' care. I don' want nothin' to do with nothin' of Henry Ford's. I don' like 'im. Never did. Got a brother worked in the plant. Oughta hear him tell.

Well, a Zephyr got sap.

The big cars on the highway . . . The big car cruising along at sixty.

I want a cold drink.

Well, there's something up ahead. Want to stop?

Do you think it would be clean?

Clean as you're going to find in this God-forsaken country.

Well, maybe the bottled soda will be all right.

The great car squeals and pulls to a stop. The fat worried man helps his wife out.

Mae looks at and past them as they enter. Al looks up from his griddle, and down again. Mae knows. They'll drink a five-cent soda and crab that it ain't cold enough. The woman will use six paper napkins and drop them on the floor. The man will choke and try to put the blame on Mae. The woman will sniff as though she smelled rotting meat and they will go out again and tell forever afterward that the people in the West are sullen.

Truck drivers. That's the stuff.

Here's a big transport comin'. Hope they stop; take away the taste of them—. When I worked in that hotel in Albuquerque, Al, the way they steal—ever' darn thing. An' the bigger

the car they got, the more they steal
—towels, silver, soap dishes. I can't
figger it.

And Al, morosely, Where ya think
they get them big cars and stuff? Born
with 'em? You won't never have
nothin'.

The transport truck, a driver and
relief. How 'bout stoppin' for a cup
a Java? I know this dump.

How's the schedule?

Oh, we're ahead!

Pull up, then. They's a ol' war
horse in here that's a kick. Good Java,
too.

The truck pulls up. Two men in
khaki riding trousers, boots, short
jackets, and shiny-visored military
caps. Screen door—slam.

H'ya, Mae?

Well, if it ain't Big Bill the Rat!
When'd you get back on this run?

Week ago.

The other man puts a nickel in the
phonograph, watches the disk slip
free and the turntable rise up under it.
Bing Crosby's voice—golden. "Thanks
for the memory, of sunburn at the
shore— You might have been a headache, but you never were a bore—"
And the truck driver sings for Mae's
ears, you might have been a haddock
but you never was a whore—

Mae laughs. Who's ya frien', Bill?
New on this run, ain't he?

The other puts a nickel in the slot
machine, wins four slugs, and puts
them back. Walks to the counter.

Well, what's it gonna be?

Oh, cup a Java. Kinda pie ya got?

Banana cream, pineapple cream,
chocolate cream—an' apple.

Make it apple. Wait— Kind is that
big thick one?

Mae lifts it out and sniffs it. Banana cream.

Cut off a hunk; make it a big hunk.

Man at the slot machine says, Two
all around.

Two it is. . . .

Al, slicing onions carefully on a
board, looks up and smiles, and then
looks down again. Truck drivers,
that's the stuff. Gonna leave a quarter
each for Mae. Fifteen cents for pie
an' coffee an' a dime for Mae. . . .

Sitting together on the stools,
spoons sticking up out of the coffee
mugs. Passing the time of day. And
Al, rubbing down his griddle, listening but making no comment. Bing
Crosby's voice stops. The turntable
drops down and the record swings into
its place in the pile. The purple light
goes off. The nickel, which has caused
all this mechanism to work, has caused
Crosby to sing and an orchestra to
play—this nickel drops from between
the contact points into the box where
the profits go. This nickel, unlike
most money, has actually done a job
of work, has been physically responsible for a reaction.

Steam spurts from the valve of the
coffee urn. The compressor of the ice
machine chugs softly for a time and
then stops. The electric fan in the
corner waves its head slowly back and
forth, sweeping the room with a
warm breeze. On the highway, on 66,
the cars whiz by.

They was a Massachusetts car
stopped a while ago, said Mae.

Big Bill grasped his cup around the
top so that the spoon stuck up between his first and second fingers. He
drew in a snort of air with the coffee,
to cool it. "You ought to be out on 66.
Cars from all over the country. All
headin' west. Never seen so many
before. Sure some honeys on the
road."

"We seen a wreck this mornin'," his
companion said. "Big car. Big Cad',
a special job and a honey, low, cream-
color, special job. Hit a truck. Folded
the radiator right back into the driver.
Must a been doin' ninety. Steerin'

wheel went right on through the guy an' lef' him a-wigglin' like a frog on a hook. Peach of a car. A honey. You can have her for peanuts now. Drivin' alone, the guy was."

Al looked up from his work. "Hurt the truck?"

"Oh, Jesus Christ! Wasn't a truck. One of them cut-down cars full a stoves an' pans an' mattresses an' kids an' chickens. Goin' west, you know. This guy come by us doin' ninety—r'ared up on two wheels just to pass us, an' a car's comin' so he cuts in an' whangs this here truck. Drove like he's blin' drunk. Jesus, the air was full a bed clothes an' chickens an' kids. Killed one kid. Never seen such a mess. We pulled up. Ol' man that's drivin' the truck, he jus' stan's there lookin' at that dead kid. Can't get a word out of 'im. Jus' rum-dumb. God Almighty, the road is full a them families goin' west. Never seen so many. Gets worse all a time. Wonder where the hell they all come from?"

"Wonder where they all go to," said Mae. "Come here for gas sometimes, but they don't hardly never buy nothin' else. People say they steal. We ain't got nothin' layin' around. They never stole nothin' from us."

Big Bill, munching his pie, looked up the road through the screened window. "Better tie your stuff down. I think you got some of 'em comin' now."

A 1926 Nash sedan pulled wearily off the highway. The back seat was piled nearly to the ceiling with sacks, with pots and pans, and on the very top, right up against the ceiling, two boys rode. On the top of the car, a mattress and a folded tent; tent poles tied along the running board. The car pulled up to the gas pumps. A dark-haired, hatchet-faced man got slowly out. And the two boys slid down from the load and hit the ground.

Mae walked around the counter and stood in the door. The man was dressed in gray wool trousers and a blue shirt, dark blue with sweat on the back and under the arms. The boys in overalls and nothing else, ragged patched overalls. Their hair was light, and it stood up evenly all over their heads, for it had been roached. Their faces were streaked with dust. They went directly to the mud puddle under the hose and dug their toes into the mud.

The man asked, "Can we git some water, ma'am?"

A look of annoyance crossed Mae's face. "Sure, go ahead." She said softly over her shoulder, "I'll keep my eye on the hose." She watched while the man slowly unscrewed the radiator cap and ran the hose in.

A woman in the car, a flaxen-haired woman, said, "See if you can't git it here."

The man turned off the hose and screwed on the cap again. The little boys took the hose from him and they upended it and drank thirstily. The man took off his dark, stained hat and stood with a curious humility in front of the screen. "Could you see your way to sell us a loaf of bread, ma'am?"

Mae said, "This ain't a grocery store. We got bread to make san'-widges."

"I know, ma'am." His humility was insistent. "We need bread and there ain't nothin' for quite a piece, they say."

"'F we sell bread we gonna run out." Mae's tone was faltering.

"We're hungry," the man said.

"Why'n't you buy a san'widge? We got nice san'widges, hamburgs."

"We'd sure admire to do that, ma'am. But we can't. We got to make a dime do all of us." And he said embarrassedly, "We ain't got but a little."

Mae said, "You can't get no loaf a bread for a dime. We only got fifteen-cent loafs."

From behind her Al growled, "God Almighty, Mae, give 'em bread."

"We'll run out 'fore the bread truck comes."

"Run out, then, goddamn it," said Al. And he looked sullenly down at the potato salad he was mixing.

Mae shrugged her plump shoulders and looked to the truck drivers to show them what she was up against.

She held the screen door open and the man came in, bringing a smell of sweat with him. The boys edged in behind him and they went immediately to the candy case and stared in—not with craving or with hope or even with desire, but just with a kind of wonder that such things could be. They were alike in size and their faces were alike. One scratched his dusty ankle with the toe nails of his other foot. The other whispered some soft message and then they straightened their arms so that their clenched fists in the overall pockets showed through the thin blue cloth.

Mae opened a drawer and took out a long waxpaper-wrapped loaf. "This here is a fifteen-cent loaf."

The man put his hat back on his head. He answered with inflexible humility, "Won't you—can't you see your way to cut off ten cents' worth?"

Al said snarlingly, "Goddamn it, Mae. Give 'em the loaf."

The man turned toward Al. "No, we want ta buy ten cents' worth of it. We got it figgered awful close, mister, to get to California."

Mae said resignedly, "You can have this for ten cents."

"That'd be robbin' you, ma'am."

"Go ahead—Al says to take it." She pushed the waxpapered loaf across the counter. The man took a deep leather pouch from his rear pocket, untied the strings, and spread it open. It was heavy with silver and with greasy bills.

"May soun' funny to be so tight," he apologized. "We got a thousan' miles to go, an' we don' know if we'll make it." He dug in the pouch with a forefinger, located a dime, and pinched in for it. When he put it down on the counter he had a penny with it. He was about to drop the penny back into the pouch when his eye fell on the boys frozen before the candy counter. He moved slowly down to them. He pointed in the case at big long sticks of striped peppermint. "Is them penny candy, ma'am?"

Mae moved down and looked in. "Which ones?"

"There, them stripy ones."

The little boys raised their eyes to her face and they stopped breathing; their mouths were partly open, their half-naked bodies were rigid.

"Oh—them. Well, no—them's two for a penny."

"Well, gimme two then, ma'am." He placed the copper cent carefully on the counter. The boys expelled their breath softly. Mae held the big sticks out.

"Take 'em," said the man.

They reached timidly, each took a stick, and they held them down at their sides and did not look at them. But they looked at each other, and their mouth corners smiled rigidly with embarrassment.

"Thank you, ma'am." The man picked up the bread and went out the door, and the little boys marched stiffly behind him, the red-striped sticks held tightly against their legs. They leaped like chipmunks over the front seat and onto the top of the load, and they burrowed back out of sight like chipmunks.

The man got in and started his car, and with a roaring motor and a cloud of blue oily smoke the ancient Nash climbed up on the highway and went on its way to the west.

From inside the restaurant the truck drivers and Mae and Al stared after them.

Big Bill wheeled back. "Them wasn't two-for-a-cent candy," he said.

"What's that to you?" Mae said fiercely.

"Them was a nickel apiece candy," said Bill.

"We got to get goin'," said the other man. "We're droppin' time." They reached in their pockets. Bill put a coin on the counter and the other man looked at it and reached again and put down a coin. They swung around and walked to the door.

"So long," said Bill.

Mae called, "Hey! Wait a minute. You got change."

"You go to hell," said Bill, and the screen door slammed.

Mae watched them get into the great truck, watched it lumber off in low gear, and heard the shift up the whining gears to cruising ratio. "Al—" she said softly.

He looked up from the hamburger he was patting thin and stacking between waxed papers. "What ya want?"

"Look there." She pointed at the coins beside the cups—two half-dollars. Al walked near and looked, and then he went back to his work.

"Truck drivers," Mae said reverently . . .

Flies struck the screen with little bumps and droned away. The compressor chugged for a time and then stopped. On 66 the traffic whizzed by, trucks and fine streamlined cars and jalopies; and they went by with a vicious whiz. Mae took down the plates and scraped the pie crusts into a bucket. She found her damp cloth and wiped the counter with circular sweeps. And her eyes were on the highway, where life whizzed by.

Al wiped his hands on his apron. He looked at a paper pinned to the wall over the griddle. Three lines of marks in columns on the paper. Al counted the longest line. He walked along the counter to the cash register, rang "No Sale," and took out a handful of nickels.

"What ya doin'?" Mae asked.

"Number three's ready to pay off," said Al. He went to the third slot machine and played his nickels in, and on the fifth spin of the wheels the three bars came up and the jack pot dumped out into the cup. Al gathered up the big handful of coins and went back of the counter. He dropped them in the drawer and slammed the cash register. Then he went back to his place and crossed out the line of dots. "Number three gets more play'n the others," he said. "Maybe I ought to shift 'em around." He lifted a lid and stirred the slowly simmering stew.

"I wonder what they'll do in California?" said Mae.

"Who?"

"Them folks that was just in."

"Christ knows," said Al.

"S'pose they'll get work?"

"How the hell would I know?" said Al.

She stared eastward along the highway. "Here comes a transport, double. Wonder if they stop? Hope they do." And as the huge truck came heavily down from the highway and parked, Mae seized her cloth and wiped the whole length of the counter. And she took a few swipes at the gleaming coffee urn too, and turned up the bottle-gas under the urn. Al brought out a handful of little turnips and started to peel them. Mae's face was gay when the door opened and the

two uniformed truck drivers entered.
"Hi, sister!"

"I won't be a sister to no man," said
Mae. They laughed and Mae laughed.
"What'll it be, boys?"

"Oh, a cup a Java. What kinda pie
ya got?"

"Pineapple cream an' banana cream
an' chocolate cream an' apple."

"Give me apple. No, wait—what's
that big thick one?"

Mae picked up the pie and smelled
it. "Pineapple cream," she said.

"Well, chop out a hunk a that."

The cars whizzed viciously by on
66.

                                        1939

MAXWELL ANDERSON
(1888–   )
WINTERSET *

CHARACTERS

TROCK	2ND GIRL	LUCIA	*Non-speaking*
SHADOW	JUDGE GAUNT	PINY	URCHINS
GARTH	MIO	A SAILOR	TWO MEN IN
MIRIAMNE	CARR	STREET URCHIN	BLUE SERGE
ESDRAS	HERMAN	POLICEMAN	
THE HOBO		RADICAL	
1ST GIRL		SERGEANT	

ACT I

SCENE ONE

The scene is the bank of a river
under a bridgehead. A gigantic span
starts from the rear of the stage and
appears to lift over the heads of the
audience and out to the left. At the
right rear is a wall of solid supporting
masonry. To the left an apartment
building abuts against the bridge and
forms the left wall of the stage with a
dark basement window and a door in
the brick wall. To the right, and in
the foreground, an outcropping of
original rock makes a barricade behind
which one may enter through a cleft.
To the rear, against the masonry, two

sheds have been built by waifs and
strays for shelter. The river bank, in
the foreground, is black rock worn
smooth by years of trampling. There
is room for exit and entrance to the
left around the apartment house, also
around the rock to the right. A single
street lamp is seen at the left—and a
glimmer of apartment lights in the
background beyond. It is an early,
dark December morning.

TWO YOUNG MEN IN SERGE *lean
against the masonry, matching bills.*
TROCK *and* SHADOW *come in from the
left.*

TROCK. Go back and watch the car.
[*The* TWO YOUNG MEN *go out.* TROCK

walks to the corner and looks toward the city.]

You roost of punks and gulls! Sleep, sleep it off,

whatever you had last night, get down in warm,

one big ham-fat against another—sleep,

cling, sleep and rot! Rot out your pasty guts

with diddling, you had no brain to begin. If you had

there'd be no need for us to sleep on iron

who had too much brains for you.

SHADOW. Now look, Trock, look,

what would the warden say to talk like that?

TROCK. May they die as I die!

By God, what life they've left me they shall keep me well! I'll have that out of them—

these pismires that walk like men!

SHADOW. Because, look, chief,

it's all against science and penology

for you to get out and begin to cuss that way

before your prison vittles are out of you. Hell,

you're supposed to leave the pen full of high thought,

kind of noble-like, loving toward all mankind,

ready to kiss their feet—or whatever parts

they stick out toward you. Look at me!

TROCK. I see you.

And even you may not live as long as you think.

You think too many things are funny. Well, laugh.

But it's not so funny.

SHADOW. Come on, Trock, you know me.

Anything you say goes, but give me leave

to kid a little.

TROCK. Then laugh at somebody else!

It's a lot safer! They've soaked me once too often

in that vat of poisoned hell they keep up-state

to soak men in, and I'm rotten inside, I'm all

one liquid puke inside where I had lungs

once, like yourself! And now they want to get me

and stir me in again—and that'd kill me—

and that's fine for them. But before that happens to me

a lot of these healthy boys'll know what it's like

when you try to breathe and have no place to put air—

they'll learn it from me!

SHADOW. They've got nothing on you, chief.

TROCK. I don't know yet. That's what I'm here to find out.

If they've got what they might have. It's not a year this time—

no, nor ten. It's screwed down under a lid.—

I can die quick enough, without help.

SHADOW. You're the skinny kind

that lives forever.

TROCK. He gave me a half a year,

the doc at the gate.

SHADOW. Jesus.

TROCK. Six months I get,

and the rest's dirt, six feet.

[LUCIA, *the street-piano man, comes in right from behind the rock and goes to the shed where he keeps his piano.* PINY, *the apple-woman, follows and stands in the entrance.* LUCIA *speaks to* ESTRELLA, *who still stands facing* SHADOW.]

LUCIA. Morning.

[TROCK *and* SHADOW *go out round the apartment house without speaking.*]

PINY. Now what would you call them?

LUCIA. Maybe someting da river
    washed up.
PINY. Nothing ever washed him—that
    black one.
LUCIA. Maybe not, maybe so. More
    like his pa and ma raise-a heem
    in da cellar. [*He wheels out the
    piano.*]
PINY. He certainly gave me a turn.
[*She lays a hand on the rock.*]
LUCIA. You don' live-a right, ol' gal.
    Take heem easy. Look on da
    bright-a side. Never say-a die.
    Me, every day in every way I
    getta be da regular heller. [*He
    starts out.*]

CURTAIN

SCENE TWO

*A cellar apartment under the apart-
ment building, floored with cement
and roofed with huge boa constrictor
pipes that run slantwise from left to
right, dwarfing the room. An outside
door opens to the left and a door at
the right rear leads to the interior of
the place. A low squat window to the
left. A table at the rear and a few
chairs and books make up the furniture.* GARTH, *son of* ESDRAS, *sits alone,
holding a violin upside down to inspect a crack at its base. He lays the
bow on the floor and runs his fingers
over the joint.* MIRIAMNE *enters from
the rear, a girl of fifteen.* GARTH *looks
up, then down again.*

MIRIAMNE. Garth—
GARTH. The glue lets go. It's the
    steam, I guess.
It splits the hair on your head.
MIRIAMNE. It can't be mended?
GARTH. I can't mend it.
No doubt there are fellows somewhere
who'd mend it for a dollar—and glad
    to do it.
That is if I had a dollar.—Got a
    dollar?
No, I thought not.

MIRIAMNE. Garth, you've sat at home
    here
three days now. You haven't gone
    out at all.
Something frightens you.
GARTH. Yes?
MIRIAMNE. And father's frightened.
He reads without knowing where.
    When a shadow falls
across the page he waits for a blow
    to follow
after the shadow. Then in a little
    while
he puts his book down softly and goes
    out
to see who passed.
GARTH. A bill collector, maybe.
We haven't paid the rent.
MIRIAMNE. No.
GARTH. You're a bright girl, sis.—
You see too much. You run along and
    cook.
Why don't you go to school?
MIRIAMNE. I don't like school.
They whisper behind my back.
GARTH. Yes? about what?
MIRIAMNE. What did the lawyer
    mean that wrote to you?
GARTH [*rising*].
What lawyer?
MIRIAMNE. I found a letter
on the floor of your room. He said,
    "Don't get me wrong,
but stay in out of the rain the next
    few days,
just for instance."
GARTH. I thought I burned that letter.
MIRIAMNE. Afterward you did. And
    then what was printed
about the Estrella gang—you hid it
    from me,
you and father. What is it—about this
    murder—?
GARTH. Will you shut up, you fool!
MIRIAMNE. But if you know
why don't you tell them, Garth?
If it's true—what they say—
you knew all the time Romagna
    wasn't guilty,

and could have said so—

GARTH. Everybody knew
Romagna wasn't guilty! But they
    weren't listening
to evidence in his favor. They didn't
    want it.
They don't want it now.

MIRIAMNE. But was that why
they never called on you?—

GARTH. So far as I know
they never'd heard of me—and I can
    assure you
I knew nothing about it—

MIRIAMNE. But something's wrong—
and it worries father—

GARTH. What could be wrong?

MIRIAMNE. I don't know.

[*A pause.*]

GARTH. And I don't know. You're a
    good kid, Miriamne,
but you see too many movies. I
    wasn't mixed up
in any murder, and I don't mean to be.
If I had a dollar to get my fiddle fixed
and another to hire a hall, by God
    I'd fiddle
some of the prodigies back into Sun-
    day School
where they belong, but I won't get
    either, and so
I sit here and bite my nails—but if
    you hoped
I had some criminal romantic past
you'll have to look again!

MIRIAMNE. Oh, Garth, forgive me—
But I want you to be so far above such
    things
nothing could frighten you. When
    you seem to shrink
and be afraid, and you're the brother
    I love,
I want to run there and cry, if there's
    any question
they care to ask, you'll be quick and
    glad to answer,
for there's nothing to conceal!

GARTH. And that's all true—

MIRIAMNE. But then I remember—
how you dim the lights—

and we go early to bed—and speak in
    whispers—
and I could think there's a death
    somewhere behind us—
an evil death—

GARTH [*hearing a step*].
Now for God's sake, be quiet!

[ESDRAS, *an old rabbi with a kindly
    face, enters from the outside. He
    is hurried and troubled.*]

ESDRAS. I wish to speak alone with
    someone here
if I may have this room. Miriamne—

MIRIAMNE. [*turning to go*].
Yes, father.

[*The outer door is suddenly thrown
    open.* TROCK *appears.*]

TROCK [*after a pause*].
You'll excuse me for not knocking.

[SHADOW *follows* TROCK *in.*]
Sometimes it's best to come in quiet.
    Sometimes
it's a good way to go out. Garth's
    home, I see.
He might not have been here if I
    made a point
of knocking at doors.

GARTH. How are you, Trock?

TROCK. I guess
you can see how I am.

[*To* MIRIAMNE.]
    Stay here. Stay where you are.
We'd like to make your acquaintance.
—If you want the facts
I'm no better than usual, thanks. Not
    enough sun,
my physician tells me. Too much close
    confinement.
A lack of exercise and an overplus
of beans in the diet. You've done well,
    no doubt?

GARTH. I don't know what makes you
    think so.

TROCK. Who's the family?

GARTH. My father and my sister.

TROCK. Happy to meet you.
Step inside a minute. The boy and I
have something to talk about.

ESDRAS. No, no—he's said nothing—

nothing, sir, nothing!

TROCK. When I say go out, you go—

ESDRAS [*pointing to the door*].
Miriamne—

GARTH. Go on out, both of you!

ESDRAS. Oh, sir—I'm old—
old and unhappy—

GARTH. Go on!

[MIRIAMNE *and* ESDRAS *go inside.*]

TROCK. And if you listen
I'll riddle that door!

[SHADOW *shuts the door behind them
and stands against it.*]
I just got out, you see,
and I pay my first call on you.

GARTH. Maybe you think
I'm not in the same jam you are.

TROCK. That's what I do think.
Who started looking this up?

GARTH. I wish I knew,
and I wish he was in hell! Some
damned professor
with nothing else to do. If you saw his
stuff
you know as much as I do.

TROCK. It wasn't you
turning state's evidence?

GARTH. Hell, Trock, use your brain!
The case was closed. They burned
Romagna for it
and that finished it. Why should I
look for trouble
and maybe get burned myself?

TROCK. Boy, I don't know,
but I just thought I'd find out.

GARTH. I'm going straight, Trock.
I can play this thing, and I'm trying
to make a living.
I haven't talked and nobody's talked
to me.
Christ—it's the last thing I'd want!

TROCK. Your old man knows.

GARTH. That's where I got the money
that last time
when you needed it. He had a little
saved up,
but I had to tell him to get it. He's as
safe
as Shadow there.

TROCK [*looking at* SHADOW].
There could be people safer
than that son-of-a-bitch.

SHADOW. Who?

TROCK. You'd be safer dead
along with some other gorillas.

SHADOW. It's beginning to look
as if you'd feel safer with everybody
dead,
the whole god-damn world.

TROCK. I would. These Jesus-bitten
professors! Looking up their half-ass
cases!
We've got enough without that.

GARTH. There's no evidence
to reopen the thing.

TROCK. And suppose they called on
you
and asked you to testify?

GARTH. Why then I'd tell 'em
that all I know is what I read in the
papers.
And I'd stick to that.

TROCK. How much does your sister
know?

GARTH. I'm honest with you, Trock.
She read my name
in the professor's pamphlet, and she
was scared
the way anybody would be. She got
nothing
from me, and anyway she'd go to the
chair
herself before she'd send me
there.

TROCK. Like hell.

GARTH. Besides, who wants to go to
trial again
except the radicals?—You and I won't
spill
and unless we did there's nothing to
take to court
as far as I know. Let the radicals go
on howling
about getting a dirty deal. They always howl
and nobody gives a damn. This professor's red—
everybody knows it.

TROCK. You're forgetting the judge.
Where's the damn judge?

GARTH. What judge?

TROCK. Read the morning papers.
It says Judge Gaunt's gone off his nut.
  He's got
that damn trial on his mind, and been
  going round
proving to everybody he was right all
  the time
and the radicals were guilty—stopping
  people
in the street to prove it—and now he's
  nuts entirely
and nobody knows where he is.

GARTH. Why don't they know?

TROCK. Because he's on the loose somewhere! They've got
the police of three cities looking for
  him.

GARTH. Judge Gaunt?

TROCK. Yes. Judge Gaunt.

SHADOW. Why should that worry you?
He's crazy, ain't he? And even if he
  wasn't
he's arguing on your side. You're jit-
  tery, chief.
God, all the judges are looney. You've
  got the jitters,
and you'll damn well give yourself
  away some time
peeing yourself in public.

[TROCK half turns toward SHADOW in
  anger.]
  Don't jump the gun now,
I've got pockets in my clothes, too.

[His hand is in his coat pocket.]

TROCK. All right. Take it easy.

[He takes his hand from his pocket,
  and SHADOW does the same.]

[To GARTH.]
  Maybe you're lying to me and maybe
  you're not.
Stay at home a few days.

GARTH. Sure thing. Why not?

TROCK. And when I say stay home I
  mean stay home.
If I have to go looking for you you'll
  stay a long time

wherever I find you.

[To SHADOW.] Come on. We'll get out
  of here.

[To GARTH.] Be seeing you.

[SHADOW and TROCK go out. After a
  pause GARTH walks over to his
  chair and picks up the violin.
  Then he puts it down and goes
  to the inside door, which he
  opens.]

GARTH. He's gone.

[MIRIAMNE enters, ESDRAS behind
  her.]

MIRIAMNE [going up to GARTH].
Let's not stay here.

[She puts her hands on his arms.]
I thought he'd come for something—
  horrible.
Is he coming back?

GARTH. I don't know.

MIRIAMNE. Who is he, Garth?

GARTH. He'd kill me if I told you who
  he is,
that is, if he knew.

MIRIAMNE. Then don't say it—

GARTH. Yes, and I'll say it! I was with
  a gang one time
that robbed a pay roll. I saw a murder
  done,
and Trock Estrella did it. If that got
  out
I'd go to the chair and so would he—
  that's why
he was here today—

MIRIAMNE. But that's not true—

ESDRAS. He says it
to frighten you, child.

GARTH. Oh, no I don't! I say it
because I've held it in too long! I'm
  damned
if I sit here forever and look at the
  door,
waiting for Trock with his sub-ma-
  chine gun, waiting
for police with a warrant!—I say I'm
  damned, and I am,
no matter what I do! These piddling
  scales
on a violin—first position, third, fifth,

arpeggios in E—and what I'm thinking
is Romagna dead for the murder—
dead while I sat here
dying inside—dead for the thing Trock
did
while I looked on—and I could have
saved him, yes—
but I sat here and let him die instead
of me
because I wanted to live! Well, it's no
life,
and it doesn't matter who I tell, because
I mean to get it over!

MIRIAMNE. Garth, it's not true!

GARTH. I'd take some scum down with
me if I died—
that'd be one good deed—

ESDRAS. Son, son, you're mad—
someone will hear—

GARTH. Then let them hear! I've lived
with ghosts too long, and lied too
long. God damn you
if you keep me from the truth!—
[He turns away.] Oh, God damn the
world!
I don't want to die!

ESDRAS. I should have known.
I thought you hard and sullen,
Garth, my son. And you were a child,
and hurt
with a wound that might be healed.
—All men have crimes,
and most of them are hidden, and
many are heavy
as yours must be to you.
[GARTH sobs.]
They walk the streets
to buy and sell, but a spreading crimson stain
tinges the inner vestments, touches
flesh,
and burns the quick. You're not alone.

GARTH. I'm alone
in this.

ESDRAS. Yes, if you hold with the
world that only

those who die suddenly should be revenged.
But those whose hearts are cancered,
drop by drop
in small ways, little by little, till
they've borne
all they can bear, and die—these
deaths will go
unpunished now as always. When
we're young
we have faith in what is seen, but
when we're old
we know that what is seen is traced in
air
and built on water. There's no guilt
under heaven,
just as there's no heaven, till men believe it—
no earth, till men have seen it, and
have a word
to say this is the earth.

GARTH. Well, I say there's an earth,
and I say I'm guilty on it, guilty as
hell.

ESDRAS. Yet till it's known you bear no
guilt at all—
unless you wish. The days go by like
film,
like a long written scroll, a figured
veil
unrolling out of darkness into fire
and utterly consumed. And on this
veil,
running in sounds and symbols of
men's minds
reflected back, life flickers and is
shadow
going toward flame. Only what men
can see
exists in that shadow. Why must you
rise and cry out:
That was I, there in the ravelled tapestry,
there, in that pistol flash, when the
man was killed.
I was there, and was one, and am
bloodstained!
Let the wind

and fire take that hour to ashes out of
    time
and out of mind! This thing that men
    call justice,
this blind snake that strikes men down
    in the dark,
mindless with fury, keep your hand
    back from it,
pass by in silence—let it be forgotten,
    forgotten!—
Oh, my son, my son—have pity!
MIRIAMNE. But if it was true
and someone died—then it was more
    than shadow—
and it doesn't blow away—
GARTH. Well, it was true.
ESDRAS. Say it if you must. If you
    have heart to die,
say it, and let them take what's left—
    there was little
to keep, even before—
GARTH. Oh, I'm a coward—
I always was. I'll be quiet and live.
    I'll live
even if I have to crawl. I know.
[*He gets up and goes into the inner
    room.*]
MIRIAMNE. Is it better
to tell a lie and live?
ESDRAS. Yes, child. It's better.
MIRIAMNE. But if I had to do it—
I think I'd die.
ESDRAS. Yes, child. Because you're
    young.
MIRIAMNE. Is that the only reason?
ESDRAS. The only reason.

CURTAIN

SCENE THREE

*Under the bridge, evening of the
same day. When the curtain rises*
MIRIAMNE *is sitting alone on the ledge
at the rear of the apartment house. A
spray of light falls on her from a street
lamp above. She shivers a little in her
thin coat, but sits still as if heedless
of the weather. Through the rocks on
the other side a* TRAMP *comes down
to the river bank, hunting a place to
sleep. He goes softly to the apple-
woman's hut and looks in, then turns
away, evidently not daring to pre-
ëmpt it. He looks at* MIRIAMNE *doubtfully. The door of the street-piano
man is shut. The vagabond passes it
and picks carefully among some rags
and shavings to the right.* MIRIAMNE
*looks up and sees him but makes no
sign. She looks down again, and the
man curls himself up in a makeshift
bed in the corner, pulling a piece
of sacking over his shoulders.* TWO
GIRLS *come in round the apartment
house.*

1ST GIRL. Honest, I never heard of
    anything so romantic. Because
    you never liked him.
2ND GIRL. I certainly never did.
1ST GIRL. You've got to tell me how it
    happened. You've got to.
2ND GIRL. I couldn't. As long as I live
    I couldn't. Honest, it was terrible.
    It was terrible.
1ST GIRL. What was so terrible?
2ND GIRL. The way it happened.
1ST GIRL. Oh, please—not to a soul,
    never.
2ND GIRL. Well, you know how I
    hated him because he had such
    a big mouth. So he reached over
    and grabbed me, and I began all
    falling to pieces inside, the way
    you do—and I said, "Oh no you
    don't mister," and started scream-
    ing and kicked a hole through
    the windshield and lost a shoe,
    and he let go and was cursing
    and growling because he bor-
    rowed the car and didn't have
    money to pay for the windshield,
    and he started to cry, and I got
    so sorry for him I let him, and
    now he wants to marry me.
1ST GIRL. Honest, I never heard of
    anything so romantic! [*She sees*

the sleeping TRAMP.] My God, what you won't see!

[*They give the* TRAMP *a wide berth, and go out right. The* TRAMP *sits up looking about him.* JUDGE GAUNT, *an elderly, quiet man, well dressed but in clothes that have seen some weather, comes in uncertainly from the left. He holds a small clipping in his hand and goes up to the* HOBO.]

GAUNT [*tentatively*]. Your pardon, sir. Your pardon, but perhaps you can tell me the name of this street.

HOBO. Huh?

GAUNT. The name of this street?

HOBO. This ain't no street.

GAUNT. There, where the street lamps are.

HOBO. That's the alley.

GAUNT. Thank you. It has a name, no doubt?

HOBO. That's the alley.

GAUNT. I see. I won't trouble you. You wonder why I ask, I daresay.— I'm a stranger.—Why do you look at me? [*He steps back.*] I— I'm not the man you think. You've mistaken me, sir.

HOBO. Huh?

JUDGE. Perhaps misled by a resemblance. But you're mistaken—I had an errand in this city. It's only by accident that I'm here——

HOBO [*muttering*]. You go to hell.

JUDGE [*going nearer to him, bending over him*]. Yet why should I deceive you? Before God, I held the proofs in my hands. I hold them still. I tell you the defense was cunning beyond belief, and unscrupulous in its use of propaganda—they gagged at nothing —not even—[*He rises.*] No, no— I'm sorry—this will hardly interest you. I'm sorry. I have an errand.

[*He looks toward the street.* ESDRAS *enters from the basement and goes to* MIRIAMNE. *The* JUDGE *steps back into the shadows.*]

ESDRAS. Come in, my daughter. You'll be cold here.

MIRIAMNE. After a while.

ESDRAS. You'll be cold. There's a storm coming.

MIRIAMNE. I didn't want him to see me crying. That was all.

ESDRAS. I know.

MIRIAMNE. I'll come soon.

[ESDRAS *turns reluctantly and goes out the way he came.* MIRIAMNE *rises to go in, pausing to dry her eyes.* MIO *and* CARR, *road boys of seventeen or so, come round the apartment house. The* JUDGE *has disappeared.*]

CARR. Thought you said you were never coming east again.

MIO. Yeah, but—I heard something changed my mind.

CARR. Same old business?

MIO. Yes, just as soon not talk about it.

CARR. Where did you go from Portland?

MIO. Fishing—I went fishing. God's truth.

CARR. Right after I left?

MIO. Fell in with a fisherman's family on the coast and went after the beautiful mackerel fish that swim in the beautiful sea. Family of Greeks—Aristides Marinos was his lovely name. He sang while he fished. Made the pea-green Pacific ring with his bastard Greek chanties. Then I went to Hollywood High School for a while.

CARR. I'll bet that's a seat of learning.

MIO. It's the hind end of all wisdom. They kicked me out after a time.

CARR. For cause?

MIO. Because I had no permanent address, you see. That means nobody's paying school taxes for

you, so out you go. [*To* MIRI-
AMNE.] What's the matter, Kid?

MIRIAMNE. Nothing. [*She looks up
at him, and they pause for a
moment.*] Nothing.

MIO. I'm sorry.

MIRIAMNE. It's all right. [*She with-
draws her eyes from his and goes
out past him. He turns and looks
after her.*]

CARR. Control your chivalry.

MIO. A pretty kid.

CARR. A baby.

MIO. Wait for me.

CARR. Be a long wait? [MIO *steps
swiftly out after* MIRIAMNE, *then
returns.*] Yeah?

MIO. She's gone.

CARR. Think of that.

MIO. No, but I mean—vanished. Presto
—into nothing—prodigioso.

CARR. Damn good thing, if you ask
me. The homely ones are bad
enough, but the lookers are fatal.

MIO. You exaggerate, Carr.

CARR. I doubt it.

MIO. Well, let her go. This river
bank's loaded with typhus rats,
too. Might as well die one death
as another.

CARR. They say chronic alcoholism is
nice but expensive. You can always starve to death.

MIO. Not always. I tried it. After the
second day I walked thirty miles
to Niagara Falls and made a
tour of the plant to get the
sample of shredded wheat biscuit on the way out.

CARR. Last time I saw you you couldn't
think of anything you wanted to
do except curse God and pass
out. Still feeling low?

MIO. Not much different. [*He turns
away, then comes back.*] Talk
about the lost generation, I'm the
only one fits that title. When
the State executes your father,
and your mother dies of grief,

and you know damn well he was
innocent, and the authorities of
your home town politely inform
you they'd consider it a favor if
you lived somewhere else—that
cuts you off from the world—
with a meat-axe.

CARR. They asked you to move?

MIO. It came to that.

CARR. God, that was white of them.

MIO. It probably gave them a headache just to see me after all that
agitation. They knew as well as
I did my father never staged a
holdup. Anyway, I've got a new
interest in life now.

CARR. Yes—I saw her.

MIO. I don't mean the skirt.—No, I
got wind of something, out west,
some college professor investigating the trial and turning up new
evidence. Couldn't find anything
he'd written out there, so I beat
it east and arrived on this blessed
island just in time to find the
bums holing up in the public
library for the winter. I know
now what the unemployed have
been doing since the depression
started. They've been catching
up on their reading in the main
reference room. Man, what a
stench! Maybe I stank, too, but a
hobo has the stench of ten because his shoes are poor.

CARR. Tennyson.

MIO. Right. Jeez, I'm glad we met up
again! Never knew anybody else
that could track me through the
driven snow of Victorian literature.

CARR. Now you're cribbing from some
half-forgotten criticism of Ben
Jonson's Roman plagiarisms.

MIO. Where did you get your education, sap?

CARR. Not in the public library, sap.
My father kept a news-stand.

MIO. Well, you're right again. [*There

is a faint rumble of thunder.]
What's that? Winter thunder?

CARR. Or Mister God, beating on His little tocsin. Maybe announcing the advent of a new social order.

MIO. Or maybe it's going to rain coffee and doughnuts.

CARR. Or maybe it's going to rain.

MIO. Seems more likely. [*Lowering his voice.*] Anyhow, I found Professor Hobhouse's discussion of the Romagna case. I think he has something. It occurred to me I might follow it up by doing a little sleuthing on my own account.

CARR. Yes?

MIO. I have done a little. And it leads me to somewhere in that tenement house that backs up against the bridge. That's how I happen to be here.

CARR. They'll never let you get anywhere with it, Mio. I told you that before.

MIO. I know you did.

CARR. The State can't afford to admit it was wrong, you see. Not when there's been that much of a row kicked up over it. So for all practical purposes the State was right and your father robbed the pay roll.

MIO. There's still such a thing as evidence.

CARR. It's something you can buy. In fact, at the moment I don't think of anything you can't buy, including life, honor, virtue, glory, public office, conjugal affection and all kinds of justice, from the traffic court to the immortal nine. Go out and make yourself a pot of money and you can buy all the justice you want. Convictions obtained, convictions averted. Lowest rate in years.

MIO. I know all that.

CARR. Sure.

MIO. This thing didn't happen to you. They've left you your name
and whatever place you can take. For my heritage
they've left me one thing only, and that's to be
my father's voice crying up out of the earth
and quicklime where they stuck him. Electrocution
doesn't kill, you know. They eviscerate them
with a turn of the knife in the dissecting room.
The blood spurts out. The man was alive. Then into
the lime pit, leave no trace. Make it short shrift
and chemical dissolution. That's what they thought
of the man that was my father. Then my mother—
I tell you these county burials are swift
and cheap and run for profit! Out of the house
and into the ground, you wife of a dead dog. Wait,
here's some Romagna spawn left.
Something crawls here—
something they called a son. Why couldn't he die
along with his mother? Well, ease him out of town,
ease him out, boys, and see you're not too gentle.
He might come back. And, by their own living Jesus,
I will go back, and hang the carrion around their necks that made it!
Maybe I can sleep then.
Or even live.

CARR. You have to try it?

MIO. Yes.
Yes. It won't let me alone. I've tried to live
and forget it—but I was birthmarked with hot iron

into the entrails. I've got to find out
  who did it
and make them see it till it scalds
  their eyes
and make them admit it till their
  tongues are blistered
with saying how black they lied!

[HERMAN, *a gawky shoe salesman,
enters from the left.*]

HERMAN. Hello. Did you see a couple
  of girls go this way?

CARR. Couple of girls? Did we see a
  couple of girls?

MIO. No.

CARR. No. No girls.

[HERMAN *hesitates, then goes out
right.* LUCIA *comes in from the
left, trundling his piano.* PINY
follows him, weeping.]

PINY. They've got no right to do it——

LUCIA. All right, hell what, no matter,
  I got to put him away, I got to
  put him away, that's what the
  hell! [TWO STREET URCHINS *follow him in.*]

PINY. They want everybody on the
  relief rolls and nobody making a
  living?

LUCIA. The cops, they do what the big
  boss say. The big boss, that's the
  mayor, he says he heard it once
  too often, the sextette——

PINY. They want graft, that's all. It's
  a new way to get graft——

LUCIA. Oh, no, no, no! He's a good
  man, the mayor. He's just don't
  care for music, that's all.

PINY. Why shouldn't you make a
  living on the street? The National Biscuit Company ropes off
  Eighth Avenue—and does the
  mayor do anything? No, the
  police hit you over the head if
  you try to go through!

LUCIA. You got the big dough, you get
  the pull, fine. No big dough, no
  pull, what the hell, get off
  the city property! Tomorrow I
  start cooking chestnuts . . . [*He*

strokes the piano fondly. The
TWO GIRLS *and* HERMAN *come
back from the right.*] She's a
good little machine, this baby.
Cost plenty—and two new records I only played twice. See this
one. [*He starts turning the crank,
talking while he plays.*] Two
weeks since they play this one
in a picture house. [*A* SAILOR
*wanders in from the left. One
of the* STREET URCHINS *begins
suddenly to dance a wild
rhumba, the others watch.*] Good
boy—see, it's a lulu—it itches in
the feet!

[HERMAN, *standing with his girl,
tosses the boy a penny. He bows
and goes on dancing; the other*
URCHIN *joins him. The* SAILOR
tosses a coin.]

SAILOR. Go it, Cuba! Go it!

[LUCIA *turns the crank, beaming.*]

2ND GIRL. Oh, Herman! [*She throws
her arms round* HERMAN *and
they dance.*]

1ST URCHIN. Hey, pipe the professionals!

1ST GIRL. Do your glide, Shirley! Do
  your glide!

LUCIA. Maybe we can't play in front,
  maybe we can play behind! [*The*
HOBO *gets up from his nest and
comes over to watch.* A YOUNG
RADICAL *wanders in.*] Maybe you
don't know, folks! Tonight we
play good-bye to the piano! Good-
bye forever! No more piano on
the streets! No more music! No
more money for the music-man!
Last time, folks! Good-bye to the
piano—good-bye forever! [MIRI-
AMNE *comes out the rear door of
the apartment and stands watching. The* SAILOR *goes over to the*
1ST GIRL *and they dance together.*] Maybe you don't know,
folks! Tomorrow will be sad as
hell, tonight we dance! Tomor-

row no more Verdi, no more
rhumba, no more good time! To-
night we play good-bye to the
piano, good-bye forever! [*The*
RADICAL *edges up to* MIRIAMNE
*and asks her to dance. She shakes
her head and he goes to* PINY,
who dances with him. The HOBO
*begins to do a few lonely curvets
on the side above.*] Hoy! Hoy!
Pick 'em up and take 'em around!
Use the head, use the feet! Last
time forever! [*He begins to sing
to the air.*]

MIO. Wait for me, will you?

CARR. Now's your chance.

[MIO *goes over to* MIRIAMNE *and holds
out a hand, smiling. She stands
for a moment uncertain, then
dances with him.* ESDRAS *comes
out to watch.* JUDGE GAUNT
*comes in from the left. There is a
rumble of thunder.*]

LUCIA. Hoy! Hoy! Maybe it rains to-
night, maybe it snows tomorrow!
Tonight we dance good-bye.
[*He sings the air lustily.* A
POLICEMAN *comes in from the
left and looks on.* TWO OR THREE
PEDESTRIANS *follow him.*]

POLICEMAN. Hey you! [LUCIA *goes on
singing.*] Hey, you!

LUCIA [*still playing*]. What you want?

POLICEMAN. Sign off!

LUCIA. What you mean? I get off the
street!

POLICEMAN. Sign off!

LUCIA [*still playing*]. What you mean?
[*The* POLICEMAN *walks over to
him.* LUCIA *stops playing and the
DANCERS pause.*]

POLICEMAN. Cut it.

LUCIA. Is this a street?

POLICEMAN. I say cut it out.

[*The* HOBO *goes back to his nest and
sits in it, watching.*]

LUCIA. It's the last time. We dance
good-bye to the piano.

POLICEMAN. You'll dance good-bye to

something else if I catch you
cranking that thing again.

LUCIA. All right.

PINY. I'll bet you don't say that to the
National Biscuit Company!

POLICEMAN. Lady, you've been selling
apples on my beat for some time
now, and I said nothing about
it——

PINY. Selling apples is allowed——

POLICEMAN. You watch yourself— [*He
takes a short walk around the
place and comes upon the* HOBO.]
What are you doing here? [*The*
HOBO *opens his mouth, points
to it, and shakes his head.*] Oh,
you are, are you? [*He comes back
to* LUCIA.] So you trundle your
so-called musical instrument to
wherever you keep it, and don't
let me hear it again.

[*The* RADICAL *leaps on the base of the
rock at right. The* 1ST GIRL *turns
away from the* SAILOR *toward the
2ND GIRL *and* HERMAN.]

SAILOR. Hey, captain, what's the matter with the music?

POLICEMAN. Not a thing, admiral.

SAILOR. Well, we had a little party
going here——

POLICEMAN. I'll say you did.

2ND GIRL. Please, officer, we want to
dance.

POLICEMAN. Go ahead. Dance.

2ND GIRL. But we want music!

POLICEMAN [*turning to go*]. Sorry.
Can't help you.

RADICAL. And there you see it, the
perfect example of capitalistic oppression! In a land where music
should be free as air and the
arts should be encouraged, a uniformed minion of the rich, a
guardian myrmidon of the Park
Avenue pleasure hunters, steps
in and puts a limit on the innocent enjoyments of the poor! We
don't go to theatres! Why not?
We can't afford it! We don't go

to night clubs, where women dance naked and the music drips from saxophones and leaks out of Rudy Vallee—we can't afford that either!—But we might at least dance on the river bank to the strains of a barrel organ—!

[GARTH *comes out of the apartment and listens.*]

POLICEMAN. It's against the law!

RADICAL. What law? I challenge you to tell me what law of God or man—what ordinance—is violated by this spontaneous diversion? None! I say none! An official whim of the masters who should be our servants!——

POLICEMAN. Get down! Get down and shut up!

RADICAL. By what law, by what ordinance do you order me to be quiet?

POLICEMAN. Speaking without a flag. You know it.

RADICAL [*pulling out a small American flag*]. There's my flag! There's the flag of this United States which used to guarantee the rights of man—the rights of man now violated by every statute of the commonweal——

POLICEMAN. Don't try to pull tricks on me! I've seen you before! You're not making any speech, and you're climbing down——

JUDGE GAUNT [*who has come quietly forward*]. One moment, officer. There is some difference of opinion even on the bench as to the elasticity of police power when applied in minor emergencies to preserve civil order. But the weight of authority would certainly favor the defendant in any equitable court, and he would be upheld in his demand to be heard.

POLICEMAN. Who are you?

GAUNT. Sir, I am not accustomed to answer that question.

POLICEMAN. I don't know you.

GAUNT. I am a judge of some standing, not in your city but in another with similar statutes. You are aware, of course, that the Bill of Rights is not to be set aside lightly by the officers of any municipality——

POLICEMAN [*looking over* GAUNT'S *somewhat bedraggled costume*]. Maybe they understand you better in the town you come from, but I don't get your drift. —[*To the* RADICAL.] I don't want any trouble, but if you ask for it you'll get plenty. Get down!

RADICAL. I'm not asking for trouble, but I'm staying right here. [*The* POLICEMAN *moves towards him.*]

GAUNT [*taking the* POLICEMAN'S *arm, but shaken off roughly*]. I ask this for yourself, truly, not for the dignity of the law nor the maintenance of precedent. Be gentle with them when their threats are childish—be tolerant while you can—for your least harsh word will return on you in the night—return in a storm of cries!—[*He takes the* POLICEMAN'S *arm again.*] Whatever they may have said or done, let them disperse in peace! It is better that they go softly, lest when they are dead you see their eyes pleading, and their outstretched hands touch you, fingering cold on your heart!—I have been harsher than you. I have sent men down that long corridor into blinding light and blind darkness! [*He suddenly draws himself erect and speaks defiantly.*] And it was well that I did so! I have been an upright judge! They are all liars! Liars!

POLICEMAN [*shaking* GAUNT *off so*

that he falls]. Why, you fool,
you're crazy!

GAUNT. Yes, and there are liars on the
force! They came to me with
their shifty lies! [*He catches at
the* POLICEMAN, *who pushes him
away with his foot.*]

POLICEMAN. You think I've got nothing better to do than listen to a
crazy fool?

1ST GIRL. Shame, shame!

POLICEMAN. What have I got to be
ashamed of? And what's going
on here, anyway? Where in hell
did you all come from?

RADICAL. Tread on him! That's right!
Tread down the poor and the
innocent! [*There is a protesting
murmur in the crowd.*]

SAILOR [*moving in a little*]. Say, big
boy, you don't have to step on
the guy.

POLICEMAN [*facing them, stepping
back*]. What's the matter with
you! I haven't stepped on anybody!

MIO [*at the right, across from the
POLICEMAN*].
Listen now, fellows, give the badge a
chance.
He's doing his job, what he gets paid
to do,
the same as any of you. They're all
picked men,
these metropolitan police, hand
picked
for loyalty and a fine up-standing pair
of shoulders on their legs—it's not so
easy
to represent the law. Think what he
does
for all of us, stamping out crime!
Do you want to be robbed and murdered in your beds?

SAILOR. What's eating you?

RADICAL. He must be a capitalist.

MIO. They pluck them fresh,
from Ireland, and a paucity of head-
piece

is a prime prerequisite. You from Ireland, buddy?

POLICEMAN [*surly*].
Where are you from?

MIO. Buddy, I tell you flat
I wish I was from Ireland, and could
boast
some Tammany connections. There's
only one drawback
about working on the force. It infects
the brain,
it eats the cerebrum. There've been
cases known,
fine specimens of manhood, too, where
autopsies,
conducted in approved scientific fashion,
revealed conditions quite incredible
in policemen's upper layers. In some,
a trace,
in others, when they've swung a stick
too long,
there was nothing there!—but nothing! Oh, my friends,
this fine athletic figure of a man
that stands so grim before us, what
will they find
when they saw his skull for the last
inspection?
I fear me a little puffball dust will
blow away
rejoining earth, our mother—and this
same dust,
this smoke, this ash on the wind, will
represent
all he had left to think with!

THE HOBO. Hooray!

[*The* POLICEMAN *turns on his heel
and looks hard at the* HOBO, *who
slinks away.*]

POLICEMAN. Oh, yeah?

MIO. My theme
gives ears to the deaf and voice to the
dumb! But now
forgive me if I say you were most
unkind
in troubling the officer. He's a simple
man
of simple tastes, and easily confused

when faced with complex issues. He
    may reflect
on returning home, that is, so far as he
is capable of reflection, and conclude
that he was kidded out of his uniform
    pants,
and in his fury when this dawns on
    him
may smack his wife down!

POLICEMAN. That'll be about enough
from you, too, professor!

MIO. May I say that I think you have
managed this whole situation
rather badly, from the beginning?——

POLICEMAN. You may not!

[TROCK *slips in from the background.
The* TWO YOUNG MEN IN SERGE
come with him.]

MIO. Oh, but your pardon, sir! It's apparent to the least competent
among us that you should have
gone about your task more subtly
—the glove of velvet, the hand
of iron, and all that sort of
thing——

POLICEMAN. Shut that hole in your
face!

MIO. Sir, for that remark I shall be
satisfied with nothing less than
an unconditional apology! I have
an old score to settle with policemen, brother, because they're
fools and fat-heads, and you're
one of the most fatuous fat-heads
that ever walked his feet flat collecting graft! Tell that to your
sergeant back in the booby-
hatch——

POLICEMAN. Oh, you want an apology, do you? You'll get an
apology out of the other side of
your mouth! [*He steps toward*
MIO. CARR *suddenly stands in his
path.*] Get out of my way! [*He
pauses and looks round him; the
crowd looks less and less friendly.
He lays a hand on his gun and
backs to a position where there*

is nobody behind him.] Get out
of here, all of you! Get out!
What are you trying to do—start
a riot?

MIO. There now, that's better! That's
in the best police tradition. Incite a riot yourself and then accuse the crowd.

POLICEMAN. It won't be pleasant if I
decide to let somebody have it!
Get out!

[*The onlookers begin to melt away.
The* SAILOR *goes out left with
the* GIRLS *and* HERMAN. CARR
and MIO *go out right,* CARR
*whistling "The Star-Spangled
Banner." The* HOBO *follows
them. The* RADICAL *walks past
with his head in the air.* PINY
and LUCIA *leave the piano where
it stands and slip away to the
left. At the end the* POLICEMAN
is left standing in the center, the
JUDGE *near him.* ESDRAS *stands
in the doorway.* MIRIAMNE *is left
sitting half in shadow and unseen by* ESDRAS.]

JUDGE GAUNT [*to the* POLICEMAN].
Yes, but should a man die,
should it be necessary that one
man die for the good of many,
make not yourself the instrument of death, lest you sleep to
wake sobbing! Nay, it avails
nothing that you are the law—
this delicate ganglion that is the
brain, it will not bear these
things—!

[*The* POLICEMAN *gives the* JUDGE *the
once-over, shrugs, decides to leave
him there and starts out left.*
GARTH *goes to his father—a fine
sleet begins to fall through the
street lights.* TROCK *is still visible.*]

GARTH. Get him in here, quick.

ESDRAS. Who, son?

GARTH. The Judge, damn him!

ESDRAS. Is it Judge Gaunt?

GARTH. Who did you think it was?
He's crazy as a bedbug and tell-
ing the world. Get him inside.
[*He looks round.*]

ESDRAS [*going up to* GAUNT]. Will
you come in, sir?

GAUNT. You will understand, sir.
We old men know how softly
we must proceed with these
things.

ESDRAS. Yes, surely, sir.

GAUNT. It was always my practice—always. They will tell you that of
me where I am known. Yet even
I am not free of regret—even I.
Would you believe it?

ESDRAS. I believe we are none of us
free of regret.

GAUNT. None of us? I would it were
true. I would I thought it were
true.

ESDRAS. Shall we go in, sir? This is
sleet that's falling.

GAUNT. Yes. Let us go in.

[ESDRAS, GAUNT *and* GARTH *enter the
basement and shut the door.*
TROCK *goes out with his men.
After a pause* MIO *comes back
from the right, alone. He stands
at a little distance from* MIRI-
AMNE.]

MIO. Looks like rain. [*She is silent.*]
You live around here? [*She nods
gravely.*] I guess
you thought I meant it—about waiting here to meet me. [*She nods
again.*]
I'd forgotten about it till I got that
winter
across the face. You'd better go inside.
I'm not your kind. I'm nobody's kind
but my own.
I'm waiting for this to blow over.
[*She rises.*]
    I lied. I meant it—
I meant it when I said it—but there's
too much black
whirling inside me—for any girl to
know.

So go on in. You're somebody's angel
child
and they're waiting for you.

MIRIAMNE. Yes. I'll go. [*She turns.*]

MIO. And tell them
when you get inside where it's warm,
and you love each other,
and mother comes to kiss her darling,
tell them
to hang on to it while they can, believe while they can
it's a warm safe world, and Jesus finds
his lambs
and carries them in his bosom.—I've
seen some lambs
that Jesus missed. If they ever want
the truth
tell them that nothing's guaranteed in
this climate
except it gets cold in winter, nor on
this earth
except you die sometime.
[*He turns away.*]

MIRIAMNE. I have no mother.
and my people are Jews.

MIO. Then you know something about
it.

MIRIAMNE. Yes.

MIO. Do you have enough to eat?

MIRIAMNE. Not always.

MIO. What do you believe in?

MIRIAMNE. Nothing.

MIO. Why?

MIRIAMNE. How can one?

MIO. It's easy if you're a fool. You see
the words
in books. Honor, it says there, chivalry, freedom,
heroism, enduring love—and these
are words on paper. It's something to
have them there.
You'll get them nowhere else.

MIRIAMNE. What hurts you?

MIO. Just that.
You'll get them nowhere else.

MIRIAMNE. Why should you want
them?

MIO. I'm alone, that's why. You see
those lights,

along the river, cutting across the
rain—?
those are the hearths of Brooklyn, and
up this way
the love-nests of Manhattan—they
turn their points
like knives against me—outcast of the
world,
snake in the streets.—I don't want a
hand-out.
I sleep and eat.

MIRIAMNE. Do you want me to go
with you?

MIO. Where?

MIRIAMNE. Where you go.

[*A pause. He goes nearer to her.*]

MIO. Why, you god-damned little
fool—
what made you say that?

MIRIAMNE. I don't know.

MIO. If you have a home
stay in it. I ask for nothing. I've
schooled myself
to ask for nothing, and take what I
can get,
and get along. If I fell for you, that's
my look-out,
and I'll starve it down.

MIRIAMNE. Wherever you go, I'd go.

MIO. What do you know about loving?
How could you know?
Have you ever had a man?

MIRIAMNE [*after a slight pause*]. No.
But I know.
Tell me your name.

MIO. Mio. What's yours?

MIRIAMNE. Miriamne.

MIO. There's no such name.

MIRIAMNE. But there's no such name
as Mio!

M.I.O. It's no name.

MIO. It's for Bartolomeo.

MIRIAMNE. My mother's name was
Miriam,
so they called me Miriamne.

MIO. Meaning little Miriam?

MIRIAMNE. Yes.

MIO. So now little Miriamne will go
in

and take up quietly where she
dropped them all
her small housewifely cares.—When I
first saw you,
not a half-hour ago, I heard myself
saying,
this is the face that launches ships for
me—
and if I owned a dream—yes, half a
dream—
we'd share it. But I have no dream.
This earth
came tumbling down from chaos, fire
and rock,
and bred up worms, blind worms that
sting each other
here in the dark. These blind worms
of the earth
took out my father—and killed him,
and set a sign
on me—the heir of the serpent—and
he was a man
such as men might be if the gods were
men—
but they killed him—
as they'll kill all others like him
till the sun cools down to the stabler
molecules,
yes, till men spin their tent-worm
webs to the stars
and what they think is done, even in
the thinking,
and they are the gods, and immortal,
and constellations
turn for them all like mill wheels—
still as they are
they will be, worms and blind. Enduring love,
oh gods and worms, what mockery!—
And yet
I have blood enough in my veins. It
goes like music,
singing, because you're here. My body
turns
as if you were the sun, and warm.
This men called love
in happier times, before the Freudians
taught us
to blame it on the glands. Only go in

before you breathe too much of my
    atmosphere
and catch death from me.

MIRIAMNE. I will take my hands
and weave them to a little house, and
    there
you shall keep a dream——

MIO. God knows I could use a dream
and even a house.

MIRIAMNE. You're laughing at me,
    Mio!

MIO. The worms are laughing.
I tell you there's death about me
and you're a child! And I'm alone and
    half mad
with hate and longing. I shall let you
    love me
and love you in return, and then, why
    then
God knows what happens!

MIRIAMNE. Something most unpleas-
    ant?

MIO. Love in a boxcar—love among
    the children.
I've seen too much of it. Are we to
    live
in this same house you make with
    your two hands
mystically, out of air?

MIRIAMNE. No roof, no mortgage!
Well, I shall marry a baker out in
    Flatbush,
it gives hot bread in the morning! Oh,
    Mio, Mio,
in all the unwanted places and waste
    lands
that roll up into the darkness out of
    sun
and into sun out of dark, there should
    be one empty
for you and me.

MIO. No.

MIRIAMNE. Then go now and leave
    me.
I'm only a girl you saw in the tene-
    ments,
and there's been nothing said.

MIO. Miriamne.

[*She takes a step toward him.*]

MIRIAMNE. Yes. [*He kisses her lips
    lightly.*]

MIO. Why, girl, the transfiguration on
    the mount
was nothing to your face. It lights
    from within—
a white chalice holding fire, a flower
    in flame,
this is your face.

MIRIAMNE. And you shall drink the
    flame
and never lessen it. And round your
    head
the aureole shall burn that burns
    there now,
forever. This I can give you. And so
    forever
the Freudians are wrong.

MIO. They're well-forgotten
at any rate.

MIRIAMNE. Why did you speak to
    me
when you first saw me?

MIO. I knew then.

MIRIAMNE. And I came back
because I must see you again. And we
    danced together
and my heart hurt me. Never, never,
    never,
though they should bind me down
    and tear out my eyes,
would I ever hurt you now. Take me
    with you, Mio,
let them look for us, whoever there is
    to look,
but we'll be away.

[MIO *turns away toward the tene-
    ment.*]

MIO. When I was four years old
we climbed through an iron gate, my
    mother and I,
to see my father in prison. He stood
    in the death-cell
and put his hand through the bars
    and said, My Mio,
I have only this to leave you, that I
    love you,
and will love you after I die. Love me
    then, Mio,

when this hard thing comes on you,
    that you must live
a man despised for your father. That
    night the guards,
walking in flood-lights brighter than
    high noon,
led him between them with his trou-
    sers slit
and a shaven head for the cathodes.
    This sleet and rain
that I feel cold here on my face and
    hands
will find him under thirteen years of
    clay
in prison ground. Lie still and rest,
    my father,
for I have not forgotten. When I for-
    get
may I lie blind as you. No other love,
time passing, nor the spaced light-
    years of suns
shall blur your voice, or tempt me
    from the path
that clears your name—
till I have these rats in my grip
or sleep deep where you sleep.
[*To* MIRIAMNE.] I have no house,
nor home, nor love of life, nor fear of
    death,
nor care for what I eat, or who I sleep
    with,
or what color of calcimine the Gov-
    ernment
will wash itself this year or next to
    lure
the sheep and feed the wolves. Love
    somewhere else,
and get your children in some other
    image
more acceptable to the State! This
    face of mine
is stamped for sewage!
[*She steps back, surmising.*]
MIRIAMNE. Mio——
MIO. My road is cut
in rock, and leads to one end. If I hurt
    you, I'm sorry.
One gets over hurts.
MIRIAMNE. What was his name—

your father's name?
MIO. Bartolomeo Romagna.
I'm not ashamed of it.
MIRIAMNE. Why are you here?
MIO. For the reason
I've never had a home. Because I'm a
    cry
out of a shallow grave, and all roads
    are mine
that might revenge him!
MIRIAMNE. But Mio—why here—why
    here?
MIO. I can't tell you that.
MIRIAMNE. No—but—there's someone
lives here—lives not far—and you
    mean to see him—
you mean to ask him——[*She pauses.*]
MIO. Who told you that?
MIRIAMNE. His name
is Garth—Garth Esdras——
MIO [*after a pause, coming nearer*].
Who are you, then? You seem
to know a good deal about me.—Were
    you sent
to say this?
MIRIAMNE. You said there was death
    about you! Yes,
but nearer than you think! Let it be
    as it is—
let it all be as it is, never see this place
nor think of it—forget the streets you
    came
when you're away and safe! Go be-
    fore you're seen
or spoken to!
MIO. Will you tell me why?
MIRIAMNE. As I love you
I can't tell you—and I can never see
    you——
MIO. I walk where I please——
MIRIAMNE. Do you think it's easy for
    me
to send you away? [*She steps back as
    if to go.*]
MIO. Where will I find you then
if I should want to see you?
MIRIAMNE. Never—I tell you
I'd bring you death! Even now. Lis-
    ten!

[SHADOW *and* TROCK *enter between the bridge and the tenement house.* MIRIAMNE *pulls* MIO *back into the shadow of the rock to avoid being seen.*]

TROCK. Why, fine.

SHADOW. You watch it now—just for the record, Trock—

you're going to thank me for staying away from it

and keeping you out. I've seen men get that way,

thinking they had to plug a couple of guys

and then a few more to cover it up, and then

maybe a dozen more. You can't own all

and territory adjacent, and you can't

slough all the witnesses, because every man

you put away has friends——

TROCK. I said all right.

I said fine.

SHADOW. They're going to find this judge,

and if they find him dead it's just too bad,

and I don't want to know anything about it—

and you don't either.

TROCK. You all through?

SHADOW. Why sure.

TROCK. All right.

We're through, too, you know.

SHADOW. Yeah? [*He becomes wary.*]

TROCK. Yeah, we're through.

SHADOW. I've heard that said before, and afterwards

somebody died.

[TROCK *is silent.*] Is that what you mean?

TROCK. You can go.

I don't want to see you.

SHADOW. Sure, I'll go.

Maybe you won't mind if I just find out

what you've got on you. Before I turn my back.

I'd like to know.

[*Silently and expertly he touches* TROCK'S *pockets, extracting a gun.*]

Not that I'd distrust you.

but you know how it is. [*He pockets the gun.*]

So long, Trock.

TROCK. So long.

SHADOW. I won't talk.

You can be sure of that.

TROCK. I know you won't.

[SHADOW *turns and goes out right, past the rock and along the bank. As he goes the* TWO YOUNG MEN IN BLUE SERGE *enter from the left and walk slowly after* SHADOW. *They look toward* TROCK *as they enter and he motions with his thumb in the direction taken by* SHADOW. *They follow* SHADOW *out without haste.* TROCK *watches them disappear, then slips out the way he came.* MIO *comes a step forward, looking after the two men. Two or three shots are heard, then silence.* MIO *starts to run after* SHADOW.]

MIRIAMNE. Mio!

MIO. What do you know about this?

MIRIAMNE. The other way,

Mio—quick!

[CARR *slips in from the right, in haste.*]

CARR. Look, somebody's just been shot.

He fell in the river. The guys that did the shooting

ran up the bank.

MIO. Come on.

[MIO *and* CARR *run out right.* MIRIAMNE *watches uncertainly, then slowly turns and walks to the rear door of the tenement. She stands there a moment, looking after* MIO, *then goes in, closing the door.* CARR *and* MIO *return.*]

CARR. There's a rip tide past the point.

You'd never find him.

MIO. No.

CARR. You know a man really ought to carry insurance living around here.—God, it's easy, putting a fellow away. I never saw it done before.

MIO [*looking at the place where* MIRIAMNE *stood*]. They have it all worked out.

CARR. What are you doing now?

MIO. I have a little business to transact in this neighborhood.

CARR. You'd better forget it.

MIO. No.

CARR. Need any help?

MIO. Well, if I did I'd ask you first. But I don't see how it would do any good. So you keep out of it and take care of yourself.

CARR. So long, then.

MIO. So long, Carr.

CARR [*looking down-stream*]. He was drifting face up. Must be half-way to the island the way the tide runs. [*He shivers.*] God, it's cold here. Well——

[*He goes out to the left.* MIO *sits on the edge of the rock.* LUCIA *comes stealthily back from between the bridge and the tenement, goes to the street-piano and wheels it away.* PINY *comes in. They take a look at* MIO, *but say nothing.* LUCIA *goes into his shelter and* PINY *into hers.* MIO *rises, looks up at the tenement, and goes out to the left.*]

CURTAIN

ACT II

The basement as in Scene Two of Act I. The same evening. ESDRAS *sits at the table reading,* MIRIAMNE *is seated at the left, listening and intent. The door of the inner room is half open and* GARTH'S *violin is heard. He is playing the theme from the third movement of Beethoven's Archduke Trio.* ESDRAS *looks up.*

ESDRAS. I remember when I came to the end
of all the Talmud said, and the commentaries,
then I was fifty years old—and it was time
to ask what I had learned. I asked this question
and gave myself the answer. In all the Talmud
there was nothing to find but the names of things,
set down that we might call them by those names
and walk without fear among things known. Since then
I have had twenty years to read on and on
and end with Ecclesiastes. Names of names,
evanid days, evanid nights and days
and words that shift their meaning. Space is time,
that which was is now—the men of to-morrow
live and this is their yesterday. All things
that were and are and will be, have their being
then and now and to come. If this means little
when you are young, remember it. It will return
to mean more when you are old.

MIRIAMNE. I'm sorry—I
was listening for something.

ESDRAS. It doesn't matter.
It's a useless wisdom. It's all I have,
but useless. It may be there is no time,
but we grow old. Do you know his name?

MIRIAMNE. Whose name?

ESDRAS. Why, when we're young and listen for a step
the step should have a name——

[MIRIAMNE, *not hearing, rises and goes to the window.* GARTH *enters from within, carrying his*

*violin and carefully closing the
door.]*

GARTH [*as* ESDRAS *looks at him*].
Asleep.

ESDRAS. He may
sleep on through the whole night—
    then in the morning
we can let them know.

GARTH. We'd be wiser to say noth-
    ing—
let him find his own way back.

ESDRAS. How did he come here?

GARTH. He's not too crazy for that.
    If he wakes again
we'll keep him quiet and shift him off
    tomorrow.
Somebody'd pick him up.

ESDRAS. How have I come
to this sunken end of a street, at a
    life's end——?

GARTH. It was cheaper here—not to be
    transcendental—
So—we say nothing——?

ESDRAS. Nothing.

MIRIAMNE. Garth, there's no place
in this whole city—not one—
where you would be safer
than here—tonight—or tomorrow.

GARTH [*bitterly*]. Well, that may be.
What of it?

MIRIAMNE. If you slipped away and
    took
a place somewhere where Trock
    couldn't find you——

GARTH. Yes—
using what for money? and why do
    you think
I've sat here so far—because I love
    my home
so much? No, but if I stepped round
    the corner
it'd be my last corner and my last
    step.

MIRIAMNE. And yet—
if you're here—they'll find you here—
Trock will come again—
and there's worse to follow——

GARTH. Do you want to get me killed?

MIRIAMNE. No.

GARTH. There's no way out of it.
    We'll wait
and take what they send us.

ESDRAS. Hush! You'll wake him.

GARTH. I've done it.
I hear him stirring now.

[*They wait quietly.* JUDGE GAUNT
    opens the door and enters.]

GAUNT [*in the doorway*]. I beg your
    pardon—
no, no, be seated—keep your place—
    I've made
your evening difficult enough, I fear;
and I must thank you doubly for your
    kindness,
for I've been ill—I know it.

ESDRAS. You're better, sir?

GAUNT. Quite recovered, thank you.
    Able, I hope,
to manage nicely now. You'll be re-
    warded
for your hospitality—though at this
    moment
[*He smiles.*] I'm low in funds.
[*He inspects his billfold.*] Sir, my em-
    barrassment
is great indeed—and more than mon-
    etary,
for I must own my recollection's
    vague
of how I came here—how we came to-
    gether—
and what we may have said. My
    name is Gaunt,
Judge Gaunt, a name long known in
    the criminal courts,
and not unhonored there.

ESDRAS. My name is Esdras—
and this is Garth, my son. And Mir-
    iamne,
the daughter of my old age.

GAUNT. I'm glad to meet you.
Esdras. Garth Esdras.
[*He passes a hand over his eyes.*]
    It's not a usual name.
Of late it's been connected with a
    case—
a case I knew. But this is hardly the
    man.

Though it's not a usual name.
[*They are silent.*] Sir, how I came
    here,
as I have said, I don't well know.
    Such things
are sometimes not quite accident.
ESDRAS. We found you
outside our door and brought you in.
GAUNT. The brain
can be overworked, and weary, even
    when the man
would swear to his good health. Sir,
    on my word
I don't know why I came here, nor
    how, nor when,
nor what would explain it. Shall we
    say the machine
begins to wear? I felt no twinge of
    it.—
You will imagine how much more
    than galling
I feel it, to ask my way home—and
    where I am—
but I do ask you that.
ESDRAS. This is New York City—
or part of it.
GAUNT. Not the best part, I presume?
[*He smiles grimly.*] No, not the best.
ESDRAS. Not typical, no.
GAUNT. And you—[*To* GARTH.]
you are Garth Esdras?
GARTH. That's my name.
GAUNT. Well, sir, [*To* ESDRAS.]
I shall lie under the deepest obliga-
    tion
if you will set an old man on his path,
for I lack the homing instinct, if the
    truth
were known. North, east and south
    mean nothing to me
here in this room.
ESDRAS. I can put you in your way.
GARTH. Only you'd be wiser to wait a
    while—
if I'm any judge.——
GAUNT. It happens I'm the judge—
[*With stiff humor.*]
in more ways than one. You'll forgive
    me if I say

I find this place and my predicament
somewhat distasteful.
[*He looks round him.*]
GARTH. I don't doubt you do;
but you're better off here.
GAUNT. Nor will you find it wise
to cross my word as lightly as you
    seem
inclined to do. You've seen me ill and
    shaken—
and you presume on that.
GARTH. Have it your way.
GAUNT. Doubtless what information is
    required
we'll find nearby.
ESDRAS. Yes, sir—the terminal,—
if you could walk so far.
GAUNT. I've done some walking—
to look at my shoes.
[*He looks down, then puts out a hand
    to steady himself.*] That—that
    was why I came—
never mind—it was there—and it's
    gone.
[*To* GARTH.] Professor Hobhouse—
that's the name—he wrote some trash
    about you
and printed it in a broadside.
—Since I'm here I can tell you
it's a pure fabrication—lacking facts
and legal import. Senseless and im-
    pudent,
written with bias—with malicious in-
    tent
to undermine the public confidence
in justice and the courts. I knew it
    then—
all he brings out about this testimony
you might have given. It's true I
    could have called you,
but the case was clear—Romagna was
    known guilty,
and there was nothing to add. If I've
    endured
some hours of torture over their at-
    tacks
upon my probity—and in this torture
have wandered from my place, wan-
    dered perhaps

in mind and body—and found my
    way to face you—
why, yes, it is so—I know it—I beg of
    you
say nothing. It's not easy to give up
a fair name after a full half century
of service to a state. It may well rock
the surest reason. Therefore I ask of
    you
say nothing of this visit.

GARTH. I'll say nothing.

ESDRAS. Nor any of us.

GAUNT. Why, no—for you'd lose, too.
    You'd have nothing to gain.

ESDRAS. Indeed we know it.

GAUNT. I'll remember you kindly.
    When I've returned,
there may be some mystery made of
    where I was—
we'll leave it a mystery?

GARTH. Anything you say.

GAUNT. Why, now I go with much
    more peace of mind—if I can call
    you friends.

ESDRAS. We shall be grateful
for silence on your part, Your Honor.

GAUNT. Sir—
if there were any just end to be
    served
by speaking out, I'd speak! There is
    none. No—
bear that in mind!

ESDRAS. We will, Your Honor.

GAUNT. Then—
I'm in some haste. If you can be my
    guide,
we'll set out now.

ESDRAS. Yes, surely.

[*There is a knock at the door. The
    four look at each other with some
    apprehension.* MIRIAMNE *rises.*]
I'll answer it.

MIRIAMNE. Yes.

[*She goes into the inner room and
    closes the door.* ESDRAS *goes to
    the outer door. The knock is re-
    peated. He opens the door.* MIO
    is there.*]

ESDRAS. Yes, sir.

MIO. May I come in?

ESDRAS. Will you state your business,
    sir?
It's late—and I'm not at liberty——

MIO. Why, I might say
that I was trying to earn my tuition
    fees
by peddling magazines. I could say
    that,
or collecting old newspapers—paying
    cash—
highest rates—no questions asked—
[*He looks round sharply.*]

GARTH. We've nothing to sell.
What do you want?

MIO. Your pardon, gentlemen.
My business is not of an ordinary
    kind,
and I felt the need of this slight in-
    troduction
while I might get my bearings. Your
    name is Esdras,
or they told me so outside.

GARTH. What do you want?

MIO. Is that the name?

GARTH. Yes.

MIO. I'll be quick and brief.
I'm the son of a man who died many
    years ago
for a pay roll robbery in New Eng-
    land. You
should be Garth Esdras, by what I've
    heard. You have
some knowledge of the crime, if one
    can believe
what he reads in the public prints,
    and it might be
that your testimony, if given, would
    clear my father
of any share in the murder. You may
    not care
whether he was guilty or not. You
    may not know.
But I do care—and care deeply, and
    I've come
to ask you face to face.

GARTH. To ask me what?

MIO. What do you know of it?

ESDRAS. This man Romagna,

did he have a son?

MIO. Yes, sir, this man Romagna,
as you choose to call him, had a son,
    and I
am that son, and proud.

ESDRAS. Forgive me.

MIO. Had you known him,
and heard him speak, you'd know
    why I'm proud, and why
he was no malefactor.

ESDRAS. I quite believe you.
If my son can help he will. But at this
    moment,
as I told you—could you, I wonder,
    come tomorrow,
at your own hour?

MIO. Yes.

ESDRAS. By coincidence
we too of late have had this thing in
    mind—
there have been comments printed,
    and much discussion
which we could hardly avoid.

MIO. Could you tell me then
in a word?—What you know—
is it for him or against him?—
that's all I need.

ESDRAS. My son knows nothing.

GARTH. No.
The picture-papers lash themselves to
    a fury
over any rumor—make them up when
    they're short
of bedroom slops.—This is what hap-
    pened. I
had known a few members of a gang
    one time
up there—and after the murder they
    picked me up
because I looked like someone that
    was seen
in what they called the murder car.
    They held me
a little while, but they couldn't iden-
    tify me
for the most excellent reason I wasn't
    there
when the thing occurred. A dozen
    years later now

a professor comes across this, and sees
    red
and asks why I wasn't called on as a
    witness
and yips so loud they syndicate his
    picture
in all the rotos. That's all I know
    about it.
I wish I could tell you more.

ESDRAS. Let me say too
that I have read some words your
    father said,
and you were a son fortunate in your
    father,
whatever the verdict of the world.

MIO. There are few
who think so, but it's true, and I
    thank you. Then—
that's the whole story?

GARTH. All I know of it.

MIO. They cover their tracks well, the
    inner ring
that distributes murder. I came three
    thousand miles
to this dead end.

ESDRAS. If he was innocent
and you know him so, believe it, and
    let the others
believe as they like.

MIO. Will you tell me how a man's
to live, and face his life, if he can't
    believe
that truth's like a fire,
and will burn through and be seen
though it takes all the years there
    are?
While I stand up and have breath in
    my lungs
I shall be one flame of that fire;
it's all the life I have.

ESDRAS. Then you must live so.
One must live as he can.

MIO. It's the only way
of life my father left me.

ESDRAS. Yes? Yet it's true
the ground we walk on is impacted
    down
and hard with blood and bones of
    those who died

unjustly. There's not one title to land
   or life,
even your own, but was built on rape
   and murder,
back a few years. It would take a fire
   indeed
to burn out all this terror.
MIO. Then let it burn down,
all of it!
ESDRAS. We ask a great deal of the
   world
at first—then less—and then less.
We ask for truth
and justice. But this truth's a thing
   unknown
in the lightest, smallest matter—and
   as for justice,
who has once seen it done? You loved
   your father,
and I could have loved him, for every
   word he spoke
in his trial was sweet and tolerant, but
   the weight
of what men are and have, rests heavy
   on
the graves of those who lost. They'll
   not rise again,
and their causes lie there with
   them.
GAUNT. If you mean to say
that Bartolomeo Romagna was innocent,
you are wrong. He was guilty.
There may have been injustice
from time to time, by regrettable
   chance, in our courts,
but not in that case, I assure you.
MIO. Oh, you assure me!
You lie in your scrag teeth, whoever
   you are!
My father was murdered!
GAUNT. Romagna was found guilty
by all due process of law, and given
   his chance
to prove his innocence.
MIO. What chance? When a court
panders to mob hysterics, and the
   jury
comes in loaded to soak an anarchist

and a foreigner, it may be due process
   of law
but it's also murder!
GAUNT. He should have thought of
   that
before he spilled blood.
MIO. He?
GAUNT. Sir, I know too well
that he was guilty.
MIO. Who are you? How do you
   know?
I've searched the records through, the
   trial and what
came after, and in all that million
   words
I found not one unbiased argument
to fix the crime on him.
GAUNT. And you yourself,
were you unprejudiced?
MIO. Who are you?
ESDRAS. Sir,
this gentleman is here, as you are
   here,
to ask my son, as you have asked, what
   ground
there might be for this talk of new
   evidence
in your father's case. We gave him
   the same answer
we've given you.
MIO. I'm sorry. I'd supposed
his cause forgotten except by myself.
   There's still
a defense committee then?
GAUNT. There may be. I
am not connected with it.
ESDRAS. He is my guest,
and asks to remain unknown.
MIO [*after a pause, looking at*
   GAUNT].
The judge at the trial
was younger, but he had your face.
   Can it be
that you're the man?—Yes—Yes.—The
   jury charge—
I sat there as a child and heard your
   voice,
and watched that Brahminical mouth.
   I knew even then

you meant no good to him. And now
   you're here
to winnow out truth and justice—the
   fountain-head
of the lies that slew him! Are you
   Judge Gaunt?

GAUNT. I am.

MIO. Then tell me what damnation to
   what inferno
would fit the toad that sat in robes
   and lied
when he gave the charge, and knew
   he lied! Judge that,
and then go to your place in that hell!

GAUNT. I know and have known
what bitterness can rise against a
   court
when it must say, putting aside all
   weakness,
that a man's to die. I can forgive you
   that,
for you are your father's son, and you
   think of him
as a son thinks of his father. Certain
   laws
seem cruel in their operation; it's
   necessary
that we be cruel to uphold them. This
   cruelty
is kindness to those I serve.

MIO. I don't doubt that.
I know who it is you serve.

GAUNT. Would I have chosen
to rack myself with other men's de-
   spairs,
stop my ears, harden my heart, and
   listen only
to the voice of law and light, if I had
   hoped
some private gain for serving? In all
   my years
on the bench of a long-established
   commonwealth
not once has my decision been in
   question
save in this case. Not once before or
   since.
For hope of heaven or place on earth,
   or power

or gold, no man has had my voice, nor
   will
while I still keep the trust that's laid
   on me
to sentence and define.

MIO. Then why are you here?

GAUNT. My record's clean. I've kept
   it so. But suppose
with the best intent, among the myriad tongues
that come to testify, I had missed my
   way
and followed a perjured tale to a
   lethal end
till a man was forsworn to death?
   Could I rest or sleep
while there was doubt of this,
even while there was question in a
   layman's mind?
For always, night and day,
there lies on my brain like a weight,
   the admonition:
see truly, let nothing sway you; among
   all functions
there's but one godlike, to judge.
   Then see to it
you judge as a god would judge, with
   clarity,
with truth, with what mercy is found
   consonant
with order and law. Without law men
   are beasts,
and it's a judge's task to lift and hold
   them
above themselves. Let a judge be once
   mistaken
or step aside for a friend, and a gap is
   made
in the dykes that hold back anarchy
   and chaos,
and leave men bond but free.

MIO. Then the gap's been made,
and you made it.

GAUNT. I feared that too. May you be
   a judge
sometime, and know in what fear,
through what nights long
in fear, I scanned and verified and
   compared

the transcripts of the trial.

MIO. Without prejudice,

no doubt. It was never in your mind
    to prove

that you'd been right.

GAUNT. And conscious of that, too—

that that might be my purpose—
    watchful of that,

and jealous as his own lawyer of the
    rights

that should hedge the defendant!

And still I found no error,

shook not one staple of the bolts that
    linked

the doer to the deed! Still following
    on from step to step, I watched
    all modern comment,

and saw it centered finally on one
    fact—

Garth Esdras was not called. This is
    Garth Esdras,

and you have heard him. Would his
    deposition

have justified a new trial?

MIO. No. It would not.

GAUNT. And there I come, myself. If
    the man were still

in his cell, and waiting, I'd have no
    faint excuse

for another hearing.

MIO. I've told you that I read

the trial from beginning to end.
    Every word you spoke

was balanced carefully to keep the
    letter

of the law and still convict—convict,
    by Christ,

if it tore the seven veils! You stand
    here now

running cascades of casuistry, to prove

to yourself and me that no judge of
    rank and breeding

could burn a man out of hate! But
    that's what you did

under all your varnish!

GAUNT. I've sought for evidence,

and you have sought. Have you found
    it? Can you cite

one fresh word in defence?

MIO. The trial itself

was shot full of legerdemain, prear-
    ranged to lead

the jury astray——

GAUNT. Could you prove that?

MIO. Yes!

GAUNT. And if

the jury were led astray, remember it's

the jury, by our Anglo-Saxon custom,

that finds for guilt or innocence. The
    judge

is powerless in that matter.

MIO. Not you! Your charge

misled the jury more than the evi-
    dence,

accepted every biased meaning, dis-
    tilled

the poison for them!

GAUNT. But if that were so

I'd be the first, I swear it, to step down

among all men, and hold out both my
    hands

for manacles—yes, publish it in the
    streets,

that all I've held most sacred was de-
    filed

by my own act. A judge's brain be-
    comes

a delicate instrument to weigh men's
    lives

for good and ill—too delicate to bear

much tampering. If he should push
    aside

the weights and throw the beam, and
    say, this once

the man is guilty, and I will have it so

though his mouth cry out from the
    ground,

and all the world

revoke my word, he'd have a short
    way to go

to madness. I think you'd find him in
    the squares,

stopping the passers-by with argu-
    ments,—

see, I was right, the man was guilty
    there—

this was brought in against him, this
    —and this—

and I was left no choice! It's no light
    thing
when a long life's been dedicate to
    one end
to wrench the mind awry!

MIO. By your own thesis
you should be mad, and no doubt you
    are.

GAUNT. But my madness
is only this—that I would fain look
    back
on a life well spent—without one
    stain—one breath
of stain to flaw the glass—not in men's
    minds
nor in my own. I take my God as
    witness
I meant to earn that clearness, and
    believe
that I have earned it. Yet my name
    is clouded
with the blackest, fiercest scandal of
    our age
that's touched a judge. What I can
    do to wipe
that smutch from my fame I will. I
    think you know
how deeply I've been hated, for no
    cause
that I can find there. Can it not be—
and I ask this
quite honestly—that the great injustice
    lies
on your side and not mine? Time and
    time again
men have come before me perfect in
    their lives,
loved by all who knew them, loved at
    home,
gentle, not vicious, yet caught so ripe
    red-handed
in some dark violence there was no
    denying
where the onus lay.

MIO. That was not so with my father!

GAUNT. And yet it seemed so to me.
    To other men
who sat in judgment on him. Can you
    be sure—

I ask this in humility—that you,
who were touched closest by the
    tragedy,
may not have lost perspective—may
    have brooded
day and night on one theme—till your
    eyes are tranced
and show you one side only?

MIO. I see well enough.

GAUNT. And would that not be part
    of the malady—
to look quite steadily at the drift of
    things
but see there what you wish—not
    what is there—
not what another man to whom the
    story
was fresh would say is there?

MIO. You think I'm crazy.
Is that what you meant to say?

GAUNT. I've seen it happen
with the best and wisest men. I but
    ask the question.
I can't speak for you. Is it not true
    wherever
you walk, through the little town
    where you knew him well,
or flying from it, inland or by the
    sea,
still walking at your side, and sleeping
    only
when you too sleep, a shadow not your
    own
follows, pleading and holding out its
    hands
to be delivered from shame?

MIO. How you know that
by God I don't know.

GAUNT. Because one spectre haunted
    you and me—
and haunts you still, but for me it's
    laid to rest
now that my mind is satisfied. He
    died
justly and not by error. [*A pause.*]

MIO [*stepping forward*]. Do you care
    to know
you've come so near to death it's mir-
    acle

that pulse still beats in your splotchy
    throat?
Do you know
there's murder in me?

GAUNT. There was murder in your
    sire,
and it's to be expected! I say he died
    justly, and he deserved it!

MIO. Yes, you'd like too well
to have me kill you! That would prove
    your case
and clear your name, and dip my
    father's name
in stench forever! You'll not get that
    from me!
Go home and die in bed, get it under
    cover,
your lux-et-lex putrefaction of the
    right thing,
you man that walks like a god!

GAUNT. Have I made you angry
by coming too near the truth?

MIO. This sets him up,
this venomous slug, this sets him up
    in a gown,
deciding who's to walk above the
    earth
and who's to lie beneath! And giving
    reasons!
The cobra giving reasons; I'm a god,
by Buddha, holy and worshipful my
    fang,
and can I sink it in!
[*He pauses, turns as if to go, then sits.*]
This is no good.
This won't help much.
[*The* JUDGE *and* ESDRAS *look at each
    other.*]

GAUNT. We should be going.

ESDRAS. Yes. [*They prepare to go.*]
I'll lend you my coat.

GAUNT [*looking at it with distaste.*]
No, keep it. A little rain
shouldn't matter to me.

ESDRAS. It freezes as it falls,
and you've a long way to go.

GAUNT. I'll manage, thank you.
[GAUNT *and* ESDRAS *go out,* ESDRAS
    obsequious, closing the door.]

GARTH [*looking at* MIO's *back*]. Well?

MIO [*not moving*]. Let me sit here a
    moment.
[GARTH *shrugs his shoulders and goes
    toward the inner door.* MIRIAMNE
    opens it and comes out.* GARTH
    looks at her, then at* MIO, *then
    lays his fingers on his lips. She
    nods.* GARTH *goes out.* MIRIAMNE
    sits and watches* MIO. *After a
    little he turns and sees her.*]

MIO. How did you come here?

MIRIAMNE. I live here.

MIO. Here?

MIRIAMNE. My name is Esdras. Garth
is my brother. The walls are thin.
I heard what was said.

MIO [*stirring wearily*]. I'm going. This
    is no place for me.

MIRIAMNE. What place
would be better?

MIO. None. Only it's better to go.
Just to go.
[*She comes over to him, puts her arm
    around him and kisses his fore-
    head.*]

MIRIAMNE. Mio.

MIO. What do you want?
Your kisses burn me—and your arms.
    Don't offer
what I'm never to have! I can have
    nothing. They say
they'll cross the void sometime to the
    other planets
and men will breathe in that air.
Well, I could breathe there,
but not here now. Not on this ball of
    mud.
I don't want it.

MIRIAMNE. They can take away so
    little
with all their words. For you're a king
    among them.
I heard you, and loved your voice.

MIO. I thought I'd fallen
so low there was no further, and now
    a pit
opens beneath. It was bad enough
    that he

should have died innocent, but if he
    were guilty—
then what's my life—what have I left
    to do—?
The son of a felon—and what they
    spat on me
was earned—and I'm drenched with
    the stuff.
Here on my hands
and cheeks, their spittle hanging! I
    liked my hands
because they were like his. I tell you
    I've lived
by his innocence, lived to see it flash
and blind them all—
MIRIAMNE. Never believe them, Mio,
never. [*She looks toward the inner
    door.*]
MIO. But it was truth I wanted, truth—
not the lies you'd tell yourself, or tell
    a woman,
or a woman tells you! The judge with
    his cobra mouth
may have spat truth—and I may be
    mad! For me—
your hands are too clean to touch me.
    I'm to have
the scraps from hotel kitchens—and
    instead of love
those mottled bodies that hitch them-
    selves through alleys
to sell for dimes or nickels. Go, keep
    yourself chaste
for the baker bridegroom—baker and
    son of a baker,
let him get his baker's dozen on you!
MIRIAMNE. No—
say once you love me—say it once;
    I'll never
ask to hear it twice, nor for any kind-
    ness,
and you shall take all I have!
[GARTH *opens the inner door and
    comes out.*]
GARTH. I interrupt
a love scene, I believe. We can do
    without
your adolescent mawkishness.
[*To* MIRIAMNE.] You're a child.

You'll both remember that.
MIRIAMNE. I've said nothing to harm
    you—
and will say nothing.
GARTH. You're my sister, though,
and I take a certain interest in you.
    Where
have you two met?
MIRIAMNE. We danced together.
GARTH. Then
the dance is over, I think.
MIRIAMNE. I've always loved you
and tried to help you, Garth. And
    you've been kind.
Don't spoil it now.
GARTH. Spoil it how?
MIRIAMNE. Because I love him.
I didn't know it would happen. We
    danced together.
And the world's all changed. I see
    you through a mist,
and our father, too. If you brought
    this to nothing
I'd want to die.
GARTH [*to* MIO]. You'd better go.
MIO. Yes, I know.
[*He rises. There is a trembling knock
    at the door.* MIRIAMNE *goes to it.
    The* HOBO *is there shivering.*]
HOBO. Miss, could I sleep under the
    pipes tonight, miss?
Could I, please?
MIRIAMNE. I think—not tonight.
HOBO. There won't be any more
    nights—
if I don't get warm, miss.
MIRIAMNE. Come in.
[*The* HOBO *comes in, looks round
    deprecatingly, then goes to a
    corner beneath a huge heating
    pipe, which he crawls under as if
    he'd been there before.*]
HOBO. Yes, miss, thank you.
GARTH. Must we put up with that?
MIRIAMNE. Father let him sleep there
    —last winter.
GARTH. Yes, God, yes.
MIO. Well, good night.
MIRIAMNE. Where will you go?

MIO. Yes, where? As if it mattered.

GARTH. Oh, sleep here, too.
We'll have a row of you under the
    pipes.

MIO. No, thanks.

MIRIAMNE. Mio, I've saved a little
    money. It's only
some pennies, but you must take it.
*[She shakes some coins out of a box
    into her hand.]*

MIO. No, thanks.

MIRIAMNE. And I love you.
You've never said you love me.

MIO. Why wouldn't I love you
when you're clean and sweet,
and I've seen nothing sweet or clean
this last ten years? I love you. I leave
    you that
for what good it may do you. It's none
    to me.

MIRIAMNE. Then kiss me.

MIO *[looking at GARTH]*.
With that scowling over us? No.
When it rains, some spring
on the planet Mercury, where the
    spring comes often,
I'll meet you there, let's say. We'll
    wait for that.
It may be some time till then.

*[The outside door opens and ESDRAS
    enters with JUDGE GAUNT, then,
    after a slight interval, TROCK fol-
    lows. TROCK surveys the interior
    and its occupants one by one,
    carefully.]*

TROCK. I wouldn't want to cause you
    inconvenience,
any of you, and especially the Judge.
I think you know that. You've all got
    things to do—
trains to catch, and so on. But trains
    can wait.
Hell, nearly anything can wait, you'll
    find,
only I can't. I'm the only one that
    can't
because I've got no time. Who's all
    this here?
Who's that? *[He points to the HOBO.]*

ESDRAS. He's a poor half-wit, sir,
that sometimes sleeps there.

TROCK. Come out. I say come out,
whoever you are.
[The HOBO stirs and looks up.]
Yes, I mean you. Come out.
[The HOBO emerges.]
What's your name?

HOBO. They mostly call me Oke.

TROCK. What do you know?

HOBO. No, sir.

TROCK. Where are you from?

HOBO. I got a piece of bread.
[He brings it out, trembling.]

TROCK. Get back in there!
*[The HOBO crawls back into his
    corner.]*
Maybe you want to know why I'm
    doing this.
Well, I've been robbed, that's why—
robbed five or six times;
the police can't find a thing—so I'm
    out for myself—
if you want to know.
[To MIO.] Who are you?

MIO. Oh, I'm a half-wit,
came in here by mistake. The differ-
    ence is
I've got no piece of bread.

TROCK. What's your name?

MIO. My name?
Theophrastus Such. That's respect-
    able.
You'll find it all the way from here to
    the coast
on the best police blotters.
Only the truth is we're a little touched
    in the head,
Oke and me. You'd better ask some-
    body else.

TROCK. Who is he?

ESDRAS. His name's Romagna. He's
the son.

TROCK. Then what's he doing here?
You said you were on the level.

GARTH. He just walked in. On account
    of the stuff in the papers. We
    didn't ask him.

TROCK. God, we are a gathering. Now

if we had Shadow we'd be all here, huh? Only I guess we won't see Shadow. No, that's too much to ask.

MIO. Who's Shadow?

TROCK. Now you're putting questions. Shadow was just nobody, you see. He blew away. It might happen to anyone. [*He looks at* GARTH.] Yes, anyone at all.

MIO. Why do you keep your hand in your pocket, friend?

TROCK. Because I'm cold, punk. Because I've been outside and it's cold as the tomb of Christ. [*To* GARTH.] Listen, there's a car waiting up at the street to take the Judge home. We'll take him to the car.

GARTH. That's not necessary.

ESDRAS. No.

TROCK. I say it is, see? You wouldn't want to let the Judge walk, would you? The Judge is going to ride where he's going, with a couple of chauffeurs, and everything done in style. Don't you worry about the Judge. He'll be taken care of. For good.

GARTH. I want no hand in it.

TROCK. Anything happens to me happens to you too, musician.

GARTH. I know that.

TROCK. Keep your mouth out of it then. And you'd better keep the punk here tonight, just for luck. [*He turns toward the door. There is a brilliant lightning flash through the windows, followed slowly by dying thunder.* TROCK *opens the door. The rain begins to pour in sheets.*] Jesus, somebody tipped it over again! [*A cough racks him.*] Wait till it's over. It takes ten days off me every time I step into it. [*He closes the door.*] Sit down and wait.

[*Lightning flashes again. The thunder*

is fainter. ESDRAS, GARTH *and the* JUDGE *sit down.*]

GAUNT. We were born too early. Even you who are young

are not of the elect. In a hundred years

man will put his finger on life itself, and then

he will live as long as he likes. For you and me

we shall die soon—one day, one year more or less,

when or where, it's no matter. It's what we call

an indeterminate sentence. I'm hungry.

[GARTH *looks at* MIRIAMNE.]

MIRIAMNE. There was nothing left tonight.

HOBO. I've got a piece of bread.

[*He breaks his bread in two and hands half to the* JUDGE.]

GAUNT. I thank you, sir. [*He eats.*] This is not good bread. [*He rises.*] Sir, I am used

to other company. Not better, perhaps, but their clothes

were different. These are what it's the fashion to call

the underprivileged.

TROCK. Oh, hell!

[*He turns toward the door.*]

MIO [*to* TROCK]. It would seem that you and the Judge know each other.

[TROCK *faces him.*]

TROCK. I've been around.

MIO. Maybe you've met before.

TROCK. Maybe we have.

MIO. Will you tell me where?

TROCK. How long do you want to live?

MIO. How long? Oh, I've got big ideas about that.

TROCK. I thought so. Well, so far I've got nothing against you but your name, see? You keep it that way.

[*He opens the door. The rain still falls in torrents. He closes the door.*

*As he turns from it, it opens
again, and* SHADOW, *white, bloodstained and dripping, stands in
the doorway.* GARTH *rises.* TROCK
turns.]

GAUNT [*to the* HOBO]. Yet if one were
careful of his health, ate sparingly, drank not at all, used himself wisely, it might be that even
an old man could live to touch
immortality. They may come on
the secret sooner than we dare
hope. You see? It does no harm
to try.

TROCK [*backing away from* SHADOW].
By God, he's out of his grave!

SHADOW [*leaning against the doorway, holding a gun in his hands*].
Keep your hands where they belong, Trock.

You know me.

TROCK. Don't! Don't! I had nothing to
do with it!

[*He backs to the opposite wall.*]

SHADOW. You said the doctor gave
you six months to live—well, I
don't give you that much. That's
what you had, six months, and
so you start bumping off your
friends to make sure of your
damn six months. I got it from
you.

I know where I got it.

Because I wouldn't give it to the
Judge.

So he wouldn't talk.

TROCK. Honest to God—

SHADOW. What God?

The one that let you put three holes
in me

when I was your friend? Well, He let
me get up again

and walk till I could find you. That's
as far as I get,

but I got there, by God! And I can
hear you

even if I can't see!

[*He takes a staggering step forward.*]

A man needs blood

to keep going.—I got this far.—And
now I can't see!

It runs out too fast—too fast—

when you've got three slugs

clean through you.

Show me where he is, you fools! He's
here!

I got here! [*He drops the gun.*]

    Help me! Help me! Oh, God!
    Oh, God!

I'm going to die! Where does a man
lie down?

I want to lie down!

[MIRIAMNE *starts toward* SHADOW.
GARTH *and* ESDRAS *help him into
the next room.* MIRIAMNE *following.* TROCK *squats in his
corner, breathing hard, looking
at the door.* MIO *stands, watching* TROCK. GARTH *returns, wiping his hand with a handkerchief.* MIO *picks up and pockets
the gun.* MIRIAMNE *comes back
and leans against the door
jamb.*]

GAUNT. You will hear it said that an
old man makes a good judge,
being calm, clear-eyed, without
passion. But this is not true.
Only the young love truth and
justice. The old are savage, wary,
violent, swayed by maniac desires, cynical of friendship or
love, open to bribery and the
temptations of lust, corrupt and
dastardly to the heart. I know
these old men. What have they
left to believe, what have they
left to lose? Whorers of daughters, lickers of girls' shoes, contrivers of nastiness in the night,
purveyors of perversion, wor-
shippers of possession! Death is
the only radical. He comes late,
but he comes at last to put away
the old men and give the young
their places. It was time.

[*He leers.*]

Here's one I heard yesterday:

Marmaduke behind the barn
    got his sister in a fix;
he says damn instead of darn;
    ain't he cute? He's only six!

THE HOBO. He, he, he!

GAUNT.

And the hoot-owls hoots all night,
    and the cuckoo cooks all day,
and what with a minimum grace
    of God
we pass the time away.

THE HOBO. He, he, he—I got ya!
[*He makes a sign with his thumb.*]

GAUNT [*sings*].

And he led her all around
    and laid her on the ground
and he ruffled up the feathers of
    her cuckoo's nest!

HOBO. Ho, ho, ho!

GAUNT. I am not taken with the way
you laugh. You should cultivate
restraint.

[ESDRAS *reënters*.]

TROCK. Shut the door.

ESDRAS. He won't come back again.

TROCK. I want the door shut! He was
dead, I tell you! [ESDRAS *closes
the door.*] And Romagna was
dead, too, once! Can't they keep
a man under ground?

MIO. No. No more! They don't stay
under ground any more, and
they don't stay under water!
Why did you have him killed?

TROCK. Stay away from me! I know
you!

MIO. Who am I, then?

TROCK. I know you, damn you! Your
name's Romagna!

MIO. Yes! And Romagna was dead,
too, and Shadow was dead, but
the time's come when you can't
keep them down, these dead
men! They won't stay down!
They come in with their heads
shot off and their entrails dragging! Hundreds of them! One by
one—all you ever killed! Watch
the door! See!—It moves!

TROCK [*looking, fascinated, at the
door*]. Let me out of here! [*He
tries to rise.*]

MIO [*the gun in his hand*]. Oh, no!
You'll sit there and wait for
them! One by one they'll come
through that door, pulling their
heads out of the gunny-sacks
where you tied them—glauming
over you with their rotten hands!
They'll see without eyes and
crawl over you—Shadow and the
paymaster and all the rest of
them—putrescent bones without
eyes! Now! Look! Look! For I'm
first among them!

TROCK. I've done for better men than
you! And I'll do for you!

GAUNT [*rapping on the table*]. Order,
gentlemen, order! The witness
will remember that a certain decorum is essential in the court-
room!

MIO. By God, he'll answer me!

GAUNT [*thundering*]. Silence! Silence!
Let me remind you of courtesy
toward the witness! What case
is this you try?

MIO. The case of the state against
Bartolomeo Romagna for the
murder of the paymaster!

GAUNT. Sir, that was disposed of long
ago!

MIO. Never disposed of, never, not
while I live!

GAUNT. Then we'll have done with it
now! I deny the appeal! I have
denied the appeal before and I
do so again!

HOBO. He, he!—He thinks he's in the
moving pictures! [*A flash of lightning.*]

GAUNT. Who set that flash! Bailiff,
clear the court! This is not
Flemington, gentlemen! We are
not conducting this case to make
a journalistic holiday! [*The thunder rumbles faintly.* GARTH *opens
the outside door and faces a*

solid wall of rain.] Stop that man! He's one of the defendants!

[GARTH *closes the door.*]

MIO. Then put him on the stand!

GARTH. What do you think you're doing?

MIO. Have you any objection?

GAUNT. The objection is not sustained. We will hear the new evidence. Call your witness.

MIO. Garth Esdras!

GAUNT. He will take the stand!

GARTH. If you want me to say what I said before I'll say it!

MIO. Call Trock Estrella then!

GAUNT. Trock Estrella to the stand!

TROCK. No, by God!

MIO. Call Shadow, then! He'll talk! You thought he was dead, but he'll get up again and talk!

TROCK [*screaming*]. What do you want of me?

MIO. You killed the paymaster! You!

TROCK. You lie! It was Shadow killed him!

MIO. And now I know! Now I know!

GAUNT. Again I remind you of courtesy toward the witness!

MIO. I know them now!
Let me remind you of courtesy toward the dead!
He says that Shadow killed him! If Shadow were here
he'd say it was Trock! There were three men involved
in the new version of the crime for which
my father died! Shadow and Trock Estrella
as principals in the murder—Garth as witness!—
Why are they here together?—and you—the Judge—
why are you here? Why, because you were all afraid
and you drew together out of that fear to arrange
a story you could tell! And Trock killed Shadow

and meant to kill the Judge out of that same fear—
to keep them quiet! This is the thing I've hunted
over the earth to find out, and I'd be blind
indeed if I missed it now!

[*To* GAUNT.] You heard what he said:
It was Shadow killed him! Now let the night conspire
with the sperm of hell! It's plain beyond denial
even to this fox of justice—and all his words
are curses on the wind! You lied! You lied!
You knew this too!

GAUNT [*low*]. Let me go. Let me go!

MIO. Then why
did you let my father die?

GAUNT. Suppose it known,
but there are things a judge must not believe
though they should head and fester underneath
and press in on his brain. Justice once rendered
in a clear burst of anger, righteously,
upon a very common laborer,
confessed an anarchist, the verdict found
and the precise machinery of law
invoked to know him guilty—think what furor
would rock the state if the court then flatly said:
all this was lies—must be reversed? It's better,
as any judge can tell you, in such cases,
holding the common good to be worth more
than small injustice, to let the record stand,
let one man die. For justice, in the main,
is governed by opinion. Communities
will have what they will have, and it's quite as well,

after all, to be rid of anarchists. Our rights
as citizens can be maintained as rights
only while we are held to be the peers
of those who live about us. A vendor of fish
is not protected as a man might be
who kept a market. I own I've sometimes wished
this was not so, but it is. The man you defend
was unfortunate—and his misfortune bore
almost as heavily on me.—I'm broken—
broken across. You're much too young to know
how bitter it is when a worn connection chars
and you can't remember—can't remember.
[*He steps forward.*] You
will not repeat this? It will go no further?
MIO. No.
No further than the moon takes the tides—no further
than the news went when he died—
when you found him guilty
and they flashed that round the earth. Wherever men
still breathe and think, and know what's done to them
by the powers above, they'll know. That's all I ask.
That'll be enough.
[TROCK *has risen and looks darkly at* MIO.]
GAUNT. Thank you. For I've said some things
a judge should never say.
TROCK. Go right on talking.
Both of you. It won't get far, I guess.
MIO. Oh, you'll see to that?
TROCK. I'll see to it. Me and some others.
Maybe I lost my grip there just for a minute.
That's all right.

MIO. Then see to it! Let it rain!
What can you do to me now when the night's on fire
with this thing I know? Now I could almost wish
there was a god somewhere—I could almost think
there was a god—and he somehow brought me here
and set you down before me here in the rain
where I could wring this out of you! For it's said,
and I've heard it, and I'm free! He was as I thought him,
true and noble and upright, even when he went
to a death contrived because he was as he was
and not your kind! Let it rain! Let the night speak fire
and the city go out with the tide, for he was a man
and I know you now, and I have my day!
[*There is a heavy knock at the outside door.* MIRIAMNE *opens it, at a glance from* GARTH. *The* POLICE-MAN *is there in oilskins.*]
POLICEMAN. Evening.
[*He steps in, followed by a* SERGEANT, *similarly dressed.*]
We're looking for someone
might be here. Seen an old man around
acting a little off?
[*To* ESDRAS.] You know the one
I mean. You saw him out there. Jeez! You've got
a funny crowd here!
[*He looks round. The* HOBO *shrinks into his corner.*] That's the one I saw.
What do you think?
SERGEANT. That's him. You mean to say you didn't know him by his pictures? [*He goes to* GAUNT.] Come on, old man. You're going home.

GAUNT. Yes, sir. I've lost my way.
I think I've lost my way.
SERGEANT. I'll say you have.
About three hundred miles. Now
don't you worry.
We'll get you back.
GAUNT. I'm a person of some rank
in my own city.
SERGEANT. We know that. One look
at you
and we'd know that.
GAUNT. Yes, sir.
POLICEMAN. If it isn't Trock!
Trock Estrella. How are you,
Trock?
TROCK. Pretty good,
Thanks.
POLICEMAN. Got out yesterday again,
I hear?
TROCK. That's right.
SERGEANT. Hi'ye, Trock?
TROCK. O. K.
SERGEANT. You know we got orders
to watch you pretty close. Be good
now, baby,
or back you go. Don't try to pull any-
thing,
not in my district.
TROCK. No, sir.
SERGEANT. No bumping off.
If you want my advice quit carrying a
gun.
Try earning your living for once.
TROCK. Yeah.
SERGEANT. That's an idea.
Because if we find any stiffs on the
river bank
we'll know who to look for.
MIO. Then look in the other room!
I accuse that man of murder! Trock
Estrella!
He's a murderer!
POLICEMAN. Hello. I remember you.
SERGEANT. Well, what murder?
MIO. It was Trock Estrella
that robbed the pay roll thirteen years
ago
and did the killing my father died for!
You know

the Romagna case! Romagna was in-
nocent,
and Trock Estrella guilty!
SERGEANT [*disgusted*]. Oh, what the
hell!
That's old stuff—the Romagna case.
POLICEMAN. Hey, Sarge!
[*The* SERGEANT *and* POLICEMAN *come
closer together.*]
The boy's a professional kidder. He
took me over
about half an hour ago. He kids the
police
and then ducks out!
SERGEANT. Oh, yeah?
MIO. I'm not kidding now.
You'll find a dead man there in the
next room
and Estrella killed him!
SERGEANT. Thirteen years ago?
And nobody smelled him yet?
MIO [*pointing*]. I accuse this man
of two murders! He killed the pay-
master long ago
and had Shadow killed tonight. Look,
look for yourself!
He's there all right!
POLICEMAN. Look boy. You stood out
there
and put the booby sign on the dumb
police
because they're fresh out of Ireland.
Don't try it twice.
SERGEANT [*to* GARTH]. Any corpses
here?
GARTH. Not that I know of.
SERGEANT. I thought so.
[MIO *looks at* MIRIAMNE.]
[*To* MIO.] Think up a better one.
MIO. Have I got to drag him
out here where you can see him?
[*He goes toward the inner door.*]
Can't you scent a murder
when it's under your nose? Look in!
MIRIAMNE. No, no—there's no one—
there's no one there!
SERGEANT [*looking at* MIRIAMNE].
Take a look inside.
POLICEMAN. Yes, sir.

[*He goes into the inside room. The* SERGEANT *goes up to the door. The* POLICEMAN *returns.*]

He's kidding, Sarge. If there's a cadaver
in here I don't see it.

MIO. You're blind then!

[*He goes into the room, the* SERGEANT *following him.*]

SERGEANT. What do you mean?

[*He comes out,* MIO *following him.*]
When you make a charge of murder
it's better to have
the corpus delicti, son. You're the
kind puts in
fire alarms to see the engine!

MIO. By God, he was there.
He went in there to die.

SERGEANT. I'll bet he did.
And I'm Haile Selassie's aunt! What's
your name?

MIO. Romagna. [*To* GARTH.] What
have you done with him?

GARTH. I don't know what you mean.

SERGEANT [*to* GARTH]. What's he
talking about?

GARTH. I wish I could tell you.
I don't know.

SERGEANT. He must have seen something.

POLICEMAN. He's got
the Romagna case on the brain. You
watch yourself,
chump, or you'll get run in.

MIO. Then they're in it together!
All of them!

[*To* MIRIAMNE.] Yes, and you!

GARTH. He's nuts, I say.

MIRIAMNE [*gently*].
You have dreamed something—isn't
it true?
You've dreamed—
But truly, there was no one—

[MIO *looks at her comprehendingly.*]

MIO. You want me to say it. [*He pauses.*]
Yes, by God, I was dreaming.

SERGEANT [*to* POLICEMAN]. I guess
you're right.

We'd better be going. Haven't you
got a coat?

GAUNT. No, sir.

SERGEANT. I guess I'll have to lend
you mine.

[*He puts his oilskins on* GAUNT.]
Come on, now. It's getting late.

[GAUNT, *the* POLICEMAN *and the* SERGEANT *go out.*]

TROCK. They're welcome to him.
His fuse is damp. Where is that walking fool
with the three slugs in him?

ESDRAS. He fell in the hall beyond
and we left him there.

TROCK. That's lucky for some of us. Is
he out this time
or is he still butting around?

ESDRAS. He's dead.

TROCK. That's perfect.
[*To* MIO.] Don't try using your fire-
arms, amigo baby,
the Sarge is outside. [*He turns to go.*]
Better ship that carrion
back in the river! The one that walks
when he's dead;
maybe he'll walk the distance for you.

GARTH. Coming back?

TROCK. Well, if I come back
you'll see me. If I don't, you won't.
Let the punk
go far as he likes. Turn him loose and
let him go.
And may you all rot in hell.

[*He pulls his coat around him and goes to left.* MIRIAMNE *climbs up to look out a window.*]

MIRIAMNE. He's climbing up to the
street, along the bridgehead.

[*She turns.*] Quick, Mio! It's safe now!
Quick!

GARTH. Let him do as he likes.

MIRIAMNE. What do you mean?
Garth! He means to kill him!
You know that!

GARTH. I've no doubt Master Romagna
can run his own campaign.

MIRIAMNE. But he'll be killed!

MIO. Why did you lie about Shadow?

[*There is a pause.* GARTH *shrugs,
    walks across the room, and sits.*]
    You were one of the gang!
GARTH. I can take a death if I have to!
    Go tell your story,
only watch your step, for I warn you,
    Trock's out gunning
and you may not walk very far. Oh,
    I could defend it
but it's hardly worth while.
If they get Trock they get me too.
Go tell them. You owe me nothing.
ESDRAS. This Trock you saw,
no one defends him. He's earned his
    death so often
there's nobody to regret it. But his
    crime,
his same crime that has dogged you,
    dogged us down
from what little we had, to live here
    among the drains,
where the waterbugs break out like a
    scrofula
on what we eat—and if there's lower
    to go
we'll go there when you've told your
    story. And more
that I haven't heart to speak—
MIO [*to* GARTH]. My father died
in your place. And you could have
    saved him!
You were one of the gang!
GARTH. Why, there you are.
You certainly owe me nothing.
MIRIAMNE [*moaning*]. I want to die.
I want to go away.
MIO. Yes, and you lied!
And trapped me into it!
MIRIAMNE. But Mio, he's my brother.
I couldn't give them my brother.
MIO. No. You couldn't.
You were quite right. The gods were
    damned ironic
tonight, and they've worked it out.
ESDRAS. What will be changed
if it comes to trial again? More blood
    poured out
to a mythical justice, but your father
    lying still

where he lies now.
MIO. The bright, ironical gods!
What fun they have in heaven! When
    a man prays hard
for any gift, they give it, and then one
    more
to boot that makes it useless.
[*To* MIRIAMNE.] You might have
    picked
some other stranger to dance with!
MIRIAMNE. I know.
MIO. Or chosen
some other evening to sit outside in
    the rain.
But no, it had to be this. All my life
    long
I've wanted only one thing, to say to
    the world
and prove it: the man you killed was
    clean and true
and full of love as the twelve-year-old
    that stood
and taught in the temple. I can say
    that now
and give my proofs—and now you
    stick a girl's face
between me and the rites I've sworn
    the dead
shall have of me! You ask too much!
    Your brother
can take his chance! He was ready
    enough to let
an innocent man take certainty for
    him
to pay for the years he's had. That
    parts us, then,
but we're parted anyway, by the same
    dark wind
that blew us together. I shall say what
    I have to say.
[*He steps back.*] And I'm not welcome
    here.
MIRIAMNE. But don't go now! You've
    stayed
too long! He'll be waiting!
MIO. Well, is this any safer?
Let the winds blow, the four winds
    of the world,
and take us to the four winds.

[*The three are silent before him. He turns and goes out.*]

CURTAIN

ACT III

The river banks outside the tenement, a little before the close of the previous act. The rain still falls through the street lamps. The TWO NATTY YOUNG MEN IN SERGE AND GRAY *are leaning against the masonry in a ray of light, concentrating on a game of chance. Each holds in his hand a packet of ten or fifteen crisp bills. They compare the numbers on the top notes and immediately a bill changes hands. This goes on with varying fortune until the tide begins to run toward the* 1ST GUNMAN, *who has accumulated nearly the whole supply. They play on in complete silence, evidently not wishing to make any noise. Occasionally they raise their heads slightly to look carefully about. Luck begins to favor the* 2ND GUNMAN, *and the notes come his way. Neither evinces the slightest interest in how the game goes. They merely play on, bored, half-absorbed. There is a slight noise at the tenement door. They put the bills away and watch.* TROCK *comes out, pulls the door shut and comes over to them. He says a few words too low to be heard, and without changing expression the* YOUNG MEN *saunter toward the right.* TROCK *goes out to the left, and the* 2ND PLAYER, *catching that out of the corner of his eye, lingers in a glimmer of light to go on with the game. The* 1ST, *with an eye on the tenement door, begins to play without ado, and the bills again shift back and forth, then concentrate in the hands of the* 1ST GUNMAN. *The* 2ND *shrugs his shoulders, searches his pockets, finds one bill, and playing with it begins to win heavily. They hear the door opening, and putting the notes away, slip* out in front of the rock. MIO *emerges, closes the door, looks around him and walks to the left. Near the corner of the tenement he pauses, reaches out his hand to try the rain, looks up toward the street, and stands uncertainly a moment. He returns and leans against the tenement wall.* MIRIAMNE *comes out.* MIO *continues to look off into space as if unaware of her. She looks away.*

MIO. This rather takes one off his high horse.—What I mean, tough weather for a hegira. You see, this is my sleeping suit, and if I get it wet—basta!

MIRIAMNE. If you could only hide here.

MIO. Hide?

MIRIAMNE. Lucia would take you in. The street-piano man.

MIO. At the moment I'm afflicted with claustrophobia. I prefer to die in the open, seeking air.

MIRIAMNE. But you could stay there till daylight.

MIO. You're concerned about me.

MIRIAMNE. Shall I ask him?

MIO. No. On the other hand there's a certain reason in your concern. I looked up the street and our old friend Trock hunches patiently under the warehouse eaves.

MIRIAMNE. I was sure of that.

MIO. And here I am, a young man on a cold night, waiting the end of the rain. Being read my lesson by a boy, a blind boy—you know the one I mean. Knee-deep in the salt-marsh, Miriamne, bitten from within, fought.

MIRIAMNE. Wouldn't it be better if you came back in to house?

MIO. You forget my claustrophobia.

MIRIAMNE. Let me walk with you, then. Please. If I stay beside you he wouldn't dare.

MIO. And then again he might.—We

don't speak the same language, Miriamne.

MIRIAMNE. I betrayed you. Forgive me.

MIO. I wish I knew this region. There's probably a path along the bank.

MIRIAMNE. Yes. Shadow went that way.

MIO. That's true, too. So here I am, a young man on a wet night, and blind in my weather eye. Stay and talk to me.

MIRIAMNE. If it happens—it's my fault.

MIO. Not at all, sweet. You warned me to keep away. But I would have it. Now I have to find a way out. It's like a chess game. If you think long enough there's always a way out.—For one or the other.—I wonder why white always wins and black always loses in the problems. White to move and mate in three moves. But what if white were to lose— ah, what then? Why, in that case, obviously black would be white and white would be black.—As it often is.—As we often are.—Might makes white. Losers turn black. Do you think I'd have time to draw a gun?

MIRIAMNE. No.

MIO. I'm a fair shot. Also I'm fair game.

[*The door of the tenement opens and* GARTH *comes out to look about quickly. Seeing only* MIO *and* MIRIAMNE *he goes in and comes out again almost immediately carrying one end of a door on which a body lies covered with a cloth. The* HOBO *carries the other end. They go to the right with their burden.*]

This is the burial of Shadow, then; feet first he dips, and leaves the haunts of men.

Let us make mourn for Shadow, wetly lying,

in elegiac stanzas and sweet crying.

Be gentle with him, little cold waves and fishes;

nibble him not, respect his skin and tissues—

MIRIAMNE. Must you say such things?

MIO. My dear, some requiem is fitting over the dead, even

for Shadow. But the last rhyme was bad.

Whittle him not, respect his dying wishes.

That's better. And then to conclude:

His aromatic virtues, slowly rising

will circumnamb the isle, beyond disguising.

He clung to life beyond the wont of men.

Time and his silence drink us all. Amen.

How I hate these identicals. The French allow them, but the French have no principles anyway. You know, Mariamne, there's really nothing mysterious about human life. It's purely mechanical, like an electric appliance. Stop the engine that runs the generator and the current's broken. When we think the brain gives off a small electrical discharge—quite measurable, and constant within limits. But that's not what makes your hair stand up when frightened.

MIRIAMNE. I think it's a mystery.

MIO. Human life? We'll have to wear veils if we're to keep it a mystery much longer. Now if Shadow and I were made up into sausages we'd probably make very good sausages.

MIRIAMNE. Don't——

MIO. I'm sorry. I speak from a high place, far off, long ago, looking down. The cortège returns. [GARTH *and the* HOBO *return, carrying the door, the cloth lying loosely over it.*] I hope you placed an obol in his mouth to pay the ferryman? Even among the Greeks a little money was prerequisite to Elysium. [GARTH *and the* HOBO *go inside, silent.*] No? It's grim to think of Shadow lingering among lesser shades on the hither side. For lack of a small gratuity.

[ESDRAS *comes out the open door and closes it behind him.*]

ESDRAS. You must wait here, Mio, or go inside. I know
you don't trust me, and I haven't earned your trust.
You're young enough to seek truth—and there is no truth;
and I know that—
but I shall call the police and see that you
get safely off.

MIO. It's a little late for that.

ESDRAS. I shall try.

MIO. And your terms? For I daresay you make terms?

ESDRAS. No.

MIO. Then let me remind you what will happen.
The police will ask some questions.
When they're answered
they'll ask more, and before they're done with it
your son will be implicated.

ESDRAS. Must he be?

MIO. I shall not keep quiet.

[*A pause.*]

ESDRAS. Still, I'll go.

MIO. I don't ask help, remember. I made no truce.
He's not on my conscience, and I'm not on yours.

ESDRAS. But you
could make it easier, so easily.
He's my only son. Let him live.

MIO. His chance of survival's

better than mine, I'd say.

ESDRAS. I'll go.

MIO. I don't urge it.

ESDRAS. No. I put my son's life in your hands.
When you're gone,
that may come to your mind.

MIO. Don't count on it.

ESDRAS. Oh,
I count on nothing.

[*He turns to go.* MIRIAMNE *runs over to him and silently kisses his hands.*]

Not mine, not mine, my daughter!
They're guilty hands.

[*He goes out left.* GARTH's *violin is heard within.*]

MIO. There was a war in heaven
once, all the angels on one side, and all
the devils on the other, and since that time
disputes have raged among the learned, concerning
whether the demons won, or the angels. Maybe
the angels won, after all.

MIRIAMNE. And again, perhaps
there are no demons or angels.

MIO. Oh, there are none.
But I could love your father.

MIRIAMNE. I love him. You see,
he's afraid because he's old. The less one has
to lose the more he's afraid.

MIO. Suppose one had
only a short stub end of life, or held
a flashlight with the batteries run down
till the bulb was dim, and knew that he could live
while the glow lasted. Or suppose one knew
that while he stood in a little shelter of time
under a bridgehead, say, he could live, and then,

from then on, nothing. Then to lie
    and turn
with the earth and sun, and regard
    them not in the least
when the bulb was extinguished or
    he stepped beyond
his circle in the cold? How could
    he live
that last dim quarter-hour, before he
    went,
minus all recollection, to grow in grass
between cobblestones?

MIRIAMNE. Let me put my arms round
    you, Mio.
Then if anything comes, it's for me,
    too. [*She puts both arms round
    him.*]

MIO. Only suppose
this circle's charmed! To be safe until
    he steps
from this lighted space into dark!
    Time pauses here
and high eternity grows in one quar-
    ter-hour
in which to live.

MIRIAMNE. Let me see if anyone's
    there—
there in the shadows.
[*She looks toward the right.*]

MIO. It might blast our eternity—
blow it to bits. No, don't go. This is
    forever,
here where we stand. And I ask you,
    Miriamne,
how does one spend a forever?

MIRIAMNE. You're frightened?

MIO. Yes.
So much that time stands still.

MIRIAMNE. Why didn't I speak—
tell them—when the officers were
    here? I failed you
in that one moment!

MIO. His life for mine? Oh, no.
I wouldn't want it, and you couldn't
    give it.
And if I should go on living we're cut
    apart
by that brother of yours.

MIRIAMNE. Are we?

MIO. Well, think about it.
A body lies between us, buried in
    quicklime.
Your allegiance is on the other side of
    that grave and not to me.

MIRIAMNE. No, Mio! Mio, I love
    you!

MIO. I love you, too, but in case my
    life went on
beyond that barrier of dark—then
    Garth
would run his risk of dying.

MIRIAMNE. He's punished, Mio.
His life's been torment to him. Let
    him go,
for my sake, Mio.

MIO. I wish I could. I wish
I'd never seen him—or you. I've
    steeped too long
in this thing. It's in my teeth and
    bones. I can't
let go or forget. And I'll not add my
    lie
to the lies that cumber his ground.
    We live our days
in a storm of lies that drifts the truth
    too deep
for path or shovel; but I've set my foot
    on a truth
for once, and I'll trail it down!
[*A silence.* MIRIAMNE *looks out to the
    right.*]

MIRIAMNE. There's someone there—
I heard—
[CARR *comes in from the right.*]

MIO. It's Carr.

CARR. That's right. No doubt about it.
Excuse me.

MIO. Glad to see you. This is Mir-
    iamne.
Carr's a friend of mine.

CARR. You're better employed
than when I saw you last.

MIO. Bow to the gentleman,
Miriamne. That's meant for you.

MIRIAMNE. Thank you, I'm sure.
Should I leave you, Mio? You want
    to talk?

MIO. Oh, no,

we've done our talking.

MIRIAMNE. But—

CARR. I'm the one's out of place—
I wandered back because I got worried about you,
that's the truth.—Oh—those two fellows with the hats
down this way, you know, the ones that ran
after we heard the shooting—they're back again,
lingering or malingering down the bank,
revisiting the crime, I guess. They may
mean well.

MIO. I'll try to avoid them.

CARR. I didn't care
for the way they looked at me.—No luck, I suppose,
with that case history? The investigation
you had on hand?

MIO. I can't say. By the way,
the stiff that fell in the water and we saw swirling
down the eddy, he came trudging up, later on,
long enough to tell his name. His name was Shadow
but he's back in the water now. It's all in an evening.
These things happen here.

CARR. Good God!

MIO. I know.
I wouldn't believe it if you told it.

CARR. But—
the man was alive?

MIO. Oh, not for long! He's dunked
for good this time. That's all that's happened.

CARR. Well,
if you don't need me——

MIRIAMNE. You had a message to send—
have you forgotten——?

MIO. I?—Yes, I had a message—
but I won't send it—not now.

MIRIAMNE. Then I will——!

MIO. No.
Let it go the way it is! It's all arranged
another way. You've been a good scout, Carr,
the best I ever knew on the road.

CARR. That sounds
like making your will.

MIO. Not yet, but when I do
I've thought of something to leave you. It's the view
of Mt. Ranier from the Seattle jail,
snow over cloud. And the rusty chain in my pocket from a pair of handcuffs my father wore. That's all the worldly goods I'm seized of.

CARR. Look, Mio—hell—
if you're in trouble——

MIO. I'm not. Not at all. I have
a genius that attends me where I go, and guards me now. I'm fine.

CARR. Well, that's good news.
He'll have his work cut out.

MIO. Oh, he's a genius.

CARR. I'll see you then.
I'll be at the Grand Street place. I'm lucky tonight,
and I can pay. I could even pay for two.

MIO. Thanks, I may take you up.

CARR. Good night.

MIO. Right, Carr.

CARR [to MIRIAMNE]. Good night.

MIRIAMNE [after a pause]. Good night.

[CARR goes out to the left.]
Why did you do that? He's your genius, Mio,
and you let him go.

MIO. I couldn't help it.

MIRIAMNE. Call him.
Run after him and call him!

MIO. I tried to say it
and it strangled in my throat. I might have known
you'd win in the end.

MIRIAMNE. Is it for me?

MIO. For you?

It stuck in my throat, that's all I
    know.
MIRIAMNE. Oh, Mio,
I never asked for that! I only hoped
Garth could go clear.
MIO. Well, now he will.
MIRIAMNE. But you—
It was your chance!
MIO. I've lost
my taste for revenge if it falls on you.
    Oh, God,
deliver me from the body of this death
I've dragged behind me all these
    years! Miriamne!
Miriamne!
MIRIAMNE. Yes!
MIO. Miriamne, if you love me
teach me a treason to what I am, and
    have been,
till I learn to live like a man! I think
    I'm waking
from a long trauma of hate and fear
    and death
that's hemmed me from my birth—
    and glimpse a life
to be lived in hope—but it's young in
    me yet, I can't
get free, or forgive! But teach me how
    to live
and forget to hate!
MIRIAMNE. He would have forgiven.
MIO. He?
MIRIAMNE. Your father. [*A pause.*]
MIO. Yes. [*Another pause.*]
You'll think it strange, but I've never
    remembered that.
MIRIAMNE. How can I help you?
MIO. You have.
MIRIAMNE. If I were a little older—
    if I knew
the things to say! I can only put out
    my hands
and give you back the faith you bring
    to me
by being what you are. Because to me
you are all hope and beauty and
    brightness drawn
across what's black and mean!
MIO. He'd have forgiven—

Then there's no more to say—I've
    groped long enough
through this everglades of old re-
    venges—here
the road ends.—Miriamne, Miriamne,
the iron I wore so long—it's eaten
    through
and fallen from me. Let me have your
    arms.
They'll say we're children—Well—the
    world's made up of children.
MIRIAMNE. Yes.
MIO. But it's too late for me.
MIRIAMNE. No.
[*She goes into his arms, and they kiss
    for the first time.*]
Then we'll meet again?
MIO. Yes.
MIRIAMNE. Where?
MIO. I'll write—
or send Carr to you.
MIRIAMNE. You won't forget?
MIO. Forget?
Whatever streets I walk, you'll walk
    them, too,
from now on, and whatever roof or
    stars
I have to house me, you shall share
    my roof
and stars and morning. I shall not
    forget.
MIRIAMNE. God keep you!
MIO. And keep you. And this to re-
    member!
if I should die, Miriamne, this half-
    hour
is our eternity. I came here seeking
light in darkness, running from the
    dawn,
and stumbled on a morning.
[*One of the* YOUNG MEN IN SERGE
    *strolls in casually from the right,
    looks up and down without ex-
    pression, then, seemingly having
    forgotten something, retraces his
    steps and goes out.* ESDRAS *comes
    in slowly from the left. He has
    lost his hat, and his face is bleed-
    ing from a slight cut on the tem-*

ple. *He stands abjectly near the tenement.*]

MIRIAMNE. Father—what is it?

[*She goes toward* ESDRAS.]

ESDRAS. Let me alone.

[*He goes nearer to* MIO.]

He wouldn't let me pass.
The street's so icy up along the bridge
I had to crawl on my knees—he kicked me back
three times—and then he held me there—I swear
what I could do I did! I swear to you
I'd save you if I could.

MIO. What makes you think
that I need saving?

ESDRAS. Child, save yourself if you can!
He's waiting for you.

MIO. Well, we knew that before.

ESDRAS. He won't wait much longer.
He'll come here—
he told me so. Those damned six months of his—
he wants them all—and you're to die
—you'd spread
his guilt—I had to listen to it——

MIO. Wait—

[*He walks forward and looks casually to the right, then returns.*]

There must be some way up through the house and out
across the roof——

ESDRAS. He's watching that. But come in—
and let me look.——

MIO. I'll stay here, thanks. Once in
and I'm a rat in a deadfall—I'll stay here—
look for me if you don't mind.

ESDRAS. Then watch for me—
I'll be on the roof——

[*He goes in hurriedly.*]

MIO [*looking up*]. Now all you silent powers
that make the sleet and dark, and never yet
have spoken, give us a sign, let the throw be ours

this once, on this longest night, when the winter sets
his foot on the threshold leading up to spring
and enters with remembered cold— let fall
some mercy with the rain. . We are two lovers
here in your night, and we wish to live.

MIRIAMNE. Oh, Mio—
if you pray that way, nothing good will come!
You're bitter, Mio.

MIO. How many floors has this building?

MIRIAMNE. Five or six. It's not as high as the bridge.

MIO. No, I thought not. How many pomegranate seeds did you eat, Persephone?

MIRIAMNE. Oh, darling, darling,
if you die, don't die alone.

MIO. I'm afraid I'm damned
to hell, and you're not damned at all.
Good God,
how long he takes to climb!

MIRIAMNE. The stairs are steep.

[*A slight pause.*]

MIO. I'll follow him.

MIRIAMNE. He's there—at the window —now.
He waves you to go back, not to go in.
Mio, see, that path between the rocks—
they're not watching that—they're out at the river—
I can see them there—they can't watch both—
it leads to a street above.

MIO. I'll try it, then.
Kiss, me. You'll hear. But if you never hear—
then I'm the king of hell, Persephone,
and I'll expect you.

MIRIAMNE. Oh, lover, keep safe.

MIO. Good-bye.

[*He slips out quickly between the rocks. There is a quick machine*

gun rat-tat. The violin stops.
MIRIAMNE *runs toward the path.*
MIO *comes back slowly, a hand
pressed under his heart.*]
It seems you were mistaken.
MIRIAMNE. Oh, God, forgive me!
[*She puts an arm around him. He
sinks to his knees.*]
Where is it, Mio? Let me help you
in! Quick, quick, let me help
you!
MIO. I hadn't thought to choose—this
—ground—
but it will do. [*He slips down.*]
MIRIAMNE. Oh, God, forgive me!
MIO. Yes?
The king of hell was not forgiven
then,
Dis is his name and Hades is his
home—
and he goes alone——
MIRIAMNE. Why does he bleed so?
Mio, if you go
I shall go with you.
MIO. It's better to stay alive.
I wanted to stay alive—because of
you—
I leave you that—and what he said
to me dying:
I love you, and will love you after I
die.
Tomorrow, I shall still love you, as
I've loved
the stars I'll never see, and all the
mornings
that might have been yours and mine.
Oh, Miriamne,
you taught me this.
MIRIAMNE. If only I'd never seen you
then you could live——
MIO. That's blasphemy—Oh, God,
there might have been some easier
way of it.
You didn't want me to die, did you,
Miriamne—?
You didn't send me away——?
MIRIAMNE. Oh, never, never——
MIO. Forgive me—kiss me—I've got
blood on your lips—

I'm sorry—it doesn't matter—I'm
sorry——
[ESDRAS *and* GARTH *come out.*]
MIRIAMNE. Mio—
I'd have gone to die myself—you must
hear this, Mio,
I'd have died to help you—you must
listen, sweet,
you must hear it—[*She rises.*]
I can die, too, see! You! There!
You in the shadows!—You killed him
to silence him!
[*She walks toward the path.*]
But I'm not silenced! All that he knew
I know,
and I'll tell it tonight! Tonight—
tell it and scream it
through all the streets—that Trock's
a murderer
and he hired you for this murder!
Your work's not done—
and you won't live long! Do you hear?
You're murderers, and I know who
you are!
[*The machine gun speaks again. She
sinks to her knees.* GARTH *runs
to her.*]
GARTH. You little fool!
[*He tries to lift her.*]
MIRIAMNE. Don't touch me!
[*She crawls toward* MIO.]
Look, Mio! They killed me, too. Oh,
you can believe me
now, Mio. You can believe I wouldn't
hurt you,
because I'm dying! Why doesn't he
answer me?
Oh, now he'll never know!
[*She sinks down, her hand over her
mouth, choking.* GARTH *kneels
beside her, then rises, shuddering. The* HOBO *comes out.* LUCIA
and PINY *look out.*]
ESDRAS. It lacked only this.
GARTH. Yes.
[ESDRAS *bends over* MIRIAMNE, *then
rises slowly.*]
Why was the bastard born? Why did
he come here?

ESDRAS.   Miriamne—Miriamne—yes,
  and Mio,
one breath shall call you now—forgive
  us both—
forgive the ancient evil of the earth
that brought you here——
GARTH. Why must she be a fool?
ESDRAS. Well, they were wiser than
  you and I. To die
when you are young and untouched,
  that's beggary
to a miser of years, but the devils
  locked in synod
shake and are daunted when men set
  their lives
at hazard for the heart's love, and
  lose. And these,
who were yet children, will weigh
  more than all
a city's elders when the experiment
is reckoned up in the end. Oh, Miriamne,
and Mio—Mio, my son—know this
  where you lie,
this is the glory of earth-born men
  and women,
not to cringe, never to yield, but
  standing,
take defeat implacable and defiant,
die unsubmitting. I wish that I'd
  died so,
long ago; before you're old you'll wish
that you had died as they have. On
  this star,

in this hard star-adventure, knowing
  not
what the fires mean to right and left,
  nor whether
a meaning was intended or presumed,
man can stand up, and look out blind,
  and say:
in all these turning lights I find no
  clue,
only a masterless night, and in my
  blood
no certain answer, yet is my mind my
  own,
yet is my heart a cry toward something dim
in distance, which is higher than I am
and makes me emperor of the endless
  dark
even in seeking! What odds and ends
  of life
men may live otherwise, let them live,
  and then
go out, as I shall go, and you. Our
  part
is only to bury them. Come, take her
  up.
They must not lie here.
[LUCIA *and* PINY *come near to help.*
  ESDRAS *and* GARTH *stoop to carry*
  MIRIAMNE.]
                    CURTAIN
                              1935

WILLIAM SAROYAN
(1908–   )

HELLO OUT THERE *

A ONE-ACT PLAY
FOR GEORGE BERNARD SHAW

This play was written early in August,
1941. It was produced at the Lobero
Theatre in Santa Barbara on Wednesday,

* From *Razzle-Dazzle* by William
Saroyan, copyright, 1942, by Harcourt,
Brace and Company, Inc.

September 10, 1941, as the curtain
raiser to George Bernard Shaw's *The
Devil's Disciple*. Miss Phyllis Walker
played the part of the girl, and Harry
Bratsburg the part of the young man.
John Houseman staged the play and

Kate Drain Lawson did the set. Harry Bratsburg, who played the part of the mailman in *My Heart's in the Highlands,* is in my opinion one of the finest actors in the American theatre. Miss Walker is a newcomer for whom good things are predicted.

Before this play was written I had spent almost four months loafing. When I came home from New York after having produced and directed *The Beautiful People* I decided not to work for a while and if possible to get out in the sun. I hadn't gotten out in the sun in years. I hadn't had any time to get out in it. I had always planned to get out, but I had always had the bad luck of getting a story or a play going just when I wanted to quit work and start loafing, and I had always stayed with the story or play until it had been written. Then I had planned to rush right out and get in the sun, only to run headlong into another story or play, and I had always gone to work and written this one, too. That is the only way I have ever been able to take care of anything that wanted to be written. Beginning any time of the day or night I have gone to work and written it—all at once if possible, but if not, as soon as possible. I have never given myself time to sit down and not have anything else on my mind.

I have never worked at writing, although I have come to refer to writing as my work. I am as excited about writing as I was when I was a kid, and I have not been able to write anything expressly for the purpose of making money. This is so because I cannot write that way. I have given away any number of pieces especially written on specific themes, but I have written these pieces because I have not been able to resist them. Furthermore, I have never had any limitations imposed on my writing other than my own. Every new piece I see in a magazine makes me happy, and every new book that comes from the

presses is something I behold with wonder, awe and amazement. I shall probably never get over the delight of writing and being published.

Even so, a good deal of my interest is away from writing, and for over ten years now I have been planning to spend a winter somewhere in the woods, camping and hunting, but have not done so; I have planned to spend a year driving all over America slowly, with special interest in out-of-the-way towns, but have never done so; I have planned to take a leisurely trip around the world, and have never done so; I have planned to go back to work on a vineyard for a winter, and have never done so; I have planned to read all the books I have always wanted to read, and have never done so; I have planned to study the works of every composer of the world, the music of all the peoples of the world, and the songs of all the folk of the world, and I have never done so; I have planned to take a year out to learn from actual painting how to paint, and I have never done so; I have planned to learn to read and write Armenian, and perhaps translate the works of my favorite Armenian writers, and have never done so; I have wanted to buy an expensive microscope and study the forms of the smallest things, and have never done so; I have planned to perfect my new theatre—a globe device with the basic colors and forms, capable of creating an inexhaustibly varied drama of objects and colors and relationships, accompanied by their related sounds—and have never done so; I have planned to walk from San Francisco to Mexico City, and have never done so; I have planned to ride a bicycle from San Francisco to New York, by way of El Paso, New Orleans, Jacksonville and Oceana, and have never done so; I have planned to marry the most beautiful woman in the world and bring up a family, and have never done so; I have never met her—

how could I do so? I have planned to read *The Bible* and the books of all other religions, and have never done so; and I have planned to buy a hundred acres of fertile land with a stream running through it, have the house I have always wanted built on it, and on the land plant as many kinds of trees as I can get hold of, and watch them grow, and I have never done it.

I have also planned to get out in the sun and get rid of the urban pallor which has become my normal complexion, and until this summer I have not done so. But this summer I managed to make it. Of course I was temporarily side-tracked in this ambition by the writing of the play *Jim Dandy*, by the reading and correcting of manuscript and proofs of two books, by a simultaneous hunger for loafing in San Francisco dives, and by cards, horses and dice. But finally I got away and went to Fresno and got out in the sun.

During the four months since my return from New York I have gone to Fresno four times—the shortest visit being a three-day visit, and the longest being a one-month one. Gradually the pallor gave way to a fairly deep tan, but nothing like the tan of Young Corbett, with whom I went fishing a number of times at Mendota and Friant.

Young Corbett runs the best saloon (or cocktail lounge) in my home town. The sun is very close to the earth in Fresno, its rays very direct and penetrating, the heat very great and magnificent, but if you expose yourself to all of this very suddenly, you are apt to be cooked. I know, because that is what happened to me every day until Corbett explained that you had to rub yourself with a mixture composed of two parts olive oil and one part vinegar. After that, instead of getting cooked every day and not being able to sleep all night and having the skin peel off after a week or so, taking the color with it and

bringing out a fresh layer of pallor, the sun-color moved in slower and deeper and stayed there. I still have some of this color, although it is beginning to fade, and now winter is coming. But I got out into the sun, just as I had planned, and had a lot of fun watching Corbett try to catch a fish, which he never did. Later, though, he got a big one off the coast of Santa Cruz, and to prove it he had the photograph printed in the papers. I hadn't talked to Corbett since we sold the *Fresno Evening Herald* together, along about twenty-five years ago, when Buzz Martin was our boss and pal, Mr. York in charge of street sales, and Mayor Toomey a big easygoing man who made a special trip to the sand-lot at Kern and L Streets to give an informal talk to the newsboys of the town. I remember that this man, Mayor Toomey, is the first important man in the world whom I didn't dislike. He came to the sand-lot, the kids all gathered around, and he stood there and talked to them. He didn't make a speech and he didn't say anything momentous, but his coming down that way, bothering with a bunch of hoodlums, made me like him and remember him as a great man. Maybe he wasn't really great, but as I *remember* it he was. I don't think Corbett remembered me as well as I remembered him, but after loafing around together a while it was practically the same as in the old days. After having been the best fighter of his time in his division, I found him great-hearted, easy-going, boyishly eager about fishing and getting out to the country, full of high spirits, a fair singer of popular ballads, and a good drinking companion. I have found few places as pleasant to loaf around in, anywhere in the world, as my home town, no bar with a better atmosphere than Young Corbett's, and no company more pleasant than his.

By the end of July I figured it was

time for me to go back to San Francisco. After I got home this play was one of the first things I wrote.

Now having a play on the same bill with a play by the one and only, the good and great, the impish and noble, the man and superman, George Bernard Shaw, is for me an honor, and I think a most fitting thing. While I have never read *The Devil's Disciple*, and while the only play of Shaw's I have ever seen has been St. Joan—and I saw that from the last row of the gallery from whence it was a pageant and not a play, since I could hear nothing said—I have long known of Mr. Shaw, read his plays and prefaces, and loved him. I admire heroic effort. Accomplishment I love. What I am about to say is no invention, and I am putting it down for whatever it may be worth to the historian of literature and for the student of influences of men on men, and because it is true and must therefore be made known. As a boy, charging pell-mell through literature, reading everything I could lay my hands on in the Public Library of Fresno, I found many men to whom I felt deeply grateful—especially Guy de Maupassant, Jack London and H. L. Mencken—but the first man to whom I felt definitely related was George Bernard Shaw. This is a presumptuous or fatuous thing to mention, perhaps, but even so it must be mentioned.

I myself, as a person, have been influenced by many writers and many things, and my writing has felt the impact of the writing of many writers, some relatively unknown and unimportant, some downright bad. But probably the greatest influence of them all when an influence is the most effective —when the man being influenced is nowhere near being solid in his own right—has been the influence of the great tall man with the white beard, the lively eyes, the swift wit and the impish chuckle. I have read Dickens with fas-

cination and wonder. I have read Schopenhauer at the age of twelve with no bewilderment and no contempt for his contempt for the world and its strange inhabitant, and no contempt for the strange inhabitant himself. I have read writing without regard for the name or quality of the writer—just writing, just print, just books. I have read Mark Twain and Walt Whitman. I have read the Russians, Chekhov, Andreyev and Gorki. I have read Sherwood Anderson and Carl Sandburg, Gertrude Stein and Ernest Hemingway. I have read Ibsen and Oscar Wilde. I have read *Poetry Magazine* and any of the little magazines I have been able to find in the second-hand bookstores of Fresno. I have read anything and everything—Ambrose Bierce and Bret Harte, and books in French and German and Spanish without being able to understand a word of it, simply because they were books and because something was being said, even if it was in a language I did not know. I have read books about the behavior of mobs—*The Mob* by Le Bon, if I remember rightly, was one—about crime in children, and genius in them, about the greatest bodies of things, and about the littlest of them. I have been fascinated by it all, grateful for it all, grateful for the sheer majesty of the existence of ideas, stories, fables and paper and ink and print and books to hold them all together for a man to take aside and examine alone. But the man I liked most and the man who seemed to remind me of myself—of what I really was and would surely become—was George Bernard Shaw.

When, at the age of eighteen, I was night manager of the Postal Telegraph office at 21 Taylor Street in San Francisco I remember having been asked by the clerk there, a man named Clifford, who the hell I thought I was. And I remember replying very simply and earnestly somewhat as follows: If you have ever heard of George Bernard Shaw, if you have ever read his plays or prefaces, you will know what I mean when I tell you that I am that man by another name.

Who is *he*? I remember the clerk asking.

George Bernard Shaw, I replied, is the tonic of the Christian peoples of the world. He is health, wisdom, and comedy, and that's what I am, too.

How do you figure? the clerk said.

Don't bother me, I said. I'm night manager of this office and when I tell you something it's final.

H. L. Mencken's *Prejudices* and George Jean Nathan's suave and lively spoofing had a fine effect on me, too. I liked the men who were most like bad boys, having fun all the time, playing pranks, talking out of turn, acting up, making fun of fools and frauds, ridiculing the pompous and phoney, howling with laughter or sitting by after ruining the works and being dead-pan and innocent about the whole thing—and beyond all this being very wise and very serious, and knowing how to write—knowing that you couldn't be serious and dull at the same time and still be effective. Mencken's stuff made me bust out laughing in the Public Library. Sometimes it even made me jump out of my chair and walk around the place whispering things at people I didn't know.

This is not the place or time, however, for me to go into detail about the men and writing and ideas which have influenced my life and writing.

All that I know is that it is right for a one-act play by William Saroyan to serve as a curtain-raiser to a play by George Bernard Shaw. To show you the importance of this, the inevitability of it in fact, let me reveal how, finally, this event came to be, and how close it came not to be. Let me reveal the series of accidental and fortuitous events—all of them always closer to not taking place

than to taking place—which finally, one by one, resulted in this most appropriate and inevitable circumstance.

When I stepped out of the sun of Fresno and came home to the gloom of San Francisco, although I felt the time was ripe for the writing of something good, nothing presented itself to me. Therefore, I made no effort, but spent my time loafing, playing pin-ball games for hours, sitting around in little bars, listening to juke-box music, drinking and talking. After three days of this I sat down one night at two o'clock in the morning with the intention of typing a title and a few ideas I didn't want to forget. But I did not get up until I had written this play. I had been drinking a good deal, but I was not drunk. There are nights of such drinking. Instead of getting drunk a man gets sober. He gets very sober. That was how it was that night. I didn't know at the time that I had a play to write, but I must have had it to write, because I wrote it.

The very writing of the play was an accident, even if it was an inevitable one. Of course we all know that accidents are compelled. I know this from having read in my Public Library days an essay about the mystical behavior of Hindus, and from having watched this matter carefully, and considered it from one year to another. I know accidents are avoidable. Even when I was the fastest messenger in Fresno, and the one who took the most chances, I had very few accidents, and these only mild. I was once forced to knock down a brewery horse by butting it with my head because I was going too fast and couldn't stop and the horse was blocking the alley down which I was racing. While racing down the alley I had reasoned that if somebody stepped out into my path I would have no trouble going through with no harm to him or to myself; if an automobile crossed this path I would pace my speed to swerve around it and go on my way; if something immovable blocked my way I would lift the whole front part of my bicycle, fall backwards, and probably hurt my back but not be instantly killed; and if something moving slowly appeared in my way and I could not pace around it I would—at this point, while I was going about twenty miles an hour, a brewery horse appeared and completely blocked the alley, moving much too slowly. Without any further reasoning I tightened up on the bicycle, feet tight in toeclips, muscles taut, head down. It was an accident and there was nothing else to do. My head butted the horse in the side, the horse exhaled, its front feet buckled and it went down. I was a little scared—especially of the horse, which was very big—but I wasn't hurt.

There were some other accidents. Chains broke on me a couple of times when I was sprinting and sprawled me out on the pavement. A cop intentionally caught my arm as I shot through between him and a truck, spinning me around and almost ruining my bicycle. And a couple of bad drivers ran into me from behind and knocked me off my bicycle. Each of these accidents could have been avoided. I know it. The one involving the horse could have been avoided but only if I was willing to agree not to speed, and I wasn't. The chains that broke had been weak and should have been attended to. The cop was a dog anyway; I knew it, and I could have avoided the accident by not challenging him and thinking I could get away with it. And the people who drove their cars into my bike should never have been credited with wakefulness by me. I had overestimated them and I had been recklessly optimistic. But the accidents could have been avoided.

Getting the title of the play was an accident too. A clownish friend of mine named Stanley Rose one night on a street corner in Fresno began calling out as if he were in the wilderness—Hello

out there! Hello out there! I liked the sound and enjoyed the absurdity of it, but immediately forgot all about it.

Next, it was an accident that I went to the opening of *Anna Christie* in San Francisco; an accident that I met the director of the play, John Houseman; an accident that he asked if I had a one-act play; an accident that I had one, *this* one, just written; and an accident that I promised to put it in the mail for him the next day. It was no accident that I did, though.

On the other side of things, to begin with I had no idea what other plays would be presented with my play. I imagined they would be new plays by one or another of the American writers of plays. It turned out there would be only one other play, and that this play was *The Devil's Disciple* by George Bernard Shaw. But this was also an accident. It seems that Mr. Shaw was allowing no further production of his plays until after the war. The production of this play had just barely gotten under the wire, but under the wire is under the wire, and my work has finally appeared on the same bill with the work of George Bernard Shaw.

Such progressions as these are important to record. A few critics with bad breath and fallen arches and a few other things of this sort are going to come forward with an attack upon Mr. Shaw himself, by way of once again annihilating me, as they have been doing these seven years. It shall seem to these critics most frightful of me to associate my name with George Bernard Shaw's, but let me simplify everything by making known very clearly that if it matters which of the writing men I have felt close to, and by whom my writing has been influenced, that man has not been Ernest Hemingway, as Mr. Edmund Wilson seems to feel, but George Bernard Shaw. Now, if Mr. Shaw and Mr. Saroyan are poles apart, no comparison between the two, one great and the other nothing, one a genius and the other a charlatan, let me repeat that if you must know which writer has influenced my writing when influences are real and for all I know enduring, then that writer has been George Bernard Shaw. I shall in my own day influence a young Shaw or two somewhere or other, and you need not worry about that.

Young Shaw, hello out there.

THERE *is a fellow in a small-town prison cell, tapping slowly on the floor with a spoon. After tapping half a minute, as if he were trying to telegraph words, he gets up and begins walking around the cell. At last he stops, stands at the center of the cell, and doesn't move for a long time. He feels his head, as if it were wounded. Then he looks around. Then he calls out dramatically, kidding the world.*

YOUNG MAN. Hello—out there!
[*Pause.*]
Hello—out there! Hello—out there!
[*Long pause.*]
Nobody out there.
[*Still more dramatically, but more comically, too.*]
Hello—out there! Hello—out there!
[*A* GIRL'S VOICE *is heard, very sweet and soft.*]
THE VOICE. Hello.
YOUNG MAN. Hello—out there.
THE VOICE. Hello.
YOUNG MAN. Is that you, Katey?
THE VOICE. No—this here is Emily.
YOUNG MAN. Who? [*Swiftly.*] Hello out there.
THE VOICE. Emily.
YOUNG MAN. Emily who? I don't know anybody named Emily. Are you the girl I met at Sam's in Salinas about three years ago?
THE VOICE. No—I'm the girl who cooks here. I'm the cook. I've never been in Salinas. I don't even know where it is.
YOUNG MAN. Hello out there. You say you cook here?
THE VOICE. Yes.

YOUNG MAN. Well, why don't you study up and learn to cook? How come I don't get no jello or anything good?
THE VOICE. I just cook what they tell me to. [*Pause.*] You lonesome?
YOUNG MAN. Lonesome as a coyote. Hear me hollering? Hello out there!
THE VOICE. Who you hollering to?
YOUNG MAN. Well—nobody, I guess. I been trying to think of somebody to write a letter to, but I can't think of anybody.
THE VOICE. What about Katey?
YOUNG MAN. I don't know anybody named Katey.
THE VOICE. Then why did you say, Is that you, Katey?
YOUNG MAN. Katey's a good name. I always did like a name like Katey. I never *knew* anyone named Katey, though.
THE VOICE. *I* did.
YOUNG MAN. Yeah? What was she like? Tall girl, or little one?
THE VOICE. Kind of medium.
YOUNG MAN. Hello out there. What sort of a looking girl are you?
THE VOICE. Oh, I don't know.
YOUNG MAN. Didn't anybody ever tell you? Didn't anybody ever talk to you that way?
THE VOICE. What way?
YOUNG MAN. You know. Didn't they?
THE VOICE. No, they didn't.
YOUNG MAN. Ah, the fools—they should have. I can tell from your voice you're O.K.

THE VOICE. Maybe I am and maybe I ain't.

YOUNG MAN. I never missed yet.

THE VOICE. Yeah, I know. That's why you're in jail.

YOUNG MAN. The whole thing was a mistake.

THE VOICE. They claim it was rape.

YOUNG MAN. No—it wasn't.

THE VOICE. That's what they claim it was.

YOUNG MAN. They're a lot of fools.

THE VOICE. Well, you sure are in trouble. Are you scared?

YOUNG MAN. Scared to death. [*Suddenly.*] Hello out there!

THE VOICE. What do you keep saying that for all the time?

YOUNG MAN. I'm lonesome. I'm lonesome as a coyote.

[*A long one.*]

Hello—out there!

[THE GIRL *appears, over to one side. She is a plain girl in plain clothes.*]

THE GIRL. I'm kind of lonesome, too.

YOUNG MAN. [*Turning around and looking at her.*] Hey—No fooling? Are you?

THE GIRL. Yeah—I'm almost as lonesome as a coyote myself.

YOUNG MAN. Who *you* lonesome for?

THE GIRL. I don't know.

YOUNG MAN. It's the same with me. The minute they put you in a place like this you remember all the girls you ever knew, and all the girls you didn't get to know, and it sure gets lonesome.

THE GIRL. I bet it does.

YOUNG MAN. Ah, it's awful. [*Pause.*] You're a pretty kid, you know that?

THE GIRL. You're just talking.

YOUNG MAN. No, I'm not just talking—you *are* pretty. Any fool could see that. You're just about the prettiest kid in the whole world.

THE GIRL. I'm not—and you know it.

YOUNG MAN. No—you are. I never saw anyone prettier in all my born days, in all my travels. I knew Texas would bring me luck.

THE GIRL. Luck? You're in jail, aren't you? You've got a whole gang of people all worked up, haven't you?

YOUNG MAN. Ah, that's nothing. I'll get out of this.

THE GIRL. Maybe.

YOUNG MAN. No, I'll be all right— *now.*

THE GIRL. What do you mean— now?

YOUNG MAN. I mean after seeing you. I got something now. You know for a while there I didn' care one way or another. Tired. [*Pause.*] Tired of trying for the best all the time and never getting it. [*Suddenly.*] Hello out there!

THE GIRL. Who you calling now?

YOUNG MAN. You.

THE GIRL. Why, I'm right here.

YOUNG MAN. I know. [*Calling.*] Hello out there!

THE GIRL. Hello.

YOUNG MAN. Ah, you're sweet. [*Pause.*] I'm going to marry you. I'm going away with you. I'm going to take you to San Francisco or some place like that. I *am*, now. I'm going to win myself some real money, too. I'm going to study 'em real careful and pick myself some winners, and we're going to have a lot of money.

THE GIRL. Yeah?

YOUNG MAN. Yeah. Tell me your

name and all that stuff.

THE GIRL. Emily.

YOUNG MAN. I know that. What's the rest of it? Where were you born? Come on, tell me the whole thing.

THE GIRL. Emily Smith.

YOUNG MAN. Honest to God?

THE GIRL. Honest. That's my name —Emily Smith.

YOUNG MAN. Ah, you're the sweetest girl in the whole world.

THE GIRL. Why?

YOUNG MAN. I don't know why, but you are, that's all. Where were you born?

THE GIRL. Matador, Texas.

YOUNG MAN. Where's that?

THE GIRL. Right here.

YOUNG MAN. Is this Matador, Texas?

THE GIRL. Yeah, it's Matador. They brought you here from Wheeling.

YOUNG MAN. Is that where I was— Wheeling?

THE GIRL. Didn't you even know what town you were in?

YOUNG MAN. All towns are alike. You don't go up and ask somebody what town you're in. It doesn't make any difference. How far away is Wheeling?

THE GIRL. Sixteen or seventeen miles. Didn't you know they moved you?

YOUNG MAN. How could I know, when I was out—cold? Somebody hit me over the head with a lead pipe or something. What'd they hit me for?

THE GIRL. Rape—that's what they said.

YOUNG MAN. Ah, that's a lie. [*Amazed, almost to himself.*] She wanted me to give her money.

THE GIRL. Money?

YOUNG MAN. Yeah, if I'd known

she was a woman like that—well, by God, I'd have gone on down the street and stretched out in a park somewhere and gone to sleep.

THE GIRL. Is that what she wanted —money?

YOUNG MAN. Yeah. A fellow like me hopping freights all over the country, trying to break his bad luck, going from one poor little town to another, trying to get in on something good somewhere, and she asks for money. I thought she was lonesome. She *said* she was.

THE GIRL. Maybe she was.

YOUNG MAN. She was *something*.

THE GIRL. I guess I'd never see you, if it didn't happen, though.

YOUNG MAN. Oh, I don't know— maybe I'd just mosey along this way and see you in this town somewhere. I'd recognize you, too.

THE GIRL. Recognize me?

YOUNG MAN. Sure, I'd recognize you the minute I laid eyes on you.

THE GIRL. Well, who would I be?

YOUNG MAN. Mine, that's who.

THE GIRL. Honest?

YOUNG MAN. Honest to God.

THE GIRL. You just say that because you're in jail.

YOUNG MAN. No, I mean it. You just pack up and wait for me. We'll high-roll the hell out of here to Frisco.

THE GIRL. You're just lonesome.

YOUNG MAN. I been lonesome all my life—there's no cure for that—but you and me—we can have a lot of fun hanging around together. You'll bring me luck. I know it.

THE GIRL. What are you looking for luck for all the time?

YOUNG MAN. I'm a gambler. I don't work. I've got to have luck, or I'm a bum. I haven' had any decent luck in years. Two whole years now—one place to another. Bad luck all the time. That's why I got in trouble back there in Wheeling, too. That was no accident. That was my bad luck following me around. So here I am, with my head half busted. I guess it was her old man that did it.

THE GIRL. You mean her father?

YOUNG MAN. No, her husband. If I had an old lady like that, I'd throw her out.

THE GIRL. Do you think you'll have better luck, if I go with you?

YOUNG MAN. It's a cinch. I'm a good handicapper. All I need is somebody good like you with me. It's no good always walking around the streets for anything that might be there at the time. You got to have somebody staying with you all the time—through winters when it's cold, and springtime when it's pretty, and summertime when it's nice and hot and you can go swimming—through *all* the times—rain and snow and all the different kinds of weather a man's got to go through before he dies. You got to have somebody who's right. Somebody who knows you, from way back. You've got to have somebody who even knows you're wrong but likes you just the same. I know I'm wrong, but I just don't want anything the hard way, working like a dog—working's the hard way and the easy way both. All I got to do is beat the price, always—and then I don't feel lousy and don't hate anybody. If you'll go along with me, I'll be the finest guy anybody ever saw. I won't be wrong any more. You know when you get enough of that money, you *can't* be wrong any more—you're right because the money says so. I'll have

a lot of money and you'll be just about the prettiest, most wonderful kid in the whole world. I'll be proud walking around Frisco with you on my arm and people turning around to look at us.

THE GIRL. Do you think they will?

YOUNG MAN. Sure they will. When I get back in some decent clothes, and you're on my arm—well, Katey, they'll turn around and look, and they'll see something, too.

THE GIRL. Katey?

YOUNG MAN. Yeah—that's your name from now on. You're the first girl I ever called Katey. I've been saving it for you. O.K.?

THE GIRL. O.K.

YOUNG MAN. How long have I been here?

THE GIRL. Since last night. You didn't wake up until late this morning, though.

YOUNG MAN. What time is it now? About nine?

THE GIRL. About ten.

YOUNG MAN. Have you got the key to this lousy cell?

THE GIRL. No. They don't let me fool with any keys.

YOUNG MAN. Well, can you get it?

THE GIRL. No.

YOUNG MAN. Can you try?

THE GIRL. They wouldn't let me get near any keys. I cook for this jail, when they've got somebody in it. I clean up and things like that.

YOUNG MAN. Well, I want to get out of here. Don't you know the guy that runs this joint?

THE GIRL. I know him, but he wouldn't let you out. They were talking of taking you to another jail in another town.

YOUNG MAN. Yeah? Why?

THE GIRL. Because they're afraid.

YOUNG MAN. What are they afraid of?

THE GIRL. They're afraid these people from Wheeling will come over in the middle of the night and break in.

YOUNG MAN. Yeah? What do they want to do that for?

THE GIRL. Don't *you* know what they want to do it for?

YOUNG MAN. Yeah, I know all right.

THE GIRL. Are you scared?

YOUNG MAN. Sure I'm scared. Nothing scares a man more than ignorance. You can argue with people who ain't fools, but you can't argue with fools—they just go to work and do what they're set on doing. Get me out of here.

THE GIRL. How?

YOUNG MAN. Well, go get the guy with the key, and let me talk to him.

THE GIRL. He's gone home. Everybody's gone home.

YOUNG MAN. You mean I'm in this little jail all alone?

THE GIRL. Well—yeah—except me.

YOUNG MAN. Well, what's the big idea—doesn't anybody stay here all the time?

THE GIRL. No, they go home every night. I clean up and then I go, too. I hung around tonight.

YOUNG MAN. What made you do that?

THE GIRL. I wanted to talk to you.

YOUNG MAN. Honest? What did you want to talk about?

THE GIRL. Oh, I don't know. I took care of you last night. You were talking in your sleep. You liked me, too. I didn't think you'd like me when you woke up, though.

YOUNG MAN. Yeah? Why not?

THE GIRL. I don't know.

YOUNG MAN. Yeah? Well, you're wonderful, see?

THE GIRL. Nobody ever talked to me that way. All the fellows in town —[*Pause.*]

YOUNG MAN. What about 'em? [*Pause.*] Well, what about 'em? Come on—tell me.

THE GIRL. They laugh at me.

YOUNG MAN. Laugh at *you.* They're fools. What do they know about anything? You go get your things and come back here. I'll take you with me to Frisco. How old are you?

THE GIRL. Oh, I'm of age.

YOUNG MAN. How old are you?— Don't lie to me! Sixteen?

THE GIRL. I'm seventeen.

YOUNG MAN. Well, bring your father and mother. We'll get married before we go.

THE GIRL. They wouldn't let me go.

YOUNG MAN. Why not?

THE GIRL. I don't know, but they wouldn't. I know they wouldn't.

YOUNG MAN. You go tell your father not to be a fool, see? What is he, a farmer?

THE GIRL. No—nothing. He gets a little relief from the government because he's supposed to be hurt or something—his side hurts, he says. I don't know what it is.

YOUNG MAN. Ah, he's a liar. Well, I'm taking you with me, see?

THE GIRL. He takes the money I earn, too.

YOUNG MAN. He's got no right to do that.

THE GIRL. I know it, but he does it.

YOUNG MAN. [*Almost to himself.*] This world stinks. You shouldn't have been born in this town, anyway, and you shouldn't have had a man like that for a father, either.

THE GIRL. Sometimes I feel sorry for him.

YOUNG MAN. Never mind feeling sorry for him. [*Pointing a finger.*] I'm going to talk to your father some day. I've got a few things to tell that guy.

THE GIRL. I know you have.

YOUNG MAN. [*Suddenly.*] Hello—out there! See if you can get that fel-with the keys to come down and let me out.

THE GIRL. Oh, I couldn't.

YOUNG MAN. Why not?

THE GIRL. I'm nobody here—they give me fifty cents every day I work.

YOUNG MAN. How much?

THE GIRL. Fifty cents.

YOUNG MAN. [*To the world.*] You see? They ought to pay money to *look* at you. To breathe the *air* you breathe. I don't know. Sometimes I figure it never is going to make sense. Hello—out there! I'm scared. You try to get me out of here. I'm scared them fools are going to come out here from Wheeling and go crazy, thinking they're heroes. Get me out of here, Katey.

THE GIRL. I don't know what to do. Maybe I could break the door down.

YOUNG MAN. No, you couldn't do that. Is there a hammer out there or anything?

THE GIRL. Only a broom. Maybe they've locked the broom up, too.

YOUNG MAN. Go see if you can find anything.

THE GIRL. All right. [*She goes.*]

YOUNG MAN. Hello—out there! Hello—out there!
[*Pause.*]

Hello—out there! Hello—out there! [*Pause.*]

Putting me in jail. [*With contempt.*]

Rape! Rape? *They* rape everything good that was ever born. His side hurts. They laugh at her. Fifty cents a day. Little punk people. Hurting the only good thing that ever came their way.
[*Suddenly.*]

Hello—out there!

THE GIRL. [*Returning.*] There isn't a thing out there. They've locked everything up for the night.

YOUNG MAN. Any cigarettes?

THE GIRL. Everything's locked up —all the drawers of the desk, all the closet doors—everything.

YOUNG MAN. I ought to have a cigarette.

THE GIRL. I could get you a package maybe, somewhere. I guess the drugstore's open. It's about a mile.

YOUNG MAN. A mile? I don't want to be alone that long.

THE GIRL. I could run all the way, and all the way back.

YOUNG MAN. You're the sweetest girl that ever lived.

THE GIRL. What kind do you want?

YOUNG MAN. Oh, any kind—Chesterfields or Camels or Lucky Strikes—any kind at all.

THE GIRL. I'll go get a package. [*She turns to go.*]

YOUNG MAN. What about the money?

THE GIRL. I've got some money. I've got a quarter I've been saving. I'll run all the way. [*She is about to go.*]

YOUNG MAN. Come here.

THE GIRL. [*Going to him.*] What?

YOUNG MAN. Give me your hand. [*He takes her hand and looks at it, smiling. He lifts it and kisses it.*] I'm scared to death.

THE GIRL. I am, too.

YOUNG MAN. I'm not lying—I don't care what happens to me, but I'm scared nobody will ever come down here to this God-forsaken broken-down town and find you. I'm scared you'll never get to Frisco and have 'em all turning around to look at you. Listen—go get me a gun, because if they come, I'll kill 'em. They don't understand. Get me a gun!

THE GIRL. I could get my father's gun. I know where he hides it.

YOUNG MAN. Go get it. Never mind the cigarettes. Run all the way. [*Pause, smiling but seriously.*] Hello, Katey.

THE GIRL. *Hello.* What's your name?

YOUNG MAN. Photo-Finish is what they call me. My races are always photo-finish races. You don't know what that means, but it means they're very close. So close the only way they can tell which horse wins is to look at a photograph after the race is over. Well, every race I bet turns out to be a photo-finish race, and my horse never wins. It's my bad luck, all the time. That's why they call me Photo-Finish. Say it before you go.

THE GIRL. Photo-Finish.

YOUNG MAN. Come here.

[THE GIRL *moves close and he kisses her.*]

Now, hurry. Run all the way.

THE GIRL. I'll run.

[THE GIRL *turns and runs.* THE YOUNG MAN *stands at the center of the cell a long time.* THE GIRL *comes running back in. Almost crying.*]

I'm afraid. I'm afraid I won't see you again. If I come back and you're not here, I—

YOUNG MAN. Hello—out there!

THE GIRL. It's so lonely in this town. Nothing here but the lonesome wind all the time, lifting the dirt and blowing out to the prairie. I'll stay *here*. I won't *let* them take you away.

YOUNG MAN. Listen, Katey. Do what I tell you. Go get that gun and come back. Maybe they won't come tonight. Maybe they won't come at all. I'll hide the gun and when they let me out you can take it back and put it where you found it. And then we'll go away. But if they come, I'll kill 'em! Now, hurry—

THE GIRL. All right. [*Pause.*] I want to tell you something.

YOUNG MAN. O.K.

THE GIRL. [*Very softly.*] If you're not here when I come back, well, I'll have the gun and I'll know what to do with it.

YOUNG MAN. You know how to handle a gun?

THE GIRL. I know how.

YOUNG MAN. Don't be a fool. [*Takes off his shoe, brings out some currency.*] Don't be a fool, see? Here's some money. Eighty dollars. Take it and go to Frisco. Look around and find somebody. Find somebody alive and halfway human, see? Promise me —if I'm not here when you come back, just throw the gun away and get the hell to Frisco. Look around and find somebody.

THE GIRL. I don't want to find anybody.

YOUNG MAN. [*Swiftly, desperately.*] Listen, if I'm not here when you come back, how do you know I haven't gotten away? Now, do what I tell you. I'll meet you in Frisco. I've got a couple dollars in my other shoe. I'll see you in San Francisco.

THE GIRL. [*With wonder.*] San Francisco?

YOUNG MAN. That's right—San Francisco. That's where you and me belong.

THE GIRL. I've always wanted to go to some place like San Francisco—but how could I go alone?

YOUNG MAN. Well, you're not alone any more, see?

THE GIRL. Tell me what it's like.

YOUNG MAN. [*Very swiftly, almost impatiently at first, but gradually slower and with remembrance, smiling, and* THE GIRL *moving closer to him as he speaks.*] Well, it's on the Pacific to begin with—ocean water all around. Cool fog and sea-gulls. Ships from all over the world. It's got seven hills. The little streets go up and down, around and all over. Every night the fog-horns bawl. But they won't be bawling for you and me.

THE GIRL. What else?

YOUNG MAN. That's about all, I guess.

THE GIRL. Are people different in San Francisco?

YOUNG MAN. People are the same everywhere. They're different only when they love somebody. That's the only thing that makes 'em different. More people in Frisco love somebody, that's all.

THE GIRL. Nobody anywhere loves anybody as much as I love you.

YOUNG MAN. [*Shouting, as if to the world.*] You see? Hearing you say that, a man could die and still be ahead of the game. Now, hurry. And don't forget, if I'm not here when you come back, get the hell to San Francisco where you'll have a chance. Do you hear me?

[THE GIRL *stands a moment looking at him, then backs away, and runs. The* YOUNG MAN *stares after her, troubled and smiling. Then he turns away from the image of her and walks about like a lion in a cage. After a while he sits down suddenly and buries his head in his hands. From a distance the sound of several automobiles approaching is heard. He listens a moment, then ignores the implications of the sound, whatever they may be. Several automobile doors are slammed. He ignores this also. A wooden door is opened with a key and closed, and footsteps are heard in the hall. Walking easily, almost casually and yet arrogantly, a* MAN *comes in. The* YOUNG MAN *jumps up suddenly and shouts at the man, almost scaring him.*]

What the hell kind of a jail-keeper are you, anyway? Why don't you attend to your business? You get paid for it, don't you? Now, get me out of here.

THE MAN. But I'm not the jail-keeper.

YOUNG MAN. Yeah? Well, who are you, then?

THE MAN. I'm the husband.

YOUNG MAN. What husband you talking about?

THE MAN. You know what husband.

YOUNG MAN. Hey! [*Pause, looking at* THE MAN.] Are you the guy that hit me over the head last night?

THE MAN. I am.

YOUNG MAN. [*With righteous indignation.*] What do you mean going around hitting people over the head?

THE MAN. Oh, I don't know. What do you mean going around—the way you do?

YOUNG MAN. [*Rubbing his head.*] You hurt my head. You got no right to hit anybody over the head.

THE MAN. [*Suddenly angry, shouting.*] Answer my question! What do you mean?

YOUNG MAN. Listen, you—don't be hollering at me just because I'm locked up.

THE MAN. [*With contempt, slowly.*] You're a dog!

YOUNG MAN. Yeah? Well, let me tell you something. You *think* you're the husband. You're the husband of nothing. [*Slowly.*] What's more, your wife—if you want to call her that—is a tramp. Why don't you throw her out in the street where she belongs?

THE MAN. [*Draws a pistol.*] Shut up!

YOUNG MAN. Yeah? Go ahead, shoot—[*Softly.*] and spoil the fun. What'll your pals think? They'll be disappointed, won't they? What's the fun in hanging a man who's already dead?

[THE MAN *puts the gun away.*]

That's right, because now you can have some fun yourself, telling me what you're going to do. That's what you came here for, isn't it? Well, you don't need tell me. I *know* what you're going to do. I've read the papers and I know. They have fun. A mob of 'em fall on one man and beat him, don't they? They tear his clothes off and kick him, don't they? And women and little children stand around watching, don't they? Well, before you go on *this* picnic, I'm going to tell you a few things. Not that that's

going to send you home with your pals—the other heroes. No. You've been outraged. A stranger has come to town and violated your women. Your pure, innocent, virtuous women. You fellows have got to set this thing right. You're men, not mice. You're home-makers, and you beat your children. [*Suddenly.*] Listen, you— I didn't know she was your wife. I didn't know she was anybody's wife.

THE MAN. You're a liar!

YOUNG MAN. Sometimes—when it'll do somebody some good—but not this time. Do you want to hear about it?

[THE MAN *doesn't answer.*]

All right, I'll tell you. I met her at a lunch counter. She came in and sat next to me. There was plenty of room, but she sat next to me. Somebody put a nickel in the phonograph and a fellow was singing *New San Antonio Rose.* Well, she got to talking about the song. I thought she was talking to the waiter, but *he* didn't answer her, so after a while *I* answered her. That's how I met her. I didn't think anything of it. We left the place together and started walking. The first thing I knew she said, This is where I live.

THE MAN. You're a dirty liar!

YOUNG MAN. Do you want to hear it? Or not?

[THE MAN *does not answer.*]

O.K. She asked me to come in. Maybe she had something in mind, maybe she didn't. Didn't make any difference to me, one way or the other. If she was lonely, all right. If not, all right.

THE MAN. You're telling a lot of dirty lies!

YOUNG MAN. I'm telling the truth. Maybe your wife's out there with your pals. Well, call her in. I got nothing against her, or you—or any of you. Call her in, and ask her a few questions. Are you in love with her?

[THE MAN *doesn't answer.*]

Well, that's too bad.

THE MAN. What do you mean, too bad?

YOUNG MAN. I mean this may not be the first time something like this has happened.

THE MAN. [*Swiftly.*] Shut up!

YOUNG MAN. Oh, you know it. You've always known it. You're afraid of your pals, that's all. She asked me for money. That's all she wanted. I wouldn't be here now if I had given her the money.

THE MAN. [*Slowly.*] How much did she ask for?

YOUNG MAN. I didn't ask her how much. I told her I'd made a mistake. She said she would make trouble if I didn't give her money. Well, I don't like bargaining, and I don't like being threatened, either. I told her to get the hell away from me. The next thing I knew she'd run out of the house hollering. [*Pause.*] Now, why don't you go out there and tell 'em they took me to another jail—go home and pack up and leave her. You're a pretty good guy, you're just afraid of your pals.

[THE MAN *draws his gun again. He is very frightened. He moves a step toward the* YOUNG MAN, *then fires three times. The* YOUNG MAN *falls to his knees.* THE MAN *turns and runs, horrified.*]

Hello—out there! [*He is bent forward.* THE GIRL *comes running in, and halts suddenly, looking at him.*]

THE GIRL. There were some people in the street, men and women and kids—so I came in through the back, through a window. I couldn't find the gun. I looked all over but I couldn't find it. What's the matter?

YOUNG MAN. Nothing—nothing. Everything's all right. Listen. Listen, kid. Get the hell out of here. Go out the same way you came in and run— run like hell—run all night. Get to another town and get on a train. Do you hear me?

THE GIRL. What's happened?

YOUNG MAN. Get away—just get away from here. Take any train that's going—you can get to Frisco later.

THE GIRL. [*Almost sobbing.*] I don't want to go any place without you.

YOUNG MAN. I can't go. Something's happened. [*He looks at her.*] But I'll be with you always—God damn it. Always!

[*He falls forward.* THE GIRL *stands near him, then begins to sob softly, walking away. She stands over to one side, stops sobbing, and stares out. The excitement of the mob outside increases.* THE MAN, *with two of his pals, comes running in.* THE GIRL *watches, unseen.*]

THE MAN. Here's the son of a bitch!

ANOTHER MAN. O.K. Open the cell, Harry.

[*The* THIRD MAN *goes to the cell door, unlocks it, and swings it open.*]

[*A* WOMAN *comes running in.*]

THE WOMAN. Where is he? I want to see him. Is he dead? [*Looking down at him as the* MEN *pick him up.*] There he is. [*Pause.*] Yeah, that's him.

[*Her husband looks at her with contempt, then at the dead man.*]

THE MAN. [*Trying to laugh.*] All right—let's get it over with.

THIRD MAN. Right you are, George. Give me a hand, Harry.

[*They lift the body.*]

THE GIRL. [*Suddenly, fiercely.*] Put him down!

THE MAN. What's this?

SECOND MAN. What are you doing here? Why aren't you out in the street?

THE GIRL. Put him down and go away.

[*She runs towards the* MEN. THE WOMAN *grabs her.*]

THE WOMAN. Here—where do you think *you're* going?

THE GIRL. Let me go. You've no right to take him away.

THE WOMAN. Well, listen to her, will you?

[*She slaps* THE GIRL *and pushes her to the floor.*]

Listen to the little slut, will you?

[*They all go, carrying the* YOUNG MAN's *body.* THE GIRL *gets up slowly, no longer sobbing. She looks around at everything, then looks straight out, and whispers.*]

THE GIRL. Hello—out—there! Hello —out there!

NOTES

In these Notes a concise biographical sketch of each author is provided, with occasional critical material, followed by a list of the author's publications, a selected bibliography, and details of publication for each selection. It has been necessary to use only the first few words sometimes in very long titles. Fuller titles can be got in most cases from F. B. Millett, *Contemporary American Authors*, 1940, and from Vol. III of the *L.H.U.S.* The more difficult allusions and passages are annotated.

Theodore Dreiser (1871–1945)

In a period characterized by a strong interest in naturalism, the chief American naturalist was Theodore Dreiser, whose reputation grew impressively during the years following World War I. Critics have constantly directed attention to his puerile style and circumscribed outlook on life, but they have rightly insisted, also, that his long, detailed novels impart a convincing impression of the turbulent world of living, erring, suffering, struggling men and women.

Dreiser was born in Terre Haute, Ind., on Aug. 27, 1871. He attended the public schools of Warsaw, Ind., and for a few months was a student at the University of Indiana. Most of his boyhood years, however, were spent in hard work, largely in Chicago, to which city he first came in his sixteenth year. He was employed in turn by a hardware company, in a real estate office, and as a collector for a furniture dealer. In 1891 he became a newspaper man, first as a reporter for the *Chicago Daily Globe*, then as a correspondent for the *St. Louis Globe-Democrat*, and lastly as a writer for the *St. Louis Republic*. From 1895 to 1898 he edited *Every Month*, a musical magazine in New York City, and after holding other editorial positions, became in 1907 the editor-in-chief of the Butterick Publications, which included *The Delineator, The Designer,* and *The New Idea*. In 1900 appeared his first novel, *Sister Carrie,* which, because it seemed to the wife of one of the publishers immoral in tone, was promptly withdrawn from the market. Not until 1911 was another novel published— *Jennie Gerhardt. The "Genius,"* 1915, and *An American Tragedy,* 1925, were both severely criticized by the morally indignant. These attacks drew much attention to his fiction, some of it unfortunate, although they also aroused critical champions to speak in his behalf. Besides novels, Dreiser wrote verse, short stories, character sketches, plays, several volumes of autobiography, and books dealing with his travels and his views on social matters. He was married in 1898. Finding the conditions of married life unbearable, however, he begged freedom of his wife, who released him. He lived in several parts of the country, particularly in New York and California. Dreiser's death occurred on December 29, 1945.

Sister Carrie, 1900; *Jennie Gerhardt,* 1911; *The Financier,* 1912; *A Traveler at Forty,* 1913; *The Titan,* 1914; *The "Genius,"* 1915; *Plays of the Natural and the Supernatural,* 1916; *A Hoosier Holiday,* 1916; *Free and Other Stories,* 1918; *The Hand of the Potter,* 1919; *Twelve Men,* 1919; *Hey Rub-a-Dub-Dub,* 1920; *A Book about Myself,* 1922 (repub. as *Newspaper Days,* 1931); *The Color of a Great City,* 1923; *An American Tragedy,* 1925; *Moods Cadenced and Declaimed,* 1926; *Chains,* 1927; *Dreiser Looks at Russia,* 1928; *A Gallery of Women,* 1929; *The Aspirant,* 1929; *The Carnegie Works at Pittsburgh,* 1929; *My City,* 1929; *Epitaph,* 1929;

Fine Furniture, 1930; *Dawn, a History of Myself*, 1931; *Tragic America*, 1932; *America Is Worth Saving*, 1941; *The Bulwark*, 1946; *Best Short Stories* (ed. by Howard Fast), 1947; *The Stoic*, 1948.

For life and criticism, see: Burton Rascoe, *Theodore Dreiser*, 1925; Dorothy Dudley, *Forgotten Frontiers: Dreiser and the Land of the Free*, 1932; Robert H. Elias, *Theodore Dreiser: Apostle of Nature*, 1948; and Dreiser's autobiographical volumes, particularly *Newspaper Days* (formerly called *A Book about Myself*) and *Dawn*. For criticism, see: Stuart P. Sherman, *On Contemporary Literature*, 1917, pp. 85–102; H. L. Mencken, *A Book of Prefaces*, 1917, pp. 67–149; Percy H. Boynton, *Some Contemporary Americans*, 1924, pp. 126–45; Stuart P. Sherman, *The Main Stream*, 1927, pp. 134–45; Milton Waldman, in *Contemporary American Authors* (ed. J. C. Squire), 1928, pp. 97–118; Régis Michaud, *The American Novel To-Day*, 1928, pp. 71–128; T. K. Whipple, *Spokesmen*, 1928, pp. 70–93; Robert Shafer, in *Humanism and America* (ed. Norman Foerster), 1930, pp. 149–69; Fred Lewis Pattee, *The New American Literature*, 1930, pp. 180–93; Joseph Warren Beach, *The Twentieth Century Novel*, 1932, pp. 321–32; C. C. Walcutt, *PMLA*, Nov., 1940, pp. 266–89; J. T. Flanagan, *Southwest Rev.*, XXXI, pp. 408–11; W. A. Ross, *Am. Lit.*, XVIII, pp. 233–43. See also: E. D. McDonald, *A Bibliography of the Writings of Theodore Dreiser*, 1928.

27. [A BOY AND A SQUID] and [THE DAMNABLE SCHEME OF THINGS] are Chapters I and XLIII, respectively, of *The Financier*, 1912, the first volume in Dreiser's "Trilogy of Desire," which includes also *The Titan* and *The Stoic*. ¶27. *"Frank Algernon Cowperwood."* "The story of Cowperwood parallels the history of Charles T. Yerkes, traction magnate, operating first in Philadelphia and then in Chicago, New York, and London."—Dudley, p. 293. Dreiser believed that Harper's withdrew the sequel to this novel after contracting to publish it because Col. Harvey, of Harper's board, did not wish to offend the second Mrs. Yerkes who was still alive. *The Titan* was published by John Lane. In *The Financier* Cowperwood, who has got into streetcar-line financing, after arriving at independence through whole-

sale marketing, is checked in his career by Jim Butler, Philadelphia political boss, who had sworn to "get even" after learning that Cowperwood had seduced his daughter, Aileen. Cowperwood saves part of his fortune but serves a prison term. Upon his early release, he leaves his wife and goes to Chicago with Aileen, where his career is taken up in *The Titan*.

40. OLD ROGAUM AND HIS THERESA. In *Free and Other Stories*, 1918. Published much earlier in a popular magazine as "The Butcher Rogaum and His Door" (Dudley).

53. [DISCOURAGING DAYS IN NEW YORK.] From *A Book about Myself*, 1922 (called since 1931 *Newspaper Days*). Originally appeared, however, in *Bookman*, Apr., 1922, in which magazine *A Book about Myself* was serialized, 1921–22. ¶54. *"my brother Paul."* Paul Dresser, a composer of many popular songs, among them "Just Tell Them That You Saw Me," "On the Banks of the Wabash," "The Blue and the Grey," "On the Bowery," and "The Letter That Never Came." Incidentally, Dreiser himself collaborated with his brother in writing the words for "On the Banks of the Wabash." For an account of Paul Dresser, see *Twelve Men*, pp. 76–110. ¶55. *"Perhaps . . . life as I saw it . . . was never to be written about."* For Dreiser's comment on the changed conditions in the field of fiction which he had witnessed since 1915, see "America and the Artist," *Nation*, Apr. 25, 1925. Although not satisfied with life in America, the author indicates that human affairs are fundamentally the same in all countries. "Life is life," he writes, "wherever you find it—in whatever land or clime."

Gamaliel Bradford (1863–1932)

Gamaliel Bradford was born on Oct. 9, 1863, in Boston, Mass. He was trained in the local schools in Wellesley Hills, and attended Harvard University for a few months, leaving because of poor health. In 1886 he married Miss Helen Hubbard Ford, and set out to win his way as a man of letters. He first wrote verse, fiction, and drama with but little success; almost by accident he entered the field of biographical writing in which he succeeded and in which his influence was strongly felt. With *Lee the American*, 1912, and *Confederate*

Portraits, 1914, came his first conspicuous success, which increased as other volumes of the kind appeared. He called himself a "psychographer"—a "portrait-painter of souls"; he acknowledged indebtedness to Sainte-Beuve, yet showed originality in the handling of the human personalities and characters treated in his books. He died on Apr. 11, 1932.

Types of American Character, 1895; *A Pageant of Life,* 1904; *The Private Tutor,* 1904; *Between Two Masters,* 1906; *Matthew Porter,* 1908; *Lee the American,* 1912; *Confederate Portraits,* 1914; *Union Portraits,* 1916; *Portraits of Women,* 1916; *A Naturalist of Souls,* 1917; *Unmade in Heaven,* 1917; *Portraits of American Women,* 1919; *A Prophet of Joy,* 1920; *Shadow Verses,* 1920; *American Portraits,* 1922; *Damaged Souls,* 1923; *The Soul of Samuel Pepys,* 1924; *Bare Souls,* 1924; *Wives,* 1925; *Darwin,* 1926; *D. L. Moody,* 1927; *The Haunted Biographer: Dialogues of the Dead,* 1927; *Life and I,* 1928; *As God Made Them,* 1929; *Daughters of Eve,* 1930; *The Quick and the Dead,* 1931; *Saints and Sinners,* 1932; *Biography and the Human Heart,* 1932; *Journal: 1883–1932* (ed. by Van Wyck Brooks), 1933; *Portraits and Personalities* (ed. by Mabel Bessey), 1933; *Letters: 1918–31* (ed. by Van Wyck Brooks), 1934; *Elizabethan Woman* (ed. by H. O. White), 1936.

For criticism, see: Joseph Warren Beach, *The Outlook for American Prose,* 1926, pp. 54–9; Samuel C. Chew, *Nation,* CXVII, p. 196; Percy H. Boynton, *New Republic,* XXXVI, pp. 184–85; Allan Nevins, *Sat. Rev. Lit.,* IV, p. 570; Henry Hazlitt, "Gamaliel Bradford," *Nation,* CXXXIV, p. 494. See also Bradford's letter about himself in Josephine K. Piercy, *Modern Writers at Work,* 1930, pp. 230–33.

56. [HENRY ADAMS'S BOOK], [ESTIMATE OF ADAMS], [IN THE FULL TIDE OF PORTRAITS] and [SPENGLER] are from *The Journal of Gamaliel Bradford,* ed. by Van Wyck Brooks in 1933. ¶56. "*Sainte-Beuve,*" Charles Augustin (1804–69), French literary critic, self-styled "naturalist of souls." ¶56. "*Hegel,*" George Wilhelm Friedrich (1770–1831), German philosopher. ¶57. "*The Stuart and Sherman.*" Portraits of J. E. B. Stuart, cavalry officer of the Confederacy, and W. T. Sherman, union general of the famous march through Georgia, done by Bradford. ¶57. "*Joel Benton.*" Author of *Life of Phineas T. Barnum,* 1891. ¶57. "*Spengler.*" Oswald (1880–1936), German philosopher. A statement of his cyclical theory of history is found in Van Wyck Brooks' *The Flowering of New England.* See pp. 524–25 in this text.

George Santayana (1863–   )

Son of Augustin Ruiz de Santayana and Josefina Borrás; born in Madrid, Spain, Dec. 16, 1863. When only nine, he was brought by his mother to U. S. to be educated. He attended Harvard College, 1882–86, spent two years abroad, then took his Ph.D. at Harvard, 1889. In the same year he was appointed instructor in philosophy at Harvard, and except for two interruptions he served the University twenty-two years. He spent 1896–97 in study at King's College, Cambridge, Eng., and during the winter of 1905–06 was Hyde lecturer at the Sorbonne, Paris. His professional advancement was surprisingly slow: he did not become assistant professor until 1898, and not until both Royce and Münsterberg advocated his promotion. A professorship was not given him until 1907. In part, this was due to neglect, and in part to Santayana's retiring and modest disposition. He had a preference for solitude; during his early years at Cambridge he had adopted solipsism, the belief that he was the only soul alive. Out of this consciousness of personality in chaos or Nature his own philosophy was born, a thorough-going materialistic naturalism. Fundamentally a poet and idealist—he had published a very subjective volume of verse in 1894—he now found poetry and idealism needed explanation. They are the highest manifestations of the life of reason, of matter become conscious and rational. Of will, Santayana was skeptical, holding it a delusion peculiarly American; this skepticism made him the opponent, never openly announced, of William James. Meanwhile he had published the foremost American treatise on aesthetics, *The Sense of Beauty,* and had begun his *Life of Reason,* not published until 1905–06.

He resigned from Harvard, 1911; on Aug. 25, 1911, he delivered his famous attack, "The Genteel Tradition in American Philosophy," before the Philosophical Union, University of California. The Emersonian doctrine of self-reliance and the pragmatism of James (both dependent on the will) chiefly received his scorn; above the will he placed the intellect. After this outburst, he made his residence abroad, during World War I in England, and after its close in Paris. He delivered the Herbert Spencer lectures at Oxford University in 1923. Prior to this he had become dissatisfied with the statement of his philosophy in *The Life of Reason*, declaring "there is hardly a page that would not need to be rewritten" if it were to express his new opinion faithfully. With *Skepticism and Animal Faith*, 1923, he began a new system, fully stated in *Realms of Being*, 1942. During World War II he lived in Italy. He now resides in the convent of the Little Company of Mary, in Rome, and is working on two MSS which he expects will be published after his death, *Posthumous Poems* and *Dominions and Powers*, the latter to be a study of politics.

Sonnets and Other Poems, 1894; *The Sense of Beauty*, 1896; *Lucifer, a Theological Tragedy*, 1898; *Interpretations of Poetry and Religion*, 1900; *The Hermit of Carmel and Other Poems*, 1901; *The Life of Reason*, 5 vols., 1905–06, rev. 1922–28; *Sonnets and Other Verses*, 1902; *Three Philosophical Poets*, 1910; *Winds of Doctrine*, 1914; *Egotism in German Philosophy*, 1916; *Philosophical Opinion in the United States*, 1920; *Soliloquies in England and Later Soliloquies*, 1922; *Skepticism and Animal Faith*, 1923; *Dialogues in Limbo*, 1925; *Platonism and the Spiritual Life*, 1927; *The Realm of Essence*, 1928; *The Realm of Matter*, 1930; *The Genteel Tradition at Bay*, 1931; *Some Turns of Thought in Modern Philosophy*, 1933; *The Last Puritan*, 1935; *Obiter Scripta*, 1935; *The Works*, 14 vols., 1936–37; *The Realm of Truth*, 1937; *Realm of Spirit*, 1940; *Realms of Being*, 1942; *Persons and Places*, 1944; *Middle Span*, 1945; *Idea of Christ in the Gospels*, 1946.

Little Essays Drawn from the Writings of George Santayana, ed. L. P. Smith, 1921; *Poems* (collected), Scribner's, 1923; *Lucifer*, Dunster House, 1924.

For life, see: *Persons and Places; Middle Span*; "Dilly Tante," *Living Authors*, 1931; Margaret Münsterberg, "Santayana at Cambridge," *Am. Merc.*, Jan., 1924. For criticism, see: M. R. Cohen, "George Santayana," *New Re-*

pub., July 21, 1920; Percy Litell, "George Santayana," *New Repub.*, Feb. 9, 1921; A. MacLeish, "Santayana, the Poet," *Am. Merc.*, Oct., 1925; Lewis Mumford, "Life of Reason," *Freeman*, May 23, 1923; J. B. Rittenhouse, *Younger American Poets*, 1904; Marten ten Hoor, *George Santayana's Theory of Knowledge*, Univ. Mich. diss.; Carl Van Doren, "Tower of Irony," *Century*, Oct., 1923.

58. ODES, II. In *Sonnets and Other Poems*, 1894. As the apostrophe to Nature ("O silent Mother") would indicate, this poem is probably inspired by Lucretius' *De rerum natura*. Santayana values classical poets above modern because of "the breadth, sanity, and happy vigor" of the ancients, and because of their idealism. The moderns are barbarians and worship the senses. See: *Interpretations of Poetry and Religion*, 1900.

59. SONNETS. From the 1894 volume. The first suggests Santayana's love of medieval Catholic poets and schoolmen. Dante, for example, has a "riper intellect" than Homer. The second sonnet, although in the Petrarchian tradition, is addressed to no known deity.

59. ON MY FRIENDLY CRITICS. From *Soliloquies in England and Later Soliloquies*, 1924 edition; first published in *The Journal of Philosophy*, Dec. 22, 1921. ¶60. *"Spinoza"*: Baruch (1632–77), Spanish Jew, whose *Ethics*, 1670, supplies the first modern Biblical criticism. ¶61. *"Kant,"* Immanuel (1724–1804), German philosopher. ¶63. *"Plato in his doctrine."* The *Theaetetus* of the Greek philosopher (c. 428–c. 348 B.C.) contains one discussion of the doctrine stated here. ¶63. *"Sheherazad"*: lady in *The Arabian Nights*, who nightly postpones her execution through her ability to entertain the king, a homicidal maniac, with her "continued" tales. ¶64. *"stocks"*: "all our fathers worshipped,"–Milton, "On the Late Massacre in Piedmont." ¶66. *"Leibniz"*: Gottfried Wilhelm Leibnitz (1646–1716), German philosopher who as early as 1663 defended the nominalistic doctrine that individuality is constituted by the whole entity or *essence* of a thing (in *De principio individui*).

As basis for criticism, see statement that investigation and reasoning are, in philosophy, but preparatory to "insight or theory."–"Three Philosophical Poets."

James T(homas) Farrell
(1904–　　)

Son of James Francis and Mary
(Daly) Farrell, James T. Farrell was
born in Chicago on Feb. 27, 1904. He
attended St. Anselm Grammar School,
where his chief interest was in baseball;
later, at St. Cyril High School, he found
himself more interested in football and
basketball (he won his letters) than in
books. After trying DePaul University,
he transferred to the University of Chicago, where his liking for writing was
encouraged by Professor James Weber
Linn (see "The Professor" in *Can All
This Grandeur Perish?*). Meanwhile he
had clerked for the American Railway
Express Company and in a cigar store,
experiences much utilized in his later
fiction; he also was a filling station attendant before he secured his first writing job as a part-time reporter (see *My
Days of Anger*). Haldeman-Julius
printed his first literary work in the
Debunker, but his career really began
with the publication of *Young Lonigan*,
the first volume in his trilogy, in 1932.
Since then, with prodigal energy, he has
averaged better than a book a year. Recently he has made his home in New
York, although, like many another
writer, he has lived in Paris. Farrell has
been twice married, first to Dorothy P.
Butler in 1931, from whom he was
divorced, and next, to Hortense Alden.
He has a son, Kevin James.

*Young Lonigan—A Boyhood in Chi-
cago Streets*, 1932; *Gas-House McGinty*,
1933; *The Young Manhood of Studs
Lonigan*, 1934; *Calico Shoes*, 1934;
Judgment Day, 1935; *Guillotine Party
and Other Stories*, 1935; *Studs Lonigan,
A Trilogy*, 1935; *A Note on Literary
Criticism*, 1936; *A World I Never Made*,
1936; *Can All This Grandeur Perish?*,
1937; *The Collected Short Stories*, 1937;
No Star Is Lost, 1938; *Tommy Gal-
lagher's Crusade*, 1939; *Father and Son*,
1940; *Ellen Rogers*, 1941; *$1000 a
Week and Other Stories*, 1942; *My
Days of Anger*, 1943; *To Whom It May
Concern*, 1944; *The League of Frightened Philistines*, 1945; *Bernard Clare*,
1946; *The Fate of Writing in America*,
1946; *When Boyhood Dreams Come
True*, 1946; *Literature and Morality*,
1947.

For life and criticism, see: J. T. Far-
rell, "A Novelist Begins," *Atlantic*,
Sept., 1938 (also in Mod. Lib. ed. *Studs*
Lonigan); R. M. Lovett, "James T.
Farrell," *English Journal*, May, 1937;
O. Cargill, *Intellectual America*, 1941;
J. W. Beach, *American Fiction, 1920–
40*, 1941.

68. STUDS. From *Guillotine Party and
Other Stories*, 1935, "originally published in *This Quarter*." "One of the
stories which I wrote for Professor Linn's
course was titled 'Studs.' . . . Professor
Linn read this story in class and praised
it most enthusiastically. . . . I asked
Professor Robert Morss Lovett to read
it. . . . After doing so, . . . he suggested that the story should be developed
at greater length. . . . Studs Lonigan is
neither a tough nor a gangster. He is a
normal young American of his time and
class."–"A Novelist Begins." Of course,
this story should be compared with the
trilogy.

Gertrude Stein (1874–1946)

Gertrude Stein was born in Allegheny,
Pa., on Feb. 3, 1874, the daughter of
"comfortably wealthy" German-Jewish
parents, Daniel and Amelia (Keyser)
Stein. She was taken to Paris and
Vienna when she was very small and
then went to live with her family in
California. After preliminary schooling
in Oakland and San Francisco, she attended Radcliffe from 1893 to 1897.
Her English themes still survive, painstakingly corrected by William Vaughn
Moody and Frank Farley. They show
none of the novelties of style which distinguish her later work, but were sufficiently interesting to solicit the encouragement of her teachers to write. Nevertheless her most memorable undergraduate experience was her participation in
an experiment, conducted by William
James and Hugo Münsterberg, to discover the character of subconscious
thought. Her particular venture was into
automatic writing, but her later style,
which reflects the results of this form of
composition, should be compared with
those obtained by James when a steno-
graphic record was made of his return
to consciousness after inhaling nitrous
oxide. Francis Galton had already surmised that the subconscious mind and
the primitive mind might have something of the same character, and it was
this analogy which Miss Stein was to
exploit much later in her writing. After
leaving Radcliffe, Miss Stein enrolled in
the Johns Hopkins Medical School, where

she "liked" her first two years "well enough," but "the last two years . . . she was bored, frankly openly bored." Failed by one professor in her "graduation examinations," she rejected the idea of a medical career, rather than make up her deficiency, and went to London in 1902 where she read English literature for a year, especially Elizabethan prose. The following year she joined her brother Leo in Paris, and this cosmopolitan city and the little town of Bilignin were her homes for the remainder of her life. In Paris her Montparnasse salon was famous as a meeting place for artistic celebrities. She counted Matisse and Picasso as her friends, but she had a select group of American admirers which at one time included Carl Van Vechten, Sherwood Anderson, F. Scott Fitzgerald, Ernest Hemingway, Louis Bromfield, Elliot Paul, Thornton Wilder, and others. She had begun to write in London and continued to pile up manuscript until in 1909 she decided to publish *Three Lives* at her own expense. Though this book was to revolutionize American primitivistic writing it made little impression at the time, and her first volume of verse, *Tender Buttons* (1914), was regarded as the most absurd of efforts at creating a "new" poetry. Sherwood Anderson "discovered" and promoted her; in the late twenties her worth became more generally recognized, but there is no doubt that her triumphal tour of the U. S., following the popular reception of *The Autobiography of Alice B. Toklas* in 1932, was more a tribute to her capacity to stimulate interest as a supposed "eccentric" than to substantial accomplishment. Returning to France, she lived unmolested during the German occupation and the Vichy regime. She died there on July 27, 1946.

Have They Attacked Mary. He Giggled (n.d.); *Portrait of Mary Dodge* (n.d.); *Three Lives*, 1909; *Tender Buttons*, 1914; *Geography and Plays*, 1922; *The Making of Americans*, 1925; *As a Wife Has a Cow, A Love Story*, 1926; *Composition as Explanation*, 1926; *An Elucidation*, 1927; *Useful Knowledge*, 1928; *A Village*, 1928; *An Acquaintance with Description*, 1929; *Dix portraits*, 1930; *Lucy Church Amiably,*, 1930; *Before the Flowers of Friendship Faded*, 1930; *How to Write*, 1931; *Operas and Plays*, 1932; *The Autobiography of Alice B. Toklas*, 1933; *Matisse, Picasso*

and Gertrude Stein, 1933; *Four Saints in Three Acts*, 1933; *Portraits and Prayers*, 1934; *Lectures in America*, 1935; *Narration*, 1935; *The Geographical History of America*, 1936; *Everybody's Autobiography*, 1937; *Picasso*, 1938; *The World Is Round*, 1939; *Paris, France*, 1940; *Wars I Have Seen*, 1945; *Brewsie and Willie*, 1946; *Selected Writings* (ed. Carl Van Vechten), 1946; *Four in America*, 1947; *First Reader*, 1948; *Last Operas and Plays* (ed. Carl Van Vechten), 1949.

For life and criticism, see: *The Autobiography of Alice B. Toklas* and *Everybody's Autobiography*; Sherwood Anderson, "The Work of Gertrude Stein" in *Geography and Plays*; Laura Riding, *Contemporaries and Snobs*, 1928; B. F. Skinner, "Has Gertrude Stein a Secret?" *Atlantic*, August, 1935; Georges Braque, Eugene Jolas, Maria Jolas, Henri Matisse, André Salmon, Tristan Tzara, *Testimony Against Gertrude Stein*, 1935; M. D. Luhan, *European Experiences*, 1935; O. Cargill, *Intellectual America*, 1941; Leo Stein, *Appreciation*, 1947; W. G. Rogers, *When This You See Remember Me*, 1948. For bibliography, see: "Gertrude Stein: Bibliography," *Transition*, Feb., 1929.

74. MELANCTHA. First published in *Three Lives*, 1909. "It was then [during her last year at medical school] that she had to take her turn in the delivering of babies and it was at that time that she noticed the negroes and the places that she afterwards used in the second of the Three Lives stories, Melanctha Herbert, the story that was the beginning of her revolutionary work." *Toklas*, p. 100.

Sherwood Anderson (1876–1941)

An author whose name strongly suggests the individualism of the post-war period, Sherwood Anderson was a self-educated man, the author of fiction showing a rich subjective vein. His work is uneven, most of it being crude and unformed by a disciplined mind or sure tastes; but a number of his short stories bear on them the stamp of an unusual narrative talent.

Anderson was born in Camden, Ohio, on Sept. 13, 1876, one of a large family of boys and girls. His father was a likable, irresponsible man who drifted from place to place and allowed his children little opportunity to attend schools. Sherwood worked at numerous odd jobs as a boy, and at the age of sixteen moved on to Chicago, where he continued to lead an unsettled existence. During the Spanish-American War he served in the army, and upon his return to the United States was surprised to find himself considered a hero. He married and settled down to serious work, becoming in a few years the manager of a paint factory in Elyria, Ohio. He was dissatisfied with his life, however, and after giving up his position went again to Chicago. Through the influence of the then existing "Chicago group" of authors, particularly Theodore Dreiser, Ben Hecht, and Floyd Dell, he was encouraged to continue with his plans to embark on a literary career, despite the refusal of editors and publishers to accept his work. Some of his earliest writing was published in *The Little Review* and *The Dial;* and in 1916 appeared his novel, *Windy McPherson's Son. Winesburg, Ohio,* 1919, a volume of stories and sketches, largely established his reputation with both readers and critics. He took a trip to Europe, lived for some time in New York City, and spent a year in New Orleans. In 1925 he purchased a farm near Marion, Virginia, where he soon settled and became the local newspaper editor. He died on March 8, 1941.

Windy McPherson's Son, 1916; *Marching Men,* 1917; *Mid-American Chants,* 1918; *Winesburg, Ohio,* 1919; *Poor White,* 1920; *The Triumph of the Egg,* 1921; *Many Marriages,* 1923; *Horses and Men,* 1923; *A Story Teller's Story,* 1924; *The Modern Writer,* 1925; *Dark Laughter,* 1925; *Tar,* 1926; *Sherwood Anderson's Notebook,* 1926; *A New Testament,* 1927; *Nearer the Grass Roots,* 1929; *Hello Towns!,* 1929; *American County Fair,* 1930; *Perhaps Women,* 1931; *Beyond Desire,* 1932; *Death in the Woods and Other Stories,* 1933; *No Swank,* 1934; *Puzzled America,* 1935; *Kit Brandon, a Portrait,* 1936; *Plays: Winesburg and Others,* 1937; *Home Town,* 1940; *Memoirs,* 1942; *Sherwood Anderson Reader* (ed. by Paul Rosenfeld), 1947.

For life, see: Sherwood Anderson, *A Story Teller's Story* and *Tar; Windy McPherson's Son* and several others of Anderson's works are also partly autobiographical. Also Karl James Anderson, "My Brother, Sherwood Anderson," *Sat. Rev. Lit.,* Sept. 4, 1948. For life and criticism, see: Harry Hansen, *Midwest*

Portraits, 1923, pp. 111–80; Cleveland B. Chase, *Sherwood Anderson,* 1927. For criticism, see: Stuart Sherman, *Critical Woodcuts,* 1926, pp. 3–18; Joseph Warren Beach, *The Outlook for American Prose,* 1926, pp. 247–80; Percy H. Boynton, *More Contemporary Americans,* 1927, pp. 157–78; Régis Michaud, *The American Novel To-Day,* 1928, pp. 154–200; T. K. Whipple, *Spokesmen,* 1928, pp. 115–39; Fred Lewis Pattee, *The New American Literature,* 1930, pp. 332–38.

150. THE EGG is from *The Triumph of the Egg,* 1921. ¶150. "Thomas Butterworth." A character in *Poor White,* 1920, which is also set in "Bidwell."

157. PERHAPS WOMEN. The first of two sections so entitled in the book *Perhaps Women,* 1931, the thesis of which is that woman may make a "conquest" of the machine where man has failed.

F(rancis) Scott Fitzgerald
(1896–1940)

Francis Scott Key Fitzgerald was born in St. Paul, Minn., on Sept. 24, 1896. His school days were spent largely in scribbling; his freshman year at Princeton University, which he entered in 1913, was devoted to the writing of a musical comedy for the Triangle Club. Leaving Princeton in 1917 to join the army, he served over a year as an infantry officer, spending his week-ends at work on a novel. This novel was rejected by publishers, but in 1920 a second novel, *This Side of Paradise,* was not only published but sold well to a public which found it highly entertaining. In the same year the author married Miss Zelda Sayre, of Montgomery, Ala., and settled in a home on Long Island. He continued to write fiction, much of it in the form of the short story, until his death in 1940. The last decade of his life was spent in Europe and in Hollywood, Calif.

Fitzgerald chose as his especial theme life among the unsettled post-war generation of young men and women, his own generation, and came to be regarded as the most understanding interpreter of a frenzied "jazz age," which he said came to an end about 1929.

This Side of Paradise, 1920; *Flappers and Philosophers,* 1920; *The Beautiful and Damned,* 1922; *Tales of the Jazz Age,* 1922; *The Vegetable,* 1923; *The*

Great Gatsby, 1925; *All the Sad Young Men*, 1926; *Tender Is the Night*, 1934; *Taps at Reveille*, 1935; *The Last Tycoon*, 1941; *The Portable F. Scott Fitzgerald* (ed. by Dorothy Parker), 1945; *Crack-up* (ed. by Edmund Wilson), 1945.

For criticism, see: *Bookman*, LV, pp. 20–25; Vivian Shaw, *Dial*, LXXII, pp. 419–22; Gilbert Seldes, *Dial*, LXXIX, pp. 162–65; Robert Littell, *New Repub.*, XXX, p. 348; William Rose Benét, *Sat. Rev. Lit.*, I, pp. 739–40.

162. THE JELLY-BEAN. From *Tales of the Jazz Age*, 1922.

Ring(gold Wilmer) Lardner (1885–1933)

Ringgold Wilmer Lardner was born in Niles, Mich., on Mar. 6, 1885. He attended the local schools, and in 1901–02 was a student at the Armour Institute of Technology in Chicago. In 1905 he joined the staff of the *Times*, at South Bend, Ind., and after 1907 served as a writer on sports in Chicago, working in turn for the *Inter-Ocean*, the *Examiner*, and the *Tribune*. From 1910 to 1919 he contributed to the sports pages of newspapers in St. Louis, Boston, and elsewhere; after 1919 he was employed by the Bell Syndicate. About 1915 he began producing comical skits and short stories which, more and more, brought him literary renown. In 1911 he married Miss Ellen Abbott of Goshen, Ind., and to them four sons were born. In 1920 the family settled in Great Neck, Long Island. Lardner contracted tuberculosis and, after a long fight, died on Sept. 25, 1933.

Lardner's employment of the American idiom has been widely praised, as has his satirical treatment of human stupidity and selfishness. His writings are only superficially humorous, containing an undertone of biting ridicule.

Bib Ballads, 1915; *You Know Me Al*, 1916; *Gullible's Travels*, 1917; *Treat 'Em Rough*, 1918; *My Four Weeks in France*, 1918; *Own Your Own Home*, 1919; *The Real Dope*, 1919; *Regular Fellows I Have Met*, 1919; *The Young Immigrunts*, 1920; *Symptoms of Being 35*, 1921; *The Big Town*, 1921; *Say It with Oil* (contains *Say It with Bricks*, by Nina Wilcox Putnam), 1923; *How to Write Short Stories*, 1924; *What of It?*, 1925; *The Love Nest and Other Stories*, 1926; *The Story of a Wonder Man*, 1927; *Round Up*, 1929; *June Moon* (with George S. Kaufman), 1930; *Lose with a Smile*, 1933; *First and Last*, 1934; *Best Stories*, 1938; *The Portable Ring Lardner* (ed. by Gilbert Seldes), 1946.

For criticism, see: Thomas L. Masson, *Our American Humorists*, 1922, pp. 186–209; Carl Van Doren, *Many Minds*, 1924, pp. 167–81; H. L. Mencken, *Prejudices, Fifth Series*, 1926, pp. 49–56; Stuart P. Sherman, *The Main Stream*, 1927, pp. 168–76; Thomas Boyd, *Bookman*, LIX, pp. 601–2; Edmund Wilson, *Dial*, LXXVII, pp. 69–73; Donald Douglas, *Nation*, CXXII, pp. 584–85; Clifton F. Fadiman, *Nation*, CXXVIII, pp. 536–37; Robert Littell, *New Repub.*, XXXXII, Apr. 15, p. 1; T. S. Matthews, *New Repub.*, LIX, pp. 35–36.

174. SOME LIKE THEM COLD. In *Sat. Eve. Post*, Oct. 1, 1921; collected in *How to Write Short Stories*, 1924. Dramatized as *June Moon*, 1930, by Lardner and G. S. Kaufman; première, Oct. 9, 1929.

Ernest Hemingway (1898–   )

Ernest Hemingway was born in Oak Park, Ill., on July 21, 1898, and spent most of his boyhood in Michigan. After completing his work in the public schools, he was a reporter for the *Kansas City Star*. During World War I he was a member of an American ambulance unit in France. Later he joined the Italian forces, saw service at the front, was severely wounded, and twice received decorations of the Italian government. After the armistice he again became a journalist, serving for the most part as a foreign correspondent for American newspapers. At the same time he familiarized himself with the ways of the demoralized generation of expatriated men and women living in Paris and other European centers after the war—a generation of which he was to become the especial chronicler. Upon returning to America, he lived in Florida, in Wyoming, and in other parts of the country. He was deeply interested in the outcome of the Spanish Civil War, and reported happenings in Spain during 1937–38. He was a war correspondent in China during 1941; and he spent the years 1944–45 in newspaper work with the R. A. F. and the Third U. S. Army. Hemingway has been married four times: to Hadley Richardson in 1921, to Pauline Pfeiffer in 1927, to Martha Gelhorn in 1940, and to Mary Welsh in 1946. His present home is in San Francisco de Paula, Cuba.

Before he was twenty-five Hemingway had begun to acquire a literary reputation; and after the appearance of *In Our Time*, 1924, and *The Sun Also Rises*, 1926, his influence became noticeably strong and widespread, especially that of his staccato style and objective primitivistic technique.

Three Stories and Ten Poems (Dijon), 1923; *In Our Time* (Paris), 1924; *The Sun Also Rises*, 1926; *The Torrents of Spring*, 1926; *Men without Women*, 1927; *Farewell to Arms*, 1929; *Death in the Afternoon*, 1932; *Winner Take Nothing*, 1933; *The Green Hills of Africa*, 1935; *To Have and to Have Not*, 1937; *The Fifth Column*, 1938; *Spanish Earth*, 1938; *For Whom the Bell Tolls*, 1940; (ed.) *Men at War*, 1942; *Essential Hemingway*, 1947.

For criticism, see: Allen Tate, *Nation*, CXXIII, pp. 642–644; Joseph Wood Krutch, *Nation*, CXXV, p. 548; Clifton Fadiman, *Nation*, CXXIX, pp. 497–98; Paul Rosenfeld, *New Repub.*, XLV, pp. 22–23; Robert Littell, *New Repub.*, LI, pp. 303–6; Edmund Wilson, *New Repub.*, LIII, pp. 102–3; Conrad Aiken, *N. Y. Herald Tribune: Books*, Oct. 31, 1926, p. 4; Malcolm Cowley, *N. Y. Herald Tribune: Books*, Oct. 6, 1929, pp. 1, 6; Cleveland B. Chase, *Sat. Rev. Lit.*, III, pp. 420–21; Lee Wilson Dodd, *Sat. Rev. Lit.*, IV, pp. 322–23; Edgar Johnson, *Sewanee Rev.*, XLVIII, pp. 284–300; Maxwell Geismar, *Va. Quar. Rev.*, XVII, pp. 517–34; Malcolm Cowley, *New Repub.*, CXI, pp. 190–95; Max Eastman, "Bull in the Afternoon" in *Art and the Life of Action*, 1934; J. P. Bishop "Homage to Hemingway" in *After the Genteel Tradition* (ed. M. Cowley), 1937. See also: L. H. Cohn, *A Bibliography of the Works of Ernest Hemingway*, 1931.

186. THE KILLERS. In *Scribner's*, Mar., 1927; collected in *Men without Women*, 1927. See Cleanth Brooks and R. P. Warren, *Understanding Fiction*, 1943, for a discussion of this story. But compare also with Stephen Crane's "The Blue Hotel." ¶186. "*Nick Adams*," central character in Hemingway's early short stories, is usually identified with Hemingway as a boy. See Philip Young,

Hemingway and Mark Twain, unpub. Iowa diss., for resemblance of Nick to Huck Finn.

192. THE SNOWS OF KILIMANJARO is from the collection *The Fifth Column and the First Forty-nine Stories*, 1939. Harry's reminiscences reveal a career that has some parallels with Hemingway's. Hospitalization in 1930 following an automobile accident furnished some substance, together with game hunting in Africa, etc. ¶193. "*Tommies.*" Thompson's gazelles, a small antelope. ¶194. "*Old Westbury.*" On Long Island, New York. The places named are those frequented by the wealthy sporting gentry. ¶194. "*Karagatch,*" suburb of Adrianople, an important railroad center, given Turkey by the Treaty of Lausanne. ¶194. "*Simplon-Orient,*" famous transcontinental express train. ¶. 194. "*Nansen,*" Fridjof (1861–1930), Norwegian Arctic explorer. ¶194. "*Schrunz,*" or Schruns, is located in the predominately Swiss-inhabited Austrian province of Voralberg (p. 196); the Tirol is reached through Blundenz (p. 196) and the Arlberg Pass. Note that Harry's mind runs on high places. ¶195. "*Sans voir,*" without looking. ¶195. "*Kaiser-Jägers,*" regiments of sharp-shooters; those referred to fought under General Krauss in the fierce battles on the left of the Italian line (some of which are here named by Hemingway) when the Austrian advance was finally checked on the Asiago-Piave front, following the retreat from Caporetto (see *A Farewell to Arms*). ¶195. "*Crillon,*" famous Parisian hotel; "*St. Germain*" is a suburb of Paris. ¶199. "*letti dui,*" bring two. ¶200. "*Anatolia,*" western part of Asia Minor. ¶200. "*Dada,*" a movement of disillusionment in French literature that reached its peak in 1920. "Dada admits nothing but instinct," wrote André Breton, "and condemns all *a priori* explanation. According to Dada, it is not our business to exert ourselves. There is no longer any question of such dogmas as morality and good taste." Tristan Tzara (1896–) gained fame as the momentary leader of the movement. ¶202. "*Triberg,*" a resort of Baden, in the Schwarzwald (Black Forest) region. ¶202. "*Place Contrescarpe,*" near the Jardin des Plantes, on the left bank of the Seine. Hemingway names actual streets, bars, and music halls in Paris. ¶202. "*Communards,*" Communists, led by Blanqui, who attempted to seize Paris

at the end of October, 1870. ¶203. *"Cole Porter,"* American composer for musical comedies, b. 1893. ¶203. *"The Forks,"* in northwestern Wyoming(?). ¶204. *"poor Julian."* The reference is supposed to be to F. Scott Fitzgerald. ¶206. *"Arusha."* In Tanganyika Territory, East Africa; Harry dreams of flying to the east coast, possibly to Mimbasa.

William Faulkner (1897–)

William Faulkner was born in New Albany, Miss., on Sept. 25, 1897, and spent most of his boyhood in the university town of Oxford. He studied at the University of Mississippi from 1919 to 1921. In 1918, he joined the British Royal Air Force, took part in the fighting on the French front, and was wounded in the wrecking of a plane. Returning to Mississippi after the armistice, he was restless and unsettled; he lived in his father's house and worked at occasional and temporary occupations. From 1922 to 1924 he was postmaster at the University of Mississippi. During a year spent in New Orleans, he lived in the home of Sherwood Anderson while writing for the *Times-Picayune* and working on a novel, *Soldier's Pay*, 1926. His fourth novel, *The Sound and the Fury*, 1929, was the first to attract the large reading public and to call striking attention to his interest in the morbid and the terrifying aspects of human nature. Having definitely made a place for himself in the world of letters, he became more settled. In 1929 he was married to Mrs. Estelle Oldham Franklin. He continues to reside in Oxford.

The Marble Faun, 1924; *Soldier's Pay*, 1926; *Mosquitoes*, 1927; *Sartoris*, 1929; *The Sound and the Fury*, 1929; *As I Lay Dying*, 1930; *Sanctuary*, 1931; *These Thirteen*, 1931; *Idyll in the Desert*, 1931; *Salmagundi*, 1932; *Miss Zilphia Gant*, 1932; *Light in August*, 1932; *The Green Bough* (poems), 1933; *Dr. Martino and Other Stories*, 1934; *Pylon*, 1935; *Absalom, Absalom!*, 1936; *The Unvanquished*, 1938; *Wild Palms*, 1939; *The Hamlet*, 1940; *Go Down, Moses, and Other Stories*, 1942; *The Portable Faulkner* (ed. by Malcolm Cowley), 1946; *Intruder in the Dust*, 1948.

For life and criticism, see: A. Wigfall Green, *Sewanee Rev.*, XL, pp. 294–306. For criticism, see: Granville Hicks, *Bookman*, LXXIV, pp. 17–24; Lionel Trilling, *Nation*, CXXXIII, pp. 491–92; Robert Cantwell, *New Repub.*, LXVIII, p. 271; Lyle Saxon, *N. Y. Herald Tribune: Books*, Oct. 13, 1929, p. 2; Edward Cushing, *Sat. Rev. Lit.*, VIII, p. 201; G. M. O'Donnell, *Kenyon Rev.*, I, pp. 285–99; Conrad Aiken, *Atlant. Mo.*, CLXIV, pp. 650–54; Warren Beck, *Antioch Rev.*, I, pp. 82–94; John M. Maclachlan, *So. Folklore Q.*, IX, pp. 153–67. See also: R. W. Daniel, *A Catalogue of the Writings of William Faulkner*, 1942.

207. A ROSE FOR EMILY. In *Forum*, Apr., 1930; collected in *These Thirteen*, 1931. ¶207. *"Colonel Sartoris."* He and *"Judge Stevens"* appear in other stories. See *Sartoris, The Unvanquished*, etc. *"Jefferson"* is the county seat of the mythical *"Yoknapatawpha County"* created by Faulkner.

213. [SPOTTED HORSES] from the section called "The Peasants" in *The Hamlet*, 1940. The title given it here is that given it by Malcolm Cowley in the *Portable Faulkner* who says, "I don't think it would be too much to call it the funniest American story since Mark Twain." Faulkner plans a history of the Snopes tribe. A short story, called "Spotted Horses," about one-third the length of the present selection, was the first product of his invention with Flem Snopes, son of a Civil War bushwhacker and horse thief, who had come to Frenchman's Bend, as his protagonist. Twelve years elapsed between the appearance of this short story and the publication of *The Hamlet*; during this time he issued four other short narratives in the saga.

Erskine (Preston) Caldwell (1903–)

White Oak, Coweta County, Ga., is the birthplace of Erskine Caldwell. Here he was born to the Reverend Ira S. and Caroline (Bell) Caldwell on Dec. 17, 1903. Because his father moved from parish to parish, Caldwell's schooling was irregular, but he gained enough to manage admission to Erskine College in South Carolina in 1920. Later he was in attendance at the University of Virginia (1922, 1925, 1926) and at the University of Pennsylvania (1924), but instead of a degree, he acquired a wife, Helen Lannigan, on March 3, 1925. Caldwell has had considerable experience as a laborer; at different times in his career, he has been a cotton picker, mill worker, hack driver, professional football player, stage hand and reporter. He was once connected with the Atlanta *Journal*. *Tobacco Road*, 1932, which first brought him to prominence, was his fourth book. Dramatized in 1933, it ran five years in New York and made him independent; before 1949 his books had sold over fourteen million copies, at home and abroad. Success did not improve his craftsmanship. With Margaret Bourke-White, the socio-photographer, he did the memorable study of poverty in the deep South, *You Have Seen Their Faces*, 1937. Separated from his wife, he was married to Miss Bourke-White on February 27, 1939. With her, he did *North of the Danube*, 1939, a study of Czecho-Slovakia. Both artists went to Russia, but there they separated. Caldwell was married to June Johnson on December 21, 1942. While in Russia, during World War II he served as correspondent for *Life*, *PM*, and the Columbia Broadcasting System. He now lives in Tucson, Arizona.

The Bastard, 1930; *Poor Fool*, 1930; *In Defense of Myself*, 1930; *American Earth*, 1931; *Tobacco Road*, 1932; *Mama's Little Girl*, 1932; *We Are the Living*, 1933; *God's Little Acre*, 1933; *A Message for Genevieve*, 1933; *Journeyman*, 1935; *Kneel to the Rising Sun*, 1935; *The Sacrilege of Alan Kent*, 1936; *You Have Seen Their Faces* (with Margaret Bourke-White), 1937; *Southways*, 1938; *North of the Danube* (with M. B.-W.), 1939; *Trouble in July*, 1940; *Jackpot*, 1940; *Say! Is This the U.S.A.?* (with M. B.-W.), 1941; *All Out on the Road to Smolensk*, 1942; *Moscow Under Fire*, 1942; *All Night Long*, 1942; *Georgia Boy*, 1943; *Stories* (ed. H. S. Canby), 1944; *Tragic Ground*, 1944; *A House in the Uplands*, 1946; *Sure Hand of God*, 1947; *This Very Earth*, 1948.

For life and criticism, see: *In Defense of Myself*; J. D. Wade, "Sweet Are the Uses of Degeneracy," *So. Rev.*, Winter, 1936; Kenneth Burke, "Caldwell, Maker of Grotesques," *New Repub.*, Apr. 10, 1935; W. T. Couch, "Landlord and Tenant," *Va. Quart. Rev.*, Spring, 1938; O. Cargill, *Intellectual America*, 1941; J. W. Beach, *American Fiction, 1920–40*, 1941.

250. KNEEL TO THE RISING SUN is from the volume by the same title, 1935.

James (Gibbons) Huneker (1860–1921)

James Gibbons Huneker was born in Philadelphia, Pa., Jan. 31, 1860. His parents were lovers of music and pictorial art, and he had the early advantage of mingling with cultivated people. His boyish imagination was fed on all kinds of books; throughout his childhood he was able to attend the best plays and musical concerts the city offered. In 1873 he was graduated from Roth's Military Academy, and for several years studied at the Law Academy in Philadelphia. Not law, however, but "the Seven Arts" (to use his own phrase) commanded his interests; and he next studied at the Sorbonne and became a student of piano under Georgies Mathias in Paris. Upon returning to America, he continued his musical studies under Rafeal Joseffy, whose assistant he became, and for ten years offered piano instruction at the National Conservatory in New York City. From 1891 to 1895 he was the music and dramatic critic for the *New York Recorder*, and from 1895 to 1897 served the *Morning Advertiser* in the same capacity. He was also for a time on the staff of the *New York Sun*, and later on those of the *New York Times* and the New York *World*. He developed into a thoroughgoing man of the world, equally at home in Europe and the United States, and acquainted with the talented and famous men and women of his generation. His gusto, his cosmopolitan taste, his receptivity to new ideas, his constant activity, all contributed to make him a resourceful and mercurial critic. His articles, dealing with numerous subjects, introduced into America many new ideas and much information about European artists and cultural activities. He died on Feb. 9, 1921.

Mezzotints in Modern Music, 1899; *Chopin: The Man and His Music*, 1900; *Melomaniacs*, 1902; *Overtones: A Book of Temperaments*, 1904; *Iconoclasts: A Book of Dramatists*, 1905; *Visionaries*, 1905; *Egoists: A Book of Supermen*, 1909; *Promenades of an Impressionist*, 1910; *Franz Liszt*, 1911; *Old Fogy: His Musical Opinions and Grotesques*, 1913; *The Pathos of Distance*, 1913; *New Cosmopolis*, 1915; *Ivory Apes and Peacocks*, 1915; *Unicorns*, 1917; *The Philharmonic Society of New York*, 1917; *The Steinway Collection of Paintings by*

American Artists, 1919; *Bedouins,* 1920; *Painted Veils,* 1920; *Steeplejack,* 1920; *Variations,* 1921; *Letters* (ed. Josephine Huneker), 1922; *Intimate Letters* (ed. Josephine Huneker), 1924.

For life, see: William J. Henderson, "James Gibbons Huneker," *D.A.B.,* IX, pp. 379–80; Huneker's autobiography, *Steeplejack,* 1920; *Letters* (ed. Josephine Huneker), 1922; and *Intimate Letters* (ed. Josephine Huneker), 1924. For criticism, see: H. L. Mencken, *A Book of Prefaces,* 1917, pp. 151–95; the Introduction by H. L. Mencken to *Essays by James Huneker,* 1929; George E. de Mille, *Literary Criticism in America,* 1931, pp. 206–45; Bernard Smith, "Huneker, Man of the Tribe," *Sat. Rev. Lit.,* Aug. 19, 1933. See also the bibliography by Joseph Lawren in Benjamin de Casseres, *James Gibbons Huneker,* 1925.

267. CRITICISM is from *Steeplejack,* 1918–20, Huneker's autobiography. ¶267. *"Brunetière."* Ferdinand (1849–1906), erudite French critic, deeply interested in classification. ¶267. *"Anatole France,"* French novelist and critic (1844–1924), very much the opposite of the conservative Roman Catholic Brunetière. Of France, it is said that "as he believed in nothing, he did not believe in a better or a worse [universe]." ¶267. *"Sainte-Beuve, Taine . . ."* etc. Nineteenth century critics, various lands. ¶268. *"Cézanne* and *Cabanel."* The former, Paul (1839–1906), was the most famous of the French post-impressionist painters; the latter, Alexandre (1823–99), a popular painter of pretty pictures, for example, "Birth of Venus." ¶268. "Alice Meynell" (1850–1922), English poet and essayist. ¶269. *"Machiavel, or Tono-Bungay . . ."* etc. characters in the fiction of H. G. Wells. ¶269. *"J. H. Rosny, Sr."* The pseudonym for the brothers Joseph and Séraphin Boëx who collaborated on scientific fiction.

H(enry) L(ouis) Mencken (1880–   )

Henry Louis Mencken was born in Baltimore, Md., on Sept. 12, 1880. He was educated in private schools and at the Baltimore Polytechnic Institute, from which he was graduated in 1896. Upon quitting the Institute, he became a journalist, which he has remained since. By 1903 he was the city editor of the *Baltimore Morning Herald,* and by 1905 the editor of the *Baltimore Evening Herald.* In 1908 he became literary editor of *The Smart Set,* and in 1914 the co-editor with George Jean Nathan. Earlier, however, he had made a number of independent literary ventures, his first volume being a collection of poems, published in 1903. In 1908 appeared *The Philosophy of Friedrich Nietzsche,* and in 1919 his important pioneer work, *The American Language.* As the years passed, however, he found in social criticism an attractive field of labor. The first volume of *Prejudices* was issued in 1919, and during the next eight years was followed by five other volumes similarly entitled. In 1924 he founded, with Nathan, the influential journal *The American Mercury,* which he edited until 1933. In 1930 he married Miss Sara Haardt, a writer and one of the contributors to *The American Mercury;* she died in 1935. His home has always been in Baltimore.

Mencken's active mind, his abounding energy, his gift for satirical utterance, his strong dislike of much in the world about him, all led him to accept the rôle of champion of the *déraciné.* During the ten years following the end of the First World War, no critical voice in America was so influential, directly and indirectly, as his.

Ventures into Verse, 1903; *George Bernard Shaw,* 1905; *The Philosophy of Friedrich Nietzsche,* 1908; *The Doll's House,* by Henrik Ibsen (ed.), 1908; *Little Eyolf,* by Henrik Ibsen (ed.), 1908; *The Gist of Nietzsche* (ed.), 1910; *Men versus the Man* (with R. R. La Monte), 1910; *The Artist,* 1912; *Europe after 8:15* (with George Jean Nathan and Willard Huntington Wright), 1914; *A Book of Burlesques,* 1916; *A Little Book in C Major,* 1916; *A Book of Prefaces,* 1917; *The Master Builder, Pillars of Society, Hedda Gabler,* by Henrik Ibsen (ed.), 1917; *Damn! A Book of Calumny,* 1918; *In Defense of Women,* 1918; *The American Language,* 1919 (rev. several times, with supplements); *Ventures in Common Sense,* by E. W. Howe (ed.), 1919; *Prejudices, First Series,* 1919; *Heliogabalus* (with George Jean Nathan), 1920; *American Credo* (with George Jean Nathan), 1920; *Antichrist,* by Friedrich Nietzsche (trans.), 1920; *Prejudices, Second Series,* 1920; *Prejudices, Third Series,* 1922; *Prejudices, Fourth*

Series, 1924; *Americana* (ed.), 1925; *Prejudices, Fifth Series*, 1926; *Notes on Democracy*, 1926; *Prejudices, Sixth Series*, 1927; *Selected Prejudices*, 1927; *James Branch Cabell*, 1927; *Essays by James Huneker* (ed.), 1929; *Treatise on the Gods*, 1930; *Making a President*, 1932; *Happy Days*, *1880–1892*, 1940; *Newspaper Days*, *1899–1906*, 1941; (ed.) *A New Dictionary of Quotations*, 1942; *Heathen Days*, 1943; *A Christmas Story*, 1946; *A Mencken Chrestomathy*, 1949.

For life, see: Ernest Boyd, *H. L. Mencken*, 1925; Isaac Goldberg, *The Man Mencken*, 1925; *Pistols for Two*, 1917, by "Owen Hatteras" (pseudonym for Mencken and George Jean Nathan; and Mencken's several autobiographical volumes, beginning with *Happy Days*, 1940. For criticism, see: Stuart P. Sherman, *Americans*, 1922, pp. 1–13; Joseph Warren Beach, *The Outlook for American Prose*, 1926, pp. 81–92; Stuart Sherman, *Critical Woodcuts*, 1926, pp. 235–44; J. B. Harrison, *A Short View of Menckenism in Menckenese*, 1927; Fred Lewis Pattee, *The New American Literature*, 1930, pp. 415–33; J. A. Clark, "H. L. Mencken: An Obituary," *Am. Spect.*, Dec., 1936–Jan., 1937; Charles Angoff, "Mencken Twilight," *No. Am. Rev.*, Winter, 1938; James Branch Cabell, *Some of Us*, 1930, pp. 107–19. See also C. Frey, *A Bibliography of the Writings of H. L. Mencken*, 1924.

270. [THE UNITED STATES, THE GREATEST SHOW ON EARTH.] This selection is taken from the long article "On Being an American," *Prejudices*, III, 1922. It appears in a preliminary form in *Nation*, Dec. 7, 1921. ¶270. "*Loyola* [Ignatius, 1491–1556, founder of the Jesuits], *Savonarola* [Girolamo, 1452–98, Florentine reformer and martyr], *and Xavier* [St. Francis, 1506–52, Jesuit missionary to India]," though zealots, are cited as representative churchmen. ¶270. "*Matterhorn*," highest peak in Swiss Alps. ¶270. "*Joseph Smith*" (1805–44), founder of the Mormon Church; "*Mother Eddy*," Mrs. Mary Baker (1821–1910) [the title is Mencken's invention], founder of Christian Science; "*John Alexander Dowie*" (1847–1907), founder of the "Christian Catholic Apostolic Church in Zion." ¶270. "*Harlequin*," buffoon in Italian comedy; "*Sganarelle*," the imaginary cuckold of Molière; "*Gobbo*," Lancelot, Shake-

spearean clown; "*Dr. Cook*" [F. A.] claimed to have reached the North Pole in his two years (1907–9) in the Arctic. ¶271. "*Martial*," Marcus Valerius (A.D. c. 40–c. 102), Roman author of epigrams.

272. [THE VOCABULARY OF BACCHANALIA IN THE REPUBLIC] is from *The American Language: Supplement I*, 1945. ¶272. "*DAE.*" *A Dictionary of American English on Historical Principles*, ed. Sir William A. Craigie and James R. Hulbert, 1938–44; "*NED*" is *A New English Dictionary*, ed. Murray, Bradley, Craigie, and Onions, 1884–1928; 1933; today known as *The Oxford English Dictionary* [*OED*].

James Branch Cabell (1879–   )

James Branch Cabell was born in Richmond, Va., on Apr. 14, 1879, of a family distinguished in the annals of the state. He attended private schools and William and Mary College, from which he was graduated in 1898. There followed a period during which he worked for newspapers. In 1898 he was employed in the press room of the *Richmond Times*; from 1899 to 1901 he was on the staff of the *New York Herald*, and in 1901 on that of the *Richmond News*. During the years 1911–13 he engaged in coal-mining in West Virginia. From 1916 to 1929 he was associated with several patriotic societies, among them the Sons of the American Revolution, as official historian and genealogist. As early as 1902 he published short stories in *The Argosy, Harper's Monthly*, and *The Smart Set*; after his marriage in 1913 to Miss Priscilla Bradley, and his permanent settlement in Richmond, he increasingly devoted his time and energy to the writing of fiction. In 1919 the suppression of the novel *Jurgen* made his name widely known, and he achieved a large reading public which has diminished in the last two decades. *The Way of Ecben*, 1929, announced his retirement as the novelist of Poictesme, although not his retirement as an author. He continues to reside in his native city.

Most of Cabell's fiction prior to 1929 forms a large work, "The Biography of Manuel," dealing with imaginary men and women, the inhabitants of an imaginary medieval country, Poictesme. Behind this elaborate fantasy lies a definite philosophy of life and of the function of literary art which the author has explained in *Beyond Life*, 1919, and *Straws and Prayer-Books*, 1924.

The Eagle's Shadow, 1904; *The Line of Love*, 1905; *Branchiana*, 1907; *Gallantry*, 1907; *The Cords of Vanity*, 1909; *Chivalry*, 1909; *Branch of Abingdon*, 1911; *The Soul of Milicent*, 1913, rev. ed. pub. as *Domnei*, 1920; *The Rivet in Grandfather's Neck*, 1915; *The Majors and Their Marriages*, 1915; *The Certain Hour*, 1916; *From the Hidden Way*, 1916; *The Cream of the Jest*, 1917; *Beyond Life*, 1919; *Jurgen*, 1919; *Figures of Earth*, 1921; *Taboo*, 1921; *The Jewel Merchants*, 1921; *The Lineage of Lichfield*, 1922; *The High Place*, 1923; *Straws and Prayer-Books*, 1924; *The Silver Stallion*, 1926; *The Music from Behind the Moon*, 1926; *Something About Eve*, 1927; *Ballads from the Hidden Way*, 1928; *The White Robe*, 1928; *The Way of Ecben*, 1929; *Sonnets from Antan*, 1929; *Works: Storisende Edition*, 1927–30; *Between Dawn and Sunrise* (ed. John Macy), 1930; *Some of Us*, 1930; *These Restless Heads*, 1932; *Special Delivery*, 1933; *Ladies and Gentlemen*, 1934; *Smirt*, 1934; *Smith*, 1935; *Preface to the Past*, 1936; *Smire*, 1937; *The King Was in the Counting House*, 1938; *Hamlet Had an Uncle*, 1940; *The First Gentleman of America*, 1942; (with A. J. Hanna) *The St. Johns*, 1943; *There Were Two Pirates*, 1946; *Let Me Lie*, 1947.

For life and criticism, see: Hugh Walpole, *The Art of James Branch Cabell*, 1920, rev. ed., 1927; Percy H. Boynton, *Some Contemporary Americans*, 1924, pp. 145–61; Don Bregenzer and Samuel Loveman, *A Round-Table in Poictesme: A Symposium*, 1924; Carl Van Doren, *James Branch Cabell*, 1925, rev. ed., 1932; Joseph Warren Beach, *The Outlook for American Prose*, 1926, pp. 63–81; H. L. Mencken, *James Branch Cabell*, 1927; Régis Michaud, *The American Novel To-Day*, 1928, pp. 200–38; Warren A. McNeill, *Cabellian Harmonics*, 1928; James Branch Cabell, *Some of Us*, 1930, pp. 85–88; G. W. Allen, "Jurgen and Faust," *Sewanee Rev.*, July–Sept., 1933; E. R. Parker, "A Key to Cabell," *Eng. Jour.*, June, 1932; P. G. Brewster, "*Jurgen* and *Figures of Earth* and the Russian Skazki," *Am. Lit.*, Jan., 1942. The best introduction to Cabell's work is found in his own *Beyond Life*, *Straws and Prayer-Books*, *The Lineage of Lichfield*,

and *Let Me Lie*. See also Guy Holt, *A Bibliography of the Writings of James Branch Cabell*, 1924; Isidore R. Brussel, *A Bibliography of the Writings of James Branch Cabell*, 1932; W. Klinefelter, *Books about Poictesme*, 1937.

285. THE LADY OF ALL OUR DREAMS. In *The Certain Hour*, 1916. An evidence of the care with which Cabell writes is found in the number of changes he made in this story before republishing it in the Storisende Edition (this text). Besides rewriting five or six paragraphs completely, he made over seventy-five minor revisions. ¶285. "John Charteris." A minor character in several of Cabell's books and the author's mouthpiece in *Beyond Life*. ¶286. "*lusus naturae*," a natural flaw. ¶288. "*You were the Empress*." One of the numerous pieces suggested by Edward Lear's "Ahkond of Swat."

Ezra (Loomis) Pound (1885–)

No more restless spirit has been found among the literati of the twentieth century than Ezra Pound, a leader in numerous literary movements, an enthusiastic experimenter, a champion of neglected artists, a poet who, without winning a popular audience, has been able to exercise a far-extending influence on the age.

Ezra Loomis Pound was born on Oct. 30, 1885, in Hailey, Idaho. He studied at the University of Pennsylvania and at Hamilton College, from which he received the Ph.B. degree in 1905. He returned to the University of Pennsylvania as a graduate student, and in 1907 set out for Spain in order to gather material for a dissertation on Lope de Vega. Attracted by European ways of life he remained abroad, although without losing contact with friends in the United States. In 1908 he published his first book in Italy, and the year following issued two others in England, where he had settled for the time being. He became the chief leader of the Imagists poets, whom he organized into a group; later, with Wyndham Lewis, he became a propagandist for the Vorticists; still later he allied himself with other artistic classes and causes. In 1914 he was married to Miss Dorothy Shakespear. From 1912 to 1919 he served as the European correspondent for Miss Monroe's magazine *Poetry*, and for three years, 1917–

20, was the London editor of *The Little Review*. In 1927 he was awarded the prize of two thousand dollars given by *The Dial* for distinguished service to American literature. In 1924 he settled at Rapallo, Italy. He came to uphold Fascism; and during World War II he worked openly for the success of Italy. For his radio speeches against his native land, he was tried for treason, after being arrested and returned to the U. S., but was acquitted upon being adjudged insane.

A Lume Spento, 1908; *A Quinzaine for This Yule*, 1908; *Exultations*, 1909; *Personæ*, 1909; *Provença*, 1910; *The Spirit of Romance*, 1910; *Canzoni*, 1911; *Ripostes* (contains poems by T. E. Hulme), 1912; *The Sonnets and Ballate of Guido Cavalcanti* (translations), 1912; *Cathay* (translations from the Chinese, from notes of Ernest Fenollosa), 1915; *Lustra*, 1915; *Gaudier-Brzeska*, 1916; *'Noh' or Accomplishment*, 1916; *Certain Noble Plays of Japan* (translations, from the MSS. of Ernest Fenollosa), 1916; *Twelve Dialogues of Fontenelle* (translations), 1917; *Letters of John Butler Yeats* (ed.), 1917; *Pavannes and Divisions*, 1918; *Quia Pauper Amavi*, 1919; *Umbra*, 1920; *Instigations*, 1920; *Poems—1918–21*, 1921; *The Natural History of Love*, by Rémy de Gourmont (translation), 1922; *Indiscretions*, 1923; *Sixteen Cantos*, 1924; *Antheil and The Treatise on Harmony*, 1924; *Personæ: Collected Poems*, 1926; *Cantos XVII–XXVII*, 1928; *Selected Poems* (ed. T. S. Eliot), 1928; *Imaginary Letters*, 1930; *A Draft of XXX Cantos*, 1930; *How to Read*, 1931; *Prolegomena*, Vol. I, 1932; *A B C of Economics*, 1933; *A B C of Reading*, 1934; *Eleven New Cantos*, 1934; *Homage to Sextus Propertius*, 1934; *Make It New*, 1934; *Jefferson and/or Mussolini*, 1935; *Fifth Decade of Cantos*, 1937; *Polite Essays*, 1937; *Culture*, 1938; *Cantos LII–LXXI*, 1940; *Selection of Poems*, 1940; *The Cantos*, 1948; *The Pisan Cantos*, 1948.

For criticism, see: T. S. Eliot, *Ezra Pound: His Metric and Poetry*, 1917; F. R. Leavis, *New Bearings in English Poetry*, 1932; Glenn Hughes, *Imagism and the Imagists*, 1931, pp. 224–50; R. P. Blackmur, "Masks of Ezra Pound," *Hound and Horn* (March, 1934), pp. 177–213; Alice Amdur, *The Poetry of Ezra Pound*, 1936; G. H. Tichenor, "This Man Is a Traitor," *PM*, Aug. 15,

1943; Charles Norman, *The Case of Ezra Pound*, 1948.

292. THE EYES. In *Exultations*, 1909. The text of this and the following five poems is from *Personæ: Collected Poems*, 1926.

292. PORTRAIT D'UNE FEMME. In *Ripostes*, 1912. ¶292. "Sargasso Sea," (l. 1) a calm area in the N. Atlantic, N.E. of the West Indies, where reputedly the débris of wrecked ships comes to rest.

293. LES MILLWIN. Also in *Ripostes*, 1912. "Slade" (l. 6), epithet applied to classes under "Slade" professors at University College, London(?). "Cleopatra" (l. 10), an opera by Massenet.

293. THE GARDEN is in *Ripostes*, 1912. The digraph "In parade dress" is from the poetry of Albert Samain (1858–1900), French symbolist, who influenced both Pound and Amy Lowell. "Kensington Gardens" (l. 2), a London park frequented thinly by the gentry.

293. VILLANELLE: THE PSYCHOLOGICAL HOUR. In *Lustra*, author's ed., 1916, pub. 1917. For the form, see Brander Matthews, *A Study of Versification*, 1911.

295. IONE, DEAD THE LONG YEAR. In *Lustra*, 1916, 1917. If "Ione" (l. 1) is the petrified maiden mentioned in Bulwer Lytton's *The Last Days of Pompeii*, the poem may be considered a symbolist lament for the decline of civilization.

295. CANTO I. From *A Draft of XXX Cantos*, 1930. Earlier drafts were published in 1910 and 1921. For the substance and allusions of this Canto generally, see Book XI of the *Odyssey* in which Ulysses describes his voyage to the infernal regions, where he encountered the soul of the unburied Elpenor who had broken his neck in a fall from the roof of the house of Circe and where he interviewed Tiresias about his safety and that of his companions. Consider: "The two works that influenced him most were, strangely enough, the two he least understood—Ernest Fenellosa's essay on the Chinese written character, and T. E. Hulme's essay on *Romanticism and Classicism*. To superimpose the nature of a Chinese written character as the organic or 'ideogrammic' form of a whole poem in English can succeed only if it is held together by something else. Pound could occasionally hold a whole Canto together by a subtle and charming rhythm, or by an occasional central theme, such as *usura*, or even

by a story, as that of Ulysses in Erebus in *Canto I*. But too often the rhythm lacked imaginative coherence, and as for imagination in the meaning, that, too, was lacking. Pound's use of the ideogrammic method too often resulted in intellectualized chop suey." J. V. Healy, "Addendum" to "The Pound Problem," *Poetry*, Dec., 1940. See also L. Zukofsky, "The Cantos of Ezra Pound," *Criterion*, X, 424–40. ¶296. *"Andreas Divus"*: "the divine Andrew" [*Divus* was a name given to emperors after their death, as in *divus Augustus,* "the divine Augustus."] Here the reference is to Andreas Wechel (d. 1600), a Parisian bookseller and publisher whose imprint follows. Pound ascribes to him one of the earliest editions of the Odyssey [*Odyssea And. Divo Justinopolitano Interprete.* . . . Paris, Wechel, 1538]. ¶296. *"Venerandam"*: "viewed with holy awe." ¶296. *"Aphrodite."* The goddess of love. ¶296. *"Cypri munimenta sortita est"*: "awarded the fastness of Cypress [an island sacred to Aphrodite]"; *"oricalchi,"* an error for *"orichalci"*: brassy. ¶296. *"the golden bough,"* a symbol of rebirth.

Wallace Stevens (1879–)

Wallace Stevens was born in Reading, Pa., on Oct. 2, 1879, and was educated at Harvard University and New York University School of Law. He began the general practice of his profession in New York City in 1904, but in 1916 he joined the legal staff of the Hartford Accident and Indemnity Co., becoming vice president of the Company in 1934. His home is in Hartford, Conn.

Stevens has not sought popular success as a poet, writing to please himself —without hurry, and with meticulous care. His poetry is highly individualized, intellectual, witty, depending largely on the subtle harmonies of sound, the delicate shadings of color, the fresh clothing of an idea.

Harmonium, 1923, enlarged ed., 1931; *Ideas of Order,* 1935; *Owl's Clover,* 1936; *Man with the Blue Guitar,* 1937; *Parts of a World,* 1942; *Notes towards a Supreme Fiction,* 1942; *Transport to Summer,* 1947.

For criticism, see: Louis Untermeyer, *American Poetry since 1900,* 1923, pp. 323–28; Harriet Monroe, *Poets and Their Art,* 1926, pp. 39–46; Gorham B. Munson, *Destinations,* 1928, pp. 75–90; Alfred Kreymborg, *Our Singing*

Strength, 1929, pp. 500–04; L. L. Martz, *Yale Poetry Rev.,* II, pp. 13–20; Wylie Sypher, *Partisan Rev.,* XIII, pp. 83–99.

296. EARTHY ANECDOTE. In *Others,* July, 1919; collected in *Harmonium,* 1923. Text of this and the next three poems from *Harmonium,* 1931.

297. OF HEAVEN CONSIDERED, etc. In *Poetry,* Oct., 1921; collected in *Harmonium,* 1923. ¶297. *"Élysée,"* Elysium.

297. THE WORMS AT HEAVEN'S GATE. In *Harmonium,* 1923. *"Badroulbadour,"* (l. 1) is apparently a fictive name for the ideal maiden and the poem is a travesty on those poems in which the poet traditionally catalogues the beauties of his mistress.

297. PETER QUINCE AT THE CLAVIER. In *Harmonium,* 1923, 1931. "Peter Quince" is self-deprecatory, for the bearer of that name was "a poet" only to buffoons. See Bottom's remark (*Midsummer Night's Dream* IV, 1, 221), "I will get Peter Quince to write a ballad of this dream." The use of "clavier" in the title is an oblique hint at the sort of composition that the poet has attempted here. To a music lover it suggests the fugues and preludes in John Sebastian Bach's *Das Wholtemperirte Klavier,* which were written expressly to encourage use of the clavichord. The story of Susannah and the Elders is an "addition" to Daniel in the Apocrypha. According to the legend, Susannah, the beautiful and pious wife of the rich Joakim, was seen walking in her garden by two elders who were also judges. Inflamed with lust, they made infamous proposals to her, and when repulsed, they charged her with adultery. Condemned to death, she was on her way to be executed when she was saved by Daniel, who separately queried her accusers.

298. BOTANIST ON AN ALP (No. 1). In *Ideas of Order,* 1935, 1936. Stevens contrasts the world seen by the French landscape painter, Claude Lorrain (1600–82), who bathed his scenes in light, with the dismal view of the world (not nature), in Stevens's eyes, taken by Karl Marx.

298. MEN MADE OUT OF WORDS. From *Transport to Summer,* 1947. A play upon the Platonic theme that only ideas have reality. For Stevens's Platonism, see J. M. Brinnin, "Plato, Phoebus and the Man from Hartford," *Voices,* Spring, 1945.

John Gould Fletcher (1886–   )

John Gould Fletcher was born in Little Rock, Ark., on Jan. 3, 1886. His elementary schooling was by his mother and private tutors. Later he attended Phillips Academy, Andover, Mass., and spent three years at Harvard University. In 1906 he inherited a small fortune from his father, and forthwith determined to gratify an insistent desire to write poetry. After passing a year in study in Boston, he sailed for Europe, living in turn in Venice, Rome, London, and Paris. By 1913, when several small volumes by him were published, he was in touch with the "advanced" poets of Europe and was beginning to be a devoted student of the newer forms. His first book to attract general attention was *Irradiations*, 1915. Subsequently he continued to be active in the cause of poetic innovation. From 1914 to 1916 he lived again in the United States, and after a further period of residence abroad he returned definitely to the U. S. to live, his present home being near Little Rock.

The Book of Nature, 1913; *The Dominant City*, 1913; *Fire and Wine*, 1913; *Fool's Gold*, 1913; *Visions of the Evening*, 1913; *Irradiations—Sand and Spray*, 1915; *Goblins and Pagodas*, 1916; *Japanese Prints*, 1918; *The Tree of Life*, 1918; *Breakers and Granite*, 1921; *Paul Gauguin*, 1921; *Preludes and Symphonies* (a reprint of *Irradiations* and *Goblins and Pagodas*), 1922; *Parables*, 1925; *Branches of Adam*, 1926; *The Dance over Fire and Water*, by Elie Faure (translation), 1926; *Reveries of a Solitary*, by J. J. Rousseau (translation), 1927; *The Black Rock*, 1928; *John Smith—Also Pocahontas*, 1928; *The Crisis of the Film*, 1929; *The Two Frontiers*, 1930; *XXIV Elegies*, 1935; *Life Is My Song*, 1937; *Selected Poems*, 1938; *North Star*, 1941; *Burning Mountain*, 1946; *Arkansas*, 1947.

For life, see Fletcher's autobiography, *Life Is My Song*, 1937. For criticism, see: Amy Lowell, *Tendencies in Modern American Poetry*, 1917, pp. 280–343; Conrad Aiken, *Scepticisms*, 1919, pp. 105–15; Louis Untermeyer, *American Poetry since 1900*, 1923, pp. 316–23; Harriet Monroe, *Poets and Their Art*, 1926, pp. 86–92; Alfred Kreymborg, *Our Singing Strength*, 1929, pp. 361–68; Glenn Hughes, *Imagism and the Imagists*, 1931, pp. 125–53.

299. BLUE SYMPHONY. Text from *Preludes and Symphonies*, 1930; originally in *Goblins and Pagodas*, 1916. "In two respects . . . these 'Symphonies' irritated many worthy critics of the time, and may still irritate some today. That was because to each of them I assigned a colour and because their form seemed to be entirely shapeless. As regards the colour-title, my intentions in that respect have been greatly exaggerated. My friendly critics might have assured themselves, by a glance at Galton's *Inquiry Concerning Human Faculty*, that colour-vision in certain states of excitement, is far more common than most people suppose; and in poetry of this visual type, some indication of the prevailing mood seems to be necessary. . . . I may have pushed metrical variation too far towards anarchy; for having employed it in preference to uniformity, I still feel I owe neither explanation nor apology." Preface, pp. xii–xiii.

300. MEXICAN QUARTER. In *Poetry*, Mar., 1916; collected in *Breakers and Granite*, 1921.

301. NIGHT LANDING. From the series "Down the Mississippi," in *Poetry*, Oct., 1920; collected in *Breakers and Granite*, 1921.

301. SKYSCRAPERS. In *Breakers and Granite*, 1921.

302. EXIT. In *The Black Rock*, 1928.

H. D. (Hilda Doolittle)
(1886–   )

Hilda Doolittle was born in Bethlehem, Pa., on Sept. 10, 1886. She attended schools in Bethlehem and Philadelphia, and for two years was a student at Bryn Mawr College. Her first published work consisted of short stories. In 1911 she went to Europe, and became interested in the literary activities then developing in France and England. Her meeting with Ezra Pound resulted in the publication of her verse in *Poetry: A Magazine of Verse*, in 1913. Already she was in sympathy with the Imagist group of poets; and she has remained more loyal to the program of that group than any other member. In 1913 she was married to the English poet, Richard Aldington, from whom she was later divorced. Her first book, *Sea Garden*, 1916, was published in England. Since that time she has lived principally in Europe, for the most part in Switzerland.

Sea Garden, 1916; Hymen, 1921; Heliodora and Other Poems, 1924; Collected Poems of H. D., 1925, 1940; Palimpsest, 1926; Hippolytus Temporizes, 1927; Hedylus, 1928; Red Roses for Bronze, 1931; The Hedgehog, 1937; Walls Do Not Fall, 1944; Tribute to the Angels, 1945; The Flowering of the Rod, 1946.

For criticism, see: Amy Lowell, Tendencies in Modern American Poetry, 1917, pp. 249–80; Louis Untermeyer, American Poetry since 1900, 1923, pp. 309–16; H. P. Collins, Modern Poetry, 1925, pp. 154–203; Harriet Monroe, Poets and Their Art, 1926, pp. 92–100; Alfred Kreymborg, Our Singing Strength, 1929, pp. 347–53; R. P. Blackmur, Poetry XLI, pp. 94–100; H. R. Fairclough, The Classics and Our Twentieth-Century Poetry, 1927, pp. 31–36; Glenn Hughes, Imagism and the Imagists, 1931, pp. 109–25.

302. EVENING. In Sea Garden, 1916, and Collected Poems, 1925.

302. CUCKOO SONG. In Hymen, 1921, and Collected Poems, 1925. ¶303. "Calypso." The sea nymph who detained Odysseus on the island Ogygia.

Amy Lowell (1874–1925)

Amy Lowell was born in Brookline, Mass., on Feb. 9, 1874, a member of a distinguished and wealthy family. After receiving training under her mother, attending private schools, and traveling extensively, she found her mind too restless and inquiring to allow her to lead an idle life. Deciding about 1902 to concentrate her energies on the writing of poetry, she spent several years in study with this objective in view. She read the works of the great English poets, studied the technique of verse-writing, and wrote and rewrote much before she began to publish her work. Not, in fact, until 1910 was she represented in the magazines, and not until 1912 did she publish a book of poems—A Dome of Many-Coloured Glass. The study of Albert Samain, Rémy de Gourmont, Paul Fort, and other French poets, together with a visit to England in 1913, determined her to throw in her lot with the "new poets," of whom she became an ardent and untiring champion. The years following 1913 were crowded with writing, studying, lecturing, varied activities in behalf of the "new poetry"; they were years of achievement and success. She

was invited to lecture at the Brooklyn Institute of Arts and Sciences, Yale University, and Brown University. In 1923 she received the Levinson prize offered by Poetry: A Magazine of Verse; and her volume What's O'Clock, published posthumously in 1925, was awarded a Pulitzer prize. She died on May 12, 1925.

Although much of her work represents unsuccessful experimentation, a score or more of her poems have unquestioned intrinsic merit. Her place in the literary history of the age is assured, moreover, on the ground of her work as a champion of the "new poetry."

Dream Drops, 1888; A Dome of Many-Coloured Glass, 1912; Sword Blades and Poppy Seed, 1914; Six French Poets, 1915; Men, Women and Ghosts, 1916; Tendencies in Modern American Poetry, 1917; Can Grande's Castle, 1918; Pictures of the Floating World, 1919; Fir-Flower Tablets (English version of translations from Chinese by Florence Ayscough), 1921; Legends, 1921; A Critical Fable (pub. anonymously), 1922; John Keats, 1925; What's O'Clock, 1925; East Wind, 1926; Ballads for Sale, 1927; The Madonna of Carthagena, 1927; Selected Poems (ed. John Livingston Lowes), 1928; Poetry and Poets, 1930.

For life and criticism, see: Clement Wood, Amy Lowell, 1926; Harriet Monroe, Poets and Their Art, 1926, pp. 78–86; Glenn Hughes, Imagism and the Imagists, 1931; S. Foster Damon, Amy Lowell, 1935; John Livingston Lowes, Dict. Am. Biog., XI, pp. 453–55.

303. ASTIGMATISM. In Sword Blades and Poppy Seed, 1914. Pound's intemperate castigation of weaker poets provoked this piece, but there was feeling between the two poets because Miss Lowell was not an unquestioning or natural disciple.

304. PATTERNS. In Little Review, Aug., 1915; collected, Men, Women and Ghosts, 1916. ¶305. "Duke in Flanders." Marlborough (1650–1722), Winston Churchill's ancestor, who defeated the French at Blenheim, 1704.

305. PURPLE GRACKLES. In Bookman, July, 1922; collected, What's O'Clock, 1925.

307. SUMMER NIGHT PIECE. In What's O'Clock, 1925.

307. [COMMODORE PERRY BEFORE THE DRAGON GATE.] This selection is written in what Miss Lowell called

"polyphonic prose," for an account of which see the Preface to *Can Grande's Castle*, pp. x–xv; first published entire in this book, 1918, though portions had previously appeared in *Seven Arts*, 1917. See *Narrative of the Expedition of an American Squadron to the China Seas and Japan*, 1856, the official record of Commodore Matthew C. Perry's trip, the first volume of which Miss Lowell probably used, for substance.

309. IMAGISM is from *Tendencies in Modern American Poetry*, 1917. "A certain intellectual unripeness and sketchiness, a proneness to hasty and self-satisfying conclusions without careful or accurate survey of the facts, make of Miss Lowell an amateur rather than a serious critic" (Aiken, *Scepticisms*). See Hughes (above) also.

Conrad (Potter) Aiken (1889–   )

Conrad Potter Aiken was born in Savannah, Ga., on Aug. 5, 1889, but was brought up in New England. He attended Harvard University, having as classmates T. S. Eliot, John Hall Wheelock, Alan Seegar, Van Wyck Brooks, Walter Lippmann, Robert Benchley, and Heywood Broun. After graduation in 1911, he decided upon writing as his profession, a decision by which he has resolutely stood. In 1914 appeared his *Earth Triumphant*, the prelude to more important work. He has compiled several anthologies, edited the *Selected Poems of Emily Dickinson*, 1924, for publication in England, and written numerous critical articles and several volumes of fiction. In 1930 he received the Pulitzer Prize for his *Selected Poems*, 1929. For a time he was instructor in English at Harvard, and he has lived in several parts of New England, as well as in Italy and England. His present home is in Brewster, Maine.

Aiken's verse is conspicuously rhythmic, sensuous, melodious. Although it owes much to other poets, and to Freud, many elements remain which are the poet's own. Aiken has been a resourceful experimenter, especially with the poetry of psychological analysis, dealing with man's "emotional and mental hinterland."

Earth Triumphant and Other Tales in Verse, 1914; *Turns and Movies*, 1916; *The Jig of Forslin*, 1916; *Nocturne of Remembered Spring*, 1917; *The Charnel Rose, Senlin: A Biography, and Other Poems*, 1918; *Scepticisms*, 1919; *The House of Dust*, 1920; *Punch, the Immortal Liar*, 1921; *Priapus and the Pool*, 1922; *Modern American Poets* (London), 1922; *The Pilgrimage of Festus*, 1923; *Selected Poems of Emily Dickinson* (London), 1924; *Bring! Bring! and Other Stories*, 1925; *Priapus and the Pool and Other Poems*, 1925; *Senlin, a Biography* (London), 1925; *Blue Voyage*, 1927; *Costumes by Eros*, 1928; *Prelude*, 1929; *American Poetry, 1671–1928* (ed.), 1929; *Selected Poems*, 1929; *John Deth, a Metaphysical Legend, and Other Poems*, 1930; *Gehenna*, 1930; *The Coming Forth by Day of Osiris Jones*, 1931; *Preludes for Memnon*, 1931; *The Great Circle*, 1933; *Among the Lost People* (short stories), 1934; *King Coffin*, 1935; *Landscape West of Eden*, 1935; *Time in the Rock*, 1936; *Heart for the Gods of Mexico*, 1939; *And in the Human Heart*, 1940; *Conversation, or Pilgrim's Progress*, 1940; *Brownstone Eclogues*, 1942; *Soldier*, 1944; *Comprehensive Anthology of American Poetry*, 1945; *The Kid*, 1947.

For criticism, see: Louis Untermeyer, *American Poetry since 1900*, 1923, pp. 170–83; Alfred Kreymborg, *Our Singing Strength*, 1929, pp. 429–38; Houston Peterson, *The Melody of Chaos*, 1931. See also *Scepticisms* for the light it throws on Aiken's own poetry.

315. MUSIC I HEARD. . . . In *Turns and Movies*, 1916.

315. ALL LOVELY THINGS WILL HAVE AN ENDING. In *Turns and Movies*, 1916.

315. [IT IS MORNING, SENLIN SAYS.] In *The Charnel Rose, Senlin: A Biography, and Other Poems*, 1918, 1925.

317. [GOOD VIRTUOUS SON] and [RIMBAUD AND VERLAINE] are from *Preludes for Memnon*, 1931. Arthur Rimbaud, 1854–91, and Paul Verlaine, 1844–96, were French symbolist poets. Verlaine left his wife for the company of Rimbaud; the lady accused the latter of corrupting her husband. The pair quarreled; Verlaine twice attempted to kill Rimbaud and did wound him; finally Rimbaud went off to Africa. See Verlaine's "Art poétique" for the hostility here expressed for "rhetoric" or "literarious" writing. The beautiful black Memnon, slain by Achilles, seems to be used by Aiken as the genius of the poetic lament. See Ovid's *Metamorphoses* XIII for the Memnonides.

T(homas) S(tearns) Eliot
(1888–   )

Thomas Stearns Eliot was born on Sept. 26, 1888, in St. Louis, Mo., a member of the New England family to which, among others, belonged the late President Eliot of Harvard University. After attending schools in St. Louis he went east to Harvard, from which he received the A.B. degree in 1910 and the A.M. degree in 1911. He studied at the Sorbonne in Paris and at Merton College, Oxford. In 1914 he settled in England, where he has since remained. He worked for a time in a bank, afterwards turning to lecturing, teaching, and editorial work. He steadily continued, however, the reading of French, English, and classical literature which he had begun while a student. By the time of the appearance of his widely discussed interpretation of contemporary civilization, *The Waste Land*, 1922, he was not only a finished craftsman but a poet who had already attracted a considerable number of followers. He was for a time the assistant editor of *The Egoist*; he was one of the founders of *The Criterion*, which he edited from 1923 to 1939. In 1927 Eliot became a British subject. He is a director in the London publishing firm of Faber and Faber, Ltd. The authorities at Harvard University appointed him to fill the Charles Eliot Norton Professorship of Poetry during the academic year 1932–33. He has since received several such appointments, and has been widely honored by universities and other scholarly and literary organizations. His greatest distinction came to him with the Nobel prize in 1948.

Eliot has influenced his contemporaries in both England and America as deeply as any man of the twentieth century. His poetry is intellectual in content, and for most readers difficult in manner, often depending on parallel connotative passages or allusions, which evoke bookish associations, or on the placing in juxtaposition of incongruous or contrasting elements. Since 1922 he has assumed more and more the rôle of critic, taking the lead in a movement to establish æsthetic standards in the face of romantic irresponsibility and disorder.

Prufrock and Other Observations (London), 1917; *Ezra Pound: His Metric and Poetry*, 1917; *Ara Vus Prec* (London), 1919; *Poems*, 1920; *The Sacred Wood* (London), 1920; *The Waste Land*, 1922; *Homage to John Dryden* (London), 1924; *Poems, 1909–1925* (London), 1926; *Shakespeare and the Stoicism of Seneca* (London), 1927; *For Lancelot Andrewes* (London), 1928; *Dante* (London), 1929; *Ash Wednesday* (London), 1930; *Anabasis of Xenophon* (ed. by St. J. Perse; trans. into verse by Eliot), 1930; *Thoughts after Lambeth* (London), 1931; *Charles Whibley*, 1931; *John Dryden, Poet, Dramatist, Critic*, 1932; *Selected Essays: 1917–32*, 1932; *Sweeney Agonistes*, 1932; *The Use of Poetry and the Use of Criticism*, 1933; *After Strange Gods*, 1934; *Elizabethan Essays*, 1934; *The Rock*, 1934; *Murder in the Cathedral*, 1935; *Collected Poems: 1909–1935*, 1936; *Essays, Ancient and Modern*, 1936; *Some Recent Developments in English Literature*, 1936; *The Family Reunion*, 1939; *Idea of a Christian Society*, 1939; *Old Possum's Book of Practical Cats*, 1939; *East Coker*, 1940; *Burnt Norton*, 1941; *Dry Salvages*, 1941; *Later Poems, 1925–1935*, 1941; *Points of View*, 1941; *The Classics and the Man of Letters*, 1942; *Little Gidding*, 1942; *The Music of Poetry*, 1942; *Four Quartets*, 1943; *What Is a Classic?*, 1945; *Milton*, 1947; *Notes Towards the Definition of Culture*, 1949.

For criticism, see: George Williamson, *The Talent of T. S. Eliot*, 1930; Thomas McGreevy, *Thomas Stearns Eliot: A Study*, 1931; Edmund Wilson, *Axel's Castle*, 1931, pp. 93 ff.; H. R. Williamson, *The Poetry of T. S. Eliot*, 1932; F. R. Leavis, *New Bearings in English Poetry*, 1932; F. O. Matthiessen, *The Achievement of T. S. Eliot*, 1935, 1947; David Daiches, *Poetry and the Modern World*, 1940; *T. S. Eliot: A Selected Critique* (ed. Leonard Unger), 1948; *T. S. Eliot: A Study of His Writing by Several Hands* (ed. B. Rajan), 1949; Elizabeth Drew, *T. S. Eliot: The Design of His Poetry*, 1949; D. C. Gallup, *Bibliographical Checklist of the Writings of T. S. Eliot*, 1947.

318. PORTRAIT OF A LADY. In *Others, a Magazine of the New Verse*, Sept., 1915; collected in *Poems*, 1920. Compare with Pound's "Portrait d'une Femme." ¶318. *"cauchemar."* nightmare.

320. THE LOVE SONG OF J. ALFRED PRUFROCK. In *Poetry, a Magazine of Verse*, June, 1915; collected in *Prufrock and Other Observations* (London), 1917, and *Poems*, 1920. Willis Wager, in an unpub. paper, says there was a Prufrock family in St. Louis. The epigraph in

Italian verse is from Dante's *Divine Comedy,* Inferno, Canto XXVII, 58–63. Cary's trans.:

"If I did think my answer were to one
Who ever could return unto the world
This flame should rest unshaken. But since ne'er,
If true be told me, any from this depth
Has found his upward way, I answer thee,
Nor fear lest infamy record the words."

These lines point ahead to "I am Lazarus . . . ," which, of course, Prufrock is not. That the portrait of Prufrock was suggested to Eliot by reading Constant Garnett's recent (1914) trans. of Dostoevski's *Crime and Punishment* is established by J. C. Pope in "Prufrock and Raskolnikov," *Am. Lit.,* Nov., 1945. The conventional comparison of Raskolnikov to Hamlet started the reverse reflection, "I am not Hamlet. . . ." "The curious splitting of Prufrock in two (sustained throughout) and the intimacy of the two selves have obvious parallels in schizophrenia, one of the most isolating of mental diseases and, coincidentally, one investigated by Morton Prince and 'the Boston school' at the time Prufrock was written."—R. Morgan & A. Wohlstetter, "Observations on 'Prufrock'," *Harvard Advocate,* Dec., 1938. The same authors point out that Eliot must have had in mind the profusion of hair on the severed head of Oscar Wilde's Jokanaan when, by contrast, he allows Prufrock to fancy his own bald head upon a platter. The yellow fog that rubs its back upon the window pane is a conventional symbolist image used by Baudelaire, Mallarmé, and others. For French influences upon Eliot, see O. Cargill, *Intellectual America,* 1941, and M. J. J. Laboulle, "T. S. Eliot and Some French Poets," *Revue de Littérature Comparée,* Apr.–June, 1936. Eliot came to the French through Arthur Symons, *Symbolist Movement in Literature,* as he revealed in a review of Peter Quennell's *Baudelaire and the Symbolists* in 1930: "I myself owe Mr. Symons a great debt. But for having read his book I should not, in the year 1908, have heard of Laforgue and Rimbaud; I should probably not have begun to read Verlaine, I should not have heard of Corbière. So the Symons book is one of those that have affected the course of my life." But Prufrock's portrait has elements borrowed from Moody and Aiken also.

323. MR. APOLLINAX. In *Prufrock and Other Observations,* 1917. The epigraph: "O the novelty of the thing! Hercules, what a strange saying. The man is clever." Apollinax, like Phlaccus and Channing-Cheetah, are proper names of Eliot's invention. For the first, see the line in his French poem, "Lune de Miel": "*Et Saint Apollinaire, raide et ascétique.*" Apollinax is anything but "stiff and ascetic"; Eliot recalls the etymology of Apollo ("to drive away evil"); hence Apollinax is probably "the solicitor of evil." There seems to be only one good candidate for Apollinax—Bertrand Russell whose views of sex and marriage probably gave Eliot offense. Russell was entertained by Mrs. Jack Gardner. ¶323. "*Professor Channing-Cheetah*" (6) is a feline dog, albeit he is a Brahmin.

323. GERONTION. In *Poems,* 1920. The title is of Eliot's coinage: the word is derived from the Greek, *geron,* old man. The epigraph is from *Measure for Measure,* III, i, 32–34. ¶323. "*waiting for rain*" (2). As in Coleridge's "Rime of the Ancient Mariner" and in Miss Millay's "Renascence," rain is here used as a symbol of rebirth, regeneracy. ¶323. "*The jew*" (8). Ostensibly a symbol of the commercial class who, in Eliot's view, have corrupted Western society, the slur also reflects Eliot's anti-semitism. See "Burbank with a Baedeker: Bleistein with a Cigar," etc. ¶324. "*Christ the tiger*" (20). In Revelation v.5 Christ is called "the lion of Judah," and Dante uses the leopard with benign significance; possibly Eliot has twisted the meaning of Blake's "The Tiger." The idea seems to be to endow Christ with qualities like those of the "Hound" of Heaven; see below, "the tiger springs in the new year. Us he devours." ¶325. "*Belle Isle . . . Horn.*" The straits are between Labrador and Newfoundland; [Cape] Horn is at the southern extremity of South America.

"Gerontion" marks the second stage of Eliot's development, if his first poetry may be said to have been written under the influence of Pound, the French symbolists, and the Preraphaelites. Turning to Dante under the influence of Harvard scholarship (Longfellow, Norton, Grandgent, Santayana) and especially under the influence of Pound (see: Matthiessen and Mario Praz [below]), Eliot, with the Italian as his master, made his images more "consciously concrete" than hitherto. "Gerontion" is the product of a mature theory of poetry: "The only way of expressing emotion in the form of art is by finding an 'objective correlative'; in other words, a set of objects, a situation, a chain of events which shall be the formula of that *particular* emotion; such that when the external facts, which must terminate in sensory experience, are given, the emotion is immediately evoked."—"Hamlet and His Problems." This poem is also the first to show the influence of Spengler or Hermann Hesse.

325. SWEENEY AMONG THE NIGHTINGALES. In *Poems*, 1920. The epigraph: "Alas, I am stricken by a timely blow within." For comment, see: R. P. Basler & Leo Kirschbaum, "Eliot's Sweeney Among the Nightingales," *Explicator*, Dec., 1934. ¶825. *"Apeneck Sweeney"* (1), protagonist of several poetic and dramatic pieces, reflects a Tory-hatred of the Irish. *"River Plate"* (6), an estuary between Argentina and Uruguay. *"Gloomy Orion"* (9). When the constellation arose late (and this is a time sign for the poem), it was a sign of stormy weather or winter. *"the Dog star"* (9). Star adjacent to Orion. *"Agamemnon cried aloud"* (38), from within the house when he was slain (*Agamemnon*, 1340–43). T. H. Thompson has fashioned a continuity out of all the Sweeney poems and fragments that makes "a detective story" which is the very antithesis of *Agamemnon* on the score of human dignity. See: "The Bloody Wood," *London Merc.*, Jan., 1934, and Unger, *op. cit.*, pp. 161–69.

325. THE WASTE LAND. In *The Criterion*, Oct., 1922; *The Dial*, Nov., 1922; separate publication, 1922. The poem has been much commented on. In addition to Williamson, McGreevy, Wilson, Leavis, Matthiessen, Daiches, and Unger in the general bibliography, see: W. Thomas & S. G. Brown, *Reading Poems*, 1941; Cleanth Brooks, *Modern Poetry and the Tradition*, 1939; Eric Mesterton, *The Waste Land, Some Commentaries*, 1943; E. M. Stephenson, *T. S. Eliot and the Lay Reader*, 1944; Gerhard Buck, "Uber die Anspielunger in T. S. Eliot's *Waste Land*," *Anglia*, Nov., 1940; W. A. Nitze, "The Waste Land: A Celtic Arthurian Theme," *Mod. Philol.*, Aug., 1945. The study of the poem as a musical form is somewhat aided by Eliot's "The Music of Poetry," *Partisan Rev.*, Nov.–Dec., 1942. Mario Praz, "T. S. Eliot and Dante," *So. Rev.*, Winter,

1937, has general reference, but is particularly helpful here. "Ion Blyth's" *The Redeemed Realm*, 1947, is a good antidote for an infatuation with Eliot.

The epigraph from Petronius' *Satyricon*, Ch. 38: "For the Sibyl of Cumae, hanging in a cage, I myself saw with my own eyes; and when the boys jeered at her, 'Sibyl, what do you want?' she answered, 'I want to die.'" She desires to die, in order to be born again, for she had forgotten to ask for youth when asking for eternal life. She is related to Tiresias, who may be born again, but only into the physical world.

The dedication to Pound is "To the better forger."

The spiritual poverty and cultural barrenness of contemporary times suggest the analogy of a waste land to the poet; only "a heap of broken images"—a rubble pile of the fragments of past cultures—confronts the inquirer who asks if life may ever spring from such a waste. Hope persists, however, that as rain revives a dead land, so renewed spirituality may revive the dull, clutching roots of culture. Hence the pattern of the poem is a mixture of "memory and desire" on which present fact and episode intrude and explode with devastating force. Some of the memories are personal—for example, those of Marie, in lines 8–18 of the poem; some are general, as the recollection of a lovely passage from *Tristan und Isolde* (30–34):

> Fresh the wind blows
> To the homeland;
> My Irish child,
> Where do you tarry?

Similarly some of the desires are personal —for example, Marie's hunger for love (with the quality of universality implied, however), and some are general, like that yearning for spirituality expressed by the prophet voice (21–30). Neither memory nor desire is allowed, however, uninterrupted statement; the statement of each (here, for example) impinges on the other, fragmentizes the other. And on both break in all that is disgusting or disheartening to the sensibilities or the hopes. To this pattern of discontinuity, the poet adds the difficulties of allusiveness and symbolism. He is not trying to disconcert the reader with his erudition, even if a kind of vanity may be suspected in his deliberate obscurity; his justification is that he desires to produce a sense of chaos by achieving persistent discontinuity, whilst still producing a closely knit, carefully patterned and unified work of art. One of his skills is that of utilizing the most subtle associations, of which verbal harmony is only one. The others are psychological. For instance, after the son of man has been shown "fear in a handful of dust," the poet desires to return to Marie and her remembered love, but at a different stage of that love, for the one last mentioned was her innocent attachment to her older cousin, the archduke. The elemental dust is associated with the air, and the Wagnerian fragment supplies a natural link—a transition to the romantic theme and Marie's memory of her lover who had given her hyacinths. The memory of the general for *Tristan und Isolde* is allowed to fade with the trailing line (42), "Desolate and empty the sea." In tone with this,. Tristan's disappointment, Marie's, and her lover's are blended in climactic unity.

But the introduction thus early in the poem of the *Tristan und Isolde* fragment, in association with frustration and barrenness, has large symbolic significance. Tristan had been, like Percival, Lancelot, and others, a searcher for the Grail. As Miss Jessie Weston had shown, in *From Ritual to Romance* (1920), the Grail story goes back to primitive rites celebrated to achieve fertility. Before any poetry of the Arthurian cycle was composed, a legend existed of a Fisher King, ill and feeble, who presided over a waste land. The land would become fertile only when a pure knight came to heal the King who was wounded in the genitals. Later this legend was joined to another, incorporating the Holy Grail—the chalice used to catch the blood of Christ, but originally also a ritual utensil, since it was associated always with a bleeding spear, the two symbolic of the female and male organs. In the incorporation of the second legend, the pure knight sought the Grail with which to heal the King, whereupon the land would burgeon again. Eliot explains that "the plan and a good deal of the incidental symbolism of the poem" were suggested by Miss Weston's book and advises readers to consult it. Eliot's eight pages of "Notes" in the *Collected Poems* are invaluable for allusions in the poem, only a small number of which can be explained here.

¶325. *"April."* Easter time in certain years, hence the season of the fertility rites. Lines 1–7 belong to the prophetpoet. *"Starnbergersee"* (8). A lake, famous for its resorts, 16 mi. south of Munich, where Marie met her lover. ¶326. *"Bin gar keine,"* etc. (12). "I am no Russian; I come from Litauen—a true German." The Russian revolution is one of the obscene elements to Eliot; see below p. 332 (368–69): "those hooded hordes swarming over endless plains." *"Madame Sosostris"* (43). Her reputation, "the wisest woman in Europe," is a sad commentary on the times, for she is only a vulgar fortune teller, whereas the Tarot pack of cards which she uses, was once employed to determine an event of social importance, the rising of the waters. In her deck, Eliot associates these face-cards as follows: The Hanged Man with "the hooded figure in the passage of the disciples to Emmaus" (Part V) and also with the Hanged God of Frazer; the man with the three staves (51) with the Fisher King; the one-eyed merchant apparently with "Mr. Eugenides, the Smyrna merchant," p. 329 (209) [These merchants were, with slaves and soldiers, the chief carriers of the Grail legends from the East]; and the drowned Phoenician sailor with "you" [the reader?]. Because of this card she ignorantly warns him against death by water, "not realizing any more than do the other inhabitants of the modern waste land that the way unto life may be by death itself. The drowned Phoenician sailor is a type of fertility god whose image was thrown into the sea annually as a symbol of the death of summer" (C. Brooks). Belladona the Lady of the Rocks is not associated by Eliot with any later character, but she may possibly be equated with the woman who "drew her long black hair out tight," p. 332 (387).

¶327. *"final stroke of nine"* (68). The hour when Jesus cried, "My God, my God, why hast Thou forsaken me?" *"Stetson"* (69), the average reader of sensibility—or at least the equal and brother of the poet. [This has led some to identify Stetson with Ezra Pound, but there seems no reason for doing this. Why should Pound be warned against "the Dog"?] *"The Dog"* (74). C. Brooks conjectures that New Humanism, which would "extirpate the supernatural," is meant here.

¶327. *"A Game of Chess."* This subtitle indicates the attitude of the poet towards the "common" manifestations of love in our day. It comes from Thomas

Middleton's *A Game at Chesse* in which a widow is kept so occupied while her daughter-in-law is violated. Thus modern love is nothing but a game. The section presents both an upper class love affair, in which a neurotic woman can elicit no affection from her lover, and a lower class affair, involving an abortion. *"The Chair"* (77). Ironic comparison to the barge of Cleopatra, *Antony and Cleopatra*, II, ii, 190. *"The change of Philomel"* (99). See Ovid, *Metamorphoses*, VII. ¶328. *"demobbed"* (139). Slang for *demobilized*. *"Hurry up,"* etc. (141). Traditional words of an English bartender at closing time.

¶329. *"The Fire Sermon."* A denunciation of unchastity. The reference is to Buddha's purgative Fire Sermon, which Eliot holds to correspond in importance to the Sermon on the Mount (see his note to 308). Fire is a symbol of both spiritual intensification and a destroyer of lust. *"Sweet Thames"* (175), once the subject of Spenser's "Prothalamium," is now the scene of tawdry affairs. *"By the waters of Leman I sat down and wept . . ."* (182). "An exile in a strange land, remembering Zion" would complete the passage, but does not the poet also recall from a youthful admiration of Byron—

"Clear, placid Leman! thy contrasted lake
With the wild world I dwelt in, is a thing
Which warns me, with its stillness, to forsake
Earth's troubled waters for a purer spring"

—from *Childe Harold's Pilgrimage?* *"While I was fishing"* (189). Here the poet identifies his, and the common, lot with that of the Fisher King. *"Et O ces voix . . ."* etc. (202) "And O, these voices of children, singing in the choir loft" (Verlaine, "Parsifal"). *"C.i.f. London"* (211). "Carriage and insurance free to London." Commerce has polluted the waters of life. *"Tiresias"* (228), described by Eliot as a "mere spectator" and "not a character," is "yet the most important person in the poem." All the women meet in one woman, Eliot further explains, and the two sexes meet in Tiresias. Thus he is the best of sick mankind, awaiting the Grail—"I too awaited the expected guest"—and ironically the carbuncular young man arrives on business instead. ¶330. *"Greenwich reach," "Isle of Dogs," "Richmond and Kew"* (275, 276, 293). Places on the

Thames. ¶331. *"Margate Sands"* (300). The Coney Island of England. *"To Carthage then I came"* (307)–"where a cauldron of unholy love sang all about my ears" (*Confessions of St. Augustine*). Just as unholy Carthage was destroyed, so London may be. The last lines in the section are from Buddha, who joins St. Augustine in prophetic symbolism.

¶331. *"Death by Water."* With some slight changes this section is a translation of the last seven lines of Eliot's earlier poem, *"Dans le restaurant,"* which seems to be a rebuke to a waiter who put his finger in the soup. The best effort to explain this section is Grover Smith's, in "Observations on Eliot's 'Death by Water'," *Accent*, summer, 1946. "This death is the death of the soul, through a rebirth of the body in the course of biological transformation. Such a birth is satisfactory to men desiring personal life after death. But, to retain identity after death, only one way is indicated—salvation through Christ. One must find the 'Hanged Man,' as neither Madame Sosostris, nor Ferdinand, nor Mr. Eugenides, nor the Phoenician sailor can do. . . ." Mr. Smith ingeniously relates all of the characters whom he names.

¶331. *"What the Thunder Said."* Through a scene of utter desolation, the poet and his "brother" (the "you" of the last lines of Section I) find themselves on the road to Emmaus with a third figure whom they do not recognize but who is Christ (359–65). They come to an empty chapel (387) and a cock crows —they and the world are betrayed: the Grail or spirituality will not be found in our time. Then the voice of the Thunder, speaking, gives the only formula for spiritual rebirth, pp. 332–33: *"Datta"* (401), Give; *Dayadhvam* (411), Sympathize; *"Damyata"* (418), Control. These virtues are found in *Upanishad*, V. The poem ends with a conventional *Upanishad* ending, *"Shantih"* (433), "Peace." ¶333. *"Poi s'acose. . . ."* "There he hid him in the fire which refines them." *Purgatorio*, xxvi, 148; *"Quando. . . ."* "When shall I be like the swallow [and from dumb distress be free?]" *Pervigilium Veneris; "Le Prince. . . ."* "[I am the gloomy one, the widower, the unconsoled,] the Prince of Aquitane at the ruined tower." Gerald de Nerval, "El Desdichado"; *"Why then I'll fit you. . . ."* Thomas Kyd, *The Spanish Tragedy*, IV, i, 67.

333. BURNT NORTON. In *Collected*

Poems, 1909–1935, 1936; reprinted as the first quartet in *Four Quartets*, 1943. For criticism of the quartets, see: P. M. Jack, "A Review of Reviews," *Am. Bookman*, Winter, 1944; Richard Lea, "T. S. Eliot's Four Quartets," *Adelphi*, July–Sept., 1945; F. O. Matthiessen, "Eliot's Quartets," *Kenyon Rev.*, Spring, 1943; Philip Wheelwright, "The Burnt Norton Trilogy," *Chimera*, Autumn, 1942.

The epigraph: "When reason is common, the many live as if they possess judgment" and "The path that leads up and down is one and the same." Heraclitus (*c.* 540–475 B.C.) taught all things are one—even the tension of opposites produces unity.

Eliot's quartets roughly resemble their musical prototype—each poem has five sections or movements. In the first section of each poem a theme is stated, developed, recapitulated. There are slow "movements," and in each poem there is a rhyming lyric section corresponding to a scherzo. The last "movement," like the first, has the sonata form, but it observes it less rigidly than does the first section. Eliot probably had in mind the late and very personal quartets of Beethoven, which are conceded to be an attempt to state in musical terms Beethoven's struggle for the final good, the ultimate philosophy.

"Burnt Norton" deals with the thoughts provoked by Henri Bergson's speculations about time and consciousness which resulted in the latter declaring that we can know the present only by intuition, since events and facts are already past in our awareness of them. Eliot sees, however, all life compressed in that indefinable point between time past and time future. "The dance along the artery . . . at the still point, there the dance is." All sensation, all sensibility is concentrated at that point; hence poetry, philosophy, and religion come from it. Joseph Beaver, in an unpublished paper, suggests "Burnt Norton" describes in barest terms three "epiphanies" in Eliot's career—

the moment in the rose garden
The moment in the arbour where the rain beat
The moment in the draughty church at smokefall.

The idea of an "epiphany" is found in James Joyce's *Stephen Hero*—it is the experience of seeing or hearing some scene or incident in such a manner that at one moment the scene or incident is completely understood. The three qualities which make an "epiphany" are wholeness, harmony, and radiance. (Joyce takes these from Aquinas.) But it would seem that Eliot uses his "epiphanies," if they are such, merely to emphasize the value of the sensate point. The value of values is Love. (See the end of the poem.) For the utilization of Dante's *rosa sempiterna*, of Lewis Carroll's *Alice in Wonderland*, and D. H. Lawrence's story "The Shadow in the Rose Garden," see: Louis L. Martz, "The Wheel and the Point," *Sewanee Rev.*, Winter, 1947.

336. TRADITION AND THE INDIVIDUAL TALENT. From *The Sacred Wood*, 1920. For Eliot as a critic, see: O. Cargill, *Intellectual America*, 1941; H. M. Campbell, "An Examination of Modern Critics," *Rocky Mt. Rev.*, Summer, 1944; W. E. Collin, "T. S. Eliot, the Critic," *Sewanee Rev.*, Oct.–Dec., 1931; Louis Kronenberger, "T. S. Eliot as Critic," *Nation*, Apr. 17, 1935. ¶340. "And now methinks. . . ." Cyril Tourneur, *The Revenger's Tragedy*, III, v. ¶341. "ὁδὲ νοῦ," etc. "Perhaps Mind is something divine, and not affected by impressions from without."

E(dward) E(stlin) Cummings (1894–)

One of the "bad boys" of literature, E. E. Cummings, who prefers to sign himself "e. e. cummings," is the son of a minister. His father, the Rev. Mr. Edward Cummings, was pastor of the Old South Church in Boston from 1905 to 1926. The poet, however, was born in Cambridge, Mass., on Oct. 14, 1894, when his father was then merely an English teacher at Harvard. Cummings was graduated from the College in 1915 and took his M.A. at the University in 1916. Very soon after he volunteered to serve in the Norton Harjes Ambulance Corps. In *The Enormous Room* (1922) he describes his three months imprisonment in a detention camp in France, which was an unhappy consequence of a censor's error. After his release, he volunteered for service in the American Army and was a private at Camp Devens. Since World War I he has alternated between New York and Paris, and between the paint brush and the pen. Married to Ann Barton in 1929, he was later divorced from her.

In *Eight Harvard Poets,* 1917; *The Enormous Room,* 1922; *Tulips and Chimneys,* 1923, 1937; & 1925; *XLI poems,* 1925; *Is 5,* 1926; *Him,* 1927; *By E. E. Cummings,* 1930; *CIOPW,* 1931; *W,* 1931; *Eimi,* 1933; *Tom,* 1935; *No Thanks,* 1935; *1/20 poems,* 1937; *Collected Poems,* 1938; *50 Poems,* 1941; *1 × 1,* 1944; *Anthropos—The Future of Art,* 1945; *Santa Claus: A Morality,* 1946.

For life and criticism, see: Anon. "The Great 'I am,' " *Sat. Rev. Lit.,* Apr. 15, 1933; J. P. Bishop, "The Poems and Prose of E. E. Cummings," *So. Rev.,* Summer, 1938; S. I. Hayakawa, "Is Indeed 5," *Poetry,* Aug., 1938; John Arthos, "The Poetry of E. E. Cummings," *Am. Lit.,* Jan., 1943.

341. [NEXT TO OF COURSE GOD], [NO-BODY LOSES ALL THE TIME], [MY SWEET OLD ETCETERA], and [JIMMIE'S GOT A GOIL] were all in *Is 5,* 1926; the text is from *Collected Poems,* 1938.

Marianne (Craig) Moore
(1887-   )

Marianne Moore was born in St. Louis, on Nov. 15, 1887. Her father was John Milton Moore and her mother's name before her marriage was Mary Warner. Marianne grew up in Pennsylvania, where she attended Metzger Institute, 1896–1905, in Carlisle. Her liberal education was completed at Bryn Mawr in 1909, but she took secretarial work at Carlisle Commercial College in 1910. She was employed as a teacher of commercial subjects in the Carlisle Indian School from 1911 to 1915; after an interval, she became an assistant in the New York Public Library in 1921 and remained there until 1925 when she became acting editor of *The Dial.* The next four years with this magazine brought her most of her literary acquaintance. She makes her home in Brooklyn. Miss Moore began to contribute to the London *Egoist* following a trip abroad in 1911. She was very self-conscious about her poetry and would never have published a volume had not her friends done it for her in 1921. She has been aptly characterized as a "literalist of the imagination."

Poems (London), 1921; *Observations,* 1924; *Selected Poems,* 1935; *The Pangolin and Other Verse,* 1936; *What Are Years,* 1941; *Nevertheless,* 1944.

For criticism, see: Harriet Monroe, "Symposium on Marianne Moore," *Poetry,* Jan., 1922; T. S. Eliot, "Introduction" to *Selected Poems;* Lewis May, "Marianne Moore," *Forum,* Sept. 23, 1936; M. L. Zabel, "A Literalist of the Imagination," *Poetry,* Mar., 1936; Kenneth Burke, "Motives and Motifs in the Poetry of Marianne Moore," *Accent,* Spring, 1942.

343. POETRY, TO A STEAM ROLLER, AN EGYPTIAN PULLED GLASS BOTTLE . . . , and IS YOUR TOWN NINEVEH? all follow the text of *Selected Poems,* 1935.

(Harold) Hart Crane (1899–1932)

Hart (or Harold) Crane was born on July 21, 1899, in Garrettsville, Ohio, and spent most of his boyhood in Cleveland. He began writing verse while in the schools of Cleveland, his first work appearing when he was fifteen years of age. From 1916 to 1925 he worked as a mechanic's assistant, a book clerk, a newspaper reporter, and a salesman. After 1922 he lived principally in New York City, writing advertising copy for a living, and reading Dostoevsky, the Elizabethans, Donne, T. S. Eliot, and other authors. His first book, *White Buildings,* was published in 1926, but already he was known to and admired by many of his young fellow-poets. In 1931 he was awarded a Guggenheim Fellowship to enable him to work on a long poem dealing with Mexico. While returning from Mexico to New York, on April 27, 1932, he committed suicide by leaping from the ship on which he was traveling.

Crane failed to complete the poetical work he had planned, or to develop as fully as his admirers expected him to do; but his influence alone gives him a place in the history of poetical developments since the middle nineteen-twenties. The mixed figures of speech and highly elliptical style of Crane's verse will be clearer if considered in the light of the poet's explanation of his work in *Poetry: A Magazine of Verse,* XXIX, pp. 34–41. He was, he wrote, "more interested in the so-called illogical impingements of the connotations of words on the consciousness . . . than . . . in the preservation of their logically rigid significations."

White Buildings, 1926; *The Bridge,* 1930; *The Collected Poems* (ed. by Waldo Frank), 1933; *Letters* (ed. Brom Weber) in progress.

For life and criticism, see: Philip Horton, *Hart Crane*, 1937; Brom Weber, *Hart Crane*, 1948; R. P. Blackmur, *The Double Agent*, 1935; Babette Deutsch, *This Modern Poetry*, 1935; Allen Tate, *Reactionary Essays*, 1936; Alfred Kreymborg, *Our Singing Strength*, 1929, pp. 602–07; Granville Hicks, *Nation*, CXXX, pp. 520–22; Malcolm Cowley, *New Repub.*, LXII, pp. 276–77; *New Repub.*, LXX, pp. 340–42; Waldo Frank, *New Repub.*, LXXIV, pp. 11–15; Yvor Winters, *Poetry*, XXXVI, pp. 153–65; E. L. Walton, "Hart Crane," *Nation*, May 3, 1933; Allen Tate, *Poetry*, XL, pp. 210–16. For Crane's relationship to Samuel Greenberg, see: *Poems from the Greenberg Manuscripts* (ed. J. Laughlin), 1939; *Poems by Samuel Greenberg*, (ed. H. Holden and J. McManis), 1947; P. Horton, "The Greenberg MS and Hart Crane's Poetry," *So. Rev.*, Summer, 1936, and "Identity of S. B. Greenberg," *So. Rev.*, Autumn, 1936.

344. VOYAGES II. From *White Buildings*, 1926.

345. THE BRIDGE. Title poem, volume of 1930. In his letters to Otto Kahn, Crane gives further publication facts and his aims. ¶350. *"Atlantis."* For different MSS stages of this section, see Brom Weber, *Hart Crane*, Appendix C.

353. THE AIR PLANT is from the third section of *The Collected Poems*, 1933, entitled "Key West: An Island Sheaf." Crane had assembled the twenty-two poems there gathered for a new volume just before his death.

353. TWO LETTERS ON "THE BRIDGE." In *Hound & Horn*, Jul.–Sept., 1934. Otto Kahn, the financier, was a proper Maecenas for Hart Crane. Long a patron of the Metropolitan Opera House, he was predisposed to understand Crane's symphonic aims. ¶353. *"Don Cristobal Colon,"* Columbus.

Archibald MacLeish (1892–)

Archibald MacLeish was born in Glencoe, Ill., a suburb of Chicago, on May 7, 1892. He was educated at the Hotchkiss School, Lakeville, Conn., at Yale University, and at the Harvard School of Law. While still a law student, in 1916, he married Miss Ada Hitchcock; and in 1917 appeared a volume of his "undergraduate verses," *Tower of Ivory*. During the First World War he served with a hospital unit, and after-

wards in the field artillery, attaining the rank of captain before hostilities ceased. After the Armistice he practiced law for three years in Boston, and then decided to follow the one occupation which really engaged his mind and heart: writing poetry. In 1923 he went with his family to Paris, later spending a summer in Normandy, and traveling through the Mediterranean countries. He studied the works of the French poets Laforgue, Rimbaud, Valéry, as well as those of Ezra Pound and T. S. Eliot. In 1924 he published *The Happy Marriage*; and this, like several succeeding volumes of poetry, shows him to have made great gains in skill. In 1928 he returned to the United States, and without giving up his literary career he came increasingly to be interested in political and economic affairs. From 1939 to 1944 he held the position of Librarian of the Library of Congress. During the years 1944–45 he was Assistant Secretary of State. He held other governmental posts, and acquired a position of leadership by reason both of his practical work and through his writings. In 1949 he was appointed Boylston Professor in Harvard College.

Tower of Ivory, 1917; *The Happy Marriage and Other Poems*, 1924; *The Pot of Earth*, 1925; *Nobodaddy*, 1926; *Streets in the Moon*, 1926; *The Hamlet of A. MacLeish*, 1928; *New Found Land*, 1930; *Conquistador*, 1932; *Poems: 1924–1933*, 1933; *Frescoes for Mr. Rockefeller's City*, 1933; *Panic*, 1935; *Public Speech*, 1936; *Fall of the City*, 1937; *Land of the Free* (photographs, with a poem), 1938; *Air Raid*, 1939; *America Was Promises*, 1939; *The Irresponsibles: A Declaration*, 1940; *The American Cause*, 1941; *Next Harvard*, 1941; *Prophets of Doom*, 1941; *A Time to Speak* (selections), 1941; *American Opinion and the War*, 1942; *A Time to Act*, 1943; *The American Story*, 1944; *Actfive*, 1948.

For criticism, see: Conrad Aiken, *Bookman*, LVXIII, p. 577; George Dangerfield, *Bookman*, LXXII, pp. 493–7; Malcolm Cowley, *Dial*, LXXXII, pp. 512–18; Allen Tate, *Nation*, CXXIV, pp. 185–86; Lewis Galantière, *Nation*, CXXVIII, pp. 471–72; Léonie Adams, *New Republic*, XLVIII, p. 100; Conrad Aiken, *New Republic*, XLIX, p. 337; Theodore Spencer, *New Republic*, LVII, pp. 226–27; Morton D. Zabel, *Poetry*, XXXVI, pp. 270–76; Harriet Monroe, *Poetry*, XXXVIII, pp. 150–56;

Stephen Vincent Benét, *Sat. Rev. Lit.*, II, p. 934; Louis Untermeyer, *Sat. Rev. Lit.*, III, pp. 578–79; Dayton Kohler, *So. Atl. Quar.*, XXXVIII, pp. 416–26; Arthur Mizener, *Sewanee Rev.*, XLIV, pp. 501–19; Edwin Honig, *Sewanee Rev.*, XLVIII, pp. 385–96; Eleanor M. Sickels, *Am. Lit.*, XV, pp. 223–37.

357. ARS POETICA. In *The Happy Marriage and Other Poems*, 1924. Another statement of MacLeish's conception of poetry is found in his article, "Nevertheless One Debt," *Poetry*, July, 1931.

358. [A WHITE NIGHT]. From *The Hamlet of A. MacLeish*, 1928. This poem should be compared with the *Hamlet* written by Jules Laforgue. (See O. Cargill, *Intellectual America*, 1941.) Taking himself as an adolescent (just as Kittredge contended Hamlet should be taken, and as Laforgue had contended before Kittredge), the poet identifies himself with the Danish prince, but every now and then slips out of the role and is his modern self. ¶359. "*Homs, Isfahan,*" etc. (51 ff.). Places in the Near East.

360. MEMORY GREEN. In *New Repub.*, Jan. 9, 1929; collected in *New Found Land*, 1930. "*Friedrichstrasse*" (5). A street crossing the Unter den Linden in Berlin at right angles, once a fashionable promenade and shopping center.

360. YOU, ANDREW MARVELL. In *New Found Land*, 1930. Compare with Marvell's poem "To His Coy Mistress," especially with the lines beginning, "But at my back I always hear. . . ." Note that Eliot had utilized this line in Sect. V of *The Waste Land*. ¶360. "*Ecbatan[a] . . . Kermanshah,*" etc. (9 ff.). Beginning with an ancient, non-existent city in W. Asia, then touching one in S.E. Iran, the poet moves westward through time and space with the sun. But the shade which comes is not merely that of the night but of the decline of the West. See Spengler.

361. "NOT MARBLE NOR THE GILDED MONUMENTS." In *New Found Land*, 1930. The title is from the first line of Shakespeare's fifty-fifth sonnet.

361. LINES FOR AN INTERMENT. In *Poems: 1924–1933*, 1933. MacLeish's brother was killed in Belgium in World War I. See *The Hamlet of A. Macleish*: ". . . on my young, my three times buried brother's stony grave." ¶362. "*OD silk*" (12). Olive drab.

362. SPEECH TO THOSE WHO SAY COM-

RADE. In *Public Speech*, 1936. "*Soissons . . . Meaux . . . Ypres*" (12). French and Belgian cities bitterly contended for in World War I. ¶363. "*hid in Geneva*" (36). Geneva was a famous refuge for fugitive revolutionists in the 19th century.

363. "DOVER BEACH"—A NOTE TO THAT POEM. In *Public Speech*, 1936. Compare with Matthew Arnold's "Dover Beach."

364. POLE STAR FOR THIS YEAR. The first poem in *Public Speech*, 1936. "*The Wain*" (7). Charles' Wain, the Big Dipper; alignment of the stars along its front indicates the pole star, or North Star—the orientation point for simple navigation.

365. THE FALL OF THE CITY. Pub. in 1937. Foreword gives the facts of presentation. See F.D.R.'s "First Inaugural Address" for the theme—"we have nothing to fear but fear itself."

Eugene (Gladstone) O'Neill (1888–   )

Eugene Gladstone O'Neill was born in New York City on Oct. 16, 1888. His father was a successful actor, and his first years were spent in large cities where his father's company played *Monte Cristo*. He was sent to private schools, and in 1906 entered Princeton University, but was suspended at the end of the year because of participation in a prank. For the next ten years he led an unsettled life, full of experiences which he was later to turn to dramatic account. He worked as secretary of a mail order house in New York City, served with his father's dramatic troupe during part of several seasons, prospected for gold, and spent many months as a sailor and dweller on the water front of seaports. After a period of severe illness in 1912–13, when for the first time he reviewed his life, he decided to attempt writing plays. In 1914 was published his *Thirst and Other One-Act Plays*, issued at the expense of his father. In 1914–15 he studied dramatic technique under Professor Baker at Harvard University. The year 1916 proved to be the pivotal one of his career, for he then began his connections with the Provincetown Players and secured his start as a successful playwright. His progress was rapid; he steadily established himself as the leading dramatist of the country. He has been awarded the Pulitzer Prize three times, and in 1936 he received the Nobel Prize for Literature. He has been married three times, his third wife being Carlotta Monterey. His home is in California.

Thirst and Other One-Act Plays, 1914; *Before Breakfast,* 1916; *Chris. Christopherson,* 1919; *The Moon of the Caribbees and Six Other Plays of the Sea,* 1919; *Beyond the Horizon,* 1920; *Gold,* 1920; *Straw,* 1920; *The Emperor Jones, Diff'rent, The Straw,* 1921; *The Hairy Ape, Anna Christie, The First Man,* 1922; *All God's Chillun Got Wings and Welded,* 1924; *The Complete Works of Eugene O'Neill,* 1924; *The Dreamy Kid,* 1925; *Desire under the Elms,* 1925; *Collected Plays,* 1925; *The Great God Brown, The Fountain, The Moon of the Caribbees,* 1926; *Marco Millions,* 1927; *Lazarus Laughed,* 1927; *Strange Interlude,* 1928; *Dynamo,* 1929; *Mourning Becomes Electra,* 1931; *Nine Plays* (selected), 1933; *Ah, Wilderness!,* 1933; *Days without End,* 1934; *Plays* (3 vols.), 1941; *The Iceman Cometh,* 1946.

For life and criticism, see: Barrett H. Clark, *Eugene O'Neill,* new rev. ed., 1947; A. H. Quinn, *A History of the American Drama from the Civil War to the Present Day,* II, pp. 165–207; S. K. Winther, *Eugene O'Neill,* 1934; R. D. Skinner, *Eugene O'Neill,* 1935; Theresa Helburn, "O'Neill: An Impression," *Sat. Rev. Lit.,* Nov. 21, 1936; Croswell Bowen, "Black Irishman," *PM,* Nov. 3, 1946.

379. BOUND EAST FOR CARDIFF. The best of O'Neill's early plays, and the first one to be produced. It was written in 1914, and produced by the Provincetown Players in 1916; first printed in *Provincetown Plays: First Series,* 1916, and was included in *The Moon of the Caribbees,* 1919. It is reprinted from *The Complete Works of Eugene O'Neill,* I, 1924. Cardiff is the Welsh seaport.

387. LAZARUS LAUGHED. Published, 1927; first presented at the Community Playhouse, Pasadena, Calif., Apr. 9, 1928. The story of the raising of Lazarus from the dead is found only in John 11.1–46, but see also L. J. Davidson, "Lazarus in Modern Literature," *Eng. Journ.,* June, 1929, which deals chiefly with this play. O'Neill's "Memoranda on Masks," *Am. Spect.,* Nov. 1932, is pertinent also. O. Cargill, *Intellectual America,* 1941, discusses the relation of Jung

and Nietzsche to *Lazarus Laughed.* The play appears to be a dramatic statement of the latter's *The Birth of Tragedy,* which should be read in conjunction with it. The choruses are "typed" by a scheme analogous to that used by Jung in his "type psychology." ¶387. Gaius Caligula A.D. 12–41, Roman emperor, A.D. 37–41, Tiberius Caesar 42 B.C.– A.D. 37, Roman emperor, A.D. 14–37, and Pompeia are the only historical characters; Crassus and Marcellus are common names for persons of their station, but they are without historical validity. Among O'Neill's sources was Gibbon's *Decline and Fall of the Roman Empire,* but most of the events of the play are imagined.

(John) Robinson Jeffers
(1887–   )

John Robinson Jeffers was born in Pittsburgh, Pa., on Jan. 10, 1887. He received careful training in the classics from his scholarly father, Dr. William Hamilton Jeffers, and attended schools in Switzerland and Germany. He later studied at the University of Western Pennsylvania, Occidental College, from which he received the A.B. degree in 1905, the University of Zurich, and the University of Southern California. He reads with ease French, German, Latin, and Greek. He began training for a career as physician, but his interest in poetry superseded all other interests, so that, upon receiving a legacy from his uncle, he determined to devote himself to literature. In 1913 he married Mrs. Una Call Kuster, and the following year settled on a bluff overlooking Carmel Bay, California, building a house of the granite stones on the shore, and later erecting with his own hands a stone tower in which he does much of his writing. Here he has lived in seclusion, leading with his family a self-sufficient life. His early volumes of poetry made little impression, but upon the publication of *Tamar,* 1924, attention was drawn to him, and he acquired a reputation which has been strengthened by the books which followed. He has been awarded several honorary degrees and elected to membership in the American Academy of Arts and Letters, the National Institute of Arts and Letters, and the Authors League of America.

Since 1925 his work has exerted a

direct and strong influence on the field of poetry. He is a poet of deep and elemental human passions, as well as a reverent worshiper of beauty, aware of the terrible irony in the fact that the loveliness of the world is at once so enduring and, from the point of view of the individual, so fleeting. His sternly tragic mood emanates from the realization of the great void left in the modern world by the dissipation of man's religious and philosophical illusions.

Flagons and Apples, 1912; *Californians,* 1916; *Tamar and Other Poems,* 1924; *Roan Stallion, Tamar and Other Poems,* 1925; *The Women at Point Sur,* 1927; *Cawdor and Other Poems,* 1928; *Poems,* 1928; *An Artist,* 1928; *Dear Judas and Other Poems,* 1929; *Descent to the Dead,* 1931; *Thurso's Landing and Other Poems,* 1932; *Give Your Heart to the Hawks,* 1933; *Solstice and Other Poems,* 1935; *Such Counsels You Gave to Me,* 1937; *Selected Poetry,* 1938; *Two Consolations,* 1940; *Be Angry at the Sun,* 1941; *Medea* (free trans. from Euripides), 1946; *The Double Axe,* 1948.

For life and criticism, see: George Sterling, *Robinson Jeffers,* 1926; Louis Adamic, *Robinson Jeffers,* 1929; L. C. Powell, *Robinson Jeffers, the Man and His Work* (rev. ed.), 1940. See also: S. S. Alberts, *A Bibliography of the Works of Robinson Jeffers,* 1933.

442. ODE ON HUMAN DESTINIES. In *Californians,* 1916. Compare with the odes of Shelley, the chief inspiration among English poets for Jeffers. See O. Cargill, *Intellectual America,* 1941. ¶442. *"the beautiful peninsula"* (1). The Monterey peninsula. ¶443. *"Santa Lucian summit lines"* (9). Westermost range of mountains, parallel to the coast, between Monterey and San Luis Obispo, Calif. *"Promontory of Stones"* (39) located in the third section of the poem. ¶444. *"Stonehenge"* (89). Site of prehistoric monument in So. England, near Salisbury. ¶445. *"Lyre"* (131). The northern constellation Lyra contains the bright star Vega. *"Thuban"* (136). Or Adib, a fixed star in the constellation Draconis (the dragon).

447. BOATS IN A FOG. In *Nation,* Sept. 23, 1925; collected in *Roan Stallion, Tamar, and Other Poems,* 1925. ¶447. *"Monterey"* (18). Largest town in the Jeffers country.

447. GALE IN APRIL. In *Roan Stallion, etc.,* 1925.

448. TO THE STONE CUTTERS. In *Roan Stallion, etc.,* 1925. Quarrying is extensive in the Jeffers country. See *Thurso's Landing.*

448. ROAN STALLION. The title poem in *Roan Stallion, Tamar, and Other Poems,* 1925. The heroine's name, California, suggests the symbolic significance of the poem; there nature is nobler than man. ¶449. *"Carmel valley"* (28). Breaks through the mountains near Carmel where Jeffers resides.

461. SHINE, PERISHING REPUBLIC. In *Roan Stallion, etc.,* 1925.

461. HURT HAWKS. In *The Women at Point Sur,* 1927.

462. MEDITATION ON SAVIORS. In *Poems,* 1928. ¶463. *"Point Lobos"* (ii, 1). One of two headlands (the other is Point Sur) frequently mentioned in Jeffers' poetry; both are below Monterey. ¶463. *"King Oedipus"* (ii, 5). The episode in *Oedipus Rex* by Sophocles in which the King tears out his eyes after learning that he has been the involuntary slayer of his father and the unwitting husband of his mother, made a powerful impression on Jeffers. He has borrowed it in *Cawdor* and there are many references to it. ¶465. "Gautama" (vi, 2) is another name for Buddha, 563?–483? B.C.

Daniel DeLeon (1852–1914)

Daniel DeLeon, whose dates are Dec. 14, 1852–May 11, 1914, was born to a Jewish surgeon, Salomon DeLeon and his wife Sara (Jesurun), on the island of Curaçao when the father was serving there in a unit of the Dutch colonial army. Educated till he was fourteen at home, Daniel was sent to the gymnasium at Hildesheim, Germany, in 1866. He studied later in Amsterdam and then, about 1874, emigrated to the U. S., where he was joined by his mother. DeLeon edited a Spanish-language paper in New York for a time, taught school in Westchester, and studied law at Columbia, where he received his LL.B. in 1878. Winning a lectureship in Latin-America diplomacy, he taught two three-year terms, 1883–1889, before tendering his resignation. Successively a supporter of Henry George and Edward Bellamy in the late eighties, he joined the Knights of Labor in 1888 and the Socialist Labor Party in 1890, becoming national lecturer for the Party in 1891 and editor of its organ, *The People,* in

1892. DeLeon wrote no books, and most of the pamphlets issued under his name were extracted from editorials in *The People*. DeLeon's dogmatic ways and vitriolic tongue led to dissension in the Socialist Labor Party. His opponents, unable to defeat him, withdrew and founded the Socialist Party of America. In June, 1905, he helped to found the militant International Workers of the World (the "I.W.W."), but in 1908 he was refused a seat in its convention by a still more militant faction which got control of this organization, and on this occasion it was DeLeon who withdrew. Also withdrawing from the labor movement in 1913, DeLeon retired to Pleasantville, N. Y., with his second wife, his first having died in 1882. His own death occurred in a New York hospital.

What Means This Strike?, 1898; *Two Pages from Roman History*, 1903; *Socialist Reconstruction of Society*, 1905; *The Ballot and the Class Struggle*, 1909; *Fifteen Questions* (n.d.); *Industrial Unionism*, 1920; *A Decadent Jeffersonian on the Socialist Gridiron*, 1926, 1935.

For life and criticism, see: W. H. Ghent, "Daniel DeLeon," *D.A.B.*; Morris Hillquit, *History of Socialism in the United States*, 1903; *Daniel DeLeon: A Symposium* (ed. Henry Kuhn), 1919; Olive M. Johnson, *Daniel DeLeon*, 1923.

467. [INDUSTRIAL UNIONISM AND SOCIALISM]. From *Socialist Reconstruction of Society*, 1905. An address by Daniel DeLeon at Minneapolis, Minn., during a lecture tour undertaken following the Chicago I.W.W. organizing convention. It was originally entitled, "The Preamble of the I.W.W.," when it had been presented before the convention itself on July 10, 1905. ¶469. *"William Liebknecht"* (1826–1900), German Socialist, opponent of Lassalle, supporter of Marx.

Thorstein Veblen (1856–1929)

The parents of Thorstein Veblen emigrated from Norway in 1847 and settled on the Wisconsin frontier. Veblen was born there on July 30, 1857. When he was eight his father selected a new homesite in Minnesota in the midst of a colony of Norwegians. A young "Norskie," with a scant knowledge of English, he was packed off to Carleton College, in Northfield, Minn., when he was

seventeen. In all he spent six years there, for he needed three in the preparatory department and only three to finish the normal four year course. He seems to have alienated teachers and classmates alike, for when he was graduated in 1880, only John Bates Clark, the economist, saw his promise. A year of teaching made it possible for him to study at Johns Hopkins, but he decided to transfer to Yale, where he studied under Noah Porter and W. G. Sumner. If the latter did nothing else for Veblen, he gave him a style. He received his Ph.D. in philosophy in 1884, but could get no appointment and retired to his Minnesota farm. He married Ellen M. Rolfe in 1888, hoping to advance himself through her connections. This did not happen, and Veblen and his wife went to live on a farm in Iowa. Three years later he turned up at Cornell where J. Laurence Laughlin procured him a fellowship. Called to head the department of economics at the University of Chicago, Laughlin took Veblen with him in 1891 and got him another fellowship. He became an instructor in 1896 and an assistant professor in 1900 following the publication the previous year of *The Theory of the Leisure Class*, the first important study in institutional economics. In 1904 came *The Theory of Business Enterprise*, but meanwhile Veblen's romantic entanglements had got him into trouble with his wife and the university authorities. He was told that he could not stay, but he was aided in getting an associate professorship at Stanford in 1906. His wife returned to him, but another affair of the heart terminated this connection. He was invited to the University of Missouri in 1911 and remained there seven years. Meanwhile he was divorced and remarried to Anne F. Bradley, a divorcée with two children. In 1918 he resigned from Missouri to move to New York City where, in 1919, he became a member of the New School for Social Research. He was an abominable teacher, yet he was sought out by young intellectuals. Not hitherto a doctrinaire, but rather an iconoclast, he became revolutionary shortly after coming to the city. *The Engineers and the Price System* handed the baton to the engineers. Organizing efforts of his own proved fruitless and Veblen grew despondent. His second wife died in 1920; in 1926 Ellen Rolfe passed away and Veblen returned to the cabin they had occupied in Menlo Park, Calif. There he had a fatal heart attack on Aug. 3, 1929. Shortly before this he had declared, "Naturally there will be other developments right along, but just now communism offers the best course I can see."

Theory of the Leisure Class, 1899; *The Theory of Business Enterprise,* 1904; *The Instinct of Workmanship,* 1914; *Imperial Germany and the Industrial Revolution,* 1915; *An Inquiry into the Nature of Peace,* 1917; *The Higher Learning,* 1918; *The Vested Interests and the State of the Industrial Arts,* 1919; *The Engineers and the Price System,* 1921; *Absentee Ownership and Business Enterprise in Recent Years,* 1923; *Essays in Our Changing Order* (ed. L. Ardzrooni), 1934; *The Portable Veblen* (ed. Max Lerner), 1948.

For life and criticism, see: Max Lerner, "Thorstein Veblen," *D.A.B.* and *Ideas Are Weapons,* 1939; Joseph Dorfham, *Thorstein Veblen and His America,* 1934; R. V. Teggert, "Thorstein Veblen," *Univ. of Calif. Pub. in Eco.,* XL, 1932; R. L. Duffus, *The Innocents at Cedro,* 1944; G. S. Gambo, *Beyond Supply and Demand,* 1946. For bibliography, see: H. W. Innes, "A Bibliography of Thorstein Veblen," *Southwestern Pol. & Soc. Sc. Quar.,* X, 1929–1930.

472. THE CAPTAINS OF FINANCE AND THE ENGINEERS is Chapter III of *The Engineers of the Price System,* 1921. See "The Socialist Economics of Karl Marx" in *Quar. Journ. of Eco.,* Aug., 1906, for Veblen's earlier attitude towards Marxism.

(John Griffith) Jack London
(1876–1916)

Illegitimate child of Flora Wellman, Jack London was born in San Francisco on Jan. 12, 1876. His father was possibly "Professor" W. H. Chaney, an itinerant Irish astrologer. Eight months after the birth of her son, Flora Wellman married John London, then working as a carpenter. Formerly a farmer, John London took up truck farming about 1880 in Alameda; in 1883 the family moved to a ranch in San Mateo County. Not until their return to Oakland, 1886, did Jack receive any schooling. He had been subjected to the least desirable companionship. "All the inconceivable filth a child running at large may hear men utter was mine." In Oakland, Jack sold papers before and after school, worked in bowling alleys and saloons. His newspaper route took him along the waterfront where he was soon a member, then the leader, of a boys' gang. At seventeen, he was dissolute, in his own words "a drunken bum," though he had already earned a title, "Prince of the Oyster Pirates," for the poaching parties he had led to private oyster beds. His family saved him by sending him to sea on a whaling schooner, the *Sophie Sutherland.* After this cruise (northern Pacific to Japan), he came back with the intention of earning his living soberly and honestly; he worked on the docks, in a jute mill, and as a coal heaver. Joining Kelley's "Army of Protest," 1894, he soon deserted to become a tramp. Begging from door to door, lodging in slums and jails, he came to value the tenets of socialism and resolved to return to California for an education.

Prepared for college, Oakland High, in two years; at the end of his preparation he studied 19 hours a day; janitor work paid his expenses. Stayed only a semester in the University of California, withdrawing to write; in his brief formal education, however, he must have become partially acquainted with Darwin, Spencer, Haeckel, Marx, Nietzsche. Failing after prodigious effort ("the way I wrote was enough to soften my brain") to arrive as an author, he joined the Alaska gold rush. Scurvy brought him back to civilization; in Oakland, he found his father dead; unable to get other employment he took up writing again, this time meeting with success.

Several stories in *Overland,* 1899; then the *Atlantic* introduced him to the East. First book, *The Son of the Wolf,* pub. 1900; *The Call of the Wild,* most poetic study of atavism in literature, gave him an international audience, 1903. Married an Oakland poet, Bessie Maddern, in April, 1900; later divorced, married Charmian Kittredge. Lived in disguise in the slums of London, gathering material for *People of the Abyss,* during 1902. 1904, an eventful year: correspondent in Korea during the Russo-Jap War; published *The Sea-Wolf.* Activities for the proletariat were eventually reflected in his writings; the revolutionary novel, *The Iron Heel,* pub. 1907. In the South Seas on the *Snark,* Apr.,

1907–July, 1908; twice again made long cruises, in 1912 and 1915. *Martin Eden,* a fictionized autobiography, is a product of the first voyage; *John Barleycorn,* a study of his struggle with alcohol, is a result of the second; from the third he seems to have derived chiefly discontent with the Socialist Party. Wrote from Honolulu, Mar., 1916, resigning because of the party's "lack of fire and fight, and its loss of emphasis on the class struggle." Died on Nov. 22, 1916, a suicide from morphine poisoning.

The Son of the Wolf, 1900; *The God of His Fathers,* 1901; *A Daughter of the Snows,* 1902; *The Children of the Frost,* 1902; *The Cruise of the Dazzler,* 1902; *The People of the Abyss,* 1903; *The Kempton-Wace Letters,* 1903; *The Call of the Wild,* 1903; *The Faith of Men,* 1904; *Brown Wolf,* 1904; *The Sea-Wolf,* 1904; *The Game,* 1905; *Tales of the Fish Patrol,* 1905; *The War of the Classes,* 1905; *Moon-Face and Other Stories,* 1906; *Love of Life,* 1906; *White Fang,* 1906; *Scorn of Women,* 1906; *Before Adam,* 1907; *The Road,* 1907; *The Iron Heel,* 1908; *Martin Eden,* 1909; *Lost Face,* 1909; *Revolution,* 1910; *The Cruise of the Snark,* 1911; *South Sea Tales,* 1911; *Smoke Bellew,* 1912; *The House of Pride,* 1912; *A Son of the Sun,* 1912; *The Night Born,* 1913; *The Abysmal Brute,* 1913; *John Barleycorn,* 1913; *The Valley of the Moon,* 1913; *The Strength of the Strong,* 1914; *The Mutiny of the Elsinore,* 1914; *The Scarlet Plague,* 1915; *The Star Rover,* 1915; *The Little Lady of the Big House,* 1916; *The Turtles of Tasman,* 1916; *The Acorn-Planter,* 1916; *Jerry of the Islands,* 1917; *The Human Drift,* 1917; *Michael, Brother of Jerry,* 1917; *On the Makaloa Mat,* 1919; *Hearts of Three,* 1920; *Dutch Courage,* 1922.

Sonoma Edition, Macmillan, 12 vols., 1917. *The Call of the Wild,* ed. F. L. Mott, M.R.S., 1926.

For life, see: Charmian London, *The Book of Jack London,* 2 vols., 1921, "La Jeunesse de Jack London," *Revue de Paris,* May, 1927; Irving Stone, *Sailor on Horseback,* 1938. For criticism, see: F. L. Pattee, *Sidelights on American Literature,* 1922, *The New American Literature,* 1930; Carl Van Doren, *The American Novel,* 1921; B. C. Williams, *Our Short-Story Writers,* 1921. For special criticism, see: L. A. M. Bosworth, "Is Jack London a Plagiarist?" *Ind.,* Feb. 14, 1907; G. S. Viereck, "The

Ghost of Jack London," *Liberty,* Oct. 10, 1931.

483. [HARRISON GOES ALOFT]. From Ch. VI of *The Sea-Wolf,* serialized in *Century,* Jan.–Nov., 1904. The narrator, Humphrey Van Weyden, literary critic and man of leisure, is picked up by Wolf Larsen, captain of the *Ghost,* after he has been shipwrecked. The novel is a masterpiece of dynamic strength till Larsen rescues another castaway, Maude Brewster, whereupon it degenerates into sentimental melodrama. Larsen is the personification of the Nietzschean "will-to-power." Christian Larsen, ship's carpenter, port of Newark, N. J., is alleged to have wrestled with London in a saloon and supplied the model for the study (Newark *Evening News,* Mar. 27, 1930).

488. A CURIOUS FRAGMENT. In *When God Laughs,* 1911. Illustrates London's socialistic writings. The conjectural world reminds one of the creations of H. G. Wells (closer parallel is found in "Goliah," *Bookman,* Feb., 1910). London anticipated as well as imitated others: compare Tarzan stories with *Before Adam.* For socialistic views, see also: "South of the Slot," "Dream of Debs," "What Life Means to Me," "The Class Struggle," *The Iron Heel, The Scarlet Plague.*

Upton (Beall) Sinclair (1878–   )

By birth and ancestry a Southerner. Born in Baltimore, Sept. 20, 1878, of a distinguished family; his great-grand-father, Commander Arthur Sinclair, in charge of a frigate, War of 1812; Lt.-Commander Arthur Sinclair, Jr., one of Commodore Perry's officers, went on an expedition to Japan, 1852–54, and later parted with his friend, David Farragut, to command a blockade runner in the Civil War. Upton Beall Sinclair, the novelist's father, too young to enlist, ran away to take part in the final defense of Richmond; in the debacle the family fortunes were ruined; he became a whole-sale liquor salesman; in Baltimore he met and married Priscilla Harden, daughter of the Sec.-Treas. of the Western Maryland R. R. The novelist is the only son of this marriage.

The Sinclairs moved to New York, 1888. After attending an East Side grammar school, Upton studied at the College of the City of New York, 1892–97. Began hack-writing at nineteen, contributing jokes and stories to the cheaper magazines; supported self and paid expenses for a graduate course at Columbia. Went to a lonely shack in the woods in Quebec, 1900, to work on a novel, *Springtime and Harvest* (privately printed, 1901). Married Meta H. Fuller, Oct., 1900; a son, David, born Dec., 1901. Attracted wide notice, 1902, with *The Journal of Arthur Stirling,* which purported to be the diary of an unsuccessful poet. After the hoax was discovered, interest waned.

Sinclair made the acquaintance of George D. Herron, a socialist editor who subsidized him and led him to socialistic books. Yet "what brought me to socialism was Christianity more than anything else." First realistic novel, *Manassas,* published 1904. "The best Civil War book I've read" (Jack London). He went to Chicago, 1904, to get material for a book on Packingtown. *The Jungle* was serialized in the *Appeal to Reason,* a socialist weekly. Published, 1906, it became a "best seller" and was translated into 17 languages. Roosevelt, in response to a popular demand, sent a commission to Chicago to investigate; the enactment of the Pure Food Laws resulted. *The Metropolis,* 1907, attacks the triviality of the life of the "Four Hundred"; *The Moneychangers,* 1908, exposes the causes of panics.

He founded the Intercollegiate Socialist Society, 1905; with the proceeds from the sale of *The Jungle* he established a coöperative residence, Helicon Hall, at Englewood, N. J. The residence (to which William James and John Dewey came as visitors, and young Sinclair Lewis, from Yale, as janitor) was mysteriously destroyed by fire, and Sinclair's savings went with it. In California, 1908–09, he organized a traveling theatrical company to produce socialist plays; went to live at a single-tax colony, Arden, Delaware, 1910. *Love's Pilgrimage* (a story of his own life up to 1904) was published in 1911. Went to Holland for a divorce, 1912. Married Mary Craig Kimbrough, of Greenwood, Mississippi, Apr., 1913, who developed into a poet under his tutelage (See *Sonnets by M. C. S.,* 1925).

On behalf of the Colorado coal miners, he picketed the offices of John D. Rockefeller, Jr., was arrested and fined. Went to Colorado to aid the strikers. Knowledge gained was reworked in *King Coal,* 1917. America's entrance into the World War, violently opposed by many socialists, evoked from Sinclair a pledge of support to Wilson. He had earlier published a polemic, *The Profits of Religion,* "a study of supernaturalism . . . as a source of income and shield of privilege," 1918. This was followed, 1919, by *The Brass Check: a Study of American Journalism,* not only an exposé, but a source book on Upton Sinclair. *Oil!,* 1917, and *Boston,* 1929, are on a par with *The Jungle.* In 1934, campaigning on a platform to "end poverty in California" (the "EPIC" plan), he secured the Democratic nomination for governor but was defeated in the election. Six years later he began to publish the "Lanny Budd" series of novels—a fictional treatment of contemporary history, remarkable for its inclusiveness and the ubiquity of its hero.

"The social and industrial order which has black-listed Upton Sinclair has, while increasing his rage, also increased his art. In his youth he was primarily a lyric boy storming the ears of the world which failed to detect in his romances the promise of which he himself was outspokenly confident. . . . The times have furnished Mr. Sinclair the keen, cool, dangerous art of Tom Paine." (Van Doren, *Contemp. Am. Novelists,* 1927).

Springtime and Harvest, 1901; *Prince Hagen,* 1902; *The Journal of Arthur Stirling,* 1903; *Manassas,* 1904; *The Jungle,* 1906; *The Metropolis,* 1907; *The Moneychangers,* 1908; *Samuel, the Seeker,* 1909; *Love's Pilgrimage,* 1911; *The Fasting Cure,* 1911; *The Millennium,* 1912; *Damaged Goods* (novelized from Brieux), 1913; *Sylvia,* 1913; *Sylvia's Marriage,* 1914; *The Cry for Justice* (editor), 1915; *King Coal,* 1917; *The Profits of Religion,* 1918; *Jimmie Higgins,* 1919; *100%,* 1920; *The Brass Check,* 1920; *They Call Me Carpenter,* 1922; *The Book of Life,* 1922; *Hell,* 1923; *The Goose-Step,* 1923; *The Goslings,* 1924; *Bill Porter,* 1925; *Singing Jailbirds,* 1925; *Mammonart,* 1925; *The Spokesman's Secretary,* 1926; *Letters to Judd,* 1926; *Money Writes!,* 1927; *Oil!,* 1927; *Boston,* 1928; *Oilplay,* 1929; *Mental Radio,* 1930; *Mountain City,* 1930; *Roman Holiday,* 1931; *The Wet Parade,* 1931; *American Outpost,* 1932; *William Fox,* 1933; *I, Governor of California,* 1933; *The Way Out,* 1933; *EPIC Answers,* 1934; *The EPIC Plan for California,* 1934; *I, Candidate for Gover-*

nor: *and How I Got Licked,* 1935; *Co-op,* 1936; *What God Means to Me,* 1936; *The Flivver King,* 1937; *No Parasan!,* 1937; *Little Steel,* 1938; *Our Lady,* 1938; *Expect No Peace,* 1939; *World's End,* 1940; *Between Two Worlds,* 1941; *Dragon's Teeth,* 1942; *Wide Is the Gate,* 1943; *Presidential Agent,* 1944; *Dragon Harvest,* 1945; *A World to Win,* 1946; *Presidential Mission,* 1947; *One Clear Call,* 1948; *O Shepherd, Speak!,* 1949.

For life, see: *The Brass Check,* *American Outpost,* and Floyd Dell, *Upton Sinclair: a Study in Social Protest,* 1927. For criticism, see: C. Van Doren, *Contemp. Am. Novelists,* 1927; Van Wyck Brooks, *Emerson and Others,* 1927; C. C. Baldwin, *The Men Who Make Our Novels,* 1924; Robert Cantwell, "Upton Sinclair," *N. Repub.,* Feb. 24, 1937.

For bibliography, see: Joseph Gaer, ed., *Upton Sinclair, Bibliography and Biographical Data,* SERA Project, Monograph No. 6, California Relief Administration, 1935.

493. THE JUNGLE. See Chs. III, IV, V, of *The Brass Check* for circumstances connected with publication. See also: Sinclair's article, "The Condemned Meat Industry," *Everybody's,* May, 1906; and "Is *The Jungle* True?" *Independent,* May 17, 1906, and "*The Jungle* Vindicated," *Bookman,* July, 1906. ¶497. *"all the world . . . his oyster":* Merry Wives of Windsor, Act ii, Sc. 1.

498. DEUTSCHLAND ERWACHE! From *Dragon's Teeth,* 1942, the third novel in the "Lanny Budd" series, for which Sinclair won the Pulitzer Prize. Lanny Budd is the illegitimate but acknowledged son of a Connecticut arms manufacturer and his Riviera mistress Beauty Budd. Social position and his profession of art agent give him important contacts throughout the world. Disguising his socialist sympathies, he is able to be an intimate of Goering, Hitler, and Laval, while taking up the duties of a Presidential agent for Franklin Roosevelt. Half the characters in the series are historical personages. For German vocabulary, see: Heinz Paechter, *Nazi-Deutsch,* 1944. ¶498. *"Schieber."* Climber. ¶499. *"Die Strasse frei . . ."* etc. "A free path for the Brown Battalions!" ¶499. *"Führerprinzip."* The leader-principle. ¶499. *"Deutschland Erwache!"* Germany, awake! ¶500. *Partei- und oberster S[turm]-A[bteilung] Führer, Vorsitzender der N[ational] S[ozialistische] D[eutsche]*

A[rbeiter] P[artei]." Two of Hitler's honorific titles. Party- and supreme Storm-Detachment Leader, President of the National Socialist German Workers Party. The *Sturm Abteilung* was the Brown Shirt organization as distinguished from the *Sturm Staffel,* the Black Shirts. For convenience, the full name of Hitler's party was shortened to "Nazi Party." ¶500. *"Untersuchungs-"* etc. Investigation and adjustment committee. ¶500. *"Zentralpartisverlag."* Central Party Publishing. ¶500. *"Personalamt."* Magistracy staff. ¶500. *"Deutsches Jungvolk,"* etc. The German Youth [Organization], the Young Girls League, the Student League, etc. ¶500. *"Versammlung."* Assembly. ¶500. *"Huete gehört uns,"* etc. Today Germany hears us; tomorrow the whole world! ¶501. *"Der Führer kommt!"* The Leader comes! ¶502. *"Juda verrecke!"* May Jewry croak! ¶502. *"Adi."* A nickname used only by Hitler's most intimate friends.

Charles Erskine Scott Wood
(1852–1944)

Has the double distinction of having penned the wittiest American satire, *Heavenly Discourse,* and the most revolutionary American chant, *The Poet in the Desert.* Both were written after the poet was sixty, for Wood had been a youth of the generation of Twain, Ingersoll, Miller, and Cody, and the spirit of that generation animates his work. He possessed a mysticism which they have not, and is nearer Rabelais and Voltaire than Twain.

Born in Erie, Pa., Feb. 20, 1852, a son of William Maxwell Wood, surgeon-general, U. S. Navy, and of Rose Carson. After attending Erie Academy and Baltimore City College, he entered West Point in the class of 1874. Upon his graduation at twenty-two, he became 2nd lieut. in U. S. Army. Served in the Northwest; took an active part in the Nez Percé campaign of 1877, and in the Bannock and Piute campaign of 1878. Became thoroughly acquainted with the Indians, their lore and mythology,· and was accepted into friendly tribes. Resigned commission after ten years' service. Supervised through the press Twain's outhouse story, *1601,* because of his admiration for the author, 1882. Completed a law course at Columbia, 1883. Admitted to the bar in Oregon, settled in Portland, 1884, where he practiced law till 1919. Champion of the poor and oppressed, friend of liberals and radicals. Retiring from law, he lived in Los Gatos, Calif., devoting his time to literature. Colonel Wood was married to Nannie Moale Smith, Nov. 26, 1878.

A Book of Tales, Being Myths of the North American Indians, 1901; *Masque of Love,* 1904; *The Poet in the Desert,* 1915; *Maia,* 1918; *Circe,* 1919; *Heavenly Discourse,* 1927; *Poems from the Ranges,* 1929; *Too Much Government,* 1931; *Earthly Discourse,* 1937; *Collected Poems,* 1949.

For life, see: "Dilly Tante," *Living Authors,* 1931; *Who's Who in America,* XIII, 1924–25. For criticism, see: Horace Gregory, "Veteran Iconoclast," *New Repub.,* Jan. 1, 1930; F. A. Groff, "Philosopher at Large," *Sunset,* Feb., 1912; Louis Untermeyer, *American Poetry since 1900,* 1923.

503. HEAVENLY DISCOURSE: "T.R." ENTERS HEAVEN. One of the discourses contributed to *Masses* between 1915 and Nov., 1917, when the magazine was suppressed. The editors and publishers (Max Eastman, Floyd Dell, Art Young, Merrill Rogers, Josephine Bell), who had printed other pacifistic propaganda besides Wood's satires, were tried for treason in 1918. Discourses were put in book form (Vanguard), 1927, and were immediately popular. ¶504. *"Voila les dents":* Look at his teeth! ¶504. *"Sang de Dieu":* Blood of God. ¶505. *"Ciel! les dents":* Heavens! his teeth! ¶505. *"La voix":* His voice. ¶505. *"Spare . . . the leberwurst . . . kielersprotten, sardellen . . .":* Spare . . . the white liver-sausage . . . the smoked sprats of Kiel, the anchovies. There follows a list of famous German beers. ¶505. *"an obscene old drunkard."* Popular conception of François Rabelais (*c.* 1490–*c.* 1553), physician and humorist, whose satire was excused at court because he was thought a drunkard. ¶506. *"Pardon en core . . . peut-être, chacum à son gout":* Pardon, again . . . perhaps, each to his taste. ¶506. *"Ma foi":* My faith.

Carl Sandburg (1878–   )

Carl Sandburg was born in Galesburg, Ill., on Jan. 6, 1878, the son of Swedish immigrants. As a boy he had little opportunity to attend school, but worked at many jobs; he was in turn the driver of a milk wagon, the porter in a barber shop, the operator of a truck at a brick kiln, a carpenter's helper, a harvest hand, a house painter. After serving in the Sixth Illinois Infantry during the Spanish-American war, he attended Lombard College, in Galesburg, incidentally acquiring an interest in writing. After finishing the college course in 1902, he sold films for Underwood and Underwood, and during the years 1907–08 was a district organizer for the Social-Democrat party of Wisconsin. In 1908 he married Miss Lillian Steichen of Milwaukee, Wisconsin, and in the same year he took up newspaper work, which has remained his principal occupation since. In 1914 his poem "Chicago" won for him the Levinson Prize awarded by *Poetry: A Magazine of Verse,* and in 1916 appeared his *Chicago Poems.* In response to invitations Sandburg turned to the reading of his poetry, and became a reciter of American folk songs, a narrator on the radio, and (during the Second World War) a popular defender of American civilization. For many years he has devoted much time and study to the career and thought of Abraham Lincoln, on whom he is now considered to be an authority. His home is in Flat Rock, N. C.

No poetry of the period occasioned more controversy upon its appearance than did the early volumes of Sandburg. After a brief struggle, however, the criticism stressing the slangy and vulgar in these volumes gave way to that pointing out the crude eloquence of some of the pieces and the tenderness and fancy shown in others.

In Reckless Ecstasy (pamphlet), 1904; *Chicago Poems,* 1916; *Cornhuskers,* 1918; *The Chicago Race Riots, July, 1919,* 1919; *Smoke and Steel,* 1920; *Slabs of the Sunburnt West,* 1922; *Rootabaga Stories,* 1922; *Rootabaga Pigeons,* 1923; *Selected Poems* (ed. Rebecca West), 1926; *Abraham Lincoln: The Prairie Years,* 1926; *The American Songbag* (compiler), 1927; *Good Morning, America,* 1928; *Steichen, the Photographer,* 1929; *Early Moon,* 1930; *Potato Face,* 1930; *Mary Lincoln* (with P. M. Angle), 1932; *The People, Yes,* 1936; *Lincoln and Whitman Miscellany,* 1938; *Abraham Lincoln: The War Years,* 1939; *Bronze Wood,* 1941; *Home Front Memo,* 1943; *Remembrance Rock,* 1948.

For life and criticism, see: Amy

Lowell, *Tendencies in Modern American Poetry*, 1917, pp. 200–33; Harry Hansen, *Midwest Portraits*, 1923, pp. 17–92; Conrad Aiken, *Scepticisms*, 1919, pp. 143–49; Stuart P. Sherman, *Americans*, 1922, pp. 239–46; Louis Untermeyer, *American Poetry since 1900*, 1923, pp. 67–88; Paul Rosenfeld, *Port of New York*, 1924, pp. 65–82; Carl Van Doren, *Many Minds*, 1924, pp. 136–51; Bruce Weirick, *From Whitman to Sandburg in American Poetry*, 1924, pp. 210–20; Llewellyn Jones, *First Impressions*, 1925, pp. 53–69; T. K. Whipple, *Spokesmen*, 1928, pp. 161–84; Karl Detzer, *Carl Sandburg*, 1941.

506. CHICAGO. Appeared in *Poetry*, Mar., 1914, winning Helen H. Levinson Prize; collected, with A FENCE (507), in *Chicago Poems*, 1916.

507. MAG. Also in *Chicago Poems*, 1916.

509. TO A CONTEMPORARY BUNK-SHOOTER. In *Chicago Poems*, 1916, but previously in *Masses*. The "Bunkshooter" was the Rev. William ["Billy"] Sunday, former ball-player and popular evangelist.

509. MEMOIR OF A PROUD BOY. In the Ludlow strike, soldiers turned machine guns on to a tent colony of strikers early on the morning of Apr. 19, 1914, killing men, women, and children and setting fire to the tents. Louis Tikas (10) was slain trying to lead women and children; Don Magregor led the reprisals of the miners from the hills as described by Sandburg.

511. FOUR PRELUDES ON PLAYTHINGS OF THE WIND. In *New Repub.*, July 21, 1920; collected in *Smoke and Steel*, 1920.

512. CHEAP BLUE. In *Bookman*, Oct., 1928; collected in *Good Morning, America*, 1928.

513. [THEY HAVE YARNS] and [THE PEOPLE WILL LIVE ON] are Sections 45 and 107 from *The People, Yes*, 1936. For Section 45 the notes to the Folk Lore material in vols. II and III in this series are helpful. See also F. A. Botkin, *A Treasury of American Folklore*, 1944.

518. [THE "HOUSE DIVIDED" SPEECH]. In *Abraham Lincoln: The Prairie Years*, 1926. ¶519. "*If we could first know where we are*, etc.'" The speech from which Sandburg quotes is printed in full in Nicolay and Hay, *Abraham Lincoln: Complete Works*, 1894, Vol. I, pp. 240–46.

Randolph (Silliman) Bourne
(1886–1918)

Randolph Silliman Bourne was born in Bloomfield, N. J., on May 30, 1886. He attended Columbia University, and during the years 1913–14 studied in London and Paris. Although a cripple and in poor health, he was energetic and made the force of his opinions felt among his contemporaries. He contributed to *The North American Review, The Atlantic Monthly, The New Republic*, and *Scribner's Magazine*; he served as contributing editor of *The Dial*, and helped to issue *The Seven Arts*. He fearlessly opposed America's entrance into the World War. He died on Dec. 22, 1918.

He was an ardent and engaging critic, deeply concerned with the possibilities of a richer intellectual life in America. He sought to encourage more intelligence, better taste, a greater degree of artistic and social sympathy. "His was a more corrosive mind than Croly's, . . . more deeply founded than Lippmann's, more incisive and flashing than Beard's."

Youth and Life, 1913; *The Gary Schools*, 1916; *Toward an Enduring Peace* (compilation), 1916; *Education and Living*, 1917; *Untimely Papers* (ed. James Oppenheim), 1919; *Vagabonds of the Sea*, by Maurice Larrouy (translation), 1919; *The History of a Literary Radical* (ed. Van Wyck Brooks), 1920.

For life, see: Ernest Sutherland Bates, "Randolph Bourne," *D.A.B.*, II, p. 486; Louis Filler, *Randolph Bourne*, 1943. For criticism, see: Van Wyck Brooks, *Emerson and Others*, 1927, pp. 121–46; Paul Rosenfeld, "Randolph Bourne," *Dial*, LXXV, pp. 545–61; Dorothy Teall, *Bookman*, LXV, pp. 590–99. *The History of a Literary Radical* contains autobiographical matter.

520. UNIVERSAL SERVICE AND EDUCATION. In *The New Republic*, July 1, 1916, as "A Moral Equivalent for Military Service"; reprinted as Ch. IX in *Education and Living*, 1917. ¶520. "*Moral equivalent for war*." An approximation of the title of a pamphlet which James wrote for the Association for International Conciliation (1910), collected in *Memories and Studies*, 1911. ¶521. "Plattsburg," the first volunteer Reserve Officers' Training Camp, founded by Theodore Roosevelt and Leonard Wood.

Van Wyck Brooks (1886–)

Van Wyck Brooks was born in Plain-field, N. J., on Feb. 16, 1886. After at-tending the local schools, he entered Harvard University, from which he was graduated in 1907. From 1907 to 1909 he was employed by Doubleday, Page and Company, and from 1911 to 1913 was a lecturer at Leland Stanford Uni-versity. In the meantime he had married and published his first book, *The Wine of the Puritans*, 1909, a critical volume. In 1915 appeared *America's Coming-of-Age*, which first brought him to the at-tention of a considerable body of stu-dents and readers. From 1915 to 1918 he worked for the Century Company, and during the years 1920–24 was asso-ciate editor of *The Freeman*. With Al-fred Kreymborg, Lewis Mumford, and Paul Rosenfeld, he edited the first *Amer-ican Caravan*, 1927. In 1923 he was awarded the prize of two thousand dol-lars offered by *The Dial* for distin-guished service to literature.

Brooks has unquestionably helped to direct critical thought in America during the years since 1915. He regards crit-icism as the investigation of influences and origins, and lays stress on the neces-sity of studying the general cultural background in the consideration of an author's work. His particular interest in recent years has been the completion of a series of volumes which, together, will embody the history of *belles lettres* in the U. S.

The Wine of the Puritans, 1909; *The Malady of the Ideal*, 1913; *John Adding-ton Symonds*, 1914; *America's Coming-of-Age*, 1915; *The World of H. G. Wells*, 1915; *Letters and Leadership*, 1918; *The Ordeal of Mark Twain*, 1920; *The History of a Literary Radical*, by Randolph Bourne (ed.), 1920; *The Story of Golton Connixloo*, by Camille Mayran (translation), 1920; *Paul Gauguin's Intimate Journals* (transla-tion), 1921; *Jean Jacques Rousseau*, by Henri Frédéric Amiel (translation), 1922; *Some Aspects of the Life of Jesus*, by Georges Berguer (translation, made with Mrs. Brooks), 1923; *Henry Thoreau, Bachelor of Nature*, by Léon Bazalgette (translation), 1924; *Journal of First Voyage to America*, by Christo-pher Columbus (ed.), 1924; *The Pil-grimage of Henry James*, 1925; *Summer*, by Romain Rolland (translation), 1925; *Mother and Son*, by Romain Rolland

(translation), 1927; *Emerson and Others*, 1927; *Road*, by André Chamson (translation), 1929; *Roux the Bandit*, by André Chamson (translation), 1929; *Philine*, by Henri Frédéric Amiel (trans-lation), 1930; *Crime of the Just*, by André Chamson (translation), 1930; *The Life of Emerson*, 1932; *Sketches in Criticism*, 1932; *The Flowering of New England, 1815–1865*, 1936; *New Eng-land: Indian Summer, 1865–1915*, 1940; *On Literature Today*, 1941; *Opinions of Oliver Allston*, 1941; *The World of Washington Irving*, 1944; *The Times of Melville and Whitman*, 1947; *A Chil-mark Miscellany*, 1948.

For criticism, see: Paul Rosenfeld, *Port of New York*, 1924, pp. 19–64; Joseph Warren Beach, *The Outlook for American Prose*, 1926, pp. 28–33; Edna Kenton, *Bookman*, LXII, pp. 153–58; Norman Foerster, *Bookman*, LXXII, pp. 35–45; Robert Morss Lovett, *Dial*, LXIX, pp. 293–300; Gorham B. Mun-son, *Dial*, LXXVIII, pp. 28–43; Gilbert Seldes, *Nation*, CXXI, pp. 191–92; Ed-mund Wilson, *New Repub.*, XLII, pp. 283–86; John Macy, *Sat. Rev. Lit.*, IV, p. 52; Oscar Cargill, *Coll. Eng.*, VIII, pp. 55–61; S. E. Hyman, *The Armed Vision*, 1948.

523. CONCLUSION is Chap. XXVIII of *The Flowering of New England*, 1936; revised, 1937. ¶524. "Spengler," Oswald, 1880–1936, German philosopher-histo-rian, whose cyclical theories (stated in *The Decline of the West*), Brooks uti-lizes here. ¶524. "Barrett Wendell" (1855–1921), professor at Harvard, au-thor of *A Literary History of America*. ¶524. "The querulous Lodge," Henry Cabot (1850–1924), U. S. Senator from Mass., opponent of Wilson. ¶525. "D. H. Lawrence" (1885–1930), English novelist and poet. ¶529. "Hafiz," (fl. 1350), Persian poet.

Max (Forrester) Eastman (1883–)

Max Forrester Eastman was born in Canandaigua, N. Y., on Jan. 4, 1883. He received the A.B. degree from Wil-liams College in 1905, being a friend and associate of Stuart P. Sherman; from 1907 to 1910 he studied at Colum-bia University, at the same time serving as an assistant in the department of phi-losophy. From 1913 to 1917 he was editor of *The Masses*, and during 1918–

22 editor of *The Liberator*. Since 1922 he has engaged in free lance criticism, in which field his interests are varied. In 1941 he became a roving editor for the *Reader's Digest*. He has written penetratingly of the art of the poet, and of the literary movements in contemporary America; he is even more interested in the economic and social order. He has long been a close student of the governmental experiments being made in Russia, and he was a personal friend of Leon Trotsky. His home is in Chilmark, Mass.

Child of the Amazons and Other Poems, 1913; *The Enjoyment of Poetry*, 1913; *Journalism versus Art*, 1916; *Understanding Germany*, 1916; *Colors of Life*, 1918; *The Sense of Humor*, 1921; *Leon Trotsky*, 1925; *Since Lenin Died*, 1925; *Marx and Lenin: the Science of Revolution* (London), 1926; *Venture*, 1927; *The Real Situation in Russia*, by Leon Trotsky (trans.), 1928; *Gabriel*, by Aleksandr Pushkin (trans.), 1929; *Kinds of Love*, 1931; *The Literary Mind*, 1931; *History of the Russian Revolution*, Vols. I, II, III, by Leon Trotsky (trans.), 1932–33; *Art and the Life of Action*, 1934; *Artists in Uniform*, 1934; *The Last Stand of Dialectic Materialism*, 1935; *The End of Socialism in Russia*, 1937; *Anthology for the Enjoyment of Poetry*, (ed.) 1939; *Enjoyment of Laughter*, 1939; *Marxism: Is It Science?*, 1940; *Stalin's Russia and the Crisis in Socialism*, 1940; *Heroes I Have Known*, 1942; *Lot's Wife*, 1942; *Enjoyment of Living*, 1948.

For criticism, see: George Dangerfield, *Bookman*, LXXIII, p. 445; Irwin Edman, *Nation*, CXIV, p. 373; Henry Raymond Mussey, *Nation*, CXXVII, pp. 159–60; Henry Hazlitt, *Nation*, CXXXIII, pp. 646–47; N. *Amer. Rev.*, CXCVII, pp. 858–59; Harriet Monroe, *Poetry*, II, pp. 140–42; Harriet Monroe, *Poetry*, XIII, pp. 322–26; C. I. Glicksberg, *Sewanee Rev.*, XL, pp. 323–37.

530. THE REALM OF LITERARY TRUTH. A chapter from *The Literary Mind*, 1931, which deals with "the relations between literature and science" and the advance of the latter "into fields heretofore occupied by literary eloquence." In the Preface the author points out that he has tried to "show that the neo-classic criticism and the New Humanism are both, in their essence, only a grandiose effort of the literary mind to resist this advance of science"; and that "the tend-

encies in poetic literature called 'modernism' are a retreat before this same invasion." ¶530. *"Dante"* Alighieri (1265–1321), author of the *Divine Comedy*. ¶530. *"Lucretius,"* Titus Lucretius Carus (*c.* 110–57? B.C.), Roman poet. ¶530. *"Aldous Huxley"* (1894–　　), English novelist and essayist. ¶530. *"John Donne"* (1573–1631), English metaphysical poet. ¶530. *"Einstein,"* Albert (1879–　　), German-American physicist, responsible for theory of relativity. ¶531. *"Shelley's . . . charioteers."* In *Prometheus Unbound*, II, 4. ¶531. *"Freud,"* Sigmund (1856–1939), Austrian psychoanalyst; *"John B. Watson"* (1878–　　), American behaviorist; *"Karl Marx"* (1818–83), German founder of modern Socialism. ¶531. *"Sacheverell Sitwell"* (1900–　　), English poet. ¶531. *"Julien Benda"* (1867–　　), French essayist and philosopher. ¶531. *"Descartes,"* René (1596–1650), French mathematician and philosopher; *"Galileo"* Galilei (1564–1642), Italian physicist. ¶533. *"Pascal,"* Blaise (1623–62), French mathematician and philosopher. ¶534. *"Morris Cohen"* (1880–1947), American philosopher. ¶534. *"Renan,"* Ernest (1823–92), French critic; *"Berthelot,"* Marcellin (1827–1907), French chemist. ¶535. *"Vauvenargues,"* Luc de Clapiers (1715–47), French moralist. ¶535. *"Thomas à Kempis"* (*c.* 1380–1471), author of the *Imitation of Christ*. ¶535. *"Goethe,"* Johann Wolfgang von (1749–1832), German poet and dramatist. ¶535. *"Paul Heyl"* (1872–　　), physicist, U. S. Bureau of Standards. ¶535. *"Herbert Read"* (1893–　　), English poet, essayist, novelist. ¶535. *"Gustav Lanson"* (1857–1934), French scholar. ¶536. *". . . the pretense on either side that he has spoken truth."* "In his book on *Practical Criticism*, pp. 185–6, Mr. Richards himself unintentionally brings the poet and the campaigner at a General Election into the same not very flattering category. I have criticized his books at length in a Note beginning on p. 297." (Author's note.) I. A. Richards (1893–　　), Englishman, long a teacher at Harvard, promoted "the explication of texts" and Basic English. ¶536. *"André Chénier"* (1762–1794), French revolutionary poet. ¶539. *"Kepler,"* Johann (1571–1630), German astronomer. ¶539. *"Isaac Newton"* (1642–1727), English scientist who stated the law of gravity. ¶539. *"Schell-*

ing," Friedrich W. J. (1775–1854), German philosopher. ¶539. *"Dichtung . . . Wahrheit."* Poetry . . . Truth.

540. THE SOUL OF MAN UNDER COMMUNISM is Ch. VI in *Artists in Uniform*, 1934. ¶540. *"Mensheviks."* The right, or less violent, wing of the revolutionary party in Russia. ¶540. *"Weltanshauung."* World-view or philosophy. ¶541. *"Jennings,"* Herbert Spencer (1868–　　), zoologist at Johns Hopkins University.

Lincoln Steffens (1866–1936)

The muck-raking articles of Steffens occupy a comparable place in our literature to that of the Junius Letters (though there is the distinction between a liberal and a conservative point of view). Both authors knew politics and political personalities equally well. Steffens is perhaps the greater journalist; he elicited his facts from avowed enemies and profited by no secret connections.

Born in San Francisco, Apr. 6, 1866. His father, Joseph Steffens, rose from clerkship to branch manager, then partner in a mercantile business; his mother, Elizabeth Louisa Symes, was an English immigrant girl. Boyhood was spent in the open near Sacramento, where his father was transferred in 1870. After attending a military academy in San Mateo, he failed in Greek, Latin, and "enough other studies" to be refused admission to college. Tutored for a year. Attended University of California, 1885–89; spent three years abroad, studying philosophy, in Heidelberg, Leipzig, and Paris. Married Josephine Bontecou, 1891, and returned to America, 1892. His father, unaware of his marriage, insisted he become self-supporting; thus a journalistic career began. Reporter and asst. city editor, N. Y. *Evening Post*, 1892–98; city editor, *Commercial Advertiser*, 1898–1902; managing editor, *McClure's Magazine*, 1902–06; associate editor, the *American* and *Everybody's*, 1906–11. During his connection with *McClure's* he began muck-raking. First article, "Tweed Days in St. Louis," *McClure's*, Oct., 1902. Later enterprises took him to Mexico and Europe. Member of Bullitt Commission to Russia, 1919. After the death of his first wife, he married Ella Winter in Paris, 1924. Convinced of the permanence of the Russian Revolution, Steffens became a defender of the U.S.S.R.

and a crusader for communism in the last years of his life. He died on August 9, 1936.

The Shame of the Cities, 1904; *The Struggle for Self Government*, 1906; *Upbuilders*, 1909; *The Least of These*, 1910; *Moses in Red*, 1926; *Autobiography*, 2 vols., 1931; *Lincoln Steffens Speaking*, 1936.

For life and criticism, see: *Letters of Lincoln Steffens* (ed. Ella Winter and Granville Hicks), 2 vols., 1938; Louis Filler, *Crusaders for American Liberalism*, 1939.

543. THE SHAME OF THE CITIES: PHILADELPHIA. In *McClure's*, July, 1903; collected, 1904. Later Steffens said: "Reform is the abnormal thing, and when the reformers fail, as they do and must, the city or state falls back to the norm, the corrupt norm." For reaction to *Shame of the Cities*, see: A. Hodder, *Bookman*, May, 1904; W. A. White, *McClure's*, June, 1904; Anon., *Cur. Lit.*, June, 1904. ¶544. *"James McManes and the Gas Ring."* A political boss and his fellows whose control of the city during the administration of W. S. Stokley was broken by the "Committee of 100," 1880–83. ¶544. *"Tweed Stage."* The Tweed Ring (Boss W. M. Tweed, Mayor Oakley Hall, Peter B. Sweeney, Richard B. Connolly) stole $45,000,000 from New York City, 1869–71. ¶545. *"Bullitt Law."* "An act to provide better government for cities," framed by J. C. Bullitt, 1882; in effect 1887. ¶545. *"Edwin H. Fitler."* Manufacturer (1825–96), mayor, 1887–91. ¶545. *"Matthew S. Quay."* Senator and political boss (1833–1904). ¶545. *"Edwin S. Stuart."* Mayor, 1890–94; later governor.

546. PROPHECY is the next to the last section in *The Autobiography of L. S.*, 1931. Compare Steffens' attitude towards reform with the political pessimism reflected in *The Education of Henry Adams*.

Granville Hicks (1901–　　)

Puritan and Yankee, Granville Hicks was born in Exeter, N. H., on Sept. 9, 1901. After taking his bachelor's degree at Harvard in 1923, he was instructor in English at Smith College until 1928. That year he devoted to getting his M.A. degree at Harvard, which won for him an appointment as an assistant professor at Rensselaer Polytechnic Institute in

1929. His resignation from the latter institution was forced because of his political views in 1935. The previous years he had become a member of the editorial staff of the *New Masses* magazine. He continued on the staff and in the Communist Party until 1939, when he resigned from both to emphasize his disapproval of the blind endorsement by the American Communist Party of the Russo-German pact. During the academic year 1938–39 he was counsellor to the Program in American Civilization at Harvard; and from 1941 to 1943 he was chairman of the radio program, "Speaking of Books." He lives in Grafton, N. Y., and takes a lively part in community affairs with his wife Dorothy Dyer Hicks, whom he married in 1925. They have one child, a daughter.

The Great Tradition, 1933, rev. ed., 1935; *One of Us* (with Lynd Ward), 1935; *John Reed,* 1935; *Proletarian Literature in the U. S.* (co-ed.), 1935; *I Like America,* 1938; *The Letters of Lincoln Steffens* (ed. with Ella Winter), 1938; *Figures of Transition,* 1939; *The First to Awaken,* 1940; *Only One Storm,* 1942; *Behold Trouble,* 1944; *Small Town,* 1946.

For life and criticism, see: *I Like America* and *Small Town; Cur. Biog.,* May, 1942; J. T. Farrell, "Mr. Hicks: Critical Vulgarian," *Am. Spect.,* Apr., 1936; C. I. Glicksberg, "Granville Hicks and Marxist Criticism," *Sewanee Rev.,* Apr., 1937.

551. LITERATURE AND REVOLUTION. Address before the College Conference on English, Central Atlantic States, Dec. 1, 1934; pub. in the *Eng. Jour.* (Col. ed.), Mar., 1935. ¶551. "*Baudelaire,*" Pierre Charles (1821–67), French lyric poet. ¶551. "*I. A. Richards.*" See notes to p. 536. ¶553. "*Kenneth Burke*" (1897–), abstruse left-wing critic, sometimes called "the critics' critic." ¶554. *H. G. Wells's comments.*" The British journalist-novelist held views completely antithetical to those of James. See his burlesque of the latter in *Boon* as well as in *Experiment in Autobiography.* ¶554. "*Joseph Wood Krutch*" (1893–), contemporary journalist, employed by Columbia. ¶555. "*Piaget,*" Jean (1896–), French child psychologist. ¶555. "*tabula rasa.*" A scraped tablet. ¶555. "*Ludwig Lewisohn*" (1883–), Freudian critic, author of *Expression in America.* ¶558. "*Chartist,*" English Workingmen's Movement, 1838–

48, which embodied its aspirations in the "People's Charter. ¶558. "*Harriet Martineau*" (1802–76), British bluestocking. ¶558. "*John Strachey.*" Contemporary British radical, visitor to the U. S. ¶561. "*Diego Rivera*" (1886–), Mexican muralist, professing communist, repudiated by the party. ¶564. "*Jack Conroy's first novel,*" *The Disinherited,* a "proletarian" production; "*Gladys Hasty Carroll's,*" *As the Earth Turns,* a novel about an immigrant-farmer family in Maine; "*Isidore Schneider,*" proletarian poet, author of *Comrade-Mister;* "*Yvor Winters,*" contemporary aesthete and poet.

Edmund Wilson (1895–)

Edmund Wilson was born in Red Bank, N. J., on May 8, 1895. He attended the Hill School, Pottstown, Pa., and then Princeton University, from which he was graduated in 1916. At Princeton he was a personal friend of F. Scott Fitzgerald. After spending a year and a half in a hospital unit in France during World War I, he returned to the United States and joined the staff of the *New York Sun,* later serving on those of *Vanity Fair* and *The New Republic.* Despite his journalistic work, he found time for much scholarly study, the assimilation of wide reading, and the sound development of his critical powers. His criticism shows a range of sympathy, and an intelligent interest in the whole contemporary social, economic, and cultural state of affairs. This interest led him after 1930 to join the Marxist group of critics for a time. In 1944 he became a book reviewer for *The New Yorker,* which he helped to make a surprising agency of critical guidance. His home is in Wellfleet, Mass.

The Undertaker's Garland (with J. P. Bishop), 1922; *Discordant Encounters,* 1927; *I Thought of Daisy,* 1929; *Poets, Farewell!,* 1929; *Axel's Castle,* 1931; *Foster and Fish,* 1932; *American Jitters,* 1932; *Travels in Two Democracies,* 1936; *This Room and This Gin and These Sandwiches,* 1937; *Triple Thinkers,* 1938; *To the Finland Station,* 1940; *The Boys in the Back Room,* 1941; *The Wound and the Bow,* 1941; *Note-Books of Night,* 1942; (ed.) *Shock of Recognition,* 1943; *Memoirs of Hecate County,* 1946; *Europe without Baedeker,* 1947.

For criticism, see: *Henri Peyre,*

Writers and Their Critics, 1944; Henry Hazlitt, *Nation,* CXXXII, pp. 245–46; Morton D. Zabel, *Poetry,* XXXV, pp. 222–26; *Sat. Rev. Lit.,* III, p. 700; F. O. Matthiessen, *Yale Rev.,* n.s. XX, pp. 854–56; E. K. Brown, *U. of Toronto Quar.,* XI, pp. 105–11; Christian Gauss, *Princeton U. Lib. Chron.,* V, pp. 41–50. See also: Arthur Mizener, "Edmund Wilson: A Check-List," *Princeton U. Lib. Chron.,* V, pp. 62–78.

565. SYMBOLISM. Appeared as "A Preface to Modern Literature" in *New Repub.,* Mar. 20, 1929; it forms the introductory chapter to *Axel's Castle,* 1931; to which ¶565. ". . . *in this book*" refers. ¶565. "*W. B. Yeats*" (1865–1939), leader of the Irish renascence; "*Marcel Proust*" (1871–1922), French novelist, notable for "total recall"; "*Paul Valéry*" (1871–1945), French symbolist poet. ¶565. "*Le Misanthrope*," "*Berenice*," etc. The authors are named on p. 566, as are those in the next list. ¶566. "*A. N. Whitehead*" (1861–1949), English mathematician and philosopher. ¶566. "*La Rochefoucauld,*" François de (1613–80), French fashioner of maxims. ¶567. "*Alfred de Vigny*" (1797–1863), French poet. ¶567. "*Zola,*" Émile (1840–1902), French naturalistic novelist. ¶568. "*The Origin of Species.*" Darwin's great work on evolution (1859). ¶568. "*Gautier,*" Théophile (1811–72); "*Leconte de Lisle,*" Charles Marie (1818–94); "*Hérédia,*" José Maria de (1842–1905) —all identified in the text. ¶569. "*Ibsen,*" Henrik (1828–1906), Norwegian founder of the modern drama. ¶569. "*Bouvard et Pécuchet, L'Education Sentimentale.*" Works by Gustave Flaubert (1821–80), author of *Madame Bovary* [below]. ¶569. "*Huysmans,*" Joris Karl (1848–1907), French novelist. ¶569. "*Mallarmé,*" Stéphane (1842–98), French symbolist poet; "*Rimbaud,*" Arthur (1854–91), French symbolist poet. ¶570. "*Chateaubriand,*" François René (1768–1848), Romantic primitivist; "*Musset,*" Alfred de (1810–57), French poet. ¶570. *Gérard de Nerval* (1808–55), eccentric French poet. ¶570. "*Baudelaire,*" Pierre Charles (1821–67), French lyric poet. ¶571. "*Comme de longs echos. . . .*" "As protracted echoes in the distance mingle so perfumes, colors, sounds correspond." ¶571. "*Michelet,*" Jules (1798–1874), French historian. ¶571. "*Rabelais,*" François (c. 1490–1553), French satirist; "*Ronsard,*" Pierre de (1524–85), formal French

poet. ¶573. "*Donner un sens. . . .*" "To give a purer sense to the words of the tribe." ¶573. "*Albert Thibaudet*" (1874–1936), French critic. ¶574. "*Remy de Gourmont*" (1858–1915), French critic. ¶575. "*Wagner,*" Richard (1813–83), German composer; "*Villiers de L'Isle Adam,*" Jean M. M. P. A. (1838–89), French poet; "*Maeterlinck,*" Maurice (1862–1948), Belgian symbolist playwright; "*D'Annunzio,*" Gabriele (1863–1938), Italian poet and patriot. ¶575. "*Lockhart* [John Gibson (1794–1854)] . . . *Jeffrey* [Lord Francis (1773–1850)]." Scotch reviewers. ¶576. "*fin de siècle,*" "end of the century."

576. FINAL REFLECTIONS is the last chapter in *Travels in Two Democracies,* 1936. For Mr. Wilson's later political, or non-political, views, see: Granville Hicks, "The Intransigence of Edmund Wilson," *Antioch Rev.,* Dec., 1946. ¶576. "*Komsomol.*" Intermediate training group between the Communist Party and the Young Pioneers, for aspirants for party membership.

Max Lerner (1902–   )

Son of Benjamin and Bessie (Podel) Lerner, Max Lerner was born in Minsk, Russia, on Dec. 20, 1902. He was brought to the United States when he was five. After taking his B.A. at Yale in 1923, he studied law there for a year and then transferred to Washington University in St. Louis, where he received his M.A. in 1925. He took his doctorate in political science at the Robert Brookings Graduate School of Economics and Government, Washington, D. C., in 1927. He was successively assistant editor and managing editor of the *Encyclopedia of the Social Sciences,* 1927–32. A lecturer at Sarah Lawrence College, Bronxville, N. Y., from 1932 to 1935, Lerner occupied a similar position in the department of government, Harvard University, in the academic year, 1935–36. In 1936, also, he became editor of the *Nation,* a post he held two years, resigning to become professor of political science in Williams College in 1938. Lerner left Williams to become editorial director of *PM* in 1943, a post he held until the paper was sold in 1948.

It Is Later Than You Think, 1938, rev. ed., 1943; *Ideas Are Weapons,* 1939; *Ideas for the Ice Age,* 1941; *The*

Mind and Faith of Justice Holmes, 1943; *Public Journal*, 1945.

For life, see: *Who's Who in America*, 1948–49; *Public Journal*.

578. HISTORY IS WRITTEN BY THE SURVIVORS. The "Epilogue" to *It Is Later Than You Think*, 1938. ¶578. "*Genghis*" Khan (1162–1227), conqueror of most of Asia and E. Europe. ¶580. "*T. E. Hulme*." Young Englishman associated with Pound in New Poetry movement, c. 1910. ¶580. "*Sorel*," Georges, syndicalist and author of *Reflections on Violence*, 1910. ¶580. "*Lessing*," Gotthold (1729–81), German critic. ¶581. "*sans culotte*": "without breeches," i.e., the French republicans.

Richard Wright (1908–   )

Richard Wright was born on a plantation near Natchez, Miss., on Sept. 4, 1908. His father was a mill worker and his mother was a country school teacher. When Richard was five, his father deserted his mother and for several years he experienced much hardship, a record of which he has set down in *Black Boy*. All his formal education was obtained at a Seventh Day Adventist school. At fifteen he began to work in Memphis at odd jobs; escaping to Chicago, he got such employment as he could find and counted himself lucky to be on the Federal Writers Project in 1935. Meanwhile he had joined the Communist Party primarily to have the advantages of the John Reed club; when this was liquidated in an arbitrary change of policy, he left the Party. In 1937 he came to New York City; two years later he was awarded a Guggenheim Fellowship. Since then he has lived in Brooklyn and in Paris.

Uncle Tom's Children, 1938, rev. ed., 1940; *Native Son*, 1940; *12 Million Black Voices*, 1941; *Black Boy*, 1945.

For life, see: *Black Boy*; *Who's Who in America*, 1948–49; "I Tried to Be a Communist," *Atlantic*, Aug., 1944. For criticism, see: H. L. Gloster, *Negro Voices in American Fiction*, 1948.

581. BRIGHT AND MORNING STAR. In the revised edition of *Uncle Tom's Children*, 1940; it had appeared in *New Masses* some time in 1938. To Wright and many other Negroes of his generation an "Uncle Tom" is one of his race who turns the other cheek whatever the provocation—a "Booker Washington Negro."

Horace (Victor) Gregory (1898–   )

English, Scotch-Irish, and German strains are united in the composition of Horace Gregory, who was born to Henry B. and Anna (Henkel) Gregory in Milwaukee, on Apr. 10, 1898. His early schooling was got at home, but he enjoyed the use of a large library belonging to an uncle. When he was sixteen, he was entered in both the German-English Academy in his native city and the Milwaukee Academy of Fine Arts, where he studied painting until 1919. He took his B.A. at the University of Wisconsin, where he cultivated a taste for Latin poetry. After his graduation in 1923, he supported himself rather badly at free lance writing while living in the Chelsea neighborhood in New York City. Two years later he was married to a Russian refugee and poet, Marya Zaturenska. Since 1934 he has taught writing and lectured on poetry at Sarah Lawrence College, in Bronxville, N. Y.

Chelsea Rooming House, 1930; *The Poems of Catullus* (tr.), 1931; *No Retreat*, 1933; *Pilgrim of the Apocalypse*, 1933; *Chorus for Survival*, 1935; *Poems: 1930–1940*, 1941; *Triumph of Life*, 1943; *The Shield of Achilles*, 1944; *A History of American Poetry, 1900–1940* (with Marya Zaturenska), 1946.

For life and criticism, see: *Who's Who in America, 1948–49*; R. P. Blackmur, "The Ribbon of Craft," *Poetry*, Jul., 1933; Kenneth Burke, "The Hope in Tragedy," *Poetry*, Jul., 1935.

602. COLUMBO DOMINICO. In *Chelsea Rooming House*, 1930. The text of this and other Gregory poems is that of *Poems: 1930–1940*, 1941. ¶603. "*Robespierre*" (34), Maximilien (1758–1794), French revolutionary, as was also Jean Paul "*Marat*" (35) (1743–93). "*Lesbia*" (36). Greek poetess, famous for the passion of her verse.

604. EMERSON: LAST DAYS AT CONCORD. In *No Retreat*, 1933. To epitomize: America, at the time of the Concord fight, was filled with the proper revolutionary spirit; the counter-symbol, "*Dover's beach*" (1. 6), implies that America is sunk in the universal death (see Arnold's poem). Emerson, reconciler of opposites, knows this fact and deplores it. His actual "*orchard*" is utopia.

605. NEW YORK, CASSANDRA. In *No Retreat*, 1933. Cassandra was the un-

popular prophetess of the fall of Troy. ¶605. *"Oceans of grain,"* symbol of overproduction; *"Macbeth"* here stands for the capitalist; *"Canopus"* ostensible reference to second brightest star is meant, more probably, to remind the reader of the Canopic vases used as burial urns in the ancient town of Canopus near Alexandria; *"Birnam wood,"* coupled with the leap of Macbeth, this allusion to the fulfillment of the Shakesperean prophecy, suggests the working out of the Marxian prediction that capitalism contains the seeds of its own destruction; ". . . *to Salt Lake City,"* an allusion to Western decadence, in the manner of Eliot; *Cerberus,* the unwilling watchdog of capitalism, drawn from the proletariat. ¶606. *"An old king."* Oedipus. To M. L. Rosenthal (*Chief Poets of the American Depression,* unpub. N. Y. U. dissertation) the darkness in which the poem ends—for this is the *meaning* of the allusion to Oedipus—is Laurentian rather than Marxian.

Kenneth (Flexner) Fearing (1902–   )

Born in Oak Park, Ill., to a Chicago lawyer, Harry L. Fearing, and his wife, Olive (Flexner) Fearing, Kenneth Fearing grew up in the vicinity of the great midland city and attended the University of Wisconsin, where he was a friend of Horace Gregory who was later to satirize him as "McAlpin Garfinkle, Poet." After receiving his B.A. in 1924, Fearing was first employed as a salesman and then as a mill hand; he later got some experience in newspaper work and decided to go to New York in quest of a career. In the metropolis he did reporting, editorial work, and publicity while establishing himself as a writer. He was married to Rachel Meltzer in 1933, by whom he had a son. Separated from his first wife, he married Nan Lurie in 1945. He confesses that he voted for Lafollette in 1924, for W. Z. Foster in 1932.

Angel Arms, 1929; *Poems,* 1935; *Dead Reckoning,* 1938; *The Hospital,* 1939; *Collected Poems,* 1940; *Dagger of the Mind,* 1941; *Clark Gifford's Body,* 1942; *Afternoon of a Pawnbroker,* 1943; *The Big Clock,* 1946.

For life and criticism, see: S. J. Kunitz & H. Haycraft, *Twentieth Century Authors,* 1942; Horace Gregory, "A

Contrast in Satires," *Poetry,* Feb., 1937; T. C. Wilson, "The Real Thing," *Poetry,* Apr., 1939; Macha Rosenthal, "Kenneth Fearing's Poetry," *Poetry,* Jul., 1944; C. D. Abbott, "The Politics of Mr. Fearing," *Univ. Colo. Stud.,* Oct., 1945.

606. CULTURAL NOTES. In *Angel Arms,* 1929. Texts for Fearing are those of the *Collected Poems,* 1940. *"Max Nordau"* (9). German critic, 1849–1923, author of a fantastic book, *Degeneracy,* in which he sought to prove most modern movements in art, music, and literature are degenerate.

607. DENOUEMENT. In *Poems,* 1935.

610. DIRGE. In *Poems,* 1935, reflecting, of course, the stock market crash of 1929.

Muriel Rukeyser (1913–   )

Born in New York City on Dec. 15, 1913, Muriel Rukeyser got her early education at the Ethical Culture and Fieldstone schools, then entered Vassar in 1930. She was forced to give up college (although she attended two summer sessions at Columbia after this) because of the depression. She became literary editor of *The Student Review* in 1932 and went as a committee member to investigate labor and Negro problems. Thus she was present at the second Scottsboro trial in Alabama, was arrested, and contracted typhoid. Recovered, she took the ground course in the Roosevelt School of Aviation, but was not permitted to fly since she was still a minor. She did, however, assimilate material for her long poem, "Theory of Flight." She had a quick round of office work, tried theatres and theatre magazines. Miss Rukeyser visited Gauley Bridge, the focal scene in Virginia of the silicosis "poisoning" cases, in 1936, and in that year she reached the Spanish border on the day the Civil War began. *U.S. 1* was written in California after her return; *A Turning Wind* was finished in Mexico. She joined the staff of *Decision* in 1941.

Theory of Flight, 1935; *U.S. 1,* 1938; *A Turning Wind,* 1939; *Wake Island,* 1942; *Willard Gibbs,* 1943; *Beast in View,* 1944; *The Elegies,* 1947; *The Green Wave,* 1948.

For life and criticism, see: S. J. Kunitz and H. Haycraft, *Twentieth Century Authors,* 1942; S. V. Benét, "Foreword," *Theory of Flight;* Louis Untermeyer,

"The Language of Muriel Rukeyser," *Sat. Rev. Lit.*, Aug. 10, 1940; H. Gregory and M. Zaturenska, *A History of American Poetry*, 1946.

611. CITATION FOR HORACE GREGORY. In *Theory of Flight*, 1935. This is a volume in the "Yale Series of Younger Poets," edited by Stephen Vincent Benét. The poetess and Gregory are now estranged.

612. FOUR IN A FAMILY. In *Theory of Flight*, 1935.

613. BOY WITH HIS HAIR CUT SHORT. In *U.S. 1*, 1938.

George Ade (1866–1944)

Born in Kentland, Ind., Feb. 9, 1866, George Ade was the only son of John Ade, an English emigrant, engaged in banking, and Adaline Bush. Ade was graduated from Purdue University in 1887. Reporter for Lafayette *Morning News;* when paper became defunct, sold patent medicines (see *Doc' Horne*). In 1890, "lit out" for Chicago; reported for *Morning News*, later the *Record*. Success of his World Fair stories made him head of a department called "Stories of the Street." His column appeared next to Eugene Field's "Sharps and Flats"; when Field died, Ade got his desk. Created "Artie" in 1895. In 1898 "ran up against the fable of the old serio-comic form"; created the first of the *Fables in Slang*, "The Blonde Girl Who Married a Bucket-Shop Man." Widely copied, this led to a book contract and fame.

Artie, 1896; *Pink Marsh*, 1897; *Doc' Horne*, 1899; *Fables in Slang*, 1899; *More Fables*, 1900; *Forty Modern Fables*, 1901; *The Girl Proposition*, 1902; *The Sultan of Sulu*, 1902; *People You Know*, 1903; *Circus Day*, 1903; *Peggy from Paris*, 1903; *Breaking into Society*, 1904; *True Bills*, 1904; *The Sho-Gun*, 1904; *The College Widow*, 1904; *The Bad Samaritan*, 1905; *Just Out of College*, 1905; *In Pastures New*, 1906; *Marse Covington*, 1906; *Mrs. Peckham's Carouse*, 1906; *The Slim Princess*, 1907; *Father and the Boys*, 1907; *The Fair Co-ed*, 1908; *The Old Town*, 1909; *Knocking the Neighbors*, 1912; *Ade's Fables*, 1914; *Nettie*, 1914; *Hand-Made Fables*, 1920; *Single Blessedness*, 1922; *Bang! Bang!*, 1928; *The Old-Fashioned Bar*, 1931; *The Living Writings* (ed. F. C. Kelly), 1947.

For life, see: E. F. Harkins, *Little Pilgrimages*, II, 1903; Fred C. Kelly, *George Ade, Warmhearted Satirist*, 1947. For criticism, see: George Whicher, "Minor Humorists," *CHAL;* H. L. Mencken, *Prejudices, I;* M. J. Moses, *The American Dramatist*, 1917.

614. THE FABLE OF THE SLIM GIRL. First of *Fables in Slang*, 1899. Both Ade and Dunne got suggestions from John Kendrick Bangs, but inspiration for the *Fables in Slang* is probably G. W. Carryl's *Fables for the Frivolous*, 1893. This is an important item in the so-called "revolt from the village," though not mentioned in Van Doren, *Contemp. Am. Novelists*, pp. 146 ff. Ade's relation to Mencken and others needs study. ¶614. "*Life is real . . .*": H. W. Longfellow's "A Psalm of Life," ll. 5–6. ¶614. "*Lucile*": Sentimental poem by "Owen Meredith" (Edward Robert Bulwer-Lytton, 1831–91), a great favorite in "household editions."

George Horace Lorimer (1868–1937)

Born in Louisville, Ky., Oct. 6, 1868, George Horace Lorimer was the son of Arabella Burford and the Rev. Dr. George Claude Lorimer, who was one of the most successful divines of his day, occupying pulpits in Louisville, Albany, Boston, Chicago, and New York.

Graduating from Mosely High School, Chicago, he attended Colby and Yale. After eight years' employment in the packing firm of Philip G. Armour, he became secretary to Mr. Armour—perhaps the original of "Old Gorgon" Graham. Married Alma Viola Ennis, June 6, 1893. Reporter for Boston *Post*, he was assigned to "cover the churches" because his father was then pastor of Tremont Temple. Surfeited after four years, he went to Philadelphia as literary editor of the *Sat. Eve. Post*. After a single year he became editor-in-chief, Mar. 17, 1899; vice-president of Curtis Publishing Company, 1927. Was made Chevalier of the Legion of Honor and Commander in Order of the Crown of Italy. Lorimer was in his life-time the object of violent attacks; George Sterling's "The Black Hound Bays," for example, is known to every parlor socialist.

Letters from a Self-Made Merchant to His Son, 1902; *Old Gorgon Graham*, 1904; *The False Gods*, 1906; *Jack Spurlock—Prodigal*, 1908.

For life and criticism, see: E. F. Harkins, *Little Pilgrimages*, II, 1903; F. L. Pattee, *The New American Literature*, 1930; Upton Sinclair, *Money Writes*, 1927.

615. LETTER I is from *The Letters of a Self-Made Merchant to His Son*, a series of twenty which ran in *Sat. Eve. Post*, 1901, collected, 1902; parodied in C. E. Merriman, *Letters from a Son to His Self-Made Father*, 1903.

Frederick Winslow Taylor
(1856–1915)

Born in Germantown, Pa., on Mar. 20, 1856, Frederick Winslow Taylor was the youngest son of Franklin and Emily (Winslow) Taylor, people of easy circumstance. The family was a bookish family, the father more interested in literature than in his profession of law, the mother affiliated with all the causes championed by Lucretia Mott. From his mother Taylor got his earliest education, but he had two years of study and eighteen months of travel in France and Germany before entering Phillips Exeter Academy in 1872. Graduating in two years, he injured his eyesight and had to abandon his plan to study law at Harvard. He does not appear to have reflected ever on the implications of this experience. For four years, 1874–78, Taylor was employed in the shops of the Enterprise Hydraulic Works, in Philadelphia, where he learned what were to be for him the very useful trades of machinist and pattern maker. Then he began work with the Midvale Steel Company as a common laborer. In six years, however, he was chief engineer. In 1883 he was granted the M.E. degree *in course* from Stevens Institute of Technology, having completed the work while carrying on his job. From 1890 to 1893 he was general manager of the Manufacturing Investment Company, then he set up the consulting business in Philadelphia which made him famous. The Bethlehem Steel Company utilized his full services between 1898 and 1903. Thereafter he had numerous connections with industry and was "investigated" by Congress. In addition to his pioneer consulting service, Taylor aided American industry by contributing over 100 patented inventions and numerous processes. In 1911 the Society to Promote the Science of Management was founded, which

became the Taylor Society, after his death on March 20, 1915. Married to Louise Spooner in 1884, Taylor adopted three children when his marriage was childless. He was half of the tennis doubles championship team of the U. S. in 1881.

"A Piece Rate System," *Trans. of Am. Soc. Mech. Engineers*, 1895; "Shop Management," *Ibid.*, 1903; *Principles of Scientific Management*, 1911; "Taylor System of Shop Management," *House Report 52* (62 Cong., 1 Sess.).

For life, see: F. B. Copley, *Frederick W. Taylor, Father of Scientific Management*, 2 vols., 1923.

618. FUNDAMENTALS OF SCIENTIFIC MANAGEMENT is Chapt. I in *The Principles of Scientific Management*, 1911. For an attack on Taylor, see: John Dos Passos, "The American System," pp. 1049–52, in this text.

Henry (Brooks) Adams
(1838–1918)

Born on Mt. Vernon St., in the shadow of Boston State House, Feb. 16, 1838, of a line unrivaled for individuality, if not for distinction. Son of Charles Francis Adams; grandson of John Quincy Adams; great-grandson of John Adams. His mother was Abigail Brooks, daughter of the wealthiest man in Boston. The conversation of intimates of his father—Palfrey, Dana, Sumner—was the greatest educational factor of his youth, though he was formally enrolled in the school of Mr. Dixwell. His tastes dictated the poets and historians of the 18th century. In season, he went to Harvard but made no effort to distinguish himself; was graduated in the middle of his class. Agassiz and Lowell (who permitted him to read in his study) stirred his interest without affecting his energies. In Nov., 1858, his extended travels (symbolic of a life-quest for an intellectual idol) began with a trip to Berlin to study civil law. Unfamiliar with the German language, he lost interest; after dallying in Berlin and Dresden, he drifted down into Italy in 1860. Garibaldi's red shirts were then outside Palermo; Adams managed through the American minister to meet the liberator. Two letters to the Boston *Courier* described his impressions; but his sympathies were not enlisted (like those of Margaret Fuller) in the Italian cause. He returned to the United States in Nov., 1860.

Served his father in Washington as secretary; with the Civil War came his father's appointment to London as Ambassador. Henry preferred the army, but went to England, serving his father until 1868. Though extraordinarily active, socially and in line with his duties, he yet found time for serious study of John Stuart Mill, De Tocqueville, Comte. Desire for expression led to an essay on Capt. John Smith for *N. Am. Rev.*, followed by two very solid articles, the product of reading and research, on British finance. It is plain now that Henry Adams might have made a name for himself in the field of economics had he persisted: he was shrewd and discerning; moreover, he was fearless. On his return he found a different America than he had left in 1861. He tried to adjust himself to this new world and chose Washington for a vantage point. For a few months he busied himself with finance and politics (possibly he hoped for a political career), and climaxed his economic writings with an article, "The New York Gold Conspiracy," so bold and vigorous that it was rejected by two magazines before being printed by the *Edinburgh Review*. He strangely eschewed economic writing thereafter, probably not realizing his gift and opportunity.

In 1870, at the instigation of his family, he was offered an opportunity to teach medieval history at Harvard and to conduct the *North American Review*. He bade farewell to politics with a caustic article on Grant's administration; organized the first historical seminary; and made an intensive study of Anglo-Saxon law. Bored with Cambridge, after a year's leave of absence in Europe following his marriage to Marian Hooper of Boston, he did not return to those duties, but took residence in Washington with a view to writing. The Adamses became members of a distinguished clique which included John Hay, William Evarts, and Clarence King. They became critics of the Gilded Age, Adams contributing anonymously *Democracy*, 1880, and Hay *The Bread-winners*, 1883. A second novel, *Esther*, under the pseudonym "Frances Snow Compton," 1884, indicates no ability in fiction. The major work of this period, for which he had really left teaching at Harvard, was *History of the United States during the Administrations of Jefferson and Madison*, a polemic tract in conception, vindicating John Quincy Adams for breaking with the Federalist Party; though chiefly concerned with politics, the earlier chapters treating social and economic conditions at the beginning of the 19th century are ordinarily considered his best historical writing. Mrs. Adams died suddenly, on Dec. 6, 1885, by her own hand and the work begun with great zest was pushed to a close without enthusiasm. The loss of his wife resulted in a search for Nirvana, for peace and solace, rather than for new interests. History could not absorb a man who felt life emptied of meaning.

Picturesque Japan, the atolls of the South Seas, the companionship of La-Farge and King hardly brought forgetfulness; hence philosophy enticed him. In 1863 Adams had written his brother Charles of his conviction that the same laws govern man as govern nature; idly now he speculated on these laws. He had reached the conclusion that "chaos was the law of nature; order the dream of man" when he found two integrating forces in the world, symbolized in the Virgin of Chartres and the Dynamo. It is apparent, however, that they are integrating forces in a disintegrating world. *Mont-Saint-Michel and Chartres* and *The Education of Henry Adams* are demonstrative of how he seized on these, but the letter in *The Degradation of Democratic Dogma* is indicative of his larger view of the world. His fellow was Max Nordau in France. Later years were spent (with a part of each year in Washington) in wandering; he visited Hawaii, Tahiti, Siam, the Caribbean islands, Cuba, Mexico, Sweden, Russia, and Egypt; but Paris, Chartres, Caen, Coutances, Mont-Saint-Michel were the objects of most frequent pilgrimage. Adams was studying medieval songs when he died, Mar. 28, 1918.

Essays on Anglo-Saxon Law, ed., 1876; *Documents Relating to New England Federalism*, ed., 1877; *The Writings of Albert Gallatin*, ed., 3 vols., 1879; *The Life of Albert Gallatin*, 1879; *Democracy, an American Novel*, 1880; *John Randolph*, 1882; *Esther*, 1884; *History of the United States during the Administrations of Jefferson and Madison, 1801–1817*, 9 vols., 1889–91 (condensed as *The Formative Years* by Herbert Agar, 1947); *Historical Essays*, 1891; *Memoirs of Marau Taaroa, Last*

Queen of Tahiti, privately printed, 1893; *Mont-Saint-Michel and Chartres,* privately printed, 1904, given public, 1913; *Life of George Cabot Lodge,* 1911; *The Education of Henry Adams,* privately printed, 1906, given public, 1918; *The Degradation of Democratic Dogma,* 1919; *Letters to a Niece and Prayer to the Virgin of Chartres,* ed. Mabel La-Farge, 1920. Reprints: *Democracy,* Holt, 1925; *The Education,* intro. by H. C. Lodge, Riverside Lib., 1930; Mod. Lib., 1931; *Travels in Tahiti* (ed. R. E. Spiller), 1947.

For life, see: *The Education; The Letters of Henry Adams,* 2 vols. (ed. W. C. Ford), 1930, 1938; *A Cycle of Adams Letters,* ed. W. C. Ford, 2 vols., 1920; *Henry Adams and His Friends* (ed. H. D. Cater), 1947; Ernest Samuels, *The Young Henry Adams,* 1948; Mabel LaFarge, "Henry Adams: a Niece's Memories," *Yale Rev.,* Jan., 1920, also intro. to *Letters of a Niece,* 1920; Intro. by Brooks Adams to *Democratic Dogma,* 1919; W. R. Thayer, *The Life and Letters of John Hay,* 2 vols., 1915; C. F. Adams, Jr., *Charles Francis Adams, an Autobiography,* 1916; Allan Johnson, "Henry Brooks ·Adams," *D.A.B.;* J. T. Adams, *Henry Adams,* 1933; Katherine Simonds, "The Tragedy of Mrs. Adams," *New Eng. Quar.,* Dec., 1936. For the Adams family, see: S. P. Sherman, "Evolution in the Adams Family," *Americans,* 1922, and J. T. Adams, *The Adams Family,* 1930.

For general criticism, see: Robert Shafer, "Henry Adams," *Internat. Journal of Ethics,* Oct., 1919, also *Progress and Science,* 1919; T. K. Whipple, *Spokesmen,* 1928; P. E. More, *Shelburne Essays,* XI, 1921; H. S. Commager, "Henry Adams," *So. Atlan. Quar.,* July, 1927, also review of *The Letters,* N. Y. *Herald-Tribune Books,* Sept. 28, 1930; Oscar Cargill, "The Medievalism of Henry Adams," *Essays and Studies in Honor of Carleton Brown,* 1940; V. L. Parrington, *The Beginnings of Critical Realism,* 1930; C. A. Beard, "Historians at Work," *Atlantic,* Apr., 1943.

For special criticism, see: M. E. Speare, "The Pioneer American Political Novel of Henry Adams," *The Political Novel,* 1924; J. S. Bassett, "Later Historians," *CHAL,* III; S. M. Crothers, "Education in Pursuit of Henry Adams," *Yale Rev.,* Apr., 1919; W. D. Sheldon, "Why Education Failed to Educate

Henry Adams," *Sewanee Rev.,* Jan., 1920.

627. THE TENDENCY OF HISTORY. An open letter addressed to the Sec. of the American Historical Association, of which Adams was president, printed later in *The Degradation of Democratic Dogma,* 1919. "To tell the truth, it doesn't impress me at all, save by its wit and erudition; and I ask you whether an old man soon about to meet his Maker can hope to save himself from the consequences of his life by pointing to the wit and learning he has shown in treating a tragic subject. No, sir, you can't impress God in that way." (William James, *Letters,* II, 346.) ¶627. *"Buckle's first volume."* Henry T. Buckle (1821–62), author of *History of Civilization in England,* held that, due to want of ability in historians and to complexity of social phenomena, very little has been done towards establishing a science of history. This letter raises the question of the nature and province of history; consult F. M. Fling, *The Writing of History,* 1920. ¶628. *"Adam Smith."* Scottish economist (1723–90), author of *The Wealth of Nations.* ¶630. *"Galileo . . . to recant."* Galileo Galilei (1564–1642), Italian physicist, was found to hold heretical doctrines and forced to recant on June 22, 1633. The legend that Galileo, rising from his knees, stamped on the ground, exclaiming *"Eppur si muove!"* (Nevertheless it moves!) is entirely apocryphal, possibly no older than Abbé Irailli's *Querrels littérairies,* 1761. ¶631. *"Heine's word . . . Also fragen, etc."* Passage from the German poet, Heinrich Heine (1797–1856); see "Zum Lazarus, I" (1853). A free translation:

> Thus we ask incessantly
> Until some one with a handful
> Of earth finally stops our mouths.
> But is that an answer?

631. THE DYNAMO AND THE VIRGIN (1900). Ch. XXV of *The Education of Henry Adams,* 1906; 1918. *The Education* is a study in "multiplicity" as opposed to *Mont-Saint-Michel and Chartres,* which is a study in "unity." Lodge suggests comparison with St. Augustine's *Confessions;* Adams himself refers the reader to Rousseau's *Confessions;* speaks of the Frenchman as "a great educator." ¶631. *"the Great Exposition of 1900."* The Paris Exposition; Adams had "rooms at the very door of the Troca-

dero"—one of the exhibition palaces.
¶631. *"Langley."* Samuel Pierpont Langley (1834–1906), a friend of Adams;
physicist and astronomer who demonstrated the practicability of mechanical
flight. ¶631. *"The Advancement of
Science."* More commonly called *The
Advancement of Learning*, by Lord
Bacon, in which, about 1603 (*not* "towards the year 1620") he projected the
reorganization of natural science. ¶632.
"Daimler motor." Gottlieb Daimler
(1834–1900) built in 1884 the first
gasoline engine for automotive work.
¶632. *"Radium denied its God."* First
of radio-active or "disintegrating" elements to be discovered. ¶633. *"Marconi."*
Guglielmo Marconi, Italian inventor,
who patented the wireless, 1895. ¶633.
"Branly coherer." Delicate device for
detecting electric waves, invented by
Edouard Branly, French physicist
(1846–   ), given *grand prix* at Paris.
¶634. *"like Sir Launcelot."* In Chretien
de Troyes' *Chevalier du Charette*,
Launcelot rescues Guinevere by crawling
along a knife edge into a castle. ¶634.
"Venus . . . Virgin." By equating the
two, Adams makes his meaning clearer;
both stand for the force of sex. ¶634.
"opening lines of Lucretius." From
(Titus) Lucretius (Carus', 99?–55?)
poem, *De rerum natura*, Bk. I, l. 21.
Freely translated: "[Thou, Venus] who
above all art sole governor of all the
things of nature. . . ." This poem certainly exerted an influence, with its discussion of the end of the world and the
failing fertility of Italy, upon Adams'
Degradation of Democratic Dogma.
¶634–5. *"the Virgin of the Schools . . .
Donna, sei tanto . . ."*: See Dante, *Divine Comedy; Paradise*, XXXIII, 13–16:

So mighty art thou, Lady, and so great
That he, who grace desireth, and comes
    not
To thee for aidance, fain would have
    desire
Fly without wings. (Henry Cary's trans.)

¶635. *"Herodias."* Wife of Herod An-
tipas, who caused the death of John the
Baptist (Matt. xiv). ¶635. *"St. Gaudens's General Sherman."* Augustus St.
Gaudens (1848–97), American sculptor, began the statue at the 59th St. entrance to Central Park in 1892; it was
dedicated in 1903. St. Gaudens' best
piece of work is commonly thought to
be the memorial to Mrs. Adams in Rock
Creek Cemetery, Washington, D. C.

Also sculptor of the Shaw memorial (see
Moody). ¶635. *" 'Don' Cameron."* Sen.
J. D. Cameron (1833–1918), of Pa.;
friend of Adams. ¶635. *"the Hunts,
Richardson, etc."* William Morris Hunt
(1824–78), painter, brought the Bar-
bizon influence to America; Richard
Morris Hunt (1828–95), with H. H.
Richardson (1838–86), both trained in
the Paris École des Beaux-Arts, greatly
improved the civic architecture of their
time; John LaFarge 1835–   ), chiefly
noted for his murals; and Stanford
White (1853–1906), most talented
architect of his day—all Americans.
¶635. *"Whistler."* J. A. McNeill Whistler (1834–1903), dabbler in art and
epigram, most feared man of his day.
¶636. *"Mont Parnasse."* Elevated section
above Latin Quarter, Left Bank of the
Seine. ¶636. *"Isis with cow's horns at
Edfoo."* The cow was sacred to the
Egyptian goddess; consequently her later
statues, like that at Edfu, in Upper
Egypt, are adorned with horns. Adams
visited Egypt with the Hays. ¶636.
"Louis XI." King of France, 1461–83
(1423–83). ¶637. *"at Cnidos . . .
Aphrodite of Praxiteles."* The most famous work of the Greek sculptor Praxiteles, fl. 340 B.C., was a nude figure of
Aphrodite about to enter the sea, which
was long admired in the temple of the
goddess at Cnidos. ¶637. *"Matthew
Arnold at the Grande Chartreuse."* See
"Stanzas from the Grande Chartreuse."
Awed by his first glimpse of "the Car-
thusians' world famed home," Arnold
wrote,

All are before me! I behold
The House, the Brotherhood austere!
—And what am I, that I am here?

638. PRAYER TO THE VIRGIN OF
CHARTRES. Found after Adams' death
among his papers. First published by his
niece, Mabel LaFarge, in *Letters to a
Niece, etc.*, 1920. Worship of the Virgin
Mary (called *Mariolatry* by dissenters,
and *hyperdulia* by the Roman Church)
in myth dates back to Mary's own time;
St. Trophinius at Arles, it is believed by
some, dedicated a chapel to her while
she was still living; Adams himself more
accurately picks the thirteenth as *her*
century, contrasting it with the masculine eleventh century, in *Mont-Saint-
Michel and Chartres*. ¶638. *"my master
Abailard."* Pierre Abelard (1079–1142),
philosopher and teacher, drew thousands
from western Europe and the British

Isles to Paris to his lectures. ¶638. *"Ave Maris Stella"*: ". . . Saint Bernard in his time was regarded as the apple of the Virgin's eye. Tradition as old as the twelfth century, which long afterwards gave to Murillo the subject of a famous painting, told that once, when he was reciting before her statue the *Ave Maris Stella,* and came to the words, *Monstra te esse Matrem,* the image, pressing its breast, dropped on the lips of her servant three drops of the milk which had nourished the Saviour" (*Mont-St.-Michel and Chartres,* pp. 92–93). The title is translated, "Hail, Star of the Sea!" ¶638. *"Blanche."* Mother of Saint Louis (Louis IX of France), responsible for the construction of the great Rose Window, Chartres Cathedral. The Virgin therein depicted is said to be a likeness of her. ¶639. *"Sphinx . . . old riddle."* The query (What is man?) put to Œdipus by the Sphinx:

Tell me, what animal is that
Which has four feet at morning bright,
Has two at noon, and three at night?

¶639. *"leap across to Alpha Centauri."* One of two stars, α and β, known as the Southern Pointers, since they point to the Southern Cross. Centauri is the third brightest star in the sky, and is found to be our nearest neighbor, 4½ light-years away. ¶640. *"Troglodytes."* Name given cave dwellers by ancient writers.

W(illiam) C(rary) Brownell
(1851–1928)

Born in New York City, Aug. 30, 1851, son of Isaac Wilbour Brownell, a commission merchant with New England forebears, and Lucia Emilie Brownell, another branch of the Brownell family which had produced Henry Howard Brownell, Civil War poet. The family moved to Buffalo when the boy was five. He attended dame school, then Miss Gardner's school, where P. R. Spencer taught him "Spencerian" hand and M. Liard, his drawing teacher, inspired a lasting love of France. After the death of his mother, he went to her parents in Adamsville, R. I. Sent two years to country school, then to Mr. Fay's school, Newport. Entered Amherst at sixteen; was graduated in 1871. Became a reporter for the New York *World;* was city editor at twenty-one. On the staff of the *Nation* under E. L. Godkin, 1879–81. Married Virginia Shields Swinburne, of Newport, Jan., 1878. Lived abroad for three years; chiefly in Paris, 1881. On staff of Philadelphia *Press,* 1884. In Jan., 1888, became editor and adviser to Charles Scribner's Sons, a position which he held to his death, July 22, 1928.

Defining Brownell as "the last of the Victorians," E. S. Bates points out the critic's failure to question the virtues of industrialism, his impatience with Carlyle and Ruskin who dared to doubt, his ignorance of philosophy (he held "a smattering of philosophy" to be enough for a critic), and his incomprehension of the basis of the revolt which disturbed his later years. Yet, Bates adds, ". . . if he was unable to justify the Victorian attitude theoretically, he illustrated it in his practise most attractively. The quiet self-respect and reticence of his style were in themselves a rebuke to contemporary vulgarity; his devotion to high, even though often vaguely defined, ideals, gave the cast of nobility to his work; his instinct for the avoidance of extremes, accompanied by a gracious worldly wisdom and a kind of enlightened common sense, lent weight to his judgments." He is "the connecting link between the Sainte-Beuve-Arnold tradition and the New Humanism" of Babbitt, More, and Sherman.

French Traits, 1889; *French Art,* 1892; *Newport,* 1896; *Victorian Prose Masters,* 1901; *American Prose Masters,* 1909; *Criticism,* 1914; *Standards,* 1917; *The Genius of Style,* 1924; *Democratic Distinction in America,* 1927; *The Spirit of Society,* 1927.

For life and criticism, see: E. S. Bates, "William Crary Brownell," *D.A.B.;* Stuart Sherman, *Woodcuts,* 1927; Edith Wharton, "William C. Brownell," *Scribner's,* Nov., 1928; G. H. Brownell, *William Crary Brownell,* 1933.

641. TASTE. Selection from essay in *Scribner's,* Apr., 1917; collected in *Standards,* 1917. ¶641. *"an American dilettante."* James McNeil Whistler, artist and wit (1834–1903). ¶642. *"Victor Hugo's* Cromwell." Preface to this play (pub. Oct., 1827) is called "the Declaration of Rights of the French Romantic movement"; attacked stagnation of literature, and Boileau's rules. ¶642. *"gens de goût":* Men of taste. ¶642. *"Scudery to La Harpe."* Madeleine de Scudery (1607–1701), French novelist, priestess

of the artificial, blue-stocking; Jean
François de La Harpe (1739–1803),
critic, dramatist. ¶642. *"chevaux de
frise"*: A defense consisting of a timber
set with spikes. ¶642. *"Renan."* Ernest
Renan (1823–92), French philosopher
and Orientalist, whose *Abbesse de
Jouarre* is a philosophical drama. ¶642.
"Doudan." Ximénès Doudan (1800–
72), French critic. ¶642. *"Rivarol."*
Antoine Rivaroli (1753–1801), opponent of the French Revolution, satirist.
¶643. *"esprits délicats"*: Sensitive spirits.
¶643. *"Mr. Mather."* Frank Jewett
Mather, Jr., author and professor of
art, Princeton. ¶643. *"poètes maudits"*:
Cursed poets (Villon). ¶643. *"Greco."*
Domenico Theotocopuli (c. 1542–1614),
known as El Greco, Spanish painter.
¶501. *"Prof. Conrad Wright."* Charles
Henry Conrad Wright (1869–   ),
whose *History of French Literature* appeared, 1912. ¶643. *"Mr. Cox."* Kenyon
Cox, (1856–1919), American artist,
whose "timely book" was *Concerning
Painting,* 1917. ¶643. *"Matisse."* Henri
Matisse (1869–   ), French futurist
painter. ¶643. *"André Gide."* French
novelist and essayist (1869–   ). ¶644.
"Gibbon . . . chapter on Mahomet."
Edward Gibbon (1737–94), English historian; see *The Decline and Fall of the
Roman Empire.* ¶645. *"Achilles and Patroclus."* Hero of the *Iliad* and his companion. ¶645. *"Épater le bourgeois"*: To
astonish the bourgeois. ¶646. *"French
seer . . . on the eve of the Revolution."*
Voltaire to Marquis de Chauvelin, in letter, Apr. 2, 1764: "The young are truly
happy; they shall see beautiful things."
¶646. *"Madame Tallien."* Thérèse,
wife of Jean Lambert Tallien, French
revolutionary; formerly wife of Comte de
Fontenay; later mistress of the banker
Ouvard. ¶646. *"Virgilian motto . . . for
Brook Farm."* *Blithedale Romance,* Ch.
VIII. ¶646. *"Mr. Galsworthy."* John
Galsworthy (1867–1933), English dramatist and novelist (*Forsyte Saga*). ¶646.
"Actæon at their ease." Actæon, huntsman, gazed on Diana and her nymphs
as they bathed; changed by the goddess
into a stag, was pursued and torn by his
own dogs. ¶646. *"Shelley calls 'naked to
laughter.'"* In "Lines: When the Lamp
is Shattered," IV, 6. ¶646. *"Keats' example . . . Max Beerbohm . . . Maupassant."* Verse of John Keats (1795–
1821), was condemned by contemporary
critics for its sensuousness; Max Beerbohm, the "Incomparable," in several

passages in his essays advocates a realistic
technique, but for the truth of Brownell's conjecture that the moderns are influenced (indirectly, perhaps) by Guy
de Maupassant (1850–93), French Naturalist, see Beerbohm's "A Relic" in
Even Now, 1920.

Paul Elmer More (1864–1937)

Born in St. Louis, Mo., Dec. 12,
1864, son of Gen. Enoch Anson and
Katharine Hay (Elmer) More. Was
graduated from Washington University,
1887; took M.A. degree, 1892; M.A.
from Harvard, 1893. Asst. professor of
Sanskrit, Harvard, 1894–95; of Sanskrit
and classical literature, Bryn Mawr,
1895–97. Abandoned teaching and went
into retirement at Shelburne, N. H.;
left in 1899, "without having found the
meaning of civilization." Married Henrietta Beck, St. Louis, June 12, 1900.
Literary editor, *Independent,* 1901–03;
literary editor, N. Y. *Evening Post,*
1903–09. Editor, *Nation,* 1909–14. "As
an editor," says Stuart Sherman, "he
taught his reviewers to fear nothing but
deviations from the truth and the insidious vices of puffery and log-rolling."
After resigning from the *Nation,* he
moved to Princeton, N. J., "in order that
my children might grow up among English-speaking peoples." He gave annual
lectures there in Greek philosophy.
More died on March 9, 1937.

The *Shelburne Essays* are praised by
Norman Foerster as the "highest accomplishment in literary criticism in America." The aesthetic merits of these essays
are somewhat obscured by More's hostility to popular movements, with the result that, as he admits, he has been "the
least read and most hated author" in the
United States. Believing the sentimentality and humanitarianism of Rousseau
have robbed man and society of all dignity, he has not only flayed the Frenchman but castigated any manifestation of
"social sympathy." Society, he holds, is
more important than the individual;
property is worth more than life. Yet his
search for standards and morals, offensive to some because of the Platonic
dualism on which it is based, has won a
tardy following which claims his as the
authentic voice of order and reason. For
his philosophy, he has chosen rather
badly the name "humanism," which
calls to mind, not impeccable Gabriel
Harvey necessarily, but such a liberal as

Erasmus. The "New Humanism" became a force about 1923; More and Irving Babbitt could claim Norman Foerster, Robert Shafer, H. H. Clark, Gorham Munson, and others as converts, and point to somewhat similar movements in France and England. Platonic dualism implies in man two natures, especially a *spiritual* nature. It implies further the existence of an "inner check" upon conduct, and the necessity of careful study of man's humane tradition. The instincts of the "natural" man are to be denied, and the "naturalistic education of the senses" to be abjured. The individualism of Nietzsche is as wicked as the equalitarianism of Rousseau; consequently the humanists are strongly opposed to the general trend in literature after 1914. In American criticism in the twenties, one group rallied around More, Babbitt, and Sherman; another (and larger) gathered about H. L. Mencken. Charles Eliot Norton (1827–1903), professor of history of art at Harvard, probably is the father of the "new humanism."

Helena and Occasional Poems, 1890; *The Great Refusal*, 1894; *A Century of Indian Epigrams*, 1898; *Judgment of Socrates*, 1898; *Benjamin Franklin*, 1900; *The Jessica Letters* (with Mrs. L. H. Harris), 1904; *Shelburne Essays*, 11 vols., 1904–21; *Nietzsche*, 1912; *Platonism*, 1917; *The Religion of Plato*, 1921; *Hellenistic Philosophies*, 1923; *The Christ of the New Testament*, 1924; *Christ, the Word*, 1927; *New Shelburne Essays*, 3 vols., 1928–36; *The Catholic Faith*, 1931; *Selected Shelburne Essays*, 1935; *Pages from an Oxford Diary*, 1937.

For life, see: Robert Shafer, *Paul Elmer More and American Criticism*, 1935. For criticism, see: P. J. Bart, "The Christianity of Paul Elmer More," *Cath. World*, Aug., 1932; Ludwig Lewisohn, *Expression in America*, 1932; H. L. Mencken, *Prejudices, III*, 1922; Stuart Sherman, *Americans*, 1922; Bernard Smith, *Forces in American Criticism*, 1939; Edmund Wilson, *The Triple Thinkers*, 1938.

For the "new humanism," see: Irving Babbitt, *Literature and the American College*, 1908, *The New Laokoön*, 1910, *Rousseau and Romanticism*, 1919; T. S. Eliot, *The Sacred Wood*, 1920; G. R. Elliott, *The Cycle of Modern Poetry*, 1929; Norman Foerster, *The American Scholar*, 1929; *Towards Standards*, 1930;

Humanism and America, ed. N. Foerster, 1930; C. H. Grattan, *The Critique of Humanism*, 1930; Folke Leander, *Humanism and Naturalism*, 1937; Louis J. A. Mercier, *Le Mouvement humaniste aux États-Unis*, 1928; L. T. Moore, *The Limitations of Science*, 1915; G. B. Munson, *Destinations*, 1928; W. S. Knickerbocker, "Humanism and Scholarship," *Sewanee Rev.*, xxxviii, 81–103; George Santayana, *The Genteel Tradition at Bay*, 1931; Robert Shafer, *Progress and Science*, 1922; *Christianity and Naturalism*, 1926; S. P. Sherman, *On Contemporary Literature*, 1917; Paul Shorey, *The Assault on Humanism*, 1917; Allen Tate, "The Fallacy of Humanism," *Hound & Horn*, iii, 234–58; S. E. Wolff, "Scholars," *CHAL*, IV; J. Zeitlin & H. Woodbridge, *Life and Letters of Stuart Sherman*, 2 vols., 1929.

647. THE NEW MORALITY. In *The Unpopular Review*, Jan.–Mar., 1914; collected, *Aristocracy and Justice*, Shelburne Essays, IX, 1915. ¶647. "young woman . . . wrote a novel." Florence Converse (1871–   ), wrote *The Burden of Christopher*, 1900. ¶647. "limbo large and broad": Paradise Lost, iii, 495. ¶647. "Embryos and idiots . . .": Paradise Lost, iii, 474. ¶648. "Harry Thaw[s]." Murderer of Stanford White, the architect. ¶648–9. "the warning of the lady Una": The Faerie Queene, Bk. I, Canto I, Stanza 13. ¶649. "Henry Vaughn." Mystical poet (c. 1621–95). ¶649. ". . . lives and speaks aloft by those pure eyes": Lycidas, 81–82; description of Fame. ¶650. "E. 'L Primo Amore." On the gate of hell was writ, "To rear me was the task of . . . primeval love. . . . All hope abandon, ye who enter here." (Dante, *Inferno* III.) ¶650. "says Warburton of Bolingbroke." William Warburton (1698–1779), bishop of Gloucester, enemy of the deists, of whom Henry St. John, Viscount Bolingbroke, was as celebrated by any. ¶650. "Baxter to Hume." Andrew Baxter (1686–1750), metaphysician, author: *An Inquiry into the Nature of the Human Soul*, 1730; David Hume (1711–76), Scotch philosopher, greatest skeptic of his day. ¶651. "La Harpe's Lycée." Lectures on ancient and modern writers given at the Lycée by Jean-François de La Harpe (1739–1803), in 1786. ¶651. "Diderot or Helvétius." Denis Diderot (1713–84), editor of the famous encyclopedia; Claude Adrien Helvétius (1715–71), French philos-

opher. ¶651. *"Les passions amorties
. . ."*: Dull passions degrade unusual
men. ¶651. *"Ellen Key."* Swedish author
(1849–1926), interested in welfare of
women and children. ¶651. *"Toussaint's
religion."* François Dominique (1743–
1803), who as Toussaint L'Ouverture,
attempted to liberate Haiti. His religion:
"One loves equally God and his mistress." ¶651. *"le désir du bien public"*:
The desire for the public good. ¶652.
"Cessavere vices rerum . . .": "Things
have ceased from changing, and the
river from flowing as it was wont to do."
(Lucan, *Bellum Civile*, VI, ll. 461,
472–73). ¶653. *"Appian."* Writer of
Roman history in Greek in reigns of
Trajan and Adrian, dates uncertain.
¶655. *"Lebon and his kind."* Joseph Le
Bon (1765–95), French politician who
led bloody attacks against counter-revo-
lutionists. ¶655. *"Putumayo Indians."*
Headhunters in the valley of the Putumayo, northeastern Peru. "All this was
written and printed, I need scarcely say,
before the outbreak of the European
war. I should not to-day refer to the
Congo and the Putumayo Indians for
the savagery underlying civilization"
(Author's note). ¶655. *"Floud of poyson . . . spewed on Spenser's Knight"*:
Faerie Queene, Bk. I, Canto I, Stanza
20. ¶656. *"Away with charity that
soothes a lie . . ."*: "The couplet is from
the first edition of Cowper's *Expostula-
tion*. You will find it in a note to that
poem in Southey's edition" (P. E.
More).

Stuart P(ratt) Sherman
(1881–1926)

Stuart Pratt Sherman was born in
Anita, Iowa, on Oct. 1, 1881. His
boyhood was spent in California and
New England, and he attended Williams College, receiving the A.B. degree from that institution in 1903. The
next year he proceeded to Harvard
University on a fellowship which allowed him three years of graduate
study; in 1904 Harvard granted him
the A.M. degree and in 1906 the Ph.D.
degree. He was an instructor in English
at Northwestern University in 1906–07;
then he accepted the position of associate
in English at the University of Illinois,
where he was an assistant professor during 1908–09, an associate professor from
1909 to 1911, and a professor from 1911
to 1924. In the meantime he had gained

considerable renown as a scholar and
lecturer, an engaging writer on literature, and a critic of contemporary America. In 1924 he accepted the position of
editor of *Books,* a new literary supplement to the *New York Herald Tribune,*
which position he held until his death
two years later. He died from heart failure while swimming on Aug. 21, 1926.

Sherman helped to raise the standard
of book-reviewing in New York, and
like Matthew Arnold, whose disciple he
was, attempted to judge of books against
a background of ideas and a full knowledge of life. In his critical position he
avoided going to extremes. Although his
training and bent of mind caused him
to hold largely with the academic and
conservative among his colleagues, he
nevertheless responded sympathetically
to the changing literary scene, and was
often in agreement with the rebellious
critics. He was, in fact, the mediator *par
excellence* between the two camps, as
well as in his own right a critic of dis-
cernment.

Stevenson's Treasure Island (ed.),
1911; *The Tragedy of Coriolanus*, by
Shakespeare (ed.), 1912; *A Book of
Short Stories,* (ed.), 1914; *'Tis Pity
She's a Whore* and *The Broken Heart,*
by John Ford (ed.), 1915; *Cambridge
History of American Literature* (co-ed.
with W. P. Trent, John Erskine, and
Carl Van Doren), 1917–21; *Matthew
Arnold: How to Know Him*, 1917; *On
Contemporary Literature,* 1917; *Essays
and Poems of Emerson* (ed.), 1921;
Americans, 1922; *The Genius of Amer-
ica,* 1923; *Poetical Works of Joaquin
Miller* (ed.), 1923; *American Prose
Masters,* by W. C. Brownell (ed.),
1923; *My Dear Cornelia,* 1924; *Points
of View,* 1924; *Letters to a Lady in the
Country* (with Garreta Busey), 1925;
Critical Woodcuts, 1926; *The Main
Stream,* 1927; *Shaping Men and
Women* (ed. Jacob Zeitlin), 1928;
The Emotional Discovery of America,
1932.

For life, see: Jacob Zeitlin and Homer
Woodbridge, *Life and Letters of Stuart
P. Sherman,* 1929; this work also contains an excellent bibliography. For criticism, see: Carl Van Doren, *Many
Minds,* 1924, pp. 67–82; V. F. Calver-
ton, *The Newer Spirit,* 1925, pp. 159–
165; Joseph Warren Beach, *The Outlook for American Prose,* 1926, pp. 92–
105; George E. de Mille, *Literary Criticism in America,* 1931, pp. 245–77.

657. THE EMOTIONAL DISCOVERY OF AMERICA. An address delivered before the American Academy of Arts and Letters on December 11, 1924. Printed in Academy Publication No. 54. Title essay, 1932 volume.

Edwin Arlington Robinson
(1869–1935)

To many critics Edwin Arlington Robinson appears to be first among American poets of the present century. His work is distinguished for its artistry, particularly for its use of the rhythms of the spoken language and the employment of an indirect mode of expression; it is even more distinguished for its weighty themes, dealing with human tragedies, human destiny, the nature of man.

Robinson was born on Dec. 22, 1869, in Head Tide, Me., but grew up in the town of Gardiner, the "Tilbury Town" of the poems. After studying at Harvard for two years, from 1891 to 1893, he worked at various occupations while attempting to make his way as a poet. In 1905 he was appointed, through President Roosevelt, to a position in the New York Customs House, where he remained until 1909. After that year he devoted his energies to the writing of poetry, living in New York City and Boston except during the summer months, which he spent at the MacDowell Colony, Peterboro, N. H. Honors and praise came to him. He received the Pulitzer Prize three times, and in 1922 was awarded the prize of the Poetry Society. He held membership in the National Academy of Arts and Letters and the international P.E.N. Club. He died on April 6, 1935; and his body was cremated and his ashes buried in Gardiner, Me.

The Torrent and the Night Before, 1896; *The Children of the Night,* 1897; *Captain Craig,* 1902; *The Town Down the River,* 1910; *Van Zorn,* 1914; *The Porcupine,* 1915; *The Man Against the Sky,* 1916; *Merlin,* 1917; *Lancelot,* 1920; *The Three Taverns,* 1920; *Avon's Harvest,* 1921; *Collected Poems,* 1921, also in 1927, 1929, 1937; *Roman Bartholow,* 1923; *The Man Who Died Twice,* 1924; *Dionysus in Doubt,* 1925; *Tristram,* 1927; *Sonnets (1889–1927),* 1928; *Three Poems,* 1928; *Fortunatus,* 1928; *The Prodigal Son,* 1929; *Cavender's House,* 1929; *Modred, a Fragment,* 1929; *The Glory of the Nightingales,* 1930; *Matthias at the Door,* 1931; *Poems* [selected], 1931; *Nicodemus,* 1932; *Talifer,* 1933; *Amaranth,* 1934; *King Jasper,* 1935; *Selected Letters* (comp. by Ridgely Torrence), 1940; *Letters to Howard George Schmitt,* 1943; *Untriangulated Stars* (letters), 1947.

For life and criticism, see: Lloyd Morris, *The Poetry of Edwin Arlington Robinson,* 1923; Mark Van Doren, *Edwin Arlington Robinson,* 1927; Charles Cestre, *An Introduction to Edwin Arlington Robinson,* 1930; R. Brown, *Next Door to a Poet,* 1937; Hermann Hagedorn, *Edwin Arlington Robinson,* 1938; Y. Winters, *Edwin Arlington Robinson,* 1946; E. E. Neff, *E. A. Robinson,* 1948. See also: L. M. Beebe and R. J. Bulkley, *A Bibliography of the Writings of Edwin Arlington Robinson,* 1931; C. B. Hogan, *A Bibliography of Edwin Arlington Robinson,* 1936; Lillian Lippincott, *A Bibliography of the Writings and Criticisms of Edwin Arlington Robinson,* 1937.

668. AARON STARK. In *The Torrent and the Night Before,* 1896, with its famous dedication: "This book is dedicated to any man, woman or critic who will cut the edges of it. I have done the top." Only 312 copies were published privately at a cost of $50.

668. THE CLERKS. In *The Torrent and the Night Before,* 1896.

668. ZOLA. In *The Torrent and the Night Before,* 1896. Émile Zola (1840–1902) was the most discussed of all French naturalists.

669. RICHARD CORY. In *Children of the Night,* 1897.

669. ISAAC AND ARCHIBALD. In *Captain Craig,* 1902.

677. AUNT IMOGEN. In *Captain Craig,* 1902.

680. MINIVER CHEEVY. In *The Town Down the River,* 1910.

680. CASSANDRA. In *Boston Evening Transcript,* Dec. 21, 1914; collected, *Man Against the Sky,* 1916.

681. BEWICK FINZER. In *Man Against the Sky,* 1916.

681. BEN JONSON ENTERTAINS, etc. In *Drama* mag., Nov., 1915; collected in *The Man Against the Sky,* 1916. ¶684. "Poor Greene," Robert (1558–92), who, in *Greene's Groat's Worth of Wit,* wrote of "an upstart crow . . . with his Tygers heart . . . the onlie Shakescene." ¶684. "He's put one there."

The so-called "dark lady of the Sonnets," subject of 28 stanzas out of 154.

689. EROS TURANNOS. In *Poetry*, Mar., 1914; collected in *The Man Against the Sky*, 1916. The title is a transliteration of the Greek; it means "Love, the Tyrant."

690. THE MAN AGAINST THE SKY. In *New Repub.*, May 27, 1916; collected in *The Man Against the Sky*, 1916.

695. MR. FLOODY'S PARTY. In *Nation*, Nov. 24, 1920; collected *Avon's Harvest*, 1921.

696. THE MILL. In *New Repub.*, Jul. 2, 1919; collected *The Three Taverns*, 1920.

696. DEMOS. In *N. Am. Rev.*, Jan., 1919; collected in *The Three Taverns*, 1920. For further exposition of Robinson's political views, see: "On the Way," "Demos and Dionysus," etc. *Demos* were the people, or commons, of an ancient Greek state. See Louise Dauner, "Vox Clamantis" *N. Eng. Quar.*, Sept., 1942, for Robinson as critic of democracy.

697. THE MAN WHO DIED TWICE. Published, 1924. ¶708. *"Bach,"* Johann Sebastian (1685–1750), German composer. ¶709. *"Achilles' heel."* By which he was held when immersed to make him invulnerable.

Robert (Lee) Frost (1875–   )

Robert Lee Frost was born on Mar. 26, 1875, in San Francisco, Calif., of New England parents, and at the age of ten was brought to the East by his widowed mother. He was educated in New England schools, but found the drudgery of college life uncongenial. A few months at Dartmouth College, and two years at Harvard University, from 1897 to 1899, represent his efforts to submit himself to the influences of higher education. He tried a number of occupations; he worked as a mill hand, a newspaper reporter, a shoemaker, a farmer, a teacher. In 1895 he married Miss Elinor Miriam White. Beginning in his early years, he had written verse, but had met with little encouragement from editors and the public until 1913, when his first volume of poetry was published in England, whither he had gone with his family, after first selling a farm given him by his grandfather. A second book of poems appeared in England in 1914, and upon returning to America Frost found himself already

favorably known. Henceforth his reputation as a poet grew rapidly; and he has since become one of the most highly regarded and honored men of letters of the twentieth century. He has held a number of academic positions, including that of Professor of English at Amherst College, Associate Fellow, Pierson College, Yale University, Fellow in Letters at the University of Michigan, and Charles Eliot Norton Professor of Poetry at Harvard University. Numerous honorary degrees have been conferred upon him, and he has won the Pulitzer Poetry Prize four times. He suffered the loss of his wife in 1938. His present home is in Cambridge, Mass.

Like Edwin Arlington Robinson and Amy Lowell, Frost has identified himself with New England. A lyrist, whose verse imparts a highly personal attitude toward life, he is a sympathetic observer of humanity and an enthusiastic seeker after the satisfactions which come from knowing the out-of-doors.

A Boy's Will (London), 1913; *North of Boston* (London), 1914; *Mountain Interval*, 1916; *New Hampshire*, 1923; *Selected Poems*, 1923; *West-Running Brook*, 1928; *A Way Out*, 1929; *The Cow's in the Corn*, 1929; *The Lovely Shall Be Choosers*, 1929; *Collected Poems*, 1930, 1939, 1943, 1949; *From Snow to Snow*, 1936; *A Further Range*, 1936; *A Witness Tree*, 1942; *Come In*, 1943; *Masque of Reason*, 1945; *Steeple Bush*, 1947; *Masque of Mercy*, 1947.

For life and criticsm, see: Gorham B. Munson, *Robert Frost*, 1927; Carl Van Doren, *Many Minds*, 1924, pp. 50–67; Harriet Monroe, *Poets and Their Art*, 1926, pp. 56–63; T. K. Whipple, *Spokesmen*, 1928, pp. 94–115; Sidney Cox, *Robert Frost*, 1929; L. R. Thompson, *Fire and Ice*, 1942. See also: W. B. S. Clymer and C. R. Green, *Robert Frost: A Bibliography*, 1937; Louis & Esther Mertins, *The Intervals of Robert Frost*, 1947.

720. MENDING WALL. In *North of Boston* (London, 1914), 1915. "Running in a straight line eastward down the slope, the stone wall of the Derry farm *is* . . . the Derry farm. Come spring, the poet, calling to his French-Canadian neighbor on the north, would go forth to repair the damage done. . . ." L. & E. Mertins, *The Intervals, etc.* 1947.

721. THE BLACK COTTAGE. In *North of Boston* (London, 1914), 1915. ¶723.

"*It will turn true again*" (108 ff.). The cyclical theory of human history expressed at the end of this poem Frost got from his reading of the Latin poets, possibly from Horace. See Dean W. R. Inge's famous essay, "The Idea of Progress," in *Outspoken Essays*, 1919. Useful: G. O. Aykroyed, "The Classical in Robert Frost," *Poet Lore*, Winter, 1929.

723. DEATH OF THE HIRED MAN. In *North of Boston* (London, 1914), 1915.

727. HOME BURIAL. In *North of Boston* (London, 1914), 1915.

728. THE ROAD NOT TAKEN. In *Atlantic*, Aug., 1915; collected, *Mountain Interval*, 1916.

729. THE SOUND OF THE TREES. In *Poetry and Drama*, Dec., 1914; also in *Atlantic*, Aug., 1915; collected, *Mountain Interval*, 1916. L. Mertins dissents from "the critics'" opinion that "the sound was that of the Ryton firs in the West Midlands [Eng.]." See R. P. Eckert, Jr., "Robert Frost in England," *Mark Twain Quar.*, Spring, 1940, for his English residence.

729. STOPPING BY WOODS ON A SNOWY EVENING. In *N. Repub.*, Mar. 7, 1923; collected in *Several Short Poems*, n.d. [1924].

729. FIRE AND ICE. In *Harper's*, Dec., 1920; collected *New Hampshire*, 1923.

729. NEW HAMPSHIRE was published in 1923. ¶730. "*Steffanson*" (22). Vilhjalmur Stefannson, Canadian arctic explorer of Icelandic descent, wrote *The Northward Course of Empire*, 1922, to which Frost refers. ¶730. "*Volstead Act*," inaugurated prohibition in 1919. ¶731. "*Purse*." Franklin Pierce (1804–69), fourteenth President. ¶731. "*John Smith remarked them*" in *A Description of New England* (1616). ¶733. "*They taunt the lofty land*" (264). See R. W. Emerson, "Ode Inscribed to W. H. Canning." ¶736. "*Birnam Wood*" (343). See *Macbeth*, V. 3. "*Ahaz' sin*" (393). From the previous line from Bryant's "A Forest Hymn," Ahaz' sin (for there are several enumerated in II Kings 16) was that he "sacrificed and burnt incense . . . on the hills and *under every green tree*" instead of in the temples.

737. ONCE BY THE PACIFIC. In *New Repub.*, Dec. 29, 1926; collected, *West Running Brook*, 1928.

737. A LONE STRIKER. Published separately, 1933; collected, *A Further Range*, 1936. "This was Lawrence, and the youth who was a bobbin watch and a night watchman in these same factories was remembering them. . . . How many lone strikers he must have known!" L. Mertins, *The Intervals, etc.*, 1947. But the reader should suspect a more current application.

738. TWO TRAMPS IN MUD-TIME. Used by Elinor and Robert Frost as their Christmas card in 1934; collected, *A Further Range*, 1936.

739. TO A THINKER. In *A Further Range*, 1936. For Frost's politics, see: R. G. Berkelman, "Robert Frost and the Middle Way," *Col. Eng.*, Nov., 1945; Malcolm Cowley, "Frost: A Dissenting Opinion," *New Repub.*, Sept. 11, 18, 1944.

Sara Teasdale (1884–1933)

Sara Teasdale was born in St. Louis, Mo., on Aug. 8, 1884. She was educated in a private school, and as a girl was an assiduous reader and scribbler of verse and prose. In 1907 some of her work appeared in *Reedy's Mirror*, and in the same year she issued *Sonnets to Duse and Other Poems*. More distinctive work, however, was seen in subsequent volumes. She also compiled several anthologies, the most successful being *The Answering Voice*, 1917. In 1914 she was married to Mr. Ernest B. Filsinger, from whom, however, she was divorced in 1929. She travelled extensively, and lived several seasons in California and Arizona. She died in New York City on Jan. 29, 1933.

Her poems are of the pure lyric type, reflections of a mood or state of mind. A number of them, rightly called songs, have been set to music.

Sonnets to Duse and Other Poems, 1907; *Helen of Troy and Other Poems*, 1911, rev. ed., 1922; *Rivers to the Sea*, 1915; *Love Songs*, 1917; *The Answering Voice: One Hundred Love Lyrics by Women* (compilation), 1917; *Vignettes of Italy* (songs; music by W. Watts), 1919; *Flame and Shadow*, 1920; *Rainbow Gold: Poems Old and New Selected for Boys and Girls*, 1922; *Dark of the Moon*, 1926; *Stars To-night: Verses New and Old for Boys and Girls*, 1930; *Strange Victory*, 1933; *Collected Poems*, 1937.

For criticism, see: Harriet Monroe, *Poetry*, XLII, pp. 30–33; Jessie B. Rittenhouse, *Bookman*, LXV, pp. 290–95; Eunice Tietjens, *Poetry*, XVII, pp. 272–

76; Louis Untermeyer, *Sat. Rev. of Lit.*, IX, p. 426.

740. PIERROT. In *Harper's*, Mar., 1910; collected in *Helen of Troy and Other Poems*, 1911.

740. BARTER. In *Poetry*, June, 1917, collected, *Love Songs*, 1917.

740. THERE WILL COME SOFT RAINS. In *Harper's*, July, 1918; collected in *Flame and Shadow*, 1920.

741. I HAVE LOVED HOURS AT SEA. In *Harper's*, Mar., 1919; collected in *Flame and Shadow*, 1920.

741. COMPENSATION. In *Bookman*, Apr., 1920; collected in *Flame and Shadow*, 1920.

741. THE FLIGHT. In *Poetry*, Apr., 1924, and *The Dark of the Moon*, 1926. The other "eagle" is reputed to have been Vachel Lindsay.

Elinor (Hoyt) Wylie (1887–1928)

Elinor Hoyt Wylie was born in 1887 at Rosemont, Pa., the daughter of an old and distinguished American family. She was educated at Miss Baldwin's School, Bryn Mawr, Pa., and the Holton Arms School, Washington, D. C., where she spent a large part of her childhood. After suffering some disillusioning personal experiences which probably helped to intensify her sensitiveness, and after serving a long apprenticeship in the writing of verse, she issued in 1921 *Nets to Catch the Wind*, the first volume published under her own name. Earlier a small book of verse by her had appeared anonymously. During the seven years remaining before her death, she developed steadily in strength as an artist. Besides her several volumes of poetry, she published also four works of fiction. In 1923 she became the wife of William Rose Benét. She died in London on Dec. 16, 1928.

Elinor Wylie's work is distinguished for its restrained expression of emotion, often intense emotion, and for deftness, exquisiteness, elegance of style.

Nets to Catch the Wind, 1921; *Black Armour*, 1923; *Jennifer Lorn*, 1923; *The Venetian Glass Nephew*, 1925; *The Orphan Angel*, 1926; *Trivial Breath*, 1928; *Mr. Hodge and Mr. Hazard*, 1928; *Angels and Earthly Creatures*, 1929; *Collected Poems*, 1932; *Last Poems*, 1943; *Collected Prose*, 1946.

For life and criticism, see: Clement Wood, *Poets of America*, 1925, pp. 262–75; Alfred Kreymborg, *Our Sing-*

ing Strength, 1929, pp. 459–66; James Branch Cabell, *Some of Us*, 1930, pp. 15–27; Harriet Monroe, *Poetry*, XXX, 266–72; Nancy Hoyt, *Elinor Wylie: The Portrait of an Unknown Lady*, 1935; Carl Van Doren, *Three Worlds*, 1936.

741. THE EAGLE AND THE MOLE. In *Nets to Catch the Wind*, 1921. The text for Elinor Wylie's verses is that of the *Collected Poems*, 1932.

742. [PURITAN SONNET] is the last sonnet of four gathered under the title "Wild Peaches" in *Nets to Catch the Wind*, 1921.

742. BEAUTY. In *Nets to Catch the Wind*, 1921. See Carl Van Doren, *Three Worlds*, 1936, for an impression of Miss Wylie's own beauty.

742. CASTILIAN. In *New Repub.*, Nov. 2, 1921; collected in *Black Armour*, 1923. ¶742. "Velasquez," Diego Rodríguez de Silva y (1599–1660), Spanish court painter. Poem inspired by the portrait of "The Unknown Man" at Aspley House(?).

743. LET NO CHARITABLE HOPE. In *Lit. Rev.* of N. Y. *Eve. Post*, July 1, 1922; reprinted in *Black Armour*, 1923.

743. HYMN TO EARTH. In *Sat. Rev. Lit.*, Jan. 26, 1929; collected in *Angels and Earthly Creatures*, 1929.

John Crowe Ransom (1888–   )

John Crowe Ransom was born in Pulaski, Tenn., on Apr. 30, 1888. He attended Vanderbilt University, from which he received the A.B. degree in 1909. The following year he went to Oxford University as a Rhodes Scholar from his native state. On his return he became a teacher of English, finding time incidentally to devote to the writing of poetry. He was one of the founders of the verse journal, *Fugitive*, published in Nashville from 1922 to 1925, and the most important of the group of poets whose organ it was. During 1931–32 he held a Guggenheim Fellowship. He was a member of the faculty at Vanderbilt University from 1914 to 1937; since the latter year he has been on the staff of Kenyon College. He is editor of *The Kenyon Review*. His home is in Gambier, Ohio.

Ransom's poetry reflects a wide range of interests and stylistic variations; it shows challenging allusiveness, irony, contrasting points of view; in manner it is sometimes involved, seemingly pedantic, but precise and subtly pliable.

Poems about God, 1919; *Chills and Fever,* 1924; *Grace after Meat* (London), 1924; *Two Gentlemen in Bonds,* 1927; *God without Thunder,* 1930; *The World's Body,* 1938; *New Criticism,* 1941; *Poetics,* 1942; *Selected Poems,* 1945.

For criticism, see: Alfred Kreymborg, *Our Singing Strength,* 1929, pp. 568–71; Allen Tate, *Nation,* CXXIV, p. 346; Edmund Wilson, *New Repub.,* XLIX, p. 310; Genevieve Taggard, *N. Y. Herald Tribune: Books,* June 26, 1927, p. 12; Robert Penn Warren, *Poetry,* XL, pp. 110–13; Robert Graves, *Sat. Rev. Lit.,* I, p. 412. See also a number of passages in *A Survey of Modernist Poetry,* 1928, by Laura Riding and Robert Graves. For criticism of Ransom's social and economic views, see William S. Knickerbocker, *Sewanee Rev.,* XXXIX, pp. 222–39.

744. CAPTAIN CARPENTER. In *Chills and Fever,* 1924; reprinted in *Fugitives: An Anthology of Verse,* 1928, to which Donald Davidson, W. V. Elliott, J. M. Frank, Stanley Johnson, Merrill Moore, Laura Riding, A. B. Stevenson, Allen Tate, R. P. Warren, and Jesse Wills were also contributors. The anthology represented the best that had appeared in *Fugitive.*

745. MISS EUPHEMIA. Also in *Chills and Fever,* 1924, but not in *Fugitives,* 1928. ¶746. "Pentecost," Whitsunday, seventh Sunday after Easter.

746. PIAZZA PIECE. In *Fugitive,* March, 1925; collected in *Two Gentlemen in Bonds,* 1927.

746. SOMEWHERE IS SUCH A KINGDOM. In *Two Gentlemen in Bonds,* 1927.

(John Orley) Allen Tate
(1899–   )

Named for his father, Allen Tate was born in Winchester, Ky., on Nov. 19, 1899. He received his early education from his mother, who was Nellie Varnell before her marriage. At nine he was sent to a private school in Louisville and at nineteen to the University of Vanderbilt, from which he was graduated with honors in 1922. He described himself as "a free lance writer since 1924." In the interval between his graduation and 1924 he was a contributor to *Fugitive* and was recognized as one of the most brilliant members of the group. He won

a Guggenheim award in 1928, which was renewed the next year. From 1934 to 1936 he was lecturer in English literature at Southwestern College in Memphis; for the academic year 1938–39 he was professor of English at Woman's College, University of North Carolina. Princeton appointed him a fellow in her creative arts program in 1939, from which sinecure he resigned in 1942, only to occupy another very shortly, the chair of poetry at the Library of Congress, 1943–44. Tate was editor of the *Sewanee Review* from 1944 to 1946; at present he is an editor of Henry Holt & Co., publishers. He was married to Caroline Gordon, the novelist, in 1924; they have a daughter.

Stonewall Jackson, 1928; *Mr. Pope and Other Poems,* 1928; *Jefferson Davis,* 1929; *The Critique of Humanism* (contrib.), 1930; *I'll Take My Stand* (contrib.), 1930; *Three Poems,* 1930; *Poems, 1928–1931,* 1932; *The Mediterranean and Other Poems,* 1935; *Who Owns America* (ed. with H. Agar), 1936; *Reactionary Essays,* 1936; *Selected Poems,* 1937; *The Fathers,* 1938; *Reason in Madness,* 1941; *Invitation to Learning* (ed. with H. Cairns & M. Van Doren), 1941; *The Language of Poetry* (ed.), 1942; *The Winter Sea,* 1944; *Poems, 1920–1945,* 1946.

For life and criticism, see: *Who's Who in America, 1948–1949;* Cleanth Brooks, *Modern Poetry and Tradition,* 1939; D. Abel, "Intellectual Criticism," *Am. Schol.,* Oct., 1943. For bibliography, see: W. Thorp, "Allen Tate: A Check List," *Princeton Univ. Lib. Chron.,* Apr., 1942.

747. ODE TO THE CONFEDERATE DEAD. In *Fugitives: An Anthology of Verse,* 1928; also in *Mr. Pope and Other Poems,* 1928. The text of Tate's verse is that of *Poems, 1920–1945,* 1946. "Of muted Zeno and Parmenides" (33). This line has given the poet trouble: originally it read "Of Heraclitus and Parmenides," then "The rage of Zeno," etc. Zeno (fl. 475 B.C.) and Parmenides (fl. 475 B.C.) were Greek philosophers of the Eleatic school.

748. MR. POPE. In *Fugitives, etc.,* 1928, and *Mr. Pope, etc.,* 1928. ¶748. "Pope's tight back": the poet was a hunchback.

749. IDIOT. In *Fugitives, etc.,* 1928, and *Mr. Pope, etc.,* 1928. ¶749. "Appomattox," a symbol of defeat, surrender.

Ellen (Anderson Gholson) Glasgow
(1874–1945)

Ellen Glasgow was an unusual figure among the authors of her region. A Southern aristocrat, she clearly saw and ridiculed the faults of her own social class; and although apparently destined to lead a sheltered life, from the first she insisted on knowing the world about her and on taking an independent part in its activities.

Ellen Anderson Gholson Glasgow was born in Richmond, Va., on Apr. 22, 1874. She was educated at home, under the direction of her mother and of tutors, and at the University of Virginia. While in her early twenties she surreptitiously wrote a novel, *The Descendant,* which was published in 1897 after months of delay. Thus began her literary career. In *The Voice of the People,* 1900, *The Battle-Ground,* 1902, and *The Deliverance,* 1904, she proved her merit as an honest interpreter of life; and the novels which followed improved in quality with the passing of the years. Miss Glasgow traveled widely, and lived periodically in New York City. From the beginning of her career, however, she made her home in the city of her birth, where she owned a sedate old mansion, filled with treasured possessions, and with a flower garden attached—a mansion in which she entertained both personal friends and distinguished visitors. She died on Nov. 22, 1945.

The Descendant, 1897; *Phases of an Inferior Planet,* 1898; *The Voice of the People,* 1900; *The Battle-Ground,* 1902; *The Freeman and Other Poems,* 1902; *The Deliverance,* 1904; *The Wheel of Life,* 1906; *The Ancient Law,* 1908; *The Romance of a Plain Man,* 1909; *The Miller of Old Church,* 1911; *Virginia,* 1913; *Life and Gabriella,* 1916; *The Builders,* 1919; *One Man in His Time,* 1922; *The Shadowy Third,* 1923; *Barren Ground,* 1925; *The Romantic Comedians,* 1926; *They Stooped to Folly,* 1929; *The Sheltered Life,* 1932; *The Vein of Iron,* 1935; *Works* (12 vols.), 1938; *In This Our Life,* 1941; *A Certain Measure,* 1943.

For criticism, see: Stuart Sherman, *Critical Woodcuts,* 1926, pp. 73–83; Grant Overton, *The Women Who Make Our Novels,* rev. ed., 1928, pp. 157–67; James Branch Cabell, *Some of Us,* 1930, pp. 47–59; Fred Lewis Pattee, *The New American Literature,* 1930,

pp. 256–60; Dorothea Lawrence Mann, "Ellen Glasgow: Citizen of the World," *Bookman,* LXIV, pp. 265–72; Sara Haardt, "Ellen Glasgow and the South," *Bookman,* LXIX, pp. 133–40.

750. [A SOUTHERN LADY.] From *The Romantic Comedians,* 1926. Is it not obvious that Annabel contemplates an action of which Amanda may not approve?

753. THE MILLER OF OLD CHURCH is from *A Certain Measure,* 1943, a volume containing the prefaces Miss Glasgow had written for the "Virginia" edition of her *Works,* 1938. ¶754. "John Esten Cooke" (1830–86), romantic novelist, wrote *The Virginia Comedians;* "Tom Jones," masterpiece of Henry Fielding (1707–54), p. 755; "Cavaliers of Virginia," by W. A. Caruthers (1800–46), author also of *Knights of the Horseshoe.* ¶755. "Mrs. Radcliffe," Anne (1764–1823), author of Gothic romances; "Jane Porter" (1776–1850), romancer of Scottish history; "Charlotte Smith" (1749–1806) mixed clandestine marriages, banditti, ghosts, earthquakes, revolutions in her novels. ¶755. "The Adventures of Peregrine Pickle" by Tobias Smollet (1721–71). *The Mysteries of Udolpho* and *Thaddeus of Warsaw* are by Mrs. Radcliffe and Miss Porter, respectively. ¶757. "katharsis," purgation. ¶759. "Stark Young" (1881–), contemporary romancer (*So Red the Rose*). ¶760. "Giants in the Earth," novel of pioneering by Ole Rölvaag (1876–1931). ¶760. "Caroline Gordon," author of *Penhally* (1931); "Marjorie Rawlings," author of *The Yearling* (1938); "Hamilton Basso," author of *Days Before Lent* (1939); "Margaret Mitchell," author of *Gone With the Wind* (1936); "Clifford Dowdey," author of *Gamble's Hundred* (1939). ¶762. "Proust," Marcel (1871–1922), author of *Á la recherche du Temps Perdu* [*Remembrance of Things Past*].

(Newton) Booth Tarkington
(1869–1946)

Born in Indianapolis, July 29, 1869, son of John Stevenson and Elizabeth (Booth) Tarkington. Named for an uncle, a former governor of California. Father had a long and active career (died, 1922): he was captain, 132 Infantry, in Civil War; member Ind. House of Rep.; judge in Seventh Circuit. James Whitcomb Riley, a neighbor, possibly exerted strong influence on the boy after he was eleven (Pattee). Riley later praised *Penrod* but did not approve of *Monsieur Beaucaire*.

Tarkington attended Phillips Exeter Academy, spent two years at Purdue, but finished his college career at Princeton in 1893. Popular and active undergraduate: in dramatics, Triangle Club; edited *Nassau Lit.* and illustrated *Princeton Tiger;* wrote an opera and set Poe's "Raven" to music; was the soloist of the glee club. Failed to become an illustrator (after *Life* printed one drawing in 1895, it rejected thirty-one). Tried to write; for five years all he wrote was rejected. *McClure's* accepted *The Gentleman from Indiana;* that and the publication of *Monsieur Beaucaire,* 1900, brought fame; whereupon H. M. Alden printed *Cherry* in *Harper's,* purchased some time previously.

In legislature 1902–03. "When I left Princeton, I was a Socialist." Colleagues probably regarded him as an Insurgent Republican. Responsible for introduction of "practically all the labor bills." Broom Makers' Union defeated his measure to teach the blind of the state a trade; consequently he renounced radicalism. His earlier attitude is reflected in *In the Arena,* 1905; later, in closing chapters of *The Turmoil,* 1916.

Entered a period of greater fidelity to fact with *The Flirt,* 1913. To this period belong *The Turmoil, The Magnificent Ambersons, Alice Adams* (last two were Pulitzer Prize winners); also *Penrod* and *Seventeen.* Criticism grants Tarkington more ability than accomplishment. It is one of the dire calamities, according to Cabell, that the commercial success of *The Gentleman from Indiana* was followed by the popular triumph of *Monsieur Beaucaire,* for it bred in Mr. Tarkington the concession to being "pleasant." Cabell thinks "no living manipulator of English . . . has a better style." Yet "nothing, apparently, so much gives Mr. Tarkington the horrors as the idea of the 'literary.' He does not want to be 'caught,' he declared, writing 'prose'" (Holliday).

Made home in Indianapolis and Kennebunkport, Me. Twice married: to Laura Louisa Fletcher, June 18, 1902; to Susannah Keifer Robinson, Nov. 6, 1912. About 1917, began to go blind; in August, 1930, became completely so. After a series of operations, his sight was (in 1932) in a measure restored. Died, May 20, 1946.

The Gentleman from Indiana, 1899; *Monsieur Beaucaire,* 1900; *The Two Van Revels,* 1902; *Cherry,* 1903; *In the Arena,* 1905; *The Conquest of Canaan,* 1905; *The Beautiful Lady,* 1905; *His Own People,* 1907; *The Quest of the Quesney,* 1908; *Beasley's Christmas Party,* 1909; *Beauty and the Jacobin,* 1911; *The Flirt,* 1913; *Penrod,* 1914; *The Turmoil,* 1915; *Penrod and Sam,* 1916; *Seventeen,* 1916; *The Magnificent Ambersons,* 1918; *Ramsey Milholland,* 1919; *Alice Adams,* 1921; *Gentle Julia,* 1922; *The Fascinating Stranger,* 1923; *The Midlander,* 1924; *Women,* 1925; *The Plutocrat,* 1927; *Looking Forward,* 1927; *Claire Ambler,* 1928; *The World Does Move,* 1928; *Young Mrs. Greeley,* 1929; *Mirthful Haven,* 1930; *Mary's Neck,* 1932; *Wanton Mally,* 1932; *Presenting Lily Mars,* 1933; *Little Orvie,* 1934; *Mr. White, The Red Barn, Hell and Bridewater,* 1935; *The Lorenzo Bunch,* 1936; *Rumbin Galleries,* 1937; *Some Old Portraits,* 1939; *The Heritage of Hatcher Ide,* 1940; *The Fighting Littles,* 1941; *Kate Fennigate,* 1943; *Image of Josephine,* 1945; *Show Piece,* 1947; *Three Selected Short Novels,* 1947.

Plays: with E. G. Sutherland, *Monsieur Beaucaire,* 1901; with H. L. Wilson, *The Man from Home,* 1906; *Cameo Kirby,* 1907; *Your Humble Servant,* 1908; *Springtime,* 1908; *Getting a Polish,* 1909; *Mister Antonio,* 1916; *The Gibson Upright,* 1919; *Up from Nowhere,* 1919; *Tweedles,* 1923; *How's Your Health?,* 1930; with Julian Street, *The Country Cousin,* 1917; without collab.: *Clarence,* 1919; *Poldekin,* 1920; *The Wren,* 1921; *The Intimate Strangers,* 1921; *Rose Brier,* 1922; *The Trysting Place,* 1923; *Colonel Satan,* 1930.

For life, see: *The World Does Move;* R. C. Holliday, *Booth Tarkington,* 1918; A. D. Dickinson, *Booth Tarkington: a Sketch,* 1925. For criticism, see C. C. Baldwin, *The Men Who Make Our Novels,* 1924; P. H. Boynton, *Some Contemporary Americans,* 1924; Meredith Nicholson, *The Hoosiers,* 1900; Grant Overton, *American Nights Entertainment,* 1923; F. L. Pattee, *The New American Literature,* 1930; Carl Van Doren, *Contemporary American Novelists,* 1922; M. O. Williams, *Indiana Authors,* 1916; J. B. Cabell, *Be-*

yond Life, 1919. For bibliography, see: B. W. Currie, *Booth Tarkington: a Bibliography,* 1932.

762. BRIDEWATER'S HALF DOLLAR. In the *Sat. Eve. Post,* June 15, 1935; collected in *Mr. White, The Red Barn, Hell and Bridewater,* 1935. ¶763. *"two-hundred-dollar-a-month plan."* The so-called "Townsend Plan."

Willa (Sibert) Cather (1876–1947)

Willa Sibert Cather was born near Winchester, Va., on Dec. 7, 1876, but at the age of eight was brought to Nebraska, where she lived for several years on a ranch. She saw much of the country, and mingled with the children of the Scandinavian, Bohemian, French, and Russian settlers who were neighbors. Later her family moved to the town of Red Cloud, where she attended the high school. In 1892 she entered the University of Nebraska, and after receiving the A.B. degree in 1895 went east in search of employment and further cultural advantages. She secured the position of telegraph editor of the Pittsburgh [Pa.] *Daily Leader,* remaining with this newspaper until 1901, when she became the head of the English department in the Allegheny High School. She had already begun to contribute to the magazines, however, and in 1903 appeared her volume of verse, *April Twilights.* After the success of the book of stories, *The Troll Garden,* 1905, she was appointed to the staff of *McClure's Magazine,* becoming the managing editor in 1908. In 1912 she resigned from the position, and after that time allowed no other occupation to interfere with her literary labors. Her reputation did not reach a flowering, however, until after 1918, when *My Antonia* was published. Throughout the years following her departure from Nebraska, she kept in close contact with life in the state, through regular visits to her family and to familiar scenes. She was elected to membership in the American Academy of Arts and Letters, and in 1944 received the award of the National Institute of Arts and Letters. She died on April 25, 1947.

Her early fiction is based on real happenings and the personalities of actual people. The originals of the characters in *My Antonia,* for example, are recognizable by citizens of Red Cloud, and the situations in other of her novels owe their existence to circumstances well known locally. *Death Comes for the Archbishop* and *Shadows on the Rock* are more pictorial in method and reflect an interest in experiences far removed from her own life, yet they gain from the careful study of historical documents which preceded their writing. *A Lost Lady* and *My Mortal Enemy,* studies done under the influence of Flaubert, are her best work.

April Twilights, 1903; *The Troll Garden,* 1905; *Alexander's Bridge,* 1912; *O Pioneers!,* 1913; *The Song of the Lark,* 1915; *My Antonia,* 1918; *Youth and the Bright Medusa,* 1920; *One of Ours,* 1922; *A Lost Lady,* 1923; *The Professor's House,* 1925; *Best Stories of Sarah Orne Jewett* (ed.), 1925; *My Mortal Enemy,* 1926; *Death Comes for the Archbishop,* 1927; *Shadows on the Rock,* 1931; *Obscure Destinies,* 1932; *Lucy Gayheart,* 1935; *Not Under Forty,* 1936; *Novels and Stories,* 1937–38; *Sapphira and the Slave Girl,* 1940; *Old Beauty and Others,* 1948.

For life and criticism, see: René Rapin, *Willa Cather,* 1930. For criticism, see: Percy H. Boynton, *Some Contemporary Americans,* 1924, pp. 162–78; Stuart Sherman, *Critical Woodcuts,* 1926, pp. 32–49; Régis Michaud, *The American Novel To-day,* 1928, pp. 238–48; Grant Overton, *The Women Who Make Our Novels,* rev. ed., 1928, pp. 76–98; Alexander Porterfield, *Contemporary American Authors* (ed. by J. C. Squire), 1928, pp. 45–68; T. K. Whipple, *Spokesmen,* 1928, pp. 139–59; Fred Lewis Pattee, *The New American Literature,* 1930, pp. 260–65; R. H. Footman, *Am. Lit.,* X, pp. 123–42; F. B. Adams, Jr., *Colophon,* n.g.s. I, no. 3, 1–10 pp., and no. 4, pp. 103–8; George L. White, *Sewanee Rev.,* L, pp. 18–25; E. K. Brown, *Yale Rev.,* XXXVI, pp. 77–92. Brown has a biography in preparation.

775. NEIGHBOUR ROSICKY. In *Obscure Destinies,* 1932. ¶779. *"Bohunk,"* a contemptuous term for a Bohemian or Czech worker. ¶780. *"kolache,"* a kind of coffee cake. ¶782. *"Cheapside,"* London street, but the usual reference is to the East End. ¶782. *"Castle Garden,"* one-time fort, later opera house and aquarium, was used for a time as a disembarkment and inspection point for immigrants. ¶790. *"Strand . . . New Oxford St.,"* area of fashionable shops and restaurants.

Thornton (Niven) Wilder
(1897–   )

Thornton Niven Wilder was born on Apr. 17, 1897, at Madison, Wis. He attended schools in China, where his father went as American consul-general in 1906, in Berkeley, Calif., and in Ojai, Calif. He spent two years at Oberlin College, but received the A.B. degree from Yale University in 1920. During the First World War, he served in the Coast Artillery at Narragansett Bay. During 1920–21 he worked at the American Academy in Rome. In 1925 he was a graduate student at Princeton University, receiving the M.A. degree in 1925. For seven years was a teacher of French at the Lawrenceville School, Lawrenceville, N. J., where he remained until 1928. His novel, *The Bridge of San Luis Rey*, 1927, was an immense and surprising success, and brought him large sums of money and a reputation. In 1929 he made an extended lecture tour, and the following year accepted a position as lecturer at the University of Chicago. During 1942–45 he served with the U. S. Air Corps Intelligence Service, becoming a lieutenant colonel in 1944. His home is in Hamden, Conn.

The Cabala, 1926; *The Trumpet Shall Sound*, 1926; *The Bridge of San Luis Rey*, 1927; *The Angel That Troubled the Waters and Other Plays*, 1928; *The Woman of Andros*, 1930; *The Long Christmas Dinner and Other Plays in One Act*, 1931; *Love and How to Cure It*, 1932; *Happy Journey*, 1934, rev. ed., 1947; *Heaven's My Destination*, 1935; *Our Town*, 1938; *Merchant of Yonkers*, 1939; *Skin of Our Teeth*, 1942.

For criticism, see: Clifton Fadiman, *Nation*, CXXV, p. 687; Henry Hazlitt, *Nation*, CXXX, p. 246; Edmund Wilson, *New Repub.*, LV, pp. 303–5; Carl Van Doren, *N. Y. Herald Tribune Books*, Feb. 23, 1930, pp. 1–2; Lee Wilson Dodd, *Sat. Rev. Lit.*, IV, p. 371; Edith Isaacs, *Theatre Arts*, XXVII, pp. 21–30; Henry Adler, *Horizon*, XII, pp. 89–98; Michael Gold, "Wilder, Prophet of the Genteel Christ," *New Repub.*, Oct. 22, 1930.

796. PERHAPS AN ACCIDENT. Forms the introductory section of *The Bridge of San Luis Rey*, 1927. ¶796. "Osier," a variety of willow; "Incas," Peruvian Indians (loosely used here).

Thomas (Clayton) Wolfe
(1900–1938)

The "Altamont" of Thomas Wolfe's novels is Asheville, N. C., where he was born on Oct. 3, 1900, to William Oliver Wolfe, a stonecutter, and his wife, Julia Elizabeth (Westall) Wolfe, who bear a close resemblance to W. O. Gant of *Look Homeward, Angel* and his wife, Liza. The episodes of Wolfe's early life are not dissimilar to those of Eugene, the hero of his first novel. He ran errands, sold papers and the *Saturday Evening Post*, and listened to his father spout Shakespeare. Later his mother ran the boarding house depicted in several of his novels. Asheville is a health resort, and one of the things glanced at in his novels, but of deeper consequence in his life, was the fact that he associated rather constantly with sick, neurotic, and abnormal people. This in part accounted for his protestations of health, his demonstrative big appetite, etc., but only partly. Wolfe went to the University of North Carolina and was graduated at twenty. As a student he had been editor of the college paper and had written plays for Koch of Carolina Playmaker fame and had acted the lead in one of them (see "Return of Buck Gavin," *Carolina Folk Plays*, second series (ed. F. H. Koch), 1924). This encouraged him to enroll in the 47 Workshop course at Harvard. Wolfe got his M.A. at Harvard but was discouraged as a dramatist by Professor Baker, whom he never forgave. He brought the MS of a play to New York with him and went through the gruelling experience of being kept on tenter hooks interminably by the producers. Meanwhile he had a tempestuous but unfortunate love affair with Arline Bernstein, the brilliant stage designer. When nothing developed with his play, he sought employment successfully as an instructor at New York University and had an irregular connection with this institution teaching English till 1930. Mr. Maxwell Perkins of Scribner's discovered the substance of several novels in the mass of MS Wolfe had accumulated by writing every day and helped this book first to shape a portion of this book into *Look Homeward, Angel* which immediately raised the raw boy from Carolina into fame. Thereafter Wolfe's life consisted of Prose. He wrote and wrote and wrote, writing whether he "hived up" in a Brooklyn room or in the Hotel Chelsea, whether he traveled to Germany to spend the royalties which his popularity brought him there or journeyed about the United States with every faculty sensate and hungry. The state of constant excitement in which he lived enervated him; he was an easy victim to cerebral infection after contracting influenza. His death occurred in the Johns Hopkins hospital on September 15, 1938.

Look Homeward, Angel, 1929; *Of Time and the River*, 1935; *From Death to Morning*, 1935; *The Story of a Novel*, 1936; *The Web and the Rock*, 1939; *The Face of a Nation* (selections), 1939; *You Can't Go Home Again*, 1940; *The Hills Beyond*, 1941; *Thomas Wolfe's Letters to His Mother* (ed. J. S. Terry), 1943.

For life and criticism, see: Obituary, *N. Y. Times*, Sept. 15, 1938; Thomas Wolfe, "What a Writer Reads," *Bk. Buyer*, Dec., 1935; *The Story of a Novel; Thomas Wolfe's Letters to His Mother;* "Writing Is My Life" [Letters], *Atlantic*, Dec., 1946, Jan., Feb., 1947; E. C. Aswell, "A Note on Thomas Wolfe" in *The Hills Beyond;* H. J. Miller, *Thomas Wolfe*, 1947; P. H. Johnson, *Hungry Gulliver*, 1948; Hayden Norwood, *The Marble Man's Wife*, 1947; J. R. Meade, "Thomas Wolfe on the Use of Fact and Fiction," *N. Y. Her.-Trib. Books*, Apr. 14, 1935; T. G. Ehrsam, "I Knew Thomas Wolfe," *Bk. Col. Jour.*, June, 1936; P. M. Jack, "Remembering Thomas Wolfe," *N. Y. Times Bk. Rev.*, Oct. 2, 1938; H. T. Volkenning, "Penance No More," *Va. Quar. Rev.*, Spring, 1939; Desmond Powell, "Of Thomas Wolfe," *Ariz. Quar.*, Spring, 1945; J. D. Wade, "Prodigal," *So. Rev.*, Jul., 1935; R. P. Warren, "A Note on the Hamlet of Thomas Wolfe," *Am. Rev.*, May, 1935.

For bibliography, see: G. R. Preston, *Thomas Wolfe: A Bibliography*, 1943; Bernice Kauffman, "Bibliog. of Periodical Art. by T. W.," *Bul. Bibl.*, May–Aug., 1942.

798. A PORTRAIT OF BASCOM HAWKE. In *Scribner's*, Apr., 1932. It has been reworked for incorporation in *Of Time and the River*, 1935. The magazine text is followed here. ¶802. "*Pahkeh House*," Parker House, a hotel famous for its restaurant. ¶808. "*The isles of Greece. . . .*" From Byron's *Don Juan*. ¶814. "*Malden . . . Dorchester,*" sub-

urbs of Boston. ¶818. "*give this ass a tongue.*" II Peter 2. 16. ¶820. "*our own former governor.*" Calvin Coolidge. ¶824. "*Hegel,*" Georg W. F. (1770–1831) German philosopher. ¶827. "*Faustian web,*" a hunger for all knowledge, such as Faust had. ¶828. "*Old Catawba.*" Wolfe's name for North Carolina. ¶833. "*the Fifth Symphony.*" Ludwig van Beethoven's Symphony No. 5 in C Minor [Opus 67]. ¶833. "*Richard Wagner*" (1813–83), German composer. ¶833. "*Critique of Pure Reason.*" By Immanuel Kant (1724–1804). ¶833. "*Goethe,*" Johann Wolfgang von (1749–1832), German novelist, poet, and dramatist. "*Voltaire,*" François Marie Arouet de (1694–1778), French philosopher. This diatribe, assigned to Bascom Hawke, was one that Wolfe himself frequently uttered. ¶834. "*Nordau's book.*" *Degeneracy* by Max Nordau (1849–1923). ¶836. "*William McDougall,*" author of *Social Psychology*, then lecturing at Harvard.

841. "THE HOLLOW MEN" is Chapter 29 in *You Can't Go Home Again*, 1940. It constitutes a "reply" to T. S. Eliot's "The Hollow Men," which should be read in conjunction. ¶841. "*Fox.*" Foxhall Edwards, fictive name for Maxwell Perkins, friend whose cynical philosophy is repudiated in this novel. Perkins was editor for Scribner's publishing house. ¶841. "*[All the] news that's 'fit to print.*'" Slogan of *The New York Times*. ¶842. "*Penn-Pitt,*" etc., a list synthesized from the *Hotel Red Book*. ¶844. "*Lefty Grove,*" great pitcher for the Philadelphia Athletics. ¶845. "*Cape St. Vincent.*" Southwestern promontory, Portugal. ¶845. "*Scilly Isles.*" Off Cornwall, England. ¶846. "*Smokies.*" Great Smoky Mountains in N. Car. and Tenn. ¶847. "*Plymouth harbor.*" To which Drake returned after his cruise around world. ¶848. "*Borough Hall.*" Area about, as well as the Borough administration building in Brooklyn.

William James (1842–1910)

Born in New York City, Jan. 11, 1842, son of Rev. Henry James, a man of leisure and means, regarded as an eccentric because of his strong interest in Swedenborg and Mesmer. Interest in mesmerism probably directed the attention of his sons, William and Henry (the novelist), to psychology. William's youth was spent in schools in Switzerland, France, and England. He studied painting, winter of 1860–61, with Holman Hunt at Newport; though gifted, he abandoned art for medicine. Two years were spent in Lawrence Scientific School, two in Harvard Medical, one on Thayer Expedition to Brazil with Agassiz, then a winter at University of Berlin, before he took an M.D. degree, Harvard, 1869. As instructor at Harvard, he offered a comparative course in psychology and physiology, and founded the first psychological laboratory in America. From his investigations he formulated the James-Lange theory that emotion is an effect, not a cause, of its organic expression. Married Alice H. Gibbens, 1878. Made asst. professor of philosophy, 1880; professor, 1885. In 1884, helped establish American Society for Psychical Research; in 1889, became professor of psychology. Exchanged title for professor of philosophy, 1897. A weakness of the heart kept him from duties, 1899–1901; but he gave the Gifford Lectures, Edinburgh, 1901–02. Lectured at Lowell Institute and Columbia, 1906–07; gave Hibbert lectures, Oxford, 1908. Died of heart failure, Cambridge, Mass., Aug. 26, 1910.

For his philosophy, James adopted the name "Pragmatism" (Grk. πρᾶγμα = action) from Charles Saunders Pierce. He held that truth must be judged by action and not by abstract concepts. His theory of life was that mankind is struggling in a world "not made for it, but in which it grew." Each thing in this world, which is increasingly complex, is self-governed, but exists only because it has made some sort of adjustment to other things. This adjustment is never permanent, for the world is constantly changing, therefore it is not *being* or existing which is important, but *becoming* or persisting. Pragmatism is the philosophy of "making good." Whatever idealism there is in James is traced to the influence of Swedenborg.

All that he wrote is well written. It is said of him and Henry his brother, the novelist, that the former wrote psychology like a novelist, the latter, fiction like a psychologist. William James was vivid, colloquial, humorous, and direct; never was there such a wealth of illustration and anecdote—at least, never in scientific treatises. A textbook in psychology is his best production! Though he abjured the "grand style," the eloquent address at Emerson Centenary Exercises, Concord,

May 25, 1903, proves he could have controlled it admirably. His Robert Gould Shaw oration inspired Moody's famous "Ode."

The Literary Remains of Henry James, Sr., 1885; *Principles of Psychology*, 2 vols., 1891; *Text-Book of Psychology*, 1892; *The Will to Believe*, 1897; *Talks to Teachers of Psychology*, 1899; *The Varieties of Religious Experience*, 1902; *Pragmatism*, 1907; *The Meaning of Truth*, 1909; *A Pluralistic Universe*, 1909; *Memories and Studies*, 1911; *Essays in Empiricism* (ed. R. B. Perry), 1912.

Selected Papers on Philosophy, ed. C. M. Bakewell, Everyman's, 1917; *The Philosophy of William James*, ed. H. Kallen, Mod. Lib., 1925.

For life, see: Émile Boutroux, *William James* (trans. A. & B. Henderson), 1912; *The Letters of William James*, ed. Henry James (his son), 2 vols., 1920; Henry James, *Notes of a Son and Brother*, 1914; R. B. Perry, *Thought and Character of William James*, 1935. For criticism, see: M. H. Cohen, "Later Philosophy," *CHAL*, III; John Macy, *The Spirit of American Literature*, 1911; Ethel Sabin, *William James and Pragmatism*, 1916; George Santayana, *Character and Opinion in the U. S.*, 1920; Woodbridge Riley, *American Thought*, rev., 1923; W. T. Bush, "William James and Panpsychism," *Studies in the History of Ideas*, II, 1925; F. C. S. Schiller, "William James and Empiricism," *Jour. of Philos.*, XXV (1928), 155–62; H. W. Schneider, *A History of American Philosophy*, 1946. For bibliography, see: R. B. Perry, *An Annotated Bibliography of the Writings of William James*, 1920.

855. WHAT PRAGMATISM MEANS. In *Pragmatism*, 1907. It was originally the second lecture which James gave at the Lowell Institute in Boston in 1906. The eight lectures make the book. ¶856. "Charles Peirce." The father (1839–1914) of the school of philosophers to which James belonged. He was a Cambridge, Mass., mathematician and logician. See H. W. Schneider, *A History of American Philosophy*, 1946. ¶856. "Howison," George H., philosophical idealist. James' lecture, "Philosophical Conceptions and Practical Results," was delivered in 1897. ¶856. "Ostwald," Wilhelm (1853–   ), pioneer physical chemist. ¶857. "Shadworth Hodgson" (1832–1912), British philosopher, influenced James. ¶857. "ultramontane

. . . *priest.* One who believes that the Pope is the spiritual head of the Church in all countries. ¶858. *"nominalism"* holds that universals are reducible to names without any objective existence corresponding to them; *"utilitarianism,"* action should be determined by what will bring the greatest happiness to the largest number; *"positivism,"* phenomena and facts should influence courses not ultimates. ¶859. *"Kepler,"* Johann (1571–1630), German astronomer. ¶859. *"Schiller,"* Ferdinand C. S., sole British pragmatist. ¶861. *"Ramsay,"* Sir William (1852–1916), English chemist, author of the theory of transmutation. ¶863. *"nulla vestigia retrorsum,"* no trace of return.

John Dewey (1859–   )

John Dewey was born in Burlington, Vt., on Oct. 20, 1859. At the age of twenty he received the A.B. degree from the University of Vermont, and in 1884 the Ph.D. degree from Johns Hopkins University. Forthwith he began the career as university teacher and author in which he was to be distinguished. From 1884 to 1894 he served in the departments of philosophy at the Universities of Michigan and Minnesota. During the years 1894–1904 he was the head of the department of philosophy at the University of Chicago, acting also as the Director of the School of Education from 1902 to 1904. In 1904 he became a professor of philosophy at Columbia University. The influence of his teaching and his writings in the fields of philosophy and education has been impressive, and has extended to the whole country.

Selections from the Writings of George MacDonald, 1885; *Psychology,* 1887; *Leibniz's New Essays Concerning the Human Understanding,* 1888; *Applied Psychology* (with J. A. McLellan), 1889; *Outlines of a Critical Theory of Ethics,* 1891; *The Study of Ethics,* 1894; *The Psychology of Number* (with J. A. McLellan), 1895; *The School and Society,* 1899; *The Educational Situation,* 1902; *Studies in Logical Theory* (with others), 1903; *The School and the Child* (selections ed. by J. J. Findlay, London), 1907; *Ethics* (with J. H. Tufts), 1908; *Moral Principles in Education,* 1909; *How We Think,* 1910; *The Influence of Darwin on Philosophy and Other Essays,* 1910; *Educational Essays by John Dewey* (ed. by J. J. Findlay, London), 1910; *Interest and Effort in Education,* 1913; *German Philosophy and Politics,* 1915; *Schools of Tomorrow* (with Evelyn Dewey), 1915; *Democracy and Education,* 1916; *Essays in Experimental Logic,* 1916; *Reconstruction in Philosophy,* 1920; *Letters from China and Japan* (with Mrs. Dewey; ed. by Evelyn Dewey), 1920; *China, Japan, and the U. S. A.,* 1920; *Human Nature and Conduct,* 1922; *Experience and Nature,* 1925; *The Public and Its Problems,* 1927; *The Philosophy of John Dewey* (ed. by Joseph Ratner), 1928; *Characters and Events* (ed. by Joseph Ratner), 1929; *Impressions of Soviet Russia and the Revolutionary World, Mexico–China–Turkey,* 1929; *The Quest for Certainty,* 1929; *The Sources of a Science of Education,* 1929; *Individualism, Old and New,* 1930; *The Way Out of Educational Confusion,* 1931; *Philosophy and Civilization,* 1931; *Art as Experience,* 1934; *Common Faith,* 1934; *Liberalism and Social Action,* 1935; *Experience and Education,* 1938; *Freedom and Culture,* 1939; *Education Today,* 1940; *German Philosophy and Politics,* 1942; *Problems of Men,* 1946; *The Public and Its Problems,* 1946.

For criticism, see: Delton Thomas Howard, *John Dewey's Logical Theory,* 1918; Arthur K. Rogers, *English and American Philosophy since 1800,* 1922, pp. 388–406; R. S. Arndt, *John Dewey's Philosophy of Education,* 1929; James Henry O'Hara, *The Limitations of the Educational Theory of John Dewey,* 1929; *John Dewey, the Man and His Philosophy: Addresses Delivered in New York in Celebration of His Seventieth Birthday,* 1930; W. T. Feldman, *The Philosophy of John Dewey,* 1934; Sidney Hook, *John Dewey,* 1939; M. G. White, *Origin of Dewey's Instrumentalism,* 1943. See also Milton Halsey Thomas and Herbert Wallace Schneider, *A Bibliography of John Dewey,* 1929.

866. EXPERIENCE AND THE PHILOSOPHIC METHOD is Chapter I of *Experience and Nature,* 1925. See H. W. Schneider, *A History of American Philosophy,* 1946, for Dewey's position in the development of American philosophy. ¶869. *"dog of Odysseus."* Though unable to rise, the old dog recognized his disguised master by thumping his tail. ¶872. *"Descartes,"* René (1596–1650). French mathematician and philosopher; *"Spinoza,"* Baruch (1632–77), Dutch

philosopher; *"Locke,"* John (1632–1704), British political writer and philosopher; *"Hume,"* David (1711–76), Scottish historian and philosopher. ¶873. *"Epictetus"* (A.D. 60?–120?), Greek stoic. ¶874. *"Kant,"* Immanuel (1724–1804) German philosopher. ¶883. *"the unum, verum, et bonum,"* the one, the true, and the good.

Finley Peter Dunne (1867–1936)

Son of Peter and Ellen (Finley) Dunne; born in St. Patrick's parish, Chicago, July 10, 1867. Newspaper reporter at eighteen, after a public school education. While working for the *Tribune,* Dunne made the acquaintance of an Irish barkeep named McGarrey in a saloon on Dearborn St. McGarrey discoursed on local politics; Dunne turned one of his speeches into an article, giving him the name "McNeery." Eventually this was dropped for "Martin Dooley," and the interlocutor "Mr. Hennessey" was created. Meanwhile, after acting as city-editor of the *Times,* 1891–98, Dunne became managing editor of the Chicago *Journal,* 1898. During the Spanish-American War the opinions of "Mr. Dooley" were awaited with as much interest as those of the nation's leaders. The genial Irishman understood perfectly the national psychology:

"We're a gr-reat people," said Mr. Hennessey earnestly.
"We ar-re," said Mr. Dooley. "We ar-re that. An' th' best iv it is, we know we ar-re."

At 33, Dunne came to New York City as editor of the *American Magazine.* Married Margaret Abbott, Dec. 9, 1902; had four children. "Mr. Dooley" continued a power through the muck-raking era.

Mr. Dooley in Peace and War, 1898; *Mr. Dooley in the Hearts of His Countrymen,* 1899; *What Dooley Says,* 1899; *Mr. Dooley's Philosophy,* 1900; *Mr. Dooley's Opinions,* 1901; *Observations by Mr. Dooley,* 1902; *Dissertations by Mr. Dooley,* 1906; *Mr. Dooley Says,* 1910; *New Dooley Book,* 1911; *Mr. Dooley on Making a Will,* 1919; *Finley Peter Dunne: Mr. Dooley at His Best* (ed. Elmer Ellis), 1938.

For life, see: E. F. Harkins, *Little Pilgrimages, II,* 1903; Elmer Ellis, *Mr. Dooley's America,* 1941. For criticism, see: J. B. Fletcher, *Col. Univ. Course in Lit.,* XVIII, 1929; W. D. Howells, "Work of Finley Peter Dunne," *N. Am. Rev.,* May, 1903; F. L. Pattee, *The New American Literature,* 1930; H. H. McClure, "Mr. Dooley, Ph.D.," *Am. Mag.,* Dec., 1907; G. F. Whicher, "Minor Humorists," *CHAL,* III.

885. A BOOK REVIEW. In Chicago *Journal,* "last week in Nov., 1898"; collected in *Mr. Dooley in the Hearts of His Countrymen,* 1899. The book "reviewed" is, of course, Theodore Roosevelt's *The Rough Riders,* 1898. "I regret to state," Roosevelt wrote Dunne on Nov. 28, "that my family and intimate friends are delighted with your review of my book." ¶886. *"Ant Hills."* The Antilles, the chain of islands which includes Cuba. ¶886. *"Richard Harding Davis"* (1864–1916), American journalist who accompanied the Rough Riders to Cuba. ¶886. *"Gin'ral Tamale."* Hardly a respectful allusion to General Vara del Rey, gallant defender of El Caney, who was slain—but not by T. R. ¶886. *"Miles,"* General Nelson A. (1839–1925), who (contrary to Mr. Dooley) had no personal share in the Cuban campaign. ¶886. *"San Joon hill."* San Juan hill was captured on July 1, 1898, by troops under Wheeler and Kent, including the Rough Riders. ¶887. *"Shafter's histhry."* General William R. (1835–1906) had promised a history of the war, but if he were no swifter with the pen than with the sword, Dooley intimates, it would never get done.

Theodore Roosevelt (1858–1919)

Born at No. 28 E. 20th St., New York City, Oct. 27, 1858, a son of Theodore, descendant from Claes M. Van Roosevelt (who came to New Amsterdam in 1644), prosperous merchant, and Martha Bulloch, related to the first governor of Georgia. The boy was privately educated; he was not precocious; suffered from asthma. His father fitted up a gymnasium, and encouraged horseback riding. He entered Harvard in 1876 ("I am sure it did me good, but only in general effect, for there was very little in my actual studies which helped me in after life"). Interested in natural science; later admitted a genuine debt to the rhetorician, A. S. Hill. In sophomore year, his father died; during senior year became engaged to Alice Hathaway Lee, of Chestnut Hill, Mass. Stood among first ten in his class; Phi Beta Kappa.

Began the study of law and joined 21st Dist. Repub. Club, 1880. A laggard at law, wrote *A History of the Naval War of 1812* (pub. 1882). Married Miss Lee Oct. 27, 1880. Elected Assemblyman, 1881; three terms at Albany, marked by strenuous efforts for reform in New York City, linked his name with crusading governor, Grover Cleveland. His mother died Feb. 12, 1884, and his wife the following day. Spent the next two years at the Chimney Butte and Elkhorn ranches on the Little Missouri. Ran as independent candidate for mayor of New York City against Henry George and Abram S. Hewitt. After defeat went to Europe; in London married Edith Kermit Carow, childhood friend. Settled at Sagamore Hill, Oyster Bay, L. I. In 1892, began publication of the *Winning of the West* which eventually extended to ten vols. Had contributed to American Statesmen Series: *Thomas Hart Benton*, 1886; *Gouverneur Morris*, 1887. (One other attempt at biography, aside from *Autobiography*, 1913, *Oliver Cromwell*, 1900.) Extraordinarily active with his pen from 1884 to end of his life.

Appointed Civil Service Commissioner by Harrison, 1888; his fine record induced Cleveland to reappoint him, 1892. Resigned to become president of Board of Police Commissioners, New York City, 1895. Reformed the department; cleaned up slums; attracted national attention. "You are doing the greatest work of which any American to-day is capable," E. L. Godkin wrote him. McKinley offered him the position of Assistant Secretary of the Navy. In Navy Dept. was chiefly responsible for a program displacing obsolete ships; when war broke out, 1898, the Navy was prepared. Gave the order to Dewey which led to the victory at Manila. Resigned to raise at San Antonio, Texas, a regiment of volunteer cavalry (the "Rough Riders"), serving as Lt. Col.; they were in the thick of Cuban fighting (Las Guasimas, San Juan Hill, Santiago). After Leonard Wood's promotion, Roosevelt was in command.

His popularity forced Sen. Platt, "boss" of N. Y. State, to accept him as candidate for governor. When elected, he began a war to tax corporations holding public franchises. To get rid of him Platt got him nominated for Vice-Presidency; was elected with McKinley,

1900. Became President on McKinley's death, Sept. 14, 1901.

In 1899 James Bryce observed, "Theodore Roosevelt is the hope of American politics"; in two terms Roosevelt fulfilled that hope. His conviction was that "governmental agencies find their justification in the way in which they are used for the practical betterment of living and working conditions among the mass of the people." His term was remarkable for incessant war on "privilege" and for the inculcation of "the Jackson-Lincoln theory of the presidency," which called for the assumption of extra-constitutional powers on the part of the Chief Executive in times of emergency. Wielding the "Big Stick," he forced conciliations and reforms before unparalleled. In international affairs, secured settlement of Alaskan boundary, arbitration in Venezuela, early termination of Russo-Jap War, and arrangements necessary to the construction of the Panama Canal. Was granted the Nobel Peace Prize. At home, he advocated conservation and reclamation.

Sponsored Taft for presidency, 1908. After a hunting trip in Africa, and receptions in European capitals, was accorded an ovation in New York; felt the administration lacked vigor. Embittered at the renomination of Taft, he became Progressive nominee, 1912; the platform contained planks made laws by Wilson who defeated him. Led an expedition into the Brazilian wilderness for Museum of Natural History; contracted a fever which caused complications at death. At outbreak of the Great War, alarmed by Wilson's pacifism, he tried to arouse the country, and aided organization of the R.O.T.C. camp at Plattsburg, N. Y. Offered his services in 1917, but was debarred from military activity. The loss of his son, Quentin, killed in an air battle in France, July 14, 1918, was a severe blow. Died from a blood clot in the heart, Jan. 6, 1919.

Writings were marked by force and cogency; had a trick of coining new phrases and of giving life to old ones: "Pussyfoot," "the Big Stick," "the square deal," "the Ananias Club," "the strenuous life," "malefactors of great wealth," "muck-raker," etc. As an historian, followed his admired master, Parkman, in further opening the West for scholarly investigation. If popular suffrage is any indication, his ideals were those of the American people between 1898 and 1912.

Other titles: *Hunting Trips of a Ranchman,* 1885; *Ranch Life and the Hunting Trail,* 1888; *New York* (*Hist. Towns Series*), 1890; *The Winning of the West,* 1889–96; *American Ideals,* 1897; *The Rough Riders,* 1898; *The Strenuous Life,* 1900; *Outdoor Pastimes of an American Hunter,* 1902; *African Game Trails,* 1910; *History as Literature,* 1913; *Through the Brazilian Wilderness,* 1914; *A Booklover's Holiday,* 1916; *Fear God and Take Your Own Part,* 1916; *The Great Adventure,* 1918.

Best editions: *Elkhorn,* 28 vols., 1906; *Memorial,* ed. Herman Hagedorn, 24 vols., 1923–25; *National,* 20 vols., 1926. For ideas, see: *Theodore Roosevelt Cyclopedia* (ed. A. B. Hart and H. R. Ferleger), 1941. For bibliography, see: J. H. Wheelock, *A Bibliography of Theodore Roosevelt,* 1920.

For life, see: *Autobiography,* 1913 (also scattered reminiscences); *Theodore Roosevelt's Letters to His Children* (ed. J. B. Bishop), 1919; *Selections from the Correspondence of Theodore Roosevelt and Henry Cabot Lodge,* 2 vols., 1925; *Letters to Kermit,* 1946; Jacob A. Riis, *Theodore Roosevelt, Citizen,* 1904; John Burroughs, *Camping and Tramping with Roosevelt,* 1907; W. R. Thayer, *Theodore Roosevelt,* 1919; J. B. Bishop, *Theodore Roosevelt and His Times,* 2 vols., 1920; Corinne Roosevelt Robinson, *My Brother, Theodore Roosevelt,* 1921; Bradley Gilman, *Roosevelt the Happy Warrior,* 1921; Lord Charnwood, *Theodore Roosevelt,* 1923; Owen Wister, *Roosevelt, the Story of a Friendship,* 1930; H. F. Pringle, *Theodore Roosevelt,* 1931. For literary criticism, see: C. W. Ferguson, "Roosevelt—Man of Letters," *Bookman,* LXIV, 726–29; Anon., "Mr. Roosevelt in Literature," *Lit. Digest,* Jan. 25, 1919; H. A. Beers, "Roosevelt as a Man of Letters," *Four Americans,* 1919.

887. THE NEW NATIONALISM. Address at Ossawatomie, Kansas, on August 31, 1910. The text is from the volume *Social Justice and Popular Rule* in the National Edition of the *Works of Theodore Roosevelt,* 1926. Having already declared himself in New York for the direct primary, Roosevelt here outlined the remainder of his "Progressive" program. ¶892. *"The Hepburn Act."* An act, passed in 1906, providing extensive regulation for the railroads under the Interstate Commerce Commission.

Charles A(ustin) Beard (1874–1948)

Charles Austin Beard was born near Knightstown, Ind., on Nov. 27, 1874. He was graduated from De Pauw University in 1898, and during the next two years continued his training at Oxford University and at Cornell University. In 1903 he received the A.M. degree, and in 1904 the Ph.D. degree, from Columbia University. From 1907 to 1910 he was an adjunct professor of politics at Columbia University; he was then promoted to associate professor, and from 1915 to 1917 was professor. He resigned his professorship on Oct. 8, 1917 in protest at the expulsion of Professors J. McK. Cattell and H. W. L. Dana for their opposition to our participation in World War I. From 1917 to 1922 he was Director of the Training School for Public Service, New York City. He was also one of the founders of the New School for Social Research. In 1922 he was appointed adviser to the Institute for Municipal Research in Tokyo, Japan, and after the earthquake, in 1923, was the adviser to the Japanese Minister of Home Affairs. He was one of the authorities in the field of American government and civilization. He died on September 1, 1948, in the midst of the discussion provoked by his last book, *President Roosevelt and the Coming of the War, 1941,* in which he charges that Franklin Roosevelt deliberately led us into World War II.

The Office of Justice of Peace in England, 1904; *An Introduction to the English Historians,* 1906; *The Development of Modern Europe* (with J. H. Robinson), 1907–08; *Readings in Modern European History,* 1908–09; *Readings in American Government and Politics,* 1909; *American Government and Politics,* 1910; *American City Government,* 1912; *The Supreme Court and the Constitution,* 1912; *Documents on the State-Wide Initiative, Referendum and Recall* (with B. E. Shultz), 1912; *An Economic Interpretation of the Constitution of the United States,* 1913; *Contemporary American History,* 1914; *American Citizenship* (with Mrs. Beard), 1914; *Economic Origins of Jeffersonian Democracy,* 1915; *History of the American People: For Grammar Grades and Junior High School* (with W. C. Bagley), 1918; *First Book in American History* (with W. C. Bagley),

1920; *History of the American People* (with W. C. Bagley), 1920; *History of the United States* (with Mrs. Beard), 1921; *History of Europe* (with J. H. Robinson), 1921; *Cross Currents in Europe Today*, 1922; *The Economic Basis of Politics*, 1922; *Our Old World Background* (with W. C. Bagley), 1922; *The Administration and Politics of Tokyo*, 1923; *The Rise of American Civilization* (with Mrs. Beard), 1927; *The American Party Battle*, 1928; *Whither Mankind* (ed.), 1928; *The Balkan Pivot: Yugoslavia* (with George Radin), 1929; *The American Leviathan* (with William Beard), 1930; *Toward Civilization* (ed.), 1930; *The Navy: Defense or Portent?*, 1932; *America Faces the Future* (ed.), 1932; *Charter for the Social Sciences in the Schools*, 1932; *The Nature of the Social Sciences*, 1934; *Presidents in American History*, 1935; *The Devil Theory of War*, 1936; *Discussion of Human Affairs*, 1936; *Jefferson, Corporations and the Constitution*, 1936; *Giddy Minds and Foreign Quarrels*, 1939; *Foreign Policy for America*, 1940; *Old Deal and New*, 1940; *Public Policy and the General Welfare*, 1941; *The American Spirit* (with Mrs. Beard), 1942; *The Republic*, 1943; *American Foreign Policy in the Making: 1932–40*, 1946; *President Roosevelt and the Coming of the War, 1941*, 1947.

For criticism, see: William E. Dodd, *Am. Hist. Rev.*, XIX, pp. 162–63; J. P. Bretz, *Am. Hist. Rev.*, XXXIII, pp. 140–42; John H. Latané, *Am. Pol. Science Rev.*, VII, pp. 697–700; T. V. Smith, *Internat. Jour. Ethics*, XXXVIII, pp. 112–14; Carl Becker, *Nation*, CXV, pp. 552–53; Lewis Mumford, *New Repub.*, L., pp. 338–40; Hubert Herring, "Charles A. Beard," *Harper's*, May, 1939; S. E. Morison, "Did Roosevelt Start the War?", *Atlan.*, Aug., 1948.

898. HISTORICAL INTERPRETATION IN THE UNITED STATES is from *An Economic Interpretation of the Constitution of the United States*, 1913, rev., 1935 (latter text followed). In explaining his novel use (for 1913) of the economic interpretation of history, Beard writes, in his Introduction to the 1935 edition, "In particular I was impressed by the philosophy of politics set forth by James Madison in Number X of the *Federalist*. . . ." But see also his *Economic Basis of Politics* and note especially the publication by his colleague E. A. R. Seligman of *The Economic Interpreta-*

tion of History, 1909, in which the ideas of Karl Marx in relation to history are discussed. ¶893. "*Bancroft*," George (1800–91). ¶899. "*Stubbs*," Bishop William (1825–1901), British historian. ¶900. "*Turgot*," Anne Robert Jacques (1727–81), French statesman; "*Voltaire*," François Marie Arouet (1694–1778), French satirist. ¶900. "*Metternich*," Prince Klemens W. L. N. von (1773–1859), Austrian statesman; "*Joseph de Maistre*" (1754–1821), French diplomat and anti-revolutionary. ¶900. "*Pascal*," Blaise (1623–62), French philosopher. ¶900. "*Turner*." See Vol. III in this series. ¶902. "*Pollock*," Sir Frederick (1845–1937), English jurist; "*Maitland*," Frederick William (1850–1906), English jurist—their "*monumental work*" is the *History of English Law* (1895). ¶903. "*Chief Justice Marshall*" [John (1755–1835)] of the U. S. Supreme Court. ¶905. "*Jhering*," Rudolph von (1818–92), German jurist; "*Der Zweck im Recht*," *The Purpose of Justice* was published in 1872. ¶905. "*Lassalle*," Ferdinand (1825–1864), German socialist; "*Das System der erworbenen Rechte*," *The System of Vested Rights* [the German of the text is not correct] was published in 1861.

(Thomas) Woodrow Wilson
(1856–1924)

Born in Staunton, Va., Dec. 28, 1856. Inherited from Scotch-Irish ancestors "a strenuously logical mind" and invincible fixity of purpose. His father, Joseph Ruggles Wilson, at various times a college teacher, was Presbyterian pastor at the time of his son's birth. His mother, Janet Woodrow, was the daughter of a Scotch Presbyterian minister. Wilson passed an uneventful boyhood in Augusta, Ga. The Civil War interfered with his early education; he could not read at nine. Entered academy, Columbia, S. C., 1870; Davidson College, N. C., 1873; Princeton University, 1875. Deeply interested in English political thought—Chatham, Burke, Brougham, Macaulay, and especially Bagehot. While a junior, he contributed to *North American Review*; wrote Henry Cabot Lodge, the editor, that the latter had supplied the first encouragement to his own ambition to become a writer.

Was graduated from Princeton, 1879; studied law, University of Virginia,

1879–80; spent year, 1880–81, recuperating from ill health. Failed to secure clients after opening a law office, Atlanta; began graduate work at Johns Hopkins, where he took a Ph.D. His dissertation, *Congressional Government,* was his first book. Instructor Bryn Mawr, 1885–88; married Ellen Louise Axson, of Savannah, 1885. Professor of history (and strategist for football team) at Wesleyan, 1888–90. Appointed professor of jurisprudence and politics, Princeton, 1890. Out of his lectures grew the pioneer book, *The State: Elements of Historical and Practical Politics,* 1889. There followed *The State and Federal Governments of the U. S.,* 1891; *Division and Reunion,* 1893; *An Old Master and Other Political Essays,* 1893; *Mere Literature,* 1896; *George Washington,* 1896; *A History of the American People,* 1902; *The New Freedom,* 1913.

President of Princeton, 1902–10. Established preceptorial system, but failed to replace campus club houses by residential halls; his policies attracted wide attention. Nominated for governor of New Jersey, 1910; elected by 50,000 votes. Reform program and victories over bosses gave him national prominence; Democratic presidential nominee and victor, 1912. Set precedent by delivering first message to Congress in person, Apr. 6, 1913. Signed Underwood Tariff Act, Oct. 3; Federal Reserve Act, Dec. 23, 1913. At his direction, Vera Cruz was occupied, Apr. 21, 1914. Coincident with the outbreak of World War came the death, Aug. 14, 1914, of Mrs. Wilson. Aug. 18 he pronounced: "The U. S. must be neutral in fact as well as name. We must be impartial in thought as well as in action." *Lusitania* torpedoed, May 7, 1915; Wilson took the position "we are too proud to fight," yet demanded reparations. Married Mrs. Edith Bolling Galt, Dec. 18, 1915.

Reelected in 1916 on the ground he had kept U. S. out of war. As late as Dec. 18, 1916, he pointed out there was little choice in the objectives of the belligerents, yet on Feb. 3, 1917, he severed relations with Germany. Declared war on "Imperial German Government," April 2, 1917. High water mark of his career, the "Fourteen Points" address to Congress, Jan. 18, 1918. His call for "open covenants of peace, openly arrived at," for "absolute freedom of navigation upon the seas, alike in peace and war," and for "a general association of nations [guaranteeing] . . . political independence and territorial integrity to great and small states alike," probably had an effect, even upon the enemy, of shortening the War. Armistice declared, Nov. 11, 1918. Sailed on Dec. 4 to take part in Peace Conference. Whether he succeeded in that conference, whether he was tricked by European politicians, or whether he made the best of a bad bargain, are controversial issues. He saw the League of Nations Covenant adopted, Feb. 14, 1919. Submitted Versailles Treaty to Senate, July 10. To force its adoption Wilson began a speaking tour in the West Sept. 3; he fell ill Sept. 26, and was stricken by paralysis Oct. 5. The Senate, under the leadership of Lodge, defeated the Treaty, Mar. 20, 1920, and placed a barrier to entrance into the League. Awarded Nobel Peace Prize, Dec. 20, 1920; retired to private life Mar. 4, 1921. Last public utterance, Nov. 11, 1923; "That we shall prevail is as sure as God reigns." Died at his home on S Street, Washington, D. C., Feb. 3, 1924.

Opinion about the man is, and probably always will be, conflicting. "The tragedy of it all," said Lloyd George, "is that Woodrow Wilson's failing was his inability to subdue personalities, his refusal to give up personal animosity. . . . Mr. Wilson walked on his weaker opponents—a dangerous policy for a great man. One can trample on great men, but not on little men—there are too many of them." Chicago *Daily News,* Feb. 3, 1924: "He was the most radical magistrate the U. S. has ever had. He has had fervent supporters, but few friends. He had vision and idealism, but lacked gifts requisite to the gradual translation of ideals into consecute realities." Philadelphia *Record,* same day: "We mourn one of whom it is not enough to say that he was the greatest American. He stood head and shoulders above the great men of the world."

President Wilson's Addresses, ed. G. McL. Harper, Holt, 1918; *Selected Addresses and Public Papers of Woodrow Wilson,* ed. A. B. Hart, Mod. Lib., 1918; *The Public Papers,* ed. R. S. Baker and W. E. Dodd, 1925–27, 6 vols.; *An Essay toward a Bibliography of the Published Writings of Woodrow Wilson,* issued in three parts, Princeton Lib., 1913, 17, 22.

For life, see: William Archer, *The Peace President,* 1919; R. S. Baker,

Woodrow Wilson, Life and Letters, 1927–39, 8 vols.; Josephus Daniels, *The Wilson Era,* 2 vols., 1945–46; W. E. Dodd, *Woodrow Wilson and His Work,* 1920; J. P. Tumulty, *Woodrow Wilson as I Knew Him,* 1920, and *Woodrow Wilson, the Man, His Times, and His Task,* 1924; W. A. White, *Life of Woodrow Wilson,* 1924; *The Intimate Papers of Colonel House,* 4 vols., 1926–29; *Life and Letters of Walter Hines Page,* 1922–25; Stephen Bonsal, *Unfinished Business,* 1944. For criticism, see: Bliss Perry, *The Praise of Folly,* 1923; William Diamond, *Economic Thought of Woodrow Wilson,* 1944.

907. THE CONDITIONS OF PEACE. Address to the Senate, Jan. 22, 1917.

Oliver Wendell Holmes, Jr.
(1841–1935)

Son of the Cambridge poet and wit who bore the same name, Oliver Wendell Holmes, Jr., was born in Boston on Mar. 8, 1841. In the due course of events he was graduated from Harvard in 1861, but putting aside whatever cherished plans he had for his own future, he immediately enlisted and served three years in the 20th Massachusetts Volunteers, becoming lieutenant-colonel of his regiment. He was three times wounded—at Ball's Bluff, Antietam, and Fredericksburg—twice very severely. (See his father's "My Hunt After 'The Captain,'" *Atlantic,* Nov., 1862.) At the very end of the war he was serving as aide-de-camp on the staff of the 6th Division. In 1864, following his discharge, he began the study of law at Harvard and was awarded his LL.B. two years later. He was admitted to the bar in 1867 and practiced law in Boston. In 1870 he began to lecture on Constitutional law at Harvard and was made editor of the *American Law Review.* Holmes was lecturer on jurisprudence in 1871–72 and in 1873 he brought out the 12th edition of Kent's *Commentaries.* Returning to the practice of law in 1873 he became a member of the firm of Shattuck, Holmes and Munroe. During his Harvard years he had belonged to the informal and unnamed "Peirce Society" and had gained the knowledge of Experimentalism which formed the basis of the "social jurisprudence" of which he was later advocate. After lecturing in the Lowell Institute in 1880, he turned his lectures into *The Common Law,* 1881, a work which established him as one of the most penetrating thinkers in his field. Though reappointed to Harvard, he resigned in 1882 to become associate justice of the Massachusetts Supreme Court. He became chief justice of this court in 1899. On December 4, 1902, he was appointed by Theodore Roosevelt to the Supreme Court of the United States. Roosevelt was aggrieved that Holmes' first decision went against him. Serving on the court until just before his death, Holmes had the satisfaction of seeing his dissenting opinions come to have as much weight as the majority reports. On his death in 1935, he willed to his country his total salary as associate justice. Modesty was his essence: "All I mean by truth is what I can't help thinking. But I have learned . . . that my *can't helps* are not necessarily cosmic."

Kent's *Commentaries* (ed., 1873); *The Common Law,* 1891; *Speeches,* 1891, 1913; *Collected Legal Papers,* 1920; *The Dissenting Opinions* (ed. A. Lief), 1929; *Representative Opinions* (ed. A. Lief), 1931; *Holmes-Pollock Letters* (ed. M. De W. Howe), 1941; *Touched with Fire: Civil War Letters and Diary* (ed. M. A. De W. Howe), 1947.

For life and criticism, see: Silas Bent, *Justice Oliver Wendell Holmes,* 1932; Felix Frankfurter, *Mr. Justice Holmes and the Constitution,* 1927, and *Mr. Justice Holmes and the Supreme Court,* 1938; Max Lerner, *Mind and Faith of Justice Holmes,* 1943; F. B. Biddle, *Mr. Justice Holmes,* 1943; C. S. D. Bowen, *Yankee from Olympus,* 1944; E. S. Sergeant, *Fire Under the Andes,* 1927.

912. ABRAMS *et al.* v. u. s. In *250 U. S. 616,* 1919. In this case "the Court upheld the sentence imposed upon five ignorant Russians in New York City who had expressed their resentment at the invasion of their native land [Vladivostok, Archangel] by U. S. troops in a leaflet in which they had quoted a few hackneyed phrases from the Communist Manifesto of 1848. The repetition of Marx's well-worn words was considered by Justice Clarke, speaking for the Court, to have been 'clearly an appeal to the "workers" of this country to arise and put down by force the government of the U. S.'" E. S. Bates, *The Story of the Supreme Court,* 1938.

Lewis Mumford (1895–   )

Lewis Mumford was born on Oct. 19, 1895, in Flushing, Long Island. He was graduated from the Stuyvesant High School in 1912, and studied at Columbia University and New York University. While in his teens he began contributing to the magazines, a practice which he has steadily continued. In 1918 he served as a radio operator in the United States Navy, and the year· 1920 he spent in England. He was one of the editors of *The American Caravan,* 1927–36. In 1932, and again in 1938, he was awarded a Guggenheim Fellowship. He has served on a number of city and regional planning commissions, and has taught at Dartmouth College, Stanford University, and Harvard University. His home is in Amenia, N. Y.

His central interest as a critic has been the cultural background of peoples, especially the American people, and the problems engendered by urban living in an age of technology.

The Story of Utopias, 1922; *Sticks and Stones,* 1924; *The Golden Day,* 1926; *Herman Melville,* 1929; *American Taste,* 1929; *The Brown Decades,* 1931; *Technics and Civilization,* 1934; *The Culture of Cities,* 1938; *Men Must Act,* 1939; *Regional Planning in the Pacific Northwest,* 1939; *Faith for Living,* 1940; *The South in Architecture,* 1941; *Social Foundations for Post-War Building,* 1943; *Condition of Man,* 1944; *City Development,* 1945; *The Plan of London County,* 1945; *A Programme for Survival,* 1946; *Values for Survival,* 1946; *Green Memories,* 1947.

For criticism, see: Norman Foerster, *Bookman,* LXXII, pp. 35–45; Thomas Craven, *Dial,* LXXVIII, pp. 153–57; Ernest Boyd, *Independent,* CXVII, p. 680; T. F. Hamlin, *Nation,* CXIX, pp. 604–05; Mark Van Doren, *Nation,* CXXIII, pp. 601–02; Robert Morss Lovett, *New Repub.,* XXXIII, pp. 73–74; Aymar Embury, *Sat. Rev. Lit.,* I, pp. 413–14; Lloyd Morris, *Sat. Rev. Lit.,* III, p. 544.

916. THE DEFEAT OF ROMANTICISM [IN AMERICAN ARCHITECTURE]. This discussion forms Chapter V of the volume *Sticks and Stones,* 1924, which Mumford characterizes as an attempt "to evaluate architecture in America in terms of our civilization," and which might also be said to be in part an attempt to evaluate American civilization in terms

of architecture. ¶916. *"The Stones of Venice,"* a book by John Ruskin; *"Ashmolean Museum"* at Oxford, founded in 1677; *"Albert Memorial"* erected to the memory of Victoria's Prince Consort. ¶916. *"H. H. Richardson"* (1838–86), American architect. ¶917. *Viollet-le-Duc,"* Eugene E. (1814–79), French archeologist and architect. ¶917. *"John La Farge"* (1835–1910), American painter and worker in stained glass; *"St. Gaudens,"* Augustus (1848–1907), Irish-born American sculptor. ¶918. *"William Morris Hunt"* (1824–79), American painter and muralist. ¶921. *"Thomas Hardy"* (1840–1928), British novelist and poet. ¶921. *"Black Friday,"* the day of the Gould-Fisk gold-corner fiasco. ¶921. *"John Roebling"* (1806–69), American civil engineer, inventor of the long-span, wire suspension bridge. ¶922. *"Mr. Samuel Smiles' heroes."* The British equivalent of the Alger stories, by Samuel Smiles (1812–1904). ¶922. *"McKim and White,"* New York firm of architects.

James G(rover) Thurber (1894–   )

Seemingly far removed from the "Western" humorist, James Thurber is still quite as native as he. His father was a Columbus, Ohio, politician, and ever since he could wield a pencil, Thurber himself has been a caricaturist. He was born in Columbus on Dec. 8, 1894, and completely educated there, topping the public schools with work at Ohio State University. A code clerk in the State Department from 1918 to 1920, he turned to journalism afterwards. Thurber worked for the Columbus *Dispatch* (1920–24), the Chicago *Tribune* (Paris, 1924–25), and the New York *Evening Post* (1925). Since 1926 his contributions to the *New Yorker* and his books have supported him. He works under great handicap for his vision is seriously impaired. Thurber's home is in Connecticut.

Is Sex Necessary? (with E. B. White), 1929; *The Owl in the Attic,* 1931; *The Seal in the Bedroom,* 1932; *My Life and Hard Times,* 1933; *The Middle-Aged Man on the Flying Trapeze,* 1935; *Let Your Mind Alone!,* 1937; *The Last Flower,* 1937; *Fables for Our Time,* 1940; *My World—and Welcome to It,* 1942; *Many Moons,* 1942; *Men,*

Women, and Dogs, 1943; *The Great Quillow,* 1944; *The Thurber Carnival,* 1944; *The White Deer,* 1945.

For criticism, see: Leonard Bacon, "Humors and Careers," *Sat. Rev. Lit.,* Apr. 29, 1939; Anon., "James Thurber: The Comic Prufrock," *Poetry,* Dec., 1943; Francis Dowling, "Thurber," *Commonweal,* Mar. 9, 1945.

923. SEX EX MACHINA. In *Let Your Mind Alone!,* 1937; the text is that of *The Thurber Carnival,* 1944.

Franklin Delano Roosevelt (1882–1945)

Franklin Delano Roosevelt was a relative of Theodore Roosevelt. His parents were James and Sara (Delano) Roosevelt, of Hyde Park, N. Y., where he was born on Jan. 30, 1882. He was sent to Groton and Harvard for his education, graduating from the latter institution in 1904. By common report, he had difficulties in Columbia Law School, whither he turned next, but he received his LL.B. in 1907. If his studies were upset it was because of his courtship of, and marriage to (on Mar. 17, 1905), his cousin Eleanor Roosevelt. Admitted to the bar in 1907 he practiced with Carter, Ledyard & Milburn until 1910 when he resigned to take his seat in the Senate of New York, to which he had been elected. As a legislator, he is remembered for a certain arrogance of which later illness cured him. On Mar. 17, 1913, he resigned from the State Senate to accept an appointment as Assistant Secretary of the Navy in the Wilson administration. His seven years in this post taught him to avoid some of the mistakes made by Wilson. In 1920, Roosevelt went down to defeat as running mate of Governor James M. Cox, the Democratic nominee for the Presidency. The next year marked the low point in his fortunes, for he was stricken with infantile paralysis. Months of immobility followed, with a painful struggle back to activity in which he was aided by his wife. "Once I spent two years lying in bed, trying to move my big toe," he remembered afterwards. "That was the hardest job I ever had to do. After that anything else seems easy." Returning to the practice of law, he founded the firm of Roosevelt & O'Connor in 1924; this partnership was not dissolved until 1933 when Roosevelt be-

came President of the United States. He reentered politics in 1928, largely on Mrs. Roosevelt's urging, and secured the nomination for Governor of the State of New York, which post he won after a vigorous campaign despite his handicap. Reelected in 1930, he had a considerable experience with problems of the very depression he was to find still gripping the country when he became Chief Executive. A logical selection for his party in 1932, Roosevelt was swept into the Presidency by an overwhelming majority. Calling to his aid an augmented "Brains Trust," like that which had advised him during his campaign, he planned a "New Deal" for the American people, but the "New Deal" was perforce chiefly emergency measures to save the country in the midst of the worst depression it had ever known. There is no point in enumerating all the agencies created for this purpose, but the CCC, the PWA, the WPA, etc., demonstrated that the democratic system has an elasticity and vitality that will not allow it to be easily destroyed under economic stress, if the leadership is at all enlightened and resourceful. Roosevelt's success in meeting the protracted emergency resulted in his reelection in 1936 and the threat of war and war itself caused the American people to ask him to lead them again in 1940 and 1944; thus he became the first President to occupy the post for more than two terms. Keenly aware that our own safety was threatened with the triumph of dictatorship in World War II he secretly began rearming out of relief funds and then, when the time was opportune, proposed Lend-Lease for hard-pressed Britain. Once we were attacked at Pearl Harbor, he made the necessary commitments to potential allies (including Russia, which he had recognized in his first term) to secure their survival as well as our own. These commitments he extended by a series of international conferences over which there is a difference of opinion as to whether he yielded too much. It was natural, however, that he should look to the transmutation of these arrangements into a permanent world organization for peace. Worn out by unremitting anxieties and the strain of fencing for advantage in both domestic and foreign affairs, Roosevelt succumbed to a paralytic stroke at Warm Springs, Georgia, on Apr. 12, 1945, with the end of

World War II in sight and on the eve of the San Francisco Conference called to draft a charter for the United Nations.

Whither Bound, 1926; *The Happy Warrior—Alfred E. Smith*, 1928; *Government—Not Politics*, 1932; *Looking Forward*, 1933; *On Our Way*, 1934; *The Public Papers and Addresses of Franklin D. Roosevelt*, 9 vols. (ed. S. I. Rosenman), 1938– ; *F. D. R. Columnist* (ed. D. S. Carmichael), 1947; *Roosevelt's Foreign Policy* (ed. Douglas Lurton), 1943; *F. D. R. His Personal Letters* (ed. Elliott Roosevelt), 1948– ; *Wartime Correspondence Between Pres. Roosevelt and Pope Pius XII* (ed. M. C. Taylor), 1947.

For life and criticism, see: E. K. Lindlay, *The Roosevelt Revolution*, 1933, and *Half Way with Roosevelt*, 1936; J. A. Farley, *Behind the Ballots*, 1938, and *Jim Farley's Story*, 1948; Raymond Moley, *After Seven Years*, 1939; J. T. Flynn, *Country Squire in the White House*, 1940, and *The Roosevelt Myth*, 1948; A. M. Schlesinger, *The New Deal in Action*, 1940; *Franklin Delano Roosevelt: A Memorial* (ed. D. P. Geddes), 1945; Frances Perkins, *The Roosevelt I Knew*, 1946; Louis Adamic, *Dinner at the White House*, 1946; Elliott Roosevelt, *As He Saw It*, 1946; R. T. MacIntire, *White House Physician*, 1946; Gerald Johnson, *Roosevelt, Dictator or Democrat*, 1946; G. C. Marshall, H. H. Arnold, & E. J. King, *The War Reports*, 1947; J. F. Byrnes, *Speaking Frankly*, 1947; H. L. Stimson & McG. Bundy, *On Active Service in Peace and War*, 1948; Cordell Hull, *Memoirs of C. H.*, 1948; C. A. Beard, *President Roosevelt and the Coming of the War, 1941*, 1948; R. E. Sherwood, *Roosevelt and Hopkins*, 1948.

927. FIRST INAUGURAL ADDRESS. Delivered on Mar. 4, 1933. Text from *The Public Papers, etc.*, Vol. II, "The Year of Crisis," 1938. ¶928. *"lending more money,"* an animadversion on the Hoover R.F.C. loans.

Reinhold Niebuhr (1892–   )

The son of Gustave and Lydia (Hosto) Niebuhr, Reinhold Niebuhr was born in Wright City, Mo., on Nov. 21, 1892. He got his undergraduate education at the small sectarian coeducational college of Elmhurst, in Illinois. After his graduation in 1910 he attended Eden Theological Seminary, in St. Louis, but transferred to Yale Divinity School from which he received his B.D. in 1915. In the same year he was ordained a minister in the Evangelical Synod of North America. Niebuhr's first and only pastorate was in Detroit, where he preached from 1915 to 1928 and where he acquired his deep interest in social problems. His own religious philosophy, a modified Barthism, attracted wide attention through his books and he was invited to give the Gifford lectures at the University of Edinburgh in 1946.

Does Civilization Need Religion?, 1927; *Leaves from the Notebook of a Tamed Cynic*, 1929; *Moral Man and Immoral Society*, 1932; *Reflections on the End of an Era*, 1934; *An Interpretation of Christian Ethics*, 1935; *Beyond Tragedy*, 1937; *Christianity and Power Politics*, 1940; *The Nature and Destiny of Man*, 2 vols., 1941, 1943; *The Children of Light and the Children of Darkness*, 1944; *Discerning the Signs of the Times*, 1946.

For life and criticism, see: *Leaves from the Notebook of a Tamed Cynic*; H. Henel, "Modern Philosophy," *Queens Quar.*, May, 1941; C. C. Morrison, "Dr. Niebuhr's Unorthodox Orthodoxy," *Christ. Cent.*, Mar. 17, 1943; E. L. Allen, "Theology of Reinhold Niebuhr," *19th Cent.*, Dec. 27, 1944; Anon., "Niebuhr v. Sin," *Time*, Apr. 29, 1946; Albert Guerard, "World Comes of Age," *Nation*, Apr. 20, 1946.

930. IS RELIGION COUNTER-REVOLUTIONARY? From *Radical Religion*, Autumn, 1935, a quarterly founded by Dr. Niebuhr. ¶931. *"Augustine,"* Saint (A.D. 354–430), bishop of Hippo, author of the *City of God*.

William Vaughn Moody
(1869–1910)

"A more Catholic mysticism than Santayana's and a larger, more liberal Americanism than Hovey's enriched the poetry of William Vaughn Moody, easily the best poet of his time" (Weirick). Promise of this is not apparent in Moody's origin. His father, Francis Burdette Moody, a river boat captain before the Civil War, was in business in Spencer, Ind., when his son was born, July 8, 1869; later he was secretary of the Ohio Falls Iron Works at New Albany, Ind., where the boy grew up. His mother, Henrietta Emily Stoy, immortalized in "The Daguerreotype," died in 1884, when her son was fifteen; she took a special interest in her children's religious education, sending them regularly to church and Sunday school. It is a disturbing thought that Moody's later mysticism had its source in the conventional evangelical faith. He was apparently the only literary man of his day who believed he had visions.

Though devoting much time to art and music, he led his high school class. Study at the Pritchett Institute of Design, Louisville, Ky., was ended by the death of his father. He taught a district school near New Albany; then he was sent to Riverview Academy by an Eastern cousin as tutor for his son. Entered Harvard, 1889, an uncle advancing the fees. Finished the requirements in three years; spent the fourth traveling in Europe with a young companion whom he had tutored for college. Toured Germany and Switzerland, wintered in Florence, visited Greece in the spring. Moody participated in Class Day exercises in June. Harvard College drew out Moody the poet. Moody knew a brilliant company of undergraduates: George Pierce Baker, Bernhard Berenson, Norman Hapgood, R. M. Lovett, Robert Herrick, and younger faculty men: George Santayana, Edward Cummings, Lewis E. Gates. His scholarship (he stood second in his class) attracted older men: William James, C. C. Everett, C. H. Toy. Was a member of the board of the *Harvard Monthly*, to which he contributed. He was a harsh critic of his own verse, destroying much that he wrote.

Graduate study at Harvard, 1893–94; reader in composition for Gates, 1894–95. With Herrick and Lovett, went to University of Chicago. Suffered nostalgia for Cambridge, yet his new and crude surroundings stimulated him. He had the companionship not only of Herrick and Lovett but of Paul Shorey, Ferdinand Schevill, and J. M. Manly; he was also a welcome guest at the home of Harriet Brainerd, a meeting place for the literati of Chicago where Harriet Monroe, Fuller, Garland, and others came. Though very successful teacher, Moody was irked by the routine of the profession, testimony to the immortal character of his soul. He did things expected of the English teacher: edited *Pilgrim's Progress* and Milton's *English and Latin Poems*, collaborated with R. M. Lovett on *A History of English Literature*. The success of this last volume made it possible for him to give up teaching in 1902.

Made New York his home, but spent much time in travel. His reputation as a poet was established before the *History* appeared: he had already published *The Masque of Judgment*, "On a Soldier Fallen in the Philippines," "Gloucester Moors," and other poems. *Poems* (collected verse) appeared, 1901. In New York, Moody was the leader of a group of younger poets: Percy MacKaye, E. A. Robinson, Ridgely Torrence. Took up painting again as recreation. Completed a poetic drama, *The Fire Bringer*, 1904; began a prose play, first called *The Sabine Woman*, but later, *The Great Divide*. He made two visits to the West, with Garland and with Scheville; these provided whatever semblance of reality there is in the play, which was a success of 1906. *The Faith Healer*, produced 1909, was a stage failure. He had suffered from a cancerous ailment since 1905; in 1908, he had a severe attack of typhoid but seemed to recover completely. Married Mrs. Brainerd, May, 1909. A summer in England was followed by a trip to Colorado for an illness which nothing could check; the poet died at Colorado Springs, Oct. 17, 1910. At the end, he regretted the "time wasted" on hack work and prose dramas.

The Masque of Judgment, 1900; *Poems*, 1901; *The Fire-Bringer*, 1904; *The Great Divide*, 1909; *The Faith Healer*, 1909. *The Poems and Plays of William Vaughn Moody*, ed. J. M. Manly, 2 vols., 1912; *The Selected Poems*, ed. R. M. Lovett, 1931.

For life, see sketches in the vols. edited by Manly and Lovett; D. G. Mason, *Some Letters of William Vaughn Moody*, 1913; *Letters to Harriet* (ed. Percy MacKaye), 1935; R. M. Lovett, *All Our Years*, 1948. For criticism, see: N. F. Adkins, "The Poetic Philosophy of William V. Moody," *Texas Rev.*, Jan., 1924; Percy Boynton, *American Poetry*, 1918; Norman Foerster, "Later Poets," *CHAL*; J. B. Gilder, "New Poet," *Critic*, Sept., 1901; A. H. Quinn, *A History of the American Drama . . . to the Present Day*, II, 1927; May Sinclair, "American Poet," *Atlan.*, 98:326–30; Bruce Weirick, *From Whitman to Sandburg*, 1924.

936. GLOUCESTER MOORS. In *Scribner's*, Dec., 1900. "It is a clear-eyed criticism of the harsh capitalism and cheaplabor days of McKinley and 16 to 1, and is the expression of the feelings that Bryan was said to rouse and Roosevelt to use in the service of social and industrial reform . . ." (Weirick). Hamlin Garland first turned Moody's thoughts to social justice (Lovett). Compare poem with Lanier's "The Ship of Earth."

938. THE MENAGERIE. From *Poems*, 1901. In many respects Moody's most original poem. Compare such a line as "a little man in trousers, slightly jagged" (75) with similar lines in Aiken and Eliot. ¶939. *"Forepaugh,"* Adam, was the proprietor of a circus, rival to Barnum & Bailey in 1900.

940. AN ODE IN TIME OF HESITATION. In *Atlantic*, May, 1900, when the agitation for Philippine independence was at its height. Compare with Fuller's verses written at the same time. Moody's interest in Robert Gould Shaw was stimulated by receiving a copy of William James' address at the dedication of the statue. ¶940. *"Saint Gaudens."* See note on p. 917. ¶941. *"the Pictured Rocks."* Sandstone cliff on southern shore of Lake Superior; extends northeast from Munising 25 mi. ¶941. *"Mariposa."* A county in Calif. which contains Yosemite Valley and sequoia trees. ¶941. *"East and West are twain."* Answers Kipling's "The Ballad of East and West." ¶943. *"the eagle nation Milton saw."* See "Areopagitica."

944. THE DEATH OF EVE. Epic fragment on same subject as his unfinished poetic drama; published in *Century*, Dec., 1906. Selected as nearest approximation to the poetic dramas. It does not represent the mystical and other-worldly poet, however, and the student should read "Road Hymn for the Start" and "Old Pourquoi." For background, see Genesis i–iv.

Lizette Woodworth Reese
(1865–1935)

Born in Waverly (now a part of Baltimore), Jan. 9, 1856, daughter of David and Louisa Reese. The father, of Welsh stock, was a Confederate soldier. The mother, of German descent, definitely molded the character of her daughter; she loved song and sang "with youthful volume and sweetness" until she was eighty, keeping a simple faith in God to

the end. Other inspiration came from books: Mother Goose, *Pilgrim's Progress*, *Pickwick Papers* (she cried when Dickens died), Richard Baxter's *The Saints' Rest*, Stevenson, Henley, Kipling, Housman. Received public school education. Was teacher at St. John's Parish School, Waverly, 1873. Her first poem pub. 1874. Transferred to No. 3 English Grammar School, 1876; teacher of English Literature at Colored High School, Baltimore, 1897; Western High School, 1901. A bronze tablet in the latter school bears her sonnet, "Tears." Retired after 45 years of teaching, in 1921.

Branch of May, pub. 1887. One reviewer declared her "a poet by the grace of God," yet the volume did not sell. Thomas Bird Mosher issued her later volumes with better results. Pen idle, 1909–20; her explanation, "had nothing to say." After a period of renewed activity, she died on Dec. 17, 1935. Untermeyer holds Miss Reese the true forerunner of Sara Teasdale, Edna Millay, and others.

Branch of May, 1887, 1920; *A Handful of Lavender*, 1891; *A Quiet Road*, 1896; *Wayside Lute*, 1909; *Spicewood*, 1920; *Wild Cherry*, 1923; *Little Henrietta*, 1927; *A Victorian Village*, 1929; *White April*, 1930; *The York Road*, 1931; *Selected Poems*, 1926; *Pastures*, 1933; *The Old House in the Country*, 1936; *Worleys* [an unfinished novel], 1936.

For life, see: *A Victorian Village* and *The York Road*. For criticism, see: J. B. Rittenhouse, *The Younger American Poets*, 1904; Louis Untermeyer, *American Poetry since 1900*, 1923; L. H. Wrenshall, "Lizette Woodworth Reese," *Lib. So. Lit.*; Harriet Monroe, "Honor to Lizette Reese," *Poetry*, Feb., 1936.

949. TEARS. In *Scribner's*, Nov., 1899. This sonnet was awarded $300 Shelley Memorial Fund Prize, 1931. ¶949. *"David his little lad!"*: Absalom. II Sam. 18.33.

949. WILD GEESE. In *Lippincott's*, Sept., 1900; collected, *A Wayside Lute*, 1909. ¶950. *"Camelot,"* mythical capital, Arthur's kingdom.

950. THE PLOWMAN. In *A Wayside Lute*, 1909.

950. NOCTURNE. From *Selected Poems*, 1926.

950. IN PRAISE OF COMMON THINGS. In *A Wayside Lute*, 1909.

950. TRAGIC BOOKS. In "New Poems," *Selected Poems*, 1926.

Percy (Wallace) MacKaye
(1875–   )

Son of Steele MacKaye, dramatist, designer, and director; and Mary Medbury, who had dramatized *Pride and Prejudice;* born in New York City, Mar. 16, 1875. Brother to William Payson MacKaye, the actor-poet. Rehearsals so much a part of his life as a boy that he was surprised when a schoolmate confided *"his* father was not a dramatist and never read aloud his plays to the family at home." Graduated, Harvard, 1897. After marriage to Marion H. Morse, of Cambridge, Oct. 8, 1898, he spent two years abroad, part of the time in study at Leipzig. Taught in a private school, 1900–04, but continued to write plays. E. H. Sothern accepted *Canterbury Pilgrims* in 1903; MacKaye then resigned to devote his full time to literature and the theatre, making his home in Cornish, N. H. Appointed Fellow in Poetry, Miami University, Oxford, Ohio, 1920.

Best "occasional" poet of his day ("Three-fourths of my work, like that of a sculptor, architect, mural or portrait painter, has been imagined and executed for definite commissions."). Particularly luminous achievements: "Ode on the Centenary of Abraham Lincoln," "Ticonderoga" (ballad composed for the 300th anniversary of the discovery of Lake Champlain), and "Browning to Ben Ezra" (read at Brooklyn Institute, Browning Centennial Meeting, May 7, 1912). Related to this accomplishment are the two masques: *St. Louis* (given at the 150th anniversary of the founding of St. Louis, by 7,500 performers before 500,000 people); and *Caliban* (presented at the tercentenary of Shakespeare's death, New York City, 1916, when 135,000 people saw ten performances).

Plays: *The Canterbury Pilgrims,* 1903; *Fenris the Wolf,* 1905; *Jeanne d'Arc,* 1906; *Sappho and Phaon,* 1907; *The Scarecrow,* 1908; *Mater,* 1908; *A Garland to Sylvia,* 1910; *Anti-Matrimony,* 1910; *Tomorrow,* 1911; *A Thousand Years Ago,* 1914; *Washington,* 1919; *This Fine-Pretty World,* 1924; *Napoleon Crossing the Rockies,* 1924. One-act plays: *Yankee Fantasies,* 1912; *Kentucky Mountain Fantasies,* 1928. Masques and pageants: *Gloucester Pageant,* 1903; *Saint Gaudens Masque-Prologue,* 1909; *A Masque of Labor,* 1912; *Sanctuary,* 1914; *St. Louis,* 1914; *The New Citizenship,* 1916; *Caliban,* 1916; *The Evergreen Tree,* 1917; *The Roll Call,* 1918. Operas: with F. S. Converse, *The Immigrants,* 1915, *Sinbad the Sailor,* 1917; with Reginald de Koven, *The Canterbury Pilgrims,* 1916, *Rip Van Winkle,* 1919. Communal dramatic song service, *The Will of Song* (with Harry Barnhart), 1919. Writings on Theatre: *The Playhouse and the Play,* 1909; *The Civic Theatre,* 1912; *The Community Drama,* 1917; *Epoch, the Life of Steele MacKaye,* 2 vols., 1927. Verse: *Collected Poems,* 1916; *Poems and Plays* (Macmillan), 2 vols., 1916; *Dogtown Common,* 1921. (Other titles below.)

For life and criticism, see: "Preface," *Poems and Plays;* A. H. Quinn, *History of the American Drama from the Civil War to the Present Day,* II, 1927; T. H. Dickinson, *Playwrights of the New American Theatre,* 1924; E. O. Grover (ed.), *Annals of an Era: Percy Mackaye and the Mackaye Family, 1826–1931,* 1932.

951. TO GEORGE PIERCE BAKER. From *Poems,* 1909. "When I graduated from Harvard in 1897, there were no courses there, technical or otherwise, in the modern drama. The official acceptance of my own commencement part, 'On the Need of Imagination in the Drama To-day,' was the first official sanction of the subject, which was commented on by the Boston *Transcript* as being unprecedented in the annals of university discussion, especially at Harvard. Not till some seven or eight years later did Professor George P. Baker begin his excellent work there in his courses on dramatic technique—itself a pioneering work which has spread to many other universities" ("Preface," *Poems and Plays*). ¶951. "Praise-God Barebones": A London tanner (*c.* 1596–1679), fanatical leader of the Parliament of 1653. ¶951. "Prospero . . . Caliban": Characters in *The Tempest.*

951. TO THE FIRE-BRINGER. From *Uriel and Other Poems,* 1912. "On the death of the author of *The Fire-Bringer,* the body of the poet was cremated, Oct., 1910. These verses were written at that time" (author's note).

951. THREE DANCE MOTIVES. From *The Present Hour,* 1914. "Composed for dances of Isadora Duncan, and recited by Augustin Duncan at the Metropolitan Opera House and the Century Theatre, New York, March, 1915"

(author's note). Isadora Duncan devoted her life to a study and interpretation of the Greek dance, hence the classical content of these "motives" (see Isadora Duncan, *My Life*, 1927). ¶951. *"Lethe . . . Dionysus . . . Diana"*: The river of forgetfulness; the god of wine and revelry; the goddess of the chase.

952. WILSON. Fourth of six sonnets, called "The Conflict," all in the Boston *Evening Transcript*, Aug. 29, 1914; written in response to a cabled sonnet rebuking America's pacificism by William Watson. Following the murder of Madero, difficulties with Huerta led Wilson to order the occupation of Vera Cruz, Mar., 1914.

953. NIETZSCHE. In *The Present Hour*, 1914. Though Nietzsche's Superman was an intellectual hero rather than a hero of blood and iron, this did not prevent the German Youth from adopting *Also Sprach Zarathustra* as the source of inspiration for the physical Superman and "the will to power." See R. B. Perry, *The Present Conflict of Ideals*, 1919.

953. LOUVAIN. In *The Present Hour*, 1914. These poems, "occasioned by the course of the Great War, were written during the first two months of the war, under the compulsion of an irresistible reaction which prevented my thinking or expressing anything else than its own impulse to expression. . . . The chief value of the war poems remains, I think, that they record the sincere reactions of an American poet towards events of the most ominous 'hour' in the world's history, and that those reactions are in a large measure representatively American. As such they may make their slight contribution to the historical psychology of the hour . . ." ("Preface," *Poems and Plays*). The destruction of the university town of Louvain is admirably reported by R. H. Davis, New York *Tribune*, Aug. 31, 1914.

(Nicholas) Vachel Lindsay
(1879–1931)

Nicholas Vachel Lindsay was born in Springfield, Ill., on Nov. 10, 1879. After completing the course in the local high school and attending Hiram College, in Ohio, for three years, he went to Chicago to study at the Art Institute. Three years of such study and two others at the New York School of Art failed to prepare him to earn a living by his drawings, and he turned reluctantly to other occupations. From 1905 to 1910 he lectured for the Y.M.C.A. in New York and Springfield, and for the Anti-Saloon League throughout Illinois. In the meantime he had written some verse, and had made the first of several tramping tours through the country, coming into contact with all kinds of people. On subsequent trips of the kind he distributed poetical pamphlets and preached "the gospel of beauty" to those who would listen. In 1913 appeared his *General William Booth Enters into Heaven*, which marked him as a striking figure among the rising group of authors. He published other books of poems and became a successful reader of his own verse, particularly during the period from 1920 to 1925. In the latter year he married Miss Elizabeth Conner and settled in Spokane, Washington. The closing years of his life were spent in his native city of Springfield, where he died from drinking Lysol on Dec. 5, 1931.

Lindsay regarded himself not chiefly as a poet but as a crusader in the cause of beauty. An art student whose energies were directed into the channel of verse-writing almost by accident, he attempted to bring the significance of poetry home to the people; he desired to restore poetry to its place in communal life by writing work designed for communal enjoyment and communal recitation. He wrote vigorous verse to be declaimed or chanted, verse which often dealt with exciting happenings or striking characters; but he strenuously objected to the characterization of his work as "jazz poetry."

The Tramp's Excuse and Other Poems, 1909; *The Village Magazine*, 1910; *Rhymes to Be Traded for Bread* (pamphlet), 1912; *The Wedding of the Rose and the Lotus* (pamphlet), 1912; *General William Booth Enters into Heaven and Other Poems*, 1913; *The Congo and Other Poems*, 1914; *Adventures While Preaching the Gospel of Beauty*, 1914; *The Art of the Moving Picture*, 1915; *A Handy Guide for Beggars*, 1916; *The Chinese Nightingale and Other Poems*, 1917; *The Daniel Jazz and Other Poems* (London), 1920; *The Golden Whales of California and Other Rhymes in the American Language*, 1920; *The Golden Book of Springfield*, 1920; *Going-to-the-Sun*,

1923; *Collected Poems,* 1923, rev. ed., 1925; *The Candle in the Cabin,* 1926; *Going-to-the-Stars,* 1926; *Johnny Appleseed and Other Poems,* 1928; *The Litany of Washington Street,* 1929; *Every Soul Is a Circus,* 1929; *Rigamarole, Rigamarole,* 1929; *Selected Poems,* 1931; *Letters to A. Joseph Armstrong,* 1940.

For life, see: A. E. Trombly, *Vachel Lindsay, Adventurer,* 1929; Stephen Graham, *Tramping with a Poet in the Rockies,* 1922; Vachel Lindsay, *Adventures While Preaching the Gospel of Beauty* and *A Handy Guide for Beggars;* Edgar Lee Masters, *Vachel Lindsay: A Poet in America,* 1935. For criticism, see: Theodore Maynard, *Our Best Poets: English and American,* 1922, pp. 181–94; A. Williams-Ellis, *An Anatomy of Poetry,* 1922, pp. 233–40; Robert Lynd, *Books and Authors,* 1923, pp. 237–44; Louis Untermeyer, *American Poetry since 1900,* 1923, pp. 88–113; Carl Van Doren, *Many Minds,* 1924, pp. 151–67; Llewellyn Jones, *First Impressions,* 1925, pp. 85–97; Harriet Monroe, *Poets and Their Art,* 1926, pp. 21–29; Alfred Kreymborg, *Our Singing Strength,* 1929, pp. 368–79; H. M. Robinson, *Bookman,* LXXV, pp. 6–9.

954. THE EAGLE THAT IS FORGOTTEN. In *General William Booth Enters into Heaven,* 1913; it had been in *Poetry* the previous year. John P. Altgeld, 1847–1902, was the governor of Illinois who had pardoned the Chicago anarchists imprisoned for the Haymarket outrage.

954. WHY I VOTED THE SOCIALIST TICKET. In *General William Booth Enters into Heaven,* 1913. Lindsay was a somewhat inconsistent Democrat, who, however, was also an intense admirer of Tolstoy and certain other socialists.

954. A NET TO SNARE THE MOONLIGHT. In *American Mag.,* Apr., 1913; collected in *General William Booth,* 1913.

955. GENERAL WILLIAM BOOTH ENTERS INTO HEAVEN. In *Poetry,* Jan., 1913; title poem of collection, 1913. Lindsay relates in the *Collected Poems* how he came to write this poem, and what he attempted in it. See the section "Adventures While Singing These Songs," pp. 21–22.

956. ABRAHAM LINCOLN WALKS AT MIDNIGHT. In *Independent,* Sept. 21, 1914; collected in *The Congo and Other Poems,* 1914. ¶956. *"the old courthouse"* in Springfield is the former state capitol.

957. THE MOON'S THE NORTH WIND'S COOKY. In *The Congo and Other Poems,* 1914.

957. FACTORY WINDOWS, etc. In *The Congo and Other Poems,* 1914.

957. THE CONGO. Title poem, collection of 1914. ¶958. *"Leopold's ghost."* The Belgian king, Leopold II (1835–1909), was charged with countenancing atrocities in the administration of the Congo.

961. THE BRONCHO, etc. In *The Chinese Nightingale and Other Poems,* 1917.

962. [RULES TO BE OBSERVED ON A POETICAL PILGRIMAGE] and (963) [THE TALE OF THE FIVE LITTLE CHILDREN EATING MUSH] are from *Adventures While Preaching the Gospel of Beauty,* 1914, which appeared in serial form, except for the concluding proclamations, in *Forum,* Sept., 1913–Feb., 1914. The poet wrote of this work as "a summary of all I have to say . . . for audiences." "My life," he wrote further, "is not an attempt to recite, but an attempt to re-apply in various ways till I find the right way, the sharpest sentences of the proclamations in *Adventures While Preaching the Gospel of Beauty.*" See the *Collected Poems,* p. xlvi. The "rules" were first published and discussed by Lindsay in *American Mag.,* May, 1912.

Edgar Lee Masters (1869–   )

Edgar Lee Masters was born in Garnett, Kan., on Aug. 23, 1869, but grew up in central Illinois, in the heart of "the Lincoln country." His father was a prominent lawyer of the state; Masters himself entered the legal profession and for over twenty years was a successful attorney in Chicago. As a boy he delighted in books and wrote verse and stories; in 1898 he published *A Book of Verses,* his first volume. This was followed by other volumes, and in 1915 by *Spoon River Anthology,* one of the most striking and influential literary works of the early twentieth century. A full-voiced arraignment of human nature in the setting of a small Middle Western village, *Spoon River Anthology* was so successful with the public and critics that it overshadowed Masters' earlier works, and has overshadowed as well his later poetical volumes, which contain numerous pieces of high merit.

He has also written a half-dozen novels, several plays, many critical articles, and a study of Lincoln, *Lincoln the Man,* 1931. His work, prose and verse alike, shows learning, an independent and fearless spirit, a hatred of shams and cowardice, an enthusiasm for the beautiful. In 1920 Masters gave up the practice of law, and since that time has resided for the most part in New York City.

A Book of Verses, 1898; *Maximilian,* 1902; *The New Star Chamber,* 1904; *Blood of the Prophets* (pseud. "Dexter Wallace"), 1905; *Althea,* 1907; *The Trifler,* 1908; *Eileen,* 1910; *The Locket,* 1910; *Songs and Sonnets,* 1910; *Songs and Sonnets: Second Series,* 1911; *The Leaves of the Tree,* 1911; *The Bread of Idleness,* 1911; *Spoon River Anthology,* 1915; *Songs and Satires,* 1916; *The Great Valley,* 1916; *Toward the Gulf,* 1918; *Starved Rock,* 1919; *Domesday Book,* 1920; *Mitch Miller,* 1920; *The Open Sea,* 1921; *Children of the Market Place,* 1922; *Skeeters Kirby,* 1923; *The Nuptial Flight,* 1923; *The New Spoon River,* 1924; *Mirage,* 1924; *Selected Poems,* 1925; *Lee,* 1926; *Kit O'Brien,* 1927; *Levy Mayer and the New Industrial Era,* 1927; *Jack Kelso,* 1928; *The Fate of the Jury,* 1929; *Lichee Nuts,* 1930; *Gettysburg, Manila, Acoma,* 1930; *Lincoln the Man,* 1931; *Godbey,* 1931; *The Serpent in the Wilderness,* 1933; *Tale of Chicago,* 1933; *Dramatic Dialogues,* 1934; *Richmond,* 1934; *Invisible Landscapes,* 1935; *Vachel Lindsay,* 1935; *The Golden Fleece of California,* 1936; *Poems of People,* 1936; *Across Spoon River,* 1936; *New World,* 1937; *Tide of Time,* 1937; *Mark Twain,* 1938; *More People,* 1939; *Illinois Poems,* 1941; *Along the Illinois,* 1942; *The Sangamon,* 1942.

For life and criticism, see: Amy Lowell, *Tendencies in Modern American Poetry,* 1917, pp. 139–200; Harry Hansen, *Midwest Portraits,* 1923, pp. 243–52; Harriet Monroe, *Poets and Their Art,* 1926, pp. 46–56; Alfred Kreymborg, *Our Singing Strength,* 1929, pp. 379–85; and Masters' own *Across Spoon River: An Autobiography,* 1936.

965. PETIT, THE POET. This, and the next nine poems, including ANNE RUTLEDGE (968) are all from *Spoon River Anthology,* 1915. William Herndon, Lincoln's partner, is responsible for the Anne Rutledge legend. See Lloyd Lewis, *Myths After Lincoln.*

968. JOHNNY APPLESEED. In *Toward the Gulf,* 1918. Cf. poems on the same theme by Vachel Lindsay. For an account of John Chapman ["Johnny Appleseed"], see *Ohio Archæl. & Hist. Pubs.,* VI, 1898, pp. 290–95.

969. MOURNIN' FOR RELIGION. In *Starved Rock,* 1919.

Edna St. Vincent Millay
(1892–)

Edna St. Vincent Millay was born in Rockland, Me., on Feb. 22, 1892, and began writing verse when a small girl. Her literary talents in time attracted the attention of a lady of means who helped her to attend college. In 1912, while she was yet a schoolgirl, her poem "Renascence" appeared in the anthology *The Lyric Year,* being the most noteworthy poem included. She continued to write verse during her career at Vassar College, from which she was graduated in 1917, the year of the publication of her first slender book, *Renascence and Other Poems.* After leaving Vassar, she went to New York City and undertook to earn a living by writing, establishing herself among the artists of Greenwich Village. She became associated with the Provincetown Players as actress and playwright, and steadily gained a reputation among discerning students of contemporary poetry. In 1923 her volume *The Harp-Weaver* won her the Pulitzer Prize. She has been awarded honorary degrees by Tufts College, Russell Sage Foundation College, Colby College, New York University, and the University of Wisconsin. She holds membership in the American Academy of Arts and Letters. She was married, in 1923, to Mr. Eugen Jan Boissevain, an importer.

From the first Miss Millay eschewed the writing of free verse and the use of experimental forms so eagerly defended during the years when she was developing. Her strength as a poet lies in the Elizabethan freshness of her language, and the skill with which, at her best, she realizes for the reader a mood, a state of mind, an experience.

Renascence, 1917; *Aria da Capo,* 1921; *A Few Figs from Thistles,* 1920; *The Lamp and the Bell,* 1921; *Second April,* 1921; *Two Slatterns and a King,* 1921; *The Ballad of the Harp-Weaver,* 1922; *The Harp-Weaver and Other Poems,* 1923; *Poems* (London), 1923;

Distressing Dialogues (pseud. "Nancy Boyd"), 1924; *Three Plays* (reprints), 1926; *The King's Henchman*, 1927; *The Buck in the Snow and Other Poems*, 1928; *Poems: Selected for Young People*, 1929; *Fatal Interview*, 1931; *The Princess Marries the Page*, 1932; *Wine from These Grapes*, 1934; *Conversation at Midnight*, 1937; *Huntsman, What Quarry?*, 1939; *Make Bright the Arrows*, 1940; *There Are No Islands, Any More*, 1940; *Collected Sonnets*, 1941; *Murder of Lidice*, 1942; *Collected Lyrics*, 1943.

For criticism, see: Theodore Maynard, *Our Best Poets: English and American*, 1922, pp. 226–32; Louis Untermeyer, *American Poetry since 1900*, 1923, pp. 214–21; Carl Van Doren, *Many Minds*, 1924, pp. 105–20; Clement Wood, *Poets of America*, 1925, pp. 199–214; Harriet Monroe, *Poets and Their Art*, 1926, pp. 63–72; Alfred Kreymborg, *Our Singing Strength*, 1929, pp. 438–46; Elizabeth Atkins, *Edna St. Vincent Millay and Her Times*, 1936; K. Yost, *A Bibliography of the Works of Edna St. Vincent Millay*, 1937.

970. RENASCENCE. In the anthology *The Lyric Year*, 1912; collected in *Renascence*, 1917. The opening lines are a description of the environs of Rockland, Me. ¶971. *"Capri."* An island in the Bay of Naples, famous for its grottoes and scenery. ¶972. *"O God, . . . give me new birth."* Compare Coleridge, "The Rime of the Ancient Mariner."

973. OH, THINK NOT I AM FAITHFUL, etc. In *A Few Figs from Thistles*, 1920, this poem is representative of Miss Millay's iconoclastic assault at that time upon the double standard.

973. ELEGY. In *Second April*, 1921, "Elegy" appears as one of a group of six elegiac pieces entitled "Memorial to D. C. [Vassar College, 1918]."

973. EUCLID ALONE HAS LOOKED, etc. In *The Harp Weaver and Other Poems*, 1923. Euclid (fl. 300 B.C.) was the father of geometry.

974. JUSTICE DENIED IN MASSACHU-SETTS. In *The Buck in the Snow and Other Poems*, 1928, but it had received pamphlet publication the previous year. The poem was occasioned by the execution of the anarchists, Sacco and Vanzetti, for a hold-up in Braintree, Mass. Miss Millay joined the protest march around the Charlestown jail on the eve of the execution and was arrested. See G. L. Joughin & E. M. Morgan, *The Legacy of Sacco and Vanzetti*, 1948. ¶974. *"The glittering bay,"* Massachusetts Bay.

974. EPITAPH FOR THE RACE OF MAN was published as Volume I in a two volume limited edition of *Wine from These Grapes*, 1934.

975. CZECHO-SLOVAKIA. In *Collected Lyrics*, 1943. At the Munich Conference with Hitler of Sept. 29–30, 1938, the premiers of Great Britain and France, Chamberlain and Daladier, abandoned Czecho-Slovakia to her fate. In March, 1939, Hitler sent his armies into the country. ¶975. *"Peter warms him."* See Mark 14:67.

Stephen Vincent Benét (1898–1943)

Stephen Vincent Benét was born in Bethlehem, Pa., on July 22, 1898. The son of an army officer, he lived as a boy in various parts of the country, and attended schools in California and Georgia. He published his first book, *Five Men and Pompey*, 1915, at the age of seventeen. In 1919 he was graduated from Yale University, afterwards studying on a fellowship at the Sorbonne in Paris. While in France he met Miss Rosemary Carr, whom he married in 1921. Turning to literary work for a living, he wrote verse, short stories, and novels, and in 1928 became widely known for his *John Brown's Body*, a volume filled with related poems on the theme of the Civil War. This called forth much critical praise, and is a moving poetical work despite its unevenness and an imperfect blending of its narrative elements. For *John Brown's Body* Benét was awarded the Pulitzer Prize in 1929. He received the award of the National Institute of Arts and Letters posthumously in 1943. He died on March 14, 1943.

Five Men and Pompey, 1915; *The Drug-Shop*, 1917; *Young Adventure*, 1918; *Heavens and Earth*, 1920; *The Beginning of Wisdom*, 1921; *Young People's Pride*, 1922; *Jean Huguenot*, 1923; *King David*, 1923; *Tiger Joy*, 1925; *Spanish Bayonet*, 1926; *John Brown's Body*, 1928; *Barefoot Saint*, 1929; *Litter of Rose Leaves*, 1930; *Ballads and Poems, 1915–30*, 1931; *James Shore's Daughter*, 1934; *Burning City*, 1936; *The Devil and Daniel Webster*, 1937; *Johnny Pye and the Fool-Killer*, 1938; *Ballad of the Duke's Mercy*, 1939; *Tales Before Midnight*, 1939; *Nightmare at Noon*, 1940; *Zero Hour*, 1940; *Sum-*

mons to the Free, 1941; *Selected Works*, 1942; *They Burned the Books*, 1942; *A Child Is Born*, 1942; *Twenty-Five Short Stories*, 1943; *Western Star*, 1943; *America*, 1944; *We Stand United*, 1945; *Last Circle*, 1946.

For criticism, see: Alfred Kreymborg, *Our Singing Strength*, 1929, pp. 607–11; Max Eastman, *Bookman*, LXVIII, pp. 362–64; Allen Tate, *Nation*, CXXVII, p. 274; Robert Morss Lovett, *New Repub.*, LVI, pp. 51–52; Hervey Allen, *Sat. Rev. Lit.*, II, p. 428; Thomas Beer, *Sat. Rev. Lit.*, II, p. 698; Hervey Allen, *Yale Rev.*, n.s. XVIII, pp. 391–93; H. W. Wells, *Coll. Eng.*, V, pp. 8–13; Christopher LaFarge, *Sat. Rev. of Lit.*, XXVII, pp. 106–8; W. R. Benét, *Sat. Rev. of Lit.*, XXVI, pp. 5–7; Paul L. Wiley, *Am. Lit.*, XVII, pp. 231–42.

976. KING DAVID. Won the *Nation's* poetry prize in 1923 and was separately published in that year. See 2 Samuel 11 ff. for the Biblical story.

980. PRELUDE—THE SLAVER. Opening section in *John Brown's Body*, 1928. ¶984. "*Guinea Coast.*" Western coast of equatorial Africa, notorious for slave trade.

985. LITANY FOR DICTATORSHIPS. In *Atlantic Mo.*, Sept. 1935; collected in *Burning City*, 1936.

Edith (Newbold Jones) Wharton
(1862–1937)

"Life," wrote Mrs. Wharton (*Fruit of the Tree*), "is not a matter of abstract principles, but a succession of pitiful compromises with fate, of concessions to old tradition, old beliefs, old tragedies, and frailties." Some of her critics have felt that, whatever life was to her, art was its antithesis. Too harsh a view: Mrs. Wharton was the disciple of form in an age abjuring it, consequently she suffered out of proportion to her sins; in 1902 H. W. Boynton felt that she was too concerned with art and predicted she would never outgrow this concern; in 1906 H. D. Sedgwick found her too "clever"; and in 1928 Osbert Burdett declared of her novels, "they possess more form than feeling." Critics were possibly so censorious because they considered only the novelist. To be sure, she did distinguished work in the novel: her first attempt, *The Valley of Decision* (an historical romance of Italy in the 18th century), was

praised beyond *Romola* and *Salammbô*; her *House of Mirth* was the literary sensation of 1905 (perhaps her best piece of characterization is the heroine of this book, Lily Bart, a woman "who is a little too weak to do without money and what it buys, or to earn it for herself, and a little too good to sell herself"); her *Custom of the Country* is the best piece of "flaying alive" in our literature, worth reading, said Phelps, if only "for the spectacle of a woman of genius in a state of exasperation"; and her *Age of Innocence* is a monument to the New York she knew as a girl. Yet her work in the novel is uneven and imitative. In her best novels, one lacks a sense of movement: the episodes are "in a state of celibate self-sufficiency."

Critical dissatisfaction with novels will ultimately fix attention on her shorter work. Already *Madame de Treymes*, the four tales in *Old New York*, and *Ethan Frome* have won high praise. Short-stories contain some of her best and most varied work. Perhaps the most distinguished are: "The Journey," done in a technique (the "stream of consciousness") which she later renounced; "The Pelican," a remarkable study in character; "The Duchess at Prayer"; "The Choice"; "Autres Temps . . ." on the tragedy of changing convention; "Xingu," a masterpiece of flippancy; and "After Holbein," perhaps best of all. She is unconvincing in the short-story only when she deals with the supernatural, never having quite attained the horror of "The Turn of the Screw."

Edith Newbold Jones was born in a mansion on Washington Sq., New York City, Jan. 24, 1862. Her mother, Lucretia Stevens Rhinelander, was a granddaughter of the distinguished Revolutionary soldier, Gen. Ebenezer Stevens. Her father, George Frederick Jones, had no profession but lived on his income. Governesses and tutors were responsible for her early education. Half her youth was spent abroad where she acquired remarkable facility in language and cosmopolitan tastes in literature. Her first literary idol was Goethe; but the influence of George Eliot, Gustave Flaubert, Paul Bourget, Marcel Proust, and especially of Henry James (best example, *The Reef*) is seen in her work. When her sister-in-law sent the collection *Crucial Instances* to James in 1901, the latter declared, "I must get hold of the little lady and pump the pure essence of my wisdom and experience into her." Thus began a friendship terminated only by James' death, 1916.

In 1885 she married Edward Wharton, a Boston merchant, whose later mental illness was a severe burden to her and whom she ultimately divorced. She enjoyed an intimate friendship with Walter Berry before separating from her husband and regarded him as "the support of her career." First published work, sonnet "Happiness," *Scribner's*, Dec., 1889. First short-story, "Mrs. Manstey's View," *Scribner's*, July, 1891. Mrs. Wharton made her home in France after 1906; in summer near Paris, at St. Brice; in winter at Hyeres, Provence. Did heroic work with Belgian and French refugees in Great War; made Chevalier of Order of Leopold, 1916; decorated with cross of the Legion of Honor, 1924; member, American Academy, 1934; died at St. Brice, August 11, 1937.

The Greater Inclination, 1899; *The Touchstone*, 1900; *Crucial Instances*, 1901; *The Decoration of Houses* (with Ogden Camden), 1901; *The Valley of Decision*, 1902; *Sanctuary*, 1903; *The Descent of Man*, 1904; *Italian Villas and Their Gardens*, 1904; *Italian Backgrounds*, 1905; *The House of Mirth*, 1905; *Madame de Treymes*, 1907; *The Fruit of the Tree*, 1907; *The Hermit and the Wild Woman*, 1908; *A Motor-Flight Through France*, 1908; *Artemis to Actæon*, 1909; *Tales of Men and Ghosts*, 1910; *Ethan Frome*, 1911; *The Reef*, 1912; *The Custom of the Country*, 1913; *Fighting France*, 1915; *Xingu and Other Stories*, 1916; *Summer*, 1917; *The Marne*, 1918; *French Ways and Their Meaning*, 1919; *In Morocco*, 1920; *The Age of Innocence*, 1920; *Glimpses of the Moon*, 1922; *A Son at the Front*, 1923; *Old New York: False Dawn, The Old Maid, The Spark, New Year's Day*, 1924; *The Writing of Fiction*, 1925; *The Mother's Recompense*, 1925; *Here and Beyond*, 1926; *Twelve Poems*, 1926; *Twilight Sleep*, 1927; *The Children*, 1928; *Hudson River Bracketed*, 1929; *Certain People*, 1930; *The Gods Arrive*, 1932; *Human Nature*, 1933; *A Backward Glance*, 1934; *The World Over*, 1936; *Ghosts*, 1937; *The Buccaneers*, 1938.

For life, see: *A Backward Glance* and Percy Lubbock, *Portrait of Edith Wharton*, 1947. For general criticism, see: P. H. Boynton, *Some Contemporary Americans*, 1924; Osbert Burdett, "Edith Wharton" in *Contemp. Am. Authors*, ed. J. C. Squire, 1928; F. T. Cooper, *Some American Story Tellers*, 1911; W. L. Cross, "Edith Wharton," *Bookman*, Aug. 19, '29; H. T. & Wilson Follett, *Some Modern Novelists*, 1918; K. F. Gerould, *Edith Wharton, a Critical Study*, 1922; R. M. Lovett, *Edith Wharton*, 1925; Percy Lubbock, "Novels of Edith Wharton," *Quar.*, Jan., 1915; Régis Michaud, *The American Novel Today*, 1928; Grant Overton, *American Nights Entertainment*, 1923, *The Women Who Make Our Novels*, rev. 1928; Carl Van Doren, *Contemp. Am. Novelists*, 1922; J. H. Van Klooster, *Moderne amerikaansche letterkunde: Edith Wharton*, 1924.

For special criticism, see: H. W. Boynton, "Books, New and Old," *Atlan.*, May, 1902, and "Mrs. Wharton's Manner," *Nation*, Oct. 30, 1913; H. D. Sedgwick, "Novels of Mrs. Wharton," *Atlan.*, Aug., 1906; C. L. Franklin, "A Note on *The House of Mirth*," *Bookman*, Nov., 1906; H. E. Woodbridge, "Fruit of the Tree and Ibsen's *Rosmersholm*," *Nation*, Dec. 5, 1907; James Huneker, "Undine, Heroine," *Bookman*, Nov., 1914; Edwin Björkman, *Voices of Tomorrow*, 1913; J. C. Underwood, *Literature and Insurgency*, 1914; Robert Sencourt, "The Poetry of Edith Wharton," *Bookman*, July, 1931. For bibliography, see: L. M. Melish, *A Bibliography of the Collected Writings of Edith Wharton*, 1927.

987. THE CHOICE. In *Century*, Nov., 1908; collected in *Xingu and Other Stories*, 1916. Written when Mrs. Wharton's mind was most occupied with the breakdown of the old aristocracy before the invasion of the new "Goths."

Robert Herrick (1868–1938)

Born in Cambridge, Mass., Apr. 28, 1868, son of William A. Herrick, a Boston lawyer and author of legal books, and Harriet Emery, related through the Mannings to Hawthorne. The five months spent each year in Boxford, Mass., were pleasanter to him than his Cambridge home. After graduating from Latin School he entered Harvard, where Child, Hill, and Wendell ripened an already formed taste for literature. Was one of a brilliant set of young men: Norman Hapgood, George Santayana, Moody, Lovett, and George Carpenter. Editor of the Harvard *Advocate* and the newly-founded *Monthly,* which he nearly wrecked financially by publishing in it the first translation of Ibsen's *Lady from the Sea.* Absented self from study to tour West and Alaska, 1887. After graduation in 1890, he taught three years in M.I.T. At twenty-six, he was called to organize the English dept., University of Chicago, on the Harvard plan, 1893. Soon he was relieved of many teaching and administrative duties. After 1909, he spent only a part of each year at the University and in 1923 he resigned. A dozen years were devoted to travel and writing, then he accepted appointment as government secretary of the Virgin Islands. His death occurred three years later in St. Thomas, on Dec. 23, 1938.

Before leaving Boston, he had published short-stories in *Atlantic* and *Scribner's,* but his chief interest was the novel, to which form he began devoting vacations. His masters were Howells, Zola, Sudermann, and Ibsen; his primary object was not to entertain. Success in the competitive system and its influence upon men and women interested him. With Mrs. Wharton he was the first to study the effect of bourgeois society upon womanhood; he exposed evils of the stockyards a year before Sinclair in a book which is one of our best studies of the financier. Herrick divided his novels into two classes: "those strictly of realistic technique," like *The Memoirs of an American Citizen;* and "those of a freer, more poetic technique," like *A Life for a Life* and *Clark's Field.* Confessed the latter were nearer his heart.

The Man Who Wins, 1895; *Literary Love-Letters,* 1896; *The Gospel of Freedom,* 1898; *Love's Dilemmas,* 1898; *The Web of Life,* 1900; *The Real World,* 1901; *Their Child,* 1903; *The Common Lot,* 1904; *The Memoirs of an American Citizen,* 1905; *The Master of the Inn,* 1908; *Together,* 1908; *A Life for a Life,* 1910; *The Healer,* 1911; *One Woman's Life,* 1913; *His Great Adventure,* 1913; *Clark's Field,* 1914; *The World Decision,* 1916; *The Conscript Mother,* 1916; *Homely Lilla,* 1923; *Waste,* 1924; *Wanderings,* 1925; *Chimes,* 1926; *The End of Desire,* 1932; *Sometime,* 1933.

For life, see autobiographical sketch in C. C. Baldwin, *The Men Who Make Our Novels,* 1924; R. M. Lovett, *All Our Years,* 1948. For criticism, see: Edwin Björkman, *Voices of Tomorrow,* 1913; Russell Blankenship, *American*

Literature, 1931; F. T. Cooper, *Some American Story Tellers,* 1911, also *Bookman,* Dec., 1908; Harry Hansen, *Midwest Portraits,* 1923; Carl Van Doren, *Contemp. Am. Novelists,* 1922; Granville Hicks, "Robert Herrick, Liberal," *N. Repub.,* June 17, 1931.

996. "SHINING PALACES ON SAND." From *The Common Lot,* serialized in *Atlantic,* Jan.–Aug., 1904.

O. Henry
(William Sydney Porter)
(1862–1910)

Born in Greensboro, N. C., Sept. 11, 1862, the son of Dr. Algernon Sidney Porter, a physician who could not collect his bills, and Mary V. Swaim, who died when he was three. Attended "Miss Lina's school" (presided over by his aunt, Evalina Maria Porter) from three to fifteen. Worked in drugstore of his uncle, Clarke Porter, until 1882, when he had an opportunity to go to Texas. Herded sheep on the ranch of Dick Hall, captain of the Rangers, for two years. "Let a man herd sheep for a spell and you'll see him splitting his ribs laughing at 'Curfew Shall Not Ring To-night,' or really enjoying himself playing cards with ladies." Went to Austin, where he learned bookkeeping; then became draftsman in the General Land Office, 1887–91; these were the happiest years of his life. Married Athol Estes, seventeen-year-old daughter of Mrs. P. G. Roach, July 5, 1887. Began to contribute humorous items to Detroit *Free Press,* the New York *Truth,* and an occasional story to S. S. McClure Newspaper Syndicate. Became teller, First National Bank, Austin, Jan. 21, 1891; resigned, 1894, to become editor of a humorous weekly, *The Rolling Stone,* which ceased to appear Apr. 27, 1895.

Though he wished to go East, he accepted a position as reporter and columnist on the Houston *Daily Post,* to be near Mrs. Porter who had developed tuberculosis. Fled arrest, June 22, 1896, when a shortage was discovered in the Austin bank accounts. Loose banking methods of the day were responsible for his difficulties, but O. Henry could not legally establish his innocence. Returned from Honduras, 1897, to the bedside of his dying wife. Stood trial, Feb., 1898, was convicted and sent to Ohio Penitentiary, Columbus, where he remained Apr. 25,

1898–July 24, 1901. Acted as drug clerk in prison; he devoted his leisure time to writing. First story under his famous pseudonym, "Whistling Dick's Christmas Stocking," in *McClure's*, Dec., 1899. Good conduct shortened his sentence. After release, he lived with his little daughter and her grandparents in Pittsburgh and devoted himself to fiction. Moved to an apartment house on Twenty-third St., New York City, 1902. His work was now much sought after. Had a contract with N. Y. *World* to write a story a week for $100 a story and kept the contract. First collection, *Cabbages and Kings*, appeared in 1904; his most famous, *The Four Million*, in 1906.

Despite fame and popularity, he lived in obscurity. Married Sallie Coleman, of Asheville, N. C., Nov. 27, 1907. Illness was twisted into themes for stories. His last complete story, "Let Me Feel Your Pulse," was heralded by the magazine announcement, "If you want to get well, read this story"; O. Henry was dead before it was published. Died at the Polyclinic Hospital, June 5, 1910.

Cabbages and Kings, 1904; *The Four Million*, 1906; *The Trimmed Lamp*, 1907; *The Heart of the West*, 1907; *The Voice of the City*, 1908; *The Gentle Grafter*, 1908; *Roads of Destiny*, 1909; *Options*, 1909; *Strictly Business*, 1910; *Whirligigs*, 1910; *Sixes and Sevens*, 1911; *Rolling Stones*, 1913; *Waifs and Strays*, 1917. *Works of O. Henry: Biographical Edition*, 18 vols., Doubleday, 1925; *Selected Stories of O. Henry*, ed. C. A. Smith, 1922.

For life and criticism, see: C. A. Smith, *O. Henry*, 1916; A. J. Jennings, *Through the Shadows with O. Henry*, 1921; R. H. Davis and A. B. Maurice, *The Caliph of Bagdad*, 1931; Russell Nye, "Social Criticism in O. Henry," *Modern Quarterly*, Summer, 1939.

999. AN UNFINISHED STORY. In *McClure's*, Aug., 1905; collected in *The Four Million*, 1906. ¶1000. *"A fly cop."* Slang for a smartly dressed and worldly-wise policeman; flashy plain clothes man. ¶1000. *"The Hoffman House."* Famous for its cuisine, stood on Madison Sq. at 1111 Broadway, in the heart of O. Henry land; now displaced by an Automat—an O. Henry ending! ¶1001. *"Pictures of General Kitchener, William Muldoon, the Duchess of Marlborough, and Benvenuto Cellini."* Horatio Herbert Kitchener (1850–1916), idol of the British Empire, had opened Sudan; William Muldoon, dictator of pugilism, N. Y. State (evidently Dulcie was Irish); the Duchess was Consuelo Vanderbilt, American beauty, who, in 1895, had married Richard John Spencer-Churchill, the ninth duke; Benvenuto Cellini (1500–71), sculptor, poet, and adventurer. ¶1002. *"Sammy"*: Music-hall hit, 1904. ¶1003. *"Not on your immortality"*: Improvement on Ade's "Not on your previous existence" ("The Good Fairy," *Fables*).

(Harry) Sinclair Lewis (1885–   )

The first American author to be awarded the Nobel Prize for Literature was Sinclair Lewis, whose satirical novels on American life have been read by a public international in extent. For the vividness of his description and characterization, unquestionably, and for the ability to mass detail so as to secure a desired satirical effect, he is equalled by few novelists of the twentieth century.

Lewis was born in Sauk Center, Minn., on Feb. 7, 1885. His mother was of Canadian stock, his father a New Englander who had settled in the town as a physician. He was educated at Yale University, from which he received the A.B. degree in 1907. After leaving the university, he drifted for a time, then entered upon a career as journalist and editor, attempting as the years passed to establish himself as a novelist. From 1914 to 1919 six of his novels appeared; but it was not until *Main Street* was published in 1920 that his work became popular. This book proved to be sensationally successful, and brought Lewis a reputation which grew steadily with the appearance of his later novels. In 1926 he refused the Pulitzer Prize voted for *Arrowsmith* as a protest against the basis on which the award is made. In 1930, however, when the much more coveted award—the Nobel Prize—was offered him, he accepted. In 1914 Lewis married Miss Grace Livingston Hegger, from whom he was divorced in 1925. Three years later he married Miss Dorothy Thompson, a journalist and lecturer, from whom he was subsequently separated also. He resides in New York City for the most part.

Hike and the Aeroplane (pseud. "Tom Graham"), 1912; *Our Mr. Wrenn*, 1914; *The Trail of the Hawk*, 1915; *The Job*, 1917; *The Innocents*, 1917;

Free Air, 1919; *Main Street*, 1920; *Babbitt*, 1922; *Arrowsmith*, 1925; *Mantrap*, 1926; *Elmer Gantry*, 1927; *The Man Who Knew Coolidge*, 1928; *Dodsworth*, 1929; *Ann Vickers*, 1933; *Work of Art*, 1934; *Selected Short Stories*, 1935; *It Can't Happen Here*, 1935; *Jayhawker* (with L. Lewis), 1935; *Bethel Merriday*, 1940; *Gideon Planish*, 1943; *Cass Timberlane*, 1945; *Kingsblood Royal*, 1947; *The God-Seeker*, 1949.

For life and criticism, see: Stuart P. Sherman, *The Significance of Sinclair Lewis*, 1922 (reprinted, without biographical sketch, in *Points of View*, 1924, pp. 189–218); O. Harrison, *Sinclair Lewis*, 1927; Carl Van Doren, *Sinclair Lewis*, 1933. For criticism, see: Vernon Louis Parrington, *Sinclair Lewis, Our Own Diogenes*, 1927; Percy H. Boynton, *More Contemporary Americans*, 1927, pp. 179–99; Milton Waldman, *Contemporary American Authors* (ed. by J. C. Squire), 1928, pp. 71–95; Régis Michaud, *The American Novel Today*, 1928, pp. 128–54; T. K. Whipple, *Spokesmen*, 1928, pp. 208–30; Fred Lewis Pattee, *The New American Literature*, 1930, pp. 338–45; James Branch Cabell, *Some of Us*, 1930, pp. 61–74; T. D. Horton, *No. Am. Rev.*, CCXLVIII, pp. 374–93; Benjamin Stolberg, *Am. Mercury*, LIII, pp. 450–60; L. & M. Gurko, *Coll. Eng.*, IV, pp. 289–92.

1003. [TWO NEWCOMERS ON MAIN STREET.] Secs. II and III, Ch. IV, of *Main Street*, 1920. ¶1008. *"Bill Hart."* [William S.] Star of "Western" motion pictures in the twenties.

1008. [MR. BABBITT STARTS THE DAY.] All except last three pages of Ch. III, of *Babbitt*, 1922.

1014. [MAX GOTTLIEB] and (1019) DR. ALMUS PICKERBAUGH are Chapters IV and XIX, respectively, of *Arrowsmith*, 1925. ¶1015. *"Die goldene Zeit":* The Golden Age. ¶1015. *"Dummkopfe":* Thickheads. ¶1016. *"Bernard Shaw"* (1856–　　), British satiric dramatist of Irish birth. ¶1016. *"Pater's 'Marius the Epicurean.'"* A stylistic novel of the decline of Rome by the English aesthete Walter Pater (1839–94). ¶1018. *"Die Wacht am Rhein."* The Watch on the Rhine, German national anthem. ¶1018. *"Kerl":* fellow. ¶1019. *"Nietzsche,"* Friedrich Wilhelm (1844–1900), German evolutionary philosopher who predicted the coming of the Superman;

"Schopenhauer," Arthur (1788–1860), German pessimistic philosopher; *"Koch,"* Robert (1843–1910), German bacteriologist; *"Pasteur,"* Louis (1822–95), French bacteriologist, advocate of pasteurization, little used in France; *"Jacques Loeb"* (1859–1924), German-born American experimental biologist whose life appears to have furnished Lewis with some of the materials for the study of Max Gottlieb; *"Arrhenius,"* Svante August (1859–1927), Swedish physicist and chemist—a curious addition to this list. ¶1020. *"Billy Sunday"* (1862–1935), contemporary revivalist, ex-baseball player. ¶1025. *"Mens Sana in the Corpus Sano":* "A sound mind in a sound body"; Pickerbaugh has taken some liberties with the Latin *mens sana in corpore sano.* If Jacques Loeb provided a model for Max Gottlieb, the late Senator Copeland of New York supplied a few hints for Pickerbaugh.

John (Roderigo) Dos Passos
(1896–　　)

John Roderigo Dos Passos was born in Chicago, Ill., on Jan. 14, 1896. He studied at Harvard University, receiving the A.B. degree in 1916. For two years during World War I he served in ambulance units; after the armistice he became associated with the group of expatriated Americans gathered around Gertrude Stein in Paris. Upon returning to the United States, he lived successively in several parts of the country; his knowledge of the classes of American society was gained at first hand.

In 1921 his novel *Three Soldiers* called forth much discussion, both friendly and hostile. *Manhattan Transfer*, 1925, brought him to the front rank among experimental novelists because of the "kaleidoscopic technique" employed in it. This novel, like several others which followed, also drew attention on account of its harsh and challenging interpretation of capitalistic society. Yet Dos Passos has described himself as a middleclass liberal and has attacked Marxism. He now lives in Provincetown, Mass.

One Man's Initiation, 1920; *Three Soldiers*, 1921; *A Pushcart at the Curb*, 1922; *Rosinante to the Road Again*, 1922; *Streets of Night*, 1923; *Manhattan Transfer*, 1925; *The Garbage Man*, 1926; *Orient Express*, 1927; *Airways, Inc.*, 1928; *The 42nd Parallel*, 1930;

Panama, by Blaise Cendrars (trans.), 1931; *1919,* 1932; *In All Countries,* 1934; *Three Plays,* 1934; *The Big Money,* 1936; *Journeys Between Wars,* 1938; *Adventures of a Young Man,* 1939; *The Ground We Stand On,* 1941; *Number One,* 1943; *The State of the Nation,* 1944; *First Encounter,* 1945; *Tour of Duty,* 1946; *The Grand Design,* 1949.

For criticism, see: Joseph Warren Beach, *The Twentieth Century Novel,* 1932, pp. 437–39, 501–12; Granville Hicks, *Bookman,* LXXV, pp. 32–43; Henry Hazlitt, *Nation,* CXXX, p. 298; Henry Hazlitt, *Nation,* CXXXIV, p. 344; Francis Hackett, *New Repub.,* XXVIII, pp. 162–63; Edmund Wilson, *New Repub.,* LXII, pp. 157–58; Malcolm Cowley, *New Repub.,* LXX, pp. 303–05; Sinclair Lewis, *Sat. Rev. Lit.,* II, p. 361; Matthew Josephson, *Sat. Rev. Lit.,* VIII, p. 600; Delmore Schwartz, *So. Rev.,* IV, pp. 351–67; R. H. Footman, *Sewanee Rev.,* XLVII, pp. 365–82; Milton Rugoff, *Sewanee Rev.,* XLIX, pp. 453–68; C. B. Bredford, *Univ. Rev.,* VIII, pp. 267–72.

1030. [TWO FATHERS.] From *Manhattan Transfer,* 1925. ¶1032. *"hypothecations,"* new pledges for loans.

1033. THE CAMERA EYE. From *The 42nd Parallel,* 1930. One of the three "timing" devices used in trilogy *U.S.A.,* the "camera eye" represents the consciousness of the novelist. The scene here is Holland in the time of the Boer War. ¶1033. *"Kruger,"* Stephanus Johannes Paulus (1825–1904), president of Transvaal; *"Bloemfontein,"* Boer stronghold, under siege; *"Ladysmith,"* English stronghold which had been relieved; *"Queen Victoria"* (1819–1901), British ruler.

1034. NEWSREEL II. Another type of "timing" device made up of scraps of news and bits of popular songs. ¶1034. *"Hazen S. Pingree"* (1840–1901) retired as governor on January 1, 1901; the citation of Pingree links "The Camera Eye" above to this "Newsreel," for Pingree was an Anglophobe and pro-Boer. ¶1043. *"Kruger"* (see note to p. 1033) was ill from his flight in October, 1900, until he died on July 14, 1904; *"Queen Victoria"* died on Jan. 22, 1901; *"Carry Nation"* (1846–1911), fanatical prohibition crusader; *"Carnegie,"* Andrew (1835–1919), Scotch-born American businessman and philanthropist; *"Alexanders ragtime band,"* popular hit; *"Jesse James"* (1847–82), American

outlaw; *"Santos Dumont,"* French balloonist, later an aviator.

1035. LOVER OF MANKIND. The third type of "timing" device—the free-verse apposite biography. Eugene Victor Debs' dates are 1855–1926.

1036. JOE WILLIAMS [3] is the third "panel" in the discontinuous narrative of a "working-class stiff" in the second novel in Dos Passos' trilogy, *1919,* 1932. ¶1036. *"Wilson had just declared war,"* April 2, 1917. ¶1036. *"C'est la guerre":* "It's the war"; *"On les aura":* "They will have them"; *"Je m'en fiche":* "It's nothing to me." ¶1037. *"petit lapin":* "little rabbit." ¶1037. *"fiddles."* A rack of cords to keep dishes from sliding in rough weather. ¶1037. *"banker."* Fishing schooner from the Great Banks. ¶1039. *"St. Thomas."* On one of the Virgin Islands, east of Puerto Rico; *"dengue,"* breakbone fever. ¶1040. *"Janey,"* Joe's sister. ¶1040. *"Redhook,"* a section of Brooklyn, N. Y. ¶1041. *"Gironde,"* 40 mi. estuary, formed by the junction of the Dordogne and Garonne [text, below] rivers near Bordeaux. ¶1041. *"Finisterre,"* most southern cape in northwest Spain. ¶1042. *"Viva los Aliados":* "Long live the Allies!"; *"Viva Maura":* "Long live Maura [Antonio Montaner (1853–1925), Spanish prime-minister, thought to be friendly toward the Central Powers.]!"

1049. THE AMERICAN PLAN. From *The Big Money,* 1936, the final novel in the trilogy. This should be compared with the earlier material on Frederick Winslow Taylor in this volume, see pp. 618–27 and 1212.

Robert Nathan (1894–   )

Robert Nathan was born in New York City on Jan. 2, 1894. He attended private schools both in the United States and in Switzerland, and for a year or two studied at Harvard University, where he began his career as a writer of verse and fiction. After leaving Harvard he worked in the office of an advertising agency; during 1924–25 he lectured in the School of Journalism, New York University. His first novel, *Peter Kindred,* appeared in 1919, but it was *Autumn,* published two years later, which first brought him considerable praise from readers and critics. Both novels were written with great care, as all of his books have been. He is, incidentally, an illustrator, a musician, and a composer. He has been married several times. His home is in New York City.

The particular qualities which lend distinction to his fiction are whimsicality, subdued irony, quiet satire, a subtly sophisticated tone blended with a strain of the idyllic.

Peter Kindred, 1919; *Autumn*, 1921; *Youth Grows Old*, 1922; *The Puppet Master*, 1923; *Jonah*, 1925; *The Fiddler in Barly*, 1926; *The Woodcutter's House*, 1927; *The Bishop's Wife*, 1928; *A Cedar Box*, 1929; *There Is Another Heaven*, 1929; *The Orchid*, 1931; *One More Spring*, 1933; *The Road of Ages*, 1935; *Selected Poems*, 1935; *Enchanted Voyage*, 1936; *Journey of Tapiola*, 1938; *Winter in April*, 1938; *Portrait of Jennie*, 1940; *Winter Tide: Sonnets and Poems*, 1940; *Tapiola's Brave Regiment*, 1941; *They Went On Together*, 1941; *Sea-Gull Cry*, 1942; *But Gently Day*, 1943; *Journey for Josephine*, 1943; *Morning in Iowa*, 1944; *Darkening Meadows*, 1945; *Mr. Whittle and the Morning Star*, 1947.

For criticism, see: Ben Ray Redman, *Nation*, CXIV, p. 624; Laura Benét, *Nation*, CXXIX, p. 634; Genevieve Taggard; *N. Y. Herald Tribune: Books*, Dec. 11, 1927, p. 2; *N. Y. Times Book Rev.*, Oct. 16, 1928, p. 6; Walter H. Kohn, *Sat. Rev. Lit.*, I, p. 627; Charles E. Noyes, *Sat. Rev. Lit.*, III, p. 335; *Times Lit. Supplement* (London), Sept. 10, 1925, p. 582.

1052. [THE PUPPET MASTER AND HIS POET ASSISTANT.] From *The Puppet Master*, 1923. ¶1054. *"Molière"* [Jean Baptiste Poquelin (1622–73)], French actor and writer of comedies. ¶1052. *"Sancho Panza,"* comic puppet named for Don Quixote's servant.

1054. [METABEL MEETS THE LITTLE GREEN MAN.] From *The Woodcutter's House*, 1927.

Louis Bromfield (1896–   )

Louis Bromfield was born in Mansfield, Ohio, on Dec. 27, 1896. He attended the local schools, and then entered Cornell University, enrolling in the Agricultural College. Originally he intended to settle on a farm in Ohio— a project he was not long in abandoning. During the World War he served with the French army, and after the armistice lived for six months in Paris. Returning to the United States, he found employment with the New York City News Association and later with the Associated Press. Next he became the foreign editor of *Musical America*. He worked for a publishing firm, and also for a theatrical producer. After completing four novels which have never appeared in print, in 1924 he published *The Green Bay Tree*, which pleased the reading public, as did the novels which have followed it. For *Early Autumn*, 1926, he was awarded the Pulitzer Prize in 1927. He was in France when the Second World War began, but was able to return to the U. S., where he settled on Malabar Farm, near Lucas, Ohio, not far from his boyhood home. His interest in soil conservation and the need of preserving the best in the life of rural America has turned his literary efforts more and more towards social and economic criticism.

The Green Bay Tree, 1924; *Possession*, 1925; *Early Autumn*, 1926; *A Good Woman*, 1927; *The House of Women*, 1927; *The Strange Case of Miss Annie Spragg*, 1928; *Awake and Rehearse*, 1929; *Twenty-Four Hours*, 1930; *Tabloid News*, 1930; *A Modern Hero*, 1932; *Lilli Barr*, 1932; *The Farm*, 1933; *Here Today and Gone Tomorrow*, 1934; *The Man Who Had Everything*, 1935; *It Had to Happen*, 1936; *The Rains Came*, 1937; *It Takes All Kinds*, 1939; *Night in Bombay*, 1940; *Wild Is the River*, 1941; *Until the Day Breaks*, 1942; *Mrs. Parkington*, 1943; *Bitter Lotus*, 1944; *What Became of Anna Bolton*, 1944; *The World We Live In*, 1944; *Pleasant Valley*, 1945; *A Few Brass Tacks*, 1946; *Kenny*, 1947; *Colorado*, 1947; *Malabar Farm*, 1948; *The Wild Country*, 1948.

For criticism, see: Henry B. Fuller, *Bookman*, LXV, pp. 200–04; Louise Maunsell Field, *Bookman*, LXXV, pp. 43–49; Alice Beal Parsons, *Nation*, CXIX, pp. 78–79; Alice Beal Parsons, *Nation*, CXXV, pp. 258, 260; Geoffrey T. Hellman, *New Repub.*, LXXI, pp. 25–26; Stuart P. Sherman, *N. Y. Herald Tribune: Books*, Oct. 11, 1925, pp. 1–3; Grace Frank, *Sat. Rev. Lit.*, IV, p. 22; Henry Seidel Canby, *Sat. Rev. Lit.*, VIII, p. 713.

1056. [OLIVIA REVIEWS HER PAST.] From Ch. III, *Early Autumn*, 1926. This novel, *The Green Bay Tree*, *Possession*, and *A Good Woman* all belong to a study of "Escape" and are given that collective title. ¶1060. *"The City,"* Clyde Fitch's last play (1909).

Pearl S(ydenstricker) Buck
(1892–   )

Pearl Sydenstricker, who was to gain world fame as Pearl S. Buck, was born in Hillsboro, W. Va., on July 26, 1892. But her parents, Absalom and Caroline (Stulting) Sydenstricker, to whom she has devoted two passionate but critical biographies, were missionaries; consequently her girlhood was passed in China. She returned to the United States for her higher education and was graduated from Randolph-Macon Woman's College in 1914. Returning to China she was married to John Lossing Buck, an American missionary interested in soil conservation, on May 13, 1917. By him she had two children, both girls. Separated from her husband, she became a college English teacher on the faculties simultaneously of the University of Nanking, 1921–31, of Southeastern University, 1925–27, and of Chung Yang University, 1928–31. (The last two are also in Nanking.) On leave from her appointments, she was awarded her M.A. degree by Cornell in 1926. She left China permanently after the success of *The Good Earth*. On July 11, 1935, having obtained a divorce, she was married to Richard J. Walsh, her publisher. In 1938 she became the third American to win the Nobel Prize for literature. Although many demands are made upon her, Pearl Buck and her husband have adopted four children.

East Wind–West Wind, 1930; *The Young Revolutionist*, 1931; *The Good Earth*, 1931; *Sons*, 1932; *The First Wife and Other Stories*, 1933; *All Men Are Brothers* (tr.), 1933; *The Mother*, 1934; *A House Divided*, 1935; *House of Earth*, 1935; *The Exile*, 1936; *Fighting Angel*, 1936; *This Proud Heart*, 1938; *The Patriot*, 1939; *The Chinese Novel*, 1939; *Other Gods*, 1940; *Stories for Little Children*, 1940; *Today and Forever*, 1941; *Of Men and Women*, 1941; *Dragon Seed*, 1942; *American Unity and Asia*, 1942; *The Chinese Children Next Door*, 1942; *What America Means to Me*, 1943; *The Water-Buffalo Children*, 1943; *The Promise*, 1943; *The Dragon Fish*, 1944; *Tell the People* (with James Yen), 1945; *Yu-Lar*, 1945; *Portrait of a Marriage*, 1945; *Talk About Russia* (with Marsha Scott), 1945; *Pavilion of Women*, 1946; *How It Hap-* *pens* (with Erna von Pristom), 1946; *Far and Near*, 1947; *Peony*, 1947; *Big Wave*, 1948.

For life and criticism, see: *The Exile, Fighting Angel; Portrait of a Marriage;* Cornelia Spencer, *The Exile's Daughter*, 1944; S. V. and Rosemary Benét, "Two-World Success Story," *N. Y. Her.-Trib. Books*, Jan. 18, 1942; Kyrle Crichton, "Preacher's Daughter," *Collier's*, Feb. 7, 1942; E. C. Ince, "Will the Twain Meet?" *Chris. Sci. Mag.*, Feb. 5, 1944.

1061. THE ENEMY. From *Harper's*, Nov., 1942; collected, *Far and Near*, 1947.

Katherine Anne Porter (1894–   )

It is hard to think of Katherine Anne Porter as a Texan, yet she was born at Indian Creek, Tex., on May 15, 1894. Her parents were Harrison B. and Mary A. (Jones) Porter. She got her total education at "various small convent schools" in Texas and Louisiana. She remembers herself, probably unfairly, as "precocious, nervous, rebellious, untractable." Early familiar with books she began to compose stories at three, but she waited a good many years for success. In 1933 she was married to Eugene Pressly, attached to the American embassy in Paris; later, divorced from Pressly, she was married in 1938 to Albert R. Erskine, Jr., a professor of English in the University of Louisiana, whom she also divorced. Since 1920, when she left the South, she has lived in New York, Paris, Mexico, and California. Her home is now Santa Monica, Calif.

Flowering Judas, 1930; *Hacienda*, 1934; *Noon Wine*, 1937; *Pale Horse, Pale Rider*, 1929; *No Safe Harbor*, 1942; *The Itching Parrot* (tr.), 1942; *The Leaning Tower*, 1944.

For life and criticism, see: *Who's Who in America*, 1948–49; S. J. Kunitz & Howard Haycraft, *Twentieth Century Authors*, 1942; Lodwick Hartly, "Katherine Anne Porter," *Sewanee Rev.*, Apr., 1940; R. P. Warren, "Katherine Anne Porter (Irony with a Center)," *Kenyon Rev.*, Winter, 1942; V. A. Young, "The Art of Katherine Anne Porter," *New Mex. Quar. Rev.*, Autumn, 1945.

1074. THE WITNESS. From *The Leaning Tower*, 1944. "Spoofing" has been appropriated by the Yankees as a Yankee trait, but this story seems to supply a good Southern example.

John (Ernst) Steinbeck (1902–   )

Of mixed German and Irish stock, John Steinbeck was named after his father when he was born on February 27, 1902, at Salinas, Calif. His mother was Olive Hamilton before her marriage. Steinbeck did much hard work as a boy but was graduated from Salinas High School in 1918. He entered Stanford University the following year, but did not follow a regular program. He abandoned all effort to get a degree in 1925. Having determined to write, he worked his way to New York on a freight boat and labored at whatever was offered (this included laying bricks at Madison Square Garden) while assailing the literary markets futilely with his product. Returning to California, he was watchman on an estate in the Sierras and workman in a fish hatchery. On the strength of getting his first novel, *A Cup of Gold* published, he married Carol Henning in 1930, but it was five years before *Tortilla Flat* brought him independence. During World War II he was in Italy as a correspondent; after the war he and Robert Capa, the photographer, made a journey to Russia. He was divorced in 1943 and married to Gwyn Conger.

Cup of Gold, 1929; *The Pastures of Heaven*, 1932; *To a God Unknown*, 1933; *Tortilla Flat*, 1935; *In Dubious Battle*, 1936; *Nothing So Monstrous*, 1936; *Katy the Virgin*, 1936; *Of Mice and Men*, 1937; *The Red Pony*, 1937; *Their Blood Is Strong*, 1938; *The Long Valley*, 1938; *Grapes of Wrath*, 1939; *The Sea of Cortez* (with E. F. Ricketts), 1941; *The Moon is Down*, 1942; *The Forgotten Village*, 1942; *Cannery Row*, 1945; *The Wayward Bus*, 1947; *The Pearl*, 1947; *A Russian Journal*, 1948. For life and criticism, see: H. T. Moore, *The Novels of John Steinbeck*, 1939; Lewis Gannett, "John Steinbeck, Novelist at Work," *Atlantic*, Dec., 1945; M. S. Shockley, "The Reception of *The Grapes of Wrath* in Oklahoma," *Am. Lit.*, Jan., 1944; S. E. Hyman, "Some Notes on John Steinbeck," *Antioch Rev.*, Summer, 1942; C. E. Jones, "Proletarian Writing and John Steinbeck," *Sewanee Rev.*, Oct., 1940. For bibliography, see: L. C. Powell, "Toward a Bibliography of John Steinbeck," *Colophon*, Autumn, 1938.

1076. THE GIFT is from *The Red Pony*, 1937. Text is from the illustrated edition of 1944. ¶1078. "*Salinas,*" inland town about 15 mi. from Monterey, Calif. ¶1078. "*pigs were scalded,*" so that the bristles might be removed. ¶1081. "*Gabilan Mountains*" are near Salinas.

1094. TWO FOR A CENT is Chapter XV in *The Grapes of Wrath*, 1939. ¶1094. "*Along 66.*" Route U. S. 66, "the Okie route," heads west from Oklahoma, passes through Amarillo, Tex., Albuquerque, N. Mex., Flagstaff, Ariz., crosses the Mohave desert, and terminates in Los Angeles, Calif. ¶1095. "*Zephyr,*" a Lincoln model manufactured by "*Henry Ford*" (1863–1947). ¶1097. "*families goin' west,*" the Okies.

Maxwell Anderson (1888–   )

It is not wholly a disadvantage to be the son of a minister in a sect which requires its preachers to move from charge to charge: the experience which Maxwell Anderson had enriched and broadened his vision. Born on Dec. 15, 1888, in Atlantic, Pa., he traveled westward through Ohio and Iowa to North Dakota with his Baptist preacher father, the Reverend William L. Anderson, getting his education at various places, but finally graduating in 1911 from the University of North Dakota. There he was one of the first members of the Sock and Buskin Society which Professor Frederick Koch founded before he was called to North Carolina. Maxwell Anderson was married to Margaret Haskett in the year of his graduation and taught in secondary schools in North Dakota and California in the next three years. In 1914 he had an opportunity to teach English at Stanford University while completing work for his M.A. degree. A year of this decided him to go into journalism and he was successively with the Grand Forks [N. D.] *Herald*, the San Francisco *Chronicle*, and the San Francisco *Bulletin*. In 1918 he arrived in New York City, where he did editorial work for the next six years on the *New Republic*, the New York *Evening Globe*, and the New York *Morning World*. After the success of *What Price Glory* it was not necessary for him to supplement his income. Margaret H. Anderson died in 1931 and in 1933 he was married to Gertrude Maynard. Anderson has a child by each marriage.

You Who Have Dreams, 1925; *Three*

American Plays (with Lawrence Stall-
ings), 1926; *Saturday's Children*, 1927;
Gods of the Lightning (with Harold
Hickerson), 1928; *Outside Looking In*
[based on "Beggars of Life" by Jim
Tully], 1928; *Elizabeth the Queen*, 1930;
Night Over Taos, 1932; *Both Your
Houses*, 1933; *Mary of Scotland*, 1933;
Valley Forge, 1934; *Winterset*, 1935; *The
Masque of Kings*, 1936; *The Wingless
Victory*, 1936; *High Tor*, 1937; *The
Star Wagon*, 1937; *The Feast of Or-
tolans*, 1938; *Knickerbocker Holiday*,
1938; *The Essence of Tragedy*, 1939;
Candle in the Wind, 1941; *Eve of St.
Mark*, 1942; *Storm Operation*, 1944;
Truckline Cafe, 1945; *Joan of Lorraine*,
1946; *Off Broadway*, 1947.

For life and criticism, see: B. H.
Clark, *Maxwell Anderson*, 1933; A.ᐧ H.
Quinn, *A History of the American
Drama from the Civil War*, 1936;
Eleanor Flexner, *American Playwrights,
1918–1938*, 1938; Carl Carmer, "Max-
well Anderson, Poet and Champion,"
Theatre Arts, June, 1933; Horace Greg-
ory, "Poets in the Theatre," *Poetry*,
July, 1936; E. J. R. Isaacs, "Maxwell
Anderson," *Eng. Jour.*, Dec. 1936;
Joseph Mersand, "Speech in New
Plays," *Col. Eng.* Mar.–Apr. 1937;
Vincent Wall, "Maxwell Anderson: the
Last Anarchist," *Sewanee Rev.*, July–
Sept. 1941; H. E. Woodbridge, "Max-
well Anderson," *So. Atlan. Quar.*, Jan.,
1945.

1100. WINTERSET. First presented at
the Martin Beck Theatre, Sept. 25,
1935; published 1935. This was Anderson's second working over of the material
of the Sacco-Vanzetti case, which he
dramatized first with Harold Hickson, as
Gods of the Lightning. This earlier play
failed. For material on Sacco and Vanzetti, see note to Miss Millay's "Justice
Denied in Massachusetts" (above p.
1247). ¶1101. *"Stir me in,"* "stir" is
criminal argot for "prison." ¶1102. *"Estrella gang."* Suggested by Joe Morelli
gang of the Sacco-Vanzetti case. ¶1109.
"stench of ten." Compare Tennyson's
"Sir Galahad":

My strength is as the strength of ten
  Because my heart is pure.

¶1111. *"the mayor heard it too often."*
Fiorella LaGuardia secured an ordinance
against street organs, etc.; *"the sextette"*
from *Lucia di Lammermoor*, popular
street-organ piece. ¶1112. *"Verdi,"*
Guiseppe (1813–1901) Italian composer.
¶1118. *"Flatbush,"* area in Brooklyn.

¶1125. *"rotos,"* rotogravure sections of
Sunday papers. ¶1126. *"Brahminical
mouth."* Holmes' "Brahmin caste" now
includes in popular application all New
England upper classes. ¶1130. *"lux-et-
lex":* "light and law." ¶1130. *"Buddha,"*
the deified founder of the Buddhists,
Gautama Siddhartha (563–483 B.C.).
¶1132. *"Theophrastus Such."* A minor
creation of George Eliot's. ¶1139. *"Haile
Selassie"* (1891–   ), the then ousted
emperor of Ethiopia. ¶1141. *"a young
man on a cold night."* See T. S. Eliot's
"Gerontion." ¶1142. *"This is the burial
of Shadow. . . ."* Mio's versifying in
times of tension is a trick Anderson
learned from Rostand. ¶1143. *"an obol
in his mouth,"* the smallest Greek coin
for payment to the ferryman Charon
for crossing the Acheron. ¶1147. *"pomegranate seeds."* Mio, remembering that
Persephone, forbidden to eat, had consumed a pomegranate and was doomed,
suggests that Miriamne is trying to conceal her fate by eating the seeds.

William Saroyan (1908–   )

Son of American immigrants, Armenag
and Takoohi Saroyan (who were also
cousins), William Saroyan was born in
Fresno, Calif., on Aug. 31, 1908. His
father had been a writer and teacher in
the old country; but he died when William was still very young, leaving his
family impoverished. At eight, Saroyan
sold papers, at thirteen he became a
telegraph messenger, and at sixteen,
abandoning school, he got work in his
uncle's vineyard. Through the public
library he early had access to books and
read voraciously if capriciously. Getting
the use of a typewriter he began to write.
An Armenian newspaper published his
first tale in 1933; he was "found" by
Story magazine in 1934 and *The Daring Young Man on the Flying Trapeze*—
still personified by Saroyan at 40—made
him famous. He poured a prodigal
energy into all forms of prose work.
Only one interruption has occurred in
his career since he began to write: his
call to the service in World War II, in
which he was a private soldier throughout his term.

*The Daring Young Man on the Flying
Trapeze and Other Stories*, 1934; *Inhale
and Exhale*, 1936; *Three Times Three*,
1936; *The Gay and Melancholy Flux*,
1937; *Little Children*, 1937; *Love, Here
Is My Hat*, 1938; *A Native American*,

1938; *The Trouble with Tigers,* 1938; *My Heart's in the Highlands,* 1939; *The Time of Your Life,* 1939; *Peace, It's Wonderful,* 1939; *My Name Is Aram,* 1940; *Fables,* 1941; *Razzle-Dazzle,* 1942; *Human Comedy,* 1943; *Dear Baby,* 1944; *Get Away Old Man,* 1944; *The Adventures of Wesley Jackson,* 1946; *Jim Dandy,* 1947.

For life and criticism, see: Clifton Fadiman, "71 Varieties," *New Yorker,* Feb. 22, 1936; Harlan Hatcher, "William Saroyan," *Eng. Jour.,* Mar., 1939; G. J. Nathan, "Saroyan: Whirling Dervish of Fresno," *Am. Merc.,* Sept., 1943; Edmund Wilson "The Boys in the Back Room," *New Repub.,* Nov. 18, 1940; E. B. Burgum, "The Lonesome Young Man on the Flying Trapeze," *Va. Quar. Rev.,* Summer 1944.

1149. HELLO OUT THERE. In *Razzle-*

Dazzle, 1942. ¶1150. "*Oceana,*" a mythical isle imagined by John Harrington. ¶1151. "*Young Corbett, . . . best fighter in his division,*" held the welterweight title in 1933. ¶1152. "*Guy de Maupassant*" (1850–93), French short-story writer. ¶1152. "*Chekhov,*" Anton (1860–1904), "*Andreyev,*" Leonid (1871–1919), and "*Gorki,*" Maxim (1868–1936)—all Russian dramatists. ¶1052. "*Ibsen,*" Henrik (1828–1906), Norwegian dramatist; "*Oscar Wilde,*" (1856–1900), Irish-born English dramatist. ¶1152. "*'The Mob' by Le Bon.*" Gustav Le Bon, French psychologist, wrote *La Psychologie des Foules* (1895). ¶1053. "*George Jean Nathan*" (1882–   ), American dramatic critic. ¶1155. "*Salinas.*" See notes to p. 1078. ¶1158. "*handicapper,*" one who sets the odds at racetracks.

INDEX

Non-italic numbers refer to pages in text; italic numbers to pages in notes.